PRAISE FOR
THE BANTAM NEW COLLEGE
ITALIAN AND ENGLISH DICTIONARY

". . . thorough, accurate, well-organized, clear, and up to date . . . Relevant to the student's contemporary life . . . It is bound to become a mainstay in the field."
—Albert N. Mancini, Professor of Romance Languages, The Ohio State University

"Both the method and the execution seem to me excellent . . . It would be impossible to find elsewhere as good a dictionary of this size."
—Beatrice Corrigan, Professor Emeritus, Editor, University of Toronto Press

"Apart from its accurate philological approach, its most useful grammatical apparatus, and other singular features, this concise dictionary is the first which is based primarily on *American* English usage . . . It contains numerous up-to-date colloquial and technical terms which cannot be found in any other similar dictionary."
—M. Ricciardelli, Professor of Italian and Comparative Literatures, Editor of *Forum Italicum*

Comprehensive, authoritative, and completely modern, **THE BANTAM NEW COLLEGE ITALIAN AND ENGLISH DICTIONARY** is a landmark in foreign language reference works.

THE BANTAM NEW COLLEGE DICTIONARY SERIES

Robert C. Melzi, Author

ROBERT C. MELZI, D. in L., A.M., Ph.D., was trained in Italy, at the University of Padua, and in the United States, at the University of Pennsylvania. He has done extensive linguistic research, traveling frequently to his native country. Now professor of Romance Languages at Widener College, he has contributed articles and reviews to many learned journals, is the author of *Castelvetro's Annotations to the Inferno,* The Hague and Paris, 1966 (Castelvetro was one of Italy's foremost philologists), and is an associate editor of *The Scribner-Bantam English Dictionary* (Scribner's, 1977; Bantam Books, 1979). Professor Melzi is a Cavaliere in the Order of Solidarity of the Republic of Italy.

Edwin B. Williams, General Editor

EDWIN B. WILLIAMS (1891–1975), A.B., A.M., Ph.D., Doct. d'Univ., LL.D., L.H.D., was chairman of the Department of Romance Languages, dean of the Graduate School, and provost of the University of Pennsylvania. He was a member of the American Philosophical Society and the Hispanic Society of America. Among his many lexicographical works are *The Williams Spanish and English Dictionary* (Scribner's, formerly Holt) and *The Bantam New College Spanish and English Dictionary*. He created and coordinated the Bantam series of original dictionaries—English, French, German, Italian, Latin, and Spanish. The University of Pennsylvania named "Williams Hall" in honor of Edwin B. Williams and his wife, Leonore, and is establishing the "Williams Chair in Lexicography," as the first chair in lexicography in an English-speaking country.

THE BANTAM NEW COLLEGE
ITALIAN & ENGLISH
DICTIONARY

ROBERT C. MELZI, Ph.D.
Widener College, Philadelphia

BANTAM BOOKS
NEW YORK · TORONTO · LONDON · SYDNEY · AUCKLAND

THE BANTAM NEW COLLEGE
ITALIAN & ENGLISH DICTIONARY
A Bantam Book / April 1976

ISBN 0-553-27947-5

Published simultaneously in the United States and Canada

Bantam Books are published by Bantam Books, a division of Random
House, Inc. Its trademark, consisting of the words "Bantam Books" and
the portrayal of a rooster, is Registered in U.S. Patent and Trademark
Office and in other countries. Marca Registrada. Bantam Books, 1540
Broadway, New York, New York 10036.

PRINTED IN THE UNITED STATES OF AMERICA

OPM   29

CONTENTS

Preface   vii

Prefazione   vii

Labels and Abbreviations   xii

Sigle ed abbreviazioni   xii

Part One   Italian-English

Italian Spelling and Pronunciation   3

Grammatical Tables   7

Table of Regular Endings of Italian Verbs   15

Model Verbs   17

ITALIAN-ENGLISH   37–364

Part Two   Inglese-Italiano

La pronunzia dell'inglese   3

La pronunzia delle parole composte   5

La pronunzia dei participi passati   5

INGLESE-ITALIANO   7–355

PREFACE

Inasmuch as the basic function of a bilingual dictionary is to provide semantic equivalences, syntactical constructions are shown in both the source and the target languages on both sides of the Dictionary. In performing this function, a bilingual dictionary must fulfill six purposes. That is, an Italian and English dictionary must provide (1) Italian words which an English-speaking person wishes to use in speaking and writing (by means of the English-Italian part), (2) English meanings of Italian words which an English-speaking person encounters in listening and reading (by means of the Italian-English part), (3) the spelling, pronunciation, and inflection of Italian words and the gender of Italian nouns which an English-speaking person needs in order to use Italian words correctly (by means of the Italian-English part), (4) English words which an Italian-speaking person wishes to use in speaking and writing (by means of the Italian-English part), (5) Italian meanings of English words which an Italian-speaking person encounters in listening and reading (by means of the English-Italian part), and (6) the spelling, pronunciation, and inflection of English words which an Italian-speaking person needs in order to use English words correctly (by means of the English-Italian part).

It may seem logical to provide the pronunciation and inflection of English words and the pronunciation and inflection of Italian words and the gender of Italian nouns where these words appear as target words inasmuch as these words, according to (1) and (4) above, are sought for the purpose of speaking and writing. Thus the user would find not only the words he seeks but all the information he needs about them in one and the same place. But this technique is impractical because target words are not alphabetized and could, therefore, be found only by the roundabout and uncertain way of seeking them through their translations in

PREFAZIONE

Dato che la funzione principale di un dizionario bilingue è quella di fornire all'utente equivalenze semantiche, le costruzioni sintattiche sono indicate in entrambe le lingue, quella di partenza e quella di arrivo, in entrambe le parti del Dizionario. Per compiere questa funzione, un dizionario bilingue deve raggiungere sei scopi differenti. Cioè, un dizionario italiano e inglese deve fornire (1) nella parte inglese-italiano, le parole italiane che la persona anglofona vuole adoperare parlando e scrivendo l'italiano; (2) nella parte italiano-inglese, il significato in inglese delle parole italiane che tale persona oda nella lingua parlata o legga in libri o giornali; (3) nella parte italiano-inglese, l'ortografia, la pronunzia, la flessione delle parole italiane e il genere dei nomi italiani che la persona anglofona deve conoscere per servirsi correttamente della lingua italiana; (4) nella parte italiano-inglese, le parole inglesi che la persona italofona vuole adoperare parlando o scrivendo l'inglese; (5) nella parte inglese-italiano, il significato in italiano delle parole inglesi che tale persona oda nella lingua parlata o legga in libri o giornali; (6) nella parte inglese-italiano, l'ortografia, la pronunzia figurata e la flessione delle parole inglesi che la persona italofona deve conoscere per servirsi correttamente della lingua inglese.

A prima vista potrebbe sembrare logico che la pronunzia e la flessione delle parole inglesi e la pronunzia e la flessione delle parole italiane e il genere dei nomi italiani fossero indicati dove queste parole si trovano nella lingua d'arrivo, dato che le parole della lingua d'arrivo, secondo i punti (1) e (4) enunciati più sopra, sono consultate da coloro che vogliono parlare e scrivere in lingua straniera. In questa maniera l'utente troverebbe non solo le parole che cerca, ma tutte le informazioni che gli sono necessarie, nello stesso luogo. Questa tecnica, peraltro, non è pratica poiché le parole della lingua d'arrivo non si trovano in ordine

the other part of the dictionary. And this would be particularly inconvenient for persons using the dictionary for purposes (2) and (5) above. It is much more convenient to provide immediate alphabetized access to pronunciation and inflection where the words appear as source words.

alfabetico e potrebbero quindi essere trovate solo in maniera complicata nella parte opposta del dizionario. E ciò sarebbe specialmente scomodo per coloro che usano il dizionario per gli scopi (2) e (5) menzionati più sopra. È molto più semplice aggiungere la pronunzia e la flessione nella serie alfabetica in cui le parole si trovano nella loro lingua di partenza.

Since Italian is an almost perfectly phonetic language, IPA transcription of Italian words has been omitted. The only elements of pronunciation not shown by standard spelling are the values of tonic e and o (§1; pp. 3, 4) the stress of words stressed on the third syllable from the end (§3,3; p. 5), the value of intervocalic s when unvoiced, and the values of z and zz when voiced (§1; p. 4); these are shown in the entry words themselves.

Dato che l'italiano è una lingua quasi perfettamente fonetica, non si è data la trascrizione delle parole italiane nell'alfabeto dell'Associazione Fonetica Internazionale. Considerando che l'ortografia comune non mostra il vario timbro della e (§1, p. 3) e della o (§1, p. 4) quando esse sono toniche, l'accento delle parole sdrucciole (§3,3, p. 5), la pronunzia della s sorda (§1, p. 4) e la pronunzia delle z e zz sonore (§1, p. 4), si è data tale informazione nell'esponente stesso.

All words are treated in a fixed order according to the parts of speech and the functions of verbs, as follows: adjective, article, substantive, pronoun, adverb, preposition, conjunction, transitive verb, intransitive verb, reflexive verb, auxiliary verb, impersonal verb, interjection.

Ogni singola voce è trattata secondo uno schema fisso che si riferisce alle parti del discorso o alle funzioni del verbo, nel seguente ordine: aggettivo, articolo, sostantivo, pronome, avverbio, preposizione, congiunzione, verbo transitivo, verbo intransitivo, verbo riflessivo, verbo ausiliare, verbo impersonale e interiezione.

Meanings with labels come after more general meanings. Labels (printed in roman and in parentheses) refer to the preceding entry or phrase (printed in boldface).

I significati accompagnati da sigle si trovano dopo quelli di accezione più generale. Tali sigle (che sono sempre stampate in carattere romano e in parentesi) si riferiscono all'esponente precedente, stampato in grassetto, o alla frase precedente, ugualmente stampata in grassetto.

In view of the fact that the users of this Italian and English bilingual dictionary are for the most part English-speaking people, definitions and discriminations are provided in English. They are printed in italics and in parentheses and refer to the English word which they particularize:

Dato che gli utenti di questo dizionario bilingue italiano e inglese sono per lo più anglofoni, definizioni e locuzioni esplicative sono apportate in inglese. Sono stampate in corsivo e in parentesi e si riferiscono sempre alla parola inglese il cui significato cercano di spiegare:

porter ['porter] *s* (*doorman*) portiere *m;* (*man who carries luggage*) facchino; ...
órdine *m* order; ... series (*e.g., of years*); college (*e.g., of surgeons*); ...

English adjectives are always translated by the Italian masculine form

Gli aggettivi inglesi sono sempre tradotti in maschile italiano, anche se il

regardless of whether the translation of the exemplary noun modified would be masculine or feminine:

nome che qualificano sia un femminile italiano:

tough [tʌf] *adj* duro; . . . ; *(luck)* cattivo; . . .

In order to facilitate the finding of the meaning and use sought for, changes within a vocabulary entry in part of speech and function of verb, in irregular inflection, in the use of an initial capital, in the gender of Italian nouns, and in the pronunciation of English words are marked with parallels: ‖, instead of the usual semicolons.

Per facilitare l'uso del Dizionario, i raggruppamenti sono stati fatti secondo le parti del discorso, la funzione del verbo, la flessione irregolare, l'uso della maiuscola iniziale, il genere dei nomi italiani e la pronunzia delle parole inglesi e sono separati da sbarrette verticali: ‖, invece del punto e virgola che è stato generalmente usato.

Since vocabulary entries are not determined on the basis of etymology, homographs are included in a single entry. When the pronunciation of an English homograph changes, this is shown in the proper place after parallels:

Dato che gli esponenti in questo Dizionario non sono stati selezionati su base etimologica, tutti gli omografi sono inclusi sotto il medesimo esponente. Il cambio di pronunzia di un omografo inglese è indicato al posto adatto dopo sbarrette verticali:

frequent [ˈfrikwənt] *adj* frequente ‖ [frɪˈkwent] or [ˈfrikwənt] *tr* . . .

However, when the pronunciation of an Italian homograph changes, the words are entered separately:

Però, quando la pronunzia di un omografo italiano cambia, si hanno esponenti separati:

retina *f* small net
rètina *f* (anat) retina
tóc·co -ca (-chi -che) *adj* . . . ‖ *m* touch; . . .
tòc·co *m* (-chi) chunk, piece; . . .

Periods are omitted after labels and grammatical abbreviations and at the end of vocabulary entries.

Il punto è stato omesso dopo sigle, abbreviazioni grammaticali, ed alla fine di ogni articolo.

Proper nouns are listed in their alphabetical position in the main body of the Dictionary. Thus **Svezia** and **svedese** do not have to be looked up in two different sections of the book. And all subentries are listed in strictly alphabetical order.

Tutti i nomi propri sono posti nella loro posizione alfabetica nel corpo del Dizionario: quindi **Svezia** e **svedese** non si trovano in sezioni separate di questo libro. Per la medesima ragione di semplicità d'uso, le parole e frasi contenute sotto ogni esponente sono poste in ordine alfabetico.

The gender of Italian nouns is shown on both sides of the Dictionary, except that the gender of masculine nouns ending in -o, feminine nouns ending in -a and -ione, masculine nouns modified by an adjective ending in -o, and feminine nouns modified by an adjective

Il genere dei nomi italiani è indicato in entrambe le parti del Dizionario, eccezion fatta nella parte inglese-italiano, per le parole maschili che terminano in -o, per le parole femminili che terminano in -a e in -ione, per i nomi maschili accompagnati da un

ending in -a is not shown on the English-Italian side.

aggettivo che termina in -o e per i nomi femminili accompagnati da un aggettivo che termina in -a.

The feminine form of an Italian adjective used as a noun (or an Italian feminine noun having identical spelling with the feminine form of an adjective) which falls alphabetically in a separate position from the adjective is treated in that position and is listed again as a cross reference under the adjective:

Quando un nome femminile italiano ha la medesima grafia della forma femminile di un aggettivo o quando tale forma femminile di aggettivo è usata come nome, lo si trova elencato nella sua posizione alfabetica come nome e poi di nuovo come rinvio interno sotto l'aggettivo:

nòta *f* mark, score, . . .
nò·to -ta *adj* . . . ‖ *m* . . . ‖ *f* see **nota**

The centered period is used in vocabulary entries of inflected words to mark off, according to standard orthographic principles in the two languages, the final syllable that has to be detached before the syllable showing the inflection is added:

Qualora l'esponente italiano o inglese sia un vocabolo a flessione, un punto leggermente elevato sopra il rigo è stato usato per separare, secondo le regole ortografiche di ciascuna delle due lingue, la sillaba finale che dev'essere rimossa prima che la nuova desinenza di flessione possa essere attaccata al corpo dell'esponente, per es.:

vèc·chio -chia (-chi -chie) *adj* . . .
put·ty [ˈpʌti] *s* (-ties) . . . ‖ *v* (*pret & pp* -tied) . . .
hap·py [ˈhæpi] *adj* (-pier; -piest) . . .

If the entry word cannot be divided by a centered period the full form is given in parentheses:

Se l'esponente non può essere scisso a mezzo del suddetto punto, la forma completa è indicata in parentesi:

mouse [maʊs] *s* (**mice** [maɪs]) . . .
mouth [maʊθ] *s* (**mouths** [maʊðz]) . . .
die [daɪ] *s* (**dice** [daɪs]) . . . ‖ *s* (**dies**) . . . ‖ *v* (*pret & pp* **died**; *ger* **dying**) *intr* . . .

Many Italian verbs which take an indirect object have, as their equivalent, English verbs which take a direct object. This is shown on both sides of this Dictionary by the insertion of (with *dat*) after the Italian verb, e.g.,

Molti verbi italiani che reggono un oggetto indiretto hanno come equivalenti inglesi verbi che reggono un oggetto diretto. Questa equivalenza è indicata in entrambe le parti del Dizionario con l'aggiunta di (with *dat*) dopo il verbo italiano, per es.:

ubbidire §176 *intr* . . . ; (with *dat*) to obey
obey [oˈbe] *tr* ubbidire (with *dat*)

On the Italian-English side inflection is shown by: a) numbers that refer to the grammatical tables of articles, pronouns, etc., and to the tables of model verbs; they are placed before the abbreviation indicating the part of speech:

Nella parte italiano-inglese la flessione si indica: a) con numeri che si riferiscono alle tavole grammaticali degli articoli, dei pronomi, ecc., e alle tavole dei verbi modello; questi numeri sono posti innanzi all'abbreviazione indicante la parte del discorso:

mì·o -a §6 *adj & pron poss*
lui §5 *pron pers*
congiùngere §183 *tr & ref*

x

b) the first person singular of the present indicative of verbs in which the stess falls on either an e or an o not stressed in the infinitive or on the third syllable from the end, whatever the vowel may be:

b) con la prima persona singolare del presente dell'indicativo dei verbi non sdruccioli all'infinito in cui l'accento tonico cade o su una e o su una o, o su qualsiasi vocale di una parola sdrucciola:

> ritornare (ritórno) *tr* ...
> visitare (vìsito) *tr* ...

---

c) the feminine endings of all adjectives which end in -o:

c) con la desinenza femminile di tutti gli aggettivi che terminano in -o nel maschile:

> laborió•so -sa [s] *adj* ...

---

d) the plural endings of nouns and adjectives which are formed irregularly:

d) con la desinenza plurale dei nomi e aggettivi che si formano in maniera irregolare:

> bràc•cio *m* (-cia *fpl*) ... || *m* (-ci) ...
> cit•tà *f* (-tà) ...
> dià•rio -ria (-ri -rie) *adj* ... || *m* ... || *f* ...
> fotogram•ma *m* (-mi) ...
> fràn•gia *f* (-ge) ...
> laburi•sta (-sti -ste) *adj* ... || *mf* ...
> la•go *m* (-ghi) ...
> òr•co *m* (-chi) ...
> òtti•co -ca (-ci -che) *adj* ... || *m* ... || *f* ...

---

e) the full plural forms of all nouns that cannot be divided by a center period or whose plural cannot be shown by such division:

e) con la completa forma plurale di quei nomi che non possono essere scissi col suddetto punto o che hanno mutamenti interni:

> re *m* (re) ...
> caporeparto *m* (capireparto) ...

I wish to express my gratitude to many persons who helped me in the production of this book and particularly to Dr. Edwin B. Williams who, ever since graduate school, has been a constant inspiration and who has established the principles upon which this book was compiled, to my wife and children, who patiently aided and abetted me through ten years of research and compilation, to Richard J. Nelson, Sebastiano DiBlasi, Walter D. Glanze, and to Giacomo De Voto, Miro Dogliotti, and Michele Ricciardelli.

Labels and abbreviations

Sigle ed abbreviazioni

abbr abbreviation—abbreviazione
(acronym) word formed from the initial letters or syllables of a series of words—parola costituita dalle lettere o sillabe iniziali di una serie di parole
adj adjective—aggettivo
adv adverb—avverbio
(aer) aeronautics—aeronautica
(agr) agriculture—agricoltura
(alg) algebra—algebra
(anat) anatomy—anatomia
(archaic) arcaico
(archeol) archeology—archeologia
(archit) architecture—architettura
(arith) arithmetic—aritmetica
art article—articolo
(astr) astronomy—astronomia
(astrol) astrology—astrologia
(aut) automobile—automobile
aux auxiliary verb—verbo ausiliare
(bact) bacteriology—batteriologia
(baseball) baseball
(basketball) pallacanestro
(bb) bookbinding—legatoria
(Bib) Biblical—biblico
(billiards) biliardo
(biochem) biochemistry—biochimica
(biol) biology—biologia
(bot) botany—botanica
(bowling) bowling
(boxing) pugilato
(bridge) bridge
(Brit) British—britannico
(cards) carte da gioco
(carp) carpentry—falegnameria
(checkers) gioco della dama
(chem) chemistry—chimica
(chess) scacchi
(coll) colloquial—familiare
(com) commercial—commerciale
comb form elemento di parola composta
comp comparative—comparativo
cond conditional—condizionale
conj conjunction—congiunzione
(cricket) cricket
(culin) cooking—cucina
dat dative—dativo
def definite—determinativo, definito
dem demonstrative—dimostrativo
(dentistry) medicina dentaria
(dial) dialectal—dialettale
(dipl) diplomacy—diplomazia

(disparaging) sprezzante
(eccl) ecclesiastical—ecclesiastico
(econ) economics—economia
(educ) education—istruzione
e.g., or *e.g.,* per esempio
(elec) electricity—elettricità
(electron) electronics—elettronica
(ent) entomology—entomologia
(equit) horseback riding—equitazione
f feminine noun—nome femminile
(fa) fine arts—belle arti
fem feminine—femminile
(fencing) scherma
(fig) figurative—figurato
(fin) financial—finanziario
(football) football americano
fpl feminine noun plural—nome femminile plurale
fut future—futuro
(geog) geography—geografia
(geol) geology—geologia
(geom) geometry—geometria
ger gerund—gerundio
(golf) golf
(gram) grammar—grammatica
(herald) heraldry—araldica
(hist) history—storia
(hort) horticulture—orticoltura
(hunt) hunting—caccia
(ichth) ichthyology—ittiologia
i.e., cioè
imperf imperfect—imperfetto
impers impersonal verb—verbo impersonale
impv imperative—imperativo
ind indicative—indicativo
indef indefinite—indefinito, indeterminativo
inf infinitive—infinito
(ins) insurance—assicurazione
interj interjection—interiezione
interr interrogative—interrogativo
intr intransitive verb—verbo intransitivo
invar invariable—invariabile
(Italian cards) carte italiane
(jewelry) gioielleria
(joc) jocular—faceto
(journ) journalism—giornalismo
(law) diritto, legge
(letterword) word in the form of an abbreviation which is pronounced by sounding the names of its letters in

succession and which functions as a part of speech—parola in forma di abbreviazione che si ottiene pronunziando consecutivamente la denominazione di ciascuna lettera e che funziona come parte del discorso
(lexicography) lessicografia
(ling) linguistics—linguistica
(lit) literary—letterario
(log) logic—logica
m masculine noun—nome maschile
(mach) machinery—macchinario
masc masculine—maschile
(math) mathematics—matematica
(mech) mechanics—meccanica
(med) medicine—medicina
(metallurgy) metallurgia
(meteor) meteorology—meteorologia
mf masculine or feminine noun according to sex—nome maschile o nome femminile secondo il sesso
m & f see below between (mythol) and (naut)
(mil) military—militare
(min) mining—lavorazione delle miniere
(mov) moving pictures—cinematografo
mpl masculine noun plural—nome maschile plurale
(mus) music—musica
(mythol) mythology—mitologia
m & f masculine and feminine noun without regard to sex—nome maschile e femminile senza distinzione di sesso
(naut) nautical—nautico
(nav) naval—navale
neut neuter—neutro
num number—numero
(obs) obsolete—in disuso
(obstet) obstetrics—ostetricia
(opt) optics—ottica
(orn) ornithology—ornitologia
(painting) pittura
(pathol) pathology—patologia
(pej) pejorative—peggiorativo
perf perfect—perfetto, passato
pers personal—personale; person—persona
(pharm) pharmacy—farmacia
(philately) filatelia
(philol) philology—filologia
(philos) philosophy—filosofia
(phonet) phonetics—fonetica
(phot) photography—fotografia
(phys) physics—fisica
(physiol) physiology—fisiologia
pl plural—plurale
(poet) poetical—poetico
(poker) poker
(pol) politics—politica
pp past participle—participio passato
poss possessive—possessivo
pref prefix—prefisso
prep preposition—preposizione

prep phrase prepositional phrase—frase preposizionale
pres present—presente
pret preterit—passato remoto
pron pronoun—pronome
(pros) prosody—prosodia
(psychoanal) psychoanalysis—psicanalisi
(psychol) psychology—psicologia
(psychopath) psychopathology—psicopatologia
qlco or *qlco* qualcosa—something
qlcu or *qlcu* qualcuno—someone
(racing) corse
(rad) radio—radio
ref reflexive verb—verbo riflessivo o pronominale
rel relative—relativo
(rel) religion—religione
(rhet) rhetoric—retorica
(rok) rocketry—studio dei razzi
(rowing) canottaggio
(rr) railroad—ferrovia
(rugby) rugby
s substantive—sostantivo
(scornful) sprezzante
(Scot) Scottish—scozzese
(sculp) sculpture—scultura
(sew) sewing—cucito
sg singular—singolare
(slang) gergo
s.o. or *s.o.* someone—qualcuno
(soccer) calcio
spl substantive plural—sostantivo plurale
(sports) sport
ssg substantive singular—sostantivo singolare
s.th or *s.th* something—qualcosa
subj subjunctive—congiuntivo
suf suffix—suffisso
super superlative—superlativo
(surg) surgery—chirurgia
(surv) surveying—agrimensura, topografia
(taur) bullfighting—tauromachia
(telg) telegraphy—telegrafia
(telp) telephone—telefonia
(telv) television—televisione
(tennis) tennis
(tex) textile—tessile
(theat) theater—teatro
(theol) theology—teologia
tr transitive verb—verbo transitivo
(trademark) marchio di fabbrica
(typ) printing—tipografia
(U.S.A.) S.U.A.
v verb—verbo
var variant—variante
(vet) veterinary medicine—medicina veterinaria
(vulg) vulgar—volgare, ordinario
(wrestling) lotta
(zool) zoology—zoologia

PART ONE

Italian-English

Italian Spelling and Pronunciation

§1. The Italian Alphabet. 1. The twenty-one letters of the Italian alphabet are listed below with their names and their sounds in terms of approximate equivalent English sounds. Their gender is masculine or feminine.

LETTER	NAME	APPROXIMATE SOUND
a	a	Like *a* in English *father*, e.g., **facile, padre.**
b	bi	Like *b* in English *boat*, e.g., **bello, abate.**
c	ci	When followed by **e** or **i**, like *ch* in English *cherry*, e.g., **cento, cinque;** if the **i** is unstressed and followed by another vowel, its sound is not heard, e.g., **ciarla, cieco.** When followed by **a, o, u,** or a consonant, like *c* in English *cook*, e.g., **casa, come, cura, credere.** The digraph **ch,** which is used before **e** and **i,** has likewise the sound of *c* in English *cook*, e.g., **chiesa, perché.**
d	di	Like *d* in English *dance*, e.g., **dare, madre.**
e	e	Has two sounds. One like *a* in English *make*, shown on stressed syllables in this DICTIONARY by the acute accent, e.g., **séra, trénta;** and one like *e* in English *met*, shown on stressed syllables in this DICTIONARY by the grave accent, e.g., **fèrro, fèsta.**
f	effe	Like *f* in English *fool*, e.g., **farina, efelide.**
g	gi	When followed by **e** or **i**, like *g* in English *general*, e.g., **gelato, ginnasta;** if the **i** is unstressed and followed by another vowel, its sound is not heard, e.g., **giallo, giorno.** When followed by **a, o, u,** or a consonant, like *g* in English *go*, e.g., **gamba, goccia, gusto, grado.** The digraph **gh,** which is used before **e** and **i,** has likewise the sound of *g* in English *go*, e.g., **gherone, ghisa.** When the combination **gli** (a) is a form of the definite article or the personal pronoun, (b) is final in a word, or (c) is intervocalic, it has the sound of Castilian *ll*, which is somewhat like *lli* in English *million*, e.g., (a) **gli uomini, gli ho parlato ieri,** (b) **battagli,** (c) **figlio, migliore.** When it is (a) initial in the word **gli,** above), (b) preceded by a consonant, or (c) followed by a consonant, it is pronounced like *gli* in English *negligence*, e.g., (a) **glioma,** (b) **ganglio,** (c) **negligenza.** The combination **gl** followed by **a, e, o,** or **u** is pronounced like *gl* in English *globe*, e.g., **glabro, gleba, globo, gluteo, inglese, poliglotto.** The digraph **gn** has the sound of Castilian *ñ*, which is somewhat like *ni* in English *onion*, e.g., **signore, gnocco.**
h	acca	Always silent, e.g., **ah, hanno.** See **ch** under **c** above and **gh** under **g** above.
i	i	Like *i* in English *machine*, e.g., **piccolo, sigla.** When unstressed and followed by another vowel, like *y* in English *yes*, e.g., **piatto, piede, fiore, flume.** For **i** in **ci,** see **c** above, in **gi,** see **g** above, and in **sci,** see **s** below.

3

LETTER	NAME	APPROXIMATE SOUND
l	elle	Like *l* in English *lamb*, e.g., **labbro, lacrima.**
m	emme	Like *m* in English *money*, e.g., **mano, come.**
n	enne	Like *n* in English *net*, e.g., **nome, cane.**
o	o	Has two sounds. One like *o* in English *note*, shown on stressed syllables in this DICTIONARY by the acute accent, e.g., **dópo, sóle;** and one like *ou* in English *ought*, shown on stressed syllables in this DICTIONARY by the grave accent, e.g., **còsa, dònna.**
p	pi	Like *p* in English *pot*, e.g., **passo, carpa.**
q	cu	This letter is always followed by the letter **u** and the combination has the sound of *qu* in English *quart*, e.g., **quanto, questo.**
r	erre	Like *r* in English *rubber*, with a slight trill, e.g., **roba, carta.**
s	esse	Has two sounds. When initial and followed by a vowel, when preceded by a consonant and followed by a vowel, and when followed by **c** [k] **f, p, q,** or **t,** like *s* in English *see*, e.g., **sale, falso, scappare, spazio, stoffa;** and when standing between two vowels and when followed by **b, d, g** [g], **l, m, n, r** or **v,** like *z* in English *zero*, e.g., **paese, sbaglio, svenire.** However, **s** standing between two vowels in some words and initial **s** followed by **b, d, g** [g], **l, m, n, r,** or **v** in some foreign borrowings are pronounced like *s* in *see*, e.g., **casa*, tesa, smoking, slam.** In this DICTIONARY this is indicated by the insertion of [s] immediately after the entry word. However, when initial **s** stands between two vowels in a compound, its pronunciation remains that of initial **s,** e.g., **autoservizio** and this is not indicated. The digraph **sc,** when followed by **e** or **i** has the sound of *sh* in English *shall*, e.g., **scelta, scimmia;** if the **i** is unstressed and followed by another vowel, its sound is not heard, e.g., **sciame, sciopero.** The trigraph **sch** has the sound of *sc* in English *scope*, e.g., **scherzo, schiavo.**
t	ti	Like *t* in English *table*, e.g., **terra, pasto.**
u	u	Like *u* in English *rule*, e.g., **luna, mulo.** When followed by a vowel, like *w* in English *was*, e.g., **quanto, guerra, nuovo.**
v	vu	Like *v* in English *vain*, e.g., **vita, uva.**
z	zeta	Has two sounds. One like *ts* in English *nuts*, e.g., **grazia, zucchero;** and one like *dz* in English *adze*, e.g., **zero, mezzo.** In this DICTIONARY the sound of *dz* in *adze* is indicated by the insertion of [dz] immediately after the entry word. If the sound is long, [ddzz] is inserted

* Intervocalic **s** is generally voiced in the north of Italy.

2. The following five letters are found in borrowings from other languages.

LETTER	NAME	EXAMPLES
j	i lunga	**jazz, jingo**
k	cappa	**kiosco, kodak**
w	doppia vu	**water-polo, whisky**
x	ics	**xenofobo, xilofono**
y	ìpsilon	**yacht, yoghurt**

3. Consonants written double are longer than consonants written single, that is, it takes a longer time to pronounce them, e.g., **camino** *chimney* and **cam-**

mino *road*, **capello** *hair* and **cappello** *hat*. Special attention is called to the following double consonants: **cc** followed by **e** or **i** has the sound of **ch ch** in English *beach chair*, that is, a lengthened **ch** (not the sound of **ks**), e.g., **accento**; **cch** has the sound of **kk** in English *bookkeeper*, e.g., **becchino**; **cq** has the sound of **kk** in English *bookkeeper*, e.g., **acqua**; **gg** followed by **e** or **i** has the sound of **ge j** in English *carriage joiner*, e.g., **peggio**; **ggh** has the sound of **g g** in English *tag game*, e.g., **agghindare**.

§2. Division of Syllables. In the application of the following rules for the syllabic division of words, the digraphs **ch, gh, gl, gn,** and **sc** count as single consonants.

(a) When a single consonant stands between two vowels it belongs to the following syllable, e.g., **ca·sa, fu·mo, ami·che, la·ghi, fi·glio, biso·gno, la·sciare.**

(b) When a consonant group consisting of two consonants of which the second is **l** or **r** stands between two vowels, the group belongs to the following syllable, e.g., **nu·cleo, so·brio, qua·dro.**

(c) When a consonant group consisting of two or more consonants of which the first or the second is **s** stands between two vowels, that part of the group beginning with **s** belongs to the following syllable, e.g., **ta·sca, bo·schi, fine·stra, super·sti·zione, sub·strato.**

(d) When a consonant group consisting of two or three consonants of which the first is **l, m, n,** or **r** stands between two vowels, the **l, m, n,** or **r** belongs to the preceding syllable, the other consonant or consonants to the following syllable, e.g., **al·bero, am·pio, prin·cipe, mor·te, in·flazione, com·pleto.**

(e) When a double consonant stands between two vowels or between a vowel and **l** or **r**, the first belongs to the preceding syllable, the second to the following syllable, e.g., **bab·bo, caval·lo, an·no, car·ro, mez·zo, sup·plica, lab·bro, quat·tro.**

§3. Stress and Accent Marks. 1. Whenever stress is shown as part of regular spelling, it is shown on **a, i,** and **u** by the grave accent mark, e.g., **libertà, giovedì, gioventù,** on close **e** and **o** by the acute accent mark, e.g., **perché,** and on open **e** and **o** by the grave accent mark, e.g., **caffè, parlò.** This occurs (a) in words ending in a stressed vowel, as in the above examples, (b) in stressed monosyllables in which the vocalic element is a diphthong of which the first letter is unstressed **i** or **u**, e.g., **già, più, può,** and (c) on the stressed monosyllable of any pair of monosyllables of which one is stressed and the other unstressed, in order to distinguish one from the other, e.g., **dà** *he gives* and **da** *from*, **è** *is* and **e** *and*, **sé** *himself* and **se** *if*, **sì** *yes* and **si** *himself*.

2. Whenever stress is not shown as part of regular spelling, it is often difficult to determine where it falls.

(a) In words of two syllables, the stress falls on the syllable next to the last, e.g., **ca'sa, mu'ro, ter'ra.** If the syllable next to the last contains a diphthong, that is, a combination of a strong vowel (**a, e,** or **o**) and a weak vowel (**i** or **u**), the strong vowel is stressed, regardless of which vowel comes first, e.g., **da'ino, ero'ico, ne'utro, fia'to, dua'le, sie'pe, fio're, buo'no.**

(b) In words of more than two syllables, the stress may fall on the syllable next to the last, e.g., **anda'ta, canzo'ne, pasto're** or on a preceding syllable, e.g., **fis'sile, gon'dola, man'dorla.** In these positions also the stressed syllable may contain a diphthong, e.g., **inca'uto, idra'ulico, fio'cina.**

(c) If a weak vowel in juxtaposition with a strong vowel is stressed, the two vowels constitute two separate syllables, e.g., **abba·i'no, ero·i'na, pa·u'ra, miri'ade, vi'a.**

(d) Two strong vowels in juxtaposition constitute two separate syllables, e.g., **pa·e'se, aure'ola, ide'a, oce'ano.**

(e) Two weak vowels in juxtaposition generally constitute a diphthong in which the first vowel is stressed in some words, e.g., **flu'ido** and the second vowel in others, e.g., **piu'ma.**

(f) If a word ends in a diphthong, the diphthong is stressed, e.g., **marina'i, parla'i, ero'i.**

3. In this DICTIONARY, stress is understood or shown on all words that do not bear an accent mark as part of regular spelling according to the following principles. In the application of these principles, individual vowels and not diphthongs are counted as units. In some words in which it is not necessary to show stress, an accent mark is used to show the quality of the stressed vowels **e** and **o**.

As in regular Italian spelling, stress is shown on **a, i,** and **u** by the grave accent mark, on close **e** and **o** by the acute accent mark, and on open **e** and **o** by the grave accent mark.

(a) It is understood that in words of more than one syllable in which no accent mark is shown, the stress falls on the vowel next to the last, e.g., **casa,**

5

fiato, duale, abbaino, paura. In such words as sièpe, fióre, buòno, paése, fluènte, eròe, nói, pòi, the accent mark is used to show the quality of the vowel.

(b) An accent mark is placed on the stressed vowel if the word is stressed on the third vowel from the end, e.g., mùsica, sìmbolo, dàino, incàuto, marinàio, contìnuo, infànzia. If this vowel is e or o, the acute or grave accent mark must correspond to the quality of the vowel, e.g., fiòcina, rómpere, nèutro, eròico, assèdio, filatóio.

(c) Contrary to the above-mentioned principle of counting vowels, an accent mark is placed on the strong vowel of a final diphthong, e.g., marinài, assài.

(d) Contrary to the above-mentioned principle of counting vowels, an accent mark is placed on the i of final ia, ie, ii, and io, e.g., farmacìa, scìa, farmacìe, mormorìi, gorgoglìo, fìo.

(e) An accent mark is placed on some borrowings ending in a consonant, e.g., hàrem, revòlver.

(f) The loss of the last vowel or last syllable of a word does not alter the position of the stress of the word, e.g., la maggior parte, in alcun modo, fan bene.

§4. The Definite Article and Combinations with Prepositions.

		MASC BEFORE CONSONANT	MASC BEFORE S IMPURE OR Z[1]	MASC BEFORE VOWEL	FEM BEFORE CONSONANT	FEM BEFORE VOWEL
	SG	il	lo	l'	la	l'
	PL	i	gli	gli[2]	le	le[3]
WITH a	SG	al	allo	all'	alla	all'
	PL	ai	agli	agli[2]	alle	alle[3]
WITH di	SG	del	dello	dell'	dell'	dell'
	PL	dei	degli	degli[2]	delle	delle[3]
WITH con	SG	col	collo	coll'	colla	coll'
	PL	coi	cogli	cogli[2]	colle	colle[3]
WITH da	SG	dal	dallo	dall'	dalla	dall'
	PL	dai	dagli	dagli[2]	dalle	dalle[3]
WITH in	SG	nel	nello	nell'	nella	nell'
	PL	nei	negli	negli[2]	nelle	nelle[3]
WITH su	SG	sul	sullo	sull'	sulla	sull'
	PL	sui	sugli	sugli[2]	sulle	sulle[3]

[1] Other letters and groups of letters, which occur in a few words, are gn, pn, ps, sc, x, and i before a vowel, sometimes spelled j or y.

[2] These forms may drop the i before words beginning with i, e.g., gl'inglesi.

[3] The e of these forms is not elided, e.g., le erbe.

7

§5. Personal and Reflexive Pronouns.

PERSONS	SUBJECT	PERSONAL DIRECT OBJECT	PERSONAL INDIRECT OBJECT	REFLEX. & RECIPROCAL DIRECT & INDIRECT OBJECT	PERSONAL PREPOSITIONAL OBJECT	REFLEX. & RECIPROCAL PREPOSITIONAL OBJECT
SG						
1	io *I*	mi *me*	mi *to me*	mi *myself; to myself*	me *me*	me *myself*
2	tu *you*	ti *you*	ti *to you*	ti *yourself; to yourself*	te *you*	te *yourself*
3 MASC	egli, lui *he*	lo *him or it*	gli *to him*	si *himself; to himself*	lui *him*	sé *himself*
3 FEM	lei, essa *she*	la *her or it*	le *to her*	si *herself; to herself*	lei, essa *her*	sé *herself*
2 FORMAL	Lei *you*	La *you*	Le *to you*	si *yourself; to yourself*	Lei *you*	sé *yourself*
PL						
1	noi *we*	ci *us*	ci *to us*	ci *ourselves; to ourselves; each other; to each other*	noi *us*	noi *ourselves; each other*
2	voi *you*	vi *you*	vi *to you*	vi *yourself; yourselves; to yourself; to yourselves; each other; to each other*	voi *you*	voi *yourself; yourselves; each other*
3 MASC	loro, essi *they*	li *them*	loro *to them*	si *themselves; to themselves; each other; to each other*	loro, essi *them*	sé *themselves; each other*
3 FEM	loro, esse *they*	le *them*	loro *to them*	si *themselves; to themselves; each other; to each other*	loro, esse *them*	sé *themselves; each other*
2 FORMAL	Loro *you*	Li } *you* Le }	Loro *to you*	si *yourselves; to yourselves; each other; to each other*	Loro *you*	sé *yourselves; each other*

ci and **vi** both mean also *here, there, to it, in it, to them, in them, about it.*
ne means *of, from, or with him, her, it, them; some, any; from here, from there, thence, about it.*

meco *with me,* **teco** *with you,* and **seco** *with him, with himself; with her, with herself; with you, with yourself, with yourselves; with them, with themselves; with each other* may be used instead of **con me, con te,** and **con sé** respectively.

8

COMBINATION OF DIRECT AND INDIRECT OBJECT

PERSONS	
1 SG & 3 SG	me lo / me la } *him, her, it to me*
1 SG & 3 PL	me li / me le } *them to me*
2 SG & 3 SG	te lo / te la } *him, her, it to you*
2 SG & 3 PL	te li / te le } *them to you*
3 SG & 3 SG	glielo / gliela } *him, her, it to him / him, her, it to her*
3 SG & 3 PL	glieli / gliele } *them to him / them to her*
2 SG FORMAL & 3 SG	Glielo / Gliela } *him, her, it to you*
2 SG FORMAL & 3 PL	Glieli / Gliele } *them to you*

PERSONS	
1 PL & 3 SG	ce lo / ce la } *him, her, it to us*
1 PL & 3 PL	ce li / ce le } *them to us*
2 PL & 3 SG	ve lo / ve la } *him, her, it to you*
2 PL & 3 PL	ve li / ve le } *them to you*
3 SG & 3 PL	lo / la } VERB loro *him, her, it to them*
3 PL & 3 PL	li / le } VERB loro *them to them*
3 SG & 2 PL FORMAL	lo / la } VERB Loro *him, her, it to you*
3 PL & 2 PL FORMAL	li / le } VERB Loro *them to you*

The form **si** (third singular and plural reflexive and reciprocal indirect object) changes to **se** before one of the direct objects **lo, la, li,** and **le,** and before **ne,** e.g., **se lo mette** he puts it on; **se n'è andato** he went away.

In combinations, **ne** occupies the same position as **lo, la, li,** and **le,** e.g., **me ne,** and forms one word with **gli,** namely, **gliene.**

9

§6 Possessive Adjectives and Pronouns

PERSON, NUMBER & SEX OF POSSESSOR	GENDER & NUMBER OF POSSESSIVE ADJECTIVE OR PRONOUN ACCORDING TO THE GENDER & NUMBER OF THE PERSON OR THING POSSESSED				MEANING OF ADJECTIVE	MEANING OF PRONOUN
	MSG	MPL	FSG	FPL		
SG						
1	il mio	i miei	la mia	le mie	my	mine
2	il tuo	i tuoi	la tua	le tue	your	yours
3 MASC	il suo	i suoi	la sua	le sue	his	his
3 FEM	il suo	i suoi	la sua	le sue	her	hers
3 NEUT	il suo	i suoi	la sua	le sue	its	its
2 FORMAL	il Suo	i Suoi	la Sua	le Sue	your	yours
PL						
1	il nostro	i nostri	la nostra	le nostre	our	ours
2	il vostro	i vostri	la vostra	le vostre	your	yours
3	il loro	i loro	la loro	le loro	their	theirs
2 FORMAL	il Loro	i Loro	la Loro	le Loro	your	yours

The definite article, shown here, is not generally used (a) in direct address, e.g., mio caro amico *my dear friend*, (b) after the verb essere, e.g., la casa è nostra *the house is ours*, and (c) when a singular form modifies the name of a relative, e.g., sua sorella *his sister*.

With forms of the indefinite article, the possessive adjective, whether standing before or after the noun, is translated by *of*

plus the possessive pronoun, e.g., un amico mio *a friend of mine*; una sua zia *an aunt of his* (or *of hers*).

The forms of the possessive pronouns also have the force of nouns, e.g., Il mio *my property, my belongings*; I suoi *his people, relatives, followers, troops, retinue*, etc.; la mia *my letter*; la sua *his opinion*.

§7. The Demonstrative Adjective.

	MASC	MASC	MASC	FEM	FEM
	BEFORE CONSONANT	BEFORE S IMPURE OR z (see note 1, p. 7)	BEFORE VOWEL	BEFORE CONSONANT	BEFORE VOWEL
SG	quel *that*	quello	quell'	quella	quell'
PL	quei *those*	quegli	quegli	quelle	quelle
SG	questo *this*	questo	questo or quest'	questa	questa or quest'
PL	questi *these*	questi	questi	queste	queste

11

§8. The Demonstrative Pronoun.

	MASC	FEM	MASC
SG	**quello** *that one*	**quella**	**quegli** *that one;*
PL	**quelli** *those*	**quelle**	*the former*
SG	**questo** *this one*	**questa**	**questi** *this one;*
PL	**questi** *these*	**queste**	*the latter*

The demonstrative pronoun **quello** is often followed by **che, di,** or **da** and the masculine singular form may be shortened to **quel** before these words.

SG	**colui** *that one*	**colei**
PL	**coloro** *those*	**coloro**
SG	**costui** *this one*	**costei**
PL	**costoro** *these*	**costoro**

code·sto -sta -sti -ste and **cote·sto -sta -sti -ste** are demonstrative adjectives and demonstrative pronouns and mean *that (of yours).*

§9. Indefinite Article and Numeral Adjective.

MASC BEFORE CONSONANT	MASC BEFORE **s** IMPURE OR **z** (see note 1, p. 7)	MASC BEFORE VOWEL	FEM BEFORE CONSONANT	FEM BEFORE VOWEL
un *a, an; one*	uno	un	una	un'

13

§10. Indefinite Pronoun uno.

MASC	FEM
uno *one*	una

§11. Correlative Indefinite Pronoun.

	MASC	FEM
SG	l'uno . . . l'altro *one . . . the other*	l'una . . . l'altra
PL	gli uni . . . gli altri *some . . . the others*	le une . . . le altre

§12. Reciprocal Indefinite Pronoun.

	MASC	FEM
SG	l'un l'altro *each other, one another*	l'una l'altra
PL	gli uni gli altri	le une le altre

Table of Regular Endings of Italian Verbs

The stem to which the endings of the gerund, past participle, present participle, imperative, present indicative, present subjunctive, imperfect indicative, preterit indicative, and imperfect subjunctive are attached is obtained by dropping the ending of the infinitive, viz., -are, -ere, -ire.

The stem to which the endings of the future indicative and present conditional are attached is obtained by dropping the -e of the ending of the infinitive of all conjugations and changing the a of the ending of the infinitive of the first conjugation to e.

The letters before the names of some of the tenses of this table correspond to the designation of the tenses shown on the following page.

Letters printed in italics have a written accent that is not part of the regular spelling.

TENSE	FIRST CONJUGATION	SECOND CONJUGATION	THIRD CONJUGATION
inf	-are	-ére (or -ere)	-ire
ger	-ando	-èndo	-èndo
pp	-ato	-uto	-ito
pres part	-ante	-ènte	-ènte
(a) *impv*	-a -ate	-i -éte	-i -ite
(b) *pres ind*	-o -i -a -iamo -ate -ano	-o -i -e -iamo -éte -ono	-o -i -e -iamo -ite -ono
(c) *pres subj*	-i -i -i -iamo -iate -ino	-a -a -a -iamo -iate -ano	-a -a -a -iamo -iate -ano
(d) *imperf ind*	-avo -avi -ava -avamo -avate -àvano	-évo -évi -éva -evamo -evate -évano	-ivo -ivi -iva -ivamo -ivate -ìvano
(e) *pret ind*	-ài -asti -ò -ammo -aste -àrono	-éi -ésti -è -émmo -éste -érono	-ìi -isti -ì -immo -iste -ìrono
imperf subj	-assi -assi -asse -àssimo -aste -àssero	-éssi -éssi -ésse -éssimo -éste -éssero	-issi -issi -isse -ìssimo -iste -ìssero
(f) *fut ind*	-er-ò -er-ài -er-à -er-émo -er-éte -er-anno	-ò -ài -à -émo -éte -anno	-ò -ài -à -émo -éte -anno

TENSE	FIRST CONJUGATION	SECOND CONJUGATION	THIRD CONJUGATION
pres cond	-er-èi	-èi	-èi
	-er-ésti	-ésti	-ésti
	-er-èbbe	-èbbe	-èbbe
	-er-émmo	-émmo	-émmo
	-er-éste	-éste	-éste
	-er-èbbero	-èbbero	-èbbero

MODEL VERBS
ORDER OF TENSES

(a) imperative
(b) present indicative
(c) present subjunctive

(d) imperfect indicative
(e) preterit indicative
(f) future indicative

In addition to the infinitive, gerund, and past participle, which are shown in line one of these tables, all simple tenses are shown if they contain at least one irregular form, except (1) the present conditional, which is always formed on the stem of the future indicative, (2) the imperfect subjunctive, which is always formed on the stem of the *2nd sg* of the preterit indicative, and (3) the present participle, which is generally formed by changing the final -do of the gerund to -te (exceptions being shown in parentheses after the gerund).

Letters printed in italics have a written accent that is not part of the regular spelling.

§100 **ACCÈDERE**—accedèndo—acceduto
   (e) accedètti *or* accedéi *or* accèssi; accedésti; accedètte *or* accedé *or* accèsse; accedémmo; accedéste; accedèttero *or* accedérono *or* accèssero

§101 **ACCÈNDERE**—accendèndo—accéso
   (e) accési, accendésti, accése, accendémmo, accendéste, accésero

§102 **ADDURRE**—adducèndo—addótto
   (b) adduco, adduci, adduce, adduciamo, adducéte, addùcono
   (c) adduca, adduca, adduca, adduciamo, adduciate, addùcano
   (d) adducévo, adducévi, adducéva, adducevamo, adducevate, adducévano
   (e) addussi, adducésti, addusse, adducémmo, adducéste, addùssero

§103 **AFFÌGGERE**—affiggèndo—affisso
   (e) affissi, affiggésti, affisse, affiggémmo, affiggéste, affìssero

§104 AFFLÌGGERE—affliggèndo—afflitto
(e) afflissi, affliggésti, afflisse, affliggémmo, affliggéste, afflìssero

§105 ALLÙDERE—alludèndo—alluso
(e) allusi, alludésti, alluse, alludémmo, alludéste, allùsero

§106 ANDARE—andando—andato
(a) va *or* va' *or* vai, andate
(b) *vò or* vado, vai, va, andiamo, andate, vanno
(c) vada, vada, vada, andiamo, andiate, vàdano
(f) andrò, andrài, andrà, andrémo, andréte, andranno

§107 ANNÈTTERE—annettèndo—annèsso *or* **annéttere,** annetténdo, annésso
(e) annettéi *or* annèssi *or* annéssi; annettésti; annetté *or* annèsse *or* annésse; annettémmo; annettéste; annettérono *or* annèssero *or* annéssero

§108 APPARIRE—apparèndo—apparso
(a) apparisci *or* appari; apparite
(b) apparisco *or* appàio; apparisci *or* appari; apparisce *or* appare; appariamo; apparite; apparìscono *or* appàiono
(c) apparisca *or* appàia; apparisca *or* appàia; apparisca *or* appàia; appariamo; appariate; apparìscano *or* appàiano
(e) apparvi *or* apparìi *or* apparsi; apparisti; apparve *or* apparì *or* apparse; apparimmo; appariste; appàrvero *or* apparìrono *or* appàrsero

§109 APPÈNDERE—appendèndo—appéso
(e) appési, appendésti, appése, appendémmo, appendéste, appésero

§110 APRIRE—aprèndo—apèrto
(e) aprìi *or* apèrsi; apristi; aprì *or* apèrse; aprimmo; apriste; aprìrono *or* apèrsero

§111 ÀRDERE—ardèndo—arso
(e) arsi, ardésti, arse, ardémmo, ardéste, àrsero

§112 ASPÈRGERE—aspergèndo—aspèrso
(e) aspèrsi, aspergésti, aspèrse, aspergémmo, aspergéste, aspèrsero

§113 ASSÌDERE—assidèndo—assiso
(e) assisi, assidésti, assise, assidémmo, assidéste, assìsero

§114 ASSÌSTERE—assistèndo—assistito
(e) assistéi *or* assistètti; assistésti; assisté *or* assistètte; assistémmo; assistéste; assistérono *or* assistèttero

§115 ASSÒLVERE—assolvèndo—assòlto *or* assoluto
(e) assolvéi *or* assolvètti *or* assòlsi; assolvésti; assolvé *or* assolvètte *or* assòlse; assolvémmo; assolvéste; assolvérono *or* assolvèttero *or* assòlsero

§116 ASSÙMERE—assumèndo—assunto
(e) assunsi, assumésti, assunse, assumémmo, assuméste, assùnsero

§117 ASSÙRGERE—assurgèndo—assurto
(e) assursi, assurgésti, assurse, assurgémmo, assurgéste, assùrsero

§118 AVÈRE—avèndo—avuto
(a) abbi, abbiate
(b) ho, hai, ha, abbiamo, avete, hanno
(c) *a*bbia, *a*bbia, *a*bbia, abbiamo, abbiate, *a*bbiano
(e) *è*bbi, avésti, *è*bbe, avémmo, avéste, *è*bbero
(f) avrò, avr*a*i, avrà, avrémo, avréte, avranno

§119 AVVIARE—avviando—avviato
(b) avvìo, avvìi, avvìa, avviamo, avviate, avvìano
(c) avvìi, avvìi, avvìi, avviamo, avviate, avvìino

§120 BÉRE—bevèndo—bevuto
(a) bévi, bevéte
(b) bévo, bévi, béve, beviamo, bevéte, bévono
(c) béva, béva, béva, beviamo, beviate, bévano
(d) bevévo, bevévi, bevéva, bevevamo, bevevate, bevévano
(e) bévvi *or* bevéi *or* bevètti; bevésti, bévve *or* bevé *or* bevètte; bevémmo; bevéste; bévvero *or* bevérono *or* bevèttero
(f) berrò, berr*a*i, berrà, berrémo, berréte, berranno

§121 CADÉRE—cadèndo—caduto
(e) caddi, cadésti, cadde, cadémmo, cadéste, c*a*ddero
(f) cadrò, cadr*a*i, cadrà, cadrémo, cadréte, cadranno

§122 CECARE—cecando—cecato
(a) cièca *or* cèca; cecate
(b) cièco *or* cèco; cièchi *or* cèchi; cièca *or* cèca; cechiamo; cecate; ciècano *or* cècano
(c) cièchi *or* cèchi; cièchi *or* cèchi; cièchi *or* cèchi; cechiamo; cechiate; cièchino *or* cèchino
(f) cecherò, cecher*a*i, cecherà, cecherémo, cecheréte, cecheranno

§123 CÈDERE—cedèndo—ceduto
(e) cedéi *or* cedètti; cedésti; cedé *or* cedètte; cedémmo; cedéste; cedérono *or* cedèttero

19

§124 CHIÈDERE—chiedèndo—chièsto
(e) chièsi, chiedésti, chièse, chiedémmo, chiedéste, chièsero

§125 CHIÙDERE—chiudèndo—chiuso
(e) chiusi, chiudésti, chiuse, chiudémmo, chiudéste, chiùsero

§126 CÌNGERE—cingèndo—cinto
(e) cinsi, cingésti, cinse, cingémmo, cingéste, cìnsero

§127 CÒGLIERE—coglièndo—còlto
(a) cògli, cogliéte
(b) còlgo, cògli, còglie, cogliamo, cogliéte, còlgono
(c) còlga, còlga, còlga, cogliamo, cogliate, còlgano
(e) còlsi, cogliésti, còlse, cogliémmo, cogliéste, còlsero

§128 COMINCIARE—cominciando—cominciato
(b) comìncio, cominci, comìncia, cominciamo, cominciate, comìnciano
(c) cominci, cominci, cominci, cominciamo, cominciate, comìncino
(f) comincerò, comincerài, comincerà, comincerémo, cominceréte, cominceranno

§129 COMPÈTERE—competèndo—*pp* missing

§130 CÒMPIERE—compièndo—compiuto
(a) cómpi, compite
(b) cómpio, cómpi, cómpie, compiamo, compite, cómpiono
(c) cómpia, cómpia, cómpia, compiamo, compiate, cómpiano
(d) compivo, compivi, compiva, compivamo, compivate, compìvano
(e) compiéi *or* compìi; compiésti *or* compisti; compié *or* compì; compiémmo *or* compimmo; compiéste *or* compiste; compiérono *or* compìrono

§131 COMPRÌMERE—comprimèndo—comprèsso
(e) comprèssi, comprimésti, comprèsse, compримémmo, compriméste, comprèssero

§132 CONCÈDERE—concedèndo—concèsso
(e) concedéi *or* concèssi *or* concedètti; concedésti; concedé *or* concèsse *or* concedètte; concedémmo; concedéste; concedérono *or* concèssero *or* concedèttero

§133 CONCÈRNERE—concernèndo—*pp* missing
(e) concernéi *or* concernètti; concernésti; concerné *or* concernètte; concernémmo; concernéste; concernérono *or* concernèttero

20

§134 CONÓSCERE—conoscèndo—conosciuto
   (e) conóbbi, conoscésti, conóbbe, conoscémmo, conoscéste, conóbbero

§135 CONQUÌDERE—conquidèndo—conquiso
   (e) conquisi, conquidésti, conquise, conquidémmo, conquidéste, conquìsero

§136 CONSÙMERE—*ger* missing—consunto
   (a) missing
   (b) missing
   (c) missing
   (d) missing
   (e) consunsi, consunse, consùnsero
   (f) missing

§137 CONVÈRGERE—convergèndo—convèrso
   (e) convèrsi *or* convergéi; convergésti; convèrse *or* convergé; convergémmo; convergéste; convèrsero *or* convergérono

§138 CONVERTIRE—convertèndo—convertito
   (e) convertìi *or* convèrsi; convertisti; convertì or convèrse; convertimmo; convertiste; convertìrono *or* convèrsero

§139 CÓRRERE—corrèndo—córso
   (e) córsi, corrésti, córse, corrémmo, corréste, córsero

§140 COSTRUIRE—costruèndo—costruito
   (a) costruisci, costruite
   (b) costruisco, costruisci, costruisce, costruiamo, costruite, costruìscono
   (c) costruisca, costruisca, costruisca, costruiamo, costruiate, costruìscano
   (e) costruìi *or* costrussi; costruisti; costruì *or* costrusse; costruimmo; costruiste; costruìrono *or* costrùssero

§141 CRÉDERE—credèndo—creduto
   (e) credéi *or* credètti; credésti; credé *or* credètte; credémmo; credéste; credérono *or* credèttero

§142 CRÉSCERE—crescèndo—cresciuto
   (e) crébbi, crescésti, crébbe, crescémmo, crescéste, crébbero

§143 CUCIRE—cucèndo—cucito
   (b) cùcio, cuci, cuce, cuciamo, cucite, cùciono
   (c) cùcia, cùcia, cùcia, cuciamo, cuciate, cùciano

§144a CUÒCERE—cuocèndo *or* cocèndo (cocènte)—còtto *or* cociuto

    (a) cuòci, cocéte
    (b) cuòcio, cuòci, cuòce, cociamo, cocéte, cuòciono
    (c) cuòcia, cuòcia, cuòcia, cociamo, cociate, cuòciano
    (d) cocévo, cocévi, cocéva, cocevamo, cocevate, cocévano
    (e) còssi, cocésti, còsse, cocémmo, cocéste, còssero
    (f) cocerò, cocerài, cocerà, cocerémo, coceréte, coceranno

§144b DARE—dando—dato
    (a) dà *or* dài *or* da'; date
    (b) dò *or* dò; dài; dà; diamo; date; danno
    (c) dìa, dìa, dìa, diamo, diate, dìano
    (e) dièdi *or* dètti; désti; diède *or* dètte *or* diè; démmo;
        déste; dièdero *or* dèttero
    (f) darò, darài, darà, darémo, daréte, daranno

§145 DECÌDERE—decidèndo—deciso
    (e) decisi, decidésti, decise, decidémmo, decidéste, decìsero

§146 DELÌNQUERE—delinquèndo—*pp* missing
    (a) missing
    (c) missing
    (e) missing

§147 DEVÒLVERE—devolvèndo—devoluto
    (e) devolvéi *or* devolvètti; devolvésti; devolvé *or* devolvètte;.
        devolvémmo; devolvéste; devolvérono *or* devolvèttero

§148 DIFÈNDERE—difendèndo—diféso
    (e) difési, difendésti, difése, difendémmo, difendéste,
        difésero

§149 DILÌGERE—diligèndo—dilètto
    (a) missing
    (b) missing
    (c) missing
    (d) missing
    (e) dilèssi, diligésti, dilèsse, diligémmo, diligéste, dilèssero
    (f) missing

§150 DIPÈNDERE—dipendèndo—dipéso
    (e) dipési, dipendésti, dipése, dipendémmo, dipendéste,
        dipésero

§151 DIRE—dicèndo—détto
    (a) di' *or* dì; dite
    (b) dico, dici, dice, diciamo, dite, dìcono
    (c) dica, dica, dica, diciamo, diciate, dìcano
    (d) dicévo, dicévi, dicéva, dicevamo, dicevate, dicévano
    (e) dissi, dicésti, disse, dicémmo, dicéste, dìssero
    (f) dirò, dirài, dirà, dirémo, diréte, diranno

§152 DIRÌGERE—dirigèndo—dirètto
(e) dirèssi, dirigésti, dirèsse, dirigémmo, dirigéste, dirèssero

§153 DISCÈRNERE—discernèndo—*pp* missing
(e) discernéi; discernésti; discerné *or* discernètte; discernémmo; discernéste; discernérono *or* discernèttero

§154 DISCÙTERE—discutèndo—discusso
(e) discussi, discutésti, discusse, discutémmo, discutéste, discùssero

§155 DISSÒLVERE—dissolvèndo—dissòlto
(e) dissòlsi *or* dissolvéi *or* dissolvètti; dissolvésti; dissòlse *or* dissolvé *or* dissolvètte; dissolvémmo; dissolvéste; dissòlsero *or* dissolvérono *or* dissolvèttero

§156 DISTÌNGUERE—distinguèndo—distinto
(e) distinsi, distinguésti, distinse, distinguémmo, distinguéste, distìnsero

§157 DIVÈRGERE—divergèndo—*pp* missing
(e) obsolete

§158 DIVÌDERE—dividèndo—diviso
(e) divisi, dividésti, divise, dividémmo, dividéste, divìsero

§159 DOLÉRE—dolèndo—doluto
(a) duòli, doléte
(b) dòlgo, duòli, duòle, doliamo, doléte, dòlgono
(c) dòlga, dòlga, dòlga, doliamo, doliate, dòlgano
(e) dòlsi, dolésti, dòlse, dolémmo, doléste, dòlsero
(f) dorrò, dorrài, dorrà, dorrémo, dorréte, dorranno

§160 DOVÉRE—dovèndo—dovuto
(b) dèbbo *or* dèvo; dèvi; dève; dobbiamo; dovéte; dèbbono *or* dèvono
(c) dèva *or* dèbba; dèva *or* dèbba; dèva *or* dèbba; dobbiamo; dobbiate; dèvano *or* dèbbano
(e) dovéi *or* dovètti; dovésti; dové *or* dovètte; dovémmo; dovéste; dovérono *or* dovèttero

§161 ELÌDERE—elidèndo—eliso
(e) elisi, elidésti, elise, elidémmo, elidéste, elìsero

§162 EMÈRGERE—emergèndo—emèrso
(e) emèrsi, emergésti, emèrse, emergémmo, emergéste, emèrsero

§163 ÉMPIERE & EMPIRE—empièndo—empito *or* empiuto
(a) émpi, empite

(b) émpio, émpi, émpie, empiamo, empite, émpiono
(c) émpia, émpia, émpia, empiamo, empiate, émpiano
(d) empivo, empivi, empiva, empivamo, empivate, empìvano
(e) empiéi or empìi; empiésti; or empisti; empié or empì; empiémmo or empimmo; empiéste or empiste; empiérono or empìrono
(f) empirò, empirài, empirà, empirémo, empiréte, empiranno

§164 **ÈRGERE**—ergèndo—èrto
(e) èrsi, ergésti, èrse, ergémmo, ergéste, èrsero

§165 **ESÌGERE**—esigèndo—esatto
(e) esigéi or esigètti; esigésti; esigé or esigètte; esigémmo; esigéste; esigérono or esigèttero

§166 **ESÌMERE**—esimèndo—pp missing
(e) esiméi or esimètti; esimésti; esimé or esimètte; esimémmo; esiméste; esimérono or esimèttero

§167 **ESPÀNDERE**—espandèndo—espanso
(e) espandéi or espandètti or espansi; espandésti; espandé or espandètte or espanse; espandémmo; espandéste; espandérono or espandèttero or espànsero

§168 **ESPÈLLERE**—espellèndo—espulso
(e) espulsi, espellésti, espulse, espellémmo, espelléste, espùlsero

§169 **ESPLÒDERE**—esplodèndo—esplòso
(e) esplòsi, esplodésti, esplòse, esplodémmo, esplodéste, esplòsero

§170 **ÈSSERE**—essèndo—stato
(a) sii, siate
(b) sóno, sèi, è, siamo, siète, sóno
(c) sìa, sìa, sìa, siamo, siate, sìano
(d) èro, èri, èra, eravamo, eravate, èrano
(e) fui, fósti, fu, fummo, fóste, fùrono
(f) sarò, sarài, sarà, sarémo, saréte, saranno

§171 **ESTÒLLERE**—estollèndo—pp missing
(e) missing

§172 **EVÀDERE**—evadèndo—evaso
(e) evasi, evadésti, evase, evadémmo, evadéste, evàsero

§173 **FARE**—facèndo—fatto
(a) fa or fài or fa'; fate

24

(b) fàccio *or* fò; fài; fa; facciamo; fate; fanno
(c) fàccia, fàccia, fàccia, facciamo, facciate; fàcciano
(d) facévo, facévi, facéva, facevamo, facevate, facévano
(e) féci, facésti, féce, facémmo, **facé**ste, fécero
(f) farò, farài, farà, farémo, faréte, faranno

§174 **FÈNDERE**—fendèndo—fenduto *or* fésso
(e) fendéi *or* fendètti; fendésti; fendé *or* fendètte; fendémmo; fendéste; fendérono *or* fendèttero

§175 **FÈRVERE**—fervèndo—*pp* missing
(e) fervéi *or* fervètti; fervésti; fervé *or* fervètte; fervémmo; fervéste; fervérono *or* fervèttero

§176 **FINIRE**—finèndo—finito
(a) finisci, finite
(b) finisco, finisci, finisce, finiamo, finite, finìscono
(c) finisca, finisca, finisca, finiamo, finiate, finìscano

§177 **FLÈTTERE**—flettèndo—flèsso
(e) flettéi *or* flèssi; flettésti; fletté *or* flèsse; flettémmo; flettéste; flettérono *or* flèssero

§178 **FÓNDERE**—fondèndo—fuso
(e) fusi, fondésti, fuse, fondémmo, fondéste, fùsero

§179 **FRÀNGERE**—frangèndo—franto
(e) fransi, frangésti, franse, frangémmo, frangéste, frànsero

§180 **FRÌGGERE**—friggèndo—fritto
(e) frissi, friggésti, frisse, friggémmo, friggéste, frìssero

§181 **GIACÉRE**—giacèndo—giaciuto
(b) giàccio; giaci; giace; giacciamo *or* giaciamo; giacete; giàcciono
(c) giàccia, giàccia, giàccia, giacciamo, giacciate, giàcciano
(e) giàcqui, giacésti, giàcque, giacémmo, giacéste, giàcquero

§182 **GIOCARE**—giocando—giocato
(a) giuòca *or* giòca; giocate
(b) giuòco *or* giòco; giuòchi *or* giòchi; giuòca *or* giòca; giochiamo; giocate; giuòcano *or* giòcano
(c) giuòchi *or* giòchi; giuòchi *or* giòchi; giuòchi *or* giòchi; giochiamo; giochiate; giuòchino *or* giòchino
(f) giocherò, giocherài, giocherà, giocherémo, giocheréte, giocheranno

§183 **GIÙNGERE**—giungèndo—giunto
(e) giunsi, giungésti, giunse, giungémmo, giungéste, giùnsero

§184 GODÉRE—godèndo—goduto
  (e) godéi *or* godètti; godésti; godé *or* godètte; godémmo; godéste; godérono *or* godèttero
  (f) godrò, godràì, godrà, godrémo, godréte, godranno

§185 IMBÉVERE—imbevèndo—imbevuto
  (e) imbévvi, imbevésti, imbévve, imbevémmo, imbevéste, imbévvero

§186 INCÓMBERE—incombèndo—*pp* missing
  (e) incombéi *or* incombètti; incombésti; incombé *or* incombètte; incombémmo; incombéste; incombérono *or* incombèttero

§187 INDÙLGERE—indulgèndo—indulto
  (e) indulsi, indulgésti, indulse, indulgémmo, indulgéste, indùlsero

§188a INFERIRE—inferèndo—inferito *or* infèrto
  (a) inferisci, inferite
  (b) inferisco, inferisci, inferisce, inferiamo, inferite, inferìscono
  (c) inferisca, inferisca, inferisca, inferiamo, inferiate, inferìscano
  (e) inferìi *or* infèrsi; inferisti; inferì *or* infèrse; inferimmo; inferiste; inferìrono *or* infèrsero

§188b INSTARE—instando—*pp* missing

§189 INTRÌDERE—intridèndo—intriso
  (e) intrisi, intridésti, intrise, intridémmo, intridéste, intrìsero

§190 INTRÙDERE—intrudèndo—intruso
  (e) intrusi, intrudésti, intruse, intrudémmo, intrudéste, intrùsero

§191 IRE—*ger* missing—ito
  (a) *sg* missing, ite
  (b) missing
  (c) missing
  (d) ivo, ivi, iva, ivamo, ivate, ìvano
  (e) *1st sg* missing, isti, *3rd sg* missing, *1st pl* missing, iste, ìrono

§192 LÈDERE—ledèndo—léso *or* lèso
  (e) lési, ledésti, lése, ledémmo, ledéste, lésero

§193 LÈGGERE—leggèndo—lètto
  (e) lèssi, leggésti, lèsse, leggémmo, leggéste, lèssero

§194 LIQUEFARE—liquefacèndo—liquefatto
- (a) liquefà, liquefate
- (b) liquefò or liquefàccio; liquefài; liquefà liquefacciamo; liquefate; liquefanno
- (c) liquefàccia, liquefàccia, liquefàccia, liquefacciamo, liquefacciate, liquefàcciano
- (d) liquefacévo, liquefacévi, liquefacéva, liquefacevamo, liquefacevate, liquefacévano
- (e) liqueféci, liquefacésti, liqueféce, liquefacémmo, liquefacéste, liquefécero
- (f) liquefarò, liquefaràì, liquefarà, liquefarémo, liquefaréte, liquefaranno

§195 MALEDIRE—maledicèndo—maledétto
- (a) maledici, maledite
- (b) maledico, maledici, maledice, malediciamo, maledite, maledìcono
- (c) maledica, maledica, maledica, malediciamo, malediciate, maledìcano
- (d) maledicévo or maledivo; maledicévi or maledivi; maledicéva or malediva; maledicevamo or maledivamo; maledicevate or maledivate; maledicévano or maledìvano
- (e) maledìi or maledissi; maledisti or maledicésti; maledì or maledisse; maledimmo or maledicémmo; malediste or maledicéste; maledìrono or maledìssero
- (f) maledirò, maledirài, maledirà, maledirémo, malediréte, malediranno

§196 MALVOLÉRE—*ger* missing—malvoluto
- (a) missing
- (b) missing
- (c) missing
- (d) missing
- (e) missing
- (f) missing

§197 MANCARE—mancando—mancato
- (b) manco, manchi, manca, manchiamo, mancate, màncano
- (c) manchi, manchi, manchi, manchiamo, manchiate, mànchino
- (f) mancherò, mancheràì, mancherà, mancherémo, mancheréte, mancheranno

§198 MÉTTERE—mettèndo—mésso
- (e) misi, mettésti, mise, mettémmo, mettéste, mìsero

§199 MÌNGERE—mingèndo—minto
- (e) minsi, mingésti, minse, mingémmo, mingéste, mìnsero

27

§200 MÒRDERE—mordèndo—mòrso
(e) mòrsi, mordésti, mòrse, mordémmo, mordéste, mòrsero

§201 MORIRE—morèndo—mòrto
(a) muòri, morite
(b) muòio, muòri, muòre, moriamo, morite, muòiono
(c) muòia, muòia, muòia, moriamo, moriate, muòiano
(f) morrò or morirò; morròi or morirài; morrà or morirà;
morrémo or morirémo; morréte or moriréte; mor-
ranno or moriranno

§202 MUÒVERE—muovèndo or movèndo (movènte)—mòsso
(a) muòvi, movéte
(b) muòvo, muòvi, muòve, moviamo, movéte, muòvono
(c) muòva, muòva, muòva, moviamo, moviate, muòvano
(d) movévo, movévi, movéva, movevamo, movevate,
movévano
(e) mòssi, movésti, mòsse, movémmo, movéste, mòssero
(f) moverò, moverài, moverà, moverémo, moveréte, move-
ranno

§203 NÀSCERE—nascèndo—nato
(e) nàcqui, nascésti, nàcque, nascémmo, nascéste, nàcquero

§204 NASCÓNDERE—nascondèndo—nascósto
(e) nascósi, nascondésti, nascóse, nascondémmo, nas-
condéste, nascósero

§205 NEGLÌGERE—negligèndo—neglètto
(a) missing
(b) missing
(c) missing
(e) neglèssi, negligésti, neglèsse, negligémmo, negligéste,
neglèssero

§206 NUÒCERE—nuocèndo—nociuto
(a) nuòci, nocéte
(b) nuòccio or nòccio; nuòci; nuòce; nociamo; nocéte;
nuòcciono or nòcciono
(c) nòccia, nòccia, nòccia, nociamo, nociate, nòcciano
(d) nocévo, nocévi, nocéva, nocevamo, nocevate, nocévano
(e) nòcqui, nocésti, nòcque, nocémmo, nocéste, nòcquero
(f) nocerò, nocerài, nocerà, nocerémo, noceréte, noceranno

§207 OFFRIRE—offrèndo (offerènte)—offèrto
(e) offrìi or offèrsi; offristi; offrì or offèrse; offrimmo;
offriste; offrìrono or offèrsero

§208 OTTÙNDERE—ottundèndo—ottuso
(e) ottusi, ottundésti, ottuse, ottundémmo, ottundéste,
ottùsero

§209 PAGARE—pagando—pagato
(b) pago, paghi, paga, paghiamo, pagate, pàgano
(c) paghi, paghi, paghi, paghiamo, paghiate, pàghino
(f) pagherò, pagheràì, pagherà, pagherémo, pagheréte, pagheranno

§210 PARÉRE—parèndo (parvènte)—parso
(a) missing
(b) pàio; pari; pare; pariamo *or* paiamo; paréte; pàiono
(c) pàia; pàia; pàia; pariamo *or* paiamo; pariate *or* paiate; pàiano
(e) parvi, parésti, parve, parémmo, paréste, pàrvero
(f) parrò, parràì, parrà, parrémo, parréte, parranno

§211 PÀSCERE—pascèndo—pasciuto
(a) pascéi *or* pascètti; pascésti; pascé *or* pascètte; pascémmo; pascéste; pascérono *or* pascèttero

§212 PÈRDERE—perdèndo—pèrso *or* perduto
(e) perdéi *or* pèrsi *or* perdètti; perdésti; perdé, *or* pèrse *or* perdètte; perdémmo; perdéste; perdérono *or* pèrsero *or* perdèttero

§213 PERSUADÉRE—persuadèndo—persuaso
(e) persuasi, persuadésti, persuase, persuadémmo, persuadéste, persuàsero

§214 PIACÉRE—piacèndo—piaciuto
(b) piàccio, piaci, piace, piacciamo, piacéte, piàcciono
(c) piàccia, piàccia, piàccia, piacciamo, piacciate, piàcciano
(e) piàcqui, piacésti, piàcque, piacémmo, piacéste, piàcquero

§215 PIÀNGERE—piangèndo—pianto
(e) piansi, piangésti, pianse, piangémmo, piangéste, piànsero

§216 PIÒVERE—piovèndo—piovuto
(e) piòvvi, piovésti, piòvve, piovémmo, piovéste, piòvvero

§217 PÒRGERE—porgèndo—pòrto
(e) pòrsi, porgésti, pòrse, porgémmo, porgéste, pòrsero

§218 PÓRRE—ponèndo—pósto
(a) póni, ponéte
(b) póngo, póni, póne, poniamo, ponéte, póngono
(c) pónga, pónga, pónga, poniamo, poniate, póngano
(d) ponévo, ponévi, ponéva, ponevamo, ponevate, ponévano
(e) pósi, ponésti, póse, ponémmo, ponéste, pósero

§219 POTÉRE—potèndo (potènte *or* possènte)—potuto
(a) missing
(b) pòsso, puòi, può, possiamo, potéte, pòssono

(c) pòssa, pòssa, pòssa, possiamo, possiate, pòssano

(e) potéi *or* potètti; potésti, poté *or* potètte; potémmo; potéste; potérono *or* potèttero

(f) potrò, potrài, potrà, potrémo, potréte, potranno

§220 **PRÈNDERE**—prendèndo—préso

(e) prési, prendésti, prése, prendémmo, prendéste, présero

§221 **PROVVEDÉRE**—provvedèndo—provveduto *or* provvisto

(e) provvidi, provvedésti, provvide, provvedémmo, provvedéste, provvìdero

§222 **PRÙDERE**—prudèndo—*pp* missing

(e) *1st sg* missing; *2nd sg* missing; prudé *or* prudètte; *1st pl* missing; *2nd pl* missing; prudérono *or* prudèttero

§223 **RÀDERE**—radèndo—raso

(e) rasi, radésti, rase, radémmo, radéste, ràsero

§224 **REDÌGERE**—redigèndo—redatto

(e) redassi, redigésti, redasse, redigémmo, redigéste, redàssero

§225 **REDÌMERE**—redimèndo—redènto

(e) redènsi, redimésti, redènse, redimémmo, rediméste, redènsero

§226 **RÈGGERE**—reggèndo—rètto

(e) rèssi, reggésti, rèsse, reggémmo, reggéste, rèssero

§227 **RÈNDERE**—rendèndo—réso

(e) rési *or* rendéi *or* rendètti; rendésti; rése *or* rendé *or* rendètte; rendémmo; rendéste; résero *or* rendérono *or* rendèttero

§228 **RETROCÈDERE**—retrocedèndo—retrocèsso *or* retroceduto

(e) retrocèssi *or* retrocedéi *or* retrocedètti; retrocedésti; retrocèsse *or* retrocedé *or* retrocedètte; retrocedémmo; retrocedéste; retrocèssero *or* retrocedérono *or* retrocedèttero

§229 **RIAVÉRE**—riavèndo—riavuto

(a) riabbi, riabbiate

(b) riò, riài, rià, riabbiamo, riavéte, rianno

(c) riàbbia, riàbbia, riàbbia, riabbiamo, riabbiate, riàbbiano

(e) rièbbi, riavésti, rièbbe, riavémmo, riavéste, rièbbero

(f) riavrò, riavrài, riavrà, riavrémo, riavréte, riavranno

§230 **RIDARE**—ridando—ridato

(a) ridài *or* ridà; ridate

(b) ridò, ridài, ridà, ridiamo, ridate, ridanno

(c) ridìa, ridìa, ridìa, ridiamo, ridiate, ridìano

(e) ridièdi *or* ridètti; ridésti; ridiède *or* ridètte; ridémmo; ridéste; ridièdero *or* ridèttero

(f) ridarò, ridarài, ridarà, ridarémo, ridaréte, ridaranno

§231 RÌDERE—ridèndo—riso
(e) risi, ridésti, rise, ridémmo, ridéste, rìsero

§232 RIFLÈTTERE—riflettèndo—riflèsso *or* riflettuto

§233 RIFÙLGERE—rifulgèndo—rifulso
(e) rifulsi, rifulgésti, rifulse rifulgémmo, rifulgéste, rifùlsero

§234 RILÙCERE—rilucèndo—*pp* missing

§235 RIMANÉRE—rimanèndo—rimasto
(b) rimango, rimani, rimane, rimaniamo, rimanéte, rimàngono
(c) rimanga, rimanga, rimanga, rimaniamo, rimaniate, rimàngano
(e) rimasi, rimanésti, rimase, rimanémmo, rimanéste, rimàsero
(f) rimarrò, rimarrài, rimarrà, rimarrémo, rimarréte, rimarranno

§236 RINCORARE—rincorando—rincorato
(a) rincuòra, rincorate
(b) rincuòro, rincuòri, rincuòra, rincoriamo, rincorate, rincuòrano
(c) rincuòri, rincuòri, rincuòri, rincoriamo, rincoriate, rincuòrino

§237 RISOLARE—risolando—risolato
(a) risuòla, risolate
(b) risuòlo, risuòli, risuòla, risoliamo, risolate, risuòlano
(c) risuòli, risuòli, risuòli, risoliamo, risoliate, risuòlino

§238 RISPÓNDERE—rispondèndo—rispósto
(e) rispósi, rispondésti, rispóse, rispondémmo, rispondéste, rispósero

§239 RÓDERE—rodèndo—róso
(e) rósi, rodésti, róse, rodémmo, rodéste, rósero

§240 RÓMPERE—rompèndo—rótto
(e) ruppi, rompésti, ruppe, rompémmo, rompéste, rùppero

§241 ROTARE—rotando—rotato
(a) ruòta, rotate
(b) ruòto, ruòti, ruòta, rotiamo, rotate, ruòtano
(c) ruòti, ruòti, ruòti, rotiamo, rotiate, ruòtino

§242 **SALIRE**—salèndo—salito
    (b) salgo, sali, sale, saliamo, salite, sàlgono
    (c) salga, salga, salga, saliamo, saliate, sàlgano

§243 **SAPÉRE**—sapèndo (sapiènte)—saputo
    (a) sappi, sappiate
    (b) sò, sai, sa, sappiamo, sapéte, sanno
    (c) sàppia, sàppia, sàppia, sappiamo, sappiate, sàppiano
    (e) sèppi, sapésti, sèppe, sapémmo, sapéste, sèppero
    (f) saprò, saprài, saprà, saprémo, sapréte, sapranno

§244 **SCÉGLIERE**—sceglièndo—scélto
    (a) scégli, scegliéte
    (b) scélgo, scégli, scéglie, scegliamo, scegliéte, scélgono
    (c) scélga, scélga, scélga, scegliamo, scegliate, scélgano
    (e) scélsi, scegliésti, scélse, scegliémmo, scegliéste, scélsero

§245 **SCÉNDERE**—scendèndo—scéso
    (e) scési, scendésti, scése, scendémmo, scendéste, scésero

§246 **SCÈRNERE**—scernèndo—*pp* missing
    (e) scernéi *or* scernètti; scernésti; scerné *or* scernètte; scer-
       némmo; scernéste; scernérono *or* scernèttero

§247 **SCÌNDERE**—scindèndo—scisso
    (e) scissi, scindésti, scisse, scindémmo, scindéste, scìssero

§248 **SCOIARE**—scoiando—scoiato
    (a) scuòia, scoiate
    (b) scuòio, scuòi, scuòia, scoiamo, scoiate, scuòiano
    (c) scuòi, scuòi, scuòi, scoiamo, scoiate, scuòino

§249 **SCÒRGERE**—scorgèndo—scòrto
    (e) scòrsi, scorgésti, scòrse, scorgémmo, scorgéste, scòrsero

§250 **SCRÌVERE**—scrivèndo—scritto
    (e) scrissi, scrivésti, scrisse, scrivémmo, scrivéste, scrìssero

§251 **SCUÒTERE**—scotèndo—scòsso
    (a) scuòti, scotéte
    (b) scuòto, scuòti, scuòte, scotiamo, scotéte, scuòtono
    (c) scuòta, scuòta, scuòta, scotiamo, scotiate, scuòtano
    (d) scotévo, scotévi, scotéva, scotevamo, scotevate, scoté-
       vano
    (e) scòssi, scotésti, scòsse, scotémmo, scotéste, scòssero

§252 **SEDÉRE**—sedéndo—seduto
    (a) sièdi, sedéte
    (b) sièdo *or* sèggo; sièdi; siède; sediamo; sedéte; sièdono
       or sèggono
    (c) sièda *or* sègga; sièda *or* sègga; sièda *or* sègga; sediamo;
       sediate; sièdano *or* sèggano
    (e) sedéi *or* sedètti; sedésti; sedé *or* sedètte; sedémmo;
       sedéste; sedérono *or* sedèttero

§253 SEPPELLIRE—seppellèndo—sepólto *or* seppellito
(a) seppellisci, seppellite
(b) seppellisco, seppellisci, seppellisce, seppelliamo, seppellite, seppellìscono
(c) seppellisca, seppellisca, seppellisca, seppelliamo, seppel-
liate, seppellìscano

§254 SODDISFARE—soddisfacèndo—soddisfatto
(a) soddisfa *or* soddisfài *or* soddisfa'
(b) soddisfàccio *or* soddisfò *or* soddisfo; soddisfài *or*
soddisfi; soddisfà *or* soddisfa; soddisfacciamo; sod-
disfate; soddisfanno *or* soddìsfano
(c) soddisfàccia *or* soddisfi; soddisfàccia *or* soddisfi; soddi-
sfàccià *or* soddisfi; soddisfacciamo; soddisfacciate;
soddisfàcciano *or* soddìsfino
(d) soddisfacévo, soddisfacévi, soddisfacéva, soddisface-
vamo, soddisfacevate, soddisfacévano
(e) soddisféci, soddisfacésti, soddisféce, soddisfacémmo,
soddisfacéste, soddisfécero
(f) soddisfarò, soddisfarài, soddisfarà, soddisfarémo, soddi-
sfaréte, soddisfaranno

§255 SOLÉRE—solèndo—sòlito
(a) missing
(b) sòglio, suòli, suòle, sogliamo, soléte, sògliono
(c) sòglia, sòglia, sòglia, sogliamo, sogliate, sògliano
(e) missing
(f) missing

§256 SÒLVERE—solvèndo—soluto
(e) solvéi *or* solvètti; solvésti; solvé *or* solvètte; solvémmo;
solvéste; solvérono *or* solvèttero

§257 SONARE—sonando—sonato
(a) suòna, sonate
(b) suòno, suòni, suòna, soniamo, sonate, suònano
(c) suòni, suòni, suòni, soniamo, soniate, suònino

§258 SÓRGERE—sorgèndo—sórto
(e) sórsi, sorgésti, sórse, sorgémmo, sorgéste, sórsero

§259 SOSPÈNDERE—sospendèndo—sospéso
(e) sospési, sospendésti, sospése, sospendémmo, sospendéste,
sospésero

§260 SPÀNDERE—spandèndo—spanto
(e) spandéi *or* spandètti *or* spansi; spandésti; spandé *or*
spandètte *or* spanse; spandémmo; spandéste; spandé-
rono *or* spandèttero *or* spànsero

§261 SPÀRGERE—spargèndo—sparso
(e) sparsi, spargésti, sparse, spargémmo, spargéste, spàrsero

§262 SPÈGNERE—spegnèndo—spènto
(b) spéngo *or* spèngo; spégni *or* spègni; spégne *or* spègne; spegniamo; spegnéte; spéngono *or* spèngono
(c) spénga *or* spènga; spénga *or* spènga; spénga *or* spènga; spegniamo; spegniate; spéngano *or* spèngano
(e) spènsi, spegnésti, spènse, spegnémmo, spegnéste, spènsero

§263 STARE—stando—stato
(a) sta *or* stai *or* sta'; state
(b) stò, stài, sta, stiamo, state, stanno
(c) stìa, stìa, stìa, stiamo, stiate, stìano
(e) stètti, stésti, stètte, stémmo, stéste, stèttero
(f) starò, starài, starà, starémo, staréte, staranno

§264 STRÌDERE—stridèndo—*pp* missing
(e) stridéi *or* stridètti; stridésti; stridé *or* stridètte; stridémmo; stridéste; stridérono *or* stridèttero

§265 STRÌNGERE—stringèndo—strétto
(e) strinsi, stringésti, strinse, stringémmo, stringéste, strìnsero

§266 STRÙGGERE—struggèndo—strutto
(e) strussi, struggésti, strusse, struggémmo, struggéste, strùssero

§267 SVÈLLERE—svellèndo—svèlto
(b) svèllo *or* svèlgo; svèlli; svèlle; svelliamo; svelléte; svèllono *or* svèlgono
(c) svèlla *or* svèlga; svèlla *or* svèlga; svèlla *or* svèlga; svelliamo; svelliate; svèllano *or* svèlgano
(e) svèlsi, svellésti, svèlse, svellémmo, svelléste, svèlsero

§268 TACÉRE—tacèndo—taciuto
(b) tàccio, taci, tace, taciamo, tacéte, tàcciono
(c) tàccia, tàccia, tàccia, taciamo, taciate, tàcciano
(e) tàcqui, tacésti, tàcque, tacémmo, tacéste, tàcquero

§269 TÀNGERE—tangèndo—pp missing
(a) missing
(b) *1st sg* missing; *2nd sg* missing; tange; *1st pl* missing; *2nd pl* missing; tàngono
(c) *1st sg* missing; *2nd sg* missing; tanga; *1st pl* missing; *2nd pl* missing; tàngano
(d) *1st sg* missing; *2nd sg* missing; tangéva; *1st pl* missing; *2nd pl* missing; tangévano
(e) missing
(f) *1st sg* missing; *2nd sg* missing; tangerà; *1st pl* missing; *2nd pl* missing; tangeranno

§270 **TÈNDERE**—tendèndo—téso
(e) tési, tendésti, tése, tendémmo, tendéste, tésero

§271 **TENÉRE**—tenèndo—tenuto
(a) tièni, tenéte
(b) tèngo, tièni, tiène, teniamo, tenéte, tèngono
(c) tènga, tènga, tènga, teniamo, teniate, tèngano
(e) ténni, tenésti, ténne, tenémmo, tenéste, ténnero
(f) terrò, terràì, terrà, terrémo, terréte, terranno

§272 **TÒRCERE**—torcèndo—tòrto
(e) tòrsi, torcésti, tòrse, torcémmo, torcéste, tòrsero

§273 **TRARRE**—traèndo—tratto
(a) tràì, traéte
(b) traggo, tràì, trae, traiamo, traéte, tràggono
(c) tragga, tragga, tragga, traiamo, traiate, tràggano
(d) traévo, traévi, traéva, traevamo, traevate, traévano
(e) trassi, traésti, trasse, traémmo, traéste, tràssero

§274 **UCCÌDERE**—uccidèndo—ucciso
(e) uccisi, uccidésti, uccise, uccidémmo, uccidéste, uccìsero

§275 **UDIRE**—udèndo *or* udièndo—udito
(a) òdi, udite
(b) òdo, òdi, òde, udiamo, udite, òdono
(c) òda, òda, òda, udiamo, udiate, òdano
(f) udirò *or* udrò; udiràì *or* udràì; udirà *or* udrà; udirémo
   or udrémo; udiréte *or* udréte; udiranno *or* udranno

§276 **ÙRGERE**—urgèndo—*pp* missing
(a) missing
(e) missing

§277 **USCIRE**—uscèndo—uscito
(a) èsci, uscite
(b) èsco, èsci, èsce, usciamo, uscite, èscono
(c) èsca, èsca, èsca, usciamo, usciate, èscano

§278 **VALÉRE**—valèndo—valso
(b) valgo, vali, vale, valiamo, valéte, vàlgono
(c) valga, valga, valga, valiamo, valiate, vàlgano
(e) valsi, valésti, valse, valémmo, valéste, vàlsero
(f) varrò, varràì, varrà, varrémo, varréte, varranno

§279 **VEDÉRE**—vedèndo—veduto *or* visto
(e) vidi, vedésti, vide, vedémmo, vedéste, vìdero
(f) vedrò, vedràì, vedrà, vedrémo, vedréte, vedranno

§280 **VEGLIARE**—vegliando—vegliato
(b) véglio, végli, véglia, vegliamo, vegliate, végliano
(c) végli, végli, végli, vegliamo, vegliate, véglino

§281 VÉNDERE—vendèndo—venduto
   (e) vendéi *or* vendètti; vendésti; vendé *or* vendètte; ven-
     démmo; vendéste; vendérono *or* vendèttero

§282 VENIRE—venèndo (veniènte)—venuto
   (a) vièni, venite
   (b) vèngo, vièni, viène, véniamo, venite, vèngono
   (c) vènga, vènga, vènga, veniamo, veniate, vèngano
   (e) vénni, venisti, vénne, venimmo, veniste, vénnero
   (f) verrò, verrài, verrà, verrémo, verréte, verranno

§283 VÈRTERE—vertèndo—*pp* missing

§284 VÌGERE—vigèndo—*pp* missing
   (a) missing
   (b) *1st sg* missing; *2nd sg* missing; vige; *1st pl* missing;
     2d pl missing; vìgono
   (c) *1st sg* missing; *2d sg* missing; viga; *1st pl* missing;
     2d pl missing; vìgano
   (d) *1st sg* missing; *2d sg* missing; vigéva; *1st pl* missing;
     2d pl missing; vigévano
   (e) missing

§285 VÌNCERE—vincèndo—vinto
   (e) vinsi, vincésti, vinse, vincémmo, vincéste, vìnsero

§286 VÌVERE—vivèndo—vissuto
   (e) vissi, vivésti, visse, vivémmo, vivéste, vìssero
   (f) vivrò, vivrài, vivrà, vivrémo, vivréte, vivranno

§287 VIZIARE—viziando—viziato
   (b) vìzio, vizi, vìzia, viziamo, viziate, vìziano
   (c) vizi, vizi, vizi, viziamo, viziate, vìzino

§288 VOLÉRE—volèndo—voluto
   (a) vògli, vogliate
   (b) vòglio, vuòi, vuòle, vogliamo, voléte, vògliono
   (c) vòglia, vòglia, vòglia, vogliamo, vogliate, vògliano
   (e) vòlli, volésti, vòlle, volémmo, voléste, vòllero
   (f) vorrò, vorrài, vorrà, vorrémo, vorréte, vorranno

§289 VÒLGERE—volgèndo—vòlto
   (e) vòlsi, volgésti, vòlse, volgémmo, volgéste, vòlsero

§290 VOLTEGGIARE—volteggiando—volteggiato
   (b) voltéggio, voltéggi, voltéggia, volteggiamo, volteggiate,
     voltéggiano
   (c) voltéggi, voltéggi, voltéggi, volteggiamo, volteggiate,
     voltéggino
   (f) volteggerò, volteggerài, volteggerà, volteggerémo, vol-
     teggeréte, volteggeranno

A

A, a [a] *m* & *f* first letter of the Italian alphabet

a *prep* (**ad** in front of a vowel) to, e.g., **diede il libro a Giovanni** he gave the book to John; in, e.g., **a Milano** in Milan; at, e.g., **a casa** at home; within, e.g., **a tre miglia da qui** within three miles from here; on, e.g., **portare una catena al collo** to wear a chain on one's neck; e.g., **al sabato** on Saturdays; for, e.g., **a vita** for life; by, e.g., **fatto a mano** made by hand; with, e.g., **una gonna a pieghe** a skirt with pleats; as, e.g., **eleggere a presidente** to elect as chairman; into, e.g., **fu gettato a mare** he was thrown into the sea; of, e.g., **un quarto alle due** fifteen minutes of two

àba·co *m* (**-chi**) (archit) abacus

abate *m* abbot

abbacchiare §287 *tr* to knock down (*e.g., olives*); to sell too cheap || *ref* to lose courage; to be dejected

abbacchia·to -ta *adj* (coll) dejected

abbàc·chio *m* (**-chi**) baby lamb (*slaughtered*)

abbacinare (**abbàcino**) *tr* to dazzle; to deceive

abbadéssa *f* var of **badessa**

abbagliante *adj* dazzling || *m* (aut) bright light, high beam

abbagliare §280 *tr* to dazzle; to deceive; to blind (*with the lights of a car*)

abbà·glio *m* (**-gli**) error; **prendere abbaglio** to make a mistake

abbaiaménto *m* bark (*of dog*)

abbaiare §287 *intr* to bark; to yelp

abbaino *m* dormer window; skylight; attic

abbambinare *tr* to walk (*a heavy piece of furniture*)

abbandonare (**abbandóno**) *tr* to abandon; to give up; to let go (*e.g., the reins*); to let fall; (sports) to withdraw from || *ref* to yield; to lose courage

abbandóno *m* abandon, abandonment; desertion; neglect; relaxation; renunciation (*of a right*); cession (*of property*); withdrawal (*from a fight*)

abbarbicare §197 (**abbàrbico**) *intr* & *ref* to cling; to hold on

abbassalin·gua *m* (**-gua**) tongue depressor

abbassaménto *m* lowering; reduction; drop, fall

abbassare *tr* to lower; to dim (*lights*); to turn (*the radio*) lower; **abbassare le armi** to surrender; **abbassare la cresta** to yield || *ref* to lower oneself; to drop

abbas·so *m* (**-so**) angry shout (*of a crowd*) || *adv* down, below; downstairs || *interj* down with!

abbastanza *adj invar* enough || *adv* enough; rather, fairly

abbàttere *tr* to demolish; to fell; to shoot down; to refute (*an argument*); to depress || *ref* to be depressed, be downcast

abbattiménto *m* demolition; felling; shooting down; chill; (fig) depression; **abbattimento a:lla base** (econ) basic exemption (*from taxes*)

abbattu·to -ta *adj* dejected, downcast || *f* clearing (*of trees*)

abbazia *f* abbey; abbacy

abbecedà·rio *m* (**-ri**) speller, primer

abbelliménto *m* embellishment, ornamentation

abbellire §176 *tr* to embellish, adorn; to landscape

abbeverare (**abbévero**) *tr* to water (*animals*) || *ref* to quench one's thirst

abbevera·tóio *m* (**-tói**) watering trough

abbic·cì *m* (**-cì**) alphabet; speller; primer; ABC's, rudiments

abbiènte *adj* well-to-do || *m*—**gli abbienti** the haves; **gli abbienti e nullatenenti** the haves and the have-nots

abbiettézza or **abiettézza** *f* abjectness, baseness

abbièt·to -ta or **abièt·to -ta** *adj* abject, base, low

abbiezióne or **abiezióne** *f* wretchedness, baseness

abbigliaménto *m* attire, wear

abbigliare §280 *tr* & *ref* to dress; to dress up

abbinaménto *m* coupling; merger

abbinare *tr* to couple; to join, merge

abbindolare (**abbìndolo**) *tr* to dupe, deceive

abbiosciare §128 *ref* to fall down; to lose heart, be downcast

abbisognare (**abbisógno**) *intr* to be in need

abboccaménto *m* interview, conversation

abboccare §197 (**abbócco**) *tr* to swallow (*the hook*); to fit (*pipes*) || *intr* to bite (*said of fish*); to fall; to fit (*said of pipes*) || *ref* to confer

abbocca·to -ta *adj* palatable; slightly sweet (*wine*)

abbonacciare §128 *ref* to calm down, abate (*said of weather*)

abbonaménto *m* subscription; **abbonamento postale** m:iling permit

abbonare (**abbòno**) *tr* to take out a subscription for (*s.o.*) || *ref* to subscribe || §257 *tr* to remit (*a debt*); to forgive

abbona·to -ta *mf* subscriber; commuter

abbondante *adj* abundant, plentiful; heavy (*rain*)

abbondanza *f* abundance, plenty

abbondare (**abbóndo**) *intr* (ESSERE & AVERE) to abound; to exceed; **abbondare di** or **in** to abound in

abbonire §176 *tr* to calm; to placate || *ref* to calm down

abbordàbile *adj* accessible, approachable; negotiable (*curve*)

abbordàg·gio m (-gi) boarding (of an enemy ship); **andare all'abbordàggio di** to board

abbordare (abbórdo) tr to board (an enemy ship); to negotiate (a curve); to face (a problem); (fig) to button-hole

abborracciare §128 tr to botch, bungle

abborracciatura f botch, bungle

abbottonare (abbottóno) tr to button || ref (coll) to keep to oneself

abbottonatura f buttoning; row of buttons

abbozzare (abbòzzo) tr to sketch; to hew (e.g., a statue); (naut) to tie up || intr (coll) to take it

abbòzzo m sketch, draft

abbracciabò·sco m (-schi) (bot) wood-bine

abbracciare embrace, embracing || §128 tr to embrace, hug; to seize (an opportunity); to become converted to (e.g., Christianity); to enter (a profession); to span, encompass || ref to cling; to embrace one another

abbràc·cio m (-ci) embrace, hug

abbrancare §197 tr to grab; to herd || ref to cling; to join a herd

abbreviaménto m abbreviation, shortening

abbreviare §287 (abbrèvio) tr to abbreviate, shorten, abridge

abbreviatura f shortening, abridgment

abbreviazióne f abbreviation

abbrivo or **abbrìvio** m headway (of a ship); **prendere l'abbrivio** to gather momentum

abbronzante [dz] adj suntanning || m suntan lotion

abbronzare [dz] (abbrónzo) tr & ref to bronze; to tan

abbronza·to -ta [dz] adj tanned, suntanned

abbronzatura [dz] f tan, suntan

abbruciacchiare §287 tr to singe

abbrunare tr to brown; to hang crepe on || ref to wear mourning

abbrunire §176 tr to turn brown; to tan; to burnish

abbrustolire §176 tr to toast; to singe || ref to tan; to become sunburned

abbrutiménto m degradation, brutishness

abbrutire §176 tr to degrade; to brutalize || intr & ref to become brutalized

abbuiare §287 tr to darken; to hush up, hide || ref to grow dark; to become gloomy || impers—abbuia it's growing dark

abbuòno m allowance, discount; handicap (in racing)

abburattaménto m sifting

abburattare tr to sift, bolt

abdicare §197 (àbdico) tr & intr to abdicate; **abdicare a** to give up, renounce; to abdicate (e.g., the throne)

abdicazióne f abdication

aberrare (abèrro) intr to deviate

aberrazióne f aberration

abéte m fir

abetina f forest of fir trees

abiàti·co m (-ci) (coll) grandson

abièt·to -ta adj abject, base, low

abigeato m (law) cattle rustling

àbile adj able, clever, capable; (mil) fit

abili·tà f (tà) ability, skill

abilitare (abìlito) tr to certify (e.g., a teacher); to qualify, license

abilita·to -ta adj certified (teacher)

abilitazióne f qualification; certification (of teachers)

abissale adj abysmal

Abissìnia, l' f Abyssinia

abissi·no -na adj & mf Abyssinian

abisso m abyss; fountain (of knowledge); slough (of degradation)

abitàbile adj inhabitable

abitàcolo m (aer) cockpit; (aut) cab, interior; (naut) compass bowl; **abitacolo eiettabile** (aer) ejection capsule

abitante mf inhabitant; resident

abitare (àbito) tr to inhabit; to occupy || intr to dwell, live, reside

abitati·vo -va adj living, e.g., **condizioni abitative** living conditions

abita·to -ta adj inhabited, populated || m built-up area

abita·tóre -trice mf dweller

abitazióne f dwelling; housing

àbito m suit (for men); dress (for women); garb, attire; habit; **abiti** clothes; **abito da ballo** evening gown; **abito da cerimonia** formal dress; **abito da inverno** winter suit; winter clothes; **levarsi l'abito** to doff the cassock; **prender l'abito** to enter the Church

abituale adj habitual

abituare (abìtuo) tr to accustom || ref to grow accustomed

abitudinà·rio -ria adj (-ri -rie) set in his ways

abitùdine f habit, custom

abituro m (poet) shanty, hut

abiura f abjuration

abiurare tr to abjure

ablati·vo -va adj & m ablative

ablazióne f (med) removal; (geol) erosion

abluzióne f ablution

abnegare §209 (abnégo & abnègo) tr to renounce, abnegate

abnegazióne f abnegation, self-denial

abnòrme adj abnormal

abolire §176 tr to abolish

abolizióne f abolition

abominàbile adj abominable

abominare (abòmino) tr to abominate, detest

abominazióne f abomination

abominévole adj abominable

aborìge·no -na adj aboriginal || m aborigine; **aborigeni** aborigines

aborrire §176 & (abòrro) tr to abhor, loathe || intr—**aborrire da** to shun, shrink from

abortire §176 intr to abort

abòrto m abortion, miscarriage; **aborto di natura** monstrosity

abrasióne f abrasion; erosion

abrasi·vo -va adj & m abrasive

abrogare §209 (àbrogo) tr to abrogate

abrogazióne f abrogation

abruzzése adj of the Abruzzi || mf person of the Abruzzi || m dialect of the Abruzzi

àbside f (archit) apse

abusare intr—abusare di to go to excesses in (e.g., smoking); to take advantage of; to impose on

abusi·vo -va adj illegal, abusive; unwarranted

abuso m abuse, excess

acà·cia f (-cie) acacia

acanto m acanthus

àcaro m (ent) acarus, mite, tick; **acaro della scabbia** itch mite

ac·ca m & f (-ca or -che) h (letter); **non valere un'acca** (coll) to not be worth a fig

accadèmia f academy

accadèmi·co -ca (-ci -che) adj academic || mf academician

accadére §121 intr (ESSERE) to happen, occur

accadu·to -ta adj happened, occurred || m fact, event; what has taken place

accagliare §280 tr, intr (ESSERE) & ref to curdle, coagulate

accalappia·ni m (-ni) dogcatcher

accalappiare §287 tr to catch (a dog); to snare; (fig) to fool

accalcare §197 tr to crowd || ref to throng

accaldare ref to get hot; to become flushed

accalda·to -ta adj hot; perspired

accalorare (accalóro) tr to excite || ref to get excited

accalora·to -ta adj excited, animated

accampaménto m encampment, camp; camping

accampare tr to encamp; to advance, lay (a claim) || ref to camp, encamp

accanimento m animosity, bitterness, obstinacy, stubbornness

accanire §176 tr to persist; to work doggedly; **accanirsi contro** to harass

accani·to -ta adj obstinate, persistent; furious; fierce, ruthless, bitter (fight)

accanto adv near, nearby; **accanto a** near

accantonaménto m tabling (e.g., of a discussion); reserve (of money); (mil) billeting; (sports) camping

accantonare (accantóno) tr to set aside (money); (mil) to billet

accaparraménto m cornering (of market)

accaparrare tr to corner (merchandise); to hoard; to put a down payment on (e.g., a house); (coll) to gain (somebody's affection)

accaparra·tóre -trice mf monopolizer; hoarder

accapigliare §280 ref to pull each other's hair; to scuffle; to come to blows

accapo or **a capo** m paragraph

accappa·tóio m (-tói) bathrobe

accapponare (accappóno) tr to castrate (a rooster) || ref to wrinkle; **mi si accappona la pelle** I get gooseflesh

accarezzare (accarézzo) tr to caress, fondle; to pet; to nurture (e.g., a hope); **accarezzare le spalle di** to strike; to club

accartocciare §128 (accartòccio) tr to wrap up in a cone || ref to curl up

accartoccia·to -ta adj curled up

accasare [s] tr & ref to marry

accasciaménto m dejection

accasciare §128 tr to weaken, enfeeble; to depress || ref to weaken; to lose heart

accasermare [s] (accasèrmo) tr to quarter, billet

accatastare tr to register (real estate); to pile, heap up

accattabri·ghe mf (-ghe) quarrelsome person, scrapper

accattare tr to beg for; to borrow (e.g., ideas) || intr to beg

accattonàg·gio m (-gi) begging, mendicancy

accattó·ne -na mf mendicant, beggar

accavalcare §197 tr to straddle; to go over

accavalciare §128 tr to bestride

accavallare tr to superimpose; to cross (one's legs) || ref to pour forward, run high (said of waves)

accecaménto m blinding

accecare §122 tr to blind; to countersink || intr (ESSERE) to become blind || ref to blind oneself

acceca·tóio m (-tói) countersink

accèdere §100 intr (ESSERE) to enter, approach; to accede

acceleraménto m acceleration

accelerare (accèlero) tr & intr to accelerate

accelera·to -ta adj accelerated; intensive (course); local (train) || m local train

acceleratóre m accelerator

accelerazióne f acceleration

accèndere §101 tr to kindle; to turn on (e.g., the light); to light (e.g., a match, a cigar) || ref to catch fire; to become lit; **accendersi in viso** to become flushed

accendisìgaro m lighter

accendi·tóio m (-tói) candle lighter

accenditóre m lighter

accennare (accénno) tr to nod; to point at; to sketch || intr to refer; to hint

accénno m nod; sign; allusion

accensióne f lighting, kindling; (aut) ignition; (law) contraction (of a debt); **accensione improvvisa** spontaneous combustion

accentare (accènto) tr to accent

accènto m accent; stress; (poet) accent (word); **accento tonico** stress accent

accentraménto m centralization

accentrare (accèntro) tr to concentrate, centralize

accentuare (accèntuo) tr to accentuate || ref to become aggravated

accentuazióne f accentuation

accerchiaménto m encirclement

accerchiare §287 (accérchio) tr to encircle, surround

accertàbile adj verifiable

accertaménto m ascertainment, verification; determination (e.g., of taxes)

accertare (accèrto) *tr* to assure; to ascertain, verify; to determine (*the tax due*) || *ref* to make sure

accè·so -sa [s] *adj* lit; turned on; on (*e.g., radio*); excited, aroused; bright (*color*)

accessìbile *adj* accessible; moderate (*price*)

accessióne *f* accession

accèsso *m* access, approach; admittance, entry; fit (*of anger, of coughing*)

accessò·rio -ria (-ri -rie) *adj* accessory || *m* accessory; (mach) accessory, attachment

accétta *f* hatchet, axe, cleaver; **tagliato con l'accetta** rough-hewn

accettàbile *adj* acceptable

accettare (accètto) *tr* to accept

accettazióne *f* acceptance; receiving room; (econ) acceptance

accèt·to -ta *adj* agreeable; welcome; **male accetto** unwelcome

accezióne *f* meaning, acceptation

acchiappafarfal·le *m* (-le) butterfly net

acchiappamó·sche *m* (-sche) fly catcher

acchiappare *tr* to grab, seize; (coll) to catch in the act

acchito *m* (billiards) break; **di primo acchito** at first

acciaccare §197 *tr* to crush; to trample upon; (coll) to lay low (*e.g., by illness*)

acciac·co *m* (-chi) illness, infirmity, ailment

acciaiare §287 *tr* to convert into steel; to strengthen with steel

acciaierìa *f* steel mill, steelworks

ac·ciàio *m* (-ciài) steel; **acciaio inossidabile** stainless steel

acciaiòlo *m* whetstone

acciambellare (acciambèllo) *tr* to shape in the form of a doughnut || *ref* to curl up

acciarino *m* flintlock; linchpin; (nav) war nose (*of a torpedo*)

accidèmpoli *interj* (slang) darn it!

accidentale *adj* accidental

accidenta·to -ta *adj* paralyzed; uneven, rough (*road*); broken (*ground*)

accidènte *m* accident; crack-up; (coll) paralytic stroke; (coll) hoot, fig; (coll) pest, menace (*child*); (mus) accidental; **accidenti!** (coll) darn!, damn!; **correre come un accidente** to run like the devil; **mandare un accidente a** to wish ill luck to; **per accidente** perchance

accidia *f* sloth

accidió·so -sa [s] *adj* slothful

acciglìare §280 *ref* to frown, knit one's brow

accìngere §126 *ref*—**accingersi a** to get ready to

-àccio -àccia *suf adj & mf* (-acci -acce) no good, e.g., **gentaccia** no good people; good-for-nothing, e.g., **ragazzacció** good-for-nothing boy

acciò or **acciocché** *conj* (poet) so that

acciottolare (acciòttolo) *tr* to pave with cobblestones

acciottola·to -ta *adj* cobblestone || *m* cobblestone pavement

acciottolì·o *m* (-ìi) clatter (*e.g., of dishes*)

accipìcchia *interj* (coll) darn it!

acciuffare *tr* to seize, grab, pinch (*a thief*)

acciu·ga *f* (-ghe) anchovy

acclamare *tr* to acclaim || *intr* to voice one's approval

acclamazióne *f* acclamation

acclimatare (acclìmato) *tr & ref* to acclimate

acclimatazióne *f* acclimatation

acclìve *adj* (poet) steep

acclivi·tà *f* (-tà) acclivity

acclùdere §105 *tr* to enclose

acclu·so -sa *adj* enclosed

accoccare §197 (accòcco & accócco) *tr* (poet) to nock (*the arrow*)

accoccolare (accòccolo) *ref* to squat down

accodare (accódo) *tr* to line up || *ref* to line up, queue

accogliènte *adj* cozy, hospitable, inviting

accogliènza *f* reception, welcome

accògliere §127 *tr* to receive; to welcome; to grant (*a request*) || *ref* (poet) to gather

accoglitrice *f* receptionist

accòlito *m* acolyte, altar boy; follower

accollare (accòllo) *tr* to overload (*a cart*); **accollare qlco a qlcu** to charge s.o. with s.th || *intr* to go up to the neck (*said of a dress*) || *ref* to assume, take upon oneself

accolla·to -ta *adj* high-necked (*dress*); high-cut (*shoes*) || *f* accolade

accollatùra *f* neck, neckhole

accòlta *f* (poet) gathering

accoltellare (accoltèllo) *tr* to knife

accomandante *m* limited partner

accomandatà·rio *m* (-ri) (law) general partner

accomàndita *f* (law) limited partnership

accomiatare *tr* to dismiss || *ref* to take leave

accomodaménto *m* arrangement; compromise; settlement

accomodante *adj* accommodating, obliging

accomodare (accòmodo) *tr* to arrange; to fix; to settle || *intr* to be convenient || *ref* to adapt oneself; to agree; to sit down; **si accomodi** have a seat, make yourself comfortable

accomodatùra *f* arrangement; repair

accompagnaménto *m* retinue; cortege; (mus) accompaniment; (law) writ of mandamus; (mil) softening-up (*by gunfire*)

accompagnare *tr* to accompany; to escort; to follow; to match || *ref*—**accompagnarsi a** or **con** to join

accompagna·tóre -trice *mf* escort; guide; (mus) accompanist

accomunare *tr* to mingle, mix; to unite, associate; to share

acconciaménto *m* arrangement

acconciare §128 (accóncio) *tr* to prepare for use; to arrange; to set (*e.g., the hair*) || *ref* to adorn oneself; to dress one's hair; to adapt oneself

acconcia·tóre -trice *mf* hairdresser

acconciatura *f* hairdo; headdress

accón·cio -cia *adj* (-ci -ce) proper, fitting

accondiscendènte *adj* acquiescing, acquiescent

accondiscendènza *f* acquiescence

accondiscéndere §245 *intr* to acquiesce, consent; to yield

acconsentire (acconsènto) *intr* to consent, acquiesce

acconsenziènte *adj* consenting, acquiescing

accontentare (accontènto) *tr* to satisfy, please ‖ *ref* to be satisfied, be pleased

accónto *m* installment

accoppare (accòppo) *tr* (coll) to kill; (coll) to beat to death ‖ *ref* (coll) to get killed

accoppiaménto *m* pairing; mating; (mach) parallel operation

accoppiare §287 **(accòppio)** *tr* to couple, pair, cross (*e.g., animals*) ‖ *ref* to mate, copulate

accoppiata *f* daily double (*in races*)

accoraménto *m* sadness, sorrow

accorare (accòro) *tr* to stab to death; to sadden ‖ *ref* to sadden, grieve

accora·to -ta *adj* saddened, grieving

accorciare §128 **(accórcio)** *tr & ref* to shorten; to shrink

accorciatura *f* shortening; shrinking

accordare (accòrdo) *tr* to harmonize (*colors*); to reconcile (*people*); to tune up; to grant; (gram) to make agree ‖ *ref* to agree; to match

accorda·to -ta *adj* tuned up ‖ *m* (econ) credit limit

accorda·tóre -trice *mf* (mus) tuner

accordatura *f* tuning

accòrdo *m* agreement, accordance; (law) mutual consent; (mus) harmony; **d'accordo** O.K., agreed; **d'accordo con** in accord with; **di comune accordo** with one accord; **essere d'accordo** to agree; **mettersi d'accordo** to come to an agreement

accòrgere §249 *ref* to perceive; notice; **accorgersi di** to become aware of, realize; **senza accorgersi** inadvertently

accorgiménto *m* smartness; device, trick

accórrere §139 *intr* (ESSERE) to run up, rush up

accortézza *f* alertness; shrewdness, perspicacity

accòr·to -ta *adj* alert; shrewd, perspicacious

accosciare §128 **(accòscio)** *ref* to squat

accostàbile *adj* approachable

accostaménto *m* approach; combination (*e.g., of colors*)

accostare (accòsto) *tr* to approach; to bring near; to leave (*a door*) ajar ‖ *intr* to be near; to cling, adhere; (naut) to come alongside; (naut) to maneuver alongside a pier; (naut) to change direction, haul ‖ *ref* to approach, come near; to cling (*e.g., to a faith*)

accosta·to -ta *adj* ajar

accò·sto -sta *adj* (coll) near ‖ *m* approach; help ‖ **accosto** *adv* near; **accosto a** near, close to

accovacciare §128 *ref* to crouch

accovonare (accovóno) *tr* to sheave

accozzàglia *f* hodgepodge; motley crowd

accozzare (accòzzo) *tr* to jumble up; to collect, gather (*people*) together ‖ *ref* to collect, congregate

accòzzo *m* jumble, medley

accreditàbile *adj* chargeable (*e.g., account*); creditable

accreditaménto *m* crediting

accreditare (accrédito) *tr* to credit, believe; to accredit (*an ambassador*); to credit (*one's account*)

accredita·to -ta *adj* confirmed (*news*); accredited

accréscere §142 *tr & ref* to increase

accresciménto *m* increase

accucciare §128 *ref* to curl up (*said of dogs*)

accudire §176 *tr* (coll) to attend (*a sick person*) ‖ *intr—accudire a* to take care of

acculturazióne *f* acculturation

accumulare (accùmulo) *tr, intr & ref* to accumulate; to gather

accumulatóre *m* storage battery

accumulazióne *f* accumulation

accuratézza *f* care, carefulness

accura·to -ta *adj* careful, painstaking

accusa *f* accusation, charge; **pubblica accusa** (law) public prosecutor

accusare *tr* to accuse, charge; to betray; to acknowledge (*receipt*); (cards) to declare, bid

accusati·vo -va *adj & m* accusative

accusa·to -ta *adj* accused ‖ *mf* defendant

accusató·re -trice *mf* accuser; **pubblico accusatore** (law) public prosecutor, district attorney

accusatò·rio -ria *adj* (-ri -rie) accusatory, accusing

acèfa·lo -la *adj* headless; without the first page (*said of a manuscript*)

acèr·bo -ba *adj* unripe, green, sour

àcero *m* maple tree, sugar maple

acèrri·mo -ma *adj* bitter, fierce

acetato *m* acetate

acèti·co -ca *adj* (-ci -che) acetic

acetificare §197 **(acetífico)** *tr* to acetify

acetilène *m* acetylene

acéto *m* vinegar; **aceto aromatico** aromatic spirits; **sotto aceto** pickled

acetóne *m* acetone

acetósa [s] *f* (bot) sorrel

acetosèlla [s] *f* wood sorrel

acetó·so -sa [s] *adj* vinegarish ‖ *f* see **acetosa**

Acherónte *m* Acheron

Achille *m* Achilles

acidificare §197 **(acidìfico)** *tr* to acidify

acidi·tà *f* (-tà) acidity; **acidità di stomaco** heartburn

àci·do -da *adj* acid, sour ‖ *m* acid; **sapere d'acido** to taste sour

acìdu·lo -la *adj* acidulous

àcino *m* berry (*of grapes*); bead (*of rosary*)

acme *f* acme; crisis

acne *f* acne

acònito m (bot) monkshood

àcqua f water; rain; purity (e.g., of a diamond); acqua a catinelle pouring rain; acqua alta high water; acqua corrente running water; acqua dolce fresh water; drinking water; acqua in bocca! mum's the word!; acqua morta stagnant water; acqua ossigenata hydrogen peroxide; acqua potabile drinking water; acqua salata salt water; acqua viva spring; all'acqua di rose very mild; avere l'acqua alla gola to be in dire straits; della più bell'acqua of the first water; fare acqua to leak (said of a boat); fare un buco nell'acqua to waste one's efforts; portare acqua al mare to carry coals to Newcastle; prendere l'acqua to get wet; sott'acqua (fig) underhand; tirare l'acqua al proprio mulino to be grist to one's mill; versare acqua in un cesto to waste one's efforts

acquafòrte f (acquefòrti) etching

acquaforti•sta mf (-sti -ste) etcher

ac•quàio -quàia (-quài -quàie) adj watering (trough) || m sink

acqualò•lo -la adj water || m water carrier; (sports) water boy

acquamarina f (acquemarine) aquamarine

acquaplano m aquaplane

acquaràgia f turpentine

acquarèllo m var of acquerello

acquà•rio m (-ri) aquarium || Acquario m (astr) Aquarius

acquartierare (acquartièro) tr (mil) to quarter || ref to be quartered

acquasanta f holy water

acquasantièra f (eccl) stoup

acquàti•co -ca adj (-ci -che) aquatic, water

acquattare ref to crouch, squat

acquavite f brandy; liquor, rum

acquazzóne m downpour, heavy shower

acquedótto m aqueduct

àcque•o -a adj aqueous, watery

acquerelli•sta mf (-sti -ste) watercolorist

acquerèllo m watercolor; watered-down wine

acquerùgiola f fine drizzle

acquiescènte adj acquiescent

acquietare (acquièto) tr to pacify, placate || ref to quiet down

acquirènte mf buyer, purchaser; il miglior acquirente the highest bidder

acquisire §176 tr to acquire

acquisi•tóre -trice mf salesperson, agent || m salesman || f saleswoman

acquistare tr to purchase, buy; to acquire; to gain (e.g., ground) || intr to improve

acquisto m buy, purchase; acquisition

acquitrino m marsh

acquitrinó•so -sa [s] adj marshy

acquolina f—far venire l'acquolina in bocca a to make one's mouth water

acquó•so -sa [s] adj watery

acre adj sour; pungent; acrid; bitter (words)

acrèdine f acrimony, sourness

acrimònia f acrimony

acro m acre

acròba•ta mf (-ti -te) acrobat

acrobàti•co -ca (-ci -che) adj acrobatic || f acrobatics

acrobatismo m acrobatics

acrobazia f acrobatics; stunt, feat

acroèdro m plateau

acrònimo m acronym

acròpo•li f (-li) acropolis

acròsti•co m (-ci) acrostic

acuire §176 tr to sharpen, whet

acuità f acuity

acùle•o m (-i) quill; prickle, thorn; stinger (of an insect)

acume m acumen

acuminare (acùmino) tr to sharpen, whet

acumina•to -ta adj pointed, sharp

acùsti•co -ca (-ci -che) adj acoustic(al) || f acoustics

acutézza f acuteness, sharpness

acutizzare [ddzz] tr & ref to sharpen

acu•to -ta adj acute, sharp || m high note

ad prep var of a before words beginning with a vowel

adagiare §290 tr to lay down gently; to lower gently || ref to lie down; to stretch out

adà•gio m (-gi) adage; (mus) adagio || adv slowly; gently; (mus) adagio

Adamo m Adam

adattàbile adj adaptable

adattaménto m adaptation; adaptability

adattare tr to adapt, fit || ref to adapt oneself; to become adapted; adattarsi a to go with; to match; to be becoming to

adat•to -ta adj suitable, adequate

addebitaménto m debiting

addebitare (addébito) tr to debit; addebitare una spesa a qlcu to debit s.o. with an expense

addébito m charge; (com) debit; elevare l'addebito di qlco a qlcu (law) to charge s.o. with s.th

addènda mpl addenda

addèndo m (math) addend

addensare (addènso) tr to thicken || ref to thicken; to gather, throng

addentare (addènto) tr to bite || ref (mach) to mesh

addentatura f bite; (carp) tongue (of tongue and groove)

addentella•to -ta adj toothed, notched || m chance, occasion; (archit) toothing

addentrare (addéntro) tr to penetrate || ref to penetrate; to proceed

addèntro adv inside; addentro in into; inside of

addestraménto m training

addestrare (addèstro) tr & ref to train

addestra•tóre -trice mf trainer

addét•to -ta adj assigned; attached; pertaining || m attaché; addetto stampa press secretary

addì adv the (+ a certain date), e.g., addì 27 gennaio the 27th of January

addiàc•cio m (-ci) sheepfold; bivouac

addiètro m (naut) stern; per l'addietro in the past || adv behind; ago; dare

addietro to back up; **lasciarsi addietro** to delay; **tempo addietro** some time ago; **tirarsi addietro** to back away

addìo *m* (**-i**) farewell; **dare l'addìo a** to say good-bye; **dare l'estremo addìo a** to pay one's last respects; **fare gli addìi** to say good-bye || *interj* farewell!, good-bye!

addire §151 *tr* (poet) to consecrate || *ref* to be suitable, be becoming; **addirsi a** to be becoming to

addirittura *adv* directly; even, without hesitation; absolutely, positively

addirizzare *tr* to straighten up; **addirizzare le gambe ai cani** to try the impossible

additare *tr* to point out

additì·vo -va *adj* & *m* additive

addivenire §282 *intr* (ESSERE)—**addivenire a** to come to, reach (*e.g., an agreement*)

addizionale *adj* additional || *f* supplementary tax

addizionare (**addizióno**) *tr* & *intr* to add

addizionatrice *f* adding machine

addizióne *f* addition

addobbaménto *m* adornment, decoration

addobbare (**addòbbo**) *tr* to adorn, bedeck, decorate

addobba·tóre -trice *mf* decorator

addòbbo *m* adornment, decoration; hangings (*in a church*)

addocilire §176 *tr* to soften up

addolcire §176 *tr* to sweeten; to calm down || *ref* to mellow, soften

addolorare (**addolóro**) *tr* & *ref* to grieve; **addolorarsi per** to grieve over, lament

addolora·to -ta *adj* sorrowful || **l'Addolorata** *f* (eccl) Our Lady of Sorrows

addòme *m* abdomen

addomesticàbile *adj* tamable

addomesticaménto *m* taming

addomesticare §197 (**addomèstico**) *tr* to tame; to accustom || *ref* to become accustomed

addomestica·to -ta *adj* tame, domesticated

addominale *adj* abdominal

addormentare (**addorménto**) *tr* to put to sleep; to numb || *ref* to fall asleep; to be asleep (*said of a limb*)

addormenta·to -ta *adj* asleep; numbed

addossare (**addòsso**) *tr* to put on; **addossare qlco a qlco** to lean s.th against s.th; **addossare qlco a qlcu** to put s.th on s.o.; (fig) to entrust s.o. with s.th || *ref* to take upon oneself; to crowd together; **addossarsi a** to lean against; to crowd

addòsso *adv* on; on oneself, on one's back; about oneself; **addosso a** on, upon; against; **avere la sfortuna addosso** to be always unlucky; **dare addosso a qlcu** to assail s.o.; **levarsi d'addosso** to get rid of; **levarsi i panni d'addosso** to take the shirt off one's back

addót·to -ta *adj* adduced, alleged

addottorare (**addottóro**) *tr* to confer the doctor's degree on || *ref* to receive the doctor's degree

addurre §102 *tr* to adduce; to allege; (poet) to bring

Ade *m* Hades

adeguare (**adéguo**) *tr* to equalize; to bring in line || *ref* to conform, adapt oneself

adeguazióne *f* equalization

adegua·to -ta *adj* adequate

adémpiere §163 *tr* to fulfill, accomplish || *ref* to come true

adempiménto *m* fulfillment, discharge (*of one's duty*)

adempire §176 *tr* to fulfill, accomplish || *ref* to come true

adenòide *adj* adenoid || **adenoidi** *fpl* adenoids

adèpto *m* follower; initiate

aderènte *adj* adherent || *mf* adherent, supporter

aderènza *f* adherence; (mach) friction; (pathol) adhesion; **aderenze** connections

aderire §176 *intr* to adhere; to stick; **aderire a** to grant (*e.g., a request*); to concur with; to subscribe to

adescare §197 (**adésco**) *tr* to lure, bait, entice; (mach) to prime (*a pump*)

adesióne *f* adhesion; support; (phys) adherence

adesì·vo -va *adj* & *m* adhesive

adèsso *adv* now, just now; **da adesso in poi** from now on; **per adesso** for the time being

adiacènte *adj* adjacent

adiacènza *f* adjacency; **adiacenze** vicinity

adianto *m* (bot) maidenhair

adibire §176 *tr* to assign; to use

àdipe *m* fat

adipó·so -sa [s] *adj* adipose

adirare *ref* to get angry

adira·to -ta *adj* angry, mad

adire §176 *tr* to apply to (*the court*); to enter into possession of (*an inheritance*)

adocchiare §287 (**adòcchio**) *tr* to eye; to ogle; to spot

adolescènte *adj* & *mf* adolescent

adolescènza *f* adolescence

adombrare (**adómbro**) *tr* to shade; to hide, veil || *ref* to shy (*said of a horse*); (fig) to take umbrage

Adóne *m* Adonis

adontare (**adónto**) *tr* (obs) to offend || *ref* to take offense

adoperare (**adòpero** & **adópero**) *tr* to use, employ || *ref* to exert oneself; to do one's best

adoràbile *adj* adorable

adorare (**adóro**) *tr* to adore; to worship || *intr* (archaic) to pray

adora·tóre -trice *mf* worshiper || *m* (joc) admirer, suitor

adorazióne *f* adoration, worship

adornare (**adórno**) *tr* to adorn || *ref* to bedeck oneself

adór·no -na *adj* adorned, bedecked; (poet) fine, beautiful

adottante *mf* (law) adopter

adottare (adòtto) *tr* to adopt

adotti·vo -va *adj* adoptive; foster (*child*)

adozióne *f* adoption

Adriàti·co -ca *adj* (*-ci -che*) Adriatic || **Adriatico** *m* Adriatic

adulare (àdulo) *tr* to flatter; to fawn on

adula·tóre -trice *mf* flatterer

adulatò·rio -ria *adj* (*-ri -rie*) flattering; fawning

adulazióne *f* adulation; fawning

adulterante *adj & m* adulterant

adulteri·no -na *adj* bastard; adulterated

adultè·rio *m* (*-ri*) adultery

adùlte·ro -ra *adj* adulterous || *m* adulterer || *f* adulteress

adul·to -ta *adj & mf* adult

adunanza *f* assembly

adunare *tr & ref* to assemble, gather

adunata *f* reunion, meeting; (mil) muster

adun·co -ca *adj* (*-chi -che*) hooked, crooked

adunghiare §287 *tr* (poet) to claw

adu·sto -sta *adj* skinny; (poet) burnt

aerare (àero) *tr* to air, ventilate

aerazióne *f* aeration; airing

aère·o -a *adj* aerial; air; overhead; high, lofty; airy, fanciful || *m* airplane; (rad & telv) aerial

aerobrigata *f* (mil) wing

aerocistèrna *f* (aer) tanker

aerodinàmi·co -ca (*-ci -che*) *adj* aerodynamic(al); streamlined || *f* aerodynamics

aeròdromo *m* airfield, airdrome

aerofaro *m* airport beacon

aerofotogram·ma *m* (*-mi*) aerial photograph

aerogiro *m* helicopter

aerògrafo *m* spray gun (*for painting*)

aerolìnea *f* airline; **aerolinea principale** trunkline

aeròlito *m* aerolite, meteorite

aeromarìtti·mo -ma *adj* air-sea

aeròmetro *m* aerometer

aeromòbile *m* aircraft; **aeromobile senza pilota** drone, pilotless aircraft

aeromodellismo *m* model-airplane building

aeromodelli·sta *mf* (*-sti -ste*) model-airplane builder

aeromodèllo *m* model airplane

aeromotóre *m* windmill; aircraft motor

aeronàu·ta *m* (*-ti*) aeronaut

aeronàuti·co -ca (*-ci -che*) *adj* aeronautic(al) || *f* aeronautics

aeronave *f* airship, aircraft

aeroplano *m* airplane

aeropòrto *m* airport, airfield

aeroportuale *adj* airport

aerorazzo [ddzz] *m* rocket spaceship

aeroriméssa *f* hangar

aerosbar·co *m* (*-chi*) landing of airborne troops

aeroservì·zio [s] *m* (*-zi*) air service

aerosilurante [s] *f* torpedo plane

aerosiluro [s] *m* aerial torpedo

aerosòl [s] *m* aerosol

aerosostenta·to -ta [s] *adj* airborne

aerospaziale *adj* aerospace

aerospà·zio *m* (*-zi*) aerospace

aerostàti·co -ca (*-ci -che*) *adj* aerostatic(al) || *f* aerostatics

aeròstato *m* aerostat

aerostazióne *f* air terminal

aerotas·sì *m* (*-sì*) taxiplane

aerotrasportare (aerotraspòrto) *tr* to airlift

aerotrasporta·to -ta *adj* airlifted; airborne

aerovia *f* (aer) beam (*course indicated by a radio beam*); (aer) air lane

afa *f* sultriness; **fare afa a** (coll) to be a pain in the neck to

afèresi *f* apheresis

affàbile *adj* affable, agreeable

affaccendare (affaccèndo) *tr* to busy || *ref* to busy oneself, bustle

affaccenda·to -ta *adj* busy, bustling; occupied with busywork

affacciare §128 *tr* to show or display at the window; to bring forward (*e.g., an objection*); to raise (*a doubt*) || *ref* to show oneself (*at the door or window*); to present itself (*said of a doubt*)

affaccia·to -ta *adj* facing

affagottare (affagòtto) *tr* to bundle || *ref* to bundle up; to dress sloppily

affamare *tr* to starve

affama·to -ta *adj* starved, ravenous || *mf* starveling; hungry person; wretch

affannare *tr* to worry, to afflict || *intr* to pant; to be out of breath || *ref* to worry; to bustle around

affanna·to -ta *adj* panting; out of breath; worried

affanno *m* shortness of breath; grief, sorrow

affannó·so -sa [s] *adj* panting; wearisome

affardellare (affardèllo) *tr* to bundle together; (mil) to pack

affare *m* affair, matter; business; condition, quality; deal; **affari** business; **affari esteri** foreign affairs; **un buon affare** a good deal; a bargain

affarismo *m* sharp business practice

affari·sta *mf* (*-sti -ste*) unscrupulous operator

affaristi·co -ca *adj* (*-ci -che*) sharp

affascinante *adj* fascinating, charming

affascinare (affàscino) *tr* to fascinate, charm; to seduce; to spellbind || (affàscino) *tr* to bundle, to sheave

affascina·tóre -trice *adj* fascinating, charming || *mf* charmer, spellbinder

affastellare (affastèllo) *tr* to fagot (*twigs*): to sheave, bundle (*e.g., hay*); to pile, heap (*wood, crops, etc*); (fig) to jumble up

affaticare §197 *tr* to fatigue, tire, weary || *ref* to get tired; to weary; to toil

affatica·to -ta *adj* weary, tired

affatto *adv* quite, entirely; **niente affatto** not at all; **non . . . affatto** not at all

affatturare *tr* to bewitch; to adulterate (*e.g., food*)

affermare (affèrmo) *tr* to affirm, assert || *intr* to nod assent || *ref* to take hold (*said, e.g., of a new product*)

affermati·vo -va *adj & f* affirmative

affermazióne *f* affirmation; assertion,

statement; success (*e.g.*, *of a new product*); (sports) victory

afferrare (**affèrro**) *tr* to grab, grasp; to catch, nab || *ref* to cling

affettare (**affètto**) *tr* to slice; to cut up || (**affètto**) *tr* to affect

affetta·to -ta *adj* affected || *m* cold cuts

affettatrice *f* slicing machine

affettazióne *f* affectation

affetti·vo -va *adj* emotional

affèt·to -ta *adj* afflicted, burdened || *m* affection, love; feeling

affettuosi·tà [s] *f* (-tà) love, affection

affettuó·so -sa [s] *adj* affectionate, loving, tender

affezionare (**affezióno**) *tr* to inspire affection in || *ref*—**affezionarsi a** to become fond of

affeziona·to -ta *adj* affectionate, loving; Suo affezionatissimo best regards; tuo affezionatissimo love, as ever

affezióne *f* affection

affiancare §197 *tr* to place next; to favor, help; (mil) to flank

affiatamènto *m* harmony; teamwork

affiatare *tr* to harmonize

affibbiare §287 *tr* to buckle, fasten; to deliver (*a blow*); to play (*a trick*); to slap (*a fine*)

affidamènto *m* consignment, delivery; trust, confidence; dare affidamento to be trustworthy; fare affidamento su to rely upon

affidare *tr* to entrust; to commit (*to memory*); affidare qlco a qlcu to entrust s.o with s.th || *ref* to trust; affidarsi a to trust in

affievolimènto *m* weakening

affievolire §176 *tr* to weaken || *ref* to grow weaker

affiggere §103 *tr* to post; to fix (*one's eyes or glance*) || *ref* to gaze, stare

affigliare §280 *tr & ref* var of affiliare

affilacoltèl·li *m* (-li) steel (*for sharpening knives*)

affilara·sóio *m* (-sói) strop

affilare *tr* to sharpen, hone, whet; to make thin || *ref* to become thin

affila·to -ta *adj* sharp, sharpened; thin || *f* sharpening

affila·tóio *m* (-tói) sharpener

affilatrice *f* grindstone

affiliare §287 *tr* to affiliate || *ref* to become affiliated; affiliarsi a to become a member of

affilia·to -ta *adj* affiliated || *mf* affiliate; foster child; member of a secret society

affiliazióne *f* affiliation

affinare *tr* to sharpen; to refine, purify; to improve (*e.g.*, *one's style*) || *ref* to improve

affinché *conj* so that, in order that; affinché non lest

affine *adj* akin, related; similar || *mf* in-law || *m* kinsman || *f* kinswoman || *adv*—affine di in order to

affini·tà *f* (-tà) affinity

affiochire §176 *tr* to make hoarse; to weaken || *ref* to become hoarse; to grow dim (*said of a candle*)

affioramènto *m* surfacing; (min) outcrop

affiorare (**affióro**) *intr* to surface, emerge; to appear, to show

affissare *tr* (poet) to fix || *ref* to concentrate; (poet) to gaze

affissióne *f* posting, bill posting

affìs·so -sa *adj* fixed; posted || *m* bill, poster; door or window; (gram) affix

affittacàme·re *m* (-re) landlord || *f* landlady

affittanza *f* rent

affittare *tr* to rent || *ref*—si affitta for rent

affitto *m* rent, rental; dare in affitto to rent (*to grant by lease*); prendere in affitto to rent (*to take by lease*)

affittuà·rio -ria *mf* (-ri -rie) renter; tenant

affliggènte *adj* tormenting, distressing

affliggere §104 *tr* to afflict, distress || *ref* to grieve

afflìt·to -ta *adj* afflicted, grieving || *mf* afflicted person, wretch

afflizióne *f* affliction, distress

afflosciare §128 (**afflòscio**) *tr* to cause to sag; to weaken || *ref* to droop; to sag; to be deflated; to faint

afflosciare §176 *tr & ref* var of afflosciare

affluènte *adj & m* confluent

affluènza *f* confluence; abundance; crowd

affluire §176 *intr* (ESSERE) to flow (*said of river*); to flock (*said of people*); to pour in (*said of earnings*)

afflusso *m* flow

affogamènto *m* drowning

affogare §209 (**affógo**) *tr* to drown; to smother || *intr* (ESSERE) to drown

affoga·to -ta *adj* drowned; poached (*egg*)

affollamènto *m* crowd, throng

affollare (**affòllo & affóllo**) *tr* to crowd; to overcome || *ref* to crowd

affolla·to -ta *adj* crowded

affondamènto *m* sinking

affondami·ne *m* (-ne) mine layer

affondare (**affóndo**) *tr* to sink; to stick || *ref* to sink

affondata *f* (aer) nosedive

affóndo *m* (fencing) lunge || *adv* deeply

afforestare (**afforèsto**) *tr* to reforest

affossare (**affòsso**) *tr* to ditch; (fig) to table (*e.g.*, *a proposal*); to hollow out || *ref* to become sunken or hollow (*said, e.g., of cheeks*)

affossatóre *m* ditchdigger; gravedigger

affrancare §197 *tr* to set free; to free; to redeem (*a property*); to stamp || *ref* to free oneself; to take heart

affrancatrice *f* postage meter

affrancatura *f* stamp, stamping

affràngere §179 *tr* to weary; (obs) to break down (*the spirit*)

affran·to -ta *adj* weary; broken down, broken-hearted

affratellamènto *m* fraternization

affratellare (**affratèllo**) *tr* to bind in brotherly love || *ref* to fraternize

affrescare §197 (**affrésco**) *tr* to fresco; to paint in fresco

affré·sco *m* (**-schi**) fresco
affrettare (**affrétto**) *tr & ref* to hurry, hasten
affretta· to -ta *adj* hurried
affrontare (**affrónto**) *tr* to face, confront ‖ *ref* to meet in combat; to come to blows
affronta·to -ta *adj*—**affrontati** (herald) combattant
affrónto *m* affront, offense
affumicare §197 (**affùmico**) *tr* to smoke; to blacken; to smoke out; to smoke (*meat or fish*)
affumica·to -ta *adj* smoked; dark (*glasses*)
affusolare [s] (**affùsolo**) *tr & ref* to taper
affusola·to -ta [s] *adj* tapered; slender
affusto *m* gun carriage
afga·no -na *adj & mf* Afghan
àfo·no -na *adj* voiceless
afori·sma *m* (**-smi**) aphorism
afó·so -sa [s] *adj* sultry
Africa, l' *f* Africa
africa·no -na *adj & mf* African
afrodisìa·co -ca *adj & m* (**-ci -che**) aphrodisiac
afta *m* mouth ulcer; **afta epizootica** (vet) foot-and-mouth disease
àgata *f* agate ‖ **Agata** *f* Agatha
agènda *f* notebook; agenda
agènte *adj* active ‖ *m* agent; broker; merchant; officer; **agente delle tasse** tax collector; **agente di cambio** stockbroker; money changer; **agente di commercio** broker, commission merchant; **agente di custodia** jailer; **agente di polizia** police officer, policeman; **agente di spionaggio** informer; **agente provocatore** agent provocateur
agenzìa *f* agency; office, branch; **agenzia immobiliare** real-estate office
agevolare (**agévolo**) *tr* to facilitate, help
agevolazióne *f* facility; **agevolazione di pagamento** easy terms
agévole *adj* easy
agevolézza *f* facility
agallare *intr* to come to the surface
agganciaménto *m* docking (*in space*); (rr) coupling
agganciare §128 *tr* to hook; (rr) to couple; (mil) to engage (*the enemy*)
aggàn·cio *m* (**-ci**) docking (*in space*); (rr) coupling
aggég·gio *m* (**-gi**) gadget
aggettivale *adj* adjectival
aggettivo *m* adjective
agghiacciaménto *m* freezing
agghiacciante *adj* hair-raising, frightful
agghiacciare §128 *tr* to freeze ‖ *ref* to freeze; to be horrified
agghiaccia·to -ta *adj* frozen, icy
agghindare *tr & ref* to preen, primp
àg·gio *m* (**-gi**) agio; **fare aggio** to be at a premium
aggiogare §209 (**aggiógo**) *tr* to yoke
aggiornaménto *m* adjournment (*e.g., of a meeting*); bringing up to date
aggiornare (**aggiórno**) *tr* to bring up to date; to adjourn ‖ *ref* to keep up with the times

aggiraménto *m* surrounding, outflanking
aggirare *tr* to surround, outflank; to swindle ‖ *ref* to roam, wander; **aggirarsi su** to approximate; to be almost
aggiudicare §197 (**aggiùdico**) *tr* to adjudicate, award ‖ *ref* to win
aggiudicazióne *f* adjudication, award
aggiùngere §183 *tr* to add; to join, connect ‖ *ref* to be added; to join
aggiunta *f* addition
aggiuntare *tr* to attach, join
aggiun·to -ta *adj & m* associate, assistant, deputy ‖ *f* see **aggiunta**
aggiustàbile *adj* repairable
aggiustaménto *m* settlement; adjustment; (mil) correction (*of fire*)
aggiustare *tr* to fix, repair; to adjust; (mil) to correct (*cannon fire*); **aggiustare per le feste** (coll) to fix; (coll) to give a good beating to ‖ *ref* (archaic) to come closer; (coll) to manage; (coll) to come to an agreement
aggiusta·tóre -trice *mf* repairer, fixer ‖ *m* repairman
aggiustatura *f* fixing, repairing, repair
agglomerare (**agglòmero**) *tr & ref* to pile up; to crowd together
agglomerato *m* built-up area; **agglomerato urbano** urban center
agglutinare (**agglùtino**) *tr & ref* to agglutinate
agglutinazióne *f* agglutination
aggobbire §176 *tr* to bend, bend over ‖ *intr* (ESSERE) & *ref* to hunch over
aggomitolare (**aggomìtolo**) *tr* to coil ‖ *ref* to curl up
aggradare *intr* (with *dat*) (poet) to please; **come Le aggrada** as you please
aggradire §176 *tr* to appreciate ‖ *intr* (poet) (with *dat*) to please
aggraffare *tr* to hook; to grab; to join (*metal sheets*) with a double seam; to stitch, staple
aggraffatrice *f* folding machine; (mach) can sealer
aggranchire §176 *tr* to benumb; to deaden, stupefy ‖ *intr* to become numb
aggrappare *tr* to grab; to clamp ‖ *ref* to cling
aggravaménto *m* aggravation
aggravante *adj* (law) aggravating (*circumstances*)
aggravare *tr* to aggravate; to overload (*e.g., one's stomach*) ‖ *ref* to get worse
aggrà·vio *m* (**-vi**) burden (*e.g., of taxes*); **fare aggravio a qlcu di qlco** to impute s.th to s.o.
aggraziare §287 *tr* to embellish; to render graceful ‖ *ref* to win, gain; to ingratiate oneself
aggrazia·to -ta *adj* graceful; polite
aggredire §176 *tr* to assail, attack, assault
aggregare §209 (**aggrègo**) *tr & ref* to join, unite
aggrega·to -ta *adj* adjunct ‖ *m* aggregation
aggressióne *f* aggression

aggressi·vo -va *adj* aggressive ‖ *m* (mil) poison gas

aggressóre *m* aggressor

aggricciare §128 *tr* to wrinkle; (slang) to knit (*e.g., the brow*) ‖ *ref* (poet) to shiver

aggrinzare *tr & ref* to wrinkle

aggrinzire §176 *tr & ref* var of **aggrinzare**

aggrondare (**aggróndo**) *tr* to knit (*the brow*)

aggrottare (**aggròtto**) *tr* to knit (*the brow*)

aggrovigliare §280 *tr* to tangle, entangle ‖ *ref* to become entangled

aggrumare *tr & ref* to clot; to coagulate

aggruppare *tr* to group

agguagliare §280 *tr* to level; to equalize; to compare

agguantare *tr* to grab; to nab; (coll) to hit; **agguantare per il collo** to grab by the neck ‖ *ref*—**agguantarsi a** to get hold of

agguato *m* ambush; **cadere in un agguato** to fall into a trap; **stàre in agguato** to wait in ambush

agguerrire §176 *tr* to train for war; to inure to war; to inure

aghétto *m* shoestring; (mil) lanyard

agiatézza *f* comfort, wealth; **vivere nell'agiatezza** to live in comfort

agia·to -ta *adj* well-to-do, comfortable

àgile *adj* agile, nimble; prompt

agili·tà *f* (**-tà**) agility, nimbleness; promptness

à·gio *m* (**-gi**) comfort; opportunity; ease; **agi** conveniences, comforts; **a Suo agio** at your convenience; **aver agio** to have time; **stare a proprio agio** to feel at ease; to be comfortable; **vivere negli agi** to live comfortably

agiografia *f* hagiography

agiògrafo *m* hagiographer

agire §176 *intr* to act; to work; (theat) to act, perform

agitare (**àgito**) *tr* to agitate, shake; to stir; to stir up; to discuss (*e.g., a problem*) ‖ *ref* to toss; to shake; to stir; to get excited

agita·to -ta *adj* rough, choppy (*sea*); troubled, upset ‖ *mf* violently insane person

agita·tóre -trice *mf* agitator ‖ *m* shaker

agitazióne *f* agitation

agli §4

agliàce·o -a *adj* garlicky

à·glio *m* (**-gli**) garlic

agnellino *m* little lamb, lambkin

agnèllo *m* lamb

agnizióne *f* recognition

agnòsti·co -ca *adj & mf* (**-ci -che**) agnostic

a·go *m* (**-ghi**) needle; pointer (*of scales*); stem (*of valve*)

agognare (**agógno**) *tr* to covet

agóne *m* contest; arena

agonía *f* agony, death struggle; anguish

agonìsti·co -ca *adj* (**-ci -che**) competitive, aggressive (*spirit*); athletic (*competition*) ‖ *f* athletics

agonizzare [ddzz] *intr* to agonize, be in agony; (fig) to die out

agopuntura *f* acupuncture

ago·ràio *m* (**-rài**) needle case

agosta·no -na *adj* August, e.g., **pomeriggio agostano** August afternoon

agostinia·no -na *adj & m* Augustinian

agósto *m* August

agrà·rio -ria (**-ri -rie**) *adj & m* agrarian ‖ *m* landlord ‖ *f* agriculture

agrèste *adj* country

agrìco·lo -la *adj* agricultural

agricoltóre *m* farmer; agriculturist

agricoltura *f* agriculture

agrifò·glio *m* (**-gli**) holly

agrimensóre *m* surveyor

agrimensura *f* surveying

a·gro -gra *adj* sour, bitter ‖ *m* citrus juice; sourness, bitterness; surrounding country

agrodólce *adj* sweet and sour; (fig) acidulous (*tone*)

agronomia *f* agronomy

agrònomo *m* agronomist

agrume *m* citrus (*tree and fruit*); **agrumi** citrus fruit

agucchiare §287 *intr* to knit or sew idly

agùglia *f* spire; top; (ichth) gar; (poet) eagle; (obs) needle

aguzzare *tr* to sharpen; to whet (*the appetite*)

aguzzino [ddzz] *m* slave driver; jailer

aguz·zo -za *adj* sharp, pointed

ah *interj* ah!, aha!; ha!

ahi *interj* ouch!

ahimè *interj* alas!

àia *f* yard, barnyard; threshing floor; governess ‖ **L'Àia** *f* the Hague

Aiace *m* Ajax

àio *m* (**ài**) tutor

aiòla *f* lawn; flower bed

àire *m* push; short run (*preparing for a jump*); **dare l'àire a** to start off; **prendere l'àire** to take off

airóne *m* heron

aitante *adj* robust, stalwart

aiuòla *f* (poet) var of **aiola**

aiutante *adj* helping ‖ *mf* assistant ‖ *m* (mil) adjutant; **aiutante di campo** aide-de-camp; **aiutante di sanità** orderly

aiutare *tr* to help ‖ *ref* to strive; to help oneself; to help one another

aiutato *m* first assistant (*e.g., of a surgeon*)

aiuto *m* aid, help; assistant; first assistant (*of a surgeon*)

aizzare (**aìzzo**) *tr* to incite, to incite to riot; to sic (*a dog*)

al §4

a·la *f* (**-li & -le**) wing; sail, vane (*of windmill*); blade (*e.g., of fan*); brim (*of hat*); (football) end; **ala a freccia** backswept wing; **ala di popolo** throng; **fare ala a** to line up along

alabarda *f* halberd

alabardière *m* halberdier

alabastri·no -na *adj* alabaster; white as alabaster

alabastro *m* alabaster

àlacre *adj* eager, lively

alacrità *f* alacrity

alàg·gio *m* (**-gi**) hauling, towing
alamaro *m* braid, gimp
alambic·co *m* (**-chi**) still
alano *m* Great Dane
alare *adj* wing (*e.g.*, *span*) ‖ *m* andiron ‖ *tr* to haul
Alasca, l' *f* Alaska
ala·to -ta *adj* winged, sublime
alba *f* dawn, daybreak
albagìa *f* haughtiness
albanése [s] *adj & mf* Albanian
Albanìa, l' *f* Albania
àlbatro *m* (orn) albatross
albeggiaménto *m* dawning
albeggiare §290 (**albéggio**) *intr* (ESSERE) to dawn; (poet) to sparkle (*said, e.g., of ice*) ‖ *impers* (ESSERE)—**albeggia** the day dawns
alberare (**àlbero**) *tr* to plant (*trees*); to reforest; to hoist (*a mast*); to mast (*a ship*)
albera·to -ta *adj* tree-lined; (naut) masted
alberèllo *m* small tree; apothecary's jar
albergare §209 (**albèrgo**) *tr* to lodge; to put up at a hotel; (fig) to harbor ‖ *intr* to lodge; to put up
alberga·tóre -trice *mf* hotelkeeper
alberghiè·ro -ra *adj* hotel
albèr·go *m* (**-ghi**) hotel; refuge; hospitality; **albergo diurno** day hostel; **albergo per la gioventù** youth hostel
àlbero *m* tree; poplar; (mach) shaft; (naut) mast; **albero a camme** (aut) camshaft; **albero a gomito** (aut) crankshaft; **albero di distribuzione** (aut) camshaft; **albero di Natale** Christmas tree; **albero di trasmissione** (aut) transmission; **albero genealogico** family tree
albicòc·ca *f* (**-che**) apricot
albicòc·co *m* (**-chi**) apricot tree
al·bo -ba *adj* (poet) white ‖ *m* album; bulletin board; (law) roll; comic book; **albo d'onore** honor roll ‖ *f* see **alba**
albóre *m* (poet) whiteness; (poet) dawn
album *m* (album) album, scrapbook
albume *m* albumen
albumina *f* albumin
àlca·li *m* (**-li**) alkali
alcali·no -na *adj* alkaline
alce *m* moose; elk
alchìmia *f* alchemy
alchimi·sta *m* (**-sti**) alchemist
alcióne *m* halcyon
alciò·nio -nia *adj* (**-ni -nie**) halcyon
àlco·le *m* alcohol
alcolici·tà *f* (**-tà**) alcoholic content
alcòli·co -ca *adj* (**-ci -che**) alcoholic ‖ *m* alcoholic beverage
alcolismo *m* alcoholism
alcolizzare [ddzz] *tr* to intoxicate ‖ *ref* to become intoxicated
alcolizza·to -ta [ddzz] *adj* intoxicated ‖ *mf* alcoholic
alcool *m* (alcool) var of **alcole**
alcoolici·tà *f* (**-tà**) var of **alcolicità**
alcòoli·co -ca (**-ci -che**) *adj & m* var of **alcolico**
alcoolismo *m* var of **alcolismo**
alcoolizzare [ddzz] *tr* var of **alcolizzare**

alcoolizza·to -ta [ddzz] *adj & mf* var of **alcolizzato**
alcòva *f* bedroom; bed; alcove
alcunché *pron* something, anything
alcu·no -na *adj & pron* some; **alcu·ni -ne** some; quite a few, several, a good many
aldilà *m* life beyond, afterlife
àlea *f* chance, hazard; **correre l'alea** to try one's luck
aleggiare §290 (**aléggio**) *intr* to flutter; to flap the wings; to hover
aleróne *m* var of **alettone**
alesàg·gio *m* (**-gi**) (mach) bore
alesare (**aléso**) *tr* (mach) to bore
alesatóre *m* reamer
alesatrice *s* boring machine
Alessandria d'Egitto *f* Alexandria
alessandri·no -na *adj & mf* Alexandrian ‖ *m* Alexandrine (*verse*)
Alessandro *m* Alexander; **Alessandro Magno** Alexander the Great
alétta *f* small wing; fin (*of fish*); (aer) tab; **aletta di compensazione** trim tab; **aletta parasole** (aut) sun visor
alettóne *m* (aer) aileron, flap
Aleuti·no -na *adj*—**Isole Aleutine** Aleutian Islands
al·fa *m* (**-fa**) alpha ‖ *f* esparto
alfabèti·co -ca *adj* (**-ci -che**) alphabetical
alfabetizzazióne [ddzz] *f* teaching to read; learning to read
alfabèto *m* alphabet; code (*e.g., Morse*)
alfière *m* flagbearer, standardbearer; (chess) bishop
alfine *adv* finally, at last
al·ga *f* (**-ghe**) alga; **alga marina** seaweed
àlgebra *f* algebra
algèbri·co -ca *adj* (**-ci -che**) algebraic
Algèri *f* Algiers
Algerìa, l' *f* Algeria
algeri·no -na *adj & mf* Algerian
aliante *m* (aer) glider
alianti·sta *mf* (**-sti -ste**) glider pilot
àli·bi *m* (**-bi**) alibi
alice *f* anchovy
alienàbile *adj* alienable
alienare (**alièno**) *tr* to alienate; to transfer, convey ‖ *ref*—**alienarsi dalla ragione** to go out of one's mind
aliena·to -ta *adj* alienated ‖ *mf* insane person; dispossessed person
alienazióne *f* alienation
alieni·sta *mf* (**-sti -ste**) alienist
alièno -na *adj* disinclined; (poet) foreign, alien
alimentare *adj* alimentary ‖ **alimentari** *mpl* food, foodstuff ‖ *v* (**aliménto**) *tr* to feed; to fuel
alimentari·sta *m* (**-sti**) food merchant; food-industry worker
alimenta·tóre -trice *mf* stoker ‖ *m* (mach) stoker, feeder
alimentazióne *f* nourishment; feeding; (mil) loading; **alimentazione artificiale** intravenous feeding
aliménto *m* food, nourishment; feed; **alimenti** alimony (*maintenance*)
alimònia *f* alimony
alìnea *f* (law) paragraph, section

aliquota *f* share; parcel, quota

aliscafo *m* hydrofoil

alisè·o -a *adj* trade (*wind*) ‖ *m* trade wind

alitare (àlito) *intr* to breathe; to blow gently; **non alitare** to not breathe a word

àlito *m* breath; (fig) breeze

alivo·lo -la *adj* (poet) winged; (fig) swift

alla §4

allacciaménto *m* binding; connection, linking

allacciare §128 *tr* to bind, tie; to connect; to buckle; (fig) to deceive

allacciatura *f* lacing; buckling

allagare §209 *tr* to flood, overflow

allampana·to -ta *adj* tall and lean, lanky

allargare §209 *tr* to broaden, widen; **allargare la mano** to be lenient; to be liberal; **allargare il freno** to give free rein ‖ *ref* to widen, spread out; **mi si allarga il cuore** I feel relieved

allargatura *f* widening

allarmante *adj* alarming

allarmare *tr* to alarm ‖ *ref* to worry, become alarmed

allarme *m* alarm; **allarme aereo** air-raid warning; **cessato allarme** all clear; **falso allarme** false alarm; **stare in allarme** to be alarmed

allascare §197 *tr* (naut) to ease, slacken (*a rope*)

allato *adv* (poet) near; **allato a** near; beside; in comparison with

allattaménto *m* nursing, feeding; **allattamento artificiale** bottle feeding

allattare *tr* to nurse (*at the breast*); to feed (*with a bottle*)

alle §4

alleanza *f* alliance

alleare (allèo) *tr* to ally ‖ *ref* to become allied; to be connected

allea·to -ta *adj* allied ‖ *mf* ally

allegare §209 (allégo) *tr* to enclose; to adduce; to allege; **allegare i denti** to set the teeth on edge ‖ *intr* (hort) to ripen

allega·to -ta *adj* enclosed ‖ *m* enclosure

alleggeriménto *m* lightening, easing

alleggerire §176 *tr* to lighten; to alleviate ‖ *ref* to put on lighter clothes; **alleggerirsi di** (naut) to jettison

allegoria *f* allegory

allegòri·co -ca *adj* (-ci -che) allegorical

allegraménte *adv* cheerfully, merrily; thoughtlessly

allegrézza *f* joy, cheerfulness

allegria *f* cheer, gaiety; **stare in allegria** to be merry ‖ *interj* good cheer!

allé·gro -gra *adj* cheerful, merry, gay ‖ *m* (mus) allegro

alleluia *m* hallelujah

allenaménto *m* training

allenare (allèno) *tr & ref* to train

allena·tóre -trice *adj* training ‖ *mf* trainer, coach

allentare (allènto) *tr* to loosen, slacken; to mitigate; (coll) to deliver (*a blow*); **essere allentato** to have a hernia ‖ *ref* to slow up; to loosen up; to diminish

allergia *f* allergy

allèrgi·co -ca *adj* (-ci -che) allergic

allérta *f* alert ‖ *adv* alert, on the alert

allessare (allésso) *tr* to boil

allés·so -sa *adj* boiled ‖ *m* boiled meat, boiled beef

allestire §176 *tr* to prepare, make ready; to rig (*e.g., a ship*); to produce (*e.g., a play*)

allettaménto *m* allure, fascination

allettante *adj* alluring, enticing

allettare (allètto) *tr* to allure, entice; to confine to bed; to bend (*plants*) to the ground ‖ *ref* to be confined to bed

allevaménto *m* raising, breeding; flock

allevare (allèvo) *tr* to raise, breed; to rear

alleva·tóre -trice *mf* raiser, breeder

alleviare §287 (allèvio) *tr* to alleviate, lighten

allibire §176 *intr* (ESSERE) to turn pale; to be astonished, be dismayed

allibraménto *m* registration, entry; booking (*of bets*)

allibrare *tr* to register, enter; to book (*a bet*) on a horse

allibratóre *m* bookmaker (*at races*)

allietare (allièto) *tr* to cheer, enliven

alliè·vo -va *mf* pupil, student; follower, disciple ‖ *m* trainee; **allievo ufficiale** cadet

alligatóre *m* alligator

allignare *intr* to take root; to do well, prosper

allineaménto *m* alignment; falling in line

allineare (alline̊o) *tr* to align; (typ) to justify ‖ *ref* to align oneself, be aligned

allinea·to -ta *adj* aligned; **non allineato** nonaligned, uncommitted

allitterazióne *f* alliteration

allo §4

allòc·co·m (-chi) horned owl; (fig) dolt, nincompoop

allocuzióne *f* (poet) speech, address

allòdola *f* lark, skylark

allogare §209 (allògo) *tr* to place; to let, lease; to find employment for; to invest (*money*); to marry off (*a daughter*)

allòge·no -na *adj* minority ‖ *mf* member of an ethnic minority

alloggiaménto *m* (mil) lodging, quarters; (carp, mach) housing

alloggiare §290 (allòggio) *tr* to lodge, put up ‖ *intr* to lodge, stay

allòg·gio *m* (-gi) lodging, living quarters; accommodations

allontanaménto *m* removal; estrangement

allontanare *tr* to remove; to send away; to exonerate; to dismiss; to alienate ‖ *ref* to go away; to withdraw; to become estranged

allóra *adj* (inv) ‖ *adv* then; at that time; in that case; **da allora** ever since; **da allora in poi** from that time on; **fino allora** until then; **per allora** at that time

allorché *conj* when

allòro *m* laurel; **riposare sugli allori** to rest on one's laurels

allorquando *conj* (poet) when

àlluce *m* big toe

allucinante *adj* hallucinating; dazzling; deceptive

allucinare (**allùcino**) *tr* to hallucinate; to dazzle; to deceive

allucinazióne *f* hallucination

allùdere §105 *intr* to allude

allume *m* alum

alluminare (**allùmino**) *tr* to illuminate (*a manuscript*); (poet) to light

allumìnio *m* aluminum

allunàg·gio *m* (-gi) lunar landing; **allunaggio morbido** soft lunar landing

allunare *intr* to land on the moon

allunga *f* (mach) adapter

allungàbile *adj* extensible; extension (*table*)

allungaménto *m* lengthening

allungare §209 *tr* to lengthen; to stretch out (*e.g., the hand*); to dilute (*e.g., wine*); (coll) to deliver (*e.g., a slap*); (sports) to pass (*the ball*); **allungare il collo** to crane the neck; **allungare il passo** to walk faster ‖ *ref* to grow longer; to stretch; to grow taller

allun·go *m* (-ghi) (sports) sprint; (sports) forward pass

allusióne *f* allusion

alluvióne *m* flood

almanaccare §197 *tr* to dream of ‖ *intr* to dream, muse

almanac·co *m* (-chi) almanac

alméno *adv* at least; if only

alno *m* (bot) alder

àloe *m & f* aloe

alògeno *m* halogen

alogenuro *m* halide

alóne *m* halo

alòsa *f* (ichth) shad

alpacca *f* German silver

alpe *f* high mountain, alp ‖ **le Alpi** the Alps

alpèstre *adj* mountainous; (fig) uncouth

alpigia·no -na *adj* mountain, mountainous; (fig) uncouth ‖ *mf* mountaineer

alpinismo *m* mountain climbing

alpini·sta *mf* (-sti -ste) mountain climber

alpinìsti·co -ca *adj* (-ci -che) mountainclimbing

alpi·no -na *adj* alpine; Alpine ‖ *m* alpine soldier

alquan·to -ta *adj & pron* some; **alquanti -te** some; quite a few, several, a good many ‖ **alquanto** *adv* somewhat, rather

Alsàzia, l' *f* Alsace

alsazia·no -na *adj* & *mf* Alsacian

alt *m* (alt) halt, stop ‖ *interj* halt!, stop!

altaléna *f* seesaw; swing; (fig) ups and downs; **altalena a bilico** seesaw; **altalena sospesa** swing

altalenare (**altaléno**) *intr* to seesaw; to swing

altana *f* roof terrace

altare *m* altar

altarino *m* small altar; **svelare gli alta-** **rini** (joc) to expose the skeleton in the closet

altèa *f* marsh mallow

alterare (**àltero**) *tr* to alter; to falsify; to adulterate; to anger ‖ *ref* to alter; to become adulterated; to get angry

altera·to -ta *adj* altered; adulterated; feverish; angry

alterazióne *f* change, alteration; adulteration; slight fever

altercare §197 (**altèrco**) *intr* to dispute, quarrel

altèr·co *m* (-chi) altercation; **venire a un alterco** to get into a quarrel

alterigia *f* haughtiness

alternare (**altèrno**) *tr & ref* to alternate

alternati·vo -va *adj* alternating ‖ *f* alternative; choice

alterna·to -ta *adj* alternate; alternating (*current*)

alternatóre *m* (elec) alternator

altèr·no -na *adj* alternate

altè·ro -ra *adj* proud, haughty

altézza *f* height; width (*of cloth*); depth (*of water*); pitch (*of sound*); (astr, geom) altitude; (fig) loftiness, nobility; (naut) latitude; (typ) size; **essere all'altezza di** to be up to, be equal to; (naut) to be off ‖ **Altezza** *f* Highness

altezzó·so -sa [s] *adj* haughty

altìc·cio -cia *adj* (-ci -ce) tipsy

altìmetro *m* altimeter

altipiano *m* var of **altopiano**

altisonante [s] *adj* high-sounding

altìssi·mo -ma *adj* very high, highest ‖ **l'Altissimo** *m* the Most High

altitùdine *f* altitude

al·to -ta *adj* high; tall; wide (*cloth*); deep (*water*); upper; full (*day*); late (*e.g., Easter*); deep (*sleep*); early (*Middle Ages*); loud (*voice*); lofty (*peak*) ‖ *m* top; upper part; high quarters; **alti e bassi** ups and downs; **fare alto e basso** to be the undisputed boss; **guardare qlcu dall'alto in basso** to look down one's nose at s.o.; **in alto** up ‖ **alto** *adv* up

altofórno *m* (**altifórni**) blast furnace

altoloca·to -ta *adj* high-placed, highranking

altoparlante *m* loudspeaker

altopiano *m* (**altipiani**) plateau

altrettan·to -ta *adj & pron* as much; the same; **altrettanti -te** as many ‖ **altrettanto** *adv* as much; the same

altri *indef pron invar* someone; someone else; **non altri che** no one else but

altrièri *m & adv* day before yesterday

altriménti *adv* otherwise

al·tro -tra *adj* other; next (*world*); **altro ieri** day before yesterday; **chi altro?** who else?; **domani l'altro** the day after tomorrow; **fra l'altro** among other things; **ieri l'altro** the day before yesterday; **l'altro anno** last year; **l'altro giorno** the other day; **noi altri** we; **qualcun altro** somebody else; anybody else; **quest'altro** (**giorno, mese, anno**) next (**day, month, year**) ‖ *pron* other; anything else; **altro che!** why yes! || **l'altro** §11 correlative indef pron || **l'altro** §12 reciprocal pron

altrónde adv (poet) somewhere else; **d'altronde** besides; on the other hand

altróve adv elsewhere, somewhere else

altrui adj invar somebody else's, other people's || pron invar somebody else || **m—l'altrui** what belongs to someone else

altrui·sta (-sti -ste) adj altruistic || mf altruist

altura f height; (naut) high seas

alun·no -na mf pupil, student

alveare m beehive

àlveo m bed (of a river)

alvèolo m alveolus; socket (of tooth); cell (of honeycomb)

alzabandiè·ra m (-ra) raising of the flag

alzacristal·li m (-li) (aut) crank (to raise a window)

alzàia f tow line; towpath

alzare tr to lift, raise; to cut (cards); to shrug (one's shoulders); to set (sail); **alzare al cielo** to praise to the sky; **alzare i tacchi** to show a clean pair of heels; **alzare la cresta** to get cocky || ref to rise; to get up; **alzarsi in piedi** to stand up

alzata f raising, lifting; shrugging (of shoulders); standing up; riser (of step); three-tier candy tray; **alzata di scudi** rebellion; **alzata di testa** whim, caprice

alzavàlvo·le m (-le) (aut) valve lifter

alzo m gunsight

amàbile adj amiable; sweetish (wine)

amabili·tà f (-tà) amiability, kindness

ama·ca f (-che) hammock

amàlga·ma m (-mi) amalgam

amalgamare (amàlgamo) tr to amalgamate || ref to amalgamate; to blend

amalgamazióne f amalgamation

amante adj loving, fond || m lover || f mistress

amanuènse m amanuensis, scribe

amare tr to love; to like || ref to love one another

amareggiare §290 (amaréggio) tr to make bitter; to sadden || ref to become bitter; to sadden

amarèna f sour cherry

amarétto m macaroon

amarézza f bitterness

ama·ro -ra adj bitter || m bitters; bitterness

amarógno·lo -la adj bitterish

amarra f (naut) hawser

amarrare tr & intr var of **ammarrare**

ama·tóre -trice mf lover; amateur

amató·rio -ria adj (-ri -rie) amatory, of love

amàzzone [ddzz] f horsewoman; female jockey; (obs) riding habit; **cavalcare all'amazzone** to ride sidesaddle || **Amazzone** f (myth) Amazon

ambage f winding path; **ambagi** circumlocutions; **senz'ambagi** without beating about the bush

ambasceria f embassy

ambà·scia f (-sce) shortness of breath; grief, sorrow

ambasciata f embassy; ambassadorship; errand, mission

ambasciatóre m ambassador

ambasciatrice f ambassadress

ambedùe adj invar—**ambedue i** or **le** both || pron invar both

ambiare §287 intr to amble, pace (said of a horse)

ambiatura f pacing (said of a horse)

ambidè·stro -stra adj ambidextrous

ambidùe adj & pron invar var of **ambedue**

ambientare (ambiènto) tr to accustom; to place (a story in a certain period) || ref to get accustomed to one's surroundings; to orient oneself

ambienta·tóre -trice mf interior decorator; (theat) decorator

ambiènte adj room, e.g., **temperatura ambiente** room temperature || m environment; habitat; milieu; room; **trovarsi fuori del proprio ambiente** to be out of one's element

ambigui·tà f (-tà) ambiguity

ambì·guo -gua adj ambiguous

àm·bio m (-bi) amble, pacing

ambire §176 tr to be eager for || intr to be ambitious; **ambire a** to be ambitious for

àmbito m range, circle; (mus) range; **nell'ambito di** within

ambizióne f ambition

ambizióso -sa [s] adj ambitious || mf ambitious person

ambo or **am·bi -be** adj pl—**ambo i, ambo le, ambi i, ambe le** both

ambosèssi adj invar of both sexes, e.g., **giovani ambosessi** young people of both sexes

ambra f amber; **ambra grigia** ambergris

ambròsia f ambrosia; (bot) ragweed

ambulante adj itinerant; circulating; ambulant || m mail car

ambulanza f ambulance

ambulare (àmbulo) intr (coll) to ambulate

ambulatò·rio -ria (-ri -rie) adj ambulatory || m clinic, first-aid department

Amburgo m Hamburg

amèba f amoeba

a·men m (-men) amen || interj amen!

ameni·tà f (-tà) amenity; pleasantry

amèno -na adj pleasant, agreeable; amusing (fellow)

América, l' f America; **l'America del Nord** North America; **l'America del Sud** South America

americana f bicycle race between pairs

americanismo m Americanism

americanizzare [ddzz] tr to Americanize || ref to become Americanized

america·no -na adj & mf American || m vermouth with bitters || f see **americana**

ametista f amethyst

amianto m asbestos

amicale adj (poet) friendly

amichévole adj friendly; (sports) noncompetitive

amicìzia f friendship; **stringere amicizia con** to make friends with

ami·co -ca (-ci -che) *adj* friendly ‖ *mf* friend; beloved ‖ *m* boy friend; lover, paramour; **amico del cuore** bosom friend ‖ *f* girl friend; mistress

amidàce·o -a *adj* starchy

amidatura *f* starching

àmido *m* starch

Amlèto *m* Hamlet

ammaccare §197 *tr* to crush; to pound; to bruise; to dent

ammaccatura *f* bruise; dent

ammaestraménto *m* instruction, teaching; training

ammaestrare (ammaèstro & ammaéstro) *tr* to teach, to educate; to train (*animals*)

ammainare (ammàino) *tr* to lower (*e.g., a flag*)

ammalare *intr* (ESSERE) to fall ill ‖ *ref* to fall ill; **ammalarsi di** to come down with

ammala·to -ta *adj* ill, sick ‖ *mf* patient

ammaliare §287 *tr* to cast a spell on; to charm, enchant, fascinate; to bewitch

ammalia·tóre -trice *adj* charming, enchanting ‖ *mf* charmer ‖ *m* enchanter, sorcerer ‖ *f* enchantress, sorceress

amman·co m (-chi) shortage

ammanettare (ammanétto) *tr* to handcuff

ammaniglia·to -ta *adj* shackled; (fig) closely bound, closely tied

ammannare *tr* to sheave (*grain*)

ammannire §176 *tr* to prepare (*a dish*); to dish up (*a meal*)

ammansare *tr & ref* var of **ammansire**

ammansa·tóre -trice *mf* (poet) tamer

ammansire §176 *tr* to tame; to calm ‖ *ref* to become tamed; to calm down

ammantare *tr* to mantle, clothe; to cover; to hide (*the truth*)

ammanto *m* mantle, cloak; (fig) authority

ammaràg·gio m (-gi) landing on water; splashdown (*of a space vehicle*)

ammaraménto *m* var of **ammaraggio**

ammarare *intr* (aer) to land on water; (rok) to splash down

ammarrare *tr* (naut) to moor

ammassare *tr* to amass ‖ *ref* to crowd, throng

ammasso *m* heap, pile; cluster (*of stars*); government stockpile

ammattiménto *m* worry, nuisance

ammattire §176 *intr* (ESSERE) to go crazy; **fare ammattire** to drive crazy

ammattonare (ammattóno) *tr* to floor with bricks

ammattona·to -ta *adj* floored with bricks ‖ *m* brick floor; bricklaying

ammazzare *tr* to kill ‖ *ref* to kill oneself; to get killed

ammazzasèt·te m (-te) braggart

ammazza·tóio m (-tói) slaughterhouse

ammènda *f* fine; satisfaction (*for injury*); **fare ammenda** to make amends

ammendaménto *m* emendation: improvement (*of land*)

ammendare (ammèndo) *tr* to emendate; to improve (*land*)

ammennìcolo *m* excuse; trifle; **ammennìcoli** extras

ammés·so -sa *adj* admitted; **ammesso che** supposing that; **ammesso e non concesso** for the sake of argument

amméttere §198 *tr* to admit; to accept, suppose

ammezzare [ddzz] **(ammèzzo)** *tr* to leave half-finished (*a piece of work*); to fill halfway; to empty halfway

ammezzato [ddzz] *m* mezzanine

ammiccare §197 *intr* to wink; to cock one's eye

amministrare *tr* to administer, manage

amministra·tóre -trice *mf* administrator, manager; **amministratore delegato** chairman of the board

amministrazióne *f* administration, management; **ordinaria amministrazione** run-of-the-mill business

ammiràbile *adj* admirable

ammiràglia *f* (nav) flagship

ammiragliato *m* admiralty

ammirà·glio m (-gli) admiral; **ammiraglio d'armata** admiral; **ammiraglio di divisione** rear admiral; **ammiraglio di squadra** vice admiral; **grande ammiraglio** admiral of the fleet

ammirare *tr* to admire ‖ *intr* to wonder

ammirati·vo -va *adj* admiring; exclamation (*mark*)

ammira·tóre -trice *mf* admirer ‖ *m* suitor

ammirazióne *f* admiration

ammirévole *adj* admirable

ammissibile *adj* admissible; permissible

ammissióne *f* admission; (mach) intake; **ammissione comune** consensus

ammobiliaménto *m* furnishing; furniture

ammobiliare §287 *tr* to furnish

ammodernare (ammodèrno) *tr* to modernize

ammòdo *adj invar* well-mannered, polite ‖ *adv* properly

ammogliare §280 **(ammóglio)** *tr* to marry, give in marriage ‖ *ref* to marry, get married

ammoglia·to *adj* married ‖ *m* married man

ammollare (ammòllo) *tr* to soften; to soak; to slacken (*e.g., a hawser*); to deliver (*a slap*) ‖ *ref* to get soaked

ammollire §176 *tr* to soften; to weaken ‖ *ref* to soften; to mellow

ammonìaca *f* ammonia

ammoniménto *m* warning

ammonire §176 *tr* to admonish, reprimand

ammoni·tóre -trice *adj* warning

ammonizióne *f* admonition, warning

ammontare *m* amount, total ‖ *v* **(ammónto)** *tr* to pile up ‖ *intr* (ESSERE) to amount

ammonticchiare §287 *tr* to pile up, heap up

ammorbare (ammòrbo) *tr* to infect, contaminate

ammorbidènte *m* softener

ammorbidire §176 *tr* to soften; to mitigate ‖ *ref* to soften

ammortaménto *m* amortization; payment, redemption (*of a loan*)

ammortare (ammòrto) *tr* to amortize
ammortire §176 *tr* to deaden; to weaken, soften
ammortizzaménto [ddzz] *m* amortization, amortizement
ammortizzare [ddzz] *tr* to amortize; (aut) to absorb (*shocks*)
ammortizzatóre [ddzz] *m* (aut) shock absorber
ammosciare §128 (ammóscio) *tr, intr & ref* var of **ammoscire**
ammoscia·to -ta *adj* (coll) downcast
ammoscire §176 *tr* to make sag; to make flabby || *intr & ref* to sag; to become flabby; to droop
ammucchiare §287 *tr* to heap up, pile up || *ref* to crowd together
ammuffire §176 *intr* (ESSERE) to become moldy
ammusare *tr & intr* to nuzzle
ammutinaménto *m* mutiny, riot
ammutinare (ammùtino & ammutino) *tr* to incite to riot || *ref* to mutiny
ammutinato *m* mutineer
ammutolire §176 *intr* (ESSERE) to become silent; to be dumbfounded
amnesia *f* amnesia
amnistia *f* amnesty
amnistiare §287 or §119 *tr* to amnesty
amo *m* hook; **abboccare all'amo** to bite, to swallow the hook
amorale *adj* immoral; amoral
amorali·tà *f* (-tà) immorality; amorality
amóre *m* love; eagerness; **amor proprio** amour-propre, self-esteem; **con amore** with pleasure; **d'amore e d'accordo** in perfect agreement; **fare all'amore** to make love; **fare l'amore** to flirt; **per amor del cielo** for heaven's sake; **per amore di** for the sake of; **un amore di bambino** a charming child; **un amore di cappello** a darling hat
amoreggiare §290 (amoréggio) *intr* to flirt; to play around
amorévole *adj* loving; kindly
amòr·fo -fa *adj* amorphous; **safety** (*match*)
amorino *m* cupid; cute child; love seat; (bot) mignonette
amoró·so -sa [s] *adj* loving; kindly; amorous; love (*e.g., life*) || *mf* lover || *m* fiancé || *f* fiancée
amovìbile *adj* removable
amperàg·gio *m* (-gi) amperage
ampère *m* ampere
amperòmetro *m* ammeter
amperóra *f* ampere-hour
ampièzza *f* width, breadth; trajectory (*of a missile*); amplitude; **ampiezza di vedute** open-mindedness
àm·pio -pia *adj* (-pi -pie) ample; wide; roomy
amplèsso *m* (poet) embrace
ampliaménto *m* amplification, extension
ampliare §287 *tr* to enlarge, widen || *ref* to widen
amplificare §197 (amplìfico) *tr* to amplify; to widen; to exaggerate
amplifica·tóre *m* (rad & telv) amplifier
amplificazióne *f* amplification
amplitùdine *f* amplitude
ampòlla *f* cruet; (eccl) ampulla
ampollièra *f* cruet stand

ampollosi·tà [s] *f* (-tà) grandiloquence, turgidity
ampolló·so -sa [s] *adj* grandiloquent, turgid
amputare (àmputo) *tr* to amputate
amputazióne *f* amputation
amulèto *m* amulet, charm
anabbagliante *m* (aut) low beam; **anabbaglianti** (aut) dimmers
anacàr·dio *m* (-di) cashew
ànace *m* var of **anice**
anacorè·ta *m* (-ti) anchorite, hermit
anacronismo *m* anachronism
anacronìsti·co -ca *adj* (-ci -che) anachronistic(al)
anàgrafe *m* bureau of vital statistics; registry of births, deaths, and marriages
anagram·ma *m* (-mi) anagram
analcòli·co -ca (-ci -che) *adj* nonalcoholic; soft (*drink*) || *m* soft drink
analfabè·ta *mf* (-ti -te) illiterate
analfabèti·co -ca *adj* (-ci -che) unalphabetized, unalphabetic
analfabetismo *m* illiteracy
analgèsi·co -ca *adj & m* (-ci -che) analgesic
anàli·si *f* (-si) analysis; breakdown; **analisi grammaticale** parsing; **analisi dell'urina** urinalysis
anali·sta *mf* (-sti -ste) analyst; **analista finanziario** financial analyst; **analista tempi e metodi** efficiency expert, efficiency engineer
analìti·co -ca *adj* (-ci -che) analytic(al)
analizzare [ddzz] *tr* to analyze; to assay (*ores*); (telv) to scan
analogìa *f* analogy
anàlo·go -ga *adj* (-ghi -ghe) analogous; similar
anamnè·si *f* (-si) (med) case history
ananasso *m* pineapple
anarchìa *f* anarchy
anàrchi·co -ca (-ci -che) *adj* anarchical || *m* anarchist
anatè·ma or **anàte·ma** *m* (-mi) anathema
anatomìa *f* anatomy
anatòmi·co -ca *adj* (-ci -che) anatomic(al)
ànatra *f* duck; drake
anatròccolo *m* duckling
an·ca *f* (-che) hip; (coll) thigh (*e.g., of a chicken*); **dare d'anche** to run away; **menare anca** to walk
ancèlla *f* maidservant
ancestrale *adj* ancestral
anche *adv* also, too; even; (poet) yet; **anche a** + *inf* even if + *ind*
anchilosare (anchilòso) *tr* to paralyze || *ref* to become paralyzed
anchilòsto·ma *m* (-mi) hookworm
àn·cia *f* (-ce) (mus) reed
ancillare *adj* servant
ancóra *adv* still, yet; again; more e.g., **ancora cinque minuti** five minutes more
àncora *f* anchor; keeper (*of magnet*); armature (*of buzzer or electric bell*); **ancora di salvezza** last hope; **gettar l'ancora** to cast anchor; **salpare** or **levar l'ancora** to weigh anchor
ancoràg·gio *m* (-gi) anchorage, berth

ancorare (àncoro) tr to anchor; to tie (e.g., a currency to gold) || ref to anchor; to hold fast

ancorché conj although

andalu·so -sa adj & mf Andalusian

andaménto m course, progress

andante adj ordinary, common; continuous

andare m going; gait; a lungo andare in the long run || §106 intr (ESSERE) to go; to spread (said of news); to be (e.g., proud); to work (said of machinery); (with dat) to fit, e.g., quel vestito non gli va that suit does not fit him; (with dat) to please, e.g. quel vestito non le va that dress does not please her; andare a cavallo to go horseback riding; andare a finire to wind up; andare a male to spoil; andare a picco to sink; andare d'accordo to agree; andare in cerca di to seek; andare in macchina to be in press; andare in onda (rad & telv) to go on the air; andare per i vent'anni to be bordering on twenty years; andare pazzo per to be crazy about; andare soldato to be drafted; andare via to go away; come va? how are things?; mi va il vino dolce I like sweet wine; ne va della vita life is at stake; va da sé it goes without saying || ref—andarsene to go away, leave

anda·to -ta adj gone, past; finished; (coll) spoiled (e.g., meat) || f going; journey, trip; a lunga andata in the long run; andata e ritorno round trip; dare l'andata a to give the go-ahead to

andatura f gait; pace; fare l'andatura to set the pace

andazzo m bad practice, bad habit; fad

Ande, le the Andes

andicappare tr to handicap

andi·no -na adj Andean

andirivìe·ni m (-ni) coming and going; maze; ado

àndito m corridor, hallway

andróne m hall, lobby

aneddòti·co -ca adj (-ci -che) anecdotal

anèddoto m anecdote

anelante adj panting

anelare (anèlo) tr to long for || intr to yearn; (poet) to pant

anèlito m last breath; yearning; (poet) panting; mandare l'ultimo anelito to breathe one's last

anellino m ringlet

anèllo m ring; link (of a chain); traffic circle; segment (of a worm); (sports) track; ad anello ring-shaped; anello di congiunzione (fig) link; anello di fidanzamento engagement ring || anella fpl (poet) ringlets; (archaic) rings

anemìa f anemia

anèmi·co -ca adj (-ci -che) anemic

anestesìa f anesthesia

anestesi·sta mf (-sti -ste) anesthetist

anestèti·co -ca adj & m (-ci -che) anesthetic

anestetizzare [ddzz] tr to anesthetize

aneuri·sma m (-smi) aneurysm

anfi·bio -bia (-bi -bie) adj amphibian; (fig) ambiguous || m amphibian

anfiteatro m amphitheater

anfitrióne m (lit) generous host

anfratto m ravine; narrow, winding, rugged spot

anfrattuosi·tà [s] f (-tà) rough broken ground; winding, rough spot

anfrattuó·so -sa [s] adj winding, rough, craggy

angariare §287 tr to pester, oppress

angèli·co -ca adj (-ci -che) angelic(al)

àngelo m angel; angelo custode guardian angel

angherìa f vexation; outrage; imposition

angina f quinsy; angina pectoris angina pectoris

angipòrto m blind alley; narrow lane

anglica·no -na adj & mf Anglican

anglicismo m Anglicism

anglicizzare [ddzz] tr to Anglicize || ref to become Anglicized

anglòfo·no -na adj English-speaking || m English-speaking person

anglosàssone adj & mf Anglo-Saxon

angolare adj angular; corner (stone) || m angle iron || v (àngolo) tr to take an angle shot of; (sports) to kick (the ball) into the corner of the goal

angolazióne f (mov) angle shot

angolièra f corner shelving; corner cupboard

àngolo m angle; corner

angoló·so -sa [s] adj angular

àngora f Angora cat; Angora goat

angò·scia f (-sce) anxiety, distress, anguish

angosciare §128 (angòscio) tr to distress

angoscia·to -ta adj tormented, distressed

angosció·so -sa [s] adj agonizing

anguilla f eel

anguillé·sco -sca adj (-schi -sche) as slippery as an eel

angùria f watermelon

angùstia f narrowness; scarcity; stare in angustia to be worried

angustiare §287 tr to distress, grieve || ref to worry

angu·sto -sta adj narrow

ànice m anise

anicino m anise cookie

anidride f anhydride

àni·dro -dra adj anhydrous

anilina f aniline

ànima f soul; life (e.g., of the party); core; kernel; bore (of gun); mold (of button); mind; enthusiasm; pith (of fruit); sounding post (of violin); web (of rail); anima dannata evil counselor; anima mia! darling!; anima nera villain; anima viva living soul; buon'anima late, e.g., mio padre, buon'anima my late father; dannare l'anima to lose patience; la buon'anima di the late; rompere l'anima a to annoy

animale adj animal; (poet) of the soul; (poet) animate || m animal; (fig) boor, lout

animalé·sco -sca *adj* (**-schi -sche**) animal, bestial

animare (**ànimo**) *tr* to animate, to enliven; to promote || *ref* to become lively or heated

anima·to -ta *adj* animated (*cartoon*); animated, lively; animal

anima·tóre -tríce *adj* animating || *m* moving spirit; (*mov*) animator

animazióne *f* animation

animèlla *f* sweetbread

ànimo *m* mind; heart, affection; courage; **aprire l'animo** to open one's heart; **avere in animo di** to have a mind to; **mal animo** ill will; **mettersi l'animo in pace** to resign oneself; **perdersi d'animo** to lose heart; **serbare nell'animo** to keep in mind

animosi·tà *f* (**-tà**) animosity, ill will

animó·so -sa [s] *adj* bold; spirited (*animal*); hostile

anióne *m* anion

anisétta *f* anisette

ànitra *f* var of **anatra**

anitròccolo *m* var of **anatroccolo**

annacquare (**annàcquo**) *tr* to water; to water down

annaffiare §287 *tr* to sprinkle; to water (*wine*)

annaffia-tóio *m* (**-tói**) sprinkling can

annaffia·tóre -trice *adj* watering, sprinkling

annali *mpl* annals *spl*

annaspare *tr* to reel || *intr* to gesticulate; to grope; to flounder

annata *f* year; year's activity; year's rent; year's issues (*of a magazine*)

annebbiare §287 (**annébbio**) *tr* to befog; to dim || *ref* to become foggy; to become dim

annegaménto *m* drowning

annegare §209 (**annégo**) *tr* & *intr* (ESSERE) to drown

anneriménto *m* blackening

annerire §176 *tr* to blacken || *ref* to turn black

annessióne *f* annexation

annès·so -sa *adj* united, attached || *m* annex; **con tutti gli annessi e connessi** everything included

annèttere §107 *tr* to annex; to attach, enclose; to unite; to ascribe (*importance*)

annichilante *adj* annihilating; devastating (*e.g., reply*)

annichilare (**annìchilo**) *tr* to annihilate || *ref* to destroy oneself; (fig) to humble oneself

annichilire §176 *tr* & *ref* var of **annichilare**

annidare *tr* to nest; (fig) to nourish, cherish || *ref* to nest; to hide; (fig) to settle

annientaménto *m* annihilation

annientare (**anniènto**) *tr* to annihilate; to knock down, demolish; (fig) to crush || *ref* to humble oneself

anniversà·rio -ria *adj* & *m* (**-ri -rie**) anniversary

anno *m* year; **anno bisestile** leap year; **anno luce** light-year; **anno nuovo** New Year; **anno scolastico** school year; **avere . . . anni** to be . . . years old; **l'anno che viene** next year; **l'anno corrente** this year; **quest'altr'anno** next year; **un anno dopo l'altro** year in, year out

annobilire §176 *tr* to ennoble

annodare (**annòdo**) *tr* to knot, tie; (fig) to tie up || *ref* to get entangled

annoiare §287 (**annòio**) *tr* to bore || *ref* to become bored

annòna *f* food; food-control agency

annonà·rio -ria *adj* (**-ri -rie**) food; rationing (*card*)

annó·so -sa [s] *adj* old, aged

annotare (**annòto**) *tr* to jot down; to chalk up; to annotate; to comment

annotazióne *f* note; notation, annotation

annottare (**annòtta**) *impers* (ESSERE) & *ref* to grow dark, e.g., **si annotta** it's growing dark; **è annottato** it grew dark

annoverare (**annòvero**) *tr* to count, number

annuale *adj* annual || *m* anniversary

annuà·rio *m* (**-ri**) annual, yearbook

annuire §176 *intr* to nod assent; to consent

annullaménto *m* nullification, annulment

annullare *tr* to annul, nullify; cancel; to call off || *ref* to cancel one another

annunciare §128 *tr* var of **annunziare**

Annunciazióne *f* Annunciation

annunziare §287 *tr* to announce; (fig) to forecast, foreshadow

annunzia·tóre -trice *mf* announcer, newscaster

annùn·zio *m* (**-zi**) announcement, notice; **annunzio economico** classified ad; **annunzio pubblicitario** advertisement; **annunzio pubblicitario radiofonico** (rad) commercial

ànnu·o -a *adj* yearly, annual

annusare [s] *tr* to smell; to snuff (*tobacco*)

annuvolaménto *m* cloudiness

annuvolare (**annùvolo**) *tr* to cloud, becloud || *ref* to become cloudy; to turn somber

anòdi·no -na *adj* pain-relieving; ineffective; weak, colorless (*person*)

ànodo *m* anode

anomalìa *f* anomaly

anòma·lo -la *adj* anomalous

anonimìa *f* anonymity

anòni·mo -ma *adj* anonymous || *m* anonymous author; **serbare l'anonimo** to preserve one's anonymity

anormale *adj* abnormal || *m* queer fellow

anormali·tà *f* (**-tà**) abnormality

ansa *f* handle (*of vase*); pretext; bend (*of a river*)

ansante *adj* panting

ansare *intr* to pant

ànsia *f* anxiety; **essere in ansia** to be worried

ansie·tà *f* (**-tà**) anxiety

ansimare (**ànsimo**) *intr* to pant

ansió·so -sa [s] *adj* anxious

antagonismo *m* antagonism

antagoni·sta (-sti -ste) *adj* antagonistic ‖ *mf* antagonist, opponent

antagonìsti·co -ca *adj* (-ci -che) antagonistic

antàrti·co -ca *adj* (-ci -che) antarctic ‖ **Antartico** *m* Antarctic

antecedènte *adj* preceding ‖ *m* antecedent

antecedènza *f* antecedence

antecessóre *m* predecessor

antefatto *m* background, antecedents

anteguèr·ra (-ra) *adj* prewar ‖ *m* prewar period

anteluca·no -na *adj* (poet) predawn

antenato *m* ancestor

antènna *f* lance; (naut) yard; (rad & telv) aerial, antenna; (zool) antenna

antepórre §218 *tr* to prefer; to place before

anteprima *f* (mov & theat) preview

anterióre *adj* fore, front; previous; earlier

antesignano [s] *m* forerunner

anti- *pref adj* anti-, e.g., **anticomunistico** anticommunist; un-, e.g., **antieconomico** uneconomical ‖ *pref mf* anti-, e.g., **anticomunista** anticommunist

antiabbagliante *adj* antiglare ‖ *m* low beam

antiàci·do -da *adj & m* antacid

antiaère·o -a *adj* antiaircraft ‖ *f* antiaircraft defense

antibattèri·co -ca (-ci -che) *adj* antibacterial ‖ *m* bactericide

antibiòti·co -ca *adj & m* (-ci -che) antibiotic

anticà·glia *f* (-glie) antique, curio; rubbish, junk

anticàmera *f* waiting room, anteroom; **fare anticamera** to cool one's heels

anticarro *adj invar* antitank

antichi·tà *f* (-tà) antiquity; **antichità** *fpl* antiques

anticipare (antìcipo) *tr* to advance; to speed up; to pay in advance; to leak (*news*); to expect, anticipate ‖ *intr* to be early

anticipa·to -ta *adj* in advance (*e.g., payment*)

anticipazióne *f* advance; collateral loan; expectation, anticipation

antìcipo *m* advance; loan (*on accounts receivable*); **in anticipo** in advance

anti·co -ca *adj* (-chi -che) antique, ancient, old; **all'antica** in the old-fashioned manner; **gli antichi** the ancients; the forefathers; **in antico** in olden times

anticoncezionale *adj & f* contraceptive

anticonformi·sta *mf* (-sti -ste) nonconformist

anticonformìsti·co -ca *adj* (-ci -che) unconventional

anticongelante *adj & m* antifreeze

anticongiunturale *adj* crisis, emergency

anticòrpo *m* antibody

anticristo *m* Antichrist

antidatare *tr* to predate

antiderapante *adj* nonskid

antidetonante *adj* antiknock ‖ *m* antiknock compound

antidiluvia·no -na *adj* antediluvian

antìdoto *m* antidote

antievanescènza *f* (rad) antifading device

antifecondati·vo -va *adj & m* contraceptive

antìfona *f* antiphon; **capire l'antifona** (fig) to get the message

antifurto *adj invar* antitheft ‖ *m* antitheft device

antigàs *adj invar* gas (*e.g., mask*)

antigièni·co -ca *adj* (-ci -che) unsanitary

antìlope *f* antelope

antimeridia·no -na *adj* antemeridian, A.M.

antimìssile *adj invar* antimissile

antimònio *m* antimony

antincèndio *adj invar* fire-fighting; fire, e.g., **scala antincendio** fire escape

antinéb·bia *adj invar* fog ‖ *m* (-bia) fog light

antinéve *adj invar* snow, e.g., **catena antineve** snow chain

antiorà·rio -ria *adj* (-ri -rie) counterclockwise

antipatìa *f* antipathy, dislike

antipàti·co -ca *adj* (-ci -che) antipathetic; disagreeable; uncongenial

antipièga *adj invar* crease-resistant, wrinkle-proof

antìpodi *mpl* antipodes

antipòlio *adj invar* polio (*e.g., vaccine*)

antipòrta *f* stormdoor; corridor

antiquà·rio -ria *adj* (-ri -rie) antiquarian ‖ *m* antiquary, antiquarian

antiqua·to -ta *adj* obsolete; antiquated

antireligió·so -sa [s] *adj* antireligious, irreligious

antirùggine *adj invar* antirust

antirumóre *adj invar* antinoise

antisala [s] *f* anteroom, waiting room

antisassi [s] *adj invar* protecting against falling stones

antischiavi·sta *adj & mf* (-sti -ste) abolitionist

antisemì·ta [s] *adj* (-ti -te) anti-Semitic ‖ *mf* anti-Semite

antisemìti·co -ca [s] *adj* (-ci -che) anti-Semitic

antisemitismo [s] *m* anti-Semitism

antisètti·co -ca [s] *adj & m* (-ci -che) antiseptic

antisociale [s] *adj* antisocial

antisóle [s] *adj invar* sun (*glasses*); suntan (*lotion*)

antisommergìbile [s] *adj* antisubmarine

antistatale *adj* antigovernment

antitàrmi·co -ca *adj* (-ci -che) mothproof

antitèmpo *adv* early, prematurely

antìte·si *f* (-si) antithesis

antitèti·co -ca *adj* (-ci -che) antithetic(al)

antitossina *f* antitoxin

antiuòmo *adj invar* (mil) antipersonnel

antivigìlia *f*—**l'antivigilia di** two days before

antologìa *f* anthology

antònimo *m* antonym

antrace *m* anthrax

antracite *f* anthracite

antro *m* cave; den, hovel

antròpi·co -ca *adj* (**-ci -che**) human

antropofagìa *f* cannibalism

antropòfa·go -ga (**-gi -ghe**) *adj* cannibalistic || *m* cannibal

antropòide *adj* anthropoid

antropologìa *f* anthropology

antropomòrfi·co -ca *adj* (**-ci -che**) anthropomorphic

antropomòr·fo -fa *adj* see **scimmia**

anulare *adj* ring-shaped, annular || *m* ring finger

Anvèrsa *f* Antwerp

anzi *adv* on the contrary, rather; **anzi che no** rather || *prep* (*poet*) before

anziani·tà *f* (**-tà**) seniority

anzia·no -na *adj* old, elderly; senior || *m* senior

anziché *conj* rather than

anzidét·to -ta *adj* aforesaid

anzitutto *adv* above all, first of all

apatìa *f* apathy

apàti·co -ca *adj* (**-ci -che**) apathetic

ape *f* bee; **ape operaia** worker; **ape regina** queen bee

aperitivo *m* apéritif

apèr·to -ta *adj* open; frank, candid || *m* open space; **all'aperto** in the open

apertura *f* opening; aperture; approach; **ad apertura di libro** at sight; **apertura alare** (*of a bird*) wingspread; (*aer*) wingspan

apià·rio *m* (**-ri**) apiary

àpice *m* apex, top; climax

apicol·tóre -trice *mf* beekeeper, apiarist

apicoltura *f* beekeeping, apiculture

Apocalisse *f* Apocalypse, Revelation

apocalìtti·co -ca *adj* (**-ci -che**) apocalyptic(al)

apòcri·fo -fa *adj* apocryphal

apofonìa *f* ablaut

apogèo *m* apogee

apòlide *adj* stateless || *m* man without a country

apolìti·co -ca *adj* (**-ci -che**) nonpolitical, nonpartisan

apologè·ta *m* (**-ti**) apologist

apologèti·co -ca *adj* (**-ci -che**) apologetic

apologìa *f* apology

apòlo·go *m* (**-ghi**) apologue

apoplessìa *f* apoplexy

apoplètti·co -ca *adj & m* (**-ci -che**) apoplectic

apostasìa *f* apostasy

apòsta·ta *mf* (**-ti -te**) apostate

apostolato *m* apostolate

apostòli·co -ca *adj* (**-ci -che**) apostolic(al)

apòstolo *m* apostle

apostrofare (**apòstrofo**) *tr* to write with an apostrophe; to apostrophize

apòstrofe *f* apostrophe (*to a person*)

apòstrofo *m* (*gram*) apostrophe

apoteò·si *f* (**-si**) apotheosis

appagare §209 *tr* to satisfy, gratify || *ref*—**appagarsi di** to be content with

appaiare §287 *tr* to pair, couple; to match || *ref* to match (*said, e.g., of colors*)

appallottolare (**appallòttolo**) *tr* to crumple into a ball || *ref* to become lumpy

appaltare *tr* to contract for

appalta·tóre -trice *mf* contractor

appalto *m* contract; state monopoly; **appalto di sali e tabacchi** tobacco shop

appannàg·gio *m* (**-gi**) appanage; (*fig*) prerogative

appannare *tr* to tarnish; to befog, becloud || *ref* to become clouded (*said, e.g., of one's eyesight*)

apparato *m* decoration; display; appliance; leadership (*of political party*); (*rad, telv*) set

apparecchiare §287 (**apparécchio**) *tr* to prepare; to set (*the table*) || *ref* to get ready

apparecchiatura *f* sizing (*of paper; of a wall*); preparation (*of a canvas*); apparatus

apparéc·chio *m* (**-chi**) apparatus; sizing; preparation; gadget; (*rad, telv*) set; airplane; **apparecchio da caccia** fighter plane; **apparecchio telefonico** telephone

apparentare (**apparènto**) *tr* to tie, unite (*through marriage*) || *ref* to become related; to become intimate; (*pol*) to form a coalition

apparènte *adj* apparent, seeming

apparènza *f* appearance; **in apparenza** seemingly

apparigliare §280 *tr* to pair, team (*horses*)

apparire §108 *intr* (ESSERE) to appear, seem; to look

appariscènte *adj* showy, flashy, gaudy

apparizióne *f* apparition; appearance

appartaménto *m* apartment

appartare *tr* to set aside || *ref* to withdraw, retire

apparta·to -ta *adj* secluded, solitary

appartenènza *f* belonging, membership; **appartenenze** accessories; annexes

appartenére §271 *intr* (ESSERE & AVERE) to belong; to pertain || *impers* (ESSERE & AVERE)—**appartiene a it** behooves, it is up to

appassionaménto *m* excitement, interest, enthusiasm

appassionare (**appassióno**) *tr* to move; to interest; to excite || *ref* to be deeply interested

appassiona·to -ta *adj* impassioned; deep, ardent || *m* fan, amateur

appassire §176 *intr* (ESSERE) to wilt, wither; to decay; to dry up (*said, e.g., of grapes*)

appellare (**appèllo**) *tr* (*law*) to appeal; (*poet*) to call || *ref* to appeal; **appellarsi da** or **contro** (*law*) to appeal

appèllo *m* call, roll call; **fare appello a** to summon (*e.g., one's strength*); **fare l'appello** to call the roll; **mancare all'appello** to be absent

appéna *adv* hardly, scarcely; only; just || *conj* as soon as; **non appena** as soon as, no sooner

appèndere §109 *tr* to hang

appendìce *f* appendix; feuilleton

appendicectomìa *f* appendectomy

appendicite *f* appendicitis

Appennino, l' *m* the Appennines

appesantire [s] §176 *tr* to make heavy; to burden, overwhelm ‖ *ref* to get heavy; to get fat

appestare (appèsto) *tr* to infect; to stink up

appesta·to -ta *adj* plague-ridden ‖ *m* plague victim

appetire §176 *tr* to crave, long for ‖ *intr* (ESSERE & AVERE) to be appetizing

appetito *m* appetite

appetitó·so -sa [s] *adj* appetizing, tempting

appètto *adv* opposite; appetto a opposite; in comparison with

appezzaménto *m* plot, parcel (*of land*)

appianare *tr* to smooth, level; to settle (*a dispute*); to get around (*a difficulty*)

appiana·tóio *m* (-tói) road grader

appiattare *tr* & *ref* to hide

appiattiménto *m* leveling; equalization

appiattire §176 *tr* & *ref* to flatten, to level

appiccare §197 *tr* to hang; appiccare il fuoco a to set on fire; appiccare una lite to pick a fight

appicciare §128 *tr* (coll) to string together; (coll) to kindle, light

appiccicare §197 (appiccico) *tr* to stick, glue; appiccicare uno schiaffo a to slap ‖ *ref* to stick, adhere

appiccicatic·cio -cia *adj* (-ci -ce) sticky

appic·co *m* (-chi) grip; steep wall (*of mountain*); (fig) pretext

appiè *adv*—appiè di at the foot of; at the bottom of

appiedare (appièdo) *tr* to order (*a cavalryman*) off a horse; to order (*e.g., troops*) off a vehicle; to force out of a car (*said, e.g., of motor trouble*)

appièno *adv* (poet) fully

appigionare (appigióno) *tr* to rent ‖ *ref*—appigionasi for rent

appigiónasi [s] *m* for-rent sign

appigliare §280 *ref* to cling, adhere; appigliarsi a un pretesto to seize a pretext

appi·glio *m* (-gli) (fig) pretext

appiómbo *m* perpendicular ‖ *adv* plumb, perpendicularly

appioppare (appiòppo) *tr* to plant with poplar trees; to tie (*a vine*) to a poplar tree; (coll) to deliver (*a blow*); (coll) to pass off (*e.g., inferior goods*)

appisolare (appisolo) *ref* to snooze, doze

applaudire §176 & (applàudo) *tr* to applaud ‖ *intr* to applaud, clap the hands; (with *dat*) to applaud

applàuso *m* applause; applausi applause

applicàbile *adj* applicable

applicare §197 (àpplico) *tr* to apply; to attach; to give (*e.g., a slap*); to put into effect (*a law*); to assign ‖ *ref* to apply oneself

applica·to -ta *adj* applied; appliqué ‖ *m* clerk

applicazióne *f* application; appliqué

applique *m* (elec) wall fixture

appoggiaca·po *m* (-po) headrest; tidy (*on back of chair*)

appoggiagómi·ti *m* (-ti) elbowrest

appoggiama·no *m* (-no) mahlstick

appoggiare §290 (appòggio) *tr* to lean; to rest; to prop, support; to raise (*the tone of voice*); to give (*a slap*); to second (*a motion*); (fig) to back, support ‖ *intr* to lean; to rest ‖ *ref*—appoggiarsi a or su to lean on

appoggia·tóio *m* (-tói) support, rest; banister

appoggiatura *f* (mus) grace note

appòg·gio *m* (-gi) support, prop; backer; backing, support; grip; (mach) bearing

appollaiare §287 *ref* to roost

appórre §218 *tr* to affix, append

apportare (appòrto) *tr* to cause; to presage; (poet) to carry

appòrto *m* carrying; contribution; (law) share

appositaménte *adv* expressly, on purpose

appòsi·to -ta *adj* proper, fitting

apposizióne *f* apposition

appòsta *adj invar* suitable ‖ *adv* on purpose, expressly, intentionally

appostaménto *m* ambush

appostare (appòsto) *tr* to ambush ‖ *ref* to lie in ambush

apprèndere §220 *tr* to learn ‖ *ref* (poet) to take hold

apprendi·sta *mf* (-sti -ste) apprentice

apprendistato *m* apprenticeship

apprensióne *f* apprehension, fear

apprensi·vo -va *adj* apprehensive

appressare (apprèsso) *tr* (poet) to approach ‖ *ref* to come near

appresso *adj invar* next, following ‖ *adv* near; later on; appresso a near; after

apprestare (apprèsto) *tr* to prepare; to supply, provide (*e.g., help*) ‖ *ref* to prepare, get ready

apprettare (apprètto) *tr* to dress (*leather*); to size (*cloth*)

apprètto *m* tan (*for leather*); sizing (*for cloth*)

apprezzàbile *adj* appreciable

apprezzaménto *m* appreciation; estimation

apprezzare (apprèzzo) *tr* to appreciate

apprezza·to -ta *adj* esteemed

approc·cio *m* (-ci) approach; approcci advances

approdare (appròdo) *intr* (ESSERE & AVERE) to land; (with *dat*) (poet) to benefit; approdare a to come to

appròdo *m* landing

approfittare *intr*—approfittare di to capitalize on ‖ *ref*—approfittarsi di to take advantage of

approfondire §176 *tr* to make deep; to study thoroughly ‖ *ref*—approfondirsi in to go deep into

approntare (apprónto) *tr* to prepare, make ready

appropriare §287 (appròprio) *tr* to adapt; to bestow ‖ *ref*—appropriarsi a to befit; appropriarsi di to appropriate; to embezzle

appropria·to -ta *adj* appropriate
appropriazióne *f* appropriation; **appropriazione indebita** fraudulent conversion, embezzlement
approssimare (appròssimo) *tr* to bring near || *ref* to approach, come near
approssimati·vo -va *adj* approximate
approssimazióne *f* approximation
approvàbile *adj* laudable
approvare (appròvo) *tr* to approve, countenance; to subscribe to (*an opinion*); to pass (*a student; a law*); to confirm
approvazióne *f* approval; confirmation; passage (*of a law*)
approvvigionaménto *m* supply
approvvigionare (approvvigióno) *tr* to supply || *ref* to be supplied
appuntaménto *m* appointment; date; **appuntamento amoroso** assignation
appuntare *tr* to sharpen; to fasten, pin; to stick (*a pin*) in; to point; to jot down, take note of; to prick up (*one's ears*); (fig) to reproach || *ref* to be turned; to aim
appunta·to -ta *adj* sharpened || *m* corporal (*of Italian police*)
appuntellare (appuntèllo) *tr* to shore up, prop up
appuntellatura *f* shoring up, propping up
appuntino *adv* precisely, meticulously
appuntire §176 *tr* to sharpen
appunti·to -ta *adj* sharp, pointed
appunto *m* note; blame, charge; **muovere un appunto a** to blame; **per l'appunto** just, precisely || *adv* exactly, precisely
appurare *tr* to ascertain
appuzzare *tr* to befoul, pollute
apribottì·glie *m* (-glie) bottle opener
apri·co -ca *adj* (-chi -che) (poet) sunny, bright
aprile *m* April
apripi·sta *m* (-sta) blade (*of bulldozer*); bulldozer
aprire §110 *tr* to open; to turn on; to dig (*e.g., a grave*) || *ref* to open; to clear up (*said of the weather*); **aprirsi con** to open one's heart to; **aprirsi il varco fra** to press through
apriscàto·le *m* (-le) can opener
aquà·rio *m* (-ri) aquarium || **Aquario** *m* (astr) Aquarius
aquàti·co -ca *adj* (-ci -che) aquatic
àquila *f* eagle; genius
aquili·no -na *adj* aquiline
aquilóne *m* north wind; kite
aquilòtto *m* eaglet; cadet (*in Italian Air Force Academy*)
Aquinate, l' *m* Saint Thomas Aquinas
ara *f* (poet) altar; are (*100 square meters*)
arabé·sca *f* (-sche) (mus) arabesque
arabesca·to·ta *adj* arabesque
arabé·sco -sca (-schi -sche) *adj* arabesque || *m* arabesque; doodle || *f* see arabesca
Aràbia, l' *f* Arabia
aràbi·co -ca *adj* (-ci -che) Arabic
aràbile *adj* tillable

àra·bo -ba *adj* Arabic, Arabian || *mf* Arab (*person*) || *m* Arabic (*language*)
aràchide *f* peanut (*vine*)
aragonése [s] *adj* & *mf* Aragonese
aragósta *f* (*Palinurus vulgaris*) lobster
aràldi·co -ca (-ci -che) *adj* heraldic || *f* heraldry
araldo *m* herald
arancéto *m* orange grove
aràn·cia *f* (-ce) orange
aranciata *f* orangeade
aràn·cio *adj invar* orange (*in color*) || *m* (-ci) orange tree
arancióne *adj* & *m* orange (*color*)
arare *tr* to plow; (naut) to drag (*the anchor*)
aratro *m* plow
arazzo *m* tapestry, arras
arbitràg·gio *m* (-gi) (sports) umpiring; (com) arbitrage
arbitrale *adj* judge's, umpire's
arbitrare (àrbitro) *tr* to umpire, referee || *intr* to arbitrate || *ref*—**arbitrarsi di** to take the liberty to
arbitrà·rio -ria *adj* (-ri -rie) arbitrary; wanton
arbitrato *m* arbitration
arbì·trio *m* (-tri) will; abuse, violation; **libero arbitrio** free will
àrbitro *m* arbiter; judge, referee, umpire
arboscèllo *m* small tree
arbusto *m* shrub, bush
ar·ca *f* (-che) sarcophagus; ark; chest; **arca di Noè** Noah's Ark; **arca di scienza** (fig) fountain of knowledge
àrcade *adj* & *m* Arcadian
Arcàdia *f* Arcadia, Arcady
arcài·co -ca *adj* (-ci -che) archaic
arcaismo *m* archaism
arcàngelo *m* archangel
arca·no -na *adj* mysterious, arcane || *m* mystery
arcata *f* arch; arcade
archeologìa *f* archaeology
archeològi·co -ca *adj* (-ci -che) archaeological
archeòlo·go -ga *mf* (-gi -ghe) archaeologist
archètipo *m* archetype
archétto *m* (archit) small arch; (elec) trolley pole; (mus) bow
archi– *pref adj* archi–, e.g., **architettonico** architectonic || *pref m* & *f* archi–, e.g., **architettura** architecture
archibù·gio *m* (-gi) harquebus
Archimède *m* Archimedes
architettare (architétto) *tr* to plan (*a building*); (fig) to contrive, plot
architetto *m* architect
architettòni·co -ca *adj* (-ci -che) architectural
architettura *f* architecture
architetturale *adj* architectural
architrave *m* architrave; doorhead, lintel
archiviare §287 *tr* to file; to lay aside, shelve; (law) to throw out
archì·vio *m* (-vi) archives; record office; chancery, public records
archivi·sta *mf* (-sti -ste) archivist, file clerk

arci- *pref adj* archi-, e.g., **arcivescovile** archiepiscopal || *pref m & f* arch-, e.g., **arciprete** archpriest

arcicontèn·to -ta *adj* (coll) very glad

arcidiàcono *m* archdeacon

arcidu·ca *m* (**-chi**) archduke

arciduchéssa *f* archduchess

arcière *m* archer, bowman

arci·gno -gna *adj* gruff, surly

arcióne *m* saddlebow; **montare in arcioni** to mount, to mount a horse

arcipèla·go *m* (**-ghi**) archipelago

arciprète *m* archpriest; dean

arcivescovado *m* archbishopric

arcivéscovo *m* archbishop

ar·co *m* (**-chi**) bow; (archit) arch; (geom, elec) arc; **arco rampante** flying buttress

arcobaléno *m* rainbow

arco·làio *m* (**-lài**) reel; **girare come un arcolaio** to spin like a top

arcuare (**àrcuo**) *tr* to arch; to bend; to camber

arcua·to -ta *adj* bent, curved; bow (*e.g., legs*); **avere le gambe arcuate** to be bowlegged

ardènte *adj* burning; hot; ardent, impassioned

àrdere §111 *tr* to burn || *intr* to burn; to be in full swing (*said, e.g., of a war*)

ardèsia *f* slate

ardiménto *m* boldness, daring

ardire *m* boldness; presumption; impudence || §176 *intr*—**ardire + inf** or **ardire di + inf** to dare to + *inf*

arditézza *f* daring; temerity

ardi·to -ta *adj* daring; rash || *m* (hist) shock trooper

ardóre *m* intense heat; ardor

àr·duo -dua *adj* arduous

àrea *f* area, surface; group, camp; area **arretrata** backward area

àrem *m* (**àrem**) harem

arèna *f* arena; **scendere nell'arena** to throw one's hat in the ring

aréna *f* sand

arenare (**aréno**) *intr* (ESSERE) & *ref* to run aground

arenària *f* sandstone

arén·go *m* (**-ghi**) (hist) town meeting

arenile *m* sandy beach

arenó·so -sa [s] *adj* sandy

areòmetro *m* hydrometer

aeronàuti·co -ca *adj & f* (**-ci -che**) var of **aeronautico**

areoplano *m* var of **aeroplano**

areopòrto *m* var of **aeroporto**

areòstato *m* var of **aerostato**

àrgano *m* winch; (naut) capstan

argentare (**argènto**) *tr* to silver; to silver-plate; to back (*a mirror*) with foil

argenta·to -ta *adj* silver; silvery; silver-plated

argentatura *f* silver plating; silver plate; foil (*of mirror*)

argènte·o -a *adj* silver, silvery

argenterìa *f* silverware

argentière *m* silversmith; jeweler

argenti·no -na *adj* silver, silvery; Argentine || *mf* Argentine || *f* high-necked sweater || **l'Argentina** *f* Argentina

argènto *m* silver; (archaic) money; **argenti** silverware; **argento vivo** quicksilver

argentóne *m* German silver

argilla *f* clay

argilló·so -sa [s] *adj* clayey

arginare (**àrgino**) *tr* to dam, dike; to hold back, check

àrgine *m* embankment, dam; (fig) defense

ar·go *m* (**-ghi**) (chem) argon; (orn) grouse || **Argo** *m* Argus

argomentare (**argoménto**) *tr & intr* to argue

argomentazióne *f* argumentation, discussion

argoménto *m* argument; pretext; subject; **fuori dell'argomento** beside the point

argonàu·ta *m* (**-ti**) Argonaut

arguire §176 *tr* to deduce, infer; (archaic) to denote

argutézza *f* wit; witty remark

argu·to -ta *adj* keen, acute; witty

argùzia *f* keenness; wit

ària *f* air; climate; look; mien; aria, tune; poem; **all'aria aperta** in the open air; **a mezz'aria** in midair; halfway; **andare all'aria** to fail; **aria condizionata** air conditioning; **avere l'aria di** to seem to; to look like; **dare aria a** to air; **in aria** in the air; **tira un'aria pericolosa** a mean wind is blowing

aria·nó -na *adj & mf* Aryan

aridi·tà *f* (**-tà**) dryness, aridity; dearth

àri·do -da *adj* arid, dry, barren; (fig) dry

arieggiare §290 (**ariéggio**) *tr* to air; to imitate || *ref*—**arieggiarsi a** to give oneself the airs of

ariète *m* ram; (mil) battering ram || **Ariete** *m* (astr) Aries

ariétta *s* breeze; (mus) short aria

arin·ga *f* (**-ghe**) herring; **aringa affumicata** kippered herring, kipper

arin·go *m* (**-ghi**) assembly; field; joust; **scendere nell'aringo** to throw one's hat in the ring

arió·so -sa [s] *adj* airy, breezy; (fig) of wide scope

àrista *f* loin of pork

arista *f* (bot) awn

aristocràti·co -ca (**-ci -che**) *adj* aristocratic || *mf* aristocrat

aristocrazìa *f* aristocracy

Aristòtele *m* Aristotle

aristotèli·co -ca *adj & m* (**-ci -che**) Aristotelian

aritmèti·co -ca (**-ci -che**) *adj* arithmetical || *m* arithmetician || *f* arithmetic

arlecchino *adj invar* harlequin; fiesta (*e.g., dishes*) || **Arlecchino** *m* Harlequin

ar·ma *f* (**-mi**) arm, weapon; (fig) army; (mil) corps, service; **alle prime armi** at the beginning; **arma bianca** steel blade; **arma da taglio** cutting weapon; **arma delle trasmissioni** signal corps

armacòllo *m*—**ad armacollo** slung across the shoulders (*said of a rifle*)

armà·dio *m* (**-di**) cabinet; closet; **armadio a muro** built-in closet; **armadio**

d'angolo corner cupboard; **armadio farmaceutico** medicine cabinet; **armadio guardaroba** armoire

armaiòlo *m* gunsmith

armamentà·rio *m* (**-ri**) outfit, set (*of tools*)

armaménto *m* armament; crew; gun crew; crew (*of rowboat*); outfit, equipment

armare *tr* to arm; to dub (*s.o. a knight*); to outfit, commission (*a ship*); to cock (*a gun*); to brace, shore up (*a building*); (rr) to furnish with track || *ref* to arm oneself; to outfit oneself

arma·to -ta *adj* armed; reinforced (*concrete*) || *m* soldier || *f* army; navy; fleet; (nav) task force

arma·tóre -trice *adj* outfitting || *m* shipowner; (min) carpenter; (rr) trackwalker

armatura *f* armor; scaffold; framework; support; reinforcement (*for concrete*); (elec) plate (*of condenser*)

armeggiare §290 (**arméggio**) *intr* to fumble, fool around; to scheme; (archaic) to handle arms; (archaic) to joust

armeggì·o *m* (**-i**) fooling around; scheming, intriguing

armè·no -na *adj* & *mf* Armenian

arménto *m* herd

armerìa *f* armory

armière *m* (aer) gunner

armìge·ro -ra *adj* warlike, bellicose || *m* warrior; bodyguard

armistiziale *adj* armistice

armistì·zio *m* (**-zi**) armistice

armonìa *f* harmony; **in armonia con** according to

armòni·co -ca (**-ci -che**) *adj* harmonic; resonant; harmonious || *f* harmonica; **armonica a bocca** mouth organ

armonió·so -sa [s] *adj* harmonious

armonizzare [ddzz] *tr* & *intr* to harmonize

arnése [s] *m* tool, implement; garb, dress; (coll) gadget; **bene in arnese** well-heeled; **male in arnese** down at the heels

àrnia *f* beehive

arò·ma *m* (**-mi**) aroma, odor; zest

aromàti·co -ca *adj* (**-ci -che**) aromatic

aromatizzare [ddzz] *tr* to flavor; to spice

arpa *f* harp

arpeggiare §290 (**arpéggio**) *intr* to play arpeggios; to play a harp; to strum

arpég·gio *m* (**-gi**) arpeggio

arpìa *f* Harpy; (coll) harpy

arpionare (**arpióno**) *tr* to harpoon

arpióne *m* hinge (*of door*); hook; harpoon; spike (*for mountain climbing*)

arpionismo *m* ratchet

arpi·sta *mf* (**-sti -ste**) harpist

arrabattare *ref* to exert oneself, to strive, to endeavor

arrabbiare §287 *intr* (ESSERE) to go mad (*said of dogs*) || *ref* to become angry (*said of people*)

arrabbia·to -ta *adj* mad (*dog*); angry; obstinate; confirmed

arrabbiatura *f* rage; **prendersi un'arrabbiatura** to burn up (*with rage*)

arraffare *tr* to snatch

arrampicare §197 (**arràmpico**) *ref* to climb, climb up

arrampicata *f* climbing

arrampica·tóre -trice *mf* climber; mountain climber; **arrampicatore sociale** social climber

arrancare §197 *intr* to hobble, limp; to struggle, work hard; to row hard

arrangiaménto *m* agreement; (mus) arrangement

arrangiare §290 *tr* to arrange; to fix; (coll) to steal || *ref* to manage, get along

arrecare §197 (**arrèco**) *tr* to cause; to carry, deliver

arredaménto *m* furnishing; furnishings; equipment

arredare (**arrèdo**) *tr* to furnish; to equip

arreda·tóre -trice *mf* interior decorator; upholsterer; (mov) property man

arrèdo *m* furnishings, furniture; piece of furniture; **arredi sacri** church supplies

arrembàg·gio *m* (**-gi**) boarding (*of a ship*)

arrenare (**arréno**) *tr* to sand

arrèndere §227 *tr* (archaic) to surrender || *ref* to surrender; **arrendersi a discrezione** to surrender unconditionally

arrendévole *adj* yielding, compliant, flexible

arrendevolézza *f* suppleness; compliance

arrestare (**arrèsto**) *tr* to stop; to arrest || *ref* to stop, stay

arrèsto *m* arrest; stop; pause; (mach) stop, catch; **arresti** (mil) house arrest; **in stato d'arresto** under arrest

arretrare (**arrètro**) *tr* to withdraw || *intr* (ESSERE & AVERE) & *ref* to withdraw

arretra·to -ta *adj* withdrawn; backward; back (*issue*); overdue || **arretrati** *mpl* arrears

arricchiménto *m* enrichment

arricchire §176 *tr* to enrich || *intr* (ESSERE) & *ref* to get rich

arricchi·to -ta *mf* nouveau riche

arricciacapél·li *m* (**-li**) curler

arricciare §128 *tr* to curl; to wrinkle; to screw up (*one's nose*); **arricciare il pelo** to bristle (*said of a person*); to bristle up (*said of an animal*) || *ref* to curl up

arriccia·to -ta *adj* curled up || *m* first coat (*of cement*)

arricciatura *f* curling (*of hair*); pleating (*of a skirt*); kink (*in a rope*)

arrìdere §231 *tr* (poet) to grant || *intr* to smile

arrìn·ga *f* (**-ghe**) harangue; (law) lawyer's plea

arringare §209 *tr* to harangue; (law) to plead

arrischiare §287 *tr* to endanger; to risk || *ref* to dare, venture

arrischia·to -ta *adj* risky; daring

arrivare *tr* to reach || *intr* (ESSERE) to arrive; to happen; to get along, be successful; **arrivare a** to reach; to succeed in

arrivà·to -ta *adj* arrived; successful; **ben arrivato** welcome

arrivedér·ci *m* (**-ci**) good-bye ‖ *interj* good-bye!, so long!

arrivedérla *interj* good-bye!

arrivismo *m* social climbing, ruthless ambition

arrivi·sta *mf* (**-sti -ste**) social climber

arrivo *m* arrival; (sports) goal line; (sports) finishing line

arroccare §197 (arròcco) *tr* to put (*e.g.*, *f.ax*) on the distaff ‖ §197 (arròcco) *tr* to shelter; (chess) to castle ‖ *ref* to seek shelter; (chess) to castle

arròc·co *m* (**-chi**) castling

arrochire §176 *tr* to make hoarse ‖ *intr* (ESSERE) to become hoarse

arrogante *adj* arrogant, insolent

arroganza *f* arrogance, insolence

arrogare §209 (arrògo) *tr*—**arrogare a sé** to arrogate to oneself ‖ *ref* to arrogate to oneself

arrolare §237 *tr* var of **arruolare**

arrossare (arrósso) *tr* to redden

arrossire §176 *intr* (ESSERE) to blush; to change color

arrostire §176 *tr* to roast; to toast; **arrostire allo spiedo** to barbecue on the spit ‖ *intr* (ESSERE) & *ref* to roast

arrò·sto *m* (**-sto** & **-sti**) roast

arrotare (arròto) *tr* to grind, hone; to smooth; to strike, run over; to grit (*one's teeth*) ‖ *ref* to grind (*to work hard*); to sideswipe

arrotatrice *f* floor sander

arrotatura *f* sharpening

arrotino *m* grinder

arrotolare (arròtolo) *tr* to roll

arrotondaménto *m* rounding; rounding out; increase (*in salary*)

arrotondare (arrotóndo) *tr* to make round; to round out; to supplement (*a salary*) ‖ *ref* to round out, become plump

arrovellare (arrovèllo) *tr* to vex ‖ *ref* to become angry; to strive, endeavor; **arrovellarsi il cervello** to rack one's brains

arroventare (arrovènto) *tr* to make red-hot ‖ *ref* to become red-hot

arroventire §176 *tr* & *ref* var of **arroventare**

arruffapòpo·li *m* (**-li**) rabble-rouser

arruffare *tr* to tangle; to muss, rumple; to confuse

arruf·fio *m* (**-fii**) tangle; confusion, mess

arruffó·ne -na *mf* blunderer; swindler

arrugginire §176 *tr*, *intr* (ESSERE) & *ref* to rust

arruolaménto *m* enlistment; draft

arruolare (arruòlo) *tr* to recruit; to draft ‖ *ref* to enlist

arruvidire §176 *tr* to make rough, roughen ‖ *intr* (ESSERE) to become rough

arsenale *m* arsenal; navy yard

arsèni·co -ca ca (**- chi**) *adj* arsenic, arsenical ‖ *m* arsenic

ar·so -sa *adj* burnt; dry, parched; **arso di** consumed with

arsura *f* sultriness; dryness

arte *f* art; ability; guile; **ad arte** on purpose; **arti e mestieri** arts and crafts

artefare §173 *tr* to adulterate

artefat·to -ta *adj* adulterated; artificial

artéfice *m* craftsman; creator

artèria *f* artery

arterioscleròsi *m* arteriosclerosis

arterió·so -sa [s] *adj* arterial

artesia·no -na *adj* artesian

àrti·co -ca *adj* (**-ci -che**) arctic ‖ **Artico** *m* Arctic

articolare *adj* articular ‖ *v* (**artìcolo**) *tr* & *ref* to articulate

articola·to -ta *adj* articulated; articulate; (gram) combined; jagged (*coastline*)

articolazióne *f* articulation

articoli·sta *mf* (**-sti -ste**) columnist; feature writer

articolo *m* article; item; paragraph; **articolo di fondo** editorial; **articolo di spalla** comment

artificiale *adj* artificial

artificière *m* pyrotechnist; (mil) demolition expert

artifi·cio *m* (**-ci**) artifice; sophistication, affectation; **artificio d'illuminazione** (mil) flare

artificiosi·tà [s] *f* (**-tà**) artfulness, craftiness; artificiality

artifició·so -sa [s] *adj* artful, crafty; artificial, affected

artigianato *m* craftsmanship

artigia·no -na *adj* of craftsmen ‖ *m* craftsman

artigliare §280 *tr* (poet) to claw

artiglière *m* artilleryman

artiglierìa *f* artillery; **artiglieria a cavallo** mounted artillery

artì·glio *m* (**-gli**) claw; **cadere negli artigli di** to fall into the clutches of

arti·sta *mf* (**-sti -ste**) artist; actor

artìsti·co -ca *adj* (**-ci -che**) artistic

ar·to -ta *adj* (poet) narrow ‖ *m* limb

artrite *f* arthritis

artrìti·co -ca *adj* & *mf* (**-ci -che**) arthritic

arturia·no -na *adj* Arthurian

arzigogolare [dz] (arzigògolo) *intr* to muse; to cavil

arzigògolo [dz] *m* fantasy; cavil

arzìl·lo -la [dz] *adj* lively, sprightly; (coll) sparkling (*wine*)

arzin·ga *f* (**-ghe**) tong (*of a blacksmith*)

asbèsto *m* asbestos

ascèlla *f* armpit

ascendènte *adj* ascendant ‖ *m* upper hand, ascendancy; **ascendenti** forefathers

ascendènza *f* ancestry, lineage

ascéndere §245 *tr* to climb ‖ *intr* (ESSERE & AVERE) to ascend, climb

ascensionale *adj* rising; lifting

ascensióne *f* ascent, climb ‖ **Ascensione** *f* Ascension, Ascension Day

ascensóre *m* elevator

ascésa [s] *f* ascent

ascèsso *m* abscess

ascè·ta *mf* (**-ti -te**) ascetic

ascèti·co -ca *adj* (**-ci -che**) ascetic

ascetismo *m* asceticism

à·scia *f* (**-sce**) adze

asciugacapél·li *m* (**-li**) hair drier

asciugamano *m* towel; **asciugamano spugna** Turkish towel

asciugante *adj* drying; blotting; soaking || *m* dryer

asciugare §209 *tr* to dry, dry up; to wipe; to drain (*e.g., a glass of wine*) || *ref* to dry oneself; to dry, dry up

asciuga·tóio *m* (**-tói**) towel; bath towel

asciugatrice *f* dryer

asciut·to -ta *adj* dry; skinny; blunt (*in speech*) || *m* dry land; dry climate; **all'asciutto** pennyless

ascoltare (**ascólto**) *tr* to listen to || *intr* to listen

ascolta·tóre -trice *mf* listener

ascólto *m* listening; **stare in ascolto** to listen

ascòrbi·co -ca *adj* (**-ci -che**) ascorbic

ascrit·to -ta *adj* ascribed; belonging || *m* member

ascrìvere §250 *tr* to inscribe, register; to ascribe, attribute

ascultare *tr* to sound (*s.o.'s chest*)

asèpsi [s] *f* asepsis

asètti·co -ca [s] *adj* (**-ci -che**) aseptic

asfaltare *tr* to tar, pave

asfalto *m* asphalt

asfissìa *f* asphyxia

asfissiante *adj* asphyxiating; poison (*gas*); boring

asfissiare §287 *tr* to asphyxiate; to bore || *intr* (ESSERE) to be asphyxiated

asfodèlo *m* asphodel

Àsia, l' *f* Asia; **l'Asia Minore** Asia Minor

asiàti·co -ca *adj* & *mf* (**-ci -che**) Asian, Asiatic

asilo *m* shelter; asylum; home; **asilo di mendicità** poorhouse; **asilo infantile** kindergarten; **asilo per i vecchi** old-age home, nursing home

asimmetria [s] *f* asymmetry

asimmètri·co -ca [s] *adj* (**-ci -che**) asymmetric(al)

asinàggine [s] *f* stupidity, asininity

asi·nàio [s] *m* (**-nài**) donkey driver

asinata [s] *f* stupidity, folly

asineria [s] *f* asininity

asiné·sco -sca [s] *adj* (**-schi -sche**) asinine

asini·no -na [s] *adj* asinine

àsino [s] *m* ass, donkey; **fare l'asino a** (slang) to play up to; **qui casca l'asino** here is the rub

asma *f* asthma

asmàti·co -ca *adj* & *mf* (**-ci -che**) asthmatic

àsola *f* buttonhole; buttonhole hem

aspàra·go *m* (**-gi**) asparagus; piece of asparagus; **asparagi** asparagus (*as food*)

aspèrgere §112 *tr* to sprinkle

aspersióne *f* aspersing, sprinkling

aspettare (**aspètto**) *tr* to wait for, await; to expect; **aspettare al varco** to be on the lookout for || *intr* to wait; **fare aspettare** to keep waiting || *ref* to expect

aspettativa *f* expectancy, expectation; leave of absence without pay

aspètto *m* waiting; aspect, look; **al primo aspetto** at first sight

àspide *m* asp

aspirante *adj* suction (*pump*) || *m* aspirant; applicant, candidate; suitor; upperclassman (*in naval academy*)

aspirapólve·re *m* (**-re**) vacuum cleaner

aspirare *tr* to inhale, breathe in; to suck (*e.g., air*); (phonet) to aspirate || *intr* to aspire

aspiratóre *m* exhaust fan

aspirazióne *f* aspiration; (aut) intake

aspirina *f* aspirin

aspo *m* reel

asportàbile *adj* removable

asportare (**aspòrto**) *tr* to remove, take away

asportazióne *f* removal

asprézza *f* sourness; roughness, harshness

a·spro -spra *adj* sour; rough, harsh

assaggiare §290 *tr* to taste; to sample, test; **assaggiare il terreno** (fig) to see how the land lies

assaggia·tóre -trice *mf* taster

assàg·gio *m* (**-gi**) taste, sample; tasting; test, trial

assài *adj invar* a lot of || *m* much || *adv* enough; fairly; very

assale *m* axle

assalire §242 *tr* to attack, assail; (fig) to seize

assali·tóre -trice *mf* assailant

assaltare *tr* to assault; **assaltare a mano armata** to stick up

assalto *m* assault, attack; (law) battery; **cogliere d'assalto** to catch unawares; **prendere d'assalto** to assault

assaporare (**assapóro**) *tr* to taste; to relish, enjoy

assassinare *tr* to assassinate; (fig) to murder

assassì·nio *m* (**-ni**) assassination, murder

assassi·no -na *adj* murderous || *mf* assassin, murderer

asse *m* axle, shaft, spindle; (geom, phys) axis; **asse ereditario** estate; **asse stradale** median strip || *f* plank; **asse da stiro** ironing board

assecondare (**assecóndo**) *tr* to help; to second; to uphold

assediante *adj* besieging || *m* besieger

assediare §287 (**assèdio**) *tr* to lay siege to, besiege

assè·dio *m* (**-di**) siege; **assedio economico** economic sanctions; **cingere d'assedio** to besiege

assegnaménto *m* awarding; allowance; faith, reliance; **fare assegnamento su** to rely upon

assegnare (**asségno**) *tr* to assign; to prescribe; to distribute; to award

assegnatà·rio -ria *mf* (**-ri -rie**) assignee

assegnazióne *f* assignment; awarding

asségno *m* allowance; check; **assegni fringe benefits; **assegni familiari** family allowance; **assegno a copertura garantita** certified check; **assegno a vuoto** worthless check; **assegno di studio** (educ) stipend; **assegno turistico** traveler's check; **assegno vademecum** certified check; **contro asségno** C.O.D.

assemblàg·gio m (-gi) (mach) assembling, assembly

assemblèa f assembly

assembraménto m gathering

assembrare (assémbro) tr & ref to gather

assennatézza f good judgment, discretion

assenna·to -ta adj sensible, prudent

assènso m approval, consent

assentare (assènto) ref to be absent, to absent oneself

assènte adj absent || mf absentee

assenteìsmo m absenteeism

assentìre (assènto) tr (poet) to grant || intr to assent, acquiesce; **assentire con un cenno** to nod assent

assènza f absence

assenziènte adj consenting, approving

assèn·zio m (-zi) absinthe; (bot) wormwood

asserìre §176 tr to affirm, assert

asserragliare §280 tr to barricade || ref to barricade oneself

assèrto m (poet) assertion

asser·tóre -trice mf advocate, supporter

asserviménto m enslavement

asservìre §176 tr to enslave; to subjugate

asserzióne f assertion

assessóre m councilman; alderman

assestaménto m arrangement; settling (of a building)

assestare (assèsto) tr to arrange; to adapt, regulate; to deliver, deal (a blow) || ref to become organized; to settle (said of a building)

assesta·to -ta adj sensible, prudent

assetare (assèto) tr to make thirsty; (fig) to inflame

asseta·to -ta adj thirsty; parched; eager || mf thirsty person

assettare (assètto) tr to tidy, straighten up || ref to straighten oneself up

assetta·to -ta adj tidy

assètto m arrangement; order; (naut) trim; **assetto longitudinale** (aer) pitch, attitude; **in assetto di guerra** ready for war; **male in assetto** in poor shape

asseverare (assèvero) tr to asseverate, assert

assicèlla f roofing board, lath; batten

assicuràbile adj insurable

assicurare tr to assure; to insure; to protect; to fasten; to deliver (e.g., a thief) || ref to make sure; to take out insurance

assicura·to -ta adj & mf insured || f insured letter

assicura·tóre -trice mf insurer

assicurazióne f assurance; insurance; **assicurazione contro gli infortuni sul lavoro** workman's compensation insurance; **assicurazione contro i danni** casualty insurance; **assicurazione incendio** fire insurance; **assicurazione infortuni** accident insurance; **assicurazione per la vecchiaia** old age insurance; **assicurazione sociale** social security; **assicurazione sulla vita** life insurance

assideraménto m freezing; frostbite

assiderare (assìdero) ref to freeze; to become frostbitten

assìdere §113 ref (poet) to take one's seat (e.g., on the throne)

assì·duo -dua adj assiduous, diligent

assième m ensemble || adv together; **assieme a** together with

assiepare (assièpo) tr & ref to crowd

assillante adj disturbing, troublesome

assillare tr to beset, trouble

assillo m gadfly; (fig) stimulus, goad

assimilare (assìmilo) tr to assimilate; to compare

assimilazióne f assimilation

assiòlo m horned owl

assiò·ma m (-mi) axiom

assiomàti·co -ca adj (-ci -che) axiomatic

assì·ro -ra adj & mf Assyrian

assìsa f (poet) uniform, livery; (geol) layer; (archaic) duty, tax; **assise** criminal court; assembly, session; (hist) assises

assistènte mf assistant; **assistente sanitario** practical nurse; **assistente sociale** social worker || m—**assistente ai lavoro** foreman || f—**assistente di volo** (aer) hostess

assistènza f assistance, help; intervention; **assistenza pubblica** relief

assistenziale adj welfare, charity

assistère §114 tr to assist, help || intr—**assistere a** to attend, be present at

assìto m flooring, boarding

assiuòlo m var of assiolo

asso m ace; **asso del volante** speed king; **piantare in asso** to walk out on

associare §128 (assòcio) tr to associate; **associare alle carceri** to take to prison || ref to associate; to become a member; to subscribe; to participate

associa·to -ta adj associate || mf associate, partner

associazióne f association; union; subscription; membership

assodare (assòdo) tr to solidify; to strengthen; to ascertain || ref to solidify; to strengthen

assoggettare (assoggètto) tr to subject, subdue || ref to submit

assola·to -ta adj sunny, exposed to the sun

assolcare §197 (assólco) tr to furrow

assoldare (assòldo) tr to hire, recruit

assólo m (mus) solo

assolutìsmo m absolutism

assolutìsti·co -ca adj (-ci -che) absolutist, despotic

assolu·to -ta adj & m absolute

assoluzióne f absolution

assòlvere §115 tr to absolve; to fulfill

assomigliare §280 tr to compare; to make similar, make equal || intr (ESSERE & AVERE) (with dat) to resemble, to look like; to be like || ref to resemble each other, look alike; **assomigliarsi a** to resemble

assommare (assómmo) tr to add; to be the epitome of; (archaic) to complete || intr (ESSERE) to amount

assonna·to -ta adj sleepy

assopìre §176 tr to lull to sleep; to

soothe ‖ *ref* to drowse, to nod; to calm down

assorbènte *adj* absorbent ‖ *m* sanitary napkin

assorbiménto *m* absorption

assorbire §176 & (assòrbo) *tr* to absorb

assorbi·to -ta *adj* absorbed; **assorbito da** consumed with

assordare (assórdo) *tr* to deafen ‖ *ref* to become deaf; to dim; to lessen

assortiménto *m* assortment; **avere in assortimento** (com) to carry, stock

assortire §176 *tr* to assort, sort out; to stock

assorti·to -ta *adj* assorted; **bene assortito** well matched

assòr·to -ta *adj* engrossed, absorbed

assottigliare §280 *tr* to thin; to sharpen; to reduce ‖ *ref* to grow thinner

assuefare §173 *tr* to accustom ‖ *ref* to become accustomed

assuefazióne *f* habit, custom

assùmere §116 *tr* to assume; to hire; to raise, elevate; (law) to accept in evidence

Assunta *f* Assumption

assunto *m* thesis, argument; (poet) task

assun·tóre -trice *mf* contractor

assunzióne *f* assumption; hiring; (law) examination ‖ **Assunzione** *f* Assumption

assurdi·tà *f* (-tà) absurdity

assur·do -da *adj* absurd ‖ *m* absurdity

assùrgere §117 *intr* (ESSERE) (poet) to rise

asta *f* staff; rod; arm (*e.g., of scale*); lance; leg (*of compass*); stroke (*in handwriting*); shaft (*of arrow*); auction; (naut) boom; (naut) mast; (elec) trolley pole; **a mezz'asta** half-mast; **vendere all'asta** to auction, auction off

astante *mf* bystander ‖ *m* physician on duty (*in a hospital*)

astanterìa *f* receiving ward

astato *m* (chem) astatine

astè·mio -mia *adj* abstemious, temperate ‖ *mf* teetotaler

astenére §271 *ref* to abstain

astensióne *f* abstension

astenuto *m* person who abstains from voting; abstention (*vote withheld*)

astèrgere §164 (*pp* astèrso) *tr* to wipe

asteri·sco m (-schi) asterisk

asticcìòla *f* penholder; rib (*of umbrella*); temple (*of eyeglasses*)

àstice *m* (*Hommarus vulgaris*) lobster

asticèlla *f* (sports) bar

astinènte *adj* abstinent

astinènza *f* abstinence

à·stio m (-sti) grudge, rancor

astió·so -sa [s] *adj* full of malice, spiteful

astóre *m* goshawk

astràgalo *m* astragalus, anklebone

astrakàn *m* Persian lamb

astrarre §273 *tr* to abstract ‖ *intr*—**astrarre da** to leave aside, overlook

astrat·to -ta *adj* abstract ‖ *m* abstract

astrazióne *f* abstraction

astringènte *adj* & *m* astringent

-astro -astra *suf adj* -ish, e.g., **verdastro**

greenish ‖ *suf mf* -aster, e.g., **poetastro** poetaster

astro *m* star, heavenly body; (bot) aster; (fig) star

astrologìa *f* astrology

astrològi·co -ca *adj* (-ci -che) astrological

astròlo·go m (-gi or -ghi) astrologer

astronàu·ta *mf* (-ti -te) astronaut

astronàuti·co -ca (-ci -che) *adj* astronautic(al) ‖ *f* astronautics

astronautizzare [ddzz] *intr* (ESSERE) to be an astronaut

astronave *f* spaceship, spacecraft

astronomìa *f* astronomy

astrònomo *m* astronomer

astronòmi·co -ca *adj* (-ci -che) astronomic(al)

astruserìa *f* abstruseness

astrusi·tà *f* (-tà) abstruseness

astru·so -sa *adj* abstruse

astùc·cio m (-ci) case, box

astu·to -ta *adj* astute, crafty

astùzia *f* astuteness, craftiness

àta·vo -va *mf* ancestor

ateismo *m* atheism

atei·sta *mf* (-sti -ste) atheist

Atène *f* Athens

atenèo *m* athenaeum; university

ateniése [s] *adj* & *mf* Athenian

àte·o -a *adj* atheistic ‖ *mf* atheist

atlante *m* atlas ‖ **Atlante** *m* Atlas

atlànti·co -ca *adj* (-ci -che) Atlantic ‖ **Atlantico** *m* Atlantic

atlè·ta *mf* (-ti -te) athlete

atletéssa *f* female athlete

atlèti·co -ca (-ci -che) *adj* athletic ‖ *f* athletics; **atletica leggera** track and field

atmosfèra *f* atmosphere

atmosfèri·co -ca *adj* (-ci -che) atmospheric

atòllo *m* atoll

atòmi·co -ca *adj* (-ci -che) atomic; (coll) stunning

atomizzare [ddzz] *tr* to atomize

atomizzatóre [ddzz] *m* atomizer

àtomo *m* atom

atòni·co -ca *adj* (-ci -che) (pathol) weak

àto·no -na *adj* (gram) atonic

atout *m* (atouts) trump

à·trio m (-tri) entrance hall, lobby

atróce *adj* atrocious

atroci·tà *f* (-tà) atrocity

atrofìa *f* atrophy

atròfi·co -ca *adj* (-ci -che) atrophied

atrofizzare [ddzz] *tr* & *ref* to atrophy

attaccabottó·ni *mf* (-ni) bore, pest, buttonholer

attaccabri·ghe *mf* (-ghe) (coll) quarrelsome person, scrapper

attaccaménto *m* attachment, affection

attaccapan·ni *m* (-ni) coathanger

attaccare §197 *tr* to attach; to bind, unite; to sew on; to stick; to hitch (*a horse*); to hang; to attack; to strike up (*a conversation*); to begin; to communicate (*a disease*); **attaccare un bottone a** (fig) to buttonhole ‖ *intr* to stick; to gain a foothold, take root; to begin ‖ *ref* to stick; to cling; to spread (*said of a disease*); (fig) to become attached

attaccatìc·cio -cia *adj* (**-ci -ce**) sticky

attacchìno *m* billposter

attac·co *m* (**-chi**) attachment; onslaught; fastening; beginning; seizure (*e.g., of epilepsy*); spell (*e.g., of coughing*); (elec) plug; (rad) jack; (sports) forward line; **attacco cardìaco** heart attack

attagliàre §280 *ref*—**attagliàrsi a** to fit, become

attanagliàre §280 *tr* to grip; to seize; to hold (*e.g., with tongs*)

attardàre *ref* to tarry, delay

attecchìre §176 *intr* to take root; to take hold

atteggiaménto *m* attitude

atteggiàre §290 (**attéggio**) *tr* to compose (*e.g., one's face*); to place ‖ *ref* to pose; to strike an attitude

attémpa·to -ta *adj* elderly

attendaménto *m* camping; jamboree (*of Boy Scouts*)

attendàre (**attèndo**) *ref* to encamp; to pitch one's tent

attendènte *m* (mil) orderly

attèndere §270 *tr* to await; (archaic) to keep; **attendere l'ora propìzia** to bide one's time ‖ *intr*—**attendere a** to attend to

attendìbile *adj* reliable

attendìsmo *m* wait-and-see attitude

attendì·sta (**-sti -ste**) *adj* wait-and-see ‖ *mf* fence-sitter

attenére §271 *tr* (pret) to keep (*a promise*) ‖ *intr*—**attenere** (with *dat*) to concern, e.g., **ciò non gli attiene** this does not concern him ‖ *ref*—**attenèrsi a** to conform to

attentàre (**attènto**) *intr*—**attentare a** to attempt (*s.o.'s life*) ‖ *ref* to make an attempt, dare

attentàto *m* attempt

attenta·tóre -trice *mf* would-be murderer; attacker

attèn·ti *m* (**-ti**) attention ‖ *interj* (mil) attention!

attèn·to -ta *adj* attentive; careful

attenuàre (**attènuo**) *tr* to extenuate, play down; to attenuate; to mitigate

attenzióne *f* attention; **fare attenzione** to take care; **prestàre attenzione** to pay attention

atterràg·gio *m* (**-gi**) landing; **atterraggio di fortùna** emergency landing; **atterraggio sènza carrèllo** crash-landing

atterraménto *m* landing; pinning, pin (*in wrestling*); (boxing) knocking down; **atterramento frenàto** (aer) arrested landing

atterràre (**attèrro**) *tr* to fell; to knock down; to pin (*in wrestling*); (fig) to humiliate ‖ *intr* to land; **atterrare scassàndo** *or* **atterrare sènza carrèllo** to crash-land

atterrìre §176 *tr* to frighten, terrify ‖ *ref* to become frightened

atté·so -sa [s] *adj* awaited, expected; **atteso che** considering that ‖ *f* waiting; expectation; **in attèsa (di)** waiting (for)

attestàre (**attèsto**) *tr* to certify, attest; to prove; to join; (mil) to deploy ‖ *ref* (mil) to take a stand

attestàto *m* certificate

attestazióne *f* testimony; affidavit; attestation, proof

àtti·co -ca (**-ci -che**) *adj* & *mf* Attic ‖ *m* attic

attìguo -gua *adj* adjacent, contiguous

attillàre *tr* & *ref* to preen

attillà·to -ta *adj* tight, close-fitting; tidy, all dressed up

àttimo *m* moment, split second; **di attimo in attimo** any moment

attinènte *adj* related, pertinent

attinènza *f* relation; **attinènze** appurtenances; annexes

attìngere §126 *tr* to draw (*water*); to get; (poet) to attain (*e.g., glory*)

attingitóio *m* (**-tói**) ladle

attiràre *tr* to draw, attract

attitùdine *f* aptitude; attitude

attivàre *tr* to activate; to expedite

attivazióne *f* activation; reassessment

attivi·tà *f* (**-tà**) activity; **attività** *fpl* assets

attì·vo -va *adj* active; profit-making ‖ *m* assets

attizzàre *tr* to stir, poke (*a fire*); (fig) to stir up

attizza·tóio *m* (**-tói**) poker

at·to -ta *adj* apt, fit ‖ *m* act, action; gesture; (law) instrument; **all'atto pràtico** in reality; **atti** proceedings (*of a learned society*); **atti notàrili** legal proceedings; **atto di nàscita** birth certificate; **fare atto di presènza** to put in a brief formal appearance; **atto di véndita** bill of sale; **nell'atto** *o* **sull'atto** in the act

attòni·to -ta *adj* astonished

attorcigliàre §280 *tr* to twist ‖ *ref* to wind; to coil up

attóre *m* actor; (law) plaintiff; **attore giòvane** (theat) juvenile; **primo attore** (theat) lead

attorniàre §287 (**attórnio**) *tr* to surround; (fig) to dupe

attórno *adv* around; **andàre attorno** to walk around; **attorno a** around, near; **dàrsi d'attorno** to busy oneself; **levàrsi qlcu d'attorno** to get rid of s.o.

attortigliàre §280 *tr* to twist ‖ *ref* to wind; to coil up

attraccàre §197 *tr* & *intr* to moor, dock

attràc·co *m* (**-chi**) mooring, docking

attraènte *adj* attractive

attràrre §273 *tr* to attract, draw

attratti·vo -va *adj* attractive; alluring ‖ *f* attraction, charm

attraversaménto *m* crossing; **attraversaménto pedonàle** pedestrian crossing

attraversàre (**attravèrso**) *tr* to cross; to go through; to thwart; **attraversàre il passo a** to stand in the way of

attravèrso *adv* across; crosswise; **andàre attraverso** to go down the wrong way (*said of food or drink*); (fig) to go wrong; **attravèrso a** through, across ‖ *prep* through, across

attrazióne *f* attraction

attrezzàre (**attrézzo**) *tr* to outfit, equip

attrezzatura *f* outfit; gear, equipment; **attrezzatura di una nave** rigging; **attrezzature** facilities

attrezzi·sta (-sti -ste) *mf* gymnast ‖ *m* toolmaker; (theat) property man

attrézzo *m* tool, utensil; **attrezzi** gymnastic equipment

attribuire §176 *tr* to award; to attribute; **attribuire qlco a qlcu** to credit s.o. with s.th ‖ *ref* to ascribe to oneself, claim for oneself

attributo *m* attribute

attribuzióne *f* attribution

attrice *f* actress; (law) plaintiff; **prima attrice** (theat) lead

attristare *tr* (poet) to sadden ‖ *ref* to become sad

attri·to -ta *adj* worn, worn-out ‖ *m* attrition; disagreement

attruppare *tr* to band, group ‖ *ref* to mill about, throng

attuàbile *adj* feasible

attuale *adj* present; present-day, current

attuali·tà *f* (-tà) timeliness; reality; **attualità** *fpl* current events; **di viva attualità** newsworthy; timely; in the news

attualizzare [ddzz] *tr* to bring up to date ‖ *ref* to become a reality

attuare (àttuo) *tr* to carry out, make come true ‖ *ref* to come true

attuà·rio -ria (-ri -rie) *adj* (hist) transport (*e.g., ship*) ‖ *m* actuary

attuazióne *f* realization

attutire §176 *tr* to mitigate; to deaden (*a sound, a blow*) ‖ *ref* to diminish (*said of a sound*)

audace *adj* audacious

audàcia *f* audacity

audiofrequènza *f* audio frequency

audiovisi·vo -va *adj* audio-visual

auditi·vo -va *adj* var of **uditivo**

auditóre *m* var of **uditore**

auditò·rio *m* (-ri) auditorium

audizióne *f* program; audition; (law) hearing

àuge *f* acme; **essere in auge** to enjoy a great reputation; to be in vogue; to be on top of the world

augurale *adj* well-wishing; salutatory

augurare (àuguro) *tr* to wish; to bid (*good day*) ‖ *intr* to augur ‖ *ref* to hope; to expect

àugure *m* augur

augù·rio *m* (-ri) wish; augury, omen

augustè·o -a *adj* Augustan

augu·sto -sta *adj* august, venerable

àula *f* hall; classroom; (poet) chamber (*of a palace*)

àuli·co -ca *adj* (-ci -che) courtly; noble, elevated

aumentare (auménto) *tr* to augment, increase ‖ *intr* (ESSERE) to increase, rise

aménto *m* increase

àura *f* (poet) breeze; (poet) breath

àure·o -a *adj* golden, gold

aurèola *f* halo

auricolare *adj* ear; first-hand ‖ *m* (telp) receiver; (rad) earphone

auròra *f* dawn; (fig) aurora

ausiliare *adj* auxiliary ‖ *m* collaborator, helper

ausilià·rio -ria (-ri -rie) *adj* auxiliary; (mil) supply ‖ *m* helper; (mil) reserve officer ‖ *f* female member of the armed forces

ausì·lio *m* (-li) (poet) help

auspicare §197 (àuspico) *tr* to wish, augur

àuspice *m* sponsor; (hist) augur

auspi·cio *m* (-ci) sponsorship; (hist, poet) augury, omen; **sotto gli auspici di** under the auspices of

austeri·tà *f* (-tà) austerity

austè·ro -ra *adj* austere

australe *adj* austral, southern

Austràlia, l' *f* Australia

australia·no -na *adj & mf* Australian

Austria, l' *f* Austria

austrìa·co -ca *adj & mf* (-ci -che) Austrian

autarchìa *f* autarky; autonomy (*of an administration*)

autàrchi·co -ca *adj* (-ci -che) autonomous, independent

autènti·ca *f* (-che) authentication of a signature or a document

autenticare §197 (autèntico) *tr* to authenticate

autentici·tà *f* (-tà) authenticity

autènti·co -ca (-ci -che) *adj* authentic, genuine ‖ *f* see **autentica**

autière *m* (mil) driver

auti·sta *mf* (-sti -ste) (aut) driver

au·to *f* (-to) auto

autoabbronzante [dz] *adj* tanning ‖ *m* tanning lotion

autoaffondaménto *m* scuttling

autoambulanza *f* ambulance

autobiografìa *f* autobiography

autobiogràfi·co -ca *adj* (-ci -che) autobiographical

autoblinda·to -ta *adj* armored

autoblin·do *m* (-do) armored car

autobótte *f* tank truck

àuto·bus *m* (-bus) bus

autocarro *m* truck, motor truck

autocèntro *m* (mil) motor pool

autocistèrna *f* tank truck

autocivétta *f* unmarked police car

autocolónna *f* row of cars

autocombustióne *f* spontaneous combustion

autocontròllo *m* self-control

autocorrièra *f* intercity bus, highway bus

autocrazìa *f* autocracy

autocrìti·ca *f* (-che) self-criticism

autòcto·no -na *adj* autochthonous, independent

autodecisióne *m* free will

autodeterminazióne *f* self-determination

autodidat·ta *mf* (-ti -te) self-taught person

autodidàtti·co -ca *adj* (-ci -che) self-instructional

autodifésa [s] *f* self-defense

autodisciplina *f* self-discipline

autòdromo *m* automobile race track

autoemotè·ca *f* (-che) bloodmobile

autofilettante *adj* self-threading

autofurgóne *m* van; **autofurgone cellu-**

lare police van; **autofurgone funebre** hearse
autogiro *m* autogyro
autogovèrno *m* self-government
autògra·fo -fa *adj* autographic(al) ‖ *m* autograph
auto·grù *f* (**-grù**) tow truck
autolesioni·sta *mf* (**-sti -ste**) person who wounds himself to avoid the draft or collect insurance
autoletti·ga *f* (**-ghe**) ambulance
autolibro *m* bookmobile
autolìnea *f* bus line
autò·ma *m* (**-mi**) automaton, robot
automàti·co -ca (**-ci -che**) *adj* automatic ‖ *m* snap
automatizzare [ddzz] *tr* to automate
automazióne *f* automation
automèzzo [ddzz] *m* motor vehicle
automòbile *f* automobile, car; **automobile da corsa** racing car; **automobile di serie** stock car; **automobile fuori serie** custom-made car
automobilismo *m* motoring
automobili·sta *mf* (**-sti -ste**) motorist
automobilìsti·co -ca *adj* (**-ci -che**) car, automobile
automo·tóre -trice *adj* self-propelled ‖ *f* (**rr**) automotor
autonolég·gio *m* (**-gi**) car rental agency
autonomìa *f* autonomy; (aer, naut) cruising radius
autonomi·sta *adj* (**-sti -ste**) autonomous
autòno·mo -ma *adj* autonomous, independent
autoparchég·gio *m* (**-gi**) parking; parking lot
autopar·co *m* (**-chi**) parking; parking lot
autopiano *m* player piano
autopilò·ta *m* (**-ti**) (aer) automatic pilot
autopómpa *f* fire engine
autopsìa *f* autopsy
autorà·dio *f* (**-dio**) car radio
autóre *m* author; perpetrator; creator, maker
autoreattóre *m* ramjet engine
autorespiratóre *m* aqualung
autorévole *adj* authoritative
autoriméssa *f* garage
autori·tà *f* (**-tà**) authority
autorità·rio -ria *adj* (**-ri -rie**) authoritarian
autoritratto *m* self-portrait
autorizzare [ddzz] *tr* to authorize
autorizzazióne [ddzz] *f* authorization
autoscàla *f* hook and ladder; ladder (*of hook and ladder*)
autoscuòla *f* driving school
autoservi·zio *m* (**-zi**) bus service, bus line; self-service
autosilo *m* parking garage
autostazióne *f* bus station
autostèllo *m* roadside motel
auto·stòp *m* (**-stòp**) hitchhiking; **fare l'autostop** to hitchhike
autostoppi·sta *mf* (**-sti -ste**) hitchhiker
autostrada *f* highway, turnpike
autosufficiènte *adj* self-sufficient
autote·làio *m* (**-lài**) (aut) frame
autotrasportare (**autotraspòrto**) *tr* to truck

autotrasportatóre *m* trucker
autotreni·sta *m* (**-sti**) truck driver, teamster
autotrèno *m* tractor trailer
autoveìcolo *m* motor vehicle
autovettura *f* car, automobile
autrice *f* authoress
autunnale *adj* autumnal, fall
autunno *m* autumn, fall
avallare *tr* to endorse (*a promissory note*); to guarantee
avallo *m* endorsement (*of a promissory note*)
avambràc·cio *m* (**-ci**) forearm
avampósto *m* outpost
avancàrica *f*—**ad avancarica** muzzle-loading
avanguàrdia *f* vanguard; avant-garde
avanguardismo *m* avant-garde
avanguardi·sta *m* (**-sti**) avant-gardist; (hist) member of Fascist youth organization
avannòtto *m* small fry (*young freshwater fish*)
avanti *adj* preceding ‖ *m* forward ‖ *adv* forward, ahead; **andare avanti** to proceed, to go ahead; **andare avanti negli anni** to be up in years; **avanti a** in front of; **avanti che** rather than; **avanti di** before; **essere avanti** to be advanced (*in work or study*); **in avanti** ahead ‖ *prep*—**avanti Cristo** before Christ; **avanti giorno** before daybreak ‖ *interj* come in!
avantièri *adv* day before yesterday
avantrèno *m* (aut) front-axle assembly; (mil) limber
avanzaménto *m* advancement
avanzare *tr* to advance; to overcome; to be creditor for, e.g., **avanza cento dollari da suo fratello** he is his brother's creditor for one hundred dollars; to save ‖ *intr* (mil) to advance ‖ *intr* (ESSERE) to advance; to stick out; to be abundant; to be left over, e.g., **avanzano due polpette** two meatballs are left over; **avanzare negli anni** to grow older ‖ *ref* to advance, come forward
avanza·to -ta *adj* advanced; progressive ‖ *f* (mil) advance
avanzo *m* remainder; **avanzi** remains
avarìa *f* damage, breakdown; (naut) average
avariare §287 *tr* to damage, spoil ‖ *intr* to spoil
avarià·to -ta *adj* damaged, spoiled
avarìzia *f* avarice, greed
ava·ro -ra *adj* avaricious, stingy ‖ *mf* miser
avellana *f* filbert
avellano *m* filbert tree
avèllo *m* (poet) tomb
avéna *f* oats
avére *m* belongings, property; assets, credit; amount due ‖ §118 *tr* to have; to hold; to wear; to receive, get; to stand (*a chance*); to be, e.g., **avere . . . anni** to be . . . years old; **avere caldo** to be hot; to be warm; **avere fame** to be hungry; **avere freddo** to be cold; **avere fretta** to be in a hurry;

avere paura to be afraid; **avere ragione** to be right; **avere sete** to be thirsty; **avere sonno** to be sleepy; **avere torto** to be wrong; **avere vergogna** to be ashamed; **avere voglia di** to be anxious to; **avere qlco da** + *inf* to have s.th to + *inf*, e.g., **ho molto lavoro da fare** I have a lot of work to do; **averla con** to be angry at; **non avere niente a che fare con** to have nothing to do with || *impers*— **v'ha** there is || *aux* to have, e.g., **ha letto il giornale** he has read the newspaper; **avere da** + *inf* to have to + *inf*, e.g., **avevo da lavorare** I had to work; **to be to** + *inf*, e.g., **ha da venire alle cinque** he is to arrive at five o'clock

avià·rio -ria (-ri -rie) *adj* bird || *m* aviary
avia·tóre -trice *mf* aviator || *f* aviatrix
aviazióne *f* aviation
avicoltóre *m* bird raiser; poultry farmer
avidi·tà *f* (-tà) avidity, greediness
àvi·do -da *adj* avid, greedy
avière *m* airman
aviogètto *m* jet plane
aviolínea *f* airline
aviopista *f* (aer) airstrip
avioriméssa *f* (aer) hangar
aviotrasporta·to -ta *adj* airborne
avi·to -ta *adj* ancestral
a·vo -va *mf* grandparent; ancestor || *m* grandfather || *f* grandmother
avocare §197 (àvoco) *tr* to demand (*jurisdiction*); to expropriate
avò·rio *m* (-ri) ivory
avul·so -sa *adj* (poet) torn, uprooted; (poet) separated
avvalére §278 *ref*—**avvalersi di** to avail oneself of
avvallaménto *m* sinking, settling
avvallare (poet) to lower (*e.g., one's eyes*) || *ref* to sink; (lit) to humiliate oneself
avvalorare (avvalóro) *tr* to strengthen, confirm || *ref* to gain strength
avvampare *tr* (poet) to inflame || *intr* (ESSERE) to burn
avvantaggiare §290 *tr* to be profitable to; to benefit || *ref* to profit; **avvantaggiarsi su** to overcome; to beat
avvedére §279 *ref*—**avvedersi di** to notice, become aware of
avvedutézza *f* discernment; shrewdness
avvedu·to -ta *adj* prudent; shrewd; **fare qlcu avveduto di** to inform s.o. of
avvelenaménto *m* poisoning
avvelenare (avveléno) *tr* to poison || *ref* to take poison; to be poisoned
avveniménto *m* happening, event
avvenire *adj invar* future, to come || *m* future; **in avvenire** in the future || **§282** *intr* (ESSERE) to happen, occur; **avvenga quel che vuole** come what may
avventare (avvènto) *tr* to hurl; to deliver (*a blow*); to venture (*an opinion*) || *ref* to throw oneself
avventatézza *f* thoughtlessness, heedlessness

avventa·to -ta *adj* thoughtless, heedless; **all'avventata** heedlessly
avventì·zio -zia *adj* (-zi -zie) outside, exterior; temporary, occasional
avvènto *m* advent; elevation, rise
avven·tóre -tóra *mf* customer, consumer
avventura *f* adventure
avventuriè·ro -ra *adj* adventurous || *m* adventurer || *f* adventuress
avventuró·so -sa [s] *adj* adventurous, adventuresome
avverare (avvéro) *tr* to make true || *ref* to come true
avvèr·bio *m* (-bi) adverb
avversà·rio -ria (-ri -rie) *adj* opposing, contrary || *mf* adversary, opponent
avversióne *f* aversion
avversi·tà *f* (-tà) adversity
avvèr·so -sa *adj* adverse; (obs) opposite || **avverso** *prep* (law) against
avvertènza *f* prudence, caution; advice; **avvertenze** instructions, directions
avvertiménto *m* caution, warning; advice
avvertire (avvèrto) *tr* to caution, warn; to notice
avvezzare (avvézzo) *tr* to accustom; to inure; to train; **avvezzar male** to spoil || *ref* to get accustomed
avvéz·zo -za *adj* accustomed
avviaménto *m* starting; introduction; trade school; good shape (*of a business*); (mach) starting; (typ) adjustment (*of printing press*)
avviare §119 *tr* to start, set in motion; to introduce; to initiate; to begin || *ref* to set out
avvia·to -ta *adj* going, thriving (*concern*)
avvicendaménto *m* alteration, rotation (*of crops*)
avvicendare (avvicèndo) *tr & ref* to alternate
avvicinaménto *m* approach; rapprochement
avvicinare *tr* to bring near or closer; to approach, go or come near to || *ref* to approach, come near; **avvicinarsi a** to come closer, approach
avviliménto *m* discouragement, dejection
avvilire §176 *tr* to degrade; to deject || *ref* to become dejected, become discouraged
avviluppare *tr* to entangle, snarl; to wrap
avvinazza·to -ta *adj & mf* drunk
avvincènte *adj* fascinating
avvìncere §285 *tr* to fascinate, charm; (poet) to twine
avvinghiare §287 *tr* to claw; to clasp, clutch || *ref* to grip one another
avvì·o *m* (-i) beginning
avviságlia *f* skirmish; **prime avvisaglie** onset; first signs
avvisare *tr* to inform, advise; (archaic) to observe, notice
avvisa·tóre -trice *mf* announcer, messenger || *m* alarm; (theat) callboy; **avvisatore acustico** (aut) horn; **avvisatore d'incendio** fire alarm
avviso *m* advise; notice, poster; opinion; **avviso di chiamata alle armi**

notice of induction; **sull'avviso** on one's guard

avvistare *tr* to sight

avvitaménto *m* (aer) tailspin

avvitare *tr* to screw; to fasten || *ref* (aer) to go into a tailspin

avviticchiare §287 *tr* to entwine || *ref* to cling

avvivare *tr* to revive; to stir up

avvizzire §176 *tr & intr* (ESSERE) to wither

avvocatéssa *f* woman lawyer

avvocato *m* lawyer, attorney

avvòcatura *f* law, legal profession

avvòlgere §289 *tr* to wind; to wrap up; to spread over, surround || *ref* to wind around; to wrap oneself up

avvolgiménto *m* winding; wrapping; (elec) coil; (mil) envelopment

avvol·tóio *m* (-tói) vulture

avvoltolare (avvòltolo) *tr* to roll up || *ref* to roll around, wallow

aziènda [dz] *f* business, firm

azionare (azióno) *tr* to start; to drive, propel

aziona·rio -ria *adj* (-ri -rie) (com) stock

azióne *f* action, act; (law) suit; (com) share (*of stock*); **azione legale** prosecution; **azione privilegiata** preferred stock

azioni·sta *mf* (-sti -ste) stockholder, shareholder

azòto [dz] *m* nitrogen

azoturo [dz] *m* nitride

aztè·co -ca *adj & mf* (-chi -che) Aztec

azzannare *tr* to seize with the fangs

azzardare [ddzz] *tr* to risk; to advance || *ref* to dare

azzarda·to -ta [ddzz] *adj* daring

azzardo [ddzz] *m* chance, hazard

azzardó·so -sa [ddzz] [s] *adj* hazardous, risky

azzeccagarbu·gli *m* (-gli) shyster

azzeccare §197 (azzécco) *tr* to hit; to deliver; to pass off (*counterfeit money*); **azzeccarla** (coll) to hit the mark

azzimare [ddzz] (àzzimo) *tr & ref* to spruce up

àzzi·mo -ma [ddzz] *adj* unleavened (*bread*)

azzittare & azzittire §176 *tr* to hush || *ref* to keep quiet

Azzòrre [ddzz] *fpl* Azores

azzuffare *ref* to come to blows; to scuffle

azzur·ro -ra [ddzz] *adj* blue || *m* blue; Italian athlete (*in international competition*)

azzurrógno·lo -la [ddzz] *adj* bluish

B

B, b [bi] *m & f* second letter of the Italian alphabet

ba·bàu *m* (-bàu) bogey, bugbear

babbè·o -a *adj* foolish || *mf* fool

babbo *m* (coll) daddy, father

babbù·cia *f* (-ce) babouche; bedroom slipper

babbuino *m* baboon

babèle *f* babel || **Babele** *f* Babel

babilònia *f* confusion || **Babilònia** *f* Babylon

babórdo *m* (naut) port

bacare §197 *ref* to become worm-eaten

baca·to -ta *adj* worm-eaten; rotten

bac·ca *f* (-che) berry

bacca·là *m* (-là) dried codfish; (coll) skinny person; (coll) lummox

baccalaureato *m* baccalaureate, bachelor's degree

baccanale *m* bacchanal

baccano *m* noise, hubbub; **fare baccano** to carry on

baccante *f* bacchant

baccellière *m* (hist) bachelor

baccèllo *m* pod

baccellóne *m* simpleton, fool

bacchétta *f* rod, wand, baton; **bacchetta magica** magic wand; **bacchette del tamburo** drumsticks

bacchétto *m* stick; handle (*of a whip*)

bacchettó·ne -na *mf* bigot

bàcchi·co -ca *adj* (-ci -che) Bacchic

Bacco *m* Baccus

bachè·ca *f* (-che) showcase

bachelite *f* bakelite

bacheròzzo *m* worm; earthworm; (coll) cockroach

bachicoltura *f* silkworm raising

baciama·no *m* (-ni) kissing of the hand

baciapi·le *mf* (-le) bigot

baciare §128 *tr* to kiss; **baciare la polvere** to bite the dust || *ref* to kiss one another

bacia·to -ta *adj* kissed; rhymed (*couplet*)

bacile *m* basin

bacillo *m* bacillus

bacinèlla *f* small basin; (phot) tray

bacino *m* basin; reservoir; cove; (anat) pelvis; **bacino carbonifero** coal field; **bacino di carenaggio** drydock; **bacino fluviale** river basin

bà·cio *m* (-ci) kiss; **a bacio** with a northern exposure

baciucchiare §287 *tr* to keep on kissing || *ref* to pet

ba·co *m* (-chi) worm; **baco da seta** silkworm

bacuc·co -ca *adj* (-chi -che)—**vecchio bacucco** dotard

bada *f*—**tenere a bada** to stave off; to delay

badare *tr* to tend, take care of || *intr* to attend; to take care; to pay attention; **badare a** to mind; to watch over; to attend to; **badare alla salute** to take care of one's health

badéssa *f* abbess

badìa *f* abbey

badilata *f* shovelful

badile *m* shovel

baffo *m* whiskers; whisker; **baffi** mustache; whiskers; **baffo di gatto** (rad) cat's whiskers; **leccarsi i baffi** to lick one's chops; **sotto i baffi** up one's sleeve

baga·gliàio *m* (**-gliài**) (rr) baggage car; (rr) baggage room; (aut) baggage rack

bagaglièra *f* baggage room

bagaglière *m* baggage master

bagà·glio *m* (**-gli**) baggage, luggage; *(of knowledge)* fund

bagagli·sta *m* (**-sti**) porter *(in a hotel)*

bagarinàg·gio *m* (**-gi**) profiteering; (theat) scalping

bagarino *m* profiteer; scalper

bagà·scia *f* (**-sce**) harlot, prostitute

bagattèlla *f* trifle, bauble

baggiano *m* nitwit, simpleton

bà·glio *m* (**-gli**) (naut) beam

baglióre *m* shine, gleam

bagnante *mf* bather, swimmer; vacationer at the seashore

bagnare *tr* to bathe; to wet; to soak; to water, sprinkle; to moisten; (fig) to celebrate || *ref* to bathe; to wet one another

bagnaròla *f* (coll) bathtub

bagnasciu·ga *f* (**-ghe**) (naut) waterline

bagnino *m* lifeguard

bagno *m* bath; bathroom; bathtub; **bagno di luce** diathermy; **bagno di schiuma** bubble bath; **bagno di sole** sun bath; **bagno di vapore** steam bath; **bagno turco** Turkish bath; **essere in un bagno di sudore** to be soaked with perspiration; **fare il bagno** to take a bath

bagnomaria *m* (**bagnimaria**) double boiler; bain-marie; **a bagnomaria** in a double boiler

bagórdo *m* carousal, revelry; **far bagordi** to carouse, revel

bàio bàia (**bài bàie**) *adj & m* bay || *f* bay; jest; trifle; **dare la baia a** to make fun of, tease

baionétta *f* bayonet; **baionetta in canna** with fixed bayonet

bàita *f* mountain hut

balaustrata *f* balustrade

balaùstro *m* baluster

balbettaménto *m* stammering

balbettare (**balbétto**) *tr* to stammer; to speak poorly *(a foreign language)* || *intr* to stammer; to babble *(said of a baby)*

balbetti·o *m* (**-i**) babble *(of a baby)*; stammering

balbùzie *f* stammering

balbuziènte *adj* stammering || *mf* stammerer

Balcani, i the Balkans

balcàni·co -ca *adj* (**-ci -che**) Balkan

balconata *f* balcony; (theat) upper gallery

balcóne *m* balcony

baldacchino *m* canopy, baldachin

baldanza *f* boldness; aplomb, assurance

baldanzó·so -sa [s] *adj* bold; self-assured

bal·do -da *adj* bold; self-assured

baldòria *f* carousal, revelry; **fare baldoria** to carouse, revel

baldrac·ca *f* (**-che**) harlot, prostitute

baléna *f* whale

balenare (**baléno**) *intr* to stagger || *intr* (ESSERE) to flash, e.g., **gli balena un pensiero** a thought flashes through his mind || *impers* (ESSERE)—**balena,** it is lightning

balenièra *f* whaler, whaleboat

baléno *m* flash; flash of lightning; **in un baleno** in a flash

balenòttera *f* rorqual

balèstra *f* crossbow; (aut) spring, leaf spring

balestrière *m* crossbowman

bàlia *f* wet nurse; **balia asciutta** dry nurse; **prendere a balia** to wet-nurse

balìa *f* power; **in balia di** at the mercy of

balìsti·co -ca (**-ci -che**) *adj* ballistic || *f* ballistics

balla *f* bale; (vulg) lie

ballàbile *adj* dance || *m* dance tune

ballare *tr* to dance || *intr* to dance; to shake; to be loose; to wobble *(said, e.g., of a chair)*

ballata *f* ballad; (mus) ballade

balla·tóio *m* (**-tói**) gallery; perch *(in birdcage)*

balleri·no -na *adj* dancing || *m* ballet dancer; dancer; dancing partner || *f* dancing girl; ballerina; chorus girl; ballet slipper; (orn) wagtail

ballétto *m* ballet; chorus

ballo *m* dance; chorus; ball; stake; **ballo di San Vito** Saint Vitus's dance; **ballo in maschera** masked ball; **ballo** at stake; in question; **tirare in ballo** to drag in

ballonzolare (**ballónzolo**) *intr* to hop around

ballottàg·gio *m* (**-gi**) runoff

ballottare (**ballòtto**) *tr* to ballot *(e.g., a candidate)*

balneare *adj* bathing; water, watering

baloccare §197 (**balòcco**) *tr* to amuse with toys || *ref* to play; to trifle, to fool around

balòc·co *m* (**-chi**) toy; hobby

balordàggine *f* silliness

balór·do -da *adj* silly, foolish

balsàmi·co -ca *adj* (**-ci -che**) balmy; antiseptic

balsamina *f* balsam

bàlsamo *m* balm, balsam

bàlti·co -ca *adj* (**-ci -che**) Baltic

baluardo *m* bastion, bulwark

baluginare (**balùgino**) *intr* (ESSERE) to flicker; to flash *(through one's mind)*

balza *f* crag, cliff; flounce *(on dress)*; fringe *(on curtains, bedspreads, etc.)*

balza·no -na *adj* white-footed *(horse)*; odd, funny || *f* flounce; fringe; white mark *(on horse's feet)*

balzare *tr* to throw *(a rider; said of a horse)* || *intr* (ESSERE) to jump, leap;

to bounce; **balzare in mente a to** suddenly dawn on

balzellare (balzèllo) *intr* to hop

balzèllo *m* hop; tribute; tax; toll; **stare a balzello** to lie in wait

balzellóni *adv*—**a balzelloni** leaping, skipping

balzo *m* leap; bounce; **pigliare la palla al balzo** to take time by the forelock

bambàgia *f* cotton wool

bambinàggine *f* childishness

bambinàia *f* nursemaid; **bambinaia ad ore** baby sitter

bambiné·sco -sca *adj* (**-schi -sche**) childish

bambi·no -na *adj* childish || *mf* child

bambòc·cio -cia *m* (**-ci**) fat baby; doll; rag doll

bàmbola *f* doll; **bambola di pezza** ragdoll

bam·bù *m* (**-bù**) bamboo

banale *adj* banal, commonplace

banali·tà *f* (**-tà**) banality, commonplaceness, triviality

banana *f* banana; hair with curls shaped as rolls

bananièra *f* banana boat

banano *m* banana plant

ban·ca *f* (**-che**) bank; embankment

bancàbile *adj* negotiable

bancarèlla *f* cart, pushcart; stall

bancà·rio -ria (**-ri -rie**) *adj* bank, banking || *m* bank clerk

bancarótta *f* bankruptcy; **fare bancarotta** to go bankrupt

banchettare (**banchétto**) *intr* to feast, banquet

banchétto *m* banquet

banchière *m* banker

banchina *f* garden bench; bicycle path; sidewalk; shoulder (*of highway*); dock, pier; (**rr**) platform; (**mil**) banquette

ban·co *m* (**-chi**) bench; seat; bank; witness stand; school (*of fish*); **banco di coralli** coral reef; **banco di ghiaccio** ice pack; **banco di nebbia** fog bank; **banco di prova** (**mach**) bench; **banco di sabbia** sandbar; **banco d'ostriche** oyster bed; **banco lotto** lottery office

bancogiro *m* (**com**) transfer of funds

bancóne *m* counter; bench

banconòta *f* banknote

banda *f* band; **andare alla banda** (**naut**) to list; **da ogni banda** from every side; **mettere da banda** to put aside

bandèlla *f* hinge (*of door or window*); hinged leaf (*of table*)

banderuòla *f* banderole; weather vane

bandièra *f* flag; banner; **battere la bandiera** (*e.g.,* **italiana**) to fly the (*e.g Italian*) flag; **mutar bandiera** to change sides

bandierare (**bandièro**) *tr* (**aer**) to feather

bandire §176 *tr* to announce (*e.g., a competitive examination*); to banish

bandìsti·co -ca *adj* (**-ci -che**) (**mus**) band

bandi·to -ta *adj* announced; open (*house*) || *m* bandit || *f* preserve (*for hunting or fishing*)

bandi·tóre -trice *mf* town crier; auctioneer; barker

bando *m* announcement; banishment; **bandi matrimoniali** (**eccl**) banns; **mandare in bando** to exile, banish

bandolièra *f* bandoleer; **a bandoliera** slung across the shoulders

bàndolo *m* end of a skein; **perdere il bandolo** to lose the thread (*e.g., of a story*)

bara *f* bier, coffin

barac·ca *f* (**-che**) hut, cabin; (**fig**) household; **fare baracca** to carouse around

baracca·to -ta *adj* lodged in a hut or a cabin; slum (*e.g., section*) || *m* dweller in a hut or a cabin; slum dweller

baraccóne *m* big circus tent

baraónda *f* hubbub; mess

barare *intr* to cheat (*e.g., at cards*)

bàratro *m* abyss, chasm

barattare *tr* to barter; **barattare le carte in mano a uno** to distort someone's words; **barattar parole** to chat, talk || *intr* to barter

barattière *m* grafter

baratto *m* barter

baràttolo *m* can, canister, jar

barba *f* beard; whiskers; barb, vane (*of feather*); (**naut**) line; **barba a punta** imperial, goatee; **fare la barba** (**a**) to shave; **farla in barba a qlcu** to act in spite of s.o.; to dupe s.o.; **mettere barbe** to take root; **radersi la barba** to shave

barbabiètola *f* beet; sugar beet

barbafòrte *m* horseradish

barbagian·ni *m* (**-ni**) owl; (**fig**) jackass

barbà·glio *m* (**-gli**) glitter, dazzle

barbaré·sco -sca (**-schi -sche**) *adj* Barbary || *m* inhabitant of the Barbary States

barbàri·co -ca *adj* (**-ci -che**) barbaric

barbà·rie *f* (**-rie**) barbarism, barbarity

barbarismo *m* barbarism

bàrba·ro -ra *adj* barbarous, barbaric || *m* barbarian

barbazzale *m* curb (*of bit*)

Barberìa, la Barbary States

barbétta *f* fetlock (*tuft of hair on horse*); goatee; (**mil**) barbette; (**naut**) painter

barbière *m* barber

barbierìa *f* barbershop

barbi·glio *m* (**-gli**) barb (*of arrow*)

barbi·no -na *adj* shoddy; botched; stingy

bàr·bio *m* (**-bi**) (**ichth**) barbel

barbiturato *m* barbiturate

barbitùri·co -ca (**-ci -che**) *adj* barbituric || *m* barbiturate

barbo *m* var of **barbio**

barbò·gio -gia *adj* (**-gi -gie**) senile

barbóne *m* long beard, thick beard; poodle; (**coll**) bum, hobo

barbó·so -sa [**s**] *adj* boring

barbugliare §280 *tr* to stutter (*e.g., a word*) || *intr* to stutter; to bubble, gurgle

barbu·to -ta *adj* bearded

bar·ca *f* (**-che**) boat; heap; (**fig**) family

affairs; **barca a motore** motorboat; **barca da pesca** fishing boat; **barca a remi** rowboat

barcàc·cia f (**-ce**) (theat) stage box

barcaiòlo m boatman

barcamenare (barcaméno) ref to manage, get along

barcarizzo m (naut) gangway

barcaròla f barcarole

barcata f boatful

barchéssa f tool shed

barchétta f small boat; (naut) log chip

barcollare (barcòllo) intr to totter, stagger

barcollóni adv staggering, tottering

barcóne m barge

bardare tr to harness ‖ ref to get dressed

bardatura f harnessing; harness

bardo m bard

bardòsso m **—a bardosso** (archaic) bareback

barèlla f stretcher

barellare (barèllo) tr to carry on a stretcher ‖ intr to totter, stagger

barenatura f (mach) boring

bargèllo m (hist) chief of police; (hist) police headquarters

bargi·glio m (**-gli**) wattle

baricèntro m center of gravity; (fig) essence, gist

barile m barrel, cask

barilòtto m keg

bàrio m barium

bari·sta mf (**-sti -ste**) bartender, barkeeper ‖ m barman ‖ f barmaid

baritonale adj baritone

barìto·no -na adj barytone ‖ m baritone

barlume m glimmer, gleam

baro m cheat, cardsharp

baròc·co -ca adj & m (**-chi -che**) baroque

baròmetro m barometer

baróne m baron

baronéssa f baroness

barra f bar; link; rod; sandbar; **andare alla barra** to plead a case; **barra del timone** (naut) tiller; **barra di torsione** (aut) torsion bar; **barra spaziatrice** space bar (of typewriter)

barrare tr to cross, draw lines across (a check)

barrétta f bar (e.g., of chocolate)

barricare §197 (bàrrico) tr to barricade ‖ ref to barricade oneself

barricata f barricade

barrièra f barrier; bar; **barriera corallina** barrier reef

barrire §176 intr to trumpet (said of elephant)

barrito m trumpeting, cry of an elephant

barroc·ciàio m (**-ciài**) cart driver

barròc·cio m (**-ci**) cart

baruffa f fight, quarrel

barzellétta [dz] f joke

basale adj basal

basalto m basalt

basaménto m foundation (of building); baseboard; base (of column)

basare tr to base ‖ ref—**basarsi su** to be based on; to rest on

ba·sco -sca adj & mf (**-schi -sche**) Basque

basculìa f balance, scale

base f base, foundation; (fig) basis; **a base di** composed of, made of; **base navale** naval base, naval station; **in base a** according to

basétta f sideburns

bàsi·co -ca adj (**-ci -che**) (chem) basic

basilare adj basic, fundamental

Basilèa f Basel

basìli·ca f (**-che**) basilica

basìli·co m (**-ci**) basil

basilissa f (fig) queen bee

bàsolo m large paving stone

bassacórte f barnyard

bassézza f baseness

bas·so -sa adj low; shallow; late (e.g., date); (fig) base, vile; **basso di statura** short ‖ m bottom; hovel (in Naples); (mus) basso ‖ **basso** adv low; down; **a basso, da basso** or **in basso** downstairs

bassofóndo m (**bassifóndi**) (naut) shallows, shallow water; **bassifondi** underworld, slums

bassopiano m lowland

bassorilièvo m bas-relief

bassòt·to -ta adj stocky ‖ m basset hound

bassotuba m bass horn

bassura f lowland; (fig) baseness

basta f hem; basting (with long stitches) ‖ interj enough!

bastante adj sufficient, adequate; comfortable (income)

bastar·do -da adj bastard; irregular ‖ m bastard

bastare intr to suffice, be enough; **basta!** enough!; **basta che + subj** as long as + ind; **bastare a sé stesso** to be self-sufficient; **non basta che + subj** not only + ind

bastévole adj sufficient

bastiménto m ship; shipload

bastióne m bastion; (fig) defense, rampart

basto m packsaddle; (fig) burden

bastonare (bastóno) tr to club, cudgel; **bastonare di santa ragione** to give a good thrashing to

bastonata f clubbing, cudgeling; **darsi bastonate da orbi** to thrash one another soundly

bastoncino m small stick; roll; (anat) rod

bastóne m stick, cane; pole; club; baton; staff; French bread; **bastone a leva** crowbar; **bastone animato** sword cane; **bastone da golf** club; **bastone da montagna** alpenstock; **bastone da passeggio** walking stick; **bastone da sci** ski pole; **bastoni** suit in Neapolitan cards corresponding to clubs; **mettere il bastone tra le ruote** to throw a monkey wrench into the machinery

batàc·chio m (**-chi**) clapper (of bell); cudgel

batata f sweet potato

batisfèra f bathysphere
batista f batiste, cambric
batòsta f blow; (fig) blow
bàtrace or **batrace** m batrachian
battà·glia f (-glie) battle; campaign
battagliare §280 intr to fight
battaglièro -ra adj fighting, warlike
battà·glio m (-gli) clapper (of bell); knocker
battaglióne m battalion
battèllo m boat; **battello di salvataggio** lifeboat; **battello pneumatico** rubber raft
battènte m leaf (e.g., of door); knocker; tapper (of alarm clock)
bàttere m—**in un batter d'occhio** in the twinkling of an eye ‖ tr to beat; to hit; to strike; **to strike** (the hour; said of a clock); to click (teeth, heels); to clap (hands); to stamp (one's foot); to mint (coins); to fly (a flag); to beat (time); to scour (the countryside); to flap (the wings); (sports) to bat; (sports) to kick (a penalty); **battere a macchina** to type; **battere il naso in** to chance upon; **battere la fiacca** to goof off; **battere la grancassa per** to ballyhoo; **battere la strada** to be a streetwalker; **senza batter ciglio** without batting an eye ‖ intr (ESSERE) to beat down (said, e.g., of rain); to beat (said of the heart); to chatter (said of teeth); to knock (at the door); **battere in ritirata** to beat a retreat; **battere in testa** (aut) to knock
batterìa f battery; set (of utensils); (sports) heat
batterici·da (-di -de) adj bactericidal ‖ m bactericide
battèri·co -ca adj (-ci -che) bacterial
battè·rio m (-ri) bacterium
batteriologìa f bacteriology
batteriòlo·go -ga mf (-gi -ghe) bacteriologist
batterì·sta mf (-sti -ste) jazz drummer
battesimale adj baptismal
battésimo m baptism; **tenere a battesimo** to christen
battezzare (battézzo) [dzz] tr to christen ‖ ref to receive baptism; to assume the name of
battibaléno m—**in un battibaleno** in the twinkling of an eye
battibéc·co m (-chi) squabble
batticuòre m palpitation; (fig) trepidation
battilò·ro m (-ro) goldsmith; silversmith
battimano m applause
battimuro m—**giocare a battimuro** to pitch pennies (against a wall)
battipalo m pile driver
battipan·ni m (-ni) clothes beater
battira·me m (-me) coppersmith
battiscó·pa m (-pa) washboard, baseboard
batti·sta adj & mf (-sti -ste) Baptist
battistèro m baptistry
battistra·da m (-da) outrider; (sports) leader; (aut) tread
battitappéto m carpet sweeper
bàttito m beating; palpitation; ticking;

wink; pitter-patter (of rain)
batti·tóio m (-tói) leaf (e.g., of door); casement; cotton beater
battitóre m (hunt) beater; (baseball) batter
battitrice f threshing machine
battitura f thrashing, whipping; threshing (e.g., of wheat)
battu·to -ta adj beaten; hammered ‖ m pavement ‖ f beat; stroke, keystroke; meter (in poetry); witticism, quip; (hunt) battue; (mus) bar; (tennis) service; (theat) line; (theat) cue; **battuta d'aspetto** (mus) pause; **dare la battuta** to give the cue
batùffolo m wad; (fig) bundle
baule m trunk; **baule armadio** wardrobe trunk; **fare i bauli** to be on one's way; **fare il baule** to pack one's trunk
baulétto m small trunk; handbag; jewel case
bava f slobber; foam, froth; burr (on metal edge); **avere la bava alla bocca** to be frothing at the mouth; **bava di vento** breath of air, soft breeze
bavaglino m bib
bavà·glio m (-gli) gag
bavarése [s] adj & mf Bavarian ‖ f Bavarian cream; chocolate cream
bàvero m collar
bavièra f beaver (of helmet) ‖ **la Baviera** Bavaria
bavó·so -sa [s] adj slobbering, slobbery
bazza [ddzz] f protruding chin; windfall
bazzana [ddzz] f sheepskin
bazzècola [ddzz] f trifle, bauble
bazzicare §197 (bàzzico) tr to frequent
bazzòt·to -ta [ddzz] adj soft-boiled; uncertain (weather)
beare (bèo) tr to delight ‖ ref to be delighted, be enraptured
beatificare §197 (beatìfico) tr to beatify
beatitùdine f beatitude, bliss
bea·to -ta adj blissful, happy; blessed ‖ mf blessed
be·bè m (-bè) baby
beccàc·cia f (-ce) woodcock
beccaccìno m snipe
beccafì·co m (-chi) figpecker, beccafico
bec·càio m (-càl) butcher
beccamòr·ti m (-ti) gravedigger
beccare §197 (bécco) tr to peck; to pick; (coll) to catch ‖ ref to peck one another; to quarrel
beccata f peck
beccheggiare §290 (becchéggio) intr (naut) to pitch
becchég·gio m (-gi) (naut) pitching
beccherìa f butcher shop
becchìme m food for poultry
becchìno m gravedigger
béc·co m (-chi) beak, bill; tip, point; nozzle (e.g., of teapot); billy goat; (vulg) cuckold; **bagnarsi il becco** (joc) to wet one's whistle; **mettere il becco in** (coll; joc) to stick one's nose into; **non avere il becco di un quattrino** to not have a red cent
beccùc·cio m (-ci) small bill; lip, spout
beccuzzare tr to peck ‖ ref to bill (said of doves)

béce·ro -ra *adj* (coll) boorish || *m* (coll) boor

bedui·no -na *adj & m* Bedouin

befana *f* (coll) Epiphany; old hag

bèffa *f* jest, mockery; **farsi beffa di** to make fun of

beffar·do -da *adj* mocking

beffare (**bèffo**) *tr* to mock, deride || *ref* —**beffarsi di** to make fun of

beffeggiare §290 (**befféggio**) *tr* to scoff at, deride

bè·ga *f* (**-ghe**) quarrel; trouble

beghina *f* Beguine; bigoted woman

begònia *f* begonia

bèl *adj* apocopated form of **bello**, used only before masculine singular nouns beginning with a consonant except impure **s**, **z**, **gn**, **ps**, and **x**, e.g., **bel ragazzo**

belare (**bèlo**) *tr* to croon || *intr* to bleat, baa; to moan

belato *m* bleat, baa

bèl·ga *adj & mf* (**-gi -ghe**) Belgian

Bèlgio, il Belgium

bèll' *adj* apocopated form of **bello**, used only before singular nouns of both genders beginning with a vowel, e.g., **bell'amico**; **bell'epoca**

bèlla *adj fem* of **bello** || *f* belle; girl-friend; final draft; (sports) final game; (sports) rubber match; **alla bell'e meglio** the best one could; **bella di notte** (bot) four-o'clock

belladònna *f* belladonna

bellétto *m* rouge, makeup

bellézza *f* beauty; **che bellezza!** how lovely!; **la bellezza di** as much as

bellici·sta *adj* (**-sti -ste**) bellicose

bèlli·co -ca *adj* (**-ci -che**) war, warlike

bellicó·so -sa [s] *adj* bellicose

belligerante *adj & m* belligerent

belligeranza *f* belligerence

bellimbusto *m* fop, dandy, beau

bèl·lo -la (declined like **quello** §7) *adj* beautiful; lovely; handsome; good-looking; pleasing; fine; quite a, e.g., **una bella cifra** quite a sum; fair; pretty; **bell'e fatto** ready-made; taken care of; **farla bella** to start trouble; (coll) to do it, e.g., **l'hai fatta bella** you've done it; **farsi bello** to dress up; **farsi bello di** to appropriate || *m* beauty; beautiful; climax; fine weather; beau; **il bello è** the funny thing is; **sul più bello** just then; **sul più bello che** just when || *f* see **bella** || **bello** *adv*—**bel bello** slowly

bellospìrito *m* (**begli spiriti**) wit, bel-esprit

bellui·no -na *adj* wild, fierce

bellumóre *m* (**begli umori**) jolly fellow

bel·tà *f* (**-tà**) beauty (**woman**); (lit) beauty

bélva *f* wild beast

belvedére *f* (**rr**) observation (**car**) || *m* belvedere; (naut) topgallant

Belzebù *m* Beelzebub

bemòlle *m* (mus) flat

benama·to -ta *adj* beloved

benarriva·to -ta *adj* welcome

benché *conj* although, albeit

bènda *f* bandage; band; blindfold; **benda gessata** cast, surgical dressing

bendàg·gio *m* (**-gi**) bandage

bendare (**bèndo**) *tr* to bandage; **bendare gli occhi a** to blindfold

bendispó·sto -sta *adj* well-disposed

bène *adj* well; well-born || *m* goal, aim; good; love; sake; **bene dell'anima** profound affection; **beni** (econ) assets, goods; **beni di consumo** consumer goods; **beni immobili** real estate; **beni mobili** personal property, chattels; **beni rifugio** hedge (*e.g., against inflation*); **è un bene** it is a blessing; **fare del bene** to do good; **per il Suo bene** for your sake; **voler bene a** to love, like; to care for || *adv* well; all right; properly; **ben bene** quite carefully; **star bene** to be well; **va bene** O.K., all right

benedetti·no -na *adj & m* Benedictine

benedét·to -ta *adj* blessed; holy

benedire §195 *tr* to bless; to praise; **andare a farsi benedire** (coll) to go to wrack and ruin; **mandare a farsi benedire** (coll) to get rid of, dump

benedizióne *f* benediction; boon

beneduca·to -ta *adj* well-behaved

benefattóre *m* benefactor

benefattrice *f* benefactress

beneficare §197 (**benèfico**) *tr* to benefit, help

beneficènza *f* welfare; charity, benefi-cence

beneficiale *adj* beneficial

beneficiare §128 *intr* to benefit

beneficià·rio -ria *adj & mf* (**-ri -rie**) beneficiary

beneficiata *f* benefit performance; streak of good luck; streak of bad luck

benefì·cio *m* (**-ci**) benefice; profit; favor; benefit

benèfi·co -ca *adj* (**-ci -che**) beneficial; beneficent

benemerènte *adj* deserving, well-deserving

benemèri·to -ta *adj* worthy, deserving || *m*—**benemerito della patria** national hero || *f*—**la Benemerita** the Carabinieri

beneplàcito *m* approval, consent; **a beneplacito di** at the pleasure of

benèssere *m* well-being, comfort; prosperity

benestante *adj* well-to-do || *mf* well-to-do person

benestare *m* approval; prosperity; **dare il benestare a** to approve

benevolènte *adj* benevolent

benevolènza *f* benevolence

benèvo·lo -la *adj* well-meaning; benev-olent

benfat·to -ta *adj* well-done; well-favored; shapely

benga·la *m* (**-li & -la**) fireworks

benga·li *adj & m* (**-li**) Bengalese

beniami·no -na *mf* favorite child; favo-rite

benigni·tà *f* (**-tà**) benignity; gracious-ness; mildness (*of climate*)

beni-gno -gna *adj* benign; gracious; mild (*climate*)

benintenziona-to -ta *adj* well-meaning

benintéso [s] *adv* of course, naturally

bènna *f* bucket, scoop (*e.g., of dredge*)

benna-to -ta *adj* (lit) well-born

benpensante *m* sensible person; conformist

benportante *adj* well-preserved

benservito *m* testimonial, recommendation; **dare il benservito a** to dismiss, fire

bensì *adv* indeed || *conj* but

bentorna-to -ta *adj & m* welcome. || *interj* welcome back!

benvenu-to -ta *adj & m* welcome; **dare il benvenuto a** to welcome

benvi-sto -sta *adj* well-thought-of

benvolére *tr*—**farsi benvolere da qlcu** to enter the good graces of s.o.; **prendere a benvolere qlcu** to be well-disposed toward s.o.

benvolu-to -ta *adj* liked, loved

benzina *f* gasoline, gas; benzine; **far benzina** (coll) to get gas

benzi-nàio *m* (**-nài**) gasoline dealer; gas-station attendant

benzòlo *m* benzene

beóne *m* drunkard, toper

bequadro *m* (mus) natural

berciare §128 (**bèrcio**) *intr* (coll) to yell

bére *m* drink, drinking || §120 *tr* to drink; (fig) to swallow; **bere come una spugna** to drink like a fish; **darla a bere** to make believe

bergamòt-to -ta *adj* bergamot || *m* bergamot orange || *f* bergamot pear

berìllio *m* beryllium

berlina *f* pillory; berlin, coach; (aut) sedan; **mettere alla berlina** to pillory

berlinése [s] *adj* Berlin || *mf* Berliner

Berlino *m* Berlin

bermuda *mpl* Bermuda shorts || **le Bermude** *f* Bermuda

bernòccolo *m* bump, protuberance; (fig) knack

berrétta *f* biretta

berrétto *m* cap; **berretto a sonagli** cap and bells; **berretto da notte** nightcap; **berretto goliardico** student cap

bersagliare §280 *tr* to harass, pursue; to bomb, bombard

bersà-glio *m* (**-gli**) target; butt (*of a joke*); target (*of criticism*)

bèrta *f* pile driver; **dar la berta a** to ridicule

bertùc-cia *f* (**-ce**) Barbary ape; **fare la bertuccia di** to ape

bestémmia *f* blasphemy

bestemmiare §287 (**bestémmio**) *tr* to blaspheme, curse

bestemmia-tóre -trice *adj* blasphemous || *mf* blasphemer

béstia *f* beast, animal; **andare in bestia** to fly into a rage; **bestia da soma** beast of burden; **bestia nera** pet aversion, bête noire; **bestie grosse** cattle

bestiale *adj* beastly, bestial

bestiali-tà *f* (**-tà**) beastliness; blunder

bestiame *m* livestock; **bestiame da cortile** barnyard animals; **bestiame grosso** cattle

bestino *m* gamy odor; stench of perspiration

bestiòla *f* tiny animal; pet

bestsèl-ler *m* (**-ler**) best seller

Betlèmme *f* Bethlehem

betonièra *f* cement mixer

béttola *f* tavern

bettolière *m* tavern keeper

bettònica *f* betony; **conosciuto più della bettonica** very well-known

betulla *f* birch

bèuta *f* flask

bevanda *f* drink, beverage

beveràg-gio *m* (**-gi**) beverage, potion

bevìbile *adj* drinkable

bevi-tóre -trice *mf* drinker

bevuta *f* drink, drinking

bezzicare §197 (**bézzico**) *tr* to peck; to vex || *ref* to fight one another

biacca *f* white lead

biada *f* feed; **biade** harvest

bianca-stro -stra *adj* whitish

biancheria *f* laundry; linen; underwear; **biancheria da letto** bed linen; **biancheria da tavola** table linen; **biancheria di bucato** freshly laundered clothes; **biancheria intima** underclothes

bianchézza *f* whiteness

bianchire §176 *tr* to blanch; to bleach; to polish

bian-co -ca (**-chi -che**) *adj* white; clean; **bianco come un cencio lavato** as white as a ghost || *m* white; **dare il bianco a** to whitewash; **in bianco** blank (*paper*); **mangiare in bianco** to eat a bland or non-spicy diet; **ricamare in bianco** to embroider

biancóre *m* whiteness

biancospino *m* hawthorn

biascicare §197 (**biàscico**) *tr* to chew with difficulty; to peck at (*one's food*); to mumble

biasimare (**biàsimo**) *tr* to blame

biasimévole *adj* blamable, censurable

biàsimo *m* blame, censure; **dare una nota di biasimo a** to censure

biauricolare *adj* binaural

Bìbbia *f* Bible

bibe-rón *m* (**-rón**) nursing bottle

bibita *f* soft drink

bìbli-co -ca *adj* (**-ci -che**) Biblical

bìblio-bus *m* (**-bus**) bookmobile

bibliòfi-lo -la *mf* bibliophile

bibliografia *f* bibliography

bibliotè-ca *f* (**-che**) library; bookshelf; stack; collection (*of books*); **biblioteca ambulante** walking encyclopedia

bibliotecà-rio -ria *mf* (**-ri -rie**) librarian

bìbu-lo -la *adj* absorbent (*e.g., paper*)

bi-ca *f* (**-che**) pile of sheaves

bicarbonato *m* bicarbonate; **bicarbonato di soda** bicarbonate of soda, baking soda

bicchierata *f* glassful; wine party

bicchière *m* glass

bicchierino *m* small glass, liquor glass; **bicchierino da rosolio** whiskey glass, jigger

biciclétta *f* bicycle

bicilìndri-co -ca *adj* (**-ci -che**) two-cylinder

bicìpite adj two-headed || m biceps

bicòc·ca f (-che) castle built on a hill; shanty, hut

bicolóre adj two-color

bicòrno m two-cornered hat

bidèllo m school janitor, caretaker

bidènte m two-pronged pitchfork

bidimensionale adj two-dimensional

bidóne m can (for milk); drum (for gasoline or oil); jalopy; (slang) fraud

bidon·ville f (-ville) shantytown

biè·co -ca adj (-chi -che) awry; sullen; cross; fierce; **guardar bieco** to look askance (at)

bièlla f connecting rod

biennale adj biennial || f biennial show

biènne adj biennial

bièn·nio m (-ni) biennium

biètola f Swiss chard

biétta f wedge, chock; (naut) batten

bifase adj diphase

biffa f (surv) rod

biffare tr to cross out; (surv) to level

bifi·do -da adj bifurcate

bifocale adj bifocal

bifól·co m (-chi) ox driver; clodhopper, boor

biforcaménto m bifurcation

biforcare §197 (bifórco) tr to bifurcate

biforcazióne f bifurcation, branching off; fork (of a road)

biforcu·to -ta adj forked; cloven (e.g., hoof)

bifrónte adj two-faced

bi·ga f (-ghe) chariot

bigamìa f bigamy

bìga·mo -ma adj bigamous || mf bigamist

bighellonare (**bighellóno**) intr to idle, dawdle, dally

bighelló·ne -na mf idler, dawdler

bigino m (slang) pony (used to cheat)

bì·gio -gia adj (-gi -gie) gray, grayish; (fig) undecided

bigiotterìa f costume jewelry; costume jewelry store

bigliardo m billiards

bigliet·tàio m (-tài) ticket agent; (rr) conductor

bigletterìa f ticket office; (theat) box office

bigliétto m note; card; ticket; **biglietto d'abbonamento** commutation ticket; season ticket; **biglietto d'andata e ritorno** round-trip ticket; **biglietto di banca** banknote; **biglietto di lotteria** lottery ticket, chance; **biglietto d'invito** invitation; **biglietto di visita** calling card; business card; **biglietto di Stato** banknote; **mezzo biglietto** half fare

bigné m (bigné) puff, creampuff

bigodino m curler; roller

bigón·cia f (-ce) vat; bucket; **a bigonce** abundantly

bigón·cio m (-ci) vat; tub; (theat) ticket box (for stubs)

bigottismo m bigotry

bigòt·to -ta adj bigoted || mf bigot

bilàn·cia f (-ce) balance, scale; **bilancia commerciale** balance of trade; **bilancia dei pagamenti** balance of payments || **Bilancia** f (astr) Libra

bilanciare §128 tr & ref to balance

bilancière m balance; balance wheel; rope-walker's balancing rod

bilàn·cio m (-ci) balance; **bilancio consuntivo** balance sheet; **bilancio preventivo** budget; **fare il bilancio** to balance; to strike a balance

bile f bile; **rodersi dalla bile** to burn with anger

bìlia f billiard ball; marble; (billiards) pocket

biliardino m pocket billiards; pinball machine

biliardo m billiards

biliare adj bile; gall (stone)

bili·co m (-chi) balance, equipoise; **in bilico** in balance; **tenere in bilico** to balance

bilìngue adj bilingual

bilióne m billion; trillion (Brit)

bilió·so -sa [s] adj bilious

bìm·bo -ba mf child

bimensile adj bimonthly

bimèstre m period of two months

bimotóre adj twin-engine || m twin-engine plane

binà·rio -ria (-ri -rie) adj binary || m (rr) track; **binario morto** (rr) siding; **uscire dai binari** (rr) to run off the track; (fig) to go astray

bina·to -ta adj binary; twin (e.g., guns)

binda f (aut) jack

binòcolo m binoculars; **binocolo da teatro** opera glasses

binò·mio -mia (-mi -mie) adj binomial || m binomial; couple, pair

biòccolo m wad (of cotton); flake (of snow); flock (of wool)

biochìmi·co -ca (-ci -che) adj biochemical || m biochemist || f biochemistry

biodegradàbile adj biodegradable

biofisica f biophysics

biografìa f biography

biogràfi·co -ca adj (-ci -che) biographic(al)

biògra·fo -fa mf biographer

biologìa f biology

biòlo·go m (-gi) biologist

biondeggiare §290 (**biondéggio**) intr to be or become blond; to ripen (said of grain)

bión·do -da adj blond, fair || m blond; blondness || f blonde

biopsìa f biopsy

biòssido m dioxide

bipartìti·co -ca adj (-ci -che) two-party, bipartisan

biparti·to -ta adj bipartite || m two-party government

bìpede adj & m biped

bipènne f double-bitted ax

biplano m biplane

bipòsto adj invar having seats for two || m two-seater

birba f rascal, rogue

birbante m scoundrel, rascal; (joc) madcap, wild young fellow

birbanterìa f knavery; trick

birbonata f trick

birbó·ne -na *adj* wicked ‖ *mf* rascal, rogue, scoundrel

bireattóre *m* twin jet

birichinata *f* prank

birichi·no -na *adj* prankish; spirited ‖ *mf* rogue; urchin

birillo *m* pin; **birilli** ninepins; tenpins

Birmània, la Burma

birra *f* beer; **birra chiara** light beer; **birra scura** dark beer

bir·ràio *m* (**-rài**) brewer; beer distributor

birrerìa *f* brewery; tavern; beer saloon

bis *adj invar*—**treno bis** (**rr**) second section ‖ *m* (**bis**) encore ‖ *interj* encore!

bisàc·cia *f* (**-ce**) knapsack; saddlebag; bag (*of mendicant friar*)

Bisànzio *m* Byzantium

bisa·vo -va *mf* great-grandparent; ancestor ‖ *m* great-grandfather ‖ *f* great-grandmother

bisbèti·co -ca (**-ci -che**) *adj* shrewish; crotchety; cantankerous ‖ *f* (*fig*) shrew

bisbigliare §280 *tr & intr* to whisper

bisbì·glio *m* (**-gli**) whisper

bisbòccia *f*—**fare bisboccia** to revel

bisboccióne *m* reveler

bis·ca *f* (**-che**) gambling house

Biscàglia *f* Biscay, e.g., **Baia di Biscaglia** Bay of Biscay; **la Biscaglia** Biscay

biscaglina *f* (*naut*) Jacob's ladder

biscazzière *m* gaming-house operator; habitué of a gaming house; marker (*at billiards*)

bischero *m* (*mus*) peg

bì·scia *f* (**-sce**) snake; **biscia d'acqua** water snake

biscottare (**biscòtto**) *tr* to toast

biscotterìa *f* cookie factory; cookie store

biscottièra *f* cookie jar

biscottifi·cio *m* (**-ci**) cookie factory

biscòt·to -ta *adj* twice-baked ‖ *m* cookie

biscròma *f* (*mus*) demisemiquaver

bisdòsso *m*—**a bisdosso** bareback

bisecare [s] §197 (**bìseco**) *tr* to bisect

bisènso [s] *m* double meaning

bisessuale [s] *adj* bisexual

bisestile [s] *adj* leap (*year*)

bisettimanale [s] *adj* biweekly

bisettrice [s] *f* bisector

bisezióne [s] *f* bisection

bisìlla·bo -ba [s] *adj* disyllabic

bislac·co -ca *adj* (**-chi -che**) queer, extravagant

bislun·go -ga *adj* (**-ghi -ghe**) oblong

bismuto *m* bismuth

bisnòn·no -na *mf* great-grandparent; **bisnonni** ancestors ‖ *m* great-grandfather ‖ *f* great-grandmother

bisógna *f* (*lit*) task, job

bisognare (**bisógna**) *intr* (with *dat*) to need, e.g., **gli bisognavano tre litri di benzina** he needed three liters of gasoline ‖ *impers*—**bisogna + inf** it is necessary to, e.g., **bisogna partire** it is necessary to leave; **bisogna che + subj** must, to have to, e.g., **bisogna che me ne vada** I must go,

I have to go; **bisognando** if need be; **non bisogna** one should not; **più che non bisogna** more than necessary

bisognévole *adj* needy

bisógno *m* need; want, lack; **aver bisogno di** to need; **c'è bisogno di** there is need of; **se ci fosse bisogno** if need be

bisognó·so -sa *adj* needy ‖ **i bisognosi** the needy

bisolfato [s] *m* bisulfate

bisolfito [s] *m* bisulfite

bisolfuro [s] *m* bisulfide

bisónte *m* bison

bistec·ca *f* (**-che**) beefsteak, steak; **bistecca al sangue** rare steak

bisticciare §128 *intr & ref* to quarrel, bicker

bistic·cio *m* (**-ci**) quarrel, bickering; play on words, pun

bistrattare *tr* to mistreat

bìstu·ri *m* (**-ri**) bistouri, surgical knife

bisul·co -ca [s] *adj* (**-chi -che**) cloven

bisun·to -ta *adj* greasy

bitagliènte *adj* double-edged

bitórzolo *m* wart (*on humans, plants, or animals*); pimple (*on human face*)

bitta *f* (*naut*) bollard

bitume *m* bitumen, asphalt

bituminó·so -sa [s] *adj* bituminous

bivaccare §197 *intr* to bivouac; to spend the night

bivac·co *m* (**-chi**) bivouac

bì·vio *m* (**-vi**) fork (*of road*); **essere al bivio** (*fig*) to be at the crossroads

bizanti·no -na [dz] *adj* Byzantine

bizza [ddzz] *f* tantrum; **fare le bizze** to go into a tantrum

bizzarrìa [ddzz] *f* extravagance, oddity

bizzar·ro -ra [ddzz] *adj* bizarre, odd; skittish (*e.g., horse*)

bizzèffe [ddzz] *adv*—**a bizzeffe** plenty, in abundance

bizzó·so -sa [ddzz] [s] *adj* irritable

blandire §176 *tr* to blandish, coax; to soothe, mitigate

blandizie *fpl* blandishment

blan·do -da *adj* bland

blasfemare (**blasfèmo**) *tr & intr* to blaspheme

blasfè·mo -ma *adj* blasphemous

blasona·to -ta *adj* emblazoned

blasóne *m* coat of arms, blazon

blaterare (**blàtero**) *intr* to babble

blatta *f* water bug, cockroach

blenoraggìa *f* gonorrhea

blè·so -sa *adj* lisping

blindàg·gio *m* (**-gi**) armor

blindare *tr* to armor

bloccare §197 (**blòcco**) *tr* to block; to blockade; to stop; to jam; to close up; to freeze (*e.g., prices*); (*sports*) to block ‖ *intr*—**bloccare su** to vote as a block for ‖ *ref* to stop

blòc·co *m* (**-chi**) block; blockade; notebook, pad; freezing (*e.g., of wages*); **in blocco** in bulk

bloc-notes *m* (**-notes**) notebook

blu *adj invar & m* blue

blua·stro -stra *adj* bluish

bluffare *intr* to bluff

blusa *f* blouse; smock

bò·a *m* (-a) boa ‖ *f* buoy
boà·rio -ria *adj* (-ri -rie) cattle
boa·ro -ra *adj* ox ‖ *m* stable boy
boato *m* roar; **boato sonico** sonic boom
bobina *f* spool (*of thread*); coil (*of wire*); reel (*of movie film; of magnetic tape*); roll (*of film*); cylinder, bobbin; (elec) coil; **bobina d'accensione** spark coil
bóc·ca *f* (-che) mouth; nozzle; muzzle (*of gun*); pit (*of the stomach*); opening; straits; pass; **a bocca aperta** agape; **bocca da fuoco** cannon; **di buona bocca** easily pleased; **in bocca al lupo!** good luck!; **per bocca** orally; **rimanere a bocca asciutta** to be foiled; to be left high and dry; **tieni la bocca chiusa!** shut up!
boccaccé·sco -sca *adj* (-schi -sche) written by or in the style of Boccaccio; bawdy, licentious
boccàc·cia *f* (-ce) ugly mouth; grimace; **fare le boccacce** to make faces
boccà·glio *m* (-gli) nozzle (*of hose or pipe*); mouthpiece (*of megaphone*)
boccale *adj* oral ‖ *m* jug, tankard
boccapòrto *m* hatch; port; mouth (*of oven or furnace*); **chiudere i boccaporti** to batten the hatches
boccascè·na *m* (-na) proscenium, front (*of stage*)
boccata *f* mouthful; **andare a prendere una boccata d'aria** to go out for a breath of fresh air
boccétta *f* small bottle, vial; small billiard ball
boccheggiante *adj* gasping; moribund
boccheggiare §290 (**bocchéggio**) *intr* to gasp
bocchétta *f* nozzle (*of sprinkling can*); mouthpiece (*of wind instrument*); opening (*of drainage or ventilation system*); **bocchetta stradale** manhole
bocchino *m* cigarette holder; mouthpiece (*of cigarette or of musical instrument*)
bòc·cia *f* (-ce) decanter; ball (*for bowling*); **bocce** bowls
bocciare §128 (**bòccio**) *tr* to score (*at bowling*); to reject (*a proposal*); to flunk (*a student*)
bocciatura *f* failure
boccino *m* jack (*at bowls*)
bocciòlo *m* bud
bóccola *f* buckle; earring; (mach) bushing
bocconcino *m* morsel; (culin) stew
boccóne *m* mouthful; piece; morsel; **buttar giù un boccone amaro** to swallow a bitter pill; **levarsi il boccone di bocca** to take the bread out of one's mouth (*to help someone*); **mangiare un boccone** to have a bite ‖ **bocconi** *adv* flat on one's face
boè·mo -ma *adj & mf* Bohemian
boè·ro -ra *adj & m* Boer
bofonchiare §287 (**bofónchio**) *intr* to snort, grumble
bò·ia *m* (-ia) hangman, executioner
boiata *f* (slang) infamy; (slang) trash
boicottàg·gio *m* (-gi) boycott
boicottare (**boicòtto**) *tr* to boycott

bòl·gia *f* (-ge) pit (*in hell*)
bólide *m* (astr) bolide, fireball; (aut) racer; (joc) lummox; **andare come un bolide** to go like a flash
bolina *f* (naut) bowline; **di bolina** (naut) close-hauled
bolivia·no -na *adj & mf* Bolivian
bólla *f* bubble; blister; ticket; **bolla di consegna** receipt; **bolla di spedizione** delivery ticket; **bolla di sapone** soap bubble; **bolla papale** papal bull
bollare (**bóllo**) *tr* to stamp; to brand
bolla·to -ta *adj* stamped; sealed
bollatura *f* stamp; brand; postage
bollènte *adj* boiling, scalding hot
bollétta *f* ticket; receipt; bill; **essere in bolletta** (coll) to be broke
bollettà·rio *m* (-ri) receipt book
bollettino *m* bulletin; receipt; **bollettino dei prezzi correnti** price list; **bollettino di versamento** (com) deposit ticket; **bollettino meteorologico** weather forecast
bollire (**bóllo**) *tr & intr* to boil
bolli·to -ta *adj* boiled ‖ *m* boiled beef
bollitura *f* boiling
bóllo *m* mark, cancellation; revenue stamp; postmark; seal; **bollo a freddo** seal (*embossed*); **bollo postale** cancellation, postmark
bollóre *m* boiling; sultriness; (fig) passion, excitement; **alzare il bollore** to begin to boil
bollò·so -sa [s] *adj* blistery
bolscevi·co -ca *adj & mf* (-chi -che) Bolshevik
bolscevismo *m* Bolshevism
ból·so -sa *adj* broken-winded (*horse*); asthmatic
bòma *f* (naut) boom
bómba *f* bomb; bubble gum; fireworks; (aer) double loop; (journ) scandal; **bomba a idrogeno** hydrogen bomb; **bomba a mano** hand grenade; **bomba antisommergibile** depth charge; **bomba a orologeria** time bomb; **bomba atomica** atom bomb; **bomba H** (*acca*) H bomb; **tornare a bomba** (fig) to get back to the point
bombàggio *m* swelling (*of a spoiled can of food*)
bombardaménto *m* bombing, bombardment
bombardare *tr* to bomb, bombard; to besiege (*with questions*)
bombardière *m* (aer) bomber; (mil) artilleryman
bombétta *f* derby (*hat*)
bómbola *f* bottle, cylinder; **bombola d'ossigeno** oxygen tank
bombonièra *f* candy box
bomprèsso *m* (naut) bowsprit
bonàc·cia *f* (-ce) calm; calm sea; (fig) normalcy; (com) stagnation
bonacció·ne -na *adj* good-hearted, good-natured
bonarie·tà *f* (-tà) kindheartedness, good nature
bonà·rio -ria *adj* (-ri -rie) kindhearted, good-natured
boncinèllo *m* hasp
bonìfi·ca *f* (-che) reclamation; re-

claimed land; improvement (*e.g., of morals*); clearing of mines; (metallurgy) hardening and tempering

bonificare §197 (bonìfico) *tr* to reclaim; to discount, make a reduction of; to clear of mines

bonìfi·co *m* (-ci) discount

bonomìa *f* good nature; simple-heartedness

bon·tà *f* (-tà) goodness; kindness; **avere la bontà di** to be kind enough to; **bontà mia** (sua, etc.) through my (his, her, etc.) kindness; **per mia** (sua, etc.) **bontà** through my (his, her, etc.) efforts

bòra *f* northeast wind

borace *m* borax

borbogliare §280 (borbóglio) *intr* to gurgle; to rumble

borbòni·co -ca (-ci -che) *adj* Bourbon ‖ *m* Bourbonist

borbottare (borbòtto) *tr* to mutter ‖ *intr* to mutter; to gurgle; to rumble (*said, e.g., of thunder*)

borbottì·o *m* (-ì) mutter; gurgle; rumble

bòrchia *f* upholsterer's nail; boss, stud

bordare (bórdo) *tr* to border, hem

bordata *f* (naut) tack; (nav) broadside

bordatura *f* border, hem

bordeggiare §290 (bordéggio) *intr* (naut) to tack

bordèllo *m* brothel

borde·rò *m* (-rò) list; note; (theat) box office, receipts

bórdo *m* side (*of ship*); border, hem; edge, rim; (naut) tack; (naut) board; **a bordo** on board; **a bordo di** on board; on, in; **bordo d'entrata** (aer) leading edge; **bordo d'uscita** (aer) trailing edge; **d'alto bordo** (naut) big, sea-going; (fig) high-toned; **virare di bordo** (naut) to change course

bordóne *m* staff; bass stop (*of organ*); drone (*of insect*); **tener bordone a** (mus) to accompany; (fig) to hold the bag for

bordura *f* hem, edge; rim

borgata *f* hamlet, village

borghése [s] *adj* middle-class ‖ *mf* bourgeois, person of the middle class; civilian; **in borghese** in civilian clothes; in plainclothes

borghesìa *f* bourgeoisie, middle class; **alta borghesia** upper middle class

bór·go *m* (-ghi) borough; small town; suburb

borgógna *m* Burgundy (*wine*) ‖ **la Borgogna** Burgundy

borgognóne *m* iceberg

borgomastro *m* burgomaster

bòria *f* haughtiness, vainglory

bòri·co -ca *adj* (-ci -che) boric

borió·so -sa [s] *adj* haughty, puffed-up; blustery

bòro *m* boron

borotal·co *m* (-chi) talcum powder

bórra *f* flock (*for pillows*); (fig) rubbish, filler

borràc·cia *f* (-ce) canteen (*e.g., for carrying water*)

bórro *m* gully

bórsa *f* bag; pouch; bourse, exchange; (sports) purse; **borsa da viaggio** traveling bag; **borsa dell'acqua** hot-water bag; **borsa della spesa** shopping bag; **borsa di ghiaccio** ice bag; **borsa di studio** scholarship; **borsa merci** commodity exchange; **borsa nera** black market; **borsa valori** stock exchange; **essere di borsa larga** to be generous; **o la borsa o la vita!** your money or your life!; **pagare di borsa propria** to pay out of one's own pocket

borsaiòlo *m* pickpocket

borsanéra *f* black market

borsaneri·sta *mf* (-sti -ste) black marketeer

borseggiare §290 (borséggio) *tr* to pick the pocket of; to rob

borseggia·tóre -trice *mf* pickpocket

borség·gio *m* (-gi) theft

borsellino *m* purse

borsétta *f* handbag, pocketbook

borsétto *m* man's purse

borsi·sta *mf* (-sti -ste) recipient of a scholarship; stockbroker

borsìsti·co -ca *adj* (-ci -che) stock-exchange

borsite *f* bursitis

boscàglia *f* thicket, underbrush

boscaiòlo *m* woodcutter

boscheréc·cio -cia *adj* (-ci -ce) wood, woodland; rustic; pastoral

boschétto *m* coppice, copse

boschi·vo -va *adj* wooded, wood

bò·sco *m* (-schi) woods, forest; **bosco ceduo** or **da taglio** tree farm

boscó·so -sa [s] *adj* wooded, woody

bòsforo *m* (lit) straits ‖ **Bosforo** *m* Bosphorus

bòsso *m* boxwood

bòssolo *m* box; cartridge case

botàni·co -ca (-ci -che) *adj* botanic(al) ‖ *m* botanist ‖ *f* botany

bòtola *f* trap door

bòtolo *m* small snarling dog

bòtta *f* hit; bump; rumble (*e.g., of an explosion*); thrust, lunging (*in fencing*); (fig) disaster; **botta dritta** (fencing) lunge; **botta e risposta** give-and-take; **botte da orbi** severe beating

bot·tàio *m* (-tài) cooper

bótte *f* barrel, cask, casket

botté·ga *f* (-ghe) store, shop; **chiudere bottega** to close up shop

botte·gàio -gàia (-gài -gàie) *adj* store, shop ‖ *mf* storekeeper, shopkeeper

botteghino *m* box office; lottery agency

bottiglia *f* bottle; **bottiglia Molotov** Molotov cocktail

bottiglierìa *f* wine store, liquor store

bottino *m* booty, spoil; capture; cesspool; sewage

bòtto *m* hit, bump; explosion; noise; toll (*of bell*); **di botto** all of a sudden

bottoncino *m* small button; cuff button; **bottoncino di rosa** rosebud

bottóne *m* button; bud; **attaccare un bottone a** (fig) to buttonhole; **botton d'oro** (bot) buttercup; **bottone automatico** snap; **bottone della**

luce (elec) pushbutton; **bottoni gemelli** cuff links; **bottoni gustativi**
taste buds
bottonièra f row of buttons; buttonhole; (elec) panel (with buttons)
bova·ro -ra adj & m var of **boaro**
bovile m ox stable
bovi·no -na adj cattle, cow; bovine ||
m bovine
box m (**box**) locker (e.g., in a station);
box stall (for a horse); pit (in auto
racing); garage (on the ground floor
of a split-level); play pen
boxare (bòxo) intr to box
boxe f boxing
bòzza f stud, boss; bump (caused by
blow); rough copy, draft; **bozze** (typ)
galleys, galley proof
bozzèllo m (mach) block and tackle
bozzétto m sketch
bòzzolo m cocoon; lump (of flour)
bra·ca f (**-che**) safety belt; (naut) sling;
brache (archaic) breeches; (joc)
trousers
braccare §197 tr to stalk; to hunt out
braccétto—a braccetto arm in arm
bracciale m armlet, armband; arm rest
braccialétto m bracelet
bracciante m laborer
bracciata f armful; stroke (in swimming); **bracciata a rana** breaststroke;
bracciata sul dorso backstroke
bràc·cio m (**-cia** fpl) arm (of body);
unit of length (about 60 centimeters);
a braccia aperte with open arms;
avere le braccia legate to have one's
hands tied; **braccia** laborers; **braccio
destro** right-hand man; **braccio di
ferro** Indian wrestling; **fare a braccio
di ferro** to play at Indian wrestling;
sentirsi cascare le braccia to lose
courage || m (**-ci**) arm (e.g., of sea,
chair, lamp, etc.); beam (of balance);
braccio diretto cutoff (of river)
bracciòlo m arm; arm rest; banister
brac·co m (**-chi**) hound, beagle
bracconàg·gio m (**-gi**) poaching
bracconière m poacher
brace f embers; (coll) charcoal; **farsi
di brace** to blush
brachétta f flap (of trousers); (bb) joint;
brachette shorts
brachière m truss (for hernia)
bracière m brazier
braciòla f chop, cutlet
bra·do -da adj wild, untamed
bra·go m (**-ghi**) (lit) mud, slime
brama f ardent desire; covetousness;
longing
bramare tr to desire intensely; to covet;
to long for
bramino m Brahmin
bramire §176 intr to roar; to bell (said
of a deer)
bramito m bell (of deer)
bramosia [s] f covetousness; greed
bramó·so -sa [s] adj (lit) covetous,
greedy
bran·ca f (**-che**) branch (of tree); flight
(of stairs); **branche** (poet) clutches
brànchia f gill
brancicare §197 (brància) tr to finger,
handle || intr to grope

bran·co m (**-chi**) flock, herd; (pej)
crowd
brancolare (bràncolo) intr to grope
branda f cot
brandèllo m tatter, shred
brandire §176 tr to brandish
brando m (lit) sword
brano m shred, bit; excerpt; **cadere a
brani** to fall apart; **fare a brani** to
tear apart
brasare tr to braze (to solder with
brass); (culin) to braise
brasile m brazil (nut) || **il Brasile**
Brazil
brasilia·no -na adj & mf Brazilian
bravàc·cio m (**-ci**) braggart, swaggerer
bravare tr to challenge; to threaten ||
intr to brag
bravata f swagger, bluster; boast; stunt
bra·vo -va adj good, able; honest; good-
hearted; brave; **alla brava** rapidly;
bravo ragazzo good boy; **fare il bravo**
to boast, be a braggart || m mer-
cenary soldier; bravo, hired assassin
|| **bravo!** interj well done!, bravo!
bravura f ability; bravery; bravura
brèc·cia f (**-ce**) breach, gap; crushed
stone
brefotrò·fio m (**-fi**) foundling hospital
Bretagna, la Britanny
bretèlla f suspenders; strap, shoulder
strap
brètone adj Breton; Arthurian
bréve adj brief, short; **in breve** in a nut-
shell; **per farla breve** in short || m
(eccl) brief || adv (lit) in short
brevettare (brevétto) tr to patent
brevétto m patent; (aer) license; (obs)
commission
brevià·rio m (**-ri**) compendium; handbook, vade mecum; (eccl) breviary
brevi·tà f (**-tà**) brevity
brézza [ddzz] f breeze
brezzare (brézzo) [ddzz] tr to winnow
|| intr to blow gently
bricchétta f briquet
bric·co m (**-chi**) kettle, pot
bricconata f rascality
briccó·ne -na m f rascal
bricconeria f rascality
brìciola f crumb; **ridurre in briciole** to
crumb, crumble
brìciolo m bit, fragment; (fig) least bit;
andare in bricioli to crumble; **mandare in bricioli** to crumble
bri·ga f (**-ghe**) worry, trouble, attaccar
briga to pick a fight; **darsi la briga di**
to worry about; **trovarsi in una briga**
to be in trouble
brigadière m noncommissioned officer
(in carabinieri); (hist) brigadier
brigantàg·gio m (**-gi**) brigandage
brigante m brigand
brigantino m (naut) brig, brigantine;
brigantino goletta (naut) brigantine
brigare §209 tr to plot; to scheme to get
|| intr to plot, scheme
brigata f company; (mil) brigade
bri·glia f (**-glie**) bridle; harness (for
holding baby); (naut) bobstay; **a
briglia sciolta** at full speed; **tirare le
briglie a** to bridle
brillante adj brilliant || m cut diamond

brillare tr to husk, hull (rice); to explode (e.g., a mine) ‖ intr to shine, sparkle; **far brillare** to explode, blow up

brilli·o m (-i) shine, sparkle

bril·lo -la adj tipsy

brina f frost

brinare tr to frost; to turn (e.g., hair) gray ‖ impers (ESSERE)—**è brinato** there was frost; **brina** there is frost

brinata f frost

brindare intr to toast; **brindare alla salute di** to toast

brindisi m (-si) toast; pledge; **fare un brindisi a** to toast

bri·o m (-i) sprightliness, liveliness, verve, spirit

briò·scia f (-sce) brioche

briò·so -sa [s] adj sprightly, lively

briscola f briscola (game); trump (card)

britànni·co -ca adj (-ci -che) British, Britannic

britan·no -na adj British ‖ mf Briton

brìvido m shake, shiver; thrill; **brivido di freddo** chill, shiver

brizzola·to -ta adj grizzled

bròc·ca f (-che) pitcher; pitcherful; shoot, bud; hobnail

broccatèllo m brocatel

broccato m brocade

bròc·co m (-chi) twig; shoot; center pin (of shield or target); (coll) nag; **dar nel brocco** to hit the bull's eye

bròccolo m (bot) broccoli; **broccoli** broccoli (as food)

bròda f slop, thin or tasteless soup; mud

brodàglia f slop

brodétto m fish soup

bròdo m broth; **andar in brodo di giuggiole** (fig) to swoon with joy; **brodo in dadi** cube bouillon; **brodo ristretto** consommé

brodó·so -sa [s] adj thin, watery (soup)

brogliàc·cio m (-ci) (com) daybook, first draft; (naut) first draft of logbook

brò·glio m (-gli) plot, intrigue; maneuver; **broglio elettorale** political maneuver

bròlo m (archaic) garden; (lit) garland

bromìdri·co -ca adj (-ci -che) hydrobromic

bròmo m bromine

bromuro m bromide

bronchite f bronchitis

brón·cio m (-ci) pout, pouting; **fare il broncio** to sulk; **tenere il broncio a** to harbor a grudge against

brón·co m (-chi) bronchial tube; thorny branch; ramification (of antlers)

brontolare (bróntolo) tr to grumble (to express with a grumble) ‖ intr to grumble, mutter; to rumble; to gurgle (said of water)

brontolí·o m (-i) grumble, mutter; rumble; gurgle

brontoló·ne -na mf grumbler; curmudgeon

bronzare [dz] (brónzo) tr to bronze

brónze·o -a [dz] adj bronze; tanned

bronzina [dz] f little bell; (mach) bearing; (mach) bushing

brónzo [dz] m bronze

brossura f brochure; **in brossura** paperback

brucare §197 tr to browse, graze

bruciacchiare §287 tr to singe

bruciante adj burning

bruciapélo m—**a bruciapelo** point-blank

bruciare §128 tr to burn; to burn down; to singe; to scorch; to cauterize (a wound); (sports) to overcome with a burst of speed; **bruciare le tappe** to go straight ahead; to press on ‖ intr (ESSERE) to burn; to smart, sting ‖ ref to burn (e.g., one's fingers); to get burnt; to blow (one's brains) out; to burn out (said of an electric light or fuse); **bruciarsi i vascelli alle spalle** to burn one's bridges behind one

bruciatíc·cio m (-ci) burnt material; **sapere di bruciaticcio** to taste burnt

brucia·to -ta adj burnt; burnt out ‖ m burnt taste or smell ‖ f roast chestnut

bruciatóre m burner; heater; **bruciatore a gas** gas burner; **bruciatore a nafta** oil burner

bruciatorí·sta m (-sti) oil burner mechanic

bruciatura f burn

brucióre m burning; burn; inflammation; **bruciore agli occhi** eye inflammation; **bruciore di stomaco** heartburn

bru·co m (-chi) caterpillar; worm

brùffolo m (coll) small boil

brughièra f waste land; heath

brulicare §197 (brùlico) intr to crawl; to swarm (e.g., with bees); to teem (with people)

brulichí·o m (-i) crawling; swarming; teeming

brul·lo -la adj barren, bare

bruma f shipworm; (lit) fog; (lit) winter

bruna·stro -stra adj brownish

brunire §176 tr to burnish

bru·no -na adj brown; dark (bread; complexion) ‖ m brown; dark; brunet; **vestire a bruno** to dress in black ‖ f brunette

bru·sca f (-sche) horse brush; **con le brusche** curtly

bruschézza f brusqueness

bruschino m scrub brush

bru·sco -sca (-schi -sche) adj sour; curt, gruff; sharp (weather); dangerous; sudden ‖ m twig ‖ f see **brusca**

brùscolo m speck, mote; **fare di un bruscolo una trave** to make a mountain out of a molehill

brusí·o m (-i) buzz, buzzing; (fig) whispering (gossip)

brutale adj brutal

brutali·tà f (-tà) brutality

brutalizzare [ddzz] tr to brutalize

bru·to -ta adj & m brute

brùtta f rough copy

bruttare tr (lit) to soil

bruttézza f ugliness; (fig) lowliness

brut·to -ta adj ugly, homely; foul (weather); bad (news); **alle brutte** at the worst; **con le brutte** harshly; **farla brutta a** to play a mean trick on;

guardare **brutto** to look irritated; **vedersela brutta** to foresee trouble ‖ *m* worst; bad weather ‖ *f* see **brutta**

bruttura *f* ugliness

bùbbola *f* lie; trifle

bùbbolo *m* jingle bell (*on horse*)

bubbòni·co -ca *adj* (**-ci -che**) bubonic

bu·ca *f* (**-che**) hole; pit; hollow; **buca cieca** trap (*for hunting*); **buca del biliardo** pocket; **buca delle lettere** mailbox; **buca del suggeritore** prompter's box; **buca sepolcrale grave**

bucané·ve *m* (**-ve**) snowdrop

bucanière *m* buccaneer

bucare §197 *tr* to pierce; to prick; to puncture (*a tire*)

bucato *m* wash; laundry; **di bucato** freshly laundered; **fare il bucato in famiglia** (fig) to not air one's family affairs, to not wash one's dirty linen in public

bucatura *f* piercing; puncturing; puncture; **bucatura di una gomma** flat tire

bùc·cia *f* (**-ce**) rind, peel; skin (*of a person; of fruit and vegetables*); tender bark; **fare le bucce a** (coll) to thwart, frustrate

bucherellare (**bucherèllo**) *tr* to riddle

bu·co *m* (**-chi**) hole; **fare un buco nell'acqua** to fail miserably

bucòli·co -ca *adj* (**-ci -che**) bucolic, pastoral

Budda *m* Buddha

buddismo *m* Buddhism

buddi·sta *mf* (**-sti -ste**) Buddhist

budèl·lo *m* (**-la** *fpl*) bowel; **budella** bowels; guts ‖ *m* (**-li**) casing (*for salami*); pipe; blind alley

budino *m* pudding

bùe *m* (**buòi**) ox (*for draft*); steer (*for meat*); **bue muschiato** musk ox

bùfalo *m* buffalo

bufèra *f* storm; **bufera di neve** snowstorm; **bufera di pioggia** rainstorm; **bufera di vento** windstorm

buffa *f* cowl; gust of wind; (archaic) trick, jest

buffare *tr* to huff (*at checkers*) ‖ *intr* to joke; (archaic) to blow

buffetteria *f* (mil) accouterments

buffétto *m* tap, slight blow

buf·fo -fa *adj* funny, comical ‖ *m* gust of wind; comic ‖ *f* see **buffa**

buffonata *f* buffoonery; antics

buffóne *m* buffoon, clown; (hist) jester; **buffone di corte** court jester

buffoneria *f* buffoonery

buffoné·sco -sca *adj* (**-schi -sche**) clownish

bugia *f* lie; candlestick; **bugia ufficiosa** white lie

bugiar·do -da *adj* lying, false ‖ *mf* liar

bugigàttolo *m* cubbyhole

bugna *f* ashlar; (naut) clew

bugnato *m* ashlar; (archit) boss

bù·io -ia (*pl* **-i -ie**) *adj* dark ‖ *m* darkness; **buio pesto** pitch dark

bulbo *m* bulb

bùlga·ro -ra *adj & mf* Bulgarian ‖ *m* Russian leather

bulinare *tr* to engrave

bulino *m* burin

bullétta *f* tack

bullonare (**bullóno**) *tr* to bolt

bullóne *m* bolt

buon *adj* apocopated form of **buono**, used before masculine singular nouns except those beginning with impure **s, z, gn, ps,** and **x**

buon' *adj* apocopated form of **buona** used before feminine singular nouns beginning with a vowel, e.g., **buon'ora**

buonagràzia *f* (**buonegràzie**) courtesy, good manners; **con Sua buonagrazia** with your permission

buonamano *f* (**buonemani**) tip, gratuity

buonànima *f* departed; **la buonanima di** the late lamented

buonavò·glia *m* (**-glia**) intern (*in a hospital*); (coll) lazybones ‖ *f* good will

buoncostume *m* morals

buongu·stàio *m* (**-stài**) gourmet; connoisseur

buò·no -na *adj* good; kind; high (*society*); cheap (*price*); **alla buona** plainly; without ceremony; **buono a nulla** good-for-nothing; **con le buone** kindly, gently; **che Dio la mandi buona** a may God be kind with; **essere in buona con** to be on good terms with ‖ *m* good person; bond; ticket; **buono a nulla** ne'er-do-well; **buono del tesoro** government bond; **buono di consegna** delivery order; **buono premio** trading stamp

buonsènso *m* common sense

buontempó·ne -na *adj* jolly ‖ *m* playboy ‖ *f* fun-loving girl; playgirl

buonumóre *m* good humor, good cheer

buonuscita *f* indemnity, bonus; severance pay

burattare *tr* to sift

buratti·nàio *m* (**-nài**) puppeteer; puppet maker

burattinata *f* clowning

burattino *m* puppet

buratto *m* sifter, sifting machine

burbanza *f* haughtiness, arrogance

burbanzó·so -sa [s] *adj* haughty, arrogant

bùrbe·ro -ra *adj* gruff, surly

bùr·chio *m* (**-chi**) (naut) lighter

burgun·do -da *adj & mf* Burgundian

burla *f* joke, jest; prank; **mettere in burla** to ridicule; **fuori di burla** joking aside

burlare *tr* to ridicule ‖ *intr* to be joking ‖ *ref*—**burlarsi di** to make fun of

burlé·sco -sca *adj* (**-schi -sche**) funny; mocking; burlesque; jocose ‖ *m* burlesque; mock-heroic

burlétta *f* joke, jest; **mettere in burletta** to ridicule

burló·ne -na *mf* joker, jester

buròcrate *m* bureaucrat

burocràti·co -ca *adj* (**-ci -che**) bureaucratic; clerical (*error*)

burocrazìa *f* bureaucracy; red tape

burra·sca *f* (**-sche**) storm

burrascó·so -sa [s] *adj* stormy

burrièra *f* butter dish

burrifi·cio *m* (**-ci**) butter factory, dairy

burro *m* butter

burróne *m* canyon, ravine

burró·so -sa [s] *adj* buttery

buscare §197 *tr* to get; to catch ‖ *intr* to be damaged ‖ *ref*—**buscarsi un malanno** to catch a cold

busécchia *f* casing (*for sausage*)

busillis *m*—**qui sta il busillis** here's the rub, that's the trouble

bussa *f* hit, blow; **venire alle busse to** come to blows

bussare *intr* to knock; **bussare a quattrini** (fig) to hit somebody for a loan

bussata *f* knock (*at the door*)

bussa•tòio *m* (-tòi) knocker

bùssola *f* sedan chair; door; revolving door; swinging door; ballot box; (mach) bushing; (aer & naut) compass; **perdere la bussola** to lose one's bearings

bussolòtto *m* dice box

busta *f* envelope; briefcase; **busta a finestrella** window envelope; **busta primo giorno** first-day cover; **in busta a parte** under separate cover

bustapa•ga *f* (-ga) pay envelope

bustarèlla *f* bribery; kickback

bustina *f* powder, dose; small envelope; (mil) cap, fatigue cap

busto *m* chest, trunk; bust; corset

butirró•so -sa [s] *adj* buttery

buttafuò•ri *m* (-ri) bouncer (*in a night club*); (theat) callboy; (naut) outrigger

buttare *tr* to throw; to waste (*e.g., time*); to give off (*e.g., smoke*); **buttar giù** to demolish; to swallow; (fig) to discredit; to jot down; **buttar via** to throw away; to cast aside ‖ *intr* to secrete, ooze ‖ *ref* to throw oneself; to let oneself fall; **buttarsi giù** (fig) to become downcast

butterare (bùttere) *tr* to pock, pit

bùttero *m* pockmark; cowboy

buzzo [ddzz] *m* (vulg) belly; **di buzzo buono** with energy; willingly

C

C, c [t∫i] *m & f* third letter of the Italian alphabet

càbala *f* cabala; cabal, intrigue

cabina *f* cabin, stateroom; car, cage (*of elevator*); cockpit (*of airplane*); booth (*of telephone*); cab (*of locomotive*)

cablàg•gio *m* (-gi) (elec) cable (*in auto or radio*)

cablare *tr* to cable

cablografare (cablògrafo) *tr* to cable

cablogram•ma *m* (-mi) cablegram, cable

cabotàg•gio *m* (-gi) coasting trade, coastal traffic

cabrare *intr* to zoom

cabrata *f* zoom

cacào *m* cocoa

cacasènno *m* (slang) wiseacre

cacató•a *m* (-a) cockatoo

càc•cia *f* (-cia) pursuit plane, fighter; (nav) destroyer ‖ *f* chase, hunt; pursuit; **caccia alle streghe** witch hunt

cacciagióne *f* small game; venison; kill (*e.g., of game birds*)

cacciapiè•tre *m* (-tre) (rr) cowcatcher

cacciare §128 *tr* to hunt; to chase; to rout; to send out; to stick, thrust; to utter (*e.g., a cry*); **cacciar fuori** to pull out; **cacciar via** to chase away ‖ *ref* to hide; to intrude; to get; to wind up; to thrust oneself; **cacciarsi negli affari di** to butt into the affairs of

cacciasommergìbi•li *m* (-li) subchaser, submarine chaser

cacciata *f* hunting party; expulsion

cacciatóra *f* hunting jacket; **alla cacciatora** (culin) stewed with herbs

cacciatóre *m* hunter; (aer) fighter pilot; **cacciatore di frodo** poacher; **cacciatore di teste** headhunter

cacciatorpediniè•re *m* (-re) destroyer

cacciatrice *f* huntress

cacciavi•te *m* (-te) screwdriver

càccola *f* gum (*on edge of eyelid*); (slang) snot

caccoló•so -sa [s] *adj* gummy (*eyelid*); (slang) snotty

ca•chi (-chi) *adj* khaki ‖ *m* Japanese persimmon; khaki

cacíc•co *m* (-chi) Indian chief; boss (*in Latin America*)

cà•cio *m* (-ci) cheese; **come il cacio sui maccheroni** (coll) at the right moment

cacofóni•co -ca *adj* (-ci -che) cacophonous

cac•tus *m* (-tus) cactus

cadau•no -na *adj* each ‖ *pron* each one

cadàvere *m* corpse, cadaver

cadavèri•co -ca *adj* (-ci -che) cadaverous

cadènte *adj* falling (*star*); rickety (*house*); run-down, decrepit (*person*)

cadènza *f* cadence, rhythm; accent (*peculiar to a region*)

cadére §121 *intr* (ESSERE) to fall; to sink; to slough (*said, e.g., of crust*); to fail; (gram) to end; **cadere a proposito** to come in handy; to come at the right moment; **cadere dalle nuvole** to be dumfounded

cadétto *m* cadet

càdmio *m* cadmium

caducità *f* transiency, brevity

cadu•co -ca *adj* (-ci -che) fleeting; deciduous

cadu•no -na *adj & pron* var of **cadauno**

cadu•to -ta *adj* fallen; lost, gone astray; **i caduti** the fallen, the dead ‖ *f* fall; crash (*of stock market*); slump (*of prices*)

caf•fè *m* (-fè) coffee; café

caffcina *f* caffeine

caffetteria *f* cafeteria

caffettièra *f* coffeepot

cafó·ne -na *adj* loud, gaudy ‖ *m* boor, lout

cagionare (cagióno) *tr* to cause, produce

cagióne *f* cause, reason; **a cagione di** because of

cagionévole *adj* sickly, delicate

cagliare §280 *tr, intr* (ESSERE) & *ref* to curdle, curd

cagliata *f* curd

cà·glio *m* (**-gli**) rennet

cagna *f* bitch

cagnara *f* barking (*of dogs*); uproar, confusion

cagné·sco -sca (**-schi -sche**) *adj* dog-like, doggish ‖ *m*—**guardare in cagnesco** to look askance at; **stare in cagnesco con** to be angry with

Caíno *m* Cain

Càiro, il Cairo

cala *f* cove; (naut) hold

calabrése [s] *adj* & *mf* Calabrian

calabróne *m* hornet

calafatare *tr* (naut) to caulk

cala·màio *m* (**-mài**) inkwell

calamaro *m* squid

calamita *f* magnet; (*mineral*) loadstone; (fig) magnet, attraction

calami·tà *f* (**-tà**) calamity, disaster

calamitare *tr* to magnetize

calamitó·so -sa [s] *adj* calamitous

càlamo *m* reed, quill

calandra *f* calender; (aut) grille

calandrare *tr* to calender

calante *adj* waning (*moon*)

calàp·pio *m* (**-pi**) snare; noose

calapran·zi *m* (**-zi**) dumbwaiter

calare *tr* to lower; to strike (*sails*) ‖ *intr* (ESSERE) to fall, sag (*said, e.g., of prices*); to grow shorter (*said of days*); to come down; to shrink (*said, e.g., of meat*); to lose weight; to set (*said, e.g., of the sun*); to wane (*said of the moon*); (mus) to drop in pitch ‖ *ref* to let oneself down; to dive

calata *f* lowering; descent; invasion; fall; wharf; (coll) intonation; **calata del sole** sunset

cal·ca *f* (**-che**) crowd, throng

calca·gno *m* (**-gni**) heel ‖ *m* (**-gna** *fpl*) (fig) heel; **alle calcagna di** at the heels of

calcare *m* limestone ‖ §197 *tr* to trample; to trace (*on paper*); to tread (*the boards*); to emphasize; **calcare la mano** to exaggerate; **calcare le orme di** to follow in the footsteps of

calce *m*—**in calce** at the foot of the page; **in calce a** at the foot of ‖ *f* lime; **calce viva** quicklime

calcedònio *m* chalcedony

calcestruzzo *m* concrete

calciare §128 *tr* & *intr* to kick

calciatóre *m* soccer player; football player

calcificare §197 (**calcìfico**) *tr* & *ref* to calcify

calcificazióne *f* calcification

calcina *f* mortar; lime

calcinàc·cio *m* (**-ci**) flake of plaster; **calcinacci** ruins, rubble

calci·nàio *m* (**-nài**) lime pit

calcinare *tr* to calcine; to lime (*e.g., a field*)

càl·cio *m* (**-ci**) kick; soccer; calcium; (*e.g., of rifle*) butt; **calcio d'inizio** (sports) kickoff

calciocianamide *m* calcium cyanamide

cal·co *m* (**-chi**) tracing; cast; imprint

calcografia *f* copper engraving

calcolare (càlcolo) *tr* to calculate; to estimate, reckon; to compute; to consider

calcola·tóre -trice *adj* calculating ‖ *m* calculator; computer; schemer ‖ *f* calculating machine, adding machine

càlcolo *m* calculation; estimate; planning; calculus; (pathol) calculus, stone; **calcolo biliare** gallstone; **calcolo errato** miscalculation; **fare calcolo su** to count upon

calcolò·si *f* (**-si**) (pathol) stones

calcomania *f* decalcomania

caldàia *f* boiler

cal·dàio *m* (**-dài**) cauldron, boiler

caldalléssa *f* boiled chestnut

caldana *f* flush

caldano *m* brazier

caldarròsta *f* roast chestnut

caldeggiare §290 (**caldéggio**) *tr* to favor, support; to recommend

calde·ràio *m* (**-rài**) coppersmith; boiler-maker

calderóne *m* cauldron

cal·do -da *adj* warm; hot; rich (*voice*); **caldo, caldo** quite recent ‖ *m* heat; warmth; **aver caldo** to be warm (*said of people*); to be hot (*said of people*); **fa caldo** it is warm; it is hot; **non mi fa nè caldo nè freddo** it leaves me cold, it does not move me

calefazióne *f* heating

caleidoscò·pio *m* (**-pi**) kaleidoscope

calendà·rio *m* (**-ri**) calendar

calènde *fpl*—**calende greche** Greek calends

calendimàggio *m* May Day

calèsse *m* buggy, gig

calére *impers*—**non mi cale** (lit) I don't care

calettare (calétto) *tr* to dovetail, mortise ‖ *intr* to fit

calibrare (càlibro) *tr* to gauge, calibrate

càlibro *m* caliber; (mach) calipers; (fig) quality, importance

càlice *m* wine cup; (bot) calyx; (eccl) chalice

cali·cò *m* (**-cò**) calico

califfo *m* caliph

calígine *f* fog, mist; (fig) darkness

caliginó·so -sa [s] *adj* foggy, misty; (fig) dark, gloomy

calla *f*—**calla dei fioristi** calla lily

calle *f* lane, alley

callìfu·go m (**-ghi**) corn remedy

calligrafia *f* penmanship; handwriting

calli·sta *mf* (**-sti -ste**) chiropodist

callo *m* corn; callus; **fare il callo a** to get used to; **pestare i calli a qlcu** to step on s.o.'s feet

callosi·tà [s] *f* (**-tà**) callosity; callus

calló·so -sa [s] *adj* corny; callous; hard

calma *f* calm, tranquillity

calmante *adj* sedative, calming, soothing ‖ *m* sedative

calmare *tr* to calm, soothe, appease ‖ *ref* to calm down; to subside, abate

calmierare (calmièro) *tr* to fix the price of

calmière *m* ceiling price; price control

cal·mo -ma *adj* calm, quiet, still ‖ *f see* **calma**

calo *m* decrease; shrinkage

calomelano *m* calomel

calóre *m* heat; warmth; fervor, ardor; (pathol) rash, inflammation; (vet) rut, mating season

caloria *f* calorie

calòri·co -ca *adj* (*-ci -che*) caloric

calorífero *m* heater, radiator

caloró·so -sa [s] *adj* warm; hot; cordial; heated

calò·scia *f* (*-sce*) var of **galoscia**

calòtta *f* skullcap; case (*e.g., of watch*); (aut) hubcap; (mach) cap; **calotta cranica** skull

calpestare (calpésto) *tr* to trample

calpestì·o *m* (*-i*) trampling

calùgine *f* down (*of bird*)

calùnnia *f* calumny, slander

calunniare §287 *tr* to calumniate, slander

calunnia·tóre -trice *mf* slanderer

calunnió·so -sa [s] *adj* slanderous

Calvàrio *m* (Bib) Calvary

calvìzie *f* baldness

cal·vo -va *adj* bald

calza *f* sock; stocking; wick; **calza da donna** stocking; **calze** hose, hosiery; **fare la calza** to knit

calzamàglia *f* tights

calzare *m* footwear ‖ *tr* to wear, put on (*shoes, gloves, or socks*) ‖ *intr* to fit (*said of any garment*); to suit

calzascar·pe *m* (*-pe*) shoehorn

calza·tóio *m* (*-tói*) shoehorn

calzatura *f* footwear; **calzature** footwear

calzaturière *m* shoe manufacturer

calzaturiè·ro -ra *adj* shoe (*e.g., industry*) ‖ *m* shoe worker

calzaturifi·cio *m* (*-ci*) shoe factory

calzeròtto *m* woolen sock

calzet·tàio *m* (*-tài*) hosier

calzettóne *m* knee-high woolen sock (*for mountain boots*)

calzifi·cio *m* (*-ci*) hosiery mill

calzino *m* sock; **calzini corti** socks; half hose; **calzini lunghi** knee-high socks

calzo·làio *m* (*-lài*) shoemaker; cobbler

calzolerìa *f* shoemaker's shop; shoe store

calzoncini *mpl* shorts

calzóne *m* trouser leg; **calzoni** trousers, pants; slacks; **calzoni a zampe d'elefante** bell-bottom trousers, flares

camaleònte *m* chameleon

camarilla *f* cabal, clique

cambiadi·schi *m* (*-schi*) record changer

cambiale *f* promissory note, IOU

cambiaménto *m* change, modification

cambiare §287 *tr* to change, exchange; to shift (*gears*) ‖ *intr* to change, switch ‖ *ref* to change (*clothing*); **cambiarsi in** to turn into

cambiavalu·te *m* (*-te*) moneychanger

càm·bio *m* (*-bi*) change; switch; rate of exchange; (mil) relief; **cambio a cloche** shift lever, stick; **cambio di velocità** gearshift; **in cambio di** in exchange for, in place of

cambrètta *f* staple (*to hold a wire*)

cam·brì *m* (*-brì*) cambric

cambusa *f* (naut) galley

cambusière *m* steward

càmera *f* room; bedroom; chamber; **camera ardente** funeral parlor; **Camera dei comuni** House of Commons; **Camera dei deputati** House of Representatives; **camera d'aria** inner tube; **camera di sicurezza** detention cell; vault (*of bank*)

camera·ta *m* (*-ti*) friend, comrade ‖ *f* dormitory; barracks; roomful (*of students or soldiers*)

cameratismo *m* comradeship

camerièra *f* waitress; maid, chambermaid

camerière *m* waiter; steward; valet

camerino *m* small room; toilet, lavatory; (nav) noncommissioned officer's quarters; (theat) dressing room

càmice *m* gown (*of physician*); smock (*of painter*); (eccl) alb

camiceria *f* shirt store; shirt factory

camicétta *f* blouse

camìcia *f* shirt; casing, jacket (*e.g., of boiler*); lining (*e.g., of furnace*); vest (*of sailor*); folder; **camicia da giorno** chemise; **camicia da notte** nightgown; **camicia di forza** strait jacket; **camicia di maglia** coat of mail; **camicia nera** black shirt (*Fascist*); **camicia rossa** red shirt (*Garibaldine*); **dare la camicia** to give the shirt off one's back; **essere nato con la camicia** to be born with a silver spoon in one's mouth; **perdere la camicia** to lose one's shirt

cami·ciàio -ciàia *mf* (*-ciài -ciàie*) shirtmaker, haberdasher

camiciòla *f* sport shirt; undershirt; T-shirt; (obs) vest

camiciòtto *m* smock (*of mechanic*); jumper; sport shirt

caminétto *m* small fireplace; fireplace

camino *m* fireplace; chimney, smokestack; shaft (*in mountain*); mouth (*of volcano*); (naut) funnel

cà·mion *m* (*-mion*) truck

camionale *f* highway

camioncino *m* small truck; panel truck, pickup truck

camionétta *f* small truck; van (*e.g., of police*)

camioni·sta *m* (*-sti*) truckdriver, teamster

camma *f* (mach) cam; (mach) wiper

cammellière *m* camel driver

cammèllo *m* camel

cammèo *m* cameo

camminaménto *m* (mil) communication trench

camminare *intr* to walk; to go, run

camminata *f* walk; gait; (obs) hall with fireplace

cammina·tóre -trice *mf* walker; runner

cammino *m* road, way, route; path (*e.g., of the moon*); course; journey; **cammin facendo** on the way; **cammino battuto** beaten path; **cammino coperto** (mil) covered way; **mettersi in cammino** to set out, start out

camomilla *f* camomile

camòrra *f* underworld

camò·scio *m* (**-sci**) chamois

campagna *f* country; countryside; country property; season (*for harvesting*); campaign; **andare in campagna** to go on vacation (in the country)

campagnò·lo -la *adj* country, rural ‖ *mf* peasant

campale *adj* field (*artillery*); pitched, decisive (*battle*)

campana *f* bell; bell glass, bell jar; lamp shade; (archit) bell; **a campana** bell-bottomed; **campana a martello** alarm bell, tocsin; **campana di vetro** bell glass; **campana pneumatica** caisson

campanàc·cio *m* (**-ci**) cowbell

campanaro *m* bell ringer; (archaic) bell founder

campanèlla *f* small bell; door knocker; curtain ring; (bot) bluebell

campanèllo *m* bell; small bell; doorbell, chimes; **campanello d'allarme** alarm bell

campanile *m* steeple, belfry; native city or town

campanilismo *m* parochialism

campano *m* cowbell

campare *tr* to keep alive; to save; to bring out the details of ‖ *intr* (ESSERE) to live; to survive; **si campa** one ekes out a living

campa·to -ta *adj*—**campato in aria** without any foundation ‖ *f* span

campeggiare §290 (**campéggio**) *intr* to camp, encamp; to stand out

campeggia·tóre -trice *mf* camper

campég·gio *m* (**-gi**) camping, outing; campground; (bot) logwood

campeggi·sta *mf* (**-sti -ste**) camper

campèstre *adj* field, country; (sports) cross-country

campidò·glio *m* (**-gli**) capitol ‖ **Campidoglio** *m* Capitoline (*hill*); Capitol (*temple*)

campionare (**campióno**) *tr* to sample

campionà·rio -ria (**-ri -rie**) *adj* of samples; trade (*exposition*) ‖ *m* sample book, catalogue, pattern book

campionato *m* championship, title

campióne *m* champion; sample; specimen; standard; **campione senza valore** uninsured parcel, sample post

campionéssa *f* championess

campionissimo *m* world champion, ace

campo *m* field; camp; ground; tennis court; golf course; center (*e.g., for refugees*); **campo addestramento** training camp; **campo d'aviazione** airfield, airport; **campo di battaglia** battlefield; **campo petrolifero** oil field; **lasciare il campo** to retreat; **mettere in campo** to bring up, adduce; **piantare il campo** to pitch camp

camposanto *m* cemetery, churchyard

camuffare *tr* to disguise, mask; to camouflage ‖ *ref* to disguise oneself

camu·so -sa *adj* snub-nosed

Canadà, il Canada

canadése [s] *adj & mf* Canadian

canàglia *f* scoundrel; rabble

canagliata *f* knavery, mean trick

canale *m* canal; irrigation ditch; network (*of communications*); pipe, drain; (anat) duct, tract; (rad, telv) channel; (theat) aisle; **Canale della Manica** English Channel; **Canale di Panama** Panama Canal; **Canale di Suez** Suez Canal

canalizzare [ddzz] *tr* to channel; to install pipes in; (elec) to wire

canalizzazióne [ddzz] *f* channeling; piping; ductwork; (elec) wiring

canalóne *m* ravine

cànapa *f* hemp

cana·pè *m* (**-pè**) sofa, couch; (culin) canapé

cànapo *m* rope, cable

Canàrie, le the Canaries

canarino *m* canary

cancàn *m* noise, racket

cancellare (**cancèllo**) *tr* to cancel, erase; to obliterate; to write off (*a debt*); to scratch (*a horse*) ‖ *ref* to vanish, fade

cancellata *f* railing

cancellatura *f* erasure

cancellazióne *f* cancellation; erasure (*of a tape*)

cancellerìa *f* chancellery; stationery

cancellière *m* chancellor; court clerk; registrar, recorder

cancèllo *m* gate, railing, grating

canceró·so -sa [s] *adj* cancerous ‖ *mf* cancer victim

cànchero *m* trouble; troublesome person; (coll) cancer

cancrèna *f* gangrene; **andare in cancrena** to become gangrenous

cancrenó·so -sa [s] *adj* gangrenous

cancro *m* cancer; (bot) canker ‖ **Cancro** *m* (astr) Cancer

candeggiante *adj* bleaching ‖ *m* bleaching agent, bleach

candeggiare §290 (**candéggio**) *tr* to bleach

candeggina *f* bleach

candég·gio *m* (**-gi**) bleaching

candéla *f* candle; candlestick; candlepower; (aut) spark plug; **studiare a lume di candela** to burn the midnight oil; **tenere la candela a** to favor the love affair of

candelabro *m* candelabrum

candellère *m* candlestick

candelòra *f* Candlemas

candelòtto *m* big wax candle; **candelotto lacrimogeno** tear-gas canister

candida·to -ta *mf* candidate

candidatura *f* candidature, candidacy

càndi·do -da *adj* white; candid

candire §176 *tr* to candy

candi·to -ta *adj* candied ‖ *m* candied fruit

candóre *m* whiteness; candor

cane *m* dog; hound; hammer, cock (*of gun*); ham actor; **cane barbone**

poodle; **cane bastardo** mongrel; **cane da ferma** setter; **cane da guardia** watchdog; **cane da presa** retriever; **cane da punta** pointer; **cane grosso** big shot; **cane guida per ciechi** seeing eye dog; **cane sciolto** (pol) lone wolf; **come un cane** all alone; **come un cane in chiesa** as an unwelcome guest; **da cani** poorly; **menare il can per l'aia** to beat around the bush; **non c'è un cane** there is nobody there; **raddrizzare le gambe ai cani** to perform an impossible task

canèstro m basket

cànfora f camphor

cangiante adj changeable (color); changing, iridescent

canguro m kangaroo

canicola f dog days

canile m doghouse, kennel

canino adj canine ‖ m canine tooth

canizie f gray hair; head of gray hair; old age

canna f cane, reed; rod (for fishing or measuring); pipe (of organ); barrel (of gun); **canna da zucchero** sugar cane; **canna di caduta** disposal chute; **canna fumaria** chimney; **canna della gola** (coll) windpipe

cannèlla f small tube; tap (of barrel); cinnamon

cannèllo m pipe, tube; stick (e.g., of licorice); (chem) pipette; **cannello ossiacetilenico** acetylene torch; **cannello ossidrico** oxyhydrogen blowpipe

cannellóni mpl cannelloni

cannéto m cane field

cannibale m cannibal

cannìc·cio m (-ci) wicker frame; shade made out of rushes

cannocchiale m spyglass; **cannocchiale astronomico** telescope

cannonata f cannonade, cannon shot; (slang) hit

cannoncino m small gun; **cannoncino antiaereo** antiaircraft gun

cannóne m gun, cannon; pipe, stovepipe; box pleat; shin (of cattle); **è un cannone** (coll) he's the tops

cannoneggiare §290 (cannonéggio) tr to cannonade, shell

cannonièra f gunboat

cannonière m gunner, artilleryman; kicker (in soccer)

cannùc·cia f (-ce) reed; thin tube; stem (e.g., of pipe); straw (for drinking); (chem) pipette

canòa f canoe; launch

canòcchia f mantis shrimp

cànone m canon; rule; rent; fee, charge (for use of radio)

canonicato m canonry

canòni·co -ca (-ci -che) adj canonical, canon (law) ‖ m priest ‖ f parsonage, rectory

canonizzare [ddzz] tr to canonize

canò·ro -ra adj song (bird); melodious

canottàg·gio m (-gi) boating, rowing

canottièra f undershirt, T-shirt; skimmer, boater

canottière m oarsman

canòtto m skiff, scull, shell

canovàc·cio m (-ci) dishcloth; embroidery cloth; plot (of novel or play)

cantàbile adj singable; songlike; cantabile ‖ m song

cantamban·co m (-chi) jongleur, wandering minstrel; mountebank

cantante adj singing, song ‖ mf singer

cantare m song; chant; laisse, epic strophe ‖ tr to sing; to chant ‖ intr to sing; to chant; (coll) to squeal

cantàride f Spanish fly

càntaro m urn

cantastò·rie mf (-rie) minstrel

canta·tóre -trice adj singing ‖ mf singer

cantau·tóre -trice mf singer composer

canterano m chest of drawers

canterellare (**canterèllo**) tr & intr to sing in a low voice, hum

canteri·no -na adj singing, warbling; decoy (bird) ‖ mf songster, singer

càntero m urinal

canticchiare §287 tr & intr to hum

cànti·co m (-ci) canticle

cantière m shipyard, dockyard; navy yard; undertaking, work in progress; **avere in cantiere** to have in hand, be working at; **cantiere edile** building site; builder's yard

cantilèna f singsong; **la stessa cantilena** the same old tune

cantimban·co m (-chi) var of **cantambanco**

cantina f cellar; wine cellar; wine shop, canteen

cantinière m cellarman; butler; wineshop keeper; sommelier

canto m song, singing; chant; canto; crow (of rooster); chirping (of grasshopper); corner, edge; (mus) voice part; **canto del cigno** swan song; **dal canto mio** for my part; **d'altro canto** on the other hand; **da un canto** on the one hand

cantonata f corner (of street); **prendere una cantonata** to make a blunder

cantóne m corner (of room or building); canton

cantonièra f corner cupboard; (rr) section worker's house

cantonière m road laborer; (rr) section hand

cantóre m choir singer; cantor; (poet) singer

cantù·cio m (-ci) nook, niche

canutézza f hoariness

canutiglia f gold thread

canu·to -ta adj gray-haired; whitehaired; (poet) white

canzonare (**canzóno**) tr to mock, ridicule

canzonatò·rio -ria adj (-ri -rie) mocking

canzonatura f mockery, gibe

canzóne f song; canzone

canzonétta f canzonet; popular song

canzonetti·sta mf (-sti -ste) singer (e.g., in a nightclub) ‖ m songster ‖ f songstress

canzonière m songbook; collection of poems; song writer

caolino m kaolin

caos *m* chaos

caòti·co -ca *adj* (**-ci -che**) caotic

capace *adj* capacious; capable, intelligent; legally qualified; **capace di** with a capacity of (*e.g., fifty people*); **essere capace di** to be able to; **fare capace di** to convince of

capaci·tà *f* (**-tà**) capacity; capability

capacitare (capàcito) *tr* to persuade ‖ *ref* to become convinced

capanna *f* hut, cabin; thatched cottage; bathhouse

capannèllo *m* group, crowd

capanno *m* hunting box; cabana, bathhouse

capannóne *m* large shed; hangar

caparbiàggine *f* var of **caparbietà**

caparbie·tà *f* (**-tà**) obstinacy, stubborness

capàr·bio -bia *adj* (**-bi -bie**) stubborn, hard-headed

caparra *f* down payment, deposit; performance bond

capatina *f* short visit

capeggiare §290 (capéggio) *tr* to lead

capeggia·tóre -trice *mf* leader

capellini *mpl* small vermicelli

capéllo *m* hair; **averne fin sopra i capelli** to have one's fill; **capelli lisci** straight hair; **capelli a spazzola** crew cut; **c'è mancato un capello che** + *subj* he came close to + *ger*; **far rizzare i capelli a qlcu** to make s.o.'s hair stand on end

capellóne *m* hippie, beatnik

capellu·to -ta *adj* hairy; long-haired

capelvènere *m* maidenhair

capèstro *m* halter; gallows

capezzale *m* bolster; (fig) bedside

capézzolo *m* nipple, teat; udder

capidò·glio *m* (**-gli**) var of **capodoglio**

capiènza *f* capacity (*e.g., of bus*)

capigliatura *f* head of hair

capillare *adj* capillary; (fig) far-reaching

capinéra *f* (orn) blackcap

capintè·sta *m* (**-sta**) boss; (sports) head, leader

capire §176 *tr* to understand; **capire a volo** to grasp immediately ‖ *intr*—**non capire dalla contentezza** to be bursting with joy ‖ *ref* to understand each other; to agree

capitale *adj* capital; mortal (*sin*) ‖ *m* capital; principal; **capitale sociale** capital stock ‖ *f* capital (*of country*)

capitalismo *m* capitalism

capitali·sta *mf* (**-sti -ste**) capitalist

capitalisti·co -ca *adj* (**-ci -che**) capitalistic

capitalizzare [ddzz] *tr* to capitalize; to compound (*interest*)

capitana *f* flagship

capitanare *tr* to lead, captain

capitaneria *f* (hist) captaincy; **capitaneria di porto** harbor-master's office; coast guard office; port authority's office

capitano *m* captain; skipper, master (*of ship*); commander (*in air force*); **capitano di corvetta** or **capitano di fregata** (nav) lieutenant commander;

capitano di gran cabotaggio master; **capitano di lungo corso** master; **capitano di porto** harbor master; **capitano di vascello** (nav) commander

capitare (càpito) *intr* (ESSERE) to arrive; to happen, occur; to happen to get, e.g., **capitò a casa mia alle tre** he happened to get to my house at three; **capitare bene** to be lucky; **dove capita** at random

capitazióne *f* poll tax

capitèllo *m* (archit) capital; (bb) headband

capitolare *adj & m* capitular ‖ *v* (**capìtolo**) *intr* to capitulate, surrender

capitolato *m* (com) specifications

capitolazióne *f* capitulation

capitolo *m* chapter; article, paragraph (*of contract*)

capitombolare (capitómbolo) *intr* to tumble

capitómbolo *m* tumble; **fare un capitombolo** (fig) to collapse

capitóne *m* big eel

capitozzare (capitòzzo) *tr* to poll (*a tree*)

capo *m* head; chief; boss, leader; top; (geog) cape; (nav) chief petty officer; **a capo scoperto** bareheaded; **capo d'accusa** (law) charge; **capo del governo** prime minister; **capo dello stato** president, chief of state; **capo di vestiario** garment; **capo scarico** scatterbrain; **col capo nel sacco** (fig) heedlessly; **da capo** all over (again); **fare capo a** to flow into; **in capo a** at the end of (*e.g., one month*); **in capo al mondo** at the end of the world; **per sommi capi** briefly; **rompersi il capo** to rack one's brain; **scoprirsi il capo** to take one's hat off; **senza capo né coda** without rhyme or reason; **venire a capo di** to come to the end of

capobanda *m* (**capibanda**) bandmaster; ringleader

capocamerière *m* headwaiter

capocannonière *m* (**capicannonièri**) petty gunnery officer; (soccer) leader in number of goals

capòcchia *f* head (*e.g., of a match*)

capòc·cia *m* (**-ci & -cia**) head of household; foreman, boss (*e.g., of road-workers or farmers*)

capocòmi·co *m* (**-ci**) head of dramatic company

capocor·da *m* (**capicòrda**) (elec) binding post, terminal

capocrònaca *m* (**capicrònaca**) leading article

capocronista *m* (**capicronisti**) city editor

capocuòco *m* (**capocuòchi & capicuòchi**) chef

capodanno *m* (**capodanni & capi d'anno**) New Year's Day

capodò·glio *m* (**-gli**) sperm whale

capofàbbrica *m* (**capifàbbrica**) foreman, superintendent

capofabbricato *m* (**capifabbricato**) air-raid warden

capofamìglia *m* (**capifamìglia**) head of the family

capofila *m* (**capifila**) head of a line ‖ *f* (**capofila**) head of a line

capofitto *adj invar*—a capofitto headlong

capogiro *m* vertigo, dizziness; **da capogiro** dizzying, e.g., **prezzi da capogiro** dizzying prices

capolavó·ro *m* (**-ri**) masterpiece

capolèttera *m* (**capilèttera**) letterhead; (typ) first large bold letter of a paragraph

capolìnea *m* (**capilìnea**) terminal, terminus

capolino *m*—fare capolino to peep

capolista *m* (**capilista**) first (*of a list*); (sports) leader ‖ *f* (**capolista**) first (*of a list*)

capoluò·go *m* (**-ghi**) capital (*of province*); county seat

capomacchini·sta *m* (**-sti**) chief engineer

capomastro *m* (**capomastri** & **capimastri**) foreman; building contractor

capomùsica *m* (**capimùsica**) bandmaster

capoofficina *m* (**capiofficina**) superintendent (*of shop*)

capopàgina *m* (**capipàgina**) heading (*of newspaper*)

capopèzzo *m* (**capipèzzo**) gunnery sergeant

capopòpolo *m* (**capipòpolo**) demagogue

caporale *m* corporal

caporeparto *m* (**capireparto**) department manager, floor walker; shop foreman

caporióne *m* ringleader

caposaldo *m* (**capisaldi**) (fig) main point, basis; (mil) stronghold; (surv) datum

caposezióne *m* (**capisezione**) department head

caposquadra *m* (**capisquadra**) group leader; (sports) team captain

capostazióne *m* (**capistazióne**) station master

capostìpite *m* founder (*of family*); prototype, archetype

capotaménto *m* var of cappottamento

capotare (**capòto**) *intr* var of cappottare

capotasto *m* nut (*of violin*)

capotàvola *m* (**capitàvola**) head of the table, honored guest

capòte *f* (aut) top

capotrèno *m* (**capitrèno** & **capotrèni**) (rr) conductor

capottaménto *m* var of cappottamento

capottare (**capòtto**) *intr* var of cappottare

capoufficio *m* (**capiufficio**) office manager

capovèrso *m* paragraph; (typ) indentation

capovòlgere §289 *tr* to overturn; (fig) to upset ‖ *ref* to overturn; (fig) to be or become reversed

capovolgiménto *m* upset; (fig) reversal

capovòlta *f* overturn; turn (*in swimming*)

cappa *f* cápe, cloak; mantle; letter K; shroud (*of clouds*); (naut) trysail;

cappa del cielo vault of heaven; **navigare alla cappa** (naut) to lay to

cappèlla *f* chapel; **cappella mortuaria** undertaker's parlor ‖ **Cappella Sistina** Sistine Chapel

cappel·làio *m* (**-lài**) hatter, hat maker or dealer

cappellano *m* chaplain

cappellata *f* hatful

cappellerìa *f* hat store

cappellièra *f* hatbox

cappèllo *m* hat; bonnet; cap (*of mushroom*); head (*of nail*); cowl (*of chimney*); preamble (*of newspaper article*); **cappello a cencio** slouch hat; **cappello a cilindro** top hat; **cappello a cono** dunce cap; **cappello a due punte** cocked hat; **cappello a tre punte** three-cornered hat; **cappello del lume** lampshade; **cappello di feltro** felt hat; **cappello di paglia** straw hat; **cappello floscio** fedora; **fare di cappello** to take one's hat off; **prendere cappello** to take offense

cappellóne *adj invar* Western (*movie*) ‖ *m* big hat; (coll) recruit; (mov) Western character

càppero *m* (bot) caper; **capperi!** (coll) wow!

càp·pio *m* (**-pi**) bow; noose; loop

capponàia *f* chicken coop

cappóne *m* capon

cappòtta *f* cape; navy coat; hood (*of car*)

cappottaménto *m* upset, rolling over

cappottare (**cappòtto**) *intr* to upset, roll over

cappottatura *f* (aer) cowl

cappòtto *m* overcoat; lurch (*at the close of game*); (cards) slam; **cappotto da mezza stagione** lightweight coat

cappuccino *m* espresso with cream; Capuchin (*friar*)

Cappuccétto *m*—**Cappuccetto Rosso** Little Red Ridinghood

cappùc·cio *m* (**-ci**) hood, cowl; cabbage; cap (*of fountain pen*)

capra *f* goat; nanny goat; tripod

ca·pràio -pràia *m* (**-prài -pràie**) goatherd

caprét·to -ta *mf* kid

capriata *f* truss (*to support roof*)

capric·cio *m* (**-ci**) whim, fancy, caprice; tantrum; flirting; (mus) capriccio

capriccio·so -sa [*s*] *adj* whimsical, capricious; naughty; fanciful, bizarre

Capricòrno *m* (astr) Capricorn

caprifò·glio *m* (**-gli**) honeysuckle

caprimul·go *m* (**-gi**) (orn) goatsucker

capri·no -na *adj* goatlike, goatish ‖ *m* smell of goat

capriòla *f* female roe deer; caper, somersault; **fare capriole** to cut capers, to caper

capriòlo *m* roe deer; roebuck

capro *m* he-goat, billy goat; **capro espiatorio** scapegoat

capróne *m* he-goat, billy goat

càpsula *f* capsule; percussion cap; cap (*of bottle*); (rok) capsule

captare *tr* to captivate; to catch, intercept; to harness (*a waterfall*); (rad, telv) to pick up (*a signal*)

captazióne *f* undue influence (*to secure an inheritance*)

capzió·so -sa [s] *adj* insidious, treacherous

carabàttola *f* (coll) trifle

carabina *f* carbine

carabinière *m* carabineer; Italian military policeman, carabiniere; (*hist*) cavalryman

caracollare (caracòllo) *intr* to caracole, caper; (coll) to trot along

caracòllo *m* caracole, caper

caraffa *f* carafe, decanter

caràmbola *f* carom

carambolare (caràmbolo) *intr* to carom

caramèlla *f* piece of hard candy; taffy; (coll) monocle; **caramelle** hard candy

caramellare (caramèllo) *tr* to caramel; to candy

caramèllo *m* caramel (*burnt sugar*)

caramènte *adv* affectionately

carati·sta *m* (**-sti**) shareholder (*in ship or business*)

carato *m* carat; share (*of ship*)

caràttere *m* character; type; handwriting; characteristic; disposition; **carattere corsivo** (typ) italic; **carattere maiuscolo** capital; **carattere minuscolo** small letter, lower case; **carattere neretto** or **grassetto** (typ) boldface

caratteri·sta *m* (**-sti**) character actor ‖ *f* (**-ste**) character actress

caratterìsti·co -ca (**-ci -che**) *adj & f* characteristic

caratterizzare [ddzz] *tr* to characterize

caratura *f* share (*in business or ship*)

cara·vàn *m* (**-vàn**) trailer, mobile home

caravanserrà·glio *m* (**-gli**) caravansary

caravèlla *f* caravel; carpenter's glue

carbo·nàio -nàia (**-nài -nàie**) *adj* coal ‖ *m* coal man, coal dealer ‖ *f* charcoal pit; coalbin, bunker; coal yard

carbonato *m* carbonate

carbón·chio *m* (**-chi**) (agr) smut (*on wheat*); (jewelry) carbuncle

carboncino *m* charcoal (*pencil and drawing*)

carbóne *m* coal; charcoal; carbon (*of arc light or primary battery*); **carbone bianco** hydroelectric power; **carbone dolce** charcoal; **carbone fossile** coal; **fare carbone** to coal

carbòni·co -ca *adj* (**-ci -che**) carbonic

carbonièra *f* coal yard; (naut) collier; (rr) tender

carbonile *m* (naut) bunker

carbònio *m* (chem) carbon

carbonizzare [ddzz] *tr* to carbonize; to char

carbùncolo *m* boil, carbuncle; (archaic) ruby

carburante *m* fuel

carburatóre *m* carburetor

carburazióne *f* (aut) mixture

carburo *m* carbide

carcassa *f* carcass; framework; (aut) jalopy; (fig) wreck

carcerare (càrcero) *tr* to jail

carcerà·rio -ria *adj* (**-ri -rie**) jail, prison

carcera·to -ta *adj* imprisoned ‖ *mf* prisoner

càrce·re *m* (**-ri** *fpl*) jail, prison

carcerière *m* jailer, prison guard

carciòfo *m* artichoke

cardàni·co -ca *adj* (**-ci -che**) universal (*e.g., joint*)

cardano *m* universal joint

cardatrice *f* carding machine

cardellino *m* goldfinch

cardìa·co -ca (**-ci -che**) *adj* heart, cardiac ‖ *m* heart patient

cardinale *adj* cardinal ‖ *m* (eccl, orn) cardinal

cardinalì·zio -zia *adj* (**-zi -zie**) cardinal, cardinal's

càrdine *m* hinge; (fig) pivot, mainstay (*e.g., of theory*)

càr·dio *m* (**-di**) cockle (*mollusk*)

cardiochirurgìa *f* heart surgery

cardiogram·ma *m* (**-mi**) cardiogram

cardiòlo·go *m* (**-gi**) cardiologist

cardiopalmo *m* tachycardia

cardiopatìa *f* heart disease

cardo *m* (bot) thistle; (bot) cardoon

carèna *f* ship's bottom; (aer) outer cover (*of airship*); (bot) rib

carenàg·gio *m* (**-gi**) careening a ship; careen

carenare (carèno) *tr* to careen (*a ship*)

carenatura *f* streamlining; **carenatura di fusoliera** (aer) turtleback

carènza *f* lack, want

carestìa *f* famine; scarcity (*e.g., of manpower*)

carézza *f* caress; **fare una carezza a** to caress

carezzare (carézzo) *tr* to caress

carezzévole *adj* caressing, fondling; sweet, suave; blandishing

cariare §287 *tr* to cause (*a tooth*) to decay; to corrode ‖ *ref* to decay; to rot

cariàtide *f* caryatid

cària·to -ta *adj* decayed

càri·ca *f* (**-che**) office, appointment; charge; (fig) insistence

caricaménto *m* loading

caricare §197 (**càrico**) *tr* to load; to burden; to wind (*a watch*); to fill (*a pipe*); to charge (*a battery*); to deepen (*a color*); **caricare la mano** to exceed; **caricare le dosi** to exaggerate ‖ *ref* to burden oneself

carica·to -ta *adj* exaggerated, affected

carica·tóre -trice *adj* loading ‖ *m* clip, magazine (*for rifle*); loader (*of gun*); cassette (*of tape recorder*); charger (*of battery*); longshoreman; (phot) cartridge, cassette

caricatura *f* caricature, cartoon; **mettere in caricatura** to ridicule

caricaturi·sta *mf* (**-sti -ste**) cartoonist, caricaturist

càrice *m* (bot) sedge

càri·co -ca (**-chi -che**) *adj* loaded; burdened; vivid (*color*); strong (*tea*); charged (*battery*) ‖ *m* loading; load, burden; charge; cargo ‖ *f* see **carica**

càrie *f* caries, decay

cari·no -na *adj* nice, pretty, cute; **questa è carina!** this is funny!

cari·tà *f* (**-tà**) charity; alms; (poet) love; **per carità** please

caritatévole *adj* charitable

caritati·vo -va *adj* (obs) charitable

carlin·ga *f* (**-ghe**) fuselage

Carlo *m* Charles

Carlomagno *m* Charlemagne

carlóna *f*—**alla carlona** carelessly, haphazardly

carlòtta *f* charlotte ‖ **Carlòtta** Charlotte

carme *m* poem, lyric poem

carmi·nio *m* (**-ni**) carmine

carnagióne *f* complexion

car·nàio *m* (**-nài**) carnage; slaughter house; mass of humanity

carnale *adj* carnal, sensual; full (*e.g.*, *brother, cousin*)

carname *m* carrion

carne *f* flesh; meat; **bene in carne** plump; **carne da macello** cannon fodder; **carne suina** pork; **carne viva** open wound; **essere solo carne ed ossa** to be nothing but skin and bones; **in carne ed ossa** in person, in the flesh; **troppa carne al fuoco** too many irons in the fire

carnéfice *m* executioner

carneficina *f* slaughter, carnage

càrne·o -a *adj* fleshy, meaty; flesh-colored

carnet *m* (**carnet**) notebook; checkbook; backlog

carnevale *m* carnival

carnièra *f* hunting jacket; gamebag

carnière *m* gamebag

carnìvo·ro -ra *adj* carnivorous ‖ *mpl* carnivores; Carnivora

carnò·so -sa [*s*] *adj* fleshy

ca·ro -ra *adj* dear (*beloved; high in price*) ‖ **caro** *adv* dear ‖ *m* high price; beloved; **i miei cari** my parents; my relatives; my friends

carógna *f* carcass; cad, rotter; **carogne** carrion

carosèllo *m* tournament; carousel, merry-go-round

caròta *f* carrot; (fig) lie

caròtide *f* carotid artery

carovana *f* caravan; group, crowd; union of longshoremen; apprenticeship; (naut, nav) convoy; **far carovana** to join a tour; **fare la carovana** to be an apprentice

carovaniè·ro -ra *adj* caravan ‖ *f* desert trail

carovi·ta *m* (**-ta**) high cost of living; cost-of-living increase

carovìve·ri *m* (**-ri**) high cost of living; cost-of-living increase

carpa *f* (ichth) carp

carpentière *m* carpenter

carpire §176 *tr* to snatch, seize; to extract, worm (*a secret*)

carpóni *adv* on all fours; **avanzare carponi** to crawl

carradóre *m* cart maker, wheelwright

car·ràio -ràia (**-rài -ràie**) *adj* passable for vehicles ‖ *f* cart road

carrarèc·cia *f* (**-ce**) country road; rut

carreggiata *f* paved road; track (*of vehicles*); (fig) right path

carrellare (**carrèllo**) *intr* (mov, telv) to dolly

carrellata *f* (mov) dolly shot, tracking shot

carrèllo *m* car (*for narrow-gauge track*); carriage (*of typewriter*); cart (*for shopping*); (aer) landing gear; (mach, rr) truck; (mov, telv) dolly; **carrello d'atterraggio** (aer) undercarriage, landing gear; **carrello elevatore** fork-lift truck

carrétta *f* cart; tramp steamer

carrettata *f* cartful; **a carrettate** abundantly

carrettière *m* cart driver, drayman; teamster

carrétto *m* small cart; **carretto a mano** pushcart

carriàg·gio *m* (**-gi**) wagon; **carriaggi** (mil) baggage train

carrièra *f* career; **di gran carriera** at top speed

carrieri·sta *mf* (**-sti -ste**) unscrupulous go-getter

carriòla *f* wheelbarrow

carro *m* wagon; cart; wagonload; cartload; carload; (rr) car; (astr) Plough; (poet) chariot; **carri armati** (mil) armor; **carro allegorico** float (*in a pageant*); **carro armato** (mil) tank; **carro attrezzi** (aut) tow truck, wrecker; **carro bestiame** (rr) cattle car; **carro botte** or **carro cisterna** (aut) tank truck; (rr) tank car; **carro di Tespi** traveling show; **carro funebre** hearse; **carro gru** (rr) wrecking crane; **carro masnquo** (rr) double decker (*used to transport automobiles*); **carro merci** (rr) freight car; **Gran Carro** (astr) Big Dipper; **mettere il carro innanzi ai buoi** to put the cart before the horse; **Piccolo Carro** (astr) Little Dipper ‖ *m* (**carra** *fpl*) carload; wagonload; cartload

carròzza *f* wagon carriage; **carrozza letti** (rr) sleeping car; **carrozza ristorante** (rr) dining car; **carrozza salone** (rr) club car; **con la carrozza di S. Francesco** on shank's mare; **signori, in carrozza!** (rr) all aboard!

carrozzàbile *adj* open to vehicular traffic ‖ *f* road open to vehicular traffic

carrozzèlla *f* small wagon; baby carriage; wheelchair; hackney

carrozzino *m* baby carriage; sidecar

carrozzóne *m* wagon; hearse; caravan (*e.g.*, *of gypsies*); (rr) car

carruba *f* carob

carrubo *m* carob tree

carrùcola *f* pulley

carta *f* paper; document (*e.g.*, *of identification*); **alla carta** à la carte; **carta assorbente** blotter; **carta astronomica** astronomical map; **carta bianca** carte blanche; **carta bollata** stamped paper (*for official documents*); **carta carbone** carbon paper; **carta catramata** tar paper; **carta da disegno** drawing paper; **carta da gioco** playing card; **carta da giornale** newsprint; **carta da imballaggio** or **da impacco** wrapping paper; **carta da lettera** or **da lettere** writing paper; **carta geografica** map, chart; **carta igienica** toilet paper; **carta oleata** wax paper; **carta torna-**

sole litmus paper; **carta velina** India paper; tissue paper; **carta vetrata** sandpaper; **carte papers**, writings; **carte francesi** cards in the four suits spades, hearts, diamonds, and clubs; **carte napoletane** cards in the four suits gold coins, cups, swords, and clubs; **fare le carte** to shuffle the cards; **fare le carte a qlcu** to tell s.o.'s fortune with cards

cartacarbóne f (**cartecarbóne**) carbon paper

cartàc·cia f (**-ce**) waste paper

cartàce·o -a adj (**-i -e**) paper

Cartàgine f Carthage

car·tàio m (**-tài**) papermaker; paper dealer; (cards) dealer

cartamonéta f paper money

cartapècora f parchment

cartapésta f papier-mâché

cartà·rio adj (**-ri -rie**) paper

cartastràccia f (**cartestracce**) wrapping paper; wastepaper

cartég·gio m (**-gi**) correspondence; (aer, naut) reckoning

cartèlla f lottery ticket; card (e.g., of bingo); page of manuscript; Manila folder; schoolbag; briefcase; binding (of book); **cartella clinica** clinical chart; **cartella di rendita** government bond; **cartella esattoriale** tax bill; **cartella fondiaria** bond certificate

cartellino m label; nameplate (on door); file; (sports) contract; **cartellino di presenza** timecard; **cartellino signaletico** criminal record

cartèllo m poster; sign (on store); (com) cartel, trust; **cartello di sfida** challenge; **cartello stradale** traffic sign

cartellóne m show bill, theater poster; bill (for advertising); **tenere il cartellone** to find public favor, make a hit, be the rage

car·ter m (**-ter**) chain guard (of bicycle); (aut) crankcase

cartièra f papermill

cartilàgine f cartilage, gristle

cartina f dose; cigarette paper; small map

cartòc·cio m (**-ci**) paper cone; charge (of gun); cornhusk; (archit) scroll

cartògrafo m cartographer

carto·làio m (**-lài**) stationer

cartoleria f stationery store

cartolina f card, post card; **cartolina precetto** induction notice

cartomante mf fortuneteller

cartoncino m light cardboard, calling card; **cartoncino natalizio** Christmas card

cartóne m cardboard, carton; **cartone animato** (mov) animated cartoon

cartùc·cia f (**-ce**) cartridge; shot, shell; **mezza cartuccia** (fig) half pint

cartuccièra f cartridge belt

casa [s] f house; dwelling; home; household; **andare a casa** to go home; **casa base** (baseball) home base; **casa colonica** farm house; **casa da gioco** gambling house; **casa del diavolo** faraway place; **casa di bambole** playhouse, doll's house; **casa di correzione** reform school; **casa di cura** sanatorium, private clinic; **casa di riposo** convalescent home, nursing home; **casa di spedizione** shipping agency; **casa di tolleranza** bawdy-house; **casa madre** home office, headquarters; **esser di casa** to be intimate; **fuori casa** (sports) away; **in casa** (sports) home; **metter su casa** to set up housekeeping; **sentirsi a casa** to feel at home; **stare a casa** to stay at home; **star di casa** to dwell, live

casac·ca f (**-che**) coat; **voltar casacca** to be a turncoat

casàccio m—**a casaccio** at random; heedlessly

casalin·go -ga (**-ghi -ghe**) [s] adj home, domestic; stay-at-home; homey; home-made ‖ **casalinghi** mpl household articles ‖ f housewife

casamatta [s] f casemate, bunker

casaménto [s] m apartment house, tenement; tenants

casata [s] f house, lineage

casato [s] m birth, family; (obs) family name

cascame m waste; remnants (e.g., of silk)

cascante adj flabby, loose; (poet) languid, dull

cascare §197 intr (ESSERE) to fall, droop; to fit (said of clothes); **cascare dalla noia** to be bored to death; **cascare dal sonno** to be overwhelmed with sleep; **cascare diritto** to escape unscathed; **non casca il mondo** the world is not coming to an end

cascata f fall, waterfall; necklace (e.g., of pearls); **a cascata** flood of, e.g., **telefonate a cascata** flood of telephone calls ‖ **le Cascate del Niagara** Niagara Falls

cascina f farm house; dairy barn

ca·sco m (**-schi**) helmet, crash helmet; electric hairdrier; cluster (e.g., of bananas)

caseggiato [s] m built-up zone; block, row of houses; apartment house

caseifi·cio m (**-ci**) dairy, creamery, cheese factory

casèlla [s] f pigeonhole; square (of paper); **casella postale** post-office box

casellante [s] mf gatekeeper ‖ m (rr) trackwalker

casellà·rio [s] m (**-ri**) filing cabinet; row of post-office boxes; **casellario giudiziale** criminal file

casèllo [s] m tollgate (on turnpike); (rr) trackwalker's house

casèrma f barracks; fire station

casino [s] m country house; clubhouse; (slang) whorehouse; (slang) noise, racket

casisti·ca f (**-che**) case study; (eccl) casuistry

caso m case; chance; fate; vicissitude; opportunity; **a caso** inadvertently; **al caso** eventually; **caso fortuito** (law) act of God; **caso mai** assuming that, in the event that; **è il caso** it is the moment; **far caso a qlco** to notice s.th; **in ogni caso** in any event; **mettere il caso che** suppose; **mi fa caso** I am surprised; **non fare caso a** to make nothing of, pay no attention to; **per caso** perchance

casolare [s] *m* hut, hovel; isolated farmhouse

casòtto [s] *m* cabana, bathhouse; sentry box

Càspio *adj* Caspian

càspita *interj* you don't say!

cassa *f* box; chest; case; stock (*of rifle*); cash; cash register; desk (*e.g., in hotel*); check-out (*in a supermarket*); **a pronta cassa** by cash; **cassa acustica** loudspeaker; **cassa di risparmio** savings bank; **cassa malattia** health insurance; **cassa rurale** farmers' credit cooperative; **in cassa** in hand (*said of money*)

cassafórma *f* (**casseforme**) (archit) form (*for cement*)

cassafòrte *f* (**cassefòrti**) safe

cassapanca *f* (**cassapanche & cassepanche**) wooden chest

cassare *tr* to erase, cancel; to cross off; (law) to annull

cassata *f* Neapolitan ice cream with soft core; Sicilian cake

cassazióne *f* annulment, abolition; cancellation

casserétto *m* (naut) poop

càssero *m* (naut) quarterdeck; **cassero di poppa** (naut) cockpit

casseruòla *f* saucepan

cassétta *f* small box; coach box; (theat) box office; **cassetta dei ferri** workbox; **cassetta delle lettere** mail box; **cassetta di cottura** dish warmer; **cassetta di sicurezza** safe-deposit box; **cassetta per ugnature** miter box

cassettièra *f* chest of drawers

cassétto *m* drawer; **cassetto di distribuzione** (mach) slide valve

cassettóne *m* chest of drawers; (archit) coffer, caisson

cassiè·re -ra *mf* cashier; teller

cassóne *m* large case, large box; chest; caisson (*for underwater construction*); body (*of truck*); (mil) caisson

cassonétto *m* cornice

cast *m* cast (*of actors*)

casta *f* caste

castagna *f* chestnut; **castagna d'India** horse chestnut

castagnéto *m* chestnut grove

castagno *m* chestnut tree; chestnut (*lumber*); **castagno d'India** horse chestnut tree

casta·no -na *adj* chestnut (*color*)

castellana *f* chatelaine

castellano *m* lord of the castle, squire

castellétto *m* scaffold; (min) gallows, headframe

castèl·lo *m* castle; works (*e.g., of watch*); scaffold; jungle gym; hydraulic boom, bucket lift (*on truck*); (naut) forecastle; **castello di menzogne** pack of lies; **castello in aria** castle in Spain ‖ *m* (**-la** *fpl*) (archaic) castle

castigare §209 *tr* to punish; (poet) to correct, castigate

castigatézza *f* purity (*e.g., of style*)

castiga·to -ta *adj* decent, modest; pure (*language*)

Castìglia, la Castile

castìglia·no -na *adj & mf* Castilian

castì·go *m* (**-ghi**) punishment; (fig) scourge; **mettere in castigo** (coll) to punish

casti·tà *f* (**-tà**) chastity; (fig) purity

ca·sto -sta *adj* chaste; pure, elegant (*language or style*)

castóne *m* setting (*of stone*)

castòro *m* beaver

castrare *tr* to castrate; to spay; (fig) to expurgate

castra·to -ta *adj* castrated; spayed; (fig) effeminate ‖ *m* mutton (of castrated sheep); eunuch

castróne *m* wether (*sheep*); gelding (*horse*); (fig) nincompoop

castroneria *f* (vulg) stupidity

casuale *adj* fortuitous, casual; sundry (*e.g., expenses*)

casuali·tà *f* (**-tà**) chance, accident

casùpola [s] *f* hut, hovel

catacli·sma *m* (**-smi**) cataclysm

catacómba *f* catacomb

catafal·co *m* (**-chi**) catafalque

catafàscio *adv*—**a catafascio** topsy-turvy

catalès·si *f* (**-si**) catalepsy

catàli·si *f* (**-si**) catalysis

catalizza·tóre -trice [ddzz] *adj* catalytic ‖ *m* catalyst

catalogare §209 (**catàlogo**) *tr* to catalogue

catàlo·go *m* (**-ghi**) catalogue

catapècchia *f* hovel

catapla·sma *m* (**-smi**) poultice, plaster; (fig) bore

catapulta *f* catapult

catapultare *tr* to catapult

cataratta *f* cataract; sluice (*of canal*)

catarro *m* catarrh

catar·si *f* (**-si**) catharsis

catàrti·co -ca *adj* (**-ci -che**) cathartic

catasta *f* pile, heap

catastale *adj* land (*office*)

catasto *m* real-estate register; land office

catàstrofe *f* catastrophe; wreck

catastròfi·co -ca *adj* (**-ci -che**) catastrophic

catechismo *m* catechism

catechizzare [ddzz] *tr* to catechize

categoria *f* category; weight (*in boxing*); (sports) class

categòri·co -ca *adj* (**-ci -che**) categorical; classified (*telephone directory*)

caténa *f* chain; range (*of mountains*); (archit) tie beam; **catene da neve** tire chains; **mordere la catena** to champ the bit

catenàc·cio *m* (**-ci**) bolt; (fig) jalopy; (journ) giant-size headline

catenèlla *f* chain

cateratta *f* var of **cataratta**

catèrva *f* great quantity, large number

catètere *m* catheter

cateterizzare [ddzz] *tr* to catheterize

catinèlla *f* water basin; **piovere a catinelle** (coll) to rain cats and dogs

catino *m* basin

càtodo *m* cathode

Catóne *m* Cato; **Catone il Maggiore** Cato the Elder

catòr·cio *m* (**-ci**) (coll) piece of junk

catramare *tr* to tar
catramatrice *f* asphalt-paving machine
catrame *m* tar, coal tar
càttedra *f* desk (*of teacher*); chair, professorship
cattedrale *adj & f* cathedral
cattedràti•co -ca (**-ci -che**) *adj* pedantic || *m* professor
catte•gù *m* (**-gù**) catgut
cattivare *tr* to captivate
cattivèria *f* wickedness; piece of wickedness
cattivi•tà *f* (**-tà**) captivity
catti•vo -va *adj* bad; wicked; vicious (*animal*); worthless; poor (*reputation; condition*); nasty; naughty; (*archaic*) cowardly || *mf* wicked person || *m* bad taste; **sapere di cattivo** to taste bad
cattolicità *f* catholicity
cattòli•co -ca (**-ci -che**) *adj* catholic || *adj & mf* Catholic
cattura *f* capture, seizure; arrest
catturare *tr* to capture, seize; to arrest
caucàsi•co -ca *adj & mf* (**-ci -che**) Caucasian
caucciù *m* (**caucciù**) rubber
càusa *f* cause, motive; fault; lawsuit, action; **a causa di** on account of; **causa civile** civil suit; **causa penale** criminal suit; **fare causa** to take legal action; **intentare causa a** to bring suit against
causale *adj* causal || *f* cause
causare (**càuso**) *tr* to cause
causìdi•co *m* (**-ci**) amicus curiae; (joc) pettifogger
càusti•co -ca *adj* (**-ci -che**) caustic
cautèla *f* caution; precaution, care
cautelare *adj* guaranteeing, protecting || *v* (**cautèlo**) *tr* to guarantee, protect *ref* to take precautions
cauterizzare [ddzz] *tr* to cauterize
càu•to -ta *adj* cautious, prudent; cagey
cauzióne *f* security, bail; **dare cauzione** to give bail
cava *f* quarry; cave; (fig) mine
cavadènti *m* (**-ti**) (coll) tooth puller, poor dentist
cavagno *m* (coll) basket
cavalcare §197 *tr* to ride; to cross over (*e.g., a river*) || *intr* to ride; **cavalcare a bisdosso** to ride bareback; **cavalcare all'amazzone** to ride sidesaddle
cavalcata *f* ride; cavalcade
cavalcatura *f* mount
cavalca•vìa *m* (**-vìa**) bridge (*between two buildings*); overpass
cavalcióni *adj*—**a cavalcioni** (**di**) astride
cavalierato *m* knighthood
cavalière *m* rider (*on horseback*); knight; cavalier; chevalier; **a cavaliere astride**; **cavaliere d'industria** adventurer; **cavaliere errante** knight errant; **essere a cavaliere di** to overlook (*e.g., a valley*); to stretch over (*e.g., two centuries*)
cavalla *f* mare
cavalleggièro *m* cavalryman
cavalleré•sco -sca *adj* (**-schi -sche**) chivalrous, knightly

cavallerìa *f* cavalry; chivalry, knighthood; (fig) chivalry
cavallerizza *f* manège, riding school; horsemanship; horsewoman
cavallerizzo *m* horseman; riding master
cavallétta *f* grasshopper
cavallétto *m* tripod; easel; trestle (*of ski lift*); scaffold (*e.g., of stonemason*); sawhorse, sawbuck
cavalli•no -na *adj* horse, horse-like || *m* foal, colt || *f* foal, filly; **correre la cavallina** to be on the loose; to sow one's wild oats
cavallo *m* horse; knight (*in chess*); crotch (*of pants*); **a cavallo** on horseback; **a cavallo di astride**; **andare col cavallo di San Francesco** to ride shank's mare; **cavallo a dondolo** hobbyhorse; **cavallo di battaglia** battle horse; (fig) specialty, forte; **cavallo da corsa** race horse; **cavallo da tiro** draft horse; **cavallo di Frisia** cheval-de-frise; **cavallo di ritorno** confirmed news; **cavallo vapore** metric horsepower; **essere a cavallo** (fig) to have turned the corner
cavallóne *m* big horse; billow
cavallùc•cio *m* (**-ci**) little horse; **a cavalluccio** on one's shoulders; **cavalluccio marino** (ichth) sea horse
cavare *tr* to dig; to extract (*e.g., a tooth*); to pull out (*e.g., money*); to draw; **cavare il cuore a qlcu** to move s.o. to compassion; **cavare una spina dal cuore a qlcu** to ease s.o.'s mind || *ref* to take off (*e.g., one's hat*); **cavarsela** to overcome an obstacle; to get out of trouble; **cavarsi la camicia di dosso** to give the shirt off one's back; **cavarsi la fame** to eat one's fill; **cavarsi la voglia** to satisfy one's wishes
cavastiva•li *m* (**-li**) bootjack
cavatap•pi *m* (**-pi**) corkscrew
cavaturàccio•li *m* (**-li**) corkscrew
cavèrna *f* cave, cavern
cavernó•so -sa [s] *adj* cavernous; deep (*voice*)
cavézza *f* halter; (fig) check
càvia *f* guinea pig; **cavia umana** (fig) guinea pig
caviale *m* caviar
cavic•chio *m* (**-chi**) peg
cavi•glia *f* (**-glie**) ankle; bolt; pin, dowel, peg
caviglièra *f* ankle support
cavillare *intr* to cavil, quibble
cavillo *m* quibble
cavilló•so -sa [s] *adj* quibbling, captious
cavi•tà *f* (**-tà**) cavity
ca•vo -va *adj* hollow || *m* hollow; cable; trough (*between two waves*); (naut) hawser; **cavo di rimorchio** towline; **cavo telefonico** telephone cable || *f* see cava
cavolfióre *m* cauliflower
càvolo *m* cabbage; **cavolo di Bruxelles** Brussels sprouts (*food*); (bot) Brussels sprout; **non capire un cavolo** (vulg) to not understand a blessed thing
cazzòtto *m* (vulg) punch, sock
cazzuòla *f* trowel

ce §5

cecare §122 *tr* to blind

cèc·ca *f* (-che) magpie; **fare cecca** to misfire

cecchino *m* sniper

céce *m* chickpea

ceci·tà *f* (-tà) blindness

cè·co -ca *adj & mf* (-chi -che) Czech

Cecoslovàcchia, la Czechoslovakia

cècoslovac·co -ca *adj & mf* (-chi -che) Czechoslovak

cèdere §123 *tr* to cede; to give up; to sell at cost; **cedere il passo** to let s.o. through; **cedere la strada** to yield the right of way; **non cederla** to be second to none ‖ *intr* to give in, yield; to give way, succumb; to sag

cedévole *adj* yielding; soft; pliable

cedìglia *f* cedilla

cedimento *m* cave-in; (fig) yielding

cèdola *f* slip; coupon

cedri·no -na *adj* citron; citron-like; cedar, cedar-like

cédro *m* (*Citrus medica*) citron; (*Cedrus*) cedar; **cedro del Libano** cedar of Lebanon

CEE *m* (letterword) (**Comunità Economica Europea**) EEC (*European Economic Community - Common Market*)

cefalèa *f* slight headache; headache

cèfalo *m* (ichth) mullet

cèffo *m* snout; (pej) face; **brutto ceffo** ugly mug

ceffone *m* slap in the face

celare (cèlo) *tr* to hide, conceal

cela·to -ta *adj* hidden ‖ *f* sallet

celebèrri·mo -ma *adj* very famous, renowned

celebrare (cèlebro) *tr & intr* to celebrate

celebrazióne *f* celebration

cèlebre *adj* famous, renowned, celebrated

celebri·tà *f* (-tà) celebrity

cèlere *adj* swift, rapid; express (*train*); short, quick; prompt ‖ **Celere** *f* special police

celeri·tà *f* (-tà) swiftness, rapidity; speed (*e.g., of a machine gun*)

celèste *adj* heavenly, celestial; blue, sky-blue ‖ *m* blue, sky blue; **celesti** heavenly spirits; (mythol) gods

celestiale *adj* celestial, heavenly

cèlia *f* jest; **mettere in celia** to deride; **per celia** in jest

celiare §287 (cèlio) *intr* to jest, joke

celibatà·rio -ria (-ri -rie) *adj* single ‖ *m* old bachelor

celibato *m* celibacy; bachelorhood

cèlibe *adj* single, unmarried ‖ *m* bachelor

cèlla *f* cell; **cella frigorifera** walk-in refrigerator; **cella campanaria** belfry

cèllofan or cèllofàn *m* cellophane

cèllula *f* cell; **cellula fotoelettrica** photoelectric cell

cellulare *adj* cellular; ventilated (*fabric*); solitary (*confinement*)

cellulòide *f* celluloid

celluló·so -sa [s] *adj* cell-like, cellular ‖ *f* cellulose

cèl·ta *mf* (-ti -te) Celt

cèlti·co -ca *adj* (-ci -che) Celtic; venereal (*disease*)

cementare (ceménto) *tr* to cement

ceménto *m* cement, concrete; **cemento armato** reinforced concrete

céna *f* supper; **Ultima Cena** Last Supper

cenàcolo *m* cenacle

cenare (céno) *intr* to sup, have supper

cenciaiò·lo -la *mf* ragpicker

cén·cio *m* (-ci) rag, duster (*for cleaning*)

cenció·so -sa [s] *adj* tattered, ragged

cénere *adj* ashen ‖ *f* ash; cinder; **andare in cenere** to go up in smoke; **ceneri** ashes (*of a person*); **ridurre in cenere** to burn to ashes ‖ **le Ceneri** Ash Wednesday

cenerèntola *f* (fig) Cinderella ‖ **Cenerèntola** *f* Cinderella (*of the fable*)

cén·gia *f* (-ge) ledge (*of a mountain*)

cénno *m* sign; wave (*with hand*); nod; wag; wink; gesture; hint; notice; **ai cenni di** at the orders of; **fare cenno a** or **di** to mention; **fare cenno di no** to shake one's head; **fare cenno di sì** to nod assent

cenò·bio *m* (-bi) monastery

cenobi·ta *m* (-ti) monk, cenobite

censiménto *m* census

censire §176 *tr* to take the census of

cènso *m* wealth, income; census (*in ancient Rome*)

censóre *m* censor; faultfinder; (educ) proctor

censuà·rio -ria (-ri -rie) *adj* income; tax (*register*) ‖ *m* taxpayer

censura *f* censure; censorship; faultfinding

censurare *tr* to censure; to criticize, find fault with

centàuro *m* centaur

centellinare *tr* to sip; to take a nip of

centellino *m* sip, nip

centenà·rio -ria (-ri -rie) *adj & mf* centenary, centennial ‖ *m* centenary, centennial (*anniversary*)

centèsi·mo -ma *adj* hundredth ‖ *m* hundredth; centime; cent; penny

centìgrado *m* centigrade

centigrammo *m* centigram

centimetro *m* centimeter; tape measure

cèntina *f* (archit) centering; (aer) rib

centi·nàio *m* hundred; **un centinaio di** about a hundred ‖ *m* (-nàia *fpl*)—a **centinaia** by the hundreds

cènto *adj, m & pron* a hundred, one hundred; **per cento** per cent

centomila *adj, m & pron* a hundred thousand, one hundred thousand

centóne *m* cento

centopiè·di *m* (-di) centipede

centrale *adj* central ‖ *f* headquarters, home office; powerhouse, generating station; telephone exchange; **centrale di conversione** (elec) transformer station; **centrale telefonica** central

centralini·sta *mf* (-sti -ste) telephone operator

centralino *m* telephone exchange

centralizzare [ddzz] *tr* to centralize

centrare (cèntro) *tr* to center; to hit the center of

centrattac·co m (**-chi**) (sports) center forward

centrifu·go -ga adj (**-ghi -ghe**) centrifugal || f centrifuge

centrino m centerpiece

centripe·to -ta adj centripetal

centri·sta mf (**-sti -ste**) (pol) centrist

cèntro m center; **al centro** downtown; **far centro** to hit the mark

centrocampo m (soccer) midfield

centuplicare §197 (**centùplico**) tr to multiply a hundredfold

cèntu·plo -pla adj & m hundredfold

cèppo m trunk, stump; log; block (for beheading); brake shoe; stock (of anchor); **ceppi** stocks, fetters || **il Ceppo** (coll) Christmas

céra f wax; face, aspect, air, look; **di cera** waxen; pale; **cera da scarpe** shoe polish; **avere buona cera** to look well; **fare buona cera a** to welcome

ceralac·ca f (**-che**) sealing wax

ceràmi·co -ca (**-ci -che**) adj ceramic || f ceramics

cerare (**céro**) tr to wax

Cèrbero m Cerberus

cerbiatto m fawn

cerbottana f blowgun, peashooter

cer·ca f (**-che**) search, quest; **in cerca di** in search of

cercare §197 (**cérco**) tr to seek, look for; to desire, yearn for; **cercare il pelo nell'uovo** to be a faultfinder, to nitpick || intr to try

cerca·tóre -trice adj seeking || mf seeker; mendicant || m prospector

cérchia f coterie; compass, limits (of a wall); circle (of friends)

cerchiare §287 (**cérchio**) tr to hoop (a barrel); to circle, encircle

cér·chio m (**-chi**) circle; hoop; loop; **fare il cerchio della morte** (aer) to loop the loop; **in cerchio in a circle** || m (**-chia** fpl) (archaic) circle

cerchióne m rim; tire (of metal)

cereale adj & m cereal

cerebrale adj cerebral

cère·o -a adj waxen; wax-colored; pale

cerfò·glio m (**-gli**) chervil

cerimònia f ceremony; **fare cerimonie** to stand on ceremony; to make a fuss

cerimoniale adj & m ceremonial

cerimonière m master of ceremonies (at court)

cerimonió·so -sa [s] adj ceremonious

cerino m wax match; taper

cernéc·chio m (**-chi**) tuft (of hair)

cernièra f hinge; clasp (of handbag); **a cerniera** hinged; **cerniera lampo** zipper

cèrnita f sorting, selection, grading

céro m church candle; **offrire un cero** to light a candle

ceróne m make-up (of actor)

ceròtto m adhesive tape; (fig) bore; **cerotto per i calli** corn plaster

certame m (poet) combat; competition, contest (of poets)

certézza f certitude, assurance, conviction, certainty

certificare §197 (**certìfico**) tr to certify, certificate

certificato m certificate

cèr·to -ta adj such, some; convinced; certain; real, positive || m certainty; **di certo** or **per certo** for certain || **certi** pron some || **certo** adv undoubtedly

certósa f Carthusian monastery, charterhouse

certosi·no m Carthusian monk; chartreuse (liquor); **da certosino** with great patience

certu·no -na adj (obs) some || **certuni** pron some

cerùle·o -a adj cerulean

cerume m ear wax

cervellétto m cerebellum

cervelli·no -na adj & mf scatterbrain

cervèllo m (**cervèlli & cervèlla** fpl) brain; head; mind; **dare al cervello** to go to one's head

cervellòti·co -ca adj (**-ci -che**) queer, extravagant

cervice f (anat) cervix; (poet) nape of the neck

cerviè·ro -ra adj lynx-like; || m lynx

cervi·no -na adj deer-like || **Cervino** m Matterhorn

cèrvo m deer; (ent) stag beetle; **cervo volante** kite

Cèsare m Caesar

cesàre·o -a adj Caesarean; (poet) courtly

cesellare (**cesèllo**) tr to chase, chisel; to carve, engrave; to polish (e.g., a poem)

cesella·tóre -trice mf chaser, engraver, chiseler

cesellatura f chasing, engraving; polished writing

cesèllo m burin, graver

cesóia f shears, metal shears; **cesoie** shears (for gardening)

cesoiatrice f shearing machine

cèspite m source (of income); (poet) tuft

céspo m tuft

cespù·glio m (**-gli**) bush, shrub, thicket

cèssa f—**senza cessa** without letup

cessare (**cèsso**) tr to stop, interrupt || intr to cease, stop; **cessare di + inf** to stop + ger

cessazione f cessation, discontinuance; **cessazione d'esercizio** going out of business

cessionà·rio m (**-ri**) assignee

cèsso m (vulg) privy, outhouse

césta f basket, hamper

cestinare tr to throw into the wastebasket; to reject (a book, article, etc.)

césto m basket; tuft; head (e.g., of lettuce)

cesura f caesura

cetàceo m cetacean

cèto m class; **ceto medio** middle class

cétra f lyre; cither; inspiration

cetriolino m gherkin

cetriòlo m cucumber; (fig) dolt

che adj what; which; what a, e.g., **che bella giornata!** what a beautiful day! || pron interr what || pron rel who; whom; that; which; (coll) in which || m—**essere un gran che** to be a big

shot, to be somebody || *adv* how,
e.g., **che bello!** how nice!; **non . . .
che** only, e.g., **non venne che Luigi**
only Luigi came; no one but, e.g.,
non restò che mio cugino no one but
my cousin stayed || *conj* that; (*after
comparatives*) than, as
ché *adv* (coll) why || *conj* (coll) be-
cause; (coll) so that
checché *pron* (lit) whatever, no matter
what
checchessìa *pron* (lit) anything, everything
chèla *f* claw
che·pì *m* (**-pì**) kepi
cherubino *m* cherub
chetare (**chéto**) *tr* to quiet; to placate ||
ref to quiet down, become quiet
chetichèlla *f*—**alla chetichella** surrepti-
tiously, stealthily
ché·to -ta *adj* quiet, still
chi *pron interr* who; whom || *pron rel*
who; whom; **chi . . . chi** some . . .
some
chiàcchiera *f* chatter, idle talk; gossip;
glibness; **fare quattro chiacchiere** to
have a chat
chiacchierare (**chiàcchiero**) *intr* to chat;
to gossip
chiacchierata *f* talk, chat; **fare una
chiacchierata** to visit
chiacchieri·no -na *adj* talkative, loquacious
chiacchierì·o *m* (**-i**) chattering, jabber-
ing (*of a crowd*)
chiacchieró·ne -na *adj* talkative, loqua-
cious || *mf* chatterbox
chiama *f* roll call; **fare la chiama** to call
the roll; **mancare alla chiama** to be
absent at the roll call
chiamare *tr* to call; to hail (*a cab*);
to invoke, call upon; **chiamare al
telefono** to call up; **esser chiamato a**
to have the vocation for || *ref* to be
named; **si chiama Giovanni** his name
is John
chiamata *f* call; (law) designation (*of
an heir*); (telp) ring; (theat) curtain
call; (typ) catchword
chiappa *f* (vulg) buttock; (slang) catch
(*e.g., of fish*)
chiarét·to -ta *adj & m* claret
chiarézza *f* clarity, clearness
chiarificare §197 (**chiarìfico**) *tr* to
clarify
chiarificazióne *f* clarification
chiariménto *m* explanation
chiarire §176 *tr* to clear up, explain;
to unravel || *intr* (ESSERE) to clear,
become clear || *ref* to make oneself
clear; to assure oneself
chia·ro -ra *adj* clear; bright; light
(*color*); honest; clear-cut; plain (*lan-
guage*); illustrious, famous || *m* light;
bright color; brightness; **chiaro di
luna** moonlight; **con questi chiari di
luna** in these troubled times; **mettere
in chiaro** to clarify, explain || **chiaro**
adv plainly; **chiaro e tondo** bluntly,
frankly
chiaróre *m* light, glimmer
chiaroveggènte *adj & mf* clairvoyant

chiaroveggènza *f* clairvoyance
chiassata *f* uproar, disturbance, racket;
noisy scene
chiasso *m* noise; uproar; alley; **fare
chiasso** to cause a sensation
chiassó·so -sa [s] *adj* noisy; gaudy
chiatta *f* barge; pontoon
chiavarda *f* bolt
chiave *f* key; wrench; (archit) keystone;
(mus) clef; **avere le chiavi di** to own;
chiave a rollino adjustable wrench;
chiave a tubo socket wrench; **chiave
di volta** keystone; **chiave inglese**
monkey wrench; **fuori chiave** off
key; **sotto chiave** under lock and key
chiavétta *f* key; cock; cotter pin
chiàvi·ca *f* (**-che**) sewer
chiavistèllo *m* bolt
chiazza *f* spot, blotch
chiazzare *tr* to spot, blotch; to mottle
chiazza·to -ta *adj* spotted, mottled
chic·ca *f* (**-che**) sweet, candy
chìcchera *f* cup
chicchessìa *pron indef* anyone, anybody
chicchirichì *m* cock-a-doodle-doo
chic·co *m* (**-chi**) grain, seed; bead (*of
rosary*); bean (*of coffee*); **chicco di
grandine** hailstone; **chicco d'uva**
grape
chièdere §124 *tr* to ask; to ask for; to
beg (*pardon*); to require; to ask (*for
damages or peace*); **chiedere a qlcu
di + inf** to ask s.o. to + *inf*; **chiedere
in prestito** to borrow; **chiedere qlco
a qlcu** to ask s.o. for s.th || *ref* to
wonder
chiéri·ca *f* (**-che**) tonsure; priesthood
chiéri·co *m* (**-ci**) clergyman; altar boy;
(archaic) clerk
chièsa *f* church
chiesuòla *f* small church; clique, set
(*e.g., of artists*); (naut) binnacle
chì·glia *f* (**-glie**) keel; **chiglia mobile**
(naut) centerboard
chilo *m* kilo, kilogram; **fare il chilo** to
take a siesta
chilociclo *m* kilocycle
chilogrammo *m* kilogram
chilohèrtz *m* kilohertz
chilometràg·gio *m* (**-gi**) distance in
kilometers
chilomètri·co -ca *adj* (**-ci -che**) kilo-
metric; interminable (*e.g., speech*)
chilòmetro *m* kilometer
chilo·watt *m* (**-watt**) kilowatt
chimèra *f* chimera; daydream, utopia
chimèri·co -ca *adj* (**-ci -che**) chimerical
chìmi·co -ca (**-ci -che**) *adj* chemical ||
m chemist || *f* chemistry
chimòno *m* kimono
china *f* slope, decline; India ink; cin-
chona
chinare *tr* to bend; to lower (*one's
eyes*); **chinare il capo** to nod assent;
chinare la fronte to yield, give in ||
ref to bend, stoop
china·to -ta *adj* bent, lowered; bitter;
with quinine, e.g., **vino chinato** wine
with quinine
chincàglie *fpl* notions, knicknacks, sundries

chincaglière *m* notions or knicknack dealer

chincaglierìa *f* knicknack; **chincaglierie** knicknacks, notions

chinina *f* quinine (*alkaloid*)

chinino *m* quinine (*salt of the alkaloid*)

chi·no -na *adj* bent, lowered || *f* see **china**

chiòc·cia *f* (-ce) brooding hen

chiocciare §128 (**chiòccio**) *intr* to cluck; to sit, brood; to crouch

chiocciata *f* brood

chiòc·cio -cia (-ci -ce) *adj* hoarse || *f* see **chioccia**

chiòcciola *f* snail; (anat) cochlea; (mach) nut

chioccolì·o *m* (-i) cackle (*of hen*); gurgle (*of water*)

chiodare (**chiòdo**) *tr* to nail

chioda·to -ta *adj* nailed shut; hobnailed

chiòdo *m* nail; spike; obsession; craze; (coll) debt; **chiodi** climbing irons; **chiodo a espansione** expansion bolt; **chiodo da cavallo** horseshoe nail; **chiodo di garofano** clove; **chiodo ribattino** rivet

chiòma *f* hair; mane; foliage; (astr) coma

chioma·to -ta *adj* hairy, long-haired; leafy

chiòsa *f* gloss

chiosare (**chiòso**) *tr* to gloss, comment on

chiò·sco *m* (-schi) kiosk, stand, newsstand; pavilion, bandstand

chiòstra *f* circular range (*of mountains*); (poet) enclosure; (poet) set (*of teeth*); (poet) zone, region

chiòstro *m* cloister

chiòt·to -ta *adj* quiet, still; **chiotto chiotto** still as a mouse

chiromante *mf* palmist

chiromanzìa *f* palmistry

chiropràtica *f* chiropractice

chirurgìa *f* surgery

chirùrgi·co -ca *adj* (-ci -che) surgical

chirur·go *m* (-ghi & -gi) surgeon

chissà *adv* maybe

chitarra *f* guitar; **chitarra hawaiana** ukulele

chitarri·sta *mf* (-sti -ste) guitar player

chiùdere §125 *tr* to shut, close; to lock; to turn off; to fasten; to block (*a road*); to fence in; to nail shut (*a box*); to strike (*a balance*); to conclude, wind up; **chiudere a chiave** to lock; **chiudere bottega** to go out of business; **chiudere il becco** (slang) to shut up || *intr* to shut, close; to lock || *ref* to shut, close; to lock; to withdraw; to cloud over

chiùnque *pron indef invar* anybody, anyone || *pron rel invar* whoever, whomever; anyone who, anyone whom

chiurlo *m* (orn) curlew

chiusa [s] *f* fence; lock (*of canal*); end, conclusion (*e.g., of letter*)

chiusino [s] *m* manhole

chiu·so -sa [s] *adj* shut, closed, locked; stuffy (*air*); high-bodiced (*dress*)

close (*vowel*) || *m* enclosure, corral; **close** || *f* see **chiusa**

chiusura [s] *f* closing, end; fastener; lock; **chiusura lampo** zipper, slide fastener

ci §5

ciabatta *f* slipper; old shoe

ciabat·tàio *m* (-tài) cobbler

ciabattare *intr* to shuffle along

ciabattino *m* cobbler, shoemaker

ciàc *f* (mov) clappers

cialda *f* wafer; thin waffle

cialdóne *m* cone (*for ice cream*)

cialtró·ne -na *mf* rogue, scoundrel; slovenly person

ciambèlla *f* doughnut; **ciambella di salvataggio** life saver

ciambellano *m* chamberlain

ciampicare §197 (**ciàmpico**) *intr* to stumble along

ciana *f* (slang) fishwife

cianamide *f* cyanamide

ciàn·cia *f* (-ce) chatter, prattle, idle gossip

cianciare §128 (**ciàncio**) *intr* to chatter, prattle

cianciafrùscola *f* trifle, bagatelle

cianfrusà·glia *f* (-glie) trifle, trinket; rubbish, trash, junk

cianìdri·co -ca *adj* (-ci -che) hydrocyanic

cianògeno *m* cyanogen

cianuro *m* cyanide

ciao *interj* (coll) hi!, hello!; (coll) goodbye!, so long!

ciarla *f* chatter, prattle, idle talk; gossip

ciarlare *intr* to chatter, prattle

ciarlatanata *f* charlatanism, quackery

ciarlataneria *f* charlatanism

ciarlatané·sco -sca *adj* (-schi -sche) charlatan

ciarlatano *m* charlatan, quack

ciarliè·ro -ra *adj* talkative, garrulous

ciarpame *m* rubbish, junk

ciaschedu·no -na *adj indef* each || *pron indef* each one, everyone

ciascu·no -na *adj indef* each || *pron indef* each one, everyone

cibare *tr* & *ref* to feed

cibà·rio -ria (-ri -rie) *adj* alimentary || **cibarie** *fpl* foodstuffs, victuals

cibo *m* food; meal; (fig) dish

cicala *f* cicada; grasshopper; locust; (fig) chatterbox; (naut) anchor ring

cicalare *intr* to prattle, babble; to chatter

cicalec·cio *m* (-ci) prattle, babble; chatter

cicatrice *f* scar

cicatrizzare [ddzz] *tr* to heal (*a wound*) || *intr* (ESSERE) & *ref* to heal, scar

cicatrizzazióne [ddzz] *f* closing, healing (*of a wound*)

cic·ca *f* (-che) butt (*of cigar or cigarette*); (slang) chewing gum

ciccare §197 *intr* to chew tobacco; (coll) to boil with anger

cicchettare (**cicchétto**) *tr* (slang) to prime (*a carburetor*); (slang) to dress down, reprimand || *intr* to tipple

cicchétto *m* nip (*of liquor*); (slang) dressing down

cìc·cia *f* (-ce) (joc) flesh; (joc) fat
cicció·ne -na *mf* fatty
ciceróne *m* guide ‖ **Cicerone** *m* Cicero
ciclàbile *adj* open to bicycles; bicycle, e.g., **pista ciclabile** bicycle trail
cìcli·co -ca *adj* (-ci -che) cyclic(al)
cicli·sta *mf* (-sti -ste) cyclist, bicyclist
ciclo *m* cycle; (coll) bicycle; **ciclo operativo** (econ) turnover
ciclomotóre *m* motorbike
ciclomotorì·sta *mf* (-sti -ste) driver of motorbike
ciclóne *m* cyclone
ciclòpe *m* cyclops
ciclòpi·co -ca *adj* (-ci -che) cyclopean, gigantic
ciclopista *f* bicycle trail
ciclostilare *tr* to mimeograph
ciclostile or **ciclostìlo** *m* mimeograph
ciclotróne *m* cyclotron
cicógna *f* stork
cicòria *f* chicory; endive
cicuta *f* hemlock
ciè·co -ca (-chi -che) *adj* blind; **alla cieca** blindly ‖ *mf* blind person ‖ *m* blind man; **i ciechi** the blind
cièlo *m* sky; heaven; weather, climate; roof (e.g., of wagon); **a ciel sereno** in the open air; **cielo a pecorelle** mackerel or fleecy sky; **dal cielo** from above; **non stare né in cielo né in terra** to be utterly absurd; **per amor del cielo** for heaven's sake; **portare al cielo** to praise to the skies; **santo cielo!** good heavens!; **volesse il cielo che . . . !** would that . . . !
cifra *f* number, figure; Arabic numeral; sum, total; digit; initial, monogram; cipher, code; **cifra d'affari** amount of business, turnover; **cifra tonda** round number
cifrare *tr* to cipher, code; to embroider (a monogram)
cifrà·rio *m* (-ri) code, cipher
ci·glio *m* (-glia *fpl*) eyelash; eyebrow; **a ciglio asciutto** with dry eyes; **ciglia** (zool) cilia; **senza batter ciglio** without batting an eye ‖ *m* (-gli) (fig) edge, brow
ciglióne *m* bank, embankment
cigno *m* swan; cob
cigolante *adj* creaky, squeaky
cigolare (**cìgolo**) *intr* to squeak, creak
cigolì·o *m* (-ìi) squeak, creak
Cile, il Chile
cilécca *f*—**fare cilecca** to misfire
cileccare §197 (**cilécco**) *intr* to goof, blunder; to fail
cilè·no -na *adj* & *mf* Chilean
cilè·stro -stra *adj* (poet) azure, blue
cilì·cio *m* (-ci) sackcloth
ciliè·gia *f* (-gie & -ge) cherry
ciliè.gio *m* (-gi) cherry tree
cilindrare *tr* to calender (e.g., paper); to roll (a road)
cilindrata *f* (aut) cylinder capacity, piston displacement
cilìndri·co -ca *adj* (-ci -che) cylindric(al)
cilindro *m* cylinder; top hat; roll, roller
cima *f* top, summit; tip (e.g., of a pole); peak (of mountain); edge, end; rope, cable; head (e.g., of let-

tuce); (coll) genius; **da cima a fondo** from top to bottom
cimare *tr* to cut the tip off; to shear; (agr) to prune
cimasa *f* (archit) coping
cimbalo *m* gong; (obs) cymbal; **in cimbali** tipsy; in a tizzy
cimè·lio *m* (-li) relic, souvenir, memento
cimentare (**ciménto**) *tr* to risk (e.g., one's life); to provoke; (archaic) to assay ‖ *ref* to expose oneself; to venture
ciménto *m* risk, danger; (archaic) assay
cìmice *f* bug; bedbug; (coll) thumbtack
cimièro *m* crest; (poet) helmet
ciminièra *f* chimney (of factory); smokestack (of locomotive); funnel (of steamship)
cimitèro *m* cemetery, graveyard; (fig) ghosttown
cimósa [s] or **cimóssa** *f* selvage; blackboard eraser
cimurro *m* distemper; (joc) cold
Cina, la China
cinabro *m* cinnabar; crimson; red ink
cìn·cia *f* (-ce) titmouse
cinciallégra *f* great titmouse
cincilla *f* chinchilla
cincischiare §287 *tr* to shred; to wrinkle, crease; to waste (time); to mumble (words) ‖ *intr* to wrinkle, crease
cine *m* (coll) cinema
cineamatóre *m* amateur movie maker
cine·asta *m* (-sti) motion-picture producer; movie fan; movie actor ‖ *f* movie actress
cinecàmera *f* movie camera
cinedilettante *mf* amateur movie maker
cinegiornale *m* newsreel
cinelàndia *f* movieland
cìne·ma *m* (-ma) movies; movie house
cinematografare (**cinematògrafo**) *tr* to film, shoot
cinematografìa *f* cinema, motion pictures, movie industry
cinematogràfi·co -ca *adj* (-ci -che) movie, motion-picture; movie-like
cinematògrafo *m* motion picture; movie theater; (fig) hubbub; (fig) funny sight
cineparchég·gio *m* (-gi) drive-in movie
cinepar·co *m* (-chi) drive-in movie
cineprésa [s] *f* movie camera
cinère·o -a *adj* ashen
cinescò·pio *m* (-pi) kinescope, TV tube
cinése [s] *adj* & *mf* Chinese
cineteatro *m* movie house; **cineteatro all'aperto** outdoor movie
cinetè·ca *f* (-che) film library
cinèti·co -ca (-ci -che) *adj* kinetic ‖ *f* kinetics
cingallégra *f* var of **cinciallegra**
cìngere §126 *tr* to surround; to gird (e.g., the head); to gird (e.g., the sword); **cingere cavaliere** to dub a knight; **cingere d'assedio** to besiege
cìnghia *f* belt, strap; **tirare la cinghia** to tighten one's belt
cinghiale *m* wild boar
cinghiata *f* lash
cingola·to -ta *adj* track-driven, caterpillar

cìngolo *m* endless metal belt, track; girdle, belt (*of a priest*)

cinguettare (cinguétto) *intr* to chirp, twitter; to babble

cinguettì·o *m* (-i) chirp, twitter; (fig) babble

cìni·co -ca (-ci -che) *adj* cynical || *m* cynic

ciniglia *f* chenille

cinismo *m* cynicism

cinòfilo *m* dog lover

cinquanta *adj, m & pron* fifty

cinquantenà·rio -ria (-ri -rie) *adj* fifty-year-old; occurring every fifty years || *m* fiftieth anniversary

cinquantènne *adj* fifty-year-old || *mf* fifty-year-old person

cinquantèn·nio *m* (-ni) period of fifty years, half century

cinquantèsi·mo -ma *adj, m & pron* fiftieth

cinquantina *f* about fifty; sulla cinquantina about fifty years old

cìnque *adj & pron* five; le cinque five o'clock || *m* five; fifth (*in dates*)

cinquecenté·sco -sca *adj* (-schi -sche) sixteenth-century

cinquecènto *adj, m & pron* five hundred || *f* small car || il Cinquecento the sixteenth century

cinquina *f* set of five; five numbers (*drawn at Italian lotto*); (mil) pay

cinta *f* fence, wall; circuit, enclosure; circumference (*of a city*)

cintare *tr* to surround; to fence in; to hold (*in wrestling*)

cin·to -ta *adj* surrounded, girded || *m* belt; girdle; cinto erniario truss || *f* see cinta

cìntola *f* waist; belt; con le mani alla cintola idling, loafing

cintura *f* belt; waist; waistband; lock (*in wrestling*); cintura di salvataggio life preserver; cintura di sicurezza safety belt

cinturare *tr* to surround

cinturino *m* strap (*of watch or shoes*); hem (*e.g., of cuffs*)

cinturóne *m* belt; Sam Browne belt

ciò *pron* this; that; a ciò for that purpose; a ciò che so that; ciò nondimeno or ciò nonostante though, nevertheless; con tutto ciò in spite of everything; per ciò therefore

ciòc·ca *f* (-c̄he) lock (*of hair*); cluster (*e.g., of cherries*)

ciòc·co *m* (-chi) log; dormire come un ciocco to sleep like a log

cioccolata *adj invar* chocolate || *f* chocolate (*beverage*)

cioccolatino *m* chocolate candy

cioccolato *m* chocolate; cioccolato al latte milk chocolate

cioè *adv* that is to say, namely; to wit; rather

ciondolare (cióndolo) *tr* to dangle || *intr* to dawdle; to stroll, saunter

cióndolo *m* pendant, charm

ciondolóne *m* idler || *adv* dangling

ciòtola *f* bowl

ciòttolo *m* pebble, small stone; cobblestone

ciottoló·so -sa [s] *adj* pebbly

cip *m* (cip) chip (*in gambling*)

cipì·glio *m* (-gli) frown

cipólla *f* onion; bulb (*e.g., of a lamp*); nozzle (*of sprinkling can*)

cippo *m* column; bench mark

ciprèsso *m* cypress

cìpria *f* face powder; cipria compatta compact

cipriò·ta *adj & mf* (-ti -te) Cypriot

Cipro *m* Cyprus

circa *adv* about, nearly || *prep* concerning, regarding, as to

cir·co *m* (-chi) circus; circo equestre circus; circo glaciale cirque; circo lunare walled plain

circolante *adj* circulating; lending (*library*) || *m* available cash (*of a corporation*)

circolare *adj* circular; cashier's (*check*) || *f* circular (*letter*); (rr) beltline || *v* (cìrcolo) *intr* to circulate

circolazióne *f* circulation; traffic; currency; circolazione sanguigna bloodstream; circulation of blood

cìrcolo *m* circle; circulation (*of blood*); reception (*e.g., at court*); club, set, group

circoncìdere §145 *tr* to circumcise

circoncisióne *f* circumcision

circonci·so -sa *adj* circumcised

circondare (circóndo) *tr* to surround, encircle; to overwhelm (*e.g., with kindness*) || *ref* to surround oneself; to be surrounded

circondà·rio *m* (-ri) district; surrounding territory

circonduzióne *f* rotation (*e.g., of the body in calisthenics*)

circonferènza *f* circumference

circonflès·so -sa *adj* circumflex

circonlocuzióne *f* circumlocution

circonvallazióne *f* city-line road; (rr) beltline

circonvenìre §282 *tr* to circumvent; to outwit

circonvenzióne *f* circumvention

circonvici·no -na *adj* neighboring, nearby

circoscrìt·to -ta *adj* circumscribed

circoscrìvere §250 *tr* to circumscribe

circoscrizióne *f* district; circuit

circospèt·to -ta *adj* circumspect, cautious

circospezióne *f* circumspection

circostante *adj* neighboring, surrounding, nearby || *m* circostanti *mpl* neighbors; bystanders, onlookers

circostanza *f* circumstance

circostanziale *adj* circumstantial

circostanziare §287 *tr* to describe in detail; to circumstanciate

circostanzia·to -ta *adj* detailed, circumstantial

circuire §176 *tr* to circumvent

circùito *m* circuit; race (*of automobiles or bicycles*); circuito stampato (rad, telv) printed circuit

circumnavigare §209 (circumnàvigo) *tr* to circumnavigate

circumnavigazióne *f* circumnavigation

cirìlli·co -ca *adj* (-ci -che) Cyrillic

Ciro *m* Cyrus
cirro *m* cirrus
cirrò·si *f* (**-si**) cirrhosis
cispa *f* gum (*on edge of eyelids*)
cisposità [s] *f* gum; gumminess
cispó·so -sa [s] *adj* gummy
ciste *f* cyst
cistèrna *f* cistern; tank
cisti *f* cyst
cistifèllea *f* gall bladder
citante *mf* (law) plaintiff
citare *tr* to cite, quote; to mention; (law) to summon, subpoena
citazióne *f* citation, quotation; mention; (law) summons, subpoena; (mil) commendation
citillo *m* (zool) gopher
citòfono *m* intercom
citostàti·co -ca *adj* (**-ci -che**) (biochem) cancer-inhibiting
citrato *m* citrate
cìtri·co -ca *adj* (**-ci -che**) citric
citrul·lo -la *adj* simple, foolish || *mf* simpleton, fool
cit·tà *f* (**-tà**) city, town || **Città del Capo** Cape Town; **Città del Messico** Mexico City; **Città del Vaticano** Vatican City; **città fungo** boom town
cittadèlla *f* citadel
cittadinanza *f* citizenship
cittadi·no -na *adj* city, town, civic || *mf* citizen; city dweller, urbanite || *m* townsman
ciù·co -ca *m* (**-chi**) (coll) donkey, ass
ciuffo *m* lock, forelock; tuft; (bot) tassel
ciuffolòtto *m* (orn) bullfinch
ciurlare *intr*—**ciurlare nel manico** to play fast and loose
ciurma *f* crew, gang, mob
ciurmare *tr* (archaic) to charm; (archaic) to trick, inveigle
ciurmatóre *m* swindler, charlatan
civètta *f* barn owl, little owl; unmarked police car; ship used as decoy; (fig) coquette, flirt
civettare (**civétto**) *intr* to flirt
civetterìa *f* coquettishness, coquetry
civettuò·lo la *adj* coquettish; attractive
cìvi·co -ca *adj* (**-ci -che**) civic; town, city
civile *adj* civil; civilian || *mf* civilian
civili·sta *mf* (**-sti -ste**) attorney, solicitor
civilizzare [ddzz] *tr* to civilize || *ref* to become civilized
civilizzazióne [ddzz] *f* civilizing (*e.g., of barbarians*); civilization
civil·tà *f* (**-tà**) civilization; civility
civismo *m* good citizenship
clac·son *m* (**-son**) horn (*of a car*)
claire *f* (**claire**) grating (*in front of a store window*)
clamóre *m* clamor, uproar
clamoró·so -sa [s] *adj* noisy; clamorous
clan *m* (**clan**) clan; clique
clandesti·no -na *adj* clandestine
clangóre *m* clangor, clang
clarinétti·sta *mf* (**-sti -ste**) clarinet player
clarinétto *m* clarinet
clarino *m* clarion
classe *f* class

classicheggiante *adj* classicistic
classicismo *m* classicism
classici·sta *mf* (**-sti -ste**) classicist
classici·tà *f* (**-tà**) classical spirit; classical antiquity
clàssi·co -ca (**-ci -che**) *adj* classic(al) || *m* classic
classifi·ca *f* (**-che**) rank, rating (*in competitive testing*); classification; (sports) rating
classificare §197 (**classìfico**) *tr* to classify; to rate, rank || *ref* to score
classificazióne *f* classification
claudicante *adj* lame, limping
claudicare §197 (**clàudico**) *intr* to limp
clauné·sco -sca *adj* (**-schi -sche**) clownish
clàusola *f* provision, proviso; clause; close, conclusion (*e.g., of a speech*); **clausola rossa** instructions for payment (*in bank-credit documents*); **clausola verde** shipping instructions (*in bank-credit documents*)
clausura *f* (eccl) seclusion; (fig) secluded place
clava *f* club, bludgeon
clavicémbalo *m* harpsichord
clavìcola *f* clavicle, collarbone
clemàtide *f* clematis
clemènte *adj* clement, indulgent; mild (*climate*)
clemènza *f* clemency; mildness
cleptòmane *adj & mf* kleptomaniac
clericale *adj* clerical || *m* clericalist
clericalismo *m* clericalism
clèro *m* clergy
clessidra *f* water clock; sandglass
clicchettì·o *m* (**-ì**) clicking, click-clack (*e.g., of a typewriter*)
cli·ché *m* (**-ché**) cliché; stereotype (*plate*)
cliènte *m* client, customer, patron
clientèla *f* clientele, customers; practice (*of a professional man*)
cli·ma *m* (**-mi**) climate
climatèri·co -ca *adj* (**-ci -che**) climacteric; crucial
climatè·rio *m* (**-ri**) climacteric; crucial period
climàti·co -ca *adj* (**-ci -che**) climatic
climatizzazióne [ddzz] *f* air conditioning
clìni·co -ca (**-ci -che**) *adj* clinic || *m* clinician; highly skilled physician || *f* clinic; private hospital
cli·sma *m* (**-smi**) enema
clistère *m* enema; **clistere a pera** fountain syringe
cloa·ca *f* (**-che**) sewer
cloche *f* (**cloche**) woman's wide-brimmed hat; (aer) stick; (aut) floor gearshift
clorare (**clòro**) *tr* to chlorinate
clorato *m* chlorate
clorìdri·co -ca *adj* (**-ci -che**) hydrochloric
clòro *m* chlorine
clorofilla *f* chlorophyll
clorofòr·mio *m* (**-mi**) chloroform
cloroformizzare [ddzz] *tr* to chloroform
cloruro *m* chloride

coabitare (coàbito) *intr* to live together; to cohabit

coabitazióne *f* sharing (*of an apartment*)

coaccusa·to -ta *adj* jointly accused ‖ *m* codefendant

coacèrvo *m* accumulation (*e.g., of interest*)

coadiutóre *m* coadjutor

coadiuvante *adj* helping ‖ *m* helper

coadiuvare (coàdiuvo) *tr* to assist, advise

coagulare (coàgulo) *tr & ref* to coagulate, clot

coagulazióne *f* coagulation, clotting

coàgulo *m* clot

coalescènza *f* coalescence

coalizióne *f* coalition

coalizzare [ddzz] *tr & ref* to unite, rally

coartare *tr* to coerce, force

coartazióne *f* coercion, forcing

coatti·vo -va *adj* forceful, compelling

coat·to -ta *adj* coercive

coautóre *m* coauthor

coazióne *f* coercion

cobalto *m* cobalt

cocaina *f* cocaine

cocainòmane *mf* cocaine addict

coc·ca *f* (-che) notch (*of arrow*); corner, edge (*e.g., of a handkerchief*); three-mast galley

coccarda *f* cockade

cocchière *m* coachman, cab driver

còc·chio *m* (-chi) coach; chariot

cocchiume *m* bung

còc·cia *f* (-ce) sword guard; (coll) head, noggin

còccige *m* coccyx

coccinèlla *f* ladybug

coccinìglia *f* cochineal

còc·cio *m* (-ci) earthenware; broken piece of pottery

cocciutàggine *m* stubbornness

cocciu·to -ta *adj* stubborn

còc·co *m* (-chi) coconut (*tree and nut*); (bact) coccus; (coll) egg; (coll) darling, favorite

cocco·dè *m* (-dè) cackle

coccodrillo *m* crocodile

còccola *f* berry (*of cypress*); darling girl

coccolare (còccolo) *tr* to fondle, cuddle ‖ *ref* to nestle, cuddle up; to bask

còcco·lo -la *adj* (coll) nice, darling ‖ *m* darling boy ‖ *f see* **coccola**

coccolóne *or* **coccolóni** *adv* squatting

cocènte *adj* burning

cocktail *m* (cocktail) cocktail; cocktail party

còclea *f* dredge; (anat) cochlea

cocómero *m* watermelon; (coll) simpleton

cocorita *f* parakeet

cocuzza *f* (coll) pumpkin; (coll) head, noggin

cocùzzolo *m* crown (*of hat*); peak (*of mountain*)

códa *f* tail; train (*of skirt*); pigtail (*of hair*); **coda di paglia** (coll) uneasy conscience; **con la coda dell'occhio** out of the corner of the eye; **con la coda tra le gambe** with its tail between its legs; (fig) crestfallen; **di**
coda last; **fare la coda** to stand in line; **in coda** in a row; at the tail end

codardìa *f* (lit) cowardice

codar·do -da *adj* cowardly ‖ *mf* coward

codazzo *m* (pej) trail (*of people*)

codeina *f* codein

codé·sto -sta §7 *adj* ‖ §8 *pron*

còdice *m* code; codex; **codice della strada** traffic laws; **codice di avviamento postale** zip code

codicillo *m* codicil

codificare §197 (codìfico) *tr* to codify

codi·no -na *adj* reactionary; conformist ‖ *m* pigtail (*of a man*); (fig) reactionary; conformist ‖ *f* small tail

códolo *m* tang, shank (*e.g., of knife*); handle (*of spoon or knife*); head (*of violin*)

coeducazióne *f* coeducation

coefficiènte *m* coefficient

coerciti·vo -va *adj* coercive

coercizióne *f* coercion

coerède *mf* coheir

coerènte *adj* coherent; consistent

coerènza *f* coherence; consistency

coesióne *f* cohesion

coesistènza *f* coexistence

coesìstere §114 *intr* to coexist

coesi·vo -va *adj* cohesive

coetàne·o -a *adj & m* contemporary

coè·vo -va *adj* contemporaneous, coeval

cofanétto *m* small chest, small coffer

còfano *m* chest, coffer; box, case (*for ammunition*); (aut) hood

còffa *f* masthead, crow's-nest

cofirmatà·rio -ria *adj & mf* (-ri -rie) cosigner

cogitabón·do -da *adj* (poet & joc) thoughtful, meditative

cogitare (cògito) *tr & intr* (poet & joc) to cogitate

cògli §4

cògliere §127 *tr* to gather; to hit (*the target*); to pluck (*flowers*); to grab, seize; (fig) to guess; **cogliere in flagrante** to catch in the act; **cogliere la palla al balzo** to seize time by the forelock; **cogliere nel giusto** to hit the nail on the head; **cogliere qlcu alla sprovvista** to catch s.o. napping; **cogliere sul fatto** to catch in the act

cogliòne *m* (vulg) testicle; (vulg) simpleton, fool

coglionerìa *f* (vulg) great stupidity

cognata *f* sister-in-law

cognato *m* brother-in-law

cògni·to -ta *adj* (poet & law) wellknown

cognizióne *f* cognition, knowledge

cognóme *m* surname, family name

coguaro *m* cougar

cói §4

coibènte *adj* nonconducting ‖ *m* nonconductor

coincidènza *f* coincidence; harmony, identity; transfer (*from one streetcar or bus to another*); (rr) connection

coincìdere §145 *intr* to coincide

coinquilino *m* fellow tenant

cointeressare (cointerèsso) *tr* to give a share (*of profit*) to

cointeressa·to -ta *adj* jointly interested || *mf* party having a joint interest

cointeressènza *f* interest, share

coinvòlgere §289 *tr* to involve

còito *m* coitus, intercourse

cól §4

colà *adv* over there

colabròdo *m* colander, strainer

colàg·gio *m* (-gi) loss, leak

colapa·sta *m* (-sta) colander

colare (cólo) *tr* to filter, strain; to sift (*wheat*); to cast (*metals*); **colare a picco** to sink || *intr* to leak, drip; to flow (*said of blood*); **colare a picco** to sink

colata *f* casting (*of metal*); stream of lava; slide (*of snow or rocks*)

colafic·cio *m* (-ci) drip, dripping

cola·tói·o *m* (-tói) colander, strainer

colazióne *f* breakfast; lunch; **colazione al sacco** picnic; **prima colazione** breakfast; **seconda colazione** lunch

colbac·co *m* (-chi) busby

colèi §8 *pron dem*

colèn·do -da *adj* (archaic) honorable

colè·ra *m* (-ra) cholera

colesterina *f* cholesterol

coli·brì *m* (-brì) hummingbird

còli·co -ca *adj & f* (-ci -che) colic

colino *m* strainer

cólla §4

còlla *f* glue; paste; **colla di pesce** isinglass

collaborare (collàboro) *intr* to collaborate; to contribute (*to newspaper or magazine*)

collaboratóre *m* collaborator; contributor (*to newspaper or magazine*)

collaborazióne *f* collaboration

collaborazioni·sta *mf* (-sti -ste) collaborationist

collana *f* necklace; series, collection (*of literary works*)

collante *adj & m* adhesive

collare *m* collar || *v* (còllo) *tr* to lift or lower (*with a rope*)

collasso *m* collapse

collaterale *adj & m* collateral

collaudare (collàudo) *tr* to test; to approve; to pass

collauda·tóre -trice *mf* tester

collàudo *m* test

collazionare (collazióno) *tr* to collate

cólle §4

còlle *m* hill; low peak; mountain pass

collè·ga *mf* (-ghi -ghe) colleague, associate

collegaménto *m* connection, telephone connection; contact; (mil) liaison

collegare §209 (collégo) *tr* to join, connect || *intr* to agree, be in harmony || *ref* to become allied; to make contact, make connection (*e.g., by phone*)

collegiale *adj* collegiate || *mf* boarding-school student

collegiata *f* collegiate church

collè·gio *m* (-gi) college (*e.g., of surgeons*); boarding school, academy

còllera *f* anger, wrath; **montare in collera** to become angry

collèri·co -ca *adj* (-ci -che) hot-tempered, choleric

collètta *f* collection; collect (*in church*)

collettivismo *m* collectivism

collettivi·tà *f* (-tà) collectivity, community

colletti·vo -va *adj* collective || *m* party worker (*of leftist party*)

collétto *m* collar; flank (*of a tooth*)

collet·tóre -trice *adj* connecting; collecting (*pipe*) || *m* collector; tax collector; manifold; (elec) commutator (*of D.C. device*); (elec) collector (*of A.C. device*); **collettore d'ammissione** intake manifold; **collettore di scarico** exhaust manifold

collettoria *f* tax office; small post office

collezionare (collezióno) *tr* to collect (*e.g., stamps*)

collezióne *f* collection; collection, series (*of literary works*)

collezioni·sta *mf* (-sti -ste) collector

collìdere §135 *intr* to collide

collimare *tr* to point (*a telescope*) || *intr* to coincide, match; to dovetail

collina *f* hill; **in collina** in the hill country

collinó·so -sa [*s*] *adj* hilly

colli·rio *m* (-ri) eyewash

collisióne *f* collision; (fig) conflict: **entrare in collisione** to collide

cóllo §4

còllo *m* neck; piece (*of baggage*); package, parcel; **al collo** in a sling; (fig) downhill; **collo del piede** instep; **collo d'oca** crankshaft; **in collo** in one's arms (*said of a baby*)

collocaménto *m* placement, employment; **collocamento a riposo** retirement; **collocamento in aspettativa** leave of absence without pay; **collocamento in malattia** sick leave

collocare §197 (còlloco) *tr* to place; to find employment for; to sell; **collocare a riposo** to retire; **collocare in aspettativa** to give a leave of absence without pay; **collocare in malattia** to grant sick leave to

collocazióne *f* location (*of a book in a library*); catalogue card

colloidale *adj* colloidal

collòide *m* colloid

colloquiale *adj* colloquial

collò·quio *m* (-qui) talk, conference; colloquy; colloquium, symposium

collosò·so [*s*] *adj* gluey, sticky

collotòrto *m* (collitòrti) bigot, hypocrite

collòttola *f* nape or scruff of the neck

collùdere §105 *intr* to be in collusion

collusióne *f* collusion

collutó·rio *m* (-ri) mouthwash

colluttare *intr* to scuffle, fight

colluttazióne *f* scuffle, fight

cólma *f* high-water level (*during high tide*)

colmare (cólmo) *tr* to fill, fill up; to fill in (*with dirt*); to overwhelm; **colmare una lacuna** to bridge a gap

colmata *f* silting; reclaimed land; sand bank

cól·mo -ma *adj* full, filled up || *m* top, peak, summit; (archit) ridgepole; (fig) acme; **al colmo di** at the height of; **è il colmo** that's the limit ‖ *f* see **colma**

colofóne *m* colophon

colofònia *f* rosin

colombàia *f* dovecot

colombèlla *f* ingenue; **a colombella** vertically

colóm·bo -ba *mf* pigeon, dove ‖ **Colombo** *m* Columbus

colònia *f* colony; cologne; settlement; summer camp; **colonia penale** penal colony; penitentiary ‖ **Colonia** *f* Cologne

coloniale *adj* colonial ‖ *m* colonial; colonist; **coloniali** imported foods

colòni·co -ca *adj* (-ci -che) farm (*e.g., house*)

colonizzare [ddzz] *tr* to colonize; to settle

colonizzazióne [ddzz] *f* colonization

colonna *f* column; row; **colonna sonora** sound track; **Colonne d'Ercole** Pillars of Hercules

colonnato *m* colonnade

colonnèllo *m* colonel

colonnétta *f* small column; gasoline pump

colò·no -na *mf* sharecropper; colonist; settler; (poet) farmer

colorante *adj* coloring ‖ *m* dye; stain

colorare (colóro) *tr* & *ref* to color; to stain

colora·to -ta *adj* colored; stained (*glass*)

colorazióne *f* coloring

colóre *m* color; paint; suit (*of cards*); flush (*at poker*); shade; character (*of a deal*); **di colore** colored (*man*); **farne di tutti i colori** to be up to all kinds of devilry; **farsi di tutti i colori** to change countenance

colorifi·cio *m* (-ci) paint factory; dye factory

colorire §176 *tr* to color

colori·to -ta *adj* colored, flushed; expressive ‖ *m* color, complexion; (fig) expression

coloritura *f* coloring; characteristic; political complexion

colóro §8

colossale *adj* colossal

Colossèo *m* Coliseum

colòsso *m* colossus

cólpa *f* fault; sin; guilt; (law) injury; **avere la colpa** to be guilty; to be wrong; **essere in colpa** to be guilty

colpévole *adj* guilty ‖ *mf* guilty person, culp.it

colpevoli·sta *mf* (-sti -ste) person who prejudges s.o. guilty

colpire §176 *tr* to hit, strike; to harm; to impress; **colpire nel segno** to hit the mark

cólpo *m* hit, blow; strike; tip, rap; knock; shot; round (*of gun*); cut, slash (*of knife*); thrust (*e.g., of spear*); lash (*of animal's tail*); toot (*of car's horn*); **andare a colpo sicuro** to know where to hit; **colpo apoplettico** stroke; **colpo da maestro** master stroke; **colpo d'aria** draft; **colpo d'ariete** water hammer; **colpo di fortuna** stroke of luck; **colpo di fulmine** love at first sight; **co:po di**

grazia coup de grâce; **colpo di mano** surprise attack; **colpo di scena** dramatic turn of events; **colpo di sole** sunstroke; **colpo di spugna** wiping the slate clean; **colpo di stato** coup d'état; **colpo di telefono** telephone call; **colpo di testa** sudden decision, inconsiderate action; **colpo di vento** gust of wind; **colpo d'occhio** view; glance, look; **di colpo** at once; **fallire il colpo** to miss the mark; **fare colpo** to make a hit; **sul colpo** then and there; **tutto in un colpo** all at once

colpó·so -sa [s] *adj* unpremeditated; involuntary (*e.g., manslaughter*)

coltèlla *f* butcher knife; (elec) knife switch

coltellàc·cio *m* (-ci) hunting knife; butcher knife; (naut) studding sail

coltellata *f* stab, gash, slash; **fare a coltellate** to fight with knives

coltelleria *f* cutlery

coltelli·nàio *m* (-nài) cutler

coltèllo *m* knife; **a coltello** edgewise (*said of bricks*); **avere il coltello per il manico** to have the upper hand; **coltello a serramanico** switchblade knife; pocketknife

coltivare *tr* to cultivate

coltiva·to -ta *adj* cultivated

coltivatóre *m* farmer

coltivazióne *f* cultivation

cól·to -ta *adj* cultivated; learned (*word*) ‖ *m* garden; (archaic) worship

cóltre *f* blanket; comforter; (fig) pall; **coltri** bedclothes

coltróne *m* quilt

coltura *f* cultivation; crop; culture (*e.g., of silkworms, bacteria*)

colubrina *f* culverin

colùi §8 *pron dem*

comandaménto *m* commandment

comandante *m* commanding officer; commandant; (nav) captain; **comandante del porto** harbor master; **comandante in seconda** (naut) first mate

comandare *tr* to command, order; to direct (*employees*); to register (*a letter*); (mach) to regulate; (mach) to control; (poet) to overlook, command the view of (*e.g., a valley*); **comandare a bacchetta** to command in a dictatorial manner ‖ *intr* to command; **comandi!** (mil) at your orders!

comando *m* command, order

comare *f* godmother; (coll) friend, neighbor; (coll) gossip

combaciare §128 *tr* (archaic) to gather ‖ *intr* to fit closely together; to tally, dovetail; to coincide

combattènte *adj* fighting ‖ *m* combatant

combàttere *tr* & *intr* to combat ‖ *ref* to fight one another

combattiménto *m* combat; fight; battle; **fuori combattimento** knockout, K.O.; **fuori combattimento tecnico** technical knockout, T.K.O.; **mettere fuori combattimento** to knock out; (fig) to weaken

combatti·vo -va *adj* pugnacious, combative

combattu·to -ta *adj* heated (*discussion*); overcome (*by doubt*); torn (*between two opposing feelings*)

combinare *tr* to combine; to match (*e.g., colors*); to organize ‖ *intr* to agree; **combinare a** to succeed in ‖ *ref* to agree; to chance, happen; to combine

combinazióne *f* combination; chance; coverall (*for mechanics or flyers*)

combriccola *f* gang

combustibile *adj* combustible ‖ *m* fuel, combustible

combustióne *f* combustion; (poet) upheaval

combutta *f* gang, band; **essere in combutta** to be in cahoots

cóme *m* manner, way; **il come e il perché** the why and the wherefore ‖ *adv* as; like; as for; how; **come mai?** why?; **e come!** and how!; **ma come?** what?, how is it? ‖ *conj* as; as soon as; while; how; because; since; **come se** as if

comecché *conj* (lit) although; (poet) wherever

comedóne *m* blackhead

cométa *f* comet

comici·tà *f* (-tà) comicalness

còmi·co -ca (-ci -che) *adj* comic(al) ‖ *m* comic; author of comedies; comic actor

comignolo *m* chimney pot; ridge (*of roof*)

cominciare §128 *tr & intr* to begin, start, commence

comitato *m* committee

comitiva *f* group, party; (poet) retinue

comi·zio *m* (-zi) (pol) meeting, rally; (hist) comitia

còm·ma *m* (-mi) paragraph, article (*of law or decree*)

commèdia *f* comedy; play, drama; (fig) farce; **commedia di carattere** comedy of character; **commedia d'intreccio** comedy of intrigue; **far la commedia** to pretend, feign; **finire in commedia** to end ludicrously; **finire la commedia** to stop faking

commediante *mf* actor; comedian (*amusing person*); (fig) hypocrite

commediògra·fo -fa *mf* playwright, comedian

commemorare (**commèmoro**) *tr* to commemorate

commemorati·vo -va *adj* commemorative, memorial

commemorazióne *f* commemoration

commènda *f* commandership (*of an order*); (eccl) commendam

commendàbile *adj* commendable

commendare (**commèndo**) *tr* (lit) to commend, praise; (obs) to entrust

commendati·zio -zia (-zi -zie) *adj* introductory ‖ *f* letter of introduction; recommendation

commendatóre *m* commander (*of an order*)

commendévole *adj* commendable

commensale *mf* guest; table companion

commensurare (**commènsuro & commensuro**) *tr* to compare; to proportion, prorate

commentare (**comménto**) *tr* to comment, comment on

commentà·rio *m* (-ri) commentary; diary, journal

commenta·tóre -trice *mf* commentator

comménto *m* comment; **fare commenti** to criticize; **non far commenti!** don't waste your time talking!

commerciàbile *adj* marketable

commerciale *adj* commercial; common, ordinary

commerciali·sta *mj* (-sti -ste) business-administration major; attorney specializing in commercial law

commerciante *mf* merchant, dealer

commerciare §128 (**commèrcio**) *tr* to deal in; to buy and sell ‖ *intr* to deal

commèr·cio *m* (-ci) commerce, trade; illegal traffic; (poet) intercourse; **commercio all'ingrosso** wholesale (trade); **commercio al minuto** retail (trade); **fuori commercio** not for sale; **in commercio** for sale

commés·so -sa *adj* committed ‖ *mf* clerk (*in a store*) ‖ *m* salesman; clerk (*in a court*); janitor (*in a school*); **commesso viaggiatore** traveling salesman ‖ *f* saleslady; order (*of merchandise*)

commestibile *adj* edible ‖ **commestibili** *mpl* staples, groceries; foodstuffs

commèttere §198 *tr* to join, connect; to commit; to charge, commission; to peg; (poet) to entrust ‖ *intr* to join, fit

commettitura *f* joint, seam

commiato *m* leave; **dare commiato a** to dismiss; **prender commiato** to take one's leave

commilitóne *m* comrade, comrade in arms

comminare *tr* (law) to determine, fix (*a penalty*)

comminatò·rio -ria *adj* threatening

commiserare (**commìsero**) *tr* to pity, feel sorry for

commiserazióne *f* commiseration

commissariale *adj* commissioner's, e.g., **funzioni commissariali** commissioner's functions; commissar's functions

commissariato *m* commissary; inspector's office

commissà·rio *m* (-ri) commissary; inspector; commissioner; **commissario del popolo** commissar; **commissario di bordo** purser; **commissario di pubblica sicurezza** police inspector; **commissario tecnico** (sports) soccer commissioner

commissionare (**commissióno**) *tr* to commission, order

commissionà·rio -ria (-ri -rie) *adj* commission ‖ *m* commission merchant

commissióne *f* commission, agency; order (*of merchandise*); committee; errand; commitment (*of an act*)

commisurare *tr* to proportion (*e.g., crime to punishment*)

committènte *mf* buyer, customer

commodòro *m* commodore

commòs·so -sa *adj* moved; moving

commovènte *adj* moving, touching

commozióne *f* commotion; emotion; **commozione cerebrale** (pathol) concussion

commuòvere §202 *tr* to move; to touch; to stir || *ref* to be moved; to be touched

commutare *tr* to commute; to switch || *ref* to turn

commuta·tóre -trice *adj* commutative || *m* (elec) change-over switch; (elec) commutator (*switch*); (telp) plugboard || *f* converter

commutatori·sta *mf* (**-sti -ste**) (telp) operator

commutazióne *f* commutation; (telp) selection; (elec) switchover

co·mò *m* (**-mò**) chest; chest of drawers

còmoda *f* commode

comodare (**còmodo**) *tr* to lend || *intr* (with *dat*) to please, e.g., **non le comoda** it doesn't please her

comodino *m* night table; (theat) bit player; **fare il comodino a** (coll) to follow sheepishly

comodi·tà *f* (**-tà**) comfort; convenience; opportunity

còmo·do -da *adj* comfortable; convenient; easy; loose-fitting; calm || *m* convenience; ease; advantage; comfort; opportunity; **a Suo comodo** at your convenience; **comodo di cassa** credit (*at the bank*); **con comodo** without hurrying; **fare comodo** to come in handy; (with *dat*) to please, e.g., **non gli fa comodo** it doesn't please him; **fare il proprio comodo** to think only of oneself; **stia comodo!** make yourself at home! || *f* see **comoda**

compaesa·no -na *mf* fellow citizen || *m* fellow countryman || *f* fellow countrywoman

compàgine *f* strict union; connection; assemblage; (fig) cohesion

compagna *f* companion, mate; (archaic) company

compagnìa *f* company; **Compagnia di Gesù** Society of Jesus; **compagnia stabile** (theat) stock company

compa·gno -gna *adj* like, similar || *m* fellow; companion, comrade; mate; partner; **compagno d'armi** comrade in arms; **compagno di viaggio** fellow traveler || *f* see **compagna**

companàti·co *m* (**-ci**) food to eat with bread

comparàbile *adj* comparable

comparati·vo -va *adj & m* comparative

compara·to -ta *adj* comparative

comparazióne *f* comparison

compare *m* godfather; best man (*at wedding*); fellow; confederate

comparire §108 *intr* to appear; to be known; to cut a figure

comparizióne *f* appearance (*in court*)

comparsa *f* appearance; (theat) extra, supernumerary; (law) petition, brief; **far comparsa** to cut a figure

compartecipare (**compartécipo**) *intr* to share

compartecipazióne *f* sharing; **compartecipazione agli utili** profit sharing

compartécipe *adj* sharing

compartimènto *m* circle, clique; district; (naut, rr) compartment

compartire §176 & (**comparto**) *tr* to divide up, distribute

compassa·to -ta *adj* measured; stiff, formal; reserved; self-controlled

compassionare (**compassióno**) *tr* to pity

compassióne *f* compassion, pity

compassionévole *adj* compassionate; pitiful

compasso *m* compass; **compasso a grossezza** calipers

compatìbile *adj* excusable; compatible

compatimènto *m* compassion; condescension

compatire §176 *tr* to pity; to forgive, overlook; to bear with; **farsi compatire** to become an object of ridicule || *intr* to pity

compatriò·ta *mf* (**-ti -te**) compatriot

compattézza *f* compactness

compat·to -ta *adj* compact, tight

compendiare §287 (**compèndio**) *tr* to epitomize, summarize

compèn·dio *m* (**-di**) compendium, summary; **fare un compendio di** to abstract

compendió·so -sa [s] *adj* compendious, brief, succinct

compenetràbile *adj* penetrable

compenetrabilità *f* penetrability

compenetrare (**compènetro**) *tr* to penetrate; to permeate; to pervade || *ref* to be overcome; **compenetrarsi di** to be conscious of

compensare (**compènso**) *tr* to compensate, pay; to balance, offset; to clear (*checks*)

compensa·to -ta *adj* compensated; laminated || *m* laminate; plywood

compensazióne *f* compensation; offset; (com) clearing (*of checks*)

compènso *m* reward; retribution, pay; **in compenso** on the other hand

cómpera *f* var of **compra**

comperare (**cómpero**) *tr & intr* var of **comprare**

competènte *adj* competent

competènza *f* competence; jurisdiction; **competenze honoraria**

compètere §129 *intr* to compete; to concern; to have jurisdiction

competiti·vo -va *adj* competitive

competi·tóre -trice *mf* competitor, contender

competizióne *f* competition, contest

compiacènte *adj* complaisant, obliging

compiacènza *f* complaisance, kindness; pleasure

compiacére §214 *tr* to gratify || *intr* (with *dat*) to please, e.g., **non posso compiacere a tutti** I cannot please everybody || *ref* to be pleased; **compiacersi con** to congratulate; **compiacersi di** to be kind enough to

compiaciménto *m* pleasure; congratulation; approval

compiaciu·to -ta *adj* pleased, satisfied

compiàngere §215 *tr* to pity || *ref* to feel sorry

compian·to -ta *adj* lamented (*departed person*) || *m* sympathy; (poet) sorrow; (poet) lament

compiegare §209 (compiègo) *tr* to enclose (*in a letter*)

cómpiere §130 *tr* to complete, finish; to fulfill, accomplish; compiere . . . anni to be . . . years old; compiere gli anni to have a birthday || *ref* to happen; to come true

compilare *tr* to compile

compila·tóre -trice *mf* compiler

compilazióne *f* compilation

compiménto *m* fulfillment, accomplishment

compire §176 *tr* to complete, finish; to fulfill, accomplish; per compir l'opera as if it weren't enough || *ref* to happen; to come true

compitare (cómpito) *tr* to syllabify; to read poorly; to spell, spell letter by letter

compitazióne *f* spelling letter by letter

compitézza *f* courtesy, politeness

cómpito *m* task; exercise; homework

compi·to -ta *adj* courteous, polite; (poet) adequate

compiu·to -ta *adj* accomplished

compleanno *m* birthday; buon compleanno happy birthday

complementare *adj* complementary; additional (*tax*) || *f* graduated income tax

compleménto *m* complement; (mil, nav) reserve

complessióne *f* build, physique

complessi·tà *f* (-tà) complexity

complessi·vo -va *adj* total, aggregate

complès·so -sa *adj* complex, complicated; compound (*fracture*) || *m* whole; complex; in complesso in general

completare (complèto) *tr* to complete, carry through; to supplement, round off

complè·to -ta *adj* complete, full; overall, thoroughgoing; al completo full (*e.g., bus*) || *m* set (*of matching items*); suit of clothes; completo femminile lady's tailor-made suit; completo maschile suit

complicare §197 (còmplico) *tr* to complicate || *ref* to become complicated

complica·to -ta *adj* complicated, complex

complicazióne *f* complication

còmplice *mf* accomplice, accessory

complici·tà *f* (-tà) complicity

complimentare (compliménto) *tr* to compliment || *ref*—complimentarsi con to congratulate

compliménto *m* compliment; congratulation; favor; complimenti regards; complimenti! congratulations!; fare complimenti to stand on ceremony; senza complimenti without ceremony; without any further ado

complimentó·so -sa [s] *adj* ceremonious; complimentary

complottare (complòtto) *intr* to plot

complòtto *m* plot, machination

complù·vio *m* (-vi) valley (*of roof*)

componènte *adj* component || *mf* member || *m* component (*component part*) || *f* component (*force*)

componibile *adj* sectional (*e.g., bookcase*)

componiménto *m* composition, settlement (*of a dispute*)

compórre §218 *tr* to compose; to arrange; to settle (*a quarrel*); to lay out (*a corpse*); (typ) to set

comportaménto *m* behavior

comportare (compòrto) *tr* to allow, tolerate; to entail || *ref* to behave; to handle (*said, e.g., of a motor*); comportarsi male to misbehave

compòrto *m* (com) delay

compòsi·to -ta *adj* composite || composite *fpl* (bot) Compositae

composi·tóio *m* (-tói) (typ) composing stick

composi·tóre -trice *mf* compositor, typesetter; composer || *f* typesetting machine

composizióne *f* composition; settlement

compósta *f* compote; composta di frutta stewed fruit

compostézza *f* neatness, tidiness; good behavior; orderliness

compostièra *f* compote, compotier

compó·sto -sta *adj* compound; neat, tidy; well-behaved || *m* compound || *f* see composta

cómpra *f* purchase; shopping; compre shopping

comprare (cómpro) *tr* to buy, purchase; to buy off || *intr* to buy, shop; to trade

compra·tóre -trice *mf* buyer, purchaser

compravèndere §281 *tr* to make a deal in, to transfer (*e.g., a house*)

compravèndita *f* transaction; transfer (*e.g., of real estate*)

comprèndere §220 *tr* to comprehend, include, comprise; to overwhelm; to understand; to forgive

comprendò·nio *m* (-ni) (joc) understanding

comprensibile *adj* understandable, comprehensible

comprensióne *f* comprehension, understanding

comprensi·vo -va *adj* comprehensive; understanding

comprensò·rio *m* (-ri) land to be reclaimed; area, zone, e.g., comprensorio turistico tourist area

comprè·so -sa [s] *adj* comprised, included; understood; deeply touched; immersed

comprèssa *f* compress

compressióne *f* compression

comprès·so -sa *adj* compressed; (fig) repressed; (aut) supercharged || *f* see compressa

compressóre *m* compressor; compressore stradale road roller

comprimà·rio *m* (-ri) (med) associate chief of staff; (theat) second lead

comprìmere §131 *tr* to compress; to repress, restrain; to tamp

compromés·so -sa *adj* jeopardized, in danger ‖ *m* compromise; referral (*to arbitration*)

compromettènte *adj* compromising

comprométtere §198 *tr* to compromise; to endanger; to involve, commit; (law) to refer (*to arbitration*)

comproprie·tà *f* (*-tà*) joint ownership

comproprietà·rio -ria *mf* (*-ri -rie*) joint owner

compròva *f* confirmation

comprovare (compròvo) *tr* to confirm; to circumstantiate

compulsare *tr* to consult, peruse; to summon (*to appear in court*)

compulsi·vo -va *adj* compulsive

compun·to -ta *adj* contrite, repentant

compunzióne *f* compunction

computàbile *adj* computable

computare (còmputo) *tr* to compute

computi·sta *mf* (*-sti -ste*) bookkeeper

computisterìa *f* bookkeeping

còmputo *m* computation, reckoning

comunale *adj* municipal, town (*e.g., hall*); community-owned; (poet) common

comunanza *f* community; **in comunanza** in common

comune *adj* common ‖ *m* normalcy; commune, municipality, town; town hall; (hist) guild; (nav) common seaman; **in comune** in common ‖ *f* commune (*in communist countries*); (theat) main stage entrance; **andare per la comune** to follow the crowd; **per la comune** commonly

comunèlla *f* cabal, clique; passkey (*in a hotel*); (law) mutual insurance (*of cattlemen*); **fare comunella con** to consort with

comunicàbile *adj* communicable

comunicante *adj* communicant; communicating ‖ *m* priest who gives communion

comunicare §197 (**comùnico**) *tr* to communicate; to administer communion to ‖ *intr* to communicate ‖ *ref* to spread; to receive communion, to commune

comunicati·vo -va *adj* communicable, spreading; communicative

comunicato *m* communiqué; **comunicato commerciale** advertisement, ad; **comunicato stampa** press release

comunicazióne *f* communication; statement; (telp) connection; **comunicazioni** communications

comunióne *f* community; (law) community property ‖ **Comunione** *f* Communion

comunismo *m* communism

comuni·sta (*-sti -ste*) *adj* communist ‖ *mf* communist; (law) joint tenant

comunìsti·co -ca *adj* (*-ci -che*) communistic

comuni·tà *f* (*-tà*) community

comunità·rio -ria *adj* (*-ri -rie*) community, e.g., **interessi comunitari** community interests

comùnque *adv* however, nevertheless ‖ *conj* however, no matter how

cón §4 *prep* with; by (*e.g., boat*); **con + art + inf** by + *ger*, e.g., **col leggere** by reading

conato *m* effort, attempt

cón·ca *f* (*-che*) washbowl, washbasin; copper water jug; valley, hollow; (poet) shell; **conca idraulica** drydock

concatenaménto *m* (poet) concatenation

concatenare (concaténo) *tr* to link ‖ *ref* to unfold, ensue

concatenazióne *f* concatenation

concàusa *f* joint cause; (law) aggravation

cònca·vo -va *adj* concave; hollow ‖ *m* hollow

concèdere §132 *tr* to grant, concede; to stretch (*a point*) ‖ *ref* to let oneself go, give oneself over

concènto *m* harmony; (fig) agreement

concentraménto *m* concentration

concentrare (concèntro) *tr* to concentrate; to center ‖ *ref* to concentrate, focus; to center

concentra·to -ta *adj* concentrated; condensed (*e.g., milk*) ‖ *m* purée (*e.g., of tomatoes*)

concentrazióne *f* concentration; (chem) condensation

concèntri·co -ca *adj* (*-ci -che*) concentric

concepìbile *adj* conceivable

concepiménto *m* conception; (fig) formulation

concepire §176 *tr* to conceive; (fig) to nurture

concerìa *f* tannery

concèrnere §133 *tr* to concern

concertare (concèrto) *tr* to scheme, concert; (mus) to orchestrate, arrange ‖ *ref* to agree

concerta·to -ta *adj* agreed upon; (mus) with accompaniment ‖ *m* ensemble (*of orchestra, soloists, and chorus*)

concerta·tóre -trice *mf* arranger ‖ *m* plotter, schemer

concertazióne *f* (mus) arrangement

concerti·sta *mf* (*-sti -ste*) concert performer, soloist

concèrto *m* concert; concerto; (fig) choir

concessionà·rio *m* (*-ri*) sole agent, concessionaire; dealer; lessee (*of business establishment*)

concessióne *f* concession; dealership; admission

concessi·vo -va *adj* concessive

concès·so -sa *adj* granted, admitting

concètto *m* concept; opinion

concettó·so -sa [*s*] *adj* concise; full of ideas; full of conceits

concettuale *adj* conceptual

concezióne *f* conception; formulation

conchìglia *f* shell, conch; (sports) jock guard, protective cup

conchiùdere §125 *tr, intr & ref* var of concludere

cón·cia *f* (*-ce*) tanning

conciapèl·li *m* (*-li*) tanner

conciare §128 (**cóncio**) *tr* to tan; to cure (*e.g., tobacco*); to arrange; to straighten up; to reduce; to cut (*a precious stone*); **conciare per le feste** (coll) to give a good beating to ‖ *ref* to get messed up, get dirty

conciatét·ti *m* (-ti) roofer

conciató·re -trice *mf* tanner

conciliàbile *adj* reconcilable

conciliàbolo *m* conventicle, secret meeting

conciliante *adj* conciliatory

conciliare *adj* council ‖ *m* member of an ecclesiastical council ‖ §287 *tr* to conciliate, reconcile; to settle (*a fine*); to promote (*e.g., sleep*); to obtain (*a favor*) ‖ *ref* to become reconciled

concilia·tóre -trice *adj* conciliatory ‖ *mf* conciliator, peacemaker ‖ *m* justice of the peace

conciliazióne *f* conciliation ‖ **la Conciliazione** the Concordat (*of 1929 between Italy and the Vatican*)

conci·lio *m* (-li) council; church council

concimàia *f* manure pit

concimare *tr* to manure

concimazióne *f* spreading of manure; chemical fertilization

concime *m* manure; fertilizer

cón·cio -cia (-ci -ce) *adj* tanned ‖ *m* ashlar; dung, manure; (archaic) agreement; **concio di scoria** cinder block ‖ *f* see **concia**

conciofossecosaché *conj* (archaic) since

concionare (concióno) *intr* (archaic) to harangue

concióne *f* (archaic) harangue; (archaic) assembly

conciossiacosaché *conj* (archaic) since

concisióne *f* concision, brevity

conci·so -sa *adj* concise, brief

concistòro *m* consistory; (fig) assembly

concitare (còncito) *tr* to excite, stir up

concita·to -ta *adj* excited; (poet) decisive

concitazióne *f* impetus; excitement

concittadi·no -na *mf* fellow citizen

conclave *m* conclave

conclùdere §105 *tr* to conclude ‖ *intr* to conclude; to be convincing ‖ *ref* to conclude, end; **concludersi con** to end with; to result in

conclusionale *adj* (law) summary

conclusióne *f* conclusion; **conclusioni** (law) summation

conclusi·vo -va *adj* conclusive

conclu·so -sa *adj* concluded; terminated; (poet) closed

concomitante *adj* concomitant

concordanza *f* concordance, agreement; (gram) concord; **concordanze** concordance (*e.g., to the Bible*)

concordare (concòrdo) *tr* to agree on; to make agree ‖ *intr* & *ref* to come to an agreement

concordato *m* agreement; concordat; settlement (*with creditors*)

concòrde *adj* in agreement

concòrdia *f* concord, harmony

concorrènte *adj* competitive ‖ *m* (com) competitor; (sports) contestant

concorrènza *f* competition

concorrenziale *adj* competitive (*e.g., price*)

concórrere §139 *intr* to converge; to concur; to compete

concórso *m* attendance; concurrence; combination (*of circumstances*); competition; competitive examination; contest; **concorso di bellezza** beauty contest; **concorso di pubblico** turnout; **fuori concorso** not entering the competition; in a class by itself

concretare (concrèto) *tr* to realize (*e.g., a dream*); to conclude, accomplish ‖ *ref* to come true

concretézza *f* concreteness, consistency

concrè·to -ta *adj* concrete, real; practical ‖ *m* practical matter; **in concreto** really, in reality

concubina *f* concubine

concubinàg·gio *m* (-gi) concubinage

concubinato *m* var of **concubinaggio**

conculcare §197 *tr* (lit) to trample under foot; (lit) to violate

concupire §176 *tr* (poet) to lust for

concupiscènza *f* concupiscence, lust

concussióne *f* extortion, shakedown; **concussione cerebrale** (pathol) concussion

condanna *f* conviction; sentence; (fig) blame, condemnation

condannare *tr* to condemn; to find guilty, convict; to sentence; to damn (*to eternal punishment*); to declare incurable; to wall up

condanna·to -ta *adj* condemned ‖ *m* convict

condensare (condènso) *tr* & *ref* to condense

condensa·to -ta *adj* condensed (*e.g., milk*)

condensatóre *m* condenser

condensazióne *f* condensation

condiménto *m* condiment, seasoning

condire §176 *tr* to season

condiret·tóre -trice *mf* associate manager

condiscendènte *adj* condescending

condiscendènza *f* condescension

condiscéndere §245 *intr* to condescend

condiscépo·lo -la *mf* schoolmate, school companion

condivìdere §158 *tr* to share

condizionale *adj* & *m* conditional ‖ *f* (law) suspended sentence

condizionare (condizióno) *tr* to condition; to treat (*to prevent spoilage*)

condizionatóre *m* air conditioner

condizióne *f* condition; term (*of sale*); **a condizione che** provided that; **condizioni** condition, shape (*e.g., of a shipment*); **essere in condizione di** to be in a position to

condoglianza *f* condolence; **fare le condoglianze a** to extend one's sympathy to

condolére §159 *ref* to condole

condomi·nio *m* (-ni) condominium

condòmi·no -na *mf* joint owner (*of real estate*)

condonare (condóno) *tr* to condone; to remit

condóno *m* pardon, parole

condót·to -ta *adj* country (*doctor*) ‖ *m* duct, canal; conduit ‖ *f* behavior, conduct; district (*of country doctor*); transportation; pipeline; (theat) baggage; **condotta forzata** flume

conducènte *m* driver; bus driver; motorman

condù·plex *mf* (-plex) (telp) party-line user

condurre §102 *tr* to lead; to drive (*a car*); to round up (*cattle*); to pipe (*e.g., gas*); to conduct; to trace (*a line*); to take; to bring; to manage; **condurre a termine** to bring to fruition, realize || *intr* to lead || *ref* to behave; to betake oneself, go; **condursi a** (poet) to be reduced to (*e.g., poverty*)

conduttivi·tà *f* (-tà) conductivity

condutti·vo -va *adj* conductive

condut·tóre -trice *adj* guiding, leading || *m* operator (*of a bus*); driver (*of a car*); (rr) engineer; (rr) ticket collector; (phys) conductor

conduttura *f* conduit, pipeline

conduzióne *f* conduction; leasing

conestàbile *m* constable (*keeper of a castle*)

confabulare (confàbulo) *intr* to confabulate, commune; to connive, scheme

confacènte *adj* suitable, appropriate; helpful

confare §173 *ref*—confarsi a to agree with, e.g., **la uova non gli si confanno** eggs do not agree with him

confederare (confèdero) *tr & ref* to confederate

confedera·to -ta *adj & m* confederate

confederazióne *f* confederation

conferènza *f* conference; lecture; **conferenza illustrata** chalk talk; **conferenza stampa** press conference

conferenziè·re -ra *mf* speaker, lecturer

conferimento *m* conferring, bestowal

conferire §176 *tr* to confer, bestow; to add; to contribute || *intr* to confer; to contribute; **conferire alla salute** to be healthful

confèrma *f* confirmation; **a conferma di** (com) in reply to, confirming

confermare (confèrmo) *tr* to confirm; to verify; to retain (*in office*) || *ref* to become more sure of oneself; to prove to be; to remain (*in the conclusion of a letter*)

confessare (confèsso) *tr & ref* to confess

confessionale *adj* confessional; church; church-related, parochial (*e.g., school*) || *m* confessional

confessióne *f* confession

confès·so -sa *adj* acknowledged, self-admitted; **confesso e comunicato** having made one's confession and taken communion

confessóre *m* confessor

confetterìa *f* candy store, confectioner's shop

confettièra *f* candy box

confettière *m* candy maker; candy dealer, confectioner

confètto *m* sugar-covered nut, sweetmeat; losenge, drop

confettura *f* candy; preserves, jam; **confetture** confectionery

confezionare (confezióno) *tr* to make; to tailor (*a suit*)

confezióne *f* preparation, manufacturing; packaging; **confezioni** ready-made clothes

confezioni·sta *mf* (-sti -ste) ready-made clothier

conficcare §197 *tr* to drive (*a nail*); to thrust (*a knife*) || *ref* to become embedded

confidare *tr* to trust (*a secret*) || *intr* to trust || *ref* to confide

confidènte *adj* confident || *mf* confident; informer

confidènza *f* confidence; secret; familiarity

confidenziale *adj* confidential; friendly

configgere §104 *tr* to plunge, thrust

configurazióne *f* configuration

confinante *adj* bordering || *mf* neighbor

confinare *tr* to exile; to confine || *intr* to border

confinà·rio -ria *adj* (-ri -rie) border (*e.g., zone*)

Confindùstria *f* (acronym) **Confederazione Nazionale degli Industriali** National Confederation of Industrialists

confine *m* border, boundary line; boundary mark, landmark

confino *m* exile (*in a different town*)

confi·sca *f* (-sche) confiscation

confiscare §197 *tr* to confiscate

confit·to -ta *adj* nailed; bound; tied; **confitto in croce** nailed to the cross

conflagrazióne *f* conflagration

conflitto *m* conflict

conflittualità *f* confrontation; belligerent attitude

confluènte *m* confluent

confluènza *f* confluence

confluire §176 *intr* to flow together, join; to converge

confóndere §178 *tr* to confuse; to overwhelm (*with kindness*); to humiliate; **confondere con** to mistake for || *ref* to mix; to become confused

conformare (confórmo) *tr* to shape; to conform || *ref* to conform

conformazióne *f* conformation

confórme *adj* faithful, exact; in agreement; true (*copy*)

conformeménte *adv* in conformity

conformi·sta *mf* (-sti -ste) conformist

conformi·tà *f* (-tà) conformity; **in conformità di** in conformity with, in accord with

confortante *adj* comforting

confortare (confòrto) *tr* to comfort

confortévole *adj* comforting, consoling; comfortable

confòrto *m* comfort, solace; convenience; corroboration; **conforti religiosi** last rites

confratèllo *m* brother, confrere

confratèrnita *f* brotherhood

confricare §197 *tr* to rub

confrontare (confrónto) *tr* to compare, confront; to consult || *intr* to correspond

confrónto *m* comparison; (law) cross examination; **a confronto di** or **in confronto a** in comparison with; with regard to

confusaménte *adv* vaguely, hazily

confusionale *adj* confusing; confused

confusionà·rio -ria (-ri -rie) *adj* blundering; scatterbrain ‖ *mf* blunderer; scatterbrain

confusióne *f* confusion, disorder; noise; error; embarrassment; shambles

confu·so -sa *adj* confused, mixed; vague, hazy; **in confuso** indistinctly

confutare (confúto) *tr* to confute

confutazióne *f* confutation

congedare (congèdo) *tr* to dismiss; to let (*a tenant*) go; (mil) to discharge ‖ *ref* to take leave

congedà·to -ta *adj* discharged ‖ *m* discharged soldier

congèdo *m* dismissal; leave; permission to leave; (mil) discharge, envoy, envoi; **congedo per motivi di salute** sick leave; **dare il congedo a** to discharge; **prender congedo** to take leave

congegnare (congégno) *tr* to assemble (*machinery*); to contrive, cook up

congégno *m* contrivance, gadget; mechanism; design (*of a play*)

congelaménto *m* freezing; frostbite

congelare (congèlo) *tr & ref* to freeze, congeal

congela·tóre -trice *adj* freezing ‖ *m* freezer; freezer unit; freezing compartment (*of a refrigerator*)

congènere *adj* similar, alike

congeniale *adj* congenial

congèni·to -ta *adj* congenital

congèrie *f* congeries

congestionare (congestióno) *tr* to congest

congestióne *f* congestion

congettura *f* conjecture

congetturare *tr* to conjecture

congiùngere §183 *tr & ref* to unite, join

congiuntiva *f* (anat) conjunctiva

congiuntivite *f* (pathol) conjunctivitis

congiunti·vo -va *adj* conjunctive; subjunctive ‖ *m* subjunctive ‖ *f* see **congiuntiva**

congiun·to -ta *adj* joined; joint ‖ *m* relative

congiuntura *f* juncture; joint; circumstance, situation; **bassa congiuntura** (econ) unfavorable circumstance; (econ) crisis

congiunzióne *f* conjunction

congiura *f* conspiracy, plot

congiurare *intr* to conspire, plot

congiura·to -ta *adj & m* conspirator

conglobare (conglòbo) *tr* to lump together

conglomerare (conglòmero) *tr & ref* to pile up, conglomerate

conglomera·to -ta *adj & m* conglomerate

congratulare (congràtulo) *intr* to rejoice ‖ *ref*—**congratularsi con** to congratulate

congratulazióne *f* congratulation

congrèga *f* gang; cabal; religious brotherhood

congregare §209 (congrègo) *tr & ref* to congregate

congregazióne *f* congregation

congressi·sta *mf* (**-sti -ste**) delegate ‖ *m* congressman ‖ *f* congresswoman

congrèsso *m* congress, assembly; conference; convention

congruènte *adj* congruous

congruènza *f* congruence

còn·gruo -grua *adj* congruous; congruent

conguagliare §280 *tr* to adjust; to make up (*what is owed*)

conguà·glio *m* (**-gli**) balance; adjustment (*of wages*)

coniare §287 (cònio) *tr* to mint, coin

coniatura *f* mintage, coinage

còni·co -ca (-ci -che) *adj* conic(al) ‖ *f* conic section

conifera *f* conifer

coniglièra *f* warren, rabbit hutch

conì·glio *m* (**-gli**) rabbit

cò·nio *m* (**-ni**) die (*to mint coins*); mintage; wedge; **dello stesso conio** (fig) of the same feather; **di nuovo conio** newly-minted; new-fangled

coniugale *adj* conjugal

coniugare §209 (cóniugo) *tr* to conjugate ‖ *ref* to marry, get married

coniuga·to -ta *adj* coupled, paired ‖ *mf* spouse, consort

coniugazióne *f* conjugation

còniuge *mf* spouse; **coniugi** *mpl* husband and wife

connaturale *adj* inborn, innate

connatura·to -ta *adj* deep-seated, deep-rooted; congenital

connazionale *mf* fellow countryman

connessióne *f* connection

connès·so -sa & connès·so -sa *adj* connected, tied

connéttere & connèttere §107 *tr* to connect, link ‖ *ref* to refer

connetti·vo -va *adj* connective

connivènte *adj* conniving

connivènza *f* connivance

connotare (connòto) *tr* to connote

connotato *m* personal characteristic

connù·bio *m* (**-bi**) wedding, union

còno *m* cone

conòcchia *f* distaff

conoscènte *mf* acquaintance

conoscènza *f* knowledge; acquaintance; understanding; consciousness; **conoscenza di causa** full knowledge; **essere a conoscenza di** to be acquainted with; **prendere conoscenza di** to take cognizance of

conóscere §134 *tr* to know; to recognize; **conoscere i propri polli** to know one's onions; **conoscere per filo e per segno** to know thoroughly; **conoscere ragioni** to listen to reason; **darsi a conoscere** to make oneself known; to reveal oneself ‖ *intr* to reason ‖ *ref* to acknowledge oneself to be; to know one another

conoscibile *adj* knowable

conosci·tóre -trice *mf* connoisseur, expert

conosciu·to -ta *adj* known, well-known; proven

conquìdere §135 *tr* (poet) to conquer

conquista f conquest

conquistare tr to conquer, win

conquista·tóre -trice adj conquering ‖ m conqueror; lady killer

consacrare tr to consecrate ‖ ref to dedicate oneself

consacrazióne f consecration

consanguineità f consanguinity

consanguìne·o -a adj consanguineous; **fratello consanguineo** half brother on the father's side ‖ m kin

consapévole adj aware, conscious

consapevolézza f awareness, consciousness

còn·scio -scia adj (-sci -sce) conscious

consecutì·vo -va adj consecutive

conségna f delivery; (mil) order; (mil) confinement (to barracks); **in consegna** (com) on consignment

consegnare (conségno) tr to deliver; to entrust; (mil) to confine (to barracks)

consegnatà·rio m (-ri) consignee

conseguènte adj consequent; consistent; **conseguente a** resulting from; consistent with

conseguènza f consequence; consistency; **in conseguenza di** as a result of

conseguìbile adj attainable

conseguiménto m attainment

conseguire (conséguo) tr to attain; to obtain ‖ intr to ensue, result

consènso m consent, approval; consensus

consensuale adj mutual-consent (e.g., agreement)

consentiménto m consent

consentire (consènto) tr to allow, permit ‖ intr to agree, consent; to yield; to admit

consenziènte adj consenting

consèr·to -ta adj intertwined; folded (arms); **di conserto** in agreement

consèrva f preserve; purée (e.g., of tomatoes); tank (for water); sauce (e.g., of cranberries); **conserve alimentari** canned goods; **di conserva** together, in a group; **far conserva di** to preserve

conservare (consèrvo) tr to preserve; to keep; to cure (e.g., meat); to cherish (a memory) ‖ ref to keep; to remain; to keep in good health

conservatì·vo -va adj preserving; conservative ‖ m conservative

conserva·tóre -trice adj preserving; conservative ‖ mf keeper, curator; conservative

conservatoria f registrar's office (in a court house)

conservatò·rio m (-ri) conservatory; girl's boarding school (run by nuns)

conservatorismo m conservatism

conservazióne f conservation; preservation; self-preservation; canning

consèsso m assembly

consideràbile adj considerable; large, important

considerare (consìdero) tr to consider; to rate; (law) to provide for

considera·to -ta adj considered; **siderato che** considering that, since;

tutto considerato all in all, considering

considerazióne f consideration

considerévole adj considerable

consigliare adj council, councilmanic ‖ §280 tr to advise, counsel ‖ ref to consult

consigliè·re -ra mf counselor, advisor ‖ m chancellor (of embassy); councilman; **consigliere delegato** chairman of the board

consì·glio m (-gli) advice, counsel; will (of God); decision, idea; council; **consiglio d'amministrazione** (com) board of directors; **consiglio dei ministri** cabinet; **consiglio municipale** city council; **l'eterno consiglio** the will of God; **venire a più miti consigli** to become more reasonable

consìmile adj similar

consistènte adj consistent, solid; trustworthy

consistènza f consistency, resistance; foundation, grounds

consistere §114 intr to consist; **consistere in** to consist of

consociare §128 (consòcio) tr to syndicate, unite

consocia·to -ta adj syndicated, united

consociazióne f syndicate, association, group

consò·cio -cia mf (-ci -cie) fellow shareholder; associate, partner

consolare adj consular ‖ v (consòlo) tr to console, cheer, comfort ‖ ref to rejoice; to take comfort

consolato m consulate

consola·tóre -trice adj comforting ‖ mf comforter

consolazióne f consolation

cònsole m consul

consò·le f (-le) console

consòlida f—**consolida maggiore** comfrey; **consolida reale** field larkspur

consolidaménto m consolidation

consolidare (consòlido) tr to consolidate ‖ ref to consolidate; to harden

consolida·to -ta adj consolidated; joint (e.g., balance sheet); hardened ‖ m funded public debt; government bonds

consonante adj & f consonant

consonànti·co -ca adj (-ci -che) consonant

consonanza f consonance; agreement; (mus) harmony

cònso·no -na adj consonant

consorèlla adj sister (e.g., company) ‖ f sister of charity; sister branch; sister firm

consòrte adj (poet) equally fortunate; (poet) united ‖ mf consort, mate, spouse

consorterìa f political clique

consòr·zio m (-zi) syndicate, consortium; (poet) society

constare (cònsto) intr to consist ‖ impers to be known; to be proved; to understand, e.g., **gli consta che Lei ha torto** he understands that you are wrong

constatare (constato & cònstato) tr to verify, ascertain, establish

constatazióne f ascertainment, verification

consuè·to -ta adj usual, customary; **consueto a** accustomed to, used to ‖ m manner, custom; **di consueto** generally

consuetudinà·rio -ria adj (-ri -rie) customary; common (law)

consuetùdine f custom; common law; (poet) familiarity

consulènte adj advising, consulting ‖ mf adviser, expert

consulènza f expert advice

consulta f council

consultare tr to consult ‖ ref to take counsel; to counsel with one another; **consultarsi con** to take counsel with

consultazióne f consultation; reference; **consultazione popolare** referendum

consulti·vo -va adj advisory

consulto m consultation (of physicians); legal conference

consul·tóre -trice mf adviser, expert ‖ m councilman

consultò·rio m (-ri) clinic, dispensary

consumare tr to consume; to perform, to consummate ‖ ref to be consumed, to waste away

consuma·to -ta adj consummate, accomplished; consummated (marriage); consumed, worn out

consuma·tóre -trice adj consuming ‖ mf consumer; customer (of a restaurant)

consumazióne f consummation (e.g., of a crime); consumption (of food); food or drink

consumismo m consumerism

consumo m consumption; wear

consunti·vo -va adj end-of-year (e.g., report); (econ) consumption ‖ m balance sheet

consun·to -ta adj worn-out

consunzióne f consumption

contàbile adj bookkeeping ‖ mf accountant; bookkeeper, clerk; **esperto contabile** certified public accountant

contabili·tà f (-tà) accounting, bookkeeping; accounts

contachilòme·tri m (-tri) odometer; (coll) speedometer

contadiné·sco -sca adj (-schi -sche) farm, farmer; rustic

contadi·no -na adj rustic ‖ mf peasant, farmer

contado m country, countryside

contagiare §290 tr to infect

contà·gio m (-gi) contagion

contagió·so -sa [s] adj contagious

contagi·ri m (-ri) tachometer

contagóc·ce m (-ce) dropper, eyedropper

contaminare (**contàmino**) tr to contaminate; to pollute

contaminazióne f contamination; pollution

contante adj & m cash; **in contanti** cash

contare (**cónto**) tr to count; to limit; to regard, value; to propose; **contarle grosse** (coll) to tell tall tales ‖ intr to count; **contare su** to count on

contasecón·di m (-di) watch with second hand

conta·to -ta adj limited; numbered (e.g., days)

conta·tóre -trice adj counting ‖ mf counter ‖ m meter; **contatore dell'acqua** water meter; **contatore della luce** electric meter

contattare tr to contact

contatto m contact

cónte m count

contèa f county

conteggiare §290 (**contéggio**) tr to charge (e.g., a bill) ‖ intr to count

contég·gio m (-gi) reckoning, calculation; (sports) count; **conteggio alla rovescia** countdown

contégno m behavior; reserve, reserved attitude; air

contegnó·so -sa [s] adj reserved, dignified

contemperare (**contèmpero**) tr to adapt; to mitigate, moderate

contemplare (**contèmplo**) tr to contemplate

contemplati·vo -va adj contemplative

contemplazióne f contemplation

contèmpo m—nel contempo meanwhile

contemporaneaménte adv at the same time

contemporàne·o -a adj contemporaneous ‖ mf contemporary

contendènte adj fighting ‖ m contender, fighter; (law) contestant

contèndere §270 tr to contest, oppose ‖ intr to contend, fight ‖ ref to fight

contenére §271 tr to contain ‖ ref to restrain oneself; to behave

conteniménto m containment

contenitóre m container

contentare (**contènto**) tr to satisfy, content ‖ ref to be satisfied

contentézza f gladness, contentedness, contentment

contentino m gratuity, makeweight, gift to a customer

contèn·to -ta adj contented, glad, happy; satisfied ‖ m (poet) happiness, contentedness

contenuto m content; contents

contenzióne f contention

contenzióso [s] m legal matter; legal department (of a corporation)

conterìe fpl beads, sequins

conterrà·neo -nea adj from the same country ‖ m fellow countryman ‖ f fellow countrywoman

conté·so -sa [s] adj coveted ‖ f contest; dispute; **venire a contesa** to dispute

contéssa f countess

contestare (**contèsto**) tr to serve (e.g., a summons); to deny; to challenge, contest; **contestare qlco a qlcu** to charge s.o. with s.th

contestazióne f notification, summons; dispute, confrontation; challenge

contè·sto -sta adj (poet) intertwined ‖ m context

conti·guo -gua adj contiguous

continentale adj continental

continènte adj & m continent

continènza f continence

contingentaménto m import quota

contingentare (**contingènto**) tr to assign a quota to (imports)

contingènte *adj* possible, contingent; (obs) due ‖ *m* contingent; import quota; **contingente di lèva** draft quota

contingènza *f* contingency

continuare (**continuo**) *tr* to continue ‖ *intr* to last, continue; **continuare a** + *inf* to keep on + *ger*

continuazióne *f* continuation

continui·tà *f* (**-tà**) continuity

contì·nuo -nua *adj* continuous; direct (*current*); **di continuo** continuously

cón·to -ta *adj* (archaic) well-known; (poet) gentle; (poet) narrated ‖ *m* figuring; account; bill, invoice; check (*in a restaurant*); opinion; worth, value; **a conti fatti** everything considered; **chiedere conto di** to call to account; **conto all'indietro** countdown; **di conto** valuable; **estratto conto** (com) statement; **fare conto di** + *inf* to intend to + *inf*; **fare conto su** to count on; **fare di conto** to count; **fare i conti senza l'oste** to reckon without one's host; **il conto non torna** the sums do not jibe; **in conto** on account; **in conto di** in one's position as; **per conto in** the name of; **per conto mio** as far as I am concerned; **render conto di** to give an account of; **rendersi conto di** to realize, be aware of; **tener conto di** to reckon with; **tener di conto** to treat with care; **torna conto** it is worthwhile

contòrcere §272 *tr* to twist ‖ *ref* to writhe

contorciménto *m* contortion, writhing

contornare (**contórno**) *tr* to surround

contórno *m* outline; contour; circle (*of people*); side dish (*of vegetables*)

contorsióne *f* contorsion; gyration (*e.g., of a dancer*); squirm

contòr·to -ta *adj* twisted (*e.g., face*)

contrabbandare *tr* to smuggle

contrabbandiè·re -ra *adj* smuggling ‖ *mf* smuggler; bootlegger

contrabbando *m* contraband; smuggling; **di contrabbando** by smuggling; (fig) without paying

contrabbasso *m* contrabass, bass viol

contraccambiare §287 *tr* to reciprocate, return ‖ *intr* to reciprocate

contraccàm·bio *m* (**-bi**) exchange; **in contraccambio di** in exchange for, in return for

contraccólpo *m* shock, rebound; recoil (*of a rifle*); backlash (*of a machine*)

contrada *f* road; (poet) region

contraddire §151 (*impv sg* **contraddici**) *tr* to contradict ‖ *ref* to contradict oneself; to contradict one another

contraddistìnguere §156 *tr* to earmark ‖ *ref* to stand out

contraddittò·rio -ria (**-ri -rie**) *adj* contradictory; incoherent ‖ *m* open discussion, debate

contraddizióne *f* contradiction

contraènte *adj* contracting; acting ‖ *mf* contractor (*person who makes a contract*); (law) party

contraère·o -a *adj* antiaircraft

contraffare §173 *tr* to counterfeit; to fake, sham ‖ *intr* (archaic) to disobey ‖ *ref* to camouflage oneself, disguise oneself

contraffat·to -ta *adj* counterfeit; adulterated; apocryphal

contraffat·tóre -trice *mf* counterfeiter; falsifier

contraffazióne *f* forgery; fake; imitation; piracy (*of book*); mockery (*of justice*)

contrafforte *m* spur (*of mountain*); crossbar (*to secure door*); (archit) buttress

contraggènio *m*—**a contraggenio** against one's will

contral·to (**-to**) *adj* alto ‖ *m* contralto (*voice*) ‖ *f* contralto (*singer*)

contrammirà·glio *m* (**-gli**) rear admiral

contrappasso *m* retributive justice

contrappesare [s] (**contrappéso**) *tr* to counterweight, counterbalance

contrappéso [s] *m* counterweight, counterpoise

contrappórre §218 *tr* to oppose; to compare ‖ *ref*—**contrapporsi a** to oppose

contrappó·sto -sta *adj* opposing ‖ *m* opposite, antithesis

contrappunto *m* counterpoint

contrare (**cóntro**) *tr* (boxing) to counter; (bridge) to double

contrariare §287 *tr* to oppose, counter; to thwart; to contradict; to bother, vex

contrarie·tà *f* (**-tà**) contrariety, vexation; setback

contrà·rio -ria (**-ri -rie**) *adj* contrary, opposite ‖ *m* opposite; **al contrario** on the contrary; **al contrario di** unlike; **avere qlco in contrario** to have some objection, object

contrarre §273 *tr & ref* to contract

contrassegnare (**contrasségno**) *tr* to earmark, mark

contrasségno *m* earmark; proof

contrastare *tr* to oppose; to obstruct; to prevent ‖ *intr* to contrast; to disagree; (poet) to quarrel ‖ *ref* to contend

contrasto *m* contrast; fight, dispute; (telv) contrast knob

contrattàbile *adj* negotiable

contrattaccare §197 *tr* to counterattack

contrattac·co *m* (**-chi**) counterattack

contrattare *tr* to contract for, negotiate a deal for ‖ *intr* to bargain

contrattèmpo *m* mishap

contrat·to -ta *adj* contracted ‖ *m* contract

contrattuale *adj* contractual

contraveléno *m* antidote

contravenire §282 *intr* (with *dat*) to contravene; **contravvenire a** to infringe upon

contravvenzióne *f* violation; ticket, fine; **in contravvenzione** in the wrong; **intimare una contravvenzione a** to give a ticket to

contrazióne *f* contraction

contribuènte *mf* taxpayer

contribuire §176 *intr* to contribute

contributo *m* contribution

contribu·tóre -trice *mf* contributor

contribuzióne *f* contribution
contristare *tr & ref* to sadden
contri·to -ta *adj* contrite
contrizióne *f* contrition
cóntro *m* con, contrary opinion || *adv*
—contro di against, versus; dar contro a to oppose; di contro opposite,
facing; per contro on the other hand
|| *prep* against, versus; at; contro
pagamento upon payment; contro
vento into the wind; contro voglia
unwillingly
controbàttere *tr* (mil) to counterattack;
(fig) to contest
controbilanciare §128 *tr* to counterpoise, counterbalance
controcanto *m* (mus) counterpoint
controcarro *adj invar* antitank
controchìglia *f* keelson
controcorrènte *f* countercurrent; under-
tow; (fig) undercurrent || *adv* up-
stream
controdado *m* lock nut
controffensiva *f* counteroffensive
controfigura *f* (mov) stand-in; (mov)
stuntman
controfilo *m*—a controfilo against the
grain
controfinèstra *f* storm window
controfirma *f* countersign
controfirmare *tr* to countersign
controfòdera *f* inner facing (*of a suit,
between lining and cloth*)
controfuò·co *m* (-chi) backfire (*to check
the advance of a forest fire*)
controindicare §197 (controindico) *tr*
to contraindicate
controllare (contròllo) *tr* to control,
check || *ref* to control oneself
contròllo *m* control, check; restraint;
(rad, telv) knob
controllóre *m* (com) comptroller; (rr)
ticket collector, conductor
controluce *f* picture taken against the
light || *adv* against the light
contromano *adv* against traffic
contromar·ca *f* (-che) check, stub (*e.g.,
of ticket*)
contromàr·cia *f* (-ce) countermarch;
(aut) reverse, reverse gear
contromezzana [ddzz] *f* (naut) topsail
contronòta *f* countermanding note
contropalo *m* strut
controparte *f* (law) opponent
contropedale *m* foot brake (*of a bicycle*)
contropélo *m* close shave (*in the oppo-
site direction of hair's growth*) || *adv*
against the grain; the wrong way
(*said of the nap*); against the nap;
accarezzare contropelo to stroke the
wrong way
contropiède *m* counterattack; cogliere
in contropiede to catch off balance
contropòrta *f* storm door
controproducènte *adj* counterproduc-
tive, self-defeating
contropropósta *f* counterproposition
contropròva *f* proof; second balloting
contrórdine *m* countermand
controrèplica *f* retort; (law) rejoinder
controrifórma *f* Counter Reformation

controrivoluzióne *f* counterrevolution
controsènso *m* nonsense; mistranslation
controspallina *f* (mil) epaulet
controspionàg·gio *m* (-gi) counter-
espionage
controvalóre *m* equivalent
controvènto *m* (archit) strut; (archit)
crossbrace || *adv* windward
controvèrsia *f* controversy
controvèr·so -sa *adj* controversial, moot
controvòglia *adv* unwillingly
contumace *adj* (archaic) contumacious;
(law) absent from court; (law) guilty
of nonappearance
contumàcia *f* quarantine; (archaic) con-
tumacy; (law) nonappearance; in
contumacia (law) in absentia
contumèlia *f* contumely
contundènte *adj* blunt
conturbante *adj* disturbing, upsetting
conturbare *tr* to disturb, upset || *ref*
to become perturbed
contusióne *f* bruise, contusion
contu·so -sa *adj* bruised
contuttoché *conj* although
contuttociò *conj* although
convalescènte *adj* convalescent
convalescènza *f* convalescence
convalescenzià·rio *m* (-ri) convalescent home
convàlida *f* validation; confirmation
convalidare (convàlido) *tr* to validate;
to confirm; to strengthen (*e.g., a
suspicion*)
convégno *m* meeting, convention
conveniènte *adj* convenient; adequate;
useful; profitable (*business*); cheap,
reasonable
conveniènza *f* convenience; suitability,
fitness; propriety; profit; convenienze
conventions
convenire §282 *tr* to fix (*e.g., a price*);
(law) to summon || *intr* (ESSERE) to
convene; to agree; to fit, be appro-
priate; (poet) to flow together || *ref*
to be proper; (with *dat*) to behoove,
befit, e.g., gli si conviene it behooves
him || *impers*—conviene it is neces-
sary
convènto *m* convent; monastery
convenu·to -ta *adj* agreed upon || *m*
agreement; (law) defendant; conve-
nuti conventioners, delegates
convenzionale *adj* conventional
convenzióne *f* convention
convergènte *adj* converging, convergent
convergènza *f* convergence
convèrgere §137 *intr* to converge
convèrsa *f* lay sister; flashing (*on a
roof*)
conversare (convèrso) *intr* to converse
conversazióne *f* conversation
conversióne *f* conversion; change of
heart; (mil) wheeling
convèrso *m* lay brother
convertìbile *adj* convertible || *m* (aer)
fighter-bomber || *f* (aut) convertible
convertibili·tà *f* (-tà) convertibility
convertire §138 *tr* to convert, change;
to translate || *ref* to convert, change;
(poet) to address oneself

converti·to -ta *adj* converted ‖ *mf* convert
convertitóre *m* converter
convès·so -sa *adj* convex
convincènte *adj* convincing
convincere §285 *tr* to convince; to convict ‖ *ref* to become convinced
convinciménto *m* conviction
convin·to -ta *adj* convinced, confirmed; convicted
convinzióne *f* conviction
convita·to -ta *adj* invited ‖ *mf* guest (*at a banquet*)
convito *m* banquet
convitto *m* boarding school
convit·tóre -trice *mf* boarding-school student
convivènte *adj* living together
convivènza *f* living together; **convivenza illecita** cohabitation; **convivenza umana** human society
convivere §286 *intr* to live together; to cohabit
conviviale *adj* convivial
convi·vio *m* (-vi) banquet
convocare §197 (**cònvoco**) *tr* to summon, convoke; to convene
convocazióne *f* convocation
convogliare §280 (**convòglio**) *tr* to convoy, escort; to convey, carry
convò·glio *m* (-gli) convoy; cortege; (rr) train
convolare (**convólo**) *intr*—**convolare a nozze** to get married
convòlvolo *m* (bot) morning-glory
convulsióne *f* convulsion
convul·so -sa *adj* convulsive; convulsed; choppy (*style*)
coonestare (**coonèsto**) *tr* to justify, palliate
cooperare (**coòpero**) *intr* to cooperate
cooperati·vo -va *adj & f* cooperative
coopera·tóre -trice *adj* coadjutant, cooperating ‖ *m* coadjutor
cooperazióne *f* cooperation
coordinaménto *m* coordination
coordinare (**coórdino**) *tr* to coordinate; to collect (*ideas*)
coordinati·vo -va *adj* (gram) coordinate
coordina·to -ta *adj & f* coordinate
coordinazióne *f* coordination
coòrte *f* cohort
copèr·chio *m* (-chi) lid, cover; top (*of box*)
copertina *f* small blanket, child's blanket; cover (*of book*)
copèr·to -ta *adj* covered; protected; cloudy; obscure ‖ *m* cover; shelter; **al coperto** under cover; indoors; secure ‖ *f* blanket, cover; seat cover; case; sheath; (naut) deck; **coperta da viaggio** steamer rug, lap robe; **far coperta a** to cover up for
copertóne *m* canvas; casing, shoe (*of tire*); **copertone cinturato** belted tire
copertura *f* covering; cover; coverage; whitewash; (boxing) defensive stance; (archit) roof
còpia *f* copy; (poet) abundance; (archaic) opportunity; **brutta copia** first draft; **copia a carbone** carbon copy; **copia dattiloscritta** typescript; **per**

copia conforme certified copy (*formula appearing on a document*)
copialètte·re *m* (-re) letter file; copying press
copiare §287 (**còpio**) *tr* to copy
copiati·vo -va *adj* indelible; copying
copiatura *f* copying; copy; plagiarism
copìglia *f* cotterpin
copilò·ta *mf* (-ti -te) copilot
copióne *m* (theat) script
copiosi·tà [s] *f* (-tà) copiousness
copió·so -sa [s] *adj* copious
copi·sta *mf* (-sti -ste) scribe; copyist
copistería *f* copying office; public typing office
còppa *f* cup, goblet; bowl; pan (*of balance*); trophy; (aut) crankcase; (aut) housing; **coppe** suit of Neapolitan cards corresponding to hearts
coppàia *f* chuck (*of lathe*)
còppia *f* couple; pair; **a coppie** two by two; **far coppia fissa** to go steady
coppière *m* cupbearer
coppìglia *f* var of **copiglia**
cóppo *m* earthenware jar (*for oil*); roof tile
copribu·sto *m* (-sto) bodice
copricapo *m* headgear
copricaté·na *m* (-na) chain guard (*on bicycle or motorcycle*)
coprifuò·co *m* (-chi) curfew
coprinu·ca *m* (-ca) havelock
coprire §110 *tr* to cover; to occupy (*a position*); to coat (*e.g., a wall*); to drown (*a noise*) ‖ *ref* to cover oneself; (econ) to hedge
copriteiè·ra *m* (-ra) cozy
coprivan·de *m* (-de) dish cover
cò·pto -pta *adj* Coptic ‖ *mf* Copt
còpula *f* copulation; (gram) copula
coque *f* see **uovo**
coràg·gio *m* (-gi) courage; effrontery; (obs) heart; **fare coraggio a** to hearten, encourage; **prendere il coraggio a quattro mani** to screw up one's courage
coraggió·so -sa [s] *adj* courageous
corale *adj* choral; (archaic) cordial; (fig) unanimous ‖ *m* chorale
coralli·no -na *adj* coral
corallo *m* coral
corame *m* engraved leather
coramèlla *f* razor strop
Corano *m* Koran
corata *f* haslet
coratèlla *f* giblets
corazza *f* breastplate, cuirass; shoulder pad (*in football*); armor plate; carapace, shell
corazzare *tr* to armor ‖ *ref* to armor, protect oneself
corazza·to -ta *adj* armor-plated, armored; plated; protected ‖ *f* battleship, dreadnought
corazzière *m* cuirassier; mounted carabineer
còrba *f* basket
corbellería *f* (coll) blunder
corbèllo *m* basket; basketful
corbézzolo *m* (bot) arbutus; **corbezzoli!** gosh!
còrda *f* rope; tightrope; string (*of an*)

instrument); chord; woof; cord; plumbline; **dare la corda a** to wind (*a clock*); **essere con la corda al collo** to have a rope around one's neck; **mostrare la corda** to be threadbare; **tagliare la corda** to take off, leave; **tenere sulla corda** to keep in suspense

cordame *m* cordage

cordata *f* group of climbers tied together

cordellina *f* (mil) braided cord, braid; (mil) lanyard

cordiale *adj* & *m* cordial

cordiali·tà *f* (-tà) cordiality

cordièra *f* (mus) tailpiece

cordò·glio *m* (-gli) sorrow, grief

cordonata *f* gradient

cordóne *m* cordon; (anat, elec) cord; curbstone; **cordone litorale** sandbar; **cordone sanitario** sanitary cordon

corèa *f* St. Vitus's dance || **Corea** *f* Korea

corea·no -na *adj* & *mf* Korean

coréggia *f* leather strap

coreografìa *f* choreography

coreògrafo *m* choreographer

coriàce·o -a *adj* tough, leathery

coriàndolo *m* (bot) coriander; **coriandoli** confetti

coricare §197 (**còrico**) *tr* to put to bed || *ref* to lie down, go to bed

corindóne *m* corundum

corìn·zio -zia *adj* & *mf* (-zi -zie) Corinthian

corì·sta *mf* (-sti -ste) choir singer, choirmaster || *m* chorus man; (mus) tuning fork; (mus) pitch pipe

coriza [dz] or **corizza** [ddzz] *f* coryza

cormorano *m* cormorant

cornàcchia *f* rook, crow

cornamusa *f* bagpipe

cornata *f* butt; hook, goring (*by bull*)

còrne·o -a *adj* horn, horn-like || *f* cornea

cornétta *f* (mus) cornet; (mus) cornet player; (telp) receiver; (hist) pennon (*of cavalry*)

cornétto *m* little horn; amulet (*in shape of horn*); crescent (*bread*); ear trumpet

cornìce *f* cornice; frame; (typ) box; (archit) pediment

cornicióne *m* (archit) ledge; (archit) cornice

cornificare §197 (**cornìfico**) *tr* (joc) to cuckold

cornìola *f* carnelian

còrniola *f* (bot) dogberry

còrniolo *m* (bot) dogwood

còrno *m* horn; wing (*of army*); edge, end; (mus) horn; **corno da caccia** hunting horn; **corno da scarpe** shoe horn; **corno dell'abbondanza** horn of plenty; **corno dogale** (hist) Doge's hat; **corno inglese** (mus) English horn; **non capire un corno** to not understand a blessed thing; **non valere un corno** to not be worth a fig; **un corno!** (slang) heck no! || *m* (**còrna** *fpl*) horn (*of animal*); **alzare le corna** to raise one's head; to be-

come rambunctious; **dire corna di** to speak evil of; **fare le corna** to make horns, to touch wood (*to ward off the evil eye*); **mettere le corna a** to cuckold (*one's husband*); to be unfaithful to (*one's wife*); **portare le corna** to be cuckolded; **rompersi le corna** to get the worst of it

cornu·to -ta *adj* horny; horn-shaped; (vulg) cuckolded

còro *m* choir; chorus; chancel

corollà·rio *m* (-ri) corollary

coróna *f* crown; coronet; wreath, garland; range (*of mountains*); collection (*e.g., of sonnets*); stem (*of watch*); felloe (*of wheel*); (astr) corona; (rel) string (*of beads*); (mus) pause; **fare corona a** to surround

coronaménto *m* crowning; (archit) capstone; (naut) taffrail

coronare (**coróno**) *tr* to crown; to top, surmount

coronà·rio -ria *adj* (-ri -rie) coronary; (hist) rewarded with a garland

corpétto *m* baby's shirt; waistcoat, vest

corpino *m* bodice; vest

còrpo *m* body; substance; staff (*of teachers*); (mil) corps; (typ) em quad; **a corpo a corpo** hand-to-hand (*fight*); (sports) in a clinch; **a corpo morto** heavily; doggedly; **andare di corpo** to have a bowel movement; **avere in corpo** (fig) to have inside; **corpo del reato** corpus delicti; **corpo di Bacco!** good Heavens!; **corpo di ballo** ballet; **corpo di commissariato** (mil) supply corps; **corpo di guardia** guard, guardhouse; **corpo semplice** (chem) simple substance; **prendere corpo** to materialize

corporale *adj* bodily, body || *m* (eccl) corporal, Communion cloth

corporativismo *m* corporatism (*e.g., of Fascist Italy*)

corporati·vo -va *adj* corporative, corporate

corpora·to -ta *adj* corporate

corporatura *f* size, build

corporazióne *f* corporation

corpòre·o -a *adj* corporeal

corpó·so -sa [s] *adj* heavy-bodied

corpulèn·to -ta *adj* corpulent

corpùscolo *m* particle; (phys) corpuscle

Corpus Dòmini *m* (eccl) Corpus Christi

corredare (**corrèdo**) *tr* to provide, furnish; to annotate, accompany

corredino *m* layette

corrèdo *m* trousseau; outfit, garb; actor's kit; furniture; equipment; apparatus (*e.g., footnotes*)

corrèggere §226 *tr* to correct; to straighten (*e.g., a road*); to rewrite, revise (*news*); to touch up the flavor of || *ref* to reform

corrég·gia *f* (-ge) leather strap

corregionale *adj* fellow || *mf* person of the same section of the country

correità *f* complicity

correlare (**corrèlo**) *tr* to correlate

correlati·vo -va *adj* correlative

correla·tóre -trìce *mf* second reader (*of a doctoral dissertation*)

correlazióne *f* correlation; (gram) sequence

corrènte *adj* current; running; fluent; recurring; run-of-the-mill ‖ *m*—**essere al corrente di** to be acquainted with; to be abreast of; **mettere al corrente di** to acquaint with ‖ *f* current; draft (*of air*); stream (*of water*); mass (*of lava*); (elec) current; (fig) tide; **contro corrente** upstream; **corrente alternata** (elec) alternating current; **corrente continua** (elec) direct current; **corrente di rete** (elec) house current

córrere §139 *tr* to travel; to run (*a risk; a race*); **correre la cavallina** to sow one's wild oats ‖ *intr* (ESSERE & AVERE) to run; to speed; to race; to flow; to fly (*said of time*); to elapse; to be (*e.g., the year 1820*); to be current (*said of coins*); to spread (*said of gossip*); to mature (*said of interest*); to intervene (*said of distance*); to have dealings; **ci corre!** there is quite a difference!; **ci corre poco che cadesse** he narrowly escaped falling; **correre a gambe levate** to run at breakneck speed; **corre l'uso** it is the fashion; **corrono parole grosse** they are having words; **non corre buon sangue fra loro** there is bad blood between them

corrensàbile *adj* jointly responsible

corresponsióne *f* payment; (fig) gratitude

correttézza *f* correctness

corretti·vo -va *adj* corrective ‖ *m* flavoring

corrèt·to -ta *adj* correct; flavored; spiked

corret·tóre -trice *mf* corrector; **correttore di bozze** proofreader

correzionale *adj* correctional

correzióne *f* correction

còrri còrri *m* rush

corri·dóio *m* (-dói) corridor; hallway; (tennis) alley; (theat) aisle

corridóre *adj* running ‖ *m* racer; runner (*in baseball*)

corrièra *f* mail coach; bus

corrière *m* courier; mail; carrier (*of merchandise*)

corrispetti·vo -va *adj* equivalent, proportionate ‖ *m* requital, compensation

corrispondènte *adj* corresponding, equivalent ‖ *mf* correspondent

corrispondènza *f* correspondence

corrispóndere §238 *tr* to pay, compensate ‖ *intr* to correspond

corri·vo -va *adj* rash; indulgent

corroborante *adj* corroborating ‖ *m* tonic

corroborare (corròboro) *tr* to corroborate; to invigorate

corroborazióne *f* corroboration

corródere §239 *tr* to corrode; to erode

corrómpere §240 *tr* to spoil; to corrupt; to suborn ‖ *ref* to putrefy, rot

corrosióne *f* corrosion

corrosi·vo -va *adj* & *m* corrosive

corró·so -sa *adj* corroded; eroded

corrót·to -ta *adj* corrupted, corrupt; putrefied, rotten ‖ *m* (archaic) lament

corrucciare §128 *tr* to anger, vex ‖ *ref* to get angry

corrùc·cio *m* (-ci) anger, vexation

corrugaménto *m* wrinkling; (geol) fold

corrugare §209 *tr* to wrinkle, knit (*one's brow*) ‖ *ref* to frown

corruscare §197 *intr* (poet) to shine

corruttèla *f* corruption

corruttibile *adj* corruptible

corrut·tóre -trice *adj* corrupting, depraving ‖ *m* seducer; briber

corruzióne *f* corruption; putrefaction, decomposition

córsa *f* race; run; trip; fare; (mach) stroke; (hist) privateering; **a tutta corsa** at full speed; **corsa al galoppo** flat race; **corsa al trotto** harness racing; **corsa semplice** one-way ticket; **corse horse racing; da corsa** race, for racing, e.g., **cavallo da corsa** race horse; **di corsa** running, in a hurry; **fare una corsa** to run an errand; **prendere la corsa** to begin to run

corsalétto *m* corselet

corsa·ro -ra *adj* privateering ‖ *m* privateer, corsair, pirate

corsétto *m* corset

corsìa *f* aisle; ward (*in hospital*); runner (*of carpet*); lane (*of highway*); **corsia d'accesso** entrance lane; **corsia d'uscita** exit lane

Còrsica, la Corsica

corsivi·sta *mf* (-sti -ste) (journ) political writer

corsi·vo -va *adj* cursive; (poet) running; (poet) current ‖ *m* cursive handwriting; (typ) italics

córso *m* course; navigation (*by sea*); path (*of stars*); parade; large street; boulevard; tender (*of currency*); current rate, current price (*of stock at the exchange*); **corso d'acqua** watercourse; **fuori corso** (coin) no longer in circulation; **in corso** in circulation; in progress; **in corso di** in the course of; **in corso di stampa** in press

còr·so -sa *adj* & *m* Corsican

cor·sóio -sóia (-sói -sóie) *adj* running (*knot*); (mach) on rollers ‖ *m* slide (*of slide rule*); (mach) slide

córte *f* court; **corte bandita** open house; **Corte d'appello** appellate court; **Corte di cassazione** Supreme Court; **fare la corte a** to pay court to, woo

cortéc·cia *f* (-ce) bark; crust (*of bread*); (fig) appearance; (anat) cortex

corteggiaménto *m* courtship

corteggiatóre *m* wooer, suitor

cortég·gio *m* (-gi) retinue; cortege

cortèo *m* procession; parade; funeral train; wedding party

cortése *adj* courteous, polite; (lit) liberal; (poet & hist) courtly

cortesìa *f* courtesy, politeness; (lit) liberality; (poet & hist) courtliness; **per cortesia** please

còrtice *f* cortex

cortigia·no -na *adj* flattering; courtly ‖ *mf* courtier; flatterer ‖ *f* courtesan

cortile *m* courtyard; barnyard

cortina f curtain; **cortina di ferro** iron curtain; **cortina di fumo** smoke screen; **oltre cortina** behind the iron curtain

cortisóne m cortisone

cór·to -ta adj short; close (*haircut*); **alle corte** in short; **essere a corto di** to be short of; **per farla corta in short**

cortocircùito m short circuit

cortometràg·gio m (-gi) (mov) short

cor·vè f (-vè) tiresome task, drudgery; **corvè di cucina** kitchen police

corvétta f corvette

corvi·no -na adj raven-black

còrvo m raven; crow

còsa [s] f thing; **belle cose!** or **buone cose!** regards!; **che cosa** what; **cosa da nulla** a mere trifle, nothing at all; **cos'ha?** what's the matter with you (him, her)?; **cosa pubblica** commonweal; **cosa strana** no wonder; **cose belongings**; **per la qual cosa** wherefore; **per prima cosa** first of all; **sopra ogni cosa** above all; **tante belle cose!** best regards!; **una cosa** something; **una cosa nuova** a piece of news

cosac·co -ca (-chi -che) adj Cossack's ‖ mf Cossack

cò·scia f (-sce) thigh; haunch; leg (*of gun*); (archit) abutment; **coscia di montone** leg of lamb

cosciènte adj conscious; sensible; aware

cosciènza f conscience; consciousness; conscientiousness; awareness

coscienzió·so -sa [s] adj conscientious

cosciòtto m leg; leg of lamb

coscrit·to -ta adj conscript ‖ m conscript, recruit, draftee

coscrivere §250 tr to conscript

coscrizióne f conscription, draft

così [s] adj invar—**un così...** or **un... così such a** ‖ adv thus; like this; so; **così ... come as ... as; così così** so so; **e così via** and so on, and so forth; **per così dire** so to speak

cosicché [s] conj so that

cosiddét·to -ta [s] adj so-called

cosiffat·to -ta [s] adj such, similar

cosino [s] m (coll) little fellow

cosmèti·co -ca adj & m (-ci -che) cosmetic

còsmi·co -ca adj (-ci -che) cosmic; outer (*space*)

còsmo m cosmos; outer space

cosmòdromo m space center

cosmologìa f cosmology

cosmonàu·ta mf (-ti -te) cosmonaut, astronaut

cosmopoli·ta adj & mf (-ti -te) cosmopolitan

cóso [s] m (coll) thing, what-d'you-call-it

cospàrgere §261 tr to spread; to sprinkle

cospèrgere §112 tr (poet) to wet, sprinkle

cospètto m presence; **al cospetto di** in the presence of

cospì·cuo -cua adj distinguished, outstanding; huge, immense; (poet) conspicuous

cospirare intr to conspire, plot

cospira·tóre -trice mf conspirator

cospirazióne f conspiracy, plot

còsta f side; rib; coast, seashore; slope; welt (*along seam*); wale (*in fabric*); (naut) frame

costà adv there; over there

costaggiù adv down there

costante adj & f constant

Costantinòpoli f Constantinople

costanza f constancy ‖ **Costanza** f Constance

costare (còsto) intr (ESSERE) to cost; to be expensive; **costare caro** to cost dear; **costare un occhio della testa** to cost a fortune

costarica·no -na or costaricènse adj & mf Costa Rican

costassù adv up there

costata f rib roast; side

costeggiare §290 (costéggio) tr to sail along; to run along; to border on ‖ intr to coast

costèi §8 pron dem

costellare (costèllo) tr to stud, star

costellazióne f constellation

costernare (costèrno) tr to dismay, cause consternation to

costernazióne f consternation

costì adv there

costiè·ro -ra adj coast, coastal; offshore ‖ f coastline; gentle slope

costipare tr to constipate; to heap, pile ‖ ref to become constipated

costipazióne f constipation

costituènte adj constituent; constituting ‖ m member of constituent assembly; (chem) constituent

costituire §176 tr to constitute; to form ‖ ref to become; to appoint oneself; to give oneself up (*to justice*); **costituirsi in giudizio** (law) to sue (*in civil court*); **costituirsi parte civile** (law) to appear as a plaintiff (*in civil court*)

costituto m (law) pact, agreement; (naut) master's declaration (*to health authorities*)

costituzionale adj constitutional

costituzióne f constitution; charter; composition; (law) appearance; surrender (*to justice*)

còsto m cost; **a costo di** at the price of; **ad ogni costo** at any cost; **a nessun costo** by no means; **a tutti i costi** at any cost, in any event; **costo della vita** cost of living; **sotto costo** below cost

còstola f rib; spine (*of book*); back (*of knife*); **avere qlcu alle costole** to have s.o. at one's heels; **rompere le costole a** (fig) to break the bones of; **stare alle costole di** to be at the back of

costolétta f chop, cutlet

costolóne m (archit) groin

costóro §8 pron dem

costó·so -sa [s] adj costly

costrìngere §265 tr to force, constrain; (poet) to compress

costritti·vo -va adj constrictive

costrizióne f constriction

costruire §140 tr to construct, build

costrut·to -ta *adj* constructed ‖ *m* profit; sense; (gram) construction; **dov'è il costrutto?** what's the point?

costruttóre *m* builder

costruzióne *f* construction; building

costùi §8 *pron dem*

costumanza *f* custom

costumare *intr* (+ *inf*) to be in the habit of (+ *ger*) ‖ *intr* (ESSERE) to be the custom; to be in use

costumatézza *f* good manners

costuma·to -ta *adj* polite, well-bred

costume *m* custom, manner; costume, dress; bathing suit

costumi·sta *mf* (*-sti -ste*) (theat) costumer

costùra *f* seam

cotale *adj* & *pron* such ‖ *adv* (archaic) thus

cotan·to -ta *adj* & *pron* (poet) so much ‖ **cotanto** *adv* (poet) such a long time

còte *f* flint

coténna *f* pigskin; rind; (coll) hide, skin

coté·sto -sta §7 *adj dem* ‖ §8 *pron dem*

cóti·ca *f* (*-che*) (coll) hide, skin (*of porker*)

cotógna *f* quince (*fruit*)

cotognata *f* quince jam

cotógno *m* quince (*tree*)

cotolétta *f* chop, cutlet

cotóne *m* cotton; thread; **cotone fulminante** guncotton; **cotone idrofilo** absorbent cotton; **cotone silicato** mineral wool

cotonière *m* cotton manufacturer

cotonie·ro -ra *adj* cotton ‖ *mf* cotton worker

cotonifi·cio *m adj* (*-ci*) cotton mill

cotonó·so -sa [s] *adj* cotton; cottony

còtta *f* cooking; baking; drying (*of bricks*); (sports) exhaustion; (coll) drunkenness; (joc) infatuation; love; (eccl) surplice; **cotta d'armi** coat of mail

cottimi·sta *mf* (*-sti -ste*) pieceworker

còttimo *m* piecework

còt·to -ta *adj* cooked; baked; burnt; suntanned; (joc) half-baked; (joc) in love; (sports) exhausted ‖ *m* brick ‖ *f* see **cotta**

cottùra *f* cooking; **a punto di cottura** (culin) done just right

coutènte *mf* (law) joint user; (telp) party-line user

cóva *f* brooding; nest

covare (**cóvo**) *tr* to brood, to hatch; to harbor or nurse (*an enmity*); to nurture (*a disease*); **covare con gli occhi** to look fondly at; **covare le lenzuola** to loll around ‖ *intr* to smolder (*said of fire or passion*)

covata *f* brood, covey

covile *m* doghouse; den

cóvo *m* shelter; den, lair; **farsi il covo** (fig) to gather a nestegg; **uscire dal covo** to stick one's nose out of the house

covóne *m* sheaf; cock (*of hay*)

còzza *f* cockle

cozzare (**còzzo**) *tr* to hit; to butt (*one's head*) ‖ *intr* to butt; (fig) to clash;

cozzare contro to bump into ‖ *ref* to hit one another; to fight

còzzo *m* butt; clash, conflict

crac *m* crash

crampo *m* cramp

crâni·co -ca *adj* (*-ci -che*) cranial

crà·nio *m* (*-ni*) cranium, skull

cràpula *f* excess (*in eating and drinking*)

cras·so -sa *adj* crass, gross; large (*intestine*)

cratère *m* crater; bomb crater

cràuti *mpl* sauerkraut

cravatta *f* tie, necktie; **cravatta a farfalla** bow tie; **fare cravatte** to be a usurer

creanza *f* politeness; **buona creanza** good manners

creare (**crèo**) *tr* to create; to name, elect

creati·vo -va *adj* creative

crea·to -ta *adj* created ‖ *m* creation, universe

creazióne *f* creation; (poet) election

crea·tóre -trice *adj* creative ‖ *mf* creator

creatùra *f* creature; baby; **povera creatura!** poor thing!

credènte *adj* believing ‖ *mf* believer

credènza *f* credence, faith, belief; sideboard, buffet; (coll) credit

credenziale *f* letter of credit; **credenziali** credentials

credenzière *m* butler

crédere §141 *tr* to believe; to think; **lo credo bene! I should say so!** ‖ *intr* to believe; to trust; **credere a** to believe in; **credere in Dio** to believe in God ‖ *ref* to believe oneself to be

credìbile *adj* credible

credibilità *f* credibility

crédito *m* credit

credi·tóre -trice *mf* creditor

crèdo *m* credo, creed

credulità *f* credulity

crèdu·lo -la *adj* credulous

crèma *f* cream; custard; **crema da scarpe** shoe polish; **crema di bellezza** beauty cream; **crema di pomodoro** cream of tomato soup; **crema evanescente** vanishing cream; **crema per barba** shaving cream

cremaglièra *f* rack; cogway, cograil

cremare (**crèmo**) *tr* to cremate

crema·tóio *m* (*-tói*) crematory

cremató·rio *m* (*-ri*) crematory

cremazióne *f* cremation

cremerìa *f* creamery

crèmisi *adj* & *m* crimson

Cremlino *m* Kremlin

cremlinologìa *f* Kremlinology

cremortàrtaro *m* cream of tartar

cremó·so -sa [s] *adj* creamy

crèn *m* horseradish

creolina *f* creolin

crè·o·lo -la *adj* & *mf* Creole

creosòto *m* creosote

crèpa *f* crack, crevice; rift

crepàc·cio *m* (*-ci*) crevasse; fissure

crepacuòre *m* heartbreak

crepapància *m*—**mangiare a crepapancia** to burst from eating too much

crepapèlle *m*—**ridere a crepapelle** to split one's sides laughing

crepare (crèpo) *intr* to burst; to crack; to chip; (slang) to croak; **crepare dalla sete** to die of thirst; **crepare dalle risa** to die laughing; **crepare d'invidia** to be green with envy

crepitare (crèpito) *intr* to crackle (*said of fire or weapons*); to rustle (*said of leaves*)

crepìti·o *m* (**-ì**) crackle; rustle; pitter-patter (*of rain*)

crepuscolare *adj* twilight; (fig) dim

crepùscolo *m* twilight

crescènte *adj* rising, growing; crescent (*moon*) ‖ *m* (astr & heral) crescent

crescènza *f* growth

créscere §142 *tr* to grow, raise; to increase ‖ *intr* (ESSERE) to grow; to increase; to rise (*said, e.g., of prices*); to wax (*said of the moon*); **farsi crescere** to grow (*a beard*)

crescióne *m* watercress

créscita *f* growth; outgrowth; rise (*of water*)

crèsima *f* confirmation

cresimare (crèsimo) *tr* to confirm

Crèso *m* (mythol) Croesus

cré·spo -spa *adj* crispy, kinky; (archaic) wrinkled ‖ *m* crepe ‖ *f* wrinkle; ruffle

crésta *f* comb (*of chicken*); crest; abbassare la cresta to come down a peg or two; alzare la cresta to become insolent

crestàia *f* (coll) milliner

créta *f* clay

cretése [s] *adj & mf* Cretan

cretinerìa *f* idiocy

creti·no -na *adj & mf* idiot, cretin

cribro *m* (poet) sieve

crìc·ca *f* (-che) clique, gang; group; crevice

cric·co *m* (-chi) (aut) jack

cricéto *m* hamster

cri crì *m* chirping (*of crickets*)

criminale *adj* criminal; (law) penal ‖ *mf* criminal

criminali·sta *mf* (-sti -ste) penal lawyer, criminal lawyer

criminalità *f* criminality

crìmine *m* crime

criminologìa *f* criminology

criminòlo·go *m* (-gi) criminologist

criminó·so -sa [s] *adj* criminal

crinale *adj* (poet) hair ‖ *m* ridge (*of mountains*)

crine *m* horsehair; (poet) hair; (poet) sunbeam

crinièra *f* mane

crinolina *f* crinoline

cripta *f* crypt

criptocomuni·sta *mf* (-sti -ste) fellow traveler

crisàlide *f* chrysalis

crisantèmo *m* chrysanthemum

crì·si *f* (-si) crisis; shortage (*of houses*); attack (*e.g., of fever*); outburst (*of tears*); (econ) slump; **crisi ancillare** or **domestica** servant problem; **in crisi** in difficulties

cristallerìa *f* glassware; crystal service; glassware shop; glassworks

cristallièra *f* china closet

cristalli·no -na *adj* crystalline ‖ *m* crystalline lens

cristallizzare [ddzz] *tr & ref* to crystallize

cristallo *m* crystal; glass; pane (*of glass*); windshield; **cristallo di rocca** rock crystal; **cristallo di sicurezza** (aut) safety glass

cristianaménte *adv* in a Christian manner, like a Christian; (coll) decently; **morire cristianamente** to die in the faith

cristianésimo *m* Christianity

cristianità *f* Christendom

cristia·no -na *adj & mf* Christian

Cristo *m* Christ; **avanti Cristo** before Christ (B.C.); **dopo Cristo** after Christ (A.D.); **un povero cristo** (slang) a poor guy

critè·rio *m* (-ri) criterion; judgment

crìti·ca *f* (-che) criticism; critique; slur

criticare §197 (crìtico) *tr* to criticize, censure; to find fault with

crìti·co -ca (-ci -che) *adj* critical ‖ *mf* critic; (coll) faultfinder ‖ *f* see critica

crittografìa *f* cryptography

crittogram·ma *m* (-mi) cryptogram

crivellare (crivèllo) *tr* to riddle

crivèllo *m* sieve, riddle

croa·to -ta *adj & mf* Croatian

Croàzia, la Croatia

croccante *adj* crisp, crunchy ‖ *m* almond brittle, peanut brittle

crocchétta *f* croquette

cròcchia *f* chignon, topknot

crocchiare §287 (cròcchio) *intr* to crackle; to sound cracked or broken; to cluck (*said of a hen*); to crack (*said of joints*)

cròc·chio *m* (-chi) group (*of people*); far crocchio to gather around

cróce *f* cross; x (*mark made by illiterate person*); tail (*of coin*); (fig) trial; **Croce del Sud** Southern Cross; **croce di Malta** Maltese cross; **Croce Rossa** Red Cross; **croce uncinata** swastika; **fare una croce sopra** to forget about; **gettare la croce addosso** (fig) to put the blame on; **mettere in croce** to crucify

crocefisso *m* crucifix

crocerossina *f* Red Cross worker

croceségno *m* cross, x (*mark made instead of signature*)

crocétta *f* (naut) crosstree

croce·vìa *m* (-vìa) crossroads, intersection

crocia·to -ta *adj* crossed; crusading; see parola ‖ *m* crusader ‖ *f* crusade

crocièra *f* cruise; (archit) cross (*vault*); (mach) cross (*of universal joint*)

crocière *m* (orn) crossbill

crocifìggere §104 *tr* to crucify

crocifissióne *f* crucifixion

crocifìs·so -sa *adj* crucified ‖ *m* crucifix

cròco *m* (-chi) crocus

crogiolare (ceògiolo) *tr* to cook on a low fire; to simmer; to temper (*glass*) ‖ *ref* to bask; to snuggle (*e.g., in bed*)

crògiolo *m* cooking on a low fire; simmering; tempering (*of glass*)

crogiòlo *m* crucible; (fig) melting pot

crollare (cròllo) *tr* to shake (*e.g., one's head*) ‖ *intr* (ESSERE) to fall down, collapse ‖ *ref* to shake

cròllo *m* shake; fall, collapse

cròma *f* (mus) quaver

cromare (**cròmo**) *tr* to plate with chromium

croma·to **-ta** *adj* chromium-plated; chrome ‖ *m* chrome yellow

cromatura *f* chromium plating

cròmo *m* chrome, chromium

cromosfèra *f* chromosphere

cromosò·ma [s] *m* (-mi) chromosome

cròna·ca *f* (-che) chronicle; report, news; **cronaca bianca** news of the day; **cronaca giudiziaria** court news; **cronaca mondana** social column; **cronaca nera** police and accident report; **cronaca rosa** wedding column; stork news

cròni·co **-ca** (-ci -che) *adj* chronic ‖ *mf* incurable

croni·sta *mf* (-sti -ste) reporter; chronicler

cronistòria *f* chronicle

cronologìa *f* chronology

cronològi·co **-ca** *adj* (-ci -che) chronologic(al)

cronometrare (**cronòmetro**) *tr* to time

cronomètri·co **-ca** *adj* (-ci -che) chronometric(al); split-second

cronometri·sta *m* (-sti) (sports) timekeeper

cronòmetro *m* stopwatch; chronometer

crosciare §128 (**cròscio**) *tr* (archaic) to heave, throw ‖ *intr* to rustle (*said of dry leaves*); to pitter-patter (*said of rain*)

cròsta *f* crust; bark (*of tree*); scab; slough; shell (*of crustacean*); poor painting

crostàceo *m* crustacean

crostata *f* pie

crostino *m* toast

crostó·so **-sa** [s] *adj* crusty

croupier *m* (**croupier**) croupier

crucciare §128 *tr* to worry, vex; to chagrin ‖ *ref* to worry; to become angry

cruccia·to **-ta** *adj* afflicted; worried; angry; chagrined

crùc·cio *m* (-ci) sorrow; (obs) anger; **darsi cruccio** to fret

cruciale *adj* crucial

crucivèr·ba *m* (-ba) crossword puzzle

crudèle *adj* cruel

crudel·tà *f* (-tà) cruelty

crudézza *f* crudity; harshness

cru·do **-da** *adj* raw; rare (*meat*); (poet) cruel

cruèn·to **-ta** *adj* (lit) bloody

crumiro *m* scab (*in strikes*)

cruna *f* eye (*of a needle*)

cru·sca *f* (-sche) bran; (coll) freckles

cruscante *adj* Della-Cruscan; affected ‖ *m* member of the Accademia della Crusca

cruschèllo *m* middlings

cruscòtto *m* (aut) dashboard; (aer) instrument panel

cuba·no **-na** *adj* & *mf* Cuban

cubatura *f* volume

cùbi·co **-ca** *adj* (-ci -che) cubic; cube (*root*)

cubitale *adj* very large (*handwriting or type*)

cùbito *m* cubit; (poet) elbow

cubo *m* cube

cuccagna *f* plenty; windfall; Cockaigne

cuccétta *f* berth

cucchiàia *f* large spoon; ladle; trowel; bucket (*of power shovel*); **cucchiaia bucata** skimmer

cucchiaiàta *f* spoonful; tablespoonful

cucchiaino *m* teaspoon; teaspoonful; spoon (*lure*)

cuc·chiàio *m* (-chiài) spoon; spoonful; tablespoon; **cucchiaio da minestra** soupspoon

cucchiaióne *m* ladle

cùc·cia *f* (-ce) dog's bed; **a cuccia!** lie down!

cucciare §128 *intr* (ESSERE) & *ref* to lie down (*said of a dog*)

cucciolata *f* litter (*e.g., of puppies*)

cùcciolo *m* puppy; cub; (fig) greenhorn

cuc·co *m* (-chi) cuckoo; simpleton; darling (*child*)

cuccuru·cù *m* (-cù) cock-a-doodle-doo

cucina *f* kitchen; cuisine; kitchen range; **cucina componibile** kitchen with sectional cabinets; **cucina economica** kitchen range; **fare da cucina** to prepare a meal

cucinare *tr* to cook; (fig) to fix

cucinétta *f* kitchenette

cuciniè·re **-ra** *mf* cook

cucire §143 *tr* to sew; to stitch ‖ *ref*— **cucirsi la bocca** to keep one's mouth shut

cucirino *m* sewing thread

cuci·tóre **-trice** *adj* sewing ‖ *mf* sewing machine operator ‖ *f* seamstress; sewing machine (*for bookbinding*); **cucitrice a grappe** stapler

cuci·to **-ta** *adj* sewn ‖ *m* sewing; needle work

cucitura *f* seam; sewing; stitches

cu·cù *m* (-cù) cuckoo

cuculo or **cùculo** *m* cuckoo

cùffia *f* bonnet (*for baby*); coif; (rad) headset; (telp) headpiece; (theat) prompter's box

cugi·no **-na** *mf* cousin

cui *pron invar* whose; to which; whom; which; of whom; of which; **per cui** (coll) therefore

culatta *f* breech (*of a gun*)

culinà·rio **-ria** (-ri -rie) *adj* culinary ‖ *f* gastronomy

culla *f* cradle

cullare *tr* to rock (*a baby*); (fig) to delude ‖ *ref* to have delusions

culminante *adj* highest; culminating

culminare (**cùlmino**) *intr* to culminate

cùlmine *m* top, summit

culo *m* (vulg) behind; (slang) bottom (*of glass or bottle*): **culi di bicchiere** (coll) fake diamonds

cul·to **-ta** *adj* cultivated; learned (*e.g., word*) ‖ *m* cult, worship

cul·tóre **-trice** *mf* devotee

cultura *f* culture; **cultura fisica** physical culture

culturale *adj* cultural

cumino *m* (bot) caraway seed; (bot) cumin

cumulati·vo **-va** *adj* cumulative

cùmulo *m* heap, pile; concurrence (*of penal sentences*); cumulus

cuna *f* cradle

cùneo *m* wedge; chock; (archit) voussoir

cunétta *f* ditch; gutter

cunìcolo *m* small tunnel; burrow

cuòcere §144a *tr* to cook; to bake (*bricks*); to burn, dry up; (fig) to stew || *intr* to cook; to burn; to dry up; (with *dat*) to grieve, to pain

cuò·co -ca *mf* (*-chi -che*) cook

cuòio *m* (**cuòi**) leather; **avere il cuoio duro** to have a tough hide; (**cuoio capelluto** scalp || *m* (**cuoia** *fpl*) (archaic) leather; **tirare le cuoia** (slang) to croak, to kick the bucket

cuòre *m* heart; **avere il cuore da coniglio** to be chicken-hearted; **avere il cuore da leone** to be lion-hearted; **cuori** (cards) hearts; **di cuore** gladly; heartily; **fare cuore a** to encourage; **stare a cuore** to be important

cupidìgia *f* cupidity, greed, covetousness

Cupido *m* Cupid

cùpi·do -da *adj* greedy, covetous

cu·po -pa *adj* dark; deep (*color, voice*); sad, gloomy

cùpola *f* dome, cupola; crown (*of hat*)

cura *f* care; interest; cure; ministry; (poet) anxiety; **a cura di** edited by (*e.g., text*)

curare *tr* to take care of; to heed || *intr* to see to it || *ref* to take care of oneself; to care; to deign; **curarsi di** to care for

curatèla *f* (law) guardianship

curati·vo -va *adj* curative

cura·to -ta *adj* cured; healed || *m* curate

cura·tóre -trìce *mf* curator; trustee; editor (*of critical edition*); receiver (*in bankruptcy*)

curculióne *m* (ent) weevil

cur·do -da *adj & mf* Kurd

cùria *f* curia; bar

curiale *adj* curia; legal

curialé·sco -sca *adj* (*-schi -sche*) hair-splitting, legalistic

curiosare [s] *intr* (**curióso**) to pry around, snoop; to browse around

curiosi·tà [s] *f* (*-tà*) curiosity; whim; curio

curió·so -sa [s] *adj* curious; bizarre, quaint

curro *m* roller

cursóre *m* process server; court messenger; slide (*of slide ruler*)

curva *f* curve, bend; sweep; **curva di livello** contour line

curvare *tr* to curve, bend; **curvare la fronte** to bow down, yield || *intr* to curve (*said of a road*); to take a curve, negotiate a curve || *ref* to curve, bend; to bow; to become bent; to warp

curvatura *f* curving, bending; warp; stoop, curvature; camber

cur·vo -va *adj* bent, curved || *f* see **curva**

cuscinétto *m* small pillow; pad (*for ink*); buffer (*zone*); (mach) bearing; **cuscinetto a rulli** roller bearing; **cuscinetto a sfere** ball bearing

cuscino *m* pillow; cushion

cùspide *f* point (*of arrow*); (archit) steeple

custòde *adj* guardian (*angel*) || *m* custodian; janitor; warden; guard; (coll) policeman, cop

custòdia *f* safekeeping, custody; case (*e.g., of violin*); trust; (mach) housing

custodire §176 *tr* to keep; to protect, guard; to be in charge of (*prisoners*); to take care of; to cherish (*a memory*)

cutàne·o -a *adj* cutaneous

cute *f* (anat) skin

cuticagna *f* (joc) nape of the neck

cutìcola *f* epidermis; cuticle; dentine

cutireazióne *f* skin test (*for allergic reactions*)

cutréttola *f* (orn) wagtail

D

D, d [di] *m & f* fourth letter of the Italian alphabet

da *prep* from; to; at; on; through; between; since; with; by, e.g., **è stato arrestato dalla polizia** he was arrested by the police; worth, e.g., **un libro da mille lire** a book worth a thousand lire; worthy of, e.g., **azione da gentiluomo** action worthy of a gentleman; at the house, office, shop, etc., of, e.g., **dal pittore** at the house of the painter; **da Giovanni** at John's; **dall'avvocato** at the lawyer's office; **d'altro lato** on the other hand; **d'ora in poi** from now on

dabbasso *adv* downstairs; down below

dabbenàggine *f* simplicity, foolishness

dabbène *adj invar* honest, upright, e.g., **un uomo dabbene** an honest man;

simple, foolish, e.g., **un dabben uomo** a Simple Simon

daccanto *adv* near, nearby

daccapo *adv* again, all over again; **andar daccapo** to begin a new paragraph; **daccapo a piedi** from top to bottom

dacché *conj* since

dado *m* cube; pedestal (*of column*); (mach) nut; (mach) die (*to cut threads*); **dadi** dice; **giocare ai dadi** to shoot craps; **il dado è tratto** the die is cast

daffare *m* things to do; bustle; **darsi daffare** to bustle, bustle about

da·ga *f* (*-ghe*) dagger

dagli §4 || *interj*—**dagli al ladro!** stop thief!; **e dagli!** cut it out!

dài §4

dài·no -na *mf* fallow deer ‖ *m* fallow deer; buckskin

dal §4

dàlia *f* dahlia

dalla §4

dallato *adv* aside; sideways

dalle §4

dalli *interj*—**dalli al ladro!** stop thief!; e **dalli!** cut it out!

dallo §4

dàlma·ta *adj* & *mf* (**-ti -te**) Dalmatian

Dalmàzia, la Dalmatia

daltòni·co -ca *adj* (**-ci -che**) color-blind

daltonismo *m* color blindness

dama *f* lady; dancing partner; checkers; andare a dama (checkers) to be crowned; **dama di compagnia** companion; **dama di corte** lady-in-waiting

damare *tr* (checkers) to crown

damascare §197 *tr* to damask

damaschinare *tr* to damascene

dama·sco *m* (**-schi**) damask ‖ **Damasco** *f* Damascus

damerino *m* fop, dandy

damigèlla *f* (lit) damsel; (orn) demoiselle; **damigella d'onore** bridesmaid

damigiana *f* demijohn

danaro *m* var of denaro

danaró·so -sa [s] *adj* wealthy, rich

dande *fpl* leading strings

danése [s] *adj* Danish ‖ *mf* Dane ‖ *m* Danish (*language*); Great Dane

Danimarca, la Denmark

dannare *tr* to damn; to bedevil ‖ *ref* to be damned; to fret

danna·to -ta *adj* damned; wicked; terrible (*e.g., fear*) ‖ *m* damned soul

dannazióne *f* damnation

danneggiare §290 (**dannéggio**) *tr* to damage; to injure, impair

danneggia·to -ta *adj* damaged; injured, impaired ‖ *mf* victim

danno *m* damage; injury; (ins) loss; **chiedere i danni** to ask for indemnification; **far danni a** to damage; **rifare i danni a** to indemnify; **tuo danno** so much the worse for you

dannó·so -sa [s] *adj* damaging, harmful

dante *m*—**pelle di dante** buckskin

danté·sco -sca *adj* (**-schi -sche**) Dantean, Dantesque

danti·sta *mf* (**-sti -ste**) Dante scholar

Danùbio *m* Danube

danza *f* dance; dancing

danzare *tr* & *intr* to dance

danza·tóre -trice *mf* dancer

dappertutto *adv* everywhere

dappiè *adv*—**dappiè di** at the foot of

dappiù *adv*—**dappiù di** more than

dappòco *adj* invar worthless

dappòi *adv* (obs) afterwards, after

dapprèsso *adv* near, nearby, close

dapprima *adv* first, in the first place

dapprincipio *adv* first, in the beginning; over again

dardeggiare §290 (**dardéggio**) *tr* to hurl darts at; to beat down on; to look daggers at ‖ *intr* to hurl darts; to beat down

dardo *m* dart, arrow; tip (*of blow-torch*)

da·re *m* (**-re**) (com) debit; **dare e avere** debit and credit ‖ §144b *tr* to give; to set (*fire*); to hand over; to lay down (*one's life*); to render (*e.g., unto Caesar*); to give away (*a bride*); to take (*an examination*); to tender (*one's resignation*); to say (*good night*); to shed (*tears*); **dare acqua a** to water; **dare alla luce** to give birth to; to bring out (*e.g., a book*); **dare aria a** to air; **dare . . . anni a qlcu** to think that s.o. is . . . years old; **dare a ridire** to give rise to complaint; **dare da intendere** to lead to believe; **dare fastidio a** to bother, annoy; **dare fondo a** to use up; **dare gli otto giorni a** to dismiss, fire; **dare il benvenuto a** to welcome; **dare il via a** to start (*e.g., a race*); **dare la colpa a** to declare guilty; to put the blame on; **dare la mano a** to shake hands with; **dare l'assalto a** to assault; **dare luogo a** to give rise to; **dare noia a** to bother; **dare per certo a** to assure; **dare ragione a** to agree with; **dare torto a** to disagree with; **dare via** to give away ‖ *intr* to burst; to begin; to beat down (*said of the sun*); **dare a** to verge on; to face, overlook; **dare addosso a** to attack, persecute; **dare ai** or **sui nervi di** to irritate, irk; **dare alla testa a** to go to one's head, e.g., **il vino gli dà alla testa** wine goes to his head; **dare contro a** to disagree with; **dare del ladro a** to call (s.o.) a thief; **dare del Lei a** to address formally; **dare del tu a** to address familiarly; **dare di volta il cervello a** to go raving mad, e.g., **gli ha dato di volta il cervello** he went raving mad; **dare giù** to abate; **dare in** to hit; **dare in affitto** to rent, lease; **dare nell'occhio** to attract attention; to hit the eye; **dare nel segno** to hit the target ‖ *ref* to put on, e.g., **darsi la cipria** to put powder on; **darsela a gambe** to take to one's heels; **darsela per intesa** to become convinced; to take for granted; **darsele** to strike one another; **darsi a** to give oneself over to; **darsi delle arie** to put on airs; **darsi il vanto di** to boast of; **darsi un bacio** to kiss one another; **darsi la mano** to shake hands; **darsi la morte** to commit suicide; **darsi pace** to resign oneself; **darsi pensiero** to worry; **darsi per malato** to declare oneself ill; to fall ill; **darsi per vinto** to give in, submit; **può darsi** it's possible, maybe; **si dà il caso** it happens

dàrsena *f* dock; basin

data *f* date; deal (*of cards*); **a . . . data** (com) . . . days hence, on or before . . . days; **di fresca data** new (*e.g., friend*); **di vecchia data** old (*e.g., friend*)

datare *tr* to date ‖ *intr*—**a datare da** beginning with

datà·rio *m* (**-ri**) date stamp

dati·vo -va *adj* & *m* dative

da·to -ta *adj* inclined, bent; addicted; given; appointed (*date*); **dato e non concesso** assumed for the sake of argument; **dato che** since || *m* datum || *f* see **data**

da·tóre -trice *mf* giver, donor; **datore di lavoro** employer; **datore di sangue** blood donor; **datori di lavoro** management

dàttero *m* date; (zool) date shell

dattilografare (dattilògrafo) *tr* to typewrite, type

dattilografia *f* typewriting

dattilògra·fo -fa *mf* typist

dattiloscopia *f* examination of fingerprints

dattiloscrit·to -ta *adj* typewritten || *m* typescript

dattórno *adv* near, nearby; **darsi dattorno** to strive; **stare dattorno a** to cling to; **togliersi dattorno qlcu** to get rid of s.o.

davanti *adj invar* fore, front || **davan·ti** *m* (**-ti**) front, face || **davanti** *adv* ahead, in front; **davanti a** in front of; **levarsi davanti a qlcu** to get out of someone's way; **passare davanti a** to pass, outstrip

davanzale *m* window sill

davanzo *adv* more than enough

davvéro *adv* indeed; **dire davvero** to speak in earnest

daziare §287 *tr* to levy a duty on

dà·zio *m* (**-zi**) duty, custom; custom office

dèa *f* goddess

debellare (debèllo) *tr* (lit) to crush

debilitare (debìlito) *tr* to debilitate

debilitazióne *f* debilitation

débi·to -ta *adj* due || *m* debit; debt; **debito pubblico** national debt

debi·tóre -trice *mf* debtor

débole *adj* weak; faint; gentle (*sex*); **debole di mente** feeble-minded || *m* weakness, weak point; weakness, foible; weakling

debolézza *f* weakness, debility

debordare (debórdo) *intr* (ESSERE & AVERE) to overflow

debòscia *f* debauchery

deboscia·to -ta *adj* debauched || *mf* debauchee

debuttante *adj* beginning || *mf* beginner || *f* debutante

debuttare *intr* to come out, make one's debut; (theat) to perform for the first time; (theat) to open

debutto *m* debut; (theat) opening night, opening

dècade *f* ten; period of ten days; (mil) ten days' pay

decadènte *adj & m* decadent

decadènza *f* decadence; lapse (*of insurance policy*); (law) forfeiture

decadére §121 *intr* (ESSERE) to decline; to lose one's standing; (ins) to lapse; **decadere da** (law) to forfeit

decadiménto *m* decadence; (law) forfeiture

decadu·to -ta *adj* fallen upon hard times

decaffeinizzare [ddzz] *tr* to decaffeinate

decalcificatóre *m* water softener

decalcomania *f* decalcomania

decàlo·go *m* (**-ghi**) decalogue

decampare *intr* to decamp; **decampare da** to abandon (*a plan*)

decano *m* dean

decantare *tr* to praise, extol; to decant; (lit) to purify || *intr* to undergo decantation

decapàggio *m* (metallurgy) pickling

decapitare (decàpito) *tr* to behead, decapitate

decapitazióne *f* beheading

decappottàbile *adj & f* (aut) convertible

decèdere §123 *intr* (ESSERE) to die; to decease

decelerare (decèlero) *tr & intr* to decelerate

decennale *adj & m* decennial

decènne *adj & mf* ten-year-old

decèn·nio *m* (**-ni**) decade

decènte *adj* decent; proper

decentralizzare [ddzz] *tr* to decentralize

decentrare (decèntro) *tr* to decentralize

decènza *f* decency; propriety

decèsso *m* decease, demise

decìdere §145 *tr* to decide; to persuade || *intr & ref* to decide; **deciditi!** make up your mind!

decifràbile *adj* decipherable

decifrare *tr* to decipher, decode; (fig) to puzzle out (*e.g., somebody's intentions*); (mus) to sight-read

dècima *f* tithe

decimale *adj & m* decimal

decimare (dècimo) *tr* to decimate

decimetro *m* decimeter; **doppio decimetro** ruler

dèci·mo -ma *adj, m & pron* tenth || *f* see **decima**

decisionale *adj* decision-making

decisióne *f* decision

decisi·vo -va *adj* decisive, conclusive

deci·so -sa *adj* determined, resolute; appointed (*time*)

declamare *tr* to declaim || *intr* to declaim; to inveigh

declamazióne *f* declamation

declaratò·rio -ria *adj* (**-ri -rie**) declarative

declinare *tr* to decline; to declare, show; (gram) to decline; (lit) to bend || *intr* to set (said, *e.g., of a star*); to slope; to diminish

declinazióne *f* declination; (gram) declension

declino *m* decline

declì·vio *m* (**-vi**) declivity, slope

decollàg·gio *m* (**-gi**) take-off; lift-off

decollare (decòllo) *tr* to decapitate || *intr* (aer) to take off; (rok) to lift off

decòllo *m* take-off; lift-off

decolorante *adj* bleaching || *m* bleach

decompórre §218 *tr, intr & ref* to decompose

decomposizióne *f* decomposition

decompressióne *f* decompression

decongelare (decongèlo) *tr* to thaw; (com) to unfreeze

decontaminare (decontàmino) *tr* to decontaminate

decorare (decòro) *tr* to decorate

decorati·vo -va *adj* decorative

decora·tóre -trice *mf* decorator

decorazióne *f* decoration

decòro *m* decorum, propriety; decor; dignity; decoration

decoró·so -sa [s] *adj* fitting, decorous, proper; dignified

decorrènza *f* beginning, effective date; lapse

decórrere §139 *intr* (ESSERE) to elapse; to begin; (lit) to run; **a decorrere da** effective, beginning with

decór·so -sa *adj* past || *m* period, span; course; development; **nel decorso di** in the course of

decòt·to -ta *adj* (com) insolvent || *m* decoction

decozióne *f* (com) insolvency

decrèpi·to -ta *adj* decrepit

decréscere §142 *intr* (ESSERE) to decrease

decretare (**decréto**) *tr* to decree

decréto *m* decree; **decreto legge** decree law

decùbito *m* recumbency

decuplicare §197 (**decùplico**) *tr* to multiply tenfold

dècu·plo -pla *adj* tenfold || *m* tenfold part

decurtare *tr* to diminish, decrease

decurtazióne *f* decrease

dèda·lo -la (lit) ingenious || *m* maze, labyrinth

dèdi·ca *f* (-**che**) dedication; inscription (*in a book*)

dedicare §197 (**dèdico**) *tr* to dedicate; to inscribe (*a book*) || *ref* to devote oneself

dèdi·to -ta *adj* devoted; addicted

dedizióne *f* devotion; (obs) surrender

dedurre §102 *tr* to deduce; to deduct; to derive; (hist) to found (*a colony*)

deduzióne *f* deduction

defalcàbile *adj* deductible

defalcare §197 *tr* to deduct, withhold

defal·co *m* (-**chi**) deduction, withholding

defecare §197 (**deféco**) *tr* (chem) to purify || *intr* to defecate

defenestrare (**defenèstro**) *tr* to throw out of the window; (fig) to fire; (pol) to unseat

defenestrazióne *f* defenestration; (fig) firing, dismissal

deferènte *adj* deferential; (anat) deferent

deferènza *f* deference

deferire §176 *tr* to submit; (law) to commit; **deferire il giuramento a qlcu** to put s.o. under oath || *intr* to defer

defezionare (**defezióno**) *intr* to desert, defect

defezióne *f* defection

deficiènte *adj* deficient, lacking || *mf* idiot

deficiènza *f* deficiency; idiocy

dèfi·cit *m* (-**cit**) deficit

deficità·rio -ria *adj* (-**ri -rie**) lacking; deficit (*e.g., budget*)

defilare *tr* to defilade || *ref* to protect oneself

denfinìbile *adj* definable

definire §176 *tr* to define; to settle (*an argument*)

definiti·vo -va *adj* definitive; **in definitiva** after all

defini·to -ta *adj* definite

definizióne *f* definition; settlement (*of an argument*)

deflagrare *intr* to burst into flame; (fig) to burst out

deflazionare (**deflazióno**) *tr* (com) to deflate

deflazióne *f* deflation

deflèttere §177 *intr* to deflect

deflettóre *m* (aut) vent window; (mach) baffle

deflorare (**deflòro**) *tr* to deflower

defluire §176 *intr* (ESSERE) to flow down; (fig) to pour out

deflusso *m* flow; outflow, outpour; ebbtide

deformare (**defórmo**) *tr* to deform; to cripple; to alter (*a word*)

defórme *adj* deformed, crippled

deformi·tà *f* (-**tà**) deformity

defraudare (**defràudo**) *tr* to defraud, bilk

defun·to -ta *adj* dead; deceased; defunct; late || *mf* dead person, deceased || *m* deceased; **i defunti** the deceased

degenerare (**degènero**) *intr* (ESSERE & AVERE) to degenerate; to worsen

degenera·to -ta *adj* degenerate, perverted || *mf* degenerate, pervert

degenerazióne *f* degeneracy, degeneration

degènere *adj* degenerate

degènte *adj* bedridden; hospitalized || *mf* patient; inpatient

degènza *f* confinement; hospitalization

dégli §4

deglutire §176 *tr* to swallow

degnare (**dégno**) *tr* to honor || *ref* to deign, condescend

degnazióne *f* condescension

dé·gno -gna *adj* worthy; **degno di nota** noteworthy

degradante *adj* degrading

degradare *tr* to degrade; to downgrade; (mil) to break || *ref* to become degraded

degradazióne *f* degradation

degustare *tr* to taste

degustazióne *f* tasting

dèh *interj* oh!

déi §4

deiezióne *f* excrement; (geol) detritus

deificare §197 (**deìfico**) *tr* to deify

dei·tà *f* (-**tà**) deity

dél §4

dela·tóre -trice *mf* informer

delazióne *f* informing; (law) administration of an oath

dèle·ga *f* (-**ghe**) proxy, power of attorney

delegare §209 (**dèlego**) *tr* to delegate

delega·to -ta *adj* delegated || *m* delegate; (eccl) legate

delegazióne *f* delegation

deletè·rio -ria *adj* (-**ri -rie**) deleterious

delfino *m* dolphin; (hist) dauphin

delibare *tr* to relish; to touch on; to ratify (*a foreign decree*)

delibazióne f ratification (of a foreign decree)

deliberare (delìbero) tr to deliberate; to decide; to award (at auction) || intr to deliberate

delibera·to -ta adj deliberate; resolved

deliberazióne f deliberation; decision

delicatézza f delicacy; gentleness; tactfulness; luxury

delica·to -ta adj delicate; gentle; tactful

delimitare (delìmito) tr to delimit

delineare (delìneo) tr to outline, sketch || ref to take shape; to appear

delinquènte m criminal

delinquènza f delinquency; **delinquenza minorile** juvenile delinquency

delìnquere §146 intr to commit a crime

deli·quio m (-qui) fainting spell, swoon; **cadere in deliquio** to faint

delirare intr to be delirious; to rave; (lit) to stray

deli·rio m (-ri) delirium; frenzy; **andare in delirio** to go wild; **cadere in delirio** to become delirious

delitto m crime

delittuó·so -sa [s] adj criminal

delizia f delight; (hort) Delicious (variety of apple)

deliziare §287 tr & ref to delight

delizió·so -sa [s] adj delicious; delightful

délla §4

délle §4

déllo §4

dèl·ta m (-ta) delta

delucidare (delùcido) tr to elucidate; to remove the sheen from

delucidazióne f elucidation; removal of sheen

delùdere §105 tr to disappoint; to deceive; to foil

delusióne f disappointment; deception

delu·so -sa adj disappointed; deceived

demagnetizzare [ddzz] tr to demagnetize

demagogìa f demagogy

demagò·go·m (-ghi) demagogue

demandare tr (law) to commit

demà·nio m (-ni) state land, state property

demarcare §197 tr to demarcate

demarcazióne f demarcation

demènte adj demented, crazy; idiotic || mf insane person; idiot

demènza f insanity, madness; idiocy

demèrito m demerit

demilitarizzare [ddzz] tr to demilitarize

democrà·ti·co -ca (-ci -che) adj democratic || mf democrat

democrazìa f democracy || **Democrazia Cristiana** Christian Democratic Party

democristia·no -na adj Christian Democratic || mf Christian Democrat

demogrà·fi·co -ca adj (-ci -che) demographic

demolire §176 tr to demolish

demoli·tóre -trice adj wrecking; destructive || mf wrecker

demolizióne f demolition

dèmone m demon

demonìa·co -ca adj (-ci -che) fiendish; demoniacal

demò·nio m (-ni) demon; **avere il demonio addosso** to be full of the devil

demoralizzare [ddzz] tr to demoralize || ref to become demoralized

demoralizza·to -ta [ddzz] adj demoralized, dejected

denaro m money; denier (of nylon thread); **avere il denaro contato** to be short of money; **denari** suit of Neapolitan cards corresponding to diamonds

denatura·to -ta adj denatured

denegare §209 (dènego or denégo) tr to deny

denigrare tr to denigrate; to backbite

denominare (denòmino) tr to call, designate

denomina·tóre -trice adj designating || m denominator

denominazióne f denomination; designation

denotare (denòto) tr to denote

densi·tà f (-tà) density

dèn·so -sa adj dense, thick

dentale adj & f dental

dentare (dènto) tr to notch, scallop || intr to teethe

dentaruòlo m teething ring

denta·to -ta adj toothed

dentatura f set of teeth; teeth (of gear)

dènte m tooth; peak (of mountain); pang (of jealousy); fluke (of anchor); prong (of fork); **battere i denti** to shiver; **dente canino** canine tooth; **dente del giudizio** wisdom tooth; **dente di latte** baby tooth; **dente di leone** (bot) dandelion; **mettere i denti** to teethe

dentellare (dentèllo) tr to notch, scallop; to perforate (stamps)

dentellatura f notch; perforation (of postage stamps); (archit) denticulation

dentèllo m notch, scallop; lace; (archit) dentil

dentièra f denture, plate; cog

dentifrì·cio -cia (-ci -cie) adj tooth || m dentifrice

denti·sta mf (-sti -ste) dentist

dentizióne f teething

déntro adv inside, in; **dentro di** inside of; within; **essere dentro** (coll) to be behind bars; **in dentro** inward || prep inside of

denuclearizzare [ddzz] tr to denuclearize

denudare tr to denude; to strip; (lit) to unveil

denunciare §128 tr var of denunziare

denùnzia f denunciation; announcement; report

denunziare §287 tr to denounce; to accuse; to announce; to report

denutri·to -ta adj undernourished

denutrizióne f undernourishment

deodorante adj & m deodorant

deodorare (deodóro) tr to deodorize

depauperare (depàupero) tr to impoverish

depennare (depénno) tr to strike out, expunge

deperìbile adj perishable

deperiménto *m* deterioration; decline
deperire §176 *intr* (ESSERE) to deteriorate; to perish; to decay
depilatò·rio -ria *adj & m* (**-ri -rie**) depilatory
deplorare (deplòro) *tr* to deplore; to reproach
deplorévole *adj* deplorable; reproachable
depolarizzare [ddzz] *tr* to depolarize
depórre §218 *tr* to lay; to lay down (*crown, arms*); to depose (*e.g., a king*); to take off (*clothes*); to give up (*hope*); to renounce; **deporre l'abito talare** to doff the cassock
deportare (depòrto) *tr* to deport
deporta·to -ta *adj* deported ‖ *mf* deportee
deportazióne *f* deportation
depositare (depòsito) *tr* to deposit; to register, check ‖ *intr* to settle (*said, e.g., of sand*)
deposità·rio -ria (**-ri -rie**) *adj* deposit ‖ *mf* depositary
depòsito *m* deposit; checking (*e.g., of a suitcase*); registration; heap (*e.g., of refuse*); warehouse; morgue; receiving ward; (mil) depot; **deposito bagagli** baggage room
deposizióne *f* deposition; Descent from the Cross
deprava·to -ta *adj* depraved
depravazióne *f* depravation
deprecare §197 **(deprèco)** *tr* to deprecate
depredare (deprèdo) *tr* to plunder
depredazióne *f* depredation
depressióne *f* depression
deprès·so -sa *adj* depressed
deprezzaménto *m* depreciation
deprezzare (deprèzzo) *tr* to depreciate; to underestimate ‖ *intr* (ESSERE) to depreciate
deprimènte *adj* depressing
deprìmere §131 *tr* to humble, discourage; to depress
depurare *tr* to purify
deputare (dèputo) *tr* to deputize, delegate
deputa·to -ta *mf* deputy, delegate; representative
deputazióne *f* deputation, delegation
deragliaménto *m* derailment
deragliare §280 *intr* to be derailed, to run off the track
derapàg·gio *m* (**-gi**) skidding
derapare *intr* to skid
derelìt·to -ta *adj & mf* derelict
derelizióne *f* dereliction
dereta·no -na *adj & m* posterior
derìdere §231 *tr* to deride, mock
derisióne *f* derision, ridicule
derisò·rio -ria *adj* (**-ri -rie**) derisory, derisive
deriva *f* (aer) vertical stabilizer; (aer, naut) leeway; (naut) drift; **alla deriva** adrift
derivare *tr* to derive; to branch off (*e.g., a canal*) ‖ *intr* (ESSERE) to be derived, arise; to drift
deriva·to -ta *adj* derivative ‖ *m* derivative (*word*) ‖ *f* (math) derivative

derivazióne *f* derivation; (elec) shunt; (telp) extension
dermatòlo·go *m* (**-gi**) dermatologist
dermòide *f* imitation leather
dèro·ga *f* (**-ghe**) exception; **in deroga a** deviating from
derogare §209 **(dèrogo)** *intr* to transgress; **derogare a** to deviate from
derrata *f* foodstuff; **derrate** foodstuff, produce
derubare *tr* to rob
dèr·vis *m* (**-vis**) or **dervì·scio** *m* (**-sci**) dervish
desalazióne [s] *f* desalinization
desalificare [s] §197 **(desalìfico)** *tr* to desalt
dé·sco *m* (**-schi**) dinner table; meal
descrittì·vo -va *adj* descriptive
descrìvere §250 *tr* to describe
descrizióne *f* description
desegregazióne [s] *f* desegregation
desensibilizzare [s] [ddzz] *tr* to desensitize
desèrti·co -ca *adj* (**-ci -che**) desert, wild
desèr·to -ta *adj* deserted; **andare deserto** to be unattended ‖ *m* desert
desideràbile [s] *adj* desirable
desiderare (desìdero) [s] *tr* to desire; **farsi desiderare** to make oneself scarce; to be dilatory
desidè·rio [s] *m* (**-ri**) desire; craving; lust; **lasciar desiderio di sé** to be greatly missed
desideró·so -sa [s] *adj* desirous
designare [s] *tr* to designate
designazióne [s] *f* designation
desinare *m* dinner ‖ *intr* to dine
desinènza *f* (gram) ending
desì·o *m* (**-i**) (lit) desire
desìstere [s] §114 *intr* to desist
desolante *adj* distressing
desolare (dèsolo) *tr* to distress; (lit) to devastate
desola·to -ta *adj* desolate; distressed
desolazióne *f* desolation; distress
dèspo·ta *m* (**-ti**) despot
despòti·co -ca *adj* (**-ci -che**) var of dispotico
despotismo *m* var of dispotismo
des·sèrt *m* (**-sèrt**) dessert
destare (désto) *tr* to awaken; to stir up ‖ *ref* to wake up
destinare *tr* to destine; to assign; to address
destinatà·rio -ria *mf* (**-ri -rie**) consignee; addressee
destinazióne *f* destination; assignment
destino *m* destiny; (com) destination
destituire §176 *tr* to demote; to dismiss; to deprive
destituzióne *f* demotion; dismissal
dé·sto -sta *adj* awake; (fig) wide-awake
dèstra *f* right, right hand
destreggiare §290 **(destréggio)** *intr* to maneuver ‖ *ref* to manage shrewdly
destrézza *f* skill, dexterity
destrière or **destrièro** *m* (lit) steed
dè·stro -stra *adj* right; skillful ‖ *f* see **destra**
destròr·so -sa *adj* clockwise; right-hand; (bot) dextrorse
destròsio *m* dextrose

desùmere [s] §116 *tr* to obtain; to infer

detecti‧ve *m* (-ve) detective

detèc‧tor *m* (-tor) (rad) detector

detenére §271 *tr* to hold; to detain

deten‧tóre -trice *mf* holder; receiver (*of stolen goods*)

detenu‧to -ta *mf* prisoner

detenzióne *f* illegal possession; detention

detergènte *adj* & *m* detergent

detèrgere §164 (*pp* **detèrso**) *tr* to cleanse; to wipe

deterioràbile *adj* perishable

deteriorare (deterióro) *tr* to spoil ‖ *intr* (ESSERE) & *ref* to deteriorate, spoil

determinare (detèrmino) *tr* to determine; to fix; to decide; to cause ‖ *ref* to decide; to happen

determinatézza *f* determination; precision

determinati‧vo -va *adj* (gram) definite

determina‧to -ta *adj* given; resolved, determined

determinazióne *f* determination

deterrènte *adj* & *m* deterrent

detersi‧vo -va *adj* cleansing ‖ *m* cleanser; detergent

detestàbile *adj* detestable

detestare (detèsto) *tr* to detest

detettóre *m* detector; **detettore di bugie** lie detector

detonare (detòno) *intr* to explode, detonate

detonatóre *m* blasting cap, detonator

detonazióne *f* detonation; report

detrarre §273 *tr* to take away; (lit) to detract

detrat‧tóre -trice *mf* detractor

detrazióne *f* detraction; deduction

detriménto *m* detriment

detrito *m* debris; detritus; (fig) outcast, outlaw

detronizzare [ddzz] *tr* to dethrone

détta *f*—**a detta di** according to

dettagliante *m* retailer

dettagliare §280 *tr* to tell in detail; to itemize; to retail ‖ *intr*—**pregasi dettagliare** please send detailed information

dettà‧glio *m* (-gli) detail; retail

dettame *m* (lit) law, norm

dettare (détto) *tr* to dictate; (lit) to compose, write; **dettar legge** to impose one's will

dettato *m* dictation; (lit) style

dettatura *f* dictation

dét‧to -ta *adj* called, named; **detto (e) fatto** no sooner said than done ‖ *m* saying ‖ *v* see **detta**

deturpare *tr* to disfigure, mar

deturpazióne *f* disfigurement, disfiguration

devalutazióne *f* devaluation

devastare *tr* to devastate, lay waste; (fig) to disfigure

devasta‧tóre -trice *adj* devastating ‖ *m* devastator

devastazióne *f* devastation

deviaménto *m* switching; derailment; (fig) straying

deviare §119 *tr* to turn aside; to lead astray; (rr) to switch; (rr) to derail

‖ *intr* to deviate; to wander; to go astray; (rr) to run off the track

deviatóre *m* (rr) switchman; (elec) two-way switch

deviazióne *f* deviation; detour; curvature (*of the spine*); (phys) declination; (phys) deflection; (rr) switching

deviazionismo *m* deviationism

dev'azioni‧sta *mf* (-sti -ste) deviationist

devoluzióne *f* transfer

devòlvere §147 *tr* to transfer ‖ *intr* & *ref* (lit) to roll down

devò‧to -ta *adj* devoted; devout, pious ‖ *m* devout person; worshiper

devozióne *f* devotion

di §4 *prep* of; in, e.g., **la più bella della famiglia** the prettiest one in the family; (*with definite article*) some, e.g., **mi occorrono dei fiammiferi** I need some matches; than, e.g., **più veloce del baleno** faster than lightning; from, e.g., **è di Milano** he is from Milan; off, e.g., **smontare di sella** to get off the saddle; about, e.g., **discutere di politica** to talk about politics; with, e.g., **ornare di fiori** to adorn with flowers; made of, e.g., **una casa di mattoni** a house made of bricks; by, e.g., **di notte** by night; for, e.g., **amor di patria** love for one's country; worth, e.g., **casa di dieci milioni** house worth ten million; in the amount of, e.g., **multa di mille lire** fine in the amount of one thousand lire; son of, e.g., **Carlo Giovannini di Filippo** Carlo Giovannini son of Philip; daughter of, e.g., **Anna Ponti di Antonio** Anna Ponti daughter of Anthony; **di corsa** running; **di gran lunga** greatly; by far; **di . . . in** from . . . to; **di là da** beyond; **di nascosto** stealthily; **di qua da** on this side of; **di quando in quando** from time to time; **di tre metri** three meters long or wide or high

dì *m* (dì) day; **a dì** (e.g., **ventisei**) this (e.g., twenty-sixth) day; **conciare per il dì delle feste** (coll) to beat up

diabète *m* diabetes

diabèti‧co -ca *adj* & *mf* (-ci -che) diabetic

diabòli‧co -ca *adj* (-ci -che) diabolic(al)

diàcono *m* deacon

diadè‧ma *m* (-mi) diadem (*of king*); tiara (*of lady*)

diàfa‧no -na *adj* diaphanous

diafonia *f* (telp) cross talk

diafram‧ma *m* (-mi) diaphragm; (fig) partition

diàgno‧si *f* (-si) diagnosis

diagnosticare §197 (diagnòstico) *tr* to diagnose

diagonale *adj* & *f* diagonal

diagram‧ma *m* (-mi) diagram; chart

diagrammare *tr* to diagram

dialettale *adj* dialectal

dialètti‧co -ca (-ci -che) *adj* dialectic(al) ‖ *m* dialectician ‖ *f* dialectic; (philos) dialectics

dialètto *m* dialect

dialettòfo‧no -na *adj* dialect-speaking ‖ *m* dialect-speaking person

dialogare §209 (**diàlogo**) *intr* to carry on a dialogue

dialoga·to -ta *adj* written in the form of a dialogue || *m* dialogue

diàlo·go *m* (**-ghi**) dialogue

diamante *m* diamond; **diamante tagliavetro** glass cutter

diametrale *adj* diametric(al)

diàmetro *m* diameter

diàmine *interj* good heavens!; the devil!; sure!

diana *f* (mil) reveille || **Diana** *f* Diana

dianzi *adv* (lit) a short while ago

diàpa·son *m* (**-son**) (mus) pitch; (mus) tuning fork

diapositiva *f* (phot) slide, transparency

dià·rio -ria *f* (**-ri -rie**) *adj* daily || *m* diary; journal; **diario scolastico** homework book || *f* per diem

diarrèa *f* diarrhea

diascò·pio *m* (**-pi**) slide projector

diaspro *m* jasper

diàstole *f* diastole

diatermìa *f* diathermy

diatriba *f* diatribe

diavolàc·cio *m* (**-ci**) devil; **buon diavolaccio** good fellow

diavolerìa *f* deviltry; devilment; evil plot

diavolè·rio *m* (**-ri**) hubbub, uproar

diavolèto *m* hubbub, uproar

diavolétto *m* little devil, imp

diàvolo *m* devil; **avere il diavolo in corpo** to be nervous; **avere un diavolo per capello** to be in a horrible mood; **buon diavolo** good fellow; **essere come il diavolo e l'acqua santa** to be at opposite poles; **fare il diavolo a quattro** to make a racket; to try very hard

dibàttere *tr* to debate || *ref* to struggle; to writhe

dibattiménto *m* debate; (law) pleading, trial

dibàttito *m* debate

dicastèro *m* department, ministry

dicèmbre *m* December

dicerìa *f* rumor, gossip

dichiarare *tr* to declare, state; to find (*guilty*); to proclaim; to nominate, name || *ref* to declare oneself to be; to declare one's love; to plead (*e.g., guilty*)

dichiarazióne *f* declaration; avowal (*of love*); return (*of income tax*); **dichiarazioni** representations

diciannòve *adj* & *pron* nineteen; **le diciannove** seven P.M. || *m* nineteen; nineteenth (*in dates*)

diciannovèsi·mo -ma *adj, m* & *pron* nineteenth

diciassètte *adj* & *pron* seventeen; **le diciassette** five P.M. || *m* seventeen; seventeenth (*in dates*)

diciassettèsi·mo -ma *adj, m* & *pron* seventeenth

diciottèsi·mo -ma *adj, m* & *pron* eighteenth

diciòtto *adj* & *pron* eighteen; **le diciotto** six P.M. || *m* eighteen; eighteenth (*in dates*)

dici·tóre -trice *mf* reciter

dicitura *f* caption, legend; (lit) wording, language

dicotomìa *f* dichotomy

didascalìa *f* note, notice; caption; legend (*e.g., on coin*); (mov) subtitle

didascàli·co -ca *adj* (**-ci -che**) didactic

didàtti·co -ca (**-ci -che**) *adj* didactic; elementary school (*director, principal*) || *f* didactics

didéntro *m* (coll) inside

didiètro *m* behind; back (*of house*) || *adv* behind

dièci *adj* & *pron* ten; **le dieci** ten o'clock || *m* ten; tenth (*in dates*)

diecimila *adj, m* & *pron* ten thousand

diecina *f* about ten

dière·si *f* (**-si**) dieresis

diè·sis *m* (**-sis**) (mus) sharp

dièta *f* diet; **dieta idrica** fluid diet

dietèti·co -ca (**-ci -che**) *adj* dietetic || *f* dietetics

dieti·sta *mf* (**-sti -ste**) dietitian

diètro *adj invar* back, rear || *m* back, rear || *adv* back, behind; **dal di dietro** from behind; **di dietro** hind (*legs*); back (*side*); behind, back (*e.g., of cupboard*) || *prep* behind; beyond; after; upon; **dietro a** behind; beyond; after; according to; **dietro consegna** on delivery; **dietro domanda** upon application; **dietro versamento** upon payment; **essere dietro a** to be in the process of

dietrofrónt *m* (mil) about face

difatti *adv* indeed

difèndere §148 *tr* to defend, protect || *ref* to protect oneself; (coll) to get along

difensi·vo -va *adj* & *f* defensive

difen·sóre -sóra *or* **difenditrice** *adj* defense || *mf* defender

difesa [s] *f* defense; bulwark; protection; **legittima difesa** self-defense; **pigliare le difese di** to defend, back up; **venire in difesa di** to go to the defense of

difettare (**difétto**) *intr* to be lacking; to be defective; **difettare di** to lack

difetti·vo -va *adj* defective

difètto *m* lack; blemish; fault; defect; **essere in difetto** to be at fault; **far difetto a** to lack, e.g., **gli fa difetto il denaro** he lacks money

difettó·so -sa [s] *adj* defective

diffamare *tr* to defame, slander

diffama·tóre -trice *mf* defamer, slanderer

diffamazióne *f* defamation, slander

differènte *adj* different

differènza *f* difference; spread; variance; **a differenza di** unlike; **c'è una bella differenza** it's a horse of another color

differenziale *adj* & *m* differential

differenziare §287 (**differènzio**) *tr* to differentiate

differiménto *m* deferment

differire §176 *tr* to postpone, defer || *intr* to be different; to differ

difficile *adj* hard, difficult; awkward (*situation*); hard-to-please; unlikely

‖ *mf* hard-to-please person ‖ *m—* **fare il difficile** to be hard to please; **qui sta il difficile!** here's the trouble!

difficol·tà *f* (**-tà**) difficulty; defect; obstacle; objection

difficoltó·so -sa [s] *adj* difficult, troublesome; fastidious

diffida *f* notice; warning

diffidare *tr* to give notice to; to warn ‖ *intr* to mistrust

diffidènte *adj* distrustful

diffidènza *f* mistrust

diffóndere §178 *tr* to spread; to circulate; to broadcast ‖ *ref* to spread; to dwell at length

diffórme *adj* unlike; (obs) deformed

diffrazióne *f* diffraction

diffusióne *f* spreading; circulation (*of a newspaper*); diffusion; (rad) broadcast

diffu·so -sa *adj* diffuse; widespread

diffusóre *m* diffuser (*to soften light*); baffle (*of loudspeaker*); (mach) choke

difilato *adv* forthwith, right away

difrónte *adj invar* in front

difterite *f* diphtheria

di·ga *f* (**-ghe**) dike; dam

digerènte *adj* alimentary (*canal*), digestive (*tube*)

digerìbile *adj* digestible

digerire §176 *tr* to digest; to tolerate, stand

digestióne *f* digestion

digesti·vo -va *adj* digestive

digèsto *m* digest

digitale *adj* digital ‖ *f* (bot) digitalis

digitalina *f* (pharm) digitalin

digiunare *intr* to fast

digiu·no -na *adj* without food; deprived; **digiuno di cognizioni** ignorant; **tenere digiuno** to keep in ignorance ‖ *m* fast; **a digiuno** on an empty stomach; **fare digiuno** to fast

digni·tà *f* (**-tà**) dignity; **dignità** *fpl* dignitaries

dignitó·so -sa [s] *adj* dignified

digradare *tr* to shade (*colors*) ‖ *intr* to slope; to fade

digredire §176 *intr* to digress

digressióne *f* digression

digrignare *tr* to show (*one's or its teeth*); to grit (*one's teeth*)

digrossare (**digròsso**) *tr* to rough-hew; to whittle down; (fig) to refine ‖ *ref* to become refined

diguazzare *tr* to beat (*a liquid*) ‖ *intr* to wallow; to splash

dilagare §209 *intr* to flood, to overflow; to spread abroad

dilaniare §287 *tr* to tear to pieces ‖ *ref* to slander one another

dilapidare (**dilàpido**) *tr* to squander

dilatare *tr* to expand; to dilate ‖ *ref* to expand; to spread

dilatazióne *f* expansion; dilation

dilatò·rio -ria *adj* (**-ri -rie**) delaying; dilatory

dilavare *tr* to wash away, erode

dilava·to -ta *adj* dull, flat; wan

dilazionare (**dilazióno**) *tr* to delay, put off; (com) to extend

dilazióne *f* delay; (com) extension

dileggiare §290 (**diléggio**) *tr* to mock

dilég·gio *m* (**-gi**) mockery, scoffing; **mettere in dileggio** to scoff at

dileguare (**diléguo**) *tr* to scatter ‖ *intr* (ESSERE) to disappear, vanish; to melt

dilèm·ma *m* (**-mi**) dilemma

dilettante *mf* amateur; dilettante

dilettanté·sco -sca *adj* (**-schi -sche**) amateurish

dilettare (**dilètto**) *tr* to delight ‖ *ref* to delight; **dilettarsi a + inf** to delight in + *ger*; **dilettarsi di** to pursue as a hobby, e.g., **si diletta di pittura** he pursues painting as a hobby

dilettévole *adj* delectable, delightful

dilèt·to -ta *adj* beloved ‖ *m* loved one; pleasure; hobby

diligènte *adj* diligent

diligènza *f* diligence; stagecoach

dilucidare (**dilùcido**) *tr* to elucidate

diluire §176 *tr* to dilute

dilungare §209 *tr* (archaic) to stretch ‖ *ref* to expatiate; to be ahead by several lengths (*said of a race horse*)

dilungo *m*—**a un dilungo** more or less

diluviare §287 *tr* to devour ‖ *intr* (ESSERE & AVERE) to rain (*said, e.g., of bullets*) ‖ *impers* (ESSERE)—**diluvia** it is pouring

dilù·vio *m* (**-vi**) deluge, flood; **diluvio universale** Flood

dimagrante *adj* reducing

dimagrare *tr* to thin down ‖ *intr* (ESSERE) to become thin; to lose weight; to become exhausted (*said of land*); (fig) to become meager

dimagrire §176 *intr* (ESSERE) to become thin; to lose weight, reduce

dimanda *f* var of **domanda**

dimane *adv* (coll) tomorrow

dimani *m & adv* var of **domani**

dimenare (**diméno**) *tr* to wag (*the tail*); to beat (*eggs*); to wave (*one's arms*); to stir up (*a question*) ‖ *ref* to toss; to busy oneself

dimensióne *f* dimension; (fig) nature

dimenticanza *f* oversight, neglect; **andare in dimenticanza** to be forgotten

dimenticare §197 (**diméntico**) *tr* to forget; to forgive ‖ *ref* to forget; **dimenticarsi di** to forget; to neglect

dimenticatóio *m*—**mettere nel dimenticatoio** (coll) to forget

diménti·co -ca *adj* (**-chi -che**) forgetful; neglectful

dimés·so -sa *adj* humble, modest (*demeanor*); low (*voice*); shabby (*clothes*)

dimestichèzza *f* familiarity

diméttere §198 *tr* to dismiss; to release ‖ *ref* to resign

dimezzare [ddzz] (**dimèzzo**) *tr* to halve

diminuire §176 *tr* to lessen, reduce; to lower (*prices*) ‖ *intr* (ESSERE) to diminish

diminuti·vo -va *adj & m* diminutive

diminuzióne *f* diminution

dimissionare (**dimissióno**) *tr* to dismiss, discharge ‖ *ref* to resign

dimissionà·rio -ria *adj* (**-ri -rie**) resigning, outgoing

dimissióne *f* resignation; **dare le dimis-si**... *to resign*

dimól·to -ta *adj* & *m* (coll) much ‖ **dimolto** *adv* (coll) much

dimòra *f* stay; residence; (lit) delay; **mettere a dimora** to install; to plant (*trees*); **senza dimora** (lit) without delay; **senza fissa dimora** vagrant

dimorare (dimòro) *intr* to stay; to reside; (lit) to delay

dimostràbile *adj* demonstrable

dimostrante *m* demonstrator

dimostrare (dimóstro) *tr* to demonstrate; to register (*e.g.,* anger); **dimostrare trent'anni** to look thirty ‖ *intr* to demonstrate ‖ *ref* to prove oneself to be

dimostrati·vo -va *adj* demonstrative; (mil) diverting

dimostra·tóre -trice *mf* demonstrator

dimostrazióne *f* demonstration

dinàmi·co -ca (-ci -che) *adj* dynamic ‖ *f* dynamics

dinamismo *m* dynamism

dinamite *f* dynamite

dìna·mo *f* (-mo) generator, dynamo

dinanzi *adj invar* front, e.g., **la porta dinanzi** the front door; preceding, e.g., **il mese dinanzi** the preceding month ‖ *adv* ahead; beforehand; (lit) before; **dinanzi a** before, in front of

dina·sta *m* (-sti) dynast

dinastìa *f* dynasty

dinàsti·co -ca *adj* (-ci -che) dynastic

dindo *m* (coll) turkey

dindòn *m* ding-dong ‖ *interj* ding-dong!

dinìè·go *m* (-ghi) denial

dinoccola·to -ta *adj* gangling; clumsy (*gait*)

dinosàuro [s] *m* dinosaur

dintórno *m*—**dintorni** surroundings, neighborhood ‖ *adv* around; **dintorno a** around

dì·o -a *adj* (-i -e) (poet) godly ‖ *m* (**dèi**) god; **gli dei the gods** ‖ **Dio** *m* God; **che Dio la manda** cats and dogs (*said of rain*); **come Dio volle** at long last; **come Dio vuole** botched (*piece of work*); **Dio ci scampi!** God forbid!; **Dio santo!** good heavens!; **grazie a Dio** God willing; thank God; **voglia Dio** God grant

diòce·si *f* (-si) diocese

diodo *m* (electron) diode

diomedèa *f* (orn) albatross

diottrìa *f* (opt) diopter

dipanare *tr* to unravel, unwind

dipartiménto *m* department

dipartire §176 *tr* (archaic) to divide ‖ *intr* (**diparto**) (ESSERE) & *ref* (lit) to depart

dipartita *f* (lit) departure; (lit) demise

dipendènte *adj* dependent ‖ *mf* employee

dipendènza *f* dependence; employment; annex; (com) branch; **in dipendenza di** as a consequence of

dipèndere §150 *intr* (ESSERE) to depend; **dipendere da** to depend on

dipìngere §126 *tr* to paint; **dipingere a olio** to paint in oils; **dipingere a tempera** to distemper ‖ *ref* to paint one-

self; to put make-up on; to appear, e.g., **gli si dipinse in volto la paura** fear appeared on his face

dipìn·to -ta *adj* painted ‖ *m* painting, picture

diplò·ma *m* (-mi) diploma, certificate

diplomare (diplòmo) *tr* to grant a degree to; to graduate ‖ *ref* to receive a degree; to graduate

diplomàti·co -ca (-ci -che) *adj* diplomatic; true, faithful (*copy*) ‖ *m* diplomat ‖ *f* diplomatics

diploma·to -ta *adj* graduated ‖ *mf* graduate ‖ *m* alumnus ‖ *f* alumna

diplomazìa *f* diplomacy

dipòi *adv* after, thereafter

diportare (dipòrto) *ref* (lit) to behave; (obs) to have a good time

dipòrto *m* recreation; (obs) sport; **andare a diporto** to go on an outing; to go for a walk

diprèsso *adv*—**a un dipresso** about, approximately

diradare *tr* to thin out (*vegetation*); to disperse; to space out (*one's visits*) ‖ *intr* (ESSERE) & *ref* to diminish; to disperse

diramare *tr* to prune; to circulate (*notices*); to issue (*a communiqué*) ‖ *ref* to branch out; to spread

diramazióne *f* branch; ramification; issuance

dire *m* talk; **per sentito dire** by hearsay; **stando al dire** according to his words ‖ §151 *tr* & *intr* to say; to tell; to call (*e.g., s.o. a genius*); to talk; **detto (e) fatto** no sooner said than done; **dica pure!** go ahead!; speak up!; **dire bene di** to speak well of; **dire di no** to say no; **dire di sì** to say yes; **direi quasi** I dare say; **dire la sua** to have one's say; **dire male di** to speak ill of; **dirla grossa** to make a blunder; to tell a tall tale; **dirlo chiaro e tondo** to speak bluntly; **dirne un sacco e una sporta a** to pour insults upon; **è tutto dire** that's all; **non c'è che dire** it's a fact; **non fo per dire** I do not want to boast; **per così dire** so to speak; **per meglio dire** rather; **trovarci a dire** to find fault with; **trovare da dire con** to have words with; **voler ben dire** to be sure; **voler dire** to mean ‖ *ref*—**dirsela con** to connive with; **si dice** it is said

dirètro *m* & *adv* (archaic) behind, back

direttìssima *f* (rr) high-speed line; **per direttissima** straight up (*in mountain climbing*)

direttìssimo *m* express train

diretti·vo -va *adj* managerial ‖ *m* board of directors ‖ *f* directive; direction; guideline

dirèt·to -ta *adj* direct; **diretto a** addressed to; directed at; bound for ‖ *m* through train

diret·tóre -trice *mf* manager; principal ‖ *m* director; **direttore di macchina** (naut, nav) chief engineer; **direttore di tiro** (nav) gunnery officer; **direttore di un giornale** editor; **direttore d'or-**

chestra orchestra leader; **direttore responsabile** publisher; **direttore tecnico** (sports) manager ‖ *f* see **direttrice**

direttò·rio -ria (-ri -rie) *adj* directorial ‖ *m* directory

direttrice *adj fem* directing; guiding; front (*wheels*) ‖ *f* directress; line of action

direzionale *adj* directional; managerial

direzione *f* direction; management; run (*of events*)

dirigènte *adj* leading; managerial ‖ *m* employer; boss; leader; executive

dirìgere §152 *tr* to direct; to turn; to lead ‖ *ref* to address oneself; **dirigersi verso** to head for

dirigìbile *adj & m* dirigible

dirimpètto *adj invar & adv* opposite; **dirimpetto a** opposite to; in comparison with

dirit·to -ta *adj* straight; right; unswerving; (coll) smart ‖ *m* law; obverse, face (*of coin*); fee, dues; (fin) right; **a buon diritto** rightly so; **di diritto** by law; **diritti d'autore** copyright; **diritti di segreteria** registration fee; **diritti doganali** customs duty; **diritti speciali di prelievo** (econ) special drawing rights; **diritto canonico** canon law; **diritto consuetudinario** common law; **diritto internazionale** international law; **in diritto** according to law ‖ *f* right, right hand ‖ **diritto** *adv* straight; **tirare diritto** to go straight ahead

dirittura *f* direction; uprightness; (sports) straightaway, home stretch

dirizzóne *m* blunder

diroccare §197 (**diròcco**) *tr* to knock down ‖ *intr* (ESSERE) (archaic) to fall down

dirocca·to -ta *adj* dilapidated, rickety

dirompènte *adj* fragmentation (*bomb*)

dirottaménto *m* hijacking; skyjacking (*of an airplane*)

dirottare (**diròtto**) *tr* to detour (*traffic*); to hijack (*e.g., a ship*); to skyjack (*an airplane*) ‖ *intr* to change course

dirottatóre *m* hijacker; skyjacker (*of a plane*)

diròt·to -ta *adj* copious, heavy (*rain, tears*); (lit) craggy; **a dirotto** cats and dogs (*said of rain*)

dirozzare [ddzz] (**diròzzo**) *tr* to roughhew; to refine ‖ *ref* to become polished

dirugginire §176 *tr* to take the rust off; to limber up; to gnash (*one's teeth*); to clear (*one's mind*)

dirupa·to -ta *adj* rocky, craggy

dirupo *m* rock; crag, cliff

disabbigliare §280 *tr & ref* to undress, disrobe

disabita·to -ta *adj* uninhabited

disabituare (**disabìtuo**) *tr* to disaccustom ‖ *ref* to become unaccustomed

disaccenta·to -ta *adj* unaccented

disaccòrdo *m* disagreement

disadat·to -ta *adj* unfit

disadór·no -na *adj* unadorned, bare

disaffezionare (**disaffezióno**) *tr* to alienate the affection of; to estrange ‖ *ref* to become estranged

disaffezióne *f* dislike

disagévole *adj* troublesome, uncomfortable

disagiare §290 *tr* to trouble, inconvenience

disagia·to -ta *adj* uncomfortable; needy

disà·gio *m* (-gi) discomfort; need

disalberare (**disàlbero**) *tr* to dismast

disambienta·to -ta *adj* bewildered, strange

disàmina *f* examination, scrutiny

disaminare (**disàmino**) *tr* to scrutinize; to weigh

disamorare (**disamóro**) *tr* to alienate the affection of; to estrange ‖ *ref* to become estranged

disancorare (**disàncoro**) *tr* to weigh anchor; to leave port ‖ *ref* to weigh anchor; (fig) to free oneself

disanimare (**disànimo**) *tr* to dishearten

disappetènza *f* loss of appetite

disapprovare (**disappròvo**) *tr* to disapprove

disapprovazióne *f* disapproval

disappunto *m* disappointment

disarcionare (**disarcióno**) *tr* to unsaddle, unhorse; to kick out

disarmare *tr* to disarm; to dismantle (*a scaffold*); to ship (*oars*); (naut) to unrig ‖ *ref* to disarm; (fig) to give up

disarma·to -ta *adj* unarmed, defenseless

disarmo *m* disarmament; dismantling; unrigging

disarmonìa *f* discord; contrast

disarmòni·co -ca *adj* (-ci -che) discordant

disarticolare (**disartìcolo**) *tr* to limber up; to disjoint ‖ *ref* to become dislocated

disassociare §128 (**disassòcio**) *tr* to disassociate

disastra·to -ta *adj* damaged ‖ *mf* victim

disastro *m* disaster, calamity; wreck

disastró·so -sa [s] *adj* disastrous

disattèn·to -ta *adj* inattentive; careless

disattenzióne *f* inattention; carelessness

disattivare *tr* to deactivate (*e.g., a mine*)

disavanzo *m* (com) deficit

disavvedu·to -ta *adj* heedless

disavventura *f* misfortune

disavvertènza *f* inadvertence

disavvezzare (**disavvézzo**) *tr* to break (*s.o.*) of a habit ‖ *ref*—**disavvezzarsi da** to give up or lose the habit of

disavvéz·zo -za *adj* unaccustomed

disbórso *m* disbursement, outlay

disboscare §197 (**disbòsco**) *tr* to deforest

disbrigare §209 *tr* to dispatch ‖ *ref* to extricate oneself

disbrì·go *m* (-ghi) prompt execution, dispatch

discacciare §128 *tr* (lit) to chase away

discanto *m* (mus) harmonizing

discàpito *m* damage; **tornare a discapito di** to be detrimental to

discàri·ca *f* (-che) discharge (*e.g., of pollutants*); dumping (*of refuse*); unloading (*of a ship*)

discàri·co *m* (**-chi**) exculpation; **a discarico di** in defense of

discatóre *m* hockey player; discus thrower

discendènte *adj* descending; sloping; down (*train*) || *mf* descendant

discendènza *f* descent; pedigree

discéndere §245 *tr* to go down || *intr* (ESSERE & AVERE) to descend, go down; to slope; to fall (*said, e.g., of thermometer*); to get off; **discendere in picchiata** (aer) to nose-dive

discènte *mf* student, pupil

discépo·lo -la *mf* disciple

discèrnere §153 *tr* to discern

discernìbile *adj* discernible

discerniménto *m* discernment

discésa [s] *f* descent; slope; drop

discettare (**discètto**) *tr* (lit) to d.scuss

dischiodare (**dischiòdo**) *tr* to take the nails out of

dischiùdere §125 *tr* to open; to reveal

discin·to -ta *adj* scantily dressed; untidy; in disarray

disciògliere §127 *tr* to dissolve, melt; (lit) to untie || *ref* to dissolve, melt

disciplina *f* discipline; whip, scourge

disciplinare *adj* disciplinary || *m* regulation || *tr* to discipline

disciplina·to -ta *adj* obedient

di·sco *m* (**-schi**) disk; (phonograph) record; bob (*of pendulum*); (ice hockey) puck; (sports) discus; (rr) signal; (pharm) tablet; **disco combinatore** (telp) dial; **disco microsolco** microgroove record; **disco volante** flying saucer

discòfilo *m* record lover

discòide *m* (pharm) tablet, pill

disco·lo -la *adj* undisciplined, wild || *m* rogue, rascal

discolorare (**discolóro**) *tr* to discolor || *ref* to pale

discolorazióne *f* discoloration; paleness

discólpa *f* defense

discolpare (**discólpo**) *tr* to defend

disconnèttere §107 *tr* to disconnect

disconóscere §134 *tr* to ignore, to disregard; to be ungrateful for

discontinuare (**discontìnuo**) *tr* to perform sporadically || *intr* to lose continuity

disconti·nuo -nua *adj* uneven

disconvenire §282 *intr* (ESSERE) (lit) to disagree || *impers* (ESSERE) (lit) to be improper

discoprire §110 (**discòpro**) *tr* to discover

discordante *adj* discordant

discordare (**discòrdo**) *intr* (ESSERE) to disagree, differ

discòrde *adj* discordant; opposing

discòrdia *f* discord, dissension

discórrere §139 *intr* to talk, chat; (coll) to keep company; **discorrere del più e del meno** to make small talk; **e via discorrendo** and so forth

discórso *m* discourse; conversation; speech; **pochi discorsi!** (coll) cut it out!

discostare (**discòsto**) *tr* to remove || *ref* to withdraw; to differ

discò·sto -sta *adj* distant || **discosto** *adv* far

discotè·ca *f* (**-che**) record library; discotheque

discreditare (**discrédito**) *tr* to discredit

discrédito *m* discredit

discrepanza *f* discrepancy

discretaménte *adv* rather; fairly well

discré·to -ta *adj* discreet; fairly large; fair

discrezióne *f* discretion

discriminante *adj* discriminatory; extenuating || *m* (math) discriminant

discriminare (**discrìmino**) *tr* to discrim'-nate; to extenuate

discriminazióne *f* discrimination

discussióne *f* discussion; argument

discus·so -sa *adj* controversial

discùtere §154 *tr* to discuss || *intr* to discuss; to argue

discutìbile *adj* moot, debatable

disdegnare (**disdégno**) *tr* to disdain, scorn || *ref* (obs) to be angry

disdégno *m* disdain, scorn

disdegnó·so -sa [s] *adj* disdainful

disdétta *f* ill luck; (law) notice

disdicévole *adj* unbecoming, unseemly

disdire §151 *tr* to retract; to belie; to cancel; to countermand; to terminate the contract of || *ref* to retract; **disdire a** to be unbecoming to

disdòro *m* shame; **tornare a disdoro di** to bring shame on

disegnare [s] (**diségno**) *tr* to draw; to sketch; to design; (obs) to elect

disegna·tóre -trice [s] *mf* cartoonist; designer || *m* draftsman

diségno [s] *m* drawing; sketch; outline; plan; design; **disegno animato** (mov) cartoon; **disegno di legge** (law) bill

disellare [s] (**disèllo**) *tr* var of **dissellare**

diserbante *adj* weed-killing || *m* weed-killer

diseredare (**diserèdo**) *tr* to disinherit

disereda·to -ta *adj* disinherited || **i diseredati** the underprivileged

disertare (**disèrto**) *tr* to desert; (lit) to lay waste || *intr* to desert

disertóre *m* deserter

diserzióne *f* desertion

disfaciménto *m* disintegration

disfare §173 *tr* to undo; to defeat; to melt; to unknit; to break up (*housekeeping*); **disfare il letto** to remove the bedclothes || *ref* to spoil (*said, e.g., of meat*); **disfarsi di** to get rid of

disfatta *f* defeat

disfattismo *m* defeatism

disfatti·sta *mf* (**-sti -ste**) defeatist

disfat·to -ta *adj* undone; defeated; melted; broken up; ravaged || *f* see **disfatta**

disfida *f* (lit) challenge

disfunzióne *f* malfunction

disgelare (**disgèlo**) *tr & intr* to thaw

disgèlo *m* thaw

disgiùngere §183 *tr & ref* to separate

disgiunti·vo -va *adj* disjunctive

disgràzia *f* disfavor; bad luck, misfortune; accident; **per disgrazia** unfortunately

disgrazia·to -ta *adj* unlucky; wretched
disgregaménto *m* disintegration
disgregare §209 (disgrègo) *tr & ref* to disintegrate
disgregazióne *f* disintegration
disguido *m* miscarriage, missending (*of a letter*)
disgustare *tr* to disgust, sicken ‖ *ref* to become disgusted, sicken; to have a falling-out, to part company
disgusto *m* disgust, repugnance
disgustó·so -sa [*s*] *adj* disgusting
disidratare *tr* to dehydrate
disilla·bo -ba *adj* disyllabic ‖ *m* disyllable
disillùdere §105 *tr* to delude, deceive ‖ *ref* to become disillusioned
disillusióne *f* disillusion
disimboscare §197 (disimbòsco) *tr* to put back in circulation
disimparare *tr* to unlearn, forget
disimpegnare (disimpégno) *tr* to release; to free, to open; to loosen; to redeem (*a pledge*); to clear; to perform ‖ *ref* to succeed
disimpégno *m* release; redemption; performance; disengagement; di disimpegno for every day (*e.g., a suit*); main (*e.g., hallway*)
disimpiè·go *m* (-ghi) unemployment; (mil) withdrawal
disincagliare §280 *tr* to set afloat; (fig) to disentangle
disincantare *tr* to disenchant
disinfestare (disinfèsto) *tr* to exterminate
disinfestazióne *f* extermination
disinfettante *adj & m* disinfectant
disinfettare (disinfètto) *tr* to disinfect
disingannare *tr* to disillusion ‖ *ref* to become disillusioned
disinganno *m* disillusion
disinnescare §197 (disinnésco) *tr* to defuse
disinnestare (disinnèsto) *tr* to disconnect; to throw out, disengage
disinserire §176 *tr* (elec) to disconnect; (aut) to disengage
disintasare [*s*] *tr* to unclog
disintegrare (disìntegro) *tr & ref* to disintegrate
disintegrazióne *f* disintegration
disinteressare (disinterèsso) *tr* to make (*s.o.*) lose interest ‖ *ref* to lose interest; to take no interest
disinteressa·to -ta *adj* selfless, unselfish
disinterèsse *m* disinterest; unselfishness
disintossicare §197 (disintòssico) *tr* to free of poison; (fig) to clean the air in ‖ *ref* to shake the drug habit
disinvòl·to -ta *adj* free and easy; fresh, forward
disinvoltura *f* naturalness, ease of manners, offhandedness; freshness; impudence
disì·o *m* (-ì) (poet) desire
disìstima *f* scorn, low regard, disesteem
disistimare *tr* to scorn, hold in low regard
dislivèllo *m* difference of level; disparity
dislocaménto *m* transfer of troops; (naut) displacement

dislocare §197 (dislòco) *tr* to transfer (*troops*); to post (*sentries*); (naut) to displace
dislocazióne *f* (mil) transfer; (geog, naut, psychol) displacement
dismisura *f* excess; a dismisura excessively
disobbedire §176 *intr* var of disubbidire
disobbligare §209 (disòbbligo) *tr* to free from an obligation ‖ *ref* to repay a favor
disoccupa·to -ta *adj* unemployed, jobless; idle; unoccupied ‖ *m* unemployed person; i disoccupati the jobless
disoccupazióne *f* unemployment
disone·stà *f* (-stà) dishonesty; shamelessness
disonè·sto -sta *adj* dishonest; shameless; immoral
disonorante *adj* disgraceful
disonorare (disonóro) *tr* to dishonor, disgrace; to seduce
disonóre *m* dishonor, shame
disonorévole *adj* dishonorable; shameful
disoppilare (disòppilo) *tr* to clear of obstructions
disópra *adj invar* upper ‖ *m* (disópra) upper part, top; prendere il disopra to have the upper hand ‖ *adv* above; al disopra di above
disordinare (disórdino) *tr* to cancel, countermand; to confuse; to mess up ‖ *intr* to indulge ‖ *ref* to become disorganized
disordina·to -ta *adj* confused; messy; untidy; intemperate
disórdine *m* confusion; mess; disarray; disorder; intemperance
disorganizzare [ddzz] *tr* to disorganize; to disrupt
disorganizzazióne [ddzz] *f* disorganization, disorder; disruption
disorientaménto *m* disorientation; confusion, bewilderment
disorientare (disoriènto) *tr* to cause (*s.o.*) to lose his way; to confuse; to disorient ‖ *ref* to be bewildered; to lose one's bearings
disorienta·to -ta *adj* disoriented; confused, bewildered; lost, astray
disormeggiare §290 (disorméggio) *tr* to unmoor
disossare (disòsso) *tr* to bone ‖ *ref* (lit) to lose weight
disótto [*s*] *adj invar* below ‖ *m* (disótto) lower part, bottom ‖ *adv* below; al disotto di below, underneath
disotturare *tr* to unclog
dispàc·cio *m* (-ci) dispatch; urgent letter; dispaccio telegrafico telegram
dispara·to -ta *adj* disparate
disparére *m* disagreement
dìspari *adj invar* odd, uneven
dispari·tà *f* (-tà) disparity
dispàrte *adv*—in disparte apart, aside; starsene in disparte to keep aloof
dispèn·dio *m* (-di) expenditure; waste
dispendió·so -sa [*s*] *adj* expensive; wasteful

dispènsa *f* cupboard; pantry; distribution; number (*of magazine*); installment (*of book*); dispensation; (naut) storeroom; (coll) store

dispensare (**dispènso**) *tr* to exempt, free; to distribute ‖ *ref*—**dispensarsi da** to get out of

dispensà·rio *m* (**-ri**) dispensary

dispensa·tóre -tríce *mf* dispenser

dispensiè·re -ra *mf* dispenser ‖ *m* steward

dispepsìa *f* dyspepsia

dispèpti·co -ca *adj* & *mf* (**-ci -che**) dyspeptic

disperare (**dispèro**) *intr* to despair; **fare disperare** to drive crazy ‖ *ref* to despair

dispera·to -ta *adj* hopeless ‖ *m* poor wretch; **come un disperato** desperately ‖ *f*—**alla disperata** with all one's might

disperazióne *f* desperation, despair

dispèrdere §212 *tr* to scatter; to waste ‖ *ref* to disperse; (fig) to waste one's energies

dispersióne *f* dispersion; loss; (elec) leakage

dispersività *f* tendency toward disorganization

dispersi·vo -va *adj* dispersive; disorganized

dispèr·so -sa *adj* scattered; lost; dispersed; missing in action

dispersóre *m* (elec) leakage conductor

dispètto *m* spite; (lit) haughtiness; **a dispetto di** in spite of; **far dispetto a** to provoke

dispettó·so -sa [s] *adj* pestiferous; spiteful, resentful

dispiacènte *adj* sorry; distressing

dispiacére *m* sorrow, displeasure ‖ §214 *intr* (ESSERE) to be displeasing; to be sorry, e.g., **mi dispiace** I am sorry; (with *dat*) to displease; (with *dat*) to dislike, e.g., **le mìe parole gli dispiacciono** he dislikes my words; **Le dispiace?** would you please?; **se non Le dispiace** if you don't mind

dispiegare §209 *tr* to manifest; (lit) to unfurl ‖ *ref* to spread out; to flow out

displù·vio *m* (**-vi**) divide, watershed; ridge (*of roof*)

disponìbile *adj* available; open-minded

disponibili·tà *f* (**-tà**) availability; inactive status; **disponibilità** *fpl* available funds

dispórre §218 *tr* to dispose; to prepare ‖ *intr* to provide; to dispose; **disporre di** to have (*available*) ‖ *ref* to get ready

dispositivo *m* gadget; device; (mil) deployment

disposizióne *f* arrangement; inclination, disposition; disposal; instruction; (law) provision

dispó·sto -sta *adj* arranged; disposed; provided; willing; **ben disposto** disposed ‖ *m* (law) proviso

dispòti·co -ca *adj* (**-ci -che**) despotic

dispotismo *m* despotism

dispregiati·vo -va *adj* disparaging; (gram) pejorative

disprè·gio *m* (**-gi**) contempt; disrepute

disprezzàbile *adj* contemptible; negligible

disprezzare (**disprèzzo**) *tr* to despise

disprèzzo *m* contempt, scorn

dìsputa *f* dispute; debate

disputàbile *adj* debatable

disputare (**dìsputo**) *tr* to contest; to discuss; to vie for (*victory*) ‖ *intr* to dispute, debate; to vie ‖ *ref* to vie for

disqualificare §197 (**disqualìfico**) *tr* to disqualify

disquisizióne *f* disquisition

dissacrare *tr* to desecrate

dissacrazióne *f* desecration

dissaldare *tr* to unsolder

dissanguare (**dissànguo**) *tr* to bleed ‖ *ref* to bleed; to ruin oneself

dissangua·to -ta *adj* bled white; **morire dissanguato** to bleed to death

dissapóre *m* disagreement

disseccare §197 (**dissécco**) *tr* to dry ‖ *ref* to dry; to dry up

disselciare §128 (**dissélcio**) *tr* to remove the cobblestones from

dissellare (**dissèllo**) *tr* to unsaddle

disseminare (**dissémino**) *tr* to disseminate; to scatter

dissensióne *f* dissension

dissènso *m* dissent; disagreement

dissenterìa *f* dysentery

dissentire (**dissènto**) *intr* to dissent

dissenziènte *adj* dissenting ‖ *mf* dissenter

disseppellire §176 *tr* to exhume

dissertare (**dissèrto**) *intr* to discourse

dissertazióne *f* dissertation

disservì·zio *m* (**-zi**) poor service

dissestare (**dissèsto**) *tr* to unsettle; to disarrange

dissesta·to -ta *adj* financially embarrassed; mentally deranged

dissèsto *m* financial embarrassment; mental derangement

dissetante *adj* thirst-quenching

dissetare (**dissèto**) *tr* to quench the thirst of ‖ *ref* to quench one's thirst

dissezióne *f* dissection

dissidènte *adj* & *m* dissident

dissidènza *f* dissent

dissì·dio *m* (**-di**) dissent; disagreement

dissigillare *tr* to unseal ‖ *ref* (lit) to melt

dissìmile *adj* unlike

dissimulare (**dissìmulo**) *tr* to dissimulate, disguise ‖ *intr* to dissimulate

dissimulazióne *f* dissimulation

dissipare (**dìssipo**) *tr* to dissipate; to squander; to clear up (*a doubt*) ‖ *ref* to dissipate

dissipa·to -ta *adj* & *mf* profligate

dissipa·tóre -trice *mf* squanderer

dissipazióne *f* dissipation

dissociare §128 (**dissòcio**) *tr* to dissociate, disassociate ‖ *ref* to dissociate or disassociate oneself

dissociazióne *f* dissociation

dissodare (dissòdo) *tr* to cultivate

dissolutézza *f* profligacy

dissolu·to -ta *adj* & *mf* profligate

dissoluzióne *f* dissolution

dissolvènza *f* (mov) fade-out; dissolvenza incrociata (mov) lap dissolve

dissòlvere §155 *tr* to dissolve; to clear up (*a doubt*); (obs) to untie || *ref* to dissolve

dissomiglianza *f* dissimilarity

dissonanza *f* dissonance

dissotterrare (dissottèrro) *tr* to exhume; to unearth

dissuadére §213 *tr* to dissuade

dissuè·to -ta *adj* (lit) unaccustomed

dissuggellare (dissuggèllo) *tr* to unseal

distaccaménto *m* (mil) detachment

distaccare §197 *tr* to detach; to remove; to transfer; to outdistance || *ref* to stand out; to withdraw, become separated

distacca·to -ta *adj* detached; branch (*office*)

distac·co *m* (-chi) detachment; separation; (sports) spread (*in points*)

distante *adj* distant; aloof; different || *adv* far away

distanza *f* distance; mantenere le distanze to keep one's distance; tenere a distanza to keep at arm's length

distanziare §287 *tr* to outdistance

distare *intr* to be distant

distèndere §270 *tr* to stretch; to spread; to unfurl; to relax; to knock down; to write || *ref* to stretch; to spread out; to relax

distensióne *f* relaxation; relaxation of tension

disté·so -sa [s] *adj* stretched out; full (*voice*); lank (*hair*) || *m*—per disteso in full || *f* expanse; row; a distesa with full voice; at full peal

distillare *tr* to distill; to exude; to pour; to trickle || *intr* (ESSERE) to trickle || *ref*—distillarsi il cervello to rack one's brain

distilla·to -ta *adj* distilled || *m* distillate

distilla·tóre -trice *mf* distiller || *m* still

distilleria *f* distillery

distinguíbile *adj* distinguishable

distinguere §156 *tr* to distinguish; to make out; to tell (*one thing from another*); to divide

distinta *f* note, list; distinta di versamento deposit slip

distintaménte *adv* distinctly; sincerely yours

distinti·vo -va *adj* distinctive || *m* emblem, insignia, badge

distìn·to -ta *adj* distinct; distinguished; sincere (*greetings*); reserved (*seat*); Distinto Signor . . . (*on an envelope*) Mr. . . . || *f* see distinta

distinzióne *f* distinction

distògliere §127 *tr* to dissuade; to deter; to distract; to turn (*one's eyes*) away

distòrcere §272 *tr* to distort; to twist || *ref* to become distorted; to sprain (*e.g., one's ankle*)

distorsióne *f* distortion; sprain; distorsione acustica wow

distrarre §273 *tr* to distract; to divert;

to amuse; to pull (*a muscle*) || *ref* to become distracted; to relax

distrat·to -ta *adj* absent-minded

distrazióne *f* absent-mindedness; distraction; diversion (*of money*); pull (*of muscle*)

distrét·to -ta *adj* (obs) close; (obs) hardpressed || *m* district; precinct (*e.g., of police*); circuit (*of court*); ward (*in city*); distretto militare draft board; distretto postale postal zone || *f* stricture; necessity

distrettuale *adj* district

distribuíre §176 *tr* to distribute; to pass out; to allot; to deploy (*troops*); (theat) to cast (*roles*); (mov) to release; (mil) to issue (*e.g., clothing*)

distribu·tóre -trice *adj* distributing, dispensing || *mf* distributor, dispenser || *m* distributor; distributore automatico vending machine; distributore di benzina gasoline pump

distribuzióne *f* distribution; issue; delivery; (aut) timing gears; (mov) release; (fig) dispensation

districare §197 *tr* to unravel || *ref* to extricate oneself

distrofia *f* dystrophy

distrùggere §266 *tr* to destroy; to ruin

distrutti·vo -va *adj* destructive

distruzióne *f* destruction

disturbare *tr* to disturb, bother; disturbo? may I come in? || *ref* to bother; to go out of one's way

disturba·tóre -trice *mf* disturber; disturbatore della quiete pubblica disturber of the peace

disturbo *m* trouble, bother; disturbance; (rad) interference; disturbi atmosferici static, atmospherics; togliere il disturbo a to take leave of

disubbidiènte *adj* disobedient

disubbidiènza *f* disobedience

disubbidíre §176 *intr* to disobey; (with *dat*) to disobey

disuguaglianza *f* inequality; disparity

disuguale *adj* uneven; unequal

disumá·no -na *adj* inhumane; unbearable

disunióne *f* disunion

disuníre §176 *tr* to disunite

disusá·to -ta *adj* obsolete, out of use

disuso *m* disuse; in disuso obsolete

disùtile *adj* useless; burdensome || *m* worthless fellow; (com) loss

disvì·o *m* (-i) miscarriage, missending (*of a letter*)

ditale *m* thimble; fingerstall

ditata *f* poke with a finger; finger mark; dab (*with a finger*)

dito *m* (dita *fpl*) finger; toe; avere le dita d'oro to have a magic touch; dita della mano fingers; dita dei piede toes; legarsela al dito to never forget || *m* (diti) finger, e.g., dito indice index finger; dito anulare ring finger; dito medio middle finger; dito mignolo little finger; dito pollice thumb

ditta *f* firm, house; office

dittàfono *m* intercom; dictaphone

dittatóre *m* dictator

dittatura f dictatorship
dittongare §209 (dittòngo) tr to diphthongize
dittòn·go m (-ghi) diphthong
diurèti·co -ca adj & m (-ci -che) diuretic
diur·no -na adj daily; daytime ‖ f (theat) matinée
diutur·no -na adj long-lasting
diva f diva; (mov) star; (lit) goddess
divagare §209 tr to amuse; to distract ‖ intr to digress ‖ ref to relax
divagazióne f distraction; digression; relaxation
divampare intr (ESSERE & AVERE) to blaze, flare
divano m divan; couch, sofa
divaricare §197 (divàrico) tr to spread (one's legs); to open up (an incision)
divà·rio m (-ri) difference
divèllere §267 tr to eradicate, uproot
diveni·re (-re) (philos) becoming ‖ §282 intr (ESSERE) (lit) to become; (archaic) to come
diventare (divènto) intr (ESSERE) to become; **diventare di tutti i colori** to blush; to be embarrassed; **diventare grande** to grow up; **diventare matto** to go mad; **diventare pallido** to turn pale; **diventare piccolo** to grow smaller; **diventare rosso** to blush
divèr·bio m (-bi) argument; **venire a diverbio** to have an altercation
divergènza f divergency
divèrgere §157 intr to diverge
diversificare §197 (diversìfico) tr to diversify ‖ ref to be diversified; to differ
diversióne f diversion
diversi·tà f (-tà) diversity
diversi·vo -va adj diverting ‖ m diversion
divèrso -sa adj different; **diver·si -se** several, e.g., **diverse ragazze** several girls ‖ **diver·si -se** pron several
divertènte adj diverting, amusing
divertiménto m amusement, pastime; fun; (mus) divertimento
divertire (divèrto) tr to amuse, entertain; (lit) to turn aside ‖ ref to have fun, enjoy oneself; (lit) to go away
diverti·to -ta adj amused; amusing
divètta f starlet
divezzare (divèzzo) tr to wean ‖ ref— **divezzarsi da** to get out of the habit of
dividèndo m dividend
dividere §158 tr to divide; to partition; to split; to share in (e.g., s.o.'s grief) ‖ ref to be divided; to become separated; **dividersi fra** to divide one's time between
divièto m prohibition; **divieto d'affissione** post no bills; **divieto di parcheggio** no parking; **divieto di sosta** no stopping; **divieto di svolta** no turns; **divieto di transito** no thoroughfare
divinare tr (lit) to divine
divina·tóre -trice adj divining ‖ m diviner

divinazióne f divination
divincolare (divìncolo) tr & ref to wriggle
divini·tà f (-tà) divinity
divinizzare [ddzz] tr to deify
divi·no -na adj divine
divisa f uniform; motto; part (in hair); **divise foreign** exchange
divisare tr (lit) to intend
divisìbile adj divisible
divisióne f division; partition; (sports) league
divismo m (painting) divisionism; (pol) separatism
divismo m (mov) star system; (mov) adulation of stars
divisóre m (math) divisor
divisò·rio -ria (-ri -rie) adj dividing ‖ m partition; (math) divisor
di·vo -va adj (lit) divine ‖ m (theat, mov) star; (lit) god ‖ f see diva
divolgare §209 (divólgo) tr & ref var of divulgare
divorare (divóro) tr to devour; to gulp down; to consume; **divorare la via** to burn up the road
divora·tóre -trice adj consuming ‖ mf consumer (e.g., of food, books)
divorziare §287 (divòrzio) intr to become divorced; **divorziare da** to divorce
divorzia·to -ta adj divorced ‖ m divorcé ‖ f divorcée
divòr·zio m (-zi) divorce
divulgare §209 tr to divulge; to publicize; to popularize ‖ ref to spread; to become popular
divulga·tóre -trice adj popularizing ‖ mf popularizer; **divulgatore di calunnie** scandalmonger; **divulgatore di notizie** telltale
divulgazióne f publicizing; popularization
divulsióne f (surg) dilation
dizionà·rio -rio m (-ri) dictionary; **dizionario geografico** gazetteer
dizióne f diction; reading (of poetry)
do [dɔ] m (do) (mus) do; (mus) C
dóc·cia f (-ce) shower; gutter (on roof); spout; (fig) dash of cold water; **fare la doccia** to take a shower
docciare §128 (dóccio) tr, intr (ESSERE) & ref to shower
doccióne m trough, gutter; gargoyle
docènte adj teaching ‖ m teacher; **libero docente** certified university teacher
docènza f teaching post; **libera docenza** lectureship
dòcile adj docile; tame; amenable (person); workable (material)
documentare (documénto) tr to document ‖ ref to gather information
documentà·rio -ria adj & m (-ri -rie) documentary
documènto m document; paper; **documenti di bordo** ship's papers
dodecafonìa f twelve-tone system
dodecasìlla·bo -ba adj twelve-syllable, dodecasyllable
dodicèsi·mo -ma adj, m & pron twelfth
dódici adj & pron twelve; **le dodici**

twelve o'clock ‖ *m* twelve; twelfth (*in dates*)

dó·ga *f* (-ghe) stave

dogale *adj* (hist) of the doge

dogana *f* duty; customs; custom house

doganière *m* customs officer

dòge *m* (hist) doge

dò·glia *f* (-glie) (lit) pain, pang; **doglie** labor pains

dò·glio *m* (-gli) barrel; (lit) large jar

doglió·so -sa [s] *adj* (lit) sorrowful

dòg·ma *m* (-mi) dogma

dogmàti·co -ca (-ci -che) *adj* dogmatic ‖ *mf* dogmatist

dogmatismo *m* dogmatism

dólce *adj* sweet; soft; gentle; fresh (*water*); mild (*climate*); delicate (*feet*); **dolce far niente** sweet idleness ‖ *m* sweet; sweet dish; **dolci** candy

dolceama·ro -ra *adj* bittersweet

dolcézza *f* sweetness; mildness; gentleness

dolcia·stro -stra *adj* sweetish

dolcière *m* candy maker; pastry baker

dolcificare §197 (**dolcífico**) *tr* to sweeten

dolciume *m* sweet; **dolciumi** candy

dolènte *adj* aching; sorrowful; sorry

dolére §159 *intr* (ESSERE & AVERE) to ache, e.g., **gli dolgono i denti** his teeth ache ‖ *ref* to grieve ‖ *impers* (ESSERE) to be sorry, e.g., **mi duole che Lei non possa venire** I am sorry that you won't be able to come

dolicònice *m* bobolink

dòllaro *m* dollar

dòlo *m* fraud, malice, guile

dolomite *f* dolomite ‖ **Dolomiti** *fpl* Dolomites

dolorante *adj* aching

dolorare (**dolóro**) *intr* (lit) to ache

dolóre *m* ache; sorrow; contrition

doloró·so -sa [s] *adj* painful; sorrowful

doló·so -sa [s] *adj* intentional, fraudulent; (law) felonious

domàbile *adj* tamable

domanda *f* question; application; appeal; (econ) demand; **domanda suggestiva** (com) leading question; **fare una domanda** to ask a question

domandare *tr* to ask; to ask for; **domandare la parola** to ask for the floor ‖ *intr* to inquire ‖ *ref* to wonder; (lit) to be called

doma·ni *m* (-ni) tomorrow ‖ *adv* tomorrow; **a domani** until tomorrow; **domani a otto** a week from tomorrow; **domani l'altro** the day after tomorrow

domare (**dómo**) *tr* to tame; to extinguish; to quell

doma·tóre -trice *mf* tamer

domattina *adv* tomorrow morning

doméni·ca *f* (-che) Sunday

domenicale *adj* Sunday (*e.g., rest*)

domenica·no -na *adj* & *m* Dominican (*e.g., order*)

domesticare §197 (**domèstico**) *tr* to domesticate

domèsti·co -ca (-ci -che) *adj* family; household; familiar; domestic ‖ *mf* domestic, servant ‖ *f* maid; **alla**

domestica family style; **domestica a mezzo servizio** part-time domestic

domiciliare *adj* house ‖ §287 *tr* (com) to draw ‖ *ref* to dwell; to settle

domicilia·to -ta *adj* residing

domicì·lio *m* (-li) domicile, residence; principal office; **domicilio coatto** imprisonment; **franco domicilio** free delivery

dominare (**dòmino**) *tr* to dominate, rule; to master; to overlook ‖ *intr* to prevail; to reign ‖ *ref* to control oneself

domina·tóre -trice *mf* ruler

dominazióne *f* domination; rule

domineddìo *m invar* (coll) the Lord God

dominica·no -na *adj* & *mf* Dominican (*e.g., Republic*)

domì·nio *m* (-ni) dominion; domain

dòmi·no *m* (-no) domino (*cloak*); dominoes (*game*)

dòn *m* (used only before singular Christian name) don (*Spanish title*); Don (*priest*); uncle (*familiar title of elderly man*)

donare (**dóno**) *tr* to donate; to give as a present ‖ *intr*—**donare a** to be becoming to

dona·tóre -trice *mf* donor; **donatore di sangue** blood donor

donazióne *f* gift, donation

donchisciotté·sco -sca *adj* (-schi -sche) quixotic

dónde *adv* wherefrom, whence

dondolare (**dóndolo**) *tr* to swing, rock ‖ *ref* to swing, rock; to loaf around

dondolì·o *m* (-i) swinging, rocking

dóndolo *m*—**a dondolo** rocking (*chair, horse*); **andare a dondolo** to loaf around

dondoló·ne -na *mf* idler, loafer

dongiovan·ni *m* (-ni) Don Juan

dònna *f* woman; ladyship; (lit) lady; (coll) Mrs.; (coll) maid; (cards) queen; **da donna** woman's, e.g., **scarpe da donna** woman's shoes; **donna cannone** fat lady (*of circus*); **donna di casa** housewife; **Nostra Donna** Our Lady

donnaiòlo *m* ladies' man, philanderer

donné·sco -sca *adj* (-schi -sche) womanly, feminine

dònnola *f* weasel

dòno *m* gift; **in dono** as a gift

donzèlla [dz] *f* (lit) damsel

donzèllo [dz] *m* (coll) doorman; (lit) page

dópo *adv* afterwards, later; **dopo che** after; **dopo di** after ‖ *prep* after; **dopo + pp** after having + *pp*

dopobar·ba *adj invar* after-shaving ‖ *m* (-ba) after-shaving lotion

dopodomani *m* & *adv* the day after tomorrow

dopoguèr·ra *m* (-ra) postwar era

dopolavóro *m* government office designed to organize workers' leisure time

dopopranzo *m* afternoon ‖ *adv* in the afternoon

doppiàg·gio *m* (-gi) (mov) dubbing

doppiare §287 (**dóppio**) *tr* to double; (mov) to dub

doppière *m* candelabrum

doppiétta *f* double-barreled shotgun; (aut) double shift

doppiézza *f* duplicity

dóp·pio -pia (-pi -pie) *adj* double; coupled; double-dealing || *adv* twice, twofold || *m* double; twice as much; (tennis) doubles; (theat) understudy

doppióne *m* duplicate; (philol) doublet

doppiopèt·to *adj invar* double-breasted || *m* (**-to**) double-breasted suit

dorare (**dòro**) *tr* to gild; (culin) to brown; **dorare la pillola** to sugar-coat the pill

dora·to -ta *adj* gilt, golden

doratura *f* gilding

dormicchiare §287 *intr* to doze

dormiènte *adj* sleeping || *mf* sleeper

dormiglió·ne -na *mf* sleepyhead

dormire (**dòrmo**) *tr & intr* to sleep; **dormire a occhi aperti** to be overcome with sleep; **dormire della grossa** to sleep profoundly; **dormire tra due guanciali** to be safe and secure

dormita *f* long sleep; **fare una bella dormita** to have a long sleep

dormitò·rio *m* (**-ri**) dormitory

dormivé·glia *m* (**-glia**) drowsiness

dorsale *adj* dorsal; back (*bone*) || *m* head (*of bed*); back (*of chair*) || *f* (geog) ridge

dòrso *m* back; (sports) backstroke

dosàg·gio *m* (**-gi**) dosage

dosare (**dòso**) *tr* to dose

dosatura *f* dosage

dòse *f* dose

dòsso *m* back; (lit) summit; **levarsi di dosso** to take off; **mettersi in dosso** to put on

dotare (**dòto**) *tr* to provide with a dowry; to endow; to bless

dotazióne *f* dowry; endowment; supply

dòte *f* dowry; gift; endowment

dòt·to -ta *adj* learned, erudite || *m* scholar; (anat) duct

dottorale *adj* doctoral

dottó·re -réssa *mf* doctor

dottrina *f* doctrine; Christian doctrine

dóve *m* where; **per ogni dove** everywhere || *adv* where; **da dove** or **di dove** from where; which way; **fin dove** up to what point; **per dove** which way || *conj* where; whereas

dovère *m* duty, obligation; homework; a dovere properly; **doveri** regards; **farsi un dovere di** to feel duty-bound to; **mettere qlcu a dovere** to put s.o. in his place; **più del dovere** more than one should; **sentirsi in dovere di** to feel duty-bound to || §160 *tr & intr* to owe || *aux* (ESSERE & AVERE) must, e.g., **deve farlo** you must do it; to have to, e.g., **dovei partire** I had to leave; ought to, e.g., **dovrebbe lucidare la macchina** he ought to polish the car; should, e.g., **dovresti immaginarti** you should imagine; to be to, e.g., **il treno doveva arrivare alle sei** the train was to arrive at six; to be supposed to, e.g., **deve aver**

fatto un lungo viaggio he is supposed to have taken a long journey

doveró·so -sa [s] *adj* proper, right

dovizia *f* (lit) abundance, wealth

dovunque *adv* wherever, anywhere; everywhere

dovu·to -ta *adj & m* due

dozzina [ddzz] *f* dozen; room and board; **da** or **di dozzina** common, ordinary; **tenere a dozzina** to board

dozzinale [ddzz] *adj* common, ordinary

dozzinante [ddzz] *mf* boarder

dra·ga *f* (**-ghe**) dredge

dragàg·gio *m* (**-gi**) dredging

dragami·ne *m* (**-ne**) minesweeper

dragare §209 *tr* to dredge

dràglia *f* (naut) stay

dra·go *m* (**-ghi**) dragon; **drago volante** kite

dragóna *f* sword strap

dragoncèllo *m* (bot) tarragon

dragóne *m* dragon; dragoon

dram·ma *m* (**-mi**) drama, play; **dramma musicale** (hist) melodrama || *f* drachma; dram

drammàti·co -ca (-ci -che) *adj* dramatic || *f* drama, dramatic art

drammatizzare [ddzz] *tr* to dramatize

drammatur·go *m* (**-ghi**) playwright, dramatist

drappég·gio *m* (**-gi**) drape; pleats

drappeggiare §290 (**drappéggio**) *tr* to drape || *ref* to be draped

drappèlla *f* pennon (*on bugler's trumpet*)

drappèllo *m* squad, platoon

drapperia *f* dry goods; dry-goods store

drappo *m* cloth, silk cloth; (billiards) green cloth, baize

dràsti·co -ca *adj* (**-ci -che**) drastic

drenàg·gio *m* (**-gi**) drainage

drenare (**drèno**) *tr* to drain

dressàg·gio *m* (**-gi**) *m* training (*of animals*)

dribblare *tr & intr* (sports) to dribble

drit·to -ta *adj* straight; (lit) correct; **dritto come un fuso** straight as a ramrod || *m* (fig) old fox || *f* right; (naut) starboard

drizza *f* (naut) halyard

drizzare *tr* to straighten; to address; to erect; to cock (*the head*); to direct (*a blow*); **drizzare le gambe ai cani** to do the impossible; **drizzare le orecchie** to prick up one's ears || *intr* (naut) to hoist the halyard || *ref* to stand erect

dró·ga *f* (**-ghe**) drug; spice; seasoning

drogare §209 (**drògo**) *tr* to drug; to spice, season

drogheria *f* grocery (store)

droghière *m* grocer

dromedà·rio *m* (**-ri**) dromedary

dru·do -da *adj* (archaic) faithful; (lit) strong || *m* (obs) vassal; (lit) lover

drùi·da *m* (**-di**) druid

drupa *f* (bot) drupe, stone fruit

duale *adj & m* dual

dualismo *m* dualism

duali·tà *f* duality

dùb·bio -bia (-bi -bie) *adj* doubtful || *m* doubt; misgiving; **mettere in dub-**

bio to question; to risk; **senza dubbio** no doubt

dubbió‧so -sa [s] *adj* dubious; doubtful; (lit) dangerous

dubitare (dùbito) *intr* to doubt; to suspect; **dubitare di** to mistrust; to doubt; **non dubitare!** don't worry!

du‧ca m (-chi) duke; (lit) leader

ducato *m* duchy; ducat

duce *m* leader; duce

duchéssa *f* duchess

duchessina *f* young duchess

duchino *m* young duke

due *adj & pron* two; **le due** two o'clock ‖ *m* two; second (*in dates*) ‖ *f*—**fra le due** between two alternatives

duecenté‧sco -sca *adj* (**-schi -sche**) thirteenth-century

duecentèsi‧mo -ma *adj, m & pron* two hundredth

duecènto *adj, m & pron* two hundred ‖ **il Duecento** the thirteenth century

duellante *adj* dueling ‖ *m* duelist

duellare (duèllo) *intr* to duel

duèllo *m* duel; contest; debate; **sfidare a duello** to challenge to a duel

duemila *adj, m & pron* two thousand ‖ **Duemila** *m* twenty-first century

duepèz‧zi m (-zi) two-piece bathing suit

duétto *m* (mus) duet

dulcamara *f* (bot) bittersweet

dulcina *f* artificial sweetening

duna *f* dune

dunque *m*—**venire al dunque** to come

to the point ‖ *adv* then ‖ *conj* therefore, hence ‖ *interj* well!

duodèno *m* (anat) duodenum

duòlo *m* (lit) grief

duòmo *m* cathedral; dome (*e.g., of a boiler*)

du‧plex m (-plex) (telp) party line

duplicare §197 (dùplico) *tr* to duplicate

duplica‧to -ta *adj & m* duplicate

duplicatóre *m* duplicator

dùplice *adj* twofold, double ‖ *f* (racing) daily double

duplici‧tà f (-tà) duplicity

duràbile *adj* durable, lasting

duràci‧no -na *adj* clingstone ‖ *f* clingstone peach

duralluminio *m* duralumin

durare *tr* to endure, bear ‖ *intr* to last; **durare a** + *inf* to keep on + *ger*; **durare in carica** to remain in office

durata *f* duration; lasting quality; **di lunga durata** long-lasting

dùrante *prep* during; throughout

duratu‧ro -ra *adj* enduring, lasting

durévole *adj* lasting, durable

durézza *f* hardness; toughness; rigidity

du‧ro -ra *adj* hard; hard-boiled (*egg*); durum (*wheat*); tough (*skin*); harsh; (phonet) voiceless ‖ *m* hard part; hard floor; hard soil; **il duro sta che . . .** the trouble is that . . . ; **tener duro** to hold out

duróne *m* callousness, callosity

dùttile *adj* ductile; tractable

E

E, e [e] *m & f* fifth letter of the Italian alphabet

e *conj* and

ebani‧sta m (-sti) cabinetmaker

ebanisterìa *f* cabinetmaking; cabinetmaker's shop

ebanite *f* ebonite, vulcanite

èbano *m* ebony

ebbène *interj* well!

ebbrézza *f* intoxication, drunkenness

èb‧bro -bra *adj* intoxicated ‖ *mf* drunk

ebdomadà‧rio -ria *adj & m* (**-ri -rie**) weekly

èbete *adj* stupid, dull, dumb

ebollizióne *f* boil, boiling

ebrài‧co -ca (**-ci -che**) *adj* Hebrew, Hebraic ‖ *m* Hebrew (*language*)

ebrè‧o -a *adj & mf* Hebrew ‖ *m* Hebrew (*language*); Jew; **ebreo errante** Wandering Jew

è‧bro -bra *adj & mf* var of **ebbro**

ebùrne‧o -a *adj* (lit) ivory

ecatòmbe *f* hecatomb, slaughter

eccedènte *adj* exceeding ‖ *m* excess

eccedènza *f* excess, surplus

eccèdere §123 *tr* to exceed ‖ *intr* to go too far

eccellènte *adj* excellent

eccellènza *f* excellence ‖ **Eccellenza** *f* Excellency

eccèllere §162 *intr* (ESSERE) to excel

eccèl‧so -sa *adj* unexcelled; very high ‖ —**l'Eccelso** *m* the Most High

eccentrici‧tà f (-tà) eccentricity

eccèntri‧co -ca (**-ci -che**) *adj* eccentric; suburban ‖ *mf* vaudeville performer ‖ *m* (mach) eccentric

eccepìbile *adj* objectionable

eccepire §176 *tr* (law) to take exception to ‖ *intr* (law) to object

eccessi‧vo -va *adj* excessive; overweening (*opinion*)

eccèsso *m* excess; **all'eccesso** excessively; **andare agli eccessi** to go to extremes; **dare in eccessi** to fly into a rage; **eccesso di peso** excess weight

eccètera *adv* and so forth, et cetera

eccètto *prep* except, but; **eccetto che** except that; unless

eccettuare (eccèttuo) *tr* to except

eccettua‧to -ta *adj* excepted ‖ **eccettuato** *prep* except

eccezionale *adj* exceptional

eccezióne *f* exception; objection; **ad eccezione di** with the exception of; **d'eccezione** extraordinary; **sollevare un'eccezione** (law) to take exception

ecchimò‧si f (-si) bruise

ecci‧dio m (-di) massacre

eccitàbile *adj* excitable

eccitaménto m instigation; excitement
eccitante adj stimulating || m stimulant
eccitare (**èccito**) tr to excite || ref to become excited or aroused; (sports) to warm up
eccitazióne f excitement; (elec) excitation
ecclesiàsti·co -ca (**-ci -che**) adj ecclesiastical || m clergyman
ècco tr invar here is (are), there is (are); **ecco che here, e.g., ecco che viene** here he comes; **eccoci** here we are; **ecco fatto** that's it; **eccola** here she is; here it is; **eccomi** here I am; **eccone** here are some || intr invar here I am; here it is; **quand'ecco** suddenly || interj look!
eccóme interj and how!, indeed!
echeggiare §290 (**echéggio**) intr (ESSERE & AVERE) to echo
eclètti·co -ca adj & mf (**-ci -che**) eclectic
eclissare tr to eclipse || ref to be eclipsed; (coll) to vanish, sneak away
eclìs·si f (**-si**) eclipse
eclìtti·ca f (**-che**) ecliptic
èclo·ga f (**-ghe**) var of egloga
è·co m & f (**-chi** mpl) echo; **far eco a** to echo
ecogoniòmetro m sonar
ecologìa f ecology
economato m comptroller's or administrator's office
economìa f administration; management; economy; economics; **economia aziendale** business management; **economia di mercato** free enterprise; **economia domestica** home economics; **economia politica** political economy; economics; **economie** savings; **fare economia** to save
econòmi·co -ca adj (**-ci -che**) economic(al); cheap
economi·sta mf (**-sti -ste**) economist
economizzare [ddzz] tr & intr to economize, save
econo·mo -ma adj thrifty || m comptroller; administrator
ecosistè·ma [s] m (**-mi**) ecosystem
ecumèni·co -ca adj (**-ci -che**) ecumenical
eczè·ma [dz] m (**-mi**) eczema
édera f ivy
edìcola f shrine; newsstand
edificante adj edifying
edificare §197 (**edìfico**) tr to build; to edify || intr to build
edifica·tóre -trice adj building || mf builder
edificazióne f building; edification
edifì·cio m (**-ci**) building, edifice; pack (e.g., of lies); structure
edìle adj building, construction || m builder, construction worker
edilì·zio -zia (**-zi -zie**) adj building, construction || f building trade
edìpi·co -ca adj (**-ci -che**) Oedipus (e.g., complex)
Edipo m Oedipus
èdi·to -ta adj published
edi·tóre -trice adj publishing || mf publisher; editor (e.g., of a text)
editorìa f publishing; publishers

editoriale adj editorial; publishing || m editorial
editoriali·sta mf (**-sti -ste**) editorial writer
editto m edict
edizióne f edition; performance; (fig) vintage
edonismo m hedonism
edoni·sta mf (**-sti -ste**) hedonist
edòt·to -ta adj (lit) informed, acquainted; **rendere qlcu edotto su qlco** (lit) to inform s.o. of s.th
edredóne m eider, eider duck
educanda f boarding-school girl; convent-school girl
educandato m (convent) boarding school for girls
educare §197 (**èduco**) tr to educate; to rear, bring up; to train; to accustom, inure; (lit) to grow
educatì·vo -va adj educational
educa·to -ta adj educated; polite, well-bred
educa·tóre -trice mf educator
educazióne f education; breeding, manners; **educazione civica** civics
edule adj edible
efèbo m (coll) sissy
efèlide f freckle
effeminatézza f effeminacy
effemìna·to -ta adj effeminate; frivolous
efferatézza f savagery
effervescènte adj effervescent
effervescènza f effervescence
effettivaménte adv really
effettì·vo -va adj real, true; effective; full (e.g., member); regular (e.g., army officer) || m effective; total amount; (mil) manpower
effètto m effect, result; (com) promissory note; (billiards) English; (sports) spin; **a questo effetto** for this purpose; **effetti** effects, belongings; **effetto di luce** play of light; **effetto ottico** optical illusion; **fare effetto** to make a sensation; **fare l'effetto di** to give the impression of; **in effetto** in fact; **mandare a effetto** to carry out; **porre in effetto** to put into effect
effettuàbile adj feasible
effettuare (**effèttuo**) tr to bring about; to contrive; to actuate; **effettuare** (**una corsa, un servizio**) to run, e.g., **l'autobus effettua una corsa ogni mezz'ora** the bus runs every half hour
efficace adj effective; forceful (writer)
efficà·cia f (**-cie**) effectiveness, efficacy; (law) validity
efficiènte adj efficient
efficiènza f efficiency; **in piena efficienza** in full working order; in top condition
effigiare §290 tr to portray, represent
effì·gie f (**-gie** or **-gi**) effigy; image
effìme·ro -ra adj ephemeral
efflusso m flow, outflow
efflù·vio m (**-vi**) effluvium; emanation (e.g., of light)
effrazióne f (law) burglary
effusióne f effusion; outflow; shedding (of blood); effusiveness
egemonìa f hegemony

egè·o -a *adj* Aegean
ègida *f* aegis
Egitto, l' *m* Egypt
egizìa·no -na *adj & mf* Egyptian
eglantina *f* sweetbrier
eglefino *m* haddock
égli §5 *pron* pers he
èglo·ga *f* (**-ghe**) eclogue
egocèntri·co -ca *adj & mf* (**-ci -che**) egocentric
egoismo *m* egoism, selfishness
egoì·sta (**-sti -ste**) *adj* selfish || *mf* egoist
egoìsti·co -ca *adj* (**-ci -che**) egoistic(al)
egotismo *m* egotism
egotì·sta (**-sti -ste**) *adj* egotistic || *mf* egotist
egrè·gio -gia *adj* (**-gi -gie**) (lit) outstanding; **Egregio Signore** Mr. (*before a man's name in an address on a letter*); Dear Sir
eguaglianza *f* equality
eguale *adj* var of **uguale**
egualità·rio -ria *adj & m* (**-ri -rie**) equalitarian
éhi *interj* hey!
éi *pron* (lit) he; (archaic) they
eiaculazióne *f* ejaculation
eiettàbile *adj* ejection (*seat*)
eiezióne *f* ejection
él *pron* (archaic) he
elaborare (**elàboro**) *tr* to elaborate; to digest; to secrete
elabora·to -ta *adj* elaborate || *m* written exercise
elaboratóre *m* computer
elaborazióne *f* elaboration; data processing
elargire §176 *tr* to donate
elargizióne *f* donation
elastici·tà *f* (**-tà**) elasticity; agility; (com) oscillation; (com) range
elàsti·co -ca (**-ci -che**) *adj* elastic || *m* rubber band; bedspring
élce *m & f* holm oak
elefante *m* elephant; **elefante marino** sea elephant
elefantéssa *f* female elephant
elegante *adj* elegant, fashionable
elegantó·ne -na *mf* fashion plate || *m* dandy, dude
eleganza *f* elegance, stylishness
elèggere §193 *tr* to elect
eleggìbile *adj* eligible
elegia *f* elegy
elegìa·co -ca *adj* elegiac
elementare *adj* elementary || **elementari** *fpl* elementary schools
eleménto *m* element; rudiment; member; cell (*of battery*); **elementi personnel**, e.g., **elementi femminili** female personnel
elemòsina *f* alms; (eccl) collection; **chiedere l'elemosina** to beg; **vivere d'elemosina** to live on charity
elemosinare (**elemòsino**) *intr* to beg
Èlena *f* Helen
elencare §197 (**elènco**) *tr* to list; to enumerate
elèn·co *m* (**-chi**) list; **elenco telefonico** telephone directory
elettì·vo -va *adj* elective
elèt·to -ta *adj* elect; distinguished

(*audience*); precious (*metal*); chosen (*people*)
elettorato *m* electorate, constituency
elet·tóre -trice *mf* voter; elector
elettràuto *m* automobile electrician; automotive electric shop
elettrici·sta *mf* (**-sti -ste**) electrician
elettrici·tà *f* (**-tà**) electricity
elèttri·co -ca (**-ci -che**) *adj* electrical || *m* electrical worker
elettrificare §197 (**elettrìfico**) *tr* to electrify
elettrizzare [**ddzz**] *tr* to electrify (*e.g., a person*) || *ref* to become electrified
ellètro *m* amber
elettrocalamita *f* electromagnet
elettrocardiògrafo *m* electrocardiograph
elettrocardiogram·ma *m* (**-mi**) electrocardiogram
elettrodinàmi·co -ca (**-ci -che**) *adj* electrodynamic || *f* electrodynamics
elèttrodo *m* electrode
elettrodomèsti·co -ca (**-ci -che**) *adj* electric household || *m* electric household appliance
elettroesecuzióne *f* electrocution
elettròge·no -na *adj* generating (*unit*)
elettròli·si *f* (**-si**) electrolysis
elettrolìti·co -ca *adj* (**-ci -che**) electrolytic
elettròlito *m* electrolyte
elettromagnèti·co -ca *adj* (**-ci -che**) electromagnetic
elettromo·tóre -trice *adj* electromotive || *m* electric motor || *f* electric train; electric railcar
elettróne *m* electron
elettróni·co -ca (**-ci -che**) *adj* electronic || *f* electronics
elettropómpa *f* electric pump
elettrosquasso *m* electroshock
elettrostàti·co -ca (**-ci -che**) *adj* electrostatic || *f* electrostatics
elettrotècni·co -ca (**-ci -che**) *adj* electrotechnical || *m* electrician; electrical engineer || *f* electrical engineering
elettrotrèno *m* electric train
elevaménto *m* elevation
elevare (**èlevo & elèvo**) *tr* to lift, elevate; (math) to raise || *ref* to rise
elevatézza *f* loftiness, dignity
eleva·to -ta *adj* high, lofty
eleva·tóre -trice *adj* elevating || *m* elevator
elevazióne *f* elevation; (sports) jump; (math) raising
elezióne *f* election; choice
èlfo *m* elf
èli·ca *f* (**-che**) propeller; (geom) helix
elicoidale *adj* helicoidal
elicòttero *m* helicopter
elìdere §161 *tr* to annul; to elide || *ref* to neutralize one another
eliminare (**elìmino**) *tr* to eliminate
eliminatò·rio -ria (**-ri -rie**) *adj* eliminating || *f* (sports) heat
eliminazióne *f* elimination; extermination
èlio- *comb form adj* helio-, e.g., **eliocentrico** heliocentric || *comb form*

m & f helio-, e.g., **elioterapìa** heliotherapy

èlio *m* helium

eliocèntri·co -ca *adj* (**-ci -che**) heliocentric

eliògrafo *m* heliograph

elioteràpi·co -ca *adj* (**-ci -che**) sunshine (*treatment*); sunbathing (*establishment*)

eliotrò·pio *m* (**-pi**) heliotrope; bloodstone

elipòrto *m* heliport

elisabettia·no -na *adj* Elizabethan

elì·sio -sia *adj* (**-si -sie**) Elysian

elisióne *f* elision

elì·sir *m* (**-sir**) elixir

èlitra *f* elytron, shard

élla *pron* (lit) she || **Ella** *pron* (lit) you

ellèboro *m* hellebore

ellèni·co -ca *adj* (**-ci -che**) Hellenic

ellisse *f* ellipse

ellìs·si *f* (**-si**) (gram) ellipsis

ellìtti·co -ca *adj* (**-ci -che**) elliptical

-èllo -èlla *suf adj* little, e.g., **poverello** poor little

elmétto *m* helmet; tin hat

élmo *m* helmet

elogiare §290 *tr* to praise

elò·gio *m* (**-gi**) praise, encomium; write-up; **elogio fùnebre** eulogy

eloquènte *adj* eloquent

eloquènza *f* eloquence

elò·quio *m* (**-qui**) (lit) speech, diction

élsa *f* hilt

elucidare (**elùcido**) *tr* to elucidate

elùdere §105 *tr* to elude, evade

elusì·vo -va *adj* elusive

elvèti·co -ca *adj & mf* (**-ci -che**) Helvetian

elzevì·ro -ra [dz] *adj* Elzevir || *m* Elzevir book; (journ) literary article

emacià·to -ta *adj* emaciated, lean

emanare *tr* to send forth; to issue || *intr* (ESSERE) to emanate; to come forth

emanazióne *f* emanation; issuance

emancipare (**emàncipo**) *tr* to emancipate || *ref* to become emancipated

emancipazióne *f* emancipation

emarginare (**emàrgino**) *tr* to note in the margin; (fig) to put aside, neglect

emarginato *m* marginal note

emàti·co -ca *adj* (**-ci -che**) blood, hematic

ematìte *f* hematite

embàr·go *m* (**-ghi**) embargo

emblè·ma *m* (**-mi**) emblem

emblemàti·co -ca *adj* (**-ci -che**) emblematic

embolìa *f* embolism

èmbrice *m* flat roof tile; shingle

embriologìa *f* embryology

embrionale *adj* embryonic

embrióne *m* embryo

emendaménto *m* emendation (*of a text*); amendment (*to a law*)

emendare (**emèndo**) *tr* to correct; to emend; to amend (*a law*) || *ref* to reform

emergènza *f* emergence; emergency

emèrgere §162 *intr* (ESSERE) to emerge;

to surface (*said of a submarine*); to loom; to stand out

emèri·to -ta *adj* emeritus (*professor*); famous

emerotè·ca *f* (**-che**) periodical library

emersióne *f* emersion; surfacing

emèr·so -sa *adj* emergent

emèti·co -ca *adj & m* (**-ci -che**) emetic

eméttere §198 *tr* to emit, send forth; to utter (*a statement*); (com) to issue

emicìclo *m* hemicycle; floor (*of legislative body*)

emicrània *f* migraine, headache

emigrante *adj & mf* emigrant

emigrare *intr* (ESSERE & AVERE) to emigrate

emigra·to -ta *adj & mf* emigrant

emigrazióne *f* emigration; migration (*e.g., of birds*)

eminènte *adj* eminent

eminènza *f* eminence; (eccl) Eminence

emisfèro *m* hemisphere

emissà·rio *m* (**-ri**) emissary; outlet (*river or lake*); drain

emissióne *f* emission; issuance; (rad) broadcast

emistì·chio *m* (**-chi**) hemistich

emittènte *adj* emitting; issuing; (rad) broadcasting || *f* (rad) transmitting set; broadcasting station

emofilìa *f* hemophilia

emoglobìna *f* hemoglobin

emolliènte *adj & m* emollient

emoluménto *m* fee, emolument

emorragìa *f* hemorrhage

emorròidi *fpl* hemorrhoids, piles

emostàti·co -ca *adj* (**-ci -che**) hemostatic || *m* hemostat

emotè·ca *f* (**-che**) blood bank

emotivi·tà *f* (**-tà**) emotionalism

emotì·vo -va *adj* emotional || *mf* emotional person

emottìsi *f* (pathol) hemoptysis

emozionante *adj* emotional, moving

emozionare (**emozióno**) *tr* to move, stir; to thrill

emozióne *f* emotion

empiastro *m* var of **impiastro**

émpiere §163 *tr & ref* var of **empìre**

empie·tà *f* (**-tà**) impiety; cruelty

èm·pio -pia *adj* (**-pi -pie**) impious; pitiless, wicked

empìre §163 *tr* to fill; (lit) to fulfill; **empìre qlcu di insulti** to heap insults on s.o. || *ref* to get full

empìre·o -a *adj* heavenly, sublime || *m* empyrean

empìri·co -ca *adj* (**-ci -che**) empirical || *mf* empiricist

empirìsmo *m* empiricism

empirì·sta *mf* (**-sti -ste**) empiricist

émpito *m* (lit) rush; fury

empò·rio *m* (**-ri**) emporium, mart

emulare (**èmulo**) *tr* to emulate

emulazióne *f* emulation, rivalry; (law) evil intent

èmu·lo -la *adj* emulous || *mf* emulator

emulsionare (**emulsióno**) *tr* to emulsify

emulsióne *f* emulsion

encefalìte *f* encephalitis

encìcli·ca *f* (**-che**) encyclical

enciclopedìa *f* encyclopedia

enciclopèdi·co **-ca** *adj* (**-ci -che**) encyclopedic
enclave *f* enclave
enclìti·co **-ca** *adj* & *f* (**-ci -che**) enclitic
encomiàbile *adj* praiseworthy
encomiare §287 (**encòmio**) *tr* to praise
encò·mio *m* (**-mi**) encomium, praise
endecasìlla·bo **-ba** *adj* hendecasyllabic ‖ *m* hendecasyllable
endemìa *f* endemic
endèmi·co **-ca** *adj* (**-ci -che**) endemic
èndice *m* nest egg; (obs) souvenir
endocàr·dio *m* (**-di**) (anat) endocardium
endocarpo *m* (bot) endocarp
endòcri·no **-na** *adj* endocrine
endourbà·no **-na** *adj* inner-city
endovenó·so **-sa** [s] *adj* intravenous
energèti·co **-ca** (**-ci -che**) *adj* energy (*e.g.*, *crisis*); (med) tonic ‖ *m* (med) tonic
energia *f* energy, power
enèrgi·co **-ca** *adj* (**-ci -che**) energetic
energùme·no **-na** *mf* wild or mad person
ènfa·si *f* (**-si**) emphasis; forcefulness
enfàti·co **-ca** *adj* (**-ci -che**) emphatic
enfiare §287 (**énfio**) *tr* & *ref* to swell
enfisè·ma *m* (**-mi**) emphysema
enfitèu·si *f* (**-si**) lease (*of land*)
enìg·ma *m* (**-mi**) enigma, riddle, puzzle
enigmàti·co **-ca** *adj* (**-ci -che**) enigmatic, puzzling
-ènne *suf adj* -year-old, *e.g.*, **ragazzo diciassettenne** seventeen-year-old boy ‖ *suf mf* -year-old person, *e.g.*, **diciassettenne** seventeen-year-old person
ennèsi·mo **-ma** *adj* nth
-èn·nio *suf m* (**-ni**) period of . . . years, *e.g.*, **ventennio** period of twenty years
enòlo·go **-ga** *mf* (**-gi -ghe**) oenologist
enórme *adj* enormous
enormeménte *adv* enormously
enormi·tà *f* (**-tà**) enormity; outrage; absurdity
Enrico *m* Henry
ènte *m* being; entity; córporation; agency, body
enteroclì·sma *m* (**-smi**) enema
enti·tà *f* (**-tà**) entity; value, importance
entomologìa *f* entomology
entram·bi **-be** *adj*—**entrambi i** both ‖ *pron* both
entrante *adj* next (*e.g.*, *week*)
entrare (**éntro**) *intr* (ESSERE) to enter; to go (*said of numbers*); to get (*into one's head*); **entrarci** to make it, *e.g.*, **con questi soldi non c'entro** I can't make it with this money; **entrarci come i cavoli a merenda** to be completely out of line; **entrare a** to begin to; **entrare in** to enter (*e.g.*, *a room*); to fit in; to go in (*said of a number*); to get into (*one's head*); **entrare in amore** to be in heat (*said of animals*); **entrare in ballo** to come into play; **entrare in carica** to take up one's duties; **entrare in collera** to get angry; **entrare in collisione** to collide; **entrare in contatto** to establish contact; **entrare in gioco** to come into play; **entrare in guerra** to go to war; **entrare in società** to make one's debut; **entrare nella parte di** (theat)

to play the role of; **entrare in vigore** to become effective; **Lei non c'entra** this is none of your business; **questo non c'entra** this is beside the point
entrata *f* entry; entrance; **entrata di favore** (theat) complimentary ticket; **entrate** income
entratura *f* entry; entrance; assumption (*of a position*); familiarity
éntro *adv* inside ‖ *prep* within; **entro di** within, inside of
entrobórdo *m* inboard motorboat
entrotèrra *f* inland, hinterland
entusiasmare *tr* to carry away, enthuse ‖ *ref* to be carried away, to become enthused
entusiasmo *m* enthusiasm
entusia·sta **-sti -ste**) *adj* enthusiastic ‖ *mf* enthusiast, devotee
entusiàsti·co **-ca** *adj* (**-ci -che**) enthusiastic
enucleare (**enùcleo**) *tr* to elucidate; (surg) to remove
enumerare (**enùmero**) *tr* to enumerate
enumerazióne *f* enumeration
enunciare §128 *tr* to enunciate, state
enunciati·vo **-va** *adj* (gram) declarative
enunciazióne *f* enunciation, statement
erzi·ma [dz] *m* (**-mi**) enzyme
èpa *f* (lit) belly, paunch
epàti·co **-ca** *adj* (**-ci -che**) hepatic, liver
epatite *f* (pathol) hepatitis
epènte·si *f* (**-si**) epenthesis
eperlano *m* (ichth) smelt
èpi·co **-ca** *adj* (**-ci -che**) epic
epicurè·o **-a** *adj* & *m* epicurean
epidemìa *f* epidemic
epidèmi·co **-ca** *adj* (**-ci -che**) epidemic (al)
epidèrmi·co **-ca** *adj* (**-ci -che**) epidermal; (fig) superficial, skin-deep
epidèrmide *f* epidermis
Epifanìa *f* Epiphany
epiglòttide *f* (anat) epiglottis
epìgono *m* follower; descendant
epìgrafe *f* epigraph
epigram·ma *m* (**-mi**) epigram
epigrammàti·co **-ca** *adj* (**-ci -che**) epigrammatic
epilessìa *f* (pathol) epilepsy
epilètti·co **-ca** *adj* & *m* (**-ci -che**) epileptic
epìlo·go *m* (**-ghi**) epilogue; conclusion
episcopale *adj* episcopal
episcopalia·no **-na** *adj* & *mf* Episcopalian
episcopato *m* episcopate, bishopric
episòdi·co **-ca** *adj* (**-ci -che**) episodic
episò·dio *m* (**-di**) episode
epìstola *f* epistle
epistolà·rio *m* (**-ri**) letters, correspondence
epitàf·fio *m* (**-fi**) epitaph
epitè·lio *m* (**-li**) epithelium
epìteto *m* epithet; insult
epitomare (**epìtomo**) *tr* to epitomize
epìtome *f* epitome
èpo·ca *f* (**-che**) epoch; period; moment; **fare epoca** to be epoch-making
epopèa *f* epic
eppure *conj* yet, and yet
epsomite *f* Epsom salt

epurare *tr* to cleanse; to purge
epurazióne *f* purification; purge
equànime *adj* calm, composed; impartial
equanimità *f* equanimity; impartiality
equatóre *m* equator
equatoriale *adj & m* equatorial
equazióne *f* equation
equèstre *adj* equestrian
equilàte·ro -ra *adj* equilateral
equilibrare *tr* to balance; (aer) to trim || *ref* to balance one another
equilibra·to -ta *adj* level-headed
equilibra·tóre -trice *adj* stabilizing || *m* (aer) horizontal stabilizer
equilì·brio *m* (**-bri**) equilibrium, balance; (fig) proportion; **equilibrio politico** balance of power
equilibrì·sta *mf* (**-sti -ste**) acrobat, equilibrist
equi·no -na *adj & m* equine
equinoziale *adj* equinoctial
equinò·zio *m* (**-zi**) equinox
equipaggiaménto *m* equipment, outfit
equipaggiare §290 *tr* to equip, outfit; (naut) to fit out; (naut) to man
equipàg·gio *m* (**-gi**) equipage; (naut) crew, complement; (sports) team; (rowing) crew
equiparare *tr* to equalize (*e.g., salaries*)
équipe *f* team
equipollènte *adj* equivalent
equi·tà *f* (**-tà**) equity, fair-mindedness
equitazióne *f* horsemanship
equivalènte *adj & m* equivalent
equivalére §278 *intr* (ESSERE & AVERE) —**equivalere a** to be equivalent to || *ref* to be equal
equivocare §197 (**equìvoco**) *intr*—**equivocare su** to mistake, misunderstand
equìvo·co -ca (**-ci -che**) *adj* equivocal; ambiguous || *m* misunderstanding
è·quo -qua *adj* equitable, fair
èra *f* era, age; **era spaziale** space age
erà·rio *m* (**-ri**) treasury
èrba *f* grass; **erba limoncina** lemon verbena; **erba medica** alfalfa; **erbe vegetables**; **erbe aromatiche** herbs; **far l'erba** to cut the grass; **in erba** (fig) budding; **metter a erba** to put to pasture
erbàc·cia *f* (**-ce**) weed
erbaggi *mpl* vegetables
erbaiò·lo -la *mf* fresh vegetable retailer
erbici·da *m* (**-di**) weed-killer
erbivéndo·lo -la *mf* fresh fruit and vegetable retailer
erbìvo·ro -ra *adj* herbivorous
erborì·sta *mf* (**-sti -ste**) herbalist
erbó·so -sa [s] *adj* grassy
Èrcole *m* Hercules
ercùle·o -a *adj* Herculean
erède *m* heir || *f* heiress
eredità *f* (**-tà**) inheritance; heredity
ereditare (**erèdito**) *tr* to inherit
eredità·rio -ria *adj* (**-ri -rie**) hereditary; crown (*prince*)
ereditièra *f* heiress
eremì·ta *m* (**-ti**) hermit
eremitàg·gio *m* (**-gi**) hermitage
èremo *m* hermitage
eresìa *f* heresy

eresìar·ca *m* (**-chi**) heretic
erèti·co -ca (**-ci -che**) *adj* heretical || *mf* heretic
erèt·to -ta *adj* erect, straight
erezióne *f* erection
ergastola·no -na *mf* lifer
ergàstolo *m* life imprisonment; prison for persons sentenced to life imprisonment
èrgere §164 *tr* (lit) to erect; (lit) to lift || *ref* to rise (*said, e.g., of a mountain*)
èrgo *m* *invar*—**venire all'ergo** to come to a conclusion || *adv* thus, hence
èri·ca *f* (**-che**) heather
erìgere §152 *tr* to erect, build || *ref* to rise; **erigersi a** to set oneself up as
eritrè·o -a *adj & mf* Eritrean
ermafrodì·to -ta *adj & m* hermafrodite
ermellino *m* ermine
ermèti·co -ca *adj* (**-ci -che**) airtight; watertight; hermetic
èrnia *f* hernia; **ernia del disco** (pathol) herniated disk
eródere §239 *tr* to erode
eròe *m* hero
erogare §209 (**èrogo**) *tr* to distribute; to bestow
erogazióne *f* distribution; bestowal
eròi·co -ca *adj* (**-ci -che**) heroic
eroicòmi·co -ca *adj* (**-ci -che**) mock-heroic
eroìna *f* heroine; (pharm) heroin
eroismo *m* heroism
erómpere §240 *intr* to erupt, burst out
erosióne *f* erosion
eròti·co -ca *adj* (**-ci -che**) erotic
erotismo *m* eroticism
èrpete *m* (pathol) herpes, shingles
erpicare §197 (**érpico**) *tr* to harrow
érpice *m* harrow
errabón·do -da *adj* (lit) wandering
errante *adj* errant; wandering
errare (**èrro**) *intr* to wander; to err; (lit) to stray
erra·to -ta *adj* mistaken, wrong
erròne·o -a *adj* erroneous
erróre *m* error, mistake; fault; (lit) wandering; **errore di lingua** slip of the tongue; **errore di scrittura** slip of the pen; **errore di stampa** misprint; **errore giudiziario** miscarriage of justice; **salvo errore od omissione** barring error or omission
ér·to -ta *adj* arduous, steep; erect || *f* arduous ascent; **all'erta** on the alert
erudire §176 *tr* to educate, instruct
erudì·to -ta *adj* erudite, learned || *m* scholar, savant
erudizióne *f* erudition, learning
eruttare *tr* to belch forth (*e.g., lava*); to utter (*obscenities*) || *intr* to belch
erutti·vo -va *adj* eruptive
eruzióne *f* eruption
esacerbare (**esacèrbo**) *tr* to embitter; to exacerbate || *ref* to become embittered
esagerare (**esàgero**) *tr & intr* to exaggerate
esagera·to -ta *adj* exaggerated, excessive || *mf* exaggerator
esagerazióne *f* exaggeration

esagitare (esàgito) tr to perturb

esàgono m hexagon

esalare tr to exhale; esalare l'ultimo respiro to breathe one's last || intr to spread (said of odors)

esalazióne f exhalation; fume, vapor

esaltare tr to exalt; to excite || ref to glorify oneself; to become excited

esalta·to -ta adj frenzied, excited || mf hothead

esame m examination; checkup; test; dare gli esami to take an examination; esame attitudinale aptitude test; esame del sangue blood test; esame di riparazione make-up test; fare gli esami to prepare a test (for a student); prendere in esame to take in consideration

esàmetro m hexameter

esaminan·do -da mf candidate; examinee

esaminare (esàmino) tr to examine; to test

esamina·tóre -trice mf examiner

esàngue adj bloodless; (fig) pale

esànime adj lifeless

esasperante adj exasperating

esasperare (esàspero) tr to exasperate || ref to become exasperated

esasperazióne f exasperation

esattézza f exactness; punctuality

esat·to -ta adj exact; punctual

esattóre m tax collector; bill collector

esattorìa f tax collector's office; bill collector's office

esaudire §176 tr to grant

esauriènte adj exhaustive; convincing

esaurimento m depletion (e.g., of merchandise); (pathol) exhaustion; (naut) drainage

esaurire §176 tr to exhaust; to play out (e.g., a hooked fish); to use up || ref to be exhausted; to be depleted; to be sold out

esauri·to -ta adj exhausted; depleted; sold out; out of print

esau·sto -sta adj exhausted; empty

esautorare (esàutoro) tr to deprive of authority; to discredit (a theory)

esazióne f exaction; collection

é·sca f (-sche) bait; punk (for lighting fireworks); tinder (for lighting powder); dare esca a to foment

escandescènza f—dare in escandescenze to fly off the handle

escava·tóre -trice mf excavator, digger || m excavator; escavatore a vapore steam shovel || f (mach) excavator

escavazióne f excavation

eschimése [s] adj & mf Eskimo

esclamare tr & intr to exclaim

esclamati·vo -va adj exclamatory; exclamation (mark)

esclùdere §105 tr to exclude; to keep or shut out

esclusióne f exclusion; a esclusione di with the exception of

esclusìva f sole right, monopoly; (journ) scoop

esclusivì·sta (-sti -ste) adj clannish; bigoted || mf bigot; (com) sole agent

esclusi·vo -va adj exclusive; intolerant, bigoted || f see esclusiva

esclu·so -sa adj excluded, excepted

escogitare (escògito) tr to think up, invent; to think out

escoriare §287 (escòrio) tr & ref to skin

escoriazióne f abrasion

escremènto m excrement

escrescènza f excrescence

escrè·to -ta adj excreted || m excreta

escursióne f excursion; (mach) sweep; (mil) transfer; escursione termica (meteor) temperature range

escursionì·sta mf (-sti -ste) excursionist, sightseer

escussióne f (law) examination, cross-examination

esecrare (esècro) tr to execrate

esecrazióne f execration

esecuti·vo -va adj & m executive

esecu·tóre -trice mf (mus) performer || m executor; esecutore di giustizia executioner || f executrix

esecuzióne f accomplishment, completion; performance; execution; esecuzione capitale capital punishment

esegè·si f (-si) exegesis

eseguire (eséguo) & §176 tr to execute, carry out; to perform

esèm·pio m (-pi) example; a mo' d'esempio as an illustration; dare il buon esempio to set a good example; per esempio for instance

esemplare adj exemplary || m copy; specimen || v (esémpio) tr (lit) to copy

esemplificare §197 (esemplìfico) tr to exemplify

esentare (esènto) tr to exempt

esènte adj exempt, free

esenzióne f exemption

esèquie fpl obsequies, funeral rites

esercènte adj practicing || mf dealer, merchant

esercire §176 tr to practice; to run (a store)

esercitare (esèrcito) tr to exercise; to tax (e.g., s.o.'s patience); to practice, ply (a trade); to wield (e.g., power) || ref to practice

esercitazióne f exercise, training; esercitazioni militari drilling

esèrcito m army; (fig) flock; Esercito della Salvezza Salvation Army

esercì·zio m (-zi) exercise; practice; training; homework; occupation; drill; d'esercizio (com) administrative (expenses); esercizio finanziario fiscal year; esercizio provvisorio (law) emergency appropriation; esercizio pubblico establishment open to the public; esercizio spirituale (eccl) retreat

esibire §176 tr to exhibit || ref to show oneself, appear; esibirsi di to offer to

esibizióne f exhibition

esigènte adj demanding, exigent

esigènza f demand, requirement, exigency

esìgere §165 tr to demand; to require; to exact; to collect

esigìbile adj due; collectable

esigui·tà f (-tà) meagerness, scantiness

esì·guo -gua adj meager, scanty

esilarante *adj* exhilarating; laughing (*gas*)

esilarare (**esìlaro**) *tr* to amuse || *ref* to be amused

èsile *adj* slender, thin; weak

esiliare §287 *tr* to exile || *ref* to go into exile; to withdraw

esìlia·to -ta *adj* exiled || *m* exile (*person*)

esì·lio *m* (**-li**) exile, banishment

esìmere §166 *tr* to exempt || *ref*—**esìmersi da** to avoid (*an obligation*)

esì·mio -mia *adj* (**-mi -mie**) distinguished, eminent

-èsi·mo -ma *suf adj & pron* -eth, e.g., **ventesimo** twentieth; -th, e.g., **diciannovesimo** nineteenth

esistènte *adj* existent; extant

esistènza *f* existence

esistenzialismo *m* existentialism

esìstere §114 *intr* (ESSERE) to exist

esitante *adj* hesitant

esitare (**èsito**) *tr* to retail || *intr* to hesitate; (med) to resolve itself

esitazióne *f* hesitation; haw (*in speech*)

èsito *m* result, outcome; sale; outlet; (philol) late form; **dare esito a** (com) to reply

esiziale *adj* ruinous, fatal

èsodo *m* exodus, flight

esòfa·go *m* (**-gi**) esophagus

esonerare (**esònero**) *tr* to exempt, release

esònero *m* exemption, release

Esòpo *m* Aesop

esorbitante *adj* exorbitant

esorbitare (**esòrbito**) *intr*—**esorbitare da** to go beyond

esorcismo *m* exorcism

esorcizzare [ddzz] *tr* to exorcise

esordiènte *adj* beginning, budding || *mf* beginner || *f* debutante

esòr·dio *m* (**-di**) beginning

esordire §176 *intr* to make a start; (theat) to debut; (theat) to open

esortare (**esòrto**) *tr* to exhort

esortazióne *f* exhortation

esò·so -sa *adj* greedy, avaricious; hateful; exorbitant (*price*)

esòti·co -ca *adj* (**-ci -che**) exotic

esotismo *m* exoticism; borrowing (*from a foreign language*)

espàndere §167 *tr* to expand || *ref* to spread out; to confide

espansióne *f* expansion; effusiveness

espansionismo *m* expansionism

espansivi·tà *f* (**-tà**) effusiveness

espansi·vo -va *adj* expansive; effusive

espan·so -sa *adj* flared; expanded, dilated

espatriare §287 *intr* to emigrate

espà·trio *m* (**-tri**) emigration

espediènte *m* expedient, makeshift; ruse; **vivere di espedienti** to live by one's wits

espedire §176 *tr* to expedite || *ref*—**espedirsi di** to get rid of

espèllere §168 *tr* to expel, eject

esperiènza *f* experience; experiment

esperiménto *m* experiment; test

espèr·to -ta *adj & m* expert

espettorare (**espèttoro**) *tr & intr* to expectorate

espiare §119 *tr* to expiate; to placate (*the gods*); **espiare una pena** to serve a sentence

espiató·rio -ria *adj* (**-ri -rie**) expiatory

espiazióne *f* expiation

espirare *tr & intr* to breath out, to exhale

espirazióne *f* exhaling

espletare (**esplèto**) *tr* to dispatch, complete

esplicare §197 (**èsplico**) *tr* to carry out; (lit) to explain

esplicati·vo -va *adj* explanatory

esplìci·to -ta *adj* explicit

esplòdere §169 *tr* to shoot; to fire (*a shot*) || *intr* (ESSERE & AVERE) to explode; to burst forth

esploditóre *m* blasting machine

esplorare (**esplòro**) *tr* to explore; to search, probe; (telv) to scan

esplora·tóre -trice *mf* explorer || *m* (nav) gunboat; **giovane esploratore** boy scout

esplorazióne *f* exploration; (telv) scanning

esplosióne *f* explosion, blast; (fig) outburst

esplosi·vo -va *adj & m* explosive

esponènte *adj* (typ) superior || *m* spokesman; dictionary entry; catchword (*of dictionary*); (math) exponent; (naut) net weight

espórre §218 *tr* to expose, show; to expound; to abandon (*a baby*); to lay out (*a corpse*); to lay open (*to danger*) || *intr* to show, exhibit || *ref* to expose oneself

esportare (**espòrto**) *tr* to export

esporta·tóre -trice *mf* exporter

esportazióne *f* export, exportation

esposìmetro *m* exposure meter

esposi·tóre -trice *mf* commentator; exhibitor

esposizióne *f* exposition; abandonment (*of a baby*); exhibit, fair; line (*of credit*); exposure (*of a house*); (phot) exposure

espó·sto -sta *adj* exposed; aforementioned || *m* petition, brief; foundling

espressióne *f* expression; feeling

espressi·vo -va *adj* expressive

esprès·so -sa *adj* manifest; express; prepared on the spot || *m* espresso; messenger; special-delivery letter; special-delivery stamp

esprìmere §131 *tr* to express; to convey (*an opinion*); (lit) to squeeze || *ref* to express oneself

espropriare §287 (**espròprio**) *tr* to expropriate || *ref* to deprive oneself; **espropriarsi di** to divest oneself of

espròprio *m* (**-pri**) expropriation

espugnare *tr* to take by storm

espulsióne *f* expulsion; (mach) ejection

espulsóre *m* ejector

espurgare §209 *tr* to expurgate

éssa §5 *pron pers* she; it

ésse §5 *pron pers* they

essènza *f* essence

essenziale *adj* essential || *m* main point

èssere *m* being; existence; condition; (coll) character; **in essere** in good shape || §170 *intr* (ESSERE) to be;

c'è there is; **ci sono** there are; **ci sono!** I get it!; **come sarebbe a dire?** what do you mean?; **come se nulla fosse** as if nothing had happened; **esserci** to have arrived, to be there; **essere di** to belong to; **essere per** to be about to; **può essere** maybe; **sarà** maybe; **sia . . . sia** both . . . and; **whether . . . or** || *aux* (ESSERE) to (form passive) to be, e.g., **fu investito da un tassametro** he was run over by a taxi; (to form the compound tenses of certain intransitive verbs and all reflexive verbs) to have, e.g., **sono arrivati** they have arrived; **mi sono appena alzato** I have just got up || *impers* (ESSERE) to be, e.g., **è giusto** it is fair

éssi §5 *pron pers* they
essiccare §197 *tr* to dry || *ref* to dry up
essicca·tóio *m* (-tói) drier
essiccazióne *f* drying
èsso §5 *pron pers* he; it; **chi per esso** his representative
essudare *intr* to exude
èst *m* east
èsta·si *f* (-si) ecstasy; **andare in estasi** to become enraptured
estasiare §287 *tr* to enrapture, delight || *ref* to become enraptured
estate *f* summer
estàti·co -ca *adj* (-ci -che) ecstatic, enraptured
estemporàne·o -a *adj* extemporaneous
estèndere §270 *tr* to extend; to broaden (*e.g., one's knowledge*); to draw up (*a document*) || *ref* to extend
estensìbile *adj* applicable; **inviare saluti estensìbili a** to send greetings to be extended to (*e.g., another person*)
estensióne *f* extension; extent; expanse (*e.g., of water*); (mus) compass, range
estensì·vo -va *adj* extensive
estèn·so -sa *adj*—**per esteso** fully
estensóre *adj* extensible || *m* compiler (*e.g., of a dictionary*); (sports) exerciser, chest expander
estenuante *adj* exhausting
estenuare (estènuo) *tr* to exhaust || *ref* to become exhausted
esterióre *adj* exterior || *m* outside appearance
esteriori·tà *f* (-tà) appearance
esternare (estèrno) *tr* to reveal, manifest || *ref* to confide
estèr·no -na *adj* external; outside; day (*student*) || *m* exterior, outside; (baseball) outfielder; **all'esterno** outside; **in esterno** (mov) on location
èste·ro -ra *adj* foreign || *m* foreign countries; **all'estero** abroad
esterrefat·to -ta *adj* terrified
esté·so -sa [s] *adj* extended, wide; **per esteso** in full
estèta *mf* (-ti -te) aesthete
estèti·co -ca (-ci -che) *adj* aesthetic || *f* aesthetics
esteti·sta *mf* (-sti -ste) beautician
estima·tóre -trice *mf* appraiser; admirer
èstimo *m* appraisal; assessment
estinguere §156 *tr* to extinguish; to quench (*thirst*); to pay off (*a debt*) || *ref* to die out

estinguìbile *adj* extinguishable; payable
estìn·to -ta *adj* extinguished; extinct || *m* deceased, dead person
estintóre *m* fire extinguisher
estirpare *tr* to uproot; to eradicate; to pull (*a tooth*)
estirpa·tóre -trice *mf* eradicator || *m* (agr) weeder
estivare *tr & intr* to summer
estì·vo -va *adj* summer; summery
estòllere §171 *tr* to extol
èstone *adj & mf* Estonian
estòrcere §272 *tr* to extort; **estorcere qlco a qlcu** to extort s.th from s.o.
estorsióne *f* extortion
estradare *tr* (law) to extradite
estradizióne *f* extradition
estràne·o -a *adj* extraneous, foreign; aloof || *mf* outsider
estrapolare (estràpolo) *tr* to extrapolate
estrarre §273 *tr* to extract, draw; to pull (*a tooth*)
estrat·to -ta *adj* extracted || *m* extract; abstract; certified copy; (typ) offprint; **estratto conto** bank statement; **estratto dell'atto di nascita** copy of one's birth certificate
estrazióne *f* extraction; drawing (*of lottery*)
estrèma *f* (sports) wing, end
estremi·sta *adj & mf* (-sti -ste) extremist
estremi·tà *f* (-tà) end; tip, top; extremity; **le estremità** the extremities
estrè·mo -ma *adj* extreme; **esalare l'estremo respiro** to breath one's last || *m* extremity; end, extreme; **essere agli estremi** to be near the end; **estremi** essentials || *f* see **estrema**
estrìnse·co -ca *adj* (-ci -che) extrinsic
èstro *m* horsefly; whim, fancy; inspiration; **estro venereo** heat (*of female animal*)
estrométtere §198 *tr* to oust, expel
estró·so -sa [s] *adj* fanciful, whimsical; inspired
estrovèr·so -sa or estroverti·to -ta *adj & mf* extrovert
estrùdere §190 *tr* to extrude
estuà·rio m (-ri) estuary
esuberante *adj* exuberant; buoyant
esuberanza *f* exuberance; buoyancy; **a esuberanza** abundantly
esulare (èsulo) *intr* (ESSERE & AVERE) to go into exile; **esulare da** to be alien to
esulcerare (esùlcero) *tr* to ulcerate on the surface; (fig) to exacerbate
esulcerazióne *f* superficial ulceration; (fig) exasperation, exacerbation
èsule *mf* exile (*person*)
esultante *adj* exultant, jubilant
esultare *intr* to exult
esumare *tr* to exhume; to revive (*e.g., a custom*)
esumazióne *f* exhumation; revival
e·tà *f* (-tà) age; **che età ha?** how old is he (or she)?; **ha la sua età** he (or she) is no longer a youngster; **l'età di mezzo** Middle Ages; **maggiore età** majority; **mezza età** middle age; **minore età** minority
etamine *f* cheesecloth
ètere *m* ether

etère·o -a *adj* ethereal
eternare (etèrno) *tr* to immortalize ‖ *ref* to become immortal
eterni·tà *f* (**-tà**) eternity
etèr·no -na *adj* eternal, everlasting ‖ *m* eternity; **in eterno** forever
eterodòs·so -sa *adj* heterodox
eterogène·o -a *adj* heterogeneous
èti·ca *f* (**-che**) ethics
etichétta *f* label; card (*e.g.*, *of a library*); etiquette; **etichetta gommata** sticker
etichettare (etichétto) *tr* to label
èti·co -ca (**-ci -che**) *adj* ethical; consumptive ‖ *m* consumptive ‖ *f* see **etica**
etile *m* ethyl
etilène *m* ethylene
etìli·co -ca *adj* (**-ci -che**) ethyl
ètimo *m* etymon
etimologia *f* etymology
etìope *adj & mf* Ethiopian
Etiòpia, *l'* *f* Ethiopia
etiòpi·co -ca *adj* (**-ci -che**) Ethiopian
etisia *f* tuberculosis
ètni·co -ca *adj* (**-ci -che**) ethnic(al)
etnografia *f* ethnography
etnologia *f* ethnology
etru·sco -sca *adj & mf* (**-schi -sche**) Etruscan
ettàgono *m* heptagon
èttaro *m* hectare
ètte *m* (coll) particle, jot, whit, tittle
ètto or **ettogrammo** *m* hectogram
-étto -étta *suf adj* rather, e.g., **piccoletto** rather small; -ish, e.g., **rotondetto** roundish
ettòlitro *m* hectoliter
eucalipto *m* eucalyptus
eucaristia *f* Eucharist
eufemismo *m* euphemism
eufonia *f* euphony
eufòni·co -ca *adj* (**-ci -che**) euphonic
euforia *f* euphoria
eufòri·co -ca *adj* (**-ci -che**) euphoric
eufuismo *m* euphuism
eugenèti·co -ca (**-ci -che**) *adj* eugenic ‖ *f* eugenics
eunu·co *m* (**-chi**) eunuch
europè·o -a *adj & mf* European
Euròpa, *l'* *f* Europe
eurovisióne *f* European television chain
eutanasia *f* euthanasia
Èva *f* Eve
evacuaménto *m* evacuation
evacuare (evàcuo) *tr* to evacuate ‖ *intr* to evacuate; to have a bowel movement
evacuazióne *f* evacuation; bowel movement

evàdere §172 *tr* to evade; to complete (*a deal*); to answer (*a letter*); to execute (*orders*) ‖ *intr* (ESSERE) to flee, escape
evanescènza *f* evanescence; (rad) fading
evanescènte *adj* evanescent; vanishing
evangèli·co -ca *adj* (**-ci -che**) evangelic(al)
evangeli·sta *m* (**-sti**) evangelist
evangelizzare [ddzz] *tr* to evangelize; to campaign for; to subject to political propaganda
evaporare (evapóro) *tr & intr* to evaporate
evaporatóre *m* evaporator; humidifier
evaporazióne *f* evaporation
evasióne *f* evasion, escape; (com) reply; **dare èvasione a** to complete (*an administrative matter*)
evasi·vo -va *adj* evasive
eva·so -sa *adj* escaped ‖ *m* escapee
evasóre *m* tax dodger
eveniènza *f* eventuality, contingency; **nell'evenienza che** in the event (that); **per ogni evenienza** just in case
evènto *m* event; **eventi correnti** current events; **fausto** or **lieto evento** happy event
eventuale *adj* contingent
eventuali·tà *f* (**-tà**) eventuality
eversi·vo -va *adj* upsetting; destructive
evidènte *adj* evident; clear
evidènza *f* evidence; clearness; **mettersi in evidenza** to make oneself conspicuous; **tenere in evidenza** (com) to keep active
evirare *tr* to emasculate
evitare (èvito) *tr* to avoid, shun; **evitare qlco a qlcu** to spare s.o. s.th, to save s.o. from s.th
èvo *m* age, era; **evo antico** ancient times; **evo moderno** modern times; **medio evo** Middle Ages
evocare §197 (**èvoco**) *tr* to evoke
evoluire §176 *intr* (aer, nav) to maneuver
evoluto -ta *adj* developed; progressive; modern
evoluzióne *f* evolution
evòlvere §115 *tr* to develop ‖ *ref* to evolve
evvi·va *m* (**-va**) cheer ‖ *interj* long live!, hurrah for!
èx *adj invar* ex-, e.g., **la sua ex moglie** his ex-wife; ex, e.g., **ex dividendo** ex dividend
ex li·bris *m* (**-bris**) bookplate
extraconiugale *adj* extramarital
extraeuropè·o -a *adj* non-European
ex vó·to *m* (**-to**) votive offering
eziologìa *f* etiology

F

F, f ['effe] *m & f* sixth letter of the Italian alphabet
fa *m* (fa) (mus) F, fa
fabbisógno *m invar* need; requirement
fàbbri·ca *f* (**-che**) building, construction; factory, plant

fabbricante *mf* builder, manufacturer
fabbricare §197 (**fàbbrico**) *tr* to manufacture; to fabricate
fabbrica·to -ta *adj* built ‖ *m* building
fabbricazióne *f* building; erection; manufacturing; fabrication (*invention*)

fabbro *m* blacksmith; locksmith; (fig) master; **fabbro ferraio** blacksmith

faccènda *f* business, matter; **faccende domestiche** household chores

faccendiè·re -ra *mf* operator, schemer

faccétta *f* small face; face, facet

facchinàg·gio *m* (-gi) porterage; (fig) drudgery

facchino *m* porter; **lavorare come un facchino** to work like a slave

fàc·cia *f* (-ce) face; countenance; **avere la faccia di** to have the gall to; **di faccia a** opposite; **faccia da galeotto** (coll) gallows bird; **faccia tosta** cheek, gall; **in faccia a** in front of

facciale *adj* facial

facciata *f* façade; page; (fig) surface appearance

face *f* (lit) torch

facè·to -ta *adj* facetious

facèzia *f* pleasantry, banter; **scambiar facezie** to banter with each other

fachiro *m* fakir

fàcile *adj* easy; inclined; loose (*morals*); glib (*tongue*); **è facile** it is probable ‖ *m* something easy

facili·tà *f* (-tà) facility, ease; inclination; **facilità di pagamento** easy payments, easy terms; **facilità di parola** glibness

facilitare (**facìlito**) *tr* to facilitate; to grant (*credit*); to give (*easy terms*)

facilitazióne *f* facilitation; easy terms; cut rate

facinoró·so -sa [s] *adj* criminal ‖ *m* hoodlum, thug

facoltà *f* (-tà) faculty; power; school (*of a university*); **facoltà** *fpl* means, wealth

facoltati·vo -va *adj* optional

facoltó·so -sa [s] *adj* wealthy, affluent

facóndia *f* loquacity, gift of gab

facón·do -da *adj* loquacious

facsìmi·le -le (-le) facsimile

faènza *f* faïence ‖ **Faenza** *f* Faenza

fàg·gio *m* (-gi) (bot) beech

fagia·na -na *mf* pheasant

fagiolino *m* string bean

fagiòlo *m* bean; (coll) sophomore; **andare a fagiolo a** (coll) to fit perfectly; **fagiolo bianco** lima bean

fà·glia *f* (-glie) (geol) fault

fagòtto *m* bundle; (mus) bassoon; **far fagotto** (coll) to pack up

fàida *f* vengeance, vendetta

faìna *f* stone marten

falange *f* phalanx

fal·bo -ba *adj* tawny

falcata *f* step, stride; bucking

falce *f* scythe; crescent (*of moon*); **falce messoria** sickle

falcétto *m* sickle

falciare §128 *tr* to mow

falcia·tóre -trice *mf* mower ‖ *f* mowing machine

falcidiare §287 *tr* to reduce; to cut down

fal·co *m* (-chi) hawk; **falco pescatore** osprey

falcóne *m* falcon

falconerìa *f* falconry

falconière *m* falconer

falda *f* band, strip; flake (*of snow*); gable (*of roof*); brim (*of hat*); foot (*of mountain*); slab (*of stone*); waist plate (*of armor*); hem (*of suit*); flounce (*of dress*); layer (*of rock*); flap, coattail; **falda della camicia** shirttail; **falde straps** (*to hold a baby*); **mettersi in falde** to wear tails

falegname *m* carpenter; cabinetmaker

falegnamerìa *f* carpentry; cabinetmaking; carpenter shop; woodworker shop

falèna *f* moth

falla *f* hole, leak; (archaic) fault

fallace *adj* fallacious, deceptive

fallà·cia *f* (-cie) fallacy

fallare *intr* & *ref* (lit) to be mistaken

fallìbile *adj* fallible

fallimentare *adj* bankrupt; ruinous

falliménto *m* bankruptcy; (fig) collapse, failure

fallire §176 *tr* to miss (*the target*) ‖ *intr* (ESSERE) to go bankrupt; to fail ‖ *intr* (AVERE) (lit) to be mistaken

falli·to -ta *adj* & *mf* bankrupt

fallo *m* error, fault; sin; flaw; phallus; (sports) penalty; (sports) foul; **cadere in fallo** to make the wrong move; **to be mistaken; cogliere in fallo** to catch in the act; **far fallo a** to fail, e.g., **gli faccio fallo** I fail him; **senza fallo** without fail

fa·lò *m* (-lò) bonfire

falpa·là *f* (-là) flounce, furbelow

falsare *tr* to falsify, alter; (lit) to forge

falsarì·ga *f* (-ghe) guideline (*for writing*); model, pattern; **seguire la falsariga di** to follow in the footsteps of

falsà·rio *m* (-ri) forger; counterfeiter

falsétto *m* falsetto

falsificare §197 (**falsìfico**) to falsify; to forge, fake

falsificazióne *f* falsification; forgery; misrepresentation

falsi·tà *f* (-tà) falsehood; falsity

fal·so -sa *adj* false; wrong (*step*); assumed (*name*); bogus, counterfeit, fake (*money*); phony ‖ *m* falsehood; perjury; forgery; **commettere un falso** to perjure oneself; to commit forgery; **giurare il falso** to bear false witness; to perjure oneself

fama *f* fame; reputation; **cattiva fama** notoriety

fame *f* hunger; dearth; **aver fame** to be hungry; **avere una fame da lupo** to be as hungry as a wolf, to be as hungry as a bear; **morire di fame** to starve to death; to be ravenous

famèli·co -ca *adj* (-ci -che) starving, famished

famigera·to -ta *adj* notorious

famìglia *f* family; community; **di famiglia** intimate; **in famiglia** at home

famì·glio *m* (-gli) beadle, usher; hired man

familiare *adj* family; familiar, intimate; homelike ‖ *m* member of the family

familiari·tà *f* (-tà) familiarity; **avere familiarità con** to be familiar with

familiarizzare [ddzz] *tr* to familiarize
famó·so -sa [s] *adj* famous, illustrious
fanale *m* lamp, lantern; (rr) headlight;
fanale di coda taillight
fanalino *m* small light; (aut) parking
light; (aut) tail light
fanàti·co -ca (**-ci -che**) *adj* fanatic,
fanatical || *mf* fanatic
fanatismo *m* fanaticism
fanatizzare [ddzz] *tr* to make a fanatic
of
fanciulla *f* girl; spinster; bride
fanciullè·sco -sca *adj* (**-schi -sche**)
childish; children's
fanciullézza *f* childhood; (fig) infancy
fanciulo·lo -la *adj* childish; childlike
|| *mf* child || *m* boy || *f* see **fanciulla**
fandònia *f* fib, tale, yarn
fanèllo *m* (orn) linnet; (orn) finch
fanfara *f* military band; fanfare
fanfaróne *m* braggart
fangatura *f* mud bath
fanghiglia *f* mud, slush
fan·go *m* (**-ghi**) mud; **fare i fanghi** to
take mud baths
fangó·so -sa [s] *adj* muddy
fannullo·ne -na *mf* idler, loafer
fanóne *m* whalebone
fantaccino *m* infantryman, foot soldier
fantascientìfi·co -ca *adj* (**-ci -che**)
science-fiction
fantasciènza *f* science fiction
fantasìa *f* fantasy, fancy, whim; (mus)
fantasia; **di fantasia** fancy
fantasió·so -sa [s] *adj* fanciful; imaginative
fanta·sma *m* (**-smi**), ghost, spirit; phantom; **fantasma poetico** poetic fancy
fantasticare §197 (**fantàstico**) *tr* to
imagine, dream up || *intr* to day-
dream
fantasticherìa *f* imagination, daydreaming
fantàsti·co -ca *adj* (**-ci -che**) fantastic ||
fantàstico *interj* unbelievable!
fante *m* infantryman, foot soldier;
(cards) jack; (obs) youth
fanterìa *f* infantry
fantè·sca *f* (**-sche**) (joc, lit) housemaid
fantino *m* jockey
fantòc·cio *m* (**-ci**) puppet
fantomàti·co -ca *adj* (**-ci -che**) ghostly;
mysterious
farabutto *m* scoundrel, heel
faraóna *f* guinea fowl
faraóne *m* Pharaoh; (cards) faro
farcire §176 *tr* to stuff
fardèllo *m* bundle; burden; **far fardello**
to pack one's bags
fare *m* doing; break (*of day*); way (*of
acting*); **sul far della sera** at nightfall
|| §173 *tr* to do; to make; to work;
to take (*e.g., a walk, a step*); to give
(*a sigh*); to deal (*cards*); to suffer
(*hunger*); to lead (*a good or bad life*);
to render (*service*); to log (*e.g., 15
m.p.h.*); to be, e.g., **tre volte tre fa
nove** three times three is nine; to
build (*e.g., a house*); to put together
(*a collection*); to prepare (*dinner*);
to say, utter (*a word*); to have (*a
dream*); to give (*fruit*); to pay (*atten-

tion*); to play (*a role*); to stir up
(*pity*); to mention (*a name*); **fare
il** (or **la**) to be a (*e.g., carpenter*);
fare + *inf* to have + *inf*, e.g., **gli
ho fatto . . .** I had him . . . ; to
make + *inf*, e.g., **il medico mi
fece . . .** the doctor made me . . . ; to
have + *pp*, e.g., **farò fare . . .** I shall
have . . . done; **fare acqua** to leak,
to take in water; to get a supply of
water; (coll) to urinate; **fare a metà**
to divide in half; **fare a pugni** to come
to blows; **fare a tempo** to be on time;
fare benzina to buy gasoline; **fare
caldo** a to keep warm, e.g., **questa
coperta gli fa caldo** this blanket keeps
him warm; **fare carbone** to coal; **fare
. . . che** to have been . . . since, e.g.,
**fanno tre mesi che siamo in questa
città** it has been three months since
we have been in this city; **fare che +
*subj*** to see to it that + *ind*, e.g.,
**faccia che comincino a lavorare su-
bito** see to it that they begin to work
at once; **fare colpo** to make an impression; **fare corona** to crown; **fare
cuore** a to encourage; **fare del
male** a to harm; **fare di + *inf*** to see
to it that + *inf*; **fare di tutto** to do
one's best; **fare festa** a to cheer; **fare
fiasco** to fail; **fare finta di** to pretend
to; **fare fronte** a to face, meet; **fare
fuoco su** to fire upon; **fare il gioco di**
to play into the hands of; **fare il
pappagallo** to parrot, ape; **fare il
pieno** to fill up (*with gasoline*); **fare
la bocca** a to get used to; **fare la
calza** to knit; **fare la coda** to queue
up, line up; **fare la festa** a to kill;
fare la guardia to stand guard; **fare
la mano** a to get used to; **fare le cose
in famiglia** to wash one's dirty linen
at home; **fare le cose in grande stile**
to splurge; **fare legna** to gather firewood; **fare l'occhio** to become accustomed; **fare mente** to pay attention;
fare onore a to do honor to; **fare
paura** a to frighten; **fare sangue** to
bleed; **fare sapere** a **qlcu** to let s.o.
know; **fare scalo** (aer, naut) to make
a call; **fare sì che** to act in such a
way that; to see to it that; **fare silenzio** to keep silent; **fare specie** a to
amaze, e.g., **il tuo comportamento
gli fa specie** your behavior amazes
him; **fare tesoro di** to prize; **fare una
bella figura** to look good; to make a
fine appearance; **fare una mala figura**
to look bad; to make a bad showing;
fare una malattia (coll) to get sick;
fare vela to set sail; **fare venire** to
send for; **fare vigilia** to fast; **farla
corta** to cut it short; **farla franca**
to get off scot-free; **farla grossa** to
commit a blunder; **farla in barba** a
to outwit; **farne di cotte e di crude,
farne di tutti i colori,** or **farne più
di Carlo in Francia** to engage in all
sorts of mischief; to paint the town
red; **non fare che + *ind*** to do nothing
but + *inf* || *intr*—**averla a che fare
con** to have words with; to have to

deal with; **fare a coltellate** to have a fight with knives; **fare a girotondo** to play ring-around-the-rosy; **fare al caso di** to fit; to suit; **fare a meno di** to do without; **fare da** to serve as, e.g., **fare da cuscino** to serve as a pillow; **fare da cena** to fix dinner; **fare di cappello** to take one's hat off; **fare presto** to hurry; **fare per** to be just the thing for; **fare tardi** to be late ‖ *ref* to become; to cut (e.g., one's hair); to move, e.g., **farsi in là** to move farther; **farsi avanti** to come forward; **farsi beffe di** to make fun of; **farsi bello** to bedeck oneself; to dress up; **farsi bello di** to boast about; to appropriate; **farsi gioco di** to make fun of; **farsi le labbra** to put lipstick on; **farsi strada** to make one's way; **farsi una ragione di** to rationalize, explain to oneself; **farsi un baffo** to not give a hoot; **si fa giorno** it is getting light ‖ *impers—che tempo fa?* what's the weather like?; **fa ago**, e.g., **alcune settimane fa** a few weeks ago; **fa estate** it is like summer; **fa fino** it is smart; **fa freddo** it is cold; **fa luna** there is moonlight, the moon is out; **fa nebbia** it is foggy; **fa notte** it is nighttime; it is dark; it is getting dark; **fa sole** it is sunny, the sun is out; **fa tipo** or **fa tono!** that's classy!; **non fa nulla** it doesn't matter, never mind

farètra *f* quiver

farfalla *f* butterfly; bow tie; (mach) butterfly valve; (coll) promissory note

farfallóne *m* large butterfly; blunder; Don Juan

farfugliare §280 *intr* to mumble, mutter

farina *f* flour; **farina d'avena** oatmeal; **farina di legno** sawdust; **farina di ossa** bone meal; **farina gialla** yellow corn meal

farinàce·o -a *adj* farinaceous ‖ **farinacei** *mpl* flour-yielding cereals

farinata *f* porridge

faringe *f* pharynx

faringite *f* pharingitis

farinó·so -sa [s] *adj* floury; powdery (snow); crumbly, friable

farisèo *m* Pharisee; (fig) pharisee

farmacèuti·co -ca *adj* (-ci -che) pharmaceutical, drug

farmacia *f* pharmacy; drugstore; medicine cabinet; **farmacia di guardia** or **di turno** drugstore open all night and Sunday

farmaci·sta *mf* (-sti -ste) pharmacist, druggist

fàrma·co *m* (-ci or -chi) remedy, medicine

farneticare §197 (farnètico) *intr* to rave

farnèti·co -ca (-chi -che) *adj* raving ‖ *m* delirium; craze

faro *m* lighthouse, beacon; (aut) headlight; **faro retromarcia** (aut) back-up light

farràgine *f* hodgepodge

farraginó·so -sa [s] *adj* confused, mixed

farsa *f* farce; burlesque

farsè·sco -sca *adj* (-schi -sche) farçical, ludicrous

farsétto *m* sweater; (hist) doublet

fascétta *f* girdle; band; wrapper; clamp; **fascetta editoriale** advertising band (of book)

fà·scia *f* (-sce) band; belt; bandage; newspaper wrapper; **fascia del cappello** hatband; **fascia di garza** gauze bandage; **fascia elastica** abdominal supporter; (aut) piston ring; **fasce del neonato** swaddling clothes; **in fasce** newborn; **sotto fascia** in a wrapper

fasciame *m* (naut) planking; (naut) plating

fasciare §128 to bind; to bandage; to wrap; to surround

fasciatura *f* bandaging, dressing

fascìcolo *m* number, issue; pamphlet; file, dossier; (bb) fasciculus

fascina *f* fagot

fascina·tóre -trice *mf* charmer

fàscino *m* fascination, charm

fà·scio *m* (-sci) bundle; sheaf; bunch (of flowers); pencil or beam (of rays); fascist party

fascismo *m* fascism

fasci·sta *adj* & *mf* (-sti -ste) fascist

fase *f* phase, stage; (aut) cycle; (astr, elec, mach) phase

fastèllo *m* bundle, fagot

fasti *mpl* records, annals; notable events; (hist) Roman calendar

fastì·dio *m* (-di) annoyance; (coll) loathing, nausea; **avere in fastidio** to loathe; **dar fastidio a** to annoy; **fastidi** troubles, worries

fastidió·so -sa [s] *adj* annoying, irksome; irritable; (obs) disgusting

fastì·gio *m* (-gi) top, summit

fa·sto -sta *adj* (lit) propitious ‖ *m invar* pomp, display ‖ *mpl* see **fasti**

fastó·so -sa [s] *adj* pompous, ostentatious

fata *f* fairy; **buona fata** fairy godmother; **Fata Morgana** Fata Morgana (mirage; Morgan le Fay)

fatale *adj* fatal; inevitable; irresistible (woman)

fatalismo *m* fatalism

fatali·sta *mf* (-sti -ste) fatalist

fatali·tà *f* (-tà) fatality, fate

fatalóna *f* vamp

fata·to -ta *adj* fairy, enchanted; (lit) predestined

fati·ca *f* (-che) fatigue, weariness; labor; **a fatica** with difficulty; **da fatica** draft (e.g., horse); of burden (beast); **durar fatica a** + *inf* to have trouble in + *ger*

faticare §197 *intr* to toil; **faticare a** to be hardly able to

faticó·so -sa [s] *adj* burdensome, heavy; (lit) weary

fatìdi·co -ca *adj* (-ci -che) fatal

fato *m* fate, destiny

fatta *f* kind, sort; **essere sulla fatta di** to be on the trail of

fattàc·cio *m* (-ci) (coll) crime

fattézze *fpl* features

fattìbile adj feasible, possible
fattispècie f—nella fattispecie in this particular case
fàt·to -ta adj made, e.g., **fatto a mano** handmade; broad (daylight); deep (night); ready-made (e.g., suit); ben fatto well-done; shapely; **esser fatto per** to be cut out for; **fatto di** made of; venir fatto a to happen, chance, e.g., **gli venne fatto d'incontrarmi** he happened to meet me || m fact; act, deed; feat; action; business, affair; **badare ai fatti propri** to mind one's own business; **cogliere sul fatto** to catch in the act; **dire a qlcu il fatto suo** to give s.o. a piece of one's mind; **fatto compiuto** fait accompli; **fatto d'arme** feat of arms; **fatto sì è** the fact remains that; **in fatto di** concerning; as of; **sapere il fatto proprio** to know one's business; **venire al fatto** to come to the point || f see **fatta**
fat·tóre -tóra or **-toréssa** mf farm manager || m maker; factor; steward || f stewardess; manager's wife
fattorìa f farm; stewardship
fattorìno m delivery boy, messenger boy; conductor (of streetcar)
fattrìce f (zool) dam
fattucchiè·re -ra mf magician || m sorcerer || f sorceress, witch
fattùra f preparation; workmanship; bill, invoice; (coll) witchcraft; (lit) creature
fatturàre tr to adulterate; to invoice, bill
fattura·to -ta adj adulterated || m (com) turnover
fatturì·sta mf (-sti -ste) billing clerk
fà·tuo -tua adj fatuous
fàuci fpl jaws; (fig) mouth
fàuna f fauna
fàuno m faun
fàu·sto -sta adj propitious, lucky
fau·tóre -trìce mf supporter, promoter
fàva f broad bean; **pigliare due piccioni con una fava** to catch two birds with one stone
favèlla f speech; (lit) tongue
favìlla f spark; **far** or **mandare faville** to sparkle
favo m honeycomb
fàvola f fable; tale; **favola del paese** talk of the town
favoló·so -sa [s] adj fabulous; mythical
favóre m favor; help; cover (e.g., of night); **a favore di** for the benefit of; **di favore** special (price); complimentary (ticket); **favore politico** patronage; **per favore** please; **per favore di** courtesy of
favoreggiaménto m abetting, support
favoreggiàre §290 (favoréggio) tr to abet, support
favoreggia·tóre -trìce mf abettor, supporter, backer
favorévole adj favorable; propitious
favorìre §176 tr to favor; to accept; to oblige, accommodate; **favorire qlcu di qlco** to oblige s.o. with s.th; **favorisca** + inf please + inf, be kind

enough to + inf; **favorisca alla cassa** please pay the cashier; **favorisca uscire!** please leave!; **tanto per favorire** just to keep you company; **vuol favorire?** won't you please join us (at a meal)?; please help yourself!
favorìta f royal mistress
favoritìsmo m favoritism
favorì·to -ta adj & mf favorite || m protegé; **favoriti** sideburns || f see **favorita**
faziōne f faction; **essere di fazione** to be on guard duty
fazió·so -sa [s] adj factious || m partisan
fazzolétto m handkerchief; **fazzoletto da collo** neckerchief
fé f var of **fede**
feb·bràio m (-brài) February
fèbbre f fever; fever blister; **febbre da cavallo** (coll) very high fever; **febbre da fieno** hay fever; **febbre dell'oro** gold fever
febbricitànte adj feverish
febbrìle adj feverish
Fèbo m Phoebus
féc·cia f (-ce) dregs; (fig) dregs (of society); **fino alla feccia** to the bitter end
fèci fpl feces
fècola f starch
fecondàre (fecóndo) tr to fecundate
fecondazióne f fecundation; **fecondazione artificiale** artificial insemination
fecondi·tà f (-tà) fecundity
fecón·do -da adj fecund, prolific
féde f faith; certificate; wedding ring; faithfulness; **far fede** to bear witness; **in fede di** che in testimony whereof; **in fede mia!** upon my word! **prestar fede a** to put one's faith in; **tener fede alla parola data** to keep one's word
fedecommésso m fideicommissum; trusteeship
fedéle adj faithful, devoted || mf faithful person; **i fedeli** the faithful
fedel·tà f (-tà) faithfulness, allegiance; fidelity; **ad alta fedeltà** hi-fi
fèdera f pillowcase
federàle adj federal
federalì·sta mf (-sti -ste) federalist
federatì·vo -va adj federative
federà·to -ta adj federate, federated
federazióne f federation; (sports) league
Federìco m Frederick
fedìfra·go -ga adj (-ghi -ghe) unfaithful, treacherous
fedìna f police record; **avere la fedina sporca** to have a bad record; **fedine** sideburns
fégato m liver; courage; **fegato d'oca** pâté de foie gras; **rodersi il fegato** to be consumed with rage
félce f fern
feldspàto m feldspar
felìce adj happy; blissful; glad; felicitous
felici·tà f (-tà) happiness; bliss
felicitàre (felìcito) tr to make happy; **che Dio vi feliciti!** God bless you! ||

ref to rejoice; **felicitarsi con qlcu per qlco** to congratulate s.o. for or on s.th

felicitazióne *f* congratulation

feli·no -na *adj & m* feline

fellóne *m* (lit) traitor

félpa *f* plush

felpa·to -ta *adj* covered with plush; soft (*e.g., step*)

féltro *m* felt; felt hat

felu·ca *f* (-che) two-cornered hat; (naut) felucca

fémmina *adj & f* female

femminile *adj* feminine, female || *m* feminine gender

femminili·tà *f* (-tà) femininity, womanliness

femminismo *m* feminism

fèmore *m* femur; thighbone

fendènte *m* slash with a sword

fèndere §174 *tr* to split, cleave; to plow (*water*); to rend (*air*); to make one's way through (*a crowd*) || *ref* to split; to come apart

fenditura *f* split, breach, fissure

fenice *f* phoenix

feni·cio -cia (-ci -cie) *adj & mf* Phoenician || **la Fenicia** Phoenicia

fèni·co -ca *adj* (-ci -che) carbolic

fenicòttero *m* flamingo

fenòlo *m* phenol

fenomenale *adj* phenomenal

fenòmeno *m* phenomenon; freak, monster; **essere un fenomeno** to be unbelievable

ferace *adj* (lit) fertile

ferale *adj* (lit) mortal, deadly

fèretro *m* bier, coffin

feriale *adj* working (*day*); weekday

fèrie *fpl* vacation; **ferie retribuite** vacation with pay

ferire §176 *tr* to wound; to strike; **senza colpo ferire** without striking a blow || *ref* to wound oneself

feri·to -ta *adj* wounded, injured || *m* wounded person; injured person; **i feriti** the wounded; the injured || *f* wound, injury

feritóia *f* loophole; embrasure

feri·tóre -trice *mf* assailant

férma *f* setting (*of setter or pointer*); (mil) service; (mil) enlistment

fermacarro *m* (rr) buffer

fermacar·te *m* (-te) paperweight; large paper clip

fermacravat·ta *m* (-ta) tiepin

fermà·glio *m* (-gli) clasp; buckle; clip; brooch

fermare (**férmo**) *tr* to stop; to pay (*attention*); to fasten; to close, shut; to detain (*in police station*); to set (*game*); to reserve (*seats*) || *ref* to stop; to stay

fermata *f* stop; **fermata a richiesta** or **facoltativa** stop on signal

fermentare (**ferménto**) *tr & intr* to ferment

fermentazióne *f* fermentation

ferménto *m* ferment

fermézza *f* firmness; steadfastness

fér·mo -ma *adj* firm; stopped; quiet (*water*); (fig) steadfast; **fermo in**

posta general delivery; **fermo restando che** seeing that; **stare fermo** to be quiet || *m* stop; detention; **mettere il fermo a** to stop (*a check*)

fermopòsta *m* general delivery || *adv* care of general delivery

feróce *adj* fierce; wild

feró·cia *f* (-cie) ferocity, ferociousness, fierceness

feròdo *m* (aut) brake lining

ferragósto *m* Assumption; mid-August holiday

ferrame *m* ironware

ferramén·to *m* (-ti) iron or metal bracket; iron or metal trimming || *m* (-ta *fpl*)—**ferramenta** hardware

ferrare (**fèrro**) *tr* to shoe (*a horse*); to hoop (*a barrel*)

ferra·to -ta *adj* iron; ironclad; shod (*horse*); spiked (*shoe*); well-versed || *f* pressing, ironing; mark or burn (*caused by ironing*); (coll) iron grate

ferravèc·chio *m* (-chi) scrap-iron dealer, junkman

fèrre·o -a *adj* iron; ironclad

ferrièra *f* ironworks; (obs) iron mine

fèrro *m* iron; tool; anchor; sword; **ai ferri** on the grill, broiled (*e.g., steak*); **essere sotto i ferri del chirurgo** to go under the knife; **ferri** shackles; **ferri del mestiere** tools of the trade; **ferro battuto** wrought iron; **ferro da arricciare** curling iron; **ferro da calza** knitting needle; **ferro da cavallo** horseshoe; **ferro da stiro** iron, flatiron; **ferro fuso** cast iron; **ferro grezzo** pig iron; **mettere a ferro e fuoco** to put to fire and sword; **venire ai ferri corti** to get into close quarters

ferromodellismo *m* hobby of model railroads

ferrotranvièri *mpl* transport workers

ferrovìa *f* railroad; **ferrovia a dentiera** rack railway; **ferrovia sopraelevata** elevated railroad

ferrovià·rio -ria *adj* (-ri -rie) railroad

ferrovière *m* railroader

fèrtile *adj* fertile

fertilizzante [ddzz] *adj* fertilizing || *m* fertilizer

fertilizzare [ddzz] *tr* to fertilize

fervènte *adj* fervent

fèrvere §175 *intr* to be fervent; to rage (*said, e.g., of a battle*); to go full blast

fèrvi·do -da *adj* fervent

fervóre *m* fervor; (fig) heat

fervorino *m* lecture, sermon

fesserìa *f* (slang) stupidity, nonsense; (slang) trifle

fés·so -sa *adj* cracked; cleft; (slang) dumb || *m* (lit) cranny; **fare fesso qlcu** (slang) to play s.o. for a sucker

fessura *f* crack; cranny

fèsta *f* feast; holiday; birthday; saint's day; **a festa** festively; **buone feste!** happy holiday!; **conciare per le feste** to drub the daylights out of; **fare festa a** to welcome; **fare le feste** to spend the holidays; **far festa** to celebrate; to take the day off; **far la festa**

a to do in, kill; **festa del ceppo** Christmas; **festa da ballo or danzante** dancing party; **festa della mamma** Mother's Day; **festa del papà** Father's Day; **festa di precetto** (eccl) day of obligation; **festa nazionale** national holiday; **mezza festa** half holiday

festante adj cheerful

festeggiaménto m celebration

festeggiare §290 (festéggio) tr to celebrate, fete; to cheer

festi·no -na adj (lit) rapid || m party

festivi·tà f (-tà) festivity

festi·vo -va adj festive, holiday

festóne m festoon

festó·so -sa [s] adj cheerful, merry

festu·ca f (-che) straw; (fig) mote

fetènte adj stinking; stink (bomb) || mf (fig) stinker, louse

fetíc·cio m (-ci) fetish

feticismo m fetishism

fèti·do -da adj stinking, fetid

fèto m fetus

fetóre m stench

fétta f slice; **tagliare a fette** to slice

fettina f thin slice; twist (of lemon); **fettina di vitello** veal cutlet

fettùc·cia f (-ce) tape, ribbon

fettuccíne fpl noodles

feudale adj feudal

feudalismo m feudalism

feudatà·rio -ria (-ri -rie) adj feudatory || m feudal vassal

fèudo m fief

fiaba f fairy tale; tale, yarn

fiacca f tiredness; sluggishness; **batter la fiacca** to loaf, to goof off

fiaccare §197 tr to weaken; to weary; to break || ref to weaken; to break (e.g., one's neck)

fiacche·ràio m (-rài) (coll) hackman, cabman

fiacchézza f weakness; sluggishness

fiac·co -ca adj (-chi -che) weak; sluggish; slack || f see fiacca

fiàccola f torch; **fiaccola della discordia** firebrand

fiaccolata f torchlight procession

fiala f vial, phial

fiamma f flame; blaze; (mil) insignia; (nav) pennant; **alla fiamma** (culin) flaming; **dare alle fiamme** to set on fire; **diventare di fiamma** to blush; **in fiamme afire**

fiammante adj blazing; **nuovo fiammante** brand-new

fiammata f blaze; flare-up

fiammeggiante adj flaming, blazing; (archit) flamboyant

fiammeggiare §290 (fiamméggio) tr to singe || intr to flame, blaze

fiammífero m match

fiammin·go -ga (-ghi -ghe) adj Flemish; Dutch (e.g., master) || mf Fleming || m Flemish (language); (orn) flamingo

fiancata f blow with one's hip; dig, sarcastic remark; side, flank; (nav) broadside

fiancheggiare §290 (fianchéggio) tr to flank; to border (a road); to support

fiancheggia·tóre -trice mf supporter, backer

fian·co m (-chi) flank, side; hip; **di fianco** sideways; **fianco a fianco** side by side; **fianco destr'!** (mil) right face!; **fianco destro** (naut) starboard; **fianco sinistr'!** (mil) left face!; **fianco sinistro** (naut) port; **prestare il fianco a** to leave oneself wide open to; **tenersi i fianchi dal ridere** to split one's sides laughing

Fiandre, le fpl Flanders

fia·sca f (-sche) flask

fiaschetteria f tavern, wine shop

fia·sco m (-schi) straw-covered wine bottle; flask; fiasco

fiata f (archaic) time

fiatare intr to breathe; **senza fiatare** without breathing a word

fiato m breath; (archaic) stench; **avere il fiato grosso** to be out of breath; **bere d'un fiato** to gulp down; **col fiato sospeso** holding one's breath; **dare fiato a** to blow, sound (a trumpet); **d'un fiato or in un fiato** without interruption; in one gulp; **fiati** (mus) winds; **senza fiato** out of breath

fiatóne m—**avere il fiatone** to be out of breath

fìbbia f clasp, buckle

fibra f fiber

fibró·so -sa [s] adj fibrous

ficcana·so [s] mf (-si mpl -so fpl) (coll) busybody, meddler; nosy person

ficcare §197 tr to stick; to drive (e.g., a nail); to push; **ficcare gli occhi addosso a** to gaze at, stare at; **ficcare il naso negli affari degli altri** to poke one's nose in other people's business || ref to hide; to butt in; to get involved

fì·co m (-chi) fig; fig tree

ficodìndia m (pl fichidìndia) prickly pear

fidanzaménto m engagement, betrothal

fidanzare tr to betroth || ref to become engaged

fidanza·to -ta adj engaged || m fiancé || f fiancée

fidare tr to entrust || intr to trust || ref to have confidence; **fidarsi a** (coll) to dare to; **fidarsi di** to trust, rely on

fida·to -ta adj trustworthy, reliable

fì·do -da adj (lit) faithful, trusted || m loyal follower; credit; **far fido** to extend credit

fidùcia f faith, confidence; (com) credit; **di fiducia** trustworthy

fiducià·rio -ria (-ri -rie) adj fiduciary || mf fiduciary, trustee

fidució·so -sa [s] adj confident, hopeful

fièle m invar gall, bile; acrimony

fienile m hayloft

fièno m hay

fieristi·co -ca adj (-ci -che) of a fair, e.g., **attività fieristica** activity of a fair

fiè·ro -ra adj fierce; dignified; proud || f fair; exhibit; wild beast

fièvole *adj* feeble, weak

fifa *f* (coll) scare; **avere la fifa** (coll) to be chicken; **avere una fifa blu** (coll) to be scared stiff

fifó·ne -na *mf* (coll) scaredy-cat

fìggere §104 *tr* (lit) to drive, thrust || *ref*—**figgersi in capo** to get into one's head

figlia *f* daughter; (com) stub; **figlia consanguinea** stepdaughter on the father's side

figliare §280 *tr & intr* to whelp (*said of animals*)

figlia·stro -stra *mf* stepchild || *m* stepson || *f* stepdaughter

figliata *f* litter (*e.g., of pigs*)

fi·glio -glia *mf* child, offspring || *m* son; **figli** children; **figlio consanguineo** stepson on the father's side || *f* see **figlia**

figliòc·cio -cia (**-ci -ce**) *mf* godchild || *m* godson || *f* goddaughter

figliolanza *f* children, offspring

figliò·lo -la *mf* child || *m* son, boy || *f* daughter, girl

figura *f* figure; illustration; figurehead; face card; **far bella figura** to make a good showing; **far cattiva figura** to make a poor showing; **far figura** to look good; **figura retorica** figure of speech

figurante *mf* (theat) extra, super

figurare *tr* to feign; to represent || *intr* to figure; to appear; to make a good showing || *ref* to imagine; **si figuri!** imagine!

figurati·vo -va *adj* (fa) figurative

figura·to -ta *adj* figurative (*speech*); transcribed (*pronunciation*); illustrated (*book*)

figurina *f* figurine; card, picture (*of a series of athletes or entertainment celebrities*)

figurini·sta *mf* (**-sti -ste**) dress designer; costume designer

figurino *m* fashion plate; fashion magazine

figuro *m* scoundrel; gangster

figurone *m*—**fare un figurone** to make a very good showing

fila *f* row; file, line; series; **di fila** in a row; **fare la fila** to wait in line; **file ranks**

filàc·cia *f* (**-ce**) lint

filacció·so -sa [s] or **filacció·so -sa** [s] *adj* thready, stringy

filaménto *m* filament

filamentó·so -sa [s] *adj* thready, stringy; thread-like

filanda *f* spinning mill; silk spinning mill

filante *adj* spinning; shooting (*star*); thready; flowing (*e.g., line*)

filantropìa *f* philanthropy

filantròpi·co -ca *adj* (**-ci -che**) philanthropic

filàntro·po -pa *mf* philanthropist

filare *m* row, line || *tr* to spin; to drip, ooze; to rest on (*one's oars*); to make (*e.g., ten knots*); (naut) to pay out; (mus) to hold (*a note*); **filare l'amore** to be in love || *intr* to spin (*said of a spider*); to rope, thread (*said of wine*

or syrup*); to make sense; to drip; **fare filare dritto qlcu** to keep s.o. in line; **filare a to do** (*e.g., twenty miles an hour*); **filare all'inglese** to take French leave; **fila via!** (coll) get out!

filarmòni·co -ca (**-ci -che**) *adj* philharmonic || *f* philharmonic society

filastròc·ca *f* (**-che**) rigmarole; nursery rhyme

filatelìa *f* philately

filatèli·co -ca (**-ci -che**) *adj* philatelic(al) || *mf* philatelist

fila·to -ta *adj* spun; well-constructed (*speech*) || *m* yarn

fila·tóio *m* (**-tói**) spinning wheel

filatura *f* spinning; spinning mill

filettare (**filétto**) *tr* to fillet; (mach) to thread

filettatura *f* stripe (*on a cap*); (mach) thread

filétto *m* fillet; stripe; snaffle (*on a horse's bit*); fine stroke (*in handwriting*); (mach) thread; (typ) ornamental line, headband; (typ) rule

filiale *adj* filial || *f* branch office

filiazióne *f* filiation

filibustière *m* filibuster, buccaneer; adventurer

filièra *f* (mach) drawplate; (mach) die (*to cut threads*)

filigrana *f* filigree; watermark (*in paper*)

filippi·no -na *adj* Philippine || *m* Filipino || **le Filippine** the Philippines

Filippo *m* Philip

filistè·o -a *adj & m* philistine; Philistine

Fillide *f* Phyllis

film *m* (film) film; movie, motion picture; **film parlato** or **sonoro** talking picture

filmare *tr* to film

filmina *f* filmstrip

filmisti·co -ca *adj* (**-ci -che**) movie, motion-picture

filmotè·ca *f* (**-che**) film library

fi·lo *m* (**-li**) thread; wire; yarn; blade (*of grass*); breath (*of air*); string (*of pearls*); edge (*of razor*); **dare del filo da torcere** to cause trouble; **essere ridotto a un filo** to be only skin and bones; **fil di voce** thin voice; **filo a piombo** plumb line; **filo d'acqua** thin stream; **filo della schiena** or **delle reni** spine; **filo spinato** barbed wire; **passare a fil di spada** to put to the sword; **per filo e per segno** in detail; from beginning to end; **senza fili** wireless; **stare a filo** to stand upright; **tenere i fili** (fig) to pull wires; **tenere in filo** to keep s.o. in line; **un filo di** a bit of || *m* (**-la** *fpl*) string (*e.g., of cooked cheese*); (archaic) file, row

filo·bus *m* (**-bus**) trolley bus

filodiffusióne *f* wired wireless; cable TV

filodrammàti·co -ca *adj & mf* (**-ci -che**) (theat) amateur

filogovernati·vo -va *adj* on the government side

filologìa *f* philology

filòlo·go -ga (**-gi -ghe**) *adj* philologic(al) || *m* philologist

filóne *m* vein (*of ore*); ripple (*of a cur-*

rent); stream; loaf (*of bread*); (lit) mainstream; **filone d'oro** gold lode
filó·so -sa [s] *adj* stringy
filosofìa *f* philosophy
filosòfi·co -ca *adj* (**-ci -che**) philosophic(al)
filòso·fo -fa *mf* philosopher
filovìa *f* trolley bus line
filtrare *tr* to filter; to percolate (*coffee*) || *intr* to filter, permeate
filtrazióne *f* filtering, filtration
filtro *m* filter; philter
filugèllo *m* silkworm
filza *f* string (*of pearls*); series (*of errors*); row; dossier, file; basting (*of dress*)
finale *adj* final, last; consumer (*goods*) || *m* end, ending; (mus) finale; (sports) finish || *f* end, ending; (sports) finals
finali·sta *mf* (**-sti -ste**) finalist
finali·tà *f* (**-tà**) end, purpose
finanche *adv* even
finanza *f* finance
finanziaménto *m* financing
finanziare §287 *tr* to finance
finanzià·rio -ria (**-ri -rie**) *adj* finance, financial || *f* (com) holding company
finanzia·tóre -trice *mf* financial backer
finanzièra *f* frock coat; **alla finanziera** with giblet gravy
finanzière *m* financier; (coll) customs officer
fin·ca *f* (**-che**) column, row (*of ledger*)
finché *conj* until, as long as; **finché non** until
fine *adj* fine, thin; choice, nice || *m* end, purpose; conclusion; (lit) limit, border; **a fin di bene** to good purpose, for the best; **secondo fine** ulterior motive || *f* end, conclusion; **condurre a fine** to bring to fruition; **fine di settimana** weekend; **in fin dei conti** after all; **senza fine** endless
fine-settimà·na *m* or *f* (**-na**) weekend
finèstra *f* window; (lit) gash, wound; **finestra a gangheri** casement window; **finestra a ghigliottina** sash window; **finestra panoramica** picture window; **finestre** (lit) eyes
finestrino *m* (aut, rr) window
finézza *f* thinness; delicacy; finesse; kindness
fingere §126 *tr* to feign, pretend; (lit) to invent || *intr* to feign, pretend || *ref* to pretend to be
finiménto *m* finishing touch; **finimenti** harness
finimóndo *m* fracas, uproar
finire §176 *tr* to end; to put an end to; **finiscila!** cut it out! || *intr* (ESSERE) to end, to be over; to abut; to wind up; **finire con** + *inf* to wind up + *ger*; **finire di** + *inf* to finish + *ger*, e.g., **ho finito di farmi la barba** I have finished shaving
fini·to -ta *adj* finished; accomplished; finite; exhausted; **aver finito** to be through; **falla finita!** cut it out!; **farla finita con** to be through with; **farla finita con la vita** to end one's life
finitura *f* finish, finishing touch

finlandése [s] *adj* Finnish || *mf* Finlander, Finn || *m* Finnish (*language*)
Finlàndia, la Finland
fìnni·co -ca *adj* & *mf* (**-ci -che**) Finnic
fi·no -na *adj* fine, thin; refined; pure; sheer; **fare fino** (coll) to be refined || *adv* even; **fin a quando?** till when?; **fin da domani** beginning tomorrow; **fin da ora** beginning right now; **fin dove?** how far?; **fin in cima** up to the top; **fino a** until; down to; up to; as far as; **fin qui** up to now; up to this point
finòc·chio *m* (**-chi**) fennel; (vulg) fairy, queer
finóra *adv* up to now, heretofore
finta *f* pretense; fly (*of trousers*); (sports) feint; **far finta di** + *inf* to pretend to + *inf*, to feign + *ger*
fintantoché *conj* until
fin·to -ta *adj* false (*teeth*); fake; fictitious; sham (*battle*) || *mf* hypocrite || *f* see **finta**
finzióne *f* pretense; fiction; figment
fio *m*—**pagare il fio** to pay the piper; **pagare il fio di** to pay the penalty for
fioccare §197 (**fiòcco**) *intr* (ESSERE) to fall (*said of snow*); to flow (*said, e.g., of complaints*) || *impers* (ESSERE) —**fiocca** it is snowing
fiòc·co *m* (**-chi**) bow, knot; flake (*of snow*); flock, tuft (*of wool*); (naut) jib; **coi fiocchi** excellent; made to perfection; **fiocco pallone** (naut) spinnaker
fioccó·so -sa [s] *adj* flaky
fiòcina *f* harpoon
fiò·co -ca *adj* (**-chi -che**) feeble, faint
fiónda *f* sling; slingshot
fioràio -ràia (**-rài -ràie**) *mf* florist || *f* flower girl
fiorami *mpl*—**a fiorami** with flower design
fiordalìso *m* fleur-de-lis; (bot) iris; (lit) lily
fiòrdo *m* fjord
fióre *m* flower; prime (*of life*); best, pick; bloom; **a fior d'acqua** on the surface; skimming the water; **a fior di labbra** in a low tone, sottovoce; **a fior di pelle** skin-deep, superficial; **fior di** (coll) a lot of; **fiore di latte** cream; **fiori** (cards) clubs; **primo fiore** down (*soft hairy growth*)
fiorènte *adj* flourishing, thriving
fiorentì·no -na *adj* & *mf* Florentine
fiorettare (**fiorétto**) *tr* (fig) to overembellish
fiorétto *m* little flower; choice, pick; overembellishment; choice passage (*from life of saint*); foil; button of foil
fioricoltóre *m* var of **floricoltore**
fioricoltura *f* var of **floricoltura**
fiorino *m* florin
fiorire §176 *tr* to cause to flower; to adorn with flowers || *intr* (ESSERE) to flower, bloom; to flourish; to break out (*said of skin eruption*); to get moldy
fiori·sta *mf* (**-sti -ste**) florist
fiorì·to -ta *adj* flowering; flowery;

mottled; moldy; studded (*e.g.*, *with errors*)

fioritura *f* flowering; flourish; mold; (pathol) eruption

fiorrancino *m* (orn) kinglet, firecrest

fiorràn·cio *m* (-**ci**) marigold

fiòtto *m* gush, surge; (obs) wave

Firènze *f* Florence

firma *f* signature; power of attorney; good reputation; (mil) enlisted man; **buona firma** famous writer; **farci la firma** (coll) to accept quite willingly; **firma di favore** guarantor's signature

firmaiòlo *m* (mil) enlisted man

firmaménto *m* firmament

firmare *tr* to sign

firmatà·rio -ria (-**ri -rie**) *adj* signatory || *mf* signer, signatory

fisarmòni·ca *f* (-**che**) accordion

fiscale *adj* fiscal, tax

fischiare §287 *tr* to whistle; to boo || *intr* to whistle; to ring (*said of ears*); to blow (*said, e.g., of a factory whistle*)

fischiettare (**fischiétto**) *tr* & *intr* to whistle

fischiétto *m* whistle (*instrument*)

fi·schio *m* (-**schi**) whistle; hiss, boo; blow (*of whistle*); ringing (*in the ears*)

fi·sciù *m* (-**sciù**) kerchief, fichu

fisco *m invar* treasury; internal revenue service

fisi·co -ca (-**ci -che**) *adj* physical; bodily || *m* physicist; physique; (obs) physician || *f* physics

fisima *f* whim, fancy, caprice

fisiologìa *f* physiology

fisiològi·co -ca *adj* (-**ci -che**) physiological

fisionomìa or **fisonomìa** *f* physiognomy; countenance, face; appearance

fisionomi·sta *mf* (-**sti -ste**) person good at faces; physiognomist

fi·so -sa *adj* (lit) fixed

fissàg·gio *m* (-**gi**) (phot) fixing

fissare *tr* to fix; to fasten; to gaze at; to reserve; to hire; **fissare lo sguardo** to gaze || *ref* to gaze, stare; to become obsessed; to settle down

fissati·vo -va *adj* fixing

fissa·to -ta *adj* fixed; (coll) cracked || *mf* (coll) crackpot

fissa·tóre -trice *adj* (phot) fixing || *m* fixer; **fissatore per capelli** hair spray; hair dressing

fissazióne *f* fixation; fixed idea

fissile *adj* fissionable

fissionàbile *adj* fissionable

fissióne *f* fission

fis·so -sa *adj* fixed; regular || *m* pay

fìstola *f* (pathol) fistula; (lit) pipe

fitta *f* pang, stitch; crowd; great amount; (coll) blow; (obs) quagmire

fittàvolo *m* tenant farmer

fitti·zio -zia *adj* (-**zi -zie**) fictitious

fit·to -ta *adj* fixed, dug in; thick, dense; pitch (*dark*) || *m* thick; rent; tenancy || *f* see **fitta**

fittóne *m* (bot) taproot

fiuma·no -na *adj* river; from Fiume || *m* person from Fiume || *f* flood, stream

fiumara *f* torrent

fiume *m* river; **a fiumi** like a river

fiutare *tr* to snuff, sniff; to smell

fiutata *f* snuff, sniff

fiuto *m* sense of smell; snuff; flair

flàcci·do -da *adj* flabby

flacóne *m* flacon

flagellare (**flagèllo**) *tr* to scourge, lash; flagellate

flagèllo *m* whip, scourge; pest, plague; (coll) mess

flagrante *adj* flagrant; **in flagrante** (**delitto**) in the act

flan *m* (**flan**) pudding; (typ) mat

flanèlla *f* flannel

flato *m* gas, flatus

flatulènza *f* flatulence

flautino *m* flageolet

flauti·sta *mf* (-**sti -ste**) flutist

flàuto *m* flute; **flauto diritto** or **dolce** (mus) recorder

fla·vo -va *adj* (lit) blond, golden

flèbile *adj* mournful

flebite *f* phlebitis

flèmma *f* apathy; coolness; phlegm

flemmàti·co -ca *adj* (-**ci -che**) phlegmatic(al)

flessìbile *adj* flexible, pliable

flessióne *f* bending; (com) fall, drop; (gram) inflection

flessuó·so -sa [*s*] *adj* lithe, willowy; winding; flowing (*style*)

flèttere §177 *tr* to flex; (gram) to inflect

flirtare *intr* to flirt

flòra *f* flora

floreale *adj* floral

floricoltóre *m* floriculturist

floricoltura *f* floriculture

flòri·do -da *adj* florid; flourishing

flò·scio -scia *adj* (-**sci -sce**) flabby; soft (*hat*)

flòtta *f* fleet

flottante *adj* floating || *m* (com) floating stock

flottare (**flòtto**) *tr* & *intr* to float

flottìglia *f* flotilla

fluènte *adj* flowing

fluidità *f* fluidity

flùi·do -da *adj* & *m* fluid; fluent (*style*)

fluire §176 *intr* (ESSERE) to flow; to pour

fluitazióne *f* log driving

fluorescènte *adj* fluorescent

fluorescènza *f* fluorescence

fluorìdri·co -ca *adj* (-**ci -che**) hydrofluoric

fluorite *f* fluor, fluorite

fluorizzazióne [*ddzz*] *f* fluoridation

fluòro *m* fluorine

fluoruro *m* fluoride

flusso *m* flow; flood (*of tide*); high tide; (pathol) flow (*e.g., of blood*); (phys) flux

flutto *m* (lit) wave

fluttuare (**flùttuo**) *intr* to fluctuate; to bob, toss; to waver; to surge, stream

fluviale *adj* fluvial, river

fobìa *f* phobia

fò·ca *f* (-**che**) seal; sealskin

focàc·cia *f* (-**ce**) flat, rounded loaf; cake

focaccina *f* bun

fo·càia *adj fem* **(-càie) flint**
focale *adj* focal
fóce *f* mouth (*of river*)
focèna *f* porpoise
fochi·sta *m* **(-sti) fireman, stoker; fireworks manufacturer
foco·làio *m* **(-lài) (pathol) focus; (fig)
hotbed
focolare *m* hearth; firebox; fireside,
home
focó·so -sa [s] *adj* fiery, high-spirited
fòdera *f* lining (*of suit*); cover, case
foderare (**fòdero**) *tr* to line; to cover
fòdero *m* sheath, scabbard; raft
fó·ga *f* **(-ghe) ardor, impetus
fòg·gia *f* **(-ge) fashion, shape; a foggia
di shaped like**
foggiare §290 (**fòggio**) *tr* to shape, fashion
fòglia *f* leaf; petal; foil (*of gold*); **mangiare la foglia** (fig) to get wise, catch
on
fogliame *m* foliage
fò·glio *m* **(-gli) sheet; bill, banknote;
folio; newspaper; permit; foglio
d'avviso notice; foglio di congedo
(mil) discharge; foglio d'iscrizione
application; foglio di via (mil) travel
orders; foglio modello blank form;
foglio rosa (aut) permit; foglio volante flier, handbill**
fógna *f* sewer, drain
fognatura *f* sewerage
fòla *f* tale, fable
fola·ga *f* **(-ghe) (zool) coot
folata *f* gust; (lit) flight (*of birds*)
folclóre *m* folklore
folgorante *adj* striking; flashing; meteoric (*career*)
folgorare (**fólgoro**) *tr* to strike (with
lightning) || *intr* to flash by || *impers*
—**folgora** it is thundering
fólgore *m* (lit) thunderbolt || *f* flash of
lightning; thunderbolt
fólla *f* crowd; (fig) flock
follare (**fóllo**) *tr* to full
fòlle *adj* mad, crazy; (aut) neutral;
(mach) loose (*pulley*)
folleggiare §290 (**folléggio**) *intr* to act
foolishly; to frolic
folleménte *adv* desperately, madly
follétto *m* elf; little imp
follìa *f* madness, lunacy; folly; **alla
follia madly; far follie per to be
crazy about**
follicolo *m* follicle
fól·to -ta *adj* thick; beetle (*brow*); deep
(*night*) || *m* depth (*e.g., of the night*);
thick (*e.g., of the battle*)
fomentare (**foménto**) *tr* to foment
fòmite *m* (lit) instigation; impetus
fónda *f* anchorage; lowland; saddlebag;
alla fonda at anchor
fónda·co *m* **(-chi) (hist) warehouse
fondale *m* depth (*of river, sea*); (theat)
backdrop
fondamentale *adj* fundamental, basic
fondamén·to *m* **(-ti) ground, foundation; basis; fare fondamento su to
count on; fondamenti elements;
senza fondamento baseless; without
getting anywhere || *m* (-ta *fpl*)—fon-
damenta foundations (*of a building*)**

fondare (**fóndo**) *tr* to found; to build;
to charter || *ref*—**fondarsi su** to rely
on; to be based upon
fondatézza *f* basis, ground, foundation
fonda·to -ta *adj* well-founded
fonda·tóre -trice *mf* founder
fondazióne *f* foundation
fondèllo *m* bottom, base
fondènte *m* flux
fóndere §178 *tr* to smelt; to melt; to
blow (*a fuse*); to cast (*a statue*); to
blend (*colors*) || *intr* to melt; to blend
|| *ref* to melt; to blend; to burn out
fonderìa *f* foundry
fondià·rio -ria (-ri -rie) *adj* real-estate,
land || *f* real-estate tax
fondìna *f* holster; (coll) soup dish
fondi·sta *mf* **(-sti -ste) editorialist;
(sports) long-distance runner**
fóndita *f* (typ) font
fonditóre *m* smelter, founder
fón·do -da *adj* deep || *m* bottom; fund;
innermost nature; seat; end; background; land, property; **a doppio
fondo with a false bottom; a fondo
thoroughly; a fondo perduto as an
outright grant; dar fondo (naut)
to cast anchor; dar fondo a to exhaust; di fondo (journ) editorial;
(sports) long-distance; fondi funds;
lees; fondi di bottega remnants; fondi
di caffè coffee grounds; fondo comune d'investimento mutual fund;
fondo d'ammortamento sinking fund;
fondo di beneficenza community
chest; fondo tinta foundation (*in
make-up*); in fondo in the end; at the
bottom; after all**
fonèma *m* **(-mi) phoneme
fonèti·co -ca (-ci -che) *adj* phonetic ||
f phonetics
fonògeno *m* pickup (*of record player*)
fonògrafo *m* phonograph, Gramophone
fonogram·ma *m* **(-mi) telegram deliv-
ered by telephone**
fonologìa *f* phonology
fonorivelatóre *m* pickup (*of record
player*)
fonovalìgia *f* portable phonograph
fontana *f* fountain; spring; source
fónte *m* (lit) spring, source; **fonte bat-
tesimale font** || *f* spring; fountain;
source; **da fonte autorevole on good
authority**
foraggiare §290 *tr* to subsidize || *intr*
to forage
foràg·gio *m* **(-gi) forage, provender,
fodder
foràne·o -a *adj* rural; outer; (naut)
outer (*dock*)
forare (**fóro**) *tr* to pierce; to bore; to
puncture || *intr* to have a flat tire ||
ref to be punctured
foratura *f* puncture
fòrbice *f*—**a forbice (sports) scissors
(*e.g., kick*); forbici scissors; clippers;
forbici per le unghie nail clippers**
forbire §176 *tr* to wipe; to polish; to
shine
fór·ca *f* **(-che) fork; pitchfork; gallows; mountain pass; fare la forca a
qlcu (slang) to betray s.o.; (slang) to
do s.o. dirt; fatto a forca V-shaped**

forcèlla f fork (of bicycle or motor-cycle); mountain pass; fork-shaped pole; hairpin; cradle (of handset); (coll) wishbone (of chicken)

forchétta f fork; (coll) wishbone (of chicken); **alla forchetta** (culin) cold (e.g., lunch)

forchettata f forkful; blow with a fork

forchettóne m carving fork

forcina f hairpin

fòrcipe m forceps

forcóne m pitchfork

forellino m pinhole

forèsta f forest

forestale adj forest, park

foresterìa f guest quarters (in college or monastery)

forestierismo m borrowing (from another language)

forestiè·ro -ra adj foreign || mf foreigner; stranger; outsider

forfètta·rio -ria adj (-ri -rie) job, e.g., **contratto forfettario** job contract; all-inclusive, e.g., **combinazione forfettaria** all-inclusive price agreement

fórfora f dandruff

fòr·gia f (-ge) forge; smithy

forgiare §290 (fòrgio) tr to forge

foriè·ro -ra adj forerunning || mf forerunner, harbinger

fórma f shape; form; mold (e.g., for cakes); wheel (of cheese); (typ) form; **forma da cappelli** hat block; **forma da scarpe** shoe tree; shoe last (used by shoemaker); **forme** shape, body; good manners; **salvare le forme** to save face

formaggièra f dish for grated cheese

formàg·gio m (-gi) cheese

formaldèide f formaldehyde

formale adj formal; prim

formalismo m formality

formali·tà f (-tà) formality

formalizzare [ddzz] tr to scandalize || ref to be shocked

formare (fórmo) tr & ref to form

forma·to -ta adj formed || m format

formazióne f formation

fòrmica f (trademark) Formica

formi·ca f (-che) ant

formi·càio m (-cài) anthill; (fig) swarm

formichière m anteater

formicolare (formìcolo) intr to swarm; to crawl || intr (ESSERE) to creep (said, e.g., of a leg)

formicolì·o m (-i) swarm; creeping sensation, numbness

formidàbile adj formidable

formó·so -sa [s] adj shapely, buxom

fòrmula f formula; (aut) category, class; **formula dubitativa** (law) lack of evidence; **formula piena** (law) acquittal

formulare (fórmulo) tr to formulate

formulà·rio m (-ri) formulary; form

fornace f furnace, kiln

for·nàio -nàia mf (-nài -nàie) baker

fornèllo m stove, range; (of boiler) firebox; bowl (of pipe); (min) shaft; **fornello a gas** gas range; **fornello a spirito** kerosene stove; chafing dish

fornire §176 tr to furnish, supply

forni·tóre -trice mf supplier, purveyor

fornitura f supply; order; delivery

fórno m oven; furnace; kiln; bakery; (theat) empty house; **al forno** or **in forno** baked; **alto forno** blast furnace; **forno crematorio** crematorium; **far forno** (theat) to play before an empty house

fóro m hole

fòro m forum; (law) bar

forosétta [s] f (lit) peasant girl

fórse m doubt; **mettere in forse** to endanger; to put in doubt || adv perhaps, maybe

forsenna·to -ta adj mad, insane || mf lunatic

fòrte adj strong; firm; bad (cold); fat, hefty; fast (color); offensive (joke); hard (smoker); main (dish); (lit) thick || m strong person; fortress; bulk, main body; forte; (lit) thick; **sapere di forte** to have a strong flavor; **farsi forte** to bear up; **farsi forte di** to appropriate, use; to be cocksure of || adv hard, strong; much; loud; openly; a lot; fast; swiftly

fortézza f fortress; strength; fortitude

fortificare §197 (fortìfico) tr to fortify || ref to be strengthened; to dig in

fortificazióne f fortification

fortino m blockhouse, redoubt

fortùi·to -ta adj fortuitous

fortuna f fortune; luck; good luck; fate, destiny; (lit) storm; **avere fortuna** to be lucky; to be a hit; buona **fortuna!** good luck!; **di fortuna** makeshift, emergency; **non aver la fortuna di** to not be fortunate enough to; **per fortuna** luckily

fortunale m storm, tempest

fortuna·to -ta adj fortunate, lucky

fortunó·so -sa [s] adj eventful

forùncolo m boil; pimple

forviare §119 tr to mislead, lead astray || intr to go astray

fòrza f strength; force; power; police; (phys) force; **a forza di** by dint of; **a tutta forza** at full speed; **bassa forza** (mil) enlisted personnel; **di forza** by force; **di prima forza** first-rate; **far forza a** to encourage; to force; **fare forza a sè stesso** to restrain oneself; **forza!** courage!; **forza di corpo** (typ) height-to-paper; **forza maggiore** force majeure, act of God; **forza muscolare** brawn; **forza pubblica** police; **forza viva** kinetic energy; **per forza** of course; under duress

forzare (fòrzo) tr to force; to strain; to rape; to tamper with (a lock); **forzare il passo** to hasten one's step; **forzare la consegna** (mil) to violate orders

forza·to -ta adj forced; force (e.g., feed) || m convict

forzière m chest, coffer

forzó·so -sa [s] adj compulsory; imposed by law

forzu·to -ta adj husky, robust

foschìa f smog; mist; haze

fó·sco -sca *adj* (**-schi -sche**) dark; gloomy; misty

fosfato *m* phosphate

fosforeggiare §290 (**fosforéggio**) *intr* to phosphoresce; to glow

fosforescènte *adj* phosphorescent

fòsforo *m* phosphorus

fòssa *f* grave; hollow; hole, ditch; moat; pit; den (*of lions*); **fossa biologica** sewage-treatment plant; **fossa di riparazione** (aut) pit; **fossa settica** septic tank

fossato *m* ditch; moat

fossétta *f* dimple

fòssile *adj* & *m* fossil

fossilizzare [ddzz] *tr* to fossilize || *ref* to become fossilized

fòsso *m* ditch; moat

fò·to *f* (**-to**) photo

fotocòpia *f* photocopy

fotocopiare §287 (**fotocòpio**) *tr* to photocopy

fotoelèttri·co -ca (**-ci -che**) *adj* photoelectric || *f* (mil) searchlight

fotogèni·co -ca *adj* (**-ci -che**) photogenic

fotogiornale *m* pictorial magazine

fotografare (**fotògrafo**) *tr* to photograph

fotografia *f* photography; photograph

fotogràfi·co -ca *adj* (**-ci -che**) photographic

fotògrafo *m* photographer

fotogram·ma *m* (**-mi**) (phot) frame

fotoincisióne *f* photoengraving

fotolampo *m* flashlight

fotòmetro *m* exposure meter

fotomontàg·gio *m* (**-gi**) photomontage

fototubo *m* phototube

fra *m invar* brother, e.g., **fra Cristoforo** Brother Christopher || *prep* among; between; in, within

frac *m* (**frac**) swallow-tailed coat

fracassare *tr* to crash, smash || *ref* to crash

fracasso *m* crash; uproar; (coll) slew

fràdi·cio -cia (**-ci -cie**) *adj* rotten; soaked || *m* rotten part; decay; wet ground

fràgile *adj* fragile; brittle; frail

fragilità *f* fragility, frailty

fràgola *f* strawberry

fragóre *m* din; peal; roar

fragoró·so -sa [s] *adj* noisy

fragrante *adj* fragrant

fraintèndere §270 *tr* to misunderstand

frammassóne *m* Freemason

frammassonería *f* Freemasonry

frammentare (**framménto**) *tr* to fragment

frammentà·rio -ria *adj* (**-ri -rie**) fragmentary

framménto *m* fragment

framméttere §198 *tr* to interpose || *ref* to meddle; **frammettersi in** to intrude in, to butt into

frammèzzo [ddzz] *adv* in the middle || *prep* in the midst of

frammischiare §287 *tr* to mix || *ref* to concern oneself

frana *f* landslide; (fig) collapse

franare *intr* to slide; to collapse

francésca·no -na *adj* & *mf* Franciscan

francé·sco -sca (**-schi -sche**) *adj* (archaic) French || **Francesco** *m* Francis || **Francesca** *f* Frances

francése *adj* French || *m* French (*language*); Frenchman (*person*); **i francesi** the French || *f* Frenchwoman

francesismo *m* gallicism

francesizzare [ddzz] *tr* to Frenchify

franchézza *f* frankness

franchi·gia *f* (**-gie**) franchise; exemption; deductible insurance; (naut) shore leave; **franchigia postale** franking privilege

Frància, la France

fran·co -ca (**-chi -che**) *adj* free; frank; Frankish; **farla franca** to get off scot free; **franco di porto** prepaid, postpaid; **franco domicilio** home delivery, free delivery || *m* franc || **Franco** *m* Frank

francobóllo *m* postage stamp, stamp

frangènte *m* breaker, surf; **essere nei frangenti** to be in bad straits

fràngere §179 *tr* to crush; (lit) to break || *ref* to break, comb (*said of waves*)

frangétta *f* bangs

fràn·gia *f* (**-ge**) fringe; embellishment; shoreline; bangs; **frangia di corallo** coral reef

frangìbile *adj* breakable

frangiflut·ti *m* (**-ti**) breakwater

frangi·vènto *m* (**-vènto**) windbreak

frangizòl·le *m* (**-le**) disc harrow

Frankfur·ter *m* (**-ter**) hot dog

fran·tóio *m* (**-tói**) crusher; **frantoio a mascelle** jawbreaker

frantumare *tr* to crush; to break to pieces || *ref* to be crushed; to go to pieces

frantume *m* fragment; **andare in frantumi** to go to pieces

frappé *m* (**frappé**) shake; frappé; **frappé alla menta** mint julep; **frappé di latte** milk shake

frappórre §218 *tr* to interpose || *ref* to interfere; to intervene

frasà·rio *m* (**-ri**) language, speech

fra·sca *f* (**-sche**) branch; bush; ornament; whim; frivolous woman, flirt

frase *f* sentence; (mus) phrase; **frase fatta** cliché; **frase idiomatica** idiom; **frasi** words; **frasi di commiserazione** condolences

fraseggiare §290 (**fraséggio**) *intr* to use phrasing; to use big words; (mus) to phrase

fraseologìa *f* phraseology

fràssino *m* ash tree

frastagliare §280 *tr* to cut out (*e.g., paper*)

frastaglia·to -ta *adj* indented, jagged; ornamented

frastornare (**frastórno**) *tr* to disturb; (lit) to prevent

frastuòno *m* din, roar

frate *m* friar, monk, brother

fratellanza *f* brotherhood

fratellastro *m* stepbrother; half brother

fratèllo *m* brother; **fratelli** brothers and sisters; **fratello consanguineo** half brother on the father's side; **fratello**

di latte foster brother; **fratello ge-mello** twin
fraterni·tà *f* (**-tà**) fraternity
fraternizzare [ddzz] *intr* to fraternize
fratèr·no -na *adj* fraternal, brotherly
fratrici·da (-di -de) *adj* fratricidal ‖ *mf* fratricide
fratrici·dio *m* (**-di**) fratricide
fratta *f* brushwood; (coll) hedge
fràttàglie *fpl* giblets, chitterlings, offal
frattanto *adv* meantime, meanwhile
frattèmpo *m*—**nel frattempo** meanwhile
frattura *f* fracture; break; breach
fratturare *tr* & *ref* to fracture, break
fraudolènto *adj* fraudulent
frazionare (**fraziòno**) *tr* to fractionate; to break up
frazionà·rio -ria *adj* (**-ri -rie**) fractional
frazióne *f* fraction; hamlet; (eccl) breaking of the host
fréc·cia *f* (**-ce**) arrow, bolt; steeple, spire; clock (*on hosiery*); (archit) rise; (fig) aspersion; **freccia consen-siva** arrow (*on traffic light*); **freccia direzionale** (aut) turn signal
frecciata *f* arrow shot; taunt, gibe; **dare una frecciata a** to hit for a loan
freddare (**fréddo**) *tr* to chill; to kill
freddézza *f* chill; cold, coldness; coolness, cold shoulder; sang-froid
fréd·do -da *adj* cold; cool, chilly; frigid ‖ *m* cold, cold weather; chill; **a freddo** cold; cooly; **avere freddo** to be cold (*said of people*); **fare freddo** to be cold (*said of weather*); **freddo cane** biting cold; **sentire freddo** to feel cold; **sudare freddo** to be in a cold sweat
freddolό·so -sa [s] *adj* chilly (*person*)
freddura *f* joke, pun; cold weather
freddurì·sta *mf* (**-sti -ste**) punster
fregagióne *f* rubbing, rubdown, massage
fregare §209 (**frégo**) *tr* to rub; to strike (*a match*); (slang) to steal; (slang) to cheat, dupe; (vulg) to make love with ‖ *ref* to rub (*e.g., one's hands*); **fregarsene di** (vulg) to not give a hoot about
fregata *f* rubbing; (nav) frigate; (orn) frigate bird; (slang) cheating
fregatura *f* (slang) cheating; (slang) hitch, halt
fregiare §290 (**frégio**) *tr* to decorate; to fret
fré·gio *m* (**-gi**) decoration; insignia (*on cap of officer*); (archit) frieze
fré·go *m* (**-ghi**) line, stroke
frégola *f* rut, heat; (slang) mania, craze
fremènte *adj* throbbing; thrilling
frèmere §123 *tr* (lit) to beg insistently ‖ *intr* to throb; to be thrilled; to shake, tremble, rustle; to shudder (*with horror*); (fig) to boil; (fig) to fret
frèmito *m* throb; thrill; shudder; roar; quiver
frenare (**fréno**) *tr* to brake, stop; to bridle (*a horse*); to curb (*passions*); to restrain (*e.g., laughter*); **frenare la corsa** to slow down ‖ *intr* to put the brakes on ‖ *ref* to control oneself

frenatóre *m* (**rr**) brakeman
frenesìa *f* frenzy; (fig) craze, fever; (lit) thought
frenèti·co -ca *adj* (**-ci -che**) frenzied; frantic; crazy, enthusiastic
fréno *m* bit, bridle; brake; (fig) check; (mach) lock; **freno ad aria compressa** air brake; **mordere il freno** to champ the bit; **senza freno** wild, unbridled; **tenere a freno** to keep in check
frenologìa *f* phrenology
frequentare (**frequènto**) *tr* to frequent; to attend ‖ *intr* to associate
frequenta·tóre -trice *mf* patron, customer; frequenter, habitué
frequènte *adj* frequent; rapid (*pulse*); (lit) crowded
frequènza *f* frequency; attendance; **frequenza ultraelevata** ultrahigh frequency
frèsa *f* milling cutter; burr (*of dentist's drill*)
fresatrice *f* milling machine
fresatura *f* (mach) milling
freschézza *f* freshness; coolness
fré·sco -sca (**-schi -sche**) *adj* fresh; cool; **fresco di malattia** just recovered; **fresco di stampa** fresh off the press; **fresco di studi** fresh out of school; **star fresco** to be in a fix; to be all wrong ‖ *m* cool weather; tropical fabric; **di fresco** recently; **fare fresco** to be cool (*said of weather*); **mettere al fresco** (coll) to put in the clink; **per il fresco** in cool weather
frescό·ne -na *mf* (slang) dumbell
frescura *f* coolness, freshness
frétta *f* hurry, haste; **avere fretta** to be in a hurry; **in fretta** in a hurry; **in fretta e furia** in a rush
frettazzo *m* plasterer's wooden trowel; steel brush
frettolό·so -sa [s] *adj* hurried, hasty
freudismo *m* Freudianism
friàbile *adj* friable, crumbly
friabilità *f* friableness
fricassèa *f* fricassee
friggere §180 *tr* to fry; **mandare qlcu a farsi friggere** to tell s.o. to go to the devil ‖ *intr* to fry; to sizzle; to fret
friggitorìa *f* fried-food shop
frigidézza *f* frigidity
frigidi·tà *f* (**-tà**) coldness; frigidity
frìgi·do -da *adj* cold; frigid
frì·gio -gia *adj* (**-gi -gie**) Phrygian
frignare *intr* to whimper
frigorìfe·ro -ra *adj* refrigerating ‖ *m* refrigerator; (journ) morgue
fringuèl·lo -la *mf* chaffinch, finch
frinire §176 *intr* to chirp
frisata *f* gunnel
frittata *f* omelet; **fare la frittata** (coll) to make a mess of it
frittèlla *f* fritter; pancake; (coll) grease spot
frit·to -ta *adj* fried; cooked, ruined ‖ *m* fry, fried platter
frittura *f* frying; fry, fried platter
frivolézza *f* frivolity
frìvo·lo -la *adj* frivolous; flighty
frizionare (**friziόno**) *tr* to massage

frizióne *f* friction; massage; (aut) clutch

frizzante [ddzz] *adj* crisp, brisk (*weather*); sparkling (*wine*)

frizzare [ddzz] *intr* to tingle; to sparkle, fizz (*said of wine*); (fig) to sting

frizzo [ddzz] *m* jest, witticism; gibe, dig

frodare (**fròdo**) *tr* to cheat, swindle

fròde *f* fraud; **frode fiscale** tax evasion or fraud

fròdo *m invar* customs evasion; **di frodo** smuggled

frò·gia *f* (-ge or -gie) nostril (*of horse*)

fròl·lo -**la** *adj* high (*meat*); soft, tender; (fig) weak

frónda *f* branch, bough; political opposition; **fronde** foliage; ornaments

frondó·so -**sa** [s] *adj* leafy

frontale *adj* front; frontal

frónte *m* (mil, pol) front; **far fronte a** to face; to face up to; to meet (*expenses*); **tenere fronte a** to face, resist || *f* forehead, brow; countenance; title page; headline; (fig) face; **a fronte** opposite, facing; **a fronte di** (com) in reference to; **dietro front!** (mil) about face!; **di fronte a** in the face of; facing; **di fronte a tutti** in plain view; **fronte destr'!** (mil) right face!; **mettere a fronte** to compare; **tenere a fronte** to have in front of one's eyes

fronteggiare §290 (**frontéggio**) *tr* to face, front || *ref* to face one another

frontespì·zio *m* (-zi) title page

frontièra *f* border, frontier

frontóne *m* (archit) pediment; (archit) gable

frónzolo *m* bauble, gewgaw; **fronzoli** finery, frippery

fròtta *f* crowd; swarm; flock

fròttola *f* fib; popular poem; **frottole** humbug

frugale *adj* frugal (*meal; life*); temperate (*in eating or drinking*)

frugare §209 *tr* to rummage through; to search (*a person*) || *intr* to rummage, poke around

frùgo·lo -**la** *mf* restless child, imp

fruire §176 *tr* to enjoy || *intr*—**fruire di** to enjoy

fruitóre *m* user

frullare *tr* to beat, whip || *intr* to flutter; to spin; **frullare per il capo a** to get into the head of, e.g., **cosa gli è frullato per il capo?** what got into his head?

frulla·to -**ta** *adj* whipped || *m* shake (*drink*)

frullatóre *m* electric beater

frullino *m* egg beater

fruménto *m* wheat

frumentóne *m* corn

frusciare §128 *intr* to rustle

frusci·o *m* (-i) rustle, rustling

frusta *f* whip; egg beater

frustare *tr* to whip, lash; (fig) to censure; (coll) to wear out (*clothes*)

frustata *f* lash; (fig) censure

frustino *m* whip, crop

fru·sto -**sta** *adj* worn out, threadbare || *f* see **frusta**

frustrare *tr* to frustrate, baffle; to discomfit

frut·ta *f* (-ta & -te) fruit; **essere alle frutta** to be at the end of the meal, to be having one's dessert

fruttare *tr* & *intr* to yield

fruttéto *m* orchard

frutticoltóre *m* fruit grower

fruttièra *f* fruit dish

fruttìfe·ro -**ra** *adj* fruit-bearing; fruitful, profitable; (lit) fecund

fruttificare §197 (**fruttìfico**) *intr* to fructify; to yield

fruttivéndo·lo -**la** *mf* fruit dealer

frutto *m* fruit; **frutti di mare** shellfish; **mettere a frutto** to make yield

fruttuó·so -**sa** [s] *adj* fruitful, profitable

fu *adj invar* late (*deceased*); son of the late . . . ; daughter of the late . . .

fucilare *tr* to shoot

fucilata *f* rifle shot

fucilazióne *f* execution by a firing squad

fucile *m* rifle, gun; **fucile ad aria compressa** air gun; **fucile da caccia** shotgun; **un buon fucile** a good shot

fucilerìa *f* fusillade

fucilière *m* rifleman

fucina *f* forge, smithy

fu·co *m* (-chi) (bot) rockweed; (zool) drone

fùcsia *f* fuchsia

fu·ga *f* (-ghe) flight; leak; row (*e.g., of rooms*); spurt (*in bicycle race*); (mus) fugue; **di fuga** hastily; **prendere la fuga** to take flight; **volgere in fuga** to put to flight; to take flight

fugace *adj* passing, fleeting

fugare §209 *tr* (lit) to avoid; (lit) to put to flight; (lit) to dispel

fuggènte *adj* passing, fleeting

fuggévole *adj* fleeting

fuggia·sco -**sca** (-schi -sche) *adj* fleeing, fugitive || *mf* fugitive; refugee

fuggi **fug·gi** *m* (-gi) stampede

fuggire *tr* to flee; to avoid || *intr* (ESSERE) to flee, run away; (sports) to take the lead; **fuggire a** to flee from

fuggiti·vo -**va** *adj* & *mf* fugitive

fulcro *m* fulcrum; (fig) pivot

fulgènte *adj* (lit) resplendent

fùlgi·do -**da** *adj* resplendent

fulgóre *m* resplendency, radiance

fulìggine *f* soot

fuligginó·so -**sa** [s] *adj* sooty

fulmicotóne *m* guncotton

fulminante *adj* crushing (*illness*); withering (*look*); explosive || *m* exploding cap; (coll) match

fulminare (**fùlmino**) *tr* to strike by lightning; to strike down; to confound, dumfound || *ref* (elec) to burn out, to blow out || *impers* (ESSERE)—**fulmina** it is lightning

fùlmine *m* lightning, thunderbolt; **fulmine a ciel sereno** bolt out of the blue

fulmìne·o -**a** *adj* swift, instant

ful·vo -**va** *adj* tawny

fumaiòlo *m* chimney; smokestack; (naut) funnel

fumante *adj* smoking; steaming; dusty

fumare *tr* to smoke; (lit) to exhale ‖ *intr* to smoke; to steam; to fume; **fumare come un turco** to smoke like a chimney

fumata *f* smoking; smoke signal; **fare una fumata** to have a smoke

fuma·tóre -trice *mf* smoker

fumetti·sta *mf* (**-sti -ste**) cartoonist

fumétto *m* cartoon; **fumetti comics**

fumigare §209 (**fùmigo**) *tr* (obs) to fumigate ‖ *intr* to steam, smoke

fumigazióne *f* fumigation

fumi·sta *m* (**-sti**) heater man; joker, hoaxer

fumisteria *f* fondness for practical jokes; bamboozling

fumo *m* smoke; vapor, steam; smoking; (coll) hot air; **andare in fumo** to go up in smoke; **fumi vapors, fumes; mandare in fumo** to squander; to thwart; **sapere di fumo** to taste smoky; **vedere qlcu come il fumo negli occhi** to not be able to stand s.o.; **vender fumo** to peddle influence

fumòge·no -na *adj* smoke, e.g., **cortina fumogena** smoke curtain

fumó·so -sa [s] *adj* smoky; obscure

funambolismo *m* tightrope walking; (fig) acrobatics

funàmbo·lo -la *mf* tightrope walker; (fig) acrobat

fune *f* rope, cable; **fune portante** suspension cable

fùnebre *adj* funeral; funereal, gloomy

funerale *adj* & *m* funeral

funerà·rio -ria *adj* (**-ri -rie**) funeral

funère·o -a *adj* funereal; funeral

funestare (**funèsto**) *tr* to afflict

funè·sto -sta *adj* baleful; mournful

fungàia *f* mushroom farm; mushroom bed; flock, swarm

fùngere §183 *intr*—**fungere da** to act as

fun·go *m* (**-ghi**) mushroom; fungus; **fungo atomico** mushroom cloud; **venir su come i funghi** to mushroom

fungó·so -sa [s] *adj* fungous

funicolare *adj* cable, cable-driven ‖ *f* funicular railway

funivia *f* cableway

funzionale *adj* functional

funzionalità *f* functionalism

funzionaménto *m* working order; functioning

funzionare (**funzióno**) *intr* to work; to function; **funzionare da** to act as

funzionà·rio -ria *mf* (**-ri -rie**) functionary, official; public official

funzióne *f* function; office; duty; (eccl) service; **facente funzione** acting; **mettere in funzione** to make (*s.th*) work

fuò·co *m* (**-chi**) fire; burner (*of gas range*); focus; (fig) home; (lit) thunderbolt; **al fuoco!** fire! (*warning*); **andare per il fuoco** (culin) to boil over; **cuocere a fuoco lento** (culin) to simmer; **dar fuoco a** to set fire to; **di fuoco** fiery; blushing; **far fuoco** to fire; **fuochi artificiali** fireworks; **fuoco di fila** enfilade; **fuoco!** (mil) fire!; **fuoco di paglia** (fig) flash in the pan; **fuoco di segnalazione** flare; **fuoco fatuo** will-o'-the-wisp; **fuoco**

incrociato cross fire; **fuoco nutrito** drumfire; **mettere a fuoco** to focus; **mettere una mano sul fuoco** to be absolutely sure, to swear by it

fuorché *prep* except; **fuorché di** except to

fuòri *adv* outside, out; aside; e.g., **lasciar fuori** to leave aside; **andar di fuori** (culin) to boil over; **dar fuori** to do away with; to squander; **di fuori** outside; **far fuori** to publish; **fuori di** out of; outside of; beyond (*a. doubt*); off (*the road*); beside (*oneself*); **fuori d'uso** out of style; obsolete; **il di fuori** the outside; **in fuori** protruding; forward; **mettere fuori** to throw out; to spread; to exhibit ‖ *prep* beyond; out of; outside; **fuori commercio** not for sale; **fuori concorso** in a class by itself (himself, etc.); **fuori luogo** untimely, out of place; **fuori (di) mano** far away; solitary; **fuori testo** inserted, tipped in

fuoribór·do *m* (**-do**) outboard; outboard motor

fuoricombattimén·to (**-to**) *adj* knocked out ‖ *m* knockout

fuorigió·co *m* (**-co**) (sports) offside

fuorilég·ge *mf* (**-ge**) outlaw

fuorisè·rie (**-rie**) *adj* custom-built ‖ *m* & *f* custom model ‖ *f* custom-built car

fuoristra·da *m* (**-da**) land rover

fuoriusci·to -ta *adj* exiled ‖ *mf* political exile ‖ *f* leak; flow; protrusion

fuorvia·to -ta *adj* mislead, misguided

furbacchió·ne -na *mf* slippery person

furberia *f* slyness, cunning

fur·bo -ba *adj* sly, cunning ‖ *mf* knave; **furbo di tre cotte** slicker

furènte *adj* furious

fureria *f* (mil) company headquarters

furétto *m* ferret

furfante *m* sharper, scoundrel

furfanteria *f* rascality

furgoncino *m* small delivery van

furgóne *m* truck; patrol wagon; hearse; **furgone cellulare** prison van

furgoni·sta *mf* (**-sti -ste**) truck driver, teamster

fùria *f* fury; strength, violence; hurry; **a furia di** by dint of; **con furia** in a hurry; **far furia a** to urge; **montare in furia** to go berserk; **to fly off the handle**

furibón·do -da *adj* furious, wild

furière *m* soldier attached to company headquarters

furió·so -sa [s] *adj* furious; fierce; mad

furóre *m* furor, frenzy; violence; longing; **far furore** to be a hit, to be all the rage

furoreggiare §290 (**furoréggio**) *intr* to be a hit, to be all the rage

furti·vo -va *adj* stealthy; furtive; stolen (*e.g., goods*)

furto *m* theft; stolen goods; **di furto** stealthily; **furto con scasso** burglary

fusa [s] *fpl*—**fare le fusa** to purr

fuscèllo *m* twig

fusciac·ca *f* (**-che**) sash (*around the waist*)

fusèllo [s] *m* spindle; axle, shaft
fusìbile *adj* fusible ‖ *m* (elec) fuse
fusióne *f* fusion; melting; merger; blending (*of colors*)
fu·so -sa *adj* melted; molten
fuso [s] *m* spindle; shank (*of anchor*); shaft (*of column*); (aut) axle; **fuso orario** time zone
fusolièra *f* (aer) fuselage
fustagno *m* fustian
fustàia *f* adult forest, full-grown forest
fustèlla *f* (perforating) punch; (pharm) price stub

fustigare §209 (fùstigo) *tr* to whip
fusto *m* trunk (*of tree*); stalk; stem (*of key*); beam (*of balance*); butt (*of gun*); trunk, body; frame (*of arm-chair*); tank (*for holding liquids*); drum (*metal receptacle*); holding stick (*of umbrella*); shaft (*of column*); **d'alto fusto** full-grown (*tree*)
fùtile *adj* futile, trifling
futilità *f* futility
futurismo *m* futurism
futuri·sta *mf* (-sti -ste) futurist
futu·ro -ra *adj* & *m* future

G

G, g [dʒi] *m* & *f* seventh letter of the Italian alphabet
gabardi·ne *f* (-ne) gabardine; gabardine raincoat or topcoat
gabbamón·do *m* (-do) cheat, sharper
gabbanèlla *f* gown (*of physician or patient*); robe
gabbano *m* cloak; frock; **mutare gab-bano** to be a turncoat
gabbare *tr* to dupe, cheat ‖ *ref*—**gab-barsi di** to make fun of
gàbbia *f* cage; ox muzzle; dock (*in courtroom*); (mach) housing; (naut) top; (naut) topsail; **gabbia d'imbal-laggio** crate; **gabbia toracica** rib cage
gabbiano *m* sea gull
gabbo *m*—**farsi gabbo di** to make fun of; **prendere a gabbo** to make light of
gabèlla *f* (obs) customs, duty
gabellare (gabèllo) *tr* to palm off; to swallow (*e.g., a tall story*); (obs) to tax
gabinétto *m* office (*of doctor, dentist, lawyer*); cabinet; chamber (*of judge*); toilet; closet; laboratory; **gabinetto da bagno** bathroom; **gabinetto di decenza** toilet, bathroom
ga·gà *m* (gà) fop, dandy; lounge lizard
gaggìa *f* acacia
gagliardétto *m* pennon; pennant
gagliardìa *f* (lit) vigor; (lit) prowess
gagliar·do -da *adj* vigorous; stalwart; hearty (*e.g., voice*)
gagliòf·fo -fa *adj* loutish; rascal ‖ *mf* lout; rascal
gaiézza *f* gaiety, vivacity
gàio gàia *adj* (gài gàie) gay, vivacious
gala *m* & *f* gala; gala affair; **di gala** formal; **mettersi in gala** to dress up ‖ *f* frill; bow tie (*for formal attire*); (naut) bunting
galalite *f* casein plastic, galalith
galante *adj* gallant, courtly; amorous; pretty, graceful
galanterìa *f* gallantry, courtliness
galantuò·mo *m* (-mini) honest man; (coll) my good fellow
galàssia *f* galaxy
galatèo *m* good manners
galèna *f* (min) galena
galeóne *m* galleon
galeòt·to -ta *adj* (archaic) intermediary

(*in love affairs*) ‖ *m* galley slave; convict; (archaic) procurer
galèra *f* galley; forced labor
gali·lèo -lèa (-lèi -lèe) *adj* & *m* Galilean
galla *f* (bot) gall; (pathol) blister; **a galla** afloat; **tenersi a galla** (fig) to keep alive; to manage; **venire a galla** to come to the surface
galleggiante *adj* floating ‖ *m* float
galleggiare §290 (galléggio) *intr* to float
gallerìa *f* tunnel; gallery; balcony; mall, arcade; wind tunnel
Galles, il Wales
gallése [s] *adj* Welsh ‖ *m* Welshman; Welsh (*language*) ‖ *f* Welsh woman
gallétta *f* cracker; hardtack; (naut) ball on top of flagpole
gallétto *m* cockerel; (fig) gallant; (fig) whippersnapper; (mach) wing nut; **fare il galletto** to swagger
gàlli·co -ca *adj* & *m* (-ci -che) Gallic
gallina *f* hen; **gallina faraona** guinea fowl
gal·lo -la *adj* Gallic; (sports) Bantam (*weight*) ‖ *m* rooster, cock; weather-cock; Gaul; Gallic (*language*); **fare il gallo** to strut; **gallo cedrone** wood grouse; **gallo d'India** turkey
gallòc·cia *f* (-ce) (naut) cleat
gallóne *m* braid; stripe; chevron; gallon
galoppare (galòppo) *intr* to gallop; (fig) to rush around
galoppata *f* gallop
galoppi·no *m* errand boy; **galoppino elettorale** ward heeler
galòppo *m* gallop; **andare al piccolo galoppo** to canter; **di gran galoppo** at full speed; **piccolo galoppo** canter
galò·scia *f* (-sce) overshoe, rubber
galvanizzare [ddzz] *tr* to electroplate; (fig) to galvanize
galvanoplàsti·ca *f* (-che) electroplating
gamba *f* leg; stem; (aer) shock strut; **a gambe all'aria** upside down; **a gambe levate** at top speed; upside down; **darsela a gambe** to take to one's heels; **essere in gamba** to be in good shape; to be on the ball; **essere male in gamba** to be in bad shape; **gamba di legno** peg leg; **gambe a ciambella** bowlegs; **le gambe mi fanno giacomo** my knees shake;

prendere qlcu sotto gamba to make light of s.o.; **raddrizzare le gambe ai cani** to try the impossible

gambale *m* legging, gaiter; boot last; leg (*of boot*)

gamberétto *m* shrimp

gàmbero *m* (*Astacus, Cambarus*) crawfish

gambétto *m* stumble; trip; (chess) gambit

gambo *m* stem

gamèlla *f* (mil) mess kit, mess tin

gamma *f* gamut; range; **gamma d'onda** (rad) wave band

ganà·scia *f* (-sce) jaw; (aut) brake shoe; **mangiare a quattro ganasce** to eat like a horse

gàn·cio *m* (-ci) hook; clasp; hanger

gan·ga *f* (-ghe) gang; (min) gangue

gànghero *m* hinge; clasp; **uscire dai gangheri** to fly off the handle

gàn·glio *m* (-gli) ganglion

ganzo [dz] *m* (slang) lover; (coll) slicker

gara *f* competition, match; **fare a gara** to compete; **gara d'appalto** competitive bidding

garagi·sta *m* (-sti) garage man

garante *adj* responsible ‖ *m* guarantor; **farsi garante per** to vouch for

garantire §176 *tr* to guarantee; to secure (*a mortgage*)

garanti·to -ta *adj* guaranteed, warranted; downright, absolute (*liar*)

garanzìa *f* guarantee, warranty; insurance, assurance

garbare *tr* (naut) to shape (*a hull*) ‖ *intr* (ESSERE) (with *dat*) to like, e.g., **non gli garbano le Sue parole** he does not like your words

garbatézza *f* politeness, courtesy

garba·to -ta *adj* polite, courteous

garbo *m* politeness, good manners; gesture; act; shape (*of a hull*); good cut (*of clothes*); elegance (*in painting or writing*); **a garbo** correctly

garbù·glio *m* (-gli) tangle, confusion; mess

gardènia *f* gardenia

gareggiare §290 (garéggio) *intr* to compete, vie

garétta *f* var of **garitta**

garétto *m* var of **garretto**

garganèlla *f*—**bere a garganella** to gulp down

gargarismo *m* gargling; gargle

gargarizzare [ddzz] *intr* & *ref* to gargle

gargaròzzo *m* throat, gullet

garitta *f* railroad-crossing box; (mil) sentry box; (rr) brakeman's box

garòfano *m* carnation, pink

garrése [s] *m* withers

garrétto *m* ankle (*of man*); hock (*of horse*)

garrire §176 *intr* to chirp, twitter; to flap; (archaic) to quarrel

garrito *m* chirp, twitter

garròtta *f* garrote

gàrru·lo -la *adj* garrulous

garza [dz] *f* gauze

garzonato [dz] *m* apprenticeship

garzó·ne -na [dz] *mf* helper ‖ *m*

helper, boy; apprentice; (archaic) bachelor; **garzone di stalla** stableboy

gas *m* (gas) gas; gasoline; **gas asfissiante** poison gas; **gas delle miniere** firedamp; **gas esilarante** laughing gas; **gas illuminante** illuminating gas; **gas lacrimogeno** tear gas

gasdótto *m* gas pipeline

gasificare §197 (gasìfico) *tr* var of **gassificare**

gasòlio *m* Diesel oil

gasòmetro *m* var of **gassometro**

gassificare §197 (gassìfico) *tr* to gasify

gassi·sta *m* (-sti) gasworker; gas fitter; gas-meter reader

gassòmetro *m* gasholder, gas tank

gassó·so -sa [s] *adj* gaseous, gassy ‖ *f* soda, pop

gastronomìa *f* gastronomy

gatta *f* she-cat, tabby; **comprare la gatta nel sacco** to buy a pig in a poke; **gatta ci cova** something is rotten in Denmark; **pigliare una gatta da pelare** to take on a heavy burden, to get a tiger by the tail

gattabùia *f* (coll) clink, lockup

gattamòrta *f* (gattemòrte) hypocrite

gattino *m* kitten; (bot) catkin

gat·to -ta *mf* cat ‖ *m* tomcat; tamper, pile driver; **gatto a nove code** cat-o'-nine-tails; **gatto soriano** tortoiseshell cat; **quattro gatti** a handful of people ‖ *f* see **gatta**

gattóni *adv* on all fours

gattopardo *m* (zool) serval; **gattopardo americano** ocelot

gattùc·cio *m* (-ci) compass saw; (ichth) small dotted dogfish

gaudènte *adj* jovial ‖ *m* bon vivant

gàu·dio *m* (-di) joy, happiness

gavazzare *intr* (lit) to revel

gavétta *f* mess kit, mess gear; **venire dalla gavetta** to come up through the ranks

gavitèllo *m* buoy

gazza [dz] *f* magpie

gazzarra [ddzz] *f* racket, uproar

gazzèlla [ddzz] *f* gazelle

gazzétta [ddzz] *f* newspaper; gazette; newsmonger, gossip; **Gazzetta Ufficiale** Official Gazette (*in Italy*); Congressional Record (*U.S.A.*)

gazzettino [ddzz] *m* small newspaper; column, e.g., **gazzettino rosa** social column; newsmonger, gossip

gazzósa [ddzz] *f* var of **gassosa**

gèl *m* gel

gelare (gèlo) *tr* to freeze; to nip ‖ *intr* (ESSERE) & *ref* to freeze ‖ *impers* (ESSERE & AVERE)—**gela** it is freezing

gelata *f* frost

gela·tàio -tàia *mf* (-tài -tàie) ice-cream dealer

gelaterìa *f* ice-cream parlor

gelatièra *f* ice-cream freezer

gelatière *m* ice-cream dealer

gelatina *f* gelatin; jelly; **gelatina di frutta** fruit jelly; gum drop

gelatinizzare [ddzz] *tr* & *ref* to gelatinize; to jell

gela·to -ta *adj* frozen ‖ *m* ice cream;

gelato da passeggio ice cream on a stick, popsicle

gèli·do -da adj icy, ice-cold

gèlo m frost; ice; cold; **diventare di gelo** to remain dumfounded; **farsi di gelo** to be cold or aloof; **sentirsi il gelo addosso** to get a chill

gelóne m chilblain

gelosìa [s] f jealousy; great care; shutter

geló·so -sa [s] adj jealous; solicitous

gèlso m mulberry

gelsomino m jasmine

gemebón·do -da adj (lit) moaning

gemellàggio m sisterhood (of two cities)

gemèl·lo -la adj twin; sister (ship) ‖ mf twin ‖ **gemelli** mpl cufflinks ‖ **Gemelli** mpl (astr) Gemini

gèmere §123 tr (lit) to lament ‖ intr (ESSERE & AVERE) to moan, groan; to suffer; to squeak (said of a wheel); to ooze; to coo (said of a dove)

gèmito m moan; howl (of wind)

gèmma f gem; (bot) bud

gemma·to -ta adj gemmate; jeweled

gendarme m gendarme, policeman

genealogìa f genealogy

generalato m generalship

generale adj general ‖ m general; **generale d'armata** (mil) general; **generale di brigata** brigadier general; **generale di corpo d'armata** lieutenant general; **generale di divisione** major general ‖ f (mil) assembly; **stare sulle generali** to speak in vague generalities

generali·tà f (-tà) generality; majority; **generalità** fpl personal data

generalizzare [ddzz] tr to generalize; to bring into general use ‖ intr to generalize, deal in generalities

generare (gènero) tr to beget; to generate ‖ ref to occur

genera·tóre -trice adj generating ‖ m generator ‖ f generatrix

generazióne f generation

gènere m genus; kind, type; genre; (gram) gender; **del genere** similar, alike; **farne di ogni genere** to commit all sorts of mischief; **genere umano** mankind; **generi alimentari** foodstuffs; **generi diversi** sundries, assorted articles; **in genere** generally

genèri·co -ca (-ci -che) adj generic; vague; all-round; general (e.g., practitioner) ‖ mf (theat) actor playing bit parts ‖ m vagueness, imprecision

gènero m son-in-law

generosi·tà [s] f (-tà) generosity

generó·so -sa [s] adj generous; rich (wine)

gène·si f (-si) genesis ‖ **il Genesi** Genesis

genèti·co -ca (-ci -che) adj genetic(al) ‖ f genetics

genetlìa·co -ca (-ci -che) adj birth ‖ m birthday

gengiva f (anat) gum

genìa f set, gang; (lit) breed

geniale adj clever; genial; inspired, genius-like

geniali·tà f (-tà) cleverness, ingeniousness; genius; (lit) geniality

genière m (mil) engineer

gè·nio m (-ni) genius; (mil) corps of engineers; **andare a genio** (with dat) to like, e.g., **la musica moderna non gli va a genio** he does not like modern music; **fare qlco di genio** to do s.th willingly

genitale adj genital ‖ **genitali** mpl genitals

geniti·vo -va adj & m genitive

geni·tóre -trice mf parent

gen·nàio m (-nài) January

genocìdio m genocide

Gènova f Genoa

genovése [s] adj & mf Genoese

gentàglia f riffraff, rabble, scum

gènte adj (archaic) gentle ‖ f people; nation; family; (nav) crew; **gente d'arme** soldiers; **gente di mal affare** riffraff; **gente di mare** sailors

gentildònna f gentlewoman

gentile adj gentle; nice; genteel ‖ **Gentili** mpl heathen

gentilézza f gentleness; kindness; **per gentilezza** kindly, please

gentilì·zio -zia adj (-zi -zie) of noble family; (lit) ancestral

gentiluò·mo m (-mini) gentleman, nobleman

genuflèttere §177 ref to kneel down

genuì·no -na adj genuine

genziana f gentian

geofìsi·co -ca (-ci -che) adj geophysical ‖ f geophysics

geografìa f geography

geogràfi·co -ca adj (-ci -che) geographic(al)

geògra·fo -fa mf geographer

geologìa f geology

geòlo·go -ga mf (-gi -ghe) geologist

geòme·tra m (-tri) geometrician; land surveyor

geometrìa f geometry

gerà·nio m (-ni) geranium

gerar·ca m (-chi) leader

gerarchìa f hierarchy

geràrchi·co -ca adj (-ci -che) hierarchical; **per via gerarchica** through proper channels

Geremìa f Jeremiah

geremìade f jeremiad

gerènte m manager, director; **gerente responsabile** (journ) managing editor

gèr·go m (-ghi) jargon

geriatrìa f geriatrics

Gèrico f Jericho

gèrla f pannier (carried on the back)

Germània, la Germany

germàni·co -ca adj (-ci -che) Germanic

germànio m germanium

germanizzare [ddzz] tr to Germanize

germa·no -na adj german, e.g., **fratello germano** brother-german; Germanic ‖ m (lit) brother-german; **germano nero** (orn) coot; **germano reale** (orn) mallard

gèrme m germ; (lit) offspring

germici·da (-di) adj germicidal ‖ m germicide

germinare (gèrmino) *intr* (ESSERE & AVERE) to germinate

germogliare §280 (germóglio) *tr* to put forth || *intr* (ESSERE & AVERE) to bud, sprout

germó·glio *m* (-gli) bud, sprout

geroglifi·co -ca *adj* & *m* (-ci -che) hieroglyphic

Geròlamo *m* Jerome

gerontocò·mio *m* (-mi) or gerotrò·fio *m* (-fi) old people's home, nursing home

gerùn·dio *m* (-di) gerund

Gerusalèmme *f* Jerusalem

gessare (gèsso) *tr* to plaster; to lime (*a field*)

gèsso *m* gypsum; plaster; chalk; (sculp) plaster cast

gessó·so -sa [s] *adj* plastery, chalky; chalklike

gèsta *f* (archaic) army; gesta *fpl* deeds, exploits

gestante *f* pregnant woman

gestazióne *f* gestation

gesticolare (gestícolo) *intr* to gesticulate

gestióne *f* management, operation; data processing

gestire §176 *tr* to manage, operate || *intr* to gesticulate; (theat) to make gestures

gèsto *m* gesture; attitude; act, deed

ge·stóre -strice *mf* manager, operator; gestore di stazione (rr) station agent

gestualità *f* bodily movements (*e.g., of an actor*)

Gesù *m* Jesus; Gesù Cristo Jesus Christ

gesuì·ta *m* (-ti) Jesuit

gesuìti·co -ca *adj* (-ci -che) Jesuitic(al)

gettare (gètto) *tr* to throw; to cast; to pour; to lay (*e.g., a floor*); to send forth; to yield; to broadcast (*seed*); to risk (*one's life*); gettare la colpa addosso a qlcu to lay the blame on s.o.; gettare le armi to lay down one's arms; gettar giù to fell, knock down; gettar sangue to bleed || *ref* to throw oneself; to plunge; to flow, empty (*said of a river*)

gettata *f* pour, pouring; jetty, shoot, sprout; cast; range (*of a gun*); gettata cardiaca (med) rate of flow of blood

gèttito *m* yield; waste; far gettito di to waste

gètto *m* throw; gush; shoot, sprout; cast; precast concrete slab; (aer) jet; a getto (aer) jet; a getto continuo continuously; di getto spontaneously; far getto di to waste; primo getto first draft

gettonare (gettóno) *tr* (coll) to call up from a pay station; (coll) to make the selection of (*a record in a juke-box*)

gettóne *m* counter, token; attendance fee; (cards) chip

gettopropulsióne *f* jet propulsion

ghepardo *m* cheetah

ghép·pio *m* (-pi) kestrel

gheri·glio *m* (-gli) kernel, meat (*of nut*)

gherlino *m* (naut) warp, line

gherminèlla *f* trick, sleight of hand; trickery

ghermire §176 *tr* to claw; to seize

gheróne *m* gusset

ghétta *f* gaiter; ghette spats

ghétto *m* ghetto

ghiacciàia *f* icebox, cooler

ghiac·ciàio *m* (-ciài) glacier; ghiacciaio continentale polar cap

ghiacciare §128 *tr* to freeze || *intr* (ESSERE) to freeze || *impers* (ESSERE) —ghiaccia it is freezing

ghiaccià·to -ta *adj* iced; ice-cold; frozen || *f* flavored crushed ice

ghiàc·cio -cia (-ci -ce) *adj* icy, ice-cold || *m* ice; ghiaccio secco dry ice

ghiacciò·lo -la *adj* crumbly, breakable || *m* icicle; popsicle

ghiàia *f* gravel, crushed stone

ghianda *f* fringe (*on a curtain*); (bot) acorn; ghiande mast (*for swine*)

ghiandàia *f* (orn) jay

ghiàndola *f* gland

ghibelli·no -na *adj* & *m* Ghibelline

ghièra *f* ferrule; ring

ghigliottina *f* guillotine; a ghigliottina sash (*window*)

ghigliottinare *tr* to guillotine

ghigna *f* (coll) grimace

ghignare *intr* to grimace; to sneer

ghigno *m* sneer, smirk; grin

ghinèa *f* guinea

ghìngheri *m invar*—in ghìngheri dressed up

ghiòt·to -ta *adj* fond; gluttonous; eager; dainty (*food*) || *f* (culin) dripping pan

ghiottó·ne -na *mf* glutton; (zool) glutton, wolverine

ghiottonerìa *f* gluttony; tidbit; (fig) rarity

ghiòzzo [ddzz] *m* dolt; (ichth) gudgeon

ghirba *f* jar; (coll) skin, life

ghiribìzzo [ddzz] *m* (coll) whim, caprice

ghirigòro *m* doodle, curlicue

ghirlanda *f* garland, wreath

ghiro *m* dormouse; dormire come un ghiro to sleep like a log

ghisa *f* cast iron

già *adv* already; once upon a time; formerly || *interj* indeed!

giac·ca *f* (-che) jacket, coat; giacca a due petti double-breasted coat; giacca a vento windbreaker

giacché *conj* since

giacènte *adj* lying; idle (*capital*); unclaimed (*letter*); in abeyance

giacènza *f* lying; stay, abeyance; giacenze di capitali idle capital; giacenze di magazzino unsold stock of merchandise

giacére §181 *intr* (ESSERE) to lie; to be in abeyance; (lit) to be prostrate

giacì·glio *m* (-gli) pallet, cot

giacimento *m* field, bed; giacimento petrolifero oil field

giacinto *m* hyacinth

Giàcomo *m* James

giaculatòria *f* ejaculation (*prayer*); litany (*monotonous account*); curse

giada *f* jade

giaggiòlo *m* (bot) iris

giaguaro *m* jaguar

giaiétto *m* jet (*black coal*)

gialappa *f* (pharm) jalap

gialla·stro -stra *adj* yellowish

gial·lo -la *adj* yellow; detective (*book or picture*); white (*with fear*) || *m* yellow; detective story, whodunit; suspense movie; giallo dell'uovo egg yolk

giamaica·no -na *adj* & *mf* Jamaican

giàmbi·co -ca *adj* (-ci -che) iambic

giambo *m* iamb

giammài *adv* never

giansenismo *m* Jansenism

Giappóne, il Japan

giapponése [s] *adj* & *mf* Japanese

giara *f* crock, jar

giardinàg·gio *m* (-gi) gardening

giardinétta *f* station wagon

giardiniè·re -ra *mf* gardener || *f* jardiniere; mixed pickles; mixed salad; wagonette; station wagon

giardino *m* garden; giardino d'infanzia kindergarten; giardino pensile roof garden; giardino zoologico zoological garden

giarrettièra *f* garter

Giasóne *m* Jason

giavanése [s] *adj* & *mf* Javanese

giavellòtto *m* javelin

gibbó·so -sa [s] *adj* gibbous, humped, humpbacked; rough (*ground*)

gibèrna *f* cartridge box; cartridge belt

gi·bus *m* (-bus) opera hat

gi·ga *f* (-ghe) gigue, jig

gigante *adj* & *m* giant

giganté·sco -sca *adj* (-schi -sche) gigantic

gigantéssa *f* giantess

gigióne *m* ham actor

gì·glio *m* (-gli) Madonna lily; fleur-de-lys

gilda *f* guild

gi·lè *f* (-lè) vest, waistcoat

gimnòto *m* electric eel

ginecologìa *f* gynecology

ginecòlo·go -ga *mf* (-gi -ghe) gynecologist

gine·pràio *m* (-prài) juniper thicket; (fig) mess

ginépro *m* juniper

ginèstra *f* (bot) Spanish broom

Ginèvra *f* Geneva

ginevri·no -na *adj* & *mf* Genevan

gingillare *ref* to trifle; to idle

gingillo *m* trifle, bauble

ginna·sio *m* (-si) secondary school; gymnasium

ginna·sta *mf* (-sti -ste) gymnast

ginnàsti·co -ca (-ci -che) *adj* gymnastic || *f* gymnastics; ginnastica a corpo libero or ginnastica da camera calisthenics

ginni·co -ca *adj* (-ci -che) gymnastic

ginocchiata *f* blow with the knee; blow on the knee

ginocchièra *f* kneepad; elastic bandage (*for knee*); kneepiece (*of armor*)

ginòc·chio *m* (-chi) knee; avere il ginocchio valgo to be bowlegged; avere il ginocchio varo to be knockkneed; in ginocchio on one's knees

|| *m* (-chia *fpl*) knee; fino alle ginocchia knee-deep; gettarsi alle ginocchia di to go down on one's knees to; mettere qlcu in ginocchio to bring s.o. to his knees

ginocchióni *adv* on one's knees

giocare §182 *tr* to play; to stake, bet, risk, gamble; to make a fool of || *intr* to play; to gamble; to circulate (*said of air*); (fig) to play a role; giocare a to play; to wager; giocare a mosca cieca to play blindman's buff; giocare con to risk; giocare d'armi to fence; giocare d'azzardo to gamble; giocare di to use (*e.g., one's wits*); giocare di gomiti to elbow one's way; giocare di mano to steal; giocare sulle parole to play on words; to pun || *ref* to risk (*e.g., one's life*); to gamble away

giocata *f* wager, stake; game, play

gioca·tóre -trice *mf* player; gambler; speculator

giocàttolo *m* toy, plaything

giocherellare (giocherèllo) *intr* to play, trifle

giochétto *m* children's game; child's play; dirty trick

giò·co *m* (-chi) game; gambling; play; wager, stake; set; joke; (cards) hand; entrare in gioco to come into play; fare gioco a to come in handy to; fare il doppio gioco to be guilty of duplicity; fare il gioco di to play into the hands of; giochi di equilibrio balancing act; gioco da ragazzi child's play; gioco d'azzardo gambling; game of chance; gioco del bussolotti (fig) jugglery; gioco di destrezza game of skill; gioco di parole play on words, pun; gioco di prestigio sleight of hand; gioco di società parlor game; metter in gioco to risk; to stake; per gioco for fun; prendersi gioco di to make fun of

giocofòrza *m*—è giocoforza + *inf* it is necessary + *inf*

giocolière *m* juggler

giocón·do -da *adj* merry, joyful

giocó·so -sa [s] *adj* jocose, jolly

giogàia *f* dewlap; chain of mountains

gió·go *m* (-ghi) yoke; beam (*of balance*); rounded peak; pass

giòia *f* joy, happiness; darling; jewel; darsi alla pazza gioia to have a wild time

gioiellerìa *f* jewelry; jewelry store

gioiellière *m* jeweler

gioièllo *m* jewel

gioió·so -sa [s] *adj* joyful

gioire §176 (*pres part* missing) *intr* to rejoice

Giòna *m* Jonas

Giordània, la Jordan (*country*)

giorda·no -na *adj* & *mf* Jordanian || Giordano *m* Jordan (*river*)

Giórgio *m* George

giorna·làio -làia *mf* (-lài -làie) newsdealer

giornale *m* newspaper; magazine; (com) journal; giornale di bordo log, logbook; giornale murale poster; giornale radio newscast

giornaliè·ro -ra *adj* daily ‖ *mf* day laborer

giornalismo *m* journalism

giornali·sta *mf* (**-sti -ste**) journalist; **giornalista pubblicista** free-lance writer ‖ *m* newspaperman ‖ *f* newspaperwoman

giornalménte *adv* daily

giornata *f* day; day's work; birthday; pay, salary; battle; day's march; **giornata campale** pitched battle; **giornata della mamma** Mother's Day; **giornata lavorativa** workday; **vivere alla giornata** to live from hand to mouth

giórno *m* day; **a giorni** within the next few days; **a giorni . . . a giorni** some days . . . others; **a giorno** open, open-work (*needlework*); full (*light*); **ai giorni nostri** nowadays; **al giorno d'oggi** nowadays; **buon giorno** good day; good morning; good-bye; **dare gli otto giorni a** to dismiss, fire; **di ogni giorno** everyday (*e.g., clothes*); **essere a giorno** to be up to date; **giorno dei morti** All Souls' Day; **giorno di lavoro** workday; **giorno di paga** payday; **giorno fatto** broad daylight; **giorno feriale** weekday; **giorno festivo** holiday; **mettere a giorno** to bring up to date; **otto giorni oggi** one week from today; **passare un brutto giorno** to have a bad time; **un giorno o l'altro** one of these days

giòstra *f* joust; merry-go-round

giostrare (**giòstro**) *intr* to joust; to get along, manage; to idle, loiter

Giosuè *m* Joshua

Giotté·sco -sca *adj* (**-schi -sche**) of the school of Giotto

giovaménto *m* benefit, advantage

gióvane *adj* young; youthful; fresh (*e.g., cheese*); Younger, e.g., **Plinio il Giovane** Pliny the Younger ‖ *m* young man; boy, apprentice; **i giovani** the young ‖ *f* young woman

giovanile *adj* youthful

Giovanni *m* John; **Giovanni Battista** John the Baptist

giovanòtta *f* young woman

giovanòtto *m* young man; (*coll*) bachelor

giovare (**gióvo**) *tr* (lit) to help ‖ *intr* (with *dat*) to help, to be of use to ‖ *ref* to avail oneself ‖ *impers* (ESSERE) —**non giova** it's no use

Giòve *m* Jupiter

giove·dì *m* (**-dì**) Thursday; **giovedì santo** Maundy Thursday

giovèn·ca *f* (**-che**) heifer

gioventù *f* youth

giovévole *adj* helpful, beneficial

gioviale *adj* jovial

giovinézza *f* youth

gip *f* (**gip**) jeep

gippóne *m* large jeep, panel truck

giràbile *adj* endorsable

giradi·schi *m* (**-schi**) record player

giradito *m* (pathol) felon

giraffa *f* giraffe; (mov, telv) boom, crane

girafilièra *f* diestock

giramà·schio *m* (**-schi**) tap wrench

giraménto *m*—**giramento di testa** vertigo, dizziness

giramón·do *m* (**-do**) globetrotter

giràndola *f* girandole; pinwheel; (fig) weathercock

girandolare (**giràndolo**) *intr* to stroll, saunter

girante *mf* endorser ‖ *f* blade (*e.g., of fan*)

girare *tr* to turn; to tour; to go around, travel over; to switch (*the conversation*); to film, shoot; to transfer (*a phone call*); to endorse; (mil) to surround ‖ *intr* to turn; to circulate; to spin (*said of one's head*) ‖ *ref* to turn; to toss and turn

girarròsto *m* turnspit; **girarrosto a motore** rotisserie

girasóle *m* sunflower

girata *f* turn; walk, ramble; (com) endorsement; (cards) deal; (coll) tongue-lashing

giratà·rio -ria *mf* (**-ri -rie**) endorsee

giravòlta *f* turn, pirouette; bend; sudden change of mind

girellare (**girèllo**) *intr* to stroll, wander around

girèllo *m* rump; go-cart, walker

girévole *adj* revolving

girino *m* tadpole; bicycle rider competing on the Tour of Italy

giro *m* periphery; turn, revolution; ride; size (*of hat*); edge (*of glass*); round (*of a doctor*); (sports) tour; (sports) lap; (com) transfer; (cards) hand; (theat) tour; **a giro di posta** by return mail; **andare in giro** to poke along; **giro collo** neckline; **giro d'affari** volume of business, turnover; **giro di parole** circumlocution; **fare il giro di** to tour; **mettere in giro** to spread (*news, gossip*); **nel giro di** within (*a period*); **prendere in giro** to poke fun at

girobùssola *f* gyrocompass

girondolare (**giróndolo**) *intr* var of girandolare

giróne *m* (sports) conference; (sports) division; (sports) league; (archaic) circle

gironzolare [dz] (**girónzolo**) *intr* to stroll, saunter

giropilò·ta *m* (**-ti**) gyropilot

giroscò·pio *m* (**-pi**) gyroscope

girotóndo *m* ring-around-a-rosy

giròtta *f* weather vane

girovagare §209 (**giròvago**) *intr* to roam, wander

giròva·go -ga (**-ghi -ghe**) *adj* wandering; strolling (*player*) ‖ *m* vagrant, hobo

gita *f* trip, excursion, outing

gita·no -na *adj & mf* Gypsy

gitante *mf* excursionist, vacationist

gittata *f* range (*of gun*)

giù *adv* down; **andar giù** to go down; to deteriorate; to get worse; **buttar giù** to throw down; (culin) to start to cook, e.g., **buttar giù gli spaghetti** to start to cook the spaghetti; (fig) to jot down; **da . . . in giù** for the past . . . ; **dar giù** to look worse (*said* *of a sick person*); **esser giù** to be downcast; **giù di lì** thereabouts; **in giù** down; downstream; **mandar giù** to swallow; **non andar giù** to not be able to stomach or swallow, e.g., **non gli vanno giù i bugiardi** he cannot stomach liars; **venire giù** to come down; to crumble; to collapse

giubba *f* coat, jacket; mane

giubbétto *m* small coat; bodice; jerkin

giubbòtto *m* jacket (*e.g., of a motorcyclist*); **giubbotto salvagente** (aer, naut) life jacket

giubilare (**giùbilo**) *tr* to retire, to pension || *intr* to rejoice

giubilèo *m* jubilee

giùbilo *m* jubilation, exultation

giuda *m* Judas || **Giuda** *m* Judas

giudài·co **-ca** *adj* (**-ci -che**) Judaic

giudaismo *m* Judaism

giudè·o **-a** *adj* Judean; Jewish || *mf* Judean; Jew

giudicare §197 (**giùdico**) *tr* to judge; to find (*e.g., s.o. innocent*); to try (*a case*) || *intr* to judge, deem

giudicato *m* (hist) Sardinian region; **passare in giudicato** (law) to become final

giùdice *m* judge; magistrate, justice; **giudice conciliatore** justice of the peace; **giudice popolare** member of the jury

giudizià·rio **-ria** *adj* (**-ri -rie**) judicial, judiciary

giudì·zio *m* (**-zi**) judgment; wisdom; trial; sentence; **giudizio di Dio** (hist) ordeal; **giudizio finale** Last Judgment; **metter giudizio** to mend one's ways

giudizió·so **-sa** [s] *adj* judicious, wise

giùggiola *f* jujube; (joc) trifle; **andare in brodo di giuggiole** to swoon, become ecstatic

giugno *m* June

giugulare *adj* jugular || *v* (**giùgolo**) *tr* to cut the throat of

giulèbbe *m* julep

giuliana *f* (culin) julienne || **Giuliana** *f* Juliana

giuli·vo **-va** *adj* gay

giullare *m* jongleur; (pej) mountebank

giumén·to **-ta** *mf* beast of burden || *f* female saddle horse

giun·ca *f* (**-che**) (naut) junk

giunchìglia *f* (bot) jonquil

giun·co *m* (**-chi**) (bot) rush

giùngere §183 *tr* to join (*e.g., one's hands*) || *intr* (ESSERE) to arrive; **giungere a** or **in** to arrive at, reach; **giungere a** + *inf* to succeed in + *ger*; **mi giunge nuovo** it's news to me

giungla *f* jungle

Giunóne *f* Juno

giunòni·co **-ca** *adj* (**-ci -che**) Junoesque

giunta *f* addition; makeweight; strip (*of cloth*); junta; committee; **di prima giunta** at the very beginning; **per giunta** in addition

giuntare *tr* to join

giuntatrice *f* (mov) splicer

giunto *m* (mach) joint, coupling;

giunto a sfere ball-and-socket joint; **giunto cardanico** universal joint

giuntura or **giunzióne** *f* joint; juncture, seam

giuò·co *m* (**-chi**) var of **gioco**

giuraménto *m* oath; **deferire il giuramento a** to put under oath

giurare *tr* to swear, pledge || *intr* to swear

giura·to **-ta** *adj* sworn || *m* juror

giurìa *f* committee; jury

giurìdi·co **-ca** *adj* (**-ci -che**) juridical

giurisdizióne *f* jurisdiction

giurisprudènza *f* jurisprudence

giurì·sta *mf* (**-sti -ste**) jurist

Giusèppe *m* Joseph

Giuseppina *f* Josephine

giusta *prep* according to; in accordance with

giustappórre §218 *tr* to juxtapose

giustézza *f* correctness, justness; (typ) measure

giustificàbile *adj* justifiable

giustificare §197 (**giustìfico**) *tr* to justify || *ref* to excuse oneself

giustificazióne *f* justification

giustizia *f* justice; **far giustizia a** to execute; **farsi giustizia da sé** to take the law into one's own hands; **render giustizia a** to do justice to

giustiziare §287 *tr* to execute

giustizière *m* executioner; (obs) judge

giu·sto **-sta** *adj* just; opportune || *m* just man; just price; rights, due || *giusto adv* just, justly

gla·bro **-bra** *adj* smooth (*face*)

glaciale *adj* glacial; (fig) icy

gladiatore *m* gladiator

gladiòlo *m* gladiolus

glàndola *f* var of **ghiandola**

glassa *f* glaze, icing

glassare *tr* to glaze, ice

glèba *f* clod, lump of earth

gli §4 *art* || §5 *pers pron*

glicerina *f* glycerin

glìcine *m* wistaria

gliéla; gliéle; gliéli; gliélo; gliéne §5

globale *adj* total, aggregate

glòbo *m* globe; **globo oculare** eyeball

globulare *adj* globular, global

glòbulo *m* globule; (physiol) corpuscle

gloglottare (**gloglòtto**) *intr* to gobble; to gurgle

gloglottì·o *m* (**-i**) gobble, gobbling; gurgle

glòria *f* glory

gloriare §287 (**glòrio**) *tr* (lit) to exalt || *ref* to boast; to glory

glorificare §197 (**glorìfico**) *tr* to glorify

glorió·so **-sa** [s] *adj* glorious; proud

glòssa *f* gloss

glossà·rio *m* (**-ri**) glossary

glòttide *f* glottis

glottòlo·go **-ga** *mf* (**-gi -ghe**) linguist

glucòsio *m* glucose

glùtine *m* gluten

gnòc·co *m* (**-chi**) potato dumpling

gnòmo *m* gnome

gnòrri *m invar*—**fare lo gnorri** to feign ignorance

gòb·bo **-ba** *adj* hunchbacked || *mf*

hunchback ‖ *f* hump; hunch; hump (*of gibbous moon*); hook (*of nose*)

góc·cia *f* (-ce) drop; bead; **avere la goccia al naso** to have a runny nose; **goccia d'acqua** raindrop

góc·cio *m* (-ci) drop, swallow

gócciola *f* drop; bead

gocciolare (**gócciolo**) *tr* & *intr* to drip

gocciola·tóio *m* (-tói) dripstone

gocciolì·o *m* (-i) drip, trickle

godére §184 *tr* to enjoy ‖ *intr* to take pleasure; to revel; to profit ‖ *ref* to enjoy; **godersela** to have a good time

godìbile *adj* enjoyable

godiménto *m* enjoyment, pleasure

goffàggine *f* clumsiness

gòf·fo -fa *adj* awkward; ill-fitting

gógna *f* pillory; **mettere alla gogna** to pillory

góla *f* throat; neck; gluttony; gorge (*of mountain*); mouth (*of cannon*); flue (*of chimney*); (archit) ogee; **far gola a** to tempt; **mentire per la gola** to lie shamelessly; **tornare a gola** to repeat (*said of food*)

golétta *f* neck (*of shirt*); (naut) schooner

gòlf *m* (**gòlf**) sweater, cardigan; (sports) golf

gólfo *m* gulf; **golfo mistico** orchestra pit ‖ **Golfo Persico** Persian Gulf

Gòlgota, il Golgotha

goliardo *m* goliard; university student

golosi·tà [s] *f* (-tà) gluttony; tidbit

goló·so -sa [s] *adj* gluttonous; appetizing

gómena *f* hawser

gomitata *f* blow with the elbow; nudge

gómito *m* elbow; bend; **alzare il gomito** to crook the elbow; **dare di gomito a** to nudge

gomìtolo *m* skein, clew

gómma *f* gum; rubber; eraser; tire; **bucare una gomma** to have a flat tire; **gomma arabica** gum arabic; **gomma a terra** flat tire; **gomma da masticare** chewing gum; **gomma lacca** shellac

gommapiuma *f* foam rubber

gomma·to -ta *adj* gummed; with tires

gommatura *f* gumming; (aut) tires

gommi·sta *m* (-sti) tire dealer; tire repairman

gommó·so -sa [s] *adj* gummy

góndola *f* gondola; (aer) pod

gonfalóne *m* gonfalon

gonfiare §287 (**gónfio**) *tr* to inflate, blow up; to bloat; to swell; to exaggerate; to puff up ‖ *intr* (ESSERE) to swell ‖ *ref* to swell; to puff up; to bulge, balloon

gonfiatura *f* inflation; exaggeration

gonfiézza *f* swelling; grandiloquence

gón·fio -fia (-fi -fie) *adj* inflated, swollen; conceited ‖ *m* swelling, bulge

gonfióre *m* swelling

gongolare (**góngolo**) *intr* to rejoice; to be elated

goniòmetro *m* goniometer; protractor

gònna *f* skirt; **gonna pantaloni** culottes

gonnèlla *f* skirt; (fig) petticoat

gonnellino *m* kilt; ballerina skirt

gón·zo -za [dz] *mf* simpleton, fool

gòra *f* millpond; marsh; (coll) spot

górbia *f* tip (*of umbrella*)

gorgheggiare §290 (**gorghéggio**) *tr* & *intr* to warble; to trill

gorghég·gio *m* (-gi) warbling; trill

gór·go *m* (-ghi) whirlpool; (lit) river

gorgogliare §280 (**gorgóglio**) *intr* to gurgle

gorgó·glio *m* (-gli) gurgle

gorgoglì·o *m* (-i) gurgling

goril·la *m* (-la) gorilla

gòta *f* cheek; (lit) side

gòti·co -ca *adj* & *m* (-ci -che) Gothic

Gòto *m* Goth

gótta *f* (pathol) gout

gottazza *f* (naut) scoop

gottó·so -sa [s] *adj* gouty

governale *m* fin (*of bomb*); (obs) rudder

governante *adj* governing ‖ *m* ruler ‖ *f* governess; housekeeper

governare (**govèrno**) *tr* to rule, govern; to steer (*a ship*); to tend (*animals*); to wash and dry (*dishes*); to run (*e.g., a bank*) ‖ *intr* to steer

governatì·vo -va *adj* government

govèrno *m* government; tending (*e.g., of animals*); running (*of household*); cleaning (*of house*); blending (*of wine*); (archaic) steering

gózzo *m* crop, craw (*of bird*); (pathol) goiter

gozzovigliare §280 *intr* to go on a spree

gracchiare §287 *intr* to caw

gràc·chio *m* (-chi) caw; (orn) chough

gracidare (**gràcido**) *intr* to croak; to honk (*said, e.g., of a goose*)

gràcile *adj* weak, frail; thin, delicate

gradasso *m* swaggerer; braggadocio

grada·to -ta *adj* graded; gradual

gradazióne *f* gradation; alcoholic proof; **gradazione vocalica** (phonet) ablaut

gradévole *adj* pleasant

gradiménto *m* pleasure; acceptance (*of a product*); liking

gradinata *f* steps; tier (*of seats*)

gradino *m* step; (fig) stepping stone

gradire §176 *tr* to like; to welcome

gradi·to -ta *adj* agreeable; welcome (*guest*); kind (*letter*)

grado *m* degree; rank; (nav) rating; (archaic) step; **a buon grado o a mal grado** willy-nilly; **a grado a grado** little by little; **a grado** according to your wishes; **di buon grado** willingly; **di secondo grado** secondary (*school*); **essere in grado di** to be in a position to; **saper grado a** (lit) to be grateful to

graduale *adj* & *m* gradual

graduare (**gràduo**) *tr* to graduate

gradua·to -ta *adj* graduated ‖ *m* noncommissioned officer

graduatòria *f* ranking; rank

graffa *f* clamp; brace, bracket

graffiare §287 *tr* to scratch; (coll) to swipe

graffiétto *m* tiny scratch; marking gage

gràf·fio *m* (-fi) scratch

grafìa *f* writing, spelling; (gram) graph

gràfi·co -ca (-ci -che) adj graphic || m graph, diagram; designer (for printing industry); member of printers' union || f graphic arts

grafite f graphite

grafologia f graphology

gragnòla f hail

gramàglia f crepe; widow's weeds; in gramaglie in mourning

gramigna f couch grass; weed

grammàti·co -ca (-ci -che) adj grammatical || m grammarian || f grammar

grammo m gram

grammofòni·co -ca adj (-ci -che) phonograph, recording

grammòfono m phonograph, record player

gra·mo -ma adj poor, sad; wretched, miserable; frail, sickly

gran adj apocopated form of grande, used before singular and plural nouns beginning with a consonant sound other than gn, pn, ps, impure s, x, and z

gra·na m (-na) Parmesan cheese || f (-ne) cochineal; grain (of wood, metal, etc); (slang) dough; (coll) trouble

granàglie fpl grain, cereals

gra·nàio m (-nài) granary, barn

granata adj invar & m garnet (color) || f pomegranate (fruit); garnet; broom; grenade

granatière m grenadier

granatina f grenadine

Gran Bretagna, la Great Britain

grancassa f bass drum

grancèvola f spider crab

gràn·chio m (-chi) crab; claw (of hammer); (coll) cramp; prendere un granchio to make a blunder

grandangolare adj wide-angle

grande adj big, large; great; tall; high (mass; voice); long (time); capital (letter); full (speed); grown-up || m grownup; grandeur; grandee; fare il grande to show off; i grandi the great; in grande on a large scale; lavishly

grandézza f size; enormity; greatness; quantity; in grandezza naturale life-size; grandezze ostentatiousness

grandezzó·so -sa [s] adj ostentatious

grandiloquènza f grandiloquence

grandinare (gràndino) tr (obs) to hail || intr to hail || impers (ESSERE & AVERE)—grandina it is hailing

grandinata f hailstorm

gràndine f hail

grandiosi·tà [s] f (-tà) grandeur, magnificence

grandió·so -sa [s] adj grandiose, grand

grandu·ca m (-chi) grand duke

granduchéssa f grand duchess

granèllo m grain, seed; speck

grànfia f clutch

granìco·lo -la adj grain, wheat

granire §176 tr to grain; to stipple; (mus) to make (the notes) clear-cut || intr to teethe

granita f sherbet, water ice

granito m granite

granitura f knurl, milled edge

grano m wheat; grain of wheat; grain; speck; grano duro durum wheat; grano saraceno buckwheat; grano turco corn

granturco m corn

granulare adj granular || v (grànulo) tr to granulate

granulatóre m crusher

grànulo m granule, pellet, bud

granuló·so -sa [s] adj granular; lumpy; gritty; friable, crumbly

grappa f eau de vie; clamp, brace

grappétta f staple; crampon

grappino m (naut) grapnel

gràppolo m bunch, cluster

grassàg·gio m (-gi) (aut) lubrication

grassatóre m highwayman

grassazióne f holdup

grassétto m boldface

grassézza f fatness; richness

gras·so -sa adj fat; rich; greasy; risqué || m fat, suet; grease; shortening

grassòc·cio -cia adj (-ci -ce) pudgy, plump

grata f grate, grating

gratèlla f strainer; sieve; broiler

grati·cia f (-ce) (theat) gridiron

grati·cio m (-ci) lattice, trellis

graticola f gridiron; grating; graticule

gratifi·ca f (-che) bonus

gratificare §197 (gratìfico) tr to give a bonus to; (fig) to pelt (with insults)

gratificazióne f bonus

gratis adv gratis, free, for nothing

gratitùdine f gratitude

gra·to -ta adj grateful, appreciative || f see grata

grattacapo m trouble, worry

grattacièlo m skyscraper

grattare tr to scratch; to scrape; to grate; (slang) to snitch || intr to scratch; to grate

grattùgia f grater

grattugiare §290 tr to grate

gratùi·to -ta adj gratuitous, free

gravame m burden; tax; (law) appeal; fare gravame a qlcu di qlco to impute s.th to s.o.

gravare tr to burden, oppress; (obs) to seize || intr (ESSERE & AVERE) to weigh; to lie; to be sorry, e.g., gli grava d'avermi disturbato he is sorry to have bothered me || ref—gravarsi di to take upon oneself

grave adj heavy; burdensome; grave, serious || m (phys) body; stare sul grave to put on airs

graveolènte adj stinking

gravézza f heaviness; burden; oppression; (obs) taxation

gravidanza f pregnancy

gràvi·do -da adj pregnant; fraught

gravi·tà f (-tà) gravity

gravitare (gràvito) intr to gravitate; to weigh, lie

gravitazióne f gravitation

gravó·so -sa [s] adj heavy; hard, burdensome; oppressive

gràzia f grace; pardon, mercy; delicacy; kindness; di grazia! please!;

essere nelle grazie di qlcu to be in s.o.'s good graces; fare grazia di qlco a qlcu to spare s.o. s.th; grazia di Dio abundance, bounty; grazie! thank you!; grazie tante! thanks a lot!; in grazia di thanks to; male grazie bad manners; per grazie as a favor; render grazia a to thank; saper grazia a to be thankful to

graziare §287 tr to pardon; graziare qlcu di qlco to grant s.th to s.o.

grazió·so -sa [s] adj graceful, pretty; gracious; (lit) free, gratuitous

Grècia, la Greece

grè·co -ca (-ci -che) adj & mf Greek || f fret, fretwork; bullion (on Italian general's hat); tunic

grega·rio -ria (-ri -rie) adj gregarious || m private; follower

grég·ge m (-gi or -ge fpl) flock, herd

grég·gio -gia (-gi -ge) adj coarse; raw, unrefined || m crude oil

gregoria·no -na adj Gregorian

grembiale m var of grembiule

grembiule m apron; frock; smock

grembiulino m pinafore

grèmbo m lap; womb; bosom

gremire §176 tr to crowd || ref to become crowded

gremi·to -ta adj overcrowded

gréppia f manger, crib

gréto m dry gravel bed of a river

grettézza f stinginess; narrow-mindedness

grét·to -ta adj stingy; narrow-minded

grève adj heavy; uncouth; (lit) grievous

gréz·zo -za [ddzz] adj raw, crude; coarse

gridare tr to cry out; to cry for (help); (coll) to scold || intr to cry out, shout

grido m cry (of animal) || m (grida fpl) cry; scream; shout; yell; fame; di grido famous; grido di guerra war cry; ultimo grido latest fashion

grifa·gno -gna adj rapacious, fierce

griffa f hobnail; (mov, phot) sprocket

grifo m snout (of pig); (pej) snoot; (lit) griffin

grifóne m vulture; (mythol) griffin

grigia·stro -stra adj grayish

grì·gio -gia -gia & m (-gi -gie) grey

grigiovérde adj invar olive-drab || m olive-drab uniform

grìglia f gridiron, broiler; grate, grille; (elec) grid (of vacuum tube)

grillare tr to grill, broil || intr to sizzle; to bubble (said of fermenting wine); to have a sudden whim

grillétto m trigger

grillo m cricket; whim, fancy

grimaldèllo m picklock

grìnfia f claw, clutch; grinfie clutches

grinta f grim or forbidding face

grinza f wrinkle; crease; non fare una grinza to be perfect

grinzó·so -sa [s] adj wrinkled; creased

grippare intr & ref to bind, jam

grisèlla f (naut) ratline

gri·sou m (-sou) firedamp

grissino m breadstick

Groenlàndia, la Greenland

grómma f incrustation, deposit

grónda f eaves; slope (of ground)

grondàia f gutter (of roof)

grondare (gróndo) tr to drip || intr (ESSERE) to ooze (said, e.g., of perspiration); to drip; grondare di sangue to stream with blood

gròppa f back (of animal); top (of mountain); restare sulla groppa a to be stuck with, e.g., gli sono restati sulla groppa cento esemplari he is stuck with one hundred copies

groppata f bucking (of horse)

gróppo m knot, tangle; lump (in throat); squall

groppóne m back, rump

gròssa f gross; dormire della grossa to sleep like a log

grossézza f bigness; thickness; density; swelling (of river); (fig) coarseness; grossezza d'udito hardness of hearing

grossi·sta mf (-sti -ste) wholesaler

gròs·so -sa adj big, large; thick; heavy (seas); swollen (river); hard (breathing); offensive (words); coarse (e.g., salt); pregnant; deep (voice); (coll) important; alla grossa approximately; di grosso a lot, very much; dirla grossa to talk nonsense; farla grossa to make a blunder; grosso d'udito hard of hearing; in grosso wholesale; sparare grosse to tell tall tales || m bulk; main body (e.g., of an army) || f see grossa

grossola·no -na adj coarse; boorish, uncouth; big (blunder)

gròtta f grotto; (coll) inn

grotté·sco -sca (-schi -sche) adj & m grotesque || f (hist) grotesque painting

grovièra f Gruyère cheese

grovì·glio m (-gli) tangle, snarl

gru f (gru) (orn, mach) crane

grùc·cia f (-ce) crutch; clothes hanger; (obs) wooden leg

grufolare (grùfolo) intr to nuzzle || ref to wallow (in mud)

grugnire §176 tr & intr to grunt

grugnito m grunt

grugno m snout; (pej) snoot; fare il grugno to sulk

grui·sta m (-sti) crane operator

grullerìa f foolishness

grul·lo -la adj silly, simple

gruma f deposit, incrustation

grumo m lump; clot

grùmolo m heart (e.g., of lettuce); small lump

grumó·so -sa [s] adj lumpy; incrusted, scaly

gruppo m group; main body (e.g., of runners); club; gruppo elettrogeno generating unit; gruppo motore (aut) power plant

gruzzolo m hoard, pile; farsi il gruzzolo to feather one's nest

guadagnare intr to earn; to win; to gain; to pick up (speed); to reach (port) || intr to win; to look better || ref to win; to win over; guadagnarsi il pane or la vita to earn one's living

guadagno m earnings; profit; a basso

guadagno (rad, telv) low-gain; **ad alto guadagno** (rad, telv) high-gain
guadare tr to wade, ford
guado m ford; (bot) woad; **passare a guado** to ford
guài interj woe!
guaina f case; scabbard, sheath; corset; (aut) seat cover
guàio m (**guài**) trouble || interj see **guài**
guaire §176 intr to yelp; to whine
guaito m yelp, whine
gualcire §176 tr to crumple
gualdrappa f saddlecloth
Gualtièro m Walter
guàn·cia f (-ce) cheek; moldboard; cheek side (of gunstock)
guanciale m pillow; **dormire tra due guanciali** to sleep safe and sound
guan·tàio -tàia mf (-tài -tàie) glove maker; glove merchant
guanterìa f glove factory
guantièra f glove case; tray
guanto m glove; **gettare il guanto** to fling down the gauntlet; **raccogliere il guanto** to take up the gauntlet; **trattare con i guanti gialli** to handle with kid gloves
guantóne m big glove; **guantoni da pugilato** boxing gloves
guardabarrière m (-re) (rr) gatekeeper, crossing watchman
guardabò·schi m (-schi) forester
guardacàc·cia m (-cia) gamekeeper
guardacò·ste m (-ste) coast guard; coast-guard cutter
guardafi·lì m (-li) (elec) lineman
guardali·nee m (-nee) (rr) trackwalker; (sports) linesman
guardama·no m (-no) guard (of sabre or rifle); work glove; (naut) handrail
guardaportò·ne m (-ne) doorman
guardare tr to look at; to protect, watch; to pay attention to; to face, overlook; (obs) to keep to (one's bed); (obs) to keep (a holiday); **guardare a vista** to keep under close watch; **guardare dall'alto in basso** to look down one's nose at; **guardare di sotto in su** to leer at || intr to look; to pay attention; **Dio guardi!** God forbid!; **guardare a** to face (said, e.g., of a room); **guardare di non + inf** to be careful not to + inf; **guardare in faccia** to face (e.g., danger); **stare a guardare** to keep on the sidelines || ref to look at one another; to look at oneself; **guardarsi da** to keep from; to guard against
guardarò·ba m (-ba) wardrobe; linen closet; checkroom, cloakroom
guardarobiè·re -ra mf checkroom attendant || f hatcheck girl
guardasigil·lì m (-li) minister of justice (in Italy); (Brit) Lord Privy Seal; (U.S.A.) attorney general; (hist) keeper of the seals
guardaspal·le m (-le) bodyguard
guardata f quick look, glance
guarda·vìa m (-vìa) guardrail; median strip
guàrdia f watch; guard; top water level; flyleaf; **di guardia** on duty;

fare la guardia a to watch; **guardia campestre** forester; **guardia carceraria** prison guard; **guardia del corpo** guard, body guard; **guardia di finanza** customs officer; **guardia d'onore** honor guard; **guardia forestale** forester; park guard; **guardia giurata** private policeman; **guardia medica** emergency clinic; **guardia municipale** police officer; **guardia notturna** night watch; **mettere qlcu in guardia** to warn s.o.; **montare la guardia** to be on guard duty, keep guard; **stare in guardia** to be on one's guard
guardiamari·na m (-na) (nav) ensign
guardiano m keeper; warden; watchdog; (eccl) superior; **guardiano notturno** night watchman
guardìna f lockup; **in guardìna** in jail
guardinfante m bustle (worn under the back of a woman's skirt)
guardin·go -ga adj (-ghi -ghe) wary
guàrdolo m welt (in shoe)
guardóne m peeping tom
guarenti·gìa f (-gìe) guarantee
guarìbile adj curable
guarigióne f cure, recovery
guarire §176 tr to cure; to heal || intr (ESSERE) to recover; to heal
guaritóre m healer; quack
guarnigióne f (mil) garrison
guarnire §176 tr to equip; to rig; to trim; (naut) to rig; (culin) to garnish || intr to add beauty
guarnizióne f decoration; trimming; lining; (culin) garniture; (mach) gasket; (mach) washer
Guascógna, la Gascony
guascó·ne -na adj & mf Gascon
guastafè·ste mf (-ste) kill-joy
guastare tr to ruin, spoil; to undo; to wreck; (obs) to lay waste; **guastare le uova nel paniere a** to spoil the plans of || ref to spoil; to worsen (said, e.g., of the weather); (mach) to break down; **guastarsi con qlcu** to quarrel with s.o.; **guastarsi il sangue** to blow one's top
guastatóre m commando
gua·sto -sta adj ruined, spoiled; wrecked || m breakdown; corruption; discord
guatare tr (lit) to look askance or with fear at
Guayana, la Guyana
guazza f dew
guazzabù·glio m (-gli) muddle, mess
guazzare tr to make (an animal) wade in a river || intr to wallow
guazzétto m stew, ragout
guazzo m puddle, pool; gouache
guèl·fo -fa adj & mf Guelph
guèr·cio -cia (-ci -ce) adj cross-eyed; one-eyed; almost blind || mf cross-eyed person; one-eyed person
guèrra f war; warfare; **guerra a coltello** internecine feud; **guerra di Troia** Trojan war; **guerra fredda** cold war; **guerra lampo** blitzkrieg; **guerra mondiale** world war

guerrafon·dàio -dàia (-dài -dàie) *adj* warmongering || *mf* warmonger

guerreggiare §290 (guerréggio) *tr* to fight, war against || *intr* to fight || *ref* to make war on one another

guerré·sco -sca *adj* (-schi -sche) warlike

guerriè·ro -ra *adj* war, warlike || *mf* fighter || *m* warrior

guerrìglia *f* guerrilla

guerriglièro *m* guerrilla (*soldier*)

gufo *m* misanthrope; (orn) horned owl

gùglia *f* spire; peak

gugliata *f* needleful

Guglièlmo *m* William

guida *f* guide; guidance; driving; runner (*rug*); guidebook; manual (*of instruction*); (aut) steering; guida a destra right-hand drive; guide reins (*of horse*); (mach) slide

guidaiòlo *m* leader (*among animals*)

guidare *tr* to guide, lead; to steer; to drive || *intr* to drive || *ref* to restrain oneself

guida·tóre -trice *mf* driver

guiderdóne *m* (lit) premium, prize

guidóne *m* pennant, pennon

guidoslitta *f* bobsled

guidovìa *f* ski lift

Guinèa, la Guinea

guinzà·glio *m* (-gli) leash; (fig) fetter, shackle

guisa *f* way, manner; in guisa che so that; in guisa di under the guise of

guit·to -ta *adj* miserly, niggardly || *m* strolling player

guizzare *intr* to dart; to wriggle; to flash (*said of lightning*); (naut) to yaw || *intr* (ESSERE) to slip away

guizzo *m* dart; wriggle; flash

gù·scio *m* (-sci) shell; pod (*of pea*); tick (*of mattress*); guscio di noce nutshell; guscio d'uovo eggshell

gustare *tr* to taste; to relish || *intr* (ESSERE & AVERE) to please; to like, e.g., gli gustano le gite in barca he likes boat rides

gusto *m* taste; pleasure; fun; whim; style; di cattivo gusto tasteless; di gusto gladly, with gusto; prendere gusto per to take a liking for; prendersi il gusto di to relish; provar gusto to have fun

gustó·so -sa [s] *adj* tasty

guttapèrca *f* gutta-percha

gutturale *adj & f* guttural

H

H, h ['ɑkkɑ] *m & f* eighth letter of the Italian alphabet

handicappare *tr* var of andicappare

hangar *m* (hangar) hangar

havaia·no -na *adj & mf* Hawaiian

henné *m* henna

hertz *m* hertz

hertzia·no -na *adj* Hertzian

hi-fi *f* (coll) hi-fi

hockei·sta *m* (-sti) hockey player

hollywoodia·no -na *adj* Hollywood, Hollywood-like

hurrà *interj* hurrah!

I

I, i, [i] *m & f* ninth letter of the Italian alphabet

i §4 *def art* the

iarda *f* yard

iattanza *f* boasting, bragging

iattura *f* misfortune, calamity

ibèri·co -ca *adj* (-ci -che) Iberian

ibernare (ibèrno) *intr* to hibernate

ibi·sco *m* (-schi) hibiscus

ibridare (ìbrido) *tr & intr* to hybridize

ìbri·do -da *adj & m* hybrid

icàsti·co -ca *adj* (-ci -che) figurative; realistic

-ìccio -ìccia *suf adj* -ish, e.g., giallìccio yellowish

iconocla·sta *mf* (-sti -ste) iconoclast

iconografìa *f* iconography

iconoscò·pio *m* (-pi) iconoscope

iddì·o *m* (-i) god || Iddìo *m* God

idèa *f* idea; goal, purpose; bit; touch; avere idea di to have a mind to; dare l'idea di to seem; farsi un'idea di to grasp the notion of; idea fissa fixed idea; neanche per idea not in the least

ideale *adj & m* ideal

idealismo *m* idealism

ideali·sta *mf* (-sti -ste) idealist

idealìsti·co -ca *adj* (-ci -che) idealistic

idealizzare [ddzz] *tr* to idealize

ideare (idèo) *tr* to conceive

idea·tóre -trice *mf* inventor

idem *adv* ditto

idènti·co -ca *adj* (-ci -che) identical

identificare §197 (identìfico) *tr* to identify || *ref* to resemble each other; identificarsi con to identify with

identificazióne *f* identification

identi·tà *f* (-tà) identity

ideologìa *f* ideology

idi *mpl & fpl* ides

idillìa·co -ca *adj* (-ci -che) idyllic

idìl·lio *m* (-li) idyll; romance

idiò·ma *m* (-mi) language, idiom

idiomàti·co -ca *adj* (-ci -che) idiomatic

idiosincrasìa f aversion; (med) idiosyncrasy
idiò·ta (-ti -te) adj idiotic ‖ mf idiot
idiotismo m idiom; idiocy
idiozìa f idiocy
idolatrare tr & intr to idolize
idolatrìa f idolatry
ìdolo m idol
idonei·tà f (-tà) fitness, aptitude; qualification
idòne·o -a adj fit; qualified; opportune
idra f hydra
idrante m hydrant, fireplug
idratante adj moisturizing
idratare tr & ref to hydrate
idrato m hydrate
idràuli·co -ca (-ci -che) adj hydraulic ‖ m plumber ‖ f hydraulics
ìdri·co -ca adj (-ci -che) water, e.g., **forza idrica** water power
idrocarburo m hydrocarbon
idroelèttri·co -ca adj (-ci -che) hydroelectric
idròfi·lo -la adj absorbent
idrofobìa f hydrophobia, rabies
idròfo·bo -ba adj hydrophobic, rabid
idròfu·go -ga adj (-ghi -ghe) waterproof
idrogenare (idrògeno) tr to hydrogenate
idrògeno m hydrogen
idròpi·co -ca (-ci -che) adj dropsical ‖ mf patient suffering from dropsy
idropisìa f dropsy
idroplano m hydroplane (boat)
idropòrto m seaplane airport
idrorepellènte adj water-repellent
idroscalo m seaplane airport
idro·scì m (-scì) water ski
idroscivolante m (naut) hydroplane
idrosilurante m torpedo plane
idròssido m hydroxide
idroterapìa f hydrotherapy
idrovìa f inland waterway
idrovolante m seaplane, hydroplane
idròvo·ro -ra adj suction (pump) ‖ f suction pump
ièna f hyena
ièri m & adv yesterday; **ieri l'altro** the day before yesterday; **ieri notte** last night; **ieri sera** last evening, last night, yesterday evening
ietta·tóre -trice mf hoodoo
iettatura f evil eye; bad luck, jinx
igiène f hygiene; sanitation
igièni·co -ca adj (-ci -che) hygienic, sanitary
igname m yam
igna·ro -ra adj unaware; inexperienced
igna·vo -va adj (lit) slothful
ignizióne f ignition
ignòbile adj (lit) ignoble
ignomìnia f ignominy; outrage
ignominió·so -sa [s] adj ignominious
ignorante adj ignorant; illiterate ‖ mf ignoramus
ignoranza f ignorance
ignorare (ignòro) tr to not know; to ignore
ignò·to -ta adj & m unknown
ignu·do -da adj (lit) naked ‖ m (lit) naked person
il §4 def art the
ìlare adj cheerful

ilari·tà f (-tà) cheerfulness; laughter
ìlice f (lit) ilex, holm oak
ìlio m (anat) ilium
illanguidire §176 tr to weaken ‖ intr (ESSERE) to get weak
illazióne f inference
illéci·to -ta adj illicit, unlawful ‖ m unlawful act
illegale adj illegal
illeggiadrire §176 tr to embellish
illeggìbile adj illegible
illegìtti·mo -ma adj illegitimate
illé·so -sa adj unhurt, unharmed
illettera·to -ta adj & mf illiterate
illibà·to -ta adj spotless, pure
illimita·to -ta adj unlimited
illìri·co -ca adj (-ci -che) Illyrian
illògi·co -ca adj (-ci -che) illogical
illùdere §105 tr to delude
illuminare (illùmino) tr to illuminate; to brighten; to enlighten ‖ ref to grow bright
illumina·to -ta adj illuminated; enlightened; educated
illuminazióne f illumination; enlightenment
illuminismo m Age of Enlightenment
illusióne f illusion; delusion; **farsi illusioni** to indulge in wishful thinking
illusionismo m sleight of hand; magic
illusioni·sta mf (-sti -ste) magician
illu·so -sa adj deluded ‖ mf deluded person
illusò·rio -ria adj (-ri -rie) illusory, illusive
illustrare tr to illustrate; to explain, elucidate ‖ ref to become famous
illustra·to -ta adj illustrated, pictorial
illustra·tóre -trice mf illustrator
illustrazióne f illustration; illustrious person
illustre adj illustrious, famous
illustrìssi·mo -ma adj distinguished; honorable; **Illustrissimo Signore** Dear Sir; Mr. (addressing a letter)
imbacuccare §197 tr & ref to muffle up; to wrap up
imbaldanzire §176 tr to embolden ‖ intr (ESSERE) & ref to grow bold
imballàg·gio m (-gi) wrapping, packaging
imballare tr to wrap up, package; to bale; to race (the motor); **imballare in una gabbia** to crate ‖ ref to race (said of a motor)
imballa·tóre -trice mf packer
imballo m packing; packaging, wrapping; racing (of motor)
imbalsamare (imbàlsamo) tr to embalm; to stuff (animals)
imbambola·to -ta adj gazing, staring; stunned, dumfounded; sleepy-eyed; sluggish
imbandierare (imbandièro) tr to bedeck with flags
imbandire §176 tr to prepare (food, a meal, a table) lavishly
imbarazzante adj embarrassing, awkward
imbarazzare tr to embarrass; to encumber, hamper; to upset (the stomach)

imbarazza·to -ta *adj* embarrassed, perplexed; upset (*stomach*); ill-at-ease

imbarazzo *m* embarrassment; annoyance; **imbarazzo di stomaco** upset stomach

imbarbari·re §176 *tr* & *ref* to make barbarous; to corrupt (*a language*)

imbarcadèro *m* landing pier

imbarcare §197 *tr* to ship; to load, embark; to ship (*water*) ‖ *ref* to sail; to embark; to curve (*said of furniture*)

imbarca·tóio *m* (**-tói**) landing pier

imbarcazióne *f* boat; **imbarcazione di salvataggio** lifeboat

imbar·co *m* (**-chi**) embarkation; port of embarkation

imbardare *intr* & *ref* (aer) to yaw; (aut) to swerve, lurch

imbardata *f* (aer) yaw; (aut) swerve, lurch

imbarilare *tr* to barrel

imbastardire §176 *tr* to corrupt ‖ *ref* to become corrupt

imbastire §176 *tr* (sew) to baste; (fig) to sketch out

imbastitura *f* (sew) basting

imbàttere *ref*—**imbattersi bene** to be lucky; **imbattersi in** to come across; **imbattersi male** to have bad luck

imbattibile *adj* unbeatable

imbavagliare §280 *tr* to gag

imbeccare §197 (**imbécco**) *tr* to feed (*a fledgling*); (fig) to prompt

imbeccata *f* beakful; (fig) prompting

imbecillàggine *f* imbecility

imbecille *adj* & *mf* imbecile

imbecilli·tà *f* (**-tà**) imbecility

imbèlle *adj* unwarlike; cowardly

imbellettare (**imbellétto**) *tr* to apply rouge to, apply make-up on ‖ *ref* to put on make-up

imbellire §176 *tr* to embellish

imbèrbe *adj* beardless; callow

imbestialire §176 *tr* to enrage ‖ *intr* (ESSERE) & *ref* to become enraged

imbévere §185 *tr* to soak; to soak up; to imbue ‖ *ref* to become soaked; to become imbued

imbiancare §197 *tr* to whiten; to bleach; to whitewash ‖ *intr* (ESSERE) & *ref* to turn white (said, *e.g.*, of *hair*); to clear up (*said of weather*)

imbiancatura *f* bleaching (of *laundry*); whitening; whitewashing

imbianchiménto *m* bleaching

imbianchino *m* whitewasher; house painter; (pej) dauber

imbianchire §176 *tr* to whiten; to bleach ‖ *ref* to turn white

imbiondire §176 *tr* to bleach (*hair*) ‖ *intr* to become blond; to ripen (*said of wheat*)

imbizzarrire [ddzz] *intr* (ESSERE) & *ref* to become skittish (*said of a horse*); to become infuriated

imbizzire [ddzz] §176 *intr* (ESSERE) to get angry

imboccare §197 (**imbócco**) *tr* to feed by mouth; to put (*an instrument*) in one's mouth; to take, enter (*a road*); to prompt ‖ *intr* (ESSERE) to

flow; to open (*said of a road*); (mach) to fit

imboccatura *f* entrance (of *street*); inlet; opening, top (*e.g.*, of *bottle*); bit (of *bridle*); (mus) mouthpiece; **avere l'imboccatura a** to be experienced in

imbóc·co *m* (**-chi**) entrance; inlet; opening

imboniménto *m* claptrap

imbonire §176 *tr* to lure, entice (*s.o.* to buy or enter)

imbonitóre *m* barker

imborghesire §176 *tr* to render middle-class ‖ *intr* (ESSERE) to become middle-class

imboscare §197 (**imbòsco**) *tr* to hide; to hide (*s.o.*) underground ‖ *ref* to shirk; to be a slacker

imbosca·to -ta *adj* (mil) shirking, draft-dodging ‖ *m* (mil) slacker; (mil) goldbrick ‖ *f* ambush; **tendere un'imboscata** to set an ambush

imboscatóre *m* accomplice of a draft dodger; hoarder (of *scarce items*)

imboschire §176 *tr* to forest

imbottare (**imbótto**) *tr* to barrel

imbottigliare §280 *tr* to bottle; to bottle up ‖ *ref* to get bottled up (*said of traffic*)

imbottire §176 *tr* to pad, fill; to stuff; to pad (*a speech*)

imbottita *f* bedspread, quilt

imbottitura *f* padding

imbra·ca *f* (**-che**) breeching strap (of *harness*); safety belt; (naut) sling

imbracare §197 *tr* to sling

imbracciare §128 *tr* to fasten (*shield*); to level (*gun*)

imbrancare §197 *tr* & *ref* to herd

imbrattacar·te *mf* (**-te**) scribbler

imbrattamu·ri *mf* (**-ri**) dauber

imbrattare *tr* to soil, dirty; to smudge, smear

imbrattaté·le *mf* (**-le**) dauber

imbratto *m* dirt; smudge, smear; daub; scribble; swill

imbrigliare §280 *tr* to bridle

imbroccare §197 (**imbròcco**) *tr* to hit (*the target*); to guess right

imbrodare (**imbròdo**) *tr* to soil

imbrogliare §280 (**imbròglio**) *tr* to cheat; to mix up; to tangle; to confuse; **imbrogliare le vele** (naut) to take in the reef ‖ *ref* to get tangled up; to get confused; to turn bad (*said of weather*)

imbrò·glio *m* (**-gli**) cheat; tangle; (naut) reef; **cacciarsi in un imbroglio** to get involved in a mess

imbrogliό·ne -na *mf* swindler

imbronciare §128 (**imbróncio**) *intr* (ESSERE) & *ref* to pout, sulk ‖ *ref* to lower (*said of the weather*)

imbroncia·to -ta *adj* sulky, surly; cloudy, overcast

imbrunire *m*—**sull'imbrunire** at nightfall ‖ §176 *intr* (ESSERE) to turn brown ‖ *impers* (ESSERE)—**imbrunisce** it is growing dark

imbruttire §176 *tr* to mar; to make ugly ‖ *intr* (ESSERE) & *ref* to grow ugly

imbucare §197 *tr* to mail; to put in a hole ‖ *ref* to hide

imburrare *tr* to butter
imbuto *m* funnel
imène *m* (anat) hymen, maidenhead
imitare (ímito) *tr* to imitate
imita·tóre -trice *mf* imitator; (theat) mimic
imitazióne *f* imitation
immacola·to -ta *adj* immaculate
immagazzinare [ddzz] *tr* to store, store up
immaginare (immàgino) *tr* to imagine; to guess; to invent || *ref*—**si immagini!** of course!; not at all!
immaginà·rio -ria *adj* (-**ri** -**rie**) imaginary
immaginativa *f* imagination
immaginazióne *f* imagination
immàgine *f* image; picture
immaginó·so -sa [s] *adj* imaginative
immalinconire §176 *tr* to sadden || *intr* (ESSERE) & *ref* to become melancholy
immancàbile *adj* unfailing; certain
immane *adj* monstruous; gigantic
immangiàbile *adj* uneatable, inedible
immantinènte *adv* (lit) immediately
immarcescìbile *adj* incorruptible
immateriale *adj* immaterial
immatricolare (immatrícolo) *tr* to matriculate
immatricolazióne *f* matriculation
immatu·ro -ra *adj* immature; premature
immedesimare (immedésimo) *tr* to identify; to blend || *ref* to identify oneself
immediatamente *adv* immediately
immediatézza *f* immediacy
immedia·to -ta *adj* immediate
immemoràbile *adj* immemorial
immèmore *adj* forgetful
immèn·so -sa *adj* immense, huge
immèrgere §162 *tr* to immerse; to plunge || *ref* to plunge; to become absorbed
immerita·to -ta *adj* undeserved
immeritévole *adj* undeserving
immersióne *f* immersion; submersion (*of a submarine*); (naut) draft
immèttere §198 *tr* to let in; **immettere qlcu nel possesso di** (law) to grant s.o. possession of
immigrante *adj* & *mf* immigrant
immigrare *intr* (ESSERE) to immigrate
immigrazióne *f* immigration; (biol) migration
imminènte *adj* imminent
imminènza *f* imminence
immischiare §287 *tr* to involve || *ref* to meddle; to become involved
immiserire §176 *tr* to impoverish || *intr* (ESSERE) & *ref* to become impoverished; to become debased
immissà·rio *m* (-**ri**) tributary
immissióne *f* letting in, introduction; intake; insertion (*in lunar orbit*)
immòbile *adj* motionless, immobile; real (*property*) || **immobili** *mpl* real estate
immobiliare *adj* real, e.g., **proprietà immobiliare** real estate; real-estate, e.g., **imposta immobiliare** real-estate tax
immobilizzare [ddzz] *tr* to immobilize; to pin down; to tie up (*capital*)

immodè·sto -sta *adj* indecent; immodest
immolare (immòlo) *tr* to immolate
immondézza *f* filth; impurity
immondez·zàio *m* (-**zài**) rubbish heap, dump; garbage can
immondìzia *f* trash; garbage; filth
immón·do -da *adj* filthy, dirty; unclean
immorale *adj* immoral
immorali·tà *f* (-**tà**) immorality
immortalare *tr* to immortalize
immortale *adj* immortal
immortalità *f* immortality
immò·to -ta *adj* (lit) motionless
immune *adj* immune
immunizzare [ddzz] *tr* to immunize
immutàbile *adj* immutable
immuta·to -ta *adj* unchanged
i·mo -ma *adj* (lit) bottom, lowest || *m* (lit) bottom; (lit) depth
impaccare §197 *tr* to pack, wrap up
impacchettare (impacchétto) *tr* to pack, bundle
impacciare §128 *tr* to hamper; to embarrass || *ref* to meddle
impaccia·to -ta *adj* hampered; clumsy
impàc·cio *m* (-**ci**) embarrassment; hindrance; trouble; **essere d'impaccio** to be in the way
impac·co *m* (-**chi**) wrapping; (med) compress
impadronire §176 *ref*—**impadronirsi di** to seize; to take possession of; to master (*a language*)
impagàbile *adj* invaluable, priceless
impaginare (impàgino) *tr* (typ) to make up (*in pages*), paginate
impaginato *m* (typ) page proof
impagliare §280 *tr* to cane (*a chair*); to stuff (*an animal; a doll*); to pack in straw
impalare *tr* to impale; to tie to a pole or stake || *ref* to stiffen up
impala·to -ta *adj* stiff, rigid
impalcatura *f* scaffold; frame, framework
impallidire §176 *intr* to turn pale; to blanch; to grow dim (*said of a star*); (fig) to wane
impalmare *tr* (lit) to wed
impalpàbile *adj* impalpable
impaludare *tr* to make swampy or marshy || *intr* to become marshy
impanare *tr* to bread; to thread (*a screw*) || *intr* to screw in
impaniare §287 *tr* to trap, ensnare || *ref* to fall into the trap
impantanare *tr* to turn into a swamp || *ref* to get stuck, to sink (*in vice*)
impaperare (impàpero) *ref* to fluff, make a slip
impappinare *tr* to confuse || *ref* to blunder; to stammer
imparare *tr* to learn; **imparare a memoria** to learn by heart || *intr* **imparare a** to learn to, to learn how to
impareggiàbile *adj* peerless, unmatched
imparentare (imparènto) *tr* to bring into the family || *ref*—**imparentarsi con** to marry into
ìmpari *adj* odd, uneven
imparrucca·to -ta *adj* bewigged
impartire §176 *tr* to impart
imparziale *adj* impartial

impasse *f* blind alley; deadlock; (cards) finesse

impassìbile *adj* impassible, impassive

impastare *tr* to knead; to mix; to smear with paste

impasta·to ‑ta *adj* kneaded; smeared; **impastato di** .tainted with; overwhelmed with (*sleep*)

impasto *m* paste; pastiche

impastoiare §287 (**impastóio**) *tr* to fetter, hamstring

impataccare §197 *tr* to besmear, soil

impattare *tr* to even up; to tie (*a game*); **impattarla con** to tie (*a person*)

impatto *m* impact

impaurire §176 *tr* to scare || *ref* to get scared

impàvi·do ‑da *adj* fearless

impaziènte *adj* impatient

impazientire §176 *intr* (ESSERE) & *ref* to get impatient

impaziènza *f* impatience

impazzare *intr* (ESSERE) to be wild with excitement; to go mad; (culin) to curdle

impazzata *f*—**all'impazzata** at top speed; berserk

impazzire §176 *intr* (ESSERE) to go crazy; **fare impazzire** to drive crazy

impeccàbile *adj* impeccable

impeciare §128 (**impécio**) *tr* to tar

impedènza *f* impedance

impediménto *m* hindrance, obstacle, impediment

impedire §176 *tr* to impede, hinder; to obstruct || *intr* to prevent; **impedire** (with *dat*) **di** + *inf* or **che** + *subj* to prevent from + *ger*

impegnare (**impégno**) *tr* to pawn; to reserve (*a room*); to engage (*the enemy*); to keep occupied; to pledge || *ref* to obligate oneself; to go all out; to become entangled

impegnati·vo ‑va *adj* demanding (*activity*); binding (*promise*)

impegna·to ‑ta *adj* pawned; pledged; occupied; committed

impégno *m* commitment; obligation; task; zeal; **senza impegno** without promising

impegolare (**impégolo**) *tr* to tar || *ref* to become entangled

impelagare §209 (**impèlago**) *ref* to bog down; to become entangled

impellicciare §128 *tr* to fur; to veneer

impenetràbile *adj* impenetrable

impenitènte *adj* impenitent; confirmed

impennàg·gio *m* (**‑gi**) (aer) empennage

impennare (**impénno**) *tr* to feather; (fig) to give wings to || *ref* to rear (*said of a horse*); to take umbrage; (aer) to zoom

impennata *f* rearing (*of horse*); (aer) zoom

impensàbile *adj* unthinkable

impensa·to ‑ta *adj* unexpected

impensierire §176 *tr* & *ref* to worry

imperante *adj* prevailing

imperare (**impèro**) *intr* to rule, reign; to prevail; **imperare su** to rule over

imperati·vo ‑va *adj* & *m* imperative

imperatóre *m* emperor

imperatrice *f* empress

impercettìbile *adj* imperceptible

imperdonàbile *adj* unforgivable

imperfèt·to ‑ta *adj* & *m* imperfect

imperfezióne *f* imperfection

imperiale *adj* imperial || *m* upper deck (*of bus or coach*); **imperiali** imperial troops

imperiali·sta *adj* & *mf* (**‑sti ‑ste**) imperialist

impèrio *m* (**‑ri**) empire; rule

imperió·so ‑sa [s] *adj* imperious; imperative

imperi·to ‑ta *adj* (lit) inexperienced

imperitu·ro ‑ra *adj* immortal; everlasting, imperishable

imperizia *f* inexperience

imperlare (**imperlo**) *tr* to bead; to cover with beads (*of perspiration*)

impermalire §176 *tr* to provoke || *ref* to become provoked

impermeàbile *adj* waterproof || *m* raincoat

imperniare §287 (**impèrnio**) *tr* to pivot; (fig) to base

impèro *adj invar* Empire || *m* empire; control, sway

imperscrutàbile *adj* inscrutable

impersonale *adj* impersonal

impersonare (**impersóno**) *tr* to impersonate || *ref*—**impersonarsi in** to be the embodiment of; (theat) to impersonate

impertèrri·to ‑ta *adj* undaunted

impertinènte *adj* impertinent, pert

impertinènza *f* impertinence

imperturbàbile *adj* imperturbable

imperturba·to ‑ta *adj* unperturbed

imperversare (**impervèrso**) *intr* to storm, rage; to be the rage

impèr·vio ‑via *adj* (**‑vi ‑vie**) impassable

impeto *m* impetus; onslaught; violence; outburst; **d'impeto** rashly

impetrare (**impètro**) *tr* to beg for; to obtain by entreaty || *intr* (ESSERE) (lit) to turn to stone

impetti·to ‑ta *adj* puffed up with pride

impetuó·so ‑sa [s] *adj* impetuous

impiallacciare §128 *tr* to veneer

impiallacciatura *f* veneer, veneering

impiantare *tr* to install (*a machine*); to set up (*a business*); to open (*an account*)

impiantito *m* floor, flooring

impianto *m* installation; plant; system

impiastrare *tr* to plaster; to dirty

impiastricciare §128 *tr* to plaster; to daub; to soil

impiastro *m* (med) plaster; (fig) bore

impiccagióne *f* hanging

impiccare §197 *tr* to hang

impicciare §128 *tr* to hinder; to bother || *ref* to meddle, butt in; **impicciarsi degli affari propri** to mind one's own business

impìc·cio *m* (**‑ci**) hindrance; trouble; **essere d'impiccio** to be in the way

impicció·ne ‑na *mf* meddler

impiccolire §176 *tr* to reduce in size || *ref* to shrink in size

impiegare §209 (**impiègo**) *tr* to employ;

to use; to devote (*one's energies*); to spend (*time*); to invest (*capital*); to take (*time*) ‖ *ref* to have a job

impiegatì·zio -zia *adj* (**-zi -zie**) employee, white-collar

impiega·to -ta *mf* employee; clerk

impiè·go *m* (**-ghi**) employment; use; job; place of business; investment

impietosire [s] §176 *tr* to move to pity ‖ *ref* to be moved to pity

impietrire §176 *tr, intr* (ESSERE) & *ref* to turn to stone

impigliare §280 *tr* to entangle ‖ *ref* to become entangled

impigrire §176 *tr* to make lazy ‖ *intr* (ESSERE) & *ref* to get lazy

impinguare (impìnguo) *tr* & *ref* to fatten

impinzare *tr* to stuff ‖ *ref* to stuff oneself; **impinzarsi il cervello** to stuff one's brain (*with knowledge*)

impiombare (impiómbo) *tr* to lead; to plumb, seal with lead; to fill (*a tooth*); (naut) to splice (*a cable*)

impiombatura *f* seal; filling (*of tooth*); (naut) splicing

impipare *ref*—**impiparsi di** (slang) to not give a hoot about

implacàbile *adj* implacable

implicare §197 (**ìmplico**) *tr* to implicate; to imply

implìci·to -ta *adj* implicit, implied

implorare (implòro) *tr* to implore

implume *adj* unfledged, featherless

impolìti·co -ca *adj* (**-ci -che**) unpolitical; impolitic, injudicious

impollinare (impòllino) *tr* to pollinate

impoltronire §176 *tr* to make lazy ‖ *ref* to get lazy

impolverare (impólvero) *tr* to cover with dust ‖ *ref* to get covered with dust

impomatare *tr* to pomade; to smear with pomade

imponderàbile *adj* imponderable; weightless

imponderabilità *f* imponderability; weightlessness

imponènte *adj* imposing; stately

imponìbile *adj* taxable ‖ *m* taxable income

impopolare *adj* unpopular

impopolarità *f* unpopularity

impórre §218 *tr* to place, put; to impose; to order; to compel; to give (*a name*) ‖ *intr* (ESSERE) to be imposing; (with *dat*) to order, command ‖ *ref* to command respect; to win favor; to be necessary

importante *adj* important; sizable ‖ *m* important thing

importanza *f* importance; size; **darsi importanza** to assume an air of importance

importare (impòrto) *tr* to import; to imply; to involve ‖ *intr* (ESSERE) to be of consequence ‖ *impers* (ESSERE) —**importa** it matters; **non importa** never mind

importa·tóre -trice *mf* importer

importazióne *f* importation; import

impòrto *m* amount

importunare *tr* to bother, importune

importu·no -na *adj* importunate, bothersome ‖ *mf* bore

imposizióne *f* imposition; giving (*of a name*); order, command; taxation

impossessare (impossèsso) *ref*—**impossessarsi di** to seize; to master (*a language*)

impossìbile *adj* & *m* impossible

impossibili·tà *f* (**-tà**) impossibility

impossibilitare (impossibilito) *tr* to make impossible; to make unable or incapable

impossibilita·to -ta *adj* unable

impòsta *f* tax; shutter; (archit) impost; **imposta complementare** surtax; **imposta sul valore aggiunto** value-added tax

impostare (impòsto) *tr* to start, begin; to state (*a problem*); to mail; to lay (*a stone*); to open (*an account*); to attune (*one's voice*); to lay the keel of (*a ship*) ‖ *ref* to take one's position, get ready

impostazióne *f* beginning, starting; laying; mail, mailing; (com) posting

impo·stóre -stóra *mf* impostor

impostura *f* imposture

impotènte *adj* weak; impotent

impotènza *f* impotence

impoveriménto *m* impoverishment

impoverire §176 *tr* to impoverish ‖ *intr* (ESSERE) & *ref* to become impoverished

impraticàbile *adj* impracticable; impassable

impratichire §176 *tr* to train, familiarize ‖ *ref* to become familiar (*e.g., with a task*)

imprecare §197 (**imprèco**) *tr* to wish (*e.g., s.o.'s death*) ‖ *intr* to curse

imprecazióne *f* imprecation, curse

imprecisàbile *adj* undefinable

imprecisióne *f* inexactness, inaccuracy

imprecì·so -sa *adj* vague, inexact

impregnare (imprégno) *tr* to impregnate

impremedita·to -ta *adj* unpremeditated

imprendìbile *adj* impregnable

imprendi·tóre -trice *mf* contractor ‖ *m*—**imprenditore di pompe funebri** undertaker

imprenditoriale *adj* managerial

imprepara·to -ta *adj* unprepared

impreparazióne *f* unpreparedness

imprésa [s] *f* enterprise; undertaking; achievement; firm, concern; (theat) management; **impresa (di) pompe funebri** undertaking establishment

impresà·rio [s] *m* (**-ri**) manager; (theat) impresario

imprescindìbile *adj* essential, indispensable; unavoidable

impresentàbile *adj* unpresentable

impressionàbile *adj* impressionable

impressionante *adj* striking, impressive; frightening

impressionare (impressióno) *tr* to impress; (phot) to expose ‖ *ref* to become frightened; (phot) to be exposed

impressióne *f* impression

imprestare (imprèsto) *tr* (coll) to lend

imprèstito *m* (philol) borrowing
imprevedìbile *adj* unforeseeable
imprevedu·to -ta *adj* unforeseen
imprevidènte *adj* improvident
imprevi·sto -sta *adj* unforeseen, unexpected || imprevisti *mpl* unforeseen events
imprigionare (imprigióno) *tr* to imprison
imprìmere §131 *tr* to impress; to imprint; to impart (*e.g., motion*)
improbàbile *adj* improbable, unlikely
impro·bo -ba *adj* dishonest; laborious
improdutti·vo -va *adj* unproductive
imprónta *f* print, imprint; mark; impronta digitale fingerprint
improntare (imprónto) *tr* to impress, imprint; to mark
improntitùdine *f* audacity, impudence
impronunziàbile *adj* unpronounceable
improprè·rio *m* (-ri) insult
improprie·tà *f* (-tà) impropriety; error
imprò·prio -pria *adj* (-pri -prie) improper, inappropriate; (math) improper
improrogàbile *adj* unextendible
improvvi·do -da *adj* improvident
improvvisare *tr* to improvise || *ref* to suddenly decide to become
improvvisa·to -ta *adj* improvised; impromptu || *f* surprise; surprise party
improvvisazióne *f* improvisation
improvvi·so -sa *adj* sudden || *m* (mus) impromptu; all'improvviso or d'improvviso suddenly
imprudènte *adj* imprudent; rash
imprudènza *f* imprudence; rashness
impudènte *adj* shameless; brazen; impudent
impudènza *f* shamelessness; impudence
impudicìzia *f* immodesty
impudi·co -ca *adj* (-chi -che) immodest, indecent
impugnare *tr* to grip, seize; to take up (*arms*); to impugn, contest
impugnatura *f* handle; grip, hold; hilt, haft
impulsi·vo -va *adj* impulsive
impulso *m* impulse; dare impulso a to promote, foment
impuneménte *adv* with impunity
impunità *f* impunity
impuni·to -ta *adj* unpunished
impuntare *intr* to stumble, trip; to stutter || *ref* to stutter; to balk; to be stubborn; impuntarsi a or di + *inf* to stubbornly insist on + *ger*
impuntigliare §280 *ref* to persist, insist
impuntire §176 *tr* to tuft (*e.g., a pillow*)
impuntura *f* backstitch
impuri·tà *f* (-tà) impurity; unchastity
impu·ro -ra *adj* impure; unchaste
imputàbile *adj* attributable
imputare (ìmputo) *tr* to impute; to charge, accuse; (com) to post
imputa·to -ta *mf* accused, defendant
imputazióne *f* imputation; charge, accusation; (com) posting
imputridire §176 *tr* & *intr* (ESSERE) to rot
in *prep* in; at; into; to; on, upon; through; during; married to, *e.g.,*

Maria Roberti in Bianchi Marie Roberti married to Bianchi; as, *e.g.,* in premio as a prize; by, *e.g.,* in automobile by car; of, *e.g.,* studente in legge student of law; essere in quattro to be four; in alto up; in breve soon; in a word; in giù down; in là there; in qua here; in realtà really; in seguito a because of
-ina *suf fem* about, *e.g.,* cinquantina about fifty
inabbordàbile *adj* unapproachable
inàbile *adj* unfit; ineligible; awkward
inabili·tà *f* (-tà) unfitness; awkwardness; inability
inabilitare (inabìlito) *tr* to incapacitate; to render unfit; to disqualify
inabilitazióne *f* disqualification
inabissare *tr* to plunge || *ref* to sink
inabitàbile *adj* uninhabitable
inabita·to -ta *adj* uninhabited
inaccessìbile *adj* inaccessible; unfathomable
inaccettàbile *adj* unacceptable
inacerbire §176 *tr* to exacerbate || *ref* to grow bitter
inacidire §176 *tr* & *ref* to sour
inadattàbile *adj* unadaptable; maladjusted
inadat·to -ta *adj* inadequate
inadegua·to -ta *adj* inadequate
inadempiènte *adj* not fulfilling; inadempiente agli obblighi di leva draft-dodging
inafferràbile *adj* that cannot be caught or captured; incomprehensible; elusive
inalare *tr* to inhale
inalatóre *m* inhaler
inalberare (inàlbero) *tr* to hoist || *ref* to rear; to fly into a rage
inalteràbile *adj* unalterable
inamidare (inàmido) *tr* to starch
inamida·to -ta *adj* starched; pompous, starchy
inammissìbile *adj* inadmissible
inamovìbile *adj* irremovable
inamovibili·tà *f* (-tà) irremovability; tenure
inane *adj* inane; futile
inanella·to -ta *adj* curly; beringed
inanima·to -ta *adj* inanimate; lifeless
inanizióne *f* starvation
inappagàbile *adj* unquenchable
inappaga·to -ta *adj* unsatisfied
inappellàbile *adj* definitive, final
inappetènza *f* lack of appetite
inapprezzàbile *adj* inappreciable, imperceptible; inestimable
inappuntàbile *adj* faultless, impeccable
inarcare §197 *tr* to arch; to raise (*one's eyebrows*)
inargentare (inargènto) *tr* to silver
inaridire §176 *tr* to dry; to parch || *ref* to dry up
inarrestàbile *adj* irresistible
inarrivàbile *adj* unattainable; inimitable
inarticola·to -ta *adj* indistinct, inarticulate
inascolta·to -ta *adj* unheeded
inaspetta·to -ta *adj* unexpected
inaspriménto *m* exacerbation

inasprire §176 *tr* to aggravate || *ref* to sour; to become embittered; to become sharper; to become fierce or furious

inastare *tr* to hoist (*flag*); to fix (*bayonets*)

inattaccàbile *adj* unattackable; unassailable; inattacabile da resistant to

inattendìbile *adj* unreliable

inattè·so -sa [s] *adj* unexpected

inattì·vo -ta *adj* inactive

inaudì·to -ta *adj* unheard-of

inaugurale *adj* inaugural; maiden (*voyage*)

inaugurare (inàuguro) *tr* to inaugurate; to usher in (*the New Year*); to open (*e.g., an exhibit*); to unveil (*a statue*); to sport for the first time

inaugurazióne *f* inauguration

inauspica·to -ta *adj* (lit) inauspicious

inavvedu·to -ta *adj* careless, rash

inavvertènza *f* inadvertence, oversight

inavvertì·to -ta *adj* unnoticed; inadvertent, thoughtless

inazióne *f* inaction

incagliare §280 *tr* to hamper; to run aground || *intr* (ESSERE) & *ref* to run aground; (fig) to get stuck

incà·glio *m* (-gli) running aground; hindrance, obstacle

incalcinare *tr* to whitewash; to lime (*a field*)

incalcolàbile *adj* incalculable

incallire §176 *tr* to make callous || *intr* (ESSERE) to become callous; to become inured

incallì·to -ta *adj* callous; inveterate

inca zante *adj* pressing

incalzare *tr* to press, pursue || *intr* to be imminent; to be pressing || *ref* to follow one another in rapid succession

incamerare (incàmero) *tr* to confiscate

incamminare *tr* to launch; to guide, direct || *ref* to set out; to be on one's way

incanagli·to -ta *adj* vile, despicable

incanalare *tr* to channel || *ref* to flow

incancrenire §176 *tr* to affect with gangrene || *ref* to become gangrenous; (fig) to become callous

incandescènte *adj* incandescent; (fig) red-hot

incandescènza *f* incandescence

incannare *tr* to reel, wind

incantare *tr* to bewitch; to auction off || *ref* to become enraptured; to be spellbound; to jam, get stuck (*said of machinery*)

incanta·tóre -trice *adj* enchanting || *m* enchanter || *f* enchantress

incantésimo *m* enchantment, spell

incantévole *adj* enchanting, charming

incanto *m* enchantment; bewitchery; auction; d'incanto marvelously well

incanutire §176 *tr, intr* (ESSERE) & *ref* to turn gray-headed, to turn gray (*said of a person*)

incanutì·to -ta *adj* hoary

incapace *adj* incapable; (law) incompetent || *mf* oaf; (law) incompetent

incapaci·tà *f* (-tà) incapacity; (law) incompetence

incaparbire §176 *intr* (ESSERE) & *ref* to be obstinate; to be determined

incaponire §176 *ref* to get stubborn; to be determined

incappare *intr* (ESSERE) to stumble

incappottare (incappòtto) *tr* to cover with a coat || *ref* to wrap oneself in a coat

incappucciare §128 *tr* to cover with a hood

incapricciare §128 *ref*—incapricciarsi di to take a fancy to; to become infatuated with

incapsulare (incàpsulo) *tr* to encapsulate; to cap

incarcerare (incàrcero) *tr* to jail, incarcerate; (fig) to confine

incaricare §197 (incàrico) *tr* to charge || *ref*—incaricarsi di to take charge of; to take care of

incarica·to -ta *adj* in charge; visiting (*professor*) || *mf* deputy; incaricato d'affari chargé d'affaires

incàri·co *m* (-chi) task; appointment, position; per incarico di on behalf of

incarnare *tr* to incarnate, embody

incarna·to -ta *adj* incarnate || *m* pink complexion

incarnazióne *f* incarnation

incarnire §176 *intr* (ESSERE) & *ref* to grow in (*said of a toenail*)

incarni·to -ta *adj* ingrown (*toenail*)

incartaménto *m* file, dossier

incartapecorì·to -ta *adj* shriveled up

incartare *tr* to wrap up (*in paper*)

incasellare [s] (incasèllo) *tr* to file; to sort out

incasellatóre [s] *m* post-office file clerk

incassare *tr* to box up; to put (*a watch*) in a case; to mortise (*a lock*); to channel (*a river*); to cash (*a check*); (fig) to take (*e.g., blows*) || *intr* to fit; to take it

incasso *m* receipts

incastellatura *f* scaffolding

incastonare (incastóno) *tr* to set, mount (*a gem*); incastonare citazioni in un discorso to stud a speech with quotations

incastrare *tr* to insert; to mortise; (fig) to corner || *intr* to fit || *ref* to fit; to become imbedded; to telescope (*said, e.g., of a train in a collision*)

incastro *m* joint; insertion; (carp) tenon; (carp) mortise

incatenare (incaténo) *tr* to chain, put in chains; to tie down, restrain

incatramare *tr* to tar

incàu·to -ta *adj* unwary, careless

incavallatura *f* truss (*to support roof*)

incavare *tr* to hollow out; to groove

incava·to -ta *adj* hollow

incavatura *f* hollow

incavicchiare §287 *tr* to peg

incavigliare §280 *tr* to peg

incavo *m* hollow; cavity; incavo dell'ascella armpit

incazzottare (incazzòtto) *tr* (naut) to furl

incèdere *m* stately walk || §123 *intr* to walk stately

incendiare §287 (incèndio) *tr* to set on fire; (fig) to inflame || *ref* to catch fire

incendià·rio -ria *adj & mf* (-ri -rie) incendiary

incèn·dio *m* (-di) fire; **incendio doloso** arson

incenerire §176 *tr* to reduce to ashes; to wither (*e.g., with a look*) || *ref* to turn to ashes

inceneritóre *m* incinerator

incensare (incènso) *tr* (eccl) to incense; (fig) to flatter

incensa·tóre -trice *mf* incense burner; (fig) flatterer

incensière *m* incense burner

incènso *m* incense

incensura·to -ta *adj* uncensured; (law) having no previous record

incentivo *m* incentive

inceppare (incèppo) *tr* to hinder; to shackle || *ref* to jam (*said of firearm*)

incerare (incèro) *tr* to wax

incerata *f* oilcloth; (naut) raincoat

incernierare (incernièro) *tr* to hinge

incertézza *f* uncertainty, incertitude

incèr·to -ta *adj* uncertain; irresolute || *m* uncertainty; **incerti extras; incerti del mestiere** cares of office, occupational annoyances, occupational hazards

incespicare §197 (incéspico) *intr* to stumble

incessàbile *adj* (lit) ceaseless

incessante *adj* unceasing, incessant

incèsto *m* incest

incestuó·so -sa [s] *adj* incestuous

incètta *f* cornering (*of market*)

incettare (incètto) *tr* to corner (*market*)

incetta·tóre -trice *mf* monopolizer

inchiavardare *tr* to key, bolt

inchièsta *f* probe, inquest; (journ) inquiry

inchinare *tr* to bend; to bow (*the head*) || *intr* (lit) to go down (*said of stars*) || *ref* to bow; to yield

inchi·no -na *adj* bent; bowing || *m* bow; curtsy

inchiodare (inchiòdo) *tr* to nail; to spike; to rivet; to tie, bind; to stop (*a car*) suddenly; to transfix || *ref* to freeze (*said, e.g., of brakes*); (fig) to be tied down; (fig) to go into debt

inchiostrare (inchiòstro) *tr* (typ) to ink

inchiòstro *m* ink; **inchiostro di china** India ink, Chinese ink

inciampare *intr* to trip, stumble

inciampo *m* stumbling block, obstacle; **essere d'inciampo a** to be in the way of

incidentale *adj* incidental

incidènte *adj* incidental || *m* incident; accident; argument, question

incidènza *f* incidence

incidere §145 *tr* to engrave; to cut; to record (*a record, a tape; a song*); **incidere all'acqua forte** to etch || *intr*—**incidere su** to weigh heavily on (*expenses, a budget*); to leave a mark on

incinerazióne *f* incineration; cremation

incinta *adj fem* pregnant

incipiènte *adj* incipient

incipriare §287 *tr* to powder || *ref* to powder oneself

incirca *adv* about; **all'incirca** more or less

incisióne *f* engraving; cutting (*of a record*); recording (*of a tape; of a song*); incision; **incisione all'acquaforte** etching

incisi·vo -va *adj* incisive; sharp (*photograph*) || *m* incisor

inciso *m* (gram) parenthetical clause; (mus) theme; **per inciso** incidentally

incisóre *m* engraver, etcher

incitare *tr* to incite, provoke

incivile *adj* uncivilized; uncouth

incivilire §176 *tr* to civilize || *ref* to become civilized

inclemènte *adj* inclement, harsh

inclemènza *f* inclemency, harshness

inclinare *tr* to tilt; to bow, bend; to incline || *intr* (fig) to lean || *ref* to bend

inclinazióne *f* inclination; slope; **inclinazione laterale** (aer) bank; **inclinazione magnetica** magnetic dip

incline *adj* inclined

incli·to -ta *adj* famous; noble

inclùdere §105 *tr* to enclose, include

inclusi·vo -va *adj* including; **inclusivo di** including

inclu·so -sa *adj* enclosed; included; inclusive; *f* enclosed letter

incoerènte *adj* incoherent

incògliere §127 *tr* (lit) to catch in the act || *intr*—**incogliere a** to happen to

incògni·to -ta *adj* unknown || *m* incognito; unknown; **in incognito** incognito || *f* (math) unknown quantity; (fig) puzzle

incollare (incòllo) *tr* to glue, paste; to size (*paper*) || *intr* to stick || *ref* to stick; to take on one's shoulders

incollatura *f* neck (*of horse*); glueing, sticking

incollerire §176 *intr & ref* to get angry

incolloca·to -ta *adj* unemployed

incolonnare (incolónno) *tr* to set up in columns

incolonnatóre *m* tabulator

incolóre *adj* colorless

incolpàbile *adj* blamable; (lit) guiltless

incolpare (incólpo) *tr*—**incolpare di** to charge with

incól·to -ta *adj* uncultivated; unkempt

incòlume *adj* unharmed, unhurt

incolumità *f* safety, security

incombènte *adj* (*danger*) impending; (*duty*) incumbent

incombènza *f* task, charge, incumbency

incómbere §186 *intr* (ESSERE) to be impending; to be incumbent

incombustibile *adj* incombustible

incominciare §128 *tr & intr* (ESSERE) to begin

incommensuràbile *adj* immeasurable; (math) incommensurable

incomodare (incòmodo) *tr* to bother, disturb || *ref* to bother; **non s'incomodi!** don't bother!

incòmo·do -da *adj* bothersome, inconvenient || *m* inconvenience; ailment;

levare l'incomodo a to get out of the way of

incomparàbile *adj* incomparable

incompatibile *adj* incompatible; unforgivable

incompetènte *adj & mf* incompetent

incompiu·to -ta *adj* unfinished

incomplè·to -ta *adj* incomplete

incompó·sto -sta *adj* untidy; unkempt; unbecoming (*behavior*)

incomprensìbile *adj* incomprehensible

incomprensióne *f* lack of understanding

incomprè·so -sa [s] *adj* misunderstood

incomprimìbile *adj* irrepressible; incompressible

inconcepìbile *adj* inconceivable

inconciliàbile *adj* irreconcilable

inconcludènte *adj* inconclusive; insignificant

inconcus·so -sa *adj* (lit) unshaken

incondiziona·to -ta *adj* unconditional

inconfessàbile *adj* unspeakable, vile

inconfes·sa·to -ta *adj* unavowed

inconfondìbile *adj* unmistakable

inconfutàbile *adj* irrefutable

incongruènte *adj* inconsistent

incòn·gruo -grua *adj* incongruous

inconoscìbile *adj* unknowable

inconsapèvole *adj* unaware, unconscious

incòn·scio -scia *adj & m* (-sci -sce) unconscious

inconseguènte *adj* inconsistent, inconsequential

inconsidera·to -ta *adj* inconsiderate

inconsistènte *adj* flimsy; inconsistent

inconsistènza *f* flimsiness; inconsistency

inconsolàbile *adj* inconsolable

inconsuè·to -ta *adj* unusual

inconsul·to -ta *adj* ill-advised, rash

incontamina·to -ta *adj* uncontaminated

incontenìbile *adj* irrepressible

incontentàbile *adj* insatiable; hard to please; exacting

incontinènza *f* incontinence

incontrare (**incóntro**) *tr* to meet; to encounter, meet with ‖ *intr* (ESSERE) to catch on (*said, e.g., of fashions*) ‖ *ref* to meet; to agree ‖ *impers* (ESSERE) to happen

incontrastàbile *adj* indisputable

incontrasta·to -ta *adj* undisputed

incóntro *m* meeting; encounter; success; meet; game, fight, match; occasion, opportunity; **all'incontro** on the other hand; opposite; **andare incontro a** to go towards; to go to meet; to face; to meet (*expenses*); to accommodate; **farsi incontro a** to advance toward

incontrollàbile *adj* uncontrollable

incontrolla·to -ta *adj* unchecked

incontrovertìbile *adj* incontrovertible

inconveniènte *adj* inconvenient ‖ *m* inconvenience, disadvantage

incoraggiante *adj* encouraging

incoraggiare §290 *tr* to encourage

incorare §257 (**incuòro**) *tr* to hearten

incordare (**incòrdo**) *tr* to string (*e.g., a racket*); to tie up (*with a cord*) ‖ *ref* to stiffen (*said of a muscle*)

incornare (**incòrno**) *tr* (taur) to gore

incorniciare §128 *tr* to frame; (journ) to border; (slang) to cuckold

incoronare (**incoróno**) *tr* to crown

incoronazióne *f* coronation

incorporàbile *adj* absorbable; adaptable

incorporare (**incòrporo**) *tr* to incorporate; to absorb ‖ *ref* to incorporate

incorpòre·o -a *adj* incorporeal

incorreggìbile *adj* incorrigible

incórrere §139 *intr* (ESSERE)—**incorrere in** to incur

incorrot·to -ta *adj* uncorrupt

incosciènte *adj* unconscious; unaware; irresponsible ‖ *mf* irresponsible person

incosciènza *f* unconsciousness; irresponsibility; madness

incostante *adj* inconstant, fickle

incredìbile *adj* incredible, unbelievable

incrèdu·lo -la *adj* incredulous ‖ *mf* disbeliever; doubter

incrementare (**increménto**) *tr* to increase, boost

increménto *m* increase, increment, boost

incresció·so -sa [s] *adj* disagreeable, unpleasant

increspare (**incréspo**) *tr* to ripple; to wrinkle; to knit (*the brow*); to pleat ‖ *ref* to ripple

incretinire §176 *tr* to make stupid; (fig) to deafen ‖ *intr* (ESSERE) to become stupid; to lose one's mind

incriminare (**incrìmino**) *tr* to incriminate

incrinare *tr* to flaw; to ruin

incrinatura *f* crack, flaw

incrociare §128 (**incròcio**) *tr* to cross ‖ *intr* (naut) to cruise ‖ *ref* to cross one another; to interbreed

incrociatóre *m* (nav) cruiser

incró·cio *m* (-ci) crossing; cross; crossroads; crossbreed

incrollàbile *adj* unshakable

incrostare (**incròsto**) *tr* to incrust; to inlay (*e.g., with mosaic*) ‖ *ref* to become incrusted

incrostazióne *f* incrustation

incrudelire §176 *tr* to enrage ‖ *intr* to commit cruelties ‖ *intr* (ESSERE) to become cruel; **incrudelire su** to commit cruelties upon

incruèn·to -ta *adj* bloodless

incubare (**incubo & incùbo**) *tr* to incubate

incubatrice *f* incubator; brooder

incubazióne *f* incubation; **in incubazione** brewing (*said of an infectious disease*)

incubo *m* nightmare

incùdine *f* anvil; **essere tra l'incudine e il martello** to be between the devil and the deep blue sea

inculcare §197 *tr* to inculcate

incunàbolo *m* incunabulum

incuneare (**incùneo**) *tr & ref* to wedge

incuràbile *adj & mf* incurable

incurante *adj* careless, indifferent

incuria *f* malpractice; neglect

incuriosire [s] §176 *tr* to intrigue ‖ *ref* to be intrigued

incursióne *f* incursion; **incursione aerea** air raid

incurvare *tr* to bend; (lit) to lower || *intr* (ESSERE) & *ref* to bend; to warp

incurvatura *f* bend, curve

incustodi·to -ta *adj* unguarded, unwatched

incùtere §154 *tr* to inspire; **incutere terrore a** to strike with terror

ìndaco *adj & m* indigo

indaffara·to -ta *adj* busy

indagare §209 *tr & intr* to investigate; **indagare su** to investigate

indaga·tóre -trice *adj* probing, searching || *mf* investigator

indàgine *f* investigation, inquiry

indarno *adv* (lit) in vain

indebitare (indébito) *tr* to burden with debts || *ref* to run into debt

indebita·to -ta *adj* indebted

indébi·to -ta *adj* undue; unjust; fraudulent (*conversion*) || *m* what one does not owe; excess payment

indebolimènto *m* weakening

indebolire §176 *tr, intr* (ESSERE) & *ref* to weaken

indecènte *adj* indecent

indecènza *f* indecency; outrage

indecifràbile *adj* indecipherable

indecisióne *f* indecision

indeci·so -sa *adj* uncertain; undecided; indecisive

indecoró·so -sa [s] *adj* indecorous, unseemly

indefès·so -sa *adj* indefatigable

indefinìbile *adj* indefinable

indefini·to -ta *adj* indefinite; undefined

indegni·tà *f* (-tà) indignity

indé·gno -gna *adj* unworthy; disgraceful

indelèbile *adj* indelible

incèlica·to -ta *adj* indelicate

indemagliàbile *adj* runproof

indemonia·to -ta *adj* possessed by the devil; restless

indènne *adj* undamaged, unscathed; **tener indenne** to guarantee against harm or damage

indenni·tà *f* (-tà) indemnity; indemnification; **indennità di carica** special emolument; bonus; **indennità di carovita** cost-of-living allowance; **indennità di preavviso** severance pay; **indennità di trasferta** per diem

indennizzare [ddzz] *tr* to indemnify

indennizzo [ddzz] *m* indemnification; indemnity

inderogàbile *adj* inescapable

indescrivìbile *adj* indescribable

indesideràbile *adj* undesirable

indesidera·to -ta *adj* unwished-for; undesirable

indeterminati·vo -va *adj* indefinite

indetermina·to -ta *adj* indeterminate; (gram) indefinite

indi *adv* (lit) then; (lit) thence; **da indi innanzi** (lit) from that moment on

India, l' *f* India; **le Indie Occidentali** the West Indies; **le Indie Orientali** the East Indies

india·no -na *adj & mf* Indian; **fare l'indiano** to feign ignorance || *f* printed calico

indiavola·to -ta *adj* devilish, fierce; impish (*child*)

indicare §197 (ìndico) *tr* to indicate; to show

indicati·vo -va *adj & m* indicative

indica·to -ta *adj* appropriate, fitting; recommended, advisable

indica·tóre -trice *adj* indicating, pointing || *m* indicator; **indicatore di direzione** (aut) turn signal; **indicatore di livello** gauge; **indicatore di pressione** pressure gauge; **indicatore di velocità** (aut) speedometer; **indicatore stradale** road sign; **indicatore telefonico** telephone directory

indicazióne *f* indication; direction; **indicazioni per l'uso** instructions

ìndice *m* index finger; pointer, gauge; indicator; sign, indication; index; (typ) fist; **indice delle materie** table of contents || **Indice** *m* Index; **mettere all'Indice** to put on the Index; to ban, index

indicìbile *adj* inexpressible, unspeakable

indietreggiare §290 (indietréggio) *intr* (ESSERE & AVERE) to withdraw

indiètro *adv* back; behind; **all'indietro** backwards; **dare indietro** to return, give back; **domandare indietro** to ask back; **essere indietro** to be slow (*said of a watch*); to be behind; to be backward, be slow; **tirarsi indietro** to withdraw; to step back

indifendìbile *adj* indefensible

indifé·so -sa [s] *adj* defenseless

indifferènte *adj* indifferent; **essere indifferente a** to be the same to; **lasciare indifferente** to leave cold

indifferènza *f* indifference

indige·no -na *adj* indigenous || *m* native

indigènte *adj* indigent, poor

indigestìbile *adj* indigestible

indigestióne *f* indigestion

indigè·sto -sta *adj* indigestible; (fig) dull, boring

indignare *tr* to anger, shock || *ref* to be aroused, be indignant

indigna·to -ta *adj* indignant, outraged

indignazióne *f* indignation

indigni·tà *f* (-tà) indignity

indimenticàbile *adj* unforgettable

indipendènte *adj & m* independent

indipendènza *f* independence

indire §151 *tr* to announce publicly; (lit) to declare (*war*)

indirèt·to -ta *adj* indirect

indirizzare *tr* to direct; to address

indirizzà·rio *m* (-ri) mailing list

indirizzo *m* address; direction

indiscernìbile *adj* indiscernible

indisciplina *f* lack of discipline

indisciplina·to -ta *adj* undisciplined

indiscré·to -ta *adj* indiscreet; tactless

indiscrezióne *f* indiscretion; gossip; news leak

indiscus·so -sa *adj* unquestioned

indiscutìbile *adj* indisputable

indispensàbile *adj* indispensable || *m* essential

indispettire §176 *tr* to annoy || *ref* to get annoyed

indisponènte *adj* vexing, irritating

indispórre §218 *tr* to indispose; to disgust

indisposizióne *f* indisposition

indispó·sto -sta *adj* indisposed

indissolùbile *adj* indissoluble

indistín·to -ta *adj* indistinct

indistruttìbile *adj* indestructible

indisturba·to -ta *adj* undisturbed

indìvia *f* endive

individuàbile *adj* distinguishable

individuale *adj* individual

individuali·tà *f* (-tà) individuality

individuare (**indivìduo**) *tr* to individuate; to outline; to single out

individuo *m* individual; fellow

indivisìbile *adj* indivisible

indivi·so -sa *adj* undivided

indiziare §287 *tr* to cast suspicion on

indizià·rio -ria *adj* (-ri -rie) circumstancial

indì·zio *m* (-zi) clue; token; symptom

indòcile *adj* indocile, unteachable

Indocìna, l' *f* Indochina

indocinése [s] *adj & mf* Indochinese

indoeuropè·o -a *adj & m* Indo-European

indolcire §176 *tr* to sweeten || *ref* to become sweet

ìndole *f* temper, disposition; nature

indolènte *adj* indolent

indolenziménto *m* soreness, stiffness; numbness

indolenzire §176 *tr* to make sore or stiff; to benumb || *ref* to become sore or stiff

indolenzi·to -ta *adj* sore, stiff; numb

indolóre *adj* painless

indomàbile *adj* indomitable

indoma·ni *m* (-ni) morrow, next day; **l'indomani di . . .** the day after . . .

indòma·to -ta *adj* (lit) indomitable, untamed

indòmi·to -ta *adj* (lit) indomitable, untamed

Indonèsia, l' *f* Indonesia

indonesia·no -na *adj & mf* Indonesian

indorare (**indòro**) *tr* to gild; (culin) to brown; (fig) to sugar-coat

indoratura *f* gilding

indossare (**indòsso**) *tr* to wear; to put on

indossatrice *f* mannequin, model

indòsso *adv* on, on one's back; **avere indosso** to have on, wear

Indostàn, l' *m* Hindustan

indosta·no -na *adj & mf* Hindustani

indòtto *m* (elec) armature (*of motor*)

indottrinare *tr* to indoctrinate

indovinare *tr* to guess; **indovinarla** to guess right; **non indovinarne una** to never hit the mark

indovina·to -ta *adj* felicitous

indovinèllo *m* puzzle, riddle

indovi·no -na *mf* soothsayer, fortune-teller

indù *adj invar & mf* Hindu

indùb·bio -bia *adj* (-bi -bie) undoubted, undisputed

indubita·to -ta *adj* undeniable

indugiare §290 *tr* to delay || *intr* to linger; to hesitate || *ref* to linger

indù·gio *m* (-gi) delay; **rompere gli**

indugi to come to a decision; **senza ulteriore indugio** without further delay

indulgènte *adj* indulgent

indulgènza *f* indulgence

indùlgere §187 *tr* to grant; to forgive || *intr* to be indulgent; **indulgere a** to indulge; to yield to

indulto *m* (law) pardon

induménto *m* garment; **indumenti intimi** undergarments, unmentionables

indurire §176 *tr* to harden || *intr* (ESSERE) to harden; to get stiff

indurre §102 *tr* to induce

indùstria *f* industry; **grande industria** heavy industry

industriale *adj* industrial || *m* industrialist

industrializzare [ddzz] *tr* to industrialize

industriare §287 *ref* to try, try hard; **industriarsi a** or **per** + *inf* to try to + *inf*, to do one's best to + *inf*

industrió·so -sa [s] *adj* industrious

indut·tóre -trice *adj* inducing, provoking || *m* (elec) field (*of motor*)

induzióne *f* induction

inebetire §176 *tr* to dull; to stun || *intr* (ESSERE) & *ref* to become dull; to be stunned

inebriare §287 (**inèbrio**) *tr* to intoxicate || *ref* to get drunk

inebriante *adj* intoxicating

ineccepìbile *adj* unexceptionable

inèdia *f* starvation, inanition; boredom

inèdi·to -ta *adj* unpublished; new, novel

ineduca·to -ta *adj* uneducated; ill-mannered

ineffàbile *adj* ineffable

inefficace *adj* ineffectual, ineffective

inefficàcia *f* inefficacy

inefficiènte *adj* inefficient

ineguale *adj* unequal; uneven

inelegante *adj* inelegant; shabby

ineleggìbile *adj* ineligible

ineluttàbile *adj* inevitable, inescapable

inenarràbile *adj* unspeakable

inerènte *adj* inherent

inèrme *adj* unarmed, defenseless

inerpicare §197 (**inérpico**) *ref* to clamber

inèrte *adj* inert

inèrzia *f* inertia; inactivity

inesattézza *f* inaccuracy

inesat·to -ta *adj* inaccurate, inexact; uncollected

inesaudi·to -ta *adj* unanswered

inesauribile *adj* inexhaustible

inescusàbile *adj* inexcusable

inesigìbile *adj* uncollectable

inesistènte *adj* inexistent

inesoràbile *adj* inexorable

inesperiènza *f* inexperience

inespèr·to -ta *adj* inexperienced; unskilled

inesplicàbile *adj* inexplicable

inesplica·to -ta *adj* unexplained

inesplora·to -ta *adj* unexplored

inesplò·so -sa *adj* unexploded

inespressi·vo -va *adj* inexpressive

inesprimìbile *adj* inexpressible

inespugnàbile *adj* impregnable; incorruptible

inespugna·to -ta *adj* unconquered

inestimàbile *adj* priceless, invaluable

inestinguìbile *adj* inextinguishable

inestirpàbile *adj* ineradicable

inestricàbile *adj* inextricable

inèt·to -ta *adj* inept

ineva·so -sa *adj* unfinished (*business*); unanswered (*mail*)

inevitàbile *adj* unavoidable, inevitable

inèzia *f* trifle, bagatelle

infagottare (**infagòtto**) *tr & ref* to bundle up

infallìbile *adj* infallible

infamante *adj* shameful, disgraceful

infamare *tr* to disgrace; to slander

infame *adj* infamous; villainous; (coll) horrible || *m* villain

infàmia *f* infamy; (coll) botch, bungle

infangare §209 *tr* to splash with mud; (fig) to stain, spot

infante *adj & mf* infant, baby || *m* infante || *f* infanta

infantile *adj* infantile, childish

infànzia *f* infancy, childhood

infarcire §176 *tr* to cram; (culin) to stuff

infarinare *tr* to sprinkle with flour; to powder; (fig) to cram || *ref* to be covered with flour

infarinatura *f* sprinkling with flour; (fig) smattering

infastidire §176 *tr* to annoy || *ref* to be annoyed, lose one's patience

infaticàbile *adj* indefatigable, tireless

infatti *adv* indeed; really

infatuare (**infàtuo**) *tr* to infatuate || *ref* to become infatuated

infatua·to -ta *adj* infatuated

infàu·sto -sta *adj* unlucky, fatal

infecón·do -da *adj* barren

infedéle *adj* unfaithful; inaccurate || *mf* infidel

infedel·tà *f* (-**tà**) unfaithfulness; inaccuracy; infidelity

infelice *adj* unhappy, unfortunate; unfavorable || *mf* wretch

infelici·tà *f* (-**tà**) unhappiness

inferióre *adj* inferior; lower; **inferiore a** a lower than; less than; smaller than

inferiorità *f* inferiority

inferire §188a *tr* to inflict; to infer; (naut) to bend (*a sail*)

infermare (**inférmo**) *tr* (lit) to weaken || *intr* (ESSERE) to get sick

infermerìa *f* infirmary

infermiè·re -ra *adj* nursing || *m* male nurse || *f* nurse; **infermiera diplomata** trained nurse

infermieristi·co -ca *adj* (-**ci -che**) nursing

infermi·tà *f* (-**tà**) infirmity

infér·mo -ma *adj* infirm; sick || *m* patient

infernale *adj* infernal

infèr·no -na *adj* (lit) lower (*region*) || *m* hell; inferno

inferocire §176 *tr* to infuriate || *intr*— **inferocire su** to be pitiless to || *intr* (ESSERE) to become infuriated

inferriata *f* grating, grill

infervorare (**infèrvoro & infervóro**) *tr* to excite, stir up || *ref* to get excited; to become absorbed

infestare (**infèsto**) *tr* to infest

infettare (**infètto**) *tr* to infect

infetti·vo -va *adj* infectious

infèt·to -ta *adj* infected; corrupted

infezióne *f* infection

infiacchire §176 *tr* to weaken || *intr* (ESSERE) & *ref* to grow weak

infiammàbile *adj* inflammable

infiammare *tr* to inflame; to ignite || *ref* to catch fire, ignite

infiamma·to -ta *adj* burning; aflame; inflamed, excited

infiammazióne *f* inflammation

infi·do -da *adj* untrustworthy

infierire §176 *intr* to become cruel; to be merciless to; to rage (*said, e.g., of a disease*)

infievolire §176 *tr* to weaken

infìggere §103 *tr* to thrust, stick, sink || *ref*—**infìggersi in** to creep in; to work in

infilare *tr* to thread (*a needle*); to insert (*a key*); to transfix (*with a sword*); to put on (*e.g., a coat*); to pull on (*one's pants*); to slip on (*a dress*); to slip (*e.g., one's arm into a sleeve*); to string (*beads*); to hit (*the target*); to take (*a road*); to enter through (*a door*); **infilare l'uscio** to slip away; **infilarle tutte** to succeed all the time; **non infilarne mai una** to never succeed || *ref* to slip; to sink; to slide (*e.g., through a crowd*)

infilata *f* row; string (*e.g., of insults*); (mil) enfilade; **d'infilata** lengthwise

infiltrare *ref* to infiltrate; to seep; (fig) to creep

infilzare *tr* to pierce; to string; (sew) to baste

infilzata *f* string (*of pearls, of lies, etc.*)

ìnfi·mo -ma *adj* lowest, bottom

infine *adv* finally

infingar·do -da *adj* lazy, slothful

infini·tà *f* (-**tà**) infinity

infinitèsi·mo -ma *adj & m* infinitesimal

infiniti·vo -va *adj* (gram) infinitive

infini·to -ta *adj* infinite || *m* infinite; infinity; (gram) infinitive; (math) infinity; **all'infinito** ad infinitum

infino *adv* (lit)—**infino a** until; as far as; **infino a che** as long as

infinocchiare §287 (**infinòcchio**) *tr* (coll) to fool, bamboozle

infioccare §197 (**infiòcco**) *tr* to adorn with tassels

infiorare (**infióro**) *tr* to adorn with flowers; (fig) to sprinkle; (fig) tö embellish || *ref* to be covered with flowers

infiorescènza *f* inflorescence

infirmare *tr* to weaken; to invalidate

infischiare §287 *ref*—**infischiarsi di** to not care a hoot about

infisso *m* frame (*e.g., of door*); fixture

infittire §176 *tr*, *intr* (ESSERE) & *ref* to thicken

inflazionare (**inflazióno**) *tr* to inflate

inflazióne *f* inflation

inflessìbile *adj* inflexible

inflessióne *f* inflection
inflèttere §177 *tr* (lit) to inflect
infliggere §104 *tr* to inflict
influènte *adj* influential
influènza *f* influence; (pathol) influenza
influenzare (**influènzo**) *tr* to influence, sway
influíre §176 *intr* to have an influence; **influíre su** to influence || *intr* (ESSERE) —**influíre in** to flow into
influsso *m* influence; (lit) plague
infocare §182 *tr* to make glow with heat || *ref* to catch fire; to get excited
infocà·to -ta *adj* red-hot; sultry
infognare (**infógno**) *ref* (coll) to sink (*e.g., in vice*); (coll) to get stuck (*e.g., in debt*)
infoltíre §176 *tr & intr* (ESSERE) to thicken
infondà·to -ta *adj* unfounded, groundless
infóndere §178 *tr* to infuse, instill
inforcare §197 (**infórco**) *tr* to pitch (*hay*); to bestride; to mount (*a horse or bicycle*); to put on (*one's eyeglasses*)
inforcatura *f* pitching with a fork; crotch
informare (**infórmo**) *tr* to inform; (fig) to mold || *ref* to conform; to inquire; **informarsi da** to seek or get information from; **informarsi di** or **su** to inquire about; to find out about
informatí·vo -va *adj* informative, informational
informa·tóre -trice *adj* underlying || *mf* informer; (journ) reporter || *m* informant (*of a foreign language*)
informazióne *f* piece of information; **chiedere informazioni sul conto di** to inquire about; **informazioni** information
infórme *adj* shapeless
informicolíre §176 *ref* to tingle; **informicolírsi** a to go to sleep, *e.g.,* **gli si è informicolíta la gamba** his leg went to sleep
infornare (**infórno**) *tr* to put in the oven; to bake
infornata *f* batch (*of bread*); (coll) flock
infortunare *ref* to get hurt
infortuna·to -ta *adj* injured || *mf* casualty, victim
infortù·nio *m* (-**ni**) accident, mishap; **infortunio sul lavoro** job-connected injury
infossare (**infòsso**) *tr* to bury || *ref* to cave in, settle; to become sunken (*said of eyes or cheeks*)
infracidare (**infràcido**) *tr* var of **infradiciare**
infracidíre §176 *intr* to rot
infradiciare §128 (**infràdicio**) *tr* to drench || *ref* to get drenched; to rot (*said of fruit*)
inframmettènza *f* interference, meddling
inframméttere §198 *tr* to interpose || *ref* to meddle, interfere
inframmezzare [ddzz] (**inframmèzzo**) *tr* to intersperse

infràngere §179 *tr & ref* to break
infrangìbile *adj* unbreakable
infran·to -ta *adj* broken, shattered
infraròs·so -sa *adj & m* infrared
infrascrit·to -ta *adj* mentioned below
infrastruttura *f* underpinning; infrastructure; (rr) roadbed
infrazióne *f* infraction, breach
infreddatura *f* mild cold
infreddolíre §176 *ref* to feel cold, to be chilled
infrenàbile *adj* irrepressible
infrequènte *adj* infrequent
infrollíre §176 *tr* to make (*meat*) high || *intr* (ESSERE) & *ref* to get high (*said of meat*); (fig) to soften
infruttuó·so -sa [s] *adj* unprofitable
infuòri *adv* out; **all'infuòri** outward; **all'infuòri di** except
infuriare §287 *tr* to infuriate, enrage || *intr* to get blustery; to rage || *intr* (ESSERE) to lose one's temper
infusióne *f* infusion; sprinkling (*of holy water*)
infuso *m* infusion
ingabbiare §287 *tr* to cage; to jail; to corner; to build the framework of
ingabbiatura *f* frame, framework
ingaggiare §290 *tr* to hire; to engage || *ref* to sign up; to get tangled up
ingàg·gio *m* (-**gi**) engagement; (sports) bonus (*for signing up*)
ingagliardíre §176 *tr* to strengthen || *ref* to become strong
ingannare *tr* to deceive; to cheat; to elude; to beguile || *ref* to be mistaken
inganna·tóre -trice *adj* deceptive || *mf* impostor
ingannévole *adj* deceitful; deceptive
inganno *m* deception; illusion
ingarbugliare §280 *tr* to entangle; to jumble || *ref* to get mixed up; to become embroiled
ingegnare (**ingégno**) *ref* to manage; to scheme
ingegnère *m* engineer
ingegnería *f* engineering; **ingegneria civile** civil engineering; **ingegneria meccanica** mechanical engineering
ingégno *m* brain, intelligence; talent; genius; expediency; (lit) machinery
ingegnosità [s] *f* ingeniousness
ingegnó·so -sa [s] *adj* ingenious; euphuistic
ingelosíre [s] §176 *tr* to make jealous || *intr* (ESSERE) & *ref* to become jealous
ingemmare (**ingèmmo**) *tr* to adorn or stud with gems
ingenerare (**ingènero**) *tr* to engender
ingèni·to -ta *adj* inborn
ingènte *adj* huge, vast
ingentilíre §176 *tr* to refine
ingenui·tà *f* (-**tà**) ingenuousness; ingenuous act
ingè·nuo -nua *adj* ingenuous, artless || *m* (theat) artless character || *f* (theat) ingénue
ingerènza *f* interference
ingerire §176 *tr* to ingest, swallow || *ref* to meddle

ingessare (ingèsso) tr to put in a plaster cast; to plaster up

ingessatura f (surg) plaster cast

inghiaiare §287 tr to gravel, cover with gravel

Inghilterra, l' f England; **la Nuova Inghilterra** New England

inghiottire (inghiótto) & §176 tr to swallow; to swallow up; to pocket (one's pride)

inghirlandare tr to bedeck with garlands; (lit) to encircle

ingiallire §176 tr & intr (ESSERE) to turn yellow

ingigantire §176 tr to exaggerate || intr (ESSERE) to grow larger, increase

inginocchiare §287 (inginòcchio) ref to kneel down

inginocchia·tóio m (-tói) prie-dieu

ingioiellare (ingioièllo) tr to bejewel; (fig) to stud

ingiù adv down; **all'ingiù** downwards

ingiùngere §183 tr to order, command || intr (with dat) to order, command, e.g., **il giudice ingiunse all'imputato di rispondere** the judge ordered the accused to answer

ingiunzióne f order; (law) injunction

ingiùria f insult, abuse; damage, wear

ingiuriare §287 tr to insult

ingiurió·so -sa [s] adj insulting

ingiustificàbile adj unjustifiable

ingiustifica·to -ta adj unjustified

ingiustizia f injustice

ingiù·sto -sta adj unjust, unfair || m unjust person

inglése [s] adj English; **all'inglese** in the English fashion; **andarsene all'inglese** to take French leave || m Englishman; English (language) || f Englishwoman

ingoiare §287 (ingóio) tr to swallow; to gulp down; **ingoiare un rospo** (fig) to swallow one's pride

ingolfare (ingólfo) tr (aut) to flood || ref to form a gulf; to get involved; (aut) to flood

ingollare (ingòllo) tr to swallow, gulp down

ingolosire [s] §176 tr to make the mouth of (s.o.) water || intr (ESSERE) & ref to have a craving

ingombrante adj cumbersome

ingombrare (ingómbro) tr to clutter

ingóm·bro -bra adj encumbered, cluttered || m encumbrance; **essere d'ingombro** to be in the way

ingommare (ingómmo) tr to glue

ingordìgia f greed

ingór·do -da adj greedy, covetous

ingorgare §209 (ingórgo) ref to get clogged up

ingór·go m (-ghi) blocking, congestion; **ingorgo stradale** traffic jam

ingovernàbile adj uncontrollable

ingozzare (ingózzo) tr to gobble, gulp down; to swallow; to cram (e.g., a goose for fattening)

ingranàg·gio m (-gi) gear, gearwheel; (fig) meshes; **ingranaggio di distribuzione** (aut) timing gear; **ingranaggio elicoidale** worm gear

ingranare tr to engage (a gear); **ingranare la marcia** to throw into gear || intr to be in gear; to succeed

ingrandiménto m enlargement; increase

ingrandire §176 tr to enlarge; to increase; || intr (ESSERE) & ref to increase, get larger

ingrassare tr to fatten; to lubricate || intr (ESSERE) & ref to get fat; to get rich

ingrassa·tóre -trice mf greaser, lubricator || f grease gun; lubricating machine

ingratitùdine f ingratitude

ingra·to -ta adj ungrateful; thankless || mf ingrate

ingraziare §287 ref to ingratiate oneself with

ingrediénte m ingredient

ingrèsso m entrance; admittance, entry; **ingressi hallway furniture**; **primo ingresso** debut

ingrossaménto m enlargement; swelling

ingrossare (ingròsso) tr to enlarge; to swell; to make bigger; to dull (the mind); to raise (one's voice) || intr (ESSERE) & ref to swell; to thicken; to become fat; to become pregnant; to become important

ingròsso m—**all'ingrosso** wholesale; approximately, more or less

ingrullire §176 tr to drive crazy || intr (ESSERE) & ref to become silly; **fare ingrullire** to drive crazy

inguadàbile adj not fordable

inguainare (inguaìno) tr to sheathe

ingualcìbile adj wrinkle-free, wrinkleproof

inguanta·to -ta adj with gloves on; **con le mani inguantate** with gloves on

inguarìbile adj incurable

inguine f (anat) groin

ingurgitare (ingùrgito) tr to swallow, gulp down

inibire §176 tr to inhibit

inibi·tóre -trice adj inhibiting || m inhibitor

inidòne·o -a adj unfit, unqualified

iniettare (iniètto) tr to inject || ref to become bloodshot; **iniettarsi di sangue** to become bloodshot

iniezióne f injection

inimicare §197 tr to make an enemy of; to alienate || ref—**inimicarsi con** to fall out with

inimicìzia f enmity

inimitàbile adj inimitable, matchless

ininterrót·to -ta adj uninterrupted

iniqui·tà f (-tà) injustice; iniquity

ini·quo -qua adj unjust; wicked

iniziale adj & f initial

iniziare §287 tr to initiate || ref to begin

iniziativa f initiative; sponsorship; **iniziativa privata** private enterprise

inizia·tóre -trice adj initiating || mf initiator, promoter

iniziazióne f initiation

ini·zio m (-zi) beginning, start

innaffiare §287 tr var of **annaffiare**

innaffia·tóio m (-tói) var of **annaffiatoio**

innalzaménto m elevation

innalzare *tr* to raise; to elevate; **innalzare al cielo** to praise to the sky ‖ *ref* to rise; to tower

innamorare (**innamóro**) *tr* to charm, fascinate; to inspire with love ‖ *ref* to fall in love

innamora·to -ta *adj* in love, enamored; fond ‖ *mf* sweetheart ‖ *m* boyfriend ‖ *f* girl friend

innanzi *adj invar* previous, prior (*e.g.*, *day*) ‖ *adv* ahead, before; **innanzi a** in front of; **innanzi di** + *inf* before + *ger*; **mettere innanzi** to prefer; to place before; to advance (*an excuse*); **per l'innanzi** before, in the past; **tirare innanzi** to get along ‖ *prep* before; above; **innanzi tempo** ahead of time; **innanzi tutto** above all

innà·rio -m (**-ri**) hymnal

inna·to -ta *adj* inborn, innate

innegàbile *adj* undeniable

inneggiare §290 (**innéggio**) *intr*—**inneggiare a** to sing the praises of

innervosire [s] §176 *tr* to make nervous

innescare §197 (**innésco**) *tr* to bait (*a hook*); to prime (*a bomb*)

inné·sco m (**-schi**) primer; detonator

innestare (**innèsto**) *tr* (hort & surg) to graft; (surg) to implant; (med) to inoculate (*a vaccine*); (mach) to engage; (elec) to plug in (*e.g., a plug*); **innestare la marcia** (aut) to throw into gear ‖ *ref* to be grafted; **innestarsi in** to merge with; **innestarsi su** to connect with

innèsto m (hort & surg) graft; (surg) implant; (med) inoculation; (mach) engagement; (mach) coupling; (elec) plug

inno m hymn; **inno nazionale** national anthem

innocènte *adj* innocent ‖ *m* innocent; **innocenti** foundlings

innocènza *f* innocence

innò·cuo -cua *adj* innocuous, harmless

innominàbile *adj* unmentionable

innomina·to -ta *adj* unnamed

innovare (**innòvo**) *tr* to innovate

innovazióne *f* innovation

innumerévole *adj* countless, innumerable

-ino -ina *suf adj* little, e.g., **poverino** poor little; hailing from, e.g., **fiorentino** hailing from Florence, Florentine ‖ *suf f* see **-ina**

inoccupa·to -ta *adj* unoccupied ‖ *m* person looking for his first job

inoculare (**inòculo**) *tr* to inoculate

inoculazióne *f* inoculation

inodó·ro -ra *adj* odorless

inoffensi·vo -va *adj* inoffensive

inoltrare (**inóltro**) *tr* (com) to forward (*e.g., a request*) ‖ *ref* to advance

inóltre *adv* besides, in addition

inóltro m (com) forwarding

inondare (**inóndo**) *tr* to inundate, flood; to swamp

inondazióne *f* flood, inundation

inoperosità [s] *f* idleness

inoperó·so -sa [s] *adj* idle

inopina·to -ta *adj* (lit) unexpected

inopportu·no -na *adj* inopportune, untimely

inoppugnàbile *adj* incontestable; indisputable

inorgàni·co -ca *adj* (**-ci -che**) inorganic

inorgoglire §176 *tr* to make proud ‖ *intr* (ESSERE) & *ref* to grow proud

inorridire §176 *tr* to horrify ‖ *intr* (ESSERE) to be horrified

inospitale *adj* inhospitable

inosservante *adj* unobservant

inosserva·to -ta *adj* unnoticed; unperceived

inossidàbile *adj* stainless

inquadrare *tr* to frame; to arrange

inquadratura *f* framing; (mov, phot) frame

inqualificàbile *adj* unspeakable

inquietante *adj* disquieting

inquietare (**inquièto**) *tr* to worry ‖ *ref* to worry; to get angry

inquiè·to -ta *adj* worried; restless; angry; (lit) stormy

inquietùdine *f* worry; restlessness; preoccupation

inquili·no -na *mf* tenant

inquinaménto *m* pollution

inquinare *tr* to pollute

inquirènte *adj* investigating

inquisi·tóre -trice *adj* inquiring ‖ *m* inquisitor

inquisizióne *f* inquisition

insabbiare §287 *tr* to cover with sand; to pigeonhole; to shelve ‖ *ref* to get covered with sand; to bury oneself in sand; to get stuck

insaccare §197 *tr* to bag; to stuff (*e.g., salami*); (mil) to hem in; (fig) to bundle up; (coll) to gulp down ‖ *ref* to be packed in; to crumple up; to disappear behind a thick bank of clouds (*said, e.g., of the sun*)

insaccato *m* participant in a sack race; **insaccati** cold cuts, lunch meat

insalata *f* salad; (fig) mess

insalatièra *f* salad bowl

insalubre *adj* unhealthy

insaluta·to -ta *adj* unsaluted; **andarsene insalutato ospite** to take French leave

insanàbile *adj* incurable; implacable

insanguinare (**insànguino**) *tr* to bloody; to cover with blood; to bathe in blood

insa·no -na *adj* insane

insaponare (**insapóno**) *tr* to soap; to lather; (fig) to soft-soap

insaporire §176 *tr* to flavor ‖ *intr* (ESSERE) to become tasty

insaputa *f*—**all'insaputa di** without the knowledge of, unbeknown to

insaziàbile *adj* insatiable

insazia·to -ta *adj* insatiate, unsatisfied

inscatolare (**inscàtolo**) *tr* to can

inscenare (**inscèno**) *tr* to stage

inscindìbile *adj* inseparable

inscrìvere §250 *tr* (geom) to inscribe

inscrutàbile *adj* inscrutable

inscurire §176 *tr, intr* (ESSERE) & *ref* to darken

insecchire §176 *tr* to dry ‖ *intr* (ESSERE) & *ref* to dry up

insediaménto *m* installation (*into an office*); assumption (*of an office*)

insediare §287 (**insèdio**) *tr* to install ‖ *ref* to be installed; to take one's seat; to settle

inségna *f* badge, insignia, emblem; ensign, flag; coat of arms; motto; sign (*e.g., on a restaurant*); traffic sign

insegnaménto *m* education, instruction

insegnante *adj* teaching ‖ *mf* teacher

insegnare (**inségno**) *tr* to teach; to show ‖ *intr* to teach

inseguiménto *m* pursuit

inseguire (**inséguo**) *tr* to pursue, chase; to chase after

insellare (**insèllo**) *tr* to saddle; to put on (*e.g., one's glasses*); to bend

insellatura *f* saddling; bending

insenatura *f* inlet, cove

insensatézza *f* nonsense, folly

insensa·to -ta *adj* nonsensical, foolish ‖ *mf* scatterbrain

insensibile *adj* insensible; unresponsive; insensitive

inseparàbile *adj* inseparable ‖ *m* (*orn*) lovebird

insepól·to -ta *adj* unburied

inserire §176 *tr* to insert; to plug in ‖ *ref* to slip in; to butt in

inseri·tóre -trice (*elec*) connecting ‖ *m* (*elec*) connector, plug ‖ *f* sorter (*of punch cards*)

insèrto *m* file, folder; insert; spliced film

inservìbile *adj* useless, worthless

inserviènte *m* attendant, porter; (*eccl*) server

inserzionare (**inserzióno**) *intr* to advertise

inserzióne *f* insertion; advertisement

inserzioni·sta (**-sti -ste**) *adj* advertising ‖ *mf* advertiser

insettici·da *adj & m* (**-di -de**) insecticide

insettìfu·go m (**-ghi**) insect repellent

insètto *m* insect; **insetti** vermin

insìdia *f* trap, ambush; insidie lure

insidiare §287 *tr* to ensnare; to try to trap; to try to seduce; to attempt (*someone's life*)

insidió·so -sa [s] *adj* insidious

insième *m* whole, entirety; harmony; ensemble; set; **d'insieme** general, comprehensive; **nell'insieme** as a whole ‖ *adv* together

insigne *adj* famous; notable; arrant (*knave*)

insignificante *adj* insignificant; petty

insignire §176 *tr* to decorate; **insignire qlcu di un titolo** to bestow a title upon s.o.

insignorire §176 *tr* (*lit*) to invest with a fief ‖ *intr* (ESSERE) to enrich oneself ‖ *ref* to enrich oneself; **insignorirsi di** to seize; to take possession of

insilare *tr* to silo, ensile

insilato *m* ensilage

insincè·ro -ra *adj* insincere

insindacàbile *adj* final, indisputable

insino *adv* (*lit*)—**insino a** until; as far as; **insino a che** as long as

insinuante *adj* insinuating

insinuare (**insìnuo**) *tr* to stick, thrust; to insinuate; (*law*) to register ‖ *ref* to creep, filter; to ingratiate oneself; **insinuarsi in** to worm one's way into

insinuazióne *f* insinuation, hint

insìpi·do -da *adj* insipid, vapid

insistènte *adj* insistent

insìstere §114 *intr* to insist

insi·to -ta *adj* inborn, inherent

insociévole *adj* unsociable

insoddisfat·to -ta *adj* dissatisfied

insofferènte *adj* intolerant

insoffrìbile *adj* unbearable, insufferable

insolazióne *f* sunning; sun bath; sunstroke; sunny exposure

insolènte *adj* insolent

insolentire §176 *tr* to insult, abuse ‖ *intr* to be insolent

insolènza *f* insolence; insult

insòli·to -ta *adj* unusual

insolùbile *adj* insoluble

insolu·to -ta *adj* unsolved; not dissolved; unpaid

insolvènza *f* insolvency

insolvìbile *adj* insolvent; bad (*debt*)

insómma *adv* in conclusion ‖ *interj* well!

insommergìbile *adj* unsinkable

insondàbile *adj* unfathomable

insònne *adj* sleepless

insònnia *f* insomnia

insonnoli·to -ta *adj* sleepy, drowsy

insonorizzazióne [ddzz] *f* soundproofing

insopportàbile *adj* unbearable

insorgènte *adj* appearing ‖ *mf* insurgent

insorgènza *f* appearance (*of illness*)

insórgere §258 *intr* (ESSERE) to rise up, revolt; to appear

insormontàbile *adj* unsurmountable, insurmountable

insór·to -ta *adj & m* insurgent

insospettàbile *adj* above suspicion; unexpected

insospetta·to -ta *adj* not suspect; unexpected

insospettire §176 *tr* to make suspicious ‖ *intr* (ESSERE) & *ref* to become suspicious

insostenìbile *adj* indefensible; unbearable

insostituìbile *adj* irreplaceable

insozzare (**insózzo**) *tr* to soil, sully

inspera·to -ta *adj* unexpected; unhoped-for

inspiegàbile *adj* unexplainable

inspirare *tr* to inhale, breathe in

inspirazióne *f* inhalation

instàbile *adj* unstable

installare *tr* to install; to set up, settle; to induct (*in an office*) ‖ *ref* to settle

installatóre *m* plumber; erector

installazióne *f* installation; plumbing

instancàbile *adj* untiring

instante *adj* insistent; impending ‖ *m* petitioner

instare (*pp* missing) *intr* to insist; to threaten, be imminent

instaurare (**instàuro**) *tr* to establish

instaurazióne *f* establishment

instigare §209 *tr* var of **istigare**

instillare *tr* var of **istillare**

instituire §176 *tr* var of **istituire**

instruire §176 *tr* var of **istruire**
instrumento *m* var of **istrumento**
instupidire §176 *tr* var of **istupidire**
insù *adv* up; **all'insù** up
insubordina·to -ta *adj* insubordinate
insuccèsso *m* failure
insudiciare §128 (**insùdicio**) *tr* to soil, dirty; to sully || *ref* to get dirty
insufficiènte *adj* insufficient; failing (*in school*)
insufficiènza *f* insufficiency; failure (*in school*)
insulare *adj* insular
insulina *f* insulin
insulsàggine *f* silliness, nonsense
insul·so -sa *adj* insipid; simple, silly
insultante *adj* insulting
insultare *tr* to insult || *intr* (with *dat*) to insult
insulto *m* insult; (pathol) attack
insuperàbile *adj* insuperable; unparalleled
insupera·to -ta *adj* unsurpassed
insuperbire §176 *tr, intr* (ESSERE) & *ref* to swell with pride
insurrezióne *f* insurrection
insussistènte *adj* nonexistent, unfounded
intabarrare *tr* to wrap up
intaccare §197 *tr* to notch; to corrode; to scratch; to attack (*said of a disease*); to damage (*e.g., a reputation*); to cut into (*capital*) || *intr* to stutter
intaccatura *f* notch; (carp) mortise
intagliare §280 *tr* to carve; to engrave
intà·glio *m* (**-gli**) carving; intaglio
intanare *ref* to hide
intangibile *adj* intangible; inviolable
intanto *adv* meanwhile; (coll) yet; (coll) finally; **intanto che** while; **per intanto** at present; in the meantime
intarsiare §287 *tr* to inlay; (fig) to stud
intarsia·to -ta *adj* inlaid
intàr·sio *m* (**-si**) inlay; inlaid work
intasare [s] *tr* to clog; to tie up (*traffic*); to stop up || *ref* to be clogged up; to be tied up; to be stopped up (*said of nose*)
intascare §197 *tr* to pocket
intat·to -ta *adj* intact, untouched
intavolare (**intàvolo**) *tr* to start (*a conversation*); to broach (*a subject*); to launch (*negotiations*)
intavolato *m* boarding, planking
integèrri·mo -ma *adj* of the utmost honesty
integrale *adj* integral; whole; wholewheat (*bread*); built-in || *m* integral
integralismo *m* policy of the complete absorption of the body politic by an ideology
integrante *adj* constituent, integral
integrare (**intègro**) *tr* to integrate || *ref* to complement each other
integrazióne *f* integration
integrità *f* integrity
ìnte·gro -gra *adj* whole, complete; honest, upright; intact
intelaiatura *f* frame; framework
intellètto *m* intellect, mind; understanding
intellettuale *adj* & *mf* intellectual

intellettuali·tà *f* (**-tà**) intelluality; intelligentsia
intellettualòide *mf* highbrow
intelligènte *adj* intelligent; clever
intelligènza *f* intelligence; understanding; **essere d'intelligenza con** to be in collusion with
intellighènzia *f* intelligentsia
intelligìbile *adj* intelligible
intemera·to -ta *adj* pure, spotless || *f* reprimand, scolding; long, boring speech
intemperante *adj* intemperate
intemperanza *f* intemperance
intempèrie *fpl* inclement weather
intempesti·vo -va *adj* untimely
intendènte *m* district director; **intendente di finanza** director of customs office; **intendente militare** commissary, quartermaster
intendènza *f* office of the district director; intendance; **intendenza militare** quartermaster corps
intèndere §270 *tr* to understand; to hear; to intend; to turn (*e.g., one's eyes*); to mean; **dare ad intendere a** to lead (*s.o.*) to believe (*s.th*); **far intendere** to give to understand; **farsi intendere** to force obedience; to make oneself understood; **intender dire che** to hear that; **intèndere a rovescio** to misunderstand; **intèndere a volo** to catch on quickly (to); **intèndere ragione** to listen to reason; **lasciare intèndere** to give to understand || *intr* to aim (*toward a goal*) || *ref* to come to an agreement; **intendersela con** to be in collusion with; to have an affair with; **intendersi di** to be a good judge of; to be an expert in
intendiménto *m* understanding, comprehension; aim, goal
intenerire §176 *tr* to soften; (fig) to move || *ref* to soften; (fig) to be moved
intensificare §197 (**intensìfico**) *tr* & *ref* to intensify
intensi·tà *f* (**-tà**) intensity
intensi·vo -va *adj* intensive
intèn·so -sa *adj* intense
intentare (**intènto**) *tr* (law) to bring (*action*)
intenta·to -ta *adj* unattempted
intèn·to -ta *adj* intent || *m* intent, goal; **coll'intento di** with the purpose of
intenzionale *adj* intentional
intenziona·to -ta *adj*—**bene intenzionato** well-meaning; **essere intenzionato di** to intend to
intenzióne *f* intention; purpose; **con intenzione** on purpose
intepidire §176 *tr* & *ref* var of **intiepidire**
interbase *f* (baseball) shortstop
intercalare *m* refrain; pet word or phrase || *tr* to intercalate; to inset
intercalazióne *f* intercalation; inset
intercapèdine *f* air space
intercèdere §123 *tr* to seek, get (*a par-*

don for s.o.) ‖ *intr* to intercede ‖ *intr* (ESSERE)—**intercedere tra** to intervene or elapse between; to extend between; to exist between

intercettare (intercètto) *tr* to intercept; to tap (*a phone*)

intercettatóre -trice *mf* interceptor

intercettóre *m* (aer) interceptor

intercomunale *adj* long-distance (*call*)

intercórrere §139 *intr* (ESSERE) to elapse; to happen; to be, to stand

interdét·to -ta *adj* dumbfounded; forbidden ‖ *m* interdict; (coll) dumbell

interdire §151 *tr* to prohibit; (eccl) to interdict; (law) to disqualify

interessaménto *m* interest, concern

interessante *adj* interesting; **in stato interessante** in the family way

interessare (interèsso) *tr* to interest; to concern ‖ *intr* to be of interest ‖ *ref*—**interessarsi a** to take an interest in; **interessarsi di** to concern oneself with

interessa·to -ta *adj* interested; selfish ‖ *m* interested party

interèsse *m* interest; self-interest

interessènza *f* (com) share, interest

interferènza *f* interference

interferire §176 *intr* to interfere

interfogliare §280 (interfòglio) *tr* to interleave

interiezióne *f* interjection

interinato *m* temporary office or tenure

interi·no -na *adj* acting ‖ *m* temporary appointee

interióra *fpl* entrails

interióre *adj* interior ‖ **interiori** *mpl* entrails

interlínea *f* interlining; (typ) leading

interlineare *adj* interlinear ‖ *v* (interlìneo) *tr* (typ) to lead

interlocu·tóre -trice *mf* participant (*in a discussion*); person speaking

interloquire §176 *intr* to take part in a discussion; to chime in

interlù·dio *m* (-di) interlude

intermedià·rio -ria (-ri -rie) *adj* & *mf* intermediary ‖ *m* middleman

intermè·dio -dia (-di -die) *adj* intermediate ‖ *mf* supervisor

intermèzzo [ddzz] *m* intermezzo; entr'acte; interval

interminàbile *adj* interminable, endless

intermissióne *f* intermission

intermittènte *adj* intermittent

internaménto *m* internment

internare (intèrno) *tr* to intern; to confine; to commit (*an insane person*) ‖ *ref* to go deep (*into a problem*)

interna·to -ta *adj* interned ‖ *m* internee; inmate; boarder; boarding school

internazionale *adj* international

internazionalizzare [ddzz] *tr* to internationalize

interni·sta *mf* (-sti -ste) internist

intèr·no -na *adj* inside, internal; inland; interior; boarding (*student*) ‖ *m* inside; interior; (med) intern; lining (*of coat*); **all'interno** inside; **interni** (mov) indoor shots ‖ **gli Interni** the Italian Ministry of Internal Affairs

inté·ro -ra *adj* entire, whole; full (*price*); (lit) upright, honest ‖ *m* whole; **per intero** completely

interpellare (interpèllo) *tr* to interpellate; to question; to consult

interpetrare (intèrpetro) *tr* var of interpretare

interplanetà·rio -ria *adj* (-ri -rie) interplanetary

interpolare (intèrpolo) *tr* to interpolate

interpolazióne *f* interpolation

interpónte *m* (naut) between-deck

interpórre §218 *tr* to interpose ‖ *ref* to intervene

interpretare (intèrpreto) *tr* to interpret

interpretazióne *f* interpretation

intèrprete *mf* interpreter

interpunzióne *f* punctuation

interrare (intèrro) *tr* to bury, inter; to fill in (*e.g., a marsh*) ‖ *ref* to become silted

interra·to -ta *adj* underground; **piano interrato** basement

interrogare §209 (intèrrogo) *tr* to question; to interrogate

interrogati·vo -va *adj* interrogative ‖ *m* why; question

interrogatò·rio -ria (-ri -rie) *adj* questioning ‖ *m* (law) interrogatory; **interrogatorio di terzo grado** third degree

interrogazióne *f* interrogation; quiz, examination; **interrogazione retorica** rhetorical question

interrómpere §240 *tr* to interrupt

interruttóre *m* (elec) switch; **interruttore di linea** (elec) controller

interruzióne *f* interruption

interscàm·bio *m* (-bi) interchange

interscolàsti·co -ca *adj* (-ci -che) interscholastic; intercollegiate

intersecare §197 (intèrseco) *tr* & *ref* to intersect

intersezióne *f* intersection

interstellare *adj* interstellar

interstì·zio *m* (-zi) interstice

interurba·no -na *adj* interurban, intercity; (telp) long-distance ‖ *f* (telp) long-distance call

intervallo *m* interval; pause; (educ) recess; (theat) intermission

intervenire §282 *intr* (ESSERE) to intervene; (surg) to operate; **intervenire a** to take part in

interventi·sta *mf* (-sti -ste) interventionist

intervènto *m* intervention; attendance; (surg) operation

intervenzióne *f* intervention

intervista *f* interview; **fare un'intervista a** to interview

intervistare *tr* to interview

inté·so -sa *adj* understood; intended, designed; **bene inteso** of course; **non darsene per inteso** to not pay attention; **rimanere inteso** to agree ‖ *f* understanding, agreement; entente

intèssere (intèsso) *tr* to interweave; to wreathe (*a garland*)

intestardire §176 *tr* to get obstinate; to be determined

intestare (intèsto) *tr* to caption; to label; (typ) to head (*a page*); **intestare qlco a qlcu** to register s.th in the name of s.o.; **intestare una fattura a** to issue a bill in the name of || *ref* to become obstinate; to take it into one's head

intesta·to -ta *adj* headed; registered (*stock*); obstinate; (law) intestate

intestazióne *f* heading; registration (*of stock*)

intestinale *adj* intestinal

intesti·no -na *adj & m* intestine; **intestino crasso** large intestine; **intestino tenue** small intestine

intiepidire §176 *tr & ref* to warm up; to cool off

intiè·ro -ra *adj & m* var of **intero**

intimare (intimo & intimo) *tr* to intimate; to order, command; to declare (*war*); to impose (*a fine*); (law) to enjoin

intimazióne *f* intimation; order; (law) injunction

intimidazióne *f* intimidation

intimidire §176 *tr* to intimidate; to threaten || *ref* to become bashful

intimi·tà *f* (-tà) intimacy; privacy

ìnti·mo -ma *adj* intimate; inmost; **biancheria intima** underwear, lingerie || *m* intimate friend; depth (*of one's heart*)

intimorire §176 *tr* to frighten

intingere §126 *tr* to dip || . *intr*—**intingere in** to dip in || *ref*—**intingersi in un affare** to have a finger in the pie

intingolo *m* sauce, gravy; fancy dish

intirizzire [ddzz] §176 *tr* to benumb || *intr* (ESSERE) *& ref* to become numb or stiff; to become stiff and frostbitten

intirizzi·to -ta [ddzz] *adj* numb

intisichire §176 *tr* to make tubercular; (fig) to weaken || *intr* (ESSERE) to become tubercular; to wither

intitolare (intitolo) *tr* to title; to dedicate || *ref* to be named; to assume the title of

intoccàbile *adj & m* untouchable

intolleràbile *adj* intolerable

intollerante *adj* intolerant

intonacare §197 (intònaco) *tr* to plaster; to whitewash; to cover (*e.g., with tar*) || *ref*—**intonacarsi la faccia** (joc) to put on one's warpaint

intòna·co m (-chi) plaster; roughcast

intonare (intòno) *tr* to intone; to harmonize; (mus) to tune || *ref* to harmonize, go

intonazióne *f* intonation; harmony

intòn·so -sa *adj* uncut; (lit) unsheared

intontire §176 *tr* to stun || *intr* (ESSERE) *& ref* to become stunned

intoppare (intòppo) *tr* to stumble upon || *intr* (ESSERE) *& ref* to stumble

intòppo *m* obstacle, hindrance

intorbidare (intórbido) *tr* to cloud; to muddy; to obfuscate; to upset (*friendship*); to stir up (*passions*) || *ref* to become cloudy or muddy; to become obfuscated

intorbidire §176 *tr & ref* to cloud; to muddy

intormentire §176 *tr* to benumb || *intr* (ESSERE) to become numb

intórno *adv* around, about; **all'intorno** all around; *intorno a* around; about; **levarsi qlcu d'intorno** to get rid of s.o.

intorpidire §176 *tr* to benumb || *ref* to become numb

intossicare §197 (intòssico) *tr* to poison, intoxicate

intossicazióne *f* poisoning, intoxication

intraducìbile *adj* untranslatable; inexpressible

intrafèrro *m* spark gap; air gap

intralciare §128 *tr* to hamper; to intertwine || *ref* to become hampered

intràl·cio m (-ci) hindrance; **essere d'intralcio** to be in the way; **intralcio del traffico** traffic congestion

intralicciatura *f* lattice truss (*of high-tension tower*)

intrallazzare *intr* to deal in the black market

intrallazza·tóre -trice *mf* black marketeer

intrallazzo *m* black-market dealing; kickback

intramezzare [ddzz] (intramèzzo) *tr* to alternate

intramontàbile *adj* undying, immortal

intransigènte *adj & mf* intransigent, die-hard

intransitàbile *adj* impassable

intransiti·vo -va *adj* intransitive

intrappolare (intràppolo) *tr* to entrap

intraprendènte *adj* enterprising

intraprendènza *f* enterprise, initiative

intraprèndere §220 *tr* to undertake

intrattàbile *adj* unmanageable, intractable

intrattenére §271 *tr* to entertain || *ref* to linger; **intrattenersi su** to dwell upon

intrattenimént̀o *m* entertainment

intravedére §279 *tr* to glimpse, catch a glimpse of; to foresee

intravenó·so -sa [s] *adj* intravenous

intrecciare §128 (intréccio) *tr* to braid; to twine; to cross (*one's fingers*); (fig) to weave; to begin (*a dance*) || *ref* to become embroiled; to become intertwined; to crisscross

intréc·cio m (-ci) knitting; intertwining; plot (*of novel*); (theat) intrigue

intrepidézza *f* intrepidness, intrepidity

intrèpi·do -da *adj* intrepid

intricare §197 *tr* (lit) to entangle

intrica·to -ta *adj* tangled; intricate

intrì·co m (-chi) tangle, jumble

intrìdere §189 *tr* to soak; to knead

intrigante *adj* intriguing || *mf* schemer

intrigare §209 *tr* to tangle · || *intr* to intrigue || *ref* (coll) to meddle

intrì·go m (-g·i) intrigue; trouble

intrìnse·co -ca (-ci -che) *adj* intrinsic; intimate || *m* intimate nature, core

intrì·so -sa *adj* soaked || *m* mash

intristire §176 *intr* (ESSERE) to wither; to waste away

introdót·to -ta *adj* introduced; well-known; knowledgeable, expert

introdurre §102 *tr* to introduce; to insert; to open (*a speech*); to show in || *ref* to slip in

introdutti·vo -va *adj* introductory

introduzióne *f* introduction

introitare (intròito) *tr* to collect, take in

intròito *m* receipts, collection; (eccl) introit

intromèttere §198 *tr* to insert; to introduce; to involve || *ref* to meddle; to pry

intromissióne *f* meddling; intrusion; intervention

intronare (intròno) *tr* to deafen; to stun

intronizzare [ddzz] *tr* to enthrone

introspetti·vo -va *adj* introspective

introspezióne *f* introspection

introvàbile *adj* unobtainable; inaccessible

introvèr·so -sa *adj & mf* introvert

intrùdere §190 *tr* (lit) to slip in || *ref* to intrude; to trespass

intrufolare (intrùfolo) *tr* (coll) to slip (*e.g., one's hand into somebody's pocket*) || *ref* to slip in, intrude

intrù·glio *m* (-gli) concoction, brew; hodgepodge; imbroglio; mess

intrusióne *f* intrusion

intru·so -sa *adj* intrusive || *mf* intruder

intuire §176 *tr* to know by intuition; to guess; to sense

intuiti·vo -va *adj* intuitive; obvious

intùito *m* intuition; insight

intuizióne *f* intuition

inturgidire §176 *intr* (ESSERE) & *ref* to swell

inuma·no -na *adj* inhuman; inhumane

inumare *tr* to bury, inhume

inumazióne *f* burial, inhumation

inumidire §176 *tr* to moisten || *ref* to get wet

inurbaménto *m* migration to the city

inurba·no -na *adj* uncouth, unmannerly

inurbare *ref* to move into the city; to become citified

inusa·to -ta *adj* unused; unusual

inusita·to -ta *adj* unusual; out-of-the-way

inùtile *adj* useless; worthless

inutilizzàbile [ddzz] *adj* unusable

inutilizzare [ddzz] *tr* to waste (*e.g., time*)

inutilizza·to -ta [ddzz] *adj* unused

inutilménte *adv* needlessly, to no purpose || *interj* no use!

invadènte *adj* meddlesome, intrusive

invàdere §172 *tr* to invade; to encroach on; to spread over; to overcome

invaghire §176 *tr* to charm || *ref* to fall in love

invalére §278 *intr* (ESSERE) to become established; to prevail

invalicàbile *adj* impassable, unsurmountable

invalidàbile *adj* voidable

invalidaménto *m* invalidity; invalidation

invalidare (invàlido) *tr* to void, invalidate; to negate (*e.g., evidence*)

invalidi·tà *f* (-tà) invalidity; invalidation; sickness, disability

invàli·do -da *adj* void, invalid; sick, disabled || *m* disabled person; invalid

inval·so -sa *adj* prevailing

invano *adv* in vain, vainly

invariàbile *adj* invariable

invaria·to -ta *adj* unchanging; unchanged

invasare *tr* to pot (*a plant*); to fill up (*a reservoir*); to possess, obsess

invasa·to -ta *adj* possessed, obsessed

invasióne *f* invasion

inva·so -sa *adj* invaded || *m* potting (*of plant*); capacity (*of reservoir*)

inva·sóre **-ditrice** *adj* invading || *m* invader

invecchiaménto *m* aging

invecchiare §287 (invècchio) *tr & intr* (ESSERE) to age

invéce *adv* on the contrary, instead; **invece di** instead of

inveire §176 *intr* to inveigh, rail

invelenire §176 *tr* to envenom; to embitter || *intr* (ESSERE) & *ref* to grow bitter

invendìbile *adj* unsalable

invendica·to -ta *adj* unavenged

invendu·to -ta *adj* unsold

inventare (invènto) *tr* to invent

inventariare §287 *tr* to inventory

inventà·rio *m* (-ri) inventory

inventi·vo -va *adj* inventive || *f* inventiveness

inven·tóre **-trice** *adj* inventive || *mf* inventor

invenzióne *f* invention; (lit) find

inverdire §176 *intr* (ESSERE) to turn green

inverecóndia *f* immodesty

inverecón·do -da *adj* immodest

invernale *adj* winter; wintry

inverniciare §128 *tr* to paint; to varnish

invèrno *m* winter

invéro *adv* (lit) truly, indeed

inverosimiglianza [s] *f* unlikelihood

inverosìmile [s] *adj* unlikely

inversióne *f* inversion

invèr·so -sa *adj* inverse, opposite; (coll) cross || *m* inverse

inversóre *m* inverter; **inversore di spinta** (aer) thrust reverser

invertebra·to -ta *adj & m* invertebrate

invertire §176 & (invèrto) *tr* to invert; to reverse

inverti·to -ta *adj* inverted || *m* invert

investigare §209 (invèstigo) *tr* to investigate

investiga·tóre **-trice** *adj* investigating || *mf* investigator; detective

investigazióne *f* investigation

investiménto *m* investment; collision

investire (invèsto) *tr* to invest; to collide with; **investire di insulti** to cover with insults || *ref*—**investirsi di** to become conscious of (*e.g., one's authority*); (theat) to become identified with (*a character*)

investi·tóre **-trice** *mf* investor

investitura *f* investiture

invetera·to -ta *adj* inveterate, confirmed

invetria·to **-ta** *adj* glazed ‖ *f* window; window pane

invettiva *f* invective

inviare §119 *tr* to send

invia·to **-ta** *mf* envoy; correspondent

invidia *f* envy

invidiàbile *adj* enviable

invidiare §287 *tr* to envy; to begrudge; **non aver niente da invidiare a** to be just as good as

invidió·so **-sa** [s] *adj* envious

invigorire §176 *tr* to strengthen, invigorate ‖ *intr* (ESSERE) & *ref* to grow stronger

invilire §176 *tr* to dishearten; to vilify; to lower (*prices*) ‖ *intr* (ESSERE) & *ref* to lose heart; to lose one's reputation

inviluppare *tr* to envelop; to wrap up

invincibile *adj* invincible

invi·o *m* (**-i**) dispatch; shipment; remittance; envoy (*of a poem*)

inviolàbile *adj* inviolable

inviperire §176 *ref* to become enraged

invischiare §287 *tr* to smear with birdlime; to ensnare ‖ *ref* to become ensnared

invisibile *adj* invisible

invi·so **-sa** *adj* disliked, hated

invitante *adj* attractive, inviting

invitare *tr* to invite; to summon; (*cards*) to bid; (*cards*) to open; (*mach*) to screw (*e.g., a light bulb*) in; to screw (*e.g., a lid*) on

invita·to **-ta** *adj* invited ‖ *m* guest

invito *m* invitation; inducement; bottom of stairway; (*cards*) opening

invit·to **-ta** *adj* unvanquished

invocare §197 (**invòco**) *tr* to invoke

invocazióne *f* invocation

invogliare §280 (**invòglio**) *tr* to induce, entice ‖ *ref* to yearn, long

involare (**invólo**) *tr* to steal; to abduct ‖ *intr* (ESSERE) (aer) to take off ‖ *ref* to disappear; to fly away

invòlgere §289 *tr* to wrap, envelop; to involve ‖ *ref* to become entangled

invólo *m* (aer) take-off

involontà·rio **-ria** *adj* (**-ri -rie**) involuntary

invòlto *m* bundle; wrapper

invòlucro *m* wrapping; shell (*of boiler*); (aer) envelope

involu·to **-ta** *adj* (fig) involved; (lit) enveloped

invòlvere §147 (*pret* missing; *pp* also **invòlto**) *tr* (lit) to envelop

invulneràbile *adj* invulnerable

inzaccherare (**inzàcchero**) *tr* to bespatter

inzeppare (**inzéppo**) *tr* to cram, stuff

inzuccherare (**inzùcchero**) *tr* to sweeten

inzuppare *tr* to soak ‖ *ref* to get drenched

ìo *m* ego; self ‖ §5 *pron pers*

iòdio *m* iodine

iodìdri·co **-ca** *adj* (**-ci -che**) hydriodic

ioduro *m* iodide

iògurt *m* yogurt

iò·le *f* (**-le**) (naut) yawl; (sports) shell

ióne *m* ion

iòni·co **-ca** *adj* & *m* (**-ci -che**) Ionic

ionizzare [ddzz] *tr* to ionize

iòsa [s] *f*—**a iosa** in abundance

iperacidità *f* hyperacidity

ipèrbole *f* (geom) hyperbola; (rhet) hyperbole

iperbòli·co **-ca** *adj* (**-ci -che**) hyperbolic(al)

ipereccita·to **-ta** *adj* overexcited

ipermercato *m* shopping center

ipersensibile *adj* hypersensitive; supersensitive

ipersostentatóre *m* landing flap

ipertensióne *f* hypertension

ipnò·si *f* (**-si**) hypnosis

ipnòti·co **-ca** *adj* & *m* (**-ci -che**) hypnotic

ipnotismo *m* hypnotism

ipnotizzare [ddzz] *tr* to hypnotize

ipnotizza·tóre **-trice** [ddzz] *adj* hypnotizing ‖ *m* hypnotizer

ipocondrìa·co **-ca** *adj* & *mf* (**-ci -che**) hypochondriac

ipocrisìa *f* hypocrisy

ipòcri·ta (**-ti -te**) *adj* hypocritical ‖ *mf* hypocrite

ipodèrmi·co **-ca** *adj* (**-ci -che**) hypodermic

iposolfito [s] *m* hyposulfite

ipotè·ca *f* (**-che**) mortgage

ipotecare §197 (**ipotèco**) *tr* to mortgage

ipotecà·rio **-ria** *adj* (**-ri -rie**) mortgage

ipotenusa *f* hypotenuse

ipòte·si *f* (**-si**) hypothesis; **nella miglior delle ipotesi** at best; **nell'ipotesi che** in the event; **per ipotesi** by supposition

ipotèti·co **-ca** *adj* (**-ci -che**) hypothetic(al)

ipotizzare [ddzz] *tr* to hypothesize

ìppi·co **-ca** *adj* (**-ci -che**) horse, horseracing ‖ *f* horse racing

ippocampo *m* sea horse

ippocastano *m* horse chestnut tree

ippòdromo *m* race track

ippoglòsso *m* (ichth) halibut

ippopòtamo *m* hippopotamus

iprite *f* mustard gas

ira *f* wrath, anger, ire

irachè·no **-na** *adj* & *mf* Iraqi

iracóndia *f* wrath, anger

iracón·do **-da** *adj* wrathful

irania·no **-na** *adj* & *mf* Iranian

irascibile *adj* irascible

ira·to **-ta** *adj* irate, angry

ire §191 *intr* (ESSERE) (lit) to go

irida·to **-ta** *adj* rainbow-hued ‖ *m* world bicycle champion

ìride *f* rainbow; (anat, bot) iris

Irlanda, l' *f* Ireland

irlandése [s] *adj* Irish ‖ *m* Irishman; Irish (*language*) ‖ *f* Irishwoman

ironìa *f* irony

iròni·co **-ca** *adj* (**-ci -che**) ironic(al)

iró·so **-sa** [s] *adj* angry, wrathful

irradiare §287 *tr* to illuminate; to irradiate, radiate; to brighten; (rad) to broadcast ‖ *intr* to radiate ‖ *ref* to radiate; to spread

irraggiare §290 *tr* to illuminate; to irradiate, radiate, beam; to brighten; (rad) to broadcast ‖ *intr* to radiate ‖ *ref* to radiate; to spread

irraggiungìbile adj unattainable
irragionévole adj unreasonable
irrancidire §176 intr (ESSERE) & ref to get rancid
irrazionale adj irrational
irreale adj unreal
irreconciliàbile adj irreconcilable
irrecuperàbile adj irretrievable, irrecoverable
irredentismo m irredentism
irredenti·sta mf (-sti -ste) irredentist
irredèn·to -ta adj not yet redeemed
irredimìbile adj irredeemable
irrefrenàbile adj unrestrainable
irrefutàbile adj irrefutable
irregimentare (irregiménto) tr to regiment
irregolare adj irregular
irregolari·tà f (-tà) irregularity
irreligió·so -sa [s] adj irreligious
irremovìbile adj irremovable; obstinate
irreparàbile adj irreparable; unavoidable
irreperìbile adj not to be found; unaccounted for (e.g., soldier)
irreprensìbile adj irreproachable
irreprimìbile adj irrepressible
irrequiè·to -ta adj restless, restive
irresistìbile [s] adj irresistible
irresolùbile [s] adj unbreakable (bond; contract); insoluble; unsolvable
irresolu·to -ta [s] adj irresolute
irrespiràbile adj unbreathable
irresponsàbile adj irresponsible
irrestringìbile adj unshrinkable
irretire §176 tr to ensnare, entrap
irrevocàbile adj irrevocable
irriconoscìbile adj unrecognizable
irriducìbile adj irreducible; stubborn
irriflessì·vo -va adj thoughtless, rash
irrigare §209 tr to irrigate
irrigazióne f irrigation
irrigidire §176 tr to chill || intr & ref to stiffen, harden; to get cool
irri·guo -gua adj well-watered; irrigating
irrilevante adj irrelevant
irrilevanza f irrelevance
irrimediàbile adj irremediable
irripetìbile adj unrepeatable
irrisióne f (lit) derision, mockery
irrisò·rio -ria adj (-ri -rie) mocking; paltry
irritàbile adj peevish; irritable
irritante adj irritating || m irritant
irritare (irrìto) tr to irritate; to anger; to chafe || ref to become irritated
irritazióne f irritation
irriverènte adj irreverent
irrobustire §176 tr & ref to strengthen
irrómpere §240 (pp missing) intr to burst
irrorare (irròro) tr to sprinkle; to bathe, wet; to spray
irroratrice f sprayer; **irroratrice a zaino** portable sprayer
irruènte adj impetuous, rash
irruzióne f foray, raid; irruption
irsu·to -ta adj hairy, bristling
ir·to -ta adj prickly; shaggy (hair); **irto di** bristling with
iscrìvere §250 tr to inscribe; to register || ref to register; to sign up

iscrizióne f inscription; registration
Islam, l' m Islam
Islanda, l' f Iceland
islandése [s] adj Icelandic || mf Icelander || m Icelandic (language)
ìsola f island; block; **ìsola spartitraffico** traffic island
isolaménto m isolation; (elec) insulation
isola·no -na adj island || mf islander
isolante adj insulating || m (elec) insulation
isolare (ìsolo) tr to isolate; (elec) to insulate || ref to keep apart
isola·to -ta adj isolated; (elec) insulated || m city block; (sports) independent
isolatóre m (elec) insulator
isolazionismo m isolationism
isolazioni·sta mf (-sti -ste) isolationist
isolétta f isle
isòscele adj isosceles
isòto·po -pa adj isotopic || m isotope
ispani·sta mf (-sti -ste) Hispanist
ispa·no -na adj Hispanic
ispanoamerica·no -na adj & mf Spanish-American
ispessire §176 tr & ref to thicken
ispettorato m inspectorship
ispet·tóre -trice mf inspector; **ispettore di produzione** (mov) production manager
ispezionare (ispezióno) tr to inspect
ispezióne f inspection
ìspi·do -da adj bristly
ispirare tr to inspire || ref to be inspired
ispirazióne f inspiration
Israèle m Israel
israelia·no -na adj & mf Israeli
israeli·ta adj & mf (-ti -te) Israelite
issare tr to hoist
issòpo m hyssop
istallare tr & ref var of **installare**
istantàne·o -a adj instantaneous || f snapshot
istante m instant, moment; petitioner
istanza f petition; request, application; (law) instance; **in ultima istanza** as a final decision
istèri·co -ca (-ci -che) adj hysteric(al) || mf hysteric
isterilire §176 tr to make barren || ref to become barren
isterismo m hysteria, hysterics
istigare §209 tr to instigate, prompt
istiga·tóre -trice mf instigator
istillare tr to instill, implant; **istillare il collirio negli occhi** to put drops in the eyes
istinti·vo -va adj instinctive
istinto m instinct
istituire §176 tr to institute, found; (lit) to decide
istituto m institute; institution; bank; **istituto di bellezza** beauty parlor
istitu·tóre -trice mf founder; teacher, instructor || m tutor || f governess; nurse
istituzionalizzare [ddzz] tr to institutionalize
istituzióne f institution
istmo m isthmus
istologìa f histology

istoriare §287 (istòrio) *tr* to adorn with historical figures

istradare *tr* to direct ‖ *ref* to wend one's way

ìstrice *m & f* (European) porcupine

istrióne *m* ham actor; buffoon

istriòni·co -ca *adj* (-ci -che) histrionic

istrionismo *m* histrionics

istruire §176 *tr* to instruct; to train; (law) to draw up, prepare (*a case*) ‖ *ref* to learn

istruì·to -ta *adj* learned, educated

istruménto *m* (law) instrument

istrutti·vo -va *adj* instructive

istrut·tóre -trice *mf* instructor; (sports) coach

istruttò·rio -ria (-ri -rie) *adj* investigating, preliminary ‖ *f* (law) preliminary investigation

istruzióne *f* instruction; (law) prelimi-nary investigation; **istruzioni** instruc-tions; directions

istupidire §176 *tr* to make dull; to stupefy

Itàlia, l' *f* Italy

italia·no -na *adj & mf* Italian

itàli·co -ca *adj* (-ci -che) italic; Italic; (lit) Italian ‖ *m* italics

italòfo·no -na *adj* Italian-speaking ‖ *m* Italian-speaking person

itinerante *adj* itinerant

itinerà·rio *m* (-ri) itinerary

ittèri·co -ca *adj* (-ci -che) jaundiced

itterìzia *f* jaundice

ittiologìa *f* ichthiology

Iugoslàvia, la Yugoslavia

iugoslà·vo -va *adj & mf* Yugoslav

iugulare *adj & tr* var of **giugulare**

iuta *f* jute

ivi *adv* (lit) there

J
K
L

L, l ['elle] *m & f* tenth letter of the Italian alphabet

la §4 *def art* the ‖ *m* (mus) la, A; **dare il la** to set the tone ‖ §5 *pers pron*

là *adv* there; **al di là** ‖ *m* (mus) la, A; **dare future; al di là da venire** to come, future; **al di là** (**di**) beyond; **andare di là** to go in the next room; **andare troppo in là** to go too far; **farsi in là** to move aside; **in là con gli anni** advanced in years; **l'al di là** the life beyond; **più in là** further; **più in là di** beyond; **va' là!** come on!

làb·bro *m* (-bri) edge (*of wound*); (lit) lip ‖ *m* (-bra *fpl*) lip; **labbro lepo-rino** harelip

labiale *adj & f* labial

làbile *adj* (coll) weak; (lit) fleeting

labiolettura *f* lip reading

labirinto *m* labyrinth, maze

laboratò·rio *m* (-ri) laboratory; work-shop; **laboratorio linguistico** lan-guage laboratory

laborió·so -sa [s] *adj* hard-working, laborious; labored (*e.g., digestion*)

laburì·sta (-sti -ste) *adj* Labour ‖ *mf* Labourite

lac·ca *f* (-che) lacquer

laccare §197 *tr* to lacquer; to japan; to polish (*nails*)

lac·chè *m* (-chè) lackey

lac·cio *m*·(-ci) lasso; snare; noose; string; (fig) bond; **laccio delle scarpe** shoelace; **laccio emostatico** tourni-quet

lacciòlo *m* snare

lacerare (làcero) *tr* to lacerate; to tear ‖ *ref* to tear

làce·ro -ra *adj* torn; tattered

lacèrto *m* (-ti) shred of flesh; (lit) biceps

lacòni·co -ca *adj* (-ci -che) laconic

làcrima *f* tear; drop

lacrimare (làcrimo) *tr* (lit) to weep

over ‖ *intr* to water (*said of the eyes*); (lit) to weep

lacrima·to -ta *adj* (lit) lamented

lacrimévole *adj* pitiful

lacrimòge·no -no *adj* tear (*e.g., gas*)

lacrimó·so -sa [s] *adj* teary, watery (*eyes*); tearful; lachrymose

lacuna *f* gap, lacuna; blank (*in one's mind*); **colmare una lacuna** to bridge a gap

lacustre *adj* lake

laddóve *conj* while, whereas

ladré·sco -sca *adj* (-schi -sche) thievish

la·dro -dra *adj* thieving; foul (*weather*); bewitching (*eyes*) ‖ *mf* thief; **ladro di strada** highwayman ‖ *f* inside pocket (*of suit*)

ladróne *m* thief; highwayman; **ladrone di mare** pirate

ladrùncolo *m* petty thief, pilferer

laggiù *adv* down there

lagnanza *f* complaint

lagnare *ref* to complain; to moan

lagno *m* complaint, lament

la·go *m* (-ghi) lake; pool (*of blood*)

làgrima *f* var of **lacrima**

laguna *f* lagoon

lai *m* (lai) lay; **lai** *mpl* (lit) lamen-tations

laicato *m* laity

lài·co -ca *adj* (-ci -che) lay ‖ *m* layman

lài·do -da *adj* foul; obscene

la·ma *m* (-ma) llama; lama ‖ *f* (-me) blade (*of knife*); marsh; (lit) lowland

lambiccare §197 *tr* to distill ‖ *ref* to strive; **lambiccarsi il cervello** to rack one's brains

lambì·co·m (-chi) still

lambire §176 *tr* to lap; to graze, to touch lightly

lamèlla *f* thin sheet

lamentare (laménto) *tr* to bemoan, lament ‖ *ref* to moan; to complain

lamentazióne *f* lamentation

lamentévole *adj* plaintive; lamentable

laménto *m* complaint, lament; moan

lamento·so -sa [s] *adj* plaintive, doleful

lamétta *f* razor blade

lamièra *f* plate; armor plate

lamierino *m* sheet metal, lamina

làmina *f* sheet, lamina

laminare (làmino) *tr* to laminate; to roll (*steel*)

lamina·tóio *m* (**-tói**) rolling mill

làmpada *f* lamp, light; **lampada al neon** neon lamp; **lampada a petrolio oil** lamp; **lampada a stelo pole** lamp; **lampada di sicurezza** (min) safety lamp; **lampada fluorescente** fluorescent lamp; **lampada lampo** (phot) flash bulb

lampadà·rio *m* (**-ri**) chandelier

lampadina *f* bulb; **lampadina tascabile** flashlight

lampante *adj* shiny; clear; lamp (*oil*)

lampeggiare §290 (**lampéggio**) *tr* (lit) to flash (*a smile*) ‖ *intr* to flash; (aut) to blink; (coll) to flash the turn signals ‖ *impers* (ESSERE & AVERE)— **lampeggia** it lightens, it is lightning

lampeggiatóre *m* (aut) turn signal; (phot) flashlight

lampio·nàio *m* (**-nài**) lamplighter

lampióne *m* street lamp

lampìride *f* glowworm

lampo *m* lightning; flash of lightning; (fig) flash

lampóne *m* raspberry

lana *f* wool; **buona lana** (coll) rogue, rascal; **lana d'acciaio** steel wool; **lana di vetro** fiberglass, glass wool

lancétta *f* lancet; hand (*of watch*); pointer (*of instrument*)

làn·cia *f* (**-ce**) lance, spear; nozzle (*of fire hose*); launch; **lancia di salvataggio** lifeboat

lanciabóm·be *m* (**-be**) trench mortar

lanciafiam·me *m* (**-me**) flamethrower

lanciamìssi·li (**-li**) *adj* missile-launching ‖ *m* missile launcher

lanciaraz·zi [ddzz] *m* (**-zi**) rocket launcher

lanciare §128 *tr* to throw, hurl; to drop (*from an airplane*); to launch (*e.g., an advertising campaign*) ‖ *ref* to hurl oneself; (rok) to blast off; **lanciarsi col paracadute** to parachute, bail out

lanciasilu·ri *m* (**-ri**) torpedo tube

lancia·to -ta *adj* hurled, flung; flying, e.g., **partenza lanciata** flying start

lancia·tóre -trice *mf* hurler, thrower; (baseball) pitcher

lancière *m* lancer

lancinante *adj* piercing

làn·cio *m* (**-ci**) throw; publicity campaign; (aer) drop; (aer) release (*of bombs*); (baseball) pitch; (rok) launch; **lancio del peso** shot put

landa *f* moor; wasteland

lanerìe *fpl* woolens

languidézza *f* languidness, languor

làngui·do -da *adj* languid; sad (*eyes*)

languire (**lànguo**) & §176 *intr* to languish

languóre *m* languor; languishing; weakness; tenderness

laniè·ro -ra *adj* wool (*industry*)

lanifi·cio *m* (**-ci**) woolen mill

lanó·so -sa [s] *adj* woolly; kinky (*hair*); bushy (*face*)

lantèrna *f* lantern

lanùgine *f* down

lanzichenéc·co *m* (**-chi**) landsknecht

laónde *conj* (lit) wherefore

laotia·no -na *adj & mf* Laotian

lapalissia·no -na *adj* self-evident

lapidare (**làpido**) *tr* to stone (to death); (fig) to pick to pieces

làpide *f* stone tablet; tombstone

lapillo *m* lapillus

là·pis *m* (**-pis**) pencil

lappare *intr* to lap

làppola *f* (bot) burdock; (bot) bur

lappóne *adj* Lappish ‖ *mf* Lapp ‖ *m* Lapp (*language*)

Lappónia, la Lapland

lardellare (**lardèllo**) *tr* to lard; to stuff with bacon

lardo *m* lard; **nuotare nel lardo** to live on easy street

largheggiare §290 (**larghéggio**) *intr* to be liberal; to be lavish

larghézza *f* width; liberality; abundance; **larghezza di vedute** broadmindedness

largire §176 *tr* (lit) to bestow liberally

largizióne *f* bestowal; donation

lar·go -ga (**-ghi -ghe**) *adj* broad, wide; ample; liberal; abundant; (phonet) open; **prenderla larga** to keep away ‖ *m* width; open sea; square; (mus) largo; **al largo** di (naut) off; **fare largo a** to open the way to; **farsi largo** to elbow one's way; **prendere il largo** to run away; (naut) to put to sea; **tenersi al largo** to keep at a distance ‖ *f*—**alla larga!** keep away! ‖ **largo** *adv*—**girare largo** to keep away

làrice *m* larch

laringe *f* larynx

laringite *f* laryngitis

laringoia·tra *mf* (**-tri -tre**) laryngologist

laringoscò·pio *m* (**-pi**) laryngoscope

larva *f* (ent) larva; (lit) ghost; (lit) skeleton; (lit) sham

lasagne *fpl* lasagne

lasciapassa·re *m* (**-re**) safe-conduct; permit

lasciare §128 *tr* to leave; to let; to let go of; **lasciar cadere** to drop; **lasciarci le penne** (coll) to die; (coll) to be skinned alive; **lasciar correre** to let go; **lasciar detto** to leave word; **lasciar fare** to leave alone; **lasciare in pace** to leave alone; **lasciare libero** to let go; **lasciare scritto** to leave in writing ‖ *ref* to abandon oneself; to abandon one another

làscito *m* (law) bequest

lascìvia *f* lasciviousness

lascì·vo -va *adj* lascivious

lassati·vo -va *adj* mildly laxative ‖ *m* mild laxative

lassìssimo *m* laxity

las·so -sa *adj* lax ‖ *m* lasso; **lasso di tempo** period of time

lassù *adv* up there, up above

lastra *f* slab; paving stone; (phot)

plate; exposed X-ray film; **farsi le lastre** (coll) to be X-rayed

lastricare §197 (làstrico) *tr* to pave

lastricato *m* paving, pavement

làstri·co *m* (**-ci** or **-chi**) pavement; roadway; **ridursi sul lastrico** to fall into abject poverty

lastróne *m* slab; plate glass

latènte *adj* latent

laterale *adj* lateral || *m* (soccer) halfback

laterì·zio -zia (-zi -zie) *adj* brick || **laterizi** *mpl* bricks, tiles

làtice *m* latex

latifondi·sta *mf* (**-sti -ste**) rich landowner

latifóndo *m* large landed estate

lati·no -na *adj* Latin; lateen (*sail*) || *m* Latin

latitante *adj* hiding || *mf* fugitive

latitanza *f* flight from justice

latitùdine *f* latitude

la·to -ta *adj* wide; broad (*meaning*) || *m* side; **d'altro lato** on the other hand

la·tóre -trice *mf* bearer

latrare *intr* to bark

latrato *m* bark

latrina *f* toilet, lavatory, washroom

latta *f* tin; can

lattàia *f* milkmaid

lat·tàio *m* (**-tài**) milkman, dairyman

lattante *adj* & *m* suckling

latte *m* milk; **latte detergente** cleansing cream; **latte di gallina** flip; (bot) star-of-Bethlehem; **latte in polvere** powdered milk; **latte magro** or **scremato** skim milk

lattemièle *m* whipped cream

làtte·o -a *adj* milky

latterìa *f* dairy; creamery

làttice *m* var of latice

latticèllo *m* buttermilk

lattici·nio *m* (**-ni**) dairy product

lattignó·so -sa (**-si**) *adj* milky

lattonière *f* tinsmith

lattu·ga *f* (**-ghe**) lettuce; head of lettuce; frill

làudano *m* paregoric, laudanum

laudati·vo -va *adj* laudatory

làurea *f* wreath; doctorate; doctoral examination

laurean·do -da *mf* candidate for the doctorate

laureare (làureo) *tr* to confer the doctorate on; to award (*s.o.*) the title of; (lit) to wreathe || *ref* to receive the doctorate; (sports) to get the tile of

laurea·to -ta *adj* laureate || *m* alumnus, graduate

làuro *m* laurel

làu·to -ta *adj* sumptuous, rich

lava *f* lava

lavabianche·rìa *f* (**-rìa**) washing machine

lavàbile *adj* washable

lavabo *m* washstand; lavatory

lavacristallo *m* windshield washer

lavacro *m* washing; font; purification; **santo lavacro** baptism

lavàg·gio *m* (**-gi**) washing; **lavaggio a secco** dry cleaning; **lavaggio del cervello** brainwashing

lavagna *f* slate; blackboard; **lavagna di panno** felt board; **lavagna luminosa** overhead projector

lavama·no *m* (**-no**) washstand

lavanda *f* washing; pumping (*of stomach*); lavender

lavandàia *f* laundrywoman; **lavandaia stiratrice** laundress (*woman who washes and irons*)

lavan·dàio *m* (**-dài**) laundryman; **lavandaio stiratore** launderer

lavanderìa *f* laundry; **lavanderia a gettone** laundromat; **lavanderia a secco** dry-cleaning establishment

lavandino *m* sink

lavapiat·ti *mf* (**-ti**) dishwasher (*person*)

lavare *tr* to wash; to cleanse; **lavare a secco** to dry-clean; **lavare il capo a** to scold || *ref* to wash oneself; **lavarsi le mani** to wash one's hands

lavastovì·glie *m* (**-glie**) dishwasher || *m & f* dishwasher (*machine*)

lavata *f* washing; **lavata di capo** scolding

lavativo *m* (coll) enema; (coll) bore; (coll) goldbricker

lava·tóio *m* (**-tói**) laundry room; washtub

lava·tóre -trice *mf* washer || *m* washerman; (mach) purifier || *f* washerwoman; washing machine

lavatura *f* washing; **lavatura a secco** dry cleaning; **lavatura di piatti** dishwater; washing of dishes; (fig) watery soup

lavèllo *m* wash basin; sink

lavoràbile *adj* workable

lavorante *mf* helper, apprentice

lavorare (lavóro) *tr* to work; to till || *intr* to work; to perform; to be busy; to trade; **lavorare ai ferri** to knit; **lavorare di fantasia** to daydream; **lavorare di ganasce** to eat voraciously; **lavorare di gomiti** to elbow one's way; **lavorare di mano** to pilfer; **lavorare di traforo** to work with a jig saw

lavorati·vo -va *adj* working; workable

lavora·to -ta *adj* wrought; tilled

lavora·tóre -trice *mf* worker || *m* workman; workingman || *f* workingwoman

lavorazióne *f* working; manufacturing; tilling

lavorì·o *m* (**-i**) bustle; steady work; scheming

lavóro *m* work; labor; steady work; homework; piece of work; (coll) trouble; **a lavori ultimati** when the work is finished; **lavori forzati** hard labor; **lavori in economia** time and material contract work; **lavori teatrali** theatrical productions; **lavoro a cottimo** piecework; **lavoro a maglia** knitting; **lavoro di cucito** needlework; **mettere al lavoro** to press into service

lazzarétto [ddzz] *m* lazaretto

lazzaróne [ddzz] *m* cad; (coll) goldbricker

le §4 *def art* the || **§5** *pers pron*

leale *adj* loyal; sincere

leali·sta *mf* (**-sti -ste**) loyalist

leal·tà *f* (**-tà**) loyalty; sincerity

lébbra f leprosy
lebbró·so -sa [s] adj leprous || mf leper
lécca-léc·ca m (-ca) (coll) lollypop
leccapiat·ti m (-ti) glutton; sponger
leccapiè·di mf (-di) bootlicker
leccarda f dripping pan
leccare §197 (lécco) tr to lick; to fawn
on; (fig) to polish || ref to make one-
self up
lecca·to -ta adj affected; polished ||
f licking
léc·cio m (-ci) holm oak
leccornìa f dainty morsel, delicacy
léci·to -ta adj licit, permissible; **mi sia
lecito** may I || m right
lèdere §192 tr to damage, injure
lé·ga f (-ghe) league; alloy; **di bassa
lega** poor, in poor taste; **fare lega**
to unite
legale adj legal; lawyer's; official || m
lawyer
legali·tà f (-tà) legality, lawfulness
legalità·rio -ria adj (-ri -rie) (pol) observing the rule of law
legalizzare [ddzz] tr to legalize; to authenticate
legame m bond; connection; relationship
legaménto m tie, bond; ligament;
(phonet) liaison
legare §209 (légo) tr to tie; to bind; to
unite; to set (a stone); to bequeath;
to alloy; (bb) to bind || intr to bond;
to mix (said of metals); to go to-
gether || ref to unite; **legàrsela al
dito** to never forget
legatà·rio -ria mf (-ri -rie) legatee
lega·to -ta adj muscle-bound || m
legate; bequest; (mus) legato
lega·tóre -trice mf bookbinder
legatorìa f bookbindery
legatura f typing; binding; ligature;
bookbinding; (mus) tie
legazióne f legation
légge f law; act; **dettar legge** to lay
down the law; **è fuori della legge**
he is an outlaw; **legge stralcio** emergency law
leggènda f legend; story, tall tale;
(journ) caption
leggendà·rio -ria adj (-ri -rie) legendary
lèggere §193 tr, intr & ref to read
leggerézza f lightness; nimbleness;
thoughtlessness; fickleness
leggè·ro -ra adj light; nimble; thoughtless; slight; fickle; **alla leggera** lightly
|| **leggero** adv lightly
leggia·dro -dra adj graceful, lovely
leggìbile adj legible, readable
leggì·o m (-ìi) lectern; music stand
legiferare (legìfero) intr to legislate
legionà·rio -ria adj & m (-ri -rie) legion-
ary
legióne f legion
legislatì·vo -va adj legislative
legisla·tóre -trice mf legislator
legislatura f legislature
legittimare (legìttimo) tr to legitimize
legittimi·tà f (-tà) legitimacy
legìtti·mo -ma adj legitimate; pure;
just, right || f (law) legitim
lé·gna f (-gna & -gne) firewood; (fig)
fuel

legnàia f woodpile; woodshed
legname m timber, lumber
legnata f clubbing, thrashing
légno m wood; stick; ship; coach;
timber; **legno compensato** plywood;
legno dolce softwood; **legno forte**
hardwood
legnòlo m ply (e.g., of a cable)
legnó·so -sa [s] adj wooden; tough
(meat); dry (style)
legu·lèio m (-lèi) pettifogger
legume m legume; **legumi** vegetables;
legumes
leguminósa [s] f leguminous plant;
leguminose legumes
lèi §5 pron pers; **dare del Lei a** to
address formally
lémbo m edge, border; patch (of land)
lèm·ma m (-mi) entry (in a dictionary)
lèmme lèmme adv (coll) slowly
léna f energy; enthusiasm; (lit) breath
lèndine m nit
lène adj (lit) light, soft, gentle; (phonet)
voiced
lenire §176 tr to soothe, assuage
lenóne m panderer, procurer
lenóna f procuress
lènte f lens; bob, pendulum bob; **lente
d'ingrandimento** magnifying glass;
lenti glasses
lentézza f slowness
lentìcchia f lentil
lentìggine f freckle
lentigginó·so -sa [s] adj freckly
lèn·to -ta adj slow; slack; (lit) loose
(hair); (lit) loose-fitting (garment) ||
lento adv slowly
lènza f fishline
lenzuò·lo m (-li) sheet; (fig) blanket;
lenzuolo a due piazze double sheet;
lenzuolo funebre winding sheet,
shroud || m (-la fpl) sheet; **lenzuola**
pair of sheets (in a bed)
leoncino m lion cub
leóne m lion; **leone d'America** cougar;
leóne marino sea lion || **Leone** m
(astr) Leo
leonéssa f lioness
leopardo m leopard
lepidézza f wit; witticism
lèpi·do -da adj witty, facetious
lepisma f (ent) silverfish
lèpre adj invar rendezvous, e.g., **razzo
lepre** rendezvous rocket || f hare
lepròtto m leveret, young hare
lèr·cio -cia adj (-ci -ce) filthy
lerciume m filth, dirt
lèsbi·co -ca (-ci -che) adj & mf Lesbian
|| f Lesbian (female homosexual)
lésina f awl; stinginess; miser
lesinare (lésino & lèsino) tr to begrudge
|| intr to be miserly
lesionare (lesióno) tr to damage; to
crack open
lesióne f damage; injury; lesion
lé·so -sa adj damaged; injured
lessare (lésso) tr to boil
lessicale adj lexical
lèssi·co m (-ci) lexicon
lessicografìa f lexicography
lessicogràfi·co -ca adj (-ci -che) lexico-
graphic(al)
lessicògrafo m lexicographer

lessicologìa f lexicology
lés·so -sa adj boiled || m boiled meat; soup meat
lè·sto -sta adj swift; nimble; quick; **alla lesta** hastily; **lesto di lingua** ready-tongued; **lesto di mano** light-fingered
lestofante m swindler
letale adj lethal, deadly
leta·màio m (-mài) dunghill
letame m manure, dung
letàrgi·co -ca adj (-ci -che) lethargic
letar·go m (-ghi) lethargy; hibernation
letìzia f happiness, joy
lèttera f letter; **alla lettera** literally; **lettera morta** unheeded, e.g., **le sue parole rimasero lettera morta** his words remained unheeded; **lettere** literature; **lettere credenziali** credentials; **scrìvere in tutte lettere** to spell out
letterale adj literal
lettera·rio -ria adj (-ri -rie) literary; learned (word)
lettera·to -ta adj literary; literate || m man of letters; (coll) literate, learned person
letteratura f literature
lettièra f litter, bedding
letti·ga f (-ghe) sedan chair; stretcher
lètto m bed; bedding; **di primo letto** born of the first marriage; **letti gemelli** twin beds; **letto a castello** bunk bed; **letto a due piazze** double bed; **letto a scomparsa** Murphy bed; **letto a una piazza** single bed; **letto bastardo** oversize bed; **letto caldo** hotbed; **letto di morte** deathbed; **letto operatorio** operating table
lèttone or **lettóne** adj Lettish || mf Lett || m Lett, Lettish (language)
Lettònia, La Latvia
let·tóre -trice mf reader; lecturer; meter reader || m reader (e.g., for microfilm); **lettore perforatore** reader (of punch cards)
lettura f reading; lecture; **lettura del pensiero** mind reading
letturi·sta m (-sti) meter reader
leucemìa f leukemia
leucorrèa f leucorrhea
lèva f lever; (mil) draft; (mil) class; **essere di leva** to be of draft age; **fare leva su** to use (s.o.'s emotions)
levachio·di m (-di) claw hammer
levante adj rising || m east; Levant
levanti·no -na adj & mf Levantine
levare (lèvo) tr to lift, raise; to weigh (anchor); to pull (a tooth); to break (camp); to collect (mail); to remove, take away; to subtract; **levare alle stelle** to praise to the sky; **levare il disturbo** a to take leave of || ref to arise; to get up; to take off; to satisfy (e.g., one's hunger); to rise (said of wind); **levarsi dai piedi** to get out of the way; **levarsi dai piedi** or **di mezzo qlcu** to get rid of s.o.
levata f rise; reveille; collection (of mail); withdrawal (of merchandise from warehouse); **levata di scudi** uprising
levatàc·cia f (-ce) getting up at an im-

possible hour; **ho dovuto fare una levataccia I** had to get up way too early
leva·tóio -tóia adj (-tói -tóie)—**ponte levatoio** drawbridge
levatrice f midwife
levatura f intellectual breadth
leviatano m leviathan
levigare §209 (lèvigo) tr to polish
levigatrice f sander; buffer
levi·tà f (-tà) (lit) levity
levitazióne f levitation
levrière m greyhound
lezióne f lesson; lecture; reading
lezió·so -sa [s] adj affected, mincing
lézzo [ddzz] m stench; filth
li def art masc plur (obs) the; **li tre novembre** the third of November (in official documents) || §5 pers pron
lì adv there; **di lì** that way; **di lì a un anno** a year hence; **essere lì lì per** to be about to; **fin lì** up to that point; **giù di lì** more or less; **lì per lì** on the spot
libanése [s] adj & mf Lebanese
Libano, il Lebanon
libare tr to toast; to taste || intr to toast
libazióne f libation
libbra f pound
libéc·cio m (-ci) southwest wind
libèllo m libel; (law) brief
libèllula f dragonfly
liberale adj & m liberal
liberali·tà f (-tà) liberality
liberare (lìbero) tr to free; to pay in full for; to open into (said, e.g., of a hall opening into a room); to clear, empty (a room) || ref—**liberarsi da** or **di** to get rid of
libera·tóre -trice adj liberating || mf liberator
liberismo m free trade
lìbe·ro -ra adj free; vacant; without a revenue stamp (document); open (syllable; heart); outspoken
liber·tà f (-tà) freedom; release (e.g., from mortgage); **libertà provvisoria** bail, parole; **libertà vigilata** probation; **mettersi in libertà** to put comfortable house clothes on; **rimettere in libertà** to set free
liberti·no -na adj & mf libertine
Lìbia, la Libya
lìbi·co -ca adj & mf (-ci -che) Libyan
libìdine f lust; greed
libidinó·so -sa [s] adj lustful
libido f libido
li·bràio m (-brài) bookseller
librare ref to balance; to soar; (aer) to glide
libratóre m (aer) glider
librerìa f bookstore; library (room); bookshelf; book collection
libré·sco -sca adj (-schi -sche) bookish
librétto m booklet; card; (mus) libretto; **libretto di banca** passbook; **libretto degli assegni** checkbook; **libretto di circolazione** car registration; **libretto ferroviario** railroad pass; **libretto di risparmio** passbook (of savings bank)
libro m book; ledger; register (e.g., of births); **a libro** folding; **libro di**

bordo log; **libro in brossura** paperback; **libro mastro** ledger; **libro paga** (com) payroll

liceale *adj* high-school || *mf* high-school student

licènza *f* permit; license; diploma; (mil) leave; **con licenza parlando!** excuse my language!; **dar licenza a** to dismiss; **prender licenza da** to take leave of

licenziaménto *m* dismissal; **licenziamento in tronco** firing on the spot

licenziare §287 (licènzio) *tr* to dismiss; to O.K. (*a book to be published*); to graduate || *ref* to take leave; to give notice, resign; to graduate

licenzió·so -sa [s] *adj* licentious

licèo *m* high school; lycée

lichène *m* lichen

licitazióne *f* auction; (bridge) bidding

lido *m* shore; sand bar

liè·to -ta *adj* glad; blessed (*event*)

lième *adj* light; slight

lievitare (lièvito) *tr* to leaven || *intr* (ESSERE & AVERE) to rise; to ferment

lièvito *m* yeast; leaven; **lievito in polvere** baking powder

lì·gio -gia *adj* (-gi -gie) devoted

lignàg·gio *m* (-gi) ancestry, lineage

ligustro *m* privet

lil·la (-la) *adj invar & m* lilac

lillipuzia·no -na *adj & mf* Lilliputian

lima *f* file; **lima per le unghie** nail file

limacció·so -sa [s] *adj* miry, muddy

limare *tr* to file; to polish (*e.g., a speech*); to gnaw, plague

limatura *f* filing; filings

limbo *m* (lit) edge; (fig) limbo || **Limbo** *m* (theol) Limbo

limétta *f* nail file; (bot) lime

limitare *m* threshold || *v* (lìmito) *tr* to limit; to bound

limitazióne *f* limitation

lìmite *m* limit; boundary; check; (soccer) penalty line; **limite di carico massimo** maximum weight; **limite di età retirement** age; **limite di velocità** speed limit; **senza limiti** limitless

limìtro·fo -fa *adj* neighboring (*country*)

limo *m* mud, mire

limonare (limóno) *intr* (coll) to spoon

limonata *f* lemonade; (med) citrate of magnesia

limóne *m* lemon tree; lemon

limó·so -sa [s] *adj* slimy

lìmpi·do -da *adj* limpid, clear

lince *f* lynx, wildcat

linciàg·gio *m* (-gi) lynching

linciare §128 *tr* to lynch

lìn·do -da *adj* neat; clean

linea *f* line; degree (*of temperature*); **conservare la linea** to keep one's figure; **in linea** abreast; (telp) connected; **in linea d'aria** as the crow flies; **linea del fuoco** firing line; **linea del cambiamento di data** international date line; **linea di circonvallazione** (rr) beltline; **linea di condotta** policy; **linea di partenza** starting line; **linea laterale** (sports) side line

lineaménti *mpl* lineaments; elements

lineare *adj* linear || *v* (lìneo) *tr* to delineate

lineétta *f* dash; hyphen

linfa *f* (anat) lymph; (bot) sap; **dar linfa** (bot) to bleed

lingòtto *m* (metallurgy) pig, ingot; **lingotto d'oro** bullion

lingua *f* tongue; language; strip (*of land*); **essere di due lingue** to speak with a forked tongue; **in lingua** in the correct language; **lingua di gatto** ladyfinger; **lingua lunga** backbiter; **lingua sciolta** glib tongue; **mala lingua** wicked tongue

linguacciu·to -ta *adj* talkative; sharp-tongued

linguàg·gio *m* (-gi) language

linguèlla *f* (philately) gummed strip

linguétta *f* tongue (*of shoe*); (mach) pin; (mus) reed

linguìsti·co -ca (-ci -che) *adj* linguistic || *f* linguistics

linifì·cio *m* (-ci) flax-spinning mill

liniménto *m* liniment

lino *m* flax; linen

linòsa [s] *f* flaxseed, linseed

linotipì·sta *mf* (-sti -ste) linotypist

liocòrno *m* unicorn

liofilizzare [ddzz] *tr* to freeze-dry

liquefare §194 *tr & ref* to liquefy

liquefazióne *f* liquefaction

liquidare (lìquido) *tr* to liquidate; to close out; to dismiss; to settle

liquidazióne *f* liquidation; clearance; **liquidazione del danno** (ins) adjustment

liquidità *f* liquidity

lìqui·do -da *adj* liquid; (com) due || *m* liquid; cash || *f* liquid

lìqui·gàs *m* (-gàs) liquid gas

liquirìzia *f* licorice

liquóre *m* liqueur; (pharm) liquor

liquorì·sta *mf* (-sti -ste) liqueur manufacturer or dealer

lira *f* lira; pound; (mus) lyre || **Lira** *f* (astr) Lyra

lìri·co -ca (-ci -che) *adj* lyric; (mus) operatic || *m* lyric poet || *f* lyric; lyric poetry; opera

lirismo *m* lyricism

Lisbóna *f* Lisbon

lì·sca *f* (-sche) fishbone; lisp

lisciare §128 *tr* to smooth; **lisciare il pelo a** to butter up, flatter; to beat up || *ref* to preen

lì·scio -scia *adj* (-sci -sce) smooth; straight (*drink*); black (*coffee*); **passarla liscia** to get away scot-free

lisciviare *tr* lye; bleach

lisciviatrice *f* washing machine

lì·so -sa *adj* worn-out, threadbare

lista *f* list; strip, band; stripe; **lista delle spese** shopping list; **lista delle vivande** bill of fare; **lista elettorale** slate (*of candidates*)

listare *tr* to border; to stripe

listèllo *m* lath; (archit) listel

listino *m* price list; market quotation

litania *f* litany

lite *f* quarrel; lawsuit

litigante *adj* quarreling || *mf* quarreler; (law) litigant

litigare §209 (lìtigo) *tr*—**litigare qlco a qlcu** to fight with s.o. for s.th ‖ *intr* to quarrel; to litigate ‖ *ref*—**litigarsi qlco** to strive for s.th
liti·gio *m* (-gi) quarrel, litigation
litigió·so -sa [s] *adj* quarrelsome
litio *m* lithium
litografia *f* lithography
litògrafo *m* lithographer
litorale *adj* littoral ‖ *m* seashore, coastline
litro *m* liter
Lituània, la Lithuania
litua·no -na *adj* & *mf* Lithuanian ‖ *m* Lithuanian (*language*)
liturgìa *f* liturgy
litùrgi·co -ca *adj* (-ci -che) liturgical
liu·tàio *m* (-tài) lute maker
liuto *m* lute
livèlla *f* level; **livella a bolla d'aria** spirit level
livellaménto *m* leveling; equalization
livellare (livèllo) *tr* to level; to equalize; to survey ‖ *intr* (ESSERE) & *ref* to become level
livella·tóre -trice *adj* leveling ‖ *mf* surveyor ‖ *f* bulldozer
livellazióne *f* leveling
livèllo *m* level; **livello delle acque** sea level
lìvi·do -da *adj* livid, black-and-blue ‖ *m* bruise
lividóre *m* bruise
livóre *m* grudge; hatred
Livórno *f* Leghorn
livrèa *f* livery
lizza *f* tilting ground; **entrare in lizza** to enter the lists
lo §4 *def art* the ‖ §5 *pers pron*
lòb·bia *m* & *f* (-bia *mpl* & *fpl*) homburg
lòbo *m* lobe
locale *adj* local ‖ *m* room; place (*of business*); (naut) compartment; **locale notturno** night spot
locali·tà *f* (-tà) locality, spot
localizzare [ddzz] *tr* to localize; to locate ‖ *ref* to become localized
localizzazióne [ddzz] *f* localization; **localizzazione dei guasti** troubleshooting
locanda *f* inn
locandiè·re -ra *mf* innkeeper
locandina *f* playbill; flyer; small poster
locare (§197 (lòco) *tr* to rent, lease
locatà·rio -ria *mf* (-ri -rie) lessee, renter
loca·tóre -trice *mf* lessor
locazióne *f* rent; lease; **dare in locazione** to rent
locomotiva *f* locomotive, engine
locomo·tóre -trice *adj* locomotive ‖ *m* & *f* (rr) electric locomotive
locomotori·sta *m* (-sti) (rr) engineer
locomozióne *f* locomotion; transportation
lòculo *m* burial niche
locusta *f* locust
locuzióne *f* locution, expression; phrase; idiom
lodàbile *adj* praiseworthy
lodare (lòdo) *tr* to praise ‖ *ref* to praise oneself, brag; **lodarsi di** (poet) to be pleased with

lodatì·vo -va *adj* laudatory
lòde *f* praise; **con la lode cum laude; con lode** plus (*on a report card*)
lodévole *adj* praiseworthy, commendable
lòdo *m* arbitration
logaritmo *m* logarithm
lòg·gia *f* (-ge) lodge; (archit) loggia
loggióne *m* (theat) upper gallery
lògi·co -ca (-ci -che) *adj* logical; **esser logico** to think logically ‖ *m* logician ‖ *f* logic
logìsti·co -ca (-ci -che) *adj* logistic ‖ *f* logistics
lò·glio *m* (-gli) cockle
logoraménto *m* wear; attrition
logorare (lógoro) *tr* to wear out; to fray ‖ *ref* to wear away; to become threadbare
logorì·o *m* (-ì) wear and tear
lógo·ro -ra *adj* worn out; threadbare
lòlla *f* chaff
lombàggine *f* lumbago
lombar·do -da *adj* & *mf* Lombard
lombata *f* loin, sirloin
lómbo *m* loin; hip; (lit) ancestry
lombrì·co *m* (-chi) earthworm
londinése [s] *adj* London ‖ *mf* Londoner
Londra *f* London
longànime *adj* patient, forbearing
longanimi·tà *f* (-tà) patience, forbearance
longevità *f* longevity
longè·vo -va *adj* long-lived
longherina *f* beam, girder
longheróne *m* (aer) longeron; (aer) spar; (aut) main frame member
longitùdine *f* longitude
longobar·do -da *adj* & *mf* Lombard
lontananza *f* distance
lonta·no -na *adj* distant, remote; vague; indirect ‖ *m* (lit) far-away place ‖ *f*—**alla lontana** from a distance; vaguely; distant (*e.g., relative*) ‖ **lontano** *adv* far; **da lontano** from afar; **lontano da** away from; far from; **rifarsi da lontano** to start from the very beginning
lóntra *f* otter
lónza *f* pork loin; (poet) leopard
lòppa *f* chaff; skin (*of plant*); slag, dross
loquace *adj* loquacious; (fig) eloquent
loquèla *f* (lit) tongue; (lit) style
lordare (lórdo) *tr* to soil, dirty
lór·do -da *adj* soiled, dirty; gross (*weight*)
lordume *m* dirt, filth
lordura *f* dirt, filth; soil
lóro §5 *pron pers* ‖ §6 *adj poss* & *pron*
losan·ga *f* (-ghe) rhombus; (herald) lozenge
ló·sco -sca *adj* (-schi -sche) squint-eyed; cross-eyed; (fig) shady
lóto *m* mud
lòto *m* lotus
lòtta *f* fight; struggle; wrestling; **essere in lotta** to be at war; **lotta libera** catch-as-catch-can
lottare (lòtto) *intr* to fight; to quarrel; to struggle; to wrestle

lotta·tóre -trice *mf* fighter; wrestler
lotteria *f* lottery
lottizzare [ddzz] *tr* to divide into lots
lòtto *m* lotto; parcel, lot
lozióne *f* lotion
lùbri·co -ca *adj* (-ci -che) lewd; (lit) slippery
lubrificante *adj & m* lubricant
lubrificare §197 (lubrìfico) *tr* to lubricate
lucchétto *m* padlock
luccicare §197 (lùccico) *intr* to sparkle; to shine
luccichi·o *m* (-i) glittering; shining; sparkle
luccicóne *m* big tear
lùc·cio *m* (-ci) pike
lùcciola *f* firefly; usherette (*in movie*); **prendere lucciole per lanterne** to make a blunder; to be seeing things
luce *f* light; sunlight; opening; glass (*of mirror*); leaf (*e.g., of door*); (archit) span; (coll) electricity; **alla luce del sole** in plain view; **fare luce** to shed light; **luce degli occhi** eyesight; **luce del giorno** daylight; **luce della luna** moonlight; **luce di arresto** (aut) stoplight; **luce di incrocio** (aut) dimmer, low beam; **luce di posizione** (aut) parking light; **luce di profondità** (aut) high beam; **luci** (poet) eyes; **luci della ribalta** (fig) stage, boards; **mettere alla luce** to give birth to; **mettere in luce** to reveal; to publish; **venire alla luce** to be born; to come to light
lucènte *adj* shiny, shining
lucentézza *f* brightness; sheen
lucèrna *f* lamp; light; **lucerne** (lit) eyes ‖ **Lucerna** *f* Lucerne
lucernà·rio *m* (-ri) skylight
lucèrtola *f* lizard
lucherino *m* (orn) siskin
Lucia *f* Lucy
lucidare (lùcido) *tr* to shine, polish; to trace (*a figure*)
lucida·tóre -trice *mf* polisher (*person*) ‖ *f* (mach) floor polisher
lucidatura *f* polish; tracing (*on paper*)
lucidi·tà *f* (-tà) polish; lucidity
lùci·do -da *adj* bright; lucid ‖ *m* shine; tracing; **lucido per le scarpe** shoe polish
lucife·ro -ra *adj* (poet) light-bringing ‖ **Lucifero** *m* Lucifer, morning star
lucìgnolo *m* wick
lucrare *tr* to win, acquire
lucrati·vo -va *adj* lucrative
lucro *m* gain, earnings, lucre; **lucro cessante** (law) loss of earnings
lucró·so -sa [s] *adj* lucrative
ludì·brio *m* (-bri) mockery; laughingstock
lù·glio *m* (-gli) July
lùgubre *adj* gloomy, dismal
lui §5 *pron pers*
luìgi *m* louis ‖ **Luigi** *m* Louis
luma·ca *f* (-che) snail
lume *m* light; lamp; **lume degli occhi** eyesight; **lume delle stelle** starlight; **lumi** eyesight; **lumi di luna** hard times; **perdere il lume degli occhi** to lose one's self-control; **reggere il lume a** to close one's eyes to; **studiare al lume di candela** to burn the midnight oil
lumeggiare §290 (luméggio) *tr* to illuminate, to shed light on
lumicino *m* faint light; **essere al lumicino** to be on one's last legs
luminare *m* star; luminary
luminària *f* illumination
lumino *m* night light; votive light; rush light
luminó·so -sa [s] *adj* luminous; bright (*idea*)
luna *f* moon; **andare a lune** to be fickle; **avere la luna di traverso** to be in a bad mood; **luna calante** waning moon; **luna crescente** crescent moon; **luna di miele** honeymoon
lunare *adj* lunar, moon
lunària *f* (min) moonstone; (bot) honesty
lunà·rio *m* (-ri) almanac; **sbarcare il lunario** to live from hand to mouth
lunàti·co -ca *adj* (-ci -che) moody; whimsical
lune·dì *m* (-dì) Monday
lunétta *f* lunette; fanlight
lunga *f*—**alla lunga** in the long run; **alla più lunga** at the latest; **andare per le lunghe** to last a long time, drag on; **di gran lunga** by far; **farla lunga** to dillydally
lungàggine *f* delay, procrastination
lunghézza *f* length; **lunghezza d'onda** wave length; **prendere la lunghezza di** to measure
lungi *adv* (lit) far
lungimirante *adj* (fig) far-sighted
lun·go -ga (-ghi -ghe) *adj* long; sharp (*tongue*); nimble (*fingers*); tall; thin (*soup*); (coll) slow; **a lungo** for a long time; at length; **a lungo andare** in the long run; **lungo disteso** sprawling ‖ *m* length; **in lungo e in largo** far and wide; **per il lungo** lengthwise ‖ *f* see **lunga** ‖ **lungo** *prep* along; during
lungofiume *m* river road
lungola·go *m* (-ghi) lakeshore road
lungomare *m* seashore road
lungometràg·gio *m* (-gi) full-length movie, feature film
lunòtto *m* (aut) rear window
luò·go *m* (-ghi) place; passage; site; (geom) locus; **aver luogo** to take place; **aver luogo in** to be laid in (*e.g., a certain place*); **dar luogo a** to give rise to; **del luogo** local; **far luogo** to make room; **fuori luogo** inopportune(ly); **in alto luogo** highplaced; **in luogo di** instead of; **luogo comune** commonplace; **luogo di decenza** toilet; **luogo di nascita** birthplace; **luogo di pena** penitentiary; **non luogo a procedere** (law) no ground for prosecution; (law) nolle prosequi; **sul luogo** on the spot; on the premises
luogotenènte *m* lieutenant
lupa *f* she-wolf
lupanare *m* (lit) brothel

lupé·sco -sca *adj* (**-schi -sche**) wolfish
lupétto *m* young wolf; cub (*in Boy Scouts*)
lupinèlla *f* sainfoin
lupi·no -na *adj* wolfish
lu·po -pa *mf* wolf; **lupo cerviero** lynx; **lupo di mare** seadog; **lupo mannaro** werewolf || *f* see **lupa**
làppolo *m* hops
lùri·do -da *adj* filthy, dirty
lusco *m*—**tra il lusco e il brusco** at twilight
lusin·ga *f* (**-ghe**) flattery; illusion
lusingare §209 *tr* to flatter || *ref* to be flattered; to hope
lusinghiè·ro -ra *adj* flattering; promising
lussare *tr* to dislocate
lussazióne *f* dislocation

lusso *m* luxury; **di lusso** de luxe; **lusso di** abundance of
lussuó·so -sa [s] *adj* luxurious, sumptuous
lussureggiante *adj* luxuriant
lussùria *f* lust
lussurió·so -sa [s] *adj* lustful, lecherous
lustrare *tr* to polish, shine; to lick (*s.o.'s boots*) || *intr* to shine, be shiny
lustrascar·pe *m* (**-pe**) bootblack
lustrino *m* sequin; tinsel
lu·stro -stra *adj* shiny, polished || *m* shine, polish; period of five years; **dare il lustro a** to shine, polish
lutto *m* mourning; bereavement; **a lutto** black-edged (*e.g., stationery*); **lutto stretto** deep mourning
luttuó·so -sa [s] *adj* mournful

M

M, m ['emme] *m & f* eleventh letter of the Italian alphabet
ma *m* but; **ma e se** ifs and buts || *conj* but; yet || *interj* who knows?; too bad!
màca·bro -bra *adj* macabre
maca·co *m* (**-chi**) macaque; (fig) dumbbell
macadàm *m* macadam
macadamizzare [ddzz] *tr* to macadamize
mac·ca *f* (**-che**) abundance; **a macca** (coll) abundantly; (coll) without paying
maccarèllo *m* mackerel
maccheróni *mpl* macaroni
màcchia *f* spot, stain; brushwood; thicket; (fig) blot; **alla macchia** clandestinely; (painting) done in pointillism; **darsi alla macchia** to join the underground; to escape the law; **macchia solare** sunspot; **senza macchia** spotless
macchiare §287 *tr* to stain, soil || *ref* to become stained; **macchiarsi d'infamia** to soil one's reputation
macchiétta *f* caricature; comedian; **fare la macchietta di** to impersonate, to parody
macchiettare (**macchiétto**) *tr* to speckle
macchietti·sta *mf* (**-sti -ste**) cartoonist; comedian; impersonator
màcchina *f* machine; engine; car, automobile; machination; **andare in macchina** to go to press; **fatto a macchina** machine-made; **macchina da presa** (mov) camera; **macchina da proiezione** projector; **macchina fotografica** camera; **macchina per o da cucire** sewing machine; **macchina per o da scrivere** typewriter; **scrivere a macchina** to typewrite
macchinale *adj* mechanical
macchinare (**màcchino**) *tr* to plot
macchinà·rio *m* (**-ri**) machinery
macchinazióne *f* machination

macchinétta *f* gadget; **macchinetta del caffè** coffee maker
macchini·sta *m* (**-sti**) engineer; (theat) stagehand
macchinó·so -sa [s] *adj* heavy, ponderous; complicated
macedònia *f* fruit salad, fruit cup
macel·làio *m* (**-lài**) butcher
macellare (**macèllo**) *tr* to butcher
macelleria *f* butcher shop
macèllo *m* slaughterhouse; butchering; carnage; disaster
macerare (**màcero**) *tr* to soak; to mortify (*the flesh*) || *ref* to waste away
maceria *f* low wall; **macerie** ruins
màce·ro -ra *adj* emaciated; skinny || *m* soaking vat (*for papermaking*)
machiavèlli·co -ca *adj* (**-ci -che**) Machiavellian
macigno *m* boulder
macilèn·to -ta *adj* emaciated, pale, wan
màcina *f* millstone; (coll) grind
macinacaf·fè *m* (**-fè**) coffee grinder
macinapé·pe *m* (**-pe**) pepper mill
macinare (**màcino**) *tr* to grind, mill; to burn up (*e.g., the road*)
macina·to -ta *adj* ground || *m* grindings; ground meat || *f* grinding
macinino *m* grinder; (coll) jalopy
mà·cis *m & f* (**-cis**) mace (*spice*)
maciste *m* strong man (*in circus*)
maciullare *tr* to brake (*flax or hemp*); to crush
macrocòsmo *m* macrocosm
màdia *f* bread bin; kneading trough
màdi·do -da *adj* wet, perspiring
madònna *f* lady || **Madonna** *f* Madonna
madornale *adj* huge; gross (*error*)
madre *f* mother; stub; mold; **madre nubile** unwed mother
madreggiare §290 (**madréggio**) *intr* to take after one's mother
madrelingua *f* mother tongue
madrepàtria *f* mother country
madrepèrla *f* mother-of-pearl
madresélva *f* (coll) honeysuckle

madrevite f (mach) nut; die; **madrevite ad alette** wing nut

madrigna f stepmother

madrina f godmother; **madrina di guerra** war mother

mae·stà f (-stà) majesty; **lesa maestà** lese majesty

maestó·so -sa [s] adj majestic, stately

maèstra f teacher; (fig) master; **maestra giardiniera** kindergarten teacher

maestrale m northwest wind (in Mediterranean)

maestranze fpl workmen

maestrìa f skill, mastery

maè·stro -stra adj masterly; main || m teacher; master; instructor; northwester (in Mediterranean); **maestro di cappella** choirmaster || f see **maestra**

mafió·so -sa [s] adj Mafia || mf member of the Mafia; gaudy dresser

ma·ga f (-ghe) sorceress

magagna f fault, weak spot

magagna·to -ta adj spoiled (fruit)

magari adv even, maybe || conj even if || interj would that . . . !

magazzinàg·gio [ddzz] m (-gi) storage

magazziniè·re -ra [ddzz] mf stockroom attendant || m warehouseman

magazzino [ddzz] m warehouse; store; inventory; (phot, journ) magazine; **grandi magazzini** department store

maggése [s] adj May || m (agr) fallow

màg·gio m (-gi) May; May Day

maggiolino m cockchafer

maggiorana f sweet marjoram

maggioranza f majority

maggiorare (**maggióro**) tr to increase

maggiorazióne f increase, appreciation

maggiordòmo m butler; majordomo

maggióre adj bigger, greater; major; main; higher (bidder); older, elder; (mil) master (e.g., sergeant); biggest, greatest; highest; oldest, eldest; **andare per la maggiore** to be all the rage; **maggiore età** majority || m (mil) major; oldest one; **maggiori** ancestors

maggiorènne adj of age || mf grown-up, adult

maggiorènte mf notable

maggiori·tà f (-tà) (mil) C.O.'s office

maggioità·rio -ria adj (-ri -rie) majority

magìa f magic

màgi·co -ca adj (-ci -che) magic

Magi mpl Magi, Wise Men

magióne f (lit) home, dwelling

magistèro m education, teaching, mastery; (chem) precipitation

magistrale adj teacher's; masterly || f teacher's college

magistrato m magistrate

magistratura f judiciary

màglia f knitting; stitch; link; undershirt; sports shirt; (hist) mail; (fig) web; **lavorare a maglia** to knit

maglierìa f knitting mill; yarn shop; knitwear store

magliétta f polo shirt, T-shirt; buckle (to secure rifle strap); picture hook; buttonhole

maglifì·cio m (-ci) knitwear factory

mà·glio m (-gli) sledge hammer; mallet; drop hammer

maglióne m heavy sweater, jersey

magnàni·mo -ma adj magnanimous

magnano m (coll) locksmith

magnate m (lit) magnate, tycoon

magnèsio m magnesium

magnète m magnet; magneto

magnèti·co -ca adj (-ci -che) magnetic

magnetismo m magnetism

magnetìte f loadstone

magnetizzare [ddzz] tr to magnetize

magnetòfono m tape recorder

magnificare §197 (**magnìfico**) tr to extol, praise; to magnify (to exaggerate)

magnificènza f magnificence

magnìfi·co -ca adj (-ci -che) magnificent; munificent; wonderful, splendid

ma·gno -gna adj (lit) great; the Great, e.g., **Alessandro Magno** Alexander the Great

magnòlia f magnolia

ma·go m (-ghi) magician; wizard

magóne m (coll) gizzard; (coll) grief; **avere il magone** (coll) to be in the dumps

magra f low water; (fig) dearth, want

magrézza f leanness; scarcity

ma·gro -gra adj lean, thin; meager || m lean meat; meatless day || f see **magra**

mài adv never; ever; **non . . . mai** never, not ever; **come mai?** how come?

maia·le -la mf pig; hog || m pork || f sow

maialé·sco -sca adj (-schi -sche) piggish

maiòli·ca f (-che) majolica

maionése [s] f mayonnaise

mà·is m (-is) corn, maize

maiuscolétto m (typ) small capital

maiùsco·lo -la adj capital || m—**scrivere in maiuscolo** to capitalize || f capital letter

Malacca, la Malay Peninsula

malaccèt·to -ta adj unwelcome

malaccòr·to -ta adj imprudent; awkward

malacreanza f (**malecreanze**) instance of bad manners; **malecreanze** bad manners

malafatta f (**malefatte**) defect; **malefatte** evildoings

malaféde f (**malefédi**) bad faith

malaffare m—**donna di malaffare** prostitute; **gente di malaffare** underworld

malagévole adj rough (road); hard (work)

malagràzia f (**malegràzie**) rudeness, uncouthness

malalìngua f (**malelìngue**) slanderer, backbiter

malanda·to -ta adj run-down; shabby

malandri·no -na adj dishonest; bewitching (eyes) || m highwayman

malànimo m ill will; **di malanimo** reluctantly

malanno m misfortune; illness; (joc) menace

malaparata f (coll) danger, dangerous situation

malapéna f—**a malapena** hardly

malària *f* malaria

malàtic·cio -cia *adj* (**-ci -ce**) sickly

mala·to -ta *adj* sick, ill; **essere malato agli occhi** to have sore eyes; **fare il malato** to play sick || *mf* patient; **i malati** the sick

malattìa *f* sickness; illness; disease; **malattie del lavoro** occupational diseases

malaugura·to -ta *adj* unfortunate; ill-omened

malaugù·rio *m* (**-ri**) ill omen

malavita *f* underworld

malavòglia *f* (**malevòglie**) unwillingness; **di malavoglia** reluctantly

malcapita·to -ta *adj* unlucky || *m* unlucky person

malcàu·to -ta *adj* rash, heedless

malcón·cio -cia *adj* (**-ci -ce**) battered

malcontèn·to -ta *adj* dissatisfied, malcontent || *mf* malcontent || *m* dissatisfaction

malcostume *m* immorality; bad practice

malcrea·to -ta *adj* ill-bred

maldè·stro -stra *adj* clumsy, awkward

maldicènte *adj* gossipy, slanderous || *mf* gossip, slanderer, backbiter

maldicènza *f* gossip, slander

male *m* evil; ill; trouble; **andare a male** to go to pot; **aversela a male** to take offense; **di male in peggio** from bad to worse, worse and worse; **fare del male** to do ill; **fare male** to be in error; **fare male a** to hurt; **farsi male** to get hurt; to hurt oneself; **far venire il mal di mare a** to make seasick; (fig) to nauseate; **Lei fa male** you should not; **mal d'aereo** airsickness; **mal di capo** headache; **mal di cuore** heart disease; **mal di denti** toothache; **mal di gola** sore throat; **mal di mare** sea-sickness; **mal di montagna** mountain sickness; **mal di pancia** bellyache; **mal di schiena** backache; **mandare a male** to spoil; **mettere male** to sow discord; **prendere a male** to take amiss; **voler male a** to bear a grudge against || *adv* badly, poorly; **male educato** ill-bred; **meno male!** fortunately!; **restar male** to be disappointed; **sentirsi male** to feel sick; **stare male** to be ill; **star male a** to not fit, e.g., **questo vestito gli sta male** this suit does not fit him; **veder male qlco** to disapprove of s.th; **veder male qlcu** to dislike s.o.

maledettaménte *adv* (coll) damned

maledét·to -ta *adj* cursed, damned

maledire §195 *tr* to curse

maledizióne *f* malediction, curse *ǁ interj* damn it!, confound it!

maleduca·to -ta *adj* ill-bred || *mf* boor

malefatta *f* var of malafatta

malefì·cio *m* (**-ci**) curse, spell; witchcraft; wickedness

malèfi·co -ca *adj* (**-ci -che**) maleficent

maleolènte *adj* (lit) malodorous

malèrba *f* weed, weeds

malése *adj* & *mf* Malay

Malésia, la Malaysia

malèssere *m* malaise; uneasiness; worry

malevolènza *f* malevolence; malice

malèvo·lo -la *adj* malevolent; malicious

malfama·to -ta *adj* ill-famed; notorious

malfat·to -ta *adj* botched; misshapen || *m* misdeed

malfat·tóre -trice *mf* malefactor

malfér·mo -ma *adj* wobbly, unsteady

malfì·do -da *adj* untrustworthy

malgarbo *m* bad manners, rudeness

malgovèrno *m* misrule; mismanagement; neglect

malgrado *prep* in spite of; **mio malgrado** in spite of me || *conj* although

malìa *f* spell, charm

maliar·do -da *adj* enchanting, charming || *mf* magician || *f* enchantress, witch

malignare *intr* to gossip

maligni·tà *f* (**-tà**) maliciousness; malevolence; malignancy

mali·gno -gna *adj* malicious, evil; unhealthy; malignant || **il Maligno** the Evil One

malinconìa *f* melancholy; melancholia

malincòni·co -ca *adj* (**-ci -che**) melancholy, wistful

malincuòre *m*—**a malincuore** unwillingly, against one's will

malintenziona·to -ta *adj* evil-minded || *mf* evildoer

malinté·so -sa [s] *adj* misunderstood; misapplied || *m* misunderstanding

maliò·so -sa [s] *adj* malicious; cunning; mischievous; bewitching

malìzia *f* malice; trick; mischief

maliziò·so -sa [s] *adj* malicious; clever, artful; mischievous

malleàbile *adj* malleable; manageable

malleva·dóre -drice *mf* guarantor

malleverìa *f* surety

mallo *m* hull, husk

mallòppo *m* bundle; (aer) trail cable; (coll) lump (*in one's throat*); (slang) swag, booty

malmenare (**malméno**) *tr* to manhandle

malmés·so -sa *adj* shabby, seedy; tasteless

malna·to -ta *adj* uncouth; unfortunate; harmful

malnutri·to -ta *adj* undernourished

malnutrizióne *f* malnutrition

ma·lo -la *adj* (lit) bad

malòc·chio *m* (**-chi**) evil eye

malóra *f* ruin; **mandare in malora** to ruin; **va in malora!** go to the devil!

malóre *m* malaise; fainting spell

malpràti·co -ca *adj* (**-ci -che**) inexperienced

malsa·no -na *adj* unhealthy; unsound

malsicu·ro -ra *adj* unsafe; insecure

malta *f* mortar; plaster; (obs) mud

maltèmpo *m* bad weather

malto *m* malt

maltòlto *m* ill-gotten gains

maltrattaménto *m* mistreatment

maltrattare *tr* to mistreat, maltreat

malumóre *m* bad humor; **di malumore** in a bad mood

malva *f* mallow

malvà·gio -gia (**-gi -gie**) *adj* wicked || *mf* wicked person || **il Malvagio** the Evil One

malversare (malvèrso) *tr* to embezzle; to misappropriate

malversazióne *f* embezzlement; misappropriation

malvestì·to -ta *adj* shabby, seedy

malvi·sto -sta *adj* disliked; unpopular

malvivènte *mf* criminal; (*lit*) profligate

malvolentièri *adv* unwillingly

malvolére *m* malevolence; indolence || §196 *tr* to dislike

mamma *f* mother, mom; (*lit*) breast; **mamma mia** dear me!

mammalùc·co *m* (*-chi*) simpleton

mammèlla *f* breast; udder

mammìfe·ro -ra *adj* mammalian || *m* mammal

màmmola *f* violet; (*fig*) shrinking violet

mam·mùt *m* (*-mut*) mammoth

manàta *f* slap; handful; **dare una manata a** to slap

man·ca *f* (*-che*) left hand, left

mancante *adj* missing, lacking; unaccounted for

mancànza *f* lack; absence; defect; mistake; **in mancanza di** for lack of

mancare §197 *tr* to miss || *intr* (AVERE) to be at fault; **mancare a** to break (*e.g.*, *one's word*); **mancare di** to be wanting; to lack; **mancare di parola** to break one's word || *intr* (ESSERE) to fail (*said, e.g., of electric power*); to be lacking, *e.g.*, **manca il sale nell'arrosto** salt is lacking in the roast; to be missing; to be absent, *e.g.*, **mancano tre soci** three members are absent; to be, *e.g.*, **mancano dieci minuti alle quattro** it is ten minutes to four; (*with dat*) to lack, *e.g.*, **gli mancano le forze** he lacks the strength; to miss, *e.g.*, **mi manca la sua compagnia** I miss his company; **mancare a** to be absent from (*e.g.*, *the roll call*); to be ... from, *e.g.*, **dieci chilometri all'arrivo** we are ten kilometers from the journey's end; **mancare ai vivi** (*lit*) to pass away; **sentirsi mancare** to feel faint || *impers*—**mancare poco che** + *subj* to narrowly miss + *ger*, *e.g.*, **ci mancò poco che fosse investito da un'automobile** he narrowly missed being hit by a car; **non ci mancherebbe altro!** that would be the last straw!, I should say not!

manca·to -ta *adj* unsuccessful; missed (*opportunity*); abortive (*attempt*), *e.g.*, **omicidio mancato** abortive attempt to murder; manqué, *e.g.*, **un poeta mancato** a poet manqué

manchévole *adj* faulty

manchevolézza *f* fault, shortcoming

màn·cia *f* (*-ce*) tip, gratuity; **mancia competente** reward

manciàta *f* handful

manci·no -na *adj* left-handed; underhanded || *mf* left-handed person || *f* left hand, left; (*mach*) floating crane

man·co -ca (*-chi -che*) *adj* left; (*lit*) sinister, ill-omened; (*lit*) lacking || *m* (*lit*) lack; **senza manco** (*coll*) without fail || **manco** *adv*—**manco male!**

(*coll*) at least!; **manco per idea!** (*coll*) not at all! || *f* see **manca**

mandaménto *m* jurisdiction

mandante *m* (*law*) principal

mandare *tr* to send; to condemn (*to death*); to commit (*to memory*); to send forth (*e.g.*, *smoke, buds*); to operate (*a machine*); **che Dio ce la mandi buona!** may God help us!; **mandare ad effetto** to carry out; **mandare all'altro mondo** to dispatch, kill; **mandare a monte** to ruin; **mandare a picco** to sink; **mandare a quel paese** to send to the devil; **mandare a spasso** to fire, dismiss; to get rid of; **mandar giù** to swallow; **mandare in malora** to ruin; **mandare in pezzi** to break to pieces; **mandare per le lunghe** to delay || *intr*—**mandare a chiamare** to send for; **mandare a dire** to send word

mandarino *m* mandarin; (*Citrus nobilis*) tangerine; (*Citrus reticulata*) mandarin orange

mandàta *f* sending; delivery (*of merchandise*); group; gang (*e.g.*, *of thieves*); turn (*of key*); **chiudere a doppia mandata** to double-lock

mandatà·rio *m* (*-ri*) mandatary, trustee

mandato *m* mandate; order; **mandato di cattura** arrest warrant; **mandato di comparizione** subpoena; **mandato di perquisizione** search warrant

mandìbola *f* jaw

mandolino *m* mandolin

màndorla *f* almond; kernel (*of fruit*)

mandorla·to -ta *adj* almond || *m* nougat

màndorlo *m* almond tree

mandràgola *f* mandrake

màndria *f* herd

mandriano *m* herdsman

mandrillo *m* mandrill

mandrino *m* (*mach*) mandrel; (*mach*) driftpin

mandritta *f*—**a mandritta** to the right

mane *f*—**da mane a sera** from morning till night

maneggévole *adj* usable; manageable; accessible to small craft (*sea*)

maneggiare §290 (*manéggio*) *tr* to work (*e.g.*, *clay*); to handle; to wield (*a sword*); to knead (*dough*); to manage; (*equit*) to train

manég·gio *m* (*-gi*) handling; intrigue; horsemanship; management; riding school; manège

manè·sco -sca *adj* (*-schi -sche*) ready-fisted; hand (*e.g.*, *weapons*)

manétta *f* throttle (*on a motorcycle*); **manette** handcuffs, manacles

manfòrte *f*—**dar manforte a** to help

manganèllo *m* bludgeon, cudgel

manganése [s] *m* manganese

màngano *m* calender; mangle

mangeréc·cio -cia *adj* (*-ci -ce*) edible

mangerìa *f* graft, peculation

mangiàbile *adj* edible

mangiana·stri *m* (*-stri*) tape recorder

mangia-pane *m* (*-pane*) idler

mangia-prèti *m* (*-prèti*) priest hater

mangiare *m* eating; food || *v* §290 *tr*

to eat; to bite, gnaw; to erode; to
embezzle, graft; (cards, chess) to
take; **mangiar la foglia** to get wise ||
intr to eat; **mangiare alle spalle di
qlcu** to eat at the expense of s.o. ||
ref to eat up; **mangiarsi il fegato** to
be green with envy; **mangiarsi la
parola** to break one's promise; **mangiarsi le unghie** to bite one's nails;
mangiarsi una promessa to break
one's promise

mangiasòldi *adj invar* money-eating,
e.g., **macchina mangiasoldi** money-
eating contraption

mangiàta *f* (coll) fill, hearty meal,
bellyful

mangiatóia *f* manger, crib

mangime *m* fodder; feed; poultry feed

mangimistì·co -ca *adj* (-ci -che) feed,
e.g., **attrezzature mangimistiche** feed
machinery

mangió·ne -na *mf* great eater, glutton

mangiucchiare §287 (mangiùcchio) *tr*
to nibble

mangusta *f* mongoose

manìa *f* mania, craze; complex; whim;
mania di grandezza delusions of
grandeur

manìa·co -ca (-ci -che) *adj* maniacal;
enthusiastic || *m* maniac; fan, en-
thusiast

mànì·ca *f* (-che) sleeve; hose; (coll)
crowd, bunch; **essere di manica larga**
to be broad-minded; **essere nelle
maniche di qlcu** to be in the favor of
s.o.; **è un altro paio di maniche** this
is a horse of another color; **in maniche di camicia** in shirt sleeves;
manica a vento air sleeve, windsock;
manica per l'acqua hose || **la Manica**
the English Channel

manicarétto *m* dainty, delicacy

manichino *m* mannequin; cuff; (obs)
handcuff; **fare il manichino** to model

mànì·co *m* (-chi & -ci) handle; stock
(*of rifle*); shaft (*of golf club*); stem
(*of spoon*); (mus) neck; **manico di
scopa** broomstick

manicò·mio *m* (-mi) insane asylum,
madhouse

manicòtto *m* muff; (mach) collar;
(mach) nipple; (mach) sleeve

manicù·re *mf* (-re) manicure, manicur-
ist (*person*) || *f* (-re) manicure (*treat-
ment*)

manicurì·sta *mf* (-sti -ste) manicurist

manièra *f* manner, fashion, way; **belle
maniere** good manners; **di maniera**
(lit, painting) Manneristic; **di maniera che** so that; **in nessuna maniera**
by no means; **maniere** bad manners

manierà·to -ta *adj* mannered, affected;
genteel

maniè·ro -ra *adj* tame, gentle || *m*
manor house, mansion || *f* see
maniera

manieró·so -sa [*s*] *adj* genteel; mannered

manifattura *f* manufacture; factory;
product; ready-made wear

manifestare (manifèsto) *tr* to manifest

|| *intr* to demonstrate || *ref* to turn
out to be

manifestazióne *f* manifestation; demonstration

manifestino *m* leaflet, handbill

manifè·sto -sta *adj* manifest, clear || *m*
poster, placard; manifest; (pol) manifesto; **manifesto di carico** (naut)
manifest

manìglia *f* handle; knob; (naut) link
(*of chain*)

manigòldo *m* criminal; scoundrel

manipolare (manìpolo) *tr* to concoct;
to adulterate; (telg) to transmit

manipola·tóre -trice *mf* schemer || *m*
telegraph key

manìpolo *m* sheaf; (eccl; hist) maniple;
(fig) handful

maniscal·co *m* (-chi) blacksmith

manna *f* manna; godsend

mannàia *f* axe; knife (*of guillotine*)

mano *f* hand; way (*in traffic*); coat (*of
paint*); (lit) handful; (fig) finger;
fingertip; **alla mano** plain, affable;
a mani nude barehanded; **a mano** by
hand; **a mano a mano** little by little;
a mano armata armed (*e.g., robbery*); at gunpoint; **andare contro
mano** to buck traffic; **a quattro mani**
four-handed; **avere le mani bucate**
to be a spendthrift; **avere le mani in
pasta** to have one's fingers in the pie;
avere le mani lunghe to be light-
fingered; **battere le mani** to clap;
con le mani in mano idle; **dare la
mano a** to shake hands with; **dare
man forte a** to help; **dare una mano**
to pitch in; **dare una mano a** to lend
a hand to; **di lunga mano** beforehand; **essere colto con le mani nel
sacco** to be caught red-handed;
essere svelto di mano to be light-
fingered; **far man bassa (su)** to plunder; **fuori mano** out of the way;
mani di burro butterfingers; **mani in
alto!** hands up!; **man mano (che)** as;
mettere mano a to begin; **mettere le
mani sul fuoco** to guarantee; to
swear; **per mano di** at the hands of;
prendere la mano to balk; to get out
of hand; **tenere la mano a** to abet;
venire alle mani to come to blows

manodòpera *f* labor, manpower; **manodopera qualificata** skilled labor

manòmetro *m* manometer

manométtere §198 *tr* to tamper with

manomissióne *f* tampering

manomòrta *f* (law) mortmain

manòpola *f* mitten; handgrip; strap
(*to hold on to*); (rad, telv) knob;
(hist) gauntlet

manoscrìt·to -ta *adj & m* manuscript

manoscrìvere §250 *intr* to write in one's
own handwriting

manovale *m* laborer, helper; hod carrier

manovèlla *f* handle, crank; lever

manòvra *f* maneuver; (rr) shifting; **fare
manovra** to maneuver; (rr) to shift

manovrare (manòvro) *tr* to maneuver;
to handle, drive; (rr) to shift || *intr*
to maneuver; (rr) to shunt, shift;
(fig) to plot

manovratóre *m* motorman; driver; (rr) brakeman; (rr) flagman

manrovè·scio *m* (-sci) backhanded slap

mansalva *f*—**rubare a mansalva** to help oneself freely (*e.g., to the till*)

mansarda *f* mansard

mansióne *f* duty, function

mansuè·to -ta *adj* tame; meek

mansuetùdine *f* tameness; meekness

mantèlla *f* coat; (mil) cape

mantellìna *f* (mil) cape

mantèllo *m* woman's coat; coat (*of animal*); (fig) cloak; (mil) cape; (mach) casing

mantenére §271 *tr* to keep; to maintain; to hold (*e.g., a position*) ‖ *ref* to stay alive; to last; to remain, stay, continue

mantenimènto *m* keeping; maintenance

mantenu·to -ta *adj* kept ‖ *m* gigolo ‖ *f* kept woman

màntice *m* bellows; folding top (*of carriage*); (aut) convertible top

manto *m* mantle; coat; cloak

Màntova *f* Mantua

mantovana *f* valance

manuale *adj* & *m* manual

manualizzare [ddzz] *tr* to make (*e.g., a machine*) hand-operated; to include in a manual; to prepare a manual of

manù·brio *m* (-bri) handlebar; handle; dumbbell

manufat·to -ta *adj* manufactured ‖ *m* manufactured product; manufacture

manutèngolo *m* accomplice

manutenzióne *f* maintenance, upkeep

manza [dz] *f* heifer

manzo [dz] *m* steer; beef

maomettà·no -na *adj & mf* Mahometan, Mohammedan

maomettìsmo *m* Mahometanism, Mohammedanism

Maométto *m* Mahomet

maóna *f* barge

mappa *f* map; bit (*of key*)

mappamóndo *m* globe; map of the world

marachèlla *f* mischief

maramèo *m*—**fare marameo** to thumb one's nose

mara·sma *m* (-smi) utter confusion; (pathol) decrepitude, feebleness

maratóna *f* marathon

maratonè·ta *m* (-ti) Marathon runner

mar·ca *f* (-che) mark, label; make, brand; token; ticket; (hist, geog) march; **di marca** of quality; **marca da bollo** revenue stamp; **marca di fabbrica** trademark

marcare §197 *tr* to mark; to label; to brand; to keep the score of; to score (*e.g., a goal*); to accentuate

marcatèm·po *m* (-po) timekeeper

marca·to -ta *adj* marked, pronounced

marchésa *f* marchioness, marquise

marchése *m* marquess, marquis

marchia·no -na *adj* gross (*error*)

marchiare §287 *tr* to brand

màr·chio *m* (-chi) brand; initials; characteristic; trademark

màr·cia *f* (-ce) march; operation; pus; (aut) gear, speed; (mil) hike; (sports)

walk; **far marcia indietro** to back up; (naut) to back water; **marcia indietro** (aut) reverse; **marcia nuziale** wedding march

marciapiède *m* sidewalk; (rr) platform

marciare §128 *intr* to march; (mil) to advance; (sports) to walk; (coll) to function; **far marciare qlcu** to keep s.o. in line

màr·cio -cia (-ci -ce) *adj* rotten; infected; corrupt ‖ *m* rotten part; decayed part; corruption ‖ *f* see **marcia**

marcire §176 *intr* (ESSERE) to rot

marciume *m* rot; pus; decay

mar·co *m* (-chi) mark

marconigram·ma *m* (-mi) radiogram

marconi·sta *mf* (-sti -ste) radio operator

mare *m* sea; bunch, heap; **al mare** at the seashore; **alto mare** high sea; **fa mare** the sea is rough; **gettare a mare** to throw overboard; **mare grosso** rough sea; **mare territoriale** territorial waters; **promettere mari e monti** to promise the moon; **tenere il mare** to be seaworthy

marèa *f* tide; sea (*e.g., of mud*); **alta marea** high tide; **bassa marea** low tide; **marea di quadratura** neap tide; **marea di sizigia** spring tide

mareggiata *f* coastal storm

maremòto *m* seaquake

mareògrafo *m* tide-level gauge

maresciallo *m* marshall; warrant officer

marétta *f* choppy sea; instability

margarina *f* margarine

margherita *f* daisy; **margherite** beads

marginale *adj* marginal

marginatóre *m* margin stop (*of typewriter*); (typ) try square

màrgine *m* margin; edge; **margine a scaletta** thumb index

marijuana *f* marijuana, marihuana

marina *f* seashore; seascape; navy; **marina mercantile** merchant marine

mari·nàio *m* (-nài) seaman, sailor

marinara *f* middy blouse

marinare *tr* to marinate; **marinare la scuola** to cut school, play truant

marinaré·sco -sca *adj* (-schi -sche) sailor, seamanlike

marina·ro -ra *adj* sea, sailor; seamanlike; nautical ‖ *m* (coll) sailor ‖ *f* see **marinara**

mari·no -na *adj* marine, nautical ‖ *f* see **marina**

mariòlo *m* rascal

marionétta *f* puppet, marionette

maritale *adj* marital

maritare *tr* to marry ‖ *ref* to get married

marito *m* husband

marìtti·mo -ma *adj* maritime, sea ‖ *m* merchant seaman

marmàglia *f* riffraff, rabble

marmellata *f* jam, preserves; **marmellata di arancia** orange marmalade

marmi·sta *m* (-sti) marble worker; marble cutter

marmitta *f* pot, kettle; (aut) muffler

marmittóne *m* (coll) sad sack

marmo *m* marble

marmòc·chio *m* (-chi) brat

marmòre·o -a *adj* marble

marmorizzare [ddzz] *tr* to marble

marmòtta *f* marmot; woodchuck; (fig) sluggard; (rr) switch signal

marmottina *f* salesman's sample case

marna *f* marl

marnare *tr* to marl

marocchi·no -na *adj & mf* Moroccan || *m* morocco leather

Maròcco, il Morocco

maróso [s] *m* billow, surge

marra *f* hoe; fluke (*of anchor*)

marrano *m* Marrano; (fig) scoundrel; (lit) traitor

marronata *f* (coll) blunder, boner

marróne *adj invar* maroon, tan || *m* chestnut; (coll) blunder

Marsìglia *f* Marseille

marsigliése [s] *adj* Marseilles || *m* native or inhabitant of Marseilles || *f* Marseillaise

marsina *f* swallow-tailed coat

Marte *m* Mars

marte·dì *m* (**-dì**) Tuesday; **martedì grasso** Shrove Tuesday

martellare (**martèllo**) *tr* to hammer; to pester (*with questions*) || *intr* to throb; (fig) to insist

martellata *f* hammer blow

martellétto *m* hammer (*of piano or bell*); lever (*of typewriter*)

martèllo *m* hammer; **martello dell'uscio** knocker; **martello perforatore** jack-hammer

martinétto *m* jack; **martinetto a vite** screw jack

martingala *f* half belt (*sewn in back of sports jacket*); martingale (*of harness*)

martinic·ca *f* (**-che**) wagon brake

martìn pescatóre *m* kingfisher

màrtire *m* martyr

marti·rio *m* (**-ri**) martyrdom

martirizzare [ddzz] *tr* to martyrize

màrtora *f* marten

martoriare §287 (**martòrio**) *tr* to torment

marxi·sta *adj & mf* (**-sti -ste**) Marxist

marzapane *m* marzipan

marziale *adj* martial

marzia·no -na *adj & mf* Martian

marzo *m* March

mas *m* (**mas**) torpedo boat

mascalzóne *m* cad, rascal

mascèlla *f* jaw; jawbone

màschera *m* usher || *f* mask; masque; **maschera antigas** gas mask; **maschera di bellezza** beauty pack; **maschera respiratoria** oxygen mask; **maschera subacquea** diving helmet

mascheraménto *m* camouflage

mascherare (**màschero**) *tr, intr & ref* to mask; to camouflage

mascherata *f* masquerade

mascherina *f* little mask, loup; tip (*of shoe*); (aut) grille; (phot) mask

maschiare §287 *tr* (mach) to tap

maschiétta *f* tomboy; **alla maschietta** bobbed (*hair*); **tagliare i capelli alla maschietta** to bob the hair

maschiétto *m* baby boy; pintle

maschile *adj* masculine; manly; men's;

male (*sex*); boys' (*school*) || *m* masculine

mà·schio -schia *adj* manly, virile; male || *m* male; keep, donjon; tenon; (mach) tap; (carp) tongue

mascolinizzare [ddzz] *tr* to make masculine or mannish || *ref* to act like a man

mascoli·no -na *adj* masculine; mannish (*woman*)

masnada *f* mob, gang; (obs) group

masnadière *m* highwayman

massa *f* mass; body (*of water*); (elec) ground; **mettere a massa** (elec) to ground; **in massa** in a body; **massa ereditaria** (law) estate

massacrante *adj* killing, fatiguing

massacrare *tr* to massacre; to ruin; to wear out, fatigue

massacro *m* massacre

massaggiare §290 *tr* to massage

massaggiatóre *m* masseur

massaggiatrice *f* masseuse

massàg·gio *m* (**-gi**) massage

massàia *f* housewife

massèllo *m* block (*of stone*); (metallurgy) pig, ingot

masseria *f* farm

masserizie *fpl* household goods

massicciata *f* roadbed; (rr) ballast

massìc·cio -cia (**-ci -ce**) *adj* massive; bulky; heavy; (fig) gross || *m* massif

màssi·mo -ma *adj* maximum; top || *m* maximum; limit; **al massimo** at the most || *f* maxim; maximum temperature

massi·vo -va *adj* massive

masso *m* rock, boulder

Massóne *m* Mason

Massoneria *f* Masonry

mastèllo *m* washtub

masticare §197 (**màstico**) *tr* to chew, masticate; to mumble (*words*); to speak (*a language*) poorly; **masticare amaro** to grumble

masticazióne *f* mastication

màstice *m* mastic; glue; putty

mastino *m* mastiff

mastodònti·co -ca *adj* (**-ci -che**) mammoth

ma·stro -stra *adj* master || *m* ledger; master, e.g., **mastro meccanico** master mechanic

masturbare *tr & ref* to masturbate

matassa *f* skein; trouble

matemàti·co -ca (**-ci -che**) *adj* mathematical || *m* mathematician || *f* mathematics

materassino *m* (sports) mat; **materassino pneumatico** air mattress

materasso *m* mattress; (boxing) sparring partner

matèria *f* matter; substance; subject; (coll) pus; **dare materia a** to give ground for; **materia grigia** gray matter; **materie coloranti** dyestuffs; **materie prime** raw materials

materiale *adj* material; rough, bulky || *m* material; equipment, supplies; (fig) makings, stuff; **materiale ferroviario** (rr) rolling stock; **materiale stabile** (rr) permanent way

materni·tà _f_ (-tà) maternity; maternity hospital; maternity ward

matèr·no -na _adj_ maternal; mother (_tongue, country_)

matita _f_ pencil; **matita per gli occhi** eye-shadow pencil; **matita per le labbra** lipstick; cosmetic pencil

matrice _f_ matrix; stub

matrici·da _mf_ (-di -de) matricide

matrici·dio _m_ (-di) matricide

matricola _f_ register, roll; registration (_number_); registry; beginner, novice; freshman (_in university_); **far la matricola a** to haze

matricola·to -ta _adj_ notorious, arrant

matrigna _f_ stepmother

matrimoniale _adj_ matrimonial; double (_bed_); married (_life_)

matrimonialmente _adv_ as husband and wife

matrimò·nio _m_ (-ni) matrimony, marriage; wedding

matròna _f_ matron

matronale _adj_ matronly

matta _f_ joker, wild card

mattacchió·ne -na _mf_ jester, prankster

mattana _f_ tantrum; fit of laughter

matta·tóio _m_ (-tói) slaughterhouse

matterèllo _m_ rolling pin

mattina _f_ morning; **di prima mattina** early in the morning; **la mattina in the morning**

mattinale _adj_ morning ǁ _m_ morning report

mattinata _f_ morning; (_theat_) matinée

mattiniè·ro -ra _adj_ early-rising

mattino _m_ morning; **di buon mattino** early in the morning

mat·to -ta _adj_ crazy; whimsical; dull; false (_jewelry_); wild (_desire_); **andare matto per** to be crazy about; **da matti** unbelievable; **fare il matto** to cut a caper; **matto da legare** raving mad ǁ _f_ see **matta**

mattòide _adj_ & _mf_ madcap

mattonare (**mattóno**) _tr_ to pave with bricks

mattonato _m_ brick floor; **restare sul mattonato** to be utterly destitute

mattóne _m_ brick; (_fig_) bore

mattonèlla _f_ tile; cushion (_of billiard table_)

mattuti·no -na _adj_ morning ǁ _m_ matins

maturan·do -da _mf_ lycée student who has to take the baccalaureate examination

maturare _tr_ to ripen; to ponder; to pass (_a lycée pupil_) ǁ _intr_ (ESSERE) to ripen, mature; to fall due

maturazióne _f_ ripening

maturi·tà _f_ (-tà) maturity; ripening; lycée final

matu·ro -ra _adj_ ripe; mature; due

Matusalèmme _m_ Methuselah

mausolèo _m_ mausoleum

mazza _f_ club; mallet; sledge hammer; cane; mace; golf club; (baseball) bat

mazzacavallo _m_ well sweep

mazzapic·chio _m_ (-chi) mallet; sledge

mazzata _f_ heavy blow, wallop (_with club_)

mazzeran·ga _f_ (-ghe) (mach) tamper

mazzière _m_ macer; (cards) dealer

mazzo _m_ bunch; bouquet; deck (_of cards_); **fare il mazzo** to shuffle the cards

mazzuòla _f_ sledge hammer

mazzuòlo _m_ sledge; mallet; wedge (_of golf club_); drumstick (_for bass drum_)

me §5 _pron pers_

meandro _m_ meander; labyrinth

MEC _m_ (letterword) (**Mercato Europeo Comune**) European Economic Community, Common Market

Mècca, la Mecca; (fig) the Mecca

meccàni·co -ca (-ci -che) _adj_ mechanical ǁ _m_ mechanic ǁ _f_ mechanics; process (_e.g., of digestion_); machinery

meccanismo _m_ machinery; mechanism; movement (_of watch_)

meccanizzare [ddzz] _tr_ to mechanize ǁ _ref_ to become mechanized

mecenate _m_ patron (_of the arts_)

méco §5 _prep phrase_ (lit) with me

medàglia _f_ medal

medaglióne _m_ medallion; locket; biographical sketch

medèsi·mo -ma _adj_ & _pron_ same; -self, e.g., **egli medesimo** he himself; very e.g., **la verità medesima** the very truth

mèdia _f_ average; secondary school, middle school; (math) mean; **media oraria** average speed ǁ **mèdia** _mpl_ media (_of communication_)

mediana _f_ median; (soccer) middle line

mediàni·co -ca _adj_ (-ci -che) medium

media·no -na _adj_ median ǁ _m_ (sports) halfback ǁ _f_ see **mediana**

mediante _prep_ by means of

mediare §287 (**mèdio**) _tr_ & _intr_ (ESSERE) to mediate

media·to -ta _adj_ indirect

media·tóre -trice _adj_ mediating ǁ _mf_ mediator; broker; commission merchant

mediazióne _f_ mediation; brokerage; broker's fee, commission

medicaménto _m_ medicine

medicamentó·so -sa [s] _adj_ medicinal

medicare §197 (**mèdico**) _tr_ to medicate; to treat

medicastro _m_ quack

medicazióne _f_ medication; dressing

medichéssa _f_ (pej) lady doctor

medicina _f_ medicine

medicinale _adj_ medicinal ǁ _m_ medicine

mèdi·co -ca (-ci -che) _adj_ medical ǁ _m_ doctor, physician; healer; **fare il medico** to practice medicine; **medico chirurgo** surgeon; **medico condotto** board-of-health doctor; country doctor; **medico curante** family physician

medievale _adj_ medieval

medievali·sta _mf_ (-sti -ste) medievalist

mè·dio -dia (-di -die) _adj_ average; median; middle; secondary (_school_); medium ǁ _m_ middle finger ǁ _f_ see **media**

mediòcre _adj_ mediocre

mediocri·tà _f_ (-tà) mediocrity

medioèvo _m_ Middle Ages

medioleggèro _m_ welterweight

mediomàssimo *m* light heavyweight
meditabón·do -da *adj* meditative
meditare (mèdito) *tr & intr* to meditate
medita·to -ta *adj* considered
meditazióne *f* meditation
mediterrà·neo -nea *adj* inland (*sea*) ‖ **Mediterraneo** *adj & m* Mediterranean
mè·dium *mf* (**-dium**) medium
medusa *f* jellyfish
mefistofèli·co -ca *adj* (**-ci -che**) Mephistophelian
mefíti·co -ca *adj* (**-ci -che**) mephitic
megaciclo *m* megacycle
megàfono *m* megaphone
megalomania *f* megalomania
megalòpo·li *f* (**-li**) megalopolis
mega·òhm *m* (**-òhm**) megohm
megèra *f* hag, termagant, vixen
mèglio *adj invar* better; (coll) best ‖ *m*—**il meglio** the best; **nel meglio di** (coll) in the middle of ‖ *f*—**avere la meglio** to get the upper hand; **avere la meglio di** to get the better of ‖ *adv* better; best; rather; **stare meglio** to feel better; to be becoming; to fit better; **stare meglio a** to be becoming to; to fit; **tanto meglio!** so much the better!
méla *f* apple; nozzle (*of sprinkling can*); **mela cotogna** quince (*fruit*); **mela renetta** pippin
melagrana *f* pomegranate
melanzana [dz] *f* eggplant
melassa *f* molasses, treacle
mela·to -ta *adj* honey, honeyed
melèn·so -sa *adj* dull, silly
melissa *f* (bot) balm
mellìflu·o -a *adj* mellifluous
mélma *f* mud, slime
melmó·so -sa [s] *adj* muddy, slimy
mélo *m* apple tree
melodìa *f* melody
melòdi·co -ca *adj* (**-ci -che**) melodic
melodió·so -sa [s] *adj* melodious
melodram·ma *m* (**-mi**) melodrama; lyric opera; (fig) melodrama
melodrammàti·co -ca *adj* (**-ci -che**) melodramatic
melograno *m* pomegranate tree
melóne *m* melon; cantaloupe; **melone d'acqua** watermelon
membrana *f* membrane; parchment; diaphragm (*of telephone*); (zool) web
membratura *f* frame
mèm·bro *m* (**-bri**, *considered individually*) limb; member; penis ‖ *m* (**-bra** *fpl*, *considered collectively*) limb (*of human body*)
membru·to -ta *adj* burly, husky
memoràbile *adj* memorable
memoràn·dum *m* (**-dum**) memorandum; agenda, calendar; note; note paper
mèmore *adj* (lit) mindful, grateful
memòria *f* memory; souvenir; memoir; dissertation; (law) brief
memoriale *m* memoir; memorial
memorizzare [ddzz] *tr* to memorize
ména *f* intrigue
mena·bò *m* (**-bò**) (typ) layout, dummy
menadito *m*—**a menadito** at one's fingertips; perfectly
menare (méno) *tr* to lead; to bring

(*luck*); to wag (*the tail*); to deliver (*a blow*); (coll) to hit; **menare a effetto** to carry out; **menare buono di** to approve of; **menare il can per l'aia** to beat around the bush; **menare per le lunghe** to delay; **menare vanto** to boast
mènda *f* (lit) fault, flaw
mendace *adj* lying, false, mendacious
mendà·cio *m* (**-ci**) (law) falsehood
mendicante *adj & m* mendicant
mendicare §197 (**méndico**) *tr & intr* to beg
mendici·tà *f* (**-tà**) indigence, poverty
mendi·co -ca *adj & mf* (**-chi -che**) mendicant
menefreghismo *m* I-don't-care attitude
menestrèllo *m* minstrel
méno *adj invar* less ‖ *m* less; least; minus (*sign*); **i meno** the few; **per lo meno** at least ‖ *adv* less; least; minus; **a meno che** unless; **meno** inferior; **fare a meno di** to do without; to spare; **meno . . . di** less . . . than; **meno male** fortunately; **meno . . . meno** the less . . . the less; **non poter fare a meno di** + *inf* to not be able to help + *ger*, e.g., **la conferenza non poteva fare a meno di essere un successo** the conference could not help being a success; **quanto meno** at least; **senza meno** without fail; **venir meno** to swoon, pass out; to fail; to lose, e.g., **gli venne meno il cuore** he lost his courage; **venir meno di** to break (*one's word*) ‖ *prep* except; less, minus; of, e.g., **le sette meno dieci** ten minutes of seven
menomare (mènomo) *tr* to lessen, diminish; (fig) to hurt, damage
mèno·mo -ma *adj* least
menopàusa *f* menopause
mènsa *f* (prepared) table; mess, mess hall; (eccl) altar; communion table; (poet) mass; (poet) altar; **mensa aziendale** company cafeteria
mensile *adj* monthly ‖ *m* monthly salary or allowance
mensili·tà *f* (**-tà**) monthly installment
mènsola *f* bracket; corner shelf; neck (*of harp*); mantel (*of chimney*); console
ménta *f* mint
mentale *adj* mental; (anat) chin
mentali·tà *f* (**-tà**) mentality, mind
ménte *f* mind; **a mente di** according to; **avere in mente** to mean; to intend; **di mente** mental; **mente direttiva** mastermind; **scappare di mente a qlcu** to escape s.o.'s mind, e.g., **gli è scappato di mente** it escaped his mind; **uscire di mente** to go out of one's mind; **venire in mente a qlcu** to remember, e.g., **non gli è venuto in mente di spedire la lettera** he did not remember to mail the letter
mentecat·to -ta *adj & mf* lunatic
mentina *f* mint; **mentina digestiva** after-dinner mint
mentire §176 & (**mènto**) *intr* to lie;

mentire per la gola to lie through one's teeth

menti·to -ta *adj* false; disguised

menti·tóre -trice *adj* lying || *mf* liar

ménto *m* chin

mentòlo *m* menthol

méntre *m*—**in quel mentre** at that very moment; **nel mentre che** at the time when || *conj* while; whereas

me·nù *m* (**-nù**) menu

menzionare (menzióno) *tr* to mention

menzióne *f* mention

menzógna *f* lie

menzognè·ro -ra *adj* false, deceptive; lying, untruthful

meraviglia *f* marvel, wonder; **a meraviglia** wonderfully; **destare le meraviglie di** to amaze; **dire meraviglie di** to praise to the skies; **fare meraviglia (with** *dat***)** to amaze; **far meraviglie** to work wonders

meravigliare §280 **(meraviglio)** *tr* to amaze; to astonish || *ref* to be astonished

meravigliò·so -sa [s] *adj* marvelous, wonderful || *m* (lit) supernatural

mercan·te -téssa *mf* merchant, dealer

mercanteggiare §290 **(mercantéggio)** *tr* to sell || *intr* to deal; to haggle

mercantile *adj* mercantile; merchant (*marine*) || *m* cargo boat, freighter

mercanzia *f* merchandise; (coll) junk

mercato *m* market; trafficking; **a buon mercato** cheap; **far mercato di** to traffic in; **sopra mercato** besides; into the bargain

mèrce *f* merchandise, goods; commodity

mercé *f* favor, grace; mercy; **alla mercé di** at the mercy of; **mercé a** thanks to; **mercé sua** thanks to him (her, etc.)

mercéde *f* pay; (lit) reward

mercenà·rio -ria *adj & m* (**-ri -rie**) mercenary

merceria *f* notions store; **mercerie** notions

mercerizzare [ddzz] *tr* to mercerize

mèr·ci *adj invar* freight (*train, car, etc.*) || *m* (**-ci**) freight train

mer·ciàlo -ciàia *mf* (**-ciài -ciàie**) notions store owner

merciaiòlo *m* small businessman; **merciaiolo ambulante** peddler

mercole·dì *m* (**-dì**) Wednesday

mercuriale *f* market report; price ceiling

mercùrio *m* mercury || **Mercurio** *m* Mercury

merènda *f* afternoon snack, bite

meretrice *f* harlot

meridia·no -na *adj & m* meridian || *f* sundial

meridionale *adj* meridional, southern || *mf* southerner

meridióne *m* south; South

merìg·gio *m* (**-gi**) noon

merin·ga *f* (**-ghe**) meringue

meritare (mèrito) *tr* to deserve; to win || *intr* (eccl) to merit; **bene meritare di** to deserve the gratitude of || *impers*—**merita** it is worth while to

meritévole *adj* deserving, worthy

mèrito *m* merit; **in merito a** concerning; **per merito di** thanks to; **render merito a** to reward

meritò·rio -ria *adj* (**-ri -rie**) meritorious

merlan·go *m* (**-ghi**) whiting

merlatura *f* battlement

merlétto *m* lace, needlepoint

mèrlo *m* blackbird; merlon; (fig) simpleton

merluzzo *m* cod

mè·ro -ra *adj* bare, mere; (poet) pure

merovìngi·co -ca (**-ci -che**) *adj* Merovingian || *f* Merovingian script

mesata [s] *f* month's wages

méscere (*pp* mesciuto) *tr* to pour (*e.g., wine*); (poet) to mix

meschini·tà *f* (**-tà**) pettiness; narrowmindedness; meanness, stinginess

meschi·no -na *adj* petty; narrowminded; wretched; puny || *mf* wretch

méscita *f* pouring; counter; bar

mescolanza *f* mixture, blend

mescolare (méscolo) *tr* to mix, blend; to shuffle (*cards*); to stir (*e.g., coffee*) || *ref* to mix, blend; to mingle; to consort; **mescolarsi in** to mind (*somebody else's business*)

mescolatrice *f* mixer, blender

mése [s] *m* month; month's pay

mesétto [s] *m* short month

mesóne *m* (phys) meson

méssa *f* (eccl & mus) Mass; **messa a fuoco** (phot) focusing; **messa a punto** adjustment; clear statement, outline of a problem; (aut) tune-up; **messa a terra** (elec) grounding; **messa cantata** high mass; **messa in marcia** or **in moto** (mach) starting; **messa in orbita** (rok) orbiting; **messa in piega** waving (*of hair*); **messa in scena** staging; **messa in vendita** putting up for sale

messaggerìe *fpl* delivery service

messaggè·ro -ra *mf* messenger; postal clerk

messàg·gio *m* (**-gi**) message

messale *m* missal

mèsse *f* harvest; crop

Messìa *m* Messiah

messiàni·co -ca *adj* (**-ci -che**) Messianic

messica·no -na *adj & mf* Mexican

Mèssico, il Mexico

messinscèna *f* staging; faking

mésso *m* clerk; (poet) messenger

mestare (mésto) *tr* to stir || *intr* to intrigue

mesta·tóre -trice *mf* ringleader; schemer

mèstica *f* (painting) filler

mesticare §197 **(mèstico)** *tr* to prime (*a canvas*); to mix (*colors*)

mestierante *mf* potboiler (*person*); tradesman, craftsman

mestière *m* trade, craft; (archaic) task; **di mestiere** by trade; habitual; **essere del mestiere** to be up in one's line

mestièri *m*—**essere di** or **far mestièri** to be necessary

mestizia *f* sadness

mè·sto -sta *adj* sad

méstola *f* ladle; trowel

méstolo *m* kitchen spoon; **avere il mestolo in mano** to be the boss

mèstruo *m* menses, menstruation

mèta f goal, aim; (rugby) goal line

méta f heap, stack (e.g., of hay)

me·tà f (-tà) half; middle; halfway; better half; **a metà** halfway, in the middle; **aver qlco a metà con qlcu** to go half and half with s.o.

metabolismo m metabolism

metafìsi·co -ca (-ci -che) adj metaphysical || m metaphysician || f metaphysics

metafonèsi f umlaut, metaphony

metafonìa f umlaut, metaphony

metàfora f metaphor

metafòri·co -ca adj (-ci -che) metaphoric(al)

metàlli·co -ca adj (-ci -che) metallic

metallizzare [ddzz] tr to cover with metal

metallo m metal; timbre (of voice); (poet) metal object; **il vile metallo** filthy lucre

metallòide m nonmetal

metallurgìa f metallurgy

metallùrgi·co -ca (ci -che) adj metallurgic(al) || m metalworker

metalmeccàni·co -ca (-ci -che) adj metallurgic(al) and mechanical || m metalworker

metamòrfo·si f (-si) metamorphosis

metanizzare [ddzz] tr to provide with methane

metano m methane

metanodótto m natural gas pipeline

metàte·si f (-si) metathesis

metèora f meteor; atmospheric phenomenon

meteorìte m & f meteorite

meteorologìa f meteorology

meteorològi·co -ca adj (-ci -che) meteorologic(al); weather (forecast)

meteoròlo·go -ga mf (-gi -ghe) meteorologist

metìc·cio -cia adj & mf (-ci -ce) half-breed

meticoló·so -sa [s] adj meticulous

metìli·co -ca adj (-ci -che) methyl

metòdi·co -ca (-ci -che) adj methodical; subject (e.g., index) || mf methodical person || f methodology

metodì·sta adj & mf (-sti -ste) Methodist

mètodo m method

metràg·gio m (-gi) length in meters; **corto metraggio** short; **lungo metraggio** full-length movie, feature film

metratura f length in meters

mètri·co -ca (-ci -che) adj metric(al) || f metrics, prosody

mètro m meter; (fig) yardstick; (lit) words

métro m (coll) subway

metrònomo m (mus) metronome

metronòt·te m (-te) night watchman

metròpo·li f (-li) metropolis

metropolità·no -na adj metropolitan || m policeman, traffic cop || f subway

metrovìa f subway

méttere §198 tr to put, place; to set (e.g., foot); to run (e.g., a nail into a board); to cause (fear; fever); to employ; to admit; to put forth; to give out; (coll) to charge; (coll) to install; (aut) to engage (a gear); **metterci** to take (e.g., an hour); **mettere a confronto** to compare; **mettere a freno** to check; **mettere a fuoco** (phot) to focus; **mettere al bando** to banish; **mettere all'asta** to auction off; **mettere al mondo** to give birth to; **mettere a nudo** to lay bare; **mettere fuori** to pull out; to give out (news); to throw (s.o.) out; **mettere giù** to lower; **mettere in onda** to broadcast; **mettere in pericolo** to endanger; **mettere la pulce nell'orecchio a** to put a bug in the ear of; **mettere qlco alla porta** to show s.o. the door; **mettere su** to set up; (coll) to put (e.g., a coat) on; **mettere su qlcu contro qlcu** to excite s.o. against s.o. || intr to sprout; to lead (said, e.g., of a road) || ref to put on, to don; to place oneself, put oneself; to take shape; **mettersi a** to begin to: **mettersi al bello** to clear up (said of weather); **mettersi a letto** to go to bed; **mettersi a sedere** to sit down; **mettersi con** to start to work with; **mettersi in ferie** to take one's vacation; **mettersi in malattia** to fall ill; **mettersi in mare** to put to sea; **mettersi in maschera** to wear a masked costume; **mettersi in salvo** to get out of danger; to save oneself; **mettersi in viaggio** to set out on a journey; **mettersi in vista** to make oneself conspicuous || impers—**mette conto** it is worth while

mettìma·le mf (-le) troublemaker

mezzadrìa [ddzz] f sharecropping

mezza·dro -dra [ddzz] mf sharecropper

mezzaluna [ddzz] f (mezzelune) half-moon; crescent (symbol of Turkey and Islam); curved chopping knife; lunette (of fortification)

mezzana [ddzz] f procuress; (naut) mizzen

mezzanave [ddzz] f—**a mezzanave** amidships

mezzanino [ddzz] m mezzanine

mezza·no -na [ddzz] adj median; medium; middle || m procurer || f see mezzana

mezzanòtte [ddzz] f (mezzenòtti) midnight

mezzatinta [ddzz] f (mezzetinte) half-tone

méz·zo -za adj overripe, rotten

mèz·zo -za [ddzz] adj half; middle || m half; middle; medium; means; vehicle; **a mezzo (di)** by (e.g., messenger); **andar di mezzo** to suffer the consequences; to be the loser; **entrare di mezzo** to interpose oneself; **esserci di mezzo** to be present; to be at stake; **giusto mezzo** happy medium; **in mezzo a** among; in the lap of, e.g., **in mezzo alle delicatezze** in the lap of luxury; **in quel mezzo** meanwhile; **levar di mezzo** to get rid of; **mezzi** means; facilities; **mezzi di comunicazione di massa** mass media; **per mezzo di** by means of

mezzobusto [ddzz] m (mezzibusti) (sculp) bust; **a mezzobusto** half-length (e.g., portrait)

mezzo·dì [ddzz] *m* (**-dì**) noon; south; South

mezzogiórno [ddzz] *m* noon; south; South

mezzùc·cio [ddzz] *m* (**-ci**) expedient

mi §5 *pron*

miagolare (**miàgolo**) *intr* to meow

miagolì·o *m* (**-i**) meow, mew

mi·ca *f* (**-che**) mica; (obs) crumb ‖ *adv*—**mica male** (coll) not too bad!; **non . . . mica** not . . . ever; not at all

mìc·cia *f* (**-ce**) fuse

michelàc·cio *m* (**-ci**) (coll) lazy bum

micidiale *adj* deadly; (fig) unbearable

mì·cio -cia *mf* (**-ci -cie**) (coll) pussy cat

micrò·bio *m* (**-bi**) microbe

microbiologìa *f* microbiology

mìcrobo *m* microbe

microfà·rad *m* (**-rad**) microfarad

microferrovìa *f* model railroad

micro·film *m* (**-film**) microfilm

microfilmare *tr* to microfilm

micròfono *m* microphone

microlettóre *m* microfilm reader

micromotóre *m* small motor; motorcycle

micrónda *f* microwave

microschèda *f* microcard

microscòpi·co -ca *adj* (**-ci -che**) microscopic(al)

microscò·pio *m* (**-pi**) microscope

microsól·co *adj invar* microgroove ‖ *m* (**-chi**) microgroove; microgroove, long-playing record

microtelèfono *m* French telephone, handset

midólla *f* crumb; (coll) marrow

midól·lo *m* (**-la** *fpl*) marrow; (bot & fig) pith; **midollo spinale** (anat) spinal cord

mièle *m* honey

miètere (**mièto**) *tr* to reap; (lit) to kill

mietitrebbiatrice *f* combine

mieti·tóre -trice *mf* reaper, harvester

mietitura *f* harvesting

mi·gliàio *m* (**-gliàia** *fpl*) thousand

mì·glio *m* (**-glia** *fpl*) mile; milestone; **miglio marino** nautical mile; **miglio terrestre** mile ‖ *m* (**-gli**) millet

miglioraménto *m* improvement

migliorare (**miglióro**) *tr*, *intr* (ESSERE & AVERE) & *ref* to improve

miglióre *adj* better; best

miglioría *f* improvement (*e.g.*, *of real estate*)

mignatta *f* leech

mignolo *adj masc* little (*finger or toe*) ‖ *m* little finger; little toe

migrare *intr* to migrate

migra·tóre -trice *adj* & *m* migrant

migrazióne *f* migration

Milano *f* Milan

miliardà·rio -ria *adj* & *mf* (**-ri -rie**) billionaire

miliardo *m* billion

milionà·rio -ria *adj* & *mf* (**-ri -rie**) millionaire

milióne *m* million

milionèsi·mo -ma *adj* & *m* millionth

militante *adj* & *m* militant

militare *adj* military ‖ *m* soldier ‖ *v* (**mìlito**) *intr* to be a member; to militate; to be in the armed forces; **militare in** to be a member of (*e.g.*, *a party*)

militaré·sco -sca *adj* (**-schi -sche**) military, soldierly

militarismo *m* militarism

militari·sta -sti -ste) *adj* militaristic ‖ *mf* militarist

militarizzare [ddzz] *tr* to militarize; to fortify

mìlite *m* militiaman; soldier; **milite del fuoco** fireman; **Milite Ignoto** Unknown Soldier

militesènte *adj* exempt from military service ‖ *m* man exempt from military service

milìzia *f* militia; (mil) service; struggle; **milizie celesti** heavenly host

miliziano *m* militiaman

millantare *tr* to boast of ‖ *ref* to brag, boast

millanta·tóre -trice *mf* braggart

millanterìa *f* bragging

mille *adj*, *m* & *pron* (**mila**) thousand, a thousand, one thousand ‖ **il Mille** the eleventh century; the year one thousand

millecènto *m* eleven hundred ‖ *f* car with a 1100 cc. motor

millefò·glie *m* (**-glie**) puff-paste cake

millenà·rio -ria (**-ri -rie**) *adj* millennial ‖ *m* millennium

millèn·nio *m* (**-ni**) millennium

millepiè·di *m* (**-di**) millipede

millèsi·mo -ma *adj* & *m* thousandth

milliam·père *m* (**-père**) milliampere

milligrammo *m* milligram

millimetra·to -ta *adj* divided into squares of one millimeter square

millìmetro *m* millimeter

milli·vòlt *m* (**-vòlt**) millivolt

milza *f* spleen

mimare *tr* & *intr* to mime

mimetizzare [ddzz] *tr* (mil) to camouflage

mimetizzazióne [ddzz] *f* (mil) camouflage

mìmi·co -ca (**-ci -che**) *adj* mimic; sign (*language*) ‖ *f* mimicry; (theat) gestures; (theat) miming

mì·mo -ma *mf* mime ‖ *m* (orn) mockingbird

mina *f* lead (*of pencil*); (mil) mine; **mina anticarro** antitank mine; **mina antiuomo** antipersonnel mine

minaccévole *adj* (lit) threatening

minàc·cia *f* (**-ce**) threat, menace

minacciare §128 *tr* to threaten, menace

minacció·so -sa [s] *adj* threatening

minare *tr* to mine; to undermine

minaréto *m* minaret

minatóre *m* miner

minatò·rio -ria *adj* (**-ri -rie**) threatening

minchionare (**minchióno**) *tr* (slang) to make a sucker of

minchióne *m* (slang) sucker

minerale *adj* & *m* mineral; ore

mineralogìa *f* mineralogy

minerà·rio -ria *adj* (**-ri -rie**) mining

minèr·va *m* (**-va**) safety match

minèstra *f* vegetable soup

minestróne *m* minestrone; hodgepodge

mìngere §199 *intr* to urinate

mingherli·no -na *adj* frail, thin

miniare §287 *tr* to paint in miniature; to illuminate

miniatura *f* miniature

miniaturizzare [ddzz] *tr* to miniaturize

miniaturizzazióne [ddzz] *f* miniaturization

minièra *f* mine

mini·gòlf *m* (-gòlf) miniature golf

minigònna *f* miniskirt

mìnima *f* lowest temperature; (mus) minim

minimizzare [ddzz] *tr* to minimize

mìni·mo -ma *adj* smallest, least; minimum || *m* minimum; **al minimo** at the least; **girare al minimo** or **tenere il minimo** (aut) to idle || *f* see **minima**

mìnio *m* red lead; rouge

ministeriale *adj* ministerial

ministèro *m* ministry; cabinet; department; **pubblico ministero** public prosecutor

ministra *f* (joc) wife of minister; (joc) female minister; (poet) minister

ministro *m* minister; secretary; administrator; **ministro degli Esteri** foreign minister; (U.S.A.) Secretary of State

minoranza *f* minority

minorare (minóro) *tr* to lessen; to disable

minora·to -ta *adj* disabled || *mf* disabled person

minorazióne *f* reduction; disability

minóre *adj* smaller, lesser; minor; smallest, least; younger; youngest || *m* minor

minorènne *adj* underage || *mf* minor

minorile *adj* juvenile (*e.g.*, *court*)

minori·tà *f* (-tà) minority

minuétto *m* minuet

minù·gia *f* (-gia & -gie) (mus) catgut

minùsco·lo -la *adj* small (*letter*); diminutive || *m & f* small letter

minuta *f* first draft, rough copy

minutàglia *f* trifles; small fry

minutante *m* secretary; retailer

minuterìa *f* trinkets, notions

minu·to -ta *adj* minute; small (*change*); common (*people*) || *m* minute; **al minuto** retail; **di minuto in minuto** at any moment; **minuto secondo** second; **nel minuto** in detail; **per minuto** minutely || *f* see **minuta**

minùzia *f* trifle; **minuzie** minutiae

minuzió·so -sa [s] *adj* meticulous

minùzzolo *m* scrap, crumb; small boy

mìo mìa §6 *adj & pron poss* (mièi mìe)

mìope *adj* nearsighted || *mf* nearsighted person

miopìa *f* nearsightedness

mira *f* aim; sight; target, goal; **prendere di mira** to aim at; to torment

miràbile *adj* admirable || *m* wonder

mirabìlia *fpl* wonders; **far mirabilia** to perform wonders; **dir mirabilia di** to speak highly of

mirabolante *adj* amazing, astonishing

miracola·to -ta *adj* miraculously cured || *mf* miraculously cured person

miràcolo *m* miracle; wonder; **dir miracoli di** to praise to the skies; **per miracolo** by mere chance

miracoló·so -sa [s] *adj* miraculous; wonderful

miràg·gio *m* (-gi) mirage

mirare (lit) *tr* to look at; (lit) to aim at || *intr* to aim; **mirare a** to aim at; **mirare a + inf** to aim to + *inf*; to intend to + *inf*

mìriade *f* myriad

mirino *m* sight (*of gun*); (phot) finder

mirra *f* myrrh

mirtillo *m* blueberry; whortleberry, huckleberry

mirto *m* myrtle

misantropìa *f* misanthropy

misàntro·po -pa *adj* misanthropic || *mf* misanthrope

miscèla *f* mixture, blend

miscelare (miscèlo) *tr* to mix, blend

miscellàne·o -a *adj* miscellaneous || *f* miscellany

mìschia *f* fight; (sports) scrimmage

mischiare §287 *tr* to mix, blend; to shuffle (*cards*) || *ref* to mix

misconóscere §134 *tr* to not appreciate, undervalue

miscredènte *adj* misbelieving || *mf* misbeliever

miscù·glio *m* (-gli) mixture, blend

miseràbile *adj* pitiful, miserable; poor, wretched

miseran·do -da *adj* pitiable

miserère *m* Miserere; **essere al miserere** to be in one's last hours

miserévole *adj* pitiful; pitiable

misèria *f* destitution, misery; wretchedness; lack, want; trifle; **piangere miseria** to cry poverty

misericòrdia *f* mercy

misericordió·so -sa [s] *adj* merciful

mìse·ro -ra *adj* unhappy, wretched; poor; meager; mean; too small, too short

misfatto *m* misdeed, misdoing

misiriz·zi [s] *m* (-zi) tumbler (*toy*); (fig) chameleon

misògi·no -na *adj* misogynous || *m* misogynist

missìle *adj & m* missile; **missile antimissile** antimissile missile; **missile intercontinentale** I.C.B.M.; **missile teleguidato** guided missile

missilìsti·co -ca *adj* (-ci -che) missile

missionà·rio -ria *adj & m* (-ri -rie) missionary

missióne *f* mission

missiva *f* missive

misterió·so -sa [s] *adj* mysterious

mistèro *m* mystery

mìstica *f* mysticism; mystical literature

misticismo *m* mysticism

mìsti·co -ca (-ci -che) *adj & mf* mystic || *f* see **mistica**

mistificare §197 (mistìfico) *tr* to hoax

mistificazióne *f* hoax

mi·sto -sta *adj* mixed || *m* mixture; mixed train

mistura *f* mixture

misura *f* measure; size; bounds; fitting; **a misura che** in proportion as; **di**

misura (sports) with a narrow margin; **su misura** made-to-order

misuràbile adj measurable

misurare tr to measure; to deliver (e.g., a slap); to budget (expenses); to try on (clothes); to weigh (the outcome) || intr to measure || ref to compete; to limit oneself; **misurarsi con** to try conclusions with

misura·to -ta adj moderate; scanty

misurino m measuring spoon or cup

mite adj mild; tame; low (price)

mìti·co -ca adj (-ci -che) mythical

mitigare §209 (mìtigo) tr to mitigate; to assuage, allay || ref to abate

mìtilo m mussel

mito m myth

mitologìa f mythology

mitològi·co -ca adj (-ci -che) mythologic(al)

mitòmane mf compulsive liar

mi·tra m (-tra) submachine gun || f miter

mitràglia f grapeshot; scrap iron; (coll) machine gun

mitragliare §280 (mitràglio) tr to machine-gun

mitragliatrice f machine gun

mitraglièra f heavy machine gun

mitraglière m machine gunner

mittènte mf sender; shipper

mo' m—apocopated form of **modo** by way of; **a mo' d'esempio** as an illustration

mòbile adj movable; personal (property); (fig) fickle; (rr) rolling (stock) || m piece of furniture; cabinet; (phys) body; **mobili** furniture

mobìlia f furniture

mobiliare adj (fin) security; (law) movable || §287 (mobìlio) tr to furnish

mobilière m furniture maker; furniture dealer

mobilità f mobility

mobilitare (mobìlito) tr & intr to mobilize

mobilitazióne f mobilization

mò·ca m (-ca) mocha; **caffè moca** Mocha coffee

mocassino m mocassin

moccicare §197 (móccico) intr (slang) to snivel; (slang) to run (said of the nose); (slang) to whimper

moccicó·so -sa [s] adj (slang) snotty

móc·cio m (-ci) snot, snivel

mocció·so -sa [s] adj (slang) snotty || m brat

mòccolo m end of candle, snuff; (joc) snot; (slang) curse word; **reggere il moccolo a qlcu** to be a third party to a couple's necking

mòda f fashion, vogue; **andar di moda** to be fashionable; to be all the rage; **fuori moda** outdated

modalità f (-tà) modality; method

modanatura f molding

mòdano m mold

modèlla f model

modellare (modèllo) tr to model; to mold || ref to pattern oneself

modella·tóre -trice mf pattern maker; molder

modellino m (archit) model, maquette

modèllo adj invar model || m model; fashion; style; pattern

moderare (mòdero) tr to moderate, control

moderatézza f moderation

modera·to -ta adj moderate; (mus) moderato || m middle-of-the-roader

modera·tóre -trice adj moderating || m moderator

modernizzare [ddzz] tr & ref to modernize

modèr·no -na adj & m modern

modèstia f modesty; scantiness, meagerness

modè·sto -sta adj modest; humble

mòdi·co -ca adj (-ci -che) reasonable

modìfi·ca f (-che) modification; alteration

modificare §197 (modìfico) tr to modify; to change; to alter

modiglióne m (archit) modillion

modista f milliner

modisterìa f millinery; millinery shop

mòdo m manner, mode, way; custom; idiom; (gram) mood; (mus) mode; **ad ogni modo** anyhow; nevertheless; **ad un modo** equally; **a modo** proper; properly; **a suo modo** in his own way; **bei modi** good manners; **di modo che** so that; **in malo modo** poorly; **in modo da** so as to; **in nessun modo** by no means; **in ogni modo** anyhow; **in qualche modo** somehow; **modo di dire** idiom; turn of phrase; **modo di fare** behavior; **modo di vedere** opinion; **per modo di dire** so to speak

modulare (mòdulo) tr to modulate

modulazióne f modulation; **modulazione d'ampiezza** amplitude modulation; **modulazione di frequenza** frequency modulation

mòdulo m module; blank, form

moffétta f skunk

mògano m mahogany

mòg·gio m (-gi) bushel

mò·gio -gia adj (-gi -gie) downcast, crestfallen

mó·glie f (-gli) wife

moìne fpl blandishments

mòla f grindstone; (coll) millstone

molare adj grinding; molar || m molar || v (mòlo) tr to grind

molassa f molasse, sandstone

molatóre m grinder (person); sander (person)

molatrice f grinder (machine); sander (machine); **molatrice di pavimenti** floor sander

mòle f size; pile; bulk, mass; huge structure

molècola f molecule

molestare (molèsto) tr to bother, annoy

molèstia f bother, trouble, annoyance

molè·sto -sta adj bothersome, troublesome

molibdèno m molybdenum

molinétto m (naut) winch

mòlla f spring; (fig) mainspring; **molla a balestra** leaf spring; **molle** tongs; **molle del letto** bedspring; **prendere**

qlco con le molle to keep at a reasonable distance from s.th

mollare (mòllo) tr to let go; to slacken; to drop (anchor); (coll) to soak || intr to give up; (coll) to soak; **molla!** (coll) cut it out!

mòlle adj wet, soaked; soft; mild; easy (life); weak (character); flexible || m softness; soft ground; **tenere a molle** to soak

mollécca f soft-shell crab

molleggiaménto m suspension; springiness

molleggiare §290 **(molléggio)** tr to provide with springs, to make elastic; (aut) to provide with suspension || intr to be springy, to have bounce || ref to bounce along

mollég·gio m (-gi) springs; (aut) suspension; springiness

mollétta f hairpin; clothespin; **mollette sugar tongs**

mollettièra f puttee

mollettóne m swansdown

mollézza f softness

molli·ca f (-che) crumb (soft inner portion of bread); **molliche crumbs**

mollificare §197 **(mollìfico)** tr & ref to mollify; to soften

mòl·lo -la adj soft || m—**mettere a mollo** to soak || f see **molla**

mollu·sco m (-schi) mollusk

mòlo m pier, wharf

moltéplice adj multiple, manifold

moltilaterale adj multilateral, many-sided

moltìpli·ca f (-che) front sprocket (of bicycle)

moltiplicare §197 **(moltìplico)** tr & ref to multiply

moltitùdine f multitude, crowd

mól·to -ta adj much, a lot of; very, e.g., **ho molta sete** I am very thirsty || pron much; a lot; **a dir molto** mostly; **ci corre molto** there is a great difference || **mol·ti -te** adj & pron many || **molto** adv very; quite; much; a lot; widely; long; **fra non molto** before long; **non . . . molto** (coll) not . . . at all

momentàne·o -a adj momentary

moménto m moment; opportune time; (slang) trifle; (phys) momentum; **dal momento che** since; **per il momento** for the time being; **sul momento** this very moment

mòna·ca f (-che) nun

monacale adj monachal, conventual

monacato m monkhood

monachésimo m monachism, monasticism

monachina f little nun; **monachine sparks**

mòna·co m (-ci) monk; (archit) king post || **Monaco** m Monaco || f Munich

monar·ca m (-chi) monarch

monarchìa f monarchy

monàrchi·co -ca adj (-ci -che) monarchical; monarchist(ic) (advocating a monarch) || mf monarchist

monastèro m monastery

monàsti·co -ca adj (-ci -che) monastic(al)

moncherino m stump (without hand)

món·co -ca (-chi -che) adj one-handed; one-armed; incomplete || mf cripple

moncóne m stump

mondana f prostitute

mondani·tà f (-tà) worldliness

monda·no -na adj mundane; worldly; society; fashionable || m playboy || f see **mondana**

mondare (móndo) tr to peel, pare; to thresh; to weed; to prune; (fig) to cleanse

mondari·so mf (-so) rice weeder

mondez·zàio m (-zài) dump

mondiale adj world, world-wide; (coll) stupendous

mondìglia f chaff; trash; refuse

mondìna f rice weeder

món·do da adj clean-peeled; (lit) pure || m world; hopscotch; (coll) heap, bunch; **bel mondo** smart set; **cascasse il mondo!** (coll) come what may!; **da che mondo è mondo** since the world began; **essere nel mondo della luna** to be absent-minded; **mandare all'altro mondo** (coll) to send packing; **mettere al mondo** to give birth to; **mondo della luna** world of fancy; **un mondo a lot; **venire al mondo** to be born || **Mondo** m—**Terzo Mondo** Third World

monega·sco -sca adj & mf (-schi -sche) Monacan

monellerìa f prank

monèl·lo -la mf urchin, brat || f romp

monéta f money; coin; piece of money; purse (in horse races); change; **batter moneta** to mint money; **moneta sonante** cash

monetà·rio -ria (-ri -rie) adj monetary || m—**falso monetàrio** counterfeiter

monetizzare [ddzz] tr to express in money; to transform into cash

mòngo·lo -la adj & mf Mongolian

monile m necklace; jewel

mònito m admonition, warning

monitóre m monitor

mònna f (obs) lady; (coll) monkey

monoàlbero adj invar (aut) single-camshaft, valve-in-head (distribution)

monoaurale adj monaural

monoblòc·co (-co) adj single-block || m (aut) cylinder block

monocilìndri·co -ca adj (-ci -che) (mach) single-cylinder

monòco·lo -la adj one-eyed || m monocle

monocolóre adj invar one-color; one-party

monofa·se adj (-si & -se) single-phase

monogamìa f monogamy

monòga·mo -ma adj monogamous || m monogamist

monografìa f monograph

monogram·ma m (-mi) monogram

monolìti·co -ca adj (-ci -che) monolithic

monolito m monolith

monòlo·go m (-ghi) monologue

monomanìa f monomania

monò·mio m (-mi) monomial
monopàttino m scooter
monopèt·to (-to) adj single-breasted ‖ m single-breasted suit
monoplano m (aer) monoplane
monopò·lio m (-li) monopoly
monopolizzare [ddzz] tr to monopolize
monopósto adj invar one-man ‖ m single-seater
monorotàia adj invar single-track ‖ f monorail
monoscò·pio m (-pi) (telv) test pattern
monosìlla·bo -ba adj monosyllabic ‖ m monosyllable
monòssido m monoxide
monoteìsti·co -ca adj (-ci -che) monotheistic
monotipìa f monotype
monotipo m monotype
monotonìa f monotony
monòto·no -na adj monotonous
monsignóre m monsignor
monsóne m monsoon
mónta f horseback riding; stud; jockey
montacàri·chi m (-chi) freight elevator
montàg·gio m (-gi) (mach) assembly; (mov) editing; (mov) montage
montagna f mountain; **montagna di ghiaccio** iceberg; **montagne russe** roller coaster
montagnó·so -sa [s] adj mountainous
montana·ro -ra adj mountain ‖ mf mountaineer
monta·no -na adj mountain
montante adj rising ‖ m riser, upright; (football) goal post; (aer) strut; (boxing) uppercut; (com) aggregate amount
montare (mónto) tr to mount; to go up (the stairs); to set (jewels); to frame (a painting); to whip (e.g., eggs); to excite; to exaggerate (news); to decorate (a house); to cover (said of a male animal); (mach) to assemble; (mov) to edit; **montare la testa a** to excite; to give a swell head to ‖ intr (ESSERE) to jump; to climb; to go up; to rise; to swell; **montare alla testa a** to go to the head of; **montare in collera** to get angry ‖ impers—**non monta** it doesn't matter, never mind
monta·tóre -trice mf (mach) assembler; (mov) editor
montatura f assembly; frame (of glasses); appliqué; setting (of gem); (journ) ballyhoo; (mov) editing; **montatura pubblicitaria** publicity stunt
montavivan·de m (-de) dumbwaiter
mónte m mountain; bank; mount (in palmistry); (cards) discard; **a monte** uphill; upstream; **andare a monte** to fail; **mandare a monte** to cause to fail; **monte di pietà** pawnbroker's; **monte di premi** pot (in a lottery)
montenegri·no -na adj & mf Montenegrin
montessoria·no -na adj Montessori
montóne m ram; mutton; rounded stone
montuó·so -sa [s] adj mountainous
montura f uniform

monumentale adj monumental
monuménto m monument
moquètte f (**moquètte**) wall-to-wall carpeting
mòra f mulberry; blackberry; brunette; Moorish woman; arrears; penalty (for arrears); (archaic) heap of stones
morale adj moral ‖ m morale; **giù di morale** downcast; **su di morale** in high spirits ‖ f morals, ethics; moral (of a fable)
moraleggiare §290 (**moraléggio**) intr to moralize
moralismo m moralism
morali·tà f (-tà) morality; morals
moralizzare [ddzz] tr & intr to moralize
moratòria f moratorium
morbidézza f softness
mòrbi·do -da adj soft; sleek; pliable ‖ m soft ground
morbillo m measles
mòrbo m disease; plague
morbó·so -sa [s] adj morbid
mòrchia f sediment; dregs of oil
mordace adj biting, mordacious
mordènte adj biting (chem) mordant; (mach) interlocking ‖ s strength; (chem) mordant
mòrdere §200 tr to bite; to grab; to corrode; **mordere il freno** to champ the bit
mordicchiare §287 (**mordìcchio**) tr to nibble
morèl·lo -la adj blackish; black (horse) ‖ m black horse
morènte adj dying ‖ mf dying person
moré·sco -sca (-schi -sche) adj Moresque, Moorish ‖ f Moorish dance
morét·to -ta adj brunet ‖ m Negro boy; dark-skinned boy; chocolate-covered ice-cream bar ‖ f Negro girl; dark-skinned girl; mask; (orn) scaup duck
morfè·ma m (-mi) morpheme
morfina f morphine
morfinòmane mf morphine addict
morfologìa f morphology
morìa f pestilence; high mortality
moribón·do -da adj moribund
morigera·to -ta adj temperate, moderate
morire §201 intr (ESSERE) to die; to be out; to end (said of a street); **morire di noia** to be bored to death
moritu·ro -ra adj about to die, doomed
mormóne mf Mormon
mormorare (**mórmoro**) tr to murmur; to whisper ‖ intr to murmur; to whisper; to babble (said of a brook); to rustle; to gossip
mormorì·o m (-i) whisper; murmur
mò·ro -ra adj Moorish; dark-skinned; dark-brown ‖ mf Moor ‖ m mulberry tree ‖ f see **mora**
morosi·tà [s] f (-tà) delinquency (in paying one's bills)
moró·so -sa [s] adj delinquent (in paying one's bills) ‖ m (coll) boyfriend; **i morosi** (coll) the lovers ‖ f (coll) girl friend
mòrsa f vise; (archit) toothing
morsétto m clamp; (elec) binding post

morsicare §197 (mòrsico) *tr* to bite
morsicatura *f* bite
morsicchiare §287 (morsìcchio) *tr* to nibble
mòrso *m* bite; bit
mor·tàio *m* (-tài) mortar
mortale *adj* mortal; deadly ‖ *m* mortal
mortali·tà *f* (-tà) mortality
mortarétto *m* firecracker
mòrte *f* death; end; averla a morte con to harbor hatred for; morte civile (law) attainder, loss of civil rights
mortèlla *f* myrtle
mortificare §197 (mortìfico) *tr* to mortify ‖ *ref* to feel ashamed
mòr·to -ta *adj* dead; still (*life*); morto di fame dying of hunger; morto di paura scared to death ‖ *mf* dead person, deceased ‖ *m* hidden treasure; (cards) dummy, widow; fare il morto to float on one's back; to play possum; morto di fame ne'er-do-well, good-for-nothing; suonare a morto to toll
mortò·rio *m* (-ri) funeral
mortuà·rio -ria *adj* (-ri -rie) mortuary
mosài·co -ca (-ci -che) *adj* Mosaic ‖ *m* mosaic
mó·sca *f* (-sche) fly; imperial (*beard*); mosca bianca one in a million; mosca cieca blindman's buff; fare venire la mosca al naso a to make angry ‖ Mosca *f* Moscow
moscaiòla *f* fly netting; flytrap
moscardino *m* dandy; (zool) dormouse
moscatèl·lo -la *adj* muscat ‖ *m* muscatel
moscato *m* muscat grape; muscat wine
moscerino *m* gnat
moschèa *f* mosque
moschettière *m* musketeer; Italian National soccer player
moschétto *m* musket
moschettóne *m* snap hook
moschici·da *adj* (-di -de) fly-killing
mó·scio -scia *adj* (-sci -sce) flabby, soft
moscóne *m* big fly; pesky suitor
moscovi·ta *adj & mf* (-ti -te) Muscovite
Mosè *m* Moses
mòssa *f* gesture; movement; move; fake; post; fare la mossa to sprout (*said of plants*); mossa di corpo bowel movement; prendere le mosse to begin; stare sulle mosse to be about to begin; to be eager to take off (*said of a horse*)
mossière *m* starter (*in a race*)
mòs·so -sa *adj* moved; in motion; plowed; rough (*sea*); blurred (*picture*); wavy (*hair; ground*) ‖ *f* see mossa
mostarda *f* mustard; candied fruit
mósto *m* must
móstra *f* show; pretense, simulation; exhibit; display window; lapel; face (*of watch*); sample; (mil) insignia; (obs) military parade; far mostra di sé to show off; mettersi in mostra to show off
mostrare (móstro) *tr* to show; to put on; mostrare a dito to point to;

mostrare la corda to be threadbare ‖ *ref* to show up; to show oneself
mostreggiatura *f* lapel; cuff
mostrina *f* (mil) insignia
móstro *m* monster
mostruó·so -sa [s] *adj* monstrous
mòta *f* mud, mire
mo·tèl *m* (-tèl) motel
motivare *tr* to cause; to justify
motivazióne *f* justification, reason
motivo *m* motive, reason; motif; theme; (coll) tune; a motivo di because of; motivo per cui wherefore
mò·to *m* (-ti) motion; movement; emotion; riot; mettere in moto to start ‖ *f* (-to) (coll) motorcycle
motobar·ca *f* (-che) motorboat
motocannonièra *f* gunboat
motocarro *m* three-wheeler (*truck*)
motocarrozzétta *f* three-wheeler (*vehicle with sidecar*)
motociclétta *f* motorcycle
motocicli·sta *mf* (-sti -ste) motorcyclist
motocorazza·to -ta *adj* armored, panzer
motofalciatrice *f* power mower
motofurgóne *m* delivery truck
motolàn·cia *f* (-ce) motorboat, speedboat
motonàuti·co -ca (-ci -che) *adj* motorboat ‖ *f* motorboating
motonave *f* motor ship
motopescheréc·cio *m* (-ci) motor fishing boat
mo·tóre -trice *adj* motive (*power*); (mach) drive ‖ *m* motor; engine; car; a motore motorized, motor; motore rotativo (aut) rotary engine; primo motore prime mover ‖ *f* see motrice
motorétta *f* motor scooter
motorino *m* small motor; motor bicycle; motorino d'avviamento (aut) starter
motori·sta *mf* (-sti) mechanic
motoristi·co -ca *adj* (-ci -che) motor
motorizzare [ddzz] *tr* to motorize
motoscafo *m* motorboat; motoscafo da corsa speedboat
motosé·ga *f* (-ghe) chain saw
motosilurante *f* torpedo boat
motoveicolo *m* motor vehicle
motovelièro *m* motor sailer
motrice *f* (rr) engine, motor; (aut) tractor; motrice a vapore steam engine
motteggiare §290 (mottéggio) *tr* to mock, jeer at ‖ *intr* to jest
mottég·gio *m* (-gi) mockery, jest
mòtto *m* witticism; motto; (lit) word
movènte *m* stimulus, motive
movènza *f* bearing, carriage; flow (*of a sentence*); cadence
movìbile *adj* movable
movimenta·to -ta *adj* lively; eventful
moviménto *m* motion, movement; traffic; movimento di cassa cash turnover
moviòla *f* (mov) viewer and splicer
mozióne *f* motion; (lit) movement
mozzare (mózzo) *tr* to lop off; to sever; mozzare la testa a to cut off the head of

mozzicóne *m* stump; butt (*e.g., of cigar*)

móz·zo -za *adj* cut off; truncated; cropped (*ears*); docked (*tail*); hard (*breathing*) ‖ *m* cabin boy; **mozzo di stalla** stable boy

mòzzo [ddzz] *m* hub

muc·ca *f* (**-che**) milch cow

mùc·chio *m* (**-chi**) pile, heap; bunch

mucillàgine *f* mucilage

mu·co *m* (**-chi**) mucus, phlegm

mucó·so -sa [s] *adj* mucous ‖ *f* mucous membrane

muda *f* molt

muffa *f* mold; mildew; **fare la muffa** to be musty

muffire §176 *intr* (ESSERE) to be musty

mùffola *f* mitten; muffle (*of furnace*)

muflóne *m* mouflon

mugghiare §287 (**mùgghio**) *intr* to bellow; to roar

mùggine *m* (ichth) mullet

muggire §176 & (**muggo**) *intr* to moo, low; to roar; to howl

muggito *m* bellow; moo, low; roar

mughétto *m* lily of the valley

mu·gnàio -gnàia *mf* (**-gnài -gnàie**) miller

mugolare (**mùgolo**) *intr* to yelp; to moan

mugolì·o *m* (**-i**) yelp; moan

mugò·lio *m* (**-li**) pine tar

mugugnare *intr* (coll) to mumble; (coll) to grumble

mugugno *m* (coll) grumble

mulattière *m* mule driver, muleteer

mulattiè·ro -ra *adj* mule ‖ *f* mule track

mulat·to -ta *adj* & *mf* mulatto

muliebre *adj* womanly, feminine

mulinare *tr* to twirl; to scheme ‖ *intr* to whirl; to muse; to buzz (*in the mind*)

mulinèllo *m* twirl; whirlpool; whirlwind; fishing reel; whirligig; **fare mulinello con** to twirl

mulino *m* mill; **mulino ad acqua** water mill; **mulino a vento** windmill

mu·lo -la *mf* mule; (slang) bastard

multa *f* penalty, fine

multare *tr* to fine

multilaterale *adj* multilateral, many-sided

mùlti·plo -pla *adj* & *m* multiple

mùmmia *f* mummy

mummificare §197 (**mummìfico**) *tr* to mummify

mùngere §183 *tr* to milk

mungi·tóre -trice *mf* milker ‖ *f* milking machine; milk maid

mungitura *f* milking

municipale *adj* municipal, city

municipalizzazióne [ddzz] *f* municipalization; city management

munici·pio *m* (**-pi**) municipality; city council; city hall

munificènza *f* munificence

munìfi·co -ca *adj* (**-ci -che**) munificent

munire §176 *tr* to fortify; to provide; **munire di** to equip with ‖ *ref* to provide oneself

munizióne *f* (obs) fortification; **munizioni** ammunition; building supplies

muòvere §202 *tr* to move; to wag; to propel, run; to lift (*one's finger*); to take (*a step*); to pose (*a question*); to stir up (*laughter*); to institute (*a lawsuit*); **muovere accusa a** to reproach ‖ *intr* (ESSERE) to begin; to move, start ‖ *ref* to move; to travel; to stir; to set out; to be moved; **muoviti!** hurry up!

mura *fpl* see **muro**

muràglia *f* wall; (fig) obstacle; **muraglia cinese** Chinese Wall

muraglióne *m* high wall, rampart

murale *adj* & *m* mural

murare *tr* to wall; to wall in ‖ *intr* to build a wall; **murare a secco** to build a dry wall ‖ *ref* to close oneself in

murata *f* (naut) bulwark

muratóre *m* bricklayer, mason

muratura *f* bricklaying, stonework

muriàti·co -ca *adj* (**-ci -che**) muriatic

mu·ro *m* (**-ri**) wall; **muro del pianto** Wailing Wall; **muro del suono** sound barrier ‖ *m* (**-ra** *fpl*)—**mura** walls (*of a city*)

musa *f* muse

muschia·to -ta *adj* musk (*e.g., ox*)

mù·schio *m* (**-schi**) musk; (coll) moss

mu·sco *m* (**-schi**) moss

mùscolo *m* muscle; (fig) sinew; (coll) mussel

muscoló·so -sa [s] *adj* muscular

muscó·so -sa [s] *adj* (lit) mossy

musèo *m* museum

museruòla *f* muzzle

musétta *f* nose bag

mùsi·ca *f* (**-che**) music; band; **cambiare musica** to change one's tune

musicale *adj* musical

musicante *adj* music-playing (*angels*) ‖ *mf* band player; second-rate musician

musicare §197 (**mùsico**) *tr* to set to music

musicassétta *f* cassette, tape cartridge

music-hall *m* (**-hall**) *m* vaudeville, burlesque

musici·sta *mf* (**-sti -ste**) musician

musicologìa *f* musicology

musicòlo·go *m* (**-gi**) musicologist

muso *m* muzzle, snout; (coll) mug; (fig) nose; **avere il muso lungo** to make a long face; **mettere il muso** to pout

musó·ne -na *mf* pouter, sulker

mussare *tr* to publish with great fanfare (*a piece of news*) ‖ *intr* to foam (*said of wine*)

mùssola or **mussolina** *f* muslin

mussolinia·no -na *adj* of Mussolini

mùssolo *m* mussel

mustàc·chio *m* (**-chi**) shroud (*of bowsprit*); **mustacchi** moustache

musulma·no -na [s] *adj* & *mf* Moslem

muta *f* change; shift; molt; set (*of sails*); pack (*of hounds*); (mil) watch

mutàbile *adj* changeable

mutande *fpl* shorts, briefs, drawers

mutandine *fpl* panties; **mutandine da bagno** trunks

mutare *tr, intr* (ESSERE) & *ref* to change

mutazióne *f* mutation; (biol) mutation, sport

mutévole *adj* changeable; fickle

mutilare (**mùtilo**) *tr* to mutilate, maim
mutila·to -ta *adj* mutilated ‖ *mf* cripple; amputee; mutilato di guerra disabled veteran
mutismo *m* silence, willful silence;
(pathol) dumbness
mu·to -ta *adj* mute; dumb; silent
(*movie*); unexpressed ‖ *mf* mute ‖ *f*
see **muta**
mùtria *f* sulking attitude; proud demeanor

mùtua *f* mutual benefit society; medical insurance; **mettersi in mutua** to
go on sick leave
mutuali·tà *f* (**-tà**) mutuality; mutual
benefit institutions
mutuare (**mùtuo**) *tr* to borrow; to lend
mutua·to -ta *mf* person insured by
mutual benefit society; person insured by medical insurance
mù·tuo -tua *adj* mutual; borrowing ‖
m loan ‖ *f* see **mutua**

N

N, n ['enne] *m & f* twelfth letter of the
Italian alphabet
nababbo *m* nabob
Nabucodònosor *m* Nebuchadnezzar
nàcchera *f* castanet
nafta *f* crude oil; naphtha; Diesel oil
naftalina *f* naphthalene
nàia *f* cobra; (slang) army discipline;
(slang) military service
nàiade *f* naiad
nàilon *m* nylon
nanna *f* sleep (*of child*); **fare la nanna**
to sleep (*said of child*)
na·no -na *adj & mf* dwarf
nàpalm *m* napalm
napoleòne *m* napoleon (*gold coin*) ‖
Napoleone *m* Napoleon
napoleòni·co -ca *adj* (**-ci -che**) Napoleonic
napoleta·no -na *adj & mf* Neapolitan ‖
f espresso coffee machine
Nàpoli *f* Naples
nappa *f* tassel; tuft; kid (*leather*)
narciso *m* narcissus
narcòti·co -ca *adj & m* (**-ci -che**) narcotic
narcotizzare [ddzz] *tr* to drug, dope;
to anesthetize
narghi·lè *m* (**-lè**) hookah
narice *f* nostril
narrare *tr* to narrate, tell, recount
narrati·vo -va *adj* narrative; fictional
‖ *f* narrative; fiction
narra·tóre -trice *mf* narrator, storyteller
narrazióne *f* narration; tale, story; narrative
nasale [s] *adj & f* nasal
nascènte *adj* nascent; budding; rising
(*sun*); dawning (*day*)
nàscere *m* beginning, origin ‖ §203 *intr*
(ESSERE) to be born; to bud; to shoot;
to dawn; to rise; to spring up; **nascere con la camicia** to be born with
a silver spoon in one's mouth
nàscita *f* birth; birthday; origin
nascitu·ro -ra *adj* unborn, future ‖ *mf*
unborn child
nascóndere §204 *tr* to hide; **nascondere
a** to hide from ‖ *ref* to hide; to lurk
nascondì·glio *m* (**-gli**) hiding place;
hideout; cache
nascondino *m* hide-and-seek; **giocare a
nascondino** to play hide-and-seek
nascó·sto -sta *adj* hidden, concealed;
secret; **di nascosto** secretly

nasèllo [s] *m* catch (*of latch*); (ichth)
hake
nasièra [s] *f* nose ring
naso [s] *m* nose; (fig) face; **aver buon
naso** to have a keen sense of smell;
ficcare il naso negli affari degli altri
to pry into the affairs of others;
menare per il naso to lead by the
nose; **naso adunco** hooknose; **restare
con un palmo di naso** to be duped
nassa *f* pot (*for fishing*); **nassa per
aragoste** lobster pot
nastrino *m* ribbon; badge
nastro *m* ribbon; band; tape; streamer;
tape measure; **nastro del cappello**
hatband; **nastro isolante** friction
tape; **nastro per capelli** hair ribbon
nastùr·zio *m* (**-zi**) nasturtium
natale *adj* native, natal ‖ **natali** *mpl*
birth; birthday; **dare i natali a** to be
the birthplace of ‖ **Natale** *m* Christmas
natali·tà *f* (**-tà**) birth rate
natalì·zio -zia (**-zi -zie**) *adj* natal;
Christmas ‖ *m* birthday
natante *adj* swimming; floating ‖ *m*
craft
natatóia *f* fin
natató·rio -ria *adj* (**-ri -rie**) swimming
nàti·ca *f* (**-che**) buttock
natì·o -a *adj* (**-i -e**) (poet) native
nativi·tà *f* (**-tà**) birth, nativity ‖ **Nati-
vità** *f* Nativity
nati·vo -va *adj* native; natural, inborn
‖ *mf* native
N.A.T.O. *f* (acronym) (North Atlantic
Treaty Organization)—**la N.A.T.O.**
NATO
na·to -ta *adj* born; **nata** née; **nato e
sputato** the spit and image of; **nato
morto** stillborn ‖ *mf* child
natura *f* nature; **natura morta** still life;
in natura in kind
naturale *adj* natural ‖ *m* nature, disposition; **al naturale** life-size
naturalézza *f* naturalness; spontaneity
naturalismo *m* naturalism
naturali·sta *mf* (**-sti -ste**) naturalist
naturali·tà *f* (**-tà**) naturalization
naturalizzare [ddzz] *tr* to naturalize ‖
ref to become naturalized
naturalizzazióne [ddzz] *f* naturalization
naturalménte *adv* naturally; of course
naufragare §209 (**nàufrago**) *intr* (ESSERE

& AVERE) to be shipwrecked; to sink, to fail

naufrà·gio m (-gi) shipwreck; failure

nàufra·go -ga (-ghi -ghe) adj shipwrecked ‖ mf shipwrecked person; (fig) outcast

nàusea f nausea; disgust; **avere la nausea** to be sick at one's stomach

nauseabón·do -da adj sickening, nauseating; (fig) unsavory

nauseante adj sickening, nauseous

nauseare (nàuseo) tr to nauseate, sicken

nàusea·to -ta adj sickened, disgusted

nàuti·co -ca (-ci -che) adj nautical ‖ f sailing, navigation

navale adj naval, navy, sea

navata f nave; **navata centrale** nave; **navata laterale** aisle

nave f ship, vessel, boat; craft; **nave ammiraglia** flagship; **nave a motore** motorboat; **nave appoggio** tender; **nave a vela** sailboat; **nave da carico** freighter; **nave da guerra** warship; **nave petroliera** tanker; **nave portaerei** aircraft carrier; **nave rompighiaccio** icebreaker; **nave traghetto** ferryboat

navétta f shuttle; **fare la navetta** to shuttle

navicèlla f nacelle, cabin (of airship); car (of balloon)

navigàbile adj navigable

navigabili·tà f (-tà) navigability; seaworthiness

navigante adj sailing ‖ m sailor

navigare §209 (nàvigo) tr & intr to navigate, to sail

naviga·to -ta adj seawise; wordly-wise

naviga·tóre -trice mf navigator

navigazióne f navigation

navi·glio m (-gli) ship, craft, boat; fleet; navy; canal; **naviglio mercantile** merchant marine

nazionale adj national ‖ f national team

nazionalismo m nationalism

nazionali·sta mf (-sti -ste) nationalist

nazionalìsti·co -ca adj (-ci -che) nationalistic

nazionali·tà f (-tà) nationality

nazionalizzare [ddzz] tr to nationalize

nazionalizzazióne [ddzz] f nationalization

nazióne f nation

nazi·sta adj & mf (-sti -ste) Nazi

nazzarè·no -na [ddzz] adj & mf Nazarene ‖ **il Nazzareno** the Nazarene

ne §5 pron & adv

né conj neither, nor; **né . . . né** neither . . . nor

neanche adv not even; nor; not . . . either

nébbia f fog, haze, mist; **fa nebbia** it is foggy; **nebbia artificiale** smoke screen

nebbióne m thick fog, pea soup

nebbió·so -sa [s] adj foggy, hazy, misty

nebulare adj nebular

nebulizzare [ddzz] tr to atomize

nebulizzatóre [ddzz] m atomizer

nebulósa [s] f nebula

nebulosi·tà [s] f (-tà) fogginess, haziness, mistiness

nebuló·so -sa [s] adj foggy, hazy, misty ‖ f see nebulosa

néces·saire m (-saire) vanity case; sewing kit

necessariaménte adv necessarily

necessà·rio -ria (-ri -rie) adj necessary, needed; essential ‖ m necessity; necessities (of life)

necessi·tà f (-tà) necessity; need, want; **di necessità** necessarily

necessitare (necèssito) tr to require; to force ‖ intr to be in want; to be necessary; **necessitare di** to need

necrologìa f necrology, obituary

necrològi·co -ca adj (-ci -che) obituary

necromanzìa f necromancy

necròsi f necrosis, gangrene

nefan·do -da adj heinous, nefarious

nefa·sto -sta adj ill-fated; ominous

nefrìte f nephritis

negare §209 (négo & nègo) tr to deny, negate; to refuse

negatì·vo -va adj & f negative

nega·to -ta adj unfit, unsuited

negazióne f negation, denial; (gram) negative

neghittó·so -sa [s] adj lazy, slothful

neglèt·to -ta adj neglected; untidy

négli §4

negligènte adj negligent, careless

negligènza f negligence, carelessness; dereliction (of duty)

neglìgere §205 tr to neglect

negoziàbile adj negotiable

negoziante mf merchant, shopkeeper; dealer; **negoziante all'ingrosso** wholesaler; **negoziante al minuto** retailer; shopkeeper, storekeeper

negoziare §287 (negòzio) tr to negotiate, transact ‖ intr to negotiate, deal

negoziati mpl negotiations

negozia·tóre -trice mf negotiator

negò·zio m (-zi) business; transaction; store, shop; **negozio di cancelleria** stationery store

negrière m slave trader; slave driver

negriè·ro -ra adj slave ‖ m slave trader; slave driver

né·gro -gra adj & mf Negro

negromante m sorcerer

néi §4

nél §4

nélla §4

nélle §4

néllo §4

némbo m rain cloud; cloud (e.g., of dust)

Nembròd m Nimrod

nèmesi f invar nemesis ‖ **Nemesi** f Nemesis

nemì·co -ca (-ci -che) adj inimical, hostile, unfriendly; enemy; (fig) adverse ‖ mf enemy, foe; **Il Nemico** the Evil One

nemméno adv not even; nor; not . . . either

nènia f funeral dirge; lamentation

nenùfaro m water lily

nèo m mole (on the skin); flaw, blemish; neon; beauty spot

neoclassicheggiante adj in the direction of the neoclassical

neòfi·ta *mf* (-ti -te) neophite
neolati·no -na *adj* Neo-Latin, Romance
neologismo *m* neologism
neomicina *f* neomycin
nèon *m* neon
neona·to -ta *adj* newborn || *mf* infant, baby; newborn child
neozelandése [dz][s] *adj* New Zealand || *mf* New Zealander
nepènte *f* nepenthe
Nepóte *m* Nepos
neppure *adv* not even; nor; not . . . either
nequìzia *f* iniquity, wickedness
nera·stro -stra *adj* blackish
nerbata *f* heavy blow
nèrbo *m* whip; sinew; bulk; strength (*of an opposing force*)
nerboru·to -ta *adj* muscular, sinewy
nereggiare §290 (neréggio) *intr* to look black; to be blackish
nerétto *m* (*typ*) boldface
né·ro -ra *adj* black; dark; gloomy; dark-red (*wine*) || *mf* black; Negro || *m* black
nerofumo *m* lampblack
Neróne *m* Nero
nervatura *f* ribbing
nervi·no -na *adj* nerve (*gas*); nervine (*medicine*)
nèrvo *m* nerve; sinew; **avere i nervi to** be in a bad mood
nervosismo [s] *m* nervousness, irritability
nervó·so -sa [s] *adj* nervous, irritable; sinewy, vigorous (*style*) || *m* bad mood; **avere il nervoso to** be in a bad mood
nèsci *m*—**fare il nesci** to feign ignorance
nèspola *f* medlar; **nespole** (*coll*) blows
nèspolo *m* medlar tree
nèsso *m* connection, link; **avere nesso to** cohere
nessu·no -na *adj* no, not any || **nessuno** *pron* nobody, no one; none; not anybody; not anyone; **nessuno dei due** neither one
nettapén·ne *m* (-ne) penwiper
nettare (nétto) *tr* to clean, to cleanse
nèttare (nétto) *tr* nectar
nettézza *f* cleanness, cleanliness; neatness; **nettezza urbana** department of sanitation; garbage collection
nét·to -ta *adj* clean; clear; sharp; net || **netto** *adv* clearly, distinctly
nettùnio *m* neptunium
Nettuno *m* Neptune
netturbino *m* street cleaner
neurologìa *f* neurology
neurò·si *f* (-si) neurosis
neuròti·co -ca *adj* (-ci -che) neurotic
neutrale *adj* & *mf* neutral
neutrali·sta *adj* & *mf* (-sti -ste) neutralist
neutrali·tà *f* (-tà) neutrality
neutralizzare [ddzz] *tr* to neutralize
nèu·tro -tra *adj* neuter; neutral
neutróne *m* neutron
ne·vàio *m* (-vài) snowfield; snowdrift
néve *f* snow; **neve carbonica** dry ice
nevicare §197 (névica) *impers* (ESSERE) —**nevica** it is snowing

nevicata *f* snowfall
nevìschio *m* sleet
nevó·so -sa [s] *adj* snowy
nevralgìa *f* neuralgia
nevrastèni·co -ca *adj* & *mf* (-ci -che) neurasthenic
nevvéro (i.e., **n'è vero** for **non è vero**) see **non**
niacina *f* niacin
nìb·bio *m* (-bi) (*orn*) kite
nìcchia *f* niche; nook, recess
nicchiare §287 (nìcchio) *intr* to waver
nìc·chio *m* (-chi) shell; nook
nichel *m* nickel
nichelare (nìchelo) *tr* to nickel, to nickel-plate
nichelatura *f* nickel-plating
nichelino *m* nickel (*coin*)
nichèlio *m* var of **nichel**
Nicòla *m* Nicholas
nicotina *f* nicotine
nidiata *f* nestful; brood
nidificare §197 (nidìfico) *intr* to build a nest, to nest
nido *m* nest; home; nursery; den (*of thieves*)
niènte *m* nothing; nothingness; **dal niente** from scratch; **di niente** you're welcome || *pron* nothing; not . . . anything; **quasi niente** next to nothing
nientediméno *adv* no less, nothing less
Nilo *m* Nile
ninfa *f* nymph
ninfèa *f* white water lily
ninnananna *f* lullaby, cradlesong
nìnnolo *m* toy; trinket
nipóte *mf* grandchild || *m* grandson; nephew; **nipoti** descendants || *f* granddaughter; niece
nippòni·co -ca *adj* (-ci -che) Nipponese
nirvana, il nirvana
nìti·do -da *adj* clear, distinct
nitóre *m* brightness; elegance
nitrato *m* nitrate
nitrire §176 *intr* to neigh
nitrito *m* neigh; (*chem*) nitrite
nitro *m* niter; **nitro del Cile** Chile saltpeter
nitroglicerina *f* nitroglycerin
nitruro *m* nitride
niu·no -na *adj* (*poet*) var of **nessuno**
nìve·o -a *adj* snow-white
Nizza *f* Nice
no *adv* no; not; **come no?** why not; certainly; **dire di no** to say no; **no?** is it not so?; **non dir di no** to consent; **proprio no** certainly not
nòbile *adj* noble; second (*floor*) || *m* nobleman || *f* noblewoman
nobiliare *adj* noble, of nobility
nobilitare (nobìlito) *tr* to ennoble
nobil·tà *f* (-tà) nobility
nòc·ca *f* (-che) knuckle
nocchière *m* or **nocchièro** *m* petty officer; (*poet*) pilot, helmsman
nocchieru·to -ta *adj* knotty
nòc·chio *m* (-chi) knot (*in wood*)
nocciòla *adj invar* hazel (*in color*) || *f* hazelnut; filbert
nocciolina *f* little nut; **nocciolina americana** peanut; roasted peanut
nòcciolo *m* stone, pit, kernel; **il noc-**

ciolo della questione the crux of the matter

nocciòlo *m* hazel (*tree*); filbert (*tree*)

nóce *m* walnut tree ‖ *f* walnut (*fruit*); **noce del collo** Adam's apple; **noce di cocco** coconut; **noce di vitello** filet of veal; **noce moscata** nutmeg

nocévole *adj* harmful

noci·vo -va *adj* harmful, detrimental

nòdo *m* knot; crux, gist (*of a question*); junction; lump (*in one's throat*); (*naut*) knot; (*phys*) node; **lì è il nodo** there's the rub; **nodo d'amore** true-love knot; **nodo ferroviario** rail center, junction; **nodo scorsoio** noose; **nodo stradale** highway center, crossroads

nodó·so -sa [*s*] *adj* knotty

Noè *m* Noah

noi §5 *pron pers* we; us; **noi altri** we, e.g., **noi altri italiani** we Italians

nòia *f* boredom; bother, trouble; bug (*in a motor*); **venire a noia** (with *dat*) to weary; **dar noia** (with *dat*) to bother

noial·tri -tre *pron* we; us; **noialtri italiani** we Italians

noió·so -sa [*s*] *adj* boring, annoying

noleggiare §290 (**noléggio**) *tr* to rent; to hire, to charter ‖ *ref*—**si noleggia, si noleggiano** for rent

noleggiatóre *m* hirer; lessor (*e.g., of a car*)

nolég·gio *m* (**-gi**) rent, lease; car rental; chartering; freightage

nolènte *adj* unwilling

nòlo *m* rent, hire; **a nolo** for hire

nòmade *adj* nomad, nomadic ‖ *mf* nomad

nóme *m* name; fame; reputation; (*gram*) noun; **a nome di** on behalf of; **in nome di** in the name of; **nome commerciale** firm name; **nome depositato** registered name; **nome di battesimo** Christian name; **nome e cognome** full name

nomèa *f* name, reputation; notoriety

nomìgnolo *m* nickname; **affibbiare un nomignolo a** to nickname

nòmina *f* appointment; **di prima nomina** newly appointed

nominale *adj* nominal; noun

nominare (**nòmino**) *tr* to name, call; to mention; to elect; to appoint

nominati·vo -va *adj* nominative; with names in alphabetical order; (*fin*) registered ‖ *m* nominative; name; model number

non *adj* no, not; none, e.g., **non troppo presto** none too soon; **non appena** as soon as; **non c'è di che** you are welcome; **non . . . che** but, only; **non è vero?** is it not so?, isn't it so? La traduzione in inglese di questa domanda dipende generalmente dalla proposizione che la precede. Se la proposizione è affermativa, l'interrogazione sarà negativa, p.es. **Lei mi scriverà, non è vero?** You will write me. Won't you? Se la proposizione è negativa, l'interrogazione sarà positiva, p.es. **Lei non beve birra, non è**

vero? You do not drink beer. Do you? Se il soggetto della proposizione è un nome sostantivo, sarà rappresentato nell'interrogazione da un pronome personale, p.es. **Giovanni ha finito, non è vero?** John has finished. Hasn't he?

nonagenà·rio -ria *adj & mf* (**-ri -rie**) nonagenarian

nonagèsi·mo -ma *adj, pron & m* nine-tieth

nonconformi·sta *mf* (**-sti -ste**) nonconformist

noncurante *adj* careless, indifferent

noncuranza *f* carelessness, indifference

nondiméno *conj* yet, nevertheless

nòn·no -na *mf* grandparent ‖ *m* grandfather ‖ *f* grandmother

nonnulla *m invar* nothing, trifle

nò·no -na *adj, m & pron* ninth

nonostante *prep* in spite of, notwithstanding; **nonostante che** although, even though

nonpertanto *adv* nevertheless, still, yet

non plus ultra *m* ne plus ultra, acme

nonsènso *m* nonsense

non so ché *adj invar* indefinable ‖ *m invar* something indefinable

nontiscordardi·mé *m* (**-mé**) forget-me-not

nòrd *m* north

nòrdi·co -ca (**-ci -che**) *adj* Nordic; northern, north ‖ *mf* northerner

nòrma *f* rule, regulation; **a norma di legge** according to law; **per Sua norma** for your guidance

normale *adj* normal; normative; perpendicular ‖ *f* perpendicular line

normali·tà *f* (**-tà**) normality, normalcy

normalizzare [*ddzz*] *tr* to normalize, to standardize

Normandìa, la Normandy

normàn·no -na *adj & mf* Norman ‖ *m* Norseman

normati·vo -va *adj* normative ‖ *f* normativeness

normògrafo *m* stencil

norvegése [*s*] *adj & mf* Norwegian

Norvègia, la Norway

nosocò·mio *m* (**-mi**) hospital

nossignóra (*i.e.*, **no signora**) *adv* no, Madam

nossignóre (*i.e.*, **no signore**) *adv* no, Sir

nostalgìa *f* nostalgia, longing; homesickness

nostàlgi·co -ca (**-ci -che**) *adj* nostalgic; homesick ‖ *m* worshiper of the good old days (*esp. of Fascism*)

nostra·no -na *adj* domestic, national; home-grown; regional

nò·stro -stra §6 *adj & pron poss*

nostròmo *m* boatswain

nòta *f* mark; score; memorandum; list; bill, invoice; report (*on a subordinate*); (*mus*) note; **note caratteristiche** personal folder, efficiency report (*of an employee*); **prender nota di** to take down

notàbile *adj* notable, noteworthy ‖ *m* notable

no·tàio *m* (**-tài**) notary (public); lawyer

notare (**nòto**) *tr* to mark, check; to note, to jot down; to observe; to bring out; **farsi notare** to attract attention, make oneself conspicuous; **nota bene** note well, take notice

notariale or **notarile** *adj* notarial

notazióne *f* notation; annotation; observation

nò·tes *m* (**-tes**) notebook

notévole *adj* noteworthy, remarkable

notìfi·ca *f* (**-che**) notification, notice; service (*e.g., of a summons*)

notificare §197 (**notìfico**) *tr* to report; to serve (*a summons*); to declare . . (*e.g., one's income*)

notificazióne *f* notification, notice; service (*e.g., of a summons*)

notìzia *f* knowledge; report; piece of news; **aver notizie di** to hear from; **notizie** news; **una notizia** a news item

notizià·rio *m* (**-ri**) news; news report, news bulletin; (rad) newscast; **notiziario sportivo** sports page; (rad, telv) sports news

nò·to -ta *adj* known, well-known ‖ *m* south wind; (coll) swimming ‖ *f* see **nota**

notorie·tà *f* (**-tà**) general knowledge; affidavit; notoriety

notò·rio -ria *adj* (**-ri -rie**) well-known

nottàmbu·lo -la *adj* nighttime; night-wandering ‖ *mf* nightwalker; night owl

nottata *f* night; **far nottata bianca** to spend a sleepless night

nòtte *f* night; **buona notte** good night; **di notte** at night, by night, in the nighttime; **la notte di lunedì** Sunday night; Monday night; **lunedì notte** Monday night; **notte bianca** sleepless night; **notte di San Silvestro** New Year's Eve; watch night

nottetèmpo *adv*—**di nottetempo** at night, in the nighttime

nòttola *f* wooden latch; (zool) bat

nottolino *m* small wooden latch; ratchet, catch

nottur·no -na *adj* nocturnal, night ‖ *m* nocturne

novanta *adj, m & pron* ninety

novantènne *adj* ninety-year-old ‖ *mf* ninety-year-old person

novantèsi·mo -ma *adj, m & pron* ninetieth

novantina *f* about ninety; **sulla novantina** about ninety years old

nòve *adj & pron* nine; **le nove** nine o'clock ‖ *m* nine; ninth (*in dates*)

novecentismo *m* twentieth-century arts and letters

novecenti·sta (**-sti -ste**) *adj* twentieth-century ‖ *mf* artist of the twentieth century

novecènto *adj, m & pron* nine hundred ‖ **il Novecento** the twentieth century

novèlla *f* short story; (poet) news

novelliè·re -ra *f* storyteller; short-story writer

novelli·no -na *adj* early, tender; inexperienced, green

novellìstica *f* storytelling; fiction

novèl·lo -la *adj* fresh, young, tender; new ‖ *f* see **novella**

novèmbre *m* November

novenà·rio -ria *adj* (**-ri -rie**) nine-syllable

noverare (**nòvero**) *tr* to count; to enumerate; (poet) to remember

nòvero *m* number; class

novilù·nio *m* (**-ni**) new moon

novìssi·mo -ma *adj* (lit) last, newest

novi·tà *f* (**-tà**) newness, originality; novelty, innovation; latest idea; late news

noviziato *m* novitiate; apprenticeship

novì·zio -zia (**-zi -zie**) *mf* novice; apprentice ‖ *f* novice (*in a convent*)

novocaina *f* novocaine

nozióne *f* notion, conception

nòzze *fpl* wedding, marriage; **nozze d'argento** silver wedding; **nozze d'oro** golden wedding

nube *f* cloud

nubifrà·gio *m* (**-gi**) cloudburst

nùbile *adj* unmarried, single (*woman*); marriageable ‖ *f* unmarried girl

nu·ca *f* (**-che**) nape of the neck, scruff

nucleare *adj* nuclear

nùcleo *m* nucleus; group; (elec) core

nudismo *m* nudism

nudi·sta *adj & mf* (**-sti -ste**) nudist

nudi·tà *f* (**-tà**) nudity, nakedness

nu·do -da *adj* naked, bare; barren; simple; **mettere a nudo** to lay bare; **nudo e crudo** stark-naked; destitute ‖ *m* nude

nùgolo *m* cloud; throng, swarm

nulla *pron* nothing ‖ *m invar* nothing; nothingness

nulla òsta *m* permission; visa

nullatenènte *adj* poor ‖ *mf* have-not

nullificare §197 (**nullìfico**) *tr* to nullify

nulli·tà *f* (**-tà**) nothingness; nonentity; invalidity (*of a document*)

nul·lo -la *adj* void, worthless ‖ *pron* (poet) none, no one ‖ **nulla** *m & pron* see **nulla**

nume *m* divinity, deity

numerare (**nùmero**) *tr* to number

numeratóre *m* numerator; numbering machine

numèri·co -ca *adj* (**-ci -che**) numerical

nùmero *m* number; lottery ticket; size (*of shoes*); **numero dispari** odd number; **numero legale** quorum; **numero pari** even number

numeró·so -sa [s] *adj* numerous, large; harmonious

nùn·zio *m* (**-zi**) nuncio; (poet) news

nuòcere §206 *intr* to be harmful; (with *dat*) to harm

nuòra *f* daughter-in-law

nuotare (**nuòto**) *intr* to swim; to float; to wallow (*in wealth*)

nuotata *f* swim, dip, plunge

nuota·tóre -trice *mf* swimmer

nuòto *m* swimming; **gettarsi a nuoto** to jump into the water; **traversare a nuoto** to swim across

nuòva *f* news; late news

Nuòva York f New York
Nuòva Zelanda, la [dz] New Zealand
nuòvo -va adj new; **di nuovo** again; **nuovo di zecca** brand-new; **nuovo fiammante** brand-new; **nuovo venuto** new arrival ‖ m—**il nuovo** the new ‖ f see **nuova**
nùtria f coypu
nutrice f wet nurse; (lit) provider
nutriènte adj nourishing
nutriménto m nourishment
nutrire §176 & (**nutro**) tr to nourish;

to nurture; to harbor (e.g., hatred) ‖ ref—**nutrirsi di** to feed on or upon
nutrìti·vo -va adj nutritious, nutritive
nutri·to -ta adj well-fed; strong; rich (food); brisk, heavy (gunfire)
nutrizióne f nutrition; food
nùvo·lo -la adj cloudy ‖ m cloudy weather; (lit) cloud; (fig) swarm ‖ f cloud
nuvoló·so -sa [s] adj cloudy
nuziale adj wedding, nuptial
nuzialità f marriage rate

O

O, o [o] m & f thirteenth letter of the Italian alphabet
o conj or; now; **o . . . o** either . . . or; whether . . . or ‖ interj oh!
òa·si f (-si) oasis
obbediènte adj var of **ubbidiènte**
obbediènza f obedience
obbedire §176 tr & intr var of **ubbidire**
obbiettare (**obbiètto**) tr & intr var of **obiettare**
obbligare §209 (**òbbligo**) tr to oblige; to compel, to force ‖ ref to obligate oneself
obbligatìssi·mo -ma adj much obliged
obbligatò·rio -ria adj (-ri -rie) compulsory, obligatory
obbligazióne f obligation; burden; (com) debenture, bond
obbligazioni·sta mf (-sti -ste) bondholder
òbbli·go m (-ghi) obligation; duty; **d'obbligo** obligatory, mandatory; **fare d'obbligo a qlcu** + inf to be necessary for s.o. to + inf, e.g., **gli fa d'obbligo lavorare** it is necessary for him to work
obbrò·brio m (-bri) opprobrium, disgrace; **obbrobri** insults
obbrobrió·so -sa [s] adj opprobrious, disgraceful
obeli·sco m (-schi) obelisk
obera·to -ta adj overburdened
obesità f obesity
obè·so -sa adj obese, stout
òbice m howitzer
obiettare (**obiètto**) tr & intr to argue; to object
obietti·vo -va adj & m objective
obiettóre m objector; **obiettore di coscienza** conscientious objector
obiezióne f objection
obitò·rio m (-ri) morgue
oblare (**òblo**) tr to willingly pay (a fine)
obla·tóre -trice mf donor
oblazióne f donation; (eccl) oblation; (law) payment of a fine
obliare §119 tr (lit) to forget
oblì·o m (-i) (lit) oblivion
oblì·quo -qua adj oblique
obliterare (**oblìtero**) tr to obliterate, cancel
o·blò m (-blò) (naut) porthole; **oblò di accesso** door (of space capsule)

oblun·go -ga adj (-ghi -ghe) oblong
òbo·e m (-e) oboe
oboi·sta mf (-sti -ste) oboist
òbolo m mite
ò·ca f (-che) goose; gander
ocarina f ocarina, sweet potato
occasionale adj chance; immediate (cause)
occasionare (**occasióno**) tr to occasion
occasióne f occasion; opportunity; ground, pretext; bargain; **all'occasione** on occasion; **d'occasione** second-hand; occasional (verses)
occhiàia f eye socket; **occhiaie** rings under the eyes
occhia·làio m (-lài) optician
occhiale adj eye, ocular ‖ **occhiali** mpl glasses; goggles; **occhiali antisole** sunglasses; **occhiali a stringinaso** nose glasses
occhialétto m lorgnon; monocle
occhiata f glance
occhieggiare §290 (**occhiéggio**) tr to eye ‖ intr to peep
occhièllo m buttonhole; boutonniere; eyelet; half title; subhead
occhièra f eyecup
òc·chio m (-chi) eye; speck of grease (in soup); handle (of scissors); ring (of stirrup); (typ) face; (fig) bit; **a occhio e croce** at a rough guess; **a quattr'occhi** in private; **battere gli occhi** to blink; **cavarsi gli occhi** to strain one's eyes; **dar nell'occhio** to attract attention; **di buon occhio** favorably; **fare l'occhio a** to get used to; **fare tanto d'occhi** to be amazed, to open one's eyes wide; **lasciare gli occhi su** to covet; **non chiudere un occhio** to not sleep a wink; **occhio!** watch out!; **occhio della testa** outrageous price; **occhio di bue** (naut) porthole; **occhio di cubia** (naut) hawsehole; **occhio di pavone** (zool) peacock butterfly; **occhio di triglia** sheep's eyes; **occhio pesto** black eye; **occhio pollino** corn (on toes); **tenere d'occhio** to keep an eye on
occhiolino m small eye; **far l'occhiolino** to wink
occidentale adj western, occidental
occidènte adj (poet) setting (sun) ‖ m west, occident

occìpite *m* occipital bone

occlusióne *f* occlusion

occlusi·vo -va *adj & f* occlusive

occlu·so -sa *adj* occluded

occorrènte *adj* necessary ‖ *m* necessary; (lit) occurrence

occorrènza *f* necessity; **all'occorrenza** if need be

occórrere §139 *intr* (ESSERE) to happen; (with *dat*) to need, e.g., **gli occorre dell'olio** he needs oil ‖ *impers* (ESSERE)—**occorre** it is necessary

occultaménto *m* concealment

occultare *tr & ref* to hide

occul·to -ta *adj* occult; (lit) hidden

occupante *adj* occupying ‖ *m* occupant

occupare (**òccupo**) *tr* to occupy; to employ ‖ *ref* to take employment; **occuparsi di** to busy oneself with, to mind; to attend to

occupa·to -ta *adj* occupied; busy

occupazionale *adj* occupational

occupazióne *f* occupation

oceàni·co -ca *adj* (**-ci -che**) oceanic

ocèano *m* ocean

òcra *f* ocher

oculare *adj* ocular; see **testimone** ‖ *m* eyepiece

oculatézza *f* circumspection, prudence

ocula·to -ta *adj* circumspect, prudent

oculi·sta *mf* (**-sti -ste**) oculist

od *conj* or

odali·sca *f* (**-sche**) odalisque

òde *f* ode

odepòri·co -ca (**-ci -che**) *adj* (lit) travel ‖ *m* (lit) travelogue

odiare §287 (**òdio**) *tr* to hate

odièr·no -na *adj* today's, current

ò·dio *m* (**-di**) hatred; **avere in odio** to hate; **essere in odio a** to be hated by

odió·so -sa [s] *adj* hateful, odious

odissèa *f* odyssey ‖ **Odissea** *f* Odyssey

Odissèo *m* Odysseus

odontòra *mf* (**-tri -tre**) doctor of dental surgery, dentist

odontoiatrìa *f* odontology, dentistry

odorare (**odóro**) *tr & intr* to smell

odora·to -ta *adj* (poet) fragrant ‖ *m* smell

odóre *m* smell, odor, scent; **cattivo odore** bad odor; **odori** herbs, spice

odoró·so -sa [s] *adj* odorous, fragrant

offèndere §148 *tr & intr* to offend ‖ *ref* to take offense

offensi·vo -va *adj & f* offensive

offensóre *m* offender

offerènte *mf* bidder; **miglior offerente** highest bidder

offèrta *f* offer; offering, donation; (at an auction) bid; (com) supply

offésa [s] *f* offense; wrongdoing; ravage (of time); **da offesa** (mil) offensive; **recarsi a offesa** qlco to regard s.th as offensive

officìna *f* shop, workshop; **officìna meccànica** machine shop

offició·so -sa [s] *adj* helpful, obliging

offrire §207 *tr* to offer; to sponsor (a radio or TV program); to dedicate (a book); to bid (at an auction); (com) to tender ‖ *ref* to offer oneself, to volunteer

offuscare §197 *tr* to darken, obscure; to obfuscate; to dim (mind; eyes) ‖ *ref* to grow dark; to grow dim

oftàlmi·co -ca *adj* (**-ci -che**) opthalmic

oftalmòlo·go -ga *mf* (**-gi -ghe**) ophthalmologist

oggettività *f* objectivity

oggetti·vo -va *adj & m* objective

oggètto *m* object; subject, argument; article; **oggetti preziosi** valuables

òggi *m* today; **dall'oggi al domani** suddenly; overnight ‖ *adv* today; **d'oggi in poi** henceforth; **oggi a otto** a week hence; **oggi come oggi** at present; **oggi è un anno** one year ago

oggidì *m invar & adv* nowadays

oggigiórno *m invar & adv* nowadays

ogiva *f* ogive, pointed arch; nose cone

ógni *adj indef invar* each; every, e.g., **ogni due giorni** every two days; **ogni cosa** everything; **ogni tanto** every now and then; **per ogni dove** (lit) everywhere

ogniqualvòlta *conj* whenever

Ognissan·ti *m* (**-ti**) All Saints' Day

ognitèmpo *adj invar* all-weather

-ógno·lo -la *suf adj* -ish, e.g., **giallognolo** yellowish

ognóra *adv* (lit) always

ognu·no -na *adj* (obs) each ‖ *pron* each one, everyone

oh *interj* oh!

òhi *interj* ouch!

ohibò *interj* fie!

ohimè *interj* alas!

o·hm *m* (**ohm**) ohm

olanda *f* Dutch linen ‖ **l'Olanda** *f* Holland

olandése [s] *adj* Dutch ‖ *m* Dutch (language); Dutchman; Dutch cheese ‖ *f* Dutch woman

oleandro *m* oleander

oleà·rio -ria *adj* (**-ri -rie**) oil

olea·to -ta *adj* oiled

oleifì·cio *m* (**-ci**) oil mill

oleodótto *m* pipeline

oleó·so -sa [s] *adj* oily

olezzare [ddzz] (**olézzo**) *intr* (lit) to smell sweet

olézzo [ddzz] *m* perfume, fragrance

olfatto *m* smell

oliare §287 (**òlio**) *tr* to oil

oliatóre *m* oiler, oil can

olìbano *m* frankincense

olièra *f* cruet

oligarchìa *f* oligarchy

olìmpìade *f* Olympiad

olìmpi·co -ca *adj* (**-ci -che**) Olympic; Olympian

olimpiòni·co -ca *adj* (**-ci -che**) Olympic ‖ *mf* Olympic athlete

ò·lio *m* (**-li**) oil; **ad olio** oil, e.g., **quadro ad olio** oil painting; **olio di fegato di merluzzo** cod-liver oil; **olio di lino** linseed oil; **olio di ricino** castor oil; **olio solare** sun-tan lotion

oliva *f* olive

oliva·stro -stra *adj* livid; swarthy ‖ *m* wild olive (tree)

olivéto *m* olive grove

Olivièro *m* Oliver

olivo *m* olive tree

ólmo *m* elm tree

olocàu·sto -sta *adj* (lit) burnt; (lit) sacrificed || *m* holocaust; sacrifice

ològra·fo -fa *adj* holographic

olóna *f* sailcloth, canvas

oltracciò *adv* besides

oltraggiare §290 *tr* to outrage; to insult

oltràg·gio *m* (-gi) outrage; offense; ravages (*of time*); **oltraggio al pudore** offense to public morals; **oltraggio al tribunale** contempt of court

oltraggió·so -sa [s] *aaj* outrageous

oltranza *f*—**a oltranza** to the bitter end

oltranzi·sta *mf* (-sti -ste) (pol) extremist

óltre *adv* beyond; ahead; further; **oltre a** apart from; in addition to; **troppo oltre** too far || *prep* beyond; past; more than

oltrecortina *adj invar* beyond-the-iron-curtain || *m* country beyond the iron curtain

oltremare *m invar* country overseas || *adv* overseas

oltremisura *adv* (lit) beyond measure

oltremòdo *adv* (lit) exceedingly

oltrepassare *tr* to overstep; to cross (*a river*); to be beyond (. . . *years old*); (sports) to overtake

oltretómba *m*—**l'oltretomba** the life beyond

omàg·gio *m* (-gi) homage; compliment; **in omaggio** complimentary; **rendere omaggio a** to pay tribute to

òmaro *m* Norway lobster

ombelì·co *m* (-chi) navel

ómbra *f* shade; shadow; umbrage; form, mass; **nemmeno per ombra** not in the least

ombreggiare §290 (**ombréggio**) *tr* to shade

ombrèlla *f* shade (*of trees*); (bot) umbel; (coll) umbrella

ombrel·làio *m* (-lài) umbrella maker

ombrellino *m* parasol

ombrèllo *m* umbrella

ombrellóne *m* beach umbrella

ombró·so -sa [s] *adj* shady; touchy; skittish (*horse*)

omelette *f* (**omelette**) omelet

omelía *f* homily

omeopàti·co -ca (-ci -che) *adj* homeopathic || *m* homeopathist

omèri·co -ca *adj* (-ci -che) Homeric

òmero *m* (anat) humerus; (lit) shoulder

omertà *f* code of silence of underworld

ométtere §198 *tr* to omit

omètto *m* little man; (coll) clothes hanger; (billiards) pin; (archit) king post

omici·da (-di -de) *adj* homicidal, murderous || *mf* homicide, murderer

omici·dio *m* (-di) homicide; murder; **omicidio colposo** (law) manslaughter; **omicidio doloso** (law) first-degree murder

ominó·so -sa [s] *adj* (lit) ominous

omissióne *f* omission

òmni·bus *m* (-bus) omnibus; way train

omnisciènte *adj* all-knowing, omniscient

omogène·o -a *adj* homogeneous

omologare §209 (**omòlogo**) *tr* to con-

firm, ratify; to probate (*a will*); (sports) to validate

omòni·mo -mo -ma *adj* of the same name || *m* namesake; homonym

omosessuale [s] *adj* & *mf* homosexual

ón·cia *f* (-ce) ounce; **oncia a oncia** little by little

ónda *f* wave; **a onde** wavy; wavily; **essere in onda** (rad, telv) to be on the air; **farsi le onde** to have one's hair waved; **mettere in onda** (rad, telv) to put on the air; **onda crespa** whitecap; **onda portante** (rad, telv) carrier wave

ondata *f* wave, billow; gust (*e.g., of smoke*); rush (*of blood*); wave (*of cold weather*)

ondatra *f* muskrat

ónde *pron* from which; of which || *adv* whereof; hence; (poet) wherefrom || *prep* **onde** + *inf* in order to || *conj* **onde** + *subj* so that

ondeggiante *adj* waving, swaying

ondeggiare §290 (**ondéggio**) *intr* to wave, sway; to waver

ondìna *f* mermaid; (mythol) undine; (mythol) mermaid

ondó·so -sa [s] *adj* wavy

ondulare (**óndulo** & **òndulo**) *tr* to wave; to corrugate (*e.g., metal*) || *intr* to sway

ondula·to -ta *adj* wavy (*hair*); corrugated (*e.g., metal*); bumpy (*road*)

ondulazióne *f* undulation; **ondulazione permanente** permanent wave

-óne -óna *suf mf* big, e.g., **librone** big book; **dormigliona** big sleeper || **-óne** *suf m* (applies to both sexes) big, e.g., **donnone** *m* big woman

ònere *m* (lit) onus, burden

oneró·so -sa [s] *adj* onerous, burdensome

onestà *f* honesty; (poet) modesty

onè·sto -sta *adj* honest; fair; (poet) modest || *m* moderate amount; honest gain; honest person

ónice *m* onyx

onnipossènte & onnipotènte *adj* almighty, omnipotent

onnisciènte *adj* omniscient

onniveggènte *adj* all-seeing

onnìvo·ro -ra *adj* omnivorous

onomàsti·co -ca (-ci -che) *adj* onomastic || *m* name day || *f* study of proper names

onomatopèi·co -ca *adj* (-ci -che) onomatopeic

onoràbile -le *adj* honorable

onoranza *f* honor; **onoranze** homage; **onoranze funebri** obsequies

onorare (**onóro**) *tr* to honor || *ref* to deem it an honor

onorà·rio -ria (-ri -rie) *adj* honorary || *m* fee, honorarium

onora·to -ta *adj* honored; honest; honorable

onóre *m* honor; **d'onore** honest, e.g., **uomo d'onore** honest man; **estremi onori** last rites; **fare gli onori di casa** to receive guests; **fare onore a** to honor; **onore al merito** credit where credit is due; **onor del mento** (lit) beard

onoré·vole *adj* honorable || *m* honorable member (*of parliament*)

onorificènza *f* dignity; decoration

onorifi·co -ca *adj* (**-ci -che**) honorific; honorary (*e.g., title*)

ónta *f* dishonor, shame; **a onta di** in spite of; **avere onta** to be ashamed; **fare onta a** to bring shame upon; **in onta a** against

** untano** *m* alder

O.N.U. (acronym) *f* (**Organizzazione delle Nazioni Unite**) United Nations, U.N.

onu·sto -sta *adj* (poet) laden

opa·co -ca *adj* (**-chi -che**) opaque

opale *m* opal

opali·no -na *adj* opaline || *f* shiny cardboard; luster (*fabric*)

òpera *f* work; organization, foundation; day's work; (mus) opera; **mettere in opera** to install; to start work on; to make ready; to begin using; **opera di consultazione** reference work; **opera morta** (naut) upper works; **opera viva** (naut) quickwork; **per opera di** thanks to

ope·ràio -ràia (**-rài -ràie**) *adj* workman's, worker's; working || *m* workman, worker; **operaio a cottimo** pieceworker; **operaio a giornata** day laborer; **operaio specializzato** craftsman, skilled workman || *f* workwoman

operante *adj* actively engaged; operative

operare (**òpero**) *tr* to operate; to work (*a miracle*); (surg) to operate on || *intr* to operate; to be actively engaged || *ref* to be operated on; to occur, take place

operati·vo -va *adj* operative; operations, e.g., **ricerca operativa** operations research

opera·to -ta *adj* operated; embossed || *m* behavior; patient operated on

opera·tóre -trice *mf* operator || *m* (mov) cameraman

operatò·rio -ria *adj* (**-ri -rie**) surgical (*operation*); operating (*room*); (math) operational

operazióne *f* operation; transaction

operétta *f* short work; (mus) operetta

operìsti·co -ca *adj* (**-ci -che**) operatic

operosità [s] *f* (**-tà**) industry

operó·so -sa [s] *adj* industrious; active

opi·mo -ma *adj* (lit) fat; rich, fertile

opinare *intr* to opine, deem

opinióne *f* opinion

opòs·sum *m* (**-sum**) opossum

oppia·to -ta *adj* opiate (*mixed with opium*); dulled by drugs || *m* opiate (*medicine containing opium*)

òppio *m* opium

oppiòmane *adj* opium-eating; opiumsmoking || *mf* opium addict

oppórre §218 *tr* to oppose; to offer, put up (*resistance*) || *ref* to be opposite; **opporsi a** to oppose, to be against

opportuni·sta *mf* (**-sti -ste**) opportunist

opportuni·tà *f* (**-tà**) opportunity; opportuneness

opportu·no -na *adj* opportune

opposi·tóre -trice *mf* opponent

opposizióne *f* opposition; (law) appeal; **fare opposizione a** to object to

oppó·sto -sta *adj* opposite; contrary || *m* opposite; **all'opposto** on the contrary

oppressióne *f* oppression

oppressi·vo -va *adj* oppressive

opprès·so -sa *adj* oppressed; overcome, overwhelmed || **oppressi** *mpl* oppressed people

oppressóre *m* oppressor

opprimènte *adj* oppressive

opprimere §131 *tr* to oppress; to overcome, overwhelm; to weigh down

oppugnare *tr* to refute, contradict

oppure *adv* otherwise || *conj* or else; or rather

optare (**òpto**) *intr* to choose; (com) to exercise an option

optometri·sta *mf* (**-sti -ste**) optometrist

opulèn·to -ta *adj* opulent

opùscolo *m* booklet, brochure, pamphlet; **opuscolo d'informazioni** instruction manual

opzióne *f* option

ór *adv* now; **or ora** right now; **or sono** ago

óra *f* hour; time; period (*in school*); **alla buon'ora!** finally!; **a ore by the hour; **a tarda ora** late; **che ora è?** or **che ore sono?** what time is it?; **da un'ora all'altra** from one moment to the next; **dell'ultima ora** up-to-date (*news*); **di buon'ora** early; early in the morning; **di ora in ora** at any moment; **d'ora in avanti** from this moment on; **d'ora in poi** from now on; **far l'ora** to kill time; **fin ora** until now; **non vedere l'ora di** + *inf* to be hardly able to wait until + *ind*; **ora di cena** suppertime; **ora di punta** rush hour, peak hour; **ora legale** daylight-saving time; **ore piccole** late hours; **un'ora di orologio** one full hour || *adv* now

oràcolo *m* oracle

òra·fo -fa *adj* goldsmith's || *m* goldsmith

orale *adj* & *m* oral

oralménte *adv* orally; by word of mouth

oramài *adv* now; already

oran·go *m* (**-ghi**) orangutan

orà·rio -ria (**-ri -rie**) *adj* hourly; per hour; clockwise || *m* timetable; schedule; roster; **essere in orario** to be on time; **orario di lavoro** working hours; **orario d'ufficio** office hours

ora·tóre -trice *mf* orator

oratò·rio -ria (**-ri -rie**) *adj* oratorical || *m* (eccl) oratory; (mus) oratorio || *f* oratory, public speaking

orazióne *f* oration; prayer; **orazione domenicale** Lord's Prayer

orbare (**òrbo**) *tr* (lit) to bereave; (lit) to deprive

òrbe *f* (lit) orb; (lit) world

orbène *adv* well

òrbita f orbit; (fig) sphere

orbitare (**òrbito**) intr to orbit

orbitazióne f orbiting

òr·bo -ba adj bereaved; deprived; blind || m blind man

òrca f killer whale

Òrcadi fpl Orkney Islands

orchèstra f orchestra; band; orchestra pit

orchestrale adj orchestral || mf orchestra player, orchestra performer

orchestrare (**orchèstro**) tr to orchestrate; (fig) to organize

orchestrina f dance band; dance-band music

orchidèa f orchid

ór·cio m (-ci) jar, jug, crock

orciòlo m—a **orciolo** puckered up (lips)

òr·co m (-chi) ogre

òrda f horde

ordàlia f (hist) ordeal

ordigno m gadget, contrivance; tool; **ordigno esplosivo** infernal machine

ordinale adj & m ordinal

ordinaménto m disposition; regulation

ordinanza f ordinance; (mil) orderly; **d'ordinanza** regulation (e.g., uniform); **in ordinanza** (mil) in formation

ordinare (**órdino**) tr to order; to straighten up; to range; to regulate; to ordain; to trim

ordinà·rio -ria (-ri -rie) adj ordinary; plain; inferior; workday (suit) || m ordinary; full professor; **d'ordinario** ordinarily, usually

ordina·to -ta adj orderly, tidy; ordained || f ordinate; straightening up; (aer) frame; (naut) bulkhead

ordinazióne f order; ordination

órdine m order; row; tier; series (e.g., of years); college (e.g., of surgeons); nature (of things); (law) warrant, writ; **in ordine a** concerning; **ordine del giorno** order of the day; **ordine d'idee** train of thought

ordire §176 tr to warp (cloth); to hatch (a plot)

ordi·to -ta adj plotted || m warp (of fabric)

orécchia f ear; dog-ear; **con le orecchie tese** all ears

orecchiale m earphone (of sonar equipment)

orecchiétta f (anat) auricle

orecchino m earring

oréc·chio m (-chi) ear; hearing; dog-ear; moldboard; **fare orecchio da mercante** to turn a deaf ear || m (orécchia fpl) (archaic) ear

orecchióne m long-eared bat; (mil) trunnion; **orecchioni** (pathol) mumps

oréfice m goldsmith; jeweler

oreficeria f goldsmith shop; jewelry shop

orfanézza f orphanage (condition)

òrfa·no -na adj orphaned || mf orphan

orfanotrò·fio m (-fi) orphanage (institution)

Orfèo m Orpheus

organdi m organdy

organétto m hand organ; mouth organ; **organetto di Barberia** hand organ

orgàni·co -ca (-ci -che) adj organic || m personnel, staff || f (mil) organization

organigram·ma m (-mi) organization chart

organino m hand organ, barrel organ

organismo m organism

organi·sta mf (-sti -ste) organist

organizzare [ddzz] tr to organize

organizza·tóre -trice [ddzz] mf organizer

organizzazióne [ddzz] f organization; **Organizzazione delle Nazioni Unite** United Nations

òrgano m organ; part (of a machine); **organo di stampa** mouthpiece

orgasmo m orgasm; agitation, excitement

òr·gia f (-ge) orgy

orgó·glio m (-gli) pride

orgoglió·so -sa [s] adj proud

orientale adj & mf oriental; Oriental

orientaménto m orientation; bearing; trend; trim (of sail); **orientamento scolastico e professionale** aptitude test; vocational guidance

orientare (**oriènto**) tr to orient; to guide; to trim (a sail) || ref to find one's bearings

oriènte m orient; **grand'oriente** grand lodge || **Oriente** m Orient, East; **Estremo Oriente** Far East; **Medio Oriente** Middle East; **Vicino Oriente** Near East

orifì·zio m (-zi) orifice, opening

orìgano m wild marjoram

originale adj original; odd || mf queer character, odd person || m original; copy (for printer)

originare (**orìgino**) tr to originate || intr (ESSERE) & ref to originate

originà·rio -ria adj (-ri -rie) originating; native; original

orìgine f origin; source; extraction

origliare §280 intr to eavesdrop

origlière m (lit) pillow

orìna f var of **urina**

orinale m chamber pot, urinal

orinare tr & intr to urinate

orina·tóio m (-tói) urinal, comfort station

oriòlo m (orn) oriole

oriun·do -da adj native || m (sports) native son

orizzontale [ddzz] adj horizontal || **orizzontali** fpl horizontal words (in crossword puzzle)

orizzontare [ddzz] (**orizzónto**) tr to orient || ref to get one's bearings

orizzónte [ddzz] m horizon

Orlando m Roland

orlare (**órlo**) tr to hem, border; **orlare a zigzag** to pink

órlo m edge; brim; hem, border; (fig) brink; **orlo a giorno** hemstitch

órma f footprint; **orme** remains, vestiges; **calcare le orme di** to follow the footsteps of

ormeggiare §290 (**orméggio**) tr & ref (naut) to moor

ormég·gio m (-gi) mooring; **mollare gli ormeggi** (naut) to cast off

ormóne m hormone

ornamentale *adj* ornamental

ornaménto *m* ornament

ornare (órno) *tr* to adorn

orna·to -ta *adj* adorned; ornate ‖ *m* ornament; ornamental design

ornitòlo·go -ga *mf* (-gi -ghe) ornithologist

òro *m* gold; (fig) money; **d'oro** gold, golden; **ori** gold objects; jewels; suit of Neapolitan cards corresponding to diamonds; **oro zecchino** pure gold; **per tutto l'oro del mondo** for all the world

orologerìa *f* watchmaking; clockmaking; watchmaker's shop

orolo·giàio *m* (-giài) watchmaker; clockmaker

orolò·gio *m* (-gi) watch; clock; **orologio a pendolo** clock; **orologio a polvere** sandglass; **orologio a scatto** digital clock; **orologio da polso** wristwatch; **orologio della morte** deathwatch; **orologio solare** sundial

oròscopo *m* horoscope

orpèllo *m* Dutch gold; (fig) tinsel

orrèndo *m* horrible

orrìbile *adj* horrible

òrri·do -da *adj* horrid ‖ *m* horridness; gorge, ravine

orripilante *adj* bloodcurdling, hairraising

orróre *m* horror; awe; **aver in** or **per orrore** to loath; **fare orrore a** to horrify

órsa *f* she-bear ‖ **Orsa** *f*—**Orsa maggiore** Great Bear; **Orsa minore** Little Bear

orsacchiòtto *m* bear cub; Teddy bear

ór·so -sa *mf* bear; **orso bianco** polar bear; **orso grigio** grizzly bear ‖ *f* see **orsa**

orsù *interj* come on!

ortàg·gio *m* (-gi) vegetable

ortàglia *f* vegetable garden; vegetable

ortènsia *f* hydrangea

orti·ca *f* (-che) nettle; hives

orticària *f* hives, nettle rash

orticoltóre *m* truck gardener; horticulturist

òrto *m* garden, vegetable garden; (lit) sunrise; **orto botanico** botanical garden; **orto di guerra** Victory garden

ortodòs·so -sa *adj* orthodox ‖ *m* Greek Catholic

ortografìa *f* orthography; spelling

ortola·no -na *adj* garden ‖ *m* truck farmer, gardener

ortopèdi·co -ca (-ci -che) *adj* orthopedic ‖ *m* orthopedist

òrza *f* bowline; windward; **andare all'orza** to sail close to the wind

orzaiòlo [dz] *m* (pathol) sty

orzare (òrzo) *intr* to sail close to the wind; to luff

orzata [dz] *f* orgeat

orzata *f* (naut) luff

òrzo [dz] *m* barley

osannare *intr* to cry or sing hosanna; **osannare a** to acclaim, applaud

osare (òso) *intr* to dare

oscenità *f* obscenity

oscè·no -na *adj* obscene; (coll) horrible

oscillante *adj* oscillating

oscillare *intr* to oscillate; to swing; to wobble; to waver, hesitate

oscillazióne *f* oscillation; fluctuation

oscuraménto *m* darkening, dimming; blackout

oscurare *tr* to darken; to blot out; to dim ‖ *ref* to get dark; **oscurarsi in volto** to frown

oscurità *f* (-tà) obscurity; darkness; ignorance

oscu·ro -ra *adj* obscure, dark; opaque (*style*) ‖ *m* obscurity, darkness; **essere all'oscuro di** to be in the dark about

osmòsi *f* osmosis

ospedale *m* hospital

ospedalière *m* hospital worker

ospedaliè·ro -ra *adj* hospital ‖ *m* hospitaler

ospedalizzare [ddzz] *tr* to hospitalize

ospitale *adj* hospitable ‖ *m* hospital

ospitalità *f* (-tà) hospitality

ospitare (òspito) *tr* to lodge, shelter, accommodate; to entertain; (sports) to play (*an opposing team*) at home

òspite *mf* host; guest; **andarsene insalutato ospite** to take French leave; **ospiti** company (*guests at home*)

ospì·zio *m* (-zi) hospice; hostel; (lit) hospitality; **ospizio dei vecchi** nursing home; **ospizio di mendicità** poorhouse

ossatura *f* frame, framework; skeleton

òsse·o -a *adj* bony

ossequènte *adj* (lit) respectful; (lit) reverent

ossequiare §287 (ossèquio) *tr* to pay one's respects to; to honor

ossè·quio *m* (-qui) respect; reverence; **i miei ossequi** my best regards; **in ossequio a** in conformity with; **porgere i propri ossequi a** to pay one's respects to

ossequió·so -sa [s] *adj* obsequious; respectful

osservante *adj* & *m* observant

osservanza *f* observance; deference

osservare (ossèrvo) *tr* to observe

osserva·tóre -trice *adj* observing, observant ‖ *mf* observer

osservatò·rio *m* (-ri) observatory

osservazióne *f* observation; rebuke

ossessionare (ossessióno) *tr* to obsess; to harass, bedevil

ossessióne *f* obsession

ossès·so -sa *adj* possessed ‖ *mf* person possessed

ossìa *conj* or; to wit

ossidante *adj* oxidizing ‖ *m* oxidizer

ossidare (òssido) *tr* & *ref* to oxidize

òssido *m* oxide; **ossido di carbone** carbon monoxide

ossìdulo *m* protoxide; **ossidulo di azoto** nitrous oxide

ossificare §197 (ossìfico) *tr* & *ref* to ossify

ossigenare (ossìgeno) *tr* to oxygenate; to bleach (*the hair*); to infuse strength into ‖ *ref* to bleach (*the hair*)

ossìgeno *m* oxygen; (fig) transfusion, shot in the arm

ossìto·no -na *adj* & *m* oxytone

òs·so *m* (-si) bone (*of animal*); stone (*of fruit*); **osso di balena** whalebone; **osso di seppia** cuttlebone; **osso duro da rodere** hard nut to crack; **osso sacro** sacrum; **rimetterci l'osso del collo** to be thoroughly ruined; **rompersi l'osso del collo** to break one's neck ‖ *m* (-sa *fpl*) bone (*of a person*); **avere le ossa rotte** to be dead-tired

ossu·to -ta *adj* bony; scrawny

ostacolare (ostàcolo) *tr* to hinder; to obstruct; **ostacolare l'azione** (*sports*) to interfere

ostàcolo *m* obstacle; obstruction; (*golf*) hazard; (*sports*) hurdle

ostàg·gio *m* (-gi) hostage

ostare (òsto) *intr* (*lit*) to be in the way; (with *dat*) to hinder; **nulla osta** no objection, permission granted

òste ostéssa *mf* innkeeper ‖ **oste** *m & f* (*lit*) army in the field ‖ *m* (*poet*) enemy

ostèllo *m* hostel; (*poet*) abode

ostentare (ostènto) *tr* to show, display; to affect, feign

ostenta·to -ta *adj* affected, ostentatious

ostentazióne *f* show, ostentation

osteopatìa *f* osteopathy

osterìa *f* tavern, inn, taproom

ostéssa *f* see **òste**

ostètri·ca *f* (-che) midwife

ostetricia *f* obstetrics

ostètri·co -ca *adj* (-ci -che) obstetrical ‖ *m* obstetrician ‖ *f* see **ostetrica**

òstia *f* wafer; Host; sacrificial victim

òsti·co -ca *adj* (-ci -che) hard; (*lit*) repugnant, distasteful

ostile *adj* hostile

ostili·tà *f* (-tà) hostility

ostinare *ref* to be stubborn; to persist

ostina·to -ta *adj* obstinate; persistent

ostinazióne *f* obstinacy

ostracismo *m* ostracism; **dare l'ostracismo a** to ostracize

ostracizzare [ddzz] *tr* (*poet*) to ostracize

òstri·ca *f* (-che) oyster; **ostrica perlifera** pearl oyster

ostri·càio *m* (-cài) oyster bed; oysterman

ostruire §176 *tr* to obstruct; to stop up

ostruzióne *f* obstruction

Otèllo *m* Othello

otorinolaringoia·tra *mf* (-tri -tre) ear, nose, and throat specialist, otorhinolaryngologist

ótre *f* wineskin; **otre di vento** windbag (*person*)

ottàni·co -ca *adj* (-ci -che) octane

ottano *m* octane

ottanta *adj, m & pron* eighty

ottantènne *adj* eighty-year-old ‖ *mf* eighty-year-old person

ottantèsi·mo -ma *adj, m & pron* eightieth

ottantina *f* about eighty; **essere sull'ottantina** to be about eighty years old

ottava *f* octave

Ottaviano *m* Octavian

ottavino *m* (*mus*) piccolo; (*com*) commission of ⅛ of 1%

otta·vo -va *adj & pron* eighth ‖ *m* eighth; octavo ‖ *f* see **ottava**

ottemperare (ottèmpero) *intr* (with *dat*) to obey; **ottemperare a** to comply with

ottenebrare (ottènebro) *tr* to becloud

ottenére §271 *tr* to obtain, get

ottétto *m* octet

òtti·co -ca *adj* optic(al) ‖ *m* optician ‖ *f* optics

ottimismo *m* optimism

ottimi·sta *mf* (-sti -ste) optimist

ottimìsti·co -ca *adj* (-ci -che) optimistic

òtti·mo -ma *adj* very good, excellent ‖ *m* best; highest rating

òtto *adj & pron* eight; **le otto** eight o'clock ‖ *m* eight; eighth (*in dates*); (*sports*) racing shell with eight oarsmen; **otto giorni** a week; **otto volante** roller coaster

ottóbre *m* October

ottocenté·sco -sca *adj* (-schi -sche) nineteenth-century

ottocènto *adj, m & pron* eight hundred ‖ **l'Ottocento** the nineteenth century

ottoma·no -na *adj & m* Ottoman ‖ *m* ottoman (*fabric*) ‖ *f* ottoman (*sofa*)

ottomila *adj, m & pron* eight thousand

ottoname *m* brassware

ottonare (ottóno) *tr* to coat with brass

ottóne *m* brass; **ottoni** (*mus*) brasses ‖ **Ottone** *m* Otto

ottuagenà·rio -ria *adj & mf* (-ri -rie) octogenarian

ottùndere §208 *tr* (*fig*) to deaden; (*lit*) to blunt

otturare *tr* to fill; to plug; to stop; to obstruct, stop up (*e.g., a channel*) ‖ *ref* to clog up

otturatóre *m* breechblock; (*phot, mov*) shutter; (*mach*) cutoff (*of cylinder*)

otturazióne *f* filling (*of tooth*)

ottu·so -sa *adj* obtuse; blunt

ovàia *f* ovary

ovale *adj* oval ‖ *m* oval; oval face

ovatta *f* wadding; absorbent cotton

ovattare *tr* to pad, wad; to muffle

ovazióne *f* ovation

óve *adv* (*lit*) where ‖ *conj* (*lit*) if; (*poet*) while

òvest *m* west

Ovìdio *m* Ovid

ovile *m* sheepcote, fold

ovi·no -na *adj* ovine ‖ **ovini** *mpl* sheep

òvo *m* var of **uovo**

ovoidale *adj* egg-shaped

òvulo *m* pill shaped like an egg; (*biol*) ovum; (*bot*) ovule

ovùnque *adv* (*lit*) wherever; (*lit*) everywhere

ovvéro *conj* or; to wit

ovvìa *interj* come on!

ovviare §119 *intr*—(with *dat*) to obviate

òv·vio -via *adj* (-vi -vie) obvious

oziare §287 (òzio) *intr* to idle, loiter

ò·zio *m* (-zi) idleness; leisure

oziosi·tà [s] *f* (-tà) idleness

ozió·so -sa [s] *adj* idle; useless, vain

ozòno [dz] *m* ozone

P

P, p [pi] *m & f* fourteenth letter of the Italian alphabet

pacare §197 *tr* (poet) to placate

pacatézza *f* tranquillity, serenity

paca·to -ta *adj* serene, tranquil

pac·ca *f* (-che) slap

pacchétto *m* parcel, package; book (of matches); pack (of cigarettes)

pàcchia *f* (coll) hearty meal; (coll) godsend, windfall

pacchia·no -na *adj* boorish, uncouth || *mf* boor

pacciamantura *f* mulching

pacciame *m* mulch

pac·co *m* (-chi) package; **pacchi postali** parcel post (service); **pacco dono** gift package; **pacco postale** parcel by mail

paccottìglia *f* shoddy goods, junk; trinkets

pace *f* peace; **lasciare in pace** to leave alone; **mettersi il cuore in pace** to resign oneself

pachidèr·ma *m* (-mi) pachyderm

pachista·no -na *adj & mf* Pakistani

paciè·re -ra *mf* peacemaker

pacificare §197 (pacìfico) *tr* to pacify; to appease; to mediate || *ref* to make one's peace

pacifica·tóre -trice *adj* pacifying || *mf* peacemaker

pacificazióne *f* pacification; appeasement

pacìfi·co -ca (-ci -che) *adj* peaceful, pacific; **è pacifico che** it goes without saying that || *m* peaceable person || **Pacìfico** *adj & m* Pacific

pacifismo *m* pacifism

pacifi·sta *mf* (-sti -ste) pacifist

pacioccó·ne -na *mf* chubby, easygoing person

padèlla *f* frying pan; bedpan; **cadere dalla padella nella brace** to jump from the frying pan into the fire

padiglióne *m* pavilion; hunting lodge; roof (of car); ward (of a hospital); (naut) rigging, tackle; **padiglione auricolare** (anat) auricle of the ear

Pàdova *f* Padua

padre *m* father; sire; **padre di famiglia** provider; (law) head of household; **Padre Eterno** Heavenly Father

padreggiare §290 (padréggio) *intr* to resemble one's father

padrino *m* godfather; second (in duel)

padrona *f* owner, boss, mistress; **padrona di casa** lady of the house

padronale *adj* proprietary; private (e.g., car)

padronanza *f* command; **padronanza di sé stesso** self-control

padró·ne *m* owner, boss, master; **essere padrone di** + *inf* to have the right to + *inf*; **padrone di casa** landlord; **padrone di** to be cool and collected

padroneggiare §290 (padronéggio) *tr* to master, control

paesàg·gio *m* (-gi) landscape

paesaggi·sta *mf* (-sti -ste) landscapist

---

paesa·no -na *adj* country || *mf* villager || *m* countryman || *f* countrywoman; **alla paesana** according to local tradition

paése *m* country; village; **i Paesi Bassi** the Netherlands; (hist) the Low Countries; **mandare a quel paese** to send to blazes

paesi·sta *mf* (-sti -ste) landscapist

paffu·to -ta *adj* chubby, plump

pa·ga *f* (-ghe) salary; wages; repayment; **mala paga** poor pay (person)

pagàbile *adj* payable

pagàia *f* paddle

pagaménto *m* payment; **pagamento alla consegna** c.o.d.

paganésimo *m* paganism

paga·no -na *adj & mf* pagan, heathen

pagare §209 *tr* to pay; to pay for; **far pagare** to charge; **pagare di egual moneta** to repay in kind; **pagare il fio per** to pay (the penalty) for; **pagare in natura** to pay in kind; **pagare salato** to pay dearly; **pagare un occhio della testa** to pay through the nose || *intr* to pay

paga·tóre -trice *mf* payer

pagèlla *f* report card

pàg·gio *m* (-gi) page (boy attendant)

paghe·rò *m* (-rò) promissory note, I.O.U.

pàgina *f* page (e.g., of book)

paginatura *f* pagination

pàglia *f* straw; thatch (for roof); **paglia di ferro** steel wool; **paglia di legno** excelsior

pagliaccé·sco -sca *adj* (-schi -sche) clownish

pagliaccétto *m* rompers

pagliacciata *f* buffoonery, antics

pagliàc·cio *m* (-ci) clown, buffoon; **fare il pagliaccio** to clown

pa·gliàio *m* (-gliài) heap of straw; haystack

paglierìc·cio *m* (-ci) straw mattress

paglieri·no -na *adj* straw-colored

pagliétta *f* skimmer, boater; steel wool; (coll) pettifogger

pagnòtta *f* loaf of bread; (coll) bread

pa·go -ga *adj* (-ghi -ghe) satisfied || *f* see **paga**

paguro *m* (zool) hermit crab

pà·io *m* (-ia *fpl*) pair, couple; **è un altro paio di maniche** this is a horse of another color; **fare il paio** to match perfectly

paiòlo *m* caldron, kettle; (mil) platform

Pakistan, il Pakistan

pala *f* shovel; blade (e.g., of turbine); paddle (of waterwheel); peel (of baker); **pala d'altare** altarpiece

paladi·no -na *mf* champion || *m* paladin; **farsi paladino di** to champion

palafitta *f* pile dwelling; piles (to support a structure)

palafrenière *m* groom

palafréno *m* palfrey

palan·ca *f* (-che) beam, board; (naut)

gangplank; copper coin; **palanche** (coll) money

palanchino *m* palanquin; (naut) pulley

palandrana *f* (joc) long, full coat

palata *f* shovelful; stroke (*of oar*); **a palate** by the bucketful

palatale *adj* & *f* palatal

palati·no -na *adj* palatine; (anat) palatal

palato *m* palate

palazzina *f* villa

palazzo *m* palace; large office or government building; mansion; **palazzo dello sport** sports arena; **palazzo di città** city hall; **palazzo di giustizia** courthouse

palchetti·sta (-sti -ste) *mf* (theat) box-holder ‖ *m* person who lays floors

palchétto *m* shelf; (theat) small box; (journ) box

pal·co *m* (**-chi**) flooring; scaffold; stand, platform; (theat) box; (theat) stage

palcoscèni·co *m* (**-ci**) (theat) stage

palesare (paléso) *tr* to reveal, manifest ‖ *ref* to show oneself

palése *adj* plain, manifest; **fare palese** to manifest, reveal

palèstra *f* gymnasium; palestra

palétta *f* small shovel, scoop; blade (*of turbine*)

palettata *f* shovelful

palétto *m* stake; bolt (*of door*)

palificazióne *f* pile work (*in the ground for foundation*); line of telephone poles

pà·lio *m* (**-lii**) embroidered cloth (*given as prize*); **metter in palio** to offer as a prize; **palio di Siena** colorful horserace at Siena

palissandro *m* Brazilian rosewood

palizzata *f* palisade; picket fence

palla *f* ball; bullet; sphere; **dar palla nera** a to blackball; **palla da cannone** cannon ball; **palla di neve** snowball; **prendere la palla al balzo** to seize the opportunity

pallabase *f* baseball

pallacanè·stro *f* (**-stro**) basketball

pallamuro *m* handball

pallanuòto *f* water polo

pallavó·lo *f* (**-lo**) volleyball

palléggiare §290 (**palléggio**) *tr* to toss (*e.g., a javelin*); to shift from one hand to another ‖ *intr* (tennis) to knock a few balls; (soccer) to dribble ‖ *ref*—**palleggiarsi la responsabilità** to shift the responsibility

pallég·gio *m* (**-gi**) (tennis) knocking back and forth; (soccer) dribbling

palliati·vo -va *adj* & *m* palliative

pallidézza *f* paleness

pàlli·do -da *adj* pale; faint

pallina *f* marble; small ball; **pallina antitarmica** mothball

pallino *m* little ball; (bowling) jack; bullet; **a pallini** polka-dot; **avere il pallino di** to be crazy about; **pallini** buckshot; polka dots

pallòncino *m* child's balloon; Chinese lantern

pallóne *m* (soccer) ball; (aer) balloon;

pallone di sbarramento barrage balloon; **pallone gonfiato** (fig) stuffed shirt; **pallone sonda** trial balloon

pallonétto *m* (tennis) lob

pallóre *m* pallor, paleness

pallòttola *f* pellet; ball; bullet

pallottolière *m* abacus

pallovale *f* rugby

palma *f* palm; **tenere in palma di mano** to hold in the highest esteem

palmare *adj* evident, plain

palménto *m* millstone; **mangiare a quattro palmenti** (coll) to stuff oneself eating

palméto *m* palm grove

palmìpede *adj* palmate, web-footed

palmì·zio *m* (**-zi**) palm

palmo *m* span; palm (*of hand*); foot (*measure*); **a palmo a palmo** little by little; **restare con un palmo di naso** to be disappointed

palo *m* pole (*of wood or metal*); beam; pile; (soccer, football) goal post; **fare il palo** to be on the lookout (*said of thieves*); **palo indicatore** signpost; **saltare di palo in frasca** to digress

palombaro *m* diver

palómbo *m* dogfish

palpàbile *adj* palpable

palpare *tr* to touch; to palpate

pàlpebra *f* eyelid; **battere le palpebre** to blink

palpeggiare §290 (**palpéggio**) *tr* to finger, touch repeatedly

palpitante *adj* throbbing; burning (*question*); fluttering (*e.g., with love*)

palpitare (pàlpito) *intr* to palpitate, pulsate; (fig) to pine

palpitazióne *f* palpitation

pàlpito *m* heartbeat; (fig) throb

pal·tò *m* (**-tò**) overcoat

paltoncino *m* child's winter coat; lady's topcoat

paludaménto *m* (joc) array, attire

palude *f* marsh, bog

paludó·so -sa [*s*] *adj* marshy

palustre *adj* marshy

pàmpino *m* grape leaf

panacèa *f* panacea, cure-all

pàna·ma *m* (**-ma**) Panama hat

panamé·gno -gna *adj* & *mf* Panamenian

panamènse *adj* & *mf* Panamenian

panare *tr* (culin) to bread

pan·ca *f* (**-che**) bench; **scaldare le panche** (coll) to loaf around; (coll) to waste one's time at school

pancétta *f* potbelly; bacon

panchétto *m* footstool

panchina *f* bench

pàn·cia *f* (**-ce**) belly; **a pancia all'aria** on one's back; **mangiare a crepa pancia** to stuff oneself like a pig; **mettere su pancia** to grow a potbelly; **salvar la pancia per i fichi** to not take any chances; **tenersi la pancia dalle risate** to split one's side laughing

panciata *f* belly flop

pancièra *f* bellypiece; body girth

panciòlle *m*—**in panciolle** frittering one's time away

panciòtto m waistcoat; vest; **panciotto a maglia** cardigan

panciu·to -ta adj potbellied

pàncre·as m (-as) pancreas

pandemò·nio m (-ni) pandemonium

pane m bread; thread (of screw); cake (e.g., of butter); loaf (of sugar); (metallurgy) pig; **a pane di zucchero** conic(al); **dire pane al pane e vino al vino** to call a spade a spade; **essere come pane e cacio** to be hand and glove; **essere pane per i propri denti** to be a match for s.o.; **guadagnarsi il pane** to earn one's living; **pane a cassetta** sandwich bread; **pane azzimo** unleavened bread, matzoth; **pan di Spagna** angel food cake, sponge cake; **pane integrale** graham bread; **render pan per focaccia** to give tit for tat

panegìri·co m (-ci) panegyric

panetterìa f bakery

panettière m baker

panétto m pat (e.g., of butter)

pànfilo m yacht

panfrutto m plum cake

pangrattato m bread crumbs

pània f birdlime; **cadere nella pania** to fall into the trap

pàni·co -ca (-ci -che) adj panicky || m panic

pani·co m (-chi) (bot) Italian millet

panièra f basket; basketful

panière m basket; basketful

panificazióne f breadmaking

panifi·cio m (-ci) bakery

panino m roll, bun; **panino imbottito** sandwich

panna f cream, heavy cream; **essere in panna** (naut) to lie to; (aut) to have a breakdown; **mettere in panna** (naut) to heave to; **panna montata** whipped cream

panne f (aut) breakdown; **essere in panne** (aut) to have a breakdown

pannèllo m linen cloth; pane; panel (of machine); (archit; elec) panel

pannìcolo m (anat) membrane, tissue

panno m cloth; woolen cloth; film, membrane; **bianco come un panno as white as a ghost; **mettersi nei panni di** to put oneself in the boots of; **non stare più nei propri panni** to be beside oneself with joy; **panni** clothes; **panno verde** baize

pannòcchia f ear (of corn)

pannolino m linen cloth; diaper; sanitary napkin

panòplia f panoply

panora·ma m (-mi) panorama

panoràmi·co -ca adj (-ci -che) panoramic || f panoramic view; (mov) panoramic scene

pantaloncìni mpl trunks

pantalóni mpl trousers; **pantaloni da donna** slacks

pàntano m bog, quagmire

panteismo m pantheism

pànteon m pantheon

pantèra f panther; (slang) police car

pantòfola f slipper

pantomima f pantomine, mimicry

panzana f (lit) fib, lie

Pàolo m Paul

paonaz·zo -za adj & m purple

pa·pa m (-pi) pope; **ad ogni morte di papa** once in a blue moon; **morto un papa se ne fa un altro** nobody is indispensable

pa·pà m (-pà) daddy, papa

papàbile adj likely to be elected || mf front runner || m cardinal likely to be elected to the papacy

papale adj papal (e.g., benediction); Papal (States)

papali·no -na adj papal || m advocate of papal temporal power || f skullcap

paparazzo m freelance photographer

papato m papacy

papàvero m poppy; **alto papavero** (fig) big shot

pàpera f young goose; slip of the tongue; spoonerism; **fare una papera** to make a boner

pàpero m gander

papiro m papyrus

pappa f bread soup, farina, pap; **pappa molla** (fig) jellyfish

pappafi·co m (-chi) (naut) topgallant; (slang) goatee

pappagallo m parrot; bedpan; (slang) masher

pappagòr·gia f (-ge) double chin, jowl

pappare tr (coll) to gulp; (fig) to gobble up fraudulently

pappata·ci m (-ci) gnat

pappina f light pap; poultice

pàpri·ca f (-che) paprika

para f crepe rubber

paràbola f parable; (geom) parabola

parabórdo m (naut) fender

parabréz·za [ddzz] m (-za) windshield

paracadutare tr to parachute, airdrop || ref to parachute

paracadu·te·m (-te) parachute

paracadutismo m parachute jumping; (sports) sky diving

paracaduti·sta mf (-sti -ste) parachutist; skydiver || m paratrooper

paracarro m spur stone

paracól·pi m (-pi) doorstop

paràcqua m (paràcqua) umbrella

paradèn·ti m (-ti) (sports) mouthpiece

paradisìa·co -ca adj (-ci -che) heavenly

paradiso m paradise

paradossale adj paradoxical

paradòsso m paradox

parafa f initials

parafan·go m (-ghi) fender, mudguard

parafare tr to initial

paraffina f paraffin

parafiam·ma m (-ma) fire-proof partition

parafrasare (paràfraso) tr to paraphrase

paràfra·si f (-si) paraphrase

parafùlmine m lightning rod

parafuò·co m (-co) screen, fender (in front of fireplace)

paràg·gio m (-gi) lineage; **paraggi** neighborhood, vicinity

paragonàbile adj comparable

paragonare (paragóno) tr to compare

paragóne m comparison; **a paragone di**

in comparison with; **mettere a paragone** to compare; **senza paragone** beyond compare

paragrafare (paràgrafo) *tr* to paragraph

paràgrafo *m* paragraph

paraguaià·no -na *adj & mf* Paraguayan

paràli·si *f* (**-si**) paralysis

paralìti·co -ca *adj & mf* (**-ci -che**) paralytic

paralizzare [ddzz] *tr* to paralyze

parallè·lo -la *adj & m* parallel || *f* (geom) parallel line; **parallele** (sports) parallel bars

paralume *m* lamp shade

paramano *m* cuff, wristband; (archit) facing brick

paraménto *s* facing (*of a wall*); (eccl) vestment

parami·ne *m* (**-ne**) (nav) paravane

paramó·sche *m* (**-sche**) fly net

paran·co *m* (**-chi**) tackle

paranìn·fo -fa *mf* matchmaker

paranòi·co -ca *adj & mf* (**-ci -che**) paranoiac

paraòc·chi *m* (**-chi**) blinker (*on horse*)

parapètto *m* parapet

parapì·glia *m* (**-glia**) hubbub

parapiòg·gia *m* (**-gia**) umbrella

parare *tr* to adorn; to hang; to protect; to parry (*a thrust*); to offer; to drive (*e.g., cattle*) || *intr*—**dove va a parare?** what are you driving at? || *ref* to protect oneself; (eccl) to don the vestments; **pararsi dinanzi a** to loom up in front of

parasóle *m* parasol; (aut) sun visor

paraspal·le *m* (**-le**) (sports) shoulder pad

parassi·ta (**-ti -te**) *adj* parasitic || *m* parasite

parassità·rio -ria *adj* (**-ri -rie**) parasitic(al)

parassìti·co -ca *adj* (**-ci -che**) parasitic(al)

parastatale *adj* government-controlled || *mf* employee of government-controlled agency

parastin·chi *m* (**-chi**) (sports) shin guard

parata *f* fence, bar; (fencing) parry; (soccer) catch; (mil) parade; **mala parata** dangerous situation

paratìa *f* bulkhead

parato *m* hangings; **parati** hangings; (naut) bilgeways

paratóia *f* sluice gate

paraur·ti *m* (**-ti**) (aut) bumper; (rr) buffer

paravènto *m* screen

Par·ca *f* (**-che**) Fate

parcare §197 *tr & intr* to park

parcèlla *f* bill, fee, honorarium; parcel, lot (*of land*)

parcheggiare §290 (**parchéggio**) *tr & intr* to park

parchég·gio *m* (**-gi**) parking; parking lot

parchìmetro *m* parking meter

par·co -ca (**-chi -che**) *adj* frugal; parsimonious || *m* park; parking; parking lot; **parco dei divertimenti** amusement park

paréc·chio -chia (**-chi -chie**) *adj indef*

a good deal of, a lot of; **parecchi** several || *pron* a good deal, a lot; **parecchi** several || **parecchio** *adv* a lot; rather

pareggiare §290 (**paréggio**) *tr* to level; to equal; to match; to balance; to recognize || *intr* (sports) to tie

pareggia·to -ta *adj* accredited (*school*)

parég·gio *m* (**-gi**) leveling; matching; (sports) tie; **pareggio del bilancio** balancing of the budget

parentado *m* kinsfolk, kindred; relationship; **concludere il parentado di** to arrange for the wedding of

parènte *mf* relative; (lit) parent; **parenti** kin

parentèla *f* relationship; relations

parènte·si *f* (**-si**) parenthesis; break, interval; **fra parentesi** parenthetically; in parentheses; **parentesi quadra** bracket

parére *m* opinion, mind; advice; **a mio parere** in my opinion || §210 *intr* (ESSERE) to seem; **che Le pare?** what is your opinion?; **ma Le pare!** not at all!; **mi pare che** + *subj* it seems to me that + *ind*; I guess that + *ind*; **non Le pare?** don't you think so?; **non mi pare vero** I can't believe it

paréte *f* wall; **tra le pareti domestiche** within the four walls of the home

pargolét·to -ta *adj* (poet) infantile || *mf* (poet) child

pàrgo·lo -la *adj* (poet) infantile || *mf* (poet) child

pari *adj invar* equal, even; **camminare di pari passo** to walk at the same rate; **essere pari** to be quits; **essere pari al proprio compito** to be equal to the task; **fare un salto a piè pari** to jump with feet together; **pari pari** verbatim; **rimanere pari con** (sports) to be tied with; **saltare a piè pari** to skip (*e.g., a page*); to dodge (*a difficulty*); **trattare da pari a pari** to treat as an equal || *m* peer; **al pari di** as, like; **del pari** aɪso; **in pari** even, leveled; **senza pari** matchless, peerless || *f*—**stare alla pari con** to be an even match for

parìa *f* peerage

pà·ria *m* (**-ria**) pariah

parificare §197 (**parìfico**) *tr* to level; to match; to accredit (*a school*); to balance

Parigi *f* Paris

parigi·no -na *adj & mf* Parisian || *f* slow-burning stove; Parisian woman; (rr) switching spur

pariglia *f* pair, couple; team (*of horses*); (cards) two of a kind; **rendere la pariglia** to give tit for tat

parimènti *adv* likewise

pari·tà *f* (**-tà**) parity

paritèti·co -ca *adj* (**-ci -che**) joint (*e.g., committee*)

parlamentare *adj* parliamentary || *mf* member of parliament || *m* (mil) envoy || *v* (**parlaménto**) *intr* to parley

parlaménto *m* parliament

parlante *adj* talking; life-like || *mf* speaker

parlantina *f* glibness

parlare *m* talk, speech; dialect ‖ *tr* to speak (*a language*) ‖ *intr* to speak, talk; to discuss; **chi parla?** (telp) hello!; **far parlare di sé** to be talked about; **parlare chiaro** to speak bluntly; **parlare del più e del meno** to make small talk; **parlare tra sé e sé** to talk to oneself ‖ *ref* to talk to one another

parla·to **-ta** *adj* spoken; current (*speech*); talking (*movie*) ‖ *m* talkie; (mov) sound track; (theat) dialogue ‖ *f* speech, talk; dialect

parla·tóre **-trice** *mf* speaker

parlatò·rio *m* (**-ri**) visting room (*e.g., in jail*)

parlottare (**parlòtto**) *intr* to whisper in secret

parmigia·no **-na** *adj & mf* Parmesan ‖ *m* Parmesan cheese

parnaso *m* Parnassus (*poetry, poets*) ‖ **il Parnaso** Mount Parnassus

paro *m*—**in un par d'ore** in a couple of hours ‖ *adv*—**andare a paro** to keep abreast; **mettere a paro** to compare

parodìa *f* parody; **fare la parodìa di** to parody

parodiare §287 (**paròdio**) *tr* to parody

paròla *f* word; speech; **avere parole con** to have words with; **buttare la mezza parola** to make an allusion; **dare la parola a** to give the floor to; **di poche parole** of few words; **domandare la parola a** to ask for the floor; **essere di parola** to keep one's word; **essere in parola con** to have dealings with; **mangiarsi la parola** to break one's word; **mangiarsi le parole** to slur one's words; **non far parola** to not breathe a word; **parola crociata** crossword puzzle; **parola d'ordine** password; **parola macedonia** acronym **parola sdrucciola** proparoxytone; **parole** lyrics; **parole di circostanza** occasional words; **prendere la parola** to take the floor; **rivolgere la parola a** to address; **venire a parole** to begin to quarrel

parolàc·cia *f* (**-ce**) dirty word; swear-word

paro·làio **-làia** (**-lài** **-làie**) *adj* wordy, verbose ‖ *mf* windbag

parolière *m* lyricist

parossismo *m* paroxysm; climax

parossito·no **-na** *adj* paroxytone

parotite *f* (pathol) parotitis; **parotite epidemica** (pathol) mumps

parrici·da *mf* (**-di** **-de**) patricide

parrocchétto *m* parakeet; (naut) fore-topsail; (naut) fore-topmast

parròcchia *f* parish

parrocchia·no **-na** *mf* parishioner

pàrro·co *m* (**-ci**) rector, parson

parruc·ca *f* (**-che**) wig; (fig) old fogey

parsimònia *f* parsimony

parsimonió·so **-sa** [s] *adj* parsimonious

partàc·cia *f*—**fare una partaccia** to break one's word; **fare una partaccia a** to make a scene in front of; to rebuke loudly

parte *f* part; share; section; side; party; partiality; (theat) role; **a parte** sepa-

rately; (theat) aside; **d'altra parte** on the other hand; **da parte** aside; **da parte mia** as for me; **fare le parti** to divide in shares; **gran parte di** a great deal of; **in parte** partially; **la maggior parte di** most of; **parte civile** (law) plaintiff; **parte . . . parte** some . . . some; part . . . part; **prendere in mala parte** to take amiss

partecipante *adj* participating ‖ *mf* participant; (sports) contestant

partecipare (**partécipo**) *tr* to announce; (lit) to share in ‖ *intr*—**partecipare a** to share in; to participate in; **partecipare di** to partake of (*e.g., the nature of an animal*)

partecipazióne *f* announcement; card; announcement (*of a wedding*); share (*in a business*); participation (*in some action*)

partécipe *adj* sharing, partaking

parteggiare §290 (**partéggio**) *intr* to side; **parteggiare per** to side with

Partenóne *m* Parthenon

partènte *adj* departing ‖ *mf* person departing, traveler; (sports) starter

partènza *f* departure; sailing; (sports) start; **di partenza** or **in partenza** about to leave; **partenza lanciata** (sports) running start

particèlla *f* particle

partici·pio *m* (**-pi**) participle

particolare *adj* particular; private; **in particolare** especially ‖ *m* detail

particolareggiare §290 (**particolaréggio**) *tr* to detail

particolarismo *m* regionalism, particularism

particolarìsti·co **-ca** *adj* (**-ci** **-che**) particularistic; individualistic

particolari·tà *f* (**-tà**) peculiarity; detail

partigianerìa *f* partisanship, factionalism

partigia·no **-na** *adj & mf* partisan

partire §176 *tr* (lit) to divide ‖ *v* (parto) *intr* to depart; (fig) to arise; **a partire da** beginning with; **far partire** to start (*e.g., a car*) ‖ *ref* to depart, leave

parti·to **-ta** *adj* parted ‖ *m* match (*in marriage*); (pol) party; **ridotto a mal partito** in bad shape; **mettere la testa a partito** to reform; **partito preso** parti pris; **prendere partito** to take sides; to make up one's mind; **trarre il miglior partito da** to make the best of ‖ *f* panel (*e.g., of door*); lot (*of goods*); game; match; party; round (*of golf*); (com) entry; **partita di caccia** hunting party; **partita doppia** (com) double entry; **partita semplice** (com) single entry

partitura *f* (mus) score

partizióne *f* partition, division

parto *m* birth, childbirth

partorire §176 *tr* to bear, bring forth

parvènza *f* (lit) appearance

parziale *adj* partial, one-sided

parziali·tà *f* (**-tà**) partiality

pàscere §211 *tr, intr & ref* to pasture, graze

pa·scià *m* (**-scià**) pasha

pasciu·to **-ta** *adj* well-fed

pascolare (pàscolo) *tr & intr* to pasture

pàscolo *m* pasture

Pàsqua *f* Easter; **contento come una Pasqua** as happy as a lark; **Pasqua fiorita** Palm Sunday

pasquale *adj* paschal (*e.g., lamb*)

passàbile *adj* passable, tolerable

passàg·gio *m* (**-gi**) passage; transfer; crossing; traffic; passageway; ride; promotion; (sports) pass; **aprirsi il passaggio** to make one's way; **di passaggio in passing**; transient (*visitor*); **essere di passaggio** to be passing by; **passaggio a livello** railroad crossing; **passaggio zebrato** zebra crossing; **vietato il passaggio** no thoroughfare

passamano *m* passing from hand to hand; ribbon; (coll) railing, handrail

passante *adj* passing (*shot*) ‖ *mf* passer-by ‖ *m* strap

passapòrto *m* passport

passare *tr* to cross; to pass; to undergo (*a medical examination*); to move; to hand; to pay; to send (*word*); to pierce; to spend (*time*); to strain; to go over; to let have (*e.g., a slap*); to overstep (*the bounds*); **passare in rassegna** to pass in review; **passare per le armi** to execute; **passare un brutto quarto d'ora** to have a bad ten minutes; **passare un guaio** to have a hard time; **passarla a qlcu** (coll) to forgive s.o.; **passarla liscia** (coll) to get off unscathed; **passarsela bene** (coll) to have a good time ‖ *intr* (ESSERE) to pass; to go; to filter (*said of air, light*); to move; to spoil (*said of food*); to be overcooked; to be promoted; to become; to enter; (lit) to be over; **fare passare qlcu** to let s.o. come in; **passare a nozze** to get married; **passare a seconde nozze** to remarry; **passare avanti a** to overcome; **passare di mente a** to forget, e.g., **gli è passata di mente la riunione** he forgot the meeting; **passare di moda** to go out of style; **passare in giudicato** (law) to be no longer appealable; **passare per** to pass as; **passare per il rotto della cuffia** to barely make it; **passare sopra qlco** to overlook s.th; **passi! come in!; passo!** (rad) over!; **passo** (cards) pass

passata *f* purée; **dare una passata a** to glance at; **dare una passata di straccio a** to rub lightly with a rag; to give a lick and a promise to; **di passata** hurriedly

passatèmpo *m* pastime; hobby

passati·sta *mf* (**-sti -ste**) traditionalist

passa·to -ta *adj* past; last; overcooked; **essere passato** (coll) to be no longer in one's prime; **passato di moda** out of fashion ‖ *m* past; purée; **passato prossimo** present perfect; **passato remoto** preterit ‖ *f see* **passata**

passatóia *f* runner (*rug*)

passa·tóio *m* (**-tói**) stepping stone

passeggè·ro -ra *adj* passing ‖ *mf* passenger; **passeggero clandestino** stowaway

passeggiare §290 (**passéggio**) *tr* to walk (*e.g., a horse*) ‖ *intr* to walk, promenade

passeggiata *f* promenade; walk; drive, ride; drive, road; **fare una passeggiata** to take a walk; to take a ride

passeggiatrice *f* streetwalker

passég·gio *m* (**-gi**) walk; promenade; **andare a passeggio** to take a walk

passerèlla *f* gangway; catwalk; footbridge

pàsse·ro -ra *mf* sparrow ‖ *f*—**passera di mare** (ichth) flounder

passìbile *adj*—**passìbile di** subject to, liable to

passiflòra *f* passionflower

passino *m* colander, strainer

passióne *f* passion

passivi·tà *f* (**-tà**) passivity; (com) deficit

passi·vo -va *adj* passive ‖ *m* (com) liabilities; (com) debit side; (gram) passive

pas·so -sa *adj*—*see* **uva** ‖ *m* step; passage; pass (*in mountain*); pace; footstep; pitch (*of screw, helix, etc.*); (aut) wheelbase; (phot) tread; (phot) size (*of roll*); **a grandi passi** with great strides; **andare al passo** to march in step; to walk (*said of a horse*); **a passi di gigante** by leaps and bounds; **a passo di corsa** running; **a passo d'uomo** walking, at a walk; **aprire il passo** to open the way; **di buon passo** at a good clip; **di pari passo** at the same rate; **fare quattro passi** to take a stroll; **passo doppio** paso doble; **passo d'uomo** manhole; step; **passo falso** misstep; (fig) stumble; **sbarrare il passo** to block the way; **seguire i passi di** to walk in the footsteps of ‖ *interj* (cards) pass!; over!

pasta *f* paste; dough; **di pasta grossa** uncouth, coarse; **pasta alimentare** pasta, macaroni products; **pasta all'uovo** egg noodles; **pasta asciutta** pasta with sauce and cheese; **pasta dentifricia** toothpaste; **una pasta d'uomo** a good-natured man

pastasciutta *f* pasta with sauce and cheese

pasteggiare §290 (**pastéggio**) *intr* to dine

pastèllo *adj invar & m* pastel ‖ *m* crayon

pastétta *f* batter; (coll) trickery

pastic·ca *f* (**-che**) lozenge, tablet; **pasticche per la tosse** cough drops

pasticceria *f* pastrymaking; pastry; pastry shop

pasticciare §128 (**pastìccio**) *tr & intr* to bungle; to scribble

pasticciè·re -ra *mf* pastry cook; confectioner

pasticcino *m* cookie; patty

pastìc·cio *m* (**-ci**) pie (*of meat, macaroni, etc*); bungle; mess; **cacciarsi nei pasticci** to wind up in the soup

pasticció·ne -na *mf* bungler

pastifì·cio *m* (**-ci**) spaghetti and macaroni factory

pastìglia *f* lozenge, tablet; **pastiglia per la tosse** cough drop

pastina·ca *f* (**-che**) parsnip
pa·sto -sta *adj* (archaic) fed || *m* meal; **pasto a prezzo fisso** table d'hôte || *f* see **pasta**
pastóia *f* hobble; (fig) shackle
pastóne *m* mash
pastóra *f* shepherdess
pastorale *adj* pastoral
pastóre *m* shepherd; pastor
pastorì·zio -zia (**-zi -zie**) *adj* shepherd || *f* sheep raising
pastorizzare [ddzz] *tr* to pasteurize
pastó·so -sa [s] *adj* pasty; mellow
pastrano *m* overcoat
pastura *f* pasture; hay; fodder
patac·ca *f* (**-che**) large, worthless coin; fake; (coll) medal; (coll) spot
patata *f* potato
patatràc *m* (**patatràc**) crash
patèlla *f* kneecap; (zool) limpet
patè·ma *m* (**-mi**) affliction; **patema d'animo** anxiety
patenta·to -ta *adj* licensed; (coll) well-known
patènte *adj* patent || *f* license; driver's license; **patente sanitaria** (naut) bill of health
patentino *m* (aut) permit
pateréc·cio *m* (**-ci**) whitlow
paternale *adj* (obs) paternal || *f* reprimand
paterni·tà *f* (**-tà**) paternity; authorship
patèr·no -na *adj* paternal; fatherly
paternòstro *m* Lord's Prayer; **è vero come il paternostro** it is the gospel truth
patèti·co -ca (**-ci -che**) *adj* pathetic; mawkish || *m* pathos; mawkishness
pathos *m* pathos
patìbile *adj* endurable
patibolare *adj* gallows
patìbolo *m* executioner's instrument; scaffold
patiménto *m* suffering
pàtina *f* patina; coating (*on paper*); varnish; fur (*on tongue*)
patinare (**pàtino**) *tr* to gloss, glaze (*e.g., paper*)
patire §176 *tr* to suffer; (gram) to be the recipient of (*an action*) || *intr* to suffer
patì·to -ta *adj* suffering, sickly || *mf* fan || *m* boyfriend || *f* girlfriend
patòge·no -na *adj* pathogenic
patologìa *f* pathology
patològi·co -ca *adj* (**-ci -che**) pathologic(al)
patos *m* var of **pathos**
patrasso *m*—**andare a patrasso** to die; to go to ruin; **mandare a patrasso** to kill; to ruin
pàtria *f* fatherland, native land
patriar·ca *m* (**-chi**) patriarch
patriarcale *adj* patriarchal
patrigno *m* stepfather
patrimoniale *adj* patrimonial; property (*tax*); capital (*e.g., transaction*)
patrimò·nio *m* (**-ni**) patrimony; estate; fortune; (fig) heritage
pà·trio -tria (**-tri -trie**) *adj* paternal; of one's country (*e.g., love*) || *f* see **patria**

patriò·ta *mf* (**-ti -te**) patriot; (coll) fellow citizen
patriòtti·co -ca *adj* (**-ci -che**) patriotic
patriottismo *m* patriotism
patrì·zio -zia (**-zi -zie**) *adj* & *m* patrician || **Patrizio** *m* Patrick
patrocinante *adj* pleading (*lawyer*)
patrocinare *tr* to favor, sponsor; to plead
patrocina·tóre -trice *mf* defender; pleader
patrocì·nio *m* (**-ni**) support; sponsorship; (law) defense; **patrocinio gratuito** public defense
patronato *m* patronage; charitable institution, foundation; **patronato scolastico** state aid fund
patronéssa *f* sponsor; trustee (*of charitable institution*)
patròno *m* patron saint; patron; sponsor; trustee (*of charitable institution*); (law) counsel
patta *f* flap (*of garment*); bill (*of anchor*); (coll) potholder; **essere** or **far patta** to be even, tie
patteggiaménto *m* negotiation
patteggiare §290 (**pattéggio**) *tr* & *intr* to negotiate
pattinàggio *m* skating
pattinare (**pàttino**) *intr* to skate; to skid (*said of a car*)
pattina·tóio *m* (**-tói**) skating rink
pattina·tóre -trice *mf* skater
pàttino *m* skate; guide block (*of an elevator*); (aer) skid, runner; **pattino a rotelle** roller skate
pattino *m* racing shell with outrigger floats
patto *m* pact; **a nessun patto** by no means; **a patto che** provided (that); **patto sociale** social contract; **venire a patti** to come to terms
pattùglia *f* patrol
pattugliare §280 *tr* & *intr* to patrol
pattuire §176 *tr* & *intr* to negotiate
pattuì·to -ta *adj* agreed || *m* agreement
pattume *m* litter, garbage
pattumièra *f* dustpan; trash bin
patùrnie *fpl*—**avere le paturnie** (coll) to be in the dumps
paura *f* fear; **aver paura di** to be afraid of; **da far paura** frightful; **dar** or **metter paura a** to frighten; **per paura che** for fear that, lest
pauró·so -sa [s] *adj* fearful
pàusa *f* pause
pausare (**pàuso**) *tr* (lit) to interrupt || *intr* (lit) to pause
paventare (**pavènto**) *tr* & *intr* to fear
pavesare (**pavéso**) *tr* to deck with flags; to dress (*a ship*)
pavé·se [s] *adj*—see **zuppa** || *m* pavis (*shield*); (naut) bunting
pàvi·do -da *adj* cowardly, timid
pavimentare (**paviménto**) *tr* to pave
pavimentazióne *f* paving, pavement
paviménto *m* floor; bottom (*of sea*); paving (*of street*)
pavoncèlla *f* lapwing
pavó·ne -na or **-néssa** *mf* peacock
pavoneggiare §290 (**pavonéggio**) *ref* to swagger, strut
pazientare (**paziènto**) *intr* to be patient

paziènte adj & mf patient

paziènza f patience; **fare scappare la pazienza a** to drive mad; **pazienza!** too bad!

pazzé·sco -sca adj (-schi -sche) crazy, wild

pazzia f madness, insanity; folly; **fare pazzie** to act like a fool

paz·zo -za adj crazy, insane; **andar pazzo per** to be crazy about || mf crazy person

pèc·ca f (-che) imperfection

peccamino·so -sa [s] adj sinful

peccare §197 (pècco) intr to sin; to be lacking; to be at fault

peccato m sin; **che peccato!** what a pity!; **è un peccato** it's a shame

pecca·tóre -trice mf sinner

pécchia f bee

pecchióne m drone

péce f pitch; **pece greca** rosin

pechinése [s] adj & mf Pekingese

Pechino f Peking

pècora f sheep

peco·ràio m (-rài) shepherd

pecorèlla f small sheep, lamb

pecori·no -na adj sheep; sheepish || m sheep-milk cheese || f sheep manure

peculato m embezzlement, peculation

peculiare adj peculiar

peculiari·tà f (-tà) peculiarity

pecù·lio m (-li) nest egg, savings; (obs) cattle

pecùnia m (lit) money

pecunià·rio -ria adj (-ri -rie) pecuniary

pedàg·gio m (-gi) toll

pedagogia f pedagogy, pedagogics

pedagògi·co -ca adj (-ci -che) pedagogic(al)

pedagò·go -ga mf (-ghi -ghe) pedagogue

pedalare intr to pedal

pedale m trunk (of tree); pedal; treadle (e.g., of sewing machine)

pedalièra f pedals, pedal keyboard; (aer) rudder bar

pedalino m (coll) sock, short stocking

pedana f footrest; platform; bedside rug; hem (of skirt); (aut) running board; (sports) springboard

pedante adj pedantic || m pedant

pedanteria f pedantry

pedanté·sco -sca adj (-schi -sche) pedantic

pedata f kick; footprint; tread (of step)

pedèstre adj pedestrian

pedia·tra mf (-tri -tre) pediatrician

pediatria f pediatrics

pedicu·re mf (-re) pedicure

pedicu·ro -ra mf var of **pedicure**

pedilù·vio m (-vi) foot bath

pedina f (checkers) checker, man; (chess) pawn

pedinare tr to shadow, follow about

pedìsse·quo -qua adj servile

pedivèlla f pedal crank

pedóne m pedestrian; (chess) pawn

pedule m stocking foot || fpl climbing shoes, sneakers

pedùncolo m (anat, bot, zool) peduncle

pegamòide f imitation leather

pèggio adj invar worse; **il peggio** the worst, e.g., **il peggio ragazzo** the worst boy; || m worst; **andare per il peggio** to be getting worse || f worst; **alla peggio** if worst comes to worst; **averne la peggio** to get the worst of it || adv worse; worst; at worst; **peggio + pp** less + pp; least + pp; **tanto peggio** so much the worse

peggioraménto m deterioration, worsening

peggiorare (peggióro) tr & intr to worsen

peggió·re (-ri) adj worse; worst || m worst

pégli §4

pégno m pledge, pawn

pégola f pitch; (coll) bad luck

péi §4

pél §4

pèla·go m (-ghi) (poet) open sea; (coll) mess; **pelago di guai** sea of trouble

pelame m hair, coat

pelandróne m (coll) shirker, do-nothing

pelapata·te m (-te) potato peeler

pelare (pélo) tr to fleece; to pluck; to pare, peel; to clear (land); (fig) to strip; to scald, burn || ref (coll) to shed; to become bald

pela·to -ta adj peeled; hairless, bald; barren || m (coll) baldy; **pelati** peeled tomatoes || f fleecing, plucking; (joc) baldness, bald spot

pélla §4

pellàc·cia f (-ce) tough hide

pellame m skins, hides

pèlle f skin, hide; **a fior di pelle** slightly, superficially; **essere nella pelle di** to be in the boots of; **fare la pelle a** to bump off; **non stare più nella pelle** to be beside oneself with joy; **pelle di dante** buckskin; **pelle d'oca** goose skin, goose flesh; **pelle d'uovo** mull; **pelle pelle** skin-deep, superficial

pélle §4

pellegrinàg·gio m (-gi) pilgrimage

pellegrinare intr (lit) to go on a pilgrimage

pellegri·no -na adj wandering; (lit) foreign; (lit) strange, quixotic || mf pilgrim, traveler

pelleróssa mf (pellirosse) redskin

pelletteria f leather goods; leather goods store

pellicano m pelican

pellicceria f furrier's store; furrier's trade, fur industry

pellìc·cia f (-ce) fur

pellic·ciàio -ciàia mf (-ciài -ciàie) furrier

pelliccióne m fur jacket

pellìcola f film; **pellicola in rotolo** roll film; **pellicola piana** film pack; **pellicola sonora** sound film; **pellicola vergine** unexposed film

pellirós·sa mf (-se) var of **pellerossa**

pélo m hair (of beard); pile (of carpet); fur; **avere pelo sul cuore** not to be easily moved; **cercare il pelo nell'uovo** to split hairs; **di primo pelo** green, inexperienced; **non avere peli sulla lingua** to not mince one's words; **pelo dell'acqua** water surface; **per un pelo** by a hair's breadth

peloponnesìa·co **-ca** *adj* (**-ci** **-che**)
Peloponnesian
peló·so **-sa** [s] *adj* hairy; self-serving
(*e.g., charity*)
péltro *m* pewter
pelùria *f* down, soft hair
péna *f* penalty; concern; compassion;
pain, suffering; grief; **a mala pena**
barely; **essere in pena per** to worry
about; **fare pena** to arouse compassion; **pena infamante** degrading punishment; loss of civil rights; **sotto
pena di** under penalty of; **valere la
pena** to be worthwhile
penale *adj* penal || *f* penalty
penali·sta *mf* (**-sti** **-ste**) criminal lawyer
penali·tà *f* (**-tà**) penalty
penalizzare [ddzz] *tr* (sports) to penalize
penare (**péno**) *intr* to suffer; to find it
difficult
pencolare (**pèncolo**) *intr* to totter; to
waver
pendà·glio *m* (**-gli**) pendant; **pendaglio
da forca** gallows bird
pendènte *adj* leaning; hanging; pending
|| *m* pendant
pendènza *f* inclination, pitch; controversy; balance; **in pendenza** pending
pèndere §123 *intr* to hang; to lean; to
slope; to pitch
pendìce *f* slope, declivity
pen·dìo *m* (**-dìi**) slant; slope
pèndola *f* clock
pendolare *adj* pendulum-like; commut-
ing; transient (*tourist*) || *mf* com-
muter || *v* (**pèndolo**) *intr* to sway
back and forth; to waver; (nav) to
cruise back and forth
pèndolo *m* pendulum; clock
pèndu·lo **-la** *adj* (lit) hanging
penetrante *adj* penetrating, piercing
penetrare (**pènetro**) *tr* to penetrate,
pierce || *intr* to penetrate || *ref*—
penetrarsi di to be convinced of; to
become aware of
penicillìna *f* penicillin
peninsulare *adj* peninsular
penìsola *f* peninsula
penitènte *adj* & *mf* penitent
penitènza *f* penitence; punishment
penitenzià·rio **-ria** *adj* & *mf* (**-ri** **-rie**)
penitentiary
pénna *f* feather; pen; peen (*of hammer*); (mus) plectrum; **penna a sfera**
ball-point pen; **penna d'oca** quill;
penna stilografica fountain pen
pennàc·chio *m* (**-chi**) panache; plume,
tuft; cloud (*of smoke*)
pennaiòlo *m* hack writer
pennarèllo *m* felt-tip pen
pennellare (**pennèllo**) *intr* to brush;
(med) to pencil
pennellata *f* brush stroke
pennèllo *m* brush; (naut) signal flag;
(naut) kedge; **pennello per la barba**
shaving brush; **stare a pennello** to fit
to a T
pennìno *m* pen; penpoint, nib
pennóne *m* flagpole; (naut) yard; (mil)
pennant

pennu·to **-ta** *adj* feathered || **pennuti**
mpl birds
penómbra *f* penumbra; semidarkness;
faint light; **vivere in penombra** to
live in obscurity
penó·so **-sa** [s] *adj* painful
pensàbile *adj* thinkable
pensante *adj* thinking
pensare (**pènso**) *tr* to think; to think of
|| *intr* to think; to worry; **dar da
pensare a** to cause worry to, e.g.,
suo figlio gli dà da pensare his son
causes him worry; **pensa ai fatti tuoi**
(coll) mind your own business; **pensa
alla salute** (coll) don't worry!; **pensare a** to think of; **pensare di** to plan,
intend to
pensata *f* bright idea, brainstorm
pensa·tóre **-trice** *mf* thinker
pensièro *m* thought; **dare pensiero a**
to cause worry to; **darsi pensiero per**
to worry about; **essere sopra pensiero**
to be absorbed in thought
pensieró·so **-sa** [s] *adj* thoughtful, pensive
pènsile *adj* hanging, overhead
pensilina *f* marquee
pensionaménto *m* retirement
pensionante *mf* boarder, paying guest
pensionare (**pensióno**) *tr* to pension
pensiona·to **-ta** *adj* pensioned || *mf*
pensioner || *m* boarding school
pensióne *f* pension; boarding house;
in pensione retired; **tenere a pensione**
to board (*a lodger*); **vivere a pensione** to board (*said of a lodger*)
pensó·so **-sa** [s] *adj* thoughtful, pensive
pentàgono *m* pentagon
pentagram·ma *m* (**-mi**) (mus) staff,
stave
pentàmetro *m* pentameter
Pentecòste, la Pentecost, Whitsunday
pentiménto *m* repentance; correction
(*e.g., in a manuscript*); change of
heart
pentire (**pènto**) *ref* to repent; to change
one's mind; **pentirsi di** to repent
penti·to **-ta** *adj* repentant, repenting;
pentito e contrito in sackcloth and
ashes
péntola *f* pot, kettle; potful; **pentola a
pressione** pressure cooker
penùlti·mo **-ma** *adj* next to the last ||
f penult
penùria *f* shortage, scarcity
penzolare (**pènzolo**) [dz] *intr* to dangle,
hang down
penzolóni [dz] *adv* dangling
peònia *f* peony
pepaiòla *f* pepper shaker; pepper mill
pepare (**pépo**) *tr* to pepper
pepa·to **-ta** *adj* peppered; peppery
pépe *m* pepper; **pepe della Giamaica**
allspice; **pepe di Caienna** red pepper,
cayenne pepper
peperóne *m* (bot) pepper
pepìta *f* nugget
per *prep* by; through; throughout; for;
because of; to, in order to; in favor
of; considering; **essere per** to be
about to; **per** + *adj* or *adv* + **che** +
subj however + *adj* or *adv* + *ind*,

e.g., **per intelligente che sia** however intelligent he is; **per caso** perchance; **per che cosa?** what for?; **per l'appunto** exactly, just; **per lungo** lengthwise; **per me** as for me; **per ora** now; **per parte mia** as for me; **per poco** hardly, scarcely, **per quanto** + *adj* or *adv* + *subj* however + *adj* or *adv* + *pres ind*, e.g., **per quanto disperatamente provi** however desperately he attempts; **per tempo** early; **per traverso** diagonally; **per via che** (coll) because; **stare per** to be about to

péra *f* pear *(fruit)*; bulb, light bulb; (joc) head

peraltro *adv* besides, moreover

peranco *adv* yet

perbacco *interj* by Jove!

perbène *adj invar* nice, well brought up

percalle *m* percale

percènto *m* percent; percentage

percentuale *adj* percentage ‖ *f* percent; commission, bonus

percepìbile *adj* collectable

percepire §176 *tr* to perceive; to receive *(a salary)*

percettìbile *adj* perceptible

percetti·vo -va *adj* perceptive

percezióne *f* perception

perché *m* why, reason; **il perché e il percome** the why and the wherefore ‖ *pron rel* for which ‖ *adv* why ‖ *conj* because; so that

perciò *conj* therefore, accordingly

percóme *m & conj* wherefore

percorrènza *f* stretch, distance

percórrere §139 *tr* to cross; to cover, go through

percórso *m* crossing, distance

percòssa *f* hit, blow; contusion

percuòtere §251 *tr* to hit, beat; (fig) to shake ‖ *intr* to strike

percussióne *f* percussion

percussóre *m* firing pin

perdènte *adj* losing ‖ *mf* loser

pèrdere §212 *tr* to lose; to waste; to miss *(e.g., a train)*; to ruin; to leak ‖ *intr* to lose; to leak; to be inferior ‖ *ref* to get lost; to waste one's time; **perdersi d'animo** to lose heart; **perdersi in un bicchier d'acqua** to become discouraged for nothing

perdifiato *m*—**a perdifiato** at the top of one's lungs

perdigiór·no *mf* (-no) idler

perdinci *interj* good Heavens!

pèrdita *f* loss; leak; **a perdita d'occhio** as far as the eye can see; **perdite** (mil) casualties

perditèm·po *mf* (-po) idler ‖ *m* waste of time

perdizióne *f* perdition

perdonàbile *adj* pardonable

perdonare (**perdóno**) *tr* to forgive; to spare; **perdonare a qlcu qlco** or **perdonare qlcu di qlco** to forgive s.o. for s.th ‖ *intr* (with *dat*) to pardon

perdóno *m* forgiveness, pardon

perdurare *intr* (ESSERE & AVERE) to last; to persevere

perdu·to -ta *adj* lost; **andar perduto** to be desperately in love; to get lost

peregrinare *intr* to wander

peregrinazióne *f* wandering

peregri·no -na *adj* far-fetched, outlandish

perènne *adj* everlasting; perennial

perentò·rio -ria *adj* (-ri -rie) peremptory

perequare (**perèquo**) *tr* to equalize

perequazióne *f* equalization

perfèt·to -ta *adj & m* perfect

perfezionaménto *m* improvement; (educ) specialization

perfezionare (**perfezióno**) *tr* to improve, polish up; to perfect ‖ *ref* to improve; (educ) to specialize

perfezióne *f* perfection; **a** or **alla perfezione** to perfection

perfidia *f* perfidy

pèrfi·do -da *adj* perfidious, treacherous; (coll) foul, nasty

perfini·re *m* (-re) punch line

perfino *adv* even

perforante *adj* piercing, perforating

perforare (**perfóro**) *tr* to pierce; to perforate; to punch; to bore

perfora·tóre -trice *mf* key-punch operator ‖ *m* drill ‖ *f* punch; drill; pneumatic drill, rock drill

perforazióne *f* perforation

pergamèna *f* parchment, vellum

pèrgamo *m* (lit) pulpit

pèrgola *f* bower, pergola

pergolato *m* arbor, pergola; grape arbor

pericolante *adj* tottering, unsafe

perìcolo *m* danger; **non c'è pericolo** don't worry

pericoló·so -sa [*s*] *adj* dangerous

periferìa *f* periphery; suburbs

perifèri·co -ca *adj* (-ci -che) peripheral

perìfra·si *f* (-si) periphrasis

perìmetro *m* perimeter

periodare *m* writing style ‖ *v* (**perìodo**) *intr* to turn a phrase

perìòdi·co -ca (-ci -che) *adj* periodic(al) ‖ *m* periodical

perìodo *m* period; age; (gram) sentence; (phys) cycle; **il periodo delle feste** holiday time

peripezìa *f* vicissitude

pèriplo *m* circumnavigation

perire §176 *intr* (ESSERE) to perish

periscò·pio *m* (-pi) periscope

peritale *adj* expert

peritare (**pèrito**) *ref* (lit) to hesitate

peri·to -ta *adj* expert, skilled ‖ *mf* expert; **perito agrario** land surveyor; **perito calligrafo** handwriting expert; **perito chimico** chemist; **perito industriale** industrial engineer

peritonèo *m* peritoneum

perizia *f* skill; survey; appraisal

periziare §287 (**perizio**) *tr* to estimate, appraise

pèrla *f* pearl; (med) capsule

perlàce·o -a *adj* pearly

perla·to -ta *adj* pearly, smooth

perlìfe·ro -ra *adj* pearl-producing

perlina *f* bead

perlomèno *adv* at least

perlopiù *adv* mostly, generally

perlustrare *tr* to patrol

perlustrazióne *f* patrol, patrolling

permaló·so -sa [s] *adj* touchy, grouchy
permanènte *adj* permanente || *f* permanent wave
permanènza *f* permanence; stay; continuance (*in office*); duration (*of a disease*); **in permanenza** permanent (*employee*); **buona permanenza!** may your stay be happy!
permanére §235 (*pp* **permaso**) *intr* (ESSERE) to remain, stay
permeàbile *adj* permeable
permeare (**pèrmeo**) *tr* to permeate
permés·so -sa *adj* permitted, allowed; **è permesso?** may I come in? || *m* permit; (*mil*) pass, leave
perméttere §198 *tr* to permit, allow, let; **permette?** do you mind? || *ref* to take the liberty; to afford
permissíbile *adj* permissible
pèrmuta *f* barter; exchange
permutàbile *adj* tradable, exchangeable
permutare (**pèrmuto**) *tr* to barter; (*math*) to permute
pernàcchia *f* (*vulg*) raspberry
pernice *f* partridge
perniciό·so -sa [s] *adj* pernicious || *f* pernicious malaria
pèr·nio *m* (**-ni**) var of **perno**
pèrno *m* pivot; pin; kingbolt; swivel; heart (*of the matter*); kernel (*of the story*); support (*of the family*); (*mach*) journal; **fare perno** to pivot
pernottare (**pernòtto**) *intr* to spend the night, stay overnight
péro *m* pear tree
però *conj* but, yet; however, nevertheless; **e però** (*lit*) therefore
peróne *m* fibula
peronòspora *f* downy mildew
perorare (**pèroro**) *tr & intr* to perorate; (*law*) to plead
perorazióne *f* peroration; (*law*) pleading
perὸssido *m* peroxide; **perossido d'idrogeno** hydrogen peroxide
perpendicolare *adj & f* perpendicular
perpendìcolo *m* plumb line; **a perpendicolo** perpendicularly
perpetrare (**pèrpetro & perpètro**) *tr* (*lit*) to perpetrate
perpètua *f* priest's housekeeper
perpetuare (**perpètuo**) *tr* to perpetuate
perpè·tuo -tua *adj* perpetual, life || *f* see **perpetua**
perplessi·tà *f* (**-tà**) perplexity
perplès·so -sa *adj* perplexed; (*lit*) ambiguous
perquisire §176 *tr* to search
perquisizióne *f* search
persecu·tóre -trice *mf* persecutor, oppressor
persecuzióne *f* persecution
perseguire (**perséguo**) *tr* to pursue; to persecute; to pester
perseguitare (**perséguito**) *tr* to persecute; to pursue; to pester
perseveranza *f* perseverance
perseverare (**persèvero**) *intr* to persevere
persia·no -na *adj* Persian || *m* Persian; Persian lamb || *f* slatted shutter; **persiana avvolgibile** Venetian blind

pèrsi·co -ca (**-ci -che**) *adj* Persian || *m* (*ichth*) perch; (*obs*) peach || *f* (*coll*) peach
persino *adv* var of **perfino**
persistènte *adj* persistent
persistènza *f* persistence
persistere §114 *intr* to persist
pèr·so -sa *adj* lost, wasted; (*archaic*) reddish-brown; **a tempo perso** in one's spare time
persóna *f* person; **per persona** apiece; per capita; **persona di servizio** servant; **persone people**
personàg·gio *m* (**-gi**) personage; character
personale *adj* personal || *m* figure, body; personnel, staff; crew || *f* one-man show
personali·tà *f* (**-tà**) personality; personage
personificare §197 (**personìfico**) *tr* to personify
perspicace *adj* perspicacious; far-sighted
perspicàcia *f* perspicacity
perspì·cuo -cua *adj* perspicuous
persuadére §213 *tr* to persuade || *ref* to become convinced
persuasióne *f* persuasion
persuasí·vo -va *adj* persuasive; pleasing || *f* persuasiveness
persua·so -sa *adj* convinced; resigned
pertanto *conj* therefore; **non pertanto** nevertheless
pèrti·ca *f* (**-che**) perch; pole
pertinace *adj* pertinacious, persistent
pertinà·cia *f* (**-cie**) pertinacity, obstinacy
pertinènte *adj* pertinent, relevant
pertinènza *f* pertinence; competence
pertósse *f* whooping cough
pertù·gio *m* (**-gi**) hole
perturbare *tr* to perturb || *ref* to be perturbed
perturbazióne *f* perturbation; disturbance
Perù, il Peru; **valere un Perù** to be worth a king's ransom
peruvia·no -na *adj & mf* Peruvian
pervàdere §172 *tr* (*lit*) to pervade
pervenire §282 *intr* (ESSERE) to arrive; to come; **pervenire a** to reach
perversióne *f* perversion
perversi·tà *f* (**-tà**) perversity
pervèr·so -sa *adj* perverse; wicked
pervertiménto *m* perversion
pervertire (**pervèrto**) *tr* to pervert || *ref* to become perverted
perverti·to -ta *adj* perverted || *mf* pervert
pervicace *adj* (*lit*) obstinate
pervìn·ca *f* (**-che**) periwinkle
pésa [s] *f* weighing; scale
pesage *m* (**pesage**) weigh-in; place for weighing in jockeys
pesalètte·re [s] *m* (**-re**) postal scale
pesante [s] *adj* heavy
pesantézza [s] *f* heaviness; weight
pesare (**péso**) [s] *tr* to weigh || *intr* to weigh; **pesare a qlcu** to weigh upon s.o.
pesa·tóre -trice [s] *mf* scale or weigh-

bridge operator; **pesatore pubblico** inspector for the department of weights and measures

pesatura [s] *f* weighing

pé·sca *f* (-sche) fishing; catch (*of fish*) **pesca alla traina** trawling; **pesca d'altura** deep-sea fishing; **pesca di beneficenza** benefit lottery

pè·sca *f* (-sche) peach

pescàg·gio *m* (-gi) (naut) draft

pescàia *f* dam, weir

pescare §197 (**pésco**) *tr* to fish; to draw (*a card*); to dig up (*a piece of news*); to dive for (*pearls*); **pescare con la lenza** to angle for (*fish*) || *intr* to fish; (naut) to displace; **pescare con la lenza** to angle; **pescare di frodo** to poach; **pescare nel torbido** to fish in troubled waters

pesca·tóre -trice *mf* fisher; **pescatore di canna** angler; **pescatore di frodo** poacher

pésce *m* fish; (typ) omission; (coll) biceps; **a pesce** headlong; **non sapere che pesci pigliare** to not know which way to turn; **pesce d'aprile** April fool; **pesce gatto** catfish; **pesce martello** hammerhead || **Pesci** *mpl* (astr) Pisces

pescecane *m* (**pescecani** & **pescicani**) shark; (fig) war profiteer

pescheréc·cio -cia (-ci -ce) *adj* fishing || *m* fishing boat

pescheria *f* fish market

peschièra *f* fishpond; fishpound (*net*)

pescivéndo·lo -la *mf* fishmonger, fish dealer || *f* fishwife, fishwoman

pè·sco *m* (-schi) peach tree

pesi·sta [s] *m* (-sti) (sports) weight lifter

péso -sa [s] *adj* (coll) heavy || *m* weight; burden; bob (*of clock*); (racing) weigh-in; (sports) shot; **di peso** bodily; **peso lordo** gross weight; **peso massimo** (sports) heavyweight; **peso specifico** specific gravity; **rubare sul peso** to give short weight; **usare due pesi e due misure** to have a double standard || *f* see **pesa**

pessimismo *m* pessimism

pessimi·sta *mf* (-sti -ste) pessimist

pessimistico -ca *adj* (-ci -che) pessimistic

pèssi·mo -ma *adj* very bad, very poor

pésta *f* track, footprint; **lasciar nelle peste** to leave in the lurch; **seguir le peste di** to follow in the footsteps of

pestàggio *m* beating, clubbing

pestare (**pésto**) *tr* to pound; to trample; to step on; **pestare le orme di** to follow in the footsteps of; **pestare i piedi** to stamp the feet; **pestare sodo** to beat up

pèste *f* plague, pest

pestèllo *m* pestle

pestife·ro -ra *adj* pestiferous

pestilènza *f* pestilence; stench

pestilenziale *adj* pestilential; pernicious

pé·sto -sta *adj* crushed; thick (*darkness*) || *m* Genoese sauce || *f* see **pesta**

pètalo *m* petal

petardo *m* petard, firecracker

petènte *mf* petitioner

petizióne *f* petition; **petizione di principio** begging the question

péto *m* wind, gas

Petrarca *m* Petrarch

petrarché·sco -sca *adj* (-schi -sche) Petrarchan

petrolièra *f* (naut) tanker

petrolière *adj* incendiary || *m* petroleum-industry worker; incendiary; oilman (*producer*)

petrolife·ro -ra *adj* oil-yielding

petrò·lio *m* (-li) petroleum; coal oil, kerosene

petró·so -sa [s] *adj* (lit) stony

pettegolare (**pettégolo**) *intr* to gossip

pettegolézzo [ddzz] *m* gossip, rumor

pettégo·lo -la *adj* gossipy || *mf* gossip

pettinare (**pèttino**) *tr* to comb; to card; (coll) to scold

pettinatóre *m* carder

pettinatrice *f* hairdresser; carding machine

pettinatura *f* coiffure, hairstyling

pèttine *m* comb; (zool) scallop; **a pettine perpendicular** (*parking*)

pettino *m* dickey; bib (*of an apron*); plastron

pettirósso *m* robin redbreast

pètto *m* breast, chest; bust; bosom; **a un petto** single-breasted; **avere al petto** to feed at the breast; **a due petti** or **a doppio petto** double-breasted; **stare a petto** to be equal

pettorale *adj* pectoral || *m* pectoral; breast collar (*of horse*)

pettorina *f* var of **pettino**

pettoru·to -ta *adj* strutting, haughty

petulante *adj* importunate; impertinent

petulanza *f* importunity; impertinence

petùnia *f* petunia

pèzza *f* piece (*of cloth*); diaper; patch (*in suit or tire*); bolt (*of paper or cloth*); **pezza d'appoggio** supporting document, voucher; **trattare come una pezza da piedi** to wipe one's boots on

pezza·to -ta *adj* spotted, dappled

pezzatura *f* dapple (*on a horse*); size (*e.g., of a loaf of bread*)

pezzènte *mf* beggar

pezzétto *m* little bit; scrap, snip

pèzzo *m* piece; cut (*of meat*); coin; (journ) article; **andare** or **cadere a pezzi** to fall apart; **a pezzi e bocconi** by fits and starts; **fare a pezzi** to break to pieces; to blow to bits; **pezzo di ricambio** spare part; **pezzo d'uomo** hunk of a man; **pezzo duro** brick ice cream; **pezzo forte** forte; **pezzo fuso** cast, casting; **un bel pezzo** a good while; **un pezzo grosso** a big shot

pezzuòla *f* small piece of cloth; (coll) handkerchief

phy·lum *m* (-lum) phylum

piacènte *adj* attractive, pleasant

piacére *m* pleasure; **a piacere** at will; **a Suo piacere** as you please; **fare piacere a** to do a favor for; to please; **per piacere** please; **piacere!**

pleased to meet you! || §214 *intr* (ESSERE) to please; to be pleasing; (with *dat*) to please, e.g., **come piace a Dio** as it pleases God; to like, e.g., **gli piace il ballo** he likes dancing

piacévole *adj* pleasant, pleasing

piacevolézza *f* pleasantness; off-color joke

pia·ga *f* (-ghe) sore; ulcer; wound; plague; (joc) bore; **piaga di decubito** bedsore

piagare §209 *tr* to make sore, injure

piàg·gia *f* (-ge) (archaic) declivity; (lit) clime, country

piaggiare §290 *tr* (lit) to flatter, blandish || *intr* (archaic) to coast

piagnistèo *m* whining

piagnó·ne -na *mf* (coll) weeper, crybaby

piagnucolare (**piagnùcolo**) *intr* to whimper, whine

piagnucoló·ne -na *mf* whimperer, crybaby

piagnucoló·so -sa [s] *adj* whimpering, whining

pialla *f* (carp) plane

piallàc·cio *m* (-ci) veneer

piallare *tr* (carp) to plane

piallatrice *f* (carp) planer

piallatura *f* (carp) planing

piana *f* plain; wide table

pianale *m* plain; platform; (rr) flatcar, platform car

pianeggiante *adj* plane, level

pianèlla *f* mule (*slipper*); tile

pianeròttolo *m* landing (*of stairs*); ledge

pianè·ta *m* (-ti) planet; horoscope || *f* (eccl) chasuble

piàngere §215 *tr* to shed (*tears*); to mourn, lament; **piàngere miseria** to cry poverty || *intr* to cry, weep

piangimisè·ria *mf* (-ria) poverty-crying penny pincher

piangiucchiare §287 *intr* to whimper

pianificare §197 (**pianìfico**) *tr* to level; (econ) to plan

pianifica·tóre -trice *mf* planner

pianino *m* (coll) barrel organ

piani·sta *mf* (-sti -ste) pianist

pia·no -na *adj* plane; plain, flat || *m* plain; plane; floor; plateau; plan; map; (mus) piano; **di primo piano** first-class; **in piano** horizontal; **piano di coda** (aer) tail assembly; **piano di studio** curriculum; **piano regolatore** building plan; **piano terra** ground floor; **primo piano** (phot) close-up; (theat) foreground || *f* see **piana** || **piano** *adv* slowly; softly

pianofòrte *m* piano; **pianoforte a coda** grand piano

pianòla *f* player piano

pianòro *m* plateau

pianotèr·ra *m* (-ra) ground floor

pianta *f* sole (*of foot*); plan, map; floor plan; **di sana pianta** wholly; **in pianta stabile** permanent (*employee*); **pianta rampicante** (bot) climber

piantagióne *f* plantation

piantana *f* scaffolding

piantare *tr* to plant; to set up (*e.g., a gun emplacement*); to pitch (*a tent*); **piantala!** (slang) cut it out!; **piantare baracca e burattini** (coll) to clear out; **piantar chiodi** (coll) to go into debt; **piantare gli occhi addosso a** to stare at; **piantare in asso** to leave in the lurch || *ref* to place oneself; to abandon one another

pianta·to -ta *adj* planted; stuck; driven; **bien piantato** well-built (*person*)

pianta·tóre -trice *mf* planter

pianterréno *m* ground floor

piantito *m* (coll) floor

pianto *m* weeping, tears; sadness; (bot) sap; (coll) sight, mess

piantonare (**piantóno**) *tr* to watch, guard

piantóne *m* watchman; (mil) orderly; (mil) sentry; (bot) cutting, shoot; **piantone di guida** (aut) steering wheel column

pianura *f* plain

piastra *f* plate; piaster (*coin*)

piastrèlla *f* tile; small flat stone; bounce (*of an airplane on landing*)

piastrellaménto *m* bump, bounce (*of motorboat or airplane*)

piastrelli·sta *m* (-sti) tiler, tile layer

piastrina *f* or **piastrino** *m* small plate; (mil) dog tag; (biol) platelet

piatire §176 *intr* (lit) to argue; (coll) to beg insistently

piattafórma *f* platform; roadbed (*of highway*); (rr) turntable; (pol) plank; **piattaforma di lancio** launching pad

piattèllo *m* small dish; bobêche; clay pigeon

piattina *f* electric cord; metal band; (min) wagon

piattino *m* saucer

piat·to -ta *adj* flat || *m* dish, plate; pan (*of scale*); pot (*in gambling*); course (*of meal*); cover (*of book*); flat (*e.g., of blade*); **piatti** (mus) cymbals; **piatto del grammofono** turntable; **piatto del giorno** plat du jour; **piatto di lenticchie** (Bib & fig) mess of pottage; **piatto fondo** soup dish; **piatto forte** pièce de résistance

piàttola *f* (zool) crab louse; (coll) cockroach; (vulg) bore

piazza *f* square; plaza; crowd; market; fortress; **andare in piazza** (coll) to become bald; **di piazza** common, ordinary; **di piazza** for hire (*e.g., cab*); **fare la piazza** (com) to canvass for customers; **far piazza pulita di** to get rid of; to clean out; **mettere in piazza** to noise abroad; **piazza d'armi** parade ground; **scendere in piazza** to take to the streets

piazzafòrte *f* (**piazzefòrti**) stronghold, fortress

piazzale *m* large square, esplanade, plaza

piazzaménto *m* placement; (sports) position (*of a team*)

piazzare *tr* to place; to sell || *ref* to place; to show (*said of a racing horse*)

piazza·to -ta adj placed; arrived (at a high position) || f row, brawl

piazzi·sta m (-sti) salesman; traveling salesman

piazzòla f court, place; rest area (off a highway); (mil) emplacement; **piazzola di partenza** (golf) tee

pi·ca f (-che) (orn) magpie

picaré·sco -sca adj (-schi -sche) picaresque

pic·ca f (-che) pike; pique; **per picca** out of spite; **picche** (cards) spades; **rispondere picche** (fig) to answer no

piccante adj piquant, racy

piccare §197 tr (obs) to prick || ref to become angry; **piccarsi di** to pride oneself on

pic·chè f (-chè) piqué

picchettaménto m picketing

picchettare (picchétto) tr to stake out; to picket

picchétto m stake; picket; (mil) detail

picchiare §287 tr to hit, strike || intr to knock; to strike; to tap (said, e.g., of rain); (aer) to nose-dive; **picchiare in testa** (aut) to knock || ref to hit one another

picchiata f hit, blow; (aer) nose dive

picchia·tóre -trice mf hitter || m (boxing) puncher

picchierellare (picchierèllo) tr & intr to tap

picchiettare (picchiétto) tr to tap; to scrape; to speckle || intr to tap

picchiet·tìo m (-tìi) patter (e.g., of rain)

pìc·chio m (-chi) knock; (orn) woodpecker; **di picchio** all of a sudden

picchiòtto m knocker (on door)

piccinerìa f pettiness

picci·no -na adj little, tiny; petty || mf child; baby

picciòlo -na m stem (e.g., of cherry); leaf-stalk, petiole

piccionàia f dovecote; loft; attic; (theat) upper gallery

piccióne -na mf pigeon; **pigliare due piccioni con una fava** to hit two birds with one stone

pic·co m (-chi) peak; (naut) gaff; **andare a picco** to sink; to go to ruin; **a picco** vertically; **picco di carico** (naut) derrick

piccolézza f smallness; trifle

pìcco·lo -la adj small; low (speed); short (distance); young; petty; **da piccolo** when young; **in piccolo** on a small scale; **nel mio piccolo** with my modest abilities || mf child

piccóne m pick

piccòzza f mattock (for mountain climbing)

pidocchierìa f stinginess; meanness

pidòc·chio m (-chi) louse; **pidocchio rifatto** (slang) parvenu

pidocchió·so -sa [s] adj lousy; stingy

piè m (piè) (lit) foot; **ad ogni piè sospinto** on every occasion; **saltare a piè pari** to skip with the feet together; (fig) to skip over

piède m foot; leg (of table); stalk (of salad); bottom (of column); trunk (of tree); footing; **alzarsi in piedi** to stand up; **a piede libero** free; **a piedi** on foot; **a piedi nudi** barefooted; **con i piedi di piombo** cautiously; **essere in piedi** to be up and around; **fare con i piedi** to botch; **mettere un piede in fallo** to stumble; **piede di porco** crowbar; **prendere piede** to take hold; **puntare i piedi** to balk; **su due piedi** offhand; **tenere il piede in due staffe** to carry water on both shoulders

piedestallo or **piedistallo** m pedestal

piedritto m buttress

piè·ga f (-ghe) bend; crease; pleat; crimp; wrinkle; (fig) turn; **prendere una cattiva piega** to take a turn for the worse

piegare §209 (**piègo**) tr to bend; to wave (hair); to fold; to pleat; to bow (head) || intr to turn || ref to bow; to bend; to buckle; to yield

piega·tóre -trice mf folder || f folding machine

piegatura f fold, crease

pieghettare (pieghétto) tr to pleat

pieghévole adj folding; pliant; (fig) versatile || m folder

pieghevolézza f flexibility

piè·go m (-ghi) folder; bundle of papers

pièna f flood; rise (of river); crowd; (fig) overflow; **in piena** overflowing

pienézza f plenitude, fullness

piè·no -na adj full; solid; broad (daylight); full (honors); **a pieno** or **in pieno** to the full; **colpire nel pieno** to hit the bull's eye; **pieno di** alive with; **pieno di sé** conceited; **pieno zeppo** replete, chock-full || m fullness; height (e.g., of winter); **fare il pieno** (aut) to fill up || f see **piena**

pie·tà f (-tà) mercy; pity; (lit) piety

pietanza f main course

pietó·so -sa [s] adj pitiful, piteous; merciful

piètra f stone; rock; **pietra angolare** cornerstone; **pietra da affilare** whetstone; **pietra da sarto** French chalk; **pietra dello scandalo** source of scandal; **pietra di paragone** touchstone; **pietra focaia** flint; **pietra miliare** milestone; **pietra tombale** tombstone; **posare la prima pietra** to lay the cornerstone

pietrificare §197 (**pietrìfico**) tr & ref to petrify

pietrina f flint (for lighter)

pietrì·sco m (-schi) rubble; (rr) ballast

Piètro m Peter

pietró·so -sa [s] adj (lit) stony

pievano m parish priest

pìffero m pipe, fife

pìgia m — **pigia pigia** crowd, throng

pigia·ma m (-ma & -mi) pajamas

pigiare §290 tr to squeeze, press || intr to insist || ref to squeeze

pigia·tóre -trice mf presser (of grapes) || f wine press

pigiatura f pressing, squeezing

pigionante mf tenant

pigióne f rent, rental; **dare a pigione** to rent; to grant the possession of; **prendere a pigione** to rent; to hold for payment

pigliamó·sche *m* (**-sche**) flypaper; fly-trap; (orn) flycatcher

pigliare §280 *tr* to take, catch; to mistake; **che Le piglia?** what's the matter with you? || *ref*—**pigliarsela (con)** to get angry (at)

pì·glio *m* (**-gli**) hold; countenance; **dar di piglio a** to grab

pigménto *m* pigment

pigmè·o -a *adj & mf* pygmy; Pygmy

pigna *f* strainer (*at the end of a suction pipe*); bunch (*of grapes*); (bot) pine cone

pignatta *f* pot

pignò·lo -la *adj* finicky, fussy || *m* pine nut

pignóne *m* pinion; embankment

pignoraménto *m* (law) seizure

pignorare (**pìgnoro**) *tr* (law) to seize

pigolare (**pìgolo**) *intr* to peep (*said, e.g., of young birds*)

pigolì·o *m* (**-i**) peep (*e.g., of a young bird*)

pigrìzia *f* laziness

pì·gro -gra *adj* lazy; (lit) sluggish

pila *f* pier; buttress (*of bridge*); heap; sink; font; (elec) cell; (elec) battery; **pila atomica** atomic pile

pilastro *m* pier, pillar

pillàcchera *f* mud splash; (fig) fault

pillola *f* pill; (slang) bullet; **addolcire la pillola** to sugar-coat the pill

pilóne *m* pier; pylon

pilò·ta (**-ti -te**) *adj* pilot || *mf* pilot; (aut) driver

pilotàg·gio *m* (**-gi**) piloting; steering

pilotare (**pilòto**) *tr* to pilot; to drive

pilotina *f* (naut) pilot boat

piluccare §197 *tr* to pluck (*e.g., grapes one by one*); to nibble, pick at; to scrounge; (lit) to consume

piménto *m* allspice

pinacotè·ca *f* (**-che**) picture gallery

pinéta *f* pine grove

pìngue *adj* fat; rich

pinguédine *f* fatness, corpulence

pinguino *m* penguin

pinna *f* fin (*of fish*); flipper; (zool) pen shell (*mussel*)

pinnàcolo *m* pinnacle

pino *m* pine tree; **pino marittimo** pinaster; **pino silvestre** Scotch fir

pinòlo *m* pine nut

pinta *f* pint

pinza *f* claw (*of lobster*); **pinza emostatica** hemostat; **pinza tagliafili** wire cutter; **pinze clippers; pliers; pincers

pinzatrice *f* stapler

pinzétte *fpl* tweezers, pliers

pinzòche·ro -ra *mf* bigot

pì·o -a *adj* (**-i -e**) pious; charitable || **Pio** *m* Pius

piòg·gia *f* (**-ge**) rain

piòlo *m* peg; rung (*of ladder*); picket, stake

piombàggine *f* graphite

piombare (**piómbo**) *tr* to lead; to seal; to knock down; to fill (*a tooth*) || *intr* to fall; to swoop down

piombatura *f* leading; filling (*of tooth*)

piombino *m* weight; seal; plumb; plumb bob

piómbo *m* lead; **a piombo** perpendicularly; **di piombo** suddenly

pioneristi·co -ca *adj* (**-ci -che**) pioneering

pionière *m* pioneer

piòppo *m* poplar; **pioppo tremolo** aspen

piorrèa *f* pyorrhea

piotare (**piòto**) *tr* to sod

piova·no -na *adj* rain (*water*)

piova·sco *m* (**-schi**) rain squall

piovènte *m* pitch, slope

piòvere §216 *intr* (ESSERE) to rain; to pour; to flock (*said of people*); **piovere addosso a** to rain down on; **piovere su** to flow down over || *impers* (ESSERE & AVERE)—**piove** it is raining; it is leaking (*from rain*); **piove a catinelle** or **a dirotto** it is raining cats and dogs

piovigginare (**piovìggina**) *impers* (ESSERE & AVERE)—**pioviggina** it is drizzling

piovigginó·so -sa [s] *adj* drizzling, drizzly

piovór·no -na *adj* (lit) var of **piovoso**

piovosi·tà [s] *f* (**-tà**) raininess; rainfall

piovó·so -sa [s] *adj* rainy

piòvra *f* octopus; (fig) leech

pipa *f* pipe; **non valere una pipa di tabacco** to not be worth a tinker's dam

pipare *intr* to smoke a pipe

pipata *f* pipe, pipeful

pipistrèllo *m* (zool) bat

pipita *f* hangnail; (vet) pip

pira *f* (lit) pyre

piràmide *f* pyramid

pira·ta *adj invar* pirate || *m* (**-ti**) pirate; **pirata dell'aria** skyjacker; **pirata della strada** hit-and-run driver

pirateggiare §290 (**piratéggio**) *intr* to pirate

pirateria *f* piracy; **pirateria letteraria** piracy of literary works

Pirenèi *mpl* Pyrenees

pìri·co -ca *adj* (**-ci -che**) fireworks; **polvere pirica** gunpowder

pirite *f* pyrite

piroétta *f* pirouette

pirò·ga *f* (**-ghe**) pirogue

pirolisi *f* (chem) cracking

piróne *m* (mus) tuning pin

piròscafo *m* steamship; **piroscafo da carico** (naut) freighter; **piroscafo da passeggeri** passenger ship

piroscissióne *f* (chem) cracking

pirotècni·co -ca (**-ci -che**) *adj* pyrotecnic || *m* pyrotecnist || *f* fireworks, pyrotechnics

pisciare §128 *intr* (vulg) to urinate

piscia-tóio *m* (**-tói**) (vulg) street urinal

piscina *f* swimming pool

pisèllo [s] *m* pea; **pisello odoroso** sweet pea

pisolare (**pìsolo**) *intr* (coll) to doze

pìsolo *m* (coll) nap; **schiacciare un pisolo** (coll) to take a nap

pìsside *f* (eccl) pyx; (bot) pyxidium

pista *f* track; ring (*of circus*); race track, speedway (*for car races*); ski run; (aer) runway; **pista ciclabile** bicycle trail; **pista da ballo** dance floor; **seguire una pista** to follow a clue

pistàc·chio m (-chi) pistachio

pistillo m (bot) pistil

pistòla f pistol

pistolettata f pistol shot

pistolòtto m lecture, talking-to; theatrical peroration

pistóne m piston; plunger

pitagòri·co -ca adj & m (-ci -che) Pythagorean

pitale m (coll) chamber pot

pitoccare §197 (**pitòcco**) intr to beg

pitòc·co m (-chi) beggar; miser

pitóne m python

pittima f plaster; (fig) bore

pit·tóre -trice mf painter

pittoré·sco -sca adj (-schi -sche) picturesque

pittòri·co -ca adj (-ci -che) pictorial

pittura f painting; picture; (coll) paint

pitturare tr to paint; to varnish || ref to put on make-up

più adj invar more; several || m (**più**) plus; most; **credersi da più** to believe oneself superior; **dal più al meno** about, more or less; **i più** most, the majority; **parlare del più e del meno** (coll) to make small talk || adv more; again; **a più non posso** to the very utmost; **in più** besides; **mai più** never again; **non poterne più** to be exhausted; **per di più** besides; **per lo più** for the most part; **più o meno** more or less; **tanto più** moreover; **tutt'al più** mostly

piuma f feather, plume; **piume** (fig) bed

piumàc·cio m (-ci) feather pillow

piumàg·gio m (-gi) plumage

piumino m down; comforter; puff, powder puff; feather duster

piuttòsto adv rather; somewhat

piva f bagpipe; **tornare con le pive nel sacco** to return bitterly disappointed

pivèllo m greenhorn; whippersnapper

pivière m (orn) plover

pizza f pizza; (mov) canister; (coll) bore

pizzaiò·lo -la mf owner of pizzeria || m pizza baker | f—**alla pizzaiola** prepared with tomato and garlic sauce

pizzardóne m (coll) cop, officer

pizzicàgno·lo -la mf grocer; sausage dealer

pizzicare §197 (**pìzzico**) tr to pinch; to pluck; to bite, burn; (mus) to pick, twang

pizzicherìa f delicatessen, grocery

pìzzi·co m (-chi) pinch

pizzicóre m itch

pizzicòtto m pinch; **dar pizzicotti a** to pinch

pizzo m peak (of mountain); goatee; lace

placare §197 tr to placate || ref to calm down

plac·ca f (-che) plate; plaque; tag, badge; (elec, rad) plate; (pathol) blotch, spot

placcare §197 tr to plate; (sports) to tackle

plàci·do -da adj placid

plafond m (**plafond**) ceiling; (aer) ceiling; (com) top credit

pla·ga f (-ghe) (lit) clime, region

plagiare §290 tr to plagiarize

plagià·rio -ria (-ri -rie) adj plagiaristic || mf plagiarist

plà·gio m (-gi) plagiarism

planare intr to glide

planata f (aer) gliding

plàn·cia f (-ce) (naut) gangplank; (naut) bridge

planetà·rio -ria (-ri -rie) adj planetary || m planetarium; (aut) planetary gear

plantare m arch support

pla·sma m (-smi) plasma

plasmare tr to mold, shape

plàsti·ca f (-che) plastic art; plastics; plastic surgery; plastic

plasticare §197 (**plàstico**) tr to mold, shape; to cover with plastic

plàsti·co -ca (-ci -che) adj plastic || m relief map; maquette; plastic bomb || f see **plastica**

plastilina f modeling clay

plastron m (plastron) ascot

plàtano m plane tree; **platano americano** buttonwood tree

platèa f audience; (theat) orchestra; (archit) foundation

plateale adj obvious; plebeian

plàtina f (typ) platen

platinare (**plàtino**) tr to platinize; to bleach (hair)

plàtino m platinum

Platóne m Plato

plaudènte adj enthusiastic

plàudere (**plàudo**) & **plaudire** (**plàudo**) intr to applaud; (with dat) to applaud, e.g., **plaudere alla generosità** to applaud the generosity

plausìbile adj plausible

plàuso m (lit) applause, praise

plebàglia f rabble

plèbe f populace; (lit) crowd

plebè·o -a adj & mf plebeian

plebiscito m plebiscite

plenà·rio -ria adj (-ri -rie) plenary

plenilù·nio m (-ni) full moon

plenipotenzià·rio -ria adj & m (-ri -rie) plenipotentiary

plètora f plethora

plèttro m (mus) pick, plectrum

pleurite f (pathol) pleurisy

pli·co m (-chi) sealed document; bundle of papers; **in plico a parte** or **in plico separato** under separate cover

plotóne m platoon; **plotone d'esecuzione** firing squad

plùmbe·o -a adj lead, leaden

plurale adj & m plural; **al plurale** in the plural

plurilìngue adj multilingual

plurimotóre adj multimotored || m multimotor

pluristàdio adj invar (rok) multistage

plusvalènza f unearned increment

plusvalóre m; surplus value (in Marxist economics)

Plutarco m Plutarch

plutocrazìa f plutocracy

Plutóne m Pluto

plutònio m plutonium
pluviale adj rain ‖ m waterspout
pneumàti·co -**ca** (-**ci** -**che**) adj pneumatic, air ‖ m tire; **pneumatico da neve** snow tire
po' m see **poco**
pochézza f lack, scarcity
pò·co -**ca** (-**chi** -**che**) adj little; short (distance); poor (health; memory); (with collective nouns) few, e.g., **poca gente** few people; (with plural nouns) a few, e.g., **fra pochi mesi** in a few months; (with plural nouns having singular meaning in English) little, e.g., **pochi quattrini** little money ‖ m invar little; short distance; short time; **a ogni poco** often; **da poco a little while ago**; of no account; **da un bel po'** quite a while; quite a while ago; **fra poco** in a little while; **manca poco a** it won't be long till; **manca poco che** (e.g., il ragazzo) non + subj (e.g., the boy) almost + ind; **per poco non** almost; **poco di buono** good-for-nothing; **poco fa** a little while ago; **saper di poco** to taste flat; **un poco di** or **un po' di** a little ‖ f—**poca di buono** hussy ‖ **poco** adv little; **poco bene** poorly; **poco dopo** shortly after; **poco male** not too poorly
podagra f gout
podére m farm, country property
poderó·so -**sa** [s] adj powerful
pode·stà m (-**stà**) (hist) mayor; (hist) podesta
podia·tra mf (-**tri** -**tre**) chiropodist
pò·dio m (-**di**) podium; platform; (archit) base
podismo m foot racing
podi·sta mf (-**sti** -**ste**) foot racer
poè·ma m (-**mi**) long poem
poesìa f poetry; poem
poè·ta m (-**ti**) poet
poetéssa f poetess
poèti·co -**ca** (-**ci** -**che**) adj poetic(al) ‖ f poetics
pòg·gia f (-**ge**) leeward
poggiare §290 (**pòggio**) tr to lean ‖ intr to be based; (mil) to move; (naut) to sail before the wind; (archaic) to rise
poggiatè·sta m (-**sta**) headrest; (aut) head restrainer
pòg·gio m (-**gi**) hillock, knoll
poggiòlo m balcony
pòi m future ‖ f adv then; later; **a poi** until later; **poi dopo** later on
poiana f buzzard
poiché conj since, as; (lit) after
pòker m poker (game); four of a kind; **poker di re** four kings
polac·co -**ca** (-**chi** -**che**) adj Polish ‖ mf Pole ‖ f (mus) polonaise
polare adj pole, polar
polarizzare [ddzz] tr to polarize
pòl·ca f (-**che**) polka
polèmi·co -**ca** (-**ci** -**che**) adj polemical ‖ f polemics
polemizzare [ddzz] intr to engage in polemics
polèna f (naut) figurehead
polènta f corn mush

polentina f poultice
poliambulanza f clinic, emergency ward
policlìni·co m (-**ci**) polyclinic
polifonìa f polyphony
polìga·mo -**ma** adj polygamous ‖ m polygamist
poliglòt·ta adj & mf (-**ti** -**te**) polyglot
poliglòt·to -**ta** adj & mf polyglot
polìgono m polygon; **poligono di tiro** shooting range
polìgrafo m author skilled in many subjects; multigraph
polinesia·no -**na** adj & mf Polynesian
polinò·mio m (-**mi**) polynomial
pòlio f (coll) polio
poliomielite f poliomielitis, infantile paralysis
pòlipo m (pathol, zool) polyp
polisìlla·bo -**ba** adj polysyllabic ‖ m polysyllable
poli·sta m (-**sti**) polo player
politea·ma m (-**mi**) theater
politècni·co -**ca** (-**ci** -**che**) adj polytechnic ‖ m polytechnic institute
politei·sta adj (-**sti** -**ste**) polytheistic ‖ mf polytheist
politeìsti·co -**ca** adj (-**ci** -**che**) polytheistic
politézza f smoothness
polìti·ca f (-**che**) politics; policy
politicante mf petty politician
polìti·co -**ca** (-**ci** -**che**) adj political ‖ m politician ‖ f see **politica**
polìtti·co m (-**ci**) polyptych
polizìa f police; **polizia sanitaria** health department; **polizia stradale** highway patrol; **polizia tributaria** income-tax investigation department
polizié·sco -**sca** adj (-**schi** -**sche**) police (car); detective (story)
poliziòtto adj masc police (dog) ‖ m policeman; detective; **poliziotto in borghese** plain-clothes man
pòlizza f policy; ticket (e.g., of pawnbroker); **polizza di carico** bill of lading
pólla f spring (of water)
pol·làio m (-**lài**) chicken coop
pollaiò·lo -**la** mf chicken dealer
pollame m poultry
pollastra f pullet; (coll) chick
pollerìa f poultry shop
pòllice m thumb; big toe; inch
pollicoltura f poultry raising
pòlline m pollen
pollivéndo·lo -**la** mf poultry dealer
póllo m chicken; (fig) sucker; **conoscere i propri polli** (fig) to know one's onions; **pollo d'India** turkey
pollóne m (bot) shoot; (fig) offspring
polmóne m lung; **a pieni polmoni** at the top of one's lungs; **polmone d'acciaio** iron lung
polmonite f pneumonia
pòlo m pole; polo shirt; (sports) polo
Polònia, la Poland
pólpa f meat; pulp; flesh (of fruit); (fig) gist; **in polpe** (hist) in knee breeches
polpàc·cio m (-**ci**) calf (of leg); cut of meat; ball of thumb

polpastrèllo *m* finger tip
polpétta *f* meat ball; meat patty, cutlet
polpettóne *m* meat loaf; (fig) hash
pólpo *m* (zool) octopus
polpó·so -sa [s] *adj* pulpy, fleshy
polpu·to -ta *adj* meaty
polsino *m* cuff
pólso *m* pulse; wrist; cuff, wristband; strong hand, energy; **di polso** energetic
poltiglia *f* mash; slush
poltrire §176 *intr* to idle; to loll in bed
poltróna *f* armchair; (theat) orchestra seat; **poltrona a orecchioni** wing chair; **poltrona a sdraio** chaise longue; **poltrona letto** day bed
poltroncina *f* parquet-circle seat
poltró·ne -na *mf* lazybones, sluggard || *f* see **poltrona**
poltroneria *f* laziness
poltronissima *f* (theat) first-row seat
pólvere *f* dust; powder; **in polvere** powdered; **polvere da sparo** gunpowder; **polvere di stelle** stardust; **polvere nera** or **pirica** gunpowder; **polveri** gunpowder
polverièra *f* powder magazine; (fig) tinderbox, trouble spot
polverifi·cio *m* (-**ci**) powder works
polverina *f* (pharm) powder
polverino *m* pounce, sand
polverizzare [ddzz] *tr* to crush, powder; to atomize; to pulverize
polverizza·to -ta [ddzz] *adj* powdered (*sugar*)
polverizzatóre [ddzz] *m* atomizer
polveróne *m* dust cloud
polveró·so -sa [s] *adj* dusty; powdery (*snow*)
pomata *f* ointment; pomade
pomella·to -ta *adj* dapple-grey
pomèllo *m* cheek; cheekbone; pommel, knob
pomeridia·no -na *adj* afternoon, P.M.
pomerig·gio *m* (-**gi**) afternoon
pomiciare §128 (**pómicio**) *tr* to pumice || *intr* (slang) to spoon
pomicióne *m* (slang) spooner
pomidòro *m* var of **pomodoro**
pómo *m* apple; knob; pommel (*of saddle*); **pomo della discordia** apple of discord; **pomo di Adamo** Adam's apple; **pomo di terra** potato
pomodòro *m* tomato; **pomodoro di mare** (zool) sea anemone
pómolo *m* (coll) knob, handle
pómpa *f* pump; pomp; state; **in pompa magna** all dressed up; **pompa aspirante** suction pump; **pompa premente** force pump; see **imprenditore** and **impresa**
pompare (**pómpo**) *tr* to pump; to pump up
pompèlmo *m* grapefruit
pompière *m* fireman
pompó·so -sa [s] *adj* pompous
pòn·ce *m* (-**ci**) punch
ponderare (**pòndero**) *tr* to weigh, ponder; to weight || *intr* to think it over
pondera·to -ta *adj* considerate, careful
ponderó·so -sa [s] *adj* ponderous

ponènte *m* west; west wind; West; West Wind
pónte *m* bridge; metal scaffolding; (aut) axle; (naut) deck; **fare il ponte** to take the day off between two holidays; **fare ponti d'oro** a to offer a good way out to; **ponte aereo** airlift; **ponte delle segnalazioni** (rr) gantry; **ponte di chiatte** pontoon bridge; **ponte di comando** (naut) bridge; **ponte di volo** flight deck; **ponte levatoio** drawbridge; **ponte radio** radio communication; **ponte sospeso** suspension bridge
pontéfice *m* pontiff; (hist) pontifex
pontéggio *m* scaffolding
ponticèllo *m* small bridge; nosepiece (*of eyeglasses*); (mus) bridge
pontière *m* (mil) engineer
pontificale *adj* pontifical || *m* pontifical mass
pontifi·cio -cia *adj* (-**ci** -**cie**) papal
pontile *m* pier
pontóne *m* pontoon, barge
ponzare (**pónzo**) *tr* (coll) to strain to accomplish || *intr* (coll) to rack one's brains
popeli·ne *f* (-**ne**) broadcloth
popola·no -na *adj* popular || *mf* commoner
popolare *adj* popular || *v* (**pòpolo**) *tr* to people, populate || *ref* to be inhabited
popolarità *f* popularity
popola·to -ta *adj* peopled; crowded
popolazióne *f* population
pòpolo *m* people; crowd; **popolo grasso** (hist) rich bourgeoisie; **popolo minuto** (hist) artisans, common people
popoló·so -sa [s] *adj* populous
popóne *m* (coll) melon
póppa *f* breast; (naut) stern; (lit) ship; **a poppa** astern, aft
poppante *adj* & *mf* suckling
poppare (**póppo**) *tr* to suckle
poppa·tóio *m* (-**tói**) nursing bottle
poppavia *f* a **poppavia** astern, aft
pòr·ca *f* (-**che**) ridge (*between furrows*); sow
porcacció·ne -na *m* cad, rake || *f* slut
por·càio -cài (-**cài**) swineherd; pigsty
porcellana *f* porcelain, china; (bot) purslane
porcellino *m* piggy; **porcellino d'India** guinea pig
porcheria *f* dirt; (coll) dirty trick; (coll) botch
porchétta *f* roast suckling pig
porcile *m* pigsty
porci·no -na *adj* pig || *m* (bot) boletus
pòr·co -ca *mf* (-**ci** -**che**) pig, hog, swine; pork; **porco mondo!** (slang) heck! || *f* see **porca**
porcospino *m* porcupine
pòrfido *m* porphyry
pòrgere §217 *tr* to hand, offer; to relate; **porgere l'orecchio** to lend an ear || *intr* to declaim || *ref* to appear, show up
pornografia *f* pornography
pòro *m* pore
poró·so -sa [s] *adj* porous
pórpora *f* purple

porpora·to -ta *adj* purple ‖ *m* purple; cardinal

porpori·no -na *adj* purple

pórre §218 *tr* to put; to repose (*trust*); to set (*a limit; one's foot*); to lay (*a stone*); to pose (*a question*); to pay (*attention*); to suppose; to advance (*the candidacy*); **porre gli occhi addosso a** to lay one's eyes on; **porre in dubbio** to cast doubt on; **porre mano a** to set to work at; **porre termine a** to put an end to; **posto che** since, provided ‖ *ref* to place oneself; **porsi in cammino** to set out or forth; **porsi in salvo** to reach safety

pòrro *m* wart; (bot) leek

pòrta *f* door; gate; (cricket) wicket; (sports) goal; **di porta in porta** door-to-door; **fuori porta** outside the city limits; **mettere alla porta** to dismiss, fire; **porta di servizio** delivery entrance; **porta scorrevole** sliding door; **porta stagna** (naut; theat) safety door

portabagà·gli *m* (**-gli**) porter; baggage rack

portabandiè·ra *m* (**-ra**) standard-bearer

portàbile *adj* portable

portàbi·ti *m* (**-ti**) coat hanger

portabottí·glie *m* (**-glie**) bottle rack

portacar·te *adj invar* & *m* (**-te**) folder

portacati·no *adj invar* washstand-supporting ‖ *m* (**-no**) washstand

portacéne·re *m* (**-re**) ashtray

portachia·vi *m* (**-vi**) key ring

portaci·pria *m* (**-pria**) compact

portadí·schi *m* (**-schi**) record cabinet, record rack; turntable

portadól·ci *m* (**-ci**) candy dish

portaère·i *f* (**-i**) aircraft carrier

portaferi·ti *m* (**-ti**) (mil) stretcher bearer

portafinèstra *f* (**portefinèstre**) French window

portafió·ri *m* (**-ri**) flower vase

portafò·gli *m* (**-gli**) or **portafò·glio** *m* (**-gli**) billfold, wallet; pocketbook; portfolio

portafortu·na *m* (**-na**) charm, amulet

portafrut·ta *m* (**-ta**) fruit dish

portafusíbi·li *m* (**-li**) fuse box

portagiò·ie *m* (**-ie**) jewel box

portaimmondí·zie *m* (**-zie**) trash can, garbage can

portainsé·gna *m* (**-gna**) standard-bearer

portalàmpa·da *m* (**-da**) (elec) socket

portale *m* portal

portalèt·te·re (**-re**) *mf* letter carrier ‖ *m* postman, mailman

portamaz·ze *m* (**-ze**) caddie

portaménto *m* posture; gait; (fig) behavior

portami·na *m* (**-na**) mechanical pencil

portamìssi·li (**-li**) *adj invar* missile-carrying ‖ *m* missile carrier

portamoné·te *m* (**-te**) purse

portamùsi·ca *m* (**-ca**) music stand

portante *adj* carrying; (archit) weight-bearing; (aer) lifting; (rad) carrier ‖ *m* amble

portantìna *f* sedan chair; stretcher

portantíno *m* bearer (*of sedan chair*); stretcher bearer

portanza *f* (archit) capacity; (aer) lift

portaombrèl·li *m* (**-li**) umbrella stand

portaórdi·ni *m* (**-ni**) (mil) messenger

portapac·chi *m* (**-chi**) parcel delivery man; basket (*on bicycle*)

portapén·ne *m* (**-ne**) penholder

portapiat·ti *m* (**-ti**) dish rack

portaposa·te [s] *m* (**-te**) silverware chest

portapran·zi [dz] *m* (**-zi**) dinner pail

portaraz·zi (**-zi**) [ddzz] *adj invar* missile-carrying ‖ *m* missile carrier

portare (**pòrto**) *tr* to carry; to bring; to take; to carry along; to lead; to herald; to praise; to wear; to drive (*car*); to run (*a candidate*); to adduce; to nurture (*hatred*); (aut) to hold (*e.g., five people*); **portare a conoscenza di** to let know; **portare avanti** to carry forward; **portare in alto** to lift; **portare via** to steal; to take away ‖ *intr* to carry (*said of a gun*) ‖ *ref* to move; to behave; to be (*a candidate*)

portaritrat·ti *m* (**-ti**) picture frame

portasapó·ne *m* (**-ne**) soap dish

portasigarét·te *m* (**-te**) cigarette case

portasiga·ri *m* (**-ri**) cigar case; humidor

portaspíl·li *m* (**-li**) pincushion

portata *f* course (*of a meal*); capacity; flow (*of river*); compass (*of voice*); range (*of voice or gun*); importance; (naut) burden; (naut) tonnage; **a portata di mano** within reach; **a portata di voce** within call, within earshot

portatèsse·re *m* (**-re**) card case

portàtile *adj* portable

porta·to -ta *adj* worn; **portato a** leaning toward ‖ *m* result, effect ‖ *f* see **portata**

porta·tóre -trice *mf* bearer

portavagliòlo *m* napkin ring

portauò·vo *m* (**-vo**) eggcup

portavó·ce *m* (**-ce**) megaphone; (fig) mouthpiece

porte-enfant *m* (**porte-enfant**) baby bunting

portèllo *m* wicket; leaf (*of cabinet door*); (naut) porthole

portènto *m* portent

portica·to -ta *adj* arcaded ‖ *m* arcade

pòrti·co *m* (**-ci**) portico, arcade, colonnade; shed

portiè·re -ra *mf* concierge ‖ *m* janitor, doorman; (sports) goalkeeper ‖ *f* portiere (*in church door*); (aut) door

porti·nàio -nàia (**-nài -nàie**) *adj* door-, door-keeping ‖ *mf* doorkeeper, concierge

portinerìa *f* janitor's quarters

pòrto *m* port, harbor; transportation charge; port wine; goal; **condurre a buon porto** to carry to fruition; **franco di porto** prepaid, postpaid; **porto a carico del mittente** postage prepaid; **porto assegnato** charges to be paid by addressee; **porto d'armi** permit to carry arms; **porto franco** free port

Portogallo, il Portugal

portoghése [s] *adj* & *mf* Portuguese;

fare il portoghese (theat) to crash the gate

portóne *m* portal

portorica·no -na *adj & nf* Puerto Rican

Portorico *m* Puerto Rico

portuale *adj* port, harbor || *m* dock worker, longshoreman

porzióne *f* portion

pòsa [s] *f* laying (*e.g., of cornerstone*); posing (*for portrait*); posture, affectation, pose; dregs; (phot) exposure; (lit) rest; **senza posa** relentless; relentlessly

posami·ne (-ne) [s] *adj invar* minelaying || *f* minelayer

posare [s] (**pòso**) *tr* to lay, put down || *intr* to lie; to settle; to pose; **posare a** to pose as || *ref* to settle; to alight; (lit) to rest

posata [s] *f* cover, place (*at table*); table utensil (*knife, fork or spoon*); **posate** knife, fork and spoon

posateria [s] *f* service (*of knives, forks, and spoons*)

posa·to -ta [s] *adj* sedate, quiet; placed || *f* see **posata**

posa·tóre -trice [s] *mf* poseur || *m* layer, installer (*of cables or pipes*)

pòscia *adv* then, afterwards; **poscia che** after

poscritto *m* postscript

posdatare *tr* var of **postdatare**

posdomani *adv* (lit) day after tomorrow

positivaménte *adv* for sure

positi·vo -va *adj* positive || *f* (phot) positive, print

posizióne *f* position; status; (fig) stand

pospórre §218 *tr* to put off, postpone; to put last; **posporre qlco a qlco** to put or place s.th after s.th

pòssa *f* (lit) strength, vigor

possanza *f* (lit) power

possedére §252 *tr* to possess; to own; to master (*a language*); **essere posseduto da** to be enthralled with; to be possessed by

possediménto *m* possession, property

posseditrice *f* owner, possessor

possènte *adj* (lit) powerful

possessióne *f* possession

possessi·vo -va *adj* possessive

possèsso *m* possession

possessóre *m* owner, possessor

possíbile *adj* possible || *m*—**fare il possibile** to do one's best

possibili·sta (-sti -ste) *adj* pragmatically flexible || *mf* pragmatically flexible person, possibilist

possibili·tà *f* (-tà) possibility; opportunity; **possibilità** *fpl* means

possidènte *mf* proprietor, owner; **possidente terriero** landowner

pòsta *f* post; mail; post office; box (*in stable*); ambush; bet; **a giro di posta** by return mail; **a posta** on purpose; **darsi la posta** to set up an appointment; **fare la posta a** to have under surveillance; **fermo in posta** general delivery; **levare la posta** to pick up the mail; **posta aerea** air mail; **posta dei lettori** (journ) letters to the editor; **poste** postal department

pósta *f* (archaic) planting; (archaic) footprint

postagi·ro *m* (-ro & -ri) postal transfer of funds

postale *adj* postal, mail || *m* mail; mail train (boat, bus, or plane)

postare (**pòsto**) *tr* (mil) to post || *ref* (mil) to take a position

postazióne *f* (mil) emplacement

postbèlli·co -ca *adj* (-ci -che) postwar

postbruciatóre *m* (aer) afterburner

postdatare *tr* to postdate

posteggiare §290 (**postéggio**) *tr & intr* to park

posteggia·tóre -trice *mf* parking-lot attendant; customer (*in a parking lot*); (coll) outdoor merchant; **posteggiatore abusivo** parking violator

postég·gio *m* (-gi) parking lot; stand (*in outdoor market*); **posteggio di tassì** cabstand

posterióre *adj* back; subsequent, later

posteri·tà *f* (-tà) posterity

pòste·ro -ra *adj* later, subsequent || **posteri** *mpl* posterity, descendants

postíc·cio -cia (-ci -ce) *adj* artificial; false (*e.g., tooth*); temporary || *m* wiglet, ponytail || *f* row of trees

posticipare (**postícipo**) *tr* to postpone

posticipa·to -ta *adj* deferred

postièria *f* postern

postiglióne *m* postilion

postilla *f* marginal note

postillare *tr* to annotate

posti·no -na *mf* letter carrier || *m* mailman, postman

pósto *m* place; room; seat; job, position; spot; (mil) post; **a posto in** order; orderly; **al posto di** instead of; **essere a posto** to have a good job; **mettere a posto** to find a good job for; (coll) to keep quiet; **quel posto** (coll) seat of the pants; (coll) toilet; **posto a sedere** seat; **posto di blocco** road block; (rr) signal tower; **posto di guardia** (mil) guardhouse; **posto di medicazione** or **di pronto soccorso** first-aid station; **posto in piedi** standing room; **posto letto** bed (*e.g., in hospital*); **posto telefonico pubblico** public telephone, pay station; **rimettere a posto** to fix, repair; **saper stare al proprio posto** to know one's place; **sul posto** on the spot

postrè·mo -ma *adj* (lit) last

postríbolo *m* (lit) brothel

postulante *adj* petitioning || *mf* petitioner, applicant; (eccl) postulant

postulare (**pòstulo**) *tr* to postulate

pòstu·mo -ma *adj* posthumous || **postumi** *mpl* sequel; (pathol) sequelae

potàbile *adj* drinkable

potare (**póto**) *tr* to trim, prune

potassa *f* potash

potàssio *m* potassium

potatura *f* pruning, polling

potentato *m* (lit) potentate

potènte *adj* powerful; influential || **I potenti** the powers that be

potènza *f* power, might; (math) power; **all'ennesima potenza** (math) to the nth power; (fig) to the nth degree; **in potenza** potential; potentially

potenziale _adj & m_ potential
potére _f_ ability; authority, power; **in potere di** in the hands of; **potere d'acquisto** purchasing power; **potere esecutivo** executive; **potere giudiziario** judiciary; **quarto potere** fourth estate ‖ §219 _intr_ to be powerful; **non ne posso più** I am at the end of my rope; **sì può?** may I come in? ‖ _aux_ (ESSERE & AVERE) to be able; **non posso fare a meno di + _inf_** I can't help + _ger_; **non potere fare a meno di** to not be able to do without; **posso,** etc. I can; I may, etc.; **potrei,** etc. I could; I might, etc.
pote·stà _f_ (-stà) power, authority
poveràc·cio -cia _mf_ (-ci -ce) poor guy, poor soul
pòve·ro -ra _adj_ poor; needy, wretched; lean (_gasoline mixture_); **povero in canna** as poor as a church mouse ‖ _mf_ pauper; beggar; poor devil ‖ **i poveri** the poor
pover·tà _f_ (-tà) poverty; paucity, scantiness
poveruòmo _m_ (used only in _sg_) poor devil
pozióne _f_ potion, brew
pózza _f_ pool, puddle
pozzànghera _f_ puddle
pozzétto _m_ small well; manhole; forecastle (_in small boat_)
pózzo _m_ well; shaft; **pozzo artesiano** artesian well; **pozzo delle catene** (naut) chain locker; **pozzo di scienza** fountain of knowledge; **pozzo di ventilazione** (min) air shaft; **pozzo nero** cesspool; **pozzo petrolifero** oil well; **pozzo trivellato** deep well; **un pozzo di** (fig) a barrel of
Praga _f_ Prague
prammàti·co -ca (-ci -che) _adj_ pragmatic ‖ _f_ social custom; **di prammatica** obligatory, de rigueur
pranzare [dz] _intr_ to dine
pranzo [dz] _m_ dinner; **dopo pranzo** afternoon
pras·si _f_ (-si) practice, praxis
prateria _f_ prairie
pràti·ca _f_ (-che) practice; knowledge; matter; file, dossier; business; experience; (naut) pratique; **aver pratica con** to be familiar with (_people_); **aver pratica di** to be familiar with (_things_); **far pratica** to be an apprentice; **fare le pratiche** to make an application; **in pratica** practically; **insabbiare una pratica** to pigeonhole a matter
praticàbile _adj_ practicable; passable ‖ _m_ (theat) raised platform
praticante _adj_ practicing ‖ _mf_ apprentice; novice; churchgoer
praticare §197 (**pràtico**) _tr_ to practice; to frequent; to be familiar with; to make (_e.g., a hole_); to grant (_a discount_) ‖ _intr_ to practice; **praticare in** to frequent
pratici·tà _f_ (-tà) utility; practicality
pràti·co -ca (-ci -che) _adj_ practical; experienced ‖ _f_ see **pratica**
praticó·ne -na _mf_ (pej) old hand
prato _m_ meadow

pratolina _f_ daisy
pra·vo -va _adj_ (lit) wicked
preaccennare (**preaccénno**) _tr_ to mention in advance
preaccenna·to -ta _adj_ aforementioned
preallarme _m_ early warning
Prealpi _fpl_ foothills of the Alps
preàmbolo _m_ preamble
preannunziare §287 (**preannùnzio**) _tr_ to foretell, forebode
preannùn·zio _m_ (-zi) advance information; foreboding
preautunnale _adj_ pre-fall
preavvertire (**preavvèrto**) _tr_ to forewarn
preavvisare _tr_ to give advance notice to; to forewarn
preavviso _m_ forewarning; notification of dismissal
prebèlli·co -ca _adj_ (-ci -che) prewar
prebènda _f_ prebend; (fig) easy money, sinecure
precà·rio -ria _adj_ (-ri -rie) precarious
precauzióne _f_ precaution
precedènte _adj_ preceding ‖ _m_ precedent; **precedenti** background; **precedenti penali** previous offenses, record
precedènza _f_ precedence; (aut) right of way; (fig) priority
precèdere §123 _tr & intr_ to precede
precettare (**precètto**) _tr_ (mil) to call back from furlough
precètto _m_ precept; (eccl) obligation
precettóre _m_ tutor
precipitare (**precipito**) _tr_ to precipitate; to hasten; (chem) to precipitate ‖ _intr_ (ESSERE) to fall; to fail; to rush (_said of events_); (chem) to precipitate ‖ _ref_ to rush
precipitó·so -sa [s] _adj_ hasty, headlong
precipi·zio _m_ (-zi) precipice, cliff; ruin; **a precipizio** headlong
preci·puo -pua _adj_ chief, principal, primary
precisare _tr_ to say exactly, specify, clarify; to fix (_a date_)
precisazióne _f_ clarification
precisióne _f_ precision
preci·so -sa _adj_ precise, exact; punctilious; identical, same; sharp, e.g., **alle sette precise** at seven o'clock sharp
precla·ro·ra _adj_ (lit) illustrious
preclùdere §105 _tr_ to preclude
precòce _adj_ precocious, premature
preconcèt·to -ta _adj_ preconceived ‖ _m_ preconception; prejudice, bias
preconizzare [ddzz] _tr_ to foretell, forecast; (eccl) to preconize
precórrere §139 _tr_ (lit) to precede ‖ _intr_ (lit) to occur before
precursóre _m_ precursor
prèda _f_ booty, prize; prey
predace _adj_ (lit) preying, predatory
predare (**prèdo**) _tr_ to pillage; to prey upon
preda·tóre -trice _adj_ predacious, rapacious ‖ _mf_ plunderer
predecessóre _m_ predecessor
predèlla _f_ dais; altar step; platform
predellino _m_ footboard
predestinare (**predestino** & **predèstino**) _tr_ to predestine

predét·to -ta adj aforementioned
prediale adj field, rural ‖ f land tax
prèdi·ca f (-che) sermon
predicare §197 (prèdico) tr & intr to preach
predicato m predicate; **essere in predicato di** + inf to be rumored to + inf; **essere predicato per** to be considered for
predica·tóre -trice mf preacher
predicazióne f preaching; sermon
predicòzzo m (coll) lecture, scolding
predilèt·to -ta adj & m favorite
predilezióne f predilection
prediligere §149 (pres part missing) tr to prefer; to like best
predire §151 tr to foretell
predispórre §218 tr to predispose, prearrange ‖ ref to prepare oneself
predisposizióne f predisposition
predizióne f prediction
predominare (predòmino) tr to overcome ‖ intr to predominate; to prevail
predomì·nio m (-ni) predominance
predóne m marauder; **predone del mare** pirate
preesistere §114 intr (ESSERE) to preexist
prefabbricare §197 (prefàbbrico) tr to prefabricate
prefazióne f preface
preferènza f preference; **a preferenza** rather; **usar preferenze a** to favor
preferìbile adj preferable
preferire §176 tr to prefer
preferì·to -ta adj preferred, favored ‖ mf favorite; pet
prefètto m prefect
prefettura f prefecture
prèfi·ca f (-che) professional mourner, paid mourner; (coll) crybaby
prefiggere §103 tr to set, fix; (gram) to prefix ‖ ref to plan
prefis·so -sa adj appointed; prefixed ‖ m (gram) prefix; (telp) area code
prefissòide m prefixed combining form
pregare §209 (prègo) tr to beg, pray; to ask, request; **farsi pregare** to take a lot of asking; **La prego** please; **prego!** please!; beg your pardon!; you are welcome!
pregévole adj valuable
preghièra f entreaty; prayer
pregiare §290 (prègio) tr (lit) to praise, esteem ‖ ref to be honored, to have the pleasure
pregia·to -ta adj precious; esteemed; **la Sua pregiata** (lettera) your favor, your kind letter; **pregiatissimo Signore** (com) dear Sir; **pregiato Signore** (com) dear Sir
prè·gio m (-gi) value, worth; esteem; **avere in pregio** to value
pregiudicare §197 (pregiùdico) tr to damage, harm, jeopardize
pregiudica·to -ta adj prejudged; prejudiced; compromised; bound to fail ‖ m previous offender
pregiudiziale adj (law) pretrial; (pol) essential ‖ f (law) pretrial
pregiudiziévole adj prejudicial, detrimental

pregiudì·zio m (-zi) prejudice, bias; harm, damage
pregnante adj pregnant
pré·gno -gna adj pregnant; saturated
prè·go m (-ghi) (lit) prayer ‖ interj please!; beg your pardon!; you are welcome!
pregustare tr to foretaste, anticipate with pleasure
preistòri·co -ca adj (-ci -che) prehistoric(al)
prelato m prelate
prelazióne f (law) preemption; (obs) privilege
prelevaménto m (com) withdrawal
prelevare (prelèvo) tr to withdraw (money); to capture
prelìba·to -ta adj excellent, delicious
prelièvo m withdrawal; (med) specimen
preliminare adj preliminary ‖ **preliminari** mpl preliminary negotiations
prelùdere §105 intr to make an introductory statement; (with dat) to precede, usher in
prelù·dio m (-di) prelude; (of an opera) overture
prematu·ro -ra adj premature
premeditare (premèdito) tr to premeditate
premeditazióne f premeditation; **con premeditazione** (law) with malice prepense
prèmere §123 tr to press; to push; to squeeze ‖ intr (ESSERE & AVERE) to press; to be urgent; **premere a** to matter to, e.g., **gli preme** it matters to him; **premere su** to press, put pressure on
preméssa f premise; introduction (to a book)
preméttere §198 tr to state at the onset; to place at the beginning
premiare §287 (prèmio) tr to award a prize to, reward
premiazióne f awarding of prizes
preminènte adj prominent, preeminent
prè·mio m (-mi) prize; premium; bonus; award
prèmito m straining (to defecate)
premolare adj & m premolar
premonire §176 tr (lit) to foretell
premonizióne f premonition
premorire §201 intr (ESSERE) (with dat) to predecease
premunire §176 tr to fortify ‖ ref—**premunirsi contro** to provide against; **premunirsi di** to provide oneself with
premura f haste; attention, care; **aver premura (di)** to be in a hurry (to); **di premura** hastily; **far premura (with** dat) to urge
premuró·so -sa [s] adj attentive, careful
prèndere §220 tr to take; to catch; to lift; to pick up; to fetch; to get; to receive; **prendere a calci** to kick; **prendere a pugni** to punch; **prendere a servizio** to employ, hire; **prendere commiato** to take leave; **prendere con le buone** to treat with kid gloves; **prendere in castagna** to catch in the act; **prendere il sole** to sun oneself; **prendere la fuga** to take flight;

prendere la mano to run away (*said of a horse*); **prendere le mosse** to begin (*said, e.g., of a story*); **prendere lucciole per lanterne** to commit a gross error; **prender paura** to get scared; **prendere per** to take for; **prendere per il naso** to lead by the nose; **prendere quota** (aer) to gain altitude; **prendere sonno** to fall asleep; **prendere un granchio** to make a blunder || *intr* to take root; to set (*said of cement*); to catch (*said of fire*); to turn (*left or right*); **prendere a** + *inf* to begin to + *inf* || *ref* to grab one another; to get along together; **prendersela con** to become angry with; to lay the blame on; **prendersi a** to take hold of

prendi·tóre -tríce *mf* receiver; payee (*of a note*); margin buyer || *m* (baseball) catcher

prenóme *m* first name, given name

prenotare (**prenòto**) *tr* to reserve, book || *ref* to register

prenotazióne *f* reservation, booking

preoccupare *adj* worrisome

preoccupare (**preòccupo**) *tr* to preoccupy; **preoccupare la mente di** to win the favor of || *ref* to worry

preoccupazióne *f* preoccupation, worry

preordinare (**preórdino**) *tr* to foreordain; to prearrange

preparare *tr* to prepare; to prime; to steep, brew || *ref* to be prepared; to brew (*said, e.g., of a storm*)

peparati·vo -va *adj* preparatory || **preparativi** *mpl* preparations

prepara·to -ta *adj* prepared; well-equipped || *m* patent medicine; (med) preparation; **preparato anatomico** dissection, anatomical specimen

preparatò·rio -ria *adj* (**-ri -rie**) preparatory

preparazióne *f* preparation

preponderante *adj* preponderant, prevailing

preponderanza *f* preponderance

prepórre §218 *tr* to prefix; to place before; to prefer; **preporre** (**qlcu**) **a** to place (*s.o.*) at the head of

preposizióne *f* preposition

prepósto *m* chief; (eccl) provost

prepotènte *adj* arrogant, overbearing; urgent (*desire*) || *m* bully

prepotènza *f* arrogance; outrage; **di prepotenza** by force

prerogativa *f* prerogative

présa [s] *f* hold, grip; handle; potholder; capture; pinch (*e.g., of salt*); setting (*of cement*); intake; (cards) trick; (elec) jack; (mov) take; **a pronta presa** quick-setting (*cement*); **dar presa a** to give rise to; **essere alle prese** to come to grips; **far presa** to stick (*said of glue*); to set (*said of cement*); to take root; **far presa su** to impress; **mettere alle prese** to pit (*e.g., animals*); **presa d'acqua** spigot, faucet; **presa d'aria** outlet (*of air hose*); air shaft; **presa di corrente** (elec) wall socket, outlet, receptacle; **presa di terra** (elec) ground; presa

in giro kidding, joke; **venire alle prese** to come to grips

presà·gio *m* (**-gi**) forecast; portent

presagire §176 *tr* to forecast; to portend

presalà·rio [s] *m* (**-ri**) (educ) stipend

prèsbite *adj* far-sighted || *mf* far-sighted person

presbiteria·no -na *adj* & *mf* Presbyterian

prescégliere §244 *tr* to choose, select

prescìndere §247 (*pret* **prescindéi** & **prescissi**) *intr*—**a prescindere da** except for; **prescindere da** to leave out

prescolàsti·co -ca *adj* (**-ci -che**) preschool

prescrit·to -ta *adj* prescribed

prescrìvere §250 *tr* to prescribe || *intr* (ESSERE) (law) to prescribe, to lapse

prescrizióne *f* prescription; (law) extinctive prescription

presegnale [s] *m* warning sign

presentàbile *adj* presentable

presentare (**presènto**) *tr* to present; to introduce; **presentare la candidatura di** to nominate; **presentat'arm!** present arms! || *ref* to show up, appear; to come, arise (*said, e.g., of an opportunity*)

presenta·tóre -trice *mf* presenter; (rad, telv) announcer || *m* master of ceremonies

presentazióne *f* presentation; introduction

presènte *adj* present; **avere presente** to have in mind; **fare presente qlco a qlcu** to bring s.th to s.o.'s attention; **tenere presente** to keep in mind || *m* present; bystander, onlooker; **al presente** at present; **di presente** immediately || *interj* here!

presentimento [s] *m* presentiment, foreboding

presentire [s] (**presènto**) *tr* to have a presentiment of

presènza *f* presence; attendance; **di presenza** in person; **presenza di spirito** presence of mind

presenziare §287 (**presènzio**) *tr* to attend; to witness || *intr*—**presenziare a** to be present at; to witness

presè·pio *m* (**-pi**) Nativity, crèche

preservare [s] (**presèrvo**) *tr* to preserve, protect

preservati·vo -va [s] *adj* & *m* prophylactic

prèside [s] *m* principal (*of secondary school*); **preside di facoltà** dean

presidènte [s] *m* president; chairman; **presidente del Consiglio** premier

presidentéssa [s] *f* president; chairwoman

presidènza [s] *f* presidency; chairmanship

presi·dio [s] *m* (**-di**) garrison; (fig) defense, help; **presidi medical aids**

presièdere §141 (**presièdo**) *tr* to preside over || *intr* to preside; **presiedere a** to preside over

prèssa *f* crowd; haste; (mach) press; **far pressa** (poet) to urge

pressacar·te [s] (**-te**) paperweight

pressaforàg·gio *m* (**-gio**) baler, hay baler

pressante *adj* pressing, urgent
pressappòco *adv* more or less
pressare (**prèsso**) *tr* to press; to urge
pressióne *f* pressure; **far pressione su** to put pressure on; **pressione sanguigna** blood pressure; **sotto pressione** under steam
prèsso *m*—**nei pressi di** in the neighborhood of || *adv* near, nearby; **a un di presso** approximately; **da presso** close; **press'a poco** more or less || *prep* near; about; at; according to; at the house of; at the office of; care of; with, e.g., **godere fama presso** to enjoy popularity with
pressoché *adv* almost, about, nearly
pressurizzare [ddzz] *tr* to pressurize
prestabilire §176 *tr* to preestablish
prestabilì·to -ta *adj* appointed
prestanó·me *m* (**-me**) straw man, figurehead
prestante *adj* strong, vigorous; comely
prestanza *f* vigor; (*lit*) comeliness
prestare (**prèsto**) *tr* to lend; to loan; to give (*ear*; *help*); to pay (*attention*); to render (*obedience*); to take (*oath*); to keep (*faith*); **prestar man forte** to give aid; **prestar servizio** to work || *ref* to lend oneself; to be suitable; to be willing; to volunteer
presta·tóre -trice *mf* lender; **prestatore d'opera** worker; **prestatori d'opera** labor
prestazióne *f* service; performance
prestigia·tóre -trice *mf* magician, juggler
presti·gio *m* (**-gi**) prestige; spell, influence; ledgerdemain
prestigió·so -sa [s] *adj* captivating, spellbinding; illusory
prèstito *m* loan; (*philol*) borrowing; **dare a prestito** to lend; **prendere a prestito** to borrow
prè·sto -sta *adj* (*archaic*) quick || *m* (*mus*) presto || **presto** *adv* soon; fast; quick, quickly; early; **al più presto** at the earliest possible time; **ben presto** soon; **far presto** to hurry; **più presto che può** as soon as you can; **presto detto** easy to say
presùmere §116 *tr* & *intr* to presume
presunti·vo -va *adj* presumptive; budgeted, estimated (*expenditure*)
presun·to -ta *adj* alleged, supposed; estimated (*expenditure*)
presuntuó·so -sa [s] *adj* presumptuous; bumptious
presunzióne *f* presumption; conceit
presuppórre [s] §218 *tr* to presuppose
presuppósto [s] *m* assumption
prète *m* priest; minister; wooden frame (*to hold bed warmer*)
pretendènte *m* suitor; pretender
pretèndere §270 *tr* to demand, claim; **pretenderla a** to pretend to be || *intr*—**pretendere a** to be a suitor for; to claim (*e.g., a throne*)
pretensióne *f* demand; pretention; pretense
pretensió·so -sa [s] or **pretenzió·so -sa** [s] *adj* pretentious
preterintenzionale *adj* (*law*) unintentional; (*law*) justifiable

pretèri·to -ta *adj* & *m* preterit
preté·so -sa [s] *adj* alleged, ostensible; assumed (*name*) || *f* pretense; pretension
pretèsto *m* pretext, excuse; **sotto il pretesto di** under pretense of
pretòni·co -ca *adj* (**-ci -che**) pretonic
pretóre *m* judge, magistrate (*of lower court*)
prèt·to -ta *adj* pure, genuine
pretura *f* lower court
prevalènte *adj* prevalent, prevailing
prevalènza *f* prevalence; **essere in prevalenza** to be in the majority; **in prevalenza** for the most part
prevalére §278 *intr* (ESSERE & AVERE) to prevail || *ref* to take advantage
prevaricare §197 (**prevàrico**) *intr* to transgress; to graft
prevarica·tóre -trice *mf* grafter
prevedére §279 *tr* to foresee; to provide for (*said of a statute*)
prevedìbile *adj* foreseeable
prevenire §282 *tr* to precede; to anticipate; to forewarn; to prejudice
preventivi·sta *mf* (**-sti -ste**) estimator
preventi·vo -va *adj* preventive; prior; estimated (*budget*) || *m* estimate
prevenu·to -ta *adj* forewarned; biased, prejudiced || *m* defendant
prevenzióne *f* prevention; prejudice, bias
previdènte *adj* provident, prudent
previdènza *f* providence; foresight; **previdenza sociale** social security
previdenziale *adj* social (*e.g., responsibility*); social-security (*e.g., contribution*)
prè·vio -via *adj* (**-vi -vie**) with previous, e.g., **previo accordo** with previous agreement
previsióne *f* foresightedness; **in previsione di** anticipating; **previsioni del tempo** weather forecast
previ·sto -sta *adj* foreseen, expected || *m* expected time; estimated amount
prezió·so -sa [s] *adj* precious, valuable; affected; **fare il prezioso** (*coll*) to play hard to get || **preziosi** *mpl* valuables, jewels
prezzare (**prèzzo**) *tr* to care about; to price
prezzémolo *m* parsley
prèzzo *m* price; cost; **mettere a prezzo** (*fig*) to sell; **prezzo di favore** special price; **prezzo d'ingresso** admission; **tenere in gran prezzo** to value highly, to esteem highly; **ultimo prezzo** rock-bottom price
prezzolare (**prèzzolo**) *tr* to hire (*e.g., a gunman*); to bribe
prigióne *f* prison, jail; (*naut*) brig
prigionìa *f* imprisonment; bondage
prigioniè·ro -ra *adj* imprisoned || *mf* prisoner || *m* stud bolt
prillare *intr* to spin, whirl
prima *f* first grade (*in school*); (*rr*) first class; (*theat*) first night; (*aut*) first (*gear*); **alla prima** or **sulle prime** at the outset || *adv* before; first; prior; ahead; **di prima** previous; **prima che** before; **prima di** ahead of; before;

prima o poi sooner or later; **quanto prima** as soon as possible

primàrio -ria (-ri -rie) *adj* primary ‖ *m* (elec) primary; (med) chief of staff

primati·sta *mf* (**-sti -ste**) (sports) record holder

primato *m* primacy; (sports) record

primavèra *f* spring; springtime; (bot) primrose

primaverile *adj* spring; spring-like

primeggiare §290 (**priméggio**) *intr* to excel

primiè·ro -ra *adj* (lit) prior; (lit) pristine ‖ *f* (cards) meld

primiti·vo -va *adj & m* primitive

primizia *f* first fruits; scoop, beat

pri·mo -ma *adj* first; early (*dawn*); prime (*cost*); raw (*material*); **sulle prime** at first ‖ *m* first; minute; **primo arrivato** first comer ‖ *f see* **prima**

primogèni·to -ta *adj* first-born; (fig) beloved ‖ *mf* first-born child

primòrdi *mpl* beginning, origin

primordiale *adj* primordial, primeval

prìmula *f* primrose ‖ **Primula** *f*—**la Primula Rossa** the Scarlet Pimpernel

principale *adj* principal, main ‖ *m* (coll) boss, chief

principalménte *adv* chiefly, mainly

principato *m* principality

prìncipe *adj* princeps ‖ *m* prince; **il principe di Galles** the Prince of Wales; **principe ereditario** crown prince

principé·sco -sca *adj* (**-schi -sche**) princely

principéssa *f* princess

principiante *adj* beginning ‖ *mf* beginner

principiare §287 *tr & intr* (ESSERE & AVERE) to begin; **a principiare da** beginning with

princì·pio *m* (**-pi**) beginning; principle; **in principio** at the beginning, at first

princisbécco *m* pinchbeck; **restare or rimanere di princisbecco** to be dumfounded

prióre *m* prior

priori·tà *f* (**-tà**) priority

prioritá·rio -ria *adj* (**-ri -rie**) priority, e.g., **progetto prioritario** priority project

pri·sma *m* (**-smi**) prism

privare *tr* to deprive; to remove

privativa *f* government monopoly; salt and tobacco store; patent

priva·to -ta *adj* private ‖ *m* private individual

privazione *f* privation, loss

privilegiare §290 (**privilègio**) *tr* to privilege; (fig) to endow

privilegia·to -ta *adj* privileged; preferred (*stock*) ‖ *m* privileged person

privilè·gio *m* (**-gi**) privilege

pri·vo -va *adj* deprived; **privo di** lacking

prò *m* (**pro**) profit, advantage; **a che pro?** what's the use?; **buon pro!** good appetite!; **far pro** to be good for the health; **il pro e il contro** the pros and the cons ‖ *prep* pro, in favor of

probàbile *adj* probable

probabili·tà *f* (**-tà**) probability; chance; odds

probante *adj* proving; evidential

probatò·rio -ria *adj* (**-ri -rie**) probative, evidential

problè·ma *m* (**-mi**) problem

prò·bo -ba *adj* (lit) honest

procàc·cia *mf* (**-cia**) messenger; mail carrier

procacciare §128 *tr* to get, procure ‖ *ref* to eke out (*a living*); to get into (*trouble*)

procace *adj* buxom, sexy; saucy, petulant

procèdere §123 (**procèdo**) *intr* to proceed, take action ‖ *intr* (ESSERE) to proceed, go ahead

procediménto *m* procedure; behavior

procedura *f* procedure

procèlla *f* (lit) storm, tempest

procellària *f* (orn) petrel

processare (**procèsso**) *tr* to try, prosecute

processióne *f* procession

procèsso *m* process; trial; **processo verbale** minutes

processuale *adj* trial

procinto *m*—**in procinto di** on the point of

procióne *m* raccoon

procla·ma *m* (**-mi**) proclamation

proclamare *tr* to proclaim

proclamazióne *f* proclamation

proclìti·co -ca *adj & f* (**-ci -che**) proclitic

proclive *adj* inclined, disposed

proclivi·tà *f* (**-tà**) proclivity

procrastinare (**procràstino**) *tr* to procrastinate, put off ‖ *intr* to procrastinate

procreare (**procrèo**) *tr* to procreate

procura *f* agency; power of attorney; **Procura della Repubblica** attorney general's office; district attorney's office

procurare *tr* to procure, to get; to cause; **procurare che** to see to it that; **procurare di** to try to ‖ *ref* to get, acquire

procura·tóre -trice *mf* proxy; agent; attorney-at-law; (sports) manager; **Procuratore della Repubblica** district attorney

pròda *f* shore, bank; (archaic) prow

pròde *adj* brave ‖ *m* brave person, hero

prodézza *f* prowess; accomplishment

prodiè·ro -ra *adj* prow; **cannone prodiero** prow gun; preceding (*in a row of ships*)

prodigare §209 (**pròdigo**)—*tr* to squander, lavish ‖ *ref* to do one's best

prodì·gio *m* (**-gi**) prodigy; wonder

prodigió·so -sa [s] *adj* prodigious; wonderful

pròdi·go -ga *adj* (**-ghi -ghe**) lavish, prodigal; **prodigo di** profuse in

prodìto·rio -ria *adj* (**-ri -rie**) traitorous

prodótto *m* product; result; **prodotti in scatola** canned goods; **prodotti (ortofrutticoli)** produce

produrre §102 *tr* to produce; to turn out; to yield; to breed; to cause; (lit)

to prolong; (law) to exhibit || *ref*
(theat) to perform, appear
produtti·vo -va *adj* productive
produttivísti·co -ca *adj* (**-ci -che**) productivity, e.g., **fine produttivístico**
productivity policy
produt·tóre -trice *adj* producing || *mf*
producer; agent; manufacturer's rep-
resentative || *m* salesman || *f* sales-
woman
produzióne *f* production; output; **produzione in massa** or **in serie** mass
production
proè·mio *m* (**-mi**) preamble, proem
profanare *tr* to profane, desecrate
profanazióne *f* profanation, desecration
profa·no -na *adj* profane; lay, unin-
formed || *m* layman; **il profano** the
profane
proferire §176 *tr* (lit) to utter; (lit) to
proffer
professare (professo) *tr* to profess; to
practice (*e.g., law*) || *intr* to practice
|| *ref* to profess oneself to be
professionale *adj* professional; occupational (*disease*); trade (*school*)
professióne *f* profession; **fare il ladro
di professione** to be a confirmed
thief; **fare qlco di professione** to pursue the trade of s.th, e.g., **fa il falegname di professione** he pursues the
trade of carpenter
professioni·sta *mf* (**-sti -ste**) professional
professorale *adj* professorial; pedantic
profes·sóre -soréssa *mf* professor;
teacher; **professore d'orchestra** orchestra member
profè·ta *m* (**-ti**) prophet
profetéssa *f* prophetess
profèti·co -ca *adj* (**-ci -che**) prophetic
profetizzare [ddzz] *tr* to prophesy
profezía *f* prophecy
profferire §176 (*pp* **profferto**; *pret* **prof-
ferii** & **proffersi**) *tr* to offer; (lit) to
utter
profi·cuo -cua *adj* profitable
profilare *tr* to outline; to sketch; to
hem; (mach) to shape || *ref* to be
outlined; to loom
profilas·si *f* (**-si**) prophylaxis
profila·to -ta *adj* outlined; hemmed;
(mach) shaped || *m* structural piece
profilàtti·co -ca *adj* (**-ci -che**) prophylactic
profilatura *f* hemming; (mach) shaping
profilo *m* profile; sketch; outline
profittare *intr* to profit, benefit
profitta·tóre -trice *mf* profiteer
profittévole *adj* (lit) profitable
profitto *m* profit; progress; **profitti e
perdite** profit and loss
profiù·vio *m* (**-vi**) overflow; (pathol)
discharge
profondare (profóndo) *tr* & *intr* to sink
profóndere §178 *tr* to squander, lavish
|| *ref* to be profuse
profondi·tà *f* (**-tà**) depth
profón·do -da *adj* deep; profound;
searching (*e.g., investigation*) || *m*
bottom; depth; subconscious
pro fórma *adj* invar pro forma; per-
functory || *m* (coll) formality

pròfu·go -ga (**-ghi -ghe**) *adj* fugitive ||
mf refugee
profumare *tr* to perfume || *intr* to smell
profumataménte *adv* lavishly
profuma·to -ta *adj* perfumed, fragrant
profumería *f* perfumery; perfume shop
profumo *m* perfume; bouquet (*of wine*)
profusióne *f* profusion; **a profusione**
in profusion
profu·so -sa *adj* profuse
progè·nie *f* (**-nie**) progeny, offspring;
(pej) breed
progeni·tóre -trice *mf* ancestor
progettare (progètto) *tr* to plan; to
design
progetti·sta *mf* (**-sti -ste**) planner; designer; wild dreamer
progètto *m* project; plan; draft (*of
law*); **far progetti** to plan; **progetto
di scala reale** (cards) possible
straight flush
prògno·si *f* (**-si**) prognosis
program·ma *m* (**-mi**) program; plan;
curriculum; cycle (*of washing machine*); (mov) feature; (theat) playbill; **programma politico** platform
programmare *tr* to program; to plan
programma·tóre -trice *mf* programmer
programmazióne *f* programming
progredire §176 *intr* (ESSERE & AVERE)
to progress, advance
progredi·to -ta *adj* advanced
progressióne *f* progression
progressi·sta *adj* & *mf* (**-sti -ste**) progressive
progressi·vo -va *adj* progressive
progrèsso *m* progress; progression, advance; **fare progressi** to progress
proibire §176 *tr* to prohibit; to prevent
proibi·to -ta *adj* forbidden; **è proibito
entrare** no admission; **è proibito fumare** no smoking
proibizióne *f* prohibition
proibizionismo *m* prohibition
proiettare (proiètto) *tr* to project; to
cast (*a shadow*) || *intr* to project ||
ref to be projected, project
proièttile *m* projectile, missile
proiettóre *m* projector, projection machine; searchlight; (aut) headlight;
proiettore acustico sonar projector
proiezióne *f* projection; **proiezione ral-
lentata** slow motion
pròle *f* invar offspring, progeny
proletariato *m* proletariat
proletà·rio -ria *adj* & *mf* (**-ri -rie**)
proletarian
proliferare (prolìfero) *intr* to proliferate
prolificare §197 (**prolìfico**) *intr* to proliferate
prolìfi·co -ca *adj* (**-ci -che**) prolific
prolis·so -sa *adj* prolix, long-winded;
long (*e.g., beard*)
pròlo·go *m* (**-ghi**) prologue; preface
prolun·ga·ga *f* (**-ghe**) extension
prolungaménto *m* prolongation, extension
prolungare §209 *tr* to prolong, extend
|| *ref* to extend; to speak at great
length
prolunga·to -ta *adj* extended, protracted
prolusióne *f* inaugural lecture

promemò·ria or **pro memò·ria** *m* (-ria) reminder

promés·so -sa *adj* promised || *mf* betrothed || *f* promise; promising individual

promettènte *adj* promising

promèttere §198 *tr* to promise; to threaten (*e.g., a storm*) || *intr* to promise; **promettere bene** to be very promising || *ref*—**promettersi a Dio** to make a vow to God; **promettersi in matrimonio** to become engaged

prominènte *adj* prominent

promì·scuo -scua *adj* promiscuous; coeducational; mixed (*marriage; races*); (*gram*) epicene

promontò·rio *m* (-ri) promontory, cliff

promo·tóre -trice *adj* promoting || *mf* promoter

promozióne *f* promotion

promulgare §209 *tr* to promulgate

promuòvere §202 *tr* to promote; to pass (*a student*); to initiate (*legal suit*); to induce (*e.g., perspiration*)

pronipóte *mf* great-grandchild || *m* great-grandson; grandnephew; **pronipoti** descendants || *f* great-granddaughter; grandniece

prò·no -na *adj* (lit) prone

pronóme *m* pronoun

pronominale *adj* (gram) pronominal; (gram) reflexive (*verb*)

pronosticare §197 (pronòstico) *tr* to prognosticate, forecast

pronòsti·co *m* (-ci) prognostication, forecast; sign, omen

prontézza *f* readiness; quickness, promptness

prón·to -ta *adj* ready; first (*aid*); quick; prompt; ready (*cash*) || **pronto** *interj* (telp) hello!

prontuà·rio *m* (-ri) handbook

pronùn·cia *f* (-cie) or **pronunzia** *f* pronunciaton; (law) judgment

pronunziare §287 *tr* to pronounce; to utter; to pass (*sentence*); to make (*a speech*) || *ref* to pass judgment

pronunzià·to -ta *adj* pronounced, marked; prominent (*nose, chin, beard*) || *m* (law) sentence

propaganda *f* propaganda; advertisement; advertising

propagandì·sta *mf* (-sti -ste) propagandist; advertiser; agent; detail man

propagandìsti·co -ca *adj* (-ci -che) advertising

propagare §209 *tr* to propagate; to spread || *ref* to spread

propàggine *f* offspring; (geog) spur, counterfor; (hort) layer

propalare *tr* (lit) to spread, divulge

propellènte *adj* & *m* propellent

propèllere §168 *tr* to propel

propèndere §123 (*pp* propènso) *intr* to incline, tend

propensióne *f* propensity, inclination

propèn·so -sa *adj* inclined, bent

propinare *tr* to administer (*e.g., poison*); **propinare qlco a qlcu** to put s.th over on s.o.

propìn·quo -qua *adj* (lit) near; (lit) related

propiziare §287 *tr* to propitiate, appease

propì·zio -zia *adj* (-zi -zie) propitious, favorable

proponiménto *m* intention, plan

propórre §218 *tr* to propose, present; to propound; **proporre come candidato** to nominate || *ref*—**proporsi di** to propose to, resolve to

proporzionare (proporzióno) *tr* to proportion, prorate

proporzióne *f* proportion

propòsito *m* purpose; **a proposito** opportune; opportunely; proper; by the way; **a proposito di** on the subject of; **di proposito** deliberately; **fuor di proposito** out of place; **parlare a proposito** to speak to the point

proposizióne *f* proposition; (gram) clause; **proposizione subordinata** dependent clause

propósta *f* proposal; **proposta di legge** bill

propriaménte *adv* exactly; properly

proprie·tà *f* (-tà) propriety; ownership; property; **la proprietà** property owners; **proprietà immobiliare** real estate; **proprietà letteraria** copyright; **sulla proprietà** on the premises

proprietà·rio -ria *mf* (-ri -rie) owner, proprietor

prò·prio -pria (-pri -prie) *adj* peculiar, characteristic; proper (*e.g., name*); own, e.g., **il mio proprio libro** my own book || *m* one's own; **i propri** one's folks; **lavorare in proprio** to work for oneself || **proprio** *adv* just, really, exactly; **non . . . proprio** not . . . at all; **proprio adesso** just, just now

propugnare *tr* to advocate; (lit) to fight for

propugna·tóre -trice *mf* (lit) advocate

propulsare *tr* to propel; (lit) to repulse

propulsióne *f* propulsion

propulsóre *m* propeller, motor

pròra *f* prow, bow

proravìa *f*—**a proravia** (naut) fore

pròro·ga *f* (-ghe) delay, extension

prorogare §209 (pròrogo) *tr* to extend; to put off, delay

proròmpere §240 *intr* to overflow; to burst (*into tears*)

prosa *f* prose

prosài·co -ca *adj* (-ci -che) prose; prosaic

prosàpia *f* (lit) ancestry

prosa·tóre -trice *mf* prose writer

proscè·nio *m* (-ni) forestage

prosciògliere §127 *tr* to free; to exonerate

prosciugare §209 *tr* to drain, reclaim || *ref* to dry up

prosciutto *m* ham; **prosciutto cotto** boiled ham; **prosciutto crudo** prosciutto

proscrìvere §250 *tr* to proscribe, outlaw

prosecuzióne [s] *f* prosecution, pursuit

proseguiménto [s] *m* prosecution, pursuit

proseguire [s] (proséguo) *tr* to follow, pursue || *intr* (ESSERE & AVERE) to continue

prosèlito *m* proselyte

prosodìa *f* prosody

prosopopèa *f* conceit

prosperare (pròspero) *intr* to prosper, thrive

prosperi·tà *f* (-tà) prosperity || *interj* gesundheit!

pròspe·ro -ra *adj* prosperous, thriving; flourishing; successful || *m* (coll) match

prosperó·so -sa [s] *adj* flourishing; healthy; buxom

prospettare (prospètto) *tr* to face, overlook; to outline || *intr*—**prospettare su** to face || *ref* to look; to appear; to loom up

prospetti·vo -va *adj* prospective || *f* perspective; prospect; view

prospètto *m* prospect, view; front (*of building*); diagram; outline; prospectus

prospettóre *m* prospector

prospiciènte *adj* facing

prossimaménte *adv* shortly

prossimi·tà *f* (-tà) proximity, nearness; **in prossimità di** near

pròssi·mo -ma *adj* near, close; next; immediate (*cause*) || *m* neighbor, fellow man

pròstata *f* prostate

prosternare (prostèrno) *ref* to prostrate oneself

prostituire §176 *tr* to prostitute

prostituta *f* prostitute

prostituzióne *f* prostitution

prostrare (pròstro) *ref* to prostrate oneself

prostrazióne *f* prostration

protagoni·sta *mf* (-sti -ste) protagonist

protèggere §193 *tr* to protect; to help, defend; to favor, promote

proteina *f* protein

protèndere §270 *tr & ref* to stretch

pròte·si *f* (-si) (philol) prothesis; (surg) prosthesis

protèsta *f* protest, protestation

protestante *adj & mf* protestant; Protestant

protestare (protèsto) *tr* to protest; to reject (*faulty merchandise*) || *intr & ref* to protest

protestatà·rio -ria (-ri -rie) *adj* protesting || *m* protester

protèsto *m* (com) protest

protèt·to -ta *adj* protected || *m* protegé || *f* protegée

protettorato *m* protectorate

protet·tóre -trice *adj* patron || *mf* protector, guardian || *m* patron || *f* patroness

protezióne *f* protection; patronage

pròto·m (typ) foreman

protocòllo *adj invar* commercial (*size*) || *m* protocol; **mettere a protocollo** to register, record

protopla·sma *m* (-smi) protoplasm

protòtipo *m* prototype; (fig) epitome

protozòi [dz] *mpl* protozoa

protrarre §273 *tr* to protract, extend || *ref* to continue

protrùdere §190 *intr* to protrude (*said, e.g., of a broken bone*)

pròva *f* test, examination; proof; try, attempt; probationary period (*of employment*); trial; token (*e.g., of friendship*); (sports) competition, event; (theat) rehearsal; **a prova di bomba** bombproof; foolproof; **a tutta prova** thoroughly tested; **in prova** on approval; **mettere a dura prova** to test (*e.g., one's patience*); **mettere alla prova** to test (*e.g., one's ability*); **mettere in prova** to fit (*a suit*); **prova del fuoco** trial by fire; **prova dell'acido** acid test; **prova generale** dress rehearsal; **prova indiziaria** circumstantial evidence

provare (pròvo) *tr* to test; to try; to try on; to try out; to taste; to prove; to feel (*e.g., anger*); (theat) to rehearse || *intr* to try || *ref* to compete

proveniènza *f* origin

provenire §282 *intr* (ESSERE) to stem, originate

provènto *m* income, proceeds

provenzale *adj & mf* Provençal

prover·bio *m* (-bi) proverb; byword

provétta *f* test tube

provèt·to -ta *adj* (lit) masterful

provìn·cia *f* (-ce) province; **in provincia** outside of the big cities

provinciale *adj* provincial || *mf* smalltown person || *f* provincial highway, state highway

provino *m* gauge; (mov) screen test

provocare §197 (pròvoco) *tr* to provoke; to bring about, cause; to arouse; to entice

provoca·tóre -trice *adj* provoking || *mf* provoker

provocatò·rio -ria *adj* (-ri -rie) provoking, provocative

provocazióne *f* provocation; challenge

provvedére §221 *tr* to prepare; to supply; **provvedere che** to see to it that || *intr* to take the necessary steps; **provvedere a** to provide for; **provvedere a + inf** to provide for + *ger*; **provvedere nei confronti di** to take steps against

provvediménto *m* measure, step

provvedi·tóre -trice *mf* provider || *m* superintendent; **provveditore agli studi** superintendent of schools

provvedu·to -ta *adj* supplied; careful

provvidènza *f* providence; windfall; **provvidenze** provisions, help

provvidenziale *adj* providential

pròvvi·do -da *adj* (lit) provident

provvigióne *f* (com) commission

provvisò·rio -ria *adj* (-ri -rie) provisional, temporary

provvi·sto -sta *adj* supplied || *f* supply, provision; **fare le provviste** to shop

prozìa *f* grandaunt

prozì·o·m (-i) granduncle

prua *f* bow, prow

prudènte *adj* prudent, cautious

prudènza *f* prudence, discretion

prùdere §222 *intr* to itch; **sentirsi prudere le mani** to feel like giving s.o. a beating

prugna *f* plum; **prugna secca** prune

prugno *m* plum tree
prùgnola *f* sloe
prùgnolo *m* sloe, blackthorn
pruno *m* thorn
prurito *m* itch
pseudònimo *m* pseudonym; alias; pen name
psicanàlisi *f* psychoanalysis
psicanali•sta *mf* (-sti -ste) psychoanalyst
psicanalizzare [ddzz] *tr* to psychoanalyze
psiche *f* psyche; cheval glass
psichia•tra *mf* (-tri -tre) psychiatrist
psichiatrìa *f* psychiatry
psìchi•co -ca *adj* (-ci -che) psychic
psicologìa *f* psychology
psicològi•co -ca *adj* (-ci -che) psychological
psicòlo•go -ga *mf* (-gi -ghe) psychologist
psicopàti•co -ca *adj* (-ci -che) psychopathic || *mf* psychopath
psicò•si *f* (-si) psychosis
psicosomàti•co -ca *adj* (-ci -che) psychosomatic
psicotècni•co -ca *adj* (-ci -che) psychotechnical || *m* industrial psychologist || *f* industrial psychology
psicòti•co -ca *adj* (-ci -che) psychotic
pubblicare §197 (pùbblico) *tr* to publish
pubblicazióne *f* publication; **pubblicazioni di matrimonio** marriage banns
pubblicismo *m* communications; advertising
pubblici•sta *mf* (-sti -ste) free-lance newspaper writer; publicist
pubblicìsti•co -ca *adj* (-ci -che) advertising; political-science || *f* newspaper business
pubblicità *f* publicity; advertising
pubblicità•rio -ria (-ri -rie) *adj* advertising || *mf* advertising agent
publicizzare [ddzz] *tr* to publicize
publicizzazióne *f* publicizing
pùbbli•co -ca *adj* & *m* (-ci -che) public; **mettere in pubblico** to publish
pubertà *f* puberty
pudibón•do -da *adj* (lit) modest, bashful; (lit) prudish
pudicìzia *f* modesty; prudery
pudi•co -ca *adj* (-chi -che) modest, chaste; bashful; (lit) reserved
pudóre *m* modesty; decency; shame
puericoltóre *m* pediatrician
puerile *adj* puerile, childish
puerili•tà *f* (-tà) puerility, childishness
puèrpera *f* lying-in patient
pugilato *m* boxing
pugilatóre *m* boxer, prize fighter
pùgile *m* boxer, prize fighter
pugili•sta *m* (-sti) boxer, prize fighter
pù•glia *f* (-glie) stake (*in gambling*)
pugnace *adj* (lit) pugnacious
pugnalare *tr* to stab
pugnalata *f* stab
pugnale *m* dagger
pugno *m* fist; fistful; punch; **avere in pugno** to have in one's grasp; **di proprio pugno** in one's own hand; **fare a pugni** to fight; to clash

pula *f* chaff
pulce *f* flea; **mettere una pulce nell'orecchio di** to put a bug in the ear of; **pulce tropicale** jigger, chigger
pulcèlla *f* maid, maiden
pulcinèlla *f*—**pulcinella di mare** (orn) Atlantic puffin || **Pulcinel•la** *m* (-la) buffoon; Punch, Punchinello
pulcino *m* chick
pulédra *f* filly
pulédro *m* colt, foal
pulég•gia *f* (-ge) pulley
pulire §176 *tr* to clean; to shine (*shoes*); to wipe; to polish
puliscìpie•di *m* (-di) doormat
puli•to -ta *adj* clean; polished; clear (*conscience*) || *f*—**dare una pulita a** to give a lick and a promise to
pulitura *f* cleaning; **pulitura a secco** dry cleaning
pulizìa *f* cleaning; cleanliness; **fare le pulizie** to clean house
pullulare (pùllulo) *intr* to swarm
pùlpito *m* pulpit
pulsante *m* knob; push button
pulsare *intr* to throb; to pulsate
pulvìscolo *m* fine dust; haze
pulzèlla *f* var of **pulcella**
pu•ma *m* (-ma) cougar
pungènte *adj* pungent; bitter (*cold*)
pùngere §183 *tr* to sting; (fig) to goad
pungiglióne *m* stinger (*of bee*); (fig) sting; (obs) goad
pungitòpo *m* (bot) butcher's broom
pungolare (pùngolo) *tr* to goad, prod
punire §176 *tr* to punish
punizióne *f* punishment; penalty
punta *f* point, tip; prong; brad; bit, trifle; needle (*of phonograph*); avantgarde; point (*of dog*); (lit) wound; (fig) peak; (mach) broach; **averne fino alla punta dei capelli** to be sick and tired; **fare la punta a** to sharpen; **in punta di penna** elegantly; **prendere di punta** to treat roughly; to face up to; **punta delle dita** fingertip; **punta di piedi** tiptoe
puntale *m* tip, ferrule
puntaménto *m* aiming
puntare *tr* to aim; to aim at; to point; to thrust; to dot; to bet; to stare at; to fix (*one's eyes*); **puntare i piedi** to stiffen up; (fig) to balk || *intr* to aim; to point; to pin; to bet; **puntare su** to count on; **puntare verso** to march on; to sail toward
puntaspìl•li *m* (-li) pincushion
puntata *f* jab (*with weapon*); excursion; bet; issue, number (*of magazine*); installment (*of story*); (mil) incursion
punteggiare §290 (puntéggio) *tr* to dot; (gram) to punctuate
punteggiatura *f* dotting; punctuation
puntég•gio *m* (-gi) score
puntellare (puntèllo) *tr* to prop, brace; to support
puntèllo *m* prop, brace; support
punterìa *f* aiming; aiming gear; (aut) tappet
punteruòlo *m* punch; awl
punti•glio *m* (-gli) obstinacy, stubbornness; punctilio

puntiglió·so -sa [s] *adj* punctilious, scrupulous; obstinate, stubborn
puntina *f* brad; needle; thumbtack
puntino *m* small dot; G-string; **a puntino** to a T
punto *m* point; period; dot; place, spot; extent; stitch; **dare dei punti a** to be superior to; **di punto in bianco** all of a sudden; **di tutto punto** thoroughly; **due punti** colon; **essere a buon punto** to be well advanced; **essere sul punto di** + *inf* to be about to + *inf*; **fare il punto** (fig; naut) to take one's bearings; **in punto on the dot; in punto franco** in bond; **in un punto** together; **mettere a punto** to get in working order; (aut) to tune up; **mettere i punti sulle i** to dot one's i's; **dare dei punti** service agency; **punto di partenza** starting point; **punto di vista** viewpoint; **punto esclamativo** exclamation point; **punto e virgola** semicolon; **punto fermo** full stop; **punto interrogativo** question mark; **punto morto** (mach) dead center; **punto stimato** (naut) dead reckoning; **qui sta il punto!** here's the rub!; **vincere ai punti** (boxing) to win by points, win by decision || *adv*—**né punto né poco** not at all; **non . . . punto** not at all
puntóne *m* rafter
puntuale *adj* punctual, prompt
puntuali·tà *f* (-tà) punctuality, promptness
puntura *f* sting; stitch (*sharp pain*); (coll) injection; **puntura lombare** spinal anesthesia
punzecchiare §287 (**punzécchio**) *tr* to keep on stinging; to tease, torment
punzecchiatura *f* sting, bite
punzonare (**punzóno**) *tr* to mark or stamp with a punch
punzonatrice *f* punch press
punzóne *m* punch; nailset
pupa *f* doll; (zool) pupa
pupazzetti·sta *mf* (-sti -ste) cartoonist
pupazzétto *m* caricature; cartoon; **pupazzetto di carta** paper doll
pupazzo *m* puppet; **pupazzo di stoffa** rag doll

pupil·lo -la *mf* pupil; ward, protégé || *f* pupil (*of eye*); protégée
pupo *m* (coll) baby
purché *conj* provided, providing
pure *adv* too, also; indeed; (lit) only; **pur di** only in order to; **quando pure** even if; **se pure** even if || *conj* though, although; but, yet
pu·rè *m* (-rè) purée; **purè di patate** mashed potatoes
purézza *f* purity
pur·ga *f* (-ghe) laxative; purification; purge
purgante *adj* purging || *m* laxative
purgare §209 *tr* to purge; to purify; **to expurgate** || *ref* to take a laxative
purgati·vo -va *adj* laxative
purgatò·rio *m* (-ri) purgatory
purificare §197 (**purìfico**) *tr* to purify
purismo *m* purism
purità *f* purity
purita·no -na *adj & m* puritan; Puritan
pu·ro -ra *adj* pure; clear; simple, mere
purosàn·gue *adj invar & m* (-gue) thoroughbred
purpùre·o -a *adj* (lit) purple
purtròppo *adv* unfortunately
purulèn·to -ta *adj* purulent
pus *m* pus
pusillànime *adj* pusillanimous
pùstola *f* pustule; pimple
puta caso *adv* possibly, maybe
putifè·rio *m* (-ri) hubbub
putrefare §173 *intr* (ESSERE) & *ref* to putrefy, rot
putrefazióne *f* putrefaction
putrèlla *f* I beam
pùtri·do -da *adj* putrid || *m* corruption
putta *f* (coll) girl; (lit) prostitute
puttana *f* (vulg) whore
put·to -ta *adj* (archaic) meretricious || *m* figure of a child || *f* see **pu̇tta**
puzza *f* var of **puzzo**
puzzare *intr* to stink, smell
puzzo *m* stench, smell, bad odor
pùzzola *f* polecat, skunk
puzzolènte *adj* stinking, smelly
puzzonata *f* (coll) contemptible action; (coll) botch, bungle
puzzóne *m* (coll) skunk (*person*)

Q

Q, q [ku] *m & f* fifteenth letter of the Italian alphabet
qua *adv* here; **da un** (**giorno, mese, anno**) **in qua** for the past (day, month, year); **di qua da** on this side of; **in qua** on this side; here
quàcche·ro -ra or **quàcque·ro -ra** *adj & mf* Quaker; **alla quacquera** in a plain fashion
quadèrno *m* copybook; **quaderno di cassa** cash book
quadràngo·lo -la *adj* quadrangular || *m* quadrangle
quadrante *m* quadrant; dial; face (*of watch*); **quadrante solare** sundial

quadrare *tr* to square || *intr* (ESSERE & AVERE) to square; **quadrare a** to be satisfactory; **quadrare con** to fit
quadra·to -ta *adj* square; sound (*mind*) || *m* square; diaper; (boxing) ring; (nav) wardroom
quadratura *f* squaring; concreteness; (astr) quadrature
quadrèl·lo *m* (-li) square ruler; square tile || *m* (-la *fpl*) (lit) bolt, arrow
quadreria *f* picture gallery; collection
quadretta·to -ta *adj* checkered
quadrétto *m* small painting; checker, small square; (fig) picture

quadriennale *adj* four-year ‖ *f* quadrennial

quadrifò·glio *m* (-gli) four-leaf clover; **a quadrifoglio** cloverleaf

quadri·glio *m* (-gli) (cards) quadrille

quadrimensionale *adj* four-dimensional

quadrimestrale *adj* four-month

quadrimèstre *m* four-month period; four-month payment

quadrimotóre *adj* four-motor ‖ *m* four-motor plane

quadrireattóre *m* four-motor jet

qua·dro -dra *adj* square; (fig) solid ‖ *m* picture; painting; sight; square; table, summary; panel, switchboard; (theat) scene; **quadri** bulletin board; (mil) cadres; (cards) diamonds

quadrùmane *adj* quadrumanous ‖ *m* monkey; ape

quadruplicare §197 (**quadrùplico**) *tr & ref* to quadruple

quadrùplice *adj* quadruple; **in quadruplice copia** in four copies

quàdru·plo -pla *adj & m* quadruple

quaggiù *adv* down here

quàglia *f* quail

quagliare §280 *tr, intr* (ESSERE) *& ref* var of **cagliare**

qualche *adj invar* some, e.g., **qualche giorno** some day; some, e.g., **qualche elefante è bianco** some elephants are white; any, e.g., **ha qualche libro da vendere?** do you have any books to sell?; a few, e.g., **qualche giorno** a few days

qualchedu·no -na *pron indef* var of **qualcuno**

qualcòsa [s] *m* (fig) something; (fig) somebody ‖ *pron indef* something; anything; **qualcosa di buono** something good

qualcu·no -na *pron indef* some; any; somebody; anybody ‖ *m* somebody

quale *adj* which, what; what a, e.g., **quale onore!** what an honor!; as, e.g., **il pane, quale vedi, è fresco** the bread, as you can see, is fresh; **quale che sia** regardless of ‖ *pron* which; what; (archaic) who; **il quale** who, whom; **per la quale** o.k.; well-bred; commendable; terrific; **quale . . . quale** some . . . some ‖ *prep* as, e.g., **quale ministro** as a minister

qualìfi·ca *f* (-che) rating; position; quality, qualification

qualificare §197 (**qualìfico**) *tr* to qualify; to classify; to rate, give a rating to ‖ *ref* to introduce oneself; to qualify

qualifica·to -ta *adj* aggravated (*assault*); qualified (*personnel*); specialized (*worker*)

quali·tà *f* (-tà) quality; capacity

qualóra *conj* if; (lit) whenever

qualsìasi [s] *adj invar* any; whatever; ordinary

qualunque *adj invar* any; whatever; common, ordinary; **in qualunque modo** anyway, anyhow; **qualunque altro** anybody else; **qualunque cosa** anything; no matter what

qualvòlta *conj* (lit) whenever

quando *m* when ‖ *adv* when; **di quando in quando** from time to time; **quando . . . quando** sometimes . . . sometimes ‖ *conj* when; whenever; while; **da quando** since

quantìsti·co -ca *adj* (-ci -che) quantum

quanti·tà *f* (-tà) quantity; number

quantitativo *m* quantity

quan·to -ta *adj* how much; as much; how great; how great a; what a; **quan·ti -te** how many; as many ‖ *m* quantum ‖ *pron* how much; as much; how great; how long; that which; what; whatever; **a quanto si dice** according to what is rumored; **da quanto** from what; for how long; **fra quanto** how soon; **per quanto io ne sappia** as far as I know; **quanto più** (or **meno**) **. . . tanto più** (or **meno**) the more (or the less) . . . the more (or the less); **quan·ti -te** how many; all those; as many as; **quanti ne abbiamo?** what's the date? ‖ **quanto** *adv* how much; as much as; in quanto as; **in quanto che** inasmuch as; **per quanto** although; no matter; nevertheless; **quanto** a as to, as for; **quanto mai** as never before; **quanto meno** at least; **quanto prima** as soon as possible

quantunque *conj* although, though

quaranta *adj, m & pron* forty; **gli anni quaranta** the forties; **i quaranta** the forties (*in age*)

quarantèna *f* quarantine

quarantènne *adj* forty-year-old ‖ *mf* forty-year-old person

quarantèsi·mo -ma *adj, m & pron* fortieth

quarantina *f* about forty; **essere sulla quarantina** to be about forty years old

quarantòtto *adj* forty-eight ‖ *m* forty-eight; (coll) hubbub, uproar

quarésima *f* Lent

quartabuòno *m* triangle (*in drafting*); **tagliare a quartabuono** to miter

quartétto *m* quartet; **quartetto d'archi** string quartet

quartière *m* quarter, district; (mil) quarters; (coll) apartment; **quartier generale** headquarters; **senza quartiere** (*fight*) without quarter

quar·to -ta *adj & pron* fourth ‖ *m* fourth; quarter; quarter of a kilo; quarter of a liter; (naut) watch; **l'una e un quarto** a quarter after one; **l'una meno un quarto** a quarter to one

quarzo *m* quartz

quasi *adv* almost, nearly; **quasi che** as if; **quasi mai** hardly ever; **senza quasi** without any ifs and buts

quassù *adv* up here

quat·to -ta *adj* crouching; squatting; **quatto quatto** stealthy, silent; **star-sene quatto quatto** to not make a sound

quattordicènne *adj* fourteen-year-old ‖ *mf* fourteen-year-old person

quattordicèsi·mo -ma *adj, m & pron* fourteenth

quattórdici *adj & pron* fourteen; **le**

quattordici two P.M. ‖ *m* fourteen; fourteenth (*in dates*)
quattrino *m* penny; (fig) bit; **quattrini** money
quattro *adj* four; a few, e.g., **quattro gatti** a few people; **a quattro mani** (mus) for four hands ‖ *pron* four; **dirne quattro a** to upbraid; **farsi in quattro** to go all out; **in quattro e quattr'otto** in a few minutes; **le quattro** four o'clock ‖ *m* four; fourth (*in dates*); racing shell with four oarsmen
quattrocènto *adj, m & pron* four hundred ‖ **il Quattrocento** the fifteenth century
quattromila *adj, m & pron* four thousand
quégli §7 *adj* ‖ §8 *pron*
quéi §7 *adj*
quél §7 *adj* ‖ §8 *pron*
quéll' §7 *adj*
quél·lo **-la** §7 *adj* ‖ §8 *pron*—**per quello che so io** as far as I know
quèr·cia *f* (**-ce**) oak tree
querci·no **-na** *adj* oaken
querèla *f* complaint
querelante *adj* complaining ‖ *mf* plaintiff
querelare (**querèlo**) *tr* to sue ‖ *ref* (law) to sue; (lit) to complain
querela·to **-ta** *adj* accused ‖ *mf* defendant
quèru·lo **-la** *adj* (lit) plaintive
quesito *m* question; problem; (lit) request
quésti §7 *pron*
questionare (**questióno**) *intr* to quarrel
questionà·rio *m* (**-ri**) questionnaire
questióne *f* question; (coll) quarrel; **questione di gabinetto** call for a vote of confidence; **venire a questione** to quarrel
qué·sto **-sta** §7 *adj* ‖ §8 *pron*—**e con questo?** so what?; **per questo** therefore; **questa** this matter; **questo . . . quello** the former . . . the latter
questóre *m* police commissioner; sergeant at arms (*of congress*)
quèstua *f* begging; collection of alms; **andare alla questua** to go begging; **vietata la questua** no begging
questura *f* police department; police headquarters

questurino *m* (coll) policeman
què·to **-ta** *adj* var of **quieto**
qui *adv* here; **di qui** hence, from here; this way; **di qui a un anno** one year hence; **di qui in avanti** from now on; **qui vicino** nearby
quiescènza *f* quiescence; retirement
quietanza *f* receipt
quietanzare *tr* to receipt
quietare (**quièto**) *tr* to quiet, calm; to satisfy (*e.g., thirst*) ‖ *ref* to quiet down
quiète *f* quiet, calmness
quiè·to **-ta** *adj* quiet, calm; still; **stia quieto!** don't worry! ‖ *m* quiet life
quindi *adv* then; therefore; (archaic) thence, from there
quindicènne *adj* fifteen-year-old ‖ *mf* fifteen-year-old person
quindicèsi·mo **-ma** *adj, m & pron* fifteenth
quìndici *adj & pron* fifteen; **le quindici** three P.M. ‖ *m* fifteen; fifteenth (*in dates*)
quindicina *f* about fifteen; two weeks, fortnight; semimonthly pay
quindicinale *adj* fortnightly
quinquennale *adj* five-year
quinta *f* (theat) wing; (mus) fifth; **dietro le quinte** behind the scenes
quintale *m* quintal (*100 kilos*)
quintèrno *m* signature of five sheets; (bb) quire
quintessènza *f* quintessence
quintétto *m* quintet
quin·to **-ta** *adj, m & pron* fifth ‖ *f* see **quinta**
quisquìlia *f* trifle
quivi *adv* (lit) over there; (lit) then
quòrum *m* quorum
quòta *f* quota; share; altitude; elevation; level (*of stock market*); market average; odds (*in betting*); subscription (*to club*); **quota zero** (fig) point of departure
quotare (**quòto**) *tr* to quote (*a price*); to value, esteem ‖ *ref* to sign up for, e.g., **si quotò duemila lire** he signed up for two thousand lire
quotazióne *f* quotation
quotidia·no **-na** *adj & m* daily
quoziènte *m* quotient; (sports) percentage; **quoziente d'intelligenza** I.Q.

R

R, r ['erre] *m & f* sixteenth letter of the Italian alphabet
rabàrbaro *m* rhubarb
rabberciare §128 (**rabbèrcio**) *tr* (coll) to patch up
ràbbia *f* rage, anger; rabies
rabbino *m* rabbi
rabbió·so **-sa** [s] *adj* furious; rabid
rabbonire §176 *tr* to pacify ‖ *ref* to calm down
rabbrividire §176 *intr* (ESSERE) to shiver, shudder

rabbuffare *tr* to rebuke; to dishevel
rabbuffo *m* rebuke; **fare un rabbuffo a** to rebuke
rabbuiare §287 *ref* to darken, turn dark
rabdomante *m* dowser, diviner
rabé·sco *m* (**-schi**) arabesque; scrawl, scribble
ràbi·do **-da** *adj* rabid
raccapezzare (**raccapézzo**) *tr* to put together; to gather (*news*); to find (*one's way*); to make out (*what is*

meant) ‖ _ref_—**non raccapezzarsi** to not be able to get one's bearings

raccapricciante _adj_ bloodcurdling

raccapric·cio _m_ (-ci) horror

raccartocciare §128 (**raccartòccio**) _tr_ & _ref_ to shrivel

raccattare _tr_ to pick up; to gather

racchétta _f_ racket; **racchetta da neve** snowshoe; **racchetta da sci** ski pole

ràc·chio -chia _adj_ (-chi -chie) (coll) ugly, homely

racchiùdere §125 _tr_ to contain, hold

raccògliere §127 _tr_ to pick up; to gather; to collect (_e.g., stamps_); to take up (_the gauntlet_); to receive; to reap; to furl (_sail_); to draw in (_a net_); to fold (_the wings_); to shelter (_e.g., foundlings_); **raccogliere i passi** to stop walking ‖ _ref_ to gather; to concentrate

raccoglimento _m_ concentration; meditation

raccogli·tóre -trice _mf_ collector, compiler ‖ _m_ folder

raccòl·to -ta _adj_ crouched; collected; engrossed; snug, intimate ‖ _m_ harvest ‖ _f_ harvest; collection; **chiamare a raccolta** to rally

raccomandàbile _adj_ recommendable; **poco raccomandabile** unreliable

raccomandare _tr_ to recommend; to secure (_e.g., a boat_); to register (_mail_); to exhort ‖ _ref_ to recommend oneself; to entreat; **mi raccomando** please; **raccomandarsi a** to beg, implore; **raccomandarsi alle gambe** to take to one's heels

raccomanda·to -ta _adj_ recommended; registered ‖ _m_ protégé ‖ _f_ protégée; registered letter

raccomandazióne _f_ recommendation; registration (_of mail_); exhortation

raccomodare (**raccòmodo**) _tr_ to fix; to mend

racconciare §128 (**raccóncio**) _tr_ to fix; to mend ‖ _ref_ to clear up (_said of the weather_); to tidy oneself up

raccontare (**racconto**) _tr_ to tell; **raccontarla bene** to be good at telling lies

raccónto _m_ tale; story; narrative

raccorciamento _m_ shortening

raccorciare §128 (**raccòrcio**) _tr_ to shorten

raccordare (**raccòrdo**) _tr_ to link, connect

raccòrdo _m_ link, connection; **raccordo a circolazione rotatoria** traffic circle; **raccordo anulare** (rr) belt line; **raccordo ferroviario** junction; spur; siding; **raccordo stradale** connecting road

raccostare (**raccòsto**) _tr_ & _ref_ to draw near

raccozzare (**raccòzzo**) _tr_ to scrape together

ràchide _m_ & _f_ backbone; midrib (_of leaf_); shaft (_of feather_)

rachìti·co -ca _adj_ (-ci -che) stunted; weak; (pathol) rickety

rachitismo _m_ rickets

racimolare (**racìmolo**) _tr_ to glean; to scrape together

rada _f_ roadstead; cove

ràdar _m_ radar

addobbare (**raddòbbo**) _tr_ (naut) to refit

raddolcire §176 _tr_ & _ref_ to sweeten; to mellow

raddoppiare §287 (**raddóppio**) _tr, intr_ (ESSERE) & _ref_ to double, redouble

raddrizzare _tr_ to straighten; (elec) to rectify ‖ _ref_ to straighten up

raddrizzatóre _m_ (elec) rectifier

ràdere §223 _tr_ to shave; to raze; to graze, skim ‖ _ref_ to shave

radézza _f_ rarity, rareness; thinness; sparsity (_of vegetation_); space, distance (_e.g., between trees_)

radiante _adj_ radiating

radiare §287 _tr_ to strike off; to expel; to condemn (_a ship_); **radiare dall'albo degli avvocati** to disbar

radiatóre _m_ radiator

radiazióne _f_ radiation; expulsion

ràdi·ca _f_ (-che) brier; (coll) root

radicale _adj_ & _mf_ radical ‖ _m_ & _f_ (philol) radical, root ‖ _m_ (chem, math) radical

radicare §197 (**ràdico**) _tr_ & _intr_ to root

radice _f_ root; base or foot (_e.g., of a mountain or tower_); **mettere radice** to take root; **svellere dalle radici** to pull up by the roots; to eradicate

rà·dio _adj invar_ radio ‖ _m_ (-di) (anat) radius; (chem) radium ‖ _f_ (-dio) radio; **radio fante** (mil) grapevine

radioabbonato _m_ (rad) subscriber (_to radio broadcasting_)

radioama·tóre -trice _mf_ radio fan; radio ham

radioannunciatóre _m_ radio announcer

radioascolta·tóre -trice _mf_ radio listener

radioatti·vo -va _adj_ radioactive

radiobùssola _f_ radio compass

radiocanale _m_ radio channel

radiocomanda·to -ta _adj_ radio-controlled

radiocròna·ca _f_ (-che) newscast

radiocroni·sta _mf_ (-sti -ste) newscaster

radiodiffóndere §178 _tr_ to broadcast

radiodiffusióne _f_ broadcasting

radiofaro _m_ radio beacon

radiofòni·co -ca _adj_ (-ci -che) radio

radiofonògrafo _m_ radiophonograph

radiofò·to _f_ (-to) radiophoto

radiofrequènza _f_ radiofrequency

radiologìa _f_ radiology

radiomontatóre _m_ radio assembler

radioónda _f_ radio wave; **radioonde** airwaves

radioricevènte _adj_ radio ‖ _f_ radio set; radio station

radioriparatóre _m_ radio repairman

radiosegnale _m_ radio signal

radiosentièro _m_ range of a radio beacon

radió·so -sa [s] _adj_ radiant

radiosorgènte _f_ quasar

radiostazióne _f_ radio station

radiostélla _f_ quasar

radiotas·sì _m_ (-sì) radio-dispatched taxi

radiotelescò·pio _m_ (-pi) radiotelescope

radiotrasméttere §198 _tr_ & _intr_ to broadcast, radio

radiotrasmissióne _f_ broadcast

radiotrasmittènte *adj* broadcasting ‖ *f* broadcasting station

ra·do -da *adj* rare; thin; sheer; sparse, scattered; **di rado** seldom, rarely

radunare *tr* & *ref* to assemble, gather

radunata *f* gathering; (mil) assembly; **radunata sediziosa** unlawful assembly

raduno *m* assembly, gathering

radura *f* clearing, glade

ràfano *m* (bot) radish

raffazzonare (raffazzóno) *tr* to mend, patch up

raffazzonatura *f* patchwork, hodgepodge

rafférma *f* confirmation; stay (*in office*); return to office; (mil) reenlistment

raffermare (raffèrmo) *tr* to reaffirm; to secure; (coll) to reconfirm; to reappoint, reelect; to return (*e.g., a mayor*) to office ‖ *intr* (ESSERE) & *ref* to reenlist; (coll) to harden

raffér·mo -ma *adj* stale (bread) ‖ *f* see **rafferma**

ràffi·ca *f* (-che) gust; blast; burst (*e.g., of machine gun*); **a raffiche** gusty

raffigurare *tr* to represent; to symbolize

raffinare *tr* to refine; to polish ‖ *intr* (ESSERE) to become refined

raffinatézza *f* refinement, polish

raffinatura *f* refinement (*of oil*)

raffinazióne *f* refining

raffinerìa *f* refinery

ràf·fio *m* (-fi) hook; grappling iron

rafforzare (raffòrzo) *tr* to strengthen

raffreddaménto *m* cooling

raffreddare (raffréddo) *tr* to make cold; to cool; **raffreddare gli spiriti di qlcu** to dampen s.o.'s enthusiasm ‖ *intr* (ESSERE) & *ref* to get cold; to cool

raffreddóre *m* cold

raffrontare (raffrónto) *tr* to compare; (law) to bring face to face

raffrónto *m* comparison; confrontation

ràfia *f* raffia

raganèlla *f* rattle; (zool) tree frog

ragazza *f* girl; spinster; (coll) girl friend; **ragazza copertina** cover girl; **ragazza squillo** call girl

ragazzata *f* boyish prank

ragaz·zo -za *mf* youth, young person ‖ *m* boy; (coll) boyfriend ‖ *f* see **ragazza**

raggelare (raggèlo) *intr* (ESSERE) to freeze

raggiante *adj* radiant; beaming

raggiare §290 *tr* & *intr* to radiate

raggièra *f* rayed halo; **a raggiera** radially

ràg·gio *m* (-gi) ray; beam; spoke; (geom) radius; **raggio d'azione** radius, range of action; **raggio di sole** sunbeam

raggiornare (raggiórno) *tr* (coll) to bring up to date ‖ *intr* (ESSERE) to dawn ‖ *impers* (ESSERE)—**raggiorna** it is dawning

raggirare *tr* to trick, swindle ‖ *ref* to roam, wander; **raggirarsi su** to turn on (*e.g., a certain subject*)

raggiro *m* trickery, swindle

raggiùngere §183 *tr* to reach; to catch up with, rejoin

raggiungìbile *adj* attainable

raggomitolare (raggomìtolo) *tr* to roll up ‖ *ref* to curl up; to cuddle

raggranellare (raggranèllo) *tr* to gather; to scrape together

raggrinzire §176 *tr* & *ref* to crease, wrinkle

raggrumare *tr* & *ref* to clot, coagulate

raggruppaménto *m* grouping; group

raggruppare *tr* & *ref* to group, assemble

ragguagliare §280 *tr* to compare; to balance; to inform in detail; to level

ragguà·glio *m* (-gli) comparison; detailed report

ragguardévole *adj* considerable, notable

ragionaménto *m* reasoning; discussion

ragionare (ragióno) *intr* to reason; to discuss ‖ *impers ref*—**si ragiona** it is rumored

ragióne *f* reason; account; rate; justice; (math) ratio; **a maggior ragione** with all the more reason; **a ragione** within reason; **aver ragione** to be right; **aver ragione di** to get the best of; **dar ragione a qlcu** to admit that s.o. is right; **di santa ragione** hard, a great deal; **farsi ragione** to be resigned; **in ragione di** at the rate of; **ragion per cui** and therefore; **ragione sociale** (com) trade name; **rendere di pubblica ragione** to publicize

ragionerìa *f* accounting; bookkeeping

ragionévole *adj* reasonable

ragioniè·re -ra *mf* accountant; bookkeeper

ragliare §280 *intr* to bray

rà·glio *m* (-gli) bray

ragnatéla *f* spider web

ragno *m* spider

ra·gù *m* (-gù) meat gravy; stew

ràion *m* rayon

rallegraménto *m* congratulation, act of congratulating; **rallegramenti** congratulations

rallegrare (rallègro) *tr* to cheer up; to rejoice, gladden ‖ *ref* to cheer up; to rejoice; **rallegrarsi con** to congratulate

rallentare (rallènto) *tr, intr* & *ref* to slow down; to lessen

rallentatóre *m* slow-motion projector; **al rallentatore** slow-motion

ra·màio *m* (-mài) tinker, coppersmith

ramaiòlo *m* ladle

ramanzina [dz] *f* reprimand

ramare *tr* to copperplate; (agr) to spray with copper sulfate

ramarro *m* green lizard

ramazza *f* broom; (mil) cleaning detail; (mil) soldier on cleaning detail

rame *m* copper; etching

ramerino *m* (coll) rosemary

ramificare §197 (ramìfico) *intr* & *ref* to branch; to branch off; to branch out, ramify

ramìn·go -ga *adj* (-ghi -ghe) wandering

ramino *m* copper pot; rummy (*card game*)

rammagliare §280 *tr* to reknit; to mend a run in (*a stocking*)

rammaricare §197 (rammàrico) *tr* to afflict ‖ *ref* to be sorry, regret; **rammaricarsi di** to be sorry for rammàri·co *m* (-chi) regret

rammendare (rammèndo) *tr* to darn

rammèndo *m* darn

rammentare (rammènto) *tr* to remember; to remind ‖ *ref*—rammentarsi di to remember

rammenta·tóre -trice *mf* prompter

rammollire §176 *tr & ref* to soften

rammolli·to -ta *adj* soft; soft-headed ‖ *m* dodo, jellyfish

ramo *m* branch; bough; point (*of antler*); ramo di pazzia streak of madness

ramoscèllo *m* twig; ramoscello d'olivo olive branch

rampa *f* ramp; flight (*of stairs*); launching platform

rampicante *adj* climbing ‖ *m* (ichth) perch; (órn) climber

rampino *m* hook; tine, prong; pretext

rampógna *f* (lit) reprimand

rampòllo *m* spring (*of water*); scion; shoot (*of a plant*); (joc) offspring

rampóne *m* harpoon; crampon

rana *f* frog

rànci·do -da *adj* rancid

ràn·cio -cia (-ci -ce) *adj* (poet) orange ‖ *m* (mil) mess

rancóre *m* rancor; grudge; serbar rancore to bear rancor

randa *f* (naut) spanker; (obs) edge

randà·gio -gia *adj* (-gi -gie) wandering; stray

randellare (randèllo) *tr* to cudgel; to bludgeon; to blackjack

randèllo *m* cudgel; bludgeon

ran·go *m* (-ghi) rank; station

rannicchiare §287 *tr* to cause to curl up ‖ *ref* to crouch; to cower; to cuddle up

ranno *m* lye; buttar via il ranno e il sapone to waste one's time and effort

rannuvolare (rannùvolo) *tr & ref* to cloud; to darken

ranòcchia *f* frog

ranòc·chio *m* (-chi) frog

rantolare (ràntolo) *intr* to wheeze

ràntolo *m* wheezing; death rattle

ranùncolo *m* buttercup

rapa *f* turnip; valere una rapa to be not worth a fig

rapace *adj* rapacious ‖ rapaci *mpl* birds of prey

rapare *tr* to shave (*s.o.'s head*) ‖ *ref* to shave one's head; to have one's head shaved

rapidi·tà *f* (-tà) rapidity, swiftness

ràpi·do -da *adj* rapid, swift ‖ *m* (rr) express ‖ rapide *fpl* rapids

rapiménto *m* rape, abduction; rapture

rapina *f* pillage, plunder; misappropriation; prey; (lit) fury; rapina a mano armata armed robbery

rapinare *tr* to rob, plunder; to hold up; rapinare qlco a qlcu to rob s.o. of s.th

rapina·tóre -trice *mf* robber, plunderer

rapire §176 *tr* to rape, abduct; to kidnap; to enrapture

rapi·tóre -trice *mf* kidnaper

rappacificare §197 (rappacìfico) *tr* to reconcile ‖ *ref* to become reconciled

rappezzare (rappèzzo) *tr* to patch; to

piece; rappezzarla to get out of trouble

rappèzzo *m* patch; patchwork

rapportare (rappòrto) *tr* to report; to transfer (*a design*) ‖ *ref* to refer

rapporta·tóre -trice *mf* reporter ‖ *m* protractor

rappòrto *m* report; relation; relationship; (math) ratio; chiamare a rapporto to summon; chiedere di mettersi a rapporto to ask for a hearing; fare rapporto to report; in rapporto a concerning; mettersi a rapporto to report; sotto ogni rapporto in every respect

rapprèndere §220 *tr & ref* to coagulate

rappresàglia [s] *f* reprisal; retaliation

rappresentante *adj* representing; representative ‖ *mf* representative; agent; rappresentante di commercio agent

rappresentanza *f* delegation; proxy; agency; representation

rappresentare (rappresènto) *tr* to represent; to play; to portray

rappresentati·vo -va *adj* representative

rappresentazióne *f* representation; description; (theat) performance; rappresentazione teatrale diurna matinée; sacra rappresentazione (theat) mystery, miracle play

rapsodia *f* rhapsody

raraménte *adv* seldom, rarely

rarefare §173 *tr* to rarefy ‖ *ref* to become rarefied

rari·tà *f* (-tà) rarity

ra·ro -ra *adj* rare; di raro seldom

rasare [s] *tr* to shave; to mow; to trim; to smooth ‖ *ref* to shave

raschiare §287 (ràschio) *tr* to scrape; to scratch ‖ *intr* to clear one's throat

raschiétto *m* scraper; erasing knife; footscraper

rà·schio *m* (-schi) clearing one's throat; hoarseness; frog in the throat

rasentare (rasènto) *tr* to graze; to scrape; to border on; to come close to

rasènte *adv* close; rasente a close to ‖ *prep* close to

ra·so -sa [s] *adj* shaved; trimmed; brimful; disreputable (*clothes*); flush ‖ *m* satin ‖ *adv*—raso terra down-to-earth; volare raso terra to skim the ground; to hedgehop

ra·sóio [s] *m* (-sói) razor; rasoio a mano libera straight razor; rasoio di sicurezza safety razor

raspa *f* rasp

raspare *tr* to rasp; to irritate; to stamp, paw; (coll) to steal ‖ *intr* to rasp; to scratch (*said of a chicken*); to scrawl

raspo *m* grape stalk; scraper; (vet) mange

rasségna *f* review; exposition

rassegnare (rasségno) *tr* to resign; rassegnare le dimissioni to resign ‖ *ref* to resign oneself; to submit

rassegnazióne *f* resignation

rasserenare (rasseréno) *tr & ref* to brighten; to cheer up

rassettare (rassètto) *tr & ref* to tidy up

rassicurare *tr* to reassure ‖ *ref* to be reassured

rassodare (**rassòdo**) *tr* to harden; to strengthen ‖ *intr* (ESSERE) & *ref* to harden

rassomigliare §280 (**rassomìglio**) *tr* to compare ‖ *intr* (ESSERE) & (with *dat*) to resemble ‖ *ref* to resemble each other

rastrellaménto *m* roundup; mop-up operation

rastrellare (**rastrèllo**) *tr* to rake; to round up; to mop up; to drag (*e.g.*, *the bottom*)

rastrellièra *f* rack; crib

rastrèllo *m* rake

rastremare (**rastrèmo**) *tr* to taper

rata *f* installment; quota; **a rate on time; by installments**

rateale *adj* installment

rateizzare [ddzz] *tr* to pròrate; to divide (*a payment*) into installments

ratifi·ca *f* (**-che**) ratification

ratificare §197 (**ratìfico**) *tr* to ratify

rat·to -ta *adj* (lit) swift ‖ *m* rat; (lit) rape ‖ **ratto** *adv* (lit) swiftly

rattoppare (**rattòppo**) *tr* to patch, patch up

rattrappire §176 *tr* to cramp; to make numb, benumb ‖ *ref* to become cramped; to become numb

rattristare *tr* & *ref* to sadden

raucèdine *f* hoarseness

ràu·co -ca *adj* (**-chi -che**) hoarse, raucous

ravanèllo *m* radish

ravizzóne *m* (bot) rape

ravvedére §279 (*fut* **ravvedrò** & **ravvederò**; *pp* **ravveduto**) *ref* to repent; to mend one's ways

ravvedu·to -ta *adj* repentant; reformed

ravviare §119 *tr* to arrange, adjust; to poke (*fire*) ‖ *ref* to tidy up; (lit) to reform

ravvicinaménto *m* approach; reconciliation; rapprochement

ravvicinare *tr* to bring up; to reconcile ‖ *ref* to approach; to become reconciled; **ravvicinarsi a** to approach

ravviluppare *tr* to wrap up; to wind up; to bamboozle ‖ *ref* to become tangled

ravvisare *tr* to recognize

ravvivare *tr* to revive; to enliven; to brighten; to stir (*fire*) ‖ *ref* to revive

ravvòlgere §289 *tr* to wrap up

razioci·nio *m* (**-ni**) reasoning; reason; common sense

razionale *adj* rational

razionalizzare [ddzz] *tr* (com, math) to rationalize

razionaménto *m* rationing

razionare (**razióno**) *tr* to ration

razióne *f* ration; portion

razza [ddzz] *f* race; breed; kind; **di razza** purebred; **far razza** to reproduce; **passare a razza** to go to stud

razza [ddzz] *f* (ichth) ray; **razza cornuta** manta ray

razzia *f* raid; foray; insect powder

razziale *adj* racial

razziare §119 *tr* & *intr* to foray

razzismo *m* racism

razzi·sta *mf* (**-sti -ste**) racist

razzo [ddzz] *m* rocket; (coll) spoke; (mil) flare

razzolare (**ràzzolo**) *intr* to scratch (*said of chickens*); (coll) to rummage

re [e] *m* (**re**) king

re [e] *m* (**re**) (mus) re

reagènte *m* reagent

reagire §176 *intr* to react

reale *adj* real, actual; royal, regal

realismo *m* royalism

reali·sta *mf* (**-sti -ste**) realist; royalist

realìsti·co -ca *adj* (**-ci -che**) realistic

realizzare [ddzz] *tr* to carry out; to realize; to build ‖ *ref* to come true

realizzazióne [ddzz] *f* realization; **realizzazione scenica** production

realizzo [ddzz] *m* conversion into cash; profit taking; forced sale

realménte *adv* really, indeed

real·tà *f* (**-tà**) reality; actuality; **realtà romanzesca** truth stranger than fiction

reato *m* crime

reatti·vo -va *adj* reactive

reattóre *m* reactor; jet plane; jet engine

reazionà·rio -ria (**-ri -rie**) *adj* & *mf* reactionary

reazióne *f* reaction; (mach) backlash; **a reazione** jet-propelled

réb·bio *m* (**-bi**) prong

recalcitrante *adj* balky, restive; **essere recalcitrante a** to be opposed to, to resist

recalcitrare (**recàlcitro**) *intr* to be balky; to kick; (with *dat*) to buck, resist

recapitare (**recàpito**) *tr* to deliver

recàpito *m* address; delivery; **far recapito in** to be domiciled in; **recapiti** (com) notes

recare §197 (**rèco**) *tr* to bring; to cause; **recare ad effetto** to carry out; **recare qlco alla memoria di qlcu** to remind s.o. of s.th; **recare qlco a lode di qlcu** to praise s.o. for s.th ‖ *ref* to go, betake oneself

recèdere §123 *intr* (ESSERE & AVERE) to recede

recensióne *f* book review; collation

recensire §176 *tr* to review; to collate

recensóre *m* reviewer

recènte *adj* recent; **di recente** recently

recessióne *f* recession

recèsso *m* recess; subsiding (*of fever*); ebb tide

recìdere §145 *tr* to cut off; to chop off

recidiva *f* relapse; second offense

recìngere §126 *tr* to enclose, pen in

recìnto *m* enclosure; pen, yard; compound; playpen; paddock; **recinto delle grida** floor of the exchange

recipiènte *m* container

reciprocità *f* reciprocity

recìpro·co -ca *adj* (**-ci -che**) reciprocal

reci·so -sa *adj* cut off; abrupt

rècita *f* show, performance

recitare (**rècito**) *tr* to recite; to portray, play; **recitare la commedia** to put on an act ‖ *intr* to perform, play; **recitare a soggetto** (theat) to improvise

recitazióne *f* recitation; diction; acting

reclamare *tr* to claim, demand ‖ *intr* to complain

récla·me *f* (-me) advertising; advertisement; **fare réclame a** to advertise; to boost

reclami·sta *mf* (-sti -ste) advertising agent; show-off ‖ *m* advertising man

reclamìsti·co -ca *adj* (-ci -che) advertising

reclamo *m* complaint; **fare reclamo** to complain

reclinare *tr* to bow ‖ *intr* to recline

reclusióne *f* seclusion; imprisonment

reclu·so -sa *adj* recluse ‖ *mf* recluse; prisoner

reclusò·rio *m* (-ri) penitentiary

rècluta *f* recruit; rookie

reclutaménto *m* recruitment

reclutare (**rècluto**) *tr* to recruit

recòndi·to -ta *adj* concealed; inmost; recondite

recriminare (**recrìmino**) *intr* to recriminate

recuperare (**recùpero**) *tr* see **ricuperare**

redarguire §176 *tr* to berate

redat·tóre -trice *mf* compiler; newspaper editor; **redattore capo** managing editor; **redattore pubblicitario** copywriter; **redattore responsabile** publisher; **redattore viaggiante** correspondent

redazionale *adj* editorial, editor's (*e.g., policy*)

redazióne *f* writing; draft; version; (journ) city room

redazza *f* mop; (naut) swab

redditi·zio -zia *adj* (-zi -zie) lucrative

rèddito *m* income, revenue; yield; **reddito nazionale** gross national product

redén·to -ta *adj* redeemed, set free

reden·tóre -trice *mf* redeemer ‖ **Redentore** *m*—**il Redentore** the Redeemer

redenzióne *f* redemption

redìgere §224 *tr* to compile; to write up, compose

redimere §225 *tr* to redeem; to ransom; to save

rèdine *f* rein

redivi·vo -va *adj* come back to life

rèduce *adj* back (*from war*) ‖ *mf* veteran

réfe *m* thread

referèn·dum *m* (-dum) referendum; **referendum postale** mail questionnaire

referènza *f* reference

referenziare (**referènzio**) *tr* to give references to; to write references for ‖ *intr* to have good references

referenzia·to -ta *adj* with good references, e.g., **impiegato referenziato** employee with good references

referto *m* report (*of a physician*)

refettò·rio *m* (-ri) refectory

refezióne *f* lunch, light meal; **refezione scolastica** school lunch

refrattà·rio -ria *adj* (-ri -rie) refractory

refrigerante *adj* cooling ‖ *m* refrigerator; (chem) condenser

refrigerare (**refrìgero**) *tr* to refrigerate; to cool ‖ *ref* to cool off

refrigè·rio *m* (-ri) relief, comfort

refurtiva *f* stolen goods

refuso *m* misprint

regalare *tr* to present; to deliver (*a slap*); to throw away (*money*); **è regalato** it's a steal

regale *adj* regal; royal; imposing

regalìa *f* gratuity; bonus

regalità *f* regality, royalty

regalo *m* present, gift

regata *f* regatta

reggènte *adj & m* regent

reggènza *f* regency

règgere §226 *tr* to hold, hold up; to stand, withstand; to guide; (gram) to govern; **reggere il sacco a** to connive with; **reggere l'ànimo di** + *inf* to bear or stand + *ger*, e.g., **non gli regge l'ànimo di vederla piangere** he cannot stand seeing her cry ‖ *intr* to hold; to be valid; to last, hold out (*said of weather*); **reggere** (with *dat*) to withstand (*e.g., the cold*); **reggere al paragone** to bear comparison ‖ *ref* to stand up; to hold; to be ruled; **reggersi a** to hold on to; to be governed as (*e.g., a republic*); **reggersi a galla** to float

règ·gia *f* (-ge) royal palace

reggical·ze *m* (-ze) girdle

reggilibro *m* book end

reggimentale *adj* regimental

reggiménto *m* regiment

reggipètto *m* brassiere

reggisé·no *m* (-ni & -no) brassiere

regìa *f* monopoly; (mov) direction; (theat) production

regici·da *mf* (-di -de) regicide

regici·dio *m* (-di) regicide

regime *m* regime; diet; flow (*e.g., of river*); government; authoritarian government; (mach) rate; **regime secco** total abstinence

regina *f* queen; **regina claudia** greengage; **regina madre** queen mother

reginétta *f* young queen; queen (*of a beauty contest*)

rè·gio -gia *adj* (-gi -gie) royal ‖ **i regi** the king's soldiers

regióne *f* region

regi·sta *mf* (-sti -ste) coordinator; (theat) producer; (mov) director

registrare *tr* to register, record; to enter; to tally, log; to adjust; to tune up (*a musical instrument*) ‖ *ref* to register

registra·tóre -trice *mf* registrar ‖ *m* recorder; **registratore di cassa** cash register

registrazióne *f* registration; record, entry; adjustment; (aut) tune-up; (telv) videotaping; (telv) video-taping studio; (telv) video-taped program

registro *m* register; registration; classbook; regulator (*of watch*); stop (*of organ*); **cambiar registro** to change one's tune; **dar registro a** to regulate (*a watch*)

regnante *adj* reigning; prevailing ‖ **i regnanti** the rulers

regnare (**régno**) *intr* to reign, rule; to prevail; to take hold (*said of a root*)

régno *m* kingdom; reign

règola f rule; regulation; moderation; **a regola d'arte** to a T; **di regola** as a rule; **in regola** in good order; **mettere in regola** to put in order; **regole** menstruation; **secondo le regole** by the book

regolamentare adj regulation || v (**regolaménto**) tr to regulate

regolaménto m regulation; settlement; **regolamento edilizio** building code

regolare adj regular; steady (employment); stock (material) || v (**règolo**) tr to regulate; to adjust; to set (a watch); to focus (a lens); to settle (an account) || ref to behave; to control oneself

regolari·tà f (-tà) regularity

regolarizzare [ddzz] tr to regularize

regolatézza f regularity; moderation

regola·to -ta adj regular, orderly

regola·tóre -trice adj regulating; see **piano** || m ruler; regulator (of watch); (mach) governor; **regolatore dell'aria** register; **regolatore di volume** (rad, telv) volume control

regolazióne f regulation

regolizia f (coll) licorice

règolo m ruler; slat; (orn, hist) kinglet; **regolo calcolatore** slide rule

regredire §116 (pres participle **regrediènte**; pp **regredito** & **regrèsso**) intr (ESSERE & AVERE) to retrogress

regrèsso m regression; abatement (of fever); (com) recourse

reiè t·to -ta adj rejected || mf outcast

reimbarcare §197 tr & ref to reship; to transship

reimbar·co m (-chi) reshipment; transshipment

reincarnare tr to reincarnate || ref to become reincarnated

reincarnazióne f reincarnation

reinseriménto m integration

reintegrare (**reintegro**) tr to restore; to reinstate; to indemnify

reità f guilt

reiterare (**reìtero**) tr to reiterate

relativi·tà f (-tà) relativity

relati·vo -va adj relative

rela·tóre -trice adj reporting || mf relator (of proceedings); presenter (of a bill); dissertation supervisor

relazióne f relation; relationship; report; **relazione amorosa** affair; **relazioni** relations; connections

re·lè m (-lè) (elec) relay

relegare §209 (**rèlego**) tr to banish; to store away

religióne f religion

religió·so -sa [s] adj religious || m clergyman || f nun

reliquia f relic

relit·to -ta adj residual || m shipwreck; air crash; derelict; shoal, bar

remare (**rèmo** & **rémo**) intr to row

rema·tóre -trice mf rower || m oarsman

reminiscènza f reminiscence

remissióne f submissiveness; remission

remissi·vo -va adj submissive

rèmo m oar; **remo alla battana** paddle

rèmora f hindrance; (lit) delay

remò·to -ta adj remote; **passato remoto** (gram) preterit

réna f sand

Renània, la the Rhineland

Renata f Renée

rèndere §227 tr to return, give back; to give (thanks); to render (justice); to yield; to translate; to make (known); **render conto di** to give an account of; **rendere di pubblica ragione** to publicize; **rendere l'anima a Dio** to give up the ghost; **rendere pan per focaccia** to give tit for tat || intr to pay, yield || ref to make oneself; to betake oneself; to become; (lit) to surrender; **rendersi conto di** to realize

rendicónto m account; report; **rendiconti** proceedings

rendiménto m rendering; yield; output; (mech) efficiency

rèndita f private income; yield; Italian Government bond

rène m kidney

renèlla f (pathol) gravel

renétta f pippin

réni fpl loins; **spezzare le reni a** to break the back of

renitènte adj opposed || m—**renitente alla leva** draft dodger

rènna f reindeer; reindeer skin

Rèno m Rhine

rè·o -a adj guilty; (lit) wicked || m guilty person; accused

reòstato m (elec) rheostat

reparto m department; (mil) unit; **reparto d'assalto** shock troops

repèllere §168 tr to repel

repentàglio m jeopardy; **mettere a repentaglio** to jeopardize

repènte adj—**di repente** suddenly

repenti·no -na adj sudden

reperìbile adj available

reperiménto m finding

reperire §176 tr to find

repèrto m (archeol) find; (law) evidence; (law) exhibit; (med) report

repertò·rio m (-ri) repertory; catalogue

rèpli·ca f (-che) repetition; replica; (law) rebuttal; (theat) repeat performance; **in replica** in reply

replicare §197 (**rèplico**) tr to repeat; to reply, answer; (theat) to repeat (a performance)

reportàg·gio m (-gi) news coverage; reporting

repòr·ter m (-ter) reporter

repressióne f repression; constraint

repressi·vo -va adj repressive; controlling, checking (e.g., a disease)

reprìmere §131 tr to repress; to hold back (tears) || ref to restrain oneself

rèpro·bo -ba adj & m reprobate

repùbbli·ca f (-che) republic

repubblica·no -na adj & mf republican

repulisti m—**fare repulisti** (coll) to make a clean sweep

repulsióne f repulsion

repulsi·vo -va adj var of **ripulsivo**

reputare (**rèputo**) tr to think, esteem, repute

reputazióne f reputation

rèquie m & f (eccl) requiem || f rest, respite

Rèquiem m & f Requiem

requisire §176 *tr* to requisition, commandeer

requisito *m* requisite, requirement

requisitòria *f* scolding, reproach; (law) summation

requisizióne *f* requisition

résa [s] *f* surrender; rendering (*of an account*); delivery (*of merchandise*); return (*e.g., of newspapers*); yield; **resa a discrezione** unconditional surrender

rescìndere §247 *tr* to rescind

resezióne [s] *f* (surg) resection

residènte [s] *adj & mf* resident

residènza [s] *f* residence

residenziale [s] *adj* residential

residua·to·ta [s] *adj* residual

resì·duo -dua [s] *adj* residual ‖ *m* residue; remainder; balance

rèsina *f* resin

resipiscènza [s] *f* (lit) repentance

resistènte [s] *adj* resistant; strong; fast (*color*) ‖ *mf* member of the Resistance

resistènza [s] *f* resistance ‖ **Resistenza** *f* Resistance

resìstere [s] §114 *intr* to resist; (with *dat*) to withstand; (with *dat*) to endure; (with *dat*) to resist

rèso [s] *m* rhesus

resocónto [s] *m* report, relation

respingènte *m* (rr) bumper, buffer

respìngere §126 *tr* to drive back, beat off; to reject; to fail (*a student*); to vote down

respìn·to -ta *adj* rejected ‖ *mf* failure (*pupil*)

respirare *tr & intr* to breathe, respire

respiratò·rio -ria *adj* (-ri -rie) respiratory

respirazióne *f* breathing

respiro *m* breath; breathing; respite

responsàbile *adj* responsible; **responsabile di** responsible for

responsabili·tà *f* (-tà) responsibility

respònso *m* decision (*of an oracle*); report (*of a physician*); return (*of an election*); (lit) response

rèssa *f* crowd; **far ressa** to crowd

rèsta *f* string (*of garlic or onions*); awn (*e.g., of wheat*); (coll) fishbone; (*for a lance*) (hist) rest

restante *adj* remaining ‖ *m* remainder

restare (**rèsto**) *intr* (ESSERE) to remain; to stay; to be located; (lit) to stop; **non restare a...che** to have no alternative but to, e.g., **non gli resta che andarsene** he has no alternative but to go; **non restare a qlcu qlco da** + *inf* to not have s.th + to + *inf*, e.g., **non gli resta molto da finire** he does not have much to finish; **resta a vedere** it remains to be seen; **restare qlco a qlcu** to have s.th left, e.g., **gli restano tre dollari** he has three dollars left; **restare sul colpo** to die on the spot; **resti comodo** please don't get up!

restaurare (**restàuro**) *tr* to restore, renovate

restaurazióne *f* restoration

restàuro *m* restoration (*of a building*)

restì·o -a (-ì -e) *adj* balky, restive ‖ *m* balkiness

restituire §176 *tr* to give back, return; (lit) to restore ‖ *ref* (lit) to return

restituzióne *f* restitution, return

rèsto *m* remainder; change; balance; **del resto** besides, after all; **resti** remains

restrìngere §265 (*pp* **ristrétto**) *tr* to narrow down; to shrink; to take in (*a suit*); to limit (*expenses*); to tighten (*a knot*); to bind (*the bowels*); to restrict ‖ *ref* to contract; to narrow

restrizióne *f* restriction

retàg·gio *m* (-gi) (lit) heritage

retata *f* haul; (fig) roundup

réte *f* net; network; (soccer) goal; **rete a strascico** trawl; **rete da pesca** fishing net; **rete del letto** bedspring; **rete metallica** wire mesh; window screen; **rete per i capelli** hair net; **rete viaria** highway network

reticèlla *f* small net; hair net; mantle (*of gas jet*)

reticènte *adj* secretive, dissembling; evasive, noncommittal

reticènza *f* secretiveness; evasiveness

reticolato *m* grid (*on map*); wire entanglement

reticolo *m* grid

retina *f* small net

rètina *f* (anat) retina

retino *m* small net; (typ) screen

retòri·co -ca (-ci -che) *adj* rhetorical ‖ *m* rhetorician ‖ *f* rhetoric

retràttile *adj* retractile

retribuire §176 *tr* to remunerate

retributì·vo -va *adj* retributive; salary (*e.g., conditions*)

retrì·vo -va *adj* backward

rètro *m* back; verso; back of store ‖ *adv* (lit) behind; **retro a** (lit) behind

retroattì·vo -va *adj* retroactive

retrobottè·ga *m & f* (-ga *mpl* -ghe *fpl*) back of store

retrocàmera *f* back room

retrocàrica *f*—**a retrocarica** breechloading

retrocèdere §228 *tr* to demote; (com) to return; (com) to give a discount to ‖ *intr* (ESSERE & AVERE) to retreat

retrocessióne *f* demotion; (sports) assignment to a lower division

retrodatare *tr* to antedate, predate

retrògra·do -da *adj* backward; retrograde

retroguàrdia *f* rearguard

retromàr·cia *f* (-ce) (aut) reverse

retrorazzo [ddzz] *m* retrorocket

retrosapóre *m* aftertaste

retroscè·na *m* (-na) intrigue, maneuver ‖ *f* backstage

retrospettì·vo -va *adj* retrospective

retrotèr·ra *m* (-ra) hinterland; (fig) background

retrotrèno *m* rear end (*of vehicle*); (aut) rear assembly

retroversióne *f* retroversion; retranslation

retrovìe *fpl* zone behind the front

retrovisì·vo -va *adj* rear-view, e.g., **specchietto retrovisivo** rear-view mirror retrovisóre *m* rear-view mirror

rètta *f* board and lodging; straight line; dar retta a to pay attention to

rettangolare *adj* rectangular

rettàngolo *m* rectangle

rettìfi·ca *f* (-che) straightening; rectification; (mach) grinding; (mach) reboring

rettificare §197 (rettífico) *tr* to straighten; to rectify; (mach) to grind; (mach) to rebore

rettifica·tóre -tríce *adj* rectifying ‖ *mf* rectifier (*person*) ‖ *m* rectifier (*apparatus*)

rettifilo *m* straightaway

rèttile *m* reptile

rettilì·neo -nea *adj* rectilinear ‖ *m* straightaway ‖ *f* straight line

rettitùdine *f* straightness; uprightness, rectitude

rèt·to -ta *adj* straight; correct; upright; (geom) right ‖ *m* right; recto; (anat) rectum ‖ *f* see retta

rettóre *m* rector; president (*of university*)

reumàti·co -ca *adj* (-ci -che) rheumatic

reumatismo *m* rheumatism

reverèn·do -da *adj* & *m* reverend

reverènte *adj* var of riverente

reverènza *f* var of riverenza

revisióne *f* revision; (mach) overhaul

revisionismo *m* revisionism

revisóre *m* inspector; revisore dei conti auditor; revisore di bozze proofreader

reviviscènza *f* rebirth

rèvo·ca *f* (-che) revocation; recall; repeal

revocare §197 (rèvoco) *tr* to revoke; to recall; to repeal

revól·ver *m* (-ver) revolver

revolverata *f* gun shot

revulsióne *f* (med) revulsion

ri- *pref* re-, e.g., rivivere to relive; again, e.g., rifare to do again; back, e.g., riandare to go back

riabbonare (riabbòno) *tr* to renew the subscription of ‖ *ref* to renew one's subscription

riabbracciare §128 (riabbràccio) *tr* to embrace again; to greet again

riabilitare (riabìlito) *tr* to rehabilitate ‖ *ref* to reestablish one's good name

riaccèndere §101 *tr* to rekindle ‖ *ref* to become rekindled

riaccompagnare *tr* to take home

riaccostare (riaccòsto) *tr* to bring near; to bring together ‖ *ref* to draw near

riacquistare *tr* to buy back; to recover

riaddormentare (riaddormènto) *tr* to put back to sleep ‖ *ref* to go back to sleep

riaffacciare §128 (riaffàccio) *tr* to present again ‖ *ref* to reappear

riaffermare (riaffèrmo) *tr* to reaffirm

riaggravare *tr* to make worse ‖ *ref* to get worse again

rialesare (rialèso) *tr* to rebore

riallacciare §128 (riallàccio) *tr* to tie again ‖ *ref* to be tied or connected

rialto *m* knoll, height; fare rialto (coll) to eat better than usual

rialzare *tr* to lift, raise; to increase ‖ *ref* to rise

rialzi·sta *mf* (-sti -ste) bull (*in stock market*)

rialzo *m* rise; raise; knoll, height; giocare al rialzo to bull the market

riammobiliare §287 *tr* to refurnish

rianimare (rιànimo) *tr* to revive; to encourage ‖ *ref* to revive; to recover one's spirits, to rally

riapertura *f* reopening

riapparire §108 *intr* (ESSERE) to reappear

riapparizióne *f* reappearance

riaprire §110 *tr* & *ref* to reopen

riarmare *tr* to rearm; to reinforce; to refit ‖ *intr* & *ref* to rearm

riarmo *m* rearmament

riar·so -sa *adj* dry, parched

riassaporare (riassapóro) *tr* to relish again

riassettare (riassètto) *tr* to tidy up

riassicurare *tr* to reinsure; to fasten again; to reassure

riassorbire §176 & (riassòrbo) *tr* to reabsorb

riassùmere §116 *tr* to hire again; to summarize, sum up

riassunto *m* précis, abstract; résumé

riassunzióne *f* rehiring; resumption

riattaccare §197 *tr* to attach again; (coll) to begin again; (telp) to hang up

riattare *tr* to repair, fix

riattivare *tr* to reactivate

riavére §229 *tr* to get again; to recover; to get back ‖ *ref* to recover

riavvicinaménto *m* var of ravvicinamento

riavvicinare *tr* & *ref* var of ravvicinare

ribadire §176 *tr* to clinch (*a nail*); to rivet; to drive home (*an idea*); to back up (*a statement*)

ribaldo *m* scoundrel, rogue

ribalta *f* lid with hinge; trap door; (theat) footlights; (theat) forestage; (fig) limelight; a ribalta hinged

ribaltàbile *adj* collapsible (*e.g., seat*) ‖ *m* dump-truck lift; dump truck

ribaltare *tr* & *ref* to upset, turn over

ribassare *tr* & *intr* (ESSERE) to lower

ribassi·sta *mf* (-sti -ste) bear (*in stock market*)

ribasso *m* fall, decline; discount, rebate; giocare al ribasso to be a bear

ribàttere *tr* to clinch (*a nail*); to return (*a ball*); to iron smooth; to belabor (*a point*) ‖ *intr* to answer back

ribattezzare [ddzz] (ribattézzo) *tr* to rebaptize

ribattino *m* rivet

ribellare (ribèllo) *tr* to rouse to rebellion ‖ *ref* to rebel; ribellarsi a to rebel against

ribèlle *adj* rebellious ‖ *mf* rebel

ribellióne *f* rebellion

ri·bes *m* (-bes) currant; gooseberry

ribobinazióne *f* rewind (*of a tape*)

riboccare §197 (ribócco) *intr* (ESSERE & AVERE) to overflow

ribollíre (ribóllo) *tr* to boil again ‖

intr to boil over; to simmer; to ferment

ribrézzo [ddzz] *m* repugnance, disgust

ributtare *tr* to return (*a ball*); to throw up; to reject; to push back ‖ *intr* to sprout; (with *dat*) to disgust, nauseate

ricacciare §128 *tr* to drive back ‖ *intr* to sprout ‖ *ref* to sneak away, disappear

ricadére §121 *intr* (ESSERE) to fall back; to fall down; to relapse; **ricadere su** to devolve upon

ricaduta *f* relapse

ricalcare §197 *tr* to transfer (*a design*); to imitate; **ricalcare le orme di** to follow in the footsteps of

rical·co *m* (**-chi**) copy, copying; **a ricalco** multiple-copy

ricamare *tr* to embroider

ricambiare §287 *tr* to return; to repay ‖ *ref* to change clothes

ricàm·bio *m* (**-bi**) exchange; spare part; refill; metabolism; **di ricambio** spare (*part*)

ricamo *m* embroidery; needlework; **ricami** (*fig*) embellishments

ricapitolare (**ricapitolo**) *tr* to recapitulate

ricaricare §197 (**ricàrico**) *tr* to reload; to wind (*a watch*); to charge (*a battery*)

ricattare *tr* to blackmail

ricatta·tóre -trice *mf* blackmailer

ricatto *m* blackmail

ricavare *tr* to draw, extract; to obtain, derive

ricavato *m* proceeds; (fig) fruit, yield

ricavo *m* proceeds

ricchézza *f* wealth; **ricchezza mobile** income from personal property; **ricchezze** riches

ric·cio -cia (**-ci -ce**) *adj* curly ‖ *m* curl; shaving; burr; scroll (*of violin*); crook (*of crozier*); (zool) hedgehog; **riccio di mare** (zool) sea urchin

ricciolo *m* curl

ricciolu·to -ta *adj* curly

ricciu·to -ta *adj* curly

ric·co -ca *adj* (**-chi -che**) rich ‖ **i ricchi** the rich

ricér·ca *f* (**-che**) search; research; **ricerca operativa** operations research

ricercare §197 (**ricérco**) *tr* to search for again; to seek; to investigate; (poet) to pluck (*a musical instrument*)

ricercatézza *f* affectation; sophistication

ricerca·to -ta *adj* sought after, wanted; affected; sophisticated

ricetrasmettitóre *m* two-way radio

ricètta *f* prescription; recipe

ricettàcolo *m* receptacle; depository

ricettare (**ricètto**) *tr* to receive (*stolen goods*); to prescribe

ricettà·rio *m* (**-ri**) recipe book; prescription pad

ricetta·tóre -trice *mf* fence, receiver of stolen goods

ricetti·vo -va *adj* receptive

ricètto *m* (poet) refuge

ricévere §141 *tr* to receive; to get; to contain; to withstand

ricevimén to *m* reception; receipt

ricevi·tóre -trice *mf* addressee ‖ *m* receiver; collector; registrar of deeds; **ricevitore postale** postmaster

ricevitoria *f* collection office; **ricevitoria postale** post office

ricevuta *f* receipt; **accusare ricevuta di** to acknowledge receipt of

ricezióne *f* (rad, telv) reception; **accusare ricezione** to acknowledge receipt

richiamare *tr* to call back; to recall; to call (*e.g., attention*); to quote; to chide ‖ *ref* to refer

richiamato *m* soldier recalled to active duty

richiamo *m* call; recall; admonition; cross reference; advertisement

richièdere §124 *tr* to ask again; to demand; to require; to apply for ‖ *ref* to be required

richiè·sto -sta *adj*—**essere richiesto** to be in demand ‖ *f* request; demand; petition, application

richiùdere §125 *tr* & *ref* to shut again

riciclare *tr* to recycle (*e.g., in the chemical industry*)

ricino *m* castor-oil plant

ricognitóre *m* scout; reconnaissance plane; (law) recognition

ricognizióne *f* recognition; (mil) reconnaissance

ricollegare §209 (**ricollégo**) *tr* to connect ‖ *ref* to be connected; to refer

ricolmare (**ricólmo**) *tr* to fill to the brim; to overwhelm

ricominciare §128 *tr* & *intr* (ESSERE) to begin again, resume

ricomparire §108 *intr* (ESSERE) to reappear

ricomparsa *f* reappearance

ricompènsa *f* compensation, recompense; reward; (mil) award

ricompensare (**ricompènso**) *tr* to compensate, recompense; to reward

ricomperare (**ricómpero**) *tr* var of **ricomprare**

ricompórre §218 *tr* to recompose; to plan again ‖ *ref* to regain one's composure

ricomprare (**ricómpro**) *tr* to buy again; to buy back

riconcentrare (**riconcèntro**) *tr* to concentrate again; to gather (*one's thoughts*) ‖ *ref* to be withdrawn

riconciliare §287 (**riconcìlio**) *tr* to reconcile ‖ *ref* to become reconciled

ricondurre §102 *tr* to bring back; to take back ‖ *ref* to go back

riconfermare (**riconfèrmo**) *tr* to reconfirm

riconfortare (**riconfòrto**) *tr* to comfort

ricongiùngere §183 *tr* & *ref* to reunite

riconoscènte *adj* grateful

riconoscènza *f* gratitude

riconóscere §134 *tr* to recognize; (mil) to reconnoiter

riconoscimén to *m* recognition; **in riconoscimento di** in recognition of

riconquistare *tr* to reconquer

riconsegnare (**riconségno**) *tr* to give back, to return

riconsiderare (**riconsìdero**) *tr* to reconsider

ricontare (**ricónto**) *tr* to recount, count again

riconversióne *f* reconversion

riconvertire §138 *tr* to reconvert; to recycle

ricopèr·to -ta *adj* covered; coated

ricopertura *f* covering; seat cover

ricopiare §287 (**ricòpio**) *tr* to make a fair copy of; to recopy; to copy

ricoprire §110 *tr* to cover; to coat; to hide || *ref* to become covered

ricordanza *f* (poet) memory

ricordare (**ricòrdo**) *tr* to remember; to remind; to mention || *ref* to remember; **ricordarsi di** to remember

ricòrdo *m* memory; souvenir; **ricordo marmoreo** marble statue

ricorrènte *adj* recurrent, recurring

ricorrènza *f* recurrence; anniversary

ricórrere §139 *intr* (ESSERE & AVERE) to run again; to run back; to resort; to recur; (law) to appeal; **ricorrere a** to have recourse to

ricórso *m* recurrence; recourse; appeal

ricostituènte *adj* invigorating || *m* tonic

ricostituire §176 *tr* to reconstitute, to reform; to reinvigorate

ricostruire §140 *tr* to rebuild; to reconstruct

ricostruzióne *f* rebuilding; reconstruction

ricòtta *f* Italian cottage cheese; **di ricotta** weak

ricoverare (**ricòvero**) *tr* to shelter || *ref* to take shelter

ricòvero *m* shelter; nursing home; (med) admission; **ricovero antiaereo** air-raid shelter

ricreare (**ricrèo**) *tr* to recreate; to refresh || *ref* to relax

ricreati·vo -va *adj* refreshing; recreational

ricreatò·rio -ria (-**ri** -**rie**) *adj* recreation, recreational || *m* recreation room; playground

ricreazióne *f* recreation; recess

ricrédere §141 *intr*—**far ricredere qlcu** to make s.o. change his mind || *ref* to change one's mind

ricréscere §142 *intr* (ESSERE) to grow again; to swell

ricucire §143 *tr* to sew up

ricuòcere §144a *tr* to cook again; to anneal

ricuperare (**ricùpero**) *tr* to recover; (naut) to salvage; (sports) to make up for (*rained-out game*)

ricùpero *m* recovery; salvage; rally; making up for (*for lost time or postponed game*)

ricur·vo -va *adj* bent; bent over

ricusare *tr* to refuse

ridacchiare §287 *intr* to titter, giggle

ridancia·no -na *adj* prone to laughter; amusing

ridare §230 (*1st sg pres ind* **ridò**) *tr* to give back; to give again; **ridare fuori** to vomit || *intr* (coll) to reappear, e.g., **gli ha ridato il foruncolo** his boil has reappeared || *intr*

(ESSERE)—**ridare giù** to have a relapse

ridda *f* round; confusion; throng

ridènte *adj* laughing; bright, pleasant

ridere §231 *tr* (poet) to laugh at || *intr* to laugh; (poet) to shine; **far ridere i polli** to be utterly ridiculous; **ridere sotto i baffi** to laugh up one's sleeve || *ref*—**ridersi di** to laugh at

ridestare (**ridèsto**) *tr & ref* to reawaken

ridicolizzare [ddzz] *tr* to ridicule; to twit

ridìco·lo -la *adj* ridiculous || *m* ridicule; ridiculousness

ridipìngere §126 *tr* to paint again

ridire §151 *tr* to tell again; to repeat; to tell (*to express*); **avere** or **trovare a** or **da ridire** (**su**) to find fault (with)

ridistribuzióne *f* redistribution

ridivenire §282 or **ridiventare** (**ridivènto**) *intr* (ESSERE) to become again

ridonare (**ridóno**) *tr* to give back

ridondante *adj* redundant

ridondare (**ridóndo**) *intr* (ESSERE & AVERE) (fig) to overflow; **ridondare a** or **in** to redound to

ridòsso *m* back; shelter; **a ridosso** sheltered; **as a shelter; behind, close behind**

ridót·to -ta *adj* reduced; **mal ridotto** down at the heel || *m* lounge; (theat) foyer || *f* (mil) redoubt

ridurre §102 *tr* to reduce; to adapt; to translate; to lead; to curtail; (mus) to arrange || *ref* to be reduced; to retire

riduttóre *m* (mach) reduction gear

riduzióne *f* reduction; (mus) arrangement

riecheggiare §290 (**riechéggio**) *tr & intr* to echo

riedificare §197 (**riedìfico**) *tr* to rebuild

rieducare §197 (**rièduco**) *tr* to reeducate

rielèggere §193 *tr* to reelect

rielezióne *f* reelection

riemèrgere §162 *intr* to resurface

riempiménto *m* fill

riempire §163 *tr* to fill; to stuff

riempiti·vo -va *adj* expletive || *m* expletive; fill-in

rientrante *adj* hollow (*cheeks*); (mil) reentrant

rientranza *f* recess

rientrare (**rièntro**) *intr* (ESSERE) to reenter; to come back; to recede; (coll) to shrink; **rientrare in** to recover (*one's expenses*); **rientrare in sé** to come to one's senses

rièntro *m* reentry

riepilogare §209 (**riepìlogo**) *tr* to sum up, recapitulate

riepìlo·go *m* (-**ghi**) recapitulation

riesame *m* reexamination

riesaminare (**riesàmino**) *tr* to reexamine

riesumare *tr* to exhume; (fig) to dig up; (fig) to bring back

rievocare §197 (**rièvoco**) *tr* to recall

rifaciménto *m* adaptation; recasting

rifare §173 (*3d sg pres ind* **rifà**) *tr* to do again, redo; to remake; to imitate; to indemnify; to prepare again; to repeat;

to make (a bed) || ref to recover; to
become again; to recoup one's losses;
to begin; **rifarsi con** to get even with;
rifarsi da to begin with

rifasciare §128 tr to rebind

riferiménto m reference

riferire §176 tr to wound again; to
refer; to relate || ref—**riferirsi a** to
refer to; to concern

riffa f raffle; lottery; (coll) violence;
di riffa o di raffa by hook or crook

rifilare tr to trim; (coll) to reel off
(a list of names); (coll) to deal (a
blow); (coll) to palm off

rifinire §176 tr to give the finishing
touch to; to wear out || .intr to stop
|| ref to wear oneself out

rifiorire §176 tr (lit) to revive || intr
to bloom again || intr (ESSERE) to
flourish; to grow better; to reappear

rifischiare §287 tr to whistle again;
(coll) to report || intr to talk, gossip

rifiutare tr to refuse; (lit) to reject ||
intr (cards) to renege, renounce || ref
to refuse, deny

rifiuto m refusal; refuse, rubbish; rejection; rebuff, spurn; (fig) wreck;
(cards) renege; **di rifiuto** waste, e.g.,
materiale di rifiuto waste material

riflessióne f reflexion

riflessi·vo -va adj thoughtful; (gram)
reflexive

riflès·so -sa adj reflex, e.g., **azione
riflessa** reflex action || m reflection;
(physiol) reflex; **di riflesso** vicarious

riflèttere §177 (pp **riflettuto & riflèsso**)
tr & intr to reflect || ref to be re-
flected

riflettóre m searchlight; reflector

rifluire §176 intr (ESSERE & AVERE) to
flow; to flow back

riflusso m flow; ebb, ebb tide

rifocillare tr to refresh (with food) ||
ref to take refreshment

rifóndere §178 tr to melt again; to recast; to refund; to reedit

rifórma f reform; (mil) rejection ||
Riforma f—**la Riforma** the Reformation

riformare (rifórmo) tr to reform; to
amend; (mil) to reject

riformati·vo -va adj reformatory

riforma·tóre -trice adj reforming || mf
reformer

riformatò·rio m (-ri) reform school,
reformatory

riforniménto m supply; refueling; **fare
rifornimento di** to fill up with; **rifornimenti** supplies

rifornire §176 tr to supply; to restock;
rifornire di benzina to refuel

rifràngere §179 tr to crush || ref to
break (said of waves) || §179 (pp
rifratto) tr to refract || ref to be
refracted

rifrat·tóre -trice adj refracting || m
refractor

rifrazióne f refraction

rifriggere §180 tr to fry again; to rehash
|| intr to fry too long or in too much
oil

rifrit·to -ta adj fried again; (fig) hack-

neyed || m taste of stale fat; (fig)
rehash

rifuggire tr to avoid || intr—**rifuggire
da** to abhor || intr (ESSERE) to take
refuge

rifugiare §290 ref to take refuge, take
shelter

rifugiato m refugee

rifù·gio m (-gi) refuge; **rifugio alpino**
mountain hut; **rifugio antiaereo** air-
raid shelter; **rifugio antiatomico** fall-
out shelter

rifùlgere §233 intr (ESSERE & AVERE) to
shine

rifusióne f recast; refund, reimburse-
ment

ri·ga f (-ghe) line; row; rank; ruler;
part (in hair); stripe; (fig) quality

rigàglie fpl giblets

rigàgnolo m rivulet; gutter (at the side
of a road)

rigare §209 tr to rule, line; to stripe; to
mark; to rifle (gun) || intr—**rigare
diritto** to toe the line

rigatino m gingham

rigattière m second-hand dealer

rigatura f ruling; rifling (of gun)

rigenerare (rigènero) tr to regenerate;
to reclaim; to recycle || ref to be-
come regenerate

rigenera·tóre m—**rigeneratore per i capelli** hair restorer

rigettare (rigètto) tr to throw back; to
reject; to recast; (slang) to throw up
|| intr to sprout

rigètto m rejection

righèllo m ruler

rigidi·tà f (-tà) rigidity; rigor; stiffness;
rigidità cadaverica rigor mortis

rigi·do -da adj rigid, stiff; severe

rigirare tr to keep turning; to dupe; to
invest; to encircle || intr to ramble ||
ref to turn around; to tumble

ri·go m (-ghi) line; **rigo musicale** (mus)
staff

rigò·glio m (-gli) luxuriance; bloom;
gurgling

rigonfiare §287 (rigónfio) tr to inflate
|| intr (ESSERE) & ref to swell up

rigóre m rigor; severity; precision; **a
rigor di termini** strictly speaking;
di rigore de rigueur; (sports) penalty
(e.g., kick)

rigorismo m rigorism, strictness, severity

rigori·sta mf (-sti -ste) rigorist || m
(soccer) kicker of penalty goal

rigoró·so -sa [s] adj rigorous, strict

rigovernare (rigovèrno) tr to clean,
wash (dishes); to groom, tend (animals)

riguadagnare tr to regain

riguardare tr to look again; to look
back; to examine; to consider; to
take care of; to concern || intr—
riguardare a to look out for; to face
(said of a window) || ref to take care
of oneself; **riguardarsi da** to keep
away from

riguardo m care; esteem; regard; **a
questo riguardo** in this regard; **ri-**

guardo a as far as . . . is concerned; senza riguardo a irrespective of

riguardó·so -sa [s] *adj* considerate

rigurgitare (rigùrgito) *tr & intr* to regurgitate

rilanciare §128 *tr* to toss back; to re-establish (*e.g., fashions*); (poker) to raise

rilasciare §128 *tr* to free, let go; to relax; to grant || *ref* to relax

rilà·scio *m* **(-sci)** release; delivery; granting, issue (*of a document*)

rilassante *adj* relaxing

rilassare *tr & ref* to relax

rilassatézza *f* laxity

rilegare §209 **(rilégo)** *tr* to tie again; to bind, rebind (*a book*); to set (*a stone*)

rilega·tóre -trice *mf* binder

rilegatura *f* binding

rilèggere §193 *tr* to reread

rilènto *m*—a rilento slowly

rilevaménto *m* survey; (naut) bearing

rilevare (rilèvo) *tr* to lift again; to observe; to draw; to bring out; to survey; to take over; to pick up; (mil) to relieve || *intr* to be delineated; to be of import || *ref* to rise again; to recover

rileva·tà·rio *m* **(-ri)** successor; (law) assignee

rilièvo *m* relief; survey; remark; assumption (*of debts*); taking over (*of business*); mettere in rilievo to bring out; to set off

rillò·ga *f* **(-ghe)** traverse hole

rilucente *adj* shiny, shining

rilùcere §234 *intr* to shine

riluttante *adj* reluctant

riluttanza *f* reluctance

rima *f* rhyme; slit; crevice; rispondere per le rime to answer in kind, to retort

rimandare *tr* to send back; to refer; to dismiss; to put off, postpone; to refer; rimandare a ottobre to condition (*a student*)

rimando *m* delay; reference; footnote; repartee; postponement; (sports) return

rimaneggiare §290 **(rimanéggio)** *tr* to rearrange; to reshuffle; to shake up (*personnel*); to rewrite (*news*)

rimanènte *adj* remaining || *m* remainder; remnant; i rimanenti the rest

rimanènza *f* remainder

rimanère §235 *intr* (ESSERE) to remain, stay; to be in agreement; to have left, e.g., mi sono rimasti solo tre dollari I only have three dollars left; to be located; (poet) to stop; rimanerci (coll) to be killed; (coll) to be duped; rimanere da to depend on, e.g., questo rimane da Lei this depends on you

rimangiare §290 *tr* to eat again || *ref*—rimangiarsi la parola to go back on one's word

rimarcare §197 *tr* to mark again; to point out

rimar·co *m* **(-chi)** remark, notice

rimare *tr & intr* to rhyme

rimarginare (rimàrgino) *tr, intr & ref* to heal

rimaritare *tr & ref* to marry again

rimasù·glio *m* **(-gli)** leftover

rima·tóre -trice *mf* poet; rhymster

rimbalzare *intr* (ESSERE & AVERE) to bounce back, rebound

rimbalzo *m* rebound

rimbambire §176 *intr* (ESSERE) & *ref* to become feeble-minded (*from old age*)

rimbambì·to -ta *adj* feeble-minded || *mf* dotard

rimbeccare §197 **(rimbécco)** *tr* to peck; to retort

rimbecilli·to -ta *adj* feeble-minded

rimboccare §197 **(rimbócco)** *tr* to tuck up; to tuck in; to fill to the brim

rimbombare (rimbómbo) *intr* (ESSERE & AVERE) to thunder, boom

rimbómbo *m* thunder, boom

rimborsare (rimbórso) *tr* to reimburse, pay back

rimbórso *m* repayment

rimboscare §197 **(rimbòsco)** *tr* to reforest || *ref* to take to the woods

rimboschiménto *m* reforestation

rimboschire §176 *tr* to reforest || *intr* (ESSERE) to become wooded

rimbrottare (rimbròtto) *tr* to scold

rimbròtto *m* scolding

rimediare §287 **(rimèdio)** *tr* (coll) to scrape together; (coll) to patch up || *intr* (with *dat*) to remedy; to make up (*lost time*)

rimè·dio *m* **(-di)** remedy

rimembranza *f* remembrance

riméritare (rimèrito) *tr* to reward

rimescolare (riméscolo) *tr* to stir; to shuffle (*cards*)

riméssa *f* remittance; shipment; harvest; store; loss; sprout; carriage house; garage; (sports) return; (sports) putting in play; rimessa del tram carbarn

rimestare (rimésto) *tr* to stir

riméttere §198 *tr* to remit; to put back; to set back; to sprout; to postpone, defer; to ship; to vomit; to recover; to deliver; to straighten up; (sports) to return; rimetterci to lose; rimettere a nuovo to renovate; rimettere in ordine to tidy up; rimettere in piedi to rebuild, restore || *intr* (coll) to sprout; (coll) to grow; (lit) to abate || *ref* to recover; to quiet down; to defer; to be clearing (said of weather); rimettersi a to go back to (*e.g., bed*); rimettersi a + *inf* to start + *ger* + again; rimettersi in cammino to start off again

rimirare *tr* to stare at

rìmmel *m* mascara

rimodellare (rimodèllo) *tr* to remodel

rimodernare (rimodèrno) *tr* to modernize; to remodel; to bring up to date || *ref* to become modern

rimónta *f* reassembly; return (*of migratory birds*); revamping (*of shoes*); (mil) remount

rimontare (rimónto) *tr* to rewind; to go up (*a stream*); to vamp (*shoes*); to

renovate; to regain; to reassemble
(*a machine*); (mil) to remount || *intr*
(ESSERE & AVERE) to climb again; to
go back (*in time*)

rimorchiare §287 (**rimòrchio**) *tr* to tow;
to drag along

rimorchiatóre *m* tugboat; tow car

rimòr·chio *m* (-chi) tow; trailer; **prendere a rimorchio** to take in tow

rimòrdere §200 *tr* to bite again; to
prick (*said, e.g., of conscience*)

rimòrso *m* remorse

rimostranza *f* remonstrance

rimostrare (**rimòstro**) *tr* to show again
|| *intr* to remonstrate; **rimostrare a**
to remonstrate with

rimozióne *f* removal; demotion

rimpannucciare §128 *tr* to outfit better
|| *ref* to be better dressed; to be
better off

rimpastare *tr* to knead again; to reshuffle, remake

rimpasto *m* reshuffling, rearrangement

rimpatriare §287 *tr* to repatriate || *intr*
to be repatriated

rimpà·trio *m* (-tri) repatriation

rimpètto *adv* opposite; **di rimpetto a**
opposite to; in comparison with

rimpiàngere §215 *tr* to regret; to mourn

rimpianto *m* regret

rimpiattare *tr* & *ref* to hide; **giocare a
rimpiattarsi** to play hide-and-seek

rimpiattino *m* hide-and-seek

rimpiazzare *tr* to replace

rimpiazzo *m* replacement, substitute

rimpiccolíre §176 *tr* to make smaller ||
intr (ESSERE) to get smaller

rimpinzare *tr* to stuff, cram

rimproverare (**rimpròvero**) *tr* to chide,
reproach; **rimproverare qlco di qlco**
or **rimproverare qlco a qlcu** to reproach s.o. for s.th

rimpròvero *m* reproach, rebuke

rimuginare (**rimùgino**) *tr* & *intr* to
rummage; to stir; to ruminate

rimunerare (**rimùnero**) *tr* to reward ||
intr to pay

rimunerati·vo -va *adj* remunerative,
rewarding

rimunerazióne *f* remuneration

rimuòvere §202 *tr* to remove; to demote; to move

rinàscere §203 *intr* (ESSERE) to be born
again; to grow again; to revive; far
rinascere to revive

rinasciménto *m* rebirth || **Rinascimento**
m Renaissance

rinàscita *f* rebirth

rincagna·to -ta *adj* snub (*nose*)

rincalzare *tr* to hill (*plants*); to underpin; to tuck in

rincalzo *m* reinforcement; support

rincantucciare §128 *tr* & *ref* to hide in
a corner

rincarare *tr* to raise the price of; to
raise; **rincarare la dose** to add insult
to injury || *intr* (ESSERE) to rise, go
up (*said of prices*)

rincasare [s] *intr* (ESSERE) to return
home

rinchiùdere §125 *tr* to enclose, shut in

rinchiu·so -sa [s] *adj* shut in; musty ||
m—**saper di rinchiuso** to smell musty

rincitrullíre §176 *intr* (ESSERE) to grow
stupid

rincontro *m*—**a rincontro** opposite

rincorare §236 *tr* to encourage || *ref*
to take heart

rincórrere §139 *tr* to pursue, chase

rincórsa *f*—**prendere la rincorsa** to take
off (*for a jump*); to get a running
start

rincréscere §142 *intr* (ESSERE) (with *dat*)
to displease; to be sorry, e.g., **gli
rincresce** he is sorry; to mind, **Le
rincresce?** do you mind?

rincresciménto *m* regret

rincrudíre §176 *tr* to sharpen; to embitter || *intr* (ESSERE) to become
bitter; to get worse

rinculare *intr* (ESSERE & AVERE) to back
up; to recoil

rínculo *m* recoil

rinfacciare §128 *tr* to throw in one's
face

rinfarcíre §176 *tr* to stuff

rinfiancare §197 *tr* to support

rinfocolare (**rinfòcolo**) *tr* to rekindle;
to revive

rinfoderare (**rinfòdero**) *tr* sheathe

rinforzare (**rinfòrzo**) *tr* to reinforce;
strengthen || *intr* (ESSERE) & *ref* to
become stronger

rinfòrzo *m* reinforcement

rinfrancare §197 *tr* to reassure || *ref*
to buck up

rinfrescante *adj* refreshing || *m* mild
laxative

rinfrescare §197 (**rinfrésco**) *tr* to refresh; to restore; to renew || *intr*
(ESSERE & AVERE) to cool off (*said of
the weather*) || *ref* to have some
refreshments; to cool off

rinfré·sco *m* (-schi) refreshment

rinfusa *f*—**alla rinfusa** at random; pellmell; in bulk

ringalluzzíre §176 *tr* & *ref* to perk up

ringhiare §287 *intr* to growl, to snarl

ringhièra *f* railing

rín·ghio *m* (-ghi) growl, snarl

ringiovaniménto *m* rejuvenation

ringiovaníre §176 *tr* to rejuvenate ||
intr (ESSERE) to grow or look younger

ringraziaménto *m* thanks

ringraziare §287 *tr* to thank; to dismiss

ringuainare (**ringuàino**) *tr* to sheathe

rinnegare §209 (**rinnègo** & **rinnégo**) *tr*
to forswear; to repudiate

rinnega·to -ta *adj* & *m* renegade

rinnovaménto *m* renewal; reawakening

rinnovare (**rinnòvo**) *tr* to renew; to
renovate; to restore; to replace || *ref*
to occur again; to renew

rinnovellare (**rinnovèllo**) *tr* to repeat;
(poet) to renew || *intr* (ESSERE) & *ref*
to change; to renew

rinnòvo *m* renewal

rinocerónte *m* rhinoceros

rinomanza *f* renown

rinoma·to -ta *adj* renowned, famous

rinsaldare *tr* to starch; (fig) to
strengthen || *ref* to become confirmed
(*in one's opinion*)

rinsanguare (rinsànguo) *tr* to give new strength to ‖ *ref* to regain strength; to recover

rinsavire §176 *intr* (ESSERE) to return to reason

rintanare *ref* to burrow; to hide

rintóc·co *m* (**-chi**) toll (*of bell*)

rintontire §176 *tr* to stun, to daze

rintracciare §128 *tr* to track down

rintronare (rintròno) *tr* to deafen; to make rumble ‖ *intr* (ESSERE & AVERE) to thunder; to rumble

rintuzzare *tr* to dull, blunt; to repel; to repress

rinùn·cia *f* (**-ce**) or **rinùnzia** *f* renunciation

rinunziare §287 *tr* to renounce ‖ *intr* (with *dat*) to give up, renounce, e.g., **rinunziò al trono** he renounced the throne

rinvangare §209 *tr* & *intr* var of **rivangare**

rinvenire §282 *tr* to find ‖ *intr* (ESSERE) to come to; **far rinvenire** to bring to, revive

rinviare §119 *tr* to send back; to postpone; to refer; to adjourn; to remit (*to a lower court*)

rinvigorire §176 *tr* to strengthen ‖ *intr* (ESSERE) & *ref* to regain strength

rinvì·o *m* (**-i**) return; postponement; adjournment; reference; (*law*) continuance

rì·o *m* (**-i**) (lit) sin; (lit) brook; (coll) canal

rioccupare (riòccupo) *tr* to reoccupy

rioccupazióne *f* reoccupation

rionale *adj* neighborhood

rióne *m* district; neighborhood

riordinare (riórdino) *tr* to rearrange; to reorganize; to order again

riorganizzare [ddzz] *tr* to reorganize

riottó·so -sa [s] *adj* (lit) quarrelsome; (lit) unruly, rebellious

ripa *f* (lit) bank (*of river*); (lit) escarpment

ripagare §209 *tr* to repay; to pay again

riparare *tr* to protect; to mend, fix, repair; to make up (*an exam*) ‖ *intr* —**riparare a** to make up for ‖ *intr* (ESSERE) & *ref* to take refuge; to betake oneself

riparazióne *f* repair; reparation; redress; (educ) make-up

riparlare *intr* to speak again; **ne riparleremo!** you will see!

riparo *m* repair; shelter

ripartire §176 *tr* to divide; to distribute; to share ‖ (**riparto**) *intr* (ESSERE) to leave again; to start again ‖ §176 *ref* to split up

ripartizióne *f* division; distribution

riparto *m* division; distribution; allotment

ripassare *tr* to cross again; to brush up, review; to repass; to sift again; to check; to read over; (mach) to overhaul ‖ *intr* (ESSERE) to go by; to come by

ripassata *f* checkup; review; (coll) rebuke

ripassa·tóre -trice *mf* checker

ripasso *m* return (*of birds*); (coll) review

ripensare (ripènso) *intr* to keep thinking; **ripensare a** to think of again; to think over again

ripentire (ripènto) *ref* to repent; **ripentirsi di** to repent

ripercórrere §139 *tr* to retrace

ripercuòtere §251 *tr* to reflect; to strike again ‖ *ref* to reverberate

ripescare §197 (**ripésco**) *tr* to fish again; (fig) to dig up

ripètere *tr* & *intr* to repeat ‖ *ref* to be repeated

ripeti·tóre -trice *mf* repeater; coach; tutor ‖ *m* (rad, telv) rebroadcasting station; (rad) relay

ripetizióne *f* repetition; review; tutoring; **a ripetizione** repeating (*firearm*)

ripiano *m* terrace; ledge; shelf; landing; (com) balancing

ripic·co *m* (**-chi**) pique; spite

ripì·do -da *adj* steep

ripiegaménto *m* bend; (mil) withdrawal, retreat

ripiegare §209 (**ripiègo**) *tr* to fold, fold over ‖ *intr* to do better; (mil) to fall back ‖ *ref* to bend over; to withdraw into oneself

ripiè·go m (**-ghi**) expedient

ripiè·no -na *adj* full; stuffed ‖ *m* stuffing; (culin) filling

ripigliare §280 *tr* to reacquire; to catch again; to begin again ‖ *intr* to recover ‖ *ref* to renew a quarrel

ripiombare (ripiómbo) *tr* to make plumb; (fig) to plunge back ‖ *intr* (ESSERE) (fig) to plunge back

ripopolare (ripòpolo) *tr* to repopulate; to restock (*e.g., a pond*)

ripórre §218 *tr* to put back; to place (*one's hope*); to repose (*one's trust*) ‖ *ref* to back down; **riporsi a** + *inf* to start + *ger* again

riportare (ripòrto) *tr* to bring back; to report; to get; to transfer (*a design*); (com) to carry forward; (hunt) to retrieve; (math) to carry ‖ *ref* to go back

ripòrto *m* filler; retrieving; (com) balance carried forward; (math) number carried

riposante [s] *adj* restful

riposare [s] (**ripòso**) *tr, intr* & *ref* to rest

ripòso [s] *m* rest; repose; Requiem; retirement; **buon riposo!** sleep well!; **mettere a riposo** to retire; **riposo!** (mil) at ease

riposti·glio *m* (**-gli**) closet

ripó·sto -sta *adj* innermost ‖ *m* (coll) pantry

riprèndere §220 *tr* to take back; to take up again; to get back; to take in (*a garment*); to catch (*s.th thrown in the air*); to take up (*arms*); to get; to reconquer; to start again, resume; to reprehend; to recover; (mov, telv) to shoot; **riprendere moglie** to remarry ‖ *intr* to start again; to recover, improve; to pick up (*said of a* *motor*) ‖ *ref* to recover; to catch oneself up

riprésa [s] *f* resumption; (aut) pickup; (theat) revival; (mov) shooting, take; (boxing) round; (soccer) second half; (mus, pros) refrain; **a più riprese** several times

ripresentare (ripresènto) *tr* to present again

ripristinare (ripristino) *tr* to restore; to reestablish

ripristino *m* revival, restoration

riprodurre §102 *tr* to reproduce; to express ‖ *ref* to reproduce; to occur

riprodut-tóre -trice *adj* reproducing ‖ *mf* reproducer ‖ *m* reproducer (*e.g., of sound*)

riproduzióne *f* reproduction; playback (*e.g., of tape*)

riprométtere §198 *tr* to promise again ‖ *ref* to hope; to propose; to hope for

ripròva *f* new proof; confirmation

riprovare (ripròvo) *tr* to try again; to try on again; to feel, experience again; to flunk; to censure ‖ *ref* to try again

riprovazióne *f* disapproval

ripudiare §287 *tr* to repudiate

ripugnante *adj* repugnant, repulsive

ripugnanza *f* repugnance; aversion

ripugnare *intr* (with *dat*) to disgust, revolt, be repugnant to

ripulire §176 *tr* to clean again; to tidy up; to clean up; to polish ‖ *ref* to be dressed up; to become polished

ripulita *f*—**dare una ripulita a** to give a lick and a promise to; **fare una ripulita** (fig) to clean house

ripulsi·vo -va *adj* repulsive

riquadrare *tr* to square; to decorate (*a room*) ‖ *intr* to measure; to square

riquadro *m* square

risac·ca [s] *f* (**-che**) undertow; backwash

risàia [s] *f* rice field

risalire [s] §242 *tr* to go up again; to stem (*the tide*); **risalire la corrente** to go upstream ‖ *intr* (ESSERE) to climb again; to reascend; (com) to appreciate; to date back

risaltare [s] *tr* to jump again ‖ *intr* (ESSERE & AVERE) to rebound ‖ *intr* to stand out; **far risaltare** to emphasize

risalto [s] *m* emphasis; prominence; relief; foil

risanare [s] *tr* to heal; to reclaim (*land*); to redevelop (*urban areas*); to reorganize ‖ *intr* (ESSERE) to heal; to improve

risapére [s] §243 *tr* to find out

risapu·to -ta [s] *adj* well-known

risarciménto [s] *m* indemnification, redress

risarcire [s] §176 *tr* to indemnify; to compensate

risata [s] *f* outburst of laughter

risatina [s] *f* chuckle

riscaldaménto *m* heating; inflammation

riscaldare *tr* to heat; to warm up; to inflame ‖ *ref* to warm up; to go in heat; to perspire; to get excited

riscaldo *m* inflammation; prickly heat; padding (*for clothes*)

riscattare *tr* to ransom; to redeem ‖ *intr* (ESSERE) to click again (*said, e.g., of a ratchet*)

riscatto *m* ransom; redemption

rischiarare *tr*, *intr* (ESSERE) & *ref* to clear, clear up

rischiare §287 *tr* to risk ‖ *intr* to run a risk

ri·schio *m* (**-schi**) risk

rischió·so -sa [s] *adj* risky

risciacquare (risciàcquo) *tr* to rinse

risciacquatura *f* rinse; swill

risciàcquo *m* rinsing (*of mouth*); mouthwash

riscónto *m* (com) discount

riscontrare (riscóntro) *tr* to compare, collate; to check; to reply to ‖ *intr* to reply; to tally ‖ *ref* to tally

riscóntro *m* comparison; check, control; draft; correspondence; reply; **far riscontro** to correspond; **far riscontro con** to correspond to; **far riscontro di** to check; **mettere a riscontro** to compare; **riscontri** drafts (*of air*); parts (*that fit together*)

riscoprire §110 *tr* to rediscover

riscòssa *f* insurrection; recovery, reconquest; (mil) counterattack

riscossióne *f* collection

riscrivere §250 *tr* to rewrite; to write back

riscuòtere §251 *tr* to shake; to wake up; to collect; to get; to redeem ‖ *ref* to wake up; to come to one's senses

riseccare [s] §197 (**risécco**) *tr*, *intr* (ESSERE) & *ref* to dry up

risecchire [s] §176 *intr* (ESSERE) & *ref* to dry up

risentiménto [s] *m* resentment, pique

risentire [s] (**risènto**) *tr* to hear again; to feel ‖ *intr*—**risentire di** to feel the effects of ‖ *ref* to take offense; to wake up; to come to one's senses; (telp) to talk again; **a risentirci!** (telp) until we talk again!; **risentirsi con** to resent (*a person*); **risentirsi di** to feel the effects of; **risentirsi per** to resent (*an act*)

risenti·to -ta [s] *adj* heard again; resentful; strong; swift; incisive

riserbare [s] (**risèrbo**) *tr* var of **riservare**

risèrbo [s] *m* var of **risèrvo**

risèrva [s] *f* preservation; exclusive rights; preserve; reserve; supply; backlog; reservation; circumspection; vintage

riservare [s] (**risèrvo**) *tr* to reserve

riservatézza [s] *f* reservedness

riserva·to -ta [s] *adj* reserved; private; classified

riservista [s] *m* (**-sti**) reservist

risèrvo [s] *m* discretion

risguardo *m* end paper

risièdere [s] *intr* to reside

risma [s] *f* ream; (fig) type

riso [s] *m* rice ‖ *m* (**risa** *fpl*) laugh; laughter; jest; cheer; (lit) smile

risolare [s] §257 *tr* to resole

risolino [s] *m* smile; giggle

risollevare [s] (**risollèvo**) *tr* to raise again; to lift ‖ *ref* to rise
risolutézza [s] *f* resoluteness
risolu·to -ta [s] *adj* resolved, determined
risoluzióne [s] *f* resolution; resolve; dissolution
risòlvere [s] §256 (*pret ind* **risolvéi** or **risolvètti** or **risòlsi**; *pp* **risòlto**) *tr* to resolve; to solve; to dissolve; to persuade ‖ *ref* to dissolve; to resolve
risolvìbile [s] *adj* solvable
risonante [s] *adj* resounding
risonanza [s] *f* resonance; (fig) sensation
risonare [s] §257 *tr* to ring again; (lit) to repeat ‖ *intr* (ESSERE & AVERE) to resonate; to resound; to ring again; to echo
risórgere [s] §258 *intr* (ESSERE) to rise again; to revive, to come back to life; to recover
risorgiménto [s] *m* renaissance; resurgence ‖ **Risorgimento** *m* Risorgimento
risórsa [s] *f* resource
risór·to -ta [s] *adj* arisen; reborn
risòtto [s] *m* risotto, rice cooked with broth
risparmiare §287 *tr* to save; to spare
rispàr·mio -mia (**-mi**) saving; sparing; savings; **risparmi** savings; **senza risparmio** lavishly
rispecchiare §287 (**rispècchio**) *tr* to reflect
rispedire §176 *tr* to send back; to forward; to reship
rispedizióne *f* reshipment
rispettàbile *adj* respectable
rispettare (**rispètto**) *tr* to respect; **farsi rispettare** to command respect; **rispettare sé stesso** to have self-respect
rispetti·vo -va *adj* respective
rispètto *m* respect; observance; restriction (*e.g.*, in building); comparison; regard; **con rispetto parlando** excuse the word; **di rispetto** (naut) spare (*e.g.*, *parts*); **rispetti** regards; **rispetto di sé medesimo** self-respect; **rispetto umano** fear of what people will say
rispettó·so -sa [s] *adj* respectful; respectable (*distance*)
risplendènte *adj* resplendent
risplèndere §281 *intr* (ESSERE & AVERE) to shine
rispóndere §238 *tr* to answer; **risponder picche** (coll) to say no ‖ *intr* to answer; **rispondere a** to answer (*e.g.*, *a letter*); **rispondere con un cenno del capo** to nod assent; **rispondere di** to be responsible for; **rispondere in** to face, overlook
risposare (**rispòso**) *tr* & *ref* to marry again, remarry
rispósta *f* answer, reply, response
rissa *f* scuffle, brawl
rissó·so -sa [s] *adj* quarrelsome
ristabilire §176 *tr* to reestablish ‖ *ref* to recover
ristagnare *tr* to tin; to solder ‖ *intr* to stagnate
ristampa *f* reprint

ristampare *tr* to reprint
ristorante *m* restaurant
ristorare (**ristòro**) *tr* & *ref* to refresh
ristora·tóre -trice *adj* refreshing ‖ *m* restaurant
ristòro *m* refreshment; compensation
ristrettézza *f* narrowness; scarcity; **ristrettezza d'idee** narrow-mindedness
ristrét·to -ta *adj* narrow; limited; in straitened circumstances; concentrated, condensed (*e.g.*, *broth*)
ristrutturazióne *f* restructuring
risù·chio -chi [s] *m* (**-chi**) whirlpool
risultante [s] *adj* resulting ‖ *m* & *f* resultant; (phys) resultant
risultare [s] *intr* (ESSERE) to result; to prove to be, turn out to be; to appear
risultato [s] *m* result
risurrezióne [s] *f* resurrection
risuscitare [s] (**risùscito**) *tr* to resurrect; to revive ‖ *intr* to be resurrected; to be revived
risvegliare §280 (**risvéglio**) *tr* & *ref* to awaken; to reawaken
risvé·glio *m* (**-gli**) awakening, reawakening
risvòlto *m* cuff; lapel; inside flap (*of book*); minor aspect (*of a question*)
ritagliare §280 *tr* to cut again; to clip; to trim
rità·glio *m* (**-gli**) clipping (*of paper*); scrap (*of meat*); cutting (*of fabric*); bit (*of time*); **al ritaglio** retail
ritappezzare (**ritappézzo**) *tr* to repaper
ritardare *tr* to delay; to slow down, retard; ‖ *intr* to tarry; to be late; to be slow (*said of a watch*)
ritardatà·rio -ria *mf* (**-ri -rie**) latecomer; (com) delinquent
ritardo *m* delay; retard; lateness; **essere in ritardo** to be late
ritégno *m* reservation; discretion; **senza ritegno** shamelessly
ritemprare (**ritèmpro**) *tr* to temper again; to invigorate ‖ *ref* to harden
ritenére §271 *tr* to retain; to hold; to withhold; to believe, think ‖ *ref* to restrain oneself; to consider oneself; to be considered
ritentare (**ritènto**) *tr* to try again; (law) to retry
ritirare *tr* to withdraw; to pay (*a note*); to throw back; to shoot again; to accept delivery of; to take back (*a promise*) ‖ *intr* to shrink ‖ *ref* to shrink; to withdraw; to fall back, retreat; to retire
ritirata *f* toilet; (mil) retreat
ritiro *m* withdrawal; retreat; retirement; shrinkage; (metallurgy) shrinking
ritma·to -ta *adj* measured (*step*)
ritmi·co -ca *adj* (**-ci -che**) rhythmic(al)
ritmo *m* rhythm; **a ritmo serrato** at a quick pace
rito *m* rite; (fig) ritual, ceremony; **di rito** customary
ritoccare §197 (**ritócco**) *tr* to retouch; to brush up
ritóc·co *m* (**-chi**) retouch; improvement; change

ritòrcere §272 *tr* to twist, twine; to wring; to retort

ritornare (ritórno) *tr* to return, give back || *intr* (ESSERE) to return, go back, come back; **ritornare in sé** to come back to one's senses

ritornèllo *m* refrain; chorus (*of song*)

ritórno *m* return; reoccurrence; **di ritorno** reoccurring; **essere di ritorno** to be back; **far ritorno** to return; **ritorno di fiamma** backfire

ritòr·to -ta *adj* twisted || *m* twist

ritrarre §273 *tr* to retract; to draw; to portray || *intr*—**ritrarre da** to look like || *ref* to retreat; to portray oneself

ritrasméttere §198 *tr* (rad, telv) to retransmit, rebroadcast

ritrattare *tr* to treat again; to retract; (coll) to portray || *ref* to recant

ritrattazióne *f* retraction

ritratti·sta *mf* (-sti -ste) portrait painter

ritratto *m* portrait, picture; photograph; (phot) print; **ritratto parlante** spit and image

ritri·to -ta *adj* (fig) stale, trite

ritrósa [s] *f* (coll) cowlick

ritrosìa [s] *f* coyness, shyness

ritró·so -sa [s] *adj* coy, shy; **a ritroso** backwards || *f* see **ritrosa**

ritrovare (ritróvo) *tr* to discover; to find; to regain; to meet again || *ref* to meet again; to find oneself; to find one's bearings; **non ritrovarcisi** to be out of sorts

ritrovato *m* discovery, find

ritròvo *m* meeting; nightspot; **ritrovo estivo** summer resort; **ritrovo notturno** night club

rit·to -ta *adj* upright; straight; right || *m* face (*of medal*); prop; (sports) post || *f* (lit) right hand

rituale *adj* & *m* ritual

riunióne *f* reunion; meeting; assembly; **riunione alla sommità** summit conference

riunire §176 *tr* to assemble; to reunite; to reconcile || *ref* to gather together; to meet; to be reunited; to rally

riuscire §277 *intr* (ESSERE) to go out again; to turn out, turn out to be; to lead (*said, e.g., of a door*); to succeed; **riuscire a** + *inf* to succeed in + *ger* || *impers*—**riesce** (with *dat*) **di** + *inf* to succeed in + *ger*, e.g., **non gli è riuscito di farsi ricevere** he did not succeed in being received

riuscita *f* success; result; outlet

riva *f* shore; bank; (naut) board

rivale *adj* & *m* rival

rivaleggiare §290 (rivaléggio) *intr* to compete; **rivaleggiare con** to rival

rivalére §278 *ref*—**rivalersi di** to use; **rivalersi su qlcu** to resort to s.o. for compensation; to fall back on s.o., to have recourse to s.o.

rivali·tà *f* (-tà) rivalry

rivalsa *f* compensation; revenge; (com) recourse

rivalutare (rivàluto & rivaluto) *tr* to revalue

rivalutazióne *f* reassessment

rivangare §209 *tr* to rake up; to mull over || *intr* to reminisce

rivedére §279 *tr* to see again; to review; to check; to reread; to revise; to read (*proof*) || *ref* to see one another; **a rivederci!** good-bye!, au revoir!

rivedìbile *adj* deferred (*for draft*)

rivelare (rivélo) *tr* to reveal; to detect; (phot) to develop

rivela·tóre -trice *adj* revealing || *m* (phot) developer; (rad) detector; **rivelatore di mine** mine detector

rivelazióne *f* revelation

rivéndere §281 *tr* to resell; (fig) to surpass

rivendicare §197 (rivéndico) *tr* to demand; to claim

rivendicazióne *f* demand; claim

rivéndita *f* resale; shop; **rivendita sali e tabacchi** cigar store

rivendi·tóre -trice *mf* seller, dealer, retailer

rivendùgliolo *m* peddler; huckster

rivèrbero *m* reverberation; reflection; glare; echo

riverènte *adj* reverent

riverènza *f* reverence; curtsy, bow

riverire §176 *tr* to revere; to pay one's respects to

riversare (rivèrso) *tr* to pour again; to transfer || *ref* to overflow

rivèr·so -sa *adj* on one's back

rivestiménto *m* coating; covering; lining

rivestire (rivèsto) *tr* to dress again; to coat; to line; to cover; to wear; to have (*importance*); to hold (*a rank*) || *ref* to get dressed again; to wear; to be covered

rivièra *f* coast || **Riviera** *f* Riviera

riviera·sco -sca *adj* (-schi -sche) coastal; riverside

rivincere §285 *tr* to win back

rivincita *f* revenge; return match; **prendersi la rivincita** to get even

rivista *f* review; parade; magazine; journal; revue; proofreading

rivìvere §286 *tr* to relive || *intr* (ESSERE) to live again; to revive

rivo *m* (lit) rivulet, brook

rivolare (rivólo) *intr* (ESSERE & AVERE) to fly again

rivolére §288 *tr* to want back

rivòlgere §289 *tr* to turn again; to revolve; to overturn; to train (*a weapon*); to address; to deter || *ref* to turn; to turn around; **rivolgersi a** to apply to

rivolgiménto *m* turn; revolution; upheaval

rivòlta *f* revolt; cuff

rivoltante *adj* revolting

rivoltare (rivòlto) *tr* to overturn; to turn inside out; to toss (*salad*); to upset || *ref* to turn around; to revolt; to toss

rivoltèlla *f* revolver; spray gun

rivoltellata *f* revolver shot

rivoltó·so -sa [s] *adj* rebellious || *m* rioter; rebel

rivoluzionare (rivoluzióno) *tr* to revolutionize

rivoluzionà·rio -ria *adj & mf* (**-ri -rie**) revolutionary

rivoluzióne *f* revolution

rizza *f* (naut) rigging

rizzare *tr* to raise; to hoist; to pay (*attention*); to build; (naut) to lash || *ref* to rise; to bristle (*said of hair*); to rear up (*said of a horse*)

ròba *f* things, stuff; property

robìnia *f* locust tree

robivèc·chi *m* (**-chi**) junk dealer

robu·sto -sta *adj* robust; burly

róc·ca *f* (**-che**) distaff

ròc·ca *f* (**-che**) rock; crag; cliff

roccafòrte *f* (**rocchefòrti**) stronghold

rocchétto *m* spool; reel; coil; roll (*of film*); pinion, rear sprocket wheel; (eccl) rochet; **rocchetto d'accensione** ignition coil; **rocchetto d'induzione** induction coil

ròc·cia *f* (**-ce**) rock; crag; cliff

rocció·so -sa [s] *adj* rocky

rò·co -ca *adj* (**-chi -che**) hoarse; (poet) faint

rodàg·gio *m* (**-gi**) breaking in, running in; adjustment period (*to a new situation*); **in rodaggio** (aut) being run in

Ròdano *m* Rhone

rodare (**ròdo**) *tr* to break in; (aut) to run in

ródere §239 *tr* to gnaw; to bite; to corrode || *ref* to worry, to fret

Ròdi *f* Rhodes

rodì·o *m* (**-i**) gnawing

rodi·tóre -trice *adj* gnawing || *mf* rodent

rodomónte *m* braggart

rogare §209 *tr* to draw up (*a contract*); (law) to request

ròdito *m* (law) instrument, deed

rógna *f* mange; itch

rognóne *m* (culin) kidney

rognó·so -sa [s] *adj* scabby, mangy

rò·go *m* (**-ghi**) pyre; stake

rollì·o *m* (**-i**) roll (*of ship*)

Róma *f* Rome

romané·sco -sca *adj* (**-schi -sche**) Roman (*dialect*)

Romanìa, la Rumania

romàni·co -ca *adj & mf* (**-ci -che**) Romanesque

roma·no -na *adj & mf* Roman; **pagare alla romana** to go Dutch

romanticismo *m* romanticism

romànti·co -ca *adj* (**-ci -che**) *adj* romantic || *mf* romanticist

romanza *f* romance; ballad

romanzare *tr* to fictionalize

romanzé·sco -sca *adj* (**-schi -sche**) romantic; of chivalry; novelistic

romanzière *m* novelist

roman·zo -za *adj* Romance (*language*) || *m* novel; story; romance; fiction; **romanzi** fiction; **romanzo a fumetti** comic strip; comic book; **romanzo d'appendice** serial story, feuilleton; **romanzo giallo** whodunit; **romanzo rosa** love story

rombare (**rómbo**) *intr* to thunder

rómbo *m* thunder, roar

romè·no -na *adj & mf* Rumanian

romì·to -ta *adj* (lit) lonely || *m* (coll) hermit

rómpere §240 *tr* to break; to bust; **rompere la testa a** to annoy, pester || *intr* to overflow; to be wrecked; to break; **rompere in pianto** to burst out crying || *ref* to fly to pieces; **rompersi la testa** to rack one's brains

rompicapo *m* annoyance; puzzle; jig-saw puzzle

rompicòllo *m* madcap; **a rompicollo** headlong, rashly; at breakneck speed

rompighiàc·cio *m* (**-cio**) icebreaker; ice pick

rompiscàto·le *m* (**-le**) bore, pest

rónci·glio *m* (**-gli**) (poet) hook

róncola *f* pruning hook

rónda *f* patrol; beat (*of policeman*)

rondèlla *f* (mach) washer

róndine *f* swallow

rondóne *m* European swift

ronfare (**rónfo**) *intr* (coll) to snore; (coll) to purr

ronzare [dz] (**rónzo**) *intr* to buzz; to hum

ronzino [dz] *m* jade, nag

ronzì·o [dz] *m* (**-i**) buzzing; humming

ròsa *adj invar & m* pink || *f* rose; group; rosette; **rosa dei venti** compass card; **rosa del Giappone** (bot) camelia; **rosa delle Alpi** (bot) rhodo-dendron; **rosa di tiro** (mil) dispersion

ro·sàio *m* (**-sài**) rosebush

rosà·rio *m* (**-ri**) rosary; **recitare il rosario** to count one's beads

rosa·to -ta *adj* rosy

ròse·o -a *adj* rosy

roséto *m* rose garden

rosétta *f* rosette; hard roll; (mach) washer

rosicanti [s] *mpl* rodents

rosicchiare [s] §287 *tr* to gnaw; to pick (*a bone*); to bite (*one's fingernails*)

rosmarino *m* (bot) rosemary

rosolare (**ròsolo**) *tr* (culin) to brown

rosolìa *f* German measles

rosóne *m* (archit) rosette; (archit) rose window

ròspo *m* toad; ugly person; unsociable person; **ingoiare un rospo** to swallow a bitter pill

rossa·stro -stra *adj* reddish

rossétto *m* rouge; **rossetto per le labbra** lipstick

rós·so -sa *adj* red; red-headed; Red; **diventare rosso** to blush || *mf* red-head; Red (*Communist*) || *m* red

rossóre *m* redness; blush

rosticceria *f* grill; rotisserie

rotàbile *adj* open to vehicular traffic (*road*); (rr) rolling (*stock*) || *f* road open to vehicular traffic

rotàia *f* rail; rut; **uscire dalle rotaie** to jump the track; (fig) to go astray

rotare §257 *tr & intr* to rotate; to circle

rotativa *f* (typ) rotary press

rotazióne *f* rotation

roteare (**roteo**) *tr* to roll (*the eyes*); to flourish (*a sword*) || *intr* to circle

rotèlla *f* small wheel; caster; roller; kneecap; disk (*of ski pole*); **gli**

manca una rotella he has a screw loose

rotocal·co *m* (-chi) rotogravure

rotolare (ròtolo) *tr & intr* (ESSERE) to roll ‖ *ref* to turn over; to wallow

ròtolo *m* roll; bolt; coil; **a rotoli** to rack and ruin

rotolóne *m* tumble; **a rotoloni** falling down; to rack and ruin

rotón·do -da *adj* round; rotund ‖ *f* rotunda; terrace

rótta *f* break; rout; (aer, naut) course; **a rotta di collo** at breakneck speed; **mettere in rotta** to rout

rottame *m* fragment; wreck; **rottami** scraps, debris; wreckage; **rottami di ferro** scrap iron

rót·to -ta *adj* broken; shattered; inured ‖ *m* break, tear; **e rotti** odd, e.g., **duecento e rotti** two hundred odd; **per il rotto della cuffia** hardly; just about ‖ *f* see **rotta**

rottura *f* break; breakage; rupture; breakdown (*of relations*); crack

ròtula *f* kneecap

rovèllo *m* (lit) anger

rovènte *adj* red-hot

róvere *m & f* oak tree ‖ *m* oak (*lumber*)

rovè·scia *f* (-sce) cuff; **alla rovescia** inside out; upside down; the wrong way

rovesciaménto *m* upset; overturn

rovesciare §128 (rovèscio) *tr* to overturn; to upset; to throw back (*one's head*); to spill (*liquid*); to pour; to hurl (*insults*); to turn inside out ‖ *intr* to throw up ‖ *ref* to spill; to pour; to upset

rovè·scio -scia *adj* reverse; inverse; inside out; upside down; backwards ‖ *m* reverse; wrong side; downpour; upset; (com) crash; (tennis) backhand; **a rovescio** upside down; backwards ‖ *f* see **rovescia**

rovéto *m* bramble; brier patch

rovina *f* ruin; blight; **andare in rovina** to go to ruin; **mandare in rovina** to ruin; **rovine** ruins

rovinare *tr* to ruin ‖ *intr* (ESSERE) to collapse ‖ *ref* to go to ruin

rovinì·o *m* (-i) clatter; crash

rovinó·so -sa [s] *adj* ruinous

rovistare *tr* to rummage through

róvo *m* bramble

ròzza [ddzz] *f* nag

róz·zo -za [ddzz] *adj* rough; coarse

ruba *f*—**andare a ruba** to sell like hotcakes; **mettere a ruba** to plunder

rubacchiare §287 *tr* to pilfer

rubacuò·ri (-ri) *adj* ravishing ‖ *m* lady-killer ‖ *f* vamp

rubare *tr* to steal; **rubare a man salva** to pillage, loot ‖ *intr* to steal; **rubare sul peso** to give short measure

ruberìa *f* thieving, stealing

rubicón·do -da *adj* rubicund

rubinétto *m* faucet; cock

rubino *m* ruby; jewel (*of watch*)

rubiz·zo -za *adj* well-preserved (*person*)

rubri·ca *f* (-che) title, heading; directory; (journ) section

rude *adj* (lit) rough; (lit) rude

rùdere *m* ruin

rudimentale *adj* rudimentary

rudiménto *m* rudiment

ruffia·no -na *mf* go-between ‖ *m* pimp, panderer ‖ *f* bawd, procuress

ru·ga *f* (-ghe) wrinkle; (bot) rocket

rùggine *f* rust; ill-will; (bot) blight

rugginó·so -sa [s] *adj* rusty

ruggire §176 *tr & intr* to roar

ruggito *m* roar

rugiada *f* dew

rugó·so -sa [s] *adj* wrinkled, wrinkly

rullàg·gio *m* (-gi) (aer) taxiing

rullare *tr* to roll ‖ *intr* to roll; to taxi

rullì·o *m* (-i) roll; rub-a-dub

rullo *m* roll; platen (*of typewriter*); pin (*in tenpins*); **rullo compressore** road roller

rumè·no -na *adj & mf* var of **romeno**

ruminare (rùmino) *tr & intr* to ruminate

rumóre *m* noise; rumor; ado; **far molto rumore** to create a stir

rumoreggiare §290 (rumoréggio) *intr* to rumble

rumoró·so -sa [s] *adj* noisy; rumbling; controversial

ruolino *m* roster

ruòlo *m* roll; role; list; **di ruolo** regular, full-time; **fuori ruolo** temporary, part-time

ruòta *f* wheel; paddle wheel; revolving server (*in convent*); **a quattro ruote** four-wheel; **dar la ruota a** to sharpen; **esser l'ultima ruota del carro** to be the fifth wheel to a wagon; **fare la ruota** to spread its tail, strut (*said, e.g., of a peacock*); to turn cartwheels (*said, e.g., of an acrobat*); **ruota dentata** cog, cogwheel; **ruota idraulica** water wheel; **seguire a ruota** to follow closely

rupe *f* cliff

rurale *adj* rural, farm, farmer

ruscèllo *m* brook

ruspa *f* road grader

ruspante *m* barnyard chicken

russare *intr* to snore

Rùssia, la Russia

rus·so -sa *adj & mf* Russian

rustica·no -na *adj* rustic, boorish

rùsti·co -ca (-ci -chi -che) *adj* rustic; coarse ‖ *m* tool shed; cottage; (lit) peasant

rutilante *adj* (lit) shiny

ruttare *tr* (lit) to belch ‖ *intr* (vulg) to belch

rutto *m* (vulg) belch

ruttóre *m* (elec) contact breaker

ruvidézza *f* or **ruvidi·tà** *f* (-tà) coarseness; roughness

rùvi·do -da *adj* coarse; rough

ruzzare [ddzz] *intr* to romp

ruzzolare (rùzzolo) *tr* to roll ‖ *intr* (ESSERE) to tumble down; to roll

ruzzolóne *m* tumble; **a ruzzoloni** tumbling down

S

S, s ['esse] *m & f* seventeenth letter of the Italian alphabet

s- *pref* dis-, e.g., **sleale** disloyal; e.g., **sconto** discount; un-, e.g., **scatenare** to unchain, unleash

sàbato *m* Saturday; (*of Jews*) Sabbath; **sabato inglese** Saturday afternoon off

sabbàti·co -ca *adj* (**-ci -che**) sabbatical

sàbbia *f* sand; **sabbia mobile** quicksand

sabbiatura *f* sand bath; sandblast

sabbièra *f* (rr) sandbox

sabbió·so -sa [s] *adj* sandy

sabotàg·gio *m* (**-gi**) sabotage

sabotare (**sabòto**) *tr* to sabotage

sac·ca *f* (**-che**) bag; satchel; (mil) pocket; **sacca d'aria** (aer) air pocket; **sacca da viaggio** traveling bag; duffel bag

saccarina *f* saccharine

saccènte *mf* wiseacre, know-it-all

saccheggiare §290 (**sacchéggio**) *tr* to pillage, plunder

sacchég·gio *m* (**-gi**) pillage, plunder

sacchétto *m* little bag, pouch

sac·co *m* (**-chi**) bag; sack; sackcloth; pouch; (boxing) punching bag; (fig) heap, lot; **fare sacco** to sag; **mettere a sacco** to sack; **mettere nel sacco** to outwit; **sacco alpino** knapsack; **sacco a pelo** or **a piuma** sleeping bag; **sacco postale** mailbag

saccòc·cia *f* (**-ce**) (coll) pocket

sacerdòte *m* priest; (fig) devotee

sacerdotéssa *f* priestess

sacerdòzio *m* priesthood; ministry

sacramentale *adj* sacramental; (joc) habitual, ritual

sacraménto *m* sacrament

sacrà·rio *m* (**-ri**) memorial; sanctuary, shrine

sacrestìa *f* var of **sagrestia**

sacrificare §197 (**sacrìfico**) *tr* to sacrifice; to waste; to force ‖ *ref* to sacrifice oneself

sacrifì·cio *m* (**-ci**) sacrifice

sacrilè·gio *m* (**-gi**) sacrilege

sacrìle·go -ga *adj* (**-ghi -ghe**) sacrilegious

sacri·sta *m* (**-sti**) sexton

sacristìa *f* var of **sagrestia**

sa·cro -cra *adj* sacred

sacrosan·to -ta *adj* sacrosanct; sacred (*truth*)

sàdi·co -ca (**-ci -che**) *adj* sadistic ‖ *mf* sadist

sadìsmo *m* sadism

saétta *f* stroke of lightning; hand (*of watch*); (mach) bit; (lit) arrow

saettare (**saétto**) *tr* to shoot; **saettare sguardi a** to look daggers at

saettóne *m* (archit) strut

sagace *adj* sagacious, shrewd

saga·cia *f* (**-cie**) sagacity

saggézza *f* wisdom

saggiare §290 *tr* to assay; to test; (dial) to taste

saggia·tóre -trice *mf* assayer ‖ *m* assay balance

saggina *f* sorghum

sàg·gio -gia (**-gi -ge**) *adj* wise ‖ *m* sage; assay; sample; proof; theme; test; rate (*of interest*); display; **di saggio** examination (*copy*)

saggì·sta *mf* (**-sti -ste**) essayist

sagittària *f* (bot) arrowhead

sagittà·rio *m* (**-ri**) (obs) archer ‖ **Sagittario** *m* Sagittarius

sàgola *f* (naut) halyard

sàgoma *f* outline; target; model, pattern; (joc) character

sagomare (**sàgomo**) *tr* to outline; to mold; to shape

sagomato *m* billboard

sagra *f* anniversary consecration (*of church*); festival

sagrato *m* elevated square in front of a church; churchyard; (coll) curse

sagrestano *m* sexton, sacristan

sagrestìa *f* sacristy, vestry

sàia *f* serge

sàio *m* (**sài**) habit (*of monk or nun*); doublet; frock coat

sala *f* axletree; hall, room; (bot) cattail, reed mace; **sala da ballo** dance hall; **sala da pranzo** dining room; **sala d'aspetto** waiting room; anteroom; **sala operatoria** operating room

salac·ca *f* (**-che**) (coll) sardine; (coll) shad

salace *adj* salacious; pungent

salamandra *f* salamander

salame *m* salami

salamelèc·co *m* (**-chi**) salaam

salamòia *f* brine

salare *tr* to salt; (coll) to cut (*school*)

salaria·to -ta *adj* wage-earning ‖ *m* wage earner

salà·rio *m* (**-ri**) pay, wages

salassare *tr* to bleed

salasso *m* bloodletting

sala·to -ta *adj* salted; salty; dear, expensive; (fig) sharp ‖ *m* salt pork; cold cuts ‖ *f* salting

salda *f* starch solution (*used in laundering*)

saldacón·ti *m* (**-ti**) bookkeeping department; credit department; ledger; bookkeeping machine

saldare *tr* to solder; to set (*a bone*); to weld; to pay, settle ‖ *ref* to knit (*said of a bone*); (lit) to heal

saldatóre *m* solderer; welder; soldering iron

saldatura *f* soldering; setting (*of bones*); joint; continuity; **saldatura autogena** welding

saldézza *f* firmness

sal·do -da *adj* firm; valid (*reason*); flawless ‖ *m* balance; clearance sale; job lot; payment; **saldi** remnants ‖ *f* see **salda**

saldobrasatura *f* soldering

sale *m* salt; wit; (lit) sea; **restare di sale** to be dumbfounded; **sale inglese** Epsom salts; **sali aromatici** smelling salts; **sali da bagno** bath salts

salgèmma *f* rock salt

sàlice *m* willow tree; salice piangente weeping willow

salicilato *m* salicylate

saliènte *adj* projecting; (fig) salient ‖ *m* projection

salièra *f* saltcellar, salt shaker

salini·tà *f* (-tà) salinity

sali·no -na *adj* saline; salty ‖ *f* salt bed

salire §242 *tr* to climb ‖ *intr* (ESSERE) to climb; to go up; to rise; salire in or su to get on (*e.g., a train*)

saliscén·di *m* (-di) latch; saliscendi *mpl* ups and downs

salita *f* climbing; ascent, rise; slope; in salita uphill

saliva *f* saliva

salma *f* corpse, body

salma·stro -stra *adj* briny; saltish ‖ *m*—sapere di salmastro to smell or taste salty

salmerìe *fpl* wagon train; (mil) supplies

salmì *m*—in salmì (culin) in a stew

salmo *m* psalm

salmodiare §287 (salmòdio) *intr* to chant, sing hymns, intone

salmóne *m* salmon

salnitro *m* saltpeter

Salomóne *m* Solomon

salóne *m* hall; salon, drawing room; (naut) saloon; salone da barbiere barber shop; salone dell'automobile auto show

salòtto *m* drawing room; living room, parlor; reception room

salpare *tr* to weigh (*anchor*) ‖ *intr* (ESSERE) to weigh anchor

salsa *f* sauce

salsaparìglia *f* sarsaparilla

salsèdine *f* saltiness

salsic·cia *f* (-ce) sausage

salsièra *f* gravy boat

sal·so -sa *adj* salty; saline ‖ *m* saltiness ‖ *f* see salsa

saltabeccare §197 (saltabécco) *intr* to hop

saltaleóne *m* coil spring

saltare *tr* to jump; to skip; to sauté; (sports) to vault, hurdle; far saltare to kick out; to blow up (*e.g., a mine*); saltare la sbarra (coll) to go A.W.O.L. ‖ *intr* (ESSERE & AVERE) to jump; to pop off, e.g., mi è saltato un bottone one of my buttons has popped off; to blow out (*said of a fuse*); saltare agli occhi to be self-evident; saltare a piè pari to skip with both feet; saltar fuori to pop out (*said of the eyes*); to appear suddenly; saltare in mente a to come to the mind of; saltare il ticchio a (qlcu) di to feel like + *ger*, e.g., gli è saltato il ticchio di cantare he felt like singing; saltare la mosca al naso a (qlcu) to blow one's top, e.g., le è saltata la mosca al naso she blew her top; saltare per aria to blow up; saltare su to start (*to make a sudden jerk*); saltare su a + *inf* to begin suddenly to + *inf*

salta·tóre -trice *mf* jumper, hurdler

saltellare (saltèllo) *intr* to skip, hop

saltellóni *adv*—a saltelloni skipping, hopping

saltimban·co *m* (-chi) acrobat, tumbler; mountebank

salto *m* jump; leap; fall; skip; (*of animals*) mating; (fig) step; a salti skipping, jumping; al salto sauté; fare quattro salti to dance; fare un salto to hop, hurry; salto a pesce jackknife (*dive*); salto coll'asta pole vaulting; salto in altezza high jump; salto in lunghezza broad jump; salto mortale somersault; salto nel vuoto leap in the dark

saltua·rio -ria *adj* (-ri -rie) desultory, occasional

salubre *adj* salubrious, healthy, healthful

salume *m* pork product

salumerìa *f* pork butcher shop

salumiè·re -ra *mf* pork butcher

salutare *adj* healthful ‖ *tr* to greet; to salute; (lit) to proclaim

salute *f* health; salvation; safety ‖ *interj* good luck; to your health!; gesundheit!

saluto *m* salute; greeting; salutation; distinti saluti sincerely yours

salva *f* salvo; outburst; a salve with blank cartridges, with blanks

salvacondótto *m* safe-conduct

salvada·nàio *m* (-nài) piggy bank

salvagèn·te *m* (-te & -ti) life preserver; fender (*of trolley car*) ‖ *m* (-te) safety island

salvaguardare *tr* to safeguard

salvaguàrdia *f* safeguard

salvaménto *m* safety

salvamotóre *m* circuit breaker; fuse box

salvapun·te *m* (-te) pencil cap; tap (*on sole of shoe*)

salvare *tr* to save; to spare (*a life*); to rescue ‖ *ref* to save oneself; to be rescued; si salvi chi può! every man for himself!

salvatàg·gio *m* (-gi) rescue

salvatóre *m* savior, rescuer ‖ il Salvatore the Saviour

salvazióne *f* salvation

salve *interj* hello!, hail!

salvézza *f* salvation; safety

sàlvia *f* (bot) sage

salviétta *f* napkin; paper napkin; paper towel

sal·vo -va *adj* safe; saved; secure ‖ *m*—mettere in salvo to put in a safe place; mettersi in salvo to reach safety ‖ *f* see salva ‖ salvo *prep* except; salvo che unless; salvo il vero unless I am mistaken

samarita·no -na *adj & mf* Samaritan

sambu·co *m* (-chi) elder tree

san *adj* apocopated and unstressed form of santo

sanàbile *adj* curable

sanare *tr* to heal; to remedy; to reclaim (*land*); to normalize

sanatò·rio *m* (-ri) sanatorium

sancire §176 *tr* to ratify, sanction; to establish

sàndalo *m* sandal; sandalwood; flat-bottom boat

sandolino *m* canoe, skiff, kayak

sangue *m* blood; **agitarsi il sangue** to fret; **all'ultimo sangue** (*duel*) to the death; **al sangue** rare (*meat*); **a sangue freddo** in cold blood; cold-blooded; **cavar sangue da una rapa** to draw blood from a stone; **farsi cattivo sangue** to get angry; **il sangue non è acqua** blood is thicker than water; **puro sangue** thoroughbred; **sangue dal naso** nosebleed; **sangue freddo** calmness, composure

sangui·gno -gna *adj* blood (*circulation*); bloody; sanguine, ruddy ‖ *m* (lit) color of blood

sanguinante *adj* bloody, bleeding

sanguinare (**sànguino**) *intr* to bleed; to be rare (*said of meat*)

sanguinà·rio -ria *adj* (**-ri -rie**) sanguinary

sanguinó·so -sa [*s*] *adj* bloody; bleeding; (fig) stinging

sanguisu·ga [*s*] *f* (-ghe) leech

sani·tà *f* (-tà) health; healthfulness; soundness (*of body*); sanity; health department

sanità·rio -ria (-ri -rie) *adj* health; sanitary ‖ *m* physician

sa·no -na *adj* healthy; sound; **sano e salvo** safe and sound

sant' *adj* apocopated form of **santo** and **santa**

santa *f* saint

santabàrbara *f* (**santebàrbare**) (nav) powder magazine

santarellina *f* goody-goody girl

santificare §197 (**santifico**) *tr* to sanctify

santissi·mo -ma *adj* most holy ‖ *m* Eucharist

santi·tà *f* (-tà) sanctity, holiness; sainthood, saintliness

san·to -ta *adj* saintly, holy; sacred; blessed, livelong, e.g., **tutto il santo giorno** all the livelong day ‖ *m* saint; name day; (fig) someone ‖ *f* see **santa**

santorég·gia *f* (-ge) (bot) savory

santua·rio *m* (-ri) sanctuary

sanzionare (**sanzióno**) *tr* to sanction; to ratify

sanzióne *f* sanction

sapére *m* knowledge; **sapere fare** savoir-faire ‖ §243 *tr* to know; to find out; to know how to; **far sapere** to let know; **saperla lunga** to know a thing or two; **un certo non so che** a certain something, something vague ‖ *intr*— **sapere di** to know; to taste; to smell; to smack of; **mi sa che** I think that; **non voler più saperne di** to not want to have anything to do with; **sapere male** (with *dat*) to feel sorry, e.g., **gli sa male** he feels sorry ‖ *ref*—**che io mi sappia** as far as I know

sàpido -da *adj* savory; witty

sapiènte *adj* wise; talented; trained (*dog*) ‖ *m* wise man

sapientó·ne -na *mf* wiseacre, know-it-all

sapiènza *f* wisdom; knowledge

saponària *f* (bot) soapwort

saponata *f* soapsuds; lather; (fig) soft soap

sapóne *m* soap; **sapone da toletta** toilet soap; **sapone per la barba** shaving soap

saponétta *f* cake of soap

saponière *m* soap maker

saponifi·cio *m* (-ci) soap factory

saponó·so -sa [*s*] *adj* soapy

sapóre *m* taste; savor; flavor

saporire §176 *tr* to savor

saporitaménte *adv* heartily; soundly

sapori·to -ta *adj* tasty; flavorful; salty; expensive

saporó·so -sa [*s*] *adj* savory; witty

saputèl·lo -la *adj* cocksure ‖ *m* smart aleck

sarac·co *m* (-chi) hand saw

saracè·no -na *adj* Saracen, Saracenic ‖ *m* Saracen; quintain

saraciné·sca *f* (-sche) metal shutter (*of store*); sluice gate; (hist) portcullis

sarcasmo *m* sarcasm

sarcàsti·co -ca *adj* (-ci -che) sarcastic

sarchiare §287 *tr* to weed

sarchia·tóre -trice *mf* weeder ‖ *f* (agr) cultivator

sarchièllo *m* weeding hoe

sàr·chio *m* (-chi) hoe

sarcòfa·go *m* (-gi & -ghi) sarcophagus

sarcràuti *mpl* sauerkraut

Sardégna, la Sardinia

sardèlla *f* pilchard; sardine

sardina *f* pilchard; sardine

sar·do -da *adj* & *mf* Sardinian

sardòni·co -ca *adj* (-ci -che) sardonic

sarménto *m* vine shoot, running stem

sarta *f* dressmaker

sàrtie *fpl* (naut) shrouds

sarto *m* tailor

sartorìa *f* dressmaker's shop; tailor shop; dressmaking; tailoring

sassaiòla *f* shower of stones

sassata *f* blow with a stone

sasso *m* stone, rock; pebble; (poet) tombstone; **di sasso** stony; **restare di sasso** to be taken aback; **tirare sassi in colombaia** to cut one's nose to spite one's face

sassòfono *m* saxophone

sàssone *adj* & *mf* Saxon

sassó·so -sa [*s*] *adj* stony

Sàtana *m* Satan

satanasso *m* Satan; devil

satèllite *m* satellite

sa·tin *m* (-tin) sateen

satinare *tr* to gloss

sàtira *f* satire

satireggiare §290 (**satiréggio**) *tr* to satirize, lampoon ‖ *intr* to compose satires

satìri·co -ca *adj* (-ci -che) satiric(al) ‖ *m* satirist

sàtiro *m* satyr

satól·lo -la *adj* sated, full

saturare *tr* (**sàturo**) *tr* to saturate; to steep; (fig) to fill; (com) to glut (*a market*)

saturni·no -na *adj* Saturnian; saturnine

Saturno *m* (astr) Saturn

sàtu·ro -ra *adj* saturated; (fig) full; (lit) sated

sàu·ro -ra *adj & m* sorrel (*horse*)

Savèrio *m* Xavier

sà·vio -via (-vi -vie) *adj* wise || *m* wise man, sage

saviar·do -da *adj & mf* Savoyard || *m* ladyfinger

saxòfono *m* saxophone

saziare §287 *tr* to satisfy; to cloy, satiate

sazietà *f* satiety, surfeit; **mangiare a sazietà** to eat one's fill

sà·zio -zia *adj* (**-zi -zie**) sated; full; satisfied

sbaciucchiare §287 (**sbaciùcchio**) *tr* to kiss again and again || *ref* to neck

sbadatàggine *f* carelessness; oversight

sbada·to -ta *adj* careless; heedless

sbadigliare §280 *intr* to yawn

sbadì·glio *m* (**-gli**) yawn

sbafa·tóre -trice *mf* sponger

sbafo *m*—**a sbafo** sponging; **mangiare a sbafo** to sponge

sbagliare §280 *tr* to miss; to mistake; **sbagliarla** to be sadly mistaken || *intr & ref* to be mistaken; to make a mistake

sbaglia·to -ta *adj* wrong; mistaken

sbà·glio *m* (**-gli**) error, mistake

sbalestrare (**sbalèstro**) *tr* to fling with the crossbow; to send (*an employee*) far away || *intr* to speak amiss; to ramble; to blunder

sbalestra·to -ta *adj* unbalanced; ill-at-ease

sballare *tr* to unpack; **sballarle grosse** to tell tall tales || *intr* to overbid

sballa·to -ta *adj* unpacked; absurd, wild

sballottare (**sballòtto**) *tr* to toss

sbalordire §176 *tr* to stun; to amaze; to bewilder || *intr* to lose consciousness; to be dumfounded

sbalorditi·vo -va *adj* amazing

sbalzare *tr* to upset; to send far away; to overthrow; to emboss || *intr* (ESSERE) to bounce

sbalzo *m* leap, jump; climb; emboss-ment, relief; **a sbalzi** by leaps and bounds; **di sbalzo** all of a sudden

sbancare §197 *tr* to clear (*ground*) of rocks; to ruin; (*cards*) to break (*the bank*)

sbandaménto *m* skid; swerve; disband-ment; breaking up; (naut) list

sbandare *tr* to disband; (naut) to cause to list || *intr* to list; to skid; to swerve; to deviate || *ref* to disband; to break up

sbanda·to -ta *adj* disbanded; stray; alienated || *mf* alienated person || *m* straggler || *f* listing (*of ship*); skid-ding (*of vehicle*); **prendere una sbandata per** to get a crush on

sbandierare (**sbandièro**) *tr* to wave (*a flag*); to display

sbaragliare §280 *tr* to rout; to crush

sbaràglio *m*—**mettere allo sbaraglio** to endanger

sbarazzare *tr* to clear out; to free || *ref* —**sbarazzarsi di** to get rid of

sbarazzi·no -na *adj* mischievous || *mf* scamp; **alla sbarazzina** cocked, at an angle (*said of a hat*)

sbarbare *tr* to shave; to uproot || *ref* to shave

sbarbatèllo *m* greenhorn, fledgling

sbarcare §197 *tr* to unload; to dis-charge; to disembark; to pass; to strew (*fodder*); **sbarcare il lunario** to make ends meet || *intr* (ESSERE) to come ashore, land

sbarca·tóio *m* (**-tói**) landing pier

sbar·co *m* (**-chi**) unloading; landing

sbarra *f* bar; (typ) dash

sbarraménto *m* barrage; obstacle

sbarrare *tr* to bar; to block (*the way*); to open (*one's eyes*) wide, e.g., **sbarrò gli occhi** he opened his eyes wide

sbarrétta *f* bar; **sbarrette verticali** (typ) parallels

sbatacchiare §287 *tr* to slam; to flap || *intr* to slam

sbatàc·chio *m* (**-chi**) shore, prop

sbàttere *tr* to flap; to fling; to slam; to beat; to toss; to send away; to make pale; **sbatter fuori** to throw out || *intr* to flap; to slam

sbattighiàc·cio *m* (**-cio**) cocktail shaker

sbattitóre *m* electric mixer

sbattiuò·va *m* (**-va**) egg beater

sbattu·to -ta *adj* haggard, downcast

sbavare *tr* to slobber over; (mach) to trim || *intr* to drivel, slobber; to run (*said of colors*)

sbavatura *f* drivel; run (*of colors*); burr (*of metal*); deckle edge; verbosity

sbeccare §197 (**sbécco**) *tr & ref* to chip

sbeffeggiare §290 (**sbefféggio**) *tr* to make fun of

sbellicare §197 *ref*—**sbellicarsi dalle risa** to burst with laughter

sbèria *f* (coll) slap

sberlèffo *m* scar; grimace; **fare gli sberleffi a** to make faces at

sbevazzare *intr* to guzzle

sbevucchiare §287 *intr* to tipple

sbiadire §176 *tr & intr* (ESSERE) to fade

sbiadi·to -ta *adj* faded; dull

sbiancare §197 *tr* to whiten || *ref* to become white; to pale

sbianchire §176 *tr* (culin) to blanch

sbiè·co -ca (**-chi -che**) *adj* oblique; **di sbieco** on the bias; **guardare di sbieco** to look askance at || *m* cloth cut diagonally

sbigottire §176 *tr* to terrify, dismay || *intr* (ESSERE) & *ref* to be dismayed

sbilanciare §128 *tr* to unbalance; to up-set || *intr* to lose one's balance || *ref* to commit oneself

sbilàn·cio *m* (**-ci**) disequilibrium; (com) deficit

sbilèn·co -ca *adj* (**-chi -che**) twisted, crooked

sbirciare §128 *tr* to leer at, ogle; to eye closely

sbir·ro -ra *adj* (coll) smart || *m* (pej) cop

sbizzarrire [ddzz] §176 *tr* to cure the whims of || *ref* to indulge one's whims

sbloccare §197 (**sblòcco**) *tr* to unblock; to raise the blockade of; to free

sbòbba *f* slop, dishwater

sboccare §197 (**sbócco**) *tr* to break the

mouth of (*a bottle*); to remove a few drops from (*a bottle*) || *intr* (ESSERE) to flow; to open (*said of a street*); **sboccare in** to turn out to be

sbocca·to -ta *adj* foulmouthed; foul (*language*); chipped at the mouth (*said of a bottle*)

sbocciare §128 (**sbòccio**) *intr* (ESSERE) to bud, burgeon, bloom

sbóc·co *m* (**-chi**) outlet; **avere uno sbocco di sangue** to spit blood

sbocconcellare (**sbocconcèllo**) *tr* to nibble at; to chip, nick

sbollentare (**sbollènto**) *tr* to blanch

sbollire §176 *intr* to stop boiling; to calm down

sbolognare (**sbológno**) *tr* (coll) to palm off; (coll) to get rid of

sbornia *f* (coll) drunk, jag; **smaltire la sbornia** to sober up

sborsare (**sbórso**) *tr* to pay out, disburse

sbórso *m* disbursement, outlay

sbottare (**sbòtto**) *intr*—**sbottare a + inf** to burst out + *ger*

sbottonare (**sbottóno**) *tr* to unbutton || *ref* (fig) to unbosom oneself

sbozzare (**sbòzzo**) *tr* to rough-hew; to sketch, outline

sbraca·to -ta *adj* without pants; slovenly; vulgar

sbracciare §128 *intr* to gesticulate || *ref* to roll up one's sleeves; to wear sleeveless clothes; to gesticulate; to do one's best

sbraccia·to -ta *adj* bare-armed

sbraitare (**sbràito**) *intr* to scream

sbraitó·ne -na *mf* bigmouth

sbranare *tr* to tear to pieces

sbrano *m* tear, rent

sbrattare *tr* to clean; to clear

sbreccare §197 (**sbrécco**) *tr* to chip, nick

sbrecciare §128 (**sbréccio**) *tr* to open a gap in

sbréndolo *m* tatter, rag

sbriciolare (**sbriciolo**) *tr* to crumb || *ref* to crumble

sbrigare §209 *tr* to transact; to take care of || *ref* to hasten, hurry; **sbrigarsela** to get out of trouble; **sbrigarsi di** to get rid of; **sbrigati!** make it snappy!, hurry up!

sbrigativ·o -va *adj* quick, brisk; businesslike

sbrigliare §280 *tr* to unbridle; to reduce (*a hernia*); to lance (*an infected wound*) || *ref* to cut loose

sbrinare *tr* to defrost

sbrindella·to -ta *adj* tattered

sbrodolare (**sbròdolo**) *tr* to soil; (fig) to drag out || *ref* to slobber

sbrogliare §280 (**sbròglio**) *tr* to untangle; to clean up || *ref* to extricate oneself; **sbrogliarsela** to get out of a tight spot

sbronzare (**sbrónzo**) *ref* (coll) to get drunk

sbruffare *tr* to squirt out of the mouth; to spatter; to bribe || *intr* to tell tall tales

sbruffo *m* sprinkle, squirt; bribe

sbruffó·ne -na *mf* braggart

sbucare §197 *intr* (ESSERE) to pop out, come out

sbucciare §128 *tr* to peel; to skin || *ref* to slough (*said of snakes*); **sbucciarsela** (coll) to goldbrick

sbucciatura *f* slight abrasion

sbudellare (**sbudèllo**) *tr* to disembowel || *ref*—**sbudellarsi dalle risa** to burst with laughter, split one's sides laughing

sbuffare *tr & intr* to puff

sbuffo *m* puff; gust (*of wind*); **a sbuffo** puffed (*sleeve*)

sbullonare (**sbullóno**) *tr* to unbolt

sc- *pref* dis-, e.g., **sconto** discount; es-, e.g., **scalare** to escalate; ex-, e.g., **scusare** to excuse

scàbbia *f* scabies

sca·bro -bra *adj* rough; stony; tight (*style*)

scabró·so -sa [s] *adj* scabrous

scacchièra *f* checkerboard; chessboard

scacchière *m* (mil) sector; (obs) checkerboard; exchequer

scacciaca·ni *m & f* (**-ni**) toy gun; gun shooting only blanks

scacciamó·sche *m* (**-sche**) fly swatter

scacciapensiè·ri *m* (**-ri**) jew's-harp

scacciare §128 *tr* to chase away, drive away; to expel

scaccino *m* sexton, sacristan

scac·co *m* (**-chi**) chessman; checker; check; square; **a scacchi** checkered; **dare scacco matto a** to checkmate; **in scacco** or **sotto scacco** in check; **scacchi** chess; **scacco matto** checkmate

scaccomatto *m* checkmate

scadènte *adj* inferior, poor, shoddy

scadènza *f* term, maturity; obligation; **a breve scadenza** short-term; **a lunga scadenza** long-term

scadére §121 *intr* (ESSERE) to decay, to decline; to fall due; to expire; (naut) to drift

scafandro *m* diving suit; **scafandro astronautico** space suit

scaffale *m* bookcase; shelf

scafo *m* hull

scagionare (**scagióno**) *tr* to exonerate, exculpate

scàglia *f* scale (*of fish*); chip; plate (*of medieval armor*); flake (*of soap*); tile (*of slate roof*)

scagliare §280 *tr* to hurl, fling, throw; to scale (*fish*) || *ref* to dash, to rush; to flake

scaglionare (**scaglióno**) *tr* to echelon; to stagger (*e.g., payments*)

scaglióne *m* terrace (*of mountain*); echelon; scale; **a scaglioni** graded (*e.g., income tax*)

scala *f* stairs; ladder; scale; (cards) straight; (rad) dial; **a scale** scaled, graded; **fare le scale** to climb the stairs; **scala a chiocciola** spiral stairway; **scala a gradini** or **a libretto** stepladder; **scala mobile** escalator; (econ) sliding scale; **scala porta** aerial ladder; **scala reale** (poker) straight flush; **su larga scala** large-scale; **su scala nazionale** on a national scale

scalandróne *m* (naut) gangway

scalare *adj* graded, scaled; gradual || *m* (com) running balance || *tr* to climb, ascend; to scale, grade; to reduce

scalata *f* climb, ascent; **dar la scalata a** to climb; to climb up to

scalcagna·to -ta *adj* down-at-the-heel

scalcare §197 *tr* to slice, carve

scalciare §128 *intr* to kick

scalcina·to -ta *adj* (*wall or plaster*) that is peeling off; worn-out; down-at-the-heels

scalda-acqua *m* (**-acqua**) hot-water heater

scaldaba·gno *m* (**-gno**) hot-water heater; **scaldabagno a gas** gas heater

scaldalèt·to *m* (**-ti & -to**) bedwarmer

scaldare *tr* to warm, warm up; to heat, heat up || *intr* (mach) to become hot || *ref* to warm up; to heat up; **scaldarsi la testa** to get excited

scaldavivan·de *m* (**-de**) hot plate

scaldino *m* hand warmer

scalèa *f* flight of stairs, stairway

scalèo *m* stepladder

scalétta *f* small ladder; small stairs; (mov) rough draft

scalfire §176 *tr* to graze, scratch; to cut (*e.g., glass*)

scalfittura *f* graze, scratch

scalinata *f* stairway, perron

scalino *m* step (*of a stair*); (fig) ladder

scalmana *f* chill; flush; **prendere una scalmana per** to take a fancy to

scalmanare *ref* to hustle, bustle; to fuss

scalmana·to -ta *adj* panting; hotheaded

scalmo *m* (naut) oarlock

scalo *m* pier, dock; (naut) ways; (naut) port of call; **fare scalo** (naut) to call, stop; (aer) to land; **scalo di alaggio** (naut) slip; **scalo merci** (rr) freight yard; **senza scalo** (aer, naut) nonstop

scalógna *f* (coll) bad luck

scalógno *m* (bot) scallion

scalòppa *f* veal chop

scaloppina *f* veal cutlet, scallop

scalpellare (scalpèllo) *tr* to chisel

scalpellino *m* stone cutter

scalpèllo *m* chisel; (surg) scalpel; **scalpello a taglio obliquo** skew chisel

scalpicciare §128 *tr & intr* to shuffle

scalpitare (scàlpito) *intr* to paw the ground

scalpóre *m* scene; **fare scalpore** to raise a fuss

scaltrézza *f* shrewdness, cunning

scaltrire §176 *tr* to polish, refine; to sharpen the wits of || *ref* to catch on; to improve

scal·tro -tra *adj* shrewd, smart

scalzare *tr* to take the shoes or stockings off of; to undermine || *ref* to take off one's shoes or stockings

scal·zo -za *adj* barefoot

scambiare §287 *tr* to exchange; to mistake || *ref* to exchange (*presents*)

scambiévole *adj* mutual

scàm·bio *m* (**-bi**) exchange; (rr) switch;

libero scambio free trade; **scambio di persona** mistaken identity

scamicia·to -ta *adj* in shirt sleeves; extremist || *m* extremist; tunic, waist

scamoscia·to -ta *adj* chamois, suede

scampagnata *f* excursion, outing

scampanare *intr* to peal, chime; to flare (*said of a garment*)

scampanellare (scampanèllo) *intr* to ring loud and clear

scampanì·o *m* (**-i**) toll, peal

scampare *tr* to save, rescue; **scamparla bella** to have a narrow escape || *intr* (ESSERE)—**scampare a** to escape from; to take refuge in

scampo *m* escape; safety; (zool) Norway lobster; **non c'è scampo** there is no way out

scàmpolo *m* remnant; **scampoli di tempo** free moments

scanalare *tr* to channel, groove, rabbet || *intr* to overflow

scanalatura *f* channel, groove, rabbet

scandagliare §280 *tr* to sound

scandà·glio *m* (**-gli**) sounding lead; **fare uno scandaglio** to make a sounding or survey

scandalismo *m* scandalmongering, yellow journalism

scandalizzare [ddzz] *tr* to scandalize, shock || *ref* to be scandalized

scàndalo *m* scandal

scandaló·so -sa [s] *adj* scandalous

scandina·vo -va *adj & mf* Scandinavian

scandire §176 *tr* to scan; to syllabize; (telv) to scan

scàndola *f* wood shingle

scannare *tr* to slaughter, butcher

scanna-tóio *m* (**-tói**) slaughterhouse; gyp joint

scanno *m* bench; seat; sand bar

scansafati·che *mf* (**-che**) loafer

scansare *tr* to move; to avoid || *ref* to get out of the way

scansia *f* shelf; bookcase

scansióne *f* scansion; (telv) scanning

scanso *m*—**a scanso di** in order to avoid

scantinare *intr* to make a blunder; (mus) to be out of tune

scantinato *m* basement

scantonare (scantóno) *tr* to round (*a corner*) || *intr* to duck around the corner

scanzona·to -ta *adj* flippant; unconventional

scapaccióne *m* clout; **dare uno scapaccione a** to clout, slap

scapa·to -ta *adj* scatterbrained || *m* scatterbrain

scapestra·to -ta *adj & m* libertine

scapigliare §280 *tr* to dishevel || *ref* to be disheveled

scapiglia·to -ta *adj* disheveled; libertine; unconventional; free and easy

scapitare (scàpito) *intr* to lose

scàpito *m* damage; loss; **a scapito di** to the detriment of

scàpola *f* shoulder blade

scapolare *m* scapular || *v* (**scàpolo**) *tr* (coll) to escape, avoid || *intr*—**scapolare da** to get out of (*danger*)

scàpo·lo -la *adj* unmarried ‖ *m* bachelor ‖ *f* see **scapola**

scappaménto *m* escapement (*of watch, of piano*); (aut) exhaust

scappare *tr*—**scapparla bella** to have a narrow escape ‖ *intr* (ESSERE) to flee; to abscond; to run; to get away; to escape; to stick out; to burst out (*said, e.g., of sun*); **far scappare la pazienza a qlcu** to make s.o. lose his patience, to tax s.o.'s patience; **scappare a gambe levate** to run away, beat it; **scappare da** to burst out, e.g., **gli è scappato da ridere** he burst out laughing; **scappar detto di** to blurt out that, e.g., **gli scappò detto di non poterne più** he blurted out that he could not hold out; **scappare di mente** to escape one's mind; **scappar fuori con** to come out with

scappata *f* excursion; sally; escapade; bolt (*of horse*); **fare una scappata** to take a run; **scappata spiritosa** witticism

scappatóia *f* subterfuge; loophole

scappellare (**scappèllo**) *ref* to tip one's hat

scappellòtto *m* smack, slap (on the head); **entrare a scappellotto** (coll) to squeeze in; **passare a scappellotto** (coll) to squeeze through with influence

scapricciare §128 *tr* to satisfy the whims of

scarabèo *m* beetle; scarab (*stone*); **scarabeo sacro** scarab; **scarabeo stercorario** dung beetle

scarabocchiare §287 (**scarabòcchio**) *tr* to scribble; to blot (*with ink*)

scarabòc·chio *m* (**-chi**) ink blot; scribble; scrawl

scarafàg·gio *m* (**-gi**) cockroach

scaramanzia *f* exorcism; **per scaramanzia** to ward off the evil eye, for good luck

scaramazza *adj fem* irregular (*pearl*)

scaramùc·cia *f* (**-ce**) skirmish

scaraventare (**scaravènto**) *tr* to hurl, chuck; to transfer suddenly

scarcerare (**scàrcero**) *tr* to release from jail

scardinare (**scàrdino**) *tr* to unhinge

scàri·ca *f* (**-che**) discharge; volley; evacuation; (elec) discharge; (fig) shower

scaricabarili *m*—**giocare a scaricabarili** (fig) to pass the buck

scaricare §197 (**scàrico**) *tr* to unload; to discharge; to hurl (*insults*); to wreak (*anger*); to free (*from responsibility*) ‖ *ref* to unburden oneself; to flow (*said of a river*); to discharge; to run down (*said of a battery or a watch*)

scaricatóre *m* longshoreman; (elec) lightning arrester

scàri·co -ca (**-chi -che**) *adj* empty, unloaded; discharged; clear (*sky*); free; run-down (*e.g., clock*) ‖ *m* unloading; discharge; exhaust; waste, refuse; **a mio** (**tuo, etc.**) **scarico** in my (your, etc.) defense ‖ *f* see **scarica**

scarlattina *f* scarlet fever

scarlat·to -ta *adj & m* scarlet

scarmigliare §280 *tr* to dishevel

scarnificare §197 (**scarnifico**) or **scarnire** §176 *tr* to bone, take the flesh off; to make thin; to wear down to the bone

scarni·to -ta or **scar·no -na** *adj* boned; meager; skinny

scaròla *f* escarole, endive

scarpa *f* shoe; wedge, skid; scarp; **fare le scarpe a** to undercut; **scarpe al sole** violent death; **scarpe da sci** ski boots

scarpata *f* escarp, escarpment; slope (*of embankment*); blow with a shoe; **scarpata continentale** continental slope

scarpétta *f* small shoe; low shoe; **scarpette chiodate** spikes; **scarpette da ginnastica** gym shoes

scarpinare *intr* to trudge

scarpóne *m* heavy boot; clodhopper

scarròc·cio *m* (**-ci**) (aer, naut) leeway

scarrozzare (**scarròzzo**) *tr* to take for a ride ‖ *intr* to go for a ride; to go for a walk

scarrozzata *f* ride, drive

scarseggiare §290 (**scarséggio**) *intr* (ESSERE) to be scarce, be in short supply; **scarseggiare di** to be short of

scarsèlla *f* pocket; (obs) purse

scarsézza *f* or **scarsi·tà** *f* (**-tà**) scarcity, dearth, lack

scar·so -sa *adj* short; scarce; scanty, scant; weak (*wind*); **scarso a** short of

scartabellare (**scartabèllo**) *tr* to leaf through (*a book*)

scartafàc·cio *m* (**-ci**) note pad, notebook; poorly-bound copybook

scartaménto *m* (rr) gauge; **a scartamento ridotto** narrow-gauge; small-size; small-scale

scartare *tr* to unpack, unwrap; to discard (*cards*); to remove; to scrap (*e.g., a machine*); (mil) to reject ‖ *intr* to swerve; to side-step

scartata *f* unwrapping; side step; swerving; (fig) scolding

scartina *f* discard

scarto *m* discard; reject; swerve; (mil) rejected soldier; (sports) difference; **di scarto inferiore**

scartocciare §128 (**scartòccio**) *tr* to unwrap; to unfold; to husk (*corn*)

scartòffie *fpl* old papers, trash

scassare *tr* to uncrate; to plow up; (coll) to ruin, bust ‖ *ref* (coll) to break down

scassinare *tr* to pick (*a lock*); to burglarize; to break open

scassina·tóre -trice *mf* burglar; **scassinatore di casseforti** safe-cracker

scasso *m* plowing, tilling; burglary

scatenare (**scaténo**) *tr* to unchain; to trigger; to excite, stir up ‖ *ref* to break loose

scàtola *f* box; can; **a scatola chiusa** sight unseen; **in scatola** canned; **rompere le scatole a** (vulg) to bug, pester; **scatola armonica** music box; **scatola a sorpresa** jack-in-the-box;

scatola cranica cranium, skull; **scatola del cambio** (aut) transmission, gear box

scatolame *m* boxes; canned food

scatolifi·cio *m* (**-ci**) box factory

scattare *tr* to take (*a picture*) || *intr* (ESSERE & AVERE) to jump, spring; to go off (*said of a trap*); to go up (*said of the cost of living*); to go into action, begin

scatto *m* click (*of camera, gun*); outburst; sprint; automatic increase (*in salary*); shutter release; **a scatti** in jerks; **di scatto** suddenly

scaturire §176 *intr* (ESSERE) to spring; to pour, gush; to stem

scavalcare §197 *tr* to jump over; to pass over; to unsaddle; to skip (*a stitch*) || *intr* (ESSERE) to dismount || *ref* (coll) to rush

scavallare *intr* to caper, cavort

scavare *tr* to dig; to dig up, unearth

scava·tóre -trice *adj* excavating || *m* digger || *f* digger, excavator

scavezzacòllo *m* scamp; daredevil; **a scavezzacollo** headlong, at breakneck speed

scavezzare (**scavézzo**) *tr* to lop; to burst; to break; to take the halter off (*a horse*)

scavo *m* digging, excavation

scazzottare (**scazzòtto**) *tr* to beat up

scégliere §244 *tr* to choose; to pick out

sceic·co *m* (**-chi**) sheik

sceleratàggine *f* or **sceleratézza** *f* wickedness, villainy

scellera·to -ta *adj* wicked || *m* villain

scellino *m* shilling

scél·to -ta *adj* choice; selected; (mil) first-class || *f* choice; pick; selection; **di prima scelta** choice

scemare (**scémo**) *tr* to diminish, reduce; to lower the level of || *intr* (ESSERE) & *ref* to lessen, diminish

scemènza *f* foolishness, stupidity

scé·mo -ma *adj* silly, foolish || *mf* simpleton, fool

scempiàggine *f* silliness, foolishness

scém·pio -pia (**-pi -pie**) *adj* simple; single; (lit) wicked || *m* ruination; (lit) slaughter; **fare scempio di** to ruin; (lit) to slaughter

scèna *f* scene; stage; acting; scenery; **esser di scena** (theat) to be on; **mettere in scena** (theat) to stage; **scene di prossima programmazione** (mov) coming attractions

scenà·rio *m* (**-ri**) scenery; scenario, setting

scenari·sta *mf* (**-sti -ste**) scenarist; script writer

scenata *f* scene (*outbreak of anger*)

scéndere §245 *tr* to descend, go down; to bring down || *intr* (ESSERE) to descend, go down; to get off; to come (*to an agreement*); to step (*into the ring*); to put up (*at a hotel*); to check in (*at a hotel*)

scendilèt·to *m* (**-to**) scatter rug; bathrobe

sceneggiare §290 (**scenéggio**) *tr* to write a scenario for; to adapt for the stage

sceneggia·tóre -trice *mf* scenarist

sceneggiatura *f* (mov) screenplay; (rad, telv) continuity

scenètta *f* (theat) sketch

scenògrafo *m* scene designer

scenotècni·ca *f* (**-che**) stagecraft

sceriffo *m* sheriff

scèrnere §246 *tr* to discern; to distinguish; to select

scervellare (**scervèllo**) *ref* to rack one's brains

scervella·to -ta *adj* scatterbrained

scésa [s] *f* discent; slope

scespiria·no -na *adj* Shakesperean

scetticismo *m* skepticism

scètti·co -ca (**-ci -che**) *adj* skeptic(al) || *m* skeptic

scèttro *m* scepter

sceverare (**scévero**) *tr* (lit) to distinguish

scé·vro -vra *adj* (lit) free, exempt

schèda *f* card; slip, form; **scheda elettorale** ballot; **scheda perforata** punch card

schedare (**schèdo**) *tr* to file

schedà·rio *m* (**-ri**) card index, card catalogue; file cabinet

schég·gia *f* (**-ge**) splinter; chip

scheggiare §290 (**schéggio**) *tr* & *ref* to splinter

schelètri·co -ca *adj* (**-ci -che**) skeleton, skeletal; succint

schèletro *m* skeleton

schè·ma *m* (**-mi**) diagram; draft; model; scheme; **schema di montaggio** (electron) hookup

schérma *f* fencing

schermàglia *f* argument

schermare (**schérmo**) *tr* to screen; (elec) to shield

schermire §176 *tr* to protect; (obs) to fence with || *ref*—**schermirsi da** to ward off, parry; to protect oneself from

schermi·tóre -trice *mf* fencer

schérmo *m* screen; protection; (elec) shield; **farsi schermo di** to use as protection; **farsi schermo delle mani** to ward off a blow with one's hands

schernire §176 *tr* to deride

schérno *m* derision, ridicule, mockery

scherzare (**schérzo**) *tr* (coll) to mock || *intr* to play; to joke, trifle

schérzo *m* play; joke, jest; freak (*of nature*); child's play; trick; **neppure per scherzo** under no circumstances; **per scherzo** in jest; **stare allo scherzo** to take a joke

scherzó·so -sa [s] *adj* joking; playful

schiacciaménto *m* crushing; flattening

schiaccianó·ci *m* (**-ci**) nutcracker

schiacciante *adj* crushing

schiacciapata·te *m* (**-te**) ricer

schiacciare §128 *tr* to crush; to take (*a nap*); to squelch (*a rumor*); to subdue (*the details of a painting*); to mash (*potatoes*); to tread on, step on (*s.o.'s foot*); to flatten; to run (*s.o.*) over; to make (*s.o.'s figure*) look squatty; to crack (*nuts*); to flunk; (tennis) to smash

schiacciata *f* hot cake; (tennis) smash

schiaffare *tr* (coll) to fling, clap

schiaffeggiare §290 (**schiafféggio**) *tr* to slap; to buffet

schiaffo *m* slap, box

schiamazzare *intr* to squawk, cackle; to honk; to make a racket

schiamazzo *m* squawking, cackle; honk; hubbub

schiantare *tr* to crush, burst || *intr* (ESSERE) (coll) to burst; (coll) to croak || *ref* to break, crack, split

schianto *m* break, crack; crash; bang; knockout (*extraordinary, attractive person or thing*); **di schianto** all of a sudden; **schianto al cuore** heartache

schiappa *f* splinter; (coll) good-for-nothing

schiarimento *m* elucidation

schiarire §176 *tr* to make clearer; to make (*the hair*) light; to clear; to explain; to elucidate || *intr* (ESSERE) to become light || *ref* to clear up (*said of the weather*); to clear (*one's throat*); to fade || *impers* (ESSERE) —**schiarisce** it is getting light

schiarita *f* clearing (*of weather*); improvement (*in relations*)

schiatta *f* race, stock

schiattare *intr* (ESSERE) to burst

schiavi·sta (-**sti** -**ste**) *adj* slave (*e.g., state*) || *mf* antiabolitionist

schiavi·tù (-**tù**) slavery; bondage

schia·vo -**va** *adj* enslaved || *mf* slave

schiccherare (**schìcchero**) *tr* to scribble; to soil; to sketch; to dash off; to blurt out; (coll) to clean out

schidionare (**schidióno**) *tr* to put on the spit

schidióne *m* spit

schièna *f* back; divide; crown (*of road*); **giocare di schiena** to buck

schienale *m* back (*of chair; cut of meat*)

schièra *f* crowd; flock; herd; (mil) rank

schieraménto *m* alignment

schierare (**schièro**) *tr* to line up || *ref* to line up; **schierarsi dalla parte di** to side with

schièt·to -**ta** *adj* pure; frank, honest

schifare *tr* to loathe; to disgust || *ref*—**schifarsi di** to feel disgusted with

schifa·to -**ta** *adj* disgusted

schifiltó·so -**sa** [*s*] *adj* fastidious; squeamish

schifo *m* disgust, loathing; skiff; shell; **fare schifo a** to disgust; to make sick

schifó·so -**sa** [*s*] *adj* disgusting; sickening; (slang) tremendous

schioccare §197 (**schiocco**) *tr* to snap (*the fingers*); to click (*the tongue*); to smack (*the lips*); to crack (*a whip*) || *intr* to crack

schiòc·co *m* (-**chi**) crack, snap; click; smack

schiodare (**schiòdo**) *tr* to take the nails out of

schioppettata *f* gunshot; earshot

schiòppo *m* gun, shotgun; **a un tiro di schioppo** within earshot

schiùdere §125 *tr* & *ref* to open

schiuma *f* foam, froth; lather; head (*of beer*); dregs, scum; meerschaum;

---

avere la schiuma alla bocca to froth at the mouth

schiumaiòla *f* skimmer

schiumare *tr* to scum; to skim || *intr* to foam, froth; to lather

schiumó·so -**sa** [*s*] *adj* foamy

schivare *tr* to avoid; to avert || *ref* to shy

schi·vo -**va** *adj* averse; bashful, shy

schizzare *tr* to spray; to sprinkle; to ooze (*venom*); to sketch; **schizzare fuoco dagli occhi** to have fire in one's eyes || *intr* (ESSERE) to gush; to squirt; to dart; **gli occhi gli schizzano dall'orbita** his eyes are popping out of his head

schizzétto *m* sprayer; syringe; water pistol

schizzinó·so -**sa** [*s*] *adj* finicky, fastidious

schizzo *m* spray; splash; sketch; survey (*e.g., of literature*)

sci *m* (sci) ski

scìa *f* wake; track; trail; **scia di condensazione** contrail

sciàbola *f* saber

sciabordare (**sciabórdo**) *tr* to shake, agitate || *intr* to break (*said of waves*)

sciacallo *m* jackal

sciacquadi·ta *m* (-**ta**) finger bowl

sciacquare (**sciàcquo**) *tr* to rinse

sciacquatura *f* rinse

sciacquí·o *m* (-**i**) splash, dash

sciàcquo *m* rinsing (*of the mouth*); mouthwash

sciagura *f* calamity, misfortune

sciagura·to -**ta** *adj* unfortunate; wretched

scialacquare (**scialàcquo**) *tr* to squander

scialare *tr* to squander || *intr* to be well off; to live it up

scial·bo -**ba** *adj* pale, faded; wan

scialle *m* shawl; **scialle da viaggio** traveling blanket

scialo *m* squandering; opulence; **a scialo** lavishly

scialuppa *f* launch; lifeboat

sciamanna·to -**ta** *adj* slovenly

sciamannó·ne -**na** *mf* slovenly person || *f* slattern

sciamare *intr* (ESSERE & AVERE) to swarm

sciame *m* swarm; flock

sciampagna *f* champagne

scianca·to -**ta** *adj* cripple, lame; wobbly (*table*)

sciangài *m* pick-up-sticks || **Sciangài** *f* Shanghai

sciarada *f* charade

sciare §119 *intr* to ski; to back water

sciarpa *f* scarf; sash (*e.g., of an officer or of a mayor*)

scias·sì *m* (-**sì**) chassis

sciàtica *f* (pathol) sciatica

scia·tóre -**trice** *mf* skier

sciatterìa *f* or **sciattézza** *f* slovenliness

sciat·to -**ta** *adj* slovenly, sloppy

scìbile *m* knowledge

sciènte *adj* conscious; knowing

scientìfi·co -**ca** *adj* (-**ci** -**che**) scientific

sciènza *f* science; knowledge

scienzia·to -ta *mf* scientist

scilinguàgnolo *m* frenum (*of tongue*); avere lo scilinguagnolo sciolto to have a loose tongue

Scilla *f* Scylla; fra Scilla e Cariddi between Scylla and Charibdis

scimitarra *f* scimitar

scimmia *f* monkey; (coll) drunk; fare la scimmia a to ape; scimmia antropomorfa anthropoid ape

scimmie·sco -sca *adj* (-schi -sche) monkeyish; apish

scimmiottare (scimmiòtto) *tr* to ape

scimpan·zé *m* (-zé) chimpanzee

scimuni·to -ta *adj* idiotic || *mf* idiot

scìndere §247 *tr* (lit) to split; to separate

scintilla *f* spark; sparkle; (fig) scintilla; scintilla elèttrica jump spark

scintillare *intr* to sparkle, to sparkle

scintillì·o *m* (-ìi) sparkle, brilliance

scioccare §197 *tr* to shock

sciocchézza *f* silliness; trifle

sciòc·co -ca (-chi -che) *adj* silly, foolish || *mf* fool, blockhead

sciògliere §127 *tr* to loosen; to release; to unfasten, untie; to solve; to disperse; to dissolve; to limber; to fulfill (*a promise*); to unfurl (*sails*) || *ref* to loosen up; to get loose; to dissolve; to melt (*into tears*)

scioglilìn·gua *m*(-gue) tongue twister

scioglimento *m* melting; dissolution; fulfillment; denouement

sciolina *f* ski wax

scioltézza *f* nimbleness, agility; freedom (*of movement*); ease

sciòl·to -ta *adj* loose; glib; free; blank (*verse*)

scioperante *adj* striking || *mf* striker

scioperare (sciòpero) *intr* to strike

sciopera·to -ta *adj* loafing; lazy || *m* loafer

sciòpero *m* strike; walkout; sciopero a singhiozzo slowdown strike; sciopero bianco sit-down strike; sciopero della fame hunger strike; sciopero di solidarietà sympathy strike; sciopero pignolo slowdown

sciorinare *tr* to display; to tell (*lies*); to air (*laundry*)

sciovìa *f* ski lift

sciovinismo *m* chauvinism, jingoism

scipì·to -ta *adj* insipid

scippo *m* snatching (*e.g., of a bag*)

sciròc·co *m* (-chi) sirocco; southeast

sciròppo *m* syrup

sci·sma *m* (-smi) schism

scismàti·co -ca *adj* (-ci -che) schismatic

scissióne *f* split; (biol, phys) fission

scis·so -sa *adj* split, rent

scisto *m* schist

sciupare *tr* to spoil; to wear out; to waste; to rumple || *ref* to wear; to run down (*said of health*); to get rumpled

sciupa·to -ta *adj* ruined; worn out; wasted; run down

sciupì·o *m* (-ìi) waste

sciupó·ne -na *mf* waster, squanderer

sciu·scià *m* (-scià) bootblack; urchin

scìvola *f* chute

scivolare (scìvolo) *intr* (ESSERE & AVERE) to slide, glide; to steal; scivolare d'ala (aer) to sideslip

scivolata *f* slide, glide; scivolata d'ala (aer) sideslip

scìvolo *m* chute; (aer) slip (*for seaplanes*)

scivolóne *m* slip, slide

scivoló·so -sa [s] *adj* slippery

scoccare §197 (scòcco) *tr* to shoot (*an arrow*); to give (*a buss*); to strike (*the hour*) || *intr* (ESSERE) to dart; to spring; to strike (*said of a clock*); to shoot

scocciare §128 (scòccio) *tr* (coll) to break; (coll) to bother; (naut) to unhook || *ref* to be bored

scoccia·tóre -trice *mf* (coll) nuisance

scocciatura *f* (coll) bother, annoyance

scòc·co *m* (-chi) darting; stroke (*e.g., of three*); (naut) hook; scocco di baci bussing, kissing

scodèlla *f* bowl; soup plate

scodellare (scodèllo) *tr* to dish out

scodellino *m* small bowl; (mil) pan (*of musket lock*)

scodinzolare (scodìnzolo) *intr* to wag its tail; to waddle (*said of a woman*)

scogliera *f* reef (*of rocks*); scogliera corallina coral reef

scò·glio *m* (-gli) rock; reef; cliff; stumbling block

scoiare §248 *tr* to skin

scoiàttolo *m* squirrel

scolabrò·do *m* (-do) colander, strainer

scolafrit·to *m* (-to) strainer

scolapa·sta *m* (-sta) (coll) colander

scolare (scólo) *tr* to drain; (fig) to polish off || *intr* (ESSERE) to drip || *ref* to melt

scolare·sco -sca (-schi -sche) *adj* school || *f* schoolchildren; student body

scola·ro -ra *mf* pupil; student

scolàsti·co -ca (-ci -che) *adj* school; scholastic || *m* scholastic, schoolman || *f* scholasticism

scola·tóio *m* (-tói) drain; strainer

scolatura *f* drip, drippings; dregs

scollaccia·to -ta *adj* low-necked; wearing a low-cut dress; dirty, obscene

scollare (scòllo) *tr* to cut off at the neck; to unglue || *ref* to wear a low-necked dress; to come unglued

scollatura *f* neckline; ungluing; scollatura a barchetta low neck; scollatura a punta V neck

scòllo *m* neck, neckline

scólo *m* drain; drainage; (slang) clap

scolopèndra *f* centipede

scolorare (scolóro) *tr*, *intr* (ESSERE), & *ref* to fade, discolor; to pale

scolorire §176 *tr*, *intr* (ESSERE), & *ref* to fade, discolor

scolpare (scólpo) *tr* to excuse

scolpire §176 *tr* to sculpture; to engrave; to emphasize

scòlta *f* (lit) sentry; fare la scolta to stand guard

scombaciare §128 *tr* to pull apart, separate

scombinare *tr* to disarrange; to upset

scómbro *m* mackerel

scombù·glio m (-gli) (coll) disorder

scombussolare (scombùssolo) tr to upset

scomméssa f bet, wager

scomméttere §198 tr to bet; to separate

scommetti·tóre -trice mf bettor

scomodare (scòmodo) tr to trouble, disturb ‖ ref to take the trouble

scomodi·tà f (-tà) trouble, inconvenience

scòmo·do -da adj awkward, unwieldy; uncomfortable ‖ m inconvenience

scompaginare (scompàgino) tr to upset; (typ) to pi

scompagna·to -ta adj odd

scomparire §108 intr (ESSERE) to disappear; to make a bad showing

scompar·so -sa adj disappeared; extinct ‖ mf deceased ‖ f disappearance; death

scompartiménto m compartment; partition

scompènso m lack of compensation; imbalance

scompigliare §280 tr to disarray; to trouble, upset

scompì·glio m (-gli) disarray; upset

scompisciare §128 tr (vulg) to piss on ‖ ref (vulg) to wet oneself; scompisciarsi dalle risa (coll) to split one's sides laughing

scomplè·to -ta adj incomplete

scompórre §218 tr to decompose, disintegrate; to rumple; to dishevel; to upset; to dismantle, take apart; (typ) to pi ‖ ref to lose one's composure

scompó·sto -sta adj unseemly

scomùni·ca f (-che) excommunication

scomunicare §197 (scomùnico) tr to excommunicate; (joc) to ostracize

sconcertare (sconcèrto) tr to upset; to disconcert ‖ ref to become disconcerted

sconcézza f obscenity, indecency

scón·cio -cia (-ci -ce) adj dirty, filthy, obscene ‖ m obscenity; shame

sconclusiona·to -ta adj inconsequential; incoherent; rambling

sconcordanza f disagreement; (gram) lack of agreement

scondi·to -ta adj unseasoned

sconfessare (sconfèsso) tr to disavow; to retract

sconfessióne f disavowal

sconfiggere §104 tr to defeat, rout; to pull (a nail); to unfasten

sconfinare intr to cross the border; sconfinare da to stray from

sconfina·to -ta adj boundless, unlimited

sconfitta f defeat, rout

sconfortante adj discouraging

sconfortare (sconfòrto) tr to discourage; to distress ‖ ref to become discouraged

sconfòrto m depression; distress

scongelare (scongèlo) tr to thaw

scongiurare tr to conjure; to implore

scongiuro m conjuration; entreaty

sconnès·so -sa adj disconnected; incoherent

sconnèttere §107 tr to disconnect; to take apart ‖ intr to be incoherent

sconoscènte adj unappreciative

sconosciu·to -ta adj unknown ‖ mf stranger

sconquassare tr to smash, shatter

sconquassa·to -ta adj broken-down; upset

sconquasso m destruction; confusion; smash-up

sconsacrare tr to desecrate

sconsideratézza f thoughtlessness

sconsidera·to -ta adj inconsiderate

sconsigliare §280 tr to dissuade, discourage

sconsiglia·to -ta adj thoughtless

sconsola·to -ta adj disconsolate

scontare (scónto) tr to expiate; to discount; to serve (time in jail)

scontentare (scontènto) tr to dissatisfy

scontèn·to -ta adj & m discontent

scónto m discount; part payment; (fig) partial remission

scontrare (scóntro) tr to meet; (naut) to turn (the wheel) sharply ‖ ref to clash; to collide; to come to blows

scontrino m check, ticket

scóntro m collision; battle, encounter; clash; ward (of key)

scontró·so -sa [s] adj peevish, cross

sconveniènte adj unfavorable; unseemly, unbecoming; indecent

sconvenire §282 intr (ESSERE) to be unseemly or unbecoming

sconvòlgere §289 tr to upset; to disconcert

sconvolgiménto m upsetting; sconvolgimento di stomaco stomach upset; sconvolgimento tellurico upheaval

sconvòl·to -ta adj upset; disconcerted; distracted

scópa f broom; scopa per lavaggio mop

scopare (scópo) tr to sweep

scopata f sweep

scoperchiare §287 (scopèrchio) tr to uncover; to take the lid off

scopèr·to -ta adj uncovered; open; bare; exposed; unpaid ‖ m open ground; open air; overdraft; (econ) short sale; (com) balance; allo scoperto in the open; overdrawn (check); short (sale) ‖ f discovery; alla scoperta openly

scòpo m purpose, goal, aim

scoppiare §287 (scòppio) tr to uncouple ‖ intr (ESSERE) to burst; to blow; to explode; to break (said, e.g., of news); (fig) to die (e.g., of overeating); scoppiare a to burst out (laughing or crying)

scoppiettare (scoppiétto) intr to crackle

scoppietti·o m (-i) crackle

scòp·pio m (-pi) burst; explosion; outbreak; outburst; blowout (of tire); a scoppio internal-combustion (engine); scoppio di tuono clap of thunder

scòppola f drop (of plane in air pocket); (coll) rabbit punch

scopriménto m uncovering; unveiling

scoprire §110 tr to uncover; to unveil; to discover; to expose ‖ ref to take off one's clothes; to take one's hat off; to reveal oneself

scopri·tóre -trice *mf* discoverer

scoraggiaménto *m* discouragement

scoraggiante *adj* discouraging

scoraggiare §290 *tr* to discourage, dishearten ‖ *ref* to be or become discouraged

scoraménto *m* (lit) discouragement

scorbuto *m* scurvy

scorciare §128 (**scórcio**) *tr* to shorten; to foreshorten ‖ *intr* (ESSERE) to shorten, grow shorter; to look foreshortened ‖ *ref* to shorten, grow shorter

scorciatóia *f* shortcut, cutoff

scór·cio *m* (**-ci**) foreshortening; end, close (*of a period*); **di scorcio** foreshortened

scordare (**scòrdo**) *tr* to forget; to put out of tune ‖ *ref* to forget; to get out of tune

scorég·gia *f* (**-ge**) (vulg) fart

scoreggiare §290 (**scoréggio**) *intr* (vulg) to fart

scòrgere §249 *tr* to perceive, to discern

scòria *f* slag, dross; (fig) scum, dregs; **scorie atomiche** atomic waste

scorna·to -ta *adj* humiliated, ridiculed; hornless

scòrno *m* humiliation, ridicule

scorpacciata *f* bellyful; **fare una scorpacciata di** to stuff oneself with

scorpióne *m* scorpion ‖ **Scorpione** *m* (astrol) Scorpio

scorrazzare *tr* to wander over ‖ *intr* to run around; to move about; (fig) to ramble; (mil) to raid

scórrere §139 *tr* to raid; to glance over ‖ *intr* (ESSERE) to flow; to run; to glide

scorrerìa *f* raid, foray, incursion

scorrettézza *f* imprecision; impropriety

scorrèt·to -ta *adj* incorrect; improper

scorrévole *adj* sliding; flowing, fluent ‖ *m* slide (*of slide rule*)

scorribanda *f* raid, foray, incursion

scór·so -sa *adj* past, last ‖ *m* error, slip ‖ *f* glance; short stay

scor·sóio -sóia *adj* (**-sói -sóie**) slip (*knot*)

scòrta *f* escort; provision, stock; **di scorta** spare (*tire*); **fare di scorta a** to escort; **scorta d'onore** (mil) honor guard; **scorte** (com) stockpile; (com) supplies; **scorte morte** agricultural supplies; **scorte vive** livestock

scortare (**scòrto**) *tr* to escort; to foreshorten

scortecciare §128 (**scortéccio**) *tr* to strip the bark from; to peel off; to scrape ‖ *ref* to peel off

scortése *adj* discourteous, impolite

scortesìa *f* discourtesy, impoliteness

scorticare §197 (**scórtico**) *tr* to skin; to be overdemanding with (*students*); to fleece ‖ *ref* to skin (*e.g.*, *one's arm*)

scòrza *f* bark; skin, hide; (fig) appearance; **scorza di limone** lemon peel

scoscendiménto *m* landslide; cliff

scoscé·so -sa [s] *adj* sloping, steep

scòssa *f* shake; jerk; **scossa di pioggia** downpour; **scossa di terremoto** earth tremor; **scossa elettrica** electric shock; **scossa tellurica** earthquake

scossóne *m* jolt, jerk

scostaménto *m* removal; separation

scostare (**scòsto**) *tr* to move away; to try to avoid ‖ *intr* (ESSERE) to stand away ‖ *ref* to step aside; to stray

scostuma·to -ta *adj* dissolute, debauched

scotennare (**scoténno**) *tr* to scalp; to skin (*an animal*)

scòtta *f* whey; (naut) sheet

scottante *adj* burning (*question*); outrageous (*offense*)

scottare (**scòtto**) *tr* to burn; to scald; to sear; to boil (*eggs*); (fig) to sting ‖ *intr* to burn; to be hot (*said of stolen goods*) ‖ *ref* to get burnt

scottatura *f* burn; (fig) blow, jolt

scòt·to -ta *adj* overcooked, overdone ‖ *m*—**pagare lo scotto** to foot the bill; **pagare lo scotto di** to expiate ‖ *f* see **scotta**

scoutismo *m* scouting

scovare (**scóvo**) *tr* to rouse (*game*); to find, discover

scovolino *m* pipe cleaner; (mil) small swab

scóvolo *m* (mil) swab

scòzia *f* (archit) scotia ‖ **la Scozia** Scotland

scozzése [s] *adj* Scotch, Scottish ‖ *m* Scotch, Scottish (*language*); Scotchman ‖ *f* Scotchwoman

scozzonare (**scozzóno**) *tr* to break in (*a horse*); to train

scranna *f* (hist) seat

screanza·to -ta *adj* ill-mannered, rude

screditare (**scrédito**) *tr* to discredit

scremare (**scrèmo**) *tr* to cream

scrematrice *f* cream separator

screpolare (**scrèpolo**) *tr*, *intr* (ESSERE), & *ref* to crack; to chap

screpolatura *f* crack; chap (*of skin*)

screziare §287 (**scrèzio**) *tr* to mottle, variegate

scrè·zio *m* (**-zi**) tiff

scri·ba *m* (**-bi**) scribe (*Jewish scholar*)

scribacchiare §287 *tr* to scribble, scrawl

scribacchino *m* scribbler; hack

scricchiolare (**scrìcchiolo**) *intr* to crack, creak

scricchiolì·o *m* (**-i**) crack, creak

scrìcciolo *m* wren

scrigno *m* jewel box

scriminatura *f* part (*in hair*)

scrit·to -ta *adj* written ‖ *m* writing ‖ *f* sign; inscription; contract; **scritta luminosa** electric sign

scrit·tóio *m* (**-tói**) writing desk

scrit·tóre -trice *mf* writer

scrittura *f* handwriting; penmanship; writing; contract; entry; (theat) booking; **Sacra Scrittura** Holy Scripture; **scrittura privata** contract; **scrittura pubblica** deed, indenture; **scrittura a macchina** typing

scritturale *adj* scriptural ‖ *m* clerk; copyist; fundamentalist

scritturare *tr* (theat) to book, engage

scrivanìa *f* desk

scrivano *m* clerk, copyist, typist

scrìvere §250 *tr & intr* to write; **scrivere a macchina** to type

scroccare §197 (**scròcco**) *tr* to sponge (*a meal*); to manage to get (*a prize*) || *intr* to sponge

scrocca·tóre -trice *mf* sponger

scròc·co *m* (**-chi**) sponging; creaking; **a scrocco** sponging; spring (*lock*); switchblade (*knife*)

scroccó·ne -na *mf* sponger

scròfa *f* sow; slut

scrollare (**scròllo**) *tr* to shake; to shrug (*one's shoulders*) || *ref* to get into action; to pull oneself together

scrollata *f* shake; **scrollata di spalle** shrug

scrosciare §128 (**scròscio**) *intr* (ESSERE & AVERE) to pelt down; (fig) to thunder

scrò·scio *m* (**-sci**) thunder, roar; **scroscio di pioggia** downpour; **scroscio di tuono** thunderclap

scrostare (**scròsto**) *tr* to pick (*a scab*); to scrape; to peel off || *ref* to peel off

scrosta·to -ta *adj* peeling; scaly

scròto *m* scrotum

scrùpolo *m* scruple; scrupulousness

scrupoló·so -sa [s] *adj* scrupulous

scrutare *tr* to scan, scrutinize

scruta·tóre -trice *adj* inquisitive || *mf* teller (*of votes*)

scrutina·tóre -trice *mf* teller (*of votes*)

scruti·nio *m* (**-ni**) poll, vote; evaluation (*of an examination*); count (*of votes*); **scrutinio segreto** secret ballot

scucire §143 *tr* to unstitch; (coll) to cough up || *ref* to come unstitched

scucitura *f* unstitching; rip

scuderìa *f* stable

scudétto *m* badge; escutcheon; (sports) badge of victory

scudièro *m* esquire

scudisciare §128 *tr* to whip

scudi·scio *m* (**-sci**) whip

scudo *m* shield; escutcheon; **far scudo a** to shield

scùffia *f* (coll) load (*intoxication*); **fare scuffia** to capsize; **prendersi una scuffia per** to fall for, to fall in love with

scugnizzo *m* Neapolitan urchin

sculacciare §128 *tr* to spank

sculacciata *f* spank, spanking

sculacción e *m* spank, spanking

sculettare (**sculétto**) *intr* to waddle

scul·tóre -trice *mf* sculptor || *f* sculptress

scultura *f* sculpture

scuòla *f* school; **scuola allievi ufficiali** military academy; officers' candidate school; **scuola dell'obbligo** mandatory education; **scuola di danza** dancing school; **scuola di dressaggio** obedience school (*for dogs*); **scuola di guerra** war college; **scuola di guida** driving school; **scuola di perfezionamento per laureati** postgraduate school; **scuola di taglio** sewing school; **scuola materna** kindergarten; **scuola mista** coeducational school

scuòla·bus *m* (**-bus**) school bus

scuòtere §251 *tr* to shake; to shake up; **scuotere di dosso** to shake off

scure *f* ax; cleaver

scurire §176 *tr, intr* (ESSERE), & *ref* to darken

scu·ro -ra *adj dark* || *m* darkness; dark; shutter; **essere allo scuro** to be in the dark

scurrile *adj* scurrilous

scusa *f* excuse; apology; pretext; **chiedere scusa** to apologize

scusare *tr* to excuse; to pardon; to apologize for; **scusi!** pardon me! || *ref* to apologize; to beg off

sdaziare §287 *tr* to clear through customs

sdebitare (**sdébito**) *tr* to free from debt || *ref* to become free of debt; **sdebitarsi con** to repay a favor to

sdegnare (**sdégno**) *tr* to scorn; to arouse, enrage || *ref* to get mad

sdégno *m* indignation, anger; (lit) scorn

sdegnó·so -sa [s] *adj* indignant; haughty

sdenta·to -ta *adj* toothless

sdilinquire §176 *tr* to weaken || *intr* (ESSERE) & *ref* to swoon; to become mawkish

sdoganare *tr* to clear through customs

sdolcina·to -ta *adj* mawkish

sdolcinatura *f* mush, slobber

sdoppiare §287 (**sdóppio**) *tr & ref* to split

sdoppiaménto *m* splitting

sdottoreggiare §290 (**sdottoréggio**) *intr* to pontificate

sdràia *f* chaise longue; deck chair

sdraiare §287 *tr* to lay down || *ref* to stretch out (*e.g., on the ground*)

sdràio *m* (**sdrài**) stretching out; **mettersi a sdraio** to lie down

sdrucciolare (**sdrùcciolo**) *intr* (ESSERE & AVERE) to slip, slide

sdrucciolévo·le *adj* slippery

sdrùcciolo -la *adj* proparoxytone || *m* slip; slope; proparoxytone

sdruccioló·ni *adv* slipping, sliding

sdrucire (**sdrùcio**) & §176 *tr* to tear, rend, rip

sdrucitura *f* tear, rend, rip

se *m* (**se**) if || §5 *pron* || *conj* if; whether; **se mai** in the event; **se no** otherwise; **se non tu** (**lui, lei, etc.**) nobody else but you (him, her, etc.), e.g., **non puoi essere stato se non tu** it could not have been anyone else but you; **se non altro** at least; **se non che** but; be pure even if

sé §5 *pron* himself; herself; itself; yourself; themselves; yourselves; oneself; **di per sé stesso** by itself; **fuori di sé** beside oneself; **rientrare in sé** to come back to one's senses; **uscire di sé** to be beside oneself

sebbène *conj* although, though

sèbo *m* sebum, tallow

séc·ca *f* (**-che**) sand bank, shoal; drought; **dare in secca** to run aground; **in secca** hard up

seccante *adj* drying; annoying

seccare §197 (**sécco**) *tr* to dry; to bore;

to bother, annoy || *intr* (ESSERE) to dry up || *ref* to dry up; to be annoyed

secca·tóio *m* (-tói) drying room; squeegee (*to remove water from wet decks*)

secca·tóre -trice *mf* bore, pest

seccatura *f* drying; trouble, nuisance

sécchia *f* bucket, pail; **piovere a secchie** to rain cats and dogs

secchièllo *m* little bucket

séc·chio *m* (-chi) bucket, pail; bucketful; **secchio dell'immondezza** trash can

séc·co -ca (-chi -che) *adj* dry; lanky; sharp || *m* dryness; dry land; drought; **a secco** dry (*cleaning*); **dare in secco** to run aground; **in secco** hard up; **lavare a secco** to dry-clean || *f* see **secca**

secenté·sco -sca *adj* (-schi -sche) seventeenth-century

secentèsi·mo -ma *adj, m & pron* six hundredth

secèrnere §153 (*pp* secréto) *tr* to secrete

secessióne *f* secession

séco §5 *prep phrase* (lit) with oneself; along, e.g., **portare seco** to bring along

secolare *adj* secular; century-old; worldly || *m* layman

sècolo *m* century; age; world

secónda *f* second; second-year class; **a seconda** with the wind; **a seconda di** according to; **in seconda** (aut) in second; (mil) second in command

secondare (secóndo) *tr* to second

seconda·rio -ria *adj* (-ri -rie) secondary

secondino *m* prison guard, turnkey

secón·do -da *adj* second; (lit) favorable || *m* second; second course; (nav) executive officer || *f* see **seconda** || *pron* second || **secondo** *prep* according to; **secondo me** (**te**, etc.) in my (your, etc.) opinion

secondogèni·to -ta *adj* second-born

secrezióne *f* secretion

sèdano *m* celery

sedare (sèdo) *tr* to calm, placate

sedati·vo -va *adj & m* sedative

sède *f* seat; branch; residence; period; (gram) syllable; (rr) right of way; **in separata sede** in private; (law) **with change of venue; Santa Sede** Holy See; **sede centrale** main office, home office

sedentà·rio -ria (-ri -rie) *adj* sedentary || *m* sedentary person

sedére *m* sitting; rear, backside || *v* §252 *intr* (ESSERE) to sit, to be seated; to be in session; to be located || *ref* to sit down

sèdia *f* chair; seat; see; **sedia a braccioli** armchair; **sedia a dondolo** rocking chair; **sedia a pozzetto** bucket seat; **sedia a sdraio** deck chair; **sedia da posta** (hist) mail coach; **sedia di vimini** wicker chair; **sedia elettrica** electric chair; **sedia girevole** swivel chair

sedicènne *adj* sixteen-year-old || *mf* sixteen-year-old person

sedicènte *adj* so-called, self-styled

sedicèsi·mo -ma *adj, m & pron* sixteenth

sédici *adj & pron* sixteen; **le sedici** four P.M. || *m* sixteen; sixteenth (*in dates*)

sedile *m* seat; bench; bottom (*of chair*); (aut) bucket seat

sediménto *m* sediment

sediòlo *m* sulky

sedizióne *f* sedition

sedizió·so -sa [s] *adj* seditious

seducènte *adj* seductive; alluring

sedurre §102 *tr* to seduce; to allure; to lead astray; to charm, captivate

seduta *f* sitting; session, meeting; **seduta fiume** (pol) uninterrupted session; **seduta stante** on the spot

sedut·tóre -trice *adj* seductive; alluring; charming || *mf* seducer

seduzióne *f* seduction; allurement; charm

sefardì·ta (-ti -te) *adj* Sephardic || *mf* Sephardi

sé·ga *f* (-ghe) saw; **a sega** serrated; **sega a nastro** band saw; **sega circolare** buzz saw; **sega da carpentiere** lumberman's saw; **sega intelaiata a lama** bucksaw; **sega meccanica** power saw

ségala *f* rye

segali·gno -gna *adj* rye; lean, wiry

segare §209 (ségo) *tr* to saw; to cut

segatrice *f* power saw; **segatrice a disco** circular saw; **segatrice a nastro** band saw

segatura *f* cutting; sawdust

seggétta *f* commode

sèg·gio *m* (-gi) seat (*e.g., in congress*); **seggio elettorale** voting commission

sèggiola *f* chair; **seggiola a sdraio** deck chair

seggiolino *m* child's chair; stool; bucket seat; **seggiolino eiettabile** (aer) ejection seat

seggiolóne *m* highchair; easy chair

seggiovia *f* chair lift

segheria *f* sawmill

seghetta·to -ta *adj* serrated

seghétto *m* hacksaw; **seghetto da traforo** coping saw

segménto *m* segment; **segmento elastico** (aut) piston ring

segnaccènto *m* accent mark

segnàcolo *m* (lit) symbol, sign

segnalare *tr* to signal; to point out || *ref* to distinguish oneself

segnalazióne *f* signaling; sign, signal; nomination; recommendation; **dare la segnalazione a** to notify; **fare segnalazioni** to signal; **segnalazioni stradali** road signs

segnale *m* sign; signal; bookmark; **segnale di allarme** (mil) alarm; **segnale di occupato** (telp) busy signal; **segnale di via libera** (telp) dial tone; **segnale orario** (rad, telv) time signal; **segnali stradali** road signs

segnalèti·co -ca *adj* (-ci -che) identification (*mark*) || *f* road signs

segnalibro *m* bookmark

segnaline·e *m* (-e) lineman

segnapósto *m* place card

segnapun·ti *m* (-ti) scorekeeper

segnare (ségno) *tr* to mark; to underscore, underline; to jot down; to say (*e.g., five o'clock, said of a watch*); to brand; (sports) to score; **segnare a dito** to point to || *ref* to cross oneself

segnatas·se *m* (-se) postage-due stamp

segnatura *f* signing; signature; library number; (eccl) chancery; (sports) final score; (typ) signature

segnavèn·to *m* (-to) weather vane

ségno *m* mark; bookmark; symbol; sign; signal; boundary; (mus) signature; **a segno che** so that; **a tal segno** to such a point; **essere fatto segno di** to be the target of; **in segno di** as a token of; **mettere a segno** to check, control; **segno della Croce** sign of the Cross; **segno di croce** cross (*mark*); **segno d'interpunzione**, or **di punteggiatura**, or **grafico** punctuation mark; **segno di riconoscimento** identification mark

ségo *m* tallow, suet

segregare §209 (sègrego) *tr* to segregate; to secrete || *ref* to withdraw

segregazióne *f* segregation; **segregazione cellulare** solitary confinement

segregazioni·sta *mf* (-sti -ste) segregationist

segretariato *m* secretariat

segretà·rio -ria *mf* secretary; clerk

segreterìa *f* secretary's office; secretaryship

segretézza *f* secrecy

segré·to -ta *adj* secret; secretive || *m* secret; secrecy; **segreto d'alcova** boudoir secret; **segreto di Pulcinella** open secret

seguace *mf* follower

seguènte *adj* following, next

segù·gio *m* (-gi) bloodhound; (fig) private eye

seguire (séguo) *tr* to follow; to attend || *intr* (ESSERE) to continue; to follow, ensue; (with *dat*) to follow

seguitare (séguito) *intr*—**seguitare a** + *inf* to keep on + *ger*, e.g., **seguitare a parlare** to keep on talking; **seguiti!** go ahead!

séguito *m* following; retinue; followers; sequence; sequel; pursuit; **di seguito** in succession; **far seguito a** to refer to; **in seguito** thereafter; **in seguito a** as a consequence of

sèi *adj & pron* six; **le sei** six o'clock || *m* six; sixth (*in dates*)

seicènto *adj, m & pron* six hundred || *f* car with a motor displacing 600 cubic centimeters || **il Seicento** the seventeenth century

seimila *adj, m, & pron* six thousand

sélce *f* silica; flint; (lit) stone; **selci** paving blocks

selciare §128 (sélcio) *tr* to pave

selcia·to -ta *adj* paved || *m* paving

seletti·vo -va *adj* selective

selezionare (selezióno) *tr* to select, sort out

selezióne *f* selection; choice

sèlla *f* saddle

sel·làio *m* (-lài) saddler

sellare (sèllo) *tr* to saddle

sellerìa *f* saddler's shop; saddlery; (aut) upholstery

sélva *f* woods, forest

selvaggina *f* game

selvàg·gio -gia (-gi -ge) *adj* savage; vicious (*horse*) || *m* savage; unsociable person

selvàti·co -ca *adj* (-ci -che) wild

selvicoltura *f* forestry

sèlz *m* (sèlz) seltzer, club soda

semàforo *m* traffic light; semaphore

semànti·co -ca (-ci -che) *adj* semantic || *f* semantics

sembiante *m* (lit) look; **fare sembianti di** to pretend

sembianza *f* look; (lit) similarity

sembrare (sémbro) *intr* (ESSERE) to seem, look, appear || *impers*—**sembra** it seems

séme *m* seed; stone (*of fruit*); (cards) suit

seménta *f* sowing season; (lit) seed

seménte *f* seed

semènza *f* seed; brads (*used in upholstery*)

semenzà·io *m* (-zài) hotbed, seedbed

semestrale *adj* semiannual, semiyearly

semèstre *m* semester; half year

sèmi- *pref adj* semi-, e.g., **semicircolare** semicircular; half-, e.g., **semichiuso** half-closed || *pref mf* semi-, e.g., **semicerchio** semicircle; half, e.g., **semitono** half tone; demi-, e.g., **semidio** demigod

semiapèr·to -ta *adj* half-open; ajar

semiasse *m* (mach) axle (*on each side of differential*)

semicér·chio *m* (-chi) semicircle

semichiu·so -sa [s] *adj* half-closed

semicingola·to -ta *adj & m* half-track

semicìrcolo *m* semicircle

semiconduttóre *m* semiconductor

semiconvit·tóre -trice *mf* day student

semicù·pio *m* (-pi) sitz bath

semi-dìo *m* (-dèi) demigod

semidòt·to -ta *adj* semilearned

semifinale *f* semifinal

sémina *f* sowing; sowing season

seminare (sémino) *tr* to sow, seed; to plant; (coll) to leave behind

seminà·rio *m* (-ri) seminary; seminar

seminari·sta *m* (-sti) seminarian

semina·to -ta *adj* sown, seeded || *m* sown land; **uscire dal seminato** to digress

semina·tóre -trice *mf* sower || *f* (mach) seeder, seeding machine

seminterrato *m* basement

seminu·do -da *adj* half-naked

semioscurità *f* partial darkness

semirìgi·do -da *adj* semirigid; inelastic

semirimòr·chio *m* (-chi) semitrailer

semisè·rio -ria [s] *adj* (-ri -rie) serio-comic

semisfèra *f* (geom) hemisphere

semi·ta (-ti -te) *adj* Semitic || *mf* Semite

semitòno *m* (mus) semitone, half tone

semmài *conj* if ever; in the event that

sémola *f* bran; (coll) freckles

semolino *m* semolina

semovènte *adj* self-propelled

sempitèr·no -na *adj* (lit) everlasting
sémplice *adj* simple; single; plain; mere; (mil) private; (nav) ordinary ‖ *m* medicinal herb; **semplici** simple folk
semplició·ne -na *adj* simple ‖ *mf* simpleton
semplici·tà *f* (-**tà**) simplicity
semplificare §197 (**semplifico**) *tr* to simplify ‖ *ref* to become easier or simpler
sèmpre *adv* always; ever; yet; **da sempre** from time immemorial; **di sempre** same, same old; **e poi sempre** ever and ever; **ma sempre** but only; **per sempre** forever; **sempre che** provided; **sempre meglio** better and better; **sempre meno** less and less; **sempre però** but only; **sempre vostro** very truly yours
semprevérde *adj, m & f* evergreen
sènape *f* mustard
senapismo *m* mustard plaster
senato *m* senate
sena·tóre -trice *mf* senator
senése [s] *adj & mf* Sienese
senile *adj* old; of old age
senilismo *m* (pathol) senility
senilità *f* old age
senióre *adj & m* elder, senior
Sènna *f* Seine
sénno *m* wisdom; **far senno** to come back to one's senses; **senno di poi** hindsight; **uscir di senno** to go out of one's mind
séno *m* chest; breast, bosom; cove; (anat) sinus; (math) sine; (fig) heart; **in seno a** within
senonché or **se non che** *conj* but
sensale *m* broker; commission merchant
sensa·to -ta *adj* sensible, reasonable; sane
sensazionale *adj* sensational
sensazióne *f* sensation
sensibile *adj* sensible; perceptible; appreciable; sensitive; responsive (*e.g., to affection*) ‖ *m* world of the senses
sensibili·tà *f* (-**tà**) sensitivity; sensibility
sensibilizzare [ddzz] *tr* to sensitize
sensiti·vo -va *adj* sensitive ‖ *m* medium
sènso *m* sense; feeling; meaning; aspect; tone, fashion; direction; **ai sensi di legge** according to law; **a senso** free (*translation*); **doppio senso** double entendre; **in senso contrario** in the opposite direction; **perdere i sensi** to lose consciousness; **riprendere i sensi** to come to; **sensi carnali** appetite, flesh; **senso unico** one-way; **senso vietato** no entry, one-way
sensò·rio -ria *adj* (-**ri -rie**) sensory
sensuale *adj* sensual, carnal; sensuous
sensualità *f* sensuality
sentènza *f* sentence; maxim
sentenziare §287 (**sentènzio**) *tr* to pass sentence upon, sentence ‖ *intr* to pontificate
sentenzió·so -sa [s] *adj* sententious
sentièro *m* path, pathway
sentimentale *adj* sentimental; mawkish
sentimentalismo *m* sentimentalism
sentiménto *m* feeling; sentiment; sense;

uscire di sentimento (coll) to go out of one's mind
sentina *f* bilge; sink (*of vice*)
sentinèlla *f* sentry, sentinel
sentire *m* feeling ‖ *v* (**sènto**) *tr* to feel; to hear; to listen to; to consult (*a doctor*); to smell; to taste; **farsi sentire** to make oneself heard ‖ *intr* to feel; to listen; to smell; to taste; **non sentirci di quell'orecchio** to turn a deaf ear; **sentirci bene** to have keen hearing ‖ *ref* to feel; **non sentirsela di** to not have the courage to; **sentirsela** to feel up to it
senti·to -ta *adj* heartfelt
sentóre *m* inkling, feeling; sign; (lit) smell
sènza *prep* without; beyond (*e.g., comparison*); **senza + inf** without + *ger*; **senza che + subj** without + *ger*; **senza di + pron** without + *pron*, e.g., **senza di lui** without him; **senz'altro** without any doubt, of course
senza·dìo *m* (-**dìo**)—**i senzadio** the godless
senzapà·tria *m* (-**tria**) man without a country; renegade
senzatét·to *m* (-**to**) homeless person; **i senzatetto** the homeless
separare *tr & ref* to separate
separazióne *f* separation
sepolcrale *adj* sepulchral
sepolcréto *m* cemetery
sepólcro *m* sepulcher, grave
sepoltura *f* burial; grave
seppellire §253 *tr* to bury
séppia *adj invar* sepia ‖ *f* cuttlefish
seppure *conj* even if
sè·psi *f* (-**psi**) sepsis
sequèla *f* series
sequènza *f* sequence
sequestrare (**sequèstro**) *tr* to seize, confiscate; to kidnap; to confine; to quarantine; (law) to attach, sequester
sequèstro *m* seizure; attachment; **sequestro di persona** unlawful detention
séra *f* evening; night; **da mezza sera** cocktail (*dress*); dark (*suit*); **da sera** evening (*gown*); formal (*attire*)
serac·co *m* (-**chi**) serac
serafino *m* seraph
serale *adj* evening; night
seralménte *adv* in the evening; every evening
serata *f* evening; soiree, evening party; **serata d'addio** (theat) farewell performance; **di beneficenza** benefit performance
serbare (**sèrbo**) *tr* to keep; to save (*e.g., a place*); to bear (*a grudge*) ‖ *ref* to keep oneself; to stay
serba·tóio *m* (-**tói**) tank; reservoir; cartridge clip
sèr·bo -ba *adj & mf* Serbian ‖ *m*—**in serbo** in store
serbocroa·to -ta *adj & mf* Serbo-Croatian
serenata *f* serenade
serenìssi·mo -ma *adj* Serene (*Highness*)
sereni·tà *f* (-**tà**) serenity

seré·no -na *adj* serene; clear, fair (*weather*)

sergènte *m* sergeant; carpenter's clamp; **sergente maggiore** first sergeant

sèri·co -ca *adj* (-ci -che) silk

sè·rie *f* (-rie) series; (sports) division; **fuori serie** (aut) custom-built; **in serie** (aut) standard; (elec) in series

serietà *f* seriousness; gravity

serigrafìa *f* silkscreen process

sè·rio -ria (-ri -rie) *adj* serious; stern; **poco serio** unreliable (*man*); loose (*woman*) || *m* seriousness; **sul serio** in earnest; really, e.g., **bello sul serio** really beautiful

sermonare (sermóno) *tr & intr* (lit) to sermonize

sermóne *m* sermon

sermoneggiare §290 (sermonéggio) *intr* to preach; to lecture

seròti·no -na *adj* late; (lit) evening

sèrpa *f* coach box

sèrpe *f* snake, serpent; **a serpe** coiled, in a coil; **nutrirsi** or **scaldarsi la serpe in seno** to nourish a viper in one's bosom

serpeggiare §290 (serpéggio) *intr* to zigzag; to wind; to creep, spread

serpènte *m* snake, serpent; **serpente a sonagli** rattlesnake

serpenti·no -na *adj* serpentine || *m* serpentine; coil (*of pipe*) || *f* zigzag, turn (*of winding road*); coil (*of pipe*)

sérqua *f* dozen; lot, large number

sèrra *f* dike, levee; hothouse; sierra; **un serra serra** a milling crowd

serrafi·la *m* (-le) rear-guard soldier || *f* rear ship (*of convoy*)

serrafilo *m* electrician's pliers; (elec) binding post

serrà·glio *m* (-gli) menagerie; seraglio

serramànico *m—a serramanico* clasp (*knife*); switchblade (*knife*)

serrame *m* lock

serraménto *m* closing, bolting || **serra·mén·ti & -ta** *fpl* closing devices, doors, windows, and shutters

serranda *f* shutter (*of store*)

serrare (sèrro) *tr* to shut, close; to pursue (*the enemy*); to increase (*tempo*); to furl (*sails*); to lock; to clench (*one's teeth, one's fists*); to shake (*hands*) || *intr* to shut; to be tight || *ref* to be wrenched, e.g., **gli si serrò il cuore** his heart was wrenched; **serrarsi addosso a** to press (*the enemy*)

serrata *f* lockout

serrate *m—serrate finale* (sports) finish

serra·to -ta *adj* shut (*e.g., door*); concise (*style*); tight (*game*); rapid (*gallop*); closed (*ranks*); thick (*crowd*) || *f* see serrata

serratura *f* lock

sèrto *m* (poet) crown, wreath

sèrva *f* (pej) maidservant, maid

servènte *adj* (*gentleman*) in waiting || *m* gunner; (obs) servant

servìbile *adj* usable

serviènte *m* (eccl) server

servì·gio *m* (-gi) service; favor

servile *adj* servile; menial; modal (*auxiliary*)

servire (sèrvo) *tr* to serve; to wait on; **in che posso servirLa?** what can I do for you?; may I help you?; **per servirLa** at your service || *intr* to serve || *intr* (ESSERE & AVERE) to serve; to answer the purpose; to last; (with *dat*) (coll) to need, e.g., **gli serve il martello** he needs the hammer; **non servire a nulla** to be of no use; **servire da** to act as || *ref* to help oneself; **servirsi da** to patronize, deal with; **servirsi di** to avail oneself of, use

servitóre *m* servant; tea wagon; **servitor suo umilissimo** your humble servant

servi·tù *f* (-tù) servitude; captivity; servants, help; **servitù di passaggio** (law) easement

serviziévole *adj* obliging, accommodating

servì·zio *m* (-zi) service; favor; turn; **a mezzo servizio** part-time (*domestic help*); **di servizio** delivery (*entrance*); for hire (*car*); domestic (*help*); **fuori servizio** out of commission; **in servizio** in commission; **servizi** kitchen and bath; facilities; **servizi pubblici** public services; public works; **servizio attivo** active duty; **servizio permanente effettivo** service in the regular army

sèr·vo -va *adj* (lit) enslaved || *m* slave; servant; **servo della gleba** serf || *f* see serva

servoassisti·to -ta *adj* servocontrolled

servofréno *m* (aut) power brake

servomotóre *m* servomotor

servostèrzo *m* (aut) power steering

sèsamo *m* sesame; **apriti sesamo!** open sesame!

sessanta *adj, m & pron* sixty

sessantènne *adj* sixty-year-old || *mf* sixty-year-old person

sessantèsi·mo -ma *adj, m & pron* sixtieth

sessantina *f* about sixty

sessióne *f* session

sèsso *m* sex; **il sesso debole** the fair sex

sessuale *adj* sexual

sestante *m* sextant

sestétto *m* sextet

sestière *m* district, section

sè·sto -sta *adj & pron* sixth || *m* sixth; curve (*of an arch*); **fuori sesto** out of sorts; **mettere in sesto** to arrange; to set in order; **sesto acuto** (archit) ogive

sèt *m* (sèt) set; set all'aperto (mov) location

séta *f* silk; **seta artificiale** rayon

setacciare §128 *tr* to sift, sieve

setàc·cio *m* (-ci) sieve

setàce·o -a *adj* silky

séte *f* thirst; **aver sete** to be thirsty; **to** lust after; **sete di** thirst for

seterìa *f* silk mill; **seterie** silk goods

setifì·cio *m* (-ci) silk mill

sétola *f* bristle; (joc) stubble

sètta *f* sect

settanta *adj, m & pron* seventy

settantènne *adj* seventy-year-old || *mf* seventy-year-old person

settantèsi·mo -ma *adj, m & pron* seventieth

settantina *f* about seventy

settà·rio -ria *adj & mf* (-ri -rie) sectarian

sètte *adj & pron* seven; le sette seven o'clock || *m* seven; seventh (*in dates*); V-shaped tear (*in clothing*)

settecentèsi·mo -ma *adj, m & pron* seven hundredth

settecènto *adj, m & pron* seven hundred || il Settecento the eighteenth century

settèmbre *m* September

settennale *adj* seven-year (*e.g., plan*)

settènne *adj* seven-year-old || *mf* seven-year-old child

settentrionale *adj* northern || *mf* northerner

settentrióne *m* north; (astr) Little Bear

setticemia *f* septicemia

sètti·co -ca *adj* (-ci -che) septic

settimana *f* week; week's wages; settimana corta five-day week

settimanale *adj & m* weekly

settimi·no -na *adj* premature (*baby*) || *m* (mus) septet

sètti·mo -ma *adj, m & pron* seventh

sètto *m* septum

settóre *m* sector; section, branch; dissector, anatomist; coroner's pathologist

sevè·ro -ra *adj* severe, stern

seviziare §287 *tr* to torture

sevizie *fpl* cruelty

sezionale *adj* sectional

sezionare (sezióno) *tr* to cut up; to divide up; to dissect

sezióne *f* section; dissection; chapter (*of club*); department (*of agency*); (geom) cross section

sfaccenda·to -ta *adj* loafing || *mf* loafer

sfaccettare (sfaccétto) *tr* to facet

sfacchinare *intr* (coll) to toil, drudge

sfacchinata *f* (coll) drudgery, grind

sfacciatàggine *f* brazenness, impudence

sfaccia·to -ta *adj* brazen, impudent; loud, gaudy; fare lo sfacciato to be fresh

sfacèlo *m* breakdown, collapse

sfà·glio *m* (-gli) swerve (*e.g., of horse*); (cards) discard

sfaldare *tr* to exfoliate; to cut into slices || *ref* to flake, scale; (fig) to collapse, crumble

sfamare *tr* to feed (*the hungry; the family*) || *ref* to get enough to eat

sfare §173 *tr* to undo || *ref* to spoil (said, *e.g., of meat*)

sfarzo *m* pomp, display; luxury

sfarzó·so -sa [s] *adj* sumptuous, luxurious

sfasare *tr* to throw out of phase; (coll) to depress || *intr* (ESSERE) (aut) to misfire; (elec) to be out of phase

sfasciare §128 *tr* to remove the bandage from; to unswathe; to smash, shatter || *ref* to go to pieces; to lose one's figure

sfatare *tr* to discredit; to unmask

sfatica·to -ta *adj* lazy || *mf* loafer

sfat·to -ta *adj* overdone; overripe; undone (*bed*); ravaged (*by age*)

sfavillare *intr* to spark, sparkle

sfavóre *m* disfavor

sfavorévole *adj* unfavorable

sfebbra·to -ta *adj* free of fever

sfegata·to -ta *adj* (coll) rabid, fanatical

sfèra *f* sphere; (coll) hand (*of clock*); a sfera ball-point (*pen*); a sfere ball (*bearing*); sfera di cuoio (sports) pigskin

sfèri·co -ca *adj* (-ci -che) spherical

sferrare (sfèrro) *tr* to unshoe (*a horse*); to unchain; to draw (*a weapon from a wound*); to deliver (*a blow*) || *ref* to hurl oneself

sfèrza *f* whip, scourge

sferzare (sfèrzo) *tr* to whip, scourge

sfiancare §197 *tr* to break open; to tire out; to fit (*clothes*) too tight || *ref* to burst open; to get worn out

sfiatare *intr* to leak (said, *e.g., of a tire*) || *intr* (ESSERE) to leak (said *of air or gas*) || *ref* to waste one's breath

sfiata·tóio *m* (-tói) vent

sfibbiare §287 *tr* to unbuckle, unfasten; to untie (*a knot*)

sfibrante *adj* exhausting

sfibrare *tr* to grind (*wood*) into fibers; to shred (*rags*) into fibers; to weaken, wear out

sfida *f* challenge

sfidare *tr* to challenge, dare; to brave, defy; to endure (*the challenge of time*); sfidare che to bet that

sfidù·cia *f* (-cie) mistrust; (pol) no confidence

sfiducia·to -ta *adj* downcast, depressed

sfigurare *tr* to disfigure || *intr* to make a bad impression; to lose face

sfilacciare §128 *tr & ref* to ravel, fray

sfilare *tr* to unstring; to take off (*one's shoes*); to count (*beads*); to unthread; to dull (*a blade*); to ravel || *intr* (ESSERE) to march, parade; to follow one another || *ref* to become unthreaded; to become frayed; to run (said *of knitted work*); to break one's back

sfilata *f* parade; row; sfilata di moda fashion show

sfilza *f* row, sequence

sfinge *f* sphinx

sfiniménto *m* exhaustion

sfinire §176 *tr* to exhaust, wear out || *ref* to be worn out

sfintère *m* sphincter

sfiorare (sfióro) *tr* to graze; to barely touch (*a subject*); to skim; (lit) to barely reach

sfioratóre *m* spillway

sfiorire §176 *intr* (ESSERE) to wither, fade

sfit·to -ta *adj* not rented

sfocare §197 *tr* to put out of focus; to blur

sfociare §128 (sfócio) *tr* to dredge (*the mouth of a river*) || *intr* (ESSERE) to flow; sfociare in (fig) to lead to

sfoderare (sfòdero) *tr* to unsheathe; to show off, sport, display; to take the cover or lining off || *intr* to be drawn out

sfogare §209 (sfógo) *tr* to vent, give vent to || *intr* (ESSERE) to flow; to pour out; sfogare in to turn into || *ref*—sfogarsi a + *inf* to have one's fill of + *ger;* **sfogarsi con** to unburden oneself to; **sfogarsi su qlcu** to take it out on s.o.

sfoga·tóio *m* (-tói) vent

sfoggiare §290 (sfòggio) *tr* to display, sport; to show off

sfòg·gio *m* (-gi) display, ostentation

sfòglia *f* foil; skin (*of onion*); layer of puff paste; (ichth) sole

sfogliare §280 (sfòglio) *tr* to pluck (*a flower*); to defoliate (*a tree*); to leaf through (*a book*); to deal (*cards*); to husk (*corn*); to press (*dough*) into layers ‖ *ref* to shed its leaves; to flake

sfogliata *f* defoliation; puff paste; **dare una sfogliata a** to glance through

sfó·go *m* (-ghi) exhaust; outlet; vent; (coll) eruption (*of skin*)

sfolgorare (sfólgoro) *intr* (ESSERE & AVERE) to shine, blaze

sfolgorì·o *m* (-i) glittering, blazing

sfollagèn·te *m* (-te) billy

sfollaménto *m* evacuation; layoff

sfollare (sfòllo) *tr* to clear; to cut the staff of ‖ *intr* (ESSERE & AVERE) to disperse, evacuate; to cut down the staff

sfolla·to -ta *adj* driven from home ‖ *mf* evacuee

sfoltire §176 *tr* to thin out

sfondare (sfóndo) *tr* to stave in; to break through; to be heavy on (*the stomach*) ‖ *intr* to give ‖ *ref* to break open

sfóndo *m* background

sfondóne *m* (coll) blunder, error

sforbiciare §128 (sfòrbicio) *tr* to clip, shear

sforbiciata *f* clipping; (sports) scissors; (sports) scissors kick

sformare (sfórmo) *tr* to pull out of shape; to take out of the mold ‖ *intr* to get mad

sforma·to -ta *adj* out of shape ‖ *m* pudding

sfornare (sfórno) *tr* to take out of the oven

sfornire §176 *tr* to deprive; to strip

sfortuna *f* bad luck, misfortune

sfortuna·to -ta *adj* unsuccessful; unlucky, unfortunate

sforzare (sfòrzo) *tr* to strain; to force ‖ *ref* to strive, endeavor

sforza·to -ta *adj* forced, unnatural

sfòrzo *m* effort; strain; stretch (*of imagination*); **senza sforzo** effortlessly

sfóttere *tr* (vulg) to make fun of

sfracassare *tr* to smash, crash

sfracellare (sfracèllo) *tr & ref* to shatter, smash

sfrangiare §290 *tr* to ravel

sfrattare *tr* to evict; to deport ‖ *intr* to be evicted

sfratto *m* eviction; notice of eviction

sfrecciare §128 (sfréccio) *intr* (ESSERE & AVERE) to speed by

sfregaménto *m* rubbing

sfregare §209 (sfrégo) *tr* to rub; to scrape; to strike (*a match*)

sfregiare §290 (sfrégio & sfrègio) *tr* to disfigure, slash

sfregia·to -ta *adj* disfigured, slashed ‖ *m* scarface

sfré·gio or **sfrè·gio** *m* (-gi) slash, scar, gash; insult

sfrenare (sfréno & sfrèno) *tr* to take the brake off; to give free rein to ‖ *ref* to kick over the traces

sfrìggere §180 *intr* to sizzle

sfrigolì·o *m* (-i) sizzle

sfrondare (sfróndo) *tr* to defoliate; to lop off; to trim down ‖ *ref* to lose leaves

sfrontatézza *f* effrontery, impudence

sfronta·to -ta *adj* brazen, impudent

sfrusciare §128 *intr* to rustle

sfruttare *tr* to exploit; to exhaust (*e.g., a mine*); to take advantage of

sfrutta·tóre -trice *mf* exploiter, developer (*e.g., of an invention*)

sfuggènte *adj* fleeting; receding (*forehead*); shifty (*glance*)

sfuggire *tr* to avoid, flee ‖ *intr* (ESSERE) to flee, escape, get away; (with *dat*) to escape, e.g., **nulla gli sfugge** nothing escapes him; to break, e.g., **sfuggì a una promessa** he broke a promise; **lasciarsi sfuggire** to let slip

sfuggita *f*—**di sfuggita** hastily; incidentally; **dare una sfuggita** to run down (*e.g., to the post office*)

sfumare *tr* to shade down; to tone down; to trim (*hair*) ‖ *intr* (ESSERE) to vanish; to shade

sfumatura *f* nuance, shade; razor clipping

sfumino *m* stump (*in drawing*)

sfuriare §287 *tr* to vent (*one's anger*) ‖ *intr* to rave

sfuriata *f* outburst of anger; gust (*of wind*); **fare una sfuriata a** to give a scolding to

sgabèllo *m* stool, footstool

sgabuzzino *m* cubbyhole

sgambettare (sgambétto) *tr* to trip ‖ *intr* to toddle; to kick (*said of a baby*); to scamper

sgambétto *m* trip, stumble; **dare lo sgambetto a** to trip

sganasciare §128 *tr* to dislocate the jaw of; to break the jaw of; to tear apart ‖ *intr* to steal right and left ‖ *ref* to break one's jaw; **sganasciarsi dalle risa** to split one's sides laughing

sganciare §128 *tr* to unhook; to lay out (*money*); to drop (*bombs*) ‖ *intr* to drop bombs; (coll) to go away ‖ *ref* to get unhooked; (mil) to disengage oneself; **sganciarsi da** to get rid of

sgangherare (sgànghero) *tr* to unhinge; to burst ‖ *ref*—**sgangherarsi dalle risa** to split one's sides laughing

spanghera·to -ta *adj* unhinged; broken down; rickety; coarse (*laughter*)

sgarbatéz·za *f* rudeness, incivility; clumsiness

sgarba·to -ta *adj* rude; clumsy

sgarberia *f* var of **sgarbatezza**

sgarbo *m*—**fare uno sgarbo a** to be rude to

sgargiante *adj* loud, flashy, showy

sgarrare *intr* to go wrong

sgattaiolare (sgattàiolo) *intr* (ESSERE) to slip away; to wriggle out

sgelare (sgèlo) *tr & intr* to thaw, melt
sgèlo *m* thaw
sghém·bo -ba *adj* crooked; **a sghembo** askew ‖ **sghembo** *adv* askew; sideways
sghèrro *m* hired assassin; gendarme
sghiacciare §128 *tr* to thaw
sghignazzare *intr* to guffaw
sghignazzata *f* guffaw
sghimbè·scio -scia —a or di sghimbescio askew, crooked
sghiribizzo [ddzz] *m* whim, fancy
sgobbare (sgòbbo) *intr* to drudge, plod, plug
sgobbó·ne -na *mf* plugger, plodder, drudge
sgocciolare (sgócciolo) *tr* to let drip ‖ *intr* to drip (*said of container*) ‖ *intr* (ESSERE) to drip (*said of liquid*)
sgocciola·tóio *m* (-tói) dish rack; drip pan
sgocciolatura *f* dripping; drippings
sgócciolo *m* last drop; **essere agli sgoccioli** to be coming to an end
sgolare (sgólo) *ref* to shout oneself hoarse
sgomberare (sgómbero) *tr & intr* var of sgombrare
sgómbero *m* moving
sgombrané·ve *m* (-ve) snowplow (*truck*)
sgombrare (sgómbro) *tr* to clear; to vacate ‖ *intr* to move, vacate
sgóm·bro -bra *adj* clear ‖ *m* moving; (ichth) mackerel
sgomentare (sgoménto) *tr* to frighten; to dismay
sgomén·to -ta *adj* dismayed ‖ *m* dismay; **rimanere di sgomento** to be dismayed
sgominare (sgòmino) *tr* to rout
sgomma·to -ta *adj* unglued; without tires; with poor tires
sgonfiare §287 (sgónfio) *tr* to deflate; to damn with faint praise (*e.g., a play*); (coll) to bore ‖ *intr* (ESSERE) to boast; to balloon ‖ *ref* to go down (*said of swelling*); to go flat (*said of a tire*); (fig) to collapse
sgón·fio -fia *adj* deflated, flat
sgonfiòtto *m* jelly doughnut; puff (*in clothing*)
sgórbia *f* (carp) gouge
sgorbiare §287 (sgòrbio) *tr* to scribble; (carp) to gouge
sgòr·bio *m* (-bi) ink spot; scribble, scrawl
sgorgare §209 (sgórgo) *tr* to unclog ‖ *intr* (ESSERE) to gush
sgottare (sgótto) *tr* to bail out (*a boat*)
sgozzare (sgózzo) *tr* to slaughter; to slit the throat of; (fig) to bleed, fleece
sgradévole *adj* disagreeable, unpleasant
sgradire §176 *tr* to refuse ‖ *intr* to be displeasing
sgradi·to -ta *adj* unpleasant; unwelcome
sgraffignare *tr* to snitch, snatch
sgrammatica·to -ta *adj* ungrammatical
sgranare *tr* to shell (*e.g., peas*); to count (*one's beads*); to seed (*grapes*); to open (*one's eyes*); (mach) to disengage ‖ *ref* to crumble; to scratch oneself

sgranchire §176 *tr* to stretch (*e.g., one's legs*)
sgranocchiare §287 (sgranòcchio) *tr* to crunch, munch
sgrassare *tr* to remove the grease from; to skim (*broth*); to scour (*wool*)
sgravare *tr* to relieve, lighten ‖ *ref* to be relieved; to give birth
sgrà·vio *m* (-vi) lightening, lessening; **a sgravio di coscienza** to ease one's conscience
sgrazia·to -ta *adj* gawky, clumsy
sgretolare (sgrétolo) *tr & ref* to crumble
sgretola·to -ta *adj* crumbling, falling down
sgridare *tr* to scold, chide
sgridata *f* scolding, reprimand
sgrondare (sgróndo) *tr* to cause to drip ‖ *intr* to drip, trickle
sgroppare (sgróppo) *tr* to wear (*a horse*) out ‖ *intr* to buck (*said of a horse*)
sgroppare (sgróppo) *tr* to untie
sgrossare (sgròsso) *tr* to rough-hew; (fig) to refine
sgrovigliare §280 *tr* to untangle
sguaiatàggine *f* uncouthness
sguaia·to -ta *adj* crude, vulgar; uncouth ‖ *mf* vulgar person; uncouth person
sguainare *tr* to unsheathe; to show (*one's nails*)
sgualcire §176 *tr* to crumple ‖ *ref* to become crumpled
sgualdrina *f* trollop, strumpet
sguardo *m* glance, look; eyes
sguarnire §176 *tr* to untrim; (mil) to strip, dismantle
sguàtte·ro -ra *mf* dishwasher, scullion ‖ *f* kitchenmaid, scullery maid
sguazzare *tr* to waste, squander ‖ *intr* to splash; to wallow; to be lost (*in shoes too big or clothes too loose*)
sguinzagliare §280 *tr* to unleash, let loose
sgusciare §128 *tr* to shell, hull ‖ *intr* (ESSERE) to slip; **sgusciare di soppiatto** to slip away
shòp·ping *m* (-ping) shopping; shopping bag; **fare lo shopping** to go shopping
shràpnel *m* (shràpnel) shrapnel
si *m* (-si) (mus) si ‖ §5 *pron*
sì *m* (sì) yes; yea; **stare tra il sì e il no** to not be able to make up one's mind; **un . . . sì e l'altro no** every other (*e.g., day*)
sìa *conj* see essere
siamése [s] *adj & mf* Siamese
siberia·no -na *adj & mf* Siberian
sibilante *adj & f* sibilant
sibilare (sìbilo) *intr* to hiss
sibilla *f* sibyl
sìbilo *m* hiss, hissing
sicà·rio *m* (-ri) hired assassin
sicché *conj* so that
siccità *f* drought
siccóme *adv* as ‖ *conj* since; as; how
Sicilia, la Sicily
sicilia·no -na *adj & mf* Sicilian
sicomòro *m* sycamore
sicumèra *f* cocksureness, overconfidence
sicura *f* safety lock (*on gun*)

sicurézza f security; assurance; safety; certainty; reliability; **di sicurezza** safety; **sicurezza sociale** social security

sicu·ro -ra adj sure; safe; steady; **di sicuro** certainly || m safety; **camminare sul sicuro** to take no chances || **sicuro** adv certainly || f see **sicura**

sicur·tà f (**-tà**) insurance

siderale adj sidereal

sidère·o -a adj sidereal

siderùrgi·co -ca (**-ci -che**) adj iron-and-steel || m iron-and-steel worker

sidro m cider, hard cider

sièpe f hedge; (fig) wall

sièro m serum

sièsta f siesta; **fare la siesta** to take a nap, take a siesta

siffat·to -ta adj such

sifilide f syphilis

sifóne m siphon; siphon bottle; trap

siga·ràio -ràia (**-rài -ràie**) mf cigar maker || m (ent) grape hopper; || f cigarette girl

sigarétta f cigarette

sigaro m cigar

sigillare tr to seal

sigillo m seal; **avere il sigillo alle labbra** to have one's lips sealed; **sigillo sacramentale** seal of confession

sigla f acronym; initials; abbreviation; letterword; **sigla musicale** theme song

siglare tr to initial

significare §197 (**signìfico**) tr to mean; to signify; **significare qlco a qlcu** to inform s.o. of s.th

significati·vo -va adj significant; meaningful

significato m meaning; **senza significato** meaningless

signóra f Madam, Mrs.; lady; mistress; owner; wife || **Nostra Signora** Our Lady

signóre m sir, Mr.; gentleman; rich man; lord, master, owner; man; **il signore desidera?** what is your pleasure?; **per signori** stag || **Signore** m Lord

signoreggiare §290 (**signoréggio**) tr to rule over; to master; to tower over; to overshadow || intr to be the master

signorìa f seigniory; rule; **La Signoria Vostra** your Honor; **Sua Signoria** his Lordship; your Lordship

signorile adj seigniorial; gentlemanly; ladylike; elegant, refined

signorìna f miss; Miss; young lady; spinster

signorino m master, young gentleman

signornò adv no, Sir

signoró·ne -na mf (coll) rich person

signoròtto m lordling

signorsì adv yes, Sir

silenziatóre -trice m silencer (of firearm); (aut) muffler

silèn·zio m (**-zi**) silence; (mil) taps; **fare silenzio** to be silent; **ridurre al silenzio** (mil) to silence

silenzió·so -sa [s] adj silent; noiseless

sìlfide f sylphid

silfo m sylph

silhouèt·te f (**-te**) silhouette

sìlice f silica

silìcio m silicon

silicóne m silicone

siliquastro m redbud

sillaba f syllable

sillabare (**sìllabo**) tr to syllabify; **to spell**

sillabà·rio m (**-ri**) reader, primer

sìllabo m syllabus

silo m silo

silòfono m xylophone

siluétta f silhouette

silurante adj torpedoing, torpedo || f destroyer; torpedo boat

silurare tr to torpedo; (fig) to fire, dismiss; (fig) to undermine

siluro m torpedo

silva·no -na adj sylvan

silvèstre adj (lit) sylvan; (lit) wild; (lit) hard, arduous

simboleggiare §290 (**simboléggio**) tr to symbolize

simbòli·co -ca adj (**-ci -che**) symbolic

simbolismo m symbolism

sìmbolo m symbol

similari·tà f (**-tà**) similarity

sìmile adj similar; such || m like; **i propri simili** fellow men

similòro m tombac

simmetrìa f symmetry

simmètri·co -ca adj (**-ci -che**) symmetrical

simonìa f simony

simpamina f benzedrine

simpatèti·co -ca adj (**-ci -che**) sympathetic

simpatìa f like, liking; **cattivarsi la simpatia di** to make oneself well liked by

simpàti·co -ca (**-ci -che**) adj nice, pleasant, congenial || m (anat) sympathetic system

simpatizzante [ddzz] adj sympathizing || mf sympathizer

simpatizzare [ddzz] intr to sympathize; to become friends

simpò·sio m (**-si**) symposium

simulare (**sìmulo**) tr to simulate

simula·tóre -trice mf faker, impostor || m simulator

simultàne·o -a adj simultaneous

sin- pref adj syn-, e.g., **sinonimo** synonymous || pref m & f syn-, e.g., **sinonimo** synonym

sin adv—**sin da** ever since

sinagò·ga f (**-ghe**) synagogue

sincerare (**sincèro**) tr (lit) to convince || ref—**sincerarsi di** to ascertain

sincè·ro -ra adj sincere; pure

sinché conj until

sìncope f fainting spell; (phonet) syncope; (mus) syncopation

sincronismo m synchronism; **sincronismo orizzontale** (telv) horizontal hold; **sincronismo verticale** (telv) vertical hold

sincronizzare [ddzz] tr to syncronize

sìncro·no -na adj syncronous

sindacale adj mayoral; union

sindacalismo m trade unionism

sindacali·sta mf (**-sti -ste**) union member; union leader

sindacare §197 (**sìndaco**) *tr* to criticize; to scrutinize

sindaca·to -ta *adj* controlled, scrutinized ‖ *m* control; labor union; syndicate; **sindacato giallo** company union

sìnda·co *m* (**-ci**) mayor; controller; auditor

sinecura *f* sinecure

sinfonìa *f* symphony; (*of an opera*) overture; (coll) racket (*noise*)

sinfòni·co -ca *adj* (**-ci -che**) symphonic

singhiozzare (**singhiózzo**) *intr* to sob; to hiccup; to jerk

singhiózzo *m* sob; hiccups; **a singhiozzo** in jerks; by fits and spurts

singolare *adj* singular ‖ *m* singular; (tennis) singles

sìngo·lo -la *adj* single ‖ *m* individual; shell for one oarsman; (rr) roomette; (telp) private line; (tennis) singles

singulto *m* hiccups; sob

sinistra *f* left hand; left

sinistrare *tr* to ruin; to damage

sinistra·to -ta *adj* injured, damaged, ruined ‖ *mf* victim (*of bombing or flood*)

sinistrismo *m* leftism

sinistri·sta *adj* (**-sti -ste**) leftish, leftist

sini·stro -stra *adj* left; sinister ‖ *m* accident; (boxing) left ‖ *f* see **sinistra**

sinistròide *adj & mf* leftist

sino *adv* var of **fino**

sinologìa *f* Sinology

sinòni·mo -ma *adj* synonymous ‖ *m* synonym

sinò·psi *f* (**-psi**) (mov) synopsis

sinóra *adv* var of **finora**

sinòs·si *f* (**-si**) synopsis

sinòtti·co -ca *adj* (**-ci -che**) synoptic(al)

sintas·si *f* (**-si**) syntax

sìnte·si *f* (**-si**) synthesis

sintèti·co -ca *adj* (**-ci -che**) synthetic(al); concise

sintetizzare [ddzz] *tr* to synthesize

sintogram·ma *m* (**-mi**) (rad) dial

sìntomo *m* symptom

sintonìa *f* harmony; (rad) tuning

sintonizzare [ddzz] *tr* (rad) to tune

sintonizzatóre [ddzz] *m* (rad) tuner

sinuó·so -sa [s] *adj* sinuous, winding

sionismo *m* Zionism

sipà·rio *m* (**-ri**) curtain; **sipario di ferro** iron curtain

sirèna *f* siren; mermaid; **sirena da nebbia** foghorn

Sìria, la Syria

siria·no -na *adj & mf* Syrian

sirìn·ga *f* (**-ghe**) panpipe; syringe; catheter; grease gun; (orn) syrinx

siringare §209 *tr* to catheterize

siròcchia *f* (obs) sister

si·sma *m* (**-smi**) earthquake

sismògrafo *m* seismograph

sismologìa *f* seismology

sissignóre *adv* yes, Sir!

sistè·ma *m* (**-mi**) system

sistemare (**sistèmo**) *tr* to arrange; to put in order; to systematize; to settle; to find a job for; to find a husband for; (coll) to fix ‖ *ref* to settle; to get married

sistemazióne *f* arrangement; settlement; job, position

sìstole *f* systole

sitibón·do -da *adj* (lit) thirsty

si·to -ta *adj* (lit) located ‖ *m* (lit) site, spot, location; (mil) sight; (coll) musty odor

situare (**sìtuo**) *tr* to locate, place, situate

situazióne *f* situation; condition

slabbrare *tr* to chip; to open (*a wound*) ‖ *intr* to overflow ‖ *ref* to become chipped; to reopen (*said of a cut*)

slacciare §128 *tr* to untie; to unfasten; to unbutton ‖ *ref* to get undone; to get unbuttoned

sladinare *tr* (sports) to train; (mach) to run in, break in

slanciare §128 *tr* to hurl, throw ‖ *ref* to hurl oneself; to rise (*said, e.g., of a tower*)

slancia·to -ta *adj* slender; soaring

slàn·cio *m* (**-ci**) leap; outburst (*of feeling*); momentum; **di slancio** with a rush; **prendere lo slancio** to get a running start

slargare §209 *tr* to widen; to warm (*the heart*) ‖ *ref* to widen, spread out

slattare *tr* to wean

slava·to -ta *adj* pale, washed out

sla·vo -va *adj* Slav, Slavic ‖ *mf* Slav ‖ *m* Slavic (*language*)

sleale *adj* disloyal; unfair (*competition*)

sleal·tà *f* (**-tà**) disloyalty

slegare §209 (**slégo**) *tr* to untie

slega·to -ta *adj* untied; disconnected

slip *m* (**slip**) briefs; tank suit, bathing suit (*for men*)

slitta *f* sled, sleigh; (mach) carriage

slittaménto *m* skid; slide

slittare *intr* to sled; to skid; to slide

slogare §209 (**slògo**) *tr* to dislocate ‖ *ref* to become dislocated; to dislocate (*e.g., an arm*)

slogatura *f* dislocation

sloggiare §290 (**slòggio**) *tr* to dislodge; to evict ‖ *intr* to vacate

slòg·gio *m* (**-gi**) moving; eviction

slovac·co -ca *adj & mf* (**-chi -che**) Slovak

smacchiare §287 *tr* to clean; to deforest

smacchia·tóre -trice *mf* cleaner ‖ *m* cleaning fluid; spot remover

smac·co *m* (**-chi**) letdown; slap in the face

smagliante *adj* dazzling, shining

smagliare §280 *tr* to break the links of; to undo the meshes of; to remove (*a fish*) from the net ‖ *intr* to shine, dazzle ‖ *ref* to run (*said, e.g., of knitted fabric*); to free itself from the net

smagliatura *f* run (*in stockings*); (fig) break

smagrire §176 *tr* to impoverish ‖ *intr* (ESSERE) & *ref* to become thin or lean

smaliziare §287 *tr* to make wiser ‖ *ref* to get wiser

smaltare *tr* to enamel; to glaze

smaltire §176 *tr* to digest; to sleep off (*a drunk*); to swallow (*an offense*);

to sell off; to get rid of; to drain off (*water*)

smalti·tóio *m* (*-tói*) drain, sewer

smalto *m* enamel; **smalto per le unghie** nail polish

smancerie *fpl* affectation; mawkishness

smanceró·so -sa [*s*] *adj* prissy

smangiare §290 *tr* to erode, eat away ‖ *ref* to be consumed (*e.g., by hatred*)

smània *f* frenzy; craze, yearning; **dare in smanie** to be in a frenzy

smaniare §287 *intr* to be delirious; to yearn, crave

smanió·so -sa [*s*] *adj* eager; disturbing

smantellare (**smantèllo**) *tr* to dismantle; to demolish; to disable (*a ship*)

smargias·so -sa *mf* braggart, boaster

smarrimento *m* loss; bewilderment; discouragement

smarrire §176 *tr* to lose ‖ *ref* to get lost; to be discouraged

smascellare (**smascèllo**) *ref*—**smascellarsi dalle risa** to split one's sides laughing

smascherare (**smàschero**) *tr* & *ref* to unmask

smazzata *f* (cards) deal; (cards) hand

smembraménto *m* dismemberment

smembrare (**smèmbro**) *tr* to dismember

smemoratàggine *f* forgetfulness

smemora·to -ta *adj* absent-minded; forgetful ‖ *mf* absent-minded or forgetful person

smentire §176 *tr* to belie; to refute; to retract; to be untrue to ‖ *ref* to not be consistent, to contradict oneself

smentita *f* denial; retraction

smeraldo *m* emerald

smerciare §128 (**smèrcio**) *tr* to sell, sell out

smèr·cio *m* (*-ci*) sale

smèr·go *m* (*-ghi*) (zool) merganser

smerigliare §280 *tr* to grind, polish; to sand

smeriglia·to -ta *adj* polished; sand (*paper*); emery (*cloth*); frosted (*glass*)

smeri·glio *m* (*-gli*) emery; (orn) merlin; (ichth) porbeagle

smerlare (**smèrlo**) *tr* to scallop

smèrlo *m* scallop (*along the edge of a garment*)

smés·so -sa *adj* hand-me-down, castoff

sméttere §198 *tr* to stop; to stop wearing; to break up (*housekeeping*); **smetterla** to cut it out ‖ *intr*—**smettere di** + *inf* to stop + *ger*

smezzare [*ddzz*] (**smèzzo**) *tr* to halve

smidollare (**smidóllo**) *tr* to remove the marrow from; (fig) to emasculate

militarizzare [*ddzz*] *tr* to demilitarize

smil·zo -za *adj* slender; poor, worthless

sminare *tr* to remove mines from

sminuire §176 *tr* to belittle

sminuzzare *tr* to crumble; to mince; to expatiate on ‖ *ref* to crumble

smistaménto *m* sorting (*of mail*); (rr) shunting, shifting

smistare *tr* to sort; (rr) to shift; (soccer) to pass; (rad) to unscramble

smisura·to -ta *adj* immense, huge

smitizzante [*ddzz*] *adj* debunking, demythologizing

smitizzare [*ddzz*] *tr* to debunk; to demythologize

smobiliare §287 *tr* to remove the furniture from

smobilitare (**smobilito**) *tr* to demobilize

smobilitazióne *f* demobilization

smoccolare (**smòccolo** & **smóccolo**) *tr* to snuff (*a candle*) ‖ *intr* (slang) to swear, curse

smoda·to -ta *adj* excessive, immoderate

smòg *m* smog

smóking *m* (**smóking**) dinner jacket, tuxedo

smontàbile *adj* dismountable

smontàg·gio *m* (*-gi*) disassembling, dismantling

smontare (**smónto**) *tr* to take apart; to dismantle; to cause (*e.g., whipped cream*) to fall; to take (*a precious stone*) out of its setting; to dishearten; to dissuade; to drop (*s.o.*) off; **smontare la guardia** to come off guard duty ‖ *intr* (ESSERE) to dismount; to get off or out (*of a conveyance*); to fade; to drop (*said, e.g., of beaten eggs*) ‖ *ref* to become downcast

smòrfia *f* grimace; mawkishness; **fare le smorfie a** to make faces at

smorfió·so -sa [*s*] *adj* mawkish, prissy

smòr·to -ta *adj* pale, wan; faded

smorzare (**smòrzo**) *tr* to attenuate; to lessen; to tone down; to turn off (*light*); (phys) to dampen

smorzatóre *m* (mus) damper

smòs·so -sa *adj* moved; loose

smottamento *m* mud slide

smozzicare §197 (**smózzico**) *tr* to crumble; to mince; to clip, mince (*one's words*)

smun·to -ta *adj* emaciated, pale, wan

smuòvere §202 *tr* to budge; to till; (fig) to move ‖ *ref* to budge; to move away; **smuoviti!** get going!

smussare *tr* to blunt; to bevel; (fig) to soften

snaturalizzare [*ddzz*] *tr* to denaturalize; to denationalize

snaturare *tr* to change the nature of; to distort, misrepresent

snatura·to -ta *adj* distorted; monstrous, unnatural

snebbiare §287 (**snébbio**) *tr* to drive the fog from; to clear (*e.g., one's mind*)

snellézza *f* slenderness; nimbleness

snellire §176 *tr* & *ref* to slenderize

snèl·lo -la *adj* slender; nimble; lively

snervante *adj* enervating

snervare (**snèrvo**) *tr* to enervate, prostrate ‖ *ref* to become enervated

snidare *tr* to drive out, flush

snòb *adj invar* snobbish ‖ *mf* (**snòb**) snob

snobbare (**snòbbo**) *tr* to snub, slight

snobismo *m* snobbishness, snobbery

snobisti·co -ca *adj* (*-ci -che*) snobbish

snocciolare (**snòcciolo**) *tr* to spill (*a secret*); to peel off (*sums of money*); to pit, stone (*fruit*)

snodare (**snòdo**) *tr* to untie; to limber up; to exercise; to loosen up (*e.g.,* _s.o.'s tongue_) ‖ _ref_ to become loose; to wind (_said, e.g., of a road_)

snòdo _m_ (mach) joint; **a snodo** flexible

soave _adj_ sweet, gentle

sobbalzare _intr_ to jerk, jolt

sobbalzo _m_ jerk, jolt; **di sobbalzo** with a jolt

sobbarcare §197 _tr_ to overburden ‖ _ref_ —**sobbarcarsi a** to take it upon oneself to

sobbór·go _m_ (**-ghi**) suburb

sobillare _tr_ to instigate, stir up

sobilla·tóre **-trice** _mf_ instigator

sobrietà _f_ sobriety, temperance

sò·brio **-bria** _adj_ sober, temperate; plain

socchiùdere §125 _tr_ to half-shut; to leave ajar

socchiu·so **-sa** [s] _adj_ ajar

soccómbere §186 _intr_ to succumb

soccórrere §139 _tr_ to help ‖ _intr_ (lit) to occur

soccórso _m_ help, succor; **mancato soccorso** failure to render assistance; hit-and-run driving

sociale _adj_ social; company (_e.g., outing_)

socialismo _m_ socialism

sociali·sta (**-sti -ste**) _adj_ socialistic ‖ _mf_ socialist

sociali·tà _f_ (**-tà**) gregariousness; social responsibility

socie·tà _f_ (**-tà**) society; company; **in società in partnership; società anonima** corporation; **società a responsabilità limitata** limited company; **Società delle Nazioni** League of Nations; **società finanziaria** holding company; **società in accomandita** limited partnership; **società per azioni** corporation

sociévole _adj_ sociable; gregarious

sò·cio _m_ (**-ci**) member; cardholder; partner; shareholder; **socio fondatore** charter member; **socio sostenitore** patron, sustaining member

sociologìa _f_ sociology

sociòlo·go **-ga** _mf_ (**-gi -ghe**) sociologist

sòda _f_ soda

sodalì·zio _m_ (**-zi**) society; brotherhood, fraternity; friendship

soddisfacènte _adj_ satisfying, satisfactory

soddisfare §173 (2d sg pres ind **soddisfài** or **soddisfì**; 3d pl pres ind **soddisfanno** or **soddìsfano**; 1st, 2d & 3d sg pres subj **soddisfaccia** or **soddisfì**; 3d pl pres subj **soddisfàcciano** or **soddisfìno**) _tr_ to satisfy ‖ _intr_ (with _dat_) to satisfy ‖ _ref_ to be satisfied

soddisfat·to **-ta** _adj_ satisfied

soddisfazióne _f_ satisfaction

sòdi·co **-ca** _adj_ (**-ci -che**) sodium

sòdio _m_ sodium

sò·do **-da** _adj_ hard; hard-boiled; stubborn; solid; **prenderle sode** to get a good thrashing ‖ _m_ hard ground; untilled soil; solid foundation; **venire al sodo** to come to the point; **mettere in sodo** to ascertain ‖ _f_ see **soda** ‖ **sodo** _adv_ hard

sodomìa _f_ sodomy

so·fà _m_ (**-fà**) couch, sofa; **sofà a letto** sofa bed

sofferènte _adj_ sickly, ailing; (lit) longsuffering

sofferènza _f_ suffering, pain; bad debt; **in sofferenza** overdue

soffermare (**sofférmo**) _tr_—**soffermare il passo** to come to a stop ‖ _ref_ to linger, pause

soffiare §287 (**sóffio**) _tr_ to blow; to whisper; (checkers) to huff; (coll) to steal ‖ _intr_ to blow; to bellow; (slang) to squeal (_about somebody's offense_); **soffiare sul fuoco** to stir up trouble ‖ _ref_ to blow (_one's nose_)

soffia·to **-ta** _adj_ blown ‖ _m_ soufflé ‖ _f_ (slang) squealing, **darsi una soffiata di naso** to blow one's nose

soffiatóre _m_ glass blower

sòffice _adj_ soft

soffierìa _f_ glass factory; blower

soffietto _m_ bellows; hood (_of carriage_); (journ) puff, ballyhoo

sóf·fio _m_ (**-fi**) blow; breath; **in un soffio** in a jiffy; **soffio al cuore** heart murmur

soffióne _m_ blowpipe; fumarole; (bot) dandelion; (coll) spy

soffitta _f_ attic, garret

soffitto _m_ ceiling

soffocaménto _m_ choking

soffocante _adj_ stifling; oppressive

soffocare §197 (**sòffoco**) _tr_ to choke; to stifle; to suffocate; to smother; to repress

sòffo·co _m_ (**-chi**) sultriness

soffóndere §178 _tr_ (lit) to suffuse

soffregare §209 (**soffrégo**) _tr_ to rub lightly

soffriggere §180 _tr_ to fry lightly ‖ _intr_ to mutter

soffrire §207 _tr_ to suffer; to endure; **non poter soffrire** to not be able to stand ‖ _intr_ to suffer; to ail; **soffrire di** to be troubled with

soffritto _m_ fried onions and bacon

sofistica·to **-ta** _adj_ adulterated; sophisticated, studied

sofìsti·co **-ca** _adj_ (**-ci -che**) sophistic; faultfinding ‖ _f_ sophistry

soggetti·sta _mf_ (**-sti -ste**) scriptwriter

soggettì·vo **-va** _adj_ subjective

soggèt·to **-ta** _adj_ subject ‖ _m_ subject; (coll) character; (law) person; **cattivo soggetto** hoodlum; **recitare a soggetto** to improvise

soggezióne _f_ subjection; awe, embarrassment; **mettere a soggezione** to awe

sogghignare _intr_ to sneer

soggiacére §181 _intr_ (ESSERE & AVERE) to be subject; to succumb

soggiogare §209 (**soggiógo**) _tr_ to subjugate, subdue

soggiornare (**soggiórno**) _intr_ to sojourn, stay

soggiórno _m_ sojourn, stay; living room; sitting room (_in hotel_)

soggiùngere §183 _tr_ to add

soggólo _m_ wimple (_of nun_); throatlatch (_on horse_); (mil) chin strap

sòglia _f_ doorsill; threshhold

sògliola _f_ sole

sognare (**sógno**) _tr_ to dream of ‖ _intr_

to dream; **sognare ad occhi aperti** to daydream

sogna·tóre -trice *adj* dreaming || *mf* dreamer

sógno *m* dream; **nemmeno per sogno** (coll) by no means

sòia *f* (bot) soy

sòl *m* (sòl) (mus) sol

so·làio *m* (-lài) attic, loft; (agr) crib

solare *adj* solar; bright; clear || *v* §257 *tr* to sole

solàr·rio *m* (-ri) solarium

solati·o -a (-i -e) *adj* sunny || *m—a solatio* with a southern exposure

solcare §197 (sólco) *tr* to furrow; to plow (*the waves*)

sól·co *m* (-chi) furrow; rut; groove (*of phonograph record*); (fig) path; (naut) wake

solcòmetro *m* (naut) log

soldaté·sco -sca (-schi -sche) *adj* soldier || *f* soldiery; soldiers; undisciplined troops

soldatino *m* toy soldier

soldato *m* soldier; **andare soldato** to enlist; **soldato di ventura** soldier of fortune; **soldato scelto** private first class; **soldato semplice** private

sòldo *m* soldo (*Italian coin*); coin; money; (mil) pay; (fig) penny; **a soldo a soldo** a penny at a time; **al soldo di** in the pay of; **tirare al soldo** to be a tightwad

sóle *m* sun; sunshine; (fig) day, daytime; **sole artificiale** sun lamp; **sole a scacchi** (joc) hoosegow, calaboose

soleggia·to -ta *adj* sunny

solènne *adj* solemn; (joc) first-class

solenni·tà *f* (-tà) solemnity

solennizzare [ddzz] *tr* to solemnize

soléré §255 *intr* (ESSERE) + *inf* to be accustomed to + *inf*, *e.g.*, **suole arrivare alle sette** he is accustomed to arrive at seven || *impers* (ESSERE) **—suole** + *inf* it generally + 3d sg ind, *e.g.*, **suole nevicare** it generally snows

solèrte *adj* (lit) diligent, industrious

solèrzia *f* (lit) diligence

solét·to -ta *adj* (lit) alone, lonely || *f* sole; inner sole; (archit) slab, cement slab

sòlfa *f* (mus) solfeggio; **la solita solfa** the same old story

solfanèllo *m* var of **zofanello**

solfara *f* sulfur mine

solfato *m* sulfate

solfeggiare §290 (solféggio) *tr* to sol-fa

solfiè·ro -ra *adj* sulfur

solfito *m* sulfite

sólfo *m* var of **zolfo**

solfòri·co -ca *adj* (-ci -che) sulfuric

solforó·so -sa [s] *adj* sulfurous

solfuro *m* sulfide

solidale *adj* solidary; (law) joint; (law) jointly responsible; (mach) built-in; **solidale con** integral with

solidarie·tà *f* (-tà) solidarity; (law) joint liability

solidarizzare [ddzz] *intr* to make common cause, become united

solidificare §197 (solidìfico) *tr* to solidify; to settle

solidi·tà *f* (-tà) solidity; (fig) soundness

sòli·do -da *adj* solid; (law) joint || *m* solid; **in solido** jointly

solilò·quio *m* (-qui) soliloquy

solin·go -ga *adj* (-ghi -ghe) (lit) lonely; (lit) solitary (*enjoying solitude*)

solino *m* detachable collar; **solino duro** stiff collar

soli·sta *mf* (-sti -ste) soloist

solità·rio -ria (-ri -rie) *adj* solitary, lonely || *m* solitaire; solitary

sòli·to -ta *adj* usual, customary; **esser solito** to be accustomed to || *m* habit, custom; **come il solito** as usual; **di solito** usually

solitùdine *f* solitude, loneliness

sollazzare *tr* to amuse || *ref* to have a good time, amuse oneself

sollazzo *m* (lit) amusement; **essere il sollazzo di** to be the laughingstock of

sollecitare (sollécito) *tr* to solicit; to urge; to induce; (mach) to stress || *intr & ref* to hasten

sollecitazióne *f* solicitation; urging; (mach) stress

solléci·to -ta *adj* quick, prompt; diligent; solicitous, anxious || *m* (com) solicitation, urging

sollecitùdine *f* solicitude; promptness; diligence; **cortese sollecitudine** (com) prompt attention

solleóne *m* dog days

solleticare §197 (sollético) *tr* to tickle; (fig) to flatter

solléti·co *m* (-chi) tickling; stimulation; **fare il solletico a** to tickle

sollevaménto *m* lifting; **sollevamento di pesi** weight lifting

sollevare (sollèvo) *tr* to lift; to relieve; to pick up; to raise (*a question*); to excite; to elevate || *ref* to rise; to lift oneself; to pick up (*said of courage or health*)

sollevazióne *f* uprising

solliè·vo *m* relief

sollùchero *m—andare in solluchero* to become ecstatic; **mandare in solluchero** to thrill

só·lo -la *adj* lone, lonely, alone; only; single; **fare da solo** to operate all by oneself; **solo soletto** all by myself (yourself, himself, etc.); within oneself; **un solo** only one || *m* (mus) solo || **solo** *adv* only || **solo** *conj* only; **solo che** provided that

solsti·zio *m* (-zi) solstice

soltanto *adv* only

solùbile *adj* soluble

soluzióne *f* solution; installment; **soluzione di comodo** compromise; **soluzione provvisoria** stopgap

solvènte *adj & m* solvent

solvènza *f* solvency

solvìbile *adj* collectable; solvent

sòma *f* burden, load

Somàlia, la Somaliland

sòma·lo -la *adj & mf* Somali

soma·ro -ra *mf* donkey, ass

someggia·to -ta *adj* carried by pack animal; carried on mule back

somigliante *adj* similar; **essere somigliante a** to look like || *m* same thing

somiglianza *f* similarity, resemblance

somigliare §280 *tr* to resemble; (lit) to compare || *intr* (ESSERE & AVERE) (with *dat*) to resemble; to seem to be || *ref* to resemble each other

sómma *f* addition; sum; summary

sommare (**sómmo**) *tr* to add; to consider; **tutto sommato** all in all || *intr* to amount

sommà·rio -ria (-**ri** -**rie**) *adj* summary || *m* summary; abstract; (journ) subheading

sommèrgere §162 *tr* to submerge; (fig) to plunge; (fig) to flood (*with insults*) || *ref* to submerge

sommergibile *adj* & *m* submarine

sommés·so -sa *adj* submissive; subdued (*voice*)

somministrare *tr* to administer; to provide; to deliver (*a blow*); to adduce (*proof*)

somministrazióne *f* administration; provision

sommi·tà *f* (-**tà**) summit

sóm·mo -ma *adj* highest; supreme || *m* top; peak, summit || *f* see **somma**

sommòssa *f* insurrection, riot

sommoviménto *m* tremor (*of earth*); arousal (*of passions*); riot

sommozzatóre *m* skin diver; (nav) frogman

sommuòvere §202 *tr* (lit) to agitate; (lit) to stir up, excite

sonaglièra *f* collar with bells

sonà·glio -gli) bell; rattle; raindrop; pitter-patter (*of the rain*)

sonante *adj* ringing, sounding; ready (*cash*)

sonare §257 *tr* to sound; to play; to strike (*the hour*); to ring (*a bell*); (coll) to dupe, cheat; (coll) to give a sound thrashing to; **sonare le campane a distesa** to ring a full peal || *intr* (ESSERE & AVERE) to play; to ring (*said of a bell*); to sound; (lit) to spread (*said of reputation*)

sona·to -ta *adj* played; past, e.g., **le tre sonate** past three o'clock; **cinquant'anni sonati** past fifty years of age || *f* ring (*of bell*); (mus) sonata; (coll) thrashing; (coll) cheating

sona·tóre -trice *mf* (mus) player

sónda *f* sound; probe; drill

sondàg·gio *m* (-**gi**) sounding; probe; drilling; **sondaggio d'opinioni** opinion survey, public opinion poll

sondare (**sóndo**) *tr* to sound; to probe; to drill; to survey (*public opinion*)

soneria *f* alarm (*of clock*)

sonétto *m* sonnet

sonnacchió·so -sa [s] *adj* sleepy, drowsy

sonnàmbu·lo -la *mf* sleepwalker

sonnecchiare §287 (**sonnécchio**) *intr* to drowse, take a nap; to nap, nod

sonnellino *m* nap

sonnife·ro -ra *adj* soporific; narcotic || *m* sleeping medicine; narcotic

sónno *m* sleep; (lit) dream; **aver sonno** to be sleepy; **far venir sonno a** to bore; **prender sonno** to fall asleep

sonnolèn·to -ta *adj* sleepy; lazy

sonnolènza *f* drowsiness; laziness

sonori·tà *f* (-**tà**) sonority; acoustics

sonorizzare [ddzz] *tr* to voice; (mov) to dub || *ref* to voice

sonò·ro -ra *adj* sound (*wave*); sonorous; (phonet) sonant, voiced

sontuó·so -sa [s] *adj* sumptuous

sopèr·chio -chia *adj* & *m* (-**chi** -**chie**) var of **soverchio**

sopire §176 *tr* to appease, calm

sopóre *m* drowsiness

soporife·ro -ra *adj* soporific

soppanno *m* interlining; lining (*of shoes*)

sopperire §176 *intr*—**sopperire a** to provide for; to make up for

soppesare [s] (**soppéso**) *tr* to heft; (fig) to weigh

soppiantare *tr* to supplant by scheming; to kick out; to replace; to trick

soppiatto *m*—**di soppiatto** stealthily

sopportàbile *adj* bearable, tolerable

sopportare (**soppòrto**) *tr* to bear, support; to suffer, endure

sopportazióne *f* forbearance, endurance

soppressióne *f* suppression, abolition

sopprìmere §131 *tr* to suppress, do away with

sópra *adj invar* upper; above, preceding || *m* upper, upper part; **al di sopra** above; **al di sopra di** above, over; beyond; **di sopra** upper || *adv* above; up; on top || *prep* on; upon; on top of; over; beyond; above; versus; **sopra pensiero** absorbed in thought

sopràbito *m* overcoat, topcoat

sopraccàri·co -ca (-**chi** -**che**) *adj* overburdened || *m* overload; overweight; (naut) supercargo

sopraccenna·to -ta *adj* above-mentioned

sopracci·glio *m* (-**gli** & -**glia** *fpl*) brow, eyebrow; window frame

sopraccita·to -ta *adj* above-mentioned

sopraccopèrta *f* bedspread; book jacket, dust jacket || *adv* (naut) on deck

sopraddét·to -ta *adj* above-mentioned

sopraffare §173 *tr* to overcome, overpower

sopraffazióne *f* overpowering; abuse

sopraffinèstra *f* transom window

sopraffi·no -na *adj* first-class; superfine

sopraggitto *m* (sew) overcasting

sopraggiùngere §183 *intr* (ESSERE) to arrive; to happen

sopraintèndere §270 *tr* var of **soprintendere**

sopralluò·go *m* (-**ghi**) inspection, investigation on the spot

sopralzo *m* var of **soprelevazione**

soprammerca·to *m*—**per soprammercato** in addition, to boot

soprammòbile *m* knicknack

soprannaturale *adj* & *m* supernatural

soprannóme *m* nickname

soprannominare (**soprannòmino**) *tr* to nickname

soprannùmero *adj invar* in excess; overtime || *m* —**in soprannumero** extra; in excess

sopra·no -na *adj* upper; (lit) supreme

|| **sopra·no** *mf* (**-ni -ne**) soprano (*person*) || *m* soprano (*voice*)
soprappensièro *adj invar & adv* immersed in thought
soprappéso [s] *m*—**per soprappeso** besides, into the bargain
soprap·più *m* (**-più**) plus, extra; **in soprappiù** besides, into the bargain
soprapprèzzo *m* extra charge, surcharge
soprascarpa *f* overshoe
soprascrit·to -ta *adj* written above || *f* address
soprassalto *m* start, jump; **di soprassalto** with a start
soprassedére §252 *intr* to wait; (with *dat*) to postpone
soprassòldo *m* extra pay; (mil) war-zone indemnity
soprastare §263 *intr* (ESSERE) to be the boss
soprattac·co *m* (**-chi**) rubber heel
soprattassa *f* surtax; surcharge
soprattutto *adv* above all, especially
sopravanzare *tr* to overcome || *intr* (ESSERE) to be left over
sopravanzo *m* surplus
sopravvalutare *tr* to overrate
sopravvenire §282 *tr* (lit) to overrun || *intr* (ESSERE) to arrive; to happen, occur; (with *dat*) to befall
sopravvènto *m* windward; **avere il sopravvento** to have the upper hand || *adv* windward
sopravvissu·to -ta *adj* surviving || *mf* survivor
sopravvivènza *f* survival
sopravvivere §286 *intr* (ESSERE) to survive; (with *dat*) to survive, to outlive
soprelevare (**sopralèvo**) *tr* to elevate (*e.g.*, *a railroad*); to increase the height of (*building*)
soprelevazióne *f* elevation; addition of one or more floors
soprintendènte *m* superintendent
soprintendènza *f* superintendency
soprintèndere §270 *tr* to oversee
sopròsso *m* (coll) bony outgrowth
sopruso *m* abuse of power
soqquadro *m*—**a soqquadro** upside down, topsy-turvy
sòrba *f* sorb apple; (coll) hit, blow
sorbettièra *f* ice-cream freezer
sorbétto *m* ice cream; sherbet
sorbire §176 *tr* to sip; (fig) to swallow, endure
sòrbo *m* sorb; service tree
sór·cio *m* (**-ci**) mouse
sòrdi·do -da *adj* sordid; dirty
sordina *f* (mus) sordino, mute; (mus) soft pedal; **in sordina** quietly; stealthily; **mettere in sordina** (mus) to muffle
sór·do -da *adj* deaf; dull (*pain*); deep-seated (*hatred*); hollow (*sound*); (phonet) surd, voiceless; **sordo come una campana** stone-deaf || *mf* deaf person
sordomu·to -ta *adj* deaf and dumb || *mf* deafmute
sorèlla *f* sister
sorellastra *f* stepsister

sorgènte *adj* rising || *f* spring; well (*of oil*); (fig) source; **sorgente del fiume** riverhead
sórgere §258 *intr* (ESSERE) to rise; to arise; to spring forth; **sorgere su un'ancora** (naut) to lie at anchor
sorgi·vo -va *adj* spring (*water*)
sór·go *m* (**-ghi**) sorghum
sormontare (**sormónto**) *tr* to surmount; to overcome || *intr* to fit
sornió·ne -na *adj* cunning, sly || *m* sneak
sorpassare *tr* to get ahead of; to surpass; to overstep; to go above
sorpasso *m* (aut) passing
sorprendènte *adj* surprising, astonishing
sorprèndere §220 *tr* to surprise; to catch; **sorprendere la buona fede di** to take advantage of || *ref* to be surprised
sorprésa [s] *f* surprise; surprise investigation; **di sorpresa** suddenly; unprepared; by surprise
sorrèggere §226 *tr* to sustain, support; to bolster
sorrìdere §231 *tr* (lit) to say with a smile || *intr* to smile; **sorridere a** to appeal to, e.g., **le sorride l'idea di questa gita** the idea of this trip appeals to her; to smile upon, e.g., **gli sorrideva la vita** life was smiling upon him
sorriso [s] *m* smile
sorsata *f* gulp, draught
sorseggiare §290 (**sorséggio**) *tr* to sip
sórso *m* sip; **a sorso a sorso** sipping
sòrta *f* kind, sort
sòrte *f* luck, lot, fate; chance; kind; (com) principal; **per sorte** of each kind; by chance; **tirare a sorte** to cast lots
sorteggiare §290 (**sortéggio**) *tr* to choose oy lot; to raffle; **sorteggiare un premio** to draw a prize
sortég·gio *m* (**-gi**) drawing
sortile·gio *m* (**-gi**) sortilege; sorcery, magic
sortire §176 *tr* (lit) to get by lot; (lit) to have (*results*); (lit) to allot || (**sòrto**) *intr* (ESSERE) to come out (*said, e.g., of a newspaper*); (coll) to be drawn (*by lot*); (coll) to go out; (mil) to make a sally
sortita *f* witticism; (mil) sally, sortie; (theat) appearance
sorvegliante *adj* watchful || *mf* overseer, caretaker; guardian || *m* watchman; foreman
sorveglianza *f* surveillance; supervision
sorvegliare §280 (**sorvéglio**) *tr* to oversee, watch over; to check, control
sorvolare (**sorvólo**) *tr* to fly over; to overfly; (fig) to avoid, skip
sorvólo *m* overflight
sò·sia *m* (**-sia**) double, counterpart
sospèndere §259 *tr* to hang; to suspend; (chem) to prepare a suspension of; (law) to stay
sospensióne *f* suspension; suspense; (law) stay; **sospensione cardanica** gimbals

sospensò·rio *m* (**-ri**) jockstrap, supporter

sospé·so -sa [s] *adj* suspended; suspension (*bridge*); **in sospeso** in suspense; in abeyance || *m* employee who has been disciplined by suspension; (com) pending item

sospettare (**sospètto**) *tr* to suspect || *intr*—**sospettare di** to suspect; to fear

sospèt·to -ta *adj* suspected; suspicious || *m* dash; suspicion

sospettó·so -sa [s] *adj* suspicious

sospìngere §126 *tr* (fig) to drive; (lit) to push

sospirare *tr* to long for, crave; **fare sospirare** to keep waiting || *intr* to sigh

sospiro *m* sigh; longing; (lit) breath; **a sospiri** little by little

sossópra *adv* upside down

sòsta *f* stop; reprieve; (rr) demurrage

sostanti·vo -va *adj* & *m* substantive

sostanza *f* substance; **sostanza grigia** gray matter

sostanziale *adj* substantial

sostanzió·so -sa [s] *adj* substantial

sostare (**sòsto**) *intr* to stop, pause

sostégno *m* prop; (fig) support

sostenére §271 *tr* to support; to sustain; to take (*an examination*); to defend (*a thesis*); to prop up; to stand (*alcohol*); to play (*a role*) || *ref* to support oneself; to hold up (*said, e.g., of a theory*); to take nourishment

sosteni·tóre -trice *mf* backer, supporter

sostentaménto *m* sustenance, support

sostentare (**sostènto**) *tr* to support, keep || *ref* to feed, eat

sostenu·to -ta *adj* reserved, austere; rising (*prices*); bullish (*market*); starchy (*manner*)

sostituibile *adj* replaceable

sostituire §176 *tr* to replace, substitute for, take the place of; **sostituire** (*qlco* or *qlcu*) **a** to substitute (*s.th* or *s.o.*) for

sostitu·to -ta *adj* acting; associate, assistant || *m* replacement, substitute

sostituzióne *f* replacement, substitution

sostrato *m* substratum

sottàbito *m* slip

sottacére §268 *tr* (lit) to withhold

sottacéto *adj invar* pickled || **sottaceti** *mpl* pickles

sott'àcqua *adv* underwater

sotta·no -na *adj* lower (*town*) || *f* skirt; petticoat; (eccl) cassock; **gettare la sottana alle ortiche** to doff the cassock

sottécchi *adv*—**di sottecchi** stealthily, secretly; **guardare di sottecchi** to peep, look furtively (at)

sottentrare (**sottèntro**) *intr* (ESSERE) (with *dat*) to replace

sotterfù·gio *m* (**-gi**) subterfuge

sotterrà *adv* underground

sotterràne·o -a *adj* subterranean, underground; secret, clandestine || *m* cave, vault; dungeon; underground passage || *f* (rr) subway, underground

sotterrare (**sottèrro**) *tr* to bury

sottigliézza *f* thinness; subtlety

sottile *adj* thin; subtle; (naut) lightweight || *m*—**guardare troppo per il sottile** to split hairs

sottilizzare [ddzz] *intr* to quibble

sottintèndere §270 *tr* to understand || *ref* to be understood, be implied

sottinté·so -sa [s] *adj* understood, implied || *m* innuendo

sótto *adj invar* lower || *m* lower part || *adv* under; underneath; **al di sotto** below; **al di sotto di** under, below; **di sotto** lower; underneath; downstairs; **di sotto a** under, below; **farsi sotto** to sneak up; **metter sotto** to run over (*with a vehicle*); **sotto a** under; **sotto di** under || *prep* under; beneath; below; just before; **prendere sotto gamba** to underestimate; **sotto braccio** arm in arm; **sotto carico** (naut) being loaded; **sotto i baffi** up one's sleeve; **sotto le armi** in the service; **sotto mano** within reach; **sotto voce** under one's breath, sottovoce

sottoascèl·la *m* (**-la**) underarm pad

sottobanco *adv* under the counter

sottobicchière *m* coaster

sottobò·sco *m* (**-schi**) underbrush, thicket

sottobràccio *adv* arm in arm

sottòcchio *adv* under one's eyes

sottoccupa·to -ta *adj* underemployed

sottochiave *adv* under lock and key

sottocó·da *m* (**-da**) crupper

sottocommissióne *f* subcommittee

sottocopèrta *adv* (naut) below decks

sottocòp·pa *m* (**-pa**) mat; coaster; (aut) oil pan

sottocòsto *adj invar* & *adv* below cost

sottocutàne·o -a *adj* subcutaneous

sottofà·scia *m* (**-scia**) wrapper; **spedire sottofascia** to mail (*a newspaper*) in a wrapper || *f* (**-sce**) wrapper (*for cigars*)

sottogamba *adv* lightly; **prendere sottogamba** to underestimate

sottogó·la *m* & *f* (**-la**) chin strap; throatlatch (*of harness*)

sottolineare (**sottolìneo**) *tr* to underline, underscore; to emphasize

sott'òlio *adv* in oil

sottomano *m* writing pad || *adv* underhand; within reach

sottomari·no -na *adj* & *m* submarine

sottomés·so -sa *adj* conquered; subdued; submissive

sottométtere §198 *tr* to subdue, crush; to defer, postpone; to present (*a bill*); to subject || *ref* to submit, yield

sottomissióne *f* submission

sottopan·cia *m* (**-cia**) bellyband, girth

sottopassàg·gio *m* (**-gi**) underpass; lower level (*of highway*)

sottopiatto *m* saucer

sottopórre §218 *tr* to subject; to submit || *ref* to submit; **sottoporsi a** to submit to; to undergo (*e.g., an operation*)

sottopó·sto -sta *adj* subject; exposed || *m* subordinate

sottoprèzzo *adj invar* cut-rate || *adv* at a cut rate

sottoprodótto *m* by-product

sottórdine *m* suborder; **in sottordine** secondary

sottosca·la *m* (**-la**) space under the stairs; closet under the stairs

sottoscrit·to -ta *adj* & *mf* undersigned

sottoscrit·tóre -trice *mf* subscriber

sottoscrìvere §250 *tr* to subscribe; to sign, undersign; to underwrite || *intr* to subscribe

sottoscrizióne *f* subscription

sottosegretà·rio *m* (**-ri**) undersecretary

ottosópra *adj invar* upset; **mettere sottosopra** to upset; to turn upside down || *m* confusion, disorder || *adv* upside down

sottostante *adj* lower; subordinate || *m* subordinate

sottostàre §263 *intr* (ESSERE) to be located below; to be subject; to yield, submit; (with *dat*) to undergo (*e.g., an examination*)

sottosuòlo *m* subsoil; cellar

sottosvilùppa·to -ta *adj* underdeveloped

sottotenènte *m* second lieutenant; **sottotenente di vascello** (nav) lieutenant j.g.

sottotèr·ra *m* (**-ra**) basement || *adv* underground

sottotétto *m* attic, garret

sottotìtolo *m* subtitle; (mov) caption

sottovalutare *tr* to underrate

sottovènto *m* & *adv* leeward

sottovèste *f* slip (*undergarment*)

sottovóce *adv* sotto voce, under one's breath

sottrarre §273 *tr* to subtract; **sottrarre a** to take away from, steal from || *ref*—**sottrarsi a** to avoid; to escape from

sottrazióne *f* subtraction

sottufficiale *m* noncommissioned officer

sovènte *adv* often

soverchiante *adj* overwhelming

soverchiare §287 (**sovèrchio**) *tr* to overwhelm; to excel; to bully; (lit) to overflow || *intr* to be in excess

soverchia·tóre -trice *adj* overbearing || *mf* overbearing person, oppressor

sovèr·chio -chia (**-chi -chie**) *adj* excessive; overbearing || *m* overbearing action

sovè·scio *m* (**-sci**) plowing under (*of green manure*)

sovièti·co -ca (**-ci -che**) *adj* Soviet || *mf* Soviet citizen

sovrabbondante *adj* superabundant

sovrabbondare (**sovrabbóndo**) *intr* (ESSERE & AVERE) to be superabundant; to go to excesses

sovraccaricare §197 (**sovraccàrico**) *tr* to overload

sovraccàri·co -ca (**-chi -che**) *adj* overburdened || *m* overload; overweight

sovraespó·sto -sta *adj* overexposed

sovraggiùngere §183 *intr* (ESSERE) var of **sopraggiungere**

sovralimentazióne *f* (aut) supercharging

sovrani·tà *f* (**-tà**) sovereignty

sovra·no -na *adj* & *mf* sovereign

sovrappopolare (**sovrappòpolo**) *tr* to overpopulate

sovrappórre §218 *tr* to overlay; to superimpose; **sovrapporre qlco a** to lay s.th on || *ref* to be superimposed; to be added; **sovrapporsi a** to put oneself above

sovrapproduzióne *f* overproduction

sovrastampa *f* overprint

sovrastante *adj* overlooking, overhanging; impending

sovrastare *tr* to tower over; to hang over; to surpass; to excel || *intr* (ESSERE & AVERE)—**sovrastare a** to tower over; to overlook; to hang over; to surpass; to excel

sovratensióne *f* (elec) surge

sovreccitare (**sovrèccito**) *tr* to overexcite

so·vrespórre §218 *tr* to overexpose

sovrimpòsta *f* surtax

sovrimpressióne *f* double exposure

sovruma·no -na *adj* superhuman

sovvenire §282 *tr* (lit) to help || *intr* (with *dat*) to help || *impers* (ESSERE)—**sovviene** (with *dat*) **di** remember, e.g., **gli sovviene spesso dei suoi cari** he often remembers his dear ones || *ref*—**sovvenirsi di** to remember

sovvenzionare (**sovvenzióno**) *tr* to subsidize, grant a subvention to

sovvenzióne *f* subsidy, subvention

sovversi·vo -va *adj* & *m* subversive

sovvertire (**sovvèrto**) *tr* to subvert

sóz·zo -za *adj* dirty, filthy, foul

sozzura *f* dirt, filth

spaccalé·gna *m* (**-gna**) woodcutter

spaccamón·ti *m* (**-ti**) braggart

spaccaòs·sa *m* (**-sa**) butcher's cleaver

spaccare §197 *tr* to break, burst; to crack; to unpack; to chop; to split || *ref* to crack; to break; to split

spacca·to -ta *adj* broken; split; (coll) identical; (coll) true || *f* (sports, theat) splits

spaccatura *f* break; crack; cleavage; split

spacchétto *m* vent (*in jacket*)

spacciare §128 *tr* to sell out; to palm off; to spread (*reports*); to expedite; to abandon (*as hopeless*); (slang) to push (*e.g., dope*) || *ref*—**spacciarsi per** to pretend to be, pass oneself off as

spaccia·to -ta *adj* (coll) cooked, done for; (coll) hopeless

spaccia·tóre -trice *mf* passer (*of bad currency or stolen goods*); **spacciatore di notizie false** gossipmonger

spàc·cio *m* (**-ci**) sale; passing (*of counterfeit money*); spreading (*of false news*); post exchange; tobacco shop

spac·co *m* (**-chi**) break; split; tear; crack; vent (*in jacket*)

spacconata *f* brag, braggadocio

spaccó·ne -na *mf* braggart, braggadocio

spada *f* sword; **a spada tratta** doggedly; **spade** suit of Neapolitan cards corresponding to spades

spadaccino *m* swordsman; swash-buckler

spadóne *m* two-handed sword

spadroneggiare §290 (**spadronéggio**) *intr* to be domineering or bossy

spaesa·to -ta *adj* out-of-place

spaghétto *m* (coll) fear, jitters; **avere lo spaghetto** (coll) to be scared stiff; **spaghetti** spaghetti

Spagna, la Spain

spagnòla *f* Spanish woman; Spanish influenza

spagnolétta *f* espagnolette; spool; (coll) cigarette; (coll) peanut

spagnò·lo -la *adj* Spanish ‖ *m* Spaniard (*individual*); Spanish (*language*); **gli spagnoli** the Spanish ‖ *f* see **spagnola**

spa·go *m* (**-ghi**) string, twine; (coll) fear, jitters

spaiare §287 *tr* to break a pair of

spaia·to -ta *adj* unmatched

spalancare §197 *tr* to open wide ‖ *ref* to open up; to gape

spalare *tr* to shovel; to feather (*oar*)

spalla *f* shoulder; back; abutment (*of bridge*); (theat) stooge, straight man; **alle spalle di qlcu** behind s.o.'s back; **a spalla** on one's back; **fare spalla a** to help; **lavorare di spalle** to elbow one's way; (fig) to worm one's way up; **vivere alle spalle di** to sponge on

spallàrm *interj* (mil) shoulder arms!

spallata *f* push with the shoulder; shrug of the shoulders

spalleggiare §290 (**spalléggio**) *tr* to back, support; (mil) to carry on one's back

spallétta *f* parapet, retaining wall; jamb

spallièra *f* back (*of chair*); head (*of bed*); foot (*of bed*); espalier

spallina *f* epaulet; shoulder strap

spallùccia *f—***fare spallucce** to shrug one's shoulders

spalmare *tr* to spread; to smear

spalto *m* glacis; **spalti** seats (*of a stadium*)

spanare *tr* to strip the thread of ‖ *ref* to be stripped (*said, e.g., of the thread of a nut*)

spanciare §128 *tr* to disembowel, gut ‖ *intr* to belly-flop; to bulge (*said of a wall*) ‖ *ref—***spanciarsi dalle risa** to split one's sides laughing

spanciata *f* belly flop; bellyful; **fare una spanciata** to stuff oneself

spàndere §260 *tr* to spread; to spill; to shed (*tears*); to squander ‖ *ref* to spread

spanna *f* span

spannare *tr* to skim (*milk*)

spannocchiare §287 (**spannòcchio**) *tr* to husk (*corn*)

spappolare (**spàppolo**) *tr* to crush, squash ‖ *ref* to become mushy

sparadrappo *m* adhesive tape; (obs) plaster, poultice

sparagnare *tr* (coll) to save

sparare *tr* to gut, disembowel; to shoot; to let go with (*a kick*); to remove

the hangings from; **spararne delle grosse** to tell tall tales

sparato *m* shirt front, dickey

sparatòria *f* shooting

sparecchiare §287 (**sparécchio**) *tr* to clear (*the table*); to clear away (*one's tools*); to eat up

sparég·gio *m* (**-gi**) disparity; deficit; (sports) play-off

spàrgere §261 *tr* to spread; to shed; to spill ‖ *ref* to spread

spargiménto *m* spreading; **spargimento di sangue** bloodshed

spargisa·le [s] *m* (**-le**) salt shaker

spariare §280 *tr* to break a pair of; to break (*a set*)

spariglia·to -ta *adj* unmatched

sparire §176 *intr* (ESSERE) to disappear

sparlare *intr* to backbite, slander; **sparlare di** to backbite, slander

sparo *m* shot

sparpagliare §280 *tr & intr* to scatter

spar·so -sa *adj* scattered; dotted; speckled; hanging loosely (*e.g., hair*)

sparta·no -na *adj & mf* Spartan

spartiàc·que *m* (-) watershed

spartiné·ve *m* (**-ve**) snowplow

spartire §176 *tr* to divide, share; to separate; **non aver nulla da spartire con** to have nothing to do with

spartito *m* (mus) score; (mus) arrangement

spartitràffi·co *m* (**-co**) median strip

spar·to -ta *adj* (lit) spread ‖ *m* esparto grass

sparu·to -ta *adj* lean, wan; meager

sparvière *m* sparrow hawk; mortar-board

spasimante *m* (joc) lover, wooer

spasimare (**spàsimo**) *intr* to writhe; **spasimare per** to long for; to be madly in love with

spàsimo *m* pang; severe pain; longing

spasmo *m* spasm

spasmòdi·co -ca *adj* (**-ci -che**) spasmodic

spassare *tr* to amuse ‖ *ref—***spassarsela** to have a good time

spassiona·to -ta *adj* dispassionate, unbiased

spasso *m* fun, amusement; walk; (coll) funny guy; **andare a spasso** to go out for a walk; **essere a spasso** to be out of a job; **mandare a spasso** to fire, dismiss; to get rid of; **per spasso** for fun; **portare a spasso** to lead by the nose; **prendersi spasso di** to make fun of

spassó·so -sa [s] *adj* amusing, droll

spàsti·co -ca *adj & mf* spastic

spato *m* spar

spatofluòre *m* fluorspar

spàtola *f* spatula; putty knife; slapstick (*of harlequin*)

spauràc·chio *m* (**chi**) scarecrow; bugaboo, bugbear

spaurare *tr & ref* (lit) var of **spaurire**

spaurire §176 *tr* to frighten ‖ *ref* to be scared

spaval·do -da *adj* bold, swaggering

spaventapàs·seri *m* (**-ri**) scarecrow

spaventare (spavènto) *tr* to scare, frighten ‖ *ref* to be scared

spaventévole *adj* frightening, dreadful

spavènto *m* fright, fear

spaventó·so -sa [s] *adj* frightful, fearful

spaziale *adj* space

spaziare §287 *tr* (typ) to space ‖ *intr* to soar; to range, rove (*said, e.g., of eye*)

spazia·tóre -trice *adj* spacing ‖ *f* space bar (*of typewriter*)

spaziatura *f* spacing

spazientire §176 *tr* to make (*s.o.*) lose his patience ‖ *intr* (ESSERE) & *ref* to lose patience

spà·zio *m* (-zi) space; (fig) room; **spazio aereo** air space; **spazio cosmico** outer space

spazió·so -sa [s] *adj* spacious, roomy; wide

spazzacamino *m* chimney sweep

spazzami·ne *m* (-ne) mine sweeper

spazzané·ve *m* (-ve) snowplow

spazzare *tr* to sweep; to plow (*snow*); to clean up

spazzata *f*—**dare una spazzata a** to give a lick and a promise to

spazzatrice *f* street sweeper

spazzatura *f* sweeping; sweepings; rubbish, trash

spazzatu·ràio *m* (-rài) or **spazzino** *m* street / cleaner; trashman, garbage collector, trash collector

spàzzola *f* brush; **capelli a spazzola** crew cut

spazzolare (spàzzolo) *tr* to brush

spazzolino *m* little brush; (elec) brush; **spazzolino da denti** toothbrush; **spazzolino per le unghie** nailbrush

spazzolóne *m* push broom

specchiare §287 **(spècchio)** *tr* (lit) to reflect ‖ *ref* to look at oneself (*in a mirror*); to be reflected; **specchiarsi in qlcu** to model oneself on s.o.

specchièra *f* mirror; dressing table; full-length mirror

specchiétto *m* mirror; synopsis; **specchietto retrovisivo** (aut) rear-view mirror

spèc·chio *m* (-chi) mirror; synopsis; shore (*of lake or river*); panel (*of door or window*); sheet (*of water*); (sports) goal line; (sports) board; **specchio di poppa** (naut) transom; **specchio ustorio** burning glass

speciale *adj* special

speciali·sta *mf* (-sti -ste) specialist

speciali·tà *f* (-tà) specialty; (mil) special services; **specialità farmaceutica** patent or proprietary medicine

specializzare [ddzz] *tr* & *ref* to specialize

spè·cie *f* (-cie) species; kind, sort; appearance, semblance; **fare specie** (with *dat*) (coll) to be surprised, e.g., **gli fa specie** he is surprised; **in specie** especially; **sotto specie di** under pretext of

specifi·ca *f* (-che) itemized list; specification

specificare §197 **(specifico)** *tr* to specify; to itemize

specifi·co -ca (-ci -che) *adj* & *m* specific ‖ *f* see **specifica**

specillo *m* (med) probe

specló·so -sa [s] *adj* specious

spè·co *m* (-chi) (lit) cave

spècola *f* observatory

spècolo *m* (med, surg) speculum

speculare (spèculo) *tr* to observe; to meditate on ‖ *intr* to speculate

specula·tóre -trice *adj* speculating ‖ *mf* speculator; **speculatore al rialzo** bull; **speculatore al ribasso** bear

speda·to -ta *adj* footworn

spedire §176 *tr* to expedite; to prepare; to ship, send, forward; (law) to deliver

spedi·to -ta *adj* rapid; free, easy

spedi·tóre -trice *mf* shipper, sender; shipping clerk

spedizióne *f* shipment, shipping; sending, forwarding; expedition; (naut) papers; **di spedizione** expeditionary

spedizionière *m* shipper, forwarder, forwarding agent

spègnere §262 *tr* to extinguish, put out; to turn off; to slake (*lime*); to kill; to mix (*flour*) with water or milk; to quench; to obliterate (*a memory*) ‖ *ref* to burn out; to go out (*said of a light*); to fade, die away; to die

spegni·tóio *m* (-tói) snuffer

spegnitura *f* (theat) blackout

spelacchiare §287 *tr* to strip of hair ‖ *ref* to shed hair or fur

spelacchia·to -ta *adj* mangy; (pej) baldy

spelare (spélo) *tr* to strip of hair; to pluck (*e.g., a chicken*); (fig) to fleece ‖ *ref* to shed hair or fur; to get bald

spellare (spèllo) *tr* to skin; (fig) to skin, fleece

spelón·ca *f* (-che) cave; hovel, den

spème *f* (poet) hope

spendacció·ne -na *mf* spendthrift

spèndere §220 *tr* to spend

spenderéc·cio -cia *adj* (-ci -ce) spendthrift, prodigal

spennacchiare §287 *tr* to pluck; (fig) to fleece ‖ *ref* to lose its feathers

spennare (spénno) *tr* & *ref* var of **spennacchiare**

spennellare (spennèllo) *tr* to dab

spensieratézza *f* thoughtlessness

spensiera·to -ta *adj* thoughtless, careless; carefree, happy-go-lucky

spèn·to -ta *adj* extinguished; turned off; slaked (*lime*); dull (*color*); low (*tone*)

spenzolare [dz] **(spènzolo)** *tr* & *intr* to hang ‖ *ref*—**spenzolarsi da** to hang out of

speranza *f* hope; prospect, expectation

speranzó·so -sa [s] *adj* hopeful

sperare (spèro) *tr* to candle (*eggs*); to hope for; to expect ‖ *intr* to hope; to trust

spèrdere §212 *tr* (lit) to scatter; (lit) to lose (*one's way*) ‖ *ref* to lose one's way, get lost

sperdu·to -ta *adj* lost, astray; godforsaken (*place*)

sperequazióne *f* disproportion; inequality; unjust distribution

spergiurare *tr & intr* to swear falsely; **giurare e spergiurare** to swear over and over again

spergiu·ro -ra *adj* perjured ‖ *mf* perjurer ‖ *m* perjury

spericola·to -ta *adj* reckless, daring

sperimentale *adj* experimental

sperimentare (speriménto) *tr* to test, try out; to experience

sperimenta·to -ta *adj* experienced

spèr·ma *m* (-mi) sperm

speronare (speróno) *tr* (naut) to ram

speróne *m* spur; abutment; (nav) ram

sperperare (spèrpero) *tr* to squander

spèrpero *m* squandering

spèr·so -sa *adj* lost, stray

spertica·to -ta *adj* too long; too tall; exaggerated, excessive

spésa [s] *f* expense; shopping; buy, purchase; **fare la spesa** to shop; **fare le spese di** to be the butt of; **lavorare per le spese** to work for one's keep; **pagare le spese** to bear the charges; **spese** expenses; room and board; **spese di manutenzione** upkeep; **spese minute** petty expenses; **spese processuali** (law) costs

spesare [s] **(spéso)** *tr* to support

spesa·to -ta [s] *adj* with all expenses paid

spés·so -sa *adj* thick; many (*times*) ‖ **spesso** *adv* often; **spesso spesso** again and again

spessóre *m* thickness

spettàbile *adj* esteemed; **Spettabile Ditta** (com) Gentlemen

spettàcolo *m* spectacle, show; sight; **dar spettacolo di sé** to make a show of oneself; **spettacolo all'aperto** outdoor performance

spettacoló·so -sa [s] *adj* spectacular; (coll) exceptional; (coll) sensational

spettanza *f* concern; pay

spettare (spètto) *intr* (ESSERE)—**spettare a** to belong to ‖ *impers* (ESSERE) —**spetta a** it behooves, it is up to

spetta·tóre -trice *mf* spectator, bystander; **spettatori** public, audience

spettegolare (spettégolo) *intr* to gossip

spettinare (spèttino) *tr* to muss the hair of

spettrale *adj* ghost-like; spectral

spèttro *m* specter, ghost; spectrum

speziale *m* dealer in spices; (coll) pharmacist

spèzie *fpl* spices

spezieria *f* grocery; (coll) drug store, pharmacy; **spezierie** spices

spezzare (spèzzo) *tr* to break; to smash; to interrupt ‖ *ref* to break

spezzatino *m* stew; **spezzatini** change

spezza·to -ta *adj* broken; fragmentary; interrupted ‖ *m* stew; (theat) set piece; **spezzati** change

spezzettare (spezzétto) *tr* to mince

spezzóne *m* small aerial bomb; fragmentation bomb; fragment

spia *f* spy; indication; peephole; (aut) gauge; (aut) pilot light; **fare la spia** to be an informer

spiaccicare §197 **(spiàccico)** *tr* to squash, crush ‖ *ref* to be squashed

spiacènte *adj* sorry; (lit) disliked

spiacére §214 *intr* (ESSERE) (with *dat*) to dislike, e.g., **queste parole gli spiacciono** he dislikes these words; to mind, e.g., **se non Le spiace** if you don't mind ‖ *ref*—**spiacersi di** to be sorry for ‖ *impers* (ESSERE) (with *dat*)—**gli spiace** he is sorry

spiacévole *adj* unpleasant

spiàg·gia *f* (-ge) beach, shore

spianare *tr* to grade (*land*); to roll (*dough*); to pave (*the way*); to iron (*pleats*); to raze, demolish; to level (*a gun*); **spianare la fronte** to smooth one's brow ‖ *intr* (ESSERE) to be level

spianata *f* esplanade; **dare una spianata a** to level

spianatóia *f* board (*for rolling dough*)

spiana·tóio *m* (-tói) rolling pin

spianatrice *f* grader

spiano *m* leveling; esplanade; **a tutto spiano** at full blast; continuously

spiantare *tr* to uproot; to raze, level; to ruin (*financially*) ‖ *ref* to ruin oneself

spianta·to -ta *adj* ruined ‖ *m* pauper

spiare §119 *tr* to spy on; to keep an eye on

spiattellare (spiattèllo) *tr* to blurt out

spiazzo *m* square; plain; clearing

spiccare §197 *tr* to detach; to pick; to enunciate; to begin; to draw up (*a commercial paper*); to issue (*a warrant*); **spiccare il volo** (aer) to take off ‖ *intr* to stand out ‖ *ref* to separate (*said, e.g., of the stone of a peach*)

spicca·to -ta *adj* clear, distinct; typical; outstanding

spìc·chio *m* (-chi) section (*of fruit*); clove (*of garlic*); slice (*e.g., of apple*); arm (*of cross*)

spicciare §128 *tr* to clear up; to wait on; to dispatch (*business*) ‖ *intr* (ESSERE) to flow forth, gush out ‖ *ref* to hurry up, make haste

spicciati·vo -va *adj* expeditious, quick; straightforward; gruff

spiccicare §197 **(spìccico)** *tr* to unglue; to enunciate; to utter ‖ *ref* to come unglued; **spiccicarsi di** to get rid of

spìc·cio -cia (-ci -ce) *adj* expeditious, quick; unhampered; small (*change*) ‖ **spicci** *mpl* change

spicciolata *adj fem*—**alla spicciolata** little by little; a few at a time

spìccio·lo -la *adj* small (change); (coll) plain ‖ **spiccioli** *mpl* small change

spìc·co -ca (-chi -che) *adj* freestone (*e.g., peach*) ‖ *m*—**fare spicco** to stand out

spidocchiare §287 **(spidòcchio)** *tr* to delouse

spièdo *m* spit; **allo spiedo** barbecued

spiegàbile *adj* explainable

spiegaménto *m* (mil) array; (mil) deployment

spiegare §209 **(spiègo)** *tr* to unfold; to let go (*with one's voice*); to unfurl; to spread (*wings*); to deploy (*troops*); to explain; to show, demonstrate; **spiegare il volo** (aer) to take off ‖ *ref* to become unfurled or unfolded;

to make oneself understood; to come to an understanding; to realize

spiega·to -ta *adj* open; full (*voice*)

spiegazióne *f* explanation

spiegazzare *tr* to crumple, rumple

spieta·to -ta *adj* pitiless, ruthless

spifferare (spiffero) *tr* (coll) to blurt out || *intr* to blow in (*said of wind*)

spiffero *m* (coll) draft

spi·ga *f* (**ghe**) panicle (*of oats*); (bot) ear, spike; **a spiga** herringbone

spiga·to -ta *adj* herringbone

spighétta *f* braid; (bot) spikelet

spigionare (spigióno) *ref* to be or become vacant

spiglia·to -ta *adj* easy, free and easy

spi·go *m* (**-ghi**) lavender

spigolare (spìgolo) *tr* to glean

spigola·tóre -trice *mf* gleaner

spìgolo *m* corner; edge; (archit) arris

spilla *f* brooch, pin; **spilla da cravatta** tiepin; **spilla di sicurezza** safety pin

spillare *tr* to draw off, tap; to wheedle, worm (*money*) || *intr* to leak (*said of container*) || *intr* (ESSERE) to leak (*said of liquid*)

spillàti·co *m* (**-ci**) (law) pin money (*for one's wife*)

spillo *m* pin; gimlet; trifle; **a spillo** spikelike; **spillo da balia** or **di sicurezza** safety pin

spillóne *m* hatpin; bodkin

spilluzzicare §197 (spillùzzico) *tr* to pick at, nibble; to scrape together

spilorcerìa *f* stinginess

spilòr·cio -cia (-ci -ce) *adj* stingy || *mf* miser, tightwad

spilungó·ne -na *mf* lanky person

spina *f* thorn; quill, spine (*of porcupine*); bone (*of fish*); (fig) preoccupation, worry; **alla spina** (*beer*) on tap; **a spina di pesce** herringbone (*fabric*); **con una spina nel cuore** sick at heart; **essere sulle spine** to be on pins and needles; **spina della botte** tap; bunghole; **spina dorsale** spinal column; (fig) backbone; **spina elettrica** plug

spinà·cio *m* (**-ci**) spinach (*plant*); **spinaci** spinach (*as food*)

spinapésce *m*—**a spinapesce** herringbone

spina·to -ta *adj* barbed (*wire*); herringbone (*fabric*)

spìngere §126 *tr* to push, press; to prod, goad || *ref* to push; to reach

spì·no -na *adj* thorny || *m* thorn || *f* see **spina**

spinóne *m* griffon

spinó·so -sa [s] *adj* thorny

spinòtto *m* wrist pin

spinta *f* push; pressure; poke, prod; stress

spinterògeno *m* (aut) distributor unit, ignition system

spin·to -ta *adj* pushed; bent, inclined; (coll) risqué; (coll) far-out, offbeat || *f* see **spinta**

spintóne *m* (coll) push, shove

spionàg·gio *m* (**-gi**) espionage, spying

spioncino *m* peephole

spió·ne -na *mf* spy, stool pigeon

spiovènte *adj* drooping; sloping; falling || *m* slope; drainage area (*of a mountain*)

spiòvere §216 *intr* to fall, to hang down (*said, e.g., of hair*); to flow down || *impers* (ESSERE)—**è spiovuto** it stopped raining

spira *f* turn (*of a coil*); coil (*of serpent*); **a spire** spiral

spirà·glio *m* (**-gli**) small opening; gleam (*of light or hope*)

spirale *adj* spiral || *f* spiral; hairspring; wreath (*of smoke*); **spirale di fumo** smoke ring

spirare *tr* to send forth; (lit) to inspire, infuse; (lit) to show (*kindness*) || *intr* to blow; to emanate; to die; to expire

spirita·to -ta *adj* possessed; wild, mad

spirìti·co -ca *adj* (**-ci -che**) spiritual; spiritualistic

spiritismo *m* spiritualism

spìrito *m* spirit; wit; mind; spirits, alcohol; sprite; **bello spirito** wit (*person*); **fare dello spirito** to be witty; to crack jokes; **l'ultimo spirito** (lit) one's last breath; **spirito di corpo** esprit de corps; **spirito di parte** partisanship; **spirito sportivo** sportsmanship

spiritosàggine [s] *f* witticism

spiritó·so -sa [s] *adj* witty; alcoholic

spirituale *adj* spiritual

spìzzi·co *m* (**-chi**)—**a spizzico** or **a spizzichi** little by little; a little at a time

splendènte *adj* resplendent, shining

splèndere §281 *intr* (ESSERE & AVERE) to shine

splèndi·do -da *adj* splendid; gorgeous; bright || *m*—**fare lo splendido** to be a big spender

splendóre *m* splendor; brightness; beauty

splène *m* (anat) spleen

spòcchia *f* haughtiness

spodestare (spodèsto) *tr* to dispossess; to dethrone; to oust

spoetizzare [ddzz] *tr* to disillusion

spòglia *f* slough (*of snake*); skin (*of onion*); husk (*of corn*); (lit) body; (lit) outer garment; **sotto mentite spoglie** under false pretense; **spoglie** spoils

spogliare §280 (spòglio) *tr* to undress, strip; to strip of armor; to defraud, deprive; to free; to check, examine; to husk (*corn*); to go through (*e.g., correspondence*) || *ref* to undress; to slough (*said, e.g., of a snake*); **spogliarsi di** to get rid of; to divest oneself of; to shake (*a habit*)

spogliarelli·sta *f* (**-ste**) stripteaser

spogliarèllo *m* striptease

spoglia·tóio *m* (**-tói**) dressing room; locker room

spò·glio -glia (-gli -glie) *adj* stripped, bare; free || *m* cast-off clothing; sorting; scrutiny; counting (*of votes*); **di spoglio** second-hand (*material*) || *f* see **spoglia**

spòla *f* bobbin; shuttle; **fare la spola** to shuttle

spolétta *f* bobbin, spool; (mil) fuse

spolmonare (spolmóno) *ref* (coll) to talk, sing, or shout oneself hoarse

spolpare (spólpo) *tr* to gnaw (*a bone*); to eat up (*fruit*); (fig) to fleece

spolverare (spólvero) *tr* to dust off, whisk; to powder, dust; to pounce

spolveratura *f* dusting; powdering; sprinkling, smattering (*of knowledge*); **dare una spolveratura a** to brush up on

spolverina *f* (coll) duster

spolverino *m* duster, smock; powder-sugar duster; pounce; (coll) whisk broom

spolverizzaménto [ddzz] *m* sprinkling (*with powder*)

spolverizzare [ddzz] *tr* to dust, powder, pounce

spólvero *m* dusting; powdering; pounce; smattering, sprinkling (*of knowledge*); display

spónda *f* bank (*of river*); side; cushion (*of billiard table*)

sponsale *adj* (lit) wedding ‖ **sponsali** *mpl* (lit) wedding

spontàne·o -a *adj* spontaneous; artless

spopolare (spòpolo) *tr* to depopulate ‖ *intr* to be a hit; to become depopulated or deserted

spoppare (spóppo) *tr* to wean

sporàdi·co -ca *adj* (-ci -che) sporadic

sporcacció·ne -na *adj* filthy ‖ *mf* filthy person; (fig) dirty mouth

sporcare §197 (spórco) *tr* to dirty; to soil ‖ *ref* to get dirty; to soil oneself; **sporcarsi la fedina** (coll) to get a black mark on one's record

sporcizia *f* dirt, filth

spòr·co -ca (-chi -che) *adj* dirty, filthy; foul; **farla sporca** to pull a dirty trick ‖ *m* dirt, filth

sporgènte *adj* leaning; protruding; beetle (*brow*)

sporgènza *f* prominence, projection

spòrgere §217 *tr* to stick out; to stretch out; to lodge (*a complaint*) ‖ *intr* (ESSERE) to project, jut out ‖ *ref* to lean out

spòrt *m* (spòrt) sport; game; **per sport** for fun, for pleasure

spòrta *f* shopping bag; bagful; basket; basketful; shopping; **a sporta** wide-brimmed (*hat*)

sportèllo *m* door; panel; window (*in bank, station, etc.*); wicket; branch (*of a bank*); (theat) box office

sportivi·tà *f* (-tà) sportsmanship

sporti·vo -va *adj* sporting; sportsman-like; athletic ‖ *m* sportsman

spòr·to -ta *adj* projecting; jutting out ‖ *m* projection; removable shutter (*on store door or window*); ‖ *f see* **sporta**

spòsa *f* bride; wife; **andare in sposa a** to get married to; **sposa promessa** fiancée

sposali·zio -zia (-zi -zie) *adj* (lit) nuptial ‖ *m* wedding

sposare (spòso) *tr* to marry; to unite; to embrace (*a cause*); to fit perfectly; to give in marriage ‖ *ref* to get married, marry

spòso *m* bridegroom; **sposi** newlyweds

spossare (spòsso) *tr* to exhaust ‖ *ref* to become worn out

spossatézza *f* exhaustion

spostaménto *m* shift; movement; displacement; change

spostare (spòsto) *tr* to move; to change, shift; to upset ‖ *ref* to move; to shift; to get out of place; to be upset

sposta·to -ta *adj* ill-adjusted, out of place ‖ *mf* misfit

spran·ga *f* (-ghe) bar, crossbar

sprangare §209 *tr* to bar, bolt

sprazzo *m* spray; flash; burst

sprecare §197 (sprèco) *tr* to waste; to miss (*an opportunity*) ‖ *ref* to waste one's efforts

sprè·co *m* (-chi) waste; squandering

sprecó·ne -na *adj & mf* spendthrift

spregévole *adj* contemptible, despicable

spregiare §290 (sprègio) *tr* to despise

sprè·gio *m* (-gi) contempt, scorn

spregiudica·to -ta *adj* open-minded, unbiased ‖ *m* open-minded person

sprèmere §123 *tr* to squeeze, press; **spremere le lacrime a** to move to tears ‖ *ref*—**spremersi il cervello** to rack one's brain

spremifrut·ta *m* (-ta) squeezer

spremilimó·ni *m* (-ni) lemon squeezer

spremuta *f* squeezing; **spremuta d'arancia** orange juice

spretare (sprèto) *ref* to doff the cassock

sprezzante *adj* contemptuous, haughty

sprezzare (sprèzzo) *tr* (lit) to despise

sprèzzo *m* disdain, contempt

sprigionare (sprigióno) *tr* to exhale, emit; to free from prison ‖ *ref* to free oneself; to escape, come forth, issue (*said, e.g., of steam*)

sprimacciare §128 *tr* to beat, fluff (*e.g., a pillow*)

sprizzare *tr* to spout; to sparkle with (*joy, health*) ‖ *intr* (ESSERE) to spurt; to fly (*said of sparks*); to sparkle

sprizzo *m* sprinkle; spurt; spark

sprofondare (sprofóndo) *tr* to send to the bottom; to destroy, ruin; to sink ‖ *intr* (ESSERE) to sink; to founder; to cave in; to be sunk (*e.g., in meditation*)

sprolò·quio *m* (-qui) long rigmarole

spronare (spróno) *tr* to spur, goad

spróne *m* spur; prodding; example; guimpe; buttress; abutment (*of bridge*); **a sprone battuto** at full speed; at once; **dar di sprone a** to spur on; **sprone di cavaliere** (bot) rocket larkspur

sproporziona·to -ta *adj* out of proportion, disproportionate

sproporzióne *f* disproportion

sproposita·to -ta *adj* out of proportion; excessive; gross (*error*)

spropòsito *m* blunder, gross error; excessive amount; **a sproposito** out of place; inopportunely

sprovvedu·to -ta *adj* deprived; brainless, witless

sprovvi·sto -sta *adj* deprived; devoid, lacking; **alla sprovvista** suddenly; unawares, off guard

spruzzabianche·rìa *m* (-rìa) sprinkler (*to sprinkle clothes*)

spruzzare *tr* to sprinkle, spray; to powder (*sugar*)

spruzzatóre *m* sprayer; (aut) nozzle (*of carburetor*)

spruzzo *m* spray; splash (*of mud*)

spudora·to -ta *adj* shameless; impudent

spugna *f* sponge; **dare un colpo di spugna** to wipe the slate clean; **gettare la spugna** to throw in the towel

spugnare *tr* to sponge; to swab

spugnatura *f* sponge bath

spugnó·so -sa [s] *adj* spongy

spulciare §128 *tr* to pick the fleas off; to scrutinize, examine minutely

spuma *f* foam, froth

spumante *adj* sparkling || *m* sparkling wine; champagne

spumare *intr* to froth

spumeggiante *adj* sparkling; vaporous; foamy

spumeggiare §290 (**spuméggio**) *intr* to foam

spumóne *m* spumoni

spumó·so -sa [s] *adj* foamy, frothy

spunta *f* check; check list; check mark

spuntare *tr* to blunt; to unpin; to overcome; to clip, trim; to check off; **spuntarla** to come out on top; to overcome || *intr* (ESSERE) to appear; to sprout; to rise; to well up (*said of tears*); to pop out; to break through || *ref* to become blunt; to die down

spuntino *m* bite, snack; **fare uno spuntino** to have a bite

spunto *m* sourness (*of wine*); (theat) cue; (sports) sprint; (fig) starting point, origin

spuntóne *m* spike; pike; crag

spurgare §209 *tr* to purge, clear; to clean up || *ref* to expectorate

spur·go *m* (-ghi) discharge; reject (*e.g., book*)

spù·rio -ria *adj* (-ri -rie) spurious

sputacchiare §287 *tr* to spit upon || *intr* to sputter

sputacchièra *f* spittoon, cuspidor

sputare *tr* to spit; to cough up; (fig) to spew (*venom*); **sputare sangue** to spit blood; (fig) to sweat blood || *intr* to spit

sputasentènze *mf* (-ze) wiseacre

sputo *m* spit, sputum; spitting

squadernare (**squadèrno**) *tr* to leaf through; **squadernare qlco a qlcu** to put s.th under the nose of s.o. || *ref* to come apart (*said of a book*)

squadra *f* square (*for measuring right angles*); squad, group; (mil) squadron; (sports) team; **a squadra** at right angles; **fuori squadra** out of kilter; **squadra di pompieri** fire company; **squadra mobile** flying squad

squadrare *tr* to square; (fig) to examine, study

squadrìglia *f* (aer, nav) squadron

squadróne *m* squadron (*of cavalry*)

squagliare §280 *tr* to melt || *ref* to melt; **squagliarsela** to take French leave

squalifi·ca *f* (-che) disqualification

squalificare §197 (**squalìfico**) *tr* to disqualify || *ref* to disqualify oneself; to prove to be unqualified

squàlli·do -da *adj* wretched, dreary, gloomy; faint (*smile*); (lit) emaciated

squallóre *m* wretchedness, dreariness, gloominess

squalo *m* shark

squama *f* scurf (*shed by the skin*); (bot, pathol, zool) scale

squamare *tr* & *ref* to scale

squamó·so -sa [s] *adj* scaly

squarciagóla *adv*—**a squarciagóla** at the top of one's voice

squarciare §128 *tr* to rend, tear apart; to dispel (*a doubt*) || *ref* to become torn; to open

squàr·cio *m* (-ci) tear, rip; passage (*of book*)

squartare *tr* to quarter

squartatura *f* quartering

squassare *tr* to shake violently; to wreck

squattrina·to -ta *adj* penniless || *m* pauper

squilibra·to -ta *adj* unbalanced, deranged || *mf* mad or insane person

squilì·brio *m* (-bri) lack of balance; **squilibrio mentale** insanity; unbalanced mental condition

squillante *adj* ringing, shrill; sharp

squillare *intr* to ring; to ring out; to blare

squillo *m* ring; peal; blare, blast (*of horn*); || *f* call girl

squinternare (**squintèrno**) *tr* to tear (*a book*) to pieces; (fig) to upset

squisi·to -ta *adj* exquisite

squittire §176 *intr* to squeak; to squeal

sradicare §197 (**sràdico**) *tr* to uproot; to eradicate; to pull (*a tooth*)

sragionare (**sragióno**) *intr* to talk nonsense

sregola·to -ta *adj* intemperate; dissolute

srotolare (**sròtolo**) *tr* to unroll

stàb·bio *m* (-bi) pen; manure, dung

stabbiòlo *m* pigpen

stàbile *adj* stable; real (*estate*); permanent; stock (*company*) || *m* building

stabiliménto *m* plant, factory; establishment; settlement, colony; conclusion (*of a deal*)

stabilire §176 *tr* to establish; to decide || *ref* to settle

stabili·tà *f* (-tà) stability, steadiness

stabilito *m* (law) agreement of sale (*drawn up by a broker*)

stabilizzare [ddzz] *tr* & *ref* to stabilize

stabilizza·tóre -trice [ddzz] *mf* stabilizing person || *m* (aer) stabilizer; (elec) voltage stabilizer

staccare §197 *tr* to detach; to unhitch; to outdistance; to draw (*a check*); to tear off; to take (*one's eyes*) away; to begin; to enunciate (*words*) || *intr* to stand out; (coll) to stop working || *ref* to come off; **staccarsi da** to come off (*e.g., the wall*); to leave (*one's home; the shore*); (aer) to take off from

stacciare §128 *tr* to sift, sieve

stàc·cio m (-ci) sieve

staccionata f fence; hurdle; stockade

stac·co m (-chi) tearing off; cut of cloth (for a suit); interval; **fare stacco** to stand out

stadèra f steelyard; **stadera a ponte** weighbridge

stàdia f leveling rod

stà·dio m (-di) stadium; stage

staffa f stirrup; heel (of sock); gaiter strap; clamp; (mach) bracket; **perdere le staffe** to lose one's nerve

staffétta f courier, messenger; pilot (car); **a staffetta** relay

staffière m groom, footman; servant

staffilare tr to whip, belt, lash

staffilata f lash

staffile m stirrup strap; whip

stàg·gio m (-gi) stay, upright

stagionale adj seasonal ‖ mf seasonal worker

stagionare (stagióno) tr to season, cure

stagiona·to -ta adj seasoned, ripe

stagióne f season; **da mezza stagione** spring-and-fall (coat); **di fine stagione** year-end (sale)

stagliare §280 tr to hack ‖ ref to stand out

staglia·to -ta adj sheer (cliff)

sta·gnàio m (-gnài) tinsmith; plumber

stagnante adj stagnant

stagnare tr to tin; to solder; to stanch ‖ intr to stagnate

stagnaro m var of **stagnaio**

stagnina f tin can

stagnino m (coll) var of **stagnaio**

sta·gno -gna adj watertight; airtight ‖ m tin; pond, pool

stagnòla f tin foil; tin can

stàio m (stài) bushel (container); a **staio** (coll) top (hat) ‖ m (stàia fpl) bushel (measure); **a staia** in abundance

stalla f stable

stallìa f (com) lay day

stallière m stableman, stableboy

stallo m seat; stall; (chess) stalemate

stallóne m stallion

stamane, stamani or **stamattina** adv this morning

stambéc·co m (-chi) ibex

stambèr·ga f (-ghe) hovel

stambù·gio m (-gi) hole, hovel

stamburare tr to puff up, to boast about ‖ intr to drum

stame m (bot) stamen; thread; yarn

stamigna f cheesecloth

stampa f printing; print; (fig) print; (fig) mold; **stampe** printed matter

stampàg·gio m (-gi) (mach) stamping

stampare tr to stamp; to print; to impress; to publish ‖ ref (fig) to be ingraved

stampatèllo m—**in stampatello** in block letters; **scrivere in stampatello** to print (with pen or pencil)

stampa·to -ta adj printed; impressed ‖ m printed form; **stampati** printed matter

stampa·tóre -trice mf printer

stampèlla f crutch

stamperìa f print shop

stampìglia f rubber stamp; billboard; overprint

stampigliare §280 tr to stamp; to overprint

stampinare tr to stencil

stampino m stencil

stampo m mold; stencil; stamp, kind; decoy

stanare tr to flush (game); (fig) to dig up

stancare §197 tr to tire, fatigue; to bore ‖ ref to tire, weary

stanchézza f tiredness, weariness

stan·co -ca adj (-chi -che) tired; tired out; (lit) left (hand)

standardizzare [ddzz] tr to standardize

stan·ga f (-ghe) bar; shaft (of cart); beam (of plow)

stangata f blow

stanghétta f small bar; bolt (of lock); temple (of spectacles); (mus) bar

stanòtte adv tonight; last night

stante adj being; standing; **a sé stante** by itself, independent ‖ prep because of; **stante che** since

stan·tìo -tìa adj (-tìi, -tìe) stale; musty

stantuffo m piston; plunger

stanza f room; stanza; **essere di stanza** (mil) to be stationed; **stanza da bagno** bath room; **stanza di compensazione** clearing house; **stanza di soggiorno** living room

stanziare §287 tr to allocate; to appropriate; to budget ‖ ref to settle

stanzino m small room; closet

stappare tr to uncork

stare §263 intr (ESSERE) to stay; to stand; to live; to be; to be located; to linger; to last; to stick (e.g., to a rule); (poker) to stand pat; **come sta?** how are you?; **lasciar stare** to leave alone; **lasciar stare che** to leave aside that; **non stare in sé dalla gioia** to be beside oneself with joy; **sta bene!** O.K.!; **starci** to fit, e.g., **ci stanno trecento persone** three hundred people fit there; **starci** to be in favor of, e.g., **io ci starei d'andare al cine** I would be in favor of going to the movies; **stare + ger** to be + ger, e.g., **stava leggendo** he was reading; **stare a** to be up to; to stand on (ceremony); to base oneself on; to take (a joke); to cost, e.g., **a quanto sta il prosciutto?** how much does the ham cost?; **stare a + inf** to keep + ger, e.g., **stai sempre a sognare** you always keep dreaming; to take + inf, e.g., **stette poco a decidere** he took little time to decide; **stare a cuore** (with dat) to deem important, e.g., **gli sta a cuore il lavoro** he deems his work important; **stare a pancia all'aria** to not do a stroke of work; **stare al proprio posto** to keep one's place; **stare a segno** to behave properly; **stare a vedere** to be possible, e.g., **sta a vedere che non viene?** could it be possible that he won't come?; **stare bene** to be well; to be well-off; (with dat) to fit, to become, e.g., **questo vestito gli sta**

bene this suit fits him well, this suit becomes him; to serve right, e.g., **gli sta bene!** it serves him right!; **stare comodo** to be at ease; to remain seated; **stare con** (fig) to be on the side of; **starsene** to stay apart, e.g., **se ne sta solo soletto** he stays apart or all alone; **stare fermo** to be quiet; to not move; **stare in forse** to doubt; to be doubtful; **stare sulle proprie** to stand aloof; **stare su** to stand erect; **stare su tardi** to stay up late; **stia comodo!** remain seated!

starna *f* gray partridge

starnazzare *intr* to flap its wings; to flutter; to cackle

starnutare *intr* to sneeze

starnuto *m* sneeze

stasare [s] *tr* to unplug, unblock

staséra [s] *adv* tonight, this evening

sta·si *f* (-si) (com) stagnation; (pathol) stasis

statale *adj* government; state ‖ *mf* government employee

stàti·co -ca (-ci -che) static ‖ *f* statics

stati·no -na *adj* (coll) migratory ‖ *m* itemized list; (educ) registration form

stati·sta *m* (-sti) statesman

statìsti·co -ca (-ci -che) *adj* statistical ‖ *m* statistician ‖ *f* statistics; **fare una statistica** (di) to survey; **statistiche** statistics (*data*)

stati·vo -va *adj* nonmigratory; permanent ‖ *m* stand (*of microscope*)

stato *m* state; condition; plight; frame (*of mind*); status; estate (*social class*); **di stato** public (*e.g., school*); **essere in stato di arresto** to be under arrest; **stati** extracts from vital statistics; **Stati Pontifici** Papal States; **Stati Uniti** United States; **stato civile** marital status; vital statistics; **stato confessionale** state under ecclesiastical rule; **stato cuscinetto** buffer state; **stato di preallarme** state of emergency; **stato di previsione** preliminary budget; **stato interessante** pregnancy; **stato maggiore** (mil) general staff

statoreattóre *m* ramjet engine

stàtua *f* statue

statuà·rio -ria (-ri -rie) *adj* statuary; statuesque ‖ *m* sculptor

statunitènse *adj & mf* American (*U.S.A.*)

statura *f* stature; height

statuto *m* statute

stavòlta *adv* (coll) this time

stazionaménto *m* parking; **stazionamento vietato** no parking

stazionare (stazióno) *intr* to park

stazionà·rio -ria *adj* (-ri -rie) stationary

stazióne *f* station; bearing; posture; **stazione balneare** shore resort; **stazione climatica** health resort, spa; **stazione di rifornimento** service station; **stazione di tassametri** cab stand; **stazione estiva** summer resort; **stazione generatrice** power plant; **stazione orbitale** orbiting station; **stazione sanitaria** clinic

stazza *f* tonnage; (naut) displacement

stazzare *tr* (naut) to gauge; (naut) to displace

stazzonare (stazzóno) *tr* to crumple

steatite *f* French chalk

stéc·ca *f* (-che) small stick; slat (*of shutter*); rib (*of umbrella*); bone (*of whale*); carton (*of cigarettes*); rail (*of fence*); letter opener; chisel (*of sculptor*); (billiards) cue; (billiards) miscue; (surg) splint; **fare una stecca** (billiards) to miscue; (mus) to sing or play a sour note

steccadèn·ti *m* (-ti) (coll) toothpick

steccare §197 (stécco) *tr* to fence; to put in a splint ‖ *intr* to play or sing a sour note; (billiards) to miscue

steccato *m* fence; (racing) inside track

stecchétto *m* small stick; **tenere a stecchetto** to keep on a strict diet; to keep short of money

stecchino *m* toothpick

stecchi·to -ta *adj* stiff; lean, lank; dry (*twig*); dumfounded

stéc·co *m* (-chi) stick, twig

stecconata *f* stockade; fence

stélla *f* star; rowel (*of spur*); speck of fat (*in soup*); (fig) sky; **a stella** star-shaped; stellar; **montare alle stelle** to be sky-high (*said, e.g., of prices*); **portare alle stelle** to praise to the skies; **stella alpina** edelweiss; **stella cadente** shooting star; **stella di mare** starfish; **stella filante** shooting star; confetti; **stella polare** polestar, lodestar

stellare *adj* stellar; (mach) radial ‖ *v* (stéllo) *tr* to spangle with stars; to stud

stella·to -ta *adj* starry; star-spangled; star-shaped; studded

stellétta *f* (mil) star; (typ) asterisk; **guadagnarsi le stellette** (mil) to earn a promotion; **portare le stellette** (mil) to be in the service

stellina *f* starlet

stelloncino *m* (journ) short paragraph

stèlo *m* stem, stalk

stèm·ma *m* (-mi) coat of arms; genealogy (*of a manuscript*)

stemperare (stèmpero) *tr* to dilute; to blunt; to untemper; (lit) to waste ‖ *ref* to melt; to become dull or blunt

stendardo *m* banner, standard

stèndere §270 *tr* to stretch; to hang up (*laundry*); to spread; to draw up (*a document*); (mil) to deploy; **stendere a terra** to knock down ‖ *ref* to stretch out

stendibianche·rìa *m* (-rìa) clothes rack, clotheshorse

stenodattilògra·fo -fa *mf* shorthand typist

stenografare (stenògrafo) *tr* to take down in shorthand

stenografia *f* shorthand, stenography

stenogràfi·co -ca *adj* (-ci -che) stenographic, shorthand

stenògra·fo -fa *mf* stenographer

stenòsi *f* (pathol) stricture

stenotipia *f* stenotypy

stentare (stènto) *tr* to eke out (*a living*)

|| *intr* to barely make ends meet; **stentare** a. to hardly be able to; to find it hard to

stenta·to -ta *adj* hard; stunted; strained (*smile*)

stènto *m* privation; hardship; **a stento** hardly; with difficulty; **senza stento** without any trouble

stèr·co *m* (**-chi**) dung

stereofòni·co -ca *adj* (**-ci -che**) stereo, stereophonic

stereoscòpi·co -ca *adj* (**-ci -che**) stereoscopic

stereoscò·pio *m* (**-pi**) stereoscope

stereotipa·to -ta *adj* stereotyped

sterilizzare [ddzz] *tr* to sterilize

sterlina *f* pound sterling

sterminare (**stèrmino**) *tr* to exterminate

stermina·to -ta *adj* immense, boundless

stermì·nio *m* (**-ni**) extermination; (**coll**) large amount, lots

stèrno *m* breastbone

sterpàglia *f* brushwood; undergrowth

stèrpo *m* dry twig; bramble

sterrare (**stèrro**) *tr* to excavate

sterratóre *m* digger

sterzare (**stèrzo**) *tr* to diminish by one third; to thin out (*woodland*); (**aut**) to steer || *intr* to swerve

sterzata *f* swerve

stèrzo *m* handle bar; (**aut**) steering gear; (**aut**) steering wheel

stésa [s] *f* coat (*of paint*); string (*of clothes on line*)

stés·so -sa *adj* same, e.g., **lo stesso mese** the same month; very, e.g., **tuo fratello stesso** your very brother; **essere alle stesse** to be just the same; **io stesso** I myself; **lui stesso** he himself, etc.; **per sé stesso** by himself; by itself || *pron* same; same thing; **fa lo stesso** it's all the same, it makes no difference

stesura [s] *f* drawing up (*of a contract*); **prima stesura** first draft

stetoscò·pio *m* (**-pi**) stethoscope

stìa *f* chicken coop

Stige *m* Styx

stì·gio -gia *adj* (**-gi -gie**) Stygian

stigmate *fpl* stigmata

stilare *tr* to draft properly

stile *m* style

stilè *adj invar* stylish

stilétto *m* dagger, stiletto

stilizzare [ddzz] *tr* to stylize

stilla *f* (**lit**) drop, droplet

stillare *tr* to exude; to distill || *intr* (ESSERE) to ooze, drip, exude || *ref*— **stillarsi il cervello** to rack one's brains

stillicì·dio *m* (**-di**) dripping; repetition

stilo *m* stylus; arm (*of steelyard*); dagger; gnomon (*of sundial*); (**poet**) style || *f* (**coll**) fountain pen

stilogràfi·ca *f* (**-che**) fountain pen

stima *f* appraisal; esteem; (**naut**) dead reckoning; **a stima d'occhio** more or less

stimare *tr* to estimate; to deem; to esteem || *ref* (**coll**) to think a lot of oneself

stima·tóre -trice *mf* appraiser; admirer

stìmmate *fpl* var of **stigmate**

stimolante *adj* & *m* stimulant

stimolare (**stìmolo**) *tr* to stimulate

stìmolo *m* influence; stimulus

stin·co *m* (**-chi**) shinbone; shin; **stinco di santo** saintly person, saint; **rompere gli stinchi a** to annoy

stìngere §126 *tr, intr* (ESSERE) & *ref* to fade

stipa *f* kindling wood, brushwood

stipare *tr* & *ref* to crowd, jam

stipendiare §287 (**stipèndio**) *tr* to employ, hire; to pay a salary to

stipendia·to -ta *adj* salaried || *mf* salaried person

stipèn·dio *m* (**-di**) pay, salary

stipétto *m* (**naut**) closet, cabinet

stìpite *m* jamb; stock, family; (**bot**) trunk (*of palm tree*)

stipo *m* cabinet

stipulare (**stìpulo**) *tr* to draw up (*a contract*); to stipulate

stiracchiare §287 *tr* to stretch; to eke out (*a living*); to twist (*a meaning*); to haggle over || *intr* to haggle; to economize || *ref* to stretch out

stirare *tr* to stretch; to iron, press || *intr* to iron || *ref* to stretch out

stira·tóre -trice *mf* ironer, presser

stiratura *f* ironing; stretching

stirerìa *f* ironing shop

stiro *m*—**ferro da stiro** see **ferro**

stirpe *f* family; birth, origin

stitichézza *f* constipation

stìti·co -ca *adj* (**-ci -che**) constipated; (**fig**) tight

stiva *f* (**naut**) hold; (**lit**) beam (*of plow*)

stivàg·gio *m* (**-gi**) stowage

stivale *m* boot; **dei miei stivali** good-for-nothing; **lustrare gli stivali a qlcu** to lick s.o.'s boots

stivalétto *m* high shoe

stivalóne *m* boot; **stivaloni da equitazione** riding boots; **stivaloni da palude** hip boots

stivare *tr* to stow

stivatóre *m* stevedore

stizza *f* anger; irritation

stizzire §176 *tr* to anger, vex || *ref* to get angry

stizzó·so -sa [s] *adj* peevish, irritable

stoccafisso *m* stockfish

stoccata *f* thrust (*with dagger or rapier*); dig, sarcastic remark; touch (*for money*)

stòc·co *m* (**-chi**) dagger; rapier; stalk (*of corn*)

Stoccólma *f* Stockholm

stòffa *f* cloth, material; (**fig**) stuff, makings

stoicismo *m* stoicism

stòi·co -ca (**-ci -che**) *adj* stoic, stoical || *m* stoic; Stoic

stoino *m* doormat

stòla *f* stole

stòli·do -da *adj* foolish, silly

stoltézza *f* foolishness, silliness

stól·to -ta *adj* silly || *mf* fool

stomacare §197 (**stòmaco**) *tr* to disgust; to nauseate

stomachévole *adj* disgusting, sickening

stòma·co m (-ci or -chi) stomach; maw (of animal); dare di stomaco to vomit

stonare (stòno) tr to sing or play out of tune; to upset || intr to sing or play out of tune; to be out of place; to not harmonize

stona·to -ta adj out-of-tune; upset; clashing (color)

stonatura f jarring sound; clash (of colors); lack of harmony

stóppa f tow; oakum; di stoppa flaxen; weak, trembling; stoppa incatramata oakum

stoppàc·cio m (-ci) wad

stóppie fpl stubble

stoppino m wick

stoppó·so -sa [s] adj stubby; stringy

stórcere §272 tr to twist; to twitch; to wrench (one's ankle); to roll (one's eyes) || ref to twist; to writhe; to bend

stordiménto m bewilderment; dizziness || stordire §176 tr to bewilder; to daze || intr to be bewildered || ref to dull one's senses

storditàggine f carelessness; mistake, blunder

stordi·to -ta adj careless; bewildered; amazed; dizzy || mf scatterbrain

stòria f history; story, tale; fact; fare storie to stand on ceremony; un'altra storia a horse of another color

stòri·co -ca (-ci -che) adj historical || m historian

storièlla f tale, short story; joke

storiografìa f historiography

storióne m sturgeon

stormire §176 intr to rustle

stórmo m swarm, flock; (aer) group

stornare (stórno) tr to ward off; to dissuade; to divert (funds); to write off (as noncollectable)

stornèllo m Italian folksong; (orn) starling

stór·no -na adj dapple-gray || m (com) transfer; (orn) starling

storpiare §287 (stòrpio) tr to cripple; to clip (one's words)

stòr·pio -pia (-pi -pie) adj crippled || m cripple

stòr·to -ta adj twisted; crooked; crippled || f twist; dislocation; retort

stoviglie fpl dishes; lavare le stoviglie to wash the dishes

stra- pref adj extra-, e.g., straordinario extraordinary; over-, e.g., stracarico overloaded

stràbi·co -ca adj (-ci -che) crosseyed

strabiliante adj astonishing, amazing

strabiliare §287 tr to amaze || intr & ref to be amazed

strabismo m strabismus, squint

straboccare §197 (strabócco) intr to overflow

strabocchévole adj overflowing

strabuzzare [ddzz] tr (coll) to roll (one's eyes)

stracàri·co -ca adj (-chi -che) overloaded, overburdened

stracca f—pigliare una stracca to be dead tired

straccale m breeching (of harness); straccali (coll) suspenders

straccare §197 tr (coll) to tire

stracciaiò·lo -la mf ragpicker

stracciare §128 tr to tear, rend; to comb (natural silk)

stràc·cio -cia (-ci -ce) adj torn, in rags; waste (paper) || m rag, tatter; tear, rend; combed silk

stracció·ne -na mf tatterdemalion

straccivéndo·lo -la mf ragpicker; rag dealer

strac·co -ca adj (-chi -che) tired; worn-out; alla stracca lazily || f see stracca

stracòt·to -ta adj overcooked, overdone || m stew

stracuòcere §144a tr to overcook, overdo

strada f roadway; street; da strada vulgar, common; divorare la strada to burn up the road; essere in mezzo a una strada to be in a bad way; fare strada a to pave the way for; farsi strada to make one's way; prender la strada to set forth; strada carrozzabile carriage road; strada dell'orto easy way out; strada ferrata railroad; strada maestra main road; tagliare la strada a to stand in the way of; (aut) to cut in front of

stradale adj road; street; traffic (e.g., accident); highway (police) || m avenue || f highway patrol

stradà·rio m (-ri) street directory

strafalcióne m blunder, gross error

strafare §173 tr to overdo; to overcook

strafóro m drilled hole; di straforo stealthily

strafottènte adj unconcerned, nonchalant; arrogant, impudent

strafottènza f nonchalance, unconcern; arrogance, impudence

strage f butchery, massacre, carnage; (coll) multitude, lot

stragrande adj enormous, huge

stralciare §128 tr to prune, trim (grapevines); to eliminate, remove; (com) to liquidate

stràl·cio adj invar interim; emergency (e.g., law); liquidating || m (-ci) excerpt; clearance sale; a stralcio at a bargain

strale m (lit) arrow

strallo m (naut) stay

stralunare tr to roll (one's eyes)

straluna·to -ta adj upset; wild-eyed

stramazzare tr to fell || intr (ESSERE) to fall down

stramazzo m sluice; (coll) straw mattress

stramberìa f eccentricity

stram·bo -ba adj odd, queer, eccentric; crooked (legs); squint (eyes)

strame m litter; fodder

strampala·to -ta adj strange; preposterous, absurd

stranézza f strangeness; oddity

strangolare (strangolo) tr to strangle; (naut) to furl

strangola·tóre -trice mf strangler

straniare §287 tr (lit) to draw away || ref to become estranged

straniè·ro -ra *adj* foreign, alien; (lit) strange ‖ *mf* foreigner, alien

stra·no -na *adj* strange, odd; (lit) estranged

straordinà·rio -ria (-ri -rie) *adj* extraordinary; extra ‖ *mf* temporary employee ‖ *m* overtime

strapagàre §209 *tr* to overpay; to pay too much for

strapazzàre *tr* to rebuke, upbraid; to mishandle; to bungle ‖ *ref* to overwork oneself

strapazzà·to -ta *adj* crumpled; bungled; scrambled (*eggs*); overworked ‖ *j* upbraiding, rebuke; fatigue

strapazzo *m* misuse; fatigue; excess; **da strapazzo** working (*clothes*); hackneyed, second-rate

strapèrdere §212 *tr & intr* to lose hopelessly ‖ *intr* to be wiped out

strapiè·no -na *adj* chock-full

strapiombàre (strapiómbo) *intr* to overhang, jut out

strapiómbo *m* overhang; **a strapiombo** sheer (*cliff*)

strapotènte *adj* overpowerful

strappàre *tr* to pull; to tear, rend; to wring (*s.o.'s heart*); **strappare le lacrime a qlcu** to move s.o. to tears; **strappare qlco a qlcu** to pry s.th out of s.o.; to snatch s.th from s.o. ‖ *ref* to tear (*e.g., one's hair*)

strappàta *f* pull, tug, snatch

strappo *m* pull; tear, rip; infraction, breach; pulling away (*on a bicycle*); patch (*of sky*); **a strappi** in jerks; **strappo muscolare** pulled muscle; sprain

strapuntino *m* folding seat, jump seat; bucket seat; (naut) mattress

straric·co -ca *adj* (**-chi -che**) (coll) immensely rich

straripàre *intr* (ESSERE & AVERE) to overflow

strascicàre §197 (**stràscico**) *tr* to drag; to shuffle; **strascicare le parole** to drawl

strascichì·o *m* (**-i**) shuffle (*of feet*)

stràsci·co *m* (**-chi**) train (*of skirt*); trail; sequel, aftermath; **a strascico** dragging

strascinàre (stràscino) *tr* to drag ‖ *ref* to drag oneself, drag

strascinì·o *m* (**-i**) shuffle

stràscino *m* dragnet, trawl

stratagèm·ma *m* (**-mi**) stratagem

strategìa *f* strategy

stratègi·co -ca *adj* (**-ci -che**) strategic

stratè·go *m* (**-ghi**) strategist; general, commander

stratificàre §197 (**stratìfico**) *tr* to stratify

strato *m* layer; coat, coating; stratum; (meteor) stratus

stratosfèra *f* stratosphere

strattóne *m* jerk, tug

stravagante *adj* extravagant; whimsical, capricious ‖ *mf* eccentric

stravèc·chio -chia *adj* (**-chi -chie**) aged (*cheese, wine, etc.*); very old

stravìncere §285 *tr* to overpower

straviziàre §287 *intr* to be intemperate

stravì·zio *m* (**-zi**) intemperance, excess

stravòlgere §289 *tr* to roll (*the eyes*); to distort; to derange

straziante *adj* heartbreaking; excruciating (*pain*); horrible

straziàre §287 *tr* to torture; to dismay; to mangle; to murder (*a language*)

strazia·to -ta *adj* torn, stricken

strà·zio *m* (**-zi**) suffering, pain; torture; shame; boredom; **fare strazio di** to squander

stré·ga *f* (**-ghe**) witch; sorceress

stregàre §209 (**strégo**) *tr* to bewitch

stregóne *m* sorcerer; witch doctor

stregonerìa *f* witchcraft; sorcery

strègua *f* standard, criterion; **alla strègua di** on the basis of

strema·to -ta *adj* exhausted

strènna *f* Christmas gift, New Year's gift; special New Year's issue

strè·nuo -nua *adj* strenuous

strepitàre (strèpito) *intr* to make a noise; to shout, make a racket

strèpito *m* noise, racket; **fare strepito** to make a hit

strepitó·so -sa [s] *adj* loud, noisy; resounding (*success*)

streptomicìna *f* streptomycin

stressà·to -ta *adj* under stress

strétta *f* grasp, clench; tightening (*of brakes*); hold; press, crush; pang; mountain pass; **mettere alle strette** to drive into a corner; **stretta dei conti** rendering of accounts; **stretta di mano** handshake; **stretta finale** climax

strettézza *f* narrowness; **strettezze** straits, hardship

strét·to -ta *adj* narrow; tight; bare (*necessities*); pure (*e.g., dialect*); strict; clenched (*fist*); heavy (*heart*); minimum (*price*); (phonet) close ‖ *m* straits, narrows ‖ *f* see **stretta** ‖ **stretto** *adv* tightly

strettóia *f* narrow stretch; hardship; bandage

strìa *f* stripe, streak

striàre §119 *tr* to stripe, streak

stricnìna *f* strychnine

stridènte *adj* jarring, clashing (*colors*); strident (*sound*)

strìdere §264 *tr* to grit (*one's teeth*) ‖ *intr* to shriek; to squeak; to creak; to clash (*said of colors*); to croak (*said of raven*); to hoot (*said of owl*); to howl (*said of wind*) ‖ *ref* (coll) to be resigned

strido *m* (**-di & -da** *fpl*) shriek; squeak

stridóre *m* shriek; creak, squeak; gnashing (*of teeth*)

strìdu·lo -la *adj* shrill

strigàre §209 *tr* to disentangle ‖ *ref* to extricate oneself

strìglia *f* currycomb

strigliàre §280 *tr* to curry; to upbraid ‖ *ref* to groom oneself

strillàre *tr* to shout; (coll) to scold; (coll) to hawk (*newspapers*) ‖ *intr* to scream

strillo *m* shriek; shout, scream

strilló·ne -na *mf* loud-mouthed person ‖ *m* newsdealer; newsboy, paperboy

striminzi·to -ta *adj* shrunken; tight; stunted; skinny

strimpellare (strimpèllo) *tr* to thrum; to thrum on

strinare *tr* to singe; to burn (*with a flatiron*)

strin·ga *f* (-ghe) lace; shoelace

stringa·to -ta *adj* terse, concise

strìngere §265 *tr* to tighten; to grip; to shake, clasp (*a hand*); to drive into a corner; to squeeze; to embrace; to close (*an alliance, a deal*); to wring (*one's heart*); to clench (*the fist*); (lit) to gird (*a sword*); (mus) to accelerate; **stringere d'assedio** to besiege; **stringere i freni** to put the brakes on ‖ *intr* to be tight; **il tempo stringe** time is running short; **stringi, stringi** at the very end, in conclusion ‖ *ref* to squeeze close together; to shrink; to coagulate; to draw close; **stringersi a** to snuggle up to; **stringersi addosso a** to attack; **stringersi nelle spalle** to shrug one's shoulders

stringina·so [s] *m* (-so) pince-nez

strì·scia *f* (-sce) strip, band; trail; stripe; line; **a strisce** striped; **striscia d'atterramento** airstrip; **striscia di cuoio** strop

strisciante *adj* crawling; (fig) fawning

strisciare §128 *tr* to shuffle (*feet*); to graze; **strisciare una riverenza** to curtsy ‖ *intr* to creep, crawl; to graze by ‖ *ref* to fawn; **strisciarsi a** to rub one's back against

strisciata or **strisciatura** *f* sliding; trail

strì·scio *m* (-sci) rubbing; shuffling; **ballare di striscio** to shuffle; **da** or **di striscio** superficial (*wound*)

striscióne *m* festoon; festooned sign; flatterer; **striscione d'arrivo** landing (*in gymnastics*); **striscione del traguardo** (sports) tape

striscióni *adv* crawling

stritolare (strìtolo) *tr* to crush, smash

strizzalimó·ni *m*(-ni) lemon squeezer

strizzare *tr* to squeeze, press; to wink (*the eye*); **strizzare l'occhio** to wink

strizza·tóio *m* (-tói) wringer

strò·fa or **strò·fe** *f* (-fe) strophe

strofinàc·cio *m* (-ci) dust cloth

strofinare *tr* to rub; to polish ‖ *ref* to rub oneself; to fawn

strofinata *f*—**dare una strofinata a** to give a lick and a promise to

strofini·o *m* (-ii) rubbing; wiping

stròla·ga *f* (-ghe) (orn) loon

strombatura *f* embrasure

strombazzare *tr* to glorify; **strombazzare i propri meriti** to toot one's own horn ‖ *intr* to blast away on the trumpet

strombazza·tóre -trice *mf* show-off

strombettare (strombétto) *tr* to trumpet, toot

stroncare §197 **(strónco)** *tr* to break off; to break down; to eliminate; (fig) to criticize severely

stroncatura *f* devastating criticism

strònzio *m* strontium

strónzo *m* (vulg) turd

stropicciare §128 *tr* to rub (*hands*); to drag, shuffle (*feet*); (coll) to crumple ‖ *ref*—**stropicciarsene** (coll) to not give a hoot

stropicci·o *m* (-ii) rubbing; shuffling

stròzza *f* (coll) gullet, throat

strozzare (stròzzo) *tr* to strangle; to stop up; to fleece, swindle ‖ *ref* to choke; to narrow

strozza·to -ta *adj* choked; choking; strangulated (*hernia*)

strozzatura *f* narrowing

strozzinàg·gio *m* (-gi) usury

strozzino *m* usurer, loan shark

strùggere §266 *tr* to melt; to consume ‖ *ref* to melt; to pine away; to be upset; **struggersi di** to be consumed by

struggimento *m* melting; longing; torment

strumentale *adj* instrument (*flying*); capital (*goods*); instructional (*language, in multi-lingual regions*); (gram, mus) instrumental

strumentali·sta *mf* (-sti -ste) instrumentalist

strumentalizzare [ddzz] *tr* to use, take advantage of

strumentare (struménto) *tr* to orchestrate

struménto *m* instrument; tool, implement; **strumento a corda** stringed instrument; **strumento a fiato** wind instrument; **strumento di bordo** (aer) flight recorder

strusciare §128 *tr* to rub; to shuffle (*feet*); to crumple; to wear out ‖ *ref*—**strusciarsi a** to fawn on

strutto *m* lard, shortening

struttura *f* structure

strutturare *tr* to organize, structure

struzzo *m* ostrich

stuccare §197 *tr* to putty; to stucco; to surfeit ‖ *ref* to grow weary

stucchévole *adj* sickening

stuc·co -ca (-chi -che) *adj* bored; **stucco e ristucco** sick and tired ‖ *m* putty; stucco; plaster of Paris; **rimanere di stucco** to be taken aback

studèn·te -téssa *mf* student

studénte·sco -sca (-schi -sche) *adj* student; student-like ‖ *f* student body

studiare §287 *tr* to study; **studiarle tutte** to consider every angle ‖ *intr* to study; to try ‖ *ref* to try; to gaze at oneself

stù·dio *m* (-di) study; school district; office (*of professional man*); studio; (hist) university; (lit) wish; (mus) étude; **a studio** on purpose; **essere allo studio** to be under consideration

studió·so -sa [s] *adj* studious ‖ *m* scholar

stufa *f* stove, heater; hothouse

stufare *tr* to warm up, heat up; to stew; (coll) to bore

stufato *m* stew

stu·fo -fa *adj* (coll) bored, sick and tired ‖ *f* see **stufa**

stuòia *f* mat; matting

stuòlo *m* throng, crowd; flock; (lit) army

stupefacènte adj amazing; habit-forming || m dope

stupefare §173 tr to amaze, astonish

stupefazióne f amazement, astonishment; stupefaction

stupèn·do -da adj stupendous

stupidàggine f stupidity; silliness; child's play, cinch

stùpi·do -da adj stupid; silly; (lit) amazed

stupire §176 tr to amaze || ref to be amazed

stupóre m amazement

stuprare tr to rape

stura f tapping; uncorking; **dar la stura** to begin (a speech)

sturabottì·glie m (-glie) bottle opener

sturalavandi·ni m (-ni) plunger (to open up clogged sink)

sturare tr to uncork; to take the wax out of (ears); to open up (clogged line)

stuzzicadèn·ti m (-ti) toothpick

stuzzicare §197 (stùzzico) tr to pick (e.g., one's teeth); to bother; to excite, arouse; to tease; to sharpen (appetite)

su adv up; on top; upstairs; **da . . . in su** from . . . on, e.g., **dal mese scorso in su** from last month on; **di su** from upstairs; **in su** up; **metter su** to put on the fire; to instigate; **metter su bottega** to set up shop; **metter su casa** to set up housekeeping; **più su** higher; further up; **su!** come on.!; let's go!; **su di on**; **su e giù** back and forth; up and down; **su per giù** more or less; **tirarsi su** to lift oneself up; to sit up; to get better, recover; **tirar su** to pick up; to grow, raise; **venir su** to grow; to come up || §4 prep on, upon; up; towards; over, above; onto; against; at, e.g., **sul far del giorno** at daybreak; on top of; out of, e.g., **due volte su tre** two times out of three; **mettere su superbia** to become proud; **stare sulle sue** to be reserved; **sul serio** in earnest; **su misura** made to order

suaccenna·to -ta adj above-mentioned

sub m (sub) (coll) skindiver

subàcque·o -a adj submarine

subaffittare tr to sublet

subaffitto m subletting, sublet; **prendere in subaffitto** to sublet

subaltèr·no -na adj & m subaltern; subordinate

subastare tr to auction off

sùbbia f stonecutter's chisel

subbù·glio m (-gli) turmoil, hubbub

subcosciènte adj & m subconscious

sùbdo·lo -la adj treacherous, deceitful

subentrare (subéntro) intr (ESSERE) (with dat) to succeed, follow

subire §176 tr to suffer; to undergo

subissare tr to ruin; to sink; to overwhelm || intr (ESSERE) to sink; to go to rack and ruin

subisso m ruin; (coll) lots, plenty

subitàne·o -a adj sudden

sùbi·to -ta adj (lit) sudden || m—**d'un subito** all of a sudden || **subito** adv

rapidly; immediately; right away; **subito al principio** at the very beginning; **subito dopo** right after; **subito prima** right before || interj right away!

sublima·to -ta adj sublimated || m **sublimato corrosivo** corrosive sublimate

sublime adj & m sublime

subodorare (subodóro) tr to suspect; to get wind of

subordinare (subórdino) tr to subordinate

subordina·to -ta adj & m subordinate || f subordinate clause

subornare (subórno) tr to bribe

substrato m substratum

suburba·no -na adj suburban

subùr·bio m (-bi) suburb

succedàne·o -a adj & m substitute

succèdere §132 (pp succeduto or successo) intr (ESSERE) (with dat) to succede, to follow || ref to follow one another, follow one after the other || (pret succèssi; pp successo) intr (ESSERE) to happen, to come to pass; (with dat) to happen to, to come over, e.g., **che gli è successo?** what happened to him?

successióne f succession; **in successione** in succession; in a row

successi·vo -va adj successive; next

succèsso m success; outcome

successóre m successor

successò·rio -ria adj (-ri -rie) inheritance (tax)

succhiare §287 tr to suck

succhièllo m gimlet

succhiétto m pacifier

sùc·chio m (-chi) suck, sucking; (bot) sap; (coll) gimlet

succiaca·pre m (-pre) goatsucker, whippoorwill

succin·to -ta adj scanty (clothing); succinct, concise

suc·co m (-chi) juice; (fig) gist

succó·so -sa [s] adj juicy; pithy

succursale f branch, branch office

sud m south

sudafrica·no -na adj & mf South African

sudamerica·no -na adj & mf South American

sudàmina f prickly heat

sudare tr to sweat; to ooze; **sudare il pane** to earn one's living by the sweat of one's brow; **sudare sette camicie** to toil very hard || intr to perspire, sweat; to reek

sudà·rio m (-ri) shroud

suda·to -ta adj wet with perspiration; hard-earned || f sweat, sweating

suddét·to -ta adj aforesaid, above

sùddi·to -ta adj & mf subject

suddivìdere §158 tr to subdivide

sud-èst m southeast

sudicerìa f filth, filthiness; smut

sùdi·cio -cia (-ci -cie) adj dirty, filthy || m dirt, filth

sudiciume m dirt, filth

sudì·sta mf (-sti -ste) Southerner

sudóre m sweat, perspiration

sud-òvest *m* southwest

sufficiènte *adj* sufficient, adequate; self-sufficient || *m* sufficient

sufficiènza *f* sufficiency; self-sufficiency; (educ) minimum passing grade

suffisso *m* suffix

suffragare §209 *tr* to support; to pray for

suffragétta *f* suffragette

suffrà·gio *m* (-gi) suffrage

suffumicare §197 (suffùmico) *tr* to fumigate

suffumi·gio *m* (-gi) treatment by inhalation; fumigation

suggellare (suggèllo) *tr* to seal

suggèllo *m* seal

suggeriménto *m* suggestion

suggerire §176 *tr* to suggest; to prompt

suggeri·tóre -trice *mf* prompter || *m* (baseball) coach

suggestionàbile *adj* suggestible

suggestionare (suggestióno) *tr* to influence by suggestion || *ref*—suggestionarsi a + *inf* to talk oneself into + *ger*

suggestióne *f* suggestion; fascination

suggesti·vo -va *adj* suggestive; fascinating; (law) leading (*question*)

sùghero *m* cork

sugli §4

sugna *f* fat; lard

su·go *m* (-ghi) juice; gravy; gist, pith; non c'è sugo it's no fun; there's nothing to it; senza sugo pointless, dull

sugó·so -sa [s] *adj* juicy

sui §4

suici·da (-di -de) *adj* suicidal || *mf* suicide (*person*)

suicidare *ref* to commit suicide

suici·dio *m* (-di) suicide (*act*)

sui·no -na *adj* swinish; see carne || *m* swine

sul §4

sulfamìdi·co -ca (-ci -che) *adj* sulfa || *m* sulfa drug

sulla §4

sulle §4

sulli §4

sullo §4

sulloda·to -ta *adj* above-mentioned

sultano *m* sultan

summentova·to -ta, summenziona·to -ta, sunnomina·to -ta *adj* above-mentioned

sunteggiare §290 (suntéggio) *tr* to summarize

sunto *m* résumé, summary

suo sua §6 *adj* & *pron poss* (suòi sue)

suòcera *f* mother-in-law

suòcero *m* father-in-law; i suoceri the in-laws

suòla *f* sole (*of shoe*); share (*of plow*); (naut) sliding ways; (rr) flange (*of rail*)

suòlo *m* ground; soil; floor || *m* (suola *fpl*) (coll) layer; (coll) sole (*of shoe*)

suonare (suòno) *tr* & *intr* var of sonare

suòno *m* sound; (fig) ring; a suon di bastonate with a sound thrashing; a suon di fischi with loud boos; suono armonico (mus) overtone

suòno·stère·o *m* (-o) stereo tape player

suòra *f* nun, sister

super- *pref adj* & *mf* super-, e.g., supersonico supersonic; over-, e.g., superallenamento overtraining

superaffollaménto *m* overcrowding

superare (sùpero) *tr* to surpass; to cross; to overcome; to pass; to exceed; (cards) to trump

supera·to -ta *adj* out-of-date, passé

supèrbia *f* pride, haughtiness; montare in superbia to get a swelled head

superbió·so -sa [s] *adj* proud, haughty

supèr·bo -ba *adj* proud, haughty; superb; spirited || i superbi the haughty ones

supercarburante *m* high-octane gas

supercolòsso *m* supercolossal film

superdònna *f*—si da arie di superdonna she thinks she's hot stuff

supereterodina *f* superheterodyne

superficiale *adj* superficial; surface; cursory, perfunctory || *m* superficial fellow

superfi·cie *f* (-ci & cie) surface; area; superficie portante airfoil

supèr·fluo -flua *adj* superfluous || *m* surplus

super-ìo *m* (-ìo) superego

superióra *f* (eccl) mother superior

superióre *adj* superior; upper; higher; above; superiore a higher than; more than; larger than || *m* superior

superlati·vo -va *adj* & *m* superlative

superlavóro *m* overwork

supermercato *m* supermarket

supersòni·co -ca *adj* (-ci -che) supersonic

supèrstite *adj* surviving; remaining || *mf* survivor

superstizióne *f* superstition

superstizió·so -sa [s] *adj* superstitious

superstrada *f* superhighway

superuòmo *m* superman

supervisióne *f* supervision

supervisóre *m* supervisor; (mov) director

supi·no -na *adj* supine; on one's back

suppellèttile *f* furnishings; equipment; fixtures; fund (*of knowledge*)

supplementare *adj* supplementary

suppleménto *m* supplement; (mil) reinforcement

supplènte *adj* & *mf* substitute

supplènza *f* substitute assignment

suppleti·vo -va *adj* additional; (gram) suppletive

sùppli·ca *f* (-che) supplication; plea; petition

supplicante *mf* supplicant

supplicare §197 (sùpplico) *tr* to beseech; to plead with; to appeal to

supplichévole *adj* beseeching, imploring

supplire §176 *tr* to replace || *intr* (with *dat*) to supplement, make up for

suppliziare §287 *tr* to torture; to execute

suppli·zio *m* (-zi) torture, torment; estremo supplizio capital punishment

suppórre §218 *tr* to suppose

suppòrto *m* support, prop

suppositò·rio *m* (-ri) suppository

supposizióne *f* supposition; presumption

suppó·sto -sta *adj* alleged || *m* supposition || *f* suppository

suppurare *intr* (ESSERE & AVERE) to suppurate

supremazìa *f* supremacy

suprè·mo -ma *adj* supreme

surclassare *tr* to outclass

surgelare (surgèlo) *tr* to quick-freeze

surreali·sta *mf* (-sti -ste) surrealist

surrenale *adj* adrenal (*gland*)

surrène *m* (anat) adrenal gland

surriscaldare *tr* to overheat

surrogare §209 (surrògo) *tr* to replace

surroga·to -ta *adj* replaceable || *m* makeshift, substitute, ersatz

suscettìbile *adj* susceptible; touchy

suscitare (sùscito) *tr* to rouse; to give rise to; to provoke

susina *f* plum

susino *m* plum tree

susseguènte *adj* subsequent, following

susseguire (susséguo) *intr* (ESSERE) (with *dat*) to follow || *ref* to follow one after the other

sussidiare §287 *tr* to subsidize

sussidià·rio -ria (-ri -rie) *adj* subsidiary; (nav) auxiliary || *m* supplementary text book; subsidiary

sussì·dio *m* (-di) subsidy; assistance, relief; **sussidi audiovisivi** audio-visual aids; **sussidi didattici** teaching aids; **sussidio di disoccupazione** unemployment compensation

sussiè·go *m* (-ghi) stiffness, haughtiness

sussistènza *f* substance; subsistence; (mil) quartermaster corps

sussìstere §114 *intr* (ESSERE & AVERE) to subsist; to be, exist

sussultare *intr* to start, jump; to quake

sussulto *m* start, jump; **sussulto di terremoto** earth tremor

sussurrare *tr* to whisper; to murmur, mutter || *intr* to whisper; to rustle || *ref*—**si sussurra** it is rumored

sussurra·tóre -trice *mf* whisperer; grumbler

sussurrì·o *m* (-i) whispering; murmur; rustle

sussurro *m* whisper; murmur

susta *f* temple (*of spectacles*); (coll) spring

suvvìa *interj* come!, come on!

svagare §209 *tr* to entertain; to distract || *ref* to have a good time; to relax

svaga·to -ta *adj* absent-minded; inattentive

sva·go *m* (-ghi) entertainment, diversion; avocation, hobby

svaligiare §290 *tr* to ransack; to rob; to pirate

svaligia·tóre -trice *mf* thief, robber

svalutare (svàluto & svaluto) *tr* to devaluate; to depreciate; to belittle || *ref* to depreciate

svalutazióne *f* depreciation

svanire §176 *intr* (ESSERE) to evaporate; to vanish

svani·to -ta *adj* faded, evaporated; vanished; enfeebled

svantàg·gio *m* (-gi) disadvantage

svantaggió·so -sa [s] *adj* disadvantageous

svaporare (svapóro) *intr* (ESSERE) to evaporate; to vanish

svaria·to -ta *adj* varied; **svaria·ti -te** several

svarióne *m* blunder, gross error

svasare *tr* to transplant from a pot; to make (*e.g., a gown*) flare

svasa·to -ta *adj* bell-mouthed, flaring

svecchiare §287 (svècchio) *tr* to renew; to rejuvenate; to modernize

svedése [s] *adj* Swedish; safety (*match*) || *mf* Swede || *m* Swedish

svéglia *f* awakening; reveille; alarm clock; **dare la sveglia a** to wake up

svegliare §280 *tr & ref* to wake up

svegliarino *m* alarm clock; (coll) rebuke

své·glio -glia *adj* (-gli -glie) awake; alert || *f* see **sveglia**

svelare (svélo) *tr* to reveal; to unveil || *ref* to reveal oneself; **svelarsi per** to reveal oneself to be

svèllere §267 *tr* (lit) to eradicate

sveltézza *f* quickness; slenderness

sveltire §176 *tr* to make shrewd; to quicken, accelerate || *ref* to become smart

svèl·to -ta *adj* quick; slender; brisk; quick-witted; **alla svelta** quickly; **svelto di lingua** loose-tongued; **svelto di mano** light-fingered || **svelto** *interj* quick!

svenare (svéno) *tr* to bleed to death; (fig) to bleed || *ref* to bleed to death; (fig) to bleed oneself white

svéndere §281 *tr* to sell below cost; to undersell

svéndita *f* clearance sale

svenévole *adj* maudlin, mawkish

svenevolézza *f* maudlinness, mawkishness

svenimén·to *m* faint, swoon

svenire §282 *intr* (ESSERE) to faint

sventagliare §280 *tr* to fan; to flash, display

sventagliata *f* blow with a fan; volley

sventare (svènto) *tr* to foil, thwart; (naut) to spill (*a sail*)

sventa·to -ta *adj* careless, thoughtless

svèntola *f* fan (*to kindle fire*); (coll) box, slap; **a sventola** (*ears*) that stick out

sventolare (svèntolo) *tr* to wave; to fan; to winnow || *intr* to flutter || *ref* to fan oneself

sventolì·o *m* (-i) fluttering, flutter

sventramén·to *m* demolition; disembowelment; hernia

sventrare (svèntro) *tr* to demolish; to disembowel; to draw (*a fowl*)

sventura *f* misfortune, mishap; bad luck

sventura·to -ta *adj* unfortunate, unlucky

sverginare (svérgino) *tr* to deflower

svergognare (svergógno) *tr* to put to shame; to unmask

svergogna·to -ta *adj* shameless

svergolare (svérgolo) *tr & ref* to warp; (mach) to twist

svernare (svèrno) *intr* to winter

svérza [dz] *f* big splinter

sverzino [dz] *m* lash, whipcord

svestire (svèsto) *tr* to undress; to hull (*rice*); (fig) to strip ‖ *ref* to undress; **svestirsi di** to shed (*e.g., leaves*)

svettare (svétto) *tr* to pollard, top ‖ *intr* to stand out; to sway (*said of a tree*)

Svè·vo -va *adj & m* Swabian

Svèzia, la Sweden

svezzaménto *m* weaning

svezzare (svézzo) *tr* to wean; **svezzare da** to break (*s.o.*) of (*e.g., a habit*)

sviare §119 *tr* to turn aside; to lead astray ‖ *intr & ref* to go astray; to straggle; (rr) to run off the track

svignare *intr* (ESSERE) to slip away ‖ *ref*—**svignarsela** to sneak away

svilire §176 *tr* to devaluate

svillaneggiare §290 (svillanéggio) *tr* to insult, abuse

sviluppare *tr* to develop; to cause; (lit) to uncoil ‖ *intr* (ESSERE & AVERE) & *ref* to develop; to break out (*said of fire*)

sviluppo *m* development; puberty

svincolare (svìncolo) *tr* to free; to clear (*at customs*)

svìncolo *m*—**svincolo autostradale**

interchange; **svincolo doganale** customs clearance

svirilizzare [ddzz] *tr* (fig) to emasculate

svisare *tr* to alter, distort

sviscerare (svìscero) *tr* to eviscerate; to examine thoroughly ‖ *ref*—**sviscerarsi per** to be crazy about; to bow and scrape to

sviscera·to -ta *adj* ardent, passionate; obsequious

svista *f* slip, error, oversight

svitare *tr* to unscrew

svìzze·ro -ra *adj & mf* Swiss ‖ **la Svìzzera** Switzerland

svocia·to -ta *adj* hoarse

svogliatézza *f* laziness; listlessness

svoglia·to -ta *adj* lazy; listless

svolazzare *intr* to flutter, flit

svolazzo *m* flutter; short flight; curlicue, flourish

svòlgere §289 *tr* to unwrap; to unfold; to unwind; to develop; to pursue (*an activity*); to dissuade ‖ *ref* to unwind; to free oneself; to develop; to take place; to unfold

svolgiménto *m* development; composition

svòlta *f* turn; curve; turning point

svoltare (svòlto) *tr* to unwrap ‖ *intr* to turn

svotare §257 or **svuotare (svuòto)** *tr* to empty

T

T, t [ti] *m & f* eighteenth letter of the Italian alphabet

tabac·càio -càia *mf* (-cài -càie) tobacconist

tabaccare §197 *intr* to take snuff

tabaccherìa *f* cigar store

tabacchièra *f* snuffbox

tabac·co *m* (-chi) tobacco; **tabacco da fiuto** snuff

tabarro *m* winter coat; cloak

tabèlla *f* tablet; list; schedule; (coll) clapper, noisemaker; **tabella di marcia** timetable

tabellare *adj* (typ) on wooden blocks; scheduled

tabellóne *m* board; bulletin board; (basketball) backboard

tabernàcolo *m* tabernacle

ta·bù *adj invar & m* (-bù) taboo

tàbula *f*—**far tabula rasa di** to make a clean sweep of

tabulare (tàbulo) *tr* to tabulate

tabulatóre *m* tabulator

tabulatrice *f* printer (*of computer*)

tac·ca *f* (-che) notch; size; kind; tally; blemish; (typ) nick; **di mezza tacca** middle-sized; mediocre; **tacca di mira** rear sight (*of firearm*)

tacca·gno -gna *adj* stingy, closefisted ‖ *mf* miser

taccheggia·tóre -trice *mf* shoplifter ‖ *f* prostitute, streetwalker

taccheggiatura *f* or **tacchég·gio** *m* (-gi) shoplifting

tacchétto *m* high heel; cleat (*on soccer or football shoe*)

tacchina *f* turkey hen

tacchino *m* turkey

tàc·cia *f* (-ce) notoriety

tacciare §128 *tr*—**tacciare di** to accuse of, charge with

tac·co *m* (-chi) heel; block; (typ) underlay; **battere i tacchi** to take to one's heels

taccóne *m* (coll) patch; (coll) hobnail; **battere il taccone** to take to one's heels

taccuino *m* pocketbook; notebook

tacére *m* silence; **mettere a tacere** to silence ‖ **§268** *tr* to conceal, withhold; to imply, understand ‖ *intr* to keep quiet; to stop playing; to quiet down; to be silent; **far tacere** to silence; **taci!** (coll) shut up!

tachìmetro *m* tachometer; (aut) speedometer

tacitare (tàcito) *tr* to silence, satisfy (*a creditor*); to pay off

tàci·to -ta *adj* silent; tacit

tacitur·no -na *adj* taciturn

tafano *m* horsefly, gadfly

tafferù·glio *m* (-gli) scuffle

taffe·tà *m* (-tà) taffeta; **taffetà adesivo**

or **inglese** adhesive plaster, court plaster

tàglia *f* ransom, reward; size; build; tally; (mach) tackle

tagliabór·se *m* (**-se**) pickpocket

tagliabò·schi *m* (**-schi**) woodcutter, woodsman

tagliacar·te *m* (**-te**) letter opener, paper knife

tagli·àcque *m* (**-àcque**) cutwater (*of bridge*)

tagliaèrba *adj invar* grass-cutting

tagliafèr·ro *m* (**-ro**) cold chisel

taglialé·gna *m* (**-gna**) woodcutter

tagliama·re *m* (**-re**) cutwater (*of ship*)

tagliando *m* coupon

tagliapiè·tre *m* (**-tre**) stonecutter

tagliare §280 *tr* to cut; to cut down; to cut off; to pick (*a pocket*); to cross (*finish line*); to tailor (*a suit*); to blend (*wine*); to turn off (*e.g., water*); **tagliare a fette** to slice; **tagliare in due** to split; **tagliare i panni addosso a qlcu** to slander s.o.; **tagliare i ponti con** to sever relations with; **tagliare i viveri a** to cut off supplies from; **tagliare la corda** to run away; **tagliare la strada a** to stand in the way of; (aut) to cut in front of; **tagliare le gambe a** to make wobbly (*said of wine*) ‖ *intr* to cut; to bite (*said of cold*); **tagliare per una scorciatoia** to take a shortcut ‖ *ref* to cut oneself; to tear (*said of material*)

tagliasìga·ri *m* (**-ri**) cigar cutter

tagliata *f* cut; clearing; (mil) abatis; **tagliata ai capelli** haircut

tagliatèlle *fpl* noodles

taglia·to -ta *adj* cut; fashioned; **essere tagliato per** to be cut out for; **tagliato all'antica** old-fashioned; **tagliato con l'accetta** rough-hewn ‖ *f* see **tagliata**

taglia·tóre -trice *mf* cutter

tagliènte *adj* cutting ‖ *m* edge

taglière *m* carving board

taglierina *f* paper cutter

tà·glio *m* (**-gli**) cut; cutting; dressmaking; cutting edge; sharpness; blending (*of wines*); size; denomination (*of. paper money*); crossing (*of t*); (bb) fore edge; **a due tagli** double-edged; **a tagli** by the slice; **dare un taglio a** to chop; **di taglio** edgewise; **rifare il taglio a** to sharpen; **taglio cesareo** Caesarean section; **taglio d'abito** suiting; **taglio dei capelli** haircut; **venire in taglio** to come in handy

tagliòla *f* trap

tagliuzzare *tr* to shred, cut into shreds

tailandése [s] *adj & mf* Thai

Tailàndia, la Thailand

tailleur *m* (**tailleur**) woman's tailored costume

talal·tro -tra *pron indef* another, some other

tàlamo *m* (lit) nuptial bed

talare *adj* ankle-length ‖ *f* soutane, cassock

talché *conj* so that

talco *m* talcum; talcum powder

tale *adj* such; such a; that; **il tale** such and such a; **u tale** such a; a certain; **un tal quale** such a; a certain ‖ *pron* so-and-so; **il tal dei tali** so-and-so; Mr. so-and-so; **il tale** that fellow; that guy; **quel tale** that fellow, that guy; **tale e quale** like; **tali e quali** exactly, word for word; **un tale** someone, a certain person

talèa *f* (hort) cutting

talènto *m* talent; inclination; **a proprio talento** gladly, willingly; **di mal talento** grudgingly; **andare a talento a** to suit, e.g., **non gli va a talento nulla** nothing suits him

talismano *m* talisman

tallire §176 *intr* (ESSERE & AVERE) to sprout

tallonare (**tallóno**) *tr* (sports) to be at the heels of

talloncino *m* coupon, stub

tallóne *m* heel; coupon, stub; tang (*of knife*); **tallone d'Achille** Achilles heel

talménte *adv* so, so much

talóra *adv* sometimes

talpa *f* mole

talu·no -na *pron indef* some; someone, somebody ‖ **talu·ni -ne** *adj & pron indef* some

talvòlta *adv* sometimes

tamarindo *m* tamarind

tamburéggiare §290 (**tamburéggio**) *intr* to drum; to beat down (*said, e.g., of hail*)

tamburèllo *m* tambour (*for embroidering*); (mus) tambourine

tamburino *m* drummer

tamburo *m* drum; barrel (*of watch; of windlass*); **a tamburo battente** on the spot

tamerice *f* tamarisk

Tamigi *m* Thames

tampòco *adv*—**né tampoco** (archaic) nor . . . either

tamponaménto *m* stopping, plugging; rear-end collision

tamponare (**tampóno**) *tr* to tampon, plug; to collide with; to hit from the rear; (surg) to tampon

tampóne *m* plug, tampon; pad; (mus) drumstick; (rr) buffer; (surg) tampon; **tampone di vapore** vapor lock

tana *f* burrow; den; hole; hovel; base (*in children games*)

tanàglie *fpl* var of **tenaglie**

tan·ca *f* (**-che**) can, jerry can; tank

tanfo *m* musty or stuffy smell

tangènte *adj* tangent ‖ *f* tangent; (com) commission

tàngere §269 *tr* (lit) to touch

Tàngeri *f* Tangier

tànghero *m* boor, lout

tangìbile *adj* tangible

tàni·ca *f* (**-che**) var of **tanca**

tantino *m*—**un tantino** a little, e.g., **è un tantino arrabbiato** he is a little angry; a little bit, e.g., **un tantino di dolce** a little bit of cake

tan·to -ta *adj & pron indef* such; so; so much; as much; **a dir tanto** or **a far tanto** at the most; **ai tanti**

(del mese) on such and such a day (of the month); **a tanto** to such a point; to such a level; **e tanto** odd, e.g., **mille dollari e tanto** a thousand odd dollars; **è tanto** it has been a long time, e.g., **è tanto che lo conosco** it has been a long time since I made his acquaintance; **fra tanto** meanwhile; **senza tanto chiasso** without any noise; **tan-ti -te** many; so many; as many; a lot, e.g., **grazie tante!** thanks a lot! **tanti . . . che** so many . . . that; **tanti . . . quanti** as many . . . as; **tanto di guadagnato** so much the better ‖ **tanto** adv so much; so; only, e.g., **tanto per passare il tempo** only to pass the time; anyhow; anyway; **nè tanto nè quanto** at all; **tant'è** it's the same; **tanto che** so much that, e.g., **mi ha annoiato tanto che l'ho mandato via** he bothered me so much that I dismissed him; **tanto . . . che** both . . . and, e.g., **tanto Maria che Roberto** both Mary and Robert; so much . . . that; **tanto fa** or **vale** it's all the same; **tanto meglio** so much the better; **tanto meno** so much the less; **tanto per cambiare** as usual; **tanto più . . . quanto più** the more . . . the more; **tanto . . . quanto as . . . as** ‖ s—**ascoltare con tanto d'orecchie** to be all ears; **di tanto in tanto** from time to time

tapi·no -na adj (lit) wretched ‖ mf (lit) wretch

tappa f stopping place; stop; stage, leg; (sports) lap; **bruciare le tappe** to press on, keep going; **fare tappa** to stop

tappabu·chi mf (-chi) makeshift, pinch hitter, substitute

tappare tr to cork, plug; to shut up tight ‖ ref to shut oneself in; to plug (e.g., one's ears)

tapparèlla f (coll) inside rolling shutter

tappéto m rug, carpet; (sports) canvas, mat; **mettere al tappeto** (boxing) to knock out; **tappeto erboso** lawn, green; **tappeto verde** gambling table

tappezzare (tappèzzo) tr to paper (a wall); to upholster

tappezzerìa f wallpaper; upholstery; upholster's shop; tapestry; wallflower

tappezzière m paperhanger; upholsterer

tappo m cork, stopper; cap; plug; **tappo a corona** bottle cap; **tappo a vite** screw cap

tara f tare

taràntola f tarantula

tarare tr to tare; to set, adjust

tara·to -ta adj net (weight); calibrated (instrument); sickly, weak

tarchia·to -ta adj stocky, sturdy

tardare tr to delay ‖ intr to delay; to be late

tardi adv late; **al più tardi** at the latest; **a più tardi!** so long!; **fare tardi** to be late; **più tardi** later; later on; **sul tardi** in the late afternoon

tardi·vo -va adj late; retarded, slow; belated

tar·do -da adj slow; late; **di età tarda** of advanced years; **tardo d'ingegno** slow-witted

tardó·ne -na adj slow-moving ‖ mf slowpoke ‖ f old dame, middle-aged vamp

tar·ga f (-ghe) plate; nameplate; shield; (aut) license plate; (sports) trophy

targare §209 tr (aut) to register

targatura f (aut) registration

targhétta f nameplate

tariffa f tariff; rate; rates

tariffà·rio -ria (-ri -rie) adj tariff; rate ‖ m price list; rate book

tarlare tr to eat (said of woodworms or moths) ‖ intr (ESSERE) & ref to become worm-eaten; to become moth-eaten

tarlo m woodworm; moth; bookworm; (fig) gnawing

tarma f moth; clothes moth

tarmare tr to eat (said of moths) ‖ intr (ESSERE) & ref to become moth-eaten

tarmici·da (-di -de) adj moth-repelling ‖ m moth repellent

taròc·co m (-chi) tarot; tarok

tarpare tr to clip; **tarpare le ali a** to clip the wings of

tartagliare §280 tr & intr to stutter, stammer

tàrta·ro -ra adj Tartar ‖ m tartar; Tartar ‖ **Tartaro** m Tartarus

tartaru·ga f (-ghe) turtle, tortoise; tortoise shell

tartassare tr to ill-treat; to harass

tartina f slice of bread and butter; canapé

tartufo m truffle; (fig) tartuffe, hypocrite

ta·sca f (-sche) pocket; briefcase; **aver le tasche piene di** to be sick and tired of; **da tasca** pocket; **rompere le tasche a** (vulg) to bother, annoy; **tasca in petto** inside pocket

tascàbile adj pocket; vest-pocket

tascapane m knapsack, rucksack

tascata f pocketful

taschino m vest pocket, small pocket

tassa f tax; (coll) duty, fee; **tassa complementare** surtax; **tassa di circolazione** road-use tax; **tassa di registro** registration fee; **tassa scolastica** tuition

tassàbile adj taxable

tassàmetro m taximeter; **tassametro di parcheggio** parking meter

tassare tr to tax; to assess ‖ ref to pledge money

tassati·vo -va adj positive; specific; peremptory

tassazióne f taxation; tax

tassèllo m dowel; inlay; plug; patch; reinforcement

tas·sì m (-sì) taxi, taxicab

tassi·sta mf (-sti) taxi driver

tasso m stake (anvil); yew tree; (com) rate (e.g., of interest); (zool) badger; **tasso valutario fluttuante** (econ) fluctuation of currency rate

tastare tr to touch; to feel; to probe; **tastare il terreno** (fig) to see how the land lies

tastièra f keyboard; manual (of organ)

tasto *m* touch, feeling, feel; plug (*e.g.,
in watermellon*); key (*of piano or
typewriter*); sample (*in drilling*);
tasto bianco white key, natural; **toccare un tasto falso** to strike a sour
note

tastóni *adv*—**a tastóni** gropingly

tàtti·co -ca (*-ci -che*) *adj* tactical; tactful ‖ *m* tactician ‖ *f* tactics; prudence; tactfulness

tatto *m* touch; tact

tatuàg·gio *m* (*-gi*) tattoó

tatuare (**tàtuo**) *tr* to tattoo

taumatur·go *m* (*-gi* & *-ghi*) wonder-
worker

tauri·no -na *adj* taurine, bull-like; bull

tavèrna *f* tavern, inn

tavernière *m* tavernkeeper

tàvola *f* board, plank; slab; table;
tablet; bookplate; list; **tavola a ribalta** drop-leaf table; **tavola armonica** (mus) sound board; **tavola calda**
cafeteria, snack bar; **tavola da stirare** ironing board; **tavola di salvezza**
(fig) last recourse, lifesaver; **tavola
imbandita** open house; **tavola nera**
blackboard; **tavola operatoria** operating table; **tavola pitagorica** multi-
plication table; **tavola reale** back-
gammon; **tavole di fondazione** charter (*of a charitable institution*)

tavolàc·cio *m* (*-ci*) wooden board (*on
which soldiers on guard and prisoners used to sleep*)

tavolare (**tàvolo**) *tr* to board up

tavolata *f* tableful

tavolato *m* planking; plateau

tavolétta *f* small table; tablet; bar (*e.g.,
of chocolate*)

tavolière *m* chessboard table; card
table; plateau, tableland

tavolino *m* small table; desk

tàvolo *m* table; desk; **tavolo di gioco**
gambling table; **tavolo d'ufficio**
office desk

tavolòzza *f* palette

tazza *f* cup; bowl

tazzina *f* demitasse

tazzóna *f* mug

te §5 *pron pers*

tè *m* (**tè**) tea; **tè danzante** tea dance,
thé dansant

tèa *adj fem*—**rosa tea** tea rose

teatrale *adj* theatrical

teatro *m* theater; performance; drama;
stage; (fig) scene; **che teatro!** what
fun!; **teatro dell'opera** or **teatro lirico**
opera house; **teatro di posa** (mov)
studio; **teatro di prosa** legitimate
theater

teatróne *m* large theater; (coll) excellent box office

Tèbe *f* Thebes

tè·ca *f* (*-che*) case; (eccl) reliquary

tecnicismo *m* technicality

tècni·co -ca (*-ci -che*) *adj* technical ‖
m technician; engineer ‖ *f* technique;
technics

téco §5 *prep phrase* (lit) with you

tedé·sco -sca *adj* & *mf* (*-schi -sche*)

tediare §287 (**tèdio**) *tr* to bore ‖ *ref*
to get bored

tè·dio *m* (*-di*) dullness, tedium, boredom; **recare tedio a** to annoy, bother

tedió·so -sa [*s*] *adj* dull, tedious

tegame *m* pan; **al tegame** fried (*e.g.,
eggs*)

tegamino *m* small pan; **uova al tegamino** fried eggs

téglia *f* pan; baking pan

tégola *f* tile; (fig) blow

tégolo *m* tile

teièra *f* teapot, teakettle

tèk *m* teak

téla *f* linen; cloth; material; canvas,
oil painting; (fig) plot, trap; (lit)
weft; (theat) curtain; **far tela** (coll)
to beat it; **tela batista** batiste; **tela
cerata** oilcloth; **tela da imballaggio**
burlap; **tela di ragno** cobweb; **tela di
sacco** sackcloth; **tela greggia** gunny,
burlap; **tela smeriglio** emery cloth

te·làio *m* (*-lài*) loom; frame; embroidery frame; sash; stretcher (*for oil
painting*); (aut) chassis; **telaio di
finestra** window sash

teleama·tóre -trice *mf* TV viewer

telear·ma *f* (*-mi*) guided missile

telecabina *f* cable car

telecàmera *f* TV camera

telecomanda·to -ta *adj* remote-control

telecomando *m* remote control

telecommentatóre *m* TV newscaster

telecròna·ca *f* (*-che*) TV broadcast;
telecronaca diretta live broadcast

telecroni·sta *mf* (*-sti -ste*) TV news
announcer, TV newscaster

telediffusióne *f* TV broadcasting

teledram·ma *m* (*-mi*) teleplay

teleféri·ca *f* (*-che*) cableway, telpherage

telefonare (**telèfono**) *tr* & *intr* to telephone ‖ *ref* to call one another

telefonata *f* telephone call

telefòni·co -ca *adj* (*-ci -che*) telephone

telefoni·sta *mf* (*-sti -ste*) telephone
operator, central; telephone installer

telèfono *m* telephone; **telefono a gettone** pay telephone (*operated by
tokens*); **telefono a moneta** pay telephone; **telefono interno** intercom-
munication system, intercom

telegèni·co -ca *adj* (*-ci -che*) telegenic,
videogenic

telegiornale *m* TV newscast

telegrafare (**telègrafo**) *tr* & *intr* to telegraph

telegràfi·co -ca *adj* (*-ci -che*) telegraphic

telegrafi·sta *mf* (*-sti -ste*) telegrapher;
telegraph installer

telègrafo *m* telegraph; **telegrafo di
macchina** (naut) engine-room telegraph; **telegrafo ottico** heliograph;
wigwag; **telegrafo senza fili** wireless

telegram·ma *m* (*-mi*) telegram

teleguida *f* remote control

teleguidare *tr* to control from a distance, to operate by remote control

Telèmaco *m* Telemachus

telèmetro *m* telemeter; range finder

teleobbiettivo *m* (phot) telephoto lens

telepatìa *f* telepathy

teleproiètto *m* guided missile

telericévere §141 *tr* to receive by TV;
to teleview

teleschérmo *m* television screen

telescò·pio *m* (**-pi**) telescope
telescrivènte *f* teletypewriter; ticker
telescriventi·sta *mf* (**-sti -ste**) teletype operator
teleselezióne *f* (telp) direct distance dialing
telespetta·tóre -trice *mf* televiewer
teletrasméttere §198 *tr* to televise, telecast
teletrasmissióne *f* telecast
televisióne *f* television, TV
televisi·vo -va *adj* television, TV
televisóre *m* television set
tellina *f* sunset shell or clam
télo *m* piece of cloth; yardage, length of material; (mil) side (*of tent*)
tèlo *m* (lit) dart, arrow
telóne *m* canvas; (theat) curtain
tè·ma *m* (**-mi**) theme; (gram) stem
téma *f* (lit) fear; **per tema di** (lit) for fear of
temerarie·tà *f* (**-tà**) recklessness, rashness
temerà·rio -ria *adj* (**-ri -rie**) reckless, rash; ill-founded
temére (**tèmo** & **tèmo**) *tr* to fear; to respect || *intr* to fear; **temere di** to be afraid to
temeri·tà *f* (**-tà**) temerity
temibile *adj* frightening
tèmpera *f* tempera, distemper
temperala·pis *m* (**-pis**) or **temperamati·te** *m* (**-te**) pencil sharpener
temperaménto *m* middle course, compromise; temper, temperament
temperante *adj* temperate, moderate
temperanza *f* temperance
temperare (**tèmpero**) *tr* to mitigate; to temper; to sharpen (*a pencil*)
tempera·to -ta *adj* temperate; tempered (*metal*); watered (*wine*)
temperatura *f* temperature; **temperatura ambiente** room temperature
temperino *m* penknife, pocketknife
tempèsta *f* tempest, storm; **tempesta in un bicchier d'acqua** tempest in a teapot
tempestare (**tempèsto**) *tr* to pound; to pepper, pelt; to pester || *intr* to storm
tempesta·to -ta *adj* studded, spangled
tempesti·vo -va *adj* timely
tempestó·so -sa [s] *adj* stormy, tempestuous
tèmpia *f* temple (*side of forehead*); **tempie** (lit) head
tempiale *m* temple (*in loom; of spectacles*)
tempière *m* Templar
tèm·pio *m* (**-pi** & **-pli**) temple (*edifice*)
tempi·sta *mf* (**-sti -ste**) person or athlete showing good timing; (mus) rhythmist
tèmpo *m* time; weather; age; period, stage; cycle (*of internal-combustion engine*); (gram) tense; (mus) tempo, (mus) movement; (sports) period; (theat, mov) part; **ad un tempo** at the same time; **al tempo che Berta filava** long ago; **a suo tempo** in due time; long ago; **a tempo debito** in due time; **a tempo e luogo** at the opportune time; **a tempo perso** in

one's spare time; **aver fatto il proprio tempo** to be outdated; **c'è sempre tempo** we are still in time; **col tempo** in time; **dare tempo al tempo** to allow time to heal things; **darsi del bel tempo** to have a good time; **da tempo** for a long time; **del tempo di** from the time of; **è scaduto il tempo utile** the time is up; **è tanto tempo** it's been a long time; **fa bel tempo** the weather is fine; **il Tempo** Father Time; **lasciare il tempo che trova** to have no effect; **molto tempo dopo** long afterward; **nel tempo che** while; **per tempo** early; **prima del tempo** formerly; **quanto tempo** how long; **sentire il tempo** to feel the weather in one's bones; **senza por tempo in mezzo** without any delay; **tempi che corrono** present times; **tempo fa** some time ago; **tempo legale** legal time limit; **tempo libero** leisure time; **tempo supplementare** (sports) overtime; **tempo un . . . within** (*e.g., one month*); **un tempo** long ago
temporale *adj* temporal || *m* storm
temporàne·o -a *adj* temporary, provisional
temporeggiare §290 (**temporéggio**) *intr* to temporize
tèmpra *f* (metallurgy) tempering, temper; (mus) timber; (fig) fiber, timber
temprare (**tèmpro**) *tr* to temper (*metal*); to harden, inure || *ref* to become hardened or inured
tenace *adj* tenacious; tough
tenàcia *f* tenacity
tenaci·tà *f* (**-tà**) strength, resistance; tenacity
tenàglie *fpl* nippers, pincers, pliers; tongs; **a tenaglie** (mil) pincers (*e.g., action*)
tènda *f* curtain; awning; tent
tendènza *f* tendency; trend
tendenzió·so -sa [s] *adj* tendentious
tèn·der *m* (**-der**) (rr) tender
tèndere §270 *tr* to stretch; to tighten; to draw (*a bow*); to cast (*nets*); to lay (*snares*); to reach out (*one's hand*); to prick up (*one's ears*); to draw (*s.o.'s attention*); to set (*sail*) || *intr* to aim; to lean; to tend; to tend to be
tendina *f* curtain, blind
tèndine *m* (anat) tendon
tendiscar·pe *m* (**-pe**) shoetree
tenditóre *m* turnbuckle; **tenditore della racchetta** (tennis) press
tendóne *m* big curtain; canvas; tent (*of circus*); (theat) curtain
tendòpo·li *f* (**-li**) tent city
tènebre *fpl* darkness
tenebró·so -sa [s] *adj* dark, gloomy
tenènte *m* lieutenant; (mil) first lieutenant; (nav) lieutenant junior grade; **tenente colonnello** (mil) lieutenant colonel; **tenente di vascello** (nav) lieutenant senior grade
tenére §271 *tr* to hold; to have; to keep; to stand (*e.g., rough sea*); to wear; to make (*a speech*); to follow

(*a course*); **tenere a battesimo** to stand for, sponsor; **tenere al corrente** to keep informed; **tenere a memoria** to remember; **tenere da conto** to hold in high esteem; to take good care of (*s.th*); **tenere d'occhio** to keep an eye on; **tenere la destra** to keep to the right; **tenere la strada** (aut) to hug the road; **tenere la testa a partito** to mend one's ways; **tenere le distanze** to keep aloof; **tenere mano a** to connive with; **tenere presente** to bear in mind; **tenere qlco a conto** to take good care of s.th || *intr* to hold; to take root; **tenerci che** to be anxious for, e.g., **ci tengo che vinca le elezioni** I am anxious for him to win the elections; **tenere a destra** to keep to the right; **tenere alle apparenze** to stand on ceremony; to keep up appearances; **tenere da** to hail from; to take after; **tenere dietro a** to follow; to keep abreast of; **tenere duro** to hold fast; **tenere per** (sports) to be a fan of || *ref* to hold; to hold on; to keep; to keep (*e.g., ready*); to regard oneself; **tenersi a** to adhere to (*e.g., a treaty*); to hold on to; to stick to; to follow; **tenersi a galla** to stay afloat; **tenersi al largo** (naut) to keep to the open sea; **tenersi al vento** (naut) to sail to leeward; (fig) to follow a safe course; **tenersi in piedi** to stand up; **tenersi per mano** to hold hands; **tenersi sulle proprie** to keep aloof

tenerézza *f* tenderness; fondness, endearment

tène·ro -ra *adj* tender || *m* tender portion

tènia *f* tapeworm

teni·tóre -trice *mf* keeper

tènnis *m* tennis; **tennis da tavolo** table tennis, ping-pong

tenni·sta *mf* (**-sti -ste**) tennis player

tennìsti·co -ca *adj* (**-ci -che**) tennis

tenóne *m* tenon

tenóre *m* character, tone; tenor; alcoholic content; manner (*of living*); **tenore di vita** way of life; standard of living

tensióne *f* tension; **alta tensione** high tension; **tensione sanguigna** blood pressure

tentàcolo *m* tentacle

tentare (**tènto**) *tr* to try, attempt; to assay; to tempt; (lit) to touch

tentativo *m* attempt; **tentativo di furto** attempted robbery

tenta·tóre -trice *adj* tempting || *m* tempter || *f* temptress

tentazióne *f* temptation

tentennare (**tenténno**) *tr* to shake; to rock || *intr* to shake; to wobble; to hesitate; to stagger

tentóne or **tentóni** *adv* blindly; gropingly; at random

tènue *adj* small (*intestine*); (lit) tenuous, thin

tenu·to -ta *adj* bound, obliged || *f* capacity, volume; estate, farm; uniform; outfit; (sports) endurance,

resistance; **a tenuta d'acqua** watertight; **a tenuta d'aria** airtight; **tenuta dei libri** bookkeeping; **tenuta di gala** (mil, nav) full-dress uniform; **tenuta di servizio** (mil) fatigues; **tenuta di strada** (aut) roadability

tenzóne *f* combat; poetic contest

teologìa *f* theology

teòlo·go *m* (**-gi**) theologian

teorè·ma *m* (**-mi**) theorem

teorèti·co -ca *adj* (**-ci -che**) theoretic(al)

teorìa *f* theory; (lit) series, row

teòri·co -ca (**-ci -che**) *adj* theoretical || *m* theoretician

tèpi·do -da *adj* var of **tiepido**

tepóre *m* warmth

téppa *f* underworld, rabble

teppi·sta *m* (**-sti**) hoodlum, hooligan

terapèuti·co -ca (**-ci -che**) *adj* therapeutic || *f* therapeutics

terapìa *f* therapy; **terapia convulsivante** or **terapia d'urto** shock therapy

Terèsa *f* Theresa

tèrgere §162 *tr* (lit) to wipe

tergicristallo *m* windshield wiper

tergiversare (**tergivèrso**) *intr* to stall; to beat around the bush

tèr·go *m* (**-ghi**) back (*of a coin*); **a tergo** on the reverse side || *m* (**-ga** *fpl*) (lit) back; **volgere le terga** (lit) to turn one's back

termale *adj* thermal (*e.g., waters*)

tèrme *fpl* spa, hot spring

tèrmi·co -ca *adj* (**-ci -che**) thermal; heat, heating

terminale *adj* & *m* terminal

terminare (**tèrmino**) *tr* to border; to end, terminate || *intr* (ESSERE) to end, terminate

terminazióne *f* termination; completion; (gram) ending

tèrmine *m* border; marker; term; deadline; end; goal; boundary, bounds; (fig) point; **a termini di legge** according to law; **avere termine** to end; **in altri termini** in other words; **mezzo termine** half measure; **porre termine a** to put an end to; **portare a termine** to put through

terminologìa *f* terminology

termistóre *m* (elec) thermistor

tèrmite *f* termite

termoconvettóre *m* baseboard radiator

termocòppia *f* thermocouple

termodinàmi·co -ca (**-ci -che**) *adj* thermodynamic || *f* thermodynamics

termòforo *m* heating pad

termòmetro *m* thermometer

termonucleare *adj* thermonuclear

tèr·mos *m* (**-mos**) thermos bottle

termosifóne *m* radiator; hot-water heating system; steam heating system

termòstato *m* thermostat

termovisièra *f* electric defroster

tèrno *m* tern (*in lotto*); **vincere un terno al lotto** to hit the jackpot

tèrra *f* earth; land; ground; world; city, town; dirt; soil; clay; **essere a terra** to be downcast; to be broke; to be flat (*said of a tire*); **rimanere a terra** to miss the boat; **sotto terra** underground; **terra bruciata** scorched earth; **terra di nessuno** no man's land; **terra di Siena** sienna; **terra ferma** terra firma; mainland; **terra** skimming the ground; (naut) close to the shore; (fig) mediocre, second-rate

terracòtta f (**terrecòtte**) terra cotta; earthenware

terrafèrma f mainland (as distinguished from adjacent islands); terra firma (dry land, not air or water)

terràglia f crockery; **terraglie** earthenware

terranò·va m (**-va**) Newfoundland (dog) || **Terranova** f Newfoundland

terrapièno m embankment

terrazza f terrace; **a terrazza** terraced

terrazza·no -na mf villager

terrazzo m balcony; terrace; ledge, shelf; terrazzo

terremota·to -ta adj hit by an earthquake || mf earthquake victim

terremòto m earthquake

terré·no -na adj terrestrial, earthly; ground-floor; first-floor || m ground floor; first floor; ground; soil; land, plot of ground; combat zone; terrain; **preparare il terreno** to work the soil; (fig) to pave the way; **scendere sul terreno** to fight a duel; **tastare il terreno** to feel one's way; **terreno di gioco** (sports) field

tèrre·o -a adj wan, sallow

terrèstre adj terrestrial; ground, land || m earthling

terrìbile adj terrible; awesome, awful

terrìc·cio m (**-ci**) soil; top soil

terriè·ro -ra adj land; landed

terrificare §197 (**terrìfico**) tr to terrify

terrina f tureen

territò·rio m (**-ri**) territory

terróre m terror

terrorismo m terrorism

terrori·sta mf (**-sti -ste**) terrorist

terrorizzare [ddzz] tr to terrorize

terró·so -sa [s] adj dirty (e.g., spinach); dirty-earth (color); (chem) rare-earth (metal)

tèr·so -sa adj clear

tèrza f third grade; (aut) third; (eccl) tierce; (rr) third class

terzaforzì·sta (**-sti -ste**) adj of the third force || m partisan of the third force

terzaròlo m (naut) reef

terzétto m trio

terzià·rio -ria adj (**-ri -rie**) tertiary

terzina f tercet

terzino m (soccer) back

tèr·zo -za adj & pron third || m third; third party || f see **terza**

terzùlti·mo -ma adj third from the end

tésa [s] f brim (of hat); snare, net

tesare [s] (**téso**) tr to pull taut

tèschio m (**-schi**) skull

tè·si f (**-si**) thesis; dissertation

té·so -sa [s] adj taut, tight; strained; outstretched (hand); **con le orecchie tese** all ears || f see **tesa**

tesorerìa f treasury; liquid assets

tesorière m treasurer

tesòro m treasure; treasury; thesaurus; bank vault; **far tesoro di** to treasure, prize; **tesoro mio!** my darling!

Tèspi m Thespis

tèssera f card; domino (piece); tessera (of mosaic)

tessera·to -ta adj card-carrying; rationed || mf card-carrying member; holder of ration card

tèssere tr to weave; to spin

tèssile adj textile || m textile; **tessili** textile workers

tessilsac·co m (**-chi**) garment bag

tessi·tóre -trice mf weaver

tessitura f weaving; spinning mill; (mus) range; (fig) plot

tessuto m cloth, fabric; tissue

tèsta f head; mind; bulb (of garlic); spindle (of wheel); warhead (of torpedo); row (of bricks); **a testa** apiece; per capita; **a testa a testa** neck and neck; **fare di testa propria** to act on one's own; **fare la testa grossa a** to stun; to annoy; **levarsi di testa** to forget about; **mettersi in testa di** to get it into one's head to; **non avere testa di** + inf to not feel like + ger; **non sapere dove battere la testa** to know which way to turn; **per una corta testa** by a neck; **rompersi la testa** to rack one's brains; **tenere testa a** to face up to; **testa coda** (aut) spin; **testa di ponte** (mil) bridgehead; **testa di sbarco** beachhead; **testa e croce** head or tails

testaménto m will, testament || **Antico** or **Vecchio Testamento** Old Testament; **Nuovo Testamento** New Testament

testardàggine f stubborness

testar·do -da adj stubborn

testata f headboard (of bed); top; end (e.g., of beam); heading (of newspaper); butt with the head; nose (of rocket)

tèste m witness

testé adv (lit) a short time ago; (lit) presently, in a little while

testìcolo m testicle

testièra f headboard; crown (of harness); battering ram

testimòne m witness; **testimone di nozze** best man; **testimone di veduta** or **testimone oculare** eyewitness

testimonianza f testimony

testimoniare §282 (**testimònio**) tr to attest; to depose, testify; **testimoniare il falso** to bear false witness || intr to bear witness

testimò·nio m (**-ni**) (coll) witness

testina f small head; whimsical person; boiled head of veal; head (e.g., of tape recorder)

tèsto m text; pie dish; (coll) flower vase; **fare testo** to serve as a model

testó·ne -na (coll) adj dolt; stubborn person

testuale adj textual; word-for-word

testùggine f turtle; tortoise

tètano m tetanus

tè·tro -tra adj (lit) gloomy, dark

tétta f (coll) teat

tettarèlla f nipple

tétto m roof; ceiling price; home; **senza tetto** homeless; **tetto a capanna** gable roof; **tetto a padiglione** hip

roof; **tetto a una falda** lean-to roof;
　tetto di paglia thatched roof
tettóia f shed; pillared roof
tettóia-garage f (**tettóie-garage**) carport
tettùc·cio m (**-ci**) (aut) roof; (aut) top;
　tettuccio a bulbo dome; **tettuccio
　rigido** (aut) convertible top
ti §5 pron
tìbia f tibia, shinbone
tic m (**tic**) twitch; habit
ticchettì·o m (**-ì**) click (of typewriter);
　patter (of rain); tick (of clock)
fìc·chio m (**-chi**) whim; tic; viciousness
　(of animal); blemish
tièpi·do -da adj tepid, lukewarm
tifo m typhus; **fare il tifo per** to root
　for; to be a fan of
tifoidèa f typhoid fever
tifóne m typhoon
tifó·so -sa [s] adj rooting || mf fan,
　rooter
tì·glio m (**-gli**) linden, lime; bast; fiber
tiglió·so -sa [s] adj tough, fibrous
tigna f ringworm; (coll) tightwad
tignòla f clothes moth
tigra·to -ta adj striped; tabby
tigre f tiger
timballo m pie, meat pie; timbale; (lit)
　drum
timbrare tr to stamp; to cancel (stamps)
timbro m stamp; character (of a
　writer); (mus) timbre; **timbro di
　gomma** rubber stamp; **timbro po-
　stale** postmark
timidézza f shyness, bashfulness; ti-
　midity
tìmi·do -da adj shy, bashful; timid ||
　mf shy person
timo m (anat) thymus; (bot) thyme
timóne m rudder, helm; shaft, pole
　(of cart); **timone di direzione** (aer)
　rudder; **timone di profondità** (aer)
　elevator; (nav) diving plane (of sub-
　marine)
timonièra f (naut) pilot house
timonière m helmsman, steersman;
　coxswain
timoniè·ro -ra adj rudder; tail (feather)
　|| f see **timoniera**
timora·to -ta adj conscientious; timo-
　rato di Dio** God-fearing
timóre m fear; awe; **avere timore di**
　to fear
timoró·so -sa [s] adj timorous
tìmpano m (archit) tympanum; (anat)
　eardrum; (mus) kettledrum; **rom-
　pere i timpani a** to deafen
tin·ca f (**-che**) (ichth) tench
tinèllo m pantry; breakfast room
tìngere §126 tr to dye; to dirty, soil;
　to color || ref to dye (e.g., one's
　hair); to put on make-up; to become
　colored
tino m tub, vat
tinòzza f tub, washtub
tinta f paint; color; dye; shade; stain;
　calcare le tinte to exaggerate; **mezza
　tinta** halftone, shade; **vedere qlco a
　fosche tinte** to take a dim view of
　s.th; **vedere qlco a tinte rosee** to see
　s.th through rose-colored glasses
tintarèlla f (coll) suntan
tinteggiare §290 (**tintéggio**) tr to calci-

mine; to whitewash; to tint; to paint
　(e.g., a house)
tintinnare intr (ESSERE & AVERE) to
　jingle; to clink
tintinnì·o m (**-ì**) jingling; clink
tìn·to -ta adj dyed; tinged; soiled; (lit)
　dark || f see **tinta**
tintó·re -ra mf dyer; dry cleaner
tintorìa f dyeworks; dry cleaning estab-
　lishment; dyeing
tintura f dyeing; dyestuff; tincture;
　smattering; **tintura di iodio** iodine
tìpi·co -ca adj (**-ci -che**) typical
tipificare §197 (**tipìfico**) tr to standard-
　ize
tipizzare [ddzz] tr to standardize
tipo adj invar typical, e.g., **famiglia
　tipo** typical family || m type; stan-
　dard, model; fellow, guy; phylum
　(in taxonomy); **bel tipo** (coll) char-
　acter, card; **coi tipi di** printed in the
　shop of; **sul tipo di** similar to; **vero
　tipo** prototype, epitome
tipografìa f typography; print shop
tipogràfi·co -ca adj (**-ci -che**) typo-
　graphical
tipògrafo m typographer; owner of
　print shop, printer
tipòmetro m (typ) line gauge
tiptologìa f table rapping (during
　séance); tapping in code (among jail-
　birds)
tiraba·ci m (**-ci**) (coll) spitcurl
tiràg·gio m (**-gi**) draft; **a tiraggio for-
　zato** forced-draft
tiralìne·e m (**-e**) ruling pen
tirannìa f tyranny
tirànni·co -ca adj (**-ci -che**) tyrannical
tiran·no -na adj tyrannical || mf tyrant
tirante m brace; rod; strap; trace (of
　harness); **tirante degli stivali** boot-
　strap
tirapiè·di m (**-di**) hangman's assistant;
　underling
tirapu·gni m (**-gni**) brass knuckles
tirare tr to pull; to draw; to tug; to
　suck; to haul in (nets); to deserve
　(a slap); to pluck; to throw; to give
　(blows); to utter (oaths); to shoot
　(arrows, bullets); to stretch; to
　tighten (one's belt); to print; to
　make (an addition); (sports) to force
　(the pace); **tirare a lucido** to polish;
　tirare a sé to attract; **tirare a sorte**
　to draw lots for; **tirare fuori** to draw
　out; to pull out; to get out; **tirare
　giù** to lower; to jot down; (coll) to
　gulp down; **tirare gli orecchi a** to
　punish by yanking the ears of; **tirare
　il collo a** to wring the neck of; **tirare
　in ballo** to bring up (a subject);
　tirare l'acqua al proprio mulino to
　look out for number one; **tirare
　l'anima coi denti** to be at the end of
　one's rope; **tirare l'aria** to draw (said
　of a chimney); **tirare le cuoia** (slang)
　to kick the bucket; **tirare per i ca-
　pelli** to drag by the hair; to drag in;
　to push, coerce; **tirare per le lunghe**
　to stretch out; **tirare su** to lift; to
　raise (children); to pull up || intr to
　be too tight (said of clothes); to
　shoot; to blow (said of wind); to

draw (said, e.g., of chimney); **tirare a** to tend toward, lean toward; **tirare a** + inf to try to + inf; **tirare a campare** (coll) to goldbrick; **tirare avanti** to go ahead; to manage to get along; **tirare di boxe** to box; **tirare diritto** to go straight ahead; **tirare di scherma** to fence; **tirare in lungo** to delay, linger; to dillydally; **tirare innanzi** to keep on going; to go ahead; **tirare sul prezzo** to haggle; **tirare via** to hurry along ‖ ref— **tirarsi addosso** (coll) to bring upon oneself; **tirarsi dietro** to drag along; **tirarsi fuori da** to get out of (e.g., trouble); **tirarsi gente in casa** to keep open house; **tirarsi indietro** to move back; **tirarsi in là** to move aside; **tirarsi su** to get up; to recover; to roll up (one's sleeves); **tirarsi un colpo di rivoltella** to shoot oneself

tirastiva·li m (-li) bootjack
tirata f pull; stretch; tirade
tirati·ra m (-ra) (coll) yen; **fare a tiratira per** (coll) to scramble for
tira·to -ta adj taut; forced (smile); drawn (face); tight, closefisted; **tirato con** short of ‖ f see tirata
tira·tóre -trice mf shot; **tiratore scelto** sharpshooter; **franco tiratore** sniper
tiratura f printing
tirchierìa f stinginess
tìr·chio -chia (-chi -chie) adj stingy, closefisted ‖ mf miser
tirèlla f trace (of harness)
tirétto m (coll) drawer
tiritèra f rigmarole
tiro m pull; pair, brace (e.g., of oxen); throw; fire, shot; trick; **a tiro** within reach; **a un tiro di schioppo** within gunshot; **da tiro** draft; **fuori del tiro dell'orecchio** out of earshot; **tiro alla fune** tug of war; **tiro di piattello** trapshooting; **tiro a quattro** four-in-hand; **tiro a segno** rifle range; shooting gallery
tiroci·nio m (-ni) apprenticeship; internship; **tirocinio didattico** practice teaching
tiròide f thyroid
tirolése [s] adj & mf Tyrolean
tirrèni·co -ca adj (-ci -che) Tyrrhenian
Tirrèno m Tyrrhenian Sea
tisana f tea, infusion
tisi f consumption, tuberculosis
tìsi·co -ca (-ci -che) adj consumptive; stunted ‖ mf consumptive
titàni·co -ca adj (-ci -che) titanic
titànio m titanium
titillare tr to tickle
titolare adj titular; regular, full-time ‖ m owner, boss; incumbent ‖ v (titolo) tr to name, call
titolo m title; heading; name; caption; entry (in dictionary); grade; fineness (of gold); (chem) titer; (educ) credit; **avere titolo a** to have a right to; **a titolo di** as, by way of; **titoli di testa** (mov) credits; **titolo al portatore** security payable to bearer; **titolo azionario** share; **titolo corrente** subtitle; **titolo di credito** instrument of

credit; certificate; deed; conveyance; **titolo di studio** degree, diploma; credits; **titolo di trasporto** travel document
titubare (tìtubo) intr to hesitate; to waver
tiziané·sco -sca adj (-schi -sche) titian; Titian
tì·zio m (-zi) fellow, guy
tizzo or **tizzóne** m brand, firebrand
to' interj here!; well!
tobò·ga m (-ga) toboggan
toccafèrro m tag (game)
toccamano m handshake (to close a deal); bribe, under-the-table tip
toccante adj touching, moving
toccare §197 (tócco) tr to touch; to reach; to concern; to push (a button); to play (an instrument); to feel; to hit (the target); to border on (e.g., the age of forty); **toccare con mano** to make sure of; **toccare il cielo col dito** to be in seventh heaven; **toccare nel vivo** to touch to the quick; **toccare terra** to land; **toccarne molte** to get a good thrashing; **toccato!** touché! ‖ intr (ESSERE) to be touching; **toccare a** to be up to, e.g., **tocca a lui** it's up to him; to have to, e.g., **le tocca partire domani** she has to leave tomorrow; to deserve, e.g., **gli è toccato il premio** he deserved the prize ‖ ref to meet, e.g., **gli estremi si toccano** extremes meet
toccasa·na [s] m (-na) cure-all, panacea
tocca·to -ta adj touché; touched in the head, nutty; **già toccato** abovementioned ‖ f (mus) toccata
tóc·co -ca (-chi -che) adj touched, nutty; spoiled (fruit) ‖ m touch; knock; one o'clock (P.M.); (coll) stroke
tòc·co m (-chi) chunk, piece; mortarboard; toque; **un bel tocco di ragazza** a buxom lass
tò·ga f (-ghe) gown, academic gown; (hist) toga
tògliere §127 tr to remove, take away; to take; to cut (telephone connection); to deduct; to take off; to preclude, prevent; **togliere a** to take away from; **togliere al cielo** (lit) to praise to the skies; **togliere di mezzo** to remove; to do away with; **togliere la parola a** to take the floor from; **togliere l'onore a** to dishonor; **togliere una spina dal cuore a** to relieve the heart and mind of ‖ intr— **tolga Dio!** God forbid! ‖ ref to take off (e.g., one's coat); to have (e.g., a tooth) pulled; to satisfy (a whim); **togliersi di mezzo** to get out of the way; **togliersi la vita** to take one's life; **togliersi qlcu dai piedi** to get rid of s.o.
tòlda f (naut) deck
tolemài·co -ca adj (-ci -che) Ptolemaic
tolétta f dressing table; dressing room; toilet, washroom; dress, gown; **fare toletta** or **farsi la toletta** to make one's toilet
tolleràbile adj tolerable

tollerante *adj* tolerant; liberal

tolleranza *f* tolerance; leeway

tollerare (**tòllero**) *tr* to tolerate; to bear, stand

tòl·to **-ta** *adj* taken; except, leaving out, e.g., **tolta sua figlia** leaving his daughter out ‖ *m*—**il mal tolto** ill-gotten goods

to·màio *m* (**-mài** & **-màia** *fpl*) or **to·màia** *f* (**-màie**) upper (*of shoe*)

tómba *f* tomb, grave

tombale *adj* grave (*e.g., stone*)

tombino *m* sewer inlet

tómbola *f* bingo; (coll) tumble

tombolare (**tómbolo**) *tr* (coll) to tumble down (*the steps*) ‖ *intr* (ESSERE) to fall headlong; (coll) to go to rack and ruin; (aer) to tumble

tómbolo *m* fall, tumble; bolster; lace pillow; (coll) fatso; **fare un tombolo** to go to rack and ruin; to lose one's position

Tommaso *m* Thomas

tòmo *m* volume; (coll) character

tòna·ca *f* (**-che**) (eccl) frock; (eccl) soutane; **gettare la tonaca alle ortiche** to doff the cassock

tonare §257 *intr* to peal; to thunder ‖ *impers* (ESSERE & AVERE)—**tuona** it is thundering

tondeggiante *adj* round; rounded; chubby; curvaceous

tondino *m* coaster; iron rod (*for reinforced concrete*); (archit) molding (*at top or bottom of column*); (archit) astragal

tón·do **-da** *adj* round; (typ) roman ‖ *m* round; circle; plate, dish; (typ) roman; **in tondo** around

tónfo *m* splash; thump

tòni·co **-ca** (**-ci** **-che**) *adj* tonic ‖ *m* tonic (*medicine*) ‖ *f* (mus) tonic

tonificare §197 (**tonìfico**) *tr* to invigorate

tonnara *f* tuna nets

tonnellàg·gio *m* (**-gi**) tonnage

tonnellata *f* ton; **tonnellata di stazza** displacement ton

tónno *m* tuna

tòno *m* tone; tune; hue; style; (mus) pitch; (mus) key; **darsi tono** to put on airs; **di tono** stylish; **fuori di tono** out of tune

tonsilla *f* tonsil

tonsura *f* tonsure

tón·to **-ta** *adj* (coll) dumb, stupid

topàia *f* rat's nest; hovel

topà·zio *m* (**-zi**) topaz

tòpi·co **-ca** (**-ci** **-che**) *adj* topical ‖ *f* topic; (coll) blunder

tòpo *m* mouse; rat; **topo campagnolo** field mouse; **topo d'acqua** water rat; **topo d'albergo** hotel thief; **topo d'auto** car thief; **topo di biblioteca** bookworm

topografia *f* topography

topolino *m* little mouse ‖ **Topolino** *m* Mickey Mouse

toporagno *m* shrew

tòppa *f* patch; keyhole

tòppo *m* stump; headstock (*of lathe*)

torace *m* thorax

tórba *f* peat

tórbi·do **-da** *adj* cloudy; murky ‖ *m* trouble; **pescare nel torbido** to fish in troubled waters; **torbidi** disorder

torbièra *f* peatbog

tòrcere §272 *tr* to twist; to wring; to bend, curve; to curl (*the lips*); to lead astray ‖ *intr* (ESSERE) to bend, curve ‖ *ref* to writhe; to bend over; **torcersi dalle risa** to split with laughter

torchiare §287 (**tòrchio**) *tr* to press

tòr·chio *m* (**-chi**) press; printing press

tòr·cia *f* (**-ce**) torch

torcicòllo *m* stiff neck; (orn) wryneck

torcinaso [s] *m* (vet) twitch

tórdo *m* thrush; simpleton

torèllo *m* young bull; (naut) garboard

torèro *m* bullfighter

tórlo *m* yolk

tórma *f* crowd, throng; herd

torménta *f* blizzard

tormentare (**tormènto**) *tr* to torture, torment; to pester, nag ‖ *ref* to worry

tormènto *m* torture, torment; pang; bore, pest, annoyance

tornacónto *m* interest, advantage

tornante *m* curve

tornare (**tórno**) *tr* (lit) to restore; (obs) to turn ‖ *intr* (ESSERE) to return; to go back; (coll) to jibe, agree, square; **tornare a** to be profitable to; **tornare a + inf** verb + again, e.g., **tornare a essere** to become again; **tornare a fare** to do again; **tornare a bomba** to return to the point; **tornare a galla** to come back to the surface; **tornare a gola** to repeat (*said of food*); **tornare a onore** or **a qlcu** to do credit to s.o.; **tornare a pennello** to fit to a T; **tornare in sé** to come to; **tornare opportuno** or **utile a** to suit, e.g., **non gli tornò opportuno vendere la casa** it did not suit him to sell the house; **tornare utile** to come in handy; **tornare sulle proprie decisioni** to change one's mind

tornasóle *m* litmus

tornèllo *m* turnstile

tornèo *m* tournament, tourney

tór·nio *m* (**-ni**) lathe

tornire §176 *tr* to turn, turn up (*on a lathe*); to polish

tornitóre *m* lathe operator

tórno *m* turn; period (*of time*)**;** **levarsi di torno** to get rid of; **torno torno** all around

tòro *m* bull; (archit, geom) torus; (lit) marital bed ‖ **Toro** *m* (astrol) Taurus

torpèdine *f* torpedo

torpedinièra *f* destroyer escort; torpedo-boat destroyer

torpè·do *f* (**-do**) (aut) touring car

torpedóne *m* bus, motor coach

tòrpi·do **-da** *adj* torpid, sluggish; numb

torpóre *m* torpor, sluggishness; numbness

tórre *f* tower; (chess) castle; (nav) turret; **torre campanaria** bell tower; **torre d'avorio** ivory tower; **torre di**

lancio (rok) gantry; **torre pendente** leaning tower

torrefare §173 *tr* to roast (*coffee*)

torreggiante *adj* towering

torreggiare §290 (**torréggio**) *intr* to tower

torrènte *m* torrent

torrenziale *adj* torrential

torrétta *f* turret; (nav) conning tower (*of submarine*); (archit) bartizan

tòrri·do -da *adj* torrid

torrióne *m* donjon; (nav) conning tower (*of battleship*)

torróne *m* nougat

torsióne *f* torsion

tórso *m* stalk; core (*of fruit*); torso, trunk; **a torso nudo** bare-chested

tórsolo *m* core; stalk; stem; **non vale un torsolo** it's not worth a fig

tórta *f* pie; cake, tart; **torta di mele** apple pie

tòrta *f* twist

tortièra *f* baking pan

tòr·to -ta *adj* twisted; crooked; gloomy (*face*) ‖ *m* wrong; **a torto** unjustly; **avere torto** to be wrong; **avere torto marcio** to be dead wrong; **dar torto a** to lay the blame on; **fare torto a** to wrong, e.g., **fece torto al proprio fratello** he wronged his own brother; to bring discredit upon ‖ *f* see **tòrta** ‖ **torto** *adv* askance

tórtora *f* turtledove

tortuó·so -sa [s] *adj* winding; ambiguous; (fig) devious

tortura *f* torture

torturare *tr* to torture; to pester ‖ *ref* to torment oneself; **torturarsi il cervello** to rack one's brain

tosare (**tóso**) *tr* to clip, crop; to shear; (fig) to fleece

tosa·tóre -trice *mf* clipper, shearer ‖ *f* clippers; lawn mower

tosatura *f* sheepshearing; clip (*of wool*)

tosca·no -na *adj* & *m* Tuscan ‖ *m* stogy ‖ **Toscana, la** Tuscany

tósse *f* cough; **tosse asinina** or **canina** whooping cough

tòssi·co -ca (**-ci -che**) *adj* toxic ‖ *m* (archaic) poison

tossicòmane *mf* drug addict

tossicomanìa *f* drug addiction

tossina *f* toxin

tossire (**tósso**) & §176 *intr* to cough

tostapa·ne *m* (**-ne**) toaster

tostare (**tòsto**) *tr* to toast; to roast (*e.g., coffee*)

tò·sto -sta *adj* (lit) prompt; (lit) impudent; (lit) brazen (*face*) ‖ **tosto** *adv* (lit) soon; **ben tosto** (lit) very soon; **tosto che** (lit) as soon as

tòt *adj pl invar* so many, that many ‖ *pron invar* so much, that much

totale *adj* & *m* total

totalità·rio -ria *adj* (**-ri -rie**) total, complete; totalitarian

totalizzare [ddzz] *tr* to add up; to make (*so many points*)

totalizzatóre [ddzz] *m* pari-mutuel; betting window; (mach) totalizator

tòtano *m* squid; (orn) tattler

totocàlcio *m* soccer pool

tovàglia *f* tablecloth

tovagliòlo *m* napkin

tòz·zo -za *adj* stubby, stocky ‖ *m* piece (*of fresh bread*); crust (*of bread*)

tra *prep* among; between

trabàccolo *m* small fishing boat

traballare *intr* to shake; to totter; to wobble; to stagger; to toddle

trabìccolo *m* frame for bedwarmer; jalopy; hulk

traboccante *adj* overflowing

traboccare §197 (**trabócco**) *tr* to knock down ‖ *intr* to overflow (*said of container*) ‖ *intr* (ESSERE) to overflow (*said of liquid*) ‖ *intr* (ESSERE & AVERE) to tip (*said of scales*); **far traboccare** to make (*the scales*) tip

trabocchétto *m* pitfall; trapdoor

tradòc·co *m* (**-chi**)—**trabocco di sangue** internal hemorrhage

tracagnòt·to -ta *adj* stubby, stocky ‖ *mf* stocky person

tracannare *tr* to gulp down

tracchég·gio *m* (**-gi**) delay; (fencing) feint

tràc·cia *f* (**-ce**) track; trace, clue; trail; outline, plan; (lit) line, row; **buona traccia** right track; **fare la traccia a** to open the way for; **in** or **sotto traccia** concealed (*e.g., wiring*); **tracce** tinge; (chem) traces

tracciante *adj* tracer (*bullet*)

tracciare §128 *tr* to trace; to pave (*the way*); to outline; (lit) to track

tracciato *m* tracing, drawing; outline; map; layout

trachèa *f* trachea, windpipe

tracòlla *f* baldric; shoulder strap; **a tracolla** slung across the shoulders

tracòllo *m* collapse, debacle

tracotanza *f* arrogance

tradiménto *m* treason; treachery; **a tradimento** unawares, unexpectedly; treacherously

tradire §176 *tr* to betray; to fail (*a person; said of memory*) ‖ *ref* to give oneself away

tradi·tóre -trice *adj* charming, seductive; treacherous; deceitful, faithless ‖ *mf* traitor; betrayer ‖ *f* traitress

tradizionale *adj* traditional

tradizióne *f* tradition

tradòtta *f* military train

tradurre §102 *tr* to translate

tradut·tóre -trice *mf* translator

traduzióne *f* translation

traènte *mf* (com) drawer

trafela·to -ta *adj* breathless, out of breath

trafèrro *m* (elec) air gap; (elec) spark gap

trafficante *m* dealer, trader; trafficker

trafficare §197 (**tràffico**) *tr* to sell; to traffic in ‖ *intr* to trade, deal; to hustle

tràffi·co *m* (**-ci**) traffic

trafficó·ne -na *mf* hustler

trafiggere §104 *tr* to pierce, stab, transfix; to wound

trafila *f* routine; red tape; (mach) drawplate

trafilare *tr* to wiredraw

trafilétto *m* (journ) short feature, special item; (journ) notice

trafitta *f* stab wound; shooting pain

trafittura *f* stab; shooting pain

traforare (tralfòro & tralfóro) *tr* to bore; to pierce; to carve (*wood*); to pink (*leather*); to embroider with open work

tralfóro *m* boring; tunnel; open work

trafugare §209 *tr* to purloin; to sneak off with

tragèdia *f* tragedy; **far tragedie** (coll) to make a fuss

traghettare (traghétto) *tr* to ferry

traghétto *m* ferry; **traghetto spaziale** space shuttle

tràgi·co -ca (-ci -che) *adj* tragic ‖ *m* tragedian; **il tragico** (fig) the tragic

tragitto *m* journey; (obs) ferry

traguardo *m* sight; aim; goal; finish line; (phot) viewfinder; (sports) tape

traiettòria *f* trajectory; path

tràina *f* towline; **pescare alla traina** to troll

trainare (tràino) *tr* to drag, tug, pull

tràino *m* drag; load; trailer

tralasciare §128 *tr* to interrupt; to omit; **non tralasciare di** not to fail to

tràl·cio *m* (-ci) stem (*of vine*)

tralic·cio *m* (-ci) ticking, bedtick; trellis; tower (*of high-tension line*)

tralice *m*—**in tralice** askance

tralignare *intr* (ESSERE & AVERE) to degenerate

tram *m* (tram) streetcar

trama *f* woof, weft; plot (*of play*); texture (*of cloth*)

tramà·glio *m* (-gli) trammel net

tramandare *tr* to hand down

tramare *tr* & *intr* to weave; to plot

trambusto *m* bustle

tramestì·o *m* (-i) bustle, confusion

tramèzza [ddzz] *f* partition

tramezzare (tramèzzo) [ddzz] *tr* to interpose; to partition

tramezzino [ddzz] *m* small partition; sandwich; sandwich man

tramèzzo [ddzz] *m* partition; side dish; (sew) insertion ‖ *adv* in between; **tramezzo a** among

tràmite *m* intermediary; (lit) pass; **per tramite di** through ‖ *prep* (coll) by; by means of

tramòg·gia *f* (-ge) hopper

tramontana *f* north wind; **perdere la tramontana** to lose one's bearings

tramontare (tramónto) *intr* (ESSERE) to set (*said, e.g., of sun*); to end

tramónto *m* setting; sunset; decline

tramortire §176 *tr* to stun ‖ *intr* (ESSERE) to faint, swoon

trampolière *m* wading bird; (orn) stilt

tràmpoli *mpl* stilts

trampolino *m* diving board; springboard; ski jump; (fig) springboard

tramutare *tr* to transfer; to transform

tràn·cia *f* (-ce) slice; (mach) shears

tranèllo *m* trap, snare

trangugiare §290 *tr* to swallow; to gulp down

tranne *prep* except, save; **tranne che** unless

tranquillante *m* tranquilizer

tranquillare *tr* & *ref* (lit) to tranquilize; to calm down

tranquilli·tà *f* (-tà) tranquillity

tranquillizzare [ddzz] *tr* to tranquilize; to reassure ‖ *ref* to become reassured

tranquil·lo -la *adj* tranquil, calm; clear (*conscience*)

transatlànti·co -ca *adj* & *m* (-ci -che) transatlantic

transazióne *f* compromise

transènna *f* bar, barrier

transètto *m* (archit) transept

trànsfu·ga *m* (-ghi) (lit) deserter

transigere §165 *tr* to settle ‖ *intr* to compromise

transistóre *m* transistor

transitàbile *adj* passable

transitare (trànsito) *intr* to move; to walk

transiti·vo -va *adj* transitive

trànsito *m* passage; traffic; (lit) passing; **di transito** transient

transitò·rio -ria *adj* (-ri -rie) temporary; transitory; transitional

transizióne *f* transition

transoceàni·co -ca *adj* (-ci -che) transoceanic

transòni·co -ca *adj* (-ci -che) transonic

transunto *m* abstract, summary (*of a document*)

trantràn *m* routine

tran·vài *m* (-vài) (coll) streetcar

tranvìa *f* streetcar line

tranvià·rio -ria *adj* (-ri -rie) streetcar

tranvière *m* streetcar conductor; motorman

trapanare (tràpano) *tr* to drill; (surg) to trephine

tràpano *m* drill; (surg) trephine; **trapano a vite** automatic drill

trapassare *tr* to pierce; (fig) to grieve; (poet) to cross; (lit) to pass, spend ‖ *intr* (ESSERE) to go through; to pass (*said of an animate*); (lit) to pass away; **trapassare da, per** or **al di là di** to come through (*said, e.g., of a nail, light*)

trapassato *m* (lit) deceased; **trapassato prossimo** past perfect

trapasso *m* crossing; transfer; transition; (lit) passing, death

trapelare (trapélo) *intr* (ESSERE) to ooze; to trickle out; to leak through; (fig) to leak out

trapè·zio *m* (-zi) trapeze; (geom) trapezoid

trapezòide *adj* trapezoidal ‖ *m* trapezoid

trapiantare *tr* to transplant ‖ *ref* to transfer

trapianto *m* transplantation; transplant; **trapianto cardiaco** heart transplant

tràppola *f* trap; (coll) gadget; (fig) lie; **trappola esplosiva** booby trap

trapunta *f* quilt

trapuntare *tr* to quilt; to embroider

trapun·to -ta *adj* quilted; embroidered; studded ‖ *m* embroidery ‖ *f* see **trapunta**

trarre §273 *tr* to pull; to drag; to draw; to bring; to deduct; to lead; to unsheathe (*a sword*); to heave (*a sigh*); to spin (*silk, wool,* etc.); **il dado è tratto** the die is cast; **trarre dalla prigione** to free from prison; **trarre d'impaccio** to get (*s.o.*) out of trouble; **trarre fuori** to extract; **trarre in inganno** to deceive; **trarre in rovina** to ruin; **trarre per mano** to lead by the hand ‖ *intr* to kick (*said of a mule*); (lit) to run; (lit) to blow (*said of the wind*) ‖ *ref* to take off (*e.g., one's hat*); **trarsi d'impaccio** to get out of trouble; **trarsi indietro** to pull back; **trarsi in disparte** to move aside

trasalire [s] §176 *intr* (ESSERE & AVERE) to start, jump

trasanda·to -ta *adj* untidy, slovenly

trasbordare (**trasbórdo**) *tr* to transfer, transship

trasbórdo *m* transfer, transshipment

trascéndere §245 *tr* to transcend ‖ *intr* (ESSERE) to go to excesses

trascinare *tr* to drag; to stir; to enthrall; to lead astray; **trascinare la vita** to barely make ends meet ‖ *ref* to drag oneself; to drag on

trascolorare (**trascolóro**) *tr* to discolor; to change the color of ‖ *intr* (ESSERE) & *ref* to discolor; to change color

trascórrere §139 *tr* to pass (*time*); to skim through (*e.g., a book*); (lit) to go through ‖ *intr* to go to excesses ‖ *intr* (ESSERE) to elapse, pass

trascórso *m* slip (*e.g., of pen*); peccadillo

trascrìvere §250 *tr* to transcribe

trascrizióne *f* transcription; registration (*e.g., of a deed*)

trascuràbile *adj* negligible

trascurare *tr* to neglect; to fail; to disregard ‖ *ref* to not take care of oneself

trascuratézza *f* negligence, neglect; carelessness; slovenliness

trascura·to -ta *adj* neglected; careless; slovenly

trasecolare (**trasècolo**) [s] *intr* (ESSERE & AVERE) to marvel, be astonished

trasferìbile *adj* transferable

trasferiménto *m* transfer; conveyance

trasferire §176 *tr* to transfer; to assign, convey ‖ *ref* to move

trasfèrta *f* business trip; traveling expenses, per diem

trasfigurare *tr* to transfigure; to distort (*the truth*) ‖ *ref* to be transfigured; to change countenance

trasfocatóre *m* (phot) zoom lens

trasfóndere §178 *tr* to transfuse; (fig) to instill

trasformàbile *adj* transformable; (aut) convertible

trasformare (**trasfórmo**) *tr* to transform; to alter ‖ *ref* to transform oneself; to be transformed

trasformati·vo -va *adj* (gram) transformational

trasformatóre *m* transformer

trasformazióne *f* transformation

trasformi·sta *mf* (**-sti -ste**) quick-change artist

trasfusióne *f* transfusion

trasgredire §176 *tr* & *intr* to transgress

trasgressióne *f* transgression

trasgressóre *m* transgressor

trasla·to -ta *adj* figurative; metaphorical; (lit) transferred ‖ *m* figure of speech; metaphor

traslitterare (**traslìttero**) *tr* to transliterate

traslocare §197 (**traslòco**) *tr* to transfer; to move ‖ *intr* & *ref* to move

traslò·co *m* (**-chi**) moving

traslùci·do -da *adj* translucent

trasméttere §198 *tr* to transmit; (rad) to broadcast

trasmetti·tóre -trice *mf* transmitter ‖ *m* (naut) engine-room telegraph; (telg) sender

trasmigrare *intr* (ESSERE & AVERE) to transmigrate ‖ *intr* (ESSERE) to pass, pass on

trasmissióne *f* transmission; conveyance; broadcast; telecast; **trasmissione del pensiero** thought transference

trasmittènte *adj* transmitting; broadcasting ‖ *f* broadcasting station

trasmutare *tr* to transmute; to change

trasogna·to -ta [s] *adj* dreamy; daydreaming; dazed

trasparènte *adj* transparent ‖ *m* transparency

trasparènza *f* transparence; **in trasparenza** against the light

trasparire §108 *intr* (ESSERE) to appear; to shine; to show through; to show, be revealed (*said of feelings*); **far trasparire** to reveal

traspirare *intr* to perspire ‖ *intr* (ESSERE) to show, be revealed

traspirazióne *f* perspiration

traspórre §218 *tr* to transpose

trasportare (**traspòrto**) *tr* to transport; to carry away; to transfer; to translate; to postpone; (mus) to transpose; **lasciarsi trasportare** to be carried away ‖ *ref* to move; (fig) to go back

trasporta·tóre -trice *mf* carrier ‖ *m* (mach) conveyor belt; (phot) sprocket

traspòrto *m* transportation; transport; transfer; eagerness; moving; (mus) transposition; **trasporto funebre** funeral

trasposi·tóre -trice *mf* (mus) transposer

trassa·to -ta *adj* paying ‖ *m* drawee

trastullare *tr* to amuse; to entice ‖ *ref* to have a good time; to loiter

trastullo *m* play, game; fun; plaything

trasudare [s] *tr* to ooze; (fig) to exude ‖ *intr* to ooze (*said of a wall*) ‖ *intr* (ESSERE) to drip (*said of perspiration*)

trasversale *adj* transverse, cross ‖ *f* crossroad

trasvèr·so -sa *adj* transverse ‖ *m* transverse beam

trasvolare (**trasvólo**) *tr* to fly over, cross by air ‖ *intr*—**trasvolare su** to skip over

trasvolata *f* non-stop flight

tratta *f* tug, pull; (rr) stretch; (com)

draft; (lit) crowd; **tratta dei neri** slave trade; **tratta delle bianche** white slavery

trattàbile *adj* negotiable; friendly, sociable

trattaménto *m* treatment; working conditions; food, spread; reception, welcome; **trattamento di favore** special treatment; **trattamento di quiescenza** retirement benefits

trattare *tr* to treat; to deal with; to transact; to wield; to play (*an instrument*); to work (*e.g. iron*); to deal in; **trattare qlcu da bugiardo** to call s.o. a liar; **trattare da cane** to treat like a dog ‖ *intr* to bargain; **trattare di** to deal with; to take care of; to treat, handle ‖ *ref* to take good care of oneself ‖ *impers* (ESSERE) **si tratta di** it's question of

trattà·rio -ria *mf* (**ri -rie**) drawee

trattativa *f* negotiation

trattato *m* treatise; treaty

trattazióne *f* treatment

tratteggiare §290 (**trattéggio**) *tr* to sketch; to outline; to hatch

tratté•gio *m* (**-gi**) hatching

trattenére §271 *tr* to keep; to entertain; to withhold; to hold back; to detain ‖ *ref* to stop; to refrain; to remain

tratteniménto *m* entertainment, party; delay

trattenuta *f* withholding; checkoff

trattino *m* dash; hyphen

trat•to -ta *adj* drawn, extracted ‖ *m* stretch; span; passage; tract; gesture; throw (*of dice*); stroke (*of pen*); bearing; section; (chess) move; **a larghi tratti** in broad outline; **a tratti** from time to time; **a un tratto** all of a sudden; at the same time; **dare un tratto alla bilancia** to tip the scales; **tratti** features; **tratti del volto** features; **tratto di corda** strappado; **tratto di unione** hyphen; **tutto d'un tratto** all of a sudden; **un bel tratto** quite a while

trat•tóre -trice *mf* innkeeper; restaurateur ‖ *m* tractor ‖ *f* tractor (*vehicle*)

trattoria *f* inn, restaurant

tratturo *m* cow path

traumatizzare [ddzz] *tr* to traumatize

travagliare §280 *tr* to torment; to molest ‖ *intr & ref* to toil, labor

travà•glio *m* (**-gli**) suffering; toil; trave (*to inhibit horse being shod*); **travaglio di parto** labor pains; **travaglio di stomaco** upset stomach

travasare *tr* to pour off; to decant; to transfer ‖ *ref* to spill

travaso *m* pouring off; transfer; **travaso di bile** gall bladder attack; **travaso di sangue** hemorrhage

travatura *f* roof timbers; **travatura maestra** ridgepole

trave *f* beam; joist; **fare una trave d'un fuscello** to make a mountain out of a molehill

travedére §279 *tr* to glimpse ‖ *intr* to be mistaken

travéggole *fpl*—**avere le traveggole** to see things; to see one thing for another

travèrsa *f* crossbar; crossroad; crosspiece; rung; bar (*of goalpost*); dam; rail (*of fence*); transom; slat (*to hold bedspring*); rubber pad; (rr) tie

traversare (**travèrso**) *tr* to cross

traversata *f* passage, crossing

traversia *f* strong wind; **traversie** misfortunes

traversina *f* (rr) tie

travèr•so -sa *adj* cross; devious ‖ *m* width; crossbar; (naut) beam; (naut) side; **a traverso** on the beam; **capire a traverso** to misunderstand; **di traverso** askance; crosswise; the wrong way ‖ *f see* **traversa**

traversóne *m* large crossbar; westerly gale; side blow with saber

travestiménto *m* disguise; travesty

travestire (**travèsto**) *tr* to disguise; to travesty, parody ‖ *ref* to disguise oneself

traviare §119 *tr* to lead astray ‖ *intr & ref* to go astray

travicèllo *m* joist

travisare *tr* to distort

travolgènte *adj* impetuous; fascinating; sweeping

travòlgere §289 *tr* to overwhelm; to overturn; to sweep away

trazióne *f* traction

tre [e] *adj & pron* three; **le tre** three o'clock ‖ *m* three; third (*in dates*)

trébbia *f* thresher; threshing

trebbiare §287 (**trébbio**) *tr & intr* to thresh

trebbiatrice *f* thresher, threshing machine

trebbiatura *f* threshing

tréc•cia *f* (**-ce**) plait; braid; **treccia a ciambella** bun, knot

trecentèsi•mo -ma *adj, m & pron* three hundredth

trecènto *adj, m & pron* three hundred ‖ **il Trecento** the fourteenth century

tredicèsi•mo -ma *adj, m & pron* thirteenth ‖ *f* Xmas bonus

trédici *adj & pron* thirteen; **le tredici** one P.M. ‖ *m* thirteen; thirteenth (*in dates*)

trègua *f* truce; respite; **tregua atomica** nuclear test ban; **senza tregua** without letup

tremare (**trèmo**) *intr* to shake, tremble; to quiver; **far tremare** to shake

tremarèlla *f*—**avere la tremarella** (coll) to shake in one's boots

tremebón•do -da *adj* (lit) shaky

tremèn•do -da *adj* tremendous

trementina *f* turpentine

tremila *adj, m & pron* three thousand

trèmito *m* trembling; quivering

tremolare (**trèmolo**) *intr* to shake; to quiver; to flicker

trèmo•lo -la *adj* tremulous ‖ *m* (bot) aspen; (mus) tremolo

trèno *m* train; quarter (*of animal*); set (*of tires*); threnody, lamentation; **treno accelerato** local; **treno di lusso** Pullman train; **treno direttissimo** express; **treno di vita** mode of life; mode of living; **treno merci** freight train; **treno stradale** tractor-trailer

trenodìa f threnody

trénta adj & pron thirty || m thirty; thirtieth (in dates)

trentèsi·mo -ma adj, m & pron thirtieth

trentina f about thirty

Trènto f Trent

trepidare (trèpido) intr to fear; to worr'

trepidazióne f fear, trepidation

treppiède m tripod; trivet

tré·sca f (-sche) intrigue; liaison

tréspolo m stool; pedestal; stand, perch; (coll) jalopy

triàngolo m triangle; **triangolo rettangolo** right triangle

tribolare (tribolo) tr to torment, afflict || intr to suffer

tribolazióne f tribulation, ordeal

tribórdo m (naut) starboard

tri·bù f (-bù) tribe

tribuna f rostrum, platform; (sports) grandstand; **tribuna stampa** press box

tribunale m court, tribunal; courthouse; **tribunale dei minorenni** juvenile court; **tribunale di prima istanza** court of first instance

tributare tr to bestow

tributà·rio -ria (-ri -rie) adj tributary; tax || m tributary

tributo m tribute; tax

trichè·co m (-chi) walrus

triciclo m tricycle

tricolóre adj & m tricolor

tricòrno m cocked hat, tricorn

tricromìa f three-color printing; three-color print

tridènte m trident

trifase adj three-phase

trifocale adj trifocal

trifò·glio m (-gli) clover; three-leaf clover

trìfola f (coll) truffle

trìglia f red mullet

trigonometrìa f trigonometry

trilióne m trillion

trillare intr to trill; to vibrate

trillo m trill; ringing

trilogìa f trilogy

trimestrale adj quarterly

trimèstre m quarter; quarterly dues; quarterly payment; (educ) quarter, trimester

trimotóre m three-engine plane

trina f lace

trin·ca f (-che) (naut) gammoning; **di trinca** clearly, cleanly; **nuovo di trinca** brand-new

trincare §197 tr (coll) to gulp down, swill

trincèa f trench

trincerare (trincèro) tr to dig trenches in || ref to entrench oneself

trincétto m shoemaker's blade

trinchétto m (naut) foremast; (naut) foresail

trinciante adj cutting || m carving knife

trinciapóllo m meat shears

trinciare §128 tr to carve; to shred; to advance (rash opinions); to cut up

trinciato m smoking tobacco

trinciatrice f shredder; slicer

Trinità f Trinity

trionfale adj triumphal

trionfante adj triumphant

trionfare (triónfo) intr to triumph

triónfo m triumph; center piece; tidbit dish with three or four tiers; trump (in game of tarot)

tripartì·to -ta adj tripartite

triplicare §197 **(trìplico)** tr & ref to triple

trìplice adj threefold

tri·plo -pla adj & m triple

tripode m tripod

trippa f tripe; (coll) belly

tripudiare §287 intr to exult

tripù·dio m (-di) exultation

tris m (tris) (poker) three of a kind

trisàvola f great-great-grandmother

trisàvolo m great-great-grandfather; **trisavoli** great-great-grandparents

trisma m lockjaw

triste adj sad; gloomy, bleak

tristézza f sadness

tri·sto -sta adj wicked; wretched; poor (figure); (lit) sad

tritacar·ne m (-ne) meat grinder

tritaghiàc·cio m (-cio) ice crusher

tritare tr to chop; to grind; to mince, hash; to pound

tri·to -ta adj minced, hashed; worn, trite

tritòlo m T.N.T.

tritóne m (zool) newt; (fig) merman || **Tritone** m Triton

trìtti·co m (-ci) triptych; export document in triplicate; trilogy

trittòn·go m (-ghi) triphthong

triturare tr to mince, hash

trivèlla f auger, drill; post-hole digger

trivellare (trivèllo) tr to drill, bore

triviale adj vulgar

trivialì·tà f (-tà) vulgarity

trì·vio m (-vi) crossroads; trivium; **da trivio** vulgar

trofèo m trophy; (mil) insignia (on headpiece)

trògolo m trough

tròia f sow; slut || **Troia** f Troy

troia·no -na adj & m Trojan

trómba f trumpet; bugle, clarion; trunk (of elephant); leg (of boot); (anat) tube; (aut, rad) horn; **con le trombe nel sacco** crestfallen, dejected; **tromba d'aria** whirlwind; tornado; **tromba marina** waterspout; **tromba delle scale** stairwell

trombétta f trumpet

trombettière m (mil) trumpeter

trombetti·sta m (-sti) trumpet player

trombóne m trombone; blunderbuss

trombò·si f (-si) thrombosis

troncare §197 **(trónco)** tr to chop; to cut off; to clip (words); to break, sever; to block (s.o.'s progress); to apocopate

tronchése [s] m wire cutter

trón·co -ca (-chi -che) adj truncate; oxytone; apocopated; exhausted, dead-tired; incomplete; **in tronco** in the middle; (dismissal) on the spot || m trunk; stub (of receipt book);

section (*of highway*); log; strain (*of a family*); (rr) branch; **tronco di cono** truncated cone; **tronco maggiore** (naut) lower mast

troncóne *m* stump

troneggiare §290 (tronéggio) *intr* to tower; to hold forth; **troneggiare su** to lord it over

trón·fio -fia *adj* (**-fi -fie**) haughty; bombastic

tròno *m* throne

tropicale *adj* tropical

tròpi·co *m* (**-ci**) tropic

troposfèra *f* troposphere

tròp·po -pa *adj. & pron* too much; **trop·pi -pe** too many ‖ *m* too much; **questo è troppo!** enough is enough! ‖ **troppo** *adv* too; too much; **essere di troppo** to be in the way

tròta *f* trout

trottare (tròtto) *intr* to trot

trotterellare (trotterèllo) *intr* to trot along; to toddle

tròtto *m* trot; **piccolo trotto** jog trot

tròttola *f* top

trovare (tròvo) *tr* to find; to visit; **trovare a** or **da ridire** (**su**) to find fault (with); **trovi?** don't you think so? ‖ *ref* to find oneself; to meet; to be; to be located; to happen, e.g., **mi trovai a passare di fronte a casa sua** I happened to pass in front of his house

trovarò·be *m* (**-be**) (theat) property man ‖ *f* (theat) dresser

trovata *f* find; trick, gimmick

trovatèl·lo -la *mf* foundling, waif

trovatóre *m* troubadour

trovièro *m* trouvère

truccare §197 *tr* to make up; to falsify; (aut) to soup up ‖ *ref* to put on make-up

truccatura *f* make-up; trick, gimmick

truc·co *m* (**-chi**) make-up; trick, gimmick

truce *adj* fierce, cruel; menacing

trucidare (trùcido) *tr* to massacre

trùciolo *m* chip, shaving

truculènto *adj* truculent

truffa *f* cheat, fraud, swindle; **truffa all'americana** confidence game

truffare *tr* to cheat, swindle

truffa·tóre -trice *mf* cheat, swindler

truismo *m* truism

truògolo *m* var of **trogolo**

truppa *f* troop; soldiers; **di truppa** (mil) enlisted (*man or woman*); **in truppa** in a flock

tu §5 *pron pers;* **a tu per tu** face to face; **dare del tu a** to address in the familiar form

tuba *f* tuba; (hist) horn, trumpet; (joc) top hat, stovepipe; (anat) tube

tubare *intr* to coo

tubatura *f* piping, tubing; pipe, tube; pipeline

tubazióne *f* tubes, pipes

tubèrcolo *m* tubercle

tubercolosà·rio [s] *m* (**-ri**) tuberculosis sanitarium

tubercolò·si *f* (**-si**) tuberculosis

tubercoló·so -sa [s] *adj* tuberculous ‖ *mf* T.B. patient

tùbero *m* tuber

tubétto *m* tube (*for pills or toothpaste*); spool

tubino *m* small tube; derby (hat)

tubo *m* tube; pipe; (anat) canal, duct; **a tubo** tubular; **tubo di scarico** exhaust pipe; **tubo di troppopieno** overflow; **tubo di ventilazione** air shaft

tubolare *adj* tubular ‖ *m* tire (*for racing bicycle*)

tuffare *tr* to dip; to plunge ‖ *ref* to plunge; to dive

tuffa·tóre -trice *mf* diver ‖ *m* dive bomber

tuffétto *m* (orn) dabchick, grebe

tuffo *m* dive; plunge; throb; **a tuffo** (aer) diving; **scendere a tuffo** (aer) to dive; **tuffo ad angelo** (sports) swan dive; **tuffo d'acqua** downpour

tufo *m* tufa

tu·ga *f* (**-ghe**) (naut) deckhouse

tugù·rio *m* (**-ri**) hovel

tulipano *m* tulip

tumefare §173 *tr & ref* to swell

tumefazióne *f* swelling

tùmi·do -da *adj* tumid

tumóre *m* tumor

fùmulo *m* tomb; tumulus

tumulto *m* tumult, riot; commotion

tumultuó·so -sa [s] *adj* tumultuous

tungstèno *m* tungsten

tùni·ca *f* (**-che**) tunic

Tùnisi *f* Tunis

Tunisìa, la Tunisia

tunisi·no -na *adj & mf* Tunisian

tuo tua §6 *adj & pron poss* (**tuòi tue**)

tuòno *m* thunder

tuòrlo *m* yolk

turàcciolo *m* cork, stopper

turare *tr* to plug, stop; to cork

turba *f* crowd; mob; (pathol) upset

turbaménto *m* commotion, perturbation; disturbance, breach (*of law and order*)

turbante *m* turban

turbare *tr* to muddy; to disturb; to upset ‖ *ref* to become cloudy; to become upset

turba·to -ta *adj* upset; disturbed; distracted

tùrbi·do -da *adj* turbid

turbina *f* turbine

turbinare (tùrbino) *tr* to separate in a centrifuge ‖ *intr* to whirl

tùrbine *m* whirlwind; swarm; tumult

turbinó·so -sa [s] *adj* whirling; tumultuous

turboèli·ca *m* (**-ca**) turboprop

turbogètto *m* turbojet

turbolèn·to -ta *adj* turbulent

turbolènza *f* turbulence

turbomotrice *f* (rr) turbine engine

turboreattóre *m* turbojet

turcasso *m* quiver

turchése [s] *m* turquoise

Turchìa, la Turkey

turchinétto *m* bluing

turchi·no -na *adj* dark-blue ‖ *m* dark blue

tur·co -ca (**-chi -che**) *adj* Turkish; **sedere alla turca** to sit cross-legged ‖ *mf* Turk ‖ *m* Turkish (*language*); **bestemmiare come un turco** to swear like a trooper; **fumare come un turco** to smoke like a steam engine

tùrgi·do -da *adj* turgid

turibolo *m* thurible, censer

turismo *m* tourism

turi·sta *mf* (**-sti -ste**) tourist

turisti·co -ca *adj* (**-ci -che**) tourist; travel (*e.g.,* **bureau**); traveler's (*check*)

turlupinare *tr* to hoodwink, swindle

turlupinatura *f* swindle, confidence game

turno *m* turn; shift; **a turno** in turn; **di turno** on duty; **fare a turno** to take turns

turpe *adj* base, abject; (*lit*) ugly

turpilò·quio *m* (**-qui**) foul language

turpitùdine *f* turpitude

tuta *f* overalls; **tuta antigravità** anti-G suit; **tuta da bambini** jumpers; **tuta spaziale** spacesuit

tutèla *f* guardianship; defense, protection

tutelare *adj* tutelary ‖ *v* (**tutèlo**) *tr* to protect, defend

tùtolo *m* corncob

tu·tóre -trice *mf* guardian; protector

tuttavìa *adv* yet, nevertheless; (*lit*) always, continuously

tut·to -ta *adj* whole; all; full; **con tutto** in spite of, *e.g.,* **con tutto quello che ho fatto per lui** in spite of all I have done for him; **del tutto** fully, completely; **è tutt'uno** it's all the same; **tutt'altro** completely different; on the contrary; **tutt'altro che** anything but; **tutti** every, *e.g.,* **tutti gli scolari** every pupil; **tutti e due** both ‖ *m* everything; whole; **con tutto che** although; **fare di tutto** to do everything possible; **in tutto** altogether ‖ *pron* **tut·ti -te** all, everybody (*of a group*); **tutti** everybody ‖ **tutto** *adv* quite; **tutt'a un tratto** all of a sudden; **tutto al contrario** quite the opposite

tuttofa·re *adj invar* of all trades; of all work ‖ *m* (**-re**) factotum, jack-of-all-trades ‖ *f* (**-re**) maid of all work

tuttóra *adv* yet, still

tziga·no -na *adj & mf* var of **zigano**

U

U, u [u] *m & f* nineteenth letter of the Italian alphabet

ubbìa *f* prejudice, bias; complex; whim

ubbidiènte *adj* obedient

ubbidire §176 *tr* to obey ‖ *intr* to obey; to respond (*said of a car*); (with *dat*) to obey, *e.g.,* **gli ubbedì** he obeyed him

ubertó·so -sa [s] *adj* fruitful; fertile

ubicazione *f* location

ubiquità *f* ubiquity; **non ho il dono dell'ubiquità** I can't be everywhere at the same time

ubì·quo -qua *adj* ubiquitous

ubriacare §197 *tr* to make drunk, intoxicate ‖ *ref* to get drunk

ubriacatura or **ubriachézza** *f* drunkenness, intoxication

ubria·co -ca (**-chi -che**) *adj* drunk; **ubriaco fradìcio** dead drunk ‖ *mf* drunkard

ubriacó·ne -na *mf* drunkard

uccellare (**uccèllo**) *tr* to take in, cajole ‖ *intr* to snare; to fowl; to hunt birds

uccèllo *m* bird; **uccello di bosco** fugitive; **uccello di galera** gallows bird; **uccello di passo** bird of passage

uccella·tóre -trice *mf* live-bird catcher

uccellièra *f* aviary; large birdcage

uccidere §274 *tr* to kill ‖ *ref* to kill oneself; to get killed; to kill one another

-ùccio -ùccia (**-ucci -ucce**) *suf adj* not very, *e.g.,* **calduccio** not very hot; rather, *e.g.,* **magruccio** rather thin; poor little, *e.g.,* **caruccio** poor little darling ‖ *suf m & f* small *e.g.,* **cappelluccio** small hat

uccisione *f* killing; murder

ucci·so -sa *adj* killed ‖ *mf* victim

ucci·sóre -ditrice *mf* killer

ucrai·no -na *adj & mf* Ukrainian ‖ **l'Ucraina** *f* the Ukraine

udìbile *adj* audible

udiènza *f* audience; hearing; **l'udienza è aperta!** the court is now in session!

udire §275 *tr* to hear; to listen to

udito *m* hearing

uditòfono *m* hearing aid

udi·tóre -trice *adj* hearing ‖ *mf* (*educ*) auditor ‖ *m* magistrate

uditò·rio -ria (**-ri -rie**) *adj* auditory ‖ *m* audience

ufficiale *adj* official ‖ *m* official; officer; **primo ufficiale** (*naut*) first officer, mate; **ufficiale di giornata** (*mil*) officer of the day; **ufficiale di rotta** (*aer, naut*) navigator; **ufficiale giudiziario** clerk of the court; process server, bailiff; **ufficiale medico** (*mil*) medical officer

ufficiare §128 *tr* to officiate

uffi·cio *m* (**-ci**) duty; office; bureau; department (*of agency*); **d'ufficio** ex-officio; public, *e.g.,* **avvocato d'ufficio** public defender; **ufficio di collocamento** placement bureau; **ufficio di compensazione** clearing house; **ufficio d'igiene** board of health

uffició·so -sa [s] *adj* unofficial; kindly; white (*lie*)

uffi·zio *m* (**-zi**) (*eccl*) office

ufo *m*—**a ufo** gratis, without paying

ugèllo *m* nozzle

ùg·gia *f* (**-ge**) darkness; gloom; dislike; **avere in uggia** to dislike

uggiolare (**ùggiolo**) *intr* to whine (*said of a dog*)

uggió·so -sa [s] *adj* gloomy; boring

ugnare *tr* to bevel; to miter

ugnatura *f* bevel; miter

ùgola *f* uvula; **bagnarsi l'ugola** (coll) to wet one's whistle

ugonòtto *m* Huguenot

uguaglianza *f* equality

uguagliare §280 *tr* to equal; to make equal; to equalize; to level; to compare || *ref* to compare oneself; to be equal; to be compared

uguale *adj* equal; same; even; level; **per me è uguale** it's the same to me || *m* equal; (math) equal sign

ùlcera *f* ulcer; sore

ulcerare (**ùlcero**) *tr & ref* to ulcerate

uliva *f* var of **oliva**

ulterióre *adj* further, subsequent, ulterior

ùltima *f* latest news; last straw

ultimare (**ùltimo**) *tr* to complete, finish

ultimato *m* ultimatum

ultimìssima *f* latest edition (*of newspaper*); **ultimissime** late news

ùlti·mo -ma *adj* last; final; latest; latter; farthest; ultimate; least; top (*floor*); **all'ultimo, dall'ultimo, nell'ultimo** or **sull'ultimo** lately; finally, at the end || *f* see **ultima**

ultimogèni·to -ta *adj* last-born || *mf* last-born child

ultra- *pref adj* and *m & f* ultra-, e.g., **ultraelevato** ultrahigh; super-, e.g., **ultrasonico** supersonic (*speed*)

ultracór·to -ta *adj* ultrashort

ultraròs·so -sa *adj & m* infrared

ultraterrè·no -na *adj* ultramundane; unearthly

ultraviolét·to -ta *adj & m* ultraviolet

ululare (**ùlulo**) *intr* to howl

ululato *m* howl

umanésimo *m* humanism

umani·sta *mf* (**-sti -ste**) humanist

umani·tà *f* (**-tà**) humanity; **umanità** *fpl* humanities

umanità·rio -ria *adj & mf* (**-ri -rie**) humanitarian

uma·no -na *adj* human; humane || *m* human nature; **umani** human beings

um·bro -bra *adj & m* Umbrian

umettare (**umétto**) *tr* to moisten, dampen

umidìc·cio -cia *adj* (**-ci -ce**) dampish

umidi·tà *f* (**-tà**) humidity, dampness

ùmi·do -da *adj* humid, damp || *m* humidity, dampness; **in umido** stewed (*e.g., meat*)

ùmile *adj* humble || **gli umili** *mpl* the meek

umiliare §287 *tr* to humiliate, humble || *ref* to humble oneself

umiliazióne *f* humiliation

umiltà *f* humility

umóre *m* humor, mood, temper; whim; (bot) sap; **un bell'umore** (coll) quite a character

umorismo *m* humor

umori·sta *mf* (**-sti -ste**) humorist

umorìsti·co -ca *adj* (**-ci -che**) humorous; amusing, comic, funny

un (apocopated form of **uno**) §9 *indef art* a, an || §9 *numeral adj* one §12 *reciprocal indef pron*—**l'un l'altro** each other, one another

unànime *adj* unanimous

unanimità *f* unanimity

unàni·mo -ma *adj* unanimous

uncinare *tr* to hook, grapple

uncinétto *m* small hook; crochet hook

uncino *m* hook; grapnel; clasp; pothook; (fig) pretext; **a uncino** hooked

undicèsi·mo -ma *adj, m & pron* eleventh

ùndici *adj & pron* eleven; **le undici** eleven o'clock || *m* eleven; eleventh (*in dates*); (soccer) squad

ùngere §183 *tr* to grease; to oil; to smear; to anoint; to flatter || *ref* to smear oneself

Ungherìa, l' *f* Hungary

ungherése [s] *adj & mf* Hungarian

ùnghia *f* nail; fingernail; claw; hoof; fluke (*of anchor*); (fig) hairbreadth; **avere le unghie lunghe** to be lightfingered; **unghia del piede** toenail; **unghie** (fig) clutches

unghiata *f* nail scratch

unguènto *m* unguent, ointment

ùni·co -ca *adj* (**-ci -che**) only, sole; unique; single (*copy*); complete (*text*) || *f*—**l'unica** the only solution

unicòrno *m* unicorn

unificare §197 (**unìfico**) *tr* to unify; to standardize

unificazióne *f* unification; standardization

uniformare (**unifórmo**) *tr* to make uniform, standardize || *ref*—**uniformarsi** a to conform to; to comply with

unifórme *adj* uniform; standard || *f* uniform; **alta uniforme** (mil) full dress

unilaterale *adj* unilateral

unióne *f* union; agreement; **unione libera** free love

unire §176 *tr & ref* to unite

unìsono [s] *m* unison; **all'unisono** in unison

uni·tà *f* (**-tà**) unity; unit; **unità di misura** unit of measurement

unità·rio -ria (**-ri -rie**) *adj* unit (*e.g., price*); united || *m* Unitarian

uni·to -ta *adj* united; joined; compact; plain (*color*); consolidated

universale *adj* universal; last (*judgment*)

universi·tà *f* (**-tà**) university

università·rio -ria (**-ri -rie**) *adj* university; college || *mf* university or college student; university or college professor

univer·so -sa *adj* universal || *m* universe

unno *m* Hun

u·no -na §9 *indef art* a, an || §9 *numeral adj* one || *m* one §10 *pron indef* one; **le una, la una,** or **l'una** one o'clock; **l'uno e l'altro** both; **l'uno o l'altro** either, either one; **per uno** in single file; **uno per uno** one by one; each other || §11 *correlative pron* one

un·to -ta *adj* greasy || *m* grease, fat; flattery; anointed one

untuosità [s] *f* greasiness; unction, unctuousness

untuó·so -sa [s] *adj* greasy; unctuous

unzióne f unction

uò·mo m (**-mini**) man; **come un sol uomo** to a man; **uomo d'affari** businessman; **uomo del giorno** man of the hour; **uomo della strada** man of the street; **uomo di chiesa** churchman; **uomo di fatica** laborer; **uomo di fiducia** trusted man; **uomo di mare** seaman; **uomo di paglia** straw man; **uomo di parola** man of his word; **uomo in mare!** man overboard!; **uomo meccanico** automaton; **uomo morto** (rr) deadman brake; **uomo nuovo** nouveau riche; **uomo rana** frogman

uòpo m—**all'uopo** if need be; **essere d'uopo** (lit) to be necessary

uòse [s] fpl leggings

uò·vo m (**-va** fpl) egg; **meglio un uovo oggi che una gallina domani** a bird in a hand is worth two in the bush; **rompere le uova nel paniere a qlcu** to spoil s.o.'s plans; **uovo affogato** poached egg; **uovo alla coque** soft-boiled egg; **uovo all'occhio di bue** fried egg; **uovo da tè** tea ball; **uovo strapazzato** scrambled egg

uragano m hurricane; storm (of applause); **uragano di neve** blizzard

Urali mpl Ural Mountains

uraníf·ero ·ra adj uranium-bearing

urànio m uranium

urbanésimo m urbanization, migration toward the cities

urbanísti·co ·ca (**-ci -che**) adj city-planning || f city planning

urbani·tà f (**-tà**) urbanity, civility; city population

urbanizzare [ddzz] tr to urbanize

urba·no ·na adj urban; urbane

urètra f urethra

urgènte adj urgent, pressing

urgènza f urgency; **d'urgenza** urgent; emergency (e.g., operation); **fare urgenza a** to urge

ùrgere §276 tr to urge, press || intr to be urgent

urína f urine

urinà·rio ·ria adj (**-ri -rie**) urinary

urlare tr to shout; to shout down || intr to howl; to shout, yell

urla·tóre ·trice adj screaming || mf screamer; loud singer

ur·lo m howl || m (**-la** fpl) yell, scream

urna f urn; ballot box; (poet) grave; **urne** polls

-uro suf m (chem) **-ide**, e.g., **cloruro** chloride

urologìa f urology

urrà interj hurrah!

ursóne m Canada porcupine

urtare tr to hit; to bump; to annoy || intr—**urtare contro** to hit, strike against; **urtare in** to hit; to stumble into || ref to get annoyed; to clash; to bump into one another

urto m hit; bump; collision; onslaught; clash, disagreement; **urto di nervi** huff

Uruguai, l' m Uruguay

uruguaia·no ·na adj & mf Uruguayan

usanza f usage, custom; habit, practice

usare tr to use, employ; to wear out;

(lit) to frequent; **usare + inf** to be accustomed to + ger || intr to be fashionable; **usare di** to use, employ || ref to become accustomed; **si usa + inf** it is customary to + inf

usa·to ·ta adj used, second-hand; worn; worn-out; (lit) usual || m usage, custom; norm; second-hand goods

usbèr·go m (**-ghi**) hauberk, (fig) shield, protection

uscènte adj ending, terminating; retiring

uscière m receptionist; office boy, errand boy; (coll) court clerk; (coll) bailiff; (coll) tipstaff

uscìo m (**-sci**) door; **infilar l'uscio** to take French leave; **metter tra l'uscio e il muro** (fig) to corner

uscire §277 intr (ESSERE) to go out, leave; to come out; to flow out; to escape; to turn out, ensue; **essere uscito** to be out; **uscire da** to leave; to run off (the track); **uscire dai gangheri** to get mad; **uscire dal comune** to be out of the ordinary; **uscire dal segno** to go too far; **uscire dal seminato** to go astray; **uscire di mente a** to escape one's mind, e.g., **gli è uscito di mente** it escaped his mind; **uscire di sentimento** to pass out; **uscire di vita** to die; **uscire in** to lead into; **uscire per il rotto della cuffia** to barely make it

uscita f exit; outlay; quip, sally; gate (e.g., in an airport); (gram) ending; **all'uscita** on the way out; **buona uscita** severance pay; bonus; **libera uscita** day off (of servant); (mil) pass; **uscita di sicurezza** emergency exit

usignòlo m nightingale

u·so ·sa adj (lit) accustomed || m practice; usage; use; wear; faculty; power (e.g., of hearing); (lit) intimate relations; **all'uso di** in the fashion of; **avere per uso di** to be wont to; **come d'uso** as usual; **farci l'uso** to get used to it!; **fuori d'uso** worn-out, out of commission; **uso esterno!** (pharm) not to be taken internally!

ustionare (ustióno) tr to burn, scorch

ustióne f burn

usuale adj usual; ordinary, common

usufruire §176 intr—**usufruire di** to have the use of; to enjoy

usura f usury; (mach) wear and tear; **ad usura** abundantly

usu·ràio ·ràia (**-rài -ràie**) adj usurious || mf usurer, loanshark

usurpare tr to usurp

utensile adj tool, e.g., **macchina utensile** machine tool || m utensil; tool

utènte m user; customer, consumer

ùtero m uterus, womb

ùtile adj useful; usable; workable; legal, prescribed (e.g., time); **essere utile a** to help; **venire utile** to come in handy || m usefulness; profit, gain

utili·tà f (**-tà**) utility, usefulness; profit, gain

utilitària f economy car, compact

utilizzare [ddzz] tr to utilize

utopìa *f* utopia
utopi‧sta *mf* (-sti -ste) utopian
utopìsti‧co -ca *adj* (-ci -che) utopian
uva *f* grapes; **un grano di uva passa** a raisin; **uva passa** raisins

uxorici‧da *m* (-di) uxoricide ‖ *f* (-de) murderer of one's husband
uxorici‧dio *m* (-di) uxoricide; murder of one's husband
ùzzolo [ddzz] *m* whim, fancy, caprice

V

V, v [vu] *m & f* twentieth letter of the Italian alphabet
V. *abbr* (**vostro**) your
vacante *adj* vacant
vacanza *f* vacancy; vacation; **fare va-canza** to be on vacation; **vacanze** vacation
vacanzière *m* vacationer
vac‧ca *f* (-che) cow
vac‧càio *m* (-cài) cowboy; stable boy
vaccherìa *f* dairy farm
vacchétta *f* cowhide
vaccìna *f* cow manure; cow
vaccinare *tr* to vaccinate
vaccinazióne *f* vaccination
vacci‧no -na *adj* cow; bovine ‖ *m* vac-cine ‖ *f* see **vaccina**
vacillante *adj* vacillating
vacillare *intr* to totter; to vacillate; to shake; to flicker; to fail, e.g., **la memoria gli vacilla** his memory is failing; **far vacillare** to rock
vacui‧tà *f* (-tà) vacuity
và‧cuo -cua *adj* empty ‖ *m* vacuum
vademè‧cum *m* (-cum) almanac, ready-reference handbook
vagabondàg‧gio *m* (-gi) vagrancy; wandering; rambling
vagabondare (**vagabóndo**) *intr* to wan-der, rove
vagabón‧do -da *adj* wandering; vaga-bond ‖ *mf* vagrant, bum, tramp; rover
vaiata *f* valley
valle *f* valley; **a valle** downhill; down-stream
vallétta *f* (telv) assistant
vagare §209 *intr* to wander, ramble, rove
vagheggiare §290 (**vaghéggio**) *tr* to gaze fondly at; to cherish
vagìre §176 *intr* to cry, whimper
vagìto *m* cry, whimper
và‧glia *m* (-glia) money order ‖ *f*—**di vaglia** worthy, capable
vagliare §280 *tr* to sift, bolt
và‧glio *m* (-gli) sieve; **mettere al vaglio** to scrutinize
va‧go -ga (-ghi -ghe) *adj* vague; vacant (*stare*); (lit) beautiful; (lit) roving; (poet) desirous ‖ *m* vagueness; (lit) rover; (anat) vagus
vagonata *f* carload
vagóne *m* (rr) car; **vagone frigorifero** (rr) refrigerator car; **vagone letto** (rr) sleeping car, sleeper; **vagone ristorante** (rr) dining car; **vagone volante** (aer) flying boxcar
vàio vàia (**vài vàie**) *adj* dark-grey ‖ *m* dark grey; (heral) vair; (zool) Sibe-rian squirrel
vaiòlo *m* smallpox
valan‧ga *f* (-ghe) avalanche
valènte *adj* capable, skillful; clever
valentìa *f* skill; cleverness

valentino *m* Valentine (*sweetheart*)
valènza *f* (chem) valence
valére §278 *tr* to win, get (*e.g., an honor for s.o.*); **che vale?** what's the use?; **valere la pena** to be worth-while; **valere un Perù** to be worth a king's ransom ‖ *intr* (ESSERE & AVERE) to be worth: to be of avail; to be valid; to mean; to be the equivalent; **far valere** to enforce; **farsi valere** to assert oneself; **tanto vale** it's all the same; **vale a dire** that is to say; **valere meglio** to be better ‖ *ref*—**valersi di** to avail oneself of; to play on; to employ
valévole *adj* valid, good
valicare §197 (**vàlico**) *tr* to cross, pass
vàli‧co *m* (-chi) mountain pass; pas-sage; opening (*in a hedge*)
validi‧tà *f* (-tà) validity
vàli‧do -da *adj* valid; able, able-bodied; strong
valigerìa *f* luggage; luggage store
valigétta *f* valise; **valigetta diplomatica** attaché case
vali‧gia *f* (-ge) suitcase; traveling bag; **fare le valige** to pack one's bags; **va-ligia diplomatica** diplomatic pouch; attaché case; **valigia per abiti** suit carrier
vallétto *m* valet; page; (telv) assistant
vallò‧ne -na *adj* & *mf* Walloon ‖ *m* narrow valley
valóre *m* value; valor, bravery; force; (fig) jewel; (math) variable; **mettere in valore** to raise the value of; **valore di mercato** market value; **valore fac-ciale** face value; **valore locativo** ren-tal value; **valori** valuables; securities; **valori mobiliari** securities
valorizzare [ddzz] *tr* to enhance the value of
valoró‧so -sa [s] *adj* brave, valiant
valuta *f* currency; (com) effective date; (com) value (*of promissory note*)
valutare *tr* to estimate, appraise; to value, prize; to count, reckon; to take into consideration
valutazióne *f* estimation, appraisal; evaluation
valva *f* (bot, zool) valve
vàlvola *f* (anat, mach) valve; (elec) fuse; (rad, telv) tube, valve; **valvola a galleggiante** ball cock; **valvola di sicurezza** safety valve; **valvola in testa** overhead valve
vàl‧zer *m* (-zer) waltz

vamp f (vamp) vamp

vampa f flame; blaze; flash; flush

vampata f burst (of heat); blast (of hot air); flash, flush

vampiro m vampire

vanàdio m vanadium

vanaglòria f vainglory, boastfulness

vanaglorió·so -sa [s] adj vainglorious

vandalismo m vandalism

vànda·lo -la adj & m vandal ‖ **Vandalo** m Vandal

vaneggiare §290 (**vanéggio**) intr to rave; (lit) to be delirious; (lit) to open, yawn

vanè·sio -sia adj (-si -sie) vain

van·ga f (-ghe) spade

vangare §209 tr to spade up; to dig with a spade

vangèlo m gospel ‖ **Vangelo** m Gospel

vanghétto m spud

vaniglia f vanilla

vanilò·quio m (-qui) empty talk

vani·tà f (-tà) vanity

vanitó·so -sa [s] adj vain, conceited

va·no -na adj vain; (lit) empty, hollow; **in vano** in vain ‖ m empty space; room

vantàg·gio m (-gi) advantage; profit; odds, handicap; discount; (coll) extra; (typ) galley; **a vantaggio di** on behalf of

vantaggió·so -sa [s] adj advantageous

vantare tr to boast of; to set up (a claim) ‖ ref to boast; **vantarsi di** to brag about, vaunt

vanteria f brag, boast, vaunt

vanto m brag, boast; **aver vanto su** (lit) to overcome

vànvera f—**a vanvera** at random

vapóre m vapor; steam; locomotive; steamship; **a tutto vapore** at full speed

vaporétto m small river boat; vaporetto (in Venice)

vaporizzare [ddzz] tr to vaporize; to spray ‖ intr (ESSERE) & ref to evaporate

vaporizzatóre [ddzz] m vaporizer; sprayer

vaporó·so -sa [s] adj vaporous

varaménto m assemblage (of prefab pieces)

varano m monitor lizard

varare tr to launch; to pass (a law); (coll) to back, promote (a candidate)

varcare §197 tr to cross ‖ intr (poet) to pass (said of time)

var·co m (-chi) opening; mountain pass; breach; **attendere al varco** to lie in wait for; **cogliere al varco** to catch unawares; **fare varco in** to breach

varechina f (laundry) bleach

variàbile adj & f variable

variante f variant; detour; (aut) model

variare §287 tr & intr (ESSERE & AVERE) to vary

variazióne f variation

varicèlla f chicken pox

varicó·so -sa [s] adj varicose

variega·to -ta adj variegated

varie·tà m (-tà) (theat) vaudeville ‖ f variety

và·rio -ria (-ri -rie) adj varied; various; variable; different; **va·ri -rie** several ‖ m variety ‖ **varie** fpl miscellanies ‖ **va·ri -rie** pron indef several

variopìn·to -ta adj multicolored

varo m (naut) launch

vas m (vas) subchaser

va·sàio m (-sài) potter

va·sca f (-sche) tub; basin; pool; **vasca da bagno** bathtub; **vasca dei pesci** aquarium; **vasca navale** (naut) basin

vascèllo m vessel, ship

vaselina or **vaselìna** f vaseline

vasellame m dishes; set of dishes; **vasellame da cucina** kitchen ware; **vasellame d'argento** silverware; **vasellame di porcellana** chinaware

vasèllo m (lit) vessel

vasi·stas [s] m (-stas) transom

vaso m vase; vessel; jar, pot; nave (of church); hall (of building); (naut) shipway; (poet) cup; **vasi vinari** wine containers; **vaso da fiori** flowerpot; **vaso da notte** chamber pot; **vaso d'elezione** (eccl) chosen vessel (viz., Saint Paul)

vassallo m vassal; (obs) helper

vas·sóio m (-sói) tray; mortarboard

vasti·tà f (-tà) vastness

va·sto -sta adj spacious; vast; (fig) deep

vate m (lit) prophet, poet

vatica·no -na adj Vatican ‖ **Vaticano** m Vatican

vaticinare (**vatìcino** & **vaticino**) tr to prophesy

vaticì·nio m (-ni) prophecy

ve §5 pron

V.E. abbr (**Vostra Eccellenza**) Your Excellency

vècchia f old woman

vecchiàia f old age

vecchiézza f old age

vèc·chio -chia (-chi -chie) adj old; elder; **vecchio come il cucco** as old as the hills ‖ m old man; **vecchi** old people; **vecchio del mestiere** old hand ‖ f see **vecchia**

véc·cia f (-ce) vetch

véce f stead, e.g., **in vece mia** in my stead; (lit) vicissitude; **fare le veci di** to act for or as

vedére m seeing; looks; view, opinion ‖ §279 tr to see; to review; to look over; **chi s'è visto s'è visto!** good-by and good luck!; **dare a vedere** to make believe; **stare a vedere** to watch; observe; **non poter vedere** to not be able to stand; **non vedere l'ora di** to be hardly able to wait for; **vedere male** qlcu to be ill-disposed toward s.o. ‖ intr—**stare a vedere** to wait and see; **vederci bene** to see (e.g., in the dark); **vederci chiaro** to look into it; **vedere di** to try to ‖ ref to see oneself; to see each other; **vedersela brutta** to anticipate trouble

vedétta f lookout; (nav) vedette

védova f widow

vedovanza f widowhood

vedovile adj widow's; widower's ‖ m dower

védo·vo -va adj widowed ǁ m widower ǁ f see **vedova**

veduta f view; (lit) eyesight; **di corte vedute** narrowminded; **di larghe vedute** broadminded

veemènte adj vehement; violent; impassioned

veemènza f vehemence; violence

vegetale adj vegetable ǁ m plant, vegetable

vegetare (**vègeto**) intr to vegetate

vegetaria·no -na adj & mf vegetarian

vegetazióne f vegetation

vège·to -ta adj vigorous, spry

veggènte adj (obs) seeing ǁ mf fortuneteller ǁ m seer, prophet; **i veggenti** people having eyesight ǁ f seeress, prophetess

véglia f vigil, watch; wakefulness; evening party, soirée; party, crowd; **a veglia** unbelievable (tale); **veglia danzante** dance; **veglia funebre** wake

vegliardo m old man

vegliare §280 (**véglio**) tr to keep watch over ǁ intr to stay awake; to keep watch; to stay up

vegglióne m masked ball

veicolo m vehicle; carrier (of disease)

véla f sail; sailing; **alzare le vele** to set sail; **ammainare le vele** to take in sail; **a vela** under sail; **far vela** to set sail; **vela aurica** lugsail; **vela bermudiana** or **Marconi** jib; **vela maestra** mainsail

ve·làio m (-lài) sailmaker

velare adj & f (phonet) velar ǁ v (**vélo**) tr to veil; to cover; to muffle (sound); to attenuate, reduce (a shock); to dim, cloud; to conceal; (phot) to fog ǁ ref to cover oneself with a veil; to take the veil; to get dim, e.g., **gli si è velata la vista** his eyesight got dim

velà·rio m (-ri) (hist) velarium; (theat) curtain

vela·to -ta adj veiled; sheer (hosiery)

velatura f coating; (aer) airfoil; (naut) sails

veleggiare §290 (**veléggio**) tr (lit) to sail over (the sea) ǁ intr to sail; (aer) to glide

veleggiatóre m sailboat; (aer) glider

veléno m poison; (fig) venom

velenó·so -sa [s] adj poisonous; (fig) venomous

velétta f veil; (naut) topgallant

vèli·co -ca adj (-ci -che) sail, sailing

velièro m sailing ship

veli·no -na adj thin (paper) ǁ f carbon copy; onionskin; slant (given to a news item)

vellìvo·lo -la adj (lit) gliding; (lit) sailing ǁ m (lit) airplane, aircraft

velleità f (-tà) wild ambition, dream

vellicare §197 (**vèllico**) tr to tickle

vèllo m (lit) fleece; **vello d'oro** Golden Fleece

velló·so -sa [s] adj hairy

velluta·to -ta adj velvety

vellutino m thin velvet; velvet ribbon; **vellutino di cotone** velveteen

vellu·to -ta adj (lit) hairy ǁ m velvet; **velluto a coste** corduroy

vélo m veil; coating; film; skin (e.g., of onion); (anat, bot) velum; (fig) body; **fare velo a** to becloud; to fog

velóce adj speedy, quick, fast; fleeting

velocipedastro m poor or reckless bicycle rider

veloci·sta mf (-sti -ste) (sports) sprinter

veloci·tà f (-tà) velocity; speed; (aut) speed; **a grande velocità** by express; **a piccola velocità** by freight; **velocità di crociera** cruising speed; **velocità di fuga** (rok) escape velocity

velòdromo m bicycle ring or track

véna f vein; grain (in wood or stone); mood; streak (of madness); **di vena** willingly; **essere in vena di** to be in the mood to

venale adj venal

venare (**véno**) tr to vein

vena·to -ta adj veined; streaked; suffused; **venato di sangue** bloodshot

venatura f veining; (fig) streak

vendémmia f vintage

vendemmiare §287 (**vendémmio**) tr to harvest (grapes) ǁ intr to gather grapes; (fig) to make a killing

vendemmia·tóre -trice mf vintager

véndere §281 tr to sell; **da vendere** plenty, more than enough; **vendere allo scoperto** (fin) to sell short; **vendere fumo** to peddle influence ǁ intr to sell; **vendere allo scoperto** (fin) to sell short ǁ ref to sell; **si vende for sale**

vendétta f vengeance; revenge; **gridare vendetta** to cry out for retribution

vendicare §197 (**véndico**) tr to avenge ǁ ref to get revenge

vendicati·vo -va adj vengeful, vindictive

vendica·tóre -trice adj avenging ǁ mf avenger

vendifu·mo mf (-mo) influence peddler

véndita f sale; shop; **in vendita** for sale; **vendita allo scoperto** (fin) short sale; **vendita per corrispondenza** catalogue sale

vendi·tóre -trice mf seller; clerk (in store) ǁ m salesman; **venditore ambulante** peddler; **venditore di fumo** influence peddler ǁ f saleslady

venefi·cio m (-ci) poisoning

venèfi·co -ca (-ci -che) adj poisonous; unhealthy ǁ m (lit) poisonmaker

veneràbile or **venerando** adj venerable

venerare (**vènero**) tr to venerate, revere; to worship

venerazióne f veneration; worship

vener·dì m (-dì) Friday ǁ **Venerdì Santo** Good Friday

Vènere m (astr) Venus ǁ f (mythol & fig) Venus

venè·reo -rea adj (-rei -ree) venereal

Venèzia f Venice; Venetia (province)

venezia·no -na adj & mf Venetian ǁ f Venetian blind

venezola·no -na adj & mf Venezuelan

vènia f (lit) forgiveness, pardon

venire §282 intr (ESSERE) to come; to turn out (well or badly); to turn out to be; **che viene** next, e.g., **il mese che viene** next month; **come viene** as it is; **far venire** to send for; to give, cause; **un va e vieni** a backward-and-forward motion; **venire** + *ger* to keep + *ger*; **venire** + *pp* to be + *pp*, e.g., **il portone viene aperto alle tre** the gate is opened at three; **venire a capo di** to solve; **venire ai ferri corti** to come into open conflict; **venire al dunque or al fatto** to come to the point; **venire alle corte** to get down to brass tacks; **venire alle mani** or **alle prese** to come to blows; **venire a parole** to have words; **venire a patti con** to come to terms with; **venire a proposito** to come in handy; **venire incontro a** to go to meet; **venire in possesso di** to come into possession of (*s.th*); to come into the hands of (*s.o.*); **venire meno** to faint; **venir meno a** to fail to keep (*one's word*); **venir su** to grow, come up; **venire via** to give way ‖ *ref*—**venirsene** to stroll along ‖ *impers* (with *dat*)—**viene da** feel the urge to, e.g., **gli venne da starnutire** he felt the urge to sneeze; **gli è venuto da ridere** he felt the urge to laugh; **viene detto** blurt out, e.g., **gli è venuto detto che non gli piaceva quel tipo** he blurted out that he did not like that fellow; **viene fatto di**+*inf* succeed in+*ger*, e.g., **le venne fatto di convincerli** she succeeded in convincing them; happen to + *inf*, e.g., **gli venne fatto di incontrarmi per istrada** he happened to meet me on the way

ventà·glio *m* (-**gli**) fan; (fig) spread; **a ventaglio** fanlike; **diramarsi a ventaglio** to fan out
ventaròla *f* weather vane
ventata *f* gust of wind; (fig) wave
ventènne *adj* twenty-year-old ‖ *mf* twenty-year-old person
ventèsi·mo -ma *adj, m & pron* twentieth
vénti *adj & pron* twenty; **le venti** eight P.M. ‖ *m* twenty; twentieth (*in dates*)
ventidue *adj & pron* twenty-two **le ventidue** ten P.M. ‖ *m* twenty-two; twenty-second (*in dates*)
ventilare (**vèntilo**) *tr* to air, ventilate; to winnow (*grain*); to discuss minutely; to air (*a subject*); to broach (*a subject*); to unfurl (*a flag*) ‖ *ref* to fan oneself
ventilatóre *m* fan, ventilator; vent; (min) ventilation shaft; (naut) funnel
ventilazióne *f* ventilation; winnowing
ventina *f* score; **una ventina (di)** twenty, about twenty
ventino *m* twenty-cent coin
ventiquattro *adj & pron* twenty-four; **le ventiquattro** twelve P.M. ‖ *m* twenty-four; twenty-fourth (*in dates*)
ventiquattró·re *f* (-**re**) overnight bag; twenty-four-hour race; **ventiquattrore** *fpl* period of twenty-four hours
ventitré *adj & pron* twenty-three; **le ventitré** eleven P.M.; **portare il cappello alle ventitré** to wear one's hat cocked ‖ *m* twenty-three; twenty-third (*in dates*)

vènto *m* wind; air; guy wire; **presentarsi al vento** to sail into the wind; **farsi vento** to fan oneself; **a vento** windproof; wind-propelled; **col vento in prora** downwind; **col vento in poppa** upwind; favorably, famously
vèntola *f* fireside fan; lampshade; candle sconce; blade (*of fan*)
ventó·so -sa [s] *adj* windy ‖ *f* cupping glass; suction cup; (zool) sucker
vèntre *m* belly; **a ventre a terra** on one's belly; on one's face; at full speed (*said of a horse*)
ventrìcolo *m* ventricle
ventrièra *f* abdominal band or belt
ventrilòquia *f* ventriloquism
ventrìlo·quo -qua *mf* ventriloquist
ventuno *adj & pron* twenty-one; **le ventuno** nine P.M. ‖ *m* twenty-one; twenty-first (*in dates*); (cards) blackjack
ventu·ro -ra *adj* next ‖ *f* (lit) luck, fortune; (lit) good fortune; **alla ventura** at random, at a venture; **di ventura** of fortune, e.g., **soldato di ventura** soldier of fortune
venustà *f* (lit) pulchritude
venu·to -ta *mf*—**nuovo venuto** newcomer; **primo venuto** firstcomer ‖ *f* coming, arrival
véra *f* curbstone (*of well*); (coll) wedding ring
verace *adj* true; truthful, veracious
veraci·tà *f* (-**tà**) veracity, truthfulness
veranda *f* veranda; porch
verbale *adj* verbal ‖ *m* minutes; ticket (*given by a policeman*); **mettere a verbale** to enter into the record
verbèna *f* verbena
vèrbo *m* verb; (lit) word ‖ **Verbo** *m* (theol) Word
verbosità [s] *f* verbiage, verbosity
verbó·so -sa [s] *adj* windy, long-winded, verbose
verda·stro -stra *adj* greenish
vérde *adj* green; young, youthful ‖ *m* green; **al verde** (coll) broke, penniless; **nel verde degli anni** in the prime of life
verdeggiante *adj* verdant
verderame *m* blue vitriol; verdigris
verdét·to -ta *adj* greenish ‖ *m* verdict
verdógno·lo -la *adj* greenish; sallow (*face*)
verdura *f* vegetables
verecóndia *f* modesty, bashfulness
verecón·do -da *adj* modest, bashful
vér·ga *f* (-**ghe**) switch; rod; ingot, bar; pole; penis; (eccl) staff, crosier; (naut) yard; **tremare a verga a verga** to shake like a leaf
vergare §209 (**vérgo**) *tr* to switch; to rule (*paper*); to stripe; to write
vergati·no -na *adj* thin (*paper*) ‖ *m* striped cloth
verga·to -ta *adj* striped; watermarked with stripes ‖ *m* (obs) serge
verginale *adj* maidenly, virginal
vérgine *adj & f* virgin ‖ **Vergine** *f* (eccl) Virgin; (astr) Virgo
verginità *f* virginity, maidenhood
vergógna *f* shame; **aver vergogna** to be

ashamed; **vergogne** privates || *interj* for shame!

vergognare (**vergógno**) *ref* to be ashamed; to feel cheap; **vergognati!** shame on you!

vergognó·so -sa [s] *adj* ashamed; bashful; shameful

veridici·tà *f* (-**tà**) veracity

verìdi·co -ca *adj* (-**ci -che**) veracious

verìfi·ca *f* (-**che**) verification; control; **verifica fiscale** auditing (*of tax return*)

verificare §197 (**verìfico**) *tr* to verify; to control, check; to audit || *ref* to come true; to happen

verifica·tóre -trice *mf* checker, inspector

verismo *m* verism (*as developed in Italy*)

veri·sta *adj & mf* (-**sti -ste**) verist

veri·tà *f* (-**tà**) truth; **in verità** truthfully, verily

veritiè·ro -ra *adj* truthful

vèrme *m* worm; (mach) thread; **verme solitario** tapeworm

vermì·glio -glia (-**gli -glie**) *adj* vermilion; ruby (*lips*) || *m* vermilion

vèr·mut *m* (-**mut**) vermouth

vernàcolo *m* vernacular

vernice *f* varnish; paint; polish; patina; (painting) private viewing; (fig) veneer; **scarpe di vernice** patent-leather shoes; **vernice a olio** oil paint; **vernice a spruzzo** spray paint; **vernice da scarpe** shoe polish

verniciare §128 *tr* to varnish; to paint

vé·ro -ra *adj* true; real; right; pure; **non è vero?** isn't that so? La traduzione precedente è generalmente rimpiazzata da molte altre frasi. Se la prima espressione è negativa, la domanda equivalente è **non è vero?** sarà affermativa, per esempio, **Lei non lavora, non è vero?** You are not working, are you? Se la prima espressione è affermativa, la domanda sarà negativa, per esempio, **Lei lavora, non è vero?** You are working, are you not? or aren't you? Se la prima espressione contiene un ausiliare, la domanda conterrà l'ausiliare stesso senza infinito o senza participio passato, per esempio, **Arriveranno domani, non è vero?** They will arrive tomorrow, won't they? **Ha finito il compito, non è vero?** He has finished his homework, hasn't he? Se la prima espressione non contiene né un ausiliare, né una delle forme del verbo "to be" in funzione di copula, la domanda conterrà l'ausiliare "do" o "did" senza l'infinito del verbo, per esempio, **Lei è vissuto a Milano, non è vero?** You lived in Milano, did you not? **Lei non va mai al parco, non è vero?** You never go to the park, do you?; **non mi par vero** it seems unbelievable || *m* truth; actuality; a **dire il vero** to tell the truth, as a matter of fact; **dal vero** from nature; **salvo il vero** if I am not mistaken || *f* see **vera**

veróne *m* (lit) balcony

verosimiglianza *f* verisimilitude; probability, likelihood

verosìmile *adj* verisimilar; probable, likely

verricèllo *m* winch, windlass

vèrro *m* boar

verru·ca *f* (-**che**) wart

versaménto *m* spilling; payment; deposit

versante *m* depositor; slope, side

versare (**vèrso**) *tr* to pour; to spill; to shed; to pay; to deposit || *intr* to overflow; **versare in gravi condizioni** to be in a bad way || *ref* to spill; to pour (*said of people*); to empty (*said of a river*)

versàtile *adj* versatile; fickle

versa·to -ta *adj* versed; gifted; fully subscribed to (*e.g., stock of a corporation*)

verseggia·tóre -trice *mf* verse writer

versétto *m* verse (*of Bible*)

versificare §197 (**versìfico**) *tr & intr* to versify

versificazióne *f* versification

versióne *f* version; translation

vèrso *adj invar*—**pollice verso** (hist) thumbs down || *m* verse; local accent; voice, cry; reverse (*of coin*); verso (*of page*); line (*of poetry*); singsong; gesture; direction, way, manner; respect; **andare a verso** (with *dat*) to suit, e.g., **le sue maniere non gli vanno a verso** her manners do not suit him; **a verso** properly; **contro verso** against the grain; **fare un verso** to make faces; **per un verso** on one hand; **rifare il verso** (with *dat*) to mimick; **senza verso** without rhyme or reason; **verso sciolto** blank verse || *prep* toward; near, around; about; for, toward; upon, in return for; as compared with; **verso di** toward

vèrtebra *f* vertebra

vertebrale *adj* vertebral; spinal

vertebra·to -ta *adj & m* vertebrate

vertènza *f* quarrel, dispute; **vertenza sindacale** labor dispute

vèrtere §283 *intr*—**vertere su** to deal with, to turn on

verticale *adj & f* vertical

vèrtice *m* top, summit; vertex; summit conference

vertigine *f* vertigo, dizziness; **avere le vertigini** to feel dizzy

vertiginó·so -sa [s] *adj* dizzy; breathtaking

vérza [dz] *f* cabbage

verzière [dz] *m* (lit) fruit, vegetable, and flower garden; (coll) produce market

verzura [dz] *f* verdure

vescì·ca *f* (-**che**) bladder; blister; **vescica di vento** (fig) windbag; **vescica gonfiata** swellhead; **vescica natatoria** air bladder

vescichétta *f* blister; vescicle; **veschetta biliare** gall bladder

vescìcola *f* blister

vescovado *m* bishopric

véscovo *m* bishop

vè·spa *f* wasp, yellowjacket ‖ *f* (-spe & -spa) motor scooter

ve·spàio *m* (-spài) wasp's nest; (fig) hornet's nest

vespasiano *m* public urinal

Vèspero *m* Vesper

vesperti·no -na *adj* (lit) evening

vèspro *m* (eccl) vespers; (lit) vespertide

vessare (vèsso) *tr* (lit) to oppress

vessatò·rio -ria *adj* (-ri -rie) vexatious

vessazióne *f* oppression

vessillo *m* flag

vestàglia *f* negligee, dressing gown; **vestaglia da bagno** bathrobe

vèste *f* dress; cover; (lit) body; **in veste di** in the quality of; as; in the guise of; **veste da camera** negligee, dressing gown; bathrobe; **veste talare** (eccl) long vestment; **vesti** clothes

vestià·rio *m* (-ri) wardrobe

vestíbolo *m* vestibule, lobby

vestí·gio *m* (-gi & -gia *fpl*) vestige, trace; (lit) footprint

vestire (vèsto) *tr* to dress; to don; to wear; to clothe; to cover, bedeck ‖ *intr* to dress; to fit ‖ *ref* to get dressed; to dress; to dress oneself; to buy one's own clothes

vestí·to -ta *adj* dressed; covered ‖ *m* dress; suit; clothing; **vestiti** clothes; **vestito da donna** dress; **vestito da festa** Sunday best; **vestito da sera** evening clothes, formal suit; evening gown; **vestito da uomo** suit

Vesùvio, il Vesuvius

vetera·no -na *adj* & *mf* veteran

veterinà·rio -ria *adj* (-ri -rie) veterinary ‖ *m* veterinarian ‖ *f* veterinary medicine

vèto *m* veto; **porre il veto a** to veto

ve·tràio *m* (-trài) glass manufacturer; glass dealer; glass blower

vetra·to -ta *adj* glass, glass-enclosed; sand (*paper*) ‖ *m* glare ice, glaze ‖ *f* glass door; glass window; glass enclosure; **vetrata a colori** or **vetrata istoriata** stained-glass window

vetrería *f* glassworks; **vetrerie** glassware

vetria·to -ta *adj* glassy; glass-covered

vetrificare §197 (vetrífico) *tr* to vitrify ‖ *ref* to become vitrified

vetrina *f* show window; showcase, glass cabinet; **mettersi in vetrina** to show off; **vetrine** (coll) eyeglasses

vetrini·sta *mf* (-sti -ste) window dresser

vetri·no -na *adj* glass-like; brittle, fragile ‖ *m* slide (*of microscope*) ‖ *f* see **vetrina**

vetriòlo *m* vitriol

vétro *m* glass; glassware; window pane; piece of glass; **vetro aderente** contact lens; **vetro infrangibile** (aut) safety glass; **vetro smerigliato** ground glass, frosted glass

vetrorèsina *f* fiberglass

vetró·so -sa [s] *adj* vitreous, glassy

vétta *f* peak; top, tip; limb (*of tree*); (naut) end (*of hawser*); **tremare come una vetta** to shake like a leaf

vet·tóre -trice *adj* leading, guiding; spreading, carrying ‖ *m* carrier; (math, phys) vector

vettovagliare §280 *tr* to supply with food

vettovàglie *fpl* victuals, food; supplies

vettura *f* forwarding; coach; car; freight; **in vettura!** (rr) all aboard!; **prendere in vettura** to hire (*a conveyance*); **vettura belvedere** (rr) observation car; **vettura da turismo** (aut) pleasure car; **vettura di piazza** hack, hackney; **vettura letto** (rr) sleeping car; **vettura ristorante** (rr) diner

vetturétta *f* economy car, compact

vetturino *m* hackman, cab driver

vetu·sto -sta *adj* old, ancient

vezzeggiare §290 (vezzéggio) *tr* to coddle ‖ *intr* (lit) to strut

vezzeggiatí·vo -va *adj* endearing ‖ *m* endearing expression; diminutive

vézzo *m* habit; caress; necklace; bad habit; **vezzi** fondling, petting; mawkish behavior; charms

vezzó·so -sa [s] *adj* graceful, charming; affected, mincing

vi §5

via *m* (vìa) starting signal; **dare il via a** to give the go-ahead to ‖ *f* street; road, way; route; career; **dare la via a** to open the way to; **in via confidenziale** in confidence; **in via eccezionale** as an exception; **per via di** via, through; (coll) because of; **per via gerarchica** through administrative channels; **per via orale** orally; **per via rettale** rectally; **prendere la via** to be on one's way; **venire a vie di fatto** to come to blows; **Via Crucis** Way of the Cross; **via d'acqua** waterway; via di scampo (fig) way out; **via d'uscita** way out; **Via Lattea** Milky Way; **vie di fatto** assault and battery; **vie legali** legal steps ‖ *adv* away; (math) times, by; **e così via** and so on; **e via dicendo** and so on; **tirar via** to hurry along; **via via che** as ‖ *prep* via, by way of

viadótto *m* viaduct

viaggiare §290 *intr* to travel; (com) to deal

viaggia·tóre -trice *adj* traveling; homing (*pigeon*) ‖ *mf* traveler ‖ *m* traveling salesman

viàg·gio *m* (-gi) travel; journey, trip; **buon viaggio!** bon voyage!; **viaggio d'andata e ritorno** round trip; **viaggio di prova** (naut) trial run, shakedown cruise

viale *m* boulevard

viandante *mf* (lit) wayfarer

vià·rio -ria *adj* (-ri -rie) road, highway

viàti·co *m* (-ci) viaticum

viavài *m* coming and going; hustle and bustle

vibrante *adj* vibrant; wiry; (phonet) vibrant ‖ *f* (phonet) trill, vibrant

vibrare *tr* to jar; to deliver (*a blow*); to vibrate; (lit) to hurl ‖ *intr* to vibrate

vibra·to -ta *adj* vibrant; resolute, vigorous ‖ *m* vibrating sound

vibrazióne *f* vibration

vicariato *m* vicarage

vicà·rio *m* (-ri) vicar

vice- *pref adj* vice-, e.g., **vicereale** viceroyal ‖ *pref m & f* vice-, e.g., **viceammiraglio** vice-admiral; assistant, e.g., **vicegovernatore** assistant governor; deputy, e.g., **vicesindaco** deputy mayor

vicediret·tóre -trice *mf* assistant manager

vicènda *f* vicissitude; rotation (*of crops*); **a vicenda** in turn

vicendévole *adj* mutual, reciprocal

vicepresidènte [s] *mf* vice president

vice·ré *m* (**-rè**) viceroy

vicevèrsa *adv* vice versa; (coll) instead, on the contrary

vichin·go -ga *adj & mf* (**-ghi -ghe**) Viking

vicinanza *f* nearness; **in vicinanza di** in the neighborhood of; **vicinanze** vicinity, neighborhood

vicinato *m* neighborhood

vici·no -na *adj* near; neighboring; next; close (*relative*) ‖ *mf* neighbor ‖ **vicino** *adv* nearby, near; **da vicino** closely; at close quarters; **vicino a** near; next to, close to

vicissitùdine *f* vicissitude

vi·co *m* (**-chi**) alley, lane; village; (lit) region

vìcolo *m* alley, court, place; **vicolo cieco** blind alley, dead end

videocassétta *f* video cassette

vidimare (**vìdimo**) *tr* to validate, visa; to sign

vidimazióne *f* validation, visa; signature

viennése [s] *adj & mf* Viennese

viepiù *adv* (lit) more and more

vietare (**vièto**) *tr* to forbid, prohibit

vieta·to -ta *adj* forbidden; **senso vietato** one way; **sosta vietata** no parking; no stopping; **vietato fumare** no smoking

Vietnam, il Vietnam

vietnami·ta *adj & mf* (**-ti -te**) Vietnamese

viè·to -ta *adj* (lit) old-fashioned; (coll) musty-smelling, rancid

vigènte *adj* current, in force

vigere §284 *intr* to be in force

vigèsi·mo -ma *adj* twentieth

vigilante *adj* watchful, vigilant ‖ *m* watchman

vigilanza *f* vigilance; surveillance

vigilare (**vìgilo**) *tr* to watch; to watch over; to police ‖ *intr* to watch; **vigilare che** to see to it that

vigila·tóre -trice *mf* inspector ‖ *f* camp counselor; **vigilatrice sanitaria** child health inspector

vigile *adj* (lit) watchful ‖ *m* watch; **vigile del fuoco** fireman; **vigile urbano** policeman

vigìlia *f* fast; vigil; **la vigilia di** on the eve of, the night before

vigliaccherìa *f* cowardice

vigliac·co -ca (**-chi -che**) *adj* cowardly ‖ *m* coward

vigna *f* vineyard

vignaiòlo *m* vine dresser

vignéto *m* vineyard

vignétta *f* vignette; **vignetta umoristica** cartoon

vignetti·sta *mf* (**-sti -ste**) cartoonist

vigógna *f* vicuña

vigóre *m* vigor; **in vigore** in force

vigorìa *f* vigor

vigoró·so -sa [s] *adj* vigorous

vile *adj* cowardly; vile, low, cheap; base (*metal*)

vilificare §197 (**vilìfico**) *tr* to vilify

vilipèndere §148 *tr* to despise; to show scorn for

villa *f* villa; country house; one-family detached house; (lit) country

villàg·gio -gi (**-gi**) village; **villaggio del fanciullo** boys' town

villanata *f* boorishness

villanìa *f* boorishness, rudeness; insult

villa·no -na *adj* rude, churlish ‖ *mf* boor, churl; (lit) peasant

villanzó·ne -na *mf* boor, uncouth person

villeggiante *mf* vacationist

villeggiare §290 (**villéggio**) *intr* to vacation

villeggiatura *f* vacation, summer vacation

villétta *f* or **villino** *m* bungalow

villó·so -sa [s] *adj* hairy

vil·tà *f* (**-tà**) baseness; cowardice

viluppo *m* tangle, twist

vìmine *m* withe, wicker, osier

vinàcce *fpl* pressed grapes

vi·nàio *m* (**-nài**) wine merchant

vincènte *adj* winning ‖ *mf* winner

vincere §285 *tr* to overcome; to win; to convince; to check; to defeat; **vincere per un pelo** to nose out; **vincerla** to come out on top ‖ *ref* to control oneself

vincetòssi·co *m* (**-ci**) swallowwort, tame poison

vincipèr·di *m* (**-di**) giveaway

vìncita *f* gain; winnings

vinci·tóre -trice *adj* conquering, victorious ‖ *mf* winner; conqueror; victor

vincolare *adj* binding; bound ‖ *v* (**vìncolo**) *tr* to tie; to bind, obligate; to restrict the use of (*real-estate property*)

vìncolo *m* tie, bond; (law) entail; (law) restriction (*in a real-estate deed*)

vinìco·lo -la *adj* wine, wine-producing

vinile *m* vinyl

vino *m* wine; **vin caldo** mulled wine; **vino da pasto** table wine; **vino di marca** vintage wine; **vino di mele** cider

vin·to -ta *adj* vanquished, overcome, defeated; victorious (*battle*); **averla vinta su** to overcome; **darla vinta a qlcu** to let s.o. get away with murder; **darsi per vinto** to give in, yield ‖ *m* vanquished person; **i vinti** the vanquished

viò·la *adj invar* violet ‖ *m* (**-la**) violet (*color*) ‖ *f* violet; (mus) viola; **viola del pensiero** pansy; **viola mammola** sweet violet

violacciòc·ca *f* (**-che**) (bot) wallflower

violà·ceo -cea *adj* violet

violare (**vìolo**) *tr* to violate; to run (*a blockade*)

violazióne *f* violation; **violazione di**

domicilio housebreaking, burglary; **violazione di proprietà** trespass

violentare (violènto) *tr* to violate, force; to do violence to; to rape

violèn·to -ta *adj* violent ‖ *m* violent person

violènza *f* violence; **violenza carnale** rape

violét·to -ta *adj* & *m* violet ‖ *f* (bot) violet

violini·sta *mf* (-sti -ste) violinist

violino *m* violin; **primo violino** concertmaster

violoncelli·sta *mf* (-sti -ste) violoncellist

violoncèllo *m* violoncello, cello

viòttolo *m* path

vipera *f* viper, adder

viràg·gio *m* (-gi) turn; (aer) banking; (naut) tacking; (phot) toning

virare *tr* to veer; to turn (*a winch*); (aer) to bank; (phot) to tone ‖ *intr* to veer, steer; **virare di bordo** (naut) to put about; (naut) to tack

virata *f* turn, veer; (aer) banking; (naut) tacking

virginale *adj* (var of **verginale**

virgi·nia *m* (-nia) Virginia tobacco ‖ *f* (-nia) Virginia cigarette

vìrgola *f* comma; (*used in Italian to set off the decimal fraction from the integer*) decimal point; **doppia virgola** quotation mark

virgolétta *f* quotation mark

virgulto *m* (lit) shoot; (lit) shrub

virile *adj* virile

virilità *f* virility

viròla *f* (mach) male piece

virologia *f* virology

vir·tù *f* (-tù) virtue; (lit) valor

virtuale *adj* virtual

virtualménte *adv* virtually, to all intents and purposes

virtuosismo [s] *m* virtuosity; showing off

virtuosità [s] *f* virtuosity

virtuó·so -sa [s] *adj* virtuous ‖ *mf* virtuoso

virulèn·to -ta *adj* virulent

virulènza *f* virulence

vi·rus *m* (-rus) virus

vìsce·re *m* (-ri) internal organ; **visceri** entrails, viscera ‖ **viscere** *fpl* entrails, viscera; (fig) heart, feeling; (fig) bowels (*of the earth*)

vi·schio *m* (-schi) mistletoe; birdlime; (fig) trap

vischió·so -sa [s] *adj* sticky, viscous; (com) steady

vìsci·do -da *adj* viscid; clammy; (fig) unctuous

vìsciola *f* sour cherry

vìsciolo *m* sour cherry tree

viscónte *m* viscount

viscontéssa *f* viscountess

viscó·so -sa [s] *adj* viscous, sticky ‖ *f* viscose

visétto *m* small face; baby face

visìbile *adj* visible; obvious

visibì·lio *m* (-li) (coll) crowd; (coll) bunch; **andare in visibilio** to become ecstatic; **mandare in visibilio** to throw into ecstasy, enrapture

visibilità *f* visibility

visièra *f* visor; fencing mask; eyeshade; **visiera termica** (aut) electric defroster

visigò·to -ta *adj* Visigothic ‖ *mf* Visigoth

visionà·rio -ria *adj* & *mf* (-ri -rie) visionary

visióne *f* vision; sight; (mov, telv) showing; **in visione gratuita** for free examination; **mandare qlco a qlcu in visione** to send s.th to s.o. for his (or her) opinion; **prendere visione di** to examine; to peruse

visi·sìr *m* (-sìr) vizier

vìsita *f* visit; visitation; **fare una visita** to pay a visit; **marcare visita** (mil) to report sick; **visita doganale** customs inspection

visitare (vìsito) *tr* to visit; to inspect

visita·tóre -trice *mf* visitor ‖ *f* social worker

visitazióne *f* visitation

visi·vo -va *adj* visual

viso *m* face; **far buon viso a cattivo gioco** to grin and bear it

visóne *m* mink

visóre *m* (phot) viewer; (phot) viewfinder

vi·spo -spa *adj* brisk, lively

vissu·to -ta *adj* wordly-wise

vista *f* sight, eyesight; view; vista; glance; (poet) window; a vista exposed, visible; **a vista d'occhio** as far as the eye can see; **essere in vista** to be expected; to be imminent; to be in the limelight; **far vista di** to pretend to; **in vista di** in view of; **mettere in vista** to show off; **vista a volo d'uccello** bird's-eye view; **vista corta** poor eyesight

vistare *tr* to validate, visa

vi·sto -sta *adj*—**visto che** seeing that, inasmuch as ‖ *m* visa; approval ‖ *f* see vista

vistó·so -sa [s] *adj* showy, flashy; (fig) considerable

visuale *adj* visual ‖ *f* view; line of sight

visualizzare [ddzz] *tr* to visualize

vita *f* life; livelihood; living; waist; **avere breve vita** to be short-lived; **fare la vita** to be a prostitute; **vita natural durante** for life; during one's lifetime

vitaiòlo *m* man about town; playboy, bon vivant

vitale *adj* vital

vitalità *f* vitality

vitalì·zio -zia (-zi -zie) *adj* life, lifetime ‖ *m* life annuity

vitamina *f* vitamin

vite *f* (bot) grapevine; (mach) screw; **a vite** threaded; (aer) in a tailspin; **vite autofilettante** self-tapping screw; **vite del Canadà** woodbine, Virginia creeper; **vite per legno** wood screw; **vite per metallo** machine screw; **vite perpetua** (mach) endless screw, worm gear; **vite prigioniera** stud bolt

vitèllo *m* calf; veal

vitìc·cio *m* (-ci) tendril

vìtre·o -a *adj* vitreous; glassy (*eyes*)

vìttima f victim

vitto m food; diet; **vitto e alloggio** room and board

vittòria f victory; **cantar vittoria** to crow; to crow too soon

vittorió·so -sa [s] adj victorious

vituperare (**vitùpero**) tr to vituperate

vituperévole adj contemptible, shameful

vitupè·rio m (**-ri**) shame, infamy; insult; (lit) blame

viuzza f narrow street, lane

viva interj long live!

vivacchiare §287 intr (coll) to get along || ref—si vivacchia (coll) so, so

vivace adj lively, brisk; brilliant; vivacious

vivacità f liveliness, briskness; brilliancy, brightness; vivacity

vivaddìo interj yes, of course!; by Jove!

vivagno m selvage; edge

vi·vàio m (**-vài**) fishpond; fish tank; tree nursery; (fig) seedbed

vivanda f food

vivandiè·re -ra mf (mil) sutler

vìvere m life; living; cost of living; **viveri** food, provisions; allowance || §286 tr to live; **vivere un brutto momento** to spend an uncomfortable moment || intr (ESSERE) to live; **vive** (typ) stet; **vivere alla giornata** to live from hand to mouth

vivézza f liveliness

vìvi·do -da adj vivid, lively

vivificare §197 (**vivìfico**) tr to vivify

vivisezionare (**vivisezióno**) tr to vivisect; to scrutinize

vivisezióne f vivisection

vi·vo -va adj alive; living; live, vivacious; lively; vivid; high (flame); bright (light); raw (flesh); sharp, acute (pain); hearty (thanks); outright (expense); gross (weight); brute (strength); modern (language); kinetic (energy); running (water) || m living being; heart (of a question); **al vivo** lively; lifelike; **i vivi e i morti** the quick and the dead; **toccare nel vivo** to sting to the quick || **viva** interj see viva

viziare §287 tr to spoil; to ruin; (law) to vitiate || ref—si to become spoiled

vizia·to -ta adj spoiled; ruined; stale (air)

vì·zio m (**-zi**) vice; defect; flaw; (law) vitiation

vizió·so -sa [s] adj vicious; defective || mf profligate

viz·zo -za adj withered

vocabolà·rio m (**-ri**) dictionary; vocabulary

vocàbolo m word

vocale adj vocal; (lit) sonorous || f vowel

vocalizzare [ddzz] tr & ref to vocalize

vocativo m vocative

vocazióne f vocation

vóce f voice; noise, roar; word; rumor; entry; tone; **ad alta voce** aloud; **a bassa voce** in a low voice; **a viva voce** by word of mouth; **a voce** orally; **dare una voce a** (coll) to call; **dare sulla voce a** to rebuke; to con-

tradict; **fare la voce grossa** to raise one's voice; **non avere voce in capitolo** to have no say; **schiarirsi la voce** to clear one's throat; **senza voce** hoarse; **sotto voce** in a low tone; **voce bianca** child's voice (in singing)

vociare m bawl || §128 (**vócio**) intr to bawl

vociferare (**vocìfero**) intr to vociferate, shout || ref—si vocifera it is rumored

vó·ga f (**-ghe**) fashion, vogue; energy, enthusiasm; rowing

vogare §209 (**vógo**) tr & intr to row

voga·tóre -trice mf rower || m oarsman; rowing machine

vòglia f wish; whim, fancy; willingness; birthmark; **aver voglia di** to feel like, have a notion to; **di buona voglia** willingly; **di mala voglia** unwillingly

voglió·so -sa [s] adj fanciful; (lit) desirous

vói §5 pron pers you; **voi altri** you, e.g., **voi altri americani** you Americans

voial·tri -tre pron pl you, e.g., **voialtri americani** you Americans

volano m shuttlecock; (mach) flywheel

volante adj flying; loose (sheet); free (agent) || m steering wheel; (mach) hand wheel; shuttlecock

volantino m leaflet; fringe; (mach) hand wheel

volare (**vólo**) tr (soccer) to overthrow || intr (ESSERE & AVERE) to fly

volata f flight; sprint; run; mouth (of gun); (tennis) volley; **di volata** in a hurry

volàtile adj volatile; flying (animal) || **volatili** mpl birds

volatilizzare [ddzz] tr & intr (ESSERE) to volatilize

volènte adj—**Dio volente** God willing; **volente o nolente** willy-nilly

volentièri adv gladly, willingly

volére m will, wish; **al volere di** at the bidding of || §288 tr to will; to want, desire; (lit) to believe, affirm; **l'hai voluto tu** it's your fault; **non vuol dire!** never mind!; **qui ti voglio** here's the rub, that's the trouble; **senza volere** without meaning to; **voglia Dio!** may God grant!; **voler bene** (with dat) to like; **volerci** to take, e.g., **ci vorranno due anni per finire questo palazzo** it will take two years to complete this building; **ce ne vogliono ancora tre** it takes three more of them; **voler dire** to mean; to try, e.g., **vuole piovere** it is trying to rain; **volere che** + subj to want + inf, e.g., **vuole che vengano** he wants them to come; **volere piuttosto** to prefer; **volere è potere** where there is a will there is a way; **voler male** (with dat) to dislike; **volerne a** to bear a grudge against; **vorrei** I should like, I'd like; **vuoi . . . vuoi** either . . . or

volgare adj vernacular, popular, common; vulgar || m vernacular

volgari·tà f (**-tà**) vulgarity

volgarizzare [ddzz] *tr* to popularize

vòlgere §289 *tr* to turn; (lit) to translate ‖ *intr* to turn; (lit) to go by; volgere a to turn toward; to draw near, to approach; volgere in fuga to take to flight ‖ *ref* to turn; to devote oneself

vól·go *m* (-ghi) (lit) crowd, mob

volièra *f* aviary

voliti·vo -va *adj* volitional; strongminded, strong-willed

vólo *m* flight; tall; al volo on the spot; on the wing; a volo d'uccello as the crow flies; bird's-eye (*e.g.*, *view*); di volo at top speed, immediately; in volo aloft, in the air; prendere il volo to take flight; volo a vela or volo planato gliding; volo strumentale instrument flying; volo veleggiato gliding

volon·tà *f* (-tà) will; di spontanea volontà of one's own volition; pieno di buona volontà eager to please; ultime volontà last will and testament

volontariato *m* volunteer work; apprenticeship without pay; (mil) volunteer service

volontà·rio -ria (-ri -rie) *adj* voluntary ‖ *m* volunteer

volonteró·so -sa [s] *adj* willing, welldisposed

volpacchiòtto *m* fox cub; (fig) sly fox

vólpe *f* fox; (agr) smut; volpe argentata silver fox

volpi·no -na *adj* fox; fox-colored; foxy ‖ *m* Pomeranian

volpó·ne -na *mf* sly fox

vòlt *m* (vòlt) (elec) volt

vòl·ta *m* (-ta) (elec) volt ‖ *f* turn; time; vault; roof (*of mouth*); alla volta di toward; a volta di corriere by return mail; a volte sometimes; c'era una volta once upon a time there was; certe volte sometimes; dare di volta il cervello a to go crazy, e.g., gli ha dato di volta il cervello he went crazy; dar la volta to turn sour (*said of wine*); due volte twice; molte volte often; per una volta tanto only once; poche volte seldom; tante volte often; tutto in una volta at one swoop, at one stroke; in one gulp, in one swallow; una volta once; una volta che (coll) inasmuch as; una volta per sempre once and for all; una volta tanto for once; volta a crociera cross vault; volta per volta little by little; volte (math) times, e.g., cinque volte cinque five times five

voltafàc·cia *m* (-cia) volte-face; fare voltafaccia to wheel around (*said of a horse*)

voltagabbà·na *mf* (-na) turncoat

voltàg·gio *m* (-gi) voltage

voltài·co -ca *adj* (-ci -che) voltaic

voltare (vòlto) *tr, intr & ref* to turn

voltastòma·co *m* (-chi) (coll) nausea; fare venire il voltastomaco a qlcu (coll) to turn s.o.'s stomach

voltata *f* turn; curve

volteggiare §290 (voltéggio) *tr* to put (*a horse*) through its paces ‖ *intr* to hover; to flit, flutter; (sports) to vault (*e.g.*, *on horseback or trapeze*)

voltég·gio *m* (-gi) (sports) vaulting

vòltmetro *m* voltmeter

vólto *m* (lit) face

voitura *f* (com, law) transfer

volùbile *adj* fickle

volubilità *f* fickleness

volume *m* volume; bulk; mass

voluminó·so -sa [s] *adj* voluminous, bulky

volu·to -ta *adj* desired; intentional ‖ *f* (archit) volute, scroll

volut·tà *f* (-tà) pleasure, enjoyment; voluptuousness

voluttuà·rio -ria *adj* (-ri -rie) luxury (*goods*)

voluttuó·so -sa [s] *adj* voluptuous, sensuous

vòmere *m* plowshare; trail spade (*of gun*)

vòmi·co -ca *adj* (-ci -che) emetic

vomitare (vòmito) *tr & intr* to vomit

vomitati·vo -va *adj & m* emetic

vòmito *m* vomit

vóngola *f* clam

vorace *adj* voracious

voraci·tà *f* (-tà) voracity

voràgine *f* chasm, gulf, abyss

vòrtice *m* vortex, whirlpool; whirlwind

vorticó·so -sa [s] *adj* whirling, swirling

vò·stro -stra §6 *adj & pron poss*

votare (vóto) *tr* to devote; to vote ‖ *intr* to vote ‖ *ref* to devote oneself

votazióne *f* vote, voting, poll; (educ) grades

voti·vo -va *adj* votive

vóto *m* vow; wish; votive offering; vote, ballot; grade, mark; a pieni voti with highest honors; fare un voto to make a vow; pronunciare i voti to take vows; voto di fiducia vote of confidence; voto preferenziale write-in vote; preferential ballot

vudù *m* voodoo

vudui·sta *mf* (-sti -ste) voodoo (*person*)

vulcàni·co -ca *adj* (-ci -che) volcanic

vulcanizzare [ddzz] *tr* to vulcanize

vulcano *m* volcano

vulga·to -ta *adj* disseminated ‖ Vulgata *f* Vulgate

vulneràbile *adj* vulnerable

vuotare (vuòto) *tr* to empty; vuotare il sacco to speak one's mind, unburden oneself ‖ *ref* to empty

vuò·to -ta *adj* empty; devoid ‖ *m* vacuum; emptiness; empty space; empty seat; empty feeling; empty (*e.g.*, *container*); a vuoto in vain; wide of the mark; (*check*) without sufficient funds; andare a vuoto to fail; (mach) to idle; cadere nel vuoto to fall on deaf ears; mandare a vuoto to thwart; sotto vuoto in a vacuum; vuoto d'aria (aer) air pocket; vuoto di cassa deficit; vuoto di potere power vacuum

W

W, w ['doppjo 'vu] *m & f*
wà·fer *m* (-fer) wafer
water-clòset *m* (-clòset) flush toilet
watt *m* (watt) watt

watt·óra *m* (-óra) watt-hour
wèstern *m* (wèstern) (mov) western
whisky *m* (whisky) whiskey
wìgwam *m* (wìgwam) wigwam

X

X, x [ɪks] *m & f*
xèna *m* xenon
xenòfo·bo -ba *mf* xenophobe

xè·res *m* (-res) sherry
xerografia *f* xerography
xeròfito *m* xerophyte

Y

Y, y ['ɪpsɪlon] *m & f*
yacht *m* (yachts) yacht
yak *m* (yak) yak

yànkee *m* (yànkees) Yankee
yìddish *adj invar & m* Yiddish

Z

Z, z ['dzɛta] *m & f* twenty-first letter of the Italian alphabet
zabaióne [dz] *m* eggnog
zàcchera *f* splash of mud
zaffare *tr* to plug; to bung
zaffata *f* unpleasant whiff, stench; gust
zafferano [dz] *m* saffron
zaffiro [dz] *m* sapphire
zaffo *m* plug; bung; tampon
zàgara [dz] *f* orange blossom
zàino [dz] *m* knapsack; (mil) pack
zampa *f* paw; (culin) leg; **a quattro zampe** on all fours; **zampa di gallina** crow's-foot; illegible scrawl; **zampa di porco** crowbar
zampare *intr* to paw; to stamp
zampettare (zampétto) *intr* to toddle; to scamper
zampillare *intr* (ESSERE & AVERE) to spurt, gush, spring
zampillo *m* spurt, gush, spring
zampino *m* little paw; **metterci lo zampino** to put one's finger in the pie
zampiróne *m* slow-burning mosquito repellent; foul-smelling cigarette
zampógna *f* bagpipe
zampognare (zampógno) *intr* to pipe, play the bagpipe
zampóne *m* Modena salami (*stuffed forepaw of a hog*)
zanèlla *f* gully
zàngola *f* butter churn
zanna *f* tusk; fang; **mostrare le zanne** to show one's teeth
zanzara [dz] [dz] *f* mosquito
zanzarièra [dz] [dz] *f* mosquito net; window screen
zappa *f* hoe; **darsi la zappa sui piedi**

to cut one's nose off to spite one's face
zappare *tr* to hoe
zappatóre *m* hoer, digger; (mil) sapper
zar *m* (zar) czar
zàttera [dz] *f* raft; **zattera di salvataggio** life raft
zatterière *m* log driver
zavòrra [dz] *f* ballast; (fig) deadwood
zavorrare [dz] (zavòrro) *tr* to ballast
zàzzera *f* mop (*of hair*)
zèbra [dz] *f* zebra; **zebre** zebra crossing
zebra·to -ta [dz] *adj* zebra-striped
ze·bù [dz] *m* (-bù) zebu
zéc·ca *f* (-che) mint; (ent) tick; **nuovo di zecca** brand-new
zecchino *m* sequin, gold coin
zèfiro [dz] *m* zephyr
zelante [dz] *adj* zealous; studious || *mf* zealot; eager beaver
zèlo [dz] *m* zeal; **zelo pubblico** public spirit
zènit [dz] *m* zenith
zénzero [dz] [dz] *m* ginger
zép·po -pa *adj* crammed, jammed || *f* wedge; (fig) padding
zerbino [dz] *m* doormat; dandy
zerbinòtto [dz] *m* dandy, sporty fellow
zèro [dz] *m* zero
zìa *f* aunt
zibaldóne [dz] *m* notebook; collection of thoughts; (pej) hodgepodge
zibellino [dz] *m* sable
zibétto [dz] *m* civet cat; civet (*substance used in perfumery*)
zibibbo [dz] *m* raisin
ziga·no -na *adj & mf* gypsy
zìgomo [dz] *m* cheekbone

zigrinare [dz] *tr* to grain (*leather*); to mill, knurl (*metal*)

zigrina‧to -ta [dz] *adj* shagreened, grained (*leather*); knurled

zigzàg [dz] [dz] *m* (**zigzàg**) zigzag; andare a zigzag to zigzag

zigzagare §209 [dz] [dz] *intr* to zigzag

zimarra [dz] *f* cassock; (obs) overcoat

zimbèllo *m* decoy (*bird*); laughingstock

zincare §197 *tr* to zinc

zinco *m* zinc

zingaré‧sco -sca (**-schi -sche**) *adj & mf* gypsy

zìnga‧ro -ra *mf* gypsy

zinnia [dz] *f* zinnia

zìo *m* uncle; **zio d'America** rich uncle

zìpolo *m* peg, bung

zircóne [dz] *m* zircon

zircònio [dz] *m* zirconium

zirlare *intr* to warble; to squeak (*said of mouse*)

zitèlla *f* old maid

zittire §176 *tr & intr* to hoot, hiss

zit‧to -ta *adj* silent; **far stare zitto** to hush up; **stare zitto** to keep quiet || *m* whisper || **zitto** *interj* quiet!; hush!; shut up!

zizzània [dz] [ddzz] *f* (bot) darnel; seminar zizzania to sow discord

zòccolo *m* clog, sabot; clump, clod; clodhopper; base (*of column*); pedestal; wide baseboard; (zool) hoof

zodìaco [dz] *m* zodiac

zolfanèllo *m* sulfur match

zolfara *f* var of **solfara**

zólfo *m* sulfur

zòlla *f* clod, clump; turf; lump, cube (*of sugar*)

zollétta *f* lump, cube (*of sugar*)

zòna [dz] *f* zone; area; girdle; band, stripe; ticker tape; (pathol) shingles; (telg) tape; **zona glaciale** frigid zone; **zona tropicale** tropics, tropical zone

zónzo [dz] [dz] *m*—**andare a zonzo** to stroll, loiter along

zoòfito [dz] *m* zoophite

zoologìa [dz] *f* zoology

zoològi‧co -ca [dz] *adj* (**-ci -che**) zoological

zoòlo‧go -ga [dz] *mf* (**-gi -ghe**) zoologist

zootecnìa [dz] *f* animal husbandry

zootècni‧co -ca [dz] (**-ci -che**) *adj* livestock || *m* livestock specialist

zoppicante *adj* limping; halting; shaky

zoppicare §197 (**zòppico**) *intr* to limp; to be shaky (*in one's studies*); to wobble

zoppicatura *f* limp; wobble

zòp‧po -pa *adj* crippled; lame; wobbly || *mf* cripple; lame person

zòti‧co -ca [dz] (**-ci -che**) *adj* uncouth, boorish || *m* churl, boor

zuc‧ca *f* (**-che**) pumpkin; (joc) pate; (coll) empty head

zuccata *f* bump with the head

zuccherare (**zùcchero**) *tr* to sweeten, sugar

zuccherièra *f* sugar bowl

zuccherifì‧cio *m* (**-ci**) sugar refinery

zuccheri‧no -na *adj* sugary || *m* candy; sugar plum; sugar-coated pill

zùcchero *m* sugar; **zucchero filato** cotton candy; **zucchero in polvere** powdered sugar

zuccheró‧so -sa [s] *adj* sugary

zucchétto *m* scull cap; zucchetto

zucchi‧no -na *m & f* zucchini

zuccó‧ne -na *mf* dunce, dumbbell

zuffa *f* brawl, fight

zufolare (**zùfolo**) *tr & intr* to whistle

zùfolo *m* (mus) whistle, pipe

zu‧lù (**-lù**) [dz] *adj & mf* Zulu

zumare [dz] *tr & intr* (mov, telv) to zoom

zumata [dz] *f* (mov, telv) zoom

zuppa *f* soup; (fig) mess; **zuppa inglese** cake with brandy and whipped cream; **zuppa pavese** consommé with toast and eggs

zuppièra *f* tureen

zup‧po -pa *adj* drenched, soaked || *f* see **zuppa**

Zurigo *f* Zurich

zuzzurullό‧ne -na [dz] [ddzz] *mf* overgrown child, just a big kid

PART TWO

Inglese-Italiano

La pronunzia dell'inglese

I simboli seguenti rappresentano approssimativamente tutti i suoni della lingua inglese.

VOCALI

SIMBOLO	SUONO	ESEMPIO
[æ]	Più chiuso della **a** in **caso**.	**hat** [hæt]
[ɑ]	Come la **a** in **basso**.	**father** ['fɑðər] **proper** ['prɑpər]
[ɛ]	Come la **e** in **sella**.	**met** [mɛt]
[e]	Più chiuso della **e** in **ché**. Specialmente in posizione finale, si pronunzia come se fosse seguita da [ɪ].	**fate** [fet] **they** [ðe]
[ə]	Come la seconda **e** nella parola francese **gouvernement**.	**heaven** ['hɛvən] **pardon** ['pɑrdən]
[i]	Come la **i** in **nido**.	**she** [ʃi] **machine** [mə'ʃin]
[ɪ]	Come la **i** in **ritto**.	**fit** [fɪt] **beer** [bɪr]
[o]	Più chiuso della **o** in **sole**. Specialmente in posizione finale, si pronunzia come se fosse seguita da [ʊ].	**nose** [noz] **road** [rod] **row** [ro]
[ɔ]	Meno chiuso della **o** in **torre**.	**bought** [bɔt] **law** [lɔ]
[ʌ]	Piuttosto simile alla **eu** nella parola francese **peur**	**cup** [kʌp] **come** [kʌm] **mother** ['mʌðər]
[ʊ]	Meno chiuso della **u** in **insulto**.	**pull** [pʊl] **book** [bʊk] **wolf** [wʊlf]
[u]	Come la **u** in **acuto**.	**rude** [rud] **move** [muv] **tomb** [tum]

DITTONGHI

SIMBOLO	SUONO	ESEMPIO
[aɪ]	Come **ai** in **laico**.	**night** [naɪt] **eye** [aɪ]
[aʊ]	Come **au** in **causa**.	**found** [faʊnd] **cow** [kaʊ]
[ɔɪ]	Come **oi** in **poi**.	**voice** [vɔɪs] **oil** [ɔɪl]

3

SIMBOLO	SUONO	ESEMPIO
[b]	Come la **b** in **bambino.** Suono bilabiale occlusivo sonoro.	**bed** [bɛd] **robber** [ˈrɑbər]
[d]	Come la **d** in **caldo.** Suono dentale occlusivo sonoro.	**dead** [dɛd] **add** [æd]
[dʒ]	Come la **g** in **gente.** Suono palatale affricato sonoro.	**gem** [dʒɛm] **jail** [dʒel]
[ð]	Come la **d** nella pronuncia castigliana di **nada.** Suono interdentale fricativo sonoro.	**this** [ðɪs] **father** [ˈfɑðər]
[f]	Come la **f** in **fare.** Suono labiodentale fricativo sordo.	**face** [fes] **phone** [fon]
[g]	Come la **g** in **gatto.** Suono velare occlusivo sonoro.	**go** [go] **get** [get]
[h]	Come la **c** aspirata nella pronuncia toscana di **casa.**	**hot** [hɔt] **alcohol** [ˈælkə ˌhɔl]
[j]	Come la **i** in **ieri** o la **y** in **yo-yo.** Semiconsonante di suono palatale sonoro.	**yes** [jes] **unit** [ˈjunɪt]
[k]	Come la **c** in **casa** ma accompagnato da un'aspirazione. Suono velare occlusivo sordo.	**cat** [kæt] **chord** [kɔrd] **kill** [kɪl]
[l]	Come la **l** in **latino.** Suono alveolare fricativo laterale sonoro.	**late** [let] **allow** [əˈlaʊ]
[m]	Come la **m** in **madre.** Suono bilabiale nasale sonoro.	**more** [mor] **command** [kəˈmænd]
[n]	Come la **n** in **notte.** Suono alveolare nasale sonoro.	**nest** [nest] **manner** [ˈmænər]
[ŋ]	Come la **n** in **manca.** Suono velare nasale sonoro.	**king** [kɪŋ] **conquer** [ˈkɑŋkər]
[p]	Come la **p** in **patto** ma accompagnato da un'aspirazione. Suono bilabiale occlusivo sordo.	**pen** [pen] **cap** [kæp]
[r]	La **r** più comune in molte parti dell'Inghilterra e nella maggior parte degli Stati Uniti e del Canadà è un suono semivocalico articolato con la punta della lingua elevata verso la volta del palato. Questa consonante è debolissima in posizione intervocalica o alla fine di una sillaba, e può appena percepirsi. L'articolazione di questa consonante ha la tendenza di influenzare il suono delle vocali contigue. La **r**, preceduta dai suoni [ʌ] o [ə], dà il proprio colorito a questi suoni e sparisce completamente come suono consonantico.	**run** [rʌn] **far** [fɑr] **art** [ɑrt] **carry** [ˈkærɪ] **burn** [bʌrn] **learn** [lʌrn] **weather** [ˈwɛðər]
[s]	Come la **s** in **sette.** Suono alveolare fricativo sordo.	**send** [send] **cellar** [ˈsɛlər]
[ʃ]	Come **sc** in **lasciare.** Suono palatale fricativo sordo.	**shall** [ʃæl] **machine** [məˈʃin]
[t]	Come la **t** in **tavolo** ma accompagnato da un'aspirazione. Suono dentale occlusivo sordo.	**ten** [ten] **dropped** [drɑpt]
[tʃ]	Come **c** in **cibo.** Suono palatale affricato sordo.	**child** [tʃaɪld] **much** [mʌtʃ] **nature** [ˈnetʃər]
[θ]	Come la **z** castigliana in **zapato.** Suono interdentale fricativo sordo.	**think** [θɪŋk] **truth** [truθ]
[v]	Come la **v** in **vento.** Suono labiodentale fricativo sonoro.	**vest** [vest] **over** [ˈovər] **of** [ɑv]

SIMBOLO	SUONO	ESEMPIO
[w]	Come la **u** in **quadro**. Suono labiovelare fricativo sonoro.	**work** [wʌrk] **tweed** [twid] **queen** [kwin]
[z]	Come la **s** in **asilo**. Suono alveolare fricativo sonoro.	**zeal** [zil] **busy** [ˈbɪzi] **his** [hɪz]
[ʒ]	Come la seconda **g** nella parola francese **garage**. Suono palatale fricativo sonoro.	**azure** [ˈeʒər] **measure** [ˈmeʒər]

ACCENTO

L'accento tonico principale, indicato col segno grafico ˈ, e l'accento secondario, indicato col segno grafico „ precedono la sillaba sulla quale cadono, per es., **fascinate** [ˈfæsɪ ˌnet].

La pronunzia delle parole composte

Nella parte inglese-italiano di questo Dizionario la pronunzia figurata di tutte le parole inglesi semplici è indicata in parentesi quadre che seguono immediatamente l'esponente, secondo un nuovo adattamento dell'alfabeto fonetico internazionale.

Vi sono tre generi di parole composte in inglese: (1) le parole in cui gli elementi componenti si sono uniti per formare una parola solida, come per es., **steamboat** vapore; (2) la parole in cui gli elementi componenti sono uniti da un trattino, come per es., **high'-grade'** di qualità superiore; (3) le parole in cui gli elementi componenti rimangono graficamente indipendenti gli uni da gli altri, per es., **post card** cartolina postale. La pronunzia delle parole inglesi composte non è indicata in questo Dizionario qualora gli elementi componenti appaiano come esponenti indipendenti nella loro normale posizione alfabetica e mostrano quindi il loro pronunzia figurata. Solo gli accenti principali e secondari di tali parole sono indicati, come per es., **steam'boat'**, **high'-grade'**, **post' card'**. Se i due membri di una parola composta inglese solida non sono separati da un accento grafico, si usa un punto leggermente elevato sopra il rigo per indicarne la divisione, come per es., **la'dy·like'**.

Nei nomi in cui l'accento secondario cade sul membro **-man** o **-men**, le vocali di tali membri si pronunziano come nelle parole semplici **man** e **men**, come per es., **mailman** [ˈmel ˌmæn] e **mailmen** [ˈmel ˌmen]. Nei nomi in cui tali membri componenti non sono accentati, le loro vocali si pronunziano come se fossero un'e muta francese, come per es., **policeman** [pəˈlismən] e **policemen** [pəˈlismən]. In questo Dizionario la trascrizione fonetica di tali nomi non è stata indicata qualora il primo membro componente appaia come esponente con la sua pronunzia in alfabeto fonetico internazionale. Gli accenti sono ciò nondimeno indicati:

mail'man' *s* (-men')
police'man *s* (-men)

La pronunzia dei participi passati

La pronunzia di una parola la cui desinenza è **-ed** (o **-d** dopo una e muta) non è indicata nel presente Dizionario, purché la pronunzia della parola stessa senza tale suffisso appaia con il suo esponente nella sua posizione alfabetica. In tale caso la pronunzia segue le regole indicate qui sotto. Si osservi che il raddoppiamento della vocale finale dopo una semplice vocale tonica non muta la pronunzia del suffisso **-ed**, per es.: **batted** [ˈbætɪd], **dropped** [drɑpt], **robbed** [rɑbd].

La desinenza **-ed** (o **-d** dopo una e muta) del preterito, del participio passato e di certi aggettivi ha tre pronunzie differenti, che dipendono dal suono in cui il tema termina:

1) Se il tema termina in suono consonantico sonoro (che non sia [d]), cioè [b], [g], [l], [m], [n], [ŋ], [r], [v], [z], [ð], [ʒ] o [dʒ] o in un suono vocalico, l'**-ed** è pronunziato [d]:

SUONO IN CUI TERMINA IL TEMA	INFINITO	PRETERITO E PARTICIPIO PASSATO
[b]	**ebb** [ɛb] **rob** [rɑb] **robe** [rob]	**ebbed** [ɛbd] **robbed** [rɑbd] **robed** [robd]

5

SUONO IN CUI TERMINA IL TEMA	INFINITO	PRETERITO E PARTICIPIO PASSATO
[g]	egg [ɛg] sag [sæg]	egged [ɛgd] sagged [sægd]
[l]	mail [mel] scale [skel]	mailed [meld] scaled [skeld]
[m]	storm [stɔrm] bomb [bɑm] name [nem]	stormed [stɔrmd] bombed [bɑmd] named [nemd]
[n]	tan [tæn] sign [saɪn] mine [maɪn]	tanned [tænd] signed [saɪnd] mined [maɪnd]
[ŋ]	hang [hæŋ]	hanged [hæŋd]
[r]	fear [fɪr] care [ker]	feared [fɪrd] cared [kerd]
[v]	rev [rev] save [sev]	revved [revd] saved [sevd]
[z]	buzz [bʌz] fuze [fjuz]	buzzed [bʌzd] fuzed [fjuzd]
[ð]	smooth [smuð] bathe [beð]	smoothed [smuðd] bathed [beðd]
[ʒ]	massage [mə'sɑʒ]	massaged [mə'sɑʒd]
[dʒ]	page [pedʒ]	paged [pedʒd]
suono vocalico	key [ki] sigh [saɪ] paw [pɔ]	keyed [kid] sighed [saɪd] pawed [pɔd]

2) Se il tema termina in un suono consonantico sordo (che non sia [t]), cioè [f], [k], [p], [s], [θ], [ʃ] o [tʃ], l'-ed si pronunzia [t]:

SUONO IN CUI TERMINA IL TEMA	INFINITO	PRETERITO E PARTICIPIO PASSATO
[f]	loaf [lof] knife [naɪf]	loafed [loft] knifed [naɪft]
[k]	back [bæk] bake [bek]	backed [bækt] baked [bekt]
[p]	cap [kæp] wipe [waɪp]	capped [kæpt] wiped [waɪpt]
[s]	hiss [hɪs] mix [mɪks]	hissed [hɪst] mixed [mɪkst]
[θ]	lath [læθ]	lathed [læθt]
[ʃ]	mash [mæʃ]	mashed [mæʃt]
[tʃ]	match [mætʃ]	matched [mætʃt]

3) Se il tema termina in un suono dentale, cioè [t] o [d], l'-ed si pronunzia [ɪd] o [əd]:

SUONO IN CUI TERMINA IL TEMA	INFINITO	PRETERITO E PARTICIPIO PASSATO
[t]	wait [wet] mate [met]	waited ['wetɪd] mated ['metɪd]
[d]	mend [mɛnd] wade [wed]	mended ['mɛndɪd] waded ['wedɪd]

L'-ed di alcuni aggettivi aggiunto ad un tema che termina in suono consonantico (oltre a quelli che terminano in [d] o [t]), è ciò nonostante talvolta pronunziato [ɪd] e tale fenomeno è idicato con la piena pronunzia della parola in simboli dell'alfabeto fonetico internazionale, per es., blessed ['blɛsɪd], crabbed ['kræbɪd].

A, a [e] *s* prima lettera dell'alfabeto inglese

a [e] *art indef* un, uno, una, un'

aback [ə'bæk] *adv* all'indietro; **taken aback** colto alla sprovvista, sconcertato

aba·cus ['æbəkəs] *s* (**-cuses** or **-ci** [ˌsaɪ]) pallottoliere *m*; (archit) abaco

abaft [ə'bæft] or [ə'bɑft] *adv* a poppa || *prep* dietro a

abandon [ə'bændən] *s* disinvoltura || *tr* abbandonare

abase [ə'bes] *tr* umiliare, degradare

abash [ə'bæʃ] *tr* imbarazzare; sconcertare

abate [ə'bet] *tr* ridurre; omettere; (law) terminare || *intr* diminuire, calmarsi

aba·tis ['æbətɪs] or [ə'bætɪs] *s* (**-tis** or **-tises**) (mil) tagliata

abattoir ['æbəˌtwar] *s* macello

abba·cy ['æbəsi] *s* (**-cies**) abbazia

abbess ['æbɪs] *s* badessa

abbey ['æbi] *s* badia, abbazia

abbot ['æbət] *s* abate *m*

abbreviate [ə'brivɪˌet] *tr* abbreviare, raccorciare

abbreviation [əˌbrivɪ'eʃən] *s* (*abbreviated form*) abbreviazione; (*shortening*) abbreviamento

A B C [ˌeˌbi'si] *s* (letterword) abbicci *m*; **A B C's** abbecedario

abdicate ['æbdɪˌket] *tr* abdicare a || *intr* abdicare

abdomen ['æbdəmən] or [æb'domən] *s* addome *m*

abduct [æb'dʌkt] *tr* rapire

abed [ə'bed] *adv* a letto

abet [ə'bet] *v* (*pret & pp* **abetted**; *ger* **abetting**) *tr* favoreggiare

abeyance [ə'be·əns] *s* sospensione; **in abeyance** in sospeso

ab·hor [æb'hɔr] *v* (*pret & pp* **-horred**; *ger* **-horring**) *tr* aborrire

abhorrent [æb'hɑrənt] or [æb'hɔrənt] *adj* detestabile

abide [ə'baɪd] *v* (*pret & pp* **abode** or **abided**) *tr* aspettare; tollerare || *intr* —**to abide by** attenersi a; rimanere fedele a

abili·ty [ə'bɪlɪti] *s* (**-ties**) abilità *f*, bravura

abject ['æbdʒekt] or [æb'dʒekt] *adj* abietto, turpe

abjure [æb'dʒur] *tr* abiurare

ablative ['æblətɪv] *adj & s* ablativo

ablaut ['æblaut] *s* apofonia

ablaze [ə'blez] *adj* in fiamme; risplendente

able ['ebəl] *adj* abile, esperto; **to be able to** + *inf* potere + *inf*

able-bodied ['ebəl'badɪd] *adj* sano; forte

abloom [ə'blum] *adj & adv* in fiore

abnormal [æb'nɔrməl] *adj* anormale

aboard [ə'bord] *adv* a bordo; **all aboard!** (rr) signori, in vettura!; **to go aboard** imbarcarsi; **to take aboard** imbarcare || *prep* a bordo di; (*a bus, train, etc.*) in, su

abode [ə'bod] *s* abitazione, dimora

abolish [ə'balɪʃ] *tr* abolire

A-bomb ['eˌbam] *s* bomba atomica

abominable [ə'bamənəbəl] *adj* abominevole

abomination [əˌbamɪ'neʃən] *s* abominazione

aborigenes [ˌæbə'rɪdʒɪˌniz] *spl* aborigeni *mpl*

abort [ə'bɔrt] *tr* terminare prematuramente; provocare un aborto in || *intr* abortire

abortion [ə'bɔrʃən] *s* aborto

abound [ə'baund] *intr* abbondare; **abound in** or **with** abbondare di

about [ə'baut] *adv* circa, press'a poco; qua intorno; qua e là; in direzione opposta; (coll) quasi; **to be about to** star sul punto di || *prep* intorno a; circa a; addosso a; tutt'intorno a; riguardo a

about'-face' *interj* (mil) dietro front!

about'-face' or **about'-face'** *s* voltafaccia; (mil) dietro front *m* || **about'-face'** *intr* fare dietro front

above [ə'bʌv] *adj* soprammenzionato; superiore || *s*—**from above** dal cielo; dall'alto || *adv* in alto; su; più sopra || *prep* sopra, sopra a; più di; al di là di, oltre; **above all** soprattutto

above-mentioned [ə'bʌv'menʃənd] *adj* summenzionato, sunnominato

abrasive [ə'bresɪv] or [ə'brezɪv] *adj & s* abrasivo

abreast [ə'brest] *adj & adv* in fila, in linea; **to keep abreast of** tenersi alla pari con; essere al corrente di

abridge [ə'brɪdʒ] *tr* compendiare; ridurre

abroad [ə'brɔd] *adv* all'estero; all'aria aperta; **to be abroad** (*said of news*) circolare

abrupt [ə'brʌpt] *adj* brusco, improvviso; (*very steep*) scosceso

abscess ['æbses] *s* ascesso

abscond [æb'skand] *intr* scappare; **to abscond with** svignarsela con

absence ['æbsəns] *s* assenza; **in the absence of** in mancanza di

absent ['æbsənt] *adj* assente || [æb'sent] *tr*—**to absent oneself** assentarsi

absentee [ˌæbsən'ti] *s* assente *mf*

absent-minded ['æbsənt'maɪndɪd] *adj* distratto, assente

absolute ['æbsəˌlut] *adj & s* assoluto

absolutely ['æbsəˌlutli] *adv* assolutamente, certamente || [ˌæbsə'lutli] *interj* certamente!

absolve [æb'salv] *tr* assolvere

absorb [æb'sɔrb] *tr* assorbire; **to be** or **become absorbed** essere assorto

absorbent [æb'sɔrbənt] *adj* assorbente; (*cotton*) idrofilo || *s* sostanza assorbente

absorbing [æb'sɔrbɪŋ] *adj* interessantissimo

abstain [æb'sten] *intr* astenersi

abstemious [æb'stimɪ·əs] *adj* astemio

abstention [æb'stenʃən] *s* astensione; astenuto (*vote withheld*)

abstinent ['æbstɪnənt] *adj* astinente

abstract ['æbstrækt] *adj* astratto ‖ *s* compendio, sommario ‖ *tr* compendiare ‖ (æb'strækt) *tr* astrarre; (*to steal*) sottrarre

abstruse [æb'strus] *adj* astruso

absurd [æb'sʌrd] *or* [æb'zʌrd] *adj* assurdo

absurdi·ty [æb'sʌrdɪti] *or* [æb'zʌrdɪti] *s* (*-ties*) assurdità *f*

abundant [ə'bʌndənt] *adj* abbondante

abuse [ə'bjus] *s* (*misuse*) abuso; maltrattamento; insulto ‖ [ə'bjuz] *tr* (*to misuse, take unfair advantage of*) abusare di; maltrattare; insultare

abusive [ə'bjusɪv] *adj* abusivo; insultante

abut [ə'bʌt] *v* (*pret & pp* **abutted; ger abutting**) *intr*—to abut on confinare con

abutment [ə'bʌtmənt] *s* rinfianco; (*at either end of bridge*) spalla; (*of buttresses of bridge*) sprone *m*

abysmal [ə'bɪzməl] *adj* abissale; (*e.g., ignorance*) spropositato

abyss [ə'bɪs] *s* abisso

academic [,ækə'dɛmɪk] *adj* accademico

ac'ademic cos'tume *s* toga accademica

academician [ə,kædə'mɪʃən] *s* accademico

ac'adem'ic year' *s* anno scolastico

acade·my [ə'kædəmi] *s* (*-mies*) accademia

accede [æk'sid] *intr* accedere; **to accede to** salire a; accedere a

accelerate [æk'sɛlə,ret] *tr & intr* accelerare

accelerator [æk'sɛlə,rɛtər] *s* acceleratore *m*

accent ['æksɛnt] *s* accento ‖ ['æksɛnt] *or* [æk'sɛnt] *tr* accentare; (*to accentuate*) accentuare

ac'cent mark' *s* segnaccento, accento grafico

accentuate [æk'sɛntʃʊ,et] *tr* accentuare

accept [æk'sɛpt] *tr* accettare

acceptable [æk'sɛptəbəl] *adj* accettabile

acceptance [æk'sɛptəns] *s* accettazione

access ['æksɛs] *s* accesso

accessible [æk'sɛsɪbəl] *adj* accessibile; (*person*) abbordabile

accession [æk'sɛʃən] *s* accessione, acquisto; (*e.g., to the throne*) adito

accesso·ry [æk'sɛsəri] *adj* accessorio ‖ *s* (*-ries*) accessorio; (*to a crime*) complice *m*

accident ['æksɪdənt] *s* accidente *m*; **by accident** accidentalmente, per caso

accidental [,æksɪ'dɛntəl] *adj* accidentale ‖ *s* (mus) accidente *m*

acclaim [ə'klem] *s* acclamazione, applauso ‖ *tr & intr* acclamare, applaudire

acclimate ['æklɪ,met] *tr* acclimatare ‖ *intr* acclimatarsi

accolade [,ækə'led] *s* accollata; (fig) elogio

accommodate [ə'kɑmə,det] *tr* (*to adjust, make fit*) accomodare; (*to pro-*

vide with a loan) venire incontro a; (*to supply with lodging*) alloggiare; (*to oblige*) favorire; (*to have room for*) aver posto per

accommodating [ə'kɑmə,detɪŋ] *adj* servizievole, compiacente

accommodation [ə,kɑmə'deʃən] *s* (*favor*) favore *m*; (*loan*) prestito; (*adaptation*) adattamento; (*reconciliation*) conciliazione; (*compromise*) accomodamento; **accommodations** (*traveling space*) posto; (*in a hotel*) alloggio

accommoda'tion train' *s* treno accelerato

accompaniment [ə'kʌmpənɪmənt] *s* accompagnamento

accompanist [ə'kʌmpənɪst] *s* accompagnatore *m*

accompa·ny [ə'kʌmpəni] *v* (*pret & pp* **-nied**) *tr* accompagnare

accomplice [ə'kɑmplɪs] *s* complice *mf*

accomplish [ə'kɑmplɪʃ] *tr* compiere

accomplished [ə'kɑmplɪʃt] *adj* (*completed*) compiuto, terminato; (*skilled*) finito, compiuto

accomplishment [ə'kɑmplɪʃmənt] *s* (*completion*) esecuzione, realizzazione; (*something accomplished*) opera; (*acquired ability*) talento; (*military achievement*) prodezza; (*social skill*) compitezza

accord [ə'kɔrd] *s* accordo; **in accord with** in conformità con; **of one's own accord** spontaneamente; **with one accord** di comune accordo ‖ *tr* concedere ‖ *intr* accordarsi

accordance [ə'kɔrdəns] *s* accordo; **in accordance with** in conformità con

according [ə'kɔrdɪŋ] *adv*—according as a seconda che; **according to** secondo, a seconda di

accordingly [ə'kɔrdɪŋli] *adv* per conseguenza, perciò; in conformità

accordion [ə'kɔrdɪ·ən] *s* fisarmonica

accost [ə'kɔst] *or* [ə'kɑst] *tr* accostare, abbordare

accouchement [ə'kuʃmənt] *s* parto

account [ə'kaʊnt] *s* (*explanation*) versione; (*report*) resoconto; conto; (*statement*) estratto conto; **by all accounts** secondo la voce comune; **of account** d'importanza; **of no account** senza importanza; **on account** in acconto; **on account of** a causa di; per l'amor di; **on all accounts** in ogni modo; **on no account** in nessuna maniera; **to call to account** chiedere conto di; **to give a good account of** oneself comportarsi bene; **to take account of** prendere in considerazione; **to turn to account** trarre profitto da ‖ *intr*—to account for render conto di; essere responsabile per

accountable [ə'kaʊntəbəl] *adj* responsabile; (*explainable*) spiegabile

accountant [ə'kaʊntənt] *s* contabile *mf*, ragioniere *m*

accounting [ə'kaʊntɪŋ] *s* contabilità *f*, ragioneria

accouterments [ə'kutərmənts] *spl* (mil)

buffetterie *fpl;* (*trappings*) ornamenti *mpl*

accredit [ə'kredɪt] *tr* accreditare; **to accredit s.o. with s.th** ascrivere qlco a credito di qlcu

accrue [ə'kru] *intr* accumularsi; (*said of interest*) maturare

acculturation [ə,kʌltʃə'reʃən] *s* acculturazione

accumulate [ə'kjumjə,let] *tr* accumulare || *intr* accumularsi

accuracy ['ækjərəsi] *s* esattezza, precisione; fedeltà *f*

accurate ['ækjərɪt] *adj* esatto, preciso; fedele

accursed [ə'kʌrsɪd] *or* [ə'kʌrst] *adj* maledetto

accusation [,ækjə'zeʃən] *s* accusa

accusative [ə'kjuzətɪv] *adj & s* accusativo

accuse [ə'kjuz] *tr* accusare

accustom [ə'kʌstəm] *tr* abituare

ace [es] *s* asso; **to be within an ace of** essere quasi sul punto di

ace' in the hole' *s* asso nella manica

acetate ['æsɪ,tet] *s* acetato

ace'tic ac'id [ə'sitɪk] *s* acido acetico

aceti·fy [ə'setɪ,faɪ] *v* (*pret & pp* -**fied**) *tr* acetificare || *intr* acetificarsi

acetone ['æsɪ,ton] *s* acetone *m*

acetylene [ə'setɪ,lin] *s* acetilene *m*

acet'ylene torch' *s* cannello ossiacetilenico

ache [ek] *s* dolore *m* || *intr* dolere, e.g., **my tooth aches** mi duole il dente

Acheron ['ækə,ran] *s* Acheronte *m*

achieve [ə'tʃiv] *tr* compiere, conseguire

achievement [ə'tʃivmənt] *s* compimento; successo; (*exploit*) impresa, prodezza

Achil'les heel' [ə'kɪliz] *s* tallone *m* d'Achille

acid ['æsɪd] *adj & s* acido

acidi·fy [ə'sɪdɪ,faɪ] *v* (*pret & pp* -**fied**) *tr & intr* acidificare

acidity [ə'sɪdɪti] *s* acidità *f*

acid' test' *s* prova del fuoco

ack-ack ['æk'æk] *s* (slang) cannone antiaereo

acknowledge [æk'nalɪdʒ] *tr* riconoscere; (*receipt of a letter*) accusare; (*a claim*) ammettere; mostrare la gratitudine per; (*law*) certificare

acknowledgment [æk'nalɪdʒmənt] *s* riconoscimento; (*of receipt of a letter*) accusa, cenno

acme ['ækmi] *s* acme *f*

acolyte ['ækə,laɪt] *s* accolito

acorn ['ekɔrn] *or* ['ekarn] *s* ghianda

acoustic [ə'kustɪk] *adj* acustico || **acoustics** *s* acustica

acquaint [ə'kwent] *tr* mettere al corrente; **to be acquainted with** conoscere; essere al corrente di; **to become acquainted** (*with each other*) conoscersi

acquaintance [ə'kwentəns] *s* conoscenza; (*person*) conoscente *mf*, conoscenza

acquiesce [,ækwɪ'es] *intr* acconsentire, accondiscendere

acquiescence [,ækwɪ'esəns] *s* accondiscendenza

acquire [ə'kwaɪr] *tr* acquistare

acquisition [,ækwɪ'zɪʃən] *s* acquisto

acquit [ə'kwɪt] *v* (*pret & pp* **acquitted;** *ger* **acquitting**) *tr* (*to pay*) ripagare; (*to declare not guilty*) assolvere; **to acquit oneself** condursi

acquittal [ə'kwɪtəl] *s* assoluzione

acre ['ekər] *s* acro

acrid ['ækrɪd] *adj* acrido, pungente

acrobat ['ækrə,bæt] *s* acrobata *mf*

acrobatic [,ækrə'bætɪk] *adj* acrobatico || **acrobatics** *ssg* (*e.g., of a stunt pilot*) acrobazie *fpl;* **acrobatics** *spl* (*gymnastics*) acrobatica

acronym ['ækrənɪm] *s* acronimo, parola macedonia

acropolis [ə'krapəlɪs] *s* acropoli *f*

across [ə'krɔs] *or* [ə'kras] *adv* dall'altra parte; **to get an idea across** to farsi capire da || *prep* attraverso; (*on the other side of*) al di là di, dall'altra parte di; **to come across** (*a person*) imbattersi in; **to go across** attraversare

across'-the-board' *adj* generale

act [ækt] *s* atto; legge *f;* rappresentazione; **in the act** in flagrante || *tr* (*a drama*) rappresentare; (*a role*) recitare || *intr* (*on the stage*) recitare; (*to behave*) comportarsi; (*to perform special duties; to reach a decision*) agire; (*to have an effect*) reagire; **to act as** fungere da; **to act for** rimpiazzare; **to act on** eseguire; **to act up** (coll) fare il matto; non funzionare bene (*said, e.g., of a motor*); **to act up to** (coll) fare festa a

acting ['æktɪŋ] *adj* facente funzione, interino || *s* recita

action ['ækʃən] *s* azione; (*moving parts*) meccanismo; **to take action** iniziare azione; (law) intentare causa

activate ['æktɪ,vet] *tr* attivare

active ['æktɪv] *adj & s* attivo

activi·ty [æk'tɪvɪti] *s* (-**ties**) attività *f*

act' of God' *s* forza maggiore

actor ['æktər] *s* attore *m*

actress ['æktrɪs] *s* attrice *f*

actual ['æktʃu·əl] *adj* reale

actually ['æktʃu·əli] *adv* realmente, in realtà

actuar·y ['æktʃu,eri] *s* (-**ies**) attuario

actuate ['æktʃu,et] *tr* attuare, mettere in azione; (*to motivate*) stimulare

acuity [ə'kju·ɪti] *s* acuità *f*

acumen [ə'kjumən] *s* acume *m*

acupuncture ['ækju,pʌŋktʃər] *s* agopuntura

acute [ə'kjut] *adj* acuto

ad [æd] *s* (coll) inserzione pubblicitaria

Adam ['ædəm] *s* Adamo; **not to know from Adam** non conoscere affatto

adamant ['ædəmənt] *adj* saldo, inflessibile

Ad'am's ap'ple *s* pomo d'Adamo

adapt [ə'dæpt] *tr* adattare

adaptation [,ædæp'teʃən] *s* adattamento; (*e.g., of a play*) rifacimento

add [æd] *tr* aggiungere; (*numbers*)

sommare || *intr* aggiungere; far di conto; **to add up to** ammontare a; (coll) voler dire

adder ['ædər] *s* vipera

addict ['ædɪkt] *s* (*to drugs*) tossicomane *mf*; (*to a sport*) tifoso || [ə'dɪkt] *tr* abituare; rendere propenso alla tossicomania; **to addict oneself to** darsi a, abbandonarsi a

addiction [ə'dɪkʃən] *s* (*to drugs*) tossicomania; (*to sports*) tifo

add'ing machine' *s* calcolatrice *f*

addition [ə'dɪʃən] *s* addizione; (*building*) annessi *mpl*; **in addition** inoltre, per di più; **in addition to** oltre a

additive ['ædɪtɪv] *adj* & *s* additivo

address [ə'dres] *or* ['ædres] *s* (*speech*) discorso; (*place and destination of mail*) indirizzo; (*skill*) destrezza; (*formal request*) petizione; **to deliver an address** pronunciare un discorso || [ə'dres] *tr* indirizzare; (*to speak to*) rivolgere la parola a

addressee [,ædre'si] *s* destinatario

address'ing machine' *s* macchina per indirizzi

adduce [ə'djus] *or* [ə'dus] *tr* addurre

adenoids ['ædə,nɔɪdz] *spl* vegetazioni *fpl* adenoidi, adenoidi *fpl*

adept [ə'dept] *adj* & *s* esperto

adequate ['ædɪkwɪt] *adj* sufficiente; (*suitable*) conveniente

adhere [æd'hɪr] *intr* aderire

adherence [æd'hɪrəns] *s* aderenza

adherent [æd'hɪrənt] *adj* & *s* aderente *m*

adhesion [æd'hiʒən] *s* adesione; (pathol) aderenza

adhesive [æd'hisɪv] *or* [æd'hizɪv] *adj* & *s* adesivo

adhe'sive tape' *s* tela adesiva, cerotto

adieu [ə'dju] *or* [ə'du] *s* (**adieus** *or* **adieux**) addio || *interj* addio!

adjacent [ə'dʒesənt] *adj* adiacente

adjective ['ædʒɪktɪv] *adj* aggettivale; accessorio, secondario || *s* aggettivo

adjoin [ə'dʒɔɪn] *tr* confinare con || *intr* essere confinanti

adjoining [ə'dʒɔɪnɪŋ] *adj* confinante; vicino, attiguo

adjourn [ə'dʒʌrn] *tr* aggiornare, rinviare || *intr* rinviarsi

adjournment [ə'dʒʌrnmənt] *s* aggiornamento, rinvio

adjust [ə'dʒʌst] *tr* accomodare; regolare; (ins) liquidare || *intr* abituarsi

adjustable [ə'dʒʌstəbəl] *adj* regolabile

adjustment [ə'dʒʌstmənt] *s* aggiustamento; accomodamento; (ins) liquidazione del danno

adjutant [ə'dʒətənt] *s* aiutante *mf*

ad-lib [,æd'lɪb] *v* (*pret* & *pp* **-libbed;** *ger* **-libbing**) *tr* & *intr* improvvisare

administer [æd'mɪnɪstər] *tr* amministrare; (*medicine*) somministrare; (*an oath*) dare || *intr*—**to administer to** ministrare, prestare aiuto a

administrator [æd'mɪnɪs,tretər] *s* amministratore *m*

admirable ['ædmɪrəbəl] *adj* ammirabile, ammirevole

admiral ['ædmɪrəl] *s* ammiraglio

admiral·ty ['ædmɪrəlti] *s* (**-ties**) ammiragliato

admire [æd'maɪr] *tr* ammirare

admirer [æd'maɪrər] *s* ammiratore *m*

admissible [æd'mɪsɪbəl] *adj* ammissibile

admission [æd'mɪʃən] *s* ammissione; confessione; (*entrance fee*) prezzo d'ingresso; **to gain admission** arrivare a entrare

ad·mit [æd'mɪt] *v* (*pret* & *pp* **-mitted;** *ger* **-mitting**) *tr* ammettere; confessare || *intr* dare l'ingresso; **to admit of** permettere, ammettere; consentire

admittance [æd'mɪtəns] *s* ammissione; permesso di entrare; **no admittance** divieto d'ingresso

admonish [æd'mɑnɪʃ] *tr* ammonire

ado [ə'du] *s* confusione, trambusto; **much ado about nothing** molto rumore per nulla; **to make a big ado** fare cerimonie

adobe [ə'dobi] *s* mattone crudo

adolescence [,ædə'lesəns] *s* adolescenza

adolescent [,ædə'lesənt] *adj* & *s* adolescente *mf*

adopt [ə'dapt] *tr* adottare

adoption [ə'dapʃən] *s* adozione

adorable [ə'dorəbəl] *adj* adorabile

adore [ə'dor] *tr* adorare

adorn [ə'dorn] *tr* adornare

adornment [ə'dornmənt] *s* ornamento

adre'nal gland' [æd'rinəl] *s* glandola surrenale

Adriatic [,edrɪ'ætɪk] *or* [,ædrɪ'ætɪk] *adj* adriatico || *adj* & *s* Adriatico

adrift [ə'drɪft] *adj* & *adv* alla deriva

adroit [ə'drɔɪt] *adj* destro

adult [ə'dʌlt] *or* ['ædʌlt] *adj* & *s* adulto

adulterate [ə'dʌltə,ret] *tr* adulterare

adulterer [ə'dʌltərər] *s* adultero

adulteress [ə'dʌltərɪs] *s* adultera

adulter·y [ə'dʌltəri] *s* (**-ies**) adulterio

advance [æd'væns] *or* [æd'vɑns] *adj* avanzato || *s* avanzata; (*increase in price*) aumento; (*of money*) anticipo; **advances** approcci *mpl*; **in advance** in anticipo || *tr* avanzare; aumentare; (*to make earlier*) anticipare; (*money*) anticipare; (*a clock*) mettere avanti || *intr* avanzare; (*said, e.g., of prices*) aumentare

advanced [æd'vænst] *or* [æd'vɑnst] *adj* avanzato, progredito

advanced' stand'ing *s* trasferimento di voti scolastici

advancement [æd'vænsmənt] *or* [æd'vɑnsmənt] *s* progresso; promozione; (mil) avanzata

advance' public'ity *s* pubblicità *f* di lancio

advantage [æd'væntɪdʒ] *or* [æd'vɑntɪdʒ] *s* vantaggio; **to advantage in** maniera favorevole; **to take advantage of** approfittarsi di; abusare di || *tr* avantaggiare

advantageous [,ædvən'tedʒəs] *adj* vantaggioso

advent ['ædvent] *s* avvento

adventure [æd'ventʃər] s avventura ||
tr avventurare || *intr* avventurarsi

adventurer [æd'ventʃərər] s avventuriero

adventuresome [æd'ventʃərsəm] *adj*
avventuroso

adventuress [æd'ventʃərɪs] s avventu-
riera

adventurous [æd'ventʃərəs] *adj* avventuroso

adverb ['ædvʌrb] s avverbio

adversar•y ['ædvər‚sɛri] s (-ies) avversario

adverse [æd'vʌrs] or ['ædvʌrs] *adj*
avverso, contrario

adversi•ty [æd'vʌrsɪti] s (-ties) avver-
sità *f*

advertise ['ædvər‚taɪz] or [‚ædvər-
'taɪz] *tr* propagandare; reclamizzare
|| *intr* fare la pubblicità; inserire un
annuncio; inserzionare

advertisement [‚ædvər'taɪzmənt] or
[æd'vʌrtɪsmənt] s annuncio pubblicitario, inserzione

advertiser ['ædvər‚taɪzər] or [‚ædvər-
'taɪzər] s inserzionista *mf*

advertising ['ædvər‚taɪzɪŋ] s pubblicità *f*, pubblicismo

ad'vertising a'gent s pubblicista *mf*

ad'vertising campaign' s campagna
pubblicitaria

ad'vertising man' s agente *m* di pubblicità, reclamista *m*

advice [æd'vaɪs] s consiglio; a piece
of advice un consiglio

advisable [æd'vaɪzəbəl] *adj* consigliabile

advise [æd'vaɪz] *tr* consigliare; infor-
mare || *intr*—to advise with chiedere
il consiglio di; avere una conferenza
con

advisement [æd'vaɪzmənt] s considerazione; to take under advisement
prendere in considerazione

adviser [æd'vaɪzər] s consigliere *m*

advisory [æd'vaɪzəri] *adj* consultivo

advocate ['ædvə‚ket] s difensore *m*;
(*lawyer*) avvocato || *tr* sostenere, pro-
pugnare

adze [ædz] s ascia

Aege'an Sea' [ɪ'dʒiːən] s mare Egeo

aegis ['idʒɪs] s egida

Aeneid [i'niːɪd] s Eneide *f*

aerate ['eret] or ['e·ə‚rét] *tr* aerare

aerial ['ɛrɪ·əl] or [e'ɪrɪ·əl] *adj* aereo ||
['ɛrɪ·əl] s (rad & telv) antenna

aer'ial pho'tograph s aerofotogramma
m

aerodrome ['ɛrə‚drom] s aerodromo

aerodynamic [‚ɛrodaɪ'næmɪk] *adj*
aerodinamico || aerodynamics *ssg*
aerodinamica

aeronaut ['ɛrə‚nɔt] s aeronauta *m*

aeronautic [‚ɛrə'nɔtɪk] *adj* aeronautico
|| aeronautics *ssg* aeronautica

aerosol ['ɛrə‚sol] s aerosol *m*

aerospace ['ɛro‚spes] *adj* aerospaziale
|| s aerospazio

Aesop ['isap] s Esopo

aesthete ['ɛsθit] s esteta *mf*

aesthetic [ɛs'θɛtɪk] *adj* estetico ||
aesthetics *ssg* estetica

afar [ə'fɑr] *adv* lontano; from afar da
lontano

affable ['æfəbəl] *adj* affabile

affair [ə'fer] s affare *m*; (*romance*)
relazione amorosa

affect [ə'fɛkt] *tr* influenzare; (*to touch
the heart of*) commuovere; (*to pretend to have*) affettare

affectation [‚æfɛk'teʃən] s affettazione

affected [ə'fɛktɪd] *adj* affettato

affection [ə'fɛkʃən] s affezione

affectionate [ə'fɛkʃənɪt] *adj* affettuoso,
affezionato

affidavit [‚æfɪ'devɪt] s affidavit *m*, dichiarazione sotto giuramento

affiliate [ə'fɪlɪ‚et] *adj* & s affiliato || *tr*
affiliare || *intr* affiliarsi

affini•ty [ə'fɪnɪti] s (-ties) affinità *f*

affirm [ə'fʌrm] *tr* affermare; confermare

affirmative [ə'fʌrmətɪv] *adj* affermativo
|| s affermativa

affix ['æfɪks] s affisso || [ə'fɪks] *tr*
affiggere; (*a signature*) apporre; (*e.g.,
blame*) attribuire

afflict [ə'flɪkt] *tr* affliggere

affliction [ə'flɪkʃən] s afflizione

affluence ['æflu·əns] s opulenza, abbondanza

affluent ['æflu·ənt] *adj* opulento, ab-
bondante; ricco || s affluente *m*

afford [ə'ford] *tr* permettersi il lusso
di; (*to furnish*) provvedere; (*to give*)
dare

affray [ə'fre] s rissa

affront [ə'frʌnt] s affronto || *tr* fare un
affronto a

afghan ['æfgən] or ['æfgæn] s coperta
di lana all'uncinetto || Afghan *adj* &
s afgano

afield [ə'fild] *adv* sul campo; far afield
lontano

afire [ə'faɪr] *adj* ardente; in fuoco, in
fiamme

aflame [ə'flem] *adj* in fiamme

afloat [ə'flot] *adj* & *adv* a galla; a
bordo; (*drifting*) alla deriva; (*said of
a rumor*) in circolazione

afoot [ə'fut] *adj* & *adv* a piedi; in
movimento, in moto

aforementioned [ə'for‚menʃənd] or
aforesaid [ə'for‚sed] *adj* suddetto

afoul [ə'faul] *adj* & *adv* in collisione;
to run afoul of finire nelle mani di,
impigliarsi con

afraid [ə'fred] *adj* impaurito, spaven-
tato; to be afraid (of) aver paura
(di)

African ['æfrɪkən] *adj* & s africano

aft [æft] or [ɑft] *adv* a poppa; indietro

after ['æftər] or ['ɑftər] *adj* seguente;
di poppa || *adv* dopo; (*behind*) dietro
|| *prep* dopo; dopo di; (*in the manner
of*) secondo; to run after correre
dietro a || *conj* dopo che

afterburner ['æftər‚bʌrnər] or ['ɑftər-
‚bʌrnər] s (aer) postbruciatore *m*

af'ter-din'ner *adj* dopo la cena

aftereffect ['æftərɪ‚fɛkt] or ['ɑftərɪ-
‚fɛkt] s conseguenza

af'ter-hours' *adj* dopo le ore di ufficio

af'ter•life' s aldilà *m*; vita sussequente

aftermath ['æftər,mæθ] or ['ɑftər-,mæθ] s conseguenze fpl; gravi conseguenze fpl

af'ter•noon' adj pomeridiano || s pomeriggio

after-shaving ['æftər,ʃevɪŋ] or ['ɑftər-,ʃevɪŋ] adj dopobarba

af'ter-taste' s retrosapore m

af'ter-thought' s pensiero tardivo

afterward ['æftərwərd] or ['ɑftərwərd] adv dopo; **long afterward** molto tempo dopo

af'ter•while' adv fra un po'

again [ə'gɛn] adv di nuovo; ancora; un'altra volta; **again and again** ripetutamente; **as much again** due volte tanto, altrettanto; **to + inf + again** tornare a + inf, e.g., **to cook again** tornare a cuocere

against [ə'gɛnst] prep contro; (opposite) in faccia a; **to be against** opporsi a; **to go against the grain** ripugnare

agape [ə'gep] adj & adv a bocca aperta

age [edʒ] s età f; (old age) vecchiaia; (full term of life) vita; (historical or geological period) evo; generazione; **of age** maggiorenne; **to come of age** diventare maggiorenne; **under age** minorenne || tr & intr invecchiare

aged [edʒd] adj dell'età di || ['edʒɪd] adj vecchio, invecchiato

ageless ['edʒlɪs] adj eternamente giovane, che non invecchia mai

agen•cy ['edʒənsɪ] s (-cies) azione; agenzia; mediazione; (of government) ente m

agenda [ə'dʒɛndə] s agenda, ordine m del giorno

agent ['edʒənt] s agente m; (coll) commesso viaggiatore, agente m di commercio; (rr) gestore m

Age' of Enlight'enment s illuminismo

agglomeration [ə,glɑmə'reʃən] s agglomerazione

aggrandizement [ə'grændɪzmənt] s aumento, innalzamento

aggravate ['ægrə,vet] tr aggravare; (coll) irritare, esasperare

aggregate ['ægrɪ,get] adj & s aggregato, totale m; **in the aggregate** nel complesso || tr aggregare; ammontare a

aggression [ə'grɛʃən] s aggressione

aggressive [ə'grɛsɪv] adj aggressivo, attivo

aggressor [ə'grɛsər] s aggressore m

aggrieve [ə'griv] tr affliggere

aghast [ə'gæst] or [ə'gɑst] adj atterrito

agile ['ædʒɪl] adj agile

agitate ['ædʒɪ,tet] tr agitare || intr agitarsi

agitator ['ædʒɪ,tetər] s agitatore m

aglow [ə'glo] adj splendente

agnostic [æg'nɑstɪk] adj & s agnostico

ago [ə'go] adv fa, e.g., **a year ago** un anno fa; **long ago** molto tempo fa

agog [ə'gɑg] adj & adv ansioso; **to set agog** riempire di ansietà

agonize ['ægə,naɪz] intr soffrire straziantemente; (to struggle) dibattersi

ago•ny ['ægənɪ] s (-nies) agonia

agrarian [ə'grɛrɪ•ən] adj agrario || s membro del partito agrario

agree [ə'gri] intr aderire, andar d'accordo; (to consent) acconsentire; (gram) concordare; **to agree with** confarsi a, e.g., **eggs do not agree with him** le uova non gli si confanno

agreeable [ə'gri•əbəl] adj gentile; gradevole; (willing to agree) consenziente

agreement [ə'grimənt] s accordo; **in agreement** d'accordo

agriculture ['ægrɪ,kʌltʃər] s agricoltura

agriculturist [,ægrɪ'kʌltʃərɪst] s (farmer) agricoltore m; perito in agricoltura, agronomo

agronomy [ə'grɑnəmɪ] s agronomia

aground [ə'graʊnd] adv alla riva; **to run aground** andare or dare in secca

ague ['egju] s (chill) brivido; febbre f

ahead [ə'hɛd] adv davanti, avanti; **to get ahead** (coll) andare avanti, aver successo; **to get ahead of** sorpassare; **to go ahead** avanzare; continuare

ahoy [ə'hɔɪ] interj—**ship ahoy!** ehi della barca!

aid [ed] s aiuto; assistente m; (mil) aiutante m di campo || tr aiutare; **to aid and abet** essere complice di

aide [ed] s assistente m

aide-de-camp ['eddə'kæmp] s (aides-de-camp) aiutante m di campo

ail [el] tr affliggere; **what ails you?** che ha? || intr soffrire, essere malato

aileron ['elə,rɑn] s alerone m

ailing ['elɪŋ] adj ammalato

ailment ['elmənt] s malattia, indisposizione; (chronic) acciacco

aim [em] s mira; intento || tr (a gun) puntare; (words) dirigere || intr mirare; **to aim to** cercare di, aver l'intenzione di

air [ɛr] adj (e.g., pocket) d'aria; (e.g., show) aeronautico || s aria; **by air** per via aerea; **in the open air** all'aria aperta; **to be in the air** circolare; **to be on the air** (rad, telv) essere in onda; **to go on the air** (rad, telv) andare in onda; **to put on airs** darsi delle arie; **to take the air** andar fuori; **up in the air** incerto; (slang) arrabbiato || tr aerare, ventilare

airborne ['ɛr,bɔrn] or ['ɛr,born] adj aerosostentato; aerotrasportato

air' brake' s freno ad aria compressa

air' cas'tle s castello in aria

air'-condi'tion tr climatizzare

air' condi'tioner s condizionatore m

air' condi'tioning s aria condizionata, climatizzazione

air'-cool' tr raffreddare con aria

air' corps' s aviazione, arma aeronautica

air'craft' s (-craft) aeromobile m

air'craft car'rier s portaerei f

airdrome ['ɛr,drom] s aerodromo

air'drop' tr paracadutare

air'field' s campo d'aviazione

air'foil' s superficie f portante, velatura

air' force' s forza aerea

air' gap' s (elec) intraferro

airing ['ɛrɪŋ] s aerazione; passeggiata all'aria aperta; pubblica discussione

air' lane' s aerovia

air' jack'et s (aer, naut) giubbotto salvagente

air' lane' s aerovia

air'lift' s ponte aereo, aerotrasporto || tr aerotrasportare

air'line' s linea aerea; tubo dell'aria

air' mail' s posta aerea

air'-mail' adj per via aerea || s lettera per posta aerea || adv per posta aerea || tr spedire per posta aerea

air'-mail let'ter s lettera per posta aerea

air'-mail stamp' s francobollo posta aerea

air'man s (-men) aviatore m, aviere m

air' mat'tress s materassino pneumatico

air'plane' s aeroplano, aereo

air'plane car'rier s portaerei f

air' pock'et s vuoto d'aria

air' pollu'tion s contaminazione atmosferica, inquinamento atmosferico

air' port' s aeroporto

air' pump' s pompa pneumatica

air' raid' s incursione aerea

air'-raid shel'ter s rifugio antiaereo

air'-raid warn'ing s allerta

air' ri'fle s fucile m ad aria compressa

air' serv'ice s aeroservizio

air' shaft' s tubo di ventilazione

air'ship' s aeronave f

airsickness ['ɛr,sɪknɪs] s male m d'aria

air' sleeve' s manica a vento

airspace ['ɛr,spes] s aerospazio

air'strip' s aviopista

air' ter'minal s aerostazione

air'tight' adj impermeabile all'aria, ermetico

air'waves' spl onde fpl, radioonde fpl

air'way' s aerovia; **airways** (rad) onda, onde fpl

air·y ['ɛri] adj (-ier; -iest) arioso; leggero; aereo

aisle [aɪl] s (between rows of seats) corsia; (of a church) navata laterale; (theat) canale m

ajar [ə'dʒar] adj socchiuso; in disaccordo

akimbo [ə'kɪmbo] adj & adv—with arms akimbo con le mani sui fianchi

akin [ə'kɪn] adj affine; congiunto

alabaster ['ælə,bæstər] or ['ælə,bastər] s alabastro

à la carte [,alə'kart] adv alla carta

à la mode [,alə'mod] or [,ælə'mod] adv alla moda; servito con gelato

alarm [ə'larm] s allarme m || tr allarmare

alarm' clock' s sveglia

alas [ə'læs] or [ə'las] interj ahimè!; povero me!

Albanian [æl'benɪ·ən] adj & s albanese mf

albatross ['ælbə,trɔs] or ['ælbə,tras] s albatro, diomedea

album ['ælbəm] s album m

albumen [æl'bjumən] s albume m

alchemy ['ælkəmi] s alchimia

alcohol ['ælkə,hɔl] or ['ælkə,hal] s alcole m

alcoholic [,ælkə'hɔlɪk] or [,ælkə'halɪk] adj alcolico || s alcolizzato

alcove ['ælkov] s (recess) alcova; (in a garden) chiosco, padiglione m; cameretta attigua

alder ['ɔldər] s ontano, alno

al'der·man s (-men) assessore m municipale, consigliere m municipale

ale [el] s birra amara

alembic [ə'lɛmbɪk] s alambicco

alert [ə'lʌrt] adj attento; vispo || s allerta; **to be on the alert** stare allerta || tr dare l'allerta a

Aleu'tian Is'lands [ə'luʃən] spl Isole Aleutine

Alexander [,ælɪg'zændər] or [,ælɪg-'zandər] s Alessandro

Alexan'der the Great' s Alessandro Magno

Alexandrine [,ælɪg'zændrɪn] adj & s alessandrino

alfalfa [æl'fælfə] s (bot) erba medica

algae ['ældʒi] spl alghe fpl

algebra ['ældʒɪbrə] s algebra

algebraic [,ældʒɪ'bre·ɪk] adj algebrico

Algeria [æl'dʒɪrɪ·ə] s l'Algeria

Algerian [æl'dʒɪrɪ·ən] adj & s algerino

Algiers [æl'dʒɪrz] s Algeri f

alias ['elɪ·əs] s pseudonimo || adv alias

ali·bi ['ælɪ,baɪ] s (-bis) alibi m

alien ['eljən] or ['elɪ·ən] adj straniero; (strange) strano || s straniero; (outsider) estraneo

alienate ['eljə,net] or ['elɪ·ə,net] tr alienare

alight [ə'laɪt] v (pret & pp alighted or alit [ə'lɪt]) intr scendere; **to alight on** or **upon** posarsi su

align [ə'laɪn] tr allineare || intr allinearsi

alike [ə'laɪk] adj uguali; **to look alike** assomigliarsi || adv nello stesso modo

alimen'tary canal' [,ælɪ'mɛntəri] s tubo digestivo

alimony ['ælɪ,moni] s alimonia

alive [ə'laɪv] adj vivo, in vita; (lively) vivace; **alive to** conscio di; **alive with** brulicante di, pieno zeppo di; **look alive!** fa presto!

alka·li ['ælkə,laɪ] s (-lis or -lies) alcali m

alkaline ['ælkə,laɪn] or ['ælkəlɪn] adj alcalino

all [ɔl] adj indef tutto, tutto il, ogni || s tutto || pron tutto; tutti; **all of** tutti || adv completamente; **all but** quasi; **all in** (slang) stanco morto; **all in all** tutto considerato; **all the better** tanto meglio; **all the worse** tanto peggio; **far all that** per quello che, e.g., **for all that I know** per quello che io ne sappia; **in all** tutto contato; **it's all right!** va bene!; **not at all** niente affatto; prego

allay [ə'le] tr calmare, mitigare

all' clear' s fine f dell'allarme, cessato allarme

allegation [,ælɪ'geʃən] s asserzione, affermazione

allege [ə'lɛdʒ] tr asserire, affermare; addurre

allegiance [ə'lidʒəns] s fedeltà f, lealtà f

allegoric(al) [ˌælɪ'gɑrɪk(əl)] or [ˌælɪ'gɔrɪk(əl)] *adj* allegorico
allego·ry [ˈælɪˌgori] *s* (-ries) allegoria
aller·gy [ˈælərdʒi] *s* (-gies) allergia
alleviate [əˈlivɪˌet] *tr* alleviare
alley [ˈæli] *s* vicolo, calle *f*; *(for bowling)* pista; *(tennis)* corridoio
All' Fools' Day' *s* primo d'aprile
all' fours' *spl*—**on all fours** a quattro gambe
alliance [əˈlaɪ·əns] *s* alleanza
alligator [ˈælɪˌgetər] *s* alligatore *m*
alliteration [əˌlɪtəˈreʃən] *s* allitterazione
all-knowing [ˈɔlˈno·ɪŋ] *adj* onnisciente
allocate [ˈæləˌket] *tr* assegnare; *(funds)* stanziare; *(to fix the place of)* allogare
allot [əˈlɑt] *v* (*pret & pp* **allotted**) *ger* **allotting**) *tr* distribuire, assegnare
all'-out' *adj* completo; *(ruthless)* acerrimo
allow [əˈlaʊ] *tr* permettere; ammettere; concedere ‖ *intr* **to allow for** prendere in considerazione
allowance [əˈlaʊ·əns] *s* (*limited share*) assegno; concessione; *(reduction in price)* sconto; tolleranza; **to make allowance for** prendere in considerazione
alloy [ˈæləɪ] or [əˈlɔɪ] *s* lega; impurezza ‖ [əˈlɔɪ] *tr* far lega di, legare; adulterare
all-powerful [ˈɔlˈpaʊ·ərfəl] *adj* onnipotente
all' right' *adj* esatto; bene; in buona salute; (slang) dabbene
All' Saints'' Day' *s* Ognissanti *m*
All' Souls'' Day' *s* giorno dei morti
all'spice' *s* pimento, pepe *m* della Giamaica
all'-star game' *s* partita sportiva in cui tutti i giocatori sono scelti fra i migliori
allude [əˈlud] *intr* alludere
allure [əˈlʊr] *s* fascino, incanto ‖ *tr* affascinare, incantare
alluring [əˈlʊrɪŋ] *adj* affascinante, seducente
allusion [əˈluʒən] *s* allusione
al·ly [ˈælaɪ] or [əˈlaɪ] *s* (-lies) alleato ‖ [əˈlaɪ] *v* (*pret & pp* -lied) *tr* allearre; associare; **to become allied** allearsi; imparentarsi ‖ *intr* allearsi
almanac [ˈɔlmə‚næk] *s* almanacco
almighty [ɔlˈmaɪti] *adj* onnipotente
almond [ˈɑmənd] or [ˈæmənd] *s* (*nut*) mandorla; *(tree)* mandorlo
al'mond brittle' *s* croccante *m*
almost [ˈɔlmost] or [əlˈmost] *adv* quasi
alms [ɑmz] *s* elemosina
aloe [ˈælo] *s* aloe *m*
aloft [əˈlɔft] or [əˈlɑft] *adv* in alto, sopra; (aer) in volo; (naut) nell'alberatura
alone [əˈlon] *adj* solo; **let alone** senza menzionare; **to leave alone** non disturbare ‖ *adv* solo, solamente
along [əˈlɔŋ] or [əˈlɑŋ] *adv* (*lengthwise*) per il lungo; *(onward)* avanti; **all along** tutto il tempo; **along with**

con; **to get along** andar d'accordo; andarsene; avanzare; aver successo; **to take along** prendere con sè ‖ *prep* lungo
along'side' *adv* a lato; **alongside of** a lato di ‖ *prep* a lato di, vicino a
aloof [əˈluf] *adj* riservato, freddo; **to keep** or **stand aloof from** tenersi a distanza da ‖ *adv* lontano; da solo
aloud [əˈlaʊd] *adv* ad alta voce
alphabet [ˈælfəˌbet] *s* alfabeto
alpine [ˈælpaɪn] *adj* alpino
Alps [ælps] *spl* Alpi *fpl*
already [ɔlˈredi] *adv* già
Alsace [ælˈses] or [ˈælsæs] *s* l'Alsazia
Alsatian [ælˈseʃən] *adj & s* alsaziano
also [ˈɔlso] *adv* anche
altar [ˈɔltər] *s* altare *m*
al'tar boy' *s* accolito, chierico
al'tar-piece' *s* pala d'altare
alter [ˈɔltər] *tr* alterare; *(a male animal)* castrare ‖ *intr* diventare differente, cambiare
alteration [ˌɔltəˈreʃən] *s* alterazione, modifica
alternate [ˈɔltərnɪt] or [ˈæltərnɪt] *s* sostituto, supplente *mf* ‖ [ˈɔltərˌnet] or [ˈæltərˌnet] *tr* alternare ‖ *intr* alternarsi, avvicendarsi
al'ternating cur'rent *s* corrente alternata
alternator [ˈɔltərˌnetər] or [ˈæltərˌnetər] *s* alternatore *m*
although [ɔlˈðo] *conj* benchè, per quanto, malgrado
altimeter [ælˈtɪmɪtər] or [ˈæltəˌmitər] *s* altimetro
altitude [ˈæltɪˌtjud] or [ˈæltɪˌtud] *s* altitudine *f*
al·to [ˈælto] *s* (-tos) contralto
altogether [ˌɔltəˈɡeðər] *adv* completamente, affatto, tutt'insieme
altruist [ˈæltrʊ·ɪst] *s* altruista *mf*
altruistic [ˌæltrʊˈɪstɪk] *adj* altruistico
alum [ˈæləm] *s* allume *m*
aluminum [əˈlumɪnəm] *s* alluminio
alum·na [əˈlʌmnə] *s* (-nae [ni]) diplomata, laureata
alum·nus [əˈlʌmnəs] *s* (-ni [naɪ]) diplomato, laureato
alveo·lus [ælˈvi·ələs] *s* (-li [ˌlaɪ]) alveolo
always [ˈɔlwɪz] or [ˈɔlwez] *adv* sempre
amalgam [əˈmælɡəm] *s* amalgama *m*
amalgamate [əˈmælɡəˌmet] *tr* amalgamare ‖ *intr* amalgamarsi
amass [əˈmæs] *tr* ammassare
amateur [ˈæmətʃər] *adj* da dilettante ‖ *s* amatore *m*, dilettante *mf*
amaze [əˈmez] *tr* stupire, meravigliare
amazing [əˈmezɪŋ] *adj* straordinario
Amazon [ˈæməˌzɑn] or [ˈæməzən] *s* rio delle Amazzoni; (myth) Amazzone *f*
ambassador [æmˈbæsədər] *s* ambasciatore *m*
ambassadress [æmˈbæsədrɪs] *s* ambasciatrice *f*
amber [ˈæmbər] *s* ambra
ambigui·ty [ˌæmbɪˈgju·ɪti] *s* (-ties) ambiguità *f*
ambiguous [æmˈbɪgju·əs] *adj* ambiguo

ambition [æm'bɪʃən] *s* ambizione

ambitious [æm'bɪʃəs] *adj* ambizioso

amble ['æmbəl] *s* ambio || *intr* ambiare

ambulance ['æmbjələns] *s* ambulanza

ambush ['æmbʊʃ] *s* imboscata; **to lie in ambush** tendere un'imboscata || *tr* appostare || *intr* appostarsi

amelioration [ə‚miljə'reʃən] *s* miglioramento

amen ['e'mɛn] or ['ɑ'mɛn] *s* amen *m* || *interj* amen!

amenable [ə'minəbəl] or [ə'mɛnəbəl] *adj* docile, aperto; (*accountable*) responsabile

amend [ə'mɛnd] *tr* emendare || **amends** *spl* ammenda, contravvenzione; **to make amends for** fare ammenda per

amendment [ə'mɛndmənt] *s* emendamento

ameni·ty [ə'minɪti] or [ə'mɛnɪti] *s* (-ties) amenità *f*

American [ə'mɛrɪkən] *adj & s* americano

Americanize [ə'mɛrɪkə‚naɪz] *tr* americanizzare

amethyst ['æmɪθɪst] *s* ametista

amiable ['emɪ·əbəl] *adj* amabile

amicable ['æmɪkəbəl] *adj* amichevole

amid [ə'mɪd] *prep* in mezzo a, fra, tra

amidship [ə'mɪd/ɪp] *adv* a mezzanave

amiss [ə'mɪs] *adj* erroneo, sbagliato || *adv* erroneamente; **to take amiss** offendersi, prendere in mala parte

ami·ty ['æmɪti] *s* (-ties) amicizia

ammeter ['æm‚mitər] *s* amperometro

ammonia [ə'monɪ·ə] *s* ammoniaca; **acqua ammoniacale**

ammunition [‚æmjə'nɪʃən] *s* munizione, munizioni *jpl*

amnes·ty ['æmnɪsti] *s* (-ties) amnistia || *v* (*pret & pp* **-tied**) *tr* amnistiare

amoeba [ə'mibə] *s* ameba

among [ə'mʌŋ] *prep* fra, tra, in mezzo a

amorous ['æmərəs] *adj* amoroso; erotico

amortize ['æmər‚taɪz] *tr* ammortare

amount [ə'maʊnt] *s* ammontare *m* || *intr*—**to amount to** ammontare a

ampere ['æmpɪr] *s* ampere *m*

am'pere-hour' *s* amperora *m*

amphibious [æm'fɪbɪ·əs] *adj* anfibio

amphitheater ['æmfɪ‚θɪ·ətər] *s* anfiteatro

ample ['æmpəl] *adj* ampio

amplifier ['æmplɪ‚faɪ·ər] *s* amplificatore *m*

ampli·fy ['æmplɪ‚faɪ] *v* (*pret & pp* **-fied**) *tr* amplificare

amplitude ['æmplɪ‚tjud] or ['æmplɪ‚tud] *s* ampiezza

am'plitude modula'tion *s* modulazione d'ampiezza

amputate ['æmpjə‚tet] *tr* amputare

amputee [‚æmpjə'ti] *s* chi ha subito l'amputazione di un arto

amuck [ə'mʌk] *adv* freneticamente; **to run amuck** dare in un accesso di pazzia; attaccare alla cieca

amulet ['æmjəlɪt] *s* amuleto

amuse [ə'mjuz] *tr* divertire

amusement [ə'mjuzmənt] *s* divertimento

amuse'ment park' *s* parco dei divertimenti, luna park *m*

amusing [ə'mjuzɪŋ] *adj* divertente

an [æn] or [ən] *art indef* var of **a**, used before words beginning with vowel or mute *h*

anachronism [ə'nækrə‚nɪzəm] *s* anacronismo

anaemia [ə'nimɪ·ə] *s* var of **anemia**

anaesthesia [‚ænɪs'θiʒə] *s* anestesia

anaesthetic [‚ænɪs'θɛtɪk] *adj & s* anestetico

anaesthetize [æ'nɛsθɪ‚taɪz] *tr* anestetizzare

analogous [ə'næləgəs] *adj* analogo

analo·gy [ə'nælədʒɪ] *s* (-gies) analogia

analy·sis [ə'nælɪsɪs] *s* (-ses [‚siz]) analisi *f*

analyst ['ænəlɪst] *s* analista *mf*

analytic(al) [‚ænə'lɪtɪk(əl)] *adj* analitico

analyze ['ænə‚laɪz] *tr* analizzare

anarchist ['ænərkɪst] *s* anarchico

anarchy ['ænərki] *s* anarchia

anathema [ə'næθɪmə] *s* anatema *m*

anatomic(al) [‚ænə'tɑmɪk(əl)] *adj* anatomico

anato·my [ə'nætəmi] *s* (-mies) anatomia

ancestor ['ænsɛstər] *s* antenato

ances·try ['ænsɛstri] *s* (-tries) lignaggio, prosapia

anchor ['æŋkər] *s* ancora; **to cast anchor** gettare l'ancora; **to ride at anchor** stare all'ancora; **to weigh anchor** salpare l'ancora, salpare || *tr* ancorare || *intr* ancorarsi, stare all'ancora

ancho·vy ['æntʃovi] *s* (-vies) acciuga

ancient ['enʃənt] *adj* antico || *s* vecchio, anziano; **the ancients** gli antichi

ancillary ['ænsɪ‚lɛri] *adj* dipendente; ausiliario, ausiliare

and [ænd] or [ənd] *conj* e, ed; **and so on, and so forth** e così via

Andean [æn'di·ən] or ['ændɪ·ən] *adj* andino || *s* abitante *mf* della regione andina

Andes ['ændiʒ] *spl* Ande *fpl*

andiron ['ænd‚aɪ·ərn] *s* alare *m*

anecdote ['ænɪk‚dot] *s* aneddoto

anemia [ə'nimɪ·ə] *s* anemia

anemic [ə'nimɪk] *adj* anemico

an'eroid barom'eter ['ænə‚rɔɪd] *s* barometro aneroide

anesthesia [‚ænɪs'θiʒə] *s* anestesia

anesthetic [‚ænɪs'θɛtɪk] *adj & s* anestetico

anesthetize [æ'nɛsθɪ‚taɪz] *tr* anestetizzare

aneurysm ['ænjə‚rɪzəm] *s* aneurisma *m*

anew [ə'nju] or [ə'nu] *adv* di nuovo, nuovamente

angel ['endʒəl] *s* angelo; (*financial backer*) (coll) finanziatore *m*

angelic(al) [æn'dʒɛlɪk(əl)] *adj* angelico

anger ['æŋgər] *s* ira, collera || *tr* adirare || *intr* adirarsi, incollerirsi

angle ['æŋgəl] *s* angolo; punto di vista

|| *intr* intrigare; **to angle for** darsi da fare per

an'gle i'ron *s* cantonale *m*, angolare *m*

angler ['æŋglər] *s* pescatore *m* alla lenza; (fig) intrigante *m*

Anglo-Saxon ['æŋglo'sæksən] *adj* & *s* anglosassone *mf*

an·gry ['æŋgri] *adj* (**-grier; -griest**) arrabbiato; (pathol) infiammato; **to become angry at** incollerirsi per; **to become angry with** adirarsi con

anguish ['æŋgwiʃ] *s* angoscia, pena

angular ['æŋgjələr] *adj* angolare

anhydrous [æn'haidrəs] *adj* anidro

aniline ['ænilin] or ['æni‚lain] *s* anilina

animal ['æniməl] *adj* & *s* animale *m*

an'imated cartoon' ['æni ‚metid] *s* cartone animato

animation [‚æni'meʃən] *s* animazione

animosi·ty [‚æni'masiti] *s* (**-ties**) animosità *f*

animus ['æniməs] *s* odio, malanimo

anion ['æn‚ai·ən] *s* anione *m*

anise ['ænis] *s* anice *f*

anisette [‚æni'zet] *s* anisetta

ankle ['æŋkəl] *s* caviglia

an'kle-bone' *s* malleolo

an'kle support' *s* cavigliera

anklet ['æŋklit] *s* calzino corto; bracciale *m* da caviglia

annals ['ænəlz] *spl* annali *mpl*

annex ['æneks] *s* annesso, dipendenza || [ə'neks] *tr* annettere, appropriarsi di

annihilate [ə'nai·i‚let] *tr* annientare

anniversa·ry [‚æni'vʌrsəri] *adj* anniversario || *s* (**-ries**) anniversario

annotate ['ænə‚tet] *tr* annotare

announce [ə'nauns] *tr* annunciare

announcement [ə'naunsmənt] *s* annuncio, partecipazione

announcer [ə'naunsər] *s* annunziatore *m*

annoy [ə'nɔi] *tr* annoiare, seccare

annoyance [ə'nɔi·əns] *s* fastidio, seccatura

annoying [ə'nɔi·iŋ] *adj* noioso

annual ['ænju·əl] *adj* annuale || *s* annuario; pianta annuale

annui·ty [ə'nju·iti] or [ə'nu·iti] *s* (**-ties**) annualità *f*; (*for life*) vitalizio

an·nul [ə'nʌl] *v* (*pret* & *pp* **-nulled;** *ger* **-nulling**) *tr* annullare, cassare

annunciation [ə‚nʌnsi'eʃən] *s* annunzio || **Annunciation** *s* Annunciazione

anode ['ænod] *s* anodo

anoint [ə'nɔint] *tr* ungere

anomalous [ə'namələs] *adj* anomalo

anoma·ly [ə'naməli] *s* (**-lies**) anomalia

anonymi·ty [‚ænə'nimiti] *s* (**-ties**) anonimia; **to preserve one's anonymity** serbare l'anonimo

anonymous [ə'naniməs] *adj* anonimo

another [ə'nʌðər] *adj* & *pron indef* un altro

answer ['ænsər] or ['ɑnsər] *s* risposta; (*to a problem*) soluzione || *tr* rispondere a; **this will answer your purpose** questo fa per Lei; **to answer back** (slang) dare una rispostaccia a; **to answer the door** andare a rispondere

|| *intr* rispondere; corrispondere; essere responsabile; **to answer back** (slang) dare una rispostaccia

ant [ænt] *s* formica

antagonism [æn'tægə‚nizəm] *s* antagonismo

antagonize [æn'tægə‚naiz] *tr* opporsi a; creare antagonismo in

antarctic [æn't'arktik] *adj* antartico || **the Antarctic** la regione antartica

anteater ['ænt‚itər] *s* formichiere *m*

antecedent [‚ænti'sidənt] *adj* & *s* antecedente *m*; **antecedents** antenati *mpl*

antechamber ['ænti‚tʃembər] *s* anticamera

antedate ['ænti‚det] *tr* antidatare; (*to happen before*) antecedere

antelope ['ænti‚lop] *s* antilope *f*

anten·na [æn'tenə] *s* (**-nae** [ni]) (*of insect*) antenna || *s* (**-nas**) (rad, telv) antenna

antepenult [‚ænti'pinʌlt] *s* terzultima sillaba

anteroom ['ænti‚rum] or ['ænti‚rum] *s* anticamera, sala d'aspetto

anthem ['ænθəm] *s* inno

ant'hill' *s* formicaio

antholo·gy [æn'θalədʒi] *s* (**-gies**) antologia

anthracite ['ænθrə‚sait] *s* antracite *f*

anthrax ['ænθræks] *s* antrace *m*

anthropoid ['ænθrə‚pɔid] *adj* antropoide, antropomorfo

anthropology [‚ænθrə'palədʒi] *s* antropologia

antiaircraft [‚ænti'er‚kræft] or [‚ænti·'er‚kraft] *adj* antiaereo

antibiotic [‚æntibai'atik] *adj* & *s* antibiotico

antibod·y ['ænti‚badi] *s* (**-ies**) anticorpo

anticipate [æn'tisi‚pet] *tr* anticipare, prevedere; ripromettersi

anticipation [æn‚tisi'peʃən] *s* anticipazione, previsione

antics ['æntiks] *spl* pagliacciate *fpl*, buffonate *fpl*

antidote ['ænti‚dot] *s* antidoto

antifreeze ['ænti‚friz] *s* anticongelante *m*

antiglare [‚ænti'gler] *adj* antiabbagliante

anti-G' suit' *s* tuta antigravità

antiknock [‚ænti'nak] *adj* antidetonante

antimissile [‚ænti'misil] *adj* antimissile

antimony ['ænti‚moni] *s* antimonio

antinoise [‚ænti'nɔiz] *adj* antirumore

antipa·thy [æn'tipəθi] *s* (**-thies**) antipatia

antipersonnel [‚ænti‚pʌrsə'nel] *adj* (*e.g.,* mine) antiuomo

antiquarian [‚ænti'kweri·ən] *adj* & *s* antiquario

antiquar·y ['ænti‚kweri] *s* (**-ies**) antiquario

antiquated ['ænti‚kwetid] *adj* antiquato

antique [æn'tik] *adj* antico, vecchio; antiquato || *s* oggetto d'epoca, antichità *f*

antique' deal'er s antiquario
antique' store' s negozio d'antiquariato
antiqui·ty [æn'tɪkwɪtɪ] s (-ties) antichità f
anti-Semitic [ˌæntɪsɪ'mɪtɪk] adj antisemita
antiseptic [ˌæntɪ'sɛptɪk] adj & s antisettico
antislavery [ˌæntɪ'slevərɪ] adj antischiavista
antitank [ˌæntɪ'tæŋk] adj anticarro
antitheft [ˌæntɪ'θɛft] adj antifurto
antithe·sis [æn'tɪθɪsɪs] s (-ses [ˌsiz]) antitesi f
antitoxin [ˌæntɪ'taksɪn] s antitossina
antitrust [ˌæntɪ'trʌst] adj antitrust
antler ['æntlər] s corno di cervo
antonym ['æntənɪm] s antonimo
Antwerp ['æntwərp] s Anversa
anvil ['ænvɪl] s incudine m
anxie·ty [æŋ'zaɪ·ətɪ] s (-ties) ansietà f; (psychol) angoscia
anxious ['æŋk/əs] adj ansioso; **anxious about** sollecito di; **anxious for** desideroso di
any ['ɛnɪ] adj indef ogni, qualunque, qualsiasi; qualche; e.g., **do you know any boy who could help me?** conosce qualche ragazzo che possa aiutarmi?; di+art, e.g., **do you want any cheese?** vuole del formaggio?; **not . . . any** non . . . nessuno, e.g., **he does not read any newspaper** non legge nessun giornale || adv un po', e.g., **do you want any?** ne vuole un po'?; **not . . . any longer** non . . . più; **not . . . any more** non . . . più || pron ne, e.g., **do you want any?** ne vuole?
an'y·bod'y pron indef chiunque; (in interrogative sentences) qualcuno; **not . . . anybody** non . . . nessuno
an'y·how' adv in qualunque modo, comunque; in ogni caso; (haphazardly) alla rinfusa
an'y·one' pron indef chiunque; (in interrogative sentences) qualcuno; **not . . . anyone** non . . . nessuno
an'y·thing' s qualunque cosa || pron indef qualcosa; qualunque cosa; tutto quanto; checchessia; **anything at all** qualunque cosa; **not . . . anything** non . . . niente; **not . . . anything at all** non . . . niente affatto, non . . . nulla; **not . . . anything else** non . . . nient'altro
an'y·way' adv in qualunque modo, comunque; in ogni caso; (haphazardly) alla rinfusa
an'y·where' adv dovunque, in qualsiasi luogo; **not . . . anywhere** non . . . in nessun luogo
apace [ə'pes] adv presto, rapidamente
apart [ə'part] adv a parte, a pezzi; separatamente; **apart from** a parte da; oltre a; **to come apart** andare a pezzi, cadere a pezzi; **to take apart** mettere in disparte; **to tear apart** fare a pezzi; **to tell apart** distinguere
apartment [ə'partmənt] s appartamento; (single room) stanza

apart'ment house' s casa d'appartamenti
apathetic [ˌæpə'θɛtɪk] adj apatico
apathy ['æpəθɪ] s apatia
ape [ep] s scimmia antropomorfa; scimmia || tr imitare, scimmiottare
Apennines ['æpə,naɪnz] spl Appennini mpl
aperture ['æpərt/ər] s apertura
apex ['epɛks] s (apexes or apices ['æpɪ,siz]) apice m
apheresis [ə'fɛrɪsɪs] s aferesi f
aphorism ['æfə,rɪzəm] s aforisma m
aphrodisiac [ˌæfrə'dɪzɪ,æk] adj & s afrodisiaco
apiar·y ['epɪ,ɛrɪ] s (-ies) apiario
apiece [ə'pis] adv a testa, per persona; ciascuno
apish ['epɪ/] adj scimmiesco; da scimmia
aplomb [ə'plam] s disinvoltura, baldanza
apocalypse [ə'pakə,lɪps] s apocalisse f
apogee ['æpə,dʒi] s apogeo
apologetic [ə,palə'dʒɛtɪk] adj pieno di scuse
apologize [ə'palə,dʒaɪz] intr chiedere scusa, scusarsi
apolo·gy [ə'palədʒi] s (-gies) scusa; (makeshift) surrogato
apoplectic [ˌæpə'plɛktɪk] adj & s apoplettico
apoplexy ['æpə,plɛksɪ] s apoplessia
apostle [ə'pasəl] s apostolo
apostrophe [ə'pastrəfɪ] s (mark) apostrofo; (rhet) apostrofe f
apothecar·y [ə'paθɪ,kɛrɪ] s (-ies) farmacista mf
appall [ə'pɔl] tr sgomentare, sbigottire
appalling [ə'pɔlɪŋ] adj sconcertante
appara·tus [ˌæpə'retəs] or [ˌæpə'rætəs] s (-tus or -tuses) apparato
apparel [ə'pærəl] s confezioni fpl, vestiario
apparent [ə'pærənt] or [ə'perənt] adj apparente; chiaramente visibile
apparition [ˌæpə'rɪ/ən] s apparizione
appeal [ə'pil] s appello; (attraction) attrattiva, fascino || tr (a sentence) appellare contro || intr dare nell'occhio; **to appeal from** (law) appellarsi contro; **to appeal to** supplicare, pregare; piacere a, e.g., **his idea appeals to me** la sua idea mi piace
appear [ə'pɪr] intr apparire; (to seem) sembrare; (said of a book) uscire; (before the public) presentarsi; (law) comparire
appearance [ə'pɪrəns] s apparizione; (of a book) pubblicazione; (outward look) apparenza; (law) comparizione; **to keep up appearances** salvare le apparenze
appease [ə'piz] tr pacificare, placare; (a desire) soddisfare
appeasement [ə'pizmənt] s pacificazione, tranquillizzazione
appel'late court' [ə'pɛlɪt] s corte f d'appello
appellation [ˌæpə'le/ən] s denominazione, nome m
append [ə'pɛnd] tr allegare, aggiungere

appendage [ə'pɛndɪdʒ] *s* appendice *f*
appendicitis [ə,pɛndɪ'saɪtɪs] *s* appendicite *f*
appen·dix [ə'pɛndɪks] *s* (-dixes or -dices [dɪ,siz]) appendice *f*
appertain [,æpər'ten] *intr* spettare, riferirsi
appetite ['æpɪ,taɪt] *s* appetito
appetizer ['æpɪ,taɪzər] *s* (*drink*) aperitivo; (*food*) stimulante *m* dell'appetito
appetizing ['æpɪ,taɪzɪŋ] *adj* appetitoso
applaud *tr* applaudire, applaudire (with *dat*) || *intr* applaudire
applause [ə'plɔz] *s* applauso, applausi *mpl*
apple ['æpəl] *s* mela, pomo; (*tree*) melo, pomo
ap'ple-jack' *s* acquavite *f* di mele
ap'ple of dis'cord *s* pomo della discordia
ap'ple of one's eye' *s* pupilla degli occhi di qlcu, beniamino di qlcu
ap'ple pie' *s* torta di mele
ap'ple pol'isher *s* leccapiedi *mf*
ap'ple-sauce' *s* marmellata di mele; (*slang*) scemenza
appliance [ə'plaɪ·əns] *s* apparecchio, apparato; (*complicated instrument*) congegno; (*for domestic chores*) utensile *m*; (*act of applying*) applicazione
applicant ['æplɪkənt] *s* postulante *mf*, aspirante *m*, candidato
application [,æplɪ'keʃən] *s* applicazione; uso; richiesta, domanda
ap·ply [ə'plaɪ] *v* (*pret & pp* -plied) *tr* applicare; (*the brakes*) mettere; (*e.g., a nickname*) affibbiare || *intr* (*said of a rule*) essere applicabile; fare richiesta; **to apply for** sollecitare
appoint [ə'pɔɪnt] *tr* nominare; assegnare; (*to furnish*) ammobiliare
appointee [,æpɔɪn'ti] *s* persona nominata a una carica
appointive [ə'pɔɪntɪv] *adj* a nomina
appointment [ə'pɔɪntmənt] *s* nomina; (*position*) ufficio; (*agreement to meet*) appuntamento; **appointments** mobilia, arredamento; **by appointment** previo appuntamento
apportion [ə'porʃən] *tr* spartire, dividere proporzionatamente
appraisal [ə'prezəl] *s* stima, valutazione; (*of real estate*) estimo
appraise [ə'prez] *tr* stimare, valutare
appreciable [ə'priʃɪ·əbəl] *adj* apprezzabile, notevole
appreciate [ə'priʃɪ,et] *tr* apprezzare, valutare; (*to be grateful for*) gradire; (*to be aware of*) rendersi conto di; (*to raise in value*) valorizzare || *intr* aumentare di valore
appreciation [ə,priʃɪ'eʃən] *s* apprezzamento, valutazione; (*grateful recognition*) gradimento, riconoscenza; valorizzazione
appreciative [ə'priʃɪ,etɪv] *adj* grato, riconoscente
apprehend [,æprɪ'hɛnd] *tr* (*to fear*) temere; (*to understand*) comprendere; (*to arrest*) arrestare

apprehension [,æprɪ'hɛnʃən] *s* timore *m*, apprensione; comprensione; arresto
apprehensive [,æprɪ'hɛnsɪv] *adj* apprensivo
apprentice [ə'prɛntɪs] *s* apprendista *mf*, novizio || *tr* mettere in apprendistato; accettare in apprendistato
apprenticeship [ə'prɛntɪs,ʃɪp] *s* apprendistato, carovana
apprise or apprize [ə'praɪz] *tr* avvertire, avvisare; stimare, valutare
approach [ə'protʃ] *s* (*a coming near*) avvicinamento; (*of night*) avvicinarsi *m*, far *m*; approssimazione; (*access*) via d'accesso; (*to a problem*) impostazione; **approaches** approcci *mpl* || *tr* avvicinarsi a, avvicinare; fare approcci con || *intr* avvicinarsi, approssimarsi
approbation [,æprə'beʃən] *s* approvazione
appropriate [ə'propri·ɪt] *adj* appropriato, acconcio || [ə'propri,et] *tr* (*to take*) appropriarsi di; (*to set aside for some specific use*) stanziare
approval [ə'pruvəl] *s* approvazione; consenso; **on approval** in prova
approve [ə'pruv] *tr & intr* approvare
approximate [ə'prɑksɪmɪt] *adj* approssimato, approssimativo || [ə'prɑksɪ,met] *tr* approssimarsi a || *intr* approssimarsi
apricot ['eprɪ,kɑt] or ['æprɪ,kɑt] *adj* color albicocca || *s* (*fruit*) albicocca; (*tree*) albicocco
April ['eprɪl] *s* aprile *m*
A'pril fool' *s* pesce *m* d'aprile
A'pril Fools' Day' *s* primo d'aprile
apron ['eprən] *s* grembiale *m*, grembiule *m*; **tied to the apron strings of** attaccato alle sottane di
apropos [,æprə'po] *adj* opportuno || *adv*—**apropos of** a proposito di
apse [æps] *s* abside *f*
apt [æpt] *adj* atto, appropriato; (*quick*) pronto; **to be apt to** essere propenso a, portato a
aptitude ['æptɪ,tjud] or ['æptɪ,tud] *s* attitudine *f*
ap'titude test' *s* esame *m* attitudinale
Apulia [ə'pjulɪ·ə] *s* la Puglia
aqualung ['ækwə,lʌŋ] *s* autorespiratore *m*
aquamarine [,ækwəmə'rin] *s* acquamarina
aquaplane ['ækwə,plen] *s* acquaplano || *intr* andare in acquaplano
aquari·um [ə'kwɛrɪ·əm] *s* (-ums or -a [ə]) acquario, vasca dei pesci
Aquarius [ə'kwɛrɪ·əs] *s* (astr) Acquario
aquatic [ə'kwætɪk] or [ə'kwɑtɪk] *adj* acquatico || *s* animale acquatico; pianta acquatica; **aquatics** sport acquatici
aqueduct ['ækwə,dʌkt] *s* acquedotto
aqueous ['ekwɪ·əs] or ['ækwɪ·əs] *adj* acquoso
aq'uiline nose' ['ækwɪ,laɪn] *s* naso aquilino
Arab ['ærəb] *adj & s* arabo
Arabic ['ærəbɪk] *adj & s* arabo

arbiter [ˈɑrbɪtər] s arbitro
arbitrary [ˈɑrbɪˌtreri] adj arbitrario
arbitrate [ˈɑrbɪˌtret] tr arbitrare ‖ intr fare l'arbitro
arbitration [ˌɑrbɪˈtreʃən] s arbitrato
arbitrator [ˈɑrbɪˌtretər] s arbitro
arbor [ˈɑrbər] s pergola, pergolato; (mach) albero, asse m
arbore·tum [ˌɑrbəˈritəm] s (-tums or -ta [tə]) arboreto
arbutus [ɑrˈbjutəs] s (Arbutus unedc) corbezzolo
arc [ɑrk] s arco; (elec) arco voltaico ‖ intr (elec) formare un arco
arcade [ɑrˈked] s arcata, portico
arch [ɑrtʃ] adj malizioso ‖ s arco; (anat) arco del piede ‖ tr attraversare; arcuare ‖ intr inarcarsi
archaeology [ˌɑrkɪˈɑlədʒi] s archeologia
archaic [ɑrˈke·ɪk] adj arcaico
archaism [ˈɑrkeˌɪzəm] or [ˈɑrkiˌɪzəm] s arcaismo
archangel [ˈɑrkˌendʒəl] s arcangelo
archbishop [ˈɑrtʃˈbɪʃəp] s arcivescovo
archduke [ˈɑrtʃˈdjuk] or [ˈɑrtʃˈduk] s arciduca m
archene·my [ˈɑrtʃˈɛnimi] s (-mies) nemico giurato
archer [ˈɑrtʃər] s arciere m
archery [ˈɑrtʃəri] s tiro con l'arco
archetype [ˈɑrkɪˌtaɪp] s archetipo, prototipo
archipela·go [ˌɑrkɪˈpeləgo] s (-gos or -goes) arcipelago
architect [ˈɑrkɪˌtekt] s architetto
architectural [ˌɑrkɪˈtektʃərəl] adj architetturale, architettonico
architecture [ˈɑrkɪˌtektʃər] s architettura
archives [ˈɑrkaɪvz] spl archivio
arch'way' s arcata
arc' lamp' s lampada ad arco
arctic [ˈɑrktɪk] adj artico ‖ **the Arctic** la regione artica
arc' weld'ing s saldatura ad arco
ardent [ˈɑrdənt] adj ardente
ardor [ˈɑrdər] s ardore m
arduous [ˈɑrdʒʊ·əs] or [ˈɑrdju·əs] adj arduo
area [ˈɛrɪ·ə] s area
ar'ea code' s prefisso
Argentina [ˌɑrdʒənˈtinə] s l'Argentina
Argentine [ˈɑrdʒənˌtin] or [ˈɑrdʒənˌtaɪn] adj & s argentino ‖ **the Argentine** l'Argentina
Argonaut [ˈɑrgəˌnɔt] s argonauta m
argue [ˈɑrgju] tr dibattere; (to indicate) indicare, provare; **to argue out of** dissuadere da; **to argue s.o. into s.th** persuadere qlcu di qlco ‖ intr argomentare, discutere
argument [ˈɑrgjəmənt] s discussione, argomentazione; (theme) argomento
argumentative [ˌɑrgjəˈmentətɪv] adj litigioso
aria [ˈɑrɪ·ə] or [ˈɛrɪ·ə] s aria
arid [ˈærɪd] adj arido
aridity [əˈrɪdɪti] s aridità f
Aries [ˈɛriz] or [ˈɛriˌiz] s (astr) Ariete m

aright [əˈraɪt] adv correttamente; **to set aright** rettificare
arise [əˈraɪz] v (pret **arose** [əˈroz]; pp **arisen** [əˈrɪzən]) intr alzarsi; (to originate) provenire, trarre origine; (to occur) succedere, avvenire; (to be raised, as objections) avanzarsi
aristocra·cy [ˌærɪsˈtɑkrəsi] s (-cies) aristocrazia
aristocrat [əˈrɪstəˌkræt] s aristocratico
aristocratic [əˌrɪstəˈkrætɪk] adj aristocratico
Aristotelian [ˌærɪstəˈtiliˑən] adj & s aristotelico
Aristotle [ˈærɪˌstɑtəl] s Aristotele m
arithmetic [əˈrɪθmətɪk] s aritmetica
arithmetical [ˌærɪθˈmetɪkəl] adj aritmetico
arithmetician [ˌærɪθməˈtɪʃən] or [əˌrɪθməˈtɪʃən] s aritmetico
ark [ɑrk] s arca
ark' of the cov'enant s arca dell'alleanza
arm [ɑrm] s braccio; (e.g., of a bear) zampa; (of a chair) bracciolo; (weapon) arma; **arm in arm** a braccetto; **to be up in arms** essere in armi; essere indignato; **to lay down one's arms** deporre le armi; **to rise up in arms** levarsi in armi; **with open arms** a braccia aperte ‖ tr armare ‖ intr armarsi
armament [ˈɑrməmənt] s armamento
armature [ˈɑrməˌtʃər] s (of an animal) corazza; (of motor or dynamo) indotto; (of a buzzer or electric bell) ancora
arm'chair' s poltrona
Armenian [ɑrˈminɪ·ən] adj & s armeno
armful [ˈɑrmˌfʊl] s bracciata
arm'hole' s giro manica
armistice [ˈɑrmɪstɪs] s armistizio
armlet [ˈɑrmlɪt] s bracciale m
armor [ˈɑrmər] s armatura, corazza ‖ tr corazzare, blindare
ar'mored car' s carro armato
ar'mor plate' s lamiera di corazza
armor·y [ˈɑrməri] s (-ies) armeria; arsenale m
arm'pit' s ascella
arm'rest' s bracciolo
ar·my [ˈɑrmi] adj dell'esercito, militare ‖ s (-mies) esercito; (two or more army corps) armata
ar'my corps' s corpo d'armata
aromatic [ˌærəˈmætɪk] adj aromatico
around [əˈraʊnd] adv intorno; all'intorno; dappertutto; **to turn around** voltarsi ‖ prep intorno a; (coll) vicino a; (approximately) (coll) circa
arouse [əˈraʊz] tr eccitare, incitare; svegliare
arpeg·gio [ɑrˈpedʒo] s (-gios) arpeggio
arraign [əˈren] tr citare, portare in giudizio; accusare
arrange [əˈrendʒ] tr disporre, sistemare; (a dispute) comporre, accomodare; (mus) ridurre, arrangiare
arrangement [əˈrendʒmənt] s disposizione, sistemazione; composizione, accomodamento; (mus) riduzione,

arrangiamento; **arrangements** preparazione, preparativi *mpl*

array [ə're] *s* ordine *m*; (*clothes*) abbigliamento; (mil) spiegamento, schiera || *tr* disporre; abbigliare, adornare; (mil) spiegare, schierare

arrears [ə'rɪrz] *spl* arretrati *mpl*; **in arrears** in arretrato

arrest [ə'rest] *s* arresto; **under arrest** in arresto || *tr* arrestare; (*the attention*) attrarre

arresting [ə'restɪŋ] *adj* interessante, che fa colpo

arrival [ə'raɪvəl] *s* arrivo; persona arrivata

arrive [ə'raɪv] *intr* arrivare

arrogance ['ærəgəns] *s* arroganza

arrogant ['ærəgənt] *adj* arrogante

arrogate ['ærə͵get] *tr* (*to take without right*) arrogare per sé, arrogarsi; (*to claim for another*) attribuire ingiustamente

arrow ['æro] *s* freccia, saetta

ar'row-head *s* punta di freccia; (bot) sagittaria

arsenal ['ɑrsənəl] *s* arsenale *m*

arsenic ['ɑrsɪnɪk] *s* arsenico

arson ['ɑrsən] *s* incendio doloso

art [ɑrt] *s* arte *f*

arter·y ['ɑrtəri] *s* (**-ies**) arteria

artful ['ɑrtfəl] *adj* artificioso; (*clever*) destro; (*crafty*) astuto

arthritic [ɑr'θrɪtɪk] *adj* & *s* artritico

arthritis [ɑr'θraɪtɪs] *s* artrite *f*

artichoke ['ɑrtɪ͵t/ok] *s* carciofo

article ['ɑrtɪkəl] *s* articolo

articulate [ɑr'tɪkjəlɪt] *adj* articolato; facile di parola || [ɑr'tɪkjə͵let] *tr* articolare || *intr* pronunziare in modo articolato

articulation [ɑr͵tɪkjə'le/ən] *s* articolazione

artifact ['ɑrtɪ͵fækt] *s* manufatto

artifice ['ɑrtɪfɪs] *s* artificio

artificial [͵ɑrtɪ'fɪ/əl] *adj* artificiale

artillery [ɑr'tɪləri] *s* artiglieria

artil'lery-man *s* (**-men**) artigliere *m*, cannoniere *m*

artisan ['ɑrtɪzən] *s* artigiano

artist ['ɑrtɪst] *s* artista *mf*

artistic [ɑr'tɪstɪk] *adj* artistico

artistry ['ɑrtɪstri] *s* abilità artistica

artless ['ɑrtlɪs] *adj* ingenuo, naturale; ignorante; (*clumsy*) grossolano

arts' and crafts' *spl* arti *fpl* e mestieri *mpl*

art·y ['ɑrti] *adj* (**-ier; -iest**) (coll) interessato nell'arte con ostentazione

Aryan ['erɪ·ən] or ['ɑrjən] *adj* & *s* ariano

as [æz] or [əz] *pron rel* che; **the same as** lo stesso che || *adv* come; per esempio; **as . . . as** così . . . come; **as far as** fino a; **as far as I know** per quanto mi consta; **as for** in quanto a, per quanto concerne; **as is** (slang) com'è, nelle condizioni in cui si trova; **as long as** tanto che, mentre che; **as per** secondo; **as soon as** appena, non appena; **as to** per quanto concerne; **as well** pure, anche; **as yet** ancora || *prep* come; da; **as a rule** come regola ||

conj come; mentre; dato che; per quanto; **as if** come se; **as it were** per così dire; **as though** come se

asbestos [æs'bestəs] *s* asbesto, amianto

ascend [ə'send] *tr* ascendere, scalare || *intr* ascendere, salire

ascension [ə'sen/ən] *s* ascensione, scalata || **Ascension** *s* Ascensione

ascent [ə'sent] *s* scalata; salita; (*slope*) erta

ascertain [͵æsər'ten] *tr* sincerarsi di, verificare

ascertainable [͵æsər'tenəbəl] *adj* verificabile

ascetic [ə'setɪk] *adj* ascetico || *s* asceta *m*

ascor'bic ac'id [ə'skɔrbɪk] *s* acido ascorbico

ascribe [ə'skraɪb] *tr* attribuire, impufare

aseptic [ə'septɪk] or [e'septɪk] *adj* asettico

ash [æʃ] *s* cenere *f*; (bot) frassino

ashamed [ə'/emd] *adj* vergognoso; **to be or feel ashamed** vergognarsi

ash'can' *s* pattumiera; (coll) bomba antisommergibile

ashen ['æ/ən] *adj* cinereo

ashlar ['æʃlər] *s* bugna, bugnato

ashore [ə'/or] *adv* a terra; **to come ashore** andare a terra, sbarcare; **to run ashore** arenarsi

ash'tray' *s* portacenere *m*

Ash' Wednes'day *s* le Ceneri

Asia ['eʒə] or ['e/ə] *s* l'Asia *f*

A'sia Mi'nor *s* l'Asia *f* Minore

Asian ['eʒən] or ['e/ən] or **Asiatic** [͵eʒɪ'ætɪk] or [͵e/ɪ'ætɪk] *adj* & *s* asiatico

aside [ə'saɪd] *s* parola detta a parte; (theat) a parte *m* || *adv* da parte; a parte; **aside from** (coll) eccetto; separato da; **to step aside** farsi da un lato

asinine ['æsɪnaɪn] *adj* (*like an ass*) asinino; (*stupid*) asinesco

ask [æsk] or [ɑsk] *tr* chiedere (with *dat*), domandare (with *dat*); invitare; (*a question*) fare; **to ask s.o. for s.th** chiedere or domandare qlco a qlcu; **to ask s.o. to** + *inf* chiedere a qlcu di + *inf* || *intr* chiedere; **to ask about** chiedere informazioni di; **to ask for** chiedere, domandare; **to ask for it** (coll) andare in cerca di disgrazie; (coll) volerlo, e.g., **he asked for it** l'ha voluto

askance [ə'skæns] *adv* di traverso, di sbieco; (fig) con sospetto

asleep [ə'slip] *adj* addormentato; **to fall asleep** addormentarsi

asp [æsp] *s* aspide *m*

asparagus [ə'spærəgəs] *s* asparago; (*as food*) asparagi *mpl*

aspect ['æspekt] *s* aspetto; (*direction anything faces*) esposizione

aspen ['æspən] *s* pioppo tremolo, tremolo

aspersion [ə'spʌrʒən] or [ə'spʌr/ən] *s* diffamazione, calunnia; (eccl) aspersione

asphalt ['æsfɔlt] or ['æsfælt] *s* asfalto || *tr* asfaltare asphyxiate [æs'fɪksɪ‚et] *tr* asfissiare

aspirant [ə'spaɪrənt] or ['æspɪrənt] *s* aspirante *mf*

aspire [ə'spaɪr] *intr* aspirare

aspirin ['æspɪrɪn] *s* aspirina

ass [æs] *s* asino

assail [ə'sel] *tr* assalire, assaltare

assassin [ə'sæsɪn] *s* assassino

assassinate [ə'sæsɪ‚net] *tr* assassinare

assassination [ə‚sæsɪ'neʃən] *s* assassinio

assault [ə'sɔlt] *s* assalto || *tr* assaltare

assault' and bat'tery *s* vie *fpl* di fatto

assay [ə'se] or ['æse] *s* saggio, esame *m* || [ə'se] *tr* saggiare

assemblage [ə'sɛmblɪdʒ] *s* assemblea; (mach) montaggio

assemble [ə'sɛmbəl] *tr* riunire; (mach) montare, mettere insieme || *intr* assembrarsi, riunirsi

assembler [ə'sɛmblər] *s* montatore *m*

assem•bly [ə'sɛmblɪ] *s* (-blies) assemblea, riunione; (mach) montaggio

assem'bly hall' *s* sala di riunioni

assem'bly line' *s* catena di montaggio

assem'bly•man *s* (-men) membro dell'assemblea legislativa

assent [ə'sɛnt] *s* assenso || *intr* assentire

assert [ə'sʌrt] *tr* asserire; to assert oneself far valere i propri diritti

assertion [ə'sʌrʃən] *s* asserzione

assess [ə'sɛs] *tr* stimare, valutare; (for taxation or fine) tassare

assessment [ə'sɛsmənt] *s* valutazione; tassazione

assessor [ə'sɛsər] *s* agente *m* delle tasse

asset ['æsɛt] *s* vantaggio; persona di valore; assets (com) attivo; (law) beni *mpl*

assiduous [ə'sɪdʒʊ‚əs] or [ə'sɪdjʊ‚əs] *adj* assiduo

assign [ə'saɪn] *s* cessionario || *tr* assegnare; (e.g., a date) fissare; (a right) trasferire

assignation [‚æsɪg'neʃən] *s* assegnazione; trasferimento; (date) appuntamento amoroso

assignment [ə'saɪnmənt] *s* assegnamento; (of rights) trasferimento; (schoolwork) compito

assimilate [ə'sɪmɪ‚let] *tr* assimilare || *intr* essere assimilato; assimilarsi

assist [ə'sɪst] *s* aiuto || *tr* aiutare, assistere

assistance [ə'sɪstəns] *s* assistenza, aiuto

assistant [ə'sɪstənt] *adj* & *s* assistente *m*

associate [ə'soʃɪ‚et] or [ə'soʃɪ‚et] *adj* associato; *s* associato; membro limitato || [ə'soʃɪ‚et] *tr* associare || *intr* associarsi

association [ə‚soʃɪ'eʃən] *s* associazione

assort [ə'sɔrt] *tr* assortire || *intr* assortirsi

assortment [ə'sɔrtmənt] *s* assortimento

assuage [ə'swedʒ] *tr* alleviare

assume [ə'sum] or [ə'sjum] *tr* assumere; (to appropriate) usurpare; (to pretend) fingere; (to suppose) supporre

assumed [ə'sumd] or [ə'sjumd] *adj* supposto, immaginario

assumption [ə'sʌmpʃən] *s* (arrogance) aria, arroganza; (thing taken for granted) supposizione; (of an undertaking) assunzione

assurance [ə'ʊrəns] *s* assicurazione, certezza; baldanza, fiducia in sè; (too much boldness) sicumera

assure [ə'ʃʊr] *tr* assicurare

assuredly [ə'ʃʊrɪdlɪ] *adv* sicuramente

astatine ['æstə‚tin] *s* astato

asterisk ['æstə‚rɪsk] *s* asterisco, stelloncino

astern [ə'stʌrn] *adv* a poppa, a poppavia

asthma ['æzmə] or ['æsmə] *s* asma

astonish [ə'stɑnɪʃ] *tr* meravigliare, stupefare

astonishing [ə'stɑnɪʃɪŋ] *adj* stupefacente, sorprendente

astound [ə'staʊnd] *tr* stupefare, sbalordire

astounding [ə'staʊndɪŋ] *adj* stupefacente

astraddle [ə'strædəl] *adv* a cavaliere, a cavalcioni

astray [ə'stre] *adv* sulla cattiva via; to go astray traviarsi; to lead astray traviare

astride [ə'straɪd] *adj* & *adv* a cavaliere; (said of a person) a cavalcioni || *prep* a cavaliere di; a cavalcioni di

astrology [ə'strɑlədʒɪ] *s* astrologia

astronaut ['æstrə‚nɔt] *s* astronauta *mf*

astronautic [‚æstrə'nɔtɪk] *adj* astronautico || astronautics *ssg* astronautica

astronomer [ə'strɑnəmər] *s* astronomo

astronomic(al) [‚æstrə'nɑmɪk(əl)] *adj* astronomico

astronomy [ə'strɑnəmɪ] *s* astronomia

astute [ə'stjut] or [ə'stut] *adj* astuto

asunder [ə'sʌndər] *adv* a pezzi; to tear asunder separare, fare a pezzi

asylum [ə'saɪləm] *s* asilo

asymmetry [ə'sɪmɪtrɪ] *s* asimmetria

at [æt] or [ət] *prep* a; in; a ·casa di, e.g., at John's a casa di Giovanni; da, e.g., at Mary's da Maria; di, e.g., to be surprised at essere sorpreso di; to laugh at ridersi di

atheist ['eθɪ‚ɪst] *s* ateista *mf*

Athenian [ə'θɪnɪ‚ən] *adj* & *s* ateniese *mf*

Athens ['æθɪnz] *s* Atene *f*

athirst [ə'θʌrst] *adj* assetato

athlete ['æθlit] *s* atleta *mf*

athletic [æθ'lɛtɪk] *adj* atletico || athletics *ssg* & *spl* atletica

Atlantic [æt'læntɪk] *adj* atlantico || *adj* & *s* Atlantico

atlas ['ætləs] *s* atlante *m* || Atlas *s* Atlante *m*

atmosphere ['ætməs‚fɪr] *s* atmosfera

atmospheric [‚ætməs'fɛrɪk] *adj* atmosferico || atmospherics *spl* disturbi atmosferici

atom ['ætəm] *s* atomo

at'om bomb' *s* bomba atomica

atomic [ə'tɑmɪk] *adj* atomico

atom'ic age' *s* era atomica

atom'ic sub'marine *s* sommergibile *m* nucleare

atomize ['ætə‚maɪz] *tr* atomizzare

atomizer [ˈætə͵maɪzər] s nebulizzatore m

at'om smash'er s acceleratore m di particelle

atone [əˈton] intr—**to atone for** espiare

atonement [əˈtonmənt] s riparazione; espiazione

atop [əˈtɑp] adv in cima ‖ prep in cima a

atrocious [əˈtroʃəs] adj atroce

atroci·ty [əˈtrɑsɪti] s (-ties) atrocità f

atro·phy [ˈætrəfi] s atrofia ‖ v (pret & pp -phied) tr atrofizzare ‖ intr atrofizzarsi

attach [əˈtætʃ] tr attaccare; (to affix) apporre; (to attribute) attribuire; (law) sequestrare; **to be attached to** essere legato a; fare parte di ‖ intr—**to attach to** essere pertinente a

attaché [͵ætəˈʃe] or [əˈtæʃe] s attaché m., addetto

attaché' case' s valigetta diplomatica

attachment [əˈtætʃmənt] s attacco, unione; affezione; (mach) accessorio; (law) sequestro

attack [əˈtæk] s attacco ‖ tr & intr attaccare

attain [əˈten] tr raggiungere ‖ intr—**to attain to** raggiungere, conseguire

attainder [əˈtendər] s morte f civile

attainment [əˈtenmənt] s raggiungimento, realizzazione; (accomplishment) dote f

attempt [əˈtempt] s tentativo; (attack) attentato ‖ tr tentare; (s.o.'s life) attentare a

attend [əˈtend] tr (to be present at) presenziare, presenziare a, assistere a; (to accompany) accompagnare; (to take care of; to pay attention to) assistere ‖ intr—**to attend to** occuparsi di, attendere a

attendance [əˈtendəns] s (attending) presenza; (company present) concorso; **to dance attendance** essere al servizio completo

attendant [əˈtendənt] adj assistente; (accompanying) concomitante ‖ s (servant) inserviente mf; presente m

attention [əˈtenʃən] s attenzione; (mil) attenti m; **attentions** attenzioni fpl; **to call s.o.'s attention to s.th** fare presente qlco a qlcu; **to stand at attention** stare sull'attenti ‖ interj attenti!

attentive [əˈtentɪv] adj attento, premuroso

attenuate [əˈtenjuͅet] tr attenuare

attest [əˈtest] tr attestare ‖ intr—**to attest to** attestare, testimoniare

attic [ˈætɪk] s attico, solaio ‖ **Attic** adj & s attico

attire [əˈtaɪr] s vestiti mpl, vestiario ‖ tr vestire

attitude [ˈætɪ͵tjud] or [ˈætɪ͵tud] s atteggiamento, attitudine f; **to strike an attitude** atteggiarsi

attorney [əˈtʌrni] s avvocato; (proxy) procuratore m

attor'ney gen'eral s (attor'neys gen'eral or attor'ney gen'erals) procuratore m generale ‖ **Attorney General** s (U.S.A.) ministro di grazia e giustizia

attract [əˈtrækt] tr attrarre; (attention) chiamare

attraction [əˈtrækʃən] s attrazione

attractive [əˈtræktɪv] adj attrattivo

attribute [ˈætrɪ͵bjut] s attributo ‖ [əˈtrɪbjut] tr attribuire

attrition [əˈtrɪʃən] s attrito; diminuzione di numero

auburn [ˈɔbərn] adj & s biondo fulvo, rosso tizianesco

auction [ˈɔkʃən] s asta, incanto ‖ tr vendere all'asta

auctioneer [͵ɔkʃəˈnɪr] s banditore m; tr & intr vendere all'asta

audacious [ɔˈdeʃəs] adj audace

audaci·ty [ɔˈdæsɪti] s (-ties) audacia

audience [ˈɔdɪ·əns] s (hearing) udienza; uditorio, pubblico

au'dio fre'quency [ˈɔdɪ͵o] s audiofrequenza

au'dio-vis'ual aids' spl sussidi audiovisivi

audit [ˈɔdɪt] s verifica or esame m dei conti ‖ tr esaminare i conti di; (a class) assistere a, come uditore ‖ intr assistere a una classe come uditore

audition [ɔˈdɪʃən] s audizione ‖ tr dare un'audizione a

auditor [ˈɔdɪtər] s revisore m dei conti; (educ) uditore m

auditorium [͵ɔdɪˈtorɪ·əm] s auditorio

auger [ˈɔgər] s succhiello, trivella

aught [ɔt] s zero; **for aught I know** per quanto ne so ‖ adv affatto

augment [ɔgˈment] tr & intr aumentare

augur [ˈɔgər] s augure m ‖ tr & intr vaticinare

augu·ry [ˈɔgəri] s (-ries) augurio

august [ɔˈgʌst] adj augusto ‖ **August** [ˈɔgəst] s agosto

aunt [ænt] or [ɑnt] s zia

aurora [əˈrorə] s aurora

auspice [ˈɔspɪs] s auspicio; **under the auspices of** sotto gli auspici di

austere [ɔsˈtɪr] adj austero

Australia [ɔˈstreljə] s l'Australia f

Australian [ɔˈstreljən] adj & s australiano

Austria [ˈɔstrɪ·ə] s l'Austria f

Austrian [ˈɔstrɪ·ən] adj & s austriaco

authentic [ɔˈθentɪk] adj autentico

authenticate [ɔˈθentɪ͵ket] tr autenticare

author [ˈɔθər] s autore m

authoress [ˈɔθərɪs] s autrice f

authoritarian [ɔ͵θɑrɪˈterɪ·ən] or [ɔ͵θɔrɪˈterɪ·ən] adj autoritario ‖ s persona autoritaria

authoritative [ɔˈθɑrɪ͵tetɪv] or [ɔˈθɔrɪ͵tetɪv] adj autorevole; autoritario

authori·ty [ɔˈθɑrɪti] or [ɔˈθɔrɪti] s (-ties) autorità f; **on good authority** da buona fonte, da fonte autorevole

authorize [ˈɔθə͵raɪz] tr autorizzare

authorship [ˈɔθər͵ʃɪp] s paternità letteraria

au·to [ˈɔto] s (-tos) (coll) auto f

autobiogra·phy [͵ɔtobaɪˈɑgrəfi] or [͵ɔtobɪˈɑgrəfi] s (-phies) autobiografia

autobus [ˈɔto ˌbʌs] *s* autobus *m*
autocratic(al) [ˌɔtəˈkrætɪk(əl)] *adj* autocratico
autograph [ˈɔtəˌgræf] *or* [ˈɔtəˌgraf] *adj & s* autografo ‖ *tr* porre l'autografo su, firmare con firma autografa
automat [ˈɔtəˌmæt] *s* ristorante *m* self-service a distribuzione automatica
automate [ˈɔtəˌmet] *tr* automatizzare
automatic [ˌɔtəˈmætɪk] *adj* automatico ‖ *s* pistola automatica
automat'ic transmis'sion *s* trasmissione automatica
automation [ˌɔtəˈmeʃən] *s* automazione
automa·ton [ɔˈtɑməˌtɑn] *s* (-**tons** *or* -**ta** [tə]) automa *m*
automobile [ˌɔtəmoˈbil] *or* [ˌɔtəˈmobil] *adj & s* automobile *f*
automobile' show' *s* salone *m* dell'automobile
automotive [ˌɔtəˈmotɪv] *adj* (*self-propelled*) automotore; automobilistico
autonomous [ɔˈtɑnəməs] *adj* autonomo
autonomy [ɔˈtɑnəmi] *s* autonomia
autop·sy [ˈɔtɑpsi] *s* (-**sies**) autopsia
au'to trans'port rig' *s* autotreno per trasporto di automobili
autumn [ˈɔtəm] *s* autunno
autumnal [ɔˈtʌmnəl] *adj* autunnale
auxilia·ry [ɔgˈzɪljəri] *adj & s* (-**ries**) ausiliare *m*
avail [əˈvel] *s* utilità *f*; **of no avail** che non serve a nulla ‖ *tr* servire (with *dat*); **to avail oneself of** servirsi di; approfittare di ‖ *intr* servire
available [əˈveləbəl] *adj* disponibile; **to make available to** mettere alla disposizione di
avalanche [ˈævəˌlæntʃ] *or* [ˈævəˌlɑntʃ] *s* valanga
avant-garde [əvɑ̃ˈgard] *adj* d'avanguardia
avant-gardism [əˈvɑ̃ˈgardɪzəm] *s* avanguardismo
avarice [ˈævərɪs] *s* avarizia
avaricious [ˌævəˈrɪʃəs] *adj* avaro
avenge [əˈvɛndʒ] *tr* vendicare; **to avenge oneself on** vendicarsi di
avenue [ˈævəˌnju] *or* [ˈævənu] *s* viale *m*, corso
aver [əˈvʌr] *v* (*pret & pp* **averred;** *ger* **averring**) *tr* asserire, affermare
average [ˈævərɪdʒ] *adj* medio ‖ *s* media; (*naut*) avaria; (*e.g., of goals*) (*sports*) quoziente *m*; **on the average** di media ‖ *tr* fare la media di; fare . . . di media, e.g., **he averages one hundred dollars a week** fa cento dollari di media alla settimana
averse [əˈvʌrs] *adj* avverso
aversion [əˈvʌrʒən] *s* avversione
avert [əˈvʌrt] *tr* (*to ward off*) evitare; (*to turn away*) distogliere
aviar·y [ˈevɪˌɛri] *s* (-**ies**) aviario, voliera
aviation [ˌevɪˈeʃən] *s* aviazione
aviator [ˈevɪˌetər] *s* aviatore *m*
avid [ˈævɪd] *adj* avido
avidity [əˈvɪdɪti] *s* avidità *f*

avocation [ˌævəˈkeʃən] *s* svago, passatempo
avoid [əˈvɔɪd] *tr* evitare
avoidable [əˈvɔɪdəbəl] *adj* evitabile
avow [əˈvau] *tr* confessare, ammettere
avowal [əˈvau·əl] *s* confessione, ammissione
await [əˈwet] *tr* aspettare, attendere
awake [əˈwek] *adj* sveglio ‖ *v* (*pret & pp* **awoke** [əˈwok] *or* **awaked**) *tr* svegliare ‖ *intr* svegliarsi
awaken [əˈwekən] *tr* svegliare ‖ *intr* svegliarsi
awakening [əˈwekənɪŋ] *s* risveglio
award [əˈwɔrd] *s* (*prize*) premio; (*decision by judge*) sentenza ‖ *tr* aggiudicare
aware [əˈwer] *adj* conscio, consapevole; **to become aware of** rendersi conto di
awareness [əˈwernɪs] *s* coscienza
awash [əˈwɑʃ] *or* [əˈwɔʃ] *adj & adv* a fior d'acqua
away [əˈwe] *adj* distante, assente ‖ *adv* lontano; via; continuamente; **away back** (coll) molto tempo fa; **away from** lontano da; **to do away with** disfarsi di, sopprimere; **to get away** scappare, sfuggire; **to go away** andarsene; **to run away** fuggire; **to send away** mandar via; **to take away** portar via
awe [ɔ] *s* estremo rispetto; sacro timore ‖ *tr* infondere rispetto a; infondere un sacro timore a
aweigh [əˈwe] *adj* (*anchor*) levato
awesome [ˈɔsəm] *adj* grandioso, imponente
awestruck [ˈɔˌstrʌk] *adj* pieno di sacro timore
awful [ˈɔfəl] *adj* terribile; imponente ‖ *adv* (coll) terribilmente
awfully [ˈɔfəli] *adv* tremendamente, terribilmente; (coll) molto
awhile [əˈhwaɪl] *adv* un po', un po' di tempo
awkward [ˈɔkwərd] *adj* (*clumsy*) goffo, maldestro; (*unwieldly*) scomodo; (*embarrassing*) imbarazzante
awl [ɔl] *s* punteruolo
awning [ˈɔnɪŋ] *s* tenda; (*in front of a store*) tendone *m*
A.W.O.L. [ˈewəl] (acronym) *or* [ˈeˈdʌbəlˌjuˈoˈɛl] (letterword) *adj* (mil) assente al contrappello
awry [əˈraɪ] *adv*—**to go awry** andare a capovescio; **to look awry** guardare di sbieco
ax *or* **axe** [æks] *s* scure *f*; **to have an axe to grind** (coll) avere un interesse speciale
axiom [ˈæksɪ·əm] *s* assioma *m*
axiomatic [ˌæksɪ·əˈmætɪk] *adj* assiomatico
axis [ˈæksɪs] *s* (**axes** [ˈæksiz]) asse *m*
axle [ˈæksəl] *s* assale *m*, asse *m*
ax'le·tree' *s* assale *m*
ay [aɪ] *s & adv* sì *m*
Azores [əˈzorz] *or* [ˈezorz] *spl* Azzorre *fpl*
azure [ˈæʒər] *or* [ˈeʒər] *adj & s* azzurro, blu *m*

B

B, b [bi] *s* seconda lettera dell'alfabeto inglese

baa [ba] *s* belato || *intr* belare

babble [ˈbæbəl] *s* (*murmuring sound*) mormorio; (*senseless prattle*) balbettio || *tr* (*e.g., a secret*) divulgare || *intr* mormorare; balbettare; (*to talk idly*) parlare a vanvera

babe [beb] *s* bebè *m*, bambino; persona inesperta; (*slang*) ragazza

baboon [bæˈbun] *s* babbuino

ba·by [ˈbebi] *s* (**-bies**) bebè *m*, neonato; bambino; (*the youngest child*) piccolo || *v* (*pret & pp* **-bied**) *tr* coccolare, ninnare

ba'by car'riage *s* carrozzella

ba'by grand' *s* piano a mezza coda

babyhood [ˈbebi‚hud] *s* infanzia

babyish [ˈbebi‚ɪʃ] *adj* infantile

Babylon [ˈbæbɪlən] *or* [ˈbæbɪ‚lɑn] *s* Babilonia

ba'by sit'ter *s* bambinaia ad ore

ba'by teeth' *spl* denti *mpl* di latte

baccalaureate [‚bækəˈlɔrɪ‚ɪt] *s* baccalaureato; servizio religioso prima del baccalaureato

bacchanal [ˈbækənəl] *adj* bacchico || *s* baccanale *m*; (*person*) ubriacone *m*, bisboccione *m*

bachelor [ˈbætʃələr] *s* (*unmarried man*) scapolo, celibe *m*; (*holder of bachelor's degree*) diplomato; (*apprentice knight*) baccelliere *m*

bachelorhood [ˈbætʃələr‚hud] *s* celibato

bacil·lus [bəˈsɪləs] *s* (**-li** [laɪ]) bacillo

back [bæk] *adj* di dietro, posteriore; arretrato; contrario || *s* dorso, schiena; parte *f* posteriore, didietro; (*of a sheet or coin*) tergo; (*of a knife*) costola; (*of a room*) fondo; (*of a book*) fine *f*; (*of a chair*) schienale *m*; **behind one's back** dietro le spalle di uno; **to turn one's back on** volgere la schiena a || *adv* dietro; indietro; **a few weeks back** alcune settimane fa; **as far back as** sino da; **back of** dietro, dietro a; **to go back on one's word** mancare di parola; **to go back to** ritornare a; **to pay back** ripagare; **to send back** restituire || *tr* appoggiare; far indietreggiare || *intr* indietreggiare; rinculare; **to back down** rinunciarci; **to back off** or **out** ritirarsi; **to back up** (*said of a car*) fare marcia indietro

back'ache' *s* mal *m* di schiena

back'bite' *v* (*pret* **-bit**; *pp* **-bitten** or **-bit**) *tr* sparlare di || *intr* sparlare

back'bit'er *s* maldicente *mf*

back'board' *s* (basketball) tabellone *m*

back'bone' *s* spina dorsale; (*of a book*) costola, dorso; (*fig*) fermezza

back'break'ing *adj* sfiancante

back'door' *adj* segreto, clandestino

back' door' *s* porta di dietro; (*fig*) mezzo clandestino

back'drop' *s* (theat) fondale *m*

backer [ˈbækər] *s* sostenitore *m*, difensore *m*; (com) finanziatore *m*

back'fire' *s* (*for firefighting*) controfuoco; (aut) ritorno di fiamma || *intr* (aut) avere un ritorno di fiamma; (fig) raggiungere l'effetto opposto

back'ground' *s* fondo, sfondo; precedenti *mpl*; origine *f*

back'ground mu'sic *s* musica di fondo

backhand [ˈbæk‚hænd] *adj* obliquo || *s* scrittura inclinata a sinistra; (tennis) rovescio

back'hand'ed *adj* obliquo; sarcastico; insincero

backing [ˈbækɪŋ] *s* appoggio; sostegno; (bb) dorso

back'ing light' *s* (aut) faro retromarcia; (theat) luce *f* per il fondale

back'lash' *s* reazione; contraccolpo; (mach) gioco

back'log' *s* ceppo; (fig) riserva

back' num'ber *s* numero arretrato; (coll) persona all'antica

back' pay' *s* paga arretrata, arretrati *mpl*

back' scratch'er *s* manina per grattare la schiena; (coll) leccapiedi *m*

back' seat' *s* (aut) sedile *m* posteriore; (fig) posizione secondaria

back'side' *s* dorso; didietro

back'slide' *v* (*pret & pp* **-slid** [‚slɪd]) *intr* ricadere

back'spac'er *s* tasto ritorno

back'spin' *s* effetto

back'stage' *adj* dietro alle quinte || *s* retroscena *m* || *adv* a retroscena, dietro alle quinte

back'stairs' *adj* indiretto, segreto

back' stairs' *spl* scala di servizio

back'stitch' *s* impuntura || *tr & intr* impunturare

back'stroke' *s* (swimming) bracciata sul dorso

back'swept wing' *s* ala a freccia

back' talk' *s* risposta impertinente

back'track' *intr* ritornare sulle proprie tracce; (fig) fare macchina indietro

back'up light' *s* (aut) faro retromarcia

backward [ˈbækwərd] *adj* ritroso; poco progredito, retrogrado || *adv* a ritroso, all'indietro; verso il passato; alla rovescia; **backward and forward** (coll) completamente, perfettamente; **to go backward and forward** andare avanti e indietro

back'wash' *s* risacca

back'wa'ter *s* gora, ristagno; (fig) eremo

back'woods' *spl* zona boscosa lontana dai centri popolati

back'yard' *s* cortile *m* posteriore

bacon [ˈbekən] *s* pancetta

bacteria [bækˈtɪrɪ‚ə] *spl* batteri *mpl*

bacterial [bækˈtɪrɪ‚əl] *adj* batterico

bacteriologist [bæk‚tɪrɪˈɑlədʒɪst] *s* batteriologo

bacteriology [bæk‚tɪrɪˈɑlədʒi] *s* batteriologia

bad [bæd] *adj* (worse [wʌrs]; worst [wʌrst]) cattivo; (*coin*) falso; (*weather*) brutto; (*debt*) insolvibile; severo || *s* male *m*; **from bad to**

worse da male in peggio || adv male;
to be too bad essere peccato; to feel
bad esser spiacente; sentirsi male; to
look bad aver brutta cera

bad' breath' s fiato cattivo

bad' egg' s (slang) cattivo soggetto

badge [bædʒ] s divisa; decorazione;
simbolo, placca

badger ['bædʒər] s tasso || tr molestare

badly ['bædli] adv male; gravemente;
molto

bad'ly off' adj in cattive condizioni

badminton ['bædmɪntən] s badminton m

baffle ['bæfəl] s (mach) deflettore m;
(rad) schermo acustico || tr frustrare,
confondere

baffling ['bæflɪŋ] adj sconcertante

bag [bæg] s sacco; borsetta; (of a
marsupial) borsa; (hunt) presa; bag
and baggage con armi e bagagli; to
be in the bag (slang) averlo nel sacco;
to be left holding the bag (coll) es-
sere piantato in asso || v (pret & pp
bagged; ger bagging) tr insaccare;
(hunt) pigliare || intr (to hang
loosely) far pieghe

baggage ['bægɪdʒ] s bagaglio

bag'gage car' s bagagliaio

bag'gage check' s scontrino del bagaglio

bag'gage room' s deposito bagagli

bag-gy ['bægi] adj (-gier; -giest) come
un sacco

bag'pipe' s cornamusa, zampogna

bag'pip'er s zampognaro

bail [bel] s cauzione; libertà provvisoria sotto cauzione; (bucket) sassola
|| tr liberare sotto cauzione; to bail
out (a boat) sgottare || intr—to bail
out (aer) gettarsi col paracadute

bailiwick ['belɪwɪk] s (fig) sfera di
competenza

bait [bet] s esca; (fig) allettamento || tr
adescare; (fig) allettare

baize [bez] s panno verde

bake [bek] tr cuocere al forno || intr
cuocersi al forno; abbrustolirsi

bakelite ['bekə‚laɪt] s bachelite f

baker ['bekər] s fornaio, panettiere m

bak'er's doz'en s tredici per ogni dozzina

baker-y ['bekəri] s (-ies) panetteria

bak'ing pan' ['bekɪŋ] s tortiera

bak'ing pow'der s lievito in polvere

bak'ing so'da s bicarbonato di soda

balance ['bæləns] s (scales) bilancia;
equilibrio; armonia; (of watch) bilanciere m; (remainder; amount due)
resto; (of budget) pareggio; in the
balance in bilico; to lose one's balance perdere l'equilibrio; to strike a
balance fare il bilancio || tr bilan-
ciare, pesare; (com) bilanciare, pa-
reggiare || intr bilanciarsi

bal'ance of pay'ments s bilancia dei
pagamenti

bal'ance of pow'er s equilibrio politico

bal'ance of trade' s bilancia commerciale

bal'ance sheet' s bilancio

balco-ny ['bælkəni] s (-nies) balcone
m; (theat) galleria

bald [bɔld] adj calvo; (bare) nudo;
(unadorned) semplice

bald' ea'gle s aquila col capo bianco
dell'America del Nord

baldness ['bɔldnɪs] s calvizie f

baldric ['bɔldrɪk] s tracolla

bale [bel] s balla; collo || tr imballare

baleful ['belfəl] adj minaccioso, funesto

balk [bɔk] tr ostacolare || intr inte-
starsi, impuntarsi

Balkan ['bɔlkən] adj balcanico || the
Balkans i Balcani

balk-y ['bɔki] adj (-ier; -iest) caparbio,
ostinato

ball [bɔl] s palla; pallone m; sfera; (of
the thumb) polpastrello; (of wool)
gomitolo; (projectile) palla, pallottola; (dance) ballo; on the ball
(slang) capace, efficiente; (slang) in
gamba; to play ball giocare alla
palla; to play ball with essere in
cooperazione con || tr—to ball up
(slang) confondere

ballad ['bæləd] s ballata

ball' and chain' s palla di piombo;
(fig) impedimento; (slang) moglie f

ball'-and-sock'et joint' ['bɔlən'sakɪt] s
giunto a sfere

ballast ['bæləst] s zavorra; (rr) pie-
trisco || tr zavorrare

ball' bear'ing s cuscinetto a sfere

ballet ['bæle] s balletto

ballistic [bə'lɪstɪk] adj balistico || bal-
listics ssg balistica

balloon [bə'lun] s pallone m; (for children) palloncino; (in comic strip)
fumetto

ballot ['bælət] s scheda elettorale; voto
|| intr votare, ballottare

bal'lot box' s bussola, urna

ball'play'er s giocatore m di palla, giocatore m di baseball

ball'-point pen' s penna a sfera

ball'room' s salone m da ballo

ballyhoo ['bælɪ‚hu] s chiasso; monta-
tura || tr far chiasso a favore di

balm [bam] s balsamo

balm-y ['bami] adj (-ier; -iest) bal-
samico; salubre; (slang) pazzo

balsam ['bɔlsəm] s balsamo; (plant)
balsamina

Baltic ['bɔltɪk] adj baltico

baluster ['bæləstər] s balaustro

balustrade [‚bæləs'tred] s balaustrata

bamboo [bæm'bu] s bambù m

bamboozle [bæm'buzəl] tr ingannare,
raggirare

bamboozler [bæm'buzlər] s raggira-
tore m

ban [bæn] s bando; (of marriage) pubblicazione matrimoniale; (eccl) inter-
detto, scomunica || v (pret & pp
banned; ger banning) tr proibire

banal ['benəl] or [bə'næl] adj banale

banana [bə'nænə] s banana, (tree)
banano

band [bænd] s banda, striscia; (of thin
cloth) benda; (of metal, rubber) fascia, nastro; (of hat) nastro; (mus)
banda, fanfara; to beat the band
fortemente; abbondantemente || tr
unire || intr—to band together unirsi

bandage ['bændɪdʒ] *s* benda, bendaggio || *tr* fasciare

bandanna [bæn'dænə] *s* fazzolettone colorato

band'box' *s* cappelliera

bandit ['bændɪt] *s* bandito

band'mas'ter *s* capomusica *m*

bandoleer [ˌbændə'lɪr] *s* bandoliera

band' saw' *s* sega a nastro

band'stand' *s* chiosco della banda

band'wag'on *s* carrozzone *m* da circo; **to jump on the bandwagon** prendere le parti del vincitore

baneful ['benfəl] *adj* nocivo; funesto

bang [bæŋ] *s* rumore *m*, scoppio; (coll) energia; *(pleasure)* (slang) piacere *m*, eccitazione; **bangs** frangetta || *adv* tutto d'un colpo || *tr* sbattere || *intr* rimbombare || *interj* bum!

bang'-up' *adj* (slang) eccellente, di prim'ordine

banish ['bænɪʃ] *tr* sbandire, mettere al bando

banishment ['bænɪʃmənt] *s* bando, esilio

banister ['bænɪstər] *s* balaustra; **banisters** balaustrata

bank [bæŋk] *s* (*of fish; of fog*) banco; (*of a river*) sponda; (*for coins*) salvadanaio; (*financial institution*) banca, banco; (*of earth, snow*) mucchio, banco; (*of clouds*) cumulo; (aer) inclinazione laterale; (billiards) sponda || *tr* (*a fire*) coprire di cenere; (*to pile up*) ammonticchiare; (*a curve*) sopraelevare; (*money*) depositare || *intr* depositare denaro; (aer) inclinarsi lateralmente; **to bank on** (coll) contare su (di)

bank'book' *s* libretto bancario, libretto di deposito

banker ['bæŋkər] *s* banchiere *m*

banking ['bæŋkɪŋ] *adj* bancario || *s* attività bancaria; professione di banchiere

bank' note' *s* biglietto di banca

bank'roll' *s* rotolo di carta moneta; soldi *mpl* || *tr* (slang) finanziare

bankrupt ['bæŋkrʌpt] *adj & s* fallito; **to go bankrupt** andare in fallimento || *tr* dichiarare in fallimento; far fallire

bankrupt·cy ['bæŋkrʌptsi] *s* (-cies) fallimento

banner ['bænər] *adj* importante || *s* bandiera, stendardo; (journ) titolo in grassetto

banns [bænz] *spl* bandi *mpl* matrimoniali

banquet ['bæŋkwɪt] *s* banchetto || *tr* dar un banchetto a || *intr* banchettare

bantam ['bæntəm] *adj* piccolo || *s* pollo nano

ban'tam·weight' *s* peso gallo, bantam *m*

banter ['bæntər] *s* scherzo, facezia || *intr* scherzare, celiare

baptism ['bæptɪzəm] *s* battesimo

baptismal [bæp'tɪzməl] *adj* battesimale; (*certificate*) di battesimo

Baptist ['bæptɪst] *adj & s* battista *mf*

baptister·y ['bæptɪstəri] *s* (-ies) battistero

baptize [bæp'taɪz] *or* ['bæptaɪz] *tr* battezzare

bar [bar] *s* barra; sbarra; (*of soap*) saponetta; (*of chocolate*) tavoletta; (*of sand*) banco; (*obstacle*) barriera; bar *m*; (*of public opinion*) tribunale *m*; (*legal profession*) avvocatura; (*of door or window*) spranga; (*of lead*) (typ) lingotto; (mus) battuta; **behind bars** in guardina; **to be admitted to the bar** diventare avvocato; **to tend bar** fare il barista || *prep* eccetto, salvo; **bar none** senza eccezione || *v* (*pret & pp* **barred;** *ger* **barring**) *tr* sbarrare; sprangare; bloccare; escludere

bar' associa'tion *s* associazione dell'ordine degli avvocati

barb [barb] *s* (*of arrow*) barbiglio

barbarian [bar'berɪ·ən] *s* barbaro

barbaric [bar'bærɪk] *adj* barbaro

barbarism ['barbəˌrɪzəm] *s* barbarismo

barbari·ty [bar'bærɪti] *s* (-ties) barbarie *f*

barbarous ['barbərəs] *adj* barbaro, crudele

Bar'bary ape' ['barbəri] *s* bertuccia

barbecue ['barbɪˌkju] *s* arrosto allo spiedo || *tr* arrostire allo spiedo

barbed [barbd] *adj* irto di punte; mordace, pungente

barbed' wire' *s* filo spinato

barber ['barbər] *s* barbiere *m*; (*who cuts and styles hair*) parrucchiere *m*

bar'ber-shop' *s* barbieria, negozio di barbiere; negozio di parrucchiere

barbiturate [bar'bɪtʃəˌret] *s* barbiturato, barbiturico

bard [bard] *s* bardo, poeta *m*

bare [ber] *adj* nudo; (*head*) a capo scoperto; (*unconcealed*) palese; (*empty*) vuoto; (*wire*) senza isolante; (*unadorned*) semplice; **to lay bare** mettere a nudo || *tr* denudare, scoprire

bare'back' *adj & adv* senza sella

barefaced ['ber ˌfest] *adj* impudente, sfacciato, spudorato

bare'foot' *adj* scalzo

barehanded ['ber ˌhændɪd] *adj & adv* a mani nude

bareheaded ['ber ˌhedɪd] *adj* a capo scoperto

barelegged ['ber ˌlegɪd] *adj* a gambe nude

barely ['berli] *adv* appena, soltanto

bargain ['bargɪn] *s* affare *m*, buon affare *m*; contrattazione; **at a bargain** a buon prezzo; **into the bargain** in soprappiù || *tr*—**to bargain away** vendere a buonissimo prezzo || *intr* contrattare, mercanteggiare; **to bargain for** aspettarsi

bar'gain sale' *s* vendita sottoprezzo

barge [bardʒ] *s* barcone *m*, chiatta || *intr*—**to barge in** entrare senza chiedere permesso

baritone ['bærɪˌton] *adj* di baritono || *s* baritono *m*

barium ['berɪ·əm] *s* bario

bark [bark] *s* corteccia, scorza; (*of dog*) abbaiamento, latrato || *tr* (e.g., *insults*) lanciare || *intr* abbaiare, latrare

bar'keep'er *s* barista *mf*

barker ['barkər] *s* banditore *m*, imbonitore *m*

barley ['barli] *s* orzo

bar' mag'net *s* calamita a forma di barra allungata

bar'maid' *s* barista *f*

bar'man *s* (**-men**) barista *m*

barn [barn] *s* granaio; (*for hay*) fienile *m*; (*for livestock*) stalla

barnacle ['barnəkəl] *s* cirripede *m*

barn' owl' *s* civetta

barn'yard' *s* bassacorte *f*, aia

barn'yard fowl' *s* animale *m* da cortile || *spl* animali *mpl* da cortile

barometer [bə'ramıtər] *s* barometro

baron ['bærən] *s* barone *m*; (*industrialist*) cavaliere *m* d'industria

baroness ['bærənıs] *s* baronessa

baroque [bə'rok] *adj* & *s* barocco

bar'rack-room' *adj* da caserma || *s* camerata

barracks ['bærəks] *spl* caserma; camerata

barrage [bə'raʒ] *s* (mil) fuoco di sbarramento

barrel ['bærəl] *s* barile *m*, botte *f*; (*of gun*) canna; (mach) cilindro

bar'rel or'gan *s* organetto di Barberia

barren ['bærən] *adj* sterile; (*without vegetation*) brullo

barricade [,bærı'ked] *s* barricata || *tr* barricare

barrier ['bærı-ər] *s* barriera

bar'rier reef' *s* barriera corallina

barring ['barıŋ] *prep* eccetto, salvo

barrister ['bærıstər] *s* (Brit) avvocato

bar'room' *s* bar *m*, cantina, mescita

bar'tend'er *s* barista *mf*, barman *m*

barter ['bartər] *s* baratto || *tr* & *intr* barattare, permutare

basalt [bə'sɔlt] *s* basalto

base [bes] *adj* basale; basso; servile; (*morally low*) turpe; (*metal*) vile, non prezioso || *s* base *f*; (*in children's games*) tana; (*of a word*) radice *f* basale || *tr* basare

base'ball' *s* baseball *m*, pallabase *f*

base'board' *s* basamento; (*of wall*) zoccolo

Basel ['bazəl] *s* Basilea

baseless ['beslıs] *adj* infondato

basement ['besmənt] *s* scantinato, piano interrato

bashful ['bæʃfəl] *adj* timido

basic ['besık] *adj* fondamentale; (chem) basico

ba'sic commod'ities *spl* articoli *mpl* di prima necessità

basilica [bə'sılıkə] *s* basilica

basin ['besın] *s* catino; vasca; (*of balance*) piatto; (*of river*) bacino; (*of harbor*) darsena

ba·sis ['besıs] *s* (**-ses** [siz]) base *f*

bask [bæsk] *or* [bask] *intr* crogiolarsi

basket ['bæskıt] *or* ['baskıt] *s* cesta; (sports) cesto

bas'ket-ball' *s* pallacanestro *f*

Basque [bæsk] *adj* & *s* basco

bas-relief [,barı'lif] *or* [,bærı'lif] *s* bassorilievo

bass [bes] *adj* & *s* (mus) basso || [bæs] *s* (ichth) pesce persico

bass' drum' *s* grancassa

bass' horn' *s* bassotuba *m*

bassinet ['bæsə,net] *or* [,bæsə'net] *s* culla a forma di cesto; carrozzina a forma di cesto

bas·so ['bæso] *or* ['baso] *s* (**-sos** *or* **-si** [si]) basso

bassoon [bə'sun] *s* fagotto

bass' vi'ol ['vaɪ-əl] *s* contrabbasso

bastard ['bæstərd] *adj* & *s* bastardo

baste [best] *tr* (*to sew*) imbastire; (*meat*) inumidire con acqua o grasso

bastion ['bæstʃən] *or* ['bæstı-ən] *s* bastione *m*

bat [bæt] *s* mazza; (*in cricket*) maglio; (coll) colpo; (zool) pipistrello || *v* (*pret* & *pp* **batted**; *ger* **batting**) *tr* colpire con la mazza; **without batting an eye** (coll) senza batter ciglio

batch [bætʃ] *s* (*of bread*) infornata; gruppo, numero

bath [bæθ] *or* [baθ] *s* bagno; **to take a bath** fare il bagno

bathe [beð] *tr* bagnare, lavare || *intr* bagnarsi, fare il bagno

bather ['beðər] *s* bagnante *mf*

bath'house' *s* (*individual*) cabina; spogliatoio

bath'ing beau'ty *s* bellezza in costume da bagno

bath'ing cap' *s* cuffia da bagno

bath'ing resort' *s* stazione balneare

bath'ing suit' *s* costume *m* da bagno

bath'ing trunks' *spl* mutandine *fpl* da bagno

bath'robe' *s* accappatoio

bath'room' *s* stanza da bagno

bath' salts' *spl* sali *mpl* da bagno

bath'tub' *s* bagno, vasca da bagno

baton [bæ'tɑn] *or* ['bætən] *s* bastone *m*; (mus) bacchetta

battalion [bə'tæljən] *s* battaglione *m*

batten ['bætən] *tr* assicella; piccola traversa; (naut) bietta || *tr*—**to batten down the hatches** chiudere ermeticamente i boccaporti

batter ['bætər] *s* pasta, farina pastosa; (baseball) battitore *m* || *tr* battere, tempestare di colpi; (*to wear out*) logorare

bat'tering ram' *s* ariete *m*

batter·y ['bætəri] *s* (**-ies**) (*primary cell*) pila; (*secondary cell*) accumulatore *m*; (*group of batteries*) batteria; (law) assalto; (mil & mus) batteria

battle ['bætəl] *s* battaglia; **to do battle** dar battaglia || *tr* combattere contro || *intr* combattere

bat'tle cry' *s* grido di guerra

battledore ['bætəl,dɔr] *s* racchetta; **battledore and shuttlecock** gioco del volano

bat'tle-field' *s* campo di battaglia

bat'tle-front' *s* fronte *m* di combattimento

battlement ['bætəlmənt] *s* merlatura

bat'tle roy'al *s* baruffa generale, zuffa generale

bat'tle-ship' *s* corazzata

battue [bæ'tu] *or* [bæ'tju] *s* (hunt) battuta

bat·ty ['bæti] *adj* (**-tier; -tiest**) (slang) pazzo, eccentrico

bauble ['bɔbəl] *s* bazzecola, gingillo

Bavaria [bə'verɪ-ə] *s* la Baviera

Bavarian [bə'verɪ-ən] *adj & s* bavarese *mf*

bawd [bɔd] *s* ruffiano; ruffiana

bawd·y ['bɔdi] *adj* (**-ier; -iest**) indecente, osceno

bawd'y·house' *s* casa di malaffare

bawl [bɔl] *s* grido; (coll) pianto || *tr*—to bawl out (slang) fare una ramanzina a || *intr* strillare; (coll) piangere

bay [be] *adj* baio || *s* baia; vano, alcova; (recess in wall) apertura nel muro; finestra sporgente; (of dog) latrato; cavallo baio; (bot) lauro; at bay in una posizione disperata || *intr* latrare

bayonet ['be-ənɪt] *s* baionetta || *tr* dare baionettate a || *intr* dare baionettate

bay' win'dow *s* finestra sporgente; (slang) pancia

bazooka [bə'zukə] *s* bazooka *m*

be [bi] *v* (*pres am* [æm], *is* [ɪz], *are* [ɑr]; *pret was* [wɑz] *or* [wʌz], *were* [wʌr]; *pp been* [bɪn]) *intr* essere; fare, e.g., **to be a mason** fare il muratore; fare, e.g., **3 times 3 is 9** tre volte tre fa nove; **be as it may be** comunque sia; **here is** *or* **here are** ecco; **there are** ci sono; **there is** c'è; **to be** futuro, e.g., **my wife to be** la mia futura sposa; **to be ashamed** aver vergogna; **to be cold** aver freddo; **to be hot** aver caldo; **to be hungry** aver fame; **to be in** stare a casa; **to be in a hurry** aver fretta; **to be in with** (coll) essere amico intimo di; **to be off** andarsene; **to be out** essere fuori; **to be out of** (coll) non aver più; **to be right** aver ragione; **to be sleepy** aver sonno; **to be thirsty** avere sete; **to be up** essere alzato; **to be up to** essere all'altezza di; toccare, e.g., **it's up to you** tocca a Lei; **to be warm** avere caldo; **to be wrong** avere torto; sbagliarsi; **to be ... years old** avere ... anni || *aux* stare, e.g., **to be waiting** stare aspettando; essere, e.g., **the murder has been committed** l'omicidio è stato commesso; dovere, e.g., **he is to clean the stables tomorrow** domani deve pulire la stalla || *impers* essere, e.g., **it is necessary** è necessario; fare, e.g., **it is cold** fa freddo; **it is hot** fa caldo

beach [bitʃ] *s* spiaggia || *tr* (a boat) arenare || *intr* arenarsi

beach'comb' *intr* raccogliere relitti sulla spiaggia

beach'comb'er *s* girellone *m* di spiaggia

beach'head' *s* testa di sbarco

beach' robe' *s* accappatoio

beach' shoe' *s* sandalo da spiaggia

beach' umbrel'la *s* ombrellone *m* da spiaggia

beacon ['bikən] *s* faro || *tr* rischiarare; fare da guida a || *intr* brillare

bead [bid] *s* perlina; grano, chicco; (drop) goccia; **beads** (in a necklace or rosary) conterie *fpl*; **to count one's beads** recitare il rosario

beagle ['bigəl] *s* segugio, bracco

beak [bik] *s* becco; promontorio

beam [bim] *s* trave *f*; (of balance) braccio; (of light) raggio; (ship's breadth) larghezza; (smile) sorriso; (radio signal) fascio direttore; (course indicated by radio beam) aerovia; (naut) traverso || *tr* (a radio signal) dirigere; (e.g., light) irraggiare || *intr* raggiare

bean [bin] *s* fagiolo; (of coffee) chicco; (slang) testa

beaner·y ['binəri] *s* (-ies) (slang) gargotta, taverna di secondo ordine

bean'pole' *s* puntello per i fagioli; (coll) palo del telegrafo

bear [bɛr] *s* orso; (astr) orsa; (com) ribassista *m*, giocatore *m* al ribasso || *v* (*pret bore* [bor]; *pp borne* [born]) *tr* (to carry) portare; (to give birth to) partorire; (to sustain) sostenere; (to withstand) sopportare; (a grudge) serbare; (in mind) tenere; (interest) produrre; (to pay) pagare; **to bear the date** aver la data; **to bear out** confermare; **to bear witness** testimoniare || *intr* (to be productive) fruttificare; (to move) dirigersi; (to be oppressive) fare pressione; **to bear down on** fare pressione su; avvicinarsi a; **to bear up** resistere; **to bear with** tollerare

bearable ['bɛrəbəl] *adj* tollerabile

beard [bɪrd] *s* barba; (e.g., in wheat) arista

bearded *adj* barbuto

beardless ['bɪrdlɪs] *adj* imberbe

bearer ['bɛrər] *s* portatore *m*

bearing ['bɛrɪŋ] *s* portamento; relazione; importanza; (mach) bronzina, cuscinetto; **bearings** orientamento; **to lose one's bearings** perdere la bussola; perdere l'orientamento

bearish ['bɛrɪʃ] *adj* (like a bear) orsino; (e.g., prices) in ribasso; (market) al ribasso; (speculator) ribassista

bear'skin' *s* pelle *f* dell'orso; (mil) colbacco

beast [bist] *s* bestia

beast·ly ['bistli] *adj* (**-lier; -liest**) bestiale || *adv* (coll) malissimo

beast' of bur'den *s* bestia da soma

beast' of prey' *s* animale *m* da rapina

beat [bit] *s* (of heart) battito; (of policeman) ronda; (stroke) colpo; (habitual route) cammino battuto; (mus) tempo; (phys) battimento || *v* (*pret beat; pp beat or beaten*) *tr* battere; percuotere; (eggs) frullare; (to whip) frustare; (coll) confondere; **beat it!** (slang) vattene!; **to beat a retreat** battere in ritirata; **to beat back** respingere; **to beat down** sopprimere; **to beat off** respingere; **to beat up** (eggs) frullare; (people) dargliene a || *intr* battere; pulsare; **to beat around the bush** (coll) menare il can per l'aia

beat'en path' ['bitən] *s* cammino battuto

beater ['bitər] *s* frullino

beati·fy [bɪ'ætɪ,faɪ] *v* (*pret & pp -fied*) *tr* beatificare

beating ['bitɪŋ] s battitura; (*whipping*) frustatura; (*throbbing*) pulsazione, battito; (*defeat*) sconfitta

beau [bo] s (**beaus** or **beaux** [boz]) (*dandy*) bellimbusto; (*girl's sweetheart*) spasimante m

beautician [bju'tɪʃən] s estetista mf

beautiful ['bjutɪfəl] adj bello

beauti•fy ['bjutɪ,faɪ] v (pret & pp -fied) tr abbellire

beau•ty ['bjuti] s (-ties) bellezza

beau'ty con'test s concorso di bellezza

beau'ty par'lor s istituto di bellezza

beau'ty sleep' s primo sonno

beau'ty spot' s neo; posto pittoresco

beaver ['bivər] s castoro; pelle f di castoro; cappello a cilindro

because [bɪ'kɔz] conj perchè; **because of** a causa di

beck [bɛk] s gesto; **at the beck and call of** agli ordini di

beckon ['bɛkən] s gesto || tr fare gesto a || intr fare gesto

becloud [bɪ'klaʊd] tr annebbiare; oscurare

be•come [bɪ'kʌm] v (pret -came; pp -come) tr convenire a; stare bene a, e.g., **this hat becomes you** questo cappello Le sta bene || intr diventare; farsi; convertirsi, e.g., **water became wine** l'acqua si convertì in vino; succedere, e.g., **what became of my coat?** che è successo del mio pastrano?; essere, e.g., **what will become of me?** che sarà di me?; **to become accustomed** abituarsi; **to become angry** entrare in collera; **to become crazy** impazzire; **to become ill** ammalarsi

becoming [bɪ'kʌmɪŋ] adj conveniente; appropriato; acconcio; **this is very becoming to you** questo Le sta molto bene

bed [bed] s letto; (*layer*) strato; giacimento; **to go to bed** andare a letto; **to take to one's bed** mettersi a letto

bed' and board' s vitto e alloggio; pensione completa

bed'bug' s cimice f

bed'clothes' spl lenzuola fpl e coperte fpl, biancheria da letto

bed'cov'er s coperta da letto

bedding ['bedɪŋ] s lenzuola fpl e coperte fpl; (*litter*) lettiera; (*foundation*) fondamenta fpl

bedeck [bɪ'dɛk] tr ornare, adornare

bedev•il [bɪ'dɛvɪl] v (pret & pp -iled or -illed; ger -iling or -illing) tr tormentare diabolicamente; confondere

bed'fast' adj confinato a letto

bed'fel'low s compagno di letto; compagno di stanza; compagno

bedlam ['bedləm] s manicomio; pandemonio

bed' lin'en s biancheria da letto

bed'pan' s padella

bedridden ['bed,rɪdən] adj degente a letto

bed'room' s stanza da letto, camera da letto

bed'room slip'per s babbuccia, pantofola

bed'side' s capezzale m

bed'side man'ner s maniera di fare coi pazienti

bed'sore' s piaga da decubito

bed'spread' s coperta da letto

bed'spring' s rete f del letto; molla del letto

bed'stead' s fusto del letto

bed'tick' s traliccio

bed'time' s ora di coricarsi

bed'warm'er s scaldaletto

bee [bi] s ape f

beech [bitʃ] s faggio

beech'nut' s faggiola

beef [bif] s bue m, manzo; **carne** f di manzo; (coll) forza; (slang) lamentela || tr—**to beef up** (coll) rinforzare || intr (slang) lamentarsi

beef' cat'tle s manzi mpl da carne

beef'steak' s bistecca

beef' stew' s stufato di manzo

bee'hive' s alveare m

bee'keep'er s apicoltore m

bee'line' s—**to make a beeline for** (coll) andare direttamente verso

beer [bɪr] s birra

beer' saloon' s birreria

beeswax ['biz,wæks] s cera d'api

beet [bit] s barbabietola

beetle ['bitəl] adj sporgente, folto || s scarafaggio

bee'tle-browed' adj dalle sopracciglia folte

beet' su'gar s zucchero di barbabietola

be•fall [bɪ'fɔl] v (pret -fell ['fɛl]; pp -fallen ['fɔlən]) tr succedere a || intr succedere

befitting [bɪ'fɪtɪŋ] adj appropriato

before [bɪ'for] adv prima, prima d'ora || prep (in time) prima di; (in place) dinnanzi a, davanti a; **before Christ** avanti Cristo || conj prima che

before'hand' adv in anticipo; precedentemente

befriend [bɪ'frend] tr diventare amico di, proteggere, favorire; aiutare

befuddle [bɪ'fʌdəl] tr confondere

beg [beg] v (pret & pp begged; ger begging) tr chiedere; implorare; (alms) mendicare; **I beg your pardon** Le chiedo scusa; **to beg s.o. for s.th** chiedere qlco a qlcu || intr chiedere la carità; **to beg for** sollecitare; **to beg off** scusarsi; **to go begging** rimanere invenduto

be•get [bɪ'get] v (pret -got ['gat]; pp -gotten -got; ger -getting) tr generare

beggar ['begər] s accattone m, mendicante m

be•gin [bɪ'gɪn] v (pret -gan ['gæn]; pp -gun ['gʌn]; ger -ginning) tr & intr cominciare, iniziare; **beginning with** a partire da; **to begin with** per cominciare

beginner [bɪ'gɪnər] s principiante mf

beginning [bɪ'gɪnɪŋ] s inizio, origine f, principio, esordio

begrudge [bɪ'grʌdʒ] tr invidiare; concedere con riluttanza

beguile [bɪ'gaɪl] tr ingannare; sedurre; (to delight) divertire

behalf [bɪ'hæf] or [bɪ'hɑf] s—**on behalf of** nell'interesse di; a nome di

behave [bɪ'hev] *intr* comportarsi; comportarsi bene

behavior [bɪ'hevjər] *s* comportamento, condotta; funzionamento

behead [bɪ'hed] *tr* decapitare

behest [bɪ'hest] *s* ordine *m*, comando

behind [bɪ'haɪnd] *s* didietro; (slang) sedere *m* ‖ *adv* dietro; (in arrears) in arretrato; **from behind** dal didietro ‖ *prep* dietro a, dietro di; **behind time** in ritardo

be·hold [bɪ'hold] *v* (*pret & pp* **-held** ['held]) *tr* contemplare; ammirare ‖ *interj* guarda!

behoove [bɪ'huv] *impers*—**it behooves him** to gli conviene di

being ['bi·ɪŋ] *adj* esistente; **for the time being** per ora ‖ *s* essere *m*, ente *m*

belabor [bɪ'lebər] *tr* attaccare; (fig) ribattere, confutare; (fig) insistere su

belated [bɪ'letɪd] *adj* tardivo

belch [bɛltʃ] *s* rutto ‖ *tr* eruttare, vomitare ‖ *intr* ruttare

beleaguer [bɪ'ligər] *tr* assediare

bel·fry ['bɛlfrɪ] *s* (**-fries**) (*tower*) campanile *m*; (*site of bell*) cella campanaria; (slang) testa

Belgian ['bɛldʒən] *adj & s* belga *mf*

Belgium ['bɛldʒəm] *s* il Belgio

be·lie [bɪ'laɪ] *v* (*pret & pp* **-lied** ['laɪd]); *ger* **-lying** ['laɪ·ɪŋ]) *tr* (*to misrepresent*) tradire; (*to prove false*) smentire

belief [bɪ'lif] *s* fede *f*, credenza

believable [bɪ'livəbəl] *adj* credibile

believe [bɪ'liv] *tr* credere ‖ *intr* credere, aver fede; **to believe in** credere in

believer [bɪ'livər] *s* credente *mf*

belittle [bɪ'lɪtəl] *tr* menomare

bell [bɛl] *s* campana; (*for a door*) campanello; (*sound*) rintocco; (*on cattle*) campanaccio; (*of deer*) bramito ‖ *intr* bramire

belladonna [,bɛlə'dɑnə] *s* belladonna

bell'-bot'tom *adj* a campana

bell'boy' *s* cameriere *m*, ragazzo

belle [bɛl] *s* bella

belles-lettres [,bɛl'lɛtrə] *spl* belle lettere

bell' glass' *s* campana di vetro

bell'hop' *s* cameriere *m*, ragazzo

bellicose ['bɛlɪ ,kos] *adj* bellicoso

belligerent [bə'lɪdʒərənt] *adj &* s belligerante *m*

bellow ['bɛlo] *s* muggito; **bellows** mantice *m*; (*of camera*) soffietto ‖ *tr* gridare ‖ *intr* muggire

bell' ring'er ['rɪŋər] *s* campanaro

bellwether ['bɛl ,wɛðər] *s* pecora guida

bel·ly ['bɛlɪ] *s* (**-lies**) ventre *m*, pancia ‖ *v* (*pret & pp* **-lied**) *intr* far pancia

bel'ly·ache' *s* (coll) mal *m* di pancia ‖ *intr* (slang) lamentarsi

bel'ly·but'ton *s* (coll) ombelico

bel'ly dance' *s* (coll) danza del ventre

bel'ly flop' *s* panciata

bellyful ['bɛlɪ ,ful] *s*—**to have a bellyful** (slang) averne fino agli occhi

bel'ly·land' *intr* (aer) atterrare sul ventre

belong [bɪ'lɔŋ] or [bɪ'laŋ] *intr* appartenere; stare bene, e.g., **this chair belongs in this room** questa sedia sta bene in questa stanza

belongings [bɪ'lɔŋɪŋz] or [bɪ'laŋɪŋz] *spl* effetti *mpl* personali

beloved [bɪ'lʌvɪd] or [bɪ'lʌvd] *adj & s* diletto, amato

below [bɪ'lo] *adv* sotto; più sotto; sotto zero, e.g., **ten below** dieci gradi sotto zero ‖ *prep* sotto, sotto di

belt [bɛlt] *s* cintura, cinghia; (mach) nastro; (mil) cinturone *m*; (geog) fascia, zona; **to tighten one's belt** far cintura ‖ *tr* cingere; (slang) staffilare

belt'ed tire' *s* copertone cinturato

belt' line' *s* linea di circonvallazione

beltway ['bɛlt ,we] *s* raccordo anulare

bemoan [bɪ'mon] *tr* lamentare; compiangere

bench [bɛntʃ] *s* banco, panca; tribunale *m*; (mach) banco, di prova; **to be on the bench** (law) essere giudice

bend [bɛnd] *s* curva; (*e.g., of pipe*) gomito, angolo ‖ *v* (*pret & pp* **bent** [bɛnt]) *tr* curvare; piegare; far piegare ‖ *intr* deviare; piegare, piegarsi; **to bend over** inchinarsi

beneath [bɪ'niθ] *adv* sotto; più sotto ‖ *prep* sotto, sotto di

benediction [,bɛnɪ'dɪkʃən] *s* benedizione

benefactor ['bɛnɪ ,fæktər] or [,bɛnɪ'fæktər] *s* benefattore *m*

benefactress ['bɛnɪ ,fæktrɪs] or [,bɛnɪ'fæktrɪs] *s* benefattrice *f*

beneficence [bɪ'nɛfɪsəns] *s* beneficenza

beneficent [bɪ'nɛfɪsənt] *adj* caritatevole; benefico

beneficial [,bɛnɪ'fɪʃəl] *adj* benefico

beneficia·ry [,bɛnɪ'fɪʃɪ ,ɛrɪ] *s* (**-ies**) beneficiario

benefit ['bɛnɪfɪt] *s* beneficio; festa di beneficenza; **for the benefit of** a beneficio di ‖ *tr & intr* beneficiare

ben'efit perform'ance *s* beneficiata

benevolence [bɪ'nɛvələns] *s* benevolenza; carità *f*

benevolent [bɪ'nɛvələnt] *adj* benevolo; (*institution*) benefico

benign [bɪ'naɪn] *adj* benigno

bent [bɛnt] *adj* curvo; **bent on** deciso a ‖ *s* curva; tendenza, propensità *f*

Benzedrine ['bɛnzɪ ,drin] (trademark) *s* benzedrina

benzene ['bɛnzin] *s* benzolo

benzine [bɛn'zin] *s* benzina

bequeath [bɪ'kwiθ] or [bɪ'kwið] *tr* legare, lasciare in eredità

bequest [bɪ'kwɛst] *s* legato, lascito

berate [bɪ'ret] *tr* redarguire

be·reave [bɪ'riv] *v* (*pret & pp* **-reaved** or **-reft** ['rɛft]) *tr* spogliare

bereavement [bɪ'rivmənt] *s* lutto, perdita

beret [bə're] or ['bere] *s* berretto

Berlin [bər'lɪn] *adj* berlinese ‖ *s* Berlino

Berliner [bər'lɪnər] *s* berlinese *mf*

Bermuda [bər'mjudə] *s* le Bermude

ber·ry ['bɛrɪ] *s* (**-ries**) (*dry seed*) chicco; (*fruit*) bacca

berserk [bʌr'sʌrk] *adj* infuriato ‖ *adv* —**to go berserk** impazzire

berth [bʌrθ] *s (for a ship)* posto di ormeggio; *(bed)* cuccetta; *(coll)* posto

beryllium [bə'rɪlɪ·əm] *s* berillio

be·seech [bɪ'sitʃ] *v (pret & pp* -**sought** ['sɔt] *or* -**seeched)** *tr* supplicare

be·set [bɪ'sɛt] *v (pret & pp* -**set;** *ger* -**setting)** *tr* assediare, circondare; *(e.g., with problems)* assillare

beside [bɪ'saɪd] *adv* oltre, inoltre ‖ *prep* vicino a, in confronto di; oltre a; **beside oneself** fuori di sé; **beside the point** fuori del seminato

besides [bɪ'saɪdz] *adv* inoltre; d'altronde ‖ *prep* oltre a

besiege [bɪ'sidʒ] *tr* assediare; *(with questions)* bombardare

besmear [bɪ'smɪr] *tr* imbrattare, sgorbiare; sporcare

besmirch [bɪ'smʌrtʃ] *tr* insudiciare

bespatter [bɪ'spætər] *tr* inzaccherare

be·speak [bɪ'spik] *v (*-**spoke** ['spok]; -**spoken)** *tr* chiedere anticipatamente a; *(to show)* dimostrare

best [bɛst] *adj super* (il) migliore; ottimo ‖ *s* meglio; **at best** nella miglior delle ipotesi; **to do one's best** fare del proprio meglio; **to get the best of** avere la meglio di; **to make the best of** adattarsi a ‖ *adv super* meglio; **had best,** *e.g.,* **I had best** dovrei ‖ *tr* battere, riuscire superiore a

bestial ['bɛstjəl] *or* ['bɛst/əl] *adj* bestiale

be·stir [bɪ'stʌr] *v (pret & pp* -**stirred;** *ger* -**stirring)** *tr* eccitare; **to bestir oneself** darsi da fare

best' man' *s* testimone *m* di nozze

bestow [bɪ'sto] *tr* accordare; conferire

best' sell'er *s* best-seller *m*

bet [bɛt] *s* scommessa ‖ *v (pret & pp* **bet** *or* **betted;** *ger* **betting)** *tr & intr* scommettere; **I bet** ci scommetto; **you bet** (coll) evidentemente

be·take [bɪ'tek] *v (pret* -**took** ['tʊk]; *pp* -**taken)** *tr*—**to betake oneself** andare, dirigersi

be·think [bɪ'θɪŋk] *v (pret & pp* -**thought** ['θɔt]) *tr* **to bethink oneself** pensare; ricordarsi

Bethlehem ['bɛθlɪ·əm] *or* ['bɛθlɪ·hɛm] *s* Betlemme *f*

betide [bɪ'taɪd] *tr* accadere a ‖ *intr* accadere

betoken [bɪ'tokən] *tr* indicare, presagire

betray [bɪ'tre] *tr* tradire, ingannare; *(to reveal)* rivelare

betroth [bɪ'troθ] *or* [bɪ'trɔθ] *tr* promettere in matrimonio a

betrothal [bɪ'troθəl] *or* [bɪ'trɔθəl] *s* fidanzamento

betrothed [bɪ'troθd] *or* [bɪ'trɔθt] *adj* fidanzato ‖ *s* promesso sposo, fidanzato

better ['bɛtər] *adj comp* migliore; **to grow better** migliorare ‖ *s*—**betters** superiori *mpl;* ottimati *mpl;* **to get the better of** avere la meglio di ‖ *adv* meglio; **had better** dovere, *e.g.,* **I had**

better dovrei; **to be better off** stare meglio; **to think better of** riconsiderare; **you ought to know better** dovrebbe vergognarsi ‖ *tr* sorpassare; migliorare; **to better oneself** migliorare la propria situazione

bet'ter half' *s* metà *f*

betterment ['bɛtərmənt] *s* miglioramento

bettor ['bɛtər] *s* scommettitore *m*

between [bɪ'twin] *adv* in mezzo; **in between** in mezzo, fra i piedi ‖ *prep* fra, tra

between'-decks' *s* interponte *m*

bev·el ['bɛvəl] *s (instrument)* falsa squadra; *(sloping part)* augnatura ‖ *v (pret & pp* -**eled** *or* -**elled;** *ger* -**eling** *or* -**elling)** *tr* augnare

beverage ['bɛvərɪdʒ] *s* bevanda

bev·y ['bɛvi] *s* (-**ies**) *(of women)* gruppo; *(of birds)* stormo

bewail [bɪ'wel] *tr* lamentare

beware [bɪ'wɛr] *tr* fare attenzione a, guardarsi da ‖ *intr* fare attenzione, guardarsi

bewilder [bɪ'wɪldər] *tr* lasciar perplesso, confondere, disorientare

bewilderment [bɪ'wɪldərmənt] *s* perplessità *f*, disorientamento

bewitch [bɪ'wɪtʃ] *tr* stregare

beyond [bɪ'jɑnd] *s*—**the beyond** l'aldilà *m* ‖ *adv* più lontano ‖ *prep* al di là di; oltre a; più tardi di; **beyond a doubt** fuori dubbio; **beyond repair** irreparabile

bias ['baɪ·əs] *s* linea diagonale; pregiudizio; **on the bias** diagonalmente ‖ *tr* prevenire

bib [bɪb] *s* bavaglino

Bible ['baɪbəl] *s* Bibbia

Biblical ['bɪblɪkəl] *adj* biblico

bibliogra·phy [,bɪblɪ'ɑgrəfi] *s* (-**phies**) bibliografia

bibliophile ['bɪblɪ·ə,faɪl] *s* bibliofilo

bicarbonate [baɪ'kɑrbə,net] *s* bicarbonato

biceps ['baɪsɛps] *s* bicipite *m*

bicker ['bɪkər] *s* bisticcio, disputa ‖ *intr* bisticciare, disputare

bicycle ['baɪsɪkəl] *s* bicicletta

bid [bɪd] *s* offerta; *(cards)* dichiarazione; *(coll)* invito ‖ *v (pret* **bade** [bæd] *or* **bid;** *pp* **bidden** ['bɪdən] *or* **bid;** *ger* **bidding)** *tr & intr* offrire; comandare; *(cards)* dichiarare

bidder ['bɪdər] *s* offerente *mf;* *(cards)* dichiarante *mf;* **the highest bidder** il miglior offerente

bidding ['bɪdɪŋ] *s* ordine *m;* offerte *fpl;* *(cards)* dichiarazione

bide [baɪd] *tr*—**to bide one's time** attendere l'ora propizia

biennial [baɪ'ɛnɪ·əl] *adj* biennale

bier [bɪr] *s* catafalco

bifocal [baɪ'fokəl] *adj* bifocale ‖ **bifocals** *spl* occhiali *mpl* bifocali

big [bɪg] *adj* (**bigger; biggest**) grande; *(coll)* importante; *(coll)* stravagante; **big with child** incinta ‖ *adv*—**to talk big** (coll) parlare con iattanza

bigamist ['bɪgəmɪst] *s* bigamo

bigamous ['bɪgəməs] *adj* bigamo

big-bellied ['bɪg ˌbɛlid] *adj* panciuto
Big' Dip'per *s* Gran Carro
big' game' *s* caccia grossa
big-hearted ['bɪg ˌhɑrtɪd] *adj* magnanimo, generoso
big' mouth' *s* (slang) sbraitone *m*
bigot ['bɪgət] *s* bigotto, bacchettone *m*
bigoted ['bɪgətɪd] *adj* (*in religion*)
bigotto; intransigente
bigot·ry ['bɪgətri] *s* (-ries) bigottismo;
intransigenza
big' shot' *s* (slang) pezzo grosso, (un)
qualcuno
big' slam' *s* (bridge) grande slam *m*
big'-time op'erator *s* (slang) grosso
trafficante
big' toe' *s* alluce *m*
big' wheel' *s* (slang) pezzo grosso
bike [baɪk] *s* (coll) bicicletta
bile [baɪl] *s* bile *f*
bilge [bɪldʒ] *s* sentina; (*of barrel*) ventre *m*
bilge'ways' *spl* parati *mpl*
bilingual [baɪ'lɪŋgwəl] *adj* bilingue
bilious ['bɪljəs] *adj* bilioso
bilk [bɪlk] *tr* defraudare
bill [bɪl] *s* (*of bird*) becco; (*statement
of charges*) conto; (*e.g., for electricity*) bolletta; (*menu*) lista; (*money*)
biglietto; (*proposed law*) disegno di
legge; (*handbill*) annunzio; (*law*)
atto; (theat) cartellone *m*; **to fill the
bill** (coll) riempire i requisiti; **to foot
the bill** (coll) pagare lo scotto || *tr*
fare una lista di; mettere in conto a
|| *intr* (*said of doves*) beccuzzarsi;
(*said of lovers*) baciucchiarsi
bill'board' *s* cartellone *m*; titolo di testa
billet ['bɪlɪt] *s* (mil) alloggiamento;
(mil) ordine *m* d'alloggiamento || *tr*
(mil) alloggiare, accasermare
bill'fold' *s* portafoglio
bill'head' *s* intestazione di fattura
billiards ['bɪljərdz] *s* bigliardo
bil'ling clerk' *s* fatturista *mf*
billion ['bɪljən] *s* (U.S.A.) miliardo;
(Brit) bilione *m*
bill' of exchange' *s* tratta
bill' of fare' *s* menu *m*, lista delle
vivande
bill' of lad'ing ['ledɪŋ] *s* polizza di
carico
bill' of rights' *s* dichiarazione dei diritti
bill' of sale' *s* atto di vendita
billow ['bɪlo] *s* ondata, cavallone *m*
bill'post'er *s* attacchino
bil·ly ['bɪli] *s* (-lies) manganello
bil'ly goat' *s* capro, caprone *m*
bimonthly [baɪ'mʌnθli] *adj* (*occurring
every two months*) bimestrale; (*occurring twice a month*) bimensile
bin [bɪn] *s* cassone *m*; (*for bread*)
madia; (*e.g., for coal*) deposito
binaural [baɪ'nɔrəl] *adj* biauricolare
bind [baɪnd] *v* (pret & pp **bound**
[baʊnd]) *tr* legare; allacciare; (*to
bandage*) fasciare; (*to constipate*)
costipare; (*a book*) rilegare; (*to
oblige*) obbligare; (mach) grippare
binder ['baɪndər] *s* rilegatore *m*;
(*cover*) cartella

binder·y ['baɪndəri] *s* (-ies) rilegatoria
binding ['baɪndɪŋ] *adj* obbligatorio ||
s (*of book*) rilegatura; legatura; fasciatura
bind'ing post' *s* (elec) capocorda; (*e.g.,
of battery*) (elec) serrafilo
binge [bɪndʒ] *s*—**to go on a binge**
(coll) far baldoria
bingo ['bɪngo] *s* tombola
binnacle ['bɪnəkəl] *s* abitacolo
binoculars [bɪ'nɑkjələrz] or [baɪ'nɑk-
jələrz] *spl* binocolo
biochemical [ˌbaɪə'kemɪkəl] *adj* bio-
chimico
biochemist [ˌbaɪ·ə'kemɪst] *s* biochi-
mico
biochemistry [ˌbaɪə'kemɪstri] *s* biochimica
biodegradable [ˌbaɪ·odɪ'gredəbəl] *adj*
biodegradabile
biographer [baɪ'ɑgrəfər] *s* biografo
biographic(al) [ˌbaɪ·ə'græfɪk(əl)] *adj*
biografico
biogra·phy [baɪ'ɑgrəfi] *s* (-phies) biografia
biologist [baɪ'ɑlədʒɪst] *s* biologo
biology [baɪ'ɑlədʒi] *s* biologia
biophysics [ˌbaɪ·ə'fɪzɪks] *s* biofisica
biop·sy ['baɪ ˌɑpsi] *s* (-sies) biopsia
bipartisan [baɪ'pɑrtɪzən] *adj* (*system*)
bipartitico; (*government*) bipartito
biped ['baɪpɛd] *adj* & *s* bipede *m*
birch [bʌrtʃ] *s* betulla || *tr* scudisciare
bird [bʌrd] *s* uccello; **a bird in the
hand is worth two in the bush** un
uovo oggi vale meglio di una gallina
domani; **birds of a feather** gente *f*
della stessa risma; **to kill two birds
with one stone** pigliare due piccioni
con una fava
bird' cage' *s* gabbia
bird' call' *s* richiamo
birdie ['bʌrdi] *s* uccellino; (golf) giocata di un colpo sotto la media
bird'lime' *s* pania
bird' of pas'sage *s* uccello di passo
bird' of prey' *s* uccello da preda
bird'seed' *s* becchime *m*
bird's'-eye view' *s* vista a volo d'uccello
bird' shot' *s* pallini *mpl* da caccia
birth [bʌrθ] *s* nascita; **to give birth to**
dare i natali a; mettere alla luce
birth' certif'icate *s* certificato di nascita
birth' control' *s* limitazione delle na-
scite
birth'day' *s* natalizio, compleanno; (*of
an event*) anniversario
birth'mark' *s* voglia
birth'place' *s* patria; (*e.g., city*) luogo
di nascita; **to be the birthplace of**
dare i natali a
birth' rate' *s* natalità *f*
birth'right' *s* diritto acquisito sin dalla
nascita
biscuit ['bɪskɪt] *s* panino soffice; (Brit)
biscotto
bisect [baɪ'sɛkt] *tr* bisecare || *intr* (*said
of roads*) incrociarsi
bisection [baɪ'sɛkʃən] *s* bisezione
bishop ['bɪʃəp] *s* vescovo; (chess) al-
fiere *m*
bishopric ['bɪʃəprɪk] *s* vescovado

bismuth ['bɪzməθ] s bismuto
bison ['baɪsən] or ['baɪzən] s bisonte m
bisulfate [baɪ'sʌlfet] s bisolfato
bisulfite [baɪ'sʌlfaɪt] s bisolfito
bit [bɪt] s (of bridle) morso; (of key) mappa; (tool) punta, trivella; (small piece) briciolo, a bit un po'; (coll) un momento; **a good bit** una buona quantità; **bit by bit** poco a poco; **to blow to bits** fare a pezzi; **to champ the bit** mordere il freno; **two bits** (slang) quarto di dollaro, cinque soldi
bitch [bɪtʃ] s cagna; (vulg) donnaccia || intr (slang) lamentarsi
bite [baɪt] s morso; (mouthful) boccone m; **to take a bite** fare uno spuntino; mangiare un boccone || v (pret bit [bɪt]; pp bit or bitten ['bɪtən]) tr mordere, addentare; pungere; (the dust) baciare || intr mordere; (said of insects) pungere; (said of fish) abboccare
biting ['baɪtɪŋ] adj mordace; pungente
bitter ['bɪtər] adj amaro; (e.g., fight) accanito; (cold) pungente || s amaro; **bitters** amaro
bit'ter end' s—**to the bitter end** fino alla fine; fino alla morte
bit'ter·en'der s (coll) intransigente mf
bitterness ['bɪtərnɪs] s amarezza
bit'ter·sweet' adj dolceamaro; (fig) agrodolce || s dulcamara
bitumen [bɪ'tjumən] or [bɪ'tumən] s bitume m
bivou·ac ['bɪvu ,æk] or ['bɪvwæk] s bivacco || v (pret & pp -acked; ger -acking) intr bivaccare
biweekly [baɪ'wikli] adj bisettimanale; quindicinale || adv ogni due settimane
biyearly [baɪ'jɪrli] adj semestrale || adv semestralmente
bizarre [bɪ'zar] adj bizzarro
blab [blæb] s chiacchierone m || v (pret & pp blabbed; ger blabbing) tr rivelare || intr chiacchierare
black [blæk] adj nero; (without light) buio || s nero; **to wear black** vestire a lutto, vestire di nero || intr—**to black out** perdere i sensi
black'-and-blue' adj livido e pesto
black'-and-white' adj in bianco e nero
black'ball' s palla nera, voto contrario || tr dare la palla nera a
black'ber'ry s (-ries) mora
black'bird' s merlo
black'board' s lavagna, tavola nera
black'cap' s capinera
black'damp' s putizza
Black' Death' s peste bubbonica
blacken ['blækən] tr annerire; (shoes) lucidare; (reputation) sporcare
black' eye' s occhio pesto; (fig) cattiva reputazione
blackguard ['blægard] s canaglia
black'head' s comedone m
blackish ['blækɪʃ] adj nerastro
black'jack' s randello; (cards) ventuno || tr randellare
black' mag'ic s magia nera

black'mail' s ricatto || tr ricattare
blackmailer ['blæk ,melər] s ricattatore m
Black' Mari'a [mə'raɪ·ə] s (coll) furgone m cellulare
black' mar'ket s borsa nera
black' marketeer' [,markɪ'tɪr] s borsanerista mf
blackness ['blæknɪs] s nerezza
black'out' s oscuramento; (theat) spegnitura; (pathol) svenimento passeggero
black' sheep' s (fig) pecora nera
black'smith' s fabbro
black' tie' s cravatta da smoking; smoking m
bladder ['blædər] s vescica
blade [bled] s (of a leaf) pagina; (of grass) stelo, filo; (of oar) pala; (of turbine) paletta; (of fan) ventola; (of knife) lama; (coll) capposcarico
blame [blem] s colpa; **to be to blame for** aver la colpa di; **to put the blame on s.o. for s.th** attribuire a qlcu la colpa di qlco; **you are to blame è colpa Sua** || tr biasimare, incolpare
blameless ['blemlɪs] adj innocente, senza colpa
blanch [blæntʃ] or [blantʃ] tr bianchire || intr impallidire
bland [blænd] adj blando; (weather) mite
blandish ['blændɪʃ] tr blandire
blank [blæŋk] adj (not written on) in bianco; (e.g., stare) vuoto; (utter) completo || s (printed form) modulo; (cartridge) cartuccia a salve; (of the mind) lacuna; **to draw a blank** (coll) non avere alcun successo || tr—**to blank out** cancellare
blank' check' s assegno in bianco; (fig) carta bianca
blanket ['blæŋkɪt] adj generale, combinato || s coperta; (of snow) cappa || tr coprire con una coperta; oscurare
blank' verse' s verso sciolto
blare [bler] s squillo || tr proclamare; fare echeggiare || intr squillare; echeggiare
blaspheme [blæs'fim] tr & intr bestemmiare
blasphemous ['blæsfɪməs] adj bestemmiatore
blasphe·my ['blæsfɪmi] s (-mies) bestemmia
blast [blæst] or [blast] s (of air) raffica; (of a horn) squillo; (blight) rovina; scoppio, esplosione; **at full blast** a piena velocità || tr rovinare; fare scoppiare, far saltare || intr —**to blast off** (rok) lanciarsi
blast' fur'nace s altoforno
blast'off' s lancio di missile or di nave spaziale
blatant ['bletənt] adj (noisy) rumoroso; (obtrusive) palmare; (flashy) chiassoso
blaze [blez] s fiammata; splendore m; (on a horse's head) stella; **in a blaze** in fiamme || tr proclamare; **to blaze a**

trail marcare il cammino ‖ *intr* divampare

bleach [blit∫] *s* candeggio, candeggina ‖ *tr* imbiancare, candeggiare

bleachers ['blit∫ərz] *spl* posti *mpl* allo scoperto or di gradinata

bleak [blik] *adj* nudo, deserto; (*cold*) freddo; (*gloomy*) triste

blear-y ['blɪri] *adj* (**-ier; iest**) (*sight*) cisposo; confuso; offuscato

bleat [blit] *s* belato ‖ *intr* belare

bleed [blid] *v* (*pret & pp* **bled** [blɛd]) *tr* (*to draw blood from*) salassare; (*a tree*) estrare linfa da; (coll) sfruttare ‖ *intr* sanguinare; (*said of a tree*) dar linfa; **to bleed to death** morire dissanguato

blemish ['blemɪ∫] *s* difetto; macchia ‖ *tr* danneggiare; macchiare

blend [blend] *s* mescolanza, miscuglio; (*of gasoline*) miscela ‖ *v* (*pret & pp* **blended** or **blent** [blent]) *tr* mescolare, miscelare ‖ *intr* mescolarsi, miscelarsi; armonizzare; fondersi

bless [bles] *tr* benedire; (*to endow*) dotare; (*to make happy*) allietare

blessed ['blesɪd] *adj* benedetto; beato; fortunato; dotato

bless'ed event' *s* lieto evento

blessing ['blesɪŋ] *s* benedizione

blight [blaɪt] *s* (*insect; disease*) piaga; rovina; (*fungus*) ruggine *f* ‖ *tr* rovinare, guastare

blimp [blɪmp] *s* piccolo dirigibile

blind [blaɪnd] *adj* cieco; (slang) ubriaco ‖ *s* persiana; tendina; (*decoy*) mascheratura; pretesto ‖ *adv* alla cieca ‖ *tr* accecare

blind' al'ley *s* vicolo cieco

blinder ['blaɪndər] *s* paraocchi *m*

blind' fly'ing *s* (aer) volo senza visibilità

blind'fold' *adj* bendato, cogli occhi bendati ‖ *s* benda ‖ *tr* bendare gli occhi a

blindly ['blaɪndli] *adv* alla cieca

blind' man' *s* cieco

blind'man's buff' *s* mosca cieca

blindness ['blaɪndnɪs] *s* cecità *f*

blind' spot' *s* (anat) punto cieco; (rad) zona di silenzio; (fig) debole *m*

blink [blɪŋk] *s* batter *m* di ciglio; (*glimpse*) occhiata; (*glimmer*) barlume *m*; **on the blink** (slang) fuori servizio ‖ *tr*—**to blink one's eyes** batter il ciglio ‖ *intr* occhieggiare; (*to wink*) ammiccare; (*to flash on and off*) lampeggiare; **to blink at** ignorare; far finta di non vedere

blinker ['blɪŋkər] *s* (*at a crossing*) luce *f* intermittente; (*on a horse*) paraocchi *m*

blip [blɪp] *s* guizzo sullo schermo radar

bliss [blɪs] *s* beatitudine *f*, felicità *f*

blissful ['blɪsfəl] *adj* beato, felice

blister ['blɪstər] *s* vescica, bolla ‖ *tr* coprire di vesciche; (fig) bollare ‖ *intr* coprirsi di vesciche

blithe [blaɪð] *adj* gaio, giocondo

blitzkrieg ['blɪts,krig] *s* guerra lampo

blizzard ['blɪzərd] *s* tormenta, ventoneve *m*

bloat [blot] *tr* gonfiare ‖ *intr* gonfiarsi

blob [blɑb] *s* (*lump*) zolla; (*of liquid*) macchia

block [blɑk] *s* (e.g., *of wood*) blocco; (*for chopping*) ceppo; (*pulley*) puleggia; ostacolo; (*of houses*) isolato; (typ) cliché *m* ‖ *tr* bloccare; (*a hat*) mettere in forma; **to block up** tappare

blockade [blɑ'ked] *s* blocco; **to run a blockade** forzare il blocco ‖ *tr* bloccare

block' and tack'le *s* bozzello

block'bust'er *s* (coll) superbomba

block'head' *s* imbecille *mf*

block' let'ter *s* carattere *m* stampatello

block' sig'nal *s* (rr) segnale di blocco

blond [blɑnd] *adj & s* biondo

blonde [blɑnd] *s* bionda

blood [blʌd] *s* sangue *m*; **in cold blood** a sangue freddo; **to draw blood** ferire, fare sanguinare

blood' bank' *s* emoteca

bloodcurdling ['blʌd,kʌrdlɪŋ] *adj* orripilante

blood' do'nor *s* donatore *m* di sangue

blood'hound' *s* segugio

bloodless ['blʌdlɪs] *adj* esangue; (e.g., *revolution*) senza effusione di sangue

blood'mobile' [mo,bil] *s* autoemoteca

blood' poi'soning *s* avvelenamento del sangue

blood' pres'sure *s* pressione sanguigna

blood' rela'tion *s* consanguineo

blood'shed' *s* spargimento di sangue, carneficina

blood'shot' *adj* iniettato di sangue

blood'stained' *adj* macchiato di sangue

blood'stream' *s* circolazione sanguigna

blood'suck'er *s* sanguisuga

blood' test' *s* esame *m* del sangue

blood'thirst'y *adj* assetato di sangue

blood' transfu'sion *s* trasfusione di sangue

blood' type' *s* gruppo sanguigno

blood' ves'sel *s* vaso sanguigno

blood-y ['blʌdi] *adj* (**-ier; -iest**) sanguinoso; (*bloodthirsty*) avido di sangue ‖ *v* (*pret & pp* **-ied**) *tr* macchiare di sangue

bloom [blum] *s* fiore *m*; (*state of having open buds*) sboccio; (*youthful glow*) incarnato ‖ *intr* fiorire; sbocciare

bloomers ['blumərz] *spl* pantaloni *mpl* femminili larghi fermati sotto il ginocchio

blossom ['blɑsəm] *s* fiore *m*; sboccio ‖ *intr* sbocciare

blot [blɑt] *s* macchia ‖ *v* (*pret & pp* **blotted**; *ger* **blotting**) *tr* macchiare; (*with blotting paper*) asciugare; **to blot out** cancellare; oscurare ‖ *intr* macchiarsi; (*to be absorbent*) essere assorbente; (*said of a pen*) fare macchie

blotch [blɑt∫] *s* chiazza, macchia ‖ *tr* chiazzare

blotter ['blɑtər] *s* carta asciugante, carta assorbente; (*book*) registro

blouse [blaus] *s* blusa

blow [blo] *s* colpo; (*blast*) folata; (*of*

horn) squillo; (*sudden reverse*) batosta; **at one blow** d'un sol colpo; **to come to blows** venire alle mani; **without striking a blow** senza colpo ferire || v (*pret* **blew** [blu]; *pp* **blown**) *tr* soffiare, soffiare su; (*an instrument*) suonare; (*one's nose*) soffiarsi; **to blow in** sfondare; **to blow one's brains out** bruciarsi le cervella; **to blow open** aprire completamente; **to blow out** (*e.g., a candle*) spegnere; (*a fuse*) fondere; **to blow up** (*e.g., a mine*) far brillare; (*phot*) ingrandire || *intr* soffiare; (*to pant*) ansimare; (*with an instrument*) suonare; (*to puff*) sbuffare; (slang) andarsene; **to blow hot and cold** cambiare d'opinione ogni cinque minuti; **to blow in** (coll) arrivare inaspettatamente; **to blow out** (said, *e.g., of a candle*) spegnersi; (*said of a fuse*) saltare, fondersi; (*said of a tire*) scoppiare; **to blow over** passare; **to blow up** saltar per aria; (*said of a storm*) scoppiare; (coll) perdere la pazienza, scoppiare d'ira

blow′out′ *s* scoppio di un pneumatico
blow′pipe′ *s* (*tube*) soffione *m*; (*peashooter*) cerbottana
blow′torch′ *s* saldatrice *f* a benzina
blubber [ˈblʌbər] *s* grasso di balena || *intr* piangere, lamentarsi
bludgeon [ˈblʌdʒən] *s* randello || randellare
blue [blu] *adj* blu, azzurro; (*gloomy*) triste; (*e.g., laws*) puritanico || *s* blu *m*, azzurro; **out of the blue** inaspettatamente; **the blues** la malinconia; (mus) blues *m*; **to have the blues** essere giù di morale || *tr* tingere di azzurro; (*a metal*) brunire
blue′ber′ry *s* (**-ries**) mirtillo
blue′bird′ *s* uccello azzurro
blue′ blood′ *s* sangue *m* blu
blue′ cheese′ *s* gorgonzola americano
blue′ chip′ *s* (fin) azione di prim'ordine
blue′ jay′ *s* ghiandaia azzurra
blue′ moon′ *s*—**once in a blue moon** ad ogni morte di papa
blue′-pen′cil *v* (*pret & pp* **-ciled** or **-cilled**; *ger* **-ciling** or **-cilling**) *tr* correggere col lapis blu
blue′print′ *s* riproduzione cianografica; (*plan*) piano || *tr* riprodurre in cianografia; preparare dettagliatamente
blue′stock′ing *s* saccente *f*, sapientona
blue′ streak′ *s*—**like a blue streak** (coll) come un razzo
bluff [blʌf] *adj* scosceso; brusco, burbero || *s* promontorio scosceso; bluff *m*; bluffatore *m* || *intr* bluffare
bluing [ˈbluɪŋ] *s* turchinetto
bluish [ˈblu-ɪʃ] *adj* bluastro
blunder [ˈblʌndər] *s* errore *m* madornale || *intr* pigliare un granchio
blunt [blʌnt] *adj* ottuso; (*plain-spoken*) franco || *tr* rendere ottuso
bluntness [ˈblʌntnɪs] *s* ottusità *f*; franchezza
blur [blʌr] *s* macchia; offuscamento; confusione || *v* (*pret & pp* **blurred**;

ger **blurring**) *tr* macchiare; (*the view*) offuscare
blurb [blʌrb] *s* annuncio pubblicitario
blurt [blʌrt] *tr*—**to blurt out** prorompere a dire, lasciarsi sfuggire
blush [blʌʃ] *s* rossore *m*; (*pinkish natural tinge*) incarnato || *intr* arrossire; **to blush at** vergognarsi di
bluster [ˈblʌstər] *s* frastuono; (fig) boria || *intr* (*said of the wind*) infuriare; fare il bravaccio
blustery [ˈblʌstəri] *adj* tempestuoso; violento; (*swaggering*) borioso
boar [bor] *s* verro; (*wild hog*) porco selvatico, cinghiale *m*
board [bord] *s* asse *m*; (*notice*) cartello; (*pasteboard*) cartone *m*; (*table*) tavola; (*meals*) vitto; (*group of administrators*) consiglio; (naut) bordo; **above board** franco; **in boards** rilegato; **on board** a bordo; (rr) in vettura; **to go by the board** andare in rovina; **to tread the boards** fare l'attore || *tr* chiudere con assi; (*to provide with meals*) dare pensione a, tenere a dozzina; (*a ship*) salire a bordo di; (*a train*) salire su; (naut) abbordare || *intr* essere a pensione
board′ and lodg′ing *s* pensione completa
boarder [ˈbordər] *s* pensionante *mf*
board′ing house′ *s* pensione di famiglia
board′ing school′ *s* collegio di pensionanti
board′ of direc′tors *s* consiglio d'amministrazione
board′ of health′ *s* ufficio d'igiene
board′ of trade′ *s* camera di commercio
board′walk′ *s* passeggiata a mare
boast [bost] *s* millanteria, vanteria || *intr* vantarsi
boastful [ˈbostfəl] *adj* millantatore
boat [bot] *s* nave *f*, battello; (*small ship*) barca, imbarcazione; (*dish*) salsiera; **in the same boat** nella stessa situazione
boat′ hook′ *s* alighiero
boat′house′ *s* capannone *m* per i canotti
boating [ˈbotɪŋ] *s* escursione in barca
boat′man *s* (**-men**) barcaiolo
boat′ race′ *s* regata
boatswain [ˈbosən] or [ˈbot‚swen] *s* nostromo
bob [bɑb] *s* (*plumb*) piombino; (*short haircut*) taglio alla bebè; coda mozza (di cavallo); (*jerky motion*) strattone *m*; (*on pendulum of clock*) lente *f*; (*on fishing line*) sughero || *v* (*pret & pp* **bobbed**; *ger* **bobbing**) *tr* tagliare alla bebè; far muovere a scatti || *intr* muoversi a scatti; fare mossa; **to bob up** apparire
bobbin [ˈbɑbɪn] *s* bobina
bob′by pin′ [ˈbɑbi] *s* forcina
bob′by-socks′ *spl* (coll) calzini *mpl* da ragazza
bobbysoxer [ˈbɑbi‚sɑksər] *s* (coll) ragazzina
bobolink [ˈbɑbə‚lɪŋk] *s* dolconice *m*
bob′sled′ *s* guidoslitta
bode [bod] *tr & intr* presagire
bodice [ˈbɑdɪs] *s* giubbetto, copribusto

bodily ['bɑdɪli] *adj* fisico, corporeo ‖ *adv* fisicamente, corporeamente; di persona; in massa

bodkin ['bɑdkɪn] *s* punteruolo; (*for lady's hair*) spillone *m*

bod·y ['bɑdi] *s* (-ies) corpo; (*corpse*) cadavere *m*; (*of water*) massa; (*of people*) gruppo; (*of a liquid*) sostanza; (*of truck*) cassone *m*; (*of car*) carrozzeria; (*of tree*) tronco; (coll) persona; **in a body** in massa

bod'y·guard' *s* (*of a high official*) guardia del corpo; (*e.g., of a movie star*) guardaspalle *m*

bod'y suit' *s* calzamaglia

bog [bɑg] *s* pantano, palude *m* ‖ (*pret & pp* **bogged**; *ger* **bogging**) *intr*—**to bog down** impelagarsi

bogey·man ['bogɪ‚mæn] *s* (-men [‚men]) babau *m*

bogus ['bogəs] *adj* (coll) falso, finto

Bohemian [bo'himɪ·ən] *adj* boemo; da bohémien ‖ *s* boemo; (fig) bohémien *m*

boil [bɔɪl] *s* bollore *m*, ebollizione; (pathol) foruncolo; **to come to a boil** cominciare a bollire ‖ *tr* bollire; **to boil down** condensare ‖ *intr* bollire; **to boil away** evaporare completamente; **to boil down** condensarsi; **to boil over** andare per il fuoco

boiled' ham' *s* prosciutto cotto

boiler ['bɔɪlər] *s* caldaia; (*for cooking*) caldaio

boil'er·mak'er *s* calderaio

boiling ['bɔɪlɪŋ] *adj* bollente ‖ *s* bollore *m*, ebollizione

boisterous ['bɔɪstərəs] *adj* (*storm*) violento; (*loud*) rumoroso

bold [bold] *adj* (*daring*) coraggioso; (*impudent*) sfacciato; (*steep*) scosceso; (*clear, sharp*) netto

bold'face' *s* (typ) neretto, grassetto

boldness ['boldnɪs] *s* coraggio, audacia; sfacciataggine *f*, impudenza

boll' wee'vil [bol] *s* antonomo del cotone

bologna [bə'lonə] or [bə'lonjə] *s* mortadella

Bolshevik ['bɑlʃəvɪk] or ['bolʃəvɪk] *adj* & *mf* bolscevico

bolster ['bolstər] *s* cuscino; cuscinetto; (*support*) sostegno ‖ *tr* sorreggere; **to bolster up** sostenere

bolt [bolt] *s* (*arrow*) freccia; (*of lightning*) fulmine *m*; (*sliding bar*) chiavistello; (*threaded rod*) bullone *m*; (*of paper or cloth*) pezza, rotolo ‖ *adv*—**bolt upright** dritto come un fuso ‖ *tr* (*to swallow hurriedly*) ingollare; (*to fasten, e.g., a door*) sprangare; (*to fasten, e.g., two metal parts*) bullonare; (*e.g., a political party*) abbandonare ‖ *intr* (*said of people*) spiccare un salto; (*said of a horse*) prendere la mano; precipitarsi

bolt' from the blue' *s* fulmine *m* a ciel sereno

bomb [bɑm] *s* bomba; (*e.g., for spraying*) bombola ‖ *tr* bombardare

bombard [bɑm'bɑrd] *tr* bombardare; (*with questions*) bersagliare

bombardment [bɑm'bɑrdmənt] *s* bombardamento

bombast ['bɑmbæst] *s* ampollosità *f*

bombastic [bɑm'bæstɪk] *adj* ampolloso

bomb' cra'ter *s* cratere *m*

bomber ['bɑmər] *s* bombardiere *m*

bomb'proof' *adj* a prova di bomba

bomb'shell' *s* bomba; (fig) colpo di bomba, colpo di sorpresa

bomb' shel'ter *s* rifugio antiaereo

bomb'sight' *s* traguardo aereo

bona fide ['bonə‚faɪdə] *adj* sincero ‖ *adv* in buona fede

bonanza [bə'nænzə] *s* (min) ricca vena; (coll) fortuna

bond [bɑnd] *s* legame *m*, vincolo; (*contractual obligation*) obbligazione; (*interest-bearing certificate*) buono, obbligazione; (*surety*) cauzione; **bonds** catene *fpl*; **in bond** sotto cauzione; (*said of goods*) in punto franco ‖ *tr* unire, connettere

bondage ['bɑndɪdʒ] *s* schiavitù *f*

bond'ed ware'house *s* deposito in punto franco

bond'hold'er *s* obbligazionista *mf*

bonds'man *s* (-men) garante *m*

bone [bon] *s* osso; (*of fish*) spina; (*of whale*) stecca; **bones** ossa *fpl*; **to have a bone to pick with** avere un conto da regolare con; **to make no bones about** (coll) ammettere; (coll) parlare esplicitamente ‖ *tr* disossare; cavare le spine a ‖ *intr*—**to bone up on** (coll) ripassare

bone'head' *s* (coll) testa dura

boneless ['bonlɪs] *adj* senz'osso; (*fish*) senza spine

boner ['bonər] *s* (slang) errore *m* madornale

bonfire ['bɑn‚faɪr] *s* falò *m*

bonnet ['bɑnɪt] *s* cappello da donna; (*of child*) berrettino

bonus ['bonəs] *s* gratifica; indennità *f*; (*to an outgoing employee*) buonuscita

bon·y ['boni] *adj* (-ier; -iest) (*having bones*) osseo; (*emaciated*) scarno; (*fish*) spinoso

boo [bu] *s* fischio, urlaccio ‖ *tr* & *intr* fischiare, disapprovare

boo·by ['bubi] *s* (-bies) stupido

boo'by hatch' *s* (naut) portello; (slang) manicomio; (slang) prigione *f*

boo'by prize' *s* premio dato al peggior giocatore

boo'by trap' *s* (mil) trappola esplosiva; (fig) tranello

boogie-woogie ['bugi'wugi] *s* bughibughi *m*

book [buk] *s* libro; (*e.g., of matches*) pacchetto; (mus) libretto; (fig) regole *fpl*; **the Book** la Bibbia; **to be in one's book** essere nelle grazie di; **to bring s.o. to book** fare una ramanzina a ‖ *tr* registrare; (*e.g., on a horse*) allibrare; (*e.g., a room*) prenotare; (*an actor*) scritturare

book'bind'er *s* rilegatore *m*

book'bind'er·y *s* (-ies) rilegatoria

book'bind'ing *s* rilegatura

book'case' *s* scaffale *m*

book' end' *s* reggilibri *m*

bookie ['bʊki] s (coll) allibratore m

booking ['bʊkɪŋ] s (of a trip) prenotazione; (of an actor) scrittura

book'ing clerk' s impiegato alla biglietteria

bookish ['bʊkɪʃ] adj studioso; libresco

book'keep'er s contabile mf

booklet ['bʊklɪt] s libretto; (pamphlet) opuscolo

book'keep'ing s contabilità f

book'mak'er s (one who accepts bets) allibratore m

book'mark' s segnalibro

bookmobile ['bʊkmo͵bil] s bibliobus m

book'plate' s ex libris m

book' review' s rassegna, recensione

book'sell'er s libraio

book'shelf' s (-shelves) scaffale m

book'stand' s (rack) scansia; (stall) edicola

book'store' s libreria

book'worm' s (zool) tarlo dei libri; (fig) topo da biblioteca

boom [bum] s (of crane) braccio; (barrier) barriera galleggiante; (noise) bum m; (fin) boom m; (naut) boma; (mov, telv) giraffa || intr rimbombare; essere in condizioni floride

boomerang ['bumə͵ræŋ] s bumerang m

boom' town' s città f fungo

boon [bun] s fortuna, benedizione

boon' compan'ion s compagnone m

boor [bʊr] s bifolco, zotico

boorish ['bʊrɪʃ] adj grossolano

boost [bust] s aumento; (coll) spinta || tr spingere in su; sostenere; (prices) alzare; parlare a favore di

booster ['bustər] s (backer) sostenitore m; propulsore m a razzo; (rok) propulsore m del primo stadio; (med) seconda iniezione

boot [but] s stivale m; (kick) calcio; (patch) (aut) pezza; **the boot is on the other foot** la situazione è rovesciata; **to be in the boots of** essere nella pelle di; **to boot** per di più; **to get the boot** (coll) essere messo sulla strada; **to lick the boots of** leccare i piedi a; **to wipe one's boots on** trattare come una pezza da piedi || tr dare un calcio a; **to boot out** (slang) buttar fuori

boot'black' s lustrascarpe m

booth [buθ] s (stall) banco da mercato; (for telephoning, voting) cabina

boot'jack' s tirastivali m

boot'leg' adj di contrabbando || s liquore m di contrabbando || v (pret & pp -legged; ger -legging) tr vendere di contrabbando || intr vendere alcol di contrabbando

bootlegger ['but͵lɛgər] s contrabbandiere m di liquori

boot'lick'er [͵lɪkər] s (coll) leccapiedi mf

boot'strap' s tirante m degli stivali

boo-ty ['buti] s (-ties) bottino

booze [buz] s (coll) bevanda alcolica || intr (coll) ubriacarsi

borax ['boræks] s borace m

border ['bɔrdər] adj confinario, confinante || s bordo, margine m; (between two countries) confine m || tr bordare; confinare con || intr confinare

bor'der clash' s incidente m ai confini

bor'der-line' adj incerto || s frontiera

bore [bor] s (drill hole) buco, foro; (hollow part of gun) anima; (caliber) calibro; (dull person) seccatore m; (annoyance) seccatura; (mach) alesaggio || tr bucare, forare; seccare; (mach) alesare

boredom ['bordəm] s noia, tedio

boring ['borɪŋ] adj noioso || s trivellazione

born [bɔrn] adj nato, partorito; **to be born** nascere; **to be born again** rinascere; **to be born with a silver spoon in one's mouth** nascere con la camicia

borough ['bʌro] s borgata, comune m

borrow ['baro] or ['bɔro] tr chiedere a or in prestito; prendere a or in prestito; ricevere a or in prestito; (to adopt) adottare; **to borrow trouble** preoccuparsi per nulla

borrower ['baro͵ər] or ['bɔro͵ər] s chi riceve a prestito; (law) comodatario, prestatario

borrowing ['baro͵ɪŋ] or ['bɔro͵ɪŋ] s prestito; prestito linguistico, forestierismo

bosom ['bʊzəm] s petto, seno; (e.g., of the family) grembo, seno; (of shirt) pettorina

bos'om friend' s amico del cuore

Bosporus ['baspərəs] s Bosforo

boss [bɔs] or [bas] s (coll) padrone m; (coll) direttore m; (coll) capintesta m; (coll) principale m; (archit) bugna, bozza || tr fare da padrone a || intr fare da padrone

boss-y ['bɔsi] or ['basi] adj (-ier; -iest) autoritario

botanical [bə'tænɪkəl] adj botanico

botanist ['batənɪst] s botanico

botany ['batəni] s botanica

botch [batʃ] s abborracciatura || tr abborracciare

both [boθ] adj entrambi i, tutti e due i || pron entrambi, tutti e due || conj del pari, al medesimo tempo; **both . . . and** tanto . . . quanto

bother ['baðər] s (worry) noia, seccatura; (person) seccatore m || tr dar noia a, seccare || intr preoccuparsi; **to bother about** or **with** occuparsi di; **to bother to** + inf molestarsi di + inf

bothersome ['baðərsəm] adj incomodo

bottle ['batəl] s bottiglia, fiasco || tr imbottigliare; **to bottle up** imbottigliare

bot'tle cap' s tappo a corona

bot'tle-neck' s collo di bottiglia; (of traffic) congestione, imbottigliamento

bot'tle o'pener ['opənər] s apribottiglie m

bottom ['batəm] adj basso; (price, dollar) ultimo; infimo || s fondo; (of chair) sedile m; base f; (of bottle) culo; (of ship) scafo; **at bottom** in realtà; **to begin at the bottom** cominciare dalla gavetta; **to get at the bottom of** andare a fondo di; **to go to the bottom** andare a picco

bottomless [ˈbɑtəmlɪs] *adj* senza fondo

boudoir [buˈdwɑr] *s* gabinetto di toletta (da signora)

bough [bau] *s* ramo

bouillon [ˈbujan] *s* brodo schietto

boulder [ˈboldər] *s* masso, roccia

boulevard [ˈbulə ˌvɑrd] *s* corso

bounce [bauns] *s* balzo; salto; elasticità *f;* (*of boat or plane*) piastrellamento; (fig) spirito; **to get the bounce** (slang) essere licenziato || *tr* far balzare; (slang) buttar fuori || *intr* rimbalzare; saltare; (aer, naut) piastrellare

bouncer [ˈbaunsər] *s* (*in night club*) (slang) buttafuori *m*

bouncing [ˈbaunsɪŋ] *adj* forte, vigoroso; grande, rumoroso

bound [baund] *adj* legato; collegato; obbligato; (bb) rilegato; (coll) risoluto; **bound for** destinato a, diretto per; **bound up in** or **with** in strette relazioni con; assorto in || *s* salto; rimbalzo; limite *m;* **bounds** zona limitrofa; **out of bounds** fuori limiti; al di là delle convenienze || *tr* delimitare

bounda·ry [ˈbaundəri] *s* (-**ries**) confine *m*, limite *m*

bound′ary stone′ *s* pietra di confine

boundless [ˈbaundlɪs] *adj* illimitato, sconfinato

bountiful [ˈbauntɪfəl] *adj* generoso; abbondante

boun·ty [ˈbaunti] *s* (-**ties**) dono generoso; generosità *f*, abbondanza; (*reward*) premio

bouquet [buˈke] or [boˈke] *s* mazzo, mazzolino; profumo, aroma *m*

bourgeois [ˈburʒwɑ] *adj* & *s* borghese *mf*

bourgeoisie [ˌburʒwɑˈzi] *s* borghesia

bout [baut] *s* lotta, contesa; (*of illness*) attacco

bow [bau] *s* inchino, riverenza; (naut) prua; **to take a bow** ricevere gli applausi || *tr* chinare, piegare || *intr* inchinarsi; sottomettersi; **to bow and scrape** fare riverenze || [bo] *s* (*weapon*) arco; (*knot*) nodo; (mus) archetto; (*stroke of bow*) (mus) arcata || *tr* & *intr* (mus) suonare con l'archetto

bowdlerize [ˈbaudlə ˌraɪz] *tr* espurgare

bowel [ˈbau·əl] *s* budello; **bowels** viscere *fpl*

bow′el move′ment *s* evacuazione; **to have a bowel movement** andar di corpo

bower [ˈbau·ər] *s* pergolato

bowery [ˈbau·əri] *adj* frondoso

bowknot [ˈbo ˌnɑt] *s* nodo scorsoio

bowl [bol] *s* (*dish*) ciotola, tazza; (*of pipe*) fornello; (*basin*) catino; (*amphitheater*) arena; (*ball*) boccia; (*delivery of ball*) bocciata; **bowls** bocce *fpl* || *tr* bocciare; **to bowl down** or **over** abbattere || *intr* giocare alle bocce

bowlegged [ˈbo ˌlɛgd] or [ˈbo ˌlɛgɪd] *adj* con le gambe storte

bowler [ˈbolər] *s* giocatore *m* di bocce

bowling [ˈbolɪŋ] *s* bocce *fpl;* bowling *m*, birilli *mpl*

bowl′ing al′ley *s* pista per il bowling; bowling *m*

bowl′ing green′ *s* campo di bocce erboso

bowshot [ˈbo ˌʃɑt] *s* tiro d'arco

bowsprit [ˈbausprit] or [ˈbosprit] *s* (naut) bompresso

bow′ tie′ [bo] *s* cravatta a farfalla

bowwow [ˈbau ˌwau] *interj* bau bau!

box [bɑks] *s* scatola; cassa; (*for jury*) banco; (*for sentry*) garitta; (*on coach*) cassetta; (*in stable*) posta; (*slap*) ceffone *m;* (*with fist*) pugno; (bot) bosso; (theat) palco, barcaccia; (baseball) posto del battitore; (typ) riquadratura || *tr* mettere in scatola; (*to slap*) schiaffeggiare; (*to hit with fist*) fare a pugilato con; **to box in** or **up** rinchiudere || *intr* fare a pugni; combattere

box′car′ *s* vagone *m* merci coperto

boxer [ˈbɑksər] *s* pugile *m*

box′hold′er *s* palchettista *mf*

boxing [ˈbɑksɪŋ] *s* pugilato

box′ing gloves′ *spl* guantoni *mpl* da pugilato

box′ of′fice *s* sportello, biglietteria; (theat) incasso; (theat) successo

box′-of′fice hit′ *s* grande successo

box′ pleat′ *s* (*of skirt*) cannone *m*

box′ seat′ *s* posto in palco

box′wood′ *s* bosso

boy [bɔɪ] *s* ragazzo, giovane *m* || *interj* accidempoli!

boycott [ˈbɔɪkɑt] *s* boicottaggio || *tr* boicottare

boy′friend′ *s* innamorato, amico

boyhood [ˈbɔɪhud] *s* fanciullezza

boyish [ˈbɔɪ·ɪʃ] *adj* giovanile

boy′ scout′ *s* giovane esploratore *m*

bra [brɑ] *s* (coll) reggiseno

brace [bres] *s* (*couple*) paio; (*device for maintaining tension*) tirante *m;* (*prop*) sostegno; (*tool*) trapano; (typ) graffa; **braces** (Brit) bretelle *fpl* || *tr* legare; serrare; puntellare; sostenere; invigorare; **to brace oneself** pigliare animo || *intr*—**to brace up** (coll) pigliare animo

brace′ and bit′ *s* menarola, trapano

bracelet [ˈbreslɪt] *s* braccialetto

bracer [ˈbresər] *s* (coll) bicchierino

bracket [ˈbrækɪt] *s* mensola; (*for lamp*) braccio; angolo; classifica; (typ) parentesi quadra || *tr* sostenere con mensola; mettere tra parentesi quadra; classificare

brackish [ˈbrækɪʃ] *adj* salmastro

brad [bræd] *s* chiodino, punta

brag [bræg] *s* vanto || *v* (*pret* & *pp* **bragged;** *ger* **bragging**) *intr* vantare

braggart [ˈbrægərt] *s* millantatore *m*

Brah·man [ˈbrɑmən] *s* (-**mans**) bramino

braid [bred] *s* treccia; (*strip of cloth*) spighetta; (mil) cordellina || *tr* intrecciare; decorare con spighette

brain [bren] *s* cervello; **brains** cervello, intelligenza; **to rack one's brains** rompersi la testa ‖ *tr* far saltare le cervella di

brain'child' *s* (coll) parto dell'ingegno, idea geniale

brain' drain' *s* (coll) fuga di cervelli

brainless ['brenlıs] *adj* senza testa

brain' pow'er *s* intelligenza

brain'storm' *s* (coll) ispirazione

brain' trust' *s* consiglio d'esperti

brain'wash'ing *s* lavaggio del cervello

brain' wave' *s* onda encefalica; (coll) idea geniale

brain'work' *s* lavoro intellettuale

brain·y ['breni] *adj* (-ier; -iest) intelligente

braise [brez] *tr* (culin) brasare

brake [brek] *s* freno; (*thicket*) macchia ‖ *tr & intr* frenare

brake' drum' *s* tamburo del freno

brake' lin'ing *s* ferodo

brake'man *s* (-men) frenatore *m*

brake' shoe' *s* ganascia

bramble ['bræmbəl] *s* rovo

bran [bræn] *s* crusca

branch [bræntʃ] *s* (*of tree*) branca, ramo; (*of river*) braccio; (*of a family*) ramo; (*of business*) filiale *f*; (rr) diramazione ‖ *intr* biforcarsi; **to branch off** or **out** ramificarsi, diramarsi

branch' line' *s* ferrovia di diramazione

branch' of'fice *s* succursale *f*

brand [brænd] *s* (*burning stick*) tizzone *m*; (*mark; stigma*) marchio; (*label; make*) marca ‖ *tr* (*to mark with a brand*) marchiare; (*to put a stigma on*) bollare; **to brand as** tacciare di

brandied ['brændıd] *adj* conservato in acquavite

brand'ing i'ron *s* ferro da marchio

brandish ['brændıʃ] *tr* brandire

brand'-new' *adj* nuovo fiammante

bran·dy ['brændi] *s* (-dies) cognac *m*, acquavite *f*

brash [bræʃ] *adj* (*too hasty*) avventato; (*insolent*) impudente ‖ *s* frammenti *mpl*; attacco (di malattia), indigestione

brass [bræs] or [brɑs] *s* ottone *m*; (coll) faccia tosta; (slang) alti ufficiali; **brasses** (mus) ottoni *mpl*

brass' band' *s* fanfara

brassiere [brə'zɪr] *s* reggiseno

brass' knuck'les *spl* tirapugni *m*

brass' tack' *s* chiodino or borchia d'ottone; **to get down to brass tacks** (coll) venire al sodo

brass·y ['bræsi] or ['brɑsi] *adj* (-ier; -iest) fatto d'ottone; sfacciato, impudente

brat [bræt] *s* marmocchio, monello

brava·do [brə'vɑdo] *s* (-does or -dos) bravata

brave [brev] *adj* coraggioso ‖ *s* persona coraggiosa; guerriero indiano ‖ *tr* (*to defy*) sfidare; (*to meet with courage*) affrontare

bravery ['brevəri] *s* coraggio

bra·vo ['brɑvo] *s* (-vos) bravo; applauso ‖ *interj* bravo!

brawl [brɔl] *s* zuffa, rissa ‖ *intr* azzuffarsi, rissare

brawn [brɔn] *s* forza muscolare

brawn·y ['brɔni] *adj* (-ier; -iest) muscoloso

bray [bre] *s* raglio ‖ *intr* ragliare

braze [brez] *s* brasatura ‖ *tr* brasare

brazen ['brezən] *adj* d'ottone; (*shameless*) sfrontato; (*sound*) penetrante ‖ *tr*—**to brazen out** or **through** affrontare sfacciatamente

brazier ['breʒər] *s* caldano, braciere *m*; (*workman*) ottonaio

Brazil [brə'zıl] *s* il Brasile

Brazilian [brə'zıljən] *adj & s* brasiliano

Brazil' nut' *s* noce *f* del Brasile

breach [britʃ] *s* (*gap*) breccia; (*failure to observe a law*) infrazione ‖ *tr* fare breccia su, fare varco in

breach' of faith' *s* abuso di confidenza

breach' of prom'ise *s* rottura di promessa di matrimonio

breach' of the peace' *s* violazione dell'ordine pubblico

bread [bred] *s* pane *m*; **to break bread with** sedersi a tavola con ‖ *tr* impannare

bread' and but'ter *s* pane *m* e burro; (coll) pane quotidiano

bread' crumbs' *spl* pangrattato

breaded ['bredıd] *adj* impannato

bread' knife' *s* coltello da pane

bread' line' *s* coda del pane

bread' stick' *s* grissino

breadth [bredθ] *s* (*width*) larghezza; (*scope*) ampiezza

bread'win'ner *s* sostegno della famiglia

break [brek] *s* interruzione; intervallo; omissione; (*breaking*) rottura; (*of bones*) frattura; (*of day*) fare *m*, spuntare *m*; (*sudden change*) mutamento; (*from jail*) evasione; (*luck*) (coll) fortuna; **to give s.o. a break** dare a qlcu l'opportunità ‖ *v* (*pret* **broke** [brok]; *pp* **broken**) *tr* (*to smash*) rompere, spezzare; (*to tame*) domare; (*to demote*) destituire; (*a record*) superare; (*to violate*) violare; (*to make bankrupt*) mandare al fallimento; (*to interrupt*) interrompere; (*to reduce the effects of*) attutire; (*to disclose*) rivelare; (*to bring to an end by force*) battere; (*a banknote*) cambiare; (*one's word*) mancare (with *dat*); (*a law*) rompere; **to break asunder** separare; **to break down** analizzare; **to break in** forzare; **to break open** forzare, scassinare; **to break up** dissolvere ‖ *intr* (*to divide*) rompersi; (*to burst*) scoppiare; (*said of voice of youngster*) cambiare; (*said of voice*) indebolirsi; (*said of a crowd*) disperdersi; (*said of weather*) rischiararsi; (*said of prices*) ribassare; (*to come into being*) scoppiare; (boxing) separarsi; **to break asunder** separarsi; **to break away** scappare; **to break down** abbattersi; (aut) essere or rimanere in panna; **to break even** fare patta; **to break in** irrompere; interrompere; **to break into** forzare; **to break into a run** incominciare a correre; **to break loose** liberarsi; (*said of a storm*) scatenarsi; **to break off** interrompere; **to break out** (*said of the skin*) avere un'eruzione; (*said, e.g., of war*) scoppiare; **to break through** aprirsi il varco; **to break up** disperdersi; **to break with** rompere le relazioni con

breakable [ˈbrekəbəl] *adj* fragile

breakage [ˈbrekɪdʒ] *s* rottura

break′down′ *s* (*in negotiations*) rottura; (aut) panna; (chem) analisi *f*; (pathol) colasso

breaker [ˈbrekər] *s* (*wave*) frangente *m*

breakfast [ˈbrekfəst] *s* prima colazione || *intr* fare prima colazione

break′neck′ *adj* pericoloso; **at breakneck speed** a rotta di collo, a rompicollo

break′ of day′ *s* alba

break′through′ *s* (mil) penetrazione; (fig) scoperta sensazionale

break′up′ *s* dispersione; dissoluzione; (*of a friendship*) rottura

break′wa′ter *s* diga, frangiflutti *m*

breast [brest] *s* petto; (*of female*) seno; (*source of emotions*) animo; **to make a clean breast of** fare una piena confessione di

breast′bone′ *s* sterno

breast′ drill′ *s* trapano da petto

breast′feed′ *v* (*pret & pp* **-fed** [fed]) *tr* allattare

breast′pin′ *s* spilla

breast′stroke′ *s* bracciata a rana

breath [brɛθ] *s* respiro, respirazione; (*odor*) alito; (*breeze*) soffio; (*whisper*) sussurro; (fig) vita; **out of breath** ansimante; **short of breath** corto di respiro; **to gasp for breath** respirare affannosamente; **under one's breath** sottovoce

breathe [brið] *tr* respirare; (*to whisper*) sussurrare; **to breathe one's last** esalare l'ultimo sospiro; **to not breathe a word** non dire una parola || *intr* respirare; **to breathe in** inspirare; **to breathe out** espirare

breath′ing spell′ *s* attimo di respiro

breathless [ˈbrɛθlɪs] *adj* senza fiato, ansimante; soffocante

breath′tak′ing *s* emozionante, commovente

breech [britʃ] *s* (*buttocks*) natiche *fpl*; (*rear part*) parte *f* posteriore; (*of gun*) culatta; **breeches** [ˈbrɪtʃɪz] pantaloni *mpl* al ginocchio; pantaloni *mpl* da cavallo; **to wear the breeches** (coll) portare le brache

breed [brid] *s* razza; tipo; (*stock*) origine *f* || *v* (*pret & pp* **bred** [bred]) *tr* produrre; (*to raise*) allevare

breeder [ˈbridər] *s* allevatore *m*; riproduttore *m*

breeding [ˈbridɪŋ] *s* (*e.g., of livestock*) allevamento; educazione

breeze [briz] *s* brezza

breez·y [ˈbrizi] *adj* (-ier; -iest) ventilato; (*brisk*) vivace, brioso

brethren [ˈbrɛðrɪn] *spl* fratelli *mpl*

brevi·ty [ˈbrɛvɪti] *s* (-ties) brevità *f*

brew [bru] *s* pozione; bevanda || *tr* (*beer*) fabbricare; (*to steep*) preparare; (*to plot*) complottare || *intr* (*said of beer*) fermentare; (*said of a storm*) prepararsi

brewer [ˈbru·ər] *s* birraio

brew′er's yeast′ *s* lievito di birra

brewer·y [ˈbru·əri] *s* (-ies) birreria, fabbrica di birra

bribe [braɪb] *s* subornazione, bustarella || *tr* subornare, dare la bustarella a

briber·y [ˈbraɪbəri] *s* (-ies) subornazione, corruzione

bric-a-brac [ˈbrɪkə‚bræk] *s* bric-a-brac *m*, cianfrusaglia, cianfrusaglie *fpl*

brick [brɪk] *s* mattone *m* || *tr* mattonare

brick′bat′ *s* pezzo di mattone; (coll) insulto

brick′kiln′ *s* fornace *f* per mattoni

bricklayer [ˈbrɪk‚le·ər] *s* muratore *m*

brick′yard′ *s* deposito di mattoni

bridal [ˈbraɪdəl] *adj* nuziale, da sposa

brid′al wreath′ *s* serto nuziale

bride [braɪd] *s* sposa

bride′groom′ *s* sposo

bridesmaid [ˈbraɪdz‚med] *s* damigella d'onore

bridge [brɪdʒ] *s* ponte *m*; (*of violin*) ponticello; (*on a ship*) ponte *m* di comando || *tr* gettare un ponte su; congiungere; **to bridge a gap** colmare una lacuna

bridge′head′ *s* testa di ponte

bridle [ˈbraɪdəl] *s* briglia || *tr* mettere la briglia a; (fig) frenare || *intr* drizzare il capo, insuperbirsi

bri′dle path′ *s* strada cavalcabile

brief [brif] *adj* breve || *s* sommario; (law) esposto; (eccl) breve *m*; **briefs** slip *mpl* || *tr* dare istruzioni a, mettere al corrente

brief′ case′ *s* cartella, borsa d'avvocato

brier [ˈbraɪ·ər] *s* radica; pipa di radica

brig [brɪg] *s* (naut) brigantino; (naut) prigione

brigade [brɪˈged] *s* brigata

brigadier [‚brɪgəˈdir] *s* (coll) brigadier generale *m*, generale *m* di brigata

brigand [ˈbrɪgənd] *s* brigante *m*

brigantine [ˈbrɪgənˌtin] or [ˈbrɪgənˌtaɪn] *s* (naut) brigantino goletta

bright [braɪt] *adj* (*shining*) lucido; (*light*) brillante; (*lively*) vivo; intelligente; famoso; (*idea*) luminoso

brighten [ˈbraɪtən] *tr* illuminare; ravvivare || *intr* illuminarsi; ravvivarsi; rischiararsi

bright′ lights′ *spl* luci *fpl* abbaglianti; (aut) fari *mpl* abbaglianti

brilliance [ˈbrɪljəns] or **brilliancy** [ˈbrɪljənsi] *s* splendore *m*, scintillio

brilliant [ˈbrɪljənt] *adj* brillante

brim [brɪm] *s* (*e.g., of cup*) orlo, bordo; (*of hat*) ala, tesa || *v* (*pret & pp* **brimmed**; *ger* **brimming**) *intr* essere pieno sino all'orlo

brim′stone′ *s* zolfo

brine [braɪn] *s* salamoia; acqua di mare

bring [brɪŋ] *v* (*pret & pp* **brought**

[brɔt]) *tr* far venire; provocare; (*to carry along*) portare con sè; **to bring about** causare; **to bring around** persuadere; **to bring back** restituire; **to bring down** far abbassare; (fig) umiliare; **to bring forth** dare alla luce; **to bring forward** (*an excuse*) addurre; (math) riportare; **to bring in** introdurre; far entrare; **to bring off** compiere; **to bring on** causare; **to bring oneself to** rassegnarsi a; **to bring out** (*to expose*) rivelare; (*to offer to the public*) presentare al pubblico; (*a book*) far uscire; **to bring to** far rinvenire; (*a ship*) fermare; **to bring together** riunire; **to bring up** (*children*) allevare, tirar su; (*to introduce*) allegare; (*to cough up*) rigettare

bringing-up ['brɪŋɪŋ'ʌp] *s* educazìone

brink [brɪŋk] *s* orlo

briquet [brɪ'kɛt] *s* bricchetta

brisk [brɪsk] *adj* (*quick*) svelto; (*sharp*) acuto; (*invigorating*) frizzante; (*gunfire*) nutrito

bristle ['brɪsəl] *s* setola || *intr* (*to be stiff*) irrigidirsi; (*said of hair*) rizzarsi; (*with anger*) adirarsi

bris-tly ['brɪslɪ] *adj* (*-tlier; -tliest*) irto di setole

British ['brɪtɪʃ] *adj* britannico || **the British** i britannici, gl'inglesi

Britisher ['brɪtɪʃər] *s* britannico

Briton ['brɪtən] *s* britannico

Brittany ['brɪtənɪ] *s* la Bretagna

brittle ['brɪtəl] *adj* fragile, friabile; (*crisp*) croccante

broach [brotʃ] *s* (*pin*) spilla; (*spit*) spiedo; (mach) alesatore *m* || *tr* perforare; (*a subject*) intavolare

broad [brɔd] *adj* largo; tollerante, liberale; (*daylight*) pieno; (*story*) grossolano; (*extensive*) lato; (*accent*) pronunciato

broad'cast' *s* disseminazione; (rad) radiodiffusione || *v* (*pret & pp* -cast) *tr* disseminare, diffondere || (*pret & pp* -cast or -casted) *tr* radiodiffondere

broad'casting sta'tion *s* stazione radiotrasmittente

broad'cloth' *s* (*wool*) panno di lana; (*cotton*) popeline *f*

broaden ['brɔdən] *tr* allargare, estendere || *intr* allargarsi, estendersi

broad' jump' *s* salto in lunghezza

broadloom ['brɔd,lum] *adj* tessuto su telaio largo

broad-minded ['brɔd'maɪndɪd] *adj* di ampie vedute, liberale

broad-shouldered ['brɔd'ʃoldərd] *adj* largo di spalle

broad'side' *s* (nav) bordo; (nav) bordata; (*verbal criticism*) (coll) sfuriata; (*written criticism*) (coll) attacco violento

broad'sword' *s* spada da taglio

brocade [bro'ked] *s* broccato

broccoli ['brɑkəlɪ] *s* broccolo; (*as food*) broccoli *mpl*

brochure [bro'ʃur] *s* opuscolo, libriccino

brogue [brog] *s* accento irlandese; scarpa forte e comoda

broil [brɔɪl] *s* cottura alla graticola; carne *f* cotta alla graticola; (*quarrel*) rissa, zuffa || *tr* cucinare alla graticola; bruciare || *intr* cucinare alla graticola; (*to quarrel*) rissare, azzuffarsi

broiler ['brɔɪlər] *s* graticola, gratella; (*chicken*) pollo da cucinare alla gratella or allo spiedo

broke [brok] *adj* (coll) al verde

broken ['brokən] *adj* rotto; fratturato; (*e.g., English*) parlato male; (*tamed*) domato

bro'ken-down' *adj* avvilito; rovinato

broken-hearted ['brokən'hɑrtɪd] *adj* affranto

broker ['brokər] *s* sensale *m;* (*on the stock exchange*) agente *m* di cambio

brokerage ['brokərɪdʒ] *s* mediazione

bromide ['bromaɪd] *s* bromuro; (coll) banalità *f*

bromine ['bromin] *s* bromo

bronchitis [brɑŋ'kaɪtɪs] *s* bronchite *f*

bron·co ['brɑŋko] *s* (*-cos*) puledro brado

broncobuster ['brɑŋko,bʌstər] *s* domatore *m* di puledri bradi

bronze [brɑnz] *adj* bronzeo || *s* bronzo || *tr* bronzare || *intr* abbronzarsi

brooch [brotʃ] or [brutʃ] *s* spilla

brood [brud] *s* covata, nidiata || *tr* covare || *intr* chiocciare; meditare; **to brood on** or **over** meditare con tristezza (su)

brook [bruk] *s* ruscello || *tr*—**to brook no** non sopportare

broom [brum] or [brum] *s* scopa; (*shrub*) saggina

broom'corn' *s* sorgo

broom'stick' *s* manico di scopa

broth [brɔθ] or [brɑθ] *s* brodo

brothel ['brɑθəl] or ['brɑðəl] *s* postribolo, bordello

brother ['brʌðər] *s* fratello

brotherhood ['brʌðər,hud] *s* fratellanza; (*association*) confraternita

broth'er-in-law' *s* (*brothers-in-law*) cognato

brotherly ['brʌðərlɪ] *adj* fraterno || *adv* fraternamente

brow [brau] *s* ciglio; (*forehead*) fronte *f;* **to knit one's brow** aggrottare la fronte

brow'beat' *v* (*pret* -beat; *pp* -beaten) *tr* intimidire, intimorire

brown [braun] *adj* bruno; (*tanned*) abbronzato || *s* color bruno || *tr* colorare di bruno; abbronzare; (*metal*) brunire; (culin) dorare || *intr* colorarsi di bruno; abbronzarsi; brunirsi; (culin) dorarsi

brownish ['braunɪʃ] *adj* brunastro

brown' stud'y *s*—**in a brown study** assorto in fantasticherie

brown' sug'ar *s* zucchero greggio

browse [brauz] *intr* (*said of cattle*) brucare; sfogliare; **to browse around** curiosare

bruise [bruz] *s* ammaccatura, contusione || *tr* ammaccare || *intr* ammaccarsi

brunet [bru'net] *adj* bruno

brunette [bru'net] *adj & s* bruna

brunt [brʌnt] *s* forza; scontro; peso

brush [brʌʃ] *s* pennello; spazzola; (*stroke*) pennellata; (*light touch*) tocco; (*brushwood*) macchia; (*brief encounter*) scaramuccia; (elec) spazzola || *tr* spazzolare; pennellare; **to brush aside** rigettare; **to brush up** ritoccare || *intr*—**to brush by** passar vicino; **to brush up on** ripassare

brush'-off' *s* (slang) scortesia; **to give the brush-off to** (slang) snobbare

brush'wood' *s* macchia, fratta

brusque [brʌsk] *adj* brusco

brusqueness ['brʌsknɪs] *s* bruschezza

Brussels ['brʌsəlz] *s* Bruxelles *f*

Brus'sels sprouts' *spl* cavolini *mpl*

brutal ['brutəl] *adj* brutale

brutali•ty [bru'tælɪti] *s* (-ties) brutalità *f*

brute [brut] *adj & s* bruto

brutish ['brutɪʃ] *adj* bruto

bubble ['bʌbəl] *s* bolla; (fig) chimera || *intr* bollire; (*to make a bubbling sound*) barbugliare; **to bubble over** traboccare

bub'ble bath' *s* bagno di schiuma

buccaneer [,bʌkə'nɪr] *s* bucaniere *m*

buck [bʌk] *s* (*deer*) cervo; (*goat*) caprone *m*; (*sawhorse*) cavalletto; (*rabbit*) coniglio maschio; (*bucking*) groppata; (*dandy*) damerino; (slang) dollaro; **to pass the buck** (coll) giocare a scaricabarile || *tr* resistere accanitamente || *intr* (*said of a horse*) fare salti da caprone; **to buck for** (slang) cercare di ottenere; **to buck up** (coll) rianimarsi, prender animo

bucket ['bʌkɪt] *s* secchio; bigoncia; (*e.g., of dredge*) benna; **to kick the bucket** (slang) tirare le cuoia

buck'et seat' *s* sedile *m*, strapuntino

buckle ['bʌkəl] *s* (*clasp*) fibbia, boccola; piega || *tr* affibbiare || *intr* piegarsi, curvarsi; **to buckle down to** (coll) mettersi di buzzo buono a

buck' pri'vate *s* (slang) soldato semplice

buckram ['bʌkrəm] *s* tela da fusto

buck'saw' *s* cavalletto

buck'shot' *s* pallini *mpl* da caccia

buck'tooth' *s* (-teeth) dente *m* in fuori, dente *m* sporgente

buck'wheat' *s* grano saraceno

bud [bʌd] *s* bocciolo, gemma; **to nip in the bud** troncare sul nascere || *v* (*pret & pp* budded; *ger* budding) *intr* sbocciare; nascere

Buddhism ['budɪzəm] *s* buddismo

bud•dy ['bʌdi] *s* (-dies) (coll) amico, compare *m*

budge [bʌdʒ] *tr* smuovere || *intr* muoversi

budget ['bʌdʒɪt] *s* bilancio || *tr* stanziare, preventivare; (*to schedule*) anticipare; (*time*) calcolare in anticipo

budgetary ['bʌdʒɪ,tɛri] *adj* preventivo, di bilancio

buff [bʌf] *adj* bruno giallastro; di pelle || *s* (*leather*) pelle gialla; dilet-

---

tante *m*; (mil) giacca di pelle gialla; (coll) pelle nuda || *tr* lucidare; (*to reduce the force of*) ammortizzare

buffa•lo ['bʌfə,lo] *s* (-loes or -los) bufalo || *tr* (coll) intimidire

buffer ['bʌfər] *s* ammortizzatore *m*; cuscinetto; (*worker*) lucidatore *m*; (mach) lucidatrice *f*; (rr) respingente *m*

buff'er state' *s* stato cuscinetto

buffet [bu'fe] *s* (*piece of furniture*) credenza; (*counter*) buffet *m* || ['bʌfɪt] *s* pugno; schiaffo || *tr* dar pugni a; schiaffeggiare; lottare con; (*to push about*) sballottare

buffet' car' [bu'fe] *s* vagone *m* ristorante

buffoon [bə'fun] *s* buffone *m*

buffoner•y [bə'funəri] *s* (-ies) buffoneria

bug [bʌg] *s* insetto; (coll) germe *m*; (*in motor*) (slang) noia; (slang) pazzo; **to put a bug in the ear of** mettere una pulce nell'orecchio di || *v* (*pret & pp* bugged; *ger* bugging) *tr* (slang) installare un sistema d'ascolto nel telefono di; (*to annoy*) (slang) seccare || *intr*—**to bug out** (slang) andarsene

bug'bear' *s* spauracchio

bug•gy ['bʌgi] *adj* (-gier; -giest) pieno di cimici; (slang) pazzo || *s* (-gies) carrozzino

bug'house' *adj* (slang) pazzo || *s* (slang) manicomio

bugle ['bjugəl] *s* tromba, cornetta

bugler ['bjuglər] *s* trombettiere *m*

build [bɪld] *s* corporatura, taglia || *v* (*pret & pp* built [bɪlt]) *tr* costruire, edificare; fondare, basare; **to build up** sviluppare

builder ['bɪldər] *s* costruttore *m*; costruttore *m* edile

building ['bɪldɪŋ] *s* edificio, stabile *m*; costruzione; edilizia

build'ing and loan' associa'tion *s* società *f* di credito fondiario

build'ing lot' *s* (coll) terreno da costruzioni

build'ing trades' *spl* edilizia

build'-up' *s* concentrazione; sviluppo; processo di preparazione; propaganda favorevole

built'-in' *adj* (*in a wall*) murato; (*in a cabinet*) incassato, incorporato

built'-in clos'et *s* armadio a muro

built'-up' *adj* armato; popolato

bulb [bʌlb] *s* bulbo; (*lamp*) lampadina; (*of a lamp*) globo, cipolla

Bulgarian [bʌl'gɛri•ən] *adj & s* bulgaro

bulge [bʌldʒ] *s* protuberanza, sporgenza || *intr* sporgere, gonfiarsi

bulk [bʌlk] *s* volume *m*, massa; **in bulk** in blocco; sciolto || *intr* avere importanza; aumentare d'importanza

bulk'head' *s* diga; (naut) paratia

bulk•y ['bʌlki] *adj* (-ier; -iest) voluminoso

bull [bʊl] *s* toro; (*in the stockmarket*) rialzista *mf*; (slang) sciemenza; (eccl) bulla || *tr*—**to bull the market** giocare al rialzo

bull'dog' *s* molosso

bulldoze ['bʊl;doz] *tr* intimidire; (*land*) livellare

bulldozer ['bʊl,dozər] *s* livellatrice *f*, apripista *m*

bullet ['bʊlɪt] *s* palla, pallottola

bulletin ['bʊlətɪn] *s* bollettino; (*of a school*) albo; (journ) comunicato

bul'letin board' *s* tabellone *m*

bul'let-proof *adj* blindato

bull'fight' *s* corrida

bull'fight'er *s* torero

bull'finch' *s* (orn) ciuffolotto

bull'frog' *s* rana americana

bull-headed ['bʊl,hedɪd] *adj* testardo

bullion ['bʊljən] *s* lingotti *mpl* d'oro or d'argento; frangia d'oro; (*on an Italian general's hat*) greca

bullish ['bʊlɪʃ] *adj* ostinato; (*market*) al rialzo; (*speculator*) rialzista

bullock ['bʊlək] *s* manzo

bull'ring' *s* arena

bull's-eye ['bʊlz,aɪ] *s* centro, tiro in pieno sul bersaglio; **to hit the bull's-eye** fare centro

bul-ly ['bʊli] *adj* (coll) eccellente ‖ *s* (**-lies**) bravaccio ‖ *v* (*pret & pp* **-lied**) *tr* intimidire

bulrush ['bʊl,rʌʃ] *s* giunco; (Bibl) papiro

bulwark ['bʊlwərk] *s* baluardo; protezione *f* ‖ *tr* proteggere

bum [bʌm] *adj* (slang) pessimo ‖ *s* (slang) vagabondo; **on the bum** (slang) rotto, fuori servizio ‖ *v* (*pret & pp* **bummed**) *ger* **bumming**) *tr* (slang) scroccare ‖ *intr* (slang) oziare; (slang) vivere d'elemosina; (slang) fare lo scroccatore

bumble ['bʌmbəl] *tr* abborracciare ‖ *intr* abborracciare; (*to stagger*) barcollare; (*to stumble*) balbettare; (*said of a bee*) ronzare

bum'blebee' *s* calabrone *m*

bump [bʌmp] *s* botta, botto; (*collision*) colpo, urto; (*swelling*) bernoccolo ‖ *tr* urtare; **to bump off** (slang) uccidere ‖ *intr* urtare, cozzare; **to bump into** incontrarsi con; cozzare contro

bumper ['bʌmpər] *adj* (coll) abbondante ‖ *s* bicchiere pieno fino all'orlo; (aut) paraurti *m*; (rr) respingente *m*

bumpkin ['bʌmpkɪn] *s* beota *m*

bumptious ['bʌmp/əs] *adj* vanitoso, presuntuoso

bump-y ['bʌmpi] *adj* (**-ier; -iest**) (*road*) irregolare, ondulato; (*air*) agitato

bun [bʌn] *s* panino; (*of hair*) crocchia, treccia a ciambella

bunch [bʌntʃ] *s* (*of grapes*) grappolo; (*of keys*) mazzo; (*of grass*) ciuffo; (*of people*) gruppo; (*of twigs*) fastello; (*of animals*) branco ‖ *tr* (*things*) ammonticchiare; (*people*) raggruppare ‖ *intr* raggrupparsi

bundle ['bʌndəl] *s* fascio, fastello; (*package*) pacco; (*large package*) collo; (*bunch*) mucchio ‖ *tr* affastellare; impacchettare; ammucchiare; **to bundle off** or **out** cacciare precipitosamente; **to bundle up** infagottare ‖ *intr*—**to bundle up** infagottarsi

bung [bʌŋ] *s* spina, cannella

bungalow ['bʌŋgə,lo] *s* casetta, villino, bungalow *m*

bung'hole' *s* spina, foro della botte

bungle ['bʌŋgəl] *s* abborracciatura ‖ *tr* abborracciare ‖ *intr* lavorare alla carlona

bungler ['bʌŋglər] *s* abborraccione *m*

bungling ['bʌŋglɪŋ] *adj* goffo; mal fatto ‖ *s* abborracciatura

bunion ['bʌnjən] *s* gonfiore *m* dell'alluce

bunk [bʌŋk] *s* letto a castello; (nav) cuccetta; (slang) sciocchezza ‖ *intr* dormire in cuccetta

bunk' bed' *s* letto a castello

bunker ['bʌŋkər] *s* (*bin*) carbonile *m*; (mil) casamatta; (golf) ostacolo

bun-ny ['bʌni] *s* (**-nies**) coniglietto

bunting ['bʌntɪŋ] *s* ornamento di bandiere; (nav) gala; (orn) zigolo

buoy [bɔɪ] or ['bu·i] *s* boa; (*life preserver*) salvagente *m* ‖ *tr*—**to buoy up** tenere a galla; (fig) rincuorare

buoyancy ['bɔɪ·ənsi] or ['bujənsi] *s* galleggiabilità *f*; (*cheerfulness*) allegria, esuberanza

buoyant ['bɔɪ·ənt] or ['bujənt] *adj* galleggiante; allegro, esuberante

bur [bʌr] *s* riccio, aculeo

burble ['bʌrbəl] *s* gorgoglio ‖ *intr* gorgogliare

burden ['bʌrdən] *s* carico, peso, fardello; (*of a speech*) tema *m*; (*chorus*) ritornello; (naut) portata ‖ *tr* caricare

bur'den of proof' *s* onere *m* della prova

burdensome ['bʌrdənsəm] *adj* oneroso

burdock ['bʌrdɑk] *s* lappa, lappola

bureau ['bjuro] *s* comò *m*; (*agency*) ufficio, servizio

bureaucra·cy [bju'rɑkrəsi] *s* (**-cies**) burocrazia

bureaucrat ['bjurə,kræt] *s* burocrate *m*

burglar ['bʌrglər] *s* scassinatore *m*

bur'glar alarm' *s* campanello antifurto

burglarize ['bʌrglə,raɪz] *tr* scassinare

bur'glar-proof' *adj* a prova di furto

burgla·ry ['bʌrgləri] *s* (**-ries**) furto con scasso, scassinatura

Burgundy ['bʌrgəndi] *s* la Borgogna; (*wine*) borgogna *m*

burial ['berɪ·əl] *s* sepoltura

bur'ial ground' *s* cimitero

burin ['bjurɪn] *s* burino, cesello

burlap ['bʌrlæp] *s* tela di iuta

burlesque [bʌr'lesk] *adj* burlesco ‖ *s* farsa, burlesque *m* ‖ *tr* parodiare

burlesque' show' *s* spettacolo di varietà, music-hall *m*

bur-ly ['bʌrli] *adj* (**-lier; -liest**) membruto, robusto

Burma ['bʌrmə] *s* la Birmania

burn [bʌrn] *s* bruciatura, scottatura ‖ *v* (*pret & pp* **burned** or **burnt** [bʌrnt]) *tr* bruciare; (*to set on fire*) dar fuoco a; (*bricks*) cuocere; **to burn down** radere al suolo; **to burn up** consumare; (*the road*) divorare; (coll) fare arrabbiare ‖ *intr* bruciare, bruciarsi; (*said of lights*) essere acceso, e.g., **the lights were burning** la luce era accesa; **to burn out** (*said of an electric bulb or a fuse*) bruciarsi;

to burn to (fig) agognare di; **to burn up** (coll) essere arrabiato; **to burn with** (e.g., envy) ardere di

burner ['bʌrnər] s (of gas fixture or lamp) becco; (of furnace) bruciatore m

burning ['bʌrnɪŋ] adj bruciante, scottante || s incendio; (ceramic) cottura finale

burn'ing ques'tion s questione di attualità palpitante

burnish ['bʌrnɪʃ] s lucidatura || tr brunire

burnt' al'mond [bʌrnt] s mandorla tostata

burp [bʌrp] s (coll) rutto || intr (coll) ruttare

burr [bʌr] s riccio, aculeo; (rough edge) bava; (dentist's drill) fresa

burrow ['bʌro] s tana, buca || intr imbucarsi, rintanarsi

bursar ['bʌrsər] s tesoriere universitario

burst [bʌrst] s esplosione; (e.g., of machine gun) raffica; (break) crepa; (of passion) accesso; (of speed) slancio || tr far scoppiare || intr scoppiare, esplodere; **to burst into** (e.g., a room) irrompere in; (e.g., angry words) esplodere in; **to burst out crying** scoppiare in lacrime; **to burst with laughter** scoppiare dalle risa

bur·y ['bɛri] v (pret & pp -ied) tr sotterrare; **to be buried in thought** essere immerso nel pensiero; **to bury the hatchet** fare la pace

bus [bʌs] s (buses or busses) bus m, autobus m || v (pret & pp bused or bussed) ger busing or bussing) tr trasportare con autobus

bus'boy' s secondo cameriere

bus·by ['bʌzbi] s (-bies) colbacco

bus' driv'er s conducente mf di autobus

bush [bʊʃ] s cespuglio, arbusto; **to beat around the bush** menare il can per l'aia

bushed [bʊʃt] adj (coll) stanco morto

bushel ['bʊʃəl] s staio

bushing ['bʊʃɪŋ] s (mach) bronzina

bush·y ['bʊʃi] adj (-ier; -iest) ricco di arbusti; (face) barbuto

business ['bɪznɪs] adj commerciale || s occupazione; commercio; affare m, negozio; faccenda; impiego; **it is not your business** non è affare Suo; **to know one's business** sapere il fatto proprio; **to make it one's business to** proporsi di; **to mean business** (coll) farla sul serio; **to mind one's own business** impicciarsi degli affari propri

businesslike ['bɪznɪs,laɪk] adj metodico; serio; efficace

busi'ness·man' s (-men') commerciante m, uomo d'affari

busi'ness suit' s abito da passeggio

busi'ness·wom'an s (wom'en) commerciante f

bus'man s (-men) guidatore m d'autobus

buss [bʌs] s (coll) bacione sonoro || tr (coll) baciare sonoramente

bus' stop' s fermata degli autobus

bust [bʌst] s busto; petto; (slang) fallimento; (slang) pugno || tr (slang) rompere; (slang) far fallire; (slang) colpire, dare pugni a; (mil) degradare

buster ['bʌstər] s (coll) ragazzo; (coll) rompitore m

bustle ['bʌsəl] s (on a dress) guardinfante m; attività f || intr affrettarsi

bus·y ['bɪzi] adj (-ier; -iest) occupato || v (pret & pp -ied) tr occupare, tenere occupato; **to busy oneself with** occuparsi di

bus'y·bod'y s (-ies) ficcanaso

bus'y sig'nal s (telp) segnale m d'occupato

but [bʌt] s ma m || adv solo, solamente; **but for** se non . . . per || prep eccetto, ad eccezione di, meno, se non; **all but** quasi || conj ma; che non, e.g., **I never go out in the rain but I catch a cold** non esco mai con la pioggia che non mi pigli un raffreddore

butcher ['bʊtʃər] s macellaio || tr macellare; massacrare

butch'er knife' s coltello da cucina, coltella

butch'er shop' s macelleria

butcher·y ['bʊtʃəri] s (-ies) macello; carneficina

butler ['bʌtlər] s cantiniere m, credenziere m

butt [bʌt] s (butting) cornata; (of rifle or gun) calcio; (of cigar) mozzicone m; (target) bersaglio; (end) estremità f; (of ridicule) zimbello; (cask) botte f || tr dare cornate a; cozzare contro || intr—**to butt into** (slang) intromettersi in

butter ['bʌtər] s burro || tr imburrare; **to butter up** (coll) adulare

but'ter·cup' s (bot) bottone m d'oro, ranuncolo

but'ter dish' s piattino per il burro, burriera

but'ter·fat' s grasso nel latte

but'ter·fly' s (-flies) farfalla

but'ter knife' s coltello per il burro

but'ter·milk' s latticello

but'ter sauce' s burro fuso

but'ter·scotch' s caramella al burro

buttocks ['bʌtəks] spl chiappe fpl, natiche fpl

button ['bʌtən] s bottone m || tr abbottonare

but'ton·hole' s occhiello, asola || tr attaccare un bottone a

but'ton·hook' s allacciabottoni m

buttress ['bʌtrɪs] s contrafforte m; piedritto || tr rinforzare

buxom ['bʌksəm] adj avvenente, procace

buy [baɪ] s compra || v (pret & pp bought [bɔt]) tr comprare; **to buy off** corrompere; **to buy out** comprare la parte di

buyer ['baɪ·ər] s compratore m

buzz [bʌz] s brusio, ronzio || tr volare a bassa quota sopra; (coll) fare una telefonata a || intr ronzare

buzzard ['bʌzərd] s (hawk) poiana; avvoltoio americano

buzzer ['bʌzər] s suoneria ronzante

buzz' saw' *s* sega circolare, segatrice *f* a disco

by [baɪ] *adv* oltre, e.g., **to speed by** correre velocemente oltre; **by and by** fra poco; **by and large** generalmente || *prep* vicino a; di, durante, e.g., **by night** di notte, durante la notte; a, e.g., **they work by the hour** lavorano all'ora; (*not later than, through*) per; (*past*) in fronte a; *(through the agency of)* da; *(according to)* secondo; (math) per, volte; **by far di molto; by the way** a proposito

bygone ['baɪ ˌgɒn] or ['baɪ ˌgʌn] *adj & s* passato; **to let bygones be bygones** dimenticare il passato

bylaw ['baɪ ˌlɔ] *s* legge *f* locale, regolamento di una società

by'-line' *s* (journ) firma

by'pass' *s* linea secondaria; (*detour*) deviazione || *tr* fare una deviazione oltre a; (*a difficulty*) evitare

by'path' *s* sentiero secondario; sentiero privato

by'prod'uct *s* sottoprodotto

bystander ['baɪ ˌstændər] *s* astante *m*, spettatore *m*

byway ['baɪ ˌwe] *s* via traversa

byword ['baɪ ˌwʌrd] *s* proverbio; oggetto di obbrobrio

Byzantium [bɪˈzænʃɪ əm] or [bɪ ˈzæntɪ əm] *s* Bisanzio

C

C, c [si] *s* terza lettera dell'alfabeto inglese

cab [kæb] *s* vettura di piazza; tassì *m*; (*of truck or locomotive*) cabina

cabbage ['kæbɪdʒ] *s* cavolo, verza

cab' driv'er *s* autista *m* di piazza; (*of horse-drawn cab*) vetturino

cabin ['kæbɪn] *s* (*shed*) capanna; (*hut*) baracca; (aer, naut) cabina

cab'in boy' *s* mozzo

cabinet ['kæbɪnɪt] *s* (*piece of furniture*) vetrina; (*for a radio*) armadietto; (*small room; ministry of a government*) gabinetto

cab'inet-mak'er *s* ebanista *m*

cab'inet-mak'ing *s* ebanisteria

cable ['kebəl] *s* cavo; cablogramma; (elec) cablaggio || *tr* cablare, mandare un cablogramma a

ca'ble address' *s* indirizzo telegrafico

ca'ble car' *s* funicolare *f*, teleferica

cablegram ['kebəl ˌgræm] *s* cablogramma *m*

caboose [kə ˈbus] *s* (rr) vagone *m* di coda

cab'stand' *s* stazione di tassametri

cache [kæʃ] *s* nascondiglio || *tr* mettere in un nascondiglio

cachet [kæ ˈʃe] *s* sigillo; (*distinguishing feature*) impronta

cackle ['kækəl] *s* (*of chickens*) coccodè *m*; (*of people*) chiacchierio || *intr* fare coccodè; ciarlare

cac·tus ['kæktəs] *s* (-tuses or -ti [taɪ]) cactus *m*

cad [kæd] *s* mascalzone *m*

cadaver [kə ˈdævər] *s* cadavere *m*

cadaverous [kə ˈdævərəs] *adj* cadaverico

caddie ['kædi] *s* portamazze *m*

cadence ['kedəns] *s* cadenza

cadet [kə ˈdɛt] *s* cadetto

cadmium ['kædmɪ əm] *s* cadmio

cadres ['kædriz] *spl* (mil) quadri *mpl*

Caesar'ean sec'tion [sɪ ˈzɛrɪ ən] *s* taglio cesareo

café [kæ ˈfe] *s* caffè *m*, bar *m*, ristorante *m*

ca'fé soci'ety *s* bel mondo

cafeteria [ˌkæfə ˈtɪrɪ ə] *s* mensa, tavola calda, caffetteria

caffeine [kæ ˈfin] or ['kæfi ɪn] *s* caffeina

cage [kedʒ] *s* gabbia; (*of elevator*) cabina || *tr* ingabbiare

ca·gey ['kedʒi] *adj* (-gier; -giest) (coll) astuto, cauto

cahoots [kə ˈhuts] *s*—**to be in cahoots** (slang) far lega, essere in combutta; **to go cahoots** (slang) dividere in parti eguali

Cain [ken] *s* Caino; **to raise Cain** (slang) arrabbiarsi; (slang) fare una sfuriata

Cairo ['kaɪro] *s* il Cairo

caisson ['kesɑn] *s* cassone *m*; (archit) cassettone *m*

cajole [kə ˈdʒol] *tr* lusingare; persuadere con lusinghe

cajoler·y [kə ˈdʒoləri] *s* (-ies) lusinga

cake [kek] *s* dolce *m*; torta, pasta; (*with bread-like dough*) focaccia; (*of earth*) zolla; (*of soap*) saponetta; **to take the cake** (coll) essere il colmo || *tr* incrostare || *intr* indurirsi; incrostarsi

calabash ['kælə ˌbæʃ] *s* zucca a fiasca

calaboose ['kælə ˌbus] *s* (coll) gattabuia

calamitous [kə ˈlæmɪtəs] *adj* calamitoso

calami·ty [kə ˈlæmɪti] *s* (-ties) calamità *f*

calci·fy ['kælsɪ ˌfaɪ] *v* (*pret & pp* -fied) *tr* calcificare || *intr* calcificarsi

calcium ['kælsɪ əm] *s* calcio

calculate ['kælkjə ˌlet] *tr* calcolare || *intr* calcolare; **to calculate on** contare su

cal'culating machine' *s* (macchina) calcolatrice

calcu·lus ['kælkjələs] *s* (-luses or -li [ˌlaɪ]) (math, pathol) calcolo

calendar ['kæləndər] *s* calendario; (*agenda*) ordine *m* del giorno

calf [kæf] or [kɑf] *s* (calves [kævz] or [kɑvz]) vitello; (*of shoes or binding*) pelle *f* di vitello; (*of the leg*) polpaccio

calf'skin' *s* pelle *f* di vitello

caliber ['kælɪbər] *s* calibro

calibrate ['kælɪ,bret] *tr* calibrare

cali·co ['kælɪ,ko] *s* (**-coes** or **-cos**) cotone stampato, calico

California [,kælɪ'fɔrnɪ·ə] *s* la California

calipers ['kælɪpərz] *spl* compasso a grossezze, calibro

caliph ['kelɪf] or ['kælɪf] *s* califfo

calisthenic [,kælɪs'θɛnɪk] *adj* ginnastico || **calisthenics** *spl* ginnastica a corpo libero

calk [kɔk] *tr* var of **caulk**

call [kɔl] *s* chiamata; visita; (*shout*) grido, richiamo; (*of bugle*) squillo; (*of telephone*) colpo; (*of ship*) scalo; obbligo; vocazione; (com) richiesta; **on call** disponibile; **within a call** a portata di voce || *tr* chiamare; convocare; (*to awaken*) svegliare; **to call back** richiamare; **to call in** (*e.g., an expert*) fare venire; (*e.g., currency*) domandare, esigere; **to call off** annullare; **to call out** chiamare; **to call together** convocare; **to call up** chiamare per telefono || *intr* chiamare; visitare; **to call at** passare per la casa di; (naut) fare scalo a; **to call for** venire a prendere; **to call out** gridare; **to go calling** andare a fare visite

cal'la lil'y ['kælə] *s* (*Zantedeschia aethiopica*) calla dei fioristi

call'boy' *s* (*in a hotel*) fattorino; (theat) buttafuori *m*

caller ['kɔlər] *s* visitatore *m*

call' girl' *s* ragazza squillo

calling ['kɔlɪŋ] *s* appello; professione

call'ing card' *s* biglietto da visita

call' num'ber *s* numero telefonico; numero di biblioteca

callous ['kæləs] *adj* calloso; insensibile

callow ['kælo] *adj* inesperto, immaturo

call' to arms' *s* chiamata alle armi

call' to the col'ors *s* chiamata sotto la bandiera

callus ['kæləs] *s* callo

calm [kɑm] *adj* calmo, tranquillo || *s* calma || *tr* calmare, tranquillizzare || *intr*—**to calm down** calmarsi; (*said of weather*) abbonacciarsi

calmness ['kɑmnɪs] *s* calma, placidità *f*, tranquillità *f*

calomel ['kælə,mɛl] *s* calomelano

calorie ['kæləri] *s* caloria

calum·ny ['kæləmni] *s* (**-nies**) calunnia

Calvary ['kælvəri] *s* (Bib) Calvario

cam [kæm] *s* camma

camber ['kæmbər] *s* curvatura; convessità *f* || *tr* arcuare || *intr* curvarsi

cambric ['kembrɪk] *s* cambrì *m*

camel ['kæməl] *s* cammello

came·o ['kæmi,o] *s* (**-os**) cammeo

camera ['kæmərə] *s* macchina fotografica; (mov) cinepresa

cam'era·man' *s* (**-men'**) operatore *m*

camomile ['kæmə,maɪl] *s* camomilla

camouflage ['kæmə,flɑʒ] *s* mascheramento || *tr* mascherare, camuffare

camp [kæmp] *s* accampamento, campo || *intr* accamparsi

campaign [kæm'pen] *s* campagna || *intr* fare una campagna

campaigner [kæm'penər] *s* veterano; (pol) propagandista *mf*

camp' bed' *s* letto da campo, branda

camper ['kæmpər] *s* campeggiatore *m*, campeggista *mf*

camp'fire' *s* fuoco di accampamento

camp'ground' *s* terreno per campeggio

camphor ['kæmfər] *s* canfora

camp'stool' *s* seggiolino pieghevole

campus ['kæmpəs] *s* campo, terreno dell'università

cam'shaft' *s* albero di distribuzione, albero a camme

can [kæn] *s* lattina, barattolo; (*of gasoline or oil*) bidone *m* || *v* (*pret & pp* **canned;** *ger* **canning**) *tr* inscatolare; (slang) licenziare || *v* (*pret & cond* **could**) *aux* I can speak **English** so parlare inglese; **can he go now?** se ne può andare ora?

Canada ['kænədə] *s* il Canadà

Canadian [kə'nedɪ·ən] *adj* & *s* canadese *mf*

canal [kə'næl] *s* canale *m*

canar·y [kə'neri] *s* (**-ies**) canarino || **Canaries** *spl* Canarie *fpl*

can·cel ['kænsəl] *v* (*pret & pp* **-celed** or **-celled;** *ger* **-celing** or **-celling**) *tr* cancellare; annullare; revocare; (*stamps*) timbrare, annullare

cancellation [,kænsə'leʃən] *s* cancellazione, annullamento; cassazione; (*of a stamp*) bollo

cancer ['kænsər] *s* cancro || **Cancer** *s* Cancro

cancerous ['kænsərəs] *adj* canceroso

candela·brum [,kændə'lɑbrəm] *s* (**-bra** [brə] or **-brums**) candelabro

candid ['kændɪd] *adj* candido; sincero, franco

candida·cy ['kændɪdəsi] *s* (**-cies**) candidatura

candidate ['kændɪ,det] *s* candidato; (*for a degree*) laureando

can'did cam'era *s* camera fotografica indiscreta

candied ['kændid] *adj* candito

candle ['kændəl] *s* candela || *tr* (*eggs*) sperare

can'dle·hold'er *s* var of **candlestick**

can'dle·light' *s* luce *f* or lume *m* di candela

can'dle·pow'er *s* (phys) candela

can'dle·stick' *s* (*ornate*) candeliere *m*; (*plain*) bugia

candor ['kændər] *s* candore *m*; ingenuità *f*

can·dy ['kændi] *s* (**-dies**) dolciumi *mpl*; **a piece of candy** un bombon || *v* (*pret & pp* **-died**) *tr* candire

can'dy box' *s* bomboniera

can'dy dish' *s* bomboniera; (*three-tier-high*) alzata

can'dy store' *s* confetteria

cane [ken] *s* canna, giunco; (*for walking*) bastone *m* || *tr* bastonare; (*chairs*) impagliare

cane' seat' *s* sedia impagliata

cane' sug'ar *s* zucchero di canna

canine ['kenaɪn] *adj* canino || *s* (*tooth*) canino; (dog) cane *m*

canister ['kænɪstər] *s* barattolo

canned' goods' *spl* conserve *fpl* alimentari; prodotti *mpl* in scatola

canned' mu'sic *s* (slang) musica su dischi

canner·y ['kænərɪ] *s* (**-ies**) fabbrica di conserve alimentari

cannibal ['kænɪbəl] *adj & s* cannibale *mf*, antropofago

canning ['kænɪŋ] *s* conservazione

cannon ['kænən] *s* cannone *m*

cannonade [ˌkænə'ned] *s* cannonata ‖ *tr* cannoneggiare

can'non-ball' *s* palla da cannone

can'non fod'der *s* carne *f* da cannone

can·ny ['kænɪ] *adj* (**-nier; -niest**) astuto, fino; malizioso

canoe [kə'nu] *s* canoa, piroga

canon ['kænən] *s* canone *m*; (*priest*) canonico

canonical [kə'nɑnɪkəl] *adj* canonico ‖ **canonicals** *spl* paramenti liturgici

canonize ['kænəˌnaɪz] *tr* canonizzare

can'on law' *s* diritto canonico

canon·ry ['kænənrɪ] *s* (**-ries**) canonicato

can' o'pener ['opənər] *s* apriscatole *m*

cano·py ['kænəpɪ] *s* (**-pies**) tenda; baldacchino; (*of sky*) (fig) volta

cant [kænt] *adj* ipocrita ‖ *s* linguaggio ipocrita; gergo; (*slope*) inclinazione

cantaloupe ['kæntəˌlop] *s* melone *m*

cantankerous [kæn'tæŋkərəs] *adj* bisbetico, attaccabrighe

canteen [kæn'tin] *s* cantina, spaccio; (*metal bottle*) borraccia

canter ['kæntər] *s* piccolo galoppo ‖ *intr* andare al piccolo galoppo

cantilever ['kæntɪˌlivər] *adj* a cantiliver ‖ *s* trave *f* a sbalzo; (archit) trave *f* a mensola

cantle ['kæntəl] *s* arcione *m* posteriore

canton ['kæn'tɑn] *s* cantone *m*; regione ‖ *tr* accantonare

cantonment [kæn'tɑnmənt] *s* accantonamentc

cantor ['kæntər] or ['kæntər] *s* cantore *m*

canvas ['kænvəs] *s* (*cloth*) olona; (*e.g. on open truck*) copertone *m*; (*painting*) tela; (naut) vela; **under canvas** (naut) a vele spiegate

canvass ['kænvəs] *s* discussione; dibattito; (pol) sollecitazione di voti ‖ *tr* discutere; (*votes*) sollecitare; (*to investigate*) indagare; (com) fare la piazza a ‖ *intr* discutere; sollecitare voti; indagare; (com) fare la piazza

canyon ['kænjən] *s* cañon *m*

cap [kæp] *s* berretto; cuffia; (*of academic costume*) berrettone *m*; (*of bottle*) tappo, capsula; (*e.g., of fountain pen*) cappuccio ‖ *v* (*pret & pp* **capped**; *ger* **capping**) *tr* (*a person*) coprire il capo di; (*s.o.'s head*) coprire con il berretto; (*a bottle*) mettere il tappo a; terminare; **to cap the climax** essere il colmo

capabili·ty [ˌkepə'bɪlɪtɪ] *s* (**-ties**) capacità *f*, abilità *f*

capable ['kepəbəl] *adj* capace, abile

capacious [kə'peʃəs] *adj* ampio, capace

capaci·ty [kə'pæsɪtɪ] *s* (**-ties**) capacità

f; **filled to capacity** pieno zeppo; **in the capacity of** in veste di

cap' and bells' *spl* berretto a sonagli; scettro di buffone

cap' and gown' *s* costume accademico, toga e tocco

caparison [kə'pærɪsən] *s* bardatura ‖ *tr* bardare

cape [kep] *s* cappa, mantello; (mil) mantella; (geog) capo

Cape' of Good' Hope' *s* Capo di Buona Speranza

caper ['kepər] *s* capriola; (bot) cappero; **to cut capers** far capriole; (fig) fare monellerie ‖ *intr* fare capriole; saltellare

Cape' Town' *s* Città *f* del Capo

capital ['kæpɪtəl] *adj* capitale ‖ *s* (*money*) capitale *m*; (*city*) capitale *f*; (*of column*) capitello

cap'ital expen'ditures *spl* spese *fpl* d'impianto

cap'ital goods' *spl* beni *mpl* strumentali

capitalism ['kæpɪtəˌlɪzəm] *s* capitalismo

capitalize ['kæpɪtəˌlaɪz] *tr* capitalizzare; scrivere con la maiuscola ‖ *intr*—**to capitalize on** approfittare di

cap'ital let'ter *s* lettera maiuscola

cap'ital pun'ishment *s* pena capitale

cap'ital stock' *s* capitale *m* sociale

capitol ['kæpɪtəl] *s* campidoglio

capitulate [kə'pɪtʃəˌlet] *intr* capitolare

capon ['kepan] *s* cappone *m*

caprice [kə'pris] *s* capriccio, ghiribizzo

capricious [kə'prɪʃəs] *adj* capriccioso, estroso

Capricorn ['kæprɪˌkɔrn] *s* Capricorno

capsize ['kæpsaɪz] *tr* capovolgere ‖ *intr* capovolgersi

capstan ['kæpstən] *s* argano

cap'stone' *s* (archit) coronamento

capsule ['kæpsəl] *adj* in miniatura; riassuntivo ‖ *s* capsula

captain ['kæptən] *s* capitano; (naut) comandante *m*; ‖ *tr* capitanare

caption ['kæp/ən] *s* titolo; (mov) didascalia; (journ) leggenda

captivate ['kæptɪˌvet] *tr* cattivare, affascinare

captive ['kæptɪv] *adj & s* prigioniero

captivi·ty ['kæp'tɪvɪtɪ] *s* (**-ties**) cattività *f*, prigionia

captor ['kæptər] *s* persona che cattura

capture ['kæptʃər] *s* cattura, presa; (*person*) prigioniero; (*thing*) bottino ‖ *tr* catturare; prendere

car [kɑr] *s* (*of train*) vagone *m*, vettura; (*automobile*) automobile *m & f*, macchina, vettura; (*of elevator*) cabina; (*of balloon*) navicella; (*for narrow-gauge track*) carrello

carafe [kə'ræf] *s* caraffa

caramel ['kærəməl] or ['kɑrməl] *s* (*burnt sugar*) caramello; (*candy*) caramella appicciaticcia

carat ['kærət] *s* carato

caravan ['kærəˌvæn] *s* carovana; (*covered vehicle*) furgone *m*

caravansa·ry [ˌkærə'vænsərɪ] *s* (**-ries**) caravanserraglio

caraway ['kærəˌwe] *s* cumino

car'barn' *s* rimessa del tram

carbide ['karbaɪd] s carburo

carbine ['karbaɪn] s carabina

carbol'ic ac'id [kar'balɪk] s acido fenico

carbon ['karbən] s (in arc light, battery, auto cylinder) carbone m; carta carbone; (chem) carbonio

car'bon cop'y s copia a carbone, velina

car'bon diox'ide s anidride carbonica

car'bon monox'ide s ossido di carbonio, monossido di carbonio

car'bon pa'per s carta carbone

carbuncle ['karbʌŋkəl] s (stone; boil) carbonchio; (boil) foruncolo

carburetor ['karbə,retər] or ['karbjə,retər] s carburatore m

carcass ['karkəs] s carcassa; (in state of decay) carogna

card [kard] s (file) scheda; (post card) cartolina; (personal card) biglietto; (announcement) partecipazione; (playing card) carta da gioco; (coll) tipo divertente, bel tipo

card'board' s cartone m

card'-car'rying mem'ber s tesserato

card' case' s portatessere m

card' cat'alogue s schedario

card'hold'er s socio, tesserato

cardiac ['kardɪ,æk] adj & s cardiaco

cardigan ['kardɪgən] s panciotto a maglia

cardinal ['kardɪnəl] adj cardinale, fondamentale || s cardinale m

card' in'dex s schedario

cardiogram ['kardɪ.o,græm] s cardiogramma m

card' par'ty s riunione per giocare a carte

card'sharp' s baro

card' ta'ble s tavoliere m, tavolino da gioco

card' trick' s gioco di prestigio colle carte

care [ker] s cura, custodia; inquietudine f, preoccupazione; cautela; **care of** presso, e.g., **R. Smith care of Jones** R. Smith presso Jones; **to take care** fare attenzione; **to take care of** prendersi cura di, badare a; **to take care of oneself** badare alla salute || intr curarsi, badare; **I don't care** non m'importa; **to care about** preoccuparsi di; **to care for** voler bene a; curarsi di; **to care to** volere

careen [kə'rin] s carenaggio || intr sbandare

career [kə'rir] adj di carriera || s carriera

care'free' adj spensierato

careful ['kerfəl] adj attento; diligente; premuroso; **careful!** faccia attenzione!

careless ['kerlɪs] adj trascurato; imprudente; indifferente

carelessness ['kerlɪsnɪs] s trascuratezza; imprudenza; indifferenza

caress [kə'res] s carezza || tr carezzare, accarezzare

caretaker ['ker,tekər] adj interinale, provvisorio || s custode m; guardiano; (of school) bidello

care'taker gov'ernment s governo interinale

care'worn' adj accasciato dalle preoccupazioni

car'fare' s passaggio, denaro per il tram; (small sum of money) spiccioli mpl

car-go ['kargo] s (-goes or -gos) carico mercantile

car'go boat' s battello da carico

Caribbean [,kærɪ'bi·ən] or [kə'rɪbɪ·ən] s Mare m dei Caraibi

caricature ['kærɪkətʃər] s caricatura || tr mettere in caricatura

carillon ['kærɪ,lan] or [kə'rɪljən] s carillon m || intr suonare il carillon

car'load' s vagone completo, vagonata

carnage ['karnɪdʒ] s carnaio, carneficina

carnal ['karnəl] adj carnale

carnation [kar'neʃən] adj incarnato || s garofano; (color) incarnato

carnival ['karnɪvəl] adj carnevalesco || s carnevale m; festa, spettacolo all'aperto

carob ['kærəb] s (fruit) carruba; (tree) carrubo

car-ol ['kærəl] s canzone f popolare; pastorella di Natale || v (pret & ger -oled or -olled; ger -oling or -olling) tr cantare

carom ['kærəm] s carambola || intr carambolare

carousal [kə'rauzəl] s baldoria, gozzoviglia

carouse [kə'rauz] intr fare baldoria, gozzovigliare

carousel [,kærə'zel] or [,kæru'zel] s giostra, carosello

carp ['karp] s carpa || intr lagnarsi, criticare

carpenter ['karpəntər] s falegname m

carpentry ['karpəntri] s falegnameria

carpet ['karpɪt] s tappeto || tr coprire con un tappeto, tappetare

carpetbagger ['karpɪt,bægər] s avventuriero; (hist) politicante m

car'pet sweep'er s spazzolone elettrico per tappeti

car'port' s tettoia-garage f

car'-ren'tal serv'ice s servizio di autonoleggi

carriage ['kærɪdʒ] s carrozza; (of gun) affusto; (of typewriter) carrello; (bearing) portamento; (mach) slitta

carrier ['kærɪ·ər] s portatore m; (person or organization in business of carrying goods) spedizioniere m; (of mail) postino; (e.g., on top of station wagon) portabagagli m; (of a disease) veicolo

car'rier pig'eon s piccione m viaggiatore

car'rier wave' s (rad) onda portante

carrion ['kærɪ·ən] s carogne fpl

carrot ['kærət] s carota

car-ry ['kæri] v (pret & pp -ried) tr portare; trasportare; (a burden) sopportare; (an election) guadagnare; (to keep in stock) avere in assortimento; **to carry along** portare con sé; **to carry away** trasportare; entusiasmare; **to carry forward** riportare; **to carry out** eseguire; **to carry**

through completare; **to carry weight** aver importanza || *intr* avere la portata (di), e.g., **this gun carries two miles** questo cannone ha la portata di due miglia; **to carry on** continuare; (coll) fare baccano

cart [kɑrt] *s* carro, carretto; (*for shopping*) carrello; **to put the cart before the horse** mettere il carro davanti ai buoi || *tr* trasportare col carro

carte blanche [ˈkɑrtˈblɑnʃ] *s* carta bianca

cartel [kɑrˈtɛl] *s* cartello

Carthage [ˈkɑrθɪdʒ] *s* Cartagine *f*

cart' horse' *s* cavallo da tiro

cartilage [ˈkɑrtɪlɪdʒ] *s* cartilagine *f*

carton [ˈkɑrtən] *s* cartone *m*; scatola di cartone; (*of cigarettes*) stecca

cartoon [kɑrˈtun] *s* disegno; caricatura; (*comic strip*) fumetto; (*mov*) disegno animato || *tr* fare caricature di

cartoonist [kɑrˈtunɪst] *s* disegnatore *m*; caricaturista *mf*

cartridge [ˈkɑrtrɪdʒ] *s* cartuccia; (*e.g., of camera*) caricatore *m*

car'tridge belt' *s* cartucciera; (mil) giberna

car'tridge clip' *s* serbatoio

cart'wheel' *s* ruota di carro; **to turn cartwheels** fare la ruota

carve [kɑrv] *tr* (*meats*) trinciare; scolpire, intagliare

carv'ing knife' *s* trinciante *m*

car' wash'er *s* lavamacchine *m*

cascade [kæsˈked] *s* cascata || *intr* cadere a mo' di cascata

case [kes] *s* (*box*) cassetta; (*of watch*) calotta; (*outer covering*) astuccio; (*instance*) caso; (gram) caso; (law) causa; (typ) cassa; **in case** in caso, nel caso; **in no case** in nessun modo || *tr* rinchiudere; (*to package*) impaccare; (slang) ispezionare

casement [ˈkesmənt] *s* telaio di finestra; finestra a gangheri

case' stud'y *s* casistica

cash [kæʃ] *s* contante *m*; **cash on delivery** spedizione contro assegno; **for cash** in contanti; **a pronta cassa** || *tr* (*a check*) cambiare, incassare || *intr* **—to cash in on** (coll) trarre profitto da

cash' box' *s* cassa

cashew [ˈkæʃu] *s* (*tree*) anacardio; (*nut*) mandorla indiana

cashier [kæˈʃɪr] *s* cassiere *m* || *tr* (*to dismiss*) silurare

cashier's' check' *s* assegno circolare

cash' reg'ister *s* registratore *m* cassa

casing [ˈkesɪŋ] *s* rivestimento; tubo di rivestimento; (*for salami*) budello; (*of tire*) copertone *m*

cask [kæsk] or [kɑsk] *s* barile *m*, botte *f*

casket [ˈkæskɪt] or [ˈkɑskɪt] *s* scrigno, cofanetto; (*coffin*) bara, cassa da morto

casserole [ˈkæsəˌrol] *s* tegame *m* di terracotta or vetro; (*food*) pasticcio, timballo

cassette [kəˈsɛt] *s* (mus) musicassetta; (mus & phot) caricatore *m*

cassock [ˈkæsək] *s* sottana, tonaca; **to doff the cassock** gettar la tonaca alle ortiche

cast [kæst] or [kɑst] *s* getto; lancio; forma; (mach) pezzo fuso; (surg) gesso; (theat) complesso artistico, cast *m* || *v* (*pret & pp* cast) *tr* gettare; fondere; (*a ballot*) dare; (*the roles*) distribuire; (*actors*) scegliere; **to cast aside** abbandonare; **to cast down** deprimere; **to cast lots** tirare a sorte; **to cast off** abbandonare; **to cast out** buttar fuori || *intr* tirare i dadi; **to cast off** (naut) mollare gli ormeggi

castanets [ˌkæstəˈnɛts] *spl* nacchere *fpl*

cast'a·way' *adj & s* naufrago; (fig) reprobo

caste [kæst] or [kɑst] *s* casta; **to lose caste** perdere prestigio

caster [ˈkæstər] or [ˈkɑstər] *s* ampollina, saliera, pepaiola; (*roller*) rotella per i mobili

castigate [ˈkæstɪˌget] *tr* castigare, punire; correggere

Castile [kæsˈtil] *s* (la) Castiglia

Castilian [kæsˈtɪljən] *adj & s* castigliano

casting [ˈkæstɪŋ] or [ˈkɑstɪŋ] *s* getto, getto fuso; (*in fishing*) pesca a getto

cast' i'ron *s* ghisa

cast'-i'ron *adj* fatto di ghisa; (*e.g., stomach*) fatto d'acciaio, di struzzo

castle [ˈkæsəl] or [ˈkɑsəl] *s* castello; (chess) torre *f* || *tr & intr* (chess) arroccare

cas'tle in Spain' or **cas'tle in the air'** *s* castello in aria

cast'off' *adj* abbandonato || *s* rigetto; persona abbandonata; (typ) stima

cas'tor oil' [ˈkæstər] or [ˈkɑstər] *s* olio di ricino

castrate [ˈkæstret] *tr* castrare

casual [ˈkæʒʊ·əl] *adj* casuale, fortuito; (*clothing*) semplice, sportivo

casually [ˈkæʒʊ·əli] *adv* con disinvoltura; (*by chance*) fortuitamente

casual·ty [ˈkæʒʊ·əlti] *s* (-ties) accidente *m*, disastro; vittima; **casualties** (*in war*) perdite *fpl*

casuist·ry [ˈkæʒʊ·ɪstri] *s* (-ries) (*specious reasoning*) speciosità *f*; (philos) casistica

cat [kæt] *s* gatto; donna perfida; **to let the cat out of the bag** lasciarsi scappare il segreto

cataclysm [ˈkætəˌklɪzəm] *s* cataclisma *m*

catacomb [ˈkætəˌkom] *s* catacomba

catalogue [ˈkætəˌlɔg] or [ˈkætəˌlɑg] *s* catalogo || *tr* catalogare

cat'alogue sale' *s* vendita per corrispondenza

catalyst [ˈkætəlɪst] *s* catalizzatore *m*

catapult [ˈkætəˌpʌlt] *s* catapulta || *tr* catapultare

cataract [ˈkætəˌrækt] *s* cataratta

catarrh [kəˈtɑr] *s* catarro

catastrophe [kəˈtæstrəfi] *s* catastrofe *f*, disastro

cat'call' s urlo di disapprovazione

catch [kætʃ] s presa; cattura; (of door) paletto; (in marriage) partito; (trick) inganno; (of fish) pesca; (mach) nottolino ‖ v (pret & pp **caught** [kɔt] tr prendere, acchiappare; (a cold) pigliare, buscarsi; **to catch hold of** afferrare; **to catch it** (coll) prendersele; **to catch oneself** contenersi; **to catch up** sorprendere sul fatto ‖ intr agganciarsi; (said of a disease) trasmettersi; **to catch on** capire l'antifona; **to catch up** mettersi al corrente; **to catch up with** raggiungere

catch'-as-catch'-can' s lotta libera americana

catch' ba'sin s ricettacolo di fogna

catcher ['kætʃər] s ricevitore m, catcher m

catching ['kætʃɪŋ] adj (alluring) seducente; (infectious) contagioso

catch'word' s slogan m; (typ) chiamata; (typ) esponente m in testa di pagina

catch•y ['kætʃi] adj (-ier; -iest) attraente, vivo; (tricky) insidioso

catechism ['kætɪ͵kɪzəm] s catechismo

catego•ry ['kætɪ͵gɔri] s (-ries) categoria

cater ['ketər] intr provvedere cibo; **to cater to** servire

cater-cornered ['ketər͵kɔrnərd] adj diagonale ‖ adv diagonalmente

caterer ['ketərər] s provveditore m

caterpillar ['kætər͵pɪlər] s bruco

cat'fish' s pesce m gatto

cat'gut' s (mus) corda di minugia; (surg) catgut m cattegù f

cathartic [kə'θartɪk] adj & s catartico

cathedral [kə'θidrəl] s cattedrale f

catheter ['kæθɪtər] s catetere m

catheterize ['kæθɪtə͵raɪz] tr cateterizzare

cathode ['kæθod] s catodo

catholic ['kæθəlɪk] adj cattolico; (e.g., mind) liberale ‖ **Catholic** adj & s cattolico

catkin ['kætkɪn] s (bot) amento, gattino

cat'nap' s corta siesta, sonnellino

cat-o'-nine-tails [͵kætə 'naɪn ͵telz] s gatto a nove code

cat's'-paw' s gonzo; (breeze) brezzolina

catsup ['kætsəp] or ['ketʃəp] s salsa piccante di pomodoro, ketchup m

cat'tail' s stiancia

cattle ['kætəl] s bestiame grosso

cat'tle•man s (-men) allevatore m di bestiame

cat•ty ['kæti] adj (-tier; -tiest) malizioso, maligno; felino, gattesco

cat'walk' s passerella, ballatoio

Caucasian [kɔ'keʒən] or [kɔ'keʃən] adj & s caucasico

caucus ['kɔkəs] s comitato elettorale; conciliabolo politico

cauldron ['kɔldrən] s calderone m

cauliflower ['kɔlɪ͵flauər] s cavolfiore m

caulk [kɔk] tr calafatare, stoppare

cause [kɔz] s causa, cagione f ‖ tr causare, cagionare; **to cause to** + inf

fare + inf, e.g., **she caused him to fall** l'ha fatto cadere

cause'way' s strada rialzata, scarpata

caustic ['kɔstɪk] adj caustico

cauterize ['kɔtə͵raɪz] tr cauterizzare

caution ['kɔʃən] s cautela, prudenza; ammonizione f ‖ tr ammonire

cautious ['kɔʃəs] adj prudente

cavalcade ['kævəl͵ked] or [͵kævəl-'ked] s cavalcata

cavalier [͵kævə'lɪr] or ['kævə ͵lɪr] adj altero, sdegnoso; disinvolto ‖ s cavaliere m

caval•ry ['kævəlri] s (-ries) cavalleria

cav'alry•man' or **cav'alry•man** s (-men' or -men) cavalleggero, soldato di cavalleria

cave [kev] s caverna, grotta ‖ intr— **to cave in** sprofondarsi; (to give in) (coll) cedere; (to become exhausted) (coll) diventare spossato

cave'-in' s sprofondamento

cave'man' s troglodita m

cavern ['kævərn] s caverna

caviar ['kævɪ͵ar] or [͵kævɪ'ar] s caviale m

ca•vil ['kævɪl] v (pret & pp -iled or -illed; ger -iling or -illing) intr cavillare

cav•ity ['kævɪti] s (-ties) cavità f; (in tooth) carie f

cavort [kə'vɔrt] intr far capriole

caw [kɔ] s gracchiamento ‖ intr gracchiare

cease [sis] tr cessare, interrompere ‖ intr cessare, interrompersi; **to cease** + ger cessare di + inf

cease'fire' s sospensione delle ostilità

ceaseless ['sislɪs] adj incessante

cedar ['sidər] s cedro; legno di cedro

cede [sid] tr cedere, trasferire

ceiling ['silɪŋ] s soffitto; (aer) altezza massima; **to hit the ceiling** (slang) uscire dai gangheri

ceil'ing price' s calmiere m, tetto

celebrate ['selɪ ͵bret] adj celebrare ‖ intr celebrare; far festa

celebrated ['selɪ ͵bretɪd] adj celebre, famoso

celebration [͵selɪ'breʃən] s celebrazione

celebri•ty [sɪ'lɛbrɪti] s (-ties) celebrità f

celery ['sɛləri] s sedano

celestial [sɪ'lɛstʃəl] adj celestiale, celeste

celibacy ['sɛləbəsi] s celibato

celibate ['sɛlə ͵bet] or ['sɛləbɪt] adj & s celibe m; nubile f

cell [sɛl] s (e.g., of jail) cella; (of electric battery) elemento; (biol, phys, pol) cellula

cellar ['sɛlər] s cantina; (partly above ground) seminterrato

cellist or **'cellist** ['tʃɛlɪst] s violoncellista mf

cel•lo or **'cel•lo** ['tʃɛlo] s(-los) violoncello

cellophane ['sɛlə ͵fɛn] s cellofan m

celluloid ['sɛljə͵lɔɪd] s celluloide f

Celtic ['sɛltɪk] or ['kɛltɪk] adj celtico ‖ s lingua celtica cement [sɪ'ment] s cemento || tr cementare

cemete·ry ['sɛmɪ‚tɛri] s (-ries) cimitero

censer ['sɛnsər] s turibolo

censor ['sɛnsər] s censore m || tr censurare

censure ['sɛnʃər] s censura, critica || tr censurare, criticare

census ['sɛnsəs] s censo, censimento

cent [sɛnt] s centesimo di dollaro, cent m; not to have a red cent to one's name non avere il becco di un quattrino

centaur ['sɛntɔr] s centauro

centennial [sɛn'tɛnɪ·əl] adj & s centenario

center ['sɛntər] s centro || tr centrare, concentrare || intr—to center on concentrarsi su

cen'ter·board' s chiglia mobile

cen'ter·piece' s centro tavola

cen'ter punch' s punzone m, punteruolo

centigrade ['sɛntɪ‚gred] adj centigrado

centimeter ['sɛntɪ‚mitər] s centimetro

centipede ['sɛntɪ‚pid] s centopiedi m

cento ['sɛnto] s centone m

central ['sɛntrəl] adj centrale || s centrale f, centrale telefonica; (operator) telefonista mf

Cen'tral Amer'ica s l'America Centrale

centralize ['sɛntrə‚laɪz] tr centralizzare || intr centralizzarsi

centu·ry ['sɛntʃəri] s (-ries) secolo

ceramic [sɪ'ræmɪk] adj ceramico || ceramics ssg ceramica; spl oggetti mpl di ceramica

cereal ['sɪrɪ·əl] adj cerealicolo || s (grain) cereale m; (uncooked breakfast food, e.g., cornflakes) fiocchi mpl; (breakfast food to be cooked) farina

cerebral ['sɛrɪbrəl] adj cerebrale

ceremonious [‚sɛrɪ'monɪ·əs] adj cerimonioso

ceremo·ny ['sɛrɪ‚moni] s (-nies) cerimonia; to stand on ceremony fare cerimonie

certain ['sʌrtən] adj certo; for certain di o per certo; to be certain to + inf non mancare di + inf

certainly ['sʌrtənli] adv certamente, (gladly) con piacere

certain·ty ['sʌrtənti] s (-ties) certezza

certificate [sər'tɪfɪkɪt] s certificato; (com) titolo || [sər'tɪfɪ‚ket] tr certificare

cer'tified check' s assegno a copertura garantita

cer'tified cop'y s estratto; (as a formula on a document) per copia conforme

cer'tified pub'lic account'ant s esperto contabile

certi·fy ['sʌrtɪ‚faɪ] v (pret & pp -fied) tr certificare, garantire

cervix ['sʌrvɪks] s (cervices [sər'vaɪsiz] cervice f

cessation [sɛ'seʃən] s cessazione

cesspool ['sɛs‚pul] s pozzo nero

Ceylo·nese [‚silə'niz] adj & s (-nese) singalese mf

chafe [tʃef] s irritazione || tr (the hands) strofinare; irritare; (to wear away) logorare || intr irritarsi; logorarsi

chaff [tʃæf] or [tʃɑf] s lolla; pula; (joke) burla; (fig) loppa

chaf'ing dish' s fornello a spirito

cha·grin [ʃə'grɪn] s cruccio, dispiacere m || v (pret -grined or -grinned; ger -grining or -grinning) tr crucciare, affliggere

chain [tʃen] s catena; (e.g., for necklace) catenella || tr incatenare

chain' gang' s catena di forzati

chain' reac'tion s reazione a catena

chain' saw' s motosega

chain'-smoke' intr fumare come un turco

chain' store' s negozio a catena

chair [tʃer] s sedia, seggiola; (of important person) seggio; (at a university) cattedra; (chairman) presidente m, presidenza; to take the chair cominciare una riunione || tr (a meeting) presiedere

chair' lift' s seggiovia

chair'man s (-men) presidente m

chair'man·ship' s presidenza

chair'wom'an s (-wom-en) presidentessa

chalice ['tʃælɪs] s calice m

chalk [tʃɔk] s gesso || tr marcare o scrivere col gesso; to chalk up prendere appunti di; attribuire

chalk' talk' s conferenza illustrata

chalk·y ['tʃɔki] adj (-ier; -iest) gessoso

challenge ['tʃælɪndʒ] s sfida; (law) ricusazione; (mil) chi va là m || tr sfidare; (a juror) (law) ricusare; (mil) dare il chi va là a

chamber ['tʃembər] s camera, stanza; (of a palace) aula; (of a judge) gabinetto

chamberlain ['tʃembərlɪn] s ciambellano

cham'ber·maid' s cameriera

cham'ber of com'merce s camera di commercio

cham'ber pot' s orinale m

chameleon [kə'mili·ən] s camaleonte m

cham·ois ['ʃæmi] s (-ois) camoscio

champ [tʃæmp] s (slang) campione m || tr masticare rumorosamente; (the bit) mordere || intr masticare rumorosamente

champagne [ʃæm'pen] s champagne m, spumante m

champion ['tʃæmpɪ·ən] s campione m || tr difendere; farsi paladino di

championship ['tʃæmpɪ·ən‚ʃɪp] s campionato

chance [tʃæns] or [tʃɑns] adj casuale, fortuito || s occasione; caso; probabilità f; rischio; biglietto di lotteria; by chance per caso; not to stand a chance non avere la probabilità di riuscita; to take one's chances arrischiarsi; to wait for a chance attendere l'opportunità || intr succedere; to chance upon imbattersi in

chancel ['tʃænsəl] or ['tʃɑnsəl] s presbiterio, coro

chancellery ['tʃænsələri] or ['tʃɑnsələri] s (-ies) cancelleria

chancellor [ˈtʃænsələr] or [ˈtʃɑnsələr] s cancelliere m

chandelier [ˌʃændəˈlir] s lampadario

change [tʃendʒ] s cambiamento; (of clothes) muta; (of currency) cambio; (coins) spiccioli mpl; **for a change** tanto per cambiare; **to keep the change** tenere il resto || tr cambiare, rimpiazzare; (clothes) cambiare, cambiarsi di || intr cambiare, mutare

changeable [ˈtʃendʒəbəl] adj mutevole, variabile, incostante

change' of heart' s pentimento, conversione

change' of life' s menopausa

chan·nel [ˈtʃænəl] s canale m; tubo, passaggio; stretto; (of river) alveo; (groove) solco; (rad, telv) canale m; **through channels** per via gerarchica || v (pret & pp -neled or -nelled) ger -neling or -nelling) tr incanalare; (a river) incassare || **the Channel** il Canale della Manica

chant [tʃænt] or [tʃɑnt] s canto; salmodia; canzone f || tr & intr cantare

chanticleer [ˈtʃænˌklɪr] s il gallo

chaos [ˈkeˌɑs] s caos m

chaotic [keˈɑtɪk] adj caotico

chap [tʃæp] s (fellow) individuo, tipo; (of skin) screpolatura; **chaps** pantaloni mpl di cuoio || v (pret & pp chapped; ger chapping) tr screpolare || intr screpolarsi

chapel [ˈtʃæpəl] s cappella

chaperon or **chaperone** [ˈʃæpəˌron] s accompagnatrice f (di signorina) || tr accompagnare

chaplain [ˈtʃæplɪn] s cappellano

chaplet [ˈtʃæplɪt] s (wreath) corona, ghirlanda; rosario

chapter [ˈtʃæptər] s capitolo; (of a club) sezione

chap'ter and verse' s—**to give chapter and verse** citare le autorità

char [tʃɑr] v (pret & pp charred; ger charring) tr carbonizzare; bruciare

character [ˈkærɪktər] s carattere m; lettera, scrittura; indole f; (theat) personaggio; (coll) tipo; **in character** caratteristico di lui (lei, loro, etc.)

char'acter ac'tor s caratterista m

char'acter ac'tress s caratterista f

char'acter assassina'tion s linciaggio morale

characteristic [ˌkærɪktəˈrɪstɪk] adj caratteristico || s caratteristica

characterize [ˈkærɪktəˌraɪz] tr caratterizzare

char'coal' s carbone m di legna, carbone m dolce; (for sketching) carboncino; (sketch) disegno al carboncino

charge [tʃɑrdʒ] s carica; incarico; responsabilità f; (indictment) accusa; costo; prezzo; debito; **in charge** in comando; **in charge of** a cura di; **to take charge of** prendersi cura di || tr caricare; comandare; accusare; (a price) fare pagare; mettere in conto; **to charge s.o. with s.th** addebitare qlco a qlcu; accusare qlcu di qlco || intr fare una carica

charge' account' s conto corrente

chargé d'affaires [ʃɑrˈʒe dəˈfɛr] s (chargés d'affaires) incaricato d'affari

charger [ˈtʃɑrdʒər] s cavallo di battaglia; (of a battery) caricatore m

chariot [ˈtʃærɪ·ət] s cocchio

charioteer [ˌtʃærɪ·əˈtɪr] s auriga m

charis·ma [kəˈrɪzmə] s (-mata [mətə]) fascino personale; (theol) carisma m

charitable [ˈtʃærɪtəbəl] adj (person) caritatevole; (institution) caritativo

chari·ty [ˈtʃærɪti] s (-ties) carità f; associazione di beneficenza

charlatan [ˈʃɑrlətən] s ciarlatano

charlatanism [ˈʃɑrlətənˌɪzəm] s ciarlataneria

Charlemagne [ˈʃɑrləˌmen] s Carlomagno

Charles [tʃɑrlz] s Carlo

char'ley horse' [ˈtʃɑrli] s (coll) crampo

charlotte [ˈʃɑrlət] s charlotte f || **Charlotte** s Carlotta

charm [tʃɑrm] s fascino; amuleto; portafortuna m || tr incantare, stregare

charming [ˈtʃɑrmɪŋ] adj affascinante

charnel [ˈtʃɑrnəl] adj orribile || s ossario

chart [tʃɑrt] s carta geografica; lista; diagramma m || tr tracciare

charter [ˈtʃɑrtər] s statuto; privilegio || tr (a company) fondare; (a conveyance) noleggiare

char'ter mem'ber s socio fondatore

char'wom'an s (-wom'en) domestica per la pulizia

chase [tʃes] s inseguimento; caccia; (typ) telaio || tr inseguire; cacciare; (to chisel) cesellare; **to chase away** scacciare || intr—**to chase after** inseguire

chaser [ˈtʃesər] s cacciatore m; (coll) bibita da bersi dopo un liquore

chasm [ˈkæzəm] s abisso, baratro

chas·sis [ˈtʃæsi] s (-sis [siz]) telaio

chaste [tʃest] adj casto

chasten [ˈtʃesən] tr castigare

chastise [tʃæsˈtaɪz] tr castigare

chastity [ˈtʃæstɪti] s castità f

chat [tʃæt] s chiacchierata || v (pret & pp chatted; ger chatting) intr chiacchierare

chatelaine [ˈʃætəˌlen] s castellana

chattels [ˈtʃætəlz] spl beni mpl mobili

chatter [ˈtʃætər] s cicaleccio; balbettio; (of teeth) battito || intr cicalare; balbettare; (said of teeth) battere

chat'ter·box' s chiacchierone m

chauffeur [ˈʃofər] or [ʃoˈfʌr] s autista mf || intr fare l'autista

cheap [tʃip] adj a buon mercato, economico; (of poor quality) scadente; **to feel cheap** vergognarsi || adv a buon mercato

cheapen [ˈtʃipən] tr deprezzare; avvilire; rendere di cattivo gusto

cheapness [ˈtʃipnəs] s buon mercato, prezzo basso

cheat [tʃit] s truffa; truffatore m || tr imbrogliare, truffare || intr truffare; (at cards) barare

check [tʃɛk] s arresto, pausa; ostacolo;

esame *m;* verifica, controllo; (*of bank*) assegno; (*for baggage*) tagliando, scontrino; (*square pattern*) quadretto; (*fabric in squares*) tessuto a scacchi; (*in a restaurant*) conto; **in check** controllato, sotto controllo; (*chess*) sotto scacco || *tr* fermare; confrontare; ispezionare; marcare; (*e.g., a coat*) depositare; disegnare a quadretti; (*chess*) dare scacco a; **to check off** controllare marcando; **to check on** controllare, verificare || *intr* fermarsi; corrispondere perfettamente; **to check in** scendere (a un albergo); **to check out** andar via; pagare il conto; **to check up on** controllare

check′book′ *s* libretto d'assegni

checker [′t∫ɛkər] *s* ispettore *m;* quadretto; (*in game of checkers*) pedina; **checkers** dama || *tr* variegare; marcare a quadretti

check′er·board′ *s* scacchiera

check′ered *adj* (*e.g., career*) pieno di vicissitudini; (*marked with squares*) a scacchi; (*in color*) variegato

check′ing account′ *s* conto corrente

check′mate′ *s* scacco matto || *tr* dare scacco matto a || *interj* scacco matto!

check′off′ dues′ *spl* trattenute *fpl* sindacali

check′-out′ *s* (*from hotel room*) partenza; (*time*) ora della partenza; (*examination*) esame *m* di controllo; (*in a supermarket*) cassa

check′point′ *s* punto di ispezione

check′room′ *s* guardaroba *m*

check′up′ *s* (*of car*) ispezione; (*of patient*) esame *m* (fisico)

cheek [t∫ik] *s* guancia, gota; (coll) faccia tosta

cheek′bone′ *s* zigomo

cheek·y [′t∫iki] *adj* (**-ier; -iest**) (coll) impudente, sfacciato

cheer [t∫ɪr] *s* gioia, allegria; applauso; **of good cheer** di buon umore || *tr* riempire di gioia, rallegrare; applaudire; ricevere con applausi || *intr* rallegrarsi; **cheer up!** animo!, coraggio!

cheerful [′t∫ɪrfəl] *adj* allegro, di buon umore; (*willing*) volonteroso

cheerless [′t∫ɪrlɪs] *adj* tetro, triste

cheese [t∫iz] *s* formaggio || *intr*—**cheese it!** (slang) scappa via!

cheese′ cake′ *s* torta di formaggio; (slang) pin-up girl *f*

cheese′cloth′ *s* etamine *f,* stamigna

chees·y [t∫izi] *adj* (**-ier; -iest**) di formaggio; come il formaggio; (slang) meschino, di cattiva qualità

chef [∫ɛf] *s* chef *m,* capocuoco

chemical [′kɛmɪkəl] *adj* chimico || *s* prodotto chimico

chemise [∫ə′miz] *s* sottoveste *f*

chemist [′kɛmɪst] *s* chimico

chemistry [′kɛmɪstri] *s* chimica

cherish [′t∫ɛrɪʃ] *tr* accarezzare; (*a memory*) custodire; (*a hope*) nutrire

cher·ry [′t∫ɛri] *s* (**-ries**) (*tree*) ciliegio; (*fruit*) ciliegia

cher·ub [′t∫ɛrəb] *s* (**-ubim** [əbɪm] & **-ubs**) cherubino

chess [t∫ɛs] *s* scacchi *mpl*

chess′board′ *s* scacchiera

chess′man′ or **chess′man** *s* (**-men′** or **-men**) scacco

chest [t∫ɛst] *s* petto; (*box*) cassapanca; (*furniture with drawers*) cassettone *m;* (*for money*) forziere *m*

chestnut [′t∫ɛsnət] *s* (*tree, wood, color*) castagno; (*nut*) castagna

chest′ of drawers′ *s* cassettone *m*

cheval′ glass′ [∫ə′væl] *s* psiche *f*

chevalier [,∫ɛvə′lɪr] *s* cavaliere *m*

chevron [′∫ɛvrən] *s* gallone *m*

chew [t∫u] *tr* masticare; **to chew the cud** ruminare; **to chew the rag** (slang) chiacchierare || *intr* masticare

chew′ing gum′ *s* gomma da masticare

chic [∫ik] *adj* & *s* chic

chicaner·y [∫ɪ′kɛnəri] *s* (**-ies**) trucco, rigiro

chick [t∫ɪk] *s* pulcino; (slang) ragazza

chicken [′t∫ɪkən] *s* pollo, pollastro; (coll) giovane *mf;* **to be chicken** (slang) avere la fifa || *intr*—**to chicken out** (coll) indietreggiare

chick′en coop′ *s* pollaio

chick′en feed′ *s* (slang) spiccioli *mpl*

chicken-hearted [′t∫ɪkən ,hɑrtɪd] *adj* timido, fifone

chick′en pox′ *s* varicella

chick′en store′ *s* polleria

chick′en wire′ *s* rete metallica esagonale

chick′pea′ *s* cece *m*

chico·ry [′t∫ɪkəri] *s* (**-ries**) cicoria

chide [t∫aɪd] *v* (*pret* **chided** or **chid** [t∫ɪd]; *pp* **chided, chid,** or **chidden** [′t∫ɪdən]) *tr* & *intr* rimproverare, correggere

chief [t∫if] *adj* principale, sommo, supremo || *s* capo, comandante supremo; (slang) padrone *m*

chief′ exec′utive *s* capo del governo

chief′ jus′tice *s* presidente *m* di una corte; presidente *m* della corte suprema

chiefly [′t∫ifli] *adv* principalmente

chief′ of staff′ *s* capo di stato maggiore

chief′ of state′ *s* capo dello stato

chieftain [′t∫iftən] *s* capo

chiffon [∫ɪ′fɑn] *s* velo trasparente, chiffon *m;* **chiffons** trine *fpl*

chiffonier [,∫ɪfə′nɪr] *s* mobile *m* a cassettini, chiffonier *m*

chilblain [′t∫ɪl ,blen] *s* gelone *m*

child [t∫aɪld] *s* (**children** [′t∫ɪldrən]) bebè *mf,* bambino; figlio; discendente *mf;* **with child** incinta

child′birth′ *s* parto

childhood [′t∫aɪldhʊd] *s* infanzia

childish [′t∫aɪldɪʃ] *adj* infantile

childishness [′t∫aɪldɪnɪs] *s* puerilità *f,* infanzia

child′ la′bor *s* lavoro dei minorenni

childless [′t∫aɪldlɪs] *adj* senza figli

child′like′ *adj* infantile, innocente

child′s′ play′ *s* un gioco

child′ wel′fare *s* protezione dell'infanzia

Chile [′t∫ɪli] *s* il Cile

Chilean [′t∫ɪlɪ·ən] *adj* cileno

chil'i sauce' [ˈtʃɪli] s salsa di pomodoro con peperoni

chill [tʃɪl] adj freddo || s freddo; brivido di freddo; freddezza; (depression) abbattimento || tr raffreddare || (a metal) temprare; (fig) scoraggiare || intr raffreddarsi

chill·y [ˈtʃɪli] adj (-ier; -iest) fresco, freddiccio; (reception) freddo

chime [tʃaɪm] s scampanio; **chimes** campanello || intr scampanare; **to chime in** cominciare a cantare all'unisono; (coll) intromettersi

chime' clock' s orologio con carillon

chimney [ˈtʃɪmni] s camino; (of factory) ciminiera; **to smoke like a chimney** fumare come un turco

chim'ney flue' s tubo di stufa, canna del camino

chim'ney pot' s testa della canna fumaria, comignolo

chim'ney sweep' s spazzacamino

chimpanzee [tʃɪmˈpænzi] or [ˌtʃɪmpænˈzi] s scimpanzé m

chin [tʃɪn] s mento; **to keep one's chin up** (coll) non perdersi di coraggio; **to take it on the chin** (slang) subire una sconfitta || v (pret & pp **chinned**; ger **chinning**) tr—**to chin oneself** sollevarsi fino al mento (ai manubri) || intr (slang) chiacchierare

china [ˈtʃaɪnə] s porcellana || **China** s la Cina

chi'na clos'et s armadio per le stoviglie

chi'na-ware' s porcellana, stoviglie fpl

Chi·nese [tʃaɪˈniz] adj cinese || s (-nese) cinese mf

Chi'nese lan'tern s lampioncino alla veneziana

Chi'nese puz'zle s rebus m

chink [tʃɪŋk] s fessura

chin' strap' s sottogola

chintz [tʃɪnts] s chintz m

chip [tʃɪp] s scheggia; frammento; (in card games) gettone m; (of wood) truciolo; **chip off the old block** vero figlio di suo padre (di sua madre); **chip on one's shoulder** propensità f a attaccar brighe || v (pret & pp **chipped**; ger **chipping**) tr scheggiare; **to chip in** contribuire || intr scheggiarsi

chipmunk [ˈtʃɪpˌmʌŋk] s tamia

chipper [ˈtʃɪpər] adj (coll) allegro, vivo

chiropodist [kaɪˈrɑpədɪst] or [kɪˈrɑpədɪst] s callista mf, pedicure mf

chiropractic [ˌkaɪrəˈpræktɪs] s chiropratica

chirp [tʃʌrp] s (of birds) cinguettio; (of crickets) cri cri m || intr cinguettare; fare cri cri

chis·el [ˈtʃɪzəl] s (for wood and metal) scalpello; (for metal) cesello || v (pret & pp -eled or -elled; ger -eling or -elling) tr scalpellare; cesellare; (slang) imbrogliare || intr (slang) imbrogliare, fare l'imbroglione

chiseler [ˈtʃɪzələr] s scalpellino; cesellatore m; (slang) imbroglione m

chit-chat [ˈtʃɪtˌtʃæt] s chiacchierata

chivalrous [ˈʃɪvəlrəs] adj cavalleresco

chivalry [ˈʃɪvəlri] s cavalleria

chive [tʃaɪv] s cipolla porraia

chloride [ˈklɔraɪd] s cloruro

chlorine [ˈklɔrin] s cloro

chloroform [ˈklɔrəˌfɔrm] s cloroformio || tr cloroformizzare

chlorophyll [ˈklɔrəfɪl] s clorofilla

chock [tʃɑk] s (wedge) bietta, cuneo

chock-full [ˈtʃɑkˈful] adj colmo, pieno zeppo

chocolate [ˈtʃɔkəlɪt] or [ˈtʃɑkəlɪt] s (candy) cioccolato; (drink) cioccolata

choc'olate bar' s barretta di cioccolato

choice [tʃɔɪs] adj di prima scelta, superiore || s scelta; (variety) assortimento

choir [kwaɪr] s coro

choir'boy' s ragazzo cantore

choir' loft' s coro

choir'mas'ter s maestro di cappella

choke [tʃok] s strozzatura; (aut) farfalla del carburatore || tr strozzare; ostruire; (an internal-combustion engine) arricchire la miscela di; **to choke back** trattenere; **to choke up** tappare, ostruire || intr soffocarsi; **to choke up** tapparsi; (coll) soffocarsi

choker [ˈtʃokər] s (necklace) (coll) collana; (scarf) (coll) foulard m

cholera [ˈkɑlərə] s colera m

choleric [ˈkɑlərɪk] adj collerico

cholesterol [kəˈlestəˌrol] or [kəˈlestəˌrɑl] s colesterina

choose [tʃuz] v (pret **chose** [tʃoz]; pp **chosen** [ˈtʃozən]) tr scegliere || intr—**to choose to** decidere di

choos·y [ˈtʃuzi] adj (-ier; -iest) (coll) di difficile contentatura

chop [tʃɑp] s colpo; (of meat) coletta; **chops** labbra fpl, bocca || v (pret & pp **chopped**; ger **chopping**) tr tagliare; (meat) tritare; **to chop off** troncare; **to chop up** sminuzzare

chopper [ˈtʃɑpər] s (man) tagliatore m; interruttore automatico; coltello da macellaio; (slang) elicottero; **choppers** (slang) i denti

chop'ping block' s tagliere m

chop·py [ˈtʃɑpi] adj (-pier; -piest) (wind) variabile; (sea) agitato; (style) instabile

choral [ˈkorəl] adj & s corale m

chorale [koˈrɑl] s corale m

chord [kɔrd] s corda; (mus) accordo

chore [tʃor] s lavoro; lavoro spiacevole; **chores** faccende domestiche

choreography [ˌkɔriˈɑgrəfi] s coreografia

chorine [koˈrin] s (slang) ballerina

chorus [ˈkorəs] s coro; (group of dancers) corpo di ballo; (of a song) ritornello

cho'rus girl' s ballerina

cho'rus man' s (men') corista m

chow [tʃau] s (dog) chow chow m; (slang) cibo, pappa

chowder [ˈtʃaudər] s zuppa di vongole; zuppa di pesce

Christ [kraɪst] s Cristo

christen [ˈkrɪsən] tr battezzare

Christendom [ˈkrɪsəndəm] s cristianità f

christening ['krɪsənɪŋ] *s* battesimo
Christian ['krɪstʃən] *adj* & *s* cristiano
Christianity [,krɪstʃɪ'ænɪtɪ] *s* (*Christendom*) cristianità *f*; (*religion*) cristianesimo
Chris'tian name' *s* nome *m* di battesimo
Christmas ['krɪsməs] *adj* natalizio || *s* Natale *m*; **Merry Christmas!** Buon Natale!
Christ'mas card' *s* cartoncino natalizio
Christ'mas car'ol *s* pastorella di Natale
Christ'mas Eve' *s* vigilia di Natale
Christ'mas gift' *s* strenna natalizia
Christ'mas tree' *s* albero di Natale
chrome [krom] *adj* cromato || *s* cromo || *tr* cromare
chromium ['kromɪ·əm] *s* cromo
chromosome ['kromə,som] *s* cromosoma *m*
chronic ['krɑnɪk] *adj* cronico
chronicle ['krɑnɪkəl] *s* cronaca || *tr* fare la storia di
chronicler ['krɑnɪklər] *s* cronista *mf*
chronolo·gy [krə'nɑlədʒɪ] *s* (-gies) cronologia
chronometer [krə'nɑmɪtər] *s* cronometro
chrysanthemum [krɪ'sænθɪməm] *s* crisantemo
chub·by ['tʃʌbi] *adj* (-bier; -biest) paffuto
chuck [tʃʌk] *s* buffetto sotto il mento; (*cut of meat*) reale *m*; (*of lathe*) coppaia || *tr* accarezzare sotto il mento; (*to throw*) (coll) gettare
chuckle ['tʃʌkəl] *s* risatina || *intr* ridacchiare
chum [tʃʌm] *s* (coll) amico intimo; (coll) compagno di stanza || *v* (*pret* & *pp* chummed; *ger* chumming) *intr* (coll) essere amico intimo; essere compagno di stanza
chum·my ['tʃʌmi] *adj* (-mier; -miest) (coll) intimo, amicone
chump [tʃʌmp] *s* ciocco, ceppo; (coll) sciocco
chunk [tʃʌŋk] *s* grosso pezzo
church [tʃʌrtʃ] *s* chiesa
churchgoer ['tʃʌrtʃ,go·ər] *s* praticante *mf*
church'man *s* (-men) parrocchiano; (*clergyman*) sacerdote *m*
Church' of Eng'land *s* chiesa anglicana
church'yard' *s* camposanto
churl [tʃʌrl] *s* zotico, villano
churlish ['tʃʌrlɪʃ] *adj* villano
churn [tʃʌrn] *s* zangola || *tr* agitare violentemente, sbattere || *intr* (*said of water*) ribollire
chute [ʃut] *s* piano inclinato, canna; (*in a river*) cascata, rapida; paracadute *m*; (*into a swimming pool*) toboga *m*
Cicero ['sɪsə,ro] *s* Cicerone *m*
cider ['saɪdər] *s* sidro
cigar [sɪ'gɑr] *s* sigaro
cigar' case' *s* portasigari *m*
cigar' cut'ter *s* tagliasigari *m*
cigarette [,sɪgə'rɛt] *s* sigaretta
cigarette' butt' *s* cicca
cigarette' case' *s* portasigarette *m*
cigarette' hold'er *s* bocchino

cigarette' light'er *s* accendisigaro, accendino
cigarette' pa'per *s* cartina da sigarette
cigar' store' *s* tabaccheria, rivendita di sali e tabacchi
cinch [sɪntʃ] *s* (*on a horse*) sottopancia *m*; (*hold*) (coll) presa; (slang) giochetto || *tr* legare con una cinghia; (slang) agguantare
cinder ['sɪndər] *s* tizzone *m*; (*slag*) scoria; **cinders** cenere *f*
cin'der block' *s* concio di scoria
Cinderella [,sɪndə'rɛlə] *s* (la) Cenerentola
cinema ['sɪnəmə] *s* cine *m*, cinema *m*
cinnabar ['sɪnə,bɑr] *s* cinabro
cinnamon ['sɪnəmən] *s* cannella
cipher ['saɪfər] *s* zero; cifra; codice *m*; monogramma *m* || *tr* calcolare; (*to write in code*) cifrare
circle ['sʌrkəl] *s* cerchio; (*of theater*) prima galleria; (*of friends*) cerchia || *tr* cerchiare, compiere una rotazione intorno a
circuit ['sʌrkɪt] *s* circuito; (*district*) circoscrizione
cir'cuit break'er *s* salvamotore *m*, interruttore automatico
circuitous [sər'kju·ɪtəs] *adj* tortuoso
circuitry ['sʌrkɪtrɪ] *s* (*plan*) schema *m* di montaggio; (*components*) elementi *mpl* di un circuito
circular ['sʌrkjələr] *adj* & *s* circolare *f*
circulate ['sʌrkjə,let] *tr* mettere in circolazione, diffondere || *intr* circolare
cir'culating li'brary *s* biblioteca circolante
circulation [,sʌrkjə'leʃən] *s* circolazione; (*of newspaper*) diffusione
circumcise ['sʌrkəm,saɪz] *tr* circoncidere
circumference [sər'kʌmfərəns] *s* circonferenza
circumflex ['sʌrkəm,flɛks] *adj* circonflesso || *s* accento circonflesso
circumscribe [,sʌrkəm'skraɪb] *tr* circoscrivere
circumspect ['sʌrkəm,spɛkt] *adj* circospetto
circumstance ['sʌrkəm,stæns] *s* circostanza; (*fact*) dettaglio; solennità *f*; **circumstances** condizioni *fpl*; dettagli *mpl*; condizioni economiche; **under no circumstances** a nessuna condizione; **under the circumstances** le cose essendo come sono
circumstantial [,sʌrkəm'stænʃəl] *adj* circostanziale, indiziario; (*incidental*) secondario; (*complete*) circostanziato
cir'cumstan'tial ev'idence *s* prova indiziaria
circumstantiate [,sʌrkəm'stænʃɪ,et] *tr* (*to support with particulars*) comprovare; (*to describe in detail*) circonstanziare
circumvent [,sʌrkəm'vɛnt] *tr* (*to surround*) accerchiare; (*to outwit*) circuire; (*a difficulty*) eludere, scansare
circus ['sʌrkəs] *s* circo equestre
cistern ['sɪstərn] *s* cisterna, serbatoio
citadel ['sɪtədəl] *s* cittadella
citation [saɪ'teʃən] *s* citazione

cite [saɪt] tr citare
cither ['sɪðər] s cetra
citizen ['sɪtɪzən] s cittadino; (civilian) civile mf
citizenship ['sɪtɪzən ˌʃɪp] s cittadinanza
citric ['sɪtrɪk] adj citrico
citron ['sɪtrən] s cedro; cedro candito
cit'rus fruit' ['sɪtrəs] s agrumi mpl
cit·y ['sɪtɪ] s (-ies) città f
cit'y counc'll s consiglio municipale
cit'y ed'itor s capocronista m
cit'y fa'thers spl maggiorenti mpl; consiglieri mpl municipali
cit'y hall' s municipio
cit'y room' s (journ) redazione
civic ['sɪvɪk] adj civico || civics s educazione civica
civil ['sɪvɪl] adj civile
civ'il engineer'ing s genio civile
civilian [sɪ'vɪljən] adj & s civile mf, borghese mf
civili·ty [sɪ'vɪlɪtɪ] s (-ties) cortesia; civilities ossequi mpl
civilization [ˌsɪvɪlɪ'zeʃən] s civilizzazione, civiltà f
civilize ['sɪvɪ ˌlaɪz] tr civilizzare
civ'il law' s diritto civile
civ'il serv'ant s impiegato statale
civ'il war' s guerra civile || Civil War s (of the U.S.A.) guerra di secessione
claim [klem] s pretesa; richiesta; (min) concessione || tr (one's rights) rivendicare; (one's property) richiedere; dichiarare; to claim to be pretendere d'essere
claim' check' s tagliando
clairvoyance [kler'vɔɪ-əns] s chiaroveggenza
clairvoyant [kler'vɔɪ-ənt] adj chiaroveggente || s veggente mf, chiaroveggente mf
clam [klæm] s vongola || intr—to clam up (coll) essere muto come un pesce
clamber ['klæmər] intr arrampicarsi
clam·my ['klæmɪ] adj (-mier; -miest) coperto di sudore freddo; morbido
clamor ['klæmər] s clamore m || intr fare clamore
clamorous ['klæmərəs] adj clamoroso
clamp [klæmp] s graffa, morsetto; (e.g., to hold a hose) fascetta || tr assicurare con graffa, aggrappare; (a tool) montare || intr—to clamp down on (coll) fare pressione su, mettere i freni a
clan [klæn] s clan m
clandestine [klæn'dɛstɪn] adj clandestino
clang [klæŋ] s clangore m || intr risonare con clangore
clannish ['klænɪʃ] adj esclusivista, partigiano
clap [klæp] s applauso; (of thunder) scoppio || v (pret & pp clapped; ger clapping) tr (the hands) battere; (e.g., in jail) schiaffare; to clap shut sbattere || intr applaudire
clapper ['klæpər] s applauditore m; (of bell) batacchio
clap'trap' s imbonimento
claret ['klærɪt] adj & s chiaretto

clari·fy ['klærɪ ˌfaɪ] v (pret & pp -fied) tr chiarificare, chiarire
clarinet [ˌklærɪ'nɛt] s clarinetto
clarion ['klærɪ-ən] adj chiaro e metallico || s tromba, clarino
clash [klæʃ] s cozzo, urto; conflitto di opinioni || intr cozzare, urtarsi; essere in conflitto
clasp [klæsp] or [klɑsp] s gancio, fermaglio; (hold) presa; (grip) stretta || tr agganciare; (to hold in the arms) abbracciare; (to grip) stringere
class [klæs] or [klɑs] s classe f || tr classificare
class'book' s registro
classic ['klæsɪk] adj & s classico
classical ['klæsɪkəl] adj classico
classicism ['klæsɪ ˌsɪzəm] s classicismo
classicist ['klæsɪsɪst] s classicista mf
classified ['klæsɪ ˌfaɪd] adj segreto
clas'sified ad' s annunzio economico
classi·fy ['klæsɪ ˌfaɪ] v (pret & pp -fied) tr classificare
class'mate' s compagno di scuola
class'room' s aula scolastica
class' strug'gle s lotta di classe
class·y ['klæsɪ] adj (-ier; -iest) (slang) di lusso, di prim'ordine
clatter ['klætər] s (of dishes) acciottolio; vocio, schiamazzo || tr acciottolare || intr fare schiamazzo
clause [klɔz] s clausola; (gram) proposizione
clavicle ['klævɪkəl] s clavicola
claw [klɔ] s artiglio; (of lobster) pinza; (tool) raffio; (of hammer) granchio; (coll) dita fpl || tr aggraffiare; artigliare
claw' ham'mer s levachiodi m
clay [kle] s argilla, creta
clay' pipe' s pipa di terracotta
clean [klin] adj pulito; (precise) netto; (e.g., break) completo || adv completamente || tr pulire; to clean out pulire, fare repulisti di; (slang) ripulire; to clean up pulire completamente; mettere in ordine || intr pulirsi, fare pulizia
clean' bill' of health' s patente sanitaria; (fig) esonero completo
clean'-cut' adj ben delineato, deciso
cleaner ['klinər] s pulitore m, smacchiatore m; (machine) pulitrice f, smacchiatrice f; to send to the cleaners (slang) spolpare
clean'ing fluid' s smacchiatore m
clean'ing wom'an s donna di servizio per fare la pulizia
clean·ly ['klɛnlɪ] adj (-lier; -liest) pulito, netto
cleanse [klɛnz] tr pulire; detergere; purificare
cleanser ['klɛnzər] s detergente m
clean'-sha'ven adj sbarbato di fresco
clean'up' s pulizia; (slang) guadagno enorme
clear [klɪr] adj chiaro; evidente; completo; innocente; (profit) netto; clear of libero da || s posto libero; in the clear libero; esonerato; non in codice || adv chiaramente; completamente || tr (e.g., trees) rischiarare; (e.g., peo-

ple) sgombrare; (*the table*) sparecchiare; (*an obstacle*) superare; (*from guilt*) discolpare; (*a profit*) guadagnare; (*goods at customs*) svincolare; (*a ship through customs*) dichiarare il carico di; (*checks*) compensare; **to clear away or off** liberare; **to clear out** sgomberare, sbarazzare; **to clear up** spiegare; (*a doubt*) dissipare || *intr* rasserenarsi; (*said of a ship*) partire; **to clear away or off** sparire; **to clear out** (coll) andarsene; **to clear up** rasserenarsi

clearance ['klɪrəns] *s* liberazione; (*of a ship*) partenza; (*of goods through customs*) sdoganamento; (*of checks*) compensazione; (*of goods*) liquidazione; (mach) gioco

clear'ance sale' *s* liquidazione

clear'-cut' *adj* chiaro, distinto

clearing ['klɪrɪŋ] *s* (*open space*) radura; (*of checks*) compensazione

clear'ing house' *s* stanza di compensazione

cleat [klit] *s* bietta, cuneo; (*on the sole of shoe*) tacchetto; (naut) galloccia

cleavage ['klivɪdʒ] *s* divisione; fessura

cleave [kliv] *v* (*pret & pp* **cleft** [klɛft] or **cleaved**) *tr* dividere, fendere || *intr* aderire, essere fedele

cleaver ['klivər] *s* scure *f*, accetta; (*of butcher*) spaccaossa *m*, fenditoio

clef [klɛf] *s* (mus) chiave *f*

cleft [klɛft] *adj* diviso, fesso || *s* fessura, crepaccio

cleft' pal'ate *s* palato spaccato, gola lupina

clematis ['klɛmətɪs] *s* clematide *f*

clemen·cy ['klɛmənsi] *s* (**-cies**) clemenza

clement ['klɛmənt] *adj* clemente

clench [klɛntʃ] *s* stretta || *tr* stringere; afferrare

clergy ['klɜrdʒi] *s* clero

cler'gy·man *s* (**-men**) ecclesiastico

cleric ['klɛrɪk] *s* ecclesiastico, sacerdote *m*

clerical ['klɛrɪkəl] *adj* da impiegato; (*error*) burocratico; (*of clergy*) clericale || *s* ecclesiastico; **clericals** abiti ecclesiastici

cler'ical work' *s* lavoro d'ufficio

clerk [klɑrk] *s* impiegato, commesso; (*accountant*) contabile *mf*; (*e.g., in a record office*) ufficiale *m*; (*cancelliere m*; (*copyist, typist*) scrivano

clever ['klɛvər] *adj* intelligente; bravo, abile; destro

cleverness ['klɛvərnɪs] *s* intelligenza; bravura, abilità *f*

clew [klu] *s* indizio, traccia; (*of yarn*) gomitolo; (naut) bugna

cliché [kli'ʃe] *s* cliché *m*, luogo comune

click [klɪk] *s* (*of camera or gun*) scatto; (*of typewriter*) battito, ticchettio || *tr* (*the tongue*) schioccare; (*the heels*) battere || *intr* ticchettare; (slang) andare d'accordo; (slang) avere fortuna

client ['klaɪ·ənt] *s* cliente *mf*

clientele [ˌklaɪ·ənˈtɛl] *s* clientela

cliff [klɪf] *s* rupe *f*, precipizio

climate ['klaɪmɪt] *s* clima *m*

climax ['klaɪmæks] *s* apice *m*; (*acute phase*) parossismo

climb [klaɪm] *s* salita; (*of a mountain*) scalata, ascensione || *tr* (*the stairs*) salire; (*a mountain*) scalare, ascendere || *intr* salire, arrampicarsi; **to climb down** discendere a carponi; (coll) ritirarsi

climber ['klaɪmər] *s* scalatore *m*; pianta rampicante; (*ambitious person*) (coll) arrampicatore *m*

clinch [klɪntʃ] *s* stretta, presa; (*boxing*) corpo a corpo *m* || *tr* (*nails*) ribattere, ribadire

clincher ['klɪntʃər] *s* chiodo per ribaditura; argomento decisivo

cling [klɪŋ] *v* (*pret & pp* **clung** [klʌŋ]) *intr* avviticchiare, attaccarsi; aderire, rimanere attaccato

cling'stone' peach' *s* pesca duracino

clinic ['klɪnɪk] *s* clinica

clinical ['klɪnɪkəl] *adj* clinico

clinician [klɪ'nɪʃən] *s* clinico

clink [klɪŋk] *s* tintinnio; (slang) gattabuia || *tr* (*glasses*) toccare || *intr* tintinnare

clinker ['klɪŋkər] *s* clinker *m*; mattone vetrificato; (slang) sbaglio

clip [klɪp] *s* (*of hair*) taglio; (*of wool*) tosatura; (*speed*) passo rapido; clip *f*, fermaglio; (*large clip*) fermacarte *m*; (*for cartridges*) caricatore *m*; (coll) colpo || *v* (*pret & pp* **clipped**; *ger* **clipping**) *tr* tagliare, tosare; (*words*) mangiare, storpiare; (*paper*) ritagliare; ritenere; (coll) battere || *intr* andare di buon passo

clipper ['klɪpər] *s* tagliatore *m*; (aer, naut) clipper *m*; (*for hair*) tosatrice *f*; (*for nails*) **clippers** pinze *fpl* per le unghie

clipping ['klɪpɪŋ] *s* taglio; (*from newspaper*) ritaglio

clique [klik] *s* cricca, chiesuola

cloak [klok] *s* mantello, manto; (fig) velo, maschera || *tr* ammantare, velare

cloak'-and-dag'ger *adj* d'avventura

cloak'-and-sword' *adj* di cappa e spada

cloak'room' *s* guardaroba *m*

clock [klɑk] *s* orologio; (*with pendulum*) pendolo, pendola; (*on stocking*) freccia || *tr* registrare, cronometrare

clock'mak'er *s* orologiaio

clock' tow'er *s* torre *f* dell'orologio

clock'wise' *adj & adv* nella direzione delle lancette dell'orologio

clock'work' *s* movimento d'orologeria; **like clockwork** come un orologio

clod [klɑd] *s* zolla; (fig) tonto

clod'hop'per *s* (*shoe*) scarpone *m*; (fig) villano, bifolco

clog [klɑg] *s* intoppo; (*to impede movement*) pastoia; scarpa *m*, zoccolo || *v* (*pret & pp* **clogged**; *ger* **clogging**) *tr* intoppare; (*to hold back*) impastoiare || *intr* otturarsi, ostruirsi

cloister ['klɔɪstər] *s* chiostro || *tr* rinchiudere in un chiostro

close [klos] *adj* vicino; (*translation*)

fedele; (air in room) male arieggiato; (weather) soffocante; (stingy) avaro; limitato, senza gioco; (haircut) corto; (friend) intimo; (hit) preciso; (enclosed) chiuso; (narrow) stretto || adv da vicino; **close to** vicino a || [kloz] s fine f, conclusione; **to bring to a close** concludere || tr chiudere; otturare; concludere; **to close down** chiudere completamente; **to close out** vendere in liquidazione; **to close up** bloccare || intr chiudersi; serrarsi; **to close down** chiudersi completamente; **to close in on** venire alle prese con; **to close up** bloccarsi; (said of a wound) rimarginarsi

close' call' [klos] s rischio scampato per miracolo

closed' chap'ter s affare chiuso

closed' cir'cuit s circuito chiuso

closed' sea'son s periodo di caccia o pesca vietata

closefisted ['klos'fɪstɪd] adj taccagno

close'-fit'ing [klos] adj attillato

close-lipped ['klos'lɪpt] adj riservato

closely ['klosli] adv da vicino; strettamente; fedelmente; attentamente

close' quar'ters [klos] spl (cramped space) pigia pigia m; **at close quarters** a corpo a corpo

close' quote' [kloz] s fine f della citazione

close' shave' [klos] s—**to have a close shave** farsi fare la barba a contropelo; (coll) scamparla per un pelo

closet ['klazɪt] s armadio a muro; (small private room) gabinetto; (for keeping clothing) ripostiglio || tr—**to be closeted with** essere in conciliabolo con

close'-up' [klos] s (mov) primo piano

closing ['klozɪŋ] s fine f, conclusione

clos'ing price' s ultimo corso

clot [klɑt] s grumo, coagulo || v (pret & pp **clotted;** ger **clotting**) intr raggrumarsi, coagularsi

cloth [klɔθ] or [klɑθ] s panno, tessuto, stoffa; abito; (for binding books) tela; **the cloth** il clero

clothe [kloð] v (pret & pp **clothed** or **clad** [klæd]) tr vestire, rivestire, coprire

clothes [kloz] or [kloðz] spl vestiti mpl, abiti mpl; (for a bed) coltre f; **to change clothes** cambiarsi

clothes'bas'ket s cesto della biancheria

clothes'brush' s spazzola per vestiti

clothes' dry'er s asciugatrice f

clothes' hang'er s attaccapanni m

clothes'horse' s cavalletto per stendere il bucato; elegantone m

clothes'line' s corda per stendere il bucato

clothes' moth' s tarma, tignola

clothes' pin' s molletta

clothes' tree' s attaccapanni m

clothier ['kloðjər] s negoziante m di confezioni; mercante m di panno

clothing ['kloðɪŋ] s vestiti mpl, vestiario

cloud [klaud] s nuvola, nube f; (great number) nuvolo; macchia; sospetto

|| tr annuvolare; offuscare || intr annuvolarsi; offuscarsi

cloud' bank' s banco di nubi

cloud'burst' s acquazzone m, nubifragio

cloud'-capped' adj coperto di nubi

cloudless ['klaudlɪs] adj senza nubi

cloud·y ['klaudi] adj (-ier; -iest) nuvoloso, annuvolato; confuso; tenebroso

clout [klaut] s (coll) schiaffo || tr (coll) schiaffeggiare

clove [klov] s chiodo di garofano; (of garlic) spicchio

cloven-hoofed ['klovən'huft] adj dal piede biforcuto; demoniaco

clover ['klovər] s trifoglio; **in clover** come un papa

clo'ver-leaf' s (-leaves [ˌlivz]) foglia di trifoglio; incrocio stradale a quadrifoglio

clown [klaun] s pagliaccio, buffone m || intr fare il pagliaccio

clownish ['klaunɪʃ] adj buffonesco, clownesco, claunesco

cloy [klɔɪ] tr saziare fino alla nausea

club [klʌb] s bastone m; circolo, società f; (playing card) fiore m || v (pret & pp **clubbed;** ger **clubbing**) tr bastonare || intr—**to club together** unirsi

club' car' s vagone m con servizio di buffet

club'house' s sede f di un circolo

club'man' s (-men) frequentatore m di circoli

club'room' s sala delle riunioni

club' sand'wich s sandwich m a tre fette di pane con insalata

club'wom'an s (-wom'en) frequentatrice f di circoli

cluck [klʌk] s (il) chiocciare || intr chiocciare

clue [klu] s traccia, indizio

clump [klʌmp] s gruppo, massa; (of earth) zolla || intr camminare con passo pesante

clum·sy ['klʌmzi] adj (-sier; -siest) goffo, malaccorto, sgraziato

cluster ['klʌstər] s gruppo; (of grapes) grappolo; (of bees) sciame m; (of stars) ammasso; (of people) folla || tr raggruppare || intr raggrupparsi

clutch [klʌtʃ] s presa; (claw) grinfia; (of chickens) covata; (mach) innesto; (aut) frizione; **clutches** grinfie fpl; **to throw the clutch in** innestare la marcia; **to throw the clutch out** disinnestare la marcia || tr afferrare, aggrappare || intr—**to clutch at** aggrapparsi a

clutter ['klʌtər] tr—**to clutter up** ingombrare alla rinfusa

coach [kotʃ] s carrozza, vettura; vagone m; (automobile) berlina; autobus m; (trainer) allenatore m; (teacher) ripetitore m || tr allenare; preparare

coach' house' s rimessa

coaching ['kotʃɪŋ] s suggerimento; (in school) ripetizione; (sports) allenamento

coach'man s (-men) cocchiere m

coagulate [ko·'ægjə‚let] *tr* coagulare || *intr* coagularsi

coal [kol] *s* carbone *m*; *(piece of burning wood)* tizzone *m*; **to call** or **haul over the coals** rimproverare || *tr* rifornire di carbone || *intr* rifornirsi di carbone; *(naut)* fare carbone

coal'bin' *s* carbonaia

coal' deal'er *s* *(wholesale)* negoziante *m* di carbone; *(retail)* carbonaio

coal' field' *s* bacino carbonifero

coal' gas' *s* gas *m* illuminante

coalition [‚ko·ə·'lɪʃən] *s* coalizione

coal' mine' *s* miniera di carbone

coal' oil' *s* cherosene *m*

coal' scut'tle *s* secchio del carbone

coal' tar' *s* catrame *m*

coal' yard' *s* carbonaia, carboniera

coarse [kors] *adj* *(manners)* volgare, ordinario; *(unrefined)* greggio; *(lacking refinement in manners)* rozzo, grossolano

coast [kost] *s* costa; discesa a ruota libera; **the coast is clear** la via è libera || *tr* costeggiare || *intr* costeggiare; scendere a ruota libera

coastal ['kostəl] *adj* costiero

coaster ['kostər] *s* nave *f* di cabotaggio; *(amusement)* otto volante, montagna russa; *(small tray)* sottobicchiere *m*

coast'er brake' *s* freno a contropedale

coast' guard' *s* guardacoste *m*

coast'-guard cut'ter *s* guardacoste *m*

coast'ing trade' *s* cabotaggio

coast'land' *s* costa

coast'line' *s* linea costiera, litorale *m*

coast'wise' *adv* lungo la costa

coat [kot] *s* soprabito; cappotto; *(jacket)* giacca; *(hide of man and animals)* mantello; *(of paint)* mano *f*; *(layer)* strato || *tr* vestire, proteggere; ricoprire, coprire

coat'ed ['kotɪd] *adj* rivestito; *(tongue)* patinato

coat' hang'er *s* attaccapanni *m*

coating ['kotɪŋ] *s* rivestimento; *(of paint)* mano *f*; *(of cement)* strato; *(cloth)* tessuto per abiti

coat' of arms' *s* scudo, stemma *m*

coat'room' *s* guardaroba *m*

coat'tail' *s* falda

coax [koks] *tr* blandire; ottenere con lusinghe

cob [kab] *s* spiga di granturco; *(horse)* cavallo da tiro; *(swan)* cigno maschio

cobalt ['kobəlt] *s* cobalto

cobble ['kabəl] *s* ciottolo || *tr* acciottolare; *(to mend)* raccomodare, riparare

cobbler ['kablər] *s* calzolaio, ciabattino; *(pie)* torta di frutta

cob'ble-stone' *s* ciottolo

cob'web' *s* tela di ragno, ragnatela

cocaine [ko'ken] *s* cocaina

cock [kak] *s* gallo; *(faucet)* rubinetto; *(of gun)* cane *m*; *(of the eye)* ammicco; *(of nose)* angolo (del naso) rivolto all'insù; *(of hay)* covone *m* || *tr* *(a gun)* armare; *(the head)* drizzare

cockade [kɑ'ked] *s* coccarda

cock-a-doodle-doo ['kakə‚dudəl'du] *s* chicchirichì *m*

cock'-and-bull' sto'ry *s* racconto incredibile

cocked' hat' *s* tricorno, cappello tricorno; **to knock into a cocked hat** *(slang)* distruggere completamente

cockeyed ['kak‚aɪd] *adj* strabico; *(slang)* sbilenco; *(slang)* sciocco, scemo

cockle ['kakəl] *s* *(mollusk)* cardio; *(weed)* loglio; *(boat)* barchetta; *(wrinkle)* grinza; **to warm the cockles of one's heart** far bene al cuore || *intr* raggrinzirsi

cock' of the walk' *s* gallo del pollaio

cock'pit' *s* *(of boat)* cabina; *(aer)* carlinga; *(naut)* cassero di poppa

cock'roach' *s* scarafaggio, blatta

cocks'comb' *s* cresta di gallo; berretto da buffone

cock'sure' *adj* ostinato; troppo sicuro di sé stesso

cock'tail' *s* cocktail *m*

cock'tail par'ty *s* cocktail *m*

cock·y ['kaki] *adj* (-ier; -iest) impudente, presuntuoso

cocoa ['koko] *s* *(bean)* cacao; *(drink)* cioccolata; *(tree)* cocco

coconut ['kokə‚nʌt] *s* noce *f* di cocco

co'conut palm' or **tree'** *s* cocco

cocoon [kə'kun] *s* bozzolo

cod [kad] *s* merluzzo

C.O.D. ['si'o'di] *s* (letterword) **(Collect on Delivery)** contro assegno

coddle ['kadəl] *tr* vezzeggiare

code [kod] *s* codice *m*, cifra; **in code** in codice, in cifra || *tr* mettere in codice or in cifra; cifrare

codex ['kodeks] *s* (codices ['kodɪ‚siz] or ['kadɪ‚siz]) codice *m*

cod'fish' *s* merluzzo

codger ['kadʒər] *s*—**old codger** (coll) vecchietto

codicil ['kadɪsɪl] *s* codicillo

codi·fy ['kadɪ‚faɪ] or ['kodɪ‚faɪ] *v* (pret & pp -fied) *tr* codificare

cod'-liver oil' *s* olio di fegato di merluzzo

coed ['co‚ed] *s* studentessa di scuola mista

coeducation [‚ko‚edʒə'keʃən] *s* coeducazione

co'educa'tional school' [‚ko·edʒə'keʃə-nəl] *s* scuola mista

coefficient [‚ko·ɪ'fɪʃənt] *s* coefficiente *m*

coerce [ko'ʌrs] *tr* forzare, costringere

coercion [ko'ʌrʃən] *s* coercizione

coexist [‚ko·ɪg'zɪst] *intr* coesistere

coffee ['kɔfi] or ['kafi] *s* caffè *m*; **ground coffee** caffè macinato; **roasted coffee** caffè torrefatto

cof'fee bean' *s* chicco di caffè

cof'fee-cake' *s* pasticcino (da mangiarsi con il caffè)

cof'fee grind'er *s* macinino da caffè, macinacaffè *m*

cof'fee grounds' *spl* fondi *mpl* di caffè

cof'fee house' *s* caffè *m*

cof'fee mak'er *s* macchinetta del caffè

cof'fee mill' *s* macinino del caffè, macinacaffè *m*

cof'fee-pot' *s* caffettiera

cof'fee shop' *s* caffè *m*

coffer ['kɔfər] or ['kafər] *s* forziere *m*; (*ceiling*) soffitto a cassettoni; (*archit*) cassettone *m*; coffers tesoro

coffin ['kɔfɪn] or ['kafɪn] *s* bara

cog [kag] *s* dente *m* d'ingranaggio; ruota dentata; to slip a cog fare un errore

cogent ['kodʒənt] *adj* convincente, persuasivo

cogitate ['kadʒɪ,tet] *tr & intr* cogitare, ponzare

cognac ['konjæk] or ['kanjæk] *s* cognac *m*

cognate ['kagnet] *adj* consanguineo, parente, affine || *s* parola dello stesso ceppo linguistico; consanguineo, parente *mf*

cognizance ['kagnɪzəns] or ['kanɪzəns] *s* conoscenza; to take cognizance of prendere conoscenza di

cognizant ['kagnɪzənt] or ['kanɪzənt] *adj* informato, al corrente

cog'wheel' *s* ruota dentata

cohabit [ko'hæbɪt] *intr* convivere; (*archaic*) coabitare

coheir [ko'er] *s* coerede *mf*

cohere [ko'hɪr] *intr* aderire; (fig) avere nesso

coherent [ko'hɪrənt] *adj* coerente

coiffeur [kwɑ'fʌr] *s* parrucchiere *m* per signora; (Brit) parrucchiere *m*

coiffure [kwɑ'fjur] *s* pettinatura || *tr* pettinare

coil [kɔɪl] *s* (*of rope*) rotolo; (*of pipe*) serpentino; (*of wire*) bobina, avvolgimento || *tr* arrotolare || *intr* arrotolarsi

coil' spring' *s* molla a spirale, molla elicoidale

coin [kɔɪn] *s* moneta; to pay back in one's own coin pagare della stessa moneta; to toss a coin giocare a testa o croce || *tr* (*money*) coniare, battere; (*words*) inventare, creare; to coin money battere moneta; (coll) fare soldoni

coincide [,ko·ɪn'saɪd] *intr* coincidere

coincidence [ko'ɪnsɪdəns] *s* coincidenza

coke [kok] *s* coke *m*, carbone *m* coke

colander ['kʌləndər] or ['kaləndər] *s* colabrodo, colapasta *m*

cold [kold] *adj* freddo; it is cold (*said of weather*) fa freddo; to be cold (*said of a person*) avere freddo || *s* freddo; (*ailment*) raffreddore *m*; out in the cold solo soletto; to catch cold pigliare freddo, pigliarsi un raffreddore

cold' blood' *s*—in cold blood a sangue freddo

cold'-blood'ed *adj* insensibile; (*sensitive to cold*) freddoloso; (*animal*) a sangue freddo

cold' chis'el *s* tagliaferro

cold' com'fort *s* magra consolazione

cold' cream' *s* crema emolliente

cold' cuts' *spl* salumi *mpl*, affettato

cold' feet' *spl*—to get cold feet (coll) perdersi d'animo

cold'-heart'ed *adj*—to be coldhearted avere il cuore duro

coldness ['koldnɪs] *s* freddezza

cold' shoul'der *s*—to get the cold shoulder (coll) essere trattato con freddezza; to turn a cold shoulder on (coll) trattare con freddezza

cold' snap' *s* freddo breve e improvviso

cold' stor'age *s* conservazione a freddo

cold' war' *s* guerra fredda

cold' wave' *s* ondata di freddo

coleslaw ['kol,slɔ] *s* insalata di cavolo cappuccio

colic ['kalɪk] *adj* colico || *s* colica

coliseum [,kalɪ'si·əm] *s* stadio, arena || Coliseum *s* Colosseo

collaborate [kə'læbə,ret] *intr* collaborare

collaborationist [kə,læbə're∫ənɪst] *s* collaborazionista *mf*

collaborator [kə'læbə,retər] *s* collaboratore *m*

collapse [kə'læps] *s* (*of business*) fallimento; (*e.g., of a roof*) caduta; (*of a person*) collasso || *tr* piegare || *intr* (*to shrink*) restringersi, sgonfiarsi; (*said of a business*) fallire; (*said of health*) venir meno; (*said, e.g., of a roof*) cadere, crollare

collapsible [kə'læpsɪbəl] *adj* pieghevole, smontabile

collar ['kalər] *s* (*of shirt*) colletto; (*for dog or horse*) collare *m*; (*ring*) anello; (*short piece of pipe*) manicotto || *tr* afferrare per il collo, catturare

col'lar-band' *s* cinturino della camicia

col'lar-bone' *s* clavicola

collate [kə'let] or ['kalet] *tr* collazionare, confrontare

collateral [kə'lætərəl] *adj* collaterale; accessorio, addizionale || *s* collaterale *m*

colleague ['kalig] *s* collega *mf*

collect ['kalɛkt] *s* (eccl) colletta || [kə'lɛkt] *adv* contro assegno; (telp) pagamento all'abbonato chiamato || *tr* raccogliere, riunire; (*e.g., stamps*) collezionare; (*mail*) levare; (*bills*) incassare; (*ideas*) coordinare; (*thoughts*) riordinare; (*e.g., classroom papers*) raccogliere; (*taxes*) riscuotere; to collect oneself riprendersi, riprendere il controllo di sé stesso || *intr* (*for the poor*) fare la colletta; riunirsi, raccogliersi

collected [kə'lɛktɪd] *adj* raccolto; equilibrato, padrone di sè

collection [kə'lɛk∫ən] *s* collezione; (*for the poor*) colletta; (*of mail*) levata; (*heap*) deposito; (*of taxes*) esazione; (*of bills*) riscossione

collec'tion a'gency *s* agenzia di riscossione

collective [kə'lɛktɪv] *adj* collettivo

collector [kə'lɛktər] *s* (*of stamps*) collezionista *mf*; (*of taxes*) esattore *m*; (*of tickets*) controllore *m*

college ['kalɪdʒ] *s* scuola superiore,

università *f*; (*e.g., of medicine*) facoltà *f*; (*electoral*) collegio

collide [kə'laɪd] *intr* collidere, scontrarsi

collie ['kɑli] *s* collie *m*

collier ['kaljər] *s* (*ship*) carboniera; (*min*) minatore *m* di carbone

collier·y ['kaljəri] *s* (*-ies*) miniera di carbone

collision [kə'lɪʒən] *s* collisione

colloid ['kalɔɪd] *adj* colloidale || colloide *m*

colloquial [kə'lokwɪ·əl] *adj* familiare, colloquiale

colloquialism [kə'lokwɪ·ə,lɪzəm] *s* espressione familiare

collo·quy ['kaləkwi] *s* (*-quies*) colloquio

collusion [kə'luʒən] *s* collusione; **to be in collusion with** essere d'intelligenza con

cologne [kə'lon] *s* acqua di colonia, colonia || **Cologne** *s* Colonia

colon ['kolən] *s* (*anat*) colon *m*; (*gram*) due punti *mpl*

colonel ['kʌrnəl] *s* colonnello

colonist ['kalənɪst] *s* colono, coloniale *m*

colonize ['kalə,naɪz] *tr & intr* colonizzare

colonnade [,kalə'ned] *s* colonnato

colo·ny ['kaləni] *s* (*-nies*) colonia

color ['kʌlər] *s* colore *m*; **off color** sbiadito, scolorito; (*slang*) sporco, volgare; **the colors** i colori, la bandiera; **to call to the colors** chiamare in servizio militare; **to change color** cambiar colore; arrossire; impallidire; **to give or lend color to** far parere probabile; **to lose color** impallidire; **to show one's colors** mostrarsi come si è; **under color of** sotto il pretesto di || *tr* colorare; (*fig*) colorire || *intr* arrossire

col'or-blind' *adj* daltonico

colored ['kʌlərd] *adj* colorato; (*person*) di colore; esagerato

colorful ['kʌlərfəl] *adj* colorito, espressivo

col'or guard' *s* guardia d'onore alla bandiera

coloring ['kʌlərɪŋ] *s* colorazione; colore *m*; pigmento; (*fig*) specie *f*

colorless ['kʌlərlɪs] *adj* incolore, incoloro

col'or photog'raphy *s* fotografia a colori

col'or ser'geant *s* sergente *m* portabandiera

col'or tel'evision *s* televisione a colori

colossal [kə'lasəl] *adj* colossale

colossus [kə'lasəs] *s* colosso

colt [kolt] *s* puledro

Columbus [kə'lʌmbəs] *s* Colombo

column ['kaləm] *s* colonna

columnist ['kaləmɪst] *s* giornalista incaricato di una colonna speciale; articolista *mf*

coma ['komə] *s* coma *m*

comb [kom] *s* pettine *m*; (*for horse*) striglia; (*of hen or wave*) cresta; (*honeycomb*) favo || *tr* pettinare;

(*fig*) esaminare minuziosamente || *intr* (*said of waves*) frangersi

com·bat ['kambæt] *s* combattimento || ['kambæt] *or* [kəm'bæt] *v* (*pret & pp* -bated *or* -batted; *ger* -bating *or* -batting) *tr & intr* combattere

combatant ['kambətənt] *s* combattente *mf*

com'bat du'ty *s* servizio in zona di guerra

combination [,kambɪ'neʃən] *s* combinazione

combine ['kambaɪn] *s* consorzio; (*pol*) coalizione; mieto-trebbiatrice *f* || [kəm'baɪn] *tr* combinare || *intr* combinarsi

combin'ing form' *s* membro di parola composta

combo ['kambo] *s* orchestrina

combustible [kəm'bʌstɪbəl] *adj & s* combustibile *m*

combustion [kəm'bʌstʃən] *s* combustione

come [kʌm] *v* (*pret* came [kem]; *pp* come) *intr* venire; arrivare; (*to become*) diventare; (*to amount*) ammontare; **come!** macchè!; **come along!** andiamo!; **come in!** avanti!, entri!; **come on!** andiamo!, avanti!, coraggio!; **to come about** accadere, succedere; **to come across** incontrarsi con; (*slang*) pagare; **to come around** cedere; mettersi d'accordo; (*said of health*) rimettersi; **to come at** raggiungere; (*to attack*) attaccare; **to come back** ritornare; **to come between** mettersi fra; **to come by** ottenere; **to come down** scendere; decadere; essere trasmesso; **to come down with** ammalarsi di; **to come forward** farsi avanti; **to come in** entrare, passare; **to come in for** ricevere; **to come into** ricevere; ereditare; **to come off** succedere; riuscire; **to come on** migliorare; incontrarsi; **to come out** uscire; debuttare in società; andare a finire; **to come out with** uscire con; mostrare; **to come over** succedere a, e.g., **what came over him?** che gli è successo?; **to come through** riuscire; **to come to** riprendere i sensi; **to come under** essere di competenza di; appartenere a; **to come up** salire; **to come up to** salire fino a; avvicinarsi a; **to come up with** raggiungere; produrre, fornire; proporre

come'back' *s* (*coll*) ritorno; (*slang*) pronta risposta; **to stage a comeback** (*coll*) ritornare in auge

comedian [kə'midɪ·ən] *s* attore comico; (*author*) commediografo; (*amusing person*) commediante *mf*

comedienne [kə,midɪ'ɛn] *s* attrice comica

come'down' *s* (*coll*) rovescio di fortuna

come·dy ['kamədi] *s* (*-dies*) commedia

come·ly ['kʌmli] *adj* (*-lier; -liest*) bello, grazioso

comet ['kamɪt] *s* cometa

comfort ['kʌmfərt] *s* conforto, sollievo;

(ease) benessere *m* ‖ *tr* confortare, alleviare

comfortable ['kʌmfərtəbəl] *adj* comodo, agiato; *(e.g., income)* (coll) bastante ‖ *s* coltre *f*

comforter ['kʌmfərtər] *s* consolatore *m;* *(bedcover)* coltre *f;* sciarpa di lana ‖ **the Comforter** lo Spirito Santo, lo Spirito Consolatore

comforting ['kʌmfərtɪŋ] *adj* confortante

com'fort sta'tion *s* latrina pubblica

comic ['kamɪk] *adj* comico ‖ *s (actor)* comico; comicità *f;* **comics** fumetti *mpl*

comical ['kamɪkəl] *adj* comico

com'ic book' *s* libretto a fumetti

com'ic op'era *s* opera buffa

com'ic strip' *s* racconto umoristico a fumetti

coming ['kʌmɪŋ] *adj* venturo, prossimo; promettente ‖ *s* venuta

com'ing out' *s* debutto in società; *(e.g., of stock)* emissione

comma ['kamə] *s* virgola

command [kə'mænd] or [kə'mɑnd] *s* comando; *(e.g., of a language)* padronanza ‖ *tr* comandare, ordinare; *(to overlook)* dominare; *(to be able to have)* disporre di ‖ *intr* avere il comando

commandant [ˌkamən'dænt] or [ˌkamən'dɑnt] *s* comandante *m*

commandeer [ˌkamən'dɪr] *tr* requisire

commander [kə'mændər] or [kə-'mɑndər] *s (of knighthood)* commendatore *m;* (mil) comandante *m;* (nav) capitano di vascello

command'er in chief' *s* comandante *m* in capo

command'ing of'ficer *s* comandante *m*

commandment [kə'mændmənt] or [kə-'mɑndmənt] *s* comandamento

command' mod'ule *s* (rok) modulo di comando

commando [kə'mændo] *s* guastatore *m*

commemorate [kə'memə ˌret] *tr* commemorare, celebrare

commence [kə'mens] *tr & intr* cominciare

commencement [kə'mensmənt] *s* inizio, esordio; *(in a school)* cerimonia per la distribuzione dei diplomi

commend [kə'mend] *tr* lodare; *(to entrust)* raccomandare, affidare

commendable [kə'mendəbəl] *adj (person)* lodevole; *(act)* commendevole

commendation [ˌkamən'deʃən] *s* lode *f;* raccomandazione; (mil) citazione

comment ['kament] *s* commento ‖ *tr* commentare ‖ *intr* fare commenti; **to comment on** fare commenti su

commentar·y ['kamən ˌteri] *s* (-ies) commentario

commentator ['kamən ˌtetər] *s* commentatore *m*

commerce ['kamərs] *s* commercio

commercial [kə'mərʃəl] *adj* commerciale ‖ *s* (rad, telv) programma *m* di pubblicità; (rad, telv) annunzio pubblicitario

commiserate [kə'mɪzə ˌret] *intr—to*

commiserate with commiserare, compiangere

commissar ['kamɪ ˌsar] or [ˌkamɪ'sar] *s* commissario del popolo

commissar·y ['kamɪ ˌseri] *s* (-ies) *(store)* economato; *(deputy)* commissario; *(in army)* intendente *m*

commission [kə'mɪʃən] *s* commissione; *(e.g., in army)* nomina, brevetto; autorità *f;* *(of a crime)* perpetrazione; (il) fare; **in commission** in servizio, in uso; **out of commission** fuori servizio ‖ *tr* nominare, dare un brevetto a; autorizzare; *(a ship)* armare

commis'sioned of'ficer *s* (mil, nav) ufficiale *m*

commissioner [kə'mɪʃənər] *s* commissario; membro di una commissione

commis'sion mer'chant *s* sensale *m*

com·mit [kə'mɪt] *v (pret & pp -mitted; ger -mitting)* *tr* commettere, perpetrare; *(to deliver)* affidare, consegnare; *(to imprison)* mandare in prigione; *(an insane person)* internare; *(to refer)* rinviare; *(to involve)* compromettere; **to commit oneself** compromettersi; **to commit to memory** imparare a memoria; **to commit to writing** mettere in iscritto

commitment [kə'mɪtmənt] *s (act of committing)* commissione; *(to an asylum)* internamento; promessa; (law) mandato

committal [kə'mɪtəl] *s* consegna; promessa

committee [kə'mɪti] *s* comitato, commissione

commode [kə'mod] *s (chest of drawers)* cassettone *m;* *(washstand)* lavabo; seggetta, comoda

commodious [kə'modɪ·əs] *adj* spazioso; conveniente

commodi·ty [kə'madɪti] *s* (-ties) merce *f;* articolo di prima necessità

commod'ity exchange' *s* borsa merci

common ['kamən] *adj* comune ‖ *s* fondo comunale; pascolo comune; **commons** gente *f* non nobile; refettorio; **in common** in comune ‖ **the Commons** la Camera dei Comuni

com'mon car'rier *s* impresa di trasporti pubblici

commoner ['kamənər] *s* plebeo, borghese *m;* membro della Camera dei Comuni

com'mon law' *s* consuetudine *f,* diritto consuetudinario

com'mon-law mar'riage *s* matrimonio basato sulla mera convivenza

commonly ['kamənli] *adv* generalmente

com'mon-place' *adj* banale, ordinario ‖ *s* banalità *f,* cosa ordinaria

com'mon sense' *s* senso comune

com'mon-sense' *adj* giudizioso

com'mon stock' *s* azione ordinaria; azioni ordinarie

commonweal ['kamən ˌwil] *s* bene pubblico

com'mon-wealth' *s* *(citizens of a state)* cittadinanza; repubblica; *(one of the*

50 states of the U.S.A.) stato; comunità f, federazione

commotion [kə'moʃən] s agitazione

commune [kə'mjun] s comune m ‖ intr confabulare; (eccl) comunicarsi

communicate [kə'mjunɪ,ket] tr & intr comunicare

communicating [kə'mjunɪ,ketɪŋ] adj comunicante

communication [kə,mjunɪ'keʃən] s comunicazione; **communications** sistema m di comunicazione; mezzi mpl di comunicazione

communicative [kə'mjunɪ,ketɪv] adj comunicativo

Communion [kə'mjunjən] s Comunione; **to take Communion** comunicarsi

communiqué [kə,mjunɪ'ke] or [kə-'mjunɪ,ke] s comunicato

communism ['kɑmjə,nɪzəm] s comunismo

communist ['kɑmjənɪst] s comunista mf

communi·ty [kə'mjunɪti] s (-ties) (people living together) comunità f; (sharing together) comunanza f; (neighborhood) circondario

commu'nity cen'ter s centro sociale

commu'nity chest' s fondo di beneficenza

commuta'tion tick'et [,kɑmjə'teʃən] s biglietto d'abbonamento

commutator ['kɑmjə,tetər] s (switch) commutatore m; (of dynamo or motor) collettore m

commute [kə'mjut] tr commutare ‖ intr commutare; fare il pendolare

commuter [kə'mjutər] s pendolare mf

compact [kəm'pækt] adj compatto ‖ ['kɑmpækt] s (small case for face powder) portacipria m; (agreement) accordo; (small car) utilitaria

companion [kəm'pænjən] s compagno; (one of two items) pendant m; (lady) dama di compagnia

compan'ion·ship' s cameratismo

compan'ion·way' s (naut) scaletta per andare sottocoperta

compa·ny ['kʌmpəni] s (-nies) compagnia; (coll) ospite m or ospiti mpl; (naut) equipaggio; **to bear company** accompagnare; **to be good company** essere simpatico; **to keep company** (said of a couple) andare insieme; **to keep company with** accompagnare; (coll) fare la corte a; **to part company** separarsi

comparable ['kɑmpərəbəl] adj comparabile, paragonabile

comparative [kəm'pærətɪv] adj comparativo; (e.g., anatomy) comparato ‖ s (gram) comparativo

compare [kəm'per] s—**beyond compare** incomparabile ‖ tr confrontare; **compared to** a confronto di, in confronto a

comparison [kəm'pærɪsən] s confronto; (gram) comparazione; **in comparison with** in confronto a, a confronto di

compartment [kəm'pɑrtmənt] s compartimento; (naut) compartimento stagno; (rr) compartimento

compass ['kʌmpəs] s (instrument for showing direction) bussola; (boundary) limite m; (range) ambito; (range of voice) portata; (of a wall) cerchia; (circuit) circuito; (drawing instrument) compasso; **compasses** (drawing instrument) compasso ‖ tr girare intorno a; comprendere; **to compass about** accerchiare

com'pass card' s rosa dei venti

compassion [kəm'pæʃən] s compassione

compassionate [kəm'pæʃənɪt] adj compassionevole

com'pass saw' s gattuccio

com·pel [kəm'pel] v (pret & pp **-pelled**; ger **-pelling**) tr forzare, obbligare

compelling [kəm'pelɪŋ] adj imperioso, coercitivo

compendious [kəm'pendɪ·əs] adj compendioso, conciso

compensate ['kɑmpən,set] tr & intr compensare

compensation [,kɑmpən'seʃən] s compensazione; (pay) pagamento; (something given to offset a loss) risarcimento, indennità f

compete [kəm'pit] intr competere

competence ['kɑmpɪtəns] or **competency** ['kɑmpɪtənsi] s (fitness) abilità f; (money) agiatezza; (authority) competenza

competent ['kɑmpɪtənt] adj abile; competente

competition [,kɑmpɪ'tɪʃən] s competizione, gara; (in business) concorrenza

competitive [kəm'petɪtɪv] adj competitivo; (based on competition) di concorso

compet'itive pric'es spl prezzi mpl di concorrenza

competitor [kəm'petɪtər] s competitore m, concorrente mf; rivale mf

compilation [,kɑmpɪ'leʃən] s compilazione

compile [kəm'paɪl] tr compilare

complacence [kəm'plesəns] or **complacency** [kəm'plesənsi] s compiacenza; compiacenza di sé stesso

complacent [kəm'plesənt] adj compiaciuto or soddisfatto con sé stesso

complain [kəm'plen] intr lagnarsi

complainant [kəm'plenənt] s (law) querelante mf

complaint [kəm'plent] s lagnanza, reclamo; (sickness) malattia; (law) querela

complaisance [kəm'plezəns] or ['kɑmplɪ,zæns] s compiacenza

complaisant [kəm'plezənt] or ['kɑmplɪ,zænt] adj compiacente, cortese

complement ['kɑmplɪmənt] s complemento; (naut) equipaggio ‖ ['kɑmplɪ,ment] tr completare

complete [kəm'plit] adj completo; (done) finito ‖ tr completare, finire

completion [kəm'pliʃən] s completamento, compimento

complex [kəm'pleks] or ['kɑmpleks]

adj complesso, complicato ‖ ['kɑm-pleks] *s* complesso
complexion [kəm'plekʃən] *s (of skin)* carnagione; *(appearance)* aspetto; *(viewpoint)* punto di vista
compliance [kəm'plaɪ·əns] *s* condiscen- denza, arrendevolezza; **in compliance with** in conformità di
complicate ['kɑmplɪ·ket] *tr* complicare
complicated ['kɑmplɪ·ketɪd] *adj* complicato
complici·ty [kəm'plɪsɪti] *s* **(-ties)** complicità *f*
compliment ['kɑmplɪmənt] *s* compli- mento, omaggio ‖ ['kɑmplɪ·ment] *tr*—**to compliment s.o. on s.th** felici- tarsi per qlcu per qlco; **to compli- ment s.o. with s.th** regalare qlco a qlcu
complimentary [,kɑmplɪ'mentəri] *adj* complimentoso, lusinghiero; *(free)* in omaggio, gratis; *(ticket)* di favore
com·ply [kəm'plaɪ] *v (pret & pp -plied) intr* acconsentire, accondi- scendere; **to comply with** accedere a
component [kəm'ponənt] *adj* compo- nente, costituente ‖ *s (component part)* componente *m*; *(force)* com- ponente *f*
compose [kəm'poz] *tr* comporre; **to be composed of** essere composto di; **to compose oneself** calmarsi
composed [kəm'pozd] *adj* calmo, tran- quillo
composer [kəm'pozər] *s (peacemaker)* conciliatore *m*; *(mus)* compositore *m*
compos'ing stick' *s (typ)* compositoio
composite ['kɑmpəzɪt] *adj & s* com- posto, composito
composition [,kɑmpə'zɪʃən] *s* compo- sizione; *(agreement)* compromesso
compositor [kəm'pɑzɪtər] *s* composi- tore *m*
compost ['kɑmpost] *s* concime *m* natu- rale
composure [kəm'poʒər] *s* calma
compote ['kɑmpot] *s (stewed fruit)* composta; *(dish)* compostiera
compound ['kɑmpaʊnd] *adj* composto; *(fracture)* complesso; *(archit, bot)* composito ‖ *s* composto; parola com- posta; *(yard)* recinto ‖ [kɑm'paʊnd] *tr (to mix)* combinare; *(to settle)* comporre; *(interest)* capitalizzare
comprehend [,kɑmprɪ'hend] *tr* com- prendere
comprehensible [,kɑmprɪ'hensɪbəl] *adj* comprensibile
comprehension [,kɑmprɪ'henʃən] *s* comprensione
comprehensive [,kɑmprɪ'hensɪv] *adj* comprensivo
compress ['kɑmpres] *s* compressa ‖ [kəm'pres] *tr* comprimere
compressed' air' *s* aria compressa
compression [kəm'preʃən] *s* compres- sione
comprise [kəm'praɪz] *s* com-

promesso ‖ *tr (a dispute)* transigere, comporre; *(to put in danger)* com- promettere ‖ *intr* transigere, fare un compromesso
comptroller [kən'trolər] *s* economo, amministratore *m*, controllore *m*
compulsive [kəm'pʌlsɪv] *adj* obbliga- torio, coercitivo; (psychol) compul- sivo
compulsory [kəm'pʌlsəri] *adj* obbliga- torio
compute [kəm'pjut] *tr & intr.* compu- tare, calcolare
computer [kəm'pjutər] *s* calcolatore *m*; elaboratore *m*
comrade ['kɑmræd] or ['kɑmrɪd] *s* camerata *m*, compagno
com'rade in arms' *s* compagno d'armi
con [kɑn] *s* contro ‖ *v (pret & pp conned) ger* conning *tr* imparare a memoria; *(slang)* imbrogliare
concave ['kɑnkev] or [kɑn'kev] *adj* concavo
conceal [kən'sil] *tr* nascondere; *(to keep secret)* celare
concealment [kən'silmənt] *s* occulta- mento; *(place)* nascondiglio
concede [kɑn'sid] *tr* concedere
conceit [kən'sit] *s (high opinion of oneself)* presunzione; *(fanciful no- tion)* concetto sottile
conceited [kən'sitɪd] *adj* vanitoso
conceivable [kən'sivəbəl] *adj* concepi- bile
conceive [kən'siv] *tr & intr* concepire
concentrate ['kɑnsən,tret] *s* concen- trato ‖ *tr* concentrare ‖ *intr* concen- trarsi; **to concentrate on** concentrarsi in
concentra'tion camp' [,kɑnsən'treʃən] *s* campo di concentrazione
concept ['kɑnsept] *s* concetto
conception [kən'sepʃən] *s* concezione
concern [kən'sʌrn] *s* interesse *m*; *(worry)* ansietà *f*; *(firm)* ditta, com- pagnia; **of concern** d'interesse ‖ *tr* concernere; **as concerns** circa; **to concern oneself** interessarsi; **to whom it may concern** a chiunque possa averne interesse
concerning [kən'sʌrnɪŋ] *prep* riguardo a
concert ['kɑnsərt] *s* concerto ‖ [kən- 'sʌrt] *tr & intr* concertare
con'cert·mas'ter *s* primo violino
concer·to [kən'tʃerto] *s* **(-tos** or **-ti** [ti])* concerto
concession [kən'seʃən] *s* concessione
conciliate [kən'sɪlɪ,et] *tr* conciliare, conciliarsi con
concise [kən'saɪs] *adj* conciso
conclude [kən'klud] *tr* concludere ‖ *intr* concludersi, terminare
conclusion [kən'kluʒən] *s* conclusione; **in conclusion** per finire; **to try con- clusions with** misurarsi con
conclusive [kən'klusɪv] *adj* decisivo, convincente
concoct [kən'kɑkt] *tr* preparare, con- fezionare; *(a story)* inventare
concoction [kən'kɑkʃən] *s* prepara-

zione, mescolanza; (*unpleasant in taste*) intruglio

concomitant [kən'kɑmɪtənt] *adj* concomitante ‖ *s* fatto or sintomo concomitante

concord ['kɑŋkərd] *s* concordia, armonia; (*treaty*) accordo; (*gram*) concordanza

concourse ['kɑŋkors] *s* confluenza; (*crowd*) affluenza, concorso; (*boulevard*) viale *m;* (rr) salone *m* principale

concrete ['kɑnkrit] or [kɑn'krit] *adj* concreto; fatto di cemento; solido ‖ *s* cemento, calcestruzzo ‖ *tr* (e.g., a *sidewalk*) cementare

con'crete mix'er *s* betoniera

con·cur [kən'kʌr] *v* (*pret & pp* **-curred;** *ger* **-curring**) *intr* (*to work together*) concorrere; (*to agree*) essere d'accordo, aderire

concurrence [kən'kʌrəns] *s* concorso; (*agreement*) accordo

concurrent [kən'kʌrənt] *adj* concomitante, simultaneo; cooperante; armonioso

concussion [kən'kʌʃən] *s* scossa, urto; (*of brain*) commozione cerebrale

condemn [kən'dem] *tr* condannare; (*to take for public use*) espropriare

condemnation [ˌkɑndem'neʃən] *s* condanna

condense [kən'dens] *tr* condensare ‖ *intr* condensarsi

condescend [ˌkɑndɪ'send] *intr* condiscendere, degnarsi

condescending [ˌkɑndɪ'sendɪŋ] *adj* condiscendente

condescension [ˌkɑndɪ'senʃən] *s* condiscendenza, degnazione

condiment ['kɑndɪmənt] *s* condimento

condition [kən'dɪʃən] *s* condizione; clausola; **on condition that** a condizione che ‖ *tr* condizionare; mettere in buone condizioni fisiche

conditional [kən'dɪʃənəl] *adj & s* condizionale *m*

condole [kən'dol] *intr* condolersi

condolence [kən'doləns] *s* condoglianza

condone [kən'don] *tr* condonare

conduce [kən'djus] or [kən'dus] *intr* contribuire, indurre

conducive [kən'djusɪv] or [kən'dusɪv] *adj* contribuente

conduct ['kɑndʌkt] *s* condotta; direzione ‖ [kən'dʌkt] *tr* condurre; (*an orchestra*) dirigere; **to conduct oneself** condursi, comportarsi ‖ *intr* dirigere

conductor [kən'dʌktər] *s* direttore *m;* (*of a streetcar*) fattorino, conduttore *m;* (phys) conduttore *m;* (rr) capotreno

conduit ['kɑndɪt] or ['kɑnduˌɪt] *s* condotto

cone [kon] *s* cono; (bot) pigna

Con'estoga wag'on ['kɑnɪˌstogə] *s* carriaggio coperto

confectioner [kən'fekʃənər] *s* confettiere *m,* pasticcere *m*

confec'tioners' sug'ar *s* zucchero in polvere finissimo

confectioner·y [kən'fekʃəˌneri] *s* (**-ies**) confetteria, pasticceria; (*candies*) confetture *fpl*

confedera·cy [kən'fedərəsi] *s* (**-cies**) confederazione; lega

confederate [kən'fedərɪt] *s* alleato; (*in crime*) complice *mf* ‖ [kən'fedəˌret] *tr* confederare ‖ *intr* confederarsi

con·fer [kən'fʌr] *v* (*pret & pp* **-ferred;** *ger* **-ferring**) *tr* conferire ‖ *intr* conferire, abboccarsi

conference ['kɑnfərəns] *s* conferenza

confess [kən'fes] *tr* confessare, ammettere ‖ *intr* confessare, confessarsi

confession [kən'feʃən] *s* confessione

confessional [kən'feʃənəl] *s* confessionale *m*

confes'sion of faith' *s* professione di fede

confessor [kən'fesər] *s* confessore *m*

confetti [kən'feti] *s* coriandoli *mpl*

confide [kən'faɪd] *tr* confidare; (*to entrust*) affidare ‖ *intr* confidarsi

confidence ['kɑnfɪdəns] *s* fiducia; sicurezza di sé; (*boldness*) baldanza; (*secrecy*) confidenza

confident ['kɑnfɪdənt] *adj* fiducioso; baldanzoso ‖ *s* confidente *mf*

confidential [ˌkɑnfɪ'denʃəl] *adj* confidenziale

confine ['kɑnfaɪn] *s* confine *m* ‖ [kən'faɪn] *tr* limitare; confinare; **to be confined** essere in altro stato; **to be confined to bed** dover stare a letto

confinement [kən'faɪnmənt] *s* confino; (*childbirth*) parto; (*imprisonment*) prigionia

confirm [kən'fʌrm] *tr* confermare; (eccl) cresimare

confirmed [kən'fʌrmd] *adj* (e.g., *piece of news*) confermato; (*bachelor; drunkard*) impenitente; inveterato; (e.g., *invalid*) cronico

confiscate ['kɑnfɪsˌket] *tr* confiscare

conflagration [ˌkɑnflə'greʃən] *s* conflagrazione

conflict ['kɑnflɪkt] *s* conflitto ‖ [kən'flɪkt] *intr* lottare; essere in conflitto

conflicting [kən'flɪktɪŋ] *adj* contrastante; contraddittorio

confluence ['kɑnfluˌəns] *s* confluenza

conform [kən'fɔrm] *tr* conformare ‖ *intr* conformarsi

conformi·ty [kən'fɔrmɪti] *s* (**-ties**) conformità *f;* **in conformity with** in conformità di

confound [kɑn'faʊnd] *tr* confondere ‖ ['kɑn'faʊnd] *tr* maledire; **confound it!** accidenti!

confounded [kɑn'faʊndɪd] or ['kɑn'faʊndɪd] *adj* maledetto; (*hateful*) odioso

confront [kən'frʌnt] *tr* affrontare, opporsi a; (*to bring face to face*) raffrontare; (*to compare*) confrontare

confrontation [ˌkɑnfrən'teʃən] *s* contestazione

confuse [kən'fjuz] *tr* confondere; **to get confused** confondersi

confusion [kən'fjuʒən] *s* confusione

congeal [kən'dʒil] *tr* congelare; coagulare ‖ *intr* congelarsi; (*said, e.g., of blood*) coagularsi

congenial [kən'dʒinjəl] *adj* (*agreeable*) simpatico; (*having similar tastes*) affine; (*suited to one's needs or tastes*) congeniale

congenital [kən'dʒɛnɪtəl] *adj* congenito

con'ger eel' ['kaŋgər] *s* grongo

congest [kən'dʒɛst] *tr* congestionare ‖ *intr* essere congestionato

congestion [kən'dʒɛstʃən] *s* congestione

conglomerate [kən'glamərɪt] *adj & s* conglomerato ‖ [kən'glamə‚ret] *tr* conglomerare ‖ *intr* conglomerarsi

congratulate [kən'grætʃə‚let] *tr* congratularsi con

congratulation [kən‚grætʃə'leʃən] *s* congratulazione, felicitazione

congregate ['kaŋgrɪ‚get] *intr* congregarsi

congregation [‚kaŋgrɪ'geʃən] *s* congregazione; fedeli *mpl* di una chiesa

congress ['kaŋgrɪs] *s* parlamento; congresso

con'gress·man *s* (**-men**) deputato al congresso degli S.U.

con'gress·wom'an *s* (**-wom'en**) deputatessa al congresso degli S.U.

conical ['kanɪkəl] *adj* conico

conjecture [kən'dʒɛktʃər] *s* congettura ‖ *tr & intr* congetturare

conjugate ['kandʒə‚get] *tr* coniugare

conjugation [‚kandʒə'geʃən] *s* coniugazione

conjunction [kən'dʒaŋkʃən] *s* congiunzione

conjure [kən'dʒur] *tr* (*to entreat*) scongiurare ‖ ['kandʒər] *or* ['kandʒər] *tr* evocare, stregare; **to conjure up** evocare ‖ *intr* fare delle stregonerie

conk [kaŋk] *intr*—**to conk out** (slang) essere in panna; (slang) svenire

connect [kə'nɛkt] *tr* connettere, unire ‖ *intr* connettersi, essere associato; (*said of public conveyances*) operare in coincidenza

connect'ing rod' [kə'nɛktɪŋ] *s* (mach) biella

connection [kə'nɛkʃən] *s* connessione; unione, associazione; (*of trains*) coincidenza; (*relative*) parente *mf*; (*e.g., of a water pipe*) allacciamento; **in connection with** rispetto a

con'ning tow'er ['kanɪŋ] *s* (nav) torretta

conniption [kə'nɪpʃən] *s* (slang) attacco di rabbia

connive [kə'naɪv] *intr* essere connivente; **to connive at** chiudere un occhio su

connote [kə'not] *tr* indicare, suggerire

conquer ['kaŋkər] *tr & intr* conquistare

conqueror ['kaŋkərər] *s* conquistatore *m*

conquest ['kaŋkwɛst] *s* conquista

conscience ['kanʃəns] *s* coscienza; **in all conscience** a prezzo onesto; certamente

conscientious [‚kanʃɪ'ɛnʃəs] *adj* coscienzioso

conscien'tious objec'tor [ab'dʒɛktər] *s* obiettore *m* di coscienza

conscious ['kanʃəs] *adj* (*aware of one's existence*) cosciente; (*aware*) conscio, consapevole; (*lie*) consapevole; **to become conscious** riprendere i sensi

consciousness ['kanʃəsnɪs] *s* coscienza, conoscenza; **to lose consciousness** perdere la conoscenza

conscript ['kanskrɪpt] *s* coscritto ‖ [kən'skrɪpt] *tr* coscrivere, arruolare

conscription [kən'skrɪpʃən] *s* coscrizione

consecrate ['kansɪ‚kret] *tr* consacrare

consecutive [kən'sɛkjətɪv] *adj* consecutivo; di seguito

consensus [kən'sɛnsəs] *s* consenso

consent [kən'sɛnt] *s* consenso; **by common consent** per comune consenso ‖ *intr* consentire

consequence ['kansɪ‚kwɛns] *s* conseguenza

consequential [‚kansɪ'kwɛnʃəl] *adj* conseguente; importante, d'importanza; pomposo, pieno di sé

consequently ['kansɪ‚kwɛntli] *adv* conseguentemente, per conseguenza

conservation [‚kansər'veʃən] *s* conservazione; preservazione delle foreste

conservatism [kən'sʌrvə‚tɪzəm] *s* conservatorismo

conservative [kən'sʌrvətɪv] *adj* conservatore; (*cautious*) cauto; (*preserving*) conservativo; (*free from fads*) tradizionale ‖ *s* conservatore *m*

conservato·ry [kən'sʌrvə‚tori] *s* (**-ries**) (*greenhouse*) serra; (mus) conservatorio

conserve [kən'sʌrv] *tr* conservare

consider [kən'sɪdər] *tr* considerare

considerable [kən'sɪdərəbəl] *adj* (*fairly large*) considerevole; (*worth thinking about*) considerabile

considerate [kən'sɪdərɪt] *adj* riguardoso, premuroso

consideration [kən‚sɪdə'reʃən] *s* considerazione; (*reason*) motivo; (*money*) pagamento; **in consideration of** a cagione di; in cambio di; **on no consideration** in nessuna maniera, mai; **under consideration** in considerazione, sotto esame; **without due consideration** senza riflessione, alla leggera

considering [kən'sɪdərɪŋ] *adv* tutto considerato ‖ *prep* per, visto ‖ *conj* considerando che, visto che

consign [kən'saɪn] *tr* consegnare; (*to send*) inviare; (*to set apart*) assegnare

consignee [‚kansaɪ'ni] *s* consegnatario

consignment [kən'saɪnmənt] *s* consegna; **on consignment** in consegna

consist [kən'sɪst] *intr*—**to consist in** consistere in; **to consist of** consistere in, constare di

consisten·cy [kən'sɪstənsi] *s* (**-cies**) (*firmness, amount of firmness*) consistenza; (*logical connection*) coerenza

consistent [kən'sɪstənt] *adj* (*holding firmly together*) consistente; (*agree-*

ing with itself or oneself) conseguente, coerente; compatibile

consolation [ˌkɑnsəˈleʃən] *s* consolazione

console [ˈkɑnsol] *s (table)* console *f;* (rad, telv) mobile *m;* (mus) console *f* ‖ [kənˈsol] *tr* consolare

consonant [ˈkɑnsənənt] *adj* consonante, armonioso; (gram) consonantico ‖ *s* consonante *f*

consort [ˈkɑnsɔrt] *s* consorte *mf* ‖ [kənˈsɔrt] *intr* associarsi; *(to agree)* concordarsi

conspicuous [kənˈspɪkju‧əs] *adj* visibile, manifesto; notevole; *(too noticeable)* appariscente; **to make oneself conspicuous** farsi notare

conspira‧cy [kənˈspɪrəsi] *s* (-cies) cospirazione, congiura

conspire [kənˈspaɪr] *intr* cospirare, congiurare; *(to act together)* cooperare

constable [ˈkɑnstəbəl] *or* [ˈkʌnstəbəl] *s* poliziotto; *(keeper of a castle)* conestabile *m*

constancy [ˈkɑnstənsi] *s* costanza

constant [ˈkɑnstənt] *adj & s* costante *f*

constellation [ˌkɑnstəˈleʃən] *s* costellazione

constipate [ˈkɑnstɪˌpet] *tr* costipare

constipation [ˌkɑnstɪˈpeʃən] *s* costipazione

constituen‧cy [kənˈstɪtʊˌ‧ənsi] *s* (-cies) *(voters)* elettorato; *(district)* circoscrizione elettorale

constituent [kənˈstɪtʊ‧ənt] *adj* costituente ‖ *s (component)* parte *f* costituente; *(voter)* elettore *m; (of a chemical substance)* costituente *m*

constitute [ˈkɑnstɪˌtjut] *or* [ˈkɑnstɪˌtut] *tr* costituire

constitution [ˌkɑnstɪˈtjuʃən] *or* [ˌkɑnstɪˈtuʃən] *s* costituzione

constrain [kənˈstren] *tr (to force)* costringere; *(to restrain)* restringere, comprimere

constrict [kənˈstrɪkt] *tr* stringere, comprimere

construct [kənˈstrʌkt] *tr* costruire

construction [kənˈstrʌkʃən] *s* costruzione; *(meaning)* interpretazione

construe [kənˈstru] *tr (to interpret)* interpretare; *(to translate)* tradurre; (gram) analizzare

consul [ˈkɑnsəl] *s* console *m*

consular [ˈkɑnsələr] *or* [ˈkɑnsjələr] *adj* consolare

consulate [ˈkɑnsəlɪt] *or* [ˈkɑnsjəlɪt] *s* consolato

consult [kənˈsʌlt] *tr* consultare ‖ *intr* consultarsi

consultation [ˌkɑnsəlˈteʃən] *s* consultazione, conferenza

consume [kənˈsum] *or* [kənˈsjum] *tr* consumare; distruggere; **consumed with** *(passion)* arso di; *(curiosity)* assorbito da

consumer [kənˈsumər] *or* [kənˈsjumər] *s* consumatore *m*

consum'er goods' *spl* beni *mpl* di consumo

consumerism [kənˈsumər ˌɪzem] *s* consumismo

consummate [kənˈsʌmɪt] *adj* consumato ‖ [ˈkɑnsəˌmet] *tr* consumare

consumption [kənˈsʌmpʃən] *s (decay)* consunzione; *(using up)* consumo; (pathol) consunzione

consumptive [kənˈsʌmptɪv] *adj* tubercolotico, tisico; *(wasteful)* logorante ‖ *s* tisico, etico

contact [ˈkɑntækt] *s* contatto; (elec) contatto; (elec) presa di corrente ‖ *tr* (coll) mettersi in contatto con ‖ *intr* (coll) mettersi in contatto

con'tact break'er *s* ruttore *m*

con'tact lens' *s* lente *f* a contatto

contagion [kənˈtedʒən] *s* contagio

contagious [kənˈtedʒəs] *adj* contagioso

contain [kənˈten] *tr* contenere; **to contain oneself** frenarsi

container [kənˈtenər] *s* recipiente *m*, contenitore *m*

contaminate [kənˈtæmɪˌnet] *tr* contaminare

contamination [kənˌtæmɪˈneʃən] *s* contaminazione

contemplate [ˈkɑntəmˌplet] *tr* contemplare; *(to think about)* meditare; *(to have in mind)* progettare, avere in mente ‖ *intr* meditare

contemplation [ˌkɑntəmˈpleʃən] *s* contemplazione; *(intention)* intenzione

contemporaneous [kənˌtempəˈreni‧əs] *adj* contemporaneo, coevo

contemporar‧y [kənˈtempəˌreri] *adj* contemporaneo, coevo ‖ *s* (-ies) contemporaneo

contempt [kənˈtempt] *s (despising)* disprezzo; *(condition of being despised)* dispregio; *(of the law)* disprezzo

contemptible [kənˈtemptɪbəl] *adj* disprezzabile, spregevole

contempt' of court' *s* (law) offesa alla magistratura, oltraggio al tribunale

contemptuous [kənˈtemptʃu‧əs] *adj* sprezzante, sdegnoso

contend [kənˈtend] *tr* dichiarare ‖ *intr (to argue)* disputare, contendere; *(to fight)* lottare

contender [kənˈtendər] *s* competitore *m*, concorrente *m*

content [kənˈtent] *adj* contento; *(willing)* pronto ‖ *s* contentezza ‖ [ˈkɑntent] *s* contenuto; **contents** contenuto ‖ [kənˈtent] *tr* contentare

contented [kənˈtentɪd] *adj* soddisfatto

contention [kənˈtenʃən] *s* disputa, litigio; contenzione

contentious [kənˈtenʃəs] *adj* litigioso

contentment [kənˈtentmənt] *s* contentezza

contest [ˈkɑntest] *s* contesa, controversia; *(game)* gara ‖ [kənˈtest] *tr* disputare, contestare ‖ *intr* combattere, fare resistenza

contestant [kənˈtestənt] *s* concorrente *m;* (law) contendente *m*

context [ˈkɑntekst] *s* contesto

contiguous [kənˈtɪgju‧əs] *adj* contiguo

continence [ˈkɑntɪnəns] *s* continenza

continent [ˈkɑntɪnənt] *adj & s* conti-

nente *m;* **on the Continent** nel continente europeo
continental [,kɑntɪ'nentəl] *adj & s*
continentale *mf*
contingen·cy [kən'tɪndʒənsi] *s* (**-cies**)
contingenza, congiuntura; *(chance)*
eventualità *f*
contingent [kən'tɪndʒənt] *adj* eventuale; imprevisto; *(philos)* contingente; **to be contingent upon** dipendere da
continual [kən'tɪnjʊ·əl] *adj* continuo
continuance [kən'tɪnjʊəns] *s* continua-
zione; *(in office)* permanenza; *(law)*
rinvio
continue [kən'tɪnjʊ] *tr* continuare; *(to
cause to remain)* mantenere; *(to*
rinviare ‖ *intr* continuare; rimanere
continui·ty [,kɑntɪ'njʊ·ɪti] *or* [,kɑntɪ-
'nu·ɪti] *s* (**-ties**) continuità *f*; *(mov &
telv)* sceneggiatura; *(rad)* copione *m*
continuous [kən'tɪnjʊ·əs] *adj* continuo
contin'nous show'ing *s* (mov) spettacolo permanente
contortion [kən'tɔrʃən] *s* contorsione;
(of facts) distorsione
contour ['kɑntʊr] *s* contorno
con'tour line' *s* curva di livello, isoipsa
contraband ['kɑntrə,bænd] *adj* di contrabbando ‖ *s* contrabbando
contrabass ['kɑntrə,bes] *s* contrabasso
contraceptive [,kɑntrə'septɪv] *adj & s*
antifecondativo
contract ['kɑntrækt] *s* contratto ‖
['kɑntrækt] *or* [kən'trækt] *tr (a
business deal)* contrattare; *(marriage)* contrarre ‖ *intr (to shrink)*
contrarsi; **to contract for** contrattare,
appaltare
contraction [kən'trækʃən] *s* contra-
zione
contractor [kən'træktər] *s (person who
makes a contract)* contraente *m;
(person who contracts to supply material)* appaltatore *m,* imprenditore
m; (in building) capomastro
contradict [,kɑntrə'dɪkt] *tr* contraddire
contradiction [,kɑntrə'dɪkʃən] *s* con-
traddizione
contradictory [,kɑntrə'dɪktəri] *adj*
contraddittorio
contrail ['kɑn,trel] *s* (aer) scia di condensazione
contral·to [kən'trælto] *s* (**-tos**) *(person)*
contralto *mf; (voice)* contralto *m*
contraption [kən'træpʃən] *s* (coll) aggeggio
contra·ry ['kɑntreri] *adj* contrario ‖
[kən'treri] *adj* ostinato, caparbio ‖
['kɑntreri] *s* (**-ries**) contrario; **on
the contrary** al contrario ‖ *adv* con-
trariamente
contrast ['kɑntræst] *s* contrasto ‖
[kən'træst] *tr* confrontare ‖ *intr*
contrastare
contravene [,kɑntrə'vin] *tr* contraddire; *(a law)* contravvenire (with
dat)
contribute [kən'trɪbjʊt] *tr* contribuire
‖ *intr* contribuire; *(to a newspaper)*
collaborare

contribution [,kɑntrɪ'bjuʃən] *s* contribuzione; *(to a newspaper)* collaborazione
contributor [kən'trɪbjʊtər] *s* contribu-
tore *m; (to a newspaper)* collaboratore *m*
contrite [kən'traɪt] *adj* contrito
contrition [kən'trɪʃən] *s* contrizione
contrivance [kən'traɪvəns] *s* dispositivo, congegno; *(faculty)* invenzione;
(scheme) artificio, piano
contrive [kən'traɪv] *tr* inventare; *(to
scheme up)* macchinare; *(to bring
about)* effettuare; **to contrive to** trovare il modo di
con·trol [kən'trol] *s* controllo; *(check)*
freno; **controls** comandi *mpl;* **to get
under control** riuscire a controllare ‖
v (pret & pp -trolled; ger -trolling) tr
controllare
controller [kən'trolər] *s* controllore *m;*
analista *mf* di gestione; economo;
(mach) regolatore *m; (elec)* interruttore *m* di linea
control'ling in'terest *s* maggioranza
delle azioni
control' stick' *s* leva di comando
controversial [,kɑntrə'vʌrʃəl] *adj* controverso, polemico, discusso
controver·sy [,kɑntrə,vʌrsi] *s* (**-sies**)
controversia
controvert ['kɑntrə,vʌrt] *or* [,kɑntrə-
'vʌrt] *tr* contraddire
contumacious [,kɑntjʊ'meʃəs] *or*
[,kɑntʊ'meʃəs] *adj* ribelle, contumace
contuma·cy ['kɑntjʊməsi] *or* ['kɑn-
tuməsi] *s* (**-cies**) contumacia
contusion [kən'tjuʒən] *or* [kən'tuʒən]
s contusione
conundrum [kə'nʌndrəm] *s* indovinello
convalesce [,kɑnvə'les] *intr* essere convalescente
convalescence [,kɑnvə'lesəns] *s* con-
valescenza
convalescent [,kɑnvə'lesənt] *adj & s*
convalescente *mf*
con'vales'cent home' *s* convalescenziario
convene [kən'vin] *tr* convocare ‖ *intr*
convenire
convenience [kən'vinjəns] *s* convenienza; *(comfort)* agio; *(anything
that saves work)* conforto; **at your
earliest convenience** quanto prima
convenient [kən'vinjənt] *adj* conveniente, adatto; comodo; **convenient
to** *(near)* (coll) vicino a
convent ['kɑnvent] *s* convento di re-
ligiose
convention [kən'venʃən] *s* convenzione,
assemblea; **conventions** *(customs)*
convenzioni *fpl*
conventional [kən'venʃənəl] *adj* convenzionale
converge [kən'vʌrdʒ] *intr* convergere
conversant [kən'vʌrsənt] *adj* versato,
esperto, dotto
conversation [,kɑnvər'seʃən] *s* conversazione
converse ['kɑnvʌrs] *adj & s* contrario
‖ [kən'vʌrs] *intr* conversare

conversion [kən'vʌrʒən] s conversione; (*unlawful appropriation*) malversazione

convert ['kɑnvʌrt] s convertito || [kən'vʌrt] tr convertire; misappropriare || *intr* convertirsi

convertible [kən'vʌrtɪbəl] *adj* & s convertible f; (aut) trasformabile f, decappottabile f

convex ['kɑnveks] or [kən'veks] *adj* convesso

convey [kən've] tr (*to carry*) trasportare; (*liquids*) convogliare; (*sounds*) trasmettere; (*to express*) esprimere; (*e.g., property*) trasferire

conveyance [kən've·əns] s trasporto; veicolo; comuni·azione; (*of property*) trasferimento; (*deed*) titolo di proprietà

convey'or belt' [kən've·ər] s trasportatore m

convict ['kɑnvɪkt] s condannato || [kən'vɪkt] tr convincere, condannare

conviction [kən'vɪk/ən] s condanna; (*belief*) convinzione, convincimento

convince [kən'vɪns] tr convincere

convincing [kən'vɪnsɪŋ] *adj* convincente

convivial [kən'vɪvɪ·əl] *adj* (*festive*) conviviale; gioviale, bonaccione

convocation [,kɑnvə'keʃən] s convocazione, assemblea

convoke [kən'vok] tr convocare

convoy ['kɑnvɔɪ] s (*of ships*) convoglio; (*of vehicles*) carovana || tr convogliare

convulse [kən'vʌls] tr (*to shake*) scuotere; (*to throw into convulsions*) mettere in convulsioni; (*to cause to shake with laughter*) far torcere dalle risa

coo [ku] *intr* tubare, gemere

cook [kʊk] s cuoco || tr cuocere; **to cook up** (coll) preparare, macchinare || *intr* (*said of food*) cuocere; (*said of a person*) fare il cuoco

cook'book' s libro di cucina

cookie ['kʊki] s var of **cooky**

cooking ['kʊkɪŋ] s culinaria

cook'out' s picnic m, spuntino all'aperto

cook'stove' s cucina economica

cook·y ['kʊki] s (-ies) pasticcino, biscotto

cool [kul] *adj* fresco; calmo; (*not cordial*) freddo; (*bold*) sfacciato || s fresco || tr rinfrescare; **to cool one's heels** fare anticamera || *intr* rinfrescarsi; **to cool off** rinfrescarsi; calmarsi

coolant ['kulənt] s miscela refrigerante

cooler ['kulər] s ghiacciaia; (*slang*) prigione

cool'-head'ed *adj* calmo, imperturbabile

coolish ['kulɪʃ] *adj* freschetto

coon [kun] s procione m

coop [kup] s pollaio; conigliera; **to fly the coop** (slang) scapparsene || **to coop up** rinchiudere tra quattro mura

cooper ['kupər] s bottaio

cooperate [ko'ɑpə·ret] *intr* cooperare

cooperation [ko,ɑpə're/ən] s cooperazione

cooperative [ko'ɑpə,retɪv] *adj* cooperativo || s cooperativa

coordinate [ko'ɔrdɪnɪt] *adj* coordinato; (gram) coordinativo || s (math) coordinata || [ko'ɔrdɪ,net] tr & *intr* coordinare

coot [kut] s (zool) folaga; (slang) vecchio pazzo

cootie ['kuti] s (slang) pidocchio

cop [kɑp] s (slang) poliziotto || v (*pret* & *pp* **copped;** *ger* **copping**) tr (slang) rubare

copartner [ko'pɑrtnər] s consocio, socio

cope [kop] *intr*—**to cope with** tener test a

cope'stone' s pietra da cimasa

copier ['kɑpɪ·ər] s (*person*) copista *mf*; imitatore m; (*machine*) duplicatore m

copilot ['ko,paɪlət] s copilota *mf*

coping ['kopɪŋ] s coronamento, cimasa

cop'ing saw' s seghetto da traforo

copious ['kopɪ·əs] *adj* copioso

copper ['kɑpər] s rame m; (*coin*) soldo; (*boiler*) calderone m; (slang) poliziotto

cop'per·head' s vipera (*Ancistrodon contortrix*)

cop'per·smith' s battirame m, calderaio

coppice ['kɑpɪs] or **copse** [kɑps] s boschetto

copulate ['kɑpjə,let] *intr* copularsi, congiungersi carnalmente

cop·y ['kɑpi] s (-ies) copia; modello; manoscritto || v (*pret* & *pp* -**ied**) tr copiare, imitare || *intr* copiare; **to copy after** imitare

cop'y·book' s quaderno

copyist ['kɑpɪ·ɪst] s copista *mf*; imitatore m

cop'y·right' s copyright m, diritto di proprietà letteraria || tr registrare; proteggere con copyright

cop'y·writ'er s copy-writer m, redattore m pubblicitario

coquetry ['kokətri] or [ko'ketri] s (-ries) civetteria

coquette [ko'ket] s civetta

coquettish [ko'ketɪʃ] *adj* civettuolo

coral ['kɑrəl] or ['kɔrəl] *adj* corallino || s corallo

cor'al reef' s banco di coralli

cord [kɔrd] s corda, fune f; (*corduroy*) tessuto cordonato; (elec) cordone m || tr legare con corda

cordial ['kɔrdʒəl] *adj* & s cordiale m

corduroy ['kɔrdə,rɔɪ] s velluto a coste; **corduroys** pantaloni *mpl* alla cacciatora

core [kor] s (*of fruit*) torsolo; (*central part*) centro; (*of problem*) nocciolo; (*of earth*) barisfera, nucleo centrale; (phys) nucleo; **rotten to the core** guasto nelle ossa

corespondent [,korɪs'pɑndənt] s coimputato in un processo di divorzio

cork [kɔrk] s (*bark*) sughero; (*stopper*) tappo, tappo di sughero || tr tappare

cork' oak' s sughero

cork'screw' s cavatappi m
cormorant ['kɔrmərənt] s cormorano
corn [kɔrn] s granturco, mais m; (kernel) chicco; (thickening of skin) callo; (whiskey) whisky m di granturco; (Brit) grano; (Scot) avena; (slang) banalità f
corn' bread' s pane m di farina gialla
corn' cake' s omelette f di granturco
corn'cob' s tutolo
corn'cob pipe' s pipa fatta di un tutolo di pannocchia
corn'crib' s granaio per le pannocchie
corn' cure' s callifugo
cornea ['kɔrnɪ·ə] s cornea
corner ['kɔrnər] s angolo; (of street) cantonata; situazione difficile; (of the eye) coda dell'occhio; (com) accaparramento, incetta, bagarinaggio; **to cut corners** tagliare le spese; **to turn the corner** passare il punto più pericoloso || tr mettere in una situazione difficile; (the market) incettare, accaparrare
cor'ner cup'board s cantoniera, armadio d'angolo
cor'ner stone' s pietra angolare; (of new building) prima pietra
cornet [kɔr'nɛt] s cornetta
corn'exchange' s borsa dei cereali
corn'field' s (in U.S.A.) campo di granturco; (in England) campo di grano; (in Scotland) campo di avena
corn'flakes' spl fiocchi mpl di granturco
corn' flour' s farina di granturco
corn'flow'er s fiordaliso
corn'husk' s brattea, cartoccio
cornice ['kɔrnɪs] s (of house) cornicione m; (of room) cornice f
corn' liq'uor s whisky m di granturco
corn' meal' s farina di granturco
corn' on the cob' s granturco servito in pannocchia
corn' plas'ter s cerotto per i calli
corn' silk' s barba del granturco
corn'stalk' s fusto di granturco
corn'starch' s amido di granturco
corn·y ['kɔrnɪ] adj (-ier; -iest) (slang) banale, trito, triviale
coronation [,kɑrə'neʃən] or [,kɔrə-'neʃən] s incoronazione
coroner ['kɑrənər] or ['kɔrənər] s magistrato inquirente
cor'oner's in'quest s inchiesta giudiziaria dinanzi a giuria
coronet ['kɑrə,nɛt] or ['kɔrə,nɛt] s corona (non reale); diadema m
corporal ['kɔrpərəl] adj caporalesco || s caporale m
corporation [,kɔrpə'reʃən] s società anonima
corps [kor] s (corps [korz]) corpo
corps' de bal'let s corpo di ballo
corpse [kɔrps] s cadavere m
corpulent ['kɔrpjələnt] adj corpulento
corpuscle ['kɔrpəsəl] s (anat) globulo; (phys) corpuscolo
cor·ral [kə'ræl] s recinto per bestiame || v (pret & pp -ralled; ger -ralling) tr mettere in un recinto; catturare
correct [kə'rɛkt] adj corretto || tr correggere
correction [kə'rɛkʃən] s correzione

corrective [kə'rɛktɪv] adj & s correttivo
correctness [kə'rɛktnɪs] s correttezza
correlate ['kɑrə,let] or ['kɔrə,let] tr correlare || intr essere in correlazione
correlation [,kɑrə'leʃən] or [,kɔrə-'leʃən] s correlazione
correspond [,kɑrɪ'spɑnd] or [,kɔrɪ-'spɑnd] intr corrispondere
correspondence [,kɑrɪ'spɑndəns] or [,kɔrɪ'spɑndəns] s corrispondenza
correspond'ence school' s scuola per corrispondenza
correspondent [,kɑrɪ'spɑndənt] or [,kɔrɪ'spɑndənt] adj & s corrispondente mf
corridor ['kɑrɪdər] or ['kɔrɪdər] s corridoio
corroborate [kə'rɑbə,ret] tr corroborare
corrode [kə'rod] tr corrodere || intr corrodersi
corrosion [kə'roʒən] s corrosione
corrosive [kə'rosɪv] adj & s corrosivo
corrugated ['kɑrə,getɪd] or ['kɔrə-,getɪd] adj ondulato
corrupt [kə'rʌpt] adj corrotto || tr corrompere; (a language) imbarbarire || intr corrompersi
corruption [kə'rʌpʃən] s corruzione
corsage [kɔr'sɑʒ] s (bodice) corpetto; (bouquet) mazzolino di fiori da appuntarsi al vestito
corsair ['kɔr,ser] s corsaro
corset ['kɔrsɪt] s corsetto
Corsican ['kɔrsɪkən] adj & s corso
cortege [kɔr'teʒ] s corteggio
cor·tex ['kɔr,tɛks] s (-tices [tɪ,siz]) cortice f
cortisone ['kɔrtɪ,son] s cortisone m
corvette [kɔr'vɛt] s corvetta
cosmetic [kɑz'mɛtɪk] adj & s cosmetico
cosmic ['kɑzmɪk] adj cosmico
cosmonaut ['kɑzmə,nɔt] s cosmonauta mf
cosmopolitan [,kɑzmə'pɑlɪtən] adj & s cosmopolita mf
cosmos ['kɑzmɑs] s cosmo
cost [kɔst] or [kɑst] s costo, prezzo; **at all costs** or **at any cost** ad ogni costo; **costs** (law) spese fpl processuali || v (pret & pp cost) intr costare
cost·ly ['kɔstlɪ] or ['kɑstlɪ] adj (-lier; -liest) costoso; (sumptuous) lussuoso
cost' of liv'ing s costo della vita
costume ['kɑstjum] or ['kɑstum] s costume m
cos'tume ball' s ballo in costume
cos'tume jew'elry s gioielli falsi
cot [kɑt] s (narrow bed) branda; (cottage) capanna, cabina
coterie ['kotərɪ] s gruppo; (clique) chiesuola
cottage ['kɑtɪdʒ] s casetta, villino
cot'tage cheese' s ricotta americana
cot'ter pin' ['kɑtər] s copiglia, coppiglia
cotton ['kɑtən] s cotone m || intr—**to cotton up to** (coll) cominciare a provare della simpatia per; (coll) andare d'accordo con
cot'ton can'dy s zucchero filato

cot′ton gin′ s sgranatrice f
cot′ton pick′er [ˈpɪkər] s chi raccoglie
il cotone; macchina che raccoglie il
cotone
cot′tonseed oil′ s olio di semi di cotone
cot′ton waste′ s cascame m di cotone
cot′ton·wood′ s pioppo deltoide
couch [kautʃ] s canapè m, sofà m, divano ‖ tr esprimere
couch′ grass′ s gramigna
cougar [ˈkugər] s puma m
cough [kɔf] or [kɑf] s tosse f ‖ tr—to
cough up sputare, sputare tossendo;
(slang) dare, pagare ‖ intr tossire
cough′ drop′ s pastiglia per la tosse
cough′ syr′up s sciroppo per la tosse
could [kʊd] v aux—I could not come
yesterday non ho potuto venire ieri;
I could not see you tomorrow non
potrei vederLa domani; it could not
be so non potrebbe essere così
council [ˈkaunsəl] s consiglio; (eccl)
concilio
coun′cil·man s (-men) consigliere m or
assessore m municipale
coun·sel [ˈkaunsəl] s consiglio; (lawyer) avvocato; to keep one's counsel
essere riservato; to take counsel with
consultarsi con ‖ v (pret & pp -seled
or -selled; ger -seling or -selling) tr
consigliare ‖ intr consigliare; consi-
gliarsi
counselor [ˈkaunsələr] s consigliere m;
avvocato
count [kaunt] s conto; (nobleman)
conte m; (law) capo d'accusa ‖ tr
contare; to count off by (twos,
threes) contare per (due, tre); to
count out escludere; (boxing) contare
‖ intr contare; (to be worth) valere;
to count on contare su
count′down′ s conteggio alla rovescia
countenance [ˈkauntɪnəns] s espressione; (face) faccia; (approval) approvazione ‖ tr approvare, incoraggiare
counter [ˈkauntər] adj contrario ‖ s
contatore m; (token) gettone m;
(table in store) banco; (opposite)
contrario ‖ adv contro, contraria-
mente ‖ tr contrariare, opporre ‖
intr (boxing) rispondere
coun′ter·act′ tr contrariare, neutralizzare
coun′ter·attack′ s contrattacco ‖
coun′ter·attack′ tr & intr contrattaccare
coun′ter·bal′ance s contrappeso ‖
coun′ter·bal′ance tr controbilanciare
coun′ter·clock′wise′ adj antiorario ‖
adv in senso antiorario
coun′ter·es′pionage′ s controspionaggio
counterfeit [ˈkauntərfɪt] adj contraf-
fatto ‖ s contraffazione; moneta falsa
‖ tr & intr contraffare
counterfeiter [ˈkauntərˌfɪtər] s con-
traffattore m
coun′ter·feit mon′ey s moneta falsa
countermand [ˈkauntərˌmænd] or
[ˈkauntərˌmɑnd] tr (troops) dare un
contrordine a; (an order; a payment)
cancellare

coun′ter·march′ s contromarcia ‖ intr
fare contromarcia
coun′ter·offen′sive s controffensiva
coun′ter·pane′ s sopraccoperta
coun′ter·part′ s copia; (person) sosia
coun′ter·point′ s (mus) contrappunto;
(mus) controcanto
Coun′ter Reforma′tion s controriforma
coun′ter·rev′olu′tion s controrivolu-
zione
coun′ter·sign′ s (password) parola d'ordine; (signature) controfirma ‖ tr
controfirmare
coun′ter·sink′ v (pret & pp -sunk) tr
incassare, accecare
coun′ter·spy′ s (-spies) membro del
controspionaggio
coun′ter·stroke′ s contraccolpo
coun′ter·weight′ s contrappeso
countess [ˈkauntɪs] s contessa
countless [ˈkauntlɪs] adj innumerevole
countrified [ˈkʌntrɪˌfaɪd] adj rustico,
rurale
coun·try [ˈkʌntri] s (-tries) (land) terreno; (nation) paese m; (land of
one's birth) patria; (rural region)
campagna
coun′try club′ s circolo privato sportivo
situato nei sobborghi
coun′try cous′in s campagnolo
coun′try estate′ s tenuta
coun′try·folk′ s campagnoli mpl
coun′try gen′tleman s proprietario terriero, signorotto di campagna
coun′try house′ s casa di campagna
coun′try jake′ s (coll) zoticone m
coun′try life′ s vita rustica
coun′try·man s (-men) paesano, com-
paesano
coun′try·peo′ple s gente f di campagna
coun′try·side′ s campagna
coun′try-wide′ adj nazionale
coun′try·wom′an s (-wom′en) s pae-
sana, compaesana
coun·ty [ˈkaunti] s (-ties) contea, distretto
coun′ty seat′ s capoluogo di contea
coup [ku] s colpo; colpo di stato
coup de grâce [ku də ˈgrɑs] s colpo di
grazia
coup d'état [ku deˈtɑ] s colpo di stato
coupe [kup] or coupé [kuˈpe] s coupé
m
couple [ˈkʌpəl] s (of people or animals) paio, coppia; (of things) paio;
(link) unione ‖ tr accoppiare; (to
link) unire, agganciare ‖ intr accoppiarsi
couplet [ˈkʌplɪt] s coppia di versi;
(mus) couplet m
coupling [ˈkʌplɪŋ] s unione; (mach)
giunto
coupon [ˈkupɑn] or [ˈkjupɑn] s coupon m, tagliando
courage [ˈkʌrɪdʒ] s coraggio; to have
the courage of one's convictions
avere il coraggio delle proprie opinioni
courageous [kəˈredʒəs] adj coraggioso
courier [ˈkʌrɪ·ər] or [ˈkʊrɪ·ər] s corriere m
course [kors] s corso; (part of meal)
portata; (place for games) campo;

(row) fila; **in due course** a tempo debito; **in the course of** durante, nel corso di; **of course** certamente, senza dubbio

court [kort] *s (uncovered place surrounded by walls)* corte *f*, cortile *m*; *(royal residence; courtship)* corte *f*; *(short street)* vicolo; *(playing area)* campo; (law) corte *f* || *tr* corteggiare; *(e.g., disaster)* andare in cerca di

courteous [ˈkʌrtɪ·əs] *adj* cortese

courtesan [ˈkʌrtɪzən] or [ˈkortɪzən] *s* cortigiana, meretrice *f*

courte·sy [ˈkʌrtɪsi] *s* (-sies) cortesia, gentilezza; **through the courtesy of** con il gentile permesso di

court'house' *s* palazzo di giustizia

courtier [ˈkortɪ·ər] *s* cortigiano

court' jest'er *s* buffone *m* di corte

court·ly [ˈkortli] *adj* (-lier; -liest) cortese, cortigiano; ossequioso

court'-mar'tial *s* (courts-martial) corte *f* marziale || *v* (*pret & pp* -tialed or -tialled); *ger* -tialing or -tialling) *tr* sottomettere a corte marziale

court' plas'ter *s* taffettà *m*

court'room' *s* aula di giustizia

courtship [ˈkort/ɪp] *s* corte *f*, corteggiamento

court'yard' *s* corte *f*, cortile *m*

cousin [ˈkʌzɪn] *s* cugino

cove [kov] *s* piccola baia, cala

covenant [ˈkʌvənənt] *s* convenzione, patto || *tr* promettere solennemente

cover [ˈkʌvər] *s (lid)* coperchio; *(tablecloth; shelter)* coperto; *(of book)* copertina; **to take cover** nascondersi; **under cover** in segreto, segretamente; **under cover of** sotto la protezione di; **under separate cover** in busta a parte, in plico a parte || *tr* coprire; puntare un'arma verso; (journ) riferire, riportare; **to cover up** coprire completamente || *intr (said of paint)* spandersi

coverage [ˈkʌvərɪdʒ] *s* copertura; (journ) servizio giornalistico; (rad, telv) raggio di udibilità

coveralls [ˈkʌvər ˌɔlz] *spl* tuta

cov'er charge' *s* coperto

cov'ered wag'on *s* carro coperto da tendone

cov'er girl' *s* ragazza-copertina

covering [ˈkʌvərɪŋ] *s* copertura; involucro

covert [ˈkʌvərt] *adj* nascosto, segreto

cov'er-up' *s* dissimulazione; sotterfugio

covet [ˈkʌvɪt] *tr* desiderare, agognare

covetous [ˈkʌvɪtəs] *adj* cupido

covey [ˈkʌvi] *s* covata

cow [kau] *s* vacca; *(of seal, elephant etc.)* femmina *f* || *tr* spaventare, intimidire

coward [ˈkau·ərd] *s* codardo, vile *m*

cowardice [ˈkau·ərdɪs] *s* codardia, viltà *f*

cowardly [ˈkau·ərdli] *adj* codardo, vile || *adv* vilmente

cow'bell' *s* campano, campanaccio

cow'boy' *s* cowboy *m*

cow'catch'er *s* (rr) cacciapietre *m*

cower [ˈkau·ər] *intr* rannicchiarsi

cow'herd' *s* guardiano d'armenti

cow'hide' *s* pelle *f* di vacca

cowl [kaul] *s (hood)* cappuccio; *(monk's cloak)* cappa; *(of car)* sostegno del cofano; *(of chimney)* cappello; (aer) cappottatura

cow'lick' *s* ritrosa

cow'pox' *s* (vet) vaiolo bovino

coxcomb [ˈkaks ˌkom] *s* zerbinotto

coxwain [ˈkaksən] or [ˈkak ˌswen] *s* timoniere *m*

coy [kɔi] *adj* timido, ritroso

co·zy [ˈkozi] *adj* (-zier; -ziest) comodo || *s* (-zies) copriteiera *m*

C.P.A. [ˈsi'pi'e] *s* (letterword) **(certified public accountant)** esperto contabile

crab [kræb] *s* granchio; (aer) scarroccio; *(complaining person)* (coll) scontroso || *v* (*pret & pp* crabbed; *ger* crabbing) *intr* (coll) lamentarsi

crab' apple' *s* mela selvatica; *(tree)* melo selvatico

crabbed [ˈkræbɪd] *adj* sgarbato; *(handwriting)* da gallina; *(style)* oscuro, ermetico

crab' louse' *s* piattola

crab·by [ˈkræbi] *adj* (-bier; -biest) scontroso, sgarbato

crack [kræk] *adj* (slang) di prim'ordine, eccellente || *s (noise)* schiocco; *(break)* rottura, screpolatura, crepa; *(opening)* fessura; (slang) tentativo; (slang) barzelletta || *tr (e.g., a whip)* schioccare; *(to break)* rompere, screpolare; *(oil)* ridurre con distillazione; (coll) risolvere; *(a safe)* (slang) forzare; *(a joke)* (slang) dire; **cracked up to be** (slang) avendo fama di || *intr (to make a noise)* scricchiolare; *(to break)* rompersi, screpolarsi; *(said of voice)* diventare fesso; (slang) avere un esaurimento nervoso; **to crack down** (slang) essere severo; **to crack up** (slang) andare a pezzi

cracked [krækt] *adj* rotto, spezzato; *(voice)* fesso; (coll) pazzo

cracker [ˈkrækər] *s* cracker *m*, galletta

crack'er-bar'rel *adj* in piccolo, alla buona

crack'er-jack' *adj* (slang) di prim'ordine || *s* (slang) persona di prim'ordine

cracking [ˈkrækɪŋ] *s* piroscissione

crackle [ˈkrækəl] *s* crepitio, crepito || *intr* crepitare

crack'pot' *adj & s* (coll) mattoide *mf*

crack'-up' *s* accidente *m;* collisione; *(breakdown in health or in relations)* (coll) colasso; (aer) accidente *m* d'atterraggio

cradle [ˈkredəl] *s* culla; *(of handset)* forcella *f* || *tr* cullare

crad'le-song' *s* ninnananna

craft [kræft] or [krɑft] *s (skill)* abilità *f; (trade)* mestiere *m; (guile)* astuzia, furberia; *(ship)* nave *f*; aeronave

craftiness [ˈkræftɪnɪs] or [ˈkrɑftɪnɪs] *s* astuzia, furberia

crafts'man *s* (-men) operaio specializzato, artigiano

craft′ un′ion s artigianato, sindacato artigiano

craft·y [ˈkræfti] or [ˈkrɑfti] adj (-ier; -iest) astuto, furbo

crag [kræg] s roccia scoscesa, rupe f

cram [kræm] v (pret & pp crammed; ger cramming) tr (to pack full) riempire fino all'orlo; (to stuff with food) rimpinzare ‖ intr rimpinzarsi; (coll) preparare un esame alla svelta

cramp [kræmp] s (painful contraction) crampo; (bar with hooks) grappa; (fig) ostacolo ‖ tr ostacolare, restringere

cranber·ry [ˈkrænˌbɛri] s (-ries) mirtillo

crane [kren] s (orn, mach) gru f; (boom) (telv, mov) giraffa ‖ tr (one's neck) allungare ‖ intr allungarsi il collo

crani·um [ˈkrɛnɪ·əm] s (-a [ə]) cranio

crank [kræŋk] s manovella; (aut) alzacristalli m; (coll) eccentrico ‖ tr girare con la manovella; mettere in moto con la manovella

crank′case′ s coppa dell'olio, carter m

crank′shaft′ s albero a gomito

crank·y [ˈkræŋki] adj (-ier; -iest) irritabile; eccentrico

cran·ny [ˈkræni] s (-nies) (crevice) crepaccio; (crack) fessura

crape [krep] s crespo

crape′hang′er s (slang) pessimista uggioso, guastafeste mf

craps [kræps] s gioco dei dadi; **to shoot craps** giocare ai dadi

crash [kræʃ] adj (coll) d'emergenza ‖ s (noise) scoppio, schianto; accidente m; (collapse of business) crac m, rovescio; (bad landing) atterraggio senza carrello ‖ tr fracassare; **to crash the gate** (coll) entrare senza invito ‖ intr fracassarsi; (com) fallire; **to cash into** investire, cozzare contro; **to cash through** sfondare

crash′ dive′ s immersione rapida di un sottomarino

crash′ hel′met s casco

crass [kræs] adj crasso

crate [kret] s gabbia d'imballaggio ‖ tr imballare in una gabbia

crater [ˈkretər] s cratere m

cravat [krəˈvæt] s cravatta

crave [krev] tr anelare; (to beg) implorare ‖ intr—**to crave for** desiderare ardentemente

craven [ˈkrevən] adj & s codardo

craving [ˈkrevɪŋ] s anelito, desiderio

craw [krɔ] s gozzo

crawl [krɔl] s strisciamento, avanzata striscioni; (sports) crawl m ‖ intr strisciare, avanzare striscioni; (said of worms) brulicare; (said of insects) formicolare; (to feel creepy) sentirsi il formicolìo

crayfish [ˈkrefɪʃ] s (Palinurus vulgaris) aragosta; (Astacus; Cambarus) gambero

crayon [ˈkre·ən] s pastello; disegno a pastello ‖ tr disegnare a pastello

craze [krez] s mania, moda ‖ tr fare impazzire

cra·zy [ˈkrezi] adj (-zier; -ziest) pazzo, matto; **to be crazy about** (coll) esser matto per; **to drive crazy** fare impazzire

cra′zy bone′ s osso rabbioso (del gomito)

creak [krik] s scricchiolìo, cigolìo ‖ intr scricchiolare, cigolare

creak·y [ˈkriki] adj (-ier; -iest) stridente, cigolante

cream [krim] s crema, panna; (finest part) fior fiore m ‖ tr rendere di consistenza cremosa; (to remove cream from) scremare; prendere il meglio di

creamer·y [ˈkriməri] s (-ies) (factory) caseificio; (store) cremeria

cream′ puff′ s bignè m

cream·y [ˈkrimi] adj (-ier; -iest) cremoso; butirroso

crease [kris] s piega, grinza ‖ tr piegare, raggrinzire ‖ intr piegarsi, raggrinzirsi, far pieghe

crease′-resis′tant adj antipiega

create [kriˈet] tr creare

creation [kriˈeʃən] s creazione; **the Creation** il creato

creative [kriˈetɪv] adj creativo

creator [kriˈetər] s creatore m

creature [ˈkritʃər] s creatura

credence [ˈkridəns] s credenza

credentials [krɪˈdɛnʃəlz] spl lettere fpl credenziali; **documento** d'autorizzazione

credible [ˈkrɛdɪbəl] adj credibile

credit [ˈkrɛdɪt] s credito; (in a school) unità f di promozione; (com) avere m; **credits** (mov, telv) titoli mpl di testa ‖ tr accreditare; **to credit s.o. with s.th** attribuire qlco a qlcu

creditable [ˈkrɛdɪtəbəl] adj lodevole

cred′it card′ s carta di credito

creditor [ˈkrɛdɪtər] s creditore m

cre·do [ˈkrido] or [ˈkredo] s (-dos) credo

credulous [ˈkrɛdʒələs] adj credulo

creed [krid] s credo

creek [krik] s fiumicello

creep [krip] v (pret & pp crept [krept]) intr strisciare, avanzare striscioni; (to grow along a wall) arrampicarsi; (to feel creepy) sentirsi il formicolìo

creeper [ˈkripər] s strisciante m; (plant) rampicante f

creeping [ˈkripɪŋ] adj lento; (plant) rampicante

cremate [ˈkrimet] tr cremare

cremato·ry [ˈkriməˌtori] adj crematorio ‖ s (-ries) forno crematorio

Creole [ˈkri·ol] adj & s creolo

crescent [ˈkrɛsənt] s (of Islam) mezzaluna; (of moon) crescente m; (roll) cornetto

cress [krɛs] s crescione m

crest [krɛst] s cresta; (heral) stemma m, insegna

crestfallen [ˈkrɛstˌfɔlən] adj depresso

Cretan [ˈkritən] adj & s cretese mf

cretin [ˈkritən] s cretino

crevice [ˈkrɛvɪs] s fessura, fenditura

crew [kru] s (group working together) personale m; (group of workmen)

mob) ciurma; *(of a ship or racing boat)* equipaggio; (sports) canottaggio

crew′ cut′ *s* capelli *mpl* a spazzola

crib [krɪb] *s (bed)* lettino; *(rack)* rastelliera; *(building)* capanna, granaio; (coll) bigino || *v (pret & pp* **cribbed)** *ger* **cribbing** *tr* (coll) usare un bigino in || *intr* (coll) usare un bigino; (coll) commettere un plagio

cricket [′krɪkɪt] *s* grillo; (sports) cricket *m*, palla a spatola

crier [′kraɪ·ər] *s* banditore *m*

crime [kraɪm] *s* delitto, crimine *m*

criminal [′krɪmɪnəl] *adj* criminale; *(code)* penale || *s* delinquente *mf*

crimp [krɪmp] *s* piega, pieghettatura; **to put a crimp in** (slang) mettere i bastoni fra le ruote a || *tr* pieghettare; *(the hair)* arricciare

crimson [′krɪmzən] *adj & s* cremisi *m* || *intr* imporporarsi

cringe [krɪndʒ] *intr* rannicchiarsi; *(to fawn)* umiliarsi

crinkle [′krɪŋkəl] *tr* arricciare || *intr (to rustle)* sfrusciare

cripple [′krɪpəl] *s* zoppo, sciancato || *tr* storpiare; *(e.g., business)* paralizzare

cri·sis [′kraɪsɪs] *s* (**-ses** [siz]) crisi *f*

crisp [krɪsp] *adj (brittle)* croccante, friabile; *(air)* frizzante; *(sharp and clear)* acuto

criteri·on [kraɪ′tɪrɪ·ən] *s* (**-a** [ə] or **-ons)** criterio

critic [′krɪtɪk] *s* critico

critical [′krɪtɪkəl] *adj* critico

criticism [′krɪtɪ‚sɪzəm] *s* critica

criticize [′krɪtɪ‚saɪz] *tr & intr* criticare

critique [krɪ′tik] *s* critica

croak [krok] *s (of frogs)* gracidio; *(of crows)* gracchiamento || *intr* gracidare; gracchiare; (slang) crepare

Croat [′kro·æt] *s* croato

Croatian [kro′eʃən] *adj & s* croato

cro·chet [kro′ʃe] *s* lavoro all'uncinetto || *v (pret & pp* **-cheted** [′ʃed]; *ger* **-cheting** [′ʃe·ɪŋ]) *tr & intr* lavorare all'uncinetto

crock [krɑk] *s* vaso di terracotta, giara, orcio

crockery [′krɑkəri] *s* vasellame *m* di terracotta, terracotta

crocodile [′krɑkə‚daɪl] *s* coccodrillo

croc′odile tears′ *spl* lacrime *fpl* di coccodrillo

crocus [′krokəs] *s* croco

crone [kron] *s* vecchia incartapecorita

cro·ny [′kroni] *s* (**-nies)** amicone *m*, compare *m*

crook [kruk] *s (hook)* uncino; *(staff)* pastorale *m; (bend)* curva; *(bend of pipe)* gomito; (coll) imbroglione *m* || *tr* piegare || *intr* piegarsi

crooked [′krukɪd] *adj* uncinato; curvo, piegato; (coll) disonesto

croon [krun] *intr* canterellare; cantare in modo sentimentale

crop [krɑp] *s (of bird)* gozzo; *(agricultural product, growing or harvested)* messe *f; (agricultural product harvested)* raccolto; *(riding whip)* frustino; *(hair cut close)* capelli corti; gruppo || *v (pret & pp* **cropped;** *ger* **cropping)** *tr (to cut the ends off of)* spuntare; *(to reap)* raccogliere; *(to cut short)* tosare || *intr*—**to crop out** or **up** apparire inaspettatamente

crop′-dust′ing *s* fumigazione aerea

cropper [′krɑpər] *s* mietitore *m; (sharecropper)* mezzadro; **to come a cropper** (coll) fare una cascataccia; (coll) andare in rovina

croquet [kro′ke] *s* croquet *m*, pallamaglio *m & f*

croquette [kro′ket] *s* crocchetta

crosier [′kroʒər] *s* pastorale *m*

cross [krɔs] or [krɑs] *adj* trasversale, contrario, obliquo; *(irritable)* bisbetico, di cattivo umore; *(of mixed breed)* incrociato || *s* croce *f; (crossing of breeds)* incrocio; **to take the cross** farsi crociato || *tr* crociare, segnare con una croce; *(the street)* attraversare; *(e.g., the legs)* incrociare; *(to draw a line across)* barrare; *(to thwart)* ostacolare; **to cross oneself** farsi il segno della croce; **to cross one's mind** venire in mente a uno; **to cross out** cancellare || *intr* incrociarsi

cross′bones′ *spl* teschio e tibie incrociate *(simbolo della morte)*

cross′bow′ *s* balestra

cross′breed′ *v (pret & pp* **-bred** [‚brɛd]) *tr* incrociare, ibridare

cross′-coun′try *adj* campestre; attraverso il paese

cross′-examina′tion *s* (law) confronto, interrogatorio in contraddittorio

cross-eyed [′krɔs‚aɪd] or [′krɑs‚aɪd] *adj* guercio, strabico

crossing [′krɔsɪŋ] or [′krɑsɪŋ] *s* incrocio; ostacolo; *(of the sea)* traversata; *(of a river)* guado; (rr) passaggio a livello

cross′patch′ *s* (coll) bisbetico

cross′piece′ *s* traversa

cross′ ref′erence *s* richiamo, rimando

cross′road′ *s* strada trasversale; **at the crossroads** al bivio; **crossroads** crocicchio

cross′ sec′tion *s* sezione trasversale

cross′ street′ *s* traversa

cross′ talk′ *s* conversazione; (telp) diafonia

cross′word puz′zle *s* cruciverba *m*, parole incrociate

crotch [krɑtʃ] *s* inforcatura; *(of pants)* cavallo

crotchety [′krɑtʃɪti] *adj* bisbetico

crouch [krautʃ] *intr* accoccolarsi

croup [krup] *s* (pathol) crup *m*

crouton [′krutɑn] *s* crostino

crow [kro] *s* corvo, cornacchia; *(cry of rooster)* chicchirichì *m;* **as the crow flies** in linea retta, a volo d'uccello; **to eat crow** (coll) rimangiarsi le parole || *intr* fare chicchirichì; **to crow over** vantarsi di, esultare per

crow′bar′ *s* bastone *m* a leva

crowd [kraud] *s* folla; *(common people)* masse *fpl;* (coll) gruppo || *tr*

affollare; (to push) spingere || intr
affollarsi; (to press forward) spin-
gersi
crowded ['kraudɪd] adj affollato
crown [kraun] s corona; (of hat) cu-
pola; (highest point) sommo || tr
coronare; (checkers) damare; **to
crown s.o.** (coll) battere qlcu sulla
testa
crown' prince' s principe ereditario
crown' prin'cess s principessa ereditaria
crow's'-foot' s (-feet) zampa di gallina
crow's'-nest' s coffa, gabbia
crucial ['kruʃəl] adj cruciale, critico
crucible ['krusɪbəl] s crogiolo
crucifix ['krusɪfɪks] s crocefisso
crucifixion [,krusɪ'fɪkʃən] s crocifis-
sione
cruci·fy ['krusɪ,faɪ] v (pret & pp -fied)
tr crocifiggere
crude [krud] adj (raw) grezzo; (unripe) acerbo; (roughly made; uncultured) rozzo
crudi·ty ['krudɪti] s (-ties) rozzezza
cruel ['kru·əl] adj crudele
cruel·ty ['kru·əlti] s (-ties) crudeltà f
cruet ['kru·ɪt] s oliera
cruise [kruz] s crociera || tr navigare,
|| intr andare in crociera; andare
avanti e indietro
cruiser ['kruzər] s (nav) incrociatore
m
cruising ['kruzɪŋ] adj di crociera
cruis'ing ra'dius s autonomia di crociera
cruller ['krʌlər] s frittella
crumb [krʌm] s briciola || tr sbricio-
lare; (e.g., a cutlet) impannare ||
intr sbriciolarsi
crumble ['krʌmbəl] tr sbriciolare, pol-
verizzare || intr andare a pezzi, pol-
verizzarsi, sbriciolarsi
crum·my ['krʌmi] adj (-mier; -miest)
(slang) sporco; (miserable) (slang)
schifoso; (e.g., joke) (slang) povero
crumple ['krʌmpəl] tr sgualcire, spiegazzare; **to crumple into a ball** ap-
pallottolare || intr spiegazzarsi
crunch [krʌntʃ] s crocchio; (coll)
stretta, morsa || tr sgranocchiare ||
intr crocchiare
crusade [kru'sed] s crociata || intr
crociarsi; (to take up a cause) farsi
paladino
crusader [kru'sedər] s crociato; (of a
cause) paladino
crush [krʌʃ] s pigiatura, schiacciatura;
(crowd) calca; (coll) infatuazione ||
tr schiacciare; (to grind) frantumare;
(to subdue) sottomettere; (to extract
by squeezing) pigiare
crust [krʌst] s crosta; (slang) faccia
tosta || tr incrostare || intr incrostare,
incrostarsi
crustacean [krʌs'teʃən] s crostaceo
crust·y ['krʌsti] adj (-ier; -iest) crostoso; duro; rude
crutch [krʌtʃ] s gruccia, stampella;
(fig) sostegno
crux [krʌks] s difficoltà f, busillis m;
(crucial point) punto cruciale

cry [kraɪ] s (cries) (shout) grido; (fit
of weeping) pianto; (entreaty) richiamo; (of animal) urlo; **a far cry**
ben lontano, ben distinto; **to have a
good cry** sfogarsi, piangere a calde
lacrime || tr gridare; (to proclaim)
bandire; **to cry down** disprezzare; **to
cry one's heart out** piangere a calde
lacrime; **to cry out** proclamare; **to
cry up** elogiare || intr gridare, urlare;
piangere; **to cry for** implorare
cry'ba'by s (-bies) piagnucolone m
crypt [krɪpt] s cripta
cryptic(al) ['krɪptɪk(əl)] adj segreto,
occulto, misterioso
crystal ['krɪstəl] s cristallo
crys'tal ball' s globo di cristallo
crystalline ['krɪstəlɪn] or ['krɪstə,laɪn]
adj cristallino
crystallize ['krɪstə,laɪz] tr cristalliz-
zare || intr cristallizzarsi
cub [kʌb] s cucciolo; (of lion) leoncino; (of fox) volpicino, volpac-
chiotto
cubbyhole ['kʌbɪ,hol] s sgabuzzino,
bugigattolo
cube [kjub] adj cubico || s cubo; (of
sugar) zolla || tr elevare al cubo; (to
shape) tagliare in quadretti
cubic ['kjubɪk] adj cubico
cub' report'er s giornalista novello
cuckold ['kʌkəld] adj & s cornuto,
becco || tr cornificare
cuckoo ['kuku] adj (slang) pazzo || s
cuculo
cuck'oo clock' s orologio a cucù
cucumber ['kjukʌmbər] s cetriolo
cud [kʌd] s mangime masticato; **to
chew the cud** ruminare
cuddle ['kʌdəl] tr abbracciare affet-
tuosamente || intr (to lie close) gia-
cere vicino; (to curl up) rannicchiarsi, raggomitolarsi
cudg·el ['kʌdʒəl] s manganello, ran-
dello; **to take up the cudgels for** farsi
paladino di || v (pret & pp -eled or
-elled; ger -eling or -elling) tr bastonare, randellare; **to cudgel one's
brains** rompersi la testa
cue [kju] s suggerimento, imbeccata;
(billiards) stecca; **to miss a cue**
(theat) mancare la battuta; (coll)
non capire l'antifona || tr—**to cue
s.o.** (in) on (coll) dare a qlcu informazioni su
cuff [kʌf] s (of shirt) polsino; (of
trousers) risvolto; (slap) schiaffo ||
tr schiaffeggiare
cuff' links' spl bottoni doppi, gemelli
mpl
cuirass [kwɪ'ræs] s corazza
cuisine [kwɪ'zin] s cucina
culinary ['kjulɪ,nɛri] adj culinario
cull [kʌl] s scarto || tr (to gather,
pluck) cogliere; selezionare, scegliere
culminate ['kʌlmɪ,net] intr culminare
culottes [ku'lɑts] spl gonna pantaloni
culpable ['kʌlpəbəl] adj colpevole
culprit ['kʌlprɪt] s colpevole m, imputato
cult [kʌlt] s culto
cultivate ['kʌltɪ,vet] tr coltivare

cultivated ['kʌltɪ ,vetɪd] *adj* colto, coltivato

cultivation [,kʌltɪ'veʃən] *s* coltivazione, cultura

culture ['kʌltʃər] *s* cultura

cultured ['kʌltʃərd] *adj* colto

cul'tured pearl' *s* perla coltivata

culvert ['kʌlvərt] *s* chiavica

cumbersome ['kʌmbərsəm] *adj* ingombrante, incomodo; *(clumsy)* goffo

cumulative ['kjumjə ,letɪv] *adj* cumulativo

cunning ['kʌnɪŋ] *adj* *(sly)* astuto; *(skillful)* abile; *(pretty)* bello; *(created with skill)* ben fatto, fine ∥ *s* astuzia; abilità *f*, destrezza

cup [kʌp] *s* tazza; *(mach, sports)* coppa; *(eccl)* calice *m*; **in one's cups** ubriaco ∥ *v (pret & pp* **cupped;** *ger* **cupping)** *tr* mettere ventose a; **to cup one's hands** foggiare le mani a mo' di conca

cupboard ['kʌbərd] *s* armadio a muro, dispensa; *(buffet)* credenza

Cupid ['kjupɪd] *s* Cupido

cupidity [kju'pɪdɪti] *s* cupidigia

cup' of tea' *s* tazza di tè; *(coll)* forte *m*, e.g., **physics is not my cup of tea** la fisica non è il mio forte

cupola ['kjupələ] *s* cupola

cur [kʌr] *s* cane bastardo; *(despicable fellow)* canaglia, gaglioffo

curate ['kjurɪt] *s* curato

curative ['kjurətɪv] *adj* curativo

curator [kju'retər] *s* conservatore *m*

curb [kʌrb] *s* *(of bit)* barbazzale *m;* *(of pavement)* orlo del marciapiede; *(check)* freno ∥ *tr* frenare

curb'stone' *s* cordone *m;* *(of well)* sponda del pozzo

curd [kʌrd] *s* cagliata ∥ *tr* cagliare ∥ *intr* cagliarsi

curdle ['kʌrdəl] *tr* cagliare; *(the blood)* far gelare ∥ *intr* cagliarsi; *(said of custard)* impazzare

cure [kjur] *s* cura ∥ *tr* curare; *(e.g., meat)* conservare; *(wood)* stagionare

cure'-all' *s* panacea

curfew ['kʌrfju] *s* coprifuoco

curi·o ['kjurɪ ,o] *s* (-os) curiosità *f*

curiosi·ty [,kjurɪ'asɪti] *s* (-ties) curiosità *f*

curious ['kjurɪ·əs] *adj* curioso

curl [kʌrl] *s* *(of hair)* ricciolo; *(anything curled)* rotolo, spirale *f* ∥ *tr* arricciare; arrotolare; *(the lips)* torcere ∥ *intr* arricciarsi; arrotolarsi; **to curl up** raggomitolarsi

curlicue ['kʌrlɪ ,kju] *s* ghirigoro

curl'ing i'ron *s* ferro da arricciare

curl'pa·per *s* bigodino

curl·y ['kʌrli] *adj* (-ier; -iest) ricciuto

curmudgeon [kər'mʌdʒən] *s* bisbetico

currant ['kʌrənt] *s* *(seedless raisin)* uva passa di Corinto, uva sultanina; *(shrub and berry of genus Ribes)* ribes *m*

curren·cy ['kʌrənsi] *s* (-cies) *(circulation)* circolazione; *(money)* denaro circolante; *(general use)* corso

current ['kʌrənt] *adj & s* corrente *f*

cur'rent account' *s* conto corrente

cur'rent events' *spl* attualità *fpl*, eventi *mpl* correnti

curricu·lum [kə'rɪkjələm] *s* (-lums or -la [lə]) programma *m;* piano educativo

cur·ry ['kʌri] *s* (-ries) *(spice)* curry *m* ∥ *v (pret & pp* -ried) *tr (a horse)* strigliare; *(leather)* conciare; **to curry favor** cercare di compiacere

cur'ry-comb' *s* striglia ∥ *tr* strigliare

curse [kʌrs] *s* maledizione; bestemmia ∥ *tr* maledire ∥ *intr* imprecare, bestemmiare

cursed ['kʌrsɪd] or [kʌrst] *adj* maledetto; *(hateful)* odiato

cursive ['kʌrsɪv] *adj & s* corsivo

cursory ['kʌrsəri] *adj* rapido, superficiale

curt [kʌrt] *adj* *(rude)* brusco, sgarbato; *(short)* breve, conciso

curtail [kər'tel] *tr* ridurre, restringere

curtain ['kʌrtən] *s* *(in front of stage)* sipario; *(for window)* tendina; *(fig)* cortina ∥ *tr* coprire con tenda; separare con tenda; coprire, nascondere

cur'tain call' *s* (theat) chiamata

cur'tain rais'er ['rezər] *s* (theat) avanspettacolo; *(sports)* incontro preliminare

cur'tain ring' *s* campanella

cur'tain rod' *s* bastone *m* su cui si fissano le tende

curt·sy ['kʌrtsi] *s* (-sies) riverenza, inchino ∥ *v (pret & pp* -sied) *intr* fare la riverenza, inchinarsi

curve [kʌrv] *s* curva ∥ *tr* curvare ∥ *intr* curvarsi

curved [kʌrvd] *adj* curvo, curvato

cushion ['kuʃən] *s* cuscino; *(of billiard table)* mattonella ∥ *tr* proteggere, ammortizzare, attutire

cuspidor ['kʌspɪ ,dər] *s* sputacchiera

cuss [kʌs] *s* (coll) bestemmia; (coll) tipo perverso ∥ *tr* maledire ∥ *intr* bestemmiare

custard ['kʌstərd] *s* crema

custodian [kəs'todɪ·ən] *s* *(caretaker)* custode *m*, guardiano *m;* *(person who is entrusted with s.th)* conservatore *m;* *(janitor of school)* bidello

custo·dy ['kʌstədi] *s* (-dies) custodia; *(imprisonment)* arresto; **in custody** in prigione; **to take into custody** arrestare

custom ['kʌstəm] *s* costume *m;* *(customers)* clientela; **customs** dogana; **customs** dogana; diritti *mpl* doganali

customary ['kʌstə ,meri] *adj* consueto, abituale

custom-built ['kʌstəm'bɪlt] *adj* fatto su misura; *(car)* fuori serie

customer ['kʌstəmər] *s* cliente *mf*

cus'tom·house' *adj* doganale ∥ *s* dogana

custom-made ['kʌstəm'med] *adj* fatto su misura

cus'toms inspec'tion *s* visita doganale

cus'toms of'ficer *s* doganiere *m*

cus'tom work' *s* lavoro fatto su misura

cut [kʌt] *adj (prices)* ridotto; **to be cut out for** essere tagliato per ∥ *s* taglio; *(reduction)* ribasso; *(typ)* cliché *m;*

(snub) (coll) affronto; (coll) assenza non autorizzata; (coll) parte *f;* **a cut above** (coll) un po' meglio di || *tr* tagliare; *(cards)* alzare; *(prices)* ridurre; (coll) far finta di non riconoscere; (coll) marinare; **cut it out!** basta!; **to cut back** ridurre; **to cut off** tagliare; diseredare; (surg) amputare; **to cut short** interrompere; **to cut teeth** fare i denti; **to cut up** sminuzzare; criticare || *intr* tagliare, tagliarsi; **to cut across** attraversare; **to cut in** interrompere; **to cut under** vendere sottoprezzo; **to cut up** (slang) fare il pagliaccio

cut-and-dried ['kʌtən'draɪd] *adj* monotono, stantio; bell'e fatto, fatto in anticipo

cutaneous [kju'tenɪ-əs] *adj* cutaneo

cut'away' coat' ['kʌtə,we] *s* marsina da giorno

cut'back' *s* riduzione; eliminazione; (mov) ritorno dell'azione a un'epoca anteriore

cute [kjut] *adj* (coll) carino, grazioso; ˙(shrewd) (coll) furbo

cut' glass' *s* cristallo intagliato

cuticle ['kjutɪkəl] *s* cuticola

cutlass ['kʌtləs] *s* sciabola

cutler ['kʌtlər] *s* coltellinaio

cutlery ['kʌtləri] *s* coltelleria

cutlet ['kʌtlɪt] *s* cotoletta; *(flat croquette)* polpetta

cut'off' *s* taglio; *(road)* scorciatoia; *(of cylinder)* otturatore *m,* chiusura dell'ammissione; *(of river)* braccio diretto

cut'out' *s* ritaglio; (aut) valvola di scappamento libero

cut'-rate' *adj* a prezzo ridotto

cutter ['kʌtər] *s* tagliatore *m;* (naut) cutter *m*

cut'throat' *adj* spietato; *(relentless)* senza posa || *s* assassino

cutting ['kʌtɪŋ] *adj* tagliente || *s* taglio; *(from a newspaper)* ritaglio;

(e.g., of prices) riduzione; (hort) talea

cut'ting board' *s* tagliere *m;* *(of dishwasher)* piano d'appoggio

cut'ting edge' *s* taglio

cuttlefish ['kʌtəl,fɪʃ] *s* seppia

cut'wat'er *s* *(of bridge)* tagliacque *m;* *(of boat)* tagliamare *m*

cyanamide [saɪ'ænə,maɪd] *s* cianamide *f;* cianamide *f* di calcio

cyanide ['saɪ-ə,naɪd] *s* cianuro

cycle ['saɪkəl] *s* ciclo; bicicletta; *(of internal combustion engine)* tempo; (phys) periodo || *intr* andare in bicicletta

cyclic(al) ['saɪklɪk(əl)] or ['sɪklɪk(əl)] *adj* ciclico

cyclone ['saɪklon] *s* ciclone *m*

cyclops ['saɪklɑps] *s* ciclope *m*

cyclotron ['saɪklo,trɑn] or ['sɪklo,trɑn] *s* ciclotrone *m*

cylinder ['sɪlɪndər] *s* cilindro; *(container)* bombola

cyl'inder block' *s* monoblocco

cyl'inder bore' *s* alesaggio

cyl'inder head' *s* testa

cylindric(al) [sɪ'lɪndrɪk(əl)] *adj* cilindrico

cymbals ['sɪmbəls] *spl* piatti *mpl*

cynic ['sɪnɪk] *adj & s* cinico

cynical ['sɪnɪkəl] *adj* cinico

cynicism ['sɪnɪ,sɪzəm] *s* cinismo

cynosure ['saɪnə,ʃur] or ['sɪnə,ʃur] *s* centro dell'attenzione

cypress ['saɪprəs] *s* cipresso

Cyprus ['saɪprəs] *s* Cipro

Cyrus ['saɪrəs] *s* Ciro

cyst [sɪst] *s* ciste *f,* cisti *f*

czar [zɑr] *s* zar *m*

czarina [zɑ'rinə] *s* zarina

Czech [tʃɛk] *adj & s* ceco

Czecho-Slovak ['tʃɛko'slovæk] *adj & s* cecoslovacco

Czecho-Slovakia [,tʃɛkoslo'vækɪ-ə] *s* la Cecoslovacchia

D

D, d [di] *s* quarta lettera dell'alfabeto inglese

dab [dæb] *s* tocco; *(of mud)* schizzo; *(e.g., of butter)* spalmata || *v* *(pret & pp* dabbed; *ger* dabbing) *tr* toccare leggermente; *(to apply a substance to)* spennellare

dabble ['dæbəl] *tr* spruzzare || *intr* diguazzare; **to dabble in** occuparsi di; *(stocks)* speculare in

dad [dæd] *s* (coll) papà *m*

dad·dy ['dædɪ] *s (-dies)* (coll) papà *m*

daffodil ['dæfədɪl] *s* trombone *m*

daff·y ['dæfɪ] *adj (-ier; -iest)* (coll) pazzo

dagger ['dægər] *s* daga, pugnale *m;* (typ) croce *f;* **to look daggers at** fulminare con lo sguardo

dahlia ['dæljə] *s* dalia

dai·ly ['delɪ] *adj* quotidiano, diurno || *s (-lies)* quotidiano || *adv* giornalmente

dai'ly dou'ble *s* duplice *f,* accoppiata

dain·ty ['dentɪ] *adj (-tier; -tiest)* delicato || *s (-ties)* manicaretto

dair·y ['deri] *s (-ies)* *(store)* latteria; *(factory)* caseificio

dair'y farm' *s* vaccheria

dair'y·man *s (-men)* lattaio

dais ['de-ɪs] *s* predella

dai·sy ['dezɪ] *s (-sies)* margherita

dal·ly ['dælɪ] *v (pret & pp* -lied) *intr (to loiter)* bighellonare; *(to trifle)* scherzare

dam [dæm] *s* diga; *(for fishing)* pescaia; (zool) fattrice *f* || *v (pret & pp* dammed; *ger* damming) *tr* arginare; ostruire; tappare

damage ['dæmɪdʒ] *s* danno, scapito; (fig) menomazione; (com) avaria; **damages** danni *mpl* ‖ *tr* danneggiare, ledere; sinistrare

damascene ['dæmə,sin] or [,dæmə-'sin] *adj* damasceno ‖ *s* damaschinatura ‖ *tr* damaschinare

dame [dem] *s* dama, signora; (slang) donna

damn [dæm] *s*—**I don't give a damn** (slang) me ne impipo; **that's not worth a damn** (slang) non vale un fico ‖ *tr* dannare, condannare ‖ *intr* maledire ‖ *interj* maledizione!

damnation [dæm'neʃən] *s* dannazione; (theol) condanna

damned [dæmd] *adj* dannato, maledetto ‖ **the damned** i dannati ‖ *adv* maledettamente

damp [dæmp] *adj* umido ‖ *s* umidità *f*; (firedamp) grisou *m* ‖ *tr* inumidire; umettare; (to muffle) smorzare; (waves) (elec) smorzare; **to damp s.o.'s enthusiasm** raffreddare gli spiriti di qlcu; scoraggiare qlcu

dampen ['dæmpən] *tr* inumidire; umettare; smorzare; (s.o.'s enthusiasm) raffreddare

damper ['dæmpər] *s* (of chimney) valvola di tiraggio; (fig) doccia fredda; (mus) smorzatore *m*; (mus) sordina

damsel ['dæmzəl] *s* damigella

dance [dæns] or [dɑns] *s* ballo, danza ‖ *tr & intr* ballare, danzare

dance' band' *s* orchestrina

dance' floor' *s* pista da ballo

dance' hall' *s* sala da ballo

dancer ['dænsər] or ['dɑnsər] *s* danzatore *m*; (expert or professional) ballerino

danc'ing part'ner *s* cavaliere *m*; dama

danc'ing par'ty *s* festa da ballo

dandelion ['dændɪ,laɪən] *s* dente *m* di leone, soffione *m*

dandruff ['dændrəf] *s* forfora

dan·dy ['dændi] *adj* (-dier; -diest) (coll) eccellente, magnifico ‖ *s* (-dies) damerino, elegantone *m*

Dane [den] *s* danese *mf*

danger ['dendʒər] *s* pericolo

dangerous ['dendʒərəs] *adj* pericoloso

dangle ['dæŋgəl] *tr* dondolare ‖ *intr* penzolare, ciondolare

Danish ['denɪʃ] *adj & s* danese *m*

dank [dæŋk] *adj* umido

Danube ['dænjub] *s* Danubio

dapper ['dæpər] *adj* azzimato

dapple ['dæpəl] *adj* pezzato ‖ *tr* chiazzare

dap'ple-gray' *adj* storno

dare [der] *s* sfida ‖ *tr* sfidare ‖ *intr* osare; **I dare say** oserei dire; forse, e.g., **I dare say we will be done at seven** forse avremo finito alle sette; **to dare to** (to have the courage to) osare di, fidarsi a

dare'dev'il *s* scavezzacollo

daring ['derɪŋ] *adj* temerario, spericolato ‖ *s* audacia, temerarietà *f*

dark [dɑrk] *adj* scuro; (complexion) bruno; oscuro, segreto; (gloomy) tetro, fosco ‖ *s* oscurità *f*, scuro; tenebre *fpl*; **in the dark** al buio

Dark' Ag'es *spl* alto medio evo

dark-complexioned ['dɑrkkəm'plɛk-ʃənd] *adj* bruno

darken ['dɑrkən] *tr* scurire, oscurare ‖ *intr* scurirsi, oscurarsi

dark' horse' *s* vincitore imprevisto, outsider *m*

darkly ['dɑrkli] *adv* oscuramente; segretamente

dark' meat' *s* gamba o anca (di pollo o tacchino)

darkness ['dɑrknɪs] *s* oscurità *f*

dark'room' *s* camera oscura

darling ['dɑrlɪŋ] *adj & s* caro, amato

darn [dɑrn] *s* rammendo ‖ *tr* rammendare ‖ *interj* (coll) accidenti!

darned [dɑrnd] *adj* (coll) maledetto ‖ *adv* maledettamente; (coll) tremendamente

darnel ['dɑrnəl] *s* zizzania

darning ['dɑrnɪŋ] *s* rammendo

darn'ing nee'dle *s* ago da rammendo

dart [dɑrt] *s* freccia, dardo; (game) frecciolo ‖ *intr* dardeggiare; lanciarsi, precipitarsi

dash [dæʃ] *s* sciacquio; piccola quantità, sospetto; (spirit) brio; (typ, telg) trattino, lineetta ‖ *tr* lanciare; mescolare; (s.o.'s hopes) frustrare; deprimere; **to dash off** gettar giù; **to dash to pieces** fare a pezzi ‖ *intr* precipitarsi; **to dash against** gettarsi contro; **to dash by** passare a gran velocità; **to dash in** entrare come un razzo; **to dash off** or **out** andarsene in fretta; lanciarsi fuori

dash'board' *s* cruscotto; (in an open carriage) parafango

dashing ['dæʃɪŋ] *adj* impetuoso; vistoso ‖ *s* (of waves) sciacquio

dastard ['dæstərd] *adj & s* vile *mf*, codardo

da'ta proc'essing *s* elaborazione

date [det] *s* (time) data; (palm) palma da datteri; (fruit) dattero; (appointment) (coll) appuntamento; **out of date** fuori moda; **to date** sinora; **up to date** a giorno ‖ *tr* datare; (coll) avere un appuntamento con ‖ *intr*— **to date from** partire da

date' line' *s* linea del cambiamento di data

dative ['detɪv] *adj & s* dativo

datum ['detəm] or ['dætəm] *s* (data ['detə] or ['dætə]) dato

daub [dɔb] *s* imbratto ‖ *tr* imbrattare

daughter ['dɔtər] *s* figlia, figliola

daughter-in-law ['dɔtərɪn,lɔ] *s* (daughters-in-law) nuora

daunt [dɔnt] *tr* spaventare; intimidire

dauntless ['dɔntlɪs] *adj* intrepido

dauphin ['dɔfɪn] *s* delfino

davenport ['dævən,port] *s* sofà *m*, sofà *m* letto

davit ['dævɪt] *s* gru *f* per lancia

daw [dɔ] *s* cornacchia

dawdle ['dɔdəl] *intr* bighellonare

dawn [dɔn] *s* alba ‖ *intr* (said of the day) farsi, nascere, spuntare; **to dawn on** cominciare a apparire nella mente di

day [de] *adj* diurno; (student) esterno ‖ *s* giorno; (of travel, work, etc.)

giornata; **a few days ago** giorni fa; **any day now** da un giorno all'altro; **by day** di giorno; **the day after** il giorno dopo; **the day after tomorrow** dopodomani; **the day before yesterday** ieri l'altro; **to call it a day** (coll) finire di lavorare

day' bed' s sofà m letto

day'book' s brogliaccio

day'break' s far m del giorno

day'dream' s fantasticheria || intr fantasticare

day' la'borer s giornaliero

day'light s luce f del giorno; alba; **in broad daylight** alla luce del sole; **to see daylight** comprendere; vedere la fine

day'light-sav'ing time s ora legale, ora estiva

day' nurs'ery s asilo infantile

day' off' s giorno di vacanza; (of servant) libera uscita

day' of reck'oning s giorno di rendiconto; (last judgment) giorno del giudizio

day' shift' s turno diurno

day'time' adj diurno || s giornata

daze [dez] s stordimento; **in a daze** stordito || tr stordire

dazzle ['dæzəl] s abbagliamento || tr abbagliare

dazzling ['dæzlɪŋ] adj abbagliante

deacon ['dikən] s diacono

dead [dɛd] adj morto || s—**in the dead of** (e.g., night) nel pieno di; **the dead** i morti || adv (coll) completamente; (abruptly) (coll) di colpo

dead' beat' adj (coll) stanco morto

dead'beat' s (coll) scroccone m

dead' cen'ter s punto morto

dead'drunk' adj ubriaco fradicio

deaden ['dɛdən] tr attutire; (e.g., s.o.'s senses) ottundere

dead' end' s vicolo cieco

dead' let'ter s lettera morta; lettera non reclamata

dead'line s termine m

dead'lock' s punto morto || tr portare al punto morto || intr giungere al punto morto

dead·ly ['dɛdli] adj (-lier; -liest) mortale; insopportabile

dead' pan' s (slang) faccia senza espressione

dead'pan' adj senza espressione

dead' reck'oning s (naut) stima

dead'wood' s legna secca; (fig) zavorra

deaf [dɛf] adj sordo; **to turn a deaf ear** fare orecchio di mercante

deaf'-and-dumb' adj sordomuto

deafen ['dɛfən] tr assordare, intronare

deafening ['dɛfənɪŋ] adj assordante

deaf'-mute' s sordomuto

deafness ['dɛfnɪs] s sordità f

deal [dil] s accordo; quantità f; (cards) mano, girata; (coll) affare m; (coll) trattamento; **a good deal (of)** or **a great deal (of)** moltissimo || v (pret & pp dealt [dɛlt]) tr (a blow) menare; (cards) fare, sfogliare; **to deal s.o. in** (coll) includere || intr mercanteggiare, commerciare; fare le

carte; **to deal with** trattare con; trattare di

dealer ['dilər] s commerciante mf, esercente mf; (cards) mazziere m

dean [din] s decano

dear [dir] adj (beloved; expensive) caro; **dear me!** povero me!; **Dear Sir** egregio Signore || s caro

dearie ['dɪri] s (coll) caro

dearth [dʌrθ] s scarsezza; insufficienza

death [dɛθ] s morte f; **to bleed to death** morire dissanguato; **to burn to death** morire bruciato; **to choke to death** morire di soffocazione; **to freeze to death** morire di gelo; **to put to death** dare la morte a; **to shoot to death** uccidere a fucilate; **to stab to death** scannare; **to starve to death** far morire di fame; morire di fame

death'bed' s letto di morte

death'blow' s colpo mortale

deathless ['dɛθlɪs] adj immortale, eterno

deathly ['dɛθli] adj mortale || adv mortalmente; assolutamente

death' pen'alty s pena di morte

death' rate' s mortalità f

death' rat'tle s rantolo della morte

death' ray' s raggio della morte

death' sen'tence s pena di morte

death' war'rant s pena di morte; fine f di ogni speranza

death'watch' s veglia mortuaria; (zool) orologio della morte

debacle [de'bɑkəl] s disastro; (downfall) tracollo; (in a river) sgelo repentino

de·bar [dɪ'bɑr] v (pret & pp -barred; ger -barring) tr escludere; proibire (with dat)

debark [dɪ'bɑrk] tr & intr sbarcare

debarkation [,dibɑr'keʃən] s sbarco

debase [dɪ'bes] tr degradare; adulterare

debatable [dɪ'betəbəl] adj discutibile

debate [dɪ'bet] s discussione || tr & intr discutere

debauch [dɪ'bɔtʃ] s dissolutezza, corruzione || tr corrompere

debauchee [,dɛbə'ʃi] or [,dɛbə'tʃi] s degenerato, vizioso

debauch·ery [dɪ'bɔtʃəri] s (-ies) dissolutezza, corruzione

debenture [dɪ'bentʃər] s (bond) obbligazione; (voucher) buono

debilitate [dɪ'bɪlɪ,tet] tr debilitare

debili·ty [dɪ'bɪlɪti] s (-ties) debolezza

debit ['dɛbɪt] s debito; (debit side) (com) dare m || tr addebitare

debonair [,dɛbə'nɛr] adj gioviale; cortese

debris [de'bri] s detrito, rottami mpl

debt [dɛt] s debito; **to run into debt** indebitarsi

debtor ['dɛtər] s debitore m

debut [de'bju] or ['debju] s debutto; **to make one's debut** debuttare || intr debuttare

debutante [,dɛbju'tɑnt] or ['debjə-,tænt] s debuttante f, esordiente f

decade ['dɛked] s decennio

decadence [dɪ'kedəns] s decadenza

decadent [dɪ'kedənt] *adj & s* decadente *mf*

decanter [dɪ'kæntər] *s* boccia

decapitate [dɪ'kæpɪ,tet] *tr* decapitare

decay [dɪ'ke] *s (decline)* decadimento; *(rotting)* marciume *m*, putredine *f*; *(of teeth)* carie *f* || *tr* imputridire || *intr* imputridire, marcire; *(said of teeth)* cariarsi

decease [dɪ'sis] *s* decesso || *intr* decedere

deceased [dɪ'sist] *adj & s* defunto

deceit [dɪ'sit] *s* inganno, frode *f*

deceitful [dɪ'sitfəl] *adj* ingannatore, menzognero, subdolo

deceive [dɪ'siv] *tr & intr* ingannare

decelerate [dɪ'selə,ret] *tr & intr* decelerare

December [dɪ'sembər] *s* dicembre *m*

decen·cy ['disənsi] *s* (-cies) decenza, pudore *m*; **decencies** convenienze *fpl*

decent ['disənt] *adj* decente; *(proper)* conveniente

decentralize [dɪ'sentrə,laɪz] *tr* decentrare

deception [dɪ'sepʃən] *s* inganno

deceptive [dɪ'septɪv] *adj* ingannevole

decide [dɪ'saɪd] *tr* decidere || *intr* decidere, decidersi

decimal ['desɪməl] *adj & s* decimale *m*

dec'imal point' *s (in Italian the comma is used to separate the decimal fraction from the integer)* virgola

decimate ['desɪ,met] *tr* decimare

decipher [dɪ'saɪfər] *tr* decifrare

decision [dɪ'sɪʒən] *s* decisione

decisive [dɪ'saɪsɪv] *adj* decisivo; *(resolute)* fermo

deck [dek] *s (of cards)* mazzo; (naut) coperta, tolda, ponte *m*; **on deck** (coll) pronto; (coll) prossimo || *tr—* **to deck out** adornare; *(with flags)* imbandierare

deck' chair' *s* sedia a sdraio

deck' hand' *s* marinaio di coperta

deck'house' *s* (naut) tuga

deck'le edge' ['dekəl] *s* sbavatura

declaim [dɪ'klem] *tr & intr* declamare

declaration [,deklə're∫ən] *s* dichiarazione

declarative [dɪ'klærətɪv] *adj* declaratorio; (gram) enunciativo

declare [dɪ'kler] *tr* dichiarare || *intr* dichiararsi

declension [dɪ'klenʃən] *s* declinazione

declination [,deklɪ'ne∫ən] *s* declinazione

decline [dɪ'klaɪn] *s* decadenza; *(in prices)* ribasso; *(in health)* deperimento; *(of sun)* tramonto || *tr* declinare || *intr* declinare; decadere, scadere

declivi·ty [dɪ'klɪvɪti] *s* (-ties) declivio, pendice *f*

decode [di'kod] *tr* decifrare

décolleté [,dekal'te] *adj* scollato

decompose [,dikəm'poz] *tr* decomporre || *intr* decomporsi

decomposition [,dikampə'zɪʃən] *s* decomposizione

décor [de'kɔr] *s* decorazione; *(of a room)* stile *m*; (theat) scenario

decorate ['dekə,ret] *tr* decorare

decoration [,dekə're∫ən] *s* decorazione

decorator ['dekə,retər] *s* decoratore *m*

decorous ['dekərəs] or [dɪ'korəs] *adj* corretto, decoroso

decorum [dɪ'korəm] *s* decoro, correttezza

decoy [dɪ'kɔɪ] or ['dikɔɪ] *s* richiamo; *(for birds)* zimbello; *(person)* adescatore *m* || *tr (to lure)* adescare; *(to deceive)* abbindolare

decrease ['dikris] or [dɪ'kris] *s* diminuzione; *(of salary)* decurtazione || [dɪ'kris] *tr* decurtare || *intr* diminuire

decree [dɪ'kri] *s* decreto || *tr* decretare

de·cry [dɪ'kraɪ] *v* (pret & pp **-cried**) *tr* denigrare, screditare

dedicate ['dedɪ,ket] *tr* dedicare

dedication [,dedɪ'ke∫ən] *s* dedizione; *(inscription in a book)* dedica

deduce [dɪ'djus] or [dɪ'dus] *tr* dedurre

deduct [dɪ'dʌkt] *tr* dedurre, defalcare

deductible [dɪ'dʌktɪbəl] *adj* defalcabile || *s* (ins) franchigia

deduction [dɪ'dʌkʃən] *s* deduzione

deed [did] *s* fatto; *(exploit)* prodezza; (law) titolo || *tr* trasferire legalmente

deem [dim] *tr & intr* credere, giudicare

deep [dip] *adj* profondo; basso; *(woods)* folto; *(friendship)* intimo; **deep in debt** carico di debiti; **deep in thought** assorto in pensieri || *adv* profondamente; **deep into the night** a notte fatta; **to go deep into** approfondirsi in

deepen ['dipən] *tr* approfondire || *intr* approfondirsi

deep'-freeze' *tr* (pret **-froze** [froz]; pp **-frozen** [frozən]) *tr* surgelare

deep-laid ['dip,led] *adj* preparato astutamente

deep' mourn'ing *s* lutto stretto

deep-rooted ['dip,rutɪd] *adj* profondo

deep'-sea' fish'ing *s* pesca d'alto mare or d'altura

deep-seated ['dip,sitɪd] *adj* profondo, connaturato

Deep' South' *s* Profondo Sud

deer [dɪr] *s* cervo

deer'skin' *s* pelle *f* di daino

deface [dɪ'fes] *tr* sfigurare

defamation [,defə'meʃən] or [,difə'meʃən] *s* diffamazione

defame [dɪ'fem] *tr* diffamare

default [dɪ'fɔlt] *s* mancanza; *(failure to act)* inadempienza; **in default of** per mancanza di; **to lose by default** dichiarare forfeit || *tr* essere inadempiente a || *intr* essere inadempiente; (sports) dichiarare forfeit

defeat [dɪ'fit] *s* sconfitta, disfatta || *tr* sconfiggere, vincere

defeatism [dɪ'fitɪzəm] *s* disfattismo

defeatist [dɪ'fitɪst] *adj & s* disfattista *mf*

defecate ['defɪ,ket] *intr* defecare

defect [dɪ'fekt] or ['difekt] *s* vizio, difetto || [dɪ'fekt] *intr* defezionare

defection [dɪ'fekʃən] *s* defezione

defective [dɪ'fektɪv] *adj* difettivo, difettoso

defend [dɪˈfɛnd] *tr* difendere, proteggere

defendant [dɪˈfɛndənt] *s* (law) imputato, querelato

defender [dɪˈfɛndər] *s* difensore *m*

defense [dɪˈfɛns] *s* difesa

defenseless [dɪˈfɛnslɪs] *adj* indifeso

defensive [dɪˈfɛnsɪv] *adj* difensivo || difensiva

de·fer [dɪˈfʌr] *v* (*pret & pp* **-ferred;** *ger* **-ferring**) *tr* differire, rinviare || *intr* rimettersi

deference [ˈdɛfərəns] *s* deferenza

deferential [ˌdɛfəˈrɛnʃəl] *adj* deferente

deferment [dɪˈfʌrmənt] *s* differimento

defiance [dɪˈfaɪ·əns] *s* opposizione; sfida; **in defiance of** a dispetto di

defiant [dɪˈfaɪ·ənt] *adj* provocante, ostile

deficien·cy [dɪˈfɪʃənsɪ] *s* (-cies) deficienza; (com) ammanco

deficient [dɪˈfɪʃənt] *adj* deficiente

deficit [ˈdɛfɪsɪt] *adj* deficitario || *s* deficit *m,* disavanzo

defile [dɪˈfaɪl] or [ˈdɪfaɪl] *s* gola, passo || [dɪˈfaɪl] *tr* profanare || *intr* marciare in fila

define [dɪˈfaɪn] *tr* definire

definite [ˈdɛfɪnɪt] *adj* definito; (gram) determinativo, determinato

definition [ˌdɛfɪˈnɪʃən] *s* definizione

definitive [dɪˈfɪnɪtɪv] *adj* definitivo

deflate [dɪˈflet] *tr* sgonfiare; (*s.o.'s hopes*) deprimere; (*e.g., currency*) deflazionare

deflation [dɪˈfleʃən] *s* sgonfiamento; (*of prices*) deflazione

deflect [dɪˈflɛkt] *tr* far deflettere || *intr* deflettere

deflower [diˈflaʊ·ər] *tr* privare dei fiori; (*a woman*) deflorare

deforest [diˈfarɛst] or [diˈfɔrɛst] *tr* disboscare, smacchiare

deform [dɪˈfɔrm] *tr* deformare

deformed [dɪˈfɔrmd] *adj* deforme

deformi·ty [dɪˈfɔrmɪtɪ] *s* (-ties) deformità *f*

defraud [dɪˈfrɔd] *tr* defraudare

defray [dɪˈfre] *tr* pagare

defrost [diˈfrɔst] or [diˈfrast] *tr* sgelare, sbrinare

defroster [diˈfrɔstər] or [diˈfrastər] *s* (aut) visiera termica

deft [dɛft] *adj* destro, lesto

defunct [dɪˈfʌŋkt] *adj* defunto

de·fy [dɪˈfaɪ] *v* (*pret & pp* **-fied**) *tr* sfidare, provocare

degeneracy [dɪˈdʒɛnərəsɪ] *s* degenerazione

degenerate [dɪˈdʒɛnərɪt] *adj & s* degenerato || [dɪˈdʒɛnəˌret] *intr* degenerare, tralignare

degrade [dɪˈgred] *tr* degradare

degrading [dɪˈgredɪŋ] *adj* degradante

degree [dɪˈgri] *s* grado; titolo accademico; **by degrees** a grado a grado; **to a degree** fino a un certo punto; troppo; **to take a degree** ricevere un titolo di studio

dehydrate [diˈhaɪdret] *tr* disidratare

deice [diˈaɪs] *tr* sgelare

dei·fy [ˈdi·ɪˌfaɪ] *v* (*pret & pp* **-fied**) *tr* deificare

deign [den] *intr* degnarsi

dei·ty [ˈdi·ɪtɪ] *s* (-ties) deità *f;* **the Deity** Dio

dejected [dɪˈdʒɛktɪd] *adj* demoralizzato

dejection [dɪˈdʒɛkʃən] *s* (*in spirits*) demoralizzazione; (*evacuation*) deiezione

delay [dɪˈle] *s* ritardo, proroga; dilazione; **without further delay** senza ulteriore indugio || *tr* tardare; (*to put off*) differire || *intr* tardare, ritardare

delayed'-ac'tion *adj* a azione differita

delectable [dɪˈlɛktəbəl] *adj* dilettevole

delegate [ˈdɛlɪˌget] or [ˈdɛlɪgɪt] *s* delegato, incaricato; (*to a convention*) congressista *mf* || [ˈdɛlɪˌget] *tr* delegare, incaricare

delegation [ˌdɛlɪˈgeʃən] *s* delegazione

delete [dɪˈlit] *tr* cancellare, sopprimere

deletion [dɪˈliʃən] *s* cancellazione

deliberate [dɪˈlɪbərɪt] *adj* meditato; (*slow in deciding*) cauto; (*slow in moving*) lento || [dɪˈlɪbəˌret] *tr & intr* deliberare

deliberately [dɪˈlɪbərɪtlɪ] *adv* (*on purpose*) deliberatamente; (*without hurrying*) con ponderatezza

delica·cy [ˈdɛlɪkəsɪ] *s* (-cies) delicatezza; (*choice food*) leccornia

delicatessen [ˌdɛlɪkəˈtɛsən] *s* negozio di salumeria || *spl* salumerie *fpl,* articoli alimentari scelti

delicious [dɪˈlɪʃəs] *adj* delizioso

delight [dɪˈlaɪt] *s* gioia, delizia || *tr* dilettare || *intr* dilettarsi

delightful [dɪˈlaɪtfəl] *adj* delizioso

delinquen·cy [dɪˈlɪŋkwənsɪ] *s* (-cies) colpa; (*offense*) delinquenza; (*in payment of a debt*) morosità *f*

delinquent [dɪˈlɪŋkwənt] *adj* colpevole; (*in payment*) moroso; non pagato || *s* delinquente *m;* debitore moroso

delirious [dɪˈlɪrɪ·əs] *adj* in delirio

deliri·um [dɪˈlɪrɪ·əm] *s* (-ums or -a [ə]) delirio

deliver [dɪˈlɪvər] *tr* consegnare; (*a blow*) affibbiare; (*a speech*) fare; (*a letter*) recapitare; (*electricity or gas*) erogare; (*said of a pregnant woman*) partorire; (*said of a doctor*) assistere durante il parto

deliver·y [dɪˈlɪvərɪ] *s* (-ies) consegna; (*of mail*) distribuzione; (*of merchandise*) fornitura; (*of a speech*) dizione; (*childbirth*) parto; (sports) lancio

deliv'ery·man' *s* (-men') fattorino

deliv'ery room' *s* sala parto

deliv'ery truck' *s* furgoncino

dell [dɛl] *s* valletta

delouse [diˈlaʊs] or [diˈlaʊz] *tr* spidocchiare

delude [dɪˈlud] *tr* illudere, ingannare

deluge [ˈdɛljudʒ] *s* diluvio, inondazione || **the Deluge** il diluvio universale || *tr* inondare

delusion [dɪˈluʒən] *s* illusione, inganno; (*psychopath*) allucinazione;

(psychopath) idea fissa; **delusions of grandeur** mania di grandezza

de luxe [dɪˈlʊks] or [dɪˈlʌks] *adj* di lusso || *adv* in gran lusso

delve [dɛlv] *intr* frugare; **to delve into** approfondirsi in

demagnetize [diˈmægnɪˌtaɪz] *tr* smagnetizzare

demagogue [ˈdɛməˌgag] *s* demagogo

demand [dɪˈmænd] or [dɪˈmɑnd] *s* esigenza; (com) richiesta, domanda; **to be in demand** essere in richiesta || *tr* esigere

demanding [dɪˈmændɪŋ] or [dɪˈmɑndɪŋ] *adj* esigente, impegnativo

demarcate [dɪˈmarket] or [ˈdimarˌket] *tr* demarcare

démarche [deˈmarʃ] *s* progetto, piano

demean [dɪˈmin] *tr* degradare; **to demean oneself** comportarsi; degradarsi

demeanor [dɪˈminər] *s* condotta, contegno

demented [dɪˈmɛntɪd] *adj* demente

demigod [ˈdɛmɪˌgad] *s* semidio

demijohn [ˈdɛmɪˌdʒan] *s* damigiana

demilitarize [diˈmɪlɪtəˌraɪz] *tr* smilitarizzare

demimonde [ˈdɛmɪˌmand] *s* donne *fpl* della società equivoca

demise [dɪˈmaɪz] *s* decesso

demitasse [ˈdɛmɪˌtæs] or [ˈdɛmɪˌtas] *s* tazzina da caffè; (*contents*) caffè nero

demobilize [diˈmobɪˌlaɪz] *tr* smobilitare

democra·cy [dɪˈmakrəsi] *s* (**-cies**) democrazia

democrat [ˈdɛməˌkræt] *s* democratico

democratic [ˌdɛməˈkrætɪk] *adj* democratico

demolish [dɪˈmalɪʃ] *tr* demolire

demolition [ˌdɛməˈlɪʃən] or [ˌdiməˈlɪʃən] *s* demolizione

demon [ˈdimən] *s* demonio

demoniacal [ˌdiməˈnaɪˌəkəl] *adj* demoniaco

demonstrate [ˈdɛmənˌstret] *tr & intr* dimostrare

demonstration [ˌdɛmənˈstreʃən] *s* dimostrazione

demonstrative [dɪˈmanstrətɪv] *adj* dimostrativo; (*giving open exhibition of emotion*) espansivo

demonstrator [ˈdɛmənˌstretər] *s* (*of a product*) dimostratore *m*; (*in a public gathering*) dimostrante *m*; (*product*) prodotto usato da dimostratori

demoralize [dɪˈmarəˌlaɪz] or [dɪˈmɔrəˌlaɪz] *tr* demoralizzare

demote [dɪˈmot] *tr* retrocedere

demotion [dɪˈmoʃən] *s* retrocessione

de·mur [dɪˈmʌr] *v* (*pret & pp* **-murred**; *ger* **-murring**) *intr* sollevare obiezioni

demure [dɪˈmjur] *adj* modesto; sobrio

demurrage [dɪˈmarɪdʒ] *s* (com) controstallie *fpl*; (rr) sosta

den [dɛn] *s* (*of animals, thieves*) tana; (*little room*) bugigattolo; (*little room for studying or writing*) studiolo; (*of lions*) (Bib) fossa

denaturalize [diˈnætʃərəˌlaɪz] *tr* snaturalizzare; privare della nazionalità

dena′tured al′cohol [diˈnetʃərd] *s* alcole denaturato

denial [dɪˈnaɪ·əl] *s* diniego; (*disavowal*) smentita

denim [ˈdɛnɪm] *s* tessuto di cotone per tuta; **denims** tuta; (*trousers*) jeans *mpl*

denizen [ˈdɛnɪzən] *s* abitante *mf*

Denmark [ˈdɛnmark] *s* la Danimarca

denomination [dɪˌnamɪˈneʃən] *s* denominazione; categoria; (com) taglio; (eccl) confessione

denote [dɪˈnot] *tr* denotare, significare

denouement [denuˈmã] *s* scioglimento

denounce [dɪˈnauns] *tr* denunziare

dense [dɛns] *adj* denso; stupido

densi·ty [ˈdɛnsɪti] *s* (**-ties**) densità *f*

dent [dɛnt] *s* ammaccatura; (*in a gearwheel*) tacca, dente *m*; **to make a dent** fare progresso; fare impressione || *tr* ammaccare; (fig) ferire

dental [ˈdɛntəl] *adj* dentale, dentario || *s* dentale *f*

den′tal floss′ *s* filo cerato dentario

dentifrice [ˈdɛntɪfrɪs] *s* dentifricio

dentist [ˈdɛntɪst] *s* dentista *mf*

dentistry [ˈdɛntɪstri] *s* odontoiatria

denture [ˈdɛntʃər] *s* dentiera

denunciation [dɪˌnʌnsɪˈeʃən] or [dɪˌnʌnʃɪˈeʃən] *s* denunzia

de·ny [dɪˈnaɪ] *v* (*pret & pp* **-nied**) *tr* (*to declare not to be true*) negare; (*to refuse*) rifiutare; **to deny oneself to callers** sottrarsi alle visite || *intr* negare; rifiutare

deodorant [diˈodərənt] *adj & s* deodorante *m*

deo′dorant spray′ *s* deodorante *m* spray

deodorize [diˈodəˌraɪz] *tr* deodorare

depart [dɪˈpart] *intr* partire, andarsene; (*to diverge*) dipartire

departed [dɪˈpartɪd] *adj* morto, defunto || **the departed** i defunti

department [dɪˈpartmənt] *s* dipartimento; (*of government*) ministero; (*e.g., of a hospital*) reparto; (*of agency*) sezione, ufficio

depart′ment store′ *s* grandi magazzini *mpl*

departure [dɪˈpartʃər] *s* partenza; divergenza, deviazione

depend [dɪˈpɛnd] *intr* dipendere; **to depend on** (*to rely on*) contare su; dipendere da

dependable [dɪˈpɛndəbəl] *adj* sicuro, fidato

dependence [dɪˈpɛndəns] *s* dipendenza; (*trust*) fiducia

dependen·cy [dɪˈpɛndənsi] *s* (**-cies**) dipendenza; (*territory*) possessione

dependent [dɪˈpɛndənt] *adj* dipendente; a carico; **to be dependent on** dipendere da || *s* persona a carico

depend′ent clause′ *s* proposizione subordinata

depict [dɪˈpɪkt] *tr* descrivere, dipingere

deplete [dɪˈplit] *tr* esaurire

depletion [dɪˈpliʃən] *s* esaurimento

deplorable [dɪˈplorəbəl] *adj* deplorevole

deplore [dɪˈplor] *tr* deplorare

deploy [dɪˈplɔɪ] *tr* (mil) spiegare, stendere

deployment [dɪ'plɔɪmənt] *s* (mil) dispositivo, spiegamento

depolarize [di'polə,raɪz] *tr* depolarizzare

depopulate [di'pɑpjə,let] *tr* spopolare

deport [dɪ'port] *tr* deportare; **to deport oneself** comportarsi

deportation [,dipor'tefən] *s* deportazione

deportee [,dipor'ti] *s* deportato

deportment [dɪ'portmənt] *s* condotta, comportamento

depose [dɪ'poz] *tr & intr* deporre

deposit [dɪ'pɑzɪt] *s* deposito; (*down payment*) caparra || *tr* depositare || *intr* depositarsi

depos'it account' *s* conto corrente

depositor [dɪ'pɑzɪtər] *s* versante *mf*; (*to the credit of an established account*) correntista *mf*

deposi·to·ry [dɪ'pɑzɪ,tori] *s* (**-ries**) deposito; (*person*) depositario

depos'it slip' *s* distinta di versamento

depot ['dipo] *or* ['depo] *s* magazzino; (mil) deposito; (rr) stazione

depraved [dɪ'prevd] *adj* depravato

depravi·ty [dɪ'prævɪti] *s* (**-ties**) depravazione

deprecate ['deprɪ,ket] *tr* deprecare

depreciate [dɪ'prifɪ,et] *tr* svalutare, deprezzare || *intr* deprezzarsi

depreciation [dɪ,prifɪ'efən] *s* (*drop in value*) deprezzamento; (*disparagement*) disprezzo

depredation [,deprɪ'defən] *s* depredazione

depress [dɪ'pres] *tr* deprimere; avvilire; (*prices*) far abbassare

depression [dɪ'prefən] *s* depressione; (*gloom*) sconforto; (*slump*) crisi *f*

deprive [dɪ'praɪv] *tr* privare; **to deprive oneself** espropriarsi

depth [depθ] *s* profondità *f*; (*of a house or room*) lunghezza; (*of sea*) fondale *m*; (fig) vastità *f*; **in the depth of** nel cuor di; **to go beyond one's depth** non toccare più; (fig) andare oltre le proprie possibilità

depth' bomb' *s* (aer) bomba antisommergibile

depth' charge' *s* (nav) granata antisommergibile

depth' of hold' *s* (naut) puntale *m*

deputation [,depjə'tefən] *s* deputazione

deputize ['depjə,taɪz] *tr* deputare

depu·ty ['depjəti] *s* (**-ties**) deputato

derail [dɪ'rel] *tr* far deragliare || *intr* deragliare, deviare

derailment [dɪ'relmənt] *s* deragliamento, deviamento

derange [dɪ'rendʒ] *tr* (*to disarrange*) dissestare; (*to make insane*) squilibrare, render pazzo

derangement [dɪ'rendʒmənt] *s* (*disorder*) disordine *m*; (*insanity*) squilibrio mentale, pazzia

der·by ['dɑrbi] *s* (**-bies**) bombetta; (*race*) derby *m*

derelict ['derɪlɪkt] *adj* derelitto; negligente || *s* derelitto; (naut) relitto

dereliction [,derɪ'lɪkʃən] *s* (*in one's duty*) negligenza; (law) derelizione

deride [dɪ'raɪd] *tr* deridere, schernire, farsi beffe di

derision [dɪ'riʒən] *s* derisione, scherno

derisive [dɪ'raɪsɪv] *adj* derisorio

derivation [,derɪ'veʃən] *s* derivazione

derivative [dɪ'rɪvətɪv] *adj & s* derivato

derive [dɪ'raɪv] *tr & intr* derivare

dermatology [,dʌrmə'tɑlədʒɪ] *s* dermatologia

derogatory [dɪ'rɑgə,tori] *adj* dispregiativo

derrick ['derɪk] *s* gru *f*; (naut) picco di carico

dervish ['dʌrvɪʃ] *s* dervis *m*

desalinization [di,selɪnɪ'zefən] *s* desalazione

desalt [di'sɔlt] *tr* desalificare

descend [dɪ'send] *tr* discendere || *intr* discendere; **to descend on** calare su, gettarsi su

descendant [dɪ'sendənt] *adj & s* discendente *mf*

descendent [dɪ'sendənt] *adj* discendente

descent [dɪ'sent] *s* (*slope*) china; (*decline*) declino; discesa; (*lineage*) stirpe *f*, discendenza; (*sudden raid*) calata

Descent' from the Cross' *s* Deposizione dalla Croce

describe [dɪ'skraɪb] *tr* descrivere

description [dɪ'skrɪpfən] *s* descrizione

descriptive [dɪ'skrɪptɪv] *adj* descrittivo

de·scry [dɪ'skraɪ] *v* (*pret & pp* **-scried**) *tr* avvistare

desecrate ['desɪ,kret] *tr* profanare, dissacrare

desecration [,desɪ'krefən] *s* profanazione, dissacrazione

desegregate [di'segrɪ,get] *intr* sopprimere la segregazione razziale

desegregation [di,segrɪ'gefən] *s* desegregazione

desensitize [di'sensɪ,taɪz] *tr* desensibilizzare

desert ['dezərt] *adj & s* deserto || [dɪ'zʌrt] *s* merito; **he received his just deserts** ricevette quanto meritava || *tr & intr* disertare

deserter [dɪ'zʌrtər] *s* disertore *m*

deserted [dɪ'zʌrtɪd] *adj* (*person*) abbandonato; (*place*) deserto

desertion [dɪ'zʌrfən] *s* diserzione; abbandono del coniuge

deserve [dɪ'zʌrv] *tr & intr* meritare

deservedly [dɪ'zʌrvɪdli] *adv* meritatamente, meritevolmente

design [dɪ'zaɪn] *s* disegno; (*of a play*) congegno; **to have designs on** aver mire su || *tr* disegnare; progettare || *intr* disegnare; **designed for** destinato a

designate ['dezɪg,net] *tr* designare

designer [dɪ'saɪnər] *s* disegnatore *m*

designing [dɪ'zaɪnɪŋ] *adj* intrigante, macchinatore || *s* disegnazione

desirable [dɪ'zaɪrəbəl] *adj* desiderabile

desire [dɪ'zaɪr] *s* desiderio || *tr* desiderare

desirous [dɪ'zaɪrəs] *adj* desideroso

desist [dɪ'zɪst] *intr* desistere

desk [desk] *s* scrittoio; tavolo d'ufficio;

(*lectern*) leggio; (*of professor*) cattedra; (*of pupil*) banco; (*com*) cassa

desk'bound' *adj* sedentario; legato al tavolino

desk' pad' *s* blocco da tavolo; blocco per appunti

desolate ['desəlɪt] *adj* desolato, deserto; (*hopeless*) disperato; (*dismal*) lugubre ‖ ['desə‚let] *tr* desolare; devastare

desolation [‚desə'leʃən] *s* desolazione; devastazione

despair [dɪ'sper] *s* disperazione; **to be in despair** disperarsi ‖ *intr* disperare, disperarsi

despairing [dɪ'sperɪŋ] *adj* disperato

despera·do [‚despə'redo] *or* [‚despə'rɑdo] *s* (**-does** *or* **-dos**) fuorilegge disposto a tutto

desperate ['despərɪt] *adj* disposto a tutto; (*hopeless*) disperato; (*very bad*) atroce, terribile; (*bitter, excessive*) accanito; (*remedy*) estremo

desperation [‚despə'reʃən] *s* disperazione

despicable ['despɪkəbəl] *adj* spregevole, incanaglito

despise [dɪ'spaɪz] *tr* sprezzare, disprezzare, vilipendere

despite [dɪ'spaɪt] *prep* malgrado

despoil [dɪ'spɔɪl] *tr* spogliare

desponden·cy [dɪ'spɑndənsi] *s* (**-cies**) scoraggiamento, abbattimento

despondent [dɪ'spɑndənt] *adj* scoraggiato, abbattuto

despot ['despət] *s* despota *m*

despotic [des'pɑtɪk] *adj* dispotico

despotism ['despə‚tɪzəm] *s* dispotismo

dessert [dɪ'zʌrt] *s* dessert *m*

dessert' spoon' *s* cucchiaio or cucchiaino da dessert

destination [‚destɪ'neʃən] *s* destinazione

destine ['destɪn] *tr* destinare

desti·ny ['destɪni] *s* (**-nies**) destino

destitute ['destɪ‚tjut] *or* ['destɪ‚tut] *adj* (*poverty-stricken*) indigente; (*lacking*) privo

destitution [‚destɪ'tjuʃən] *or* [‚destɪ'tuʃən] *s* indigenza, miseria

destroy [dɪ'strɔɪ] *tr* distruggere

destroyer [dɪ'strɔɪ·ər] *s* (nav) cacciatorpediniere *m*

destruction [dɪ'strʌkʃən] *s* distruzione

destructive [dɪ'strʌktɪv] *adj* distruttivo

desultory ['desəl‚tori] *adj* saltuario, sconnesso

detach [dɪ'tætʃ] *tr* staccare, distaccare; (mil) distaccare

detachable [dɪ'tætʃəbəl] *adj* staccabile; separabile

detached [dɪ'tætʃt] *adj* (*e.g., stub*) staccato; (*e.g., house*) discosto; (*aloof*) riservato, freddo; imparziale

detachment [dɪ'tætʃmənt] *s* distacco; imparzialità *f*; (mil) distaccamento

detail [dɪ'tel] *or* ['ditel] *s* dettaglio, ragguaglio; (mil) distaccamento ‖ [dɪ'tel] *tr* dettagliare; (mil) distaccare

detain [dɪ'ten] *tr* detenere, trattenere

detect [dɪ'tekt] *tr* scoprire, discernere; (rad) rivelare

detection [dɪ'tekʃən] *s* scoperta; (rad) rivelazione

detective [dɪ'tektɪv] *s* detective *m*

detec'tive sto'ry *s* romanzo poliziesco, romanzo giallo

detector [dɪ'tektər] *s* (rad) detector *m*, rivelatore *m*

detention [dɪ'tenʃən] *s* detenzione

de-ter [dɪ'tʌr] *v* (*pret & pp* **-terred;** *ger* **-terring**) *tr* distogliere, impedire

detergent [dɪ'tʌrdʒənt] *adj & s* detergente *m*

deteriorate [dɪ'tɪrɪ·ə‚ret] *tr* deteriorare ‖ *intr* deteriorarsi, andar giù

determination [dɪ‚tʌrmɪ'neʃən] *s* determinazione

determine [dɪ'tʌrmɪn] *tr* determinare

determined [dɪ'tʌrmɪnd] *adj* determinato, risoluto

deterrent [dɪ'tʌrənt] *s* deterrente *m*

detest [dɪ'test] *tr* detestare, odiare

dethrone [dɪ'θron] *tr* detronizzare

detonate ['deɪə‚net] *or* ['dɪtə‚net] *tr* far scoppiare ‖ *intr* detonare

detonator ['detə‚netər] *s* innesco

detour ['ditur] *or* [dɪ'tur] *s* deviazione ‖ *tr* far deviare ‖ *intr* deviare

detract [dɪ'trækt] *tr* detrarre ‖ *intr*— **to detract from** diminuire

detractor [dɪ'træktər] *s* detrattore *m*

detriment ['detrɪmənt] *s* detrimento; **to the detriment of** a danno di

detrimental [‚detrɪ'mentəl] *adj* pregiudizievole

deuce [djus] *or* [dus] *s* (cards) due *m*; **the deuce!** diavolo!

devaluate [di'vælju‚et] *tr* svalutare

devaluation [di‚vælju'eʃən] *s* devalutazione, svalutazione

devastate ['devəs‚tet] *tr* devastare

devastating ['devəs‚tetɪŋ] *adj* devastatore, devastante; (*e.g., reply*) schiacciante, annichilante

devastation [‚devəs'teʃən] *s* devastazione

develop [dɪ'veləp] *tr* sviluppare; (phot) sviluppare, rivelare ‖ *intr* svilupparsi; manifestarsi

developer [dɪ'veləpər] *s* (*e.g., of a new engine*) sfruttatore *m*; (*in real estate*) specialista *mf* in lottizzazione; (phot) sviluppatore *m*, rivelatore *m*

development [dɪ'veləpmənt] *s* sviluppo; valorizzazione; sfruttamento; (phot) rivelazione

deviate ['divi‚et] *tr* sviare ‖ *intr* deviare, sviarsi

deviation [‚divi'eʃən] *s* deviazione

deviationism [‚divi'eʃə‚nɪzəm] *s* deviazionismo

deviationist [‚divi'eʃənɪst] *s* deviazionista *mf*

device [dɪ'vaɪs] *s* dispositivo, congegno; (*trick*) stratagemma *m*; (*motto*) divisa, emblema *m*; **to leave s.o. to his own devices** lasciare che qlcu faccia come gli pare e piace

dev-il ['devəl] *s* diavolo; **between the devil and the deep blue sea** fra l'incudine e il martello; **to raise the devil** (slang) fare diavolo a quattro ‖ *v* (*pret & pp* **-iled** *or* **-illed;** *ger*

-iling or **-illing**) *tr* condire con spezie or con pepe; (*coll*) infastidire

devilish ['dɛvəlɪʃ] *adj* diabolico

devilment ['dɛvəlmənt] *s* (*mischief*) diavoleria; (*evil*) cattiveria

devil-try ['dɛvəltri] *s* (**-tries**) malvagità *f*, crudeltà *f*; (*mischief*) diavoleria

devious ['divɪ·əs] *adj* (*tricky*) traverso; (*roundabout*) tortuoso

devise [dɪ'vaɪz] *tr* ideare, inventare; (*law*) legare, disporre per testamento

devoid [dɪ'vɔɪd] *adj* sprovvisto

devolve [dɪ'vɑlv] *intr*—**to devolve on** ricadere su

devote [dɪ'vot] *tr* dedicare

devoted [dɪ'votɪd] *adj* devoto; dedito, dedicato

devotee [,dɛvə'ti] *s* devoto; (*fan*) fanatico, tifoso, entusiasta *mf*

devotion [dɪ'voʃən] *s* devozione; (*e.g., to work*) dedizione; **devotions** orazioni *mpl*, preghiere *fpl*

devour [dɪ'vaur] *tr* divorare

devout [dɪ'vaut] *adj* devoto; sincero

dew [dju] or [du] *s* rugiada

dew'drop' *s* goccia di rugiada

dew'lap' *s* giogaia

dew·y ['dju·i] or ['du·i] *adj* (**-ier; -iest**) rugiadoso

dexterity [dɛks'tɛrɪti] *s* destrezza

diabetes [,daɪ·ə'bitis] or [,daɪ·ə'bitiz] *s* diabete *m*

diabetic [,daɪ·ə'bɛtɪk] or [,daɪ·ə-'bitɪk] *adj & s* diabetico

diabolic(al) [,daɪ·ə'bɑlɪk(əl)] *adj* diabolico

diadem ['daɪ·ə,dɛm] *s* diadema *m*

diaere·sis [daɪ'ɛrɪsɪs] *s* (**-ses** [,siz]) dieresi *f*

diagnose [,daɪ·ə'betɪk] or [,daɪ·əg-'noz] *tr* diagnosticare

diagno·sis [,daɪ·əg'nosɪs] *s* (**-ses** [siz]) diagnosi *f*

diagonal [daɪ'ægənəl] *adj & s* diagonale *f*

dia·gram ['daɪ·ə,græm] *s* diagramma *m*; (*drawing*) schema *m*; (*plan*) prospetto *m* || *v* (*pret & pp* **-gramed** or **-grammed**; *ger* **-graming** or **-gramming**) *tr* diagrammare

dial ['daɪ·əl] *s* (*of watch*) quadrante *m*; (*rad*) tabella graduata, sintogramma *m*; (*telp*) disco combinatore || *v* (*rad*) sintonizzare; (*a person*) (*telp*) chiamare; (*a number*) (*telp*) comporre; (*the phone*) (*telp*) comporre il numero di || *intr* (*telp*) comporre il numero

dialect ['daɪ·ə,lɛkt] *s* dialetto

dialing ['daɪ·əlɪŋ] *s* composizione del numero

dialogue ['daɪ·ə,lɔg] or ['daɪ·ə,lag] *s* dialogo

di'al tel'ephone *s* telefono automatico

di'al tone' *s* (*telp*) segnale *m* di via libera

diameter [daɪ'æmɪtər] *s* diametro

diametric(al) [,daɪ·ə'mɛtrɪk(əl)] *adj* diametrico, diametrale

diamond ['daɪ·əmənd] *s* diamante *m*; (*figure of a rhombus*) losanga; (*baseball*) diamante *m*; **diamonds** (*cards*) quadri *mpl*

diaper ['daɪ·pər] *s* pannolino

diaphanous [daɪ'æfənəs] *adj* diafano

diaphragm ['daɪ·ə,fræm] *s* diaframma *m*; (*teip*) membrana

diar·rhea [,daɪ·ə'ri·ə] *s* diarrea

dia·ry ['daɪ·əri] *s* (**-ries**) diario

diastole [daɪ'æstəli] *s* diastole *f*

diathermy ['daɪ·ə,θʌrmi] *s* diatermia

dice [daɪs] *spl* dadi *mpl*; (*small cubes*) cubetti *mpl*; **no dice** (*slang*) niente da fare; (*slang*) risposta a picche

dice' cup' *s* bussolotto

dichloride [daɪ'klɔraɪd] *s* bicloruro

dichoto·my [daɪ'kɑtəmi] *s* (**-mies**) di-otomia

dickey ['dɪki] *s* camiciola; (*starched insert*) sparato; (*bib*) bavaglino

dictaphone ['dɪktə,fon] *s* dittafono

dictate ['dɪktet] *s* dettato || ['dɪktet] or [dɪk'tet] *tr* dettare

dictation [dɪk'teʃən] *s* dettato; (*act of ordering*) ordine *m*; **to take dictation** scrivere sotto dettatura

dictator ['dɪktetər] or [dɪk'tetər] *s* dittatore *m*

dictatorship ['dɪktetər,ʃɪp] or [dɪk-'tetər,ɪp] *s* dittatura

diction ['dɪkʃən] *s* dizione

dictionar·y ['dɪkʃən,ɛri] *s* (**-ies**) dizionario, vocabolario

dic·tum ['dɪktəm] *s* (**-ta** [tə]) detto, sentenza

didactic(al) [daɪ'dæktɪk(əl)] or [dɪ-'dæktɪk(əl)] *adj* didattico

die [daɪ] *s* (*die* [daɪs]) dado; **the die is cast** il dado è tratto || *s* (**dies**) (*for stamping coins, medals,* etc.) stampo; (*for cutting threads*) filiera || *v* (*pret & pp* **died**; *ger* **dying**) *intr* morire; **to die hard** morire lentamente; morire lottando; **to die laughing** morire dalle risa; **to die off** morire uno per uno

die'-hard' *adj & s* intransigente *m*

die'sel oil' ['dizəl] *s* nafta, gasolio

die'stock' *s* girafiliera

diet ['daɪ·ət] *s* dieta, regime *m* || *intr* stare a dieta

dietetic [,daɪ·ə'tɛtɪk] *adj* dietetico || **dietetics** *ssg* dietetica

dietitian [,daɪ·ə'tɪʃən] *s* dietista *mf*

differ ['dɪfər] *intr* (*to be different*) differire, differenziarsi; **to differ with** dissentire da

difference ['dɪfərəns] *s* differenza; **to make no difference** fare lo stesso; **to split the difference** dividere la differenza; (*fig*) venire a un compromesso

different ['dɪfərənt] *adj* differente

differential [,dɪfə'rɛnʃəl] *adj & s* differenziale *m*

differentiate [,dɪfə'rɛnʃɪ,et] *tr* differenziare || *intr* differenziarsi

difficult ['dɪfɪ,kʌlt] *adj* difficile

difficul·ty ['dɪfɪ,kʌlti] *s* (**-ties**) difficoltà *f*

diffident ['dɪfɪdənt] *adj* timido, imbarazzato

diffuse [dɪ'fjus] *adj* diffuso || [dɪ'fjuz] *tr* diffondere || *intr* diffondersi

dig [dɪg] *s* (*poke*) botta, spintone *m*; (*jibe*) stoccata, fiancata || *v* (*pret & pp* **dug** [dʌg]; *ger* **digging**) *tr* scavare, sterrare; **to dig up** dissodare; (*to uncover*) dissotterrare || *intr* scavare; **to dig in** (mil) fortificarsi; **to dig into** (coll) sprofondarsi in

digest ['daɪdʒɛst] *s* compendio; (law) digesto || [dɪ'dʒɛst] or [daɪ'dʒɛst] *tr & intr* digerire

digestible [dɪ'dʒɛstɪbəl] or [daɪ'dʒɛstɪbəl] *adj* digeribile, digestibile

digestion [dɪ'dʒɛst/ən] or [daɪ'dʒɛst/ən] *s* digestione

digestive [dɪ'dʒɛstɪv] or [daɪ'dʒɛstɪv] *adj* (tube) digerente || *s* digestivo

digit ['dɪdʒɪt] *s* cifra, unità *f*; (*finger*) dito; (*toe*) dito del piede

dig'ital clock' *s* orologio a scatto

digitalis [,dɪdʒɪ'tælɪs] or [,dɪdʒɪ'telɪs] *s* (bot) digitale *f*; (pharm) digitalina

dignified ['dɪgnɪ,faɪd] *adj* dignitoso, fiero, contegnoso

digni•fy ['dɪgnɪ,faɪ] *v* (*pret & pp* -fied) *tr* (*to ennoble*) nobilitare; onorare, esaltare; dare la dignità a

dignitar•y ['dɪgnɪ,tɛri] *s* (-ies) dignitario; **dignitaries** dignità *fpl*

digni•ty ['dɪgnɪti] *s* (-ties) dignità *f*, decoro; **to stand on one's dignity** mantenere la propria dignità

digress [dɪ'grɛs] or [daɪ'grɛs] *intr* digredire, divagare

digression [dɪ'grɛʃən] or [daɪ'grɛʃən] *s* digressione, divagazione

dike [daɪk] *s* diga; (*in a river*) argine *m*; (*ditch*) fosso; scarpata

dilapidated [dɪ'læpɪ,detɪd] *adj* dilapidato, decrepito

dilate [daɪ'let] *tr* dilatare || *intr* dilatarsi

dilatory ['dɪlə,tori] *adj* lento, tardivo; (*e.g., strategy*) dilatorio

dilemma [dɪ'lɛmə] *s* dilemma *m*

dilettan•te [,dɪlə'tænti] *adj* dilettantesco || *s* (-tes or -ti [ti]) dilettante *mf*

diligence ['dɪlɪdʒəns] *s* diligenza

diligent ['dɪlɪdʒənt] *adj* diligente

dill [dɪl] *s* (bot) aneto

dillydal•ly ['dɪlɪ,dæli] *v* (*pret & pp* -lied) *intr* farla lunga

dilute [dɪ'lut] or [daɪ'lut] *adj* diluito || [dɪ'lut] *tr* diluire || *intr* diluirsi

dilution [dɪ'luʃən] *s* diluizione

dim [dɪm] *adj* (dimmer; dimmest) (*light*) fioco; (*sight*) debole; (*memory*) vago; (*color*) smorzato; (*sound*) sordo; **to take a dim view of** avere una visione pessimistica di || *v* (*pret & pp* dimmed; *ger* dimming) *tr* (*lights*) smorzare; **to dim the headlights** abbassare i fari

dime [daɪm] *s* moneta di dieci centesimi di dollaro

dimension [dɪ'mɛnʃən] *s* dimensione

diminish [dɪ'mɪnɪʃ] *tr & intr* diminuire, scemare

diminutive [dɪ'mɪnjətɪv] *adj* (*tiny*) minuscolo; (gram) diminutivo || *s* diminutivo

dimly ['dɪmli] *adv* indistintamente

dimmer ['dɪmər] *s* smorzatore *m*; (aut) luce *f* di incrocio; **dimmers** fari *mpl* antiabbaglianti

dimple ['dɪmpəl] *s* fossetta

dimwit ['dɪm,wɪt] *s* (slang) stupido, cretino

din [dɪn] *s* fragore *m*, frastuono || *v* (*pret & pp* dinned; *ger* dinning) *tr* assordare; **to din s.th into s.o.'s ears** rintronare qlco nelle orecchie di qlcu

dine [daɪn] *tr* offrire un pranzo a; offire una cena a || *intr* pasteggiare; cenare; **to dine out** mangiare fuori di casa

diner ['daɪnər] *s* commensale *m*; (rr) vettura ristorante; (U.S.A.) ristorante *m* a forma di vagone

ding-dong ['dɪŋ,dɔŋ] or ['dɪŋ,dɑŋ] *s* dindon *m*

din•gy ['dɪndʒi] *adj* (-gier; -giest) sporco, sbiadito

din'ing car' *s* vagone *m* ristorante

din'ing room' *s* sala da pranzo

dinner ['dɪnər] *s* cena; pranzo; (*formal meal*) banchetto

din'ner coat' or **jack'et** *s* smoking *m*

din'ner knife' *s* coltello da tavola

din'ner set' *s* servizio da tavola

din'ner ta'ble *s* desco

din'ner time' *s* ora di pranzo or di cena

dinosaur ['daɪnə,sɔr] *s* dinosauro

dint [dɪnt] *s* tacca, ammaccatura; **by dint of** a forza di || *tr* ammaccare

diocese ['daɪə,sis] or ['daɪ-əsɪs] *s* diocesi *f*

diode ['daɪ-od] *s* diodo

dioxide [daɪ'ɑksaɪd] *s* biossido

dip [dɪp] *s* immersione; (*brief swim*) tuffo, nuotata; (*in a road*) depressione; inclinazione magnetica || *v* (*pret & pp* dipped; *ger* dipping) *tr* immergere, tuffare; (*the flag*) abbassare; (*bread*) inzuppare || *intr* immergersi, tuffarsi; inclinarsi; (*to drop down*) sparire subitamente; **to dip into** (*a book*) sfogliare; (*business*) mettersi in; (*a container of liquids*) intingere; **to dip into one's purse** spendere soldi

diphtheria [dɪf'θɪrɪ-ə] *s* difterite *f*

diphthong ['dɪfθɔŋ] or ['dɪfθɑŋ] *s* dittongo

diphthongize ['dɪfθɔŋ,gaɪz] or ['dɪfθɑŋ,gaɪz] *tr & intr* dittongare

diploma [dɪ'plomə] *s* diploma *m*

diploma•cy [dɪ'ploməsi] *s* (-cies) diplomazia

diplomat ['dɪplə,mæt] *s* diplomatico

diplomatic [,dɪplə'mætɪk] *adj* diplomatico

dip'lomat'ic pouch' *s* valigia diplomatica

dipper ['dɪpər] *s* mestolo

dip'stick' *s* asta di livello

dire [daɪr] *adj* terribile, orrendo

direct [dɪ'rɛkt] or [daɪ'rɛkt] *adj* diretto; sincero || *tr* dirigere; ordinare

direct' cur'rent *s* corrente continua

direct' dis'course *s* discorso diretto

direct' dis'tance di'aling *s* (telp) teleselezione *f*

direct' hit' *s* colpo centrato

direction [dɪ'rɛkʃən] or [daɪ'rɛkʃən] *s* direzione; **directions** istruzioni *fpl*; (*for use*) indicazioni *fpl* per l'uso

directional [dɪ'rɛkʃənəl] or [daɪ-'rɛkʃənəl] *adj* direzionale

directive [dɪ'rɛktɪv] or [daɪ'rɛktɪv] *s* direttiva

direct' ob'ject *s* (gram) complemento diretto, complemento oggetto

director [dɪ'rɛktər] or [daɪ'rɛktər] *s* direttore *m*, gerente *m*; (*member of a governing body*) consigliere *m*

directorship [dɪ'rɛktər.ʃɪp] or [daɪ-'rɛktər.ʃɪp] *s* direzione; amministrazione

directo·ry [dɪ'rɛktəri] or [daɪ'rɛktəri] *s* (**-ries**) (*board of directors*) direzione, direttorio; (*list of names and addresses*) rubrica, elenco; (telp) elenco dei telefoni, guida telefonica

dirge [dʌrdʒ] *s* canto funebre

dirigible [ˈdɪrɪdʒɪbəl] *adj & s* dirigibile *m*

dirt [dʌrt] *s* (*soil*) terra, suolo; (*dust*) polvere *m*; (*mud*) fango; (*accumulation of dirt*) sudiciume *m*, lerciume *m*; (*moral filth*) porcheria, sozzura; (*gossip*) pettegolezzi *mpl*; **to do s.o. dirt** (slang) calunniare qlcu

dirt'-cheap' *adj* a prezzo bassissimo

dirt' road' *s* strada di terra battuta

dirt·y [ˈdʌrti] *adj* (**-ier; -iest**) sporco, sudicio; fangoso; polveroso; (*e.g., spinach*) terroso; (*obscene*) sconcio, lurido; immondo || *v* (*pret & pp* **-ied**) *tr* sporcare, insudiciare, imbrattare

dir'ty lin'en *s* roba sporca; **to air one's dirty linen in public** mettere i panni al sole

dir'ty trick' *s* brutto tiro

disabili·ty [ˌdɪsə'bɪlɪti] *s* (**-ties**) incapacità *f*, invalidità *f*

disabil'ity insur'ance *s* assicurazione invalidità

disable [dɪs'ebəl] *tr* mutilare, storpiare; (*a ship*) smantellare; (law) invalidare

disabuse [ˌdɪsə'bjuz] *tr* disingannare

disadvantage [ˌdɪsəd'væntɪdʒ] or [ˌdɪsəd'vɑntɪdʒ] *s* svantaggio

disadvantageous [dɪs.ædvən'tedʒəs] *adj* svantaggioso

disagree [ˌdɪsə'gri] *intr* discordare, disconvenire; (*to quarrel*) litigare, altercare; **to disagree with** non essere del parere di

disagreeable [ˌdɪsə'gri·əbəl] *adj* sgradevole

disagreement [ˌdɪsə'grimənt] *s* sconcordanza, dissidio, dissenso

disallow [ˌdɪsə'lau] *tr* non permettere, rifiutare

disappear [ˌdɪsə'pɪr] *intr* sparire, scomparire

disappearance [ˌdɪsə'pɪrəns] *s* scomparsa

disappoint [ˌdɪsə'pɔɪnt] *tr* deludere, disilludere; **to be disappointed** rimanere deluso

disappointment [ˌdɪsə'pɔɪntmənt] *s* delusione, disinganno, disappunto

disapproval [ˌdɪsə'pruvəl] *s* disapprovazione, riprova

disapprove [ˌdɪsə'pruv] *tr & intr* disapprovare

disarm [dɪs'ɑrm] *tr* disarmare || *intr* disarmare, disarmarsi

·isarmament [dɪs'ɑrməmənt] *s* disarmo

·isarming [dɪs'ɑrmɪŋ] *adj* ingraziante, simpatico

disarray [ˌdɪsə're] *s* disordine *m*, scompiglio; (*of apparel*) sciatteria || *tr* scomporre, scompigliare

disassemble [ˌdɪsə'sɛmbəl] *tr* smontare, sconnettere

disassociate [ˌdɪsə'soʃɪ‚et] *tr* dissociare, disassociare

disaster [dɪ'zæstər] or [dɪ'zɑstər] *s* disastro, sinistro

disastrous [dɪ'zæstrəs] or [dɪ'zɑstrəs] *adj* disastroso

disavow [ˌdɪsə'vau] *tr* sconfessare

disavowal [ˌdɪsə'vau‚əl] *s* sconfessione

disband [dɪs'bænd] *tr* (*an assembly*) sciogliere; (*troops*) congedare; (*any group*) sbandare || *intr* sbandarsi

dis-bar [dɪs'bar] *v* (*pret & pp* **-barred; ger -barring**) *tr* (law) radiare dall'albo degli avvocati

disbelief [ˌdɪsbɪ'lif] *s* incredulità *f*

disbelieve [ˌdɪsbɪ'liv] *tr* rifiutarsi di credere a || *intr* rifiutarsi di credere

disburse [dɪs'bʌrs] *tr* sborsare

disbursement [dɪs'bʌrsmənt] *s* sborso, disborso

discard [dɪs'kard] *s* scarto, scartina; **to put into the discard** scartare || *tr* scartare

discern [dɪ'zʌrn] or [dɪ'sʌrn] *tr* scernere, discernere, sceverare

discernible [dɪ'zʌrnəbəl] or [dɪ'sʌrnəbəl] *adj* discernibile

discerning [dɪ'zʌrnɪŋ] or [dɪ'sʌrnɪŋ] *adj* perspicace, oculato

discernment [dɪ'zʌrnmənt] or [dɪ'sʌrnmənt] *s* discernimento

discharge [dɪs'tʃardʒ] *s* (*of a load*) scarico; (*of a gun; of electricity*) scarica; (*of a prisoner*) liberazione; (*of a duty*) adempimento; (*of a debt*) pagamento; (*from a job*) licenziamento; (mil) foglio di congedo; (pathol) spurgo || *tr* scaricare; (*a duty*) adempiere; (*a prisoner*) liberare; (*a debt*) pagare; (*an employee*) licenziare; (*a patient*) lasciar uscire; (*a passenger from a ship*) sbarcare; (*a battery*) scaricare; (mil) congedare || *intr* (said, *e.g., of a liquid*) sboccare; (said *of a gun or a battery*) scaricarsi

disciple [dɪ'saɪpəl] *s* discepolo

disciplinarian [ˌdɪsɪplɪ'nɛrɪ·ən] *s* disciplinatore *m*; partigiano di una forte disciplina

disciplinary [ˈdɪsɪplɪ‚nɛri] *adj* disciplinare

discipline [ˈdɪsɪplɪn] *s* disciplina; castigo || *tr* disciplinare; castigare

disclaim [dɪs'klem] *tr* non riconoscere, negare

disclose [dɪs'kloz] *tr* rivelare, scoprire

disclosure [dɪs'kloʒər] *s* rivelazione, scoperta; divulgazione

discolor [dɪs'kʌlər] *tr* scolorare, scolorire || *intr* scolorirsi

discoloration [dɪs‚kʌlə're‚ʃən] *s* discolorazione

discomfit [dɪs'kʌmfɪt] *tr* sconcertare, turbare; frustrare, battere, mettere in fuga

discomfiture [dɪs'kʌmfɪtʃər] *s* sconcerto, turbamento; frustrazione; disfatta

discomfort [dɪs'kʌmfərt] *s* disagio || *tr* incomodare

disconcert [ˌdɪskən'sʌrt] *tr* sconcertare

disconnect [ˌdɪskə'nekt] *tr* sconnettere; (elec) disinserire

disconsolate [dɪs'kɑnsəlɪt] *adj* sconsolato, desolato

discontent [ˌdɪskən'tent] *adj & s* scontento || *tr* scontentare

discontented [ˌdɪskən'tentɪd] *adj* scontento

discontinue [ˌdɪskən'tɪnju] *tr* cessare, interrompere

discord ['dɪskɔrd] *s* discordia, dissidio

discordance [dɪs'kɔrdəns] *s* discordanza

discotheque ['dɪsko'tɛk] *s* discoteca

discount ['dɪskaunt] *s* sconto || ['dɪskaunt] or [dɪs'kaunt] *tr* scontare; (news) fare la tara a

dis'count rate' *s* tasso di sconto

discourage [dɪs'kʌrɪdʒ] *tr* scoraggiare, sconfortare; (to dissuade) sconsigliare

discouragement [dɪs'kʌrɪdʒmənt] *s* scoraggiamento; disapprovazione

discourse ['dɪskɔrs] or [dɪs'kɔrs] *s* discorso || [dɪs'kɔrs] *intr* discorrere

discourteous [dɪs'kʌrtɪ-əs] *adj* scortese

discourte·sy [dɪs'kʌrtəsi] *s* (-sies) scortesia

discover [dɪs'kʌvər] *tr* scoprire

discoverer [dɪs'kʌvərər] *s* scopritore *m*

discover·y [dɪs'kʌvəri] *s* (-ies) scoperta

discredit [dɪs'kredɪt] *s* discredito || *tr* screditare

discreditable [dɪs'kredɪtəbəl] *adj* indegno, disonorevole

discreet [dɪs'krit] *adj* discreto

discrepan·cy [dɪs'krepənsi] *s* (-cies) discrepanza, divario

discretion [dɪs'kreʃən] *s* discrezione

discriminate [dɪs'krɪmɪˌnet] *tr* discriminare || *intr*—**to discriminate against** fare delle discriminazioni contro

discrimination [dɪsˌkrɪmɪ'neʃən] *s* discriminazione

discriminatory [dɪs'krɪmɪnəˌtori] *adj* discriminante

discuss [dɪs'kʌs] *tr & intr* discutere

discussion [dɪs'kʌʃən] *s* discussione

discus thrower ['dɪskəs 'θro·ər] *s* discobolo

disdain [dɪs'den] *s* disdegno || *tr* disdegnare, sdegnare

disdainful [dɪs'denfəl] *adj* sdegnoso

disease [dɪ'ziz] *s* malattia

diseased [dɪ'zizd] *adj* malato

disembark [ˌdɪsem'bɑrk] *tr & intr* sbarcare

disembarkation [dɪsˌembɑr'keʃən] *s* sbarco

disembowel [ˌdɪsem'bau·əl] *tr* sbudellare, sventrare

disenchant [ˌdɪsen'tʃænt] or [ˌdɪsen-'tʃɑnt] *tr* disincantare

disenchantment [ˌdɪsen'tʃæntmənt] or [ˌdɪsen'tʃɑntmənt] *s* disinganno

disengage [ˌdɪsen'gedʒ] *tr* (from a pledge) svincolare; (to disconnect) sgranare, disinnestare; (mil) sganciare

disengagement [ˌdɪsen'gedʒmənt] *s* liberazione; disinnesto; svincolamento

disentangle [ˌdɪsen'tæŋgəl] *tr* disincagliare, districare

disentanglement [ˌdɪsen'tæŋgəlmənt] *s* districamento

disestablish [ˌdɪses'tæblɪʃ] *tr* (the Church) separare dallo Stato

disfavor [dɪs'fevər] *s* disfavore *m*

disfigure [dɪs'fɪgjər] *tr* sfigurare, deturpare

disfigurement [dɪs'fɪgjərmənt] *s* deturpazione

disfranchise [dɪs'fræntʃaɪz] *tr* privare dei diritti civili

disgorge [dɪs'gɔrdʒ] *tr* vomitare; (something illicitly obtained) restituire; (said of a river) scaricare || *intr* vomitare; scaricarsi

disgrace [dɪs'gres] *s* vergogna; disgrazia || *tr* disonorare; privare del favore

disgraceful [dɪs'gresfəl] *adj* infamante, disonorante

disgruntle [dɪs'grʌntəl] *tr* scontentare, irritare

disgruntled [dɪs'grʌntəld] *adj* irritato, di cattivo umore

disguise [dɪs'gaɪz] *s* travestimento || *tr* travestire, dissimulare

disgust [dɪs'gʌst] *s* disgusto, schifo || *tr* disgustare, fare schifo a

disgusting [dɪs'gʌstɪŋ] *adj* disgustoso, schifoso

dish [dɪʃ] *s* piatto, **dishes** vasellame *m*; **to wash the dishes** fare i piatti || *tr* scodellare; (to defeat) (slang) sconfiggere; **to dish out** (slang) distribuire

dish'cloth' *s* canovaccio, strofinaccio

dishearten [dɪs'hɑrtən] *tr* scoraggiare, disanimare, desolare

dishev·el [dɪ'ʃevəl] *v* (pret & pp -eled or -elled; ger -eling or -elling) *tr* scomporre, scarmigliare, scapigliare

dishonest [dɪs'ɑnɪst] *adj* disonesto

dishones·ty [dɪs'ɑnɪsti] *s* (-ties) disonestà *f*

dishonor [dɪs'ɑnər] *s* disonore *m* || *tr* disonorare; (com) rifiutare di pagare

dishonorable [dɪs'ɑnərəbəl] *adj* disonorevole, disonorante

dish'pan' *s* bacinella per lavare i piatti

dish'rack' *s* portapiatti *m*, sgocciolatoio

dish'rag' *s* canovaccio, strofinaccio

dish'towel *s* canovaccio per le stoviglie

dish'wash·er *s* (person) sguattero, lavapiatti *m*; (machine) lavastoviglie *m & f*

dish'wa'ter *s* lavatura di piatti

disillusion [ˌdɪsɪ'luʒən] *s* disillusione || *tr* disilludere

disillusionment [ˌdɪsɪ'luʒənmənt] *s* disillusione

disinclination [dɪsˌɪnklɪ'neʃən] *s* riluttanza, avversione

disinclined [ˌdɪsɪn'klaɪnd] *adj* riluttante, avverso

disinfect [ˌdɪsɪnˈfɛkt] *tr* disinfettare
disinfectant [ˌdɪsɪnˈfɛktənt] *adj* & *s* disinfettante *m*
disingenuous [ˌdɪsɪnˈdʒɛnjuˌəs] *adj* poco schietto, insincero
disinherit [ˌdɪsɪnˈhɛrɪt] *tr* diseredare
disintegrate [dɪsˈɪntɪˌgret] *tr* disintegrare, disgregare || *intr* disintegrarsi, disgregarsi
disintegration [dɪsˌɪntɪˈgreʃən] *s* disintegrazione, disgregamento
disin·ter [ˌdɪsɪnˈtʌr] *v* (*pret* & *pp* **-terred**; *ger* **-terring**) *tr* dissotterrare
disinterested [dɪsˈɪntəˌrɛstɪd] or [dɪsˈɪntrɪstɪd] *adj* disinteressato
disjunctive [dɪsˈdʒʌŋktɪv] *adj* disgiuntivo
disk [dɪsk] *s* disco; (*of ski pole*) rotella
disk′ jock′ey *s* presentatore *m* di un programma radiofonico di dischi
dislike [dɪsˈlaɪk] *s* antipatia, avversione; **to take a dislike for** prendere in uggia || *tr* non piacere (with *dat*), e.g., **he dislikes wine** non gli piace il vino
dislocate [ˈdɪsloˌket] *tr* spostare, mettere fuori posto; (*a bone*) slogare
dislodge [dɪsˈladʒ] *tr* sloggiare
disloyal [dɪsˈlɔɪˌəl] *adj* sleale
disloyal·ty [dɪsˈlɔɪˌəltɪ] *s* (-ties) slealtà *f*
dismal [ˈdɪzməl] *adj* tetro, triste; cattivo, orribile
dismantle [dɪsˈmæntəl] *tr* smontare, smantellare; (*a fortress*) sguarnire
dismay [dɪsˈme] *s* costernazione || *tr* costernare
dismember [dɪsˈmɛmbər] *tr* smembrare
dismiss [dɪsˈmɪs] *tr* congedare; (*to fire*) licenziare; (*a subject*) scartare; (*from the mind*) scacciare
dismissal [dɪsˈmɪsəl] *s* congedo; licenziamento
dismount [dɪsˈmaʊnt] *tr* disarcionare || *intr* scendere, smontare
disobedience [ˌdɪsəˈbidiˌəns] *s* disubbidienza
disobedient [ˌdɪsəˈbidiˌənt] *adj* disubbidiente
disobey [ˌdɪsəˈbe] *tr* disubbidire (with *dat*) || *intr* disubbidire
disorder [dɪsˈɔrdər] *s* disordine *m* || *tr* disordinare, confondere
disorderly [dɪsˈɔrdərlɪ] *adj* disordinato, confuso; (*unruly*) turbolento
disor′derly con′duct *s* contegno contrario all'ordine pubblico
disor′derly house′ *s* bordello, lupanare *m*
disorganize [dɪsˈɔrgəˌnaɪz] *tr* disorganizzare
disoriented [dɪsˈɔrɪˌɛntɪd] *adj* disorientato
disown [dɪsˈon] *tr* disconoscere
disparage [dɪsˈpærɪdʒ] *tr* svilire, deprezzare
disparagement [dɪsˈpærɪdʒmənt] *s* discredito, deprezzamento
disparate [ˈdɪspərɪt] *adj* disparato
dispari·ty [dɪsˈpærɪtɪ] *s* (-ties) disparità *f*, spareggio
dispassionate [dɪsˈpæʃənɪt] *adj* spassionato

dispatch [dɪsˈpætʃ] *s* dispaccio || *tr* spedire; (*to dismiss*) congedare; uccidere; (*a meal*) (coll) liquidare
dis·pel [dɪsˈpɛl] *v* (*pret* & *pp* **-pelled**; *ger* **-pelling**) *tr* dissipare
dispensa·ry [dɪsˈpɛnsərɪ] *s* (-ries) dispensario
dispensation [ˌdɪspɛnˈseʃən] *s* (*dispensing*) distribuzione, dispensa; (*exemption*) dispensa
dispense [dɪsˈpɛns] *tr* (*medicines*) distribuire; (*justice*) amministrare; (*to distribute*) dispensare; (*to exempt*) esimere || *intr*—**to dispense with** fare a meno di; esimersi da
dispenser [dɪsˈpɛnsər] *s* dispensatore *m*; (*automatic*) distributore *m*
disperse [dɪsˈpʌrs] *tr* disperdere || *intr* disperdersi
dispersion [dɪsˈpʌrʒən] or [dɪsˈpɛrʃən] *s* dispersione
dispersive [dɪsˈpʌrsɪv] *adj* dispersivo
dispirit [dɪsˈpɪrɪt] *tr* scoraggiare
displace [dɪsˈples] *tr* muovere; costringere a lasciare il proprio paese; (*to supplant*) rimpiazzare; (naut) dislocare
displaced′ per′son *s* rifugiato politico
displacement [dɪsˈplesmənt] *s* spostamento; sostituzione; (*of a piston*) cilindrata; (naut) dislocamento
display [dɪsˈple] *s* sfoggio, mostra || *tr* mostrare; (*e.g., in a store window*) mettere in mostra; (*to unfold*) spiegare; (*to show ostentatiously*) sfoggiare, ostentare; (*ignorance*) rivelare
display′ cab′inet *s* bacheca
display′ win′dow *s* mostra, vetrina
displease [dɪsˈpliz] *tr* dispiacere (with *dat*)
displeasing [dɪsˈplizɪŋ] *adj* spiacevole
displeasure [dɪsˈplɛʒər] *s* dispiacere *m*; sfavore *m*
disposable [dɪsˈpozəbəl] *adj* (*available*) disponibile; (*made to be thrown away after use*) scartabile, da gettarsi via, usa e getta
disposal [dɪsˈpozəl] *s* disposizione; eliminazione; **to have at one's disposal** disporre di
dispose [dɪsˈpoz] *tr* disporre; **to dispose of** disporre di; (*to get rid of*) sbarazzarsi di; vendere
disposed [dɪsˈpozd] *adj*—**to be disposed to** essere disposto a
disposition [ˌdɪspəˈzɪʃən] *s* disposizione; (*mental outlook*) indole *f*; tendenza; (mil) ordinamento
dispossess [ˌdɪspəˈzɛs] *tr* spodestare, bandire; (*to evict*) sfrattare
disproof [dɪsˈpruf] *s* confutazione
disproportionate [ˌdɪsprəˈpɔrʃənɪt] *adj* sproporzionato
disprove [dɪsˈpruv] *tr* confutare
dispute [dɪsˈpjut] *s* disputa; **beyond dispute** incontestabile; **in dispute** in discussione || *tr* & *intr* disputare
disquali·fy [dɪsˈkwɑlɪˌfaɪ] *v* (*pret* & *pp* **-fied**) *tr* squalificare
disquiet [dɪsˈkwaɪˌət] *s* inquietudine *f* || *tr* inquietare, turbare
disquisition [ˌdɪskwɪˈzɪʃən] *s* disquisizione

disregard [ˌdɪsrɪˈgɑrd] s (of a rule) inosservanza; (of danger) disprezzo, noncuranza ‖ tr non fare attenzione a

disrepair [ˌdɪsrɪˈpɛr] s cattivo stato, rovina

disreputable [dɪsˈrɛpjətəbəl] adj malfamato; disonorevole; (in bad condition) raso, logoro

disrepute [ˌdɪsrɪˈpjut] s cattiva fama; **to bring into disrepute** rovinare la reputazione di

disrespect [ˌdɪsrɪˈspɛkt] s mancanza di rispetto ‖ tr mancare di rispetto a

disrespectful [ˌdɪsrɪˈspɛktfəl] adj non rispettoso, irriverente

disrobe [dɪsˈrob] tr svestire ‖ intr svestirsi, spogliarsi

disrupt [dɪsˈrʌpt] tr disorganizzare; interrompere

disruption [dɪsˈrʌpʃən] s rottura; disorganizzazione

dissatisfaction [ˌdɪsætɪsˈfækʃən] s scontento, malcontento

dissatisfied [dɪsˈsætɪsˌfaɪd] adj scontento, malcontento; insoddisfatto

dissatis·fy [dɪsˈsætɪsˌfaɪ] v (pret & pp -fied) tr scontentare

dissect [dɪˈsɛkt] tr sezionare

dissemble [dɪˈsɛmbəl] tr & intr dissimulare

disseminate [dɪˈsɛmɪˌnet] tr disseminare, divulgare

dissension [dɪˈsɛnʃən] s dissensione

dissent [dɪˈsɛnt] s dissenso; (nonconformity) dissidio ‖ intr dissentire

dissenter [dɪˈsɛntər] s dissenziente m

dissertation [ˌdɪsərˈteʃən] s dissertazione

disservice [dɪˈsɜrvɪs] s danno; cattivo servizio

dissidence [ˈdɪsɪdəns] s dissidenza

dissident [ˈdɪsɪdənt] adj & s dissidente m

dissimilar [dɪˈsɪmɪlər] adj dissimile

dissimilate [dɪˈsɪmɪˌlet] tr dissimilare ‖ intr dissimilarsi

dissimulate [dɪˈsɪmjəˌlet] tr & intr dissimulare

dissipate [ˈdɪsɪˌpet] tr dissipare ‖ intr dissiparsi; (to indulge oneself) darsi alla dissipatezza

dissipated [ˈdɪsɪˌpetɪd] adj dissipato

dissipation [ˌdɪsɪˈpeʃən] s dissipazione

dissociate [dɪˈsoʊʃɪˌet] tr dissociare ‖ intr dissociarsi

dissolute [ˈdɪsəˌlut] adj dissoluto

dissolution [ˌdɪsəˈluʃən] s dissoluzione

dissolve [dɪˈzɑlv] tr sciogliere, disciogliere ‖ intr sciogliersi, disciogliersi

dissonance [ˈdɪsənəns] s dissonanza

dissuade [dɪˈswed] tr dissuadere

dissyllabic [ˌdɪsɪˈlæbɪk] adj disillabo

dissyllable [dɪˈsɪləbəl] s disillabo

distaff [ˈdɪstæf] or [ˈdɪstɑf] s rocca

dis'taff side' s ramo femminile di una famiglia

distance [ˈdɪstəns] s distanza; **a long distance** (fig) moltissimo; **in the distance** in lontananza; **to keep at a distance** or **to keep one's distance** mantenere le distanze ‖ tr distanziare

distant [ˈdɪstənt] adj distante; (relative) lontano; (aloof) freddo, riservato

distaste [dɪsˈtest] s ripugnanza

distasteful [dɪsˈtestfəl] adj ripugnante, sgradevole

distemper [dɪsˈtɛmpər] s cimurro; (painting) tempera ‖ tr dipingere a tempera

distend [dɪsˈtɛnd] tr stendere, distendere; gonfiare ‖ intr stendersi, distendersi; gonfiarsi

distension [dɪsˈtɛnʃən] s distensione; gonfiamento

distill [dɪsˈtɪl] tr distillare

distillation [ˌdɪstɪˈleʃən] s distillazione

distiller·y [dɪsˈtɪləri] s (-ies) distilleria

distinct [dɪsˈtɪŋkt] adj distinto, chiaro; (not blurred) nitido

distinction [dɪsˈtɪŋkʃən] s distinzione

distinctive [dɪsˈtɪŋktɪv] adj distintivo

distinguish [dɪsˈtɪŋgwɪʃ] tr distinguere

distinguished [dɪsˈtɪŋgwɪʃt] adj distinto

distort [dɪsˈtɔrt] tr distorcere; (the truth) svisare, snaturare

distortion [dɪsˈtɔrʃən] s deformazione; (of the truth) alterazione, svisamento; (rad) distorsione

distract [dɪsˈtrækt] tr distrarre

distracted [dɪsˈtræktɪd] adj distratto; (irrational) turbato, sconvolto

distraction [dɪsˈtrækʃən] s distrazione

distraught [dɪsˈtrɔt] adj turbato, stordito

distress [dɪsˈtrɛs] s pena, dispiacere m; pericolo; (naut) difficoltà f ‖ tr sconfortare, affliggere

distressing [dɪsˈtrɛsɪŋ] adj penoso

distress' mer'chandise s merce f sotto costo

distress' sig'nal s segnale m di soccorso

distribute [dɪsˈtrɪbjut] tr distribuire

distribution [ˌdɪstrɪˈbjuʃən] s distribuzione, erogazione

distributor [dɪsˈtrɪbjutər] s distributore m; (aut) distributore m d'accensione

district [ˈdɪstrɪkt] s regione; (of a city) rione m, quartiere m; (administrative division) distretto ‖ tr dividere in distretti

dis'trict attor'ney s procuratore m generale

distrust [dɪsˈtrʌst] s diffidenza ‖ tr diffidare di

distrustful [dɪsˈtrʌstfəl] adj diffidente

disturb [dɪsˈtɜrb] tr disturbare, turbare; disordinare

disturbance [dɪsˈtɜrbəns] s disturbo, turbamento, perturbazione; disordine m

disuse [dɪsˈjus] s disuso

ditch [dɪtʃ] s fossa, fossato ‖ tr scavare un fosso in; (rr) far deragliare; (slang) piantare in asso ‖ intr fare un ammaraggio forzato

dither [ˈdɪðər] s agitazione; **to be in a dither** (coll) essere agitato

dit·to [ˈdɪto] s (-tos) lo stesso; (ditto symbol) virgolette fpl ‖ adv ugualmente, idem ‖ tr copiare, duplicare

dit'to marks' spl virgolette fpl

dit·ty ['dɪti] s (-ties) canzonetta

diva ['divə] s (mus) diva

divan ['daɪvæn] or [dɪ'væn] s divano

dive [daɪv] s tuffo; (of a submarine) immersione; (aer) picchiata; (coll) taverna; (com) discesa || v (pret & pp **dived** or **dove** [dov]) intr tuffarsi; (said of submarine) immergersi; (to plunge) lanciarsi; (aer) scendere in picchiata; **to dive for** (e.g., pearls) pescare

dive'-bomb' tr bombardare in picchiata || intr scendere a tuffo

dive' bomb'ing s bombardamento in picchiata

diver ['daɪvər] s tuffatore m; (person who works under water) palombaro; (orn) tuffetto

diverge [dɪ'vʌrdʒ] or [daɪ'vʌrdʒ] intr divergere

divers ['daɪvərz] adj diversi, vari

diverse [dɪ'vʌrs], [daɪ'vʌrs] or ['daɪvʌrs] adj (different) diverso; (of various kinds) multiforme

diversification [dɪ,vʌrsɪfɪ'keʃən] or [daɪ,vʌrsɪfɪ'keʃən] s diversificazione

diversi·fy [dɪ'vʌrsɪ,faɪ] or [daɪ'vʌrsɪ,faɪ] v (pret & pp -fied) tr diversificare || intr diversificarsi

diversion [dɪ'vʌrʒən] or [daɪ'vʌrʒən] s diversione; (pastime) svago

diversi·ty [dɪ'vʌrsɪti] or [daɪ'vʌrsɪti] s (-ties) diversità f

divert [dɪ'vʌrt] or [daɪ'vʌrt] tr deviare; (to entertain) divertire; (money) stornare, distrarre

diverting [dɪ'vʌrtɪŋ] or [daɪ'vʌrtɪŋ] adj divertente

divest [dɪ'vest] or [daɪ'vest] tr spogliare; spossessare; **to divest oneself of** spogliarsi di, espropriarsi di

divide [dɪ'vaɪd] s spartiacque m || tr dividere || intr dividersi

dividend ['dɪvɪ,dend] s dividendo

dividers [dɪ'vaɪdərz] spl compasso a punte fisse

divination [,dɪvɪ'neʃən] s divinazione

divine [dɪ'vaɪn] adj divino || s sacerdote m, prete m || tr divinare

diviner [dɪ'vaɪnər] s divinatore m

diving ['daɪvɪŋ] s tuffo, immersione

div'ing bell' s campana da palombaro

div'ing board' s trampolino

div'ing suit' s scafandro

divin'ing rod' [dɪ'vaɪnɪŋ] s bacchetta rabdomantica

divini·ty [dɪ'vɪnɪti] s (-ties) divinità f; teologia; **the Divinity** Dio

divisible [dɪ'vɪsɪbəl] adj divisibile

division [dɪ'vɪʒən] s divisione

divisor [dɪ'vaɪzər] s divisore m

divorce [dɪ'vors] s divorzio; **to get a divorce** divorziare || tr (a married couple) divorziare; (one's spouse) divorziare da || intr divorziare

divorcé [dɪvor'se] s divorziato

divorcee [dɪvor'si] s divorziata

divulge [dɪ'vʌldʒ] tr divulgare

dizziness ['dɪzɪnɪs] s vertigine f, stordimento; confusione

diz·zy ['dɪzi] adj (-zier; -ziest) (causing dizziness) vertiginoso; (suffering diz-ziness) preso da vertigine, stordito; (coll) stupido

do [du] v (3rd pers **does** [dʌz]; pret **did** [dɪd]; pp **done** [dʌn]; ger **doing** ['du·ɪŋ]) tr fare; (a problem) risolvere; (a distance) percorrere; (to study) studiare; (to explore) attraversare; (to tire) stancare; **to do one's best** fare del proprio meglio; **to do over** tornare a fare; ripetere; **to do right by** trattare bene; **to do s.o. out of s.th** (coll) portare via qlco a qlcu; **to do to death** mettere a morte; **to do up** (coll) impacchettare; stancare; (one's hair) farsi; vestire; (a shirt) lavare e stirare; **to have done** far fare || intr fare; agire; comportarsi; servire; bastare; stare; succedere; **how do you do?** come sta?; **that will do** basta; è sufficiente; **to have done with** non aver più nulla a che fare con; **to have nothing to do with** non aver nulla a che vedere con; **to have to do with** aver a che fare con, trattarsi di; **to do away with** togliere di mezzo; **to do for** servire da; **to do well** crescere bene; **to do without** fare a meno di || v aux used 1) in interrogative sentences: **Do you speak Italian?** Parla italiano?; 2) in negative sentences: **I do not speak Italian** Non parlo italiano; 3) to avoid repetition of a verb or full verbal expression: **Did you go to church this morning? Yes, I did.** È stato in chiesa questa mattina? Sì, ci sono stato; 4) to lend emphasis to a principal verb: **I do believe what you told me** Ci credo a quello che mi ha detto; 5) in inverted constructions after certain adverbs: **Seldom does he come to see me** Mi viene a vedere di raro; 6) in a supplicating tone with imperatives: **Do come in** entri per favore

docile ['dɑsɪl] adj docile

dock [dɑk] s (wharf) molo; (waterway between two piers) darsena; (area including piers and waterways) scalo portuario; (law) gabbia degli imputati || tr (to deduct from the wages of) fare una deduzione a; (to deduct s.o.'s salary) dedurre da; (an animal) scodare; (naut) attraccare || intr (aer) agganciarsi; (naut) attraccare

dockage ['dɑkɪdʒ] s attracco; (charges) diritti mpl di porto

docket ['dɑkɪt] s ordine m del giorno; (law) ruolo delle sentenze; **on the docket** (coll) pendente, in sospeso

dock' hand' s portuale m

docking ['dɑkɪŋ] s (aer) aggancio; (naut) attracco

dock'yard' s cantiere m navale

doctor ['dɑktər] s dottore m; (physician) medico || tr curare; aggiustare; falsificare; adulterare || intr esercitare la medicina; (coll) curarsi, prendere medicine

doctorate ['dɑktərɪt] s dottorato

doctrine ['dɑktrɪn] s dottrina

document ['dɑkjəmənt] s documento || ['dɑkjə,ment] tr documentare

documenta·ry [‚dɑkjə'mɛntəri] *adj &
s* (*-ries*) documentario

documentation [‚dɑkəmɛn'teʃən] *s* do-
cumentazione

doddering ['dɑdərɪŋ] *adj* tremante,
rimbambito

dodge [dɑdʒ] *s* scarto, schivata; (fig)
stratagemma *m* ‖ *tr* schivare, evitare
‖ *intr* schivarsi; (fig) rispondere eva-
sivamente; **to dodge around the corner** scantonare

do·do ['dodo] *s* (*-dos* or *-does*) (coll)
rimbecillito

doe [do] *s* (*of deer*) cerva; (*of goat*)
capretta; (*of rabbit*) coniglia

doeskin ['do‚skɪn] *s* pelle *f* di daino,
pelle *f* di dante; lana finissima

doff [dɑf] or [dɔf] *tr* (*one's hat*) togliersi; (*clothing*) deporre

dog [dɔg] or [dɑg] *s* cane *m*; **to go to
the dogs** (coll) andare in malora; **to
put on the dog** (coll) darsi delle arie
‖ *v* (*pret & pp* **dogged**; *ger* **dogging**)
tr seguire; perseguitare

dog'catch'er *s* accalappiacani *m*

dog' days' *s* solleone *m*, canicola

dog'-ear' *s* orecchia, orecchio

dog'fight' *s* duello aereo

dogged ['dɔgɪd] or ['dɑgɪd] *adj* accanito

doggerel ['dɔgərəl] or ['dɑgərəl] *s*
versi *mpl* da colascione

dog·gy ['dɔgi] or ['dɑgi] *adj* (*-gier*;
-giest) vistoso; canino ‖ *s* (*-gies*)
cagnolino

dog'house' *s* canile *m*; **to be in the doghouse** (slang) essere in disgrazia

dog' Lat'in *s* latino maccheronico

dogma ['dɔgmə] or ['dɑgmə] *s* dogma
m

dogmatic [dɔg'mætɪk] or [dɑg'mætɪk]
adj dogmatico

dog' rac'ing *s* corse *fpl* dei cani

dog' show' *s* mostra canina

dog's' life' *s* vita da cani

Dog' Star' *s* canicola

dog' tag' *s* (mil) piastrina, piastrino

dog'-tired' *adj* (coll) stanco morto

dog'tooth' *s* (*-teeth* [‚tiθ]) canino

dog' track' *s* cinodromo

dog'watch' *s* (naut) quarto di solo due
ore, gaettone *m*

dog'wood' *s* corniolo

doi·ly ['dɔrli] *s* (*-lies*) centrino

doings ['du·ɪŋz] *spl* azioni *fpl*, fatti
mpl

do'-it-your·self' *s* il fare tutto da sé

doldrums ['dɑldrəmz] *spl* calma equatoriale; inattività *f*; depressione

dole [dol] *s* elemosina; (*to the jobless*)
sussidio di disoccupazione ‖ *tr—to
dole out** distribuire parsimoniosa-
mente

doleful ['dolfəl] *adj* lugubre, triste

doll [dɑl] *s* bambola ‖ *intr—to doll up**
(slang) agghindarsi

dollar ['dɑlər] *s* dollaro

dol'lar·wise' *adv* in termini finanziari

dol·ly ['dɑli] *s* (*-lies*) pupattola; (*low,
wheeled frame for moving heavy
loads*) carrello; (mov, telv) carrello

‖ *v* (*pret & pp* **-lied**) *intr* (mov, telv)
carrellare

dol'ly shot' *s* (mov, telv) carrellata

dolphin ['dɑlfɪn] *s* delfino

dolt [dolt] *s* gonzo, balordo

doltish ['doltɪʃ] *adj* gonzo, balordo

domain [do'men] *s* dominio; (law) proprietà *f*; (fig) campo, orbita

dome [dom] *s* cupola

dome' light' *s* lampadario

domestic [də'mɛstɪk] *adj & s* domestico

domesticate [də'mɛstɪ‚ket] *tr* domesticare

domicile ['dɑmɪsɪl] or ['dɑmɪ‚saɪl] *s*
domicilio ‖ *tr* domiciliare

dominance ['dɑmɪnəns] *s* dominio

dominant ['dɑmɪnənt] *adj & s* domi-
nante *f*

dominate ['dɑmɪ‚net] *tr & intr* dominare

domination [‚dɑmɪ'neʃən] *s* domina-
zione

domineer [‚dɑmɪ'nɪr] *intr* spadroneggiare

domineering [‚dɑmɪ'nɪrɪŋ] *adj* dispotico, tirannico

Dominican [də'mɪnɪkən] *adj & s* do-
minicano; (eccl) domenicano

dominion [də'mɪnjən] *s* dominio

domi·no ['dɑmɪ‚no] *s* (*-noes* or *-nos*)
(*costume and person*) domino;
(*piece*) tessera di domino; **dominoes**
(*game*) domino

don [dɑn] *s* signore *m*; don *m*; membro
di un collegio universitario inglese ‖
v (*pret & pp* **donned**; *ger* **donning**)
tr (*clothes*) mettersi, vestire

donate ['donet] *tr* donare, dare

donation [do'neʃən] *s* donazione

done [dʌn] *adj* fatto; finito; stanco;
(culin) ben cotto, ben rosolato

done' for' *adj* (coll) stanco morto;
(coll) rovinato; (coll) fuori combattimento; (coll) morto

donjon ['dʌndʒən] or ['dɑndʒən] *s* torrione *m*, maschio

Don Juan [dɑn 'wɑn] or [dɔn 'hwɑn]
s Don Giovanni

donkey ['dɑŋki] or ['dʌŋki] *s* asino,
somaro

donnish ['dɑnɪʃ] *adj* pedante

donor ['donər] *s* donatore *m*

doodle ['dudəl] *tr & intr* scarabocchiare, riempire di ghirigori

doom [dum] *s* destino; morte *f*, rovina;
sentenza di morte; giudizio finale ‖
tr destinare; condannare; condannare
a morte

doomsday ['dumz‚de] *s* giorno del
giudizio

door [dor] *s* porta; (*of a carriage or
automobile*) portiera, sportello; (*one
part of a double door*) battente *m*;
behind closed doors a porte chiuse;
to see to the door accompagnare alla
porta; **to show s.o. the door** mettere
qlcu alla porta

door'bell' *s* campanello della porta

door' check' *s* chiusura automatica di
porta, scontro

door'frame' *s* cornice *f*

door'head' s architrave m
door'jamb' s stipite m
door'keep'er s portinaio
door'knob' s maniglia della porta
door' knock'er s battente m
door' latch' s paletto
door'man' s (-men') portiere m, portinaio; (of large apartment house) guardaportone m
door'mat' s stoino, zerbino
door'nail' s borchione m; **dead as a doornail** morto e ben morto
door'post' s stipite m
door' scrap'er s raschietto
door'sill' s soglia
door'step' s gradino davanti la porta
door'stop' s paracolpi m
door'-to-door' adj (shipment) diretto; (selling) di porta in porta
door'way' s vano della porta; porta
dope [dop] s lubrificante m; (aer) vernice f; (slang) stupido, scemo; (slang) informazioni fpl; (slang) narcotico || tr (slang) narcotizzare; **to dope out** (slang) indovinare, decifrare, immaginare
dope' fiend' s (slang) tossicomane mf
dope'sheet' s giornaletto con le previsioni della corse ippiche
dormant ['dɔrmənt] adj dormente; latente
dor'mer win'dow ['dɔrmər] s abbaino
dormito·ry ['dɔrmɪ,tori] s (-ries) dormitorio
dor·mouse ['dɔr,maʊs] s (-mice [,maɪs]) ghiro
dosage ['dosɪdʒ] s dosatura
dose [dos] s dose f; (coll) boccone amaro || tr dosare; somministrare
dossier ['dɑsɪ,e] s incartamento
dot [dɑt] s punto; **on the dot** (coll) in punto || v (pret & pp dotted; ger dotting) tr punteggiare; **to dot one's i's** mettere i punti sulle i
dotage ['dotɪdʒ] s rimbecillimento; **to be in one's dotage** essere rimbambito
dotard ['dotərd] s vecchio rimbambito
dote [dot] intr rimbambirsi; **to dote on** essere pazzo per
doting ['dotɪŋ] adj che ama alla follia; (from old age) rimbambito, rimbecillito
dots' and dash'es spl (telg) punti mpl e tratti mpl
dot'ted line' s linea punteggiata; **to sign on the dotted line** firmare inconsideratamente
double ['dʌbəl] adj doppio || s (bridge) contre m; **doubles** (tennis) doppio || tr raddoppiare; (bridge) contrare || intr raddoppiarsi; (bridge) contrare; (mov, theat) sostenere due ruoli; (mov) doppiare; **to double up** (said of two people) dividere la stessa camera, dividere lo stesso letto; piegarsi in due
double-barreled ['dʌbəl'bærəld] adj a due canne; (fig) a doppio fine
dou'ble bass' s contrabbasso
dou'ble bed' s letto matrimoniale
dou'ble boil'er s bagnomaria m

double-breasted ['dʌbəl'brɛstɪd] adj a doppio petto, doppiopetto
dou'ble chin' s pappagorgia
dou'ble-cross' tr (coll) tradire
dou'ble date' s (coll) appuntamento amoroso di due coppie
dou'ble-deal'ing adj doppio
dou'ble-deck'er s (bed) letto a castello; (sandwich) tramezzino doppio; autobus m a due piani; (naut) nave f due ponti; (aer) aereo due ponti
double-edged ['dʌbəl'edʒd] adj a due tagli, a doppio taglio
dou'ble en'try s (com) partita doppia
dou'ble fea'ture s (mov) programma m di due lungometraggio
double-header ['dʌbəl'hɛdər] s treno con due locomotive; due partite di baseball giocate successivamente
double-jointed ['dʌbəl'dʒɔɪntɪd] adj snodato
dou'ble-park' tr & intr parcheggiare in doppia fila
dou'ble-quick' adj & adv a passo di carica
dou'ble stand'ard s—**to have a double standard** usare due pesi e due misure
doublet ['dʌblɪt] s (close-fitting jacket) farsetto; (philol) doppione m
dou'ble-talk' s discorso incomprensibile; **to give s.o. double-talk** parlare evasivamente a qlcu || intr parlare evasivamente
dou'ble time' s paga doppia; (mil) passo di carica
doubleton ['dʌbəltən] s doppio
doubly ['dʌbli] adv doppiamente
doubt [daʊt] s dubbio; **beyond doubt** senza dubbio; **if in doubt** in caso di dubbio; **no doubt** senza dubbio || tr dubitare di || intr dubitare
doubter ['daʊtər] s incredulo
doubtful ['daʊtfəl] adj incerto; dubbioso
doubtless ['daʊtlɪs] adj indubitabile || adv senza dubbio; probabilmente
douche [duʃ] s irrigazione f; (instrument) irrigatore m || tr irrigare || intr fare irrigazioni
dough [do] s pasta di pane; (money) (slang) soldi mpl, quattrini mpl
dough'boy' s fantaccino americano
dough'nut' s ciambella; (with filling) sgonfiotto
dough·ty ['dauti] adj (-tier; -tiest) forte, coraggioso
dough·y ['do·i] adj (-ier; -iest) pastoso, molle
dour [daʊr] or [dʊr] adj triste, severo
douse [daʊs] tr immergere; bagnare; (the light) (coll) spegnere
dove [dʌv] s colomba, tortora
dovecote ['dʌv,kot] s piccionaia
dove'tail' s coda di rondine || tr calettare a coda di rondine; (to make fit) adattare, far combaciare || intr (to fit) combaciare; corrispondere
dowager ['dau·ədʒər] s vedova titolata; vecchia signora austera; **queen dowager** regina madre
dow·dy ['daudi] adj (-dier; -diest) trasandato

dow·el ['dau-əl] *s* caviglia, tassello ‖
v (*pret* & *pp* **-eled** or **-elled;** *ger*
-eling or **-elling**) *tr* tassellare

dower ['dau-ər] *s* (*widow's portion*)
legittima, vedovile *m;* (*marriage portion; natural gift*) dote *f* ‖ *tr* dotare;
assegnare un vedovile a

down [daun] *adj* che discende; basso;
(*train*) che va al centro; depresso;
finito; (*money, payment*) anticipato;
(*storage battery*) esaurito ‖ *s* (*of
fruit and human body*) lanugine *f;*
(*of birds*) piumino; (*upset*) rovescio;
discesa; (*sandhill*) duna ‖ *adv* giù;
all'ingiù, in giù; dabbasso; a terra; al
sud; (*in cash*) a contanti; **down and
out** rovinato; senza un soldo; **down
from a; down on one's knees** in
ginocchio; **down to** fino a; **down
under** agli antipodi; **down with . . . !**
abasso . . . !; **to get down to work**
mettersi seriamente al lavoro; **to go
down** scendere; **to lie down** sdraiarsi;
andare a letto; **to sit down** sedersi ‖
prep giù per; **down the river** a valle;
down the street giù per la strada ‖ *tr*
abbattere; (*coll*) buttar giù, tracannare

down'cast' *adj* mogio, sfiduciato

down'fall' *s* rovina, rovescio

down'grade' *adj* & *adv* in declivio, a
valle ‖ *s* discesa; **to be on the down-
grade** essere in declino ‖ *tr* attribuire
minor importanza a; degradare

downhearted ['daun,hɑrtɪd] *adj* scoraggiato, abbattuto

down'hill' *adj* & *adv* in declivio; **to go
downhill** declinare

down' pay'ment *s* acconto

down'pour' *s* acquazzone *m*, rovescio

down'right' *adj* assoluto; completo;
franco, diretto ‖ *adv* completamente

down'stairs' *adj* del piano di sotto ‖ *s*
il piano di sotto; i piani di sotto ‖
adv dabbasso, di sotto; giù

down'stream' *adv* a valle

down'stroke' *s* corsa discendente

down'town' *adj* centrale ‖ *s* centro
della città ‖ *adv* al centro della città

down' train' *s* treno discendente, treno
che va al centro

down'trend' *s* tendenza al ribasso

downtrodden ['daun,trɑdən] *adj* cal-
pestato, oppresso

downward ['daunwərd] *adj* & *adv* al-
l'ingiù

down·y ['dauni] *adj* (**-ier; -iest**) piu-
moso, lanuginoso; (*soft*) molle, morbido

dow·ry ['dauri] *s* (**-ries**) dote *f*

doze [doz] *s* pisolo ‖ *intr* dormicchiare; **to doze off** appisolarsi

dozen ['dʌzən] *s* dozzina

dozy ['dozi] *adj* sonnolento

drab [dræb] *adj* (**drabber; drabbest**)
grigiastro; (*dull*) scialbo ‖ *s* colore
grigiastro; (*fabric*) tela naturale;
donna di malaffare

drach·ma ['drækmə] *s* (**-mas** or **-mae**
[mi]) dramma

draft [dræft] or [drɑft] *s* corrente *f*
d'aria; (*pulling*) tiro; (*in a chimney*)

tiraggio; (*sketch, outline*) schizzo;
(*first form of a writing*) prima stesura; (*drink*) sorso, bicchiere *m;*
(com) tratta, lettera di credito; (law)
progetto, disegno; (naut) pesca; (mil)
coscrizione *f*, leva; **on draft** alla
spina ‖ *tr* disegnare; fare uno schizzo
di; (*a document*) stendere; (mil) coscrivere; **to be drafted** essere di leva,
andar coscritto

draft' age' *s* età *f* di leva

draft' beer' *s* birra alla spina

draft' board' *s* consiglio di leva

draft' dodg'er ['dɑdʒər] *s* renitente *m*
alla leva, imboscato

draftee [,dræf'ti] or [,drɑf'ti] *s* coscritto

draft' horse' *s* cavallo da tiro

drafts'man *s* (**-men**) disegnatore *m;*
(*man who draws up documents*) redattore *m*

draft' trea'ty *s* progetto di trattato

drag [dræg] *s* (*sledge for conveying
heavy bodies*) traino, treggia; (*on a
cigarette*) boccata; (aer) resistenza
aerodinamica; (naut) pressione idro-
statica; (naut) draga; (fig) noia; (*influence*) (slang) aderenze *fpl;* (*a
bore*) (slang) rompiscatole *m* ‖ *v*
(*pret* & *pp* **dragged;** *ger* **dragging**) *tr*
strascinare, strascicare; (naut) rastrellare ‖ *intr* strascicare, strasci-
carsi; dilungarsi; **to drag on** andare
per le lunghe

drag'net' *s* paranza; (fig) retata

dragon ['drægən] *s* drago, dragone *m*

drag'on-fly' *s* (**-flies**) libellula

dragoon [drə'gun] *s* (mil) dragone *m*
‖ *tr* forzare, costringere

drain [dren] *s* scolo; prosciugamento;
(geog) spiovente *m;* (surg) drenaggio;
(fig) salasso ‖ *tr* (*a liquid*) scolare;
prosciugare; (*humid land; a wound*)
drenare ‖ *intr* scolare; prosciugarsi;
(geog) defluire

drainage ['drenɪdʒ] *s* drenaggio; (geog)
displuvio, spartiacque *m*

drain'board' *s* scolatoio per le stoviglie

drain' cock' *s* rubinetto di scarico

drain'pipe' *s* tubo di scarico

drake [drek] *s* anatra maschio

dram [dræm] *s* dramma; bicchierino di
liquore

drama ['drɑmə] or ['dræmə] *s*
dramma *m;* (*art and genre*) drammatica

dramatic [drə'mætɪk] *adj* drammatico
‖ **dramatics** *ssg* drammatica; *spl* rappresentazione dilettantesca; comportamento drammatico

dramatist ['dræmətɪst] *s* drammaturgo

dramatize ['dræmə,taɪz] *tr* drammatizzare

drape [drep] *s* tenda, cortina; (*of a
curtain*) drappeggio; (*of a skirt*) taglio ‖ *tr* drappeggiare

draper·y ['drepəri] *s* (**-ies**) drapperia;
negozio di tessuti; **draperies** tendaggi
mpl

drastic ['dræstɪk] *adj* drastico

draught [dræft] or [drɑft] s & tr var of **draft**

draught' beer' s birra alla spina

draw [drɔ] s (in a game) patta; (in a lottery) sorteggio; (act of drawing) tiro; (of chimney) tiraggio; (attraction) attrazione; (of a drawbridge) ala || v (pret **drew** [dru]; pp **drawn** [drɔn]) tr (a line) tirare; (to attract) richiamare; (butter) fondere; (a sword) sguainare; (a nail) estrarre; (people) attrarre; (a sigh) emettere; (a curtain) far scorrere; (a salary) pigliare; (a prize) ricevere; (a game) impattare; (in card games) pescare; (a drawbridge) sollevare; (said of a ship) pescare; (a comparison) fare; (a profit) ricavare; (a chicken) sventrare; (e.g., a picture) disegnare, ritrarre; (to sketch in words) descrivere; (a contract) stipulare; (interest) ricevere; (com) spiccare, staccare; to **draw forth** far uscire; to **draw off** estrarre; (a liquid) spillare; to **draw** (shoes) **on** mettersi; to **draw** (money) **on** ritirare da; to **draw** (a draft) **on** domiciliare presso; to **draw oneself up** raddrizzarsi; to **draw out** (to persuade to talk) far parlare, tirar fuori le parole a; to **draw up** (a document) estendere; (mil) schierare || intr (said of chimney) tirare; impattare; sorteggiare un premio; aver attrazione; disegnare; to **draw aside** scostarsi; to **draw back** retrocedere, ritirarsi; to **draw near** avvicinarsi; volgere a; to **draw to a close** essere quasi finito; to **draw together** unirsi

draw'back' s inconveniente m

draw'bridge' s ponte levatoio

drawee [ˌdrɔˈi] s trattario, trassato

drawer [ˈdrɔ‑ər] s disegnatore m; (com) traente m || [drɔr] s cassetto; **drawers** mutande fpl

drawing [ˈdrɔ‑ɪŋ] s disegno; (in a lottery) sorteggio

draw'ing board' s tavolo da disegno

draw'ing card' s attrazione

draw'ing room' s salotto, salottino

draw'knife' s (-knives [ˌnaɪvz]) coltello a petto

drawl [drɔl] s accento strascicato || tr dire con accento strascicato || intr strascicare le parole

drawn' but'ter s burro fuso

drawn' work' s lavoro a giorno

dray [dre] s carro pesante; slitta, treggia; autocarro

drayage [ˈdre‑ɪdʒ] s carreggio

dray'man s (-men) carrettiere m

dread [drɛd] adj spaventoso, terribile || s spavento, terrore m || tr & intr temere

dreadful [ˈdrɛdfəl] adj spaventevole, terribile; (coll) orribile

dread'nought' s corazzata

dream [drim] s sogno; illusione, fantasticheria; **dream come true** sogno fatto realtà || v (pret & pp **dreamed** or **dreamt** [drɛmt]) tr sognare; to **dream up** (coll) immaginare, fantasticare || intr sognare

dreamer [ˈdrimər] s sognatore m

dream'land' s paese m dei sogni

dream·y [ˈdrimi] adj (-ier; -iest) sognante; (visionary) trasognato; vago

drear·y [ˈdrɪri] adj (-ier; -iest) squallido; triste; (boring) noioso

dredge [drɛdʒ] s draga || tr dragare; (culin) infarinare

dredger [ˈdrɛdʒər] s (boat) draga; (container) spolverino

dredging [ˈdrɛdʒɪŋ] s dragaggio

dregs [drɛgz] spl feccia

drench [drɛntʃ] tr infradiciare, inzuppare

dress [drɛs] s vestito; vestiti mpl; vestito da donna; abito; abito da cerimonia; (of a bird) piumaggio || tr vestire; adornare, decorare; (hair) pettinare; (a wound) medicare; (leather) conciare; (food) condire; (a boat) pavesare; to **dress down** (coll) rimproverare; to **get dressed** vestirsi || intr vestire; vestirsi; (mil) schierarsi; to **dress up** vestirsi da sera; farsi bello, mettersi in gala

dress' ball' s ballo di gala

dress' coat' s frac m

dresser [ˈdrɛsər] s toletta; (sideboard) credenza; to be a good **dresser** vestire con eleganza

dress' goods' spl stoffa per abiti

dressing [ˈdrɛsɪŋ] s ornamento; (for food) condimento, salsa; (stuffing for fowl) ripieno; (fertilizer) concime m; (for a wound) medicazione

dress'ing down' s ramanzina

dress'ing gown' s vestaglia

dress'ing room' s spogliatoio, toletta; (theat) camerino

dress'ing sta'tion s posto di pronto soccorso

dress'ing ta'ble s toletta, specchiera

dress'mak'er s sarta, sarto per donna

dress'mak'ing s taglio, sartoria

dress' rehears'al s prova generale

dress' shirt' s camicia inamidata

dress' suit' s marsina

dress' u'niform s (mil) alta uniforme

dress·y [ˈdrɛsi] adj (-ier; iest) (coll) elegante, ricercato

dribble [ˈdrɪbəl] s goccia || tr (sports) palleggiare, dribblare || intr gocciolare; (at the mouth) sbavare; (sports) dribblare

driblet [ˈdrɪblɪt] s piccola quantità; in **driblets** col contagocce

dried' beef' [draɪd] s carne seccata

dried' fruit' s frutta secca

drier [ˈdraɪ‑ər] s (for hair) asciugacapelli m; (for clothes) asciugatrice f

drift [drɪft] s movimento; (of sand, snow, etc.) cumulo; (snowdrift) neve accumulata dal vento; tendenza, corrente f; intenzione; (aer, naut) deriva; (rad, telv) deviazione || intr andare alla deriva; (said of snow) accumularsi; (aer, naut) derivare, scadere

drift' ice' s ghiaccio alla deriva

drift'pin' s (mach) mandrino

drift'wood' s legname andato alla deriva

drill [drɪl] s esercizio; (*fabric*) tela cruda; (agr) seminatrice *f*; (mach) trapano, trivella; (mil) esercitazioni *fpl* militari ‖ *tr* trivellare; istruire; (mil) insegnare gli esercizi militari a ‖ *intr* addestrarsi; (mil) fare gli esercizi militari

drill'mas'ter s istruttore *m*

drill' press' s trapano a colonna

drink [drɪŋk] s bevanda; **the drinks are on the house!** paga il proprietario! ‖ *v* (*pret* **drank** [dræŋk]; *pp* **drunk** [drʌŋk]) *tr* bere; assorbire; **to drink down** tracannare; **to drink in** bere, assorbire; (*air*) aspirare ‖ *intr* bere; **to drink out of** bere da; **to drink to the health of** bere alla salute di

drinkable ['drɪŋkəbəl] *adj* bevibile, potabile

drinker ['drɪŋkər] s bevitore *m*

drinking ['drɪŋkɪŋ] s (il) bere

drink'ing foun'tain s fontanella pubblica

drink'ing song' s canzone bacchica

drink'ing straw' s cannuccia

drink'ing trough' s abbeveratoio

drink'ing wa'ter s acqua potabile

drip [drɪp] s sgocciolo, sgocciolatura ‖ *v* (*pret & pp* **dripped**) *ger* **dripping**) *intr* sgocciolare, stillare; (*said of perspiration*) trasudare

drip' cof'fee s caffè fatto con la macchinetta

drip'-dry' *adj* non-stiro

drip' pan' s (culin) ghiotta; (mach) coppa

dripping ['drɪpɪŋ] s gocciolio; **drippings** grasso che cola dall'arrosto

drive [draɪv] s scarrozzata; strada; passeggiata; impulso; forza, iniziativa; urgenza; spinta; campagna; (aut) trazione; (mach) trasmissione ‖ *v* (*pret* **drove** [drov]; *ger* **driven** ['drɪvən]) *tr* (*a nail*) ficcare, piantare; (*e.g., cattle*) condurre, parare; (*s.o. in a carriage or auto*) condurre, portare; spingere; stimulare; forzare; spingere a lavorare; (sports) colpire molto forte; **to drive away** scacciare; **to drive back** respingere; **to drive mad** far impazzire; **to drive out** scacciare ‖ *intr* fare una scarrozzata; **to drive at** parare a; voler dire; **to drive hard** lavorare sodo; **to drive in** entrare in automobile; (*a place*) entrare in automobile in; **to drive on the right** guidare a destra; **to drive out** uscire in macchina; **to drive up** arrivare in macchina

drive'-in' mov'ie the'ater s cineparco

drive'-in' res'taurant s ristorante *m* con servizio alla portiera

driv·el ['drɪvəl] s (*slobber*) bava; (*nonsense*) scemenza ‖ *v* (*pret* **-eled** or **-elled**; *ger* **-eling** or **-elling**) *intr* sbavare; dire scemenze

driver ['draɪvər] s guidatore *m*; (*of a carriage*) cocchiere *m*; (*of a locomotive*) macchinista *m*; (*of pack animals*) carrettiere *m*, mulattiere *m*

driv'er's li'cense s patente automobilistica

driv'er's seat' s posto di guida

drive' shaft' s albero motore

drive'way' s strada privata d'accesso; carrozzabile *f*

drive' wheel' s ruota motrice

driv'ing school' ['draɪvɪŋ] s autoscuola, scuola guida

drizzle ['drɪzəl] s pioviggine *f* ‖ *intr* piovigginare

droll [drol] *adj* buffo, spassoso

dromedar·y ['drɑmə,dɛri] s (-ies) dromedario

drone [dron] s fuco, pecchione *m*; (*hum*) ronzio; (*of bagpipe*) bordone *m*; aeroplano teleguidato ‖ *tr* dire in tono monotono ‖ *intr* (*to live in idleness*) fare il fannullone; (*to buzz, hum*) ronzare

drool [drul] s (*slobber*) bava; (slang) scemenza ‖ *intr* sbavare; (slang) dire scemenze

droop [drup] s accasciamento ‖ *intr* (*to sag*) pendere; (*to lose spirit*) accasciarsi; (*said, e.g., of wheat*) avvizzire

drooping ['drupɪŋ] *adj* (*eyelid*) abbassato; (*shoulder*) spiovente; (fig) accasciato

drop [drɑp] s goccia; (*slope*) pendenza; (*earring*) pendente *m*; (*in temperature*) discesa; (*from an airplane*) lancio; (*trap door*) botola; (*gallows*) trabocchetto della forca; (*lozenge*) pastiglia; (*slit for letters*) buca; (*curtain*) tela; (*in prices*) calo; **a drop in the bucket** una goccia nell'oceano ‖ *v* (*pret & pp* **dropped**; *ger* **dropping**) *tr* lasciar cadere; (*a letter*) imbucare; (*a curtain*) abbassare; (*a remark*) lasciar scappare; (*a note*) scrivere; omettere; abbandonare; (*anchor*) gettare; (*from an airplane*) lanciare; (*from an automobile*) lasciare; (*from a list*) cancellare ‖ *intr* cadere; lasciarsi cadere; terminare; **to drop dead** cader morto; **to drop in** entrare un momento; **to drop off** sparire; addormentarsi; morire improvvisamente; **to drop out** scomparire; ritirarsi; dare le dimissioni

drop' cur'tain s telone *m*

drop' ham'mer s maglio

drop'-leaf' ta'ble s tavola a ribalta

drop'light' s lampada sospesa

drop'out' s studente *m* che abbandona permanentemente la scuola media

dropper ['drɑpər] s contagocce *m*

dropsical ['drɑpsɪkəl] *adj* idropico

dropsy ['drɑpsi] s idropisia

dross [drɔs] or [drɑs] s scoria; (fig) feccia

drought [draut] s siccità *f*; (*shortage*) mancanza

drove [drov] s branco; folla; **in droves** in massa

drover ['drovər] s mandriano

drown [draun] *tr & intr* affogare, annegare

drowse [drauz] *intr* sonnecchiare

drow·sy ['drauzi] *adj* (-sier; -siest) sonnolento, insonnolito

drub [drʌb] *v* (*pret & pp* **drubbed**; *ger* **drubbing**) *tr* bastonare; battere

drudge [drʌdʒ] s sgobbone m ‖ intr sgobbare, sfacchinare

drudger·y ['drʌdʒəri] s (-ies) lavoro ingrato, sfacchinata

drug [drʌg] s droga, medicina; narcotico; **drug on the market** merce f invendibile ‖ v (pret & pp **drugged**; ger **drugging**) tr drogare, narcotizzare

drug' ad'dict s tossicomane mf

drug' addic'tion s tossicomania

druggist ['drʌgɪst] s farmacista mf

drug' hab'it s tossicomania

drug'store' s farmacia

drug' traf'fic s traffico in stupefacenti

druid ['dru·ɪd] s druida m

drum [drʌm] s (cylinder; instrument) tamburo; (container) fusto ‖ v (pret & pp **drummed**; ger **drumming**) tr stamburare; **to drum up** (customers) farsi; (enthusiasm) creare ‖ intr tamburegglare; (with the fingers) tamburellare

drum'beat' s rullo di tamburi

drum' corps' s banda di tamburi

drum'fire' s fuoco nutrito

drum'head' s membrana del tamburo

drum' ma'jor s tamburo maggiore

drummer ['drʌmər] s (salesman) agente m viaggiatore; (mus) tamburo; (mil) tamburino

drum'stick' s bacchetta del tamburo; (of cooked fowl) coscia

drunk [drʌŋk] adj ubriaco; **to get drunk** ubriacarsi ‖ s ubriaco; (spree) sbornia; **to go on a drunk** (coll) ubriacarsi

drunkard ['drʌŋkərd] s ubriacone m

drunken ['drʌŋkən] adj ubriaco

drunk'en driv'ing s—**to be arrested for drunken driving** esser arrestato per aver guidato in stato di ubriachezza

drunkenness ['drʌŋkənnɪs] s ubriachezza, ebbrezza

dry [draɪ] adj (drier; driest) secco; (boring) arido; **to be dry** aver sete ‖ s (drys) abolizionista mf ‖ v (pret & pp **dried**) tr seccare; (to wipe dry) asciugare ‖ intr seccarsi; **to dry up** prosciugarsi, essiccarsi; (slang) star zitto

dry' bat'tery s pila a secco; (group of dry cells) batteria a secco

dry' cell' s pila a secco

dry'-clean' tr lavare a secco, pulire a secco

dry' clean'er s tintore m

dry' clean'ing s lavaggio a secco, pulitura a secco

dry'-clean'ing estab'lishment s tintoria

dry' dock' s bacino di carenaggio

dryer ['draɪ·ər] s var of **drier**

dry'-eyed' adj a occhi asciutti

dry' farm'ing s coltivazione di terreno arido

dry' goods' spl tessuti mpl; aridi mpl

dry'-goods store' s drapperia, negozio di tessuti

dry' ice' s neve carbonica, ghiaccio secco

dry' law' s legge f proibizionista

dry' meas'ure s misura per solidi

dryness ['draɪnɪs] s siccità f; (e.g., of a speaker) aridità f

dry' nurse' s balia asciutta

dry' run' s esercizio di prova; (mil) esercitazione senza munizioni

dry' sea'son s stagione arida

dry' wash' s roba lavata e asciugata ma non stirata

dual ['dju·əl] or ['du·əl] adj & s duale m

duali·ty [dju'ælɪti] or [du'ælɪti] s (-ties) dualità f

dub [dʌb] s (slang) giocatore inesperto ‖ v (pret & pp **dubbed**; ger **dubbing**) tr chiamare, affibbiare il nome di; (a knight) armare; (mov) doppiare

dubbing ['dʌbɪŋ] s doppiaggio

dubious ['djubɪ·əs] or ['dubɪ·əs] adj dubbioso; incerto

ducat ['dʌkət] s ducato

duchess ['dʌtʃɪs] s duchessa

duch·y ['dʌtʃi] s (-ies) ducato

duck [dʌk] s anatra; mossa rapida; (in the water) tuffo; (dodge) schivata; **ducks** pantaloni mpl di tela cruda ‖ tr (one's head) abbassare rapidamente; (in water) tuffare; (a blow) schivare ‖ intr tuffarsi; **to duck out** (coll) svignarsela

duckling ['dʌklɪŋ] s anatroccolo

ducks' and drakes' s—**to play ducks and drakes** with buttar via, sperperare

duck' soup' s (slang) cosa facilissima

duct [dʌkt] s tubo, condotto

ductile ['dʌktɪl] adj duttile

duct'less gland' ['dʌktlɪs] s ghiandola a secrezione interna

duct'work' s condotto, canalizzazione

dud [dʌd] s (slang) bomba inesplosa; (person) (slang) fallito; (enterprise) (slang) fallimento; **duds** (coll) vestito; roba

dude [djud] or [dud] s elegantone m

due [dju] or [du] adj dovuto; atteso, debito; pagabile; **due to** dovuto a; **to fall due** scadere; **when is the train due?** a che ora arriva il treno? ‖ s spettanza; debito; **dues** (of a member) quota sociale; **to get one's due** ricevere quanto uno merita; **to give the devil his due** trattare ognuno con giustizia ‖ adv in direzione, e.g., **due north** in direzione nord

duel ['dju·əl] or ['du·əl] s duello; **to fight a duel** battersi a duello ‖ v (pret & pp **dueled** or **duelled**; ger **dueling** or **duelling**) intr duellare

duelist or **duellist** ['dju·əlɪst] or ['du·əlɪst] s duellante mf

dues-paying ['djuz,pe·ɪŋ] or ['duz,pe·ɪŋ] adj regolare, effettivo

duet [dju'et] or [du'et] s duetto

duf'fel bag' ['dʌfəl] s sacca da viaggio

duke [djuk] or [duk] s duca m

dukedom ['djukdəm] or ['dukdəm] s ducato

dull [dʌl] adj (not sharp) spuntato, senza filo; (color) spento, sbiadito; (sound, pain) sordo; (stupid) ebete, tonto; (business) inattivo; (boring) noioso, melenso; (flat) opaco, appannato ‖ tr spuntare; sbiadire; inebetire; ottundere; (enthusiasm) raffreddare; (pain) alleviare ‖ intr spuntarsi; sbiadirsi; inebetirsi; raffreddarsi

dullard ['dʌlərd] s stupido

duly ['djuli] or ['duli] adv debitamente

dumb [dʌm] adj (lacking the power to speak) muto; (coll) tonto, stupido

dumb′bell′ s manubrio; (slang) zuccone m, stupido

dumb′ crea′ture s animale m, bruto

dumb′ show′ s pantomima

dumb′wai′ter s montavivande m

dumfound [,dʌm'faund] tr interdire, lasciare esterrefatto

dum-my ['dʌmi] adj copiato; falso ‖ s (-mies) (dress form) manichino; (in card games) morto; (figurehead) uomo di paglia, prestanome m; (skeleton copy of a book) menabò m; copia; (slang) stupido, tonto

dump [dʌmp] s immondezzaio; mucchio di spazzature; (mil) deposito munizioni; (min) montagnetta di scarico; **to be down in the dumps** (coll) avere le paturnie ‖ tr scaricare; (to tip over) rovesciare; (com) scaricare sul mercato; (com) vendere sottocosto

dumping ['dʌmpɪŋ] s scarico; (com) dumping m

dumpling ['dʌmplɪŋ] s gnocco

dump′ truck′ s ribaltabile m

dump-y ['dʌmpi] adj (-ier; -iest) grassoccio, tarchiato

dun [dʌn] adj bruno grigiastro ‖ s creditore importuno; (demand for payment) sollecitazione di pagamento ‖ v (pret & pp dunned; ger dunning) tr sollecitare

dunce [dʌns] s ignorante mf, zuccone m

dunce′ cap′ s berretto d'asino

dune [djun] or [dun] s duna

dung [dʌŋ] s sterco, letame m ‖ tr concimare con il letame

dungarees [,dʌŋgə'riz] spl tuta di cotone blu

dungeon ['dʌndʒən] s carcere sotterraneo; (fortified tower) torrione m, maschio

dung′hill′ s letamaio

dunk [dʌŋk] tr inzuppare

du-o ['dju-o] or ['du-o] s (-os) duo

duode-num [,dju-ə'dinəm] or [,du-ə-'dinəm] s (-na [nə]) duodeno

dupe [djup] or [dup] s gonzo ‖ tr gabbare, ingannare

du′plex house′ ['djupleks] or ['dupleks] s casa di due appartamenti

duplicate ['djuplɪkɪt] or ['duplɪkɪt] adj & s duplicato ‖ ['djuplɪ,ket] or ['duplɪ,ket] tr duplicare

du′plicating machine′ s duplicatore m

duplici-ty [dju'plɪsɪti] or [du'plɪsɪti] s (-ties) duplicità f, doppiezza

durable ['djurəbəl] or ['durəbəl] adj durabile, duraturo

du′rable goods′ spl beni mpl durevoli

duration [dju'reʃən] or [du'reʃən] s durata

during ['djurɪŋ] or ['durɪŋ] prep durante

du′rum wheat′ ['durəm] or ['djurəm] s grano duro

dusk [dʌsk] s crepuscolo

dust [dʌst] s polvere f ‖ tr (to free of dust) spolverare; (to sprinkle with dust) spolverizzare; **to dust off** (slang) rimettere in uso; (slang) spolverare le spalle a

dust′ bowl′ s regione polverosissima

dust′cloth′ s strofinaccio

dust′ cloud′ s polverone m

duster ['dʌstər] s (cloth) cencio; (light overgarment) sopravveri no

dust′ jack′et s sopraccoperta

dust′pan′ s pattumiera

dust′ rag′ s strofinaccio

dust-y ['dʌsti] adj (-ier; -iest) polveroso; grigiastro

Dutch [dʌtʃ] adj olandese; (slang) tedesco ‖ s (language) olandese m; (language) (slang) tedesco; **in Dutch** (slang) in disgrazia; (slang) nei pasticci; **the Dutch** gli olandesi; (slang) i tedeschi; **to go Dutch** (coll) pagare alla romana

Dutch′man s (-men) olandese m; (slang) tedesco

Dutch′ treat′ s invito alla romana

dutiable ['djutɪ·əbəl] or ['dutɪ·əbəl] adj soggetto a dogana

dutiful ['djutɪfəl] or ['dutɪfəl] adj obbediente, doveroso

du-ty ['djuti] or ['duti] s (-ties) dovere m; (task) funzione; dazio, dogana; **off duty** libero; in libera uscita; **on duty** in servizio; di guardia; **to do one's duty** fare il proprio dovere; **to take up one's duties** entrare in servizio

du′ty-free′ adj esente da dogana

dwarf [dwɔrf] adj & s nano ‖ tr impiccolire ‖ intr rimpiccolire; apparire più piccolo

dwarfish ['dwɔrfɪʃ] adj nano, da nano

dwell [dwel] v (pret & pp dwelled or dwelt [dwelt]) intr dimorare, abitare; **to dwell on** or **upon** intrattenersi su

dwelling ['dwelɪŋ] s abitazione, residenza

dwell′ing house′ s casa d'abitazione

dwindle ['dwindəl] intr diminuire; restringersi, consumarsi

dye [daɪ] s tinta, colore m ‖ v (pret & pp dyed; ger dyeing) tr tingere

dyed-in-the-wool ['daɪdɪnðə,wul] adj tinto prima della tessitura; completo, intransigente

dyeing ['daɪ·ɪŋ] s tintura

dyer ['daɪ·ər] s tintore m

dye′stuff′ s tintura, materia colorante

dying ['daɪ·ɪŋ] adj morente

dynamic [daɪ'næmɪk] or [dɪ'næmɪk] adj dinamico

dynamite ['daɪnə,maɪt] s dinamite f ‖ tr far saltare con la dinamite

dyna-mo ['daɪnə,mo] s (-mos) dinamo f

dynast ['daɪnæst] s dinasta m

dynas-ty ['daɪnəsti] s (-ties) dinastia

dysentery ['dɪsən,teri] s dissenteria

dyspepsia [dɪs'pepsɪ·ə] or [dɪs'pepʃə] s dispepsia

E

E, e [i] *s* quinta lettera dell'alfabeto inglese

each [itʃ] *adj indef* ogni ǁ *pron indef* ognuno, ciascuno; **each other** ci; vi; si; l'un l'altro ǁ *adv* l'uno; a testa

eager ['igər] *adj (enthusiastic)* ardente; **eager for** avido di; **eager to** + *inf* desideroso di + *inf*

ea'ger bea'ver *s* zelante *mf*

eagerness ['igərnɪs] *s* ardore *m;* brama

eagle ['igəl] *s* aquila

ea'gle owl' *s* gufo reale

eaglet ['iglɪt] *s* aquilotto

ear [ir] *s* orecchio; *(of corn)* pannocchia; *(of wheat)* spiga; **to be all ears** essere tutt'orecchi; **to prick up one's ears** tendere l'orecchio; **to turn a deaf ear** far l'orecchio di mercante

ear'ache' *s* mal *m* d'orecchi

ear'drop' *s* pendente *m*

ear'drum' *s* timpano

ear'flap' *s* paraorecchi *m*

earl [ʌrl] *s* conte *m*

earldom ['ʌrldəm] *s* contea

ear·ly ['ʌrli] *adj (-lier; -liest) adj (occurring before customary time)* di buon'ora; *(first in a series)* primo; *(far back in time)* remoto, antico; *(occurring in near future)* prossimo ǁ *adv* presto; per tempo, di buon'ora; **as early as** *(a certain time of day)* già a; *(a certain time or date)* fin da, già in; **as early as possible** quanto prima possibile; **early in** *(e.g., the month)* all'inizio di; **early in the morning** di mattina presto, di buon mattino; **early in the year** all'inizio dell'anno

ear'ly bird' *s* persona mattiniera

ear'ly mass' *s* prima messa

ear'ly ris'er *s* persona mattiniera

ear'mark' *s* contrassegno ǁ *tr* contrassegnare; assegnare a scopo speciale

ear'muff' *s* paraorecchi *m*

earn [ʌrn] *tr* guadagnare, guadagnarsi; *(to get one's due)* meritarsi; *(interest)* (com) produrre ǁ *intr* trarre profitto, rendere

earnest ['ʌrnɪst] *adj* serio; fervente; **in earnest** sul serio ǁ *s* caparra

ear'nest mon'ey *s* caparra

earnings ['ʌrnɪŋz] *s* guadagno; salario

ear'phone' *s (of sonar)* orecchiale *m;* (rad, telp) cuffia

ear'piece' *s (of eyeglasses)* susta; (telp) ricevitore *m*

ear'ring' *s* orecchino

ear'shot' *s* tiro dell'orecchio; **within earshot** a portata di voce

ear'split'ting *adj* assordante

earth [ʌrθ] *s* terra; **to come back to** or **down to earth** scendere dalle nuvole

earthen ['ʌrθən] *adj* di terra; di terracotta

ear'then·ware' *s* coccio, terraglie *fpl,* terracotta

earthling ['ʌrθlɪŋ] *s* terrestre *mf*

earthly ['ʌrθli] *adj* terreno, terrestre;

to be of no earthly use non servire assolutamente a niente

earthmover ['ʌrθ͵muvər] *s* ruspa

earth'quake' *s* terremoto

earth'work' *s* terrapieno

earth'worm' *s* lombrico

earth·y ['ʌrθi] *adj (-ier; -iest)* terroso; *(coarse)* rozzo; pratico; sincero, diretto

ear' trum'pet *s* corno acustico

ear'wax' *s* cerume *m*

ease [iz] *s* facilità *f; (naturalness)* spigliatezza, disinvoltura; *(comfort)* benestare *m;* tranquillità *f;* **at ease!** (mil) riposo!; **with ease** con facilità ǁ *tr* facilitare; *(a burden)* alleggerire; *(to let up on)* rallentare; mitigare; **to ease out** licenziare con le buone maniere ǁ *intr* alleviarsi, mitigarsi, diminuire; rallentare

easel ['izəl] *s* cavalletto

easement ['izmənt] *s* attenuamento; (law) servitù *f*

easily ['izɪli] *adv* facilmente; senza dubbio; probabilmente

easiness ['izɪnɪs] *s* facilità *f;* disinvoltura; grazia, agilità *f;* indifferenza

east [ist] *s* oriente, dell'est ǁ *s* est *m* ǁ *adv* verso l'est

Easter ['istər] *s* Pasqua

East'er egg' *s* uovo di Pasqua

East'er Mon'day *s* lunedì *m* di Pasqua

eastern ['istərn] *adj* orientale

East'er·tide' *s* tempo pasquale

eastward ['istwərd] *adv* verso l'est

eas·y ['izi] *adj (-ier; -iest)* facile; *(conducive to ease)* comodo, agiato; *(free from worry)* tranquillo; *(easygoing)* disinvolto, spigliato; *(not tight)* ampio; *(not hurried)* lento, moderato ǁ *adv* (coll) facilmente; (coll) tranquillamente; **to take it easy** (coll) riposarsi; (coll) ⸱ non prendersela; (coll) andar piano

eas'y chair' *s* poltrona

eas'y-go'ing *adj (person)* comodone; *(horse)* sciolto nell'andatura

eas'y mark' *s* (coll) gonzo

eas'y mon'ey *s* denaro fatto senza fatica; soldi rubati

eas'y terms' *spl* facilitazioni *fpl* di pagamento

eat [it] *v (pret* ate [et]; *pp* eaten ['itən]) *tr* mangiare; **to eat away** smangiare; **to eat up** mangiarsi ǁ *intr* mangiare

eatable ['itəbəl] *adj* mangiabile ǁ **eatables** *spl* commestibili *mpl*

eaves [ivz] *spl* gronda

eaves'drop' *v (pret & pp* -dropped; *ger* -dropping) *intr* origliare

ebb [ɛb] *s* riflusso; decadenza ǁ *intr (said of the tide)* ritirarsi; decadere

ebb' and flow' *s* flusso e riflusso

ebb' tide' *s* riflusso, deflusso

ebon·y ['ɛbəni] *s (-ies)* ebano

ebullient [ɪ'bʌljənt] *adj* bollente

eccentric [ɛk'sɛntrɪk] *adj & s* eccentrico

eccentrici·ty [ˌeksən'trisiti] s (-ties) eccentricità f, originalità f

ecclesiastic [ɪˌklizɪ'æstɪk] adj & s ecclesiastico

echelon ['ɛʃəˌlɑn] s scaglione m; (mil) scaglione m || tr scaglionare

ech·o ['ɛko] s (-oes) eco f || tr far eco a || intr echeggiare, rieccheggiare

éclair [e'kler] s dolce ripieno di crema

eclectic [ɛk'lɛktɪk] adj & s eclettico

eclipse [ɪ'klɪps] s eclisse f, eclissi f || tr eclissare

eclogue ['ɛklɔg] or ['ɛklɑg] s egloga

ecology [ɪ'kɑlədʒɪ] s ecologia

economic(al) [ˌikə'nɑmɪk(əl)] or [ˌɛkə'nɑmɪk(əl)] adj economico

economics [ˌikə'nɑmɪks] or [ˌɛkə'nɑmɪks] s economia (politica)

economist [ɪ'kɑnəmɪst] s economista mf

economize [ɪ'kɑnəˌmaɪz] tr & intr economizzare

econo·my [ɪ'kɑnəmi] s (-mies) economia

ecosystem ['ɛkoˌsɪstəm] s ecosistema m

ecsta·sy ['ɛkstəsi] s (-sies) estasi f

ecstatic [ɛk'stætɪk] adj estatico

ecumenic(al) [ˌɛkjə'mɛnɪk(əl)] adj ecumenico

eczema ['ɛksɪmə] or [ɛg'zimə] s eczema m

ed·dy ['ɛdi] s (-dies) turbine m || v (pret & pp -died) tr & intr turbinare

edelweiss ['edəlˌvaɪs] s stella alpina

edge [ɛdʒ] s (of knife, sword, etc) filo, tagliente m; (border at which a surface terminates) orlo, bordo; (of a wound) labbro, margine m; (of a book) taglio; (of a tumbler) giro; (of clothing) vivagno; (of a table) spigolo; (slang) vantaggio; **on edge** nervoso; **to have the edge on** (coll) avere il vantaggio su; **to set the teeth on edge** far allegare i denti || tr affilare, aguzzare; orlare, bordare; **to edge out** riuscire ad eliminare || intr avanzare lentamente

edgeways ['ɛdʒˌwez] adv di taglio; **to not let s.o. get a word in edgeways** non lasciar dire una parola a qicu

edging ['ɛdʒɪŋ] s orlo, bordo

edg·y ['ɛdʒi] adj (-ier; -iest) acuto, angolare; nervoso, ansioso

edible ['ɛdɪbəl] adj mangereccio, mangiabile || **edibles** spl commestibili mpl

edict ['idɪkt] s editto

edification [ˌɛdɪfɪ'keʃən] s edificazione

edifice ['ɛdɪfɪs] s edificio

edi·fy ['ɛdɪˌfaɪ] v (pret & pp -fied) tr edificare

edifying ['ɛdɪˌfaɪɪŋ] adj edificante

edit ['ɛdɪt] tr redigere; (e.g., a manuscript) correggere; (an edition) curare; (a newspaper) dirigere; (mov) montare

edition [ɪ'dɪʃən] s edizione

editor ['ɛdɪtər] s (of a newspaper or magazine) direttore m, gerente mf; (of an editorial) redattore m, cronista mf; (of a critical edition) editore m; (of a manuscript) revisore m

editorial [ˌɛdɪ'tɔriəl] adj editoriale || s capocronaca m, articolo di fondo

ed·itor-in-chief s gerente mf responsabile

educate ['ɛdʒuˌket] tr educare, erudire

education [ˌɛdʒu'keʃən] s educazione; istruzione, insegnamento

educational [ˌɛdʒu'keʃənəl] adj educativo

educa'tional institu'tion s istituto di magistero

educator ['ɛdʒuˌketər] s educatore m

eel [il] s anguilla; **to be as slippery as an eel** guizzare di mano come un'anguilla

ee·rie or **ee·ry** ['ɪri] adj (-rier; -riest) spettrale, pauroso

efface [ɪ'fes] tr cancellare; **to efface oneself** eclissarsi, mettersi in disparte

effect [ɪ'fɛkt] s effetto; (main idea) tenore m; **in effect** in vigore; in realtà; **to go into effect** or **to take effect** andare in vigore; **to put into effect** mandare ad effetto || tr effettuare

effective [ɪ'fɛktɪv] adj efficace; (actually in effect) effettivo; (striking) che colpisce; **to become effective** entrare in vigore

effectual [ɪ'fɛktʃuəl] adj efficace

effectuate [ɪ'fɛktʃuˌet] tr effettuare

effeminacy [ɪ'fɛmɪnəsi] s effemminatezza

effeminate [ɪ'fɛmɪnɪt] adj effemminato

effervesce [ˌɛfər'vɛs] intr essere in efferves cenza

effervescence [ˌɛfər'vɛsəns] s effervescenza

effervescent [ˌɛfər'vɛsənt] adj effervescente

effete [ɪ'fit] adj esausto, sterile

efficacious [ˌɛfɪ'keʃəs] adj efficace

effica·cy [ˌɛfɪkəsi] s (-cies) efficacia

efficien·cy [ɪ'fɪʃənsi] s (-cies) efficienza; (mech) rendimento, efficacia

effi'ciency engineer' s analista mf tempi e metodi

efficient [ɪ'fɪʃənt] adj efficiente; (person) abile; (me h) efficiente

effi·gy ['ɛfɪdʒɪ] s (-gies) effigie f

effort ['ɛfərt] s sforzo

effronter·y [ɪ'frʌntəri] s (-ies) sfrontatezza, sfacciataggine f

effusion [ɪ'fjuʒən] s effusione

effusive [ɪ'fjusɪv] adj espansivo

egg [ɛg] s uovo; (slang) bravo ragazzo || tr—**to egg on** incitare

egg'beat'er s frullino, sbattiuova m

egg' cup' s portauovo

egg'head' s (coll) intellettuale mf

eggnog ['ɛgˌnɑg] s zabaione m

egg'plant' s melanzana, petonciano

egg'shell' s guscio d'uovo

egoism ['ɛgoˌɪzəm] or ['igoˌɪzəm] s egoismo

egoist ['ɛgoˌɪst] or ['igoˌɪst] s egoista mf

egotism ['ɛgoˌtɪzəm] or ['igoˌtɪzəm] s egotismo

egotist ['ɛgotɪst] or ['igotɪst] s egotista mf

egregious [ɪˈgridʒəs] *adj* gigantesco, tremendo, marchiano

egress [ˈigres] *s* uscita

Egypt [ˈidʒɪpt] *s* l'Egitto

Egyptian [ɪˈdʒɪpʃən] *adj & s* egiziano

ei'der down' [ˈaɪdər] *s* piumino

ei'der duck' *s* edredone *m*

eight [et] *adj & pron* otto ǁ *s* otto; **eight o'clock** le otto

eighteen [ˈetˈtin] *adj, s & pron* diciotto

eighteenth [ˈetˈtinθ] *adj, s & pron* diciottesimo ǁ *s* (*in dates*) diciotto

eighth [etθ] *adj & s* ottavo ǁ *s* (*in dates*) otto

eight' hun'dred *adj, s & pron* ottocento

eightieth [ˈetɪ·ɪθ] *adj, s & pron* ottantesimo

eight·y [ˈeti] *adj & pron* ottanta ǁ *s* (**-ies**) ottanta *m;* **the eighties** gli anni ottanta

either [ˈiðər] *or* [ˈaɪðər] *adj* l'uno o l'altro; l'uno e l'altro; ciascuno; entrambi i, tutti e due i ǁ *pron* l'uno o l'altro; l'uno e l'altro; entrambi ǁ *adv*—**not either** nemmeno ǁ *conj*— **either . . . or . . . o**

ejaculate [ɪˈdʒækjə‚let] *tr* esclamare; (*physiol*) emettere ǁ *intr* esclamare; (*physiol*) avère un'eiaculazione

eject [ɪˈdʒekt] *tr* espellere, gettar fuori; (*to evict*) sfrattare

ejection [ɪˈdʒekʃən] *s* espulsione; (*of a tenant*) sfratto

ejec'tion seat' *s* sedile *m* eiettabile

eke [ik] *tr*—**to eke out a living** sbarcare il lunario

elaborate [ɪˈlæbərɪt] *adj* (*done with great care*) elaborato; (*detailed*) minuzioso; (*ornate*) ornato ǁ [ɪˈlæbə‚ret] *tr* elaborare ǁ *intr*—**to elaborate on** *or* **upon** circonstanziare, particolareggiare

elapse [ɪˈlæps] *intr* passare, trascorrere

elastic [ɪˈlæstɪk] *adj & s* elastico

elasticity [ɪ‚læsˈtɪsɪti] *or* [‚ilæsˈtɪsɪti] *s* elasticità *f*

elated [ɪˈletɪd] *adj* esultante, gongolante

elation [ɪˈleʃən] *s* esultanza, gaudio

elbow [ˈelbo] *s* gomito; (*in a river*) ansa; (*of a chair*) braccio; **at one's elbow** sotto mano; **out at the elbows** coi gomiti logori; **to crook the elbow** alzare il gomito; **to rub elbows** stare gomito a gomito; **up to the elbows** fino al collo ǁ *tr*—**to elbow one's way** aprirsi il passo a gomitate ǁ *intr* dar gomitate

el'bow grease' *s* (coll) olio di gomiti

el'bow patch' *s* toppa al gomito

el'bow rest' *s* bracciolo

el'bow·room' *s* spazio sufficiente; libertà *f* d'azione

elder [ˈeldər] *adj* seniore, maggiore ǁ *s* (bot) sambuco; (eccl) maggiore *m*

el'der·ber'ry *s* (**-ries**) sambuco; (*fruit*) bacca del sambuco

elderly [ˈeldərli] *adj* attempato, anziano

eld'er states'man *s* uomo di stato esperto

eldest [ˈeldɪst] *adj* (il) maggiore; (il) più vecchio

elect [ɪˈlekt] *adj & s* eletto; **the elect** gli eletti ǁ *tr* eleggere

election [ɪˈlekʃən] *s* elezione

electioneer [ɪ‚lekʃəˈnɪr] *intr* fare una campagna elettorale

elective [ɪˈlektɪv] *adj* elettivo ǁ *s* corso facoltativo

electorate [ɪˈlektərɪt] *s* elettorato

electric(al) [ɪˈlektrɪk(əl)] *adj* elettrico

elec'tric blend'er *s* frullatore *m*

elec'tric chair' *s* sedia elettrica

elec'tric cord' *s* piattina, filo elettrico

elec'tric eel' *s* gimnoto

elec'tric eye' *s* occhio elettrico

electrician [ɪ‚lekˈtrɪʃən] *or* [‚elekˈtrɪʃən] *s* elettricista *m*

electricity [ɪ‚lekˈtrɪsɪti] *or* [‚elekˈtrɪsɪti] *s* elettricità *f*

elec'tric me'ter *s* contatore *m* della luce

elec'tric per'cola'tor *s* caffettiera elettrica

elec'tric shav'er *s* rasoio elettrico

elec'tric shock' *s* scossa elettrica, elettroshock

elec'tric tape' *s* nastro isolante

elec'tric train' *s* elettrotreno

electri-fy [ɪˈlektrɪ‚faɪ] *v* (*pret & pp* **-fied**) *tr* (*to provide with electric power*) elettrificare; (*to communicate electricity to; to thrill*) elettrizzare

electrocute [ɪˈlektrə‚kjut] *tr* fulminare con la corrente; far morire sulla sedia elettrica

electrode [ɪˈlektrod] *s* elettrodo

electrolysis [ɪ‚lekˈtrɑlɪsɪs] *or* [‚elekˈtrɑlɪsɪs] *s* elettrolisi *f*

electrolyte [ɪˈlektrə‚laɪt] *s* elettrolito

electromagnet [ɪ‚lektrəˈmægnɪt] *s* elettrocalamita

electromagnetic [ɪ‚lektrəmægˈnetɪk] *adj* elettromagnetico

electromotive [ɪ‚lektrəˈmotɪv] *adj* elettromotore

electron [ɪˈlektrɑn] *s* elettrone *m*

electronic [ɪ‚lekˈtrɑnɪk] *or* [‚elekˈtrɑnɪk] *adj* elettronico ǁ **electronics** *s* elettronica

electroplating [ɪˈlektrə‚pletɪŋ] *s* galvanostegia

electrostatic [ɪ‚lektrəˈstætɪk] *adj* elettrostatico

electrotype [ɪˈlektrə‚taɪp] *s* stereotipia ǁ *tr* stereotipare

eleemosynary [‚elɪˈmɑsɪ‚neri] *adj* caritatevole, di beneficenza

elegance [ˈelɪgəns] *s* eleganza

elegant [ˈelɪgənt] *adj* elegante

elegiac [‚elɪˈdʒaɪ‚æk] *adj* elegiaco

ele·gy [ˈelɪdʒi] *s* (**-gies**) elegia

element [ˈelɪmənt] *s* elemento; **to be out of one's element** essere fuori del proprio ambiente

elementary [‚elɪˈmentəri] *adj* elementare

elephant [ˈelɪfənt] *s* elefante *m*

elevate [ˈelɪ‚vet] *tr* elevare, innalzare

elevated [ˈelɪ‚vetɪd] *adj* elevato ǁ *s* ferrovia soprelevata, metropolitana soprelevata

elevation [‚elɪˈveʃən] *s* elevazione; (surv) quota

elevator [ˈelɪ‚vetər] *s* ascensore *m;*

(for freight) montacarichi *m; (for hoisting grain)* elevatore *m* di grano; *(warehouse for storing grain)* deposito granaglie; (aer) timone *m* di profondità

eleven [ɪˈlɛvən] *adj & pron* undici || *s* undici *m;* **eleven o'clock** le undici

eleventh [ɪˈlɛvənθ] *adj, s & pron* undicesimo || *s (in dates)* undici *m*

elev'enth hour' *s* ultimo momento

elf [ɛlf] *s (elves* [ɛlvz]*)* elfo

elicit [ɪˈlɪsɪt] *tr* cavare, sottrarre

elide [ɪˈlaɪd] *tr* elidere

eligible [ˈɛlɪdʒɪbəl] *adj* eleggibile; accettabile

eliminate [ɪˈlɪmɪ,net] *tr* eliminare

elision [ɪˈlɪʒən] *s* elisione

elite [eˈlit] *adj* eletto, scelto || *s*—**the elite** l'élite *f*

elk [ɛlk] *s* alce *m*

ellipse [ɪˈlɪps] *s* (geom) ellisse *f*

ellip·sis [ɪˈlɪpsɪs] *s (-ses* [siz]*)* (gram) ellissi *f*

elliptic(al) [ɪˈlɪptɪk(əl)] *adj* ellittico

elm [ɛlm] *s* olmo

elongate .[ɪˈlɔŋget] or [ɪˈlɔŋget] *tr* allungare, prolungare

elope [ɪˈlop] *intr* fuggire con un amante

elopement [ɪˈlopmənt] *s* fuga con un amante

eloquence [ˈɛləkwəns] *s* eloquenza

eloquent [ˈɛləkwənt] *adj* eloquente

else [ɛls] *adj*—**nobody else** nessun altro; **nothing else** nient'altro; **somebody else** qualcun altro; **something else** qualcosa .d'altro; **what else** che altro; **who else** chi altro; **whose else** di che altra persona || *adv*—**how else** in che altra maniera; **or else** se no; altrimenti; **when else** in che altro momento; in che altro periodo; **where else** dove mai, da che parte

else'where' *adv* altrove

elucidate [ɪˈlusɪ,det] *tr* dilucidare

elude [ɪˈlud] *tr* eludere

elusive [ɪˈlusɪv] *adj* elusivo; *(evasive)* fugace, sfuggente

emaciated [ɪˈmeʃɪ,etɪd] *adj* smunto, emaciato, macilento

emanate [ˈɛmə,net] *tr & intr* emanare

emancipate [ɪˈmænsɪ,pet] *tr* emancipare

embalm [ɛmˈbɑm] *tr* imbalsamare

embankment [ɛmˈbæŋkmənt] *s* terrapieno

embar·go [ɛmˈbɑrgo] *s (-goes)* embargo || *tr* mettere l'embargo a

embark [ɛmˈbɑrk] *intr* imbarcarsi

embarkation [ˌɛmbɑrˈkeʃən] *s* imbarco

embarrass [ɛmˈbærəs] *tr* imbarazzare, mettere .a disagio; *(to impede)* imbarazzare, impacciare; mettere in difficoltà economiche

embarrassing [ɛmˈbærəsɪŋ] *adj* sconcertante; imbarazzante

embarrassment [ɛmˈbærəsmənt] *s* imbarazzo, disagio, confusione; impaccio; difficoltà finanziaria, dissesto

embas·sy [ˈɛmbəsɪ] *s (-sies)* ambasciata

em·bed [ɛmˈbɛd] *s (pret & pp -bedded; ger -bedding) tr* incastrare, incassare

embellish [ɛmˈbɛlɪʃ] *tr* imbellire

embellishment [ɛmˈbɛlɪʃmənt] *s* abbellimento; (fig) fioretto

ember [ˈɛmbər] *s* brace *f;* **embers** braci *fpl*

Em'ber days' *spl* tempora *fpl*

embezzle [ɛmˈbɛzəl] *tr* appropriare, malversare || *intr* appropriarsi

embezzlement [ɛmˈbɛzəlmənt] *s* appropriazione indebita, malversazione; *(of public funds)* peculato

embezzler [ɛmˈbɛzɪər] *s* malversatore ·*m*

embitter [ɛmˈbɪtər] *tr* amareggiare

emblazon [ɛmˈblezən] *tr* blasonare; celebrare

emblem [ˈɛmbləm] *s* emblema *m*

emblematic(al) [ˌɛmbləˈmætɪk(əl)] *adj* emblematico

embodiment [ɛmˈbɑdɪmənt] *s* incarnazione, personificazione

embod·y [ɛmˈbɑdɪ] *v (pret & pp -ied) tr* incarnare, personificare; incorporare

embolden [ɛmˈboldən] *tr* imbaldanzire

embolism [ˈɛmbə,lɪzəm] *s* embolia

emboss [ɛmˈbɔs] or [ɛmˈbɑs] *tr (metal)* sbalzare; *(paper)* goffrare

embrace [ɛmˈbres] *s* abbraccio || *tr* abbracciare || *intr* abbracciarsi

embrasure [ɛmˈbreʒər] *s* (archit) strombatura; (mil) feritoia

embroider [ɛmˈbrɔɪdər] *tr* ricamare, trapuntare

embroider·y [ɛmˈbrɔɪdərɪ] *s (-ies)* ricamo, trapunto

embroil [ɛmˈbrɔɪl] *tr* ingarbugliare; *(to involve in contention)* coinvolgere

embroilment [ɛmˈbrɔɪlmənt] *s* imbroglio; *(in contention)* disaccordo

embry·o [ˈɛmbrɪ,o] *s (-os)* embrione *m*

embryology [ˌɛmbrɪˈɑlədʒɪ] *s* embriologia

embryonic [ˌɛmbrɪˈɑnɪk] *adj* embrionale

emcee [ˈɛmˈsi] *s* presentatore *m* || *tr* presentare

emend [ɪˈmɛnd] *tr* emendare

emendation [ˌimənˈdeʃən] *s* emendamento

emerald [ˈɛmərəld] *s* smeraldo

emerge [ɪˈmʌrdʒ] *intr* emergere

emergence [ɪˈmʌrdʒəns] *s* emergenza

emergen·cy [ɪˈmʌrdʒənsɪ] *s (-cies)* emergenza

emer'gency brake' *s* freno a mano

emer'gency ex'it *s* uscita di sicurezza

emer'gency land'ing *s* atterraggio di fortuna

emer'gency ward' *s* sala d'urgenza

emeritus [ɪˈmɛrɪtəs] *adj* emerito

emersion [ɪˈmʌrʒən] or [ɪˈmʌrʃən] *s* emersione

emery [ˈɛmərɪ] *s* smeriglio

em'ery cloth' *s* tela smeriglio

em'ery wheel' *s* mola a smeriglio

emetic [ɪˈmɛtɪk] *adj & s* emetico

emigrant [ˈɛmɪgrənt] *adj & s* emigrante *mf*

emigrate [ˈɛmɪ,gret] *intr* emigrare

émigré [emiˈgre] or [ˈɛmɪ,gre] *s* emigrato

eminence ['ɛmɪnəns] s eminenza; (eccl) Eminenza

eminent ['ɛmɪnənt] adj eminente

emissar·y ['ɛmɪ‚sɛri] s (-ies) emissario

emission [ɪ'mɪʃən] s emissione

emit [ɪ'mɪt] v (pret & pp **emitted;** ger **emitting**) tr emettere

emolument [ɪ'mɑljəmənt] s emolumento

emotion [ɪ'moʃən] s emozione

emotional [ɪ'moʃənəl] adj emotivo

emperor ['ɛmpərər] s imperatore m

empha·sis ['ɛmfəsɪs] s (-ses [‚sɪz]) enfasi f, risalto

emphasize ['ɛmfə‚saɪz] tr dar rilievo a, sottolineare

emphatic [ɛm'fætɪk] adj enfatico

emphysema [‚ɛmfɪ'simə] s enfisema m

empire ['ɛmpaɪr] s impero

empiric(al) [ɛm'pɪrɪk(əl)] adj empirico

empiricist [ɛm'pɪrɪsɪst] s empirista mf

emplacement [ɛm'plesmənt] s piazzola, postazione

employ [ɛm'plɔɪ] s impiego || tr impiegare, usare; valersi di

employee [ɛm'plɔɪ·i] or [‚ɛmplɔɪ'i] s impiegato, dipendente mf

employer [ɛm'plɔɪ·ər] s dirigente mf, datore m di lavoro

employment [ɛm'plɔɪmənt] s impiego, occupazione

employ'ment a'gency s agenzia di collocamento

empower [ɛm'pau·ər] tr autorizzare; permettere

empress ['ɛmprɪs] s imperatrice f

emptiness ['ɛmptɪnɪs] s vuoto

emp·ty ['ɛmpti] adj (-tier; -tiest) vuoto; (gun) scarico; (hungry) (coll) digiuno; (fig) esausto || v (pret & pp -tied) tr vuotare || intr vuotarsi

empty-handed ['ɛmpti'hændɪd] adj a mani vuote

empty-headed ['ɛmpti'hɛdɪd] adj dalla testa vuota, balordo

empyrean [‚ɛmpɪ'ri·ən] adj & s empireo

emulate ['ɛmjə‚let] tr emulare

emulator ['ɛmjə‚letər] s emulo

emulous ['ɛmjələs] adj emulo

emulsi·fy [ɪ'mʌlsɪ‚faɪ] v (pret & pp -fied) tr emulsionare

emulsion [ɪ'mʌlʃən] s emulsione

enable [ɛn'ebəl] tr abilitare; permettere (with dat)

enact [ɛn'ækt] tr decretare; (a role) rappresentare

enactment [ɛn'æktmənt] s legge f; (of a law) promulgazione; (of a play) rappresentazione

enam·el [ɪn'æməl] s smalto || v (pret & pp -eled or -elled; ger -eling or -elling) tr smaltare

enam'el·ware' s utensili mpl di cucina di ferro smaltato

enamor [ɛn'æmər] tr innamorare; **to become enamored of** innamorarsi di

encamp [ɛn'kæmp] tr accampare || intr accamparsi

encampment [ɛn'kæmpmənt] s campeggio; (mil) accampamento

encase [ɛn'kes] tr incassare

encephalitis [ɛn‚sɛfə'laɪtɪs] s encefalite f

enchain [ɛn'tʃen] tr incatenare

enchant [ɛn'tʃænt] or [ɛn'tʃɑnt] tr incantare

enchantment [ɛn'tʃæntmənt] or [ɛn'tʃɑntmənt] s incanto, malia

enchanting [ɛn'tʃæntɪŋ] or [ɛn'tʃɑntɪŋ] adj incantatore, incantevole

enchantress [ɛn'tʃæntrɪs] or [ɛn'tʃɑntrɪs] s incantatrice f, maliarda

enchase [ɛn'tʃes] tr incastonare

encircle [ɛn'sʌrkəl] tr rigirare, girare intorno a; (mil) circondare

enclave ['ɛnklev] s enclave f

enclitic [ɛn'klɪtɪk] adj enclitico || s enclitica

enclose [ɛn'kloz] tr rinchiudere; (in a letter) accludere, includere; **to enclose herewith** accludere alla presente

enclosure [ɛn'kloʒər] s (land surrounded by fence) recinto, chiuso; (e.g., letter) allegato

encomi·um [ɛn'komi·əm] s (-ums or -a [ə]) encomio, elogio

encompass [ɛn'kʌmpəs] tr circondare; racchiudere, contenere

encore ['ɑŋkor] s bis m || tr (a performance) chiedere il bis di; (a performer) chiedere il bis a || interj bis!

encounter [ɛn'kauntər] s (casual meeting) incontro; (combat) scontro || tr incontrare || intr scontrarsi

encourage [ɛn'kʌrɪdʒ] tr incoraggiare; (to foster) favorire

encouragement [ɛn'kʌrɪdʒmənt] s incoraggiamento; favoreggiamento

encroach [ɛn'krotʃ] intr—**to encroach on** or **upon** invadere; usurpare; occupare il territorio di

encumber [ɛn'kʌmbər] tr imbarazzare; ingombrare; (to load with debts, etc) gravare

encumbrance [ɛn'kʌmbrəns] s imbarazzo; ingombro; gravame m

encyclical [ɛn'sɪklɪkəl] or [ɛn'saɪklɪkəl] s enciclica

encyclopedia [ɛn‚saɪklə'pidɪ·ə] s enciclopedia

encyclopedic [ɛn‚saɪklə'pidɪk] adj enciclopedico

end [ɛnd] s (extremity; concluding part) fine f; (e.g., of the week) fine f; (purpose) fine m; (part adjacent to an extremity) lembo; (small piece) pezza, avanzo; (of a beam) testata; (sports) estrema; **at the end of** in capo a; **in the end** alla fine, all'ultimo; **no end** (coll) moltissimo; **no end of** (coll) un mucchio di; **to make both ends meet** sbarcare il lunario; **to no end** senza effetto; **to stand on end** mettere in piedi, drizzare; mettersi diritto; (said of hair) drizzarsi; **to the end that** affinché || tr finire, terminare; **to end up** andare a finire || intr finire, terminare; **to end up** finire

endanger [ɛn'dendʒər] tr mettere in pericolo

endear [en'dɪr] *tr* affezionare; **to endear oneself to** rendersi caro a

endeavor [en'devər] *s* tentativo, sforzo || *intr* tentare, sforzarsi

endemic [en'demɪk] *adj* endemico || *s* endemia

ending ['endɪŋ] *s* fine *f*, conclusione; (gram) terminazione, desinenza

endive ['endaɪv] *s* indivia

endless ['endlɪs] *adj* interminabile; sterminato; (mach) senza fine

end'most' *adj* estremo, ultimo

endorse [en'dɔrs] *tr* girare; (fig) approvare, confermare

endorsee [ˌendɔr'si] *s* giratario

endorsement [en'dɔrsmənt] *s* girata; approvazione, conferma

endorser [en'dɔrsər] *s* girante *mf*

endow [en'daʊ] *tr* dotare

endowment [en'daʊmənt] *adj* dotale || *s* (*of an institution*) dotazione; (*gift, talent*) dote *f*

end' pap'er *s* risguardo

endurance [en'djʊrəns] *or* [en'dʊrəns] *s* sopportazione, tolleranza; (*ability to hold out*) resistenza, forza; (*lasting time*) durata

endure [en'djʊr] *or* [en'dʊr] *tr* sopportare, tollerare; resistere (with *dat*) || *intr* durare, resistere

enduring [en'djʊrɪŋ] *or* [en'dʊrɪŋ] *adj* duraturo, durevole; paziente

enema ['enəmə] *s* clistere *m*

ene·my ['enəmi] *adj* nemico || *s* (*-mies*) nemico

en'emy al'ien *s* straniero nemico

energetic [ˌenər'dʒetɪk] *adj* energetico, vigoroso

ener·gy ['enərdʒi] *s* (*-gies*) energia

enervate ['enər‚vet] *tr* snervare

enfeeble [en'fibəl] *tr* indebolire

enfold [en'fold] *tr* avvolgere; abbracciare

enforce [en'fɔrs] *tr* far osservare; ottenere per forza; (*e.g., obedience*) imporre; (*an argument*) far valere

enforcement [en'fɔrsmənt] *s* imposizione; (*of a law*) esecuzione

enfranchise [en'fræntʃaɪz] *tr* liberare; concedere il diritto di voto a

engage [en'gedʒ] *tr* occupare; riservare; (*s.o.'s attention*) attrarre; (*a gear*) ingranare; (*the enemy*) ingaggiare; (*to hire*) assumere; (theat) scritturare; **to be engaged, to be engaged to be married** essere fidanzato; **to engage s.o. in conversation** intavolare una conversazione con qlcu || *intr* essere occupato; essere impiegato; assumere un'obbligazione; (mil) impegnarsi; (mach) ingranare, incastrarsi

engaged [en'gedʒd] *adj* fidanzato; occupato, impegnato; (*column*) murato

engagement [en'gedʒmənt] *s* accordo; fidanzamento; impegno, contratto; (*appointment*) appuntamento; (mil) azione; (mach) innesto

engage'ment ring' *s* anello di fidanzamento

engaging [en'gedʒɪŋ] *adj* attrattivo

engender [en'dʒendər] *tr* ingenerare

engine ['endʒɪn] *s* macchina; (aut) motore *m*; (rr) locomotiva, motrice *f*

engineer [ˌendʒə'nɪr] *s* ingegnere *m*; (rr) macchinista *m*; (mil) zappatore *m*, geniere *m* || *tr* costruire; progettare

engineering [ˌendʒə'nɪrɪŋ] *s* ingegneria

en'gine house' *s* stazione dei pompieri

en'gine-man' *s* (*-men*) (rr) macchinista *m*

en'gine room' *s* sala macchine

en'gine-room' tel'egraph *s* (naut) telegrafo di macchina, trasmettitore *m*

England ['ɪŋglənd] *s* l'Inghilterra

Englander ['ɪŋgləndər] *s* nativo dell'Inghilterra

English ['ɪŋglɪʃ] *adj* inglese || *s* inglese *m*; (billiards) effetto; **the English** gli inglesi

Eng'lish Chan'nel *s* Canale *m* della Manica

Eng'lish dai'sy *s* margherita

Eng'lish horn' *s* (mus) corno inglese

Eng'lish·man *s* (*-men*) inglese *m*

Eng'lish-speak'ing *adj* di lingua inglese, anglofono

Eng'lish·wom'an *s* (*-wom'en*) inglese *f*

engraft [en'græft] *or* [en'grɑft] *tr* (hort) innestare; (fig) inculcare

engrave [en'grev] *tr* incidere

engraver [en'grevər] *s* incisore *m*

engraving [en'grevɪŋ] *s* incisione

engross [en'gros] *tr* preoccupare, assorbire; redigere ufficialmente, scrivere a grandi caratteri; monopolizzare

engrossing [en'grosɪŋ] *adj* assorbente

engulf [en'gʌlf] *tr* sommergere, inondare

enhance [en'hæns] *or* [en'hɑns] *tr* valorizzare; far risaltare

enigma [ɪ'nɪgmə] *s* enigma *m*

enigmatic(al) [ˌenɪg'mætɪk(əl)] *adj* enigmatico

enjambment [en'dʒæmmənt] *or* [en'dʒæmbmənt] *s* inarcatura

enjoin [en'dʒɔɪn] *tr* ingiungere, intimare

enjoy [en'dʒɔɪ] *tr* godere; **to enjoy +** *ger* provar piacere in + *inf*; **to enjoy oneself** divertirsi

enjoyable [en'dʒɔɪ‚əbəl] *adj* gradevole

enjoyment [en'dʒɔɪmənt] *s* (*pleasure*) piacere *m*; (*pleasurable use*) godimento

enkindle [en'kɪndəl] *tr* infiammare

enlarge [en'lɑrdʒ] *tr* aumentare; ingrossare; (phot) ingrandire || *intr* aumentare; **to enlarge on or upon** dilungarsi su

enlargement [en'lɑrdʒmənt] *s* aumento; ingrossamento; (phot) ingrandimento

enlighten [en'laɪtən] *tr* illustrare, illuminare

enlightenment [en'laɪtənmənt] *s* spiegazione, schiarimento || **Enlightenment** *s* illuminismo

enlist [en'lɪst] *tr* (*e.g., s.o.'s favor*) guadagnarsi; (*the help of a person*) ottenere; (mil) ingaggiare || *intr* (mil) ingaggiarsi, arruolarsi; **to enlist**

in (*a cause*) dare il proprio appoggio a

enlistment [ɛn'lɪstmənt] *s* arruolamento, ingaggio

enliven [ɛn'laɪvən] *tr* ravvivare

enmesh [ɛn'mɛʃ] *tr* irretire

enmi·ty ['ɛnmɪti] *s* (*-ties*) inimicizia

ennoble [ɛn'nobəl] *tr* nobilitare

ennui ['ɑnwi] *s* noia, tedio

enormous [ɪ'nɔrməs] *adj* enorme

enormously [ɪ'nɔrməsli] *adv* enormemente

enough [ɪ'nʌf] *adj* abbastanza ‖ *s* il sufficiente ‖ *adv* abbastanza ‖ *interj* basta!

enounce [ɪ'naʊns] *tr* enunciare; (*to declare*) affermare

enrage [ɛn'redʒ] *tr* infuriare, irritare

enrapture [ɛn'ræptʃər] *tr* mandare in visibilio, estasiare

enrich [ɛn'rɪtʃ] *tr* arricchire

enroll [ɛn'rol] *tr* arruolare, ingaggiare; (*a student*) iscrivere ‖ *intr* arruolarsi, ingaggiarsi; (*said of a student*) iscriversi

enrollment [ɛn'rolmənt] *s* arruolamento, ingaggio; (*of a student*) iscrizione

en route [ɑn 'rut] *adv* in cammino; **en route to** in via per

ensconce [ɛn'skɑns] *tr* nascondere; **to esconce oneself** rannicchiarsi, istallarsi comodamente

ensemble [ɑn'sɑmbəl] *s* insieme *m*; (*mus*) concertato

ensign ['ɛnsaɪn] *s* (*standard*) bandiera, insegna; (*badge*) distintivo ‖ ['ɛnsən] *or* ['ɛnsaɪn] *s* guardamarina *m*

ensilage ['ɛnsəlɪdʒ] *s* (*preservation of fodder*) insilamento; (*preserved fodder*) insilato

ensile ['ɛnsaɪl] *or* [ɛn'saɪl] *tr* insilare

enslave [ɛn'slev] *tr* fare schiavo, asservire

enslavement [ɛn'slevmənt] *s* asservimento

ensnare [ɛn'sner] *tr* irretire

ensue [ɛn'su] *or* [ɛn'sju] *intr* risultare; seguire, conseguire

ensuing [ɛn'suɪŋ] *or* [ɛn'sjuɪŋ] *adj* risultante, conseguente; seguente

ensure [ɛn'ʃʊr] *tr* assicurare, garantire

entail [ɛn'tel] *s* (law) obbligo ‖ *tr* provocare, comportare; (law) obbligare

entangle [ɛn'tæŋgəl] *tr* intricare, imbrogliare, impigliare

entanglement [ɛn'tæŋgəlmənt] *s* groviglio, garbuglio

enter ['ɛntər] *tr* (*a house*) entrare in; (*in the customhouse*) dichiarare; (*to make a record of*) registrare; (*a student*) iscrivere; iscriversi a; fare membro; (*to undertake*) intraprendere; **to enter s.o.'s head** passare per la testa a qlcu ‖ *intr* entrare; (theat) entrare in scena; **to enter into** entrare in; (*a contract*) impegnarsi in; **to enter on** or **upon** intraprendere

enterprise ['ɛntər,praɪz] *s* (*undertak-*

ing) impresa; (*spirit, push*) intraprendenza

enterprising ['ɛntər,praɪzɪŋ] *adj* intraprendente

entertain [,ɛntər'ten] *tr* divertire, intrattenere; (*guests*) ospitare; (*a hope*) accarezzare; (*a proposal*) considerare ‖ *intr* ricevere

entertainer [,ɛntər'tenər] *s* (*host*) ospite *mf*; (*in public*) attore *m*, cantante *mf*, fine dicitore *m*

entertaining [,ɛntər'tenɪŋ] *adj* divertente

entertainment [,ɛntər'tenmənt] *s* trattenimento, svago; spettacolo, attrazione; buon trattamento

enthrall [ɛn'θrɔl] *tr* affascinare, incantare; (*to subjugate*) asservire, soggiogare

enthrone [ɛn'θron] *tr* mettere sul trono, intronizzare; esaltare, innalzare

enthuse [ɛn'θuz] *or* [ɛn'θjuz] *tr* (coll) entusiasmare ‖ *intr* (coll) entusiasmarsi

enthusiasm [ɛn'θuzɪ,æzəm] *or* [ɛn'θjuzɪ,æzəm] *s* entusiasmo

enthusiast [ɛn'θuzɪ,æst] *or* [ɛn'θjuzɪ,æst] *s* entusiasta *mf*, maniaco

enthusiastic [ɛn,θuzɪ'æstɪk] *or* [ɛn,θjuzɪ'æstɪk] *adj* entusiastico

entice [ɛn'taɪs] *tr* attrarre, provocare; tentare

enticement [ɛn'taɪsmənt] *s* attrazione, provocazione; tentazione

entire [ɛn'taɪr] *adj* intero

entirely [ɛn'taɪrli] *adv* interamente; (*solely*) solamente

entire·ty [ɛn'taɪrti] *s* (*-ties*) interezza; totalità *f*

entitle [ɛn'taɪtəl] *tr* dar diritto a; (*to give a name to*) intitolare

enti·ty ['ɛntɪti] *s* (*-ties*) (*something real; organization, institution*) ente *m*; (*existence*) entità *f*

entomb [ɛn'tum] *tr* seppellire

entombment [ɛn'tummənt] *s* sepoltura

entomology [,ɛntə'mɑlədʒi] *s* entomologia

entourage [,ɑntu'rɑʒ] *s* seguito

entrails ['ɛntrelz] *or* ['ɛntrəlz] *spl* visceri *mpl*

entrain [ɛn'tren] *tr* far salire sul treno ‖ *intr* imbarcarsi sul treno

entrance ['ɛntrəns] *s* entrata, ingresso ‖ [ɛn'træns] *or* [ɛn'trɑns] *tr* ipnotizzare, incantare

en'trance exam'ina'tion *s* esame *m* d'ammissione

entrancing [ɛn'trænsɪŋ] *or* [ɛn'trɑnsɪŋ] *adj* incantatore

entrant ['ɛntrənt] *s* nuovo membro; (sports) concorrente *mf*

en·trap [ɛn'træp] *v* (*pret* & *pp* **-trapped**; *ger* **-trapping**) *tr* intrappolare, irretire

entreat [ɛn'trit] *tr* implorare

entreat·y [ɛn'triti] *s* (*-ies*) implorazione, supplica

entree ['ɑntre] *s* entrata, ingresso; (culin) prima portata

entrench [ɛn'trɛntʃ] *tr* trincerare ‖ *intr* —**to entrench on** or **upon** violare

entrust [ɛn'trʌst] *tr* affidare, confidare

en·try ['ɛntri] *s* (**-tries**) entrata; *(item)* partita, registrazione; *(in a dictionary)* lemma, esponente *m;* (sports) concorrente *mf*

entwine [ɛn'twaɪn] *tr* intrecciare ‖ *intr* intrecciarsi

enumerate [ɪ'njumə,ret] or [ɪ'numə,ret] *tr* enumerare

enunciate [ɪ'nʌnsɪ,et] or [ɪ'nʌnʃɪ,et] *tr* enunciare, staccare

envelop [ɛn'vɛləp] *tr* involgere

envelope ['ɛnvə,lop] or ['ɑnvə,lop] *s* *(for a letter)* busta; *(wrapper)* involucro

envenom [ɛn'vɛnəm] *tr* avvelenare

enviable ['ɛnvɪ-əbəl] *adj* invidiabile

envious ['ɛnvɪ-əs] *adj* invidioso

environment [ɛn'vaɪrənmənt] *s* ambiente *m;* condizioni *fpl* ambientali

environs [ɛn'vaɪrənz] *spl* dintorni *mpl,* sobborghi *mpl*

envisage [ɛn'vɪzɪdʒ] *tr* considerare, immaginare

envoi ['ɛnvɔɪ] *s* (pros) congedo

envoy ['ɛnvɔɪ] *s* inviato; (mil) parlamentare *m;* (pros) congedo

en·vy ['ɛnvi] *s* (**-vies**) invidia ‖ *v* (*pret & pp* **-vied**) *tr* invidiare

enzyme ['ɛnzaɪm] or ['ɛnzɪm] *s* enzima *m*

epaulet or **epaulette** ['ɛpə,lɛt] *s* spallina

epenthe·sis [ɛ'pɛnθɪsɪs] *s* (**-ses** [,siz]) epentesi *f*

ephemeral [ɪ'fɛmərəl] *adj* effimero

epic ['ɛpɪk] *adj* epico ‖ *s* epica

epicure ['ɛpɪ,kjʊr] *s* epicureo

epicurean [,ɛpɪkjʊ'ri-ən] *adj & s* epicureo

epidemic [,ɛpɪ'dɛmɪk] *adj* epidemico ‖ *s* epidemia

epidermis [,ɛpɪ'dʌrmɪs] *s* epidermide *f*

epiglottis [,ɛpɪ'glatɪs] *s* epiglottide *f*

epigram ['ɛpɪ,græm] *s* epigramma *m*

epilepsy ['ɛpɪ,lɛpsi] *s* epilessia

epileptic [,ɛpɪ'lɛptɪk] *adj & s* epilettico

epilogue ['ɛpɪ,lɔg] or ['ɛpɪ,lɑg] *s* epilogo

Epiphany [ɪ'pɪfəni] *s* Epifania

Episcopalian [ɪ,pɪskə'peli-ən] *adj & s* episcopaliano

episode ['ɛpɪ,sod] *s* episodio

epistle [ɪ'pɪsəl] *s* epistola

epitaph ['ɛpɪ,tæf] *s* epitaffio

epithet ['ɛpɪ,θɛt] *s* epiteto

epitome [ɪ'pɪtəmi] *s* epitome *f;* (fig) prototipo, personificazione

epitomize [ɪ'pɪtə,maɪz] *tr* epitomare; (fig) incarnare, personificare

epoch ['ɛpək] or ['ipak] *s* epoca

epochal ['ɛpəkəl] *adj* memorabile

ep'och-mak'ing *adj*—**to be epoch-making** fare epoca

Ep'som salt' ['ɛpsəm] *s* sale *m* inglese

equable ['ɛkwəbəl] or ['ikwəbəl] *adj* uniforme; tranquillo

equal ['ikwəl] *adj* uguale; **equal to** pari a, all'altezza di ‖ *s* uguale *m* ‖ *v* (*pret & pp* **equaled** or **equalled**; *ger* **equaling** or **equalling**) *tr* uguagliare

equali·ty [ɪ'kwɑlɪti] *s* (**-ties**) uguaglianza

equalize ['ikwə,laɪz] *tr* uguagliare; *(to make uniform)* perequare, pareggiare

equally ['ikwəli] *adv* ugualmente

equanimity [,ikwə'nɪmɪti] *s* equanimità *f*

equate [i'kwet] *tr* mettere in forma di equazione; considerare uguale or uguali

equation [i'kweʒən] or [i'kweʃən] *s* equazione

equator [i'kwetər] *s* equatore *m*

equatorial [,ikwə'tɔri-əl] *adj* equatoriale

equer·ry ['ɛkwəri] or [ɪ'kwɛri] *s* (**-ries**) scudiero

equestrian [ɪ'kwɛstrɪ-ən] *adj* equestre ‖ *s* cavallerizzo

equilateral [,ikwɪ'lætərəl] *adj* equilatero

equilibrium [,ikwɪ'lɪbrɪ-əm] *s* equilibrio

equinoctial [,ikwɪ'nɑkʃəl] *adj* equinoziale

equinox ['ikwɪ,nɑks] *s* equinozio

equip [ɪ'kwɪp] *v* (*pret & pp* **equipped;** *ger* **equipping**) *tr* equipaggiare; **to equip** (*e.g., a ship*) **with** munire di

equipment [ɪ'kwɪpmənt] *s* equipaggiamento; *(skill)* attitudine *f,* capacità *f*

equipoise ['ikwɪ,pɔɪz] or ['ɛkwɪ,pɔɪz] *s* equilibrio ‖ *tr* equilibrare

equitable ['ɛkwɪtəbəl] *adj* equo

equi·ty ['ɛkwɪti] *s* (**-ties**) *(fairness)* equità *f;* valore *m* al netto; *(in a corporation)* interessenza azionaria

equivalent [ɪ'kwɪvələnt] *adj* equivalente ‖ *s* equivalente *m;* (com) controvalore *m*

equivocal [ɪ'kwɪvəkəl] *adj* equivoco

equivocate [ɪ'kwɪvə,ket] *intr* giocare sulle parole, parlare in maniera equivoca

equivocation [ɪ,kwɪvə'keʃən] *s* equivocità *f;* maniera equivoca

era ['ɪrə] or ['irə] *s* era, evo

eradicate [ɪ'rædɪ,ket] *tr* sradicare

erase [ɪ'res] *tr* cancellare

eraser [ɪ'resər] *s* gomma da cancellare; *(for blackboard)* spugna

erasure [ɪ'reʃər] or [ɪ'reʒər] *s* cancellatura; *(of a tape)* cancellazione

ere [ɛr] *prep* (lit) prima di ‖ *conj* (lit) prima che

erect [ɪ'rɛkt] *adj* dritto, eretto; *(hair)* irto ‖ *tr* *(to set in upright position)* drizzare; *(a building)* erigere, costruire; *(a machine)* montare

erection [ɪ'rɛkʃən] *s* erezione

ermine ['ʌrmɪn] *s* ermellino; (fig) carica di giudice, toga, magistratura

erode [ɪ'rod] *tr* erodere ‖ *intr* corrodersi, consumarsi

erosion [ɪ'roʒən] *s* erosione

erotic [ɪ'rɑtɪk] *adj* erotico

err [ʌr] *intr* errare; *(to be incorrect)* sbagliarsi

errand ['ɛrənd] *s* corsa, commissione; **to run an errand** fare una commissione

er'rand boy' *s* fattorino, galoppino

erratic [ɪˈrætɪk] *adj* erratico; strano, eccentrico

erra·tum [ɪˈretəm] or [ɪˈrɑtəm] *s* (-ta [tə]) errore *m* di stampa

erroneous [ɪˈronɪ·əs] *adj* erroneo

error [ˈerər] *s* errore *m*, sbaglio

erudite [ˈeruˌdaɪt] or [ˈerjuˌdaɪt] *adj* erudito, dotto

erudition [ˌeruˈdɪʃən] or [ˌerjuˈdɪʃən] *s* erudizione

erupt [ɪˈrʌpt] *intr* (*said of a volcano*) eruttare; (*said of a skin rash*) fiorire; (*said of a tooth*) spuntare; (fig) erompere

eruption [ɪˈrʌpʃən] *s* eruzione

escalate [ˈeskəˌlet] *tr & intr* aumentare

escalation [ˌeskəˈleʃən] *s* aumento

escalator [ˈeskəˌletər] *s* scala mobile

escallop [esˈkæləp] *s* (*on edge of cloth*) dentellatura, festone *m*; (*mollusk*) pettine *m* ‖ *tr* cuocere in conchiglia; cuocere al forno con salsa e pane grattugiato

escapade [ˌeskəˈped] *s* scappatella

escape [esˈkep] *s* (*getaway*) fuga; (*from responsibility, duties, etc.*) scampo ‖ *tr* sottrarsi a, eludere; **to escape s.o.** scappare da qlcu; scappar di mente a qlcu ‖ *intr* scappare; sprigionarsi; **to escape from** (*a person*) sfuggire a; (*jail*) evadere da

escapee [ˌeskəˈpi] *s* evaso

escape' lit'erature *s* letteratura di evasione

escapement [esˈkepmənt] *s* scappamento

escape' veloc'ity *s* (rok) velocità *f* di fuga

escarpment [esˈkɑrpmənt] *s* scarpata

eschew [esˈtʃu] *tr* evitare, rifuggire da

escort [ˈeskɔrt] *s* scorta; (*of a woman or girl*) compagno, cavaliere *m* ‖ [esˈkɔrt] *tr* scortare

escutcheon [esˈkʌtʃən] *s* scudo; (*plate in front of lock on door*) bocchetta

Esk·imo [ˈeskɪˌmo] *adj* eschimese ‖ *s* (-mos or -mo) eschimese *mf*

esopha·gus [iˈsɑfəgəs] *s* (-gi [ˌdʒaɪ]) esofago

espalier [esˈpæljər] *s* spalliera

especial [esˈpeʃəl] *adj* speciale

espionage [ˈespɪ·ənɪdʒ] or [ˌespɪ·əˈnɑʒ] *s* spionaggio

esplanade [ˌespləˈned] or [ˌespləˈnɑd] *s* spianata, piazzale *m*

espousal [esˈpauzəl] *s* sposalizio; (*of a cause*) adozione

espouse [esˈpauz] *tr* sposare; (*to advocate*) abbracciare, adottare

esquire [esˈkwaɪr] or [ˈeskwaɪr] *s* scudiero ‖ **Esquire** *s* titolo di cortesia usato generalmente con persone di riguardo

essay [ˈese] *s* saggio

essayist [ˈese·ɪst] *s* saggista *mf*

essence [ˈesəns] *s* essenza

essential [eˈsenʃəl] *adj & s* essenziale *m*

establish [esˈtæblɪʃ] *tr* stabilire

establishment [esˈtæblɪʃmənt] *s* stabilimento; fondazione; **the Establishment** l'autorità costituita

estate [esˈtet] *s* stato; condizione sociale; (*landed property*) tenuta; (*a*

person's possessions) patrimonio; (*left by a decedent*) massa ereditaria

esteem [esˈtim] *s* stima ‖ *tr* stimare

esthete [ˈesθit] *s* esteta *mf*

esthetic [esˈθetɪk] *adj* estetico ‖ **esthetics** *ssg* estetica

estimable [ˈestɪməbəl] *adj* stimabile

estimate [ˈestɪˌmet] or [ˈestɪmɪt] *s* stima, valutazione; (*statement of cost of work to be done*) preventivo ‖ [ˈestɪˌmet].*tr* stimare, valutare; preventivare

estimation [ˌestɪˈmeʃən] *s* stima; **in my estimation** a mio parere

estimator [ˈestɪˌmetər] *s* preventivista *mf*

estrangement [esˈtrendʒmənt] *s* alienazione, disaffezione

estuar·y [ˈestʃuˌerɪ] *s* (-ies) estuario

etch [etʃ] *tr & intr* incidere all'acquaforte

etcher [ˈetʃər] *s* acquafortista *mf*

etching [ˈetʃɪŋ] *s* acquaforte *f*

eternal [ɪˈtɑrnəl] *adj* eterno

eterni·ty [ɪˈtɑrnɪti] *s* (-ties) eternità *f*

ether [ˈiθər] *s* etere *m*

ethereal [ɪˈθɪrɪ·əl] *adj* etereo

ethical [ˈeθɪkəl] *adj* etico

ethics [ˈeθɪks] *ssg* etica

Ethiopian [ˌiθɪˈopɪ·ən] *adj & s* etiope *mf*

ethnic(al) [ˈeθnɪk(əl)] *adj* etnico

ethnography [eθˈnɑgrəfi] *s* etnografia

ethnology [eθˈnɑlədʒi] *s* etnologia

ethyl [ˈeθɪl] *s* etile *m*

ethylene [ˈeθɪˌlin] *s* etilene *m*

etiquette [ˈetɪˌket] *s* etichetta

étude [eˈtjud] *s* (mus) studio

etymology [ˌetɪˈmɑlədʒi] *s* etimologia

ety·mon [ˈetɪˌman] *s* (-mons or -ma [mə]) etimo

eucalyp·tus [ˌjukəˈlɪptəs] *s* (-tuses or -ti [taɪ]) eucalipto

Eucharist [ˈjukərɪst] *s* Eucaristia

eugenics [juˈdʒenɪks] *ssg* eugenetica

eulogistic [ˌjuləˈdʒɪstɪk] *adj* elogiativo

eulogize [ˈjuləˌdʒaɪz] *tr* elogiare

eulo·gy [ˈjulədʒi] *s* (-gies) elogio; elogio funebre

eunuch [ˈjunak] *s* eunuco

euphemism [ˈjufɪˌmɪzəm] *s* eufemismo

euphemistic [ˌjufɪˈmɪstɪk] *adj* eufemistico

euphonic [juˈfɑnɪk] *adj* eufonico

eupho·ny [ˈjufəni] *s* (-nies) eufonia

euphoria [juˈforɪ·ə] *s* euforia

euphuism [ˈjufjuˌɪzəm] *s* eufuismo

Europe [ˈjurəp] *s* l'Europa

European [ˌjurəˈpi·ən] *adj & s* europeo

euthanasia [ˌjuθəˈneʒə] *s* eutanasia

evacuate [ɪˈvækjuˌet] *tr & intr* evacuare

evacuation [ɪˌvækjuˈeʃən] *s* evacuazione

evacuee [ɪˈvækjuˌi] or [ɪˌvækjuˈi] *s* sfollato

evade [ɪˈved] *tr* eludere ‖ *intr* evadere

evaluate [ɪˈvæljuˌet] *tr* valutare

evaluation [ɪˌvæljuˈeʃən] *s* valutazione

Evangel [ɪˈvændʒəl] *s* Vangelo

evangelic(al) [ˌivænˈdʒelɪk(əl)] or [ˌevənˈdʒelɪk(əl)] *adj* evangelico

Evangelist [ɪ'vændʒəlɪst] s evangelista m

evaporate [ɪ'væpə‚ret] tr & intr evaporare

evasion [ɪ'veʒən] s evasione; (subterfuge) scappatoia

evasive [ɪ'vesɪv] adj evasivo

eve [iv] s vigilia; **on the eve of** la vigilia di

even ['ivən] adj (smooth) piano, regolare; (number) pari; uguale, uniforme; (temperament) calmo, placido; **even with** a livello di; **to be even** mettersi in pari; **to get even** prendersi la rivincita || adv anche; fino, perfino; pure; esattamente; magari; **even as** proprio mentre; **even if** anche se, quando pure; **even so** anche se così; **even though** quantunque; **even when** anche quando; **not even** neppure, nemmeno; **to break even** impattare || tr spianare; **to even up** bilanciare

evening ['ivnɪŋ] adj serale || s sera, serata; **all evening** tutta la sera; **every evening** tutte le sere; **in the evening** la sera

eve'ning clothes' spl vestito da sera

eve'ning gown' s vestito da sera da signora

eve'ning star' s espero

e'ven‐song' s (eccl) vespro

event [ɪ'vent] s avvenimento; (outcome) evenienza; (public function) manifestazione; (sports) prova; **at all events** or **in any event** in ogni caso; **in the event that** in caso che, se mai

eventful [ɪ'ventfəl] adj ricco di avvenimenti; movimentato

eventual [ɪ'ventʃʊ‐əl] adj finale

eventuali‐ty [ɪ‚ventʃʊ'ælɪti] s (‐ties) eventualità f, evenienza

eventually [ɪ'ventʃʊ‐əli] adv finalmente, alla fine

eventuate [ɪ'ventʃʊ‚et] intr risultare; accadere

ever ['evər] adv (at all times) sempre; (at any time) mai; **as ever** come sempre; **as much as ever** tanto come prima; **ever since** (since that time) sin da; da allora in poi; **ever so** molto; **ever so much** moltissimo; **hardly ever** or **scarcely ever** quasi mai; **not . . . ever** non . . . mai

ev'er‐glade' s terreno paludoso coperto di erbe

ev'er‐green' adj & s sempreverde m & f; **evergreens** decorazione di sempreverdi

ev'er‐last'ing adj eterno; incessante; (lasting indefinitely) duraturo; (wearisome) noioso || s eternità f; (bot) semprevivo

ev'er‐more' adv eternamente; **for evermore** per sempre

every ['evri] adj tutti i; (each) ogni, ciascuno; (being each in a series) ogni, e.g., **every three days** ogni tre giorni; **every bit** (coll) in tutto e per tutto, e.g., **every bit a man** un uomo in tutto e per tutto; **every now and then** di quando in quando; **every once in a while** una volta ogni tanto;

every other day ogni secondo giorno; **every which way** (coll) da tutte le parti; (coll) in disordine

ev'ery‐bod'y pron indef ognuno, tutti

ev'ery‐day' adj di ogni giorno; quotidiano; ordinario

ev'ery‐man' s l'uomo qualunque || pron chiunque

ev'ery‐one' or **ev'ery one'** pron indef ciascuno, tutti

ev'ery‐thing' pron indef tutto, ogni cosa, tutto quanto

ev'ery‐where' adv dappertutto, dovunque

evict [ɪ'vɪkt] tr sfrattare, sloggiare

eviction [ɪ'vɪkʃən] s sfratto, sloggio

evidence ['evɪdəns] s evidenza; (law) prova

evident ['evɪdənt] adj evidente

evil ['ivəl] adj cattivo, malvagio || s male m; disgrazia

evildoer ['ivəl‚dʊ‐ər] s malfattore m, malvagio

e'vil‐do'ing s malafatta, malvagità f

e'vil eye' s iettatura, malocchio

evil‐minded ['ivəl'maɪndɪd] adj malintenzionato

e'vil one', **the** il nemico

evince [ɪ'vɪns] tr mostrare, manifestare

evoke [ɪ'vok] tr evocare

evolution [‚evə'luʃən] s evoluzione

evolve [ɪ'valv] tr sviluppare || intr evolversi

ewe [ju] s pecora

ewer ['ju‐ər] s brocca

ex [eks] prep senza includere

exacerbation [ɪg‚zæsər'beʃən] s esulcerazione, esacerbazione

exacerbate [ɪg'zæsər‚bet] tr esacerbare, esulcerare

exact [eg'zækt] adj esatto || tr esigere

exacting [eg'zæktɪŋ] adj esigente

exaction [eg'zækʃən] s esazione

exactly [eg'zæktli] adv esattamente; (sharp, on the dot) in punto

exactness [eg'zæktnɪs] s esattezza

exaggerate [eg'zædʒə‚ret] tr esagerare

exalt [eg'zɔlt] tr elevare, esaltare

exam [eg'zæm] s (coll) esame m

examination [eg‚zæmɪ'neʃən] s esame m; **to take an examination** sostenere un esame

examine [eg'zæmɪn] tr esaminare

examiner [eg'zæmɪnər] s esaminatore m

example [eg'zæmpəl] or [eg'zɑmpəl] s esempio; (precedent) precedente m; (of mathematics) problema m; **for example** per esempio

exasperate [eg'zæspə‚ret] tr esasperare

excavate ['ekskə‚vet] tr scavare

exceed [ek'sid] tr eccedere

exceedingly [ek'sidɪŋli] adv estremamente, sommamente

ex‐cel [ek'sel] v (pret & pp ‐celled; ger ‐celling) tr sorpassare || intr eccellere

excellence ['eksələns] s eccellenza

excellen‐cy ['eksələnsi] s (‐cies) eccellenza; **Your Excellency** Sua Eccellenza

excelsior [ek'selsɪ‐ər] s trucioli mpl per imballaggio

except [ek'sept] prep eccetto; **except**

for tranne, ad eccezione di; **except that** eccetto che || *tr* eccettuare

exception [ɛk'sɛp/ən] *s* eccezione; **to take exception** obiettare; scandalizzarsi; **with the exception of** a esclusione di, eccetto

exceptional [ɛk'sɛp/ənəl] *adj* eccezionale

excerpt ['ɛksʌrpt] *or* [ɛk'sʌrpt] *s* brano, selezione || [ɛk'sʌrpt] *tr* scegliere, selezionare

excess ['ɛksɛs] *or* [ɛk'sɛs] *adj* eccedente || [ɛk'sɛs] *s* (*amount or degree by which one thing exceeds another*) eccedente *m*, eccedenza; (*excessive amount; immoderate indulgence; unlawful conduct*) eccesso; **in excess of** più di

ex'cess bag'gage *s* bagaglio eccedente

ex'cess fare' *s* (rr) supplemento

excessive [ɛk'sɛsɪv] *adj* eccessivo

ex'cess-prof'its tax' *s* tassa sui soprapprofitti

exchange [ɛks't/endʒ] *s* scambio; (*place for buying and selling*) borsa; (*transactions in the currencies of two different countries*) cambio; (telp) centrale *f*, centralino; **in exchange for** in cambio di || *tr* scambiare, scambiarsi; **to exchange blows** venire alle mani; **to exchange greetings** salutarsi

exchequer [ɛks't/ɛkər] *or* ['ɛkst/ɛkər] *s* erario, tesoro

ex'cise tax' [ɛk'saɪz] *or* ['ɛksaɪz] *s* imposta sul consumo

excitable [ɛk'saɪtəbəl] *adj* eccitabile

excite [ɛk'saɪt] *tr* eccitare

excitement [ɛk'saɪtmənt] *s* eccitazione

exciting [ɛk'saɪtɪŋ] *adj* emozionante; (*stimulating*) eccitante

exclaim [ɛks'klem] *tr & intr* esclamare

exclamation [ˌɛksklə'me/ən] *s* esclamazione

exclama'tion mark' *or* **point'** *s* punto esclamativo

exclude [ɛks'klud] *tr* escludere

excluding [ɛks'kludɪŋ] *prep* a esclusione di, senza contare

exclusion [ɛks'kluʒən] *s* esclusione; **to the exclusion of** tranne, salvo

exclusive [ɛks'klusɪv] *adj* esclusivo; **exclusive of** escluso, senza contare || *s* (journ) esclusiva

excommunicate [ˌɛkskə'mjunɪˌket] *tr* scomunicare

excommunication [ˌɛkskəˌmjunɪ'ke-/ən] *s* scomunica

excoriate [ɛks'korɪˌet] *tr* criticare aspramente, vituperare

excrement ['ɛkskrəmənt] *s* escremento

excruciating [ɛks'kru/ɪˌetɪŋ] *adj* (e.g., *pleasure*) estremo; (e.g., *pain*) atroce, lancinante, straziante

exculpate ['ɛkskʌlˌpet] *or* [ɛks'kʌlpet] *tr* scolpare, scagionare

excursion [ɛks'kʌrʒən] *or* [ɛks'kʌr/ən] *s* escursione, gita

excursionist [ɛks'kʌrʒənɪst] *or* [ɛks-'kʌr/ənɪst] *s* escursionista *mf*

excusable [ɛks'kjuzəbəl] *adj* scusabile

excuse [ɛks'kjus] *s* scusa || [ɛks'kjuz] *tr* scusare; esentare; (*a debt*) rimettere

execute ['ɛksɪˌkjut] *tr* (*to carry out; to produce*) eseguire; (*to put to death*) giustiziare; (law) rendere esecutorio

execution [ˌɛksɪ'kju/ən] *s* esecuzione; (e.g., *of a criminal*) esecuzione capitale

executioner [ˌɛksɪ'kju/ənər] *s* giustiziere *m*, boia *m*, carnefice *m*

executive [ɛg'zɛkjətɪv] *adj* esecutivo || *s* esecutivo; (*of a school, business, etc.*) dirigente *mf*

Exec'utive Man'sion *s* palazzo del governatore; residenza del capo del governo statunitense

executor [ɛg'zɛkjətər] *s* (law) esecutore testamentario

executrix [ɛg'zɛkjətrɪks] *s* (law) esecutrice testamentaria

exemplary [ɛg'zɛmpləri] *or* ['ɛgzəmˌplɛri] *adj* esemplare

exempli·fy [ɛg'zɛmplɪˌfaɪ] *v* (*pret & pp* -**fied**) *tr* esemplificare

exempt [ɛg'zɛmpt] *adj* esente || *tr* esimere, esentare

exemption [ɛg'zɛmp/ən] *s* esenzione

exercise ['ɛksər,saɪz] *s* esercizio; cerimonia; **to take exercise** fare del moto || *tr* esercitare; (*care*) usare; (*to worry*) preoccupare || *intr* esercitarsi

exert [ɛg'zʌrt] *tr* (e.g., *power*) esercitare; **to exert oneself** sforzarsi

exertion [ɛg'zʌr/ən] *s* sforzo, tentativo; (*active use*) uso, esercizio

exhalation [ˌɛksˌhə'le/ən] *s* (*of gas, vapors*) esalazione; (*of air from lungs*) espirazione

exhale [ɛks'hel] *or* [ɛg'zel] *tr* (*gases, vapors, etc.*) esalare; (*air from lungs*) espirare || *intr* esalare; espirare

exhaust [ɛg'zɔst] *s* scarico, scappamento; tubo di scarico or scappamento || *tr* (*to wear out*) spossare, finire; (*to use up*) esaurire, dar fondo a; vuotare

exhaust' fan' *s* aspiratore *m*

exhaustion [ɛg'zɔst/ən] *s* esaurimento; estenuazione; (sports) cotta

exhaustive [ɛg'zɔstɪv] *adj* esauriente

exhaust' man'ifold *s* collettore *m* di scarico

exhaust' pipe' *s* tubo di scarico

exhaust' valve' *s* valvola di scappamento

exhibit [ɛg'zɪbɪt] *s* esposizione; (law) documento in giudizio || *tr* esibire

exhibition [ˌɛksɪ'bɪ/ən] *s* esibizione

exhibitor [ɛg'zɪbɪtər] *s* espositore *m*

exhilarating [ɛg'zɪlə,retɪŋ] *adj* esilarante

exhort [ɛg'zɔrt] *tr* esortare

exhume [ɛks'hjum] *or* [ɛg'zjum] *tr* esumare, dissotterrare

exigen·cy ['ɛksɪdʒənsi] *s* (-**cies**) esigenza

exigent ['ɛksɪdʒənt] *adj* esigente

exile ['ɛgzaɪl] *or* ['ɛksaɪl] *s* esilio; (*person*) esule *mf* || *tr* esiliare

exist [ɛg'zɪst] *intr* esistere

existence [ɛg'zɪstəns] *s* esistenza

existing [ɛg'zɪstɪŋ] *adj* esistente

exit ['ɛgzɪt] *or* ['ɛksɪt] *s* uscita || *intr* uscire

exodus ['ɛksədəs] s esodo

exonerate [ɛg'zɑnə ˌret] tr (from an obligation) esonerare; (from blame) scagionare

exorbitant [ɛg'zɔrbɪtənt] adj esorbitante

exorcise ['ɛksɔr ˌsaɪz] tr esorcizzare

exotic [ɛg'zɑtɪk] adj esotico

expand [ɛks'pænd] tr (a metal) dilatare; (gas) espandere; (to enlarge) allargare, ampliare; (to unfold) spiegare; (math) svolgere, sviluppare ‖ intr dilatarsi; espandersi; allargarsi, ampliarsi; spiegarsi, estendersi

expanse [ɛks'pæns] s vastità f

expansion [ɛks'pænʃən] s espansione

expansive [ɛks'pænsɪv] adj espansivo

expatiate [ɛks'pe/ɪ ˌet] intr dilungarsi

expatriate [ɛks'petrɪ·ɪt] adj esiliato ‖ s esule mf ‖ [ɛks'petrɪ ˌet] tr esiliare; **to expatriate oneself** espatriare

expect [ɛks'pɛkt] tr aspettare, attendere; (coll) credere, supporre; **to expect it** aspettarselo, aspettarsela

expectan·cy [ɛks'pɛktənsɪ] s (-cies) aspettativa, aspettazione

expect'ant moth'er [ɛks'pɛktənt] s futura madre

expectation [ˌɛkspɛk'teʃən] s aspettativa

expectorate [ɛks'pɛktə ˌret] tr & intr espettorare

expedien·cy [ɛks'pidɪ·ənsɪ] s (-cies) industria, ingegno; opportunismo, vantaggio personale

expedient [ɛks'pidɪ·ənt] adj conveniente; vantaggioso; (acting with self-interest) opportunista ‖ s espediente m

expedite ['ɛkspɪ ˌdaɪt] tr sbrigare, accelerare; (a document) dar corso a

expedition [ˌɛkspɪ'dɪʃən] s spedizione; (speed) celerità f

expeditionary [ˌɛkspɪ'dɪʃən ˌɛrɪ] adj (e.g., corps) di spedizione

expeditious [ˌɛkspɪ'dɪʃəs] adj spicciativo, spiccio

ex·pel [ɛks'pɛl] v (pret & pp -pelled; ger -pelling) tr espellere, scacciare

expend [ɛks'pɛnd] tr spendere, consumare

expendable [ɛks'pɛndəbəl] adj spendibile; da buttarsi via; (mil) da sacrificare

expenditure [ɛks'pɛndɪt/ər] s spesa

expense [ɛks'pɛns] s spesa; **at the expense of** al costo di; **expenses** spese fpl; **to meet expenses** far fronte alle spese

expense' account' s conto delle spese risarcibili

expensive [ɛks'pɛnsɪv] adj caro, costoso

experience [ɛks'pɪrɪ·əns] s esperienza ‖ tr sperimentare, provare

experienced [ɛks'pɪrɪ·ənst] adj esperto, sperimentato

experiment [ɛks'pɛrɪmənt] s esperimento ‖ [ɛks'pɛrɪ ˌmɛnt] intr sperimentare

expert ['ɛkspərt] adj & s esperto

expertise [ˌɛkspər'tiz] s maestria

expiate ['ɛkspɪ ˌet] tr espiare

expiation [ˌɛkspɪ'eʃən] s espiazione

expire [ɛks'paɪr] tr espirare ‖ intr (to breathe out) espirare; (said of a contract) scadere; (to die) morire

explain [ɛks'plen] tr spiegare; **to explain away** giustificare; dar ragione di ‖ intr spiegare, spiegarsi

explainable [ɛks'plenəbəl] adj spiegabile

explanation [ˌɛksplə'neʃən] s spiegazione, delucidazione

explanatory [ɛks'plænə ˌtorɪ] adj esplicativo

explicit [ɛks'plɪsɪt] adj esplicito

explode [ɛks'plod] tr far scoppiare; (a theory) smontare ‖ intr scoppiare

exploit [ɛks'plɔɪt] or ['ɛksplɔɪt] s impresa, prodezza ‖ [ɛks'plɔɪt] tr utilizzare, sfruttare

exploitation [ˌɛksplɔɪ'teʃən] s utilizzazione, sfruttamento

exploration [ˌɛksplə'reʃən] s esplorazione

explore [ɛks'plor] tr esplorare

explorer [ɛks'plorər] s esploratore m

explosion [ɛks'ploʒən] s esplosione, scoppio; (of a theory) confutazione

explosive [ɛks'plosɪv] adj & s esplosivo

exponent [ɛks'ponənt] s esponente m

export ['ɛksport] adj di esportazione ‖ s esportazione, articolo di esportazione ‖ [ɛks'port] or ['ɛksport] tr & intr esportare

exportation [ˌɛkspor'teʃən] s esportazione

exporter [ɛks'portər] or [ɛks'portər] s esportatore m

expose [ɛks'poz] tr esporre; (to unmask) smascherare

exposé [ˌɛkspo'ze] s rivelazione scandalosa, smascheramento

exposition [ˌɛkspə'zɪʃən] s esposizione; interpretazione, commento

expostulate [ɛks'pɑst/ə ˌlet] intr protestare; **to expostulate with** lagnarsi con

exposure [ɛks'poʒər] s (disclosure) rivelazione; (situation with regard to sunlight) esposizione; (phot) esposizione

expo'sure me'ter s (phot) fotometro, esposimetro

expound [ɛks'paʊnd] tr esporre

express [ɛks'prɛs] adj espresso ‖ s (rr) celere m, rapido, direttissimo; **by express** per espresso, a grande velocità ‖ adv per espresso, a grande velocità ‖ tr esprimere; mandare per espresso; (to squeeze out) spremere; **to express oneself** esprimersi

ex'press com'pany s servizio corriere

expression [ɛks'prɛ/ən] s espressione

expressive [ɛks'prɛsɪv] adj espressivo

expressly [ɛks'prɛsli] adv espressamente

express'man s (-men) fattorino di servizio corriere

express'way s autostrada

expropriate [ɛks'proprɪ ˌet] tr espropriare

expulsion [ɛks'pʌl/ən] s espulsione

expunge [ɛks'pʌndʒ] *tr* espungere
expurgate ['ɛkspər͵get] *tr* espurgare
exquisite ['ɛkskwɪzɪt] *or* [ɛks'kwɪzɪt] *adj* squisito; intenso
ex'serv'ice-man' *s* (-men') ex combattente *m*
extant ['ɛkstənt] *or* [ɛks'tænt] *adj* ancora esistente
extemporaneous [ɛks͵tɛmpə'reni-əs] *adj* estemporaneo; (*made for the occasion*) improvvisato
extempore [ɛks'tɛmpəri] *adj* improvvisato || *adv* senza preparazione
extemporize [ɛks'tɛmpə͵raɪz] *tr & intr* improvvisare
extend [ɛks'tɛnd] *tr* allungare; estendere; (*e.g., aid*) offrire; (*payment of a debt*) dilazionare || *intr* estendersi
extended [ɛks'tɛndɪd] *adj* esteso; prolungato
extension [ɛks'tɛnʃən] *s* estensione; prolungamento; (com) proroga; (telp) derivazione
exten'sion lad'der *s* scala porta, scala a prolunga
exten'sion ta'ble *s* tavola allungabile
exten'sion tel'ephone' *s* telefono interno
extensive [ɛks'tɛnsɪv] *adj* (*wide*) vasto; (*lengthy*) lungo; (*characterized by extention*) estensivo
extent [ɛks'tɛnt] *s* estensione; **to a certain extent** fino a un certo punto; **to a great extent** in larga misura; **to the full extent** all'estremo limite
extenuate [ɛks'tɛnju͵et] *tr* (*to make seem less serious*) attenuare; (*to underrate*) sottovalutare
exterior [ɛks'tɪrɪ-ər] *adj & s* esteriore *m*
exterminate [ɛks'tʌrmɪ͵net] *tr* sterminare
external [ɛks'tʌrnəl] *adj* esterno || **externals** *spl* esteriorità *f*, di fuori *m*
extinct [ɛks'tɪŋkt] *adj* estinto
extinction [ɛks'tɪŋkʃən] *s* estinzione
extinguish [ɛks'tɪŋgwɪʃ] *tr* estinguere
extinguisher [ɛks'tɪŋgwɪʃər] *s* estintore *m*
extirpate ['ɛkstər͵pet] *or* [ɛks'tʌrpet] *tr* estirpare
ex-tol [ɛks'tol] *or* [ɛks'tal] *v* (*pret & pp* -tolled; *ger* -tolling) *tr* inneggiare
extort [ɛks'tort] *tr* estorcere
extortion [ɛks'torʃən] *s* estorsione
extra ['ɛkstrə] *adj* extra; (*spare*) di scorta || *s* (*of a newspaper*) edizione straordinaria; (*something additional*) soprappiù *m*; (theat) figurante *mf* || *adv* straordinariamente
ex'tra charge' *s* supplemento
extract ['ɛkstrækt] *s* estratto || [ɛks'trækt] *tr* (*to pull out*) estrarre; (*to take from a book*) scegliere, selezionare
extraction [ɛks'trækʃən] *s* estrazione
extracurricular [͵ɛkstrəkə'rɪkjələr] *adj* fuori del programma normale
extradition [͵ɛkstrə'dɪʃən] *s* estradizione
ex'tra-dry' *adj* molto secco, brut
ex'tra fare' *s* supplemento al biglietto

ex'tra-mar'ital *adj* extraconiugale.
extramural [͵ɛkstrə'mjurəl] *adj* fuori della scuola, interscolastico; fuori delle mura
extraneous [ɛks'trenɪ-əs] *adj* estraneo
extraordinary [͵ɛkstrə'ordɪ͵nɛri] *or* [ɛks'trordɪ͵nɛri] *adj* straordinario
extrapolate [ɛks'træpə͵let] *tr & intr* estrapolare
extrasensory [͵ɛkstrə'sɛnsəri] *adj* extrasensoriale
extravagance [ɛks'trævəgəns] *s* prodigalità *f*; (*wildness, folly*) stravaganza
extravagant [ɛks'trævəgənt] *adj* prodigo; (*wild, foolish*) stravagante
extreme [ɛks'trim] *adj & s* estremo; **in the extreme** in massimo grado; **to go to extremes** andare agli estremi
extremely [ɛks'trimli] *adv* estremamente, in sommo grado
extreme' unc'tion *s* Estrema Unzione
extremist [ɛks'trimɪst] *adj & s* estremista *mf*
extremi-ty [ɛks'trɛmɪti] *s* (-ties) estremità *f*; (*great want*) estrema necessità; **extremities** estremi *mpl*; (*hands and feet*) estremità *fpl*
extricate ['ɛkstrɪ͵ket] *tr* districare
extrinsic [ɛks'trɪnsɪk] *adj* estrinseco
extrovert ['ɛkstrə͵vʌrt] *s* estroverso
extrude [ɛks'trud] *tr* estrudere || *intr* protrudere
exuberant [ɛg'zubərənt] *or* [ɛg'zjubərənt] *adj* esuberante
exude [ɛg'zud] *or* [ɛk'sud] *tr & intr* trasudare, stillare
exult [ɛg'zʌlt] *intr* esultare, tripudiare
exultant [ɛg'zʌltənt] *adj* esultante
eye [aɪ] *s* occhio; (*of hook and eye*) occhiello; **to catch one's eye** attirare l'attenzione di qlcu; **to feast one's eyes on** deliziarsi la vista con; **to lay eyes on** riuscire a vedere; **to make eyes at** fare gli occhi dolci a; **to roll one's eyes** stralunare gli occhi; **to see eye to eye** andare perfettamente d'accordo; **to shut one's eyes to** chiudere un occhio a; far finta di non vedere; **without batting an eye** senza batter ciglio || *v* (*pret & pp* eyed; *ger* eying *or* eyeing) *tr* occhieggiare; **to eye up and down** guardare da capo a piedi
eye'ball' *s* globo oculare
eye'bolt' *s* bullone *m* ad anello
eye'brow' *s* sopracciglio; **to raise one's eyebrows** inarcare le sopracciglia
eye'cup' *s* occhiera
eye'drop'per *s* contagocce *m*
eyeful ['aɪ͵ful] *s* vista, colpo d'occhio; (coll) bellezza
eye'glass' *s* (*of optical instrument*) lente *f*, oculare *m*; (*eyecup*) occhiera; **eyeglasses** occhiali *mpl*
eye'lash' *s* ciglio
eyelet ['aɪlɪt] *s* occhiello, maglietta, asola; (*hole to look through*) feritoia
eye'lid' *s* palpebra
eye' o'pener ['opənər] *s* affare *m* che apre gli occhi; (coll) bicchierino bevuto di mattina presto

eye'piece' s oculare m

eye'shade' s visiera

eye' shad'ow s rimmel m

eye'shot' s—**within eyeshot** a portata di vista

eye'sight' s vista; (range) capacità visiva

eye' sock'et s occhiaia, orbita

eye'sore' s pugno in un occhio

eye'strain' s vista affaticata

eye'-test chart' s tabella optometrica

eye'tooth' s (-teeth) dente canino; **to cut one's eyeteeth** (coll) fare esperienza; **to give one's eyeteeth for** (coll) dare un occhio della testa per

eye'wash' s (flattery) burro, lusinga; (pharm) collirio; (slang) balla

eye' wit'ness s testimone m oculare

F

F, f [ɛf] s sesta lettera dell'alfabeto inglese

fable ['febəl] s favola

fabric ['fæbrɪk] s stoffa, tessuto; fabbrica, struttura

fabricate ['fæbrɪ‚ket] tr fabbricare

fabrication [‚fæbrɪ'keʃən] s fabbricazione; falsificazione, invenzione

fabulous ['fæbjələs] adj favoloso

façade [fə'sɑd] s facciata

face [fes] s volto, viso, faccia; (surface) superficie f; (of coin) diritto; (of precious stone) faccetta; (of watch) mostra; (grimace) smorfia; (of building) facciata; (typ) occhio; **in the face of** di fronte a; **to have a long face** fare il muso lungo; **to keep a straight face** contenere le risa; **to show one's face** farsi vedere ‖ tr far fronte a, fronteggiare; (a wall) ricoprire; (a suit) foderare; **facing** di fronte a ‖ intr—**to face about** voltarsi, fare dietro front; **to face on** dare a; **to face up to** guardare in faccia

face' card' s figura

face' lift'ing s plastica facciale

face' pow'der s cipria

facet ['fæsɪt] s faccetta, (fig) faccia

facetious [fə'siʃəs] adj faceto

face' val'ue s valore m facciale

facial ['feʃəl] adj facciale ‖ s massaggio facciale

fa'cial tis'sue s velina detergente

facilitate [fə'sɪlɪ‚tet] tr facilitare

facili-ty [fə'sɪlɪti] s (-ties) facilità f; **facilities** (installations) attrezzature fpl; (for transportation) mezzi mpl; (services) servizi mpl

facing ['fesɪŋ] s rivestimento

facsimile [fæk'sɪmɪli] s facsimile m

fact [fækt] s fatto; **in fact** in realtà; **the fact is that** il fatto si è che

faction ['fækʃən] s fazione; discordia

factional ['fækʃənəl] adj fazioso; (partisan) partigiano

factionalism ['fækʃənə‚lɪzəm] s partigianeria; parzialità f

factor ['fæktər] s fattore m ‖ tr scomporre in fattori

facto-ry ['fæktəri] s (-ries) fabbrica

factual ['fæktʃʊəl] adj effettivo, reale

facul-ty ['fækəlti] s (-ties) facoltà f

fad [fæd] s moda passeggera

fade [fed] tr stingere ‖ intr (said of colors) stingersi, sbiadire; (said of

sounds, sight, radio signals, memory, etc.) svanire, affievolirsi; (said of beauty) sfiorire

fade'-out' s affievolimento, affievolirsi m; (mov) chiusura in dissolvenza; (rad, telv) evanescenza

fading ['fedɪŋ] s affievolimento; (mov) dissolvenza; (rad, telv) evanescenza

fag [fæg] s schiavo del lavoro; (coll) sigaretta ‖ tr—**to fag out** stancare

fagot ['fægət] s fascina, fastello

fail [fel] s—**without fail** senza meno ‖ tr mancare (with dat); (a student) riprovare; (an examination) farsi bocciare in ‖ intr fallire, venire a meno; (said of a student) farsi riprovare; (said of a motor) rompersi, fermarsi; (com) cadere in fallimento; **to fail to** mancare di

failure ['feljər] s insuccesso; insufficienza; (student) bocciato; (com) fallimento

faint [fent] adj debole; **to feel faint** sentirsi mancare ‖ s svenimento ‖ intr svenire

faint-hearted ['fent'hɑrtɪd] adj codardo, timido

fair [fer] adj giusto, onesto; (moderately large) discreto; (even) liscio; (civil) gentile; (hair) biondo; (complexion) chiaro; (sky, weather) sereno ‖ s (exhibition) fiera; (carnival) sagra ‖ adv direttamente; **to play fair** agire onestamente

fair'ground' s terreno dell'esposizione, campo della fiera

fairly ['ferli] adv giustamente, imparzialmente; discretamente, abbastanza; completamente

fair-minded ['fer'maɪndɪd] adj equanime, equo, giusto

fairness ['fernɪs] s giustizia, imparzialità f; bellezza; (of complexion) bianchezza

fair' play' s comportamento leale

fair' sex' s bel sesso

fair'-weath'er adj—**a fair-weather friend** un amico del tempo felice

fair-y ['feri] adj fatato ‖ s (-ies) fata; (slang) finocchio

fair'y god'mother s buona fata

fair'y-land' s terra delle fate

fair'y tale' s favola, racconto delle fate

faith [feθ] s fede f; **to break faith with** venir meno alla parola data a; **to keep faith with** tener fede alla parola data a; **to pin one's faith on** porre tutte le proprie speranze su; **upon my faith!** in fede mia!

faithful ['feθfəl] *adj* fedele || **the faithful** i fedeli

faithless ['feθlɪs] *adj* infedele, sleale

fake [fek] *adj* falso, finto || *s* contraffazione; (*person*) imbroglione *m* || *tr & intr* contraffare, falsificare

faker ['fekər] *s* (coll) imbroglione *m*

falcon ['fɔkən] or ['fɔlkən] *s* falcone *m*

falconer ['fɔkənər] or ['fɔlkənər] *s* falconiere *m*

falconry ['fɔkənri] or ['fɔlkənri] *s* falconeria

fall [fɔl] *adj* autunnale || *s* caduta; (*of water*) cataratta, cascata; (*of prices*) ribasso; (*autumn*) autunno; **falls** cataratta, cascate *fpl* || *v* (*pret* **fell** [fel]; *pp* **fallen** ['fɔlən*]) intr* cadere; discendere; **to fall apart** farsi a pezzi; **to fall back** (mil) ripiegare; **to fall behind** rimanere indietro; **to fall down** cadere; stramazzare; **to fall due** scadere; **to fall flat** stramazzare; essere un insuccesso; **to ·fall for** (slang) lasciarsi abbindolare da; (slang) innamorarsi di; **to fall in** (*said of a building*) crollare; (mil) allinearsi; **to fall in with** imbattersi in; mettersi d'accordo con; **to fall off** ritirarsi; diminuire; **to fall out** accadere; essere in disaccordo; (mil) rompere i ranghi; **to fall out of** cadere da; **to fall out with** inimicarsi con; **to fall over** cadere; (coll) adulare; **to fall through** fallire; **to fall to** cominciare; (coll) cominciare a mangiare; (*said, e.g., of an inheritance*) ricadere su; **to fall under** rientrare in

fallacious [fə'leʃəs] *adj* fallace

falla·cy ['fæləsi] *s* (-cies) fallacia

fall' guy' *s* (slang) testa di turco

fallible ['fælɪbəl] *adj* fallibile

fall'ing star' *s* stella cadente

fall'out' *s* pulviscolo radioattivo

fall'out shel'ter *s* rifugio antiatomico

fallow ['fælo] *adj* incolto; **to lie fallow** rimanere incolto || *s* maggese *m* || *tr* maggesare

false [fɔls] *adj* falso; (*hair, teeth, etc.*) posticcio, finto || *adv* falsamente; **to play false** tradire

false' bot'tom *s* doppio fondo

false' col'ors *spl* apparenze mentite

false' face' *s* maschera; (*ugly false face*) mascherone *m*

false'-heart'ed ['fɔls'hɑrtɪd] *adj* perfido

falsehood ['fɔls·hʊd] *s* falsità *f*, falso

false' pretens'es *spl* falso, impostura; **under false pretenses** allegando ragioni false

falset·to [fɔl'seto] *s* (-tos) (*voice*) falsetto; (*person*) cantante *m* in falsetto

falsi·fy ['fɔlsɪ·faɪ] *v* (*pret & pp* -**fied**) *tr* falsificare; (*to disprove*) smentire || *intr* mentire

falsi·ty ['fɔlsɪti] *s* (-ties) falsità *f*

falter ['fɔltər] *s* vàcillamento; (*in* speech*) balbettio || *intr* vacillare; balbettare

fame [fem] *s* fama

famed [femd] *adj* famoso

familiar [fə'mɪljər] *adj* familiare; intimo; **to be familiar with** (*people*) aver pratica con; (*things*) aver pratica di

familiari·ty [fə,mɪlɪ'ærɪti] *s* (-ties) familiarità *f*, dimestichezza

familiarize [fə'mɪljə,raɪz] *tr* far conoscere

fami·ly ['fæmɪli] *adj* familiare; **in the family way** (coll) in altro stato || *s* (-lies) famiglia

fam'ily man' *s* (men') padre *m* di famiglia

fam'ily name' *s* cognome *m*

fam'ily tree' *s* albero genealogico

famine ['fæmɪn] *s* carestia

famished ['fæmɪʃt] *adj* famelico; **to be famished** avere una fame da lupo

famous ['feməs] *adj* famoso; (coll) eccellente

fan [fæn] *s* ventaglio; (elec) ventilatore *m*; (coll) tifoso, patito || *v* (*pret & pp* **fanned**) *ger* **fanning** *tr* sventagliare; (*to winnow*) vagliare; (*fire, passions*) attizzare || *intr* sventagliarsi; **to fan out** (*said of a road*) diramarsi a ventaglio

fanatic [fə'nætɪk] *adj & s* fanatico

fanatical [fə'nætɪkəl] *adj* fanatico

fanaticism [fə'nætɪ,sɪzəm] *s* fanatismo

fan' belt' *s* (aut) cinghia del ventilatore

fancied ['fænsɪd] *adj* immaginario

fancier ['fænsɪər] *s* maniaco, tifoso; (*of animals*) conoscitore *m*, allevatore *m*

fanciful ['fænsɪfəl] *adj* fantasioso, estroso; immaginario

fan·cy ['fænsi] *adj* (-cier; -ciest) immaginario; immaginativo; ornamentale; di lusso; fantasioso, estroso || *s* fantasia; (*whim*) grillo, estro; **to take a fancy to** prendere una passione per || *v* (*pret & pp* -**cied**) *tr* immaginare

fan'cy ball' *s* ballo in costume

fan'cy dress' *s* costume *m*

fan'cy foods' *spl* cibi *mpl* di lusso

fan'cy-free' *adj* libero dai lacci dell'amore

fan'cy skat'ing *s* pattinaggio artistico

fan'cy-work' *s* (sew) ricamo ornamentale

fanfare ['fænfer] *s* fanfara

fang [fæŋ] *s* zanna; (*of reptile*) dente velenoso

fan'light' *s* lunetta

fantastic(al) [fæn'tæstɪk(əl)] *adj* fantastico

fanta·sy ['fæntəzi] or ['fæntəsi] *s* (-sies) fantasia

far [fɑr] *adj* distante; **on the far side of** dall'altra parte di || *adv* lontano; **as far as** fino a; **as far as I am concerned** per quanto mi riguardi; **as far as I know** per quanto io sappia; **by far** di gran lunga; **far and near** in lungo e in largo; **far away** molto lontano; **far be it from me** Dio me ne scampi e liberi; **far better** molto meglio; molto migliore; **far different** molto differente; **far from** lontano da; **far from it** tutto al contrario; **far into** fino al fondo di; **far into the night** fino a tarda ora; **far more** molto più; **far off** lontanissimo; **how far** quanto lontano; **how far is it?** a che distanza è da qui?; **in so far as** in quanto; **thus far** sinora; **to go far towards** contribuire molto a

faraway ['farə͵we] *adj* distante, lontano; distratto

farce [fɑrs] *s* farsa

farcical ['fɑrsɪkəl] *adj* farsesco

fare [fer] *s* prezzo della corsa; passeggero; (*food*) vitto || *intr* andare, e.g., **how did you fare?** come Le è andata?

Far' East' *s* Estremo Oriente

fare'well' *s* congedo, commiato; **to bid farewell to** or **to take farewell of** prender commiato da || *interj* addio!

far-fetched ['fɑr'fɛt/t] *adj* peregrino, campato in aria

far-flung ['fɑr'flʌŋ] *adj* ampio; d'ampia distribuzione

farm [fɑrm] *adj* agricolo || *s* fattoria, tenuta || *tr* (*land*) coltivare || *intr* fare l'agricoltore or l'allevatore

farmer ['fɑrmər] *s* agricoltore *m*, contadino

farm' hand' *s* bracciante *m*

farm'house' *s* casa colonica, masseria

farming ['fɑrmɪŋ] *s* agricoltura, coltivazione

farm'yard' *s* aia

far'-off' *adj* lontano

far-reaching ['fɑr'rit/ɪŋ] *adj* di grande portata

far-sighted ['fɑr'saɪtɪd] *adj* lungimirante; perspicace; presbite

farther ['fɑrðər] *adj* più lontano; addizionale || *adv* più lontano, più in là; inoltre; **farther on** più oltre

farthest ['fɑrðɪst] *adj* (il) più lontano; ultimo || *adv* al massimo

farthing ['fɑrðɪŋ] *s* (Brit) quarto di centesimo

Far' West' *s* (U.S.A.) lontano Occidente

fascinate ['fæsɪ͵net] *tr* affascinare

fascinating ['fæsɪ͵netɪŋ] *adj* incantatore, affascinante

fascism ['fæsɪzəm] *s* fascismo

fascist ['fæsɪst] *adj* & *s* fascista *mf*

fashion ['fæ/ən] *s* voga, moda; foggia, maniera; alta società; **after a fashion** in certo modo; **in fashion** di moda; **out of fashion** fuori moda; **to go out of fashion** passare di moda || *tr* fare, foggiare

fashionable ['fæ/ənəbəl] *adj* elegante, alla moda

fash'ion design'ing *s* alta moda

fash'ion plate' *s* figurino

fash'ion show' *s* sfilata di moda

fast [fæst] or [fɑst] *adj* veloce; (*clock*) che corre, in anticipo; dissoluto; ben legato; (*color*) solido; (*friend*) fedele || *s* digiuno; **to break fast** rompere il digiuno || *adv* rapidamente; fortemente; (*asleep*) profondamente; **to hold fast** tenersi saldo; **to live fast** condurre una vita dissoluta || *intr* digiunare, fare vigilia

fast' day' *s* giorno di magro

fasten ['fæsən] or ['fɑsən] *tr* fissare; attaccare; (*a door*) sbarrare; (*a nickname; blows*) affibbiare; (*a dress*) allacciare || *intr* attaccarsi

fastener ['fæsənər] or ['fɑsənər] *s* legaccio, laccio; (*snap, clasp*) fermaglio; (*for papers*) fermacarte *m*

fastidious [fæs'tɪdɪ·əs] *adj* schizzinoso; meticoloso

fasting ['fæstɪŋ] or ['fɑstɪŋ] *s* digiuno

fat [fæt] *adj* (**fatter; fattest**) grasso; (*productive*) forte, ricco, pingue; **to get fat** ingrassare || *s* grasso, unto; (*of pork*) sugna

fatal ['fetəl] *adj* fatale

fatalism ['fetə͵lɪzəm] *s* fatalismo

fatalist ['fetəlɪst] *s* fatalista *mf*

fatal·i·ty [fe'tælɪti] *s* (**-ties**) (*in an accident*) morte *f*; accidente *m* mortale; fatalità *f*

fate [fet] *s* fato; **the Fates** le Parche || *tr* predestinare

fated ['fetɪd] *adj* destinato

fateful ['fetfəl] *adj* fatidico, fatale

fat'head' *s* (coll) zuccone *m*

father ['fɑðər] *s* padre *m*; (*male ancestor*) antenato || *tr* procreare; creare; assumere la paternità di

fatherhood ['fɑðər͵hud] *s* paternità *f*

fa'ther-in-law' *s* (**fathers-in-law**) suocero

fa'ther-land' *s* patria

fatherless ['fɑðərlɪs] *adj* orfano di padre; senza padre

fatherly ['fɑðərli] *adj* paterno

Fa'ther's Day' *s* festa del papà

Fa'ther Time' *s* il Tempo

fathom ['fæðəm] *s* braccio || *tr* sondare

fathomless ['fæðəmlɪs] *adj* senza fondo; imponderabile

fatigue [fə'tig] *s* fatica, strapazzo; (mil) comandata || *tr* stancare, affaticare

fatigue' clothes' *spl* (mil) tenuta di servizio, tenuta di fatica

fatten ['fætən] *tr* & *intr* ingrassare

fat·ty ['fæti] *adj* (**-tier; -tiest**) grasso; (pathol) adiposo || *s* (**-ties**) (coll) tombolo

fatuous ['fæt/ʊ·əs] *adj* fatuo

faucet ['fɔsɪt] *s* rubinetto

fault [fɔlt] *s* (*misdeed, blame*) colpa; (*defect*) difetto, magagna; (geol) faglia; (sports) fallo; **it's your fault** è colpa Sua; **to a fault** all'eccesso; **to find fault with** trovare a ridire sul conto di

fault'find'er *s* ipercritico, criticone *m*

fault'find'ing *adj* criticone || *s* ipercritica

faultless ['fɔltlɪs] *adj* perfetto, inappuntabile

fault·y ['fɔlti] *adj* (**-ier; -iest**) manchevole, difettuoso

faun [fɔn] *s* fauno

fauna ['fɔnə] *s* fauna

favor ['fevər] *s* favore *m*; (*letter*) pregiata; **do me the favor to** mi faccia il piacere di; **by your favor** col Suo permesso; **favors** regali *mpl* di festa; **to be in favor with** essere nelle grazie di; **to be out of favor** cadere in disgrazia ‖ *tr* favorire; (coll) assomigliare (with *dat*)

favorable [ˈfevərəbəl] *adj* favorevole

favorite [ˈfevərɪt] *adj & s* favorito

favoritism [ˈfevərɪˌtɪzəm] *s* favoritismo

fawn [fɔn] *s* cerbiatto ‖ *intr*—**to fawn on** adulare, strusciarsi a

faze [fez] *tr* (coll) perturbare

fear [fɪr] *s* paura; **for fear of** per paura di; **for fear that** per paura che; **no fear** non c'è pericolo; **to be in fear of** aver timore di ‖ *tr & intr* temere

fearful [ˈfɪrfəl] *adj* pauroso, timorato; (coll) spaventoso

fearless [ˈfɪrlɪs] *adj* impavido

feasible [ˈfizɪbəl] *adj* fattibile, possibile

feast [fist] *s* festa; (*sumptuous meal*) festino, banchetto ‖ *tr* intrattenere ‖ *intr* banchettare; **to feast on** rallegrarsi alla vista di

feat [fit] *s* fatto, prodezza

feather [ˈfeðər] *s* penna; (*soft and fluffy structure covering bird*) piuma; (*type*) qualità *f*, conio; (*tuft*) pennacchio; **in fine feather** di buon umore; **in buona salute** ‖ *tr* impennare; coprire di piume; (naut) spalare; (aer) bandierare; **to feather one's nest** arricchirsi

feath′er bed′ *s* letto di piume

feath′er·bed′ding *s* impiego di mano d'opera non necessaria richiesto da un sindacato operaio

feath′er·brain′ *s* cervello di gallina

feath′er·edge′ *s* (*of board*) augnatura; (*of sharpened tool*) filo morto

feath′er·weight′ *s* peso piuma

feathery [ˈfeðəri] *adj* piumato; leggero

feature [ˈfitʃər] *s* fattezza; caratteristica; (journ) articolo principale; (mov) attrazione; **features** fattezze *fpl* ‖ *tr* caratterizzare; mettere in evidenza; (coll) immaginare

fea′ture film′ *s* lungometraggio

fea′ture sto′ry *s* articolo di spalla

February [ˈfɛbruˌɛri] *s* febbraio

feces [ˈfisɪz] *spl* feci *fpl*

feckless [ˈfɛklɪs] *adj* debole; inetto

federal [ˈfɛdərəl] *adj* federale ‖ *s* federalista *mf*

federate [ˈfɛdəˌret] *adj* federato ‖ *tr* federare ‖ *intr* federarsi

federation [ˌfɛdəˈreʃən] *s* federazione

federative [ˈfɛdəˌretɪv] or [ˈfɛdərətɪv] *adj* federativo

fedora [fɪˈdorə] *s* cappello floscio di feltro

fed′ up′ [fɛd] *adj* stanco e stufo; **to be fed up with** averne fin sopra gli occhi di

fee [fi] *s* onorario; (*charge allowed by law*) diritto; (*tip*) mancia; (*for tuition*) tassa; (*for admission*) ingresso ‖ *tr* pagare

feeble [ˈfibəl] *adj* debole, fievole

feeble-minded [ˈfibəlˈmaɪndɪd] *adj* rimbecillito; debole, vacillante

feed [fid] *s* mangime *m*; (coll) mangiata; (mach) dispositivo d'alimentazione ‖ *v* (*pret & pp* **fed** [fɛd]) *tr* nutrire; (*a machine*) alimentare; (*cattle*) pascere; (theat) imbeccare ‖ *intr* mangiare; **to feed upon** nutrirsi di

feed′back′ *s* (*of a computer*) ritorno d'informazioni; (electron) reazione

feed′ bag′ *s* musetta

feed′ pump′ *s* pompa di alimentazione

feed′ trough′ *s* (*for cattle*) vasca; (*for hogs*) trogolo

feed′ wire′ *s* cavo di alimentazione

feel [fil] *s* sensazione; (*touch*) tocco; (*vague mental impression*) senso ‖ *v* (*pret & pp* **felt** [fɛlt]) *tr* sentire; (*e.g., with the hands*) palpare, toccare; (*s.o.'s pulse*) tastare ‖ *intr* (*sick, tired, etc.*) sentirsi; **to feel bad** sentirsi male; (*to be unhappy*) essere spiacente; **to feel cheap** vergognarsi; **to feel comfortable** sentirsi a proprio agio; **to feel for** cercare di toccare; avere compassione per; **to feel like** aver voglia di; **to feel safe** sentirsi al sicuro; **to feel sorry** essere spiacente; pentirsi; **to feel sorry for** aver compassione di; pentirsi di

feeler [ˈfilər] *s* (*hint*) sondaggio; **feelers** (*of insect*) antenne *fpl*; (*of mollusk*) tentacoli *mpl*; **to put out feelers** (fig) tastare il terreno

feeling [ˈfilɪŋ] *s* (*with senses*) senso; (*impression, emotion*) sentimento, sensazione; opinione

feign [fen] *tr* fingere; inventare; imitare ‖ *intr* far finta; **to feign to be** fingersi

feint [fent] *s* finta ‖ *intr* fare una finta

feldspar [ˈfɛldˌspɑr] *s* feldspato

felicitate [fəˈlɪsɪˌtet] *tr* felicitarsi con

felicitous [fəˈlɪsɪtəs] *adj* felice, indovinato; eloquente

fell [fɛl] *adj* crudele, mortale ‖ *tr* (*trees*) abbattere

felloe [ˈfɛlo] *s* cerchione *m*; (*part of the rim*) gavello

fellow [ˈfɛlo] *s* compagno; collega *m*; (*of a society*) membro, socio; (*holder of fellowship*) borsista *mf*; (coll) tipo, tizio; (coll) innamorato; **good fellow** buon diavolo; galantuomo

fel′low cit′izen *s* concittadino

fel′low coun′try·man *s* (-men) concittadino

fel′low crea′ture *s* prossimo

fel′low-man′ *s* (-men′) prossimo

fel′low mem′ber *s* consocio

fellowship [ˈfɛloˌʃɪp] *s* compagnia; (*for study*) borsa di studio

fel′low trav′eler *s* simpatizzante *mf*; criptocomunista *mf*; compagno di viaggio

felon [ˈfɛlən] *s* criminale *mf*; (pathol) patereccio, giradito

felo·ny [ˈfɛləni] *s* (-nies) delitto doloso

felt [fɛlt] *s* feltro

felt′ board′ *s* lavagna di panno

felt′-tip pen′ *s* pennarello

female [ˈfimel] *adj* (*sex*) femminile;

(*animal, plant, piece of a device*) femmina || *s* femmina

feminine ['fɛmɪnɪn] *adj* & *s* femminile *m*

feminism ['fɛmɪ ,nɪzəm] *s* femminismo

fence [fɛns] *s* steccato, staccionata; (*for stolen goods*) ricettatore *m*; (*carp*) squadra di guida; (*sports*) scherma; **on the fence** (coll) indeciso || *tr* recingere || *intr* tirare di scherma

fencing ['fɛnsɪŋ] *s* scherma; (fig) schermaglia

fenc'ing mask' *s* visiera

fend [fɛnd] *tr*—**to fend off** parare || *intr*—**to fend for oneself** (coll) badare a sé stesso

fender ['fɛndər] *s* (*of trolley car*) salvagente *m*; (*of fireplace*) parafuoco; (aut) parafango; (naut) parabordo

fennel ['fɛnəl] *s* finocchio

ferment ['fʌrmɛnt] *s* fermento || [fər-'mɛnt] *tr* & *intr* fermentare

fern [fʌrn] *s* felce *f*

ferocious [fə'roʃəs] *adj* feroce

ferocity [fə'rɑsɪti] *s* ferocia

ferret ['fɛrɪt] *s* furetto || *tr*—**to ferret out** scovare || *intr* indagare

Fer'ris wheel' ['fɛrɪs] *s* ruota (del parco di divertimenti)

fer·ry ['fɛri] *s* (-ries) traghetto; nave *f* traghetto || *v* (*pret* & *pp* -ried) *tr* traghettare || *intr* attraversare

fer'ry·boat' *s* nave *f* traghetto, ferryboat *m*

fertile ['fʌrtɪl] *adj* fertile

fertilize ['fʌrtɪ ,laɪz] *tr* fertilizzare; (*to impregnate*) fecondare

fertilizer ['fʌrtɪ ,laɪzər] *s* fertilizzante *m*; (*e.g., of flowers*) fecondatore *m*

fervent ['fʌrvənt] *adj* fervente, fervido

fervid ['fʌrvɪd] *adj* fervido

fervor ['fʌrvər] *s* fervore *m*

fester ['fɛstər] *s* ulcera, piaga || *tr* corrompere || *intr* suppurare; (fig) corrompersi

festival ['fɛstɪvəl] *adj* festivo || *s* festa; (*of music*) festival *m*

festive ['fɛstɪv] *adj* festivo

festivi·ty [fɛs'tɪvɪti] *s* (-ties) festività *f*

festoon [fɛs'tun] *s* festone *m* || *tr* ornare di festoni

fetch [fɛtʃ] *tr* andare a prendere; (*a price*) fruttare, vendersi per

fetching ['fɛtʃɪŋ] *adj* (coll) cattivante, attraente

fete [fet] *s* festa || *tr* festeggiare

fetid ['fɛtɪd] *or* ['fitɪd] *adj* fetido

fetish ['fitɪ/] *or* ['fɛtɪ/] *s* feticcio

fetlock ['fɛtlɑk] *s* nocca; (*tuft of hair*) barbetta

fetter ['fɛtər] *s* ceppo, catena || *tr* mettere ai ceppi, incatenare

fettle ['fɛtəl] *s* stato, condizione; **in fine fettle** in buone condizioni

fetus ['fitəs] *s* feto

feud [fjud] *s* antagonismo; odio ereditario || *intr* essere in lotta

feudal ['fjudəl] *adj* feudale

feudalism ['fjudə ,lɪzəm] *s* feudalismo

fever ['fivər] *s* febbre *f*

feverish ['fivərɪ/] *adj* febbrile

few [fju] *adj* & *pron* pochi; **a few** alcuni; **quite a few** molti

fiancé [,fi·ɑn'se] *s* fidanzato

fiancée [,fi·ɑn'se] *s* fidanzata

fias·co [fɪ'æsko] *s* (-cos *or* -coes) fiasco

fib [fɪb] *s* menzogna, frottola || *v* (*pret* & *pp* fibbed; *ger* fibbing) *intr* raccontar frottole

fiber ['faɪbər] *s* fibra; (fig) tempra

fi'ber·glass' *s* vetroresina

fibrous ['faɪbrəs] *adj* fibroso

fickle ['fɪkəl] *adj* volubile, incostante, mobile

fiction ['fɪkʃən] *s* (*invention*) finzione; (*branch of literature*) novellistica

fictional ['fɪkʃənəl] *adj* immaginario

fictionalize ['fɪkʃənə ,laɪz] *tr* romanzare

fictitious [fɪk'tɪ/əs] *adj* fittizio

fiddle ['fɪdəl] *s* violino; **fit as a fiddle** in perfetta salute || *tr* (coll) suonare sul violino; **to fiddle away** (coll) sprecare || *intr* (coll) suonare il violino; **to fiddle with** (coll) giocherellare con

fiddler ['fɪdlər] *s* (coll) violinista *mf*

fiddling ['fɪdlɪŋ] *adj* triviale, futile, insignificante

fideli·ty [faɪ'dɛlɪti] *or* [fɪ'dɛlɪti] *s* (-ties) fedeltà *f*

fidget ['fɪdʒɪt] *intr* agitarsi; **to fidget with** giocherellare con

fidgety ['fɪdʒɪti] *adj* irrequieto

fiduciar·y [fɪ'dju/ɪ ,ɛri] *or* [fɪ'du/ɪ ,ɛri] *adj* fiduciario || *s* (-ies) fiduciario

fie [faɪ] *interj* vergogna!

fief [fif] *s* feudo

field [fild] *adj* (mil) da campagna || *s* campo; (sports) terreno; (min) giacimento; (*of motor or dynamo*) (elec) induttore *m*; (phys) campo

fielder ['fildər] *s* (*outfielder*) giocatore *m* del campo esterno

field' glass'es *spl* binocolo

field' hock'ey *s* hockey *m* su prato

field' mag'net *s* induttore *m*, calamita induttrice

field' mar'shal *s* (mil) maresciallo di campo

field' mouse' *s* topo di campagna

field'piece' *s* pezzo da campagna

fiend [find] *s* diavolo; (coll) addetto, tifoso

fiendish ['findɪ/] *adj* diabolico

fierce [fɪrs] *adj* fiero, feroce; (*wind*) furioso; (coll) maledetto

fierceness ['fɪrsnɪs] *s* ferocia

fier·y ['faɪri] *or* ['faɪ·əri] *adj* (-ier; -iest) ardente, focoso

fife [faɪf] *s* piffero

fifteen ['fɪf'tin] *adj*, *s* & *pron* quindici *m*

fifteenth ['fɪf'tinθ] *adj*, *s* & *pron* quindicesimo || *s* (*in dates*) quindici *m*

fifth [fɪfθ] *adj*, *s* & *pron* quinto || *s* (*in dates*) cinque *m*

fifth' col'umn *s* quinta colonna

fiftieth ['fɪftɪ·ɪθ] *adj*, *s* & *pron* cinquantesimo

fif·ty ['fɪfti] *adj* & *pron* cinquanta || *s* (-ties) cinquanta *m*; **the fifties** gli anni cinquanta

fif′ty-fif′ty *adv*—**to go fifty-fifty** fare a metà

fig [fɪg] *s* fico

fight [faɪt] *s* lotta; baruffa; combattimento; spirito combattivo; (sports) incontro; **to pick a fight with** attaccar briga con ‖ *v* (*pret* & *pp* **fought** [fɔt]) *tr* lottare con; combattere contro; opporsi a ‖ *intr* lottare; combattere; **to fight shy of** cercar di evitare

fighter [′faɪtər] *s* lottatore *m*; (*warrior*) combattente *m*; (aer) caccia *m*

fig′ leaf′ *s* foglia di fico

figment [′fɪgmənt] *s* finzione

figurative [′fɪgjərətɪv] *adj* (fa) figurativo; (rhet) figurato

figure [′fɪgjər] *s* figura; numero; prezzo; **to be good at figures** far bene di conto; **to cut a figure** fare una buona figura; **to keep one's figure** conservare la linea ‖ *tr* figurare; immaginare; raffigurare; supporre; calcolare; **to figure out** calcolare; decifrare ‖ *intr* apparire; **to figure on** (coll) contare su

fig′ure·head′ *s* uomo di paglia, prestanome *m*; (naut) polena

fig′ure of speech′ *s* figura retorica

fig′ure skat′ing *s* pattinaggio artistico

figurine [ˌfɪgjə′rin] *s* figurina

filament [′fɪləmənt] *s* filamento

filbert [′fɪlbərt] *s* (*tree*) nocciolo, avellano; (*nut*) nocciola, avellana

filch [fɪltʃ] *tr* rubacchiare

file [faɪl] *s* (*row*) fila; (*tool*) lima; (*folder*) filza; (*room*) archivio; (*of cards*) schedario ‖ *tr* mettere in fila; limare; archiviare, schedare; (journ) trasmettere ‖ *intr* sfilare; **to file for** fare domanda di

file′ clerk′ *s* schedarista *mf*

filet [fɪ′le] *or* [′fɪle] *s* filetto ‖ *tr* tagliare in filetti

filial [′fɪlɪ·əl] *or* [′fɪljəl] *adj* filiale

filiation [ˌfɪlɪ′eʃən] *s* filiazione

filibuster [′fɪlɪˌbʌstər] *s* (*tactics*) ostruzionismo; (*speech*) discorso ostruzionista; (*person making such a speech*) ostruzionista *mf*; (*buccaneer*) filibustiere *m* ‖ *tr* fare ostruzionismo contro ‖ *intr* fare dell'ostruzionismo

filigree [′fɪlɪ ˌgri] *adj* filigranato ‖ *s* filigrana ‖ *tr* lavorare in filigrana

filing [′faɪlɪŋ] *s* (*of documents*) schedatura; limatura; **filings** limatura

fil′ing cab′inet *s* schedario

fil′ing card′ *s* cartellino, scheda

fill [fɪl] *s* sazietà *f*; (*place filled with earth*) terrapieno; **to have or get one's fill** mangiare a sazietà ‖ *tr* riempire; (*an order*) eseguire; (*a hole*) otturare; (*a tooth*) piombare; (*a tire*) gonfiare; (*a place*) occupare; (*with sand*) interrare; **to fill out** (*a form*) riempire; **to fill up** (aut) fare il pieno di ‖ *intr* riempirsi; **to fill in** prendere il posto; **to fill up** riempirsi

filler [′fɪlər] *s* ripieno; (*person*) riempitore *m*; (painting) mestica; (journ) articolo riempitivo

fillet [′fɪlɪt] *s* nastro, fascia; (*for hair*) nastro; (archit) listello ‖ *tr* filettare

‖ [′fɪle] *or* [′fɪlɪt] *s* (*of meat or fish*) filetto ‖ *tr* tagliare a filetti

filling [′fɪlɪŋ] *s* (*of a tooth*) impiombatura; (*of turkey*) ripieno

fill′ing sta′tion *s* stazione di rifornimento

fillip [′fɪlɪp] *s* stimolo; colpetto col dito ‖ *tr* dare un colpetto col dito a; (fig) stimulare

fil·ly [′fɪli] *s* (**-lies**) puledra

film [fɪlm] *s* pellicola; (mov, phot) pellicola, film *m* ‖ *tr* filmare

film′ li′brary *s* cineteca, filmoteca

film′strip′ *s* filmina

film·y [′fɪlmi] *adj* (**-ier**; **-iest**) sottile, delicato; (*look*) annebbiato

filter [′fɪltər] *s* filtro ‖ *tr* & *intr* filtrare

filtering [′fɪltərɪŋ] *s* filtrazione

fil′ter pa′per *s* carta da filtro

fil′ter tip′ *s* filtro, bocchino filtro

filth [fɪlθ] *s* sporco, sporcizia

filth·y [′fɪlθi] *adj* (**-ier**; **-iest**) sporco, sudicio

filth′y lu′cre [′lukər] *s* il vile metallo

filtrate [′fɪltret] *s* liquido filtrato ‖ *tr* & *intr* filtrare

fin [fɪn] *s* pinna; (slang) biglietto da cinque dollari

final [′faɪnəl] *adj* finale; (*last in a series*) ultimo; definitivo, insindacabile ‖ *s* esame *m* finale; **finals** (sports) finale *f*

finale [fɪ′nɑli] *s* (mus) finale *m*

finalist [′faɪnəlɪst] *s* finalista *mf*

finally [′faɪnəli] *adv* finalmente

finance [fɪ′næns] *or* [′faɪnæns] *s* finanza; **finances** finanze *fpl* ‖ *tr* finanziare

financial [fɪ′næn/əl] *or* [faɪ′næn/əl] *adj* finanziario

financier [ˌfɪnən′sɪr] *or* [ˌfaɪnən′sɪr] *s* finanziere *m*

financing [fɪ′nænsɪŋ] *or* [′faɪnænsɪŋ] *s* finanziamento

finch [fɪntʃ] *s* fringuello

find [faɪnd] *s* trovata ‖ *v* (*pret* & *pp* **found** [faʊnd]) *tr* trovare; rinvenire; (*s.o. innocent or guilty*) dichiarare; **to find out** venire a sapere ‖ *intr* (law) sentenziare; **to find out about** informarsi su

finder [′faɪndər] *s* (phot) mirino; (astr) cannochiale cercatore

finding [′faɪndɪŋ] *s* scoperta; (law) sentenza

fine [faɪn] *adj* buono; bello; fino, fine ‖ *s* multa ‖ *adv* (coll) benissimo; **to feel fine** (coll) sentirsi benissimo ‖ *tr* multare

fine′ arts′ *spl* belle arti

fineness [′faɪnnɪs] *s* finezza; (*of metal*) titolo

fine′ print′ *s* testo in caratteri minuti

finer·y [′faɪnəri] *s* (**-ies**) ornamenti *mpl*, fronzoli *mpl*; abito vistoso

fine-spun [′faɪn ˌspʌn] *adj* sottile

finesse [fɪ′nɛs] *s* finezza; (bridge) impasse *f* ‖ *tr* fare l'impasse a ‖ *intr* fare l'impasse

fine′-tooth comb′ *s* pettine fitto; **to go over with a fine-tooth comb** esaminare minuziosamente

finger [ˈfɪŋgər] s dito; **to have a finger in the pie** avere le mani in pasta; **to put one's finger on the spot** mettere il dito nella piaga; **to slip between the fingers** sfuggire di tra le dita; **to snap one's fingers at** infischiarsi di; **to twist around one's little finger** fare ciò che si vuole di || *tr* toccare con le dita; (*to pilfer*) rubacchiare; (slang) mostrare a dito

fin'ger board' s (mus) tastiera

fin'ger bowl' s sciacquadita m

fingering [ˈfɪŋgərɪŋ] s palpeggiamento; (mus) diteggiatura

fin'ger mark' s ditata

fin'ger-nail' s unghia

fin'ger-print' s impronta digitale || *tr* prendere le impronte digitali di

fin'ger-tip' s polpastrello; **to have at one's fingertips** avere sulla punta delle dita, sapere a menadito

finical [ˈfɪnɪkəl] or **finicky** [ˈfɪnɪki] *adj* pignolo, schizzinoso

finish [ˈfɪnɪʃ] s fine *f*; finitura; (sports) finale *m* || *tr* finire; **to finish off** distruggere || *intr* finire; **to finish + *ger*** finire di + *inf*; **to finish by + *ger*** finire per + *inf*

fin'ishing school' s scuola di perfezionamento per signorine

fin'ishing touch' s ultimo tocco

finite [ˈfaɪnaɪt] *adj* finito

Finland [ˈfɪnlənd] s la Finlandia

Finlander [ˈfɪnləndər] s finlandese *mf*

Finn [fɪn] s (*member of a Finnish-speaking group of people*) finnico; (*native or inhabitant of Finland*) finlandese *mf*

Finnic [ˈfɪnɪk] *adj & s* finnico

Finnish [ˈfɪnɪʃ] *adj* finlandese || s (*language*) finlandese *m*

fir [fʌr] s abete *m*

fire [faɪr] s fuoco; (*destructive burning*) incendio; **to be on fire** ardere; **to be under enemy fire** essere sotto tiro nemico; **to catch fire** infiammarsi; **to hang fire** essere in sospeso; **to open fire** aprire il fuoco; **to set on fire, to set fire to** dar fuoco a; **under fire** sotto fuoco nemico; accusato || *tr* accendere; (*an oven*) scaldare; (*bricks*) cuocere; (*a weapon*) sparare; (*the imagination*) riscaldare; (*an employee*) (coll) licenziare || *intr* accendersi; **to fire on** far fuoco su; **to fire up** attivare una caldaia

fire' alarm' s avvisatore *m* d'incendio

fire'arm' s arma da fuoco

fire'ball' s palla da cannone esplosiva; (*lightning*) lampo a forma di globo infocato; meteorite *m* a forma di globo infocato

fire'boat' s lancia dei pompieri

fire'box' s (*of a boiler*) fornello; (*to give alarm*) stazione d'allarme

fire'brand' s tizzone *m*; (fig) fiaccola della discordia

fire'brick' s mattone refrattario

fire' brigade' s corpo di pompieri volontari

fire'bug' s (coll) incendiario

fire' com'pany s corpo dei pompieri; compagnia d'assicurazioni contro gli incendi

fire'crack'er s mortaretto

fire'damp' s grisou *m*

fire' depart'ment s corpo dei pompieri

fire'dog' s alare *m*

fire' drill' s esercitazione in caso d'incendio

fire' en'gine s autopompa

fire' escape' s scala di sicurezza

fire' extin'guisher s estintore *m*

fire'fly' s (-flies) lucciola

fire'guard' s parafuoco

fire' hose' s manichetta

fire'house' s caserma dei pompieri

fire' hy'drant s bocca d'incendi

fire' insur'ance s assicurazione contro gli incendi

fire' i'rons spl arnesi mpl del camino

fire'man s (-men) (*man who extinguishes fires*) pompiere *m*, vigile *m* del fuoco; (*stoker*) fochista *m*

fire'place' s camino

fire'plug' s bocca da incendio, idrante *m*

fire'proof' *adj* incombustibile || *tr* rendere incombustibile

fire' sale' s vendita di merce avariata dal fuoco

fire' screen' s parafuoco

fire' ship' s brulotto

fire'side' s focolare *m*

fire'trap' s edificio senza mezzi adeguati per combattere incendi

fire' wall' s paratia antincendio

fire'wa'ter s (coll) acquavite *f*

fire'wood' s legna

fire'works' spl fuochi mpl artificiali

firing [ˈfaɪrɪŋ] s (*of furnace*) alimentazione; (*of bricks*) cottura; (*of a gun*) sparo; (*of soldiers*) tiro; (*of an internal-combustion engine*) accensione; (*of an employee*) (coll) licenziamento

fir'ing line' s linea del fuoco

fir'ing or'der s (aut) ordine *m* d'accensione

fir'ing pin' s percussore *m*

fir'ing squad' s (*for saluting at a burial*) plotone *m* d'onore; (*for executing*) plotone *m* d'esecuzione

firm [fʌrm] *adj* forte, fermo || s ditta, compagnia

firmament [ˈfʌrməmənt] s firmamento

firm' name' s ragione *f* sociale

firmness [ˈfʌrmnɪs] s fermezza

first [fʌrst] *adj* primo || s primo; (aut) prima; (mus) voce *f* principale; **at first** sulle prime; **from the first** da bel principio || *adv* prima; **first of all** per prima cosa

first' aid' s pronto soccorso

first'-aid' kit' s cassetta farmaceutica d'urgenza

first'-aid' sta'tion s posto di pronto soccorso

first'-born' *adj & s* primogenito

first'-class' *adj* di prim'ordine, sopraffino || *adv* in prima classe

first' cous'in s cugino primo

first'-day cov'er s busta primo giorno

first' draft' s brutta copia

first' fin'ger s dito indice
first' floor' s pianoterra m
first' fruits' spl primizie fpl
first' lieuten'ant s tenente m
firstly ['fʌrstli] adv in primo luogo
first' mate' s (naut) primo ufficiale, comandante m in seconda, secondo
first' name' s nome m. di battesimo
first' night' s (theat) prima
first' of'ficer s (naut) primo ufficiale, comandante m in seconda, secondo
first'-rate' adj di prima forza; eccellente || adv (coll) benissimo
first'-run' adj di prima visione
fiscal ['fɪskəl] adj (pertaining to public treasury) fiscale; finanziario || s avvocato fiscale
fis'cal year' s esercizio finanziario ·
fish [fɪʃ] s pesce m; to be like a fish out of water essere come un pesce fuor d'acqua; to be neither fish nor fowl non essere né carne né pesce; to drink like a fish bere come una spugna || tr pescare || intr pescare; to fish for compliments cercare di farsi dei complimenti; to go fishing andare alla pesca; to take fishing portare con sé alla pesca
fish'bone' s lisca, spina di pesce
fish'bowl' s vaschetta per i pesci rossi
fisher ['fɪʃər] s pescatore m; (zool) martora comune
fish'er·man s (-men) pescatore m; (boat) peschereccio
fisher·y ['fɪʃəri] s (-ies) (activity) pesca; (business) pescheria; (grounds) riserva di pesca, luogo dove si pesca
fish' glue' s colla di pesce
fish'hook' s amo
fishing ['fɪʃɪ] adj da pesca || s pesca
fish'ing reel' s mulinello
fish'ing rod's canna da pesca
fish'ing tack'le s attrezzatura da pesca
fish'line' s lenza
fish' mar'ket s pescheria
fish'pool' s peschiera
fish' spear' s fiocina
fish' sto'ry s (coll) fandonia; to tell fish stories sparare grosse
fish'tail' s (aut) imbardata (aer) spedalata || intr (aut) imbardare; (aer) compiere una spedalata
fish'wife' s (-wives') pescivendola; (foul-mouthed woman) ciana
fish'worm' s lombrico
fish·y ['fɪʃi] adj (-ier; -iest) che sa di pesce; (coll) dubbioso, inverosimile
fission ['fɪʃən] s (biol) scissione; (phys) fissione
fissionable ['fɪʃənəbəl] adj fissionabile
fissure ['fɪʃər] s fenditura; (in rock) crepaccio
fist [fɪst] s pugno; (typ) indice m; to shake one's fist at mostrare i pugni a
fist'fight' s scontro a pugni
fist'ful' s pugno, manciata
fisticuff ['fɪstɪ͵kʌf] s pugno; fisticuffs scontro a pugni
fit [fɪt] adj (fitter; fittest) indicato; idoneo, adatto; in buona salute; fit to be tied (coll) infuriato, arrabbia-

tissimo; fit to eat mangiabile; to feel fit sentirsi in buona salute; to see fit giudicare conveniente || s equipaggiamento; (of a suit) taglio; (of one piece with another) incastro; (of coughing) accesso; (of anger) attacco; by fits and starts a pezzi e a bocconi || v (pret & pp fitted) ger fitting) tr adattare; quadrare a; andar bene a; equipaggiare; preparare; servire a; esser d'accordo con; to fit out or up attrezzare, equipaggiare || intr stare; incastrare; (said of clothes) cascare; entrare; to fit in entrarci
fitful ['fɪtfəl] adj capriccioso; incostante, irregolare
fitness ['fɪtnɪs] s convenienza; idoneità f; buona salute
fitter ['fɪtər] s aggiustatore m; (of machinery) montatore m; (of clothing) sarto che mette in prova
fitting ['fɪtɪ] adj appropriato, adatto, conveniente || s adattamento; (of a garment) prova; tubo adattabile; (carp) incastro; fittings accessori mpl; utensili mpl; (iron trimmings) ferramenta fpl
five [faɪv] adj & pron cinque || s cinque m; five o' clock le cinque
five' hun'dred adj & pron cinquecento
five'-year plan' s piano quinquennale
fix [fɪks] s—in a tight fix (coll) nei pasticci; to be in a fix (coll) star fresco, essere nei guai || tr riparare; fissare; (a meal) preparare; (a bayonet) inastare; (attention) attrarre, fermare; (hair) mettere a posto; (coll) arrangiare || intr fissarsi, stabilirsi; to fix on scegliere
fixed [fɪkst] adj fisso; (time) improrogabile; (coll) arrangiato
fixing ['fɪksɪ] adj fissativo || s (fastening) attacco; (phot) fissaggio; with all the fixings (coll) con tutti i contorni
fix'ing bath' s bagno di fissaggio
fixture ['fɪkstʃər] s infisso; accessorio; (of a lamp) guarnizione; fixtures (e.g., of a store) suppellettili fpl
fizz [fɪz] s effervescenza; gazosa; (Brit) spumante m || intr frizzare
fizzle ['fɪzəl] s (coll) fiasco || intr crepitare; (coll) fare fiasco
flabbergast ['flæbər͵gæst] tr (coll) sbalordire, lasciare stupefatto
flab·by ['flæbi] adj (-bier; -biest) floscio, flaccido, cascante
flag [flæg] s bandiera || v (pret & pp flagged; ger flagging) tr imbandierare; segnalare; (rr) far fermare || intr ammosciarsi, afflosciarsi
flageolet [͵flædʒə'lɛt] s flautino
flag'man s (-men) (rr) manovratore m
flag' of truce' s bandiera parlamentare
flag'pole' s pennone m
flagrant ['flegrənt] adj flagrante; scandaloso
flag'ship' s nave ammiraglia
flag'staff' s pennone m
flag' sta'tion s (rr) stazione facoltativa
flag'stone' s lastra di pietra

flag′ stop′ s (rr) fermata facoltativa

flail [flel] s correggiato ‖ tr battere col correggiato; battere

flair [fler] s fiuto, istinto

flak [flæk] s fuoco antiaereo

flake [flek] s falda; (of snow) fiocco, falda; (of cereal) fiocco; ‖ tr sfaldare; (fish) scagliare ‖ intr sfaldarsi

flak·y [′fleki] adj (-ier; -iest) a falde, faldoso

flamboyant [flæm′bɔɪ·ənt] adj sgargiante; (archit) fiammeggiante

flame [flem] s fiamma ‖ tr & intr fiammeggiare

flamethrower [′flem‚θro·ər] s lanciafiamme m

flaming [′flemɪŋ] adj fiammeggiante; appassionato; (culin) alla fiamma

flamin·go [flə′mɪŋgo] s (-gos or -goes) fenicottero, fiammingo

flammable [′flæməbəl] adj infiammabile

Flanders [′flændərz] s le Fiandre

flange [flændʒ] s (e.g., on a pipe) flangia; (on 1 beam) bordo; (of a wheel) cerchione m

flank [flæŋk] s fianco ‖ tr fiancheggiare

flannel [′flænəl] s flanella

flap [flæp] s (in clothing) falda; (of hat) tesa; (of book) risvolto; (of pocket) patta; (of shoe) linguetta; (blow) colpo; (of a table) pannello; (of the counter in a store) ribalta; (of wings) alata ‖ v (pret & pp flapped; ger flapping) tr battere, sbattere; (to move violently) sbatacchiare ‖ intr penzolare

flare [fler] s vampa; scintillio; (of a dress) svasatura; (mil) fuoco di segnalazione; flares (trousers) calzoni mpl a zampe d'elefante ‖ tr svasare ‖ intr scintillare; (said of a garment) scampanare; **to flare up** divampare; (said of an illness) aggravarsi, infiammarsi

flare′-up′ s vampa, fiammata; (of an illness) recrudescenza; scoppio d'ira, accesso di collera

flash [flæʃ] s (of light) sprazzo; (of lightning) lampo, baleno; (of hope) raggio; (of joy) accesso; (journ, phot) flash m; (fig) lampo; **flash in the pan** fuoco di paglia ‖ tr (powder) accendere; (a sword) brandire; (journ) diffondere; (e.g., money) (coll) ostentare ‖ intr lampeggiare, balenare, folgorare; **to flash by** passare come un lampo

flash′back′ s flashback m

flash′ bulb′ s lampada lampo

flash′ cube′ s cuboflash m

flash′ flood′ s inondazione torrenziale

flashing [′flæʃɪŋ] s metallo per coprire la conversa; commessura metallica fra tetto e comignolo

flash′light′ s lampadina tascabile; (of a lighthouse) luce f intermittente; (phot) fotolampo, lampeggiatore m

flash′light bulb′ s lampada per fotolampo

flash·y [′flæʃi] adj (-ier; -iest) sgargiante, chiassoso, vistoso

flask [flæsk] or [flɑsk] s fiasco, fiasca; (for laboratory use) beuta

flat [flæt] adj (flatter; flattest) piano; (nose) camuso; (boat) a fondo piatto; (surface) liscio; (beer) svanito; (tire) sgonfio; (denial) deciso; (mus) bemolle; (coll) al verde ‖ s (flat surface) piatto; (flat area) piano; (apartment) appartamento; (mus) bemolle m; (coll) gomma a terra ‖ adv—**to fall flat** fallire

flat′boat′ s chiatta

flat′car′ s (rr) pianale m

flat-footed [′flæt‚fʊtɪd] adj dai piedi piatti; (coll) inflessibile

flat′head′ s (of a bolt) testa piatta; (coll) testa di legno

flat′i′ron s ferro da stiro

flat′ race′ s corsa piana

flatten [′flætən] tr schiacciare; distendere ‖ intr appiattirsi; indebolirsi; **to flatten out** appiattirsi; (aer) porsi in linea orizzontale di volo

flatter [′flætər] tr adulare, lusingare; (to make seem more attractive) favorire ‖ intr adulare

flatterer [′flætərər] s adulatore m, lusingatore m

flattering [′flætərɪŋ] adj lusinghiero

flatter·y [′flætəri] s (-ies) lusinga

flat′ tire′ s gomma a terra

flat′top′ s portaerei f

flatulence [′flætʃələns] s flatulenza

flat′ware′ s argenteria, vasellame m

flaunt [flɔnt] or [flɑnt] tr sfoggiare, ostentare

flautist [′flɔtɪst] s flautista mf

flavor [′flevər] s sapore m, gusto; condimento ‖ tr insaporire; condire; aromatizzare; profumare

flavoring [′flevərɪŋ] s condimento, sapore m

flaw [flɔ] s difetto, menda, fallo; (crack) incrinatura

flawless [′flɔlɪs] adj senza difetti

flax [flæks] s lino

flaxen [′flæksən] adj di lino; biondo

flax′seed′ s linosa

flay [fle] tr scorticare, scoiare

flea [fli] s pulce f

flea′bite′ s morso di pulce; (fig) inezia, seccatura secondaria

fleck [flek] s macchia; efelide f ‖ tr chiazzare, macchiare

fledgling [′fledʒlɪŋ] s uccellino appena nato; (fig) pivello

flee [fli] v (pret & pp fled [fled]) tr & intr fuggire, sfuggire

fleece [flis] s vello; (e.g., of clouds) bioccolo ‖ tr tosare; (fig) pelare

fleec·y [′flisi] adj (-ier; -iest) lanoso; (sky) a pecorelle

fleet [flit] adj rapido ‖ s flotta

fleeting [′flitɪŋ] adj fugace, passeggero

Fleming [′flemɪŋ] s fiammingo

Flemish [′flemɪʃ] adj & s fiammingo

flesh [fleʃ] s carne f; (of fruit) polpa; **in the flesh** in carne ed ossa; **to lose flesh** dimagrire; **to put on flesh** ingrassare

flesh′ and blood′ s (relatives) carne f della carne, i miei, i suoi, etc.; il corpo umano

flesh-colored ['fleʃ‚kʌlərd] *adj* color carne

fleshiness ['fleʃɪnɪs] *s* carnosità *f*

fleshless ['fleʃlɪs] *adj* scarno

flesh'pot' *s* piatto di carne; locale *m* di dissoluzione; **fleshpots** vita dissoluta

flesh' wound' *s* ferita superficiale

flesh·y ['fleʃi] *adj* (-ier; -iest) carnoso; polposo

flex [flɛks] *tr* piegare ‖ *intr* piegarsi

flexible ['flɛksɪbəl] *adj* flessibile; (*joint*) a snodo

flick [flɪk] *s* schiocco; (slang) pellicola cinematografica ‖ *tr* schioccare

flicker ['flɪkər] *s* fiamma tremolante; (*of eyelids*) battito; (*of hope*) bagliore *m* ‖ *intr* tremolare; vacillare

flier ['flaɪ·ər] *s* aviatore *m;* (*venture*) (coll) impresa rischiosa; (coll) foglio volante

flight [flaɪt] *s* fuga; (*of an airplane*) volo; (*of birds*) stormo; (*of stairs*) rampa; (*of fancy*) slancio; **to put to flight** mettere in fuga; **to take flight** prendere la fuga

flight' deck' *s* ponte *m* di volo

flight·y ['flaɪti] *adj* (-ier; -iest) frivolo; volubile

flim-flam ['flɪm‚flæm] *s* (coll) imbroglio, truffa ‖ *v* (*pret & pp* -flammed; *ger* -flamming) *tr* (coll) imbrogliare, truffare

flim·sy ['flɪmzi] *adj* (-sier; -siest) leggero; (*material*) di scarsa consistenza; (*excuse*) inconsistente

flinch [flɪntʃ] *intr* indietreggiare; **without flinching** senza scomporsi

fling [flɪŋ] *s* tiro; ballo scozzese; **to go on a fling** darsi alla pazza gioia; **to have a fling at** tentare di fare; **to have one's fling** correre la cavallina ‖ *v* (*pret & pp* flung [flʌŋ]) *tr* sbattere, scagliare; (*e.g., in jail*) schiaffare; **to fling open** spalancare; **to fling shut** chiudere improvvisamente

flint [flɪnt] *s* selce *f*, pietra focaia

flint'lock' *s* fucile *m* a pietra focaia

flint·y ['flɪnti] *adj* (-ier; -iest) pietroso; (*unmerciful*) spietato; duro come un macigno

flip [flɪp] *adj* (flipper; flippest) impertinente ‖ *s* buffetto; salto mortale ‖ *v* (*pret & pp* flipped; *ger* flipping) *tr* sbattere in aria; muovere d'un tratto **to flip a coin** giocare a testa e croce; **to flip shut** (*e.g., a fan*) chiudere improvvisamente

flippancy ['flɪpənsi] *s* leggerezza

flippant ['flɪpənt] *adj* scanzonato, leggero

flirt [flʌrt] *s* (*woman*) civetta; (*man*) vagheggino ‖ *intr* (*said of a woman*) civettare; (*said of a man*) fare il damerino; **to flirt with** flirtare con; (*an idea*) accarezzare; (*death*) giocare con

flit [flɪt] *v* (*pret & pp* flitted; *ger* flitting) *intr* svolazzare, volteggiare; passare rapidamente, volare

flitch [flɪtʃ] *s* fetta di pancetta

float [flot] *s* (*raft*) galleggiante *m;* (*of mason*) cazzuola; carro allegorico ‖ *tr* far galleggiare; (*a business*) lan-

ciare; (*stocks, bonds*) emettere ‖ *intr* galleggiare, tenersi a galla

floating ['flotɪŋ] *adj* galleggiante

flock [flak] *s* (*of birds*) stormo; (*of sheep*) gregge *m;* (*of people*) stuolo; (*of wool*) fiocco; (fig) mucchio ‖ *intr* affollarsi, riunirsi, radunarsi

floe [flo] *s* tavola di ghiaccio

flog [flag] *v* (*pret & pp* flogged; *ger* flogging) *tr* battere, fustigare

flood [flʌd] *s* (*caused by rain*) diluvio; (*sudden rise of river*) piena, fiumana; (*of tide*) flusso ‖ *tr* inondare; (aut) ingolfare ‖ *intr* straripare; (aut) ingolfarsi ‖ **the Flood** il diluvio universale

flood'gate' *s* (*of a canal*) chiusa; (*of a dam*) saracinesca

flood'light' *s* riflettore *m*

flood' tide' *s* flusso

floor [flor] *s* (*inside bottom surface of room*) pavimento; (*story of building*) piano; (*of the sea, a swimming pool, etc.*) fondo; (*of the exchange*) recinto delle grida; (*of an assembly hall*) emiciclo; (naut) madiere *m;* **to ask for the floor** chiedere la parola; **to have the floor** avere la parola; **to take the floor** prendere la parola ‖ *tr* pavimentare; abbattere, gettare al suolo; (coll) confondere; (coll) vincere

flooring ['florɪŋ] *s* palco, impiantito

floor' mop' *s* redazza

floor' plan' *s* pianta

floor' show' *s* spettacolo di caffè concerto

floor'walk'er *s* direttore *m* di sezione

floor' wax' *s* cera da pavimenti

flop [flap] *s* (coll) fiasco ‖ *v* (*pret & pp* flopped; *ger* flopping) *tr* lasciar cadere; sbattere ‖ *intr* lasciarsi cadere; (coll) fare fiasco; **to flop over** (*to change sides*) cambiare casacca

flora ['florə] *s* flora

floral ['florəl] *adj* floreale

Florence ['flɔrəns] *or* ['flɑrəns] *s* Firenze *f*

Florentine ['flɔrən‚tin] *or* ['flɑrən‚tin] *adj & s* fiorentino

florescence [flo'rɛsəns] *s* inflorescenza

florid ['flɔrɪd] *or* ['flɑrɪd] *adj* florido

florist ['flɔrɪst] *s* fiorista *mf*, fioraio

floss [flɔs] *or* [flɑs] *s* lanugine *f;* (*of corn*) barba

floss·y ['flɔsi] *or* ['flɑsi] *adj* (-ier; -iest) serico; (*downy*) lanuginoso; (coll) vistoso

flotsam ['flɑtsəm] *s* relitti gettati a mare

flot'sam and jet'sam *s* relitti *mpl* di naufragio; (*trifles*) cianfrusaglie *fpl;* gentaglia, vagabondi *mpl*

flounce [flaʊns] *s* balza, falda, falpalà *m* ‖ *tr* ornare di falpalà ‖ *intr*—**to flounce out** andarsene irosamente

flounder ['flaʊndər] *s* (ichth) passera ‖ *intr* dibattersi

flour [flaʊr] *adj* farinoso ‖ *s* farina ‖ *tr* infarinare

flourish ['flʌrɪʃ] *s* (*with the sword*) mulinello; (*with the pen*) ghirigoro; (*as part of signature*) svolazzo; (mus) fioritura || *tr* (*one's sword*) roteare || *intr* rifiorire, prosperare

flourishing ['flʌrɪʃɪŋ] *adj* prosperoso

flour' mill' *s* mulino per grano

floury ['flauri] *adj* farinoso; infarinato

flout [flaut] *tr* burlarsi di || *intr* burlare, motteggiare

flow [flo] *s* flusso; (*of a river*) regime *m* || *intr* fluire; (*said of tide*) montare; (*said of hair in the air*) ondeggiare; **to flow into** gettarsi in, sfociare in; **to flow over** traboccare; **to flow with** abbondare di

flower ['flau-ər] *s* fiore *m* || *tr* infiorare || *intr* fiorire

flow'er bed' *s* aiola fiorita

flow'er gar'den *s* giardino

flow'er girl' *s* fioraia; (*at a wedding*) damigella d'onore

flow'er-pot' *s* vaso da fiori

flow'er shop' *s* negozio di fiori

flow'er show' *s* esposizione di fiori

flow'er-stand' *s* portafiori *m*

flowery ['flau-əri] *adj* fiorito

flowing ['flo-ɪŋ] *adj* (*water*) corrente; (*language*) scorrevole; (*e.g., hair*) fluente; (*e.g., lines of a dress*) filante

flu [flu] *s* influenza

fluctuate ['flʌktʃu‚et] *intr* fluttuare, ondeggiare; (*said of prices*) oscillare

flue [flu] *s* gola, fumaiolo

fluency ['flu-ənsi] *s* facilità *f* di parola

fluent ['flu-ənt] *adj* (*speaker*) facondo; (*style*) fluido

fluently ['flu-əntli] *adv* correntemente

fluff [flʌf] *s* lanugine *f*; vaporosità *f*; (*of an actor*) papera || *tr* sprimacciare || *intr* sprimacciarsi; (*coll*) impaperarsi

fluff·y ['flʌfi] *adj* (-ier; -iest) lanuginoso; vaporoso

fluid ['flu-ɪd] *adj* & *s* fluido

flu'id drive' *s* trasmissione idraulica

fluidity [flu'ɪdɪti] *s* fluidità *f*

fluke [fluk] *s* (*of anchor*) marra, dente *m*; (*in billiards*) colpo fortunato; (ichth) passera

flume [flum] *s* gora; condotta forzata

flunk [flʌŋk] *s* (coll) bocciatura || *tr* (coll) bocciare; (*a course*) (coll) farsi bocciare in || *intr* (coll) fare fiasco; **to flunk out** (coll) farsi bocciare

flunk·y ['flʌŋki] *s* (-ies) valletto; parassita *m*

fluor ['flu-ər] *s* fluorite *f*

fluorescence [‚flu-ə'resəns] *s* fluorescenza

fluorescent [‚flu-ə'resənt] *adj* fluorescente

fluoridation [‚flu-ərɪ'deʃən] *s* fluorizzazione

fluoride ['flu-ə‚raɪd] *s* fluoruro

fluorine ['flu-ə‚rin] *s* fluoro

fluoroscope ['flu-ərə‚skop] *s* schermo fluorescente

fluorspar ['flu-er‚spɑr] *s* spatofluore *m*

flur·ry ['flʌri] *s* (-ries) agitazione; (*of wind*) raffica; (*of rain*) acquazzone *m*; (*of snow*) turbine *m* || *v* (pret & pp -ried) *tr* agitare

flush [flʌʃ] *s* livellato; contiguo; pro-

spero, ben provvisto; abbondante; vigoroso; (*full to overflowing*) rigurgitante; arrossito; **flush with** allo stesso livello che || *s* (*of water*) flusso improvviso; (*in the cheeks*) caldana, scalmana; (*of spring*) germogliare *m*; (*of joy*) ebbrezza; (*of youth*) rigoglio; (*in poker*) colore *m* || *adv* rasente, raso || *tr* (*to cause to blush*) far arrossire; lavare con un getto d'acqua; (*e.g., a rabbit*) snidare || *intr* essere accaldato; (*to blush*) arrossire; (*to gush*) zampillare

flush' tank' *s* sciacquone *m*

flush' toi'let *s* gabinetto a sciacquone

fluster ['flʌstər] *s* nervosismo, eccitazione || *tr* innervosire, eccitare

flute [flut] *s* (*of a column*) scanalatura; (mus) flauto || *tr* scanalare

flutist ['flutɪst] *s* flautista *mf*

flutter ['flʌtər] *s* svolazzo; agitazione; sensazione || *intr* frullare; svolazzare; agitarsi; (*said of the heart*) palpitare; (*said of the heartbeat*) essere irregolare

flux [flʌks] *s* (*flow*) flusso; (*for fusing metals*) fondente *m*

fly [flaɪ] *s* (flies) mosca; (*of trousers*) finta; (*for fishing*) mosca artificiale || *v* (pret flew [flu]; pp flown [flon]) *tr* (*an airplane*) pilotare, far volare; trasportare a volo; (*e.g., an ocean*) trasvolare; (*a flag*) battere || *intr* volare; fuggire, scappare; (*said of a flag*) ondeggiare; **to fly away** involarsi; **to fly into a rage** andare in eccessi; **to fly off** volare via; scappare; **to fly over** trasvolare; **to fly shut** chiudersi improvvisamente

fly'blow' *s* uovo di mosca

fly'-by-night' *adj* poco raccomandabile; di breve durata

fly'catch'er *s* (orn) pigliamosche *m*

flyer ['flaɪ-ər] *s* var of flier

fly'fish' *intr* pescare con le mosche artificiali

flying ['flaɪ-ɪŋ] *adj* volante; rapido; in fuga; (*start*) lanciato || *s* volo

fly'ing boat' *s* idrovolante *m* a scafo centrale

fly'ing but'tress *s* contrafforte *m*

fly'ing col'ors *spl* successo; **with flying colors** a bandiere spiegate

fly'ing field' *s* campo d'aviazione

fly'ing sau'cer *s* disco volante

fly'ing sick'ness *s* male *m* d'aria

fly'ing squad' *s* squadra mobile

fly'ing time' *s* ore *fpl* di volo

fly'leaf' *s* (-leaves') (bb) guardia

fly' net' *s* (*for a bed*) moschettiera; (*for a horse*) scacciamosche *m*

fly'pa'per *s* carta moschicida

fly'speck' *s* macchia di mosca; macchiolina

fly' swat'ter ['swɑtər] *s* scacciamosche *m*

fly'trap' *s* pigliamosche *m*

fly'wheel' *s* volano

foal [fol] *s* puledro || *intr* (*said of a mare*) figliare

foam [fom] *s* schiuma || *intr* schiumare

foam' rub'ber *s* gommapiuma

foam·y [ˈfomi] *adj* (**-ier; -iest**) spumoso, schiumeggiante

fob [fab] *s* taschino per l'orologio; (*chain*) catenina per l'orologio || *v* (*pret & pp* **fobbed;** *ger* **fobbing**) *tr—* **to fob off s.th on s.o.** rifilare qlco a qlcu

f.o.b. or **F.O.B.** [ˌefˌoˈbi] *adv* (letterword) (**free on board**) franco

focal [ˈfokəl] *adj* focale

fo·cus [ˈfokəs] *s* (**-cuses** or **-ci** [saɪ]) fuoco; (*of a disease*) focolaio || *v* (*pret & pp* **-cused** or **-cussed**) *ger* **-cusing** or **-cussing**) *tr* mettere a fuoco; (*attention*) concentrare || *intr* convergere

fodder [ˈfadər] *s* foraggio

foe [fo] *s* nemico

fog [fɑɡ] or [fɔɡ] *s* nebbia; (*phot*) velo || *v* (*pret & pp* **fogged**) *ger* **fogging**) *tr* annebbiare; (*phot*) velare || *intr* annebbiarsi; (*phot*) velarsi

fog′ bank′ *s* banco di nebbia

fog′bound′ *adj* avvolto nella nebbia

fog·gy [ˈfɑɡi] or [ˈfɔɡi] *adj* (**-gier; -giest**) annebbiato; nebbioso; (*idea*) vago; (*phot*) velato; **it is foggy** fa nebbia

fog′horn′ *s* sirena da nebbia

foible [ˈfɔɪbəl] *s* debolezza, debole *m*

foil [fɔɪl] *s* (*thin sheet of metal*) foglia; (*of mirror*) argentatura; contrasto, risalto; (*sword*) fioretto || *tr* sventare; (*a mirror*) argentare

foist [fɔɪst] *tr—* **to foist s.th on s.o.** rifilare qlco a qlcu

fold [fold] *s* piega; drappeggio; (*for sheep*) ovile *m*; (*of sheep; of the faithful*) gregge *m*; (*geol*) corrugamento || *tr* piegare; (*the arms*) incrociare; **to fold up** ripiegare || *intr* piegarsi; **to fold up** (coll) fare fallimento

folder [ˈfoldər] *s* (*pamphlet*) pieghevole *m*; (*cover*) portacarte *m*

folding [ˈfoldɪŋ] *adj* pieghevole

fold′ing cam′era *s* macchina fotografica a soffietto

fold′ing chair′ *s* sedia pieghevole

fold′ing cot′ *s* branda

fold′ing door′ *s* porta a libro

fold′ing seat′ *s* strapuntino

foliage [ˈfolɪ·ɪdʒ] *s* fogliame *m*

foli·o [ˈfolɪˌo] *adj* in-folio || *s* (**-os**) foglio; (*book*) in-folio || *tr* numerare

folk [fok] *adj* popolare || *s* (**folk** or **folks**) gente *f*; **your folks** i Suoi

folk′lore′ *s* folclore *m*

folk′ mu′sic *s* musica folcloristica

folk′ song′ *s* canzone *f* tradizionale

folk·sy [ˈfoksi] *adj* (**-sier; -siest**) socievole; alla buona, alla mano

folk′ways′ *spl* costumi *mpl* tradizionali

follicle [ˈfalɪkəl] *s* follicolo

follow [ˈfalo] *tr* seguire; (*to keep up with*) interessarsi di; **to follow suit** seguire l'esempio; (*cards*) rispondere al colore || *intr* seguire; derivare; **as follows** come segue; **it follows** ne risulta

follower [ˈfalo·ər] *s* seguace *m*; discepolo; partigiano

following [ˈfalo·ɪŋ] *adj* susseguente || *s* seguito; aderenti *mpl*

fol′low-up′ *adj* susseguente; ricordativo; da continuarsi || *s* prosecuzione; lettera ricordativa

fol·ly [ˈfali] *s* (**-lies**) follia; **follies** rivista di varietà

foment [foˈmɛnt] *tr* fomentare

fond [fand] *adj* appassionato; (*of food*) ghiotto; **to become fond of** appassionarsi di

fondle [ˈfandəl] *tr* accarezzare, vezzeggiare

fondness [ˈfandnɪs] *s* tenerezza; passione

font [fant] *s* acquasantiera, pila; fonte *f* battesimale; (typ) fondita

food [fud] *adj* alimentare || *s* cibo, vitto; (*for animals*) mangiare *m*; **food for thought** materia di che pensare

food′ store′ *s* negozio di commestibili

food′stuffs′ *spl* commestibili *mpl*

fool [ful] *s* scemo, sciocco; (*jester*) buffone *m*; (*person imposed on*) vittima, zimbello; **to make a fool of** beffarsi di; **to play the fool** fare lo stupido || *tr* infinocchiare, ingannare; **to fool away** sprecare || *intr* giocare, fare per gioco; **to fool around** perdere il proprio tempo; **to fool with** giocherellare con

fooler·y [ˈfuləri] *s* (**-ies**) pazzia, buffonata

fool′har′dy *adj* (**-dier; -diest**) temerario

fooling [ˈfulɪŋ] *s* scherzo; **no fooling** senza scherzi, parlando sul serio

foolish [ˈfulɪʃ] *adj* sciocco; matto

fool′proof′ *adj* a tutta prova; infallibile

fools′cap′ *s* berretto a sonagli; carta formato protocollo

fool′s′ er′rand *s* impresa inutile

fool′s′ par′adise *s* felicità immaginaria

foot [fut] *s* (**feet** [fit]) piede *m*; (*of an animal*) zampa; (*of horse*) zoccolo; **to drag one's feet** procedere a passo di lumaca; **to put one's best foot forward** fare del proprio meglio; **to put one's foot down** farsi valere, imporsi; **to put one's foot in it** (coll) fare una topica; **to stand on one's own two feet** agire indipendentemente; **to tread under foot** calcare || *tr* (*the bill*) pagare; **to foot it** andare a piedi; ballare

footage [ˈfutɪdʒ] *s* distanza or lunghezza in piedi; (*of film measured in meters*) metraggio

foot′-and-mouth′ disease′ *s* (vet) afta epizootica

foot′ball′ *s* (*ball*) pallone *m*; (*game*) pallovale *f*; (*soccer*) calcio, football *m*

foot′board′ *s* (*support for foot*) predellino; (*of bed*) spalliera

foot′ brake′ *s* freno a pedale

foot′bridge′ *s* passerella, ponte riservato ai pedoni

foot′fall′ *s* passo

foot′hill′ *s* collina ai piedi di una montagna

foot'hold' s stabilità f; **to gain a foot-hold** prender piede

footing ['futɪŋ] s piede m, e.g., **he lost his footing** perse piede; **on a friendly footing** in relazioni amichevoli; **on an equal footing** su un piede di parità; **on a war footing** su un piede di guerra

foot'lights' spl luci fpl della ribalta; (fig) ribalta, scena

foot'loose' adj completamente libero

foot'man s (**-men**) staffiere m

foot'mark' s orma

foot'note' s rimando, rinvio

foot'path' s sentiero

foot'print' s orma, pesta

foot' race' s corsa podistica

foot'rest' s pedana

foot' rule' s regolo di un piede

foot' soldier' s fante m, fantaccino

foot'sore' adj coi piedi stanchi

foot'step' s passo; **to follow in the footsteps of** seguire le orme di

foot'stone' s pietra tombale a piè di un sepolcro; (archit) pietra di sostegno

foot'stool' s sgabello

foot' warm'er s scaldino

foot'wear' s calzature fpl

foot'work' s allenamento delle gambe; (fig) manovra delicata

foot'worn' adj (road) battuto; (person) spedato

foozle ['fuzəl] s schiappinata || tr & intr mancare completamente

fop [fap] s bellimbusto, gagà m

for [fɔr] prep per; malgrado, e.g., **for all his wealth** malgrado tutta la sua ricchezza; come, e.g., **he uses his house for an office** adopera la casa come ufficio; di, e.g., **time for bed** ora di andare a letto; da, e.g., **he has been here for three days** è qui da tre giorni; per amor di; **to go for a walk** andare a fare una passeggiata || conj perchè, poichè

forage ['farɪdʒ] or ['fɔrɪdʒ] adj foraggero || s foraggio || tr foraggiare || intr andare in cerca di foraggio

foray ['fore] or ['fare] s razzia, scorreria || intr razziare

for·bear [fɔr'bɛr] v (pret -**bore** ['bor]; pp -**borne** ['born]) tr astenersi da || intr essere longanime

forbearance [fɔr'bɛrəns] s longanimità f, tolleranza; astensione

for·bid [fɔr'bɪd] v (pret -**bade** ['bæd] or -**bad** ['bæd]; pp -**bidden** ['bɪdən]; ger -**bidding**) tr proibire, vietare || intr—**God forbid!** Dío ci scampi!

forbidding [fɔr'bɪdɪŋ] adj severo, sinistro

force [fɔrs] s forza; (staff of workers) forza, personale m; (phys) forza; **by force of** a forza di; **by main force** con tutte le sue forze; **in force** vigente; in gran numero; **to join forces** allearsi || tr forzare; obbligare; **to force back** respingere; **to force open** forzare; **to force s.th on s.o.** obbligare qlcu a accettare qlco

forced [fɔrst] adj forzato; studiato

forced' air' s aria sotto pressione

forced' draft' s tiraggio forzato

forced' land'ing s atterraggio forzato

forced' march' s marcia forzata

forceful ['fɔrsfəl] adj vigoroso, energico

for·ceps ['fɔrsəps] s (**-ceps** or -**cipes** [sɪ‚piz]) (dent, surg) pinze fpl; (obstet) forcipe m

force' pump' s pompa premente

forcible ['fɔrsɪbəl] adj impetuoso, energico; efficace

ford [fɔrd] s guado || tr guadare

fore [fɔr] adj davanti; (naut) prodiero || s davanti m; (naut) prua; **to the fore** alla ribalta; d'attualità || adv prima; (naut) a proravia || interj attenzione!

fore' and aft' adv a poppa e a prua

fore'arm' s avambraccio || **fore·arm'** tr premunire; prevenire

fore'bears' spl antenati mpl

forebode [fɔr'bod] tr (to portend) preannunziare; (to have a presentiment of) presentire

foreboding [fɔr'bodɪŋ] s preannunzio; presentimento

fore'cast' s pronostico || v (pret & pp -**cast** or -**casted**) tr pronosticare

forecastle ['foksəl], ['fɔr‚kæsəl] or ['fɔr‚kasəl] s castello, pozzetto

fore·close' tr escludere, precludere; (a mortgage) (law) precludere il riscatto di

fore·doom' tr condannare all'insuccesso

fore' edge' s (bb) taglio

fore'fa'ther s antenato

fore'fin'ger s dito indice

fore'front' s—**in the forefront** all'avanguardia

fore·go' v (pret -**went**; pp -**gone'**) tr & intr precedere

fore·go'ing adj precedente, anteriore

fore'gone' conclu'sion s conclusione inevitabile; decisione già scontata

fore'ground' s primo piano

forehanded ['fɔr‚hændɪd] adj previdente; (thrifty) risparmiatore

forehead ['farɪd] or ['fɔrɪd] s fronte f

foreign ['farɪn] or ['fɔrɪn] adj straniero; (product; affairs) estero; **foreign to** estraneo a

for'eign affairs' spl affari esteri

for'eign-born' adj nato all'estero

foreigner ['farɪnər] or ['fɔrɪnər] s straniero, forestiero

for'eign exchange' s divise fpl; (money) valuta

for'eign min'ister s ministro degli affari esteri

for'eign of'fice s ministero degli affari esteri

for'eign serv'ice s servizio diplomatico e consolare; (Brit) servizio militare in paesi d'oltremare

fore'leg' s zampa anteriore

fore'lock' s ciuffo sulla fronte; **to take time by the forelock** acchiappare l'occasione

fore'man s (**-men**) sorvegliante m, capomastro; presidente m dei giurati

foremast ['formast], ['fɔr‚mæst] or ['fɔr‚mast] s trinchetto

foremost ['fɔr‚most] adj primo, principale, più importante

fore·noon' *adj* mattinale ‖ *s* mattina

fore'part' *s* parte *f* anteriore; prima parte

fore'paw' *s* zampa anteriore

fore'quar'ter *s* quarto anteriore

fore'run'ner *s* precursore *m*, predecessore *m*, foriero

fore·sail ['fɔrsəl] or ['fɔr‚sel] *s* trinchetto

fore·see' *v* (*pret* -saw'; *pp* -seen') *tr* prevedere

foreseeable [for'si·əbəl] *adj* prevedibile

fore·shad'ow *tr* presagire

fore·short'en *tr* scorciare

fore'sight' *s* (*prudence*) previdenza; (*foreknowledge*) previsione

fore'sight'ed *adj* previdente

fore'skin' *s* prepuzio

forest ['fɑrɪst] or ['fɔrɪst] *adj* forestale ‖ *s* foresta, bosco

fore·stall' *tr* prevenire; anticipare; (*to buy up*) accapparrare

for'est rang'er ['rendʒər] *s* guardaboschi *m*, guardia forestale

forestry ['fɑrɪstrɪ] or ['fɔrɪstrɪ] *s* selvicoltura

fore'taste' *s* pregustazione ‖ *tr* pregustare

fore·tell' *v* (*pret & pp* -told') *tr* predire, presagire, preannunziare

fore'thought' *s* premeditazione; previdenza

forever [for'ɛvər] *adv* per sempre; continuamente

fore·warn' *tr* prevenire, preavvertire

fore'word' *s* avvertenza, prefazione

forfeit ['fɔrfɪt] *adj* perduto ‖ *s* perdita, confisca; multa; (*article deposited*) pegno; **forfeits** (*game*) pegni *mpl* ‖ *tr* decadere da

forfeiture ['fɔrfɪt/ər] *s* perdita di un pegno

forgather [for'gæðər] *intr* riunirsi; incontrarsi

forge [fɔrdʒ] *s* fucina, forgia ‖ *tr* forgiare; (*a lie*) inventare; (*e.g., handwriting*) falsificare ‖ *intr* forgiare; commettere un falso; **to forge ahead** farsi strada

forger·y ['fɔrdʒərɪ] *s* (-ies) falsificazione, falso, contraffazione

for·get [for'gɛt] *v* (*pret* -got ['gɑt]; *pp* -got or -gotten ['gɑtən]) *tr* dimenticare; **forget it!** non si preoccupi!; **to forget oneself** venir meno alla propria dignità; **to forget to** passare di mente a (qlcu) di, *e.g.,* **he forgot to turn off the lights** gli è passato di mente di spegnere la luce

forgetful [for'gɛtfəl] *adj* (*apt to forget*) smemorato; (*neglectful*) dimentico, immemore

forgetfulness [for'gɛtfəlnɪs] *s* (*inability to recall*) smemorataggine *f*; (*neglectfulness*) dimenticanza

for·get'-me-not' *s* nontiscordardimé *m*

forgivable [for'gɪvəbəl] *adj* perdonabile

for·give [for'gɪv] *v* (*pret* -gave'; *pp* -giv'en) *tr* perdonare

forgiveness [for'gɪvnɪs] *s* perdono

forgiving [for'gɪvɪŋ] *adj* clemente

for·go [for'go] *v* (*pret* -went; *pp* -gone) *tr* rinunciare (*with dat*)

fork [fɔrk] *s* (*pitchfork*) forca, forcone *m*; (*of a bicycle*) forcella; (*for eating*) forchetta; (*of a tree or road*) biforcazione, diramazione ‖ *tr* muovere col forcone; inforcare; **to fork out** (*slang*) cacciar fuori ‖ *intr* biforcarsi, diramarsi

forked [fɔrkt] *adj* biforcuto

fork'-lift truck' *s* carrello elevatore a forca

forlorn [for'lɔrn] *adj* abbandonato; disperato; miserabile

forlorn' hope' *s* impresa disperata

form [fɔrm] *s* forma; (*paper to be filled out*) formulario; (*construction to give shape to cement*) cassaforma ‖ *tr* formare ‖ *intr* formarsi

formal ['fɔrməl] *adj* formale; di gala, da sera, da etichetta

for'mal attire' *s* vestito da cerimonia

for'mal call' *s* visita di prammatica

formali·ty [for'mælɪtɪ] *s* (-ties) formalità *f*; (*excessive adherence to rules*) formalismo

for'mal par'ty *s* ricevimento di gala

for'mal speech' *s* discorso ufficiale

format ['fɔrmæt] *s* formato

formation [for'me/ən] *s* formazione

former ['fɔrmər] *adj* (*preceding*) anteriore; (*long past*) passato, antico; (*having once been*) già, ex; (*of two*) primo; **the former** quello

formerly ['fɔrmərlɪ] *adv* già, prima, in tempi passati

form'fit'ting *adj* aderente al corpo

formidable ['fɔrmɪdəbəl] *adj* formidabile

formless ['fɔrmlɪs] *adj* informe

form' let'ter *s* lettera a formulario, stampato

formu·la ['fɔrmjələ] *s* (-las or -lae [‚li]) formula

formulate ['fɔrmjə‚let] *tr* formulare

for·sake [for'sek] *v* (*pret* -sook ['suk]; *pp* -saken ['sekən]) *tr* abbandonare

fort [fɔrt] *s* forte *m*, fortezza

forte [fɔrt] *s* forte *m*

forth [forθ] *adv* avanti; **and so forth** e così via; **from this day forth** da oggi in poi; **to go forth** uscire

forth'com'ing *adj* prossimo; immediatamente disponibile

forth'right' *adj* diretto ‖ *adv* direttamente; senza ambagi; immediatamente

forth'with' *adv* immediatamente

fortieth ['fɔrtɪ·ɪθ] *adj, s & pron* quarantesimo

fortification [‚fɔrtɪfɪ'ke/ən] *s* fortificazione

forti·fy ['fɔrtɪ‚faɪ] *v* (*pret & pp* -fied) *tr* fortificare; aumentare il livello alcolico di

fortitude ['fɔrtɪ‚tjud] or ['fɔrtɪ‚tud] *s* fortezza, fermezza

fortnight ['fɔrtnaɪt] or ['fɔrtnɪt] *s* quindicina, due settimane

fortress ['fɔrtrɪs] *s* fortezza, forte *m*

fortuitous [for'tju·ɪtəs] or [for'tu·ɪtəs] *adj* fortuito, occasionale

fortunate ['fɔrt/ənɪt] *adj* fortunato

fortune ['fɔrt/ən] *s* fortuna; **to make a fortune** farsi un patrimonio; **to tell**

s.o. his fortune leggere il futuro a qlcu

for'tune hunt'er s cacciatore m di dote

for'tune·tel'ler s indovino, cartomante mf

for·ty ['fɔrti] adj & pron quaranta || s (-ties) quaranta m; the forties gli anni quaranta

fo·rum ['forəm] s (-rums or -ra [rə]) foro

forward ['fɔrwərd] adj avanzato; precoce; impertinente || s (soccer) avanti m || adv avanti; to bring forward mettere in luce; riportare; to come forward avanzare; to look forward to anticipare il piacere di || tr inoltrare, trasmettere; promuovere

fossil ['fɑsɪl] adj & s fossile m

foster ['fɔstər] or ['fɑstər] adj adottivo; di latte || tr allevare; promuovere

fos'ter home' s famiglia adottiva

foul [faul] adj sporco; (air) viziato; (wind) contrario; (weather; breath) cattivo; (baseball) fuori linea di gioco || s (of boats) urto, collisione; (baseball) palla colpita fuori linea di gioco; (boxing) colpo basso; (sports) fallo || adv slealmente; (baseball) fuori linea di gioco; to fall foul of entrare in collisione con; urtarsi con; to run foul of avere una controversia con || tr sporcare; otturare; (baseball) colpire fuori linea di gioco || intr (said of two boats) entrare in collisione; (said, e.g., of a rope) imbrogliarsi

foul-mouthed ['faul'mauðd] or ['faul-'mauθt] adj sboccato, osceno

foul' play' s reato; (sports) gioco sleale

found [faund] tr fondare; (to melt, to cast) fondere

foundation [faun'defən] s fondazione; (endowment) dotazione; (charitable) patronato; (masonry support) platea, fondamenta fpl; (make-up) fondo tinta; (fig) fondatezza

founder ['faundər] s fondatore m; (of family) capostipite m; (of metals) fonditore m || intr (said of a ship) affondare; (said of a horse) azzopparsi; (to fail) fare fiasco

foundling ['faundlɪŋ] s trovatello

found'ling hos'pital s brefotrofio

found·ry ['faundrɪ] s (-ries) fonderia

found'ry·man s (-men) fonditore m

fount [faunt] s fonte f

fountain ['fauntən] s fonte f, fontana; (of knowledge) pozzo

foun'tain·head' s sorgente f

foun'tain pen' s penna stilografica

foun'tain syringe' s clistere m a pera

four [for] adj & pron quattro || s quattro; four o'clock le quattro; on all fours gattoni, carponi

four'-cy'cle adj a quattro tempi

four'-cyl'inder adj a quattro cilindri

four'-flush' intr (coll) millantarsi

fourflusher ['for,flʌʃər] s (coll) millantatore m

four-footed ['for'futɪd] adj quadrupede

four' hun'dred adj, s & pron quattrocento || the Four Hundred l'alta società

four'-in-hand' s cravatta a cappio; tiro a quattro

four'-lane' adj a quattro corsie

four'-leaf clo'ver s quadrifoglio

four-legged ['for'legɪd] or ['for'legd] adj a quattro zampe; (schooner) (coll) a quattro alberi

four'-letter word' s parolaccia di quattro lettere

four'-mo'tor plane' s quadrimotore m

four'-o'clock' s (bot) bella di notte

four' of a kind' s (cards) poker m

four'post'er s letto a baldacchino

four'score' adj ottanta

foursome ['forsəm] s gruppo di quattro giocatori

fourteen ['for'tin] adj, s & pron quattordici m

fourteenth ['for'tinθ] adj, s & pron quattordicesimo || s (in dates) quattordici m

fourth [forθ] adj, s & pron quarto || s (in dates) quattro

fourth' estate' s quarto potere

four'-way' adj a quattro orifizi; fra quattro persone; quadruplice

fowl [faul] s pollo || intr uccellare

fowl'ing piece' s fucile m da caccia

fox [fɑks] s volpe f || tr (coll) ingannare

fox'glove' s digitale f

fox'hole' s buca ricovero

fox'hound' s segugio

fox' hunt' s caccia alla volpe

fox' ter'rier s fox-terrier m

fox'-trot' s (of a horse) piccolo trotto; (dance) fox-trot m

fox·y ['fɑksi] adj (-ier; -iest) volpino, astuto

foyer ['fɔɪ·ər] s (of a private house) ingresso, vestibolo; (theat) ridotto

fracas ['frekəs] s lite f, tumulto

fraction ['frækʃən] s frazione; frammento

fractional ['frækʃənəl] adj frazionario; insignificante

fractious ['frækʃəs] adj litigioso, permaloso; indisciplinato

fracture ['fræktʃər] s frattura || tr fratturare; (e.g., an arm) fratturarsi, rompersi || intr fratturarsi

fragile ['frædʒɪl] adj fragile

fragment ['frægmənt] s frammento; (e.g., of a movie) spezzone m || tr frammentare, spezzare

fragmenta'tion bomb' [,frægmən'te-ʃən] s bomba dirompente

fragrant ['fregrənt] adj fragrante

frail [frel] adj (not robust) gracile; (easily broken) fragile; (morally weak) debole || s canestro di giunco

frail·ty ['frelti] s (-ties) fragilità f; (of a person) debolezza

frame [frem] s (of picture) cornice f; (of glasses) montatura; (structure) ossatura; (of a building) ingabbiatura, impalcatura; (for embroidering) telaio; (of a window) intelaiatura; (of mind) stato; (of government) sistema m; (mov) inquadratura; (phot) fotogramma m; (aer) ordinata;

(naut) costa || *tr (to put in a frame)* incorniciare; montare; costruire; inventare; esprimere; (slang) architettare un' accusa contro

frame' house' *s* casa con l'ossatura di legno

frame'-up' *s* (slang) complotto per incriminare un innocente

frame'work' *s* intelaiatura, impalcatura; palificazione

franc [fræŋk] *s* franco

France [fræns] or [frɑns] *s* la Francia

Frances ['frænsɪs] or ['frɑnsɪs] *s* Francesca

franchise ['fræntʃaɪz] *s* diritto di voto; concessione; *(privilege)* franchigia

Francis ['frænsɪs] or ['frɑnsɪs] *s* Francesco

Franciscan [fræn'sɪskən] *adj & s* francescano

frank [fræŋk] *adj* sincero, schietto || *s* affrancatura postale; lettera affrancata; *(franking privilege)* franchigia postale || *tr* affrancare || **Frank** *s (member of Frankish tribe)* franco; *(masculine name)* Franco

frankfurter ['fræŋkfərtər] *s* salsiccia di Francoforte, Frankfurter *m*

frankincense ['fræŋkɪn‚sens] *s* olibano

Frankish ['fræŋkɪʃ] *adj & s* franco

frankness ['fræŋknɪs] *s* franchezza

frantic ['fræntɪk] *adj* frenetico

frappé [fræ'pe] *adj & s* frappé *m*

frat [fræt] *s* (slang) associazione di studenti

fraternal [frə'tʌrnəl] *adj* fraterno

fraterni·ty [frə'tʌrnɪti] *s* (-ties) *(brotherliness)* fraternità *f;* sodalizio; (eccl) confraternita; (U.S.A.) associazione di studenti

fraternize ['frætər‚naɪz] *intr* fraternizzare

fraud [frɔd] *s* truffa, frode *f; (person)* (coll) truffatore *m*

fraudulent ['frɔdjələnt] *adj* fraudolento; *(conversion)* indebito

fraught [frɔt] *adj*—**fraught with** carico di, gravido di

fray [fre] *s* zuffa, rissa, lotta || *intr* sfilacciarsi, logorarsi

freak [frik] *s (sudden fancy)* capriccio, ticchio; *(person, animal)* fenomeno

freakish ['frikɪʃ] *adj* capriccioso; strano, grottesco

freckle ['frekəl] *s* lentiggine *f*, efelide *f*

freckle-faced ['frekəl‚fest] *adj* lentigginoso

freckly ['frekli] *adj* lentigginoso

Frederick ['fredərɪk] *s* Federico

free [fri] *adj (freer* ['fri·ər]; *freest* ['fri·ɪst]) libero; gratis; franco; sciolto; esente; generoso; to be free with essere prodigo di; to set free liberare || *adv* liberamente; in libertà; gratis || *v (pret & pp* freed [frid]; *ger* freeing ['fri·ɪŋ]) *tr* liberare; *(from customs)* svincolare; esimere

freebooter ['fri‚butər] *s* pirata *m*

free'born' *adj* nato in libertà; proprio di un popolo libero

freedom ['fridəm] *s* libertà *f*

free'dom of speech' *s* libertà *f* di parola

free'dom of the press' *s* libertà *f* di stampa

free'dom of the seas' *s* libertà *f* di navigazione

free'dom of wor'ship *s* libertà religiosa

free' en'terprise *s* economia libera

free'-for-all' *s* rissa, tafferuglio

free' hand' *s* libertà assoluta

free'-hand' *adj* a mano libera

freehanded ['fri'hændɪd] *adj* liberale, generoso

free' lance' *s* giornalista *mf* pubblicista; scrittore *m* che lavora senza contratto; soldato di ventura

free'load'er ['fri‚lodər] *s* (coll) mangiatore *m* a sbafo

free'man *s* (-men) uomo libero; cittadino

Free'ma'son *s* frammassone *m*

Free'ma'sonry *s* frammassoneria

free' of charge' *adj* gratis, senza spese

free' port' *s* porto franco

free' serv'ice *s* manutenzione gratuita

free'-spo'ken *adj* franco, aperto

free'stone' *adj* spiccagnolo || *s* pesca spicca

free'think'er *s* libero pensatore

free' thought' *s* libero pensiero

free' trade' *s* libero scambio

free'trad'er *s* liberoscambista *mf*

free'way' *s* autostrada

free' will' *s* libero arbitrio

freeze [friz] *s* gelo, gelata; *(e.g., of prices)* blocco || *v (pret* froze [froz]; *pp* frozen) *tr* gelare; *(credits, rentals, etc.)* bloccare || *intr* gelarsi; *(said of brakes)* inchiodarsi; morire assiderato; *(to become immobilized)* irrigidirsi

freeze'-dry' *v (pret & pp -dried)* *tr* liofilizzare

freezer ['frizər] *s* congelatore *m; (for making ice cream)* sorbettiera

freight [fret] *s* carico; *(charge)* porto; (naut) nolo; **by freight** come carico mercantile; (rr) a piccola velocità || *tr* spedire come carico

freight' car' *s* vagone *m* or carro merci

freighter ['fretər] *s* speditore *m;* nave *f* da carico

freight' plat'form *s* (rr) banchina adibita al traffico merci

freight' sta'tion *s* (rr) stazione merci

freight' train' *s* treno merci, merci *m*

freight' yard' *s* (rr) scalo merci

French [frentʃ] *adj & s* francese *m;* the **French** i francesi

French' bread' *s* pane *m* a bastone

French' chalk' *s* pietra da sarto

French' door' *s* porta a vetri

French' dress'ing *s* salsa verde con aceto

French' fried' pota'toes *spl* patate fritte affettate

French' horn' *s* (mus) corno

French' leave' *s*—to take **French leave** andarsene all'inglese, filare all'inglese

French'man *s* (-men) francese *m*

French' tel'ephone *s* microtelefono

French' toast' *s* pane dorato al salto

French' win'dow *s* portafinestra

French'wom'an *s* (-wom'en) francese *f*

frenzied ['frenzɪd] *adj* frenetico

fren·zy ['frenzɪ] *s* (-zies) frenesia

frequen·cy ['frikwənsɪ] *s* (-cies) frequenza

fre'quency modula'tion *s* modulazione di frequenza

frequent ['frikwənt] *adj* frequente || [frɪ'kwɛnt] *or* ['frikwənt] *tr* frequentare, praticare

frequently ['frikwəntlɪ] *adv* frequentemente

fres·co ['fresko] *s* (-coes *or* -cos) affresco || *tr* affrescare

fresh [frɛʃ] *adj* fresco; (*water*) dolce; (*new*) nuovo; (*wind*) moderato; (*inexperienced*) novizio; (*cheeky*) (slang) sfacciato || *adv* recentemente, di recente; **fresh in** (coll) appena arrivato; **fresh out** (coll) appena esaurito

freshen ['frɛʃən] *tr* rinfrescare || *intr* rinfrescarsi

freshet ['frɛʃɪt] *s* piena, crescita

fresh'man *s* (-men) (*newcomer*) novizio; (*educ*) matricola

freshness ['frɛʃnɪs] *s* freschezza; (*of air*) frescura; (*cheek*) (slang) sfacciataggine *f*

fresh'-wa'ter *adj* d'acqua dolce; poco conosciuto; piccolo

fret [frɛt] *s* (*interlaced design*) fregio, greca; irritazione; (mus) tasto || *v* (*pret & pp* **fretted**; *ger* **fretting**) *tr* fregiare || *intr* fremere, trepidare, agitarsi

fretful ['frɛtfəl] *adj* irritabile, permaloso

fret'work' *s* greca

Freudianism ['frɔɪdɪ·ə‚nɪzəm] *s* freudismo

friar ['fraɪ·ər] *s* frate *m*

friar·y ['fraɪ·ərɪ] *s* (-ies) convento di frati

fricassee [‚frɪkə'si] *s* fricassea

friction ['frɪkʃən] *s* frizione; disaccordo, dissenso

fric'tion tape' *s* nastro isolante

Friday ['fraɪdɪ] *s* venerdì *m*

fried [fraɪd] *adj* fritto

fried' egg' *s* uovo al tegame, uovo occhio di manzo

friend [frɛnd] *s* amico; **to be friends with** essere amico di; **to make friends** allacciare amicizie; **to make friends with** fare l'amicizia di

friend·ly ['frɛndlɪ] *adj* (-lier; -liest) amico, amichevole

friendship ['frɛndʃɪp] *s* amicizia

frieze [friz] *s* (archit) fregio

frigate ['frɪgɪt] *s* fregata

fright [fraɪt] *s* spavento; **to take fright at** spaventarsi di

frighten ['fraɪtən] *tr* intimorire, spaventare; **to frighten away** mettere in fuga, sgomentare || *intr* spaventarsi

frightful ['fraɪtfəl] *adj* spaventevole, orribile; (coll) enorme

frightfulness ['fraɪtfəlnɪs] *s* spavento; terrorismo

frigid ['frɪdʒɪd] *adj* freddo; (*zone*) glaciale

frigidity [frɪ'dʒɪdɪtɪ] *s* (fig) frigidezza; (pathol) frigidità *f*

frill [frɪl] *s* pieghettatura; (*of birds and other animals*) collarino; (*in dress, speech, etc.*) affettazione

fringe [frɪndʒ] *s* frangia; (*in dressmaking*) volantino; (*on curtains*) balza; **on the fringe of** all'orlo di || *tr* orlare

fringe' ben'efits *spl* assegni *mpl*, benefici *mpl* marginali

fripper·y ['frɪpərɪ] *s* (-ies) (*finery*) fronzoli *mpl*; ostentazione; (*trifles*) cianfrusaglie *fpl*

frisk [frɪsk] *tr* perquisire; (slang) derubare || *intr* fare capriole

frisk·y ['frɪskɪ] *adj* (-ier; -iest) gaio, vivace

fritter ['frɪtər] *s* frittella; frammento || *tr*—**to fritter away** sprecare

frivolous ['frɪvələs] *adj* frivolo

friz [frɪz] *s* (frizzes) ricciolo || *v* (*pret & pp* **frizzed**; *ger* **frizzing**) *tr* arricciare

frizzle ['frɪzəl] *s* ricciolo || *tr* arricciare || *intr* arricciarsi

friz·zly ['frɪzlɪ] *adj* (-zlier; -zliest) crespo, riccio

fro [fro] *adv*—**to and fro** avanti e indietro; **to go to and fro** andare e venire

frock [frɑk] *s* gabbano; (*smock*) grembiule *m*; blusa; (*of priest*) tonaca

frock' coat' *s* finanziera

frog [frɑg] *or* [frɔg] *s* rana; (*button and loop on a garment*) alamaro; (*in throat*) raschio

frog'man' *s* (-men') sommozzatore *m*, uomo rana

frol·ic ['frɑlɪk] *s* scherzo, monelleria || *v* (*pret & pp* **-icked**; *ger* **-icking**) *intr* scherzare, folleggiare

frolicsome ['frɑlɪksəm] *adj* scherzoso

from [frʌm], [frəm] *or* [frɔm] *prep* da; di, e.g., **I am from New York** sono di New York; da parte di; a, e.g., **to take s.th away from s.o.** portar via qlco a qlcu

front [frʌnt] *adj* frontale, anteriore; di fronte || *s* fronte *m & f*; (*of a building*) prospetto; (*of a book*) principio; (*of a shirt*) sparato; (*e.g., of wealth*) apparenza; (theat) boccascena *m*; (mil) fronte *m*; **in front of** dinanzi a; **to put on a front** (coll) fare ostentazione; **to put up a bold front** (coll) farsi coraggio || *tr* (*to face*) fronteggiare; (*to confront*) affrontare; (*to supply with a front*) coprire; servire da facciata a || *intr*—**to front on** dare su

frontage ['frʌntɪdʒ] *s* facciata, veduta; terreno di fronte alla casa

front' door' *s* porta d'entrata

front' drive' *s* (aut) trazione anteriore

frontier [frʌn'tɪr] *adj* limitrofo || *s* frontiera

fron'tiers'man *s* (-men) pioniere *m*

frontispiece ['frʌntɪs‚pis] *s* (*of book*) pagina illustrata di fronte al frontispizio; (*of building*) facciata

front' mat'ter *s* (*of book*) parte *f* preliminare

front'-page' *tr* stampare in prima pagina

front' porch' *s* porticato

front' room' s stanza con vista sulla strada

front' row' s prima fila

front' seat' s posto in una delle file davanti; (aut) sedile m anteriore

front' steps' spl scalinata d'ingresso

front' view' s vista sulla strada

frost [frɔst] or [frɑst] s gelo, brina, gelata; (fig) freddezza; (slang) fiasco ‖ tr agghiacciare; (with sugar) glassare; (glass) smerigliare

frost'ed glass' s vetro smerigliato

frost'bite' s congelamento

frosting ['frɔstɪŋ] or ['frɑstɪŋ] s glassatura; (of glass) smerigliatura

frost·y ['frɔsti] or ['frɑsti] adj (-ier; -iest) brinato; (hair) canuto; (fig) gelido

froth [frɔθ] or [frɑθ] s schiuma; (fig) frivolezza ‖ intr schiumare; (at the mouth) avere la schiuma

froth·y ['frɔθi] or ['frɑθi] adj (-ier; -iest) spumoso; frivolo

froward ['frowərd] adj indocile

frown [fraʊn] s aggrottare m delle ciglia; (of disapproval) cipiglio ‖ intr aggrottare le ciglia; **to frown at** or **on** disapprovare

frows·y or **frowz·y** ['fraʊzi] adj (-ier; -iest) sporco; puzzolente

fro'zen foods' ['frozən] spl cibi congelati; cibi surgelati

frugal ['frugəl] adj parsimonioso; (in food and drink) frugale

fruit [frut] adj (tree) fruttifero; (dish) da frutta ‖ s (such as apple) frutto; (collectively) frutta, e.g., **I like fruit** mi piace la frutta; (fig) frutto

fruit' cake' s torta con noci e canditi

fruit' cup' s macedonia di frutta

fruit' dish' s fruttiera, portafrutta m

fruit' fly' s moscerino del vino

fruitful ['frutfəl] adj fruttuoso

fruition [fru'ɪʃən] s realizzazione; **to come to fruition** giungere a buon fine

fruit' jar' s vaso da frutta

fruit' juice' s sugo or spremuta di frutta

fruitless ['frutlɪs] adj infruttuoso

fruit' sal'ad s macedonia di frutta

fruit' stand' s bancarella da fruttivendolo

fruit' store' s negozio di frutta

frumpish ['frʌmpɪʃ] adj trasandato

frustrate ['frʌstret] tr frustrare

fry [fraɪ] s (fries) fritto ‖ v (pret & pp fried) tr & intr friggere

fry'ing pan' s padella; **out of the frying pan into the fire** dalla padella nella brace

fudge [fʌdʒ] s dolce m di cioccolato

fuel ['fju·əl] s combustibile m; (fig) cibo ‖ v (pret & pp fueled or fuelled; ger fueling or fuelling) tr rifornire di carburante ‖ intr rifornirsi di carburante

fuel' cell' s cellula elettrogena

fu'el oil' s nafta, olio pesante

fu'el tank' s serbatoio del carburante

fugitive ['fjudʒɪtɪv] adj & s fuggiasco, fuggitivo

fugue [fjug] s (mus) fuga

ful·crum ['fʌlkrəm] s (-crums or -cra [krə]) fulcro

fulfill [ful'fɪl] tr (to carry out) eseguire; (an obligation) mantenere; (to bring to an end) completare

fulfillment [ful'fɪlmənt] s adempimento; realizzazione

full [ful] adj pieno; (speed) tutto; (garment) ampio; (voice) spiegato; (of food) sazio; (member) effettivo; **full of aches and pains** pieno d'acciacchi; **full of fun** divertentissimo; **full of play** pieno di vita ‖ s pieno; colmo; **in full** per esteso, in pieno; **to the full** completamente ‖ adv completamente; **full many (a)** moltissimi; **full well** perfettamente ‖ tr follare

full-blooded ['ful'blʌdɪd] adj vigoroso; purosangue

full-blown ['ful'blon] adj completamente sbocciato; maturo

full-bodied ['ful'badɪd] adj forte, ricco

full' dress' s vestito da sera; (mil) tenuta di gala, alta uniforme

full-faced ['ful'fest] adj paffuto; (view) intero; (typ) grassetto

full-fledged ['ful'fledʒd] adj completamente sviluppato; vero, autentico

full-grown ['ful'gron] adj completamente sviluppato, adulto

full' house' s (theat) piena; (poker) full m

full'-length' mir'ror s specchiera

full'-length mo'vie s lungometraggio

full' moon' s luna piena

full' name' s nome m e cognome m

full'-page' adj di tutta una pagina

full' pow'ers spl pieni poteri

full' sail' adv a vele spiegate

full'-scale' adj in grandezza naturale; completo

full-sized ['ful'saɪzd] adj in grandezza naturale

full' speed' adv a tutta velocità

full' stop' s fermata; (gram) punto

full' swing' s piena attività

full' tilt' adv a tutta forza

full'-time' adj a orario completo

fully ['fuli] or ['fulli] adv completamente, del tutto

fulsome ['fulsəm] or ['fʌlsəm] adj basso, volgare; nauseante

fumble ['fʌmbəl] tr (a ball) lasciar cadere ‖ intr titubare; andare a tentoni; (in one's pocket) cercare alla cieca

fume [fjum] s fumo, vapore m, esalazione ‖ tr affumicare ‖ intr fumare, esalare fumo; (to show anger) irritarsi

fumigate ['fjumɪ‚get] tr fumigare

fumigation [‚fjumɪ'geʃən] s fumigazione

fun [fʌn] s divertimento, spasso; **to be fun** essere divertente; **to have fun** divertirsi; **to make fun of** prendersi gioco di

function ['fʌŋkʃən] s funzione ‖ intr funzionare, marciare, camminare

functional ['fʌŋkʃənəl] adj funzionale

functionalism ['fʌŋkʃənəl‚ɪzəm] s funzionalismo

functionar·y ['fʌŋkʃə‚nɛri] s (-ies) funzionario

fund [fʌnd] *s* fondo; (*of knowledge*) suppellettile *f* ‖ *tr* (*debts*) consolidare

fundamental [ˌfʌndəˈmentəl] *adj* fondamentale ‖ *s* fondamento

fundamentalist [ˌfʌndəˈmentəlɪst] *adj* & *s* scritturale *m*

funeral [ˈfjunərəl] *adj* funebre, funerario ‖ *s* funerale *m*, trasporto funebre; **it's not my funeral** (slang) non sono affari miei

fu'neral direc'tor *s* imprenditore *m* di pompe funebri

fu'neral home' or **par'lor** *s* impresa di pompe funebri

fu'neral serv'ice *s* ufficio dei defunti

funereal [fjuˈnɪrɪəl] *adj* funebre

fungous [ˈfʌŋgəs] *adj* fungoso

fungus [ˈfʌŋgəs] *s* (**funguses** or **fungi** [ˈfʌndʒaɪ]) fungo

funicular [fjuˈnɪkjələr] *adj* & *s* funicolare *f*

funk [fʌŋk] *s* (coll) paura; (coll) codardo; **in a funk** (coll) con una paura matta

fun·nel [ˈfʌnəl] *s* imbuto; (*smokestack*) fumaiolo; (*for ventilation*) manica a vento ‖ *v* (*pret & pp* **-neled** or **-nelled**; *ger* **-neling** or **-nelling**) *tr* incanalare

funnies [ˈfʌniz] *spl* pagine *fpl* fumetti

fun·ny [ˈfʌni] *adj* (**-nier; -niest**) comico, buffo; (coll) strano; **to strike as funny** parere strano o buffo a

fun'ny bone' *s* osso rabbioso (del gomito); **to strike s.o.'s funny bone** far ridere qlcu

fur [fʌr] *s* pelo; (*garment*) pelliccia; (*on the tongue*) patina

furbelow [ˈfʌrbəˌlo] *s* falpalà *m*

furbish [ˈfʌrbɪʃ] *tr* lustrare; mettere a nuovo; **to furbish up** rinfrescare

furious [ˈfjurɪ·əs] *adj* furioso

furl [fʌrl] *tr* (*a flag*) incazzottare; (naut) raccogliere, strangolare

fur-lined [ˈfʌrˌlaɪnd] *adj* foderato di pelliccia

furlong [ˈfʌrlɔŋ] or [ˈfʌrlaŋ] *s* un ottavo di miglio terrestre

furlough [ˈfʌrlo] *s* licenza ‖ *tr* licenziare

furnace [ˈfʌrnɪs] *s* fornace *f*; (*to heat a house*) caldaia del calorifero

furnish [ˈfʌrnɪʃ] *tr* fornire; ammobiliare

furnishings [ˈfʌrnɪʃɪŋz] *spl* mobilia; (*things to wear*) accessori *mpl* da uomo

furniture [ˈfʌrnɪtʃər] *s* mobili *mpl*, mobilia; (naut) attrezzatura; **a piece of furniture** un mobile

fur'ni·ture deal'er *s* mobiliere *m*

furor [ˈfjurər] *s* furore *m*

furrier [ˈfʌrɪ·ər] *s* pellicciaio

furrier·y [ˈfʌrɪ·əri] *s* (**-ies**) pellicceria

furrow [ˈfʌro] *s* solco ‖ *tr* solcare

further [ˈfʌrðər] *adj* più lontano; ulteriore ‖ *adv* oltre; più; inoltre ‖ *tr* favorire, incoraggiare

furtherance [ˈfʌrðərəns] *s* avanzamento, incoraggiamento

furthermore [ˈfʌrðərˌmor] *adv* inoltre

furthest [ˈfʌrðɪst] *adj* (il) più lontano ‖ *adv* al massimo

furtive [ˈfʌrtɪv] *adj* furtivo

fu·ry [ˈfjuri] *s* (**-ries**) furia

furze [fʌrz] *s* ginestra spinosa

fuse [fjuz] *s* (*for igniting an explosive*) miccia; (*for detonating an explosive*) spoletta; (elec) fusibile *m*; **to burn out a fuse** bruciare un fusibile ‖ *tr* fondere ‖ *intr* fondersi; (elec) saltare

fuse' box' *s* valvoliera

fuselage [ˈfjuzəlɪdʒ] or [ˌfjuzəˈlaʒ] *s* fusoliera

fusible [ˈfjuzɪbəl] *adj* fusibile

fusillade [ˌfjuzɪˈled] *s* fucileria; (fig) gragnola ‖ *tr* attaccare con fuoco di fucileria

fusion [ˈfjuʒən] *s* fusione

fuss [fʌs] *s* agitazione inutile; (coll) alterco per nulla; **to make a fuss** accogliere festosamente; far molte storie; **to make a fuss over** aver un alterco su ‖ *tr* disturbare ‖ *intr* agitarsi per una nonnulla

fuss·y [ˈfʌsi] *adj* (**-ier; -iest**) (*person*) pignolo, meticoloso; (*object*) carico di fronzoli; (*writing*) complicato

fustian [ˈfʌstʃən] *s* fustagno; (fig) verbosità *f*, magniloquenza

fust·y [ˈfʌsti] *adj* (**-ier; -iest**) ammuffito, che sa di muffa; antico, sorpassato

futile [ˈfjutɪl] *adj* (*unproductive*) sterile; (*unimportant*) futile

futili·ty [fjuˈtɪliti] *s* (**-ties**) sterilità *f*; futilità *f*

future [ˈfjutʃər] *adj* futuro ‖ *s* futuro; **futures** contratto con consegna a termine; **in the near future** nel prossimo avvenire

fuze [fjuz] *s* (*for igniting an explosive*) miccia; (*for detonating an explosive*) spoletta; (elec) fusibile *m* ‖ *tr* innestare la spoletta a

fuzz [fʌz] *s* lanugine *f*, peluria; (*in corners*) polvere *f*; (slang) poliziotto; (slang) polizia

fuzz·y [ˈfʌzi] *adj* (**-ier; -iest**) lanuginoso; coperto di polvere; (*indistinct*) confuso

G

G, g [dʒi] *s* settima lettera dell'alfabeto inglese

gab [gæb] *s* (coll) parlantina ‖ *v* (*pret & pp* **gabbed**; *ger* **gabbing**) *intr* (coll) chiacchierare

gabardine [ˈgæbərˌdin] *s* gabardine *f*

gabble [ˈgæbəl] *s* barbugliamento ‖ *intr* barbugliare

gable [ˈgebəl] *s* (archit) timpano

ga'ble roof' *s* tetto a due falde, tetto a capanna

gad [gæd] *v* (*pret & pp* **gadded**; *ger* **gadding**) *intr* bighellonare

gad'about' *adj* ozioso ‖ *s* vagabondo, bighellone *m*; fannullone *m*

gad'fly' *s* (**-flies**) tafano, moscone *m*

gadget ['gædʒɪt] s congegno, dispositivo, macchinetta

Gaelic ['gelɪk] adj & s gaelico

gaff [gæf] s arpione m; (naut) picco; **to stand the gaff** (slang) aver pazienza

gag [gæg] s bavaglio; (joke) barzelletta; (theat) battuta improvvisata || v (pret & pp **gagged**) ger **gagging**) tr imbavagliare; soffocare || intr sentirsi venire la nausea

gage [gedʒ] s (pledge) pegno; (challenge) sfida

gaie·ty ['ge·ɪti] s (-ties) gaiezza

gaily ['geli] adv allegramente

gain [gen] s profitto; (increase) aumento || tr guadagnare; (to reach) raggiungere; (altitude) prendere || intr (said of a patient) migliorare; (said of a watch) correre; **to gain on** guadagnare terreno su; sorpassare

gainful ['genfəl] adj rimunerativo

gain·say v (pret & pp **-said** [‚sed] or [‚sed]) tr disdire, misconoscere; negare

gait [get] s portamento, andatura

gaiter ['getər] s ghetta

gala ['gælə] or ['gelə] adj di gala || s gala m & f, festa

galax·y ['gæləksi] s (-ies) galassia

gale [gel] s (of wind) bufera; (of laughter) scoppio; **to weather the gale** resistere alla tempesta

gall [gɔl] s fiele m; bile f; cistifellea; scorticatura; (gallnut) galla; (audacity) (coll) faccia tosta || tr irritare || intr irritarsi; (naut) logorarsi

gallant ['gælənt] or [gə'lænt] adj galante || ['gælənt] adj (brave) valoroso; (grand) magnifico; (showy) festivo || s prode m; (man attentive to women) galante m

gallant·ry ['gæləntri] s (-ries) galanteria; valore m

gall' blad'der s vescichetta biliare

gall'-blad'der attack' s travaso di bile

galleon ['gælɪ·ən] s galeone m

galler·y ['gæləri] s (-ies) galleria; tribuna; (cheapest seats in theater) loggione m

galley ['gæli] s (vessel) galera; (kitchen) (aer) cucina; (kitchen) (naut) cambusa; (galley proof) (typ) bozza in colonna; (tray) (typ) vantaggio

gal'ley proof' s bozza in colonna

gal'ley slave' s galeotto

Gallic ['gælɪk] adj gallo, gallico

galling ['gɔlɪŋ] adj irritante

gallivant ['gælɪ‚vænt] intr andare a spasso; fare il galante

gall'nut' s galla

gallon ['gælən] s gallone m

galloon [gə'lun] s gallone m, nastro

gallop ['gæləp] s galoppo; **at a gallop** al galoppo || tr far galoppare || intr galoppare

gal·lows ['gæloz] s (-lows or -lowses) forca; (min) castelletto

gal'lows bird' s (coll) remo di galera, pendaglio da forca

gall'stone' s calcolo biliare

galore [gə'lɔr] adv in abbondanza

galosh [gə'lɑʃ] s stivaletto di gomma

galvanize ['gælvə‚naɪz] tr galvanizzare

gal'vanized i'ron s ferro zincato

gambit ['gæmbɪt] s gambetto

gamble ['gæmbəl] s azzardo; (game) gioco d'azzardo || tr giocare; **to gamble away** giocarsi || intr giocare d'azzardo; (com) speculare

gambler ['gæmblər] s giocatore m; speculatore m

gambling ['gæmblɪŋ] s gioco (d'azzardo)

gam'bling den' s bisca

gam'bling house' s casa da gioco

gam·bol ['gæmbəl] s salto, capriola || v (pret & pp **-boled** or **-bolled**) ger **-boling** or **-bolling** intr saltare, far capriole

gambrel ['gæmbrəl] s garretto

gam'brel roof' s tetto a mansarda

game [gem] adj da caccia; coraggioso; (leg) (coll) zoppo; (coll) pronto || s (amusement) gioco; (contest) partita; (any sport) sport m; (wild animals hunted) selvaggina; (any pursuit) attività f; (object of pursuit) bersaglio; (bridge) manche f; **the game is up** il gioco è fallito; **to make game of** farsi gioco di; **to play the game** giocare onestamente

game' bag' s carniere m

game'cock' s gallo da combattimento

game'keep'er s guardacaccia m

game' of chance' s gioco d'azzardo

game' preserve' s bandita di caccia

game' war'den s guardacaccia m

gamut ['gæmət] s (mus, fig) gamma

gam·y ['gemi] adj (-ier; -iest) coraggioso; (culin) che sa di selvatico

gander ['gændər] s papero, oca

gang [gæŋ] adj multiplo || s (of workers) ganga; (of thugs) cricca || intr—**to gang up** riunirsi; **to gang up against** or **on** (coll) gettarsi insieme contro

gangling ['gæŋglɪŋ] adj dinoccolato

gangli·on ['gæŋglɪ·ən] s (-ons or -a [ə]) ganglio

gang'plank' s palanca, plancia

gangrene ['gæŋgrin] s cancrena || tr far andare in cancrena || intr andare in cancrena

gangster ['gæŋstər] s gangster m

gang'way' s (passageway) corridoio; (gangplank) passerella, scalandrone m; (in ship's side) barcarizzo || interj lasciar passare!

gan·try ['gæntri] s (-tries) (of crane) cavalletto; (rr) ponte m delle segnalazioni; (rok) piattaforma verticale, torre f di lancio

gap [gæp] s (pass) passo; (in a wall) breccia; (interval) lacuna; (between two points of view) abisso; (mach) gioco

gape [gep] or [gæp] s apertura; (yawn) sbadiglio; sguardo di meraviglia || intr stare a bocca aperta; **to gape at** guardare a bocca aperta

garage [gə'rɑʒ] s rimessa

garb [gɑrb] s veste f || tr vestire

garbage ['gɑrbɪdʒ] s pattume m, immondizia, immondizie fpl

gar'bage can' s portaimmondizie m

gar'bage collec'tor s spazzaturaio, spazzino, netturbino

garble ['gɑrbəl] tr falsare, mutilare

garden ['gɑrdən] s (of vegetables) orto; (of flowers) giardino

gardener ['gɑrdnər] s (of vegetables) ortolano; (of flowers) giardiniere m

gardenia [gɑr'dini·ə] s gardenia

gardening ['gɑrdnɪŋ] s orticoltura; giardinaggio

gar'den par'ty s trattenimento in giardino

gargle ['gɑrgəl] s gargarismo || intr gargarizzare

gargoyle ['gɑrgɔɪl] s doccione m, gargolla

garish ['gerɪʃ] or ['gærɪʃ] adj appariscente; abbagliante

garland ['gɑrlənd] s ghirlanda || tr inghirlandare

garlic ['gɑrlɪk] s aglio

garment ['gɑrmənt] s capo di vestiario

gar'ment bag' s tessilsacco

garner ['gɑrnər] tr mettere in granaio; (to get) acquistarsi; (to hoard) incettare

garnet ['gɑrnɪt] adj & s granata

garnish ['gɑrnɪʃ] s guarnizione; || tr guarnire; (law) sequestrare

garret ['gerɪt] s sottotetto, soffitta

garrison ['gerɪsən] s guarnigione, presidio || tr presidiare

garrote [gə'rɑt] or [gə'rot] s strangolamento; garrotta || tr strangolare; giustiziare con la garrotta

garrulous ['gærələs] or ['gærjələs] adj garrulo, loquace

garter ['gɑrtər] s giarrettiera

gas [gæs] s gas m; (coll) benzina; (slang) successo; (slang) chiacchiere fpl || v (pret & pp gassed) ger gassing) tr fornire di gas; (mil) gassare; (slang) divertire || intr emettere gas; (slang) chiacchierare; **to gas up** fare il pieno

gas'bag' s involucro per il gas; (coll) chiacchierone m

gas' burn'er s becco a gas; (on a stove) fornello a gas

Gascony ['gæskəni] s la Guascogna

gaseous ['gæsɪ·əs] adj gassoso

gas' fit'ter s gassista m

gash [gæʃ] s sfregio || tr sfregiare

gas' heat' s calefazione a gas

gas'hold'er s gassometro

gasi·fy ['gæsɪ,faɪ] v (pret & pp -fied) tr gassificare || intr gassificarsi

gas' jet' s fornello a gas; fiamma

gasket ['gæskɪt] s guarnizione

gas'light' s luce f del gas

gas' main' s tubatura principale del gas

gas' mask' s maschera antigas

gas' me'ter s contatore m del gas

gasoline ['gæsə,lin] or [,gæsə'lin] s benzina

gas'oline' deal'er s benzinaio

gas'oline' pump' s colonnetta, distributore m di benzina

gasp [gæsp] or [gɑsp] s respirazione affannosa; (of death) rantolo || tr dire affannosamente || intr boccheggiare

gas' range' s cucina a gas, fornello a gas

gas'-sta'tion attend'ant s benzinaio

gas' stove' s cucina a gas

gas' tank' s gassometro; (aut) serbatoio di benzina

gastric ['gæstrɪk] adj gastrico

gastronomy [gæs'trɑnəmi] s gastronomia

gas' works' s officina del gas

gate [get] s porta; (in fence or wall) cancello; (of sluice) saracinesca; (in an airport or station) uscita; (rr) barriera; (sports, theat) incasso totale; **to crash the gate** (coll) fare il portoghese

gate'keep'er s portiere m; (rr) guardabarriere m

gate'way' s passaggio, entrata

gather ['gæðər] tr raccogliere, cogliere; (news) raccapezzare; (dust) coprirsi di; (e.g., a shawl) avvolgere; (speed) aumentare (di); con:ludere, dedurre; (signatures) (bb) riunire; (sew) increspare || intr riunirsi; raccogliersi; accumularsi

gathering ['gæðərɪŋ] s riunione; (bb) raccolta e piegatura; (pathol) ascesso; (sew) pieghettatura

gaud·y ['gɔdi] adj (-ier; -iest) chiassoso, vistoso

gauge [gedʒ] s misura; calibro; (for liquids) indicatore m di livello; (of carpenter) graffietto; indice m; diametro; (aut) spia; (rr) scartamento || tr misurare; calibrare; (naut) stazzare

Gaul [gɔl] s gallo

gaunt [gɔnt] or [gɑnt] adj magro, emaciato; (e.g., landscape) desolato

gauntlet ['gɔntlɪt] or ['gɑntlɪt] s guanto; guanto di ferro; guantone m, manopola; **to run the gauntlet** (fig) esporsi alla critica; **to take up the gauntlet** raccogliere il guanto; **to throw down the gauntlet** gettare il guanto

gauze [gɔz] s garza

gavel ['gævəl] s martello, martelletto

gavotte [gə'vɑt] s gavotta

gawk [gɔk] s sciocco || intr guardare a bocca aperta

gawk·y ['gɔki] adj (-ier; -iest) sgraziato, goffo

gay [ge] adj gaio; brillante; dissipato; (slang) omosessuale

gaye·ty ['ge·ɪti] s (-ties) gaiezza

gaze [gez] s sguardo fisso || intr fissare lo sguardo

gazelle [gə'zel] s gazzella

gazette [gə'zet] s gazzetta

gazetteer [,gæzə'tɪr] s dizionario geografico

gear [gɪr] s utensili mpl, attrezzi mpl; (mechanism) meccanismo, dispositivo; (aut) marcia; (mach) ingranaggio **out of gear** disingranato; (fig) disturbato; **to throw into gear** ingranare; **to throw out of gear** disingranare; (fig) disturbare || tr adattare || intr adattarsi

gear' box' s scatola del cambio

gear'shift' s cambio di velocità

gear'shift lev'er s leva del cambio

gear'wheel s ruota dentata

gee [dʒi] *interj* oh!; che bellezza!; **gee up!** (*command to a draft animal*) arri!

Gei'ger count'er [ˈgaigər] s contatore *m* Geiger

gel [dʒɛl] s gel *m* || *v* (*pret & pp* **gelled**; *ger* **gelling**) *intr* gelatinizzarsi

gelatine [ˈdʒɛlətɪn] s gelatina

geld [gɛld] *v* (*pret & pp.* **gelded** or **gelt** [gɛlt]) *tr* castrare

gem [dʒɛm] s gemma, gioia

Gemini [ˈdʒɛmɪ ˌnai] *spl* i Gemelli

gender [ˈdʒɛndər] s (gram) genere *m*; (coll) sesso

gene [dʒin] s (biol) gene *m*

genealo·gy [ˌdʒɛnɪˈæ lədʒi] or [ˌdʒini-ˈæ lədʒi] s (**-gies**) genealogia

general [ˈdʒɛnərəl] *adj & s* generale *m*

gen'eral deliv'ery s fermo in posta, fermo posta *m*

generalissi·mo [ˌdʒɛnərəˈlɪsɪmo] s (**-mos**) generalissimo

generali·ty [ˌdʒɛnəˈrælɪti] s (**-ties**) generalità *f*

generalize [ˈdʒɛnərə ˌlaiz] *tr & intr* generalizzare

generally [ˈdʒɛnərəli] *adv* in genere, generalmente

gen'eral part'ner s accomandatario

gen'eral practi'tioner s medico generico

generalship [ˈdʒɛnərəl ˌʃɪp] s generalato; strategia, abilità *f* militare; abilità amministrativa

gen'eral staff' s stato maggiore

generate [ˈdʒɛnə ˌret] *tr* (*offspring*; *electricity*) generare; (math) originare

gen'erat'ing sta'tion s centrale elettrica

generation [ˌdʒɛnəˈreʃən] s generazione

generative [ˈdʒɛnə ˌretɪv] *adj* generativo

gen'erative gram'mar s grammatica generativa

generator [ˈdʒɛnə ˌretər] s generatore *m*; (elec) generatrice *f*

generic [dʒɪˈnɛrɪk] *adj* generico

generous [ˈdʒɛnərəs] *adj* generoso; abbondante, copioso

gene·sis [ˈdʒɛnɪsɪs] s (**-ses** [ˌsiz]) genesi *f* || **Genesis** s (Bib) Genesi *m*

genetic [dʒɪˈnɛtɪk] *adj* genetico || **genetics** *ssg* genetica

Geneva [dʒɪˈnivə] s Ginevra

Genevan [dʒɪˈnivən] *adj & s* ginevrino

genial [ˈdʒinɪ·əl] *adj* affabile, geniale

genie [ˈdʒini] s genio

genital [ˈdʒɛnɪtəl] *adj* genitale || **genitals** *spl* genitali *mpl*

genitive [ˈdʒɛnɪtɪv] *adj & s* genitivo

genius [ˈdʒinjəs] or [ˈdʒini·əs] s (**geniuses**) genio || s (**genii** [ˈdʒini- ˌai] (*spirit; deity*) genio

Genoa [ˈdʒɛno·ə] s Genova

genocide [ˈdʒɛnə ˌsaid] s (*act*) genocidio; (*person*) genocida *mf*

Geno·ese [ˈdʒɛno·iz] *adj* genovese || s (**-ese**) genovese *mf*

genre [ˈʒɑnrə] *adj* (*e.g., painting*) di genere || s genere *m*

genteel [dʒɛnˈtil] *adj* (*well-bred*) beneducato; (*affectedly polite*) manieroso, manierato

gentian [ˈdʒɛnʃən] s genziana

gentile [ˈdʒɛntɪl] or [ˈdʒɛntail] *adj* gentilizio || [ˈdʒɛntail] *adj & s* non circonciso; non ebreo; cristiano; (*pagan*) gentile

gentili·ty [dʒɛnˈtɪlɪti] s (**-ties**) distinzione, raffinatezza

gentle [ˈdʒɛntəl] *adj* (*e.g., manner*) gentile; (*e.g., wind*) dolce, soave; (*wellborn*) bennato; (*tap*) leggero

gen'tle-folk' s gente *f* per bene

gen'tle-man s (**-men**) signore *m*; (*attendant to a person of high rank*) gentiluomo; (*well-mannered man*) gentleman *m*

gen'tleman in wait'ing s gentiluomo di camera

gentlemanly [ˈdʒɛntəlmənli] *adj* signorile

gen'tleman of the road' s brigante *m*; vagabondo

gen'tlemen's agree'ment s accordo fondato sulla buona fede

gen'tle sex' s gentil sesso

gentry [ˈdʒɛntri] s gente *f* per bene

genuine [ˈdʒɛnju·ɪn] *adj* genuino

genus [ˈdʒinəs] s (**genera** [ˈdʒɛnərə] or **genuses**) genere *m*

geographer [dʒɪˈɑgrəfər] s geografo

geographic(al) [ˌdʒɪ·əˈgræfɪk(əl)] *adj* geografico

geogra·phy [dʒɪˈɑgrəfi] s (**-phies**) geografia

geologic(al) [ˌdʒɪ·əˈlɑdʒɪk(əl)] *adj* geologico

geologist [dʒɪˈɑlədʒɪst] s geologo

geolo·gy [dʒɪˈɑlədʒi] s (**-gies**) geologia

geometric(al) [ˌdʒɪ·əˈmɛtrɪk(əl)] *adj* geometrico

geometrician [dʒɪ ˌɑmɪˈtrɪʃən] s geometra *mf*

geome·try [dʒɪˈɑmɪtri] s (**-tries**) geometria

George [dʒɔrdʒ] s Giorgio

geranium [dʒɪˈreni·əm] s geranio

geriatrics [ˌdʒɛrɪˈætrɪks] *ssg* geriatria

germ [dʒʌrm] s germe *m*

German [ˈdʒʌrmən] *adj & s* tedesco

germane [dʒʌrˈmen] *adj* pertinente

Germanize [ˈdʒʌrmə ˌnaiz] *tr* germanizzare

Ger'man mea'sles s rosolia, rubeola

Ger'man sil'ver s alpacca

Germany [ˈdʒʌrməni] s la Germania

germ' car'rier s portatore *m* di germi

germ' cell' s cellula germinale

germicidal [ˌdʒʌrmɪˈsaidəl] *adj* germicida

germicide [ˈdʒʌrmɪ ˌsaid] s germicida *m*

germinate [ˈdʒʌrmɪ ˌnet] *intr* germinare

germ' war'fare s guerra batteriologica

gerontology [ˌdʒɛrənˈtɑlədʒi] s gerontologia

gerund [ˈdʒɛrənd] s gerundio

gestation [dʒɛsˈteʃən] s gestazione

gesticulate [dʒɛsˈtɪkjə ˌlet] *intr* gesticolare

gesticulation [dʒɛs‚tɪkjəˈleʃən] *s* gesticolazione

gesture [ˈdʒɛstʃər] *s* gesto || *intr* gestire, gesticolare

get [get] *v* (*pret* **got** [gɑt]; *pp* **got** or **gotten** [ˈgɑtən]; *ger* **getting**) *tr* ottenere; ricevere; prendere; andare a comprare; procacciare; riportare; procurarsi; riscuotere; guadagnare; **to get across** far capire; **to get back** riacquistare; **to get down** staccare; (*to swallow*) tranguiare; **to get off** togliere, cavare; **to get s.o. to** + *inf* indurre che qlcu + *subj*; **to get done** far fare; **to have got** (coll) avere; **to have got to** + *inf* (coll) dovere + *inf* || *intr* (*to become*) diventare, farsi; (*to arrive*) arrivare, venire; **to get out** (*said of a convalescent*) alzarsi; **to get along** (colla) andare avanti; tirare avanti, giostrare; aver successo; **to get along in years** essere avanti con gli anni; **to get along with** andare d'accordo con; **to get angry** arrabbiarsi; **to get around** uscire; divulgarsi; rigirare; **to get away** scappare, darsela a gambe; **to get away with s.th** scappare con qlco; (coll) farla franca; **to get back** ritornare; ricuperare; **to get back at** (coll) vendicarsi di; **to get behind** rimanere indietro; (*to support*) appoggiare, patrocinare; **to get better** migliorare; **to get by** passare oltre; (*to succeed*) arrivare a farcela; passare inosservato; **to get even with** rifarsi con, prendersi la rivincita con; **to get going** mettersi in moto; **to get in** entrare; rientrare; arrivare; **to get in deeper and deeper** cacciarsi nei pasticci; **to get in with** diventare amico di; **to get married** sposarsi; **to get off** andarsene; smontare da; **to get old** invecchiare; **to get on** andare avanti; andare d'accordo; **to get out** uscire; propagarsi; **to get out of** (*a car*) uscire da; (*trouble*) trarsi di; **to get out of the way** togliersi di mezzo; **to get run over** essere investito; **to get through** finire; arrivare; farsi capire; **to get to** be finire per essere; **to get under way** mettersi in cammino; **to get up** alzarsi; **to not get over it** (coll) non arrivare a rassegnarsi

get'a·way' *s* fuga; (sports) partenza

get'-to·geth'er *s* riunione, crocchio

get'up' *s* (coll) stile *m*, presentazione; (coll) costume *m*, abbigliamento

gewgaw [ˈgjugɔ] *s* cianfrusaglia

geyser [ˈgaɪzər] *s* geyser *m*

ghast·ly [ˈgæstlɪ] or [ˈgɑstli] *adj* (-**lier**; -**liest**) orribile, orrendo; spettrale

gherkin [ˈgʌrkɪn] *s* cetriolino

ghet·to [ˈgɛto] *s* (-**tos** or -**toes**) ghetto

ghost [gost] *s* spettro, fantasma *m*; **not a ghost of** nemmeno l'ombra di; **to give up the ghost** rendere l'anima

ghost·ly [ˈgostlɪ] *adj* (-**lier**; -**liest**) spettrale, fantomatico

ghost' sto'ry *s* storia di fantasmi

ghost' town' *s* città morta

ghost' writ'er *s* collaboratore anonimo

ghoul [gul] *s* spirito necrofago; ladro di tombe

ghoulish [ˈgulɪʃ] *adj* demoniaco, macabro

GI [ˈdʒiˈaɪ] (letterword) (**General Issue**) *s* (**GI's**) soldato degli Stati Uniti

giant [ˈdʒaɪ·ənt] *adj & s* gigante *m*

giantess [ˈdʒaɪ·əntɪs] *s* gigantessa

gibberish [ˈdʒɪbərɪ] or [ˈgɪbərɪʃ] *s* linguaggio inintelligibile

gibbet [ˈdʒɪbɪt] *s* forca || *tr* impiccare sulla forca; (*to hold up to scorn*) mettere alla berlina

gibe [dʒaɪb] *s* scherno, frecciata || *intr* schernire; **to gibe at** beffarsi di

giblets [ˈdʒɪblɪts] *spl* rigaglie *fpl*

giddiness [ˈgɪdɪnɪs] *s* vertigine *f*; frivolezza

gid·dy [ˈgɪdi] *adj* (-**dier**; -**diest**) vertiginoso; preso dalle vertigini; frivolo

gift [gɪft] *s* regalo; (*natural ability*) dono, dote *f*; (*for Christmas*) strenna

gifted [ˈgɪftɪd] *adj* dotato

gift' horse' s—never look a gift horse in the mouth a caval donato non si guarda in bocca

gift' of gab' s (coll) facondia; **to have the gift of gab** (coll) avere la lingua sciolta

gift' pack'age *s* pacco-dono

gift' shop' *s* negozio di regali

gift'-wrap' *v* (*pret & pp* -**wrapped;** *ger* -**wrapping**) *tr* incartare in carta speciale per regali

gigantic [dʒaɪˈgæntɪk] *adj* gigantesco

giggle [ˈgɪgəl] *s* risolino || *intr* ridere scioccamente, ridacchiare

gigo·lo [ˈdʒɪgə‚lo] *s* (-**los**) gigolo

gild [gɪld] *v* (*pret & pp* **gilded** or **gilt** [gɪlt]) *tr* dorare, indorare

gilding [ˈgɪldɪŋ] *s* doratura

gill [gɪl] *s* (*of fish*) branchia || [dʒɪl] *s* quarto di pinta

gilt [gɪlt] *adj & s* dorato

gilt-edged [ˈgɪlt‚ɛdʒd] *adj* a bordo dorato; di primissima qualità

gimcrack [ˈdʒɪm‚kræk] *adj* di nessun valore || *s* cianfrusaglia

gimlet [ˈgɪmlɪt] *s* succhiello

gimmick [ˈgɪmɪk] *s* (slang) trucco

gin [dʒɪn] *s* (*liquor*) gin *m*; (*trap*) trappola; (mach) arganello; (tex) sgranatrice *f* di cotone || *v* (*pret & pp* **ginned;** *ger* **ginning**) *tr* ginnare, sgranare

ginger [ˈdʒɪndʒər] *s* zenzero; (coll) energia, vivacità *f*

gin'ger ale' *s* gazosa allo zenzero

gin'ger·bread' *s* pan di zenzero; ornamento di cattivo gusto

gingerly [ˈdʒɪndʒərli] *adj* cauto || *adv* con cautela

gin'ger·snap' *s* biscotto allo zenzero

gingham [ˈgɪŋəm] *s* rigatino

giraffe [dʒɪˈræf] or [dʒɪˈrɑf] *s* giraffa

girandole [ˈdʒɪrən‚dol] *s* girandola

gird [gʌrd] *v* (*pret & pp* **girt** [gʌrt] or **girded**) *tr* cingere; (*to equip*) dotare; (*to prepare*) preparare; (*to surround*) circondare

girder [ˈgʌrdər] *s* longherina

girdle ['gʌrdəl] *s* reggicalze *m*, zona, fascetta ‖ *tr* fasciare; circondare

girl [gʌrl] *s* fanciulla; ragazza

girl' friend' *s* amica, innamorata

girlhood ['gʌrlhud] *s* adolescenza, giovinezza

girlish ['gʌrlɪʃ] *adj* fanciullesco; da ragazza

girl' scout' *s* giovane esploratrice *f*

girth [gʌrθ] *s* circonferenza; fascia; (*to hold a saddle*) sottopancia *m*

gist [dʒɪst] *s* sugo, nocciolo, essenza

give [gɪv] *s* elasticità *f* ‖ *v* (*pret* gave [gev]; *pp* given ['gɪvən]) *tr* dare; (*trouble*) causare; (*a play*) rappresentare; (*a speech; fruit; a sigh*) fare; **to give away** distribuire gratuitamente; (*to reveal*) lasciarsi sfuggire; (*a bride*) accompagnare all'altare; (*coll*) tradire; **to give back** restituire; **to give forth** (*odors*) emettere; **to give oneself up** darsi; **to give up** cedere; (*a position*) abbandonare ‖ *intr* dare; cedere; (*said, e.g., of a rope*) rompersi; **to give in** cedere; darsi per vinto; **to give out** esaurirsi; venir meno; **to give up** darsi per vinto

give'-and-take' *s* compromesso; conversazione briosa

give'a·way' *s* premio gratuito; rivelazione involontaria; (*game*) vinciperdi *m*; (*rad, telv*) programma *m* a premi

given ['gɪvən] *adj* dato; **given that** dato che, concesso che

giv'en name' *s* nome *m* di battesimo

giver ['gɪvər] *s* donatore *m*; dispensatore *m*

gizzard ['gɪzərd] *s* magone *m*

glacial ['gleʃəl] *adj* glaciale

glacier ['gleʃər] *s* ghiacciaio

glad [glæd] *adj* (**gladder; gladdest**) felice, lieto, contento; **to be glad (to)** essere felice (di)

gladden ['glædən] *tr* rallegrare

glade [gled] *s* radura

glad' hand' *s* (coll) accoglienza calorosa

gladiator ['glædɪ‚etər] *s* gladiatore *m*

gladiola [‚glædɪ'olə] or [glə'daɪ-ələ] *s* gladiolo

gladly ['glædli] *adv* volentieri, di buon grado

gladness ['glædnɪs] *s* contentezza

glad' rags' *s* (coll) panni *mpl* da festa; (coll) vestito da sera

glamorous ['glæmərəs] *adj* affascinante, attraente

glamour ['glæmər] *s* fascino, malia

glam'our girl' *s* ragazza sci-sci

glance [glæns] *or* [glɑns] *s* occhiata, guardata; **at first glance** a prima vista ‖ *intr* lanciare uno sguardo; **to glance at** dare un'occhiata a; **to glance off** sorvolare su; deviare da; **to glance over** dare una scorsa a

gland [glænd] *s* ghiandola

glanders ['glændərz] *spl* morva

glare [gler] *s* splendore *m*, luce *f* abbagliante; sguardo minaccioso ‖ *intr* risplendere; lanciare occhiatacce; **to glare at** fare la faccia feroce a

glare' ice' *s* vetrato

glaring ['glerɪŋ] *adj* risplendente, abbagliante; (*look*) torvo; evidente

glass [glæs] *or* [glɑs] *s* vetro; (*tumbler*) bicchiere *m*; (*mirror*) specchio; (*glassware*) cristalleria; **glasses** occhiali *mpl*

glass' blow'er ['blo·ər] *s* vetraio

glass' case' *s* vetrinetta

glass' cut'ter *s* tagliatore *m* di cristallo; (*tool*) diamante *m* tagliavetro

glass' door' *s* porta a vetri

glassful ['glæsful] *or* ['glɑsful] *s* bicchiere *m*

glass'house' *s* vetreria; (fig) casa di vetro

glass'ware' *s* vetreria, cristalleria

glass' wool' *s* vetro filato

glass'work'er *s* vetraio

glass'works' *s* vetreria, cristalleria

glass·y ['glæsi] *or* ['glɑsi] *adj* (**-ier; -iest**) vetriato, vetroso

glaze [glez] *s* vernice vitrea; smalto; (*of ice*) superficie invetriata; (culin) glassa ‖ *tr* smaltare; invetriare; (culin) glassare

glazier ['gleʒər] *s* vetraio

gleam [glim] *s* barlume *m*, raggio ‖ *intr* baluginare

glean [glin] *tr* spigolare, racimolare; (*to gather facts*) raccogliere

glee [gli] *s* gioia, esultanza

glee' club' *s* società *f* corale

glib [glɪb] *adj* (**glibber; glibbest**) loquace; (*tongue*) facile, sciolto

glide [glaɪd] *s* scivolata; (aer) volo a vela, volo planato; (mus) legamento ‖ *intr* scivolare; (aer) librarsi, planare; **to glide away** scorrere

glider ['glaɪdər] *s* (aer) libratore *m*, veleggiatore *m*

glimmer ['glɪmər] *s* barlume *m* ‖ *intr* brillare, luccicare; tralucere

glimmering ['glɪmərɪŋ] *adj* tenue, tremulo ‖ *s* luce fioca; barlume *m*

glimpse [glɪmps] *s* occhiata; **to catch a glimpse of** intravedere ‖ *tr* travedere

glint [glɪnt] *s* scintillio ‖ *intr* scintillare

glisten ['glɪsən] *s* scintillio, lucicchio ‖ *intr* scintillare, luccicare

glitter ['glɪtər] *s* lucicchio ‖ *intr* rilucere, sfolgorare

gloaming ['glomɪŋ] *s* crepuscolo (vespertino)

gloat [glot] *intr* guardare con maligna soddisfazione; **to gloat over** godere di

global ['globəl] *adj* globale; universale; globulare

globe [glob] *s* globo; (*with map of earth*) mappamondo

globe-trotter ['glob‚trɑtər] *s* giramondo

globule ['glɑbjul] *s* globulo

glockenspiel ['glɑkən‚spil] *s* vibrafono

gloom [glum] *s* oscurità *f*; malinconia, uggia

gloom·y ['glumi] *adj* (**-ier; -iest**) lugubre, triste, tetro

glori·fy ['glorɪ‚faɪ] *v* (*pret & pp* **-fied**) *tr* glorificare; (*to enhance*) esaltare

glorious ['glorɪ·əs] *adj* glorioso; magnifico, splendido

glo·ry ['glorɪ] *s* (**-ries**) gloria; **to go to glory** morire ‖ *v* (*pret & pp* **-ried**) *intr* gloriarsi

gloss [glɔs] *or* [glas] *s* lucentezza, patina; (*commentary*) glossa ‖ *tr* satinare, patinare; (*to annotate*) glossare; **to gloss over** nascondere, discolpare

glossa·ry ['glɑsərɪ] *s* (**-ries**) glossario

gloss·y ['glosɪ] *or* ['glasɪ] *adj* (**-ier; -iest**) lucido; (*paper*) satinato

glottal ['glɑtəl] *adj* articolato alla glottide

glottis ['glɑtɪs] *s* glottide *f*

glove [glʌv] *s* guanto

glove' compart'ment *s* cassetto portaoggetti

glow [glo] *s* fuoco, incandescenza; splendore *m*, scintillio; calore *m*; colorito acceso ‖ *intr* essere incandescente; (*said of cheeks*) avvampare; (*said of cat's eyes*) fosforeggiare

glower ['glau·ər] *s* sguardo torvo ‖ *intr* guardare col viso torvo

glowing ['glo·ɪŋ] *adj* incandescente, acceso; entusiasta, entusiastico

glow'worm' *s* lucciola; lampiride *m*

glucose ['glukos] *s* glucosio

glue [glu] *s* colla, mastice *m* ‖ *tr* incollare, ingommare

glue'pot' *s* pentolino per la colla

gluey ['glu·i] *adj* (**gluier; gluiest**) attaccaticcio; (*smeared with glue*) incollato

glum [glʌm] *adj* (**glummer; glummest**) tetro, accigliato

glut [glʌt] *s* abbondanza; eccesso; **there is a glut on the market** il mercato è saturo ‖ *v* (*pret & pp* **glutted;** *ger* **glutting**) *tr* saziare; (*the market*) saturare; (*a channel*) otturare

glutton ['glʌtən] *adj & s* ghiottone *m*

gluttonous ['glʌtənəs] *adj* ghiotto

glutton·y ['glʌtənɪ] *s* (**-ies**) ghiottoneria, golosità *f*

glycerine ['glɪsərɪn] *s* glicerina

G'-man' *s* (**-men**) agente *m* federale

gnarl [nɑrl] *s* nodo ‖ *tr* torcere ‖ *intr* ringhiare

gnarled [nɑrld] *adj* nodoso; (*wrinkled*) grinzoso

gnash [næʃ] *tr* digrignare ‖ *intr* digrignare i denti

gnat [næt] *s* moscerino, pappataci *m*

gnaw [nɔ] *tr* rosicchiare, rodere ‖ *intr* —**to gnaw at** (fig) rimordere

gnome [nom] *s* gnomo

go [go] *s* (**goes**) andata; energia; (*for traffic*) via libera; **it's all the go** (coll) è all'ultimo grido; **it's no go** (coll) è impossibile; **on the go** in continuo andare e venire; **to make a go of** (coll) aver successo con ‖ *v* (*pret* **went** [wɛnt]; *pp* **gone** [gɔn] *or* [gan]) *tr* (coll) sopportare; (coll) scommettere; (coll) pagare; **to go it alone** fare da sé ‖ *intr* andare; (*to operate*) camminare, funzionare; (*e.g., mad*) diventare; (*said of numbers*) entrare; **gone!** venduto!; **so it goes** così va il mondo; **to

be going to** + *inf* andare a + *inf*, e.g., **I am going to New York to see him** vado a New York a vederlo; (*to express futurity*) use *fut ind*, e.g., **I am going to stay home today** starò a casa oggi; **to be gone** essere andato; esser morto; **to go against** opporsi a; **to go ahead** andar avanti; tirare avanti; **to go around** andare in giro; **to go away** andarsene; **to go back** tornare; **to go by** passare per; regolarsi su; (*said of time*) passare; **to go down** discendere; (*said of a boat*) affondare; **to go fishing** andare a pescare; **to go for** vendersi per; andare a pigliare; attaccare; favorire; **to go get** andare a pigliare; **to go house hunting** andare in cerca di una casa; **to go hunting** andare a caccia; **to go in** entrare in; (*to fit in*) starci in; **to go in for** dedicarsi a; **to go into** investigare; darsi a, dedicarsi a; (*gear*) (aut) ingranare; **to go in with** associarsi con; **to go off** andarsene; aver luogo; (*said of a bomb*) esplodere; (*said of a rifle*) sparare; (*said of a trap*) scattare; **to go on** continuare, protrarsi; **to go on** + *ger* continuare a + *inf*; **to go out** uscire; passare di moda; (*said, e.g., of fire*) spegnersi; (*to strike*) mettersi in sciopero; **to go over** aver successo; leggere; esaminare; **to go over to** passare ai ranghi di; **to go skiing** andare a sciare; **to go swimming** andare a nuotare, andare al bagno; **to go through** esperimentare; (*to examine carefully*) rovistare; (*said, e.g., of a plan or a project*) aver successo; (*a fortune*) dissipare; **to go through a red light** passare la strada col semaforo rosso; **to go with** andare con, accompagnare; (*a girl*) essere l'amico di; **to go without** fare a meno di

goad [god] *s* pungolo ‖ *tr* pungolare; (fig) spronare

go'-ahead' *adj* intraprendente ‖ *s* via *m*

goal [gol] *s* meta; (football) gol *m*

goalie ['golɪ] *s* portiere *m*

goal'keep'er *s* portiere *m*

goal' line' *s* linea di porta

goal' post' *s* montante *m*

goat [got] *s* capra; (*male*) becco; (coll) capro espiatorio; **to get the goat of** (coll) irritare

goatee [go'ti] *s* barbetta, pizzo

goat'herd' *s* capraio

goat'skin' *s* pelle *f* di capra

goat'suck'er *s* caprimulgo

gob [gab] *s* massa informe; **gobs** (coll) mucchio, quantità *f* enorme

gobble ['gabəl] *s* gloglottio ‖ *tr* ingozzare; **to gobble up** (coll) trangugiare; (coll) impadronirsi di ‖ *intr* trangugiare; (*said of a turkey*) gloglottare

gobbledegook ['gabəldɪ‚guk] *s* linguaggio oscuro

go'-between' *s* intermediario; (*pander*) mezzano; (poet) pronubo

goblet ['gablɪt] *s* coppa

goblin ['gablɪn] *s* folletto

go'-by' *s*—**to give s.o. the go-by** (coll) schivare qlcu

go'-cart' *s* carrettino; (*walker*) girello

god [gɑd] *s* dio; **God forbid** Dio ci scampi; **God grant** voglia Dio; **God willing** se Dio vuole

god'child' *s* (-chil'dren) figlioccio

god'daugh'ter *s* figlioccia

goddess ['gɑdɪs] *s* dea, diva

god'fa'ther *s* padrino

God'-fear'ing *adj* timorato di Dio

God'for-sak'en *adj* miserabile; (*place*) sperduto, fuori di mano

god'head' *s* deità *f* || **Godhead** *s* Ente Supremo, Dio

godless ['gɑdlɪs] *adj* ateo; malvagio || **the godless** i senza Dio

god·ly ['gɑdli] *adj* (-lier; -liest) devoto, pio

god'moth'er *s* madrina

God's' a'cre *s* camposanto

god'send' *s* manna, provvidenza

god'son' *s* figlioccio

God'speed' *s* successo, buona fortuna

go-getter ['go ,gɛtər] *s* (coll) persona intraprendente

goggle ['gɑgəl] *intr* stralunare gli occhi

goggle-eyed ['gɑgəl ,aɪd] *adj* dagli occhi sporgenti

goggles ['gɑgəlz] *spl* occhiali *mpl* da protezione

going ['go·ɪŋ] *adj* in moto, in funzione; **going on** quasi, e.g., **it is going on seven o'clock** sono quasi le sette || *s* andata; progresso

go'ings on' *s* (coll) comportamento, contegno; (coll) avvenimenti *mpl*

goiter ['gɔɪtər] *s* gozzo

gold [gold] *adj* aureo, d'oro || *s* oro

gold'beat'er *s* battiloro

gold'brick' *s* imitazione, frode *f*; (slang) fannullone *m*

gold' dig'ger ['dɪgər] *s* cercatore *m* d'oro; (coll) donna unicamente interessata nel denaro

golden ['goldən] *adj* aureo, d'oro; (*gilt*) dorato; (fig) splendido

gold'en age' *s* età *f* dell'oro

gold'en calf' *s* vitello d'oro

Gold'en Fleece' *s* vello d'oro

gold'en mean' *s* aurea mediocrità

gold'en-rod' *s* (bot) verga d'oro

gold'en rule' *s* regola della carità cristiana

gold'en wed'ding *s* nozze *fpl* d'oro

gold-filled ['gold ,fɪld] *adj* otturato in oro

gold'finch' *s* cardellino

gold'fish' *s* pesce rosso

goldilocks ['goldɪ ,lɑks] *s* bionda; (bot) ranuncolo

gold' leaf' *s* oro in foglia

gold' mine' *s* miniera d'oro

gold' plate' *s* vasellame *m* d'oro

gold'-plate' *tr* dorare

gold' rush' *s* febbre *f* dell'oro

gold'smith' *s* orefice *m*

gold' stand'ard *s* regime aureo

golf [gɑlf] *s* golf *m* || *intr* giocare a golf

golf' cart' *s* mini-auto *f* per campi da golf

golf' club' *s* mazza; associazione di giocatori di golf

golfer ['gɑlfər] *s* giocatore *m* di golf

golf' links' *spl* campo di golf

Golgotha ['gɑlgəθə] *s* il Golgota

gondola ['gɑndələ] *s* gondola

gondolier [,gɑndə'lɪr] *s* gondoliere *m*

gone [gɔn] *or* [gɑn] *adj* partito; rovinato; andato; morto; **gone on** (coll) innamorato di

gong [gɔŋ] *or* [gɑŋ] *s* gong *m*

goo [gu] *s* (coll) sostanza appicciaticcia

good [gud] *adj* (**better; best**) buono; **good and . . .** (coll) molto, e.g., **good and cheap** molto a buon mercato; **good for** buono per; responsabile per; (*equivalent*) valido per; **to be good at** esser bravo a; **to be no good** (coll) non servire a nulla; (coll) essere un perdigiorno; **to make good** avere successo; (*one's promise*) mantenere; (*a debt*) pagare; (*damages*) indennizzare || *s* bene *m*; utile *m*, profitto; **for good** per sempre; **for good and all** una volta per sempre; **goods** merce *f*, mercanzia; **the good** il bene; i buoni; **to catch with the goods** (coll) cogliere in flagrante; **to deliver the goods** (slang) mantenere le promesse; **to do good** fare del bene; **to the good** come profitto; come attivo; **what is the good of . . . ?** a che serve . . . ?

good' afternoon' *s* buon pomeriggio

good'-by' [,gud'baɪ] *s* addio || *interj* addio!; arrivederci!

good' day' *s* buon giorno

good' deed' *s* buona azione

good' egg' *s* (slang) bonaccione *m*, gran brava persona

good' eve'ning *s* buona sera; buona notte

good' fel'low *s* buon ragazzo

good'-fel'low·ship' *s* cameratismo

good'-for-noth'ing *adj* inutile, senza valore || *s* pelandrone *m*, inetto

Good' Fri'day *s* Venerdì Santo

good' grac'es *spl* buone grazie

good-hearted ['gud 'hɑrtɪd] *adj* di buon cuore

good'-hum'ored *adj* di buon umore

good'-look'ing *adj* bello

good' looks' *s* bellezza

good·ly ['gudli] *adj* (-lier; -liest) bello; di buona qualità; ampio, considerevole

good' morn'ing *s* buon giorno

good-natured ['gud'net/ərd] *adj* bonaccione, affabile

goodness ['gudnɪs] *s* bontà *f*; **for goodness sake!** per amor di Dio!; **goodness knows!** chi sa mai! || *interj* Dio mio!

good' night' *s* buona notte

good'-sized' *adj* piuttosto grande

good' speed' *s* buona fortuna

good'-tem'pered *adj* di carattere mite, gioviale

good' time' *s* periodo gradevole; **to have a good time** divertirsi; **to make good time** andare di buon passo

good' turn' *s* favore *m*, servizio

good' will' *s* buona volontà; (com) reputazione; (com) clientela

good·y ['gudi] *adj* (coll) troppo buono || *s* (-ies) (coll) santerello; **goodies**

(coll) ghiottonerie *fpl* || *interj* (coll) bene!, benissimo!

gooey [ˈgu-i] *adj* (**gooier; gooiest**) (slang) attaccaticcio

goof [guf] *s* (slang) sciocco || *tr* (slang) rovinare; **to goof up** (*an opportunity*) (slang) mancare || *intr* (slang) pigliare un granchio; **to goof off** (slang) battere la fiacca; **to goof up** (slang) farla grossa

goof·y [ˈgufi] *adj* (**-ier; -iest**) (slang) sciocco

goon [gun] *s* (slang) scemo; (coll) crumiro, gaglioffo, terrorista *m*

goose [gus] *s* (**geese** [gis]) oca; **the goose hangs high** tutto va per il meglio; **to cook one's goose** rompere le uova nel paniere di qlcu; **to kill the goose that lays the golden eggs** uccidere la gallina delle uova d'oro || *s* (**gooses**) ferro da stiro per sarto

goose'ber'ry *s* (**-ries**) uva spina; (berry) bacca d'uva spina

goose' egg' *s* (slang) zero; (*lump on the head*) (coll) bernoccolo

goose' flesh' *s* pelle *f* d'oca

goose'neck' *s* collo d'oca

goose' pim'ples *spl* pelle *f* d'oca

goose' step' *s* passo dell'oca

gopher [ˈgofər] *s* scoiattolo di terra, citillo

gore [gor] *s* sangue coagulato; (*in a garment*) gherone *m* || *tr* (*with a horn*) incornare; inserire gheroni a

gorge [gɔrdʒ] *s* gola, burrone *m*; (*meal*) mangiata || *tr* rimpinzare || *intr* rimpinzarsi

gorgeous [ˈgɔrdʒəs] *adj* splendido, magnifico

gorilla [gəˈrɪlə] *s* gorilla *m*

gorse [gɔrs] *s* gineprone *m*

gor·y [ˈgori] *adj* (**-ier; -iest**) sanguinolento

gosh [gɑʃ] *interj* perbacco!

goshawk [ˈgɑsˌhɔk] *s* sparviere *m*, astore *m*

gospel [ˈgɑspəl] *s* vangelo || **Gospel** *s* Vangelo

gos'pel truth' *s* santissima verità

gossamer [ˈgɑsəmər] *s* ragnatela; (*variety of gauze*) garza finissima; tessuto impermeabile finissimo

gossip [ˈgɑsɪp] *s* maldicenza; (person) pettegolo; **piece of gossip** maldicenza || *intr* spettegolare

gossipy [ˈgɑsɪpi] *adj* pettegolo

Goth [gɑθ] *s* Goto

Gothic [ˈgɑθɪk] *adj* & *s* gotico

gouge [gaʊdʒ] *s* (*cut made with a gouge*) scanalatura; (*tool*) sgorbia; (coll) truffa || *tr* sgorbiare; (coll) truffare

goulash [ˈgulɑʃ] *s* gulasch *m*

gourd [gord] *or* [gʊrd] *s* zucca

gourmand [ˈgʊrmənd] *s* ghiottone *m*

gourmet [ˈgʊrme] *s* buongustaio

gout [gaʊt] *s* gotta, podagra

gout·y [ˈgaʊti] *adj* (**-ier; -iest**) gottoso

govern [ˈgʌvərn] *tr* governare; (gram) reggere

governess [ˈgʌvərnɪs] *s* governante *f*, istitutrice *f*

government [ˈgʌvərnmənt] *s* governo; (gram) reggenza

governmental [ˌgʌvərnˈmentəl] *adj* governativo

governor [ˈgʌvərnər] *s* governatore *m*; (mach) regolatore *m*

governorship [ˈgʌvərnərˌʃɪp] *s* governatorato

gown [gaʊn] *s* (*of a woman*) vestito; (academic) toga; (*of a physician or patient*) gabbanella; (*of a priest*) veste *f* talare

grab [græb] *s* presa; **up for grabs** (coll) pronto a esser pigliato || *v* (*pret & pp* **grabbed**; *ger* **grabbing**) *tr* pigliare, afferrare

grace [gres] *s* (charm; favor) grazia; (pardon) mercé *f*; (prayer) benedicite *m*; (com) dilazione; **to say grace** recitare il benedicite; **with good grace** di buona voglia || *tr* adornare

graceful [ˈgresfəl] *adj* grazioso, vezzoso, leggiadro

grace' note' *s* (mus) appoggiatura

gracious [ˈgreʃəs] *adj* grazioso; misericordioso || *interj* Dio buono!

gradation [greˈdeʃən] *s* gradazione; (*step in a series*) passo

grade [gred] *s* grado; (slope) pendenza; (*mark in school*) voto; **to make the grade** raggiungere la meta || *tr* selezionare; (*a student*) dare un voto a; (land) spianare

grade' cros'sing *s* (rr) passaggio a livello

grade' school' *s* scuola elementare

gradient [ˈgredɪ·ənt] *adj* in pendenza || *s* pendenza; (phys) gradiente *m*

gradual [ˈgrædʒʊ·əl] *adj* graduale

graduate [ˈgrædʒʊ·ɪt] *adj* graduato; superiore; (student) laureato; (*candidate for degree*) laureando || [ˈgrædʒʊ,et] *tr* graduare; laureare, diplomare || *intr* laurearsi, diplomarsi

grad'uate school' *s* facoltà *f* di studi avanzati

graduation [ˌgrædʒʊˈeʃən] *s* graduazione; laurea; cerimonia della consegna delle lauree

graft [græft] *or* [grɑft] *s* (hort) innesto; (surg) trapianto; (coll) prevaricazione || *tr* (hort) innestare; (surg) trapiantare || *intr* (coll) prevaricare

gra'ham bread' [ˈgre·əm] *s* pane *m* integrale

grain [gren] *s* chicco; (*of sand*) granello; (*cereal seeds*) granaglie *fpl*; (*in wood*) venatura; (*in stone*) grana; **against the grain** di cattivo verso || *tr* granulare; (leather) zigrinare; (metal) granire

grain' el'evator *s* elevatore *m* di grano; (building) deposito di cereali

graining [ˈgrenɪŋ] *s* venatura

gram [græm] *s* grammo

grammar [ˈgræmər] *s* grammatica

grammarian [grəˈmerɪ·ən] *s* grammatico

gram'mar school' *s* scuola elementare

grammatical [grəˈmætɪkəl] *adj* grammatico

gramophone ['græmə,fon] s (trademark) grammofono

grana·ry ['grænəri] s (-ries) granaio

grand [grænd] adj grandioso; grande, famoso

grand'aunt' s prozia

grand'child' s (-chil'dren) nipote mf

grand'daugh'ter s nipote f

grand' duch'ess s granduchessa

grand' duke' s granduca m

grandee [græn'di] s grande m

grandeur ['grændʒər] or ['grændʒur] s grande m, grandiosità f

grand'fa'ther s nonno; (forefather) antenato

grand'father's clock' s grande orologio a pendolo

grandiose ['grændɪ,os] adj grandioso

grand' ju'ry s giuria investigativa

grand' lar'ceny s furto importante

grand' lodge' s grande oriente m

grandma ['grænd,ma], ['græm,ma] or ['græmə] s (coll) nonna

grand'moth'er s nonna

grand'neph'ew s pronipote m

grand'niece' s pronipote f

grand' op'era s opera, opera lirica

grandpa ['grænd,pa], ['græn,pa] or ['græmpa] s (coll) nonno

grand'par'ent s nonno, nonna

grand' pian'o s pianoforte m a coda

grand'son' s nipote m

grand'stand' s tribuna

grand' to'tal s somma totale; importo globale

grand'un'cle s prozio

grand' vizier' s gran visir m

grange [grendʒ] s (farm) fattoria; (organization of farmers) sindacato di agricoltori

granite ['grænɪt] s granito

grant [grænt] or [grant] s concessione; (sum of money) sovvenzione; trapasso di proprietà ‖ tr concedere; (a wish) esaudire; (a permit) rilasciare; (law) trasferire; **to take for granted** ammettere come vero; trattare con indifferenza

grantee [græn'ti] or [gran'ti] s concessionario; beneficiario

grant'-in-aid' s (grants'-in-aid') sussidio governativo a un ente pubblico; borsa di studio

grantor [græn'tor] or [gran'tor] s concedente m, concessore m

granular ['grænjələr] adj granulare

granulate ['grænjə,let] tr granulare ‖ intr diventare granulato

gran'ulated sug'ar s zucchero cristallizzato

granule ['grænjul] s granulo

grape [grep] s chicco d'uva; (vine) vite f; **grapes** uva

grape' ar'bor s pergolato

grape'fruit' s pompelmo

grape' juice' s succo d'uva

grape'shot' s mitraglia

grape'vine' s vite f; **by the grapevine** di bocca in bocca; (mil) attraverso la radio fante

graph [græf] or [graf] s (diagram) grafico; (gram) segno grafico

graphic(al) ['græfɪk(əl)] adj grafico

graphite ['græfaɪt] s grafite f

graph' pa'per s carta millimetrata

grapnel ['græpnəl] s uncino; (anchor) grappino

grapple ['græpəl] s uncino; lotta corpo a corpo ‖ tr uncinare ‖ intr combattere; **to grapple with** lottare con

grap'pling i'ron s raffio, grappino

grasp [græsp] or [grasp] s impugnatura; (power) possesso; **to have a good grasp of** sapere a fondo; **within the grasp of** nei limiti della comprensione di ‖ tr (with hand) impugnare; (to get control of) impadronirsi di; (fig) capire ‖ intr—**to grasp at** cercare di afferrare

grasping ['græspɪŋ] or ['graspɪŋ] adj tenace; avido, cupido

grass [græs] or [gras] s erba; (pasture land) pastura; (lawn) tappeto erboso; **to go to grass** (said of cattle) andare al pascolo; andare in vacanza; ritirarsi; andare in rovina; morire; **to not let the grass grow under one's feet** non dormire in piuma

grass' court' s campo da tennis d'erba

grass'hop'per s cavalletta

grass'-roots' adj popolare

grass' seed' s semente f d'erba

grass' wid'ow s donna separata dal marito

grass·y ['græsi] or ['grasi] adj (-ier; -iest) erboso

grate [gret] s (for cooking) griglia; (at a window) grata ‖ tr mettere una grata a; (one's teeth) digrignare; (e.g., cheese) grattugiare ‖ intr stridere, cigolare; **to grate on one's nerves** dare sui nervi di qlcu

grateful ['gretfəl] adj riconoscente; (pleasing) piacevole, gradito

grater ['gretər] s grattugia

grati·fy ['grætɪ,faɪ] v (pret & pp -fied) tr gratificare, soddisfare

gratifying ['grætɪ,faɪ·ɪŋ] adj soddisfacente, piacevole

grating ['gretɪŋ] adj irritante; (sound) stridente ‖ s inferriata

gratis ['gretɪs] or ['grætɪs] adj gratuito ‖ adv gratis

gratitude ['grætɪ,tjud] or ['grætɪ,tud] s gratitudine f, riconoscenza

gratuitous [grə'tju·ɪtəs] or [grə'tu·ɪtəs] adj gratuito

gratui·ty [grə'tju·ɪti] or [grə'tu·ɪti] s (-ties) mancia, regalia

grave [grev] adj grave ‖ s tomba, sepolcro, fossa

gravedigger ['grev,dɪgər] s becchino

gravel ['grævəl] s ghiaia; (pathol) renella

grav'en im'age ['grevən] s idolo

grave'stone' s pietra tombale

grave'yard' s cimitero, camposanto

gravitate ['grævɪ,tet] intr gravitare

gravitation [,grævɪ'teʃən] s gravitazione

gravi·ty ['grævɪti] s (-ties) gravità f

gravure [grə'vjur] or ['grevjur] s fotoincisione

gra·vy ['grevi] s (-vies) (juice from

cooking *meat*) sugo; (*sauce made with it*) salsa, intingolo; (slang) guadagni *mpl* facili

gra'vy boat' *s* salsiera

gra'vy train' *s* (slang) greppia, mangiatoia

gray [gre] *adj* grigio; (*gray-haired*) canuto || *s* grigio; cavallo grigio || *intr* incanutire

gray'beard' *s* vecchio

gray-haired ['gre ˌherd] *adj* canuto

gray'hound' *s* levriere *m*

grayish ['greˌɪʃ] *adj* grigiastro

gray' mat'ter *s* materia grigia

graze [grez] *tr* (*to touch lightly*) sfiorare; (*to scratch lightly*) scalfire; (*grass*) brucare; (*cattle*) pascere, pascolare || *intr* pascere, brucare

grease [gris] *s* grasso, unto || [gris] *or* [griz] *tr* ingrassare, ungere

grease' cup' [gris] *s* coppa dell'olio

grease' gun' [gris] *s* ingrassatore *m*

grease' lift' [gris] *s* piattaforma di lubrificazione

grease' paint' [gris] *s* cerone *m*

grease' pit' [gris] *s* fossa di riparazione

greas·y ['grisi] *or* ['grizi] *adj* (-ier; -iest) grasso, unto, untuoso

great [gret] *adj* grande; (coll) eccellente || **the great** i grandi

great'-aunt' *s* prozia

Great' Bear' *s* Orsa Maggiore

Great' Brit'ain ['brɪtən] *s* la Gran Bretagna

Great' Dane' *s* danese *m*, alano

Great'er New York' *s* Nuova York e i suoi sobborghi

great'-grand'child' *s* (-chil'dren) pronipote *mf*

great'-grand'daugh'ter *s* pronipote *f*

great'-grand'fa'ther *s* bisnonno

great'-grand'moth'er *s* bisnonna

great'-grand'par'ent *s* bisnonno, bisnonna

great'-grand'son' *s* pronipote *m*

greatly ['gretli] *adj* molto

great'-neph'ew *s* pronipote *m*

greatness ['gretnɪs] *s* grandezza

great'-niece' *s* pronipote *f*

great'-un'cle *s* prozio

Grecian ['griʃən] *adj* & *s* greco

Greece [gris] *s* la Grecia

greed [grid] *s* avarizia, avidità *f*

greediness ['gridɪnɪs] *s* bramosia

greed·y ['gridi] *adj* (-ier; -iest) avaro, ingordo, bramoso

Greek [grik] *adj* & *s* greco

green [grin] *adj* verde; (fig) verde, inesperto || *s* verde *m*; (*lawn*) tappeto erboso; **greens** verdura, insalata

green'back' *s* (U.S.A.) biglietto di banca

green' earth' *s* verdaccio

greener·y ['grinəri] *s* (-ies) (*foliage*) vegetazione; (*hothouse*) serra

green'-eyed' *adj* dagli occhi verdi; (coll) geloso

green'gage' *s* regina claudia

green'horn' *s* (slang) pivello, sempliciotto

green'house' *s* serra

greenish ['grinɪʃ] *adj* verdastro

Greenland ['grinlənd] *s* la Groenlandia

green' light' *s* semaforo verde; (coll) via *m*

greenness ['grinnɪs] *s* verdore *m*, verdezza; inesperienza

green' pep'per *s* peperone *m* verde

greensward ['grinˌswɔrd] *s* tappeto erboso

green' thumb' *s* abilità *f* speciale per il giardinaggio

green' veg'etables *spl* verdura

green'wood' *s* bosco verde

greet [grit] *tr* salutare; ricevere; (e.g., *one's ears*) offrirsi a

greeting ['gritɪŋ] *s* saluto; accoglienza || **greetings** *interj* saluti!

greet'ing card' *s* cartolina d'auguri

gregarious [grɪˈgɛrɪ-əs] *adj* (*living in the midst of others*) gregario; (*sociable*) sociale

Gregorian [grɪˈgɔrɪ-ən] *adj* gregoriano

grenade [grɪˈned] *s* granata

grenadier [ˌgrɛnəˈdɪr] *s* granatiere *m*

grenadine [ˌgrɛnəˈdin] *s* granatina

grey [gre] *adj*, *s* & *intr* var of **gray**

grid [grɪd] *s* (network) rete *f*; (on *map*) reticolato; (electron) griglia

griddle ['grɪdəl] *s* tegame *m*

grid'dle-cake' *s* frittella cotta in teglia, crêpe *m*

grid'i'ron *s* griglia; campo di football; (theat) graticcia

grief [grif] *s* affanno, dolore *m*; disgrazia; **to come to grief** andare in rovina

grievance ['grivəns] *s* lagnanza; motivo di lagnanza

grieve [griv] *tr* affliggere || *intr* affliggersi, dolersi; **to grieve over** soffrire per

grievous ['grivəs] *adj* doloroso, penoso; (error) grave; (*deplorable*) deplorevole

griffin ['grɪfɪn] *s* grifo, grifone *m*

grill [grɪl] *s* griglia || *tr* mettere alla griglia; (coll) interrogare insistentemente

grille [grɪl] *s* inferriata; (aut) mascherina, calandra

grill'room' *s* grill-room *m*, rosticceria

grim [grɪm] *adj* (grimmer; grimmest) (stern) accigliato; (fierce) feroce; (sinister) sinistro; (unyielding) implacabile

grimace ['grɪməs] *or* [grɪˈmes] *s* smorfia, sberleffo || *intr* fare le boccacce

grime [graɪm] *s* sporco; (soot) fuliggine *f*

grim·y ['graɪmi] *adj* (-ier; -iest) sporco; fuligginoso

grin [grɪn] *s* sorriso; (*malicious in intent*) ghigno || *v* (pret & pp grinned; ger grinning) *intr* sorridere; ghignare

grind [graɪnd] *s* macinata; (*laborious work*) (coll) macina; (slang) sgobbone *m* || *v* (pret & pp ground [graund]) *tr* macinare; (to sharpen) molare; (lenses) smerigliare; (meat) tritare; opprimere; (a crank) girare; (mach) rettificare || *intr* macinare; frantumarsi; cigolare; (coll) sgobbare

grinder ['graɪndər] *s* (to sharpen tools) mola; (to grind coffee) macinino;

(*back tooth*) molare *m*; (*person*) molatore *m*

grind'stone' *s* mola; **to keep one's nose to the grindstone** lavorare senza posa

grin·go ['grɪŋgo] *s* (**-gos**) (disparaging) gringo

grip [grɪp] *s* (*grasp*) presa; (*with hand*) stretta; (*handle*) impugnatura; **to come to grips** venire alle prese ‖ *v* (*pret & pp* **gripped; ger gripping**) *tr* stringere; impugnare; attirare l'attenzione di

gripe [graɪp] *s* (coll) lamentela; (naut) rizza; **gripes** colica ‖ *intr* (coll) lamentarsi, brontolare

grippe [grɪp] *s* influenza

gripping ['grɪpɪŋ] *adj* interessantissimo, affascinante

gris·ly ['grɪzli] *adj* (**-lier; -liest**) orribile, spaventoso

grist [grɪst] *s* (*grain to be ground*) macinata; (*ground grain*) farina; (coll) mucchio; **to be grist to the mill of** (coll) fare comodo a

gristle ['grɪsəl] *s* cartilagine *f*

gris·tly ['grɪsli] *adj* (**-tlier; -tliest**) cartilaginoso

grist'mill' *s* mulino

grit [grɪt] *s* sabbia, arenaria; (fig) forza d'animo ‖ *v* (*pret & pp* **gritted; ger gritting**) *tr* (*one's teeth*) far stridere, digrignare

grit·ty ['grɪti] *adj* (**-tier; -tiest**) sabbioso, granuloso; (fig) forte, coraggioso

griz·zly ['grɪzli] *adj* (**-zlier; -zliest**) brizzolato, canuto ‖ *s* (**-zlies**) orso grigio

groan [gron] *s* gemito ‖ *intr* gemere; (*to be overburdened*) essere sovraccarico

grocer ['grosər] *s* droghiere *m*; pizzicagnolo; proprietario di negozio di generi alimentari

grocer·y ['grosəri] *s* (**-ies**) (*store selling spices, soap, etc.*) drogheria; (*store selling cheese, cold cuts, etc.*) negozio di pizzicagnolo; negozio di generi alimentari; **groceries** generi *mpl* alimentari, commestibili *mpl*

grog [grɑg] *s* grog *m*

grog·gy ['grɑgi] *adj* (**-gier; -giest**) (coll) groggy, intontito

groin [grɔɪn] *s* (anat) inguine *m*; (archit) costolone *m*

groom [grum] *s* mozzo di stalla; (*bridegroom*) sposo ‖ *tr* rassettare; (*horses*) rigovernare; (pol) preparare per le elezioni

grooms'man *s* (**-men**) compare *m* di nozze

groove [gruv] *s* scanalatura; (*of a pulley*) gola; (*of a phonograph record*) solco; (fig) routine *f* ‖ *tr* scanalare, incavare

grope [grop] *intr* brancicare; (*for words*) cercare; **to grope for** cercare a tastoni

gropingly ['gropɪŋli] *adv* a tastoni

gross [gros] *adj* (*thick*) spesso; (*coarse*) volgare; (*fat*) grosso; (*error*) mar-

chiano; (*without deductions*) lordo ‖ *s* grossa ‖ *tr* fare un incasso lordo di

grossly ['grosli] *adv* approssimativamente; totalmente

gross' na'tional prod'uct *s* reddito nazionale

grotesque [gro'tɛsk] *adj & s* grottesco

grot·to ['grɑto] *s* (**-toes** or **-tos**) grotta

grouch [grautʃ] *s* (coll) malumore *m*; (coll) persona stizzosa ‖ *intr* (coll) brontolare

grouch·y ['grautʃi] *adj* (**-ier; -iest**) (coll) stizzoso, brontolone

ground [graund] *s* (*earth, soil, land*) terra; (*piece of land*) terreno; (*basis*) causa, fondatezza; (elec) terra, massa; (fig) occasione, motivo; **grounds** giardini *mpl*, terreno; (*of coffee*) fondi *mpl*; **on the ground of** per motivo di; **to break ground** dare la prima palata; (fig) mettere la prima pietra; **to fall to the ground** cadere al suolo; (fig) fallire; **to gain ground** guadagnar terreno; **to give ground** ceder terreno; **to lose ground** perder terreno; **to stand one's ground** non indietreggiare ‖ *tr* fondare; (elec) mettere a massa; **to be grounded** (*said of an airplane*) essere forzato di rimanere a terra; **to be well grounded** essere bene al corrente ‖ *intr* incagliarsi

ground' connec'tion *s* messa a terra

ground' crew' *s* (aer) personale *m* di servizio

ground' floor' *s* pianterreno

ground' glass' *s* vetro smerigliato

ground' hog' *s* marmotta americana

ground' lead' [lid] *s* (elec) collegamento a massa

groundless ['graundlɪs] *adj* infondato

ground' meat' *s* carne tritata

ground' plan' *s* progetto, pianta

ground' swell' *s* mareggiata

ground' wire' *s* filo di terra, filo di massa

ground'work' *s* fondamento, base *f*

group [grup] *adj* collettivo ‖ *s* gruppo; (aer) stormo ‖ *tr* raggruppare ‖ *intr* raggrupparsi

grouse [graus] *s* gallo cedrone; (slang) brontolio ‖ *intr* (slang) brontolare

grout [graut] *s* stucco ‖ *tr* stuccare

grove [grov] *s* boschetto

grov·el ['grævəl] or ['grɑvəl] *v* (*pret & pp* **-eled** or **-elled; ger -eling** or **-elling**) *intr* umiliarsi

grow [gro] *v* (*pret* **grew** [gru]; *pp* **grown** [gron]) *tr* (*plants*) coltivare; (*animals*) allevare; (*a beard*) farsi crescere ‖ *intr* crescere; svilupparsi; nascere; venir su; (*to become*) diventare; farsi; **to grow angry** arrabbiarsi; **to grow old** invecchiare; **to grow out of** (*fashion*) passare di; originare da; **to grow up** svilupparsi

growing ['gro·ɪŋ] *adj* crescente; (*pains*) di crescenza; (*child*) in crescita

growl [graul] *s* ringhio; brontolio ‖ *intr* (*said of animals*) ringhiare; brontolare

grown'-up' *adj* adulto, grande ‖ *s* (grown-ups) adulto

growth [groθ] *s* crescita, sviluppo; aumento; (pathol) escrescenza

growth' stock' *s* azione *f* che promette di aumentare di valore

grub [grʌb] *s* (drudge) sgobbone *m;* larva di coleottero; (coll) mangiare *m* ‖ *v* (pret & pp grubbed; ger grubbing) *tr* scavare, zappare, dissodare ‖ *intr* cercare assiduamente; scavare; sgobbare

grub-by ['grʌbi] *adj* (-bier; -biest) sporco; bacato; infestato di larve

grudge [grʌdʒ] *s* rancore *m;* to have a grudge (to spend unwillingly) lesinare; invidiare

grudgingly ['grʌdʒɪŋli] *adv* di cattiva voglia

gru-el ['gru-əl] *s* farinata d'avena ‖ *v* (pret & pp -eled or -elled; ger -eling or -elling) *tr* estenuare

gruesome ['grusəm] *adj* raccapricciante

gruff [grʌf] *adj* brusco, burbero; (voice) rauco, roco

grumble ['grʌmbəl] *s* brontolio ‖ *intr* brontolare, borbottare

grump-y ['grʌmpi] *adj* (-ier; -iest) di cattivo umore, scontroso

grunt [grʌnt] *s* grugnito ‖ *intr* grugnire

G-string ['dʒi,strɪŋ] *s* (loincloth) perizoma *m;* (worn by a female entertainer) triangolino di stoffa; (mus) corda di sol

guarantee [,gærən'ti] *s* garanzia; (guarantor) garante *mf* ‖ *tr* garantire

guarantor ['gærən,tɔr] *s* garante *mf*

guaran-ty ['gærənti] *s* (-ties) garanzia ‖ *v* (pret & pp -tied) *tr* garantire

guard [gard] *s* guardia; (safeguard) protezione; (in a prison) guardia carceraria; (of a sword) guardamano; (football) mediano; **off guard** alla sprovvista; **on guard** in guardia; di fazione; **to mount a guard** montare la guardia; **under guard** ben custodito ‖ *tr* guardare ‖ *intr* fare la sentinella; **to guard against** guardarsi di

guard-ed ['gardɪd] *adj* (remark) prudente

guard'house' *s* locale *m* di detenzione; (mil) corpo di guardia

guardian ['gardɪ-ən] *adj* tutelare ‖ *s* guardiano; (law) tutore *m*

guard'ian an'gel *s* angelo custode

guardianship ['gardɪ-ən,ʃɪp] *s* protezione; (law) tutela

guard'rail' *s* guardavia *m;* (naut) parapetto

guard'room' *s* (mil) corpo di guardia

guards'man *s* (-men) guardia

guerrilla [gə'rɪlə] *s* guerrigliero

guerril'la war'fare *s* guerriglia

guess [gɛs] *s* congettura, supposizione ‖ *tr & intr* congetturare, supporre; (to estimate correctly) indovinare; (coll) credere; **I guess so** credo di sì

guess'work' *s* congettura

guest [gɛst] *s* invitato, ospite *m;* (of a hotel) cliente *mf;* (of a boarding house) pensionante *mf*

guest' book' *s* albo d'onore; (in a hotel) registro

guffaw [gə'fɔ] *s* sghignazzata ‖ *intr* sghignazzare

Guiana [gɪ'ɑnə] or [gɪ'ænə] *s* la Guayana

guidance ['gaɪdəns] *s* guida, governo; **for your guidance** per Sua norma

guide [gaɪd] *s* guida ‖ *tr* guidare

guide'board' *s* indicatore *m* stradale

guide'book' *s* guida

guid'ed mis'sile ['gaɪdɪd] *s* telearma, teleproietto, missile teleguidato

guide' dog' *s* cane *m* conduttore di un cieco

guide'line' *s* falsariga; corda fissa; linea di condotta, direttiva

guide'post' *s* indicatore *m* stradale

guide' word' *s* esponente *m* in testa di pagina

guidon ['gaɪdən] *s* guidone *m*

guild [gɪld] *s* associazione mutua; (hist) gilda

guild'hall' *s* palazzo delle corporazioni

guile [gaɪl] *s* astuzia, frode *f*

guileful ['gaɪlfəl] *adj* astuto, insidioso

guileless ['gaɪllɪs] *adj* sincero, innocente

guillotine ['gɪlə,tin] *s* ghigliottina ‖ [,gɪlə'tin] *tr* ghigliottinare

guilt [gɪlt] *s* colpa, reità *f*

guiltless ['gɪltlɪs] *adj* innocente

guilt-y ['gɪlti] *adj* (-ier; -iest) colpevole, reo

guimpe [gɪmp] or [gæmp] *s* sprone *m*

guinea ['gɪni] *s* ghinea; gallina faraona ‖ **Guinea** *s* la Guinea

guin'ea fowl' *s* gallina faraona

guin'ea pig' *s* porcellino d'India, cavia; (fig) cavia

guise [gaɪz] *s* aspetto; veste *f;* **under the guise of** in guisa di

guitar [gɪ'tɑr] *s* chitarra

guitarist [gɪ'tɑrɪst] *s* chitarrista *mf*

gulch [gʌltʃ] *s* burrone *m*

gulf [gʌlf] *s* golfo; abisso

Gulf' Stream' *s* corrente *f* del Golfo

gull [gʌl] *s* gabbiano; (coll) credulone *m* ‖ *tr* darla da bere a

gullet ['gʌlɪt] *s* gargarozzo; esofago

gullible ['gʌlɪbəl] *adj* credulone

gul-ly ['gʌli] *s* (-lies) borro, zanella

gulp [gʌlp] *s* sorsata ‖ *tr*—**to gulp down** (food) ingoiare; (drink) tracannare; (fig) ingoiare, tranguigiare ‖ *intr* secernere gomma

gum [gʌm] *s* gomma; (mucus on eyelids) cispa; **gums** (anat) gengive *fpl* ‖ *v* (pret & pp gummed; ger gumming) *tr* ingommare; **to gum up** (slang) guastare ‖ *intr* secernere gomma

gum' ar'abic *s* gomma arabica

gum'boil' *s* flemmone *m* gengivale

gum' boot' *s* stivale *m* da palude

gum'drop' *s* caramella alla gelatina di frutta, pasticca di gomma, drop *m*

gum-my ['gʌmi] *adj* (-mier; -miest) gommoso, vischioso; (eyelid) cisposo

gumption ['gʌmpʃən] *s* (coll) iniziativa; (coll) coraggio, fegato

gum'shoe' *s* caloscia; (slang) poliziotto ‖ *v* (pret & pp -shoed; ger -shoeing) *intr* (slang) camminare silenziosamente

gun [gʌn] *s* (*rifle*) fucile *m;* (*revolver*) revolver *m;* (*pistol*) rivoltella; (*e.g., for spraying*) rivoltella; **to stick to one's guns** tener duro || *v* (*pret & pp* **gunned;** *ger* **gunning**) *tr* far fuoco su, freddare; (*a motor*) (slang) accelerare rapidamente || *intr* andare a caccia; sparare; **to gun for** andare a caccia di

gun'boat' *s* cannoniera, esploratore *m*

gun' car'riage *s* affusto

gun'cot'ton *s* fulmicotone *m*

gun'fire' *s* fuoco, tiro

gun'man *s* (-men) bandito, sicario

gun' met'al *s* bronzo da cannoni; acciaio brunito

gunnel [ˈgʌnəl] *s* (naut) frisata

gunner [ˈgʌnər] *s* artigliere *m,* servente *m*

gunnery [ˈgʌnəri] *s* artiglieria, tiro

gunnysack [ˈgʌniˌsæk] *s* sacco di tela greggia

gunpoint [ˈgʌnˌpɔint] *s* mirino; **at gunpoint** a mano armata, e.g., **he was held up at gunpoint** subì una rapina a mano armata

gun'pow'der *s* polvere nera or pirica

gun'run'ner *s* contrabbandiere *m* di armi da fuoco

gun'shot' *s* schioppettata; revolverata; **within gunshot** a tiro di schioppo

gun'shot' wound' *s* schioppettata

gun'smith' *s* armaiolo

gun'stock' *s* cassa del fucile

gunwale [ˈgʌnəl] *s* frisata

gup·py [ˈgʌpi] *s* (-pies) lebiste *m*

gurgle [ˈgɑrgəl] *s* gorgoglio, borboglio || *intr* gorgogliare, borbogliare; (*said of a human being*) barbugliare

gush [gʌʃ] *s* getto, fiotto || *intr* zampillare, sgorgare; (coll) dare in effusioni

gusher [ˈgʌʃər] *s* pozzo di petrolio; (coll) persona espansiva

gushing [ˈgʌʃiŋ] *adj* zampillante, sgorgante; (coll) espansivo || *s* zampillio; (coll) espansione, effusione

gush·y [ˈgʌʃi] *adj* (-ier; -iest) (coll) espansivo, effusivo

gusset [ˈgʌsit] *s* gherone *m*

gust [gʌst] *s* (*of wind*) raffica; (*of smoke*) ondata, zaffata; (*of noise*) esplosione; (*of anger*) sfuriata

gusto [ˈgʌsto] *s* gusto; entusiasmo

gust·y [ˈgʌsti] *adj* (-ier; -iest) a raffiche, burrascoso

gut [gʌt] *s* budello; **guts** budello; (slang) fegato, coraggio || *v* (*pret & pp* **gutted;** *ger* **gutting**) *tr* sparare, spanciare; distruggere l'interno di

gutta-percha [ˈgʌtəˈpʌrtʃə] *s* guttaperca

gutter [ˈgʌtər] *s* (*on side of road*) cunetta; (*in street*) rigagnolo; (*of roof*) doccia, grondaia; (fig) bassifondi *mpl*

gut'ter-snipe' *s* monello

guttural [ˈgʌtərəl] *adj & s* gutturale *f*

guy [gai] *s* cavo di sicurezza; (coll) tipo, tizio || *tr* burlarsi di

guzzle [ˈgʌzəl] *tr & intr* trincare, bere a garganella

guzzler [ˈgʌzlər] *s* ubriacone *m*

gym [dʒim] *s* (coll) palestra

gymnasi·um [dʒimˈnɛziˌəm] *s* (-ums or -a [ə]) palestra

gymnast [ˈdʒimnæst] *s* ginnasta *mf*

gymnastic [dʒimˈnæstik] *adj* ginnastico || **gymnastics** *spl* ginnastica

gynecologist [ˌgainəˈkɑlədʒist], [ˌdʒainəˈkɑlədʒist] or [ˌdʒinəˈkɑlədʒist] *s* ginecologo

gyp [dʒip] *s* (coll) imbroglio; (*person*) (coll) imbroglione *m* || *v* (*pret & pp* **gypped;** *ger* **gypping**) *tr* imbrogliare

gypsum [ˈdʒipsəm] *s* gesso

gyp·sy [ˈdʒipsi] *adj* zingaresco, zingaro || *s* (-sies) zingaro || **Gypsy** *s* (*language*) zingaresco

gypsyish [ˈdʒipsiˌiʃ] *adj* zingaresco

gyrate [ˈdʒairet] *intr* turbinare

gyrocompass [ˈdʒairoˌkʌmpəs] *s* girobussola

gyroscope [ˈdʒairəˌskop] *s* giroscopio

H

H, h [etʃ] *s* ottava lettera dell'alfabeto inglese

haberdasher [ˈhæbərˌdæʃər] *s* camiciaio; (*dealer in notions*) merciaio

haberdasher·y [ˈhæbərˌdæʃəri] *s* (-ies) camiceria; merceria

habit [ˈhæbit] *s* abitudine *f;* (*addiction*) vizio; (*garb*) saio; **to be in the habit of** aver l'usanza di

habitat [ˈhæbiˌtæt] *s* habitat *m*

habitation [ˌhæbiˈteʃən] *s* abitazione

habit-forming [ˈhæbitˌfɔrmiŋ] *adj* (*e.g., drugs*) stupefacente; (*e.g., T.V.*) assuefacente, che fa venire il vizio

habitual [həˈbitʃuˌəl] *adj* abituale

habitué [həˌbitʃuˈe] *s* habitué *m*

hack [hæk] *s* (*cut*) taglio; (*notch*) tacca; (*cough*) tosse secca; cavallo da nolo; vettura di piazza; (*nag*) ronzino; (*poor writer*) scribacchino || *tr* tagliare; stagliare

hack'man *s* (-men) vetturino

hackney [ˈhækni] *s* cavallo da sella; vettura di piazza

hackneyed [ˈhæknid] *adj* banale, **trito**

hack'saw' *s* seghetto per metalli

haddock [ˈhædək] *s* eglefino

haft [hæft] or [hɑft] *s* impugnatura

hag [hæg] *s* (*ugly old woman*) megera; (*witch*) strega

haggard [ˈhægərd] *adj* sparuto, macilento; (*wild-looking*) stralunato

haggle ['hægəl] *intr* mercanteggiare

hagiographer [ˌhægiˈɑgrəfər] or [ˌhedʒiˈɑgrəfər] *s* agiografo

hagiography [ˌhægiˈɑgrəfi] or [ˌhedʒiˈɑgrəfi] *s* agiografia

Hague, The [heg] *s* L'Aia *f*

hail [hel] *s* (*precipitation*) grandine *f*; (*greeting*) saluto; **within hail** a portata di voce || *tr* salutare; accogliere; chiamare; (*e.g., blows*) far cadere || *intr* grandinare; **to hail from** venire da || *interj* salute!; salve!

hail'-fel'low *adj* gioviale

Hail' Mar'y *s* Ave Maria, avemaria

hail'stone' *s* chicco di grandine

hail'storm' *s* grandinata

hair [her] *s* capelli *mpl*; (*of animals*) pelame *m* or pelo; **a hair** (*a single filament*) un capello or un pelo; **to a hair** a perfezione; **to get in one's hair** (slang) dare sui nervi a qlcu; **to let one's hair down** (slang) parlare francamente; (slang) comportarsi alla buona; **to make one's hair stand on end** far rizzare i capelli a qlcu; **to not turn a hair** non scomporsi; **to split hairs** cercare il pelo nell'uovo

hair'breadth' *s* spessore *m* di un capello; **to escape by a hairbreadth** scamparla per un pelo

hair'brush' *s* spazzola per i capelli

hair'cloth' *s* cilicio

hair'cut' *s* taglio dei capelli; **to get a haircut** farsi tagliare i capelli

hair'do' *s* (-dos) acconciatura

hair'dress'er *s* parrucchiere *m* per signora; pettinatrice *f*

hair' dri'er *s* asciugacapelli *m*

hair' dye' *s* tintura per i capelli

hairless ['herlɪs] *adj* pelato, calvo

hair' net' *s* rete *f* per i capelli

hair'pin' *s* forcella, forcina, molletta

hair-raising ['her ˌrezɪŋ] *adj* orripilante

hair' re·mov'er *s* depilatorio

hair' restor'er [rɪˈstorər] *s* rigeneratore *m* per i capelli

hair' rib'bon *s* nastro per i capelli

hairsplitting ['her ˌsplɪtɪŋ] *adj* meticoloso, pignolo

hair'spring' *s* spirale *f*

hair' styl'ing *s* pettinatura per signora

hair·y ['heri] *adj* (-ier; -iest) peloso, villoso, irsuto

hake [hek] *s* merluzzo, nasello

halberd ['hælbərd] *s* alabarda

halberdier [ˌhælbərˈdɪr] *s* alabardiere *m*

halcyon ['hælsɪ·ən] *adj* calmo, pacifico

hale [hel] *adj* sano, robusto || *tr* trascinare a viva forza

half [hæf] or [hɑf] *adj* mezzo; **a half** or **half a** mezzo; **half the** la metà di || *s* (**halves** [hævz] or [hɑvz]) metà *f*; (arith) mezzo; **in half** a metà; **to go halves** fare a metà || *adv* mezzo, e.g., **half asleep** mezzo addormentato; a metà, e.g., **half finished** a metà finito; **half past** e mezzo or e mezza, e.g., **half past three** le tre e mezzo or le tre e mezza; **half . . . half** metà . . . metà

half'-and-half' *adj* mezzo e mezzo || *s* mezza crema e mezzo latte; mezza

birra chiara e mezza scura || *adv* a metà, in parti uguali

half'back' *s* (football) mediano; (soccer) laterale *m*

half-baked ['hæf ˌbekt] or ['hɑf ˌbekt] *adj* mezzo cotto; (*ideas*) infondato, inesperto

half' bind'ing *s* rilegatura in mezza pelle

half'-blood' *s* meticcio; fratellastro; sorellastra

half'-breed' *s* meticcio

half' broth'er *s* fratellastro

half-cocked ['hæf ˌkɑkt] or ['hɑf ˌkɑkt] *adj* immaturo, precipitato || *adv* (coll) precipitatamente

half' fare' *s* mezza corsa

half'-full' *adj* mezzo pieno

half-hearted ['hæf ˌhɑrtɪd] or ['hɑf ˌhɑrtɪd] *adj* indifferente, freddo

half'-hol'iday *s* mezza festa

half' hose' *s* calzini *mpl* corti

half'-hour' *s* mezz'ora; **on the half-hour** ogni trenta minuti allo scoccare dell'ora e della mezz'ora

half'-length' *adj* a mezzo busto || *s* ritratto a mezzo busto

half'life' *s* (phys) vita media

half'-mast' *s*—**at half-mast** a mezz'asta

half'moon' *s* mezzaluna

half' mourn'ing *s* mezzo lutto

half' note' *s* (mus) minima

half' pay' *s* mezza paga

halfpen·ny ['hepəni] or ['hepni] *s* (-nies) mezzo penny

half' pint' *s* mezza pinta; (slang) mezza cartuccia, mezza calzetta

half'-seas o'ver *adj*—**to be half-seas over** (slang) essere sbronzato

half' shell' *s*—**on the half shell** in conchiglia

half' sis'ter *s* sorellastra

half' sole' *s* mezza suola

half'-sole' *tr* mettere la mezza suola a

half'-staff' *s*—**at half-staff** a mezz'asta

half-timbered ['hæf ˌtɪmbərd] or ['hɑf ˌtɪmbərd] *adj* in legno e muratura

half' ti'tle *s* occhiello, occhietto

half'tone' *s* mezzatinta

half'-track' *s* semicingolato

half'truth' *s* mezza verità, mezza bugia

half'way' *adj* a metà strada; parziale, mezzo || *adv* a metà strada; **halfway through** nel mezzo di; **to meet halfway** fare concessioni mutue

half-witted ['hæf ˌwɪtɪd] or ['hɑf ˌwɪtɪd] *adj* mezzo scemo

halibut ['hælɪbət] *s* ippoglosso

halide ['hælaɪd] or ['helaɪd] *s* alogenuro

halitosis [ˌhælɪˈtosɪs] *s* alito cattivo, fiato puzzolente

hall [hɔl] *s* (*passageway*) corridoio; (*entranceway*) vestibolo; (*large meeting room*) salone *m*; (*assembly room of a university*) aula magna; (*building of a university*) edificio

halleluiah or **hallelujah** [ˌhælɪˈlujə] *s* alleluia *m* || *interj* alleluia!

hall'mark' *s* punzone *m* di garanzia; (fig) contrassegno, caratteristica

hal·lo [həˈlo] *s* (-los) grido || *interj* ehi!

hallow ['hælo] *tr* santificare

hallowed ['hæləd] *adj* consacrato

Halloween or **Hallowe'en** [,hælo'in] *s* vigilia di Ognissanti

hallucination [hə ,lusɪ'neʃən] *s* allucinazione

hall'way' *s* corridoio; entrata

ha·lo ['helo] *s* (**-los** or **-loes**) alone *m*

halogen ['hælədʒən] *s* alogeno

halt [hɔlt] *adj* zoppicante ‖ *s* fermata; **to call a halt** dare ordine di fermarsi; **to come to a halt** fermarsi ‖ *tr* fermare ‖ *intr* fermarsi, esitare ‖ *interj* altolà!

halter ['hɔltər] *s* (*for leading horse*) cavezza; (*noose*) capestro; (*hanging*) impiccagione; corpino bagno di sole

halting ['hɔltɪŋ] *adj* zoppicante; esitante

halve [hæv] or [hɑv] *tr* dimezzare

halyard ['hæljərd] *s* (naut) drizza

ham [hæm] *s* (*part of leg behind knee*) polpaccio; (*thigh and buttock*) coscia; (*cured meat from hog's hind leg*) prosciutto; (slang) istrione *m*; (slang) radioamatore *m*; **hams** natiche *fpl*

ham' and eggs' *spl* uova *fpl* col prosciutto

hamburger ['hæm ,bʌrgər] *s* hamburger *m*

hamlet ['hæmlɪt] *s* frazione, paese *m* ‖ **Hamlet** *s* Amleto

hammer ['hæmər] *s* martello; (*of gun*) cane *m*; (*of piano*) martelletto; **under the hammer** all'asta pubblica ‖ *tr* martellare; **to hammer out** battere; portare a fine faticosamente ‖ *intr* martellare; **to hammer away** lavorare accanitamente

hammock ['hæmək] *s* amaca

hamper ['hæmpər] *s* cesta ‖ *tr* imbarazzare, intralciare

hamster ['hæmstər] *s* criceto

ham-string ['hæm ,strɪŋ] *v* (*pret & pp* **-strung**) *tr* azzoppare; tagliare i garretti a; (fig) impastoiare

hand [hænd] *adj* manuale; fatto a mano ‖ *s* mano *f*; (*workman*) garzone *m*, operaio; (*way of writing*) scrittura; (*signature*) firma; (*clapping of hands*) applauso; (*of clock or watch*) lancetta; (*all the cards in one's hand*) gioco; (*a round of play*) smazzata, mano *f*; (*player*) giocatore *m*; (*skill*) destrezza; (*side*) lato; **all hands** (naut) tutto l'equipaggio; (coll) tutti *mpl*; **at first hand** direttamente; **at hand** a portata di mano; **hand in glove** in perfetta unione; **hand in hand** tenendosi per mano; **hands up!** le mani in alto!; **hand to hand** corpo a corpo; **in hand** tra le mani; **in his own hand** di proprio pugno; **on hand** disponibile; **on hands and knees** (*crawling*) a gattoni; (*beseeching*) in ginocchio; **on the one hand** da un canto; **on the other hand** per contro; **to change hands** cambiare di mano; **to clap hands** battere le mani; **to eat out of one's hand** essere sottomesso a qlcu; **to get out of hand** diventare incontrollabile; **to have a hand in** prender parte a; **to have one's hands**

full essere occupatissimo; **to hold hands** tenersi per mano; **to hold up one's hands** (*as a sign of surrender*) alzare le mani; **to join hands** darsi la mano; **to keep one's hands off** non mettere il naso in; **to lend a hand** dare una mano; **to live from hand to mouth** vivere alla giornata; **to not lift a hand** non alzare un dito; **to play into the hands of** fare il gioco di; **to shake hands** darsi la mano; **to show one's hand** scoprire il proprio gioco; **to take in hand** prendere in mano; (*a matter*) prendere in esame; **to throw up one's hands** darsi per vinto; **to try one's hand** mettere la propria abilità alla prova; **to turn one's hand to** dedicarsi a; **to wash one's hands of** lavarsi le mani di; **under my hand** di mia firma autografa; **under the hand and seal of** firmato di pugno da ‖ *tr* dare, porgere; **to hand down** tramandare; **to hand in** consegnare; **to hand on** trasmettere; **to hand out** distribuire

hand'bag' *s* borsetta

hand' bag'gage *s* valigie *fpl* a mano

hand'ball' *s* palla a mano

hand'bill' *s* manifestino, foglio volante

hand'book' *s* manuale *m*; guida; (*of a particular field*) prontuario

hand'breadth' *s* palmo

hand'car' *s* (rr) carrello a mano

hand'cart' *s* carretto a mano

hand'cuffs' *spl* manette *fpl* ‖ *tr* mettere le manette a

handful ['hænd ,fʊl] *s* manata, manciata

hand' glass' *s* lente *f* di ingrandimento; specchietto

hand' grenade' *s* bomba a mano

handi·cap ['hændɪ ,kæp] *s* svantaggio; (sports) handicap *m* ‖ *v* (*pret & pp* **-capped**; *ger* **-capping**) *tr* andicappare

handicraft ['hændɪ ,kræft] or ['hændɪ ,krɑft] *s* destrezza manuale; artigianato

handiwork ['hændɪ ,wʌrk] *s* lavoro fatto a mano; opera, lavoro

handkerchief ['hæŋkərtʃɪf] or ['hæŋkər ,tʃɪf] *s* fazzoletto

handle ['hændəl] *s* manico; (*of a sword*) impugnatura; (*of a door*) maniglia; (*of a drawer*) pomolo; (*of a hand organ*) manovella; espediente *m*; **to fly off the handle** (slang) uscire dai gangheri ‖ *tr* maneggiare; manovrare, dirigere; commerciare in ‖ *intr* comportarsi

handle'bar' *s* manubrio

handler ['hændlər] *s* (sports) allenatore *m*

hand'made' *adj* fatto a mano

hand'maid' or **hand'maid'en** *s* domestica, serva; (fig) ancella

hand'-me-down' *adj* smesso ‖ *s* vestito smesso or di seconda mano

hand' or'gan *s* organetto, organino, organetto di Barberia

hand'out' *s* elemosina di cibo; articolo distribuito gratis; comunicato stampa

hand-picked ['hænd ,pɪkt] *adj* colto a mano; scelto specialmente

hand'rail' s guardamano, passamano
hand'saw' s sega a mano
hand'set' s microtelefono
hand'shake' s stretta di mano
handsome ['hænsəm] adj bello; considerevole; generoso
hand'spring' s capriola, salto mortale fatto toccando il terreno con le mani
hand'-to-hand' adj corpo a corpo
hand'-to-mouth' adj precario, da un giorno all'altro
hand'work' s lavoro fatto a mano
hand'writ'ing s scrittura
hand'wrought' adj lavorato a mano
hand-y ['hændi] adj (-ier; -iest) (easy to handle) maneggevole; (within easy reach) vicino; (skillful) destro, abile; **to come in handy** tornare utile
hand'y-man s (-men') factotum m
hang [hæŋ] s maniera di cadere; **to get the hang of** (coll) imparare a adoperare; **to not give a hang** (coll) non importare un fico a || v (pret & pp **hung** [hʌŋ]) tr sospendere; (laundry) stendere; (to attach) attaccare; (a door or window) mettere sui cardini; (one's head) abbassare; **hang it!** (coll) al diavolo!; **to hang up** appendere; sospendere il progresso di || intr pendere, penzolare; esitare; essere sospeso; essere attaccato; **to hang around** ciondolare, oziare, gironzolare; **to hang on** essere sospeso a; dipendere da; persistere; (s.o.'s words) pendere; **to hang out** sporgersi; (slang) raccogliersi; (slang) vivere; **to hang over** esser sospeso; (to threaten) minacciare; **to hang together** mantenersi uniti; **to hang up** (telp) riattaccare || v (pret hanged or hung) tr (to execute) impiccare || intr impiccarsi
hangar ['hæŋər] or ['hæŋgər] s rimessa; (aer) aviorimessa, hangar m
hanger ['hæŋər] s gancio, uncino; (for clothes) attaccapanni m
hang'er-on' s (hangers-on) seguace mf; seccatore m; (sponger) parassita m
hanging ['hæŋɪŋ] adj pendente, pensile || s impiccagione; **hangings** parati mpl
hang'man s (-men) boia m
hang'nail' s pipita delle unghie
hang'out' s (coll) ritrovo abituale
hang'o'ver s mal m di testa dopo una sbornia
hank [hæŋk] s matassa
hanker ['hæŋkər] intr agognare
Hannibal ['hænɪbəl] s Annibale m
haphazard [,hæp'hæzərd] adj fortuito, a caso || adv a caso; alla carlona
hapless ['hæplɪs] adj sfortunato
happen ['hæpən] intr succedere; **to happen along** sopravvenire; **to happen on** incontrarsi per caso con; **to happen to** + inf per caso + ind, e.g., I happened to see her at the theater l'ho incontrata per caso a teatro
happening ['hæpənɪŋ] s avvenimento, fatto
happily ['hæpɪli] adv felicemente; fortunatamente

happiness ['hæpɪnɪs] s felicità f; gioia, piacere m
hap-py ['hæpi] adj (-pier; -piest) lieto, felice, contento; **to be happy to** avere il piacere di
hap'py-go-luck'y adj spensierato
hap'py me'dium s giusto mezzo
Hap'py New Year' interj buon anno!, felice anno nuovo!
harangue [hə'ræŋ] s arringa, concione || tr & intr arringare
harass ['hærəs] or [hə'ræs] tr bersagliare; tartassare, tormentare
harbinger ['harbɪndʒər] s foriero; annunzio || tr annunziare
harbor ['harbər] adj di porto, portuario || s porto || tr albergare; (love or hatred) nutrire; (e.g., a criminal) dare ricetto a
har'bor mas'ter s capitano di porto
hard [hard] adj duro; (difficult) difficile; (work) improbo; (solder) forte; (hearing or breathing) grosso; (drinker) impenitente; (liquor) fortemente alcolico; **to be hard on** essere severo con; (to wear out fast) logorare rapidamente || adv duro; forte; molto; **hard upon** subito dopo
hard'-and-fast' adj inflessibile
hard'-bitten ['hard'bɪtən] adj duro, incallito
hard-boiled ['hard'bɔɪld] adj (egg) sodo; (coll) duro
hard' can'dy s caramelle fpl; **piece of hard candy** caramella
hard' cash' s denaro contante
hard' ci'der s sidro fermentato
hard' coal' s antracite f
hard'-earned' adj guadagnato a stento
harden ['hardən] tr indurire || intr indurirsi
hardening ['hardənɪŋ] s indurimento; (metallurgy) tempra
hard' facts' spl realtà f
hard-fought ['hard'fɔt] adj accanito
hard-headed ['hard'hedɪd] adj astuto, ostinato, caparbio
hard-hearted ['hard'hartɪd] adj dal cuore duro
hardihood ['hardɪ,hud] s forza, coraggio; insolenza
hardiness ['hardɪnɪs] s ardire m; vigore m, robustezza fisica
hard' la'bor s lavori forzati
hard' luck' s mala sorte
hard'-luck' sto'ry s storia delle proprie disgrazie
hardly ['hardli] adv appena, quasi no; (with great difficulty) a malapena, a fatica; **hardly ever** quasi mai
hardness ['hardnɪs] s durezza
hard'-of-hear'ing adj duro d'orecchio
hard-pressed ['hard'prest] adj oppresso; **to be hard-pressed for** essere a corto di
hard' rub'ber s ebanite f
hard' sauce' s miscela di burro e zucchero
hard'-shell crab' s granchio con la corazza
hardship ['hardʃɪp] s pena, privazione; **hardships** privazioni fpl, strettezze fpl

hard'tack' s galletta

hard' times' spl strettezze fpl

hard' to please' adj di difficile contentatura

hard' up' adj (coll) in urgente bisogno; **to be hard up for** (coll) essere a corto di

hard'ware' s ferramenta fpl; macchinario

hard'ware store' s negozio di ferramenta

hard-won ['hard,wʌn] adj (victory, battle) conquistato con molti sforzi; (money) acquistato con molti sforzi

hard'wood' s legno forte

hard'wood floor' s pavimento di legno, parquet m

har·dy ['hardi] adj (-dier; -diest) forte, resistente; (rash) temerario; (hort) resistente al freddo

hare [her] s lepre f

harebrained ['her,brend] adj scervellato, sventato

hare'lip' s labbro leporino

harem ['herəm] s arem m

hark [hark] intr ascoltare; **to hark back** (said of hounds) ritornare sulla pista; riandare col pensiero || interj ascolta!

harken ['harkən] intr ascoltare

harlequin ['harləkwɪn] s arlecchino

harlot ['harlət] s meretrice f, baldracca

harm [harm] s danno m || tr rovinare; nuocere (with dat), fare del male (with dat)

harmful ['harmfəl] adj nocivo

harmless ['harmlɪs] adj innocuo

harmonic [har'manɪk] adj armonico || s (phys) armonica || **harmonics** ssg armonica; spl suoni armonici

harmonica [har'manɪkə] s armonica a bocca

harmonious [har'monɪ-əs] adj armonioso

harmonize ['harmə,naɪz] tr intonare; (mus) armonizzare || intr intonarsi; (mus) cantare all'unisono

harmo·ny ['harməni] s (-nies) armonia

harness ['harnɪs] s bardatura, finimenti mpl; (fig) routine f; **to die in the harness** morire sulla breccia || tr bardare, imbrigliare; (a waterfall) captare

har'ness mak'er s sellaio

har'ness race' s corsa al trotto, corsa di cavalli col sulky

harp [harp] s arpa || intr—**to harp on** ripetere ostinatamente

harpist ['harpɪst] s arpista mf

harpoon [har'pun] s rampone m || tr & intr arpionare

harpsichord ['harpsɪ,kɔrd] s arpicordo, clavicembalo

har·py ['harpi] s (-pies) arpia

harrow ['hæro] s erpice m || tr (agr) erpicare; (fig) tormentare

harrowing ['hæro·ɪŋ] adj straziante

har·ry ['hæri] v (pret & pp -ried) tr saccheggiare; tormentare

harsh [harʃ] adj (to touch) ruvido; (to taste or hearing) aspro; inclemente

harshness ['harʃnɪs] s ruvidezza; asprezza; inclemenza

hart [hart] s cervo

harum-scarum ['herəm'skerəm] adj & s scervellato

harvest ['harvɪst] s raccolta, mietitura || tr raccogliere, mietere

harvester ['harvɪstər] s (person) mietitore m; (machine) mietitrice f

har'vest home' s fine f della mietitura; festa dei mietitori; canzone f dei mietitori

har'vest moon' s luna di settembre

has-been ['hæz,bɪn] s (person) fallito; (thing) anticaglia

hash [hæʃ] s polpettone m || tr tritare

hash' house' s osteria di terz'ordine

hashish ['hæʃɪʃ] s ascisc m

hasp [hæsp] or [hasp] s boncinello

hassle ['hæsəl] s (coll) rissa, disputa

hassock ['hæsək] s cuscino poggiapiedi

haste [hest] s premura; **in haste** di premura; **to make haste** fare presto

hasten ['hesən] tr affrettare || intr affrettarsi

hast·y ['hesti] adj (-ier; -iest) frettoloso; precipitato

hat [hæt] s cappello; **to keep under one's hat** (coll) mantenere il segreto su; **to throw one's hat in the ring** (coll) dichiarare la propria candidatura

hat'band' s nastro del cappello

hat' block' s forma da cappelli

hat'box' s cappelliera

hatch [hætʃ] s (brood) nidiata; (shading line) tratteggio; (trap door) porta a ribalta; (lower half of door) mezza porta; (naut) boccaporto || tr (eggs) covare; (a drawing) tratteggiare; complottare, tramare || intr schiudersi

hat'check' girl' s guardarobiera

hatchet ['hætʃɪt] s accetta; **to bury the hatchet** fare la pace

hatch'way' s (trap door) porta a ribalta; (naut) boccaporto

hate [het] s odio || tr & intr odiare

hateful ['hetfəl] adj odioso

hat'pin' s spillone m

hat'rack' s attaccapanni m

hatred ['hetrɪd] s odio, livore m

hatter ['hætər] s cappellaio

haughtiness ['hotɪnɪs] s superbia

haugh·ty ['hoti] adj (-tier; -tiest) superbo, sprezzante

haul [hɔl] s (tug) tiro; (amount caught) retata; (distance transported) percorso, pezzo || tr trasportare; tirare; (naut) alare

haunch [hɔntʃ] or [hantʃ] s fianco; anca; (hind quarter of an animal) coscia; (same used for food) cosciotto

haunt [hɔnt] or [hant] s ritrovo, nido || tr frequentare assiduamente; perseguitare

haunt'ed house' s casa frequentata dai fantasmi

haute couture [ot ku'tyr] s alta moda

have [hæv] s—**the haves and the have-nots** gli abbienti e i nullatenenti || v (*pret & pp* had [hæd]) *tr* avere; (*a dream*) fare; (*to get, take*) prendere, ottenere, ricevere; **to have got** (coll) avere; **to have got to** + *inf* (coll) dovere + *inf;* **to have it in for** (coll) serbar rancore per; **to have it out with** avere a che dire con; **to have on** portare; **to have** (s.th) **to do with** avere (qlco) a che fare con, e.g., **I don't want to have anything to do with him** non voglio aver nulla a che fare con lui; **to have** + *inf* fare + *inf*, e.g., **I had him pay the bill** gli ho fatto pagare il conto; **to have** + *pp* fare + *inf*, e.g., **I had my watch repaired** ho fatto aggiustare l'orologio || *intr*—to have at attaccare, mettersi di buzzo buono con; **to have to** + *inf* dovere + *inf;* **to have to do with** avere a che fare con; trattare di, e.g., **this book has to do with superstition** questo libro tratta di superstizione || *v aux* avere, e.g., **he has studied his lesson** ha studiato la sua lezione

havelock [ˈhævlɑk] *s* coprinuca *m*
haven [ˈhevən] *s* porto; asilo
haversack [ˈhævərˌsæk] *s* bisaccia; (mil) zaino
havoc [ˈhævək] *s* rovina; **to play havoc with** rovinare; scompigliare
haw [hɔ] *s* (*of hawthorn*) bacca; (*in speech*) esitazione || *intr* voltare a sinistra || *interj* voltare a sinistra!
hawk [hɔk] *s* falco; (*mortarboard*) sparviere *m;* (coll) persona rapace || *tr* imbonire; (*newspapers*) strillare; **to hawk up** sputare raschiandosi la gola || *intr* fare il merciaiolo ambulante; schiarirsi la gola
hawker [ˈhɔkər] *s* merciaiolo ambulante
hawse [hɔz] *s* (naut) cubia; (*hole*) (naut) occhio di cubia; (naut) altezza di cubia
hawse'hole' *s* occhio di cubia
hawser [ˈhɔzər] *s* cavo, gomena
haw'thorn' *s* biancospino
hay [he] *s* fieno; **to hit the hay** (slang) andare a letto; **to make hay while the sun shines** battere il ferro fin ch'è caldo
hay' fe'ver *s* febbre *f* da fieno, raffreddore *m* da fieno
hay'field' *s* prato seminato a fieno
hay'fork' *s* forcone *m;* (mach) rastrello
hay'loft' *s* fienile *m*
haymow [ˈhe ˌmau] *s* fienile *m*
hay'rack' *s* rastrelliera
hay'ride' *s* gita notturna in carro da fieno
hay'seed' *s* semente *f* d'erba; (coll) semplicione *m*, campagnolo
hay'stack' *s* meta, pagliaio
hay'wire' *adj* (coll) disordinato, in confusione; (coll) impazzito || *s* filo per legare il fieno
hazard [ˈhæzərd] *s* pericolo; (*chance*) rischio; (golf) ostacolo || *tr* rischiare; (*an opinion*) arrischiare
hazardous [ˈhæzərdəs] *adj* pericoloso
haze [hez] *s* foschia; (fig) confusione || *tr* far la matricola a

hazel [ˈhezəl] *adj* nocciola || *s* (*tree*) nocciolo; (*fruit*) nocciola
ha'zel-nut' *s* nocciola
hazing [ˈhezɪŋ] *s* vessazione, angheria; (*at university*) matricola
ha-zy [ˈhezi] *adj* (-zier; -ziest) nebbioso; confuso
H-bomb [ˈetʃ ˌbam] *s* bomba H
he [hi] *s* (hes) maschio || *pron pers* (they) lui, egli, esso
head [hed] *s* testa, capo; (*of bed*) testiera; (*caption*) testata; (*of a nail*) cappello; (*on a glass of beer*) schiuma; (*of a boil*) punta purulenta; (e.g., *of cattle*) capo; **at the head of** a capo di; **from head to foot** da capo a piedi; **head over heels** a gambe levate; completamente; **heads or tails** testa o croce; **over one's head** al di sopra della capacità intellettuale di qlcu; (*going to a higher authority*) al di sopra di qlcu; **to be out of one's head** (coll) esser matto; **to bring to a head** far giungere alla crisi; **to come into one's head** passar per la mente a qlcu; **to go to one's head** dare al cervello a qlcu; **to keep one's head** non perdere la testa; **to keep one's head above water** arrivare a sbarcare il lunario; **to not make head or tail of** non riuscire a raccapezzarsi su || *tr* dirigere, comandare; essere alla testa di || *intr*—to head towards dirigersi verso
head'ache' *s* mal di capo, emicrania
head'band' *s* fascia sul capo; (bb) capitello; (typ) filetto
head'board' *s* testiera del letto
head' cheese' *s* salame *m* di testa
head'dress' *s* acconciatura
header [ˈhedər] *s*—to take a header (coll) gettarsi a capofitto
head'first' *adv* a capofitto
head'gear' *s* copricapo; (*for protection*) casco
head'hunt'er *s* cacciatore *m* di teste
heading [ˈhedɪŋ] *s* intestazione; (*of a chapter of a book*) titolo; (journ) testata, capopagina *m*
headland [ˈhedlənd] *s* promontorio
headless [ˈhedlɪs] *adj* senza testa
head'light' *s* (naut, rr) fanale *m;* (aut) faro
head'line' *s* (*of a page of a book*) titolo; (journ) testata || *tr* intestare; fare pubblicità a
head'lin'er *s* (slang) attrazione principale
head'long' *adj* precipitoso || *adv* a precipizio; a capofitto
head'man *s* (-men) capo; giustiziere *m*
head'mas'ter *s* direttore *m* di un collegio per ragazzi
head'most' *adj* primo, più avanzato
head' of'fice *s* sede *f* centrale
head' of hair' *s* capigliatura
head'-on' *adj* frontale || *adv* di fronte, frontalmente
head'phones' *spl* cuffia
head'piece' *s* (*any covering for the head*) copricapo; (*helmet*) elmo; (*brains, judgment*) testa; (*of bed*)

spalliera; *(headset)* cuffia; (typ) testata
head′quar′ters *s* sede *f* centrale, direzione; (mil) quartier *m* generale
head′rest′ *s* poggiatesta *m*, testiera
head′set′ *s* cuffia
head′ship′ *s* direzione
head′stone′ *s* pietra angolare; *(on a grave)* pietra tombale
head′stream′ *s* affluente *m* principale
head′strong′ *adj* testardo, ostinato
head′wait′er *s* capocameriere *m*
head′wa′ters *spl* fonti *fpl* or sorgenti *fpl* d'un fiume
head′way′ *s* progresso; **to make headway** progredire
head′wear′ *s* copricapo
head′wind′ *s* vento di prua
head′work′ *s* lavoro intellettuale
head·y [′hɛdi] *adj* (-ier; -iest) eccitante; impetuoso; violento; *(clever)* astuto; intossicante
heal [hil] *tr* sanare, guarire; purificare ‖ *intr* risanarsi, guarire; *(said of a wound)* rimarginare
healer [′hilər] *s* guaritore *m*
health [hɛlθ] *s* salute *f;* **to radiate health** sprizzare salute da tutti i pori; **to your health!** alla Sua salute!
health′ depart′ment *s* sanità *f*
healthful [′hɛlθfəl] *adj* salutare
health′ insur′ance *s* assicurazione malattia
health·y [′hɛlθi] *adj* (-ier; -iest) sano; salubre
heap [hip] *s* mucchio; (coll) insalata, mare *m* ‖ *tr* ammucchiare; **to heap s.th upon s.o.** colmare qlcu di qlco; **to heap with** colmare di
hear [hɪr] *v (pret & pp* **heard** [hʌrd]) *tr* udire; **to hear it said** sentirlo dire ‖ *intr* udire; **hear!, hear!** bravo!; **to hear about** sentir parlare di; **to hear from** aver notizie di; **to hear of** sentir parlare di; **to hear that** sentir dire che
hearer [′hɪrər] *s* ascoltatore *m*.
hearing [′hɪrɪŋ] *s (sense)* udito, orecchio; *(act)* udienza; **in the hearing of** in presenza di; **within hearing** a portata d'orecchio
hear′ing aid′ *s* uditofono
hear′say′ *s* diceria; **by hearsay** per sentito dire
hearse [hʌrs] *s* carro, carrozzone *m*, or furgone *m* funebre
heart [hɑrt] *s* cuore *m; (e.g., of lettuce)* grumolo; **after one's heart** di gusto di qlcu; **by heart** a memoria; **heart and soul** di tutto cuore; **to break the heart of** spezzare il cuore di; **to die of a broken heart** morire di crepacuore; **to eat one's heart out** piangere silenziosamente; **to get to the heart of** sviscerare il nocciolo di; **to have one's heart in one's work** lavorare di buzzo buono; **to have one's heart in the right place** avere buone intenzioni; **to lose heart** scoraggiarsi; **to open one's heart to** aprire il cuore a; **to take heart** prender coraggio; **to take to heart** prendersi a cuore; **to**

wear one's heart on one's sleeve parlare a cuore aperto; **with one's heart in one's mouth** col cuore in bocca
heart′ache′ *s* angustia, angoscia
heart′ attack′ *s* attacco cardiaco
heart′beat′ *s* battito del cuore
heart′break′ *s* angoscia straziante
heart′break′er *s* rubacuori *m*
heartbroken [′hɑrt‚brokən] *adj* col cuore spezzato
heart′burn′ *s* bruciore *m* di stomaco
heart′ disease′ *s* mal *m* di cuore
hearten [′hɑrtən] *tr* rincuorare
heart′ fail′ure *s (death)* arresto cardiaco; collasso cardiaco
heartfelt [′hɑrt‚fɛlt] *adj* sentito
hearth [hɑrθ] *s* focolare *m*
hearth′stone′ *s* pietra del focolare
heartily [′hɑrtɪli] *adv* di cuore, cordialmente; saporitamente
heartless [′hɑrtlɪs] *adj* senza cuore, insensibile
heart′ mur′mur *s* soffio al cuore
heart-rending [′hɑrt‚rɛndɪŋ] *adj* da far male al cuore
heart′sick′ *adj* afflitto, sconsolato
heart′strings′ *spl* precordi *mpl*
heart′-to-heart′ *adj* cuore a cuore
heart′ trans′plant *s* trapianto cardiaco
heart′wood′ *s* cuore *m* del legno
heart·y [′hɑrti] *adj* (-ier; -iest) cordiale, di cuore; abbondante; *(eater)* grande
heat [hit] *adj* termico ‖ *s* calore *m; (of room, house, etc.)* riscaldamento; (zool) fregola; (sports) batteria; (fig) fervore *m;* **in heat** (zool) in amore ‖ *tr* scaldare, riscaldare; (fig) eccitare ‖ *intr* riscaldarsi; (fig) accalorarsi
heated [′hit:d] *adj* accalorato
heater [′hitər] *s* riscaldatore *m; (for central heating)* calorifero; *(to heat hands or bed)* scaldino; *(to heat water in tub)* scaldabagno
heath [hiθ] *s* (shrub) brugo, erica; *(tract of land)* brughiera
hea·then [′hiðən] *adj* pagano; irreligioso ‖ *s* (-then or -thens) pagano
heathendom [′hiðəndəm] *s (worship)* paganesimo; *(land)* pagania
heather [′hɛðər] *s* erica, brugo
heating [′hitɪŋ] *adj* di riscaldamento ‖ *s* riscaldamento
heat′ing pad′ *s* termoforo
heat′ light′ning *s* lampo di caldo
heat′ shield′ *s* (rok) scudo termico
heat′stroke′ *s* colpo di calore
heat′ wave′ *s* ondata di caldo
heave [hiv] *s* sollevamento, sforzo; **heaves** (vet) bolsaggine *f* ‖ *v (pret & pp* **heaved** or **hove** [hov]) *tr* sollevare, alzare; rigettare; *(a sigh)* emettere ‖ *intr* alzarsi e abbassarsi; *(said of one's chest)* palpitare; avere conati di vomito
heaven [′hɛvən] *s* cielo; **for heaven's sake!** or **good heavens!** per amor del cielo!; **heavens** *(firmament)* cielo ‖ **Heaven** *s* cielo
heavenly [′hɛvənli] *adj* celeste
heav′enly bod′y *s* corpo celeste
heav·y [′hɛvi] *adj* (-ier; -iest) *(of great*

weight) pesante; *(liquid)* denso; *(cloth, sea)* grosso; *(traffic)* forte; *(serious)* grave; *(crop)* abbondante; *(rain)* dirotto; *(features)* grossolano; *(heart)* stretto; *(ponderous)* macchinoso; *(industry)* grande; *(stock market)* abbattuto || *adv* (coll) pesantemente; **to hang heavy** *(said of time)* passar lentamente

heav'y-du'ty *adj* extraforte

heavy-hearted ['hɛvɪ'hɑrtɪd] *adj* afflitto, triste

heav'y·set' *adj* forte, corpulento

heav'y·weight' *s* peso massimo

Hebrew ['hibru] *s & s* ebreo; *(language)* ebraico

hecatomb ['hɛkə,tom] *or* ['hɛkə,tum] *s* ecatombe *f*

heckle ['hɛkəl] *tr* interrompere con domande imbarazzanti

hectic ['hɛktɪk] *adj* febbrile

hedge [hɛdʒ] *s* barriera; *(of bushes)* siepe *f*; *(in stock market)* operazione controbilanciante || *tr* circondare con siepe; **to hedge in** circondare || *intr* evitare di compromettersi; (com) coprirsi

hedge'hog' *s* (zool) riccio; *(porcupine)* (zool) porcospino

hedge'hop' *v (pret & pp* **-hopped;** *ger* **hopping)** *intr* volare a volo radente

hedgehopping ['hɛdʒ,hɑpɪŋ] *s* volo radente

hedge'row' [ro] *s* siepe *f*

heed [hid] *s* attenzione; **to take heed** fare attenzione || *tr* badare a || *intr* fare attenzione, badare

heedless ['hidlɪs] *adj* sbadato

heehaw ['hi,hɔ] *s (of donkey)* raglio d'asino; *(laugh)* risata || *intr* ragliare; ridere fragorosamente

heel [hil] *s (of shoe, of foot)* calcagno, tallone *m*; *(of stocking or shoe)* tallone *m*; *(raised part of shoe below heel)* tacco; (coll) farabutto; **down at the heel** mal ridotto; **to cool one's heels** aspettare a lungo; **to kick up one's heels** darsi alla pazza gioia; **to show a clean pair of heels** *or* **to take to one's heels** battere i tacchi

heeler ['hilər] *s* politicante *mf*

heft·y ['hɛftɪ] *adj* **(-ier; -iest)** *(heavy)* pesante; *(strong)* forte

hegemon·y [hɪ'dʒɛmənɪ] *or* ['hɛdʒɪ-,monɪ] *s* **(-ies)** egemonia

hegira [hɪ'dʒaɪrə] *or* ['hɛdʒɪrə] *s* fuga

heifer ['hɛfər] *s* manza, giovenca

height [haɪt] *s* altezza; *(of a person)* altezza, statura; *(e.g., of folly)* colmo

heighten ['haɪtən] *tr* innalzare; *(to increase the amount of)* accrescere, aumentare || *intr* aumentare

heinous ['henəs] *adj* nefando, odioso

heir [ɛr] *s* erede *m*

heir' appar'ent *s* **(heirs' appar'ent)** erede necessario

heirdom ['ɛrdəm] *s* eredità *f*

heiress ['ɛrɪs] *s* ereditiera, erede *f*

heirloom ['ɛr,lum] *s* cimelio di famiglia

Helen ['hɛlən] *s* Elena

helicopter ['hɛlɪ,kɑptər] *s* elicottero

heliport ['hɛlɪ,port] *s* eliporto

helium ['hilɪ·əm] *s* elio

helix ['hilɪks] *s* **(helixes** *or* **helices** ['hɛlɪ,siz])** spirale *f*; (geom) elica

hell [hɛl] *s* inferno

hell-bent ['hɛl'bɛnt] *adj* (coll) risoluto; **to be hell-bent on** (coll) avere un chiodo in testa di

hell'cat' *s* arpia, megera

hellebore ['hɛlɪ,bor] *s* elleboro

Hellene ['hɛlin] *s* greco

Hellenic [hɛ'lɛnɪk] *or* [hɛ'linɪk] *adj* ellenico

hell'fire' *s* fuoco dell'inferno

hellish ['hɛlɪʃ] *adj* infernale

hel·lo [hɛ'lo] *s* saluto || *interj* ciao!; *(on telephone)* pronto!

helm [hɛlm] *s* barra del timone; ruota del timone; timone *m* || *tr* dirigere

helmet ['hɛlmɪt] *s* (mil) elmetto; (sports) casco; (hist) elmo

helms'man *s* **(-men)** timoniere *m*

help [hɛlp] *s* aiuto; *(relief)* rimedio, e.g., **there's no help for it** non c'è rimedio; servitù *f*; impiegati *mpl*; operai *mpl*; **to come to the help of** venire in aiuto di || *tr* aiutare; soccorrere, mitigare; *(to wait on)* servire; **it can't be helped** non c'è rimedio; **so help me God!** Dio mi sia testimonio!; **to help down** aiutare a scendere; **to help s.o. with his coat** aiutare qlcu a mettersi il cappotto; **to help oneself** servirsi da solo; **to help up** aiutare a salire; aiutare ad alzarsi; **to not be able to help** + *ger* non poter fare a meno di + *inf*, e.g., **he can't help laughing** non può fare a meno di ridere || *intr* aiutare || *interj* aiuto!

helper ['hɛlpər] *s* aiutante *m*; *(in a shop)* garzone *m*, lavorante *m*

helpful ['hɛlpfəl] *adj* utile, servizievole

helping ['hɛlpɪŋ] *s (of food)* razione *f*

helpless ['hɛlplɪs] *adj (weak)* debole; *(powerless)* impotente; senza risorse; *(confused)* perplesso; *(situation)* irrimediabile

help'mate' *s* compagno; *(wife)* compagna

helter-skelter ['hɛltər'skɛltər] *adj & adv* in fretta e furia; alla rinfusa

hem [hɛm] *s (any edge)* orlo; *(of skirt)* basta, pedana; *(of suit)* falda || *v (pret & pp* **hemmed;** *ger* **hemming)** *tr* orlare, bordare; **to hem in** insaccare || *intr* esitare; **to hem and haw** esitare; essere evasivo

hemisphere ['hɛmɪ,sfɪr] *s* emisfero

hemistich ['hɛmɪ,stɪk] *s* emistichio

hem'line' *s* orlo della gonna

hem'lock' *s (herb and poison)* cicuta; *(Tsuga canadensis)* abete *m* del Canada

hemoglobin [,hɛmə'globɪn] *or* [,himə-'globɪn] *s* emoglobina

hemophilia [,hɛmə'fɪlɪ·ə] *or* [,himə-'fɪlɪ·ə] *s* emofilia

hemorrhage ['hɛmərɪdʒ] *s* emorragia

hemorrhoids ['hɛmə,rɔɪdz] *spl* emorroidi *fpl*

hemostat ['hɛmə,stæt] *or* ['himə,stæt] *s* pinza emostatica

hemp [hɛmp] *s* canapa

hemstitch ['hem,stɪtʃ] *s* orlo a giorno || *tr & intr* orlare a giorno
hen [hen] *s* gallina
hence [hens] *adv* di qui; da ora; quindi; di qui a, e.g., **three weeks hence** di qui a tre settimane
hence'forth' *adv* d'ora innanzi
hench-man ['hentʃ/mən] *s* (**-men** [mən]) accolito; politicante *m*
hen'house' *s* pollaio
henna ['henə] *s* henna || *tr* tingere con la henna
hen'peck' *tr* (*a husband*) trovare a ridire con
hen'pecked' hus'band *s* marito dominato dalla moglie
her [hʌr] *adj poss* suo, il suo || *pron pers* la, lei; **to her** le, a lei
herald ['herəld] *s* araldo; annunziatore *m* || *tr* annunziare
heraldic [he'rældɪk] *adj* araldico
herald-ry ['herəldrɪ] *s* (**-ries**) (*office*) consulta araldica; (*science*) araldica; (*coat of arms*) blasone *m*
herb [ʌrb] or [hʌrb] *s* erba; erba medicinale
herbaceous [hʌr'beʃəs] *adj* erbaceo
herbage ['ʌrbɪdʒ] or ['hʌrbɪdʒ] *s* erba; (*law*) erbatico
herbalist ['hʌrbəlɪst] or ['ʌrbəlɪst] *s* erborista *mf*
herbari-um [hʌr'berɪ-əm] *s* (**-ums** or **-a** [ə]) erbario
herb' doc'tor *s* erborista *mf*
herculean [hʌr'kjulɪ-ən] or [,hʌrkju-'li-ən] *adj* erculeo
herd [hʌrd] *s* (*of sheep*) gregge *m*; (*of cattle*) mandria; (*of men*) torma || *tr & intr* imbrancare
herds'man *s* (**-men**) (*of cattle*) mandriano, vaccaio; (*of sheep*) pastore *m*
here [hɪr] *adj* presente || *s*—**the here and the hereafter** la vita presente e l'aldilà || *adv* qui, qua; **here and there** qua e là; **here is** or **here are** ecco; **that's neither here not there** ciò non ha nulla a che vedere || *interj* presente!
hereabouts ['hɪrə,bauts] *adv* qua vicino
here-af'ter *s* aldilà *m* || *adv* d'ora innanzi; nel futuro
here-by' *adv* con la presente
hereditary [hɪ'redɪ,terɪ] *adj* ereditario
heredi-ty [hɪ'redɪtɪ] *s* (**-ties**) eredità *f*
here-in' *adv* qui; in questo posto
here-of' *adv* di questo
here-on' *adv* in questo; su questo
here-sy ['herəsɪ] *s* (**-sies**) eresia
heretic ['herətɪk] *s* & *s* eretico
heretical [hɪ'retɪkəl] *adj* eretico
heretofore [,hɪrtu'for] *adv* sinora
here-u-pon' *adv* su questo; in questo; immediatamente dopo
here-with' *adv* accluso; con la presente
heritage ['herɪtɪdʒ] *s* eredità *f*
hermetic(al) [hʌr'metɪk(əl)] *adj* ermetico
hermit ['hʌrmɪt] *s* eremita *m*
hermitage ['hʌrmɪtɪdʒ] *s* eremitaggio
herni-a ['hʌrnɪ-ə] *s* (**-as** or **-ae** [,i]) ernia
he-ro ['hɪro] *s* (**-roes**) eroe *m*

heroic [hɪ'ro-ɪk] *adj* eroico || **heroics** *spl* linguaggio altisonante
heroin ['hero-ɪn] *s* (pharm) eroina
heroine ['hero-ɪn] *s* eroina
heroism ['hero,ɪzəm] *s* eroismo
heron ['herən] *s* airone *m*
herring ['herɪŋ] *s* aringa
her'ring-bone' *s* (*in fabrics*) spina di pesce; (*in hardwood floors*) spiga
hers [hʌrz] *pron poss* il suo; **of hers** suo
herself [hʌr'self] *pron pers* lei stessa; sé stessa; si, e.g., **she enjoyed herself** si divertì; **with herself** con sé
hertz [hʌrts] *s* hertz *m*
hesitan-cy ['hezɪtənsɪ] *s* (**-cies**) titubanza, esitanza
hesitant ['hezɪtənt] *adj* esitante
hesitate ['hezɪ,tet] *intr* esitare, titubare; (*to stutter*) balbettare
hesitation [,hezɪ'teʃən] *s* esitazione
heterodox ['hetərə,dɑks] *adj* eterodosso
heterodyne ['hetərə,daɪn] *s* eterodina
heterogeneous [,hetərə'dʒinɪ-əs] *adj* eterogeneo
hew [hju] *v* (*pret* **hewed**; *pp* **hewed** or **hewn**) *tr* tagliare; (*a passage*) aprirsi; (*a statue*) abbozzare; **to hew down** abbattere || *intr*—**to hew close to the line** (coll) filare diritto
hex [heks] *s* strega; incantesimo || *tr* stregare, incantare
hexameter [heks'æmɪtər] *s* esametro
hey [he] *interj* ehi!
hey'day' *s* apogeo
hia-tus [haɪ'etəs] *s* (**-tuses** or **-tus**) (*gap*) lacuna; (gram) iato
hibernate ['haɪbər,net] *intr* ibernare; (*said of people*) svernare
hibiscus [hɪ'bɪskəs] or [haɪ'bɪskəs] *s* ibisco
hic-cup ['hɪkəp] *s* singhiozzo || *v* (*pret & pp* **-cuped** or **-cupped**; *ger* **-cuping** or **-cupping**) *intr* singhiozzare
hick [hɪk] *adj & s* (coll) rustico
hicko-ry ['hɪkərɪ] *s* (**-ries**) hickory *m*
hidden ['hɪdən] *adj* nascosto
hide [haɪd] *s* cuoio, pelle *f*; **hides** cuoio; **neither hide nor hair** nemmeno una traccia; **to tan s.o.'s hide** (coll) dargliele sode a qlcu || *v* (*pret* **hid** [hɪd]; *pp* **hid** or **hidden** ['hɪdən]) *tr* nascondere || *intr* nascondersi; **to hide out** (coll) rintanarsi
hide'-and-seek' *s* rimpiattino; **to play hide-and-seek** giocare a rimpiattino or a nascondino
hide'bound' *adj* retrogrado, conservatore
hideous ['hɪdɪ-əs] *adj* orribile, brutto
hide'out' *s* nascondiglio
hiding ['haɪdɪŋ] *s* nascondere *m*; (*place*) nascondiglio; **in hiding** nascosto
hid'ing place' *s* nascondiglio
hie [haɪ] *v* (*pret & pp* **hied**; *ger* **hieing** or **hying**) *tr*—**hie thee home** affrettati a tornare a casa || *intr* affrettarsi
hierar-chy ['haɪ-ə,rɑrkɪ] *s* (**-chies**) gerarchia
hieroglyphic [,haɪ-ərə'glɪfɪk] *adj & s* geroglifico

hi-fi ['haɪ'faɪ] *adj* di alta fedeltà ‖ *s* alta fedeltà

higgledy-piggledy ['hɪɡəldɪ'pɪɡəldɪ] *adj* confuso ‖ *adv* alla rinfusa

high [haɪ] *adj* alto; (*color*) forte; (*merry*) allegro; (*luxurious*) lussuoso; (*coll*) ubriaco; (*culin*) frollo; **high and dry** abbandonato; **high and mighty** (coll) arrogante ‖ *adv* molto; riccamente; **to aim high** mirare in alto; **to come high** essere caro ‖ *s* (aut) quarta, diretta; **on high** in cielo

high′ al′tar *s* altare *m* maggiore

high′ball′ *s* whiskey con ghiaccio e gazosa ‖ *intr* (slang) andare di carriera

high′ blood′ pres′sure *s* ipertensione

high′born′ *adj* di nobile lignaggio

high′boy′ *s* cassettone alto

high′brow′ *s* intellettuale *mf*; (coll) intellettualoide *mf*

high′chair′ *s* seggiolino per bambini

high′ command′ *s* comando supremo

high′ cost′ of liv′ing *s* carovita *m*, caro-viveri *m*

high′er educa′tion *s* insegnamento universitario, istruzione superiore

higher-up [,haɪ·ər'ʌp] *s* (coll) superiore *m*

high′ explo′sive *s* esplosivo ad alta potenza

highfalutin [,haɪfə'lutən] *adj* (coll) pomposo, pretenzioso

high′ fidel′ity *s* high fidelity, alta fedeltà

high′-fre′quency *adj* ad alta frequenza

high′ gear′ *s* (aut) presa diretta

high′-grade′ *adj* di qualità superiore

high-handed ['haɪ'hændɪd] *adj* arbitrario

high′ hat′ *s* cappello a cilindro

high′-hat′ *adj* (coll) snob *m* ‖ *v* (*pret & pp* -hatted; *ger* -hatting) *tr* (coll) snobbare

high′-heeled′ shoe′ ['haɪ,hild] *s* scarpa coi tacchi alti

high′ horse′ *s* comportamento arrogante; **to get up on one's high horse** darsi delle grandi arie

high′ jinks′ [dʒɪŋks] *s* (slang) pagliacciata, gazzarra

high′ jump′ *s* salto in altezza

highland ['haɪlənd] *adj* montagnoso ‖ **highlands** *spl* regione montagnosa

high′ life′ *s* high-life *f*, alta società

high′light′ *s* punto culminante ‖ *tr* mettere in risalto

highly ['haɪlɪ] *adv* altamente, molto; (*paid*) profumatamente; **to speak highly of** parlar molto bene di

High′ Mass′ *s* messa cantata

high-minded ['haɪ'maɪndɪd] *adj* magnanimo

highness ['haɪnɪs] *s* altezza ‖ **Highness** *s* Altezza

high′ noon′ *s* mezzogiorno in punto; (fig) sommo

high-pitched ['haɪ'pɪtʃt] *adj* acuto; intenso, emozionante

high-powered ['haɪ'pau·ərd] *adj* ad alta potenza; (*binoculars*) ad alto ingrandimento

high′pres′sure *adj* ad alta pressione ‖ *tr* sollecitare con insistenza

high-priced ['haɪ'praɪst] *adj* caro, di alto prezzo

high′ priest′ *s* sommo sacerdote

high′ rise′ *s* edificio di molti piani

high′road′ *s* strada principale

high′school′ *s* scuola media; (*in Italy*) liceo

high′ sea′ *s* alto mare; **high seas** alto mare

high′ soci′ety *s* l'alta società

high′-sound′ing *adj* altisonante

high′-speed′ *adj* ad alta velocità

high-spirited ['haɪ'spɪrɪtɪd] *adj* fiero, vivace, focoso

high′ spir′its *spl* allegria, vivacità *f*

high-strung ['haɪ'strʌŋ] *adj* teso, nervoso

high′-test′ fuel′ *s* supercarburante *m*

high′ tide′ *s* alta marea; punto culminante

high′ time′ *s* ora, e.g., **it is high time for you to go** è proprio ora che Lei se ne vada; (coll) baldoria

high′ trea′son *s* (*against the sovereign*) lesa maestà; (*against the state*) alto tradimento

high′ wa′ter *s* alta marea; (*in a river*) straripamento

high′way′ *adj* autostradale ‖ *s* autostrada

high′way man *s* (-men) grassatore *m*

hijack ['haɪ,dʒæk] *tr* rubare; (*e.g., an airplane*) dirottare ‖ *intr* effettuare un dirottamento

hijacker ['haɪ,dʒækər] *s* ladro a mano armata; (*e.g., of an airplane*) dirottatore *m*

hijacking ['haɪ,dʒækɪŋ] *s* furto a mano armata; dirottamento

hike [haɪk] *s* (*for pleasure*) gita, camminata; (*increase*) aumento; (mil) marcia ‖ *tr* tirar su; aumentare ‖ *intr* fare una gita; (mil) fare una marcia

hiker ['haɪkər] *s* camminatore *m*

hilarious [hɪ'lɛrɪ·əs] *or* [haɪ'lɛrɪ·əs] *adj* ilare; (*e.g., joke*) allegro, divertente

hill [hɪl] *s* collina ‖ *tr* rincalzare

hillbil·ly ['hɪl,bɪlɪ] *s* (-lies) (coll) montanaro rustico

hillock ['hɪlək] *s* poggio, collinetta

hill′side′ *s* pendio

hill′top′ *s* cima

hill·y ['hɪlɪ] *adj* (-ier; -iest) collinoso; ripido

hilt [hɪlt] *s* impugnatura, elsa; **up to the hilt** completamente

him [hɪm] *pron pers* lo; lui; **to him** gli, a lui

himself [hɪm'sɛlf] *pron pers* lui stesso; sé stesso; si, e.g., **he enjoyed himself** si è divertito; **with himself** con sé

hind [haɪnd] *adj* posteriore, di dietro ‖ *s* cerva

hinder ['hɪndər] *tr* ostacolare, impedire

hindmost ['haɪnd,most] *adj* ultimo

hind′quar′ter *s* quarto posteriore

hindrance ['hɪndrəns] *s* ostacolo, impedimento

hind'sight' s senno di poi

Hindu ['hɪndu] adj & s indù mf

hinge [hɪndʒ] s cardine m; (bb) cerniera; (philately) listello gommato; punto principale || tr munire di cardini || intr—to hinge on dipendere da

hin·ny ['hɪni] s (-nies) bardotto

hint [hɪnt] s insinuazione; to take the hint capire l'antifona || tr & intr insinuare; to hint at alludere a

hinterland ['hɪntər‚lænd] s retroterra m, entroterra m

hip [hɪp] adj—to be hip to (slang) essere al corrente di || s anca, fianco; (of a roof) spigolo

hip'bone' s ileo, osso iliaco

hipped [hɪpt] adj (livestock) zoppicante; (roof) a padiglione; hipped on (coll) ossessionato per

hippie ['hɪpi] s capellone m

hip·po ['hɪpo] s (-pos) (coll) ippopotamo

hippodrome ['hɪpə‚drom] s ippodromo

hippopota·mus [‚hɪpə'pɑtəməs] s (-muses or -mi [‚maɪ]) ippopotamo

hip' roof' s tetto a padiglione

hire [haɪr] s paga, salario; nolo; for hire a nolo || tr (help) impiegare; (a conveyance) noleggiare || intr—to hire out mettersi a servizio

hired' girl' s lavorante f di campagna

hired' hand' s lavorante mf

hired' man' s (men') lavorante m di campagna

hireling ['haɪrlɪŋ] adj venale || s persona prezzolata

his [hɪz] adj poss suo, il suo || pron poss il suo

Hispanic [hɪs'pænɪk] adj ispano

Hispanist ['hɪspənɪst] s ispanista mf

hiss [hɪs] s (of fire, wind, serpent, etc.) sibilo; (of disapproval) fischio, zittio || tr zittire || intr zittire; sibilare; (said of a kettle) fischiare

histology [hɪs'tɑlədʒi] s istologia

historian [hɪs'torɪ·ən] s storico

historic(al) [hɪs'tɑrɪk(əl)] or [hɪs'tɔrɪk(əl)] adj storico

histo·ry ['hɪstəri] s (-ries) storia

histrionic [‚hɪstrɪ'ɑnɪk] adj teatrale; (artificial, affected) istrionico, teatrale || histrionics s istrionismo, teatralità f

hit [hɪt] s colpo; successo; (sarcastic remark) frecciata; to be a hit far furore; to make a hit with fare ottima impressione con || v (pret & pp hit; ger hitting) tr colpire; (to bump) cozzare; (the target) toccare, imbroccare, infilare; (with a car) metter sotto; (a certain speed) andare a || intr battere; to hit on (s.th new) imbroccare; to hit out at attaccare

hit'-and-run' adj (driver) colpevole di mancato soccorso

hit'-and-run' driv'er s pirata m della strada

hitch [hɪtʃ] s (jerk) strattone m; (knot) nodo; difficoltà f, ostacolo; || tr (to tie) attaccare; (oxen) aggiogare; (slang) sposare

hitch'hike' intr fare l'autostop

hitch'hik'er s autostoppista mf

hitch'ing post' s palo per attaccare un cavallo

hither ['hɪðər] adv qua, qui; hither and thither qua e là

hith'er·to' adv sinora

hit'-or-miss' adj fatto alla carlona

hit' rec'ord s disco di grande successo

hive [haɪv] s (box for bees) alveare m; (swarm) sciame m; hives orticaria || tr (bees) raccogliere

hoard [hɔrd] s cumulo; (of money) gruzzolo || tr & intr custodire gelosamente; tesaurizzare

hoarding ['hɔrdɪŋ] s ammassamento, tesaurizzazione

hoarfrost ['hɔr‚frɔst] s brina

hoarse [hɔrs] adj rauco, svociato

hoarseness ['hɔrsnɪs] s raucedine f

hoar·y ['hɔri] adj (-ier; -iest) canuto, incanutito

hoax [hoks] s mistificazione || tr mistificare

hob [hɑb] s mensola del focolare; to play hob with (coll) mettere a soqquadro

hobble ['hɑbəl] s zoppicamento; (to tie legs of animal) pastoia || tr far zoppicare; imbarazzare; mettere le pastoie a || intr zoppicare

hob·by ['hɑbi] s (-bies) svago, passatempo; to ride a hobby dedicarsi troppo alla propria occupazione favorita

hob'by-horse' s cavallo a dondolo

hob'gob'lin s folletto

hob'nail' s brocca, bulletta

hob·nob ['hɑb‚nɑb] v (pret & pp -nobbed; ger -nobbing) intr essere amiconi; to hobnob with essere intimo di

ho·bo ['hobo] s (-bos or -boes) girovago, vagabondo

Hob'son's choice' ['hɑbsənz] s scelta fra quanto viene offerto o niente

hock [hɑk] s garretto; (coll) pegno; in hock (coll) impegnato, al monte di pietà || tr tagliare i garretti a; (coll) impegnare

hockey ['hɑki] s hockey m

hock'ey play'er s hockeista m, discatore m

hock'shop' s (coll) negozio di prestiti su pegno

hocus-pocus ['hokəs'pokəs] s (meaningless formula) abracadabra m; gherminella

hod [hɑd] s vassoio; secchio per il carbone

hod' car'rier s manovale m

hodgepodge ['hɑdʒ‚pɑdʒ] s farragine f

hoe [ho] s marra, zappa || tr & intr zappare

hog [hɑg] or [hɔg] s suino, porco, maiale m || v (pret & pp hogged; ger hogging) tr (slang) mangiarsi il meglio di

hoggish ['hɑgɪʃ] or ['hɔgɪʃ] adj maialesco; egoista

hogs'head' s barilozzo di sessantatré galloni

hog'wash' s broda da maiali

hoist [hɔɪst] s montacarichi m; (lift)
spinta ‖ tr alzare, rizzare; (a flag)
inastare; (naut) issare
hoity-toity ['hɔɪtɪ'tɔɪtɪ] adj arrogante,
altezzoso
hokum ['hokəm] s (coll) fandonie fpl;
(coll) sentimentalismo volgare
hold [hold] s presa, piglio; (handle)
impugnatura; autorità f, ascendente
m; (wrestling) presa; (aer) cabina
bagagli; (mus) corona; (naut) cala,
stiva; **to take hold of** afferrare; impossessarsi di ‖ v (pret & pp **held**
[held]) tr tenere; (to hold up) sostenere; (e.g., with a pin) assicurare; (a
rank) rivestire; contenere; (a meeting) avere; (a note) (mus) filare; **to
hold back** trattenere; **to hold in** trattenere; **to hold one's own** non perdere terreno; **to hold over** differire;
to hold up reggere, sostenere; (to
rob) (coll) derubare, rapinare ‖ intr
stare; (to cling) reggere; restare valido; **hold on!** un momento!; **to hold
back** frenarsi; **to hold forth** fare un
discorso; **to hold off** astenersi; mantenersi a distanza; **to hold on** continuare; **to hold on to** attaccarsi a;
to hold out tener duro, resistere; **to
hold out for** mantenersi fermo per
holder ['holdər] s possessore m, detentore m; (e.g., for a cigar) bocchino;
(e.g., for a pot) manico, impugnatura
holding ['holdɪŋ] s possesso; **holdings**
valori mpl, patrimonio
hold′ing com′pany s società finanziaria
hold′up′ s (delay) interruzione; (coll)
rapina a mano armata; (fig) furto
hold′up man′ s grassatore m
hole [hol] s buco; (in cheese) occhio;
(in a road) buca; (den) tana; (burrow) fossa; **in a hole** in grane, in difficoltà; **to burn a hole in one's
pocket** (said of money) scorrere attraverso le mani bucate di qlcu; **to pick
holes in** trovare a ridire su ‖ intr—to
hole up (coll) imbucarsi
holiday ['hɑlɪ,de] s giorno festivo,
festa; vacanza
holiness ['holɪnɪs] s santità f; **his
Holiness** sua Santità
Holland ['hɑlənd] s l'Olanda f
Hollander ['hɑləndər] s olandese mf
hollow ['halo] adj vuoto, (sound)
sordo; (eyes, cheeks) infossato; vano,
futile ‖ s buca, cavità f; (small valley) valletta ‖ adv—**to beat all hollow**
(coll) battere completamente ‖ tr
scavare
hol·ly ['hali] s (-lies) agrifoglio
holly′hock′ s altea, malvone m
holm′ oak′ [hom] s leccio
holocaust ['halə,kɔst] s olocausto
holster ['holstər] s fondina
ho·ly ['holi] adj (-lier; -liest) santo;
(writing) sacro; (water) benedetto
Ho′ly Ghost′ s Spirito Santo
ho′ly or′ders spl ordini sacri; **to take
holy orders** entrare in un ordine religioso
Ho′ly Rood′ [rud] s Santa Croce
Ho′ly Scrip′ture s Sacra Scrittura

Ho′ly See′ s Santa Sede
Ho′ly Sep′ulcher s Santo Sepolcro
Ho′ly Thurs′day s l'Ascensione; il giovedì santo
ho′ly wa′ter s acqua benedetta, acquasanta
Ho′ly Writ′ s Sacra Scrittura
homage ['hamɪdʒ] or ['amɪdʒ] s
omaggio
homburg ['hambʌrg] s lobbia m & f
home [hom] adj (journey, domestico;
nazionale ‖ s casa, dimora; (fatherland) patria; (for the sick, aged; etc.)
ricovero; (sports) meta, traguardo; **at
home** a casa; (at ease) a proprio
agio; (sports) nel proprio campo;
away from home fuori di casa; **make
yourself at home** stia comodo; **to be
at home** (to receive callers) ricevere
‖ adv a casa; **to see home** accompagnare a casa; **to strike home** toccare nel vivo
home′bod′y s (-ies) persona casalinga
homebred ['hom,bred] adj domestico;
rozzo; semplice
home′brew′ s bevanda fatta in casa
home-coming ['hom,kʌmɪŋ] s ritorno
a casa
home′ coun′try s paese m natale
home′ deliv′ery s trasporto a domicilio
home′ front′ s fronte domestico
home′land′ s paese natio
homeless ['homlɪs] adj senza tetto
home′ life′ s vita familiare
home-loving ['hom,lʌvɪŋ] adj casalingo
home·ly ['homli] adj (-lier; -liest) (not
goodlooking) brutto; (not elegant)
semplice, scialbo
homemade ['hom'med] adj fatto in
casa
homemaker ['hom,mekər] s casalinga
home′ of′fice s sede f centrale ‖ **Home
Office** s (Brit) ministero degli interni
homeopath ['homɪ·ə,pæθ] or ['hamɪ·ə,pæθ] s omeopatico
home′ plate′ s casa base
home′ port′ s porto d'iscrizione (nel
registro marittimo)
home′ rule′ s autogoverno
home′ run′ s colpo che permette al battitore di percorrere tutte le basi del
diamante fino alla casa base
home′sick′ adj nostalgico; **to be homesick for** sentire la nostalgia per
home′sick′ness s nostalgia
homespun ['hom,spʌn] adj filato a
casa; semplice
home′stead s casa e terreno
home′stretch′ s (sports) dirittura
d'arrivo; (fig) fase f finale
home′town′ s città f natale
homeward ['homwərd] adj di ritorno ‖
adv verso casa; verso la patria
home′work′ s lavoro a domicilio; (of
a student) dovere m, esercizio
homey ['homi] adj (homier; homiest)
intimo, comodo
homicidal [,hamɪ'saɪdəl] adj omicida
homicide ['hamɪ,saɪd] s (act) omicidio; (person) omicida mf
homi·ly ['hamɪli] s (-lies) omelia

homing ['homɪŋ] *adj* (*pigeon*) viaggiatore; (*weapon*) cercatore del bersaglio

hominy ['hɑmɪni] *s* granturco macinato

homogenei·ty [,hɑmədʒɪ'ni·ɪti] or [,hɑmədʒɪni·ɪti] *s* (**-ties**) omogeneità *f*

homogeneous [,homə'dʒini·əs] or [,homə'dʒini·əs] *adj* omogeneo

homogenize [hə'mɑdʒə ,naɪz] *tr* omogeneizzare

homonym ['hɑmənɪm] *s* omonimo

homonymous [hə'mɑnɪməs] *adj* omonimo

homosexual [,homə'sekʃʊ·əl] *adj & s* omosessuale *mf*

hone [hon] *s* cote *f* ‖ *tr* affilare

honest ['ɑnɪst] *adj* onesto; guadagnato onestamente; integro, schietto

honesty ['ɑnɪsti] *s* onestà *f*; (bot) lunaria

hon·ey ['hʌni] *adj* melato, dolce ‖ *s* miele *m*; nettare *m*; (coll) caro ‖ *v* (*pret & pp* **-eyed** or **-ied**) *tr* dire parole melate a

hon'ey·bee' *s* ape domestica

hon'ey·comb' *s* favo ‖ *tr* crivellare

honeyed ['hʌnid] *adj* melato

hon'ey·dew' mel'on *s* melone *m* dolce dalla scorza liscia

hon'ey lo'cust *s* acacia a tre spine

hon'ey·moon' *s* luna di miele ‖ *intr* andare in viaggio di nozze

honeysuckle ['hʌni ,sʌkəl] *s* caprifoglio

honk [hɑŋk] or [hɔŋk] *s* (*of wild goose*) schiamazzo; (*of automobile horn*) suono del clacson ‖ *tr* (aut) suonare ‖ *intr* schiamazzare; (aut) suonare

honkytonk ['hɑŋki ,tɑŋk] or ['hɔŋki ,tɔŋk] *s* (coll) locale notturno rumoroso

honor ['ɑnər] *s* onore *m* ‖ *tr* onorare; (com) accettare e pagare

honorable ['ɑnərəbəl] *adj* (*upright*) onorato; (*bringing honor; worthy of honor*) onorevole

honorari·um [,ɑnə'reri·əm] *s* (**-ums** or **-a** [ə]) onorario

honorary ['ɑnə ,reri] *adj* onorario

honorific [,ɑnə'rɪfɪk] *adj* onorifico ‖ *s* titolo onorifico; formula di gentilezza

hon'or sys'tem *s* sistema scolastico basato sulla parola d'onore

hood [hud] *s* cappuccio; cappuccio di toga universitaria; (*of carriage*) soffietto; (aut) cofano; (slang) gangster *m* ‖ *tr* incappucciare

hoodlum ['hudləm] *s* (slang) facinoroso, gangster *m*, teppista *m*

hoodoo ['hudu] *s* (*body of primitive rites*) vuduismo; (*bad luck*) iettatura; (*person who brings bad luck*) iettatore *m* ‖ *tr* iettare

hood'wink' *tr* turlupinare, imbrogliare

hooey ['hu·i] *s* (coll) sciocchezze *fpl*

hoof [huf] or [huf] *s* zoccolo, unghia; **on the hoof** (*cattle*) vivo ‖ *tr*—**to hoof it** (slang) camminare; ballare

hoof'beat' *s* rumore *m* degli zoccoli

hook [huk] *s* gancio; (*for fishing*) amo;

(*to join two things*) agganciamento; (*for pulling*) raffio, rampino; (*curve*) curva; (*of hook and eye*) uncinello; (boxing) hook *m*, gancio; **by hook or by crook** di riffa o di raffa; **to swallow the hook** abboccare all'amo ‖ *tr* agganciare; (*to bend*) curvare; (*fish*) pigliare; (*to wound with the horns*) incornare; **to hook up** agganciare; (*e.g., a loudspeaking system*) montare ‖ *intr* agganciarsi; curvarsi

hookah ['hukə] *s* narghilè *m*

hook' and eye' *s* uncinello e occhiello

hook' and lad'der *s* autoscala

hooked' rug' *s* tappeto fatto all'uncinetto

hook'nose' *s* naso gobbo

hook'up' *s* (electron) diagramma *m*, schema *m* di montaggio; (rad, telv) rete *f*

hook'worm' *s* anchilostoma *m*

hooky ['huki] *s*—**to play hooky** marinare la scuola

hooligan ['hulɪgən] *s* teppista *m*

hooliganism ['hulɪgən ,ɪzəm] *s* teppismo

hoop [hup] or [hup] *s* cerchio ‖ *tr* cerchiare

hoop' skirt' *s* crinolina

hoot [hut] *s* grido della civetta; grido di derisione ‖ *tr* zittire ‖ *intr* . stridere; **to hoot at** fischiare

hoot' owl' *s* allocco

hop [hɑp] *s* salto, saltello; (aer) breve volo; (bot) luppolo; (coll) corsa; **hops** (*dried flowers of hop vine*) luppolo ‖ *v* (*pret & pp* **hopped**; *ger* **hopping**) *tr* saltare su; (aer) trasvolare ‖ *intr* saltellare; saltellare su un piede; **to hop over** saltare su; fare una corsa a

hope [hop] *s* speranza ‖ *tr & intr* sperare; **to hope for** sperare

hope' chest' *s* corredo da sposa

hopeful ['hopfəl] *adj* (*feeling hope*) fiducioso; (*giving hope*) promettente

hopeless ['hoplɪs] *adj* disperato

hopper ['hɑpər] *s* tramoggia

hop'scotch' *s* gioco del mondo

horde [hord] *s* orda

horehound ['hor ,haund] *s* marrubio; pastiglie *fpl* per la tosse al marrubio

horizon [hə'raɪzən] *s* orizzonte *m*

horizontal [,hɑri'zɑntəl] or [,hɔri'zɑntəl] *adj & s* orizzontale *f*

hormone ['hɔrmon] *s* ormone *m*

horn [hɔrn] *s* corno; (aut) clacson *m*, avvisatore acustico; (mus) corno; (*trumpet*) (slang) tromba; **to blow one's horn** cantare le proprie lodi; **to lock horns** lottare, disputare; **to pull in one's horns** battere in ritirata ‖ *intr*—**to horn in** (slang) intromettersi (in)

horned' owl' [hɔrned] *s* allocco

hornet ['hɔrnɪt] *s* calabrone *m*

hor'net's nest' *s* vespaio; **to stir up a hornet's nest** suscitare un vespaio

horn' of plen'ty *s* corno dell'abbondanza

horn'pipe' *s* clarinetto contadinesco inglese fatto di corno di bue

horn'-rimmed glass'es ['hɔrn'rɪmd] *spl* occhiali cerchiati di corno or con la montatura di corno

horn-y ['hɔrni] *adj* (**-ier; -iest**) corneo; (*callous*) calloso; (*having hornlike projections*) cornuto; (*slang*) preso da desiderio lussurioso

horoscope ['hɔrə,skop] *or* ['hɑrə,skop] *s* oroscopo

horrible ['hɑrɪbəl] *or* ['hɔrɪbəl] *adj* orrendo, orribile

horrid ['hɑrɪd] *or* ['hɔrɪd] *adj* orrido, orribile

horri-fy ['hɑrɪ,faɪ] *or* ['hɔrɪ,faɪ] *v* (*pret & pp* **-fied**) *tr* inorridire

horror ['hɑrər] *or* ['hɔrər] *s* orrore *m;* **to have a horror of** provare orrore per

hors d'oeuvre [ɔr 'dʌrv] *s* (**hors d'oeuvres** [ɔr 'dʌrvz]) *s* antipasto

horse [hɔrs] *s* cavallo; (*of carpenter*) cavalletto; **hold your horses!** (coll) aspetti un momento!; **to back the wrong horse** (coll) puntare sul perdente; **to be a horse of another color** (coll) essere un altro paio di maniche ‖ *intr*—**to horse around** (slang) giocherellare; (slang) fare tiri burloni

horse'back' *s*—**on horseback** a cavallo ‖ *adv*—**to ride horseback** montare a cavallo

horse' block' *s* montatoio
horse'break'er *s* domatore *m* di cavalli
horse'car' *s* tram *m* a cavalli
horse' chest'nut *s* (*tree*) ippocastano; (*nut*) castagna d'India
horse' deal'er *s* mercante *m* di cavalli
horse' doc'tor *s* veterinario
horse'fly' *s* (**-flies**) tafano
horse'hair' *s* crine *m* di cavallo; (*fabric*) cilicio
horse'hide' *s* cuoio di cavallo
horse'laugh' *s* risataccia
horse'man *s* (**-men**) cavallerizzo
horsemanship ['hɔrsmən,ʃɪp] *s* equitazione, maneggio
horse' meat' *s* carne equina
horse' op'era *s* western *m*
horse' pis'tol *s* pistola da sella
horse'play' *s* gioco violento, tiro burlone
horse'pow'er *s* cavallo vapore inglese
horse' race' *s* corsa ippica
horse'rad'ish *s* cren *m*, barbaforte *m*
horse' sense' *s* (coll) senso comune
horse'shoe' *s* ferro di cavallo
horse'shoe mag'net *s* calamita a ferro di cavallo
horse'shoe nail' *s* chiodo da cavallo
horse' show' *s* concorso ippico
horse' thief' *s* ladro di cavalli
horse'-trade' *intr* trafficare
horse'whip' *s* staffile *m* ‖ *v* (*pret & pp* **-whipped**) *ger* **-whipping**) *tr* staffilare
horse'wom'an *s* (**-wom'en**) amazzone *f*
hors-y ['hɔrsi] *adj* (**-ier; -iest**) equestre; (*interested in horses*) appassionato ai cavalli; (coll) goffo
horticulture ['hɔrtɪ,kʌltʃər] *s* orticoltura
horticulturist [,hɔrtɪ'kʌltʃərɪst] *s* orticoltore *m*

hose [hoz] *s* (*stocking*) calza; (*sock*) calzino corto; (*flexible tube*) manica ‖ **hose** *spl* calze *fpl*
hosier ['hoʒər] *s* calzettaio
hosiery ['hoʒəri] *s* calze *fpl;* calzificio
hospice ['hɑspɪs] *s* ospizio
hospitable ['hɑspɪtəbəl] *or* [hɑs'pɪtəbəl] *ac'j* ospitale
hospital ['hɑspɪtəl] *s* ospedale *m*
hospitali-ty [,hɑspɪ'tælɪti] *s* (**-ties**) ospitalità *f*
hospitalize ['hɑspɪtə,laɪz] *tr* ospedalizzare
host [host] *s* ospite *m;* (*at an inn*) oste *m;* (*army*) milizia; (*crowd*) folla ‖ **Host** *s* (eccl) ostia
hostage ['hɑstɪdʒ] *s* ostaggio
hostel ['hɑstəl] *s* ostello della gioventù
hostel-ry ['hɑstəlri] *s* (**-ries**) albergo
hostess ['hostɪs] *s* ospite *f*, padrona di casa; (*e.g., on a bus*) accompagnatrice *f*, guida *f;* (aer) assistente *f* di volo
hostile ['hɑstɪl] *adj* ostile
hostili-ty [hɑs'tɪlɪti] *s* (**-ties**) ostilità *f*
hostler ['hɑslər] *or* ['ɑslər] *s* stalliere *m*
hot [hɑt] *adj* (**hotter; hottest**) caldo; (*reception*) caloroso; (*e.g., pepper*) piccante; (*fresh*) fresco; (*pursuit*) impetuoso; (*in rut*) in calore; (coll) radioattivo; **to be hot** (*said of a person*) aver caldo; (*said of the weather*) fare caldo; **to make it hot for** (coll) dare del filo da torcere a
hot' air' *s* aria calda; (slang) fumo
hot'-air fur'nace *s* impianto di riscaldamento ad aria calda
hot' baths' *spl* terme *fpl*
hot'bed' *s* (*e.g., of revolt*) focolaio; (hort) semenzaio, letto caldo
hot'-blood'ed *adj* ardente; impetuoso
hot' cake' *s* frittella; **to sell like hot cakes** vendersi come se fosse regalato
hot' dog' *s* Frankfurter *m*, Würstel *m*
hotel [ho'tel] *adj* alberghiero ‖ *s* albergo
ho-tel'keep'er *s* albergatore *m*
hot'head' *s* testa calda
hotheaded ['hɑt,hedɪd] *adj* esaltato, scalmanato
hot'house' *s* serra
hot' plate' *s* fornello elettrico, scaldavivande *m*
hot' springs' *spl* terme *fpl*
hot-tempered ['hɑt'tempərd] *adj* impulsivo, irascibile
hot' wa'ter *s*—**to be in hot water** (coll) essere nei guai
hot'-wa'ter boil'er *s* caldaia del termosifone
hot'-wa'ter bot'tle *s* borsa dell'acqua calda
hot'-wa'ter heat'er *s* scaldabagno
hot'-wa'ter heat'ing *s* riscaldamento a circolazione di acqua calda
hound [haʊnd] *s* bracco; **to follow the hounds** *or* **to ride to hounds** andare a caccia alla volpe ‖ *tr* perseguitare
hour [aʊr] *s* ora; **by the hour** a ore; **in an evil hour** in un brutto momento; **on the hour** ogni ora al suonar del-

l'ora; **to keep late hours** andare a letto tardi

hour'glass' s clessidra

hour' hand' s lancetta delle ore

hourly ['aʊrli] adj orario || adv ogni ora; spesso

house [haʊs] s (**houses** ['haʊzɪz]) casa; (legislative body) camera; (size of audience) concorso di pubblico; teatro; **to keep house** fare le faccende domestiche; **to put one's house in order** migliorare il proprio comportamento; accomodare le próprie faccende || [haʊz] tr allogare

house' arrest' s arresto a domicilio

house'boat' s casa galleggiante

house'break'er s scassinatore m

housebreaking ['haʊs‚brekɪŋ] s violazione di domicilio; scasso

housebroken ['haʊs‚brokən] adj (e.g., cat) che è stato addestrato a tenersi pulito

house'clean'ing s pulizia della casa; (fig) pulizia, repulisti m

house'coat' s vestaglia da casa

house' cur'rent s corrente f di rete

house'fly' s (-flies) mosca domestica

houseful ['haʊs‚fʊl] s casa piena

house' fur'nishings spl arredi domestici

house'hold' adj domestico || s famiglia

house'hold'er s capo della famiglia

house'-hunt' intr—**to go house-hunting** andare in cerca di casa

house'keep'er s governante f

house'keep'ing s faccende domestiche; **to set up housekeeping** metter su casa

house'keeping apart'ment s appartamentino

house'maid' s domestica

house' me'ter s contatore domestico

house'moth'er s maestra in pensionato per studenti

house' of cards' s castello di carte

house' of ill' repute' s casa di malaffare

house' paint'er s imbianchino

house' physi'cian s medico residente

house'top' s tetto; **to shout from the housetops** proclamare ai quattro venti

housewarming ['haʊs‚wɔrmɪŋ] s festa per l'inaugurazione di una casa

house'wife' s (-wives') donna di casa

house'work' s faccende domestiche

housing ['haʊzɪŋ] s (of a horse) gualdrappa; (dwelling) abitazioni fpl; (carp) alloggiamento; (mach) gabbia, custodia; (aut) coppa; (of transmission) (aut) scatola

hous'ing short'age s crisi f degli alloggi

hovel ['hʌvəl] or ['hɑvəl] s catapecchia, stamberga; (shed) baracca

hover ['hʌvər] or ['hɑvər] intr librarsi; (on the lips) trapelare; (fig) ondeggiare, esitare

how [haʊ] adv come; (at what price) a quanto; **how early** quando, a che ora; **how else** in che altro modo; **how far** fino a dove; quanto, e.g., **how far is it to the station?** quanto c'è da qui alla stazione?; **how long** quanto tempo; **how many** quanti; **how much**

quanto; **how often** quante volte; **how old are you?** quanti anni ha?; **how soon** quando, a che ora; **how + adj** quanto + adj, e.g., **how beautiful she is!** quanto è bella!

how-ev'er adv comunque; in qualunque modo; per quanto . . . , e.g., **however wrong he may be** per quanto torto possa avere || conj come, e.g., **do it however you want** lo faccia come vuole

howitzer ['haʊ‚ɪtsər] s obice m

howl [haʊl] s ululato, urlo; scoppio di risa || tr gridare; **to howl down** sopraffare a grida; || intr ululare, urlare

howler ['haʊlər] s urlatore m; (coll) strafalcione m, topica

hoyden ['hɔɪdən] s ragazzaccia

hub [hʌb] s mozzo; (fig) centro

hubbub ['hʌbəb] s putiferio, fracasso

hub'cap' s (aut) calotta della ruota

huckleber·ry ['hʌkəl‚beri] s (-ries) mirtillo

huckster ['hʌkstər] s venditore m ambulante; trafficante m

huddle ['hʌdəl] s conferenza segreta || intr affollarsi, accalcarsi

hue [hju] s tono, tinta; **hue and cry** grido d'indignazione

huff [hʌf] s stizza; **in a huff** di cattivo umore || tr (checkers) buffare

hug [hʌg] s abbraccio || v (pret & pp hugged; ger hugging) tr abbracciare; (e.g., a wall) costeggiare || intr abbracciarsi

huge [hjudʒ] adj smisurato, immane

huh [hʌ] interj eh!

hulk [hʌlk] s scafo, carcassa; (unwieldy object) trabiccolo

hulking ['hʌlkɪŋ] adj grosso e goffo

hull [hʌl] s (of ship or hydroplane) scafo; (of dirigible) intelaiatura; (of airplane) fusoliera; (e.g., of a nut) guscio || tr sgusciare; (rice) brillare

hullabaloo ['hʌlǝbǝ‚lu] or ['‚hʌlǝbǝ'lu] s fracasso, baccano

hum [hʌm] s canterellio; (of bee, machine, etc.) ronzio || v (pret & pp hummed; ger humming) tr canterellare || intr canterellare; (to buzz) ronzare; (coll) vibrare, essere attivo

human ['hjumən] adj umano

hu'man be'ing s essere umano

humane [hju'men] adj umano; compassionevole

humanist ['hjumənɪst] adj umanistico || s umanista mf

humanitarian [hju‚mænɪ'tɛri·ən] adj & s umanitario

humani·ty [hju'mænɪti] s (-ties) umanità f; **humanities** (of Greece and Rome) studi umanistici; (literature, art, philosophy) scienze umanistiche

hu'man·kind' s genere umano

humble ['hʌmbəl] or ['ʌmbəl] adj umile || tr umiliare

hum'ble pie' s—**to eat humble pie** accettare un'umiliazione

hum'bug' s frottola; (person) impostore m || v (pret & pp -bugged; ger

-bugging) *tr* imbrogliare || *intr* fare l'imbroglione

hum'drum' *adj* noioso, monotono

humer·us ['hjumərəs] *s* (-i [,aɪ]) omero

humid ['hjumɪd] *adj* umido

humidifier [hju'mɪdɪ,faɪ·ər] *s* evaporatore *m*

humidi·fy [hju'mɪdɪ,faɪ] *v* (*pret & pp* -fied) *tr* inumidire

humidity [hju'mɪdɪti] *s* umidità *f*

humiliate [hju'mɪlɪ,et] *tr* umiliare

humiliating ·[hju'mɪlɪ,etɪŋ] *adj* umiliante

humility [hju'mɪlɪti] *s* umiltà *f*

hummingbird ['hʌmɪŋ,bʌrd] *s* colibrì *m*

humor ['hjumər] or ['jumər] *s* umore *m*; umorismo; **out of humor** di cattivo umore || *tr* adattarsi alle fisime di, assecondare

humorist ['hjumərɪst] or ['jumərɪst] *s* umorista *mf*

humorous ['hjumərəs] or ['jumərəs] *adj* umoristico

hump [hʌmp] *s* gobba; (*in the ground*) monticello

hump'back' *s* gobba; (*person*) gobbo

humus ['hjuməs] *s* humus *m*

hunch [hʌntʃ] *s* gobba; (*premonition*) (coll) sospetto || *tr* piegare || *intr* accovacciarsi

hunch'back' *s* gobba; (*person*) gobbo

hundred ['hʌndrəd] *adj, s & pron* cento; **a hundred or one hundred** cento; **by the hundreds** a centinaia

hundredth ['hʌndrədθ] *adj, s & pron* centesimo

hun'dred·weight' *s* cento libbre

Hungarian [hʌŋ'gerɪ·ən] *adj & s* ungherese *mf*

Hungary ['hʌŋgəri] *s* l'Ungheria *f*

hunger ['hʌŋgər] *s* fame *f* || *intr* aver fame; **to hunger for** aver un desiderio ardente di, agognare

hun'ger strike' *s* sciopero della fame

hun·gry ['hʌŋgri] *adj* (-grier; -griest) affamato; **to be hungry** aver fame; **to go hungry** andare digiuno

hunk [hʌŋk] *s* (coll) bel pezzo

hunt [hʌnt] *s* caccia; **on the hunt for** a caccia di || *tr* cacciare; (*to look for*) cercare || *intr* andare a caccia; cercare; **to go hunting** andare a caccia; **to hunt for** cercare

hunter ['hʌntər] *s* cacciatore *m*; (*dog*) cane *m* da caccia

hunting ['hʌntɪŋ] *adj* da caccia || *s* caccia

hunt'ing box' *s* capanno

hunt'ing dog' *s* cane *m* da caccia

hunt'ing ground' *s* terreno di caccia

hunt'ing horn' *s* corno da caccia

hunt'ing jack'et *s* cacciatora

hunt'ing lodge' *s* (*hut*) capanno; villino da caccia

hunt'ing sea'son *s* stagione della caccia

huntress ['hʌntrɪs] *s* cacciatrice *f*

hunts'man *s* (-men) cacciatore *m*

hurdle ['hʌrdəl] *s* (*hedge*) siepe *f*; (*wooden frame*) barriera; (*sports, fig*) ostacolo; **hurdles** corsa ad ostacoli || *tr* saltare, superare

hur'dle race' *s* corsa agli ostacoli

hurl [hʌrl] *s* lancio || *tr* lanciare; **to hurl back** respingere

hurrah [hu'rɑ] or **hurray** [hu're] *s* viva *m* || *tr* applaudire || *intr* gridare urrà || *interj* evviva!, urrà!; **hurrah for...! viva...!**

hurricane ['hʌrɪ,ken] *s* uragano

hurried ['hʌrid] *adj* frettoloso

hur·ry ['hʌri] *s* (-ries) fretta; **to be in a hurry** avere fretta || *v* (*pret & pp* -ried) *tr* affrettare, sollecitare || *intr* affrettarsi; **to hurry away** andarsene di furia; **to hurry back** ritornare presto; **to hurry up** spicciarsi

hurt [hʌrt] *adj* (*injured*) ferito; (*offended*) risentito || *s* (*harm*) danno; (*injury*) ferita; (*pain*) dolore *m* || *v* (*pret & pp* hurt) *tr* (*to harm*) fare male a; (*to injure*) ferire; (*to offend*) offendere; (*to pain*) dolere (with *dat*) || *intr* fare male, dolere; aver male, e.g., **my head hurts** ho male alla testa

hurtle ['hʌrtəl] *intr* sferrarsi, scagliarsi, precipitarsi

husband ['hʌzbənd] *s* marito || *tr* amministrare con economia

hus'band·man *s* (-men) agricoltore *m*

husbandry ['hʌzbəndri] *s* agricoltura; (*management of domestic affairs*) governo, economia domestica

hush [hʌʃ] *s* silenzio || *tr* far tacere; **to hush up** (*a scandal*) soffocare || *intr* tacere || *interj* zitto!

hushaby ['hʌʃə,baɪ] *interj* fa' la nanna!

hush'-hush' *adj* segretissimo

hush' mon'ey *s* prezzo del silenzio

husk [hʌsk] *s* guscio; (*of corn*) spoglia || *tr* sgusciare; (*rice*) brillare; (*corn*) scartocciare, spogliare

husk·y ['hʌski] *adj* (-ier; -iest) forte; (*voice*) rauco

hus·sy ['hʌzi] or ['hʌsi] *s* (-sies) poca di buono; ragazza impudente

hustle ['hʌsəl] *s* vigore *m*; (*slang*) traffico || *tr* forzare, spingere || *intr* affrettarsi, scalmanarsi; (*slang*) trafficare; (*said of a prostitute*) (*slang*) accostare un cliente

hustler ['hʌslər] *s* (*go-getter*) persona intraprendente; (*slang*) trafficone *m*, imbroglione *m*; (*slang*) passeggiatrice *f*

hut [hʌt] *s* casolare *m*, casupola

hyacinth ['haɪ·əsɪnθ] *s* giacinto

hybrid ['haɪbrɪd] *adj & s* ibrido

hybridize ['haɪbrɪ,daɪz] *tr & intr* ibridare

hy·dra ['haɪdrə] *s* (-dras or -drae [driɪ]) idra

hydrant ['haɪdrənt] *s* idrante *m*; (*water faucet*) rubinetto

hydrate ['haɪdret] *s* idrato || *tr* idratare || *intr* idratarsi

hydraulic [haɪ'drɔlɪk] *adj* idraulico || **hydraulics** *s* idraulica

hydrau'lic ram' *s* pompa idraulica

hydriodic [,haɪdrɪ'ɑdɪk] *adj* iodidrico

hydrobromic [,haɪdrə'bromɪk] *adj* bromidrico

hydrocarbon [ˌhaɪdrə'kɑrbən] s idro-carburo

hydrochloric [ˌhaɪdrə'klɔrɪk] adj clo-ridrico

hydroelectric [ˌhaɪdro·ɪ'lɛktrɪk] adj idroelettrico

hydrofluoric [ˌhaɪdrəflu'ɑrɪk] or [ˌhaɪdrəflu'ɔrɪk] adj fluoridrico

hydrofoil ['haɪdrə,fɔɪl] s superficie idrodinamica; (winglike member) aletta idrodinamica; (vessel) ali-scafo, idroplano

hydrogen ['haɪdrədʒən] s idrogeno

hy'drogen bomb' s bomba all'idrogeno

hy'drogen perox'ide s perossido d'idro-geno, acqua ossigenata

hy'drogen sul'fide s solfuro d'idrogeno

hydrometer [haɪ'drɑmɪtər] s areome-tro

hydrophobia [ˌhaɪdrə'fobɪ·ə] s idro-fobia

hydroplane ['haɪdrə,plen] s (aer) idro-volante m; (naut) idroscivolante m, idroplano

hydroxide [haɪ'drɑksaɪd] s idrossido

hyena [haɪ'inə] s iena

hygiene ['haɪdʒin] or ['haɪdʒɪ,in] s igiene f

hygienic [ˌhaɪdʒɪ'ɛnɪk] or [haɪ'dʒɪnɪk] adj igienico

hymn [hɪm] s inno

hymnal ['hɪmnəl] s innario

hyperacidity [ˌhaɪpərə'sɪdɪti] s ipera-cidità f

hyperbola [haɪ'pʌrbələ] s (geom) iper-bole f

hyperbole [haɪ'pʌrbəli] s (rhet) iper-bole f

hyperbolic [ˌhaɪpər'bɑlɪk] adj iper-bolico

hypersensitive [ˌhaɪpər'sɛnsɪtɪv] adj ipersensibile

hypertension [ˌhaɪpər'tɛnʃən] s iper-tensione

hyphen ['haɪfən] s trattino

hyphenate ['haɪfə,net] tr unire con trattino; scrivere con trattino

hypno·sis [hɪp'nosɪs] s (-ses [siz]) ipnosi f

hypnotic [hɪp'nɑtɪk] adj & s ipnotico

hypnotism ['hɪpnə,tɪzəm] s ipnotismo

hypnotize ['hɪpnə,taɪz] tr ipnotizzare

hypochondriac [ˌhaɪpə'kɑndrɪ,æk] or [ˌhɪpə'kɑndrɪ,æk] s ipocondriaco

hypocri·sy [hɪ'pɑkrəsi] s (-sies) ipo-crisia

hypocrite ['hɪpəkrɪt] s ipocrita mf

hypocritical [ˌhɪpə'krɪtɪkəl] adj ipo-crita

hypodermic [ˌhaɪpə'dʌrmɪk] adj ipo-dermico

hyposulfite [ˌhaɪpə'sʌlfaɪt] s iposolfito

hypotenuse [haɪ'pɑtɪ,nus] or [haɪ'pɑtɪ,njus] s ipotenusa

hypothesis [haɪ'pɑθɪsɪs] s (-ses [,siz]) ipotesi f

hypothesize [haɪ'pɑθɪ,saɪz] tr ipotiz-zare

hypothetic(al) [ˌhaɪpə'θɛtɪk(əl)] adj ipotetico

hyssop ['hɪsəp] s issopo

hysteria [hɪs'tɪrɪ·ə] s isterismo

hysteric [hɪs'tɛrɪk] adj isterico ‖ **hys-terics** s isterismo

hysterical [hɪs'tɛrɪkəl] adj isterico

I

I, i [aɪ] s nona lettera dell'alfabeto inglese

I [aɪ] pron pers (we [wi]) io; **it is I** sono io

iambic [aɪ'æmbɪk] adj giambico

iam·bus [aɪ'æmbəs] s (-bi [baɪ]) giambo

I'-beam' s putrella

Iberian [aɪ'bɪrɪ·ən] adj iberico ‖ s abi-tante mf dell'Iberia; lingua iberica

ibex ['aɪbeks] s (ibexes or ibices ['ɪbɪ,siz]) stambecco

ice [aɪs] s ghiaccio; **to break the ice** rompere il ghiaccio; **to cut no ice** (coll) non aver importanza; **to skate on thin ice** cacciarsi in una situazione delicata ‖ tr gelare; (to cover with icing) glassare ‖ intr gelarsi

ice' age' s epoca glaciale

ice' bag' s borsa di ghiaccio

iceberg ['aɪs,bʌrg] s borgognone m, montagna di ghiaccio

ice'boat' s slitta a vela; (icebreaker) rompighiaccio

icebound ['aɪs,baʊnd] adj chiuso dal ghiaccio

ice'box' s ghiacciaia

ice'break'er s rompighiaccio

ice' buck'et s secchiello da ghiaccio

ice'cap' s calotta glaciale

ice'-cold' adj gelido, ghiacciato

ice'-cream' s gelato, sorbetto

ice'-cream cone' s cono gelato

ice'-cream freez'er s gelatiera

ice'-cream par'lor s gelateria

ice' cube' s cubetto di ghiaccio

ice' hock'ey s hockey m su ghiaccio

Iceland ['aɪslənd] s l'Islanda f

Icelander ['aɪs,lændər] or ['aɪsləndər] s islandese mf

Icelandic [aɪs'lændɪk] adj islandese ‖ s (language) islandese m

ice'man' s (-men') venditore m di ghiaccio

ice' pack' s banco di ghiaccio; (ice bag) borsa di ghiaccio

ice' pick' s rompighiaccio

ice' shelf' s tavolato di ghiaccio

ice' skate' s pattino da ghiaccio

ice' wa'ter s acqua gelata

ichthyology [ˌɪkθɪ'ɑlədʒɪ] s ittiologia

icicle ['aɪsɪkəl] s ghiacciolo

icing ['aɪsɪŋ] s glassa; (meteor) gelo

iconoclast [aɪ'kɑnə,klæst] s icono-clasta mf

iconoscope [aɪ'kɑnə,skop] *s* (trademark) iconoscopio

icy ['aɪsi] *adj* (**icier; iciest**) ghiacciato; (*e.g., wind, hands*) gelido; (fig) glaciale

idea [aɪ'di·ə] *s* idea

ideal [aɪ'di·əl] *adj* & *s* ideale *m*

idealist [aɪ'di·əlɪst] *adj* & *s* idealista *m*

idealistic [aɪ,di·əl'ɪstɪk] *adj* idealistico

idealize [aɪ'di·ə,laɪz] *tr* idealizzare

identic(al) [aɪ'dentɪk(əl)] *adj* identico

identification [aɪ,dentɪfɪ'keʃən] *s* identificazione, riconoscimento

identifica'tion card' *s* carta d'identità

identifica'tion tag' *s* piastrina

identi-fy [aɪ'dentɪ,faɪ] *v* (*pret* & *pp* **-fied**) *tr* identificare

identi-ty [aɪ'dentɪti] *s* (**-ties**) identità *f*

ideolo-gy [,aɪdɪ'ɑlədʒi] *or* [,ɪdɪ-'ɑlədʒi] *s* (**-gies**) ideologia

ides [aɪdz] *spl* idi *mpl* & *fpl*

idio-cy ['ɪdɪ·əsi] *s* (**-cies**) idiozia

idiom ['ɪdɪ·əm] *s* (*expression that is contrary to the usual patterns of the language*) locuzione idiomatica, idiotismo; (*style of language*) lingua, idioma *m*; (*style of an author*) stile *m*; (*character of a language*) indole *f*

idiomatic [,ɪdɪ·ə'mætɪk] *adj* idiomatico

idiosyncra-sy [,ɪdɪ·ə'sɪnkrəsi] *s* (**-sies**) eccentricità *f*, originalità *f*; (med) idiosincrasia

idiot ['ɪdɪ·ət] *s* idiota *mf*

idiotic [,ɪdɪ'ɑtɪk] *adj* idiota

idle ['aɪdəl] *adj* (*unemployed*) disoccupato; (*machine*) fermo; (*capital*) giacente; (*time*) perso; (*talk*) vano; (*lazy*) fannullone, ozioso; **to run idle** girare a vuoto ‖ *tr*—**to idle away** (*time*) sprecare ‖ *intr* poltrire, fare il fannullone; (aut) girare al minimo

idleness ['aɪdəlnɪs] *s* ozio

idler ['aɪdlər] *s* fannullone *m*

idling ['aɪdlɪŋ] *s* (*of motor*) minimo

idol ['aɪdəl] *s* idolo

idola-try [aɪ'dɑlətri] *s* (**-tries**) idolatria

idolize ['aɪdə,laɪz] *tr* idolatrare

idyll ['aɪdəl] *s* idillio

idyllic [aɪ'dɪlɪk] *adj* idilliaco

if [ɪf] *conj* se; **as if** come se; **even if** anche se; **if so** se è così; **if true** se è vero

ignis fatuus ['ɪgnɪs'fætʃ·ʊ·əs] *s* (**ignes fatui** ['ɪgniz'fætʃ·ʊ,aɪ]) fuoco fatuo

ignite [ɪg'naɪt] *tr* infiammare ‖ *intr* infiammarsi

ignition [ɪg'nɪʃən] *s* ignizione; (aut) accensione

igni'tion switch' *s* (aut) chiavetta dell'accensione

igni'tion sys'tem *s* (aut) apparecchiatura d'accensione

ignoble [ɪg'nobəl] *adj* ignobile

ignominious [,ɪgnə'mɪnɪ·əs] *adj* ignominioso

ignoramus [,ɪgnə'reməs] *s* ignorante *mf*

ignorance ['ɪgnərəns] *s* ignoranza

ignorant ['ɪgnərənt] *adj* ignorante; **to be ignorant of** ignorare

ignore [ɪg'nor] *tr* (*a person; a person's kindness*) ignorare

ill [ɪl] *adj* (**worse** [wʌrs]; **worst** [wʌrst]) malato; **to take ill** cadere malato ‖ *adv* male; **to take ill** prendere in mala parte

ill-advised ['ɪləd'vaɪzd] *adj* inconsulto, sconsiderato

ill'-at-ease' *adj* imbarazzato, spaesato

ill-bred ['ɪl'brɛd] *adj* maleducato

ill-considered ['ɪlkən'sɪdərd] *adj* sconsiderato

ill-disposed ['ɪldɪs'pozd] *adj* maldisposto, malintenzionato

illegal [ɪ'ligəl] *adj* illegale

illegible [ɪ'lɛdʒɪbəl] *adj* illeggibile

illegitimate [,ɪlɪ'dʒɪtɪmɪt] *adj* illegittimo

ill' fame' *s* pessima fama

ill-fated ['ɪl'fetɪd] *adj* infausto

ill-gotten ['ɪl'gɑtən] *adj* male acquistato

ill-humored ['ɪl'hjumərd] *adj* di cattivo umore

illicit [ɪ'lɪsɪt] *adj* illecito

illitera-cy [ɪ'lɪtərəsi] *s* (**-cies**) analfabetismo; (*mistake*) solecismo; ignoranza

illiterate [ɪ'lɪtərɪt] *adj* (*uneducated*) illetterato; (*unable to read or write*) analfabeta ‖ *s* analfabeta *mf*

ill-mannered ['ɪl'mænərd] *adj* screanzato, maleducato

illness ['ɪlnɪs] *s* malattia

illogical [ɪ'lɑdʒɪkəl] *adj* illogico

ill-spent ['ɪl'spɛnt] *adj* sprecato

ill-starred ['ɪl'stɑrd] *adj* nato sotto una cattiva stella; sfortunato, funesto

ill-tempered ['ɪl'tɛmpərd] *adj* di cattivo umore

ill-timed ['ɪl'taɪmd] *adj* inopportuno

ill'-treat' *tr* maltrattare, tartassare

illuminate [ɪ'lumɪ,net] *tr* illuminare; (*a manuscript*) miniare

illumination [ɪ,lumɪ'neʃən] *s* illuminazione; (*in manuscript*) miniatura

illusion [ɪ'luʒən] *s* illusione

illusive [ɪ'lusɪv] *adj* illusorio

illusory [ɪ'lusəri] *adj* illusorio

illustrate ['ɪləs,tret] *or* [ɪ'lʌstret] *tr* illustrare

illustration [,ɪləs'treʃən] *s* illustrazione

illustrator ['ɪləs,tretər] *s* illustratore *m*

illustrious [ɪ'lʌstrɪ·əs] *adj* illustre

ill' will' *s* astio, ruggine *f*, malevolenza

image ['ɪmɪdʒ] *s* immagine *f*; **the very image of** il ritratto parlante di

image-ry ['ɪmɪdʒri] *or* ['ɪmɪdʒəri] *s* (**-ries**) (*mental images*) fantasia; (*images collectively*) immagini *fpl*; (rhet) linguaggio figurato

imaginary [ɪ'mædʒɪ,nɛri] *adj* immaginario

imagination [ɪ,mædʒɪ'neʃən] *s* immaginazione

imagine [ɪ'mædʒɪn] *tr* & *intr* immaginare; (*to conjecture*) immaginarsi; **imagine!** si figuri!

imbalance [ɪm'bæləns] *s* scompenso

imbecile ['ɪmbɪsɪl] *adj* & *s* imbecile *mf*

imbecili·ty [ˌɪmbɪ'sɪlɪti] *s* (**-ties**) imbecillità *f*, imbecillaggine *f*

imbibe [ɪm'baɪb] *tr* (*to drink*) bere; assorbire ‖ *intr* bere

imbue [ɪm'bju] *tr* imbevere

imitate ['ɪmɪ ˌtet] *tr* imitare

imitation [ˌɪmɪ'teʃən] *adj* (*e.g., jewelry*) falso ‖ *s* imitazione

imitator ['ɪmɪ ˌtetər] *s* imitatore *m*

immaculate [ɪ'mækjəlɪt] *adj* immacolato

immaterial [ˌɪmə'tɪrɪ·əl] *adj* immateriale; poco impórtante; **it's immaterial to me** a me fa lo stesso

immature [ˌɪmə'tjʊr] or [ˌɪmə'tʊr] *adj* immaturo

immeasurable [ɪ'meʒərəbəl] *adj* incommensurabile, smisurato

immediacy [ɪ'midɪ·əsi] *s* immediatezza

immediate [ɪ'midɪ·ɪt] *adj* immediato

immediately [ɪ'midɪ·ɪtli] *adv* immediatamente

immemorial [ˌɪmɪ'morɪ·əl] *adj* immemorabile

immense [ɪ'mɛns] *adj* immenso

immerge [ɪ'mʌrdʒ] *intr* sommergersi

immerse [ɪ'mʌrs] *tr* immergere

immersion [ɪ'mʌrʃən] or [ɪ'mʌrʒən] *s* immersione

immigrant ['ɪmɪgrənt] *adj & s* immigrante *mf*

immigrate ['ɪmɪ ˌgret] *intr* immigrare

immigration [ˌɪmɪ'greʃən] *s* immigrazione

imminent ['ɪmɪnənt] *adj* imminente

immobile [ɪ'mobɪl] or [ɪ'mobɪl] *adj* immobile

immobilize [ɪ'mobɪ ˌlaɪz] *tr* immobilizzare

immoderate [ɪ'madərɪt] *adj* smodato, sregolato

immodest [ɪ'madɪst] *adj* immodesto

immoral [ɪ'marəl] or [ɪ'mɔrəl] *adj* immorale

immortal [ɪ'mɔrtəl] *adj & s* immortale *mf*

immortalize [ɪ'mɔrtə ˌlaɪz] *tr* eternare, immortalare

immune [ɪ'mjun] *adj* immune

immunize ['ɪmjə ˌnaɪz] or [ɪ'mjunaɪz] *tr* immunizzare

imp [ɪmp] *s* diavoletto; (*child*) frugolo

impact ['ɪmpækt] *s* impatto

impair [ɪm'per] *tr* danneggiare; (*to weaken*) indebolire

impan·el [ɪm'pænəl] *v* (*pret & pp* **-eled** or **-elled**; *ger* **-eling** or **-elling**) *tr* iscrivere nella lista dei giurati; (*a jury*) selezionare

impart [ɪm'part] *tr* (*a secret*) far conoscere; (*knowledge*) impartire; (*motion*) imprimere

impartial [ɪm'parʃəl] *adj* imparziale

impassable [ɪm'pæsəbəl] or [ɪm'pasəbəl] *adj* impraticabile, intransitabile

impasse [ɪm'pæs] or ['ɪmpæs] *s* vicolo cieco, impasse *f*

impassible [ɪm'pæsɪbəl] *adj* impassibile

impassioned [ɪm'pæʃənd] *adj* caloroso, veemente

impassive [ɪm'pæsɪv] *adj* impassibile

impatience [ɪm'peʃəns] *s* impazienza

impatient [ɪm'peʃənt] *adj* impaziente

impeach [ɪm'pitʃ] *tr* accusare; (*a public official*) sottoporre a un'inchiesta; (*a statement*) mettere in dubbio

impeachment [ɪm'pitʃmənt] *s* accusa; inchiesta

impeccable [ɪm'pɛkəbəl] *adj* impeccabile

impecunious [ˌɪmpɪ'kjuni·əs] *adj* indigente

impedance [ɪm'pidəns] *s* impedenza

impede [ɪm'pid] *tr* impedire, intralciare

impediment [ɪm'pɛdɪmənt] *s* impedimento; ostacolo

im·pel [ɪm'pɛl] *v* (*pret & pp* **-peled** or **-pelled**; *ger* **-peling** or **-pelling**) *tr* spingere, forzare

impending [ɪm'pɛndɪŋ] *adj* imminente, incombente

impenetrable [ɪm'pɛnətrəbəl] *adj* impenetrabile

impenitent [ɪm'pɛnɪtənt] *adj* impenitente ‖ *s* persona impenitente

imperative [ɪm'pɛrɪtɪv] *adj* (*commanding*) imperativo; (*urgent*) imperioso ‖ *s* imperativo

imperceptible [ˌɪmpər'sɛptɪbəl] *adj* impercettibile

imperfect [ɪm'pʌrfɪkt] *adj & s* imperfetto

imperfection [ˌɪmpər'fɛkʃən] *s* imperfezione

imperial [ɪm'pɪrɪ·əl] *adj* imperiale ‖ *s* (*goatee*) barbetta, mosca; (*top of coach*) imperiale *m*

imperialist [ɪm'pɪrɪ·əlɪst] *adj & s* imperialista *mf*

imper·il [ɪm'pɛrɪl] *v* (*pret & pp* **-iled** or **-illed**; *ger* **-iling** or **-illing**) *tr* mettere in pericolo

imperious [ɪm'pɪrɪ·əs] *adj* imperioso

imperishable [ɪm'pɛrɪʃəbəl] *adj* imperituro, duraturo

impersonate [ɪm'pʌrsə ˌnet] *tr* (*to pretend to be*) spacciarsi per; (*on the stage*) impersonare

impertinence [ɪm'pʌrtɪnəns] *s* impertinenza

impertinent [ɪm'pʌrtɪnənt] *adj* impertinente

impetuous [ɪm'pɛtʃʊ·əs] *adj* impetuoso

impetus ['ɪmpɪtəs] *s* impeto, foga

impie·ty [ɪm'paɪ·əti] *s* (**-ties**) empietà *f*

impinge [ɪm'pɪndʒ] *intr*—**to impinge on** or **upon** violare; (*said, e.g., of the sun*) ferire; (*the imagination*) colpire

impious ['ɪmpɪ·əs] *adj* empio

impish ['ɪmpɪʃ] *adj* indiavolato

implant [ɪm'plænt] *tr* innestare; instillare, istillare

implement ['ɪmplɪmənt] *s* utensile *m*, strumento ‖ ['ɪmplɪ ˌment] *tr* completare, mettere in opera; (*to provide with implements*) attrezzare

implicate ['ɪmplɪ ˌket] *tr* implicare

implicit [ɪm'plɪsɪt] *adj* implicito; (*unquestioning*) assoluto, cieco

implied [ɪm'plaɪd] *adj* implicito

implore [ɪm'plor] *tr* (*a person; pardon*)

implorare; *(to entreat)* raccomandarsi a

im•ply [ɪm'plàɪ] *v (pret & pp* -**plied**) *tr* voler dire, significare; implicare, sottintendere

impolite [,ɪmpə'laɪt] *adj* scortese

import ['ɪmport] *s* importazione; articolo d'importazione; importanza ‖ [ɪm'port] or ['ɪmport] *tr* importare; significare ‖ *intr* importare

importance [ɪm'portəns] *s* importanza

important [ɪm'portənt] *adj* importante

importation [,ɪmpor'teʃən] *s* importazione

importer [ɪm'portər] *s* importatore *m*

importunate [ɪm'portʃənɪt] *adj* importuno

importune [,ɪmpor'tjun] or [,ɪmpor'tun] *tr* importunare

impose [ɪm'poz] *tr* imporre ‖ *intr*—**to impose on** or **upon** abusare di; abusare della gentilezza di

imposing [ɪm'pozɪŋ] *adj* imponente

imposition [,ɪmpə'zɪʃən] *s* imposizione; abuso; abuso della gentilezza; inganno

impossible [ɪm'pasɪbəl] *adj* impossibile

impostor [ɪm'pastər] *s* impostore *m*

imposture [ɪm'pastʃər] *s* impostura

impotence ['ɪmpətəns] *s* impotenza

impotent ['ɪmpətənt] *adj* impotente

impound [ɪm'paund] *tr* rinchiudere, recintare; *(water)* raccogliere; (law) sequestrare, confiscare

impoverish [ɪm'pavərɪʃ] *tr* impoverire

impracticable [ɪm'præktɪkəbəl] *adj* impraticabile; *(intractable)* intrattabile

impractical [ɪm'præktɪkəl] *adj* poco pratico

impregnable [ɪm'prɛgnəbəl] *adj* inespugnabile, imprendibile

impregnate [ɪm'prɛgnet] *tr* impregnare

impresari•o [,ɪmprɪ'sɑrɪ,o] *s* (-os) impresario

impress [ɪm'prɛs] *tr (to affect in mind or feelings)* impressionare; *(to produce by pressure; to fix on s.o.'s mind)* imprimere; (mil) arruolare

impression [ɪm'prɛʃən] *s* impressione

impressionable [ɪm'prɛʃənəbəl] *adj* impressionabile

impressive [ɪm'prɛsɪv] *adj* impressionante, imponente

imprint ['ɪmprɪnt] *s* impronta; (typ) indicazione dell'editore ‖ [ɪm'prɪnt] *tr* imprimere

imprison [ɪm'prɪzən] *tr* imprigionare

imprisonment [ɪm'prɪzənmənt] *s* prigione, prigionia

improbable [ɪm'prabəbəl] *adj* improbabile

impromptu [ɪm'pramptju] or [ɪm'pramptu] *adj* improvvisato ‖ *s* improvvisazione; (mus) impromptu *m* ‖ *adv* all'improvviso

improper [ɪm'prapər] *adj (erroneous)* improprio; *(inappropriate; unseemly)* scorretto; (math) improprio

improve [ɪm'pruv] *tr* migliorare; *(an opportunity)* approfittare di ‖ *intr* migliorare; **to improve on** or **upon** perfezionare

improvement [ɪm'pruvmənt] *s* miglioramento, perfezionamento; *(in real estate)* miglioria; *(e.g., of time)* buon uso

improvident [ɪm'pravɪdənt] *adj* improvvido, imprevidente

improvise ['ɪmprə,vaɪz] *tr & intr* improvvisare

imprudence [ɪm'prudəns] *s* imprudenza

imprudent [ɪm'prudənt] *adj* imprudente

impudence ['ɪmpjədəns] *s* impudenza, sfrontatezza, sfacciataggine *f*

impudent ['ɪmpjədənt] *adj* sfrontato, sfacciato, spudorato

impugn [ɪm'pjun] *tr* impugnare

impulse ['ɪmpʌls] *s* impulso

impulsive [ɪm'pʌlsɪv] *adj* impulsivo

impunity [ɪm'pjunɪti] *s* impunità *f*

impure [ɪm'pjur] *adj* impuro

impuri•ty [ɪm'pjurɪti] *s* (-ties) impurità *f*

impute [ɪm'pjut] *tr* imputare

in [ɪn] *adj* interno; (coll) moderno, alla moda ‖ *s* relazione; **the ins and outs** tutti i dettagli ‖ *adv* dentro; in casa; in ufficio; **in here** qui dentro; **in there** lì dentro; **to be in** essere a casa; **to be in for** essere destinato a; **to be in with** essere in intimità con ‖ *prep* in; *(within)* dentro a; *(over, through)* per; di, e.g., **the best in the class** il migliore della classe; **dressed in** vestito di; **in so far as** per quanto; **in that** per quanto, dato che

inability [,ɪnə'bɪlɪti] *s* inabilità *f*

inaccessible [,ɪnæk'sɛsɪbəl] *adj* inaccessibile

inaccura•cy [ɪn'ækjərəsi] *s* (-cies) inesattezza, imprecisione

inaccurate [ɪn'ækjərɪt] *adj* inesatto

inaction [ɪn'ækʃən] *s* inazione

inactive [ɪn'æktɪv] *adj* inattivo

inadequate [ɪn'ædɪkwɪt] *adj* inadeguato, inadatto

inadvertent [,ɪnəd'vʌrtənt] *adj* disattento; inavvertito

inadvisable [,ɪnəd'vaɪzəbəl] *adj* poco consigliabile

inane [ɪn'en] *adj* insensato, assurdo

inanimate [ɪn'ænɪmɪt] *adj* inanimato

inappreciable [,ɪnə'priʃɪ•əbəl] *adj* inapprezzabile

inappropriate [,ɪnə'propri•ɪt] *adj* non appropriato, improprio

inarticulate [,ɪnɑr'tɪkjəlɪt] *adj (sounds, words)* inarticolato; *(person)* incapace di esprimersi

inasmuch as [,ɪnəs'mʌtʃ ,æz] *conj* dato che, visto che, in quanto che

inattentive [,ɪnə'tɛntɪv] *adj* disattento

inaugural [ɪn'ɔgjərəl] *adj* inaugurale ‖ *s* discorso inaugurale

inaugurate [ɪn'ɔgjə,ret] *tr* inaugurare

inauguration [ɪn,ɔgjə'reʃən] *s* inaugurazione; *(investiture of a head of government)* assunzione dei poteri

inborn ['ɪn,bɔrn] *adj* innato, ingenito

inbreeding ['ɪn,bridɪŋ] *s* incrocio fra animali o piante affini

incandescent [,ɪnkən'dɛsənt] *adj* incandescente

incapable [ɪn'kepəbəl] *adj* incapace
incapacitate [ˌɪnkə'pæsɪˌtet] *tr* inabilitare; (law) interdire
incapaci·ty [ˌɪnkə'pæsɪti] *s* (**-ties**) incapacità *f*
incarcerate [ɪn'kɑrsəˌret] *tr* incarcerare
incarnate [ɪn'kɑrnɪt] or [ɪn'kɑrnet] *adj* incarnato || [ɪn'kɑrnet] *tr* incarnare
incarnation [ˌɪnkɑr'neʃən] *s* incarnazione
incendiarism [ɪn'sɛndɪ·əˌrɪzəm] *s* incendio doloso; (*agitation*) sobillazione
incendiar·y [ɪn'sɛndɪˌɛri] *adj* incendiario || *s* (**-ies**) incendiario; (fig) sobillatore *m*
incense ['ɪnsɛns] *s* incenso || *tr* (*to burn incense for*) incensare || [ɪn'sɛns] *tr* irritare, esasperare
in'cense burn'er *s* (*person*) incensatore *m*; (*vessel*) incensiere *m*
incentive [ɪn'sɛntɪv] *adj* & *s* incentivo
inception [ɪn'sɛpʃən] *s* principio
incertitude [ɪn'sʌrtɪˌtjud] or [ɪn'sʌrtɪˌtud] *s* incertezza
incest ['ɪnsɛst] *s* incesto
incestuous [ɪn'sɛst/ʊ·əs] *adj* incestuoso
inch [ɪntʃ] *s* pollice *m*; **to be within an inch of** essere a due dita da || *intr*—**to inch ahead** spingersi avanti poco a poco
incidence ['ɪnsɪdəns] *s* incidenza
incident ['ɪnsɪdənt] *adj* incidente, incidentale || *s* incidente *m*
incidental [ˌɪnsɪ'dɛntəl] *adj* incidentale || *s* elemento incidentale; **incidentals** piccole spese
incidentally [ˌɪnsɪ'dɛntəli] *adv* incidentalmente, per inciso; a proposito
incinerator [ɪn'sɪnəˌretər] *s* inceneritore *m*
incision [ɪn'sɪʒən] *s* incisione
incisive [ɪn'saɪsɪv] *adj* incisivo
incite [ɪn'saɪt] *tr* incitare, stimulare
inclemen·cy [ɪn'klɛmənsi] *s* (**-cies**) inclemenza
inclination [ˌɪnklɪ'neʃən] *s* inclinazione
incline ['ɪnklaɪn] or [ɪn'klaɪn] *s* declivio || [ɪn'klaɪn] *tr* inclinare || *intr* inclinarsi
inclose [ɪn'kloz] *tr* includere, accludere; **to inclose herewith** accludere alla presente
inclosure [ɪn'kloʒər] *s* (*land surrounded by fence*) recinto; (*e.g., letter*) allegato
include [ɪn'klud] *tr* includere; **including** incluso, e.g., **three books including the grammar** tre libri inclusa la grammatica
inclusive [ɪn'klusɪv] *adj* incluso, e.g., **until next Friday inclusive** fino a venerdì prossimo incluso; **inclusive of** inclusivo di, e.g., **price inclusive of freight** prezzo inclusivo delle spese di trasporto
incogni·to [ɪn'kɑgnɪˌto] *adj* incognito || *s* (**-tos**) incognito || *adv* in incognito

incoherent [ˌɪnko'hɪrənt] *adj* incoerente
incombustible [ˌɪnkəm'bʌstɪbəl] *adj* incombustibile
income ['ɪnkʌm] *s* reddito, provento
in'come tax' *s* imposta sul reddito
incoming ['ɪnˌkʌmɪŋ] *adj* entrante; futuro; (*tide*) ascendente || *s* entrata
incomparable [ɪn'kɑmpərəbəl] *adj* incomparabile, impareggiabile
incompatible [ˌɪnkəm'pætɪbəl] *adj* incompatibile
incomplete [ˌɪnkəm'plit] *adj* incompleto, tronco, scompleto
incomprehensible [ˌɪnkɑmprɪ'hɛnsɪbəl] *adj* incomprensibile
inconceivable [ˌɪnkən'sivəbəl] *adj* inconcepibile
inconclusive [ˌɪnkən'klusɪv] *adj* inconcludente
incongruous [ɪn'kɑŋgru·əs] *adj* incongruo
inconsequential [ɪnˌkɑnsɪ'kwɛnʃəl] *adj* (*lacking proper sequence of thought or speech*) inconseguente; (*trivial*) di poca importanza
inconsiderate [ˌɪnkən'sɪdərɪt] *adj* inconsiderato, sconsiderato
inconsisten·cy [ˌɪnkən'sɪstənsi] *s* (**-cies**) inconsistenza
inconsistent [ˌɪnkən'sɪstənt] *adj* inconsistente, inconseguente
inconsolable [ˌɪnkən'soləbəl] *adj* inconsolabile, sconsolato
inconspicuous [ˌɪnkən'spɪkju·əs] *adj* poco appariscente, poco apparente
inconstant [ɪn'kɑnstənt] *adj* incostante
incontinence [ɪn'kɑntɪnəns] *s* incontinenza
incontrovertible [ɪnˌkɑntrə'vʌrtɪbəl] *adj* incontrovertibile
inconvenience [ˌɪnkən'vini·əns] *s* scomodo, incomodo || *tr* scomodare
inconvenient [ˌɪnkən'vini·ənt] *adj* incomodo, inconveniente
incorporate [ɪn'kɔrpəˌret] *tr* incorporare; costituire in società anonima || *intr* incorporarsi; costituirsi in società anonima
incorrect [ˌɪnkə'rɛkt] *adj* scorretto
increase ['ɪnkris] *s* aumento; crescita; **to be on the increase** essere in aumento || [ɪn'kris] *tr* aumentare; (*by propagation*) moltiplicare || *intr* aumentare; moltiplicarsi
increasingly [ɪn'krisɪŋli] *adv* sempre più
incredible [ɪn'krɛdɪbəl] *adj* incredibile
incredulous [ɪn'krɛdʒələs] *adj* incredulo
increment ['ɪnkrɪmənt] *s* aumento, incremento
incriminate [ɪn'krɪmɪˌnet] *tr* incriminare
incrust [ɪn'krʌst] *tr* incrostare
incubate ['ɪnkjəˌbet] *tr* incubare || *intr* essere in incubazione; (*said, e.g., of a hen*) covare; (fig) covare
incubator ['ɪnkjəˌbetər] *s* incubatrice *f*
inculcate [ɪn'kʌlket] or ['ɪnkʌlˌket] *tr* inculcare

incumben·cy [ɪn'kʌmbənsi] *s* (-cies) incombenza

incumbent [ɪn'kʌmbənt] *adj*—**to be incumbent on** incombere a, spettare a ‖ *s* titolare *mf*

incunabula [ˌɪnkju'næbjələ] *spl* (*beginnings*) origini *fpl*; (*early printed books*) incunaboli *mpl*

in·cur [ɪn'kʌr] *v* (*pret & pp* **-curred**; *ger* **-curring**) *tr* incorrere in; (*a debt*) assumere, contrarre

incurable [ɪn'kjurəbəl] *adj & s* incurabile *mf*

incursion [ɪn'kʌrʒən] *or* [ɪn'kʌrʃən] *s* incursione, scorreria

indebted [ɪn'detɪd] *adj* indebitato; obbligato

indecen·cy [ɪn'disənsi] *s* (-cies) indecenza, sconcezza

indecent [ɪn'disənt] *adj* indecente, sconveniente

indecisive [ˌɪndɪ'saɪsɪv] *adj* indeciso; (*e.g., event*) non decisivo

indeed [ɪn'did] *adv* difatti, infatti ‖ *interj* davvero!

indefatigable [ˌɪndɪ'fætɪgəbəl] *adj* indefesso, infaticabile

indefensible [ˌɪndɪ'fensɪbəl] *adj* indifendibile, insostenibile

indefinable [ˌɪndɪ'faɪnəbəl] *adj* indefinibile

indefinite [ɪn'defɪnɪt] *adj* indefinito

indelible [ɪn'delɪbəl] *adj* indelebile

indemnification [ɪnˌdemnɪfɪ'keʃən] *s* indennità *f*, indennizzo

indemni·fy [ɪn'demnɪˌfaɪ] *v* (*pret & pp* **-fied**) *tr* indennizzare

indemni·ty [ɪn'demnɪti] *s* (-ties) indennità *f*, indennizzo

indent [ɪn'dent] *tr* frastagliare, dentellare; (*typ*) far rientrare

indentation [ˌɪnden'teʃən] *s* frastaglio, dentellatura; (*typ*) accapo

indenture [ɪn'dentʃər] *s* scrittura pubblica; contratto di apprendista ‖ *tr* obbligare per contratto

independence [ˌɪndɪ'pendəns] *s* indipendenza

independent [ˌɪndɪ'pendənt] *adj & s* indipendente *mf*

indescribable [ˌɪndɪ'skraɪbəbəl] *adj* indescrivibile

indestructible [ˌɪndɪ'strʌktɪbəl] *adj* indistruttibile

indeterminate [ˌɪndɪ'tʌrmɪnɪt] *adj* indeterminato

index ['ɪndeks] *s* (**indexes** or **indices** ['ɪndɪˌsiz]) indice *m*; (*typ*) indice *m* indicatore ‖ *tr* mettere un indice a; mettere all'indice ‖ **Index** *s* Indice *m*

in'dex card' *s* scheda di catalogo

in'dex fin'ger *s* dito indice

India ['ɪndɪə] *s* l'India *f*

Indian ['ɪndɪən] *adj & s* indiano

In'dia ink' *s* inchiostro di china

In'dian club' *s* clava di ginnastica

In'dian corn' *s* granoturco

In'dian file' *s* fila indiana ‖ *adv* in fila indiana

In'dian O'cean *s* Oceano Indiano

In'dian sum'mer *s* estate *f* di San Martino

In'dian wres'tling *s* braccio di ferro

In'dia pa'per *s* carta bibbia, carta d'India

In'dia rub'ber *s* caucciù *m*

indicate ['ɪndɪˌket] *tr* indicare

indication [ˌɪndɪ'keʃən] *s* indicazione

indicative [ɪn'dɪkətɪv] *adj & s* indicativo

indicator ['ɪndɪˌketər] *s* indicatore *m*, indice *m*

indict [ɪn'daɪt] *tr* accusare

indictment [ɪn'daɪtmənt] *s* accusa, atto d'accusa

indifferent [ɪn'dɪfərənt] *adj* indifferente; (*not particularly good*) passabile

indigenous [ɪn'dɪdʒɪnəs] *adj* indigeno

indigent ['ɪndɪdʒənt] *adj* indigente ‖ **the indigent** gli indigenti

indigestion [ˌɪndɪ'dʒestʃən] *s* indigestione

indignant [ɪn'dɪgnənt] *adj* indignato

indignation [ˌɪndɪg'neʃən] *s* indignazione

indigni·ty [ɪn'dɪgnɪti] *s* (-ties) indignità *f*

indi·go ['ɪndɪˌgo] *adj* indaco ‖ *s* (-gos or -goes) indaco

indirect [ˌɪndɪ'rekt] *or* [ˌɪndaɪ'rekt] *adj* indiretto

in'direct' dis'course *s* discorso indiretto

indiscernible [ˌɪndɪ'zʌrnɪbəl] *or* [ˌɪndɪ'sʌrnɪbəl] *adj* indiscernibile

indiscreet [ˌɪndɪs'krit] *adj* indiscreto

indispensable [ˌɪndɪs'pensəbəl] *adj* indispensabile, imprescindibile

indispose [ˌɪndɪs'poz] *tr* indisporre

indisposed [ˌɪndɪs'pozd] *adj* (*disinclined*) mal disposto; (*slightly ill*) indisposto

indissoluble [ˌɪndɪ'saljəbəl] *adj* indissolubile

indistinct [ˌɪndɪs'tɪŋkt] *adj* indistinto

indite [ɪn'daɪt] *tr* redigere

individual [ˌɪndɪ'vɪdʒu·əl] *adj* individuale ‖ *s* individuo

individuali·ty [ˌɪndɪˌvɪdʒu'ælɪti] *s* (-ties) individualità *f*; (*person of distinctive character*) individuo

Indochina ['ɪndo't∫aɪnə] *s* l'Indocina *f*

Indo-Chi·nese ['ɪndot∫aɪ'niz] *adj* indocinese ‖ *s* (-nese) indocinese *mf*

Indo-European ['ɪndoˌjurə'pi·ən] *adj & s* indoeuropeo

indolent ['ɪndələnt] *adj* indolente

Indonesia [ˌɪndo'niʒə] *or* [ˌɪndo'niʒə] *s* l'Indonesia *f*

Indonesian [ˌɪndo'niʒən] *or* [ˌɪndo'niʒən] *adj & s* indonesiano

indoor ['ɪnˌdor] *adj* situato in casa; da farsi in casa

indoors ['ɪn'dorz] *adv* dentro, a casa, al coperto

indorse [ɪn'dors] *tr* (com) girare; (fig) appoggiare, approvare

indorsee [ˌɪndor'si] *s* giratario

indorsement [ɪn'dorsmənt] *s* (com) girata; (fig) appoggio, approvazione

indorser [ɪn'dorsər] *s* girante *mf*

induce [ɪn'djus] *or* [ɪn'dus] *tr* indurre

inducement [ɪn'djusmənt] *or* [ɪn'dusmənt] *s* stimolo, incentivo

induct [ɪn'dʌkt] *tr* installare; iniziare; (mil) arruolare

induction [ɪn'dʌkʃən] *s* iniziazione; (elec & log) induzione; (mil) arruolamento

indulge [ɪn'dʌldʒ] *tr* indulgere (with *dat*) || *intr* cedere, lasciarsi andare; **to indulge in** abbandonarsi a; permettersi il lusso di

indulgence [ɪn'dʌldʒəns] *s* compiacenza; intemperanza, abbandono; (*leniency*) indulgenza

indulgent [ɪn'dʌldʒənt] *adj* indulgente

industrial [ɪn'dʌstrɪ·əl] *adj* industriale

industrialist [ɪn'dʌstrɪ·əlɪst] *s* industriale *m*

industrialize [ɪn'dʌstrɪ·ə‚laɪz] *tr* industrializzare

industrious [ɪn'dʌstrɪ·əs] *adj* industrioso, laborioso

indus·try ['ɪndʌstrɪ] *s* (**-tries**) industria

inebriation [ɪn‚ɪbrɪ'eʃən] *s* ubriachezza

inedible [ɪn'ɛdɪbəl] *adj* immangiabile

ineffable [ɪn'ɛfəbəl] *adj* ineffabile

ineffective [‚ɪnɪ'fɛktɪv] *adj* inefficace; (*person*) incapace

ineffectual [‚ɪnɪ'fɛkt/ʊ·əl] *adj* inefficace

inefficient [‚ɪnɪ'fɪʃənt] *adj* inefficiente

ineligible [ɪn'ɛlɪdʒɪbəl] *adj* ineleggibile

inequali·ty [‚ɪnɪ'kwɑlɪtɪ] *s* (**-ties**) disuguaglianza

inequi·ty [ɪn'ɛkwɪtɪ] *s* (**-ties**) ingiustizia

ineradicable [‚ɪnɪ'rædɪkəbəl] *adj* inestirpabile

inertia [ɪn'ʌrʃ/ɛ] *s* inerzia

inescapable [‚ɪnɛs'kepəbəl] *adj* ineluttabile, inderogabile

inevitable [ɪn'ɛvɪtəbəl] *adj* inevitabile

inexact [‚ɪnɛg'zækt] *adj* inesatto

inexcusable [‚ɪnɛks'kjuzəbəl] *adj* inescusabile

inexhaustible [‚ɪnɛg'zɔstɪbəl] *adj* inesauribile

inexorable [ɪn'ɛksərəbəl] *adj* inesorabile

inexpedient [‚ɪnɛk'spidɪ·ənt] *adj* inopportuno

inexpensive [‚ɪnɛk'spɛnsɪv] *adj* poco costoso, a buon mercato

inexperience [‚ɪnɛk'spɪrɪ·əns] *s* inesperienza

inexplicable [ɪn'ɛksplɪkəbəl] *adj* inesplicabile

inexpressible [‚ɪnɛk'sprɛsɪbəl] *adj* indicibile, inesprimibile

infallible [ɪn'fælɪbəl] *adj* infallibile

infamous ['ɪnfəməs] *adj* infame

infa·my ['ɪnfəmɪ] *s* (**-mies**) infamia

infan·cy ['ɪnfənsɪ] *s* (**-cies**) infanzia

infant ['ɪnfənt] *adj* infantile; (*in the earliest stage*) (fig) nascente || *s* neonato, bebè *m*

infantile ['ɪnfən‚taɪl] *or* [ˈɪnfəntɪl] *adj* infantile

infan·try ['ɪnfəntrɪ] *s* (**-tries**) fanteria

in'fantry·man *s* (**-men**) fante *m*

infatuated [ɪn'fæt/ʊ‚etɪd] *adj* infatuato

infect [ɪn'fɛkt] *tr* infettare

infection [ɪn'fɛkʃən] *s* infezione

infectious [ɪn'fɛkʃəs] *adj* infettivo

in·fer [ɪn'fʌr] *v* (*pret & pp* **-ferred**; *ger* **-ferring**) *tr* inferire; (coll) dedurre, supporre

inferior [ɪn'fɪrɪ·ər] *adj & s* inferiore *m*

inferiority [ɪn‚fɪrɪ'ɑrɪtɪ] *s* inferiorità *f*

inferior'ity com'plex *s* complesso di inferiorità

infernal [ɪn'fʌrnəl] *adj* infernale

infest [ɪn'fɛst] *tr* infestare

infidel ['ɪnfɪdəl] *adj & s* infedele *mf*

infideli·ty [‚ɪnfɪ'dɛlɪtɪ] *s* (**-ties**) infedeltà *f*

in'field *s* campo interno, diamante *m*

infiltrate [ɪn'fɪltret] *or* [‚ɪnfɪl'tret] *tr* infiltrarsi in || *intr* infiltrarsi

infinite ['ɪnfɪnɪt] *adj & s* infinito

infinitive [ɪn'fɪnɪtɪv] *adj* infinitivo || *s* infinito

infini·ty [ɪn'fɪnɪtɪ] *s* (**-ties**) infinità *f*; (math) infinito

infirm [ɪn'fʌrm] *adj* infermo; (*not firm*) debole

infirma·ry [ɪn'fʌrmərɪ] *s* (**-ries**) infermeria

infirmi·ty [ɪn'fʌrmɪtɪ] *s* (**-ties**) infermità *f*

inflame [ɪn'flem] *tr* infiammare || *intr* infiammarsi

inflammable [ɪn'flæməbəl] *adj* infiammabile

inflammation [‚ɪnflə'meʃən] *s* infiammazione

inflate [ɪn'flet] *tr* gonfiare; (*currency, prices*) inflazionare || *intr* gonfiarsi

inflation [ɪn'fleʃən] *s* inflazione; (*of a tire*) gonfiatura

inflect [ɪn'flɛkt] *tr* curvare; (*voice*) modulare; (gram) flettere

inflection [ɪn'flɛkʃən] *s* inflessione; (gram) flessione

inflexible [ɪn'flɛksɪbəl] *adj* inflessibile

inflict [ɪn'flɪkt] *tr* infliggere, inferire

influence ['ɪnflu·əns] *s* influenza || *tr* influire su, influenzare

influential [‚ɪnflu'ɛnʃəl] *adj* influente

influenza [‚ɪnflu'ɛnzə] *s* influenza

inform [ɪn'fɔrm] *tr* informare || *intr* dare informazioni; **to inform on** denunziare, fare la spia contro

informal [ɪn'fɔrməl] *adj* non ufficiale, ufficioso; (*unceremonious*) alla buona, familiare

informant [ɪn'fɔrmənt] *s* informatore *m*; (*informer*) delatore *m*; (ling) fonte *f* orale, informatore *m*

information [‚ɪnfər'meʃən] *s* informazioni *fpl*; conoscenze *fpl*

informational [‚ɪnfər'meʃənəl] *adj* informativo

informed' sour'ces *spl* fonti *fpl* attendibili

informer [ɪn'fɔrmər] *s* (*informant*) informatore *m*; (*spy*) delatore *m*

infraction [ɪn'frækʃən] *s* infrazione

infrared [‚ɪnfrə'rɛd] *adj & s* infrarosso

infrequent [ɪn'frikwənt] *adj* infrequente

infringe [ɪn'frɪndʒ] *tr* violare || *intr*— **to infringe on** *or* **upon** violare, contravvenire a

infringement [ɪn'frɪndʒmənt] *s* infrazione

infuriate [ɪn'fjʊrɪ ,et] *tr* infuriare
infuse [ɪn'fjuz] *tr* infondere
infusion [ɪn'fjuʒən] *s* infusione
ingenious [ɪn'dʒinjəs] *adj* ingegnoso
ingenui·ty [,ɪndʒɪ'nu·ɪti] or [,ɪndʒɪ-'nju·ɪti] *s* (**-ties**) ingegnosità *f*
ingenuous [ɪn'dʒenjʊ·əs] *adj* ingenuo
ingenuousness [ɪn'dʒenjʊ·əsnɪs] *s* ingenuità *f*
ingest [ɪn'dʒɛst] *tr* ingerire
ingoing ['ɪn ,goɪŋ] *adj* entrante
ingot ['ɪŋgət] *s* lingotto, massello
ingraft [ɪn'græft] or [ɪn'grɑft] *tr* (hort & surg) innestare; (fig) inculcare
ingrate ['ɪŋgret] *s* ingrato
ingratiate [ɪn'greʃɪ ,et] *tr*—**to ingratiate oneself with** ingraziarsi
ingratiating [ɪn'greʃɪ ,etɪŋ] *adj* attraente, affascinante, insinuante
ingratitude [ɪn'grætɪ ,tjud] or [ɪn-'grætɪ ,tud] *s* ingratitudine *f*
ingredient [ɪn'gridɪ·ənt] *s* ingrediente *m*
in'grown nail' ['ɪngron] *s* unghia incarnita
ingulf [ɪn'gʌlf] *tr* sommergere, inondare
inhabit [ɪn'hæbɪt] *tr* abitare, popolare
inhabitant [ɪn'hæbɪtənt] *s* abitante *mf*
inhale [ɪn'hel] *tr* & *intr* inspirare
inherent [ɪn'hɪrənt] *adj* inerente
inherit [ɪn'hɛrɪt] *tr* & *intr* ereditare
inheritance [ɪn'hɛrɪtəns] *s* eredità *f*
inheritor [ɪn'hɛrɪtər] *s* erede *mf*
inhibit [ɪn'hɪbɪt] *tr* inibire
inhospitable [ɪn'hɑspɪtəbəl] or [,ɪn-hɑs'pɪtəbəl] *adj* inospitale
inhuman [ɪn'hjumən] *adj* inumano
inhumane [,ɪnhju'men] *adj* inumano
inimical [ɪ'nɪmɪkəl] *adj* nemico
iniqui·ty [ɪ'nɪkwɪti] *s* (**-ties**) iniquità *f*
ini·tial [ɪ'nɪʃəl] *adj* & *s* iniziale *f* ‖ *v* (*pret* **-tialed** or **-tialled;** *ger* **-tialing** or **-tialling**) *tr* siglare
initiate [ɪ'nɪʃɪ ,et] *tr* iniziare
initiation [ɪ ,nɪʃɪ'eʃən] *s* iniziazione
initiative [ɪ'nɪʃɪ·ətɪv] or [ɪ'nɪʃətɪv] *s* iniziativa
inject [ɪn'dʒɛkt] *tr* iniettare; introdurre
injection [ɪn'dʒɛkʃən] *s* iniezione
injudicious [,ɪndʒu'dɪʃəs] *adj* avventato, sconsiderato
injunction [ɪn'dʒʌŋkʃən] *s* ingiunzione
injure ['ɪndʒər] *tr* (*to harm*) danneggiare; (*to wound*) ferire; (*to offend*) offendere, ingiuriare
injurious [ɪn'dʒʊrɪ·əs] *adj* dannoso; offensivo, ingiurioso
inju·ry ['ɪndʒəri] *s* (**-ries**) (*harm*) danno; (*wound*) ferita, lesione; offesa, ingiuria
injustice [ɪn'dʒʌstɪs] *s* ingiustizia
ink [ɪŋk] *s* inchiostro ‖ *tr* inchiostrare
inkling ['ɪŋklɪŋ] *s* sentore *m*, indizio
ink'stand' *s* (*container*) calamaio; (*stand*) calamaiera
ink'well' *s* calamaio
ink·y ['ɪŋki] *adj* (**-ier; -iest**) nero come l'inchiostro; nero d'inchiostro
inlaid ['ɪn ,led] or [,ɪn'led] *adj* intarsiato, incrostato

inland ['ɪnlənd] *adj* & *s* interno ‖ *adv* verso l'interno
in'-law' *s* affine *mf*
in·lay ['ɪn ,le] *s* intarsio, tassello ‖ [ɪn'le] or ['ɪn ,le] *v* (*pret* & *pp* **-laid**) *tr* intarsiare
in'let *s* (*of the shore*) insenatura; (*entrance*) ammissione
in'mate' *s* (*patient, e.g., in an insane asylum*) internato; (*in a jail*) prigioniero
inn [ɪn] *s* taverna, osteria
innate [ɪ'net] or ['ɪnet] *adj* innato
inner ['ɪnər] *adj* interno, interiore; intimo, profondo
in'ner·spring' mat'tress *s* materasso a molle
in'ner tube' *s* camera d'aria
inning ['ɪnɪŋ] *s* (baseball) turno
inn'keep'er *s* locandiere *m*, oste *m*
innocence ['ɪnəsəns] *s* innocenza
innocent ['ɪnəsənt] *adj* & *s* innocente *mf*
innovate ['ɪnə ,vet] *tr* innovare
innovation [,ɪnə've/ən] *s* innovazione
innuen·do [,ɪnju'endo] *s* (**-does**) sottinteso, insinuazione
innumerable [ɪ'njumərəbəl] or [ɪ'numərəbəl] *adj* innumerevole
inoculate [ɪn'akjə ,let] *tr* inoculare; (*e.g., with hatred*) inoculare; permeare
inoculation [ɪn ,akjə'le/ən] *s* inoculazione
inoffensive [,ɪnə'fensɪv] *adj* inoffensivo
inopportune [ɪn ,apər'tjun] or [ɪn-,apər'tun] *adj* inopportuno
inordinate [ɪn'ɔrdɪnɪt] *adj* smoderato
inorganic [,ɪnɔr'gænɪk] *adj* inorganico
in'pa'tient *s* degente *mf*
in'put' *s* entrata; (elec, mach) energia immessa
inquest ['ɪnkwɛst] *s* inchiesta
inquire [ɪn'kwaɪr] *tr* domandare, chiedere ‖ *intr*—**to inquire about, after, or for** chiedere di; **to inquire into** investigare
inquir·y [ɪn'kwaɪri] or ['ɪnkwɪri] *s* (**-ies**) indagine *f*, inchiesta
inquisition [,ɪnkwɪ'zɪ/ən] *s* inquisizione
inquisitive [ɪn'kwɪzɪtɪv] *adj* indagatore, curioso
in'road' *s* incursione, invasione
insane [ɪn'sen] *adj* pazzo, matto
insane' asy'lum *s* manicomio
insani·ty [ɪn'sænɪti] *s* (**-ties**) pazzia, follia, demenza
insatiable [ɪn'se/əbəl] *adj* insaziabile
inscribe [ɪn'skraɪb] *tr* iscrivere; (*a book*) dedicare; (geom) inscrivere
inscription [ɪn'skrɪp/ən] *s* scritta, iscrizione; (*of a book*) dedica
inscrutable [ɪn'skrutəbəl] *adj* imperscrutabile
insect ['ɪnsɛkt] *s* insetto
insecticide [ɪn'sɛktɪ ,saɪd] *adj* & *s* insetticida *m*
insecure [,ɪnsɪ'kjur] *adj* malsicuro
inseparable [ɪn'sɛpərəbəl] *adj* inseparabile

insert ['ɪnsʌrt] s inserzione; (*circular*) inserto ‖ [ɪn'sʌrt] *tr* inserire

insertion [ɪn'sʌrʃən] s inserzione; (*in lunar orbit*) immissione; (*of lace*) tramezzo

in·set ['ɪn ˌset] s intercalazione ‖ [ɪn-'set] or ['ɪn ˌset] *v* (*pret* & *pp* **-set**; *ger* **-setting**) *tr* intercalare

in'shore' *adj* & *adv* vicino alla spiaggia

in'side' *adj* interno; privato, confidenziale ‖ s interno; **insides** (coll) interiora *fpl*; **to be on the inside** avere informazioni confidenziali ‖ *adv* dentro; all'interno; **inside of** dentro, dentro a, dentro di; **to turn inside out** rovesciare, voltare il diritto al rovescio ‖ *prep* dentro, dentro a

in'side flap' s (bb) risvolto

insider [ˌɪn'saɪdər] s persona informata

in'side track' s (racing) steccato; **to have the inside track** (coll) trovarsi in una situazione vantaggiosa

insidious [ɪn'sɪdɪ·əs] *adj* insidioso

in'sight' s intuito, penetrazione

insigni·a [ɪn'sɪgnɪ·ə] s (**-a** or **-as**) distintivo; (*distinguishing sign*) segno

insignificant [ˌɪnsɪg'nɪfɪkənt] *adj* insignificante

insincere [ˌɪnsɪn'sɪr] *adj* insincero

insinuate [ɪn'sɪnju ˌet] *tr* insinuare

insist [ɪn'sɪst] *intr* insistere

insofar as [ˌɪnso'fɑr ˌæz] *conj* per quanto

insolence ['ɪnsələns] s insolenza

insolent ['ɪnsələnt] *adj* insolente

insoluble [ɪn'sɑljəbəl] *adj* insolubile

insolven·cy [ɪn'sɑlvənsɪ] s (**-cies**) insolvenza

insomnia [ɪn'sɑmnɪ·ə] s insonnia

insomuch [ˌɪnso'mʌtʃ] *adv* fino al punto; **insomuch as** giacché, visto che; **insomuch that** fino al punto che

inspect [ɪn'spekt] *tr* ispezionare

inspection [ɪn'spekʃən] s ispezione

inspector [ɪn'spektər] s ispettore m

inspiration [ˌɪnspɪ'reʃən] s ispirazione

inspire [ɪn'spaɪr] *tr* & *intr* ispirare

install [ɪn'stɔl] *tr* istallare

installment [ɪn'stɔlmənt] s rata; (*of a book*) dispensa; **in installments** a rate

install'ment plan' s pagamento rateale; **on the installment plan** con facilitazioni di pagamento

instance ['ɪnstəns] s esempio; (law) istanza; **for instance** per esempio

instant ['ɪnstənt] *adj* istantaneo ‖ s istante m; mese m corrente

instantaneous [ˌɪnstən'tenɪ·əs] *adj* istantaneo

instantly ['ɪnstəntlɪ] *adv* immediatamente, istantaneamente

instead [ɪn'sted] *adv* invece; **instead of** invece di

in'step' s collo del piede

instigate ['ɪnstɪ ˌget] *tr* istigare

instigation [ˌɪnstɪ'geʃən] s istigazione

in·still' *tr* instillare, istillare

instinct ['ɪnstɪŋkt] s istinto

instinctive [ɪn'stɪŋktɪv] *adj* istintivo

institute ['ɪnstɪ ˌtjut] or ['ɪnstɪ ˌtut] s istituto ‖ *tr* istituire

institution [ˌɪnstɪ'tjuʃən] or [ˌɪnstɪ-'tuʃən] s istituzione

institutionalize [ˌɪnstɪ'tjuʃənə ˌlaɪz] or [ˌɪnstɪ'tuʃənə ˌlaɪz] *tr* istituzionalizzare

instruct [ɪn'strʌkt] *tr* istruire

instruction [ɪn'strʌkʃən] s istruzione

instructive [ɪn'strʌktɪv] *adj* istruttivo

instructor [ɪn'strʌktər] s istruttore m

instrument ['ɪnstrəmənt] s strumento; (law) istrumento ‖ ['ɪnstrə ˌment] *tr* strumentare

instrumental [ˌɪnstrə'mentəl] *adj* strumentale; **to be instrumental in** contribuire a

instrumentalist [ˌɪnstrə'mentəlɪst] s strumentista *mf*

instrumentali·ty [ˌɪnstrəmən'tælɪtɪ] s (**-ties**) mediazione, aiuto

in'strument fly'ing s volo strumentale

in'strument pan'el s (aut) cruscotto

insubordinate [ˌɪnsə'bɔrdɪnɪt] *adj* insubordinato

insufferable [ɪn'sʌfərəbəl] *adj* insoffribile

insufficient [ˌɪnsə'fɪʃənt] *adj* insufficiente

insular ['ɪnsələr] or ['ɪnsjulər] *adj* insulare; (*e.g., attitude*) gretto

insulate ['ɪnsə ˌlet] *tr* isolare

in'sulating tape' ['ɪnsəletɪŋ] s nastro isolante

insulation [ˌɪnsə'leʃən] s isolamento

insulator ['ɪnsə ˌletər] s isolatore m

insulin ['ɪnsəlɪn] s insulina

insult ['ɪnsʌlt] s insulto ‖ [ɪn'sʌlt] *tr* insultare, insolentire

insulting [ɪn'sʌltɪŋ] *adj* insultante

insurance [ɪn'ʃurəns] s assicurazione

insure [ɪn'ʃur] *tr* assicurare

insurer [ɪn'ʃurər] s assicuratore m

insurgent [ɪn'sʌrdʒənt] *adj* & s insorgente *mf*

insurmountable [ˌɪnsər'mauntəbəl] *adj* insormontabile

insurrection [ˌɪnsə'rekʃən] s insurrezione

insusceptible [ˌɪnsə'septɪbəl] *adj* non suscettibile

intact [ɪn'tækt] *adj* intatto, integro

in'take' s (*place of taking in*) entrata; (*act of taking in*) ammissione; (mach) presa, immissione, aspirazione

in'take man'ifold' s collettore m d'ammissione

intangible [ɪn'tændʒɪbəl] *adj* intangibile; (fig) vago, inafferrabile

integer ['ɪntɪdʒər] s numero intero

integral ['ɪntɪgrəl] *adj* integrale; (*part of a whole*) integrante ‖ s (math) integrale m

integration [ˌɪntɪ'greʃən] s integrazione

integrity [ɪn'tegrɪtɪ] s integrità f

intellect ['ɪntə ˌlekt] s intelletto

intellectual [ˌɪntə'lektʃu·əl] *adj* & s intellettuale *mf*

intelligence [ɪn'telɪdʒəns] s intelligenza; informazione, conoscenza

intel'ligence bu'reau *s* ufficio spionaggi

intel'ligence quo'tient *s* quoziente *m* d'intelligenza

intelligent [ɪn'tɛlɪdʒənt] *adj* intelligente

intelligentsia [ɪn‚tɛlɪ'dʒɛntsɪ‑ə] or [ɪn‚tɛlɪ'gɛntsɪ‑ə] *s* intellighenzia, intellettualità *f*

intelligible [ɪn'tɛlɪdʒɪbəl] *adj* intelligibile, comprensibile

intemperance [ɪn'tɛmpərəns] *s* intemperanza, sregolatezza

intemperate [ɪn'tɛmpərɪt] *adj* intemperante; (*climate*) rigoroso

intend [ɪn'tɛnd] *tr* intendere, prefiggersi; (*to mean for a particular purpose*) destinare; (*to signify*) voler dire

intendance [ɪn'tɛndəns] *s* intendenza

intendant [ɪn'tɛndənt] *s* intendente *m*

intended [ɪn'tɛndɪd] *adj* & *s* (coll) promesso, promessa

intense [ɪn'tɛns] *adj* intenso

intensi·fy [ɪn'tɛnsɪ‚faɪ] *v* (*pret* & *pp* **‑fied**) *tr* intensificare, rinforzare; (phot) rinforzare ‖ *intr* intensificarsi, rinforzarsi

intensi·ty [ɪn'tɛnsɪti] *s* (**‑ties**) intensità *f*

intensive [ɪn'tɛnsɪv] *adj* intensivo

intent [ɪn'tɛnt] *adj* intento, attento; **intent on** deciso a ‖ *s* (*purpose*) intento, scopo; (*meaning*) significato; **to all intents and purposes** virtualmente, in realtà

intention [ɪn'tɛnʃən] *s* intenzione

intentional [ɪn'tɛnʃənəl] *adj* intenzionale, deliberato

intentionally [ɪn'tɛnʃənəli] *adv* apposta, deliberatamente

in·ter [ɪn'tʌr] *v* (*pret* & *pp* **‑terred;** *ger* **‑terring**) *tr* interrare, inumare

interact [‚ɪntər'ækt] *intr* esercitare un'azione reciproca

interaction [‚ɪntər'ækʃən] *s* azione reciproca

inter·breed [‚ɪntər'brid] *s* (*pret* & *pp* **‑bred** ['brɛd]) *tr* incrociare ‖ *intr* incrociarsi

intercalate [ɪn'tʌrkə‚let] *tr* intercalare

intercede [‚ɪntər'sid] *intr* intercedere

intercept [‚ɪntər'sɛpt] *tr* intercettare

interceptor [‚ɪntər'sɛptər] *s* (*person*) intercettatore *m;* (aer) intercettore *m*

interchange [‚ɪntər'tʃendʒ] *s* interscambio; (*on a highway*) svincolo autostradale ‖ [‚ɪntər't∫endʒ] *tr* scambiare ‖ *intr* scambiarsi

intercollegiate [‚ɪntərkə'lidʒɪ‑ɪt] *adj* interscolastico, fra università

intercom ['ɪntər‚kɑm] *s* citofono

intercourse ['ɪntər‚kɔrs] *s* comunicazione; (*of products, ideas, etc.*) scambio; (*copulation*) copula, coito; **to have intercourse** accoppiarsi sessualmente

intercross [‚ɪntər'krɔs] or [‚ɪntər'krɑs] *tr* incrociare ‖ *intr* incrociarsi

interdict ['ɪntər‚dɪkt] *s* interdetto ‖ [‚ɪntər'dɪkt] *tr* interdire; **to interdict s.o. from** + *ger* interdire a qlcu di + *inf*

interest ['ɪntərɪst] or ['ɪntrɪst] *s* interesse *m;* **the interests** i potenti ‖ ['ɪntərɪst], ['ɪntrɪst] or ['ɪntə‚rɛst] *tr* interessare

interested ['ɪntrɪstɪd] or ['ɪntə‚rɛstɪd] *adj* interessato

interesting ['ɪntrɪstɪŋ] or ['ɪntə‚rɛstɪŋ] *adj* interessante

interfere [‚ɪntər'fɪr] *intr* interferire; (sports) ostacolare l'azione; **to interfere with** interferire in

interference [‚ɪntər'fɪrəns] *s* interferenza

interim ['ɪntərɪm] *adj* interino ‖ *s* interim *m;* **in the interim** frattanto

interior [ɪn'tɪrɪ‑ər] *adj* & *s* interno

interject [‚ɪntər'dʒɛkt] *tr* interporre ‖ *intr* interporsi

interjection [‚ɪntər'dʒɛkʃən] *s* interposizione; esclamazione; (gram) interiezione

interlard [‚ɪntər'lɑrd] *tr* infiorare, lardellare

interline [‚ɪntər'laɪn] *tr* scrivere nell'interlinea di; (*a garment*) foderare con ovattina

interlining ['ɪntər‚laɪnɪŋ] *s* soppanno

interlink [‚ɪntər'lɪŋk] *tr* concatenare

interlock [‚ɪntər'lɑk] *tr* connettere ‖ *intr* connettersi

interlope [‚ɪntər'lop] *intr* intromettersi; trafficare senza permesso

interloper [‚ɪntər'lopər] *s* intruso

interlude ['ɪntər‚lud] *s* interludio; (theat) intermezzo

intermarriage [‚ɪntər'mærɪdʒ] *s* matrimonio tra consanguinei; matrimonio fra membri di razze diverse

intermediar·y [‚ɪntər'midɪ‚ɛri] *adj* intermediario ‖ (**‑ies**) *s* intermediario

intermediate [‚ɪntər'midɪ‑ɪt] *adj* intermedio

interment [ɪn'tʌrmənt] *s* inumazione

intermingle [‚ɪntər'mɪŋgəl] *tr* mescolare ‖ *intr* mescolarsi

intermission [‚ɪntər'mɪʃən] *s* interruzione; (theat) intervallo

intermittent [‚ɪntər'mɪtənt] *adj* intermittente

intermix [‚ɪntər'mɪks] *tr* mescolare ‖ *intr* mescolarsi

intern ['ɪntʌrn] *s* interno ‖ [ɪn'tʌrn] *tr* internare

internal [ɪn'tʌrnəl] *adj* interno

inter'nal‑combus'tion en'gine *s* motore *m* a combustione interna, motore *m* a scoppio

inter'nal rev'enue *s* fisco

international [‚ɪntər'næʃənəl] *adj* internazionale

in'terna'tional date' line' *s* linea del cambiamento di data

internationalize [‚ɪntər'næʃənə‚laɪz] *tr* internazionalizzare

internecine [‚ɪntər'nisɪn] *adj* micidiale, sanguinario

internee [‚ɪntər'ni] *s* internato

internist [ɪn'tʌrnɪst] *s* internista *mf*

internment [ɪn'tʌrnmənt] *s* internamento

internship ['ɪntʌrn‚ʃɪp] *s* tirocinio in un ospedale, internato

interpellate [ˌɪntər'pelet] or [ɪn'tʌrpɪˌlet] *tr* interpellare

interplanetary [ˌɪntər'plænəˌteri] *adj* interplanetario

interplay ['ɪntərˌple] *s* azione reciproca

interpolate [ɪn'tʌrpəˌlet] *tr* interpolare

interpose [ˌɪntər'poz] *tr* frapporre

interpret [ɪn'tʌrprɪt] *tr* interpretare

interpreter [ɪn'tʌrprətər] *s* interprete *mf*

interrogate [ɪn'terəˌget] *tr & intr* interrogare

interrogation [ɪn ˌterə'geʃən] *s* interrogazione

interroga'tion mark' or **point'** *s* punto interrogativo

interrupt [ˌɪntə'rʌpt] *tr* interrompere

interruption [ˌɪntə'rʌpʃən] *s* interruzione

interscholastic [ˌɪntərskə'læstɪk] *adj* interscolastico

intersect [ˌɪntər'sekt] *tr* intersecare ‖ *intr* intersecarsi

intersection [ˌɪntər'sekʃən] *s* (*of streets, roads, etc.*) crocevia *m*; (geom) intersezione

intersperse [ˌɪntər'spʌrs] *tr* cospargere, inframezzare

interstellar [ˌɪntər'stelər] *adj* interstellare

interstice [ɪn'tʌrstɪs] *s* interstizio

intertwine [ˌɪntər'twaɪn] *tr* intrecciare ‖ *intr* intrecciarsi

interval ['ɪntərvəl] *s* intervallo; **at intervals** a intervalli; **di tanto in tanto**

intervene [ˌɪntər'vin] *intr* intervenire; (*to happen*) succedere

intervening [ˌɪntər'vinɪŋ] *adj*—**in the intervening time** nel frattempo

intervention [ˌɪntər'venʃən] *s* intervenzione

interview ['ɪntərˌvju] *s* intervista ‖ *tr* intervistare

inter-weave [ˌɪntər'wiv] *v* (*pret* -wove ['wov] or -weaved; *pp* -wove, -woven or -weaved) *tr* intessere

intestate [ɪn'testet] or [ɪn'testɪt] *adj* intestato

intestine [ɪn'testɪn] *s* intestino

inthrall [ɪn'θrəl] *tr* affascinare, incantare; (*to subjugate*) asservire, soggiogare

inthrone [ɪn'θron] *tr* mettere sul trono, intronizzare; esaltare, innalzare

intima·cy ['ɪntɪməsi] *s* (-cies) intimità *f*

intimate ['ɪntɪmɪt] *adj & s* intimo ‖ ['ɪntɪˌmet] *tr* insinuare

intimation [ˌɪntɪ'meʃən] *s* insinuazione

intimidate [ɪn'tɪmɪˌdet] *tr* intimidire

into ['ɪntu] or ['ɪntu] *prep* in; verso; contro

intolerant [ɪn'tɑlərənt] *adj & s* intollerante *mf*, insofferente *mf*

intomb [ɪn'tum] *tr* inumare, seppellire

intombment [ɪn'tummənt] *s* sepoltura

intonation [ˌɪntə'neʃən] *s* intonazione

intone [ɪn'ton] *tr* intonare ‖ *intr* salmodiare

intoxicant [ɪn'tɑksɪkənt] *s* bevanda alcoolica

intoxicate [ɪn'tɑksɪˌket] *tr* ubriacare; esilarare; (*to poison*) avvelenare, intossicare

intoxication [ɪn ˌtɑksɪ'keʃən] *s* ubriachezza; ebbrezza, allegria; (*poisoning*) avvelenamento, intossicazione

intractable [ɪn'træktəbəl] *adj* intrattabile

intransigent [ɪn'trænsɪdʒənt] *adj & s* intransigente *mf*

intransitive [ɪn'trænsɪtɪv] *adj* intransitivo

intravenous [ˌɪntrə'vinəs] *adj* intravenoso, endovenoso

intrench [ɪn'trentʃ] *tr & intr* var of **entrench**

intrepid [ɪn'trepɪd] *adj* intrepido

intrepidity [ˌɪntrə'pɪdɪti] *s* intrepidezza

intricate ['ɪntrɪkɪt] *adj* intricato

intrigue [ɪn'trig] or ['ɪntrig] *s* intrigo; tresca, intrigo amoroso; (theat) intreccio ‖ [ɪn'trig] *tr* incuriosire ‖ *intr* intrigare; trescare

intrinsic(al) [ɪn'trɪnsɪk(əl)] *adj* intrinseco

introduce [ˌɪntrə'djus] or [ˌɪntrə'dus] *tr* introdurre; (*a product*) lanciare; (*a person*) presentare

introduction [ˌɪntrə'dʌkʃən] *s* introduzione; presentazione

introductory [ˌɪntrə'dʌktəri] *adj* introduttivo

introit ['ɪntro·ɪt] *s* (eccl) introito

introspective [ˌɪntrə'spektɪv] *adj* introspettivo

introvert ['ɪntrəˌvʌrt] *adj & s* introverso

intrude [ɪn'trud] *intr* intrudersi, intrufolarsi

intruder [ɪn'trudər] *s* intruso; importuno

intrusion [ɪn'truʒən] *s* intrusione

intrusive [ɪn'trusɪv] *adj* invadente

intrust [ɪn'trʌst] *tr* affidare, confidare

intuition [ˌɪntu'ɪʃən] or [ˌɪntju'ɪʃən] *s* intuizione, intuito

inundate ['ɪnənˌdet] *tr* inondare

inundation [ˌɪnən'deʃən] *s* inondazione

inure [ɪn'jur] *tr* indurire, assuefare ‖ *intr* entrare in vigore; **to inure to** ridondare in favore di

invade [ɪn'ved] *tr* invadere

invader [ɪn'vedər] *s* invasore *m*

invalid [ɪn'vælɪd] *adj* (*non valid*) invalido ‖ ['ɪnvəlɪd] *adj* (*person*) invalido; (*thing*) povero; (*diet*) per malati ‖ ['ɪnvəlɪd] *s* invalido

invalidate [ɪn'vælɪˌdet] *tr* invalidare

invalidity [ˌɪnvə'lɪdɪti] *s* invalidità *f*

invaluable [ɪn'væljuˌəbəl] *adj* inestimabile, inapprezzabile

invariable [ɪn'verɪˌəbəl] *adj* invariabile

invasion [ɪn'veʒən] *s* invasione

invective [ɪn'vektɪv] *s* invettiva

inveigh [ɪn've] *intr*—**to inveigh against** inveire contro

inveigle [ɪn'vegəl] or [ɪn'vigəl] *tr* sedurre, abbindolare

invent [ɪn'vent] *tr* inventare

invention [ɪn'venʃən] *s* invenzione

inventiveness [ɪnˈventɪvnɪs] *s* inventiva

inventor [ɪnˈventər] *s* inventore *m*

invento·ry [ˈɪnvənˌtori] *s* (**-ries**) inventario ‖ *v* (*pret* & *pp* **-ried**) *tr* inventariare

inverse [ɪnˈvʌrs] *adj* & *s* inverso

inversion [ɪnˈvʌrʒən] *or* [ɪnˈvʌrʃən] *s* inversione

invert [ˈɪnvʌrt] *s* invertito ‖ [ɪnˈvʌrt] *tr* invertire

invertebrate [ɪnˈvʌrtɪˌbret] *or* [ɪnˈvʌrtɪbrɪt] *adj* & *s* invertebrato

invest [ɪnˈvest] *tr* investire ‖ *intr* fare un investimento; fare investimenti

investigate [ɪnˈvestɪˌget] *tr* investigare

investigation [ɪnˌvestɪˈgeʃən] *s* investigazione

investigator [ɪnˈvestɪˌgetər] *s* investigatore *m*

investment [ɪnˈvestmənt] *s* (*of money*) investimento; (*e.g., with an office*) investitura; (*siege*) assedio

investor [ɪnˈvestər] *s* investitore *m*

inveterate [ɪnˈvetərɪt] *adj* inveterato

invidious [ɪnˈvɪdɪ·əs] *adj* irritante, odioso

invigorate [ɪnˈvɪgəˌret] *tr* invigorire

invigorating [ɪnˈvɪgəˌretɪŋ] *adj* ritemprante, ricostituente, rinforzante

invincible [ɪnˈvɪnsɪbəl] *adj* invincibile

invisible [ɪnˈvɪzɪbəl] *adj* invisibile

invis'ible ink' *s* inchiostro simpatico

invitation [ˌɪnvɪˈteʃən] *s* invito

invite [ɪnˈvaɪt] *tr* invitare

inviting [ɪnˈvaɪtɪŋ] *adj* invitante, attrattivo; (*food*) appetitoso; accogliente

invoice [ˈɪnvɔɪs] *s* fattura; **as per invoice** secondo fattura ‖ *tr* fatturare

invoke [ɪnˈvok] *tr* invocare; (*a spirit*) evocare

involuntary [ɪnˈvɑlənˌteri] *adj* involontario

involve [ɪnˈvɑlv] *tr* involvere, includere; occupare; (*to bring unpleasantness upon*) implicare, coinvolgere; complicare

invulnerable [ɪnˈvʌlnərəbəl] *adj* invulnerabile

inward [ˈɪnwərd] *adj* interno ‖ *adv* al di dentro, verso l'interno

iodide [ˈaɪ·əˌdaɪd] *s* ioduro

iodine [ˈaɪ·əˌdin] *s* iodio ‖ [ˈaɪ·əˌdaɪn] *s* tintura di iodio

ion [ˈaɪ·ən] *or* [ˈaɪ·ɑn] *s* ione *m*

ionize [ˈaɪ·əˌnaɪz] *tr* ionizzare

IOU [ˈaɪˌoˈju] *s* (letterword) (**I owe you**) cambiale *f*, pagherò *m*

I.Q. [ˈaɪˈkju] *s* (letterword) (**intelligence quotient**) quoziente *m* d'intelligenza

Iranian [aɪˈrenɪ·ən] *adj* & *s* iraniano

Ira·qi [ɪˈrɑki] *adj* iracheno ‖ *s* (**-qis**) iracheno

irate [ˈaɪret] *or* [aɪˈret] *adj* irato

ire [aɪr] *s* ira, collera

Ireland [ˈaɪrlənd] *s* l'Irlanda *f*

iris [ˈaɪrɪs] *s* iride *f*

I'rish·man *s* (**-men**) irlandese *m*

I'rish stew' *s* stufato all'irlandese

I'rish·wom'an *s* (**-wom'en**) irlandese *f*

irk [ʌrk] *tr* infastidire, annoiare

irksome [ˈʌrksəm] *adj* fastidioso

iron [ˈaɪ·ərn] *adj* ferreo ‖ *s* ferro; (*to press clothes*) ferro da stiro; **irons** ferri *mpl*; **strike while the iron is hot** batti il ferro fin ch'è caldo ‖ *tr* (*clothes*) stirare; **to iron out** (*a difficulty*) (coll) appianare

i'ron·bound' *adj* ferrato; (*unyielding*) ferreo, inflessibile; (*rock-bound*) roccioso, scabroso

ironclad [ˈaɪ·ərnˌklæd] *adj* corazzato, blindato; inflessibile, ferreo

i'ron constitu'tion *s* salute *f* di ferro

i'ron cur'tain *s* cortina di ferro

i'ron horse' *s* locomotiva a vapore

ironic(al) [aɪˈrɑnɪk(əl)] *adj* ironico

ironing [ˈaɪ·ərnɪŋ] *s* stiratura; roba stirata; roba da stirare

i'roning board' *s* tavolo *or* asse *m* da stiro

i'ron lung' *s* polmone *m* d'acciaio

i'ron·ware' *s* ferrame *m*

i'ron will' *s* volontà *f* di ferro

i'ron·work' *s* lavoro in ferro; **ironworks** *ssg* ferriera

i'ron·work'er *s* ferraio; metalmeccanico, siderurgico

iro·ny [ˈaɪrəni] *s* (**-nies**) ironia

irradiate [ɪˈredɪˌet] *tr* irradiare ‖ *intr* irradiare, irradiarsi

irrational [ɪˈræʃənəl] *adj* irrazionale

irrecoverable [ˌɪrɪˈkʌvərəbəl] *adj* irrecuperabile

irredeemable [ˌɪrɪˈdiməbəl] *adj* irredimibile

irrefutable [ˌɪrɪˈfjutəbəl] *adj* irrefutabile

irregular [ɪˈregjələr] *adj* irregolare ‖ *s* (mil) irregolare *m*

irrelevance [ɪˈreləvəns] *s* irrilevanza

irrelevant [ɪˈreləvənt] *adj* irrilevante

irreligious [ˌɪrɪˈlɪdʒəs] *adj* irreligioso

irremediable [ˌɪrɪˈmidɪ·əbəl] *adj* irrimediabile

irremovable [ˌɪrɪˈmuvəbəl] *adj* irremovibile, inamovibile

irreplaceable [ˌɪrɪˈplesəbəl] *adj* insostituibile

irrepressible [ˌɪrɪˈpresɪbəl] *adj* irreprimibile, incontenibile

irreproachable [ˌɪrɪˈprotʃəbəl] *adj* irreprensibile

irresistible [ˌɪrɪˈzɪstɪbəl] *adj* irresistibile

irrespective [ˌɪrɪˈspektɪv] *adj*—**irrespective of** senza riguardo a

irresponsible [ˌɪrɪˈspɑnsɪbəl] *adj* irresponsabile

irretrievable [ˌɪrɪˈtrivəbəl] *adj* irrecuperabile

irreverent [ɪˈrevərənt] *adj* irriverente

irrevocable [ɪˈrevəkəbəl] *adj* irrevocabile

irrigate [ˈɪrɪˌget] *tr* irrigare

irrigation [ˌɪrɪˈgeʃən] *s* irrigazione

irritant [ˈɪrɪtənt] *adj* & *s* irritante *m*

irritate [ˈɪrɪˌtet] *tr* irritare

irritation [ˌɪrɪˈteʃən] *s* irritazione

irruption [ɪˈrʌpʃən] *s* irruzione

isinglass [ˈaɪzɪŋˌglæs] *or* [ˈaɪzɪŋˌglɑs] *s* (*gelatine*) colla di pesce; mica

Islam [ˈɪsləm] *or* [ɪsˈlɑm] *s* l'Islam *m*

island ['aɪlənd] *adj* isolano || *s* isola; *(for safety of pedestrians)* salvagente *m*

islander ['aɪləndər] *s* isolano

isle [aɪl] *s* isoletta

isolate ['aɪsə‚let] or ['ɪsə‚let] *tr* isolare

isolation [‚aɪsə'leʃən] or [‚ɪsə'leʃən] *s* isolamento

isolationist [‚aɪsə'leʃənɪst] or [‚ɪsə'leʃənɪst] *s* isolazionista *mf*

isosceles [aɪ'sɑsə‚liz] *adj* isoscele

isotope ['aɪsə‚top] *s* isotopo

Israel ['ɪzrɪ-əl] *s* l'Israele *m*

Israe·li [ɪz'reli] *adj* israeliano || *s* (-lis [liz]) israeliano

Israelite ['ɪzrɪ-ə‚laɪt] *adj* & *s* israelita *mf*

issuance ['ɪʃu‚əns] *s* *(of stamps, stocks, bonds, etc.)* emissione; *(e.g., of clothes)* distribuzione; *(of a law)* emanazione

issue ['ɪʃu] *s* *(outlet)* uscita; distribuzione; *(result)* conseguenza; *(offspring)* prole *f*; *(of a magazine)* puntata, fascicolo; *(of a bond)* emissione; *(yield)* prodotto; *(of a law)* promulgazione; *(pathol)* flusso; **at issue** in discussione; **to face the issue** affrontare la situazione; **to force the issue** forzare la soluzione; **to take issue with** non essere d'accordo con, dissentire da || *tr* *(e.g., a book)* pubblicare; *(bonds, orders)* emettere; *(a communiqué)* diramare; *(e.g., food)* distribuire || *intr* uscire; **to issue from** provenire da

isthmus ['ɪsməs] *s* istmo

it [ɪt] *pron pers* esso, essa; lo, la; **it is**

I sono io; **it is raining** piove; **it is four o'clock** sono le quattro

Italian [ɪ'tæljən] *adj* & *s* italiano

Ital'ian-speak'ing *adj* italofono

italic [ɪ'tælɪk] *adj* (typ) corsivo || **italics** *s* (typ) corsivo || **Italic** *adj* italico

italicize [ɪ'tælɪ‚saɪz] *tr* stampare in carattere corsivo; sottolineare

Italy ['ɪtəli] *s* l'Italia *f*

itch [ɪtʃ] *s* prurito; *(pathol)* rogna; *(eagerness)* (fig) pizzicore *m* || *tr* prudere, e.g., **his foot itches him** gli prude il piede || *intr* *(said of a part of body)* prudere; *(said of a person)* avere il prurito; **to itch to** avere il pizzicore di

itch·y ['ɪtʃi] *adj* (-ier; -iest) che prude; *(pathol)* rognoso

item ['aɪtəm] *s* articolo; notizia; *(on the agenda)* questione; (slang) notizia scottante

itemize ['aɪtə‚maɪz] *tr* dettagliare, specificare

itinerant [aɪ'tɪnərənt] or [ɪ'tɪnərənt] *adj* itinerante, ambulante || *s* viaggiatore *m*, viandante *m*

itinerar·y [aɪ'tɪnə‚reri] or [ɪ'tɪnə‚reri] *adj* itinerario || *s* (-ies) itinerario

its [ɪts] *adj* & *pron poss* il suo

itself [ɪt'sɛlf] *pron pers* sé stesso; sì, e.g., **it opened itself** si è aperto

ivied ['aɪvɪd] *adj* coperto di edera

ivo·ry ['aɪvəri] *adj* d'avorio || *s* (-ries) avorio; **ivories** (slang) tasti *mpl* del piano; (slang) palle *fpl* da bigliardo; *(dice)* (slang) dadi *mpl*; (slang) denti *mpl*

i'vory tow'er *s* torre *f* d'avorio

ivy ['aɪvi] *s* (ivies) edera

J

J, j [dʒe] *s* decima lettera dell'alfabeto inglese

jab [dʒæb] *s* puntata; *(prick)* puntura; *(with elbow)* gomitata || *v* *(pret* & *pp* **jabbed;** *ger* **jabbing)** *tr* pugnalare; pungere; dare una gomitata a || *intr* dare colpi

jabber ['dʒæbər] *s* borbottamento, ciarla || *tr* & *intr* borbottare, ciarlare

jack [dʒæk] *s* *(for lifting heavy objects)* cricco, martinetto; *(jackass)* asino; *(device for turning a spit)* girarrosto; *(to remove a boot)* cavastivali *m*; *(cards)* fante *m*; *(bowling)* pallino; *(rad* & *telv)* jack *m*; *(elec)* presa; (slang) soldi *mpl*; **every man jack** ognuno, tutti *mpl* || **Jack** *s* marinaio; *(coll)* buonuomo || *tr*—**to jack up** alzare col cricco; *(prices)* (coll) alzare

jackal ['dʒækəl] *s* sciacallo

jack'ass' *s* asino

jack'daw' *s* cornacchia

jacket ['dʒækɪt] *s* giacca; *(of boiled*

potatoes) buccia; *(of book)* sopraccoperta; *(metal casing)* camicia

jack'ham'mer *s* martello perforatore

jack'-in-the-box' *s* scatola a sorpresa

jack'knife' *s* (-knives) coltello a serramanico; *(sports)* salto a pesce

jack'-of-all'-trades' *s* factotum *m*

jack-o'-lantern ['dʒækə‚læntərn] *s* lanterna a forma di testa umana fatta con una zucca; fuoco fatuo

jack'pot' *s* monte *m* premi; **to hit the jackpot** (slang) vincere un terno al lotto

jack' rab'bit *s* lepre nordamericana di taglia grande

jack'screw' *s* cricco a verme

jack'-tar' *s* (coll) marinaio

jade [dʒed] *adj* di giada, come la giada || *s* *(ornamental stone)* giada; *(worn-out horse)* ronzino; *(disreputable woman)* donnaccia || *tr* logorare

jad'ed ['dʒedɪd] *adj* logoro, stanco; *(appetite)* stucco

jag [dʒæg] *s* slabbratura; **to have a jag on** (slang) avere la sbornia

jagged ['dʒægɪd] *adj* dentato, slabbrato

jaguar ['dʒægwɑr] *s* giaguaro

jail [dʒel] *s* prigione *f*; **to break jail** evadere dal carcere || *tr* carcerare

jail'bird' *s* galeotto, remo di galera

jail'break' *s* evasione *f* dal carcere

jailer ['dʒelər] *s* carceriere *m*

jalop·y [dʒə'lɑpi] *s* (**-ies**) carcassa, trespolo, trabiccolo

jam [dʒæm] *s* stretta, compressione; (*in traffic*) imbottigliamento; (*preserve*) marmellata, confettura; (*difficult situation*) (coll) pasticcio || *v* (*pret & pp* **jammed**; *ger* **jamming**) *tr* stipare; (*e.g., one's finger*) schiacciare, schiacciarsi; (rad) disturbare; **to jam on the brakes** bloccare i freni || *intr* schiacciarsi; (*said of firearms*) incepparsi; (mach) grippare

jamb [dʒæm] *s* stipite *m*

jamboree [,dʒæmbə'ri] *s* riunione nazionale di giovani esploratori; (coll) riunione

James [dʒemz] *s* Giacomo

jamming ['dʒæmɪŋ] *s* radiodisturbo

jam-packed ['dʒæm'pækt] *adj* gremito, pieno fino all'orlo

jangle ['dʒæŋgəl] *s* suono stridente; (*quarrel*) baruffa || *tr* fare suoni stridenti con || *intr* stridere; litigare

janitor ['dʒænɪtər] *s* portiere *m*

janitress ['dʒænɪtrɪs] *s* portinaia

January ['dʒænju,eri] *s* gennaio

ja·pan [dʒə'pæn] *s* lacca giapponese; oggetto di lacca giapponese || *v* (*pret & pp* **-panned**; *ger* **-panning**) *tr* laccare || **Japan** *s* il Giappone

Japa·nese [,dʒæpə'niz] *adj* giapponese || *s* (**-nese**) giapponese *mf*

Jap'anese bee'tle *s* scarabeo giapponese

Jap'anese lan'tern *s* lampioncino alla veneziana

Jap'anese persim'mon *s* cachi *m*

jar [dʒɑr] *s* barattolo; (*earthenware container*) orcio, giara; discordanza; (*jolt*) scossa; (fig) brutta sorpresa; **on the jar** (*said of a door*) socchiuso || *v* (*pret & pp* **jarred**; *ger* **jarring**) *tr* scuotere; far stridere || *intr* vibrare; stridere; essere in conflitto; **to jar on** irritare

jardiniere [,dʒɑrdɪ'nɪr] *s* (*pot*) vaso da fiori; giardiniera

jargon ['dʒɑrgən] *s* gergo

jasmine ['dʒæsmɪn] *or* ['dʒæzmɪn] *s* gelsomino

jasper ['dʒæspər] *s* diaspro

jaundice ['dʒɔndɪs] *or* ['dʒɑndɪs] *s* itterizia; (fig) invidia

jaundiced ['dʒɔndɪst] *or* ['dʒɑndɪst] *adj* itterico; (fig) invidioso

jaunt [dʒɔnt] *or* [dʒɑnt] *s* passeggiata, gita

jaun·ty ['dʒɔnti] *or* ['dʒɑnti] *adj* (**-tier**; **-tiest**) disinvolto; elegante

Java·nese [,dʒævə'niz] *adj* giavanese *m* || *s* (**-nese**) giavanese *m*

javelin ['dʒævlɪn] *or* ['dʒævəlɪn] *s* giavellotto

jaw [dʒɔ] *s* mascella, mandibola; (mach) ganascia; **jaws** fauci *fpl*; gola, stretta || *tr* (slang) rimproverare ||

intr (slang) chiacchierare; (slang) fare la predica

jaw'bone' *s* mascella, mandibola

jaw'break'er *s* (coll) parola difficile da pronunciare; (coll) caramella durissima; (mach) frantoio a mascelle

jay [dʒe] *s* (orn) ghiandaia; (coll) sempliciotto

jay'walk' *intr* attraversare la strada contro la luce rossa del semaforo

jay'walk'er *s* (coll) pedone distratto che attraversa la strada contro la luce rossa del semaforo

jazz [dʒæz] *s* jazz *m*; (slang) spirito || *tr*—**to jazz up** (slang) dar vita a

jazz' band' *s* orchestra jazz

jealous ['dʒɛləs] *adj* geloso; (*envious*) invidioso; vigilante

jealous·y ['dʒɛləsi] *s* (**-ies**) gelosia; invidia; vigilanza

jean [dʒin] *s* tela cruda; **jeans** pantaloni *mpl* di tela cruda

jeep [dʒip] *s* gip *f*, jeep *f*

jeer [dʒɪr] *s* beffa || *tr* beffare || *intr* beffarsi; **to jeer at** motteggiare

Jeho'vah's Wit'nesses ['dʒɪ'hovəs] *spl* Testimoni *mpl* di Geova

jell [dʒel] *s* gelatina || *intr* (to congeal) gelatinizzarsi; (to become substantial) cristallizzarsi

jel·ly ['dʒeli] *s* (**-lies**) gelatina || *v* (*pret & pp* **-lied**) *tr* gelatinizzare || *intr* gelatinizzarsi

jel'ly-fish' *s* medusa; (*weak person*) (coll) fiaccone *m*

jeopardize ['dʒepər,daɪz] *tr* compromettere, mettere a repentaglio

jeopardy ['dʒepərdi] *s* pericolo, repentaglio

Jeremiad [,dʒerɪ'maɪ,æd] *s* geremiade *f*

Jericho ['dʒerɪ,ko] *s* Gerico *f*

jerk [dʒʌrk] *s* strattone *m*, scatto; tic *m*; (*stupid person*) scempio, sciocco; **by jerks** a scatti || *tr* tirare a strattoni; (*meat*) essiccare || *intr* sobbalzare

jerked' beef' *s* fetta di carne di bue essiccata

jerkin ['dʒʌrkɪn] *s* giubbetto

jerk'wa'ter *adj* di scarsa importanza

jerk·y ['dʒʌrki] *adj* (**-ier**; **-iest**) sussultante; (*style*) disuguale

Jerome [dʒə'rom] *s* Gerolamo

jersey ['dʒʌrzi] *s* jersey *m*, maglione *m*

Jerusalem [dʒɪ'rusələm] *s* Gerusalemme *f*

jest [dʒest] *s* scherzo, burla; **in jest** per celia || *intr* scherzare

jester ['dʒestər] *s* motteggiatore *m*, burlone *m*; (hist) buffone *m*

Jesuit ['dʒezʊ·ɪt] *or* ['dʒezju·ɪt] *adj & s* gesuita *m*

Jesuitic(al) [,dʒezʊ'ɪtɪk(əl)] *or* [,dʒezju'ɪtɪk(əl)] *adj* gesuitico

Jesus ['dʒizəs] *s* Gesù *m*

Je'sus Christ' *s* Gesù *m* Cristo

jet [dʒet] *adj* di giaietto || *s* (*of a fountain*) zampillo; (*stream shooting forth from nozzle*) getto; (*mineral; lustrous black*) giaietto; (aer) aereo a getto || *v* (*pret & pp* **jetted**; *ger* **jetting**) spruzzare ‖ *intr* zampillare; volare in aereo a getto

jet' age' *s* era dell'aviogetto

jet'-black' *adj* nero come il carbone

jet' bomb'er *s* bombardiere *m* a reazione

jet' coal' *s* carbone *m* a lunga fiamma

jet' en'gine *s* motore *m* a reazione

jet' fight'er *s* caccia *m* a reazione

jet'lin'er *s* aviogetto da trasporto passeggeri

jet' plane' *s* aviogetto

jet' propul'sion *s* gettopropulsione

jetsam ['dʒetsəm] *s* relitto

jet' stream' *s* corrente *f* a getto; scappamento di motore a razzo

jettison ['dʒetɪsən] *s* (naut) alleggerimento ‖ *tr* (naut) alleggerirsi di; (fig) disfarsi di

jet-ty ['dʒetɪ] *s* (-ties) gettata; (*wharf*) molo, imbarcadero

Jew [dʒu] *s* giudeo

jewel ['dʒu·əl] *s* pietra preziosa; (*valuable personal ornament*) gioia, gioiello; (*of a watch*) rubino; (*costume jewelry*) gioia finta; (fig) valore *m*, gioiello

jew'el case' *s* scrigno, portagioie *m*

jeweler or jeweller ['dʒu·ələr] *s* gioielliere *m*, orefice *m*

jewelry ['dʒu·əlrɪ] *s* gioielli *mpl*

jew'elry shop' *s* gioielleria

Jewess ['dʒu·ɪs] *s* giudea

Jewish ['dʒu·ɪʃ] *adj* giudeo

jews'-harp or jew's-harp ['dʒuz‚harp] *s* scacciapensieri *m*

jib [dʒɪb] *s* (*of a crane*) (mach) braccio (di gru); (naut) fiocco, vela Marconi

jib' boom' *s* asta di fiocco

jibe [dʒaɪb] *s* burla, beffa ‖ *intr* beffarsi; accordarsi; to jibe at beffarsi di

jif-fy ['dʒɪfɪ] *s*—in a jiffy (coll) in men che non si dica

jig [dʒɪg] *s* (*dance*) giga; the jig is up (slang) tutto è perduto

jigger ['dʒɪgər] *s* bicchierino di liquore d'un'oncia e mezza; (*flea*) pulce *f* tropicale; (*gadget*) (coll) aggeggio; (naut) bozzello; (min) crivello

jiggle ['dʒɪgəl] *s* scossa ‖ *tr* scuotere, agitare ‖ *intr* scuotersi

jig' saw' *s* sega da traforo

jig'saw puz'zle *s* gioco di pazienza, rompicapo

jilt [dʒɪlt] *tr* piantare

jim·my ['dʒɪmɪ] *s* (-mies) piccolo piede di porco ‖ *v* (*pret & pp* -mied) *tr* scassinare; to jimmy open scassinare

jingle ['dʒɪŋgəl] *s* sonaglio, bubbolo; (*sound*) rumore *m* di sonagliera; cantilena, rima infantile ‖ *tr* far suonare ‖ *intr* tintinnare

jin·go ['dʒɪŋgo] *adj* sciovinista ‖ *s* (-goes) sciovinista *mf*; by jingo! perbaccol

jingoism ['dʒɪŋgo‚ɪzəm] *s* sciovinismo

jinx [dʒɪŋks] *s* iettatura; (*person*) iettatore *m* ‖ *tr* portare la iettatura a

jitters ['dʒɪtərz] *spl* (coll) nervosismo; to have the jitters (coll) essere nervoso

jittery ['dʒɪtərɪ] *adj* nervoso

job [dʒab] *s* (*piece of work*) lavoro;

(*task*) mansione; (*employment*) posto, impiego; (slang) furto; by the job a cottimo; on the job (slang) attento, sollecito; to be out of a job essere disoccupato; to lie down on the job (slang) dormire sul lavoro

job' anal'ysis *s* valutazione delle mansioni

jobber ['dʒabər] *s* grossista *mf*; (*pieceworker*) lavoratore *m* a cottimo; funzionario disonesto

job'hold'er *s* impiegato; (*in the government*) burocrate *m*

jobless ['dʒablɪs] *adj* disoccupato

job' lot' *s* (com) saldo

job' print'er *s* piccolo tipografo non specializzato

job' print'ing *s* piccolo lavoro tipografico

jockey ['dʒakɪ] *s* fantino ‖ *tr* (*a horse*) montare; manovrare; (*to trick*) abbindolare

jockstrap ['dʒak‚stræp] *s* sospensorio

jocose [dʒo'kos] *adj* giocoso

jocular ['dʒakjələr] *adj* scherzoso

jog [dʒag] *s* spinta; piccolo trotto ‖ *v* (*pret & pp* jogged; *ger* jogging) *tr* spingere leggermente; (*the memory*) rinfrescare ‖ *intr* barcarellare; to jog along continuare col solito tran tran

jog' trot' *s* piccolo trotto; (fig) tran tran *m*

John [dʒan] *s* Giovanni *m*

John' Bull' *s* il tipico inglese; the inglesi, il popolo inglese

John' Han'cock ['hænkak] *s* (coll) la firma

johnnycake ['dʒanɪ‚kek] *s* pane *m* di granturco

John'ny-come'-late'ly *s* (coll) ultimo arrivato

John'ny-jump'-up' *s* violetta, viola del pensiero

John'ny-on-the-spot' *s* (coll) persona sempre pronta

John' the Bap'tist *s* San Giovanni Battista

join [dʒɔɪn] *tr* giungere, congiungere; associarsi a; unire; (*e.g., a party*) farsi membro di; (*the army*) arruolarsi in; (*battle*) ingaggiare; (*to empty into*) sfociare in ‖ *intr* congiungersi, unirsi; (*said, e.g., of two rivers*) confluire

joiner ['dʒɔɪnər] *s* falegname *m*; membro di molte società

joint [dʒɔɪnt] *adj* congiunto ‖ *s* (*in a pipe*) giuntura; (*of bones*) giuntura, articolazione; (*hinge of book*) brachetta; (*in woodwork*) incastro, commettitura; (*of meat*) taglio; (mach) snodo; (*gambling den*) (slang) bisca; (elec) innesto; (slang) bettola; out of joint slogato; (fig) fuori luogo; to throw (*e.g., one's arm*) out of joint slogarsi

joint' account' *s* conto in comune

joint' commit'tee *s* commissione mista

jointly ['dʒɔɪntlɪ] *adv* unitamente

joint' own'er *s* condomino

joint'-stock' com'pany *s* società *f* per azioni a responsabilità illimitata

joist [dʒɔɪst] *s* trave *f*

joke [dʒok] *s* burla, barzelletta; (*trifling matter*) cosa da nulla; (*person laughed at*) zimbello; **to tell a joke** raccontare una barzelletta; **to play a joke on** fare uno scherzo a ‖ *tr*—**to joke one's way into** ottenere dicendo barzellette ‖ *intr* burlare, dire storielle; **joking aside** senza scherzi

joker ['dʒokər] *s* burlone *m*, fumista *m*; (*wise guy*) saputello; (*hidden provision*) clausola ingannatrice; (cards) matta

jol·ly ['dʒɑli] *adj* (**-lier; -liest**) allegro, gaio ‖ *adv* (coll) molto ‖ *v* (*pret & pp* **-lied**) *tr* (coll) prendersi gioco di ‖

jolt [dʒolt] *s* scossa ‖ *tr* scuotere ‖ *intr* sobbalzare

Jonah ['dʒonə] *s* Giona; (fig) uccello di mal augurio

jongleur ['dʒɑŋglər] *s* giullare *m*

jonquil ['dʒɑŋkwɪl] *s* giunchiglia

Jordan ['dʒɔrdən] *s* (*country*) la Giordania; (*river*) Giordano

Jordanian [dʒɔr'denɪ·ən] *adj & s* giordano

josh [dʒɑʃ] *tr & intr* (coll) canzonare

jostle ['dʒɑsəl] *s* spintone *m* ‖ *tr* spingere ‖ *intr* scontrarsi; farsi strada a gomitate

jot [dʒɑt] *s*—**I don't care a jot for** non mi importa un fico di ‖ *v* (*pret & pp* **jotted**; *ger* **jotting**) *tr*—**to jot down** notare, gettar giù

jounce [dʒauns] *s* scossa ‖ *tr* scuotere ‖ *intr* sobbalzare

journal ['dʒʌrnəl] *s* (*newspaper*) giornale *m*; (*magazine*) rivista; (*daily record*) diario; (com) giornale *m*; (mach) perno; (naut) giornale *m* di bordo

journalese [ˌdʒʌrnə'liz] *s* linguaggio giornalistico

journalism ['dʒʌrnəlˌɪzəm] *s* giornalismo

journalist ['dʒʌrnəlɪst] *s* giornalista *mf*

journey ['dʒʌrni] *s* viaggio ‖ *intr* viaggiare

jour'ney·man *s* (**-men**) operaio specializzato

joust [dʒʌst] *or* [dʒust] *or* [dʒaust] *s* giostra ‖ *intr* giostrare

jovial ['dʒovɪ·əl] *adj* gioviale

jowl [dʒaul] *s* (*cheek*) guancia; (*jawbone*) mascella; (*of cattle*) giogaia; (*of fowl*) bargiglio; (*of fat person*) pappagorgia

joy [dʒɔɪ] *s* gioia, allegria; **to leap with joy** ballare dalla gioia

joyful ['dʒɔɪfəl] *adj* gioioso, festoso; **joyful over** lieto di

joyless ['dʒɔɪlɪs] *adj* senza gioia

joyous ['dʒɔɪ·əs] *adj* gioioso

joy' ride' *s* (coll) gita in auto; (coll) gita all'impazzata in auto

jubilant ['dʒubɪlənt] *adj* esultante

jubilation [ˌdʒubɪ'leʃən] *s* giubilo

jubilee ['dʒubɪˌli] *s* (*jubilation*) giubilo; (eccl) giubileo

Judaism ['dʒudeˌɪzəm] *s* giudaismo

judge [dʒʌdʒ] *s* giudice *m* ‖ *tr & intr* giudicare; **judging by** a giudicare da

judge' ad'vocate *s* avvocato militare; avvocato della marina da guerra

judgeship ['dʒʌdʒʃɪp] *s* carica di giudice

judgment ['dʒʌdʒmənt] *s* giudizio; (*legal decision*) sentenza

judg'ment day' *s* giorno del giudizio

judg'ment seat' *s* banco dei giudici; tribunale *m*

judicature ['dʒudɪkətʃər] *s* carica di giudice

judicial [dʒu'dɪʃəl] *adj* giudiziario; (*becoming a judge*) giudizioso

judiciar·y [dʒu'dɪʃɪˌeri] *adj* giudiziario ‖ *s* (**-ies**) (*judges collectively*) magistratura; (*judicial branch*) potere giudiziario

judicious [dʒu'dɪʃəs] *adj* giudizioso

jug [dʒʌg] *s* brocca, boccale *m*; (*narrow-necked vessel*) orcio; (*jail*) (slang) prigione

juggle ['dʒʌgəl] *s* gioco di prestigio ‖ *tr* fare il giocoliere con; (*documents, facts*) alterare frodolentemente; **to juggle away** ghermire, trafugare ‖ *intr* fare il giocoliere; fare l'imbroglione

juggler ['dʒʌglər] *s* giocoliere *m*, prestigiatore *m*; impostore *m*

juggling ['dʒʌglɪŋ] *s* giochi *mpl* di prestigio

Jugoslav ['jugo'slɑv] *adj & s* iugoslavo, jugoslavo

Jugoslavia ['jugo'slɑvɪ·ə] *s* la Iugoslavia, la Jugoslavia

jugular ['dʒʌgjələr] *or* ['dʒugjələr] *adj & s* giugulare *f*

juice [dʒus] *s* sugo; (*natural fluid of an animal body*) succo; (slang) elettricità *f*; (slang) benzina; **to stew in one's own juice** (coll) annegarsi nel proprio sugo

juic·y ['dʒusi] *adj* (**-ier; -iest**) sugoso, succoso; (*spicy*) piccante

jukebox ['dʒuk·bɑks] *s* grammofono a gettone, juke-box *m*

julep ['dʒulɪp] *s* bibita di menta col ghiaccio; (pharm) giulebbe *m*

julienne [ˌdʒulɪ'ɛn] *s* giuliana

July [dʒu'laɪ] *s* luglio

jumble ['dʒʌmbəl] *s* intrico, garbuglio ‖ *tr* ingarbugliare

jum·bo ['dʒʌmbo] *adj* (coll) enorme ‖ *s* (**-bos**) (*person*) (coll) elefante *m*; (*thing*) (coll) oggetto enorme

jump [dʒʌmp] *s* salto; (*in a parachute*) lancio; (*of prices*) sbalzo; (*start*) soprassalto; **on the jump** in moto; **to get** *or* **to have the jump on** (coll) avere il vantaggio su ‖ *tr* saltare; (*a horse*) far saltare; (*prices*) alzare; uscire da, e.g., **the train jumped the track** il treno uscì dalle rotaie; (*to attack*) (coll) balzare su; (checkers) suffiare ‖ *intr* saltare; (*from surprise*) trasalire; (*said of prices*) salire; (*in a parachute*) lanciarsi; **to jump at** (e.g., *an offer*) afferrare; **to jump on** saltare su; (coll) sgridare, arrabbiarsi con; **to jump over** oltrepassare; (*a page*) saltare; **to jump to a conclusion** arrivare precipitosamente a una conclusione

jumper ['dʒʌmpər] *s* saltatore *m*; camiciotto; **jumpers** tuta da bambini

jump'ing jack' ['dʒʌmpɪŋ] *s* marionetta

jump'ing-off' place' *s* fine *f* del mondo; (fig) trampolino, punto di partenza

jump' seat' *s* strapuntino

jump' spark' *s* scintilla elettrica; *(of induction coil)* (elec) scintilla d'intraferro

jump' wire' *s* filo elettrico di contatto

jump·y ['dʒʌmpi] *adj* (-ier; -iest) nervoso, eccitato

junction ['dʒʌŋktʃən] *s* congiunzione; *(of two rivers)* confluenza; (carp) commettitura; (rr) raccordo ferroviario

juncture ['dʒʌŋktʃər] *s* giuntura; *(occasion)* congiuntura; *(moment)* momento

June [dʒun] *s* giugno

jungle ['dʒʌŋgəl] *s* giungla

junglegym ['dʒʌŋgəl,dʒɪm] *s* (trademark) castello

junior ['dʒunjər] *adj* minore, di minore età; giovane; *(in American university)* del penultimo anno; figlio, e.g., **John H. Smith, Junior** Giovanni H. Smith, figlio || *s* minore *m*; socio secondario; studente *m* del penultimo anno

jun'ior col'lege *s* scuola universitaria unicamente di primo biennio

jun'ior high' school' *s* scuola media; ginnasio

juniper ['dʒunɪpər] *s* ginepro

ju'niper ber'ry *s* coccola di ginepro

junk [dʒʌŋk] *s* roba vecchia, ferro vecchio; *(Chinese ship)* giunca; (naut) carne salata || *tr* (slang) gettar via

junk' deal'er *s* robivecchi *m*

junket ['dʒʌŋkɪt] *s* budino di giuncata; *(outing)* viaggio di piacere; viaggio pagato a spese del tesoro || *intr* far un viaggio di piacere; far un viaggio a spese del tesoro

junk'man' *s* (-men') ferravecchio; rigattiere *m*

junk' room' *s* ripostiglio

junk' shop' *s* negozio di robivecchi

junk'yard' *s* cantiere *m* di ferravecchio

juridical [dʒʊ'rɪdɪkəl] *adj* giuridico

jurisdiction [,dʒʊrɪs'dɪk/ən] *s* giurisdizione

jurisprudence [,dʒʊrɪs'prudəns] *s* giurisprudenza

jurist ['dʒʊrɪst] *s* giurista *mf*

juror ['dʒʊrər] *s* giurato

ju·ry ['dʒʊri] *s* (-ries) giuria

ju'ry box' *s* banco della giuria

ju'ry·man *s* (-men) giurato

just [dʒʌst] *adj* giusto || *adv* giustamente, giusto; appena; proprio; **just as come,** proprio come; **just beyond** un po' più in là (di); **just now** poco fa, or ora; **just out** appena uscito, appena pubblicato

justice ['dʒʌstɪs] *s* giustizia; *(judge)* giudice *m*; **to bring to justice** arrestare e condannare; **to do justice to** render giustizia a; apprezzare bastantemente

jus'tice of the peace' *s* giudice *m* conciliatore

justifiable ['dʒʌstɪ,faɪ·əbəl] *adj* giustificabile

justi·fy ['dʒʌstɪ,faɪ] *v* (pret & pp **-fied**) *tr* giustificare; (typ) giustificare

justly ['dʒʌstli] *adv* giustamente

jut [dʒʌt] *v* (pret & pp **jutted**; ger **jutting**) *intr*—**to jut out** strapiombare, sporgere

jute [dʒut] *s* iuta || **Jute** *s* Iuto

juvenile ['dʒuvənɪl] or ['dʒuvə,naɪl] *adj* giovanile; minorile || *s* giovane *mf*; libro per la gioventù; (theat) amoroso

ju'venile court' *s* tribunale *m* per i minorenni

ju'venile delin'quency *s* delinquenza minorile

juvenilia [,dʒuvə'nɪlɪ·ə] *spl* opere *fpl* giovanili; libri *mpl* per ragazzi

juxtapose [,dʒʌkstə'poz] *tr* giustapporre

K

K, k [ke] *s* undicesima lettera dell'alfabeto inglese

kale [kel] *s* verza; (slang) cocuzza soldi *mpl*

kaleidoscope [kə'laɪdə,skop] *s* caleidoscopio

kangaroo [,kæŋgə'ru] *s* canguro

katydid ['ketɪdɪd] *s* grossa cavalletta verde nordamericana

kedge [kedʒ] *s* (naut) ancorotto

keel [kil] *s* chiglia || *intr*—**to keel over** (naut) abbattersi in carena, capovolgersi; (fig) svenire

keelson ['kelsən] or ['kɪlsən] *s* (naut) controchiglia

keen [kin] *adj* *(sharpened)* affilato; *(wind; wit)* tagliente, mordente; *(eyes)* penetrante; *(ears; mind)* acuto,

fine; *(eager)* entusiasta; intenso, vivo; (slang) meraviglioso; **to be keen on** essere appassionato per

keep [kip] *s* mantenimento; *(of medieval castle)* torrione *m*, maschio; **for keeps** (coll) seriamente; (coll) per sempre; **to earn one's keep** guadagnarsi la vita || *v* (pret & pp **kept** [kept]) *tr* mantenere; *(watch)* fare; *(one's word)* mantenere; *(to withhold)* trattenere; *(accounts)* tenere; *(servants, guests)* avere; *(a garden)* coltivare; *(a business)* esercitare; *(a holiday)* festeggiare; *(to support)* sostentare; *(a secret; one's seat)* serbare; *(to decide to purchase)* prendere **to keep away** tener lontano; **to keep back** trattenere; *(a secret)* mantenere; **to keep down** reprimere; (*expenses*) ridurre al minimo; **to keep s.o. from** + *ger* impedire a qlcu di + *inf*; **to keep in** tener chiuso; **to keep off** tenere a distanza; (*e.g., moisture*) non lasciar penetrare; **to keep s.o. informed about s.th** tenere qlcu al corrente di qlco; **to keep s.o. waiting** fare aspettare qlcu; **to keep up** mantenere, sostenere || *intr* **to keep** + *ger* continuare a + *inf*; **to keep away** tenersi lontano; **to keep from** + *ger* evitare di + *inf*; **to keep informed (about)** tenersi al corrente (di); **to keep in with** (coll) stare nelle buone grazie di; **to keep off** stare lontano (da); (*the grass*) non calpestare; **to keep on** + *ger* seguitare a + *inf*; **to keep out** star fuori, non entrare; **to keep out of** non entrare in; (*danger*) stare lontano da; non immischiarsi in; **to keep quiet** stare tranquillo; **to keep to** (*left or right*) tenere; **to keep to oneself** stare in disparte; **to keep up** continuare; **to keep up with** stare alla pari con; (*e.g., the news*) tenersi al corrente di

keeper ['kipər] *s* (*of a shop*) tenitore *m*; guardiano; (*of a game preserve*) guardacaccia *m*; (*of a magnet*) ancora

keeping ['kipiŋ] *s* custodia; (*of a holiday*) celebrazione; **in keeping with** in armonia con; **in safe keeping** in luogo sicuro; **out of keeping with** in cattivo accordo con

keep'sake' *s* ricordo

keg [keg] *s* barilotto, botticella

ken [ken] *s* portata; **beyond the ken of** al di là dell'ambito di

kennel ['kenəl] *s* canile *m*

kep·i ['kepi] or ['kepi] *s* (-is) chepì *m*

kept' wo'man [kept] *s* (**wom'en**) mantenuta

kerchief ['kʌrtʃɪf] *s* fisciù *m*

kernel ['kʌrnəl] *s* (*of a nut*) gheriglio; (*of wheat*) chicco; (fig) nucleo

kerosene ['kerə,sin] or ['kerə'sin] *s* cherosene *m*, petrolio da illuminazione

kerplunk [kər'plʌŋk] *interj* patapum!

ketchup ['ketʃəp] *s* salsa piccante di pomodoro, ketchup *m*

kettle ['ketəl] *s* marmitta, paiolo; (*teakettle*) bricco, teiera

ket'tle·drum' *s* timpano

key [ki] *adj* a chiave; chiave || *s* chiave *f*; (*of piano, typewriter, etc.*) tasto; (*cotter pin*) chiavetta, coppiglia; (*reef*) isolotto; (*tone of voice*) tono; (fig, mus) chiave *f*; (bot) samara; (telg) tasto trasmettitore, manipolatore *m*; **off key** stonato || *tr* aggiustare; inchiavardare; **to key up** eccitare, portare al parossismo

key'board' *s* tastiera

key'hole' *s* toppa, buco della serratura; (*of a clock*) buco della chiave

key'note' *s* (mus) tono; (fig) principio informatore

key'note address' *s* discorso d'apertura

key'punch op'era'tor *s* perforatore *m*

key' ring' *s* portachiavi *m*

key'stone' *s* chiave *f* di volta

key' word' *s* parola chiave

kha·ki ['kɑki] or ['kæki] *adj* cachi || *s* (-kis) cachi *m*

khedive [kə'div] *s* kedivè *m*

kibitz ['kɪbɪts] *intr* (coll) dare consigli non richiesti

kibitzer ['kɪbɪtsər] *s* (*at a card game*) (coll) consigliere *m* importuno; (coll) ficcanaso *mf*

kibosh ['kaɪbɑʃ] or [kɪ'baʃ] *s* (coll) sciocchezza; **to put the kibosh on** (coll) impossibilitare

kick [kɪk] *s* calcio, pedata; (*of a gun*) rinculo; (*complaint*) (slang) protesta; (*of liquor*) (slang) forza; **to get a kick out of** (slang) pigliar piacere da || *tr* prendere a calci; (*a ball*) calciare; (*one's feet*) battere; **to kick out** (coll) sbatter fuori a pedate; **to kick up a row** scatenare un putiferio || *intr* calciare; (*said of an animal*) scalciare, trarre; (*said of a firearm*) rinculare; (coll) lamentarsi; **to kick against the pricks** dar calci al vento; **to kick off** (football) dare il calcio d'inizio

kick'back' *s* (coll) contraccolpo; (coll) intrallazzo, bustarella

kick'off' *s* calcio d'inizio

kid [kɪd] *s* capretto; **kids** guanti *mpl* or scarpe *fpl* di capretto || *v* (*pret & pp* **kidded**; *ger* **kidding**) *tr* (coll) prendere in giro; **to kid oneself** (coll) farsi illusioni || *intr* (coll) dirlo per scherzo

kidder ['kɪdər] *s* (coll) burlone *m*

kid' gloves' *spl* guanti *mpl* di capretto; **to handle with kid gloves** trattare con la massima cautela

kid'nap' *v* (*pret & pp* **-naped** or **-napped**; *ger* **-naping** or **-napping**) *tr* rapire, sequestrare

kidnaper or **kidnapper** ['kɪd,næpər] *s* rapitore *m* a scopo d'estorsione

kidnaping or **kidnapping** ['kɪd,næpiŋ] *s* rapimento a scopo di estorsione

kidney ['kɪdni] *s* rene *m*; (culin) rognone *m*; (*temperament*) carattere *m*; (*kind*) tipo

kid'ney bean' *s* fagiolo

kid'ney stone' *s* calcolo renale

kill [kɪl] *s* uccisione *m*; (*game killed*) cacciagione; (coll) fiumicello; **for the kill** per il colpo finale || *tr* uccidere; eliminare; (*a bill*) bocciare; (fig) opprimere

killer ['kɪlər] *s* uccisore *m*

kill'er whale' *s* orca

killing ['kɪlɪŋ] *adj* mortale; (*exhausting*) opprimente; (coll) molto divertente || *s* uccisione; (*game killed*) cacciagione; (coll) fortuna; **to make a killing** (coll) fare una fortuna da un giorno all'altro

kill'-joy' *s* guastafeste *mf*

kiln [kɪl] or [kɪln] *s* forno, fornace *f*

kil·o ['kɪlo] or ['kilo] *s* (-os) chilogrammo; chilometro

kilocycle ['kɪlə,saɪkəl] *s* chilociclo

kilogram ['kɪlə,græm] *s* chilogrammo

kilo·hertz ['kɪlə,hʌrts] *s* (-hertz) chilohertz

kilometer ['kɪlə,mitər] *or* [kɪ'lɑmɪtər] *s* chilometro

kilowatt ['kɪlə,wɑt] *s* kilowatt *m*, chilowatt *m*

kilowatt-hour ['kɪlə,wɑt'aur] *s* (**kilowatt-hours**) chilowattora *m*

kilt [kɪlt] *s* gonnellino

kilter ['kɪltər] *s*—**to be out of kilter** (coll) essere fuori squadra

kimo·no [kɪ'monə] *or* [kɪ'mono] *s* (**-nos**) chimono

kin [kɪn] *s* (*family relationship*) parentela; (*relatives*) parenti *mpl*; **of kin** parente, affine; **the next of kin** il parente più prossimo, i parenti più prossimi

kind [kaɪnd] *adj* gentile; **kind to** buono con ‖ *s* genere *m*, specie *f*; **a kind of** una specie di; **all kinds of** (coll) ogni sorta di; **in kind** in natura; **kind of** (coll) quasi, piuttosto; **of a kind** dello stesso stampo; (*mediocre*) di poco valore

kindergarten ['kɪndər,gɑrtən] *s* scuola materna, giardino d'infanzia

kindergartner ['kɪndər,gɑrtnər] *s* allievo della scuola d'infanzia; (*teacher*) maestra giardiniera

kind-hearted ['kaɪnd'hɑrtɪd] *adj* gentile, di buon cuore

kindle ['kɪndəl] *tr* accendere ‖ *intr* accendersi

kindling ['kɪndlɪŋ] *s* accensione; legna minuta

kin'dling wood' *s* legna minuta per accendere il fuoco

kind·ly ['kaɪndli] *adj* (**-lier; -liest**) gentile; (*climate*) benigno; favorevole ‖ *adv* gentilmente; cordialmente; **per gentilezza; to not take kindly to** non accettare di buon grado

kindness ['kaɪndnɪs] *s* gentilezza; **have the kindness to** abbia la bontà di

kindred ['kɪndrɪd] *adj* imparentato; affine ‖ *s* parentela; affinità *f*

kinescope ['kɪnɪ,skop] *s* (trademark) cinescopio

kinetic [kɪ'nɛtɪk] *or* [kaɪ'nɛtɪk] *adj* cinetico ‖ **kinetics** *s* cinetica

kinet'ic en'ergy *s* forza viva, energia cinetica

king [kɪŋ] *s* re *m;* (checkers) dama; (cards, chess) re *m*

king'bolt' *s* perno

kingdom ['kɪŋdəm] *s* regno

king'fish'er *s* martin pescatore *m*

king·ly ['kɪŋli] *adj* (**-lier; -liest**) reale; (*stately*) maestoso ‖ *adv* regalmente

king'pin' *s* birillo centrale; (aut) perno dello sterzo; (fig) figura principale

king' post' *s* (archit) ometto, monaco

king's' e'vil *s* scrofola

kingship ['kɪŋʃɪp] *s* regalità *f*

king'-size' gold' *s* extra-grande

king's' ran'som *s* ricchezza di Creso

kink [kɪŋk] *s* (*in a rope*) arricciatura; (*in hair*) crespatura; (*soreness in neck*) torcicollo; (*flaw*) ostacolo; (*mental twist*) ghiribizzo ‖ *tr* attorcigliare ‖ *intr* attorcigliarsi

kink·y ['kɪŋki] *adj* (**-ier; -iest**) attorcigliato; (*hair*) crespo

kinsfolk ['kɪnz,fok] *s* parentado

kinship ['kɪnʃɪp] *s* parentela; affinità *f*

kins'man *s* (**-men**) parente *m*

kins'wom'an *s* (**-wom'en**) parente *f*

kipper ['kɪpər] *s* aringa affumicata ‖ *tr* (*herring or salmon*) affumicare

kiss [kɪs] *s* bacio; (*billiards*) rimpallo leggerissimo; (*confection*) meringa ‖ *tr* baciare; **to kiss away** (*tears*) asciugare con baci ‖ *intr* baciare, baciarsi; (billiards) rimpallare leggermente

kit [kɪt] *s* (*case*) cassetta dei ferri; (*tools*) ferri *mpl* del mestiere; (*set of supplies*) corredo; (*of small tools*) astuccio; (*of a traveler*) borsa da viaggio; (*pail*) secchio; **the whole kit and caboodle** (coll) tutti quanti

kitchen ['kɪtʃən] *s* cucina

kitchenette [,kɪtʃə'nɛt] *s* cucinetta

kitch'en gar'den *s* orto

kitch'en-maid' *s* sguattera

kitch'en police' *s* (mil) corvè *f* di cucina

kitch'en range' *s* cucina economica

kitch'en sink' *s* acquaio

kitch'en-ware' *s* utensili *mpl* di cucina

kite [kaɪt] *s* cervo volante, aquilone *m;* (orn) nibbio

kith' and kin' [kɪθ] *spl* amici *mpl* e parenti *mpl*

kitten ['kɪtən] *s* gattino

kittenish ['kɪtənɪʃ] *adj* giocattolone; civettuolo

kit·ty ['kɪti] *s* (**-ties**) gattino; (cards) piatto ‖ *interj* micio!

kleptomaniac [,klɛptə'meni,æk] *s* cleptomane *mf*

knack [næk] *s* abilità *f*, destrezza

knapsack ['næp,sæk] *s* zaino

knave [nev] *s* furfante *m;* (cards) fante *m*

knaver·y ['nevəri] *s* (**-ies**) furfanteria

knead [nid] *tr* maneggiare, intridere; (*a muscle*) massaggiare

knee [ni] *s* ginocchio; (*of trousers*) ginocchiera; (mach) gomito; **to bring s.o. to his knees** ridurre qlcu all'obbedienza; **to go down on one's knees** (**to**) gettarsi in ginocchio (davanti a)

knee' breech'es [,brɪtʃɪz] *spl* calzoni *mpl* al ginocchio

knee'cap' *s* rotula, patella; (*protective covering*) ginocchiera

knee'-deep' *adj* fino al ginocchio

knee'-high' *adj* fino al ginocchio

knee' jerk' *s* riflesso patellare

kneel [nil] *v* (*pret & pp* **knelt** [nɛlt] *or* **kneeled**) *intr* inginocchiarsi

knee'pad' *s* ginocchiera

knee'pan' *s* rotula, patella

knell [nɛl] *s* rintocco funebre, campana a morto; **to toll the knell of** annunciare la morte di ‖ *intr* suonare a morte

knickers ['nɪkərz] *spl* knickerbockers *mpl*, calzoni *mpl* alla zuava

knickknack ['nɪk,næk] *s* soprammobile *m;* gingillo, ninnolo

knife [naɪf] *s* (**knives** [naɪvz]) coltello; (*of a paper cutter*) mannaia; (*of a milling machine*) fresa; **to go under the knife** essere sulla tavola operatoria ‖ *tr* accoltellare; mettere il coltello nella schiena di

knife' sharp'ener *s* affilatoio

knife' switch' s (elec) coltella

knight [naɪt] s cavaliere m; (chess) cavallo || tr armare cavaliere

knight-errant ['naɪt'erənt] s (knights-errant) cavaliere m errante

knighthood ['naɪt·hʊd] s cavalleria

knightly ['naɪtlɪ] adj cavalleresco

knit [nɪt] v (pret & pp knitted or knit; ger knitting) tr lavorare a maglia; (to join) unire; (e.g., the brow) corrugare || intr lavorare a maglia; fare la calza; unirsi; (said of a bone) saldarsi

knitting ['nɪtɪŋ] s maglia, lavoro a maglia

knit'ting machine' s macchina per maglieria

knit'ting mill' s maglieria

knit'ting nee'dle s ferro da calza

knit'wear' s maglieria

knit'wear store' s maglieria

knob [nɑb] s (lump) bozza, protuberanza; (of a door) maniglia; (on furniture) pomolo; (hill) collinetta rotondeggiante; (rad, telv) manopola, pulsante m

knock [nɑk] s colpo; (on a door) tocco; (slang) attacco, critica || tr battere; (repeatedly) sbatacchiare; (slang) attaccare, criticare; **to knock down** (with a punch) stendere a terra; (a wall) diroccare; (to the highest bidder) aggiudicare; (e.g., a machine) smontare; **to knock off** (work) (slang) sospendere; (slang) terminare; (slang) uccidere; **to knock out** mettere fuori combattimento || intr battere; (aut) battere in testa; (slang) criticare; **to knock about** (slang) gironzolare; **to knock against** urtare contro; **to knock at** (e.g., a door) battere a, bussare a; **to knock off** (slang) cessare di lavorare

knock'down' adj (blow) knock down, che atterra; (dismountable) smontabile || s (blow) colpo che atterra; (discount) sconto

knocker ['nɑkər] s (on a door) battaglio, bussatoio; (coll) criticone m

knock-kneed ['nɑk,nid] adj con le gambe a X [iks]

knock'out' s pugno che mette fuori combattimento; fuori combattimento; (coll) pezzo di giovane

knock'out drops' spl (slang) narcotico

knoll [nol] s poggio, rialzo

knot [nɑt] s nodo; (worn as an ornament) fiocco; (in wood) nocchio; gruppo; protuberanza; (tie) nodo; (naut) nodo; **to tie the knot** (coll) sposarsi || v (pret & pp knotted; ger knotting) tr annodare; (the brow) corrugare || intr annodarsi

knot'hole' s buco lasciato da un nodo (nel legno)

knot·ty ['nɑti] adj (-tier; -tiest) nodoso; (fig) spinoso

know [no] s—**to be in the know** (coll) essere al corrente || v (pret knew [nju] or [nu]; pp known) tr & intr (by reasoning or learning) sapere; (by the senses or by perception; through acquaintance or recognition) conoscere; **as far as I know** per quanto io ne sappia; **to know about** essere al corrente di; **to know best** essere il miglior giudice; **to know how to + inf** sapere + inf; **to know it all** (coll) sapere tutto; **to know what's what** (coll) saperla lunga; **you ought to know better** dovresti vergognarti

knowable ['no·əbəl] adj conoscibile

know'-how' s sapere m, abilità f

knowingly ['no·ɪŋli] adv con conoscenza di causa; (on purpose) apposta

know'-it-all' adj & s (coll) saputello

knowledge ['nɑlɪdʒ] s (faculty) scibile m, sapere m, sapienza; (awareness, acquaintance, familiarity) conoscenza; **to have a thorough knowledge of** conoscere a fondo; **to my knowledge** per quanto io ne sappia; **with full knowledge** con conoscenza di causa; **without my knowledge** a mia insaputa

knowledgeable ['nɑlɪdʒəbəl] adj intelligente, bene informato

knuckle ['nʌkəl] s nocca; foro del cardine, cardine m; **knuckles** pugno di ferro || intr—**to knuckle down** (coll) lavorare di impegno; **to knuckle under** (coll) darsi per vinto

knurl [nʌrl] s granitura || tr godranare, zigrinare

Koran [ko'ran] or [ko'ræn] s Corano

Korea [ko'ri·ə] s la Corea

Korean [ko'ri·ən] adj & s coreano

kosher ['koʃər] adj kasher, casher, puro secondo la legge giudaica; (coll) autentico

kowtow ['kaʊ'taʊ] or ['ko'taʊ] intr inchinarsi servilmente

Kremlin ['kremlɪn] s Cremlino

Kremlinology [,kremlɪ'nɑlədʒi] s Cremlinologia

kudos ['kjudɑs] or ['kudɑs] s (coll) gloria, fama, approvazione

L

L, l [el] s dodicesima lettera dell'alfabeto inglese

la·bel ['lebəl] s marca, etichetta; (descriptive word) qualifica || v (pret & pp -beled or -belled; ger -beling or -belling) tr etichettare; qualificare

labial ['lebɪ·əl] adj & s labiale f

labor ['lebər] adj operaio || s lavoro; (toil) fatica; (childbirth) parto; (body of wage earners) manodopera; (class as contrasted with management) prestatori mpl d'opera, lavoro; **labors** fatiche fpl; **to be in labor** avere le doglie || intr lavorare; (to exert one-

self) travagliare; (*said of a ship*) rollare e beccheggiare; **to labor for** lottare per; **to labor under** soffrire di

laborato·ry ['læbərə,tori] *s* (*-ries*) laboratorio

la'bor dispute' *s* vertenza sindacale

labored ['lebərd] *adj* elaborato, artificiale; penoso, difficile

laborer ['lebərər] *s* lavoratore *m*; (*unskilled worker*) bracciante *m*, manovale *m*, uomo di fatica

laborious [lə'borɪ·əs] *adj* laborioso

la'bor un'ion *s* sindacato

Labourite ['lebə,raɪt] *s* laburista *mf*

labyrinth ['læbrrɪnθ] *s* labirinto

lace [les] *s* (*cord or string*) stringa; (*netlike ornament*) trina, merletto; (*braid*) gallone *m* ‖ *tr* stringare; merlettare; (coll) fustigare

lace'work' *s* trina, merletto, pizzo

lachrymose ['lækrɪ,mos] *adj* lacrimoso

lacing ['lesɪŋ] *s* stringa, cordone *m*; gallone *m*; (coll) battuta, frustata

lack [læk] *s* mancanza, scarsezza, difetto ‖ *tr* mancare di, scarseggiare di ‖ *intr* mancare, scarseggiare, difettare

lackadaisical [,lækə'dezɪkəl] *adj* letargico, indifferente

lackey ['læki] *s* lacchè *m*

lacking ['lækɪŋ] *prep* privo di

lack'lus'ter *adj* smorto, spento

laconic [lə'kɑnɪk] *adj* laconico

lacquer ['lækər] *s* lacca ‖ *tr* laccare

lac'quer spray' *s* lacca spray

lac'quer ware' *s* oggetti *mpl* laccati

lacu·na [le'kjunə] *s* (*-nas or -nae* [ni]) lacuna

lac·y ['lesi] *adj* (*-ier; -iest*) simile al merletto

lad [læd] *s* ragazzo, fanciullo

ladder ['lædər] *s* scala; (*stepladder hinged on top*) scaleo; (*stepping stone*) (fig) scalino

lad'der truck' *s* autocarro di pompieri munito di scale

la'dies' man' *s* beato fra le donne

la'dies' room' *s* gabinetto per signore

ladle ['ledəl] *s* ramaiolo, mestolo; (*of tinsmith*) cucchiaio ‖ *tr* scodellare

la·dy ['ledi] *s* (*-dies*) signora, dama

la'dy-bug' *s* coccinella

la'dy-fin'ger *s* savoiardo, lingua di gatto

la'dy-in-wait'ing *s* (*ladies-in-waiting*) dama di corte

la'dy-kil'ler *s* rubacuori *m*

la'dy-like' *adj* signorile; **to be ladylike** comportarsi come una signora

la'dy-love' *s* amata

la'dy of the house' *s* padrona di casa

ladyship ['ledi,ʃɪp] *s* signoria

la'dy's maid' *s* cameriera personale della signora

lag [læg] *s* ritardo ‖ *v* (*pret & pp* **lagged;** *ger* **lagging**) *intr* ritardare; **to lag behind** rimanere indietro

la'ger beer' ['lɑgər] *s* birra invecchiata

laggard ['lægərd] *s* tardo, pigro

lagoon [lə'gun] *s* laguna

laid' pa'per [led] *s* carta vergata

laid' up' *adj* messo da parte; (naut) disarmato; (coll) costretto a letto

lair [ler] *s* tana, covo

laity ['le·ɪti] *s* laicato

lake [lek] *adj* lacustre ‖ *s* lago

lamb [læm] *s* agnello

lambaste [læm'best] *tr* (*to thrash*) sferzare; (*to reprimand*) riprovare

lamb' chop' *s* cotoletta d'agnello

lambkin ['læmkɪn] *s* agnellino; (fig) innocente *mf*

lamb'skin' *s* (*leather*) pelle *f* d'agnello; (*skin with its wool*) agnello

lame [lem] *adj* zoppo; difettoso; (*disabled*) invalido; (*excuse*) debole ‖ *tr* azzoppare

lament [lə'ment] *s* lamento; lamento funebre ‖ *tr* lamentare ‖ *intr* lamentarsi

lamentable ['læməntəbəl] *or* [lə'mentəbəl] *adj* lamentevole

lamentation [,læmən'teʃən] *s* lamentazione

laminate ['læmɪ,net] *tr* laminare

lamp [læmp] *s* lampada

lamp'black' *s* nerofumo

lamp' chim'ney *s* tubo di vetro di lampada a petrolio

lamp'light' *s* luce *f* di lampada

lamp'light'er *s* lampionaio

lampoon [læm'pun] *s* satira ‖ *tr* satireggiare

lamp'post' *s* colonna del lampione

lamp'shade' *s* paralume *m*, ventola

lamp'wick' *s* lucignolo

lance [læns] *or* [lɑns] *s* lancia; (surg) lancetta ‖ *tr* (*with an oxygen lance*) tagliare col cannello ossidrico; (surg) sbrigliare, incidere col bisturi

lance' rest' *s* resta

lancet ['lænsɪt] *or* ['lɑnsɪt] *s* (surg) lancetta

land [lænd] *adj* terrestre; (*wind*) di terra ‖ *s* terra; **on land, on sea, and in the air** per mare, per terra e nel cielo; **to make land** toccare terra; **to see how the land lies** tastare terreno ‖ *tr* sbarcare; (aer) fare atterrare; (coll) pigliare ‖ *intr* sbarcare; (*to come to rest*) andare a finire; (naut) toccar terra; (aer) atterrare; **to land on one's feet** cadere in piedi; **to land on one's head** andare a gambe all'aria; **to land on the moon** allunare; **to land on the water** ammarare

land' breeze' *s* vento di terra

landed ['lændɪd] *adj* (*owning land*) terriero; (*real estate*) immobile

land'fall' *s* (*sighting land*) avvistamento; terra avvistata; (*landslide*) frana

land' grant' *s* terreno ricevuto in dono dallo stato

land'hold'er *s* proprietario terriero

landing ['lændɪŋ] *s* (*of passengers*) sbarco; (*place where passengers and goods are landed*) imbarcadero; (*of stairway*) pianerottolo; (aer, naut) atterraggio

land'ing bea'con *s* radiofaro d'atterraggio

land'ing card' *s* cartoncino di sbarco

land'ing craft' *s* imbarcazione da sbarco

land'ing field' *s* campo d'atterraggio

land'ing flap' *s* (aer) iposostentatore *m*

land'ing gear' *s* (aer) carrello d'atterraggio

land'ing strip' *s* (aer) pista d'atterraggio

land'la'dy *s* (-dies) (*of an apartment*) padrona di casa; (*of a lodging house*) affittacamere *f;* (*of an inn*) ostessa

landlocked ['lænd‚lɑkt] *adj* circondato da terra

land'lord' *s* (*of an apartment*) padrone *m* di casa; (*of a lodging house*) affittacamere *m;* (*of an inn*) oste *m*

land·lubber ['lænd‚lʌbər] *s* marinaio d'acqua dolce

land'mark' *s* (*boundary stone*) pietra di confine; (*distinguishing landscape feature*) punto di riferimento; (fig) pietra miliare

land' of'fice *s* ufficio del catasto

land'-office busi'ness *s* (coll) sacco d'affari

land'own'er *s* proprietario terriero

landscape ['lænd‚skep] *s* paesaggio ‖ *tr* abbellire

land'scape gar'dener *s* giardiniere *m* ornamentale

land'scape paint'er *s* paesista *mf*

landscapist ['lænd‚skepɪst] *s* paesista *mf*

land'slide' *s* frana; (fig) vittoria strepitosa

landward ['lændwərd] *adv* verso terra, verso la costa

land' wind' *s* vento di terra

lane [len] *s* (*narrow street*) vicolo, viuzza; (*of a highway*) corsia; (naut) rotta; (aer) corridoio

langsyne [‚læŋ'saɪn] *s* (Scotch) tempo passato ‖ *adv* (Scotch) molto tempo fa

language ['læŋgwɪdʒ] *s* lingua; (*style of language*) linguaggio; (*of a special group of people*) gergo

lan'guage lab'oratory *s* laboratorio linguistico

languid ['læŋgwɪd] *adj* languido

languish ['læŋgwɪʃ] *intr* languire; affettare languore

languor ['læŋgər] *s* languore *m*

languorous ['læŋgərəs] *adj* languido; (*causing languor*) snervante

lank [læŋk] *adj* scarnito, sparuto

lank·y ['læŋki] *adj* (-ier; -iest) scarnito, sparuto

lantern ['læntərn] *s* lanterna

lan'tern slide' *s* diapositiva

lanyard ['lænjərd] *s* (naut) drizza; (mil) aghetto, cordellina

lap [læp] *s* (*of human body or clothing*) grembo; (*with the tongue*) leccata; (*of the waves*) sciacquio; (sports) giro, tappa; **in the lap of** in mezzo a, e.g., **in the lap of luxury** in mezzo alle delicatezze ‖ *v* (*pret & pp* **lapped;** *ger* **lapping**) *tr* lappare; (*said, e.g., of waves*) lambire; (*to fold*) piegare; (*to overlap*) sovrapporre; **to lap up** lappare; (coll) accettare con entusiasmo ‖ *intr* sovrapporsi; **to lap against** (*said of the waves*) lambire; **to lap over** traboccare

lap'board' *s* tavolino da lavoro da tenersi sulle ginocchia

lap' dissolve' *s* (mov) dissolvenza incrociata

lap' dog' *s* cagnolino da salotto

lapel [lə'pɛl] *s* risvolto

Lap'land' *s* la Lapponia

Laplander ['læp‚lændər] *s* lappone *mf*

Lapp [læp] *s* lappone *mf;* (*language*) lappone *m*

lap' robe' *s* coperta da viaggio

lapse [læps] *s* (*interval*) spazio di tempo; (*fall, decline*) caduta; (*of memory*) perdita; errore *m;* (ins) risoluzione; (law) decadenza ‖ *intr* cadere, ricadere; cadere in disuso; (*said of time*) passare; (ins) risolversi; (law) decadere

lap'wing' *s* pavoncella

larce·ny ['lɑrsəni] *s* (-nies) furto

larch [lɑrtʃ] *s* larice *m*

lard [lɑrd] *s* strutto ‖ *tr* lardellare

larder ['lɑrdər] *s* dispensa

large [lɑrdʒ] *adj* grande, grosso ‖ *s—* **at large** in libertà

large' intes'tine *s* intestino crasso

largely ['lɑrdʒli] *adv* in gran parte

large'-scale' *adj* su larga scala

lariat ['læri‚ət] *s* lazo, laccio

lark [lɑrk] *s* allodola; (coll) burla; **to go on a lark** (coll) far festa

lark'spur' *s* (*rocket larkspur*) sprone *m* di cavaliere; (*field larkspur*) consolida reale

lar·va ['lɑrvə] *s* (-vae [vi]) larva

laryngitis [‚lærɪn'dʒaɪtɪs] *s* laringite *f*

laryngoscope [lə'rɪŋgə‚skop] *s* laringoscopio

larynx ['lærɪŋks] *s* (**larynxes** or **larynges** [lə'rɪndʒiz]) laringe *f*

lascivious [lə'sɪvɪ·əs] *adj* lascivo

lasciviousness [lə'sɪvɪ·əsnɪs] *s* lascivia

laser ['lesər] *s* (acronym) (**light amplification by stimulated emission of radiation**) laser *m*

lash [læʃ] *s* (*cord on end of whip*) sverzino; (*blow with whip; scolding*) staffilata; (*of animal's tail*) colpo; (*eyelash*) ciglio; (fig) assalto ‖ *tr* (*to whip*) frustare; (*to bind*) legare; (*to shake*) agitare; (*to attack with words*) staffilare ‖ *intr* lanciarsi; **to lash out at** attaccare violentemente

lashing ['læʃɪŋ] *s* legatura; (*severe scolding*) staffilata; (*fastening with a rope*) (naut) rizza

lass [læs] *s* ragazza, giovane *f;* innamorata

las·so ['læso] or [læ'su] *s* (-sos or -soes) lasso, lazo ‖ *tr* pigliare col lasso

last [læst] or [lɑst] *adj* ultimo, passato; (*most recent*) scorso; **before last** ierlaltro, e.g., **the night before last** ierlaltro notte; **every last one** tutti senza eccezione; **last but one** penultimo ‖ *s* ultima persona; ultima cosa; fine *f;* (*for holding shoes*) forma; **at last** alla fine; **at long last!** finalmente!; **stick to your last!** fa' il mestiere tuo!; **the last of the month** alla fine del mese; **to breathe one's last** dare l'ultimo sospiro; **to see the last of s.o.** vedere qlcu per l'ultima volta; **to the last** fino alla fine || *adv* ultimo, per ultimo, alla fine || *intr* durare, continuare

lasting ['læstɪŋ] or ['lɑstɪŋ] *adj* duraturo, durevole

lastly ['læstli] or ['lɑstli] *adv* finalmente, in conclusione

last'-min'ute news' *s* notizie *fpl* dell'ultima ora

last' name' *s* cognome *m*

last' night' *adv* ieri sera; la notte scorsa

last' quar'ter *s* ultimo quarto

last' sleep' *s* ultimo sonno

last' straw' *s* ultima, colmo

Last' Sup'per *s* Ultima Cena

last will' and tes'tament *s* ultime volontà *fpl*

last' word' *s* ultima parola; (*latest style*) ultima novità, ultimo grido

latch [læt/] *s* saliscendi *m*; (*wooden*) nottola || *tr* chiudere col saliscendi

latch'key' *s* chiave *f* per saliscendi

latch'string' *s*—**the latchstring is out** faccia come fosse a casa Sua

late [let] *adj* (*happening after the usual time*) tardo; (*person*) in ritardo; (*hour of the night*) avanzato; (*news*) dell'ultima ora, recente; (*incumbent of an office*) predecessore, ex, passato; (*coming toward the end of a period*) tardivo; (*deceased*) defunto, fu; **in the late 30's, 40's, etc.** verso la fine del decennio che va dal 1930, 1940, etc. al 1940, 1950, etc.; **of late** recentemente; **to be late in** + *ger* essere in ritardo a + *inf*; **to grow late** farsi tardi; **to keep late hours** fare le ore piccole || *adv* tardi; in ritardo; **late in** (*the week, the month, etc.*) alla fine di; **late in life** a un'età avanzata

latecomer ['let ˌkʌmər] *s* ritardatario

lateen' sail' [læ'tin] *s* vela latina

lately ['letli] *adv* recentemente

latent ['letənt] *adj* latente

later ['letər] *adj comp* più tardi; (*event*) susseguente; **later than** posteriore a || *adv comp* più tardi; **later on** più tardi; **see you later** (coll) arrivederci, a ben presto

lateral ['lætərəl] *adj* laterale

lath [læθ] or [lɑθ] *s* listello, striscia di legno || *tr* mettere listelli su

lathe [leð] *s* tornio

lather ['læðər] *s* schiuma di sapone; schiuma || *tr* insaponare; (coll) bastonare || *intr* schiumare

lathery ['læðəri] *adj* schiumoso

lathing ['læθɪŋ] or ['lɑθɪŋ] *s* costruzione con listelli

Latin ['lætɪn] or ['lætən] *adj & s* latino

Lat'in Amer'ica *s* l'America latina

Lat'in-Amer'ican *adj* dell'America latina

Lat'in Amer'ican *s* abitante *mf* dell'America latina

latitude ['lætɪ ˌtjud] or ['lætɪ ˌtud] *s* latitudine *f*

latrine [lə'trin] *s* latrina militare

latter ['lætər] *adj* (*more recent*) posteriore; (*of two*) secondo; **the latter** questo; **the latter part of** la fine di

lattice ['lætɪs] *s* graticcio || *tr* munire di graticcio, graticciare

lat'tice gird'er *s* trave *f* a traliccio

lat'tice-work' *s* graticcio, traliccio

Latvia ['lætvɪ‧ə] *s* la Lettonia

laud [lɔd] *tr* lodare

laudable ['lɔdəbəl] *adj* lodevole

laudanum ['lɔdənəm] or ['lɔdnəm] *s* laudano

laudatory ['lɔdə ˌtori] *adj* lodativo

laugh [læf] or [lɑf] *s* riso || *tr*—**to laugh away** dissipare ridendo; **to laugh off** prendere sotto gamba, non dare importanza a || *intr* ridere, ridersi; **to laugh at** ridersi di; **to laugh up one's sleeve** ridere sotto i baffi

laughable ['læfəbəl] or ['lɑfəbəl] *adj* risibile

laughing ['læfɪŋ] or ['lɑfɪŋ] *adj* che ride; **to be no laughing matter** non esserci niente da ridere || *s* riso

laugh'ing gas' *s* gas *m* esilarante

laugh'ing-stock' *s* ludibrio, zimbello

laughter ['læftər] or ['lɑftər] *s* riso

launch [lɔnt/] or [lɑnt/] *s* (*of a ship*) varo; (*of a rocket*) lancio; (naut) lancia, scialuppa || *tr* (*to throw; to send forth*) lanciare; (naut) varare || *intr* lanciarsi

launching ['lɔnt/ɪŋ] or ['lɑnt/ɪŋ] *s* lancio; (*of a ship*) varo

launch'ing pad' *s* piattaforma di lancio

launder ['lɔndər] or ['lɑndər] *tr* lavare e stirare || *intr* riuscire dopo il lavaggio

launderer ['lɔndərər] or ['lɑndərər] *s* lavandaio stiratore *m*

laundress ['lɔndrɪs] or ['lɑndrɪs] *s* lavandaia stiratrice *f*

laundromat ['lɔndrə ˌmæt] or ['lɑndrə ˌmæt] *s* (trademark) lavanderia a gettone

laun·dry ['lɔndri] or ['lɑndri] *s* (**-dries**) lavanderia; (*clothing*) bucato

laun'dry·man' *s* (**-men'**) lavandaio

laun'dry·wom'an *s* (**-wom'en**) lavandaia

laureate ['lɔrɪ‧ɪt] *adj* laureato || *s* laureato; poeta laureato

lau·rel ['lɔrəl] or ['lɑrəl] *s* lauro, alloro; **laurels** (fig) alloro; **to rest** or **sleep on one's laurels** dormire sugli allori || *v* (*pret & pp* **-reled** or **-relled**; *ger* **-reling** or **-relling**) *tr* laureare

lava ['lɑvə] or ['lævə] *s* lava

lavato·ry ['lævə ˌtori] *s* (**-ries**) (*room*) gabinetto da bagno; (*bowl*) lavabo; (*toilet*) gabinetto di decenza, cesso

lavender ['lævəndər] *s* lavanda

lavish ['lævɪ/] *adj* prodigo || *tr* prodigare, profondere

law [lɔ] *s* (*of man, of nature, of science*) legge *f*; (*study, profession of law*) diritto; **to enter the law** farsi avvocato; **to go to law** ricorrere alla legge; **to lay down the law** dettar legge; **to maintain law and order** mantenere la pace interna; **to practice law** fare l'avvocato

law-abiding ['lɔ‧əˌbaɪdɪŋ] *adj* osservante della legge

law'break'er *s* violatore *m* della legge

law' court' s tribunale m di giustizia
lawful ['lɔfəl] adj legale, legittimo
lawless ['lɔlɪs] adj illegale; (unbridled) sfrenato
law'mak'er s legislatore m
lawn [lɔn] s tappeto erboso; (fabric) batista
lawn' mow'er s tosatrice f
law' of'fice s ufficio d'avvocato
law' of na'tions s diritto delle genti
law' of the jun'gle s legge f della giungla
law' stu'dent s studente m di legge
law'suit' s causa, lite f, processo
lawyer ['lɔjər] s avvocato, legale m
lax [læks] adj (in morals) lasso, rilassato; (rope) lento; (negligent) trascurato; vago, indeterminato
laxative ['læksətɪv] adj purgativo ‖ s purga, purgante m
lay [le] adj (not belonging to the clergy) laico; (not having special training) non dotto, profano ‖ s configurazione, disposizione ‖ v (pret & pp laid [led]) tr mettere, collocare; (snares) tendere; (one's eyes; a stone) porre; (blame) dare, gettare; (a bet) fare; (for consideration) presentare; (the table) imbandire; (said of a hen) deporre; (plans) impostare; (to locate) disporre; (to be laid in (said of a scene) aver luogo in; **to lay aside** mettere da parte; **to lay down** dichiarare; (one's life) dare; (one's arms) deporre; **to lay low** abbattere; uccidere; **to lay off** (workers) licenziare; (to measure) marcare; (slang) lasciare in pace; **to lay open** rivelare; (to a danger) esporre; **to lay out** estendere; preparare, disporre; (a corpse) comporre; (money) (coll) sborsare; **to lay over** posporre; **to lay up** mettere da parte; obbligare a letto; (naut) disarmare ‖ intr (said of a hen) fare le uova; **to lay about** dar botte da orbi; **to lay for** (slang) attendere al varco; **to lay off** (coll) cessare di lavorare; **to lay over** trattenersi, fermarsi; **to lay to** (naut) navigare alla cappa
lay' broth'er s frate m secolare; converso
lay' day' s (com) stallia
layer ['le·ər] s (of paint) mano f; (of bricks) testa; (e.g., of rocks) strato, falda; (anat) pannicolo; (hort) propaggine f ‖ tr (hort) propagginare
lay'er cake' s dolce m a strati
layette [le'ɛt] s corredino
lay' fig'ure s manichino
laying ['le·ɪŋ] s posa; (of eggs) deporre m; (of a wire) tendere m
lay'man s (-men) (member of the laity) laico, secolare m; (not a member of a special profession) laico, profano
lay'off' s (dismissal of workers) licenziamento; (period of unemployment) disoccupazione
lay' of the land' s andamento generale
lay'out' s piano; (sketch) tracciato; (of tools) armamentario; (coll) residenza; (typ) menabò m; (coll) banchetto, festino

lay'o'ver s fermata in un viaggio
lay' sis'ter s suora al secolo; conversa
laziness ['lezɪnɪs] s pigrizia
la-zy ['lezi] adj (-zier; -ziest) pigro
la'zy-bones' s (coll) poltrone m
lea [li] s (fallow land) maggese m; (meadow) prato
lead [led] adj plumbeo ‖ s piombo; (of lead pencil) mina; (for sounding depth) (naut) scandaglio; (typ) interlinea ‖ [led] v (pret & pp leaded; ger leading) tr impiombare; (typ) interlineare ‖ [lid] s (foremost place) primato; (guidance) guida, direzione; (leash) guinzaglio; (journ) testata; (cards) mano f, prima mano; (elec) conduttore m; (mach) passo; (min) filone m; (rad, telv) filo d'entrata; (theat) ruolo principale; (theat) primo attore; (theat) prima attrice; **to take the lead** prendere il comando ‖ [lid] v (pret & pp led [led]) tr condurre, portare; (to command) comandare, essere alla testa di; (an orchestra) dirigere; (a good or bad life) fare; (s.o. into vice) trascinare; (cards) cominciare a giocare; (elec, mach) anticipare; **to lead astray** forviare ‖ intr essere in testa, guidare; prendere l'offensiva; (said of a road) condurre; (cards) cominciare a giocare; **to lead to** risultare in; **to lead up to** andare a condurre a
leaden ['ledən] adj (of lead; like lead) plumbeo; (sluggish) tardo; (with sleep) carico; triste
leader ['lidər] s capo, comandante m; (ringleader) capobanda m; (of an orchestra) direttore m; (among animals) guidaiolo; (in a dance) ballerino guidaiolo; (sports) capintesta m; (journ) articolo di fondo
lead'er dog' s cane m guida di ciechi
leadership ['lidər,ʃɪp] s comando, direzione; doti fpl di comando
leading ['lidɪŋ] adj principale; primo; dirigente, preeminente
lead'ing ar'ticle s articolo di fondo
lead'ing edge' s (aer) bordo d'attacco
lead'ing la'dy s prima attrice
lead'ing man' s (men') primo attore
lead'ing ques'tion s domanda suggestiva, domanda orientatrice
lead'ing strings' spl dande fpl
lead'-in wire' ['lid,ɪn] s filo d'antenna
lead' pen'cil [led] s lapis m, matita
leaf [lif] s (leaves [livz]) (of plant) foglia; (of vine) pampino; (of paper) foglio; (of double door) battente m; (of table) asse m a ribalta; **to turn over a new leaf** ricominciare una nuova vita ‖ intr fogliare; **to leaf through** sfogliare
leafless ['liflɪs] adj senza foglie
leaflet ['liflɪt] s manifestino, volantino; (of plant) foglietina
leaf' spring' s molla a balestra
leaf'stalk' s picciolo
leaf-y ['lifi] adj (-ier; -iest) foglioso, frondoso
league [lig] s lega ‖ tr associare ‖ intr associarsi

League' of Na'tions s Società f delle Nazioni

leak [lik] s (in a roof) stillicidio; (in a ship) falla; (of water, gas, steam) fuga; (of electricity) dispersione; buco, fessura; (of news) filtrazione; **to spring a leak** avere una perdita; (naut) cominciare a far acqua ‖ tr (gas, liquids) perdere, lasciar scappare; (news) lasciar trapelare ‖ intr (said of water, gas etc.,) perdere, scappare; (said of a barrel) spillare; (naut) fare acqua; (of water, gas of money) andarsene; **to leak away** (said of money) andarsene; **to leak out** (said of news) trapelare

leakage ['likɪdʒ] s perdita, fuoruscita, fuga; (elec) dispersione; (com) colaggio

leak·y ['liki] adj (-ier; -iest) che perde; (naut) che fa acqua; (coll) indiscreto

lean [lin] adj magro, secco; (gasoline mixture) povero ‖ v (pret & pp **leaned** or **leant** [lɛnt]) tr inclinare; appoggiare ‖ intr pendere, inclinarsi; (fig) inclinare, tendere; **to lean against** appoggiarsi a, addossarsi a; **to lean back** sdraiarsi; **to lean on** appoggiarsi su; **to lean out (of)** sporgersi (da); **to lean over backwards** fare di tutto; **to lean toward** (fig) tendere a, avere un'inclinazione per

leaning ['linɪŋ] adj inclinato, pendente ‖ s inclinazione

lean'ing tow'er s torre f pendente

lean'-to' s (-tos) tetto a una falda

leap [lip] s salto, balzo; **by leaps and bounds** a passi da gigante; **leap in the dark** salto nel vuoto ‖ v (pret & pp **leaped** or **leapt** [lɛpt]) tr saltare ‖ intr saltare; (said of one's heart) balzare

leap'frog' s cavallina; **to play leapfrog** giocare alla cavallina

leap' year' s anno bisestile

learn [lʌrn] s (pret & pp **learned** or **learnt** [lʌrnt]) tr imparare; imparare a memoria; (news) apprendere ‖ intr istruirsi, apprendere

learned ['lʌrnɪd] adj dotto; (word) colto

learn'ed jour'nal s rivista scientifica

learn'ed soci'ety s associazione di eruditi

learn'ed word' s parola dotta

learn'ed world' s mondo di dotti

learner ['lʌrnər] s apprendista mf; studente m; (beginner) principiante mf

learning ['lʌrnɪŋ] s istruzione; (scholarship) erudizione

lease [lis] s locazione, contratto d'affitto; **a new lease on life** nuove prospettive di felicità; vita nuova (dopo una malattia) ‖ tr locare; prendere in affitto ‖ intr affittare

lease'hold' adj affittato ‖ s beni mpl sotto locazione

leash [liʃ] s guinzaglio; **to strain at the leash** mordere il freno ‖ tr frenare, controllare

least [list] adj minore, menomo, minimo ‖ s (il) meno; **at least** or **at the least** per lo meno, quanto meno;

not in the least nient'affatto ‖ adv meno

leather ['lɛðər] s cuoio

leath'er-back tur'tle s tartaruga di mare

leath'er goods' store' s pelletteria

leathery ['lɛðəri] adj coriaceo

leave [liv] s (permission) permesso; (permission to be absent) licenza; (farewell) commiato; **on leave** in licenza; **to take French leave** andarsene all'inglese; **to take leave (of)** prender congedo (da) ‖ v (pret & pp **left** [lɛft]) tr (to go away from) lasciare, uscire da; (to let stay) lasciare; (to bequeath) lasciare in testamento; **leave it to me!** lasciami farei; **to be left** restare, e.g., **the door was left open** la porta restò aperta; esserci, e.g., **there is no bread left** non c'è più pane; **to leave alone** lasciare in pace; **to leave no stone unturned** cercare ogni possibilità; **to leave off** abbandonare, lasciare; **to leave out** omettere; **to leave things as they are** lasciar stare le cose ‖ intr andarsene; (said of a conveyance) partire

leaven ['lɛvən] s lievito ‖ tr lievitare; (fig) impregnare, permeare

leavening ['lɛvənɪŋ] s lievito

leave' of ab'sence s licenza; (without pay) aspettativa

leave'-tak'ing s commiato

leavings ['livɪŋz] spl rifiuti mpl

Leba·nese [ˌlɛbə'niz] adj libanese ‖ s (-nese) libanese mf

Lebanon ['lɛbənən] s il Libano

lecher ['lɛtʃər] s libertino

lecherous ['lɛtʃərəs] adj libidinoso

lechery ['lɛtʃəri] s lussuria

lectern ['lɛktərn] s leggio

lecture ['lɛktʃər] s conferenza; (tedious reprimand) pistolotto ‖ tr dare una conferenza a; sermoneggiare ‖ intr fare una conferenza; sermoneggiare

lecturer ['lɛktʃərər] s conferenziere m

ledge [lɛdʒ] s cornice f, cornicione m

ledger ['lɛdʒər] s (com) libro mastro

ledg'er line' s (mus) rigo supplementare

lee [li] s (shelter) rifugio; (naut) parte f sottovento; **lees** feccia

leech [litʃ] s mignatta, sanguisuga; **to stick like a leech** attaccarsi come una sanguisuga

leek [lik] s porro

leer [lɪr] s occhiata lussuriosa or maligna ‖ intr—**to leer at** guardare di sbieco, sbirciare

leer·y ['lɪri] adj (-ier; -iest) sospettoso

leeward ['liwərd] or ['luˑərd] adj di sottovento ‖ s sottovento, poggia ‖ adv sottovento

lee'way' s (aer, naut) deriva, scarroccio; (in time) (coll) tolleranza; (coll) libertà f d'azione

left [lɛft] adj sinistro; (pol) di sinistra ‖ s sinistra; (boxing) sinistro ‖ adv alla sinistra

left' field' s fuoricampo di sinistra

left'-hand' drive' s guida a sinistra

left-handed ['lɛft'hændɪd] adj (individual) mancino; (awkward) goffo;

(*compliment*) ambiguo; (*mach*) sinistrorso

leftish ['lɛftɪʃ] *adj* sinistrista

leftist ['lɛftɪst] *adj* di sinistra ‖ *s* membro della sinistra

left'o'ver *adj & s* rimanente *m;* **leftovers** resti *mpl*

left'-wing' *adj* di sinistra

left-winger ['lɛft'wɪŋər] *s* (coll) membro dell'estrema sinistra; (coll) membro della sinistra

leg [lɛg] *s* (*of man, animal, table, chair; of trousers*) gamba; (*of fowl; of lamb*) coscia; (*of boot*) gambale *m;* (*of a journey*) tappa; **to be on one's last legs** essere agli estremi, essere ridotto alla disperazione; **to not have a leg to stand on** (coll) non avere la minima giustificazione; **to pull the leg of** (coll) prendere in giro, burlarsi di; **to shake a leg** (coll) affrettarsi; (*to dance*) (coll) ballare; **to stretch one's legs** sgranchirsi le gambe

lega·cy ['lɛgəsi] *s* (-cies) legato

legal ['ligəl] *adj* legale

legali·ty [lɪ'gælɪti] *s* (-ties) legalità *f*

legalize ['ligə,laɪz] *tr* legalizzare

le'gal ten'der *s* denaro a corso legale

legate ['lɛgɪt] *s* legato

legatee [,lɛgə'ti] *s* legatario

legation [lɪ'geʃən] *s* legazione

legend ['lɛdʒənd] *s* leggenda

legendary ['lɛdʒən,dɛri] *adj* leggendario

legerdemain [,lɛdʒərdɪ'men] *s* gioco di prestigio; (*trickery*) imbroglio

legging ['lɛgɪŋ] *s* gambale *m*

leg·gy ['lɛgi] *adj* (-gier; -giest) dalle gambe lunghe

leg'horn' *s* cappello di paglia di Firenze; gallina bianca livornese ‖ **Leghorn** *s* Livorno

legible ['lɛdʒɪbəl] *adj* leggibile

legion ['lidʒən] *s* legione *f*

legislate ['lɛdʒɪs,let] *tr* ordinare per mezzo di legge ‖ *intr* legiferare

legislation [,lɛdʒɪs'leʃən] *s* legislazione

legislative ['lɛdʒɪs,letɪv] *adj* legislativo

legislator ['lɛdʒɪs,letər] *s* legislatore *m*

legislature ['lɛdʒɪs,letʃər] *s* legislatura; corpo legislativo

legitimacy [lɪ'dʒɪtɪməsi] *s* legittimità *f*

legitimate [lɪ'dʒɪtɪmɪt] *adj* legittimo ‖ [lɪ'dʒɪtɪ,met] *tr* legittimare

legit'imate dra'ma *s* teatro serio

legitimize [lɪ'dʒɪtɪ,maɪz] *tr* legittimare

leg' of lamb' *s* cosciotto d'agnello

legume ['lɛgjum] *or* [lɪ'gjum] *s* (*pod*) legume *m;* (*table vegetables*) legumi *mpl;* (bot) leguminose *fpl*

leg'work' *s* lavoro che involve molto cammino

leisure ['liʒər] *or* ['lɛʒər] *s* ozio; **at leisure** senza fretta; disoccupato; **at one's leisure** quando si abbia un po' di tempo libero

lei'sure class' *s* gente agiata

lei'sure hours' *spl* ore *fpl* d'ozio

leisurely ['liʒərli] *or* ['lɛʒərli] *adj* lento ‖ *adv* lentamente, a tempo perso

lei'sure time' *s* tempo libero

lemon ['lɛmən] *s* limone *m;* (*car*) (coll) catorcio

lemonade [,lɛmə'ned] *s* limonata

lem'on squeez'er *s* spremilimoni *m*

lend [lɛnd] *s* (*pret & pp* **lent** [lɛnt]) *tr* prestare; (*a hand*) dare

lender ['lɛndər] *s* prestatore *m*

lend'ing li'brary *s* biblioteca circolante

length [lɛŋθ] *s* lunghezza; (*of time*) durata; **at length** finalmente; **to go to any lengths** fare quanto è possibile; essere disposto a tutto; **to keep at arm's length** (*someone else*) tenere a distanza (qlcu); (*said of oneself*) tenere la distanza

lengthen ['lɛŋθən] *tr* allungare ‖ *intr* allungarsi

length'wise' *adj* longitudinale ‖ *adv* per il lungo

length·y ['lɛŋθi] *adj* (-ier; -iest) lungo, prolungato

lenien·cy ['linɪ·ənsi] *s* (-cies) indulgenza

lenient ['linɪ·ənt] *adj* indulgente, clemente

lens [lɛnz] *s* lente *f;* (*of the eye*) cristallino

Lent [lɛnt] *s* quaresima

Lenten ['lɛntən] *adj* quaresimale

lentil ['lɛntəl] *s* lenticchia

Leo ['li·o] *s* (astr) il Leone

leopard ['lɛpərd] *s* leopardo

leotard ['li·ə,tard] *s* calzamaglia

leper ['lɛpər] *s* lebbroso

leprosy ['lɛprəsi] *s* lebbra

leprous ['lɛprəs] *adj* lebbroso; (*of an animal or plant*) squamoso

Lesbian ['lɛzbɪ·ən] *adj* lesbico ‖ *s* lesbico; (*female homosexual*) lesbica

lesbianism ['lɛzbɪ·ə,nɪzəm] *s* lesbismo

lese majesty ['liz'mædʒɪsti] *s* delitto di lesa maestà

lesion ['liʒən] *s* lesione

less [lɛs] *adj* minore ‖ *adv* meno; **less and less** sempre meno; **less than** meno che; (*followed by numeral or personal pron*) meno di; (*followed by verb*) meno di quanto ‖ *s* meno

lessee [lɛs'i] *s* locatario; (*of business establishment*) concessionario

lessen ['lɛsən] *tr* diminuire, ridurre ‖ *intr* diminuire, ridursi

lesser ['lɛsər] *adj comp* minore

lesson ['lɛsən] *s* lezione

lessor ['lɛsər] *s* locatore *m*

lest [lɛst] *conj* per paura che

let [lɛt] *v* (*pret & pp* **let;** *ger* **letting**) *tr* permettere; (*to rent*) affittare; **let +** *inf* **che + ** *subj,* e.g., **let him go** che vada; **let alone** tanto meno; senza menzionare; **let good enough alone** essere contento dell'onesto; **let us +** *inf* **= 1st pl impv,** e.g., **let us sing** cantiamo; **to let** da affittare; **to let alone** lasciare in pace; **to let be** lasciar stare; **to let by** lasciar passare; **to let down** far scendere; deludere; tradire; abbandonare; **to let fly** (*insults*) lanciare; **to let go** lasciar libero; vendere; **to let in** fare entrare; **to let it go at that** non parlarne più; **to let know** far sapere; **to**

let loose sciogliere; **to let out** lasciar uscire; (*a secret*) divulgare; (*a scream*) lasciarsi scappare; (*to enlarge*) allargare; affittare; **to let through** lasciar passare; **to let up** lasciar salire; lasciar alzare ‖ *intr* affittare; **to let down** diminuire gli sforzi; **to let go of** disfarsi di; **one's** **to let on** (coll) fare finta; **to not let on** (coll) non lasciar trapelare; **to let out** (said, *e.g.*, *of school*) terminare; **to let up** (coll) cessare; (coll) diminuire

let'down' *s* diminuzione; smacco, umiliazione; delusione

lethal ['liθəl] *adj* letale

lethargic [lɪ'θɑrdʒɪk] *adj* letargico

lethar·gy ['lɛθərdʒi] *s* (**-gies**) letargo

Lett [lɛt] *s* lettone *mf*; (*language*) lettone *m*

letter ['lɛtər] *s* lettera; **letters** (*literature*) lettere *fpl*, letteratura; **to the letter** alla lettera ‖ *tr* marcare con lettere

let'ter box' *s* cassetta delle lettere

let'ter car'rier *s* postino

let'ter drop' *s* buca delle lettere

let'ter·head' *s* capolettera *m*; (*paper with printed heading*) carta da lettera intestata

lettering ['lɛtərɪŋ] *s* iscrizione; lettere *fpl*

let'ter of cred'it *s* lettera di credito

let'ter o'pener ['opənər] *s* tagliacarte *m*

let'ter pa'per *s* carta da lettere

let'ter-per'fect *adj* alla lettera; che sa alla perfezione

let'ter-press' *s* stampato in tipografia ‖ *adv* a stampa tipografica

let'ter scales' *spl* pesalettere *m*

let'ter-word' *s* sigla

Lettish ['lɛtɪʃ] *adj* & *s* lettone *m*

lettuce ['lɛtɪs] *s* lattuga

let'up' *s* (coll) pausa, sosta; (coll) tregua; **without letup** (coll) senza posa

leucorrhea [,lukə'ri·ə] *s* leucorrea

leukemia [lu'kimɪ·ə] *s* leucemia

Levant [lɪ'vænt] *s* levante *m*

levee ['lɛvi] *s* (*embankment*) argine *m*; (*reception*) ricevimento

lev·el ['lɛvəl] *adj* piano; livellato; equilibrato; **level with** a livello di; **one's level best** (coll) il proprio meglio ‖ *s* (*instrument*) livella; (*degree of elevation*) livello; (*flat surface*) spianata, pianura; **on the level** (slang) onesto; onestamente; **to find one's level** trovare il proprio ambiente ‖ *v* (*pret* & *pp* **-eled** or **-elled**; *ger* **-eling** or **-elling**) *tr* livellare; (*to flatten out*) spianare; (*e.g.*, *prices*) pareggiare, ragguagliare; (*a gun*) puntare; (coll) gettare a terra; (fig) dirigere ‖ *intr*— **to level off** (aer) volare orizzontalmente

level-headed ['lɛvəl'hɛdɪd] *adj* equilibrato

lev'eling rod' *s* stadia

lever ['livər] or ['lɛvər] *s* leva ‖ *tr* far leva su ‖ *intr* far leva

leverage ['livərɪdʒ] or ['lɛvərɪdʒ] *s* azione di una leva; (fig) potere *m*

leviathan [lɪ'vaɪ·əθən] *s* leviatano

levitation [,lɛvɪ'teʃən] *s* levitazione

levi·ty ['lɛvɪti] *s* (**-ties**) leggerezza

lev·y ['lɛvi] *s* (**-ies**) (*of taxes*) esazione; (*of money*) tributo; (*of troops*) leva ‖ *v* (*pret* & *pp* **-ied**) *tr* (*a tax*) imporre; (*soldiers*) reclutare; (*war*) fare

lewd [lud] *adj* (*lustful*) lascivo; osceno

lexical ['lɛksɪkəl] *adj* lessicale

lexicographer [,lɛksɪ'kɑgrəfər] *s* lessicografo

lexicographic(al) [,lɛksɪko'græfɪk(əl)] *adj* lessicografico

lexicography [,lɛksɪ'kɑgrəfi] *s* lessicografia

lexicology [,lɛksɪ'kɑlədʒi] *s* lessicologia

lexicon ['lɛksɪkən] *s* lessico

liabili·ty [,laɪ·ə'bɪlɪti] *s* (**-ties**) svantaggio; responsabilità *f*; (*e.g.*, *to disease*) tendenza; (com) passivo; **liabilities** debiti *mpl*; (com) passivo

liabil'ity insur'ance *s* assicurazione sulla responsabilità civile

liable ['laɪ·əbəl] *adj* (*e.g.*, *to disease*; *e.g.*, *to make mistakes*) soggetto; responsabile; probabile; (*e.g.*, *to a fine*) passibile

liaison ['li·ə,zɑn] or [li'ɛzən] *s* legame *m*; relazione illecita; (mil, nav) collegamento; (phonet) legamento

li'aison of'ficer *s* ufficiale *m* di collegamento

liar ['laɪ·ər] *s* bugiardo, mentitore *m*

libation [laɪ'beʃən] *s* (joc) libazione, bevuta

li·bel ['laɪbəl] *s* diffamazione; (*defamatory writing*) libello ‖ *v* (*pret* & *pp* **-beled** or **-belled**; *ger* **-beling** or **-belling**) *tr* diffamare

libelous ['laɪbələs] *adj* diffamatorio

liberal ['lɪbərəl] *adj* liberale; (*translation*) libero ‖ *s* liberale *mf*

liberali·ty [,lɪbə'rælɪti] *s* (**-ties**) liberalità *f*; (*breadth of mind*) ampiezza di vedute

liberal-minded ['lɪbərəl'maɪndɪd] *adj* liberale, tollerante

liberate ['lɪbə,ret] *tr* liberare

liberation [,lɪbə'reʃən] *s* liberazione

liberator ['lɪbə,retər] *s* liberatore *m*

libertine ['lɪbər,tin] *adj* & *s* libertino

liber·ty ['lɪbərti] *s* (**-ties**) libertà *f*; **to take the liberty** to permettersi di

liberty·loving ['lɪbərti'lʌvɪŋ] *adj* amante della libertà

libidinous [lɪ'bɪdɪnəs] *adj* libidinoso

libido [lɪ'bido] or [lɪ'baɪdo] *s* libidine *f*; (*psychoanal*) libido *f*

Libra ['laɪbrə] or ['lɑɪbrə] *s* (astr) Bilancia

librarian [laɪ'brɛrɪ·ən] *s* bibliotecario

librar·y ['laɪ,brɛri] or ['laɪbrɛri] *s* (**-ies**) biblioteca; (*room in a house*; *collection of books*) libreria

li'brary num'ber *s* segnatura

li'brary sci'ence *s* biblioteconomia

libret·to [lɪ'brɛto] *s* (**-tos**) (mus) libretto

Libya ['lɪbɪ·ə] *s* la Libia

license ['laɪsəns] *s* licenza; (aut) patente *f* ‖ *tr* dare la licenza a

li'cense num'ber *s* numero di targa di circolazione

li'cense plate' or **tag'** *s* targa di circolazione

licentious [laɪˈsɛnʃəs] *adj* licenzioso

lichen [ˈlaɪkən] *s* lichene *m*

lick [lɪk] *s* leccata, leccatura; (coll) esplosione di energia; (coll) velocità *f;* (coll) battitura; (coll) ripulita; **to give a lick and a promise to** (coll) fare rapidamente e con poca attenzione || *tr* leccare; (*said of waves, flames, etc.*) lambire; (*to defeat*) (coll) battere, vincere; (*e.g., with a stick*) (coll) bastonare

licorice [ˈlɪkərɪs] *s* liquirizia

lid [lɪd] *s* coperchio; (*eyelid*) palpebra; (*curb*) (coll) restrizione, freno; (*hat*) (slang) cappello

lie [laɪ] *s* menzogna; **to catch in a lie** pigliare in castagna; **to give the lie to** smentire || *v* (*pret* & *pp* **lied;** *ger* **lying**) *tr*—**to lie oneself out of** or **to lie one's way out of** trarsi fuori da (*un impaccio*) con una menzogna || *intr* mentire || *v* (*pret* **lay** [le]; *pp* **lain** [len]; *ger* **lying**) *intr* essere sdraiato; trovarsi; (*in the grave*) giacere; **to lie down** sdraiarsi

lie' detec'tor *s* macchina della verità

lien [lin] or [ˈli-ən] *s* diritto di pegno, diritto di garanzia

lieu [lu] *s*—**in lieu of** in luogo di

lieutenant [luˈtɛnənt] *s* luogotenente *m;* (mil) tenente *m;* (nav) tenente *m* di vascello

lieuten'ant colo'nel *s* (mil) tenente *m* colonnello

lieuten'ant command'er *s* (nav) capitano di corvetta

lieuten'ant gen'eral *s* (mil) generale *m* di corpo d'armata

lieuten'ant gov'ernor *s* (USA) vicegovernatore *m*

lieuten'ant jun'ior grade' *s* (nav) sottotenente *m* di vascello

life [laɪf] *adj* (*animate*) vitale; (*lifelong*) perpetuo; (*annuity*) vitalizio; (*working from nature*) dal vero || *s* (*lives* [laɪvz]) vita; (*of an insurance policy*) forza; **for life** a vita; **for the life of me** per quanto io provi; **the life and soul of** (*e.g., the party*) l'anima di; **to come to life** tornare a sé; riprender vita; **to depart this life** passar a miglior vita; **to run for one's life** scappare a tutta corsa

life' annu'ity *s* rendita vitalizia

life' belt' *s* cintura di salvataggio

life'boat' *s* imbarcazione di salvataggio, lancia di salvataggio

life' buoy' *s* salvagente *m*

life' float' *s* zattera di salvataggio

life'guard' *s* bagnino

life' impris'onment *s* ergastolo

life' insur'ance *s* assicurazione sulla vita

life' jack'et *s* cintura or giubbotto di salvataggio

lifeless [ˈlaɪflɪs] *adj* inanimato; (*in a faint*) esanime; senza vita

life'like' *adj* (*e.g., portrait*) parlante; naturale

life' line' *s* sagola di salvataggio; (fig) linea di comunicazioni vitale

life'long' *adj* perpetuo, a vita

life' of Ri'ley [ˈraɪli] *s* vita del michelaccio

life' of the par'ty *s* anima della festa

life' preserv'er [prɪˈzɜrvər] *s* salvagente *m*

lifer [ˈlaɪfər] *s* (slang) ergastolano

life' raft' *s* zattera di salvataggio

life'sav'er *s* salvatore *m* della vita; (*something that saves from a predicament*) ancora di salvezza

life' sen'tence *s* condanna all'ergastolo

life'-size' *adj* in grandezza naturale

life'time' *adj* vitalizio || *s* corso della vita

life' vest' *s* (air, naut) giubbotto salvagente or di salvataggio

life'work' *s* lavoro di tutta una vita

lift [lɪft] *s* sollevamento; (*act of helping*) aiuto; (*ride*) passaggio; (*apparatus*) elevatore *m;* (aer) portanza || *tr* sollevare, alzare; (*one's hat*) levarsi; rimuovere; (coll) plagiare; (coll) rubare; (*fire*) (mil) sospendere || *intr* sollevare, sollevarsi; (*said, e.g., of fog*) dissiparsi

lift'-off' *s* (aer) decollo verticale

lift' truck' *s* carrello elevatore

ligament [ˈlɪgəmənt] *s* legamento

ligature [ˈlɪgətʃər] *s* legatura

light [laɪt] *adj* (*in weight*) leggero; (*hair*) biondo; (*complexion*) chiaro; (*oil*) fluido; (naut) con poco carico; (*room*) chiaro, illuminato; (*beer*) chiaro; **light in the head** (*dizzy*) allegro; (*silly*) scimunito; **to make light of** prendere sotto gamba || *s* luce *f;* (*to light a cigarette*) fuoco; (*to control traffic*) segnale *m;* (*shining example*) luminare *m;* (*lighthouse*) faro; (*window*) luce *f;* **according to one's lights** secondo l'intelligenza che il buon Dio gli (le) ha dato; **against the light** controluce; **in this light** sotto questo punto di vista; **lights** esempio; (*of sheep*) polmone *m;* **to come to light** venire alla luce; **to shed** or **throw light on** mettere in luce; **to strike a light** accendere un fiammifero || *v* (*pret* & *pp* **lighted** or **lit** [lɪt]) *tr* (*to furnish with illumination*) illuminare; (*to ignite*) accendere; **to light up** illuminare || *intr* illuminarsi; accendersi; (*said, e.g., of a bird*) posarsi; (*from a car*) scendere; **to light into** (coll) gettarsi contro; **to light out** (slang) darsela a gambe; **to light upon** imbattersi in || *adv* senza bagagli; senza carico

light' bulb' *s* lampadina

light-complexioned [ˈlaɪtkəmˈplɛkʃənd] *adj* dal colorito chiaro

lighten [ˈlaɪtən] *tr* alleggerire, sgravare; illuminare; (*to cheer up*) rallegrare || *intr* alleggerirsi; (*to become less dark*) illuminarsi; (*to give off flashes of lightning*) lampeggiare

lighter [ˈlaɪtər] *s* accenditore *m;* (naut) burchio

light-fingered [ˈlaɪtˈfɪŋgərd] *adj* svelto di mano, con le mani lunghe

light-footed ['laɪt'futɪd] *adj* agile
light-headed ['laɪt'hɛdɪd] *adj* (*dizzy*) allegro; (*simple*) scemo
light-hearted ['laɪt'hɑrtɪd] *adj* allegro
light'house' *s* faro
lighting ['laɪtɪŋ] *s* illuminazione
lightly ['laɪtli] *adv* alla leggera
light' me'ter *s* esposimetro
lightness ['laɪtnɪs] *s* (*in weight*) leggerezza; (*in illumination*) chiarezza
light·ning ['laɪtnɪŋ] *s* lampo, fulmine *m* || *v* (*ger* -**ning**) *intr* lampeggiare
light'ning arrest'er [ə'rɛstər] *s* scaricatore *m*
light'ning bug' *s* lucciola
light'ning rod' *s* parafulmine *m*
light' op'era *s* operetta
light'ship' *s* battello faro
light-struck ['laɪt,strʌk] *adj* che ha preso luce
light'weight' *adj* leggero; da mezza stagione, e.g., **lightweight coat** cappotto da mezza stagione
light'-year' *s* anno luce
likable ['laɪkəbəl] *adj* simpatico
like [laɪk] *adj* uguale, simile; uguale a, simile a, e.g., **this hat is like mine** questo cappello è simile al mio; (*elec*) di segno uguale; **like father like son** tale il padre quale il figlio; **to feel like** + *ger* aver voglia di + *inf*; **to look like** assomigliare a; sembrare, e.g., **it looks like rain** sembra che pioverà || *s* (*liking*) preferenza; (*fellow man*) simile *m*; **and the like** e cose dello stesso genere; **to give like for like** rendere pane per focaccia || *adv* come; **like enough** (coll) probabilmente || *prep* come || *conj* (coll) come; come se; (coll) che, e.g., **it seems like he is afraid** sembra che abbia paura || *tr* voler bene (with *dat*), e.g., **I like her very much** le voglio molto bene; trovar piacere in, e.g., **I like music** trovo piacere nella musica; piacere (with *dat*), e.g., **John likes apples** le mele piacciono a Giovanni; **to like best** o **better** preferire; **to like it** in trovarsi a proprio agio in; **to like to** + *inf* piacere (with *dat*) + *inf*, e.g., **she likes to dance** le piace ballare; gradire che + *subj*, e.g., **I should like him to pay a visit to my parents** gradirei che facesse una visita ai miei genitori || *intr* volere, desiderare, e.g., **as you like** come desidera; **if you like** se vuole
likelihood ['laɪklɪ,hʊd] *s* probabilità *f*
like·ly ['laɪkli] *adj* (-**lier**; -**liest**) probabile; verosimile; a proposito; promettente; **to be likely to** + *inf* essere probabile che + *fut*, e.g., **Mary is likely to get married in the spring** è probabile che Maria si sposerà in primavera || *adv* probabilmente
like-minded ['laɪk'maɪndɪd] *adj* dello stesso parere, della stessa opinione
liken ['laɪkən] *tr* paragonare
likeness ['laɪknɪs] *s* (*picture*) ritratto; (*similarity*) rassomiglianza; apparenza
like'wise' *adv* ugualmente; inoltre; **to do likewise** fare lo stesso

liking ['laɪkɪŋ] *s* simpatia; **to be to the liking of** essere di gusto di; **to have a liking for** (*things*) prendere gusto per; (*people*) affezionarsi a
lilac ['laɪlək] *adj* & *s* lilla *m*
Lilliputian [,lɪlɪ'pjuʃən] *adj* & *s* lilliputiano
lilt [lɪlt] *s* canzone *f* a cadenza; movimento a cadenza; (*in verse*) cadenza
lil·y ['lɪli] *s* (-**ies**) giglio; **to gild the lily** cercare di migliorare quanto è già perfetto
lil'y of the val'ley *s* mughetto
li'ma bean' ['laɪmə] *s* fagiolo bianco
limb [lɪm] *s* (*of body*) membro, arto; (*of tree*) ramo; (*of cross*) braccio; **to be out on a limb** (coll) essere nei guai
limber ['lɪmbər] *adj* agile || *intr*—**to limber up** sciogliersi i muscoli, sgranchirsi le gambe
lim·bo ['lɪmbo] *s* (-**bos**) esilio; dimenticatoio; (theol) limbo
lime [laɪm] *s* (*calcium oxide*) calce *f*; (*Citrus aurantifolia*) limetta agra; (*linden tree*) tiglio || *tr* cessare
lime'kiln' *s* fornace *f* da calce
lime'light' *s*—**to be in the limelight** essere in vista
limerick ['lɪmərɪk] *s* canzoncina umoristica di cinque versi
lime'stone' *s* calcare *m*
limit ['lɪmɪt] *s* limite *m*; (coll) colmo; **to go to the limit** andare agli estremi || *tr* limitare
limitation [,lɪmɪ'teʃən] *s* limitazione
lim'ited-ac'cess high'way ['lɪmɪtɪd] *s* autostrada, strada con corsia d'accesso
lim'ited com'pany *s* società *f* a responsabilità limitata
lim'ited mon'archy *s* monarchia costituzionale
limitless ['lɪmɪtlɪs] *adj* illimitato
limousine ['lɪmə,zin] *or* [,lɪmə'zin] *s* berlina
limp [lɪmp] *adj* floscio; debole || *s* zoppicatura || *intr* zoppicare
limpid ['lɪmpɪd] *adj* limpido
linage ['laɪnɪdʒ] *s* (typ) numero di linee
linchpin ['lɪntʃ,pɪn] *s* acciarino
linden ['lɪndən] *s* tiglio
line [laɪn] *s* linea; (e.g., *of people*) fila; (*of trees*) filare *m*; (*for fishing*) lenza; (*written* or *printed*) rigo, riga; (*wrinkle*) ruga; (*of goods*) ramo; (naut) gherlino; **all along the line** su tutta la linea; **in line** allineato; sotto controllo; **in line with** secondo; **out of line** fuori d'allineamento; (slang) in disaccordo; **to bring into line** far filare; **to draw the line at** fermarsi a; stabilire il limite a; **to fall in line** conformarsi; allinearsi; **to have a line on** (coll) aver informazioni su; **to read between the lines** leggere fra le righe; **to stand in line** fare la coda; **to toe the line** filare diritto; **to wait in line** fare la fila || *tr* rigare; (e.g., *the street*) schierare lungo; (*a suit*) foderare; (*a brake*) rivestire; **to line up** allineare; trovare, scovare || *intr*

—**to line up** mettersi in fila; fare la coda

lineage ['lɪnɪ‧ɪdʒ] s lignaggio

lineaments ['lɪnɪ‧əmənts] spl lineamenti mpl

linear ['lɪnɪ‧ər] adj lineare

line'man s (-men) (elec) guardafili m; (sports) guardalinee m; (surv) assistente geometra m

linen ['lɪnən] adj di tela di lino ‖ s (fabric) tela di lino, lino; (yarn) filo di lino; biancheria

lin'en clos'et s guardaroba m per la biancheria

line' of fire' s (mil) linea di tiro

line' of least' resist'ance s principio del minimo sforzo; **to follow the line of least resistance** prendere la via più facile

line' of sight' s visuale f; (mil) linea di mira

liner ['laɪnər] s transatlantico

line'-up' s disposizione; (of prisoners) allineamento; (sports) formazione

linger ['lɪŋɡər] intr indugiare, soffermarsi; (to be tardy) tardare; rimanere in vita; **to linger over** contemplare

lingerie [‚lænʒə'ri] s biancheria intima

lingering ['lɪŋɡərɪŋ] adj prolungato

lingual ['lɪŋɡwəl] adj linguale ‖ s suono linguale

linguist ['lɪŋɡwɪst] s poliglotto; (specialist in linguistics) glottologo

linguistic [lɪŋ'ɡwɪstɪk] adj linguistico ‖ **linguistics** s linguistica, glottologia

lining ['laɪnɪŋ] s (of a coat) fodera; (of auto brake) guarnizione; (of a furnace) rivestimento interno; (of wall) rivestimento

link [lɪŋk] s anello, maglia; unione; (of sausage) nocco; **links** campo di golf ‖ tr connettere ‖ intr connettersi

linnet ['lɪnɪt] s fanello

linotype ['laɪnə‚taɪp] s linotype f ‖ tr comporre in linotipia

lin'otype op'erator s linotipista mf

linseed ['lɪn‚sid] s linosa

lin'seed oil' s olio di lino

lint [lɪnt] s peluria, sfilacciatura; (for dressing wounds) filaccia

lintel ['lɪntəl] s architrave m

lion ['laɪən] s leone m; celebrità f; **to beard the lion in his den** affrontare l'avversario a casa sua; **to put one's head in the lion's mouth** cacciarsi nei pericoli

lioness ['laɪ‧ənɪs] s leonessa

lion-hearted ['laɪ‧ən‚hɑrtɪd] adj cuor di leone, coraggioso

lionize ['laɪ‧ə‚naɪz] tr festeggiare come una celebrità

li'ons' den' s fossa dei leoni

li'on's share' s parte f del leone

lip [lɪp] s labbro; (of a jar) beccuccio; (slang) linguaggio insolente; **to smack one's lips** leccarsi le labbra

lip'read' v (pret & pp -read [‚red]) tr leggere le labbra di ‖ intr leggere le labbra

lip' read'ing s labiolettura

lip' serv'ice s omaggio non sentito

lip'stick' s rossetto per le labbra, matita per le labbra

lique-fy ['lɪkwɪ‚faɪ] v (pret & pp -fied) tr & intr liquefare

liqueur [lɪ'kʌr] s liquore m

liquid ['lɪkwɪd] adj liquido ‖ s liquido; (phonet) liquida

liquidate ['lɪkwɪ‚det] tr & intr liquidare

liquidity [lɪ'kwɪdɪtɪ] s liquidità f

liq'uid meas'ure s misura di capacità per liquidi

liquor ['lɪkər] s distillato alcolico, bevanda alcolica; (broth) brodo

Lisbon ['lɪzbən] s Lisbona

lisp [lɪsp] s pronuncia blesa ‖ intr parlare bleso

lissome ['lɪsəm] adj flessibile, agile

list [lɪst] s lista, elenco; (border) orlo; (selvage) cimossa, vivagno; (naut) sbandamento; **lists** lizza; **to enter the lists** entrare in lizza ‖ tr elencare, listare ‖ intr (naut) sbandare, andare alla banda

listen ['lɪsən] intr ascoltare; obbedire; **to listen in** ascoltare una conversazione; (rad) captare una comunicazione; **to listen to** ascoltare; obbedire a, prestare attenzione a; **to listen to reason** intendere ragione

listener ['lɪsənər] s ascoltatore m; radioascoltatore m

lis'tening post' s (mil) posto di ascolto

listless ['lɪstlɪs] adj svogliato

list' price' s prezzo di catalogo

lita-ny ['lɪtənɪ] s (-nies) litania

liter ['litər] s litro

literacy ['lɪtərəsɪ] s abilità f di leggere e scrivere; istruzione

literal ['lɪtərəl] adj letterale

literary ['lɪtə‚rɛrɪ] adj letterario; (individual) letterato

literate ['lɪtərɪt] adj che sa leggere e scrivere; (educated) istruito; (well-read) letterato ‖ s persona che sa leggere e scrivere; letterato

literature ['lɪtərət‚ʃər] s letteratura; (printed matter) opuscoli pubblicitari

lithe [laɪθ] adj flessibile, agile

lithium ['lɪθɪ‧əm] s litio

lithograph ['lɪθə‚græf] or ['lɪθə‚grɑf] s litografia f ‖ tr litografare

lithographer [lɪ'θɑgrəfər] s litografo

lithography [lɪ'θɑgrəfɪ] s litografia

Lithuania [‚lɪθu'enɪ‧ə] s la Lituania

Lithuanian [‚lɪθu'enɪ‧ən] adj & s lituano

litigant ['lɪtɪgənt] adj & s litigante mf

litigate ['lɪtɪ‚get] tr & intr litigare

litigation [‚lɪtɪ'geʃən] s litigio; (lawsuit) lite f, causa

litmus ['lɪtməs] s tornasole m

lit'mus pa'per s cartina al tornasole

litter ['lɪtər] s disordine m; (scattered rubbish) pattume m; (young brought forth at one birth) figliata; (of puppies) cucciolata; (bedding for animals) strame m; (stretcher; bed carried by men or animals) lettiga, portantina ‖ tr mettere in disordine; spargere rifiuti per; coprire di strame ‖ intr partorire

lit·ter·bug' s sparpagliatore m di rifiuti

littering ['lɪtərɪŋ] s—**no littering** vietato gettare rifiuti

little ['lɪtəl] adj (in size) piccolo; (in amount) poco, e.g., **little salt** poco sale; **a little un po' di**, e.g., **a little salt un po' di sale**; **the little ones** i piccini || s poco; **a little un po'**; **to make little of** farsi gioco di; non pigliar sul serio; **to think little of** non tener di conto || adv poco; **little by little** poco a poco, mano a mano

Lit'tle Bear' s Orsa minore

Lit'tle Dip'per s Piccolo Carro

lit'tle fin'ger s mignolo; **to twist around one's little finger** maneggiare come un fantoccio

lit'tle·neck' s piccola vongola (Venus mercenaria)

lit'tle owl' s civetta

lit'tle peo'ple spl fate fpl; folletti mpl

Lit'tle Red Rid'inghood' ['raɪdɪŋ͵hʊd] s Cappuccetto Rosso

lit'tle slam' s (bridge) piccolo slam

liturgic(al) [lɪ'tʌrdʒɪk(əl)] adj liturgico

litur·gy ['lɪtərdʒi] s (-gies) liturgia

livable ['lɪvəbəl] adj abitabile; socievole; tollerabile

live [laɪv] adj vivo; (flame) ardente; di attualità; (elec) sotto tensione; (telv) in diretta || [lɪv] tr vivere; **to live down** (one's past) far dimenticare; **to live it up** (coll) darsi alla bella vita, scialare; **to live out** (e.g., a war) sopravvivere (with dat) || intr vivere; **to live from hand to mouth** vivere alla giornata; **to live high** darsi alla bella vita; **to live on** continuare a vivere; (e.g., vegetables) vivere di; vivere alle spalle di; **to live up to** (one's promises) compiere; (one's earnings) spendere

live' coal' [laɪv] s brace f

livelihood ['laɪvlɪ͵hʊd] s vita; **to earn one's livelihood** guadagnarsi la vita

livelong ['lɪv͵lɔŋ] or ['laɪv͵lɔŋ] adj—**all the livelong day** tutto il santo giorno

live·ly ['laɪvli] adj (-lier; -liest) vivo, vivace; (color) vivido; (resilient) elastico; (tune) brioso

liven ['laɪvən] tr animare || intr animarsi, rianimarsi

liver ['lɪvər] s abitante mf; (anat) fegato

liver·y ['lɪvəri] s (-ies) livrea

liv'ery·man s (-men) stalliere m

liv'ery sta'ble s stallaggio

livestock ['laɪv͵stɑk] adj zootecnico || s bestiame m

live' wire' [laɪv] s (elec) filo carico di corrente; (slang) persona energica

livid ['lɪvɪd] adj livido; (with anger) incollerito

living ['lɪvɪŋ] adj vivo; (conditions) abitativo || s vivere m; **to earn a living** guadagnarsi la vita

liv'ing quar'ters spl abitazione, alloggio

liv'ing room' s stanza di soggiorno

liv'ing wage' s salario sufficiente per vivere

lizard ['lɪzərd] s lucertola

load [lod] s peso, carico; **loads of** (coll) un mucchio di; **to get a load of** (slang) stare a vedere; (slang) stare a sentire; **to have a load on** (slang) essere ubriaco || tr caricare || intr caricarsi

loaded ['lodɪd] adj caricato; (slang) ubriaco fradicio; (slang) ricchissimo

load'ed dice' spl dadi truccati

load'stone' s magnetite f; (fig) calamita

loaf [lof] s (loaves [lovz]) pane m; (molded mass) forma; (of sugar) pane m; (long and thin loaf) filone m || intr batter fiacca, oziare

loafer ['lofər] s fannullone m

loam [lom] s ricca argilla sabbiosa; terra da fonderia

loan [lon] s prestito; **to hit for a loan** (coll) dare una stoccata a || tr prestare

loan' shark' s (coll) strozzino

loan' word' s (ling) prestito

loath [loθ] adj poco disposto; **nothing loath** molto volentieri

loathe [loð] tr detestare, aborrire

loathsome ['loðsəm] adj abominevole, disgustoso

lob [lɑb] s (tennis) pallonetto || v (pret & pp lobbed; ger lobbing) tr (tennis) dare un pallonetto a

lob·by ['lɑbi] s (-bies) anticamera, vestibolo; sollecitazione di voti || v (pret & pp lob -bied) intr sollecitare voti, influenzare il voto dietro le quinte

lobbyist ['lɑbɪ͵ɪst] s politicante m che cerca di influenzare il voto dietro le quinte

lobe [lob] s lobo

lobster ['lɑbstər] s (Palinurus vulgaris) aragosta; (Hommarus vulgaris) astice m

lob'ster pot' s nassa per aragoste

local ['lokəl] adj locale || s treno accelerato; notizia di interesse locale; (of a union) sezione

locale [lo'kæl] s località f

locali·ty [lo'kælɪti] s (-ties) località f

localize ['lokə͵laɪz] tr localizzare

lo'cal op'tion s referendum m locale sulla vendita di alcolici

locate [lo'ket] or ['loket] tr (to discover the location of) localizzare; (to place, settle) situare, stabilire; (to ascribe a location to) individuare || intr stabilirsi

location [lo'keʃən] s localizzazione; posizione; sito; **on location** (mov) in esterno

lock [lɑk] s serratura; (of a canal) chiusa; (of hair) ciocca; (of a firearm) percussore m; (mach) freno; **lock, stock, and barrel** (coll) completamente; **under lock and key** sotto chiave || tr chiudere a chiave; serrare; (a boat) far passare per una chiusa; unire; abbracciare; **to lock in** chiudere sotto chiave; **to lock out** chiudere fuori; (workers) sbarrare dal lavoro; **to lock up** chiudere a chiave, incarcerare

locker ['lɑkər] s armadietto a chiave; (in the form of a chest) bauletto

lock′er room′ *s* spogliatoio
locket [′lɑkɪt] *s* medaglione *m*
lock′jaw′ *s* tetano, trisma *m*
lock′ nut′ *s* controdado
lock′out′ *s* serrata
lock′smith′ *s* magnano, fabbro
lock′ step′ *s—***to march in lock step** marciare a passo serrato
lock′ stitch′ *s* punto a filo doppio
lock′ ten′der *s* guardiano di chiusa
lock′up′ *s* prigione; (typ) messa in forma
lock′ wash′er *s* rondella di sicurezza
locomotive [ˌlokə′motɪv] *s* locomotiva
lo·cus [′lokəs] *s* (**-ci** [saɪ]) luogo
locust [′lokəst] *s* (ent) locusta; (*cicada*) (ent) cicala; (bot) robinia
lode [lod] *s* filone *m*, vena
lode′star′ *s* stella polare; guida
lodge [lɑdʒ] *s* casetta; padiglione *m* da caccia; albergo; (*e.g., of Masons*) loggia ‖ *tr* alloggiare, ospitare; depositare; contenere; (*a complaint*) sporgere ‖ *intr* alloggiare; essere contenuto, trovarsi; andar a finire
lodger [′lɑdʒər] *s* inquilino
lodging [′lɑdʒɪŋ] *s* alloggio
loft [lɔft] *or* [lɑft] *s* (*attic*) solaio; (*hayloft*) fienile *m*; (*in theater or church*) galleria
loft·y [′lɔftɪ] *or* [′lɑftɪ] *adj* (**-ier; -iest**) alto, elevato; (*haughty*) orgoglioso
log [lɔg] *or* [lɑg] *s* ceppo, ciocco; (naut) solcometro; (aer, naut) giornale *m* di bordo; **to sleep like a log** dormire della grossa ‖ *v* (*pret & pp* **logged;** *ger* **logging**) *tr* registrare; (*a speed*) fare; (*a distance*) percorrere
logarithm [′lɔgəˌrɪðəm] *or* [′lɑgəˌrɪðəm] *s* logaritmo
log′book′ *s* (aer, naut) libro di bordo
log′ cab′in *s* capanna di tronchi
log′ chip′ *s* (naut) barchetta
log′ driv′er *s* zatteriere *m*
log′ driv′ing [′draɪvɪŋ] *s* fluitazione
logger [′lɔgər] *or* [′lɑgər] *s* taglialegna *m;* trattore *m* per trasporto tronchi
log′ger·head′ *s* testone *m;* **at loggerheads in lite**
loggia [′lɑdʒə] *s* loggia
logic [′lɑdʒɪk] *s* logica
logical [′lɑdʒɪkəl] *adj* logico
logician [lo′dʒɪʃən] *s* logico
logistic(al) [lo′dʒɪstɪk(əl)] *adj* logistico
logistics [lo′dʒɪstɪks] *s* logistica
log′jam′ *s* ingorgo fluviale dovuto a ammasso di tronchi; (fig) ristagno
log′ line′ *s* (naut) sagola
log′roll′ *intr* barattare favori politici
log′wood′ *s* campeggio
loin [lɔɪn] *s* lombo; **to gird up one′s loins** prepararsi per l′azione
loin′cloth′ *s* perizoma *m*, copripudende *m*
loiter [′lɔɪtər] *tr—***to loiter away** (*time*) sprecare in ozio ‖ *intr* bighellonare, trastullarsi
loiterer [′lɔɪtərər] *s* perdigiorno
loll [lɑl] *intr* sdraiarsi pigramente, adagiarsi pigramente; pendere
lollipop [′lɑlɪˌpɑp] *s* caramella sullo stecchetto, lecca-lecca *m*

Lombard [′lɑmbɑrd] *or* [′lɑmbərd] *adj & s* lombardo; (hist) longobardo
Lom′bardy pop′lar *s* pioppo italico
Lon′con [′lʌndən] *adj* londinese ‖ *s* Londra
Londoner [′lʌndənər] *s* londinese *mf*
lone [lon] *adj* solo; solitario
loneliness [′lonlinɪs] *s* solitudine *f*
lone·ly [′lonli] *adj* (**-lier; -liest**) solingo, solo, solitario
lonesome [′lonsəm] *adj* solitario
lone′ wolf′ *s* (coll) orso, solitario
long [lɔŋ] *or* [lɑŋ] *adj* (**longer** [′lɔŋgər] *or* [′lɑŋgər]; **longest** [′lɔŋgɪst] *or* [′lɑŋgɪst]) *adj* lungo; **three meters long** lungo tre metri ‖ *adv* molto, molto tempo; **as long as** mentre; (*provided*) fin tanto che; (*inasmuch as*) dato che; **before long** fra poco; **how long?** quanto?; **long ago** molto tempo fa; **long before** molto prima; **long since** molto tempo fa; **no longer** non più; **so long!** (coll) ciao!, arrivederci!; **so long as** fino a che, finché ‖ *intr* anelare; **to long for** sviscerarsi per, sospirare per
long′boat′ *s* (naut) lancia
long′-dis′tance *adj* (telp) interurbano, intercomunale; (sports) di fondo; (aer) a distanza
long′-drawn′-out′ *adj* prolungato
longeron [′lɑndʒərən] *s* longherone *m*
longevity [lɑn′dʒevɪti] *s* longevità *f*
long′ face′ *s* (coll) faccia triste, muso lungo
long′hair′ *adj & s* (coll) intellettuale *mf;* (coll) musicomane *mf*
long′hand′ *adj* (scritto) a mano ‖ *s* scrittura a mano; **in longhand** scritto a mano
longing [′lɔŋɪŋ] *or* [′lɑŋɪŋ] *adj* bramoso, anelante ‖ *s* brama, anelito
longitude [′lɔndʒɪˌtjud] *or* [′lɑndʒɪˌtud] *s* longitudine *f*
long-lived [′lɔŋ′laɪvd], [′lɑŋ′laɪvd], [′lɔŋ′lɪvd] *or* [′lɑŋ′lɪvd] *adj* (*person*) longevo, di lunga vita; (*e.g., rumor*) di lunga durata
long′-play′ing rec′ord *s* disco di grande durata
long′-range′ *adj* a lunga portata
long′shore′man *s* (**-men**) portuale *m*, scaricatore *m*
long′stand′ing *adj* vecchio, che esiste da lungo tempo
long′-suf′fering *adj* paziente, longanime
long′ suit′ *s* (cards) serie lunga; (fig) forte *m*
long′-term′ *adj* a lunga scadenza
long′-wind′ed *adj* verboso; (*speech*) chilometrico
look [lʊk] *s* (*appearance*) aspetto; (*glance*) sguardo; (*search*) ricerca; **looks** aspetto, apparenza; **to take a look at** dare un′occhiata a ‖ *tr* guardare; (*one′s age*) mostrare; **to look daggers at** fulminare con lo sguardo; **to look up** (*e.g., in a dictionary*) cercare; andare a visitare; venire a visitare ‖ *intr* guardare; cercare; parere; **look out!** attenzione!; **to look after** badare a; occuparsi di; **to look at** guardare; **to look back** riguardare;

(fig) guardare al passato; **to look down** on s.o. guardare qlcu dall'alto in basso; **to look for** cercare; aspettarsi; **to look forward** to anticipare il piacere di; **to look ill** avere una brutta cera; **to look in** on passare per la casa di; **to look into** esaminare a fondo; **to look like** sembrare, parere; **to look out** fare attenzione; **to look out for** aver cura di; **to look out of** guardare da; **to look out on** dare su; **to look through** guardare per; (*a book*) sfogliare; **to look toward** dare su; **to look up to** ammirare, guardare con ammirazione; **to look well** avere una buona cera; fare figura

looker-on [ˌlʊkər'ɑn] or [ˌlʊkər'ɔn] s (**lookers-on**) astante *m*

look'ing glass' ['lʊkɪŋ] s specchio

look'out' s guardia; (*person; watch kept; place from which a watch is kept*) vedetta; (*concern*) (coll) affare *m*; **to be on the lookout** stare in guardia; **to be on the lookout for** essere in cerca di

loom [lum] s telaio || *intr* apparire indistintamente; pararsi dinanzi; apparire

loon [lun] s scemo; fannullone *m*; (orn) (*Gavia*) strolaga

loon-y ['luni] *adj* (-**ier; -iest**) (slang) pazzo || s (-**ies**) (slang) pazzo

loop [lup] s cappio; (*e.g., of a road*) tortuosità *f*; (*for fastening a button*) occhiello; (aer) cerchio or giro della morte; (phys) ventre *m*; || *tr* fare cappi in; annodare; **to loop the loop** (aer) fare il giro della morte || *intr* avanzare tortuosamente, girare

loop'hole' s (*narrow opening*) feritoia; (*means of evasion*) scappatoia

loose [lus] *adj* libero, sciolto; (*available*) disponibile; (*not firm*) rilasciato; (*tooth*) che balla; (*unchaste*) facile; (*garment*) ampio; (*soil*) smosso; (*translation*) libero; (*rein*) lento; **to become loose** sciogliersi; **to break loose** mettersi in libertà; **to have loose bowels** avere la diarrea; **to turn loose** liberare || s—**to be on the loose** (coll) essere in libertà; (coll) correre la cavallina || *tr* sciogliere; slegare; lanciare

loose' change' s spiccioli *mpl*

loose' end' s capo sciolto; **at loose ends** indeciso; disoccupato, senza nulla da fare

loose'-leaf' *adj* a fogli mobili

loosen ['lusən] *tr* snodare; rilasciare; smuovere; allentare; (*the bowels*) liberare dalla stitichezza || *intr* snodarsi; rilasciarsi; smuoversi; allentarsi

looseness ['lusnɪs] s scioltezza; (*in morals*) rilassamento

loose-tongued ['lus'tʌŋd] *adj* sciolto di lingua; linguacciuto, maldicente

loot [lut] s bottino || *tr* saccheggiare

lop [lɑp] v (*pret & pp* **lopped**; *ger* **lopping**) *tr* lasciar cadere, lasciar penzolare; **to lop off** mozzare; (*a tree*) potare; (*a vine*) stralciare || *intr* penzolare

lopsided ['lɑp'saɪdɪd] *adj* che pende da una parte; asimmetrico, sproporzionato

loquacious [lo'kweʃəs] *adj* loquace

lord [lɔrd] s signore *m*; (Brit) lord *m* || *tr*—**to lord it over** signoreggiare su

lord-ly ['lɔrdli] *adj* (-**lier; -liest**) signorile, magnifico; altero, disdegnoso, arrogante

Lord's' Day', the la domenica, il giorno del Signore

lordship ['lɔrdʃɪp] s signoria

Lord's' Prayer' s paternostro

Lord's' Sup'per s Eucarestia; Ultima Cena

lore [lor] s tradizioni *fpl* popolari; cognizioni *fpl*

lorgnette [lɔrn'jɛt] s occhialetto, lorgnette *f*; binocolo da teatro col manico

lor-ry ['lɑri] or ['lɔri] s (-**ries**) (rr) vagoncino; (Brit) camion *m*

lose [luz] v (*pret & pp* **lost** [lɔst] or [lɑst]) *tr* perdere; (*said of a physician*) non riuscire a salvare; **to lose heart** perdersi d'animo; **to lose oneself** perdersi, smarrirsi || *intr* perdere; (*said of a watch*) ritardare; **to lose out** rimettersi

loser ['luzər] s perdente *mf*

losing ['luzɪŋ] *adj* perdente || **losings** *spl* perdite *fpl*

loss [lɔs] or [lɑs] s perdita; **to be at a loss** essere perplesso; **to be at a loss to** + *inf* non saper come + *inf*; **to sell at a loss** vendere in perdita

loss' of face' s perdita di faccia

lost [lɔst] or [lɑst] *adj* perduto; **lost in thought** assorto in sé stesso; **lost to** perso per; insensibile a

lost'-and-found' depart'ment s ufficio degli oggetti smarriti

lost' sheep' s percorella smarrita

lot [lɑt] s (*for building*) lotto; (*fate*) sorte *f*; (*parcel, portion*) partita; (*of people*) gruppo; (coll) grande quantità *f*; (coll) tipo, soggetto; **a lot** (**of**) or **lots of** (coll) molto, molti; **to cast** or **to throw in one's lot with** condividere la sorte di; **to draw** or **to cast lots** tirare a sorte

lotion ['loʃən] s lozione

lotter-y ['lɑtəri] s (-**ies**) lotteria, riffa

lotto ['lɑto] s tombola, lotto

lotus ['lotəs] s loto

loud [laud] *adj* forte; (*noisy*) rumoroso; (*voice*) alto; (*garish*) sgargiante, chiassoso, appariscente; (*foul-smelling*) puzzolente || *adv* a voce alta; rumorosamente

loud-mouthed ['laud,mauθt] or ['laud,mauðd] *adj* chiassone

loud'speak'er s altoparlante *m*

lounge [laundʒ] s divano, sofà *m*; sala soggiorno; ridotto || *intr* oziare, star senza far niente; bighellonare; **to lounge around** bighellonare

lounge' liz'ard s (slang) damerino, bellimbusto, gagà *m*

louse [laus] s (*lice* [laɪs]) pidocchio || *tr*—**to louse up** (slang) rovinare

lous-y ['lauzi] *adj* (-**ier; -iest**) pidocchioso; (*mean; bungling*) (coll) schifoso; *(filthy)* (coll) sporco; **lousy with** *(e.g., money)* (slang) pieno di

lout [laut] *s* gaglioffo, tanghero

louver ['luvər] *s* sportello girevole di persiana; *(aut)* feritoia per ventilazione

lovable ['lʌvəbəl] *adj* amabile

love [lʌv] *s* amore *m*; *(tennis)* zero; **not for love nor money** a nessun prezzo; **to be in love (with)** essere innamorato (di); **to make love to** fare l'amore con ‖ *tr* amare; voler bene a; piacere (with *dat*), e.g., **she loves short skirts** le piacciono le sottane corte

love' affair' *s* passione, amóri *mpl*

love'bird' *s* (orn) inseparabile *m*; **lovebirds** (slang) amanti appassionati

love' child' *s* figlio naturale

love' feast' *s* agape *f*

loveless ['lʌvlɪs] *adj* senza amore

lovelorn ['lʌv‚lərn] *adj* abbandonato dalla persona amata

love•ly ['lʌvli] *adj* (-lier; -liest) bello; (coll) delizioso

love' match' *s* matrimonio d'amore

love' po'tion *s* filtro d'amore

lover ['lʌvər] *s* amante *m*; *(e.g., of music)* amico, appassionato

love' seat' *s* amorino

love'sick' *adj* malato d'amore

love'sick'ness *s* mal *m* d'amore

love' song' *s* canzone *f* d'amore

loving ['lʌvɪŋ] *adj* affezionato, amoroso; **your loving son** il vostro affezionato figlio

lov'ing-kind'ness *s* tenera sollecitudine

low [lo] *adj* basso; *(deep)* profondo; *(diet)* magro; *(visibility)* cattivo; *(dress)* scollato; *(dejected)* abbattuto; *(fire)* lento; *(flame; speed)* piccolo; **to lay low** ammazzare; abbattere; **to lie low** rimanere nascosto; attendere ‖ *s* punto basso; prezzo minimo; *(of cow)* muggito; (aut) prima velocità; (meteor) depressione ‖ *adv* basso, a basso, in basso ‖ *intr (said of a cow)* muggire

low'born' *adj* di umili origini

low'boy' *s* cassettone basso con le gambe corte

low'brow' *adj & s* (coll) ignorante *mf*

low'-cost' hous'ing *s* case *fpl* popolari

Low' Coun'tries, the i Paesi Bassi

low'-down' *adj* (coll) basso, vile ‖ **low'-down'** *s* (coll) semplice verità *f*, notizie *fpl* confidenziali

lower ['lo‚ər] *adj* inferiore, disotto ‖ *tr* abbassare; *(prices)* ribassare ‖ *intr* diminuire; discendere ‖ ['lau‚ər] *intr* aggrottare le ciglia; *(said of the weather)* imbronciarsi

low'er berth' ['lo‚ər] *s* cuccetta inferiore

low'er case' ['lo‚ər] *s* (typ) cassa inferiore

lower-case ['lo‚ər‚kes] *adj* (typ) minuscolo

low'er mid'dle class' ['lo‚ər] *s* piccola borghesia

lowermost ['lo‚ər‚most] *adj* (il) più basso, (l') infimo

low'-fre'quency *adj* a bassa frequenza

low' gear' *s* prima velocità, prima

lowland ['loland] *s* pianura ‖ **Lowlands** *spl* Scozia meridionale, bassa Scozia

low•ly ['loli] *adj* (-lier; -liest) umile

Low' Mass' *s* messa bassa

low-minded ['lo'maındıd] *adj* vile, basso

low-necked ['lo'nɛkt] *adj* scollato

low-pitched ['lo'pıt/t] *adj* *(sound)* basso, grave; *(roof)* poco inclinato

low'-pres'sure *adj* a bassa pressione

low-priced ['lo'praıst] *adj* a buon mercato, a basso prezzo

low' shoe' *s* scarpa bassa

low'-speed' *adj* di bassa velocità

low-spirited ['lo'spırıtıd] *adj* depresso

low' tide' *s* bassa marea; (fig) punto più basso

low' visibil'ity *s* scarsa visibilità

low' wa'ter *s* *(low tide)* bassa marea; *(of a river)* magra

loyal ['lɔı‚əl] *adj* leale

loyalist ['lɔı‚əlıst] *s* lealista *mf*

loyal•ty ['lɔı‚əlti] *s* (-ties) lealtà *f*

lozenge ['lazındʒ] *s* losanga; *(candy cough drop)* pastiglia, pastiglia

LP ['ɛl'pi] *s* (letterword) (trademark) disco di grande durata

lubricant ['lubrıkənt] *adj & s* lubrificante *m*

lubricate ['lubrı‚ket] *tr* lubrificare; *(e.g., one's hands)* ungersi

lubrication [‚lubrı'ke/ən] *s* lubrificazione

lubricous ['lubrıkəs] *adj* lubrico; incerto, incostante

lucerne [lu'sʌrn] *s* erba medica

lucid ['lusıd] *adj* lucido

Lucifer ['lusıfər] *s* Lucifero

luck [lʌk] *s* *(good or bad)* sorte *f*; *(good)* sorte *f*, fortuna; **down on one's luck** in cattive condizioni; **in luck** fortunato; **out of luck** sfortunato; **to bring luck** portare (buona) fortuna; **to try one's luck** tentare la sorte; **worse luck** disgraziatamente

luckily ['lʌkıli] *adv* fortunatamente

luckless ['lʌklıs] *adj* sfortunato

luck•y ['lʌki] *adj* (-ier; -iest) fortunato; *(supposed to bring luck)* portafortuna; *(foretelling good luck)* di buon augurio; **to be lucky** aver fortuna

luck'y hit' *s* (coll) colpo di fortuna

lucrative ['lukrətıv] *adj* lucrativo

ludicrous ['ludıkrəs] *adj* ridicolo

lug [lʌg] *s* manico; *(pull)* tiro; **to put the lug on s.o.** (slang) batter cassa a qlcu ‖ *v (pret & pp lugged; ger lugging)* *tr* tirarsi dietro; (coll) introdurre a sproposito

luggage ['lʌgıdʒ] *s* *(used in traveling)* bagaglio; *(found in a store)* valigeria

lug'gage store' *s* valigeria

lugubrious [lu'gubrı‚əs] or [lu'gjubrı‚əs] *adj* lugubre

lukewarm ['luk‚wɔrm] *adj* tiepido

lull [lʌl] *s* momento di calma, calma ‖ *tr* calmare, pacificare; addormentare

lulla•by ['lʌlə‚baı] *s* (-bies) ninnananna

lumbago [lʌm'bego] *s* lombaggine *f*

lumber ['lʌmbər] *s* legname *m*, legno da costruzione; cianfrusaglie *fpl* ‖ *intr* muoversi pesantemente

lum'ber·jack' *s* boscaiolo

lum'ber jack'et *s* giaccone *m*

lum'ber·man *s* (**-men**) (*dealer*) commerciante *m* in legname; (*man who cuts down lumber*) boscaiolo

lum'ber room' *s* ripostiglio

lum'ber·yard' *s* deposito legnami

luminar·y ['lumɪ,nɛri] *s* (**-ies**) luminare *m*

luminous ['lumɪnəs] *adj* luminoso

lummox ['lʌməks] *s* (coll) scimunito

lump [lʌmp] *s* grumo; mucchio; cumulo; (*swelling*) bernoccolo; (*of sugar*) zolletta; (*in one's throat*) groppo; (coll) stupidone *m*; **in the lump** in blocco; **nell'insieme** ‖ *tr* mescolare; (*to make into lumps*) raggrumare; **to lump it** (coll) mandarla giù

lumpish ['lʌmpɪʃ] *adj* grumoso; goffo; balordo

lump' sum' *s* ammontare unico, somma globale

lump·y ['lʌmpi] *adj* (**-ier; -iest**) grumoso; (*person*) pesante, ottuso; (*sea*) agitato

luna·cy ['lunəsi] *s* (**-cies**) pazzia

lunar ['lunər] *adj* lunare

lu'nar land'ing *s* allunaggio

lu'nar mod'ule *s* modulo lunare

lu'nar rov'er *s* auto *f* lunare

lunatic ['lunətɪk] *adj & s* demente *mf*

lu'natic asy'lum *s* manicomio

lu'natic fringe' *s* estremisti *mpl* fanatici

lunch [lʌntʃ] *s* (*regular midday meal*) seconda colazione; (*light meal*) spuntino, merenda ‖ *intr* fare colazione; fare uno spuntino

lunch' bas'ket *s* portavivande *m*

luncheon ['lʌntʃən] *s* seconda colazione; pranzo ufficiale

luncheonette [,lʌntʃə'nɛt] *s* tavola calda

lunch'eon meat' *s* insaccati *mpl*

lunch'room' *s* tavola calda

lung [lʌŋ] *s* polmone *m*

lunge [lʌndʒ] *s* slancio; (*fencing*) affondo ‖ *intr* slanciarsi

lurch [lʌrtʃ] *s* barcollamento; (*at close of a game*) cappotto; (naut) sbandata; **to leave in the lurch** piantare

in asso ‖ *intr* barcollare; (naut) sbandare

lure [lur] *s* esca; (fig) insidie *fpl* ‖ *tr* adescare; **to lure away** distogliere, sviare

lurid ['lurɪd] *adj* (*fiery*) ardente, acceso; sensazionale; (*gruesome*) orripilante

lurk [lʌrk] *intr* stare in agguato, nascondersi; (fig) essere latente

luscious ['lʌʃəs] *adj* delizioso; lussuoso, lussureggiante; voluttuoso

lush [lʌʃ] *adj* lussureggiante, lussuoso

lust [lʌst] *s* desiderio sfrenato; libidine *f*, lussuria ‖ *intr*—**to lust after or for** aver sete di

luster ['lʌstər] *s* (*gloss*) lustro, lucentezza; (*glory*) lustro, onore *m*

lus'ter·ware' *s* ceramiche smaltate

lustful ['lʌstfəl] *adj* lussurioso

lustrous ['lʌstrəs] *adj* lucido

lust·y ['lʌsti] *adj* (**-ier; -iest**) vigoroso, gagliardo

lute [lut] *s* (mus) liuto; (chem) luto

Lutheran ['luθərən] *adj & s* luterano

luxuriance [lʌg'ʒurɪ·əns] *s* rigoglio

luxuriant [lʌg'ʒurɪ·ənt] *adj* lussureggiante; (*imagery*) ridondante

luxuriate [lʌg'ʒurɪ,et] *or* [lʌk'ʃurɪ,et] *intr* lussureggiare; trovare piacere

luxurious [lʌg'ʒurɪ·əs] *or* [lʌk'ʃurɪ·əs] *adj* lussuoso, fastoso

luxu·ry ['lʌkʃəri] *or* ['lʌgʒəri] *s* (**-ries**) lusso, sfarzo

lye [laɪ] *s* ranno, lisciva

lying ['laɪ·ɪŋ] *adj* menzognero ‖ *s* il mentire

ly'ing-in' hos'pital *s* clinica ostetrica, maternità *f*

lymph [lɪmf] *s* linfa

lymphatic [lɪm'fætɪk] *adj* linfatico

lynch [lɪntʃ] *tr* linciare

lynching ['lɪntʃɪŋ] *s* linciaggio

lynx [lɪŋks] *s* lince *f*

lynx-eyed ['lɪŋks,aɪd] *adj* dagli occhi di lince

lyonnaise [,laɪ·ə'nez] *adj* (culin) alla maniera di Lione

lyre [laɪr] *s* lira

lyric ['lɪrɪk] *adj* lirico ‖ *s* lirica; (*words of a song*) parole *fpl*

lyrical ['lɪrɪkəl] *adj* lirico

lyricism ['lɪrɪ,sɪzəm] *s* lirismo

lyricist ['lɪrɪsɪst] *s* (*writer of words for songs*) paroliere *m*; (*poet*) lirico

M

M, m [em] *s* tredicesima lettera dell'alfabeto inglese

ma'am [mæm] *or* [mɑm] *s* (coll) signora

macadam [mə'kædəm] *s* macadàm *m*

macadamize [mə'kædə,maɪz] *tr* macadamizzare

macaroni [,mækə'roni] *s* maccheroni *mpl*

macaroon [,mækə'run] *s* amaretto

macaw [mə'kɔ] *s* ara

mace [mes] *s* mazza; (*spice*) macis *m & f*

mace' bear'er *s* mazziere *m*

machination [,mækɪ'neʃən] *s* macchinazione, macchina

machine [mə'ʃin] *s* macchina ‖ *tr* fare a macchina

machine' gun' *s* mitragliatrice *f*

machine'-gun' *v* (*pret & pp* **-gunned;** *ger* **-gunning**) *tr* mitragliare

machine'-made' *adj* fatto a macchina

machiner·y [mə'ʃinəri] s (-ies) macchinario, meccanismo
machine' screw' s vite f per metallo
machine' shop' s officina meccanica
machine' tool' s macchina utensile
machinist [mə'ʃinist] s meccanico; (nav) secondo macchinista
mackerel ['mækərəl] s maccarello
mack'erel sky' s cielo a pecorelle
mackintosh ['mækɪn,taʃ] s impermeabile m
mad [mæd] adj (madder; maddest) (angry; rabid) arrabbiato; (insane; foolish) pazzo, folle; furioso; **to be mad about** (coll) andar pazzo per; **to drive mad** far impazzire; **to go mad** impazzire; (said of a dog) diventare idrofobo
madam ['mædəm] s signora
mad'cap' s mattoide m, rompicollo
madden ['mædən] tr (to make angry) inferocire; (to make insane) fare impazzire
made-to-order ['medtə'ɔrdər] adj fatto apposta; (clothing) fatto su misura
made'-up' adj inventato; (using cosmetics) truccato
mad'house' s manicomio
mad'man' s (-men') pazzo
madness ['mædnɪs] s rabbia; pazzia
Madonna lily [mə'dɑnə] s giglio
maelstrom ['melstrəm] s vortice m
magazine ['mægə,zin] or [,mægə'zin] s (periodical) rivista, giornale m; (warehouse) magazzino; (for cartridges) caricatore m; (for powder) polveriera; (naut) santabarbara; (phot) magazzino
maggot ['mægət] s larva di dittero
Magi ['medʒaɪ] spl Re Magi
magic ['mædʒɪk] adj magico ‖ s magia; illusionismo; **as if by magic** come per incanto
magician [mə'dʒɪʃən] s (entertainer) illusionista mf; (sorcerer) mago
magistrate ['mædʒɪs,tret] s magistrato
magnanimous [mæg'nænɪməs] adj magnanimo
magnesium [mæg'niʃɪ·əm] or [mæg-'niʒɪ·əm] s magnesio
magnet ['mægnɪt] s calamita, magnete m
magnetic [mæg'netɪk] adj magnetico
magnetism ['mægnɪ,tɪzəm] s magnetismo
magnetize ['mægnɪ,taɪz] tr calamitare, magnetizzare
magne·to [mæg'nito] s (-tos) magnete m
magnificent [mæg'nɪfɪsənt] adj magnifico
magni·fy ['mægnɪ,faɪ] v (pret & pp -fied) tr ingrandire; (to exaggerate) magnificare
mag'nifying glass' s lente f d'ingrandimento
magnitude ['mægnɪ,tjud] or ['mægnɪ,tud] s grandezza
magpie ['mæg,paɪ] s gazza
mahlstick ['mal,stɪk] or ['mɔl,stɪk] s appoggiamano
mahoga·ny [mə'hɑgəni] s (-nies) mogano

Mahomet [mə'hɑmɪt] s Maometto
maid [med] s (girl) ragazza; (servant) cameriera, domestica
maiden ['medən] s pulzella
maid'en-hair' s (bot) capelvenere m
maid'en-head' s imene m
maidenhood ['medən,hud] s verginità f
maid'en la'dy s zitella
maid'en name' s nome m da signorina
maid'en voy'age s viaggio inaugurale
maid'-in-wait'ing s (maids-in-waiting) (of a princess) damigella d'onore; (of a queen) dama d'onore
maid' of hon'or s (attendant at a wedding; attendant of a princess) damigella d'onore; (attendant of a queen) dama d'onore
maid'serv'ant s domestica, ancella
mail [mel] s posta; (of armor) maglia; **by return mail** a volta di corriere ‖ tr impostare
mail'bag' s sacco postale
mail'boat' s battello postale
mail'box' s cassetta or buca delle lettere
mail' car' s vagone m postale
mail' car'rier s postino, portalettere m
mail'ing list' s indirizzario
mail'ing per'mit s abbonamento postale
mail'man' s (-men') portalettere m
mail' or'der s ordinazione per corrispondenza
mail'-order house' s ditta che fa affari unicamente per corrispondenza
mail'plane' s areoplano postale
mail' train' s treno postale
maim [mem] tr mutilare
main [men] adj principale, maggiore ‖ s condotta principale; **in the main** principalmente, per lo più
main' clause' s proposizione principale
main' course' s piatto forte
main' deck' s ponte m principale
mainland ['men,lænd] or ['menlənd] s terra ferma, continente m
main' line' s (rr) linea principale
mainly ['menli] adv principalmente
mainmast ['menmæst], ['men,mæst] or ['men,mɑst] s albero maestro
mainsail ['mensəl] or ['men,sel] s vela maestra
main'spring' s molla motrice; (fig) molla
main'stay' s (naut) strallo di maestra; (fig) cardine m
main' street' s strada principale
maintain [men'ten] tr mantenere
maintenance ['mentɪnəns] s mantenimento; (upkeep) manutenzione
maitre d'hôtel [,metər do'tel] s (butler) maggiordomo; (headwaiter) capocameriere m
maize [mez] s mais m
majestic [mə'dʒestɪk] adj maestoso
majes·ty ['mædʒɪsti] s (-ties) maestà f
major ['medʒər] adj maggiore ‖ s (educ) specializzazione; (mil) maggiore m ‖ intr (educ) specializzarsi
major·do·mo [,medʒər'domo] s (-mos) maggiordomo
ma'jor gen'eral s generale m di divisione

majori·ty [mə'dʒɑrɪti] or [mə'dʒɔrɪti] *adj* maggioritario ‖ *s* (-ties) (*being of full age*) maggiore età *f*; (*larger number or part*) maggioranza *f*; (mil) grado di maggiore

make [mek] *s* (*brand*) marca; (*form*) stile *m*; produzione; **on the make** (slang) tirando l'acqua al proprio mulino ‖ *v* (*pret & pp* **made** [med]) *tr* fare; (*a train*) pigliare; (*a circuit*) chiudere; essere, e.g., **she will make a good typist** sarà una buona dattilografa; **to make** + *inf* fare + *inf*, e.g., **she made him study** lo fece studiare; **to make into** trasformare in; **to make known** far sapere; **to make of** pensare di; **to make oneself known** darsi a conoscere; **to make out** decifrare; (*a prescription*) scrivere, preparare; (*a check*) riempire; **to make over** convertire; (com) trasferire; **to make up** preparare, comporre; (*a story*) inventare; (*lost time*) riguadagnare; (typ) impaginare; (theat) truccare ‖ *intr* essere fatto; **to make away with** rubare; disfarsi di; **to make believe that** + *ind* far finta di + *inf*, e.g., **he made believe (that) he was sleeping** fece finta di dormire; **to make for** avvicinarsi a; attaccare; (*better relations*) contribuire a cementare; **to make much of** (coll) fare le feste a; **to make off** andarsene; **to make off with** svignarsela con; **to make out** (coll) farcela; **to make toward** incamminarsi verso; **to make up** truccarsi; fare la pace; **to make up for** compensare per, supplire a; **to make up to** (coll) ingraziarsi; (coll) fare la corte a

make'-be·lieve' *adj* immaginario ‖ *s* finzione, sembianza

maker ['mekər] *s* fabbricante *mf*, costruttore *m* ‖ **Maker** *s* Fattore *m*

make'shift' *adj* improvvisato, di fortuna ‖ *s* espediente *m*, ripiego; (*person*) tappabuchi *mf*

make'-up' *s* composizione, costituzione; truccatura, cosmetico; (typ) impaginazione; (journ) caratteristica

make'-up man' *s* truccatore *m*

make'-up test' *s* esame *m* di riparazione

make'weight' *s* giunta, contentino; (fig) supplemento, di più *m*

making ['mekɪŋ] *s* fabbricazione; costituzione; causa del successo; **makings** materiale *m*; (*potential*) stoffa

maladjusted [ˌmælə'dʒʌstɪd] *adj* spostato

mala·dy ['mælədi] *s* (-dies) malattia

malaise [mæ'lez] *s* malessere *m*

malapropos [ˌmæləprə'po] *adj* inopportuno ‖ *adv* a sproposito

malaria [mə'lɛri·ə] *s* malaria

Malay ['mele] or [mə'le] *adj & s* malese *mf*

malcontent ['mælkən ˌtɛnt] *adj & s* malcontento

male [mel] *adj & s* maschio

malediction [ˌmælɪ'dɪkʃən] *s* maledizione

malefactor ['mælɪ ˌfæktər] *s* malfattore *m*

male' nurse' *s* infermiere *m*

malevolent [mə'lɛvələnt] *adj* malevolo

malfeasance [mæl'fizəns] *s* reato di pubblico funzionario

malice ['mælɪs] *s* malizia; (law) dolo; **to bear malice** serbar rancore; **with malice prepense** (law) con premeditazione

malicious [mə'lɪʃəs] *adj* malizioso, maligno

malign [mə'laɪn] *adj* maligno ‖ *tr* calunniare

malignan·cy [mə'lɪgnənsi] *s* (-cies) malignità *f*; (pathol) malignità *f*

malignant [mə'lɪgnənt] *adj* maligno

maligni·ty [mə'lɪgnɪti] *s* (-ties) malignità *f*

malinger [mə'lɪŋgər] *intr* fingersi ammalato, darsi malato (per sottrarsi al proprio dovere)

mall [mɔl] or [mæl] *s* viale *m*; (*strip of land in a boulevard*) aiola

mallet ['mælɪt] *s* maglio; (*of a stone cutter*) mazzuolo

mallow ['mælo] *s* malva

malnutrition [ˌmælnju'trɪʃən] or [ˌmælnu'trɪʃən] *s* malnutrizione

malodorous [mæl'odərəs] *adj* puzzolente

malpractice [mæl'præktɪs] *s* incuria, negligenza; (*of physician or lawyer*) negligenza colposa

malt [mɔlt] *s* malto

maltreat [mæl'trit] *tr* maltrattare

mamma ['mɑmə] or [mə'mɑ] *s* (coll) mamma

mammal ['mæməl] *s* mammifero

mammalian [mæ'meli·ən] *adj & s* mammifero

mammoth ['mæməθ] *adj* mastodontico ‖ *s* mammut *m*

man [mæn] *s* (men [mɛn]) uomo; (in chess) pedina; (in checkers) pezzo; **a man** uno, e.g., **a man can get lost in this town** uno può perdersi in questa città; **as one man** come un sol uomo; **man alive!** accidenti!; **man and wife** marito e moglie; **to be one's own man** essere completamente indipendente ‖ *v* (*pret & pp* **manned**; *ger* **manning**) *tr* (*a boat*) equipaggiare; (*a fortress*) guarnire; (*a cannon*) manneggiare

man' about town' *s* vitaiolo

manacle ['mænəkəl] *s*—**manacles** manette *fpl* ‖ *tr* ammanettare

manage ['mænɪdʒ] *tr* (*a business*) gestire; (*e.g., a tool*) maneggiare ‖ *intr* sbrogliarsela; **to manage to** fare in modo di; ingegnarsi a; **to manage to get along** barcamenarsi

manageable ['mænɪdʒəbəl] *adj* maneggevole

management ['mænɪdʒmənt] *s* direzione, gestione; (*executives collectively*) classe *f* dirigente; direzione; (*college course*) economia aziendale

manager ['mænədʒər] *s* direttore *m*, gerente *mf*; (theat) impresario; (sports) procuratore *m*, manager *m*

managerial [ˌmænə'dʒɪrɪ·əl] *adj* direttoriale, imprenditoriale

man'aging ed'itor *s* gerente *m* responsabile, redattore *m* in capo

mandate ['mændet] *s* mandato || *tr* dare in mandato a

mandatory ['mændə,tori] *adj* obbligatorio

mandolin ['mændəlɪn] *s* mandolino

mandrake ['mændrek] *s* mandragola

mandrel ['mændrəl] *s* (mach) mandrino

mane [men] *s* criniera

maneuver [mə'nuvər] *s* manovra || *tr* manovrare || *intr* manovrare; (aer, nav) evoluire; (fig) intrigare

manful ['mænfəl] *adj* maschile, risoluto

manganese ['mæŋgə,nis] *or* ['mæŋgə,niz] *s* manganese *m*

mange [mendʒ] *s* rogna

manger ['mendʒər] *s* presepio

mangle ['mæŋgəl] *tr* straziare, lacerare

man-gy ['mendʒɪ] *adj* (-gier; -giest) rognoso; (squalid) misero

man'han'dle *tr* malmenare, maltrattare

man'hole' *s* passo d'uomo, pozzetto

manhood ['mænhʊd] *s* virilità *f*; uomini *mpl*, umanità *f*

man'hunt' *s* caccia all'uomo

mania ['menɪ.ə] *s* mania

maniac ['menɪ,æk] *adj & s* maniaco

manicure ['mænɪ,kjur] *s* (treatment) manicure *f*; (manicurist) manicure *mf* || *tr* (a person) curare le mani di; (the hands) curare

manicurist ['mænɪ,kjurɪst] *s* manicurista *mf*, manicure *mf*

manifest ['mænɪ,fest] *adj* manifesto || *s* (naut) manifesto di carico || *tr* manifestare

manifes·to [,mænɪ'festo] *s* (-toes) manifesto

manifold ['mænɪ,fold] *adj* molteplice || *s* copia; carta velina; (aut, mach) collettore *m*

manikin ['mænɪkɪn] *s* manichino; (dwarf) nano

man' in the moon' *s* faccia di uomo che appare nella luna piena

man' in the street' *s* uomo qualunque, uomo della strada

manipulate [mə'nɪpjə,let] *tr* manipolare

man'kind' *s* genere umano || **man'kind'** *s* il sesso maschile

manliness ['mænlɪnɪs] *s* virilità *f*

man-ly ['mænlɪ] *adj* (-lier; -liest) maschio, virile

manned' space'ship *s* astronave pilotata

mannequin ['mænɪkɪn] *s* (figure) manichino; (person) indossatrice *f*

manner ['mænər] *s* maniera; **by all manner of means** in tutti i modi; **in a manner of speaking** in una certa maniera; **in the manner of** alla moda di; **manners** maniere, *fpl*, educazione; **to the manner born** avvezzo sin dalla nascita

mannish ['mænɪʃ] *adj* maschile; (woman) mascolino

man' of God' *s* santo; profeta *m*; (priest) uomo al servizio di Dio

man' of let'ters *s* letterato

man' of means' *s* uomo danaroso

man' of parts' *s* uomo di talento

man' of straw' *s* uomo di paglia

man' of the world' *s* uomo di mondo

man-of-war [,mænəv'wɔr] *s* (men-of-war [,menəv'wɔr] nave *f* da guerra

manor ['mænər] *s* maniero; feudo

man'or house' *s* maniero, palazzo

man' o'verboard *interj* uomo in mare!

man'pow'er *s* manodopera; (mil) effettivo

mansard ['mænsard] *s* mansarda

mansion ['mænʃən] *s* palazzo, palazzina; (manor house) maniero

man'slaugh'ter *s* omicidio colposo

mantel ['mæntəl] *s* parte *f* anteriore dei pilastri del camino; (shelf above it) mensola

man'tel·piece' *s* mensola del camino

man'tis shrimp' ['mæntɪs] *s* canocchia

mantle ['mæntəl] *s* mantello, cappa || *tr* ammantare; (to conceal) nascondere || *intr* (to blush) arrossire

manual ['mænju·əl] *adj* manuale || *s* (book) manuale *m*; (mil) esercizio; (mus) tastiera d'organo

man'ual train'ing *s* istruzione nelle arti e mestieri

manufacture [,mænjə'fæktʃər] *s* fabbricazione; (thing manufactured) manufatto *m* || *tr* fabbricare

manufacturer [,mænjə'fæktʃərər] *s* fabbricante *mf*, industriale *m*

manure [mə'njur] *or* [mə'nur] *s* letame *m* || *tr* concimare

manuscript ['mænjə,skrɪpt] *adj & s* manoscritto

many ['menɪ] *adj & pron* molti; **a good many** *or* **a great many** un buon numero; **as many . . . as** tanti . . . quanti; **as many as** fino a, e.g., **they sell as many as five thousand dozen** vendono fino a cinquemila dozzine; **how many** quanti; **many a** molti, e.g., **many a day** molti giorni; **many another** molti altri; **many more** molti di più; **so many** tanti; **too many** troppi; **twice as many** altrettanti, il doppio

many-sided ['menɪ,saɪdɪd] *adj* multilaterale; versatile

map [mæp] *s* mappa; (of a city) piano || *v* (pret & pp **mapped**; ger **mapping**) *tr* tracciare la mappa di; mostrare sulla mappa; **to map out** fare il piano di

maple ['mepəl] *s* acero

maquette [mɑ'ket] *s* plastico

mar [mɑr] *v* (pret & pp **marred**; ger **marring**) *tr* deturpare, sfigurare

maraud [mə'rɔd] *tr & intr* predare

marauder [mə'rɔdər] *s* predone *m*

marble ['mɑrbəl] *adj* marmoreo || *s* marmo; (little ball of glass) bilia; **marbles** bilie *fpl*; **to lose one's marbles** (slang) mancare una rotella a qlcu || *tr* marmorizzare

march [mɑrtʃ] *s* marcia; (hist) marca; **to steal a march on** guadagnare il vantaggio su ‖ *tr* far marciare ‖ *intr* marciare ‖ **March** *s* marzo

marchioness ['mɑr/ənɪs] *s* marchesa

mare [mer] *s* (*female horse*) cavalla; (*female donkey*) asina

margarine ['mɑrdʒərɪn] *s* margarina

margin ['mɑrdʒɪn] *s* margine *m*; (econ) scoperto

mar′gin stop′ *s* marginatore *m*

marigold ['mærɪ‚gold] *s* fiorrancio

marihuana or marijuana [‚mærɪ-'hwɑnə] *s* marijuana

marina [mə'rinə] *s* porto turistico di imbarcazioni, porticciolo turistico

marinate ['mærɪ‚net] *tr* marinare

marine [mə'rin] *adj* marino, marittimo ‖ *s* marina; soldato di fanteria da sbarco; **marines** fanteria da sbarco; **tell that to the marines!** (coll) va a raccontarlo ai frati!

mariner ['mærɪnər] *s* marinaio

marionette [‚mærɪ·ə'nɛt] *s* marionetta

mar′ital sta′tus ['mærɪtəl] *s* stato civile

maritime ['mærɪ‚taɪm] *adj* marittimo

marjoram ['mɑrdʒərəm] *s* origano; (*sweet marjoram*) maggiorana

mark [mɑrk] *s* segno; (*brand*) marca; (*of punctuation*) punto; (*in an examination*) voto; (*sign made by illiterate person*) croce *f*; (*landmark*) segnale *m*; (*target*) bersaglio; (*spot*) macchia; (*starting point in a race*) linea di partenza; (*of confidence*) voto; (*coin*) marco; impronta; **to be beside the mark** essere fuori del seminato; **to hit the mark** colpire il bersaglio; **to leave one's mark** lasciare la propria impronta; **to make one's mark** raggiungere il successo; **to miss the mark** fallire il colpo; **to toe the mark** mettersi in fila; filare diritto ‖ *tr* marcare, segnare, contrassegnare; (*a student*) dar il voto a; (*a test*) esaminare; improntare; notare, avvertire; **to mark down** mettere in iscritto; ribassare il prezzo di

mark′down′ *s* riduzione di prezzo

market ['mɑrkɪt] *s* mercato; **to bear the market** giocare al ribasso; **to bull the market** giocare al rialzo; **to play the market** giocare in borsa; **to put on the market** lanciare sul mercato ‖ *tr* mettere sul mercato

marketable ['mɑrkɪtəbəl] *adj* commerciabile, vendibile

marketing ['mɑrkɪtɪŋ] *s* compravendita; marketing *m*

mar′ket·place′ *s* piazza del mercato

mar′ket price′ *s* prezzo corrente

mark′ing gauge′ ['mɑrkɪŋ] *s* graffietto

marks′man *s* (-men) tiratore *m*; **a good marksman** un tiratore scelto

marksmanship ['mɑrksmən‚ʃɪp] *s* qualità *f* di tiratore scelto

mark′up′ *s* margine *m* di rivendita

marl [mɑrl] *s* marna ‖ *tr* marnare

marmalade ['mɑrmə‚led] *s* marmellata d'arance

marmot ['mɑrmət] *s* marmotta

maroon [mə'run] *adj & s* marrone *m* ‖ *tr* abbandonare (*in un luogo deserto*)

marquee [mɑr'ki] *s* pensilina

marquess ['mɑrkwɪs] *s* marchese *m*

marque·try ['mɑrkətri] *s* (-tries) intarsio

marquis ['mɑrkwɪs] *s* marchese *m*

marquise [mɑr'kiz] *s* marchesa; (Brit) pensilina

marriage ['mærɪdʒ] *s* matrimonio

marriageable ['mærɪdʒəbəl] *adj* adatto al matrimonio; (*woman*) nubile

mar′riage por′tion *s* dote *f*

mar′riage rate′ *s* nuzialità *f*

mar′ried life′ *s* vita coniugale

marrow ['mæro] *s* midollo

mar·ry ['mæri] *v* (*pret & pp* -ried) *tr* sposare; **to get married to** sposarsi con ‖ *intr* sposarsi; **to marry into** (*e.g., a noble family*) imparentarsi con; **to marry the second time** risposarsi

Mars [mɑrz] *s* Marte *m*

Marseilles [mɑr'selz] *s* Marsiglia

marsh [mɑrʃ] *s* palude *f*, lama

mar·shal ['mɑrʃəl] *s* direttore *m* di una sfilata; maestro di cerimonie; (mil) maresciallo; (U.S.A.) ufficiale *m* di giustizia ‖ *v* (*pret & pp* -shaled or -shalled; *ger* -shaling or -shalling) *tr* introdurre cerimoniosamente; mettere in buon ordine

marsh′ mal′low *s* (bot) altea

marsh′mal′low *s* dolce *m* di gelatina e zucchero

marsh·y ['mɑrʃi] *adj* (-ier; -iest) paludoso, palustre

marten ['mɑrtən] *s* (*Martes martes*) martora; (*Martes zibellina*) zibellino

martial ['mɑrʃəl] *adj* marziale

mar′tial law′ *s* legge *f* marziale

Martian ['mɑrʃən] *adj & s* marziano

martin ['mɑrtɪn] *s* rondicchio

martinet [‚mɑrtɪ'nɛt] *or* ['mɑrtɪ‚nɛt] *s* pignolo

martyr ['mɑrtər] *s* martire *mf*

martyrdom ['mɑrtərdəm] *s* martirio

mar·vel ['mɑrvəl] *s* meraviglia ‖ *v* (*pret & pp* -veled or -velled; *ger* -veling or -velling) *intr* meravigliarsi; **to marvel at** stupirsi di, meravigliarsi di

marvelous ['mɑrvələs] *adj* meraviglioso

Marxist ['mɑrksɪst] *adj & s* marxista *mf*

mascara [mæs'kærə] *s* bistro, rimmel *m*

mascot ['mæskət] *s* mascotte *f*

masculine ['mæskjəlɪn] *adj & s* maschile *m*

mash [mæʃ] *s* (*crushed mass*) poltiglia; (*to form wort*) decotto d'orzo germinato; (*e.g., for poultry*) intriso ‖ *tr* schiacciare; impastare

mashed′ pota′toes *spl* purè *m* di patate

masher ['mæʃər] *s* utensile *m* per schiacciare; (slang) pappagallo

mask [mæsk] *or* [mɑsk] *s* maschera; (phot) mascherina ‖ *tr* mascherare; (phot) mettere una mascherina a ‖ *intr* mascherarsi

masked′ ball′ *s* ballo in maschera

mason ['mesən] *s* muratore *m* ‖ **Mason** *s* massone *m*

mason·ry ['mesənri] *s* (-ries) arte *f* del

muratore; muratura || **Masonry** s
massoneria

masquerade [ˌmæskəˈred] or [ˌmɑskə-
ˈred] s mascherata; (*disguise*) ma-
schera; (*pretense*) finzione || *intr*
mascherarsi; **to masquerade as** mascherarsi da; farsi passare per

mass [mæs] s massa; (*celebration of
the Eucharist*) messa; **in the mass**
nell'insieme; **the masses** le masse ||
tr ammassare || *intr* ammassarsi, ac-
cumularsi

massacre [ˈmæsəkər] s massacro, strage
f || *tr* massacrare, trucidare

massage [məˈsɑʒ] s massaggio || *tr*
massaggiare

masseur [mæˈsœr] s massaggiatore m

masseuse [mæˈsœz] s massaggiatrice f

massive [ˈmæsɪv] *adj* massiccio; (*e.g.,
dose*) massivo; solido

mass′ me′dia [ˈmidɪ·ə] s mezzi mpl di
comunicazione di massa

mass′ meet′ing s assemblea popolare;
adunanza in massa

mass′ produc′tion s produzione in serie

mast [mæst] or [mɑst] s (*post*) palo;
(agr) ghiande fpl, faggiole fpl; (naut)
albero; **before the mast** come marinaio semplice

master [ˈmæstər] or [ˈmɑstər] s (*employer*) padrone m; (*male head of
household*) capo di casa; (*man who
possesses some special skill*) maestro;
(*title of respect for a boy*) signorino;
(naut) capitano || *tr* dominare; (*a
language*) possedere

mas′ter bed′room s camera da letto
padronale

mas′ter blade′ s foglia maestra (di una
balestra)

mas′ter build′er s capomastro

masterful [ˈmæstərfəl] or [ˈmɑstərfəl]
adj autoritario; provetto, magistrale

mas′ter key′ s chiave maestra

masterly [ˈmæstərli] or [ˈmɑstərli] *adj*
magistrale || *adv* magistralmente

mas′ter mechan′ic s mastro meccanico

mas′ter-mind′ s mente direttiva || *tr*
organizzare, dirigere

mas′ter of cer′emonies s maestro di
cerimonia; (*in a night club, radio,
etc.*) presentatore m

mas′ter-piece′ s capolavoro

mas′ter ser′geant s (mil) sergente m
maggiore

mas′ter stroke′ s colpo da maestro

mas′ter-work′ s capolavoro

master-y [ˈmæstəri] or [ˈmɑstəri] s
(-ies) (*command of a subject*) dominio; (*skill*) maestria

mast′head′ s (journ) titolo; (naut)
testa d'albero

masticate [ˈmæstɪˌket] *tr* masticare

mastiff [ˈmæstɪf] or [ˈmɑstɪf] s mastino

masturbate [ˈmæstərˌbet] *tr* mastur-
bare || *intr* masturbarsi

mat [mæt] s (*for floor*) tappeto,
stuoia; (*under a dish*) tondo, sotto-
coppa, centrino; (*before a door*)
stoino, zerbino; (*around a picture*)
bordo di cartone; (sports) materas-

sino; (typ) flan m; flano || *v* (*pret &
pp* **matted;** *ger* **matting**) *tr* coprire di
stuoie; arruffare || *intr* arruffarsi

match [mætʃ] s (*counterpart*) uguale
m; (*suitably associated pair*) paio;
(*light*) fiammifero; (*wick*) miccia;
(*prospective mate*) partito; (sports)
partita, gara; **to be a match for**
essere pari a, fare fronte a; **to meet
one's match** trovare un degno rivale
|| *tr* uguagliare, pareggiare; (*colors*)
combinare; (*in pairs*) appaiare; giocarsi, e.g., **to match s.o. for the
drinks** giocarsi le bevande con qlcu
|| *intr* corrispondersi, fare il paio

match′box′ s scatola di fiammiferi; (*of
wax matches*) scatola di cerini

matchless [ˈmætʃlɪs] *adj* incomparabile, senza pari

match′mak′er s paraninfo

mate [met] s compagno; (*husband or
wife*) consorte mf; (*to a female*) maschio; (*to a male*) femmina; (chess)
scacco matto; (naut) primo ufficiale
|| *tr* appaiare; (chess) dar scacco
matto a; **to be well mated** esser ben
appaiato || *intr* accoppiarsi

material [məˈtɪrɪ·əl] *adj* materiale;
importante || s materiale m, materia;
(*cloth, fabric*) tela, stoffa; **materials**
occorrente m

materialist [məˈtɪrɪ·əlɪst] s materialista
mf

materialize [məˈtɪrɪ·əˌlaɪz] *intr* mate-
rializzarsi

matériel [məˌtɪrɪˈɛl] s materiale m;
materiale bellico

maternal [məˈtʌrnəl] *adj* materno

maternity [məˈtʌrnɪti] s maternità f

mater′nity ward′ s maternità f

mathematical [ˌmæθɪˈmætɪkəl] *adj*
matematico

mathematician [ˌmæθɪməˈtɪʃən] s matematico

mathematics [ˌmæθɪˈmætɪks] s matematica

matinée [ˌmætɪˈne] s mattinata, diurna

mat′ing sea′son s calore m

matins [ˈmætɪnz] spl mattutino

matriarch [ˈmetrɪˌɑrk] s matrona di-
gnitosa; donna che possiede l'autorità matriarcale

matricidal [ˌmetrɪˈsaɪdəl] or [ˌmætrɪ-
ˈsaɪdəl] *adj* matricida

matricide [ˈmetrɪˌsaɪd] or [ˈmætrɪ-
ˌsaɪd] s (*act*) matricidio; (*person*)
matricida mf

matriculate [məˈtrɪkjəˌlet] *tr* immatri-
colare || *intr* immatricolarsi

matriculation [məˌtrɪkjəˈleʃən] s im-
matricolazione, iscrizione

matrimonial [ˌmætrɪˈmonɪ·əl] *adj* matrimoniale

matrimo-ny [ˈmætrɪˌmoni] s (-nies)
matrimonio

ma-trix [ˈmetrɪks] or [ˈmætrɪks] s
(-trices[trɪˌsiz] or -trixes) matrice f

matron [ˈmetrən] s matrona; direttrice
f; guardiana

matronly [ˈmetrənli] *adj* matronale

matter [ˈmætər] s (*physical substance*)
materia; (*pus*) materia; (*affair, busi-*

ness) faccenda; (*material of a book*) contenuto; (*reason*) motivo; (*copy for printer*) manoscritto; (*printed material*) stampati *mpl*; **a matter of** un caso di; **for that matter** per quanto riguarda ciò; **in the matter** al soggetto; **no matter** non importa; **no matter how** non importa come; **no matter when** non importa quando; **no matter where** non importa dove; **what is the matter?** cosa succede?; **what is the matter with you?** cosa ha? || *intr* importare

mat′ter of course′ *s*—**as a matter of course** come se nulla fosse, come se fosse una cosa naturale

mat′ter of fact′ *s*—**as a matter of fact** in realtà, a onor del vero

matter-of-fact ['mætərəv‚fækt] *adj* prosaico, pratico

mattock ['mætək] *s* piccone *m*

mattress ['mætrɪs] *s* materasso

mature [mə'tʃur] or [mə'tur] *adj* maturo; (*due*) scaduto || *tr* maturare || *intr* maturare; (*com*) scadere

maturity [mə'tʃurɪti] or [mə'turɪti] *s* maturità *f*; (*com*) scadenza

maudlin ['mɔdlɪn] *adj* sentimentale, lagrimoso; piagnucoloso e ubriaco

maul [mɔl] *tr* maltrattare, bistrattare

maulstick ['mɔl‚stɪk] *s* appoggiamano

maundy ['mɔndi] *s* lavanda

Maun′dy Thurs′day *s* giovedì santo

mausole·um [‚mɔsə'li·əm] *s* (**-ums** or **-a** [ə]) mausoleo

maw [mɔ] *s* (e.g., *of a hog*) stomaco; (*of carnivorous mammal*) fauci *fpl*; (*of fowl*) gozzo; (*fig*) bocca, fauci *fpl*

mawkish ['mɔkɪʃ] *adj* (*sickening*) nauseante; (*sentimental*) svenevole

maxim ['mæksɪm] *s* massima

maximum ['mæksɪməm] *adj & s* massimo

may [me] *v aux*—**it may be** può essere; **may I come in?** si può?; **may you be happy!** possa tu essere felice! || **May** *s* maggio

maybe ['mebi] *adv* forse

May′ Day′ *s* primo maggio; festa della primavera; (*hist*) calendimaggio (*in Florence*)

mayhem ['mehem] or ['me·əm] *s* mutilazione dolosa

mayonnaise [‚me·ə'nez] *s* maionese *f*

mayor ['me·ər] or [mer] *s* sindaco

mayoress ['me·ɔrɪs] or ['mɛrɪs] *s* donna sindaco

May′pole′ *s* maio, maggio, palo per le danze di calendimaggio

May′pole dance′ *s* ballo figurato con nastri per la festa di primavera

May′ queen′ *s* reginetta di maggio

maze [mez] *s* dedalo, labirinto

me [mi] *pron* me; mi; **to me** mi; **a me**

meadow ['mɛdo] *s* prato

mead′ow·land′ *s* prateria

meager ['migər] *adj* magro

meal [mil] *s* (*food*) pasto; (*unbolted grain*) farina

meal′time′ *s* ora del pasto

mean [min] *adj* (*intermediate*) medio; (*low in rank*) basso, umile; (*shabby*) misero; (*of poor quality*) inferiore; (*stingy*) taccagno; (*nasty*) villano; (*vicious, as a horse*) intrattabile; (*coll*) indisposto; (*coll*) vergognoso; (*slang*) splendido; **no mean** eccellente || *s* media, termine medio; **by all means** certamente, senza dubbio; **by means of** per mezzo di; **by no means** in nessuna maniera; **means** beni *mpl*; (*agency*) mezzo, maniera; **to live on one's means** vivere di rendita || *v* (*pret & pp* **meant** [ment]) *tr* significare, voler dire; **to mean to** pensare || *intr*—**to mean well** aver buone intenzioni

meander [mɪ'ændər] *s* meandro || *intr* serpeggiare, vagare

meaning ['minɪŋ] *s* senso, significato

meaningful ['minɪŋfəl] *adj* significativo

meaningless ['minɪŋlɪs] *adj* senza senso, senza significato

meanness ['minnɪs] *s* viltà *f*, bassezza; (*stinginess*) meschinità *f*; (*lowliness*) umiltà *f*, povertà *f*

mean′time′ *s*—**in the meantime** nel frattempo || *adv* frattanto, intanto

mean′while′ *s & adv* var *of* **meantime**

measles ['mizəlz] *s* morbillo; (*German measles*) rosolia

mea·sly ['mizli] *adj* (**-slier**; **-sliest**) col morbillo; (*coll*) miserabile

measurable ['mɛʒərəbəl] *adj* misurabile

measure ['mɛʒər] *s* misura; (*legislative bill*) progetto di legge; (*mus*) battuta; **in a measure** in un certo senso; **to take the measure of** prendere le misure di; giudicare accuratamente || *tr* misurare; (*a distance*) percorrere; **to measure out** somministrare || *intr* misurare; **to measure up to** essere all'altezza di

measurement ['mɛʒərmənt] *s* misura; **to take s.o.'s measurements** prendere le misure di qlcu

meas′uring cup′ *s* metro graduato

meat [mit] *s* carne *f*; (*food in general*) cibo; (*of nut*) gheriglio; (*fig*) sostanza, midollo

meat′ball′ *s* polpetta

meat′ grind′er *s* tritacarne *m*

meat′ loaf′ *s* polpettone *m*

meat′ mar′ket *s* macelleria

meat·y ['miti] *adj* (**-ier**; **-iest**) carnoso, polputo; (*fig*) sostanzioso

Mecca ['mɛkə] *s* la Mecca; **the Mecca** (fig) la Mecca

mechanic [mɪ'kænɪk] *s* meccanico; (*aut*) motorista *m*

mechanical [mɪ'kænɪkəl] *adj* meccanico; (*machinelike*) (fig) macchinale

mechan′ical engineer′ing *s* ingegneria meccanica

mechan′ical pen′cil *s* matita automatica

mechanics [mɪ'kænɪks] *s* meccanica

mechanism ['mɛkə‚nɪzəm] *s* meccanismo, congegno

mechanize ['mɛkə‚naɪz] *tr* meccanizzare

medal ['mɛdəl] *s* medaglia

medallion [mɪ'dæljən] *s* medaglione *m*

meddle ['mɛdəl] *intr* intromettersi
meddler ['mɛdlər] *s* ficcanaso
meddlesome ['mɛdəlsəm] *adj* invadente, indiscreto
median ['midɪ·ən] *adj* medio, mediano ‖ *s* punto medio, numero medio
me'dian strip' *s* spartitraffico
mediate ['midɪ‚et] *tr* (*a dispute*) comporre; (*parties*) pacificare ‖ *intr* (*to be in the middle*) mediare; fare da paciere
mediation [‚midɪ'eʃən] *s* mediazione
mediator ['midɪ‚etər] *s* mediatore *m*
medical ['mɛdɪkəl] *adj* medico; (*student*) di medicina
medicinal [mə'dɪsɪnəl] *adj* medicinale
medicine ['mɛdɪsɪn] *s* medicina
med'icine cab'inet *s* armadietto farmaceutico
med'icine kit' *s* cassetta farmaceutica
med'icine man' *s* (**men'**) stregone indiano
medieval [‚midɪ'ivəl] *or* [‚mɛdɪ'ivəl] *adj* medievale
medievalist [‚midɪ'ivəlɪst] *or* [‚mɛdɪ'ivəlɪst] *s* medievalista *mf*
mediocre ['midɪ‚okər] *or* [‚midɪ'okər] *adj* mediocre
mediocri·ty [‚midɪ'akrɪti] *s* (-**ties**) mediocrità *f*
meditate ['mɛdɪ‚tet] *tr & intr* meditare
meditation [‚mɛdɪ'teʃən] *s* meditazione
Mediterranean [‚mɛdɪtə'renɪ·ən] *adj & s* Mediterraneo
medi·um ['midɪ·əm] *adj* medio; (*heat*) moderato; (*meat*) cotto moderatamente ‖ *s* (-**ums** *or* -**a** [ə]) (*middle state; mean*) media; mezzo; (*in spiritualism*) medium *m*; media (*of communication*) media *mpl*; **through the medium of** per mezzo di
medlar ['mɛdlər] *s* (*tree*) nespolo; (*fruit*) nespola
medley ['mɛdli] *s* farragine *f*, mescolanza; (*mus*) pot-pourri *m*
medul·la [mɪ'dʌlə] *s* (-**lae** [li]) midollo
meek [mik] *adj* mansueto, umile
meekness ['miknɪs] *s* mansuetudine *f*
meerschaum ['mɪrʃəm] *or* ['mɪrʃəm] *s* schiuma; pipa di schiuma
meet [mit] *adj* conveniente ‖ *s* incontro ‖ *v* (*pret & pp* **met** [mɛt]) *tr* incontrare, incontrarsi con; (*to become acquainted with*) fare la conoscenza di; riunirsi con; (*to cope with*) sopperire a; (*one's obligations*) far fronte a; (*bad luck*) avere; **to meet the eyes of** presentarsi agli occhi di ‖ *intr* incontrarsi; riunirsi; conoscersi; **till we meet again** arrivederci; **to meet with** incontrare, incontrarsi con; (*an accident*) avere; (*said of a public carrier*) fare coincidenza con
meet'ing ['mitɪŋ] *s* riunione, ritrovo; seduta, convegno; (*political*) comizio; (*e.g., of two rivers*) confluenza; duello
meet'ing of the minds' *s* accordo, consonanza di voleri
meet'ing place' *s* luogo di riunione

megacycle ['mɛgə‚saɪkəl] *s* megaciclo
megaphone ['mɛgə‚fon] *s* megafono, portavoce *m*
megohm ['mɛg‚om] *s* megaohm *m*
melancholia [‚mɛlən'kolɪ·ə] *s* melanconia, malinconia
melanchol·y ['mɛlən‚kɑli] *adj* malinconico ‖ *s* (-**ies**) malinconia
melee ['mele] *or* ['mɛle] *s* (*fight*) mischia; confusione
mellow ['mɛlo] *adj* (*fruit*) maturo; (*wine*) pastoso; (*voice*) soave, melodioso ‖ *tr* raddolcire ‖ *intr* raddolcirsi
melodic [mɪ'lɑdɪk] *adj* melodico
melodious [mɪ'lodɪ·əs] *adj* melodioso
melodramatic [‚mɛlədrə'mætɪk] *adj* melodrammatico
melo·dy ['mɛlədɪ] *s* (-**dies**) melodia
melon ['mɛlən] *s* melone *m*, popone *m*
melt [mɛlt] *tr* sciogliere; (*metals*) fondere; (*fig*) intenerire ‖ *intr* sciogliersi; fondersi; (*fig*) intenerirsi; **to melt away** svanire; **to melt into** convertirsi in, diventare; (*tears*) struggersi in
melt'ing pot' *s* crogiolo
member ['mɛmbər] *s* membro
membership ['mɛmbər‚ʃɪp] *s* associazione; numero di membri
membrane ['mɛmbren] *s* membrana
memen·to [mɪ'mɛnto] *s* (-**tos** *or* -**toes**) oggetto ricordo
mem·o ['mɛmo] *s* (-**os**) (coll) memorandum *m*
memoir ['mɛmwar] *s* memoria, memoriale *m*; biografia; **memoirs** memorie *fpl*
memoran·dum [‚mɛmə'rændəm] *s* (-**dums** *or* -**da** [də]) memorandum *m*
memorial [mɪ'morɪ·əl] *adj* commemorativo ‖ *s* sacrario; (*petition*) memoriale *m*
Memo'rial Day' *s* giorno dei caduti
memorialize [mɪ'morɪ·ə‚laɪz] *tr* commemorare
memorize ['mɛmə‚raɪz] *tr* imparare a memoria
memo·ry ['mɛmərɪ] *s* (-**ries**) memoria; **to commit to memory** imparare a memoria
menace ['mɛnɪs] *s* minaccia ‖ *tr & intr* minacciare
ménage [me'naʒ] *s* casa; (*housekeeping*) economia domestica
menagerie [mə'næʒərɪ] *or* [mə'nædʒərɪ] *s* serraglio
mend [mɛnd] *s* riparo; **to be on the mend** migliorare ‖ *tr* (*to repair*) accomodare, riparare; (*to patch*) rammendare; (*fig*) correggere ‖ *intr* correggersi
mendacious [mɛn'deʃəs] *adj* mendace
mendicant ['mɛndɪkənt] *adj & s* mendicante *mf*
menfolk ['mɛn‚fok] *spl* uomini *mpl*
menial ['minɪ·əl] *adj* basso, servile ‖ *s* servitore *m*, servo
menses ['mɛnsiz] *spl* mestruazione, mestrui *mpl*
men's' fur'nishings *spl* articoli *mpl* d'abbigliamento maschile
men's' room' *s* gabinetto per signori

menstruate ['mɛnstru ,et] *intr* avere le mestruazioni

men'tal arith'metic ['mɛntəl] *s* calcolo mentale

men'tal hos'pital *s* manicomio

men'tal ill'ness *s* malattia mentale

men'tal reserva'tion *s* riserva mentale

men'tal test' *s* test *m* mentale

mention ['mɛnʃən] *s* menzione || *tr* menzionare; **don't mention it** non c'è di che

menu ['mɛnju] or ['menju] *s* menu *m*, lista

meow [mɪ'au] *s* miagolio || *intr* miagolare

Mephistophelian [,mɛfɪstə'fili-ən] *adj* mefistofelico

mercantile ['mʌrkən ,til] or ['mʌrkən ,taɪl] *adj* mercantile

mercenar·y ['mʌrsə ,nɛri] *adj* mercenario || *s* (-ies) mercenario

merchandise ['mʌrtʃən ,daɪz] *s* mercanzia, merce *f*

merchant ['mʌrtʃənt] *adj* mercantile || *s* mercante *m*, commerciante *mf*

mer'chant-man *s* (-men) mercantile *m*

mer'chant marine' *s* marina mercantile

merciful ['mʌrsɪfəl] *adj* misericordioso

merciless ['mʌrsɪlɪs] *adj* spietato

mercu·ry ['mʌrkjəri] *s* (-ries) mercurio || **Mercury** *s* Mercurio

mer·cy ['mʌrsi] *s* (-cies) misericordia; **at the mercy of** alla mercé di

mere [mɪr] *adj* mero, puro

meretricious [,mɛrɪ'trɪʃəs] *adj* vistoso, chiassoso, sgargiante; artificiale, falso, finto

merge [mʌrdʒ] *tr* fondere || *intr* fondersi; (*said of two roads*) convergere; **to merge into** convertirsi lentamente in

merger ['mʌrdʒər] *s* fusione

meridian [mə'rɪdɪ-ən] *adj* meridiano; culminante || *s* meridiano; apogeo

meringue [mə'ræŋ] *s* meringa

merit ['mɛrɪt] *s* merito || *tr* meritare

meritorious [,mɛrɪ'tɔri-əs] *adj* meritorio

merlon ['mʌrlən] *s* merlo

mermaid ['mʌr ,med] *s* sirena

mer'man' *s* (-men') tritone *m*

merriment ['mɛrɪmənt] *s* allegria

mer·ry ['mɛri] *adj* (-rier; -riest) allegro, giocondo; **to make merry** divertirsi

Mer'ry Christ'mas *interj* Buon Natale!

mer'ry-go-round' *s* giostra, carosello; (*of parties*) serie ininterrotta

mer'ry-mak'er *s* festaiolo

mesh [mɛʃ] *s* (*network*) rete *f*; (*each open space of net*) maglia; (mach) ingranaggio; **meshes** rete *f* || *tr* irretire; (mach) ingranare || *intr* irretirsi; (mach) ingranarsi

mess [mɛs] *s* (*dirty condition*) disordine *m*; (*meal for a group of people*) mensa, rancio, porzione; **to get into a mess** mettersi nei pasticci; **to make a mess of** rovinare || *tr* sporcare; disordinare; rovinare || *intr* mangiare in comune; **to mess around** (coll) perdersi in cose inutili

message ['mɛsɪdʒ] *s* messaggio

messenger ['mɛsəndʒər] *s* messaggero; (*person who goes on an errand*) fattorino; (mil) portaordini *m*

mess' hall' *s* mensa

Messiah [mə'saɪ-ə] *s* Messia *m*

mess' kit' *s* gavetta, gamella

mess'mate' *s* compagno di rancio

mess' of pot'tage ['pɑtɪdʒ] *s* (Bib & fig) piatto di lenticchie

Messrs. ['mɛsərz] *pl of* **Mr.**

mess·y ['mɛsi] *adj* (-ier; -iest) disordinato; sporco

metal ['mɛtəl] *adj* metallico || *s* metallo

metallic [mɪ'tælɪk] *adj* metallico

metallurgy ['mɛtə ,lʌrdʒi] *s* metallurgia

met'al pol'ish *s* lucido per metalli

met'al-work' *s* lavoro di metallo

metamorpho·sis [,mɛtə'mɔrfəsɪs] *s* -ses [,siz]) metamorfosi *f*

metaphony [mə'tæfəni] *s* metafonia, metafonesi *f*

metaphor ['mɛtəfər] or ['mɛtə ,fɔr] *s* metafora

metaphorical [,mɛtə'fɑrɪkəl] or [,mɛtə'fɔrɪkəl] *adj* metaforico

metathe·sis [mɪ'tæθɪsɪs] *s* (-ses [,siz]) metatesi *f*

mete [mit] *tr*—**to mete out** distribuire

meteor ['mitɪ-ər] *s* meteora

meteoric [,mitɪ'arɪk] or [,mitɪ'ɔrɪk] *adj* meteorico; (fig) rapidissimo, folgorante

meteorite ['mitɪ-ə ,raɪt] *s* meteorite *m* & *f*

meteorology [,mitɪ-ə'rɑlədʒi] *s* meteorologia

meter ['mitər] *s* (*unit of length; verse*) metro; (*instrument for measuring gas, water, etc.*) contatore *m*; (mus) tempo || *tr* misurare col contatore

methane ['mɛθen] *s* metano

method ['mɛθəd] *s* metodo

methodic(al) [mɪ'θɑdɪk(əl)] *adj* metodico

Methodist ['mɛθədɪst] *adj* & *s* metodista *mf*

Methuselah [mɪ'θuzələ] *s* Matusalemme *m*

meticulous [mɪ'tɪkjələs] *adj* meticoloso

metric(al) ['mɛtrɪk(əl)] *adj* metrico

metronome ['mɛtrə ,nom] *s* metronomo

metropolis [mɪ'trɑpəlɪs] *s* metropoli *f*

metropolitan [,mɛtrə'pɑlɪtən] *adj* & *s* metropolitano

mettle ['mɛtəl] *s* disposizione, temperamento; brio, animo; **to be on one's mettle** impegnarsi a fondo

mettlesome ['mɛtəlsəm] *adj* brioso

mew [mju] *s* miagolio; (orn) gabbiano; **mews** scuderie *fpl*

Mexican ['mɛksɪkən] *adj* & *s* messicano

Mexico ['mɛksɪ ,ko] *s* il Messico

mezzanine ['mɛzə ,nin] *s* mezzanino

mica ['maɪkə] *s* mica

microbe ['maɪkrob] *s* microbio

microbiology [,maɪkrəbaɪ'ɑlədʒi] *s* microbiologia

microcard ['maɪkrə ,kɑrd] *s* microscheda

microfarad [ˌmaɪkrəˈfæræd] s microfarad m

microfilm [ˈmaɪkrəˌfɪlm] s microfilm m || tr microfilmare

microgroove [ˈmaɪkrəˌgruv] adj microsolco || s microsolco; disco microsolco

microphone [ˈmaɪkrəˌfon] s microfono

microscope [ˈmaɪkrəˌskop] s microscopio

microscopic [ˌmaɪkrəˈskɑpɪk] adj microscopico

microwave [ˈmaɪkrəˌwev] s microonda

mid [mɪd] adj mezzo, la metà di, e.g., mid October la metà di ottobre

mid'day' adj di mezzogiorno || s mezzogiorno

middle [ˈmɪdəl] adj medio, mezzo || s mezzo, metà f; (of human body) cintura; about the middle of verso la metà di; in the middle of nel mezzo di

mid'dle age' s mezza età || Middle Ages spl Medio Evo

mid'dle class' s ceto medio, borghesia

Mid'dle East' s Medio Oriente

Mid'dle Eng'lish s inglese m medievale parlato fra il 1150 e il 1500

mid'dle fin'ger s dito medio

mid'dle-man's (-men') intermediario

middling [ˈmɪdlɪŋ] adj mediocre, passabile || s (coarsely ground wheat) farina grossa integrale; **middlings** articoli mpl di qualità mediocre || adv moderatamente

mid'dy [ˈmɪdi] s (-dies) aspirante m di marina

mid'dy blouse' s marinara

midget [ˈmɪdʒɪt] s nano

midland [ˈmɪdlənd] adj centrale, interno || s regione centrale

mid'night' adj di mezzanotte; **to burn the midnight oil** studiare a lume di candela || s mezzanotte f

midriff [ˈmɪdrɪf] s diaframma m; (middle part of body) cintura, vita

mid'ship'man s (-men) aspirante m di marina

midst [mɪdst] s mezzo, centro; in the midst of in mezzo a

mid'stream' s—in midstream in mezzo al fiume

mid'sum'mer s cuore m dell'estate

mid'way' adj situato a metà strada || s metà strada; viale m principale di un' esposizione || adv a metà strada

mid'week' s mezzo della settimana

mid'wife' s (-wives') levatrice f

mid'win'ter s cuore m dell'inverno

mid'year' adj nel mezzo dell'anno || s mezzo dell'anno; **midyears** (coll) esami mpl nel mezzo dell'anno scolastico

mien [min] s aspetto, portamento

miff [mɪf] s (coll) battibecco || tr (coll) offendere

might [maɪt] s forza, potenza; **with might and main** a tutta forza || v aux used to form the potential, e.g., he might change his mind è possibile che cambi opinione

might·y [ˈmaɪti] adj (-ier; -iest) po-

tente; (huge) grandissimo || adv (coll) moltissimo, grandemente

migraine [ˈmaɪgren] s emicrania

migrate [ˈmaɪgret] intr migrare

migratory [ˈmaɪgrəˌtori] adj migratore

milch [mɪltʃ] adj lattifero

mild [maɪld] adj dolce, mite, gentile; (disease) leggero

mildew [ˈmɪlˌdju] or [ˈmɪlˌdu] s (mold) muffa; (plant disease) peronospora

mile [maɪl] s miglio terrestre; miglio marino

mileage [ˈmaɪlɪdʒ] s distanza in miglia

mile'age tick'et s biglietto calcolato in miglia simile al biglietto chilometraggio

mile'post' s colonnina miliare

mile'stone' s pietra miliare

milieu [mɪlˈju] s ambiente m

militancy [ˈmɪlɪtənsi] s bellicismo; spirito militante

militant [ˈmɪlɪtənt] adj & s militante mf

militarism [ˈmɪlɪtəˌrɪzəm] s militarismo

militarist [ˈmɪlɪtərɪst] adj & s militarista mf

militarize [ˈmɪlɪtəˌraɪz] tr militarizzare

military [ˈmɪlɪˌteri] adj militare || s—the military le forze armate

mil'itary acad'emy s scuola allievi ufficiali, accademia militare

mil'itary police' s polizia militare

militate [ˈmɪlɪˌtet] intr militare

militia [mɪˈlɪʃə] s milizia

mili'tia-man s (-men) miliziano

milk [mɪlk] adj lattifero; di latte; al latte || s latte m || tr mungere; (fig) spillare || intr dare latte

milk' can' s bidone m per il latte

milk' choc'olate s cioccolato al latte

milk' diet' s regime latteo

milking [ˈmɪlkɪŋ] s mungitura

milk'maid' s lattaia

milk'man' s (-men') lattaio

milk' of hu'man kind'ness s grande compassione

milk' pail' s secchio da latte

milk' shake' s frappé m or frullato di latte

milk'sop' s effeminato

milk'weed' s vincetossico

milk·y [ˈmɪlki] adj (-ier; -iest) latteo; (whitish) lattiginoso

Milk'y Way' s Via Lattea

mill [mɪl] s (for grinding grain) mulino; (for making fabrics) filanda; (for cutting wood) segheria; (for refining sugar) zuccherificio; (for producing steel) acciaieria; (to grind coffee) macinino; (part of a dollar) millesimo; **to put through the mill** mettere a dura prova || tr (grains) macinare; (coins) zigrinare; (steel) laminare; (ore) frantumare; (with a milling machine) fresare; (chocolate) frullare || intr—**to mill about** or **around** girare intorno

millennial [mɪˈlɛnɪəl] adj millenario

milleni·um [mɪ'lɛnɪ-əm] *s* (-ums or -a [ə]) millennio

miller ['mɪlər] *s* mugnaio; (ent) tignola notturna

millet ['mɪlɪt] *s* panico, miglio

milliampere [,mɪlɪ'æmpɪr] *s* milliampere *m*

milliard ['mɪljərd] or ['mɪljɑrd] *s* (Brit) miliardo, bilione *m*

milligram ['mɪlɪ,græm] *s* milligrammo

millimeter ['mɪlɪ,mitər] *s* millimetro

milliner ['mɪlɪnər] *s* modista

milliner·y ['mɪlɪ,nɛri] or ['mɪlɪnəri] *s* (-ies) cappelli *mpl* per signora; modisteria; articoli *mpl* di modisteria

mil'linery shop' *s* modisteria

milling ['mɪlɪŋ] *s* (of grain) macinatura; (of coins) granitura; (mach) fresatura

mill'ing machine' *s* fresatrice *f*

million ['mɪljən] *adj* milione di, milioni di || *s* milione *m*

millionaire [,mɪljən'ɛr] *s* milionario

millionth ['mɪljənθ] *adj, s* & *pron* milionesimo

millivolt ['mɪlɪ,volt] *s* millivolt *m*

mill'pond' *s* gora

mill'race' *s* corrente *f* che aziona il mulino; canale *m* di presa

mill'stone' *s* mola, macina, palmento; (fig) peso, gravame *m*

mill' wheel' *s* ruota del mulino

mill'work' *s* lavoro di falegnameria; lavoro di falegnameria fatto a macchina

mime [maɪm] *s* mimo || *tr* mimare

mimeograph ['mɪmɪ-ə,græf] or ['mɪmɪə,graf] *s* (trademark) ciclostile *m* || *tr* ciclostilare

mim·ic ['mɪmɪk] *s* mimo, imitatore *m* || *v* (*pret* & *pp* **-icked**; *ger* **-icking**) *tr* imitare, scimmiottare

mimic·ry ['mɪmɪkri] *s* (-ries) mimica; (biol) mimetismo

minaret [,mɪnə'rɛt] or ['mɪnə,rɛt] *s* minareto

mince [mɪns] *tr* tagliuzzare, triturare; (words) pronunziare con affettazione; **to not mince one's words** non aver peli sulla lingua

mince'meat' *s* carne tritata; **to make mincemeat of** annientare completamente

mince' pie' *s* torta di frutta secca e carne tritata

mind [maɪnd] *s* mente *f*; opinione; to bear in mind tener presente; to be not in one's right mind essere fuori di senno; to be of one mind essere d'accordo; to be out of one's mind essere impazzito; to change one's mind cambiare d'opinione; to go out of one's mind impazzire; to have a mind to aver voglia di; to have in mind to pensare a; to have on one's mind avere in mente; to lose one's mind uscire di mente; to make up one's mind decidersi; to my mind a mio modo di vedere; to say whatever comes to one's mind dire quanto salta in testa, e.g., **John always says whatever comes to his mind** Gio-

vanni dice sempre quanto gli salta in testa; to set one's mind on risolversi a; to slip one's mind scappare di mente (with *dat*), e.g., **it slipped his mind** gli è scappato di mente; to speak one's mind dire la propria opinione; with one mind unanimamente || *tr* (to take care of) occuparsi di; obbedire (with *dat*); do you mind the smoke? Le disturba il fumo?; mind your own business si occupi degli affari Suoi || *intr* osservare, fare attenzione; rincrescere, e.g., **do you mind if I go?** Le rincresce se vado?; never mind non si preoccupi

mindful ['maɪndfəl] *adj* memore

mind' read'er *s* lettore *m* del pensiero

mind' read'ing *s* lettura del pensiero

mine [maɪn] *s* (e.g., of coal) miniera; (mil & nav) mina || *pron poss* il mio; mio || *tr* minare; (earth) scavare; (ore) estrarre || *intr* lavorare una miniera; (mil & nav) minare

mine' detec'tor *s* rivelatore *m* di mine

mine'field' *s* campo minato

mine'lay'er *s* posamine *m*

miner ['maɪnər] *s* minatore *m*

mineral ['mɪnərəl] *adj* & *s* minerale *m*

mineralogy [,mɪnə'rælədʒi] *s* mineralogia

min'eral wool' *s* cotone *m* or lana minerale

mine' sweep'er *s* dragamine *m*

mingle ['mɪŋgəl] *tr* mescolare; unire || *intr* mescolarsi, associarsi

miniature ['mɪnɪ-ətʃər] or ['mɪnɪt/ər] *s* miniatura; to paint in miniature miniare, dipingere in miniatura

min'iature golf' *s* minigolf *m*

miniaturization [,mɪnɪ-ətʃəri'zeʃən] or [,mɪnɪt/əri'zeʃən] *s* miniaturizzazione

minimal ['mɪnɪməl] *adj* minimo

minimize ['mɪnɪ,maɪz] *tr* minimizzare

minimum ['mɪnɪməm] *adj* & *s* minimo

min'imum wage' *s* salario minimo

mining ['maɪnɪŋ] *adj* minerario || *s* estrazione di minerali; (nav) posa di mine

minion ['mɪnjən] *s* servo; favorito, beniamino

min'ion of the law' *s* poliziotto

miniskirt ['mɪnɪ,skʌrt] *s* minigonna

minister ['mɪnɪstər] *s* ministro; pastore *m* protestante || *tr* & *intr* ministrare

ministerial [,mɪnɪs'tɪrɪ-əl] *adj* ministeriale

minis·try ['mɪnɪstri] *s* (-tries) ministero; sacerdozio

mink [mɪŋk] *s* visone *m*

minnow ['mɪno] *s* pesciolino; (ichth) ciprino

minor ['maɪnər] *adj* minore || *s* minore *m*, minorenne *mf*; (educ) corso secondario

minori·ty [mɪ'nɑrɪti] or [mɪ'nɔrɪti] *adj* minoritario || *s* (-ties) (smaller number or part; group differing in race, etc., from majority) minoranza; (under legal age) minorità *f*

minstrel ['mɪnstrəl] *s* (hist) menestrello; (U.S.A.) comico vestito da nero

minstrel·sy ['mɪnstrəlsi] s (-sies) giulleria; poesia giullaresca

mint [mɪnt] s zecca; (plant) menta; (losenge) mentina; (fig) miniera d'oro ‖ tr coniare

minuet [ˌmɪnjuˈɛt] s minuetto

minus ['maɪnəs] adj meno ‖ s meno, perdita ‖ prep meno, senza

minute [maɪˈnjut] or [maɪˈnut] adj minuto ‖ ['mɪnɪt] adj fatto in un minuto ‖ s minuto; momento; minutes processo verbale; to write up the minutes tenere i verbali; up to the minute al corrente; dell'ultima ora

min'ute hand' ['mɪnɪt] s sfera or lancetta dei minuti

minutiae [mɪˈnjuʃɪˌi] or [mɪˈnuʃɪˌi] spl minuzie fpl

minx [mɪŋks] s sfacciata, civetta

miracle ['mɪrəkəl] s miracolo

mir'acle play' s sacra rappresentazione

miraculous [mɪˈrækjələs] adj miracoloso

mirage [mɪˈrɑʒ] s miraggio

mire [maɪr] s limo, mota

mirror ['mɪrər] s specchio ‖ tr specchiare, riflettere

mirth [mʌrθ] s allegria, gioia

mir·y ['maɪri] adj (-ier; -iest) fangoso, limaccioso

misadventure [ˌmɪsədˈvɛntʃər] s disavventura, contrattempo

misanthrope ['mɪsənˌθrop] s misantropo

misanthropy [mɪsˈænθrəpi] s misantropia

misapprehension [ˌmɪsæprɪˈhɛnʃən] s malinteso

misappropriation [ˌmɪsəˌproprɪˈeʃən] s malversazione

misbehave [ˌmɪsbɪˈhev] intr comportarsi male

misbehavior [ˌmɪsbɪˈhevɪ·ər] s cattiva condotta

miscalculation [ˌmɪskælkjəˈleʃən] s calcolo errato

miscarriage [mɪsˈkærɪdʒ] s (of justice) errore m; (of a letter) disguido; (pathol) aborto

miscar·ry [mɪsˈkæri] v (pret & pp -ried) intr (said of a project) fallire; (said of a letter) smarrirsi; (pathol) abortire

miscellaneous [ˌmɪsəˈlenɪ·əs] adj miscellaneo

miscella·ny ['mɪsəˌleni] s (-nies) miscellanea

mischief ['mɪstʃɪf] s (harm) danno; (disposition to annoy) malizia; (prankishness) birichinata

mis'chief-mak'er s mettimale mf

mischievous ['mɪstʃɪvəs] adj dannoso; malizioso; birichino

misconception [ˌmɪskənˈsɛpʃən] s concetto erroneo

misconduct [mɪsˈkɑndəkt] s cattiva condotta; (of a public official) malgoverno ‖ [ˌmɪskənˈdʌkt] tr male amministrare; to misconduct oneself comportarsi male

misconstrue [ˌmɪskənˈstru] or [mɪsˈkɑnstru] tr fraintendere

miscount [mɪsˈkaunt] s conteggio erroneo ‖ tr & intr contare male

miscue [mɪsˈkju] s sbaglio; (in billiards) stecca ‖ intr steccare; (theat) sbagliarsi di battuta

mis-deal ['mɪsˌdil] s distribuzione sbagliata ‖ [mɪsˈdil] v (pret & pp -dealt [dɛlt]) tr & intr distribuire erroneamente

misdeed [mɪsˈdid] or ['mɪsˌdid] s misfatto, malfatto

misdemeanor [ˌmɪsdɪˈminər] s cattiva condotta; (law) delitto colposo

misdirect [ˌmɪsdɪˈrɛkt] or [ˌmɪsdaɪˈrɛkt] tr dare un indirizzo sbagliato a; (a letter) mettere un indirizzo sbagliato su

misdoing [mɪsˈdu·ɪŋ] s misfatto

miser ['maɪzər] s avaro, spilorcio

miserable ['mɪzərəbəl] adj miserabile, miserevole; (coll) malissimo; (coll) schifoso

miserly ['maɪzərli] adj spilorcio

miser·y ['mɪzəri] s (-ies) miseria

misfeasance [mɪsˈfizəns] s infrazione della legge; abuso di autorità commesso da pubblico funzionario

misfire [mɪsˈfaɪr] s difetto di esplosione; (aut) difetto d'accensione ‖ intr (said of a gun) fare cilecca; (aut) dare accensione irregolare; (fig) fallire

mis-fit ['mɪsˌfɪt] s vestito che non va bene; (person) spostato, pesce m fuor d'acqua ‖ [mɪsˈfɪt] v (pret & pp -fitted) ger -fitting) intr andar male

misfortune [mɪsˈfɔrtʃən] s disgrazia

misgiving [mɪsˈɡɪvɪŋ] s dubbio, timore m, cattivo presentimento

misgovern [mɪsˈɡʌvərn] tr amministrare male

misguided [mɪsˈɡaɪdɪd] adj fuorviato; (e.g., kindness) sconsigliato

mishap ['mɪshæp] or [mɪsˈhæp] s accidente m, infortunio

misinform [ˌmɪsɪnˈfɔrm] tr dare informazioni errate a

misinterpret [ˌmɪsɪnˈtɛrprɪt] tr interpretare male, trasfigurare

misjudge [mɪsˈdʒʌdʒ] tr & intr giudicare male

mis-lay [mɪsˈle] v (pret & pp -laid [ˌled]) tr (e.g., tile) applicare in maniera sbagliata; (e.g., papers) smarrire, mettere al posto sbagliato

mis-lead [mɪsˈlid] v (pret & pp -led [ˌled]) tr sviare, traviare

misleading [mɪsˈlidɪŋ] adj ingannatore

mismanagement [mɪsˈmænɪdʒmənt] s malgoverno

misnomer [mɪsˈnomər] s termine improprio

misplace [mɪsˈples] tr mettere fuori di posto; (trust) riporre erroneamente

misprint ['mɪsˌprɪnt] s errore m di stampa, refuso ‖ [mɪsˈprɪnt] tr stampare erroneamente

mispronounce [ˌmɪsprəˈnauns] tr pronunciare in modo erroneo

mispronunciation [ˌmɪsprəˌnʌnsɪ-

'efən] or [ˌmɪsprəˌnʌnʃɪˈefən] s errore m di pronuncia

misquote [mɪsˈkwot] tr citare incorrettamente

misrepresent [ˌmɪsrɛprɪˈzɛnt] tr travisare, snaturare; (pol) rappresentare slealmente

miss [mɪs] s sbaglio, omissione; tiro fuori bersaglio; signorina || tr (a train, an opportunity) perdere; (the target) fallire; (an appointment) mancare; (the point) non vedere, non capire; per poco, e.g., **the car missed hitting him** l'automobile non l'ha investito per poco || intr sbagliare, fallire; mancare il bersaglio || **Miss** s signorina, la signorina

missal [ˈmɪsəl] s messale m

misshapen [mɪsˈʃepən] adj deforme, malfatto

missile [ˈmɪsɪl] adj missilistico || s missile m

mis'sile launch'er s lanciamissili m

missing [ˈmɪsɪŋ] adj mancante; assente; (in action) disperso

mis'sing link' s anello di congiunzione

miss'ing per'son s disperso

mission [ˈmɪʃən] s missione f

missionary [ˈmɪʃənˌɛri] adj missionario || s (-ies) (eccl) missionario; (dipl) incaricato in missione

missive [ˈmɪsɪv] s missiva

misspell [mɪsˈspɛl] v (pret & pp -spelled or -spelt [ˈspɛlt]) tr & intr scrivere male

misspelling [mɪsˈspɛlɪŋ] s errore m di ortografia

misspent [mɪsˈspɛnt] adj sprecato

misstatement [mɪsˈstetmənt] s dichiarazione inesatta

misstep [mɪsˈstɛp] s passo falso

miss·y [ˈmɪsi] s (-ies) (coll) signorina

mist [mɪst] s caligine f, foschia; (of tears) velo; (of smoke, vapors, etc.) nuvola

mis·take [mɪsˈtek] s errore m, sbaglio; **and no mistake** (coll) di sicuro; **by mistake** per sbaglio; **to make a mistake** sbagliarsi || v (pret -took [ˈtʊk]; pp -taken) tr fraintendere; **to be mistaken for** essere preso per; **to mistake for** pigliare per

mistaken [mɪsˈtekən] adj errato, sbagliato; **to be mistaken** essere in errore, sbagliarsi

mister [ˈmɪstər] s (mil, nav) signore m; (coll) marito || interj (coll) signore!; (coll) Lei!; (coll) buonuomo! || **Mister** s Signore m

mistletoe [ˈmɪsəlˌto] s vischio

mistreat [mɪsˈtrit] tr maltrattare

mistreatment [mɪsˈtritmənt] s maltrattamento

mistress [ˈmɪstrɪs] s (of a household) signora, padrona; (paramour) amante f, ganza; (Brit) maestra di scuola

mistrial [mɪsˈtraɪəl] s processo viziato da errore giudiziario

mistrust [mɪsˈtrʌst] s diffidenza || tr diffidare di || intr diffidarsi

mistrustful [mɪsˈtrʌstfəl] adj diffidente

mist·y [ˈmɪsti] adj (-ier; -iest) fosco, brumoso; (fig) vago, confuso

misunder·stand [ˌmɪsʌndərˈstænd] v (pret & pp -stood [ˈstʊd]) tr fraintendere, equivocare

misunderstanding [ˌmɪsʌndərˈstændɪŋ] s malinteso

misuse [mɪsˈjus] s abuso; (of funds) malversazione || [mɪsˈjuz] tr abusare di; (funds) malversare

misword [mɪsˈwʌrd] tr comporre male

mite [maɪt] s obolo; (ent) acaro

miter [ˈmaɪtər] s (carp) ugnatura; (carp) giunto a quartabuono; (eccl) mitra || tr tagliare a quartabuono, ugnare; giungere a quartabuono

mi'ter box' s cassetta per ugnature

mi'ter joint' s giunto a quartabuono

mitigate [ˈmɪtɪˌget] tr mitigare

mitten [ˈmɪtən] s manopola, muffola

mix [mɪks] tr mescolare; (colors) mesticare; (dough) impastare; (salad) condire; **to mix up** confondere || intr confondersi, mescolarsi

mixed [mɪkst] adj misto; (candy) assortito; (coll) confuso

mixed' com'pany s riunione f di ambo i sessi

mixed' drink' s miscela di liquori diversi

mixed' feel'ing s sentimento ambivalente

mixed' met'aphor s metafora incongruente

mixer [ˈmɪksər] s (mach) mescolatrice f; **to be a good mixer** essere socievole

mixture [ˈmɪkstʃər] s mistura, mescolanza; (aut) miscela, carburazione

mix'-up' s confusione; (coll) baruffa

mizzen [ˈmɪzən] s mezzana

moan [mon] s gemito || intr gemere

moat [mot] s fosso, fossato

mob [mab] s turba || v (pret & pp mobbed; ger mobbing) tr assaltare; affollarsi intorno a; (a place) affollare

mobile [ˈmobɪl] or [ˈmobɪl] adj mobile

mo'bile home' s caravan m, roulotte f

mobility [moˈbɪlɪti] s mobilità f

mobilization [ˌmobɪlɪˈzefən] s mobilitazione

mobilize [ˈmobɪˌlaɪz] tr & intr mobilitare

mob' rule' s legge f della teppa

mobster [ˈmabstər] s gangster m

moccasin [ˈmakəsɪn] s mocassino

Mo'cha cof'fee [ˈmokə] s caffè m moca

mock [mak] adj finto, imitato || s dileggio, burla || tr deridere, canzonare; ingannare || intr motteggiare; **to mock at** farsi gioco di

mocker·y [ˈmakəri] s (-ies) dileggio, scherno; (subject of derision) zimbello; (poor imitation) contraffazione

mock'-hero'ic adj eroicomico

mockingbird [ˈmakɪŋˌbɑrd] s mimo

mock' or'ange s gelsomino selvatico

mock' tur'tle soup' s finto brodo di tartaruga

mock'-up' s modello dimostrativo

mode [mod] s modo, maniera; (fashion) moda; (gram) modo

mod·el [ˈmadəl] adj modello, e.g., **model student** studente modello || s modello; (*woman serving as subject for artists*) modello *f*; (*woman wearing clothes at fashion show*) indossatrice *f* ‖ *v* (*pret & pp* **-eled** or **-elled**; *ger* **-eling** or **-elling**) *tr* modellare ‖ *intr* modellarsi; fare il manichino

mod′el air′plane *s* aeromodello

mo′del-air′plane build′er *s* aeromodellista *mf*

mod′eling clay′ *s* plastilina

moderate [ˈmɑdərɪt] *adj* moderato ‖ [ˈmɑdəˌret] *tr* moderare; (*a meeting*) presiedere a ‖ *intr* moderarsi

moderator [ˈmɑdəˌretər] *s* moderatore *m*; (*mediator*) arbitro; (phys) moderatore *m*

modern [ˈmɑdərn] *adj* moderno

modernize [ˈmɑdərˌnaɪz] *tr* modernizzare, rimodernare

modest [ˈmɑdɪst] *adj* modesto

modes·ty [ˈmɑdɪsti] *s* (**-ties**) modestia

modicum [ˈmɑdɪkəm] *s* piccola quantità

modi·fy [ˈmɑdɪˌfaɪ] *v* (*pret & pp* **-fied**) *tr* modificare; (gram) determinare

modish [ˈmɑdɪʃ] *adj* alla moda

modulate [ˈmɑdʒəˌlet] *tr & intr* modulare

modulation [ˌmɑdʒəˈleʃən] *s* modulazione

mohair [ˈmoˌhɛr] *s* mohair *m*

Mohammedan [moˈhæmɪdən] *adj & s* maomettano

Mohammedanism [moˈhæmɪdəˌnɪzəm] *s* maomettismo

moist [mɔɪst] *adj* umido; lacrimoso

moisten [ˈmɔɪsən] *tr* inumidire ‖ *intr* inumidirsi

moisture [ˈmɔɪstʃər] *s* umidità *f*

molar [ˈmolər] *s* molare *m*

molasses [məˈlæsɪz] *s* melassa

mold [mold] *s* stampo, forma; (*fungus*) muffa; humus *m*; (fig) indole *f* ‖ *tr* plasmare, conformare; (*to make moldy*) fare ammuffire ‖ *intr* ammuffire

molder [ˈmoldər] *s* modellatore *m* ‖ *intr* sgretolarsi; polverizzarsi

molding [ˈmoldɪŋ] *s* modellato; (archit, carp) modanatura

mold·y [ˈmoldi] *adj* (**-ier; -iest**) ammuffito

mole [mol] *s* (*pier*) molo; (*harbor*) darsena; (*spot on skin*) neo; (*small mammal*) talpa

molecule [ˈmɑlɪˌkjul] *s* molecola

mole′hill′ *s* mucchio di terra sopra la tana di talpe

mole′skin′ *s* pelle *f* di talpa; (*fabric*) fustagno di prima qualità

molest [məˈlest] *tr* molestare; fare proposte disoneste a

moll [mɑl] *s* (slang) ragazza della malavita; (slang) puttana

molli·fy [ˈmɑlɪˌfaɪ] *v* (*pret & pp* **-fied**) *tr* pacificare, placare

mollusk [ˈmɑləsk] *s* mollusco

mollycoddle [ˈmɑlɪˌkɑdəl] *s* effeminato ‖ *tr* viziare, coccolare

Mo′lotov cock′tail [ˈmɑləˌtɔf] *s* bottiglia Molotov

molt [molt] *s* muda ‖ *intr* andare in muda

molten [ˈmoltən] *adj* fuso

molybdenum [məˈlɪbdɪnəm] or [ˌmɑlɪbˈdinəm] *s* molibdeno

moment [ˈmomənt] *s* momento; **at any moment** da un momento all'altro

momentary [ˈmomənˌteri] *adj* momentaneo

momentous [moˈmɛntəs] *adj* grave, importante

momen·tum [moˈmɛntəm] *s* (**-tums** or **-ta** [tə]) slancio; (mech) momento

monarch [ˈmɑnərk] *s* monarca *m*

monarchic(al) [məˈnɑrkɪk(əl)] *adj* monarchico

monarchist [ˈmɑnərkɪst] *adj & s* monarchico

monar·chy [ˈmɑnərki] *s* (**-chies**) monarchia

monaster·y [ˈmɑnəsˌteri] *s* (**-ies**) monastero

monastic [məˈnæstɪk] *adj* monastico, monacale

monasticism [məˈnæstɪˌsɪzəm] *s* monachesimo

Monday [ˈmʌndi] *s* lunedì *m*

monetary [ˈmɑnɪˌteri] *adj* monetario; pecuniario

money [ˈmʌni] *s* denaro; **to be in the money** esser carico di soldi; **to make money** far quattrini

mon′ey-bag′ *s* borsa per denaro; **moneybags** (coll) riccone sfondato

moneychanger [ˈmʌniˌtʃendʒər] *s* cambiavalute *m*

moneyed [ˈmʌnid] *adj* danaroso

moneylender [ˈmʌniˌlendər] *s* prestatore *m* di denaro

mon′ey-mak′er *s* capitalista *mf*; affare vantaggioso

mon′ey or′der *s* vaglia *m*

Mongolian [mɑŋˈgoliən] *adj & s* mongolo

mon·goose [ˈmɑŋgus] *s* (**-gooses**) mangusta

mongrel [ˈmʌŋgrəl] or [ˈmɑŋgrəl] *adj* ibrido ‖ *s* ibrido; cane bastardo

monitor [ˈmɑnɪtər] *s* (educ) capoclasse *mf*; (rad, telv) monitore *m* ‖ *tr* osservare; (*a signal*) controllare; (*a broadcast*) ascoltare

monk [mʌŋk] *s* monaco

monkey [ˈmʌŋki] *s* scimmia; **to make a monkey of** farsi gioco di ‖ *intr*—**to monkey around** (coll) oziare; **to monkey around with** (coll) giocherellare con

mon′key-shines′ *spl* (slang) monellerie *fpl*, pagliacciate *fpl*

mon′key wrench′ *s* chiave *f* inglese

monkhood [ˈmʌŋkhud] *s* monacato

monkshood [ˈmʌŋksˌhud] *s* (bot) aconito

monocle [ˈmɑnəkəl] *s* monocolo

monogamy [məˈnɑgəmi] *s* monogamia

monogram [ˈmɑnəˌgræm] *s* monogramma *m*

monograph [ˈmɑnəˌgræf] or [ˈmɑnəˌgrɑf] *s* monografia

monolithic [ˌmɑnəˈlɪθɪk] *adj* monolitico

monologue ['manə‚lɔg] or ['manə‚lɑg] s monologo

monomania [‚manə'menɪ‑ə] s monomania

monomial [mə'nomɪ‑əl] s monomio

monopolize [mə'napə‚laɪz] tr monopolizzare, accaparrare

monopo‧ly [mə'napəli] s (-lies) monopolio, privativa

monorail ['manə‚rel] s monorotaia

monosyllable ['manə‚sɪləbəl] s monosillabo

monotheist ['manə‚θi‑ɪst] adj & s monoteista mf

monotonous [mə'natənəs] adj monotono

monotype ['manə‚taɪp] s (method) monotipia; (typ) monotipo

monoxide [mə'naksaɪd] s monossido

monseigneur [‚mansen'jœr] s monsignore m

monsignor [man'sinjər] s (-monsignors or monsignori [‚mansɪ'njori]) (eccl) monsignore m

monsoon [man'sun] s monsone m

monster ['manstər] adj mostruoso ‖ s mostro

monstrance ['manstrəns] s ostensorio

monstrosi‧ty [man'strasɪti] s (-ties) mostruosità f

monstrous ['manstrəs] adj mostruoso

month [mʌnθ] s mese m

month‧ly ['mʌnθli] adj mensile ‖ s (-lies) rivista mensile; **monthlies** (coll) mestruazione ‖ adv mensilmente

monument ['manjəmənt] s monumento

moo [mu] s muggito ‖ intr muggire

mood [mud] s umore m, vena; (gram) modo; **moods** luna, malumore m

mood‧y ['mudi] adj (-ier; -iest) triste, malinconico; lunatico, capriccioso

moon [mun] s luna; **once in a blue moon** ad ogni morte di papa ‖ tr—**to moon away** (time) (coll) sprecare ‖ intr—**to moon about** (coll) gingillarsi, baloccarsi; (to daydream about) (coll) sognarsi di

moon′beam′ s raggio di luna

moon′light′ s chiaro m di luna

moon′light′ing s secondo lavoro notturno

moon′shine′ s chiaro m di luna; (coll) chiacchiere fpl, balle fpl; (coll) whisky m distillato illegalmente

moon′shot′ s lancio alla luna

moon′stone′ s lunaria

moor [mur] s brughiera, landa ‖ tr ormeggiare ‖ intr ormeggiarsi ‖ **Moor** s moro

Moorish ['murɪʃ] adj moresco

moor′land′ s brughiera, landa

moose [mus] s (moose) alce americano

moot [mut] adj controverso, discutibile

mop [map] s scopa di filaccie; (naut) redazza; (of hair) zazzera ‖ v (pret & pp mopped; ger mopping) tr (a floor) pulire, asciugare; (one's brow) asciugarsi; **to mop up** rastrellare

mope [mop] intr andare rattristato

mopish ['mopɪʃ] adj triste, avvilito

moral ['marəl] or ['mɔrəl] adj morale ‖ s (of a fable) morale f; **morals** (ethics) morale f; (modes of conduct) costumi mpl

morale [mə'ræl] or [mə'rɑl] s morale m

morali‧ty [mə'rælɪti] s (-ties) moralità f

mor′als charge′ s accusa di oltraggio al pudore

morass [mə'ræs] s palude f

moratori‧um [‚morə'torɪ‑əm] or [‚marə'torɪ‑əm] s (-ums or -a [ə]) moratoria

morbid ['mɔrbɪd] adj (gruesome) orribile; (feelings; curiosity; pertaining to disease; pathologic) morboso

mordacious [mɔr'deʃəs] adj mordace

mordant ['mɔrdənt] adj & s mordente m

more [mor] adj & s più m ‖ adv più; **more and more** sempre più; **more than** più di; (followed by verb) più di quanto; **the more . . . the less** tanto più . . . quanto meno

more‧o′er adv per di più, inoltre

Moresque [mo'resk] adj moresco

morgue [mɔrg] s deposito, obitorio; (journ) archivio di un giornale, frigorifero

moribund ['mɔrɪ‚bʌnd] or ['marɪ‚bʌnd] adj moribondo

morning ['mɔrnɪŋ] adj mattiniero ‖ s mattina, mattino; **good morning** buon giorno; **in the morning** di mattina

morn′ing coat′ s giacca nera a code

morn′ing‑glo′ry s (-ries) convolvolo; (Ipomea) campanella; (Convolvulus tricolor) bella di giorno

morn′ing sick′ness s vomito di gravidanza

morn′ing star′ s Lucifero, stella del mattino

Moroccan [mə'rakən] adj & s marocchino

morocco [mə'rako] s (leather) marocchino ‖ **Morocco** s il Marocco

moron ['mɔran] s deficiente mf

morose [mə'ros] adj tetro, imbronciato

morphine ['mɔrfin] s morfina

morphology [mɔr'falədʒi] s morfologia

morrow ['maro] or ['mɔro] s—**on the morrow** l'indomani, il giorno seguente; domani

morsel ['mɔrsəl] s boccone m, boccincino; pezzetto

mortal ['mɔrtəl] adj & s mortale m

mortality [mɔr'tælɪti] s mortalità f; (death or destruction on a large scale) moria

mortar ['mɔrtər] s (mixture of lime or cement) malta, calcina; (bowl) mortaio; (mil) mortaio, lanciabombe m

mor′tar‑board′ s sparviere m; (cap) tocco accademico

mortgage ['mɔrgɪdʒ] s ipoteca ‖ tr ipotecare

mortgagee [‚mɔrgɪ'dʒi] s creditore m ipotecario

mortgagor ['mɔrgɪdʒər] s debitore m ipotecario

mortician [mɔr'tɪʃən] s impresario di pompe funebri

morti‧fy ['mɔrtɪ,faɪ] v (pret & pp -fied) tr mortificare; **to be mortified** vergognarsi

mortise ['mɔrtɪs] s intaccatura, incastro || tr incassare, incastrare

mor'tise lock' s serratura incastrata

mortuar‧y ['mɔrtʃʊ,ɛri] adj mortuario || s (-ies) camera mortuaria

mosaic [mo'ze‧ɪk] s mosaico

Moscow ['mɑskau] or ['mɑsko] s Mosca

Moses ['mozɪz] or ['mozɪs] s Mosè m

Mos‧lem ['mɑzləm] or ['mɑsləm] adj musulmano || s (-lems or -lem) musulmano

mosque [mɑsk] s moschea

mosqui‧to [məs'kito] s (-toes or -tos) zanzara

mosqui'to net' s zanzariera

moss [mɔs] or [mɑs] s musco

moss'back' s (coll) ultraconservatore m, fossile m

moss‧y ['mɔsi] or ['mɑsi] adj (-ier; -iest) muscoso

most [most] adj il più di, la maggior parte di || s la maggioranza, i più; **most of** la maggior parte di; **to make the most of** trarre il massimo da || adv più, maggiormente, al massimo

mostly ['mostli] adv per lo più, maggiormente, al massimo

motel [mo'tɛl] s motel m, autostello

moth [mɔθ] or [mɑθ] s falena; (clothes moth) tarma

moth'ball' s pallina antitarmica

moth-eaten ['mɔθ,itən] or ['mɑθ,itən] adj tarmato; antiquato

mother ['mʌðər] adj (love, tongue) materno; (country) natio; (church, company) madre || s madre f; (elderly woman) (coll) zia || tr fare da madre a; creare; procreare; assumere la maternità di

moth'er coun'try s madrepatria

Moth'er Goose' s supposta autrice di una raccolta di favole infantili

motherhood ['mʌðər,hʊd] s maternità f

moth'er-in-law' s (moth'ers-in-law') suocera

moth'er-land' s madrepatria

motherless ['mʌðərlɪs] adj orfano di madre, senza madre

mother-of-pearl ['mʌðərəv'pʌrl] adj madreperlaceo || s madreperla

motherly ['mʌðərli] adj materno

Moth'er's Day' s giorno della madre, festa della mamma

moth'er supe'rior s madre superiora

moth'er tongue' s madrelingua; (language from which another language is derived) lingua madre

moth'er wit' s intelligenza nativa

moth' hole' s tarlatura

moth‧y ['mɔθi] or ['mɑθi] adj (-ier; -iest) tarmato

motif [mo'tif] s motivo

motion ['moʃən] s movimento; (e.g., of a dancer) movenza, mossa; (in parliamentary procedure) mozione; **in motion** in moto || intr fare cenno

motionless ['moʃənlɪs] adj immobile

mo'tion pic'ture s pellicola cinematografica; **motion pictures** cinematografia

mo'tion-picture' adj cinematografico

motivate ['motɪ,vet] tr animare, incitare

motive ['motɪv] adj motivo; (producing motion) motore || s motivo; (incentive) movente m

mo'tive pow'er s forza motrice; impianto motore; (rr) insieme m di locomotive

motley ['mɑtli] adj eterogeneo; variato, variopinto

motor ['motər] adj motore; (operated by motor) motorizzato; (pertaining to motor vehicles) motoristico || s motore m; (aut) macchina || intr viaggiare in macchina

mo'tor-boat' s motobarca, motoscafo

mo'tor-bus' s torpedone m; autobus m

motorcade ['motər,ked] s carovana di automobili

mo'tor-car' s automobile f

mo'tor-cy'le s motocicletta

motorist ['motərɪst] s automobilista mf

motorize ['motə,raɪz] tr motorizzare

mo'torman s (-men) guidatore m di tram; guidatore m di locomotore

mo'tor sail'er s motoveliero

mo'tor scoot'er s motoretta

mot'or ship' s motonave f

mo'tor truck' s autocarro, camion m

mo'tor ve'hicle s motoveicolo

mottle ['mɑtəl] tr chiazzare, screziare

mot‧to ['mɑto] s (-toes or -tos) motto, divisa

mould [mold] s, tr, & intr var of mold

mound [maund] s monticello, collinetta

mount [maunt] s monte m, montagna; (horse for riding) cavalcatura, monta; (setting for a jewel) montatura; supporto; (for a picture) incorniciatura || tr montare; (a wall) scalare; (theat) allestire || intr montare; (to climb) salire

mountain ['mauntən] s montagna; **to make a mountain out of a molehill** fare di un bruscolo una trave, fare d'una mosca un elefante

moun'tain climb'ing s alpinismo

mountaineer [,mauntə'nɪr] s montanaro

mountainous ['mauntənəs] adj montagnoso

moun'tain rail'road s ferrovia a dentiera

moun'tain range' s catena di montagne

moun'tain sick'ness s mal m di montagna

mountebank ['maunti,bæŋk] s ciarlatano

mounting ['mauntɪŋ] s (act) il montare, montaggio; (setting) montatura; (mach) supporto

mourn [morn] tr (the loss of s.o.) piangere; (a misfortune) lamentare || intr piangere; vestire a lutto

mourner ['mornər] s persona in lutto; (penitent sinner) penitente mf;

(woman hired to attend a funeral or funerals) prefica

mourn'er's bench' *s* banco dei penitenti

mournful ['mɔrnfəl] *adj* luttuoso, funesto; *(gloomy)* lugubre

mourning ['mɔrnɪŋ] *s* lutto; **to be in mourning** portare il lutto

mourn'ing band' *s* bracciale *m* a lutto

mouse [maʊs] *s* (**mice** [maɪs]) topo, sorcio

mouse'hole' *s* topaia; piccolo buco

mouser ['maʊzər] *s* cacciatore *m* di topi

mouse'trap' *s* trappola per topi

moustache [məs'tæʃ] or [məs'taʃ] *s* baffi *mpl*, mustacchi *mpl*

mouth [maʊθ] *s* (**mouths** [maʊðz]) bocca; **by mouth** per via orale; **to be born with a silver spoon in one's mouth** essere nato con la camicia; **to make one's mouth water** fare venire a qlcu l'acquolina in bocca

mouthful ['maʊθ,fʊl] *s* boccata

mouth' or'gan *s* armonica a bocca

mouth'piece' *s (of wind instrument)* bocchetta; *(of bridle)* imboccatura; *(of megaphone)* boccaglio; *(of cigarette)* bocchino; *(of telephone)* imboccatura; *(spokesman)* portavoce *m*

mouth'wash' *s* sciacquo, risciacquo

movable ['muvəbəl] *adj* mobile, movibile; *(law)* mobiliare

move [muv] *s* movimento; *(change of residence)* trasloco; *(step)* passo; *(e.g., in chess)* mossa; **on the move** in moto, in movimento; **to get a move on** (coll) affrettarsi ‖ *tr* muovere; *(the bowels)* provocare l'evacuazione di; *(to prompt)* spingere; *(to stir the feelings of)* emozionare, commuovere; *(law)* proporre; *(com)* svendere; **to move up** *(a date)* anticipare ‖ *intr* movimentarsi; passare; *(to another house)* traslocare; *(to another city)* trasferirsi; *(said of goods)* avere una vendita; *(said of the bowels)* evacuare; *(law)* presentare una mozione; (coll) andarsene; **to move away** andarsene; trasferirsi; **to move back** tirarsi indietro; **to move in** avanzare; *(society)* frequentare; **to move off** allontanarsi

movement ['muvmənt] *s* movimento; *(of a watch)* meccanismo; *(of the bowels)* evacuazione; *(mus)* movimento, tempo

movie ['muvi] *s* (coll) film *m*, pellicola

movie-goer ['muvi,go·ər] *s* frequentatore *m* del cinema

mov'ie house' *s* (coll) cinematografo

mov'ie·land' *s* (coll) cinelandia

moving ['muvɪŋ] *adj* commovente, emozionante ‖ *s* trasporto; *(from one house to another)* trasloco

mov'ing pic'ture *s* film *m*, pellicola

mov'ing stair'case' *s* scala mobile

mow [mo] *v (pret* **mowed***; pp* **mowed** or **mown)** *tr & intr* falciare

mower ['mo·ər] *s* falciatore *m; (mach)* falciatrice *f*

Mr. ['mɪstər] *s* (**Messrs.** ['mesərz]) Signore *m*

Mrs. ['mɪsɪz] *s* Signora

much [mʌtʃ] *adj & pron* molto; **as much . . . as** tanto . . . quanto; **too much** troppo ‖ *adv* molto; **however much** per quanto; **how much** quanto; **too much** troppo; **very much** moltissimo

mucilage ['mjusɪlɪdʒ] *s* colla; *(gummy secretion in plants)* mucillagine *f*

muck [mʌk] *s* letame *m; (dirt)* sudiciume *m; (min)* materiale *m* di scoria

muck'rake' *intr* (coll) sollevare scandali

mucous ['mjukəs] *adj* mucoso

mucus ['mjukəs] *s* muco

mud [mʌd] *s* fango, melma, limo; **to sling mud at** calunniare

muddle ['mʌdəl] *s* confusione, guazzabuglio ‖ *tr* confondere, intorbidire ‖ *intr*—**to muddle through** arrangiarsi; cavarsela alla meno peggio in

mud'dle·head' *s* (coll) semplicione *m*

mud·dy ['mʌdi] *adj* (**-dier; -diest**) fangoso, melmoso; *(obscure)* torbido ‖ *v (pret & pp* **-died)** *tr* turbare, intorbidare; *(to soil with mud)* infangare

mud'guard' *s* parafango

mud'hole' *s* pozzanghera, fangaia

mud' slide' *s* smottamento

mudslinger ['mʌd,slɪŋgər] *s* calunniatore *m*

muff [mʌf] *s* manicotto ‖ *tr* (coll) mancare; *(to handle badly)* (coll) abborracciare; *(sports)* mancare di pigliare

muffin ['mʌfɪn] *s* panino soffice

muffle ['mʌfəl] *tr* infagottare, imbacuccare; *(a sound)* velare, smorzare

muffler ['mʌflər] *s* sciarpa; *(aut)* silenziatore *m*, marmitta

mufti ['mʌfti] *s*—**in mufti** in borghese

mug [mʌg] *s* tazzona; *(slang)* muso, grugno ‖ *v (pret & pp* **mugged)** *ger* **mugging)** *tr* (slang) fotografare; *(slang)* attaccare proditoriamente ‖ *intr* fare le smorfie

mug·gy ['mʌgi] *adj* (**-gier; -giest**) afoso, opprimente

mulat·to [mju'læto] or [mə'læto] *s* (**-toes**) mulatto

mulber·ry ['mʌl,beri] *s* (**-ries**) *(tree)* gelso; *(fruit)* mora di gelso

mulct [mʌlkt] *tr* defraudare

mule [mjul] *s* mulo; *(slipper)* pianella

muleteer [,mjulə'tɪr] *s* mulattiere *m*

mulish ['mjulɪʃ] *adj* testardo

mull [mʌl] *tr (wine)* scaldare aggiungendo spezie ‖ *intr*—**to mull over** pensarci sopra, rinvangare

mulled' wine' *s* vino caldo

mullion ['mʌljən] *s* colonnina che divide una bifora

multigraph ['mʌltɪ,græf] or ['mʌltɪ,graf] *s* (trademark) poligrafo ‖ *tr* poligrafare

multilateral [,mʌltɪ'lætərəl] *adj* multilaterale

multimotor [,mʌltɪ'motər] *s* plurimotore *m*

multiple ['mʌltɪpəl] *adj & s* multiplo

multiplici·ty [,mʌltɪ'plɪsɪti] *s* (**-ties**) molteplicità *f*

multi·ply ['mʌltɪ,plaɪ] *v (pret & pp* **-plied)** *tr* moltiplicare ‖ *intr* moltiplicarsi

multistage [ˈmʌltɪ ˌstedʒ] *adj* (rok) pluristadio

multitude [ˈmʌltɪ ˌtjud] or [ˈmʌltɪ ˌtud] s moltitudine *f*

mum [mʌm] *adj* zitto; **mum's the word!** acqua in bocca!; **to keep mum** stare zitto || *interj* zitto!

mumble [ˈmʌmbəl] *tr* biascicare || *intr* farfugliare

mummer·y [ˈmʌməri] *s* (-ies) buffonata, mascherata

mum·my [ˈmʌmi] *s* (-mies) mummia

mumps [mʌmps] *s* orecchioni *mpl*

munch [mʌntʃ] *tr* sgranocchiare

mundane [ˈmʌnden] *adj* mondano

municipal [mjuˈnɪsɪpəl] *adj* municipale

municipali·ty [mjuˌnɪsɪˈpælɪti] *s* (-ties) municipio

munificent [mjuˈnɪfɪsənt] *adj* munifico

munition [mjuˈnɪʃən] *s* munizione || *tr* fornire di munizioni

muni'tion dump' *s* deposito munizioni

mural [ˈmjurəl] *adj* murale || *s* pittura murale

murder [ˈmʌrdər] *s* omicidio || *tr* assassinare

murderer [ˈmʌrdərər] *s* omicida *m*

murderess [ˈmʌrdərɪs] *s* omicida *f*

murderous [ˈmʌrdərəs] *adj* omicida, crudele, sanguinario

murk·y [ˈmʌrki] *adj* (-ier; -iest) fosco, tenebroso; brumoso, nebbioso

murmur [ˈmʌrmər] *s* mormorio || *tr & intr* mormorare

Mur'phy bed' [ˈmʌrfi] *s* letto a scomparsa

muscle [ˈmʌsəl] *s* muscolo

muscular [ˈmʌskjələr] *adj* muscolare; (*having well-developed muscles*) muscoloso

muse [mjuz] *s* musa; **the Muses** le Muse || *intr* meditare, rimuginare

museum [mjuˈzi·əm] *s* museo

mush [mʌʃ] *s* pappa, polentina; (fig) leziosaggine *f*, sdolcinatura

mush'room *s* fungo || *intr* venir su come i funghi; **to mushroom into** diventare rapidamente

mush'room cloud' *s* fungo atomico

mush·y [ˈmʌʃi] *adj* (-ier; -iest) polposo, spappolato; (fig) sdolcinato, sentimentale

music [ˈmjuzɪk] *s* musica; **to face the music** (coll) affrontare le conseguenze; **to set to music** mettere in musica

musical [ˈmjuzɪkəl] *adj* musicale

mu'sical com'edy *s* operetta, commedia musicale

musicale [ˌmjuzɪˈkæl] *s* serata musicale

mu'sic box' *s* scatola armonica

mu'sic cab'inet *s* scaffaletto per la musica

mu'sic hall' *s* salone *m* da concerti; (Brit) teatro di varietà, music-hall *m*

musician [mjuˈzɪʃən] *s* musicista *mf*

musicianship [mjuˈzɪʃən ˌʃɪp] *s* abilità *f* musicale, virtuosismo

musicologist [ˌmjuzɪˈkɑlədʒɪst] *s* musicologo

musicology [ˌmjuzɪˈkɑlədʒi] *s* musicologia

mu'sic stand' *s* portamusica *m*

musk [mʌsk] *s* muschio

musk' deer' *s* mosco

musket [ˈmʌskɪt] *s* moschetto

musketeer [ˌmʌskɪˈtɪr] *s* moschettiere *m*

musk'mel'on *s* melone *m*

musk' ox' *s* bue muschiato

musk'rat' *s* ondatra, topo muschiato

muslin [ˈmʌzlɪn] *s* mussolina

muss [mʌs] *tr* (*the hair*) scompigliare, arruffare; (*clothing*) (coll) sciupare

mussel [ˈmʌsəl] *s* mussolo

Mussulman [ˈmʌsəlmən] *adj & s* musulmano

muss·y [ˈmʌsi] *adj* (-ier; -iest) (coll) arruffato, scompigliato

must [mʌst] *s* (*new wine*) mosto; (*mold*) muffa; (coll) cosa assolutamente indispensabile || *v aux*—**I must go now** devo andarmene ora; **it must be Ann** deve essere Anna; **she must be ill** dev'essere malata; **they must have known it** devono averlo saputo

mustache [məsˈtæʃ], [ˈmʌstæʃ] or [ˈmʌstæʃ] *s* baffi *mpl*, mustacchi *mpl*

mustard [ˈmʌstərd] *s* mostarda

mus'tard plas'ter *s* senapismo

muster [ˈmʌstər] *s* adunata, rivista; **to pass muster** passar ispezione || *tr* chiamare a raccolta; riunire; **to muster in** arruolare; **to muster out** congedare; **to muster up courage** prendere coraggio a quattro mani

mus'ter roll' *s* ruolo; (naut) appello

mus·ty [ˈmʌsti] *adj* (-tier; -tiest) (*moldy*) ammuffito; (*stale*) stantio; (fig) ammuffito, stantio

mutation [mjuˈteʃən] *s* mutazione

mute [mjut] *adj & s* muto || *tr* mettere la sordina a

mutilate [ˈmjutɪ ˌlet] *tr* mutilare

mutineer [ˌmjutɪˈnɪr] *s* ammutinato

mutinous [ˈmjutɪnəs] *adj* ammutinato

muti·ny [ˈmjutɪni] *s* (-nies) ammutinamento || *v* (*pret & pp* -nied) *intr* ammutinarsi

mutt [mʌt] *s* (slang) cane bastardo; (slang) scemo

mutter [ˈmʌtər] *tr & intr* borbottare

mutton [ˈmʌtən] *s* montone *m*

mut'ton chop' *s* cotoletta di montone

mutual [ˈmutʃu·əl] *adj* mutuo, vicendevole

mu'tual aid' *s* mutualità *f*

mu'tual fund' *s* fondo comune di investimento

muzzle [ˈmʌzəl] *s* (*of animal*) muso; (*device to keep animal from biting*) museruola; (*of firearm*) bocca || *tr* mettere la museruola a; (fig) imbavagliare

my [maɪ] *adj poss* mio, il mio || *interj* (coll) corbezzoli!

myriad [ˈmɪrɪ·əd] *s* miriade *f*

myrrh [mʌr] *s* mirra

myrtle [ˈmʌrtəl] *s* mirto, mortella

myself [maɪˈself] *pron pers* io stesso; me, me stesso; mi, e.g., **I hurt myself** mi sono fatto male

mysterious [mɪsˈtɪrɪ·əs] *adj* misterioso

myster·y [ˈmɪstəri] *s* (-ies) mistero

mystic [ˈmɪstɪk] *adj & s* mistico

mystical [ˈmɪstɪkəl] *adj* mistico

mysticism [ˈmɪstɪˌsɪzəm] *s* misticismo

mystification [ˌmɪstɪfɪˈkeʃən] *s* mistificazione

mysti·fy [ˈmɪstɪˌfaɪ] *v* (*pret & pp* **-fied**) *tr* avvolgere nel mistero; (*to hoax*) mistificare

myth [mɪθ] *s* mito

mythical [ˈmɪθɪkəl] *adj* mitico

mythological [ˌmɪθəˈlɑdʒɪkəl] *adj* mitologico

mytholo·gy [mɪˈθɑlədʒi] *s* (-gies) mitologia

N

N, n [ɛn] *s* quattordicesima lettera dell'alfabeto inglese

nab [næb] *v* (*pret & pp* **nabbed**; *ger* **nabbing**) *tr* (slang) afferrare, agguantare

nag [næg] *s* ronzino *|| v* (*pret & pp* **nagged**; *ger* **nagging**) *tr & intr* tormentare, infastidire

naiad [ˈne·æd] or [ˈnaɪ·æd] *s* naiade *f*

nail [nel] *s* (*of finger or toe*) unghia; (*of metal*) chiodo; **to hit the nail on the head** cogliere nel giusto *|| tr* inchiodare

nail′brush′ spazzolino per le unghie

nail′ file′ *s* lima per le unghie

nail′ pol′ish *s* smalto per le unghie

nail′ set′ *s* punzone *m*

naïve [nɑˈiv] *adj* candido, ingenuo

naked [ˈnekɪd] *adj* nudo, ignudo; **to strip naked** denudare; denudarsi; **with the naked eye** a occhio nudo

name [nem] *s* nome *m*; (*first name*) nome *m*; (*last name*) cognome *m*; fama, reputazione; titolo; lignaggio; **in the name of** nel nome di; **to call s.o. names** coprire qlco di ingiurie; **to go by the name of** essere conosciuto sotto il nome di; **to make a name for oneself** farsi un nome; **what is your name?** come si chiama Lei? *|| tr* nominare; menzionare; battezzare; (*a price*) fissare

name′ day′ *s* onomastico

nameless [ˈnemlɪs] *adj* senza nome, anonimo

namely [ˈnemli] *adv* cioè, vale a dire

name′plate′ *s* targa, targhetta

namesake [ˈnemˌsek] *s* omonimo; persona chiamata in onore di qualcun altro

nan′ny goat′ [ˈnæni] *s* capra

nap [næp] *s* lanugine *f*; (*pile*) pelo; pisolino, sonnellino; **to take a nap** schiacciare un sonnellino *|| v* (*pret & pp* **napped**; *ger* **napping**) *intr* sonnecchiare; **to catch napping** cogliere alla sprovvista

napalm [ˈnepɑm] *s* napalm *m*

nape [nep] *s* nuca

naphtha [ˈnæfθə] *s* nafta

napkin [ˈnæpkɪn] *s* tovagliolo

nap′kin ring′ *s* portatovagliolo

Naples [ˈnepləz] *s* Napoli *f*

Napoleonic [nəˌpolɪˈɑnɪk] *adj* napoleonico

narcissus [nɑrˈsɪsəs] *s* narciso

narcotic [nɑrˈkɑtɪk] *adj & s* narcotico

narrate [næˈret] *tr* narrare

narration [næˈreʃən] *s* narrazione

narrative [ˈnærətɪv] *adj* narrativo *|| s* narrazione; (*genre*) narrativa

narrator [næˈretər] *s* narratore *m*

narrow [ˈnæro] *adj* stretto; limitato; (*illiberal*) meschino, ristretto *||* **narrows** *spl* stretti *mpl || tr* limitare, restringere *|| intr* limitarsi, restringersi

nar′row escape′ *s*—**to have a narrow escape** scamparla bella

nar′row-gauge′ *adj* a scartamento ridotto

narrow-minded [ˈnæroˈmaɪndɪd] *adj* gretto, ristretto d'idee

nasal [ˈnezəl] *adj & s* nasale *f*

nasturtium [nəˈstʌrʃəm] *s* nasturzio

nas·ty [ˈnæsti] *adj* (-tier; -tiest) brutto, cattivo; sgradevole, orribile; sudicio; (*foul*) perfido

natatorium [ˌnetəˈtorɪ·əm] *s* piscina

nation [ˈneʃən] *s* nazione

national [ˈnæʃənəl] *adj & s* nazionale *mf*

na′tional an′them *s* inno nazionale

na′tional debt′ *s* debito pubblico

na′tional hol′iday *s* festa nazionale

nationalism [ˈnæʃənəˌlɪzəm] *s* nazionalismo

nationali·ty [ˌnæʃənˈælɪti] *s* (-ties) nazionalità *f*

nationalize [ˈnæʃənəˌlaɪz] *tr* nazionalizzare

na′tion-wide′ *adj* su scala nazionale

native [ˈnetɪv] *adj* nativo, indigeno, oriundo; (*language*) materno *|| s* indigeno, nativo

na′tive land′ *s* patria, paese natio

nativi·ty [nəˈtɪvɪti] *s* (-ties) nascita, natività *f ||* **Nativity** *s* Natività *f*

Nato [ˈneto] *s* (acronym) (**North Atlantic Treaty Organization**) la N.A.T.O.

nat·ty [ˈnæti] *adj* (-tier; -tiest) accurato, elegante

natural [ˈnætʃərəl] *adj* naturale *|| s* imbecille *mf*; (mus) bequadro; (mus) tono naturale; (mus) tasto bianco; **a natural** (coll) proprio quello che ci vuole

naturalism [ˈnætʃərəˌlɪzəm] *s* naturalismo

naturalist [ˈnætʃərəlɪst] *s* naturalista *mf*

naturalization [ˌnætʃərəlɪˈzeʃən] *s* naturalizzazione

nat′uraliza′tion pa′pers *spl* documenti *mpl* di naturalizzazione

naturalize ['næt/ərə‚laɪz] *tr* naturalizzare

naturally ['næt/ərəli] *adv* naturalmente

nature ['net/ər] *s* natura; **from nature**
dal vero

naught [nɔt] *s* niente *m*; zero; **to come
to naught** ridursi al nulla; **to set at
naught** disprezzare

naugh·ty ['nɔti] *adj* (**-tier; -tiest**) cattivo, disubbidiente; (*joke*) di cattivo
genere

nausea ['nɔ/ɪ·ə] or ['nɔsɪ·ə] *s* nausea

nauseate ['nɔ/ɪ‚et] or ['nɔsɪ‚et] *tr*
nauseare || *intr* essere nauseato

nauseating ['nɔ/ɪ‚etɪŋ] or ['nɔsɪ‚etɪŋ]
adj nauseabondo, stomachevole

nauseous ['nɔ/ɪ·əs] or ['nɔsɪ·əs] *adj*
nauseabondo

nautical ['nɔtɪkəl] *adj* nautico, marittimo, marino

naval ['nevəl] *adj* navale

na'val acad'emy *s* accademia navale

na'val of'ficer *s* ufficiale *m* di marina

na'val sta'tion *s* base *f* navale

nave [nev] *s* navata centrale; (*of a
wheel*) mozzo

navel ['nevəl] *s* ombelico

na'vel or'ange *s* arancia (con depressione alla sommità)

navigability [‚nævɪgə'bɪlɪti] *s* naviga-
bilità *f*; (*of a ship*) manovrabilità *f*

navigable ['nævɪgəbəl] *adj* (*river*) navigabile; (*ship*) manovrabile

navigate ['nævɪ‚get] *tr & intr* navigare

navigation [‚nævɪ'ge/ən] *s* navigazione

navigator ['nævɪ‚getər] *s* navigatore
m; (*in charge of navigating ship or
plane*) ufficiale *m* di rotta

na·vy ['nevi] *adj* blu marino || *s* (**-vies**)
marina (da guerra)

na'vy bean' *s* fagiolo secco

na'vy blue' *s* blu marino

na'vy yard' *s* arsenale *m*

nay [ne] *s* no; voto negativo || *adv* no;
anzi

Nazarene [‚næzə'rin] *adj & s* nazzareno; **the Nazarene** il Nazzareno

Nazi ['nɑtsi] or ['nætsi] *adj & s*
nazista *mf*

N-bomb ['ɛn‚bɑm] *s* bomba al neutrone

Neapolitan [‚ni·ə'pɑlɪtən] *adj & s* na-
poletano

neap' tide' [nip] *s* marea di quadratura

near [nɪr] *adj* vicino, prossimo; intimo;
esatto || *adv* vicino, da vicino || *prep*
vicino a, accanto a; **to come near**
avvicinarsi a || *tr* avvicinarsi a || *intr*
avvicinarsi

nearby ['nɪr‚baɪ] *adj* vicino || *adv* vi-
cino, qui vicino

Near' East' *s* Medio Oriente

nearly ['nɪrli] *adv* quasi; (*a little more
or less*) press'a poco; per poco non,
e.g., **he nearly died** per poco non
morì

near-sighted ['nɪr'saɪtɪd] *adj* miope

near'-sight'ed·ness *s* miopia

neat [nit] *adj* netto, pulito; elegante,
accurato; puro

neat's'-foot oil' *s* olio di piede di bue

Nebuchadnezzar [‚nɛbjəkəd'nɛzər] *s*
Nabucodonosor *m*

nebu·la ['nɛbjələ] *s* (**-lae** [‚li] or **-las**)
nebulosa

nebular ['nɛbjələr] *adj* nebulare

nebulous ['nɛbjələs] *adj* nebuloso

necessary ['nɛsɪ‚sɛri] *adj* necessario

necessitate [nɪ'sɛsɪ‚tet] *tr* necessitare,
esigere

necessitous [nɪ'sɛsɪtəs] *adj* bisognoso

necessi·ty [nɪ'sɛsɪti] *s* (**-ties**) necessità
f

neck [nɛk] *s* collo; (*of a horse*) incollatura; (*of violin*) manico; (*of mountain*) gola, passo; **neck and neck**
testa a testa; **to stick one's neck out**
(coll) esporsi al pericolo; **to win by a
neck** vincere per una corta testa ||
intr (slang) abbracciarsi, sbaciuc-
chiarsi

neck'band' *s* colletto

neckerchief ['nɛkər‚t/ɪf] *s* fazzoletto
da collo

necklace ['nɛklɪs] *s* collana

neck'line' *s* giro collo, scollatura

necktie ['nɛk‚taɪ] *s* cravatta

neck'tie pin' *s* spilla da cravatta

necrolo·gy [nɛ'krɑlədʒi] *s* (**-gies**) necrologia

necromancy ['nɛkrə‚mænsi] *s* necro-
manzia

nectar ['nɛktər] *s* nettare *m*

née or **nee** [ne] *adj* nata

need [nid] *s* necessità *f*, bisogno; povertà *f*; **if need be** se ci fosse bi-
sogno; **in need** in strettezze || *tr* aver
bisogno di || *intr* necessitare, essere
in necessità || *v aux*—**to need (to)** +
inf dovere + *inf*

needful ['nidfəl] *adj* necessario

needle ['nidəl] *s* ago; (*of phonograph*)
puntina; **to look for a needle in a
haystack** cercare l'ago nel pagliaio ||
tr cucire; (fig) aguzzare, eccitare

nee'dle bath' *s* bagno a doccia filiforme

nee'dle·case' *s* agoraio

nee'dle·point' *s* merletto; ricamo su
canovaccio

needless ['nidlɪs] *adj* inutile

nee'dle·work' *s* lavoro di cucito; (*embroidery*) ricamo; (*needlepoint*) merletto

needs [nidz] *adv* necessariamente; **it
must needs be** dev'essere proprio
così

need·y ['nidi] *adj* (**-ier; -iest**) bisognoso,
indigente || **the needy** i bisognosi

ne'er-do-well ['nɛrdu‚wɛl] *adj & s*
buono a nulla

negate ['nɛget] or [nɪ'get] *tr* invalidare; negare

negation [nɪ'ge/ən] *s* negazione

negative ['nɛgətɪv] *adj* negativo || *s*
negativa; (elec) polo negativo;
(gram) negazione || *tr* respingere,
votare contro; neutralizzare

neglect [nɪ'glɛkt] *s* negligenza, trascu-
ratezza || *tr* trascurare; **to neglect to**
trascurare di; dimenticarsi di

neglectful [nɪ'glɛktfəl] *adj* negligente,
trascurato

négligée or **negligee** [‚nɛglɪ'ʒe] *s* veste
f da camera or vestaglia per signora

negligence ['nɛglɪdʒəns] *s* negligenza,
trascuratezza

negligent ['nɛglɪdʒənt] *adj* negligente, trascurato

negligible ['nɛglɪdʒɪbəl] *adj* trascurabile, insignificante

negotiable [nɪ'goʃɪəbəl] *adj* negoziabile; *(security)* al portatore; *(road)* transitabile

negotiate [nɪ'goʃɪ,et] *tr* negoziare; *(to overcome)* superare || *intr* negoziare

negotiation [nɪ,goʃɪ'eʃən] *s* negoziazione, negoziato

Ne-gro ['nigro] *adj* negro || *s* (**-groes**) negro, nero

neigh [ne] *s* nitrito || *intr* nitrire

neighbor ['nebər] *adj* vicino, adiacente || *s* vicino; *(fellow man)* prossimo || *tr* essere vicino a || *intr* essere vicino

neighborhood ['nebər,hʊd] *s* vicinanza, vicinato; **in the neighborhood of** nei pressi di; (coll) a un dipresso, all'incirca

neighboring ['nebərɪŋ] *adj* vicino, attiguo; *(country)* limitrofo

neighborly ['nebərli] *adj* da buon vicino, socievole

neither ['niðər] or ['naɪðər] *adj indef* nessuno dei due, e.g., **neither boy** nessuno dei due ragazzi || *pron indef* nessuno dei due, nè l'uno nè l'altro || *conj* neppure, nemmeno, e.g., **neither do I** nemmeno io; **neither . . . nor** nè . . . nè

neme-sis ['nɛmisis] *s* (**-ses** [,siz]) nemesi *f* || **Nemesis** *s* Nemesi *f*

neologism [ni'ɑlə,dʒɪzəm] *s* neologismo

neomycin [,ni-ə'maɪsɪn] *s* neomicina

ne'on lamp' ['ni-ɑn] *s* lampada al neon

neophyte ['ni-ə,faɪt] *s* neofita *mf*

nepenthe [nɪ'pɛnθi] *s* nepente *f*

nephew ['nɛfju] or ['nɛvju] *s* nipote *m*

Nepos ['nipɑs] or ['nepɑs] *s* Nipote *m*

Neptune ['nɛptʃun] or ['nɛptjun] *s* Nettuno

neptunium [nɛp'tʃunɪ-əm] or [nɛp-'tjunɪ-əm] *s* (chem) nettunio

Nero ['nɪro] *s* Nerone *m*

nerve [nʌrv] *adj* nervoso || *s* nervo; *(courage)* coraggio; *(boldness)* (coll) faccia tosta; **to get on one's nerves** dare ai nervi di qlcu; **to lose one's nerve** perdere le staffe

nerve-racking ['nʌrv,rækɪŋ] *adj* irritante, esasperante

nervous ['nʌrvəs] *adj* nervoso

nerv'ous break'down *s* esaurimento nervoso

nervousness ['nʌrvəsnɪs] *s* nervosismo

nerv-y ['nʌrvi] *adj* (**-ier; -iest**) *(strong)* forte, vigoroso; audace; (coll) insolente, sfacciato

nest [nɛst] *s* nido; *(of hen)* cova; *(retreat)* rifugio; *(hangout)* tana; *(brood)* nidiata; **to feather one's nest** farsi il gruzzolo || *tr* (e.g., *tables*) mettere l'uno nell'altro || *intr* nidificare

nest' egg' *s* endice *m*; (fig) gruzzolo

nestle ['nɛsəl] *tr* annidare || *intr* annidarsi, nidificare; *(to cuddle up)* rannicchiarsi

net [nɛt] *adj* netto || *s* rete *f*; *(snare)* laccio, trappola; guadagno netto || *tr* prendere con la rete; *(a sum of money)* fare un guadagno netto di

nether ['nɛðər] *adj* inferiore, infero

Netherlander ['nɛðər,lændər] or ['nɛð-ərləndər] *s* olandese *mf*

Netherlands, The ['nɛðərləndz] *spl* i Paesi Bassi

netting ['nɛtɪŋ] *s* rete *f*

nettle ['nɛtəl] *s* ortica || *tr* irritare, provocare

net'work' *s* rete *f*

neuralgia [nju'rældʒə] or [nʊ'rældʒə] *s* nevralgia

neurology [nju'ralədʒi] or [nʊ'ralədʒi] *s* neurologia

neuro-sis [nju'rosɪs] or [nʊ'rosɪs] *s* (**-ses** [siz]) *s* neurosi *f*

neurotic [nju'ratɪk] or [nʊ'ratɪk] *adj* & *s* neurotico

neuter ['njutər] or ['nutər] *adj* neutro || *s* genere neutro

neutral ['njutrəl] or ['nutrəl] *adj* neutro; *(not aligned)* neutrale || *s* neutrale *m*; (mach) folle *m*

neutralist ['njutrəlɪst] or ['nutrəlɪst] *adj* & *s* neutralista *mf*

neutrality [nju'trælɪti] or [nu'trælɪti] *s* neutralità *f*

neutralize ['njutrə,laɪz] or ['nutrə,laɪz] *tr* neutralizzare

neutron ['njutrɑn] or ['nutrɑn] *s* neutrone *m*

neu'tron bomb' *s* bomba al neutrone

never ['nɛvər] *adv* mai, giammai; non . . . mai; **never mind** non importa

nev'er-more' *adv* mai più

nevertheless [,nɛvərðə'lɛs] *adv* ciò nonostante, ciò nondimeno, tuttavia

new [nju] or [nu] *adj* nuovo; **what's new?** che c'è di nuovo?

new' arri'val *s* nuovo venuto; *(baby)* neonato

new'born' *adj* neonato; *(e.g., faith)* rinato

New'cas'tle *s*—**to carry coals to Newcastle** portare l'acqua al mare, portare vasi a Samo

newcomer ['nju,kʌmər] or ['nu,kʌmər] *s* nuovo venuto

New' Eng'land *s* la Nuova Inghilterra

newfangled ['nju,fæŋgəld] or ['nu,fæŋgəld] *adj* all'ultima moda; di nuovo conio, di nuova invenzione

Newfoundland ['njufənd,lænd] or ['nufənd,lænd] *s* la Terranova || [nju'faundlənd] or [nu'faundlənd] *s* *(dog)* terranova *m*

newly ['njuli] or ['nuli] *adv* di recente, di fresco

new'ly-wed' *s* sposino or sposina; **the newlyweds** gli sposi

new' moon' *s* luna nuova, novilunio

news [njuz] or [nuz] *s* notizie *fpl*; **a news item** una notizia; **a piece of news** una notizia

news' a'gency *s* agenzia d'informazioni

news'beat' *s* colpo giornalistico

news'boy' *s* strillone *m*

news'cast' *s* notiziario

news'cast'er *s* annunziatore *m*, radiocommentatore *m*, telecommentatore *m*

news' con'ference *s* conferenza stampa

news′ cov′erage s reportaggio

news′deal′er s venditore m di giornali

news′man′ s (-men′) (reporter) giornalista m; giornalaio

newsmonger [ˈnjuz ˌmʌŋɡər] or [ˈnuz ˌmʌŋɡər] s persona pettegola, gazzettino

news′pa′per adj giornalistico ‖ s giornale m

news′pa′per·man′ s (-men′) giornalista m

news′print′ s carta da giornale

news′reel′ s cinegiornale m

news′stand′ s chiosco, edicola

news′week′ly s (-lies) settimanale m d′informazione

news′wor′thy adj degno d′essere pubblicato, di viva attualità

news·y [ˈnjuzi] or [ˈnuzi] adj (-ier; -iest) (coll) informativo

New′ Tes′tament s Nuovo Testamento

New′ Year′s′ card′ s cartolina d′auguri di capodanno

New′ Year′s′ Day′ s il capo d′anno, il capodanno

New′ Year′s′ Eve′ s la vigilia di capodanno, la sera di San Silvestro

New′ York′ [jɔrk] adj nuovayorchese ‖ s New York f, Nuova York

New′ York′er [ˈjɔrkər] s nuovayorchese mf

New′ Zea′land [ˈzilənd] adj neozelandese ‖ s la Nuova Zelanda

New′ Zea′lander [ˈziləndər] s neozelandese mf

next [nɛkst] adj prossimo, seguente; (month) prossimo, entrante ‖ adv la prossima volta; dopo, in seguito; next to vicino a; next to nothing quasi nulla; to come next essere il prossimo

next′-door′ adj della casa vicina ‖ next′-door′ adv nella casa vicina

next′ of kin′ s (next′ of kin′) parente più prossimo

niacin [ˈnaɪ·əsɪn] s niacina

Niag′ara Falls′ [naɪˈægərə] spl le Cascate del Niagara

nib [nɪb] s becco; punta; his nibs (slang & pej) sua eccellenza

nibble [ˈnɪbəl] s piccolo morso ‖ tr & intr mordicchiare, sbocconcellare; (said of a fish) abboccare

nice [naɪs] adj (pleasant) simpatico, gentile; (requiring skill) buono, bello; (fine) sottile; (refined) raffinato, per bene; (fussy) esigente, difficile; rispettabile; (weather) bello; (attractive) bello; nice . . . and (coll) bello, e.g., it is nice and warm fa un bel caldo

nice-looking [ˈnaɪsˈlʊkɪŋ] adj bello, attraente

nicely [ˈnaɪsli] adv precisamente, esattamente; (coll) benissimo

nice·ty [ˈnaɪsəti] s (-ties) esattezza, precisione; to a nicety con la massima precisione

niche [nɪtʃ] s nicchia

Nicholas [ˈnɪkələs] s Nicola m

nick [nɪk] s intaccatura; (of a dish) slabbratura; in the nick of time al

momento giusto ‖ tr intaccare; (to cut) tagliare; (a dish) slabbrare

nickel [ˈnɪkəl] s nichel m; moneta americana di cinque cents ‖ tr nichelare

nick′el plate′ s nichelatura

nick′el-plate′ tr nichelare

nicknack [ˈnɪk ˌnæk] s soprammobile m; gingillo, ninnolo

nick′name′ s nomignolo, soprannome m ‖ tr soprannominare

nicotine [ˈnɪkə ˌtin] s nicotina

niece [nis] s nipote f

nif·ty [ˈnɪfti] adj (-tier; -tiest) (coll) elegante; (coll) eccellente

niggard [ˈnɪɡərd] adj & s spilorcio

night [naɪt] adj notturno ‖ s notte f; at or by night di notte; the night before last l′altra notte; to make a night of it (coll) fare le ore piccole

night′cap′ s berretto da notte; bicchierino di liquore che si beve prima di coricarsi

night′ club′ s night-club m

night′ driv′ing s il guidare di notte

night′fall′ s crepuscolo; at nightfall sul cader della notte, all′imbrunire

night′gown′ s camicia da notte

nightingale [ˈnaɪtən ˌɡel] s usignolo

night′ latch′ s serratura a molla

night′ let′ter s telegramma notturno

night′long′ adj di tutta la notte ‖ adv tutta la notte

nightly [ˈnaɪtli] adj di notte; di ogni notte ‖ adv di notte; ogni notte

night′mare′ s incubo

nightmarish [ˈnaɪt ˌmɛrɪʃ] adj raccapricciante

night′ owl′ s (coll) nottambulo

night′ school′ s scuola serale

night′shirt′ s camicia da notte

night′time′ s notte f

night′walk′er s nottambulo; vagabondo notturno; (prostitute) passeggiatrice f

night′ watch′ s guardia notturna

night′ watch′man s (-men) guardiano notturno

nihilist [ˈnaɪ·ɪlɪst] s nichilista mf

nil [nɪl] s nulla m, niente m

Nile [naɪl] s Nilo

nimble [ˈnɪmbəl] adj agile, svelto

Nimrod [ˈnɪmrɑd] s Nembrod m

nincompoop [ˈnɪnkəm ˌpup] s babbeo, tonto, semplicione m

nine [naɪn] adj & pron nove ‖ s nove m; nine o′ clock le nove

nine′ hun′dred adj, s & pron novecento

nineteen [ˈnaɪnˈtin] adj, s & pron diciannove m

nineteenth [ˈnaɪnˈtinθ] adj & s diciannovesimo; (century) decimonono ‖ s (in dates) diciannove m ‖ pron diciannovesimo

ninetieth [ˈnaɪntɪ·ɪθ] adj, s & pron novantesimo

nine·ty [ˈnaɪnti] adj & pron novanta ‖ s (-ties) novanta m; the gay nineties il decennio scapestrato dal 1890 al 1900

ninth [naɪnθ] adj, s & pron nono ‖ s (in dates) nove m

nip [nɪp] s morso, pizzicotto; freddo pungente; (of liquor) bicchierino, sorso; **nip and tuck** testa a testa ‖ *v* (*pret & pp* **nipped;** *ger* **nipping**) *tr* pizzicare, mordere; (*to squeeze*) spremere; (*to freeze*) gelare; (*liquor*) sorseggiare; **to nip in the bud** arrestare di bel principio ‖ *intr* bere a sorsi

nipple ['nɪpəl] *s* capezzolo; (*of rubber*) tettarella; (*mach*) corto tubo filettato a entrambe le estremità, manicotto, cappuccio

Nippon [nɪ'pɑn] or ['nɪpɑn] *s* il Giappone

Nippon-ese [ˌnɪpə'niz] *adj* nipponico ‖ *s* (*-ese*) Giapponese *mf*

nip-py ['nɪpi] *adj* (*-pier; -piest*) mordente, pizzicante; gelato

nirvana [nɪr'vɑnə] *s* il nirvana

nit [nɪt] *s* lendine *m;* pidocchio

niter ['naɪtər] *s* nitro

nit'-pick' *intr* (coll) cercare il pelo nell'uovo

nitrate ['naɪtret] *s* nitrato; (agr) nitrato di soda; (agr) nitrato di potassio

ni'tric ac'id ['naɪtrɪk] *s* acido nitrico

nitride ['naɪtraɪd] *s* azoturo, nitruro

nitrogen ['naɪtrədʒən] *s* azoto

nitroglycerin [ˌnaɪtrə'glɪsərɪn] *s* nitroglicerina

ni'trous ox'ide ['naɪtrəs] *s* ossidulo di azoto

nitwit ['nɪtˌwɪt] *s* (slang) baggiano

no [no] *adj* nessuno; **no admittance** vietato l'ingresso; **no doubt** senza dubbio; **no matter** non importa; **no parking** divieto di sosta; **no smoking** vietato fumare; **no thoroughfare** divieto di transito; **no use** inutilmente; **with no** senza ‖ *s* no; voto negativo ‖ *adv* no; non; **no longer** non . . . più; **no sooner** non appena

Noah ['no·ə] *s* Noè *m*

nob-by ['nɑbi] *adj* (*-bier; -biest*) (slang) elegante; (slang) eccellente

nobili-ty [no'bɪlɪti] *s* (*-ties*) nobiltà *f*

noble ['nobəl] *adj & s* nobile *m*

no'ble-man *s* (*-men*) nobile *m,* nobiluomo

no'ble-wom'an *s* (*-wom'en*) nobile *f,* nobildonna

nobod-y ['noˌbɑdi] or ['nobədi] *s* (*-ies*) nessuno, illustre sconosciuto ‖ *pron indef* nessuno; **nobody but** nessun altro che; **nobody else** nessun altro

nocturnal [nɑk'tʌrnəl] *adj* notturno

nod [nɑd] *s* cenno d'assenso, cenno del capo; (*of person going to sleep*) crollo del capo ‖ *v* (*pret & pp* **nodded;** *ger* **nodding**) *tr* (*one's head*) inclinare; **to nod assent** fare cenno di sì ‖ *intr* inclinare il capo; (*to drowse*) assopirsi

node [nod] *s* nodo; protuberanza; (phys) nodo

no'-good' *adj & s* (coll) buono a nulla

nohow ['noˌhaʊ] *adv* (coll) in nessuna maniera

noise [nɔɪz] *s* rumore *m* ‖ *tr* divulgare

noiseless ['nɔɪzlɪs] *adj* silenzioso

nois-y ['nɔɪzi] *adj* (*-ier; -iest*) rumoroso, chiassoso

nomad ['nomæd] *adj & s* nomade *m*

no' man's' land' *s* terra di nessuno

nominal ['nɑmɪnəl] *adj* nominale; simbolico

nominate ['nɑmɪˌnet] *tr* presentare la candidatura di; (*to appoint*) nominare, designare

nomination [ˌnɑmɪ'neʃən] *s* candidatura; nomina

nominative ['nɑmɪnətɪv] *adj & s* nominativo

nominee [ˌnɑmɪ'ni] *s* candidato designato

nonbelligerent [ˌnɑnbə'lɪdʒərənt] *adj & s* non belligerante *m*

nonbreakable [nɑn'brekəbəl] *adj* infrangibile

nonce [nɑns] *s*—**for the nonce** per l'occasione

nonchalance ['nɑnʃələns] or [ˌnɑnʃə'lɑns] *s* disinvoltura, indifferenza

nonchalant ['nɑnʃələnt] or [ˌnɑnʃə'lɑnt] *adj* disinvolto, indifferente

noncom ['nɑnˌkɑm] *s* (coll) sottufficiale *m*

noncombatant [nɑn'kɑmbətənt] *adj* non combattente ‖ *s* persona non combattente

non'commis'sioned of'ficer [ˌnɑnkə'mɪʃənd] *s* sottufficiale *m*

noncommittal [ˌnɑnkə'mɪtəl] *adj* ambiguo, evasivo

non compos mentis ['nɑn 'kɑmpəs 'mentɪs] *adj* pazzo; (law) incapace

nonconformist [ˌnɑnkən'fɔrmɪst] *s* anticonformista *mf,* nonconformista *mf*

nondelivery [ˌnɑndɪ'lɪvəri] *s* mancata consegna

nondescript ['nɑndɪˌskrɪpt] *adj* indefinibile, inclassificabile

none [nʌn] *pron indef* nessuno; **none of** nessuno di; **none other** nessun altro ‖ *adv* non; affatto, niente affatto; **none the less** ciò nonostante, nondimeno

nonenti-ty [nɑn'entɪti] *s* (*-ties*) inesistenza; (*person*) nullità *f*

nonfiction [nɑn'fɪkʃən] *s* letteratura non romanzesca

nonfulfillment [ˌnɑnfʊl'fɪlmənt] *s* mancanza di esecuzione

nonintervention [ˌnɑnɪntər'venʃən] *s* non intervento

nonmetal ['nɑnˌmetəl] *s* metalloide *m*

nonpayment [nɑn'pemənt] *s* mancato pagamento

non-plus ['nɑnplʌs] or [nɑn'plʌs] *s* perplessità *f* ‖ *v* (*pret & pp* **-plussed** or **plused;** *ger* **-plussing** or **-plusing**) *tr* lasciare perplesso

nonprofit [nɑn'prɑfɪt] *adj* senza scopo lucrativo

nonrefillable [ˌnɑnrɪ'fɪləbəl] *adj* (*prescription*) non ripetibile; (*e.g., bottle*) non ricaricabile

nonresident [nɑn'rezɪdənt] *s* persona di passaggio, non residente *mf*

nonresidential [ˌnɑnˌrezɪ'denʃəl] *adj* commerciale, non residenziale

nonscientific [ˌnɑnˌsaɪ·ən'tɪfɪk] *adj* non scientifico

nonsectarian [ˌnɑnsekˈterɪ·ən] *adj* che non segue nessuna confessione religiosa

nonsense [ˈnɑnsens] *s* sciocchezza, assurdità *f*, nonsenso

nonsensical [nɑnˈsensɪkəl] *adj* sciocco, assurdo, illogico

nonskid [ˈnɑnˈskɪd] *adj* antiderapante

nonstop [ˈnɑnˈstɑp] *adj & adv* senza scalo

nonsupport [ˌnɑnsəˈpɔrt] *s* mancato pagamento degli alimenti

noodle [ˈnudəl] *s* (slang) scemo; (slang) testa; **noodles** tagliatelle *fpl*

noo′dle soup′ *s* tagliatelle *fpl* in brodo

nook [nʊk] *s* angolo, cantuccio

noon [nun] *s* mezzogiorno; **at high noon** a mezzogiorno in punto

no one or no-one [ˈno ˌwʌn] *pron indef* nessuno; **no one else** nessun altro

noontime [ˈnun ˌtaɪm] *s* mezzogiorno

noose [nus] *s* laccio, nodo scorsoio

nor [nɔr] *conj* nè

Nordic [ˈnɔrdɪk] *adj* nordico

norm [nɔrm] *s* norma, media, tipo

normal [ˈnɔrməl] *adj* normale ‖ *s* condizione normale; norma; (geom) normale *f*

Norman [ˈnɔrmən] *adj & s* normanno

Normandy [ˈnɔrməndɪ] *s* la Normandia

Norse [nɔrs] *adj* norvegese; scandinavo ‖ *s* (ancient Scandinavian language) scandinavo; (language of Norway) norvegese *m*; **the Norse** gli scandinavi; i norvegesi

Norse′man *s* (-men) normanno

north [nɔrθ] *adj* del nord, settentrionale ‖ *s* nord *m* ‖ *adv* al nord, verso il nord

North′ Amer′ica *s* l'America del Nord

North′ Amer′ican *adj & s* nordamericano

north′east′ *adj* di nord-est ‖ *s* nord-est *m* ‖ *adv* al nord-est

north′east′er *s* vento di nord-est

northern [ˈnɔrðərn] *adj* settentrionale; (Hemisphere) boreale

North′ Kore′a *s* la Corea del Nord

North′ Pole′ *s* polo nord

northward [ˈnɔrθwərd] *adv* verso il nord

north′west′ *adj* di nord-ovest ‖ *s* nord-ovest *m* ‖ *adv* al nord-ovest

north′ wind′ *s* vento del nord, aquilone *m*

Norway [ˈnɔrwe] *s* la Norvegia

Norwegian [nɔrˈwidʒən] *adj & s* norvegese *mf* ‖ *s* (language) norvegese *m*

nose [noz] *s* naso; (of missile) testata; **to blow one's nose** soffiarsi il naso; **to count noses** contare il numero dei presenti; **to follow one's nose** andare a lume di naso; **to lead by the nose** menare per il naso; **to look down one's nose at** (coll) guardare dall'alto in basso; **to pay through the nose** pagare un occhio della testa; **to pick one's nose** mettersi le dita nel naso; **to speak through the nose** parlare nel naso; **to thumb one's nose** at fare maramco a; **to turn up one's nose at** guardare dall'alto in basso, guardare con disprezzo ‖ *tr* fiutare; **to nose out** vincere per un pelo ‖ *intr* fiutare; **to nose about** curiosare

nose′ bag′ *s* musetta

nose′band′ *s* museruola di cavallo

nose′bleed′ *s* sangue *m* dal naso

nose′ cone′ *s* ogiva

nose′ dive′ *s* (of prices) subita discesa; (aer) discesa in picchiata

nose′-dive′ *intr* discendere in picchiata

nosegay [ˈnoz ˌge] *s* mazzolino di fiori

nose′ glass′es *spl* occhiali *mpl* a stringinaso

nose′ ring′ *s* nasiera

nose′wheel′ *s* (aer) ruota del carrello anteriore

no′-show′ *s* (coll) passeggero che si è prenotato e non parte

nostalgia [nɑˈstældʒə] *s* nostalgia

nostalgic [nɑˈstældʒɪk] *adj* nostalgico

nostril [ˈnɑstrɪl] *s* narice *f*

nos·y [ˈnozɪ] *adj* (-ier; -iest) (coll) curioso

not [nɑt] *adv* no; non; **not at all** niente affatto; **not yet** non ancora; **to think not** credere di no; **why not?** come no?

notable [ˈnotəbəl] *adj* notevole, notabile ‖ *s* notabile *m*

notarize [ˈnotə ˌraɪz] *tr* munire di fede notarile

nota·ry [ˈnotərɪ] *s* (-ries) notaio

notch [nɑtʃ] *s* tacca; (in mountain) passo; (coll) tantino; **notches** (coll) di gran lunga, e.g., **notches above** di gran lunga migliore ‖ *tr* intaccare

note [not] *s* nota, annotazione; (currency) banconota; (communication) memorandum *m*; (of bird) canto; (tone of voice) tono; (reputation) riguardo; (short letter) biglietto, letterina; (mus) nota; (com) cambiale *f* ‖ *tr* notare, annotare; osservare

note′book′ *s* (for school) quaderno; taccuino, notes *m*

noted [ˈnotɪd] *adj* ben noto, eminente

note′ pa′per *s* carta da lettera

note′wor′thy *adj* notevole

nothing [ˈnʌθɪŋ] *s* niente *m*, nulla; **for nothing** gratis; inutilmente; **next to nothing** quasi niente ‖ *pron indef* niente, nulla, non . . . niente, non . . . nulla; **nothing else** niente'altro; **to make nothing of it** non farne caso ‖ *adv* per nulla; **nothing less** non meno

notice [ˈnotɪs] *s* attenzione; notizia, notifica; annunzio, preavviso; (in newspaper) trafiletto; (law) disdetta; **on short notice** senza preavviso; (com) a breve scadenza; **to escape the notice of** passare inavvertito a; **to serve notice to** far sapere a, far constatare a ‖ *tr* osservare, notare, prendere nota di

noticeable [ˈnotɪsəbəl] *adj* notevole; (e.g., difference) percettibile

noti·fy [ˈnotɪ ˌfaɪ] *v* (pret & pp -fied) *tr* informare, far sapere

notion [ˈnoʃən] *s* nozione; (whim) capriccio; **notions** mercerie *fpl*; **to have a notion to** aver voglia di

notorie·ty [ˌnotəˈraɪ·ɪtɪ] *s* (-ties) (state

of being well known) notorietà *f;* cattiva fama

notorious [noˈtorɪ·əs] *adj* (*generally known*) notorio; (*unfavorably known*) famigerato

no′-trump′ *adj & s* senza atout *m*

notwithstanding [ˌnɑtwɪðˈstændɪŋ] or [ˌnɑtwɪθˈstændɪŋ] *adv* ciò nonostante ‖ *prep* malgrado ‖ *conj* sebbene

nougat [ˈnugət] *s* torrone *m*

noun [naun] *s* nome *m*, sostantivo

nourish [ˈnʌrɪʃ] *tr* nutrire

nourishing [ˈnʌrɪʃɪŋ] *adj* nutriente

nourishment [ˈnʌrɪʃmənt] *s* nutrimento

novel [ˈnɑvəl] *adj* nuovo, novello, insolito, originale ‖ *s* romanzo

novelist [ˈnɑvəlɪst] *s* romanziere *m*

novel·ty [ˈnɑvəlti] *s* (**-ties**) novità *f;* **novelties** chincaglierie *fpl*

November [noˈvɛmbər] *s* novembre *m*

novice [ˈnɑvɪs] *s* novizio

novitiate [noˈvɪʃɪ·ɪt] *s* noviziato

novocaine [ˈnovə‚ken] *s* novocaina

now [nau] *s* presente *m* ‖ *adv* adesso; **from now on** d'ora in poi; **just now** un momento fa; **now and then** di tempo in tempo; **now that** visto che ‖ *conj* visto che, dato che

nowadays [ˈnau·əˌdez] *adv* al giorno d'oggi, oggidì

no′way′ *adv* in nessun modo; nient'affatto

no′where′ *adv* da nessuna parte; **nowhere else** da nessun'altra parte, in nessun altro luogo

noxious [ˈnɑkʃəs] *adj* nocivo

nozzle [ˈnɑzəl] *s* (*of hose or pipe*) boccaglio; (*of tea pot, gas burner*) becco; (*of gun*) bocca; (*of sprinkling can*) bocchetta; (aut, mach) becco; (slang) naso

nth [ɛnθ] *adj* ennesimo; **to the nth degree** all'ennesima potenza

nuance [njuˈɑns] or [ˈnju·ɑns] *s* sfumatura

nub [nʌb] *s* protuberanza; (*of coal*) pezzo; (coll) nocciolo, cuore *m*

nuclear [ˈnjuklɪ·ər] or [ˈnuklɪ·ər] *adj* nucleare

nu′clear fis′sion *s* fissione nucleare

nu′clear fu′sion *s* fusione nucleare

nu′clear test′ ban′ *s* accordo per la tregua atomica

nucle·us [ˈnjuklɪ·əs] or [ˈnuklɪ·əs] *s* (**-i** [ˌaɪ] or **-uses**) nucleo

nude [njud] or [nud] *adj* nudo ‖ *s*—**in the nude** nudo

nudge [nʌdʒ] *s* gomitatina ‖ *tr* dare di gomito a

nudist [ˈnjudɪst] or [ˈnudɪst] *adj & s* nudista *mf*

nudi·ty [ˈnjudɪti] or [ˈnudɪti] *s* (**-ties**) nudità *f*

nugget [ˈnʌgɪt] *s* pepita

nuisance [ˈnjusəns] or [ˈnusəns] *s* noia, seccatura; (*person*) seccatore *m*, pittima *mf*

null [nʌl] *adj* nullo; **null and void** invalido

nulli·fy [ˈnʌlɪˌfaɪ] *v* (*pret & pp* **-fied**) *tr* annullare, invalidare

nulli·ty [ˈnʌlɪti] *s* (**-ties**) nullità *f*

numb [nʌm] *adj* intorpidito; (*from cold*) intirizzito; **to become numb** intorpidirsi ‖ *tr* intorpidire

number [ˈnʌmbər] *s* numero; (*for sale*) articolo di vendita; (*publication*) fascicolo; (*of a serial*) dispensa, puntata; **a number of** parecchi; **beyond** or **without number** senza numero, infiniti ‖ *tr* numerare, contare; **his days are numbered** i suoi giorni sono contati ‖ *intr*—**to number among** essere tra

numberless [ˈnʌmbərlɪs] *adj* innumerevole

numeral [ˈnjumərəl] or [ˈnumərəl] *adj* numerale ‖ *s* numero

numerical [njuˈmɛrɪkəl] or [nuˈmɛrɪkəl] *adj* numerico

numerous [ˈnjumərəs] or [ˈnumərəs] *adj* numeroso

numskull [ˈnʌm‚skʌl] *s* (coll) stupido

nun [nʌn] *s* monaca, religiosa

nuptial [ˈnʌpʃəl] *adj* nuziale ‖ **nuptials** *spl* nozze *fpl*

nurse [nʌrs] *s* infermiera; (*to suckle a child*) nutrice *f;* (*to take care of a child*) bambinaia ‖ *tr* (*to minister to*) curare; allattare; allevare; (*e.g., hatred*) covare ‖ *intr* fare l'infermiera

nurser·y [ˈnʌrsəri] *s* (**-ies**) stanza dei bambini; (*shelter for children*) asilo infantile; (hort) vivaio

nurs′ery·man *s* (**-men**) orticoltore *m*

nurs′ery rhyme′ *s* canzoncina per i più piccini

nurs′ery school′ *s* scuola materna

nursing [ˈnʌrsɪŋ] *adj* infermieristico ‖ *s* allattamento; professione d'infermiera

nurs′ing bot′tle *s* biberon *m*, poppatoio

nurs′ing home′ *s* convalescenziario; ospizio dei vecchi, gerontocomio

nurture [ˈnʌrtʃər] *s* allevamento; nutrimento ‖ *tr* allevare; alimentare; (*e.g., hope*) accarezzare

nut [nʌt] *s* noce *f;* (*eccentric*) (slang) esaltato, pazzoide *m;* (mus) capotasto; (mach) madrevite *f,* dado; **a hard nut to crack** un osso duro da rodere; **to be nuts for** (coll) essere pazzo per

nut′crack′er *s* schiaccianoci *m*

nutmeg [ˈnʌt‚mɛg] *s* noce moscata

nutrition [njuˈtrɪʃən] or [nuˈtrɪʃən] *s* (*process*) nutrizione; (*food*) nutrimento

nutritious [njuˈtrɪʃəs] or [nuˈtrɪʃəs] *adj* nutriente

nut′shell′ *s* guscio di noce; **in a nutshell** in breve, in poche parole

nut·ty [ˈnʌti] *adj* (**-tier; -tiest**) che sa di noci; (slang) pazzo; **nutty about** (slang) pazzo per

nuzzle [ˈnʌzəl] *tr* toccare col muso, ammusare ‖ *intr* (*said of swine*) grufolare; (*said of other animals*) stare muso a muso, ammusare; (*to snuggle*) rannicchiarsi

nylon [ˈnaɪlɑn] *s* nailon *m*

nymph [nɪmf] *s* ninfa

O

O, o [o] *s* quindicesima lettera dell'alfabeto inglese

O *interj* o!, oh!

oaf [of] *s* balordo, scemo, imbecille *mf*

oak [ok] *s* quercia

oaken ['okən] *adj* di quercia, quercino

oakum ['okəm] *s* stoppa incatramata

oar [or] *s* remo; **to lie or rest on one's oars** dormire sugli allori; **non lavorare più** ‖ *tr* spingere coi remi ‖ *intr* remare

oar'lock' *s* scalmo

oars'man *s* (**-men**) rematore *m*

oa·sis [o'esıs] *s* (**-ses** [siz]) oasi *f*

oat [ot] *s* avena; **oats** (*seeds*) avena; **to feel one's oats** (coll) essere pieno di vita; (coll) sentirsi importante; **to sow one's wild oats** correre la cavallina

oath [oθ] *s* giuramento; **on oath** sotto giuramento; **to take an oath** giurare, prestar giuramento

oat'meal' *s* (*breakfast food*) fiocchi *mpl* d'avena; farina d'avena

obdurate ['abdjərıt] *adj* indurito, inesorabile; impenitente, incallito

obedience [o'bidɪ·əns] *s* obbedienza, ubbidienza

obedient [o'bidɪ·ənt] *adj* ubbidiente

obeisance [o'besəns] or [o'bisəns] *s* saluto rispettoso; omaggio

obelisk ['abəlısk] *s* obelisco

obese [o'bis] *adj* obeso

obesity [o'bisıti] *s* obesità *f*

obey ['obe] *tr* ubbidire (with *dat*), ubbidire ‖ *intr* ubbidire

obfuscate [ab'fʌsket] or ['abfəs‚ket] *tr* offuscare

obituar·y [o'bɪtʃu‚eri] *adj* necrologico ‖ *s* (**-ies**) necrologia

object ['abdʒɪkt] *s* oggetto ‖ [ab'dʒɛkt] *tr* obiettare ‖ *intr* fare obiezioni, obiettare

objection [ab'dʒɛkʃən] *s* obiezione

objectionable [ab'dʒɛkʃənəbəl] *adj* reprensibile; (*e.g., odor*) sgradevole; offensivo

objective [ab'dʒɛktıv] *adj* & *s* obiettivo

obligate ['ablı‚get] *tr* obbligare

obligation [‚ablı'geʃən] *s* obbligo, obbligazione

oblige [ə'blaıdʒ] *tr* obbligare; favorire; **much obliged** obbligatissimo

obliging [ə'blaıdʒıŋ] *adj* compiacente, accomodante, servizievole

oblique [ə'blik] *adj* obliquo; indiretto

obliterate [ə'blıtə‚ret] *tr* obliterare; spegnere, distruggere

oblivion [ə'blıvı·ən] *s* oblio

oblivious [ə'blıvı·əs] *adj* (*forgetful*) dimentico; (*unaware*) ignaro

oblong ['ablɔŋ] or ['ablɑŋ] *adj* oblungo

obnoxious [ab'nakʃəs] *adj* detestabile

oboe ['obo] *s* oboe *m*

oboist ['obo·ıst] *s* oboista *mf*

obscene [ab'sin] *adj* osceno

obsceni·ty [ab'senıti] or [ab'sinıti] *s* (**-ties**) oscenità *f*, sconcezza

obscure [əb'skjur] *adj* oscuro ‖ *tr* oscurare

obscuri·ty [əb'skjurıti] *s* (**-ties**) oscurità *f*

obsequies ['absıkwiz] *spl* esequie *fpl*

obsequious [əb'sikwı·əs] *adj* ossequioso, servile

observance [əb'zʌrvəns] *s* osservanza; **observances** pratiche *fpl*; cerimonie *fpl*

observation [‚abzər'veʃən] *s* osservazione; osservanza

observa'tion car' *s* (rr) vettura belvedere

observato·ry [əb'zʌrvə‚tori] *s* (**-ries**) osservatorio

observe [əb'zʌrv] *tr* osservare

observer [əb'zʌrvər] *s* osservatore *m*

obsess [əb'sɛs] *tr* ossessionare

obsession [əb'sɛʃən] *s* ossessione

obsolescent [‚absə'lɛsənt] *adj* che sta cadendo in disuso

obsolete ['absə‚lit] *adj* disusato

obstacle ['abstəkəl] *s* ostacolo

obstetrical [ab'stɛtrıkəl] *adj* ostetrico

obstetrics [ab'stɛtrıks] *s* ostetricia

obstina·cy ['abstınəsi] *s* (**-cies**) ostinazione

obstinate ['abstınıt] *adj* ostinato

obstreperous [ab'strɛpərəs] *adj* turbolento; rumoroso

obstruct [əb'strʌkt] *tr* ostruire

obstruction [əb'strʌkʃən] *s* ostruzione

obtain [əb'ten] *tr* ottenere ‖ *intr* prevalere, essere in voga

obtrusive [əb'trusıv] *adj* intruso, importuno; sporgente

obtuse [əb'tjus] or [əb'tus] *adj* ottuso

obviate ['abvı‚et] *tr* ovviare (with *dat*)

obvious ['abvı·əs] *adj* ovvio, palmare

occasion [ə'keʒən] *s* occasione; **on occasion** di quando in quando ‖ *tr* occasionare

occasional [ə'keʒənəl] *adj* saltuario; (*e.g., verses*) d'occasione

occasionally [ə'keʒənəli] *adv* occasionalmente, di tanto in tanto

occident ['aksıdənt] *s* occidente *m*

occidental [‚aksı'dɛntəl] *adj* & *s* occidentale *mf*

occlud'ed front' [ə'kludıd] *s* fronte occluso

occlusion [ə'kluʒən] *s* occlusione

occlusive [ə'klusıv] *adj* occlusivo ‖ *s* occlusiva

occult [ə'kʌlt] or ['akʌlt] *adj* occulto

occupancy ['akjəpənsi] *s* occupazione, presa di possesso; (*tenancy*) locazione

occupant ['akjəpənt] *s* occupante *m*; (*tenant*) inquilino

occupation [‚akjə'peʃən] *s* occupazione

occupational [‚akjə'peʃənəl] *adj* occupazionale; (*e.g., disease*) professionale, del lavoro

occu·py ['akjə‚paı] *v* (*pret* & *pp* **-pied**) *tr* occupare; (*to dwell in*) abitare

oc·cur [ə'kʌr] *v* (*pret* & *pp* **-curred**;

ger -curring) *intr* accadere, succedere; incontrarsi; (*to come to mind*) venir in mente, e.g., **it occurs to me** mi viene in mente

occurrence [əˈkʌrəns] *s* evento, avvenimento; apparizione

ocean [ˈoʃən] *s* oceano

o'cean lin'er *s* transatlantico

o'clock [əˈklɑk] *adv* secondo l'orologio; **it is one o'clock** è la una; **it is two o'clock** sono le due

octane [ˈɑkten] *adj* ottanico || *s* ottano

octave [ˈɑktɪv] *or* [ˈɑktev] *s* ottava

Octavian [ɑkˈtevɪ·ən] *s* Ottaviano

October [ɑkˈtobər] *s* ottobre *m*

octo·pus [ˈɑktəpəs] *s* (-puses *or* -pi [ˌpaɪ]) (*small*) polpo; (*large*) piovra; (fig) piovra

ocular [ˈɑkjələr] *adj* & *s* oculare *m*

oculist [ˈɑkjəlɪst] *s* oculista *mf*

odd [ɑd] *adj* (*number*) dispari; strambo, bizzarro; (*not matching*) scompagnato, spaiato; strano; e rotti, e.g., **three hundred odd** tre cento e rotti || **odds** *ssg or spl* probabilità *f*; (*advantage*) vantaggio, superiorità *f*; **at odds** in disaccordo; **by all odds** senza dubbio; **it makes no odds** fa lo stesso; **the odds are** la quota è; **to set at odds** seminare zizzania fra

oddi·ty [ˈɑdɪti] *s* (-ties) stranezza

odd' jobs' *spl* lavori saltuari

odd' lot' *s* (fin) compravendita di meno di cento unità

odds' and ends' *spl* un po' di tutto

odious [ˈodɪ·əs] *adj* odioso

odor [ˈodər] *s* odore *m*; **to be in bad odor** aver cattiva fama

odorless [ˈodərlɪs] *adj* inodoro

odorous [ˈodərəs] *adj* odoroso

Odysseus [oˈdɪsjus] *or* [oˈdɪsɪ·əs] *s* Odisseo

Odyssey [ˈɑdɪsi] *s* Odissea

Oedipus [ˈɛdɪpəs] *or* [ˈidɪpəs] *s* Edipo

of [əv] *or* [ɑv] *prep* di, e.g., **the lead of the pencil** la mina della matita; a, e.g., **to think of** pensare a; meno, e.g., **a quarter of ten** le dieci meno un quarto

off [ɔf] *or* [ɑf] *adj* (*wrong*) sbagliato; (*slightly abnormal*) matto, pazzo; inferiore; (*electricity*) tagliato; (*agreement*) sospeso; libero, in libertà; distante; destro; (*season*) morto || *adv* via; fuori, lontano, distante; **to be off** mettersi in marcia || *prep* da; fuori da; al disotto di; lontano da; distolto da, e.g., **his eyes were off the target** i suoi occhi erano distolti dal bersaglio; (naut) al largo di

offal [ˈɑfəl] *or* [ˈɔfəl] *s* (*of butchered animal*) frattaglie *fpl*; rifiuti *mpl*

off' and on' *adv* di tempo in tempo

off'beat' *adj* insolito, originale

off' chance' *s* possibilità remota

off'-col'or *adj* scolorito; indisposto; (*joke*) di dubbio gusto

offend [əˈfɛnd] *tr* & *intr* offendere

offender [əˈfɛndər] *s* offensore *m*

offense [əˈfɛns] *s* offesa; **to take offense (at)** offendersi (di)

offensive [əˈfɛnsɪv] *adj* offensivo || *s* offensiva

offer [ˈɔfər] *or* [ˈɑfər] *s* offerta || *tr* offrire; (*thanks*) porgere; (*resistance*) opporre || *intr* offrirsi

offering [ˈɔfərɪŋ] *or* [ˈɑfərɪŋ] *s* offerta

off'hand' *adj* fatto all'improvviso; sbrigativo, alla buona || *adv* all'improvviso; bruscamente

office [ˈɔfɪs] *or* [ˈɑfɪs] *s* ufficio; funzione, incombenza; (*of a doctor*) gabinetto; (*of a lawyer*) studio; (eccl) uffizio; **through the good offices of** per tramite di

of'fice boy' *s* fattorino

of'fice·hold'er *s* pubblico funzionario

of'fice hours' *spl* orario d'ufficio

officer [ˈɔfɪsər] *or* [ˈɑfɪsər] *s* (*in a corporation*) funzionario; (*policeman*) agente *m*; (mil, nav, naut) ufficiale *m*; **officer of the day** (mil) ufficiale *m* di giornata

of'fice seek'er [ˈsikər] *s* aspirante *m* a un ufficio pubblico

of'fice supplies' *spl* articoli *mpl* di cancelleria

official [əˈfɪʃəl] *adj* ufficiale || *s* funzionario, ufficiale *m*

officiate [əˈfɪʃɪ·et] *intr* ufficiare

officious [əˈfɪʃəs] *adj* invadente, inframettente; **to be officious** essere un impiccione

offing [ˈɔfɪŋ] *or* [ˈɑfɪŋ] *s*—**in the offing** al largo; (fig) in preparazione, probabile

off'-lim'its *adj* proibito; **off-limits to** ingresso proibito a

off'-peak' heat'er *s* (elec) scaldabagno azionato unicamente in periodi di consumo minimo

off'-peak' load' *s* (elec) carico di consumo minimo

off'print' *s* estratto

off'set' *s* compensazione; (typ) offset *m* || **off'set'** *v* (*pret* & *pp* -set; *ger* -setting) *tr* compensare; stampare in offset

off'shoot' *s* (*of plant*) germoglio; (*of family or race*) discendente *mf*; (*branch*) ramo; (fig) conseguenza

off'shore' *adj* (*wind*) di terra; (*fishing*) vicino alla costa; (*island*) costiero || *adv* al largo

off'side' *adv* (sports) fuori gioco

off'spring' *s* discendente *m*; prole *f*; figlio; figli *mpl*

off'stage' *adv* tra le quinte

off'-the-rec'ord *adj* confidenziale || *adv* confidenzialmente

often [ˈɔfən] *or* [ˈɑfən] *adv* sovente, spesso; **how often?** quante volte?; **once too often** una volta di troppo

ogive [ˈodʒaɪv] *or* [oˈdʒaɪv] *s* ogiva

ogle [ˈogəl] *tr* adocchiare, occhieggiare

ogre [ˈogər] *s* orco

ohm [om] *s* ohm *m*

oil [ɔɪl] *adj* (*pertaining to edible oil*) oleario; (*e.g., well*) di petrolio; (*e.g., lamp*) a olio; (*tanker*) petroliero; (*field*) petrolifero || *s* olio; petrolio; **to burn the midnight oil** studiare a lume di candela; **to pour oil on troubled waters** pacificare; **to strike oil** trovare petrolio || *tr* oliare; lubrificare; ungere ‖ intr (said of a motorship) fare petrolio

oil' burn'er s bruciatore m a gasolio

oil'can' s oliatore m

oil'cloth' s incerata, tela cerata

oil' field' s giacimento petrolifero

oil' lamp' s lampada a petrolio

oil'man s (-men) (retailer) mercante m di petrolio; (operator) petroliere m

oil' paint'ing s quadro a olio

oil' slick' s macchia d'olio

oil' tank'er s petroliera

oil' well' s pozzo di petrolio

oil·y ['ɔɪli] adj (-ier; -iest) oleoso; untuoso

ointment ['ɔɪntmənt] s unguento

O.K. ['o'ke] adj (coll) corretto ‖ s (coll) approvazione f ‖ adv (coll) benissimo, d'accordo ‖ v (pret & pp O.K.'d; ger O.K.'ing) tr (coll) dare l'approvazione a ‖ interj benissimo!

okra ['okrə] s (bot) ibisco esculento; (bot) baccello dell'ibisco esculento

old [old] adj vecchio; antico, vetusto; how old is . . . ? quanti anni ha . . . ?; of old anticamente; to be . . . years old avere . . . anni

old' age' s vecchiaia

old' boy' s vecchietto arzillo; (Brit) vecchio mio

old'-clothes'man' s (-men') rigattiere m

old' coun'try s madre patria

old-fashioned ['old'fæʃənd] adj all'antica; fuori moda

old' fo'gey or old' fo'gy ['fogi] s (-gies) uomo di idee antiquate, reazionario

Old' Glo'ry s la bandiera degli Stati Uniti

Old' Guard' s (U.S.A.) parte f più conservatrice di un partito

old' hand' s vecchio del mestiere

old' maid' s zitella

old' mas'ter s grande maestro; quadro di un gran maestro

old' moon' s luna calante

old' salt' s lupo di mare

old' school' s gente f all'antica

old' school' tie' s (Brit) cravatta coi colori della propria scuola; (fig) tradizionalismo

Old' Tes'tament s Antico Testamento

old'-time' adj all'antica; del tempo antico

old-timer ['old'taɪmər] s (coll) veterano; (coll) vecchio

old' wives' tale' s superstizione da donnicciole; racconto di vecchie comari

Old' World' s mondo antico

oleander [,oli'ændər] s oleandro

olig·ar·chy ['ɑlɪ,gɑrki] s (-chies) oligarchia

olive ['ɑlɪv] adj oleario; (color) olivastro ‖ s (tree) olivo; (fruit) oliva

ol'ive branch' s ramoscello d'olivo

ol'ive grove' s oliveto

ol'ive oil' s olio d'oliva

Oliver ['ɑlɪvər] s Oliviero

ol'ive tree' s olivo

Olympiad [o'lɪmpɪ,æd] s olimpiade f

Olympian [o'lɪmpɪ-ən] adj olimpico ‖ s deità olimpica; giocatore olimpico

Olympic [o'lɪmpɪk] adj olimpico, olimpionico

omelet or omelette ['ɑmələt] or ['ɑmlɪt] s frittata, omelette f

omen ['omən] s augurio

ominous ['ɑmɪnəs] adj infausto, ominoso

omission [o'mɪʃən] s omissione

omit [o'mɪt] v (pret & pp omitted; ger omitting) tr omettere

omnibus ['ɑmnɪ,bʌs] or ['ɑmnɪbəs] adj di interesse generale ‖ s bus m; volume collettivo

omnipotent [ɑm'nɪpətənt] adj onnipotente

omniscient [ɑm'nɪʃənt] adj onnisciente

omnivorous [ɑm'nɪvərəs] adj onnivoro

on [ɑn] or [ɔn] adj addosso, e.g., with his hat on col cappello addosso; in uso, in funzione; (light) acceso; (deal) fatto, concluso; (e.g., game) già cominciato; what is on at the theater? che cosa si dà al teatro? ‖ adv su; avanti; dietro, e.g., to drag on tirarsi dietro; and so on e così via; come on! va via!; farther on più in là; later on più tardi; to be on to s.o. (coll) scoprire il gioco di qlcu.; to have on avere addosso; to . . . on continuare a, e.g., the band played on la banda continuò a suonare; to put on mettersi ‖ prep su, sopra; a, e.g., on foot a piedi; on his arrival at suo arrivo; sotto, e.g., on my responsibility sotto la mia responsabilità; contro, e.g., an attack on the government un attacco contro il governo; da, e.g., on good authority da buona fonte; on all sides da tutte le parti; verso, e.g., to march on the capital marciare verso la capitale; dopo, e.g., victory on victory vittoria dopo vittoria

on' and on' adv senza cessa

once [wʌns] s una volta; volta, e.g., this once questa volta ‖ adv una volta; mai, e.g., if this once becomes known se questo si risapesse mai; at once repentinamente; at once subito; allo stesso tempo; for once almeno una volta; once and again ripetutamente; once in a blue moon ad ogni morte di papa; once in a while di tanto in tanto; once upon a time there was c'era una volta ‖ conj se appena; una volta che

once'-o'ver s (coll) occhiata rapida; to give s.th the once-over (coll) esaminare qlco rapidamente; (coll) pulire qlco superficialmente

one [wʌn] adj uno; un certo, e.g., one Smith un certo Smith; unico e.g., one price prezzo unico ‖ s uno ‖ pron uno, e.g., how can one live here? come è possibile che uno viva qui?; si, e.g., how does one go to the museum? come si va al museo?; I for one per me; it's all one and the same to me per me fa lo stesso; my little one piccolo mio; one and all tutti; one another si, e.g., they wrote one another si scrissero l'un(o) l'altro, e.g., **they looked at one another** si guardarono l'un l'altro; **one o'clock** la una; **one's** il suo, il proprio; **the blue hat and the red one** il cappello blu e quello rosso; **the one and only** l'unico; **the one that** chi, quello che; **this one** questo; **that one** quello; **to make one** unire

one'-eyed' adj monocolo

one'-horse' adj a un solo cavallo; (coll) da nulla, poco importante

one'-man' show' s personale f

onerous ['ɑnərəs] adj oneroso

one-self' pron sé stesso; se; si; **to be oneself** essere normale; comportarsi normalmente

one-sided ['wan'saɪdɪd] adj unilaterale; ingiusto, parziale

one'-track' adj a un solo binario; (coll) unilaterale, limitato

one'-way' adj a senso unico; (ticket) semplice, d'andata

onion ['ʌnjən] s cipolla; **to know one's onions** (coll) conoscere i propri polli

on'ion-skin' s carta pelle aglio, carta velina

on'look'er s presente m, spettatore m

only ['onlɪ] adj solo, unico || adv solo, soltanto, non . . . più di; **not only . . . but also** non solo . . . ma anche || conj ma; se non che

on'set' s attacco; (beginning) inizio; **at the onset** dapprincipio

onslaught ['ɑn‚slɔt] or ['ɔn‚slɔt] s attacco

on'to prep su, sopra a; **to be onto** (coll) rendersi conto del gioco di

onward ['ɑnwərd] or **onwards** ['ɑnwərdz] adv avanti, più avanti

onyx ['ɑnɪks] s onice m

ooze [uz] s trasudazione; liquido per concia || tr sudare || intr trasudare; (said, e.g., of blood) stillare; (said, e.g., of air) filtrare; (fig) trapelare

opal ['opəl] s opale m

opaque [o'pek] adj opaco; (writer's style) oscuro; stupido

open ['opən] adj aperto, scoperto; (job) vacante; (time) libero; (hunting season) legale; indeciso; manifesto; (hand) liberale; (needlework) a giorno; **to break or to crack open** forzare; **to throw open** aprire completamente || s apertura; (in the woods) radura; **in the open** all'aperto; all'aria aperta; in alto mare; apertamente || tr aprire; (an account) impostare; **to open up** spalancare; (one's eyes) sbarrare || intr aprire, aprirsi; (theat) esordire; **to open into** sboccare in; **to open on** dare su; **to open up** sbottonarsi

o'pen-air' adj all'aria aperta

open-eyed ['opən‚aɪd] adj con gli occhi aperti; meravigliato; fatto con piena conoscenza

open-handed ['opən'hændɪd] adj generoso, liberale

open-hearted ['opən'hɑrtɪd] adj franco, sincero; gentile

o'pen house' s tavola imbandita; **to keep open house** aver sempre ospiti

opening ['opənɪŋ] s apertura; (of dress) giro collo; (e.g., of sewer) imbocco; (in the woods) radura; (vacancy) posto vacante; (beginning) inizio; (chance to say something) occasione

o'pening night' s debutto, prima

o'pening num'ber s primo numero

o'pening price' s prezzo d'apertura

open-minded ['opən'maɪndɪd] adj di larghe vedute; imparziale

o'pen se'cret s segreto di Pulcinella

o'pen shop' s officina che impiega chi non è membro del sindacato

o'pen-work' s traforo

opera ['ɑpərə] s opera

op'era glass'es spl binocolo da teatro

op'era hat' s gibus m

op'era house' s teatro dell'opera

operate ['ɑpə‚ret] tr (a machine) far funzionare; (a shop) gestire; operare || intr funzionare; operare; **to operate on** (surg) operare

operatic [‚ɑpə'rætɪk] adj operistico

op'erating expens'es spl spese fpl di ordinaria amministrazione

op'erating room' s sala operatoria

op'erating ta'ble s tavola operatoria

operation [‚ɑpə're/ən] s operazione; funzionamento, marcia

opera'tions research' s ricerca operativa

operator ['ɑpə‚retər] s operatore m; (of a conveyance) conduttore m, conducente mf; (com) gestore m; (telp) telefonista mf; (surg) chirurgo operatore; (slang) faccendiere m

opiate ['opɪ‚ɪt] or ['opɪ‚et] adj & s oppiato

opinion [ə'pɪnjən] s opinione; **in my opinion** a mio modo di vedere; **to have a high opinion of** avere una grande stima di

opinionated [ə'pɪnjə‚netɪd] adj ostinato, testardo, dogmatico

opium ['opɪ‚əm] s oppio

o'pium den' s fumeria d'oppio

opossum [ə'pɑsəm] s opossum m

opponent [ə'ponənt] s avversario

opportune [‚ɑpər'tjun] or [‚ɑpər'tun] adj opportuno

opportunist [‚ɑpər'tjunɪst] or [‚ɑpər-'tunɪst] s opportunista mf

opportuni-ty [‚ɑpər'tjunɪtɪ] or [‚ɑpər-'tunɪtɪ] s (-ties) opportunità f, occasione

oppose [ə'poz] tr opporsi a

opposite ['ɑpəsɪt] adj opposto; di rimpetto, e.g., **the house opposite** la casa di rimpetto || s contrario || prep di faccia a, di rimpetto a

op'posite num'ber s persona di grado corrispondente

opposition [‚ɑpə'zɪ/ən] s opposizione

oppress [ə'pres] tr opprimere

oppressive [ə'presɪv] adj oppressivo; opprimente, soffocante

oppressor [ə'presər] s oppressore m

opprobrious [ə'probrɪ‚əs] adj obbrobrioso

opprobrium [ə'probri·əm] *s* obbrobrio
optic ['optɪk] *adj* ottico ‖ **optics** *ssg* ottica
optical ['optɪkəl] *adj* ottico
optician [ap'tɪʃən] *s* ottico, occhialaio
optimism ['optɪ,mɪzəm] *s* ottimismo
optimist ['optɪmɪst] *s* ottimista *mf*
optimistic [,optɪ'mɪstɪk] *adj* ottimistico
option ['opʃən] *s* opzione
optional ['opʃənəl] *adj* facoltativo
optometrist [ap'tomɪtrɪst] *s* optometrista *mf*
opulent ['opjələnt] *adj* opulento
or [or] *conj* o; (*or else*) oppure
oracle ['orəkəl] *or* ['orækəl] *s* oracolo
oracular [o'rækjələr] *adj* profetico; ambiguo; misterioso; sentenzioso
oral ['orəl] *adj* orale
orange ['arɪndʒ] *or* ['orɪndʒ] *adj* di arance; arancio ‖ *s* arancia
orangeade [,arɪndʒ'ed] *or* [,orɪndʒ-'ed] *s* aranciata
or'ange blos'som *s* zagara
or'ange grove' *s* aranceto
or'ange juice' *s* sugo d'arancia
or'ange squeez'er *s* spremiagrumi *m*
or'ange tree' *s* arancio
orang-outang [o'ræŋu,tæŋ] *s* orango
oration [o're/ən] *s* orazione, discorso
orator ['arətər] *or* ['orətər] *s* oratore *m*
oratorical [,arə'torɪkəl] *or* [,orə'torɪkəl] *adj* oratorio
oratori·o [,arə'torɪ,o] *or* [,orə'torɪ,o] *s* (*-os*) (mus) oratorio
orato·ry ['arə,tori] *or* ['orə,tori] *s* (*-ries*) oratoria; (eccl) oratorio
orb [orb] *s* orbe *m*
orbit ['orbɪt] *s* orbita; **to go into orbit** entrare in orbita ‖ *tr* mettere in orbita; orbitare intorno a ‖ *intr* orbitare
or'biting sta'tion *s* stazione orbitale
orchard ['ortʃərd] *s* frutteto
orchestra ['orkɪstrə] *s* orchestra; (*parquet*) platea
orchestral [or'kestrəl] *adj* orchestrale
or'chestra pit' *s* golfo mistico
or'chestra seat' *s* poltrona di platea
orchestrate ['orkɪs,tret] *tr* orchestrare
orchid ['orkɪd] *s* orchidea
ordain [or'den] *tr* predestinare; decretare; (eccl) ordinare
ordeal [or'dil] *or* [or'di·əl] *s* sfacchinata; (hist) ordalia
order ['ordər] *s* ordine *m*; compito, e.g., **a big order** un compito difficile; (com) commessa, ordinazione; (mil) consegna; **in order that** affinché; **in order to** + *inf* per + *inf*; **made to order** fatto su misura; **to get out of order** guastarsi; **to give an order** dare un ordine; (com) fare una commessa ‖ *tr* (*e.g., a drink*) ordinare; (*a person*) ordinare (with *dat*); (*a suit of clothes*) far fare; **to order around** mandare attorno; **to order s.o. away** mandar via qlcu
or'der blank' *s* cedola d'ordinazione
order·ly ['ordərli] *adj* ordinato; disciplinato ‖ *s* (*-lies*) (*in a hospital*) in-

serviente *mf*; (mil) ordinanza, attendente *m*
ordinal ['ordɪnəl] *adj & s* ordinale *m*
ordinance ['ordɪnəns] *s* ordinanza
ordinary ['ordɪ,neri] *adj* ordinario
ordnance ['ordnəns] *s* artiglieria; bocche *fpl* da fuoco; munizionamento
ore [or] *s* minerale *m* (metallifero)
organ ['orgən] *s* organo
organ·dy ['orgəndi] *s* (*-dies*) organdi *m*
or'gan grind'er *s* suonatore *m* d'organetto
organic [or'gænɪk] *adj* organico
organism ['orgə,nɪzəm] *s* organismo
organist ['orgənɪst] *s* organista *mf*
organization [,orgənɪ'zeʃən] *s* organizzazione
organize ['orgə,naɪz] *tr* organizzare
organizer ['orgə,naɪzər] *s* organizzatore *m*
or'gan loft' *s* palco, galleria per l'organo
orgasm ['orgæzəm] *s* orgasmo
or·gy ['ordʒi] *s* (*-gies*) orgia
orient ['ori·ənt] *s* oriente *m* ‖ **Orient** *s* Oriente *m* ‖ **orient** ['ori,ent] *tr* orientare, orizzontare
oriental [,ori'entəl] *adj* orientale ‖ **Oriental** *s* orientale *mf*
orifice ['arɪfɪs] *or* ['orɪfɪs] *s* orifizio
origin ['arɪdʒɪn] *or* ['orɪdʒɪn] *s* origine *f*, provenienza
original [ə'rɪdʒɪnəl] *adj & s* originale *mf*
originate [ə'rɪdʒɪ,net] *tr* originare ‖ *intr* originare, originarsi
oriole ['ori,ol] *s* oriolo, rigogolo
Ork'ney Is'lands ['orkni] *spl* Orcadi *fpl*
ormolu ['ormə'lu] *s* (*alloy*) similoro; (*gold powder*) polvere *f* d'oro; (*gilded metal*) bronzo dorato
ornament ['ornəmənt] *s* ornamento ‖ ['ornə,ment] *tr* ornamentare
ornamental [,ornə'mentəl] *adj* ornamentale
ornate [or'net] *or* ['ornet] *adj* ornato; (*style*) elaborato
ornithologist [,ornɪ'θalədʒɪst] *s* ornitologo
orphan ['orfən] *adj & s* orfano ‖ *tr* rendere orfano
orphanage ['orfənɪdʒ] *s* (*institution*) orfanotrofio; (*condition*) orfananza
Orpheus ['orfjus] *or* ['orfi·əs] *s* Orfeo
orthodox ['orθə,daks] *adj* ortodosso
orthogra·phy [or'θagrəfi] *s* (*-phies*) ortografia
oscillate ['asɪ,let] *intr* oscillare
osier ['oʒər] *s* vimine *m*; (bot) vinco
osmosis [az'mosɪs] *or* [as'mosɪs] *s* osmosi *f*
osprey ['aspri] *s* falco pescatore
ossi·fy ['asɪ,faɪ] *v* (*pret & pp* -fied) *tr* ossificare ‖ *intr* ossificarsi
ostensible [as'tensɪbəl] *adj* apparente, preteso
ostentatious [,asten'teʃəs] *adj* ostentato
osteopathy [,astɪ'apəθi] *s* osteopatia
ostracism ['astrə,sɪzəm] *s* ostracismo

ostracize ['ɑstrə‚saɪz] *tr* dare l'ostracismo a, ostracizzare

ostrich ['ɑstrɪtʃ] *s* struzzo

Othello [oˈθɛlo] or [əˈθɛlo] *s* Otello

other ['ʌðər] *adj & pron indef* altro || *adv*—other than diversamente che

otherwise ['ʌðər‚waɪz] *adv* altrimenti; differentemente

otter ['ɑtər] *s* lontra

ottoman ['ɑtəmən] *s* (*fabric*) ottomano; (*sofa*) ottomana; cuscino per i piedi || **Ottoman** *adj & s* ottomano

ouch [aʊtʃ] *interj* ahi!

ought [ɔt] *s* qualcosa; zero; **for ought I know** per quanto io sappia || *v aux* is rendered in Italian by the conditional of *dovere*, e.g., **you ought to be ashamed** dovresti vergognarti

ounce [aʊns] *s* oncia

our [aʊr] *adj poss* nostro, il nostro

ours [aʊrz] *pron poss* il nostro

ourselves [aʊrˈsɛlvz] *pron pers* noi stessi; ci, e.g., **we enjoyed ourselves** ci siamo divertiti

oust [aʊst] *tr* espellere; (*a tenant*) sfrattare

out [aʊt] *adj* erroneo; esterno; fuori pratica; svenuto; ubriaco; finito; (*book*) pubblicato; (*lights*) spento; fuori moda; introvabile; palmare; di permesso, e.g., **my night out** la mia serata di permesso; (*e.g., at the knees*) frusto; (*sports*) fuori gioco || *s* via d'uscita; **to be on the outs or at outs with** (coll) essere in disaccordo con || *adv* fuori, all'infuori; all'aria libera; **out for** in cerca di; **out of** fuori, fuori di; di; da; (*e.g., money*) a corto di, senza; su, e.g., **two students out of three** due studenti su tre || *prep* fuori di; per, lungo || *interj* fuori!

out' and away' *adv* di gran lunga

out'-and-out' *adj* perfetto, completo || *adv* perfettamente, completamente

out'bid' *v* (*pret* -bid; *pp* -bid or -bidden; *ger* -bidding) *tr* fare un'offerta migliore di; (*bridge*) fare una dichiarazione più alta di

out'board mo'tor *s* fuoribordo, motore *m* fuoribordo

out'break' *s* insurrezione; (*of hives*) eruzione; (*of anger; of war*) scoppio

out'build'ing *s* dipendenza

out'burst' *s* (*of tears; of laughter*) scoppio; (*of energy*) impeto, slancio

out'cast' *s* vagabondo reietto

out'come' *s* risultato

out'cry' *s* (-cries) grido, chiasso

out'dat'ed *adj* fuori moda

out'dis'tance *tr* distanziare

out'do' *v* (*pret* -did; *pp* -done) *tr* sorpassare; **to outdo oneself** sorpassare sé stesso

out'door' *adj* all'aria aperta

out'doors' *s* aria libera, aperta campagna || *adv* all'aria aperta, fuori di casa

out'er space' ['aʊtər] *s* spazio cosmico

out'field' *s* (baseball) campo esterno

out'field'er *s* (baseball) esterno

out'fit' *s* equipaggiamento; (*female costume*) insieme *m*; (*of bride*) corredo; (*group*) (coll) corpo; (com) compagnia || *v* (*pret & pp* -fitted; *ger* -fitting) *tr* equipaggiare

out'flow' *s* efflusso

out'go'ing *adj* in partenza; (*tide*) decrescente; (*character*) espansivo || *s* efflusso

out'grow' *v* (*pret* -grew; *pp* -grown) *tr* essere troppo grande per; sorpassare in statura; perdere l'interesse per || *intr* protrudere

out'growth' *s* risultato, conseguenza; crescita

outing ['aʊtɪŋ] *s* gita, scampagnata

outlandish [aʊtˈlændɪʃ] *adj* strano, bizzarro; dall'aspetto straniero; (*remote, far away*) in capo al mondo

out'last' *tr* sopravvivere (with *dat*)

out'law' *s* fuorilegge *mf* || *tr* proscrivere; dichiarare illegale

out'lay' *s* disborso || **out-lay'** *v* (*pret & pp* -laid) *tr* sborsare

out'let *s* uscita; (*e.g., of river*) sbocco; (com) mercato; (elec) presa di corrente; (fig) sfogo

out'line' *s* contorno; traccia, tracciato; sagoma, profilo; prospetto || *tr* delineare; tracciare, tratteggiare; sagomare, profilare; prospettare

out'live' *tr* sopravvivere (with *dat*)

out'look' *s* prospettiva; (*watch*) guardia; (*mental view*) modo di vedere, opinione

out'ly'ing *adj* lontano, fuori di mano; periferico

outmoded [‚aʊtˈmodɪd] *adj* fuori moda, antiquato

out'num'ber *tr* superare in numero

out'-of-date' *adj* fuori moda

out'-of-door' *adj* all'aria aperta

out'-of-doors' *adj* all'aria aperta || *s* aria aperta || *adv* all'aria aperta; fuori di casa

out'-of-print' *adj* esaurito

out'-of-the-way' *adj* appartato, fuori mano; inusitato, strano

out' of tune' *adj* stonato || *adv* fuori di tono

out' of work' *adj* disoccupato

out'pa'tient *s* paziente *mf* esterno

out'post' *s* (mil) posto avanzato

out'put' *s* produzione; (elec) uscita; (mach) rendimento, potenza utile

out'rage' *s* oltraggio, indecenza || *tr* oltraggiare; (*a woman*) violare

outrageous [aʊtˈredʒəs] *adj* oltraggioso; (*excessive*) eccessivo; atroce, feroce

out'rank' *tr* superare in grado

out'rid'er *s* battistrada *m*

out'right' *adj* completo, intero || *adv* completamente; apertamente; sul colpo, sull'istante

out'set' *s* inizio, principio

out'side' *adj* esterno; (*unlikely*) improbabile; (*price*) massimo || *s* esterno, di fuori *m*; aspetto esteriore; vita fuori del carcere || *adv* fuori, di fuori; **outside of** fuori di || *prep* fuori di; (coll) all'infuori di

outsider [ˌaut'saɪdər] s estraneo, intruso; (sports) outsider m

out'skirts' spl sobborghi mpl, periferia

out'spo'ken adj franco, esplicito

out'stand'ing adj saliente, eminente; (debt) arretrato, non pagato

outward ['autwərd] adj esterno, superficiale || adv al di fuori

out'weigh' tr pesare più di; eccedere in importanza

out'wit' v (pret & pp -witted; ger -witting) tr farla in barba di; (a pursuer) far perdere la traccia or la pista a

oval ['ovəl] adj & s ovale m

ova·ry ['ovəri] s (-ries) ovaia

ovation [o've/ən] s ovazione

oven ['ʌvən] s forno

over ['ovər] adj superiore; esterno; finito, concluso || adv su, sopra; dall'altra parte; dall'altra sponda; al rovescio; di nuovo; (at the bottom of a page) continua; qui, e.g., **hand over the money** dammi qui il denaro; **over again** di nuovo; **over against** contro; **over and over** ripetutamente; **over here** qui; **over there** là || prep su, sopra; dall'altra parte di; attraverso, per; (a certain number) più di; a causa di; **over and above** in eccesso di

o'ver·all' adj completo, totale || **over·alls** spl tuta

o'ver·bear'ing adj arrogante, prepotente

o'ver·board' adv in acqua; **man overboard!** uomo in mare!; **to go overboard** andare agli estremi

o'ver·cast' adj annuvolato || s cielo annuvolato || v (pret & pp -cast) tr coprire, annuvolare

o'ver·charge' s prezzo eccessivo; sovraccarico; (elec) carica eccessiva || **o'ver·charge'** tr far pagare eccessivamente; sovraccaricare

o'ver·coat' s soprabito, pastrano

o'ver·come' v (pret -came; pp -come) tr vincere, sopraffare; (e.g., passions) frenare; opprimere

o'vercon'fidence s sicumera

o'ver·crowd' tr gremire

o'ver·do' v (pret -did; pp -done) tr esagerare; strafare; esaurire; (meat) stracuocere || intr esaurirsi

o'ver·dose' s dose eccessiva

o'ver·draft' s assegno allo scoperto

o'ver·draw' v (pret -drew; pp -drawn) tr (a check) emettere allo scoperto; (a character) esagerare la descrizione di

o'ver·due' adj in ritardo; (com) in sofferenza, scaduto

o'ver·eat' v (pret -ate; pp -eaten) tr & intr mangiare troppo

o'ver·exer'tion s sforzo eccessivo

o'ver·expose' tr sovresporre

o'ver·expo'sure s sovresposizione

o'ver·flow' s (of a river) piena, straripamento; (excess) sovrabbondanza; (e.g., of a fountain) trabocco; (outlet) tubo di troppopieno || **o'ver·flow'** intr (said of a river) straripare; (said of a container) traboccare

o'ver·fly' v (pret -flew; pp -flown) tr sorvolare; (a target) oltrepassare

o'ver·grown' adj cresciuto troppo; coperto, denso

o'ver·hang' s strapiombo || **o'ver·hang'** v (pret & pp -hung) tr sovrastare (with dat); sovrastare; (to threaten) minacciare; pervadere, permeare || intr sovrastare, strapiombare

o'ver·haul' s riparazione; esame m, revisione || tr riparare; esaminare, ripassare, rivedere; raggiungere, mettersi alla pari con

o'ver·head' adj in alto, sopra la testa; aereo; elevato, pensile; generale || **o'ver·head'** adv in alto, di sopra || **o'ver·head'** s spese fpl generali

o'ver·head projec'tor s lavagna luminosa

o'ver·head valve' s valvola in testa

o'ver·hear' v (pret & pp -heard) tr sentire per caso, udire per caso

o'ver·heat' tr surriscaldare || intr surriscaldarsi; eccitarsi

overjoyed [ˌovər'dʒɔɪd] adj felicissimo; **to be overjoyed** non stare in sé dalla contentezza

overland ['ovərˌlænd] or ['ovərlənd] adj & adv per via di terra

o'ver·lap' v (pret & pp -lapped; ger -lapping) tr sovrapporre, estendersi sopra || intr sovrapporsi, estendersi; coincidere parzialmente

o'ver·load' s sovraccarico || **o'ver·load'** tr sovraccaricare, stracaricare

o'ver·look' tr sovrastare su, dominare; ispezionare, sorvegliare; passare sopra, trascurare; dare su, e.g., **the window overlooks the street** la finestra dà sulla strada

o'ver·lord' s dominatore m || tr dominare despoticamente

overly ['ovərli] adv eccessivamente

o'ver·night' adj per la notte, per solo una notte || **o'ver·night'** adv durante la notte; la notte prima

o'vernight bag' s astuccio di toletta per la notte

o'ver·pass' s cavalcavia, viadotto

o'ver·pop'ulate tr sovrappopolare

o'ver·pow'er tr sopraffare

o'ver·pow'ering adj schiacciante

o'ver·produc'tion s sovrapproduzione

o'ver·rate' tr sopravvalutare

o'ver·run' v (pret -ran; pp -run; ger -running) tr invadere, infestare; inondare; (one's time) oltrepassare, eccedere

o'ver·sea' or **o'ver·seas'** adj di oltremare || **o'ver·sea'** or **o'ver·seas'** adv oltremare, al di là dei mari

o'ver·see' v (pret -saw; pp -seen) tr sorvegliare

o'ver·seer' s sorvegliante mf

o'ver·shad'ow tr oscurare, eclissare

o'ver·shoe' s soprascarpa

o'ver·shoot' v (pret & pp -shot) tr (the target) oltrepassare; (said of water) scorrere sopra; **to overshoot oneself** andare troppo in là || intr (aer) atterrare lungo e richiamare

o'ver·sight' s sbadataggine f, svista; sorveglianza, supervisione o'ver·sleep' v (pret & pp -slept) tr (a certain hour) dormire oltre || intr dormire troppo a lungo

o'ver·step' v (pret & pp -stepped; ger -stepping) tr eccedere, oltrepassare

o'ver·stock' tr riempire eccessivamente

o'ver·sup·ply' s (-plies) fornitura superiore alla richiesta || o'ver·sup·ply' v (pret & pp -plied) tr fornire in quantità superiore alla richiesta

overt ['ovərt] or [o'vʌrt] adj palmare, chiaro, manifesto

o'ver·take' v (pret -took; pp -taken) tr raggiungere, sorpassare; sorprendere

o'ver-the-count'er adj (securities) venduto direttamente al compratore

o'ver·throw' s rovesciamento; disfatta || o'ver·throw' v (pret -threw; pp -thrown) tr rovesciare, sconfiggere

o'ver·time' adj supplementare, fuori orario || s straordinario; (sports) tempo supplementare || adv fuori orario

o'ver·tone' s (mus) suono armonico; (fig) sottinteso

o'ver·trump' s taglio con atout più alto || o'ver·trump' tr & intr tagliare con atout più alto

overture ['ovərt∫ər] s apertura; (mus) preludio, sinfonia

o'ver·turn' s rovesciamento || o'ver·turn' tr rovesciare, travolgere || intr rovesciarsi, ribaltarsi

overweening [,ovər'winiŋ] adj presuntuoso, vanitoso; esagerato, eccessivo

o'ver·weight' adj troppo grasso; oltrepassante i limiti di peso || o'ver·weight' s sovraccarico; preponderanza; eccesso di peso

overwhelm [,ovər'hwɛlm] tr schiacciare, debellare; coprire; (e.g., with kindness) colmare, ricolmare

o'ver·work' s lavoro straordinario; superlavoro || o'ver·work' tr far lavorare eccessivamente || intr lavorare eccessivamente

Ovid ['avɪd] s Ovidio

ow [au] interj ahi!

owe [o] tr dovere || intr essere in debito

owing ['o·ɪŋ] adj dovuto; owing to a causa di

owl [aul] s gufo, barbagianni m

own [on] adj proprio, e.g., my own brother il mio proprio fratello || s il proprio; on one's own (coll) per proprio conto; (without anybody's advice) di testa propria; to come into one's own entrare in possesso del proprio; essere riconosciuto per quanto si vale; to hold one's own non perdere terreno; essere pari || tr possedere; riconoscere || intr—to own up to confessare

owner ['onər] s padrone m, proprietario, titolare m

ownership ['onər,∫ɪp] s proprietà f

own'er's li'cence s permesso di circolazione

ox [aks] s (oxen ['aksən]) bue m

ox'cart' s carro tirato da buoi

oxide ['aksaɪd] s ossido

oxidize ['aksɪ,daɪz] tr ossidare || intr ossidarsi

oxygen ['aksɪdʒən] s ossigeno

ox'ygen mask' s maschera respiratoria

ox'ygen tent' s tenda ad ossigeno

oxytone ['aksɪ,ton] adj tronco, ossitono || s ossitono

oyster ['ɔɪstər] adj di ostriche || s ostrica

oys'ter bed' s ostricaio, banco di ostriche

oys'ter cock'tail s ostriche fpl servite in valva

oys'ter fork' s forchettina da ostriche

oys'ter·house' s ristorante m per la vendita delle ostriche

oys'ter·knife' s coltello per aprire le ostriche

oys'ter·man s (-men) ostricaio

oys'ter shell' s conchiglia d'ostrica

oys'ter stew' s brodetto d'ostriche

ozone ['ozon] s ozono

P

P, p [pi] s sedicesima lettera dell'alfabeto inglese

pace [pes] s passo, andatura; (of a horse) ambio; to keep pace with andare di pari passo con; to put s.o. through his paces mettere qlcu a dura prova; to set the pace for fare l'andatura per; dare l'esempio a || tr misurare a passi, percorrere; to pace the floor andare avanti e indietro per la stanza || intr camminare lentamente; andare al passo; (said of a horse) ambiare

pace'mak'er s battistrada m; (in races) chi stabilisce il passo; (med) pacemaker m

pacific [pə'sɪfɪk] adj pacifico || Pacific adj & s Pacifico

pacifier ['pæsɪ,faɪ·ər] s paciere m; (teething ring) succhietto, tettarella

pacifism ['pæsɪ,fɪzəm] s pacifismo

pacifist ['pæsɪfɪst] adj & s pacifista mf

paci·fy ['pæsɪ,faɪ] v (pret & pp -fied) tr pacificare

pack [pæk] s fardello, pacco; (of merchandise) balla; (of lies) mucchio; (of cards) mazzo; (of thieves) banda; (of dogs) muta; (of animals) branco; (of birds) stormo; (of cigarettes) pacchetto; (of ice) banchiglia; (of people) turba || tr affardellare, impaccare; (to wrap) imballare; ammucchiare; (in cans) mettere in conserva; (people) stipare; (a trunk) fare; to pack in stipare; to pack off mandare via || intr ammucchiarsi, pigiarsi, accalcarsi; **to pack up** fare il baule

package ['pækɪdʒ] *s* pacco, collo; *(small)* pacchetto ‖ *tr* impacchettare

pack' an'imal *s* bestia da soma

packer ['pækər] *s* imballatore *m*; *(of canned goods)* proprietario *(di fabbrica di conserve alimentari)*

packet ['pækɪt] *s* pacchetto; *(boat)* vapore *m* postale

packing ['pækɪŋ] *s* imballaggio; *(on shoulders of suit)* spallina; *(mach)* stoppa; *(ring) (mach)* guarnizione

pack'ing box' or **case'** *s* cassa d'imballaggio

pack'ing house' *s* fabbrica di conserve alimentari; fabbrica di carne in conserva

pack'ing slip' *s* foglio d'imballaggio

pack'sad'dle *s* basto

pack'thread' *s* spago d'imballaggio

pack'train' *s* fila di animali da soma

pact [pækt] *s* patto

pad [pæd] *s* cuscinetto, tampone *m*; imbottitura; *(of writing paper)* blocco da annotazioni; *(of an animal)* superficie *f* plantare, zampa; *(of a water lily)* foglia; *(rok)* piattaforma ‖ *v (pret & pp* **padded**; *ger* **padding)** *tr* imbottire, ovattare; *(e.g., a speech)* infarcire ‖ *intr* camminare pesantemente

pad'ding *s* imbottitura

paddle ['pædəl] *s* pagaia; *(of waterwheel)* pala ‖ *tr* remare; *(to spank)* bastonare ‖ *intr* remare; *(to splash)* diguazzare

pad'dle wheel' *s* ruota a pale

paddock ['pædək] *s* prato d'allenamento, paddock *m*

pad'lock' *s* lucchetto ‖ *tr* chiudere col lucchetto

pagan ['pegən] *adj & s* pagano

paganism ['pegə‚nɪzəm] *s* paganesimo

page [pedʒ] *s (of a book)* pagina; *(at court)* paggio; *(in hotels)* fattorino, valletto ‖ *tr* impaginare; *(in hotels)* chiamare, far chiamare

pageant ['pædʒənt] *s* parata, corteo, spettacolo

pageant·ry ['pædʒəntri] *s* (-ries) pompa, fasto

paginate ['pædʒɪ‚net] *tr* impaginare

pail [pel] *s* secchio

pain [pen] *s* dolore *m*; **on pain of** sotto pena di; **to take pains to** prendersi cura di; **to take pains not to** guardarsi da ‖ *tr & intr* dolere

painful ['penfəl] *adj* doloroso, penoso

pain'kill'er *s* (coll) analgesico

painless ['penlɪs] *adj* indolore

painstaking ['penz‚tekɪŋ] *adj* meticoloso

paint [pent] *s (for pictures)* colore *m*; *(for a house)* vernice *f*; *(make-up)* trucco ‖ *tr* dipingere; *(a house)* verniciare, tinteggiare ‖ *intr* *(with make-up)* dipingersi; essere pittore

paint'box' *s* scatola da colori

paint'brush' *s* pennello

painter ['pentər] *s (of pictures)* pittore *m*; *(of a house)* verniciatore *m*; *(naut)* barbetta

painting ['pentɪŋ] *s* pittura, dipinto

paint' remov'er [rɪ'muvər] *s* solvente *m* per levar la vernice

paint' thin'ner *s* diluente *m*

pair [per] *s* paio *m*; *(of people)* coppia ‖ *tr* appaiare, accoppiare ‖ *intr* appaiarsi, accoppiarsi

pair' of scis'sors *s* forbici *fpl*

pair' of trou'sers *s* calzoni *mpl*

pajamas [pə'dʒaməz] *or* [pə'dʒæməz] *spl* pigiama *m*

Pakistan [‚pakɪ'stan] *s* il Pakistan

Pakistani [‚pakɪ'stani] *adj & s* pachistano

pal [pæl] *s* (coll) compagno ‖ *v (pret & pp* **palled**; *ger* **palling)** *intr* (coll) essere compagni

palace ['pælɪs] *s* palazzo

palatable ['pælətəbəl] *adj* gustoso, appetitoso; accettabile

palatal ['pælətəl] *adj & s* palatale *f*

palate ['pælɪt] *s* palato

pale [pel] *adj* pallido ‖ *s* palo; *(enclosure)* recinto; *(fig)* ambito ‖ *intr* impallidire

pale'face' *s* faccia pallida

palette ['pælɪt] *s* tavolozza

palfrey ['pɔlfri] *s* palafreno

palisade [‚pælɪ'sed] *s* palizzata; *(line of cliffs)* dirupo

pall [pɔl] *s* panno mortuario; *(of smoke)* cappa ‖ *tr* saziare, infastidire ‖ *intr* saziarsi, perdere l'appetito

pall'bear'er *s* chi accompagna il feretro; chi porta il feretro

palliate ['pælɪ‚et] *tr* attenuare, alleviare

pallid ['pælɪd] *adj* pallido

pallor ['pælər] *s* pallore *m*

palm [pɑm] *s (tree and leaf)* palma; *(of hand; measure)* palmo; **to carry off the palm** riportare la palma; **to grease the palm of** ungere le ruote a ‖ *tr* far sparire nella mano; nascondere; **to palm off s.th on s.o.** rifilare qlco a qlcu

palmet·to [pæl'meto] *s* (-tos or -toes) palmeto

palmist ['pɑmɪst] *s* chiromante *mf*

palmistry ['pɑmɪstri] *s* chiromanzia

palm' leaf' *s* palma, foglia di palma

palm' oil' *s* olio di palma

Palm' Sun'day *s* Domenica delle Palme

palpable ['pælpəbəl] *adj* palpabile

palpitate ['pælpɪ‚tet] *intr* palpitare

pal·sy ['pɔlzi] *s* (-sies) paralisi *f* ‖ *v (pret & pp* **-sied)** *tr* paralizzare

pal·try ['pɔltri] *adj* (-trier; -triest) vile, meschino, irrisorio

pamper ['pæmpər] *tr* viziare; *(the appetite)* saziare

pamphlet ['pæmflɪt] *s* opuscolo, libello

pan [pæn] *s* padella, casseruola; *(of a balance)* coppa, piatto; *(phot)* bacinella ‖ *v (pret & pp* **panned**; *ger* **panning)** *tr* friggere; *(gold)* vagliare in padella; *(salt)* estrarre in salina; *(coll)* criticare ‖ *intr* essere estratto; **to pan out** (coll) riuscire ‖ **Pan** *s* Pan *m*

panacea [‚pænə'si-ə] *s* panacea

Pan'ama Canal' [‚pænə‚mɑ] *s* Canale *m* di Panama

Pan'ama hat' *s* panama *m*
Panamanian [ˌpænəˈmɛnɪ.ən] *or*
[ˌpænəˈmɑnɪ.ən] *adj & s* panamegno
pan'cake' *s* frittella ‖ *intr* (aer) atterrare a piatto
pan'cake land'ing *s* atterraggio a piatto
pancreas [ˈpænkrɪ.əs] *s* pancreas *m*
pander [ˈpændər] *s* mezzano ‖ *intr*
ruffianeggiare; **to pander to** favorire,
assecondare i desideri di
pane [pen] *s* pannello, vetro di finestra
pan-el [ˈpænəl] *s* pannello; gruppo che
discute in faccia al pubblico, telequiz
m; discussione pubblica; (*of door or
window*) specchio; (law) lista di giu-
rati ‖ *v* (*pret & pp* **-eled** *or* **-elled**; *ger*
-eling *or* **-elling**) *tr* coprire di pan-
nelli
pan'el discus'sion *s* colloquio di esperti
in faccia al pubblico
panelist [ˈpænəlɪst] *s* partecipante *mf*
a una discussione in faccia al pubblico
pan'el lights' *spl* luci *fpl* del cruscotto
pan'el truck' *s* camioncino
pang [pæŋ] *s* (*sharp pain*) spasimo;
(*of remorse*) tormento
pan'han'dle *s* manico della padella ‖
intr accattare, mendicare
pan-ic [ˈpænɪk] *adj & s* panico ‖ *v*
(*pret & pp* **-icked**; *ger* **-icking**) *tr*
riempire di panico ‖ *intr* essere colto
dal panico
pan'ic-strick'en *adj* morto di paura, in
preda al panico
pano-ply [ˈpænəplɪ] *s* (**-plies**) panoplia;
abbigliamento in pompa magna
panorama [ˌpænəˈræmə] *or* [ˌpænə-
ˈrɑmə] *s* panorama *m*
pan-sy [ˈpænzɪ] *s* (**-sies**) viola del pensiero
pant [pænt] *s* anelito, affanno; **pants**
pantaloni *mpl*, calzoni *mpl*; **to wear
the pants** portare i calzoni ‖ *intr*
ansare; (*said of heart*) palpitare
pantheism [ˈpænθɪ.ɪzəm] *s* panteismo
pantheon [ˈpænθɪ.ɑn] *or* [ˈpænθɪ.ən]
s panteon *m*, pantheon *m*
panther [ˈpænθər] *s* pantera
panties [ˈpæntɪz] *spl* mutandine *fpl*
pantomime [ˈpæntəˌmaɪm] *s* pantomima
pan-try [ˈpæntrɪ] *s* (**-tries**) dispensa
pap [pæp] *s* pappa
papa-cy [ˈpepəsɪ] *s* (**-cies**) papato
Pa'pal States' [ˈpepəl] *spl* Stati *mpl*
pontifici
paper [ˈpepər] *adj* di carta, cartaceo ‖
s carta; (*newspaper*) giornale *m*; (*of
a student*) tema *m*, saggio; (*of a
scholar*) studente; **on paper** per
iscritto ‖ *tr* (*a wall*) tappezzare
pa'per-back' *s* libro in brossura
pa'per-boy' *s* giornalaio, strillone *m*
pa'per clip' *s* fermaglio per le carte,
clip *m*
pa'per cone' *s* cartoccio
pa'per cut'ter *s* rifilatrice *f*
pa'per-hang'er *s* tappezziere *m*
pa'per knife' *s* tagliacarte *m*
pa'per mill' *s* cartiera
pa'per mon'ey *s* carta moneta

pa'per prof'its *spl* guadagni *mpl* non
realizzati su valori non venduti
pa'per tape' *s* (*of teletype*) nastro di
carta; (*of computer*) nastro perforato
pa'per-weight' *s* fermacarte *m*
pa'per work' *s* lavoro a tavolino
papier-mâché [ˌpepərmə'ʃe] *s* carta-
pesta
paprika [pæˈprikə] *or* [ˈpæprɪkə] *s*
paprica
papy-rus [pəˈpaɪrəs] *s* (**-ri** [raɪ])
papiro
par [par] *adj* alla pari, nominale; normale ‖ *s* parità *f*, valore *m* nominale;
at par alla pari
parable [ˈpærəbəl] *s* parabola
parabola [pəˈræbələ] *s* parabola
parachute [ˈpærə.ʃut] *s* paracadute *m*
‖ *intr* lanciarsi col paracadute
par'a-chute jump' *s* lancio col paracadute
parachutist [ˈpærə.ʃutɪst] *s* paracadutista *mf*
parade [pəˈred] *s* parata, sfilata; ostentazione, sfoggio ‖ *tr* ostentare, sfoggiare; disporre in parata ‖ *intr* fare
mostra di sé; (mil) sfilare
paradise [ˈpærə.daɪs] *s* paradiso
paradox [ˈpærə.dɑks] *s* paradosso
paradoxical [ˌpærə'dɑksɪkəl] *adj* paradossale
paraffin [ˈpærəfɪn] *s* paraffina
paragon [ˈpærə.gɑn] *s* paragone *m*
paragraph [ˈpærə.græf] *or* [ˈpærə-
ˌgraf] *s* paragrafo, capoverso; (*in a
newspaper*) trafiletto; (*of law*)
comma *m*.
parakeet [ˈpærə.kit] *s* parrocchetto
paral·lel [ˈpærə.lɛl] *adj* parallelo ‖ *s*
(geog, fig) parallelo; (geom) paral-
lela; **parallels** (typ) sbarrette *fpl* verticali ‖ *v* (*pret & pp* **-leled** *or* **-lelled**;
ger **-leling** *or* **-lelling**) *tr* collocare
parallelamente; correre parallelo a;
confrontare
par'allel bars' *spl* parallele *fpl*
paraly-sis [pəˈrælɪsɪs] *s* (**-ses** [ˌsiz])
paralisi *f*
paralytic [ˌpærə'lɪtɪk] *adj & s* parali-
litico
paralyze [ˈpærə.laɪz] *tr* paralizzare
paramount [ˈpærə.maunt] *adj* capitale, supremo
paramour [ˈpærə.mur] *s* amante *mf*
paranoiac [ˌpærə'nɔɪ.æk] *adj & s*
paranoico
parapet [ˈpærə.pɛt] *s* parapetto
paraphernalia [ˌpærəfər'nɛlɪ.ə] *spl*
roba, cose *fpl*; attrezzi *mpl*, aggeggi
mpl
parasite [ˈpærə.saɪt] *s* parassita *m*
parasitic(al) [ˌpærə'sɪtɪk(əl)] *adj* pa-
rassitico, parassitario
parasol [ˈpærə.sɔl] *or* [ˈpærə.sɑl] *s*
parasole *m*, ombrellino da sole
par'a-troop'er *s* paracadutista *m*
par'a-troops' *spl* truppe *fpl* paracadu-
tiste
parboil [ˈpar.bɔɪl] *tr* bollire parzialmente; (fig) far bollire
parcel [ˈparsəl] *s* pacchetto; (*of land*)
appezzamento ‖ *v* (*pret & pp* **-celed**
or **-celled**; *ger* **-celing** *or* **-celling**) *tr*

impacchettare; **to parcel out** dividere, distribuire

par'cel post' s servizio pacchi postali

parch [partʃ] tr bruciare; (*land*) inaridire; (*e.g., beans*) essiccare; **to be parched** bruciare dalla sete ‖ intr arrostirsi; inaridire

parchment ['partʃmənt] s pergamena

pardon ['pardən] s perdono, grazia; **I beg your pardon** scusi ‖ tr perdonare; (*an offense*) graziare

pardonable ['pardənəbəl] adj perdonabile, veniale

par'don board' s ufficio per la decisione delle grazie

pare [per] tr (*fruit, potatoes*) sbucciare, pelare; (*nails*) tagliare; (*expenses*) ridurre

parent ['perənt] adj madre, principale ‖ s genitore m or genitrice f; (fig) origine f; **parents** genitori mpl

parentage ['perəntɪdʒ] s discendenza, lignaggio

parenthesis [pə'renθɪsɪs] s (**-ses** [‚siz]) parentesi f; **in parenthesis** tra parentesi

parenthetically [‚pærən'θetɪkəli] adv tra parentesi

parenthood ['perənt‚hud] s paternità f or maternità f

pariah [pə'raɪə] or ['parɪə] s paria m

pari-mutuel ['pærɪ'mjutʃu‑əl] s totalizzatore m

par'ing knife' ['perɪŋ] s coltello per sbucciare

Paris ['pærɪs] s Parigi f

parish ['pærɪʃ] s parrocchia

parishioner [pə'rɪʃənər] s parrocchiano

Parisian [pə'rɪʒən] adj & s parigino

parity ['pærɪti] s parità f

park [park] s parco ‖ tr parcare, parcheggiare ‖ intr parcare, parcheggiare, stazionare

parking ['parkɪŋ] s posteggio, parcheggio; **no parking** divieto di parcheggio

park'ing lights' spl luci fpl di posizione

park'ing lot' s posteggio, parcheggio

park'ing me'ter s parchimetro

park'ing tick'et s contravvenzione per parcheggio abusivo

park'way' s boulevard m

parlay ['parli] or [par'le] tr rigiocare

parley ['parli] s trattativa, conferenza ‖ tr parlamentare

parliament ['parlimənt] s parlamento

parlor ['parlər] s salotto; (*of beautician or undertaker*) salone m; (*of convent*) parlatorio

par'lor car' s vettura salone

par'lor game' s gioco di società

par'lor pol'itics s politica da caffè

Parmesan [‚parmɪ'zæn] adj & s parmigiano

Parnassus [par'næsəs] s (*poetry; poets*) parnaso; **il Parnaso**

parochial [pə'rokɪ‑əl] adj parrocchiale; ristretto, limitato; (*school*) confessionale

paro·dy ['pærədɪ] s (**-dies**) parodia ‖ v (*pret & pp* **-died**) tr parodiare

parole [pə'rol] s parola d'onore; libertà f condizionale, condizionale f ‖ tr mettere in libertà condizionale

paroxytone [pær'aksɪ‚ton] adj parossitono ‖ s parola parossitona

par-quet [par'ke] s pavimento di legno tassellato, tassellato; (theat) platea ‖ v (*pret & pp* **-queted** ['ked]) ger **-queting** ['ke‑ɪŋ]) tr pavimentare in legno tassellato

par'quet cir'cle s poltroncine fpl

parricide ['pærɪ‚saɪd] s (*act*) patricidio, parricidio; (*person*) patricida mf, parricida mf

parrot ['pærət] s pappagallo ‖ tr scimmiottare, fare il pappagallo a

par·ry ['pærɪ] s (**-ries**) parata ‖ v (*pret & pp* **-ried**) tr parare; (fig) evitare

parse [pars] tr (gram) analizzare grammaticalmente

parsimonious [‚parsɪ'monɪ‑əs] adj parsimonioso

parsley ['parslɪ] s prezzemolo

parsnip ['parsnɪp] s pastinaca

parson ['parsən] s parroco; pastore m protestante

part [part] s parte f; (*of a machine*) pezzo, organo; (*of hair*) riga; **for my part** per parte mia; **on the part of** da parte di; **part and parcel** parte f integrante; **parts** abilità f, dote f; regione f, paesi mpl; **to do one's part** fare il proprio dovere ‖ adv parzialmente, in part ‖ tr dividere, separare; **to part company** separarsi; **to part one's hair** farsi la riga ‖ intr separarsi; **to part from** separarsi da, dividersi da; **to part with** rinunciare a

par·take [par'tek] v (*pret* **-took** ['tuk]; *pp* **-taken**) tr condividere ‖ intr—**to partake in** partecipare a; **to partake of** condividere

parterre [par'ter] s aiola; (theat) platea

Parthenon ['parθɪ‚nan] s Partenone m

partial ['parʃəl] adj parziale

participate [par'tɪsɪ‚pet] intr partecipare; **to participate in** partecipare a

participation [par‚tɪsɪ'peʃən] s partecipazione

participle ['partɪ‚sɪpəl] s participio

particle ['partɪkəl] s particella

particular [pər'tɪkjələr] adj (*belonging to a single person*) particolare; (*exacting*) esigente, fastidioso ‖ s particolare m; **in particular** specialmente, particolarmente

part'ing adj (*words*) di commiato; (*last*) ultimo ‖ s commiato; separazione

partisan ['partɪzən] adj & s partigiano

partition [par'tɪʃən] s partizione, divisione; (*or house*) tramezzo ‖ tr dividere; tramezzare

partner ['partnər] s (*in sports*) compagno; (*in dancing*) cavaliere m, dama; (*husband or wife*) consorte mf; (com) socio

partnership ['partnər‚ʃɪp] s associazione; (com) società f

part' of speech' s parte f del discorso

partridge ['partrɪdʒ] s pernice f

part' time' adj a orario ridotto, a ore

par·ty ['partɪ] adj comune; di gala ‖ s (**-ties**) festa, ricevimento, trattenimento; (*of people*) gruppo; (*indi-*

vidual) persona; *(pol)* partito; *(law)* contraente *mf;* *(mil)* distaccamento; **to be a party to** prendere parte a; essere complice di

par'ty girl' *s* ragazza che fa la vita

par'ty-go'er *s* frequentatore *m* di trattenimenti

part'y line' *s (boundary)* linea di confine; *(of Communist party)* politica del partito; *(telp)* linea in coutenza

pass [pæs] or [pɑs] *s passaggio;* *(state)* stato, situazione; *(free ticket)* ingresso gratuito; *(leave of absence given to a soldier)* congedo, permesso; *(of a hypnotist)* gesto; *(between mountains)* passo; *(slang)* tentativo d'abbraccio; **a pretty pass** (coll) un bell'affare || *tr (a course in school)* passare; *(to promote)* promuovere; *(a law)* approvare; *(a sentence)* pronunciare; *(an opinion)* esprimere, avanzare; *(to excrete)* evacuare; far muovere; **to pass by** non fare attenzione a; **to pass off** *(e.g., bogus money)* azzeccare; **to pass on** trasmettere; **to pass out** distribuire; **to pass over** omettere || *intr (to go)* passare; *(said of a law)* essere approvato; *(said of a student)* essere promosso; *(to be accepted)* farsi passare; *(said, e.g., of two trains)* incrociarsi; **to come to pass** accadere, succedere; **to pass as** passare per; **to pass away** morire; **to pass out** (slang) svenire; **to pass over** or **through** attraversare, passare per

passable ['pæsəbəl] or ['pɑsəbəl] *adj* praticabile; *(by boat)* navigabile; *(adequate)* passabile; *(law)* promulgabile

passage ['pæsɪdʒ] *s passaggio;* *(of a law)* approvazione; *(ticket)* biglietto di passaggio; *(of the bowels)* evacuazione

pass'book' *s* libretto di banca; libretto della cassa di risparmio

passenger ['pæsəndʒər] *s passeggero*

passer-by ['pæsər'baɪ] or ['pɑsər'baɪ] *s* **(passers-by)** passante *mf*

passing ['pæsɪŋ] or ['pɑsɪŋ] *adj (fleeting)* fuggente; *(casual)* incidentale; *(grade)* che concede la promozione || *s passaggio;* *(death)* morte *f;* promozione

passion ['pæʃən] *s passione*

passionate ['pæʃənɪt] *adj* appassionato; *(hot-tempered)* collerico; veemente, ardente

passive ['pæsɪv] *adj & s passivo*

pass'key' *s* chiave maestra; *(for use of hotel help)* comunella

Pass'o'ver *s* Pasqua ebraica

pass'port' *s passaporto*

pass'word' *s* parola d'ordine

past [pæst] or [pɑst] *adj* passato, scorso; ex, e.g., **past president** ex presidente || *s passato* || *adv* oltre; al di fuori; al di là || *prep* oltre; al di là di; dopo (di); **past belief** incredibile; **past cure** incurabile; **past hope** senza speranza; **past recovery** incurabile; **past three o'clock** le tre passate

paste [pest] *s (dough)* pasta; *(adhesive)* colla; diamante *m* artificiale || *tr* incollare; *(slang)* dare pugni a

paste'board' *s* cartone *m*

pastel [pæs'tɛl] *adj & s* pastello

pasteurize ['pæstə,raɪz] *tr* pastorizzare

pastime ['pæs,taɪm] or ['pɑs,taɪm] *s* diversione, passatempo

pastor ['pæstər] or ['pɑstər] *s* pastore *m,* sacerdote *m*

pastoral ['pæstərəl] or ['pɑstərəl] *adj* pastorale || *s (poem, letter)* pastorale *f;* *(crosier)* pastorale *m*

pas-try ['pestri] *s* **(-tries)** pasticceria

pas'try cook' *s* pasticciere *m*

pas'try shop' *s* pasticceria

pasture ['pæstʃər] or ['pɑstʃər] *s* pastura, pascolo || *tr* condurre al pascolo || *intr* brucare

past-y ['pesti] *adj* **(-ier; -iest)** pastoso; flaccido

pat [pæt] *s* colpetto; *(of butter)* panetto || *v (pret & pp* **patted;** *ger* **patting)** *tr* accarezzare leggermente; battere leggermente; **to pat on the back** elogiare, incoraggiare battendo sulla spalla

patch [pætʃ] *s (on a suit or shoes)* toppa; *(in a tire)* pezza; *(on wound)* benda; *(of ground)* appezzamento; *(small area)* lembo || *tr* rammendare; **to patch up** *(an argument)* comporre; *(to produce crudely)* raffazzonare

patent ['petənt] *adj* patente, palmare || ['pætənt] *adj* brevettato || *s (of invention)* brevetto; *(sole right)* privativa || *tr* brevettare

pat'ent leath'er ['pætənt] *s* copale *m & f,* pelle *f* di vernice

pat'ent med'icine ['pætənt] *s* specialità *f* medicinale

pat'ent right' ['pætənt] *s* proprietà brevettata

paternal [pə'tʌrnəl] *adj* paterno

paternity [pə'tʌrnɪti] *s* paternità *f*

path [pæθ] or [pɑθ] *s* via battuta, sentiero; *(fig)* via

pathetic [pə'θɛtɪk] *adj* patetico

path'find'er *s* esploratore *m*

pathology [pə'θɑlədʒi] *s* patologia

pathos ['peθɑs] *s* patos *m,* pathos *m*

path'way' *s* sentiero, cammino

patience ['peʃəns] *s* pazienza

patient ['peʃənt] *adj & s* paziente *mf*

patriarch ['petri,ɑrk] *s* patriarca *m*

patrician [pə'trɪʃən] *adj & s* patrizio

patricide ['pætri,saɪd] *s (act)* parricidio; *(person)* parricida *mf*

Patrick ['pætrik] *s* Patrizio

patrimo-ny ['pætri,moni] *s* **(-nies)** patrimonio

patriot ['petri-ət] or ['pætri-ət] *s* patriota *mf*

patriotic [,petri'atɪk] or [,pætri'atɪk] *adj* patriottico

patriotism ['petri-ə,tɪzəm] or ['pætri-ə,tɪzəm] *s* patriottismo

pa-trol [pə'trol] *s (group)* pattuglia; *(individual)* soldato or agente *m* di pattuglia || *v (pret & pp* **-trolled;** *ger* **-trolling)** *tr & intr* pattugliare

patrol'man *s* **(-men)** agente *m,* poliziotto

patrol' wag'on *s* carrozzone *m* cellulare, cellulare *m*

patron ['petrən] *or* ['pætrən] *s* patrono, sostenitore *m;* (*customer*) cliente *mf*

patronize ['petrə‚naɪz] *or* ['pætrə‚naɪz] *tr* (*to support*) sostenere; trattare con condiscendenza; essere cliente abituale di

pa'tron saint' *s* patrono

patter ['pætər] *s* (*e.g., of rain*) battito; (*of feet*) scalpiccio; (*speech*) chiaccherio ‖ *intr* battere, picchiettare; chiaccherare

pattern ['pætərn] *s* modello; disegno; (*of flight*) procedura ‖ *tr* modellare

pat·ty ['pæti] *s* (**-ties**) pasticcino; (*meat cake*) polpetta

paucity ['pɔsɪti] *s* pochezza, scarsità *f,* insufficienza

Paul [pɔl] *s* Paolo

paunch [pɔntʃ] *s* pancia

paunch·y ['pɔntʃi] *adj* (**-ier; -iest**) panciuto

pauper ['pɔpər] *s* povero, indigente *mf*

pause [pɔz] *s* pausa; (*of a tape recorder*) arresto momentaneo; **to give pause (to)** dar di che pensare (a) ‖ *intr* far pausa, fermarsi; (*to hesitate*) esitare, vacillare

pave [pev] *tr* pavimentare, lastricare; **to pave the way (for)** aprire il cammino (a)

pavement ['pevmənt] *s* pavimentazione, lastricato; (*sidewalk*) marciapiede *m*

pavilion [pə'vɪljən] *s* padiglione *m;* (*of circus*) tendone *m*

paw [pɔ] *s* zampa ‖ *tr* (*to touch with paws*) dar zampate a; (*to handle clumsily*) maneggiare goffamente; (*coll*) palpeggiare ‖ *intr* zampare

pawn [pɔn] *s* (*security*) pegno; (*tool of another person*) pedina; (*chess*) pedina, pedone *m;* (*fig*) ostaggio ‖ *tr* dare in pegno, impegnare

pawn'bro'ker *s* prestatore *m* su pegno

pawn'shop' *s* agenzia di prestiti su pegno, monte di pietà

pawn' tick'et *s* ricevuta di pegno, polizza del monte di pietà

pay [pe] *s* pagamento; (*wages*) paga, salario; (*mil*) soldo ‖ *v* (*pret & pp* **paid** [ped]) *tr* pagare; (*wages*) conguagliare; (*one's respects*) presentare; (*a visit*) fare; (*a bill*) saldare; (*attention*) fare, presentare; **to pay back** ripagare; (*fig*) pagare pan per focaccia a; **to pay for** pagare; **to pay off** liquidare; (*in order to discharge*) pagare e licenziare; **to pay up** saldare ‖ *intr* pagare; valere la pena; **pay as you enter** pagare all'ingresso; **pay as you go** pagare le tasse per trattenuta; **pay as you leave** pagare all'uscita

payable ['pe‚əbəl] *adj* pagabile

pay' boost' *s* aumento di salario

pay'check' *s* assegno in pagamento del salario; salario, paga

pay'day' *s* giorno di paga

payee [pe'i] *s* beneficiario

pay' en'velope *s* bustapaga

payer ['pe·ər] *s* pagatore *m*

pay'load' *s* peso utile

pay'mas'ter *s* ufficiale *m* pagatore

payment ['pemənt] *s* pagamento

pay'off' *s* pagamento, regolamento; (*coll*) conclusione

pay' phone' *s* telefono a moneta

pay'roll' *s* lista degli impiegati; libro paga

pay' sta'tion *s* telefono pubblico

pea [pi] *s* pisello

peace [pis] *s* pace *f;* **to hold one's peace** tacere, stare zitto

peaceable ['pisəbəl] *adj* pacifico

peaceful ['pisfəl] *adj* pacifico

peace'mak'er *s* paciere *m*

peace' of mind' *s* serenità *f* d'animo

peace' pipe' *s* calumet *m* della pace

peach [pitʃ] *s* pesca; (*coll*) persona **or** cosa stupenda

peach' tree' *s* pesco

peach·y ['pitʃi] *adj* (**-ier; -iest**) (*coll*) stupendo

pea'cock' *s* pavone *m*

peak [pik] *s* picco; (*of traffic*) punta; (*of one's career*) sommo

peak' hour' *s* ora di punta

peak' load' *s* carico delle ore di punta, carico massimo

peal [pil] *s* (*of bells*) squillo; (*of gun*) rombo; (*of laughter*) scoppio; (*of thunder*) scroscio ‖ *intr* scampanare, squillare

pea'nut' *s* nocciolina americana; (*plant*) arachide *f*

pea'nut but'ter *s* pasta d'arachidi

pear [per] *s* (*fruit*) pera; (*tree*) pero

pearl [pʌrl] *s* perla; (*mother-of-pearl*) madreperla; colore perlaceo

pearl' oys'ter *s* ostrica perlifera

pear' tree' *s* pero

peasant ['pezənt] *adj & s* contadino

pea'shoot'er *s* cerbottana

pea' soup' *s* minestra di piselli; (*coll*) nebbione *m*

peat [pit] *s* torba

pebble ['pebəl] *s* ciottolo

peck [pek] *s* beccata; misura di due galloni; **a peck of trouble** un mare di guai ‖ *tr* beccare ‖ *intr* beccare; **to peck at** beccucciare

peculation [‚pekjə'leʃən] *s* malversazione, peculato

peculiar [pɪ'kjuljər] *adj* peculiare; (*odd*) strano

pedagogue ['pedə‚gag] *s* pedagogo

pedagogy ['pedə‚godʒi] *or* ['pedə‚gadʒi] *s* pedagogia

ped·al ['pedəl] *s* pedale *m* ‖ *v* (*pret & pp* **-aled** *or* **-alled;** *ger* **-aling** *or* **-alling**) *tr* spingere coi pedali ‖ *intr* pedalare

pedant ['pedənt] *s* pedante *mf*

pedantic [pɪ'dæntɪk] *adj* pedantesco

pedant·ry ['pedəntri] *s* (**-ries**) pedanteria

peddle ['pedəl] *tr* vendere di porta in porta ‖ *intr* fare il venditore ambulante

peddler ['pedlər] *s* venditore *m* **or** merciaiolo ambulante

pedestal ['pedɪstəl] s piedistallo
pedestrian [pɪ'destrɪ·ən] adj pedestre || s pedone m
pediatrics [ˌpidɪ'ætrɪks] or [ˌpedɪ-'ætrɪks] s pediatria
pedigree ['pedɪˌgri] s albero genealogico; discendenza, lignaggio
pediment ['pedɪmənt] s frontone m
peek [pik] s sbirciata || intr sbirciare
peel [pil] s scorza, buccia; (of baker) pala || tr sbucciare; **to keep one's eyes peeled** (slang) tenere gli occhi aperti || intr pelarsi
peep [pip] s sbirciata; (sound) pigolio || intr guardare attraverso una fessura; (said of birds) pigolare; (to begin to appear) fare capolino
peep'hole' s spioncino
Peep'ing Tom' s guardone m
peep' show' s cosmorama m
peer [pɪr] s pari m, uguale m; (Brit) pari m || intr guardare da vicino
peerless ['pɪrlɪs] adj senza pari
peeve [piv] s (coll) seccatura, irritazione || tr (coll) seccare, irritare
peevish ['pivɪʃ] adj irritabile
peg [peg] s (to plug holes) zipolo; (pin) cavicchio; (mus) bischero; (coll) grado; **to take down a peg** (coll) fare abbassare la testa a || v (pret & pp **pegged**; ger **pegging**) tr fissare con cavicchi; (prices) stabilizzare || intr—**to peg away** lavorare di lena
peg' leg' s gamba di legno
Peking ['pi'kɪŋ] s Pechino f
Peking·ese [ˌpiki'niz] adj pechinese || s (-ese) pechinese mf
pelf [pelf] s (pej) denaro rubacchiato, maltolto
pelican ['pelɪkən] s pellicano
pellet ['pelɪt] s pallottola; (for shotgun) pallino; (pill) pillola
pell-mell ['pel'mel] adj confuso, disordinato || adv alla rinfusa
Peloponnesian [ˌpeləpə'niʃən] adj & s peloponnesiaco
pelt [pelt] s pelle grezza; (blow) colpo || tr scagliare contro; (to beat) battere violentemente || intr battere, scrosciare
pen [pen] s (enclosure) recinto; (for writing) penna; (pen point) pennino || v (pret & pp **penned**; ger **penning**) tr scrivere a penna; (to compose) redigere || v (pret & pp **penned** or **pent**; ger **penning**) tr recintare
penalize ['pinə'laɪz] tr punire; (sports) penalizzare
penal·ty ['penəltɪ] s (-ties) punizione; (fine) multa; (for late payment) penale f; **under penalty of** sotto pena di
pen'alty goal' s calcio di rigore
penance ['penəns] s penitenza
penchant ['pentʃənt] s propensione
pen·cil ['pensəl] s matita; (of rays) fascio || v (pret & pp **-ciled** or **-cilled**; ger **-ciling** or **-cilling**) tr scrivere a matita; (med) pennellare
pen'cil sharp'ener s temperalapis m
pendent ['pendənt] adj pendente, sospeso || s pendente m, ciondolo

pending ['pendɪŋ] adj imminente; in sospeso || prep durante; fino a
pendulum ['pendʒələm] s pendolo
pen'dulum bob' s lente f
penetrate ['penɪˌtret] tr & intr penetrare
penguin ['peŋgwɪn] s pinguino
pen'hold'er s portapenne m
penicillin [ˌpenɪ'sɪlɪn] s penicillina
peninsula [pe'nɪnsələ] s penisola
peninsular [pə'nɪnsələr] adj & s peninsulare
penitence ['penɪtəns] s penitenza
penitent ['penɪtənt] adj & s penitente mf
pen'knife' s (-knives) temperino
penmanship ['penmənˌʃɪp] s calligrafia
pen' name' s nome m di penna, pseudonimo
pennant ['penənt] s pennone m
penniless ['penɪlɪs] adj povero in canna, senza un soldo
pennon ['penən] s pennone m
pen·ny ['penɪ] s (-nies) (U.S.A.) centesimo || s (**pence** [pens]) (Brit) penny m
pen'ny pinch'er ['pɪntʃər] s spilorcio
pen' pal' s amico corrispondente
pen'point' s pennino; (of ball-point pen) punta
pension ['penʃən] s pensione || tr pensionare, mettere in pensione
pensioner ['penʃənər] s pensionato
pensive ['pensɪv] adj pensieroso
Pentecost ['pentɪˌkɔst] or ['pentɪˌkɑst] s la Pentecoste
penthouse ['pentˌhaʊs] s appartamento di lusso sul tetto; tettoia
pent-up ['pent'ʌp] adj represso
penult ['pinʌlt] s penultima
penum·bra [pɪ'nʌmbrə] s (-brae [bri] or -bras) penombra
penurious [pɪ'nʊrɪ·əs] adj taccagno, meschino; indigente
penury ['penjərɪ] s taccagneria; estrema povertà, miseria
pen'wip'er s nettapenne m
people ['pipəl] spl popolo, gente f; (relatives) famiglia; gente f del popolo; si, e.g., **people say** si dice || ssg (**peoples**) nazione, popolazione || tr popolare
pep [pep] s (coll) animo, brio || v (pret & pp **pepped**; ger **pepping**) tr—**to pep up** (coll) dar animo a
pepper ['pepər] s pepe m || tr pepare; (to pelt) tempestare
pep'per·box' s pepaiola
pep'per·mint' s menta piperita
per [pʌr] prep per; (for each) il, e.g., **three dollars per meter** tre dollari il metro; **as per** secondo
perambulator [pər'æmbjəˌletər] s carrozzella, carrozzino
per capita [pər 'kæpɪtə] per persona, a testa
perceive [pər'siv] tr percepire
percent [pər'sent] s percento, per cento
percentage [pər'sentɪdʒ] s percento, percentuale f; (coll) vantaggio
perception [pər'sep/ən] s percezione

perch [pʌrtʃ] s (*roost*) posatoio; (*horizontal rod*) ballatoio; (ichth) pesce persico ‖ *intr* appollaiarsi

percolator [ˈpʌrkə‚letər] s caffettiera filtro a circolazione

percus'sion cap' [pərˈkʌʃən] s capsula di percussione

per diem [pər ˈdaɪ‐əm] s assegno giornaliero

perdition [pərˈdɪʃən] s perdizione

perennial [pəˈrɛnɪ‐əl] adj perenne ‖ s pianta perenne

perfect [ˈpʌrfɪkt] adj & s perfetto ‖ [pərˈfɛkt] tr perfezionare

perfidious [pərˈfɪdɪ‐əs] adj perfido

perfi·dy [ˈpʌrfɪdɪ] s (**-dies**) perfidia

perforate [ˈpʌrfə‚ret] tr perforare

perforation [‚pʌrfəˈreʃən] s perforazione; (*of postage stamp*) dentellatura

perforce [pərˈfors] adv per forza, necessariamente

perform [pərˈfɔrm] tr (*a task*) eseguire; (*a promise*) adempiere; (*to enact*) rappresentare ‖ *intr* recitare; (*said, e.g., of a machine*) funzionare

performance [pərˈfɔrməns] s esecuzione; (*of a machine*) funzionamento; (*deed*) atto di prodezza; (theat) rappresentazione

performer [pərˈfɔrmər] s esecutore *m*; attore *m*; acrobata *mf*

perform'ing arts' spl arti *fpl* dello spettacolo

perfume [ˈpʌrfjum] s profumo ‖ [pərˈfjum] tr profumare

perfumer·y [pərˈfjuməri] s (**-ies**) profumeria

perfunctory [pərˈfʌŋktəri] adj superficiale, pro forma; indifferente

perhaps [pərˈhæps] adv forse

per·il [ˈpɛrəl] s pericolo ‖ v (*pret & pp* **-iled** or **-illed**; *ger* **-iling** or **-illing**) tr mettere in pericolo

perilous [ˈpɛrɪləs] adj pericoloso

period [ˈpɪrɪ‐əd] s periodo; mestruazione; (*in school*) ora; (sports) tempo; (gram) punto

pe'riod cos'tume s costume *m* dell'epoca

periodic [‚pɪrɪˈɑdɪk] adj periodico

periodical [‚pɪrɪˈɑdɪkəl] adj & s periodico

peripher·y [pəˈrɪfəri] s (**-ies**) periferia

periscope [ˈpɛrɪ‚skop] s periscopio

perish [ˈpɛrɪʃ] intr perire

perishable [ˈpɛrɪʃəbəl] adj deteriorabile

periwig [ˈpɛrɪ‚wɪg] s parrucca

perjure [ˈpʌrdʒər] tr—**to perjure oneself** spergiurare, giurare il falso

perju·ry [ˈpʌrdʒəri] s (**-ries**) spergiuro

perk [pʌrk] tr (*the head, the ears*) alzare; **to perk oneself up** agghindarsi ‖ intr—**to perk up** ringalluzzirsi

permanence [ˈpʌrmənəns] s permanenza

permanen·cy [ˈpʌrmənənsi] s (**-cies**) permanenza

permanent [ˈpʌrmənənt] adj permanente ‖ s permanente *f*, ondulazione permanente

per'manent fix'ture s cosa or persona permanente

per'manent ten'ure s inamovibilità *f*

per'manent way' s (rr) sede *f* stradale ed armamento

permeate [ˈpʌrmɪ‚et] tr permeare ‖ intr permearsi

permissible [pərˈmɪsɪbəl] adj permissibile

permission [pərˈmɪʃən] s permesso

per·mit [ˈpʌrmɪt] s permesso; patente *f*, licenza ‖ [pərˈmɪt] v (*pret & pp* **-mitted**; *ger* **-mitting**) tr permettere

permute [pərˈmjut] tr permutare

pernicious [pərˈnɪʃəs] adj pernicioso

pernickety [pərˈnɪkɪti] adj (coll) incontentabile, meticoloso

perorate [ˈpɛrə‚ret] intr perorare

peroxide [pərˈɑksaɪd] s perossido; perossido d'idrogeno

perox'ide blonde' s bionda ossigenata

perpendicular [‚pʌrpənˈdɪkjələr] adj & s perpendicolare *f*

perpetrate [ˈpʌrpɪ‚tret] tr (*a crime*) perpetrare; (*a blunder*) commettere

perpetual [pərˈpɛtʃʊ‐əl] adj perpetuo

perpetuate [pərˈpɛtʃʊ‚et] tr perpetuare

perplex [pərˈplɛks] tr lasciare perplesso

perplexed [pərˈplɛkst] adj perplesso

perplexi·ty [pərˈplɛksɪti] s (**-ties**) perplessità *f*

per se [pər ˈsi] di per se

persecute [ˈpʌrsɪ‚kjut] tr perseguitare

persevere [‚pʌrsɪˈvɪr] intr perseverare

Persian [ˈpʌrʒən] adj & s persiano

Per'sian Gulf' s Golfo Persico

persimmon [pərˈsɪmən] s diospiro virginiano; cachi *m*

persist [pərˈsɪst] or [pərˈzɪst] intr persistere

persistent [pərˈsɪstənt] or [pərˈzɪstənt] adj persistente

person [ˈpʌrsən] s persona; **no person** nessuno

personage [ˈpʌrsənɪdʒ] s personaggio; persona

personal [ˈpʌrsənəl] adj personale; (*goods*) mobile ‖ s inserzione personale; trafiletto di società

personali·ty [‚pʌrsəˈnælɪti] s (**-ties**) personalità *f*; offesa personale

person'ality cult' s culto della personalità

per'sonal prop'erty s beni *mpl* mobili

personi·fy [pərˈsɑnɪ‚faɪ] v (*pret & pp* **-fied**) tr personificare

personnel [‚pʌrsəˈnɛl] s personale *m*

per'son-to-per'son call' s (telp) chiamata con preavviso

perspective [pərˈspɛktɪv] s prospettiva

perspicacious [‚pʌrspɪˈkeʃəs] adj perspicace

perspire [pərˈspaɪr] intr sudare

persuade [pərˈswed] tr persuadere

persuasion [pərˈsweʒən] s persuasione; fede religiosa

pert [pʌrt] adj impertinente, sfacciato; vivace

pertain [pərˈten] intr appartenere; (*to have reference*) riferirsi

pertinacious [‚pʌrtɪˈneʃəs] adj pertinace

pertinent [ˈpʌrtɪnənt] *adj* pertinente
perturb [pərˈtʌrb] *tr* perturbare
Peru [pəˈru] *s* il Perù
perusal [pəˈruzəl] *s* attenta lettura
peruse [pəˈruz] *tr* leggere attentamente
pervade [pərˈved] *tr* pervadere
perverse [pərˈvʌrs] *adj* perverso; (*obstinate*) ostinato
perversion [pərˈvʌrʒən] *s* perversione
perversi·ty [pərˈvʌrsɪti] *s* (**-ties**) perversità *f*; contrarietà *f*
pervert [ˈpʌrvərt] *s* pervertito, degenerato || [pərˈvʌrt] *tr* pervertire, degenerare
pes·ky [ˈpeski] *adj* (**-kier; -kiest**) (coll) noioso, molesto
pessimism [ˈpesɪˌmɪzəm] *s* pessimismo
pessimist [ˈpesɪmɪst] *s* pessimista *mf*
pessimistic [ˌpesɪˈmɪstɪk] *adj* pessimistico
pest [pest] *s* peste *f*, pestilenza; insetto; animale nocivo; (*person*) peste *f*, seccatore *m*
pester [ˈpestər] *tr* seccare, annoiare
pest'house' *s* lazzaretto
pesticide [ˈpestɪˌsaɪd] *s* insetticida *m*
pestiferous [pesˈtɪfərəs] *adj* pestifero
pestilence [ˈpestɪləns] *s* pestilenza
pestle [ˈpesəl] *s* pestello
pet [pet] *s* animale favorito; beniamino || *v* (*pret & pp* **petted; ger petting**) *tr* accarezzare || *intr* (coll) pomiciare
petal [ˈpetəl] *s* petalo
petard [pɪˈtɑrd] *s* petardo
pet'cock' *s* chiavetta
Peter [ˈpitər] *s* Pietro; **to rob Peter to pay Paul** fare un buco per tapparne un altro || *intr*—**to peter out** (coll) affievolirsi
petition [pɪˈtɪʃən] *s* petizione || *tr* rivolgere un'istanza a
pet' name' *s* nomignolo vezzeggiativo
Petrarch [ˈpitrɑrk] *s* Petrarca *m*
petri·fy [ˈpetrɪˌfaɪ] *v* (*pret & pp* **-fied**) *tr* pietrificare || *intr* pietrificarsi
petrol [ˈpetrəl] *s* (Brit) benzina
petroleum [pɪˈtrolɪ·əm] *s* petrolio
pet' shop' *s* negozio di animali domestici
petticoat [ˈpetɪˌkot] *s* sottoveste *f*; (coll) sottana, gonnella
pet·ty [ˈpeti] *adj* (**-tier; -tiest**) insignificante, minore; meschino
pet'ty cash' *s* cassa delle piccole spese
pet'ty lar'ceny *s* furterello
pet'ty of'ficer *s* (nav) sottufficiale *m* di marina
petulant [ˈpetjələnt] *adj* stizzoso, irritabile
pew [pju] *s* banco di chiesa
pewter [ˈpjutər] *s* peltro; oggetti *mpl* di peltro
phalanx [ˈfelæŋks] or [ˈfælæŋks] *s* falange *f*
phantasm [ˈfæntæzəm] *s* fantasma *m*
phantom [ˈfæntəm] *s* fantasma *m*
Pharaoh [ˈfero] *s* Faraone *m*
pharisee [ˈfærɪˌsi] *s* fariseo || **Pharisee** *s* fariseo
pharmaceutical [ˌfɑrməˈsutɪkəl] *adj* farmaceutico

pharmacist [ˈfɑrməsɪst] *s* farmacista *mf*
pharma·cy [ˈfɑrməsi] *s* (**-cies**) farmacia
pharynx [ˈfærɪŋks] *s* faringe *f*
phase [fez] *s* fase *f* || *tr* mettere in fase; sincronizzare; **to phase in** mettere in operazione gradualmente; **to phase out** eliminare gradualmente
pheasant [ˈfezənt] *s* fagiano
phenobarbital [ˌfinoˈbɑrbɪˌtæl] *s* acido fenil-etilbarbiturico, barbiturato
phenomenal [fɪˈnɑmɪnəl] *adj* fenomenale
phenome·non [fɪˈnɑmɪˌnɑn] *s* (**-na** [nə]) fenomeno
phial [ˈfaɪ·əl] *s* fiala
philanderer [fɪˈlændərər] *s* donnaiolo
philanthropist [fɪˈlænθrəpɪst] *s* filantropo
philanthro·py [fɪˈlænθrəpi] *s* (**-pies**) filantropia
philatelist [fɪˈlætəlɪst] *s* filatelico
philately [fɪˈlætəli] *s* filatelia
Philip [ˈfɪlɪp] *s* Filippo
Philippine [ˈfɪlɪˌpin] *adj* filippino || **Philippines** *spl* isole *fpl* Filippine
Philistine [fɪˈlɪstɪn], [ˈfɪlɪˌstin] or [ˈfɪlɪˌstaɪn] *adj & s* filisteo
philologist [fɪˈlɑlədʒɪst] *s* filologo
philology [fɪˈlɑlədʒi] *s* filologia
philosopher [fɪˈlɑsəfər] *s* filosofo
philosophic(al) [ˌfɪləˈsɑfɪk(əl)] *adj* filosofico
philoso·phy [fɪˈlɑsəfi] *s* (**-phies**) filosofia
philter [ˈfɪltər] *s* filtro
phlebitis [flɪˈbaɪtɪs] *s* flebite *f*
phlegm [flem] *s* (*secretion*) muco, catarro; (*self-possession*) flemma; apatia
phlegmatic(al) [flegˈmætɪk(əl)] *adj* flemmatico
Phoebus [ˈfibəs] *s* Febo
Phoenician [fɪˈnɪʃən] or [fɪˈnɪʃən] *adj & s* fenicio
phoenix [ˈfinɪks] *s* fenice *f*
phone [fon] *s* (coll) telefono || *tr & intr* (coll) telefonare
phone' call' *s* chiamata telefonica
phonetic [foˈnetɪk] *adj* fonetico || **phonetics** *s* fonetica
phonograph [ˈfonəˌgræf] or [ˈfonəˌgrɑf] *s* fonografo
phonology [fəˈnɑlədʒi] *s* fonologia
pho·ny [ˈfoni] *adj* (**-nier; -niest**) (coll) falso || *s* (**-nies**) (coll) frode *f*; (*person*) (coll) impostore *m*
phosphate [ˈfasfet] *s* fosfato
phosphorescent [ˌfasfəˈresənt] *adj* fosforescente
phospho·rus [ˈfasfərəs] *s* (**-ri** [ˌraɪ]) fosforo
pho·to [ˈfoto] *s* (**-tos**) (coll) foto *f*
photo·cop·y [ˈfotəˌkɑpi] *s* (**-ies**) fotocopia || *tr* fotocopiare
pho'toelec'tric cell' [ˌfoto·ɪˈlektrɪk] *s* cellula fotoelettrica
photoengraving [ˌfoto·enˈgrevɪŋ] *s* fotoincisione
pho'to fin'ish *s* photofinish *m*, arrivo con fotografia

photogenic [‚fotoˈdʒenɪk] *adj* fotoge-
nico
photograph [ˈfotə‚græf] or [ˈfotə-
‚graf] *s* fotografia || *tr* fotografare ||
intr—**to photograph well** riuscire in
fotografia
photographer [fəˈtɑgrəfər] *s* fotografo
photography [fəˈtɑgrəfi] *s* fotografia
photojournalism [‚fotəˈdʒʌrnə‚lɪzəm]
s giornalismo fotografico
pho'to·play' *s* dramma adattato per il
cinematografo
photostat [ˈfotə‚stæt] *s* (trademark)
copia fotostatica || *tr* riprodurre foto-
staticamente
phototube [ˈfotə‚tjub] or [ˈfotə‚tub] *s*
fototubo
phrase [frez] *s* (gram) locuzione; (mus)
frase *f* || *tr* esprimere, formulare ||
intr (mus) fraseggiare
phrenology [frɪˈnɑlədʒi] *s* frenologia
Phyllis [ˈfɪlɪs] *s* Fillide *f*
phy·lum [ˈfaɪləm] *s* (-la [lə]) phylum
m, tipo
phys·ic [ˈfɪzɪk] *s* purgante *m* || *v* (pret
& pp **-icked**; ger **-icking**) *tr* dare il
purgante a, purgare
physical [ˈfɪzɪkəl] *adj* fisico
physician [fɪˈzɪʃən] *s* medico
physicist [ˈfɪzɪsɪst] *s* fisico
physics [ˈfɪzɪks] *s* fisica
physiognomy [‚fɪzɪˈɑgnəmi] or [‚fɪzɪ-
ˈɑnəmi] *s* fisionomia
physiological [‚fɪzɪ·əˈlɑdʒɪkəl] *adj* fi-
siologico
physiology [‚fɪzɪˈɑlədʒi] *s* fisiologia
physique [fɪˈzɪk] *s* fisico
pi [paɪ] *s* (math) pi greco; (typ) tipi
scartati || *v* (pret & pp **pied**; ger
piing) *tr* (typ) scompaginare, scomporre
pian·o [pɪˈæno] *s* (**-os**) piano
picaresque [‚pɪkəˈrɛsk] *adj* picaresco
picayune [‚pɪkəˈjun] *adj* meschino,
minore, di poca importanza
picco·lo [ˈpɪkə‚lo] *s* (**-los**) ottavino
pick [pɪk] *s* (tool) piccone *m*; (choice)
scelta; (the best) fiore *m*; (mus) plet-
tro || *tr* scavare; (to scratch at) grat-
tare; (to gather) cogliere; (to pluck)
spennare; (to pull apart) separare;
(one's teeth) stuzzicarsi; (a bone)
rosicchiare; (to choose) scegliere; (a
lock) scassinare; (a pocket) tagliare,
rubare; (mus) pizzicare; **to pick a
fight** attaccare briga; **to pick faults**
trovare a ridire; **to pick out** scegliere;
distinguere; discriminare; **to pick s.o.
to pieces** (coll) tagliare i panni addosso a qlcu; **to pick up** sollevare;
(to find) trovare; (to learn) arrivare
a sapere; (a radio signal) captare;
(speed) acquistare || *intr* usare il
piccone; **to pick at** (food) spilluzzicare; (coll) criticare; **to pick on**
(coll) scegliere; (coll) criticare; **to
pick up** (coll) migliorare
pick'ax' *s* piccone *m*
picket [ˈpɪkɪt] *s* picchetto || *tr* rinchiu-
dere con palizzata; (to hitch) legare;
(to post) (mil) mettere di picchetto;
(e.g., a factory) picchettare

pick'et fence' *s* steccato
pick'et line' *s* corteo di scioperanti;
corteo di dimostranti
pickle [ˈpɪkəl] *s* salamoia, sottaceto;
(cucumber) cetriolo sottaceto; **to get
into a pickle** (coll) cacciarsi in un
imbroglio || *tr* mettere sottaceto;
(metallurgy) decapare
pick-me-up [ˈpɪkmi‚ʌp] *s* (coll) spuntino; (coll) bevanda stimulante
pick'pock'et *s* borseggiatore *m*, borsaiolo
pick'up' *s* sollevamento; (in speed) accelerazione; (of phonograph) pick-up
m, fonorivelatore *m*; (aut) camioncino; (coll) persona conosciuta per
caso; (coll) miglioramento
pick'-up-sticks' *spl* sciangai *m*
pic·nic [ˈpɪknɪk] *s* picnic *m* || *v* (pret
& pp **-nicked**; ger **-nicking**) *intr* fare
merenda all'aperto
pictorial [pɪkˈtorɪ·əl] *adj* pittorico;
illustrato; vivido || *s* rivista illustrata
picture [ˈpɪktʃər] *s* illustrazione, disegno; (painting) quadro, dipinto; (of
a person) ritratto; fotografia; film
m, pellicola || *tr* fare il ritratto di;
disegnare; dipingere; fotografare; descrivere; immaginare, immaginarsi
pic'ture frame' *s* cornice *f*
pic'ture gal'lery *s* pinacoteca, galleria
di quadri, quadreria
pic'ture post' card' *s* cartolina illustrata
pic'ture show' *s* cinematografo; mostra
di quadri
picturesque [‚pɪktʃəˈrɛsk] *adj* pittoresco
pic'ture tube' *s* tubo televisivo
pic'ture win'dow *s* finestra panoramica
piddling [ˈpɪdlɪŋ] *adj* insignificante
pie [paɪ] *s* (with fruit) torta; (with
meat) timballo; (orn) pica *f* || *v* (pret
& pp **pied**; ger **pieing**) *tr* (typ) scompaginare, scomporre
piece [pis] *s* pezzo; (e.g., of cloth)
pezza; **a piece of advice** un consiglio; **a piece of baggage** un collo; **a
piece of furniture** un mobile *m*; **a
piece of news** una notizia; **by the
piece** a cottimo; **to break to pieces**
frantumare; frantumarsi; **to cut to
pieces** fare a pezzi; **to fall to pieces**
cadere a pezzi; **to fly to pieces** rompersi in mille pezzi; **to give s.o. a
piece of one's mind** dirne di tutti i
colori; **to go to pieces** perdere
il controllo di sé stesso; **to take to
pieces** confutare punto per punto || *tr*
rappezzare, mettere insieme || *intr*
(coll) mangiucchiare
piece'meal' *adv* poco a poco
piece'work' *s* lavoro a cottimo
piece'work'er *s* cottimista *mf*
pier [pɪr] *s* (of a bridge) pila; (over
water) molo; (archit) pilastro, pilone
m
pierce [pɪrs] *tr* forare, bucare; pene-
trare; (to stab) trapassare || *intr*
penetrare
piercing [ˈpɪrsɪŋ] *adj* acuto; (eyes)
penetrante; (pain) lancinante

pier′ glass′ *s* specchiera
pie·ty [′paɪ·əti] *s* (**-ties**) pietà *f*
piffle [′pɪfəl] *s* (coll) fesserie *fpl*
pig [pɪg] *s* maiale *m*, porco; (metallurgy) lingotto, massello; **to buy a pig in the poke** comprare il gatto nel sacco
pigeon [′pɪdʒən] *s* piccione *m*
pi′geon·hole′ *s* nicchia nella piccionaia; (*for filing*) casella ‖ *tr* (*to lay aside for later time*) archiviare; (*to shelve, e.g., an application*) insabbiare
pi′geon house′ *s* colombaia, piccionaia
piggish [′pɪgɪʃ] *adj* porcino, maialesco
pig′gy·back′ [′pɪgɪ ‚bæk] *adv* sulle spalle, sulla schiena; (rr) su carrello stradale per trasporto carri
pig′head′ed *adj* ostinato, cocciuto
pig′ i′ron *s* ghisa, ferro grezzo
pigment [′pɪgmənt] *s* pigmento ‖ *tr* pigmentare ‖ *intr* pigmentarsi
pig′pen′ *s* porcile *m*
pig′skin′ *s* pelle *f* di maiale; (coll) pallone *m* da football, sfera di cuoio
pig′sty′ *s* (**-sties**) porcile *m*
pig′tail′ *s* codino; (*of girl*) treccia; treccia di tabacco
pike [paɪk] *s* (*weapon*) picca; (*road*) autostrada; (ichth) luccio
piker [′paɪkər] *s* (coll) uomo piccino
pile [paɪl] *s* (*heap*) pila; (*for burning a corpse*) pira; (*large building*) mole *f*; (*beam*) palo; (*of carpet*) pelo; (*of money*) (slang) gruzzolo; (coll) mucchio; **piles** emorroidi *fpl* ‖ *tr* ammucchiare, accumulare; **to pile up ammonticchiare** ‖ *intr* accumularsi; **to pile into** pigiarsi in; **to pile up** accumularsi
pile′ driv′er *s* battipalo, berta
pilfer [′pɪlfər] *tr & intr* rubacchiare
pilgrim [′pɪlgrɪm] *s* pellegrino
pilgrimage [′pɪlgrɪmɪdʒ] *s* pellegrinaggio
pill [pɪl] *s* pillola; amara pillola; (coll) rompiscatole *mf*; **to sugar-coat the pill** addolcire la pillola
pillage [′pɪlɪdʒ] *s* saccheggio, rapina ‖ *tr & intr* saccheggiare, rapinare
pillar [′pɪlər] *s* pilastro, colonna; **from pillar to post** da Erode a Pilato
pill′box′ *s* scatoletta per le pillole; (mil) casamatta
pillo·ry [′pɪləri] *s* (**-ries**) gogna, berlina ‖ *v* (*pret & pp* **-ried**) *tr* mettere alla berlina
pillow [′pɪlo] *s* cuscino, guanciale *m*
pil′low·case′ *s* federa
pilot [′paɪlət] *adj* pilota ‖ *s* pilota *m*; (*of locomotive*) respingente *m* ‖ *tr* pilotare
pi′lot light′ *s* fiammella automatica
pimp [pɪmp] *s* ruffiano, lenone *m*
pimple [′pɪmpəl] *s* bitorzolo
pim·ply [′pɪmpli] *adj* (**-plier; -pliest**) bitorzoluto
pin [pɪn] *s* (*of metal*) spillo; (*peg*) caviglia; (*adornment*) spilla; (*linchpin*) acciarino; (*of key*) mappa; (*clothespin*) molletta; (*bowling pin*) birillo; **to be on pins and needles** stare sulle spine ‖ *tr* appuntare; (*to hold*) im-

mobilizzare; **to pin s.o. down** forzare qlcu a rivelare i propri piani; **to pin s.th on s.o.** (coll) dare la colpa a qlcu per qlco
pinafore [′pɪnə ‚for] *s* grembiulino
pinaster [paɪ′næstər] *s* pino marittimo
pin′ball machine′ *s* biliardino
pince-nez [′pæns ‚ne] *s* occhiali *mpl* a stringinaso
pincers [′pɪnsərz] *ssg or spl* tenaglie *fpl*; (zool) pinze *fpl*
pinch [pɪntʃ] *s* (*squeeze*) pizzicotto; (*of tobacco*) presa; (*of salt*) pizzico; (*hardship*) strettoia; **in a pinch** in caso di necessità ‖ *tr* stringere, pizzicare; (*to press*) comprimere; ridurre alle strettezze; (slang) rubare; (slang) arrestare ‖ *intr* stringere; (*to be stingy*) fare l'avaro
pin′cush′ion *s* puntaspilli *m*
pine [paɪn] *s* pino ‖ *intr*—**to pine away** struggersi; **to pine for** spasimare per
pine′ap′ple *s* ananas *m*
pine′ cone′ *s* pigna
pine′ nee′dle *s* ago del pino
ping [pɪŋ] *s* rumore secco; rumore metallico ‖ *intr* fare un rumore secco or metallico
pin′head′ *s* capocchia di spillo; (slang) testa quadra
pin′hole′ *s* forellino
pink [pɪŋk] *adj* rosa ‖ *s* color *m* rosa; condizione perfetta; (bot) garofano ‖ *tr* orlare a zig-zag; (*to stab*) perforare
pin′ mon′ey *s* denaro per le piccole spese
pinnacle [′pɪnəkəl] *s* pinnacolo
pin′point′ *adj* di precisione ‖ *s* punta di spillo ‖ *tr* mettere in rilievo
pin′prick′ *s* puntura di spillo
pint [paɪnt] *s* pinta
pintle [′pɪntəl] *s* maschietto
pin′up′ *s* pin-up-girl *f*
pin′wheel′ *s* girandola
pioneer [‚paɪ·ə′nɪr] *s* pioniere *m* ‖ *tr* aprire la via a ‖ *intr* fare il pioniere
pioneering [‚paɪ·ə′nɪrɪŋ] *adj* pioneristico
pious [′paɪ·əs] *adj* pio, devoto
pip [pɪp] *s* (*seed*) seme *m*; (vet) pipita
pipe [paɪp] *s* tubo, canna; (*of stove*) cannone *m*; (*for smoking*) pipa; (mus) legno; (mus) cornamusa ‖ *tr* suonare; cantare ad alta voce; fischiare; condurre in una tubatura; munire di tubatura ‖ *intr* suonare la zampogna; **to pipe down** (slang) stare zitto
pipe′ clean′er *s* scovolino
pipe′ dream′ *s* castello in aria
pipe′ line′ *s* oleodotto; (fig) fonte *f* (d'informazioni)
pipe′ or′gan *s* organo a canne
piper [′paɪpər] *s* zampognaro; **to pay the piper** pagare lo scotto
pipe′ wrench′ *s* chiave *f* per tubi
piping [′paɪpɪŋ] *adj* (*voice*) acuto; (*sound*) di cornamusa ‖ *s* tubatura; suono di cornamuse; suono acuto; (*on cakes*) fregio; (*on garments*) cor-

doncino ornamentale || *adv*—**piping hot** scottante, bollente

pippin ['pɪpɪn] *s* mela renetta; (*seed*) seme *m*; (*fig*) gran brava persona

piquant ['pikənt] *adj* piccante

pique [pik] *s* picca, ripicco || *tr* offendere, eccitare

pira·cy ['paɪrəsɪ] *s* (-cies) pirateria

pirate ['paɪrɪt] *s* pirata *mf* || *tr* derubare; (*a book*) svaligiare, pubblicare illegalmente || *intr* pirateggiare

pirouette [,pɪru'ɛt] *s* piroetta || *intr* piroettare

Pisces ['paɪsiz] or ['pɪsiz] *s* (astr) Pesci *mpl*

pistol ['pɪstəl] *s* pistola

piston ['pɪstən] *s* pistone *m*

pis'ton displace'ment *s* cilindrata

pis'ton ring' *s* segmento elastico

pis'ton rod' *s* (*of a steam engine*) biella d'accoppiamento; (*of a motor*) asta del pistone, biella

pis'ton stroke' *s* corsa dello stantuffo

pit [pɪt] *s* (*in the ground*) buca; (*trap*) trappola; (*of fruit*) nocciolo; (*of stomach*) bocca; (*scar*) buttero; (*in exchange*) recinto delle grida; (*for fights*) arena; (theat) platea; (min) miniera; (aut) fossa di riparazione || *v* (*pret & pp* **pitted;** *ger* **pitting**) *tr* infossare; butterare; opporre; (*to remove pits from*) snocciolare

pitch [pɪtʃ] *s* (*black sticky substance*) pece *f*; (*throw*) lancio; (*of a roof*) pendenza, inclinazione; (*of a boat*) beccheggio; (*of a screw*) passo; (*of sound*) altezza || *tr* lanciare; (*a tent*) rizzare || *intr* beccheggiare; **to pitch in** (coll) mettersi al lavoro; (coll) cominciare a mangiare

pitch' ac'cent *s* accento di altezza

pitch' at'titude *s* assetto longitudinale

pitch'-dark' *adj* nero come la pece

pitched' bat'tle *s* battaglia campale

pitcher ['pɪtʃər] *s* brocca; (baseball) lanciatore *m*

pitch'fork' *s* forca, tridente *m*; **to rain pitchforks** (coll) piovere a dirotto

pitch' pipe' *s* (mus) corista *m*

pit'fall' *s* trappola, trabocchetto

pith [pɪθ] *s* midollo; (*strength*) (fig) forza; (fig) succo, essenza

pith·y ['pɪθɪ] *adj* (-ier; -iest) midolloso; succoso, essenziale

pitiful ['pɪtɪfəl] *adj* pietoso

pitiless ['pɪtɪlɪs] *adj* spietato

pit·y ['pɪtɪ] *s* (-ies) pietà *f*; **it is a pity that** è un peccato che; **what a pity!** che peccato! || *v* (*pret & pp* -ied) *tr* aver pietà di

Pius ['paɪəs] *s* Pio

pivot ['pɪvət] *s* asse *m*, perno; (fig) asse *m* || *tr* imperniare || *intr* imperniarsi; **to pivot on** fare perno su; dipendere da

placard ['plækɑrd] *s* manifesto, affisso || *tr* affiggere

place [ples] *s* luogo; locale *m*; (*court*) piazzetta; (*short street*) vicolo; residenza; sito, luogo, località *f*; (*point*) punto; (*space occupied*) posto; (*office*) posto, impiego; **in no place**

da nessuna parte; **in place** a posto; **in place of** al posto di, invece di; **in the first place** in primo luogo; **in the next place** in secondo luogo; **to know one's place** saper stare al proprio posto; **to take place** aver luogo || *tr* piazzare, mettere; (*to find employment for*) collocare; (*to identify*) ravvisare || *intr* (sports) piazzarsi

place·bo [plə'sibo] *s* (-bos or -boes) rimedio fittizio

place' card' *s* segnaposto

placement ['plesmənt] *s* (*e.g., of furniture*) collocazione; (*employment*) collocamento

place' name' *s* toponimo

place' of busi'ness *s* ufficio, negozio

placid ['plæsɪd] *adj* placido

plagiarism ['pledʒə,rɪzəm] *s* plagio

plagiarize ['pledʒə,raɪz] *tr* plagiare

plague [pleg] *s* peste bubbonica; (*widespread affliction*) piaga, flagello || *tr* infestare, appestare; tormentare

plaid [plæd] *s* tessuto scozzese

plain [plen] *adj* piano; aperto; evidente, esplicito; semplice; (*undyed*) naturale; comune, ordinario; **in plain English** senz'ambagi; **in plain view** di fronte a tutti || *s* pianura

plain'-clothes' man' *s* (-men') agente *m* in borghese

plains'man *s* (-men) abitante *m* della pianura

plaintiff ['plentɪf] *s* querelante *mf*

plaintive ['plentɪv] *adj* lamentevole

plan [plæn] *s* piano, progetto || *v* (*pret & pp* **planned;** *ger* **planning**) *tr & intr* progettare

plane [plen] *adj* piano || *m* piano; (*tool*) pialla; (aer) aeroplano; (aer) ala d'aeroplano; (bot) platano || *tr* piallare || *intr* andare in aeroplano

plane' sick'ness *s* male *m* d'aria

planet ['plænɪt] *s* pianeta *m*

plane' tree' *s* platano

plan'ing mill' *s* officina di piallatura

plank [plæŋk] *s* tavola, asse *m*; (*political party*) piattaforma || *tr* coprire d'assi; cucinare sulla graticola e servire sul tagliere; **to plank down** (*e.g., money*) (coll) snocciolare

plant [plænt] or [plɑnt] *s* (*factory*) impianto, stabilimento; (*e.g., of a college*) complesso di edifici; (bot) pianta; (mach) apparato motore; (slang) trappola || *tr* (*e.g., a tree*) piantare; (*seeds*) seminare; (*to stock*) fornire

plantation [plæn'teʃən] *s* piantagione

planter ['plæntər] *s* piantatore *m*; (mach) piantatrice *f*

plaster ['plæstər] or ['plɑstər] *s* (*gypsum*) gesso; (*mixture to cover walls*) intonaco, malta; (*poultice*) impiastro || *tr* ingessare; intonacare; impiastrare; (*with posters*) affiggere, ricoprire

plas'ter·board' *s* cartone *m* di gesso

plas'ter cast' *s* (sculp) gesso; (surg) ingessatura

plas'ter of Par'is *s* gesso, stucco

plastic ['plæstɪk] *adj & s* plastico

plate [plet] *s* (*dish*) piatto; (*sheet of metal*) placca, piastra; (*thin sheet of metal*) lamina; (*of vacuum tube*) placca; (*of auto license*) targa; (*of condenser*) armatura; (*tableware*) vasellame *m* d'argento, vasellame *m* d'oro; dentiera; (*baseball*) casa base; (phot) lastra; (typ) cliché *m* ‖ *tr* (*with gold or silver*) placcare; (*with armor*) blindare, corazzare

plateau [plæˈto] *s* altipiano

plate′ glass′ *s* lastrone *m*

platen [ˈplætən] *s* rullo

platform [ˈplætˌfɔrm] *s* piattaforma; (*for speaker*) tribuna, palco; (*for passengers*) (rr) marciapiede *m*; (*at end of car*) (rr) piattaforma

plat′form car′ *s* (rr) pianale *m*

platinum [ˈplætɪnəm] *s* platino

plat′inum blonde′ *s* bionda platinata

platitude [ˈplætɪˌtjud] *or* [ˈplætɪˌtud] *s* trivialità *f*, banalità *f*

Plato [ˈpleto] *s* Platone *m*

platoon [pləˈtun] *s* plotone *m*

platter [ˈplætər] *s* piatto di portata; (slang) disco di grammofono

plausible [ˈplɔzɪbəl] *adj* plausibile; (*person*) credibile, attendibile

play [ple] *s* gioco; libertà *f* d'azione; recreazione; turno, volta; (theat) dramma *m*; (mach) gioco ‖ *tr* giocare; giocare contro; causare, produrre; (*a drama*) rappresentare; (*a character*) fare la parte di; (*to wield*) esercitare; (mus) suonare; **to play back** (*e.g., a tape*) riprodurre; **to play down** diminuire l'importanza di; **to play one off against another** mettere uno contro l'altro; **to play up** dare importanza a ‖ *intr* giocare; (*to act*) giocare, comportarsi; (theat) recitare; (mus) suonare; (mach) aver gioco; **to play on** continuare a giocare; continuare a suonare; valersi di; **to play safe** non prendere rischi; **to play sick** fare il malato; **to play up to** fare la corte a

play′back′ *s* riproduzione; apparechiatura di riproduzione

play′bill′ *s* (theat) programma *m*

play′boy′ *s* playboy *m*, gaudente *m*

player [ˈpleɔr] *s* giocatore *m*; (theat) attore *m*; (mus) suonatore *m*

play′er pian′o *s* pianola

playful [ˈplefəl] *adj* giocoso

playgoer [ˈpleˌgoɔr] *s* frequentatore *m* del teatro

play′ground′ *s* parco di ricreazione; (*resort*) posto di villeggiatura

play′house′ *s* teatro; casa di bambole

play′ing card′ [ˈple·ɪŋ] *s* carta da gioco

play′ing field′ *s* campo da gioco

play′mate′ *s* compagno di gioco

play′-off′ *s* (sports) spareggio

play′pen′ *s* recinto, box *m*

play′thing′ *s* giocattolo

play′time′ *s* ricreazione

playwright [ˈpleˌraɪt] *s* drammaturgo, commediografo

play′writ′ing *s* drammaturgia

plaza [ˈplæzə] *or* [ˈplɑzə] *s* piazzale *m*

plea [pli] *s* scusa; richiesta, domanda; (law) dichiarazione

plead [plid] *v* (*pret & pp* **pleaded** *or* **pled** [pled]) *tr* (*ignorance*) dichiarare; (*a case*) perorare ‖ *intr* supplicare; argomentare; **to plead guilty** dichiararsi colpevole

pleasant [ˈplezənt] *adj* piacevole; (*person*) simpatico

pleasant·ry [ˈplezəntri] *s* (-ries) facezia, motto

please [pliz] *tr* piacere (*with dat*) ‖ *intr* piacere; **as you please** come vuole; **if you please** per favore; **please per cortesia; to be pleased to** avere il piacere di; **to be pleased with** essere soddisfatto con; **to do as one pleases** fare come par e piace

pleasing [ˈplizɪŋ] *adj* piacevole

pleasure [ˈpleʒər] *s* piacere *m*; desiderio; **what is your pleasure?** cosa desidera?

pleas′ure car′ *s* vettura da turismo

pleat [plit] *s* piega ‖ *tr* piegare, pieghettare

plebeian [plɪˈbi·ən] *adj* & *s* plebeo

plebiscite [ˈplebɪˌsaɪt] *s* plebiscito

pledge [pledʒ] *s* pegno, promessa; voto; (*person*) ostaggio; (*toast*) brindisi *m*; **as a pledge** in pegno; **to take the pledge** giurare d'astenersi dal bere ‖ *tr* dare in pegno; (*to bind*) far promettere a

plentiful [ˈplentɪfəl] *adj* abbondante

plenty [ˈplenti] *s* abbondanza ‖ *adv* (coll) abbastanza

pleurisy [ˈplurɪsi] *s* pleurite *f*

pliable [ˈplaɪ·əbəl] *adj* flessibile, pieghevole; docile

pliers [ˈplaɪ·ərz] *ssg or spl* pinze *fpl*

plight [plaɪt] *s* condizione o situazione precaria ‖ *tr*—**to plight one's troth** fidanzarsi

plod [plɑd] *v* (*pret & pp* **plodded**; *ger* **plodding**) *tr* percorrere pesantemente ‖ *intr* camminare pesantemente; (*to drudge*) sgobbare

plot [plɑt] *s* (*of ground*) appezzamento; (*of a play*) trama, intreccio; (*evil scheme*) cospirazione, trama ‖ *v* (*pret & pp* **plotted**; *ger* **plotting**) *tr* fare il piano di; macchinare; preparare la trama di; (aer, naut) fare il punto di ‖ *intr* tramare, cospirare

plover [ˈplʌvər] *or* [ˈplovər] *s* piviere *m*

plow [plaʊ] *s* aratro; (*for snow*) spazzaneve *m* ‖ *tr* arare; (*e.g., water*) solcare; (snow) spazzare; **to plow back** reinvestire ‖ *intr* arare; aprirsi la via; camminare pesantemente

plow′man *s* (-men) aratore *m*; contadino

plow′share′ *s* vomere *m*

pluck [plʌk] *s* strattone *m*; coraggio; (*giblets*) frattaglie *fpl* ‖ *tr* (*to snatch*) tirare; (*e.g., fruit*) svellere; (*a fowl*) spennare; (mus) pizzicare ‖ *intr* tirare; **to pluck up** farsi coraggio

pluck·y [ˈplʌki] *adj* (-ier; -iest) coraggioso

plug [plʌg] *s* tappo, zaffo; tavoletta di

tabacco; bocca da incendi; (elec) spina; (horse) (slang) ronzino; (slang) raccomandazione || v (pret & pp plugged; ger plugging) tr tappare, otturare; colpire; inserire; (slang) fare la pubblicità di; **to plug in** (elec) innestare, connettere || intr (coll) sgobbare

plum [plʌm] s (fruit) susina; (tree) susino; (slang) cosa bellissima; (slang) colpo di fortuna

plumage ['plumɪdʒ] s piumaggio

plumb [plʌm] adj appiombo || s piombino || adv appiombo; (coll) completamente || tr determinare la verticale col piombino; assodare

plumb' bob' s piombino

plumber ['plʌmər] s installatore m, idraulico

plumbing ['plʌmɪŋ] s impianto idraulico; mestiere m d'idraulico; sondaggio

plumb'ing fix'tures spl rubinetteria, impianti mpl sanitari

plumb' line' s filo a piombo

plum' cake' s panfrutto

plume [plum] s piuma; (tuft of feathers) pennacchio || tr coprire di piume; **to plume oneself on** piccarsi di; **to plume one's feathers** pulirsi le penne

plummet ['plʌmɪt] s piombino || intr cadere a piombo

plump [plʌmp] adj grassoccio, paffuto; franco || s caduta || adv francamente || intr cadere a piombo

plum' pud'ding s budino con uva passa

plum' tree' s susino

plunder ['plʌndər] s (act) saccheggio; (loot) bottino || tr & intr saccheggiare

plunge [plʌndʒ] s (fall) caduta; (dive) nuotata, tuffo || tr gettare; tuffare; (e.g., a knife) configgere || intr (to rush) precipitarsi; (to gamble) (coll) darsi al gioco; (fig) ripiombare

plunger ['plʌndʒər] s tuffatore m; (for clearing clogged drains) sturalavandini m; (mach) stantuffo; (coll) giocatore temerario

plunk [plʌŋk] adv (coll) proprio; (coll) con un colpo secco || tr (coll) gettare; lasciar cadere; (mus) pizzicare || intr (coll) lasciarsi cadere

plural ['plurəl] adj & s plurale m

plus [plʌs] adj superiore; (elec) positivo; (coll) con lode || s più m; soprappiù m || prep più

plush [plʌʃ] adj di lusso || s peluche f, felpa

Plutarch ['plutɑrk] s Plutarco

Pluto ['pluto] s Plutone m

plutonium [plu'tonɪəm] s plutonio

ply [plaɪ] s (plies) spessore m; (layer) strato; (of rope) legnolo || v (pret & pp plied) tr (a trade) esercitare; (a tool) maneggiare; (to assail) premere, incalzare || intr lavorare assiduamente; **to ply between** fare la spola tra

ply'wood' s legno compensato

pneumatic [nju'mætɪk] or [nu'mætɪk] adj pneumatico

pneumat'ic drill' s martello perforatore or pneumatico

pneumonia [nju'monɪ·ə] or [nu'monɪ·ə] s polmonite f

poach [potʃ] tr (eggs) affogare || intr cacciare or pescare di frodo

poacher ['potʃər] s bracconiere m; pescatore m di frodo

pock [pak] s buttero

pocket ['pakɪt] adj tascabile || s tasca; (billiards) buca; (aer) vuoto; (min) deposito || tr intascare; (e.g., one's pride) ingoiare

pock'et·book' s portafoglio; (woman's purse) borsetta

pock'et book' s libro tascabile

pock'et·hand'kerchief' s fazzoletto

pock'et·knife' s (-knives) temperino

pock'et mon'ey s spiccioli mpl

pock'mark' s buttero

pod [pad] s baccello; (aer) contenitore m

poem ['po·ɪm] s poesia; (of some length) poema m

poet ['po·ɪt] s poeta m

poetess ['po·ɪtɪs] s poetessa

poetic [po'etɪk] adj poetico || poetics ssg poetica

poetry ['po·ɪtri] s poesia

pogrom ['pogrəm] s pogrom m

poignancy ['pɔɪnjənsi] or ['pɔɪnənsi] s strazio; intensità f

poignant ['pɔɪnjənt] or ['pɔɪnənt] adj straziante; intenso

point [pɔɪnt] s (sharp end) punta; (something essential) essenziale m; (hint) suggerimento; (dot, decimal point, spot, degree, instant, position of compass) punto; (coll) costrutto; **beside the point** fuori del seminato; **in point of** per quanto concerne; **to come to the point** venire al sodo; **to get the point** capire l'antifona; **to make a point of** dar importanza a; insistere di; **to stretch a point** fare un'eccezione, fare uno strappo alla regola; **to the point** a proposito || tr (e.g., a weapon) puntare; (to sharpen) aguzzare; (to dot) punteggiare; (to give force to) dare enfasi a; (with mortar) rinzaffare || intr puntare; **to point at** puntare il dito a; **to point to** mostrare a dito

point'blank' adj & adv a bruciapelo

pointed ['pɔɪntɪd] adj appuntito; personale, diretto, acuto

pointer ['pɔɪntər] s (rod) bacchetta; indice m, indicatore m; cane m da punta, pointer m; (coll) direttiva

poise [pɔɪz] s equilibrio, stabilità f; dignità f || tr equilibrare || intr equilibrarsi, stare in equilibrio

poison ['pɔɪzən] s veleno || tr avvelenare

poi'son i'vy s edera del Canada, tossicodendro

poisonous ['pɔɪzənəs] adj velenoso

poke [pok] s spinta, urto; (with elbow) gomitata; (slang) polentone m || tr (to prod) spingere, urtare; (the head) sporgere; (the fire) attizzare; **to poke fun at** burlarsi di; **to poke one's nose into** ficcare il naso in || intr (to jab)

urtare; (to thrust oneself) ficcarsi; (to pry) ficcare il naso; **to poke around** gironzolare; **to poke out** spuntare, protrudere
poker ['pokər] s (game) poker m; (bar) attizzatoio
pok'er face' s faccia impassibile
pok·y ['poki] adj (-ier; -iest) (coll) lento; (coll) meschino, modesto || (-ies) s (slang) gattabuia
Poland ['polənd] s la Polonia
po'lar bear' ['polər] s orso bianco
polarize ['polə ,raiz] tr polarizzare
pole [pol] s palo; (long rod) pertica; (of wagon) timone m; (for jumping) asta; (astr, biol, elec, geog, math) polo || tr (a boat) spingere con un palo || intr spingere una barca con un palo || **Pole** s polacco
pole'cat' s puzzola
pole' lamp' s lampada a stelo
pole'star' s stella polare
pole' vault' s salto coll'asta
police [pə'lis] s polizia || tr vigilare, proteggere; (mil) pulire
police'man s (-men) agente m di polizia, vigile urbano
police' state' s governo poliziesco
police' sta'tion s commissariato di polizia
poli·cy ['palisi] s (-cies) politica; (ins) polizza
polio ['poli ,o] s (coll) polio f
polish ['paliʃ] s lustro, lucentezza; (for shoes or furniture) cera; (fig) raffinatezza, eleganza || tr pulire; (e.g., a stone) levigare; **to polish off** (slang) finire; **to polish up** (slang) migliorare || intr pulirsi; diventar lucido || **Polish** ['poliʃ] adj & s polacco
polisher ['paliʃər] s lucidatore m; (mach) lucidatrice f
polite [pə'lait] adj raffinato, cortese
politeness [pə'laitnis] s cortesia
politic ['palitik] adj prudente; (expedient) diplomatico
political [pə'litikəl] adj politico
politician [,pali'tiʃən] s politico; (pej) politicante m, politicastro
politics ['palitiks] ssg or spl politica
poll [pol] s votazione; (registering of votes) scrutinio; lista elettorale; (analysis of public opinion) referendum m, sondaggio; (head) testa; **to go to the polls** andare alle urne; **to take a poll** fare un'inchiesta || tr ricevere i voti di; contare i voti di; (a tree) potare; fare un'inchiesta di
pollen ['palən] s polline m
pollinate ['pali ,net] tr fecondare col polline
poll'ing booth' ['poliŋ] s cabina elettorale
polliwog ['pali ,wag] s girino
poll' tax' s capitazione
pollute [pə'lut] tr insudiciare; (to defile) desecrare, profanare; (e.g., the environment) inquinare, contaminare
pollution [pə'luʃən] s inquinamento, contaminazione
poll' watch'er s rappresentante m di lista

polo ['polo] s polo
po'lo play'er s giocatore m di polo, polista m
po'lo shirt' s maglietta, polo
polygamist [pə'ligəmist] s poligamo
polygamous [pə'ligəməs] adj poligamo
polyglot ['pali ,glat] adj & s poliglotto
polygon ['pali ,gan] s poligono
polynomial [,pali'nomi·əl] adj polinomiale || s polinomio
polyp ['palip] s (pathol, zool) polipo
polytheist ['pali ,θi·ist] s politeista mf
polytheistic [,paliθi'istik] adj politeistico
pomade [pə'med] or [pə'mad] s pomata
pomegranate ['pam ,grænit] s (shrub) melograno; (fruit) melagrana
pom·mel ['pʌməl] or ['paməl] s (of sword) pomello; (of saddle) arcione m || v (pret & pp -meled or -melled; ger -meling or -melling) tr prendere a pugni
pomp [pamp] s pompa
pompadour ['pampə ,dor] or ['pampə ,dur] s acconciatura a ciuffo
pompous ['pampəs] adj pomposo
pon·cho ['pantʃo] s (-chos) poncho
pond [pand] s stagno
ponder ['pandər] tr & intr ponderare; **to ponder over** pensare sopra
ponderous ['pandərəs] adj ponderoso
poniard ['panjərd] s pugnale m
pontiff ['pantif] s pontefice m
pontifical [pan'tifikəl] adj pontificale
pontoon [pan'tun] s (boat) chiatta, pontone m; (aer) galleggiante m
po·ny ['poni] s (-nies) pony m; (glass and drink) bicchierino; (for cheating) (slang) bigino
poodle ['pudəl] s barbone m, cane m barbone
pool [pul] s (pond) stagno; (puddle) pozza; (for swimming) piscina; (game) biliardo; (com) cartello, consorzio; (com) fondo comune || tr mettere in un fondo comune || intr formare un cartello or un consorzio
pool'room' s sala da biliardo
pool' ta'ble s tavolo da biliardo
poop [pup] s poppa; (deck) casseretto
poor [pur] adj povero; (inferior) scadente || **the poor** spl i poveri
poor' box' s cassetta per l'elemosina
poor'house' s asilo dei poveri
poorly ['purli] adv male
pop [pap] s scoppio; (soda) gazzosa || v (pret & pp popped; ger popping) tr far scoppiare; **to pop the question** (coll) fare la domanda di matrimonio || intr esplodere con fragore; **to pop in** fare una capatina; entrare all'improvviso
pop'corn' s pop-corn m
pope [pop] s papa m
popeyed ['pap ,aid] adj con gli occhi sporgenti; con gli occhi fuori dalle orbite
pop'gun' s fucile m ad aria compressa
poplar ['paplər] s pioppo
pop·py ['papi] s (-pies) papavero
pop'py·cock' s (coll) scemenza

popsicle ['pɑpsɪkəl] *s* (trademark) gelato da passeggio

populace ['pɑpjələs] *s* gente *f*, popolino

popular ['pɑpjələr] *adj* popolare

popularize ['pɑpjələ ˌraɪz] *tr* divulgare, volgarizzare

populate ['pɑpjə ˌlet] *tr* popolare

population [ˌpɑpjə'leʃən] *s* popolazione

populous ['pɑpjələs] *adj* popoloso

porcelain ['pɔrsəlɪn] or ['pɔrslɪn] *s* porcellana

porch [pɔrtʃ] *s* portico

porcupine ['pɔrkjə ˌpaɪn] *s* (*Hystrix cristata*) istrice *m* & *f*, porcospino; (*Erethizon dorsatum*) ursone *m*, porcospino americano

pore [pɔr] *s* poro ‖ *intr*—**to pore over** studiare minutamente

pork [pɔrk] *s* carne *f* di maiale

pork' butch'er shop' *s* salumeria

pork'chop' *s* cotoletta di maiale

porous ['pɔrəs] *adj* poroso

po'rous plas'ter *s* cataplasma *m*

porphy·ry ['pɔrfɪri] *s* (**-ries**) porfido

porpoise ['pɔrpəs] *s* focena; (*dolphin*) delfino

porridge ['pɑrɪdʒ] or ['pɔrɪdʒ] *s* pappa, farinata

port [pɔrt] *adj* portuario ‖ *s* (*harbor*; *wine*) porto; (*naut*) babordo, sinistra; (*opening in side of ship*) portello; (*round opening*) (naut) oblò *m*

portable ['pɔrtəbəl] *adj* portabile

portal ['pɔrtəl] *s* portale *m*

portend [pɔr'tɛnd] *tr* presagire

portent ['pɔrtɛnt] *s* presagio

portentous [pɔr'tɛntəs] *adj* sinistro, funesto, premonitore; (*amazing*) portentoso

porter ['pɔrtər] *s* (*doorman*) portiere *m*; (*man who carries luggage*) facchino; (*of a sleeper*) conduttore *m*; (*in a store*) inserviente *mf*; (*beverage*) birra scura e amara

portfoli·o [pɔrt'folɪ ˌo] *s* (**-os**) cartella; (*office*; *holdings*) portafoglio

port'hole' *s* (*opening in side of ship*) portello; (*round opening*) (naut) oblò *m*

porti·co ['pɔrtɪ ˌko] *s* (**-cos** or **-coes**) portico

portion ['pɔrʃən] *s* porzione; (*dowry*) dote *f* ‖ *tr*—**to portion out** dividere, ripartire

port·ly ['pɔrtli] *adj* (**-lier**; **-liest**) obeso, corpulento

port' of call' *s* scalo

portrait ['pɔrtret] or ['pɔrtrɪt] *s* ritratto

portray [pɔr'tre] *tr* ritrarre

portrayal [pɔr'tre·əl] *s* delineazione; ritratto

Portugal ['pɔrtʃəgəl] *s* il Portogallo

Portu·guese ['pɔrtʃə ˌgiz] *adj* portoghese ‖ *s* (**-guese**) portoghese *mf*

pose [poz] *s* posa ‖ *tr* (*a question*) avanzare; (*a model*) mettere in posa ‖ *intr* posare; **to pose as** posare a, atteggiarsi a

posh [pɑʃ] *adj* (coll) di lusso

position [pə'zɪʃən] *s* posizione; rango; impiego, posto; **to be in a position to** essere in grado di

positive ['pɑzɪtɪv] *adj* positivo ‖ *s* positivo; (phot) positiva

possess [pə'zɛs] *tr* possedere

possession [pə'zɛʃən] *s* possedimento; (*of mental faculties*) possesso; **possessions** (*wealth*) beni *mpl*

possessive [pə'zɛsɪv] *adj* possessivo; (*e.g., mother*) opprimente, soffocante

possible ['pɑsɪbəl] *adj* possibile

possum ['pɑsəm] *s* opossum *m*; **to play possum** (coll) fare il morto

post [post] *s* (*mail*) posta; (*pole*) palo; (*in horse racing*) linea di partenza; posizione, rango; (*job*) posto; (mil) presidio ‖ *tr* mettere in una lista; impostare; tenere al corrente; **post no bills** divieto d'affissione

postage ['postɪdʒ] *s* affrancatura

post'age me'ter *s* affrancatrice *f*

post'age stamp' *s* francobollo

postal ['postəl] *adj* postale

post'al card' *s* cartolina postale

pos'tal per'mit *s* abbonamento postale

post'al sav'ings bank' *s* cassa di risparmio postale

post'al scale' *s* pesalettere *m*

post' card' *s* cartolina illustrata; cartolina postale

post'date' *tr* postdatare

poster ['postər] *s* cartellone *m*, manifesto pubblicitario

posterity [pɑs'tɛrɪti] *s* posterità *f*

postern ['postərn] *adj* posteriore ‖ *s* postierla

post' exchange' *s* spaccio militare

post'haste' *adv* al più presto possibile

posthumous ['pɑstʃʊməs] *adj* postumo

post'man *s* (**-men**) portalettere *m*

post'mark' *s* bollo, timbro postale ‖ *tr* bollare, timbrare

post'mas'ter *s* ricevitore *m* postale

post'master gen'eral *s* (**postmasters general**) ministro delle poste

post-mortem ['post'mɔrtəm] *adj* postumo ‖ *s* autopsia

post' of'fice *s* ufficio postale

post'-office box' *s* casella postale

postpaid ['post ˌped] *adj* franco di porto

postpone [post'pon] *tr* differire, posporre

postscript ['post ˌskrɪpt] *s* poscritto

postulant ['postʃələnt] *s* postulatore *m*, postulante *mf*

posture ['pɑstʃər] *s* portamento; posa ‖ *intr* posare

post'war' *adj* del dopoguerra

po·sy ['pozi] *s* (**-sies**) fiore *m*; (*nosegay*) mazzolino di fiori

pot [pɑt] *s* pentola, pignatta; pitale *m*, orinale *m*; (*in gambling*) (coll) piatto; **to go to pot** andare a gambe all'aria

potash ['pɑt ˌæʃ] *s* potassa

potassium [pə'tæsɪ·əm] *s* potassio

pota·to [pə'teto] *s* (**-toes**) patata

pota'to om'elet *s* omelette *f* con patate

potbellied ['pɑt ˌbelid] *adj* panciuto

poten·cy ['potənsi] *s* (**-cies**) potenza

potent ['potənt] *adj* potente

potentate ['potǝn͵tet] s potentato

potential [pǝ'tɛn/ǝl] adj & s potenziale m

pot'hold'er s patta, presa

pot'hook' s uncino

potion ['po/ǝn] s pozione

pot'luck' s—**to take potluck** mangiare quello che passa il convento

pot' shot' s colpo sparato a casaccio

potter ['patǝr] s vasaio

pot'ter's clay' s argilla per stoviglie

pot'ter's field' s cimitero dei poveri

potter·y ['patǝri] s (-ies) vasellame m; fabbrica di vasellame; ceramica

pouch [paut/] s sacchetto, borsa; (of kangaroo) borsa

poultice ['poltɪs] s cataplasma m

poultry ['poltri] s pollame m

poul'try·man s (-men) pollivendolo

pounce [pauns] intr—**to pounce on** balzare su

pound ['paund] s libbra; lira sterlina; (for stray animals) recinto ‖ tr battere, picchiare; tempestare di colpi; (to crush) polverizzare ‖ intr battere

pound' cake' s dolce m fatto con una libbra di burro, una di zucchero ed una di farina

pound' ster'ling s lira sterlina

pour [por] tr versare; (e.g., tea) servire; (wine) mescere; (stones upon an enemy) far piovere ‖ intr fluire; (to rain) diluviare; **to pour in** affluire; **to pour out** uscire in massa

pout [paut] s broncio ‖ intr tenere il broncio

poverty ['pavǝrti] s povertà f

POW ['pi'o'dʌbl͵ju] s (letterword) (prisoner of war) prigioniero di guerra

powder ['paudǝr] s polvere f; (for the face) cipria; (med) polverina ‖ tr incipriare; (to sprinkle with powder) spolverizzare

pow'dered sug'ar s zucchero in polvere

pow'der puff' s piumino

pow'der room' s toletta

powdery ['paudǝri] adj polveroso; fragile; (snow) farinoso

power ['pau·ǝr] s (ability, authority) potere m; forza, energia; (nation) potenza; (math, phys) potenza; **in power** al potere; **the powers that be** i potenti ‖ tr azionare

pow'er·boat' s barca a motore

pow'er brake' s (aut) servofreno

pow'er com'pany s compagnia di elettricità

pow'er drive' s picchiata

powerful ['pau·ǝrfǝl] adj poderoso

pow'er·house' s centrale elettrica

powerless ['pau·ǝrlɪs] adj impotente

pow'er line' s elettrodotto

pow'er mow'er s motofalciatrice f

pow'er of attor'ney s procura legale

pow'er plant' s stazione f generatrice; (aut) gruppo motore

pow'er steer'ing s servosterzo

pow'er tool' s apparecchiatura a motore

pow'er vac'uum s vuoto di potere

practical ['præktɪkǝl] adj pratico

prac'tical joke' s scherzo da prete

practically ['præktɪkǝli] adv (in a practical manner; virtually, really) praticamente; più o meno, quasi

practice ['præktɪs] s pratica; (of a profession) esercizio; (e.g., of a doctor) clientela; (process of doing something) prassi f; (habitual performance) abitudine f ‖ tr praticare, esercitare ‖ intr esercitarsi, praticare; (to be active in a profession) esercitare; **to practice as** esercitare la professione di

practitioner [præk'tɪ/ǝnǝr] s professionista mf

Prague [prag] or [preg] s Praga

prairie ['preri] s prateria

prai'rie dog' s cinomio

prai'rie wolf' s coyote m

praise [prez] s lode f, elogio ‖ tr lodare, elogiare; **to praise to the skies** levare alle stelle

praise'wor'thy adj lodevole

pram [præm] s (coll) carrozzella

prance [præns] or [prans] s caracollo ‖ intr caracollare; (to caper) ballonzolare

prank [præŋk] s burla, tiro

prate [pret] intr cianciare

prattle ['prætǝl] s ciancia, chiacchierio ‖ intr cianciare, parlare a vanvera

pray [pre] tr & intr pregare

prayer [prer] s preghiera

prayer' book' s libro di preghiere

preach [prit/] tr & intr predicare

preacher ['prit/ǝr] s predicatore m

preamble ['pri͵æmbǝl] s preambolo

precarious [prɪ'kɛrɪ·ǝs] adj precario

precaution [prɪ'ko/ǝn] s precauzione

precede [prɪ'sid] tr & intr precedere

precedent ['prɛsɪdǝnt] s precedente m

precept ['prisɛpt] s precetto

precinct ['prisɪŋkt] s distretto; circoscrizione elettorale; **precincts** dintorni mpl

precious ['prɛ/ǝs] adj prezioso ‖ adv—**precious little** (coll) molto poco

precipice ['prɛsɪpɪs] s precipizio

precipitate [prɪ'sɪpɪ͵tet] adj precipitoso ‖ s precipitato ‖ tr & intr precipitare

precipitous [prɪ'sɪpɪtǝs] adj precipitoso, a precipizio

precise [prɪ'saɪs] adj preciso

precision [prɪ'sɪʒǝn] s precisione

preclude [prɪ'klud] tr precludere; escludere

precocious [prɪ'ko/ǝs] adj precoce

predatory ['prɛdǝ͵tori] adj da preda, predatore

predicament [prɪ'dɪkǝmǝnt] s situazione critica or imbarazzante

predict [prɪ'dɪkt] tr predire

prediction [prɪ'dɪk/ǝn] s predizione

predispose [͵pridɪs'poz] tr predisporre

predominant [prɪ'damɪnǝnt] adj predominante

preeminent [prɪ'ɛmɪnǝnt] adj preminente

preempt [prɪ'ɛmpt] tr occupare or acquistare in precedenza

preen [prin] tr (feathers, fur) lisciarsi;

to preen oneself agghindarsi, attillarsi

prefabricate [pri'fæbri‚ket] *tr* prefabbricare

preface ['prefis] *s* prefazione ‖ *tr* prefazionare; essere la prefazione di

pre·fer [pri'fʌr] *v* (*pret & pp* **-ferred**; *ger* **-ferring**) *tr* preferire; (*to advance*) promuovere; (law) presentare, avanzare

preferable ['prefərəbəl] *adj* preferibile

preference ['prefərəns] *s* preferenza

preferred' stock' *s* azioni *fpl* privilegiate

prefix ['prifiks] *s* prefisso ‖ *tr* prefiggere

pregnan·cy ['pregnənsi] *s* (**-cies**) gravidanza

pregnant ['pregnənt] *adj* incinta, gravida; (fig) gravido

prehistoric [‚prihis'tɑrik] or [‚prihis'tɔrik] *adj* preistorico

prejudice ['predʒədis] *s* pregiudizio; preconcetto; **without prejudice** senza detrimento ‖ *tr* (*to harm*) pregiudicare; predisporre; **to prejudice against** prevenire contro

prejudicial [‚predʒə'diʃəl] *adj* pregiudizievole

prelate ['prelit] *s* prelato

preliminar·y [pri'limi‚neri] *adj* preliminare ‖ *s* (**-ies**) preliminare *m*

prelude ['preljud] or ['prilud] *s* preludio ‖ *tr* preludere a ‖ *intr* preludere

premeditate [pri'medi‚tet] *tr* premeditare

premier [pri'mir] or ['primi·ər] *s* primo ministro, presidente *m* del consiglio

premiere [prə'mjer or [pri'mir] *s* prima; prima attrice

premise ['premis] *s* premessa; **on the premises** nella proprietà, sul luogo; **premises** proprietà *f*

premium ['primi·əm] *s* premio; **at a premium** in gran richiesta; a prezzo altissimo

premonition [‚primə'niʃən] *s* presentimento; indizio

preoccupation [pri‚ɑkjə'peʃən] *s* preoccupazione

preoccu·py [pri'ɑkjə‚pai] *v* (*pret & pp* **-pied**) *tr* preoccupare; (*to occupy beforehand*) occupare prima

prepaid [pri'ped] *adj* pagato in anticipo; franco di porto

preparation [‚prepə'reʃən] *s* preparazione; (*for a trip*) preparativo; (pharm) preparato

preparatory [pri'pærə‚tɔri] *adj* preparatorio

prepare [pri'per] *tr* preparare ‖ *intr* prepararsi

preparedness [pri'peridnəs] or [pri'perdnis] *s* preparazione; preparazione militare

pre·pay [pri'pe] *v* (*pret & pp* **-paid**) *tr* pagare anticipatamente

preponderant [pri'pɑndərənt] *adj* preponderante

preposition [‚prepə'ziʃən] *s* preposizione

prepossessing [‚pripə'zesiŋ] *adj* simpatico, attraente, piacevole

preposterous [pri'pɑstərəs] *adj* assurdo, ridicolo

prep' school' [prep] *s* (coll) scuola preparatoria

prerecorded [‚priri'kɔrdid] *adj* (rad & telv) a registrazione differita

prerequisite [pri'rekwizit] *s* requisito

prerogative [pri'rɑgətiv] *s* prerogativa

presage ['presidʒ] *s* presagio ‖ [pri'sedʒ] *tr* presagire

Presbyterian [‚prezbi'tiri·ən] *adj & s* presbiteriano; Presbiteriano

prescribe [pri'skraib] *tr & intr* prescrivere

prescription [pri'skripʃən] *s* prescrizione; (pharm) ricetta

presence ['prezəns] *s* presenza; **in the presence of** alla presenza di

present ['prezənt] *adj* presente ‖ *s* presente *m*, regalo ‖ [pri'zent] *tr* presentare; **present arms!** presentat'arm!; **to present s.o. with s.th** regalare qlco a qlcu

presentable [pri'zentəbəl] *adj* presentabile

presentation [‚prezən'teʃən] or [‚prizən'teʃən] *s* presentazione; (theat) rappresentazione

presenta'tion cop'y *s* copia d'omaggio

presentiment [pri'zentimənt] *s* presentimento

presently ['prezəntli] *adv* fra poco; attualmente

preserve [pri'zʌrv] *s* (*for hunting*) riserva; **preserves** conserva, marmellata ‖ *tr* preservare; conservare

preserved' fruit' *s* frutta in conserva

preside [pri'zaid] *intr* presiedere; **to preside over** presiedere, presiedere a

presiden·cy ['prezidənsi] *s* (**-cies**) presidenza

president ['prezidənt] *s* presidente *m*; (*of a university*) rettore *m*

press [pres] *s* pressione; (*crowd*) folla; (*closet*) armadio; (mach) pressa; (typ) stampa; **to go to press** andare in macchina ‖ *tr* (*to push*) spingere, premere; (*to squeeze*) spremere; (*to embrace*) abbracciare; forzare; costringere; urgere, sollecitare; (*to iron*) stirare ‖ *intr* premere; avanzare

press' a'gent *s* agente pubblicitario

press' con'ference *s* conferenza stampa

pressing ['presiŋ] *adj* pressante, urgente ‖ *s* (*of records*) incisione

press' release' *s* comunicato stampa

pressure ['preʃər] *s* pressione; tensione, urgenza ‖ *tr* pressare, incalzare con insistenza

pres'sure cook'er ['kukər] *s* pentola a pressione

pressurize ['preʃə‚raiz] *tr* pressurizzare

prestige [pres'tiʒ] or ['prestidʒ] *s* prestigio

prestigious [pre'stidʒi·əs] or [pre'stidʒəs] *adj* onorato, stimato

presumably [pri'zuməbli] or [pri'zjuməbli] *adv* presumibilmente

presume [pri'zum] or [pri'zjum] *tr* presumere; **to presume to** prendersi la libertà di ‖ *intr* assumere; **to presume on** or **upon** abusare di

presumption [prɪˈzʌmpʃən] *s* presunzione; supposizione

presumptuous [prɪˈzʌmptʃʊ·əs] *adj* presuntuoso

presuppose [ˌprisəˈpoz] *tr* presupporre

pretend [prɪˈtɛnd] *tr* fingere, fare finta di ‖ *intr* fingere; **to pretend to** (*e.g.*, *the throne*) pretendere a

pretender [prɪˈtɛndər] *s* pretendente *mf*; impostore *m*

pretense [prɪˈtɛns] or [ˈpritɛns] *s* pretesa; finzione; **under false pretenses** allegando ragioni false; **under pretense of** sotto l'apparenza di

pretentious [prɪˈtɛnʃəs] *adj* pretenzioso

preterit [ˈprɛtərɪt] *adj* passato, preterito ‖ *s* passato remoto, preterito

pretext [ˈpritɛkst] *s* pretesto

pretonic [priˈtɑnɪk] *adj* pretonico

pret·ty [ˈprɪti] *adj* (**-tier; -tiest**) grazioso, carino; (*e.g.*, *sum of money*) (coll) bello ‖ *adv* abbastanza; molto; **sitting pretty** (slang) ben messo

prevail [prɪˈvel] *intr* prevalere; **to prevail on** or **upon** persuadere

prevailing [prɪˈvelɪŋ] *adj* prevalente

prevalent [ˈprɛvələnt] *adj* comune

prevaricate [prɪˈværɪˌket] *intr* mentire

prevent [prɪˈvɛnt] *tr* impedire; **to prevent from** + *ger* impedire (with *dat*) di + *inf* or che + *subj*

prevention [prɪˈvɛnʃən] *s* prevenzione

preventive [prɪˈvɛntɪv] *adj* preventivo ‖ *s* rimedio preventivo

preview [ˈpriˌvju] *s* indizio; (*private showing*) (mov) anteprima; (*showing of brief scenes for advertising*) (mov) scene *fpl* di prossima programmazione

previous [ˈpriviˑəs] *adj* previo, precedente ‖ *adv* precedentemente; **previous to** prima di

prewar [ˈpriˌwɔr] *adj* anteguerra

prey [pre] *s* preda; **to be prey to** essere preda di ‖ *intr* predare; **to prey on** or **upon** predare, sfruttare; preoccupare

price [praɪs] *s* prezzo; **at any price** a qualunque costo ‖ *tr* chiedere il prezzo di; fissare il prezzo di

price′ control′ *s* calmiere *m*

price′ cut′ting *s* riduzione di prezzo

price′ fix′ing *s* regolamento dei prezzi

price′ freez′ing *s* congelamento dei prezzi

priceless [ˈpraɪslɪs] *adj* inestimabile; (coll) molto divertente

price′ list′ *s* listino prezzi

price′ tag′ *s* cartellino del prezzo

price′ war′ *s* guerra dei prezzi

prick [prɪk] *s* punta; puntura; **to kick against the pricks** tirare calci al vento ‖ *tr* bucare, forare; pungere; (*to goad*) spronare; (*the ears*) ergere; (*said, e.g., of the conscience*) rimordere (with *dat*)

prick·ly [ˈprɪkli] *adj* (**-lier; -liest**) spinoso, pungente

prick′ly heat′ *s* sudamina

prick′ly pear′ *s* ficodindia *m*

pride [praɪd] *s* orgoglio; arroganza; **the**

pride of il fiore di ‖ *tr*—**to pride oneself on** or **upon** inorgoglirsi di

priest [prist] *s* prete *m*, sacerdote *m*

priesthood [ˈpristˌhʊd] *s* sacerdozio

priest·ly [ˈpristli] *adj* (**-lier; -liest**) sacerdotale

prig [prɪg] *s* pedante *mf*, moralista *mf*

prim [prɪm] *adj* (**primmer; primmest**) formale, corretto, compito

prima·ry [ˈpraɪˌmɛri] or [ˈpraɪməri] *adj* primario ‖ *s* (**-ries**) elezione preferenziale; (elec) bobina primaria; (elec) primario

prime [praɪm] *adj* primo; originale; di prima qualità ‖ *s* (*earliest part*) inizio; (*best period*) fiore *m*; (*choicest part*) fior fiore *m*; (math) numero primo; (*mark*) (math) primo ‖ *tr* preparare; (*a pump*) adescare; (*a firearm*) innescare; (*a canvas*) mesticare; (*a wall*) dare la prima mano a; (*to supply with information*) istruire

prime′ min′ister *s* primo ministro

primer [ˈprɪmər] *s* sillabario, abbecedario ‖ [ˈpraɪmər] *s* innesco, detonatore *m*

primeval [praɪˈmivəl] *adj* primordiale

primitive [ˈprɪmɪtɪv] *adj* primitivo

primp [prɪmp] *tr* agghindare ‖ *intr* agghindarsi

prim′rose′ *s* primula

prim′rose path′ *s* sentiero dei piaceri

prince [prɪns] *s* principe *m*; **to live like a prince** vivere da principe

prince′ roy′al *s* principe ereditario

princess [ˈprɪnsɪs] *s* principessa

principal [ˈprɪnsɪpəl] *adj* principale ‖ *s* (*chief*) padrone *m*, principale *m*; (*of school*) direttore *m*, preside *m*; (*actor*) primo attore; (com) capitale *m*; (law) mandante *mf*

principle [ˈprɪnsɪpəl] *s* principio; **on principle** per principio

print [prɪnt] *s* stampa; (*cloth*) tessuto stampato; (*printed matter*) stampato; (*newsprint*) giornale *m*; (*mark made by one's thumb*) impronta; (phot) positiva; **in print** stampato; disponibile; **out of print** esaurito ‖ *tr* stampare, tirare; (*to write in print*) scrivere in stampatello; (*in the memory*) imprimere

print′ed cir′cuit *s* circuito stampato

print′ed mat′ter *s* stampati *mpl*

printer [ˈprɪntər] *s* stampatore *m*; (*of computer*) tabulatrice *f*

print′er's dev′il *s* apprendista *m* tipografo

print′er's ink′ *s* inchiostro da stampa

printing [ˈprɪntɪŋ] *s* stampa; stampato; tiratura, edizione; (*writing in printed letters*) stampatello

prior [ˈpraɪ·ər] *adj* anteriore, precedente ‖ *s* priore *m* ‖ *adv* prima; **prior to** prima di

priori·ty [praɪˈɑrɪti] or [praɪˈɒrɪti] *s* (**-ties**) priorità *f*

prism [ˈprɪzəm] *s* prisma *m*

prison [ˈprɪzən] *s* prigione, carcere *m*

prisoner [ˈprɪzənər] or [ˈprɪznər] *s* prigioniero

pris′on van′ *s* furgone *m* cellulare

pris·sy [´prɪsi] *adj* (**-sier; -siest**) smanceroso, smorfioso

priva·cy [´praɪvəsi] *s* (**-cies**) ritiro; segreto; **to have no privacy** non esser mai lasciato in pace

private [´praɪvɪt] *adj* privato, personale ‖ *s* soldato semplice; **in private** privatamente; **privates** pudende *fpl*

pri´vate eye´ *s* poliziotto privato

pri´vate first´ class´ *s* soldato scelto

pri´vate hos´pital *s* clinica

priv´ate view´ing *s* (**mov**) anteprima; (**painting**) vernice *f*

privet [´prɪvɪt] *s* ligustro

privilege [´prɪvɪlɪdʒ] *s* privilegio

priv·y [´prɪvi] *adj* privato; **privy to** segretamente a conoscenza di ‖ *s* (**-ies**) latrina

prize [praɪz] *s* premio; (**nav**) preda ‖ *tr* valutare, stimare

prize´ fight´ *s* incontro di pugilato

prize´ fight´er *s* pugile *m*, pugilista *m*

prize´ ring´ *s* ring *m*, quadrato

pro [pro] *s* (**pros**) pro; voto favorevole; argomento favorevole; (**coll**) professionista *m*; **the pros and the cons** il pro e il contro

probabili·ty [ˌprɑbə´bɪlɪti] *s* (**-ties**) probabilità *f*

probable [´prɑbəbəl] *adj* probabile

probate [´probet] *s* omologazione di un testamento; copia autentica di un testamento ‖ *tr* (*a will*) omologare

probation [pro´beʃən] *s* prova; periodo di prova; (**law**) condizionale *f*, libertà vigilata; (**educ**) provvedimento disciplinare

probe [prob] *s* inchiesta; (**surg**) sonda ‖ *tr* indagare; sondare

problem [´prɑbləm] *s* problema *m*

procedure [pro´sidʒər] *s* procedura

proceed [pro´sid] *s*—**proceeds** provento ‖ [pro´sid] *intr* procedere

proceeding [pro´sidɪŋ] *s* procedimento; **proceedings** atti *mpl*; (**law**) procedimenti *mpl*

process [´prɑses] *s* processo; **in the process of time** in processo di tempo ‖ *tr* trattare

procession [pro´sɛʃən] *s* processione

proc´ess serv´er *s* ufficiale giudiziario

proclaim [pro´klem] *tr* proclamare

proclitic [pro´klɪtɪk] *adj* proclitico ‖ *s* parola proclitica

procrastinate [pro´kræstɪˌnet] *tr & intr* procrastinare

procure [pro´kjur] *tr* ottenere ‖ *intr* ruffianeggiare

prod [prɑd] *s* pungolo, stimolo ‖ *v* (*pret & pp* **prodded**; *ger* **prodding**) *tr* stimolare, pungolare, incitare

prodigal [´prɑdɪgəl] *adj & s* prodigo

prodigious [pro´dɪdʒəs] *adj* prodigioso

prodi·gy [´prɑdɪdʒi] *s* (**-gies**) prodigio

produce [´prɑdjus] or [´prɑdus] *s* produzione; prodotti *mpl* agricoli ‖ [pro-´djus] or [pro´dus] *tr* produrre; (**theat**) presentare

producer [pro´djusər] or [pro´dusər] *s* produttore *m*; (*of a play*) impresario; (**mov**) produttore *m*

product [´prɑdəkt] *s* prodotto

production [pro´dʌkʃən] *s* produzione

profane [pro´fen] *adj* profano; blasfemo ‖ *tr* profanare

profani·ty [pro´fænɪti] *s* (**-ties**) bestemmia

profess [pro´fes] *tr & intr* professare

profession [pro´fɛʃən] *s* professione

professor [pro´fesər] *s* professore *m*

proffer [´prɑfər] *s* offerta ‖ *tr* offrire

proficient [pro´fɪʃənt] *adj* abile, competente

profile [´profaɪl] *s* profilo ‖ *tr* profilare

profit [´prɑfɪt] *s* profitto; vantaggio; **at a profit** con guadagno ‖ *tr* avvantaggiare; giovare (with *dat*) ‖ *intr* avvantaggiarsi; **to profit by** approfittare di

profitable [´prɑfɪtəbəl] *adj* vantaggioso

prof´it and loss´ *s* profitti *mpl* e perdite *fpl*

profiteer [ˌprɑfɪ´tɪr] *s* profittatore *m* ‖ *intr* fare il profittatore

prof´it shar´ing *s* cointeressenza, partecipazione agli utili

prof´it tak´ing *s* realizzo

profligate [´prɑflɪgɪt] *adj & s* dissoluto; prodigo

pro for´ma in´voice [´fɔrmə] *s* fattura fittizia

profound [pro´faund] *adj* profondo

profuse [prə´fjus] *adj* profuso, abbondante; **profuse in** prodigo di

proge·ny [´prɑdʒəni] *s* (**-nies**) prole *f*

progno·sis [prɑg´nosɪs] *s* (**-ses** [siz]) prognosi *f*

prognostic [prɑg´nɑstɪk] *s* pronostico

prognosticate [prɑg´nɑstɪˌket] *tr* pronosticare

pro·gram [´progræm] *s* programma *m* ‖ *v* (*pret & pp* **-gramed** or **-grammed**; *ger* **-graming** or **-gramming**) *tr* programmare

programmer [´progræmər] *s* pannellista *mf*, programmatore *m*

progress [´prɑgres] *s* progresso; **in progress** in corso; **to make progress** fare dei progressi ‖ [prə´gres] *intr* progredire; migliorare

progressive [prə´gresɪv] *adj* (*proceeding step by step*) progressivo; progressista ‖ *s* progressista *mf*

prohibit [pro´hɪbɪt] *tr* proibire

prohibition [ˌpro·ə´bɪʃən] *s* proibizione; (**hist**) proibizionismo

project [´prɑdʒekt] *s* progetto ‖ [prə-´dʒekt] *tr* (*to propose, plan*) progettare; (*light, a shadow, etc.*) proiettare ‖ *intr* sporgere, protrudere

projectile [prə´dʒektɪl] *s* proiettile *m*

projection [prə´dʒekʃən] *s* proiezione, sporgenza

projector [prə´dʒektər] *s* (*apparatus*) proiettore *m*; (*person*) progettista *m f*

proletarian [ˌprolɪ´tɛriən] *adj & s* proletario

proliferate [prə´lɪfəˌret] *intr* proliferare

prolific [prə´lɪfɪk] *adj* prolifico

prolix [´prolɪks] or [pro´lɪks] *adj* prolisso

prologue [´prolɔg] or [´prolɑg] *s* prologo

prolong [pro'lɔŋ] or pro'laŋ] *tr* prolungare

promenade [ˌpramɪ'ned] or [ˌpramɪ'nad] *s* passeggiata; ballo di gala || *tr & intr* passeggiare

promenade' deck' *s* ponte *m* passeggiata

prominent ['pramɪnənt] *adj* prominente

promise ['pramɪs] *s* promessa || *tr & intr* promettere

prom'ising young' man' *s* giovane *m* di belle speranze

prom'issory note' ['pramɪˌsori] *s* cambiale *f*, pagherò *m*

promonto·ry ['pramənˌtori] *s* (**-ries**) promontorio

promote [prə'mot] *tr* promuovere

promotion [prə'moʃən] *s* promozione

prompt [prampt] *adj* pronto || *tr* incitare, istigare; (theat) suggerire

prompter ['pramptər] *s* suggeritore *m*, rammentatore *m*

prompt'er's box' *s* buca del suggeritore

promptness ['pramptnɪs] *s* prontezza

promulgate ['praməlˌget] or [pro'mʌlget] *tr* promulgare

prone [pron] *adj* prono

prong [prɔŋ] or [praŋ] *s* punta; (*of fork*) dente *m*; (*of pitchfork*) rebbio

pronoun ['pronaʊn] *s* pronome *m*

pronounce [prə'naʊns] *tr* pronunziare

pronounced [prə'naʊnst] *adj* pronunziato, marcato

pronouncement [prə'naʊnsmənt] *s* dichiarazione ufficiale

pronunciamen·to [prəˌnʌnsɪ·ə'mento] *s* (**-tos**) pronunciamento

pronunciation [prəˌnʌnsɪ'eʃən] or [prəˌnʌnʃɪ'eʃən] *s* pronunzia

proof [pruf] *adj*—**proof against** a prova di || *s* prova; (*of alcoholic beverages*) gradazione; (typ) bozza

proof'read'er *s* correttore *m* di bozze

prop [prap] *s* sostegno, puntello; (*pole*) palo; **props** attrezzi *mpl* teatrali || *v* (*pret & pp* **propped**; *ger* **propping**) *tr* sostenere, puntellare

propaganda [ˌprapə'gændə] *s* propaganda

propagate ['prapəˌget] *tr* propagare || *intr* propagarsi

pro·pel [prə'pɛl] *v* (*pret & pp* **-pelled**; *ger* **-pelling**) *tr* propulsare, spingere, azionare; (*a rocket*) propellere

propeller [prə'pɛlər] *s* elica

propensi·ty [prə'pɛnsɪti] *s* (**-ties**) propensione

proper ['prapər] *adj* appropriato, corretto; decente, convenevole; (gram) proprio; **proper to** proprio di

proper·ty ['prapərti] *s* (**-ties**) proprietà *f*; **properties** attrezzi *mpl* teatrali

prop'erty man' *s* trovarobe *m*, attrezzista *m*

prop'erty own'er *s* proprietario fondiario

prophe·cy ['prafɪsi] *s* (**-cies**) profezia

prophe·sy ['prafɪˌsaɪ] *v* (*pret & pp* **-sied**) *tr* profetizzare

prophet ['prafɪt] *s* profeta *m*

prophetess ['prafɪtɪs] *s* profetessa

prophylactic [ˌprofɪ'læktɪk] *adj* profilattico || *s* rimedio profilattico; preservativo

propitiate [prə'pɪʃɪˌet] *tr* propiziare

propitious [prə'pɪʃəs] *adj* propizio

prop'jet' *s* turboelica *m*

proportion [prə'porʃən] *s* proporzione; **in proportion as** a misura che; **in proportion to** in proporzione a; **out of proportion** sproporzionato || *tr* proporzionare, commensurare

proportionate [prə'porʃənɪt] *adj* proporzionato

proposal [prə'pozəl] *s* proposta; proposta di matrimonio

propose [prə'poz] *tr* proporre || *intr* fare una proposta di matrimonio; **propose to** chiedere la mano di; proporsi di + *inf*

proposition [ˌprapə'zɪʃən] *s* proposizione, proposta; (coll) progetto || *tr* fare delle proposte indecenti a

propound [prə'paʊnd] *tr* proporre

proprietary [prə'praɪ·əˌteri] *adj* padronale; esclusivo, patentato

proprietor [prə'praɪ·ətər] *s* proprietario

proprietress [prə'praɪ·ətrɪs] *s* proprietaria

proprie·ty [prə'praɪ·əti] *s* (**-ties**) correttezza, decoro; **proprieties** convenzioni *fpl* sociali

propulsion [prə'pʌlʃən] *s* propulsione

prorate [pro'ret] *tr* rateizzare

prosaic [pro'ze·ɪk] *adj* prosaico

proscribe [pro'skraɪb] *tr* proscrivere

prose [proz] *adj* prosaico || *s* prosa

prosecute ['prasɪˌkjut] *tr* eseguire; (law) processare

prosecutor ['prasɪˌkjutər] *s* esecutore *m*; (law) querelante *m*; (law) avvocato d'accusa

proselyte ['prasɪˌlaɪt] *s* proselito

prose' writ'er *s* prosatore *m*

prosody ['prasədi] *s* prosodia, metrica

prospect ['praspɛkt] *s* vista; prospettiva; candidato; probabile cliente *m*; **prospects** speranze *fpl* || *intr* fare il cercatore; **to prospect for** fare il cercatore di

prospectus [prə'spɛktəs] *s* prospetto

prosper ['praspər] *tr & intr* prosperare

prosperi·ty [pras'pɛrɪti] *s* (**-ties**) prosperità *f*, benessere *m*

prosperous ['praspərəs] *adj* prospero

prostitute ['prastɪˌtjut] or [ˌprastɪˌtut] *s* prostituta || *tr* prostituire

prostrate ['prastret] *adj* prostrato || *tr* prostrare

prostration [pras'treʃən] *s* prostrazione

protagonist [pro'tægənɪst] *s* protagonista *mf*

protect [prə'tɛkt] *tr* proteggere

protection [prə'tɛkʃən] *s* protezione

protégé ['protəˌʒe] *s* protetto, favorito

protégée ['protəˌʒe] *s* protetta, favorita

protein ['proti·ɪn] or ['protɪn] *s* proteina

pro tempore [pro'tɛmpəˌri] *adj* provvisorio, interinale

protest ['protɛst] *s* protesta; (com)

protesto || [pro'tɛst] *tr & intr* protestare

Protestant ['pratɪstənt] *adj & s* protestante *mf*

protester [prə'tɛstər] *s* protestatario

prothonotar·y [pro'θɑnə,teri] *s* (**-ies**) (law) cancelliere *m* capo

protocol ['protə,kɑl] *s* protocollo

protoplasm ['protə,plæzəm] *s* protoplasma *m*

prototype ['protə,taɪp] *s* prototipo

proto-zoon [,protə'zo-ɑn] *s* (**-zoa** ['zo-ə]) protozoo

protract [pro'trækt] *tr* prolungare

protractor [pro'træktər] *s* rapportatore *m*

protrude [pro'trud] *intr* sporgere

proud [praud] *adj* fiero; arrogante; maestoso, magnifico

proud' flesh' *s* tessuto di granulazione

prove [pruv] *v* (*pret* **proved**; *pp* **proved** or **proven**) *tr* provare; (*ore*) analizzare; (law) omologare; (math) fare la prova di || *intr* risultare

proverb ['pravərb] *s* proverbio

provide [prə'vaɪd] *tr* provvedere || *intr*—**to provide for** provvedere a; (*to be ready for*) prepararsi a

provided [prə'vaɪdɪd] *conj* a condizione che, purché; **provided that** a condizione che, purché

providence ['pravɪdəns] *s* provvidenza

providential [,pravɪ'dɛnʃəl] *adj* provvidenziale

providing [prə'vaɪdɪŋ] *conj* var of **provided**

province ['pravɪns] *s* provincia; (fig) pertinenza, competenza

provision [prə'vɪʒən] *s* provvedimento; clausola; **provisions** viveri *mpl*

provi·so [prə'vaɪzo] *s* (**-sos** or **-soes**) stipulazione, clausola

provoke [prə'vok] *tr* provocare; contrariare, irritare

prow [prau] *s* prora, prua

prowess ['prau-ɪs] *s* prodezza; maestria

prowl [praul] *intr* andare in cerca di preda; vagabondare

prowler ['praulər] *s* vagabondo; ladro

proximity [prak'sɪmɪti] *s* prossimità *f*

prox·y ['praksi] *s* (**-ies**) procura; (*person*) procuratore *m*

prude [prud] *s* pudibondo

prudence ['prudəns] *s* prudenza

prudent ['prudənt] *adj* prudente

pruder·y ['prudəri] *s* (**-ies**) attitudine pudibonda

prudish ['prudɪʃ] *adj* pudibondo

prune [prun] *s* prugna secca || *tr* potare

pry [praɪ] *v* (*pret & pp* **pried**) *tr*—**to pry open** forzare con una leva; **to pry s.th out of s.o.** strappare qlco a qlcu || *intr* intromettersi, cacciarsi

psalm [sam] *s* salmo

pseudo ['sudo] or ['sjudo] *adj* falso, finto, sedicente

pseudonym ['sudənɪm] or ['sjudənɪm] *s* pseudonimo

psychiatrist [saɪ'kaɪ-ətrɪst] *s* psichiatra *mf*

psychiatry [saɪ'kaɪ-ətri] *s* psichiatria

psychic ['saɪkɪk] *adj* psichico || *s* medium *mf*

psychoanaly·sis [,saɪko-ə'nælɪsɪs] - *s* psicanalisi *f*

psychoanalyze [,saɪko'ænə,laɪz] *tr* psicanalizzare

psychologic(al) [,saɪko'lɑdʒɪk(əl)] *adj* psicologico

psychologist [saɪ'kɑlədʒɪst] *s* psicologo

psycholo·gy [saɪ'kɑlədʒi] *s* (**-gies**) psicologia

psychopath ['saɪkə,pæθ] *s* psicopatico

psycho·sis [saɪ'kosɪs] *s* (**-ses** [siz]) psicosi *f*

psychotic [saɪ'kɑtɪk] *adj* psicotico

pub [pʌb] *s* (Brit) taverna, bar *m*

puberty ['pjubərti] *s* pubertà *f*

public ['pʌblɪk] *adj & s* pubblico

pub'lic-address' sys'tem *s* sistema *m* d'amplificazione per discorsi in pubblico

publication [,pʌblɪ'keʃən] *s* pubblicazione

pub'lic convey'ance *s* veicolo di servizi pubblici

publicity [pʌb'lɪsɪti] *s* pubblicità *f*

publicize ['pʌblɪ,saɪz] *tr* pubblicare, divulgare

pub'lic li'brary *s* biblioteca comunale

pub'lic-opin'ion poll' *s* sondaggio d'opinioni

pub'lic pros'ecutor *s* pubblico ministero

pub'lic school' *s* (U.S.A.) scuola dell'obbligo; (Brit) scuola privata, collegio

pub'lic serv'ant *s* funzionario pubblico

pub'lic speak'ing *s* oratoria

pub'lic spir'it *s* civismo

pub'lic toi'let *s* gabinetto pubblico

pub'lic util'ity *s* impresa di servizio pubblico; **public utilities** azioni emesse da imprese di servizi pubblici

publish ['pʌblɪʃ] *tr* pubblicare

publisher ['pʌblɪʃər] *s* editore *m*; (journ) direttore *m* responsabile

pub'lishing house' *s* casa editrice

pucker ['pʌkər] *s* grinza || *tr* raggrinzire || *intr* raggrinzirsi

pudding ['pudɪŋ] *s* budino, torta

puddle ['pʌdəl] *s* pozza, pozzanghera || *intr* diguazzare

pudg·y ['pʌdʒi] *adj* (**-ier; -iest**) grassoccio

puerile ['pju-ərɪl] *adj* puerile

Puerto Rican ['pwerto'rikən] *adj & s* portoricano

puff [pʌf] *s* soffio, sbuffo; (*e.g., of cigar*) boccata; (*pad*) piumino; (*exaggerated praise*) pistolotto; (culin) bignè *m* || *tr* sbuffare; gonfiare; adulare || *intr* soffiare, sbuffare; (*to breathe heavily*) ansimare, ansare; gonfiarsi; tirare boccate

puff' paste' *s* pasta sfoglia

pugilist ['pjudʒɪlɪst] *s* pugile *m*

pug-nosed ['pʌg,nozd] *adj* camuso

puke [pjuk] *tr & intr* (slang) vomitare

pull [pul] *s* tiro; (*act of drawing in*) tirata; (*handle*) tirante *m*; (slang) influenza, appoggi *mpl* || *tr* tirare; (*a tooth*) cavare; (*a muscle*) strappare;

(a punch) (coll) limitare la forza di; **to pull apart** fare a pezzi; **to pull down** abbattere; degradare; **to pull on** *(e.g., one's pants)* infilarsi; **to pull oneself together** ricomporsi; **to pull s.o.'s leg** beffarsi di qlcu || *intr* tirare; **to pull apart** andare a pezzi; **to pull at** tirare; **to pull away** andarsene; **to pull for** (coll) fare il tifo per; **to pull in** *(said of a train)* arrivare, entrare in stazione; **to pull out** *(said of a train)* partire; **to pull through** guarire, riuscire a cavarsela; **to pull up to** avanzare fino a

pullet ['pulɪt] *s* pollastra

pulley ['pulɪ] *s* puleggia, carrucola

pulp [pʌlp] *s* polpa; *(for making paper)* pasta

pulpit ['pulpɪt] *s* pulpito

pulsate ['pʌlset] *intr* pulsare

pulsation [pʌl'se/ən] *s* pulsazione

pulse [pʌls] *s* polso; **to feel or take the pulse** of tastare il polso a

pulverize ['pʌlvə‚raɪz] *tr* polverizzare

pum'ice stone' *s* ['pʌmɪs] *s* pomice *f*, pietra pomice

pum·mel ['pʌməl] *v (pret & pp -meled or -melled; ger -meling or -melling) tr* prendere a pugni

pump [pʌmp] *s* pompa; *(slipper)* scarpina || *tr* pompare; (coll) cavare un segreto a; **to pump up** pompare

pumpkin ['pʌmpkɪn] *or* ['puŋkɪn] *s* zucca

pump-priming ['pʌmp‚praɪmɪŋ] *s* stimolo governativo per sostentare l'economia

pun [pʌn] *s* gioco di parole || *v (pret & pp punned; ger punning) intr* fare giochi di parole

punch [pʌnt/] *s* pugno; *(tool)* punteruolo, punzone *m; (drink)* ponce *m;* (coll) forza || *tr* dare un pugno a; *(metal)* punzonare; *(a ticket)* perforare || **Punch** *s* Pulcinella *m;* **pleased as Punch** soddisfattissimo

punch' bowl' *s* vaso per il ponce

punch' card' *s* scheda perforata

punch' clock' *s* orologio di controllo

punch'-drunk *adj* stordito

punched' tape' *s* nastro perforato

punch'ing bag' *s* sacco

punch' line' *s* perfinire *m*, motto finale

punctilious [pʌŋk'tɪlɪ·əs] *adj* cerimonioso, pignolo

punctual ['pʌŋkt/u·əl] *adj* puntuale

punctuate ['pʌŋkt/u‚et] *tr* punteggiare

punctuation [‚pʌŋkt/u'e/ən] *s* punteggiatura

punctua'tion mark' *s* segno d'interpunzione

puncture ['pʌŋkt/ər] *s* puntura; *(hole)* bucatura; **to have a puncture** avere una gomma a terra || *tr* bucare, perforare || *intr* essere bucato

punct'ure-proof' *adj* antiperforante

pundit ['pʌndɪt] *s* esperto, autorità *f*

pungent ['pʌndʒənt] *adj* pungente

punish ['pʌnɪ/] *tr* punire

punishment ['pʌnɪ/mənt] *s* punizione, castigo

punk [pʌŋk] *adj* (slang) di pessima qualità || *s* esca; *(decayed wood)* legno marcio; (slang) malandrino

punster ['pʌnstər] *s* freddurista *mf*

punt [pʌnt] *s* (football) calcio dato al pallone prima che tocchi il terreno

pu·ny ['pjuni] *adj (-nier; -niest)* insignificante, meschino; *(weak)* debole

pup [pʌp] *s* cucciolo

pupil ['pjupəl] *s* allievo, scolaro; (anat) pupilla

puppet ['pʌpɪt] *s* marionetta, burattino; (fig) fantoccio

puppeteer [‚pʌpɪ'tɪr] *s* burattinaio

pup'pet gov'ernment *s* governo fantoccio or pupazzo

pup'pet show' *s* spettacolo di marionette

pup·py ['pʌpi] *s (-pies)* cucciolo

pup'py love' *s* amore *m* giovanile

purchase ['pʌrt/əs] *s* compra, acquisto; *(grip)* presa, leva || *tr* comprare, acquistare

pur'chasing pow'er *s* potere *m* d'acquisto

pure [pjur] *adj* puro

purgative ['pʌrgətɪv] *adj* purgativo || *s* purga

purge [pʌrdʒ] *s* purga || *tr* purgare

puri·fy ['pjuri‚faɪ] *v (pret & pp -fied) tr* purificare || *intr* purificarsi

puritan ['pjuritən] *adj & s* puritano || **Puritan** *adj & s* puritano

purity ['pjuriti] *s* purezza

purloin [pər'lɔɪn] *tr & intr* rubare

purple ['pʌrpəl] *adj* purpureo || *s* porpora

purport ['pʌrport] *s* senso, significato || [pər'port] *tr* significare; **to purport to + inf** pretendere di + *inf*

purpose ['pʌrpəs] *s* scopo, fine, *m;* **on purpose** apposta; **to good purpose** con buoni risultati; **to no purpose** inutilmente; **to serve one's purpose** fare al caso proprio

purposely ['pʌrpəsli] *adv* a bella posta, apposta

purr [pʌr] *s* ronfare *m* || *intr* fare le fusa

purse [pʌrs] *s* borsa; *(woman's handbag)* borsetta; *(for men)* borsetto || *tr (one's lips)* arricciare

purser ['pʌrsər] *s* commissario di bordo

purse' snatch'er ['snæt/ər] *s* borsaiolo

purse' strings' *spl* cordini *mpl* della borsa; **to hold the purse strings** controllare le spese

purslane ['pʌrslen] *or* ['pʌrslɪn] *s* (bot) porcellana

pursue [pər'su] *or* [pər'sju] *tr* perseguire; *(to harass)* perseguitare; *(a career)* proseguire

pursuit [pər'sut] *or* [pər'sjut] *s* inseguimento, caccia; occupazione, esercizio

pursuit' plane' *s* caccia *m*

purvey [pər've] *tr* provvedere, fornire

pus [pʌs] *s* pus *m*

push [pu/] *s* spinta; *(advance)* avanzata; (coll) impulso, energia || *tr* premere, spingere; *(a product)* promuovere la vendita di; dare impulso a; *(narcotics)* (slang) spacciare; **to**

push around (coll) dare spintoni a;
(fig) fare pressione su; **to push back**
ricacciare ‖ *intr* spingere; **to push
ahead** avanzarsi a spintoni, avanzarsi; **to push on** avanzare
push' but'ton *s* pulsante *m*, bottone *m*
push'-button con'trol *s* controllo a pul-
santi
push'cart' *s* carretto a mano
pusher ['puʃər] *adj* spingente; (aer)
propulsivo ‖ *s* spingitore *m*; (aer)
aeroplano a elica propulsiva; (slang)
spacciatore *m* di stupefacenti
pushing ['puʃɪŋ] *adj* aggressivo, intraprendente
puss [pus] *s* micio
puss' in the cor'ner *s* gioco dei quattro
cantoni
puss·y ['pusi] *s* (-ies) micio
puss'y wil'low *s* salice americano a gat-
tini
pustule ['pʌstʃul] *s* pustola
put [put] *v* (*pret & pp* **put;** *ger* **putting**)
tr mettere; (*to estimate*) stimare; (*a
question*) rivolgere; (*to throw*) lanciare; imporre; **to put across** (slang)
far accettare; **to put aside, away** or
by mettere da parte; **to put down** annotare; (*to suppress*) reprimere; **to
put off** differire; evadere; **to put on**
(*clothes*) mettersi; (*a brake*) azionare; (*to assume*) fingere; (*airs*)
darsi; **to put out** spegnere; imbarazzare; incomodare; deludere; annoiare, irritare; (*of a game*) espellere;
to put it over on s.o. fargliela a qlcu;
to put off rinviare; **to put over** mandare ad effetto; **to put to flight** mettere in fuga; **to put to shame** svergognare; **to put through** portare a

termine; **to put up** offrire; mettere
in conserva; alloggiare; costruire;
(*money*) contribuire; (coll) incitare
‖ *intr* dirigersi; **to put to sea** mettersi in mare; **to put up** prendere
alloggio; **to put up with** tollerare
put'-out' *adj* sconcertato, seccato
putrid ['pjutrɪd] *adj* putrido
Putsch [putʃ] *s* tentativo di sollevazione, sollevazione
putter ['pʌtər] *intr* occuparsi di inezie;
to putter about andare avanti e indietro
put·ty ['pʌti] *s* (-ties) stucco, mastice
m ‖ *v* (*pret & pp* -**tied**) *tr* stuccare
put'ty knife' *s* spatola
put'-up' *adj* (coll) complottato
puzzle ['pʌzəl] *s* enigma *m*; (*toy*) indovinello ‖ *tr* rendere perplesso, confondere; **to puzzle out** decifrare ‖
intr essere perplesso
puzzler ['pʌzlər] *s* enigma *m*
puzzling ['pʌzlɪŋ] *adj* enigmatico
pyg·my ['pɪgmi] *s* (-mies) pigmeo
pylon *s* pilone *m*
pyramid ['pɪrəmɪd] *s* piramide *f* ‖ *tr*
(*e.g., costs*) aumentare gradualmente;
(*one's money*) aumentare giocando in
margine
pyre [paɪr] *s* pira
Pyrenees ['pɪrɪ ,niz] *spl* Pirenei *mpl*
pyrites [paɪ'raɪtiz] or ['paɪraɪts] *s*
pirite *f*
pyrotechnics [,paɪrə'tɛknɪks] *spl* piro-
tecnica
python ['paɪθən] or ['paɪθən] *s* pitone
m
pythoness ['paɪθənɪs] *s* pitonessa
pyx [pɪks] *s* (eccl) pisside *f*

Q

Q, q [kju] *s* diciassettesima lettera del-
l'alfabeto inglese
quack [kwæk] *adj* falso ‖ *s* medicastro;
ciarlatano; qua qua *m* ‖ *intr* (*said
of a duck*) fare qua qua
quacker·y ['kwækəri] *s* (-ies) ciarlataneria
quadrangle ['kwad ,ræŋgəl] *s* quadran-
golo
quadrant ['kwadrənt] *s* quadrante *m*
quadruped ['kwadru ,pɛd] *adj & s*
quadrupede *m*
quadruple ['kwadrupəl] or [kwa'dru-
pəl] *adj* quadruplo; (*alliance*) quadruplice ‖ *s* quadruplo ‖ *tr* quadruplicare ‖ *intr* quadruplicarsi
quaff [kwaf] or [kwæf] *s* lungo sorso ‖
tr & intr bere a lunghi sorsi
quail [kwel] *s* quaglia ‖ *intr* sgomen-
tarsi
quaint [kwent] *adj* strano, strambo,
originale; all'antica ma bello
quake [kwek] *s* terremoto ‖ *intr* tremare, sussultare
Quaker ['kwekər] *adj & s* quacchero,
quacquero

Quak'er meet'ing *s* riunione di quac-
cheri; (coll) riunione in cui si parla
poco
quali·fy ['kwali ,faɪ] *v* (*pret & pp*
-**fied**) *tr* qualificare; (*for a profession*) abilitare ‖ *intr* qualificarsi; abi-
litarsi
quali·ty ['kwaliti] *s* (-ties) qualità *f*;
(*of a sound*) timbro
qualm [kwam] *s* scrupolo di coscienza;
preoccupazione; nausea
quanda·ry ['kwandəri] *s* (-ries) incertezza, perplessità *f*
quanti·ty ['kwantiti] *s* (-ties) quantità *f*
quan·tum ['kwantəm] *adj* quantistico
‖ *s* (-ta [tə]) quanto
quarantine ['kwarən ,tin] or ['kwərən-
,tin] *s* quarantena ‖ *tr* mettere in
quarantena
quar·rel ['kwarəl] or ['kwɔrəl] *s* litigio, diverbio; **to have no quarrel with**
non essere in disaccordo con; **to pick
a quarrel with** venire a diverbio con
‖ *v* (*pret & pp* -**reled** or -**relled;** *ger*
-**reling** or -**relling**) *intr* litigare

quarrelsome [ˈkwɑrəlsəm] or [ˈkwɔrəl-səm] adj litigioso, rissoso

quar·ry [ˈkwɑri] or [ˈkwɔri] s (-ries) cava; (game) selvaggina, cacciagione ‖ v (pret & pp -ried) tr cavare

quart [kwɔrt] s quarto di gallone

quarter [ˈkwɔrtər] adj quarto ‖ s quarto; moneta di un quarto di dollaro; (three months) trimestre m; (of town) quartiere m; **a quarter after one** l'una e un quarto; **a quarter of an hour** un quarto d'ora; **a quarter to one** l'una meno un quarto; **at close quarters** corpo a corpo; **quarters** quartiere m ‖ tr squartare; (soldiers) accasermare

quar'ter-deck' s cassero

quar'ter-hour' s quarto d'ora; **on the quarter-hour** ogni quindici minuti allo scoccare del quarto d'ora

quarter·ly [ˈkwɔrtərli] adj trimestrale ‖ s (-lies) pubblicazione trimestrale ‖ adv trimestralmente

quar'ter-mas'ter s (mil) intendente m militare; (nav) secondo capo

quartet [kwɔrˈtɛt] s quartetto

quartz [kwɔrts] s quarzo

quasar [ˈkwesɑr] s (astr) radiostella

quash [kwɑʃ] tr sopprimere; annullare

quaver [ˈkwevər] s tremito; (mus) tremolo; (mus) croma ‖ intr tremare

quay [ki] s molo

queen [kwin] s regina; (in cards) donna; (chess) regina

queen' bee' s ape regina; (fig) basilessa

queen' dow'ager s regina vedova

queen·ly [ˈkwinli] adj (-lier; -liest) da regina; regio

queen' moth'er s regina madre

queen' post' s monaco

queen's' Eng'lish s inglese corretto

queer [kwɪr] adj strano, curioso; poco bene, indisposto; falso; (slang) omosessuale ‖ s (slang) finocchio ‖ tr rovinare, mettere in pericolo

quell [kwɛl] tr soffocare, domare; (pain) calmare

quench [kwɛntʃ] tr (fire, thirst) spegnere, estinguere; (rebellion) soffocare; (elec) ammortizzare

que·ry [ˈkwɪri] s (-ries) domanda; punto interrogativo; dubbio ‖ v (pret & pp -ried) tr interrogare; (typ) apporre punto interrogativo a

quest [kwɛst] s ricerca; **in quest of** in cerca di

question [ˈkwɛstʃən] s domanda; problema m, quesito; (matter) questione; **beyond question** senza dubbio; **out of the question** impossibile; **this is beside the question** questo non c'entra; **to ask a question** fare una domanda; **to be a question of** trattarsi di; **to call in** or **into question** mettere in dubbio; **without question** senza dubbio ‖ tr interrogare; mettere in dubbio; (pol) interpellare

questionable [ˈkwɛstʃənəbəl] adj discutibile

ques'tion mark' s punto interrogativo

questionnaire [ˌkwɛstʃənˈɛr] s questionario

queue [kju] s (of hair) codino; (of people) coda ‖ intr fare la coda

quibble [ˈkwɪbəl] intr sottilizzare

quick [kwɪk] adj pronto, sollecito; sbrigativo; veloce, rapido; vivo ‖ s— **the quick and the dead** i vivi e i morti; **to cut to the quick** toccare nel vivo

quicken [ˈkwɪkən] tr sveltire; animare; ravvivare

quick'lime' s calce viva

quick' lunch' s tavola calda

quickly [ˈkwɪkli] adv svelto, alla svelta; presto

quick'sand' s sabbia mobile

quick'-set'ting adj a presa rapida

quick'sil'ver s argento vivo

quick'work' s (naut) opera viva

quiet [ˈkwaɪ·ət] adj quieto; silenzioso; (com) calmo; **to keep quiet** stare zitto ‖ s quiete f, tranquillità f; pace f, calma ‖ tr quietare; calmare ‖ intr— **to quiet down** quietarsi, calmarsi

quill [kwɪl] s penna d'oca; (basal part of feather) calamo; (e.g., of porcupine) aculeo

quilt [kwɪlt] s trapunta, imbottita ‖ tr trapuntare

quince [kwɪns] s cotogna; (tree) cotogno

quinine [ˈkwaɪnaɪn] s (alkaloid) chinina; (salt of the alkaloid) chinino

quinsy [ˈkwɪnzi] s angina

quintessence [kwɪnˈtɛsəns] s quintessenza

quintet [kwɪnˈtɛt] s quintetto

quintuplet [kwɪnˈtjuplət] or [kwɪnˈtuplət] s gemello nato da un parto quintuplice

quip [kwɪp] s frizzo, uscita ‖ v (pret & pp quipped; ger quipping) tr & intr uscire a dire, dire come battuta

quire [kwaɪr] s ventiquattro fogli; (bb) quinterno

quirk [kwʌrk] s stranezza, manierismo; (quibble) cavillo; (sudden turn) mutamento improvviso

quit [kwɪt] adj libero; **to be quits** esser pari; **to call it quits** finirla, farla finita ‖ v (pret & pp quit or quitted; ger quitting) tr abbandonare ‖ intr andarsene; abbandonare l'impiego; smettere (di + inf)

quite [kwaɪt] adv completamente; molto, del tutto

quitter [ˈkwɪtər] s persona che abbandona facilmente

quiver [ˈkwɪvər] s fremito; (to hold arrows) faretra, turcasso ‖ intr fremere, tremare

quixotic [kwɪksˈɑtɪk] adj donchisciottesco

quiz [kwɪz] s (quizzes) esame m; interrogatorio ‖ v (pret & pp quizzed; ger quizzing) tr esaminare; interrogare

quiz' game' s quiz m

quiz' pro'gram s programma m di quiz

quiz' sec'tion s (educ) classe f a base di esercizi (e non di conferenze)

quizzical [ˈkwɪzɪkəl] adj strano, curioso; (derisive) canzonatore

quoin [kɔɪn] or [kwɔɪn] s cantone m,

pietra angolare; (*piece of wood*) zeppa; (*typ*) serraforme *m* ‖ *tr* fissare con serraforme

quoit [kwɔɪt] *or* [kɔɪt] *s* anello di corda o di metallo da lanciarsi come gioco; **quoits** *ssg* gioco consistente nel lancio di anelli su di un piolo

quondam [ˈkwɑndæm] *adj* quondam

quorum [ˈkwɔrəm] *s* quorum *m*

quota [ˈkwotə] *s* (*share*) quota; (*of imports*) contingentamento; (*of persons*) contingente *m*

quotation [kwoˈteʃən] *s* (*from a book*) citazione; (*of prices*) quotazione

quota'tion mark' *s* doppia virgola, virgoletta

quote [kwot] *s* citazione, richiamo ‖ *tr & intr* citare, richiamare; (*com*) quotare; **quote** cito

quotient [ˈkwoʃənt] *s* quoziente *m*

R

R, r [ɑr] *s* diciottesima lettera dell'alfabeto inglese

rabbet [ˈræbɪt] *s* scanalatura, incastro ‖ *tr* scanalare, incastrare

rab·bi [ˈræbaɪ] *s* (**-bis**) rabbino

rabbit [ˈræbɪt] *s* coniglio

rab'bit ears' *spl* (telv) doppia antenna a stilo

rabble [ˈræbəl] *s* gentaglia, marmaglia

rab'ble-rous'er [ˈrauzər] *s* arruffapopoli *m*

rabies [ˈrebiz] *or* [ˈrebɪˌiz] *s* rabbia

raccoon [ræˈkun] *s* procione *m*

race [res] *s* (*branch of human stock*) razza; (*contest in speed*) corsa; (*contest of any kind*) gara; (*channel*) canale *m* di adduzione ‖ *tr* far correre; gareggiare (in velocità) con; (*a motor*) imballare ‖ *intr* correre; fare le corse; (*said of a motor*) imballarsi; (naut) fare le regate

race' horse' *s* cavallo da corsa

race' ri'ot *s* contestazione di razza

race' track' *s* pista

racial [ˈreʃəl] *adj* razziale

rac'ing car' *s* automobile *f* da corsa

rack [ræk] *s* (*to hang clothes*) attaccapanni *m*; (*framework to hold fodder, baggage, guns, etc.*) rastrelliera; (mach) cremagliera; **to go to rack and ruin** andare a rotoli ‖ *tr* tormentare, torturare; **to rack off** (*wine*) travasare; **to rack one's brains** rompersi il capo, lambiccarsi il cervello

racket [ˈrækɪt] *s* racchetta; (*noise*) chiasso, gazzarra; (*coll*) racket *m*; **to raise a racket** fare gazzarra

racketeer [ˌrækɪˈtɪr] *s* chi è nel racket; (*engaged in extortion*) ricattatore *m* ‖ *intr* essere nel racket; fare il ricattatore

rack' rail'way *s* ferrovia a cremagliera

rac·y [ˈresi] *adj* (**-ier; -iest**) pungente, vigoroso; piccante

radar [ˈredar] *s* radar *m*

radiant [ˈredɪənt] *adj* raggiante, radioso

radiate [ˈredɪˌet] *tr* irradiare ‖ *intr* irradiarsi

radiation [ˌredɪˈeʃən] *s* radiazione

radia'tion sick'ness *s* malattia causata da radiazione atomica

radiator [ˈredɪˌetər] *s* radiatore *m*

ra'diator cap' *s* tappo del radiatore

radical [ˈrædɪkəl] *adj* radicale ‖ *s* radicale *mf*; (chem, math) radicale *m*

radi·o [ˈredɪˌo] *s* (**-os**) radio *f*; radiogramma *m* ‖ *tr* radiotrasmettere

radioactive [ˌredɪ·oˈæktɪv] *adj* radioattivo

ra'dio am'ateur *s* radioamatore *m*

ra'dio announc'er *s* radioannunciatore *m*

ra'dio bea'con *s* radiofaro

ra'dio·broad'cast *s* radiodiffusione ‖ *tr* radiodiffondere

ra'dio com'pass *s* radiobussola

ra'dio·fre'quency *s* radiofrequenza

ra'dio lis'tener *s* radioascoltatore *m*

radiology [ˌredɪˈɑlədʒi] *s* radiologia

ra'dio net'work *s* rete *f*

ra'dio news'caster *s* radiocronista *mf*

ra'dio·pho'to *s* (**-tos**) (coll) radiofoto *f*

ra'dio set' *s* radioricevente *f*

ra'dio sta'tion *s* stazione radio

radish [ˈrædɪʃ] *s* ravanello

radium [ˈredɪəm] *s* radio

radi·us [ˈredɪ·əs] *s* (**-i** [ˌaɪ] *or* **-uses**) (anat) radio; (fig, geom) raggio; **within a radius of** entro un raggio di

raffle [ˈræfəl] *s* riffa ‖ *tr* sorteggiare

raft [ræft] *or* [rɑft] *s* zattera; (coll) mucchio

rafter [ˈræftər] *or* [ˈrɑftər] *s* puntone *m*

rag [ræg] *s* straccio; **to chew the rag** (slang) chiacchierare

ragamuffin [ˈrægəˌmʌfɪn] *s* straccione *m*

rag' doll' *s* bambola di pezza

rage [redʒ] *s* rabbia; **to be all the rage** furoreggiare; **to fly into a rage** montare in bestia ‖ *intr* infuriare

ragged [ˈrægɪd] *adj* cencioso; (*torn*) stracciato; (*edge*) rozzo, scabroso

ragpicker [ˈrægˌpɪkər] *s* cenciaiolo, straccivendolo

rag'weed' *s* (bot) ambrosia

raid [red] *s* irruzione, razzia ‖ *tr* scorrere ‖ *intr* scorrazzare

rail [rel] *s* (*of fence*) stecca, traversa; (*fence*) stecconata; (*railing*) ringhiera; (rr) rotaia; **by rail** per ferrovia; **rails** titoli *mpl* ferroviari ‖ *intr* inveire; **to rail at** inveire contro

rail'car' *s* automotrice *f*

rail' fence' *s* stecconata fatta di traverse piallate alla buona

rail'head' s fine f della linea ferroviaria
railing ['relɪŋ] s ringhiera
rail'road' adj ferroviario || s ferrovia ||
tr trasportare in ferrovia; (a bill) far
passare precipitosamente; (coll) imprigionare falsamente
rail'road cros'sing s passaggio a livello
rail'road'er s ferroviere m
rail'way' s ferrovia, strada ferrata
raiment ['remənt] s (lit) abbigliamento
rain [ren] s pioggia; **rain or shine** con
qualunque tempo || tr fare piovere;
(lit) piovere; **to rain cats and dogs**
piovere a catinelle; **to rain out** far
sospendere per via della pioggia ||
intr piovere
rainbow ['ren,bo] s arcobaleno
rain'coat' s impermeabile m
rain'fall' s acquazzone m; piovosità f
rain•y ['reni] adj (-ier; -iest) piovoso,
piovano
rain'y day' s giorno piovoso; (fig)
tempi mpl difficili
raise [rez] s aumento || tr levare, rial-
zare; (children, animals) allevare; (to
build) tirare su; (a question) sollevare; (the dead) risollevare; (to increase) aumentare; (money) raccogliere; (a siege) togliere; (at cards)
rilanciare; (anchor) salpare; (math)
elevare
raisin ['rezən] s grano d'uva passa,
grano d'uva secca; **raisins** uva passa,
uva secca
rake [rek] s rastrello; (person) porcac-
cione m, libertino || tr rastrellare; **to
rake in money** far soldoni
rake'-off' s (coll) compenso illecito,
bustarella; (coll) sconto
rakish ['rekɪʃ] adj libertino; brioso,
vivace; **to wear one's hat at a rakish
angle** portare il cappello sulle ventitré
ral•ly ['ræli] s (-lies) riunione, comi-
zio; adunata; ricupero || v (pret &
pp -lied) tr riunire, chiamare a rac-
colta; rianimare || intr riunirsi; riu-
marsi; (said of stock prices) rialzarsi;
rimettersi in forze; **to rally to the
side of** correre all'aiuto di
ram [ræm] s (male sheep) montone m;
(mil) ariete m; (nav) sperone m;
(mach) maglio del battipalo || v (pret
& pp **rammed**; ger **ramming**) tr battere, sbattere contro; cacciare, con-
ficcare; forzare; (nav) speronare ||
intr—**to ram into** sbattere contro
ramble ['ræmbəl] s rampa || intr (to
wander around) gironzolare; vagare;
(said of a vine) crescere disordinata-
mente; (said, e.g., of a river) serpeggiare; (fig) scorrazzare, divagare
rami•fy ['ræmɪ,faɪ] v (pret & pp
-fied) tr ramificare || intr ramificarsi
ram'jet en'gine s statoreattore m
ramp [ræmp] s rampa
rampage ['ræmpedʒ] s stato d'eccitazione; **to go on a rampage** infierire,
comportarsi furiosamente
rampart ['ræmpɑrt] s baluardo, mura-
glione m

ram'rod' s (for ramming) (mil) bacchetta; (for cleaning) (mil) scovolo
ram'shack'le adj cadente, in rovina
ranch [ræntʃ] s fattoria agricola
rancid ['rænsɪd] adj rancido
rancor ['ræŋkər] s rancore m
random ['rændəm] adj fortuito; **at random** alla rinfusa, a casaccio
range [rendʒ] s (row) fila; (rank)
classe f; (distance) portata; campo
di tiro a segno; raggio d'azione;
(scope) gamma; (for grazing) pascolo; (stove) fornello, cucina economica; **within range of** alla portata
di || tr allineare; ordinare; passare
attraverso; mandare al pascolo || intr
variare, fluttuare; estendersi; trovarsi; (mil) portare; **to range over**
percorrere; (fig) trattare
range' find'er s telemetro
rank [ræŋk] adj esuberante; grossolano; denso, spesso; puzzolente; ec-
cessivo; completo, assoluto || s
rango, grado; (row) fila, schiera;
ranks truppe fpl, ranghi mpl || tr
arrangiare, allineare; classificare;
avere rango superiore a || intr avere
il massimo rango; **to rank high** avere
un'alta posizione; **to rank low** avere
una posizione bassa; **to rank with**
essere allo stesso livello di
rank' and file' s truppa; massa
rankle ['ræŋkəl] tr irritare || intr ina-
sprirsi
ransack ['rænsæk] tr (to search thoroughly) frugare, rovistare; (to pillage) svaligiare, saccheggiare
ransom ['rænsəm] s taglia, riscatto ||
tr riscattare
rant [rænt] intr farneticare, parlare a
vanvera
rap [ræp] s colpo, colpetto; **I don't
care a rap** non m'importa un fico; **to
take the rap** (slang) prendersi la
colpa || v (pret & pp **rapped**; ger
rapping) tr dare colpi a; battere; **to
rap out** (e.g., a command) lanciare ||
intr dare colpi, bussare
rapacious [rə'peʃəs] adj rapace
rape [rep] s rapimento; (of a woman)
stupro; (bot) ravizzone m || tr rapire;
forzare, violentare
rapid ['ræpɪd] adj rapido || **rapids** spl
rapide fpl
rap'id-fire' adj a tiro rapido
rapidity [rə'pɪdəti] s rapidità f
rapier ['repɪ·ər] s spada, stocco
rapt [ræpt] adj assorto; estatico
rapture ['ræptʃər] s rapimento, estasi f
rare [rer] adj raro; (thinly distributed)
rado; (gas) rarefatto; (meat) al sangue; (gem) prezioso
rare'-earth' met'al s metallo delle terre
rare
rare•fy ['rerɪ,faɪ] v (pret & pp -fied)
tr rarefare || intr rarefarsi
rarely ['rerli] adv di rado, raramente
rascal ['ræskəl] s briccone m, birbante
m
rash [ræʃ] adj temerario, precipitato
|| s eruzione; (fig) mucchio
rasp [ræsp] or [rɑsp] s raspa; rumore

m di raspa || *tr* raspare; irritare; dire con voce roca || *intr* fare rumore raspante

raspber·ry ['ræz‚beri] *or* ['raz‚beri] *s* (-ries) lampone *m*; (slang) pernacchia

rat [ræt] *s* ratto; (*to give fullness to hair*) posticcio; (slang) traditore *m*; **to smell a rat** (coll) subodorare un inganno

ratchet ['rætʃɪt] *s* nottolino

rate [ret] *s* (*of interest*) saggio, tasso; prezzo; costo; velocità *f*; (*degree of action*) ragione; tariffa; **at any rate** ad ogni modo; **at the rate of** in ragione di || *tr* valutare, classificare || *intr* essere considerato; essere classificato

rate' of exchange' *s* corso del cambio

rather ['ræðər] *or* ['raðər] *adv* piuttosto; a preferenza; per meglio dire; bensì; discretamente; **rather than** piuttosto di || *interj* e come!

rati·fy ['rætɪ‚faɪ] *v* (*pret & pp* -fied) *tr* ratificare, sancire

rating ['retɪŋ] *s* classifica; (nav) grado; (com) valutazione

ra·tio ['reʃo] *or* ['reʃɪ‚o] *s* (-tios) ragione, rapporto; proporzione

ration ['reʃən] *or* ['ræʃən] *s* razione || *tr* razionare

rational ['ræʃənəl] *adj* razionale

ra'tion book' *s* tessera di razionamento

rat' poi'son *s* veleno per i topi

rat' race' *s* (coll) corsa dei barberi

rattle ['rætəl] *s* (*sharp sounds*) fracasso; (*child's toy*) sonaglio; (*noise-making device*) raganella; (*in throat*) rantolo || *tr* scuotere; (*to confuse*) sconcertare; **to rattle off** dire rapidamente, snocciolare || *intr* risuonare; scuotersi; cianciare

rat'tle·snake' *s* serpente *m* a sonagli

rat'trap' *s* trappola per topi; (*hovel*) topaia; (*jam*) (fig) frangente *m*

raucous ['rɔkəs] *adj* rauco

ravage ['rævɪdʒ] *s* distruzione; ravages (*of time*) oltraggio || *tr* distruggere, disfare

rave [rev] *intr* farneticare, delirare; infuriare; andare in estasi; **to rave about** levare alle stelle

raven ['revən] *s* corvo

ravenous ['rævənəs] *adj* famelico

ravine [rə'vin] *s* canalone *m*, burrone *m*

ravish ['rævɪʃ] *tr* incantare, entusiasmare; rapire; (*a woman*) stuprare

raw [rɔ] *adj* crudo; (*e.g., silk*) grezzo; (*flesh*) vivo; inesperto

raw' deal' *s* trattamento brutale e ingiusto

raw'hide' *s* pelle greggia

raw' mate'rial *s* materia prima

ray [re] *s* raggio; (*fish*) razza

rayon ['re·ɑn] *s* raion *m*

raze [rez] *tr* radere al suolo

razor ['rezər] *s* rasoio

ra'zor blade' *s* lametta

ra'zor strop' *s* coramella

razz [ræz] *s* (slang) pernacchia || *tr* (slang) prendere in giro

reach [ritʃ] *s* portata; estensione; out

of **reach** (**of**) fuori della portata (di); oltre alle possibilità (di); fuori tiro (di); **within reach of** alla portata di || *tr* raggiungere; toccare; (*customers*) guadagnare || *intr* estendere la mano; **to reach for** cercare di raggiungere

react [rɪ'ækt] *intr* reagire

reaction [rɪ'ækʃən] *s* reazione

reactionar·y [rɪ'ækʃə‚neri] *adj* reazionario || *s* (-ies) reazionario

reactor [rɪ'æktər] *s* reattore *m*

read [rid] *v* (*pret & pp* read [rɛd]) *tr* leggere; (*s.o.'s thoughts*) leggere in; **to read over** ripassare || *intr* leggere; saper leggere; essere concepito, e.g., **your cable reads thus** il vostro telegramma è concepito così; leggersi, e.g., **this books reads easily** questo libro si legge facilmente; **to read on** continuare a leggere

reader ['ridər] *s* lettore *m*; libro di lettura, sillabo

readily ['redɪlɪ] *adv* velocemente; facilmente; di buona voglia

reading ['ridɪŋ] *s* lettura; dizione

read'ing desk' *s* leggio

read'ing glass' *s* lente *f* d'ingrandimento; **reading glasses** occhiali *mpl* per la lettura

read'ing lamp' *s* lampada da scrittoio

read'ing room' *s* sala di lettura

read·y ['redi] *adj* (-ier; -iest) pronto; disponibile; **to make ready** preparare; prepararsi || *v* (*pret & pp* -ied) *tr* preparare || *intr* prepararsi

read'y cash' *s* denaro contante

read'y-made cloth'ing *s* confezioni *fpl*

read'y-made suit' *s* vestito già fatto

reaffirm [‚ri·ə'fʌrm] *tr* riaffermare

reagent [rɪ'edʒənt] *s* reagente *m*

real ['ri·əl] *adj* effettivo, reale

re'al estate' *s* beni *mpl* immobili, proprietà *f* immobiliare

re'al-estate' *adj* immobiliare, fondiario

realism ['ri·ə‚lɪzəm] *s* realismo

realist ['ri·əlɪst] *s* realista *mf*

realistic [‚ri·ə'lɪstɪk] *adj* realistico

reali·ty [rɪ'ælɪti] *s* (-ties) realtà *f*

realize ['ri·ə‚laɪz] *tr* rendersi conto di; concretare; realizzare || *intr* convertire proprietà in contanti

realm [relm] *s* regno

realtor ['ri·əl‚tɔr] *or* ['ri·əltər] *s* (trademark) agente *m* d'immobili membro dell'associazione nazionale

realty ['ri·əlti] *s* proprietà *f* immobiliare

ream [rim] *s* risma; **reams** pagine *fpl* e pagine || *tr* alesare

reamer ['rimər] *s* (mach) alesatore *m*; (dentistry) fresa

reap [rip] *tr & intr* (*to cut*) mietere; (*to gather*) raccogliere

reaper ['ripər] *s* (*person*) mietitore *m*; (mach) mietitrice *f*

reappear [‚ri·ə'pɪr] *intr* ricomparire, riapparire

reappearance [‚ri·ə'pɪrəns] *s* riapparizione, ricomparsa

reapportionment [‚ri·ə'pɔrʃənmənt] *s* ridistribuzione

rear [rɪr] *adj* posteriore, di dietro || *s*

retro, di dietro; posteriore *m;* (mil) retroguardia || *tr* alzare, elevare; allevare, educare || *intr* (*said of a horse*) impennarsi

rear' ad'miral *s* contrammiraglio

rear' drive' *s* trazione posteriore

rear' end' *s* retro, di dietro; (coll) posteriore *m;* (aut) retrotreno

rearmament [ri'arməmənt] *s* riarmo

rear'-view mir'ror *s* specchietto retrovisivo

rear' win'dow *s* (aut) lunetta posteriore

reason ['rizən] *s* ragione; **by reason of** per causa di; **to bring s.o. to reason** indurre qlcu alla ragione; **to stand to reason** esser logico || *tr & intr* ragionare

reasonable ['rizənəbəl] *adj* ragionevole

reassessment [,ri-ə'sesmənt] *s* rivalutazione

reassure [,ri-ə'ʃur] *tr* rassicurare, riassicurare

reawaken [,ri-ə'wekən] *tr* risvegliare || *intr* risvegliarsi

rebate ['ribet] *or* [ri'bet] *s* ribasso || *tr* ribassare

rebel ['rebəl] *adj & s* ribelle *mf* || **re·bel** [ri'bel] *v* (*pret & pp* **-belled;** *ger* **-belling**) *intr* ribellarsi

rebellion [ri'beljən] *s* ribellione

rebellious [ri'beljəs] *adj* ribelle

re·bind [ri'baind] *v* (*pret & pp·* **bound** ['baund]) *tr* (bb) rilegare

rebirth ['ribʌrθ] *or* [ri'bʌrθ] *s* rinascita

rebore [ri'bor] *tr* rialesare, rettificare

rebound ['ri,baund] *or* [ri'baund] *s* rimbalzo || [ri'baund] *intr* rimbalzare

rebroad'casting sta'tion *s* stazione ripetitrice

rebuff [ri'bʌf] *s* rifiuto || *tr* respingere, rifiutare

re·build [ri'bild] *v* (*pret & pp* **-built** ['bilt]) *tr* ricostruire, riedificare

rebuke [ri'bjuk] *s* rabbuffo || *tr* rabbuffare

re·but [ri'bʌt] *v* (*pret & pp* **-butted;** *ger* **-butting**) *tr* confutare

rebuttal [ri'bʌtəl] *s* confutazione

recall [ri'kɔl] *or* ['rikɔl] *s* richiamo; revoca || [ri'kɔl] *tr* richiamare; ricordare, ricordarsi di; richiamare alla memoria

recant [ri'kænt] *tr* ritrattare || *intr* ritrattarsi

re·cap ['ri,kæp] *or* [ri'kæp] *v* (*pret & pp* **-capped;** *ger* **-capping**) *tr* ricopiolare, riepilogare; (*a tire*) rifare il battistrada a

recapitulation [,rikə,pitʃə'leʃən] *s* ricapitolazione, riepilogo

re·cast ['ri,kæst] *or* ['ri,kɑst] *s* rifusione || [ri'kæst] *or* [ri'kɑst] *v* (*pret & pp* **-cast**) *tr* rifondere

recede [ri'sid] *intr* ritirarsi, allontanarsi; recedere, retrocedere; (*said, e.g., of chin*) sfuggire

receipt [ri'sit] *s* ricevimento; (*acknowledgment of payment*) ricevuta; (*recipe*) ricetta; **receipts** incasso, introito || *tr* quietanzare

receive [ri'siv] *tr* ricevere; (*stolen*

---

goods) ricettare; (*to have inflicted upon one*) subire || *intr* ricevere

receiver [ri'sivər] *s* ricevitore *m;* ricettatore *m;* (law) curatore *m* fallimentare; (telp) auricolare *m*

receiv'ing set' *s* apparecchio radioricevente

receiv'ing tell'er *s* cassiere *m* incaricato delle riscossioni

recent ['risənt] *adj* recente

recently ['risəntli] *adv* recentemente, di recente

receptacle [ri'septəkəl] *s* recipiente *m;* (elec) presa

reception [ri'sepʃən] *s* accoglienza; (*function*) ricevimento

recep'tion desk' *s* ufficio informazioni, bureau *m*

receptionist [ri'sepʃənist] *s* accoglitrice *f;* (*male*) usciere *m*

receptive [ri'septiv] *adj* ricettivo

recess [ri'ses] *or* ['rises] *s* intermezzo, interludio; ora di ricreazione; (*in a line*) rientranza; (*in a wall*) nicchia, alcova; (fig) recesso || [ri'ses] *tr* aggiornare, dare vacanza a; incassare, mettere in una nicchia || *intr* aggiornarsi, prendersi vacanza

recession [ri'seʃən] *s* ritirata; processione finale; (com) recessione

recipe ['resɪ,pi] *s* ricetta

reciprocal [ri'sɪprəkəl] *adj* reciproco

reciprocity [,resɪ'prasiti] *s* reciprocità *f*

recital [ri'saitəl] *s* narrazione; (*of music or poetry*) recital *m*

recite [ri'sait] *tr* raccontare; (*music or poetry*) recitare

reckless ['reklɪs] *adj* temerario, spericolato

reckon ['rekən] *tr* calcolare; considerare; (coll) supporre || *intr* contare; **to reckon with** prevedere, tener conto di

reclaim [ri'klem] *tr* (*land*) sanare, prosciugare; (*substances*) rigenerare; (fig) rigenerare

recline [ri'klain] *tr* reclinare || *intr* reclinarsi, adagiarsi

recluse [ri'klus] *or* ['reklus] *adj & s* recluso

recognition [,rekəg'nɪʃən] *s* riconoscimento

recognize ['rekəg,naiz] *tr* riconoscere

recoil [ri'kɔil] *s* indietreggiamento; (*of a firearm*) rinculo || *intr* indietreggiare; rinculare

recollect [,rekə'lekt] *tr & intr* ricordare

recollection [,rekə'lekʃən] *s* ricordo

recommend [,rekə'mend] *tr* raccomandare

recompense ['rekəm,pens] *s* ricompensa || *tr* ricompensare

reconcile ['rekən,sail] *tr* riconciliare; **to reconcile oneself** rassegnarsi

reconnaissance [ri'kanisəns] *s* ricognizione

reconnoiter [,rekə'nɔitər] *or* [,rikə'nɔitər] *tr & intr* perlustrare

reconsider [,rikən'sidər] *tr* riconsiderare

reconstruct [ˌrikən'strʌkt] *tr* ricostruire

reconversion [ˌrikən'vʌrʒən] *s* riconversione

record ['rekərd] *s* registrazione; annotazione; (*official report*) verbale *m*, protocollo; (*criminal*) fedina sporca; (*of a phonograph*) disco; (*educ*) documenti *mpl* scolastici; (sports) record *m*, primato; **off the record** confidenziale; confidenzialmente; **records** annali *mpl*, documenti *mpl*; **to break a record** battere un record || [rɪ'kɔrd] *tr* registrare; mettere a verbale; (*e.g., a song*) incidere

rec'ord break'er *s* (sports) primatista *mf*

rec'ord chang'er ['tʃendʒər] *s* cambiadischi *m*

recorder [rɪ'kɔrdər] *s* (*apparatus*) registratore *m*; (law) cancelliere *m*; (mus) flauto a imboccatura a tubo

rec'ord hold'er *s* (sports) primatista *mf*

recording [rɪ'kɔrdɪŋ] *s* registrazione; (*of a record*) incisione; (*record*) disco

record'ing sec'retary *s* cancelliere *m*

rec'ord play'er *s* giradischi *m*

recount ['ri,kaʊnt] *s* nuovo conteggio || [ri'kaʊnt] *tr* (*to count again*) ricontare || [rɪ'kaʊnt] *tr* (*to narrate*) raccontare

recourse [rɪ'kɔrs] or ['rikɔrs] *s* ricorso; (com) rivalsa; **to have recourse** to ricorrere a

recover [rɪ'kʌvər] *tr* ricuperare, riacquistare; (*a substance*) rigenerare; **to recover consciousness** riaversi, riprendere conoscenza || *intr* rimettersi; guadagnare una causa

recover·y [rɪ'kʌvəri] *s* (-ies) ricupero; guarigione; **past recovery** incurabile

recreant ['rekri-ənt] *adj & s* codardo, traditore *m*

recreation [ˌrekri'eʃən] *s* ricreazione

recruit [rɪ'krut] *s* recluta || *tr & intr* reclutare

rectangle ['rek,tæŋgəl] *s* rettangolo

rectifier ['rektə,faɪ-ər] *s* rettificatore *m*; (elec) raddrizzatore *m*

recti·fy ['rekti,faɪ] *v* (*pret & pp* -fied) *tr* rettificare; (elec) raddrizzare

rectitude ['rekti,tud] or ['rekti,tjud] *s* rettitudine *f*

rec·tum ['rektəm] *s* (-tums or -ta [tə]) retto

recumbent [rɪ'kʌmbənt] *adj* sdraiato

recuperate [rɪ'kjupə,ret] *tr* ricuperare || *intr* ristabilirsi, rimettersi

re·cur [rɪ'kʌr] *v* (*pret & pp* -curred; *ger* -curring) *intr* ricorrere; ritornare; tornare a mente

recurrent [rɪ'kʌrənt] *adj* ricorrente

recycle [rɪ'saɪkəl] *tr* riconvertire; (*e.g., in chemical industry*) riciclare

red [red] *adj* (**redder; reddest**) rosso || *s* rosso; **in the red** in debito , in rosso || **Red** *adj & s* (*Communist*) rosso

red'bait' *tr* dare del comunista a

red'bird' *s* cardinale *m*

red-blooded ['red,blʌdɪd] *adj* sanguigno; vigoroso

red'breast' *s* pettirosso

red'bud' *s* siliquastro

red'cap' *s* (Brit) poliziotto militare; (U.S.A.) facchino

red' cell' *s* globulo rosso

red' cent' *s*—**to not have a red cent** (coll) non avere il becco di un quattrino

Red' Cross' *s* Croce Rossa

redden ['redən] *tr* arrossare || *intr* arrossire

redeem [rɪ'dim] *tr* redimere; (*a promise*) disimpegnare

redeemer [rɪ'dimər] *s* redentore *m*

redemption [rɪ'dempʃən] *s* redenzione; disimpegno

red-handed ['red'hændɪd] *adj*—**to be caught red-handed** esser colto sul fatto or con le mani nel sacco

red'head' *s* persona dai capelli rossi

red' her'ring *s* argomento usato per sviare l'attenzione; aringa affumicata

red'-hot' *adj* rovente, incandescente; fresco fresco, appena uscito

rediscover [ˌridɪs'kʌvər] *tr* riscoprire

red'-let'ter *adj* memorabile

red'-light' dis'trict *s* quartiere *m* delle case di tolleranza

red' man' *s* pellerossa *m*

re-do ['ri'du] *v* (*pret* -did ['dɪd]; *pp* -done ['dʌn]) *tr* rifare

redolent ['redələnt] *adj* fragrante, profumato; **redolent of** che sa di

redoubt [rɪ'daʊt] *s* (mil) ridotta

redound [rɪ'daʊnd] *intr* ridondare

red' pep'per *s* pepe *m* di Caienna

redress [rɪ'dres] or ['ridres] *s* riparazione, risarcimento || [rɪ'dres] *tr* riparare, risarcire

red'skin' *s* pellerossa *mf*

red' tape' *s* trafila, burocrazia

reduce [rɪ'djus] or [rɪ'dus] *tr* ridurre; diluire; (mil) retrocedere; (*a hernia*) (surg) sbrigliare || *intr* ridursi; (*to lose weight*) dimagrire

reducing [rɪ'djusɪŋ] or [rɪ'dusɪŋ] *adj* dimagrante; (chem) riducente

reduction [rɪ'dʌkʃən] *s* riduzione

redundant [rɪ'dʌndənt] *adj* ridondante

red'wood' *s* sequoia

reed [rid] *s* (*stalk*) calamo; (*plant*) canna; (mus) linguetta; (mus) strumento a linguetta

reedit [ri'edit] *tr* rifondere

reef [rif] *s* scoglio, barriera; (naut) terzarolo; (min) vena, filone *m* || *tr* (*sail*) imbrogliare

reefer ['rifər] *s* giacchetta a doppio petto; (slang) sigaretta di marijuana

reek [rik] *intr* puzzare; sudare, evaporare, fumare

reel [ril] *s* (*spool*) bobina; (*sway*) vacillamento; (*for fishing*) mulinello; **off the reel** senza esitazione || *tr* bobinare; **to reel off** rifilare || *intr* barcollare

reelection [ˌri·ɪ'lekʃən] *s* rielezione

reenlist [ˌri·en'lɪst] *tr* arruolare di nuovo || *intr* arruolarsi di nuovo

reen·try [rɪ'entri] *s* (-tries) rientro

reexamination [ˌri·eg,zæmɪ'neʃən] *s* riesame *m*

re·fer [rɪ'fʌr] v (pret & pp **-ferred;** ger **-ferring**) tr riferire || intr riferirsi

referee [ˌrɛfə'ri] s arbitro || tr & intr arbitrare

reference ['rɛfərəns] s riferimento; (testimonial) referenza; (e.g., in a book) rinvio, rimando

ref'erence book' s libro di consultazione

referen·dum [ˌrɛfə'rɛndəm] s (**-dums** or **-da** [də]) referendum m

refill ['rɪfɪl] s ricambio || [rɪ'fɪl] tr riempire di nuovo

refine [rɪ'faɪn] tr raffinare

refinement [rɪ'faɪnmənt] s raffinatezza; (of oil) raffinatura

refiner·y [rɪ'faɪnəri] s (**-ies**) raffineria

reflect [rɪ'flɛkt] tr riflettere || intr riflettere, riflettersi

reflection [rɪ'flɛkʃən] s riflessione

reflex ['riflɛks] adj riflesso || s riflesso; (camera) reflex m

reflexive [rɪ'flɛksɪv] adj riflessivo

reforestation [ˌrifɔrɪs'teʃən] or [ˌrifɔrɪs'teʃən] s rimboschimento

reform [rɪ'fɔrm] s riforma || tr riformare || intr correggersi

reformation [ˌrɛfər'meʃən] s riforma || **Reformation** s—**the Reformation** la Riforma

reformato·ry [rɪ'fɔrmə ˌtori] adj riformativo || s (**-ries**) riformatorio

reformer [rɪ'fɔrmər] s riformatore m

reform' school' s riformatorio

refraction [rɪ'frækʃən] s rifrazione

refrain [rɪ'fren] s ritornello, intercalare m || intr astenersi

refresh [rɪ'frɛʃ] tr rinfrescare; ristorare || intr ristorarsi

refreshing [rɪ'frɛʃɪŋ] adj rinfrescante; ristoratore; ricreativo

refreshment [rɪ'frɛʃmənt] s rinfresco

refrigerate [rɪ'frɪdʒə ˌret] tr refrigerare

refrigerator [rɪ'frɪdʒə ˌretər] s refrigerante m, frigorifero

refrig'erator car' s vagone frigorifero

re·fuel [rɪ'fjul] v (pret & pp **-fueled** or **-fuelled;** ger **-fueling** or **-fuelling**) tr rifornire di carburante || intr rifornirsi di carburante

refuge ['rɛfjudʒ] s rifugio; scampo; **to take refuge (in)** rifugiarsi (in)

refugee [ˌrɛfju'dʒi] s rifugiato

refund ['rɪfʌnd] s rifusione || [rɪ'fʌnd] tr (to repay) rifondere || [rɪ'fʌnd] tr (bonds) consolidare; (to fund anew) rifondere

refurnish [rɪ'fʌrnɪʃ] tr riammobiliare

refusal [rɪ'fjuzəl] s rifiuto

refuse ['rɛfjus] s rifiuto, spazzatura || [rɪ'fjuz] tr rifiutare; **to refuse to** rifiutarsi di

refute [rɪ'fjut] tr smentire, confutare

regain [rɪ'gen] tr riguadagnare; **to regain consciousness** tornare in sé

regal ['rigəl] adj reale, regale

regale [rɪ'gel] tr intrattenere, rallegrare

regalia [rɪ'gelɪ·ə] spl (of royalty) prerogative fpl reali; alta uniforme

regard [rɪ'gard] s riguardo; (look)

sguardo; (esteem) rispetto; **in regard to** rispetto a; **regards** rispetti mpl; **warm regards** cordiali saluti mpl; **without regard to** senza considerare || tr considerare; osservare; concernere; **as regards** per quanto concerne

regarding [rɪ'gardɪŋ] prep per quanto concerne

regardless [rɪ'gardlɪs] adj incurante || adv ciò nonostante; costi quello che costi; **regardless of** malgrado

regatta [rɪ'gætə] s regata

regen·cy ['ridʒənsi] s (**-cies**) reggenza

regenerate [rɪ'dʒɛnə ˌret] tr rigenerare || intr rigenerarsi

regent ['ridʒənt] s reggente mf

regicide ['rɛdʒɪ ˌsaɪd] s (act) regicidio; (person) regicida mf

regiment ['rɛdʒɪmənt] s reggimento || ['rɛdʒɪ ˌment] tr irregimentare

regimental [ˌrɛdʒɪ'mɛntəl] adj reggimentale || **regimentals** spl uniforme f reggimentale

region ['ridʒən] s regione

register ['rɛdʒɪstər] s registro; (for controlling the flow of air) regolatore m dell'aria || tr registrare; (e.g., a student) iscrivere; (e.g., anger) dimostrare; (a letter) raccomandare || intr registrarsi; iscriversi; fare impressione

reg'istered let'ter s raccomandata

reg'istered nurse' s infermiera diplomata

registrar ['rɛdʒɪs ˌtrar] s registratore m, archivista mf; (of deeds) ricevitore m

registration [ˌrɛdʒɪs'treʃən] s registrazione; (e.g., of a student) iscrizione; (of mail) raccomandazione

registra'tion fee' s diritto di segreteria

re·gret [rɪ'grɛt] s pentimento, rammarico; **regrets** scuse fpl || v (pret & pp **-gretted;** ger **-gretting**) tr rimpiangere; **to regret to** essere spiacente di

regrettable [rɪ'grɛtəbəl] adj deplorevole

regular ['rɛgjələr] adj regolare; (life) regolato; (coll) vero || s cliente m abituale; (mil) effettivo

regularity [ˌrɛgju'lærɪti] s regolarità f

regularize ['rɛgjələ ˌraɪz] tr regolarizzare

regulate ['rɛgjə ˌlet] tr regolare

regulation [ˌrɛgjə'leʃən] s regolazione; (rule) regolamento

rehabilitate [ˌrihə'bɪlɪ ˌtet] tr riabilitare

rehearsal [rɪ'hʌrsəl] s prova

rehearse [rɪ'hʌrs] tr provare || intr fare le prove

rehiring [ri'haɪrɪŋ] s riassunzione

reign [ren] s regno || intr regnare

reimburse [ˌri·ɪm'bʌrs] tr rimborsare

rein [ren] s redine f; **to give full rein to** dare briglia sciolta a || tr guidare con le redini; frenare

reincarnation [ˌri·ɪnkar'neʃən] s reincarnazione

reindeer ['ren ˌdɪr] s renna

reinforce [ˌri·ɪn'fors] tr rinforzare; (a wall) armare

re'inforced con'crete s cemento armato

reinforcement [ˌri·ɪnˈforsmənt] s rinforzo

reinstate [ˌri·ɪnˈstet] tr reintegrare

reiterate [riˈɪtəˌret] tr reiterare

reject [ˈrɪdʒɛkt] s rigetto, rifiuto; **rejects** scarti mpl || [rɪˈdʒɛkt] tr rigettare; (to refuse) rifiutare

rejection [rɪˈdʒɛkʃən] s rigetto; rifiuto

rejoice [rɪˈdʒɔɪs] intr rallegrarsi

rejoin [rɪˈdʒɔɪn] tr raggiungere; (to reunite) riunire; (to reply) rispondere

rejoinder [rɪˈdʒɔɪndər] s risposta; (law) controreplica

rejuvenation [rɪˌdʒuvɪˈneʃən] s ringiovanimento

rekindle [riˈkɪndəl] tr riaccendere

relapse [rɪˈlæps] s ricaduta || intr ricadere

relate [rɪˈlet] tr mettere in relazione; (to tell) narrare

relation [rɪˈleʃən] s relazione; (account) resoconto; (relative) parente mf; (kinship) parentela; **in relation to** o **with** in relazione a

relationship [rɪˈleʃənˌʃɪp] s rapporto, relazione; (kinship) parentela

relative [ˈrɛlətɪv] adj relativo || s congiunto, parente mf

relativity [ˌrɛləˈtɪvɪti] s relatività f

relax [rɪˈlæks] tr rilasciare, rilassare || intr rilasciarsi, rilassarsi

relaxation [ˌrilæksˈeʃən] s distensione; (entertainment) ricreazione

relaxa'tion of ten'sion s distensione

relaxing [rɪˈlæksɪŋ] adj rilassante; divertente

relay [ˈrile] o [rɪˈle] s (elec) relè m; (rad) ripetitore m; (mil, sports) staffetta; (sports) corsa a staffetta || v (pret & pp -layed) tr trasmettere, ritrasmettere || [rɪˈle] v (pret & pp -laid) tr rimettere, porre di nuovo

re'lay race' s corsa a staffetta

release [rɪˈlis] s (e.g., from jail) liberazione; (from obligation) disimpegno; (for publication) autorizzazione; (mov) distribuzione; (journ) comunicato; (aer) lancio; (mach) scappamento || tr liberare; disimpegnare; autorizzare la pubblicazione di; (mov) distribuire; (a bomb) (aer) lanciare; **to release s.o. from a debt** rimettere un debito a qlcu

relent [rɪˈlent] intr placarsi

relentless [rɪˈlentlɪs] adj implacabile

relevant [ˈrɛlɪvənt] adj pertinente

reliable [rɪˈlaɪ·əbəl] adj (person) fidato; (source) attendibile

reliance [rɪˈlaɪ·əns] s fiducia, fede f

relic [ˈrɛlɪk] s reliquia

relief [rɪˈlif] s sollievo; sussidio; (prominence; projection) rilievo; (mil) cambio; **in relief** in rilievo; **on relief** sotto sussidio

relieve [rɪˈliv] tr (e.g., pain) alleviare; (e.g., a load) sgravare; (mil) rilevare

religion [rɪˈlɪdʒən] s religione

religious [rɪˈlɪdʒəs] adj religioso

relinquish [rɪˈlɪŋkwɪʃ] tr abbandonare

relish [ˈrɛlɪʃ] s piacere m, gusto; sapore m, aroma m; (culin) condimento || tr gustare, apprezzare; dare gusto a

reluctance [rɪˈlʌktəns] s riluttanza

reluctant [rɪˈlʌktənt] adj riluttante

re·ly [rɪˈlaɪ] v (pret & pp -lied) intr fare assegnamento; **to rely on** fidarsi di, fondarsi su

remain [rɪˈmen] s—**remains** resti mpl; resti mpl mortali || intr restare, rimanere

remainder [rɪˈmendər] s resto, restante m; (unsold books) fondi mpl di libreria || tr vendere come rimanenza

re·make [riˈmek] v (pret & pp -made [ˈmed]) tr rifare

remark [rɪˈmɑrk] s osservazione, rimarco || tr & intr osservare; **to remark on** fare osservazioni su

remarkable [rɪˈmɑrkəbəl] adj notevole

remar·ry [rɪˈmæri] v (pret & pp -ried) intr riprendere moglie, risposarsi

reme·dy [ˈrɛmɪdi] s (-dies) rimedio || v (pret & pp -died) tr rimediare (with dat)

remember [rɪˈmɛmbər] tr ricordarsi di; (to send greetings to) ricordare || intr ricordare, ricordarsi

remembrance [rɪˈmɛmbrəns] s rimembranza, ricordo

remind [rɪˈmaɪnd] tr rammentare

reminder [rɪˈmaɪndər] s promemoria

reminisce [ˌrɛmɪˈnɪs] intr ricordare il passato

reminiscence [ˌrɛmɪˈnɪsəns] s reminiscenza

remiss [rɪˈmɪs] adj negligente

re·mit [rɪˈmɪt] v (pret & pp -mitted; ger -mitting) tr rimettere; (to a lower court) (law) rinviare

remittance [rɪˈmɪtəns] s rimessa

remnant [ˈrɛmnənt] s (remaining quantity) rimanente m; (of cloth) scampolo; vestigio; **remnants** (of merchandise) rimanenze fpl, fondi mpl di magazzino

remod·el [riˈmɑdəl] v (pret & pp -eled o -elled; ger -eling o -elling) tr rimodellare; ricostruire

remonstrance [rɪˈmɑnstrəns] s rimostranza

remonstrate [rɪˈmɑnstret] intr protestare, rimostrare; **to remonstrate with** rimostrare a

remorse [rɪˈmɔrs] s rimorso

remorseful [rɪˈmɔrsfəl] adj tormentato dal rimorso, pentito

remote [rɪˈmot] adj remoto

remote' control' s telecomando

removable [rɪˈmuvəbəl] adj amovibile

removal [rɪˈmuvəl] s rimozione; trasferimento; (dismissal) destituzione

remove [rɪˈmuv] tr rimuovere; (one's jacket) togliersi, cavarsi; (from office) destituire; eliminare || intr trasferirsi; andarsene

remuneration [rɪˌmjunəˈreʃən] s rimunerazione

renaissance [ˌrenəˈsɑns] o [rɪˈnesəns] s rinascimento, rinascita || **Renaissance** s Rinascimento

rend [rend] v (pret & pp rent [rent]) tr (to tear) stracciare; (to split) fendere, squarciare

render [ˈrendər] tr (justice) rendere;

(*a service*) fare; (*aid*) prestare; (*a bill*) presentare; (*to translate*) tradurre; (*a piece of music*) interpretare; (*e.g., fat*) struggere

rendez·vous ['rɑndə,vu] *s* (**-vous** [,vuz]) appuntamento; (*in space*) incontro ‖ *v* (*pret & pp* **-voused** [,vud]; *ger* **-vousing** [,vu·ɪŋ]) *intr* incontrarsi

rendition [rɛn'dɪʃən] *s* restituzione, resa; traduzione; interpretazione

renege [rɪ'nɪg] *s* rifiuto ‖ *intr* rifiutare; (coll) venire meno

renew [rɪ'nju] or [rɪ'nu] *tr* rinnovare ‖ *intr* rinnovarsi

renewal [rɪ'nju·əl] or [rɪ'nu·əl] *s* rinnovo, rinnovamento

renounce [rɪ'nauns] *tr* rinunziare (with *dat*); ripudiare

renovate ['rɛnə,vet] *tr* rinnovare; (*a building*) restaurare; (*a room*) rimettere a nuovo

renown [rɪ'naun] *s* rinomanza

renowned [rɪ'naund] *adj* rinomato

rent [rɛnt] *adj* scisso ‖ *s* fitto, pigione; (*tear*) squarcio ‖ *tr* locare, dare a pigione ‖ *intr* prendere a pigione

rental ['rɛntəl] *s* affitto

renter ['rɛntər] *s* affittuario, locatario

renunciation [rɪ,nʌnsɪ'eʃən] or [rɪ,nʌnʃɪ'eʃən] *s* rinunzia

reopen [rɪ'opən] *tr* riaprire ‖ *intr* riaprirsi

reopening [rɪ'opənɪŋ] *s* riapertura

reorganize [rɪ'ɔrgə,naɪz] *tr* riorganizzare ‖ *intr* riorganizzarsi

repair [rɪ'pɛr] *s* riparazione; **in good repair** in buono stato ‖ *tr* riparare ‖ *intr* riparare, dirigersi

repair'man' *s* (**-men'**) aggiustatore *m*

repaper [rɪ'pepər] *tr* ritappezzare

reparation [,rɛpə'reʃən] *s* riparazione

repartee [,rɛpər'ti] *s* replica arguta, rimando

repast [rɪ'pæst] or [rɪ'pɑst] *s* pasto

repatriate [rɪ'petrɪ,et] *tr* rimpatriare

re·pay [rɪ'pe] *v* (*pret & pp* **-paid** ['ped]) *tr* ripagare

repayment [rɪ'pemənt] *s* rimborso; risarcimento, compensazione

repeal [rɪ'pil] *s* revoca, abrogazione ‖ *tr* revocare, abrogare

repeat [rɪ'pit] *s* ripetizione ‖ *tr* ripetere ‖ *intr* ripetere; (*said of food*) tornare a gola

re·pel [rɪ'pɛl] *v* (*pret & pp* **-pelled**; *ger* **-pelling**) *tr* respingere, ricacciare; ripugnare (with *dat*)

repent [rɪ'pɛnt] *tr* pentirsi di ‖ *intr* pentirsi, ravvedersi

repentance [rɪ'pɛntəns] *s* pentimento

repentant [rɪ'pɛntənt] *adj* pentito

repercussion [,rɪpər'kʌʃən] *s* ripercussione

reperto·ry ['rɛpər,torɪ] *s* (**-ries**) (com) magazzino; (theat) repertorio

repetition [,rɛpɪ'tɪʃən] *s* ripetizione

repine [rɪ'paɪn] *intr* lamentarsi

replace [rɪ'ples] *tr* (*to put back*) rimettere; (*to take the place of*) rimpiazzare

replaceable [rɪ'plesəbəl] *adj* sostituibile

replacement [rɪ'plesmənt] *s* rimpiazzo, sostituzione; **as a replacement for** al posto di

replenish [rɪ'plɛnɪʃ] *tr* rifornire

replete [rɪ'plit] *adj* pieno zeppo

replica ['rɛplɪkə] *s* replica

re·ply [rɪ'plaɪ] *s* (**-plies**) risposta ‖ *v* (*pret & pp* **-plied**) *tr & intr* rispondere

report [rɪ'port] *s* rapporto, informazione; voce *f*, rumore *m*; (*of a physician*) responso; (*of a firearm*) detonazione ‖ *tr* riportare, rapportare; denunziare ‖ *intr* fare un rapporto; fare il cronista; presentarsi; **to report sick** (mil) marcare visita

report' card' *s* pagella

reportedly [rɪ'portɪdlɪ] *adv* secondo la voce comune

reporter [rɪ'portər] *s* cronista *mf*, reporter *m*

reporting [rɪ'portɪŋ] *s* reportage *m*

repose [rɪ'poz] *s* riposo ‖ *tr* posare, riporre ‖ *intr* riposare

reprehend [,rɛprɪ'hɛnd] *tr* riprovare, rimproverare

represent [,rɛprɪ'zɛnt] *tr* rappresentare

representation [,rɛprɪzɛn'teʃən] *s* rappresentazione; protesta; **representations** dichiarazioni *fpl*

representative [,rɛprɪ'zɛntətɪv] *adj* rappresentativo ‖ *s* rappresentante *mf*; (pol) deputato

repress [rɪ'prɛs] *tr* reprimere

repression [rɪ'prɛʃən] *s* repressione

reprieve [rɪ'priv] *s* tregua temporanea; sospensione della pena capitale ‖ *tr* accordare una tregua a; sospendere l'esecuzione di

reprimand ['rɛprɪ,mænd] or ['rɛprɪ,mɑnd] *s* sgridata, ramanzina ‖ *tr* sgridare, rimproverare

reprint ['ri,prɪnt] *s* ristampa; (*off-print*) estratto ‖ [rɪ'prɪnt] *tr* ristampare

reprisal [rɪ'praɪzəl] *s* rappresaglia

reproach [rɪ'protʃ] *s* rimprovero; vituperio ‖ *tr* rimproverare; **to reproach s.o. for s.th** rimproverare qlcu di qlco, rimproverare qlco a qlcu

reproduce [,riprə'djus] or [,riprə'dus] *tr* riprodurre ‖ *intr* riprodursi

reproduction [,riprə'dʌkʃən] *s* riproduzione

reproof [rɪ'pruf] *s* rimprovero

reprove [rɪ'pruv] *tr* rimproverare; disapprovare

reptile ['rɛptɪl] *s* rettile *m*

republic [rɪ'pʌblɪk] *s* repubblica

republican [rɪ'pʌblɪkən] *adj & s* repubblicano

repudiate [rɪ'pjudɪ,et] *tr* ripudiare; rinnegare

repugnant [rɪ'pʌgnənt] *adj* ripugnante

repulse [rɪ'pʌls] *s* rifiuto; sconfitta ‖ *tr* rifiutare; (*e.g., an enemy*) sconfiggere

repulsive [rɪ'pʌlsɪv] *adj* ripulsivo

reputation [,rɛpjə'teʃən] *s* reputazione

repute [rɪ'pjut] s reputazione, fama ‖ tr reputare

reputedly [rɪ'pjutɪdlɪ] adv secondo l'opinione corrente

request [rɪ'kwɛst] s domanda, richiesta; **at the request of** su domanda di ‖ tr richiedere

Requiem ['rɪkwɪ‚ɛm] or ['rɛkwɪ‚ɛm] adj di Requiem ‖ s Requiem m & f; Messa di Requiem

require [rɪ'kwaɪr] tr richiedere

requirement [rɪ'kwaɪrmənt] s requisito; richiesta, fabbisogno

requisite ['rɛkwɪzɪt] adj requisito, richiesto ‖ s requisito

requisition [‚rɛkwɪ'zɪʃən] s requisizione

requital [rɪ'kwaɪtəl] s contraccambio

requite [rɪ'kwaɪt] tr (e.g., an injury) contraccambiare; (a person) contraccambiare (with dat)

re-read [ri'rid] v (pret & pp -read ['rɛd]) tr rileggere

resale ['ri‚sel] or [ri'sel] s rivendita

rescind [rɪ'sɪnd] tr annullare, cancellare; (law) rescindere

rescue ['rɛskju] s salvataggio, liberazione; **to go to the rescue of** andare al soccorso di ‖ tr salvare, liberare, soccorrere

research [rɪ'sʌrtʃ] or ['risʌrtʃ] s ricerca, indagine f ‖ intr investigare

re-sell [ri'sel] v (pret & pp -sold ['sold]) tr rivendere

resemblance [rɪ'zɛmbləns] s somiglianza

resemble [rɪ'zɛmbəl] tr somigliare (with dat), rassomigliare (with dat); **to resemble one another** rassomigliarsi

resent [rɪ'zɛnt] tr (a remark) risentirsi per; (a person) risentirsi con

resentful [rɪ'zɛntfəl] adj risentito

resentment [rɪ'zɛntmənt] s risentimento

reservation [‚rɛzər'veʃən] s riserva; (e.g., for a room) prenotazione

reserve [rɪ'zʌrv] s riserva; (self-restraint) riserbo, contegno ‖ tr riservare; prenotare

reservist [rɪ'zʌrvɪst] s riservista m

reservoir ['rɛzər‚vwɑr] s serbatoio, cisterna; (large storage place for supplying community with water) bacino di riserva; (fig) pozzo

re-set [ri'sɛt] v (pret & pp -set; ger -setting) tr rimettere a posto; (a watch) regolare; (a gem) incastonare di nuovo; (a machine) rimontare

re-ship [ri'ʃɪp] v (pret & pp -shipped; ger -shipping) tr rispedire; (on a ship) reimbarcare ‖ intr reimbarcarsi

reshipment [ri'ʃɪpmənt] s rispedizione; (on a ship) reimbarco

reside [rɪ'zaɪd] intr risiedere

residence ['rɛzɪdəns] s residenza

resident ['rɛzɪdənt] adj & s residente mf

residential [‚rɛzɪ'dɛnʃəl] adj residenziale

residue ['rɛzɪ‚dju] or ['rɛsɪ‚du] s residuo

resign [rɪ'zaɪn] tr rassegnare, abbandonare; **to be resigned to** rassegnarsi a ‖ intr dimettersi, rassegnare le dimissioni

resignation [‚rɛzɪg'neʃən] s (from a job) dimissione; (submission) rassegnazione

resin ['rɛzɪn] s resina

resist [rɪ'zɪst] tr resistere (with dat) ‖ intr resistere

resistance [rɪ'zɪstəns] s resistenza

resole [ri'sol] tr risolare

resolute ['rɛzə‚lut] adj risoluto

resolution [‚rɛzə'luʃən] s risoluzione; **good resolutions** buoni propositi

resolve [rɪ'zɒlv] s risoluzione ‖ tr risolvere ‖ intr risolversi

resonance ['rɛzənəns] s risonanza

resort [rɪ'zɔrt] s (appeal) ricorso; (for vacation) centro di villeggiatura ‖ intr ricorrere

resound [rɪ'zaʊnd] intr risonare

resounding [rɪ'zaʊndɪŋ] adj risonante; (success) strepitoso

resource [rɪ'sɔrs] or ['risɔrs] s risorsa

resourceful [rɪ'sɔrsfəl] adj ingegnoso

respect [rɪ'spɛkt] s rispetto; **respects** rispetti mpl, ossequi mpl; **with respect to** rispetto a ‖ tr rispettare

respectable [rɪ'spɛktəbəl] adj rispettabile; onesto, per bene

respectful [rɪ'spɛktfəl] adj rispettoso

respecting [rɪ'spɛktɪŋ] prep rispetto a

respective [rɪ'spɛktɪv] adj rispettivo

respiratory ['rɛspɪrə‚torɪ] or [rɪ'spaɪrə‚torɪ] adj respiratorio

respire [rɪ'spaɪr] tr & intr respirare

respite ['rɛspɪt] s tregua, requie f; (reprieve) proroga, dilazione

resplendent [rɪ'splɛndənt] adj risplendente

respond [rɪ'spɒnd] intr rispondere

response [rɪ'spɒns] s risposta

responsibili·ty [rɪ‚spɒnsɪ'bɪlɪtɪ] s (-ties) responsibilità f

responsible [rɪ'spɒnsɪbəl] adj responsabile; (job) di fiducia; **responsible for** responsabile di

responsive [rɪ'spɒnsɪv] adj rispondente; (e.g., to affection) sensibile; (e.g., motor) che risponde

rest [rɛst] s riposo; (what remains) resto; (mus) pausa; **at rest** in riposo; tranquillo, in pace; (dead) morto; **the rest** il resto, gli altri; **to come to rest** andare a finire; **to lay to rest** sotterrare ‖ tr riposare; (to direct one's eyes) dirigere; (faith) porre ‖ intr riposarsi, riposare; appoggiarsi; **to rest assured (that)** esser sicuro (che); **to rest on** aver fiducia in; basarsi su; (one's laurels) dormire su

restaurant ['rɛstərənt] or ['rɛstə‚rɑnt] s ristorante m

restful ['rɛstfəl] adj riposante, tranquillo

rest' home' s casa di riposo

rest'ing place' s luogo di riposo; (of a staircase) pianerottolo; (of the dead) ultima dimora

restitution [‚rɛstɪ'tjuʃən] or [‚rɛstɪ'tuʃən] s restituzione

restive ['restɪv] *adj* irrequieto; *(e.g., horse)* recalcitrante
restless ['restlɪs] *adj* irrequieto; *(night)* insonne, in bianco
restock [ri'stak] *tr* rifornire; *(e.g., with fish)* ripopolare
restoration [,restə'reʃən] *s* restaurazione
restore [rɪ'stor] *tr* restaurare, ripristinare
restrain [rɪ'stren] *tr* ritenere, frenare; limitare
restraint [rɪ'strent] *s* restrizione; controllo, ritegno; detenzione
restrict [rɪ'strɪkt] *tr* restingere, limitare
restriction [rɪ'strɪkʃən] *s* restrizione
rest' room' *s* toletta; gabinetto di decenza
restructuring [ri'strʌktʃərɪŋ] *s* ristrutturazione
result [rɪ'zʌlt] *s* risultato || *intr* risultare; **to result in** risolversi in, concludersi con
resume [rɪ'zum] *or* [rɪ'zjum] *tr* riprendere || *intr* ricominciare
résumé [,rezu'me] *or* [,rezju'me] *s* sunto, riassunto
resumption [rɪ'zʌmpʃən] *s* ripresa
resurface [ri'sʌrfɪs] *tr* mettere copertura nuova a || *intr* riemergere
resurrect [,rezə,rekt] *tr & intr* risuscitare
resurrection [,rezə'rekʃən] *s* risurrezione
resuscitate [rɪ'sʌsɪ,tet] *tr* rendere alla vita
retail ['ritel] *adj & adv* al dettaglio, al minuto || *s* dettaglio || *tr* dettagliare, vendere al minuto || *intr* vendere or vendersi al minuto
retailer ['ritelər] *s* dettagliante *mf*
retain [rɪ'ten] *tr* ritenere; *(a lawyer)* assicurarsi i servizi di
retaliate [rɪ'tælɪ,et] *intr* fare rappresaglie; **to retaliate for** ricambiare
retaliation [rɪ,tælɪ'eʃən] *s* rappresaglia
retard [rɪ'tard] *s* ritardo || *tr* ritardare
retch [retʃ] *intr* avere sforzi di vomito
reticence ['retɪsəns] *s* riservatezza
reticent ['retɪsənt] *adj* riservato, taciturno
retina ['retɪnə] *s* retina
retinue ['retɪ,nju] *or* ['retɪ,nu] *s* seguito, corteggio
retire [rɪ'taɪr] *tr* ritirare; *(an employee)* giubilare, mettere a riposo || *intr* ritirarsi; andare a riposo *(to go to bed)* andare a letto
retired [rɪ'taɪrd] *adj (employee)* in pensione; *(officer)* a riposo
retirement [rɪ'taɪrmənt] *s* ritiro; *(of an employee)* pensionamento, quiescenza
retort [rɪ'tɔrt] *s* risposta per le rime; controreplica; *(chem)* storta || *tr* rispondere per le rime a || *intr* rispondere per le rime
retouch [ri'tʌtʃ] *tr* ritoccare
retrace [ri'tres] *tr* ripercorrere; **to retrace one's steps** ritornare sui propri passi

retract [rɪ'trækt] *tr* ritrattare, disdire || *intr* disdirsi
re-tread ['ri,tred] *s* pneumatico col copertone ricostruito || [ri'tred] *v (pret & pp -treaded) tr* ricostruire il copertone di || *v (pret -trod* ['trad]; *pp -trod or -trodden) tr* ripercorrere || *intr* rimettere il piede
retreat [rɪ'trit] *s (seclusion)* ritiro; *(mil)* ritirata; *(eccl)* esercizio spirituale; **to beat a retreat** battere in ritirata || *intr* ritirarsi
retrench [rɪ'trentʃ] *tr* ridurre, tagliare; *(mil)* trincerare || *intr* ridurre le spese; *(mil)* trincerarsi
retribution [,retrɪ'bjuʃən] *s* ricompensa; *(theol)* giudizio finale
retributive [rɪ'trɪbjətɪv] *adj* retributivo
retrieve [rɪ'triv] *tr* riguadagnare, riconquistare; *(to repair)* risarcire; *(hunt)* riportare || *intr* riportare la presa
retriever [rɪ'trivər] *s* cane *m* da presa
retroactive [,retro'æktɪv] *adj* retroattivo
retrofiring [,retro'faɪrɪŋ] *s* accensione dei retrorazzi
retrogress [,retrə,gres] *intr* regredire; retrocedere
retrorocket [,retro'rakɪt] *s* retrorazzo
retrospect [,retrə,spekt] *s* esame retrospettivo; **in retrospect** retrospettivamente
retrospective [,retrə'spektɪv] *adj* retrospettivo
re-try [ri'traɪ] *v (pret & pp -tried) tr (a person)* riprocessare; *(a case)* ritentare
return [rɪ'tʌrn] *adj* di ritorno; ripetuto || *s* restituzione; ritorno; profitto; *(of income tax)* dichiarazione; risposta; rapporto ufficiale; *(of an election)* responso; (sports) rimando, rimessa; **in return (for)** in cambio (di); **many happy returns of the day!** cento di questi giorni!; **returns** *(of an election)* responso, risultato || *tr* tornare, ritornare restituire; *(a favor)* contraccambiare; *(a profit)* dare; *(thanks; a decision)* rendere; (sports) ribattere || *intr* tornare; rispondere
return' ad'dress *s* indirizzo del mittente
return' bout' *s* (boxing) rivincita
return' mail' *s*—**by return mail** a volta di corriere, a giro di posta
return' tick'et *s* biglietto di ritorno; (Brit) biglietto di andata e ritorno
reunification [ri,junɪfɪ'keʃən] *s* riunione, unificazione
reunion [ri'junjən] *s* riunione
reunite [,riju'naɪt] *tr* riunire || *intr* riunirsi
rev [rev] *s* · (coll) giro || *v (pret & pp revved; ger revving) tr*—**to rev up** (coll) imballare || *intr* (coll) accelerare, imballarsi
revamp [ri'væmp] *tr* rinnovare, rappezzare
reveal [rɪ'vil] *tr* rivelare, svelare
reveille ['revəli] *s* sveglia, levata
rev·el ['revəl] *s* baldoria || *v (pret &*

pp **-eled** or **-elled;** *ger* **-eling** or **-elling)** *intr* gozzovigliare; bearsi
revelation [ˌrɛvəˈleʃən] *s* rivelazione || **Revelation** *s* (Bib) Apocalisse *f*
revel·ry [ˈrɛvəlri] *s* (**-ries**) baldoria
revenge [rɪˈvɛndʒ] *s* vendetta || *tr* vendicare
revengeful [rɪˈvɛndʒfəl] *adj* vendicativo
revenue [ˈrɛvəˌnju] or [ˈrɛvəˌnu] *s* entrata, profitto; (*government income*) entrate *fpl* erariali
rev'enue cut'ter *s* motobarca della guardia di finanza
rev'enue stamp' *s* marca da bollo
reverberate [rɪˈvʌrbəˌret] *intr* riverberarsi; (*said, e.g., of sound*) ripercuotersi, risonare; (*said of an echo*) rimbalzare
revere [rɪˈvɪr] *tr* venerare, riverire
reverence [ˈrɛvərəns] *s* riverenza || *tr* ossequiare
reverend [ˈrɛvərənd] *adj & s* reverendo
reverent [ˈrɛvərənt] *adj* reverente
reverie [ˈrɛvəri] *s* sogno, fantasticheria
reversal [rɪˈvʌrsəl] *s* inversione, cambio; (law) annullamento
reverse [rɪˈvʌrs] *adj* rovescio, contrario; (mach) di retromarcia || *s* contrario; (*rear*) dietro; (*misfortune; side of a coin not bearing principal design*) rovescio; (mach) retromarcia || *tr* invertire; rovesciare; mettere in marcia indietro; **to reverse oneself** cambiare d'opinione; **to reverse the charges** far pagare al destinatario; (telp) far pagare al numero chiamato || *intr* invertirsi
revert [rɪˈvʌrt] *intr* ritornare
review [rɪˈvju] *s* (*critical article*) recensione; (*magazine*) rivista; (educ) ripasso, ripetizione; (mil) rivista || *tr* recensire; rivedere; (*a lesson*) ripassare; (mil) passare in rassegna
revile [rɪˈvaɪl] *tr* insultare, offendere
revise [rɪˈvaɪz] *tr* revisione; (typ) seconda bozza || *tr* rivedere, correggere
revision [rɪˈvɪʒən] *s* revisione
revisionism [rɪˈvɪʒəˌnɪzəm] *s* revisionismo
revival [rɪˈvaɪvəl] *s* ripresa delle forze; (*restoration*) ripristino; (*of learning*) rinascimento; risveglio religioso; (theat, mov) ripresa
revive [rɪˈvaɪv] *tr* ravvivare; (*a custom*) ripristinare; (theat) dare la ripresa di || *intr* ravvivarsi; risorgere
revoke [rɪˈvok] *tr* revocare
revolt [rɪˈvolt] *s* rivolta || *tr* rivoltare || *intr* rivoltarsi
revolting [rɪˈvoltɪŋ] *adj* rivoltante
revolution [ˌrɛvəˈluʃən] *s* rivoluzione
revolutionar·y [ˌrɛvəˈluʃəˌnɛri] *adj* rivoluzionario || *s* (**-ies**) rivoluzionario
revolve [rɪˈvalv] *tr* far rotare; (*in one's mind*) rivolgere || *intr* girare, rotare
revolver [rɪˈvalvər] *s* rivoltella
revolv'ing book'case *s* scaffale *m* girevole
revolv'ing cred'it *s* credito rotativo
revolv'ing door' *s* porta girevole

revolv'ing fund' *s* fondo rotativo
revue [rɪˈvju] *s* rivista
revulsion [rɪˈvʌlʃən] *s* ripugnanza, avversione; (med) revulsione
reward [rɪˈwɔrd] *s* premio, ricompensa; (*money offered for capture*) taglia; (*for return of articles lost*) mancia competente || *tr* premiare, ricompensare
rewarding [rɪˈwɔrdɪŋ] *adj* rimunerativo; gradevole
re·wind [rɪˈwaɪnd] *s* (*of a tape*) ribobinazione || *v* (*pret & pp* **-wound** [ˈwaʊnd]) *tr* ribobinare
re·write [rɪˈraɪt] *v* (*pret* **-wrote** [ˈrot]; *pp* **-written** [ˈrɪtən]) *tr* riscrivere; (*news*) rimaneggiare, correggere
rhapso·dy [ˈræpsədi] *s* (**-dies**) rapsodia
rheostat [ˈriˌə ˌstæt] *s* reostato
rhesus [ˈrisəs] *s* reso
rhetoric [ˈrɛtərɪk] *s* retorica
rhetorical [rɪˈtɑrɪkəl] or [rɪˈtɔrɪkəl] *adj* retorico
rheumatic [ruˈmætɪk] *adj & s* reumatico
rheumatism [ˈrumə ˌtɪzəm] *s* reumatismo
Rhine [raɪn] *s* Reno
Rhineland [ˈraɪnˌlænd] *s* la Renania
rhine'stone' *s* gemma artificiale
rhinoceros [raɪˈnɑsərəs] *s* rinoceronte *m*
Rhodes [rodz] *s* Rodi *f*
Rhone [ron] *s* Rodano
rhubarb [ˈrubarb] *s* rabarbaro; (slang) baruffa
rhyme [raɪm] *s* rima; **without rhyme or reason** senza capo né coda || *tr & intr* rimare
rhythm [ˈrɪðəm] *s* ritmo
rhythmic(al) [ˈrɪðmɪk(əl)] *adj* ritmico
rial·to [rɪˈælto] *s* (**-tos**) mercato || **the Rialto** il ponte di Rialto; il centro teatrale di New York
rib [rɪb] *s* costola; (*cut of meat*) costata; (*of umbrella*) stecca; (*of leaf*) nervatura; (aer, archit) centina; (naut) costa || *v* (*pret & pp* **ribbed;** *ger* **ribbing**) *tr* (slang) prendersi gioco di
ribald [ˈrɪbəld] *adj* volgare, indecente
ribbon [ˈrɪbən] *s* nastro; (*decoration*) nastrino; **ribbons** (*shreds*) brandelli *mpl*
rice [raɪs] *s* riso
rich [rɪtʃ] *adj* ricco; (*food*) nutrito, grasso; (*wine*) generoso; (*voice*) caldo; (*color*) vivo; (*odor*) forte; (coll) divertente; (coll) assurdo; **to strike it rich** trovare la miniera d'oro || **riches** *spl* ricchezze *fpl*; **the rich** i ricchi
rickets [ˈrɪkɪts] *s* rachitismo
ricket·y [ˈrɪkɪti] *adj* (*object*) sgangherato; (*person*) vacillante; (*suffering from rickets*) rachitico
rid [rɪd] *v* (*pret & pp* **rid;** *ger* **ridding**) *tr* liberare, sbarazzare; **to get rid of** liberarsi di, sbarazzarsi di
riddance [ˈrɪdəns] *s* liberazione; **good riddance!** che sollievo!
riddle [ˈrɪdəl] *s* enigma *m*, indovi-

nello; (*sieve*) crivello || *tr* crivellare; (*to sift*) vagliare; (*s.o.'s reputation*) rovinare; **to riddle with** crivellare di

ride [raɪd] *s* scarrozzata; cavalcata; gita || *v* (*pret* **rode** [rod]; *pp* **ridden** [ˈrɪdən]) *tr* cavalcare, montare, montare su; (*e.g., a bus*) andare in; (*the waves*) galleggiare su; attraversare; tiranneggiare; farsi gioco di; **to ride down** travolgere; sorpassare; **to ride out** uscire felicemente da || *intr* cavalcare; fare una passeggiata, fare una gita; (*to float*) galleggiare; **to let ride** lasciar correre; **to ride on** dipendere da

rider [ˈraɪdər] *s* cavallerizzo; ciclista *mf*; viaggiatore *m*, passeggero

ridge [rɪdʒ] *s* (*of mountains*) crinale *m*, dorsale *f*; (*of roof*) displuvio; (*agr*) porca

ridge′pole′ *s* trave maestra, colmo

ridicule [ˈrɪdɪˌkjul] *s* ridicolo; **to expose to ridicule** porre in ridicolo || *tr* ridicolizzare

ridiculous [rɪˈdɪkjələs] *adj* ridicolo

rid′ing boot′ *s* stivalone *m* d'equitazione

rid′ing school′ *s* maneggio

rife [raɪf] *adj* comune, prevalente; **rife with** pieno di

riffraff [ˈrɪfˌræf] *s* gentaglia

rifle [ˈraɪfəl] *s* fucile *m*; cannone rigato || *tr* (*a place*) svaligiare; (*a person*) derubare; (*a gun*) rigare

rifle′ range′ *s* tiro a segno

rift [rɪft] *s* crepa, fessura; disaccordo

rig [rɪg] *s* attrezzatura; equipaggio; impianto di sondaggio (per il petrolio); (*outfit*) tenuta || *v* (*pret & pp* **rigged**) *ger* **rigging**) *tr* attrezzare, equipaggiare; guarnire; abbigliare in maniera strana

rigging [ˈrɪgɪŋ] *s* (naut) padiglione *m*; (*tackle*) (naut) rizza; (coll) vestiti *mpl*

right [raɪt] *adj* giusto; corretto; (*mind*) sano, destro, diritto; (geom) retto; (geom) perpendicolare; **right or wrong** a torto o a ragione; **to be all right** star bene di salute; **to be right** aver ragione || *s* diritto; quanto è giusto, (il) giusto; (*in a company*) interessanza; (*right hand*) destra; (*turn*) giro a destra; (boxing) diritto; (tex) dritto; (pol) destra; **by right** in giustizia; **on the right** alla destra; **to be in the right** aver ragione || *adv* direttamente; completamente; immediatamente; proprio, precisamente; correttamente, giustamente; bene; alla destra; (coll) molto; **all right** benissimo || *tr* drizzare; correggere; rimettere a posto || *intr* drizzarsi

righteous [ˈraɪtʃəs] *adj* retto; virtuoso

right′ field′ *s* (baseball) campo destro

rightful [ˈraɪtfəl] *adj* giusto; legittimo

right′-hand drive′ *s* guida a destra

right-handed [ˈraɪtˈhændɪd] *adj* che usa la destra; destrorso

right′-hand man′ *s* braccio destro

rightist [ˈraɪtɪst] *adj* conservatore || *s* conservatore *m*, membro della destra

rightly [ˈraɪtli] *adv* correttamente; giustamente; **rightly or wrongly** a torto o a ragione

right′ mind′ *s*—**in one's right mind** nel pieno possesso delle proprie facoltà, con la testa a posto

right′ of way′ *s* precedenza; (law) servitù *f* di passaggio; (rr) sede *f*

rights′ of man′ *s* diritti *mpl* dell'uomo

right′-wing′ *adj* della destra

right-winger [ˈraɪtˈwɪŋər] *s* membro della destra, conservatore *m*

rigid [ˈrɪdʒɪd] *adj* rigido

rigmarole [ˈrɪgməˌrol] *s* sproloquio

rigorous [ˈrɪgərəs] *adj* rigoroso

rile [raɪl] *tr* irritare, esasperare

rill [rɪl] *s* rigagnolo

rim [rɪm] *s* orlo, bordo; (*of a wheel*) cerchione *m*

rime [raɪm] *s* brina; (*in verse*) rima || *tr* brinare; rimare || *intr* rimare

rind [raɪnd] *s* (*of animals*) cotenna; (*of fruit or cheese*) scorza

ring [rɪŋ] *s* (*for finger*) anello; (*anything round*) cerchio; (*circular course*) pista; (*of people*) crocchio; (*of evildoers*) combriccola; (*of anchor*) anello; (*sound of bell*) squillo; (*loud sound of bell*) scampanellata; (*of small bell; of glassware*) tintinnio; (*act of ringing*) sonata; (telp) chiamata; (fig) suono; (boxing) quadrato; (mach) ghiera; (fig, taur) arena; **to run rings around** essere molto migliore di || *v* (*pret & pp* **ringed**) *tr* accerchiare; mettere un anello a || *intr* formare cerchi || *v* (*pret* **rang** [ræŋ]; *pp* **rung** [rʌŋ]) *tr* sonare; squillare; tintinnare; chiamare al telefono; **to ring up** chiamare al telefono; (*a sale*) battere sul registratore di cassa || *intr* sonare; squillare; tintinnare; chiamare; (*said of one's ears*) fischiare; **to ring for** chiamare col campanello; **to ring off** terminare una conversazione telefonica; **to ring up** chiamare al telefono

ring-around-a-rosy [ˈrɪŋəˌraʊndəˈrozi] *s* girotondo

ringing [ˈrɪŋɪŋ] *adj* alto, sonoro || *s* accerchiamento; squillo; tintinnio; (*in the ears*) fischio

ring′lead′er *s* capobanda *m*

ringlet [ˈrɪŋlɪt] *s* anellino

ring′mas′ter *s* direttore *m* di circo equestre

ring′side′ *s* posto vicino al quadrato

ring′worm′ *s* tigna

rink [rɪŋk] *s* pattinatoio

rinse [rɪns] *s* risciacquatura || *tr* risciacquare

riot [ˈraɪət] *s* sommossa, tumulto; profusione; **to be a riot** (coll) essere divertentissimo; **to run riot** sfrenarsi; (*said of plants*) crescere disordinatamente || *intr* tumultuare; darsi alle gozzoviglie

rioter [ˈraɪətər] *s* rivoltoso

rip [rɪp] *s* sdrucitura; (*open seam*) scucitura || *v* (*pret & pp* **ripped**) *ger* **ripping**) *tr* sdrucire; (*to open the* *seam of*) scucire || *intr* sdrucirsi; scucirsi; **to rip out with insults** (coll) prorompere in improperi

ripe [raɪp] *adj* maturo; (*lips*) turgido; (*cheese*) stagionato; pronto

ripen [ˈraɪpən] *tr & intr* maturare

ripple [ˈrɪpəl] *s* increspatura; (*sound*) mormorio || *tr* increspare || *intr* incresparsi; mormorare

rise [raɪz] *s* (*of prices, temperature*) aumento; (*of a road*) salita; (*of ground*) elevazione; (*of a heavenly body*) levata; (*in rank*) ascesa; (*of a step*) alzata; (*of a stream*) sorgente *f*; (*of water*) crescita; **to get a rise out of** (coll) farsi rispondere per le rime da; **to give rise to** dar origine a || *v* (*pret* **rose** [roz]; *pp* **risen** [ˈrɪzən]) *intr* (*said of the sun*) sorgere; rialzarsi; (*said of plants*) crescere; (*said of the wind*) alzarsi; (*said of a building*) ergersi; (*to return from the dead*) risorgere; (*to increase*) aumentare; **to rise above** alzarsi al di sopra di; essere al di sopra di; **to rise to** sorgere all'altezza di

riser [ˈraɪzər] *s* (*of step*) alzata; (*upright*) montante *m*; **early riser** persona mattiniera; **late riser** dormiglione *m*

risk [rɪsk] *s* rischio; **to run or take a risk** correre un rischio || *tr* rischiare

risk·y [ˈrɪski] *adj* (**-ier; -iest**) rischioso

risqué [rɪsˈke] *adj* audace, spinto

rite [raɪt] *s* rito; **last rites** riti *mpl* funebri

ritual [ˈrɪtʃʊ·əl] *adj & s* rituale *m*

ri·val [ˈraɪvəl] *s* rivale *mf* || *v* (*pret & pp* **-valed** or **-valled;** *ger* **-valing** or **-valling**) *tr* rivaleggiare con

rival·ry [ˈraɪvəlri] *s* (**-ries**) rivalità *f*

river [ˈrɪvər] *s* fiume *m*; **down the river** a valle; **up the river** a monte

riv·er ba·sin *s* bacino fluviale

riv·er·bed *s* letto di fiume

riv·er front *s* riva di fiume

riv·er·head *s* sorgente *f* di fiume

riv·er·side *s* rivierasco || *s* riva del fiume

rivet [ˈrɪvɪt] *s* ribattino; (*of scissors*) perno || *tr* ribadire; (*s.o.'s attention*) concentrare

roach [rotʃ] *s* scarafaggio

road [rod] *adj* stradale || *s* strada; via; (naut) rada; **to be in the road of** ostacolare il cammino a; **to burn up the road** divorare la strada; **to get out of the road** togliersi di mezzo

roadability [ˌrodəˈbɪlɪti] *s* tenuta di strada

road·bed *s* (*of highway*) piattaforma; (rr) massicciata, infrastruttura

road·block *s* (mil) barricata; (fig) impedimento

road·house *s* taverna su autostrada

road la·borer *s* cantoniere *m*

road map *s* carta stradale

road roll·er *s* compressore *m* stradale, rullo compressore

road serv·ice *s* servizio di assistenza stradale

road·side *s* bordo della strada

road·side inn *s* taverna posta su autostrada

road sign *s* indicatore *m* stradale

road·stead *s* rada

road·way *s* carreggiata; strada

roam [rom] *s* vagabondaggio || *tr* girovagare per || *intr* girovagare

roar [ror] *s* ruggito, muggito; boato, fragore *m* || *intr* muggire; **to roar with laughter** fare una risata

roast [rost] *s* arrosto; torrefazione || *tr* arrostire; (*coffee*) tostare, torrefare; (coll) farsi beffe di || *intr* arrostirsi

roast beef *s* rosbif *m*

roast·ed pea·nut *s* nocciolina americana abbrustolita

roast pork *s* arrosto di maiale

rob [rab] *v* (*pret & pp* **robbed;** *ger* **robbing**) *tr & intr* derubare

robber [ˈrabər] *s* ladro, malandrino

robber·y [ˈrabəri] *s* (**-ies**) furto

robe [rob] *s* (*of a woman*) vestito; (*of a professor*) toga; (*of a priest*) abito talare; (*dressing gown*) vestaglia; (*for lap*) coperta da viaggio; **robes** vestiti *mpl* || *tr* vestire || *intr* vestirsi

robin [ˈrabɪn] *s* pettirosso

robot [ˈrobat] *s* robot *m*

robust [roˈbʌst] *adj* robusto

rock [rak] *s* roccia; (*any stone*) pietra; (*sticking out of water*) scoglio; (*one that is thrown*) sasso; (*hill*) rocca; (slang) pietra preziosa; **on the rocks** (coll) in rovina; (coll) al verde; (said, e.g., of whiskey) sul ghiaccio || *tr* far vacillare; dondolare || *intr* vacillare; dondolare

rock·bot·tom *adj* (l') ultimo; (il) minimo

rock can·dy *s* zucchero candito

rock crys·tal *s* cristallo di rocca

rocker [ˈrakər] *s* (*curved piece at bottom of rocking chair*) dondolo; sedia a dondolo; (mach) bilanciere *m*; **off one's rocker** (slang) matto

rocket [ˈrakɪt] *s* razzo || *intr* partire come un razzo

rock·et launch·er [ˈlɔntʃər] or [ˈlɑntʃər] *s* lanciarazzo

rock gar·den *s* giardino piantato fra le rocce

rock·ing chair *s* sedia a dondolo

rock·ing horse *s* cavallo a dondolo

rock salt *s* salgemma *m*

rock wool *s* cotone *m* or lana minerale

rock·y [ˈraki] *adj* (**-ier; -iest**) roccioso; traballante; (coll) debole

rod [rad] *s* verga, bacchetta; scettro; punizione; (*bar*) asta; (*for fishing*) canna da pesca; (anat, biol) bastoncino; (mach) biella; (surv) biffa; (Bib) razza, tribù *f*; (slang) pistola; **spare the rod and spoil the child** la madre pietosa fa la piaga cancrenosa

rodent [ˈrodənt] *adj & s* roditore *m*

rod·man *s* (**-men**) *s* aiutante *m* geometra

roe [ro] *s* capriolo; (*of fish*) uova *fpl*

rogue [rog] *s* furfante *m*; (*scamp*) picaro

rogues'' gal′lery s collezione di fotografie di malviventi

rôle or **role** [rol] s ruolo, parte f; **to play a role** fare la parte

roll [rol] s (of film, paper, etc.) rotolo, bobina; (of fat) strato; (roller) rotella; (of bread) panino; ondulazione; (noise) rullio, rullo; (of a boat) rollio; (of thunder) rombo; (list) ruolo; (of money) (slang) fascio; **to call the roll** fare la chiama ‖ tr far rotolare; (one's r's) arrotare; (one's eyes) stralunare; (e.g., dough) spianare; (steel) laminare; (to wrap) arrotolare; (a drum) rullare; **to roll back** (prices) ridurre; **to roll out** spianare; **to roll up** (one's sleeves) arrotolarsi; accumulare; aumentare ‖ intr rotolare; rullare; arrotolarsi; raggomitolarsi; **to roll on** passare; **to roll out** srotolarsi; (to get out of bed) (slang) alzarsi

roll′ call′ s chiama, appello

roll′er ['rolər] s rotella; (for hair) bigodino; rotolo; (wave) ondata lunga

roll′er bear′ing s cuscinetto a rotolamento

roll′er coast′er s montagne russe

roll′er skate′ s pattino a rotelle

roll′er-skate′ intr pattinare coi pattini a rotelle

roll′er tow′el s bandinella

roll′ing mill′ ['rolɪŋ] s laminatoio

roll′ing pin′ s matterello

roll′ing stock′ s (rr) materiale m rotabile

roll′-top desk′ s scrivania a piano scorrevole

roly-poly ['roli'poli] adj grassoccio

roman ['romən] adj (typ) romano, tondo ‖ s (typ) carattere romano, tondo ‖ **Roman** adj & s romano

Ro′man can′dle s candela romana

Ro′man Cath′olic Church′ s Chiesa Cattolica Apostolica Romana

romance [ro'mæns] or ['romæns] s romanzo; sentimentalità f; idillio, intrigo amoroso; (mus) romanza ‖ [ro'mæns] intr scrivere romanzi; raccontare romanzi; fare il romantico ‖ **Romance** ['romæns] or [ro'mæns] adj romanzo, neolatino

Ro′man Em′pire s Impero Romano

romanesque [,romən'esk] adj romantico ‖ **Romanesque** adj & s romanico

Ro′man nose′ s naso aquilino

romantic [ro'mæntɪk] adj romantico

romanticism [ro'mæntɪ,sɪzəm] s romanticismo

romanticist [ro'mæntɪsɪst] s romantico

romp [ramp] intr ruzzare

rompers ['rampərz] spl pagliaccetto

roof [ruf] or [ruf] s (of house) tetto; (of heaven) volta; (of car) tetto, padiglione m; **to hit the roof** (slang) andare fuori dai gangheri; **to raise the roof** (slang) fare molto chiasso; (slang) protestare violentemente ‖ tr ricoprire con tetto

roofer ['rufər] or ['rufər] s conciatetti

roof′ gar′den s giardino pensile

rook [ruk] s (bird) cornacchia; (in chess) torre f ‖ tr truffare

rookie ['ruki] s novizio; (mil) recluta

room [rum] or [rum] s stanza, camera; vano, locale m; posto, spazio; opportunità f; **to make room** far luogo ‖ intr alloggiare

room′ and board′ s vitto e alloggio

room′ clerk′ s impiegato d'albergo assegnato alle prenotazioni

roomer ['rumər] or ['rumər] s inquilino

room′ing house′ s casa con camere d'affittare

room′mate′ s compagno di stanza

room·y ['rumi] or ['rumi] adj (-ier; -iest) ampio, spazioso

roost [rust] s (perch) ballatoio; (house for chickens) pollaio; (place for resting) posto di riposo; **to rule the roost** essere il gallo del pollaio ‖ intr appollaiarsi; andare a dormire

rooster ['rustər] s gallo

root [rut] or [rut] s radice f; **to get to the root** of andare al fondo di; **to take root** metter radici ‖ tr inchiodare, piantare ‖ intr radicare; (said of swine) grufolare; **to root for** fare il tifo per

rooter ['rutər] or ['rutər] s tifoso

rope [rop] s fune f, corda; (of a hangman) capestro; laccio, lasso; **to know the ropes** (coll) conoscere la faccenda a fondo, saperla lunga ‖ tr legare con fune; prendere al laccio; **to rope in** (slang) imbrogliare

rope′danc′er or **rope′walk′er** s funambolo

rosa·ry ['rozəri] s (-ries) rosario

rose [roz] adj & s rosa

rose′bud′ s bottoncino di rosa

rose′bush′ s rosaio

rose′-col′ored adj color di rosa

rose′-colored glass′es spl occhiali mpl rosa

rose′ gar′den s roseto

rosemar·y ['roz,meri] s (-ies) rosmarino

rose′ of Shar′on ['ʃerən] s altea

rosette [ro'zet] s rosetta; (archit) rosone m

rose′ win′dow s rosone m

rose′wood′ s palissandro

rosin ['razɪn] s colofonia

roster ['rastər] s ruolino; orario scolastico

rostrum ['rastrəm] s tribuna

ros·y ['rozi] adj (-ier; -iest) rosa, roseo

rot [rat] s marcio; (coll) stupidaggine f ‖ v (pret & pp **rotted**; ger **rotting**) tr & intr imputridire

ro′tary en′gine ['rotəri] s motore rotativo

ro′tary press′ s rotativa

rotate ['rotet] or [ro'tet] tr & intr rotare

rotation [ro'teʃən] s rotazione; **in rotation** in successione, a turno

rote [rot] s ripetizione macchinale; **by rote** a memoria

rot′gut′ s (slang) acquavite f di infima qualità

rotisserie [ro'tɪsəri] *s* girarrosto a motore

rotten ['rɑtən] *adj* marcio, fradicio; corrotto

rotund [ro'tʌnd] *adj* (*plump*) rotondetto; (*voice*) profondo; (*speech*) enfatico

rouge [ruʒ] *s* belletto, rossetto || *tr* dare il belletto a || *intr* darsi il belletto

rough [rʌf] *adj* scabroso; (*sea*) agitato; (*crude*) rozzo, rude; (*road*) accidentato; approssimativo || *tr*—**to rough it** vivere primitivamente; **to rough up** malmenare

rough'cast' *s* intonaco; modello disgrossato || *v* (*pret & pp* -cast) *tr* (*a wall*) intonacare; disgrossare, dirozzare

rough' cop'y *s* brutta copia

rough-hew ['rʌf'hju] *tr* digrossare, dirozzare

roughly ['rʌfli] *adv* aspramente; rozzamente; approssimativamente

round [raund] *adj* rotondo || *s* tondo; (*of applause; of guns*) salva; (*of a single gun*) colpo, tiro; (*of a chair*) piolo; (*of a doctor*) giro; (*of a policeman*) ronda; serie *f*; (*of golf*) partita; (*e.g., of bridge*) mano *f*; cerchio; (*boxing*) ripresa || *adv* intorno; dal principio alla fine || *prep* intorno a; attraverso || *tr* (*to make round*) arrotondare; circondare; (*a corner*) scantonare; **to round off** arrotondare; completare, perfezionare; **to round up** raccogliere; (*cattle*) condurre

roundabout ['raundə,baut] *adj* indiretto || *s* giacca attillata; via traversa; giro di parole; (*Brit*) giostra; (*Brit*) anello stradale

round'house' *s* rimessa per locomotive

round-shouldered ['raund'ʃoldərd] *adj* dalle spalle spioventi

round'-trip tick'et *s* biglietto d'andata e ritorno

round'up' *s* (*of cattle*) riunione; (*of criminals*) retata; (*of facts*) riassunto

rouse [rauz] *tr* svegliare; suscitare; (*game*) scovare || *intr* svegliarsi

rout [raut] *s* sconfitta, rotta || *tr* sconfiggere, mettere in rotta || *intr* grufolare

route [rut] *or* [raut] *s* via, rotta; itinerario || *tr* istradare

routine [ru'tin] *adj* ordinario || *s* trafila, routine *f*

rove [rov] *intr* vagabondare, vagare

rover ['rovər] *s* vagabondo

row [rau] *s* piazzata, scenata; (*clamor*) (coll) baccano; **to raise a row** (coll) fare baccano || [ro] *s* fila; (*of figures*) finca; (*e.g., of trees*) filare *m*; **in a row** in continuazione, di seguito || *tr* vogare || *intr* remare, vogare

rowboat ['ro,bot] *s* barca a remi

row·dy ['raudi] *adj* (-dier; -diest) turbolento || *s* (-dies) attaccabrighe *mf*

rower ['ro·ər] *s* rematore *m*

rowing ['ro·ɪŋ] *s* (*action*) voga; (*sport*) canottaggio

royal ['rɔɪ·əl] *adj* reale, regio

royalist ['rɔɪ·əlɪst] *adj* sostenitore del re || *s* realista *mf*

royal·ty ['rɔɪ·əlti] *s* (-ties) regalità *f*; membro della famiglia reale; nobiltà *f*; diritto d'autore; diritto d'inventore; percentuale *f* sugli utili

rub [rʌb] *s* frizione; difficile *m*; **here's the rub** qui sta il busillis || *v* (*pret & pp* rubbed; *ger* rubbing) *tr* fregare; **to rub elbows** con stare giunto a gomiti con; **to rub out** cancellare con la gomma; (slang) togliere di mezzo || *intr* sfregare; **to rub off** venir via sfregando; cancellarsi

rubber ['rʌbər] *s* gomma, caucciù *m*; gomma da cancellare; (*overshoe*) caloscia; (*in cards*) rubber *m*; (sports) bella

rub'ber band' *s* elastico

rub'ber-neck' *s* (coll) ficcanaso; (coll) turista curioso || *intr* (coll) allungare il collo

rub'ber plant' *s* albero del caucciù

rub'ber stamp' *s* timbro di gomma; (coll) persona che approva inconsultamente

rub'ber-stamp' *tr* timbrare; (coll) approvare inconsultamente

rubbish ['rʌbɪʃ] *s* spazzatura; immondizia; (fig) detrito; (coll) sciocchezza

rubble ['rʌbəl] *s* (*broken stone*) pietrisco; (*masonry*) mistura di malta e pietrame; (*broken bits*) calcinacci *mpl*

rub'down' *s* fregagione

rube [rub] *s* (slang) contadino gonzo

ru·by ['rubi] *adj* vermiglio || *s* (-bies) rubino

rudder ['rʌdər] *s* timone *m*; (aer) timone *m* di direzione

rud·dy ['rʌdi] *adj* (-dier; -diest) rubicondo

rude [rud] *adj* rude, sgarbato

rudiment ['rudɪmənt] *s* rudimento

rue [ru] *tr* lamentare, rimpiangere

rueful ['rufəl] *adj* lamentevole; triste

ruffian ['rʌfɪ·ən] *s* ribaldo

ruffle ['rʌfəl] *s* increspatura; (*of drum*) rullo; (sew) gala, crespa || *tr* increspare; arruffare; irritare; (*a drum*) far rullare; (sew) guarnire di gala or crespa

rug [rʌg] *s* tappeto

rugged ['rʌgɪd] *adj* aspro, irregolare; rugoso; rozzo; forte; tempestoso

ruin ['ru·ɪn] *s* rovina || *tr* rovinare, mandare in rovina

rule [rul] *s* regola; dominazione; (*reign*) regno; (law) ordinanza; (typ) filetto; **as a rule** in generale || *tr* governare; dominare; (*with lines*) rigare; (law) deliberare; **to rule out** escludere || *intr* governare; regnare; **to rule over** governare

rule' of thumb' *s* regola basata sull'esperienza; **by rule of thumb** secondo la propria esperienza

ruler ['rulər] *s* governante *m*, dominatore *m*; (*for ruling lines*) riga, regolo

ruling ['rulɪŋ] *adj* dirigente || *s* (*ruled lines*) rigatura; (law) decisione

rum [rʌm] *s* rum *m*; (*any alcoholic drink*) acquavite *f*

Rumanian [ruˈmenɪ·ən] *adj & s* rumeno

rumble [ˈrʌmbəl] *s* rimbombo; (*of the intestines*) gorgoglio; (*slang*) rissa fra ganghe rivali ‖ *intr* rimbombare; gorgogliare

ruminate [ˈrumɪ ˌnet] *tr & intr* ruminare

rummage [ˈrʌmɪdʒ] *tr & intr* rovistare, frugare

rum'mage sale' *s* vendita di cianfrusaglie

rumor [ˈrumər] *s* voce *f*, diceria ‖ *tr* vociferare; **it is rumored that** corre voce che

rump [rʌmp] *s* anca; posteriore *m;* (*of beef*) quarto posteriore

rumple [ˈrʌmpəl] *s* piega ‖ *tr* spiegazzare, sgualcire ‖ *intr* sgualcirsi

rumpus [ˈrʌmpəs] *s* tumulto; rissa; **to raise a rumpus** fare baccano

run [rʌn] *s* corsa; percorso; produzione; (*e.g., in a stocking*) smagliatura; direzione; (*spell*) serie *f;* (*in cards*) scala; (*of goods*) richiesta; (*on a bank*) afflusso; **in the long run** a lungo andare; **on the run** (coll) di corsa; in fuga; **the common run of men** la media della gente; **to give s.o. a run for his money** dare a qlcu del filo da torcere; essere denaro ben speso per qlcu, e.g., **that sweater gave me a run for my money** quello sweater è stato denaro ben speso per me; **to have a long run** tenere il cartellone per lungo tempo; **to have the run of** avere la libertà di andare e venire per ‖ *v* (*pret* ran [ræn]; *pp* run; *ger* running) *tr* muovere; (*a horse*) far correre; (*the street*) vivere liberamente in; (*game*) inseguire; trasportare; (*a machine*) far camminare; (*a store*) esercire; (*a candidate*) portare; (*a risk*) correre; (*a blockade*) violare; mettere, ficcare; (*a line*) tirare; **to run down** cacciare; esaminare; trovare; (*a pedestrian*) investire; denigrare, criticare; **to run in** (*a machine*) rodare; (*slang*) schiaffare in prigione; **to run off** creare di getto; cacciare; (*typ*) tirare; **to run up** ammassare ‖ *intr* correre; scappare; (*in a race*) arrivare; (*said of a candidate*) portarsi; passare; (*said of knitted material*) smagliarsi; (*said of a liquid*) scorrere; (*said of a color*) sbavare; (*said of fish*) migrare; funzionare; (*to become*) diventare; (*to be worded*) essere del tenore; (*com*) decorrere; (*theat, mov*) durare in cartellone; **to run across** imbattersi in; **to run aground** incagliarsi; **to run away** fuggire; (*said of a horse*) prendere la mano; **to run down** (*said of a liquid*) scorrere; (*said of a battery, a watch*) scaricarsi; (*in health*) sciuparsi; **to run for** presentarsi candidato per; **to run in the family** essere una caratteristica familiare; **to run into** imbattersi in; ammontare a; (*to follow*) succedersi a; **to run off the track** (rr) uscire dalle rotaie; **to run out** aver termine; scadere; esaurirsi;

to run out of rimanere senza; **to run over** oltrepassare; (*e.g., with a car*) investire; **to run through** trapassare; (*a fortune*) dilapidare; esaminare rapidamente

run'a·way' *adj* fuggiasco; (*horse*) che ha preso la mano ‖ *s* fuggiasco; cavallo che ha preso la mano; fuga

run'-down' *adj* esausto; negletto, cadente; (*watch, battery*) scarico

rung [rʌŋ] *s* (*of chair or ladder*) piolo

runner [ˈrʌnər] *s* corridore *m;* messaggero; fattorino, messo; (*of sleigh*) pattino; (*of ice skate*) lama; (*rug*) guida; (*on a table*) striscia di pizzo; (*in stocking*) smagliatura

run'ner-up' *s* (**runners-up**) finalista *mf* secondo

running [ˈrʌnɪŋ] *adj* in corsa; da corsa; (*water*) corrente; (*vine*) rampicante; (*knot*) scorsoio; (*sore*) purulento; (*writing*) corsivo; consecutivo; (*start*) (sports) lanciato ‖ *s* corsa; (*of a business*) esercizio; direzione; funzionamento; **to be in the running** avere possibilità di vittoria

run'ning board' *s* predana

run'ning head' *s* titolo corrente

run·ny [ˈrʌni] *adj* (**-nier; -niest**) (*liquid*) scorrevole; (*color*) sbavante; **to have a runny nose** avere la goccia al naso

run'off' *s* ballottaggio

run-of-the-mill [ˈrʌnəvðəˈmɪl] *adj* ordinario, corrente

run'proof' *adj* indemagliabile

runt [rʌnt] *s* nanerottolo; animale deperito

run'way' *s* pista; (*of a stream*) letto; (*for animals*) chiusa; (aut) corsia

rupture [ˈrʌptʃər] *s* rottura; (pathol) ernia ‖ *tr* rompere; causare un'ernia a ‖ *intr* rompersi; soffrire di ernia

ru'ral free' deliv'ery [ˈrurəl] *s* distribuzione postale campestre

ruse [ruz] *s* astuzia, stratagemma *m*

rush [rʌʃ] *adj* urgente ‖ *s* fretta; slancio, corsa; (*of blood*) ondata; (*rushing of persons to a new mine*) febbre *f;* (bot) giunco; **in a rush** in fretta e furia ‖ *tr* affrettare; portare di fretta; spingere; (coll) fare la corte a; **to rush through** fare di fretta; (*e.g., a bill through Congress*) far approvare di fretta ‖ *intr* lanciarsi; affrettarsi; passare velocemente; **to rush through** (*a book*) leggere velocemente; (*one's work*) fare in fretta; (*a town*) attraversare velocemente

rush'-bot'tomed chair' *s* sedia di giunchi

rush' can'dle *s* lumicino con lo stoppino fatto di midollo di giunco

rush' hour' *s* ora di punta

russet [ˈrʌsɪt] *adj* color cannella

Russia [ˈrʌʃə] *s* la Russia

Russian [ˈrʌʃən] *adj & s* russo

rust [rʌst] *s* ruggine *f;* (fig) torpore *m* ‖ *tr* arrugginire ‖ *intr* arrugginirsi

rustic [ˈrʌstɪk] *adj & s* rusti·o

rustle [ˈrʌsəl] *s* fruscio; (*of leaves*) stormire *m* ‖ *tr* far frusciare; far stormire; *(cattle)* (coll) rubare ‖ *intr* frusciare; stormire; (coll) lavorare di buzzo buono

rust·y ['rʌsti] *adj* (**-ier; -iest**) rugginoso; color ruggine; fuori pratica

rut [rʌt] *s (track)* solco, carrareccia; *(of animals)* fregola; (il) solito tran tran.

ruthless ['ruθlɪs] *adj* spietato

rye [raɪ] *s* segala; whiskey *m* di segala

S

S, s [ɛs] *s* diciannovesima lettera dell'alfabeto inglese

Sabbath ['sæbəθ] *s (of Jews)* sabato; *(of Christians)* domenica; **to keep the Sabbath** osservare il riposo domenicale

sabbat'ical year' [sə'bætɪkəl] *s* anno di congedo; (Bib) anno sabbatico

saber ['sebər] *s* sciabola

sa'ber rat'tling *s* minacce *fpl* di guerra

sable ['sebəl] *adj* nero ‖ *s* zibellino; **sables** vestiti di lutto

sabotage ['sæbə,taʒ] *s* sabotaggio ‖ *tr & intr* sabotare

saccharin ['sækərɪn] *s* saccarina

sachet ['sæʃe] or [sæ'ʃe] *s* sacchetto profumato (per la biancheria)

sack [sæk] *s* sacco; *(of an employee)* (slang) licenziamento; (slang) letto ‖ *tr* insaccare; *(to lay waste)* saccheggiare, mettere a sacco; (slang) licenziare

sack'cloth' *s* tela di sacco; *(for penitence)* sacco, cilicio; **in sackcloth and ashes** pentito e contrito

sacrament ['sækrəmənt] *s* sacramento

sacramental [,sækrə'mentəl] *adj* sacramentale

sacred ['sekrəd] *adj* sacro

sacrifice ['sækrɪ,faɪs] *s* sacrificio; **at a sacrifice** in perdita ‖ *tr* sacrificare; (com) svendere

sacrilege ['sækrɪlɪdʒ] *s* sacrilegio

sacrilegious [,sækrɪ'lɪdʒəs] or [,sækrɪ'lidʒəs] *adj* sacrilego

sacristan ['sækrɪstən] *s* sagrestano

sacris·ty ['sækrɪsti] *s* (**-ties**) sagrestia

sad [sæd] *adj* (**sadder; saddest**) triste; *(bad)* cattivo; *(color)* tetro

sadden ['sædən] *tr* rattristare ‖ *intr* rattristarsi

saddle ['sædəl] *s* sella ‖ *tr* insellare; **to saddle with** gravare di

saddle'bag' *s* fonda

saddlebow ['sædəl,bo] *s* arcione *m* anteriore

sad'dle-cloth' *s* gualdrappa

saddler ['sædlər] *s* sellaio

sad'dle-tree' *s* arcione *m*

sadist ['sædɪst] or ['sedɪst] *s* sadico

sadistic [sæ'dɪstɪk] or [se'dɪstɪk] *adj* sadico

sadness ['sædnɪs] *s* tristezza

sad' sack' *s* (coll) marmittone *m*

safe [sef] *adj* sicuro; cauto; *(distance)* rispettoso; **safe and sound** sano e salvo ‖ *s* cassaforte *f*

safe'-con'duct *s* salvacondotto

safe'-depos'it box' *s* cassetta di sicurezza

safe'guard' *s* salvaguardia ‖ *tr* salvaguardare

safe·ty ['sefti] *adj* di sicurezza ‖ *s* (**-ties**) sicurezza; *(of a gun)* sicura; **to reach safety** mettersi in salvo

safe'ty belt' *s (of a worker)* imbraca; (aer, aut) cintura di sicurezza; (naut) cintura di salvataggio

safe'ty glass' *s* vetro infrangibile

safe'ty is'land *s* salvagente *m*

safe'ty match' *s* fiammifero svedese

safe'ty pin' *s* spillo di sicurezza

safe'ty ra'zor *s* rasoio di sicurezza

safe'ty valve' *s* valvola di sicurezza

saffron ['sæfrən] *s* zafferano

sag [sæg] *s* cedimento; depressione; *(of a rope)* allentamento ‖ *v (pret & pp sagged; ger sagging)* *intr* curvarsi; cedere, afflosciarsi; allentarsi; *(said of prices)* calare

sagacious [sə'geʃəs] *adj* sagace

sage [sedʒ] *adj* saggio, savio ‖ *s* saggio, savio; (bot) salvia

sage'brush' *s* artemisia

Sagittarius [,sædʒɪ'teri·əs] *s* Sagittario

sail [sel] *s* vela; *(of windmill)* ala; gita a vela; **to set sail** far vela; **under full sail** a piena velatura ‖ *tr* veleggiare, navigare; *(a boat)* far navigare ‖ *intr* veleggiare, navigare; far vela; volare; *(said of a vessel)* partire; **to sail into** (coll) attaccare

sail'boat' *s* nave *f* a vela, veliero

sail'cloth' *s* tela di olona

sailing ['selɪŋ] *adj* in partenza ‖ *s* partenza; navigazione; navigazione a vela

sail'ing ship' *s* veliero

sail'mak'er *s* velaio

sailor ['selər] *s* marinaio

saint [sent] *adj & s* santo ‖ *tr* santificare, canonizzare

saint'hood *s* santità *f*

saintliness ['sentlɪnɪs] *s* santità *f*

Saint' Vi'tus's dance' ['vaɪtəsəz] *s* (pathol) ballo di San Vito

sake [sek] *s* causa, interesse *m*; **for the sake of** per il bene di, per l'amor di

salaam [sə'lɑm] *s* salamelecco ‖ *tr* fare salamelecchi

salable ['seləbəl] *adj* vendibile

salacious [sə'leʃəs] *adj* salace

salad ['sæləd] *s* insalata

sal'ad bowl' *s* insalatiera

sal'ad oil' *s* olio da tavola

sala·ry ['sæləri] *s* (**-ries**) stipendio

sale [sel] *s* vendita; *(at reduced prices)* svendita, saldo; **for sale** in vendita; si vende, si vendono

sales'clerk' *s* commesso, impiegato

sales'la·dy *s* (**-dies**) commessa, impiegata

sales'man *s* (**-men**) venditore *m;* commesso; (*traveling*) piazzista *m*

sales'man·ship' *s* arte *f* di vendere

sales' promo'tion *s* promozione delle vendite, promotion *f*

sales'room' *s* sala di esposizione; sala vendite

sales' talk' *s* discorso da venditore; (*e.g., of a barker*) imbonimento

sales' tax' *s* imposta sulle vendite

saliva [sə'laɪvə] *s* saliva

sallow ['sælo] *adj* giallastro, olivastro

sal·ly ['sælɪ] *s* (**-lies**) escursione, gita; (*outburst*) esplosione; (*witty remark*) uscita; (mil) sortita ‖ *v pret & pp* **-lied**) *intr* fare una sortita; **to sally forth** balzar fuori

salmon ['sæmən] *s* salmone *m*

salon [sæ'lɑn] *s* salone *m*

saloon [sə'lun] *s* taverna; (*on a passenger vessel*) salone *m*

saloon' keep'er *s* taverniere *m*

salt [sɔlt] *s* sale *m;* **to be worth one's salt** valere il pane che si mangia ‖ *tr* salare; (*cattle*) dare sale a; **to salt away** (coll) metter via, conservare

salt' bed' *s* salina

salt'cel'lar *s* saliera

saltine [sɔl'tin] *s* galletta salata

saltish ['sɔltɪʃ] *adj* salmastro

salt'pe'ter *s* (*potassium nitrate*) salnitro; (*sodium nitrate*) nitro del Cile

salt' shak'er *s* saliera

salt·y ['sɔltɪ] *adj* (**-ier; -iest**) salato

salubrious [sə'lubrɪ·əs] *adj* salubre

salutation [ˌsæljə'teʃən] *s* saluto

salute [sə'lut] *s* saluto ‖ *tr* salutare

salvage ['sælvɪdʒ] *s* ricupero ‖ *tr* ricuperare

salvation [sæl'veʃən] *s* salvezza

Salva'tion Ar'my *s* Esercito della Salvezza

salve [sæv] *or* [sav] *s* unguento ‖ *tr* lenire, alleviare

sal·vo ['sælvo] *s* (**-vos** *or* **-voes**) salva

Samaritan [sə'mærɪtən] *adj* & *s* samaritano

same [sem] *adj* & *pron indef* medesimo, stesso; **it's all the same to me** a me fa lo stesso; **just the same** lo stesso, ugualmente; ciò nonostante; **same . . . as** lo stesso . . . che

sameness ['semnɪs] *s* uniformità *f;* monotonia

sample ['sæmpəl] *s* campione *m,* saggio ‖ *tr* (*to take a sample of*) campionare; (*to taste*) assaggiare; provare

sam'ple cop'y *s* esemplare *m* di campione

sancti·fy ['sæŋktɪˌfaɪ] *v* (*pret & pp* **-fied**) *tr* santificare

sanctimonious [ˌsæŋktɪ'monɪ·əs] *adj* che affetta devozione ipocrita

sanction ['sæŋkʃən] *s* sanzione ‖ *tr* sanzionare

sanctuar·y ['sæŋktʃʊˌɛrɪ] *s* (**-ies**) santuario; **to take sanctuary** prendere asilo, rifugiarsi

sand [sænd] *s* sabbia ‖ *tr* insabbiare;

(*to polish*) smerigliare; cospergere di sabbia

sandal ['sændəl] *s* sandalo

san'dal·wood' *s* sandalo

sand'bag' *s* sacchetto a terra

sand'bank' *s* banco di sabbia

sand' bar' *s* cordone *m* litorale, banco di sabbia

sand'blast' *s* sabbiatura ‖ *tr* pulire con sabbiatura, sabbiare

sand'box' *s* cassone *m* pieno di sabbia; (rr) sabbiera

sand'glass' *s* orologio a polvere or a sabbia

sand'pa'per *s* carta vetrata ‖ *tr* pulire con carta vetrata

sand'stone' *s* arenaria

sandwich ['sændwɪtʃ] *s* panino imbottito, tramezzino ‖ *tr* inserire

sand'wich man' *s* tramezzino, uomo sandwich

sand·y ['sændɪ] *adj* (**-ier; -iest**) sabbioso; (*hair*) biondo rossiccio

sane [sen] *adj* sensato

sanguinary ['sæŋgwɪnˌɛrɪ] *adj* sanguinario

sanguine ['sæŋgwɪn] *adj* fiducioso; (*complexion*) sanguigno

sanitary ['sænɪˌtɛrɪ] *adj* sanitario

san'itary nap'kin *s* pannolino igienico

sanitation [ˌsænɪ'teʃən] *s* sanità *f*

sanity ['sænɪtɪ] *s* sanità *f* di mente

Santa Claus ['sæntəˌklɔz] *s* Babbo Natale

sap [sæp] *s* linfa, succhio; (mil) trincea; (coll) scemo ‖ *v* (*pret & pp* **sapped**) *ger* **sapping**) *tr* scavare; insidiare, minare; (*to weaken*) indebolire

sapling ['sæplɪŋ] *s* alberello; (*youth*) giovanetto

sapphire ['sæfaɪr] *s* zaffiro

Saracen ['særəsən] *adj* & *s* saraceno

sarcasm ['sɑrkæzəm] *s* sarcasmo

sarcastic [sɑr'kæstɪk] *adj* sarcastico

sardine [sɑr'din] *s* sardina; **packed in like sardines** pigiati come le acciughe

Sardinia [sɑr'dɪnɪ·ə] *s* la Sardegna

Sardinian [sɑr'dɪnɪ·ən] *adj* & *s* sardo

sarsaparilla [ˌsɑrsəpə'rɪlə] *s* salsapariglia

sash [sæʃ] *s* sciarpa; (*around one's waist*) fusciacca; (*of window*) telaio

sash' win'dow *s* finestra a ghigliottina

sas·sy ['sæsi] *adj* (**-sier; -siest**) (coll) impertinente; (*pert*) (coll) vivace

satchel ['sætʃəl] *s* sacca; (*of schoolboy*) cartella

sateen [sæ'tin] *s* satin *m*

satellite ['sætəˌlaɪt] *s* satellite *m*

satiate ['seʃɪˌet] *tr* saziare

satin ['sætən] *s* raso

satire ['sætaɪr] *s* satira

satiric(al) [sə'tɪrɪk(əl)] *adj* satirico

satirist ['sætɪrɪst] *s* satirico

satirize ['sætɪˌraɪz] *tr* satireggiare

satisfaction [ˌsætɪs'fækʃən] *s* soddisfazione

satisfactory [ˌsætɪs'fæktərɪ] *adj* soddisfacente

satis·fy ['sætɪsˌfaɪ] *v* (*pret & pp* **-fied**) *tr* & *intr* soddisfare

saturate ['sætʃəˌret] *tr* saturare

Saturday ['sætərdi] *s* sabato

Saturn ['sætərn] *s* (astr) Saturno

sauce [sɔs] *s* salsa; (*of fruit*) conserva; (*of chocolate*) crema; (coll) insolenza, impertinenza || *tr* condire; rendere piccante || [sɔs] or [sæs] *tr* (coll) rispondere con impertinenza a

sauce'pan' *s* casseruola

saucer ['sɔsər] *s* piattino

sau·cy ['sɔsi] *adj* (-cier; -ciest) impertinente; (*pert*) vivace

sauerkraut ['saur,kraut] *s* sarcrauti *mpl*, crauti *mpl*

saunter ['sɔntər] *s* giro, bighellonata || *intr* girandolare, bighellonare

sausage ['sɔsɪdʒ] *s* salsiccia

savage ['sævɪdʒ] *adj & s* selvaggio

savant ['sævənt] *s* erudito

save [sev] *prep* tranne, salvo || *tr* salvare; (*money*) risparmiare; (*to set apart*) serbare; **to save face** salvare le apparenze || *intr* fare economia

saving ['sevɪŋ] *adj* economico; che redime || **savings** *spl* risparmi *mpl*, economie *fpl* || **saving** *prep* eccetto, salvo

sav'ings account' *s* conto di risparmio

sav'ings and loan' associa'tion *s* cassa di risparmio che concede mutui

sav'ings bank' *s* cassa di risparmio

savior ['sevjər] *s* salvatore *m*

Saviour ['sevjər] *s* Salvatore *m*

savor ['sevər] *s* sapore *m* || *tr* assaporare; (*to flavor*) saporire || *intr* odorare; **to savor of** sapere di; odorare di

savor·y ['sevəri] *adj* (-ier; -iest) saporoso; piccante; delizioso || *s* (-ies) (bot) santoreggia

saw [sɔ] *s* (*tool*) sega; detto, proverbio || *tr* segare

saw'buck' *s* cavalletto

saw'dust' *s* segatura

saw'horse' *s* cavalletto

saw'mill' *s* segheria

Saxon ['sæksən] *adj & s* sassone *m*

saxophone ['sæksə,fon] *s* sassofono

say [se] *s* dire *m*; **to have no say** non aver voce in capitolo; **to have one's say** esprimere la propria opinione; **to have the say** avere l'ultima parola || *v* (*pret & pp* **said** [sɛd]) *tr* dire; **I should say so!** certamente; **it is said** si dice; **no sooner said than done** detto fatto; **that is to say** vale a dire; **to go without saying** essere ovvio

saying ['se·ɪŋ] *s* detto, proverbio

scab [skæb] *s* crosta; (*strikebreaker*) crumiro

scabbard ['skæbərd] *s* guaina, fodero

scab·by ['skæbi] *adj* (-bier; -biest) crostoso; (*animal*) rognoso; (slang) vile

scabrous ['skæbrəs] *adj* scabroso

scads [skædz] *spl* (slang) un mucchio

scaffold ['skæfəld] *s* impalcatura; (*to execute a criminal*) patibolo

scaffolding ['skæfəldɪŋ] *s* incastellatura, ponteggio

scald [skɔld] *tr* scottare; (*e.g.*, *milk*) cuocere al disotto del punto d'ebollizione

scale [skel] *s* (*e.g.*, *of map*) scala; piatto della bilancia; (*of fish*) squama; **on a large scale** in grande scala; **scales** bilancia; **to tip the scales** far inclinare la bilancia || *tr* squamare; (*to incrust*) incrostare; (*to weigh*) pesare; scalare; graduare; ridurre a scala || *intr* squamarsi; scrostarsi

scallion ['skæljən] *s* scalogno

scallop ['skaləp] or ['skæləp] *s* (*for cooking*) conchiglia; (*mollusk*) pettine *m*; (*slice of meat*) scaloppina; (*on edge of cloth*) dentello, smerlo || *tr* (*fish*) cuocere in conchiglia; dentellare, smerlare

scalp [skælp] *s* cuoio capelluto || *tr* scotennare; (*tickets*) fare il bagarinaggio di

scalpel ['skælpəl] *s* scalpello

scalper ['skælpər] *s* bagarino

scal·y ['skeli] *adj* (-ier; -iest) squamoso; scrostato

scamp [skæmp] *s* cattivo soggetto, briccone *m*

scamper ['skæmpər] *intr* sgambettare; **to scamper away** darsela a gambe

scan [skæn] *v* (*pret & pp* **scanned**) *ger* **scanning**) *tr* scrutare; dare un'occhiata a; (*verse*) scandire; (telv) analizzare, scandire, esplorare

scandal ['skændəl] *s* scandalo

scandalize ['skændə,laɪz] *tr* scandalizzare

scandalous ['skændələs] *adj* scandaloso

Scandinavian [,skændɪ'nevi·ən] *adj & s* scandinavo

scanning ['skænɪŋ] *s* (telv) esplorazione

scan'ning line' *s* (telv) riga di analisi

scant [skænt] *adj* scarso; corto || *tr* diminuire; lesinare

scant·y ['skænti] *adj* (-ier; -iest) appena sufficiente; povero, magro; (*clothing*) succinto

scapegoat ['skep,got] *s* capro espiatorio

scar [skar] *s* cicatrice *f*; (fig) sfregio || *v* (*pret & pp* **scarred**; *ger* **scarring**) *tr* segnare, marcare; sfregiare || *intr* cicatrizzarsi

scarce [skers] *adj* scarso; raro; **to make oneself scarce** (coll) non farsi vedere

scarcely ['skersli] *adv* appena; a mala pena; non ... affatto; **scarcely ever** raramente; non ... affatto

scarci·ty ['skersɪti] *s* (-ties) scarsità *f*, scarsezza; carestia

scare [sker] *s* spavento || *tr* spaventare, impaurire; **to scare away** fare scappare per lo spavento; **to scare up** (*money*) (coll) metter insieme

scare'crow' *s* spaventapasseri *m*

scarf [skarf] *s* (**scarfs** or **scarves** [skarvz]) sciarpa; cravattone *m*; (*cover for table*) centro, striscia

scarf'pin' *s* spilla da cravatta

scarlet ['skarlɪt] *adj* scarlatto

scar'let fe'ver *s* scarlattina

scar·y ['skeri] *adj* (-ier; -iest) (*timid*) (coll) fifone; (*causing frigh.*) (coll) spaventevole

scathing ['skeðɪŋ] *adj* severo, bruciante

scatter ['skætər] *tr* disperdere, sparpagliare || *intr* disperdersi, sparpagliarsi

scatterbrained ['skætər,brend] *adj* scervellato, stordito

scenari·o [sɪ'nɛrɪ,o] *or* [sɪ'nɑrɪ,o] *s* (-os) scenario

scenarist [sɪ'nɛrɪst] *or* [sɪ'nɑrɪst] *s* scenarista *mf*, sceneggiatore *m*

scene [sin] *s* (*view*) paesaggio; (*place*) scena; (*theat*) scena, quadro; **behind the scenes** dietro le quinte; **to make a scene** fare una scenata

scener·y ['sinərɪ] *s* (-ies) paesaggio; (*theat*) scenario

scenic ['sinɪk] *or* ['sɛnɪk] *adj* pittoresco; (*pertaining to the stage*) scenico

scent [sɛnt] *s* odore *m*; profumo; (*sense of smell*) fiuto, odorato; (*trail*) traccia, pista || *tr* profumare; (*to detect*) fiutare, annusare

scepter ['sɛptər] *s* scettro

sceptic ['skɛptɪk] *adj* & *s* scettico

sceptical ['skɛptɪkəl] *adj* scettico

scepticism ['skɛptɪ,sɪzəm] *s* scetticismo

schedule ['skɛdjul] *s* lista; programma *m*; (*of trains, planes, etc.*) orario || *tr* programmare; mettere in orario

scheme [skim] *s* schema *m*; piano, progetto; (*plot*) trama || *tr* progettare; tramare

schemer ['skimər] *s* progettista *mf*; (*underhanded*) manipolatore *m*, concertatore *m*

scheming ['skimɪŋ] *adj* intrigante, scaltro

schism ['sɪzəm] *s* scisma *m*

schist [ʃɪst] *s* scisto

scholar ['skɑlər] *s* (*pupil*) alunno; detentore *m* di una borsa di studio; (*learned person*) dotto, studioso

scholarly ['skɑlərlɪ] *adj* erudito, studioso

scholarship ['skɑlər,ʃɪp] *s* erudizione; (*money*) borsa di studio

scholasticism [skə'læstɪ,sɪzəm] *s* scolastica

school [skul] *s* scuola; (*of a university*) facoltà *f*; (*of fish*) banco || *tr* istruire, insegnare

school' age' *s* età scolastica

school' bag' *s* cartella

school' board' *s* comitato scolastico

school' boy' *s* alunno, scolaro

school' bus' *s* scuolabus *m*

school' day' *s* giorno di scuola; durata della giornata scolastica

school'girl' *s* alunna, scolara

school'house' *s* scuola, edificio scolastico

schooling ['skulɪŋ] *s* istruzione

school'mas'ter *s* maestro di scuola; direttore scolastico

school'mate' *s* compagno di scuola, condiscepolo

school'room' *s* aula scolastica

school'teach'er *s* maestro

school' year' *s* anno scolastico

schooner ['skunər] *s* goletta

sciatica [saɪ'ætɪkə] *s* (pathol) sciatica

science ['saɪəns] *s* scienza

sci'ence fic'tion *s* fantascienza

sci'ence-fic'tion *adj* fantascientifico

scientific [,saɪən'tɪfɪk] *adj* scientifico

scientist ['saɪəntɪst] *s* scienziato

scimitar ['sɪmɪtər] *s* scimitarra

scintillate ['sɪntɪ,let] *intr* scintillare

scion ['saɪən] *s* rampollo, discendente *m*

scissors ['sɪzərz] *ssg or spl* forbici *fpl*

scoff [skɔf] *or* [skɑf] *s* dileggio, beffa || *intr* burlarsi; **to scoff at** burlarsi di, dileggiare

scold [skold] *s* megera || *tr* & *intr* sgridare, rimproverare

scoop [skup] *s* (*ladlelike utensil*) paletta; (*kitchen utensil*) cucchiaio, cucchiaione *m*; cucchiaiata; palettata; (*of dredge*) benna; (*hollow*) buco; (*naut*) gottazza; (*journ*) primizia, esclusiva; (*coll*) colpo || *tr* vuotare a cucchiaiate; (*journ*) battere; (*naut*) gottare; **to scoop out** (*e.g., sand*) scavare; (*soup*) scodellare

scoot [skut] *s* (coll) corsa || *intr* (coll) correre precipitosamente

scooter ['skutər] *s* monopattino

scope [skop] *s* ampiezza; lunghezza; **to give full scope to** dare piena libertà d'azione a

scorch [skɔrtʃ] *s* scottatura || *tr* bruciacchiare; bruciare, inaridire; (fig) ferire || *intr* bruciarsi

scorching ['skɔrtʃɪŋ] *adj* bruciante

score [skor] *s* (*in a game*) punteggio; (*in an examination*) nota; linea, segno, marca; (*twenty*) ventina; (mus) partitura; **scores** un mucchio; **to keep score** segnare il punteggio; **to settle a score** (fig) saldare un conto || *tr* raggiungere il punteggio di, fare; marcare; guadagnare; (*to censure*) sgridare, rimproverare; (mus) orchestrare

score'board' *s* quadro del punteggio

score'keep'er *s* segnapunti *m*

scorn [skɔrn] *s* disdegno, disprezzo || *tr* & *intr* disdegnare, disprezzare

scornful ['skɔrnfəl] *adj* disdegnoso

Scorpio ['skɔrpɪ,o] *s* Scorpione *m*

scorpion ['skɔrpɪ·ən] *s* scorpione *m*

Scot [skɑt] *s* scozzese *mf*

Scotch [skɑtʃ] *adj* scozzese || *s* scozzese *m*; whisky *m* scozzese; **the Scotch** gli scozzesi

Scotch'man *s* (-men) scozzese *m*

Scotch' pine' *s* pino silvestre

Scotch' tape' *s* (trademark) nastro autoadesivo Scotch

scot'-free' *adj* impune; **to get off scot-free** farla franca

Scotland ['skɑtlənd] *s* la Scozia

Scottish ['skɑtɪʃ] *adj* scozzese || *s* scozzese *mf*; **the Scottish** gli scozzesi

scoundrel ['skaundrəl] *s* birbante *m*, farabutto, manigoldo

scour [skaur] *tr* sgrassare fregando, pulire fregando; (*the countryside*) battere

scourge [skʌrdʒ] *s* sferza; (fig) flagello || *tr* sferzare

scout [skaut] *s* esplorazione; giovane esploratore *m*; giovane esploratrice *f*; (mil) ricognitore *m*; (nav) esploratore *m*; (slang) tipo || *tr* esplorare, riconoscere; cercar di trovare; disdegnare

scouting ['skautɪŋ] *s* scoutismo

scowl [skaul] *s* cipiglio || *intr* aggrottare le ciglia; guardare torvamente

scram [skræm] *v* (*pret & pp* **scrammed;** *ger* **scramming**) *intr* (coll) tagliare la corda; **scram!** (coll) vattene!, (coll) escimi di tra i piedi!

scramble ['skræmbəl] *s* ruffa, gara || *tr* (*to grab up*) arraffare; confondere, mescolare; (*eggs*) strapazzare || *intr* arrampicarsi; (*to struggle*) azzuffarsi

scram'bled eggs' *spl* uova strapazzate

scrap [skræp] *s* pezzetto, frammento; ritaglio, rottame *m*; (coll) baruffa; **scraps** avanzi *mpl*; || *v* (*pret & pp* **scrapped;** *ger* **scrapping**) *tr* scartare || *intr* (coll) fare baruffa

scrap'book' *s* album *m* di ritagli (di giornale o fotografie)

scrape [skrep] *s* impiccio, imbroglio; baruffa || *tr* raschiare, graffiare; **to scrape together** racimolare || *intr* raschiare; **to scrape along** vivacchiare; **to scrape through** passare per il rotto della cuffia

scraper ['skrepər] *s* raschietto

scrap' i'ron *s* rottami *mpl* di ferro

scrap' pa'per *s* carta straccia; carta da appunti

scratch [skrætʃ] *s* graffio, scalfittura; scarabocchio; (billiards) punto perduto; (sports) linea di partenza; **from scratch** da bel principio; dal niente; **up to scratch** soddisfacente || *tr* graffiare, grattare; (*e.g., a horse*) cancellare || *intr* graffiare; (*said of a chicken*) raspare; (*said of a pen*) grattare

scratch' pad' *s* quaderno per appunti

scratch' pa'per *s* carta da appunti

scrawl [skrɔl] *s* scarabocchio || *tr & intr* scarabocchiare

scraw·ny ['skrɔni] *adj* (-nier; -niest) ossuto, scarno

scream [skrim] *s* grido, strillo; cosa divertentissima; persona divertentissima || *intr* gridare, strillare

screech [skritʃ] *s* stridio || *intr* stridere

screech' owl' *s* gufo; (*barn owl*) barbagianni *m*

screen [skrin] *s* (*movable partition*) paravento; (*in front of fire*) parafuoco; rete metallica; (*sieve*) vaglio; (mov; phys) schermo; (telv) teleschermo || *tr* schermare; riparare, proteggere; (*to sieve*) vagliare; (*a film*) proiettare; (*to adapt*) (mov) sceneggiare

screen' grid' *s* (rad, telv) griglia schermo

screen' test' *s* provino

screw [skru] *s* vite *f*; giro di vite; (*of a boat*) elica; **to have a screw loose** (slang) avere una rotella fuori di posto; **to put the screws on** far pressione su || *tr* avvitare; (*to twist*)

torcere; **to screw up** (slang) rovinare; **to screw up one's courage** prendere il coraggio a quattro mani || *intr* avvitarsi

screw'ball' *s* (slang) pazzoide *m*, svitato

screw'driv'er *s* cacciavite *m*

screw' eye' *s* occhiello a vite

screw' jack' *s* martinetto a vite

screw' propel'ler *s* elica

screw·y ['skru·i] *adj* (-ier; -iest) (slang) pazzo; (slang) fuori di posto, strano

scribble ['skrɪbəl] *s* scarabocchio || *tr & intr* scarabocchiare

scribe [skraɪb] *s* (*Jewish scholar*) scriba *m*; copista *mf* || *tr* tracciare, incidere

scrimmage ['skrɪmɪdʒ] *s* ruffa; (*football*) azione

scrimp [skrɪmp] *tr & intr* lesinare

script [skrɪpt] *s* scrittura, scrittura a mano; manoscritto; testo; (*e.g., of a play*) copione *m*; (typ) carattere *m* inglese

scriptural ['skrɪptʃərəl] *adj* scritturale, biblico

scripture ['skrɪptʃər] *s* scrittura || **Scripture** *s* Scrittura

script'writ'er *s* soggettista *mf*

scrofula ['skrɑfjələ] *s* scrofola

scroll [skrol] *s* rotolo di carta, rotolo di pergamena; (*of violin*) riccio; (archit) voluta, cartoccio

scroll'work' *s* ornamentazione a voluta

scro·tum ['skrotəm] *s* (-ta [tə] or -tums) scroto

scrub [skrʌb] *s* boscaglia; alberelli *mpl*; animale bastardo; persona di poco conto; (*act of scrubbing*) fregata; (sports) giocatore *m* di riserva || *v* (*pret & pp* **scrubbed;** *ger* **scrubbing**) *tr* pulire, fregare

scrub' oak' *s* rovere basso

scrub'wom'an *s* (-wom'en) lavatrice *f*, donna a giornata

scruff [skrʌf] *s* nuca, collottola

scruple ['skrupəl] *s* scrupolo

scrupulous ['skrupjələs] *adj* scrupoloso

scrutinize ['skrutɪ͵naɪz] *tr* scrutare, disaminare

scruti·ny ['skrutɪni] *s* (-nies) attento esame, disamina

scuff [skʌf] *s* graffio, logorio || *tr* logorare, graffiare

scuffle ['skʌfəl] *s* zuffa, rissa || *intr* azzuffarsi, colluttare

scull [skʌl] *s* (*oar*) remo a bratto; (*boat*) canotto || *tr* spingere a bratto || *intr* vogare a bratto

sculler·y ['skʌləri] *s* (-ies) retrocucina

scul'lery maid' *s* sguattera

scullion ['skʌljən] *s* sguattero

sculptor ['skʌlptər] *s* scultore *m*

sculptress ['skʌlptrɪs] *s* scultrice *f*

sculpture ['skʌlptʃər] *s* scultura || *tr & intr* scolpire

scum [skʌm] *s* schiuma; (slag) scoria; (rabble) feccia, gentaglia || *v* (*pret & pp* **scummed;** *ger* **scumming**) *tr & intr* schiumare

scum·my ['skʌmi] *adj* (**-mier; -miest**) spumoso; (coll) vile, schifoso

scurf [skʌrf] *s* (*shed by the skin*) squama; incrostazione

scurrilous ['skʌrɪləs] *adj* scurrile

scur·ry ['skʌri] *v* (*pret & pp* **-ried**) *intr* affrettarsi; **to scurry around** dimenarsi

scur·vy ['skʌrvi] *adj* (**-vier; -viest**) spregevole, meschino ‖ *s* scorbuto

scuttle ['skʌtəl] *s* (*for coal*) secchio; (*trap door*) botola; corsa, fuga; (naut) boccaporto ‖ *tr* aprire una falla in, affondare ‖ *intr* affrettarsi, darsi alla corsa

scut'tle-butt' *s* (naut) barilozzo dell'acqua; (coll) rumore *m*, diceria

scuttling ['skʌtlɪŋ] *s* autoaffondamento

Scylla ['sɪlə] *s* Scilla; **between Scylla and Charybdis** fra Scilla e Cariddi

scythe [saɪð] *s* falce *f*

sea [si] *s* mare *m*; (*wave*) maroso; **at sea** in alto mare; **by the sea** a mare, sulla costa; **to follow the sea** farsi marinaio; **to put to sea** prendere il largo

sea'board' *adj* costiero ‖ *s* litorale *m*

sea' breeze' *s* brezza marina

sea'coast' *s* costa, litorale *m*

sea' dog' *s* (*seal*) foca; (*sailor*) lupo di mare

seafarer ['si,ferər] *s* marinaio; viaggiatore marittimo

sea'food' *s* pesce *m*; (*shellfish*) frutti *mpl* di mare

seagoing ['si,go·ɪŋ] *adj* di alto mare

sea' gull' *s* gabbiano

seal [sil] *s* sigillo; (*sea animal*) foca; (fig) suggello ‖ *tr* sigillare, apporre i sigilli a; (fig) suggellare

sea' legs' *spl*—**to have good sea legs** avere piede marino

sea' lev'el *s* livello del mare

seal'ing wax' *s* ceralacca

seal'skin' *s* pelle *f* di foca

seam [sim] *s* (*abutting of edges*) giuntura; (*stitches*) costura, cucitura; (*scar*) cicatrice *f*; (*wrinkle*) ruga; (in metal) commettitura; (min) filone *m*, vena

sea'man *s* (**-men**) marinaio

sea' mile' *s* miglio marino

seamless ['simlɪs] *adj* senza giuntura; (*stockings*) senza cucitura

seamstress ['simstrɪs] *s* cucitrice *f*

seam·y ['simi] *adj* (**-ier; -iest**) pieno di cuciture; basso, sordido; (*unpleasant*) spiacevole

séance ['se·ɑns] *s* seduta spiritica

sea'plane' *s* idrovolante *m*

sea'port' *s* porto di mare

sea' pow'er *s* potenza navale

sear [sɪr] *adj* secco ‖ *tr* scottare, bruciare; (*to brand*) marcare a fuoco; inaridire; (fig) indurire

search [sʌrtʃ] *s* ricerca, investigazione; (*frisking a person*) perquisizione; **in search of** in cerca di ‖ *tr* cercare, investigare; perquisire, frugare ‖ *intr* investigare; **to search for** cercare; **to search into** investigare

searching ['sʌrtʃɪŋ] *adj* (*e.g., inspec-*

tion) profondo; (*e.g., glance*) indagatore, penetrante

search'light' *s* proiettore *m*, riflettore *m*; (mil) fotoelettrica

search' war'rant *s* mandato di perquisizione

sea'scape' *s* vista del mare; (*painting*) marina

sea' shell' *s* conchiglia

sea'shore' *s* costa, marina, mare *m*

sea'sick' *adj*—**to be seasick** aver mal di mare

sea'sick'ness *s* mal *m* di mare

sea'side' *s* costa, riviera, marina

season ['sizən] *s* stagione; **in season** di stagione; **in season and out of season** sempre, continuamente; **out of season** fuori stagione ‖ *tr* (*food*) condire; (*to mature*) stagionare; (*e.g., wood*) stagionare

seasonal ['sizənəl] *adj* stagionale

seasoning ['sizənɪŋ] *s* condimento; (*of wood*) stagionamento

sea'son's greet'ings *spl* migliori auguri *mpl* per le feste natalizie

sea'son tick'et *s* biglietto d'abbonamento

seat [sit] *s* sedia; (*part of chair*) sedile *m*; (*of human body*) sedere *m*; (*of pants*) fondo; sito, posto; (*e.g., of government*) sede *f*; (*in parliament*) seggio; (*e.g., of learning*) centro; (rr, theat) posto ‖ *tr* far sedere; aver posti per; (*a chair*) mettere il sedile a; (*pants*) mettere il fondo a; (*an official*) insediare; (mach) installare; **to be seated** essere seduto; **to seat oneself** sedersi

seat' belt' *s* cintura di sicurezza

seat' cov'er *s* guaina, foderina

seat'ing room' *s* posti *mpl* a sedere

sea' wall' *s* diga

sea'way' *s* via marittima; alto mare; mare grosso; rotta percorsa; via di fiume accessibile a navi da trasporto

sea'weed' *s* alga marina; pianta marina

sea'wor'thy *adj* atto a tenere il mare

secede [sɪ'sid] *intr* separarsi, distaccarsi

secession [sɪ'sɛʃən] *s* secessione

seclude [sɪ'klud] *tr* appartare; isolare

seclusion [sɪ'kluʒən] *s* reclusione; solitudine *f*, intimità *f*

second ['sɛkənd] *adj & pron* secondo; **to be second to none** non cederla a nessuno ‖ *s* secondo; (*in a duel*) padrino; (*in dates*) due *m*; (aut, mus) seconda; **seconds** (com) articoli *mpl* di seconda qualità; **to have seconds on** servirsi una seconda volta di ‖ *tr* assecondare; (*a motion*) appoggiare ‖ *adv* in secondo luogo

secondar·y ['sɛkən,dɛri] *adj* secondario ‖ *s* (**-ies**) (elec) secondario

sec'ond-best' *adj* (il) migliore dopo il primo; **to come off second-best** arrivare secondo

sec'ond-class' *adj* di seconda qualità; (aer, naut, rr) di seconda classe

sec'ond hand' *s* lancetta dei secondi

sec'ond-hand' *adj* di seconda mano, d'occasione

sec'ond lieuten'ant s sottotenente m
sec'ond-rate' adj di seconda categoria; (inferior) da strapazzo
sec'ond sight' s chiaroveggenza
sec'ond wind' [wind] s—**to get one's second wind** riprendere fiato
secre·cy ['sikrəsi] s (-cies) segretezza; **in secrecy** in segreto
secret ['sikrit] adj & s segreto; **in secret** in segreto
secretar·y ['sɛkrɪ,tɛri] s (-ies) segretario; (desk) scrittoio
se'cret bal'lot s scrutinio segreto
secrete [sɪ'krit] tr nascondere; (physiol) secernere
secretive ['sikrɪtɪv] or [sɪ'kritɪv] adj riservato, poco comunicativo
sect [sɛkt] s setta
sectarian [sɛk'tɛrɪ·ən] adj & s settario
section ['sɛkt/ən] s sezione; (of city) rione m; (of fruit) spicchio; (of highway) tronco; (rr) tratta || tr sezionare
sectional ['sɛk/ənəl] adj (e.g., book-case) componibile; sezionale; locale, regionale
secular ['sɛkjələr] adj & s secolare m
secularism ['sɛkjələ,rɪzəm] s laicismo
secure [sɪ'kjur] adj salvo, sicuro || tr ottenere; assicurare; fissare; (law) garantire
securi·ty [sɪ'kjurɪti] s (-ties) sicurezza; protezione; garanzia; (person) garante m; **securities** valori mpl, titoli mpl
sedan [sɪ'dæn] s (aut) berlina
sedan' chair' s bussola, portantina
sedate [sɪ'det] adj calmo, posato
sedation [sɪ'de/ən] s ritorno alla calma; stato di calma mentale
sedative ['sɛdətɪv] adj & s sedativo
sedentary ['sɛdən,tɛri] adj sedentario
sedge [sɛdʒ] s carice m
sediment ['sɛdɪmənt] s sedimento
sedition [sɪ'dɪ/ən] s sedizione
seditious [sɪ'dɪ/əs] adj sedizioso
seduce [sɪ'djus] or [sɪ'dus] tr sedurre
seducer [sɪ'djusər] or [sɪ'dusər] s seduttore m, corruttore m
seduction [sɪ'dʌk/ən] s seduzione
seductive [sɪ'dʌktɪv] adj seduttore
sedulous ['sɛdjələs] adj diligente
see [si] s (eccl) sede f || v (pret **saw** [sɔ]; pp **seen** [sin]) tr vedere; **to see off** andare ad accompagnare; **to see through** portare a termine || intr vedere; **see here!** faccia attenzione!; **to see after** prender cura di; **to see through** conoscere il gioco di
seed [sid] s seme m, semenza; **to go to seed** andare in semenza; deteriorarsi || tr seminare; (fruit) togliere i semi da || intr seminare; produrre semi
seed'bed' s semenzaio; (fig) vivaio
seeder ['sidər] s (person) seminatore m; (machine) seminatrice f
seedling ['sidlɪŋ] s piantina da trapianto
seed·y ['sidi] adj (-ier; -iest) pieno di semi; (unkempt) malmesso, malvestito
seeing ['si·ɪŋ] conj visto che, dato che

See'ing Eye' dog' s cane m guida per ciechi
seek [sik] v (pret & pp **sought** [sɔt]) tr cercare, ricercare; **to be sought after** essere ricercato; **to seek to** cercare di
seem [sim] intr parere, sembrare
seemingly ['simɪŋli] adv apparentemente
seem·ly ['simli] adj (-lier; -liest) decoroso; appropriato
seep [sip] intr colare, filtrare
seer [sɪr] s profeta m, veggente m
see'saw' s altalena; (motion) viavai m || intr altalenare
seethe [sið] intr bollire
segment ['sɛgmənt] s segmento
segregate ['sɛgrɪ,get] tr segregare
segregation [,sɛgrɪ'ge/ən] s segregazione
segregationist [,sɛgrɪ'ge/ənɪst] s segregazionista mf
Seine [sen] s Senna
seismograph ['saɪzmə,græf] or ['saɪzmə,grɑf] s sismografo
seismology [saɪz'mɑlədʒi] s sismologia
seize [siz] tr afferrare; impossessarsi di; (with one's clenched fist) impugnare; comprendere; (law) sequestrare, confiscare
seizure ['siʒər] s conquista, cattura; (of an illness) attacco; (law) sequestro, pignoramento
seldom ['sɛldəm] adj di raro, raramente
select [sɪ'lɛkt] adj scelto, selezionato || tr prescegliere, selezionare
selectee [sɪ,lɛk'ti] s (mil) recluta
selection [sɪ'lɛk/ən] s selezione, scelta
selective [sɪ'lɛktɪv] adj selettivo
self [sɛlf] adj uno stesso || s (selves [sɛlvz]) sé stesso; io, personalità f; **all by one's self** senza aiuto altrui || pron sé stesso
self'-abuse' s abuso delle proprie forze; masturbazione
self'-addressed' adj col nome e l'indirizzo del mittente
self'-cen'tered adj egocentrico
self'-con'scious adj imbarazzato, vergognoso, timido
self'-control' s padronanza di sé stesso, autocontrollo
self'-defense' s autodifesa; **in self-defense** in legittima difesa
self'-deni'al s abnegazione
self'-deter'mina'tion s autodeterminazione
self'-dis'cipline s autodisciplina
self'-ed'ucat'ed adj autodidatta
self'-employed' adj che lavora in proprio
self'-ev'i·dent adj evidente, lampante
self'-ex·plan'a·tor'y adj ovvio, che si spiega da sé
self'-gov'ernment s autogoverno; controllo sopra sé stesso
self'-im·por'tant adj presuntuoso
self'-in·dul'gence s intemperanza
self'-in'terest s egoismo, interesse m
selfish ['sɛlfɪ/] adj egoista
selfishness ['sɛlfɪ/nɪs] s egoismo

selfless ['selflıs] *adj* disinteressato; altruista

self'-liq'ui·dat'ing *adj* autoammortizzabile

self'-love' *s* amor proprio

self'-made' *adj* che si è fatto da sé

self'-por'trait *s* autoritratto

self'-pos·sessed' *adj* calmo, padrone di sé

self'-pres'er·va'tion *s* conservazione

self'-pro·pelled' *adj* semovente

self'-re·li'ant *adj* pieno di fiducia in sé stesso

self'-re·spect' *s* rispetto di sé stesso

self'-right'eous *adj* che si considera più morale degli altri, ipocrita

self'-sac'ri·fice' *s* sacrificio di sé, spirito di sacrificio

self'-same' *adj* stesso e medesimo

self'-sat'is·fied' *adj* contento di sé

self'-seek'ing *s* egoista || *s* egoismo

self'-serv'ice *s* autoservizio

self'-start'er *s* motorino d'avviamento

self'-styled' *adj* sedicente

self'-support' *s* indipendenza economica

self'-tap'ping screw' *s* vite *f* autofilettante

self'-taught' *adj* autodidatta

self-threading ['self'θredıŋ] *adj* autofilettante

self'-willed' *adj* ostinato, caparbio

self'-wind'ing *adj* a carica automatica

sell [sel] *v* (*pret & pp* sold [sold]) *tr* vendere; (*an idea*) fare accettare; **to sell off** svendere, liquidare; **to sell out** smerciare; vendere a stralcio; (coll) tradire || *intr* vendere, vendersi; fare il venditore; **to sell off** (*said of the stock market*) essere in ribasso; **to sell out** vendere a stralcio; vendersi

seller ['selər] *s* venditore *m*

Selt'zer wa'ter ['seltsər] *s* selz *m*

selvage ['selvɪdʒ] *s* cimosa, vivagno

semantic [sɪ'mæntɪk] *adj* semantico || **semantics** *s* semantica

semaphore ['semə,for] *s* semaforo

semblance ['sembləns] *s* apparenza, specie *f*; apparizione

semen ['simɛn] *s* sperma *m*

semester [sɪ'mɛstər] *adj* semestrale || *s* semestre *m*

semicircle ['semɪ,sʌrkəl] *s* semicircolo

semicolon ['semɪ,kolən] *s* punto e virgola

semiconductor [,semɪkən'dʌktər] *s* semiconduttore *m*

semiconscious [,semi'kanʃəs] *adj* mezzo cosciente

semifinal [,semi'faɪnəl] *s* semifinale *f*

semilearned [,semi'lʌrnɪd] *adj* semidotto

semimonth·ly [,semi'mʌnθli] or [,semaɪ'mʌnθli] *adj* quindicinale || *s* (-lies) rivista quindicinale

seminar ['semɪ,nɑr] or [,semɪ'nɑr] *s* seminario

seminar·y ['semɪ,neri] *s* (-ies) seminario

Semite ['semaɪt] or ['simaɪt] *s* semita *mf*

Semitic [sɪ'mɪtɪk] *adj* semitico || *s* lingua semitica; (*family of languages*) semitico

semitrailer ['semɪ,trelər] *s* semirimorchio

semiweek·ly [,semi'wikli] or [,semaɪ'wikli] *adj* bisettimanale || *s* (-lies) periodico bisettimanale

semiyearly [,semi'jɪrli] or [,semaɪ'jɪrli] *adj* semestrale || *adv* due volte all'anno

senate ['senɪt] *s* senato

senator ['senətər] *s* senatore *m*

send [send] *v* (*pret & pp* sent [sent]) *tr* inviare, mandare; spedire; (*e.g., a punch*) lanciare; **to send back** rimandare; **to send forth** emettere; **to send packing** licenziare su due piedi || *intr* (rad) trasmettere; **to send for** mandare a chiamare, far venire

sender ['sendər] *s* speditore *m*, mittente *m*; (telg) trasmettitore *m*

send'-off' *s* (coll) addio affettuoso; (coll) lancio

senility [sɪ'nɪlɪti] *s* (pathol) senilismo

senior ['sinjər] *adj* maggiore, più anziano; seniore, di grado più elevato; dell'ultimo anno, laureando; senior, il vecchio || *s* maggiore *m*; seniore *m*, persona di grado più elevato; studente *m* dell'ultimo anno, laureando

sen'ior cit'izen *s* vecchio, pensionato

seniority [sin'jɔrɪti] or [sin'jɔrɪti] *s* anzianità *f*

sensation [sen'seʃən] *s* sensazione

sensational [sen'seʃənəl] *adj* sensazionale

sense [sens] *s* senso; **in a sense** in un certo senso; **to come to one's senses** riprendere il giudizio; **to make sense out of** arrivare a capire; **to take leave of one's senses** perdere il ben dell'intelletto || *tr* intuire; comprendere

senseless ['senslɪs] *adj* (*unconscious*) privo di sensi; (*meaningless*) insensato, privo di senso

sense' or'gan *s* organo di senso

sensibili·ty [,sensɪ'bɪlɪti] *s* (-ties) sensibilità *f*; **sensibilities** suscettibilità *f*

sensible ['sensɪbəl] *adj* sensato; (*keenly aware*) sensibile; cosciente

sensitive ['sensɪtɪv] *adj* sensitivo, sensibile; delicato

sensitize ['sensɪ,taɪz] *tr* sensibilizzare

sensory ['sensəri] *adj* sensorio

sensual ['senʃʊ·əl] *adj* sensuale

sensuous ['senʃʊ·əs] *adj* sensuale

sentence ['sentəns] *s* (gram) frase; (law) sentenza, condanna || *tr* sentenziare, condannare

sentiment ['sentɪmənt] *s* sentimento

sentimental [,sentɪ'mentəl] *adj* sentimentale

sentimentalism [,sentɪ'mentəl,ɪzəm] *s* sentimentalismo

sentinel ['sentɪnəl] *s* sentinella; **to stand sentinel** montare di sentinella

sen·try ['sentri] *s* (-tries) sentinella

sen'try box' *s* garitta, casotto

separate ['sepərɪt] *adj* separato ||

['sepə,ret] *tr* separare || *intr* separarsi

separation [,sepə'reʃən] *s* separazione

Sephardic [sɪ'fɑrdɪk] *adj* sefardita

September [sep'tembər] *s* settembre *m*

septic ['septɪk] *adj* settico

sep'tic tank' *s* fossa settica

sepulcher ['sepəlkər] *s* sepolcro

sequel ['sikwəl] *s* seguito

sequence ['sikwəns] *s* serie *f*, sequenza, successione; conseguenza; (cards, eccl, mov) sequenza; (gram) correlazione

sequester [sɪ'kwestər] *tr* isolare, appartare; (law) sequestrare

sequin ['sikwɪn] *s* lustrino

ser·aph ['serəf] *s* (-aphs or -aphim [əfɪm]) serafino

Serbian ['sʌrbɪ·ən] *adj & s* serbo

Serbo-Croatian [,sʌrbokro'eʃən] *adj & s* serbocroato

sere [sɪr] *adj* secco, appassito

serenade [,serə'ned] *s* serenata || *tr* fare la serenata a || *intr* fare la serenata

serene [sɪ'rin] *adj* sereno

serenity [sɪ'renɪtɪ] *s* serenità *f*

serf [sʌrf] *s* servo della gleba

serfdom ['sʌrfdəm] *s* servitù *f* della gleba

serge [sʌrdʒ] *s* saia

sergeant ['sɑrdʒənt] *s* sergente *m*

ser'geant at arms' *s* (**ser'geants at arms'**) ufficiale *m* delegato a mantenere l'ordine

ser'geant ma'jor *s* (**sergeants major** or **sergeant majors**) (*in U.S. Army*) sergente *m* maggiore; (*in Italian Army*) maresciallo

serial ['sɪrɪ·əl] *adj* a puntate, a dispense || *s* periodico; romanzo a puntate; programma *m* a serie

se'rial num'ber *s* matricola; (*of a book*) segnatura; (aut) matricola di telaio

se·ries ['sɪriz] *s* (-ries) serie *f*; (*works dealing with the same topic*) collana; **in series** (elec) in serie

serious ['sɪrɪ·əs] *adj* serio

seriousness ['sɪrɪ·əsnɪs] *s* serietà *f*; **in all seriousness** molto sul serio

sermon ['sʌrmən] *s* sermone *m*

sermonize ['sʌrmə,naɪz] *tr & intr* sermonare

serpent ['sʌrpənt] *s* serpente *m*

se·rum ['sɪrəm] *s* (-rums or -ra [rə]) siero

servant ['sʌrvənt] *s* servo, domestico; (*civil servant*) funzionario; (fig) servitore *m*

serv'ant girl' *s* serva, domestica

serv'ant prob'lem *s* crisi *f* ancillare

serve [sʌrv] *s* (*in tennis*) servizio || *tr* servire; (*a sentence*) espiare; (*to suffice*) bastare (with *dat*); (*a writ*) notificare; **to serve s.o. right** stare bene (with *dat*), e.g., **it serves him right** gli sta bene || *intr* servire; **to serve as** fare da

service ['sʌrvɪs] *s* servizio; (*of a writ*) notifica; (*branch of the armed forces*) arma; **at your service** per servirLa || *tr* rifornire, riparare

serviceable ['sʌrvɪsəbəl] *adj* utile; durevole; pratico; riparabile

serv'ice club' *s* casa del soldato

serv'ice·man' *s* (-men') militare *m*; riparatore *m*, aggiustatore *m*

serv'ice mod'ule *s* modulo di servizio

serv'ice sta'tion *s* stazione di servizio or di rifornimento

serv'ice-sta'tion attend'ant *s* benzinaio

serv'ice stripe' *s* gallone *m*

servile ['sʌrvɪl] *adj* servile

servitude ['sʌrvɪ,tjud] or ['sʌrvɪ,tud] *s* servitù *f*; lavori forzati

sesame ['sesəmɪ] *s* sesamo; **open sesame** apriti sesamo

session ['seʃən] *s* sessione *f*, seduta

set [set] *adj* determinato, preordinato; abituale; fisso, rigido; (*ready*) pronto; meditato, studiato || *s* (*e.g., of books*) collezione, serie *f*; (*e.g., of chess*) gioco; set *m*, insieme *m*, completo; (*of tires*) treno; (*of horses*) pariglia; (*of tennis*) partita; (*of dishes*) servizio; (*of kitchen utensils*) batteria; posizione, atteggiamento; (*of a garment*) linea; (*e.g., of cement*) presa; (*of people*) gruppo; (*of thieves*) genìa; (*of sails*) muta; (*of lines*) (geom) fascio; (rad, telv) apparato; (theat, mov) set *m* || *v* (*pret & pp* set; *ger* setting) *tr* porre, deporre; mettere; (*fire*) dare; (*the table*) imbandire; (*a watch*) regolare; (*s.o. a certain number of tricks*) far cadere di; (*a price*) fissare; (*a gem*) incastonare; (*a fracture*) mettere a posto; (*a saw*) allicciare; (*a trap*) tendere; (*hair*) acconciare; stabilire; insediare; (*to plant*) piantare; (*a sail*) tendere; (*e.g., milk*) rapprendere; calibrare, tarare; (*cement*) solidificare; (typ) comporre; **to set back** ritardare; (*a clock*) mettere indietro; **to set forth** descrivere; **to set one's heart on** desiderare ardentemente; **to set store by** tenere in gran conto; **to set up** metter su; impiantare; (*drinks*) (slang) pagare || *intr* (said, e.g., *of the sun*) tramontare; (*said of a liquid*) solidificarsi; (*said of cement*) fare presa; (*said of milk*) rapprendersi; (*said of a hen*) covare; (*said of a garment*) cascare; (*said of hair*) prendere la piega; **to set about** mettersi a; **to set out** porsi in cammino; **to set out to** mettersi a; **to set to work** mettersi a lavorare; **to set upon** attaccare

set'back' *s* rovescio, contrarietà *f*

set'screw' *s* vite *f* di pressione

setting ['setɪŋ] *s* (*environment*) ambiente *m*; (*of a gem*) montatura; (*of cement*) presa; (*e.g., of the sun*) tramonto; (theat) scenario; (mus) arrangiamento

set'ting-up' ex'ercises *spl* ginnastica da camera

settle ['setəl] *tr* determinare, risolvere; sistemare, regolare; (*a bill*) liquidare; installarsi in, colonizzare; calmare; (*a liquid*) far depositare; (law) conciliare || *intr* mettersi d'accordo; saldare un conto; stanziarsi, domiciliarsi; fermarsi, posare; (*said of a liquid*) depositare, calmarsi; solidificarsi; **to settle down to work** mettersi a lavorare di buzzo buono; **to settle on** scegliere, fissare

settlement ['sɛtəlmənt] *s* stabilimento; sistemazione, regolamento; colonia, comunità *f;* (*of a building*) infossamento; agenzia di beneficenza

settler ['sɛtlər] *s* fondatore *m;* colono; conciliatore *m*

set'up' *s* portamento; (*e.g., of tools*) disposizione; quanto è necessario per mescolare una bibita alcolica; (coll) incontro truccato

seven ['sɛvən] *adj & pron* sette || *s* sette *m;* **seven o'clock** le sette

sev'en hun'dred *adj, s & pron* settecento

seventeen ['sɛvən'tin] *adj, s & pron* diciassette *m*

seventeenth ['sɛvən'tinθ] *adj, s & pron* diciassettesimo || *s* (*in dates*) diciassette *m*

seventh ['sɛvənθ] *adj, s & pron* settimo || *s* (*in dates*) sette *m*

seventieth ['sɛvəntɪ-ɪθ] *adj, s & pron* settantesimo

seven·ty ['sɛvənti] *adj & pron* settanta || *s* (**-ties**) settanta *m;* **the seventies** gli anni settanta

sever ['sɛvər] *tr* tagliare, mozzare; (*relations*) troncare || *intr* separarsi

several ['sɛvərəl] *adj* parecchi, vari; rispettivi || *spl* parecchi *mpl*

sev'erance pay' ['sɛvərəns] *s* buonuscita, indennità *f* di licenziamento

severe [sɪ'vɪr] *adj* severo; (*weather*) rigido; (*pain*) acuto; (*illness*) grave

sew [so] *v* (*pret* **sewed;** *pp* **sewed** or **sewn**) *tr & intr* cucire

sewage ['su·ɪdʒ] or ['sju·ɪdʒ] *s* acque *fpl* di scolo or di rifiuto

sewer ['su·ər] or ['sju·ər] *s* fogna, chiavica

sewerage ['su·ərɪdʒ] or ['sju·ərɪdʒ] *s* fognatura; drenaggio, rimozione delle acque di rifiuto

sew'ing machine' ['so·ɪŋ] *s* macchina da cucire

sex [sɛks] *s* sesso

sex' appeal' *s* attrattiva fisica, sex appeal *m*

sextant ['sɛkstənt] *s* sestante *m*

sextet [sɛks'tɛt] *s* sestetto

sexton ['sɛkstən] *s* sagrestano

sexual ['sɛkʃu·əl] *adj* sessuale

sex·y ['sɛksi] *adj* (**-ier; -iest**) (coll) erotico; (coll) procace

shab·by ['ʃæbi] *adj* (**-bier; -biest**) (*clothes*) frusto; (*house*) malandato; (*person*) malvestito; (*deal*) cattivo

shack [ʃæk] *s* baracca

shackle ['ʃækəl] *s* ceppo; (*to tie an animal*) pastoia; (fig) ostacolo; **shackles** ceppi *mpl,* manette *fpl* || *tr* mettere in ceppi; (fig) inceppare

shad [ʃæd] *s* alosa

shade [ʃed] *s* ombra; (*of lamp*) paralume *m;* (*of window*) tendina; (*for the eyes*) visiera; (*hue*) tinta, sfumatura; **a shade of** un po' di; **shades** tenebre *fpl;* ombre *fpl* || *tr* ombreggiare; sfumare, digradare; (*a price*) ribassare leggermente

shadow ['ʃædo] *s* ombra || *tr* ombreggiare; (*to follow*) pedinare; **to shadow forth** adombrare, preannunciare

shadowy ['ʃædo·i] *adj* ombroso, ombreggiato; illusorio, chimerico

shad·y ['ʃedi] *adj* (**-ier; -iest**) ombroso; spettrale; (coll) losco; **to keep shady** (slang) starsene lontano

shaft [ʃæft] or [ʃɑft] *s* (*of arrow*) asta; (*of feather*) rachide *f;* (*of light*) raggio; (*handle*) manico; (*of wagon*) stanga, timone *m;* (*of motor*) albero; (*of column*) fusto; (*of elevator*) pozzo; (*in a mountain*) camino; (min) fornello; (fig) frecciata

shag·gy ['ʃægi] *adj* (**-gier; -giest**) peloso, irsuto; (*unkempt*) trasandato; (*cloth*) ruvido

shag'gy dog' sto'ry *s* storiella senza capo né coda

shake [ʃek] *s* scossa; stretta di mano; momento, istante *m;* **the shakes** la tremarella || *v* (*pret* **shook** [ʃʊk]; *pp* **shaken**) *tr* scuotere; scrollare; (*s.o.'s hand*) serrare; (*e.g., with a mixer*) sbattere; agitare, perturbare; eludere; disfarsi di || *intr* tremare; (*to totter*) traballare, tentennare; scuotere; darsi la mano

shake'down' *s* estorsione, concussione; (*bed*) lettuccio di fortuna

shake'down' cruise' *s* (naut) viaggio di prova

shaker ['ʃekər] *s* (*e.g., for sugar*) spolverino; (*for cocktails*) sbattighiaccio, shaker *m*

shake'-up' *s* cambiamento completo, riorganizzazione, rimaneggiamento

shak·y ['ʃeki] *adj* (**-ier; -iest**) tremebondo; traballante, zoppicante

shall [ʃæl] *v* (*cond* **should** [ʃʊd]) *v aux* si usa per formare (1) il futuro dell'indicativo, per es., **I shall do it** lo farò; (2) il futuro perfetto dell'indicativo, per es., **I shall have done it** l'avrò fatto; (3) espressioni di obbligo o necessità, per es., **what shall I do?** che devo fare?, che vuole che faccia?

shallow ['ʃælo] *adj* basso, poco profondo; leggero, superficiale

sham [ʃæm] *adj* falso, finto || *s* frode *f,* contraffazione || *v* (*pret & pp* **shammed**) *ger* **shamming**) *tr & intr* fingere

sham' bat'tle *s* finta battaglia

shambles ['ʃæmbəlz] *s* macello; confusione, disordine

shame [ʃem] *s* vergogna; **shame on you!** vergogna!; **what a shame!** che peccato! || *tr* svergognare, disonorare

shame'faced' *adj* timido, vergognoso

shameful ['ʃemfəl] *adj* vergognoso

shameless ['ʃemlɪs] *adj* sfrontato, impudente, svergognato

shampoo [ʃæm'pu] s shampoo m ‖ tr fare lo shampoo a

shamrock [ˈʃæmrɑk] s trifoglio irlandese

shanghai [ˈʃæŋhaɪ] or [ʃæŋˈhaɪ] tr imbarcare a viva forza ‖ **Shanghai** s Sciangai f

shank [ʃæŋk] s fusto; (of tool) codolo; (stem) gambo; (of bird) zampa; (of anchor) fuso; (coll) principio; (coll) fine f; **to ride shank's mare** andare col cavallo di San Francesco

shan·ty [ˈʃænti] s (-ties) bicocca

shan'ty-town' s bidonville f

shape [ʃep] s forma; **in bad shape** in cattive condizioni; **out of shape** sformato ‖ tr formare, foggiare; plasmare, conformare ‖ intr formarsi; **to take shape** prender forma

shapeless [ˈʃeplɪs] adj informe

shape·ly [ˈʃepli] adj (-lier; -liest) ben fatto, formoso

share [ʃer] s parte f; interesse m; (of stock) azione f; (of plow) suola; **to go shares** dividere in parti eguali ‖ tr (to enjoy jointly) condividere; (to apportion) ripartire ‖ intr partecipare, prender parte

sharecropper [ˈʃerˌkrɑpər] s mezzadro

share'hold'er s azionista mf

shark [ʃɑrk] s pescecane m; (schemer) piovra; (slang) esperto

sharp [ʃɑrp] adj affilato, acuto; angoloso; (e.g., curve) forte; distinto, ben delineato; (taste) pungente, salato; (pain) vivo; (words) mordace; (slang) elegante ‖ s (mus) diesis m ‖ adv acutamente; in punto, e.g., **at seven o'clock sharp** alle sette in punto

sharpen [ˈʃɑrpən] tr affilare; (a pencil) fare la punta a ‖ intr affilarsi

sharpener [ˈʃɑrpənər] s (person) affilatore m; (machine) affilatrice f

sharper [ˈʃɑrpər] s gabbamondo

sharp'shoot'er s tiratore scelto

shatter [ˈʃætər] tr frantumare; sfracellare; (health) rovinare; (nerves) sconvolgere; distruggere ‖ intr frantumarsi, andare in pezzi

shat'ter-proof' adj infrangibile

shave [ʃev] s rasatura; **to have a close shave** scapparla or scamparla bella ‖ tr (the face) radere, sbarbare; (wood) piallare; (to scrape) sfiorare; (prices) ridurre; (a lawn) tosare ‖ intr rasarsi

shaving [ˈʃevɪŋ] adj da barba, per barba, e.g., **shaving cream** crema da or per barba ‖ s rasatura; **shavings** trucioli mpl

shav'ing brush' s pennello da barba

shav'ing soap' s sapone m per la barba

shawl [ʃɔl] s scialle m

she [ʃi] s (shes) femmina ‖ pron pers (they) essa, lei

sheaf [ʃif] s (sheaves [ʃivz]) covone m; (of paper) fascio

shear [ʃɪr] s lama di cesoia; tagliatura; **shears** cesoie fpl ‖ v (pret sheared; pp sheared or shorn [ʃɔrn]) tr (sheep) tosare; (cloth) tagliare; **to shear s.o. of** privare qlcu di

sheath [ʃiθ] s (sheaths [ʃiðz]) guaina, coperta; (of a sword) fodero

sheathe [ʃið] tr rinfoderare, inguainare

shed [ʃed] s portico, tettoia; (geog) spartiacque m, versante m ‖ v (pret & pp shed; ger shedding) tr (e.g., blood) spargere, versare; (light) dare, fare; (feathers) spogliarsi di, lasciar cadere

sheen [ʃin] s lucentezza

sheep [ʃip] s (sheep) pecora; **sheep's eyes** occhio di triglia; **to separate the sheep from the goats** separare i buoni dai cattivi

sheep'dog' s cane m da pastore

sheepish [ˈʃipɪʃ] adj timido, goffo; pecoresco, pedissequo

sheep'skin' s pelle f di pecora; (parchment) cartapecora; (bb) bazzana; (coll) diploma m

sheer [ʃɪr] adj trasparente, fino, velato; puro; (cliff) stagliato ‖ adv completamente ‖ intr deviare

sheet [ʃit] s (for bed) lenzuolo; (of paper) foglio; (of metal) lamina; (of water) specchio; (naut) scotta

sheet' light'ning s lampeggio all'orizzonte

sheet' met'al s lamiera

sheet' mu'sic s spartito non rilegato

sheik [ʃik] s sceicco; (great lover) (slang) rubacuori m

shelf [ʃelf] s (shelves [ʃelvz]) scaffale m, scansia; (ledge) terrazzo, ripiano; banco di sabbia; **on the shelf** in disparte, dimenticato

shell [ʃel] s (of egg or crustacean) guscio; (of mollusk) conchiglia; (of vegetable) baccello; proietto, proiettile m; (cartridge) cartuccia; (of a cartridge) bossolo; (framework) armatura; (of boiler) involucro; (naut) imbarcazione da regata, schifo, iole f ‖ tr (vegetables) sgranare; bombardare, cannoneggiare; **to shell out** (slang) tirar fuori

shel·lac [ʃəˈlæk] s gomma lacca ‖ v (pret & pp -lacked; ger -lacking) tr verniciare con gomma lacca; (slang) dare una batosta a

shell'fish' ssg (-fish) frutto di mare; crostaceo; spl frutti mpl di mare; crostacei mpl

shell' hole' s cratere m

shell' shock' s psicosi traumatica bellica

shelter [ˈʃeltər] s rifugio, ricovero; **to take shelter** rifugiarsi ‖ tr raccogliere, ospitare, dare rifugio a

shelve [ʃelv] tr mettere sullo scaffale; (a bill) insabbiare; mettere a riposo

shepherd [ˈʃepərd] s pastore m ‖ tr guardare, curarsi di

shep'herd dog' s cane m da pastore

shepherdess [ˈʃepərdɪs] s pastora

sherbet [ˈʃɑrbət] s sorbetto

sheriff [ˈʃerɪf] s sceriffo

sher·ry [ˈʃeri] s (-ries) xeres m

shield [ʃild] s scudo; (for armpit) sottoascella m; (badge) scudetto; (elec) schermo ‖ tr proteggere; (elec) schermare

shift [ʃɪft] s cambio, cambiamento;

(*period of work*) turno; (*group of workmen*) operai *mpl* di turno, squadra di lavoro; espediente *m*, sotterfugio ‖ *tr* cambiare; spostare; (*blame*) riversare; ‖ *intr* cambiare; spostarsi; fare da sé; vivere di espedienti; (rr) manovrare; (aut) cambiare marcia

shift′ key′ *s* tasto maiuscole

shiftless [′ʃɪftlɪs] *adj* pigro, ozioso

shift·y [′ʃɪftɪ] *adj* (**-ier; -iest**) astuto; evasivo; pieno d'espedienti; (*glance*) sfuggente

shilling [′ʃɪlɪŋ] *s* scellino

shimmer [′ʃɪmər] *s* luccichio ‖ *intr* luccicare, mandare bagliori

shim·my [′ʃɪmɪ] *s* (**-mies**) (*dance*) shimmy *m*; (aut) farfallamento delle ruote, shimmy *m* ‖ *intr* ballare lo shimmy; vibrare

shin [ʃɪn] *s* stinco; (*of cattle*) cannone *m* ‖ *v* (*pret & pp* **shinned**; *ger* **shinning**) *tr* arrampicarsi su ‖ *intr* arrampicarsi

shin′bone′ *s* stinco, tibia

shine [ʃaɪn] *s* splendore *m*; luce *f*; bel tempo; lucidatura, lucido; **to take a shine to** (coll) prender simpatia per ‖ *v* (*pret & pp* **shined**) *tr* pulire, lucidare ‖ *v* (*pret & pp* **shone** [ʃon]) *tr* (*e.g., a flashlight*) dirigere i raggi di ‖ *intr* brillare, luccicare, risplendere; (*to excel*) essere brillante, eccellere

shiner [′ʃaɪnər] *s* (slang) occhio pesto

shingle [′ʃɪŋgəl] *s* assicella di copertura; (*to cover a wall*) mattoncino di rivestimento; (Brit) greto ciottoloso; (coll) capelli *mpl* alla bebé; **shingles** (pathol) erpete *m*, zona; **to hang out one's shingle** (coll) aprire un ufficio professionale ‖ *tr* coprire di assicelle or mattoncini; (*hair*) tagliare alla bebé

shining [′ʃaɪnɪŋ] *adj* brillante, lucente

shin·y [′ʃaɪnɪ] *adj* (**-ier; -iest**) lucente, lucido; (*paper*) patinato

ship [ʃɪp] *s* nave *f*, bastimento; aeronave *f*; aeroplano; (*crew*) equipaggio ‖ *v* (*pret & pp* **shipped**; *ger* **shipping**) *tr* imbarcare; mandare, spedire; (*oars*) disarmare; (*water*) imbarcare ‖ *intr* imbarcarsi

ship′board′ *s*—**on shipboard** a bordo

ship′build′er *s* costruttore *m* navale

ship′build′ing *s* architettura navale

ship′mate′ *s* compagno di bordo

shipment [′ʃɪpmənt] *s* invio, spedizione

ship′own′er *s* armatore *m*

shipper [′ʃɪpər] *s* speditore *m*, spedizioniere *m*, mittente *m*

shipping [′ʃɪpɪŋ] *s* imbarco; spedizione; (naut) trasporto marittimo

ship′ping clerk′ *s* speditore *m*

ship′ping room′ *s* ufficio impaccatura

ship′shape′ *adj & adv* in perfette condizioni

ship′side′ *s* molo

ship′s′ pa′pers *spl* documenti *mpl* di bordo

ship′wreck′ *s* naufragio; (*remains*) relitto ‖ *tr* far naufragare ‖ *intr* naufragare

ship′yard′ *s* cantiere *m* navale

shirk [ʃʌrk] *tr* (*work*) evitare; (*responsibility*) sottrarsi a ‖ *intr* imboscarsi

shirt [ʃʌrt] *s* camicia; **to keep one's shirt on** (slang) non perdere la calma; **to lose one's shirt** (slang) perdere la camicia

shirt′ front′ *s* sparato

shirt′ sleeve′ *s* manica di camicia

shirt′tail′ *s* falda della camicia

shirt′waist′ *s* blusa da donna

shiver [′ʃɪvər] *s* brivido ‖ *intr* rabbrividire, battere i denti

shoal [ʃol] *s* secca, banco di sabbia

shock [ʃɑk] *s* urto, collisione; scossa; scossa elettrica; (pathol) shock *m* ‖ *tr* scuotere; (*to strike against*) urtare; scandalizzare, indignare; dare la scossa elettrica a; (fig) scioccare

shock′ absorb′er [æb′sɔrbər] *s* ammortizzatore *m* di colpi

shocking [′ʃɑkɪŋ] *adj* disgustoso, scandalizzante

shock′ ther′apy *s* terapia d'urto

shock′ troops′ *spl* truppe *fpl* d'assalto

shod·dy [′ʃɑdɪ] *adj* (**-dier; -diest**) scadente, falso

shoe [ʃu] *s* scarpa; (*horseshoe*) ferro da cavallo; (*of a tire*) copertone *m*; (*of brake*) ganascia, ceppo ‖ *v* (*pret & pp* **shod** [ʃɑd]) *tr* calzare; (*a horse*) ferrare

shoe′black′ *s* lustrascarpe *m*

shoe′horn′ *s* corno da scarpe, calzatoio

shoe′lace′ *s* laccio delle scarpe

shoe′mak′er *s* calzolaio

shoe′ pol′ish *s* crema or cera da scarpe

shoe′shine′ *s* lucidatura, lustramento di scarpe

shoe′ store′ *s* calzoleria

shoe′string′ *s* laccio delle scarpe; **on a shoestring** con quattro soldi

shoe′tree′ *s* tendiscarpe *m*

shoo [ʃu] *tr* fare sció a ‖ *intr* fare sció

shoot [ʃut] *s* (*e.g., with a firearm*) tiro; gara di tiro; (*chute*) scivolo; (rok) lancio; (bot) getto, virgulto ‖ *v* (*pret & pp* **shot** [ʃɑt]) *tr* (*any missile*) tirare; (*a bullet*) sparare; (*to execute with a bullet*) fucilare; (*to fling*) lanciare; (*the sun*) prendere l'altezza di; (*dice*) gettare; (mov, telv) girare, riprendere; **to shoot down** (*a plane*) abbattere; **to shoot up** (coll) terrorizzare sparando a casaccio ‖ *intr* tirare, sparare; passare rapidamente; nascere; (*said of pain*) dare fitte; (mov) cinematografare; **to shoot at** tirare a; (coll) cercare di ottenere

shoot′ing gal′lery *s* tiro a segno

shoot′ing match′ *s* gara di tiro a segno; (slang) tutto, ogni cosa

shoot′ing star′ *s* stella cadente

shop [ʃɑp] *s* negozio, rivendita; (*workshop*) officina; **to talk shop** parlare del proprio lavoro ‖ *v* (*pret & pp* **shopped**; *ger* **shopping**) *intr* fare la spesa; **to go shopping** andare a fare la spesa; **to shop around** cercare un'occasione di negozio in negozio

shop′girl′ *s* venditrice *f*

shop'keep'er *s* negoziante *mf*
shoplifter ['ʃɑp‚lɪftər] *s* taccheggia-
tore *m*
shopper ['ʃɑpər] *s* compratore *m*
shopping ['ʃɑpɪŋ] *s* compra; (*pur-
chases*) compre *fpl*, shopping *m*
shop'ping bag' *s* sporta, shopping *m*
shop'ping cen'ter *s* centro d'acquisto,
ipermercato
shop'ping dis'trict *s* zona commerciale
shop'win'dow *s* vetrina
shop'worn' *adj* sciupato, usato
shore [ʃor] *s* costa, riva; spiaggia,
lido; (*fig*) regione; (*support*) sostegno, puntello ‖ *tr* puntellare
shore' din'ner *s* pranzo di pesce
shore' leave' *s* (naut) franchigia
shore'line' *s* frangia costiera
shore' patrol' *s* polizia della marina
short [ʃort] *adj* (*in stature*) piccolo,
basso; (*in space, time*) breve;
(*scanty*) scarso; succinto; (*in quantity*) poco, piccolo; (*rude*) brusco;
in a short time in breve; **in short** per
farla breve; **on short notice** senza
preavviso; **short of breath** corto di
fiato; **to be short of** scarseggiare di
‖ *s* (elec) cortocircuito; (mov) corto-
metraggio; **shorts** (*underwear*) mutande *fpl*; (*sports attire*) calzoncini
mpl, shorts *mpl* ‖ *adv* brevemente,
bruscamente; (com) allo scoperto,
e.g., **to sell short** vendere allo scoperto; **to run short of** essere a corto
di; **to stop short** fermarsi di colpo ‖
tr (elec) causare un cortocircuito in
‖ *intr* (elec) andare in cortocircuito
shortage ['ʃortɪdʒ] *s* mancanza; (*of
food*) carestia; (*from pilfering*) ammanco
short'cake' *s* torta di pasta frolla; torta
ricoperta di frutta fresca
short'-change' *tr* non dare il cambio
giusto a; (coll) imbrogliare
short' cir'cuit *s* (elec) cortocircuito
short'-cir'cuit *tr* mandare in cortocircuito; (coll) rovinare ‖ *intr* andare
in cortocircuito
short'com'ing *s* difetto, manchevolezza
short'cut' *s* scorciatoia
shorten ['ʃortən] *tr* raccorciare, abbreviare ‖ *intr* raccorciarsi, abbreviarsi
shortening ['ʃortənɪŋ] *s* raccorciamento; (culin) grasso, strutto
short'hand' *adj* stenografico ‖ *s* stenografia; **to take shorthand** stenografare
short'hand' typ'ist *s* stenodattilografo
short-lived ['ʃort'laɪvd] *or* ['ʃort'lɪvd]
adj effimero, di breve vita
shortly ['ʃortli] *adv* in breve, brevemente; fra poco; bruscamente;
shortly after poco dopo
short'-range' *adj* di corta portata
short' sale' *s* vendita allo scoperto
short-sighted ['ʃort'saɪtɪd] *adj* miope;
(fig) miope
short'stop' *s* (baseball) interbase *m*
short' sto'ry *s* novella
short-tempered ['ʃort'tempərd] *adj* irascibile
short'-term' *adj* a breve scadenza

short'wave' *adj* alle onde corte ‖ *s*
onda corta
short' weight' *s*—**to give short weight**
rubare sul peso
shot [ʃat] *s* tiro, sparo; (*cartridge*) cartuccia; (*for cannon*) palla; (*pellets
of lead*) pallini *mpl*; (*person*) tiratore
m; (*hypodermic injection*) iniezione;
(*of liquor*) bicchierino; (phot) istantanea; (sports) peso; (mov) inquadratura; **not by a long shot** nemmeno
a pensarci; **to start like a shot** partire
come una palla da cannone; **to take
a shot at** tirare un colpo a; (*to attempt to*) provarsi a
shot'gun' *s* schioppo, fucile *m* da caccia
shot' put' *s* lancio del peso
should [ʃʊd] *v aux* si usa nelle seguenti
situazioni: 1) per formare il condizionale presente, per es., **if I should
wait for him, I should miss the train**
se lo aspettassi, perderei il treno;
2) per formare il perfetto del condizionale, per es., **if I had waited for
him, I should have missed the train**
se lo avessi aspettato, avrei perso il
treno; 3) per indicare la necessità di
un'azione, per es., **he should go at
once** dovrebbe andare immediatamente; **he should have gone immediately** sarebbe dovuto andare immediatamente
shoulder ['ʃoldər] *s* spalla; (*of highway*) banchina; **across the shoulder** a
bandoliera; **to put one's shoulders
to the wheel** mettersi a lavorare di
buzzo buono; **to turn a cold shoulder
to** volgere le spalle a ‖ *tr* portare
sulle spalle; (*a responsibility*) addossarsi; spingere con le spalle
shoul'der blade' *s* scapola
shoul'der strap' *s* spallina; (mil) tracolla
shout [ʃaʊt] *s* urlo, grido ‖ *tr* urlare,
gridare; **to shout down** far tacere a
forza di strilli ‖ *intr* gridare
shove [ʃʌv] *s* spintone *m* ‖ *tr* spingere
‖ *intr* spingere, dare spintoni; **to
shove off** allontanarsi dalla riva;
(slang) andarsene
shov·el ['ʃʌvəl] *s* pala ‖ *v* (pret & pp
-eled *or* -elled; ger -eling *or* -elling)
tr spalare ‖ *intr* lavorare di pala
show [ʃo] *s* mostra; apparenza; traccia; ostentazione; (mov, telv, theat)
spettacolo; **to make a show of** dar
spettacolo di; **to steal the show from**
ricevere tutti gli applausi invece di ‖
tr mostrare, esporre; (*a movie*) presentare; dimostrare, insegnare; provare; (*to register*) segnare; (*one's
feelings*) manifestare; (*to the door*)
accompagnare; **to show in** fare entrare; **to show off** mettere in mostra
‖ *intr* mostrarsi; presentarsi, apparire; (*said of a horse*) (sports) arrivare terzo, piazzarsi; **to show off**
mettersi in mostra; **to show up** (coll)
mostrarsi; (coll) farsi vedere
show' bill' *s* cartellone *m*
show'boat' *s* battello per spettacoli teatrali

show' busi'ness s industria dello spettacolo

show'case' s bacheca, vetrina

show'down' s carte scoperte; chiarificazione

shower [ˈʃau.ər] s (of rain) acquazzone m; (shower bath) doccia; (e.g., for a bride) ricevimento cui i partecipanti devono portare un regalo; (fig) pioggia || tr inaffiare; **to shower with** colmare di || intr diluviare; fare la doccia

show'er bath' s doccia

show' girl' s ballerina, girl f

show'man s (-men) impresario teatrale; persona che ha molta scena

show'-off' s reclamista m, strombazzatore m

show'piece' s capolavoro, oggetto d'arte

show'place' s luogo celebre; **to be a showplace** (said, e.g., of a house) essere arredato perfettamente

show'room' s sala di mostra

show' win'dow s vetrina

show-y [ˈʃo-i] adj (-ier; -iest) vistoso, sgargiante

shrapnel [ˈʃræpnəl] s shrapnel m

shred [ʃred] s brano, brandello; ritaglio; (fig) granello; **to cut to shreds** fare a brandelli || v (pret & pp **shredded** or **shred**; ger **shredding**) tr fare a brandelli; (paper) tagliuzzare

shrew [ʃru] s (woman) bisbetica; (animal) toporagno

shrewd [ʃrud] adj astuto, scaltro

shriek [ʃrik] s strido; strillo; risata stridula || intr stridere; strillare

shrill [ʃrɪl] adj stridulo, squillante

shrimp [ʃrɪmp] s gamberetto; (person) omiciattolo, nanerottolo

shrine [ʃraɪn] s santuario, sacrario

shrink [ʃrɪŋk] v (pret **shrank** [ʃræŋk] or **shrunk** [ʃrʌŋk]; pp **shrunk** or **shrunken**) tr contrarre, restringere || intr contrarsi, restringersi, ritirarsi

shrinkage [ˈʃrɪŋkɪdʒ] s restringimento; (in weight) calo

shriv•el [ˈʃrɪvəl] v (pret & pp **-eled** or **-elled**; ger **-eling** or **-elling**) tr raggrinzire; (from heat) raccartocciare; (to wither) avvizzire || intr raggrinzirsi; accartocciarsi; avvizzire; **to shrivel up** incartapecorire

shroud [ʃraud] s sudario, lenzuolo funebre; (fig) cappa || tr avvolgere

Shrove' Tues'day [ʃrov] s martedì grasso

shrub [ʃrʌb] s arbusto

shrubber•y [ˈʃrʌbəri] s (-ies) arbusti mpl, cespugli mpl

shrug [ʃrʌg] s scrollata di spalle || v (pret & pp **shrugged**; ger **shrugging**) tr scrollare; **to shrug one's shoulders** scrollare le spalle || intr fare spallucce

shudder [ˈʃʌdər] s brivido, fremito || intr rabbrividire, fremere

shuffle [ˈʃʌfəl] s (of cards) mescolata; turno di fare il mazzo; (of feet) straschichio; evasione || tr mescolare; strisciare, strascicare || intr fare il mazzo; scalpicciare; ballare di striscio; **to shuffle off** strascicarsi, scalpicciare; **to shuffle out of** evadere da

shun [ʃʌn] v (pret & pp **shunned**; ger **shunning**) tr evitare, schivare

shunt [ʃʌnt] tr sviare; (elec) shuntare; (rr) deviare

shut [ʃʌt] adj chiuso || v (pret & pp **shut**; ger **shutting**) tr chiudere, serrare; **to shut in** rinchiudere; **to shut off** (e.g., gas) tagliare; **to shut up** tappare; imprigionare; (coll) fare star zitto || intr chiudersi; **to shut up** (coll) stare zitto, tacere

shut'down' s chiusura

shutter [ˈʃʌtər] s (outside a window) persiana, gelosia; (outside a store window) serranda, saracinesca; (phot) otturatore m

shuttle [ˈʃʌtəl] s spola, navetta || intr fare la spola

shut'tle-cock' s volano, volante m

shut'tle train' s treno che fa la spola fra due stazioni

shy [ʃaɪ] adj (shyer or shier; shyest or shiest) timido; (fearful) schivo, ritroso; corto, a corto, e.g., **he is shy of funds** è a corto di denaro || v (pret & pp **shied**) intr ritirarsi; schivarsi; (said of a horse) adombrarsi; **to shy away** tenersi discosto

shyster [ˈʃaɪstər] s (coll) azzeccagarbugli m

Sia-mese [ˌsaɪ-əˈmiz] adj siamese || s (-mese) siamese mf

Si'amese twins' spl fratelli mpl siamesi

Siberian [saɪˈbɪri-ən] adj & s siberiano

sibilant [ˈsɪbɪlənt] adj & s sibilante f

sibyl [ˈsɪbɪl] s sibilla

sic [sik] adv sic || [sɪk] v (pret & pp **sicked**; ger **sicking**) tr aizzare; **sick 'em!** va!; **to sick on** aizzare contro

Sicilian [sɪˈsɪljən] adj & s siciliano

Sicily [ˈsɪsɪli] s la Sicilia

sick [sɪk] adj ammalato; nauseato; (bored) stucco; **sick at heart** con una spina nel cuore; **to be sick and tired** averne sin sopra i capelli; **to be sick at one's stomach** avere la nausea; **to take sick** cader malato || tr (a dog) aizzare

sick'bed' s letto d'ammalato

sicken [ˈsɪkən] tr ammalare; disgustare || intr ammalarsi

sickening [ˈsɪkənɪŋ] adj stomachevole

sick' head'ache s emicrania accompagnata da nausea

sickle [ˈsɪkəl] s falce messoria, falcetto

sick' leave' s congedo per motivi di salute

sick•ly [ˈsɪkli] adj (-lier; -liest) cagionevole, malaticcio

sickness [ˈsɪknɪs] s malattia; nausea

side [saɪd] s lato laterale || s parte f, lato; (e.g., of a coin) faccia; (slope) versante m; (of human body, of a ship) fianco; **to take sides** parteggiare || intr parteggiare; **to side with** schierarsi dalla parte di

side'board' s credenza

side'burns' spl basette fpl, favoriti mpl

side'car' s motocarrozzetta; carrozzino laterale (di motocarrozzetta)

side' dish' s portata extra

side' door' s porta laterale

side' effect' s effetto secondario

side'-glance' s occhiata di sbieco

side' is'sue s questione secondaria

side'line' s linea laterale; impiego secondario; attività secondaria

sidereal [saɪ'dɪrɪ-əl] adj siderale

side'sad'dle adv all'amazzone

side' show' s spettacolo secondario di baraccone; affare secondario

side'slip' intr (aer) scivolare d'ala

side'split'ting adj che fa sbellicare dalle risa

side' step' s passo laterale; scartata

side'-step' v (pret & pp -stepped; ger -stepping) tr evitare || intr farsi da parte; fare una scartata

side'track' s binario morto di smistamento || tr sviare; (rr) smistare

side' view' s vista di profilo

side'walk' s marciapiede m

side'walk café' s caffè m con tavolini all'aperto

sideward ['saɪdwərd] adj obliquo, a sghembo || adv verso un lato; di sghembo

side'ways' adj sghembo || adv di sghembo; di fianco

side' whisk'ers spl favoriti mpl

siding ['saɪdɪŋ] s (rr) diramazione, binario morto, raccordo ferroviario

sidle ['saɪdəl] intr andare al lato; muoversi furtivamente

siege [sidʒ] s assedio; (of illness) ricorrenza d'attacchi; **to lay siege to** cingere d'assedio, assediare

siesta [si'estə] s siesta; **to take a siesta** fare la siesta

sieve [sɪv] s vaglio, setaccio || tr vagliare, setacciare

sift [sɪft] tr (flour) abburattare; setacciare; (to scatter with a sieve) spolverare; (fig) vagliare

sigh [saɪ] s sospiro || tr mormorare sospirando || intr sospirare; **to sigh for** sospirare

sight [saɪt] s vista, visione; spettacolo, veduta; (opt) mira, traguardo; (mil) mirino, tacca di mira; (coll) mucchio; **a sight of** (coll) molto; **at first sight** a prima vista; **at sight** ad apertura di libro; (com) a vista; **out of sight** fuori di vista; lontano dagli occhi; (prices) astronomico; **sights** luoghi mpl interessanti; **sight unseen** senza averlo visto prima, a occhi chiusi; **to be a sight** (coll) essere un orrore; **to catch sight of** arrivare a intravedere; **to know by sight** conoscere di vista; **to not be able to stand the sight of s.o.** non poter vedere qlcu nemmeno dipinto || tr avvistare; (a weapon) mirare || intr mirare, prendere di mira; osservare attentamente

sight' draft' s (com) tratta a vista

sight'-read' v (pret & pp -read [ˌred]) tr & intr leggere a libro aperto

sight'see'ing adj turistico || s turismo, visite fpl turistiche

sightseer ['saɪtˌsi·ər] s turista mf

sign [saɪn] s segno; segnale m; (e.g., on a store) insegna, cartello; **signs** tracce fpl || tr firmare; ingaggiare; indicare, segnalare || intr firmare; fare segno; **to sign off** (rad, telv) terminare la trasmissione; **to sign up** iscriversi

sig'nal ['sɪgnəl] adj insigne, segnalato || s segnale m || v (pret & pp -naled or -nalled; ger -naling or -nalling) tr segnalare || intr fare segnalazioni

sig'nal corps' s (mil) armi fpl di trasmissione

sig'nal tow'er s (rr) posto di blocco

signato·ry ['sɪgnɪˌtori] s (-ries) firmatario

signature ['sɪgnətʃər] s firma; segno musicale; (typ) segnatura

sign'board' s cartellone m

signer ['saɪnər] s firmatario

sig'net ring' ['sɪgnɪt] s anello col sigillo

significance [sɪg'nɪfɪkəns] s importanza; (meaning) significato

significant [sɪg'nɪfɪkənt] adj importante

signi·fy ['sɪgnɪˌfaɪ] v (pret & pp -fied) tr significare

sign'post' s palo indicatore

silence ['saɪləns] s silenzio || tr far tacere; (mil) ridurre al silenzio

silent ['saɪlənt] adj silenzioso, tacito

si'lent mov'ie s cinema muto

silhouette [ˌsɪlu'et] s silhouette f, siluetta

silicon ['sɪlɪkən] s silicio

silicone ['sɪlɪˌkon] s silicone m

silk [sɪlk] adj di seta || s seta; **to hit the silk** (slang) gettarsi col paracadute

silken ['sɪlkən] adj serico, di seta

silk' hat' s cappello a cilindro

silk'screen proc'ess s serigrafia

silk'-stock'ing adj & s aristocratico

silk'worm' s baco da seta, filugello

silk·y ['sɪlki] adj (-ier; -iest) di seta; come la seta

sill [sɪl] s basamento; (of a door) soglia; (of a window) davanzale m

sil·ly ['sɪli] adj (-lier; -liest) sciocco, scemo

si·lo ['saɪlo] s (-los) silo || tr insilare

silt [sɪlt] s sedimento

silver ['sɪlvər] adj d'argento; (voice) argentino; (plated with silver) argentato || s argento || tr inargentare

sil'ver·fish' s (ent) lepisma

sil'ver foil' s foglia d'argento

sil'ver fox' s volpe argentata

sil'ver lin'ing s spiraglio di speranza

sil'ver plate' s vasellame m d'argento; argentatura

sil'ver screen' s (mov) schermo

sil'ver·smith' s argentiere m

sil'ver spoon' s ricchezza ereditata; **to be born with a silver spoon in one's mouth** esser nato con la camicia

sil'ver·ware' s argenteria

sil'ver·ware' chest' s portaposate m

similar ['sɪmɪlər] adj simile

similari·ty [ˌsɪmɪ'lærɪti] s (-ties) similarità f, somiglianza

simile ['sɪmɪli] s similitudine f

simmer ['sɪmər] *tr* cuocere a fuoco lento ‖ *intr* cuocere a fuoco lento; (fig) ribollire; **to simmer down** (slang) calmarsi

simper ['sɪmpər] *s* sorriso scemo ‖ *intr* fare un sorriso scemo

simple ['sɪmpəl] *adj* semplice

simple-minded ['sɪmpəl'maɪndɪd] *adj* semplicione, scemo

simpleton ['sɪmpəltən] *s* semplicione *m*

simulate ['sɪmjə,let] *tr* simulare

simultaneous [,saɪməl'teni·əs] or [,sɪməl'teni·əs] *adj* simultaneo

sin [sɪn] *s* peccato ‖ *v* (*pret & pp* **sinned;** *ger* **sinning**) *intr* peccare

since [sɪns] *adv* da allora, da allora in poi; da tempo fa ‖ *prep* da ‖ *conj* dacché; poiché, dato che

sincere [sɪn'sɪr] *adj* sincero

sincerity [sɪn'sɛrɪti] *s* sincerità *f*

sine [saɪn] *s* (math) seno

sinecure ['saɪnɪ,kjur] or ['sɪnɪ,kjur] *s* sinecura

sinew ['sɪnju] *s* tendine *m;* (fig) nerbo

sinful ['sɪnfəl] *adj* (*person*) peccatore; (*act, intention, etc.*) peccaminoso

sing [sɪŋ] *v* (*pret* **sang** [sæŋ] or **sung** [sʌŋ];* *pp* **sung**) *tr* cantare; **to sing to sleep** ninnare ‖ *intr* cantare; (*said, e.g., of the ears*) fischiare

singe [sɪndʒ] *v* (*pret* **singeing**) *tr* strinare, bruciacchiare

singer ['sɪŋər] *s* cantante *mf;* (*in night club*) canzonettista *mf*

single ['sɪŋgəl] *adj* unico, solo; (*room*) a un letto; (*bed*) a una piazza; (*man*) celibe; (*woman*) nubile; (*combat*) corpo a corpo; semplice, sincero ‖ **singles** *ssg* singolare *m* ‖ *tr* scegliere; **to single out** individuare

single-breasted ['sɪŋgəl'brɛstɪd] *adj* a un petto, monopetto

sin'gle entry' *s* partita semplice

sin'gle file' *s* fila indiana

single-handed ['sɪŋgəl'hændɪd] *adj* da solo, senza aiuto altrui

sin'gle-phase' *adj* (elec) monofase

sin'gle room' *s* camera a un letto

sin'gle-track' *adj* (rr) a binario semplice; (fig) di corte vedute

sing'song' *adj* monotono ‖ *s* cantilena

singular ['sɪŋgjələr] *adj & s* singolare *m*

sinister ['sɪnɪstər] *adj* sinistro

sink [sɪŋk] *s* acquaio; (*sewer*) scolo, fogna; (fig) sentina ‖ *v* (*pret* **sank** [sæŋk] or **sunk** [sʌŋk];* *pp* **sunk**) *tr* sprofondare; infiggere; (*a well*) scavare; (*in tone*) abbassare; (*a boat*) mandare a picco; rovinare; investire; perdere ‖ *intr* sprofondarsi; abbassarsi; (*said, of the sun, prices, etc.*) calare; andare a picco; lasciarsi cadere; (*in vice*) impantanarsi; (*said of one's cheeks*) infossarsi; (*in thought*) perdersi; **to sink down** sedersi; **to sink in** penetrare

sink'ing fund' *s* fondo d'ammortamento

sinner ['sɪnər] *s* peccatore *m*

Sinology [si'nɑlədʒi] *s* sinologia

sinuous ['sɪnju·əs] *adj* sinuoso

sinus ['saɪnəs] *s* seno

sip [sɪp] *s* sorso ‖ *v* (*pret & pp* **sipped;** *ger* **sipping**) *tr* sorbire, sorseggiare

siphon ['saɪfən] *s* sifone *m* ‖ *tr* travasare con un sifone

si'phon bot'tle *s* sifone *m*

sir [sʌr] *s* signore *m;* (Brit) sir *m;* **Dear Sir** Illustrissimo signore; (com) Egregio signore

sire [saɪr] *s* (*king*) sire *m;* padre *m,* stallone *m* ‖ *tr* generare

siren ['saɪrən] *s* sirena

sirloin ['sʌrlɔɪn] *s* lombata, lombo

sirup ['sɪrəp] or ['sʌrəp] *tr* sciroppo

sis·sy ['sɪsi] *s* (**-sies**) effemminato

sister ['sɪstər] *adj* (*ship*) gemello; (*language*) sorella; (*corporation*) consorella ‖ *s* sorella; (*nun*) suora, monaca

sis'ter-in-law' *s* (**sis'ters-in-law'**) cognata

Sis'tine Chap'el ['sɪstɪn] *s* Cappella Sistina

sit [sɪt] *v* (*pret & pp* **sat** [sæt];* *ger* **sitting**) *intr* sedere; posare; (*said of a hen*) covare; (*said of a jacket*) stare; essere in sessione; **to sit down** sedersi; **to sit in** partecipare a; assistere a; **to sit still** stare tranquillo; **to sit up** alzarsi; (coll) essere sorpreso

sit'-down strike' *s* sciopero bianco

site [saɪt] *s* sito, luogo, posizione

sitting ['sɪtɪŋ] *s* seduta; (*of a court*) sessione; (*of a hen*) covata; (*serving of a meal*) turno

sit'ting duck' *s* (slang) facile bersaglio

sit'ting room' *s* soggiorno

situate ['sɪtʃu,et] *tr* situare

situation [,sɪtʃu'eʃən] *s* situazione, posizione; posto

sitz' bath' [sɪts] *s* semicupio

six [sɪks] *adj & pron* sei ‖ *s* sei *m;* **at sixes and sevens** in disordine; **six o'clock** le sei

six' hun'dred *adj, s & pron* seicento

sixteen ['sɪks'tin] *adj, s & pron* sedici *m*

sixteenth ['sɪks'tinθ] *adj, s & pron* sedicesimo ‖ *s* (*in dates*) sedici *m*

sixth [sɪksθ] *adj, s & pron* sesto ‖ *s* (*in dates*) sei *m*

sixtieth ['sɪkstɪ·iθ] *adj, s & pron* sessantesimo

six·ty ['sɪksti] *adj & pron* sessanta ‖ *s* (**-ies**) sessanta *m;* **the sixties** gli anni sessanta

sizable ['saɪzəbəl] *adj* considerevole

size [saɪz] *s* grandezza; quantità *f;* (*of person or garment*) taglia; (*of shoes*) numero; (*of hat*) giro; (*of a pipe*) diametro; (*for gilding*) colla; (fig) situazione ‖ *tr* misurare, classificare secondo grandezza; incollare; **to size up** (coll) stimare, giudicare

sizzle ['sɪzəl] *s* sfrigolio ‖ *intr* sfriggere

skate [sket] *s* pattino; (slang) tipo ‖ *intr* pattinare; **to skate on thin ice** andare in cerca di disgrazie

skat'ing rink' *s* pattinatoio

skein [sken] *s* gomitolo, matassa

skeleton ['skɛlɪtən] *adj* scheletrico ‖ *s* scheletro

skel'eton key' *s* chiave maestra

skeptic ['skɛptɪk] *adj & s* scettico

skeptical ['skɛptɪkəl] *adj* scettico
sketch [skɛtʃ] *s* schizzo, disegno; abbozzo, bozzetto; (theat) scenetta || *tr* schizzare, disegnare; abbozzare
sketch'book' *s* album *m* di schizzi; quaderno per abbozzi
skew [skju] *adj* obliquo || *s* movimento obliquo; (chisel) scalpello a taglio obliquo || *tr* tagliare di sghembo || *intr* (to swerve) deviare; (to look obliquely) guardare di sghembo
skew' chis'el *s* scalpello a taglio obliquo
skewer ['skju·ər] *s* spiedino || *tr* mettere allo spiedo
ski [ski] *s* (skis or ski) sci *m* || *intr* sciare
ski' boot' *s* scarpa da sci
skid [skɪd] *s* (device to check a wheel) scarpa; (skidding forward) slittamento; (skidding sideway) sbandamento; (aer, mach) pattino || *v* (pret & pp skidded; ger skidding) tr frenare || *intr* (forward) slittare; (sideways) sbandare
skid' row' [ro] *s* quartiere malfamato
skier ['ski·ər] *s* sciatore *m*
skiff [skɪf] *s* skiff *m*, singolo
skiing ['ski·ɪŋ] *s* sci *m*
ski' jump' *s* salto con gli sci; trampolino di salto
ski' lift' *s* sciovia
skill [skɪl] *s* destrezza, perizia
skilled [skɪld] *adj* abile, esperto
skilled' la'bor *s* manodopera qualificata
skillet ['skɪlɪt] *s* padella
skillful ['skɪlfəl] *adj* destro, abile
skim [skɪm] *v* (pret & pp skimmed; ger skimming) tr (milk) scremare; (e.g., broth) sgrassare; (to graze) sfiorare; (the ground) radere; (a page) trascorrere || *intr* sfiorare; to skim over scorrere
ski' mask' *s* passamontagna *m*
skimmer ['skɪmər] *s* schiumaiola; (hat) canottiera
skim' milk' *s* latte scremato or magro
skimp [skɪmp] *tr* lesinare || *intr* economizzare, risparmiare
skimp·y ['skɪmpi] *adj* (-ier; -iest) corto, scarso; taccagno
skin [skɪn] *s* pelle *f*; (rind) scorza; (of onion) spoglia; by the skin of one's teeth (coll) per il rotto della cuffia; soaked to the skin bagnato fino alle ossa; to have a thin skin offendersi facilmente || *v* (pret & pp skinned; ger skinning) tr pelare, spellare; (e.g., one's knee) spellarsi; (slang) tosare; to skin alive (slang) scotennare; (slang) battere in pieno
skin'-deep' *adj* a fior di pelle
skin'-div'er *s* nuotatore subacqueo, sub *m*; (mil) sommozzatore *m*
skin'flint' *s* avaro
skin' game' *s* truffa
skin·ny ['skɪni] *adj* (-nier; -niest) magro, scarno
skin' test' *s* cutireazione
skip [skɪp] *s* salto || *v* (pret & pp

skipped; ger skipping) *tr* (a fence; a meal) saltare; (a subject) sorvolare; (school) (coll) marinare || *intr* saltare, salterellare; (said of typewriter) saltare uno spazio; (coll) svignarsela
ski' pole' *s* racchetta da sci
skipper ['skɪpər] *s* capitano, comandante *m*
skirmish ['skɑrmɪʃ] *s* scaramuccia || *intr* battersi in una scaramuccia
skirt [skɑrt] *s* sottana, gonna; (edge) orlo; (woman) (slang) gonnella || *tr* orlare; costeggiare; (a subject) evitare
ski' run' *s* pista da sci
skit [skɪt] *s* (theat) quadretto comico
skittish ['skɪtɪʃ] *adj* bizzarro, balzano; timido; (horse) ombroso
skulduggery [skʌl'dʌgəri] *s* trucco disonesto
skull [skʌl] *s* cranio, teschio
skull' and cross'bones *s* due tibie incrociate ed un teschio
skull'cap' *s* papalina
skunk [skʌŋk] *s* puzzola, moffetta; (coll) puzzone *m*
sky [skaɪ] *s* (skies) cielo; firmamento; to praise to the skies portare al cielo
sky'div'er *s* paracadutista *mf*
sky'jack'er *s* pirata *m* dell'aria
sky'lark' *s* allodola || *intr* (coll) darsi alla pazza gioia
sky'light' *s* lucernario
sky'line' *s* linea dell'orizzonte; (of city) profilo
sky'rock'et *s* razzo || *intr* salire come un razzo
sky'scrap'er *s* grattacielo
sky'writ'ing *s* scrittura pubblicitaria aerea
slab [slæb] *s* (of stone) lastra, lastrone *m*; (of wood) tavola; (slice) fetta
slack [slæk] *adj* lento, allentato; negligente, indolente; (fig) fiacco, morto || *s* lentezza; negligenza; stagione morta, inattività *f*; **slacks** pantaloni *mpl* da donna; pantaloni sciolti || *tr* allentare; trascurare; (lime) spegnere || *intr* rilasciarsi; essere negligente; to slack up rallentare
slacker ['slækər] *s* fannullone *m*; (mil) imboscato
slag [slæg] *s* scoria
slake [slek] *tr* spegnere
slalom ['slɑləm] *s* slalom *m*
slam [slæm] *s* colpo; (of door) sbatacchiamento; (in cards) cappotto; (coll) strapazzata || *v* (pret & pp slammed; ger slamming) tr sbattere, sbatacchiare; (coll) strapazzare || *intr* sbattere, sbatacchiare
slam'bang' *adv* (coll) con gran rumore, precipitosamente
slander ['slændər] *s* calunnia, maldicenza || *tr* calunniare, diffamare
slanderous ['slændərəs] *adj* calunnioso, diffamatorio
slang [slæŋ] *s* gergo
slant [slænt] *s* inclinazione; punto di vista || *tr* inclinare; (news) snaturare || *intr* inclinarsi; deviare

slap [slæp] *s* manata; (*in the face*) schiaffo, ceffone *m*; (*noise*) rumore *m*; insulto || *v* (*pret & pp* **slapped;** *ger* **slapping**) *tr* dare una manata a; schiaffeggiare

slap'dash' *adj* raffazzonato, fatto a casaccio || *adv* a casaccio

slap'hap'py *adj* (*punch-drunk*) stordito; (*giddy*) allegro, brillo

slap'stick' *adj* buffonesco || *s* bastone *m* d'Arlecchino; buffonata

slash [slæʃ] *s* sfregio; (*of prices*) riduzione || *tr* sfregiare; (*cloth*) tagliare; (*prices*) ridurre

slat [slæt] *s* travicello, regolo; (*for bed*) traversa; (*of shutter*) stecca

slate [slet] *s* ardesia, lavagna; (*for electoral*) lista elettorale; **clean slate** buon certificato || *tr* coprire con tegole d'ardesia; proporre la nomina di; (*to schedule*) mettere in cantiere

slate' roof' *s* tetto d'ardesia

slattern ['slætərn] *s* (*slovenly woman*) sciamannona; (*harlot*) puttana

slaughter ['slɔtər] *s* eccidio, carneficina || *tr* sgozzare, scannare

slaugh'ter-house' *s* macello, scannatoio

Slav [slɑv] *or* [slæv] *adj & s* slavo

slave [slev] *adj & s* schiavo || *intr* lavorare come uno schiavo

slave' driv'er *s* negriere *m*

slavery ['slevəri] *s* schiavitù *f*

slave' trade' *s* tratta degli schiavi

Slavic ['slɑvɪk] *or* ['slævɪk] *adj & s* slavo

slay [sle] *v* (*pret* **slew** [slu]; *pp* **slain** [slen]) *tr* scannare, uccidere

slayer ['sle·ər] *s* uccisore *m*

sled [sled] *s* slittino, slitta || *v* (*pret & pp* **sledded;** *ger* **sledding**) *intr* slittare

sledge' ham'mer *s* [sledʒ] *s* mazza

sleek [slik] *adj* liscio, lustro; elegante || *tr* lisciare, ammorbidire

sleep [slip] *s* sonno; **to go to sleep** addormentarsi; **to put to sleep** addormentare; uccidere con un anestetico || *v* (*pret & pp* **slept** [slept]) *tr* dormire; aver posto a dormire per; **to sleep it over** dormirci sopra; **to sleep off a hangover** smaltire una sbornia dormendo || *intr* dormire; **to sleep in** dormire fino a tardi; passare la notte a casa; **to sleep out** passare la notte fuori di casa

sleeper ['slipər] *s* (*person*) dormiente *mf*; (*beam, timber*) trave *f*

sleep'ing bag' *s* sacco a pelo

sleep'ing car' *s* vettura letto

sleep'ing pill' *s* sonnifero

sleepless ['sliplɪs] *adj* insonne; (*night*) bianco

sleep'walk'er *s* sonnambulo

sleep·y ['slipi] *adj* (*-ier; -iest*) insonnolito, sonnolento; **to be sleepy** aver sonno

sleep'y-head' *s* dormiglione *m*

sleet [slit] *s* nevischio || *impers* **it is sleeting** cade il nevischio

sleeve [sliv] *s* manica; (*of phonograph record*) busta; (*mach*) manicotto; **to laugh in or up one's sleeve** ridere sotto i baffi

sleigh [sle] *s* slitta || *intr* andare in slitta

sleigh' bells' *spl* bubboli *mpl* da slitta, sonagliera da slitta

sleigh' ride' *s* passeggiata in slitta

sleight' of hand' [slaɪt] *s* gioco di prestigio

slender ['slɛndər] *adj* smilzo, snello; esiguo, esile

sleuth [sluθ] *s* segugio

slew [slu] *s* (coll) mucchio

slice [slaɪs] *s* fetta; (*of an orange*) spicchio || *tr* tagliare a fette; (fig) fendere

slick [slɪk] *adj* liscio, lustro; scivoloso; astuto; (slang) ottimo || *s* posto scivoloso; (coll) rivista stampata su carta patinata || *tr* lisciare, lustrare; **to slick up** (coll) acconciare

slicker ['slɪkər] *s* impermeabile *m* di tela cerata; (coll) furbo di tre cotte

slide [slaɪd] *s* scivolata, scivolone *m*; (*chute*) scivolo; (*landslide*) frana; (*for projection*) diapositiva; (*of a microscope*) vetrino; (mach) guida; (*of a slide rule*) (mach) cursore *m* || *v* (*pret & pp* **slid** [slɪd]) *tr* far scivolare || *intr* sdrucciolare, scivolare; (*said of a car*) pattinare, slittare; **to let slide** lasciar correre

slide' fas'tener *s* chiusura lampo

slide' projec'tor *s* diascopio

slide' rule' *s* regolo calcolatore

slide' valve' *s* (mach) cassetto di distribuzione

slid'ing door' *s* porta scorrevole

slid'ing scale' *s* scala mobile

slight [slaɪt] *adj* leggero, lieve; delicato || *s* noncuranza, disattenzione; affronto || *tr* fare con negligenza; (*to snub*) trattare con noncuranza, snobbare

slim [slɪm] *adj* (**slimmer; slimmest**) sottile; magro

slime [slaɪm] *s* melma; (*e.g., of a snail*) bava

slim·y ['slaɪmi] *adj* (*-ier; -iest*) melmoso; bavoso; sudicio

sling [slɪŋ] *s* (*to shoot stones*) fionda; (naut) braca; **in a sling** (*arm*) al collo || *v* (*pret & pp* **slung** [slʌŋ]) *tr* gettare; lanciare; (*freight*) imbracare; sospendere; mettere a bandoliera

sling'shot' *s* fionda

slink [slɪŋk] *v* (*pret & pp* **slunk** [slʌŋk]) *intr* andare furtivamente; **to slink away** eclissarsi

slip [slɪp] *s* scivolone *m*; svista, errore *m*; (*in prices*) discesa; (*underdress*) sottoveste *f*; (*pillowcase*) federa; (*of paper*) pezzo; (*space between two wharves*) darsena, imbarcatoio; (*form*) modulo; personcina; (*inclined plane*) (naut) scalo d'alaggio; (bot) innesto; **to give the slip to** eludere || *v* (*pret & pp* **slipped;** *ger* **slipping**) *tr* infilare; liberare; liberarsi da; ometter; **to slip off** togliersi; **to slip on** mettersi; **to slip one's mind** dimenticarsi di, e.g., **it slipped my mind** me ne sono dimenticato || *intr* scivolare, scorrere; sdrucciolare; sbagliare; peggiorare; **to let slip** lasciarsi sfuggire; **to slip away** svignarsela; **to slip by** (said of time) passare, fuggire; **to slip out of s.o.'s hands** sgusciare dalle mani di qlcu; **to slip up** sbagliarsi

slip'cov'er s fodera

slip'knot' s nodo scorsoio

slip' of the tongue' s errore m nel parlare

slipper ['slɪpər] s pantofola

slippery ['slɪpəri] adj sdrucciolevole, scivoloso; evasivo; incerto

slip'shod' adj trasandato, mal fatto

slip'-up' s (coll) sbaglio

slit [slɪt] s taglio, fenditura ‖ v (pret & pp slit; ger slitting) tr tagliare, fendere; **to slit the throat of** sgozzare

slob [slab] s (slang) rozzo, villanzone m

slobber ['slabər] s bava; sdolcinatura ‖ intr sbavare; parlare sdolcinatamente

sloe [slo] s (shrub) prugnolo; (fruit) prugnola

slogan ['slogən] s slogan m

sloop [slup] s cutter m

slop [slap] s pastone m; (slang) sbobba ‖ v (pret & pp slopped; ger slopping) tr versare, imbrodare ‖ intr rovesciarsi, scorrere; (slang) perdersi in smancerie

slope [slop] s costa, pendice f; (of mountain or roof) spiovente m ‖ tr inclinare ‖ intr digradare, scendere

slop·py ['slapi] adj (-pier; -piest) fangoso; bagnato; (slovenly) sciatto; (done badly) abborracciato

slot [slat] s scanalatura; (for letters) buca; (e.g., on a broadcasting schedule) posizione

sloth [sloθ] or [sloθ] s pigrizia; (zool) bradipo, poltrone m

slot' machine' s macchina a gettone

slouch [slautʃ] s postura goffa; persona goffa; (coll) poltrone m ‖ intr muover·i goffamente; **to slouch in a chair** sdraiarsi

slouch' hat' s cappello floscio

slough [slau] s pantano; (fig) abisso ‖ [slʌf] s (of snake) spoglia; (pathol) crosta ‖ tr—**to slough off** spogliarsi di ‖ intr sbucciarsi, cadere

Slovak ['slovæk] or [slo'væk] adj & s slovacco

sloven·ly ['slʌvənli] adj (-lier; -liest) sciatto, trasandato

slow [slo] adj lento; (sluggish) tardo; (clock) indietro, in ritardo; (in understanding) tardivo ‖ adv piano ‖ tr rallentare ‖ intr rallentarsi; (said of a watch) ritardare

slow'down' s sciopero pignolo

slow' mo'tion s—**in slow motion** al rallentatore

slow'-motion projec'tor s rallentatore m

slow'poke' s (coll) poltrone m

slug [slʌg] s (heavy piece of metal) lingotto; (metal disk) gettone m; (fig) poltrone m; (zool) lumaca; (coll) colpo, mazzata ‖ v (pret & pp slugged; ger slugging) tr picchiare sodo

sluggard ['slʌgərd] s poltrone m

sluggish ['slʌgɪʃ] adj pigro, indolente; lento, fiacco

sluice [slus] s canale m; stramazzo

sluice' gate' s paratoia

slum [slʌm] s bassifondi mpl ‖ v (pret & pp slummed; ger slumming) intr visitare i bassifondi

slumber ['slʌmbər] s dormiveglia m, sonnellino ‖ intr dormire, dormicchiare

slump [slʌmp] s depressione, crisi f; (in prices) ribasso, calo ‖ intr impantanarsi; peggiorare; (said of prices) ribassare, calare

slur [slʌr] s insulto, macchia; critica; (mus) legatura ‖ v (pret & pp slurred; ger slurring) tr pronunziare indistintamente; (a subject) sorvolare; insultare, calunniare; (mus) legare

slush [slʌʃ] s poltiglia di neve; fanghiglia; (fig) sdolcinatezza

slut [slʌt] s cagna; (slovenly woman) sciamannona; troia, puttana

sly [slar] adj (slyer or slier; slyest or sliest) furbo; insidioso; (hiding one's true feelings) sornione; **on the sly** furtivamente

smack [smæk] s schiaffo; (of whip or lips) schiocco; (taste) traccia, sapore m; (coll) bacio collo schiocco ‖ adv di colpo, direttamente ‖ tr dare uno schiaffo a; colpire; (the whip or one's lips) schioccare; schioccare un bacio a ‖ intr—**to smack of** sapere di

small [smɔl] adj piccolo; povero; basso, umile; (change) spicciolo; (typ) minuscolo

small' arms' spl armi fpl portatili

small' busi'ness s piccolo commercio

small' cap'ital s (typ) maiuscoletto

small' change' s spiccioli mpl

small' fry' s minutaglia; bambini mpl; gente f di poca importanza

small' hours' spl ore fpl piccole

small' intes'tine s intestino tenue

small-minded ['smɔl'maɪndɪd] adj di corte vedute, gretto

small' of the back' s fine f della schiena, reni fpl

smallpox ['smɔl,paks] s vaiolo

small' talk' s conversazione futile

small'-time' adj di poca importanza

small'-town' adj di provincia

smart [smart] adj intelligente; scaltro, furbo; (pain) acuto; (in appearance) elegante; (pert) impertinente; (coll) grande, abbondante ‖ s dolore acuto, sofferenza ‖ intr bruciare; dolere; soffrire

smart' al'eck ['ælɪk] s saputello

smart' set' s bel mondo

smash [smæʃ] s sconquasso; colpo; collisione; rovina, fallimento; (tennis) smash m, schiacciata ‖ tr sconquassare; sfracellare; rovinare; (tennis) schiacciare ‖ intr sconquassarsi; sfracellarsi; andare in rovina; **to smash into** scontrarsi con

smash' hit' s successone m

smash'-up' s sconquasso

smattering ['smætərɪŋ] s infarinatura, spolvero

smear [smɪr] s macchia, imbrattatura; calunnia; (bact) striscio || tr imbrattare; spalmare; calunniare

smear' campaign' s campagna di vilipendio

smell [smel] s odore m; (sense) olfatto, odorato; profumo || v (pret & pp smelled or smelt) tr fiutare, odorare || intr odorare; (to stink) puzzare; profumare; to smell of odorare di; puzzare di

smell'ing salts' spl sali aromatici

smell·y ['smelɪ] adj (-ier; -iest) puzzolente

smelt [smelt] s (ichth) eperlano || tr & intr fondere

smile [smaɪl] s sorriso || intr sorridere

smiling ['smaɪlɪŋ] adj sorridente

smirk [smʌrk] s ghigno || intr ghignare

smite [smaɪt] v (pret smote [smot]; pp smitten ['smɪtən] or smit [smɪt]) tr colpire; percuotere; affliggere, castigare

smith [smɪθ] s fabbro

smith·y ['smɪθɪ] s (-ies) fucina

smit'ten adj afflitto; innamorato

smock [smɑk] s camice m; (of mechanic) camiciotto

smock' frock' s blusa da lavoro

smog [smɑg] s foschia, smog m

smoke [smok] s fumo; to go up in smoke andare in cenere || tr affumicare; (tobacco) fumare; to smoke out cacciare col fumo; scoprire || intr fumare; (said, e.g., of the earth) fumigare

smoke'-filled room' s stanza da riunioni piena di fumo

smoke'less pow'der ['smoklɪs] s polvere f senza fumo

smoker ['smokər] s fumatore m; salone m fumatori; (rr) vagone m fumatori

smoke' rings' spl anelli mpl di fumo

smoke' screen' s cortina di fumo

smoke'stack' s fumaiolo

smoking ['smokɪŋ] s (il) fumare; no smoking vietato fumare

smok'ing car' s vagone m fumatori

smok'ing jack'et s giacca da casa

smok'ing room' s stanza per fumatori

smok·y ['smokɪ] adj (-ier; -iest) fumoso

smolder ['smoldər] s fumo derivante da fuoco che cova || intr (said of fire or passion) covare; (said of s.o.'s eyes) ardere

smooch [smutʃ] intr (coll) baciarsi, baciucchiarsi

smooth [smuð] adj liscio, levigato; (face) glabro; di consistenza uniforme; (flat) piano; senza interruzioni; tranquillo; elegante; (sound) armonioso; (taste) gradevole; (wine) abboccato; (sea) calmo; (style) fluido || tr lisciare, levigare; appianare, facilitare; calmare; to smooth away appianare

smooth-faced ['smuð'fest] adj (beardless) glabro; liscio

smooth-spoken ['smuð,spokən] adj mellifluo

smooth·y ['smuðɪ] s (-ies) galante m

smother ['smʌðər] tr affoggare, soffocare

smudge [smʌdʒ] s macchia, imbrattatura || tr macchiare, imbrattare; (a garden) affumicare

smudge' pot' s apparecchiatura per affumicare

smug [smʌg] adj (smugger; smuggest) pieno di sé stesso; liscio, lisciato

smuggle ['smʌgəl] tr contrabbandare || intr praticare il contrabbando

smuggler ['smʌglər] s contrabbandiere m

smuggling ['smʌglɪŋ] s contrabbando

smut [smʌt] s sudiciume m; oscenità f; (agr) volpe f, golpe f

smut·y ['smʌtɪ] adj (-ier; -iest) sudicio; osceno; (agr) malato di volpe

snack [snæk] s spuntino, merenda; porzione

snack' bar' s tavola calda

snag [snæg] s tronco sommerso; protuberanza, sporgenza; (tooth) dente rotto; (fig) intoppo, ostacolo; to hit a snag incontrare un ostacolo || v (pret & pp snagged; ger snagging) tr fare uno straccio a; (fig) ostacolare

snail [snel] s chiocciola, lumaca; at a snail's pace come una lumaca

snake [snek] s serpente m; (non-venomous) biscia

snake' in the grass' s pericolo nascosto; (person) serpe f in seno

snap [snæp] s (sharp sound) schiocco; (bite) morso; (fastener) bottone automatico; (of cold weather) breve periodo; (manner of speaking) tono tagliente; (phot) istantanea; (coll) vigore m; (coll) cosa da nulla || v (pret & pp snapped; ger snapping) tr schioccare; chiudere di colpo; spezzare di colpo; (a picture) scattare; to snap one's fingers at infischiarsi di; to snap up afferrare; (a person) tagliare la parola a || intr schioccare; (to crack) rompersi di colpo; to snap at cercare di mordere; (a bargain) cercare di afferrare; to snap out of it (coll) riprendersi; to snap shut chiudersi di colpo

snap'drag'on s (bot) bocca di leone

snap' fas'tener s bottone automatico

snap' judg'ment s decisione presa senza riflessione

snap·py ['snæpɪ] adj (-pier; -piest) mordente, mordace; (coll) vivo, vivace; (coll) elegante; to make it snappy (slang) sbrigarsi

snap'shot' s istantanea

snare [sner] s laccio, lacciolo; (of a drum) corda

snare' drum' s cassa rullante

snarl [snɑrl] s (of a dog) ringhio; groviglio; (of traffic) ingorgo; (fig) confusione || tr urlare con un ringhio; (to tangle) aggrovigliare; complicare || intr ringhiare; aggrovigliarsi; complicarsi

snatch [snætʃ] s strappo, strappone m; presa; pezzetto; momentino || tr &

intr strappare; **to snatch at** cercare di afferrare; **to snatch from** strappare a

sneak [snik] *s* furfante *m* || *tr* mettere di nascosto; pigliare di nascosto || *intr*—**to sneak in** entrare di nascosto; **to sneak out** svignarsela

sneaker ['snikǝr] *s* furfante *m*; scarpetta da ginnastica

sneak' thief' *s* ladro, topo

sneak·y ['sniki] *adj* (**-ier; -iest**) furtivo

sneer [snɪr] *s* ghigno || *intr* sogghignare; **to sneer at** beffarsi si

sneeze [sniz] *s* starnuto || *intr* starnutare; **not to be sneezed at** (coll) non essere disprezzabile

snicker ['snɪkǝr] *s* risatina || *intr* fare una risatina

snide [snaɪd] *adj* malizioso

sniff [snɪf] *s* fiuto, fiutata; (*scent*) odore *m* || *tr* fiutare || *intr* aspirare rumorosamente; (*with emotion*) moccicare; **to sniff at** annusare; mostrare disprezzo per

sniffle ['snɪfǝl] *s* moccio; **to have the sniffles** moccicare || *intr* moccicare

snip [snɪp] *s* taglio; pezzetto; (*person*) (coll) mezza cartuccia || *v* (*pret & pp* **snipped**; *ger* **snipping**) *tr* tagliuzzare

snipe [snaɪp] *s* tiro di nascosto; (orn) beccaccino || *intr* sparare in appostamento; attaccare da lontano

sniper ['snaɪpǝr] *s* franco tiratore, cecchino

snippet ['snɪpɪt] *s* ritaglio, frammento; (fig) mezza cartuccia

snip·py ['snɪpi] *adj* (**-pier; -piest**) frammentario; (coll) corto, brusco; (coll) arrogante

snitch [snɪtʃ] *tr & intr* (coll) graffignare, sgraffignare

sniv·el ['snɪvǝl] *s* moccio; singhiozzo, piagnisteo; falsa commozione || *v* (*pret & pp* **-eled** or **-elled**; *ger* **-eling** or **-elling**) *intr* singhiozzare, piagnucolare; (*to have a runny nose*) moccicare, avere il moccio

snob [snɑb] *s* snob *mf*

snobbery ['snɑbǝri] *s* snobismo

snobbish ['snɑbɪʃ] *adj* snobistico

snoop [snup] *s* (coll) ficcanaso || *intr* (coll) ficcare il naso

snoop·y ['snupi] *adj* (**-ier; -iest**) (coll) curioso, invadente

snoot [snut] *s* (slang) naso

snoot·y ['snuti] *adj* (**-ier; -iest**) (coll) snobistico

snooze [snuz] *s* (coll) sonnellino || *intr* (coll) fare un sonnellino

snore [snor] *s* russamento || *intr* russare

snort [snɔrt] *s* sbuffo || *intr* sbuffare

snot [snɑt] *s* (slang) moccio

snot·ty ['snɑti] *adj* (**-tier; -tiest**) (coll) snobistico; (coll) arrogante; (slang) moccioso

snout [snaut] *s* muso; (*of pig*) grugno; (*of person*) muso, grugno

snow [sno] *s* neve *f* || *intr* nevicare

snow'ball' *s* palla di neve || *tr* gettare palle di neve a || *intr* aumentare come una palla di neve

snow'blind' *adj* accecato dalla neve

snow'bound' *adj* prigioniero della neve

snow-capped ['sno‚kæpt] *adj* coperto di neve

snow'drift' *s* banco di neve

snow'fall' *s* nevicata

snow' fence' *s* barriera contro la neve

snow'flake' *s* fiocco di neve

snow' flur'ry *s* neve portata da raffiche

snow' line' *s* limite *m* delle nevi perenni

snow'man' *s* (**-men'**) uomo di neve

snow'plow' *s* spazzaneve *m*

snow'shoe' *s* racchetta da neve

snow'slide' *s* valanga

snow'storm' *s* bufera di neve

snow' tire' *s* gomma da neve, pneumatico da neve

snow'-white' *adj* bianco come la neve

snow·y ['sno·i] *adj* (**-ier; -iest**) nevoso

snub [snʌb] *s* affronto || *v* (*pret & pp* **snubbed**; *ger* **snubbing**) *tr* snobbare

snub-by ['snʌbi] *adj* (**-bier; -biest**) camuso, rincagnato

snuff [snʌf] *s* fiutata; tabacco da fiuto; (*of a candlewick*) moccolo; **up to snuff** (coll) soddisfacente; (coll) bene || *tr* fiutare; tabaccare; (*a candle*) smoccolare; **to snuff out** spegnere; (fig) soffocare

snuff'box' *s* tabacchiera

snuffers ['snʌfǝrz] *spl* smoccolatoio

snug [snʌg] *adj* (**snugger; snuggest**) comodo; (*dress*) attillato; compatto; (*well-off*) agiato; (*sum*) discreto; (*sheltered*) ben protetto; (*well-hidden*) nascosto

snuggle ['snʌgǝl] *intr* rannicchiarsi; **to snuggle up to** stringersi a

so [so] *adv* così; così or tanto + *adj or adv*; per quanto; **and so** certamente; pure; **and so on** e così via; **or so** più o meno; **to think so** credere di sì; **so as to** + *inf* per + *inf*; **so far** sinora, finora; **so long!** arrivederci!; **so many** tanti; **so much** tanto; **so so** così così; **so that** in maniera che, di modo che; **so to speak** per così dire || *conj* cosicché || *interj* bene!; basta!; così!

soak [sok] *s* bagnata; (*toper*) (slang) ubriacone *m* || *tr* bagnare, inzuppare; imbevere; (coll) ubriacare; (slang) far pagare un prezzo esorbitante a; **to soak up** assorbire; **soaked to the skin** bagnato fino alle ossa || *intr* stare a molle, macerare; inzupparsi

so'-and-so' *s* (**-sos**) tal *m* dei tali; tal cosa

soap [sop] *s* sapone *m* || *tr* insaponare

soap'box' *s* cassa di sapone; tribuna improvvisata

soap'box or'ator *s* oratore *m* che parla da una tribuna improvvisata

soap' bub'ble *s* bolla di sapone

soap' dish' *s* portasapone *m*

soap' flakes' *spl* sapone *m* a scaglie

soap' op'era *s* (coll) trasmissione radiofonica o televisiva lacrimogena

soap' pow'der *s* sapone *m* in polvere

soap'stone' *s* pietra da sarto

soap'suds' *spl* saponata

soap·y ['sopi] *adj* (**-ier; -iest**) saponoso

soar [sor] *intr* spaziare, slanciarsi; (aer) librarsi

sob [sɑb] *s* singhiozzo || *v* (*pret & pp* sobbed; *ger* sobbing) *tr* dire a singhiozzi || *intr* singhiozzare

sober ['sobər] *adj* sobrio; non ubriaco || *intr* smaltire la sbornia; to sober down calmarsi; to sober up smaltire la sbornia

sobriety [so'braɪətɪ] *s* sobrietà *f*

sobriquet ['sobrɪ͵ke] *s* nomignolo

sob' sis'ter *s* giornalista lacrimogeno

sob' sto'ry *s* storia lacrimogena

so'-called' *adj* cosiddetto

soccer ['sɑkər] *s* calcio, football *m*

sociable ['soʃəbəl] *adj* sociale, socievole

social ['soʃəl] *adj* sociale || *s* riunione sociale

so'cial climb'er ['klaɪmər] *s* arrampicatore *m* sociale

so'cial con'tract *s* patto sociale

socialism ['soʃə͵lɪzəm] *s* socialismo

socialist ['soʃəlɪst] *s* socialista *mf*

socialite ['soʃə͵laɪt] *s* persona che appartiene all'alta società

So'cial Reg'ister *s* (trademark) annuario dell'alta società

so'cial secu'rity *s* sicurezza sociale

so'cial work'er *s* visitatrice *f*, assistente *mf* sociale

socie·ty [sə'saɪətɪ] *s.* (-ties) società *f*; (*companionship or company*) compagnia

soci'ety ed'itor *s* cronista mondano

sociology [͵sosɪ'ɑlədʒi] or [͵soʃɪ-'ɑlədʒi] *s* sociologia

sock [sɑk] *s* calzino; (slang) colpo forte; (slang) attore *m* di prim'ordine; (slang) spettacolo eccezionale || *tr* (slang) dare un forte colpo a

socket ['sɑkɪt] *s* (*of eye*) occhiaia; (*of tooth*) alveolo; (*of candlestick*) bocciolo; (*wall socket*) (elec) presa di corrente; (elec) portalampada *m*

sock'et wrench' *s* chiave *f* a tubo

sod [sɑd] *s* zolla; terreno erboso || *v* (*pret & pp* sodded; *ger* sodding) *tr* piotare

soda ['sodə] *s* soda

so'da crack'er *s* galletta fatta al bicarbonato

so'da wa'ter *s* soda, gazosa

sodium ['sodɪ·əm] *adj* sodico || *s* sodio

sofa ['sofə] *s* sofà *m*, divano

so'fa bed' *s* sofà *m* letto

soft [sɔft] or [sɑft] *adj* molle; (*smooth*) morbido; (*iron*) dolce; (*hat*) floscio; (*person*) rammollito; (coll) facile

soft'-boiled' egg' ['sɔft'bɔɪld] or ['sɑft'bɑrld] *s* uovo alla coque

soft' coal' *s* carbone bituminoso

soft' drink' *s* bibita

soften ['sɔfən] or ['sɑfən] *tr* mollificare, rammollire; (fig) intenerire || *intr* intenerirsi

softener ['sɔfənər] or ['sɑfənər] *s* ammorbidente *m*

soft' land'ing *s* allunaggio morbido

soft'-ped'al *v* (*pret & pp* -aled or

-alled; *ger* -aling or -alling) *tr* mettere in sordina; (coll) moderare

soft'-shell crab' *s* mollecca

soft' soap' *s* sapone *m* molle; (coll) adulazione

soft'-soap' *tr* (coll) insaponare

sog·gy ['sɑgi] *adj* (-gier; -giest) rammollito, inzuppato

soil [sɔɪl] *s* suolo, terreno; territorio; (*spot*) macchia; (*filth*) porcheria, lordura || *tr* sporcare, macchiare || *intr* sporcarsi, macchiarsi

soil' pipe' *s* tubo di scarico

soiree or soirée [swɑ're] *s* serata

sojourn ['sodʒʌrn] *s* soggiorno || ['sodʒʌrn] or [so'dʒʌrn] *intr* soggiornare

solace ['sɑlɪs] *s* conforto || *tr* confortare, consolare

solar ['solər] *adj* solare

so'lar bat'tery *s* batteria solare

solder ['sɑdər] *s* saldatura; lega per saldatura || *tr* saldare

sol'dering i'ron *s* saldatoio

soldier ['soldʒər] *s* (*man of rank and file*) soldato; (*man in military service*) militare *m* || *intr* fare il soldato

sol'dier of for'tune *s* soldato di ventura

soldier·y ['soldʒərɪ] *s* (-ies) soldatesca

sold-out ['sold͵aut] *adj* esaurito; (*e.g., theater*) completo

sole [sol] *adj* solo, unico; esclusivo || *s* (*of foot*) pianta; (*of stocking*) soletta; (*of shoe*) suola; (*fish*) sfoglia || *tr* solare

solely ['sollɪ] *adv* solamente

solemn ['sɑləm] *adj* solenne

solicit [sə'lɪsɪt] *tr* sollecitare; adescare, accostare

solicitor [sə'lɪsɪtər] *s* sollecitatore *m*; agente *m*; (law) procuratore *m*

solicitous [sə'lɪsɪtəs] *adj* sollecito

solicitude [sə'lɪsɪ͵tjud] or [sə'lɪsɪ͵tud] *s* sollecitudine *f*

solid ['sɑlɪd] *adj* solido; (*not hollow*) sodo; (*e.g., clouds*) denso; (*wall*) pieno, massiccio; (*word*) con grafia unita; intero; unanime, solidale; (*good*) buono; (*e.g., gold*) puro, massiccio

solidity [sə'lɪdɪtɪ] *s* solidità *f*

sol'id-state' *adj* transistorizzato, senza valvole

solilo·quy [sə'lɪləkwi] *s* (-quies) soliloquio

solitaire ['sɑlɪ͵ter] *s* solitario

solitar·y ['sɑlɪ͵terɪ] *adj* solitario; unico || *s* (-ies) persona solitaria

sol'itary confine'ment *s* segregazione cellulare

solitude ['sɑlɪ͵tjud] or ['sɑlɪ͵tud] *s* solitudine *f*

so·lo ['solo] *adj* solo, solitario; (mus) solista || *s* (-los) (mus) solo

soloist ['solo·ɪst] *s* solista *mf*

so' long' *interj* (coll) ciao!; (coll) addio!; (coll) arrivederci!

solstice ['sɑlstɪs] *s* solstizio

soluble ['sɑljəbəl] *adj* solubile

solution [sə'luʃən] *s* soluzione *f*

solvable ['sɑlvəbəl] *adj* risolvibile

solve [sɑlv] *tr* risolvere, sciogliere

solvency ['salvənsi] *s* solvenza
solvent ['salvənt] *adj* & *s* solvente *m*
somber ['sambər] *adj* tetro
some [sʌm] *adj indef* qualche; di + *art*, e.g., **some apples** delle mele; (coll) forte, grande ‖ *pron indef* alcuni, taluni; ne, e.g., **I have some** ne ho
some'bod'y *pron indef* taluno, qualcuno; **somebody else** qualcun altro ‖ *s* (**-ies**) (coll) qualcuno
some'day' *adv* qualche giorno
some'how' *adv* in qualche modo; **somehow or other** in un modo o nell'altro
some'one' *pron indef* qualcuno, taluno; **someone else** qualcun altro
somersault ['sʌmər ,sɔlt] *s* salto mortale ‖ *intr* fare un salto mortale
something ['sʌmθɪŋ] *pron indef* qualcosa; **something else** qualcos'altro ‖ *adv* un po'; (coll) molto, moltissimo
some'time' *adj* antico, di un tempo ‖ *adv* un giorno o l'altro, uno di questi giorni
some'times' *adv* talora, talvolta
some'way' *adv* in qualche modo
some'what' *s* qualcosa ‖ *adv* piuttosto, un po'
some'where' *adv* in qualche luogo, da qualche parte; a qualche momento; **somewhere else** altrove
somnambulist [sam'næmbjəlɪst] *s* sonnambulo
somnolent ['samnələnt] *adj* sonnolento
son [sʌn] *s* figlio
sonar ['sonar] *s* ecogoniometro, sonar *m*
song [sɔŋ] or [saŋ] *s* canto, canzone *f*; **for a song** per un soldo
song'bird' *s* uccello canoro
Song' of Songs' *s* Cantico dei Cantici
songster ['sɔŋstər] *s* cantante *m*, canzonettista *m*
songstress ['sɔŋstrɪs] *s* cantante *f*, canzonettista *f*
song'writ'er *s* canzoniere *m*
son'ic boom' ['sanɪk] *s* boato sonico
son'-in-law' *s* (**sons'-in-law'**) genero
sonnet ['sanɪt] *s* sonetto
son'ny ['sʌni] *s* (**-nies**) figliolo
sonori·ty [sə'narɪti] or [sə'nɔrɪti] *s* (**-ties**) sonorità *f*
soon [sun] *adv* in breve, ben presto; subito, presto; **as soon as** non appena, quanto prima; **as soon as possible** quanto prima; **I had sooner** preferirei; **how soon?** quando?; **soon after** poco dopo; **sooner or later** prima o poi, tosto o tardi
soot [sut] or [sut] *s* fuliggine *f*
soothe [suð] *tr* calmare, lenire
soothsayer ['suθ ,se·ər] *s* indovino
soot·y ['suti] or ['suti] *adj* (**-ier; -iest**) fuligginoso
sop [sap] *s* (*soaked food*) zuppa; (*bribe*) dono, offa ‖ *v* (*pret* & *pp* **sopped; ger sopping**) *tr* intingere, inzuppare; **to sop up** assorbire
sophisticated [sə'fɪstɪ ,ketɪd] *adj* sofisticato, smaliziato
sophistication [sə ,fɪstɪ'keʃən] *s* eccessiva ricercatezza; gusti *mpl* raffinati

sophomore ['safə ,mor] *s* studente *m* del secondo anno, fagiolo
sophomoric [,safə'mɔrɪk] *adj* saputello, presuntuoso; ingenuo, imberbe
sopping ['sapɪŋ] *adv*—**sopping wet** inzuppato
sopran·o [sə'præno] or [sə'prano] *adj* per soprano, da soprano ‖ *s* (**-os**) soprano *mf*
sorcerer ['sɔrsərər] *s* mago, stregone *m*
sorceress ['sɔrsərɪs] *s* maga, strega
sorcer·y ['sɔrsəri] *s* (**-ies**) stregoneria
sordid ['sɔrdɪd] *adj* sordido
sore [sor] *adj* irritato; indolenzito; estremo, grave; **to be sore at** (coll) aversela con ‖ *s* piaga, ulcera; dolore *m*, afflizione; **to open an old sore** riaprire una ferita
sorely ['sorli] *adv* penosamente; gravemente, urgentemente
soreness ['sornis] *s* dolore *m*, afflizione
sore' spot' *s* (fig) piaga
sore' throat' *s* mal *m* di gola
sorori·ty [sə'rarɪti] or [sə'rɔrɪti] *s* (**-ties**) associazione femminile universitaria
sorrel ['sarəl] or ['sɔrəl] *adj* sauro
sorrow ['saro] or ['sɔro] *s* dolore *m*, cordoglio ‖ *intr* affliggersi, provar cordoglio; **to sorrow for** rimpiangere
sorrowful ['sarəfəl] or ['sɔrəfəl] *adj* doloroso
sor·ry ['sari] or ['sɔri] *adj* (**-rier; -riest**) spiacente, desolato, dolente; povero, cattivo; **to be sorry** dolersi; dispiacere a, e.g., **he is sorry** gli dispiace ‖ *interj* mi dispiace!, scusi!
sort [sɔrt] *s* tipo, specie *f*; maniera; **a sort of** una specie di; **out of sorts** depresso; ammalato; di mal umore; **sort of** (coll) piuttosto; (coll) un certo, e.g., **sort of a headache** un certo mal di testa ‖ *tr* assortire; (*mail*) smistare
so'-so' *adj* passabile ‖ *adv* così così
sot [sat] *s* ubriacone *m*
soubrette [su'bret] *s* (theat) soubrette *f*
soul [sol] *s* anima; **upon my soul!** sulla mia parola!
sound [saund] *adj* sano; solido, forte; valido, buono; (*sleep*) profondo; valido, legale; onesto ‖ *s* suono; rumore *m*; (*of an animal*) verso; (*passage of water*) stretto; (surg) sonda; (ichth) vescica natatoria; **within sound of** alla portata di ‖ *adv* profondamente ‖ *tr* (*an instrument*) sonare; pronunciare; (*e.g., s.o.'s deem*) auscultare; (*praises*) cantare; (*to measure*) sondare ‖ *intr* sonare; parere, sembrare; fare uno scandaglio; **to sound like** avere il suono di; dare l'impressione di, parere
sound' bar'rier *s* muro del suono
sound' film' *s* pellicola sonora
soundly ['saundli] *adv* solidamente; profondamente; completamente
sound'proof' *adj* a prova di suono ‖ *tr* insonorizzare

sound' track' s (mov) sonoro, colonna sonora

sound' truck' s autoveicolo con impianto sonoro

sound' wave' s onda sonora

soup [sup] s zuppa, minestra

soup' dish' s piatto fondo

soup' kitch'en s asilo dei poveri che serve zuppa gratuitamente

soup'spoon' s cucchiaio (da minestra)

sour [saur] adj acido; (fruit) acerbo || tr inacidire || intr inacidirsi

source [sors] s fonte f, sorgente f

source' lan'guage s lingua di partenza

source' mate'rial s fonti fpl originali

sour' cher'ry s (fruit) amarena; (tree) amareno

sour' grapes' interj l'uva è verde!

south [sauθ] adj meridionale, del sud || s sud m, meridione m || adv verso il sud

South' Amer'ica s l'America f del Sud

South' Amer'ican adj & s sudamericano

southeast [ˌsauθ'ist] adj di sud-est || s sud-est || adv al sud-est

southern ['sʌðərn] adj meridionale

South'ern Cross' s Croce f del Sud

southerner ['sʌðərnər] s meridionale mf

South' Kore'a s la Corea del Sud

south'paw' adj & s (coll) mancino

South' Pole' s Polo sud

South' Vietnam·ese' [vɪˌɛtnə'miz] adj vietnamita del sud || s (-ese) vietnamita mf del sud

southward ['sauθwərd] adv verso il sud

south'west' adj di sud-ovest || s sud-ovest m || adv al sud-ovest

souvenir [ˌsuvə'nɪr] or ['suvəˌnɪr] s ricordo, memoria

sovereign ['savrɪn] or ['sʌvrɪn] adj sovrano || s (king) sovrano; (queen; coin) sovrana

sovereign·ty ['savrɪnti] or ['sʌvrɪnti] s (-ties) sovranità f

soviet ['sovɪˌɛt] or [ˌsovɪ'ɛt] adj sovietico || s soviet m

So'viet Rus'sia s la Russia Sovietica

sow [sau] s porca, troia || [so] v (pret sowed; pp sown or sowed) tr seminare

soybean ['sɔɪˌbin] s soia; seme m di soia

spa [spɑ] s terme fpl

space [spes] adj spaziale || s spazio; periodo; after a space dopo un po' || tr spaziare; to space out diradare

space' bar' s barra spaziatrice, spaziatrice f

space' cen'ter s cosmodromo

space'craft' s astronave f

space' flight' s volo spaziale

space'man' s (-men') navigatore m spaziale

spacer ['spesər] s spaziatrice f, barra spaziatrice

space'ship' s astronave f

space'suit' s scafandro astronautico, tuta spaziale

spacious ['speʃəs] adj spazioso

spade [sped] s vanga; (cards) picca; **to call a spade a spade** dire pane al pane, vino al vino || tr vangare

spade'work' s lavoro preliminare

spaghetti [spə'gɛti] s spaghetti mpl

Spain [spen] s la Spagna

span [spæn] s (of the hand) spanna; (of time) tratto; (of a bridge) campata, luce f; (of horses) paio; (aer) apertura || v (pret & pp spanned; ger spanning) tr misurare a spanne; attraversare, oltrepassare; (said of time) abbracciare

spangle ['spæŋgəl] s lustrino || tr tempestare di lustrini; (with bright objects) stellare || intr brillare

Spaniard ['spænjərd] s spagnolo

Spanish ['spænɪʃ] adj & s spagnolo; **the Spanish** gli spagnoli

Span'ish-Amer'ican adj & s ispano-americano

Span'ish broom' s ginestra

Span'ish fly' s mosca cantaride

Span'ish om'elet s frittata di pomodori, cipolle e peperoni

Span'ish-speak'ing adj di lingua spagnola

spank [spæŋk] tr sculacciare

spanking ['spæŋkɪŋ] adj rapido; forte; (coll) eccellente, straordinario || s sculacciata

spar [spɑr] s (mineral) spato; (naut) asta, pennone m; (aer) longherone m || v (pret & pp sparred; ger sparring) intr fare la box

spare [sper] adj di riserva; libero, in eccesso; (e.g., diet) frugale; (lean) magro || tr salvare, risparmiare; perdonare; (to do without) fare a meno di, privarsi di; **to have . . . to spare** aver . . . d'avanzo; **to spare oneself** risparmiarsi

spare' parts' s pezzi mpl di ricambio

spare' room' s camera per gli ospiti

spare' tire' s ruota di scorta, pneumatico di scorta

spare' wheel' s ruota di scorta

sparing ['sperɪŋ] adj economico; (scanty) scarso

spark [spɑrk] s scintilla; traccia || tr (coll) rianimare; (coll) corteggiare || intr scintillare

spark' coil' s bobina d'accensione

spark' gap' s (elec) traferro, intraferro

sparkle ['spɑrkəl] s scintilla; (luster) scintillio; allegria, vivacità f || intr scintillare; (said, e.g., of eyes) brillare, luccicare; (said of wine) frizzare, spumeggiare

sparkling ['spɑrklɪŋ] adj scintillante; (wine) frizzante, spumeggiante; (water) gassoso

spark' plug' s candela

sparrow ['spæro] s passero

sparse [spɑrs] adj rado

Spartan ['spɑrtən] adj & s spartano

spasm ['spæzəm] s spasmo; sprazzo d'energia

spasmodic [spæz'mɑdɪk] adj spasmodico; intermittente, a sprazzi

spastic ['spæstɪk] adj & s spastico

spat [spæt] s litigio, battibecco; **spats**

ghette *fpl* || *v* (*pret & pp* **spatted;** *ger* **spatting**) *intr* avere un battibecco

spatial ['spe/əl] *adj* spaziale

spatter ['spætər] *tr* schizzare, spruzzare || *intr* gocciolare

spatula ['spætʃələ] *s* spatola

spawn [spɔn] *s* prole *f*, progenie *f*; risultato || *tr* produrre, generare || *intr* (ichth) deporre le uova

spay [spe] *tr* asportare le ovaie a

speak [spik] *v* (*pret* **spoke** [spok]; *pp* **spoken**) *tr* (*a language*) parlare; (*the truth*) dire || *intr* parlare; **so to speak** per così dire; **speaking!** al telefono!; **to speak of** importante, che valga parlarne; **to speak out** dire la propria opinione

speak'-eas'y *s* (-**ies**) bar clandestino

speaker ['spikər] *s* conferenziere *m*, oratore *m*; (*of a language*) parlante *mf*; (pol) presidente *m*; (rad) altoparlante *m*

speaking ['spikɪŋ] *adj* parlante; **to be on speaking terms** parlarsi || *s* parlare *m*, discorso

speak'ing tube' *s* tubo acustico

spear [spɪr] *s* lancia; (*for fishing*) arpione *m*; (*of grass*) stelo || *tr* trafiggere con la lancia

spear' gun' *s* fucile subacqueo

spear'head' *s* punta di lancia || *tr* condurre, dirigere

spear'mint' *s* menta romana spicata

special ['spe/əl] *adj* speciale || *s* prezzo speciale; treno speciale

spe'cial deliv'ery *s* espresso

spe'cial draw'ing rights' *spl* (econ) diritti *mpl* speciali di prelievo

specialist ['spe/əlɪst] *s* specialista *mf*

specialize ['spe/ə‚laɪz] *tr* specializzare || *intr* specializzarsi

spe'cial part'ner *s* accomandante *mf*

special·ty ['spe/əlti] *s* (-**ties**) specialità *f*

spe·cies ['spisiz] *s* (-**cies**) specie *f*

specific [spɪ'sɪfɪk] *adj & s* specifico

specification [‚spesɪfɪ'ke/ən] *s* specifica; (com) capitolato

specif'ic grav'ity *s* peso specifico

speci·fy ['spesɪ‚faɪ] *v* (*pret & pp* -**fied**) *tr* specificare

specimen ['spesɪmən] *s* esemplare *m*; (coll) tipo

specious ['spi/əs] *adj* specioso

speck [spek] *s* macchiolina; (*of dust*) granello; (*of hope*) filo || *tr* macchiettare

speckle ['spekəl] *s* macchiolina || *tr* macchiettare, picchiettare

spectacle ['spektəkəl] *s* spettacolo; **spectacles** occhiali *mpl*

spectator ['spektetər] *or* [spek'tetər] *s* spettatore *m*

specter ['spektər] *s* spettro

spec·trum ['spektrəm] *s* (-**tra** [trə] *or* -**trums**) spettro; (fig) gamma

speculate ['spekjə‚let] *intr* speculare

speech [spit/] *s* parola, parlata; (*before an audience*) discorso; (*of an actor*) elocuzione; **in speech** oralmente

speech' clin'ic *s* clinica per la correzione dei difetti del linguaggio

speechless ['spit/lɪs] *adj* senza parole, muto

speed [spid] *s* velocità *f*; (aut) marcia || *tr* accelerare, affrettare || *intr* accelerare, affrettarsi; guidare oltre la velocità massima

speed'boat' *s* motoscafo da corsa

speeding ['spidɪŋ] *s* eccesso di velocità

speed' king' *s* asso del volante

speed' lim'it *s* limite *m* di velocità

speedometer [spi'dɑmɪtər] *s* tachimetro; (*to record the distance covered*) contachilometri *m*

speed'-up' *s* accelerazione

speed'way' *s* (*highway*) autostrada; (*for races*) pista

speed·y ['spidi] *adj* (-**ier**; -**iest**) veloce, rapido

spell [spel] *s* malia, incantesimo; fascino; turno; attacco; periodo di tempo; **to cast a spell on** incantare || *v* (*pret & pp* **spelled** *or* **spelt** [spelt]) *tr* compitare; scrivere in tutte lettere; voler dire; **to spell out** (coll) spiegare dettagliatamente || *intr* scrivere, sillabare || *v* (*pret & pp* **spelled**) *tr* rimpiazzare

spell'bind' *v* (*pret & pp* -**bound**) *tr* affascinare

spell'bind'er *s* oratore *m* abbagliante

spelling ['spelɪŋ] *adj* ortografico || *s* (*act*) compitazione; (*way a word is spelled*) grafia; (*subject of study*) ortografia

spell'ing bee' *s* gara di ortografia

spelunker [spɪ'lʌŋkər] *s* esploratore *m* di caverne

spend [spend] *v* (*pret & pp* **spent** [spent]) *tr* spendere; (*time*) passare

spender ['spendər] *s* spenditore *m*

spend'ing mon'ey *s* denaro per le piccole spese personali

spend'thrift' *s* sprecone *m*, spendaccione *m*

sperm [spʌrm] *s* sperma *m*

sperm' whale' *s* capodoglio

spew [spju] *tr & intr* vomitare

sphere [sfɪr] *s* sfera

spherical ['sfɛrɪkəl] *adj* sferico

sphinx [sfɪŋks] *s* (**sphinxes** *or* **sphinges** ['sfɪndʒiz]) sfinge *f*

spice [spaɪs] *s*. droga; spezie *fpl*; (fig) gusto, sapore *m* || *tr* drogare; dare gusto a, rendere piccante

spick-and-span ['spɪkənd'spæn] *adj* ordinato e pulito

spic·y ['spaɪsi] *adj* (-**ier**; -**iest**) drogato; piccante

spider ['spaɪdər] *s* ragno

spi'der·web' *s* ragnatela

spiff·y ['spɪfi] *adj* (-**ier**; -**iest**) (slang) elegante, vestito a puntino

spigot ['spɪgət] *s* (*peg*) zipolo; (*faucet*) rubinetto

spike [spaɪk] *s* chiodo, chiodone *m*; (*sharp-pointed piece*) spuntone *m*; (rr) arpione *m*; (bot) spiga || *tr* inchiodare; mettere chiodi a; (*a rumor*) porre fine a; (coll) alcolizzare

spill [spɪl] *s* rovesciamento; liquido rovesciato; (coll) caduta || *v* (*pret & pp* **spilled** *or* **spilt** [spɪlt]) *tr* rovesciare, spandere; versare; (naut) sventare; (coll) far cadere; (slang) snocciolare || intr rovesciarsi; versarsi

spill'way' s sfioratore m, stramazzo

spin [spɪn] s giro; (twirl) mulinello; corsa; **to go into a spin** (aer) cadere a vite || v (pret & pp **spun** [spʌn]; ger **spinning**) tr far girare; (e.g., thread) filare; **to spin out** prolungare; **to spin a yarn** raccontare una storia || intr girare; (said of a top) prillare; filare

spinach ['spɪnɪtʃ] or ['spɪnɪdʒ] s spinacio; (leaves used as food) spinaci mpl

spi'nal col'umn ['spaɪnəl] s spina dorsale, colonna vertebrale

spi'nal cord' s midollo spinale

spindle ['spɪndəl] s (rounded rod) fuso; (shaft, axle) asse m; balaustro

spine [spaɪn] s spina; spina dorsale; (bb) costola; (fig) forza, carattere m

spineless ['spaɪnlɪs] adj senza spine; senza carattere

spinet ['spɪnɪt] s spinetta

spinner ['spɪnər] s filatore m; (machine) filatrice f

spinning ['spɪnɪŋ] adj filante || s filatura; rotazione

spin'ning mill' s filanda

spin'ning wheel' s filatoio

spinster ['spɪnstər] s zitella

spi-ral ['spaɪrəl] adj & s spirale f || v (pret & pp **-raled** or **-ralled**; ger **-raling** or **-ralling**) intr muoversi lungo una spirale

spi'ral stair'case s scala a chiocciola

spire [spaɪr] s (of a steeple) guglia, freccia; (of grass) foglia; (spiral) spirale f

spirit ['spɪrɪt] s spirito; valore m, vigore m; bevanda spiritosa; **out of spirits** giù di morale || tr—**to spirit away** portar via misteriosamente

spirited ['spɪrɪtɪd] adj brioso; (horse) superbo, vivace

spir'it lamp' s lampada a spirito

spiritless ['spɪrɪtlɪs] adj senza anima, senza vita

spir'it lev'el s livella a bolla d'aria

spiritual ['spɪrɪtʃuəl] adj spirituale; (séance) spiritico

spiritualism ['spɪrɪtʃuə‚lɪzəm] s spiritismo; (philos) spiritualismo

spiritualist ['spɪrɪtʃuəlɪst] s spiritista mf; (philos) spiritualista mf

spirituous ['spɪrɪtʃuəs] adj alcolico

spit [spɪt] s sputo; (for roasting) spiedo, schidione m; punta; **the spit and image of** (coll) il ritratto parlante di || v (pret & pp **spat** [spæt] or **spit**; ger **spitting**) tr & intr sputare

spite [spaɪt] s dispetto, ripicco; **in spite of** a dispetto di, a onta di; **out of spite** per picca || tr far dispetto a; offendere; contrariare

spiteful ['spaɪtfəl] adj dispettoso

spit'fire' s persona collerica; (woman) bisbetica

spit'ting im'age s (coll) ritratto parlante

spittoon [spɪ'tun] s sputacchiera

splash [splæʃ] s schizzo, spruzzo; (of mud) zacchera; (sound) tonfo; **to make a splash** fare molto sci-sci || tr & intr sguazzare

splash'down' s (rok) ammaraggio, urto con l'acqua

spleen [splin] s cattivo umore, bile f; (anat) milza, splene m

splendid ['splendɪd] adj splendido; ottimo, magnifico

splendor ['splendər] s splendore m

splice [splaɪs] s giuntura || tr giuntare

splint [splɪnt] s stecca || tr steccare

splinter ['splɪntər] s scheggia || intr scheggiare || intr scheggiarsi

splin'ter group' s gruppo dissidente

split [splɪt] adj spaccato; diviso || s spaccatura; fessura; rottura, divisione; **splits** (sports) spaccato || v (pret & pp **split**; ger **splitting**) tr spaccare; dividere; **to split one's sides with laughter** scoppiare dalle risa || intr scindersi, dividersi; **to split up** separarsi

split' personal'ity s sdoppiamento della personalità

splitting ['splɪtɪŋ] adj che fende; che si fende; violento, fortissimo || s—**splittings** frammenti mpl

splotch [splɑtʃ] s macchia, chiazza || tr macchiare, chiazzare

splurge [splʌrdʒ] s ostentazione || intr fare ostentazione; fare una spesa matta

splutter ['splʌtər] s crepitio; (utterance) barbugliamento || tr barbugliare || intr crepitare; barbugliare

spoil [spɔɪl] s spoglia, bottino; **spoils** (mil) spoglie fpl; (pol) profitto, vantaggio || v (pret & pp **spoiled** or **spoilt** [spɔɪlt]) tr rovinare, sciupare; (a child) viziare; (food) deteriorare || intr guastarsi, andare a male

spoilage ['spɔɪlɪdʒ] s deterioramento

spoiled [spɔɪld] adj (child) viziato; (food) andato a male, passato

spoils' sys'tem s sistema politico secondo il quale le cariche vanno al partito vincitore

spoke [spok] s (of a wheel) raggio; (of a ladder) piolo

spokes'man s (-men) portavoce m

sponge [spʌndʒ] s spugna; **to throw in the sponge** (slang) gettare la spugna || tr pulire con spugna; assorbire; (coll) scroccare || intr assorbire; **to sponge off** (coll) vivere alle spalle di

sponge' bath' s spugnatura

sponge' cake' s pan m di Spagna

sponger ['spʌndʒər] s scroccatore m

sponge' rub'ber s gommapiuma

spon-gy ['spʌndʒi] adj (-gier; -giest) spugnoso

sponsor ['spɑnsər] s patrocinatore m; (of a charitable institution) patrono; (godfather) padrino; (godmother) madrina || tr patrocinare; (rad, telv) offrire

sponsorship ['spɑnsər‚ʃɪp] s patrocinio

spontaneous [spɑn'teniəs] adj spontaneo

spoof [spuf] *s* mistificazione; parodia || *tr* mistificare; parodiare || *intr* mistificare; fare una parodia

spook [spuk] *s* (coll) spettro

spook·y ['spuki] *adj* (**-ier; -iest**) (coll) spettrale; (*horse*) (coll) nervoso

spool [spul] *s* spola, rocchetto

spoon [spun] *s* cucchiaio; (*lure*) cucchiaino; **born with a silver spoon in one's mouth** nato con la camicia || *tr* servire col cucchiaio || *intr* (coll) limonare

spoonerism ['spunə ‚rɪzəm] *s* papera

spoon'-feed' *v* (*pret & pp* **-fed**) *tr* nutrire col cucchiaino; (fig) coccolare

spoonful ['spun ‚ful] *s* cucchiaiata

spoon·y ['spuni] *adj* (**-ier; -iest**) (coll) svenevole

sporadic(al) [spə'rædɪk(əl)] *adj* sporadico

spore [spor] *s* spora

sport [sport] *adj* sportivo || *s* sport *m;* gioco; (*laughingstock*) zimbello; (*gambler*) (coll) giocatore *m;* (*person who behaves in a sportsmanlike manner*) (coll) spirito sportivo; (*flashy fellow*) (coll) tipo fino; (biol) mutazione; **to make sport of** farsi gioco di || *tr* (coll) sfoggiare; (fig) coccolare; **to sport away** dissipare || *intr* divertirsi; giocare; farsi beffe

sport' clothes' *spl* vestiti *mpl* sport

sport'ing chance' *s* pari opportunità *f* di vincere

sport'ing goods' *spl* articoli *mpl* sportivi

sport'ing house' *s* (coll) bordello

sports'cast'er *s* annunciatore sportivo

sports' fan' *s* appassionato agli spettacoli sportivi, tifoso

sports'man *s* (**-men**) sportivo

sports'man·ship *s* sportività *f,* spirito sportivo

sports' news' *s* notiziario sportivo

sports'wear' *s* articoli *mpl* d'abbigliamento sportivo

sports'writ'er *s* cronista sportivo

sport·y ['sporti] *adj* (**-ier; -iest**) (coll) elegante; (coll) sportivo; (coll) appariscente

spot [spat] *s* macchia; luogo, punto, posto; (*e.g., of tea*) goccia; **spots** locali *mpl;* **on the spot** sul posto; (*right now*) seduta stante; (slang) in difficoltà; **to hit the spot** (slang) soddisfare completamente || *v* (*pret & pp* **spotted**; *ger* **spotting**) *tr* macchiare; spargere; (coll) riconoscere || *intr* macchiare; macchiarsi

spot' cash' *s* pronta cassa

spot'-check' *tr* fare un breve sondaggio di; controllare rapidamente

spot' check' *s* breve sondaggio; rapido controllo

spotless ['spatlɪs] *adj* immacolato, senza macchia

spot'light' *s* riflettore *m;* (aut) proiettore *m;* **to be in the spotlight** (fig) essere il centro d'attenzione

spot' remov'er [rɪ'muvər] *s* smacchiatore *m*

spot' weld'ing *s* saldatura per punti

spouse [spauz] *or* [spaus] *s* consorte *mf*

spout [spaut] *s* (*to carry water from roof*) doccia; (*of jar, pitcher, etc.*) becco, beccuccio; (*jet*) zampillo, getto || *tr & intr* sprizzare, zampillare; (coll) declamare

sprain [spren] *s* distorsione || *tr* distorcere, distorcersi

sprawl [sprɔl] *intr* sdraiarsi

spray [spre] *s* spruzzo; (*of the sea*) schiuma; (*device*) spruzzatore *m;* (*twig*) ramoscello || *tr & intr* spruzzare

sprayer ['spre‚ər] *s* spruzzatore *m,* schizzetto, vaporizzatore *m;* (hort) irroratrice *f*

spray' gun' *s* pistola a spruzzo; (hort) irroratrice *f*

spray' paint' *s* vernice *f* a spruzzo

spread [spred] *s* espansione; diffusione; differenza; tappeto, coperta; elasticità *f;* (*of the wings of bird or airplane*) apertura; cibo da spalmare; (coll) festino; (journ) articolo di fondo or pubblicitario su varie colonne || *v* (*pret & pp* **spread**) *tr* tendere, estendere; (*one's legs*) divaricare; (*wings*) spiegare; spargere, cospargere; (*the table*) preparare; (*butter*) spalmare; diffondere || *intr* estendersi; spiegarsi; spargersi; spalmarsi; diffondersi

spree [spri] *s* baldoria, bisboccia; **to go on a spree** darsi alla pazza gioia

sprig [sprig] *s* ramoscello

spright·ly ['spraɪtli] *adj* (**-lier; -liest**) brioso, vivace

spring [sprɪŋ] *adj* primaverile; sorgivo; a molla || *s* (*season*) primavera; (*issue of water from earth*) fonte *f,* polla; (*elastic device*) molla; elasticità *f;* (*leap*) salto; (*crack*) fenditura; (aut) balestra || *v* (*pret* **sprang** [spræŋ] *or* **sprung** [sprʌŋ]; *pp* **sprung**) *tr* (*e.g., a lock*) far scattare; (*a leak*) aprire; (*a mine*) far brillare || *intr* saltare; (*said of a metal spring*) scattare; scaturire, zampillare; nascere, derivare; esplodere; **to spring forth** or **up** sorgere

spring'board' *s* pedana, trampolino

spring' chick'en *s* pollo giovanissimo; (slang) ragazzina

spring' fe'ver *s* indolenza primaverile

spring' mat'tress *s* materasso a molle

spring' tide' *s* marea di sizigia

spring'time' *s* primavera

sprinkle ['sprɪŋkəl] *s* spruzzo, spruzzatina; (*small amount*) pizzico || *tr* spruzzare; (*e.g., sugar*) spolverizzare || *intr* spruzzare; piovigginare

sprinkler ['sprɪŋklər] *s* annaffiatoio; (*person*) annaffiatore *m*

sprinkling ['sprɪŋklɪŋ] *s* sprizzo, spruzzo; (*with holy water*) aspersione; (*with powder*) spolverizzamento; (*e.g., of knowledge*) spolvero, spolveratura; (*of people*) piccolo numero

sprin'kling can' *s* annaffiatoio

sprint [sprɪnt] s (sports) scatto, volata || intr (sports) scattare

sprite [spraɪt] s spirito folletto

sprocket [ˈsprɑkɪt] s moltiplica; (phot) trasportatore m

sprout [spraʊt] s germoglio || intr germogliare; crescere rapidamente

spruce [sprus] adj elegante, attillato || s abete rosso || tr attillare, azzimare || intr attillarsi, azzimarsi

spry [spraɪ] adj (spryer or sprier; spryest or spriest) vegeto

spud [spʌd] s vanghetto, tagliaradici m; (coll) patata

spun' glass' s lana di vetro

spunk [spʌŋk] s (coll) coraggio, fegato

spur [spʌr] s sperone m; (rr) raccordo ferroviario; (fig) pungolo; on the spur of the moment lì per lì || v (pret & pp spurred; ger spurring) tr spronare; to spur on spronare, incitare

spurious [ˈspjʊrɪ·əs] adj spurio

spurn [spʌrn] s disprezzo, sdegno; rifiuto || tr disprezzare, sdegnare; rifiutare

spurt [spʌrt] s spruzzo, zampillo; (sudden burst) scatto repentino || intr sprizzare, zampillare; scattare

sputter [ˈspʌtər] s barbugliamento; (sizzling) crepitio || tr barbugliare || intr barbugliare; crepitare

spu·tum [ˈspjutəm] s (-ta [tə]) sputo

spy [spaɪ] s (spies) spia || v (pret & pp spied) tr spiare; osservare || intr fare la spia; spy on spiare

spy'glass' s cannocchiale m

spying [ˈspaɪ·ɪŋ] s spionaggio

squabble [ˈskwɑbəl] s battibecco || intr litigare

squad [skwɑd] s squadra

squadron [ˈskwɑdrən] s (of cavalry) squadrone m; (aer, nav) squadriglia; (mil) squadra

squalid [ˈskwɑlɪd] adj sordido; squallido, misero

squall [skwɔl] s groppo, turbine m; urlo || intr gridare, urlare

squalor [ˈskwɑlər] s sordidezza; squallore m, miseria

squander [ˈskwɑndər] tr scialacquare, dilapidare, sperperare

square [skwer] adj quadrato, e.g., two square miles due miglia quadrate; di . . . di lato, e.g., two miles square di due miglia di lato; ad angolo retto; solido; saldato; (coll) onesto; (coll) diretto; (coll) sostanzioso; (slang) all'antica; to get square with (coll) farghela pagare a || s quadrato; (small square, e.g., of checkerboard) quadretto; (city block) isolato; (open area in city) piazza, piazzale m; (of carpenter) squadra; on the square ad angolo retto; (coll) onesto || adv ad angolo retto; (coll) onestamente || tr squadrare; dividere in quadretti; elevare al quadrato; quadrare; (a debt) saldare; to square with adattare a || intr quadrare; to square off prepararsi, mettersi in posizione difensiva

square' dance' s danza figurata americana

square' meal' s (coll) pasto abbondante

square' root' s radice quadrata

square' shoot'er [ˈʃutər] s (coll) persona onesta

squash [skwɑʃ] s spappolamento; (bot) zucca; (sports) squash m || tr spappolare; spiaccicare; (e.g., a rumor) sopprimere; (a person) (coll) ridurre al silenzio || intr spiaccicarsi

squash·y [ˈskwɑʃi] adj (-ier; -iest) tenero; (ground) fangoso, pantanoso; (fruit) maturo

squat [skwɑt] adj tozzo || v (pret & pp squatted; ger squatting) intr accoccolarsi; stabilirsi illegalmente su territorio altrui; stabilirsi su terreno pubblico per ottenerne titolo

squatter [ˈskwɑtər] s intruso

squaw [skwɔ] s squaw f; (coll) donna

squawk [skwɔk] s schiamazzo; (slang) lamento stridulo || intr schiamazzare; (slang) lamentarsi strillando

squaw' man' s bianco sposato con una pellerossa

squeak [skwik] s strido; cigolio || intr stridere; cigolare; (said of a mouse) squittire; to squeak through farcela per il rotto della cuffia

squeal [skwil] s strido || intr stridere; (slang) cantare, fare il delatore

squealer [ˈskwilər] s (slang) delatore m

squeamish [ˈskwimɪʃ] adj pudibondo; scrupoloso; (easily nauseated) schifiltoso, schizzinoso

squeeze [skwiz] s spremuta; stretta, abbraccio; to put the squeeze on (coll) far pressione su || tr premere; spremere, pigiare; stringere || intr stringere; to squeeze through aprirsi il passo attraverso; (fig) farcela a pena

squeezer [ˈskwizər] s spremifrutta m

squelch [skwɛltʃ] s osservazione schiacciante || tr schiacciare

squid [skwɪd] s calamaro, totano

squint [skwɪnt] s tendenza losca; (coll) occhiata; (pathol) strabismo || tr (one's eyes) socchiudere || intr socchiudere gli occhi; guardare furtivamente

squint-eyed [ˈskwɪnt ˌaɪd] adj guercio, losco; malevolo

squire [skwaɪr] s (of a lady) cavalier m servente; (Brit) proprietario terriero; (U.S.A.) giudice m conciliatore || tr (a woman) accompagnare

squirm [skwʌrm] s contorsione || intr contorcersi; mostrare imbarazzo; to squirm out of cavarsela da

squirrel [ˈskwʌrəl] s scoiattolo

squirt [skwʌrt] s schizzo; (instrument) schizzetto; (coll) saputello || tr & intr schizzare

stab [stæb] s pugnalata; (of pain) fitta; to make a stab at (coll) provare || v (pret & pp stabbed; ger stabbing) tr pugnalare, trafiggere || intr pugnalare

stabilize [ˈstebəl ˌaɪz] tr stabilizzare

stab' in the back' s pugnalata nella schiena or alle spalle

stable ['stebəl] *adj* stabile ‖ *s* stalla; (*of race horses*) scuderia

sta'ble-boy' *s* stalliere *m*

stack [stæk] *s* pila; (*of hay or straw*) pagliaio; (*of firewood*) catasta; (*of books*) scaffale *m;* camino; (coll) mucchio, sacco ‖ *tr* ammonticchiare, accatastare

stadi·um ['stedɪ·əm] *s* (-ums *or* -a [ə]) stadio

staff [stæf] *or* [stɑf] *s* bastone *m;* asta, albero; personale *m*, corpo; (mil) stato maggiore; (mus) rigo, pentagramma *m* ‖ *tr* dotare di personale

staff' of'ficer *s* ufficiale *m* di stato maggiore

stag [stæg] *adj* per signori soli ‖ *s* (*deer*) cervo; maschio; (coll) signore *m* ‖ *adv* senza compagna

stage [stedʒ] *s* fase *f*, stadio; tappa, giornata; (*coach*) diligenza; teatro; piattaforma; (*of microscope*) piatto portaoggetti; (theat) scena, palcoscenico; **by easy stages** poco a poco; **to go on the stage** diventare attore ‖ *tr* mettere in scena; organizzare

stage'coach' *s* diligenza

stage'craft' *s* scenotecnica

stage' door' *s* (theat) ingresso degli artisti

stage' fright' *s* tremarella

stage'hand' *s* macchinista *m*

stage' left' *s* (theat) la sinistra della scena guardando il pubblico

stage' man'ager *s* direttore *m* di scena

stage' right' *s* (theat) la destra della scena guardando il pubblico

stage'-struck' *adj* innamorato del teatro

stage' whis'per *s* a parte *m*

stagger ['stægər] *tr* far traballare; impressionare; (*troops; hours*) scaglionare ‖ *intr* traballare

stag'gering *adj* traballante; impressionante, stupefacente

staging ['stedʒɪŋ] *s* impalcatura; (theat) messa in scena

stagnant ['stægnənt] *adj* stagnante

staid [sted] *adj* serio, grave

stain [sten] *s* macchia; tinta; colorante *m* ‖ *tr* macchiare; tingere; colorare ‖ *intr* macchiarsi

stained' glass' *s* vetro colorato

stained'-glass window' *s* vetrata a colori

stainless ['stenlɪs] *adj* immacolato; (*steel*) inossidabile

stair [stɛr] *s* scala

stair'case' *s* scala

stair'way' *s* scala

stair'well' *s* tromba delle scale

stake [stek] *s* picchetto; (*e.g., of cart*) staggio; (*to support a plant*) puntello; (*in gambling*) puglia, giocata; **at stake** in gioco; **to die at the stake** morire sul rogo; **to pull up stakes** (coll) andarsene, traslocare ‖ *tr* picchettare; puntellare; attaccare a un palo; arrischiare; (coll) aiutare; **to stake out** picchettare; (slang) tenere sotto sorveglianza; **to stake out a claim** avanzare una pretesa

stale [stel] *adj* stantio; (*air*) viziato; (fig) ritrito

stale'mate' *s* (chess) stallo; **to reach a**

stalemate essere in una posizione di stallo ‖ *tr* mettere in una posizione di stallo

stalk [stɔk] *s* stelo; (*of corn*) stocco; (*of salad*) piede *m* ‖ *tr* braccare ‖ *intr* avanzare furtivamente; camminare con andatura maestosa

stall [stɔl] *s* (*in a stable*) posta; (*booth in a market*) bancarella; (*seat*) stallo; (*space in a parking lot*) spazio per il parcheggio ‖ *tr* (*an animal*) stallare; (*a car*) parcheggiare; (*a motor*) far fermare; **to stall off** eludere, tenere a bada ‖ *intr* impantanarsi; stare nella posta; (*said of a motor*) fermarsi; (*to temporize*) menare il can per l'aia

stallion ['stæljən] *s* stallone *m*

stalwart ['stɔlwərt] *adj* forte, gagliardo ‖ *s* sostenitore *m*

stamen ['stemən] *s* stame *m*

stamina ['stæmɪnə] *s* forza, vigore *m*

stammer ['stæmər] *s* balbuzie *f* ‖ *tr* & *intr* balbettare

stammerer ['stæmərər] *s* balbuziente *mf*

stamp [stæmp] *s* (*postage stamp*) francobollo; (*device to show that a fee has been paid*) timbro, bollo; impressione; carattere *m*; sigillo; (*tool for stamping coins*) conio; (*tool for crushing ore*) maglio ‖ *tr* timbrare, stampigliare, bollare; sigillare; coniare; (*one's foot*) battere, pestare; imprimere; caratterizzare; (mach) stampare; **to stamp out** spegnere; sopprimere ‖ *intr* battere il piede; (*said of a horse*) zampare

stampede [stæm'pid] *s* fuga precipitosa ‖ *tr* precipitarsi verso; far fuggire precipitosamente ‖ *intr* precipitarsi

stamp'ing ground' *s* (coll) luogo di ritrovo abituale

stamp' pad' *s* tampone *m*

stamp'-vend'ing machine' *s* distributore automatico di francobolli

stance [stæns] *s* posizione

stanch [stɑntʃ] *adj* leale; forte; a tenuta d'acqua ‖ *s* chiusa ‖ *tr* arrestare il flusso da; (*blood*) stagnare

stand [stænd] *s* posizione; resistenza, difesa; tribuna, palco; sostegno, supporto; (*booth in market*) posteggio; posto di sosta ‖ *v* (*pret* & *pp* **stood** [stud]) *tr* mettere in piedi; reggere, sostenere; sopportare, tollerare; (*one's ground*) mantenere; (*a chance*) avere; (*watch*) fare; (coll) pagare; **to stand off** tenere a distanza ‖ *intr* stare; essere alto; fermarsi; stare in piedi; trovarsi; aver forza; essere; (*e.g., apart*) tenersi; **to stand back of** spalleggiare; **to stand by** appoggiare; **to stand for** rappresentare, voler dire; appoggiare, favorire; tenere a battesimo; (coll) tollerare; **to stand in line** fare la fila o la coda; **to stand in with** (coll) essere nelle buone grazie di; **to stand out** stagliarsi, distaccarsi, risaltare; **to stand up** tenersi in piedi; resistere, durare; **to stand up to** affrontare

standard ['stændərd] *adj* (*usual*) normale; uniforme, standard; (language) corretto, preferito ‖ s standard m; (model) modello, campione m; (flag) stendardo

stand·ard·bear'er s portabandiera m

standardize ['stændər ˌdaɪz] tr standardizzare

stand'ard of liv'ing s tenore m di vita

stand'ard time' s ora ufficiale, ora legale

standee [stæn'di] s passeggero in piedi; spettatore m in piedi

stand'-in' s (mov) controfigura; **to have a stand-in with** (coll) essere nelle buone grazie di

standing ['stændɪŋ] adj (jump) da fermo; in piedi; fermo; (water) stagnante; vigente, permanente; (idle) fuori uso ‖ s posizione, rango, situazione; classifica; **in good standing** riconosciuto da tutti; **of long standing** vecchio, da lungo tempo

stand'ing ar'my s esercito permanente

stand'ing room' s posto in piedi

standpatter ['stænd ˌpætər] s (coll) seguace mf dell'immobilismo

stand'point' s punto di vista

stand'still' s fermata; riposo; **to come to a standstill** fermarsi

stanza ['stænzə] s stanza

staple ['stepəl] adj principale ‖ s articolo di prima necessità; elemento indispensabile; (e.g., to hold wire) cavallottino, cambretta; (to fasten papers) grappetta; fibra tessile ‖ tr aggraffare

stapler ['steplər] s cucitrice f a grappe

star [star] s (any heavenly body, except the moon, appearing in the sky) astro; (heavenly body radiating self-produced energy) stella; (actor) divo; (actress) diva, stella (athlete) asso; (fig, mov) stella; (typ) stelletta; **to thank one's lucky stars** ringraziare la propria stella ‖ v (pret & pp starred; ger starring) tr costellare, stellare; presentare come stella; (typ) marcare con stelletta ‖ intr primeggiare

starboard ['starbərd] or ['star ˌbord] adj di dritta, di tribordo ‖ s dritta, tribordo ‖ adv a dritta, a tribordo

starch [start∫] s amido, fecola; (in laundering) salda; (coll) forza ‖ tr inamidare

starch·y ['start∫i] adj (-ier; -iest) amidaceo; (e.g., collar) inamidato; (manner) sostenuto, contegnoso

star' dust' s polveri fpl meteoriche; (fig) polvere f di stelle

stare [ster] s sguardo fisso ‖ intr rimirare; **to stare at** fissare gli occhi addosso a

star'fish' s stella di mare

star'gaze' intr guardare le stelle; sognare ad occhi aperti

stark [stark] adj completo; desolato; severo, serio; duro, rigido ‖ adv completamente

stark'-na'ked adj nudo e crudo

starlet ['starlɪt] s stellina, divetta

star'light' s lume f delle stelle

starling ['starlɪŋ] s storno, stornello

Stars' and Stripes' s bandiera stellata

Star'-Spangled Ban'ner s bandiera stellata

star' sys'tem s (mov) divismo

start [start] s inizio, principio; partenza; linea di partenza; (sudden jerk) sussulto, soprassalto; (advantage) vantaggio; (spurt) scatto ‖ tr iniziare, principiare; mettere in moto; dare il via a; (a conversation) intavolare; (game) stanare ‖ intr iniziare, principiare; mettersi in moto; incamminarsi; (to be startled) trasalire, sussultare; **to start+ger** mettersi a + inf; **to start+ger+again** rimettersi a + inf; **to start after** andare in cerca di

starter ['startər] s (of a venture) iniziatore m; partente m; (aut) motorino d'avviamento; (sports) mossiere m

starting ['startɪŋ] adj di partenza ‖ s messa in marcia

start'ing crank' s manovella d'avviamento

start'ing point' s punto di partenza

startle ['startəl] tr far trasalire ‖ intr trasalire, sussultare

startling ['startlɪŋ] adj allarmante, sorprendente

starvation [star've∫ən] s fame f, inedia, inanizione

starva'tion wag'es spl paga da fame

starve [starv] tr affamare; far morire di fame; **to starve out** prendere per fame ‖ intr essere affamato; morire di fame

starving ['starvɪŋ] adj famelico

state [stet] adj statale; ufficiale; di gala, di lusso ‖ s condizione; stato; gala, pompa; **to lie in state** essere esposto in camera ardente; **to live in state** vivere sfarzosamente ‖ tr dichiarare, affermare; (a problem) impostare

stateless ['stetlɪs] adj apolide

state·ly ['stetli] adj (-lier; -liest) maestoso, imponente

statement ['stetmənt] s dichiarazione, affermazione; comunicazione; (com) estratto conto

state' of mind' s stato d'animo

state'room' s cabina; (rr) compartimento privato

states'man s (-men) statista m, uomo di stato

static ['stætɪk] adj statico; (rad) atmosferico ‖ s disturbi mpl atmosferici

station ['ste∫ən] s stazione; rango, condizione ‖ tr stazionare

sta'tion a'gent s capostazione m

stationary ['ste∫ən ˌɛri] adj stazionario

sta'tion break' s (rad, telv) intervallo

stationer ['ste∫ənər] s cartolaio

stationery ['ste∫ən ˌɛri] s (writing paper) carta da lettere; (writing materials) cancelleria

sta'tionery store' s cartoleria

sta'tion house' s posto di polizia

sta'tion·mas'ter s capostazione m

sta'tion wag'on s giardinetta

statistical [stə'tɪstɪkəl] adj statistico

statistician [ˌstætɪs'tɪ∫ən] s statistico

statistics [stə'tɪstɪks] *ssg* (*science*) statistica; *spl* (*data*) statistiche *fpl*
statue ['stætʃu] *s* statua
statuesque [ˌstætʃu'esk] *adj* statuario
stature ['stætʃər] *s* statura
status ['stetəs] *s* stato, condizione; condizione sociale
sta'tus sym'bol *s* simbolo della posizione sociale
statute ['stætʃut] *s* legge *f;* regolamento
stat'ute of limita'tions *s* legge *f* che governa la prescrizione
statutory ['stætʃuˌtori] *adj* legale
staunch [stɔntʃ] or [stɑntʃ] *adj*, *s* & *tr* var of **stanch**
stave [stev] *s* (*of barrel*) doga; (*of ladder*) piolo; (*mus*) rigo, pentagramma *m* ‖ *v* (*pret* & *pp* **staved** or **stove** [stov]) *tr* bucare; (*to smash*) sfondare; **to stave off** tenere a bada
stay [ste] *s* permanenza, soggiorno; (*brace*) staggio; (*of corset*) stecca di balena; sostegno; (*law*) sospensione; (*naut*) strallo ‖ *tr* fermare; sospendere; poner freno a ‖ *intr* stare; mantenersi; restare, rimanere; (*at a hotel*) sostare; **to stay up** stare alzato
stay'-at-home' *adj* casalingo ‖ *s* persona casalinga
stead [stɛd] *s* posto; **in his stead** in suo luogo; **to stand in good stead** esser utile
stead'fast' *adj* fermo, risoluto
stead·y ['stɛdi] *adj* (-**ier**; -**iest**) stabile, fermo; regolare, costante; abituale; calmo, sicuro ‖ *v* (*pret* & *pp* -**ied**) *tr* rinforzare; calmare ‖ *intr* rinforzarsi; calmarsi
steak [stek] *s* bistecca
steal [stil] *s* (coll) furto ‖ *v* (*pret* **stole** [stol]; *pp* **stolen**) *tr* rubare; involare; (*the attention*) cattivare ‖ *intr* rubare; **to steal away** svignarsela; **to steal out** uscire di soppiatto; **to steal upon** approssimarsi silenziosamente a
stealth [stɛlθ] *s* clandestinità *f;* **by stealth** di straforo, di soppiatto
steam [stim] *adj* a vapore ‖ *s* vapore *m;* fumo; **to get up steam** aumentare la pressione; **to let off steam** scaricare la pressione; (slang) sfogarsi ‖ *tr* (*a steamship*) guidare; esalare; esporre al vapore; (*e.g., glasses*) appannare ‖ *intr* dar vapore, fumigare; bollire; (*to become clouded*) appannarsi; andare a vapore; **to steam ahead** avanzare a tutto vapore
steam'boat' *s* vapore *m*
steam' en'gine *s* macchina a vapore
steamer ['stimər] *s* vapore *m*
steam'er rug' *s* coperta da viaggio
steam'er trunk' *s* bauletto da cabina
steam' heat' *s* riscaldamento a vapore
steam' roll'er *s* rullo compressore; (fig) rullo compressore
steam'ship' *s* piroscafo, vapore *m*
steam' shov'el *s* escavatore *m* a vapore
steam' ta'ble *s* tavola riscaldata a vapore per mantenere calde le vivande
steed [stid] *s* destriere *m*

steel [stil] *adj* d'acciaio; (*industry*) siderurgico ‖ *s* acciaio; (*bar*) stecca d'acciaio; (*for sharpening knives*) affilacoltelli *m;* (fig) spada, brando ‖ *tr* acciaiare; **to steel oneself** corazzarsi, indurirsi; armarsi di coraggio
steel' wool' *s* paglia di ferro
steel'works' *spl* acciaieria
steelyard ['stilˌjard] or ['stiljərd] *s* stadera
steep [stip] *adj* erto, scosceso, ripido; (*price*) alto ‖ *tr* immergere, saturare, imbevere
steeple ['stipəl] *s* campanile *m;* (*spire*) cuspide *f,* guglia
stee'ple-chase' *s* corsa ad ostacoli
stee'ple-jack' *s* aggiustatore *m* di campanili
steer [stɪr] *s* bue *m,* manzo ‖ *tr* governare, guidare; (aer) pilotare ‖ *intr* governare; **to steer clear of** evitare
steerage ['stɪrɪdʒ] *s* (naut) alloggio passeggeri di terza classe
steer'ing wheel' *s* (aut) volante *m,* sterzo; (naut) ruota del timone
stellar ['stɛlər] *adj* stellare; (*role*) da stella
stem [stɛm] *s* (*of pipe, of key*) cannello; (*of goblet*) gambo; (*of column*) fusto; (*of spoon*) manico; (*of watch*) corona; (*of a word*) tema *m;* (*of note*) (mus) gamba; (bot) peduncolo, stelo; (bot) gambo; **from stem to stern** da poppa a prua ‖ *v* (*pret* & *pp* **stemmed;** *ger* **stemming**) *tr* togliere il gambo a; (*to check*) arrestare; (*to dam up*) arginare; (*to plug*) otturare; (*the tide*) risalire, andare contro ‖ *intr* originare, derivare
stem'-win'der *s* orologio a corona
stench [stɛntʃ] *s* tanfo, fetore *m*
sten·cil ['stɛnsəl] *s* stampo, stampino; parole *fpl* a stampo ‖ *v* (*pret* & *pp* -**ciled** or -**cilled;** *ger* -**ciling** or -**cilling**) *tr* stampinare
stenographer [stə'nɑgrəfər] *s* stenografo
stenography [stə'nɑgrəfi] *s* stenografia
step [stɛp] *s* passo; (*footprint*) orma, impronta; (*of ladder*) piolo; (*of staircase*) gradino; (*of carriage*) montatoio; **step by step** passo passo; **to watch one's step** fare molta attenzione ‖ *v* (*pret* & *pp* **stepped;** *ger* **stepping**) *tr* scaglionare; **to step off** misurare a passi ‖ *intr* camminare, andare a passi; mettere il piede; **to step aside** scostarsi; **to step back** indietreggiare; **to step on it** (slang) fare presto; **to step on the gas** (coll) accelerare; **to step on the starter** avviare il motore
step'broth'er *s* fratellastro, fratello consanguineo
step'child' *s* (-**children** [ˌtʃɪldrən]) figliastro
step'daugh'ter *s* figliastra
step'fa'ther *s* patrigno
step'lad'der *s* scala a gradini **or** a libretto
step'moth'er *s* matrigna
steppe [stɛp] *s* steppa

step'ping stone' s passatoio, pietra per guadare; (fig) gradino

step'sis'ter s sorellastra

step'son' s figliastro

stere·o ['stɛrɪ‚o] or ['stɪrɪ‚o] adj stereofonico; stereoscopico ‖ s (-os) musica stereofonica; sistema stereofonico; fotografia stereoscopica

stereotyped ['stɛrɪ‚ə‚taɪpt] or ['stɪrɪ‚ə‚tarpt] adj stereotipato

sterile ['stɛrɪl] adj sterile

sterilize ['stɛrɪ‚laɪz] tr sterilizzare

sterling ['stɑrlɪŋ] adj di lira sterlina; d'argento; puro; eccellente ‖ s argento .925; vasellame m d'argento puro

stern [stʌrn] adj severo ‖ s poppa

stet [stɛt] v (pret & pp **stetted;** ger **stetting**) tr marcare con la parola "vive"

stethoscope ['stɛθə‚skop] s stetoscopio

stevedore ['stivə‚dor] s stivatore m

stew [stju] or [stu] s stufato, guazzetto ‖ tr stufare ‖ intr cuocere a fuoco lento; (coll) preoccuparsi

steward ['stju‚ərd] or ['stu‚ərd] s amministratore m, agente m; maggiordomo; (aer, naut) cambusiere m, cameriere m

stewardess ['stju‚ərdɪs] or ['stu‚ərdɪs] s (naut) cameriera; (aer) hostess f, assistente f di volo

stewed' fruit' s composta di frutta

stewed' toma'toes spl pomodori mpl in umido

stick [stɪk] s stecco; legno; bacchetta; bastone m; (e.g., of candy) cannello; (naut) albero; (typ) compositoio; **in the sticks** (coll) in casa del diavolo ‖ v (pret & pp **stuck** [stʌk]) tr pungere; ficcare, infiggere; attaccare; confondere; **to be stuck** essere insabbiato; essere attaccato; (fig) essere confuso; **to stick out** (the head) sporgere; (the tongue) cacciare; **to stick up** (slang) assaltare a mano armata, rapinare ‖ intr rimanere attaccato; persistere; (said of glue) appiccicarsi; (to one opinion) tenersi; stare; **to stick out** sporgere; **to stick together** rimanere uniti; **to stick up** risaltare; (said, e.g., of quills) rizzarsi; **to stick up for** (coll) stare dalla parte di

sticker ['stɪkər] s etichetta gommata; spina; persona zelante; (coll) busillis m

stick'ing plas'ter s cerotto

stick'pin' s spilla da cravatta

stick'up' s (slang) grassazione

stick·y ['stɪki] adj (-ier; -iest) attaccaticcio; vischioso; (weather) afoso, soffocante; (fig) difficile

stiff [stɪf] adj rigido, duro; forte; (price) alto; denso ‖ s (slang) cadavere m; **poor stiff** (slang) povero diavolo

stiff' col'lar s colletto duro

stiffen ['stɪfən] tr irrigidire ‖ intr irrigidirsi

stiff' neck' s torcicollo; ostinazione

stiff'-necked adj testardo

stiff' shirt' s camicia inamidata

stifle ['staɪfəl] tr soffocare

stigma ['stɪgmə] s (-mas or -mata [mətə]) stigma m

stigmatize ['stɪgmə‚taɪz] tr stigmatizzare

still [stɪl] adj fermo, tranquillo; silenzioso; (wine) non spumante ‖ s calma; distillatore m; distilleria; (phot) fotografia singola ‖ adv ancora; tuttora ‖ conj tuttavia ‖ tr calmare ‖ intr calmarsi

still'birth' s parto di infante nato morto

still'born' adj nato morto

still' life' s (lifes') natura morta

stilt [stɪlt] s trampolo; (in water) palafitta; (orn) trampoliere m

stilted ['stɪltɪd] adj elevato; pomposo

stimulant ['stɪmjələnt] adj & s stimulante m, eccitante m

stimulate ['stɪmjə‚let] tr stimulare

stimu·lus ['stɪmjələs] s (-li [‚laɪ]) stimolo

sting [stɪŋ] s puntura; (of insect) pungiglione; (fig) scottatura ‖ v (pret & pp **stung** [stʌŋ]) tr intr pungere

stin·gy ['stɪndʒi] adj (-gier; -giest) tirchio, taccagno

stink [stɪŋk] s puzza ‖ v (pret **stank** [stæŋk] or **stunk** [stʌŋk]; pp **stunk**) tr far puzzare ‖ intr puzzare; **to stink of money** (slang) aver soldi a palate

stinker ['stɪŋkər] s (slang) puzzone m

stint [stɪnt] s limite m; lavoro assegnato, compito ‖ intr lesinarsi

stipend ['staɪpənd] s stipendio; assegno di studio, presalario

stipulate ['stɪpjə‚let] tr stipulare

stir [stʌr] s agitazione, movimento; (poke) spinta; **to create a stir** creare una sensazione ‖ v (pret & pp **stirred;** ger **stirring**) tr mescolare; muovere; (fire) ravvivare; (pity) fare; **to stir up** eccitare, svegliare; (to rebellion) sommuovere ‖ intr muoversi, agitarsi

stirring ['stʌrɪŋ] adj commovente

stirrup ['stʌrəp] or ['stɪrəp] s staffa

stitch [stɪtʃ] s punto; maglia; (pain) fitta; (bit) poco, po' m; **to be in stitches** (coll) sbellicarsi dalle risa ‖ tr cucire; aggraffare ‖ intr cucire

stock [stɑk] adj regolare, comune; banale, ordinario; di bestiame; borsistico; azionario; (aut) di serie; (theat) stabile ‖ s provvista, scorta; capitale m sociale; azione f; azioni fpl, titoli mpl; (of tree) tronco; (of family; of anchor; of anvil) ceppo; razza, famiglia; materia prima; (of rifle) cassa; (broth) brodo; (handle) manico; (livestock) bestiame m; (theat) compagnia stabile; **in stock** in magazzino, disponibile; **out of stock** esaurito; **stocks** gogna, berlina; **to take stock** fare l'inventario; **to take stock in** (coll) aver fede in ‖ tr fornire; fornire di bestiame; fornire di pesci ‖ intr—**to stock up** fare rifornimenti

stockade [stɑ'ked] s staccionata

stock'breed'er s allevatore m di bestiame

stock′bro′ker *s* agente *m* di cambio

stock′ car′ *s* automobile *f* di serie; (rr) carro bestiame

stock′ com′pany *s* (theat) compagnia stabile; (com) società anonima

stock′ div′idend *s* dividendo pagato in azioni

stock′ exchange′ *s* borsa valori

stock′fish′ *s* stoccafisso

stock′hold′er *s* azionista *mf*

stock′holder of rec′ord *s* azionista *mf* registrato nei libri della compagnia

Stockholm [′stɑkhom] *s* Stoccolma

stocking [′stɑkɪŋ] *s* calza

stock′ in trade′ *s* stock *m*; ferri *mpl* del mestiere

stock′ mar′ket *s* borsa valori

stock′pile′ *s* riserva, scorta ‖ *tr* mettere in riserva ‖ *intr* mettere in riserva materie prime

stock′ rais′ing *s* allevamento bestiame

stock′room′ *s* magazzino, deposito

stock·y [′stɑki] *adj* (-ier; -iest) tozzo, tarchiato

stock′yard′ *s* chiuso per il bestiame

stoic [′sto·ɪk] *adj & s* stoico

stoicism [′sto·ɪˌsɪzəm] *s* stoicismo

stoke [stok] *tr* (fire) attizzare; (a furnace) caricare

stoker [′stokər] *s* fochista *m*

stolid [′stɑlɪd] *adj* impassibile

stomach [′stʌmək] *s* stomaco ‖ *tr* (fig) digerire

stone [ston] *s* sasso, pietra; (of fruit) osso; (pathol) calcolo ‖ *tr* lapidare; affilare con la pietra; (fruit) snocciolare

stone′-broke′ *adj* (coll) senza un soldo, senza il becco di un quattrino

stone′-deaf′ *adj* sordo come una campana

stone′ma′son *s* tagliapietra *m*

stone′ quar′ry *s* cava di pietra

stone′s throw′ *s* tiro di sasso; **within a stone′s throw** a un tiro di schioppo

ston·y [′stoni] *adj* (-ier; -iest) di sasso, sassoso, pietroso

stooge [studʒ] *s* (theat) spalla; (slang) complice *mf*

stool [stul] *s* sgabello, seggiolino; gabinetto; (mass evacuated) feci *fpl*

stool′ pi′geon *s* piccione *m* di richiamo; (slang) spia

stoop [stup] *s* curvatura, inclinazione; scalini *mpl* d'ingresso ‖ *intr* inclinarsi, piegarsi; degnarsi, umiliarsi

stoop-shouldered [′stup′ʃoldərd] *adj* con le spalle cadenti

stop [stɑp] *s* fermata, sosta; arresto; otturazione, blocco; cessazione; ostacolo; (of a check) fermo; (restraint) freno; (of organ) registro; **to come to a stop** fermarsi; cessare; **to put a stop to** metter fine a ‖ *v* (pret & pp **stopped**; ger **stopping**) *tr* fermare, cessare; arrestare, sospendere; tappare, otturare; (a check) mettere il fermo a; **to stop up** tappare, otturare ‖ *intr* fermarsi; arrestarsi; (said of a ship) fare scalo; (at an hotel) scendere; **to stop + ger** smettere di or cessare di + *inf*

stop′cock′ *s* rubinetto di arresto

stop′gap′ *adj* provvisorio ‖ *s* soluzione provvisoria; (person) tappabuchi *m*

stop′light′ *s* (traffic light) semaforo; (aut) luce *f* di stop

stop′o′ver *s* fermata intermedia

stoppage [′stɑpɪdʒ] *s* fermata, arresto; (of work, wages, etc.) sospensione

stopper [′stɑpər] *s* tappo, turacciolo

stop′ sign′ *s* segnale *m* di fermata

stop′watch′ *s* cronometro a scatto

storage [′storɪdʒ] *s* magazzinaggio; (place for storing) magazzino; (of a computer) memoria

stor′age bat′tery *s* (elec) accumulatore *m*

store [stor] *s* negozio; magazzino; (supply) scorta; **in store** in serbo; **to set store by** dare molta importanza a ‖ *tr* immagazzinare; **to store away** accumulare

store′house′ *s* magazzino, deposito; (of knowledge) miniera

store′keep′er *s* negoziante *m*

store′room′ *s* magazzino; (naut) dispensa

stork [stɔrk] *s* cicogna

storm [stɔrm] *s* tempesta, temporale *m*; (on the Beaufort scale) burrasca; (mil) assalto; (fig) scoppio ‖ *tr* assaltare ‖ *intr* tempestare; imperversare; (mil) andare all'attacco

storm′ cloud′ *s* nuvolone *m*

storm′ door′ *s* controporta

storm′ sash′ *s* controfinestra

storm′ troops′ *spl* truppe *fpl* d'assalto

storm′ win′dow *s* controfinestra

storm·y [′stɔrmi] *adj* (-ier; -iest) tempestoso, burrascoso; (fig) inquieto, violento

sto·ry [′stori] *s* (-ries) storia, racconto, romanzo; (plot) trama; (level) piano; (coll) storia, menzogna ‖ *v* (pret & pp -ried) *tr* istoriare

sto′ry-tell′er *s* narratore *m*, novelliere *m*; (coll) mentitore *m*

stoup [stup] *s* (eccl) acquasantiera

stout [staut] *adj* grasso, obeso; forte, robusto; leale; coraggioso ‖ *s* birra nera forte

stout-hearted [′staut,hɑrtɪd] *adj* coraggioso

stove [stov] *s* (for warmth) stufa; (for cooking) fornello, cucina economica

stove′pipe′ *s* tubo della stufa, cannone *m*; (hat) (coll) tuba

stow [sto] *tr* mettere in riserva; riempire; (naut) stivare ‖ *intr*—**to stow away** imbarcarsi clandestinamente

stowage [′sto·ɪdʒ] *s* stivaggio; (place) stiva

stow′a·way′ *s* passeggero clandestino

straddle [′strædəl] *s* divaricamento ‖ *tr* (a horse) cavalcare; (the legs) divaricare; favorire entrambe le parti in ‖ *intr* cavalcare; stare a gambe divaricate; (coll) tenere il piede tra due staffe

strafe [straf] or [stref] *s* attacco violento ‖ *tr* attaccare violentemente con fuoco aereo; bombardare violentemente; (slang) punire

straggle ['strægəl] *intr* sbandarsi, sviarsi; sparpagliarsi, essere sparpagliato

straggler ['stræglər] *s* ritardatario

straight [stret] *adj* diritto, ritto; *(e.g., shoulders)* quadro; candido, franco; *(honest, upright)* retto; inalterato; *(hair; whiskey)* liscio; **to set s.o. straight** mettere qlcu sulla retta via; mostrare la verità a qlcu || *s* rettilinea; *(cards)* scala || *adv* dritto; sinceramente; rettamente; **straight ahead** sempre diritto; **straight away** immediatamente; **to go straight** vivere onestamente

straighten ['stretən] *tr* ordinare; raddrizzare || *intr* raddrizzarsi

straight' face' *s* faccia seria

straight' flush' *s* (cards) scala reale

straight'for'ward *adj* diretto; onesto

straight' man' *s* (theat) spalla

straight' ra'zor *s* rasoio a mano libera

straight'way' *adv* immediatamente

strain [stren] *s* sforzo; fatica eccessiva; tensione, pressione; strappo muscolare; tono, stile *m*; *(family)* famiglia; tendenza, vena; (coll) lavoro severo; (mus) aria, melodia || *tr* passare, colare; *e.g., a rope)* tirare al massimo; *(one's ear)* tendere; *(a muscle)* strappare; *(the ankle)* slogare; *(e.g., words)* storcere, forzare || *intr* colare, filtrare; tendersi, tirare; sforzarsi; fare resistenza; **to strain at** tirare; resistere a

strained [strend] *adj* (smile) stentato; *(relations)* teso

strainer ['strenər] *s* scolatoio

strait [stret] *s* stretto; **straits** stretto; (fig) strettezze *fpl*; **to be in dire straits** essere nei frangenti

strait' jack'et *s* camicia di forza

strait'-laced' *adj* puritano, pudibondo

strand [strænd] *s* sponda, lido; *(of metal cable)* trefolo; *(of rope)* legnolo; *(of pearls)* filo || *tr* sfilare; *(e.g., a rope)* ritorcere, intrecciare; *(e.g., a boat)* lasciare incagliato; **to be stranded** trovarsi incagliato

stranded ['strændɪd] *adj* (ship) incagliato, arenato; *(e.g., rope)* ritorto, intrecciato

strange [strendʒ] *adj* strano, straniero; non abituato; inusitato

stranger ['strendʒər] *s* forestiero, nuovo venuto, intruso

strangle ['stræŋgəl] *tr* strangolare; soffocare || *intr* strangolarsi; soffocarsi

strap [stræp] *s* (of leather) correggia; *(for holding things together)* tirante *m*; *(shoulder strap)* bretella; *(for passengers to hold on to)* manopola; *(to hold a sandal)* guigia; *(to hold a baby)* falda; *(strop)* coramella || *v* (*pret & pp* **strapped**; *ger* **strapping**) *tr* legare con correggia or tirante; *(a razor)* affilare

strap'hang'er *s* (coll) passeggero senza posto a sedere

strapping ['stræpɪŋ] *adj* robusto; (coll) grande, enorme

stratagem ['strætədʒəm] *s* stratagemma *m*

strategic(al) [strə'tidʒɪk(əl)] *adj* strategico

strategist ['strætɪdʒɪst] *s* stratego

strate·gy ['strætɪdʒɪ] *s* (-gies) strategia

strati·fy ['strætɪ‚faɪ] *v* (*pret & pp* **-fied**) *tr* stratificare || *intr* stratificarsi

stratosphere ['strætə‚sfɪr] *or* ['stretə‚sfɪr] *s* stratosfera

stra·tum ['stretəm] *or* ['strætəm] *s* (-ta [tə] *or* -tums) strato

straw [strɔ] *adj* di paglia; di nessun valore; falso, fittizio || *s* paglia; *(for drinking)* cannuccia; **I don't care a straw** non mi importa un fico; **to be the last straw** essere il colmo

straw'ber·ry *s* (-ries) fragola

straw' hat' *s* cappello di paglia; *(with hard crown)* paglietta

straw' man' *s* (figurehead) uomo di paglia; *(scarecrow)* spaventapasseri *m*

straw' mat'tress *s* pagliericcio

straw' vote' *s* votazione esplorativa

stray [stre] *adj* sbandato, randagio; casuale, fortuito || *s* animale randagio || *intr* sviarsi, (fig) sbandarsi

streak [strik] *s* stria; *(of light)* raggio; *(of madness)* ramo, vena; *(of luck)* (coll) periodo; **like a streak** (coll) come un lampo || *tr* striare, venare || *intr* striarsi, venarsi; andare come un lampo

stream [strim] *s* corrente *f*; *(of light)* raggio; *(of people)* fiumana, torrente *m*; *(of cars)* fila || *intr* colare; filtrare, penetrare; *(said of a flag)* fluttuare

streamer ['strimər] *s* pennone *m*; nastro; raggio di luce

streamlined ['strim‚laɪnd] *adj* aerodinamico; (aer) carenato

stream'lin'er *s* treno dal profilo aerodinamico

street [strit] *adj* stradale || *s* via, strada

street'car' *s* tram *m*

street' clean'er *s* spazzino; (mach) spazzatrice *f*

street' clothes' *spl* vestiti *mpl* da passeggio; vestito da passeggio

street' floor' *s* pianterreno

street'light' *s* lampione *m*

street' map' *s* pianta della città; stradario

street' sign' *s* segnale *m* stradale

street' sprin'kler *s* carro annaffiatoio

street' walk'er *s* passeggiatrice *f*

strength [strεŋθ] *s* forza; resistenza; *(of spirituous liquors)* gradazione; (com) tendenza al rialzo; (mil) numero; **on the strength of** basandosi su

strengthen ['strεŋθən] *tr* rinforzare; (fig) convalidare, rinsaldare || *intr* rinforzarsi, ingagliardirsi

strenuous ['strεnju‚əs] *adj* vigoroso; strenuo

stress [strεs] *s* enfasi *f*, importanza; spinta; tensione, preoccupazione; accento; (mech) sollecitazione; **to lay**

stress on mettere in rilievo ‖ *tr (a word)* accentare, accentuare; *(to emphasize)* accentuare; *(mech)* sollecitare

stress′ ac′cent *s* accento di intensità

stretch [strɛtʃ] *s* tiro, tirata; *(in time or space)* periodo; *(of road)* tratto, percorrenza; *(of imagination)* sforzo; *(rr)* tratta; *(slang)* periodo di detenzione; **at a stretch** di un tiro ‖ *tr* tirare; tendere, distendere; *(the imagination)* forzare; *(facts)* esagerare; *(money)* stiracchiare; *(one's legs)* sgranchirsi; *(the truth)* esagerare; **to stretch oneself** sdraiarsi ‖ *intr* estendersi; stiracchiarsi; distendersi; **to stretch out** sdraiarsi

stretcher [′strɛtʃər] *s (for a painting)* telaio; *(tool)* tenditore *m*, tenditoio; *(to carry wounded)* barella, lettiga

stretch′er-bear′er *s* portantino

strew [stru] *v (pret* **strewed;** *pp* **strewed** *or* **strewn)** *tr* spargere, cospargere; disseminare

stricken [′strɪkən] *adj* afflitto; ferito; danneggiato

strict [strɪkt] *adj* stretto, severo

stricture [′strɪktʃər] *s* aspra critica; *(pathol)* stenosi *f*

stride [straɪd] *s* passo; andatura; **rapid strides** grandi passi *mpl;* **to hit one's stride** avanzare a andatura regolare; **to take s.th in one's stride** fare qlco senza sforzi ‖ *v (pret* **strode** [strod]; *pp* **stridden** [′strɪdən]) *tr* attraversare a grandi passi; attraversare di un salto ‖ *intr* camminare a grandi passi; *(majestically)* incedere

strident [′straɪdənt] *adj* stridente

strife [straɪf] *s* discordia; concorrenza

strike [straɪk] *s (blow)* colpo; *(stopping of work)* sciopero; *(discovery of oil, ore, etc.)* scoperta; *(of fish)* abboccatura; colpo di fortuna ‖ *v (pret & pp* **struck** [strʌk]) *tr* colpire, percuotere; infiggere; *(a match)* strofinare; *(fire)* accendere; fare impressione su; incontrare improvvisamente; *(e.g., ore)* scoprire; *(roots)* mettere; *(a coin)* coniare; andare in sciopero contro; arrivare a; *(a posture)* prendere; *(the hour)* scoccare; cancellare, eliminare; *(sails)* calare; *(attention)* richiamare; **to strike it rich** scoprire una miniera; avere un colpo di fortuna ‖ *intr* dare un colpo; cadere; *(said of a bell)* suonare; accendersi; scioperare; *(mil)* attaccare; **to strike out** mettersi in marcia; *(to fail)* (fig) fallire, venir meno

strike′break′er *s* crumiro

striker [′straɪkər] *s* battitore *m; (clapper in clock)* martelletto; *(worker)* scioperante *m*

striking [′straɪkɪŋ] *adj* impressionante, sorprendente; notevole; scioperante

strik′ing pow′er *s* potere *m* d'assalto

string [strɪŋ] *s* spago, cordicella; *(e.g., of apron)* laccio; *(of pearls)* filo; *(of onions, of lies)* filza; *(row)* fila, infilata; *(mus)* corda; **no strings attached** *(coll)* senza condizioni;

strings strumenti *mpl* a corda; *(coll)* condizioni *fpl;* **to pull strings** usare influenza ‖ *v (pret & pp* **strung** [strʌŋ]) *tr* legare; allacciare; infilare; infilzare; *(a racket)* munire di corde; *(to stretch)* tendere; *(a musical instrument)* mettere le corde a; *(slang)* ingannare; **to string along** *(slang)* menare per il naso; **to string up** impiccare ‖ *intr*—**to string along with** *(slang)* andare d'accordo con

string′ bean′ *s* fagiolino

stringed′ in′strument *s* strumento a corda

stringent [′strɪndʒənt] *adj* stringente; urgente; severo

string′ quartet′ *s* quartetto d'archi

strip [strɪp] *s* striscia; *(of metal)* lamina; *(of land)* lingua ‖ *v (pret & pp* **stripped)** *ger* **stripping)** *tr* spogliare; denudare; *(a fruit)* pelare; *(a ship)* sguarnire; *(tobacco)* togliere le nervature da; scortecciare; *(thread)* spanare; **to strip of** spogliare di ‖ *intr* spogliarsi; denudarsi; fare lo spogliarello

stripe [straɪp] *s* stria, striscia, riga, lista; tipo, qualità *f; (mil)* gallone *m* ‖ *tr* striare, filettare, rigare

strip′ min′ing *s* sfruttamento minerario a cielo aperto

strip′tease′ *s* spogliarello

stripteaser [′strɪp ˌtizər] *s* spogliarellista

strive [straɪv] *v (pret* **strove** [strov]; *pp* **striven** [′strɪvən]) *intr* sforzarsi; lottare; **to strive to** sforzarsi di

stroke [strok] *s* colpo; *(of bell or clock)* rintocco; *(of pen)* tratto, frego; *(of brush)* pennellata; *(of arms in swimming)* bracciata; colpo apoplettico; *(caress)* carezza; *(with oar)* vogata; *(of oar or paddle)* palata; *(of a master)* tocco; *(of a piston)* corsa; *(keystroke)* battuta; *(of genius)* lampo; *(of the hour)* scoccio; **to not do a stroke of work** non muovere un dito ‖ *tr* accarezzare

stroll [strol] *s* passeggiata; **to take a stroll** fare una passeggiata ‖ *intr* fare una passeggiata, andare a zonzo; errare

stroller [′strolər] *s* girovago; carrozzella; *(itinerant performer)* (theat) guitto

strong [strɔŋ] *or* [strɑŋ] *adj* forte, vigoroso; valido; acceso, zelante; *(butter)* rancido; *(cheese)* piccante; *(com)* sostenuto

strong′box′ *s* cassaforte *f*

strong′ drink′ *s* bevanda alcolica

strong′hold′ *s* piazzaforte *f*

strong′ man′ *s (in a circus)* maciste *m; (leader)* anima; dittatore *m*

strong-minded [′strɔŋ ˌmaɪndɪd] *or* [′strɑŋ ˌmaɪndɪd] *adj* volitivo

strong′point′ *s* luogo fortificato

strontium [′strɑnʃɪˌəm] *s* stronzio

strop [strɑp] *s* coramella, affilarasoio ‖ *v (pret & pp* **stropped;** *ger* **stropping)** *tr* affilare

strophe [′strofi] *s* strofa, strofe *f*

struc′tural steel′ ['strʌktʃərəl] *s* profilato di acciaio

structure ['strʌktʃər] *s* struttura; edificio || *tr* strutturare

struggle ['strʌgəl] *s* lotta; sforzo || *intr* lottare; sforzare, dibattersi

strum [strʌm] *v* (*pret & pp* **strummed;** *ger* **strumming**) *tr & intr* strimpellare

strumpet ['strʌmpɪt] *s* sgualdrina, puttana

strut [strʌt] *s* controvento, puntello, saettone *m;* incedere impettito; (aer) montante || *v* (*pret & pp* **strutted;** *ger* **strutting**) *intr* pavoneggiarsi, fare la ruota

strychnine ['strɪknaɪn] or ['strɪknɪn] *s* stricnina

stub [stʌb] *s* (*of tree*) coppo; (*e.g., of cigar*) mozzicone *m;* (*of a check*) matrice *f,* madre *f* || *v* (*pret & pp* **stubbed;** *ger* **stubbing**) *tr* sradicare; **to stub one's toe** inciampare

stubble ['stʌbəl] *s* (*of beard*) pelo ispido; **stubbles** stoppie *fpl*

stubborn ['stʌbərn] *adj* (*headstrong*) testardo; (*resolute*) accanito; (*e.g., resistance*) ostinato; (*e.g., illness*) ribelle; (*soil*) ingrato

stuc·co ['stʌko] *s* (*-coes* or *-cos*) stucco || *tr* stuccare

stuck [stʌk] *adj* infisso; attaccato; (*glued*) incollato; (*unable to continue*) in panna; **stuck on** (slang) invaghito di

stuck′-up′ *adj* (coll) presuntuoso, arrogante

stud [stʌd] *s* (*in upholstery*) borchia; bottone *m* da sparato; (*of walls*) montante *m;* (*stallion*) stallone *m;* (*for mares*) monta; (archit) bugna, bugnato || *v* (*pret & pp* **studded;** *ger* **studding**) *tr* cospergere; (*with stars*) costellare; (*with jewels*) incastonare, ingioiellare

stud′ bolt′ *s* prigioniero

stud′book′ *s* registro della genealogia

student ['stjudənt] or ['studənt] *adj* studentesco || *s* studente *m;* scolaro; (*investigator*) studioso

stu′dent bod′y *s* scolaresca

stud′horse′ *s* stallone *m*

studied ['stʌdid] *adj* premeditato; (*affected*) studiato

studi·o ['studɪ,o] or ['stjudɪ,o] *s* (*-os*) studio

studious ['stjudɪ·əs] or ['studɪ·əs] *adj* studioso; assiduo, zelante

stud·y ['stʌdi] *s* (*-ies*) studio || *v* (*pret & pp* **-ied**) *tr & intr* studiare

stuff [stʌf] *s* roba, cosa; stoffa; materiale *m;* (*nonsense*) scemenze *fpl;* medicina; (coll) mestiere *m* || *tr* riempire, inzeppare; (*one's stomach*) rimpinzare; (*e.g., poultry*) farcire; (*e.g., salami*) insaccare; (*a dead animal*) impagliare; **to stuff up** intasare || *intr* rimpinzarsi

stuffed′ shirt′ *s* persona altezzosa

stuffing ['stʌfɪŋ] *s* ripieno

stuff·y ['stʌfi] *adj* (*-ier; -iest*) soffocante, opprimente; (*nose*) chiuso; pedante

stumble ['stʌmbəl] *intr* incespicare, inciampare; sbagliare, impaperarsi; **to stumble on** or **upon** intopparsi in

stum′bling block′ *s* inciampo, scoglio

stump [stʌmp] *s* (*of tree*) toppo, ceppo; (*e.g., of arm*) moncherino, moncone *m;* (*of cigar, candle*) mozzicone *m;* dente rotto; tribuna popolare; (*for drawing*) sfumino; **up a stump** (coll) completamente perplesso || *tr* mozzare; lasciare perplesso; (coll) fare discorsi politici in

stump′ speech′ *s* discorso politico

stun [stʌn] *v* (*pret & pp* **stunned;** *ger* **stunning**) *tr* tramortire; (fig) sbalordire

stunning ['stʌnɪŋ] *adj* (*blow*) che stordisce; sbalorditivo, magnifico

stunt [stʌnt] *s* atrofia; creatura striminzita; bravata, prodezza; (*for publicity*) montatura || *tr* striminzire; arrestare la crescita di || *intr* fare delle acrobazie

stunt′ed *adj* striminzito

stunt′ fly′ing *s* acrobazia aerea

stunt′ man′ *s* (mov) controfigura

stupe·fy ['stjupɪ,faɪ] or ['stupɪ,faɪ] *v* (*pret & pp* **-fied**) *tr* istupidire, intontire

stupendous [stju'pɛndəs] or [stu'pɛndəs] *adj* stupendo

stupid ['stjupɪd] or ['stupɪd] *adj* stupido, ebete, scemo

stupor ['stjupər] or ['stupər] *s* torpore *m,* stupore *m*

stur·dy ['stʌrdi] *adj* (*-dier; -diest*) forte; (*robust*) tarchiato; risoluto

sturgeon ['stʌrdʒən] *s* storione *m*

stutter ['stʌtər] *s* tartagliamento || *tr & intr* tartagliare

sty [staɪ] *s* (**sties**) porcile *m;* (pathol) orzaiolo

style [staɪl] *s* stile *m;* tono; (*mode of living*) treno || *tr* chiamare col nome di

stylish ['staɪlɪʃ] *adj* alla moda, di tono

sty·mie ['staɪmi] *v* (*pret & pp* **-mied;** *ger* **-mieing**) *tr* ostacolare, contrastare

styp′tic pen′cil ['stɪptɪk] *s* matita emostatica

Styx [stɪks] *s* Stige *m*

suave [swɑv] or [swev] *adj* soave

subaltern [səb'ɔltərn] *adj & s* subalterno

subcommittee ['sʌbkə,mɪti] *s* sottocommissione

subconscious [səb'kɑnʃəs] *adj & s* subcosciente *m*

subconsciousness [səb'kɑnʃəsnɪs] *s* subcosciente *m,* subcoscienza

sub′deb′ *s* (coll) signorina più giovane di una debuttante

subdivide [,sʌbdɪ,vaɪd] or [,sʌbdɪ'vaɪd] *tr* suddividere || *intr* suddividersi

subdue [səb'dju] or [səb'du] *tr* soggiogare, sottomettere; (*color, voice*) attenuare

subdued [səb'djud] or [səb'dud] *adj* (*voice*) sommesso; (*light*) tenue

subheading ['sʌb‚hedɪŋ] s sottotitolo; (journ) sommario

subject ['sʌbdʒɪkt] adj soggetto; **subject to** (e.g., a cold) soggetto a; (e.g., a fine) passibile di || s soggetto, materia, proposito; (of a ruler) suddito; (gram, med, philos) soggetto || [səb-'dʒɛkt] tr sottomettere

sub'ject cat'alogue s catalogo per materie

sub'ject in'dex s indice m per materie

subjection [səb'dʒɛk/ən] s soggezione

subjective ['sʌbdʒə'ktɪv] adj soggettivo

sub'ject mat'ter s soggetto

subjugate ['sʌbdʒə‚get] tr soggiogare

subjunctive [səb'dʒʌŋktɪv] adj & s congiuntivo

sublease ['sʌb‚lis] s subaffitto || [‚sʌb-'lis] tr subaffittare

sub·let ['sʌb'let] or ['sʌb‚let] v (pret & pp -let; ger -letting) tr subaffittare

sub·machine' gun' [‚sʌbmə'/in] s mitra m

submarine ['sʌbmə‚rin] adj & s sottomarino

sub'marine chas'er ['t/esər] s cacciasommergibili m

submerge [səb'mʌrdʒ] tr sommergere || intr sommergersi

submersion [səb'mʌrʒən] or [səb-'mʌr/ən] s sommersione

submission [səb'mɪ/ən] s sottomissione

submissive [səb'mɪsɪv] adj sottomesso

sub·mit [səb'mɪt] v (pret & pp -mitted; ger -mitting) tr sottomettere; presentare, deferire; osservare rispettosamente || intr sottomettersi

subordinate [səb'ɔrdɪnɪt] adj & s subordinato || [səb'ɔrdɪ‚net] tr subordinare

suborna'tion of per'jury [‚sʌbər'ne/ən] s subornazione

subplot ['sʌb‚plɑt] s intreccio secondario

subpoena or **subpena** [sʌb'pinə] or [sə-'pinə] s mandato di comparizione || tr citare

sub rosa [sʌb'rozə] adv in segreto

subscribe [səb'skraɪb] tr sottoscrivere || intr sottoscrivere; **to subscribe to** sottoscrivere a; (a magazine) abbonarsi a; (an opinion) approvare

subscriber [səb'skraɪbər] s sottoscrittore m; abbonato

subscription [səb'skrɪp/ən] s sottoscrizione; (e.g., to a newspaper) abbonamento; (e.g., to club) quota

subsequent ['sʌbsɪkwənt] adj susseguente, posteriore

subservient [səb'sʌrvɪ‚ənt] adj subordinato; ossequioso, servile

subside [səb'saɪd] intr calmarsi; (said of water) decrescere

subsidiar·y [səb'sɪdɪ‚ɛri] adj sussidiario || s (-ies) sussidiario

subsidize ['sʌbsɪ‚daɪz] tr sussidiare, sovvenzionare; (by bribery) subornare

subsi·dy ['sʌbsɪdi] s (-dies) sussidio, sovvenzione

subsist [səb'sɪst] intr sussistere

subsistence [səb'sɪstəns] s sussistenza

subsoil ['sʌb‚sɔɪl] s sottosuolo

substance ['sʌbstəns] s sostanza

substandard [sʌb'stændərd] adj inferiore al livello normale

substantial [səb'stæn/əl] adj considerevole; ricco, influente; (food) sostanzioso; (e.g., reason) sostanziale

substantiate [səb'stæn/ɪ‚et] tr provare, verificare; dare prova di, sostanziare

substantive ['sʌbstəntɪv] adj & s sostantivo

substation ['sʌb‚ste/ən] s ufficio postale secondario; (elec) sottostazione

substitute ['sʌbstɪ‚tjut] or ['sʌbstɪ‚tut] adj provvisorio, interino || s (thing) sostituto, surrogato; (person) sostituto, supplente mf; **beware of substitutes** guardarsi dalle contraffazioni || tr—**to substitute for** sostituire (qlco or qlcu) a || intr—**to substitute for** sostituire, rimpiazzare, e.g., **he substituted for the teacher** sostituì il maestro

substitution [‚sʌbstɪ'tju/ən] or [‚sʌb-stɪ'tu/ən] s sostituzione; (by fraud) contraffazione

substra·tum ['sʌb‚strætəm] s (-ta [tə]) sostrato, substrato

subterfuge ['sʌbtər‚fjudʒ] s sotterfugio

subterranean [‚sʌbtə'reni‚ən] adj & s sotterraneo

subtitle ['sʌb‚taɪtəl] s sottotitolo; (journ) titolo corrente; (mov) didascalia || tr dare una didascalia a

subtle ['sʌtəl] adj sottile

subtle·ty ['sʌtəlti] s (-ties) sottigliezza

subtract [səb'trækt] tr sottrarre

subtraction [səb'træk/ən] s sottrazione

suburb ['sʌbʌrb] s suburbio, sobborgo; **the suburbs** la periferia

suburban [sə'bʌrbən] adj suburbano

suburbanite [sə'bʌrbə‚naɪt] s abitante mf dei suburbi

subvention [səb'vɛn/ən] s sovvenzione || tr sovvenzionare

subversive [səb'vʌrsɪv] adj & s sovversivo

subvert [səb'vʌrt] tr sovvertire

subway ['sʌb‚we] s sotterranea, metropolitana, metrovia; sottopassaggio

sub'way sta'tion s stazione della metropolitana

succeed [sək'sid] tr succedere (with dat), subentrare (with dat) || intr riuscire; **to succeed to** (the throne) succedere a

success [sək'sɛs] s successo, riuscita

successful [sək'sɛsfəl] adj felice, fortunato; che ha avuto successo

succession [sək'sɛ/ən] s successione; **in succession** in seguito, uno dopo l'altro

successive [sək'sɛsɪv] adj successivo

succor ['sʌkər] s soccorso || tr soccorrere

succotash ['sʌkə‚tæ/] s verdura di fagioli e granturco

succumb [sə'kʌm] intr soccombere

such [sʌt/] adj & pron indef tale, simile; **such a** un simile, un tale; **such**

a + *adj* tanto + *adj*, e.g., **such a beautiful story** una storia tanto bella;
such as tale quale, come

suck [sʌk] *s* succhio ‖ *tr* succhiare;
(*air*) aspirare; **to suck in** (slang) ingannare

sucker ['sʌkər] *s* lattante *mf*; (bot)
succhione *m*; (mach) pistone *m*;
(coll) fesso, pollo, minchione *m*

suckle ['sʌkəl] *tr* allattare; nutrire ‖
intr poppare

suck'ling pig' ['sʌklɪŋ] *s* maiale *m*
di latte

suction ['sʌkʃən] *s* aspirazione

suc'tion cup' *s* ventosa

suc'tion pump' *s* pompa aspirante

sudden ['sʌdən] *adj* subito, improvviso; **all of a sudden** all'improvviso

suddenly ['sʌdənli] *adv* all'improvviso

suds [sʌdz] *spl* saponata; schiuma;
(coll) birra

sue [su] *or* [sju] *tr* querelare ‖ *intr*
querelarsi; **to sue for damages** chiedere i danni; **to sue for peace** chiedere la pace

suede [swed] *s* pelle scamosciata

suet ['su·ɪt] *or* ['sju·ɪt] *s* grasso, sego

suffer ['sʌfər] *tr* soffrire; (e.g., *heavy
losses*) subire ‖ *intr* soffrire, patire

sufferance ['sʌfərəns] *s* tolleranza

suffering ['sʌfərɪŋ] *adj* sofferente ‖ *s*
sofferenza, strazio, patimento

suffice [sə'faɪs] *intr* bastare

sufficient [sə'frʃənt] *adj* sufficiente

suffix ['sʌfɪks] *s* suffisso

suffocate ['sʌfə‚ket] *tr* & *intr* soffocare

suffrage ['sʌfrɪdʒ] *s* suffragio

suffragette [‚sʌfrə'dʒɛt] *s* suffragetta

suffuse [sə'fjuz] *tr* soffondere

sugar ['ʃʊgər] *adj* (water) zuccherato;
(*industry*) zuccheriero ‖ *s* zucchero ‖
tr zuccherare

sug'ar beet' *s* barbabietola da zucchero

sug'ar bowl' *s* zuccheriera

sug'ar cane' *s* canna da zucchero

sug'ar-coat' *tr* inzuccherare; (e.g., *the
pill*) addolcire

sug'ar ma'ple *s* acero

sug'ar-plum' *s* zuccherino

sug'ar spoon' *s* cucchiaino per lo zucchero

sug'ar tongs' *spl* mollette *fpl* per lo
zucchero

sugary ['ʃʊgəri] *adj* zuccherino, zuc-
cheroso

suggest [səg'dʒɛst] *tr* suggerire

suggestion [səg'dʒɛstʃən] *s* suggerimento; (psychol) suggestione; ombra,
traccia

suggestive [səg'dʒɛstɪv] *adj* suggestivo;
(*risqué*) scabroso

suicidal [‚su·ɪ'saɪdəl] *or* [‚sju·ɪ-
'saɪdəl] *adj* suicida

suicide ['su·ɪ‚saɪd] *or* ['sju·ɪ‚saɪd] *s*
(*person*) suicida *mf*; (act) suicidio;
to commit suicide suicidarsi

suit [sut] *or* [sjut] *s* vestito da uomo;
(*of a lady*) tailleur *m*; (of cards)
seme *m*, colore *m*; (for bathing) costume *m*; corte *f*, corteggiamento;
domanda, supplica; (law) causa; **to
follow suit** seguire l'esempio; (cards)

rispondere a colore ‖ *tr* adattarsi
(with *dat*); convenire (with *dat*);
suit yourself faccia come vuole ‖
intr convenire, andare a proposito

suitable ['sutəbəl] *or* ['sjutəbəl] *adj*
indicato, conveniente

suit'case' *s* valigia

suite [swit] *s* gruppo, serie *f*; serie *f*
di stanze; (of furniture) mobilia;
(*retinue*) seguito; (mus) suite *f*

suiting ['sutɪŋ] *or* ['sjutɪŋ] *s* taglio
d'abito

suit' of clothes' *s* completo maschile

suitor ['sutər] *or* ['sjutər] *s* pretendente *m*; (law) querelante *mf*

sul'fa drugs' ['sʌlfə] *spl* sulfamidici
mpl

sulfate ['sʌlfet] *s* solfato

sulfide ['sʌlfaɪd] *s* solfuro

sulfite ['sʌlfaɪt] *s* solfito

sulfur ['sʌlfər] *adj* solfiero ‖ *s* zolfo;
color *m* zolfo

sulfuric [sʌl'fjurɪk] *adj* solforico

sul'fur mine' *s* solfara

sulfurous ['sʌlfərəs] *adj* solforoso

sulk [sʌlk] *s* broncio ‖ *intr* imbronciarsi

sulk·y ['sʌlki] *adj* (-ier; -iest) imbronciato ‖ *s* (-ies) (in horse racing) se-
diolo, sulky *m*

sullen ['sʌlən] *adj* bieco, triste, tetro

sul·ly ['sʌli] *v* (pret & pp -lied) *tr* insudiciare, insozzare

sulphur ['sʌlfər] *adj* & *s* var of **sulfur**

sultan ['sʌltən] *s* sultano

sul·try ['sʌltri] *adj* (-trier; -triest) soffocante; infocato, appassionato

sum [sʌm] *s* somma; sommario; problema *m* di aritmetica ‖ *v* (pret &
pp **summed**; ger **summing**) *tr* som-
mare; **to sum up** riepilogare

sumac *or* **sumach** ['ʃumæk] *or*
['sumæk] *s* (bot) sommacco

summarize ['sʌmə‚raɪz] *tr* riassumere

summa·ry ['sʌməri] *adj* sommario ‖ *s*
(-ries) sommario, sunto

summer ['sʌmər] *adj* estivo ‖ *s* estate
f ‖ *intr* passare l'estate

sum'mer resort' *s* stazione estiva

summersault ['sʌmər‚sɔlt] *s* & *intr* var
of **somersault**

sum'mer school' *s* scuola estiva

summery ['sʌməri] *adj* estivo

summit ['sʌmɪt] *s* sommità *f*

sum'mit con'ference *s* riunione al vertice

summon ['sʌmən] *tr* convocare, invitare; evocare; (law) compulsare

summons ['sʌmənz] *s* ordine *m*, comando; (law) citazione ‖ *tr* (law)
citare

sumptuous ['sʌmptʃu·əs] *adj* sontuoso

sun [sʌn] *s* sole *m*; **place in the sun**
posto al sole ‖ *v* (pret & pp **sunned**;
ger **sunning**) *tr* esporre al sole ‖ *intr*
prendere il sole

sun' bath' *s* bagno di sole

sun'beam' *s* raggio di sole

sun'burn' *s* abbronzatura ‖ *v* (pret &
pp **-burned** or **-burnt**) *tr* abbronzare
‖ *intr* abbronzarsi

sundae ['sʌndi] s gelato con sciroppo, frutta o noci

Sunday ['sʌndi] adj domenicale || s domenica

Sun'day best' s (coll) vestito da festa

Sun'day's child' s bambino nato con la camicia

Sun'day school' s scuola domenicale della dottrina

sunder ['sʌndər] tr separare

sun'di'al s meridiana

sun'down' s tramonto

sundries ['sʌndriz] spl generi mpl diversi

sundry ['sʌndri] adj vari, diversi

sun'fish' s pesce m mola, pesce m luna

sun'flow'er s girasole m

sun'glass'es spl occhiali mpl da sole

sunken ['sʌŋkən] adj affondato, sommerso; (hollow) incavato

sun' lamp' s sole m artificiale

sun'light' s luce f del sole

sun'lit' adj illuminato dal sole

sun·ny ['sʌni] adj (-nier; -niest) solatìo, soleggiato; allegro, ridente; **it is sunny** fa sole

sun'ny side' s parte soleggiata; lato buono; **on the sunny side of** (e.g., thirty) al disotto dei . . . anni

sun' porch' s veranda a solatìo

sun'rise' s sorgere m del sole; **from sunrise to sunset** dall'alba al tramonto

sun'set' s tramonto

sun'shade' s tenda; parasole m

sun'shine' s sole m, luce f del sole; **in the sunshine** al sole

sun'spot' s macchia solare

sun'stroke' s insolazione

sun' tan' s tintarella

sun'tan lo'tion s pomata antisole, abbronzante m

sun'up' s sorgere m, levare m del sole

sun' vi'sor s (aut) aletta parasole, parasole m

sup [sʌp] v (pret & pp supped; ger supping) intr cenare

super ['supər] adj (coll) superficiale; (coll) di prim'ordine, super || s (coll) sovrintendente m; (coll) articolo di prim'ordine, super m

superabundant [,supərə'bʌndənt] adj sovrabbondante

superannuated [,super'ænju,etid] adj giubilato, pensionato; messo a riposo per limiti di età; antiquato

superb [su'pʌrb] or [sə'pʌrb] adj superbo

supercar·go ['supər,kargo] s (-goes) (naut) sopraccarico

supercharge [,supər'tʃardʒ] tr sovralimentare

supercilious [,supər'sɪlɪ·əs] adj altero, arrogante

superficial [,supər'fɪʃəl] adj superficiale

superfluous [su'pʌrflu·əs] adj superfluo

su'per·high'way s autostrada

superhuman [,supər'hjumən] adj sovrumano

superimpose [,supərɪm'poz] tr sovrapporre

superintendent [,supərɪn'tendənt] s soprintendente m; (of schools) provveditore m

superior [sə'pɪrɪ·ər] or [su'pɪrɪ·ər] adj superiore; di superiorità; (typ) esponente || s superiore m

superiority [sə'pɪrɪ'ɑrɪti] or [su,pɪrɪ·'ɑrɪti] s superiorità f

superlative [sə'pʌrlətɪv] or [su'pʌrlətɪv] adj & s superlativo

su'per·man' s (-men') superuomo

supermarket ['supər,markɪt] s supermercato

supernatural [,supər'nætʃərəl] adj soprannaturale

superpose [,supər'poz] tr sovrapporre

supersede [,supər'sid] tr rimpiazzare, sostituire

supersensitive [,supər'sɛnsɪtɪv] adj ipersensibile

supersonic [,supər'sanɪk] adj supersonico

superstition [,supər'stɪʃən] s superstizione

superstitious [,supər'stɪʃəs] adj superstizioso

supervene [,supər'vin] intr sopravvenire

supervise ['supər,vaɪz] tr sorvegliare, dirigere

supervision [,supər'vɪʒən] s supervisione, sorveglianza, direzione

supervisor ['supər,vaɪzər] s supervisore m, sorvegliante mf; ispettore m

supper ['sʌpər] s cena

sup'per·time' s ora di cena

supplant [sə'plænt] tr rimpiazzare

supple ['sʌpəl] adj flessibile; docile

supplement ['sʌplɪmənt] s supplemento || ['sʌplɪ,mɛnt] tr completare, supplire (with dat)

suppliant ['sʌplɪ·ənt] adj & s supplicante mf

supplicant ['sʌplɪkənt] s supplicante mf

supplication [,sʌplɪ'keʃən] s supplica

supplier [sʌ'plaɪ·ər] s fornitore m

sup·ply [sə'plaɪ] s (-plies) rifornimento, fornitura; provvista, scorta; (com) offerta; **supplies** rifornimenti mpl, vettovaglie fpl || v (pret & pp -plied) tr fornire, provvedere; (food) vettovagliare

supply' and demand' s domanda ed offerta

support [sə'port] s sostegno, appoggio; puntello, rincalzo; mantenimento || tr sostenere, appoggiare; puntellare; (a cause) caldeggiare; mantenere

supporter [sə'portər] s fautore m, sostenitore m; (jockstrap) sospensorio; giarrettiera; fascia elastica

suppose [sə'poz] tr supporre; ammettere; **suppose we take a walk?** che ne dice se facessimo una passeggiata?; **to be supposed to be** aver fama di essere; **to suppose so** credere di sì

supposed [sə'pozd] adj presunto

supposition [,sʌpə'zɪʃən] s supposizione

supposito·ry [sə'pazɪ,tori] s (-ries) suppositorio, supposta

suppress [sə'prɛs] tr sopprimere

suppression [sə'prɛʃən] s soppressione

suppurate ['sʌpjə,ret] intr suppurare

supreme [sə'prim] or [su'prim] adj supremo, sommo

Supreme' Court' s (in Italy) Corte f di Cassazione; (in U.S.A.) tribunale m di ultima istanza

surcharge ['sʌr,tʃɑrdʒ] s soprapprezzo; soprattassa; sovraccarico; (philately) sovrastampa || [,sʌr'tʃɑrdʒ] or ['sʌr,tʃɑrdʒ] tr sovraccaricare

sure [ʃur] adj sicuro; to be sure! certamente!, senza dubbio! || interj (coll) certamente!; sure enough! (coll) difatti

sure-footed ['ʃjur'futɪd] adj dal piede sicuro

sure' thing' s (coll) successo garantito || adv (coll) certamente || interj (coll) di sicuro!

sure-ty ['ʃurti] or ['ʃurɪti] s (-ties) malleveria

surf [sʌrf] s frangente m

surface ['sʌrfɪs] adj superficiale || s superficie f || tr rifinire; spianare; ricoprire || intr emergere

sur'face mail' s posta ordinaria

surf'board' s tavola per il surfing

surfeit ['sʌrfɪt] s eccesso; sazietà f || tr saziare, rimpinzare || intr saziarsi, rimpinzarsi

surf'ing s surfing m

surge [sʌrdʒ] s ondata; fiotto; (elec) sovratensione || tr ondeggiare, fluttuare; (said, e.g., of a crowd) affluire

surgeon ['sʌrdʒən] s (medico) chirurgo

surger-y ['sʌrdʒəri] s (-ies) chirurgia; sala operatoria

surgical ['sʌrdʒɪkəl] adj chirurgico

sur-ly ['sʌrli] adj (-lier; -liest) arcigno, imbronciato

surmise [sər'maɪz] or ['sʌrmaɪz] s congettura, supposizione || [sər'maɪz] tr & intr congetturare, supporre

surmount [sər'maunt] tr sormontare; coronare

surname ['sʌr,nem] s cognome m; (added name) soprannome m || tr dare il cognome a; soprannominare

surpass [sər'pæs] or [sər'pɑs] tr sorpassare, superare

surplice ['sʌrplɪs] s cotta

surplus ['sʌrplʌs] adj eccedente || s sopravanzo, eccedenza

surprise [sər'praɪz] adj inaspetato, improvviso || s sorpresa || tr sorprendere

surprise' par'ty s improvvisata

surprising [sər'praɪzɪŋ] adj sorprendente

surrender [sə'rɛndər] s resa || tr arrendere || intr arrendersi

surren'der val'ue s (ins) valore m di riscatto

surreptitious [,sʌrɛp'tɪʃəs] adj clandestino, nascosto, furtivo

surround [sə'raund] tr circondare, contornare; (mil) aggirare

surrounding [sə'raundɪŋ] adj circostante, circonvicino || **surroundings** spl dintorni mpl; ambiente m

surtax ['sʌr,tæks] s sovrimposta, soprattassa; imposta complementare

surveillance [sər'veləns] or [sər'veljəns] s sorveglianza, vigilanza

survey ['sʌrve] s quadro generale, schizzo; indagine f; (of opinion) sondaggio; rapporto; rilievo topografico; perizia || [sʌr've] or ['sʌr've] tr fare un'indagine di; sondare; rilevare; misurare || intr fare un rilievo

sur'vey course' s corso di rassegna generale

surveyor [sər've·ər] s livellatore m, geometra m

survival [sər'vaɪvəl] s sopravvivenza

survive [sər'vaɪv] tr sopravvivere (with dat) || intr sopravvivere

surviving [sər'vaɪvɪŋ] adj superstite

survivor [sər'vaɪvər] s sopravvissuto, superstite mf

survivorship [sər'vaɪvər,ʃɪp] s (law) sopravvivenza

susceptible [sə'sɛptɪbəl] adj suscettibile, ricettivo; impressionabile; **susceptible to** (e.g., colds) soggetto a

suspect ['sʌspɛkt] or [səs'pɛkt] adj sospetto || ['sʌspɛkt] s sospetto || [səs'pɛkt] tr sospettare

suspend [səs'pɛnd] tr sospendere || intr essere sospeso; fermarsi; fermare i pagamenti

suspenders [səs'pɛndərz] spl bretelle fpl

suspense [səs'pɛns] s sospensione; sospeso; **in suspense** in sospeso

suspen'sion bridge' [səs'pɛnʃən] s ponte sospeso

suspicion [səs'pɪʃən] s sospetto

suspicious [səs'pɪʃəs] adj (subject to suspicion) sospetto; (inclined to suspect) sospettoso

sustain [səs'ten] tr sostenere, sorreggere; (with food) sostentare; (a conversation) mantenere; (a loss) soffrire; (law) confermare

sustenance ['sʌstɪnəns] s sostentamento

sutler ['sʌtlər] s (mil) vivandiere m

swab [swab] s (mil) scovolo; (naut) redazza; (surg) batuffolo di cotone || v (pret & pp swabbed; ger swabbing) tr pulire con la redazza; spugnare; assorbire col cotone

swaddle ['swadəl] tr fasciare

swad'dling clothes' spl fasce fpl del neonato

swagger ['swægər] s spavalderia || intr fare lo spavaldo

swain [swen] s innamorato; (lad) contadinotto

swallow ['swalo] s (of liquid) sorso; (of food) boccone m; (orn) rondine f || tr & intr tranguiare, inghiottire

swal'low-tailed coat' ['swalo,teld] s frac m, marsina, abito a coda di rondine

swal'low-wort' s vincetossico

swamp [swamp] s pantano, palude f || tr inondare, sommergere

swamp-y ['swampi] adj (-ier; -iest) paludoso, pantanoso

swan [swan] s cigno

swan' dive' s volo dell'angelo

swank [swæŋk] *adj* (coll) elegante, vistoso ‖ *s* (coll) eleganza vistosa

swan's-down [ˈswɑnz͵daʊn] *s* piuma di cigno, piumino; mollettone *m*

swan' song' *s* canto del cigno

swap [swɑp] *s* scambio, baratto ‖ *v* (*pret & pp* **swapped;** *ger* **swapping**) *tr & intr* scambiare, barattare

swarm [swɔrm] *s* sciame *m* ‖ *intr* sciamare; (fig) formicolare

swarth·y [ˈswɔrði] or [ˈswɔrθi] *adj* (**-ier; -iest**) olivastro, abbronzato

swashbuckler [ˈswɑʃ͵bʌklər] *s* spadaccino, rodomonte *m*

swat [swɑt] *s* colpo ‖ *v* (*pret & pp* **swatted;** *ger* **swatting**) *tr* colpire; (*a fly*) schiacciare

sway [swe] *s* dondolio, ondeggiamento; dominio ‖ *tr* dondolare, fare oscillare; influenzare; dominare ‖ *intr* dondolarsi, ondulare; oscillare

swear [swer] *v* (*pret* **swore** [swor]; *pp* **sworn** [sworn]) *tr* giurare; (*to secrecy*) fare giurare; **to swear in** fare prestar giuramento a; **to swear off** giurare di rinunziare a; **to swear out a warrant** ottenere un atto di accusa sotto giuramento ‖ *intr* giurare; (*to blaspheme*) bestemmiare; **to swear at** maledire; **to swear by** giurare su, avere certezza di; **to swear to** dichiarare sotto giuramento; giurare di + *inf*

swear'word' *s* bestemmia, parolaccia

sweat [swet] *s* sudata; sudore *m* ‖ *v* (*pret & pp* **sweat** or **sweated**) *tr* sudare; far sudare; **to sweat it out** (slang) farcela fino alla fine; **to sweat off** (*weight*) perdere sudando ‖ *intr* sudare

sweater [ˈswetər] *s* maglione *m*, golf *m*, sweater *m*

sweat' shirt' *s* maglione *m* da ginnastica

sweat·y [ˈsweti] *adj* (**-ier; -iest**) sudato; che fa sudare

Swede [swid] *s* svedese *mf*

Sweden [ˈswidən] *s* la Svezia

Swedish [ˈswidɪʃ] *adj & s* svedese *m*

sweep [swip] *s* scopata; movimento circolare; estensione; curva; (*of wind*) soffio; (*of well*) mazzacavallo; **to make a clean sweep of** far piazza pulita di ‖ *v* (*pret & pp* **swept** [swept]) *tr* spazzare, scopare; percorrere con lo sguardo; (*eyes*) dirigere; travolgere ‖ *intr* scopare; passare; estendersi; dragare

sweeper [ˈswipər] *s* spazzino; (*machine*) spazzatrice *f;* (nav) dragamine *m*

sweeping [ˈswipɪŋ] *adj* esteso; travolgente, decisivo ‖ **sweepings** *spl* spazzatura

sweep'-sec'ond *s* lancetta dei secondi a perno centrale

sweep'stakes' *ssg* or *spl* lotteria abbinata alle corse dei cavalli

sweet [swit] *adj* dolce; (*butter*) senza sale; (*cider*) analcolico; **to be sweet on** (coll) essere innamorato di ‖

sweets *spl* dolci *mpl;* (coll) patate *fpl* dolci ‖ *adv* dolcemente; **to smell sweet** saper di buono

sweet'bread' *s* animella

sweet'bri'er *s* eglantina

sweeten [ˈswitən] *tr* inzuccherare; raddolcire; purificare ‖ *intr* raddolcirsi; purificarsi

sweet'heart' *s* innamorato; innamorata; caro, amore *m*

sweet' mar'joram *s* maggiorana

sweet'meats' *spl* dolci *mpl*, confetti *mpl*

sweet' pea' *s* pisello odoroso

sweet' pota'to *s* batata, patata americana; (mus) ocarina

sweet-scented [ˈswit͵sɛntɪd] *adj* odoroso, profumato

sweet' tooth' *s* debole *m* per i dolci

sweet-toothed [ˈswit͵tuθt] *adj* goloso

sweet' wil'liam *s* garofano barbuto

swell [swel] *adj* (slang) elegante; (slang) eccellente, di prim'ordine ‖ *s* gonfiore *m;* onda, ondata; aumento; (mus) crescendo; (slang) elegantone *m* ‖ *v* (*pret* **swelled;** *pp* **swelled** or **swollen** [ˈswolən]) *tr* gonfiare, ingrossare; aumentare ‖ *intr* gonfiare, ingrossarsi; aumentare; (*said of the sea*) alzarsi; (*with pride*) montarsi

swelled' head' *s* borioso; **to have a swelled head** montarsi, essere pieno di sé

swelter [ˈsweltər] *intr* soffocare dal caldo

swept'back wing' *s* ala a freccia

swerve [swʌrv] *s* scarto, sbandamento ‖ *tr* sviare ‖ *intr* scartare, sbandare

swift [swɪft] *adj* rapido ‖ *s* rondone *m* ‖ *adv* rapidamente

swig [swɪg] *s* (coll) sorso ‖ *v* (*pret & pp* **swigged;** *ger* **swigging**) *tr & intr* (coll) bere a grandi sorsi

swill [swɪl] *s* imbratto; risciacquatura ‖ *tr* tracannare, trincare ‖ *intr* bere a lunghi sorsi

swim [swɪm] *s* nuoto; **the swim** (*in social activities*) la corrente ‖ *v* (*pret* **swam** [swæm]; *pp* **swum** [swʌm]; *ger* **swimming**) *tr* traversare a nuoto ‖ *intr* nuotare; essere inondato; (*said of one's head*) girare, e.g., **her head is swimming** le gira la testa

swimmer [ˈswɪmər] *s* nuotatore *m*

swimming [ˈswɪmɪŋ] *s* nuoto

swim'ming pool' *s* piscina

swim'ming trunks' *spl* mutandine *fpl* da bagno

swim'suit' *s* costume *m* da bagno

swindle [ˈswɪndəl] *s* truffa, imbroglio ‖ *tr* truffare, imbrogliare

swine [swaɪn] *s* suino, maiale *m*, porco; **swine** *spl* suini *mpl*

swing [swɪŋ] *s* oscillazione; dondolio; curva; (*suspended seat*) altalena; alternarsi *m;* piena attività; (boxing) sventola; (mus) swing *m;* **free swing** libertà *f* d'azione; **in full swing** (coll) in piena attività ‖ *v* (*pret & pp* **swung** [swʌŋ]) *tr* (e.g., *one's arms*) dondolare, oscillare; (*a weapon*) brandire; (*e.g., a club*) rotare; far girare; appendere; (*a deal*) (coll) riuscire ad ottenere ‖ *intr* dondolare, dondolarsi, oscillare; girare; essere sospeso; cambiare; (boxing) dare una sventola; **to swing open** aprirsi di colpo

swing'ing door' ['swɪŋɪŋ] *s* porta oscillante

swinish ['swaɪnɪʃ] *adj* porcino

swipe [swaɪp] *s* (coll) colpo forte ‖ *tr* (coll) dare un forte colpo a; (slang) portare via, rubare

swirl [swʌrl] *s* turbine *m*, vortice *m* ‖ *tr* far girare ‖ *intr* turbinare

swirling ['swʌrlɪŋ] *adj* vorticoso

swish [swɪʃ] *s* (*of whip*) schiocco; (*of silk*) fruscìo ‖ *tr* (*a whip*) schioccare; ‖ *intr* schioccare; frusciare

Swiss [swɪs] *adj* svizzero ‖ *s* svizzero; **the Swiss** gli svizzeri

Swiss' chard' [tʃɑrd] *s* bietola

Swiss' cheese' *s* groviera

Swiss' Guards' *spl* guardie *fpl* svizzere

switch [swɪtʃ] *s* verga; vergata; (*false hair*) posticcio; cambio, trapasso; (elec) interruttore *m*; (rr) scambio ‖ *tr* battere, frustare; (elec) commutare; (rr) deviare; (fig) girare; **to switch off** (*light, radio, etc.*) spegnere; **to switch on** (*light, radio, etc.*) accendere ‖ *intr* fustigare; cambiare; (rr) deviare

switch'back' *s* strada a zigzag; (rr) tracciato a zigzag

switch'blade knife' *s* coltello a serra-manico

switch'board' *s* quadro

switch'board op'erator *s* centralinista *mf*

switch'ing en'gine *s* locomotiva da manovra

switch'man *s* (-men) deviatore *m*

switch'yard' *s* stazione smistamento

Switzerland ['swɪtsərlənd] *s* la Svizzera

swiv•el ['swɪvəl] *s* perno, gancio girevole ‖ *v* (*pret & pp* **-eled** or **-elled**; *ger* **-eling** or **-elling**) *intr* girare

swiv'el chair' *s* sedia girevole

swoon [swun] *s* deliquio, svenimento ‖ *intr* svenire

swoop [swup] *s* calata a piombo ‖ *intr* calare a piombo, piombare

sword [sord] *s* spada; **at swords' points** pronti a incrociare le spade; **to put to the sword** passare a fil di spada

sword' belt' *s* cinturone *m*

sword' cane' *s* bastone animato

sword'fish' *s* pesce *m* spada

swords'man *s* (-men) spadaccino

sword' swal'lower ['swɑlo-ər] *s* giocoliere *m* che ingoia spade

sword' thrust' *s* stoccata

sworn [sworn] *adj* giurato

sycophant ['sɪkəfənt] *s* adulatore *m*; parassita *mf*

syllable ['sɪləbəl] *s* sillaba

sylla•bus ['sɪləbəs] *s* (**-bi** [,baɪ]) sillabo, sommario scolastico

syllogism ['sɪlə,dʒɪzəm] *s* sillogismo

sylph [sɪlf] *s* silfo; silfide *f*; (fig) silfide *f*

sylvan ['sɪlvən] *adj* silvano

symbol ['sɪmbəl] *s* simbolo

symbolic(al) [sɪm'bɑlɪk(əl)] *adj* simbolico

symbolism ['sɪmbə,lɪzəm] *s* simbolismo

symbolize ['sɪmbə,laɪz] *tr* simboleggiare

symmetric(al) [sɪ'mɛtrɪk(əl)] *adj* simmetrico

symme•try ['sɪmɪtri] *s* (**-tries**) simmetria

sympathetic [,sɪmpə'θɛtɪk] *adj* simpatetico; ben disposto

sympathize ['sɪmpə,θaɪz] *intr*—**to sympathize with** aver compassione di; mostrar comprensione per; (*to be in accord with*) simpatizzare con

sympa•thy ['sɪmpəθi] *s* (**-thies**) compassione, commiserazione; **to be in sympathy with** essere d'accordo con; **to extend one's sympathy to** fare le condoglianze a

sym'pathy strike' *s* sciopero di solidarietà

symphonic [sɪm'fɑnɪk] *adj* sinfonico

sympho•ny ['sɪmfəni] *s* (**-nies**) sinfonia

symposi•um [sɪm'pozɪ-əm] *s* (**-a** [ə]) simposio, colloquio

symptom ['sɪmptəm] *s* sintomo

synagogue ['sɪnə,gɔg] or ['sɪnə,gɑg] *s* sinagoga

synchronize ['sɪŋkrə,naɪz] *tr & intr* sincronizzare

synchronous ['sɪŋkrənəs] *adj* sincrono

sincopation [,sɪŋkə'peʃən] *s* sincope *f*

syncope ['sɪŋkə,pi] *s* (phonet) sincope *f*

syndicate ['sɪndɪkɪt] *s* sindacato ‖ ['sɪndɪ,ket] *tr* organizzare in un sindacato

synonym ['sɪnənɪm] *s* sinonimo

synonymous [sɪ'nɑnɪməs] *adj* sinonimo

synop•sis [sɪ'nɑpsɪs] *s* (**-ses** [siz]) sinossi *f*; (mov) sinopsi *f*

synoptic(al) [sɪ'nɑptɪk(əl)] *adj* sinottico

syntax ['sɪntæks] *s* sintassi *f*

synthe•sis ['sɪnθɪsɪs] *s* (**-ses** [,sɪz]) sintesi *f*

synthesize ['sɪnθɪ,saɪz] *tr* sintetizzare

synthetic(al) [sɪn'θɛtɪk(əl)] *adj* sintetico

syphilis ['sɪfɪlɪs] *s* sifilide *f*

Syria ['sɪrɪ-ə] *s* la Siria

Syrian ['sɪrɪ-ən] *adj & s* siriano

syringe [sɪ'rɪndʒ] or ['sɪrɪndʒ] *s* (*fountain syringe*) schizzetto; (*for hypodermic injections*) siringa ‖ *tr* schizzettare; iniettare

syrup ['sɪrəp] or ['sʌrəp] *s* sciroppo

system ['sɪstəm] *s* sistema *m*

systematic(al) [,sɪstə'mætɪk(əl)] *adj* sistematico

systematize ['sɪstəmə,taɪz] *tr* ridurre a sistema

systole ['sɪstəli] *s* sistole *f*

T

T, t [ti] *s* ventesima lettera dell'alfabeto inglese; **to fit to a T** calzare come un guanto

tab [tæb] *s* (*strap*) linguetta; (*of a pocket*) patta; targa; (*label*) etichetta; **to keep tabs on** (coll) sorvegliare; **to pick up the tab** (coll) pagare il conto

tab·by ['tæbi] *s* (**-bies**) gatto tigrato; gatta; (*spinster*) zitella; vecchia pettegola

tabernacle ['tæbər,nækəl] *s* tabernacolo

table ['tebəl] *s* tavola; (*food*) mensa; (*people at a table*) tavolata; (*synopsis*) quadro, prospetto; (*list or catalogue*) indice *m;* **to turn the tables** rovesciare la posizione; **under the table** ubriaco fradicio || *tr* aggiornare, rinviare

tab·leau ['tæblo] *s* (**-leaus** or **-leaux** [loz]) quadro vivente

ta'ble·cloth' *s* tovaglia

table d'hôte ['tɑbəl'dot] *s* pasto a prezzo fisso

tableful ['tebəl,ful] *s* (*persons*) tavolata; (*food*) tavola apparecchiata

ta'ble·land' *s* tavoliere *m*

ta'ble lin'en *s* biancheria da tavola

ta'ble man'ners *spl* maniere *fpl* a tavola

ta'ble of con'tents *s* indice *m* delle materie

ta'ble·spoon' *s* cucchiaio

tablespoonful ['tebəl,spun,ful] *s* cucchiaiata

tablet ['tæblɪt] *s* (*writing pad*) blocco; (*slab*) lapide *f;* (*flat rigid sheet*) tabella, tavoletta; (*pharm*) disco, pastiglia

ta'ble talk' *s* conversazione familiare a tavola

ta'ble ten'nis *s* ping-pong *m*, tennis *m* da tavolo

ta'ble·ware' *s* servizio da tavola

ta'ble wine' *s* vino da pasto

tabloid ['tæbloɪd] *s* giornale *m* a carattere sensazionale

taboo [tə'bu] *adj & s* tabù *m* || *tr* proibire assolutamente

tabulate ['tæbjə,let] *tr* tabulare

tabulator ['tæbjə,letər] *s* tabulatore *m*, incolonnatore *m*

tachometer [tə'kɑmɪtər] *s* tachimetro

tacit ['tæsɪt] *adj* tacito

taciturn ['tæsɪ,tʌrn] *adj* taciturno

tack [tæk] *s* bulletta; cambio di direzione; (naut) virata; (sew) imbastitura || *tr* imbullettare; attaccare; (naut) bordeggiare; (sew) imbastire || *intr* virare; mutare di direzione

tackle ['tækəl] *s* attrezzatura; (mach) taglia, paranco; (*gear*) (naut) paddiglione *m* || *tr* attaccare, affrontare; (sports) placcare, bloccare

tack·y ['tæki] *adj* (**-ier; -iest**) appiccicaticcio; (coll) trasandato

tact [tækt] *s* tatto

tactful ['tæktfəl] *adj* pieno di tatto

tactical ['tæktɪkəl] *adj* tattico

tactician [tæk'tɪʃən] *s* tattico

tactics ['tæktɪks] *ssg* (mil) tattica || *spl* tattica

tactless ['tæktlɪs] *adj* che non ha tatto, indiscreto

tadpole ['tæd,pol] *s* girino

taffeta ['tæfɪtə] *s* taffettà *m*

taffy ['tæfi] *s* caramella, zucchero d'orzo; (coll) lisciata

tag [tæg] *s* etichetta; (*on a shoelace*) punta dell'aghetto; conclusione; (*last words of speech*) pistolotto finale; epiteto; frase fatta; (*of hair*) ciocca; (*in writing*) ghirigoro; (*game*) toccaferro || *v* (*pret & pp* **tagged**; *ger* **tagging**) *tr* etichettare; (*to fine*) multare; aggiungere; soprannominare; accusare; stabilire il prezzo di; (coll) pedinare || *intr* seguire da presso

tag' end' *s* (*e.g., of day*) fine *f;* estremità logorata; avanzo

tail [tel] *adj* di coda || *s* coda; fine *f;* (*of coin*) croce *f;* **tails** falde *fpl*, frac *m;* **to turn tails** darsela a gambe || *tr* attaccare; finire; (coll) pedinare

tail' assem'bly *s* (aer) impennaggio

tail' end' *s* coda, fine *f*

tail'light' *s* fanale *m* di coda

tailor ['telər] *s* sarto || *tr* (*a suit*) tagliare, confezionare; (*one's conduct*) adattare || *intr* fare il sarto

tailoring ['telərɪŋ] *s* sartoria

tai'lor-made' *adj* fatto su misura

tai'lor shop' *s* sartoria

tail'piece' *s* coda, estremità *f;* (mus) cordiera; (typ) fusello finale

tail'race' *s* canale *m* di scarico

tail'spin' *s* avvitamento

tail'wind' *s* (aer) vento di coda; (naut) vento in poppa

taint [tent] *s* macchia; infezione || *tr* macchiare, infettare, corrompere

take [tek] *s* presa; (*of fish*) retata; (mov) presa; ripresa; (slang) incasso || *v* (*pret* **took** [tuk]; *pp* **taken**) *tr* prendere, pigliare; ricevere, accettare; portare; (*to get by force*) portar via; (*a nap*) schiacciare; (*a bath*) fare; (*a joke*) stare a; (*an examination*) sostenere; (*one's own life*) togliersi; (*to deduct*) cavare; (*a purchase*) comprare; (*to convey*) portare; (*time*) impiegare; (*a step, a walk*) fare; (*a subject*) studiare; (*a responsibility, role, etc.*) assumere; (*an oath*) prestare; (*root*) mettere; (*exception*) sollevare; credere; (*e.g., a photograph*) fare, scattare; (slang) fregare; **it takes** ci vuole, ci vogliono; **to take amiss** prendere a male; **to take apart** scomporre; smontare; **to take back** riprendere; **to take down** abbassare; smontare; prender nota di; **to take for** prendere per; **to take from** portar via a; **to take in** (*to admit*) ammettere, ricevere; (*to encompass*) includere; (*a dress*) restringere; (*to cheat*) ingannare; (*water*) fare; (*a point of inter-*

est) visitare; **to take it** accettare, ammettere; (slang) resistere; **to take off** (*e.g., one's coat*) togliersi; portar via; scontare, defalcare; (slang) imitare; **to take on** ingaggiare; assumere; intraprendere; accettare la sfida di; **to take out** cavare, togliere; (*e.g., a girl*) portar fuori; (*e.g., a patent*) ottenere; **to take over** rilevare; (slang) imbrogliare; **to take place** aver luogo; **to take s.o.'s eye** attrarre l'attenzione di qlcu; **to take the place of** sottentrare a; **to take up** cominciare a studiare; sollevare, tirar su; (*a duty*) assumere; (*time, space*) occupare || *intr* prendere; scattare; darsi; diventare; **to take after** rassomigliare a; **to take off** (coll) partire, andarsene; (aer) decollare, involare; **to take up with** (coll) fare amicizia con; (coll) vivere con; **to take well** riuscire bene in fotografia

take'off' *s* parodia; (aer) decollaggio; (mach) presa di forza

tal'cum pow'der [ˈtælkəm] *s* talco

tale [tel] *s* storia, racconto; favola, fiaba; (*lie*) bugia, frottola; (*piece of gossip*) maldicenza

tale'bear'er *s* pettegolo

talent [ˈtælənt] *s* talento; persona di talento; gente *f* di talento

talented [ˈtæləntɪd] *adj* dotato di talento, dotato d'ingegno

tal'ent scout' *s* scopritore *m* di talenti

talk [tɔk] *s* chiacchierata; discorso, conferenza; (*language*) parlata; (*gossip*) pettegolezzo; **to cause talk** originare pettegolezzi || *tr* parlare; convincere parlando; **to talk up** elogiare || *intr* parlare; discutere; **to talk on** discutere; continuare a parlare; **to talk up** parlare apertamente

talkative [ˈtɔkətɪv] *adj* loquace

talker [ˈtɔkər] *s* parlatore *m*

talkie [ˈtɔki] *s* (coll) parlato

talk'ing machine' *s* grammofono

talk'ing pic'ture *s* film parlato

tall [tɔl] *adj* alto; (coll) stravagante, esagerato

tallow [ˈtælo] *s* sego

tal·ly [ˈtæli] *s* (-lies) tacca, taglia || *v* (*pret & pp* -lied) *tr* contare, registrare || *intr* riscontrarsi

tal'ly sheet' *s* foglio di spunta

talon [ˈtælən] *s* artiglio

tambourine [ˌtæmbəˈrin] *s* tamburello

tame [tem] *adj* addomesticato; docile, mansueto; mite || *tr* addomesticare; domare; (*water power*) captare

tamp [tæmp] *tr* pigiare, comprimere; (*e.g., ground*) costipare

tamper [ˈtæmpər] *s* (*person*) pigiatore *m*; (*tool*) mazzeranga || *intr* intrigare; **to tamper with** (*a lock*) forzare; (*a document*) manomettere; (*a witness*) corrompere

tampon [ˈtæmpɑn] *s* (surg) tampone *m* || *tr* (surg) tamponare

tan [tæn] *adj* marrone; (*by sun*) abbronzato || *v* (*pret & pp* **tanned**; *ger* **tanning**) *tr* (*leather*) conciare; abbronzare; (coll) picchiare, sculacciare

tandem [ˈtændəm] *adj & adv* in tandem || *s* tandem *m*

tang [tæŋ] *s* sapore *m* piccante; odore *m* forte; traccia; (*of knife*) tallone *m*; (*sound*) tintinnio

tangent [ˈtændʒənt] *adj* tangente || *s* tangente *f*; **to fly off at a tangent** cambiare improvvisamente d'idea

tangerine [ˌtændʒəˈrin] *s* mandarino

tangible [ˈtændʒɪbəl] *adj* tangibile

Tangier [tænˈdʒɪr] *s* Tangeri *f*

tangle [ˈtæŋɡəl] *s* intrico; (coll) litigio || *tr* intricare || *intr* intricarsi; (coll) litigare

tank [tæŋk] *s* conserva, serbatoio; (mil) carro armato

tankard [ˈtæŋkərd] *s* boccale *m*

tank' car' *s* (rr) carro botte

tanker [ˈtæŋkər] *s* petroliera; (aer) aerocisterna

tank' farm'ing *s* idroponica

tank' truck' *s* autocisterna

tanner [ˈtænər] *s* conciapelli *m*

tanner·y [ˈtænəri] *s* (-ies) conceria

tantalize [ˈtæntəˌlaɪz] *tr* stuzzicare con vane promesse

tantamount [ˈtæntəˌmaʊnt] *adj* equivalente

tantrum [ˈtæntrəm] *s* bizze *fpl*

tap [tæp] *s* colpetto, buffetto; (*in a keg*) spina, cannella; (*faucet*) rubinetto; (elec) presa; (mach) maschio; **on tap** alla spina; (coll) disponibile; **taps** (mil) silenzio || *v* (*pret & pp* **tapped**; *ger* **tapping**) *tr* battere; picchiare, picchiettare; (*from a barrel*) spillare; mettere il cannello a; (*resources*) usare; (*a telephone*) intercettare; (*water, electricity*) derivare; (mach) maschiare || *intr* picchiare

tap' dance' *s* tip tap *m*

tap'-dance' *intr* ballare il tip tap

tape [tep] *s* nastro; (sports) striscione *m* del traguardo || *tr* legare con nastro; misurare col metro a nastro; registrare su nastro magnetico

tape' meas'ure *s* metro a nastro; nastro per misurare

tape' play'er *s* riproduttore *m* a nastro magnetico

taper [ˈtepər] *s* cerino || *tr* affusolare || *intr* affusolarsi; **to taper off** rastremarsi; diminuire in intensità; diminuire a poco a poco

tape'-re·cord' *tr* registrare su nastro magnetico

tape' record'er *s* magnetofono, registratore *m* a nastro

tapes·try [ˈtæpɪstri] *s* (-tries) tappezzeria || *v* (*pret & pp* -tried) *tr* tappezzare

tape'worm' *s* verme solitario, tenia

tappet [ˈtæpɪt] *s* (aut) punteria

tap'room' *s* taverna, osteria

tap'root' *s* radice *f* a fittone

tap' wa'ter *s* acqua corrente

tap' wrench' *s* giramaschio

tar [tɑr] *s* catrame *m* || *v* (*pret & pp* **tarred**; *ger* **tarring**) *tr* incatramare

tar·dy ['tɑrdi] *adj* (-dier; -diest) in ritardo; lento

tare [ter] *s* tara ‖ *tr* tarare

target ['tɑrgɪt] *s* segno, bersaglio

tar'get date' *s* data progettata

tar'get lan'guage *s* lingua obbiettivo, lingua di arrivo

tar'get prac'tice *s* esercizio di tiro a segno

tariff ['tærɪf] *s* (*duties*) tariffa doganale; (*charge or fare*) tariffa

tarnish ['tɑrnɪʃ] *s* ossidazione; (fig) macchia ‖ *tr* appannare ‖ *intr* appannarsi, perdere il lustro

tar' pa'per *s* carta catramata

tarpaulin [tɑr'pɔlɪn] *s* telone *m* impermeabile incatramato

tarragon ['tærəgən] *s* dragoncello

tar·ry ['tɑri] *adj* incatramato ‖ ['tæri] *v* (*pret & pp* -ried) *intr* rimanere; ritardare

tart [tɑrt] *adj* acido, pungente ‖ *s* torta; (slang) puttana

tartar ['tɑrtər] *s* tartaro; cremore *m* di tartaro; (*shrew*) megera; **to catch a tartar** imbattersi in un muso duro

Tartarus ['tɑrtərəs] *s* Tartaro

task [tæsk] or [tɑsk] *s* compito, incarico; **to take to task** rimproverare

task' force' *s* gruppo formato per una missione speciale

task'mas'ter *s* sorvegliante *m*; sorvegliante severo

tassel ['tæsəl] *s* nappa; (bot) ciuffo

taste [test] (test) *s* gusto, sapore *m*; buon gusto; (*sampling, e.g., of wine*) assaggio; esperienza; **to one's taste** a genio di qlcu ‖ *tr* gustare, assaggiare ‖ *intr* sentire, sapere; **to taste of** degustare; sapere di

tasteless ['testlɪs] *adj* insipido; di cattivo gusto

tast·y ['testi] *adj* (-ier; -iest) saporito; (coll) di buon gusto

tatter ['tætər] *s* brandello, sbrendolo ‖ *tr* sbrindellare

tattered ['tætərd] *adj* sbrindellato

tattle ['tætəl] *s* chiacchiera; (*gossip*) pettegolezzo ‖ *intr* chiacchierare; spettegolare

tat'tle-tale' *adj* rivelatore ‖ *s* gazzetta, chiacchierone *m*

tattoo [tæ'tu] *s* tatuaggio; (mil) ritirata ‖ *tr* tatuare

taunt [tɔnt] or [tɑnt] *s* rimprovero sarcastico, insulto ‖ *tr* rimproverare sarcasticamente, insultare

Taurus ['tɔrəs] *s* (astr) Toro

taut [tɔt] *adj* teso, tirato

tavern ['tævərn] *s* osteria

taw·dry ['tɔdri] *adj* (-drier; -driest) vistoso, sgargiante, pacchiano

taw·ny ['tɔni] *adj* (-nier; -niest) falbo, fulvo

tax [tæks] *s* tassa, imposta ‖ *tr* tassare; (*s.o.'s patience*) mettere a dura prova

taxable ['tæksəbəl] *adj* tassabile

tax'able in'come *s* imponibile *m*

taxation [tæk'seʃən] *s* imposizione, tassazione, contribuzione

tax' collec'tor *s* esattore *m* delle imposte

tax' deduc'tion *s* detrazione

tax'-ex·empt' *adj* esente da tasse

tax' evad'er [ɪ'vedər] *s* evasore *m*

tax·i ['tæksi] *s* (-is) tassì *m* ‖ *v* (*pret & pp* -ied; *ger* -iing or -ying) *tr* far rullare ‖ *intr* andare in tassì; (aer) rullare

tax'i·cab' *s* tassì *m*

tax'i driv'er *s* tassista *m*

tax'i·plane' *s* aeroplano da noleggio, aerotassì *m*

tax' stand' *s* posteggio di tassì

tax'pay'er *s* contribuente *mf*

tax' rate' *s* imponibilità *f*

tea [ti] *s* tè *m*; (*medicinal infusion*) tisana; (*beef broth*) brodo di carne

tea' bag' *s* sacchetto di tè

tea' ball' *s* uovo da tè

tea'cart' *s* servitore *m*

teach [titʃ] *v* (*pret & pp* taught [tɔt]) *tr & intr* insegnare

teacher ['titʃər] *s* maestro, insegnante *mf*

teach'ers col'lege *s* scuola magistrale

teach'er's pet' *s* beniamino del maestro

teaching ['titʃɪŋ] *adj* insegnante ‖ *s* insegnamento, dottrina

teach'ing aids' *spl* sussidi *mpl* didattici

teach'ing staff' *s* corpo insegnante

tea'cup' *s* tazza da tè

tea' dance' *s* tè *m* danzante

teak [tik] *s* tek *m*

tea'ket'tle *s* bricco del tè

team [tim] *s* (*e.g., of horses*) pariglia; (sports) squadra, equipaggio ‖ *tr* apparigliare; tirare or trasportare con pariglia ‖ *intr*—**to team up** unirsi, associarsi

team'mate' *s* compagno di squadra

teamster ['timstər] *s* (*of horses*) carrettiere *m*; (*of truck*) camionista *m*, autotrenista *m*

team'work' *s* affiatamento, collaborazione

tea'pot' *s* teiera

tear [tɪr] *s* lacrima; **to hold back one's tears** ingoiare le lacrime; **to laugh away one's tears** cambiare dal pianto al riso ‖ [ter] *s* strappo ‖ [ter] *v* (*pret* tore [tor]; *pp* torn [torn]) *tr* strappare; stracciare; (*one's heart*) squarciare; (*to wound*) sbranare; (*one's hair*) strapparsi; **to tear apart** rompere in due; separare; **to tear down** demolire; (*a piece of equipment*) smontare; **to tear off** staccare; **to tear to pieces** dilaniare; fare a pezzi; **to tear up** (*a piece of paper*) stracciare; (*a street*) scavare ‖ *intr* strapparsi, stracciarsi; **to tear along** precipitarsi; correre all'impazzata

tear' bomb' [tɪr] *s* bomba lacrimogena

tearful ['tɪrfəl] *adj* lacrimoso

tear' gas' [tɪr] *s* gas lacrimogeno

tear-jerker ['tɪr ‚dʒʌrkər] *s* (coll) storia lacrimogena

tear-off ['ter ‚ɔf] *adj* da staccarsi, perforato

tea'room' *s* sala da tè

tear' sheet' [ter] *s* copia di annuncio pubblicitario

tease [tiz] *tr* stuzzicare, molestare;

(*hair*) accotonare; (*e.g., wool*) cardare

tea'spoon' *s* cucchiaino

teaspoonful ['ti,spun,fʊl] *s* cucchiaino

teat [tit] *s* capezzolo

tea'time' *s* l'ora del tè

tea' wag'on *s* servitore *m*

technical ['tɛknɪkəl] *adj* tecnico

technicali·ty [,tɛknɪ'kælɪti] *s* (**-ties**) tecnicismo; dettaglio tecnico

technician [tɛk'nɪʃən] *s* tecnico

technics ['tɛknɪks] *ssg* or *spl* tecnica

technique [tɛk'nik] *s* tecnica

ted'dy bear' ['tɛdi] *s* orsacchiotto

tedious ['tidɪ·əs] or ['tidʒəs] *adj* tedioso, noioso

tee [ti] *adj* fatto a T ‖ *s* giunto a tre vie; (*golf*) piazzola di partenza ‖ *tr—* **to tee off** (*slang*) cominciare ‖ *intr—* **to be teed off** (*slang*) essere arrabbiato; **to tee off** (*golf*) colpire la palla dalla piazzola di partenza; **to tee off on** (*slang*) rimproverare severamente

teem [tim] *intr* brulicare; piovere a dirotto; **to teem with** abbondare di

teeming ['timɪŋ] *adj* brulicante; (*rain*) torrenziale

teen-ager ['tin,edʒər] *s* giovane *mf* dai 13 ai 19 anni

teens [tinz] *spl* numeri inglesi che finiscono in **-teen** (dal 13 al 19); **to be in one's teens** avere dai 13 ai 19 anni

tee·ny ['tini] *adj* (**-nier; -niest**) (coll) piccolo, piccolissimo

teeter ['titər] *s* altalena, dondolio ‖ *intr* dondolarsi, oscillare

teethe [tið] *intr* mettere i denti

teething ['tiðɪŋ] *s* dentizione

teeth'ing ring' *s* dentaruolo

teetotaler [ti'totələr] *s* astemio

tele-cast ['tɛlɪ,kæst] or ['tɛlɪ,kɑst] *s* teletrasmissione ‖ *v* (*pret & pp* **-cast** or **-casted**) *tr & intr* teletrasmettere

telegram ['tɛlɪ,græm] *s* telegramma *m*

telegraph ['tɛlɪ,græf] or ['tɛlɪ,grɑf] *s* telegrafo ‖ *tr & intr* telegrafare

tel'egraph pole' *s* palo del telegrafo

Telemachus [tɪ'lɛməkəs] *s* Telemaco

telemeter [tɪ'lɛmɪtər] *s* telemetro ‖ *tr* misurare col telemetro

telepathy [tɪ'lɛpəθi] *s* telepatia

telephone ['tɛlɪ,fon] *s* telefono ‖ *tr & intr* telefonare

tel'ephone book' *s* elenco or guida dei telefoni

tel'ephone booth' *s* cabina telefonica

tel'ephone call' *s* chiamata telefonica, colpo di telefono

tel'ephone direc'tory *s* elenco or guida dei telefoni

tel'ephone exchange' *s* centrale telefonica

tel'ephone op'erator *s* centralinista *mf*, telefonista *mf*

tel'ephone receiv'er *s* ricevitore *m*

tel'ephoto lens' ['tɛlɪ,foto] *s* teleobbiettivo

teleplay ['tɛlɪ,ple] *s* teledramma *m*

teleprinter ['tɛlɪ,prɪntər] *s* telescrivente *f*

telescope ['tɛlɪ,skop] *s* telescopio ‖ *tr*

snodare; condensare ‖ *intr* essere snodabile; (*in a collision*) incastrarsi

teletype ['tɛlɪ,taɪp] *s* telescrivente *f* ‖ *tr & intr* trasmettere per telescrivente

teleview ['tɛlɪ,vju] *tr* telericevere

televiewer ['tɛlɪ,vju·ər] *s* telespettatore *m*

televise ['tɛlɪ,vaɪz] *tr* teletrasmettere

television ['tɛlɪ,vɪʒən] *adj* televisivo ‖ *s* televisione

tel'evision screen' *s* teleschermo

tel'evision set' *s* televisore *m*

tell [tɛl] *v* (*pret & pp* **told** [told]) *tr* dire; (*to narrate*) raccontare; (*to count*) contare; distinguere; **I told you so!** te l'avevo detto!; **to tell off** (coll) dire il fatto suo a ‖ *intr* dire; prevedere; avere effetto; **to tell on** (*s.o.'s health*) pesare a, e.g., **age was telling on his health** l'età pesava alla sua salute; (coll) denunciare

teller ['tɛlər] *s* narratore *m*; (*of bank*) cassiere *m*; (*of votes*) scrutatore *m*

temper ['tɛmpər] *s* indole *f*, temperamento; umore *m*; calma; (*metallurgy*) tempra; **to keep one's temper** mantenersi calmo; **to lose one's temper** perdere la pazienza ‖ *tr* temprare ‖ *intr* temprarsi

temperament ['tɛmpərəmənt] *s* indole *f*, temperamento, carattere *m*

temperamental [,tɛmpərə'mɛntəl] *adj* emotivo, capriccioso

temperance ['tɛmpərəns] *s* (*self-restraint in action*) temperanza; (*abstinence from alcoholic beverages*) sobrietà *f*

temperate ['tɛmpərɪt] *adj* temperato

temperature ['tɛmpərətʃər] *s* temperatura

tempest ['tɛmpɪst] *s* tempesta; **tempest in a teapot** tempesta in un bicchier d'acqua

tempestuous [tɛm'pɛstʃʊ·əs] *adj* tempestoso

temple ['tɛmpəl] *s* (*place of worship*) tempio; (*of spectacles*) susta, stanghetta; (*anat*) tempia

tem·po ['tɛmpo] *s* (**-pos** or **-pi** [pi]) (mus) tempo; (fig) ritmo

temporal ['tɛmpərəl] *adj* temporale

temporary ['tɛmpə,rɛri] *adj* temporaneo, provvisorio, transitorio, interino

temporize ['tɛmpə,raɪz] *intr* temporeggiare

tempt [tɛmpt] *tr* tentare

temptation [tɛmp'teʃən] *s* tentazione

tempter ['tɛmptər] *s* tentatore *m*

tempting ['tɛmptɪŋ] *adj* tentatore

ten [tɛn] *adj & pron* dieci ‖ *s* dieci *m*; **ten o'clock** le dieci

tenable ['tɛnəbəl] *adj* difendibile

tenacious [tɪ'neʃəs] *adj* tenace

tenant ['tɛnənt] *s* inquilino, pigionante *mf*; (*of land*) fittavolo

tend [tɛnd] *tr* riguardare, governare; accudire (with *dat*), e.g., **he tends the fire** accudisce al fuoco ‖ *intr* tendere; **to tend to** propendere verso; (*e.g., one's own business*) attendere a; **to tend to** + *inf* tendere a + *inf*

tenden·cy ['tɛndənsi] *s* (**-cies**) tendenza, propensione

tender ['tɛndər] *adj* tenero; sensibile, dolorante || *s* offerta; (naut) nave *f* rifornimento; (naut) lancia; (rr) carboniera || *tr* offrire

tender-hearted ['tɛndər ,hɑrtɪd] *adj* dal cuore tenero

ten'der·loin' *s* filetto || **Tenderloin** *s* rione *m* della mala vita

tenderness ['tɛndərnɪs] *s* tenerezza

tendon ['tɛndən] *s* tendine *m*

tendril ['tɛndrɪl] *s* viticcio

tenement ['tɛnɪmənt] *s* appartamento; casa; casamento

ten'ement house' *s* casamento

tenet ['tɛnɪt] *s* dogma *m*, dottrina

tennis ['tɛnɪs] *s* tennis *m*

ten'nis court' *s* campo da tennis

ten'nis play'er *s* tennista *mf*

tenor ['tɛnər] *s* tenore *m*

tense [tɛns] *adj* teso || *s* (gram) tempo

tension ['tɛnʃən] *s* tensione

tent [tɛnt] *s* tenda; (*of circus*) tendone *m*

tentacle ['tɛntəkəl] *s* tentacolo

tentative ['tɛntətɪv] *adj* a titolo di prova; (*smile*) esile

tenth [tɛnθ] *adj, s & pron* decimo || *s* (*in dates*) dieci *m*

tenuous ['tɛnju·əs] *adj* tenue

tenure ['tɛnjər] *s* (*in office*) rafferma; (*permanency of employment*) inamovibilità *f*; (law) possesso

tepid ['tɛpɪd] *adj* tiepido

tercet ['tʌrsɪt] *s* terzina

term [tʌrm] *s* vocabolo, voce *f*; periodo, durata; termine *m*; (com) scadenza; **terms** condizioni *fpl*; **to be on good terms** essere in buone relazioni; **to come to terms** venire a patti || *tr* chiamare, definire

termagant ['tʌrməgənt] *s* megera

terminal ['tʌrmɪnəl] *adj* terminale || *s* (*end or extremity*) terminale *m*; (elec) morsetto; (rr) capolinea *m*

terminate ['tʌrmɪ ,net] *tr & intr* terminare

terminus ['tʌrmɪnəs] *s* termine *m*, fine *m*; (rr) capolinea *m*

termite ['tʌrmaɪt] *s* termite *f*

terrace ['tɛrəs] *s* terrazza, terrazzo; (agr) gradino, scaglione *m*

terra firma ['tɛrə 'fʌrmə] *s* terra ferma

terrain [tɛ'ren] *s* terreno

terrestrial [tə'rɛstrɪ·əl] *adj* terrestre

terrific [tə'rɪfɪk] *adj* terrificante; (coll) tremendo

terri·fy ['tɛrɪ ,faɪ] *v* (*pret & pp* **-fied**) *tr* terrificare, inorridire

territo·ry ['tɛrɪ ,tori] *s* (**-ries**) territorio

terror ['tɛrər] *s* terrore *m*

terrorize ['tɛrə ,raɪz] *tr* terrorizzare; dominare col terrore

ter'ry cloth' ['tɛri] *s* tessuto a spugna

terse [tʌrs] *adj* conciso, terso

tertiary ['tʌrʃɪ ,ɛri] or ['tʌrʃəri] *adj* terziario

test [tɛst] *s* prova, saggio; esame *m* || *tr* provare, saggiare; esaminare; (*e.g., a machine*) collaudare

testament ['tɛstəmənt] *s* testamento || **Testament** *s* Testamento Nuovo

test' ban' *s* interdizione degli esperimenti nucleari

test' flight' *s* volo di prova

testicle ['tɛstɪkəl] *s* testicolo

testi·fy ['tɛstɪ ,faɪ] *v* (*pret & pp* **-fied**) *tr & intr* testimoniare

testimonial [,tɛstɪ'moni·əl] *s* (*certificate*) benservito, referenza; (*expression of esteem*) segno di gratitudine

testimo·ny ['tɛstɪ ,moni] *s* (**-nies**) testimonianza

test' pat'tern *s* (telv) monoscopio

test' pi'lot *s* pilota *m* collaudatore

test' tube' *s* provetta

tetanus ['tɛtənəs] *s* tetano

tether ['tɛðər] *s* cavezza, pastoia; **at the end of one's tether** al limite delle proprie risorse || *tr* legare; incavezzare, impastoiare

tetter ['tɛtər] *s* eczema *m*, impetigine *f*

text [tɛkst] *s* testo; tema *m*

text'book' *s* libro di testo

textile ['tɛkstɪl] or ['tɛkstaɪl] *adj & s* tessile *m*

textual ['tɛkstʃʊ·əl] *adj* testuale

texture ['tɛkstʃər] *s* (*of cloth*) trama; caratteristica, proprietà *f*

Thai ['tɑ·i] or ['taɪ] *adj & s* tailandese *mf*

Thailand ['taɪlənd] *s* la Tailandia

Thames [tɛmz] *s* Tamigi *m*

than [ðæn] *conj* di, e.g., **he is faster than you** è più veloce di te; (*before a verb*) di quanto, e.g., **he is smarter than I thought** è più intelligente di quanto pensavo; che, e.g., **he had barely begun to eat than it was time to leave** non aveva appena cominciato a mangiare che era ora di andarsene

thank [θæŋk] *s—***thanks** ringraziamenti *mpl*; **thanks to** grazie a, in grazie di || *tr* ringraziare || **thanks** *interj* grazie!

thankful ['θæŋkfəl] *adj* grato

thankless ['θæŋklɪs] *adj* ingrato

Thanksgiv'ing Day' [,θæŋks'gɪvɪŋ] *s* giorno del Ringraziamento

that [ðæt] *adj* dem. (*those*) quel; codesto; **that one** quello, quello là || *pron dem* (*those*) quello; codesto || *pron rel* che, quello che, il quale; **that is** cioè; **that's that** (coll) ecco fatto, ecco tutto || *adv* (coll) tanto, così; **that far** così lontano; **that many** tanti; **that much** tanto || *conj* che

thatch [θætʃ] *s* paglia, copertura di paglia; (*hair*) capigliatura || *tr* coprire di paglia

thaw [θɔ] *s* sgelo || *tr* sgelare || *intr* sgelarsi

the [ðə], [ðɪ], or [ði] *art def* il; al, e.g., **one dollar the dozen** un dollaro alla dozzina || *adv—***so much the worse for him** tanto peggio per lui; **the more . . . the more** quanto più . . . tanto più

theater ['θi·ətər] *s* teatro

the'ater·go'er *s* frequentatore *m* abituale del teatro

the'ater news' *s* cronaca teatrale

theatrical [θɪ'ætrɪkəl] *adj* teatrale

Thebes [θibz] *s* Tebe *f*

thee [ði] *pron pers* (Bib; poet) ti; te

theft [θɛft] *s* furto, ruberia

their [ðer] *adj poss* il loro, loro

theirs [ðerz] *pron poss* il loro

them [ðem] *pron pers* li; loro; **to them** loro

theme [θim] *s* tema *m*, soggetto; saggio; (mus) tema *m*

theme' song' *s* (mus) tema *m* centrale; (rad) sigla musicale

them·selves' *pron pers* essi stessi, loro stessi; si, se, **e.g., they enjoyed themselves** si divertirono

then [ðen] *adj* allora, di allora ‖ *s* quel tempo; **by then** a quell'epoca; **from then on** da quel giorno in poi ‖ *adv* allora; indi, poi; **then and there** a quel momento

thence [ðens] *adv* indi, quindi; da lì; da allora in poi

thence'forth' *adv* da allora in poi

theolo·gy [θi'ɑlədʒi] *s* (-gies) telogia

theorem ['θiərəm] *s* teorema *m*

theoretical [ˌθi·ə'rɛtɪkəl] *adj* teoretico

theo·ry ['θiəri] *s* (-ries) teoria

therapeutic [ˌθɛrə'pjutɪk] *adj* terapeutico ‖ **therapeutics** *ssg* terapeutica

thera·py ['θɛrəpi] *s* (-pies) terapia

there [ðer] *adv* lì, là; **there are** ci sono; **there is** c'è; ecco, **e.g., there it is** eccolo

there'abouts' *adv* circa, approssimativamente, giù di lì

there'af'ter *adv* in seguito, dipoi

there'by' *adv* quindi, perciò, così

therefore ['ðerfor] *adv* per questo, quindi, dunque

there'in' *adv* lì; in quel rispetto

there'of' *adv* di ciò, da ciò

Theresa [tə'risə] *or* [tə'resə] *s* Teresa

there'upon' *adv* su questo; a quel momento; come conseguenza

thermal ['θʌrməl] *adj* (water) termale; (capacity) termico

thermistor [θər'mɪstər] *s* (elec) termistore *m*

thermocouple ['θʌrmoˌkʌpəl] *s* termocoppia

thermodynamic [ˌθʌrmodaɪ'næmɪk] *adj* termodinamico ‖ **thermodynamics** *ssg* termodinamica

thermometer [θər'mɑmɪtər] *s* termometro

thermonuclear [ˌθʌrmo'njuklɪ·ər] *or* [ˌθʌrmo'nukli·ər] *adj* termonucleare

ther'mos bot'tle ['θʌrməs] *s* termos *m*

thermostat ['θʌrmoˌstæt] *s* termostato

thesau·rus [θi'sɔrəs] *s* (-ri [raɪ] *or* -ruses) tesoro, lessico, compendio

these [ðiz] *pl* of **this**

the·sis ['θisɪs] *s* (-ses [siz]) tesi *f*

Thespis ['θɛspɪs] *s* Tespi *m*

they [ðe] *pron pers* essi, loro

thick [θɪk] *adj* spesso, grosso; folto, denso; pieno, coperto; viscoso; stupido; (coll) intimo ‖ *s* spessore *m*; **in the thick of** nel folto di; **through thick and thin** nei tempi buoni e cattivi

thicken ['θɪkən] *tr* ispessire; ingrossare; infoltire ‖ *intr* ispessirsi; ingrossarsi; (said of a plot) complicarsi

thicket ['θɪkɪt] *s* boscaglia, macchia

thick-headed ['θɪkˌhɛdɪd] *adj* indietro, stupido

thick'set' *adj* tarchiato; (hedge) fitto, denso

thief [θif] *s* (thieves [θivz]) ladro

thieve [θiv] *intr* rubare

thiever·y ['θivəri] *s* (-ies) furto

thigh [θaɪ] *s* coscia

thigh'bone' *s* femore *m*

thimble ['θɪmbəl] *s* ditale *m*

thin [θɪn] *adj* (thinner; thinnest) (paper, ice) sottile; (lean) magro, smilzo; (e.g., hair) rado; (air) fine; (excuse) tenue; (voice) esile; (wine) leggero, annacquato ‖ *v* (pret & pp thinned; ger thinning) *tr* assottigliare; (paint) diluire ‖ *intr* assottigliarsi; **to thin out** (said of a crowd; one's hair) diradarsi

thine [ðaɪn] *adj & pron poss* (Bib & poet) tuo, il tuo

thing [θɪŋ] *s* cosa; **not to get a thing out of** non riuscire a capire; non cavare un briciolo d'informazione da; **of all things!** che cosa!; che sorpresa!; **the thing** l'ultima moda; **things** roba; **to see things** avere allucinazioni

think [θɪŋk] *v* (pret & pp thought [θɔt]) *tr* pensare; credere; **to think it over** ripensarci; **to think nothing of it** non darci la minima importanza; **to think of** (to have as an opinion of) pensare di, e.g., **what do you think of that doctor?** cosa ne pensa di quel medico?; **to think out** decifrare; **to think up** immaginare ‖ *intr* pensare; **to think not** credere di no; **to think of** (to turn one's thoughts to) pensare a, e.g., **he is thinking of the future** pensa al futuro; (to imagine) immaginare; **to think so** credere di sì; **to think well of** avere una buona opinione di

thinkable ['θɪŋkəbəl] *adj* pensabile

thinker ['θɪŋkər] *s* pensatore *m*

third [θʌrd] *adj, s & pron* terzo ‖ *s* terzo; (in dates) tre *m*; (aut) terza

third' degree' *s* interrogatorio di terzo grado

third' rail' *s* (rr) rotaia elettrificata di contatto

third'-rate' *adj* di terz'ordine

Third' World' *s* Terzo Mondo

thirst [θʌrst] *s* sete *f* ‖ *intr* aver sete; **to thirst for** aver sete di

thirst·y ['θʌrsti] *adj* (-ier; -iest) assetato, sitibondo; **to be thirsty** avere sete

thirteen ['θʌr'tin] *adj, s & pron* tredici *m*

thirteenth ['θʌr'tinθ] *adj, s & pron* tredicesimo ‖ *s* (in dates) tredici *m*

thirtieth ['θʌrti·ɪθ] *adj, s & pron* trentesimo ‖ *s* (in dates) trenta *m*

thir·ty ['θʌrti] *adj, s & pron* trenta ‖ *s* (-ties) trenta *m;* **the thirties** gli anni trenta

this [ðɪs] *adj dem* (these) questo; **this one** questo, questo qui ‖ *pron dem* (these) questo, questo qui ‖ *adv* (coll) tanto, così

thistle ['θɪsəl] *s* cardo

thither ['θɪðər] *or* ['ðɪðər] *adv* là, da quella parte

Thomas ['tɑməs] s Tommaso

thong [θɔŋ] or [θɑŋ] s coreggia

thorax ['θɔræks] s (-raxes or -races [rə‚siz]) torace m

thorn [θɔrn] s spina

thorn·y ['θɔrni] adj (-ier; -iest) spinoso

thorough ['θʌro] adj completo, esauriente

thor'ough·bred' adj di razza; (horse) purosangue || s individuo di razza; (horse) purosangue mf

thor'ough·fare' s passaggio; no thoroughfare divieto di passaggio

thor'ough·go'ing adj completo, esauriente

thoroughly ['θʌroli] adv a fondo

those [ðoz] pl of that

thou [ðaʊ] pron pers (Bib; poet) tu || tr dare del tu a

though [ðo] adv tuttavia || conj malgrado, sebbene; as though come se

thought [θɔt] s pensiero; perish the thought! (coll) nemmeno a pensarci!

thoughtful ['θɔtfəl] adj pensieroso, riflessivo; (considerate) sollecito

thoughtless ['θɔtlɪs] adj irriflessivo; sconsiderato; (reckless) incurante

thought' transfer'ence s trasmissione del pensiero

thousand ['θaʊzənd] adj, s & pron mille m; a thousand or one thousand mille m

thousandth ['θaʊzəndθ] adj, s & pron millesimo

thralldom ['θrɔldəm] s schiavitù f

thrash [θræʃ] tr battere; (agr) trebbiare; to thrash out discutere a fondo || intr agitarsi, dibattersi

thread [θrɛd] s filo; (mach) filetto, verme m; to lose the thread of perdere il filo di || tr infilare; (fig) pervadere; (mach) filettare, impanare; to thread one's way through aprirsi il passaggio attraverso

thread'bare' adj frusto, logoro

threat [θrɛt] s minaccia

threaten ['θrɛtən] tr & intr minacciare

threatening ['θrɛtənɪŋ] adj minaccioso; (e.g., letter) minatorio

three [θri] adj & pron tre || s tre m; three o'clock le tre

three'-cor'nered adj triangolare; (hat) a tre punte

three' hun'dred adj, s & pron trecento

threepenny ['θrɛpəni] or ['θrɪpəni] adj del valore di tre penny; di nessun valore

three'-phase' adj trifase

three'-ply' adj a tre spessori

three' R's' [ɑrz] spl lettura, scrittura e aritmetica

three'score' adj sessanta

three' thou'sand adj, s & pron tre mila mpl

threno·dy ['θrɛnədi] s (-dies) trenodia

thresh [θrɛʃ] tr (agr) trebbiare; to thresh out discutere a fondo || intr trebbiare; battere

thresh'ing machine' s trebbiatrice f

threshold ['θrɛʃold] s soglia

thrice [θraɪs] adv tre volte; molto

thrift [θrɪft] s economia

thrift·y ['θrɪfti] adj (-ier; -iest) eco-

nomo, economico; vigoroso; prospero

thrill [θrɪl] s fremito d'emozione; esperienza emozionante || tr emozionare || intr emozionarsi; vibrare

thriller ['θrɪlər] s (coll) thrilling m

thrilling ['θrɪlɪŋ] adj emozionante, thrilling

thrive [θraɪv] v (pret thrived or throve [θrov]; pp thrived or thriven ['θrɪvən]) intr prosperare, fiorire

throat [θrot] s gola; to clear one's throat schiarirsi la voce

throb [θrɑb] s battito, palpito, tuffo || v (pret & pp throbbed; ger throbbing) intr palpitare, pulsare

throe [θro] s agonia, travaglio, spasimo; in the throes of nel travaglio di; (e.g., battle) nel momento più penoso di

throne [θron] s trono

throng [θrɔŋ] or [θrɑŋ] s folla, stuolo || intr affollarsi

throttle ['θrɑtəl] s (of locomotive) leva di comando; (of motorcycle) manetta; (of car) acceleratore m; (mach) valvola di controllo || tr soffocare; (mach) regolare

through [θru] adj diretto, senza fermate; to be through aver finito; to be through with farla finita con || adv attraverso; da una parte all'altra; completamente; || prep attraverso, per; durante; fino alla fine di; per mezzo di

through·out' adv completamente, da un capo all'altro; dappertutto || prep durante tutto, e.g., throughout the afternoon durante tutto il pomeriggio; per tutto, e.g., throughout the house per tutta la casa

throw [θro] s getto, tiro, lancio; gettata; coperta leggera || v (pret threw [θru]; pp thrown) tr gettare, tirare, lanciare; (a shadow) proiettare; (the current) connettere; (said of a horse) disarcionare; (wrestling) gettare a terra; (a game) (coll) perdere intenzionalmente; (coll) stupire; to throw away gettar via; perdere; to throw back rigettare; ritardare; to throw in (the clutch) innestare; (coll) aggiungere; to throw oneself into darsi a; to throw out sbatter fuori; (the clutch) disinnestare; to throw over abbandonare || intr gettare, tirare, lanciare; to throw up vomitare

thrum [θrʌm] v (pret & pp thrummed; ger thrumming) intr tambureggiare; (mus) far scorrere la mano sulle corde di uno strumento

thrush [θrʌʃ] s tordo

thrust [θrʌst] s (push) spinta; botta; (with dagger) pugnalata; (with sword) stoccata || v (pret & pp thrust) tr spingere; conficcare, configgere; to thrust oneself (e.g., into a conversation) ficcarsi

thru'way' s autostrada

thud [θʌd] s tonfo || v (pret & pp thudded; ger thudding) intr fare un rumore sordo

thug [θʌg] s fascinoroso

thumb [θʌm] *s* pollice *m;* **all thumbs** maldestro, goffo; **thumbs down** pollice verso; **to twiddle one's thumbs** girare i pollici, essere ozioso; **under the thumb of** sotto l'influenza di ‖ *tr* sporcare con le dita; *(a book)* sfogliare; **to thumb a ride** chiedere l'autostop; **to thumb one's nose (at)** fare marameo (a)

thumb′ in′dex *s* margine *m* a scaletta

thumb′nail′ *adj* breve, conciso ‖ *s* unghia del pollice

thumb′screw′ *s* vite *f* ad aletta

thumb′tack′ *s* puntina

thump [θʌmp] *s* tonfo ‖ *tr* battere, percuotere ‖ *intr* battere; cadere con un tonfo; camminare a passi pesanti; *(said of the heart)* palpitare violentemente

thumping [′θʌmpɪŋ] *adj* (coll) straordinario, eccezionale; (coll) grande

thunder [′θʌndər] *s* tuono; *(of applause)* scroscio; *(of a cannon)* rombo ‖ *tr* lanciare ‖ *intr* tonare, rombare; (fig) scrosciare

thun′der·bolt′ *s* folgore *f,* fulmine *m*

thun′der·clap′ *s* scroscio di tuono

thunderous [′θʌndərəs] *adj* fragoroso

thun′der·show′er *s* acquazzone *m* accompagnato da tuoni

thun′der·storm′ *s* temporale *m*

thun′der·struck′ *adj* attonito

Thursday [′θʌrsdɪ] *s* giovedì *m*

thus [ðʌs] *adv* così; **thus far** sino qui

thwack [θwæk] *s* colpo ‖ *tr* colpire

thwart [θwɔrt] *adj* obliquo ‖ *adv* di traverso ‖ *tr* contrariare, sventare

thy [ðaɪ] *adj poss* (Bib; poet) tuo, il tuo

thyme [taɪm] *s* timo

thy′roid gland′ [′θaɪrɔɪd] *s* tiroide *f*

thyself [ðaɪ′self] *pron* (Bib; poet) te stesso; te, ti

tiara [taɪ′ɑrə] or [taɪ′erə] *s (female adornment)* diadema *m;* (eccl) tiara

tick [tɪk] *s (of pillow)* fodera; *(of mattress)* guscio; *(of clock)* ticchettìo; *(dot)* punto; (ent) zecca; **on tick** (coll) a credito ‖ *intr* fare ticchettìo; **to make s.o. tick** mandare avanti qlcu

ticker [′tɪkər] *s* telescrivente *f;* (slang) orologio; (slang) cuore *m*

tick′er tape′ *s* nastro della telescrivente

ticket [′tɪkɪt] *s* biglietto; *(e.g., of pawnbroker)* polizza; *(slip of paper or identifying tag)* bolletta, bollettino; *(summons)* verbale *m;* *(e.g., to indicate price)* etichetta; lista dei candidati; **that's the ticket** (coll) questo è quello che fa

tick′et a′gent *s* bigliettaio

tick′et of′fice *s* biglietteria

tick′et scalp′er [′skælpər] *s* bagarino

tick′et win′dow *s* sportello

ticking [′tɪkɪŋ] *s* traliccio

tickle [′tɪkəl] *s* solletico ‖ *tr* solleticare; divertire ‖ *intr* avere il solletico

ticklish [′tɪklɪʃ] *adj* sensibile al solletico; delicato; permaloso; **to be ticklish** soffrire il solletico

tick-tock [′tɪk ‚tɑk] *s* tic tac *m*

tid′al wave′ [′taɪdəl] *s* onda di marea; (fig) ondata

tidbit [′tɪd ‚bɪt] *s* bocconcino

tiddlywinks [′tɪdlɪ ‚wɪŋks] *s* gioco della pulce

tide [taɪd] *s* marea; **to go against the tide** andare contro la corrente; **to stem the tide** fermare la corrente ‖ *tr* portare sulla cresta delle onde; **to tide over** aiutare; *(a difficulty)* sormontare

tide′wa′ter *s* marea; costa marina

tidings [′taɪdɪŋz] *spl* notizie *fpl*

ti·dy [′taɪdɪ] *adj* [-dier; -diest] pulito, ordinato ‖ *s* (-dies) cofanetto, astuccio; appoggiacapo ‖ *v* (pret & pp -died) *tr* rassettare, mettere in ordine ‖ *intr* rassettarsi

tie [taɪ] *s* laccio, nodo, vincolo; *(in games)* patta; *(necktie)* cravatta; (archit) traversa; (rr) traversina; (mus) legatura ‖ *v* (pret & pp **tied;** ger **tying**) *tr* allacciare, annodare; legare; confinare; *(a game)* impattare; *(a person)* impattarla con; **to be tied up** essere occupato; **to tie down** confinare, limitare; **to tie up** legare; impedire; *(e.g., traffic)* intasare ‖ *intr* allacciare; *(in games)* impattare

tie′ beam′ *s* catena

tie′pin′ *s* spilla da cravatta

tier [tɪr] *s* gradinata; ordine *m,* livello

tiff [tɪf] *s* screzio, litigio

tiger [′taɪgər] *s* tigre *f*

ti′ger lil′y *s* giglio cinese

tight [taɪt] *adj* teso; stretto; compatto; impermeabile, ermetico; pieno; *(game)* (coll) serrato; (coll) tirato; (slang) ubriaco ‖ **tights** *spl* calzamaglia ‖ *adv* strettamente; **to hold tight** tenere stretto

tighten [′taɪtən] *tr* (e.g., one's belt) tirare; *(e.g., a screw)* stringere ‖ *intr* tirarsi; stringersi

tight-fisted [′taɪt′fɪstɪd] *adj* taccagno

tight′-fit′ting *adj* attillato

tight′rope′ *s* corda tesa

tight′ squeeze′ s—to be in a tight squeeze (coll) essere alle strette

tight′wad′ *s* (coll) spilorcio

tigress [′taɪgrɪs] *s* tigre femmina

tile [taɪl] *s* mattonella; *(for floor)* piastrella; *(for roof)* tegola, coppo ‖ *tr* coprire di mattonelle; coprire di piastrelle; coprire di coppi

tile′ roof′ *s* tetto di tegole

till [tɪl] *s* cassetto dei soldi ‖ *prep* fino a ‖ *conj* fino a che . . . non, fino a che, sinché . . . non, sinché ‖ *tr* lavorare, coltivare

tilt [tɪlt] *s* inclinazione; giostra, torneo; **full tilt** di gran carriera; a tutta forza ‖ *tr* inclinare; *(a lance)* mettere in resta; attaccare ‖ *intr* inclinarsi; giostrare; **to tilt at** combattere con

timber [′tɪmbər] *s* legno, legname *m* da costruzione; alberi *mpl;* (fig) tempra

tim′ber·land′ *s* bosco destinato a produrre legname

tim′ber line′ *s* linea della vegetazione

timbre ['tɪmbər] *s* (phonet & phys) timbro

time [taɪm] *s* tempo; ora, e.g., **what time is it?** che ora è?; volta, e.g., **three times** tre volte; giorni *mpl*, e.g., **in our time** ai giorni nostri; momento; ultima ora; ore *fpl* lavorative; periodo, e.g., **Xmas time** periodo natalizio; **for a long time** da lungo; **for the time be**'**ng** per ora, per il momento; **in time** presto; col tempo; **on time** a tempo, a rate; (*said, e.g., of a bus*) in orario; **times** volte, e.g., **seven times** seven sette volte sette; **to bide one's time** aspettare l'ora propizia; **to do time** (coll) essere in prigione; **to have a good time** divertirsi; **to have no time for** non poter sopportare; **to lose time** (*said of a watch*) ritardare; **to make time** avanzare rapidamente; guadagnare terreno; **to pass the time of day** fare una chiacchierata; salutarsi; **to take one's time** fare le cose senza fretta; **to tell time** leggere l'orologio || *tr* fissare il momento di; calcolare il tempo di; (sport) cronometrare

time' bomb' *s* bomba a orologeria

time' card' *s* cartellino di presenza

time' clock' *s* orologio di controllo (delle presenze)

time' expo'sure *s* (phot) posa

time' fuse' *s* spoletta a tempo

time'keep'er *s* marcatempo; orologio; (sports) cronometrista *mf*

timeless ['taɪmlɪs] *adj* senza fine, eterno

time'ly ['taɪmli] *adj* (-lier; -liest) opportuno, tempestivo

time'piece' *s* orologio; cronometro

time' sig'nal *s* segnale orario

time'ta'ble *s* orario; tabella di marcia

time'work' *s* lavoro a ore

time'worn' *adj* logorato dal tempo

time' zone' *s* fuso orario

timid ['tɪmɪd] *adj* timido, pavido

tim'ing gears' ['taɪmɪŋ] *spl* ingranaggi *mpl* di distribuzione

timorous ['tɪmərəs] *adj* timoroso

tin [tɪn] *s* (element) stagno; (tin plate; can) latta || *v* (pret & pp **tinned**; ger **tinning**) *tr* stagnare

tin' can' *s* latta

tincture ['tɪŋktʃər] *s* tintura

tin' cup' *s* tazzina metallica

tinder ['tɪndər] *s* esca

tin'der·box' *s* cassetta con l'esca e l'acciarino; persona eccitabile; (fig) polveriera

tin' foil' *s* stagnola

ting-a-ling ['tɪŋə,lɪŋ] *s* dindìn *m*

tinge [tɪndʒ] *s* sfumatura; pizzico, punta || *v* (ger **tingeing** or **tinging**) *tr* sfumare; dare una traccia di sapore a

tingle ['tɪŋgəl] *s* formicolio, pizzicore *m* || *intr* formicolirsi, pizzicare; (*said of the ears*) ronzare; (*with enthusiasm*) fremere

tin' hat' *s* (slang) elmetto

tinker ['tɪŋkər] *s* calderaio, ramaio || *intr* armeggiare

tinkle ['tɪŋkəl] *s* tintinnio || *tr* far tintinnare || *intr* tintinnare

tin' plate' *s* latta

tin' roof' *s* tetto di lamiera di latta

tinsel ['tɪnsəl] *s* orpello, lustrino

tin'smith' *s* lattoniere *m*, stagnino

tin' sol'dier *s* soldatino di piombo

tint [tɪnt] *s* tinta, sfumatura || *tr* tinteggiare

tin'ware' *s* articoli *mpl* di latta

ti·ny ['taɪni] *adj* (-nier; -niest) piccino

tip [tɪp] *s* punta; (*of mountain*) vetta; (*of umbrella*) gorbia; (*of shoe*) mascherina; (*of cigarette*) bocchino; (*of shoestring*) aghetto; colpetto; (fee) mancia; informazione confidenziale; inclinazione || *v* (pret & pp **tipped**; ger **tipping**) *tr* mettere la punta a; inclinare, rovesciare; (*one's hat*) levarsi; dare la mancia a; toccare, battere; (*the scales*) far traboccare; **to tip in** (bb) inserire fuori testo; **to tip off** (coll) dare informazioni confidenziali a || *intr* inclinarsi; dare la mancia

tip'cart' *s* carro ribaltabile

tip'-off' *s* (coll) avvertimento confidenziale

tipped'-in' *adj* (bb) fuori testo

tipple ['tɪpəl] *intr* sbevucchiare

tip'staff' *s* usciere *m*

tip·sy ['tɪpsi] *adj* (-sier; -siest) brillo

tip'toe' *s* punta di piedi || *v* (pret & pp **-toed**; ger **-toeing**) *intr* camminare in punta di piedi

tirade ['taɪred] *s* tirata

tire [taɪr] *s* gomma, pneumatico; (*of metal*) cerchione *m* || *tr* stancare || *intr* stancarsi; infastidirsi

tire' chain' *s* catena antineve

tired [taɪrd] *adj* stanco, stracco

tire' gauge' *s* manometro della pressione delle gomme

tireless ['taɪrlɪs] *adj* infaticabile

tire' pres'sure *s* pressione (delle gomme)

tire' pump' *s* pompa (per i pneumatici)

tiresome ['taɪrsəm] *adj* faticoso; (*boring*) noioso

tissue ['tɪʃju] *s* tessuto; tessuto finissimo, velina

tis'sue pa'per *s* carta velina

titanium [taɪ'teni·əm] or [tɪ'teni·əm] *s* titanio

tithe [taɪð] *s* decima || *tr* imporre la decima su; pagare la decima di

Titian ['tɪʃən] *adj* tizianesco || *s* Tiziano

title ['taɪtəl] *s* titolo; (sports) campionato || *tr* intitolare

ti'tle deed' *s* titolo di proprietà

ti'tle-hold'er *s* campione *m*, primatista *mf*

ti'tle page' *s* frontespizio

ti'tle role' *s* (theat) ruolo principale

tit'mouse' *s* (-mice) (orn) cincia

titter ['tɪtər] *s* risatina || *intr* ridacchiare

titular ['tɪtʃələr] *adj* titolare

TNT ['ti,en'ti] *s* (letterword) tritoio

to [tu], [tʊ] or [tə] *adv*—**to and fro** da una parte all'altra, avanti e indietro; **to come to** tornare in sè || *prep* a, e.g., **he is going to Rome** va a Roma; **he gave a kiss to his mother**

diede un bacio a sua madre; **she is learning to sew** impara a cucire; per, e.g., **he has been a true friend to me** è stato un vero amico per me; da, e.g., **there is still a lot of work to do** c'è ancora molto lavoro da fare; con, e.g., **she was very kind to me** è stata molto gentile con me; in, e.g., **we went to church** siamo andati in chiesa; fino a, e.g., **to see s.o. to the station** accompagnare qlcu fino alla stazione; in confronto di, e.g., **the accounts are nothing to what really happened** le storie non sono nulla, in confronto di quanto è realmente successo; meno, e.g., **ten minutes to seven** le sette meno dieci

toad [tod] *s* rospo

toad'stool' *s* agarico, fungo velenoso

to-and-fro [tu-ənd'fro] *adj* avanti e indietro

toast [tost] *s* pane tostato; (*drink to s.o.'s health*) brindisi *m*; **a piece of toast** una fetta di pane tostato || *tr* tostare; brindare alla salute di || *intr* tostarsi; brindare

toaster ['tostər] *s* (*of bread*) tostapane *m*; persona che fa un brindisi

toast'mas'ter *s* persona che annuncia i brindisi, maestro di cerimonie

tobac·co [tə'bæko] *s* (*-cos*) tabacco

tobacconist [tə'bækənɪst] *s* tabaccaio

tobac'co pouch' *s* borsa da tabacco

toboggan [tə'bagən] *s* toboga *m*

tocsin ['taksɪn] *s* campana a martello; scampanata d'allarme

today [tə'de] *s* & *adv* oggi *m*

toddle ['tadəl] *s* passo vacillante || *intr* traballare, trotterellare

tod·dy ['tadi] *s* (*-dies*) ponce *m*

to-do [tə'du] *s* (*-dos*) (coll) daffare *m*, rumore *m*

toe [to] *s* dito del piede; (*of shoe*) punta || *v* (*pret & pp* toed; *ger* toeing) *tr*—**to toe the line** filare diritto

toe'nail' *s* unghia del piede

together [tu'geðər] *adv* insieme; **to bring together** riunire; riconciliare; **to call together** chiamare a raccolta; **to stick together** (coll) rimanere uniti, stare insieme

togs [tagz] *spl* vestiti *mpl*

toil [tɔɪl] *s* travaglio, sfacchinata; **toils** reti *fpl*, lacci *mpl* || *intr* travagliare, sfacchinare

toilet ['tɔɪlɪt] *s* toletta; gabinetto, ritirata; **to make one's toilet** farsi la toletta

toi'let pa'per *s* carta igienica

toi'let pow'der *s* polvere *f* di talco

toi'let soap' *s* sapone *m* da toletta

toi'let wa'ter *s* acqua da toletta

token ['tokən] *s* segno, marca; ricordo; (*used as money*) gettone *m*; **by the same token** per di più; **in token of** in segno di, come prova di

tolerance ['talərəns] *s* tolleranza

tolerate ['talə ̩ret] *tr* tollerare

toll [tol] *s* (*of bell*) rintocco; (*e.g., for passage over bridge*) pedaggio; (*tax*) dazio; (*compensation for grinding grains*) molenda; (*number of victims*) perdite *fpl*; (telp) tariffa inter-

urbana || *tr* (*a bell*) sonare a morto; (*the faithful*) chiamare a raccolta || *intr* sonare a morto

toll' bridge' *s* ponte *m* a pedaggio

toll' call' *s* (telp) chiamata interurbana

toll'gate' *s* barriera di pedaggio; (*in a turnpike*) casello

toma·to [tə'meto] *or* [tə'mato] *s* (*-toes*) pomodoro

toma'to juice' *s* sugo di pomodoro

tomb [tum] *s* tomba

tomboy ['tam ̩bɔɪ] *s* maschietta

tomb'stone' *s* pietra tombale, lapide *f*

tomcat ['tam ̩kæt] *s* gatto maschio

tome [tom] *s* tomo

tomorrow [tu'maro] *or* [tu'mɔro] *s* domani *m*; **the day after tomorrow** dopodomani *m* || *adv* domani

tom-tom ['tam ̩tam] *s* tam-tam *m*

ton [tʌn] *s* tonnellata; **tons** (coll) montagne *fpl*

tone [ton] *s* tono; (fig) tenore *m* || *tr* intonare; **to tone down** (colors) smorzare; (sounds) sfumare || *intr* intonarsi; **to tone down** moderarsi; **to tone up** rinforzarsi

tone' po'em *s* poema sinfonico

tongs [tɔŋz] *or* [taŋz] *spl* tenaglie *fpl*; (*e.g., for sugar*) molle *fpl*

tongue [tʌŋ] *s* (*language*) lingua; (*of bell*) battaglio; (*of shoe*) linguetta; (*of wagon*) timone *m*; (anat) lingua; (carp) maschio; **tongue in cheek** poco sinceramente; **to hold one's tongue** mordersi la lingua; **to speak with forked tongue** essere di due lingue

tongue' depres'sor *s* abbassalingua *m*

tongue'-lash'ing *s* sgridata

tongue' twist'er *s* scioglilingua *m*

tonic ['tanɪk] *adj & s* tonico

tonight [tu'naɪt] *s* questa sera, questa notte || *adv* stasera; stanotte

tonnage ['tʌnɪdʒ] *s* tonnellaggio, stazza

tonsil ['tansəl] *s* tonsilla

ton·y ['toni] *adj* (*-ier; -iest*) (slang) elegante, di lusso

too [tu] *adv* (also) anche, pure; (*more than enough*) troppo; **too bad!** peccato!; **too many** troppi; **too much** troppo

tool [tul] *s* utensile *m*, attrezzo; (*person*) strumento; (*of lathe*) punta || *tr* lavorare; (bb) decorare

tool' bag' *s* borsa degli attrezzi

tool'box' *s* cassetta attrezzi

tool'mak'er *s* attrezzista *m*

tool'shed' *s* barchessa

toot [tut] *s* (*of horn*) suono; (*of locomotive*) fischio; (*of car's horn*) colpo; (coll) gazzarra || *tr* strombettare; **to toot one's own horn** strombazzare i propri meriti || *intr* strombettare

tooth [tuθ] *s* (**teeth** [tiθ]) dente *m*

tooth'ache' *s* mal *m* di denti

tooth'brush' *s* spazzolino da denti

toothless ['tuθlɪs] *adj* sdentato

tooth'paste' *s* pasta dentifricia

tooth'pick' *s* stuzzicadenti *m*

tooth' pow'der *s* polvere dentifricia

top [tap] *s* cima, sommo, vertice *m*; (*upper part of anything*) disopra *m*;

(of mountain, tree) vetta; *(of box)* coperchio; *(beginning)* principio; *(of bottle)* imboccatura; *(of a bridge)* testata; *(of wagon)* mantice *m*; *(of car)* tetto; *(of wall)* coronamento; *(toy)* trottola; *(naut)* gabbia; **at the top of one's voice** a perdifiato; **from top to bottom** daccapo a piedi, dal principio alla fine; **on top of** in cima di; subito dopo; **the tops** (coll) il migliore, il fiore; **to blow one's top** (slang) dare in escandescenze; **to sleep like a top** dormire come un ghiro || *v (pret & pp* **topped**; *ger* **topping)** *tr (a tree)* svettare; coronare; superare

topaz ['topæz] *s* topazio

top' bil'ling *s*—**to get top billing** essere artista di cartello; (journ) ricevere il posto più importante

top' boot' *s* stivale *m* a tromba

top'coat' *s* soprabito di mezza stagione

toper ['topər] *s* ubriacone *m*

topgal'lant sail' [,top'gælənt] *s* (naut) pappafico, veletta

top' hat' *s* cappello a staio or a cilindro

top'-heav'y *adj* troppo pesante in cima, sovraccarico in cima

topic ['tɑpɪk] *s* topica, tema *m*

top'knot' *s* crocchia

topless ['tɑplɪs] *adj (mountain)* di cui non si vede la vetta, eccelso; *(bathing suit)* topless

top'mast' *s* (naut) alberetto

top'most' *adj* il più alto

topog·ra·phy [tə'pɑgrəfi] *s* (-phies) topografia

topple ['tɑpəl] *tr* abbattere, rovesciare || *intr* rovesciarsi, cadere

top' prior'ity *s* priorità massima

topsail ['tɑpsəl] or ['tɑp,sel] *s* (naut) gabbia

top'-se'cret *adj* segretissimo

top'soil' *s* strato superiore del terreno

topsy-turvy ['tɑpsi'tʌrvi] *adj* rovesciato; confuso || *s* soqquadro || *adv* a soqquadro

torch [tɔrtʃ] *s* fiaccola, torcia; **to carry the torch for** (slang) amare disperatamente

torch'bear'er *s* portatore *m* di fiaccola; (fig) capo, guida *m*

torch'light' *s* luce *f* di fiaccola

torch' song' *s* canzone *f* triste d'amore non corrisposto

torment ['tɔrmɛnt] *s* tormento || [tɔr'mɛnt] *tr* tormentare

torna·do [tɔr'nedo] *s* (-dos or -does) tornado, tromba d'aria

torpe·do [tɔr'pido] *s* (-does) siluro || *tr* silurare

torpe'do boat' *s* motosilurante *f*

torpe'do-boat destroy'er *s* torpediniera

torrent ['tɔrənt] or ['tɑrənt] *s* torrente *m*

torrid ['tɑrɪd] or ['tɔrɪd] *adj* torrido

torsion ['tɔrʃən] *s* torsione

tor'sion bar' *s* barra di torsione

tor·so ['tɔrso] *s* (-sos) torso

tortoise ['tɔrtəs] *s* tartaruga

tor'toise shell' *s* tartaruga

torture ['tɔrtʃər] *s* tortura || *tr* torturare

toss [tɔs] or [tɑs] *s* lancio, getto || *tr* lanciare, gettare; *(to fling about)* sballottare; *(one's head)* alzare sdegnosamente; agitare; rivoltare; *(an opinion)* avventare; **to toss off** fare rapidamente; *(e.g., a drink)* buttar giù; **to toss up** *(a coin)* gettar in aria, gettare a testa e croce; (coll) rigettare || *intr* agitarsi, dimenarsi; **to toss and turn** *(in bed)* girarsi; **to toss up** giocare a testa e croce

toss'up' *s* testa e croce; (coll) eguale probabilità *f*

tot [tɑt] *s* bambino, piccolo

to·tal ['totəl] *adj* totale; *(e.g., loss)* completo || *s* totale *m* || *v (pret & pp* **-taled** or **-talled;** *ger* **-taling** or **-talling)** *tr* ammontare a; *(to make a total of)* sommare

totalitarian [to,tælɪ'tɛrɪ·ən] *adj* totalitario || *s* aderente *mf* al totalitarismo

totter ['tɑtər] *s* vacillamento || *intr* vacillare

touch [tʌtʃ] *s (act)* tocco; *(sense)* tatto; *(of an illness)* leggero attacco; *(slight amount)* punta; *(for money)* (slang) stoccata; **to get in touch with** mettersi in contatto con; **to lose one's touch** perdere il tocco personale || *tr* toccare; raggiungere; riguardare; *(for a loan)* (slang) dare una stoccata a; **to touch on** menzionare; **to touch up** ritoccare || *intr* toccare; **to touch down** (aer) atterrare

touching ['tʌtʃɪŋ] *adj* toccante, commovente || *prep* riguardo a

touch'stone' *s* pietra di paragone

touch' type'writing *s* dattilografia a tatto

touch·y ['tʌtʃi] *adj* (-ier; -iest) suscettibile, permaloso; delicato, precario, rischioso

tough [tʌf] *adj* duro; forte; *(luck)* cattivo; violento || *s* malvivente *m*

toughen ['tʌfən] *tr* indurire || *intr* indurirsi

tough' luck' *s* disdetta, sfortuna

tour [tur] *s* gita, viaggio; (sports) giro; (mil) turno; (theat) tournée *f* || *tr* girare; (theat) portare in tournée || *intr* girare; (theat) andare in tournée

tour'ing car' ['turɪŋ] *s* automobile *f* da turismo

tourist ['turɪst] *adj* turistico || *s* turista *mf*

tournament ['turnəmənt] or ['tʌrnəmənt] *s* torneo

tourney ['turni] or ['tʌrni] *s* torneo || *intr* giostrare

tourniquet ['turnɪ,ket] or ['tʌrnɪ,ke] *s* laccio emostatico

tousle ['tauzəl] *tr* spettinare

tow [to] *s* rimorchio; *(e.g., of hemp)* stoppa; **to take in tow** prendere a rimorchio || *tr* rimorchiare

toward(s) [tord(z)] or [tə'word(z)] *prep (in the direction of)* verso; *(in respect to)* per; *(near)* vicino a; *(a certain hour)* su, verso

tow'boat' *s* rimorchiatore *m*

tow' car' *s* rimorchiatore *m*

tow·el ['tau·əl] *s* asciugamano; *(of paper)* salvietta; **to throw in the**

towel (slang) gettare la spugna ‖ *v* (*pret & pp* -eled or -elled; *ger* -eling or -elling) *tr* asciugare

tow'el rack' *s* portasciugamani *m*

tower ['tau‐ər] *s* torre *f* ‖ *intr* torreggiare

towering ['tau‐ərɪŋ] *adj* torreggiante; gigantesco; eccessivo

towline ['to‚laɪn] *s* cavo di rimorchio

town [taun] *s* città *f;* (*townspeople*) cittadinanza; **in town** in città

town' clerk' *s* segretario municipale

town' coun'cil *s* consiglio comunale

town' cri'er *s* banditore *m* municipale

town' hall' *s* municipio

township ['taun/ɪp] *s* suddivisione di contea

towns'man *s* (-men) cittadino; concittadino

towns'peo'ple *spl* cittadini *mpl;* gente *f* di città

town' talk' *s* dicerie *fpl,* pettegolezzi *mpl*

tow'path' *s* strada d'alaggio

tow'rope' *s* corda da rimorchio

tow' truck' *s* autogru *f*

toxic ['taksɪk] *adj & s* tossico

toy [tɔɪ] *adj* giocattolo; di giocattoli ‖ *s* giocattolo; (*trifle*) nonnulla *m;* (*trinket*) gingillo ‖ *intr* giocare; **to toy with** (*to play with*) giocare con; (*to trifle, e.g., with food*) baloccarsi con; (*an idea*) accarezzare; (*to flirt with*) flirtare con

toy' bank' *s* salvadanaio

toy' sol'dier *s* soldatino di piombo

trace [tres] *s* traccia, vestigio; (*tracing*) tracciato; (*of harness*) tirella; (*fig*) ombra ‖ *tr* tracciare; (*e.g., s.o.'s ancestry*) rintracciare; (*a pattern*) lucidare

trac'er bul'let ['tresər] *s* pallottola tracciante

trache‐a ['trekɪ‐ə] *s* (-ae [‚i]) trachea

tracing ['tresɪŋ] *s* tracciato

track [træk] *s* (*of foot*) traccia, pesta; (*rut*) solco, rotaia; (*of boat*) scia; corso; (*course followed by boat*) rotta; (*of tape recorder*) pista; (*of tractor*) cingolo; (*of ideas*) successione; (*width of a vehicle measured from wheel to wheel*) (aut) carreggiata; (rr) binario; (*track and field*) (sports) atletica leggera; (*for horses*) (sports) galoppatoio; (*for running*) (sports) pista, corsia; **to keep track of** non perder di vista; **to lose track of** perder di vista; **to make tracks** (coll) affrettarsi; **to stop in one's tracks** (coll) fermarsi di colpo ‖ *tr* rintracciare, seguire le tracce di; lasciare tracce su; **to track down** rintracciare

track'ing sta'tion ['trækɪŋ] *s* (rok) stazione di avvistamento

track'less trol'ley ['træklɪs] *s* filobus *m*

track' meet' *s* incontro di atletica leggera

track'walk'er *s* (rr) guardialinee *m*

tract [trækt] *s* tratto, opuscolo, trattatello; (anat) tubo, canale *m*

traction ['trækʃən] *s* trazione

trac'tion com'pany *s* società *f* di trasporti urbani

tractor ['træktər] *s* trattore *m;* (*of a tractor-trailer*) motrice *f*

trac'tor-trail'er *s* treno stradale

trade [tred] *s* commercio; affare *m;* occupazione, mestiere *m;* (*people*) commercianti *mpl,* professionisti *mpl;* mercato; (*customers*) clientela; (*in slaves*) tratta ‖ *tr* mercanteggiare; cambiare; **to trade in** dare come pagamento parziale ‖ *intr* trafficare, commerciare; comprare; **to trade in** lavorare in; **to trade on** approfittarsi di

trade'mark' *s* marca or marchio di fabbrica

trade' name' *s* ragione sociale

trader ['tredər] *s* trafficante *m*

trade' school' *s* scuola d'avviamento professionale, scuola d'arti e mestieri

trades'man *s* (-men) commerciante *m;* artigiano

trade' un'ion *s* sindacato di lavoratori

trade' un'ionist *s* sindacalista *mf*

trade' winds' *spl* alisei *mpl*

trad'ing post' *s* centro di scambi commerciali; (*in stock exchange*) posto delle compravendite

trad'ing stamp' *s* buono premio

tradition [trə'dɪʃən] *s* tradizione

traditional [trə'dɪʃənəl] *adj* tradizionale

traduce [trə'djus] or [trə'dus] *tr* calunniare

traf-fic ['træfɪk] *s* traffico, circolazione; commercio; comunicazione ‖ *v* (*pret & pp* -ficked; *ger* -ficking) *intr* trafficare

traf'fic cir'cle *s* raccordo a circolazione rotatoria

traf'fic court' *s* tribunale *m* della polizia stradale

traf'fic is'land *s* isola spartitraffico

traf'fic jam' *s* intralcio del traffico, ingorgo stradale

traf'fic light' *s* semaforo

traf'fic man'ager *s* dirigente *m* del traffico; (rr) gestore *m* di stazione

traf'fic sign' *s* segnale *m* di circolazione stradale, cartello indicatore

traf'fic tick'et *s* contravvenzione per violazione del traffico

tragedian [trə'dʒidɪ‐ən] *s* tragico

trage‐dy ['trædʒɪdɪ] *s* (-dies) tragedia

tragic ['trædʒɪk] *adj* tragico

trail [trel] *s* sentiero; (*track*) traccia, pista; (*of robe*) strascico, coda; (*of smoke*) pennacchio; (*left by an airplane*) striscia; (*of people*) codazzo ‖ *tr* strascicare; essere sulla fatta di; (*e.g., dust on the road*) sollevare; (*mud*) lasciar cadere ‖ *intr* strascicare; (*said, e.g., of a snake*) strisciare; (*said of a plant*) arrampicarsi; **to trail off** mutare; (*to weaken*) affievolirsi

trailer ['trelər] *s* traino; (*to haul freight*) semirimorchio; (*for living*) carovana, roulotte *f;* (bot) rampicante *m*

train [tren] *s* (*of vehicles*) convoglio; (*of robe*) strascico; (*of thought*) ordine *m*; *(of people)* coda; (rr) treno || *tr* addestrare, impratichire; *(a weapon)* puntare, rivolgere; *(a horse)* scozzonare; *(e.g., a dog)* ammaestrare; *(a plant)* far crescere; (sports) allenare || *intr* addestrarsi; ammaestrarsi; (sports) allenarsi

trained' nurse' *s* infermiera diplomata

trainer ['trenər] *s* allenatore *m*

training ['trenɪŋ] *s* esercizio, esercitazione; (sports) allenamento

train'ing camp' *s* campo addestramento

train'ing school' *s* scuola di addestramento professionale; riformatorio

train'ing ship' *s* nave *f* scuola

trait [tret] *s* tratto, caratteristica

traitor ['tretər] *s* traditore *m*

traitress ['tretrɪs] *s* traditrice *f*

trajecto·ry [trə'dʒɛktəri] *s* (**-ries**) traiettoria

tramp [træmp] *s* lunga camminata; vagabondo; *(hussy)* sgualdrina || *tr* attraversare; calpestare || *intr* camminare a passi fermi; fare il vagabondo

trample ['træmpəl] *tr* calpestare; (fig) conculcare || *intr*—**to trample on or upon** calpestare

trampoline ['træmpə‚lin] *s* trampolino di olona per salti mortali

tramp' steam'er *s* carretta

trance [træns] *or* [trɑns] *s* trance *f*; *(dazed condition)* estasi *f*

tranquil ['træŋkwɪl] *adj* tranquillo

tranquilize ['træŋkwɪ‚laɪz] *tr* tranquillizzare || *intr* tranquillizzarsi

tranquilizer ['træŋkwɪ‚laɪzər] *s* tranquillante *m*

tranquillity [træn'kwɪlɪti] *s* tranquillità *f*

transact [træn'zækt] *or* [træns'ækt] *tr* sbrigare, trattare

transaction [træn'zækʃən] *or* [træns'ækʃən] *s* disbrigo, operazione

transatlantic [‚trænsət'læntɪk] *adj* & *s* transatlantico

transcend [træn'sɛnd] *tr* trascendere, sorpassare || *intr* eccellere

transcribe [træn'skraɪb] *tr* trascrivere

transcript ['trænskrɪpt] *s* copia; traduzione; (educ) copia ufficiale del certificato di studi

transcription [træn'skrɪpʃən] *s* trascrizione

transept ['trænsɛpt] *s* transetto

trans·fer ['trænsfər] *s* trasferimento; passaggio; *(pattern)* rapporto; *(of funds)* giro; *(of real estate)* compravendita; (law) voltura || [træns'fʌr] *or* ['trænsfər] *v* (*pret* & *pp* **-ferred**; *ger* **-ferring**) *tr* trasferire, trasportare; *(funds)* stornare; *(a design)* rapportare; *(real estate)* compravendere || *intr* trasferirsi; cambiare di treno

trans'fer tax' *s* tassa di successione; tassa sulla compravendita

transfix [træns'fɪks] *tr* trafiggere; paralizzare, inchiodare

transform [træns'fɔrm] *tr* trasformare; (elec) trasformare || *intr* trasformarsi

transforma'tional gram'mar [‚trænsfər-**

'mɛʃənəl] *s* grammatica trasformativa

transformer [træns'fɔrmər] *s* trasformatore *m*

transfusion [træns'fjuʒən] *s* trasfusione

transgress [træns'grɛs] *tr* trasgredire; *(a limit or boundry)* oltrepassare || *intr* peccare

transgression [træns'grɛʃən] *s* trasgressione; peccato

transient ['trænʃənt] *adj* passeggero, temporaneo; di passaggio || *s* ospite *mf* di passaggio

transistor [træn'zɪstər] *s* transistore *m*

transit ['trænsɪt] *or* ['trænzɪt] *s* transito

transition [træn'zɪʃən] *s* transizione

transitional [træn'zɪʃənəl] *adj* di transizione

transitive ['trænsɪtɪv] *adj* transitivo || *s* verbo transitivo

transitory ['trænsɪ‚tori] *adj* transitorio

translate [træns'let] *or* ['trænslet] *tr* tradurre; convertire; *(to transfer)* trasportare || *intr* tradursi

translation [træns'leʃən] *s* traduzione; trasformazione; (telg) ritrasmissione

translator [træns'letər] *s* traduttore *m*

transliterate [træns'lɪtə‚ret] *tr* traslitterare

translucent [træns'lusənt] *adj* traslucido; (fig) chiaro

transmission [træns'mɪʃən] *s* trasmissione; (aut) trasmissione

trans·mit [træns'mɪt] *v* (*pret* & *pp* **-mitted**; *ger* **-mitting**) *tr* & *intr* trasmettere

transmitter [træns'mɪtər] *s* trasmettitore *m*

transmit'ting set' *s* emittente *f*

transmit'ting sta'tion *s* stazione trasmettitrice

transmute [træns'mjut] *tr* & *intr* trasmutare

transom ['trænsəm] *s* *(crosspiece)* traversa; *(window over door)* vasistas *m*; (naut) specchio di poppa

transparen·cy ['træns'pɛrənsi] *s* (**-cies**) trasparenza; *(design on a translucent substance)* trasparente *m*; (phot) diapositiva

transparent [træns'pɛrənt] *adj* trasparente

transpire [træns'paɪr] *intr* *(to happen)* avvenire; *(to perspire)* traspirare; *(to become known)* trapelare

transplant [træns'plænt] *or* [træns-'plɑnt] *tr* trapiantare || *intr* trapiantarsi

transport ['trænsport] *s* trasporto; mezzo di trasporto || [træns'port] *tr* trasportare

transportation [‚trænspor'teʃən] *s* trasporto; trasporti *mpl*, locomozione; biglietto di trasporto

trans'port work'er *s* ferrotranviere *m*

transpose [træns'poz] *tr* trasporre; (mus) trasportare

trans·ship [træns'ʃɪp] *v* (*pret* & *pp* **-shipped**; *ger* **-shipping**) *tr* trasbordare

trap [træp] *s* trappola, tranello;

(*double-curved pipe*) sifone m; (slang) bocca; (sports) congegno lanciapiattelli || v (*pret & pp* trapped; *ger* trapping) *tr* intrappolare, accalappiare

trap' door' s trabocchetto, botola; (theat) ribalta

trapeze [trə'piz] s (sports) trapezio

trapezoid ['træpɪ‚zɔɪd] s (geom) trapezio, trapezoide m

trapper ['træpər] s cacciatore m di animali da pelliccia con trappole

trappings ['træpɪŋz] spl ornamenti mpl; (*for a horse*) gualdrappa

trap'shoot'ing s tiro al piattello

trash [træʃ] s immondizia, spazzatura; (*nonsense*) sciocchezze fpl; (*junk*) ciarpame m; (*worthless people*) gentaglia

trash' can' s portaimmondizie m

travail ['trævel] or [trə'vel] s travaglio; travaglio di parto

trav-el ['trævəl] s viaggio; traffico; (mach) corsa || v (*pret & pp* -eled or -elled; *ger* -eling or -elling) *tr* viaggiare per, percorrere || *intr* viaggiare; muoversi; (coll) andare

trav'el a'gency s ufficio turistico

traveler ['trævələr] s viaggiatore m

trav'eler's check' s assegno viaggiatori

trav'eling bag' s sacca da viaggio

trav'eling expens'es spl spese fpl di viaggio; (*per diem*) trasferta

trav'eling sales'man s (-men) commesso viaggiatore

traverse ['trævərs] or [trə'vʌrs] *tr* attraversare

traves-ty ['trævɪstɪ] s (-ties) parodia || v (*pret & pp* -tied) *tr* parodiare

trawl [trɔl] s (*fishing net*) rete f a strascico; (*fishing line*) lenza al traino || *tr & intr* pescare con la rete a strascico; pescare con la lenza al traino

trawling ['trɔlɪŋ] s pesca con la rete a strascico; pesca con la lenza al traino

tray [tre] s guantiera, vassoio; (chem, phot) bacinella

treacherous ['tretʃərəs] adj traditore, subdolo; incerto, pericoloso

treacher-y ['tretʃərɪ] s (-ies) tradimento

tread [tred] s (*step*) passo; (*of shoe*) suola; (*of tire*) battistrada m; (*of stairs*) pedata || v (*pret* trod [trɑd]; *pp* trodden ['trɑdən] or trod) *tr* calpestare; (*the boards*) calcare; accoppiarsi con || *intr* camminare; to tread on calpestare

treadle ['tredəl] s pedale m

tread'mill' s ruota azionata col camminare; (fig) lavoro ingrato

treason ['trizən] s tradimento

treasonable ['trizənəbəl] adj traditore

treasure ['trɛʒər] s tesoro || *tr* far tesoro di

treasurer ['trɛʒərər] s tesoriere m

treas'ure hunt' s caccia al tesoro

treasur-y ['trɛʒərɪ] s (-ies) tesoreria; tesoro, erario

treat [trit] s trattenimento; (*something affording pleasure*) piacere m, diletto || *tr* trattare; (*to cure*) curare, medi-

care; offrire un trattenimento a || *intr* trattare; pagare per il trattenimento

treatise ['tritɪs] s trattato

treatment ['tritmənt] s trattamento; (*of a theme*) trattazione

trea-ty ['tritɪ] s (-ties) trattato

treble ['trebəl] adj (*threefold*) triplo; (mus) soprano || s (*person*) soprano mf; (*voice*) soprano || *tr* triplicare || *intr* triplicarsi

tree [tri] s albero

tree' farm' s bosco ceduo

tree' frog' s raganella

treeless ['trilɪs] adj spoglio, senza alberi

tree'top' s cima dell'albero

trellis ['trelɪs] s traliccio, graticcio

tremble ['trembəl] s tremito || *intr* tremare

tremendous [trɪ'mendəs] adj tremendo

tremor ['tremər] or ['trimər] s tremito; (*of earth*) scossa

trench [trentʃ] s fosso, canale m; (mil) trincea

trenchant ['trentʃənt] adj mordace, caustico; vigoroso; incisivo

trench' coat' s trench m

trench' mor'tar s lanciabombe m

trend [trend] s tendenza, orientamento || *intr* tendere, dirigersi

Trent [trent] s Trento f

trespass ['trespəs] s (law) intrusione, violazione di proprietà || *intr* entrare senza diritto, intrudersi; peccare; no trespassing divieto di passaggio; to trespass against peccare contro; to trespass on entrare abusivamente in; (*e.g., s.o.'s time*) abusare di; violare

tress [tres] s treccia

trestle ['tresəl] s cavalletto; viadotto a cavalletti; ponte m a cavalletti

trial ['traɪ-əl] s tentativo, prova; tribolazione, croce f; (law) giudizio, processo; on trial in prova; (law) sotto processo; to bring to trial sottoporre a processo

tri'al and er'ror s metodo per tentativo; by trial and error a tastoni

tri'al balloon' s pallone m sonda

tri'al by ju'ry s processo con giuria

tri'al ju'ry s giuria civile or processuale

tri'al or'der s (com) ordine m di prova

tri'al run' s viaggio di prova

triangle ['traɪ‚æŋgəl] s triangolo; (in drafting) quartabuono

tribe [traɪb] s tribù f

tribunal [trɪ'bjunəl] or [traɪ'bjunəl] s tribunale m

tribune ['trɪbjun] s tribuna

tributar-y ['trɪbjə‚terɪ] adj tributario || s (-ies) tributario

tribute ['trɪbjut] s tributo; to pay tribute to (*e.g., beauty*) rendere omaggio a

trice [traɪs] s momento, istante m; in a trice in un batter d'occhio

trick [trɪk] s gherminella, inganno; trucco, tiro, scherzo; (*knack*) abilità f; (*feat*) atto; (*set of cards won*) presa; turno; (coll) piccola; to be up to one's old tricks farne una delle sue; **to play a dirty trick on** fare un brutto tiro a|| *tr* giocare, ingannare

tricker·y ['trɪkəri] *s* (-ies) gherminella, inganno

trickle ['trɪkəl] *s* goccolio, filo || *intr* gocciolare; *(said of people)* andare or venire alla spicciolata; *(said of news)* trapelare

trickster ['trɪkstər] *s* imbroglione *m*

trick·y ['trɪki] *adj* (-ier; -iest) ingannatore; *(machine)* complicato; *(ticklish to deal with)* delicato

tried [traɪd] *adj* fedele, provato

trifle ['traɪfəl] *s* bazzecola, bagattella; *(small amount of money)* piccolezza, miseria; **a trifle** un po' || *tr*—**to trifle away** sprecare || *intr* gingillarsi; **to trifle with** giocherellare con; scherzare con; divertirsi con

trifling ['traɪflɪŋ] *adj* futile; insignificante, trascurabile

trifocal [traɪ'fokəl] *adj* trifocale || **trifocals** *spl* occhiali *mpl* trifocali

trigger ['trɪgər] *s (of a firearm)* grilletto; *(of any device)* leva di sgancio || *tr (a gun)* far sparare; *(fig)* scatenare

trigonometry [,trɪgə'namɪtri] *s* trigonometria

trill [trɪl] *s* trillo, gòrgheggio; vibrazione; *(speech sound)* (phonet) vibrante *f* || *tr* gorgheggiare; pronunziare con vibrazione || *intr* trillare, gorgheggiare

trillion ['trɪljən] *s* trilione *m*

trilo·gy ['trɪlədʒi] *s* (-gies) trilogia

trim [trɪm] *adj* (**trimmer; trimmest**) lindo, azzimato || *s* condizione: buona condizione; *(dress)* vestito; *(of hair)* taglio, sfumatura; decorazione, ornamento; *(of sails)* orientamento; (aut) attrezzatura della carrozzeria || *v (pret & pp* **trimmed;** *ger* **trimming)** *tr* tagliare; *(an edge)* rifilare; adattare; arrangiare; *(Christmas tree)* decorare; *(hair)* sfumare; *(a tree)* potare; ordinare, assettare; *(a sail)* orientare; (aer) equilibrare; (mach) sbavare; (coll) rimproverare; (coll) bastonare; *(to defeat* (coll) battere, vincere

trimming ['trɪmɪŋ] *s* ornamento, guarnizione; (coll) battitura, batosta; **trimmings** guarnizioni *mpl*; (mach) sbavatura; (mach) rifilatura

trini·ty ['trɪnɪti] *s* (-ties) *(group of three)* triade *f* || **Trinity** *s* Trinità *f*

trinket ['trɪŋkɪt] *s (small ornament)* ninnolo, gingillo; **trinkets** *(trivial objects)* paccottiglia

tri·o ['tri·o] *s* (-os) terzetto

trip [trɪp] *s* viaggio; corsa; *(stumble)* inciampata; *(act of causing s.o. to stumble)* sgambetto; *(error)* passo falso; passo agile || *v (pret & pp* **tripped;** *ger* **tripping)** *tr* far inciampare, far cadere; fare lo sgambetto a; cogliere in fallo; (mach) far scattare || *intr* inciampare; fare un passo falso; avanzare saltellando, saltellare; **to trip over** inciampare in

tripartite [traɪ'partaɪt] *adj* tripartito

tripe [traɪp] *s* trippa; (slang) sciocchezze *fpl*

trip'ham'mer *s* maglio meccanico

triphthong ['trɪfθɔŋ] or ['trɪfθɑŋ] *s* trittongo

triple ['trɪpəl] *adj & s* triplo || *tr* triplicare || *intr* triplicarsi

triplet ['trɪplɪt] *s (offspring)* nato da un parto trigemino; (mus, poet) terzina

triplicate ['trɪplɪkɪt] *adj* triplicato || *s* triplice copia || ['trɪplɪ,ket] *tr* triplicare

tripod ['traɪpad] *s (e.g., for a camera)* treppiede *m; (stool with three legs)* tripode *m*

triptych ['trɪptɪk] *s* trittico

trite [traɪt] *adj* trito, ritrito

triumph ['traɪ·əmf] *s* trionfo || *intr* trionfare

trium'phal arch' [traɪ'ʌmfəl] *s* arco trionfale

trivia ['trɪvɪ·ə] *spl* banalità *f*, futilità *f*

trivial ['trɪvɪ·əl] *adj* insignificante, futile, banale

Trojan ['trodʒən] *adj & s* troiano

Tro'jan Horse' *s* cavallo di Troia

Tro'jan War' *s* guerra troiana

troll [trol] *tr & intr* pescare con la lenza al traino, pescare con il cucchiaino

trolley ['trali] *s* asta di presa, trolley *m;* carrozza tranviaria, tram *m*

trol'ley bus' *s* filobus *m*

trol'ley car' *s* vettura tranviaria, tram *m*

trol'ley pole' *s* trolley *m*

trollop ['traləp] *s (slovenly woman)* sciattona; *(hussy)* sgualdrina

trombone ['trambon] *s* trombone *m*

troop [trup] *s* truppa, gruppo; *(of animals)* branco; *(of cavalry)* squadrone *m; troops* soldati *mpl* || *intr* raggrupparsi; marciare insieme

trooper ['trupər] *s* soldato di cavalleria; poliziotto a cavallo; **to swear like a trooper** bestemmiare come un turco

tro·phy ['trofi] *s* (-phies) trofeo; *(any memento)* ricordo

tropic ['trapɪk] *adj* tropicale || *s* tropico; **tropics** zona tropicale

tropical ['trapɪkəl] *adj* tropicale

troposphere ['trapə,sfɪr] *s* troposfera

trot [trat] *s* trotto || *v (pret & pp* **trotted;** *ger* **trotting)** *tr* far trottare; **to trot out** (coll) squadernare, esibire || *intr* trottare

troth [trɔθ] or [troθ] *s* promessa di matrimonio; **by my troth** affé di Dio; **in troth** in verità; **to plight one's troth** impegnarsi; dare la parola

troubadour ['trubə,dor] or ['trubə,dur] *s* trovatore *m*

trouble ['trʌbəl] *s* disturbo, fastidio; inconveniente *m*, grattacapo; disordine *m*, conflitto; *(of a mechanical nature)* panna, guasto; **not to be worth the trouble** non valere la pena; **that's the trouble** questo è il male; **the trouble is that** il guaio è che; **to be in trouble** essere nei guai; **to be**

looking for trouble andare a cercarsi le grane; **to get into trouble** mettersi nei pasticci; **to have trouble in** + ger durar fatica a + inf; **to take the trouble** incomodarsi || tr molestare, disturbare; (e.g., water) intorbidare; dar del filo da torcere a; **to be troubled with** soffrire di; **to trouble oneself** scomodarsi

trouble' light' s lampada di soccorso

trou'ble-mak'er s mettimale mf

troubleshooter ['trʌbəl‚ʃutər] s localizzatore m di guasti; (in disputes) paciere m, conciliatore m

troubleshooting ['trʌbəl‚ʃutɪŋ] s localizzazione dei guasti; (of disputes) composizione

troublesome ['trʌbəlsəm] adj molesto; difficile

trouble' spot' s luogo di disordini, polveriera

trough [trɔf] or [traf] s (to knead bread) madia; (for feeding pigs) trogolo; (for feeding animals) mangiatoia; (for watering animals) abbeveratoio; (gutter) doccia; (between two waves) cavo

troupe [trup] s troupe f

trouper ['trupər] s membro della troupe; vecchio attore; tipo di cui ci si può fidare

trousers ['trauzərz] spl pantaloni mpl

trousseau [tru'so] or ['truso] s (-seaux or -seaus) corredo da sposa

trout [traut] s trota

trouvère [tru'ver] s troviero

trowel ['trau‚əl] s cazzuola, mestola

Troy [trɔɪ] s Troia

truant ['tru‚ənt] s fannullone m; **to play truant** marinare la scuola

truce [trus] s tregua

truck [trʌk] s autocarro, camion m; (tractor-trailer) autotreno; (van) furgone m; (to be moved by hand) carretto; verdura per il mercato; (mach, rr) carrello; (coll) robaccia; (coll) relazioni fpl || tr trasportare per autocarro, autotrasportare

truck'driv'er s camionista m

truck' farm' s fattoria agricola per la produzione degli ortaggi

truculent ['trʌkjələnt] or ['trʌkjələnt] adj truculento

trudge [trʌdʒ] intr camminare; **to trudge along** camminare laboriosamente, scarpinare

true [tru] adj vero; esatto, conforme; legittimo; infallibile; a livello; **to come true** verificarsi; **true to life** conforme alla realtà

true' cop'y s copia conforme

true-hearted ['tru‚hɑrtɪd] adj fedele

true'love knot' s nodo d'amore

truffle ['trʌfəl] or ['trufəl] s tartufo

truism ['tru‚ɪzəm] s truismo

truly ['truli] adv veramente; correttamente; **yours truly** distinti saluti

trump [trʌmp] s (cards) atout m; (Italian cards) briscola; **no trump** senza atout || tr superare; (cards) pigliare con un atout or con una briscola; **to**

trump up inventare, fabbricare || intr giocare un atout or una briscola

trumpet ['trʌmpɪt] s tromba; (toy) trombetta; **to blow one's own trumpet** cantare le proprie lodi || tr strombazzare || intr sonar la tromba; strombazzare; (said of an elephant) barrire

truncheon ['trʌntʃən] s bastone m del comando; (Brit) manganello

trunk [trʌŋk] s (of living body, tree, family, railroad) tronco; (for clothes) baule m; (of elephant) tromba; (aut) bagagliaio; (archit) fusto; (telp) linea principale; **trunks** pantaloncini mpl

trunk' hose' s (hist) brache fpl

truss [trʌs] s (to support a roof) capriata, incavallatura; (based on cantilever system) intralicciatura; (for reducing a hernia) cinto, brachiere m; (bot) infiorescenza || tr legare, assicurare

trust [trʌst] s fede f; speranza; fiducia, custodia; (com) trust m, cartello; (law) fedecommesso; **in trust** in deposito; come fedecommesso; **on trust** a credito || tr fidarsi di; credere (with dat); (to entrust) dare in deposito a; dare a credito a || intr credere; fidarsi, prestar fede; **to trust in** (e.g., a friend) fidarsi di; (God) aver fede in

trust' com'pany s compagnia fedecommissaria; banca di deposito

trustee [trʌs'ti] s amministratore m; fiduciario; (of a university) curatore m; (of an estate) fedecommissario

trusteeship [trʌs'ti‚ɪp] s amministrazione; (law) fedecommesso; (pol) amministrazione fiduciaria

trustful ['trʌstfəl] adj fiducioso

trust'wor'thy adj fidato, di fiducia

trust·y ['trʌsti] adj (-ier; -iest) fidato || s (-ies) carcerato degno di fiducia

truth [truθ] s verità f; **in truth** in verità

truthful ['truθfəl] adj verace, veritiero

try [traɪ] s (tries) tentativo, prova || v (pret & pp tried) tr provare; (s.o.'s patience) mettere a dura prova; (a person) (law) processare; (a case) (law) giudicare; **to try on** (clothes) provare; **to try out** provare; esperimentare || intr cercare, tentare; **to try out for** cercare di ottenere il posto di; (sports) cercare di farsi accettare in; **to try to** cercare di

trying ['traɪ‚ɪŋ] adj duro, penoso, difficile

tryst [trɪst] or [traɪst] s appuntamento

T'-shirt' s maglietta

tub [tʌb] s tino, bigoncia; vasca da bagno; (clumsy boat) (slang) carretta; (fat person) (slang) bombolo

tube [tjub] or [tub] s tubo; (e.g., for toothpaste) tubetto; (of tire) camera d'aria; (anat) tuba, tromba; (coll) ferrovia sotterranea

tuber ['tjubər] or ['tubər] s tubero

tubercle ['tjubərkəl] or ['tubərkəl] s tubercolo

tuberculosis [tju͵bɑːkjə'losɪs] or [tu-͵bɑːkjə'losɪs] *s* tubercolosi *f*
tuck [tʌk] *s* basta ‖ *tr* ripiegare; **to tuck away** nascondere; (slang) fare una scorpacciata di; **to tuck in** rincalzare; **to tuck up** rimboccare
tucker ['tʌkər] *s* collarino di merletto ‖ *tr*—**to tucker out** (coll) stancare
Tuesday ['tjuzdɪ] or ['tuzdɪ] *s* martedì *m*
tuft [tʌft] *s* (*of feathers*) pennacchio; (*of hair*) cernecchio; (*of flowers*) cespo; (*fluffy threads*) fiocco, nappa ‖ *tr* impuntire; adornare di fiocchi ‖ *intr* crescere a cernecchi
tug [tʌg] *s* strattone *m*, strappata; (*struggle*) lotta; (*boat*) rimorchiatore *m* ‖ *v* (*pret & pp* **tugged**; *ger* **tugging**) *tr* tirare; (*a boat*) rimorchiare ‖ *intr* tirare con forza; lottare
tug'boat' *s* rimorchiatore *m*
tug' of war' *s* tiro alla fune
tuition [tju'ɪʃən] or [tu'ɪʃən] *s* (*instruction*) insegnamento; tassa scolastica
tulip ['tjulɪp] or ['tulɪp] *s* tulipano
tumble ['tʌmbəl] *s* rotolone *m*, ruzzolone *m*; (*somersault*) salto mortale; caduta; disordine *m*, confusione; (*confused heap*) mucchio ‖ *intr* rotolare, ruzzolare; cadere, capitombolare; gettarsi; rigirarsi; **to tumble down** cadere in rovina; **to tumble to** (coll) rendersi conto di
tum'ble-down' *adj* dilapidato
tumbler ['tʌmblər] *s* (*acrobat*) saltimbanco; (*glass*) bicchiere *m*; (*in a lock*) levetta; (*toy*) misirizzi *m*
tumor ['tjumər] or ['tumər] *s* tumore *m*
tumult ['tjumʌlt] or ['tumʌlt] *s* tumulto
tun [tʌn] *s* botte *f*, barile *m*
tuna ['tunə] *s* tonno
tune [tjun] or [tun] *s* (*air*) aria; (*manner of speaking*) tono; **in tune** intonato; **out of tune** stonato; **to change one's tune** cambiare di tono ‖ *tr* intonare; **to tune in** (rad) sintonizzare; **to tune out** (rad) interrompere la sintonizzazione di; **to tune up** (*a motor*) mettere a punto; (mus) intonare
tuner ['tunər] or ['tjunər] *s* (rad) sintonizzatore *m*; (mus) accordatore *m*
tungsten ['tʌŋstən] *s* tungsteno
tunic ['tjunɪk] or ['tunɪk] *s* tunica
tun'ing coil' ['tunɪŋ] or ['tjunɪŋ] *s* bobina di sintonia
tun'ing fork' *s* diapason *m*, corista *m*
Tunis ['tjunɪs] or ['tunɪs] *s* Tunisi *f*
Tunisia [tju'nɪʒə] or [tu'nɪʒə] *s* la Tunisia
Tunisian [tju'nɪʒən] or [tu'nɪʒən] *adj & s* tunisino
tun·nel ['tʌnəl] *s* tunnel *m*, traforo, galleria; (min) galleria ‖ *v* (*pret & pp* **-neled** or **-nelled**; *ger* **-neling** or **-nelling**) *tr* costruire un passaggio attraverso or sotto a
turban ['tʌrbən] *s* turbante *m*
turbid ['tʌrbɪd] *adj* turbido

turbine ['tʌrbɪn] or ['tʌrbaɪn] *s* turbina
turbojet ['tʌrbo͵dʒɛt] *s* turboreattore *m*
turboprop ['tʌrbo͵prɑp] *s* turboelica *m*
turbulent ['tʌrbjələnt] *adj* turbolento
tureen [tu'rin] or [tju'rin] *s* terrina
turf [tʌrf] *s* zolla erbosa; (*peat*) torba; **the turf** il campo delle corse; le corse, il turf
turf'man *s* (-men) amatore *m* delle corse ippiche
Turk [tʌrk] *s* turco
turkey ['tʌrki] *s* tacchino ‖ **Turkey** *s* la Turchia
turk'ey vul'ture *s* (*Cathartes aura*) avvoltoio americano
Turkish ['tʌrkɪʃ] *adj & s* turco
Turk'ish tow'el *s* asciugamano spugna
turmoil ['tʌrmɔɪl] *s* subbuglio
turn [tʌrn] *s* giro; (*time for action*) turno, volta; (*change of direction*) voltata; (*bend*) svolta, curva; (*of events*) piega; servizio; inclinazione, attitudine *f*; (*of key*) mandata; (*of coil*) spira; (*coll*) colpo, sussulto; (aer, naut) virata; **at every turn** a ogni piè sospinto; **in turn** a tua (Sua, vostra, etc.) volta; **to be one's turn** toccare a qlcu, e.g., **it's your turn** tocca a Lei; **to take turns** fare a turno ‖ *tr* girare, voltare; (*soil*) rovesciare; cambiare; (*to make sour*) coagulare; (*to translate*) tradurre; (*e.g., ten years*) raggiungere; (*e.g., one's eyes*) volgere; (*on a lathe*) tornire; (*e.g., a coat*) rivoltare; (*to twist*) torcere; (*the wheel*) (aut) sterzare; **to turn against** mettere su contro; **to turn around** rigirare; (*s.o.'s words*) ritorcere; **to turn aside** sviare; **to turn away** cacciare via; **to turn back** ricacciare; restituire; (*the clock*) ritardare; **to turn down** ripiegare; (*the light*) abbassare; (*an offer*) rifiutare; **to turn in** ripiegare; denunziare; rassegnare; **to turn off** (*e.g., light*) spegnere, smorzare; (*gas, water, etc.*) tagliare; (*e.g., a faucet*) chiudere; **to turn on** (*e.g., light, radio, etc.*) accendere; (*e.g., a faucet*) aprire; **to turn out** mettere alla porta; (*animals*) fare uscire dalla stalla; rivoltare; (*light*) spegnere; produrre, fabbricare; **to turn up** ripiegare in su, rimboccare; (*on a lathe*) tornire; tirar su; (*a card*) scoprire; trovare; (*e.g., the radio*) alzare ‖ *intr* girare; svoltare, e.g., **turn left at the corner** svolti a sinistra all'angolo; girarsi; cambiare; fermentare; cambiare di colore; diventare; (naut) virare; **to turn against** voltarsi contro; inimicarsi con; **to turn around** fare una giravolta; **to turn aside** or **away** sviarsi; **to turn back** ritornare; retrocedere; **to turn down** piegarsi in giù; rovesciarsi; **to turn in** ripiegarsi; tornare a casa; (coll) andare a dormire; **to turn into** sfogare in; trasformarsi in; **to turn on** voltarsi contro; girarsi su; dipendere da; occuparsi di; **to turn**

out riuscire; **to turn out to be** manifestarsi; riuscire ad essere; **to turn over** rotolarsi; rovesciarsi; **to turn up** voltarsi all'insù; alzarsi; apparire, farsi vedere

turn'buck'le s tenditore m

turn'coat' s voltagabbana mf; **to become a turncoat** voltar gabbano

turn'down' adj (collar) rovesciato ‖ s rifiuto

turn'ing point' s punto decisivo

turnip ['tʌrnɪp] s rapa

turn'key' s secondino, carceriere m

turn' of life' s menopausa

turn' of mind' s disposizione naturale

turn'out' s (gathering of people) concorso; (crowd) folla; produzione; (outfit) vestito; stile m, moda; (in a road) slargo, piazzola; (horse and carriage) equipaggio; (rr) binario laterale

turn'over' s (upset) rovesciamento, ribaltamento; (of customers) movimento di clienti; (of business) giro d'affari; rotazione di lavoratori; (com) ciclo operativo

turn'pike' s autostrada a pedaggio

turn' sig'nal s (aut) indicatore m di direzione, lampeggiatore m

turnstile ['tʌrn‚staɪl] s tornello

turn'ta'ble s (of phonograph) piatto rotante; (rr) piattaforma girevole

turpentine ['tʌrpən‚taɪn] s trementina

turpitude ['tʌrpɪ‚tjud] or ['tʌrpɪ‚tud] s turpitudine f

turquoise ['tʌrkɔɪz] or ['tʌrkwɔɪz] s turchese m

turret ['tʌrɪt] s torretta

turtle ['tʌrtəl] s tartaruga; **to turn turtle** rovesciarsi, capovolgersi

tur'tle-dove' s tortora

Tuscan ['tʌskən] adj & s toscano

Tuscany ['tʌskəni] s la Toscana

tusk [tʌsk] s zanna

tussle ['tʌsəl] s lotta, zuffa ‖ intr lottare, azzuffarsi

tutor ['tjutər] or ['tutər] s istitutore privato, ripetitore m; (guardian) tutore m ‖ tr dare ripetizioni a ‖ intr dare ripetizioni; studiare con un ripetitore

tuxe·do [tʌk'sido] s (-dos) smoking m

twaddle ['twadəl] s sciocchezze fpl ‖ intr dire sciocchezze

twang [twæŋ] s (of musical instrument) suono vibrato; (of voice) timbro nasale ‖ tr pizzicare; dire con un timbro nasale ‖ intr parlare con voce nasale

twang·y ['twæŋi] adj (-ier; -iest) (tone) metallico; (voice) nasale

tweed [twid] s tweed m; **tweeds** abito di tweed

tweet [twit] s pigolio ‖ intr pigolare

tweeter ['twitər] s altoparlante m per alte audiofrequenze, tweeter m

tweezers ['twizərz] spl pinzette fpl

twelfth [twelfθ] adj, s & pron dodicesimo ‖ s (in dates) dodici m

Twelfth'-night' s vigilia dell'Epifania; sera dell'Epifania

twelve [twelv] adj & pron dodici ‖ s dodici m; **twelve o'clock** le dodici

twentieth ['twentɪ·ɪθ] adj, s & pron ventesimo ‖ s (in dates) venti m

twen·ty ['twenti] adj & pron venti ‖ s (-ties) venti m; **the twenties** gli anni venti

twice [twaɪs] adv due volte

twice'-told' adj detto più di una volta; detto e ridetto

twiddle ['twɪdəl] tr—**to twiddle one's thumbs** rigirare i pollici, oziare

twig [twɪg] s ramoscello; **twigs** sterpi mpl

twilight ['twaɪ‚laɪt] adj crepuscolare ‖ s crepuscolo

twill [twɪl] s diagonale m ‖ tr tessere in diagonale

twin [twɪn] adj & s gemello

twine [twaɪn] s spago ‖ tr intrecciare ‖ intr intrecciarsi

twinge [twɪndʒ] s punta, dolore acuto

twinkle ['twɪŋkəl] s scintillio; batter m d'occhio ‖ intr scintillare

twin'-screw' adj a due eliche

twirl [twʌrl] s giro, mulinello ‖ tr girare; (slang) lanciare ‖ intr girare rapidamente, frullare

twist [twɪst] s curva; giro; viluppo, intreccio; tendenza, inclinazione; (yarn) ritorno; (e.g., of lemon) fettina; (dance) twist m ‖ tr intrecciare; torcere; (e.g., the face) contorcere; (the meaning) stravolgere, stiracchiare; girare ‖ intr intrecciarsi; torcersi, divincolarsi; girare; seggiare; **to twist and turn** (in bed) girarsi e rigirarsi

twister ['twɪstər] s (coll) tromba d'aria

twit [twɪt] v (pret & pp **twitted**; ger **twitting**) tr ridicolizzare

twitch [twɪtʃ] s tic m; (jerk) strattone m; (to restrain a horse) torcinaso ‖ intr contrarsi; tremare; **to twitch at** tirare

twitter ['twɪtər] s garrito, cinguettio; (chatter) chiacchierio; ansia, agitazione ‖ intr garrire, cinguettare; chiacchierare; tremare d'ansia

two [tu] adj & pron due ‖ s due m; **to put two and two together** arrivare alle logiche conclusioni; **two o'clock** le due

two'-cy'cle adj a due tempi

two'-cyl'inder adj a due cilindri

two-edged ['tu‚edʒd] adj a doppio filo

two'fold' adj duplice, doppio

two' hun'dred adj, s & pron duecento

two'some ['tusəm] s coppia

two'-time' tr (slang) fare le corna a

two'-way ra'dio s ricetrasmettitore m

tycoon [taɪ'kun] s magnate m

type [taɪp] s tipo; (typ) carattere m; (pieces collectively) (typ) caratteri mpl ‖ tr scrivere a macchina; simbolizzare ‖ intr scrivere a macchina

type'face' s stile m di carattere

type'script' s dattiloscritto

typesetter ['taɪp‚setər] s (person) compositore m; (machine) compositrice f

type'write' v (pret **-wrote;** pp **-written**) tr & intr dattilografare, scrivere a macchina

type'writ'er s (machine) macchina da scrivere; (typist) dattilografo

type'writ'ing s dattilografia, scrittura a macchina; lavoro battuto a macchina

ty'phoid fe'ver ['taɪfɔɪd] s febbre f tifoide

typhoon [taɪ'fun] s tifone m

typical ['tɪpɪkəl] adj tipico

typi·fy ['tɪpɪ,faɪ] v (pret & pp **-fied**) tr simbolizzare

typist ['taɪpɪst] s dattilografo

typographic(al) [,taɪpə'græfɪk(əl)] adj tipografico

typograph'ical er'ror s errore m di stampa

typography [taɪ'pɒgrəfi] s tipografia

tyrannic(al) [tɪ'rænɪk(əl)] or [taɪ'rænɪk(əl)] adj tirannico

tyrannous ['tɪrənəs] adj tiranno

tyrant ['taɪrənt] s tiranno

ty·ro ['taɪro] s (**-ros**) principiante m

Tyrrhe'nian Sea' [tɪ'rini·ən] s Mare Tirreno

U

U, u [ju] s ventunesima lettera dell'alfabeto inglese

ubiquitous [ju'bɪkwɪtəs] adj ubiquo

udder ['ʌdər] s mammella

ugliness ['ʌglɪnɪs] s bruttezza

ug·ly ['ʌgli] adj (**-lier; -liest**) brutto

Ukraine, the ['jukren] or [ju'kren] s l'Ucraina f

Ukrainian [ju'kreni·ən] adj & s ucraino

ulcer ['ʌlsər] s piaga, ulcera; (corrupting element) (fig) piaga

ulcerate ['ʌlsə,ret] tr ulcerare ‖ intr ulcerarsi

ulterior [ʌl'tɪrɪ·ər] adj ulteriore; (motive) nascosto, secondo

ultimate ['ʌltɪmɪt] adj ultimo

ultima·tum [,ʌltɪ'metəm] s (**-tums** or **-ta** [tə]) ultimato

ultimo ['ʌltɪ,mo] adv del mese scorso

ul'tra·high fre'quency ['ʌltrə'haɪ] s frequenza ultraelevata

ultrashort [,ʌltrə'ʃɔrt] adj ultracorto

ultraviolet [,ʌltrə'vaɪ·əlɪt] adj & s ultravioletto

umbil'ical cord' [ʌm'bɪlɪkəl] s cordone m ombelicale

umbrage ['ʌmbrɪdʒ] s—**to take umbrage at** adombrarsi per

umbrella [ʌm'brelə] s ombrello, paracqua m; (mil) ombrello

umbrel'la stand' s portaombrelli m

Umbrian ['ʌmbrɪ·ən] adj & s umbro

umlaut ['umlaut] s metafonesi f; (mark) dieresi f ‖ tr cambiare il timbro di; scrivere con dieresi

umpire ['ʌmpaɪr] s arbitro ‖ tr arbitrare ‖ intr fare l'arbitro

UN ['ju'en] s (letterword) (United Nations) ONU f

unable [ʌn'ebəl] adj incapace; **to be unable to** essere impossibilitato a, non potere

unabridged [,ʌnə'brɪdʒd] adj integrale, non abbreviato

unaccented [ʌn'æksentɪd] or [,ʌnæk'sentɪd] adj non accentato, atono

unacceptable [,ʌnək'septəbəl] adj inaccettabile

unaccountable [,ʌnə'kauntəbəl] adj irresponsabile; inesplicabile

unaccounted-for [,ʌnə'kauntɪd ,fɔr]

adj (e.g., failure) inesplicato; (e.g., soldier) irreperibile, mancante

unaccustomed [,ʌnə'kʌstəmd] adj (unusual) insolito; non abituato

unafraid [,ʌnə'fred] adj impavido

unaligned [ʌnə'laɪnd] adj non impegnato

unanimity [,junə'nɪmɪti] s unanimità f

unanimous [ju'nænɪməs] adj unanime

unanswerable [ʌn'ænsərəbəl] adj per cui non vi è risposta; (argument) irrefutabile, incontestabile

unappreciative [,ʌnə'priʃɪ,etɪv] adj sconoscente, ingrato

unapproachable [,ʌnə'protʃəbəl] adj inabbordabile; incomparabile

unarmed [ʌn'ɑrmd] adj disarmato, inerme

unascertainable [ʌn,æsər'tenəbəl] adj non verificabile

unassailable [,ʌnə'seləbəl] adj inattaccabile

unassembled [,ʌnə'sembəld] adj smontato

unassuming [,ʌnə'sumɪŋ] or [,ʌnə'sjumɪŋ] adj modesto, semplice

unattached [,ʌnə'tætʃt] adj indipendente; (loose) sciolto; non sposato; non fidanzato

unattainable [,ʌnə'tenəbəl] adj inarrivabile, irraggiungibile

unattractive [,ʌnə'træktɪv] adj poco attraente

unavailable [,ʌnə'veləbəl] adj non disponibile

unavailing [,ʌnə'velɪŋ] adj futile

unavoidable [,ʌnə'vɔɪdəbəl] adj inevitabile, ineluttabile

unaware [,ʌnə'wer] adj inconsapevole, ignaro ‖ adv inaspettatamente; (unknowingly) inavvertitamente

unawares [,ʌnə'werz] adv inaspettatamente; (unknowingly) inavvertitamente

unbalanced [ʌn'bælənst] adj sbilanciato, squilibrato

unbandage [ʌn'bændɪdʒ] tr sbendare

un·bar [ʌn'bɑr] v (pret & pp **-barred;** ger **-barring**) tr disserrare il chiavistello di

unbearable [ʌn'berəbəl] adj insopportabile, insostenibile

unbeatable [ʌn'bitəbəl] *adj* imbattibile

unbecoming [ˌʌnbɪ'kʌmɪŋ] *adj* sconveniente, indegno; (*e.g., hat*) disadatto, che non sta bene

unbelievable [ˌʌnbɪ'livəbəl] *adj* incredibile

unbeliever [ˌʌnbɪ'livər] *s* miscredente *mf*

unbending [ʌn'bɛndɪŋ] *adj* inflessibile

unbiased [ʌn'baɪəst] *adj* imparziale, spassionato

un-bind [ʌn'baɪnd] *v* (*pret & pp* **-bound** ['baʊnd]) *tr* slegare

unbleached [ʌn'blitʃt] *adj* non candeggiato, al colore naturale

unbolt [ʌn'bolt] *tr* (*a door*) togliere il chiavistello a; sbullonare

unborn [ʌn'bɔrn] *adj* nascituro

unbosom [ʌn'buzəm] *tr* (*a secret*) rivelare; **to unbosom oneself** aprire il proprio animo, sfogarsi

unbound [ʌn'baʊnd] *adj* sciolto, libero; (*book*) non rilegato

unbreakable [ʌn'brekəbəl] *adj* infrangibile

unbridle [ʌn'braɪdəl] *tr* sbrigliare

unbuckle [ʌn'bʌkəl] *tr* sfibbiare

unburden [ʌn'bʌrdən] *tr* scaricare; **to unburden oneself** (**of**) vuotare il sacco (di)

unburied [ʌn'bɛrid] *adj* insepolto

unbutton [ʌn'bʌtən] *tr* sbottonare

uncalled-for [ʌn'kɔld ˌfɔr] *adj* superfluo, gratuito; fuori di posto, sconveniente

uncanny [ʌn'kæni] *adj* misterioso, straordinario

uncared-for [ʌn'kɛrd ˌfɔr] *adj* negletto, trascurato

unceasing [ʌn'sisɪŋ] *adj* incessante

unceremonious [ˌʌnsɛrɪ'monɪ-əs] *adj* senza cerimonie

uncertain [ʌn'sʌrtən] *adj* incerto

uncertain·ty [ʌn'sʌrtənti] *s* (**-ties**) incertezza

unchain [ʌn'tʃen] *tr* scatenare, sferrare

unchangeable [ʌn'tʃendʒəbəl] *adj* immutabile

uncharted [ʌn'tʃɑrtɪd] *adj* inesplorato

unchecked [ʌn'tʃɛkt] *adj* incontrollato

uncivilized [ʌn'sɪvɪˌlaɪzd] *adj* incivile

unclad [ʌn'klæd] *adj* svestito

unclaimed [ʌn'klemd] *adj* non reclamato; (*letter*) giacente

unclasp [ʌn'klæsp] *or* [ʌn'klɑsp] *tr* sfibbiare

unclassified [ʌn'klæsɪˌfaɪd] *adj* non classificato; non secreto

uncle ['ʌŋkəl] *s* zio

unclean [ʌn'klin] *adj* immondo

un-clog [ʌn'klɑg] *v* (*pret & pp* **-clogged**; *ger* **-clogging**) *tr* disintasare

unclouded [ʌn'klaʊdɪd] *adj* sereno, senza nubi

uncollectible [ˌʌnkə'lɛktɪbəl] *adj* inesigibile

uncomfortable [ʌn'kʌmfərtəbəl] *adj* scomodo, disagevole

uncommitted [ˌʌnkə'mɪtɪd] *adj* non impegnato

uncommon [ʌn'kamən] *adj* raro, straordinario

uncompromising [ʌn'kamprə ˌmaɪzɪŋ] *adj* intransigente

unconcerned [ˌʌnkən'sʌrnd] *adj* indifferente, noncurante

unconditional [ˌʌnkən'dɪʃənəl] *adj* incondizionato

uncongenial [ˌʌnkən'dʒini-əl] *adj* antipatico, sgradito

unconquerable [ʌn'kaŋkərəbəl] *adj* inconquistabile, inespugnabile

unconscionable [ʌn'kanʃənəbəl] *adj* senza scrupoli; eccessivo

unconscious [ʌn'kanʃəs] *adj* (*without awareness*) inconscio, inconsapevole; (*temporarily devoid of consciousness*) incosciente; (*unintentional*) involontario

unconsciousness [ʌn'kanʃəsnɪs] *s* incoscienza

unconstitutional [ˌʌnkanstɪ'tjuʃənəl] *or* [ˌʌnkanstɪ'tuʃənəl] *adj* incostituzionale

uncontrollable [ˌʌnkən'troləbəl] *adj* incontrollabile, ingovernabile

unconventional [ˌʌnkən'vɛnʃənəl] *adj* non convenzionale, anticonformista

uncork [ʌn'kɔrk] *tr* stappare

uncouple [ʌn'kʌpəl] *tr* sganciare, disconnettere

uncouth [ʌn'kuθ] *adj* zotico, incivile, pacchiano

uncover [ʌn'kʌvər] *tr* scoprire

unction ['ʌŋkʃən] *s* unzione; (fig) untuosità *f*

unctuous ['ʌŋktʃu-əs] *adj* untuoso

uncultivated [ʌn'kʌltɪˌvetɪd] *adj* incolto

uncultured [ʌn'kʌltʃərd] *adj* incolto, rozzo

uncut [ʌn'kʌt] *adj* non tagliato; (*book*) intonso

undamaged [ʌn'dæmɪdʒd] *adj* indenne, illeso

undaunted [ʌn'dɔntɪd] *adj* imperterrito, impavido

undeceive [ˌʌndɪ'siv] *tr* disingannare

undecided [ˌʌndɪ'saɪdɪd] *adj* indeciso

undefeated [ˌʌndɪ'fitɪd] *adj* invitto

undefended [ˌʌndɪ'fɛndɪd] *adj* indifeso

undefensible [ˌʌndɪ'fɛnsɪbəl] *adj* insostenibile

undefiled [ˌʌndɪ'faɪld] *adj* puro, immacolato

undeniable [ˌʌndɪ'naɪ-əbəl] *adj* innegabile, indubitato

under ['ʌndər] *adj* di sotto; (*lower*) inferiore; (*clothing*) intimo, personale || *adv* sotto; più sotto; **to go under** affondare; cedere; (coll) fallire || *prep* sotto; sotto a; (*e.g., 20 years old*) meno di; **under full sail** a vele spiegate; **under lock and key** sotto chiave; **under oath** sotto giuramento; **under penalty of death** sotto pena di morte; **under sail** a vela; **under separate cover** in plico separato; **under steam** sotto pressione; **under the hand and seal of** firmato di pugno di; **under the weather** (coll) un po' indisposto; **under way** già iniziato

un'der·age' *adj* minorenne

un'der·arm' pad *s* sottoascella *m*

un'der·bid' v (pret & pp -bid; ger -bidding) tr fare un'offerta inferiore a quella di

un'der·brush' s sottobosco

un'der·car'riage s (aut) telaio; (aer) carrello d'atterraggio

un'der·clothes' spl biancheria intima

un'der·consump'tion s sottoconsumo

un'der·cov'er adj segreto

un'der·cur'rent s (of water) corrente subacquea; (of air) corrente f inferiore; (fig) controcorrente f

underdeveloped [ˌʌndərdɪ'vɛləpt] adj sottosviluppato

un'der·dog' s chi è destinato ad avere la peggio; vittima; **the underdogs** i diseredati

un'der·done' adj non cotto abbastanza

un'der·es'timate tr sottovalutare

un'der·gar'ment s indumento intimo

un'der·go' v (pret -went; pp -gone) tr (a test) passare, sottostare (with dat); (surgery) subire, sottoporsi a; soffrire

un'der·grad'uate adj (student) non ancora laureato; (course) per studenti non ancora laureati || s studente universitario che non ha ancora ricevuto il primo diploma

un'der·ground' adj sotterraneo; segreto || s regione sotterranea; macchia, resistenza || adv sottoterra; alla macchia, segretamente

un'der·growth' s sterpaglia

underhanded ['ʌndər'hændəd] adj subdolo, di sottomano

un'der·line' or **un'der·line'** tr sottolineare

underling ['ʌndərlɪŋ] s tirapiedi m

un'der·mine' tr scalzare, minare

underneath [ˌʌndər'niθ] adj inferiore || s disotto || adv sotto, di sotto || prep sotto a, sotto

undernourished [ˌʌndər'nʌrɪʃt] adj denutrito, malnutrito

un'der·pass' s sottopassaggio

un'der·pay' s (pret & pp -paid) tr & intr pagare insufficientemente

un'der·pin' v (pret & pp -pinned; ger -pinning) tr rincalzare

underprivileged [ˌʌndər'prɪvɪlɪdʒd] adj derelitto, diseredato

un'der·rate' tr sottovalutare

un'der·score' tr sottolineare

un'der·sea' adj sottomarino || adv sotto il mare

un'der·seas' adv sotto il mare

un'der·sec'retar'y s (-ies) sottosegretario

un'der·sell' v (pret & pp -sold) tr vendere a prezzo minore di; (to sell for less than actual value) svendere

un'der·shirt' s camiciola, canottiera

undersigned ['ʌndər ˌsaɪnd] adj sottoscritto

un'der·skirt' s sottogonna

un'der·stand' v (pret & pp -stood) tr capire, comprendere; sottintendere; (to accept as true) constare, e.g., **he understands that you are wrong** gli consta che Lei ha torto || intr capire, comprendere

understandable [ˌʌndər'stændəbəl] adj comprensibile

understanding [ˌʌndər'stændɪŋ] adj comprensivo, tollerante || s (mind) intelletto; (knowledge) conoscenza; comprensione, intendimento; (agreement) intesa, accordo

understatement [ˌʌndər'stetmənt] s sottovalutazione

un'der·stud'y s (-ies) (theat) doppio, sostituto || v (-ied) tr (an actor) fare il doppio di

un'der·take' v (pret -took; ger -taken) tr intraprendere; (to promise) promettere

undertaker [ˌʌndər'tekər] or ['ʌndərˌtekər] s impresario || [ˌʌndərˌtekər] s impresario di pompe funebri

undertaking [ˌʌndər'tekɪŋ] s (task) impresa; (promise) promessa || ['ʌndərˌtekɪŋ] s impresa di pompe funebri

un'der·tone' s bassa voce; (background sound) ronzio di fondo; tono; colore smorzato

un'der·tow' s (on the beach) risacca; (countercurrent below surface) controcorrente f

un'der·wa'ter adj subacqueo || adv sott'acqua

un'der·wear' s biancheria intima

un'der·world' s (criminal world) malavita; teppa; (abode of spirits) ade m, averno; mondo sotterraneo; mondo sottomarino; antipodi mpl

un'der·write' v (pret -wrote; pp -written) tr sottoscrivere; (to insure) assicurare

un'der·writ'er s sottoscrittore m; (ins) assicuratore m

undeserved [ˌʌndɪ'zɑrvd] adj immeritato

undesirable [ˌʌndɪ'zaɪrəbəl] adj & s indesiderabile mf

undetachable [ˌʌndɪ'tætʃəbəl] adj non movibile

undeveloped [ˌʌndɪ'vɛləpt] adj (land) non sfruttato; (country) sottosviluppato

undigested [ˌʌndɪ'dʒɛstɪd] adj non digerito

undignified [ʌn'dɪgnɪˌfaɪd] adj poco decoroso

undiscernible [ˌʌndɪ'zɑrnɪbəl] or [ˌʌndɪ'sɑrnɪbəl] adj impercettibile

undisputed [ˌʌndɪ'spjutəd] adj indiscusso, incontrastato

un·do [ʌn'du] v (pret -did; pp -done) tr sfare, disfare; rovinare; (a package) aprire; (a knot) sciogliere

undoing [ʌn'du·ɪŋ] s rovina

undone [ʌn'dʌn] adj non finito; **to come undone** disfarsi; **to leave nothing undone** non tralasciare di fare nulla

undoubtedly [ʌn'daʊtɪdli] adv indubiamente, senza dubbio

undress ['ʌnˌdrɛs] or [ʌn'drɛs] s vestaglia; vestito da ogni giorno || [ʌn'drɛs] tr spogliare, svestire; (a *wound*) sbendare ‖ *intr* spogliarsi, svestirsi

undrinkable [ʌn'drɪŋkəbəl] *adj* imbevibile, non potabile

undue [ʌn'dju] or [ʌn'du] *adj* indebito; immeritato; eccessivo

undulate ['ʌndjə,let] *intr* ondulare

unduly [ʌn'djuli] or [ʌn'duli] *adv* indebitamente, eccessivamente

unearned [ʌn'ɑrnd] *adj* non guadagnato col lavoro; immeritato; non ancora guadagnato

un'earned in'crement *s* plusvalenza

unearth [ʌn'ɑrθ] *tr* dissotterrare

unearthly [ʌn'ɑrθli] *adj* ultraterreno; spettrale; impossibile, straordinario

uneasy [ʌn'izi] *adj* (*worried*) preoccupato; (*constrained*) scomodo; (*not conducive to ease*) inquietante, a disagio

uneatable [ʌn'itəbəl] *adj* immangiabile

uneconomic(al) [,ʌnikə'nɑmɪk(əl)] or [,ʌnekə'nɑmɪk(əl)] *adj* antieconomico

uneducated [ʌn'edʒə,ketɪd] *adj* ineducato

unemployed [,ʌnem'plɔɪd] *adj* disoccupato, incollocato; improduttivo ‖ **the unemployed** i disoccupati

unemployment [,ʌnem'plɔɪmənt] *s* disimpiego, disoccupazione

unemploy'ment compensa'tion *s* sussidio di disoccupazione

unending [ʌn'endɪŋ] *adj* interminabile

unequal [ʌn'ikwəl] *adj* disuguale, impari; **to be unequal to** (*a task*) non essere all'altezza di

unequaled or **unequalled** [ʌn'ikwəld] *adj* ineguagliato

unerring [ʌn'ɑrɪŋ] or [ʌn'erɪŋ] *adj* infallibile; corretto, preciso

unessential [,ʌne'senʃəl] *adj* non essenziale

uneven [ʌn'ivən] *adj* disuguale, ineguale; (*number*) dispari

uneventful [,ʌnɪ'ventfəl] *adj* senza avvenimenti importanti; (*life*) tranquillo

unexceptionable [,ʌnek'sepʃənəbəl] *adj* ineccepibile, irreprensibile

unexpected [,ʌnek'spektɪd] *adj* inaspettato, imprevisto

unexplained [,ʌnek'splend] *adj* inesplicato

unexplored [,ʌnek'splord] *adj* inesplorato

unexposed [,ʌnek'spozd] *adj* (phot) non esposto alla luce

unfading [ʌn'fedɪŋ] *adj* immarcescibile; imperituro

unfailing [ʌn'felɪŋ] *adj* immancabile, infallibile; (*inexhaustible*) inesauribile; (*dependable*) sicuro

unfair [ʌn'fer] *adj* ingiusto; disonesto, sleale

unfaithful [ʌn'feθfəl] *adj* infedele

unfamiliar [,ʌnfə'mɪljər] *adj* poco pratico; poco abituale, strano; non conosciuto

unfasten [ʌn'fæsən] or [ʌn'fɑsən] *tr* sfibbiare, sciogliere

unfathomable [ʌn'fæðəməbəl] *adj* insondabile

unfavorable [ʌn'fevərəbəl] *adj* sfavorevole

unfeeling [ʌn'filɪŋ] *adj* insensibile

unfetter [ʌn'fetər] *tr* sciogliere dalle catene

unfinished [ʌn'fɪnɪʃt] *adj* incompiuto; grezzo, non rifinito; (*business*) inevaso

unfit [ʌn'fɪt] *adj* disadatto; inabile

unfledged [ʌn'fledʒd] *adj* implume

unfold [ʌn'fold] *tr* schiudere; (*e.g., a newspaper*) spiegare ‖ *intr* schiudersi; svolgersi

unforeseeable [,ʌnfor'si·əbəl] *adj* imprevedibile

unforeseen [,ʌnfor'sin] *adj* imprevisto

unforgettable [,ʌnfər'getəbəl] *adj* indimenticabile

unforgivable [,ʌnfər'gɪvəbəl] *adj* imperdonabile

unfortunate [ʌn'fɔrtʃənɪt] *adj & s* disgraziato, sfortunato

unfounded [ʌn'faundɪd] *adj* infondato

un-freeze [ʌn'friz] *v* (*pret* -**froze**; *pp* -**frozen**) *tr* disgelare; (*credit*) sbloccare

unfriend-ly [ʌn'frendli] *adj* (-**lier**; -**liest**) *adj* mal disposto, ostile; sfavorevole

unfruitful [ʌn'frutfəl] *adj* infruttuoso

unfulfilled [,ʌnfəl'fɪld] *adj* incompiuto

unfurl [ʌn'fɑrl] *tr* spiegare, dispiegare

unfurnished [ʌn'fɑrnɪʃt] *adj* smobiliato

ungainly [ʌn'genli] *adj* sgraziato, maldestro

ungentlemanly [ʌn'dʒentəlmənli] *adj* indegno di un gentleman

ungird [ʌn'gɑrd] *tr* discingere

ungodly [ʌn'gɑdli] *adj* irreligioso, empio; (*dreadful*) (coll) atroce

ungracious [ʌn'greʃəs] *adj* rude, scortese; (*task*) sgradevole

ungrammatical [,ʌngrə'mætɪkəl] *adj* sgrammaticato

ungrateful [ʌn'gretfəl] *adj* ingrato

ungrudgingly [ʌn'grʌdʒɪŋli] *adv* di buon grado, volentieri

unguarded [ʌn'gɑrdɪd] *adj* incustodito, indifeso; incauto, imprudente

unguent ['ʌŋgwənt] *s* unguento

unhappiness [ʌn'hæpɪnɪs] *s* infelicità *f*

unhap-py [ʌn'hæpi] *adj* (-**pier**; -**piest**) infelice, sfortunato

unharmed [ʌn'hɑrmd] *adj* illeso

unharness [ʌn'hɑrnɪs] *tr* togliere i finimenti a

unhealth-y [ʌn'hɛlθi] *adj* (-**ier**; -**iest**) malsano

unheard-of [ʌn'hɑrd,av] *adj* (*unknown*) sconosciuto; inaudito

unhinge [ʌn'hɪndʒ] *tr* sgangherare; (fig) sconvolgere

unhitch [ʌn'hɪtʃ] *tr* sganciare; (*a horse*) staccare

unho-ly [ʌn'holi] *adj* (-**lier**; -**liest**) empio; terribile, atroce

unhook [ʌn'huk] *tr* sganciare

unhoped-for [ʌn'hopt,fɔr] *adj* insperato

unhorse [ʌn'hɔrs] *tr* disarcionare

unhurt [ʌnˈhʌrt] *adj* incolume, illeso

unicorn [ˈjunɪˌkɔrn] *s* unicorno

unification [ˌjunɪfɪˈkeʃən] *s* unificazione

uniform [ˈjunɪˌfɔrm] *adj* & *s* uniforme *f* || *tr* uniformare

uni·fy [ˈjunɪˌfaɪ] *v* (*pret* & *pp* -fied) *tr* unificare

unilateral [ˌjunɪˈlætərəl] *adj* unilaterale

unimpeachable [ˌʌnɪmˈpitʃəbəl] *adj* irrefutabile; irreprensibile

unimportant [ˌʌnɪmˈpɔrtənt] *adj* poco importante

uninhabited [ˌʌnɪnˈhæbɪtɪd] *adj* inabitato, disabitato

uninspired [ˌʌnɪnˈspaɪrd] *adj* senza ispirazione, prosaico

unintelligent [ˌʌnɪnˈtelɪdʒənt] *adj* non intelligente; stupido

unintelligible [ˌʌnɪnˈtelɪdʒɪbəl] *adj* inintelligibile

uninterested [ʌnˈɪntrɪstɪd] or [ʌnˈɪntəˌrestɪd] *adj* non interessato

uninteresting [ʌnˈɪntrɪstɪŋ] or [ʌnˈɪntəˌrestɪŋ] *adj* poco interessante

uninterrupted [ˌʌnɪntəˈrʌptɪd] *adj* ininterrotto

union [ˈjunjən] *s* unione; unione matrimoniale; (*of workers*) sindacato

unionize [ˈjunjəˌnaɪz] *tr* organizzare in un sindacato || *intr* organizzarsi in un sindacato

un'ion shop' *s* fabbrica che assume solo sindacalisti

un'ion suit' *s* combinazione

unique [juˈnik] *adj* unico

unison [ˈjunɪsən] or [ˈjunɪzən] *s* unisono; in unison all'unisono

unit [ˈjunɪt] *adj* unitario || *s* unità *f*; (mach, elec) gruppo

unite [juˈnaɪt] *tr* unire || *intr* unirsi

united [juˈnaɪtɪd] *adj* unito

Unit'ed King'dom *s* Regno Unito

Unit'ed Na'tions *spl* Organizzazione delle Nazioni Unite

Unit'ed States' *adj* statunitense || the United States *ssg* gli Stati Uniti

uni·ty [ˈjunɪti] *s* (-ties) unità *f*

universal [ˌjunɪˈvʌrsəl] *adj* universale

u'niver'sal joint' *s* giunto cardanico

universe [ˈjunɪˌvʌrs] *s* universo

universi·ty [ˌjunɪˈvʌrsɪti] *adj* universitario || *s* (-ties) università *f*

unjust [ʌnˈdʒʌst] *adj* ingiusto

unjustified [ʌnˈdʒʌstɪˌfaɪd] *adj* ingiustificato

unkempt [ʌnˈkempt] *adj* spettinato; trascurato

unkind [ʌnˈkaɪnd] *adj* scortese; duro, crudele

unknowable [ʌnˈno·əbəl] *adj* inconoscibile

unknowingly [ʌnˈno·ɪŋli] *adv* inconsapevolmente

unknown [ʌnˈnon] *adj* sconosciuto || *s* incognito; (math) incognita

Un'known Sol'dier *s* Milite Ignoto

unlace [ʌnˈles] *tr* slacciare

unlatch [ʌnˈlætʃ] *tr* tirare il saliscendi a

unlawful [ʌnˈlɔfəl] *adj* illegale

unleash [ʌnˈliʃ] *tr* sguinzagliare; (fig) scatenare

unleavened [ʌnˈlevənd] *adj* azzimo

unless [ʌnˈles] *conj* se non che, salvo che

unlettered [ʌnˈletərd] *adj* ignorante; (*illiterate*) analfabeta

unlike [ʌnˈlaɪk] *adj* dissimile, differente; dissimile da, e.g., a copy unlike the original una copia dissimile dall'originale; (elec) di segno contrario || *prep* diversamente da, a differenza di; it was unlike him to arrive late non era cosa normale per lui arrivare in ritardo

unlikely [ʌnˈlaɪkli] *adj* improbabile

unlimber [ʌnˈlɪmbər] *tr* mettere in batteria || *intr* prepararsi a fare fuoco; (fig) prepararsi

unlimited [ʌnˈlɪmɪtɪd] *adj* illimitato

unlined [ʌnˈlaɪnd] *adj* (*e.g., coat*) non foderato; (*paper*) non rigato

unload [ʌnˈlod] *tr* scaricare; (*passengers*) sbarcare; (*to get rid of*) liberarsi di || *intr* scaricare; sbarcare

unloading [ʌnˈlodɪŋ] *s* discarica; sbarco

unlock [ʌnˈlak] *tr* aprire

unloose [ʌnˈlus] *tr* rilasciare; sciogliere

unloved [ʌnˈlʌvd] *adj* poco amato

unlovely [ʌnˈlʌvli] *adj* poco attraente

unluck·y [ʌnˈlʌki] *adj* (-ier; -iest) sfortunato, disgraziato

un·make [ʌnˈmek] *v* (*pret* & *pp* -made [ˈmed]) *tr* disfare; deporre

unmanageable [ʌnˈmænɪdʒəbəl] *adj* incontrollabile

unmanly [ʌnˈmænli] *adj* non virile, effeminato; codardo

unmannerly [ʌnˈmænərli] *adj* scortese

unmarketable [ʌnˈmɑrkɪtəbəl] *adj* invendibile

unmarriageable [ʌnˈmærɪdʒəbəl] *adj* che non si può sposare; non adatto al matrimonio

unmarried [ʌnˈmærid] *adj* scapolo; (*female*) nubile

unmask [ʌnˈmæsk] or [ʌnˈmɑsk] *tr* smascherare || *intr* smascherarsi

unmatchable [ʌnˈmætʃəbəl] *adj* impareggiabile

unmatched [ʌnˈmætʃd] *adj* impareggiabile; (*unpaired*) sparigliato

unmentionable [ʌnˈmenʃənəbəl] *adj* innominabile

unmerciful [ʌnˈmʌrsɪfəl] *adj* spietato

unmesh [ʌnˈmeʃ] *tr* disingranare || *intr* disingranarsi

unmindful [ʌnˈmaɪndfəl] *adj* immemore; incurante

unmistakable [ˌʌnmɪsˈtekəbəl] *adj* inconfondibile

unmitigated [ʌnˈmɪtɪˌgetɪd] *adj* completo; assoluto, perfetto

unmixed [ʌnˈmɪkst] *adj* puro

unmoor [ʌnˈmur] *tr* disormeggiare

unmoved [ʌnˈmuvd] *adj* immoto; fisso, immobile; (fig) impassibile

unmuzzle [ʌnˈmʌzəl] *tr* togliere la museruola a

unnamed [ʌnˈnemd] *adj* innominato

unnatural [ʌnˈnætʃ/ərəl] *adj* contro natura, snaturato; innaturale, affettato

unnecessary [ʌn'nesə ,seri] *adj* inutile

unnerve [ʌn'nʌrv] *tr* snervare

unnoticeable [ʌn'notɪsəbəl] *adj* impercettibile

unnoticed [ʌn'notɪst] *adj* inosservato

unobserved [,ʌnəb'zʌrvd] *adj* inosservato

unobtainable [,ʌnəb'tenəbəl] *adj* non ottenibile, irraggiungibile

unobtrusive [,ʌnəb'trusɪv] *adj* discreto, riservato

unoccupied [ʌn'ɑkjə ,paɪd] *adj* libero, disponibile; (*not busy*) disoccupato

unofficial [,ʌnə'fɪʃəl] *adj* non ufficiale, ufficioso

unopened [ʌn'opənd] *adj* non aperto, chiuso; (*letter*) non dissuggellato; (*book*) intonso

unorthodox [ʌn'ɔrθə ,dɑks] *adj* non ortodosso

unpack [ʌn'pæk] *tr* spaccare, sballare

unpalatable [ʌn'pælətəbəl] *adj* di gusto spiacevole

unparalleled [ʌn'pærə ,lɛld] *adj* incomparabile, senza pari

unpardonable [ʌn'pardənəbəl] *adj* imperdonabile

unpatriotic [,ʌnpetri'ɑtɪk] *or* [,ʌn-pætri'ɑtɪk] *adj* antipatriottico

unperceived [,ʌnpər'sivd] *adj* inosservato

unperturbable [,ʌnpər't ʌrbəbəl] *adj* imperterrito, imperturbato

unpleasant [ʌn'plesənt] *adj* spiacevole; (*person*) antipatico

unpopular [ʌn'pɑpjələr] *adj* impopolare

unpopularity [ʌn ,pɑpjə'læriti] *s* impopolarità *f*

unprecedented [ʌn'presi ,dentɪd] *adj* senza precedenti, inaudito

unprejudiced [ʌn'predʒədɪst] *adj* senza pregiudizio, imparziale

unpremeditated [,ʌnpri'medi ,tetɪd] *adj* impremeditato

unprepared [,ʌnpri'perd] *adj* impreparato

unprepossessing [,ʌnpripə'zesɪŋ] *adj* poco attraente, antipatico

unpresentable [,ʌnpri'zentəbəl] *adj* impresentabile

unpretentious [,ʌnpri'tenʃəs] *adj* modesto, senza pretese

unprincipled [ʌn'prinsipəld] *adj* senza principi

unproductive [,ʌnprə'dʌktɪv] *adj* improduttivo

unprofitable [ʌn'prɑfitəbəl] *adj* infruttuoso

unpronounceable [,ʌnprə'naunsəbəl] *adj* impronunziabile

unpropitious [,ʌnprə'pɪʃəs] *adj* inauspicato

unpublished [ʌn'pʌblɪʃt] *adj* inedito

unpunished [ʌn'pʌnɪʃt] *adj* impunito

unqualified [ʌn'kwɑlɪ ,faɪd] *adj* inabile, inidoneo; assoluto, completo

unquenchable [ʌn'kwentʃəbəl] *adj* inappagabile, inestinguibile

unquestionable [ʌn'kwestʃənəbəl] *adj* indiscutibile

unrav·el [ʌn'rævəl] *v* (*pret & pp* -eled

or -elled; *ger* -eling *or* -elling) *tr* dipanare || *intr* districarsi; chiarirsi

unreachable [ʌn'ritʃəbəl] *adj* irraggiungibile

unreal [ʌn'ril] *adj* irreale

unreali·ty [,ʌnri'æliti] *s* (-ties) irrealità *f*

unreasonable [ʌn'rizənəbəl] *adj* irragionevole

unrecognizable [ʌn'rekəg ,naɪzəbəl] *adj* irriconoscibile

unreel [ʌn'ril] *tr* svolgere, srotolare || *intr* srotolarsi

unrefined [ʌn'raɪnd] *adj* non raffinato, greggio; volgare, ordinario

unrelenting [,ʌnri'lentɪŋ] *adj* inesorabile, inflessibile; indefesso

unreliable [,ʌnri'laɪ-əbəl] *adj* malfido; (*news*) inattendibile

unremitting [,ʌnri'mitɪŋ] *adj* incessante, costante

unrented [ʌn'rentɪd] *adj* da affittare

unrepeatable [,ʌnripitəbəl] *adj* irripetibile

unrepentant [,ʌnri'pentənt] *adj* impenitente

un'requit'ed love' [,ʌnri'kwaɪtɪd] *s* amore non corrisposto

unresponsive [,ʌnri'spɑnsɪv] *adj* apatico, insensibile

unrest [ʌn'rest] *s* agitazione

un·rig [ʌn'rig] *v* (*pret & pp* -rigged; *ger* -rigging) *tr* (naut) disarmare

unrighteous [ʌn'raɪtʃəs] *adj* ingiusto

unripe [ʌn'raɪp] *adj* immaturo

unrivaled *or* **unrivalled** [ʌn'raɪvəld] *adj* senza pari

unroll [ʌn'rol] *tr* srotolare

unromantic [,ʌnro'mæntɪk] *adj* poco romantico

unruffled [ʌn'rʌfəld] *adj* calmo, imperturbabile

unruly [ʌn'ruli] *adj* turbolento; indisciplinato, insubordinato

unsaddle [ʌn'sædəl] *tr* (*a horse*) dissellare; (*a rider*) scavalcare

unsafe [ʌn'sef] *adj* malsicuro, pericolante

unsaid [ʌn'sed] *adj* non detto, taciuto; **to leave unsaid** passare sotto silenzio

unsalable [ʌn'seləbəl] *adj* invendibile

unsanitary [ʌn'sæni ,teri] *adj* antigienico

unsatisfactory [ʌn ,sætis'fæktəri] *adj* poco soddisfacente

unsatisfied [ʌn'sætis ,faɪd] *adj* insoddisfatto, inappagato

unsavory [ʌn'sevəri] *adj* insipido; (fig) disgustoso, nauseabondo

un·say [ʌn'se] *v* (*pret & pp* -said [sed']) *tr* disdire

unscathed [ʌn'skeðd] *adj* incolume

unscheduled [ʌn'skedʒuld] *adj* non in elenco; (*event*) fuori programma; (*e.g., flight*) fuori orario; (*phase of production*) non programmato

unscientific [,ʌnsai-ən'tifik] *adj* poco scientifico

unscrew [ʌn'skru] *tr* svitare || *intr* svitarsi

unscrupulous [ʌn'skrupjələs] *adj* senza scrupoli

unseal [ʌn'sil] *tr* dissigillare

unseasonable [ʌn'sizənəbəl] *adj* fuori stagione; inopportuno

unseasoned [ʌn'sizənd] *adj* scondito; (*crop*) immaturo; (*crew*) inesperto

unseat [ʌn'sit] *tr* (*a rider*) scavalcare, disarcionare; (*e.g., a congressman*) far perdere il seggio a, defenestrare

unseemly [ʌn'simli] *adj* disdicevole, sconveniente

unseen [ʌn'sin] *adj* non visto, inosservato; nascosto, occulto; invisibile

unselfish [ʌn'selfiʃ] *adj* disinteressato

unsettled [ʌn'setəld] *adj* disabitato; disorganizzato; disordinato, erratico; indeciso; (*bill*) da pagare

unshackle [ʌn'ʃækəl] *tr* liberare

unshaken [ʌn'ʃekən] *adj* inconcusso

unshapely [ʌn'ʃepli] *adj* senza forma, deforme

unshaven [ʌn'ʃevən] *adj* non rasato

unshatterable [ʌn'ʃætərəbəl] *adj* infrangibile

unsheathe [ʌn'ʃið] *tr* sguainare

unshod [ʌn'ʃɑd] *adj* scalzo; (*horse*) sferrato

unshrinkable [ʌn'ʃrɪŋkəbəl] *adj* irrestringibile

unsightly [ʌn'saɪtli] *adj* ripugnante, brutto

unsinkable [ʌn'sɪŋkəbəl] *adj* insommergibile

unskilled [ʌn'skɪld] *adj* inesperto

un'skilled la'bor *s* lavoro manuale; mano d'opera non specializzata

unskillful [ʌn'skɪlfəl] *adj* maldestro

unsnarl [ʌn'snɑrl] *tr* sbrogliare

unsociable [ʌn'soʃəbəl] *adj* insocievole

unsold [ʌn'sold] *adj* invenduto

unsolder [ʌn'sɑdər] *tr* dissaldare

unsophisticated [ˌʌnsə'fɪstɪˌketɪd] *adj* semplice, puro

unsound [ʌn'saund] *adj* malsano, malato; (*decayed*) guasto, imputridito; falso, fallace; (*sleep*) leggero

unsown [ʌn'son] *adj* incolto, non seminato

unspeakable [ʌn'spikəbəl] *adj* indicibile; (*atrocious*) innominabile, inqualificabile

unsportsmanlike [ʌn'sportsmən ˌlaɪk] *adj* antisportivo

unstable [ʌn'stebəl] *adj* instabile

unsteady [ʌn'stedi] *adj* malfermo; incostante; irregolare

unstinted [ʌn'stɪntɪd] *adj* generoso, senza limiti

unstitch [ʌn'stɪtʃ] *tr* scucire

un-stop [ʌn'stɑp] *v* (*pret* & *pp* -stopped; *ger* -stopping) *tr* stasare

unstressed [ʌn'strest] *adj* non accentuato; (*e.g., syllable*) non accentato

unstrung [ʌn'strʌŋ] *adj* (*beads*) sfilato; (*instrument*) allentato; (*person*) snervato

unsuccessful [ˌʌnsək'sesfəl] *adj* (*person*) sfortunato; (*deal*) mancato; **to be unsuccessful** fallire

unsuitable [ʌn'sutəbəl] or [ʌn'sjutəbəl] *adj* inappropriato

unsurpassable [ˌʌnsər'pæsəbəl] or [ˌʌnsər'pɑsəbəl] *adj* insuperabile

unsuspected [ˌʌnsəs'pektɪd] *adj* insospettato

unswerving [ʌn'swʌrvɪŋ] *adj* diritto, fermo, costante

unsympathetic [ˌʌnsɪmpə'θetɪk] *adj* indifferente, che non mostra comprensione

unsystematic(al) [ˌʌnsɪstə'mætɪk(əl)] *adj* senza sistema

untactful [ʌn'tæktfəl] *adj* senza tatto

untamed [ʌn'temd] *adj* indomito

untangle [ʌn'tæŋgəl] *tr* sgrovigliare

unteachable [ʌn'titʃəbəl] *adj* indocile; refrattario agli studi

untenable [ʌn'tenəbəl] *adj* insostenibile

unthankful [ʌn'θæŋkfəl] *adj* ingrato

unthinkable [ʌn'θɪŋkəbəl] *adj* impensabile

unthinking [ʌn'θɪŋkɪŋ] *adj* irriflessivo

untidy [ʌn'taɪdi] *adj* disordinato

un-tie [ʌn'taɪ] *v* (*pret* & *pp* -tied; *ger* -tying) *tr* sciogliere; (*a knot*) slacciare, snodare || *intr* sciogliersi

until [ʌn'tɪl] *prep* fino, fino a || *conj* fino a che, finché

untillable [ʌn'tɪləbəl] *adj* incoltivabile

untimely [ʌn'taɪmli] *adj* intempestivo; (*death*) prematuro

untiring [ʌn'taɪrɪŋ] *adj* instancabile

untold [ʌn'told] *adj* non detto, non raccontato; incalcolabile; (*inexpressable*) indicibile

untouchable [ʌn'tʌtʃəbəl] *adj* & *s* intoccabile *mf*

untouched [ʌn'tʌtʃt] *adj* intatto; insensibile; non menzionato

untoward [ʌn'tord] *adj* sfavorevole; sconveniente, disdicevole

untrammeled or untrammelled [ʌn'træməld] *adj* non inceppato

untried [ʌn'traɪd] *adj* non provato

untroubled [ʌn'trʌbəld] *adj* tranquillo

untrue [ʌn'tru] *adj* falso

untrustworthy [ʌn'trʌst ˌwʌrði] *adj* infido, malfido

untruth [ʌn'truθ] *s* falsità *f*, menzogna

untruthful [ʌn'truθfəl] *adj* falso, menzognero

untwist [ʌn'twɪst] *tr* districare || *intr* districarsi

unusable [ʌn'juzəbəl] *adj* inservibile

unused [ʌn'juzd] *adj* inutilizzato; **unused to** [ʌn'justu] disavvezzo a

unusual [ʌn'juʒʊəl] *adj* insolito

unutterable [ʌn'ʌtərəbəl] *adj* impronunciabile; indicibile

unvanquished [ʌn'væŋkwɪʃt] *adj* invitto

unvarnished [ʌn'vɑrnɪʃt] *adj* non verniciato; puro, semplice

unveil [ʌn'vel] *tr* svelare; (*a statue*) scoprire, inaugurare || *intr* scoprirsi

unveiling [ˌʌn'velɪŋ] *s* scoprimento

unvoiced [ʌn'vɔɪst] *adj* non espresso; (*phonet*) sordo

unwanted [ʌn'wɑntɪd] *adj* non desiderato

unwarranted [ʌn'wɑrəntɪd] *adj* ingiustificato

unwary [ʌn'weri] *adj* incauto

unwavering [ʌn'wevərɪŋ] *adj* fermo, incrollabile

unwelcome [ʌn'welkəm] *adj* malaccetto, sgradito

unwell [ʌn'wel] *adj* poco bene; **to be**

unwell (*said of a woman*) (coll) avere le mestruazioni

unwholesome [ʌn'holsəm] *adj* malsano

unwieldy [ʌn'wildi] *adj* ingombrante

unwilling [ʌn'wɪlɪŋ] *adj* riluttante

unwillingly [ʌn'wɪlɪŋli] *adv* a malincuore, a controvoglia

un·wind [ʌn'waɪnd] *v* (*pret & pp* -wound* ['waund]) *tr* svolgere || *intr* svolgersi; (*said of a watch*) scaricarsi; (*said of a person*) rilasciarsi

unwise [ʌn'waɪz] *adj* malaccorto

unwished-for [ʌn'wɪʃt,fɔr] *adj* indesiderato, non augurato

unwitting [ʌn'wɪtɪŋ] *adj* involontario

unwonted [ʌn'wʌntɪd] *adj* insolito

unworldly [ʌn'wʌrdli] *adj* (*not of this world*) non terrestre; (*not interested in things of this world*) non mondano; (*naïve*) semplice

unworthy [ʌn'wʌrði] *adj* indegno

un·wrap [ʌn'ræp] *v* (*pret & pp* -wrapped*; *ger* -wrapping) *tr* scartare, svolgere, scartocciare

unwrinkled [ʌn'rɪŋkəld] *adj* senza una grinza

unwritten [ʌn'rɪtən] *adj* orale; non scritto; (*blank*) in bianco

unyielding [ʌn'jildɪŋ] *adj* inflessibile

unyoke [ʌn'yok] *tr* liberare dal giogo

up [ʌp] *adj* che va verso la città; diretto al nord; al corrente; finito, terminato; alto; su; (sports) pari; **to be up and about** essere in piedi || *s* salita; vantaggio; aumento; **ups and downs** alti e bassi *mpl* || *adv* su; in alto; alla pari; **to be up** essere alzato; (*in sports or games*) essere avanti; **to be up in arms** essere in armi; essere indignato; **to be up to a person** toccare a una persona; **to get up** alzarsi; **to go up** salire; **to keep up** mantenere; continuare; **to keep up with** mantenersi alla pari con; **up above** lassù; **up against** (coll) contro; **up against it** (coll) in una strettoia; **up to** fino a; (*capable of*) (coll) all'altezza di; (*scheming*) (coll) tramando; **what's up?** che succede? || *prep* su; sopra; fino a; **to go up a river** risalire un fiume

up-and-coming ['ʌpən'kʌmɪŋ] *adj* promettente

up-and-doing ['ʌpən'du.ɪŋ] *adj* (coll) intraprendente; (coll) attivo

up-and-up ['ʌpən'ʌp] *s*—**on the up-and-up** (coll) aperto; (coll) apertamente; (coll) in ascesa

upbraid *tr* rimproverare, strapazzare

upbringing ['ʌp,brɪŋɪŋ] *s* educazione

up'coun'try *adj* all'interno || *s* interno || *adv* verso l'interno

up·date *tr* aggiornare

upheaval [ʌp'hivəl] *s* sommovimento; (geol) sconvolgimento tellurico

up'hill' *adj* erto, scosceso; arduo, faticoso || *adv* in salita, all'insù

up·hold *v* (*pret & pp* -held) *tr* alzare; sostenere; difendere

upholster [ʌp'holstər] *tr* tappezzare

upholsterer [ʌp'holstərər] *s* tappezziere *m*

upholster·y [ʌp'holstəri] *s* (-ies) tappezzeria; (*e.g., of cushions*) imbottitura; (aut) selleria

up'keep' *s* manutenzione; spese *fpl* di manutenzione

upland ['ʌplənd] *or* ['ʌplænd] *adj* alto, elevato || *s* terreno elevato

up'lift' *s* elevazione; miglioramento sociale; edificazione || **up'lift'** *tr* elevare

upon [ʌ'pɑn] *prep* su, sopra, in; **upon** + *ger* non appena + *pp*, e.g., **upon arising** non appena alzato; **upon my word!** sulla mia parola!

upper ['ʌpər] *adj* superiore, disopra; (*town*) soprano; (*river*) alto || *s* disopra *m*; (*of shoe*) tomaia; (rr) (coll) cuccetta; **on one's uppers** ridotto al verde

up'per berth' *s* cuccetta superiore

up'per case' *s* (typ) cassa delle maiuscole, cassa superiore

up'per-case' *adj* (typ) maiuscolo

up'per classes' *spl* classi *fpl* elevate

up'per hand' *s* vantaggio; **to have the upper hand** prendere il disopra

up'per·most' *adj* (il) più alto; principale || *adv* principalmente, in primo luogo

uppish ['ʌpɪʃ] *adj* (coll) arrogante, snob

up·raise' *tr* alzare, tirare su

up'right' *adj* ritto, verticale; dabbene, onesto || *s* staggio, montante *m* || *adv* verticalmente

uprising [ʌp'raɪzɪŋ] *or* ['ʌp,raɪzɪŋ] *s* sollevazione, insurrezione

up'roar' *s* gazzarra, cagnara, fracasso

uproarious [ʌp'rori·əs] *adj* tumultuoso; (*noisy*) rumoroso; (*funny*) comico

up·root' *tr* sradicare

up·set' *adj* rovesciato; scompigliato; (*emotionally*) scombussolato; (*stomach*) imbarazzato || **up'set'** *s* (*overturn*) rovesciamento; (*defeat*) rovescio; (*disorder*) scompiglio; (*illness*) imbarazzo, disturbo || **up·set'** *v* (*pret & pp* -set; *ger* -setting) *tr* rovesciare; scompigliare; indisporre || *intr* rovesciarsi, ribaltarsi

upset' price' *s* prezzo minimo di vendita di un oggetto all'asta

upsetting [ʌp'setɪŋ] *adj* sconcertante

up'shot' *s* conclusione; essenziale *m*

up'side' *s* disopra *m*

up'side down' *adv* alla rovescia; a gambe all'aria; a soqquadro

up'stage' *adj* al fondo della scena; altiero, arrogante || *adv* al fondo della scena || *tr* trattare altezzosamente; (theat) rubare la scena a

up'stairs' *adj* del piano di sopra || *s* piano di sopra || *adv* su, al piano di sopra

upstanding [ʌp'stændɪŋ] *adj* diritto; forte; onorevole

up'start' *s* arrivato, nuovo ricco

up'stream' *adv* a monte, controcorrente

up'stroke' *s* (*in handwriting*) tratto ascendente; (mach) corsa ascendente

up'swing' *s* (*in prices*) ascesa; miglioramento; **to be on the upswing** migliorare

up'-to-date' *adj* recentissimo; moderno; dell'ultima ora

up'town' *adj* della parte più alta della città || *adv* nella parte più alta della città

up'trend' *s* tendenza al rialzo

up'turn' *s* rivolta; (com) rialzo

upturned [ʌpˈtʌrnd] *adj* rivolto all'insù; (*upside down*) capovolto

upward [ˈʌpwərd] *adj* ascendente || *adv* all'insù; **upward of** più di

U'ral Moun'tains [ˈjurəl] *spl* Urali *mpl*

uranium [juˈrɛnɪ·əm] *s* uranio

urban [ˈʌrbən] *adj* urbano

urbane [ʌrˈben] *adj* urbano

urbanite [ˈʌrbə‚naɪt] *s* abitante *mf* di una città

urbanity [ʌrˈbænɪti] *s* urbanità *f*

urbanize [ˈʌrbə‚naɪz] *tr* urbanizzare

ur'ban renew'al *s* ricostruzione urbanistica

urchin [ˈʌrtʃɪn] *s* monello, birichino

ure·thra [juˈriθrə] *s* (-thras or -thrae [θri]) uretra

urge [ʌrdʒ] *s* stimolo || *tr* urgere, sollecitare, spronare; (*to endeavor to persuade*) esortare; (*an enterprise*) accelerare || *intr*—**to urge against** opporsi a

urgen·cy [ˈʌrdʒənsi] *s* (-cies) urgenza

urgent [ˈʌrdʒənt] *adj* urgente; (*desire*) prepotente

urinal [ˈjurɪnəl] *s* (*receptacle*) orinale *m*; (*for a bedridden person*) pappagallo; (*place*) orinatoio, vespasiano

urinary [ˈjurɪ‚nɛri] *adj* urinario

urinate [ˈjurɪ‚net] *tr* & *intr* orinare

urine [ˈjurɪn] *s* urina

urn [ʌrn] *s* urna; (*for making coffee*) caffettiera; (*for making tea*) samovar *m*

urology [juˈrɑlədʒi] *s* urologia

Uruguay [ˈjurə‚gwe] or [ˈjurə‚gwaɪ] *s* l'Uruguai *m*

Uruguayan [‚jurə'gwe·ən] or [‚jurə'gwaɪ·ən] *adj* & *s* uruguaiano

us [ʌs] *pron pers* ci; noi; **to us** ci, a noi, per noi

U.S.A. [ˈjuˈesˈe] *s* (letterword) (**United States of America**) S.U.A. *mpl*

usable [ˈjuzəbəl] *adj* servibile, adoperabile

usage [ˈjusɪdʒ] or [ˈjuzɪdʒ] *s* uso, usanza; (*of a language*) uso

use [jus] *s* uso, impiego, usanza; **in use** in uso, in servizio; **it's no use** non giova; **out of use** disusato; **to be of no use** non servire a nulla; **to have**

no use for non aver bisogno di; non poter soffrire; **to make use of** servirsi di; **what's the use?** a che pro? || [juz] *tr* usare, impiegare, servirsi di; **to use badly** maltrattare; **to use up** consumare, esaurire || *intr*—**used to** translated in Italian in three ways: (1) by the imperfect indicative, e.g., **he used to go to church at seven o'clock** andava in chiesa alle sette; (2) by the imperfect indicative of **solere**, e.g., **he used to smoke all day** soleva fumare tutto il giorno; (3) by the imperfect indicative of **avere l'abitudine di**, e.g., **he used to go to the shore** aveva l'abitudine di andare alla spiaggia

used [juzd] *adj* uso, usato; **to get used to** [ˈjuzdtu] or [ˈjustu] fare la mano a, abituarsi a

useful [ˈjusfəl] *adj* utile

usefulness [ˈjusfəlnɪs] *s* utilità *f*

useless [ˈjuslɪs] *adj* inutile, inservibile

user [ˈjuzər] *s* utente *mf*

usher [ˈʌʃər] *s* (*doorkeeper*) portiere *m*; (hist) cerimoniere *m*; (theat) maschera; (mov) lucciola || *tr* introdurre; **to usher in** annunciare, introdurre

U.S.S.R. [ˈjuˈesˈesˈar] *s* (letterword) (**Union of Soviet Socialist Republics**) U.R.S.S. *f*

usual [ˈjuʒʊ·əl] *adj* usuale, abituale; **as usual** come il solito

usually [ˈjuʒʊ·əli] *adv* usualmente

usurp [juˈzʌrp] *tr* usurpare

usu·ry [ˈjuʒəri] *s* (-ries) usura

utensil [juˈtɛnsɪl] *s* utensile *m*

uter·us [ˈjutərəs] *s* (-i [‚aɪ]) utero

utilitarian [‚jutɪlɪ'tɛri·ən] *adj* utilitario

utili·ty [juˈtɪlɪti] *s* (-ties) utilità *f*; compagnia di servizi pubblici

utilize [ˈjutɪ‚laɪz] *tr* utilizzare

utmost [ˈʌt‚most] *adj* sommo; estremo; massimo || *s*—**the utmost** il massimo; **to do one's utmost** fare tutto il possibile; **to the utmost** al massimo limite

utopia [juˈtopɪ·ə] *s* utopia

utopian [juˈtopɪ·ən] *adj* utopistico || *s* utopista *mf*

utter [ˈʌtər] *adj* completo, totale || *tr* proferire, pronunziare; (*a sigh*) dare, fare

utterly [ˈʌtərli] *adv* completamente

uxoricide [ʌkˈsori‚saɪd] *s* (*husband*) uxoricida *m*; (*act*) uxoricidio

uxorious [ʌkˈsorɪ·əs] *adj* eccessivamente innamorato della propria moglie; dominato dalla moglie

V

V, v [vi] *s* ventiduesima lettera dell'alfabeto inglese

vacan·cy [ˈvekənsi] *s* (-cies) (*emptiness*) vuoto; (*unfilled position*) vacanza; (*unfilled job*) posto vacante; (*in a building*) appartamento libero;

(*in a hotel*) camera libera; **no vacancy** completo

vacant [ˈvekənt] *adj* (*empty*) vuoto; (*position*) vacante; (*expression of the face*) vago

vacate [ˈveket] *tr* sgombrare; (*a posi-*

tion) ritirarsi da; (*law*) annullare; **to vacate one's mind of worries** liberarsi dalle preoccupazioni || *intr* sloggiare; (*coll*) andarsene

vacation [ve'keʃən] *s* vacanza, villeggiatura; **vacanze** *fpl* || *intr* estivare, villeggiare

vacationer [ve'keʃənər] *s* villeggiante *mf*, vacanziere *m*

vacationist [ve'keʃənɪst] *s* villeggiante *mf*, vacanziere *m*

vaca'tion with pay' *s* vacanze *fpl* pagate

vaccinate ['væksɪ,net] *tr* vaccinare

vaccination [,væksɪ'neʃən] *s* vaccinazione

vaccine [væk'sin] *s* vaccino

vacillate ['væsɪ,let] *intr* vacillare

vacillating ['væsɪ,letɪŋ] *adj* vacillante

vacul·ty [væ'kjuːɪti] *s* (*-ties*) vacuità *f*

vacu·um ['vækjuəm] *s* (*-ums* or *-a* [ə]) vuoto; **in a vacuum** sotto vuoto || *tr* pulire con l'aspirapolvere

vac'uum clean'er *s* aspirapolvere *m*

vac'uum-pack'ed *adj* confezionato sotto vuoto

vac'uum tube' *s* tubo elettronico

vagabond ['vægə,bɑnd] *adj* & *s* vagabondo

vagar·y [və'geri] *s* (*-ies*) capriccio

vagran·cy ['vegrənsi] *s* (*-cies*) vagabondaggio

vagrant ['vegrənt] *adj* & *s* vagabondo

vague [veg] *adj* vago

va'gus nerve' ['vegəs] *s* (anat) vago

vain [ven] *adj* vano; (*conceited*) vanitoso; **in vain** in vano

vainglorious [ven'glorɪəs] *adj* vanaglorioso

valance ['væləns] *s* balza, mantovana

vale [vel] *s* valle *f*

valedictorian [,vælɪdɪk'torɪən] *s* studente *m* che pronuncia il discorso di commiato

valence ['veləns] *s* (chem) valenza

valentine ['vælən,taɪn] *s* (*sweetheart*) valentino; (*card*) cartolina di San Valentino

valet ['vælɪt] or ['væle] *s* valletto

valiant ['væljənt] *adj* valoroso

valid ['vælɪd] *adj* valido

validate ['vælɪ,det] *tr* convalidare, vidimare; (*sports*) omologare

validation [,vælɪ'deʃən] *s* convalida, vidimazione; (*sports*) omologazione

validi·ty [və'lɪdɪti] *s* (*-ties*) validità *f*

valise [və'lis] *s* valigetta

valley ['væli] *s* valle *f*, vallata; (*of roof*) linea di compluvio

valor ['vælər] *s* valore *m*, coraggio

valorous ['vælərəs] *adj* valoroso

valuable ['væljuəbəl] or ['væljəbəl] *adj* (*having monetary worth*) prezioso; pregevole, pregiato || **valuables** *spl* valori *mpl*

value ['vælju] *s* valore *m*; importanza; (com) valuta, valore *m*; **an excellent value** un acquisto eccellente || *tr* stimare, valutare

value'-added tax' *s* imposta sul valore aggiunto

valueless ['væljulɪs] *adj* senza valore

valve [vælv] *s* (anat, mach, rad, telv)

valvola; (bot, zool) valva; (mus) pistone *m*

valve' gears' *spl* meccanismo di distribuzione

valve'-in-head' en'gine *s* motore *m* a valvole in testa

valve' lift'er ['lɪftər] *s* alzavalvole *m*

valve' seat' *s* sede *f* della valvola

valve' spring' *s* molla di valvola

valve' stem' *s* stelo di comando della valvola

vamp [væmp] *s* parte *f* anteriore della tomaia; (*patchwork*) rabberciatura; (*female*) vamp *f* || *tr* (*a shoe*) rimontare; rabberciare; (*to concoct*) inventare, raffazzonare; (*an accompaniment*) improvvisare; (*said of a female*) sedurre

vampire ['væmpaɪr] *s* vampiro; (*female*) vamp *f*

van [væn] *s* camionetta, autofurgone *m*; (*mil* & *fig*) avanguardia

vanadium [və'nedɪəm] *s* vanadio

vandal ['vændəl] *adj* & *s* vandalo || **Vandal** *adj* & *s* Vandalo

vandalism ['vændə,lɪzəm] *s* vandalismo

vane [ven] *s* (*weathervane*) banderuola; (*of windmill, of turbine*) pala; (*of feather*) barba

vanguard ['væn,gɑrd] *s* avanguardia; **in the vanguard** all'avanguardia

vanilla [və'nɪlə] *s* vaniglia

vanish ['vænɪʃ] *intr* svanire

van'ishing cream' ['vænɪʃɪŋ] *s* crema evanescente

vani·ty ['vænɪti] *s* (*-ties*) vanità *f*; (*table*) toletta; (*case*) astuccio di toletta

vanquish ['vænkwɪʃ] *tr* superare, vincere

van'tage ground' ['væntɪdʒ] *s* posizione favorevole

vapid ['væpɪd] *adj* insipido

vapor ['vepər] *s* vapore *m*; (*visible vapor*) vapori *mpl*

vaporize ['vepə,raɪz] *tr* vaporizzare || *intr* vaporizzarsi

va'por lock' *s* tampone *m* di vapore

vaporous ['vepərəs] *adj* vaporoso

va'por trail' *s* scia di condensazione

variable ['verɪ-əbəl] *adj* & *s* variabile *f*

variance ['verɪ-əns] *s* divario, differenza; **at variance with** (*a thing*) differente da; differentemente da; (*a person*) in disaccordo con

variant ['verɪ-ənt] *adj* & *s* variante *f*

variation [,verɪ'eʃən] *s* variazione

varicose ['værɪ,kos] *adj* varicoso

varied ['verɪd] *adj* vario, svariato

variegated ['verɪ-ə,getɪd] or ['verɪ-,getɪd] *adj* variegato, screziato

varie·ty [və'raɪ-ɪti] *s* (*-ties*) varietà *f*

vari'ety show' *s* spettacolo di varietà

varnish ['vɑrnɪʃ] *s* vernice *f* || *tr* verniciare; (fig) dare la vernice a

variola [və'raɪ-ələ] *s* (pathol) vaiolo

various ['verɪ-əs] *adj* vari; (*varicolored*) vario, variegato

varsi·ty ['vɑrsɪti] *adj* (sports) universitario *f* || *s* (*-ties*) (sports) squadra numero uno

var·y ['veri] v (pret & pp **-ied**) tr & intr variare

vase [ves] or [vez] s vaso

vaseline ['væsə,lin] s (trademark) vaselina

vassal ['væsəl] adj & s vassallo

vast [væst] or [vɑst] adj vasto

vastly ['væstli] or ['vɑstli] adv enormemente

vastness ['væstnɪs] or ['vɑstnɪs] s vastità f

vat [væt] s tino, bigoncia

Vatican ['vætɪkən] adj vaticano ‖ s Vaticano

Vat'ican Cit'y s Città f del Vaticano

vaudeville ['vodvɪl] or ['vɔdəvɪl] s spettacolo di varietà; (theatrical piece) vaudeville m, commedia musicale

vault [vɔlt] s. volta; (underground chamber) cantina; (of a bank) camera di sicurezza; (burial chamber) cripta; (of heaven) cappa; (leap) salto ‖ tr formare a mo' di volta; saltare ‖ intr saltare

vaunt [vɔnt] or [vɑnt] s vanto, vanteria ‖ tr vantarsi di ‖ intr vantarsi

veal [vil] s vitello

veal' chop' s scaloppa, cotoletta di vitello

veal' cut'let s scaloppina

vedette [vɪ'dɛt] s (nav) vedetta; (mil) sentinella avanzata

veer [vɪr] s virata ‖ tr far cambiare di direzione a ‖ intr virare; (said of the wind) cambiare di direzione

vegetable ['vɛdʒɪtəbəl] adj vegetale ‖ s (plant) vegetale m; (edible plant) ortaggio; **vegetables** verdura, erbe fpl, erbaggi mpl, ortaggi mpl

veg'etable gar'den s orto

veg'etable soup' s minestra di verdura

vegetarian [,vɛdʒɪ'tɛrɪ·ən] adj & s vegetariano

vegetate ['vɛdʒɪ,tet] intr vegetare

vehemence ['vi·ɪməns] s veemenza

vehement ['vi·ɪmənt] adj veemente

vehicle ['vi·ɪkəl] s veicolo

vehic'ular traf'fic [vɪ'hɪkjələr] s circolazione stradale

veil [vel] s velo; **to take the veil** prendere il velo ‖ tr velare

vein [ven] s vena; (streak) venatura; (of ore) filone m ‖ tr venare

velar ['vilər] adj & s velare f

vellum ['vɛləm] s pergamena

veloci·ty [vɪ'lɑsɪti] s (-ties) velocità f

velvet ['vɛlvɪt] adj di velluto ‖ s velluto; (slang) guadagno al gioco; (coll) situazione all'acqua di rose

velveteen [,vɛlvɪ'tin] s vellutino di cotone

velvety ['vɛlvɪti] adj vellutato

vend [vɛnd] tr vendere; (to peddle) fare il venditore ambulante di

vend'ing machine' s distributore automatico

vendor ['vɛndər] s venditore m

veneer [və'nɪr] s impiallacciatura, piallaccio; (fig) vernice f ‖ tr impiallacciare

venerable ['vɛnərəbəl] adj venerabile

venerate ['vɛnə,ret] tr venerare

venereal [vɪ'nɪrɪ·əl] adj venereo

Venetia [vɪ'niʃɪ·ə] or [vɪ'niʃə] s (province) Venezia

Venetian [vɪ'niʃən] adj & s veneziano

Vene'tian blind' s veneziana, persiana avvolgibile

Venezuelan [,vɛnɪ'zwilən] adj & s venezolano

vengeance ['vɛndʒəns] s vendetta; **with a vengeance** violentemente; eccessivamente

vengeful ['vɛndʒfəl] adj vendicativo

Venice ['vɛnɪs] s Venezia

venire·man [vɪ'naɪrimən] s (-men) membro di un collegio di giurati

venison ['vɛnɪsən] or ['vɛnɪzən] s carne f di cervo

venom ['vɛnəm] s veleno

venomous ['vɛnəməs] adj velenoso

vent [vɛnt] s sfiatatoio; (of jacket) spacco; **to give vent to** dare sfogo a ‖ tr sfogare, sfuriare; mettere uno sfiatatoio a; **to vent one's spleen** sfogare la bile

vent' hole' s apertura di sfogo

ventilate ['vɛntɪ,let] tr ventilare

ventilator ['vɛntɪ,letər] s ventilatore m

ventricle ['vɛntrɪkəl] s ventricolo

ventriloquist [vɛn'trɪləkwɪst] s ventriloquo

venture ['vɛntʃər] s azzardo, avventura rischiosa; **at a venture** alla ventura ‖ tr avventurare ‖ intr avventurarsi, arrischiarsi

venturesome ['vɛntʃərsəm] adj (risky) rischioso; (daring) avventuroso

venturous ['vɛntʃərəs] adj avventuroso

vent' win'dow s (aut) deflettore m

venue ['vɛnju] s (law) posto dove ha avuto luogo il reato; (law) luogo dove si riunisce la corte; **change of venue** cambio di giurisdizione

Venus ['vinəs] s (very beautiful woman) venere f; (astr) Venere m; (myth) Venere f

veracious [vɪ're/əs] adj verace

veraci·ty [vɪ'ræsɪti] s (-ties) veridicità f

veranda or **verandah** [və'rændə] s veranda

verb [vʌrb] adj verbale ‖ s verbo

verbalize ['vʌrbə,laɪz] tr esprimere con parole; (gram) convertire in forma verbale ‖ intr essere verboso

verbatim [vər'betɪm] adj letterale ‖ adv parola per parola, testualmente

verbena [vər'binə] s (bot) verbena

verbiage ['vʌrbɪ·ɪdʒ] s verbosità f; (style of wording) espressione

verbose [vər'bos] adj verboso

verdant ['vʌrdənt] adj verde, verdeggiante

verdict ['vʌrdɪkt] s verdetto

verdigris ['vʌrdɪ,ɡris] s verderame m

verdure ['vʌrdʒər] s verde m

verge [vʌrdʒ] s orlo, limite m; bordo; (of a column) fusto; **on the verge of** al punto di; all'orlo di ‖ intr—**to verge on** costeggiare, rasentare

verification [,vɛrɪfɪ'ke/ən] s verifica

veri·fy ['vɛrɪ ˌfaɪ] v (pret & pp **-fied**) tr verificare, confermare

verily ['vɛrɪlɪ] adv in verità

veritable ['vɛrɪtəbəl] adj vero

vermilion [vər'mɪljən] adj & s vermiglio

vermin ['vʌrmɪn] ssg (person) persona abominevole || spl (animals or persons) insetti mpl

vermouth [vər'muθ] or ['vʌrmuθ] s vermut m

vernacular [vər'nækjələr] adj volgare || s volgare m, vernacolo; (language peculiar to a class or profession) gergo

versatile ['vʌrsətɪl] adj (person) versatile; (tool or device) a vari usi

verse [vʌrs] s verso; (Bib) versetto

versed [vʌrst] adj versato

versification [ˌvʌrsɪfɪ'keʃən] s versificazione

versi·fy ['vʌrsɪ ˌfaɪ] v (pret & pp **-fied**) tr & intr versificare

version ['vʌrʒən] s versione

ver·so ['vʌrso] s (**-sos**) (of coin) rovescio; (of page) verso

versus ['vʌrsəs] prep contro; in confronto a

verte·bra ['vʌrtɪbrə] s (**-brae** [ˌbri] or **-bras**) vertebra

vertebrate ['vʌrtə ˌbret] adj & s vertebrato

ver·tex ['vʌrteks] s (**-texes** or **-tices** [tɪ ˌsiz]) vertice m

vertical ['vʌrtɪkəl] adj & s verticale f

ver'tical hold' s (telv) regolatore m del sincronismo verticale

ver'tical sta'bilizer s (aer) deriva

verti·go ['vʌrtɪ ˌgo] s (**-goes** or **-gos**) vertigine f

verve [vʌrv] s verve f, brio

very ['vɛrɪ] adj (utter) grande, completo; (precise) vero e proprio; (mere) stesso, e.g., his **very** brother suo fratello stesso || adv molto, e.g., to be **very** rich essere molto ricco

vesicle ['vɛsɪkəl] s vescichetta

vesper ['vɛspər] s vespro; **vespers** vespri mpl || **Vesper** s Vespero

ves'per bell' s campana a vespro

vessel ['vɛsəl] s (ship) nave f, vascello; (container) vaso; (anat) vaso; (fig) vasello

vest [vɛst] s (of man's suit) panciotto, gilè m; (of woman's garment) corpino || tr vestire; to **vest** (authority) in concedere a; to **vest with** investire di || intr vestirisi; to **vest** in passare a

vest'ed in'terest s interesse acquisito

vestibule ['vɛstɪ ˌbjul] s vestibolo

vestige ['vɛstɪdʒ] s vestigio

vestment ['vɛstmənt] s (eccl) paramento

vest'-pock'et adj da tasca, tascabile

ves·try ['vɛstrɪ] s (**-tries**) sagrestia; (chapel) cappella; giunta esecutiva della chiesa episcopaliana

ves'try·man s (**-men**) membro della giunta esecutiva della chiesa episcopaliana

Vesuvius [vɪ'suvɪ·əs] or [vɪ'sjuvɪ·əs] s il Vesuvio

---

vetch [vɛtʃ] s veccia; (grass pea) cicerchia

veteran ['vɛtərən] adj & s veterano

veterinarian [ˌvɛtərɪ'nɛrɪ·ən] s veterinario

veterinar·y ['vɛtərɪ ˌnɛrɪ] adj veterinario || s (**-ies**) veterinario

ve·to ['vito] s (**-toes**) veto || tr porre il veto a

vex [vɛks] tr irritare, tormentare

vexation [vɛk'seʃən] s fastidio, contrarietà f

vexatious [vɛk'seʃəs] adj irritante, fastidioso; (law) vessatorio

vexing ['vɛksɪŋ] adj noioso, fastidioso, irritante

via ['vaɪ·ə] prep via, per via di

viaduct ['vaɪ·ə ˌdʌkt] s viadotto

vial ['vaɪ·əl] s fiala, boccetta

viand ['vaɪ·ənd] s vivanda, manicaretto

viati·cum [vaɪ'ætɪkəm] s (**-cums** or **-ca** [kə]) (eccl) viatico

vibrate ['vaɪbret] tr & intr vibrare

vibration [vaɪ'breʃən] s vibrazione

vicar ['vɪkər] s vicario

vicarage ['vɪkərɪdʒ] s residenza del vicario; (office; duties) vicariato

vicarious [vaɪ'kɛrɪ·əs] or [vɪ'kɛrɪ·əs] adj sostituto; (punishment) ricevuto in vece di altra persona; (power) delegato; (enjoyment) di riflesso

vice [vaɪs] s vizio

vice'-ad'miral s viceammiraglio, ammiraglio di squadra

vice'-pres'ident s vicepresidente m

viceroy ['vaɪsrɔɪ] s viceré m

vice versa ['vaɪsɪ 'vʌrsə] or ['vaɪsə 'vʌrsə] adv viceversa

vicini·ty [vɪ'sɪnɪtɪ] s (**-ties**) vicinanze fpl, paraggi mpl

vicious ['vɪʃəs] adj vizioso; maligno, malvagio; (dog) cattivo, che morde; (horse) selvaggio; (headache) tremendo; (reasoning; circle) vizioso

victim ['vɪktɪm] s vittima

victimize ['vɪktɪ ˌmaɪz] tr fare una vittima di; ingannare; (hist) sacrificare

victor ['vɪktər] s vincitore m

victorious [vɪk'torɪ·əs] adj vittorioso

victo·ry ['vɪktərɪ] s (**-ries**) vittoria

victuals ['vɪtəlz] spl vettovaglie fpl

vid'eo cassette' ['vɪdɪ ˌo] s videocassetta

vid'eo sig'nal s segnale m video

vid'eo tape' s nastro televisivo

vie [vaɪ] v (pret & pp vied; ger vying) intr gareggiare; to **vie for** disputarsi

Vien·nese [ˌvi·ə'niz] adj viennese || s (**-nese**) viennese mf

Vietnam [ˌviɛt'nɑm] s il Vietnam

Vietnam·ese [vɪ ˌɛtnə'miz] adj vietnamita || s (**-ese**) vietnamita mf; (language) vietnamita m

view [vju] s vista; (picture) veduta; prospetto; esame m; punto di vista; to be **on view** (said of a corpse) essere esposto; to **keep in view** non perdere di vista; to **take a dim view** of avere un'opinione scettica di; with a **view to** con lo scopo di || tr guardare, osservare; considerare

viewer ['vju·ər] s spettatore m; (telv) telespettatore m; (phot) visore m; (phot) proiettore m di diapositive

view'find'er s (phot) traguardo, visore m

view'point' s punto di vista

vigil ['vɪdʒɪl] s vigilia; **to keep vigil** vegliare

vigilance ['vɪdʒɪləns] s vigilanza

vigilant ['vɪdʒɪlənt] adj vigilante

vignette [vɪn'jet] s vignetta

vigor ['vɪgər] s vigore m, gagliardia

vigorous ['vɪgərəs] adj vigoroso

Viking ['vaɪkɪŋ] s vichingo

vile [vaɪl] adj vile, malvagio; (wretchedly bad) orribile; disgustoso, ripugnante; (filthy) sporco; (poor) povero, basso

vili·fy ['vɪlɪ,faɪ] v (pret & pp **-fied**) tr vilificare

villa ['vɪlə] s villa

village ['vɪlɪdʒ] s villaggio, paese m

villager ['vɪlɪdʒər] s paesano

villain ['vɪlən] s scellerato; (of a play) cattivo, anima nera

villainous ['vɪlənəs] adj vile, infame

villain·y ['vɪləni] s (-ies) scelleratezza, malvagità f

vim [vɪm] s vigore m, brio

vinaigrette [,vɪnə'gret] s boccetta dell'aceto aromatico

vinaigrette' sauce' s salsa verde

vindicate ['vɪndɪ,ket] tr scolpare; difendere, sostenere; (e.g., a claim) rivendicare

vindictive [vɪn'dɪktɪv] adj vendicativo

vine [vaɪn] s (climber) rampicànte f; (grape plant) vite f

vine'dress'er s vignaiolo

vinegar ['vɪnɪgər] s aceto

vinegarish ['vɪnɪgərɪʃ] adj acetoso; (fig) acre, mordace

vinegary ['vɪnɪgari] adj acetoso; (fig) irritabile, irascibile

vineyard ['vɪnjərd] s vigna, vigneto

vintage ['vɪntɪdʒ] s vendemmia; vino di annata eccezionale; (fig) edizione f

vintager ['vɪntɪdʒər] s vendemmiatore m

vin'tage wine' s vino di marca

vin'tage year' s buona annata

vintner ['vɪntnər] s produttore m di vino; vinaio

vinyl ['vaɪnɪl] or ['vɪnɪl] s vinile m

violate ['vaɪə,let] tr violare

violation [,vaɪə'leʃən] s violazione f

violence ['vaɪələns] s violenza

violent ['vaɪələnt] adj violento

violet ['vaɪəlɪt] adj violetto || s (color) violetto, viola; (bot) violetta; (Viola odorata) viola mammola

violin [,vaɪə'lɪn] s violino

violinist [,vaɪə'lɪnɪst] s violinista mf

violoncellist [,vaɪələn'tʃelɪst] or [,vɪələn'tʃelɪst] s violoncellista mf

violoncel·lo [,vaɪələn'tʃelo] or [,vɪələn'tʃelo] s (-los) violoncello

VIP ['vi'aɪ'pi] s (letterword) **(Very Important Person)** persona di maggiore riguardo

viper ['vaɪpər] s vipera; (any snake) serpe f; (spiteful person) vipera

vira·go [vɪ'rego] s (-goes or -gos) megera, donna dal caratteraccio impossibile

virgin ['vʌrdʒɪn] adj & s vergine f || **Virgin** s Vergine f

vir'gin birth' s parto verginale della Madonna; (zool) partenogenesi f

Virgin'ia creep'er [vər'dʒɪnɪ·ə] s vite f del Canada

virginity [vʌr'dʒɪnɪti] s virginità f

Virgo ['vʌrgo] s (astr) Vergine f

virility [vɪ'rɪlɪti] s virilità f

virology [vaɪ'rɑlədʒi] s virologia

virtual ['vʌrtʃu·əl] adj virtuale

virtue ['vʌrtʃu] s virtù f

virtuosi·ty [,vʌrtʃu'ɑsɪti] s (-ties) virtuosità f, virtuosismo

virtuo·so [,vʌrtʃu'oso] s (-sos or -si [si]) virtuoso

virtuous ['vʌrtʃu·əs] adj virtuoso

virulence ['vɪrjələns] s virulenza

virulent ['vɪrjələnt] adj virulento

virus ['vaɪrəs] s virus m

visa ['vizə] s visto || tr vistare

visage ['vɪzɪdʒ] s faccia; apparenza

vis-à-vis [,vizə'vi] adj l'uno di fronte all'altro || adv vis-à-vis || prep di fronte a

viscera ['vɪsərə] spl visceri mpl, viscere fpl

viscount ['vaɪkaunt] s visconte m

viscountess ['vaɪkauntɪs] s viscontessa

viscous ['vɪskəs] adj viscoso

vise [vaɪs] s morsa

visé ['vize] or [vi'ze] s & tr var of **visa**

visible ['vɪzɪbəl] adj visibile

Visigoth ['vɪzɪ,gɑθ] s visigoto

vision ['vɪʒən] s visione; (sense) vista

visionar·y ['vɪʒə,neri] adj visionario || s (-ies) visionario

visit ['vɪzɪt] s visitare; affliggere, colpire; (a punishment) far ricadere || intr visitare; (to chat) fare un chiacchierata

visitation [,vɪzɪ'teʃən] s visitazione; punizione divina, visita del Signore

vis'iting card' s biglietto da visita

vis'iting hours' spl orario delle visite

vis'iting nurse' s infermiera che visita i pazienti a domicilio

visitor ['vɪzɪtər] s visitatore m

visor ['vaɪzər] s visiera; (fig) maschera

vista ['vɪstə] s vista, prospettiva

visual ['vɪʒu·əl] adj visivo, visuale

vis'ual acu'ity s acutezza visiva

visualize ['vɪʒu·ə,laɪz] tr formare l'immagine mentale di; (to make visible) visualizzare

vital ['vaɪtəl] adj vitale; (deadly) mortale || **vitals** spl organi vitali

vitality [vaɪ'tælɪti] s vitalità f

vitalize ['vaɪtə,laɪz] tr animare, infondere vita a

vi'tal statis'tics spl statistiche fpl anagrafiche

vitamin ['vaɪtəmɪn] s vitamina

vitiate ['vɪʃɪ,et] tr viziare

vitreous ['vɪtrɪ·əs] adj vitreo, vetroso

vitriolic [,vɪtrɪ'ɑlɪk] adj di vetriolo; (fig) caustico

vituperate [vaɪ'tupə,ret] or [vaɪ'tjupə,ret] tr vituperare

viva ['vivə] *s* evviva || *interj* viva!

vivacious [vɪ'veʃəs] or [vaɪ'veʃəs] *adj* vivace

vivaci·ty [vɪ'væsɪti] or [vaɪ'væsɪti] *s* (-ties) vivacità *f*, gaiezza

viva voce ['vaɪvə 'vosi] *adv* a viva voce

vivid ['vɪvɪd] *adj* vivido

vivi·fy ['vɪvɪ,faɪ] *v* (*pret & pp* **-fied**) *tr* vivificare

vivisection [,vɪvɪ'sɛkʃən] *s* vivisezione

vixen ['vɪksən] *s* volpe femmina; (*ill-tempered woman*) megera

vizier [vɪ'zɪr] or ['vɪzjər] *s* visir *m*

vocabular·y [vo'kæbjə,lɛri] *s* (-ies) vocabolario

vocal ['vokəl] *adj* vocale; (*inclined to express oneself freely*) che si fa sentire, loquace; (*e.g., outburst*) verbale

vocalist ['vokəlɪst] *s* cantante *mf*; (*of jazz*) vocalist *mf*

vocalize ['vokə,laɪz] *tr* vocalizzare || *intr* vocalizzarsi

vocation [vo'keʃən] *s* vocazione; professione, impiego

voca'tional educa'tion *s* istruzione professionale

vocative ['vakətɪv] *s* vocativo

vociferate [vo'sɪfə,ret] *intr* vociferare

vociferous [vo'sɪfərəs] *adj* rumoroso, vociferante

vogue [vog] *s* voga, moda; **in vogue** in voga, di moda

voice [vɔɪs] *s* voce *f*; (*of animals*) verso; **in a loud voice** a voce alta; **in a low voice** a voce bassa; **to give voice to** esprimere; **with one voice** con una sola voce || *tr* esprimere; (*phonet*) sonorizzare || *intr* sonorizzarsi

voiced [vɔɪst] *adj* (phonet) sonoro

voiceless ['vɔɪslɪs] *adj* senza voce; muto; (phonet) sordo, duro

void [vɔɪd] *adj* (*useless*) inutile; (*empty*) vuoto; (law) invalido, nullo; **void of** sprovvisto di || *s* vuoto; (*gap*) buco || *tr* vuotare; (*the bowels*) evacuare; annullare || *intr* andare di corpo

volatile ['valətɪl] *adj* volatile; instabile; (*disposition*) volubile, incostante

volatilize ['valətɪ,laɪz] *tr* volatilizzare || *intr* volatilizzarsi

volcanic [val'kænɪk] *adj* vulcanico

volca·no [val'keno] *s* (-noes or -nos) vulcano

volition [və'lɪʃən] *s* volontà *f*; **of one's own volition** di propria volontà

volley ['vali] *s* (*e.g., of bullets*) scarica, sventagliata; (tennis) volata || *tr* colpire a volo || *intr* colpire la palla a volo

vol'ley·ball *s* pallavolo *f*

volplane ['val,plen] *s* planata || *intr* planare

volt [volt] *s* volt *m*

voltage ['voltɪdʒ] *s* voltaggio

volt'age divi'der [dɪ'vaɪdər] *s* divisore *m* del voltaggio

voltaic [val'te·ɪk] *adj* voltaico

volte-face [vɔlt'fas] *s* voltafaccia *m*

volt'me'ter *s* voltmetro

voluble ['valjəbəl] *adj* locuace

volume ['valjəm] *s* volume *m;* **to speak volumes** avere molta importanza; essere molto espressivo

voluminous [və'lumɪnəs] *adj* voluminoso

voluntar·y ['valən,tɛri] *adj* volontario || *s* (-ies) assolo di organo

volunteer [,valən'tɪr] *adj & s* volontario || *tr* dare or dire volontariamente || *intr* offrirsi; arruolarsi come volontario; **to volunteer to** + *inf* offrirsi di + *inf*

voluptuar·y [və'lʌptʃu,ɛri] *adj* voluttuoso || *s* (-ies) sibarita *m*, epicureo

voluptuous [və'lʌptʃu·əs] *adj* voluttuoso

volute [və'lut] *s* voluta

vomit ['vamɪt] *s* vomito || *tr & intr* vomitare, rigettare

voodoo ['vudu] *adj* di vudù || *s* (*practice*) vudù *m;* (*person*) vuduista *mf*

voracious [və'reʃəs] *adj* vorace

voracity [və'ræsɪti] *s* voracità *f*

vor·tex ['vɔrtɛks] *s* (-texes or -tices [tɪ,siz]) vortice *m*

vota·ry ['votəri] *s* (-ries) persona legata da un voto; amante *mf*, appassionato

vote [vot] *s* voto; **to put to the vote** mettere ai voti; **to tally the votes** procedere allo scrutinio dei voti || *tr* votare; dichiarare; **to vote down** respingere; **to vote in** eleggere; **to vote out** scacciare || *intr* votare

vote'get'ter ['gɛtər] *s* accaparratore *m* di voti; slogan *m* che conquista voti

voter ['votər] *s* elettore *m*

vot'ing machine' ['votɪŋ] *s* macchina per registrare lo scrutinio dei voti

votive ['votɪv] *adj* votivo

vo'tive of'fering *s* voto, ex voto, offerta votiva

vouch [vautʃ] *tr* garantire || *intr*—**to vouch for** (*s.th*) garantire; (*s.o.*) rendersi garante per, garantire per

voucher ['vautʃər] *s* garante *mf*; (*certificate*) ricevuta, pezza d'appoggio

vouch·safe' *tr* concedere, accordare || *intr*—**to vouchsafe to** + *inf* degnarsi di + *inf*

voussoir [vu'swar] *s* cuneo

vow [vau] *s* voto; **to take vows** pronunciare i voti || *tr* promettere; (*vengeance*) giurare || *intr* fare un voto

vowel ['vau·əl] *s* vocale *f*

voyage ['vɔɪ·ɪdʒ] *s* viaggio; (*by sea*) traversata || *tr* attraversare || *intr* viaggiare

voyager ['vɔɪ·ɪdʒər] *s* viaggiatore *m*, passeggero

vulcanize ['vʌlkə,naɪz] *tr* vulcanizzare

vulgar ['vʌlgər] *adj* volgare; comune, popolare

vulgari·ty [vʌl'gærɪti] *s* (-ties) volgarità *f*

Vul'gar Lat'in *s* latino volgare

Vulgate ['vʌlget] *s* Vulgata

vulnerable ['vʌlnərəbəl] *adj* vulnerabile

vulture ['vʌltʃər] *s* avvoltoio

W

W, w ['dʌbəl ˌju] *s* ventitreesima lettera dell'alfabeto inglese

wad [wɑd] *s* (*of cotton*) batuffolo, bioccolo; (*of money*) mazzetta, rotolo; (*of tobacco*) pallottola; (*in a gun*) stopp·accio || *v* (*pret & pp* **wadded;** *ger* **wadding**) *tr* arrotolare; (*shot*) comprimere; (fig) imbottire

waddle ['wɑdəl] *s* andatura a mo' di anitra || *intr* sculettare

wade [wed] *tr* guadare || *intr* guadare; avanzare faticosamente; sguazzare; **to wade into** (coll) attaccare violentemente; **to wade through** procedere a stento per; leggere con difficoltà

wad'ing bird' ['wedɪŋ] *s* trampoliere *m*

wafer ['wefər] *s* disco adesivo di carta per chiudere lettere; (*cake*) wafer *m*, cialda; (eccl, med) ostia

waffle ['wɑfəl] *s* cialda

waf'fle i'ron *s* schiacce *fpl*

waft [wæft] *or* [wɑft] *tr* portare leggermente or a volo || *intr* librarsi, spandersi

wag [wæg] *s* (*of head*) cenno; (*of tail*) scodinzolio; (*person*) burlone *m* || *v* (*pret & pp* **wagged;** *ger* **wagging**) *tr* (*the head*) scuotere; (*the tail*) dimenare || *intr* scodinzolare

wage [wedʒ] *s* salario, paga; **wages** salario, paga; ricompensa; prezzo, e.g., **the wages of sin is death la morte è il prezzo del peccato** || *tr* (*war*) fare

wage' earn'er ['ˌʌrnər] *s* salariato

wager ['wedʒər] *s* scommessa; **to lay a wager** fare una scommessa || *tr & intr* scommettere

wage'work'er *s* lavoratore salariato

waggish ['wægɪʃ] *adj* scherzoso, comico, burlone

Wagnerian [vɑgˈnɪrɪ·ən] *adj & s* wagneriano

wagon ['wægən] *s* carro, carretto; (*e.g.*, *Conestoga wagon*) carriaggio; furgone *m*; carrozzone *m*; **to be on the wagon** (slang) astenersi dal bere; **to hitch one's wagon to a star** avere altissime ambizioni

wag'tail' *s* (orn) ballerina, cutrettola

waif [wef] *s* (*foundling*) trovatello; abbandonato; animale smarrito

wail [wel] *s* gemito, lamento || *intr* gemere, lamentarsi

wain·scot ['wenskət] *or* ['wenskɑt] *s* pannello per rivestimenti || *v* (*pret & pp* **-scoted** *or* **-scotted;** *ger* **-scoting** *or* **-scotting**) *tr* rivestire di pannelli di legno

waist [west] *s* vita, cintura; blusa, camicetta, corpetto

waist'band' *s* cintola

waist'cloth' *s* perizoma *m*

waistcoat ['west ˌkot] *or* ['westkət] *s* corpetto, gilè *m*

waist'line' *s* vita, cintura; **to keep or watch one's waistline** conservare la linea

wait [wet] *s* attesa; **to lie in wait** atten-

dere al varco || *tr* (*one's turn*) attendere || *intr* attendere, aspettare; **to wait for** attendere, aspettare; **to wait on** servire; **to wait up for** (coll) aspettare alzato

wait'-and-see' pol'icy *s* attendismo

waiter ['wetər] *s* cameriere *m*; (*tray*) vassoio

wait'ing list' *s* lista di aspettativa

wait'ing room' *s* sala d'aspetto

waitress ['wetrɪs] *s* cameriera

waive [wev] *tr* (*one's rights*) rinunciare (with *dat*); differire; mettere da parte

waiver ['wevər] *s* rinuncia

wake [wek] *s* (*any watch*) veglia; (*watch by a dead body*) veglia funebre; (*of a boat*) solco, scia; **in the wake of** come risultato di; nelle orme di || *v* (*pret* **waked** *or* **woke** [wok]; *pp* **waked**) *tr* svegliare || *intr* svegliarsi; **to wake to** darsi conto di; **wake up** svegliarsi

wakeful ['wekfəl] *adj* sveglio; insonne

waken ['wekən] *tr* svegliare || *intr* svegliarsi

wale [wel] *s* segno lasciato da una frustata, vescica; (*in fabric*) riga, costa

Wales [welz] *s* la Galles

walk [wɔk] *s* (*act*) camminata; (*distance*) cammino; (*for pleasure*) passeggiata; (*gait*) andatura; (*line of work*) attività *f*, mestiere *m*; (*sidewalk*) marciapiede *m*; (*in a garden*) sentiero; (*yard for domestic animals to exercise in*) recinto; (sports) marcia; **to go for a walk** andare a fare una passeggiata || *tr* (*a street*) percorrere; (*a horse*) passeggiare; (*a patient*) far camminare; (*a heavy piece of furniture*) abbambinare; **to walk off** (*a headache*) far passare camminando || *intr* camminare; passeggiare; (*said of a horse*) andare al passo; (sports) marciare; **to walk away from** andarsene a piedi da; **to walk off with** rubare; vincere con facilità; **to walk out** uscire in segno di protesta; (coll) mettersi in sciopero; **to walk out on** (coll) piantare in asso

walkaway ['wɔkəˌwe] *s* facile vittoria

walker ['wɔkər] *s* camminatore *m*; (*to teach a baby to walk*) girello

walkie-talkie ['wɔkɪˈtɔki] *s* trasmettitore-ricevitore *m* portatile

walk'ing pa'pers *spl*—**to give s.o. his walking papers** (coll) dare gli otto giorni a qlcu

walk'-in refrig'erator *s* cella frigorifera

walk'ing stick' *s* bastone *m* da passeggio

walk'-on' *s* (*actor*) figurante *m*, comparsa; (*role*) particina

walk'out' *s* sciopero

walk'o'ver *s* facile vittoria, passeggiata

wall [wɔl] *s* muro; (*between rooms; of a vein*) parete *f*; (*rampart*) muraglia; **to drive to the wall** ridurre alla disperazione; **to go to the wall** perdere; fare fallimento ‖ *tr* murare; **to wall up** circondare con muro

wall'board' *s* pannello da costruzione

wallet ['wɑlɪt] *s* portafoglio

wall'flow'er *s* violacciocca gialla; **to be a wallflower** fare tappezzeria

Walloon [wɑ'lun] *adj* & *s* vallone *mf*

wallop ['wɑləp] *s* (coll) colpo violento; (coll) effetto *f* ‖ *tr* (coll) dare un colpo violento a; (coll) battere completamente

wallow ['wɑlo] *s* diguazzamento; (*place*) brago, pantano ‖ *intr* diguazzare; (*in wealth*) nuotare

wall'pa'per *s* tappezzeria ‖ *tr* tappezzare

walnut ['wɔlnət] *s* (*tree; wood*) noce *m*; (*fruit*) noce *f*

walrus ['wɔlrəs] *or* ['wɑlrəs] *s* tricheco

Walter ['wɔltər] *s* Gualtiero

waltz [wɔlts] *s* valzer *m* ‖ *tr* ballare il valzer con; (coll) condurre con disinvoltura ‖ *intr* ballare il valzer

wan [wɑn] *adj* (**wanner; wannest**) (*face*) smunto, sparuto, smorto; (*light*) debole

wand [wɑnd] *s* bacchetta

wander ['wɑndər] *tr* vagare per ‖ *intr* vagare, vagabondare; errare

wanderer ['wɑndərər] *s* vagabondo; pellegrino

Wan'dering Jew' *s* ebreo errante

wan'der·lust' *s* passione del vagabondaggio

wane [wen] *s* decadenza, declino; calare *m* della luna; **on the wane** in declino; (*moon*) calante ‖ *intr* decadere, declinare; (*said of the moon*) calare

wangle ['wæŋgəl] *tr* (coll) ottenere con l'astuzia, rimediare; (coll) falsificare; **to wangle one's way out of** (coll) tirarsi fuori da . . . con l'astuzia ‖ *intr* (coll) arrangiarsi

want [wɑnt] *or* [wɔnt] *s* bisogno, necessità *f*; domanda; miseria; **for want of** a causa della mancanza di; **to be in want** essere in miseria; **to be in want of** aver bisogno di ‖ *tr* volere, desiderare; mancare; aver bisogno di ‖ *intr* desiderare; **to be wanting** mancare, e.g., **three cards are wanting** mancano tre carte; **to want for** aver bisogno di

want' ad' *s* annunzio economico

wanton ['wɑntən] *adj* di proposito, deliberato; arbitrario; licenzioso, sfrenato; (*archaic*) lussureggiante

war [wɔr] *s* guerra; **to go to war** entrare in guerra; (*said of a soldier*) andare in guerra; **to wage war** fare la guerra ‖ *v* (*pret & pp* **warred**; *ger* **warring**) *intr* guerreggiare; **to war on** fare la guerra a

warble ['wɔrbəl] *s* gorgheggio ‖ *intr* gorgheggiare

warbler ['wɔrblər] *s* canterino; uccello canoro; (orn) beccafico

war' cloud' *s* minaccia di guerra

ward [wɔrd] *s* (*of city*) distretto; (*division of hospital*) corsia; (*separate building in hospital*) padiglione *m*;

(*guardianship*) tutela; (*minor*) pupillo; (*of lock*) scontro ‖ *tr*—**to ward off** stornare, schermirsi da

warden ['wɔrdən] *s* guardiano; (*of jail*) direttore *m*; (*in wartime*) capofabbricato

ward' heel'er *s* politicantuccio

ward'robe *s* guardaroba *m*

ward'robe trunk' *s* baule *m* armadio

ward'room' *s* (nav) quadrato

ware [wer] *s* vasellame *m*; **wares** merce *f*

war' ef'fort *s* sforzo bellico

ware'house' *s* deposito, magazzino

ware'house·man *s* (**-men**) magazziniere *m*

war'fare' *s* guerra

war'head' *s* (mil) testa

war'horse' *s* cavallo di battaglia; (coll) veterano

warily ['werɪli] *adv* con cautela

wariness ['werɪnɪs] *s* cautela

war'like' *adj* guerresco, guerriero

war' loan' *s* prestito di guerra

war' lord' *s* generalissimo

warm [wɔrm] *adj* caldo; (*lukewarm*) tiepido; (*clothes*) che tiene caldo; (*with anger*) acceso; **to be warm** (*said of a person*) avere caldo; (*said of the weather*) fare caldo ‖ *tr* scaldare, riscaldare; (*s.o.'s heart*) slargare; **to warm up** riscaldare ‖ *intr* scaldarsi, riscaldarsi; **to warm up** (*said, e.g., of a room*) riscaldarsi; (*with emotion*) eccitarsi, accalorarsi; **to warm up** to prender simpatia per

warm-blooded ['wɔrm'blʌdɪd] *adj* (*animal*) a sangue caldo; impetuoso, ardente

war' memo'rial *s* monumento ai caduti

warmer ['wɔrmər] *s* scaldino

warm-hearted ['wɔrm'hɑrtɪd] *adj* caloroso, cordiale

warm'ing pan' *s* scaldaletto

warmonger ['wɔr,mʌŋgər] *s* guerrafondaio

war' moth'er *s* madrina di guerra

warmth [wɔrmθ] *s* calore *m*, tepore *m*; foga, entusiasmo

warm'up' *s* preparazione; (*of radio, engine, etc.*) riscaldamento

warn [wɔrn] *tr* avvertire, mettere in guardia; (*to admonish*) ammonire; informare; **to warn off** intimare di allontanarsi (da)

warn'ing *adj* di avvertimento ‖ *s* avvertimento, ammonimento; (law) diffida

war' nose' *s* acciarino, testa

war' of nerves' *s* guerra dei nervi

War' of the Roses' *s* Guerra delle due Rose

warp [wɔrp] *s* (*of a fabric*) ordito; (*of a board*) svergolamento, curvatura; aberrazione mentale; (naut) gherlino ‖ *tr* curvare, svergolare; (*a fabric*) ordire; falsare, alterare; (naut) tirare col gherlino ‖ *intr* curvarsi; falsarsi, alterarsi; (naut) alare

war'path' *s*—**to be on the warpath** essere sul sentiero della guerra, prepararsi alla guerra; (*to be angry*) essere arrabiato, essere di cattivo umore

war'plane' s aeroplano da guerra

war' prof'iteer s pescecane m

warrant ['wɑrənt] or ['wɔrənt] s garanzia; certificato; ricevuta; (com) nota di pegno; (law) ordine m, mandato ‖ tr garantire; autorizzare

warrantable ['wɑrəntəbəl] or ['wɔrəntəbəl] adj giustificabile, legittimo

war'rant of'ficer s sottufficiale m

warran·ty ['wɑrənti] or ['wɔrənti] s (-ties) garanzia; autorizzazione

warren ['wɑrən] or ['wɔrən] s conigliera; (fig) formicaio

warrior ['wɔrjər] or ['wɑrjər] s guerriero

Warsaw ['wɔrsɔ] s Varsavia

war'ship' s nave f da guerra

wart [wɔrt] s verruca

war'time' s tempo di guerra

war'-torn' adj devastato dalla guerra

war' to the death' s guerra a morte

war·y ['weri] adj (-ier; -iest) guardingo

wash [wɑʃ] or [wɔʃ] s lavata; (clothes washed or to be washed) bucato; (rushing movement of water) sciacquio; (dirty water) lavatura; (painting) mano f di colore; (aer, naut) scia ‖ tr lavare; (dishes) rigovernare; (said of sea or river) bagnare; to be washed up essere finito; to wash away (soil of river bank) dilavare; portar via ‖ intr lavarsi; fare il bucato; essere lavabile; (said of waves) battere

washable ['wɑʃəbəl] or ['wɔʃəbəl] adj lavabile

wash'-and-wear' adj non-stiro

wash'ba'sin s conca, catinella

wash'bas'ket s cesto del bucato

wash'board' s asse m da lavanda; (baseboard) battiscopa m

wash'bowl' s conca, catinella

wash'cloth' s pezzuola per lavarsi

wash'day' s giorno del bucato

washed-out ['wɑʃt‚aut] or ['wɔʃt‚aut] adj slavato; (coll) stanco; (coll) abbattuto, accasciato

washed-up ['wɑʃt'ʌp] or ['wɔʃt'ʌp] adj (coll) finito

washer ['wɑʃər] or ['wɔʃər] s (person) lavatore m; (machine) lavatrice f; (under head of bolt) rondella, rosetta; (ring to prevent leakage) guarnizione

wash'er·man s (-men) lavatore m

wash'er·wom'an s (-wom·en) lavatrice f, lavandaia

wash' goods' spl tessuti mpl lavabili

washing ['wɑʃɪŋ] or ['wɔʃɪŋ] s lavata, lavaggio, lavanda; (of clothes) bucato; washings lavaggio

wash'ing machine' s lavabiancheria, lavatrice f

wash'ing so'da s soda da lavare

wash'out' s erosione; (aer) svergolamento negativo; (coll) rovina completa

wash'rag' s pezzuola per lavarsi; straccio di cucina

wash'room' s gabinetto, toletta

wash'stand' s lavabo, lavamano

wash'tub' s mastello, lavatoio

wash' wa'ter s lavatura

wasp [wɑsp] s vespa

waste [west] s spreco; (refuse) scarico, rifiuto; (desolate country) landa; (excess material) scarto; (for wiping machinery) cascame m di cotone; to go to waste essere sciupato; to lay waste devastare ‖ tr perdere, sciupare, sprecare ‖ intr—to waste away intristire, consumarsi

waste'bas'ket s cestino della carta straccia

wasteful ['westfəl] adj dispendioso; distruttivo

waste'pa'per s cartastraccia

waste' pipe' s tubo di scarico

waste' prod'uct s scarto; (body excretion) escremento

wastrel ['westrəl] s sciupone m; spendaccione m, prodigo

watch [wɑtʃ] s orologio; (lookout) guardia; (mil) guardia; (naut) turno; to be on the watch for essere all'erta per; to keep watch over vegliare su ‖ tr (to look at) osservare; (to oversee) vigilare; guardare; fare attenzione a ‖ intr guardare; (to keep awake) vegliare; to watch for fare attenzione a; to watch out fare attenzione; to watch out for fare attenzione a; essere all'erta per; to watch over sorvegliare; watch out! attenzione!

watch'band' s cinturino dell'orologio

watch'case' s cassa dell'orologio

watch' charm' s ciondolo dell'orologio

watch' crys'tal s cristallo dell'orologio

watch'dog' s cane m da guardia; (fig) guardiano

watch'dog' commit'tee s comitato di sorveglianza

watchful ['wɑtʃfəl] adj vigile

watchfulness ['wɑtʃfəlnɪs] s vigilanza

watch'mak'er s orologiaio

watch'man s (-men) guardiano, sorvegliante m; (at night) guardia notturna, metronotte m

watch' night' s notte f di San Silvestro; ufficio religioso della vigilia di Capodanno

watch' pock'et s taschino dell'orologio

watch'tow'er s torre f d'osservazione

watch'word' s parola d'ordine, consegna; slogan m

water ['wɔtər] or ['wɑtər] s acqua; of the first water di prim'ordine; (e.g., a thief) della più bell'acqua; to back water retrocedere; to be in deep water essere in cattive acque; to fish in troubled waters pescare nel torbido; to hold water aver fondamento; to keep above water (fig) tenersi a galla; to make water (to urinate) urinare; (naut) fare acqua; to throw cold water on scoraggiare ‖ tr bagnare; dare acqua a; (cattle) abbeverare; (wine) annacquare ‖ intr abbeverarsi; (said of the mouth) aver l'acquolina; (said, e.g., of a ship) fare acqua; (said of the eyes) lacrimare

wa'ter bug' s bacherozzolo

wa'ter car'rier s acquaiolo

wa'ter-col'or s acquerello

wa'ter-cooled' adj a raffreddamento ad acqua

wa'ter-course' s corso d'acqua

wa'ter-cress' s crescione m

wa'ter cure' s cura delle acque

wa'ter-fall' s cascata

wa'ter-front' s riva, banchina

wa'ter gap' s gola, passo

wa'ter ham'mer s colpo d'ariete

wa'ter heat'er s scaldabagno, scalda-acqua m

wa'ter ice' s granita

wa'tering can' s annaffiatoio

wa'tering place' s stabilimento balneare; stazione termale; (drinking place) abbeveratoio

wa'tering pot' s annaffiatoio

wa'tering trough' s abbeveratoio

wa'ter jack'et s camicia d'acqua

wa'ter lil'y s nenufaro

wa'ter line' s linea di galleggiamento or d'acqua; linea di livello

wa'ter main' s tubo di flusso principale

wa'ter-mark' s linea di livello massimo; (in paper) filigrana

wa'ter-mel'on s cocomero, anguria

wa'ter me'ter s contatore m dell'acqua

wa'ter mill' s mulino ad acqua

wa'ter pipe' s tubo dell'acqua

wa'ter po'lo s pallanuoto f

wa'ter pow'er s forza idrica

wa'ter-proof' adj & s impermeabile m

wa'ter-repel'lent adj idroripellente

wa'ter-shed' s spartiacque m, displuvio

wa'ter ski' s idrosci m

wa'ter sof'tener s decalcificatore m

wa'ter-spout' s (to carry water from roof) pluviale m; (meteor) tromba marina

wa'ter sys'tem s (of a river) sistema m fluviale; (of city) conduttura dell'acqua, impianto idrico

wa'ter-tight' adj stagno, ermetico; (fig) perfetto, inconfutabile

wa'ter tow'er s torre f serbatoio

wa'ter wag'on s (mil) carro dell'acqua; to be on the water wagon (slang) astenersi dal bere

wa'ter-way' s via d'acqua, idrovia

wa'ter wheel' s ruota or turbina idraulica; (of steamboat) ruota a pale

wa'ter wings' spl galleggiante m per nuotare

wa'ter-works' s impianto idrico; (pumping station) impianto di pompaggio

watery ['wotəri] or ['watəri] adj acquoso; lacrimoso; povero, insipido; umido, acquitrinoso

watt [wat] s watt m

watt'-hour' s (-hours) wattora m

wattle ['watəl] s (of bird) bargiglio

watt'me'ter s wattmetro

wave [wev] s onda; (of cold; of feeling) ondata; (of the hand) cenno; (of hair) onda, ondulazione || tr (a flag) sventolare; (the hair) ondulare; (the hand) fare cenno con; to wave aside fare cenno di allontanarsi a; (e.g., a proposal) rifiutare || intr ondeggiare; fare cenni con la mano

wave'length' s lunghezza d'onda

wave' mo'tion s movimento ondulatorio

waver ['wevər] intr ondeggiare, oscillare; (to hesitate) titubare, tentennare; (to totter) pencolare

wav·y ['wevi] adj (-ier; -iest) (sea) ondoso; (hair) ondulato

wax [wæks] s cera; (fig) fantoccio || tr incerare; (a recording) (coll) registrare || intr aumentare; diventare; (said of the moon) crescere; to wax indignant indignarsi

wax' pa'per s carta cerata, carta oleata

wax'works' s museo di statue di cera

way [we] s maniera, modo; via; condizione; across the way di fronte; a good way un buon tratto; all the way fino alla fine della strada; completamente; all the way to fino a; any way ad ogni modo; by the way a proposito; in a way in un certo modo; fino a un certo punto; in every way per ogni verso; in this way in questa maniera; one way senso unico; on the way to andando a; on the way out uscendo; diminuendo, sparendo; out of the way eliminato; fuori mano; strano; irregolare; that way in quella direzione; per di lì; in quella maniera; this way in questa direzione; per di qui; in questa maniera; to be in the way essere d'impaccio; to feel one's way avanzare a tentoni; to force one's way aprirsi il passo a viva forza; to get out of the way togliersi di mezzo; to give way ritirarsi, cedere; (said of a rope) rompersi; to give way to cedere a, darsi a; to go out of one's way darsi da fare, disturbarsi; to have one's way vincerla; to keep out of the way stare fuori dai piedi; to know one's way around conoscere bene la via; (fig) sapere il fatto proprio; to know one's way to sapere andare a; to lead the way guidare, fare da guida; prendere l'iniziativa; to lose one's way perdersi; to make one's way avanzare; fare carriera; to make way for far largo a; to mend one's ways mettere la testa a partito; to not know which way to turn non sapere a che santo votarsi; to put out of the way togliere di mezzo; to see one's way to vedere la possibilità di; to take one's way andarsene; to wind one's way through andare a zig zag per; to wing one's way andare a volo; under way in moto; in cammino, avviato; way in entrata; way out uscita; ways modi mpl, maniere fpl; (naut) scalo; which way? da che parte?; in che modo?, per dove?

way'bill' s lettera di vettura

wayfarer ['we ˌferər] s viandante m

way'lay' v (pret & pp -laid) tr tendere un agguato a; fermare improvvisamente

way' of life' s tenore m di vita

way'side' *s* bordo della strada; **to fall by the wayside** cadere per istrada; (fig) fare fiasco

way' sta'tion *s* stazione con fermata facoltativa

way' train' *s* treno omnibus

wayward ['wewərd] *adj* indocile, caparbio; irregolare; capriccioso

we [wi] *pron pers* noi; noialtri, e.g., **we Italians** noialtri italiani

weak [wik] *adj* debole

weaken ['wikən] *tr* indebolire, infiacchire ‖ *intr* indebolirsi, infiacchirsi

weakling ['wiklɪŋ] *s* debolino, rammollito

weak-minded ['wik'maɪndɪd] *adj* irresoluto; scemo

weakness ['wiknɪs] *s* debolezza, fiacchezza; (liking) debole *m*

wealth [welθ] *s* ricchezza

wealth·y ['welθɪ] *adj* (-ier; -iest) ricco

wean [win] *tr* svezzare, slattare; **to wean away from** disavvezzare da

weanling ['winlɪŋ] *adj* appena svezzato ‖ *s* bambino or animale appena svezzato

weapon ['wepən] *s* arma

weaponry ['wepənrɪ] *s* armi *fpl*, armamento

wear [wer] *s* uso, servizio; (clothing) vestiti *mpl*, indumenti *mpl*; (wasting away from use) consumo, logorìo; (lasting quality) durata, durabilità *f*; **for everyday wear** per ogni giorno ‖ *v* (pret **wore** [wor]; *pp* **worn** [worn]) *tr* portare, avere indosso; (to cause to deteriorate) logorare, consumare; (to tire) stancare; **to wear out** logorare, strusciare; (a horse) sfiancare; (one's patience) esaurire; (s.o.'s hospitality) abusare di ‖ *intr* logorarsi, consumarsi; **to wear off** diminuire, sparire; **to wear out** logorarsi; stancarsi; esaurirsi; **to wear well** essere di ottima durata

wear' and tear' [ter] *s* logorìo

weariness ['wIrInIs] *s* fatica, stanchezza

wear'ing appar'el ['werɪŋ] *s* abbigliamento, articoli *mpl* d'abbigliamento

wearisome ['wIrIsəm] *adj* affaticante; (tedious) noioso

wea·ry ['wIrɪ] *adj* (-rier; -riest) stanco ‖ *v* (pret & pp -ried) *tr* stancare ‖ *intr* stancarsi

weasel ['wizəl] *s* donnola

wea'sel words' *spl* parole *fpl* ambigue

weather ['weðər] *s* tempo; maltempo; **to be under the weather** (coll) non sentirsi bene; (to be slightly drunk) (coll) essere alticcio ‖ *tr* (lumber) stagionare; (adversities) superare, resistere (with *dat*)

weather-beaten ['weðər,bitən] *adj* segnato dalle intemperie

weath'er bu'reau *s* servizio metereologico

weath'er-cock' *s* banderuola

weath'er fore'cast *s* previsioni *fpl* del tempo, bollettino metereologico

weath'er-man' *s* (-men') metereologo

weath'er report' *s* bollettino metereologico

weath'er strip'ping ['strɪpɪŋ] *s* guarnizione a nastro per inzeppare

weath'er vane' *s* banderuola, ventarola

weave [wiv] *s* tessitura ‖ *v* (pret **wove** [wov] or **weaved**; *pp* **wove** or **woven** ['wovən]) *tr* tessere; (fig) inserire; **to weave one's way** aprirsi un varco serpeggiando ‖ *intr* tessere; serpeggiare

weaver ['wivər] *s* tessitore *m*

web [web] *s* tessuto; (of spider) tela; (of rail) anima, gambo; (zool) membrana; (fig) rete *f*, maglia

web-footed ['web,futɪd] *adj* palmipede

wed [wed] *v* (pret & pp **wed** or **wedded**; *ger* **wedding**) *tr* sposare; (said of the groom) impalmare; (said of the bride) andare in sposa a ‖ *intr* sposarsi

wedding ['wedɪŋ] *adj* nuziale ‖ *s* sposalizio, nozze *fpl*, matrimonio

wed'ding cake' *s* torta nuziale

wed'ding day' *s* giorno di nozze

wed'ding invita'tion *s* invito a nozze

wed'ding march' *s* marcia nuziale

wed'ding ring' *s* fede *f*, vera

wedge [wedʒ] *s* cuneo; (of pie) spicchio; (to split wood) bietta; (to hold a wheel) scarpa ‖ *tr* incuneare

wed'lock *s* matrimonio

Wednesday ['wenzdɪ] *s* mercoledì *m*

wee [wi] *adj* piccolo piccolo

weed [wid] *s* malerba, erbaccia; (zool) sigaretta; (slang) marijuana; **weeds** vestito da lutto, gramaglie *fpl* ‖ *tr* sarchiare, mondare

weeder ['widər] *s* (agr) estirpatore *m*

weed'ing hoe' *s* sarchio, zappa

weed'-kill'er *s* diserbante *m*

week [wik] *s* settimana; **week in, week out** una settimana dopo l'altra

week'day' *s* giorno feriale

week'end' *s* fine-settimana *m*, fine *f* di settimana, week-end *m* ‖ *intr* passare il fine-settimana

week·ly ['wiklɪ] *adj* settimanale ‖ *s* (-lies) settimanale *m* ‖ *adv* settimanalmente

weep [wip] *v* (pret & pp **wept** [wept]) *tr* piangere; **to weep oneself to sleep** addormentarsi piangendo; **to weep one's eyes out** piangere a calde lacrime ‖ *intr* piangere; **to weep for joy** piangere di gioia

weeper ['wipər] *s* piagnone *m*; (hired mourner) prefica

weep'ing wil'low *s* salice *m* piangente

weep·y ['wipɪ] *adj* (-ier; -iest) piangente, lacrimoso

weevil ['wivəl] *s* curculione *m*

weft [weft] *s* (yarns running across warp) trama; (fabric) tela, tessuto

weigh [we] *tr* pesare; (anchor) levare; (to make heavy) appesantire; (fig) soppesare, ponderare; **to weigh down** piegare ‖ *intr* pesare; gravitare; **to weigh in** (sports) pesarsi; **to weigh upon** gravare a

weigh'bridge' *s* stadera

weight [wet] *s* peso; (fig) peso; **to carry weight** aver del peso; **to lose weight** diminuire di peso; **to put on weight** crescere di peso; **to throw**

one's weight around far sentire la propria importanza || *tr* appesantire; (*statistically*) ponderare, dare un certo peso a

weightless ['wetlis] *adj* senza peso, imponderabile

weightlessness ['wetlisnis] *s* imponderabilità *f*

weight·y ['weti] *adj* (-ier; -iest) pesante; importante

weir [wir] *s* sbarramento; (*for catching fish*) pescaia

weird [wird] *adj* soprannaturale, misterioso; strano, bizzarro

welcome ['welkəm] *adj* benvenuto; gradito; you are welcome (*i.e., gladly received*) sia il benvenuto; (*in answer to thanks*) prego; you are welcome to it è a Sua disposizione; you are welcome to your opinion pensi come la vuole || *s* benvenuto || *tr* dare il benvenuto a; accettare; gradire || *interj* benvenuto!

weld [weld] *s* saldatura autogena; (bot) guaderella || *tr* saldare || *intr* saldarsi

welder ['weldər] *s* saldatore *m*; (*machine*) saldatrice *f*

welding ['welding] *s* saldatura autogena

wel'fare' *s* benessere *m*; (*effort to improve living conditions*) beneficenza, assistenza; to be on welfare ricevere assistenza pubblica

wel'fare state' *s* stato sociale or assistenziale

well [wel] *adj* bene; in buona salute || *s* pozzo; (*for ink*) pozzetto, serbatoio; (*spring*) sorgente *f*; (*shaft for stairs*) tromba || *adv* bene; as well pure; as well ... as tanto ... come; as well as tanto come, non meno che || *intr* —to well up sgorgare || *interj* beh!; bene!; allora!; dunque!

well-appointed ['welə'pɔintid] *adj* ben ammobiliato

well-attended ['welə'tendid] *adj* molto frequentato

well-behaved ['welbi'hevd] *adj* beneducato; to be well-behaved comportarsi bene

well'-be'ing *s* benessere *m*

well'born' *adj* bennato

well-bred ['wel'bred] *adj* educato, costumato

well-disposed ['weldis'pozd] *adj* bendisposto

well-done ['wel'dʌn] *adj* benfatto; (*meat*) ben cotto

well-fixed ['wel'fikst] *adj* (coll) agiato, abbiente

well-formed ['wel'fɔrmd] *adj* benfatto

well-founded ['wel'faundid] *adj* fondato

well-groomed ['wel'grumd] *adj* (*person*) curato; (*horse*) ben governato

well-heeled ['wel'hild] *adj* (coll) agiato, benestante

well-informed ['welin'fɔrmd] *adj* bene informato

well-intentioned ['welin'tenʃənd] *adj* benintenzionato

well'-kept' *adj* ben conservato; (*person*) benportante; (*secret*) ben mantenuto

well-known ['wel'non] *adj* notorio, ben noto

well-meaning ['wel'miniŋ] *adj* benevolo, benintenzionato

well-nigh ['wel'nai] *adv* quasi

well'-off' *adj* agiato, benestante

well-preserved ['welpri'zʌrvd] *adj* ben conservato; (*person*) benportante

well-read ['wel'red] *adj* colto, che ha letto molto

well-spoken ['wel'spokən] *adj* (*person*) raffinato nel parlare; (*word*) a proposito

well'spring' *s* sorgente *f*

well' sweep' *s* mazzacavallo del pozzo

well-tempered ['wel'tempərd] *adj* ben temperato

well-thought-of ['wel'θɔt,ɑv] *adj* tenuto in alta considerazione

well-timed ['wel'taimd] *adj* opportuno

well-to-do ['weltə'du] *adj* benestante

well-wisher ['wel'wiʃər] *s* amico, sostenitore *m*

well-worn ['wel'worn] *adj* (*clothing*) liso, consunto, trito; (*argument*) logoro, banale; portato con eleganza

welsh [welʃ] *intr*—to welsh on (*a promise*) (slang) mancare a; (*a person*) (slang) fregare || Welsh *adj & s* gallese *mf*; the Welsh i gallesi

Welsh'man *s* (-men) gallese *m*

Welsh' rab'bit or rare'bit ['rerbit] *s* fonduta fatta con la birra servita su pane abbrustolito

welt [welt] *s* (*finish along a seam*) costa; (*of shoe*) guardolo; (*wale from a blow*) riga, sferzata

welter ['weltər] *s* guazzabuglio; confusione; (*a tumbling about*) rotolio || *intr* rotolarsi, guazzare

wel'ter-weight' *s* (boxing) peso welter, peso medio-leggero

wench [wentʃ] *s* ragazza, giovane *f*

wend [wend] *tr*—to wend one's way dirigere i propri passi

werewolf ['wir,wulf] *s* lupo mannaro

west [west] *adj* occidentale || *s* ovest *m*, occidente *m* || *adv* verso l'ovest

western ['westərn] *adj* occidentale || *s* western *m*

West' In'dies ['indiz] *spl* Indie *fpl* Occidentali

westward ['westwərd] *adv* verso l'ovest

wet [wet] *adj* (wetter; wettest) bagnato; (*paint*) fresco; (*damp*) umido; (*rainy*) piovoso; che permette la vendita delle bevande alcoliche || *s* umidità *f*; antiproibizionista *mf* || *v* (*pret & pp* wet or wetted; *ger* wetting) *tr* bagnare || *intr* bagnarsi

wet' blan'ket *s* guastafeste *mf*

wether ['weðər] *s* castrone *m*

wet' nurse' *s* nutrice *f*, balia

whack [hwæk] *s* (slang) colpo, percossa; (slang) prova, tentativo || *tr* (slang) percuotere

whale [hwel] *s* balena; a whale of (slang) gigantesco, e.g., a whale of a lie una bugia gigantesca; enorme, e.g., a whale of a difference una differenza enorme || *tr* (coll) battere || *intr* pescare balene

whale'bone' *s* osso di balena, fanone *m*

wharf [hwɔrf] *s* (**wharves** [hwɔrvz] or **wharfs**) molo

what [hwɑt] *adj interr* che; quale || *adj rel* quello . . . che; il . . . che, e.g., **wear what tie you prefer** mettiti la cravatta che preferisci || *pron interr* che; quale; **what else?** che altro?; **what if . . . ?** e se . . . ?; **what of it?** e che me ne importa? || *pron rel* quello che; **what's what** (coll) tutta la situazione || *interj* **what a . . . !** che . . . !, e.g., **what a beautiful day!** che splendida giornata!

what-ev'er *adj* qualsiasi; qualunque || *pron* quanto; che; quello che

what'not' *s* scaffaletto

wheal [hwil] *s* vescichetta

wheat [hwit] *s* grano, frumento

wheedle ['hwidəl] *tr* adulare; persuadere con lusinghe; (*money*) spillare

wheel [hwil] *s* ruota; (*of cheese*) forma; (coll) bicicletta; **at the wheel** al volante; in controllo || *tr* roteare; portare in carrozzella || *intr* girare

wheelbarrow ['hwil,bæro] *s* carriola

wheel'base' *s* passo

wheel'chair' *s* carrozzella

wheel' col'umn *s* (aut) piantone *m* di guida

wheeler-dealer ['hwilər'dilər] *s* (slang) grande affarista *m*

wheel' horse' *s* cavallo di timone; lavoratore *m* di fiducia

wheelwright ['hwil,rɑrt] *s* carradore *m*

wheeze [hwiz] *s* affanno; (pathol) rantolo || *intr* respirare affannosamente; (pathol) rantolare

whelp [hwelp] *s* cucciolo || *tr & intr* figliare, partorire

when [hwen] *adv & conj* quando

whence [hwens] *adv* donde, di dove || *conj* donde; per che ragione

when-ev'er *conj* ogniqualvolta, qualora

where [hwer] *adv & conj* dove

whereabouts ['hwerə,bauts] *s* luogo dove uno si trova || *adv & conj* dove

whereas [hwer'æz] *conj* mentre; visto che, considerato che

where-by' *adv* per cui, col quale

wherever [hwer'evər] *adv* dove mai || *conj* dovunque

wherefore ['hwerfor] *s* perché *m* || *adv* perché || *conj* per cui, percome

where-from' *adv* donde

where-in' *adv* dove; in che modo || *conj* dove; nel quale

where-of' *adv* di che || *conj* di che; del quale

where'upon' *adv* sul che; laonde, dopodiché

wherewithal ['hwerwɪð,ɔl] *s* mezzi *mpl*

whet [hwet] *v* (*pret & pp* **whetted;** *ger* **whetting**) *tr* affilare; (*the appetite*) aguzzare

whether ['weðər] *conj* se; **whether or no** ad ogni modo, in ogni caso; **whether or not** che . . . o che non

whet'stone' *s* pietra da affilare

whey [hwe] *s* scotta

which [hwɪtʃ] *adj interr* quale || *adj rel* il (la, etc.) quale || *pron interr* che; quale; **which is which** qual'è

l'uno e qual'è l'altro || *pron rel* che; il quale; quello che

which-ev'er *adj & pron rel* qualunque

whiff [hwɪf] *s* (*of air*) soffio; fiutata; (*trace of odor*) zaffata; **to get a whiff of** sentire l'odore di || *intr* soffiare; (*said of a smoker*) dare boccate

while [hwaɪl] *s* tempo; **a long while un bel pezzo; a while ago** un tratto fa; **to be worth one's while** valere la pena || *conj* mentre || *tr*—**to while away** passare piacevolmente

whim [hwɪm] *s* capriccio, estro

whimper ['hwɪmpər] *s* piagnucolio || *tr & intr* piagnucolare

whimsical ['hwɪmzɪkəl] *adj* capriccioso, estroso, stravagante

whine [hwaɪn] *s* (*of dog*) guaito; (*of person*) piagnucolio || *intr* (*said of a dog*) guaire, uggiolare; (*said of a person*) piagnucolare

whin•ny ['hwɪni] *s* (**-nies**) nitrito || *v* (*pret & pp* **-nied**) *intr* nitrire

whip [hwɪp] *s* frusta; **uova** *fpl* sbattute con frutta || *v* (*pret & pp* **whipped** or **whipt;** *ger* **whipping**) *tr* frustare, battere; (*eggs*) frullare; (coll) vincere, sconfiggere; **to whip off** (coll) buttar giù; **to whip out** tirar fuori rapidamente; **to whip up** (coll) preparare in quattro e quatt'otto; (coll) eccitare, incitare

whip'cord' *s* cordino della frusta; (*fabric*) saia a diagonale

whip' hand' *s* mano che tiene la frusta; vantaggio, posizione vantaggiosa

whip'lash' *s* scudisciata

whipped' cream' *s* panna montata

whipper-snapper ['hwɪpər,snæpər] *s* pivello

whippet ['hwɪpɪt] *s* piccolo levriere

whip'ping boy' ['hwɪpɪŋ] *s* testa di turco

whip'ping post' *s* palo per la fustigazione

whippoorwill [,hwɪpər'wɪl] *s* caprimulgo, succiacapre *m*

whir [hwʌr] *s* ronzio || *v* (*pret & pp* **whirred;** *ger* **whirring**) *intr* ronzare; volare ronzando

whirl [hwʌrl] *s* giro improvviso; corsa; mulinello; (fig) successione || *tr & intr* mulinare; **my head whirls** mi gira la testa

whirligig ['hwʌrlɪ,gɪg] *s* turbine *m*; (*carrousel*) giostra; (*toy*) girandola; (ent) ragno d'acqua

whirl'pool' *s* risucchio, mulinello

whirl'wind' *s* turbine *m*, tromba d'aria

whirlybird ['hwʌrlɪ,bʌrd] *s* (coll) elicottero

whish [hwɪʃ] *s* fruscio || *intr* frusciare

whisk [hwɪsk] *s* scopatina || *tr* scopare, spolverare; (*eggs*) sbattere; **to whisk out of sight** far sparire || *intr* guizzare

whisk' broom' *s* scopetta per i vestiti, spolverino

whiskers ['hwɪskərz] *spl* barba; (*on side of man's face*) basette *fpl*; (*of cat*) baffi *mpl*

whiskey ['hwɪski] *s* whisky *m*

whisper ['hwɪspər] *s* sussurro, bisbiglio, mormorio; **in a whisper** in un sussurro ‖ *tr & intr* sussurrare, bisbigliare, mormorare

whisperer ['hwɪspərər] *s* sussurrone *m*

whispering ['hwɪspərɪŋ] *adj* di maldicenze ‖ *s* sussurro; maldicenza

whistle ['hwɪsəl] *s* fischio; **to wet one's whistle** (coll) bagnarsi l'ugola ‖ *tr* fischiare ‖ *intr* fischiare, zufolare; **to whistle for** chiamare con un fischio; *(money)* aspettare in vano

whis'tle stop' *s* stazioncina, paesetto

whit [hwɪt] *s*—**not a whit** niente affatto

white [hwaɪt] *adj* ‖ *s* bianco; **whites** (pathol) leucorrea

white'cap' *s* frangente *m*, cavallone *m*, onda crespa

white' coal' *s* carbone bianco

white'-col'lar *adj* impiegatizio

white' feath'er *s*—**to show the white feather** mostrarsi vile

white' goods' *spl* biancheria da casa; articoli *mpl* di cotone; apparecchi *mpl* elettrodomestici

white-haired ['hwaɪt,herd] *adj* dai capelli bianchi; (coll) favorito

white' heat' *s* calor bianco

white' lead' [led] *s* biacca

white' lie' *s* bugia innocente

white' meat' *s* bianco, carne *f* del petto

whiten ['hwaɪtən] *tr* imbiancare, sbiancare ‖ *intr* imbiancarsi, sbiancarsi; impallidire

whiteness ['hwaɪtnɪs] *s* bianchezza

white' plague' *s* tubercolosi *f*

white' slav'ery *s* tratta delle bianche

white' tie' *s* cravatta da frac; marsina, abito da cerimonia

white'wash' *s* imbiancatura; (fig) copertura ‖ *tr* imbiancare, intonacare; (fig) coprire

white' wa'ter lil'y *s* ninfea

whither ['hwɪθər] *adv* dove, a che luogo ‖ *conj* dove

whiting ['hwaɪtɪŋ] *s* (ichth) nasello; (ichth) merlango

whitish ['hwaɪtɪʃ] *adj* biancastro

whitlow ['hwɪtlo] *s* patereccio

Whitsuntide ['hwɪtsən,taɪd] *s* settimana di Pentecoste

whittle ['hwɪtəl] *tr* digrossare; **to whittle away** or **down** ridurre gradualmente

whiz or **whizz** [hwɪz] *s* sibilo; (coll) asso ‖ *v* (*pret & pp* **whizzed**; *ger* **whizzing**) *intr*—**to whiz by** passare sibilando; passare come una freccia

who [hu] *pron interr* chi; **who else?** chi altri?; **who goes there?** (mil) chi va là?; **who's who** chi è l'uno e chi è l'altro; **chi è la gente importante** ‖ *pron rel* chi; il quale

whoa [hwo] or [wo] *interj* fermo!

who·ev'er *pron rel* chiunque

whole [hol] *adj* tutto, intero; sano, intatto; **made out of the whole cloth** completamente immaginario ‖ *s* tutto; **as a whole** nell'insieme; **on the whole** in generale

wholehearted ['hol,hartɪd] *adj* molto sincero, generoso

whole' note' *s* (mus) semibreve *f*

whole'sale' *adj & adv* all'ingrosso ‖ *s* ingrosso ‖ *tr* vendere all'ingrosso ‖ *intr* vendersi all'ingrosso

wholesaler ['hol,selər] *s* grossista *mf*

wholesome ['holsəm] *adj* (*beneficial*) salutare; (*in good health*) sano

wholly ['holi] *adv* interamente

whom [hum] *pron interr* chi ‖ *pron rel* che; il quale

whom·ev'er *pron rel* chiunque

whoop [hup] or [hwup] *s* urlo; (pathol) urlo della pertosse; **to not be worth a whoop** (coll) non valere un fico secco ‖ *tr*—**to whoop it up** (slang) fare il diavolo a quattro ‖ *intr* urlare

whoop'ing cough' ['hupɪŋ] or ['hupɪŋ] *s* pertosse *f*

whopper ['hwapər] *s* (coll) enormità *f;* (coll) fandonia, bugia enorme

whopping ['hwapɪŋ] *adj* (coll) enorme

whore [hor] *s* puttana ‖ *intr*—**to whore around** puttaneggiare; andare a puttane

whortleber·ry ['hwʌrtəl,beri] *s* (-ries) mirtillo

whose [huz] *pron interr* di chi ‖ *pron rel* di chi; del quale; di cui

why [hwaɪ] *s* (whys) perché *m*; **the whys and the wherefores** il perché e il percome ‖ *adv* perché ‖ *interj* diamine!; **why, certainly!** certamente!; **why, yes!** evidentemente!

wick [wɪk] *s* stoppino, lucignolo

wicked ['wɪkɪd] *adj* malvagio; (*mischievous*) cattivo; (*dreadful*) terribile, bestiale

wicker ['wɪkər] *adj* di vimini ‖ *s* vimine *m*

wicket ['wɪkɪt] *s* (*small door*) portello; (*ticket window*) sportello; (*of a canal*) chiusa; (cricket) porta; (croquet) archetto

wide [waɪd] *adj* largo; esteso; (*eyes*) aperto; (*sense of a word*) lato ‖ *adv* largamente; completamente; lontano; **wide of the mark** lontano dal bersaglio

wide'-an'gle *adj* grandangolare

wide'-awake' *adj* sveglio

widen ['waɪdən] *tr* slargare, estendere ‖ *intr* slargarsi, estendersi

wide'-o'pen *adj* spalancato; (*to a gambler*) accessibile

wide'-spread' *adj* (*e.g., arms*) aperto; diffuso

widow ['wɪdo] *s* vedova; (cards) morto ‖ *tr* lasciar vedova

widower ['wɪdo·ər] *s* vedovo

widowhood ['wɪdo,hud] *s* vedovanza

wid'ow's mite' *s* obolo della vedova

wid'ow's weeds' *spl* gramaglie *fpl* vedovili

width [wɪdθ] *s* larghezza

wield [wild] *tr* (*e.g., a sword*) brandire; (*e.g., a hammer*) maneggiare; (*power*) esercitare

wife [waɪf] *s* (wives [waɪvz]) moglie *f*

wig [wɪg] *s* parrucca

wiggle ['wɪgəl] *s* dimenio; (*of fish*)

guizzo || *tr* dimenare || *intr* dimenarsi; guizzare

wig'wag' *s* segnalazione con bandierine || *v* (*pret & pp* -wagged; *ger* -wagging) *tr & intr* segnalare con bandierine

wigwam ['wɪgwam] *s* tenda a cupola dei pellirosse, wigwam *m*

wild [waɪld] *adj* (*animal*) feroce; (*e.g., berry*) selvatico; (*barbarous*) selvaggio; (*violent*) furioso; (*mad*) pazzo; (*unruly*) discolo, indisciplinato; (*extravagant*) pazzesco; (*shot or throw*) lanciato all'impazzata; **wild about** pazzo per || *s* regione deserta; **the wild** la foresta; **wilds** regioni selvagge || *adv* pazzamente; **to go wild** andare in delirio; **to run wild** crescere all'impazzata; correre senza freno

wild' boar' *s* cinghiale *m*

wild' card' *s* matta

wild'cat' *s* gatto selvatico; lince *f*; impresa arrischiata || *v* (*pret & pp* -catted; *ger* -catting) *tr & intr* esplorare per conto proprio

wild'cat strike' *s* sciopero non autorizzato dal sindacato

wilderness ['wɪldərnɪs] *s* deserto

wild-eyed ['waɪld ,aɪd] *adj* stralunato; (*scheme*) pazzesco

wild'fire' *s* fuoco greco; fuoco fatuo; **to spread like wildfire** crescere come la gramigna; (*said of news*) spargersi come il baleno

wild' flow'er *s* fiore *m* di campo

wild' goose' *s* oca selvatica

wild'-goose' chase' *s* ricerca della luna nel pozzo

wild'life' *s* animali *spl* selvatici

wild' oat' *s* avena selvatica; **to sow one's wild oats** correre la cavallina

wild' ol'ive *s* olivastro, oleastro

wile [waɪl] *s* stratagemma *m*, inganno; (*cunning*) astuzia || *tr* allettare; **to wile away** passare piacevolmente

will [wɪl] *s* volontà *f*, volere *m*; (*law*) testamento; **at will** a volontà || *tr* volere; (*law*) legare || *intr* volere; **do as you will** faccia come vuole || *v* (*pret & cond* would) *aux* **she will leave tomorrow** partirà domani; **a cactus plant will live two months without water** una pianta grassa può vivere due mesi senz'acqua

willful ['wɪlfəl] *adj* volontario; ostinato

willfulness ['wɪlfəlnɪs] *s* volontarietà *f*; ostinatezza

William ['wɪljəm] *s* Guglielmo

willing ['wɪlɪŋ] *adj* volonteroso; **to be willing** essere disposto

willingly ['wɪlɪŋli] *adv* di buon grado, volentieri

willingness ['wɪlɪŋnɪs] *s* buona voglia, propensione

will-o'-the-wisp ['wɪləðə'wɪsp] *s* fuoco fatuo; (*fig*) illusione, chimera

willow ['wɪlo] *s* salice *m*

willowy ['wɪlo-i] *adj* pieghevole; (*slender*) snello; pieno di giunchi

will' pow'er *s* forza di volontà

willy-nilly ['wɪli'nɪli] *adv* volente o nolente

wilt [wɪlt] *tr* far appassire || *intr* appassire

wil·y ['waɪli] *adj* (-i-er; -i-est) astuto, scaltro

wimple ['wɪmpəl] *s* soggolo

win [wɪn] *s* vittoria, vincita || *v* (*pret & pp* won [wʌn]; *ger* winning) *tr & intr* guadagnare; **to win out** vincere, aver successo

wince [wɪns] *s* sussulto || *intr* sussultare

winch [wɪntʃ] *s* verricello; (*handle*) manovella; (naut) molinello

wind [wɪnd] *s* vento; (*gas in intestines*) vento; (*breath*) fiato, tenuta; **to break wind** scoreggiare; **to get wind of** subodorare; **to sail close to the wind** (naut) andare all'orza; **to take the wind out of the sails of** sconcertare; **winds** (mus) fiati *mpl* || *tr* far perdere il fiato a || [waɪnd] *v* (*pret & pp* wound [waʊnd]) *tr* (*to wrap up*) arrotolare; (*thread, wool*) dipanare, aggomitolare; (*a clock*) caricare; (*a handle*) far girare; **to wind one's way through** serpeggiare per; **to wind up** arrotolare; eccitare; finire, portare a termine || *intr* serpeggiare, snodarsi

windbag ['wɪnd ,bæg] *s* (*of a bagpipe*) otre *m*; (fig) parolaio, otre *m* di vento

windbreak ['wɪnd ,brek] *s* frangivento

wind' cone' [wɪnd] *s* manica a vento

winded ['wɪndɪd] *adj* senza fiato

windfall ['wɪnd ,fɔl] *s* frutta abbattuta dal vento; provvidenza, manna del cielo

wind'ing sheet' ['waɪndɪŋ] *s* lenzuolo funebre

wind'ing stairs' ['waɪndɪŋ] *spl* scala a chiocciola

wind' in'strument [wɪnd] *s* (mus) strumento a fiato

windlass ['wɪndləs] *s* verricello

windmill ['wɪnd ,mɪl] *s* mulino a vento; (*air turbine*) aeromotore *m*; **to tilt at windmills** combattere i mulini a vento

window ['wɪndo] *s* finestra; (*of ticket office*) sportello; (*of car or coach*) finestrino

win'dow dress'er *s* vetrinista *mf*

win'dow dress'ing *s* vetrinistica; (fig) facciata, apparenza

win'dow en'velope *s* busta a finestrella

win'dow frame' *s* intelaiatura della finestra

win'dow·pane' *s* vetro, invetriata

win'dow sash' *s* intelaiatura della finestra

win'dow screen' *s* zanzariera

win'dow shade' *s* tendina avvolgibile

win'dow-shop' *v* (*pret & pp* -shopped; *ger* -shopping) *intr* guardare nelle vetrine senza comprare

win'dow sill' *s* davanzale *m* della finestra

windpipe ['wɪnd ,paɪp] *s* trachea

windproof ['wɪnd ,pruf] *adj* resistente al vento

windshield ['wɪnd ,ʃild] *s* parabrezza *m*

wind'shield wash'er *s* lavacristallo

wind'shield wip'er *s* tergicristallo

windsock ['wɪnd ˌsɑk] *s* (aer) manica a vento

windstorm ['wɪnd ˌstɔrm] *s* bufera di vento

wind' tun'nel [wɪnd] *s* (aer) galleria aerodinamica

wind-up ['waɪnd ˌʌp] *s* conclusione

windward ['wɪndwərd] *s* orza, sopravvento; **to turn to windward** mettersi al sopravvento

Wind'ward Is'lands *spl* Isole *fpl* Sopravvento

wind·y ['wɪndɪ] *adj* (-ier; -iest) ventoso; verboso, ampolloso; **it is windy** fa vento

wine [waɪn] *s* vino || *tr* offrire vino a || *intr* bere del vino

wine' cel'lar *s* cantina

wine'glass' *s* bicchiere da vino

winegrower ['waɪn ˌgro·ər] *s* vinificatore *m*, viticoltore *m*

wine' press' *s* torchio per l'uva

winer·y ['waɪnərɪ] *s* (-ies) stabilimento vinicolo

wine'shop' *s* fiaschetteria

wine'skin' *s* otre *m*

wine' stew'ard *s* sommelier *m*

winetaster ['waɪn ˌtestər] *s* degustatore *m* di vini

wing [wɪŋ] *s* ala; (unit of air force) aerobrigata; (theat) quinta; **to take wing** levarsi a volo; **under one's wing** sotto la protezione di qlcu || *tr* ferire nell'ala; **to wing one's way** volare, portarsi a volo

wing' chair' *s* poltrona a orecchioni

wing' col'lar *s* colletto per marsina

wing' nut' *s* (mach) galletto

wing'span' *s* (of airplane) apertura alare

wing'spread' *s* (of bird) apertura alare

wink [wɪŋk] *s* ammicco; **in a wink in** un batter d'occhio; **to not sleep a wink** non chiudere occhio; **to take forty winks** (coll) schiacciare un pisolino || *tr* (the eye) strizzare || *intr* ammiccare, strizzare l'occhio; (to blink) battere le ciglia; **to wink at** ammiccare a; far finta di non vedere

winner ['wɪnər] *s* vincitore *m*

winning ['wɪnɪŋ] *adj* vincente, vincitore; attraente, simpatico || **winnings** *spl* vincita

winnow ['wɪno] *tr* ventilare, brezzare; (fig) vagliare || *intr* svolazzare

winsome ['wɪnsəm] *adj* attraente

winter ['wɪntər] *adj* invernale || *s* inverno || *intr* svernare

win'ter-green' *s* tè *m* del Canadà; olio di gaulteria

win·try ['wɪntrɪ] *adj* (-trier; -triest) invernale; freddo

wipe [waɪp] *tr* forbire, detergere; (to dry) asciugare; **to wipe away** (tears) asciugare; **to wipe off** pulire, forbire; **to wipe out** distruggere completamente; (coll) eliminare

wiper ['waɪpər] *s* strofinaccio; (mach) camma; (elec) contatto scorrevole

wire [waɪr] *s* filo metallico; telegramma *m*; (coll) telegrafo; **to pull wires** manovrare di dietro le quinte

|| *tr* legare con filo metallico; attrezzare l'elettricità in; (coll) mandare per telegrafo; (coll) telegrafare || *intr* (coll) telegrafare

wire' cut'ter *s* pinza tagliafili

wire' entan'glement *s* reticolato di filo spinato

wire' gauge' *s* calibro da fili

wire-haired ['waɪr ˌherd] *adj* a pelo ruvido

wireless ['waɪrlɪs] *adj* senza fili || *s* telegrafo senza fili; telegrafia senza fili

wire' nail' *s* chiodo da falegname

wirepulling ['waɪr ˌpulɪŋ] *s* manovra dietro alle quinte

wire' record'er *s* magnetofono a filo

wire' screen' *s* rete metallica

wire'tap' *v* (pret & pp -tapped; ger -tapping) *tr* (a conversation) intercettare

wiring ['waɪrɪŋ] *s* sistema *m* di fili elettrici

wir·y ['waɪrɪ] *adj* (-ier; -iest) fatto di filo; (hair) ispido; (tone) metallico, vibrante; (sinewy) segaligno

wisdom ['wɪzdəm] *s* senno, sapienza, saggezza

wis'dom tooth' *s* dente *m* del giudizio

wise [waɪz] *adj* saggio, sapiente; (decision) giudizioso; **to be wise to** (slang) accorgersi del gioco di; **to get wise** (slang) mangiare la foglia; (slang) diventare impertinente || *s* modo, maniera; **in no wise** in nessun modo || *tr*—**to wise up** (slang) avvertire || *intr*—**to wise up** (slang) accorgersi

wiseacre ['waɪz ˌekər] *s* sapientone *m*

wise'crack' *s* (coll) spiritosaggine *f* || *intr* (coll) dire spiritosaggini

wise' guy' *s* (slang) sputasentenze *m*

wish [wɪʃ] *s* desiderio; augurio; **to make a wish** formulare un desiderio || *tr* desiderare; augurare; **to wish s.o. a good day** dare il buon giorno a qlcu || *intr* desiderare; **to wish for** desiderare

wish'bone' *s* forcella

wishful ['wɪʃfəl] *adj* desideroso

wish'ful think'ing *s* pio desiderio

wistful ['wɪstfəl] *adj* melanconico, pensoso, meditabondo

wit [wɪt] *s* spirito; (person) bellospirito; (understanding) senso; **to be at one's wits' end** non sapere a che santo votarsi; **to have one's wits about one** avere presenza di spirito; **to live by one's wits** vivere di espedienti

witch [wɪtʃ] *s* strega

witch'craft' *s* stregoneria

witch' doc'tor *s* stregone *m*

witch'es' Sab'bath *s* sabba *m*

witch' ha'zel *s* (shrub) amamelide *f*; (liquid) estratto di amamelide

witch' hunt' *s* caccia alle streghe

with [wɪð] or [wɪθ] *prep* con; a, e.g., **with open arms** a braccia aperte; di, e.g., **covered with silk** coperto di seta; **to be satisfied with the** performance essere contento della rappresentazione; da, e.g., **with the In-**

dians dagli indiani; **to part with** separarsi da

with·draw' v (pret **-drew;** pp **-drawn**) tr ritirare || intr ritirarsi

withdrawal [wɪð'drɔ·əl] or [wɪθ'drɔ·əl] s ritiro, ritirata; (of funds) prelevamento

wither ['wɪðər] tr intisichire; (with a glance) incenerire || intr avvizzire, intisichire

with·hold' v (pret & pp **-held**) tr trattenere; (information) sottacere; (payment) defalcare; (permission) negare

withhold'ing tax' s imposta trattenuta

with·in' adv dentro, didentro || prep entro, dentro di, dentro a, dentro di; fra; in; (a time period) nel giro di

with·out' adv fuori || prep senza; fuori, fuori di; **to do without** fare a meno di; without + ger senza + inf, e.g., without saying a word senza dire una parola; senza che + subj, e.g., she fell without anyone helping her cadde senza che nessuno l'aiutasse

with·stand' v (pret & pp **-stood**) tr resistere (with dat), reggere (with dat)

witness ['wɪtnɪs] s testimone mf; in witness whereof in fé di che; **to bear witness** far fede || tr (to be present at) presenziare; (to attest) testimoniare, firmare come testimone

wit'ness stand' s banco dei testimoni

witticism ['wɪtɪ‚sɪzəm] s motto, battuta spiritosa, spiritosaggine f

wittingly ['wɪtɪŋli] adv consapevolmente

wit·ty ['wɪti] adj (-tier; -tiest) spiritoso, divertente

wizard ['wɪzərd] s mago

wizardry ['wɪzərdri] s magia

wizened ['wɪzənd] adj raggrinzito

woad [wod] s (bot) guado

wobble ['wabəl] s oscillazione, dondolio || intr oscillare, dondolare; (said of a chair) zoppicare; (fig) titubare

wob·bly ['wabli] adj (-blier; -bliest) oscillante, zoppo, malfermo

woe [wo] s disgrazia, afflizione, sventura; || interj—**woe is me!** ahimè!

woebegone ['wobɪ‚gɔn] or ['wobɪ‚gan] adj triste, abbattuto

woeful ['wofəl] adj sfortunato, disgraziato; (of poor quality) orribile

wolf [wʊlf] s (wolves [wʊlvz]) lupo; (coll) dongiovanni m; **to cry wolf** gridare al lupo; **to keep the wolf from the door** tener lontana la miseria || tr & intr mangiare come un lupo

wolf'hound' s cane m da pastore alsaziano

wolfram ['wʊlfrəm] s wolframio

wolf's-bane or **wolfsbane** ['wʊlfs‚ben] s (bot) aconito

wolverine [‚wʊlvə'rin] s (zool) ghiottone m

woman ['wʊmən] s (women ['wɪmɪn]) donna

womanhood ['wʊmən‚hʊd] s (quality) femminilità f; (women collectively) donne fpl, sesso femminile

womanish ['wʊmənɪʃ] adj femminile; (effeminate) effeminato

wom'an·kind' s sesso femminile

womanly ['wʊmənli] adj (-lier; -liest) femminile, muliebre

wom'an suf'frage s suffragio alle donne

woman-suffragist ['wʊmən'sʌfrədʒɪst] s suffragista mf

womb [wum] s utero; (fig) seno

womenfolk ['wɪmɪn‚fok] spl le donne

wonder ['wʌndər] s (something strange and surprising) meraviglia; (feeling) ammirazione; (miracle) prodigio, miracolo; **for a wonder** cosa strana; **no wonder that** non fa meraviglia che; **to work wonders** fare miracoli || tr— **to wonder that** meravigliarsi che; **to wonder how, if, when, where, who, why** domandarsi or chiedersi come, se, quando, dove, chi, perché || intr meravigliarsi; chiedersi; **to wonder at** ammirare

won'der drug' s medicina miracolosa

wonderful ['wʌndərfəl] adj meraviglioso

won'der·land' s paese m delle meraviglie

wonderment ['wʌndərmənt] s sorpresa, meraviglia, stupore m

won'der-work'er s taumaturgo

wont [wʌnt] or [wɔnt] adj abituato, solito || s abitudine f, costume m

wonted ['wʌntɪd] or ['wɔntɪd] adj solito, abituale

woo [wu] tr (a woman) corteggiare; (to seek to win) allettare; (good or bad consequences) andare in cerca di

wood [wʊd] s legno; (firewood) legna; (keg) barile m; **out of the woods** fuori pericolo; al sicuro; **woods** bosco, selva

woodbine ['wʊd‚baɪn] s (honeysuckle) abbracciabosco; (Virginia creeper) vite f del Canadà

wood' carv'ing s intaglio in legno, statua in legno

wood'chuck' s marmotta americana

wood'cock' s beccaccia

wood'cut' s silografia

wood'cut'ter s boscaiolo

wooded ['wʊdɪd] adj legnoso, boschivo

wooden ['wʊdən] adj di legno; duro, rigido; inespressivo

wood' engrav'ing s silografia

wooden-headed ['wʊdən‚hɛdɪd] adj (coll) dalla testa dura

wood'en leg' s gamba di legno

wood'en shoe' s zoccolo

wood' grouse' s gallo cedrone

woodland ['wʊdlənd] adj boschivo || s foresta, bosco

wood'man s (-men) boscaiolo

woodpecker ['wʊd‚pɛkər] s picchio

wood'pile' s legnaia

wood' screw' s vite f per legno

wood'shed' s legnaia

woods'man s (-men) abitatore m dei boschi; boscaiolo

wood'wind' s strumento a fiato di legno

wood'work' s lavoro in legno; parti fpl di legno

wood'work'er s ebanista m, falegname m

wood'worm' s tarlo

wood·y ['wudɪ] *adj* (**-ier; -iest**) boscoso, alberato; (*like wood*) legnoso

wooer ['wu·ər] *s* corteggiatore *m*

woof [wuf] *s* (*yarns running across warp*) trama; (*fabric*) tessuto

woofer ['wufər] *s* altoparlante *m* per basse audiofrequenze, woofer *m*

wool [wul] *s* lana

woolen ['wulən] *adj* di lana ‖ *s* tessuto di lana; **woolens** laneria

woolgrower ['wul‚gro·ər] *s* allevatore *m* di pecore

wool·ly ['wulɪ] *adj* (**-ier; -liest**) di lana; lanoso; (coll) confuso

word [wʌrd] *s* parola; **by word of mouth** oralmente; **to be as good as one's word** essere di parola; **to have a word with** dire quattro parole a; **to have word from** aver notizie da; **to keep one's word** essere di parola; **to leave word** lasciar detto; **to send word that** mandare a dire che; **words** (*quarrel*) baruffa ‖ *tr* esprimere, formulare ‖ **Word** *s* (theol) Verbo

word' count' *s* conto lessicale

word' forma'tion *s* formazione delle parole

wording ['wʌrdɪŋ] *s* fraseologia, dicitura

word' or'der *s* disposizione delle parole in una frase

word'stock' *s* lessico

word·y ['wʌrdɪ] *adj* (**-ier; -iest**) verboso, parolaio

work [wʌrk] *s* lavoro; (*of art, fortification, etc.*) opera; **at work** al lavoro, in ufficio; (*in operation*) in servizio; **out of work** senza lavoro, disoccupato; **to give s.o. the works** (slang) trattare male; (slang) ammazzare; **to shoot the works** (slang) scialare; **works** opificio; meccanismo; (*of clock*) castello ‖ *tr* far funzionare, lavorare, maneggiare; (*e.g., a miracle*) operare; (*e.g., iron*) trattare; **to work up** preparare; stimulare, eccitare ‖ *intr* lavorare; (*said of a machine*) funzionare; (*said of a remedy*) avere effetto; **to work loose** sciogliersi; **to work out** andare a finire; (*said of a problem*) sciogliersi; (*said of a total*) ammontare; (sports) allenarsi

workable ['wʌrkəbəl] *adj* (*feasible*) praticabile; (*e.g., iron*) lavorabile

work'bench' *s* banco

work'book' *s* manuale *m* d'istruzioni; (*for students*) quaderno d'esercizi

work'box' *s* cassetta dei ferri del mestiere; (*for needlework*) cestino da lavoro

work'day' *adj* lavorativo; ordinario, di tutti i giorni ‖ *s* (*working day*) giorno feriale, giornata lavorativa

worked-up ['wʌrkt'ʌp] *adj* sovreccitato

worker ['wʌrkər] *s* lavorante *m*, lavoratore *m*, operaio

work' force' *s* mano *f* d'opera

work'horse' *s* cavallo da tiro; (*tireless worker*) lavoratore indefesso

work'house' *s* carcere *m* con lavoro obbligatorio; (Brit) istituto dei poveri

work'ing class' *s* classe operaia

work'ing condi'tions *spl* trattamento, condizioni *fpl* di lavoro

work'ing girl' *s* ragazza lavoratrice

work'ing hours' *spl* orario di lavoro

working'man *s* (**-men**) lavoratore *m*

work'ing or'der *s* buone condizioni, efficienza

work'ing-wom'an *s* (**-wom'en**) operaia, lavoratrice *f*

work'man *s* (**-men**) lavoratore *m*; (*skilled worker*) operaio specializzato

workmanship ['wʌrkmən‚ʃɪp] *s* fattura; (*work executed*) opera

work' of art' *s* opera d'arte

work'out' *s* (sports) esercizio, allenamento

work'room' *s* (*for manual work*) officina; (*study*) gabinetto, laboratorio

work'shop' *s* officina

work' stop'page *s* sospensione del lavoro

world [wʌrld] *adj* mondiale ‖ *s* mondo; **a world of** un monte di; **for all the world** per tutto l'oro del mondo; **in the world** al mondo; **since the world began** da che mondo è mondo; **the other world** l'altro mondo; **to bring into the world** mettere al mondo; **to see the world** conoscere il mondo; **to think the world of** tenere in altissima considerazione

world' affairs' *spl* relazioni *fpl* internazionali

world·ly ['wʌrldlɪ] *adj* (**-ier; -liest**) mondano, secolare

world'ly-wise' *adj* vissuto

world's' fair' *s* esposizione *f* mondiale

world' war' *s* guerra mondiale

world'-wide' *adj* mondiale

worm [wʌrm] *s* verme *m* ‖ *tr* liberare dai vermi; **to worm a secret out of s.o.** carpire un segreto a qlcu; **to worm one's way into** insinuarsi in

worm-eaten ['wʌrm‚itən] *adj* tarlato, bacato

worm' gear' *s* meccanismo a vite perpetua, ingranaggio elicoidale

worm'wood' *s* assenzio; (fig) amarezza

worm·y ['wʌrmɪ] *adj* (**-ier; -iest**) verminoso; (*worm-eaten*) bacato; (*groveling*) vile, strascicante

worn [wɔrn] *adj* usato; (*look*) stanco, esausto

worn'-out' *adj* logoro, scalcinato; (*by illness*) consunto; (fig) trito

worrisome ['wʌrɪsəm] *adj* preoccupante; (*inclined to worry*) preoccupato

wor·ry ['wʌrɪ] *s* (**-ries**) preoccupazione, inquietudine *f*; (*trouble*) fastidio ‖ *v* (*pret & pp* **-ried**) *tr* preoccupare, inquietare; **to be worried** essere impensierito ‖ *intr* preoccuparsi, inquietarsi; **don't worry!** non si preoccupi!

worse [wʌrs] *adj* & *s* peggiore *m*, peggio ‖ *adv* peggio; **worse and worse** di male in peggio

worsen ['wʌrsən] *tr* & *intr* peggiorare

wor·ship ['wʌr‚ʃɪp] *s* venerazione, adorazione; servizio religioso; **your Worship** La Signoria Vostra ‖ *v* (*pret &*

pp -shiped or -shipped; *ger* -shiping or -shipping) *tr* venerare, adorare

worshiper or **worshipper** [ˈwʌrʃɪpər] *s* adoratore *m*; (*in church*) devoto, fedele *m*

worst [wʌrst] *adj* (il) peggiore; pessimo ‖ *s* peggio, peggiore *m*; **at worst** alla peggio; **if worst comes to worst** alla peggio; **to get the worst** averne la peggio ‖ *adv* peggio

worsted [ˈwʊstɪd] *adj* di lana pettinata ‖ *s* tessuto di lana pettinata

wort [wʌrt] *s* mosto di malto; pianta, erba

worth [wʌrθ] *adj* che vale, da, e.g., **worth ten dollars** da dieci dollari; **to be worth** valere; essere di pregio; **to be worth** + *ger* valere la pena (di) + *inf*, e.g., **it is worth reading** vale la pena (di) leggerlo ‖ *s* pregio, valore *m*; **a dollar's worth** un dollaro di

worthless [ˈwʌrθlɪs] *adj* senza valore; inutile; inservibile; (*person*) indegno

worth'while' *adj* meritevole, meritevole d'attenzione

wor·thy [ˈwʌrði] *adj* (**-thier; -thiest**) degno, meritevole ‖ *s* (**-thies**) maggiorente *mf*

would [wʊd] *v aux* **they said they would come** dissero che sarebbero venuti; **he would buy it if he had the money** lo comprerebbe se avesse i soldi; **would you be so kind to** avrebbe la cortesia di; **he would spend every winter in Florida** passava tutti gli inverni in Florida; **would that . . . !** oh se . . . !, volesse il cielo che . . . !, magari . . . !

would'-be' *adj* preteso, sedicente; (*intended to be*) inteso

wound [wund] *s* ferita ‖ *tr* ferire

wounded [ˈwundɪd] *adj* ferito ‖ **the wounded** i feriti

wow [waʊ] *s* distorsione acustica di suono riprodotto; (slang) successone *m* ‖ *tr* (slang) entusiasmare ‖ *interj* (coll) accidenti!

wrack [ræk] *s* naufragio; vestigio; (*seaweed*) alghe marine gettate sulla spiaggia; **to go to wrack and ruin** andare interamente in rovina

wraith [reθ] *s* spettro, fantasma *m*

wrangle [ˈræŋgəl] *s* baruffa, alterco ‖ *intr* altercare, rissare

wrap [ræp] *s* sciarpa; mantello ‖ *v* (*pret & pp* **wrapped**; *ger* **wrapping**) *tr* involgere; impaccare; **to be wrapped up in** essere assorto in; **to wrap up** avvolgere; (*in paper*) incartare; (*in clothing*) imbaccucare; (coll) concludere ‖ *intr*—**to wrap up** imbaccuccarsi, avvolgersi

wrapper [ˈræpər] *s* veste *f* da camera, peignoir *m*; (*of newspaper*) fascia, fascetta; (*of cigars*) involto

wrap'ping pa'per [ˈræpɪŋ] *s* carta d'impacco or d'imballaggio

wrath [ræθ] or [rɑθ] *s* ira; vendetta

wrathful [ˈræθfəl] or [ˈrɑθfəl] *adj* collerico, iracondo

wreak [rik] *tr* (*vengeance*) infliggere; (*anger*) scaricare

wreath [riθ] *s* (**wreaths** [riðz]) ghirlanda; (*of laurel*) laurea; (*of smoke*) spirale *f*

wreathe [rið] *tr* inghirlandare; avviluppare; (*a garland*) intessere ‖ *intr* (*said of smoke*) innalzarsi in spire

wreck [rek] *s* rottame *m*, relitto; naufragio; rovina; catastrofe *f*, disastro; (fig) rottame *m*, relitto ‖ *tr* far naufragare; distruggere, rovinare; (*a train*) fare scontrare, fare deragliare; (*a building*) demolire

wreckage [ˈrekɪdʒ] *s* rottami *mpl*, relitti *mpl*; rovine *fpl*

wrecker [ˈrekər] *s* (*tow truck*) autogrù *f*; (*housewrecker*) demolitore *m*

wreck'ing ball' *s* martello demolitore

wreck'ing car' *s* autogrù *f*

wrecking crane' *s* (rr) carro gru

wren [ren] *s* scricciolo

wrench [rentʃ] *s* chiave *f*; (*pull*) tiro; (*of a joint*) distorsione ‖ *tr* torcere, distorcere; (*one's limb*) torcersi, distorcersi

wrest [rest] *tr* strappare, togliere a viva forza; (*to twist*) torcere

wrestle [ˈresəl] *s* lotta, combattimento ‖ *intr* fare la lotta, lottare

wrestler [ˈrestlər] *s* lottatore *m*

wrestling [ˈreslɪŋ] *s* lotta

wretch [retʃ] *s* disgraziato, tapino

wretched [ˈretʃɪd] *adj* (*pitiable*) misero, disgraziato, tapino; (*poor, worthless*) miserabile

wriggle [ˈrɪgəl] *s* (*e.g., of a snake*) guizzo; dondolio ‖ *tr* dondolare, dimenare ‖ *intr* guizzare; dimenarsi; **to wriggle out of** sgattaiolare da, divincolarsi da

wrig·gly [ˈrɪgli] *adj* (**-glier; -gliest**) che si contorce; (fig) evasivo

wring [rɪŋ] *s* (*pret & pp* **wrung** [rʌŋ]) *tr* torcere; (*wet clothing*) strizzare; (*one's heart*) stringersi; (*e.g., one's hands*) torcersi; **to wring the truth out of** strappare la verità a

wringer [ˈrɪŋər] *s* strizzatoio

wrinkle [ˈrɪŋkəl] *s* (*on skin*) ruga; (*on fabric*) crespa, grinza; (coll) trovata, espediente *m* ‖ *tr* corrugare, raggrinzire; (*fabric*) increspare

wrin'kle-proof' *adj* antipiega, ingualcibile

wrin·kly [ˈrɪŋkli] *adj* (**-klier; -kliest**) rugoso, grinzoso

wrist [rɪst] *s* polso

wrist'band' *s* polso

wrist' pin' *s* spinotto

wrist' watch' *s* orologio da polso

writ [rɪt] *s* scritto; (law) ordine *m*

write [raɪt] *v* (*pret* **wrote** [rot]; *pp* **written** [ˈrɪtən]) *tr* scrivere; **to write down** mettere in iscritto; (*to disparage*) menomare; **to write off** (*a debt*) cancellare; (com) stornare; **to write up** redigere, scrivere in pieno; (*to ballyhoo*) scrivere le lodi di ‖ *intr* scrivere; **to write back** rispondere per lettera

write'-in-vote' *s* voto per candidato il cui nome non è nella lista

writer [ˈraɪtər] *s* scrittore *m*

write'-up' *s* descrizione scritta, conto; stamburata, elogio; (com) valutazione eccesiva

writhe [raɪð] *intr* contorcersi, spasimare, dibattersi

writing ['raɪtɪŋ] *s* lo scrivere; (*something written*) scritto; (*characters written*) scrittura; professione di scrittore; **at this writing** scrivendo questa mia; **in one's own writing** di proprio pugno; **to put in writing** mettere in iscritto

writ'ing desk' *s* scrittoio

writ'ing mate'rials *spl* l'occorrente *m* per scrivere, oggetti *mpl* di cancelleria

writ'ing pa'per *s* carta da lettere

writ'ten ac'cent ['rɪtən] *s* accento grafico

wrong [rɔŋ] *or* [raŋ] *adj* sbagliato, erroneo; (*awry*) guasto; (*step*) falso; cattivo, ingiusto; **there is nothing wrong with him** non ha niente; **to be wrong** (*mistaken*) aver torto; (*guilty*) aver la colpa ‖ *s* torto; **to**

be in the wrong essere in errore; **to do wrong** fare del male; commettere un'ingiustizia ‖ *adv* male; (*backward*) alla rovescia; **to go wrong** andare alla rovescia; andare per la cattiva strada ‖ *tr* far torto a, offendere, maltrattare

wrongdoer ['rɔŋ,du·ər] *or* ['rɑn,du·ər] *s* peccatore *m*, trasgressore *m*

wrongdoing ['rɔŋ,du·ɪŋ] *or* ['rɑn,du·ɪŋ] *s* peccato, offesa, trasgressione

wrong' num'ber *s* (telp) numero sbagliato; **you have the wrong number** Lei si è sbagliato di numero

wrong' side' *s* rovescio; (*of street*) altra parte; **to get out of bed on the wrong side** alzarsi di malumore; **wrong side out** alla rovescia

wrought' i'ron [rɔt] *s* ferro battuto

wrought'-up' *adj* sovreccitato

wry [raɪ] (**wrier; wriest**) sbieco, storto; pervertito, alterato; ironico

wry'neck' *s* (orn & pathol) torcicollo

X

X, x [ɛks] *s* ventiquattresima lettera dell'alfabeto inglese

Xanthippe [zæn'tɪpi] *s* Santippe *f*

Xavier ['zævɪ·ər] *or* ['zevɪ·ər] *s* Saverio

xebec ['zibɛk] *s* (naut) sciabecco

xenon ['zinɑn] *or* ['zenɑn] *s* xeno

xenophobe ['zenə,fob] *s* xenofobo

Xenophon ['zenəfɑn] *s* Senofonte *m*

xerography [zɪ'rɑgrəfi] *s* xerografia

xerophyte [zɪrə,faɪt] *s* xerofito

Xerxes ['zʌrksɪs] *s* Serse *m*

Xmas ['krɪsməs] *s* Natale *m*

x-ray ['ɛks,re] *adj* radiografico ‖ *s* raggio X; (*photograph*) radiogramma *m*, radiografia ‖ *tr* radiografare

xylograph ['zaɪlə,græf] *or* ['zaɪlə,grɑf] *s* silografia

xylophone ['zaɪlə,fon] *s* silofono

Y

Y, y [waɪ] *s* venticinquesima lettera dell'alfabeto inglese

yacht [jɑt] *s* yacht *m*, panfilo

yacht' club' *s* club *m* nautico, associazione velica

yak [jæk] *s* yak *m* ‖ *v* (*pret & pp* **yakked;** *ger* **yakking**) *intr* (slang) ciarlare, chiacchierare

yam [jæm] *s* igname *m*; (*sweet potato*) patata dolce, batata

yank [jæŋk] *s* tiro, strattone *m* ‖ *tr* dare uno strattone a, tirare ‖ *intr* dare uno strattone, tirare

Yankee ['jæŋki] *adj & s* yankee *mf*

yap [jæp] *s* guaito; (slang) chiacchierio, ciancia ‖ *v* (*pret & pp* **yapped;** *ger* **yapping**) *intr* latrare, guaire; (slang) chiacchierare, ciarlare

yard [jɑrd] *s* cortile *m*; recinto; yard *m*, iarda; (naut) pennone *m*; (rr) scalo smistamento

yard'arm' *s* estremità *f* del pennone

yard' goods' *spl* tessuti *mpl* in pezza

yard'mas'ter *s* (rr) capo dello scalo smistamento

yard'stick' *s* stecca di una iarda di lunghezza; (fig) metro

yarn [jɑrn] *s* filo, filato; (coll) storia

yarrow ['jæro] *s* millefoglie *m*

yaw [jɔ] *s* (naut) straorzata; (aer) imbardata ‖ *intr* (naut) straorzare, guizzare; (aer) imbardare

yawl [jɔl] *s* barca a remi; (naut) iolla

yawn [jɔn] *s* sbadiglio ‖ *intr* sbadigliare; (*said, e.g., of a hole*) vaneggiare, aprirsi

yea [je] *s & adv* sì *m*

yean [jin] *intr* (*said of sheep or goat*) partorire

year [jɪr] *s* anno; **to be . . . years old** avere . . . anni; **year in, year out** un anno dopo l'altro

year'book' *s* annuario

yearling ['jɪrlɪŋ] *adj* di un anno di età ‖ *s* animale *m* di un anno di età

yearly ['jɪrli] *adj* annuale ‖ *adv* annualmente

yearn [jʌrn] *intr* smaniare, sospirare; **to yearn for** anelare per

yearning ['jʌrnɪŋ] *s* anelo, sospiro ardente

yeast [jist] *s* lievito

yeast' cake' *s* compressa di lievito

yell [jel] *s* urlo ‖ *tr* gridare ‖ *intr* urlare

yellow ['jelo] *adj* giallo; (*newspaper*) sensazionale; (*cowardly*) (coll) vile ‖ *s* giallo; giallo d'uovo ‖ *intr* ingiallire

yellowish ['jelo‑ɪʃ] *adj* giallastro

yel'low•jack'et *s* vespa, calabrone *m*

yel'low streak' *s* (coll) vena di codardia

yelp [jelp] *s* guaito ‖ *intr* guaire

yeo'man *s* (**-men**) (naut) sottufficiale *m*; (Brit) piccolo proprietario terriero

yeo'man of the guard' *s* guardia del servizio reale

yeo'man's serv'ice *s* lavoro onesto

yes [jes] *s* sì *m*; **to say yes** dire di sì ‖ *adv* sì ‖ *v* (*pret & pp* **yessed**; *ger* **yessing**) *tr* dire di sì a ‖ *intr* dire di sì

yes' man' *s* (coll) persona che approva sempre; (coll) leccapiedi *m*

yesterday ['jestərdi] *or* ['jestər‚de] *s & adv* ieri *m*

yet [jet] *adv* ancora; tuttavia; **as yet** sinora; **nor yet** nemmeno; **not yet** non ancora ‖ *conj* ma, però, pure

yew' tree' [ju] *s* tasso

Yiddish ['jɪdɪʃ] *adj & s* yiddish *m*

yield [jild] *s* rendimento, resa; (*crop*) raccolto; (com) reddito, gettito ‖ *tr* rendere, fruttare ‖ *intr* rendere, fruttare, produrre; (*to surrender*) cedere, arrendersi; sottomettersi; cedere il posto

yodeling *or* **yodelling** ['jodəlɪŋ] *s* tirolesa

yoke [jok] *s* (*contrivance*) giogo; (*pair, e.g., of oxen*) paio; (*of shirt*) sprone *m*; (naut) barra del timone; **to throw off the yoke** scuotere il giogo ‖ *tr* aggiogare

yokel ['jokəl] *s* zoticone *m*

yolk [jok] *s* tuorlo

yonder ['jɑndər] *adj* situato lassù; situato laggiù ‖ *adv* lassù; laggiù

yore [jor] *s*—**of yore** del tempo antico, del tempo in cui Berta filava

you [ju] *pron pers* Lei; tu; Le, La; te, ti; voi; vi; Loro ‖ *pron indef* si, e.g., **you eat at noon** si mangia a mezzogiorno

young [jʌŋ] *adj* (**younger** ['jʌŋɡər]; **youngest** ['jʌŋɡɪst]) giovane ‖ **the young** i giovani

young' hope'ful *s* giovane *m* di belle speranze

young' la'dy *s* giovane *f*; (*married*) giovane signora

young' man' *s* giovane *m*, giovanotto

young' peo'ple *s* i giovani

youngster ['jʌŋstər] *s* giovanetto; (*child*) bambino

your [jur] *adj* Suo, il Suo; tuo, il tuo; vostro, il vostro

yours [jurz] *pron poss* Suo, il Suo; tuo, il tuo; vostro, il vostro; **of yours** Suo; **very truly yours** distinti saluti

your•self [jur'self] *pron pers* (**-selves** ['sɛlvz]) Lei stesso; sé stesso; si, e.g., **are your enjoying yourself?** si diverte?

youth [juθ] *s* (**youths** [juðs] *or* [juðz]) gioventù *f*, giovinezza; (*person*) giovane *m*; i giovani

youthful ['juθfəl] *adj* giovane, giovanile

yowl [jaʊl] *s* urlo ‖ *intr* urlare

Yugoslav ['jugo'slɑv] *adj & s* iugoslavo

Yugoslavia ['jugo'slɑvɪ‑ə] *s* la Iugoslavia

Yule [jul] *s* il Natale; le feste natalizie

Yule' log' *s* ceppo

Yuletide ['jul‚taɪd] *s* le feste natalizie

Z

Z, z [zi] *s* ventiseiesima lettera dell'alfabeto inglese

za•ny ['zeni] *adj* (**-nier; -niest**) comico, buffonesco ‖ *s* (**-nies**) buffone *m*, pagliaccio

zeal [zil] *s* zelo, entusiasmo

zealot ['zelət] *s* zelante *mf*, fanatico

zealotry ['zelətri] *s* fanatismo

zealous ['zeləs] *adj* zelante, volonteroso

zebra ['zibrə] *s* zebra

ze'bra cross'ing *s* zebre *fpl*

zebu ['zibju] *s* zebù *m*

zenith ['zinɪθ] *s* zenit *m*

zephyr ['zefər] *s* zefiro

ze•ro ['ziro] *s* (**-roes**) zero ‖ *tr*—**to zero in** (mil) aggiustare il mirino di ‖ *intr*—**to zero in on** (mil) concentrare il fuoco su

ze'ro grav'ity *s* gravità *f* zero

ze'ro hour' *s* ora zero

zest [zest] *s* entusiasmo; (*flavor*) aroma *m*, sapore *m*

Zeus [zus] *s* Zeus *m*

zig-zag ['zɪg‚zæg] *adj & adv* a zigzag ‖ *s* zigzag *m*; serpentina ‖ *v* (*pret & pp* **-zagged**; *ger* **-zagging**) *intr* zigzagare; serpeggiare

zinc [zɪŋk] *s* zinco

zinnia ['zɪnɪ‑ə] *s* zinnia

Zionism ['zaɪ‑ə‚nɪzəm] *s* sionismo

zip [zɪp] *s* (coll) sibilo; (coll) energia, vigore *m* ‖ *v* (*pret & pp* **zipped**; *ger* **zipping**) *tr* chiudere con cerniera lampo; aprire con cerniera lampo; (coll) portare rapidamente; **to zip up** (*to add zest to*) dare gusto a ‖ *intr* aprirsi con cerniera lampo; sibilare; (coll) filare, correre; **to zip by** (coll) passare come un lampo

zip′ code′ s codice m di avviamento postale

zipper [ˈzɪpər] s cerniera or serratura lampo

zircon [ˈzʌrkɑn] s zircone m

zirconium [zərˈkonɪ-əm] s zirconio

zither [ˈzɪθər] s cetra tirolese

zodiac [ˈzodɪˌæk] s zodiaco

zone [zon] s zona; distretto postale || tr dividere in zone

zoo [zu] s giardino zoologico

zoologic(al) [ˌzo·əˈlɑdʒɪk(əl)] adj zoologico

zoologist [zoˈɑlədʒɪst] s zoologo

zoology [zoˈɑlədʒi] s zoologia

zoom [zum] s ronzio; (aer) cabrata, impennata; (mov, telv) zumata || tr (aer) far cabrare, fare impennare; (mov, telv) zumare || intr ronzare; (aer) cabrare, impennarsi; (mov, telv) zumare

zoom′ lens′ s (phot) transfocatore m

zoophite [ˈzo·əˌfaɪt] s zoofito

Zu·lu [ˈzulu] adj zulù || s (-lus) zulù mf

Zurich [ˈzurɪk] s Zurigo f